'Despite its comprehensive scope, this book is written with simplicity and clarity, two virtues often lacking in systematic theologies. Deeply rooted in the wealth of Bible-wisdom, and drawing on the witness of historical theology across the centuries, Dr Culver has given us a classic statement of the evangelical faith. This is a book to come back to again and and again.'

Timothy F. George,
Dean of Beeson Divinity School of Samford University, Birmingham, Alabama
and an executive editor of Christianity Today

'Dr Culver is a veteran teacher in the classic evangelical and Reformed stream of Christian understanding, and this wide-ranging, well-directed, sharp-sighted textbook, the fruit of decades of reading, thinking, and classroom encounters, is his magnum opus. Some may wonder about his traducianism, his premillennialism, his adherence to systematic theology's old look as distinct from its new look, and his evident preference for Shedd over Hodge, but all must admire his thoroughness in thinking through the main questions, fudging none and always proposing answers that stimulate, even when they do not finally convince. Within the group of recent conservative systematic theologies this one stands high as a demonstration of the biblical rationality of the Reformed faith.'

J. I. Packer,
Professor of Theology, Regent College, Vancouver, Canada

'Dr Robert Culver has been an "international treasure" in the church for years and has helped many of us in our personal walk and ministry. As a theologian, he is biblical and balanced, and he keeps reminding us that theology is for living and not just for studying. He believes that a theologian should challenge and instruct and he fulfills these ministries admirably. Both the young preacher and the veteran will find enlightenment and nourishment in these pages.'

Warren W. Wiersbe

'Here is the rich harvest of a dedicated scholar's lifetime of study, teaching, and writing. There is no area of theology which Dr Culver fails to discuss with a masterful grasp of all the relevant issues. What I especially appreciate is his command of significant literature. This exhaustive work provides a resource that pastors in particular will find of great help in dealing with doctrinal questions.'

Vernon Grounds,
Chancellor, Denver Seminary, Denver, Colorado

'In a day of reduced theological vigor, evangelicals should greet Robert Culver's new Systematic Theology with enthusiasm. Here is a bold, comprehensive, and faithful systematic theology. This work is based clearly upon a biblical foundation and is marked by genuine scholarship, doctrinal clarity, and historical insight. Culver provides his readers with an encyclopedic breadth of material, but he is also bold to write with conviction and verve. This new Systematic Theology should be warmly received by evangelical pastors, laypersons, and students.'

R. Albert Mohler, Jr.,
President, The Southern Baptist Theological Seminary,
Louisville, Kentucky

'Systematic Theology by Robert Duncan Culver, a distinguished student of Scripture and an eleventh generation descendent of a Puritan who arrived on American shores in 1635, represents the labor of a lifetime. This theological resource proves to be thoroughly biblical, soundly orthodox, and eminently readable. Thus, it receives my warm commendation to those who love and cherish God's Word.'

Richard L. Mayhue,
Executive Vice President, The Master's College and Seminary,
Santa Clarita, California

'It was my pleasure to study in Dr Culver's systematic theology courses in the 1970s at Trinity Evangelical Divinity School. Long have I cherished my set of his mimeographed notes from such classes as "sin and salvation" and "ecclesiology and eschatology." What I learned from him has served me exceptionally well as an evangelical professor (who happens to be Southern Baptist). As I perused the proof copy of the present work, it was just as if I were back in the classroom. Dr Culver's careful presentation and encyclopedic wisdom, acquired over many decades of study, preaching, and teaching, shine through these pages. I am grateful that the current generation of Bible students – and those to come – will now be able to learn from one of the American masters of theology. Dr Culver's warm evangelicalism coupled with his commitment to Reformed soteriology and historic Premillennial eschatology truly honors our Lord.'

Kendell H. Easley,
Chair, Department of New Testament and Greek, Mid-America Baptist Theological Seminary,
Memphis, Tennessee

'Culver's Systematic Theology is biblically grounded, edifying and thorough. It has the depth of a good old classic theology with an accessible style and relevant contemporary insights. As a theologian, he writes with the worshipful reverence of a Puritan, the stirring exhortation of a prophet, the logical precision of a philosopher, and the wise guidance of a pastor. His desire to ground all our theology in Scripture is obvious throughout. I anticipate this being an outstanding resource for those I teach at both the University as well as in my church. I am thankful to God for this treasure of sage theological insight.'

K. Erik Thoennes,
Associate Professor of Theology, Talbot School of Theology/Biola University,
Pastor, Grace Evangelical Free Church, La Mirada, California

'Those of us who sat under Robert Culver's classroom instruction are no strangers to his straightforward and unadorned presentation of even the most profound theological truth. This is not to say his writing is without charm and wit. Nevertheless Culver speaks plainly for the earnest Christian not merely the academician. The oft ignored doctrine of the perspicuity of Scripture has found a new champion in Robert Culver's thorough yet engaging Systematic Theology. First, last, and always he is a teacher, a teacher of the sure and certain doctrines of the Bible. He chooses to examine his subjects primarily within the parameters of their biblical terminology and the logical demands of a reasonable gospel. Though Culver is conversant with the speculative side of theology, he rarely stays long under its allure. He reminds us, by avoiding such pitfalls himself, how easily good theology can be lost in the murky waters of speculation. Culver's theology is in keeping with the best of reformation and subsequent evangelical traditions. We are eager to see Robert Culver's Systematic Theology translated into the Magyar tongue. It is hoped his words will, as they have with so many of his American students, encourage and inform sound Bible teaching in the reawakening pulpits of the Hungarian people.'

Michael A. Braun,
Director, Project Hungary

'The arrival of a new Systematic Theology from the hand of a great evangelical theologian like Dr Robert Culver is always welcome. In this case, the book will be welcomed by both evangelical audiences and those not inclined toward evangelicalism simply because of the erudition of the work. The believing community will have its life and ministry enhanced by this excellent volume.'

Paige Patterson,
President, The Southwestern Baptist Theological Seminary,
Fort Worth, Texas

Systematic Theology

Biblical and Historical

Robert Duncan Culver

MENTOR

Unless otherwise indicated, all Scripture quotations are from The Holy Bible, English Standard Version, copyright © 2001 by Crossway Bibles, a division of Good News Publishers. Used by permission. All rights reserved.

Scripture quotations marked (NIV) are taken from the HOLY BIBLE, NEW INTERNATIONAL VERSION®. NIV®. Copyright©1973, 1978, 1984 by International Bible Society. Used by permission of Zondervan. All rights reserved.

Scripture quotations marked (NKJV) are taken from the New King James Version. Copyright © 1982 by Thomas Nelson, Inc. Used by permission. All rights reserved.

Scripture quotations marked (NASB) are taken from the New American Standard Bible®, Copyright © 1960, 1962, 1963, 1968, 1971, 1972, 1973, 1975, 1977, 1995 by The Lockman Foundation. Used by permission. All rights reserved.

Scripture quotations marked (NRSV) are taken from the New Revised Standard Version Bible, copyright 1989, Division of Christian Education of the National Council of the Churches of Christ in the United States of America. Used by permission. All rights reserved.

Scripture quotations marked (RSV) are taken Revised Standard Version of the Bible, copyright 1952 [2nd edition, 1971] by the Division of Christian Education of the National Council of the Churches of Christ in the United States of America. Used by permission. All rights reserved.

© Robert Duncan Culver 2005

ISBN 1-84550-049-0

10 9 8 7 6 5 4 3 2 1

Published in 2005
in the
Mentor Imprint
by
Christian Focus Publications, Ltd.,
Geanies House, Fearn, Ross-shire,
IV20 1TW, Great Britain

www.christianfocus.com

Robert Duncan Culver asserts the moral right to be identified as the author of this book.

Cover Design by
Alister MacInnes

Printed and bound by
Bercker, Germany

All rights reserved. No part of this publication may be reproduced, stored in a retrieval system or transmitted, in any form or by any means, electronic, mechanical, photocopying, recording or otherwise, without the prior permission of the publishers.

CONTENTS

ABBREVIATIONS	IX
ABOUT THE AUTHOR	X
ACKNOWLEDGEMENTS	XI
FOREWORD BY WALTER C. KAISER JR.	XIII
A PROLOGUE TO THE READER	XV
PART 1: THEOLOGY PROPER — *INTRODUCTION AND DOCTRINE OF GOD*	1
PART 2: ANTHROPOLOGY — *MAN AS CREATED*	227
PART 3: HAMARTIOLOGY — *MAN AS SINNER*	337
PART 4: CHRISTOLOGY — *PERSON AND WORK OF CHRIST*	419
PART 5: SOTERIOLOGY — *SALVATION APPLIED*	639
PART 6: ECCLESIOLOGY — *CHURCH LOCAL AND UNIVERSAL*	799
PART 7: ESCHATOLOGY — *LAST THINGS, PERSONAL AND UNIVERSAL*	1007
BIBLIOGRAPHY	1156
SCRIPTURE INDEX	1176
GENERAL INDEX	1224

Part 1: Theology Proper: Introduction and Doctrine of God 1
1. An Introduction to Christian Theology 2
2. Preliminary to Talk about God 12
3. Special Terms of Talk about God 19
4. Why People do Believe in God 29
5. Reasons for Believing in God 36
6. How God has Revealed Himself to Mankind 44
7. The Names of God 53
8. The Attributes of God 60
9. The Spirituality of the Godhead 66
10. The Unity of the Godhead 75
11. The Greatness of the Godhead 83
12. The Goodness of the Godhead 93
13. The Triunity of the Godhead in Biblical and Christian History 104
14. The Triunity of the Godhead: Questions, Traditional Expressions, Illustrations, Values, Refinements, Cautions 113
15. Predestination or the Decrees of God: God's Eternal Plan for the Heavens and the Earth, Part I 122
16. Predestination or the Decrees of God: God's Eternal Plan for the Heavens and the Earth, Part II 131
17. God's Work of Creation, Part I 141
18. God's Work of Creation, Part II 152
19. The World of Unseen Spirits: Their Place in Creation 164
20. Satan and Demons: Fallen Created Spirits 176
21. God's Work of Preservation and Providence 181
22. Appendices on God's Preservation and Providence (Chapter 21) 202
23. God's Blessedness, or Impassibility 216

Part 2: Anthropology: Man as Created 227
1. Introduction to Anthropology 228
2. The Origin and Unity of Mankind by Creation 240
3. Mankind the Image of God 248
4. The Non-Physical Aspects of Human Nature 258
5. The Elements of Human Nature 268
6. The Origin of the Soul 275
7. Mankind's Original Environment, Circumstances and Capacities 282
8. The Divine Purpose In and For Mankind 293
9. The Apostasy of Mankind: Probation, Temptation and Fall 301
10. Consequences of the Fall of Mankind 311
11. Fallen Mankind in the order of Nature 321
12. Fallen Mankind, in their World 329

Part 3: Hamartiology: Man as Sinner 337
1. Introduction to Hamartiology 338
2. The Vocabulary, Common and Biblical, About Sin 341
3. The Nature of Sin: Sin As Moral Evil 348
4. The Nature of Sin: Sin As Disposition 358
5. Sins As Acts Committed by Sinners 364
6. Divine Control and Human Extremes 372
7. The Transmission of Sin Through the Generations of Man 378
8. Theories of the Imputation of Sin 385
9. Analysis of the Problem of Imputation of Sin and a Proposed Solution 395
10. The Worldwide Reign of Sin 406
11. The Personal Consequences of Sin 413

Part 4: Christology: Person and Work of Christ 419

1. Introduction to Christology 420
2. Preparation for the Coming of Christ 428
3. The Preexistence of Christ 438
4. The Deity of Christ, Part One: Introduction; Names and Attributes of Deity 445
5. The Deity of Christ, Part Two: Works, Claims, Honors, Assumptions, Position of Deity 453
6. Anthropotēs, The Human Nature of Christ 461
7. The Virgin Birth of Jesus 469
8. The Incarnation of the Son of God 483
9. The Incarnate Person of Jesus Christ 492
10. The Saving Work of the Incarnate Son of God: Topics, Terms, Issues, Development 501
11. Humiliation and Exaltation: Two States of the Incarnate Life of the Son of God 510
12. The Sinless Life of Jesus 520
13. The Passion and Death of Jesus 530
14. The Meaning of the Death of Christ Part One: How to Explore the Revealed Mystery 540
15. The Meaning of the Death of Jesus Christ Part Two: The Biblical Vocabulary of the Atonement 546
16. The Meaning of the Death of Christ Part Three: Atonement by Vicarious Satisfaction 560
17. The Extent of the Atonement 570
18. Further Benefits and Accomplishments of the Death of Christ in our Place 583
19. The Doctrine of Atonement before Anselm 592
20. The Resurrection of Christ I 601
21. The Resurrection of Christ II 608
22. The Ascension of Christ 616
23. Enthroned in Heaven at God's Right Hand 623
24. The Present Heavenly High Priestly Work of Christ our Lord 629

Part 5: Soteriology: Salvation Applied 639

Preface 640
1. Introduction to the Doctrine of Salvation 642
2. What Salvation Is 646
3. *Ordo Salutis*, or the Order of Salvation 652
4. The Doctrine of Grace 657
5. The Doctrine of Union with Christ 664
6. The Doctrine of Election 671
7. The Doctrine of Calling 682
8. The Doctrine of Regeneration 689
9. The Doctrine of Conversion 699
10. The Doctrine of Repentance 706
11. The Doctrine of Faith: Linguistic Factors and Specific Elements 714
12. The Doctrine of Faith: The Theological Construct 721
13. The Doctrine of Justification by Faith 733
14. The Doctrine of Adoption 744
15. The Doctrine of Sanctification: Linguistic Factors and Past Positional Aspects .. 747
16. The Doctrine of Sanctification: Present and Future Aspects 755
17. The Doctrine of Perseverance 765
18. The Doctrine of Assurance 772
19. Salvation Through Christ Alone 780
20. Is Christ Present in Non-Christian Religions? 791

Part 6: Ecclesiology: Church Local and Universal 799

1. The Critical Importance of the Doctrine of the Church 800
2. Defining Ecclesiology 808
3. The Words 'Church' and *Ekklēsia* 814
4. Metaphors, Images and Ideas Related to the Church 820
5. The Twofold Aspect of the Church, Universal and Local 826
6. Foundation for the Church 834
7. The Establishment of the Church 839
8. The Church in Relation to Israel 848
9. The Church in Relation to the Kingdom of God 857
10. The Essential Nature of the Church 869
11. The Unity of the Church 879
12. The Gifts of Christ to the Church 889
13. The Mission of the Church in the World 898
14. The Present Purposes of God for the Church and Her Destiny 908
15. The Nature of the Local Church 914
16. The Form of the Church: Organization and Governance 923
17. Church Polity: Theories of Church Government 932
18. Church Offices and Ministry, I 941
19. Church Offices and Ministry, II 950
20. Church Discipline 956
21. Public Meetings for Worship in the Church 962
22. The Ordinance of Baptism: The Church's Rite of Initation, I 976
23. The Ordinance of Baptism: The Church's Rite of Initiation, II 982
24. Worship at the Lord's Table, I 991
25. Worship at the Lord's Table, II 998

Part 7: Eschatology: Last Things, Personal and Universal 1007

1. Introduction to Eschatology 1008
2. Death, Mortality and Immortality 1018
3. Where Are the Dead Now and What is Their Condition?: the Doctrine of the Intermediate State 1030
4. The Doctrine of the Resurrection of the Dead, I. Its Main Features and Unique Position in Biblical Religion 1044
5. The Doctrine of the Resurrection of the Dead, II. Time and Order of the Resurrection of the Dead 1054
6. The Doctrine of Judgment 1066
7. The Final Destiny of the Unsaved, I 1074
8. The Final Destiny of the Unsaved, II 1085
9. Heaven, the Eternal Home of the Redeemed 1096
10. The Second Advent of Christ and Related Events 1111
11. The Time of the Lord's Return 1120
12. Precursors to the Day of the Lord: The Great Tribulation, the Great Apostasy and the Revelation of the Man of Sin 1128
13. The Thousand Years of Revelation 20 1138
14. Recent and Current Views of 'The Millennium': Postmillennial, Amillennial, Premillennial 1143
15. The Future Eternal State 1153

Abbreviations

No formal system of abbreviations except for the names of books of the Bible is employed. Most abbreviations are obvious in context of the chapter. The following are a few of the less obvious abbreviations employed. Full bibliographical data are in the Bibliography.

ABD – *Anchor Bible Dictionary*, 6 volumes
ANF – *The Ante-Nicene Fathers*, 10 volumes
Barth – Karl Barth, *Church Dogmatics*, 13 volumes
Bauer, or Arndt and Gingrich – Walter Bauer, *A Greek-English Lexicon of the New Testament and Other Early Christian Literature*, translation and adaptation from the 5th edition by W. F. Arndt & F. W. Gingrich.
Bettenson – Henry S. Bettenson, *Documents of the Christian Church*
BDB – Brown, Driver and Briggs, *A Hebrew and English Lexicon of the Old Testament*
Calvin, *Institutes,* or *Institutes* – John Calvin, *Institutes of the Christian Religion*, 2 volumes
Catholic Encyclopedia – *The Catholic Encyclopedia, An International Work of References on Constitution, Doctrine, Discipline and History of the Catholic Church*, 16 volumes
Denzinger – Henry Denzinger, *The Sources of Catholic Dogma*
EDBT – *Evangelical Dictionary of Biblical Theology,* Ed. Walter A. Elwell
EDT – *Evangelical Dictionary of Theology*, Ed. Walter A. Elwell
HDB – *A Dictionary of the Bible*, Ed. James Hastings, 5 volumes
Liddell and Scott – *A Greek-English Lexicon, Based on the German Work of Francis Passow*, by Henry G. Liddell and Robert Scott
LW – *Luther's Works*, Ed. by J. Pelican and H. T. Lehmann, 55 volumes
McClintock and Strong – *Cyclopedia of Biblical, Theological and Ecclesiastical Literature*, prepared by John McClintock and James Strong, 12 volumes
NPNF, I – *Nicene and Post-Nicene Fathers,* First Series, 14 volumes
NPNF, II – *Nicene and Post-Nicene Fathers*, Second Series, 14 volumes
OED or *Oxford English Dictionary* – *The Compact Edition of the Oxford English Dictionary*
Philo – *The Works of Philo*, New Updated Edition, Complete & Unabridged in One Volume
Strack & Billerbeck – *Kommentar Zum Neuen Testament Aus Talmud und Midrasch*, 6 volumes, Herman L. Strack and Paul Billerbeck
TDNT – *Theological Dictionary of the New Testament*, 10 volumes, Eds. G. Kittel & G. Friedrich, Trans. G. W. Bromiley
TWNT – *Theological Wordbook of the Old Testament*, 2 volumes, Eds. R. L. Harris, G. L. Archer, Jr., B. K. Waltke
ZPEB – *The Zondervan Pictorial Encyclopedia of the Bible*, 5 volumes, Ed. M. C. Tenney

About the Author

Robert Culver was born in rural Yakima County, Washington. It was there that he became, along with parents and family, part of a new small village congregation of believers, that has sent many of its sons and daughters into various missionary and pastoral careers. Early education was in the public schools. He is a graduate of Heidelberg College (A.B.), Grace Theological Seminary (B.D., Th.M., Th.D.) and did post-doctoral theological studies at Chicago Lutheran Theological Seminary and ancient Near-East languages at the Graduate School of the University of Minnesota.

Dr Culver received formal ordination to the ministry immediately after graduation from seminary but has been a preacher, pastor and teacher all his adult life, to the present. His career as a professor has taken him to Grace Theological Seminary (Professor of Old Testament and Hebrew), Wheaton College and Graduate School (Associate Professor of Bible and Theology) Trinity Evangelical Divinity School (Professor and Chairman of Theology). He was annual director of the Near-East School of Archaeology at Jerusalem (1962). He has been special or visiting lecturer at schools in Canada, several states in USA, Jordan, Hong Kong, France, the Netherlands and Argentina. Among his several publications perhaps best known are *The Life of Christ*, *Civil Government: a Biblical View*, *Daniel and the Latter Days* and the section on "Daniel" in the *Wycliffe Commentary*.

Acknowledgements

Production of this volume, by God's grace, involved the careful and persistent efforts of many competent people besides the author. Malcom Maclean, the editor of the Mentor Imprint of Christian Focus Publications, at the first, examined a portion (Part Six) of the manuscript and secured acceptance of the whole for publication. Willie MacKenzie, Editorial Manager, patiently shepherded the whole project from initial editing through indexing, printing and distribution. Colin Duriez edited the majority of the book and guided editing of the whole. He offered many helpful suggestions, notably adoption of the English Standard Version for all otherwise undesignated Bible quotations. Several typesetters and proofreaders, Jonny Sherlock, Annella MacDonald and Martin Maclean and others whose names I do not know, helped preserve the integrity of authorial intent and correct form of the final product. Susan Hart, Director of the Rushford, Minnesota Public Library has kept the author supplied with needed books and documentary information through the library search facilities and inter-library loan system over the years of the writing of this volume. Jonathan Burd prepared the lengthy Scripture Index and David Cradduck, within a narrow time frame, prepared the General Index

Special acknowledgement is due Celeste Knipmeyer Culver, my loving wife of thirty years and loving stepmother, grandmother and great grandmother. She has worked steadily on this project, almost full-time since before 1990, when we decided to devote all our best energies to it. She put every word and mark into a series of computers, having already checked my handwritten 8 ½" x 14" sheets – on through revisions, rewrites and transmission to editors and final corrections before going to press. Without her cheerful contributions and moral support this book of systematic theology would never have come to be.

Likewise my three children, Douglas, Keith and Lorraine have steadily encouraged me to complete a project begun, as they well know, long ago.

As Jesus Himself said, in another connection: "Others have labored and you have entered into their labors" (John 4:38).

Foreword
By
Walter C. Kaiser Jr.

Not every book that has seen the light of day should have been written, but this volume by the Rev Dr Robert Duncan Culver entitled Systematic Theology was one that just had to be written. Without it, we would have been deprived of one of the strongest examples of the exegetical use of the Bible in forming a Systematic Theology for our day. Parts of this line of teaching have only been known through the oral presentations of a stream of great teachers that Dr Culver represents as the highest achievement in the area of Systematic Theology of that line of godly teachers.

Even though we are seeing all of a sudden a flurry of activity in the number and size of volumes on this subject, this volume has such uniqueness about it that our generation and those that follow us, if our Lord tarries, would have been left with some major gaps in our understanding of the system of thought found in the Scriptures. I have had the privilege of hearing much of these volumes as a student, colleague and friend.

My acquaintance with Robert Culver and his teaching goes back to the latter part of the 1950s when as a graduate student I served as his teaching assistant. As I assisted him in marking the doctrinal tests of his college students and occasionally teaching a class for him, I became aware of his thought and strong Biblical approach to all of doctrine. Later I was able to take on the graduate level his course in Ecclesiology and Eschatology. But that would not be the end of our relationship or partnership in the gospel, for as a graduate student I later became an Assistant Pastor with him in a nearby Church for a year and a half until I finished my graduate work. Sometime after this we served together on two separate faculties. Culver. Therefore, I am in deep debt to him for many lines in my own thinking as I have been challenged over and over again to be more radically Biblical in my thinking while being systematic in my thought.

All too many in our day feel that Systematic Theology is a poor cousin to the newer forms of Biblical Theology with its diachronic methods as opposed to the systematic categories involving metaphysical, epistemological and logical thought. That is most unfortunate, for eventually our generation will see that, despite whatever validity may be found in the distinctive methods of Biblical theology (and there are many), nevertheless, neither discipline by itself can perform all the necessary duties laid upon it by the extraordinary issues, questions and expectations of our day. A mere perusal of this volume on Systematic Theology will demonstrate that point very readily.

It is not that Systematic Theology is indebted to Greek philosophical categories, as well as modern ones, whereas Biblical Theology is without any of these accoutrements. That is to badly understand one's own method without critically assessing the baggage that one may bring along with his or her study of the Scriptures. We must not be shy in our day of laying claim to the possibility of holding a 'correct' or 'objective meaning' or interpretation of the text of Scripture, for to deny that one can have a correct or objective meaning is objectively to state that there are none to be had! It is like saying, as one of my university professors said so blatantly, 'There are no absolutes!' When I asked him as casually as I could if he affirmed this absolutely, he unthinkingly replied, 'Absolutely!' He too had to be involved in precisely what he was disallowing!

Therefore, I am deeply grateful to my teacher, colleague, and long-standing friend for giving to all of us this extraordinary work that represents the fruit of a lifetime of studying God's word and teaching theology to collegians, seminarians, and the body of Christ. May our Lord use it to further the work of the gospel around the world in this new century when new believers are coming into the family of God at the phenomenal rate of two new believers every second, especially in the two-thirds world.

Walter C. Kaiser, Jr.
President and Colman M. Mockler Distinguished Professor of Old Testament,
Gordon-Conwell Theological Seminary,
Hamilton, Massachusetts

A Prologue to the Reader

The student or scholar who holds this large book in hand or on desktop, open to this page, likely has had strong reasons for buying or borrowing it. It was not a casual decision. Nor is a decision to proceed on to read such a large tome a casual one. The opening chapter of 'An Introduction to Christian Theology,' and the next following five chapters, though in the section of *theology proper* (the Doctrine of God), are intended to prepare the reader's mind and will for the whole discipline of systematic Christian theology. Both mind and will must be prepared, for only with clean hands and a pure heart do we ascend the hill of the Lord (Ps. 24:3, 4).

Some treatments of systematic theology preface it all with a separate book or large section called *prolegomena* (Greek for 'things said beforehand') similar to *prologue*, a Greek term from dramatics for a monologue to introduce the main action in a stage play. I share the view of many others that these recondite matters (history of the subject, theories of knowledge and of hermeneutics, competing systems, sources, etc.) fit best in two other places: when the questions and topics arise – as inevitably they do – at various places over the whole of systematic theology or, the same may be taught as apologetics and philosophy of religion concurrently with or after the theology.[1]

Source and Resources

A sound *evangelical* theology should make a distinction between the *source* of Christian doctrines (or church dogma) and *resources* for understanding these doctrines and how to formulate them in a system of thought. The only source of theological doctrine is the Word of God. Man, said Jesus, lives 'by every word that comes from the mouth of God' (Matt. 4:4). In the present time, long after the close of the ages of revelation, our only access to those words is the canonical Scriptures of the Old Testament and New Testament, the source of our theology. The chief acknowledged *resources* for deriving truth from the *source* are tradition, reason and experience.

---

1. Since the time of Schleiermacher, 1768-1834, apologetics is sometimes called *Fundamental Theology*. A large symposium of Roman Catholic scholars about how to approach theology is entitled *Problems of Fundamental Theology* (New York: Paulist Press, 1982). Louis Berkhof presents a good discussion of the relation of how and when apologetics is 'introduction' or defense and at what point in *Introduction to Systematic Theology*, Grand Rapids, MI: Baker Books, 1932, pp. 48-51. It is significant that his *Systematic Theology* is published without his *Introduction to Systematic Theology*.

Tradition – in the sense of the history of exegesis and interpretation of the words of God in the Word – is a resource all theologians depend on in one way or another. The tradition is embodied in creeds, confessions and all the commentaries and works of theology, plus the instructions of teachers, parents and pastors. No writer of theology starts from scratch. Every author of theology draws on this tradition and passes it on with his own contributions. Otherwise his book would fall as short of an adequate grasp of the Christian revelation as the faltering efforts of the first ecclesiastical writers back in the second Christian century.

I owe a debt for almost all the theology I know to all my teachers, the books of theology written by godly men of learning which I have read, and every sound lecture and sermon I ever heard – especially to my seminary professors and, of course, their teachers.

Reason is another resource for theology. Most 'reasonable' Christians assume that as beings made in the image of God our minds have a capacity for thought, of taking notice of cause and effect, of turning perceptions into conceptions, of organizing facts and truths in arrangements demonstrating relationships. We assume that the world we perceive with our senses is real and capable of being truly understood adequately if not perfectly. If we are both industrious and devout we may employ this capacity, or faculty to derive truths from Scripture, establish apparent relationships, place them in order and draw inferences. The Reformation creeds took special note of this. There are no metaphysical or epistemological commitments necessary except the common-sense realism which is spread over every page of the Bible. God would not make a world where all our sense impressions of the external world tell us lies.

Christian experience is not accepted by every orthodox theologian as a resource for theology. Some good Christians have claimed mystical experiences as revelatory. Yet mystical experiences are by definition impossible to report. Early neo-orthodox (*Krisis*) theology and successors make the whole Bible a fallible human report of ineffable (I-Thou) meetings with God. This the historic Christian theological consensus rejects. Yet the teaching of a 'seasoned' scholar or an 'experienced' pastor or professor is valued more than the opinion of novices. Further, would there be a world-wide church today if the first and succeeding generations of believers had not truly experienced 'O taste and see that the LORD is good: blessed is the man that trusteth in him' (Ps. 34:8 KJV).

Sola Scriptura

Yet, because the Bible is the only source of theology, and judges all the proposed findings of the other resources, biblical truth should pervade every paragraph of this volume and scripturally derived norms should control as well as inform every sentence.

The Bible is perspicuous in the sense that any literate person 'in due use of ordinary means, may attain to a sufficient understanding' (*Westminster Confession of Faith* I. vii). Nevertheless, deep theological insight is served by going behind translations to the original languages. This book does not assume the reader's acquaintance with Greek and Hebrew. Hence, when citing words from the original languages they are made approximately pronounceable by a non-technical, but traditional, transliteration. Theologians, I think, should practice scientific exegesis but report results rather than process in a book not designed for language specialists. A few passages, such as Romans 5:12-21 (in connection with sin and atonement) and the first verses of Genesis (in connection with creation), are exceptional and require furnishing some technical exegetical treatment of the original texts.

The formal scheme of systematic theology sometimes includes a section on the doctrine of Holy Scripture. The section may be entitled bibliology, inspiration, revelation or revelation and inspiration. One of the most successful orthodox evangelical volumes (*Systematic Theology* by Louis Berkhof) has no section on the Bible as such, yet throughout relies unapologetically on the veracity, integrity, inspiration and divine authority of the Canon of the sixty-six books of the Old Testament and New Testament. Regretfully, for several reasons, I have followed Berkhof's example. J. O. Buswell (*A Systematic Theology of the Christian Religion*) tucks in a few pages after the doctrine of God. W. G. T. Shedd (*Dogmatic Theology*, three large volumes) supplies fifty or sixty pages on the subject, while Francis Pieper (*Christian Dogmatics*), deep in Lutheran controversy about the Bible, has more pages on Holy Scripture than The Doctrine of God. The first six chapters of this volume supply some features of a doctrine of Holy Scripture, though I have included no formal section on the Doctrine of Holy Scripture. I endorse plenary, verbal inspiration, i.e., the words of Scripture though in human languages and written freely by men are also fully the words of God.

The words of Scripture, not merely the ideas, are God's words, without error in original documents, true and of divine authority.[2]

It is assumed the reader is already familiar with the entire Bible, not necessarily previous classroom courses in Bible, but the acquaintance which comes through reading the Book. With extra effort in diligently reading the Bible references furnished and use of reference works, an inadequate knowledge of Scripture may be overcome. Reading fifty pages a day in a moderately large-print Bible will take you from Genesis through Revelation in a month.

Sound doctrine will be founded on sound interpretation of the Bible. Hence many departments of systematic theology offer a course in *biblical hermeneutics*. Sadly, the contemporary field of hermeneutics is plagued with a plethora of aggressive proponents of nihilistic to weird theories of meaning and of non-meaning of documents, including the Bible.[3] We have been compelled by our times to come to terms with assaults but not to surrender to them. The same common sense realism (formal or informal) which took you through fourth grade geography and college chemistry will take you through Bible and theology. A course in hermeneutics is hardly prerequisite to theology. It can wait.

Theology must also be aware of the importance of *biblical introduction* both general (text and canon) and special (date, authorship, genuineness, sources, etc.). Several kinds of destructive scholarly criticism have relentlessly attacked Christian belief from this quarter for two centuries. These subjects are almost unbelievably complicated. They should be pursued under competent guidance and good literary sources. Yet systematic theology serves as well, perhaps better, as preliminary to critical studies than the other way around. This book takes neither a pre-critical nor an uncritical approach to Scripture, but one of informed rejection of that form of biblical criticism which assumes rejection of the Christian, theistic, *weltanschauug* (world-view) as a precondition of scholarly study. We have the canon of Holy Scripture and accept it as inspired and truthful in all its parts. We gratefully adopt and promote all the positive fruits of modern study of the science of interpretation and both special and general introduction to the Bible.

The goals in this volume do not include references in text and notes to every author or teacher who over the author's life has informed or affected my thoughts about theology. I document quotations and give credit to immediate sources even if not directly quoted and supply some guidance to further reading. Readers are pointed to far more ancient, Reformation, post-Reformation, recent and contemporary evangelical authors than to the offerings of the largely university-generated, burgeoning theological marketplace of today. It does not seem wise to let the spoilers set the agenda for constructive theology for Christians – even as we try to take due note of any positive corrections or refinements their work suggests. The hot trails of ephemeral controversies and faddish 'new theology' do not lead to the deposit of acknowledged, Christian consensual truth about God and His ways.

The program of investigation and instruction is *systematic* because God is not the author of confusion (1 Cor. 14:33). If it is God's will that in the church all things be *done* decently and in order (1 Cor. 14:40; cf. 14:2 and 34) then *thinking* about eternal truth should also be in some systematic order. The Apostle commands the interim pastor at Ephesus to 'Follow the *pattern* of sound words' which he had already heard from his systematic theology professor ('sound words... heard from me' 2 Tim. 1:13 RSV). He is to 'guard the truth that has been entrusted to you' (2 Tim. 1:14 RSV). Down through the seventy-five-plus generations of our era comes the charge:

> Do your best to present yourself to God as one approved, a workman who has no need to be ashamed, rightly handling the word of truth. Avoid... godless chatter, for it will lead people into more and more ungodliness (2 Tim. 2:15, 16 RSV).

Very early in my ministry as a pastor I found I had not achieved competence to do what these and similar passages demand. My college education had been interrupted by prolonged and acute hard times. There was no money to move a pastor from the center of things to our rather remote church. So when our young pastor resigned to finish seminary education the congregation invited me and my bride to move into the parsonage, preach, teach and shepherd the flock at the tender age of twenty-one! Things went fairly well. Youthful enthusiasm and a strong voice

---

2. I have set forth a more comprehensive summary of the doctrine as The Doctrine of Holy Scripture in a large section of a book published jointly with Dr Lloyd M. Perry, *How to Search the Scriptures* (Grand Rapids, MI: Baker Books, 1967, 1979). I intend, God enabling, to enlarge that modest effort into a book on the subject. This is only one of several writing projects that preparation of this volume has provoked.

3. A good brief survey of the subject from a non-committal point of view is *Hermeneutics* by Bernard Lategan in *The Anchor Bible Dictionary*, vol. 3, pp. 149–154, corrected somewhat by *Interpretation of the Bible* by F. F. Bruce, *EDT*, pp. 565–568. A highly recommended recent textbook is *Introduction to Biblical Interpretation* by Klein, Blomberg and Hubbard.

in a community of many loyal friends old and young carried quite a distance. The congregation was even attracting a few new people.

I already had a fair grasp of the historical structure and literary content of the Bible and was thoroughly familiar with all the notes in the most popular study Bible of the time. Some college courses in Bible, church history, Christian evidences and twenty semester hours in Greek enabled the aspirant pastor-teacher to ascertain the surface meaning of the text of the Epistle to the Ephesians and some of the depths. But in the very first chapter he came up against election, the Holy Trinity, the sovereign will of God, a present reign of Christ in heaven and a seemingly complicated doctrine of the church. Nothing in his background had provided definition and a logical structure of doctrines whereby these grand truths of revelation could be defined and related to one another and to the 'whole counsel of God.' The ancient church used *kat-holikos* (catholic) both of the whole church through all the world and the *canon of faith*, or scheme of beliefs – in other words, systematic theology. What this aspirant pastor-teacher desperately needed, in America, is usually called systematic theology, that is, 'What the church of Jesus Christ believes, teaches and confesses on the basis of the word of God: this is Christian doctrine.'[4]

No theologian or denomination has a lock-hold on all the details, though each writer or lecturer necessarily places his own distinct character on structure and details. Yet, to be of interest to any beyond the author and his immediate sympathizers, systematic theology will consist mainly of historical, consensual, orthodox, biblical doctrine – in the language of Vincent of Lerins, that which has been believed 'everywhere, always, by all' – orthodox believers, that is.

The opening 'Introduction to Theology,' follows up on the questions aroused by these opening sentences and lays ground for all to follow.

---

4. The first line repeated often afterward in Jaroslav Pelikan's, *The Christian Tradition*, 5 vols., Vol. I, p. 1.

PART 1
THEOLOGY PROPER
Introduction and Doctrine of God

PART 2
ANTHROPOLOGY
Man as Created

PART 3
HAMARTIOLOGY
Man as Sinner

PART 4
CHRISTOLOGY
Person and Work of Christ

PART 5
SOTERIOLOGY
Salvation Applied

PART 6
ECCLESIOLOGY
Church Local and Universal

PART 7
ESCHATOLOGY
Last Things, Personal and Universal

BIBLIOGRAPHY

SCRIPTURE INDEX

GENERAL INDEX

1
An Introduction to Christian Theology

I. What Theology is.

One may rightly say Christian theology is study or organized treatment of the topic, God, from the standpoint of Christianity. To leave the matter there, however, would be grossly misleading, for theology is not merely an interpretation of the meaning of God from the outside; theology is a part or aspect of Christianity itself. On a deeper level theology is of the essence of Christianity. It is so much of the essence that to dispense with theology is to dispense with Christianity.

Christianity is not merely a mixture of ceremonies, beliefs, adherents, history and the like. The Christian religion is all of these, perhaps, but that also is a misleading statement, for it is not an aggregate or mixture of things like baptism (ceremony), the Apostles' Creed (beliefs), a congregation of Baptists (adherents) and a book of church history.

Authentic Christianity is a single thing. We may compare it to a chemical compound such as sulphuric acid (H_2SO_4). H_2SO_4 is not two parts hydrogen, one of sulphur and four of oxygen, somehow mixed together in a glass beaker. It is a single thing in which there are three elements so integrally united as to form a substance different from any one of the three alone, and from anything else. The distinctive features of Christianity are really of little importance singly. They are always together in authentic Christian religion. They are each explicit in Scripture. There are four: (1) certain acts of God in history, or *redemption*; (2) the meaning of those acts of God as set forth in Holy Scripture, or *doctrines*; (3) the *lives of countless believers*, the Christians themselves through the ages but particularly those alive today; and (4) the *congregations of believers* throughout the world, the churches, or, considered in their spiritual oneness, *the church*.

Redemption – History of what God has done.

First, in historical and logical order, Christianity has been rendered what it is by what God did a long time ago. The Second Person of the Godhead became a man. He lived, suffered and died for us and for our salvation. He arose, ascended to the right hand of God where presently He reigns till His enemies are made the footstool of His feet and where He exercises certain ministries for us in the presence of the Father. Essentially, however, redemption is finished: 'After making purification for sins, he sat down at the right hand of the Majesty on high' (Heb. 1:3). His sitting down signified, in part, that His redemptive work had been completed.

What God did in the redemptive career of Jesus of Nazareth was a consummation of events of God's doing from eternity past, through all of the preparatory history of the Old Testament and up to the point when in 'the fullness of time… God sent forth his Son' (Gal. 4:4).

Christianity, one may justly say, is a history, in the sense of a finished work of redemption performed in a certain period of linear time. The events of redemption may be precisely located in time and place. The first four books of the New Testament are the only extensive authentic sources of information about those acts of God.

The four Gospels are not precisely of the genre history, but they contain a very special species of history, truthful reports of events in time. Though not very specific about the timeframe, the nature of the events themselves is clear if the records are permitted to speak for themselves.

The first Christian generation heard the story of redemption from eyewitnesses – at least the earliest ones did. We, however, depend upon the written testimony of the eyewitnesses. There is no alternate dependable source at this late date.

The element Christianity calls history (events which happened, not mere reports of them) in our religion accounts in large part for the preponderance of narrative in most of the Bible up to the Epistles in the New Testament. It also is the reason why the 'Gospels' are Gospels – more about this later.

Doctrines – The Biblical Meaning of the Redemptive History.

There is an essential second element in our religion. The events of biblical salvation history – God's acts of redemption – have meaning. They must be interpreted, and are seminally interpreted, in the same Scriptures which report God's acts. This interpretation is known as doctrine.

The late J. Gresham Machen explained this matter well:

> From the beginning, the Christian gospel, as indeed the name 'gospel' or 'good news' implies, consisted of an account of something that had happened. And when from the beginning, the meaning of the happening was set forth there was Christian doctrine. 'Christ died' – that is history. 'Christ died for our sins' – that is doctrine. Without these two elements joined in an absolutely indissoluble union there is no Christianity.[1]

The death of Christ taken as a naked fact is not a doctrine, not even a very significant fact. Julius Caesar died. So did my dear father over forty years ago and my dear mother over fifteen years ago. 'It is appointed for man to die once.' There is no special meaning for the human race in the fact that a man, even a sinless man died unless someone in a position to have the facts tells us why and what for. The death of Christ, as we sometimes hear it correctly said, had a cosmic meaning. Statement of the fact with the meaning it has for the world of sinful people is a statement of Christian doctrine. We call it the doctrine of atonement.

There is a modern approach to Christianity which holds all doctrines to be assertions of and interpretations of religious experience. My liberal-Niebuhrian college professor of religion, for example, claimed that Luther's doctrine of Justification by Faith was the Reformer's interpretation of his religious experience of forgiveness and acceptance by God. Of course, Luther himself, who found the doctrine in evangelical Psalms, Galatians and Romans as he prepared his sermons for the congregation of one of the churches of Wittenberg, said it was the other way around. First he learned the doctrine of Justification of David and Paul on the ground of Jesus' shed blood, appropriated by faith alone. After he believingly appropriated the righteousness of God he had wonderful Christian religious experiences.

The distinction between redemptive facts of Christianity and doctrine must not be pressed too far, for it does not apply to all doctrines or facts. Some teachings, which must be called doctrines, are revealed truths. Among these are the present ministry for us by Christ in heaven, His Second Advent and the present ministry of the Holy Spirit. The doctrine of the Holy Trinity is part Christian interpretation of events of history (e.g. events at Jesus' baptism) and part revealed truth.

Furthermore, there are some doctrines uniformly believed by Christians everywhere, confessed and proclaimed, that are not spelled out in any verse of the Bible, but are quite as certain as if they were. Some doctrines have comprehensive exact statement in a single text of the Bible. Some do not. Why that is true and what theologians have done about it must be reserved for later.

---

1. Gresham Machen, *Christianity and Liberalism* (Grand Rapids: Eerdmans, 1923), p. 27.

Insistence on proclamation of these two elements, the interpretation of facts, and history and its meaning, is found repeatedly in the New Testament. Yet, in spite of that, about every generation or so, another emphasis, 'another gospel', 'which is not another', is proposed. When I began to learn about such things in college the prevalent notion in Protestant centres of ministerial training in America was that the apostles' superior grasp of eternal, moral principles taught by Jesus and exemplified by Him was the gospel that conquered the empire of Rome. Another world depression, Hitler, a Second World War and general dissolution of liberalism scotched that fable. Then in America the gospel of existential experience (neo-orthodoxy) came and went. After that 'the image of God in man' theology, promoting self-fulfilment as the essential Christian gospel came along. There have been and are other theologies. A whole series of books about these and other ephemeral theologies sits on the back shelves of many a preacher's private library today. Like the rest of the world (1 John. 2:17) they are all 'passing away'.

The Lives of Countless Believers.

It probably seems obvious to anyone who thinks about it that in some manner Christianity is properly to be equated with all the Christian people one knows. This is at least partially correct. Christianity is life, human life of a very special kind. Here we must briefly consider some more biblical history and apostolic testimony.

Notice how Paul ties redemptive history and the meaning of it within his own life as essential, true religion: 'Christ will be honoured in my body, whether by life or by death. For to me to live is Christ, and to die is gain' (Phil. 1:20,21). 'I have been crucified with Christ and I no longer live, but Christ lives in me. The life I live in the body, I live by faith in the Son of God, who loved me and gave himself for me' (Gal. 2:20 NIV).

This is what Christianity has been from its beginning. The beginnings of Christianity, as reported in Acts and Epistles and Revelation, are now again acknowledged even by many critical scholars as definite historical phenomena, not mythical or imaginary. This is in spite of two centuries of every conceivable attack on the genuineness of the accounts. Christianity began a few days after Jesus' resurrection and ascension. It was not an absolute beginning for it existed in preliminary form as soon as Jesus gathered that original group of five or six who accompanied Him the first year of His public ministry. They did not even have a collective name until years later, at Antioch of Syria, their neighbours named them, 'Christians' (Acts 11:26).

Somehow the fact got abroad into public knowledge that not only was Christ their teacher, example and Savior, but that He lived in them and with them. Paul did not invent the theology of Christian life we read of in these statements quoted above from Philippians 1:20, 21 and Galatians 2:20.

Development of the idea of Christian life, individual and as a group, will come later in these studies. The dynamics of it, however, are on display beginning with the first chapter of Acts through the end of Revelation. In a nutshell, the elements were constant attention (*proskarterountes*) to apostolic doctrine (*didachē*), to the fellowship (*koinōnia*), to the special central fact of worship, i.e. 'the breaking of the bread', to their prayers together (Acts 2:41, 42 and 4:23-41) and to their public testimony (Acts 2:43-47 and 5:12-42). These were irresistible to outsiders, purifying to insiders and enviable to competitors for the hearts of mankind.

There has been much interest among historians and philosophers about what caused the Christian movement to succeed. What forces were at work in overwhelming the Roman Empire by Christianity in the three centuries from about AD 30 to about AD 315? Industrious readers will find the matter discussed learnedly in Edward Gibbon's multi-volumed *The Decline and Fall of the Roman Empire*, Adolph Harnack's *The History of Dogma*, Ernst Troelsch's *The Social Teachings of the Churches*, Kenneth Scott Latourette's *The History of Christianity* and even Arnold J. Toynbee's multi-volumed *Study of History*. There are many differences and agreements in part among these five writers. All agree, however, that moral quality of the lives of these early Christian people, in concert with their love one for another, and care for the welfare of all mankind, set them apart. These qualities came gradually to be grudgingly admired in spite of harassment by a succession of emperors, in vain hope of saving the corrupt society of ancient Roman paganism from ruin, without deigning to acknowledge any of the claims of Christianity.

The same quality of life is of the essence of biblical Christianity. Professed religion anywhere without it is less than the religion of which Jesus is the heart, life and centre.

An Institution-Church, Churches, and Organization

There is a fourth element – the public association of believers together in congregations. They have a corporate life together, partially observable to all men. In John Bunyan's classic, *The Pilgrim's Progress*, Christian is introduced, rather early in his journey from the City of Destruction to Mount Zion, to the great house 'built by the LORD of the hill, for the relief and security of pilgrims'. There he became acquainted with Prudence, Piety and Charity, was furnished companionship and nourishment and sent on his way toward the celestial destination panoplied with the full armour of God. This he found useful at every future stage of the journey.

The people in these visible local associations also think of themselves as members of a world-wide spiritual commonwealth of believers. These living believers, together with all deceased believers now in heaven, are all together 'the assembly of the firstborn who are enrolled in heaven' (Heb. 12:23) and constitute 'the church, which is his body, the fullness of him who fills all in all' (Eph. 1:22, 23).

This unity of the believers both locally and universally is so central in the New Testament protrayal of Christianity that our religion can neither be discussed nor possessed without reference to it. There is no such thing as having Christ, or loving, admiring or confessing Him without similar participation in 'the church'. This is the way Christ Himself, determined the matter to be. For reasons of space and good order an adequate exposition of the church as a doctrine will await its proper place in this treatment of doctrines. The features of the church which distinguish it from other social groups will then be examined. The church of today is inseparable, in reality and thought about it, from the church of yesterday and the church of tomorrow. It is both a heavenly reality and an earthly entity. The history of Christianity and the history of the church may be distinguished but not separated.

Christianity, to summarize, exists under four inseparable aspects: (1) *redemptive acts of God in history*; (2) *doctrines*, which are apostolic interpretation of the meaning of that history; (3) the *lives* of those who have embraced the redemptive acts of God in history and the apostolic interpretation of them; and (4) the *Church* (Heb. 12:23) 'of the firstborn who are enrolled in heaven'.

II. What Systematic Theology is.

It is apparent that a book of 'theology', even though we have not fully defined theology as yet, is connected closely with the 'doctrine' aspect of Christianity. 'What the church of Jesus Christ believes, teaches and confesses on the basis of the Word of God: this is Christian doctrine… The Christian church would not be the church as we know it without Christian doctrine.'[2]

When what the church teaches is announced as it emerges portion by portion from the Bible the discourse is properly called *exposition*. The process of exploring the texts and bringing out the meaning in preparation for exposition is *exegesis*. Particular teachings are *doctrines*. These doctrines are believed and confessed regularly by Christians in their gatherings for worship, in classes and groups as well as privately to their neighbours. When these doctrines are organized into some logically coherent arrangement there is systematic theology. As shall become evident, *systematic theology* is more than logical arrangement of biblical doctrines, but it must not ever be less if it is rightly to claim the title, Systematic Theology of the Christian Religion.[3] There are other adjectives used with 'theology' – biblical, historical, practical, dogmatic, symbolic – but for now we will attend only to systematic theology.

Sustained study of doctrines of the Word of God cannot avoid organized, coherent arrangement of the doctrines, nor should it. Meaningful study of botany, zoology, law, history, medicine, agriculture or any other topic cannot proceed without organized, coherent arrangement of the data.

If new believers are to be instructed, false doctrines exposed, described and corrected, and if the teachings of the Bible are to be seen in their wholeness, then something not in the written book called the Bible but written in human nature must be brought to it. We call it orderly arrangement or system.

To illustrate, nature has put a hundred species of plants all together in one acre of hillside forest on my small farm. But to know and use what is there – even though I was reared on a farm and my ancestors for at least ten generations have been 'yankee farmers' – I have bought several books on botany: one on flowers, others on shrubs, deciduous trees, coniferous trees and so on. I even bought several on lumber and another on firewood. Similarly the *topics* of theology loci, (Latin for 'places', in English *lo-see*, singular, *lo-kus*) were born of rational necessity for thinking people. These loci usually begin with God, then move on to revelation (Holy Scripture), mankind, sin, redemption (Christ's person and work), salvation (application of redemption), church and last things. These loci can no more be avoided than hooks in a closet, shelves in a pantry or library, or drawers in a filing cabinet.

---

2. Jaroslav Pelikan, *The Christian Tradition: A History of the Development of Doctrine* vol. I (Chicago: University of Chicago Press, 1971), p. 1.
3. J. O. Buswell, *A Systematic Theology of the Christian Religion* 2 vols. (Grand Rapids: Zondervan, 1962, 1971).

Persuading Objectors to Theology.

The moods of recent decades, even in theological schools, have not always been favourable to the study of systematic theology – not even to the study of doctrines of church, denomination or even of Christianity itself. This may be the fruit of commonly low opinions of authority of all kinds among the young – though that may be passing. Yet, even among those hardly to be regarded as lawless in spirit, there has been widespread genuine suspicion of systematic approaches to Christian doctrines. The 'pietist' flavour of popular, evangelical theology certainly has had something to do with this distrust. 'How can you say anybody's beliefs are right and another's wrong' was one new student's response to my third lecture and twenty-five pages into the textbook for the course, not long ago. I wondered who had admitted this sophomore ('wise fool') to a graduate course in theology. 'Post-modern' was not yet a respectable category.

Whatever it is that causes suspicion of systematic theology, it frequently comes out as a preference for something called 'biblical theology' even when the objector may not know what biblical theology is. It seems very intellectual and pious to assume prejudice or hoary-headed sectarian controversies control 'systematics' while to derive doctrines from fresh, inductive study of Scripture gives the Holy Spirit a chance to teach us. John 16:12 may be cited out of context to support this outlook. It is not an entirely unworthy attitude, however erroneous. If one has not yet thought through the implications of what the Bible has to say about the gift of 'teacher' and 'teachers', Christ's Lordship over truth and warnings against theological independence, an atmosphere of doctrinal non-commitment seems quite admirable. The subtlety of Satan has taken quick advantage of many who looked at revealed truth in this way.

A true story about a theological student will convey the matter neatly. He was a bright young man in a course leading to the M.A. degree in church history at the seminary. There was a required 'minor comprehensive' examination in systematic theology which, to his dismay and disgust, he failed utterly. As department chairman in charge of a second try, and with some lenity, I allowed the student to read the college level *Manual of Christian Doctrine* by Louis Berkhof, and to document and to make a satisfactory written report in lieu of a second try at the examination. Reading this standard work was his very first experience with theology and it completely changed his mind about the value of systematic theology in education for a Christian ministry of any kind. In his report I was pleased to read the following conversion – uncoerced by me, for he did not need to respond personally. 'I came to Trinity with a strong anti-theological bias and I wanted to study church history without studying theology. The fact that I imagined such a thing to be possible… indicates the extent of my ignorance of both disciplines. As one might expect, I spent an extremely foggy first year.'

He goes on to say he did poorly on his papers in church history, the area of his major, because he did not understand the theological issues involved. He acknowledged that the theology book I required him to read had not only fascinated him but compelled him to change what he now called 'unsupported dogmas' of his own. The report closed as follows:

> The greatest value of the book was in setting boundaries for discussion. When one studies church history, the field looks infinite… there is no end to the topics and this is extremely frustrating. There is something reassuring about being able to examine a book from cover to cover [Berkhof's *Manual*] and know that one has at least an introduction to all the subject area within a given discipline. I have never had a course in introduction to theology: the reading of Berkhof could not actually replace such a course, but it did provide the general overview of the field which I needed but did not want [desire]. I am not yet a theologian, but I know what I will need to become one.

It is good to know that this young man settled down to complete a standard course of education for the Christian ministry, including, of course, all the required systematic theology studies.

Biblical Mandate for Formal Theological Training.

Is there a specific biblical mandate for setting up schools of training for pastors, missionaries and evangelists and, if so, must systematic doctrinal study be a part of it? Do we really need teachers? Is it not true that if serious Christians would only gather together with Bibles on their laps, read together, and share their insights and experiences, this is all they need to understand the Word of God? Is something less explicit than formal, guided study under authorized teachers possible and, if so, is it desirable? Is there intellectual depth to Christianity which justly challenges the best minds? If so, does that require the same sorts of intellectual rigour which is the case in many other areas of human culture? The answer to all these questions is not far to seek.

Let us start with Jesus. He lived out His days as a biblical Jew, according to the requirements and instructions of the Law and the Prophets. They spoke to Jesus with authority. The synagogue, its school and rabbis were part of His youthful training. He asserted that to search the Old Testament is a part of the true way of eternal life.

This attitude of Jesus He passed on to the apostles, all of whom were already committed to the same outlook. They followed Jesus everywhere, being schooled thereby in one of the accepted pedagogical methods of the ancient world, i.e. they were true 'Peripatetics' though not quite after the Aristotelian model.

Many times He promised they would understand fully what He had been saying only after His resurrection. So, at one of His first post-resurrection meetings with the apostles He 'opened their minds that they might understand the Scriptures' (Luke 24:45). From then forward the Hebrew Scriptures became for Jesus' followers a Christian book. All the vast resources of that treasury of religious literature instantly became part of the Christian tradition with distinctly Christian meaning. All truth of Old Testament biblical religion, all that was true even in first century Judaism, became sources of Christian doctrines. This great body of truths answers the deepest questions ever to occupy human minds – about the origin of the world, the nature of humanity, about the Godhead, sin, evil, salvation, the future life and many other things.

The apostles were custodians of their Master's teachings, truths to be transmitted to those who would believe through their word. From the first the Christian congregations gathered regularly to give attention to the apostles' 'doctrine'. There is merit, if not pressed too far, in distinguishing their preaching of the good news (gospel, evangel) from their instruction in doctrine. Doctrine in the Acts and Epistles often translates *didachē*, from the Greek word to teach. *Didachē* is not usually 'proclaimed as by a herald' whereas gospel or evangel was proclaimed as by a herald; hence its preaching was *kerygma*, from *kērusso*, to proclaim. The gospel, when considered narrowly, is only a segment of the proclamation of Christianity, as Paul shows in 1 Corinthians 15. The teaching (*didachē*) contains the gospel, but the gospel does not contain all the teaching. After a lesson or two anyone can tell someone else the good news with its simple corollaries. Hence there are useful tracts like 'Four things God wants You to Know' – in use as long as most of us have been alive.

Doctrine is something else. It is like the *halakoth*, or moral precepts of rabbinical Judaism. Minimally the many passages in the New Testament, employing *didachē* and the several other words for doctrines, require that we distinguish a more complete statement of Christianity alongside the proclamation of salvation. The *didachē* may be characterized as a statement, with full explanantion, chiefly to believers, of the entire Christian revelation. Most of these doctrines were already contained in the Hebrew Scriptures, what Christians call the Old Testament. Christ had opened their minds that they might understand these Scriptures in a Christian way (see Luke 24:25, 26, 44-49).[4] This was and is the basis of Christian theology along with the New Testament revelation.

This task of instruction was of sufficient magnitude and importance that the first congregation 'devoted themselves [*proskaterountes*] to the apostles' teaching' (Acts 2:42). It was also boldly stated to unbelievers of the Jewish nation (Acts 5:28). It sometimes accompanied, even preceded, announcement of the gospel in missionary evangelism (see Acts 13:12; 17:19).

This body of doctrine was a treasure committed by the apostles to the next generation of believers. Paul, though he did not derive his message directly from any of the Twelve, nevertheless preserved the same methods and emphasis in regard to the instruction of Pauline churches. Therefore, typically a Pauline Epistle will devote the major first part to Christian doctrines and in the second turn to ethics and practices of Christian living.

In the Pastoral Epistles Paul instructs leaders of the churches to devote prior attention to this deposit of truth. These three letters (1 and 2 Tim. and Titus) are among the most conservative in tone of any literature. The last thing Paul or his corps of pastors wished to be was 'innovative' in their doctrines. They may have pioneered new methods of evangelism (though always through 'the foolishness of preaching' [1 Cor. 1:21 KJV]) but they thought of themselves as conservators of known truths not inventors of new ones.

---

4. I explain further the relevance of all the Old Testament to Christology in my book *The Life of Christ* (Grand Rapids: Baker Books, 1976, 1991), pp. 1–36. This book is now *The Earthly Career of Jesus, the Christ* (Fearn, Tain, Ross-shire, Scotland: Christian Focus Publ., 2002).

There is considerable evidence that the gist of doctrinal affirmation took on a fixed verbal form for liturgical recitation. Researches of C. H. Dodd a couple of generations ago promoted this understanding among many scholars. Whether the words were the same everywhere or not, in this early period of apostolic and Catholic Christianity, it was important to all the Fathers whose writings comment on the matter, that doctrines (what was believed, taught and confessed) be the same in every congregation. The Fathers inherited this outlook from the apostles, especially Paul whose speeches in Acts and exhortations in his Epistles show how great was his concern for uniformity of doctrines everywhere.

Paul besought the Corinthians all to 'speak the same thing... perfectly joined together in the same mind and in the same judgment'. There is but 'one faith', he said. The pastor's sermon was to contain only 'sound words', 'the trustworthy word... sound doctrine' and 'sound doctrine, in accordance with the glorious gospel of the blessed God'(1 Cor. 1:10 KJV; Eph. 4:5; 2 Tim. 1:13; Titus 1:9; 1 Tim. 1:10-11). These are some of the expressions demonstrating Paul's insistence on a uniform orthodoxy, perhaps even a standard verbal form or creed-like outline of doctrines, in the apostolic churches.

Such mandates for giving 'constant attention to the apostles' doctrine', that is, doctrines announced in the Old Testament, refined by Jesus, illuminated by the Spirit, enlarged by apostles, uniform in all the churches, would have been impossible to effect without a staff of exponents – teachers, elders – call them clergy if you like, educated for their vocation. The churches everywhere were in immediate need for the services of teachers who had mastered the body of doctrine received from the founders.

The notion that Christianity ever was for any extended period capable of maintaining itself as a 'wholly spiritual' movement bound together on spiritual, ethical and social principles only – without organization, having no recognized trained leadership and committed to no official teachings (only the word *dogma* seems to fit) – is impossible to maintain in light of the evidence. It certainly was not true of the early church. Even some Plymouth Brethren have conceded that not every new 'assembly' comes to birth with all the spiritual gifts and those gifted to be 'pastors and teachers'. Very late they have 'discovered' that their founding Fathers were all thoroughly educated and theologically trained Anglican clergymen.

If there were to be teachers who had mastered what Scripture, Jesus and the apostles taught, there had to be some programme of instruction. If so, then there were likely also recognized schools of theology. We know of several located in metropolitan churches, for example, in Caesarea, Antioch and Alexandria in the subapostolic age. How about schools for the training of pastors and teachers in Paul's time among the churches he founded? All the twelve apostles were graduates of the 'peripatetic' school of Jesus. Paul was a learned man already and mentions his private studies after conversion over several years (Gal. 1:18; see Acts 22:3; Phil. 3:4-6) before setting off on apostolic mission. He, himself, schooled his own missionary corps.

It should be expected that he would establish means of perpetuating a trained ministry to serve on after he was gone from earth – schools of theology – in any centre where Christians became numerous. Ephesus was such a place. It is close to certain Paul established such a school there. This is the significance some theologians and exegetes have found in 2 Timothy 2:1, 2: 'You then, my son, be strong in the grace that is in Christ Jesus. And the things you have heard me say in the presence of many witnesses entrust to reliable men who will also be qualified to teach others' (NIV).

I quote only two of several theologians who could be cited. Francis Pieper, a leading theologian for the Lutheran Church–Missouri Synod, wrote this summary statement, 'Timothy performed the work of a theological professor when he committed the things he had learned from the Apostle Paul "to faithful men who will be able to teach others also" (2 Tim. 2:2).' He quotes the Lutheran scholar Quenstedt on oral teaching by professors of theology to student ministers in theological schools. This text, he goes on to say, 'teaches and establishes the mysteries of the faith and refutes the errors contrary to sound doctrine more accurately and copiously, and is the province of bishops and preachers in the church'.[5]

A most convincing argument that this verse mandates a theological seminary in the ancient city of Ephesus was proposed by Alfred Plummer as now follows. I quote only certain leading statements from Plummer's comments on 2 Timothy 2:2 in *The Expositor's Bible, The Pastoral Epistles*:

---

5. Francis Pieper, *Christian Dogmatics vol. i* (St. Louis: Concordia Publ., 1950), p. 43.

> In this tenderly affectionate address we have a very early indication of the beginnings of Christian *tradition* and Christian *schools*, two subjects intimately connected with one another... He [Paul]... exhorts him [Timothy] to make proper provision for continuity of sound teaching in the church [Ephesus] committed to his care. In other words, before leaving his flock in order to visit his spiritual father and friend, he is to establish a school, – a school of picked scholars, intelligent enough to appreciate, and trustworthy enough to preserve, all that has been handed down from Christ and His Apostles respecting the essentials of the Christian faith... [the authentic and only gospel and *didachē*, Gal. 1:6-9].[6]

Plummer goes on to say that Christ in Matthew 28:19-20 'from the outset' commanded such provision for 'the tradition' and for 'Christian schools'. He further showed how 'experience has proved how entirely necessary such [schools] are' (p. 466). The doctrine and order of the churches tend to be only as sound as the sources (schools or otherwise) where their pastors receive their training.

Plummer wrote as a thoroughly informed orthodox Anglican. He was fully aware of the school of thought embodied in the Modernism of Adolph Harnack, which contended Paul had overthrown original Christianity, that continuity between Jesus' teachings and the doctrine of the second century church had been almost totally lost. This gives both importance and poignancy to Plummer's still fully revelant closing remarks on 2 Timothy 2:1-2, as follows:

> But what is certain respecting the earliest ages of the church is this, that in every Church regular instruction in the faith was given by persons in authority specially selected for this work, and frequent intercourse between Churches showed that the substance of the instruction given was in all cases the same, whether the form of the words was identical or not. These facts, which do not by any means stand alone, are conclusive against the hypothesis [Harnack's] that between the Crucifixion and the middle of the second century a complete revolution in the creed was effected; and the traditional belief of Christians is not that which Jesus of Nazareth taught, but a perversion of it which owes its origin mainly to the overwhelming influence of His professed follower, but virtual supplanter, Saul of Tarsus.[7]

In view then of the obvious importance of this text (2 Tim. 2:2), let us enlarge upon it.

Theological education for ministers is a very large undertaking. It is utterly reasonable that every seminary or department which intends to prepare pastors and missionaries will have some distinct features since its mandate, is distinct from all others. Let us therefore seek to understand in detail and as fully as possible what this, the only such text in the New Testament, has to say to the people who found or manage such schools and to tell students what they have a right to expect.

1. Mandate.

The mandate for a special theological school for the ministry is provided in Paul's 'Therefore' (KJV). He had been expressing concern for 'the pattern of the sound words that you have heard from me' throughout chapter 1 (see 2 Tim. 1:13) and was aware of a particular doctrinal peril from heresies originating in the very province (Asia) in which Ephesus was located. So this very practical Apostle has in mind two reasons for founding a school of theology. The primary one was *catechetical*, the necessity of thoroughly grounding the preachers in the doctrines of Christianity; the secondary one was *apologetical*, preparing the teacher to repel the perversions of aggressive promoters of error and heresy. There are therefore sound reasons to assume schools of Christian theology have existed from the very beginning and will of necessity always exist in some form or other for these same two reasons.

2. Subject Matter.

Nor are we without guidance as to the subject matter of a sound theological education. Timothy knew exactly what it was: the things that he had heard Paul say. As 2 Timothy 1:13 puts it, he was to 'Follow the pattern of the sound words that you have heard from me'. The content of teaching was to be a body of truth, elsewhere designated as 'teachings' (*didaskalia*), truths 'committed to... trust' imperiled by 'godless chatter and the opposing ideas of what is falsely called knowledge' (1 Tim. 6:20 NIV). No doubt Timothy knew something about inductive study and the methods of historical research, as anyone in a learned profession, but neither was particularly revelant to the heart of the Christian Theological Academy of Ephesus where Timothy served as dean. His assignment was faithful transmission

---

6. Alfred Plummer, The Pastoral Epistles. *The Expositor's Bible* (New York: A. C. Armstrong & Son, 1908), p. 466.
7. ibid., p. 469.

of truth already defined and made available to him through the Apostle Paul's oral instructions. He was not therefore directed to head up a research project – valuable as research in the present age of the world may be. Paul's *Ekousas* (aorist) 'what you have heard' sounds for all the world like listening to sermons and lectures and not at all like doing research and writing papers (again, valuable in a certain context). The origin and authority of these teachings in the Apostles, and ultimately from Christ, Himself, has been mentioned earlier and will demand extended attention again in connection with the doctrine of Holy Scripture.

3. Public Quality.

The public quality of these teachings is plain. Timothy had heard it *dia pollōn marturiōn*, 'among many witnesses' (KJV and ASV), 'before' (RSV), 'in the presence of' (NASB, NIV). The Greek preposition *dia* with the genitive, as here, ordinarily means 'through', though the translations give the necessary sense that what Paul had transmitted to a group, of which Timothy was a part, and has now become common property, is to be transmitted in similar public manner (church, classrooms, etc.) to another generation. Here is a sort of freedom of information statute for Christian doctrine. Though we do not ordinarily conduct our doctrine classes in the street (even a university setting is generally inappropriate), our lectures are open. Only the interested will come, but the information is not a *gnosticism* which only the initated may hear. Observers of all sorts may be admitted, though membership may be restricted to believers. Strictly to the point, tenets of the Christian religion have nothing in common with rituals and formulae of secret societies and mystery religions which only initiates and lodge members may know. Christ tells us not to cast our pearls before swine or give holy things to dogs, as it were, but truly interested people are neither intellectual nor spiritual swine and dogs. They are welcome to learn. This being true, no special jargon is strictly necessary to theology, however useful specific, technical terms may be. A good term, say 'Providence', may save a lot of time in discussion if everyone understands it. Such words – and there are many useful ones – are of value as they serve to conserve time, summarize or elucidate ideas, and promote clear communication of ideas. As mere marks of erudition they are useless and should be avoided. On the other hand, beginners must be both patient and industrious enough to learn the special terms as they come along. Anyone can master the ideas which they represent, given industry, a little time and spiritual inclination.

4. Pedagogical Method.

The pedagogical method is specified in 'entrust', or more exactly, *these things* (Gr. *tauta*) 'entrust to faithful men'.

The usefulness of scientific experiments, of data-gathering and inductive reasoning, in many areas of knowledge may not be questioned. There is a widely diffused notion that skills, techniques and special information basic to professions such as law, medicine, engineering and the like need not be mastered by those aspiring to be pastors and Christian teachers in the office of the ministry. Such thinking is contradictory to common sense, and here, contradictory to Scripture also. From the beginning there was a body of Christian doctrine to be learned. It was not going to be codified and organized for a long time into the future, but in seminal form it was all there, not to be researched, but mastered. The truths were to be *set before* or *put before* as food on a table. The Greek word is *paratithēmi*, also used of Jesus' setting His parables before the disciples (Matt. 13:24, 31).

5. Recipients.

The subjects, that is the ones instructed in the theological school, are 'faithful men' ('reliable men' NIV).

An important matter is present here. The word is not 'believing men' but 'faithful men'. The former would be *pisteuousi*; the latter (in the text before us) is *pistois*, dative plural of *pistos*, faithful.

Christian truths belong to all Christians, but not everyone is equipped by nature and the special gifts of the Holy Spirit to be a teacher. So the church needs to make provision that some be trained in order to be 'able to teach others also'. Paul's rhetorical question 'Are all teachers?' (1 Cor. 12:29) implies that *not* all are teachers. This is true in the home. Parents teach the children, not the other way around. Not every Christian is required to be a teacher of the Word. Only a small group *must* be 'able to teach' (1 Tim. 3:2, *didaktikon*, related to *didaskō* to teach), i.e. the bishop (=elder or pastor). It is therefore both lawful and wise that those admitted to this kind of education at church expense be approved ahead of time. Or if that is impractical, then at least, as Francis Pieper wrote: 'Therefore men must not be elected to the teaching office by lot or in any other haphazard way; only such may be chosen as possess the qualifications set down in 1 Tim. 3:1 ff; Titus 1:5-11, one of which is a special aptitude to teach [others].'[8]

6. Goal.

The goal of special theological education is that those so instructed be 'able to teach others also'. This is not, specifically, evangelism. Only by a very loose employment of language is it 'discipling'. If one wishes to speak exactly, disciples are not made by theological education, though certainly it is not irrelevant. Disciples of Christ are His confessed followers – i.e. *public* Christians. Ordinarily they become so by public baptism. Of course, the ones who are instructed and who are obedient are better disciples than those who are uninstructed and disobedient. The preparation of these men is in order to teach all the believers: 'able to teach others [other Christians] also'. There is a large body of Scripture information on the ministry of pastoral teaching. Let it await the proper locus in the doctrine of the church.

Every experienced preacher and teacher knows that there are several levels of theological teaching. The one appropriate for everyone at the same time is the sermon. Yet, as we should know, preaching good sermons takes extraordinary skill, especially when they must be delivered by the same minister one to three or four times a week to the same band of listeners, week after week, year in and year out.

The study of theology is therefore particularly important for ministers of the Word throughout their years of preaching and teaching. Since all believers are admonished by Scripture to deepen their understanding of divine things, the study of theology in a structured manner is appropriate for everyone. 'In fact, though by this time you ought to be teachers, you need someone to teach you the elementary truths of God's Word all over again. You need milk, not solid food! Anyone who lives on milk, being still an infant, is not acquainted with the teaching about righteousness. But solid food is for the mature, who by constant use have trained themselves to distinguish good from evil' (Heb. 5:12-14 NIV).

---

8. Pieper, *op. cit.*, p. 40.

2
Preliminary to Talk about God

The most striking statement in the whole Bible may be the first one: 'In the beginning, God created the heavens and the earth' (Gen. 1:1).

The Bible begins with talk about God. It also ends that way (Rev. 22:18-21).

There is no preliminary introduction to the leading person or 'idea'. God is simply encountered at the start. It is assumed those who hear the Bible read for the first time already have the idea of a person called God in their world of thought. God's name appears twenty-eight times in the first chapter – God did this or God said that – yet not a single sentence is devoted to identifying or defining Him. Nothing is said about where God came from or what He is like. Later in Scripture God is identified in contrast with other non-gods, which are regarded by mistaken people as real (Isa. 41:21-24; 44:6-17; 1 Cor. 8:4-6). There are a few very important statements about God's being (e.g. 'The LORD our God, the LORD is one') and some formal statements about His character (e.g. 'I the LORD... am a jealous God'). The clear position of the authors of Scripture is that people come to the Bible already knowing God exists. The burden of Scripture is to tell of God's dealings with mankind. In process, enough is disclosed about God and the world that it is quite correct to say Scripture tells us all we need to know about the One who is Creator, Savior and LORD and all we need to know of ourselves as well.

This spirit and outlook were shared by the Reformation Fathers who shaped the great creeds and confessions of the sixteenth and seventeenth centuries. Luther's *Small Catechism*, for the instruction of the children of believing parents, for example, begins: 'I believe that God has made me and all creatures.'[1] John Calvin, who after 400 years still informs most evangelical Protestant teachers, began the first (and archetypal) complete work of Protestant theology with the sentence: 'Nearly all the wisdom we possess, that is to say, true and sound wisdom, consists of two parts: the knowledge of God and of ourselves.'[2]

Most informed students of the Bible are convinced that people do not need to be told that God exists. We already know too painfully well He does exist. The Christian mission is, in part, to address this painful awareness, to clear up the garbled understanding of God with correct information and to relieve the conscience of its weight of guilt, provided, of course, that the 'good news' is received into the heart. To bring people true awareness of the

---

1. Dr Martin Luther, *Small Catechism* (St. Louis: Concordia Publ., ed. of 1943), p. 9.
2. John Calvin, *Institutes of the Christian Religion*, 2 vols., (Philadelphia: Westminster Press, 1960, I, 1.1.), p. 35.

living God lays them in the dust of despair. Like the Israelites before God's presence at Sinai (Exod. 19:16-20; Deut. 5:23-27; 18:16) and like that startled man in the Gospel (Luke 5:8), they are apt to cry: 'Depart from me, for I am a sinful man'. Or like Isaiah, they may exclaim: 'Woe is me! For I am lost; for I am a man of unclean lips, and I dwell in the midst of a people of unclean lips' (Isa. 6:5). According to the Apocalypse of John, everyone on earth – 'the kings of the earth and the great ones and the generals and the rich and the powerful, and everyone, slave and free' – finally shall be compelled to be present while God acts and to respond when He speaks. When that happens they will call to mountains and rocks, 'Fall on us and hide us from the face of him who is seated on the throne, and from the wrath of the Lamb' (Rev. 6:15, 16).

General Awareness of God.

But let us press the point of awareness of God among all humanity much further. Basic to all the preaching and exhortation of Scripture is the assumption that all people everywhere already know something about God. They are not unaware of their dependence upon Him or their accountability to Him. The book of Jonah furnishes a striking example. The Hebrew prophet, after obstinate delays, did finally preach his divinely imparted message in the great, pagan city of Nineveh. He cried, 'Yet forty days, and Nineveh shall be overthrown' (Jon. 3:4). Significantly, the narrative runs on: 'So the people of Nineveh believed God, and proclaimed a fast' (Jon. 3:5 KJV). Jonah obviously delivered no preliminary lectures on monotheism or biblical theism. There was already sufficient awareness of the one God even in Nineveh to produce understanding of Jonah's preachment.

When the word came to the king of Nineveh he joined in, announcing national repentance. 'Let everyone turn from his evil way… Who knows? God may turn and relent… so that we may not perish'? (Jon. 3:8-9). The pagan Ninevites evidently had a more exact understanding of divine truth as ground for evangelism than did the scripturally informed Jews of Jesus' time. For the LORD said, 'The men of Nineveh will rise up at the judgment with this generation and condemn it, for they repented at the preaching of Jonah, and behold, something greater than Jonah is here' (Luke 11:32).

This knowledge of God which sinful people have does not bring them pleasure and peace, for that knowledge is largely guilty knowledge. The prophets of Old Testament times relied on this guilty knowledge, even in heathen hearts, to rebuke their sins. Amos, for example, directed prophecies of judgment against five of the neighbour lands of Judah and Israel (Amos 1:1-2). God condemned Damascus for excessive violence in conduct of war (1:3), the Philistines of Gaza for unnecessary cruelty to a whole nation in time of war (1:6), Tyre for treaty-breaking (1:9), Edom for lack of fraternal feeling and murderous anger (1:11), Ammon for atrocities against the women of a conquered district (1:13), Moab for desecration of a neighbour people's cemetery (2:1). This last, against Moab, is very instructive, for no familiar verse in the Bible says one must respect others's graveyards. Yet people somehow know they should do so. Even though they may never have heard of God's covenant name, Jehovah, these people had some moral standards which they knew God would enforce.

On the other hand, even without the special aid of supernatural revelation, this knowledge has benefited mankind. It has improved our morals and put some restraint on our sins. Almost all of the world's best art has been creator-directed. Families have been moved by this dim awareness to dignify and beautify their homes. Parents seek the training of their children and improvement of their lives.

The Bible very quickly moves on to show that the 'creator of heaven and earth' is not some obscure principle or power. He is a certain Being who tolerates no rivals. Though there are many claimants to deity, there is but one being in the category of God. In the first chapter of the Bible God is called *Elohim* (El-o-heem). This is joined in chapter 2, with LORD to form the name LORD God or *YHWH Elohim*. The pronunciation of those four letters, rendered 'LORD' in our Bibles, will be discussed later. Several other names and name-like terms appear farther along in the Bible. But they all belong to Him that is true, 'The LORD our God, the LORD is one' (Deut. 6:4). The possible reasons for this variety of names, their meanings and significance for the doctrine of God, will be considered shortly.

Necessity and Importance of Worship of God.

A report of the earliest efforts of people to worship God is the immediate sequel of the narrative of creation and fall (Gen. 1–3). Such is the primary importance of the story of Cain and Abel (Gen. 4:1-15). Its relevance to doctrine is immediately apparent. No discussion of God's being, person or attributes precedes the story. Nor are there recorded instructions on time, manner and means of worship. The record simply states the first two men born into the fallen race were fully aware that God is and if God exists He may not be ignored, the way we have come to ignore so-called background music. If God the Creator exists (and we know He does) then man, the only visible rational creature on earth, must worship Him as also do the angels in heaven. The two sons of Eve knew this. We have no knowledge of how they came to have this information. Various explanations have been offered. But, know it they did. All generations of mankind since have known no less, however garbled and corrupted the knowledge may have become.

One God, Lost and Recovered.

Though, as we have seen, the first generations of humanity worshipped God (*Elohim*), when the narrative of redemptive history moves on to the call of Abraham that event is interpreted as a recovery from paganism. There is a certain reverence for the superiority of the religion and morality of people of Abram's origin over the Canaanites, among whom Abram and his descendants to the fourth generation dwelt for 215 years; they were nevertheless polytheists. Abram's obedience therefore involved something like a 'change of religion'. True, there were survivals of primitive monotheism (Melchizedek was priest of 'God Most High', Gen. 14) and Moses' father-in-law seems to have worshipped Him, yet passages such as Joshua 24:2 and Rachel's attachment to her father's teraphim, or household gods (Gen. 31:25-35), shows that their Aramean ancestral tribe were corrupted in some degree at least by polytheism.

This is not the place to discuss rival views of the religion of the ancient Semites from whom Abram took his origin. Nor is it the place to discuss to what degree his faith in the LORD (*YHWH*), who revealed Himself at the oak of Moreh (Gen. 12:6, 7) and whom he worshipped at Bethel (Gen. 12:8), was mixed with the false notions of Ur and Haran from which he came. The title of a once widely used book, *Hebrew Religion, Its Origin and Development* (*Oesterley and Robinson*) aptly phrases the subject, which continues to attract the interest of biblical scholars and archaeologists.

The Abrahamic (Hebrew) people became worshippers of the LORD God alone. The perfection of that new faith and its development is an emphasis of the rest of the Bible. It is appropriate now to show what the Bible itself has to say as to some of the specific means employed in divine providence to bring that to pass. What specifically convinced Abram to follow 'God Most High' and what means was employed to perpetuate that faith among his posterity?

We do not know what external means the divine Spirit employed to convince Abram belatedly to follow the initial call (Gen. 12:1-4; Heb. 11:8). We do know how God strengthened his faith, as reported in Genesis 12–25 and as interpreted by the New Testament (Rom. 4; Heb. 11).

Miracles, Prophecy and Biblical Monotheism.

Considering the utterly anti-supernatural spirit of the epoch in which we live one might wish to avoid the plain truth of the matter. Nevertheless, the biblical narrative from Genesis 12 to the end of Revelation employs what we call miracles and prophecy (in the sense of fulfilment of specific prediction) in showing how first the messengers of the LORD (Moses and the prophets) and then the people to whom they spoke came to be intellectually convinced of the LORD as the sole living and true God. Monotheism, as such, will be discussed later at greater length.

First we consider a striking exemplary case. In a time of national apostasy Elijah the Tishbite suddenly appeared before King Ahab announcing the beginning of a contest. It was to be between Jehovah (*YHWH*) and His prophet on the one hand and the fertility gods and goddesses of the Canaanite pantheon with their many so-called prophets on the other. The fascinating story composes 1 Kings, chapters 17 and 18.

The correct pronunciation of the covenant name of Israel's God is not known. Modern scholars have proposed the vowels **a** and **e** to accompany the *YHWH*, hence *Yah-weh*. There is an older, more Arabic-like pronunciation of Hebrew (Sephardic) as well as the presently preferred Eastern European (*Yiddish, Ashkenazic*). The traditional 'Jehovah' has the merit of centuries of use in English translations. I am not consistent in use of either *Jehovah* or *Yahweh*; I prefer usually to translate the name as LORD (all capitals) as in KJV, ASV, RSV and ESV.

The significance of it is pointed out near the end of Elijah's prayer and the people's response: 'Elijah the prophet came near and said, "O LORD God of Abraham, Isaac, and Israel, let it be known this day that you are God in Israel, and that I am your servant, and that I have done all these things at your word... that this people may know that you, O LORD, are God' (1 Kings 18:36, 37). Immediately the fire of God fell on the water-soaked sacrifice which Elijah had prepared and consumed it, together with the stones of the altar and the wood. Then, 'when all the people saw it, they fell on their faces and said, "The LORD, he is God" [*Jehovah* is the *Elohim*]' (1 Kings 18:39). This is not the only such contest reported in the Bible but it is certainly the most striking one. They are in the Scriptures to teach us. What do they teach? That God has demonstrated Himself to be true by the mighty acts of power which are performed at His messengers' word. In each case the messengers of God were authenticated by the same great acts of God's power. Other such incidents involving the prophets of ancient Israel are reported at 1 Kings 22 and notably at Jeremiah 28 (see also Ps. 106, esp. v. 12).

The contest of Elijah with the prophets of Baal has been mentioned first because it is such an outstanding example of the biblical method of demonstrating that the God of the Bible alone is God. God's action in omnipotence and omniscience (miracles and prophecy) are united in a remarkable way in Scripture.

It may come as a surprise to see just how thoroughly woven into the faith of ancient believers the use of prophecy and miracle really was. Let us look further in the Old Testament. Herein the Bible itself is telling why it *must* be believed. It addresses us with kinds of evidence all human beings must believe in if they are to be saved, the kind which will surely convince everyone at the end of life and at the judgment. These statements of evidence lying in the midst of narrative constitute the ancient 'apologetics' of the Bible, itself.

There is first the faith of the patriarchs. Abraham was told his wife would have a son through whom God's many promises to the family (Gen. 12:1-3; 15:14-16) would be fulfilled. When faith was weak (Gen. 18:10-12), Sarah being ninety years of age and Abraham one hundred, God promised them a son within the following year (Gen. 18:11-14). Within the year a son was born to them (Gen. 21:1, 2). Sarah had laughed in her doubt (Gen. 18:12) and, as if to rebuke her, Abraham named the child 'Laughter', for such is the meaning of the name, Isaac. Similar experiences were granted to Isaac, Jacob and especially to Joseph, as the stories of these men in the last half of Genesis report.

One may think of Moses as a veritable giant of faith and so he became, but he was not always so. When God first found him he was weak-kneed and vacillating (Exod. 3:11; 4:1, 10). The method of prophecy and miracle convinced him as it did others who heard of it. At the time of the 'burning bush' God told Moses his brother Aaron, then in Egypt far away, would meet him in the wilderness (Exod. 4:14, 27, 28); God said, 'this shall be the sign for you, that I have sent you: when you have brought the people out of Egypt, you shall serve [worship] God on this mountain' (Ex. 3:12). Both the prophecies were quickly fulfilled in detail (Exod. 19:1-25). These experiences were important parts of the enactment of the Mosaic covenant at Sinai, which in turn is the main part of the Pentateuch, the foundation of all biblical religion and written revelation.[3]

In one sense the ten plagues of Egypt and the remarkable dividing of the waters of the Red Sea were marvels of God's power. They were also each a marvel of divine omniscience – in each case a prediction fulfilled – of water turned to blood, lice, darkness, death of the first-born, etc. Each was fulfilled on schedule as announced by God's messengers, Moses and Aaron. Both the messengers and the God they claimed to represent were thus certified as genuine. This was 'apologetics' indeed! When this marvelous series of divine manifestations was over, climaxed by the Israelites' crossing of the Red Sea between walls of water, the drowning of the pursuing Egyptian army and its Pharaoh, just as Moses had predicted, there was not an Israelite who did not know in his heart that the LORD is God and Moses his servant: 'Israel saw the great power that the LORD used against the Egyptians, so the people feared [worshipped] the LORD, and they believed in the LORD and in his servant Moses' (Exod. 14:31).

Forty years later, with the migrating nation poised for the attack on Canaan, Moses was about to die. The new civil and military leader, Joshua, had already been selected. But there was no one yet to take Moses' place as God's messenger. At this juncture the aged lawgiver proclaimed the office of prophet, with a succession of men to fill it (Deut. 18:9-18). The several qualifications of the prophet need not concern us here, with one exception. There was a possibility of impostors. One of the means by which the impostor might be infallibly detected was his inability to predict the near future (Deut. 18:21, 22). These were not to be long-range prophecies of the remote future but short-range predictions that could be observed and tested by the people of the prophet's own time.

---

3. The covenant of the Law was miraculously confirmed at Sinai (=Horeb). The Old Testament historical books trace Israel's obedience and disobedience to the Law of the Pentateuch; the poetical books celebrate the Law; while the prophetical books report the prophets' efforts to rebuke disobedience of the Law and to encourage obedience to it. Jesus came to fulfil the law and to announce its successor covenant – which we have in the New Testament.

A prophet had to be an Israelite 'from among their brothers' (Deut. 18:15, 18); he spoke only in the name of Jehovah – 'in my name' (Deut 18:20); he must be able to predict near future events (Deut. 18:21, 22). Further he might be asked to perform a miracle (Deut. 13:1 ff.). But even if he met all these requirements the supposed prophet had to honour the one LORD God of Israel and his message had to be conformable to previously authenticated revelation from God, specifically the Mosaic covenant-law (Deut. 13:1-18). The utter seriousness of the matter is demonstrated by the extreme measures employed to enforce the rule. Deuteronomy 13 explains why later Elijah forthrightly demanded extermination of 500 prophets of Baal (1 Kings 18:40).

The last great prophet, the consummation of the line of the prophets, was our Lord Himself. There were others in the apostolic age who spoke by special divine revelation, but all these spoke by His authority and were but channels of His revelation. When Jesus came, He too was certified as a true messenger of God in the same way. The Jews asked for a sign of His authority, and He predicted His resurrection (Matt. 12:38-40; John 2:13-22). When John the Baptist wanted a sign that the Messiah stood before him, God let him know ahead of time that in some visible manner he would see the Spirit of God descending on the Messiah (John 1:33). When at Jesus' baptism John saw exactly that, fulfilled prophecy had again given its seal of certainty (John 1:29-32). When later, John the Baptist, from his cell in jail, asked for further assurance, Jesus only alluded to His fulfilment of ancient prophecies (Matt. 11:2-6; cf. Isa. 29:18; 35:5, 6; 61:1).

The most extensive evidential use of fulfilled prophecy in the Bible itself is in the portion of Isaiah which begins with chapter 40 and leads up to the marvelous prediction of our Lord's career in chapter 53. In this section the LORD God Himself is represented in contest with the impotent gods of paganism for human minds. The theme running through the passage, in part, is that the LORD alone is God for He alone can act. Among His mightiest acts is true prediction of the future. The entire section should be read at this point, but let us extract a few verses.

> Set forth your case, says the LORD; bring your proofs, says the King of Jacob.

Let them bring them, and tell us what is to happen. Tell us the former things, what they are, that we may consider them, that we may know their outcome or declare to us the things to come.

'Tell us what is to come hereafter, that we may know that you are gods; do good, or do harm, that we may be dismayed and terrified. [At least do something.] Behold, you are nothing and your work is less than nothing; an abomination is he who chooses you' (Isa. 41:21-24).

In this manner God demonstrates His magnificent solitary grandeur, showing that He alone is God – for He alone can either reconstruct the unknown or forgotten past, or predict the unknown future. In the same tenor, but even more emphatically, the LORD later says: 'I am God, and there is no other; I am God, and there is none like me, declaring the end from the beginning, and from ancient times things not yet done' (Isa. 46:9, 10).

Thus we have seen that from the very earliest times in the history of biblical revelation and redemption the fulfillment of prophecy has been a strong proof of the validity of God's own claims and the claims of His messengers. We have observed this in the assurance of the pre-Mosaic patriarchs, in the accreditation of Moses to the Israelites, in the support of the faith given to the Hebrews at the time of the Exodus, and from thence onward to New Testament times. The Messiah Himself and God His Father have placed their confidence in this mode of apologetical proof.

Validity of Apologetical Use of Fulfilled Prophecy.

Fulfilled prophecy, however, is only part of the base of biblical evidences. In fact, standing alone it would prove nothing except that some people in the history of the world have had a strange, inexplicable knowledge of the future. It is the connection of this supernatural power with the miracles of Scripture (i.e. those reported and authorized therein), the relation of both miracles and prophecy with the Jewish people and the claims of their prophets, apostles and Messiah, that makes the case for Christianity an infallible one.

Even so it must be remembered that even though God has declared the case a certain one, it is possible for us to deny it (Isa. 53:1-3; cf. John 12:37-41; Acts 3:1-4, 22, especially 4:13-18; Acts 17:30-32). The gospel will always remain foolishness to the minds of sinful people until the Holy Spirit enlightens them (1 Cor. 1:18; 2:14). The important thing for us to see in this connection is that if people fail at this point, the root of the failure is not in their *mental* faculties but in their *spiritual* ones: that their rejection is not based on *intellectual* obstacles but on *moral* ones. Their active resistance and arguments prove that they are vital and active mentally, but as to spiritual things are 'dead in… trespasses and sins' (Eph. 2:1-3; cf. 1 Cor. 2:14).

Sometimes people simply reject fulfillment of prophecy as impossible and, without bringing the 'case to court', refuse to examine the evidence. When the evidence is thrust upon them, various expedients are devised. In the case of people who endorse outright materialism or atheism, we must seek to convince them of the existence of a personal, transcendent creator-God. Until this is done, they will not even consider the evidence. Yet it must be admitted that the only conclusive proof of the existence of the Christian God lies in the miraculous deeds by which He has borne witness to Himself. The nature of the situation requires supernatural acts as proof. This, to use a technical phrase, is to say the rational arguments of natural theology are useful in that they may remove philosophical objections to the true Christian evidences. Fortunately, most people will at least consider the evidence. The average citizen, however this-worldly his interests, does not find it difficult to accept the possibility of the supernatural.

The common device for voiding the evidential value of biblical prophecies appears to have been invented in the third Christian century by a pagan philosopher named Porphyry (AD 233–304). This man was the most noted disciple of Plotinus, the father of the movement known as Neoplatonism, a system of thought which taught that the universe emanates out of God and that salvation is achieved by ascetic practices. St Augustine reports that Porphyry was brought up a Christian and after becoming apostate wrote against Christianity from a spirit of revenge. A very clever writer, Porphyry saw that if he could convince others that the predictions of the Old Testament, especially the detailed ones of the book of Daniel, were written after the events they predict had transpired, then he would have destroyed one of the main supports for their faith in the inspiration of Scripture and in Christianity. Little has been added to Porphyry's arguments (as far as they are known), though his method has become exceedingly popular among liberal higher critics.

Essential Features of Predictive Prophecy.

It must be recognized that prophecies of the sort under consideration will have some distinctive characteristics. They will not be mere sage remarks, or scientific prediction based on laws of nature. Neither will they reflect a humanly controlled situation wherein the prophet or his supporters fulfill the prophecy. They must be predictions of the future such as only God could know and bring to pass.

Another necessary feature is a degree of obscurity in many of the predictions. At first thought this might seem seriously to weaken the evidential value. Actually, it is the basis of its strength. The prophecy ordinarily will have a true but obscure reference to future events. Let us pursue this thought.

Jesus' predictions of His resurrection will serve as typical examples. In His prophecy of Matthew 12:40 He did not clearly say He would die, that His body would be buried, and that three days later His body would be resurrected, leaving a tomb empty. Rather He made an enigmatical reference to Jonah's experience in the 'great fish' and indicated that He would have a similar experience in the 'heart of the earth', i.e. underground. When He predicted the resurrection in connection with His cleansing of the temple (John 2:18, 19), He said, 'Destroy this temple, and in three days I will raise it up.' Actually, except for Jesus Himself, no one on earth really understood those predictions until after the resurrection and then only with considerable reflection (John 2:20, 21). When prophecy had become history, with reflection, it was then seen that our Lord was speaking of the resurrection, and that unmistakably (John 2:22). If this obscurity were not initially present, prophecy might actually produce either its non-fulfillment through the efforts of those who might wish to oppose it, or its evidential value might be destroyed by the bungling efforts of other too-helpful friends who would try to bring it to pass.

Thus, far from being a flaw in the evidence, this feature is one of the strengths of the evidence of fulfilled prophecy. It is like a case presented either by the prosecution or the defence in court when a true verdict is issued at the time of decision. As the case is being assembled, the pieces may seem difficult, disconnected and obscure. But once the truth is known, all fit a pattern. It is also like a disassembled jigsaw puzzle, which seems only dimly connected with a picture when lying in its box but assumes an unmistakable picture pattern when once it is assembled. The full design cannot be known till the pieces are put together. So the full design of prophecy, dimly seen at first, becomes clear with fulfillment.

The doctrine that God alone is God is nowhere spelled out more faithfully than by Paul in an exceedingly helpful passage. Let us lay some background. The common knowledge that God the mighty Maker does exist was important to the Greeks. This truth, however, had been perverted. The public religion of Greece was a gross, expensive, corrupting worship of many gods. At Corinth there was particularly offensive development of this feature of Greek culture. Idol worship got mixed up with the marketing of meat (the flesh of animals). It was hard even to buy a piece of fresh meat in the 'shambles' (butcher shop, 1 Cor. 10:25) that had not been previously offered to an idol. What should a Christian do? The believers there wanted to know. So Paul wrote, 'Therefore, as to the eating of food offered to idols, we know that "an idol has no real existence," and that "there is no God but one". For although there be so-called gods in heaven or on earth – as indeed there are many "gods" and many "lords" – yet for us there is one God, the Father, from whom are all things and for whom we exist, and one Lord, Jesus Christ, through whom are all things and through whom we exist' (1 Cor. 8:4-6). In view of the nonentity of gods other than the true God, Paul went on to say, the flesh of animals offered to an idol by someone else had not been harmfully affected. So the flesh could be bought in the market and eaten in all good conscience by a Christian. Idol-gods are nonentities. They cannot therefore do anything at all. The only God who acts is the God and Father of our Lord Jesus Christ.

In the following chapters our attention will be directed first to the vocabulary by which scholars discuss the subject of God and later to the names by which we may address or refer scripturally to the true and living God.

3
Special Terms of Talk about God

Through all the chapters of this book the discussion will necessarily employ a minimum of somewhat special vocabulary. Most of these terms and the ideas which they designate have been in use for centuries. If the reader already lives in a world of discourse where one is at home with theological vocabulary, fine. Unhappily, public education, now fully secularized, by simple omission of our religious culture, has about eliminated even simple theological vocabulary from discourse.

The godly wisdom of the Reformers of the sixteenth century rejected most of the ultra-refined vocabulary of late medieval scholastic philosophers and theologians. These denizens of the university faculties gave *formal* endorsement of the doctrine of grace, that is salvation from start to finish as a free gift. Most of them claimed to follow this doctrine as found in Augustine's expositions of Paul's Epistles and in his anti-Pelagian writings. Yet, following persistent streaks of *legalism* (salvation by keeping rules), *moralism* (salvation by being good), *sacerdotalism* (salvation mediated through sacred ceremonies) and accumulation of merit – all with some rootage in certain church Fathers – they mixed grace with human merit as necessary for salvation. These same philosopher-theologians created an ever-growing, never conclusive body of controversial theology – distinction after distinction, refinement after refinement – that continued up to Reformation times. In the vocabulary of this scholastic theology – petrified and perpetuated in canons of councils and decrees of popes – there are said to be innumerable kinds of faith and grace, justification and sanctification, for example. Sadly, in each distinction there was (and still is in Rome's theology) some affirmation that grace saves by enabling the Christian to accumulate merit for salvation.

The first line of Reformers – notably Luther, Melanchthon and Calvin – rejected the scholastic project of relating theology to any theory of the nature of substance (metaphysics), of epistemology (how knowledge is gained) or the status of universals, whether realism or nominalism, and the like.

The leading reformers were schooled in the learning of the day, hence well acquainted with late scholasticism, which in turn had as subject matter the philosophy-science of antiquity. They did not, however, interpret Scripture or teach theology as partisans in philosophical debate. Where some of the rich vocabulary of that learning was helpful, they used it, but only sparingly, taking care to explain. They addressed the multitudes of their time, not the university professors. Leaders of the Reformation wished to win the church people as well as the pastors and did so in plain language. Paul Althaus remarks: 'Luther recognizes the inner relationship and even identity of religious intellectualism and moralism. He shows that both are in opposition to the cross.'[1]

Melanchthon, author of the first Protestant manual of evangelical theology (1521), in the dedication of his book wrote:

> Rightly oriented teachers are needed, therefore, to clarify and preserve the proper meaning of the words of the prophets [O.T.] and apostles [N.T.]. And such true teachers do not invent new or peculiar doctrines about God; instead, they stay close to the unadulterated [*einigen*] meaning, which God himself revealed through the words which are found in the writings of the prophets and apostles and in the creeds.[2]

The creeds to which Melanchthon refers, contrary to what some unfriendly critics say, use technical terms sparingly and then only to make matters clear rather than obscure.

Calvin, in the Prefatory Address of the *Institutes*, addressed King Francis I of France, saying:

> I undertook this labor especially for our French countrymen, very many of whom I knew to be hungering and thirsting for Christ… The book [the *Institutes*] itself witnesses that this was my intention, adapted as it is to simple and, you may say, elementary form of teaching.[3]

The period of Protestant scholasticism (mainly seventeenth century) reverted somewhat to over-refinement, but since that time evangelical theologians have intended to produce a more chaste and limited special vocabulary of their specialty. As new or renewed controversies, errors and heresies have arisen, a few new terms of necessity have been borrowed or coined, and some ancient vocabulary has re-entered our discourse. Further, since philosophers also think and speak about God and some who write theology, if not philosophers, are acquainted with philosophy, some of the language of modern philosophy has been found useful.

The Bible itself furnishes most of the terms of theology and usually in such context as to be understood upon close attention. Some other terms have entered the discourse from writers critical of historic, orthodox understanding of the language of Scripture, the creeds and evangelical theology. We need to know these terms and the ideas behind them to relate our interpretation and proclamation to them.

At the end of this chapter, I propose some of the most important questions about God and His ways and hope to lead the reader into preliminary decisions about how those questions ought to be answered.

We shall discuss, firstly, the several uses of the word *theology* and modifications thereof. The most influential modern philosopher, Emmanuel Kant (1724–1804), made memorable and important a distinction between the world of *phenomena* and the world of *noumena*. This kind of distinction is at least as old as Aristotle (384–322 BC). Whether they know it or not, this distinction affects the manner in which people today, learned or not, understand all discussion of ultimate matters. Theology makes *ultimate concerns*, as Paul Tillich has taught us to say, its stock-in-trade. More recently, a distinction between *propositional* and *existential* truth has become so prevalent that one must decide early as to how to receive biblical statements about God. A very influential modern writer has introduced certain ideas about *ultimate concerns*, *essence*, *being*, *being in itself* that must be heeded if one is to read about the doctrine of God in anything other than purely Bible language. Notice must also be taken of the special use which theology makes of the words *apology* and *apologetics*. Then some more ancient questions must be raised – the relation of *faith* and *reason*, the meaning of *knowledge* when we say we have knowledge of God, and, finally, the meaning and relation of *anthropomorphism* to proper interpretation of the Bible.

Theology.

This word (Greek, *theos*, God, plus *logos*, science of a thing) and its modification, *theological*, is used in at least four distinct, somewhat technical, senses.

(1) The broadest signifies all techniques, training and information related to the Christian religion. Thus, we refer to a theological seminary, meaning a school that teaches a very broad scope of studies related to training for the Christian ministry. Sometimes *divinity* is employed as an approximate stand-in for this sense of the word theology. In former times, *divinity* was often employed rather than theology. It is in this sense John, author of the last book of the Bible, was called John the *Divine*, i.e. the theologian. This archaic use is perpetuated familiarly in Bachelor (or Master) of Divinity, the commonest theological seminary degrees.

---

1. Paul Althaus, *The Theology of Martin Luther* (Philadelphoa: Fortress Press, trans. Robert Schultz, 1966), p. 28.
2. Philipp Melanchthon, *Melanchthon on Christian Doctrine, Loci Communes*, 1555 (Grand Rapids: Baker Book, 1982, trans. Clyde L. Manschreck), p. xliii.
3. John Calvin, *The Institutes of the Christian Religion*, trans. F. L. Battles (Philadelphia: Westminster Press, vol i, 1960), p. 6.

(2) Theology is also a name for one of the four comprehensive areas within the theological seminary curriculum – biblical, historical, practical and theological. Here the word theology means the doctrines of Christianity – how they are formulated, their history in the church, their defence and organization.

(3) Still more narrowly, only the formulation and explanation of these doctrines is theology, that is, *systematic theology*. A single topic of doctrine is called a *locus* (plural *loci*). When arrangement of the topics is guided by the creed of a church, each creedal article is a *dogma*, hence a treatment of all the articles is *dogmatics*. Sometimes arrangement and treatment in creedal order is called *symbolics*, from 'symbol', an old word for a creed.

(4) Still more narrowly, a single topic of doctrine, the doctrine of God, His person, nature, attributes and works, is *theology proper*. Other doctrines (or *loci*) are mankind, sin, Christ, the church, last things and so on. This book falls particularly in the category of number three, the doctrines of Christianity, and the doctrine (*locus*) in particular now under consideration is God, that is, theology proper, the narrowest meaning of 'theology'. Study of the development of Christian doctrines through the Christian centuries is called *historical theology*.

Biblical Theology.

Biblical theology is an expression whose meaning is determined by the context in which it is used. Most generally, (a) In a non-technical sense, it simply means teachings derived from the Bible. (b) In a more special sense biblical theology is a discipline, or approach to discovering the message of the Bible. In controversies about doctrine, biblical theology is sometimes exalted in contrast with 'proof-texting', church dogmas and merely traditional interpretations of the Bible, as opposed to judging dogmas and opinions by careful interpretation of Scripture in context. (c) As a method of study, biblical theology 'seeks to discover what the Biblical writers, under divine guidance, believed, described and taught in the context of their own times'.[4] All this is for the good of sound theological expression. However, biblical theology (like Christian education and 'biblical counselling') is also the name of a recent movement with specific agenda. It produced several scholarly journals and a large literature and, though now diminished, has not fully run its course.[5] As a method it has been productive of great gains in modifying some merely inherited views of God and His ways with the world and mankind. As a movement largely in the hands of less than thoroughly faithful exponents of evangelical theology, it has drawn its world-view from worldly, elite academic cultures and plagued sound theological enterprise with unrelenting attack to the present moment.[6]

Phenomena and Noumena.

We meet the former, plural of phenomenon, in science classes, though not 'noumena'. These two terms draw distinction between the world where persons, things and events are observed by the five senses and the world of the supposedly real lying behind them. Idealistic philosophy – Christian and otherwise – affirms that whatever factuality or reality there is in the sensible, the basis of the sensible is not sensible. It is the invisible, intangible, inaudible, ineffable. There is an element of biblical truth in this. Paul expressed it succinctly: 'we look not to the things that are seen [sensed] but to the things that are unseen. For the things that are seen are transient, but the things that are unseen are eternal' (2 Cor. 4:18).

Emmanuel Kant (1724–1804) and his disciples wish to convince us that nothing of the unseen world of the *noumenal*, the unseen world of the truly real, can be known certainly by human beings. All we know are *phenomena*. Yet the Scripture quoted above does not say that. The difficulty of sensing the unseen is there quite clearly conveyed. Nothing elsewhere in the Bible tells us that the invisible God is not conveying – however dimly – certainties about unseen, eternal things (life, God, spirit, heaven, hell, angels) through the messages of prophets and their enscriptured words. Nor are the mighty works of God such as creation, miracles, preservation of the universe and the like, impossible for God to tell us about. He has, indeed, told us about them in the Bible and in many ways they speak for themselves (Ps. 19; Rom. 10). The Son of God, who was and is God and was eternally with God, became flesh so that people beheld God's glory in Him. Certain witnesses of His life and career wrote down what they saw and heard and we can read it (John 1:1, 14, 15).

---

4. Robert W. Yarbrough, *Evangelical Dictionary of Biblical Theology*, ed. Walter A. Elwell (Grand Rapids: Baker Books, 1996), p. 61.
5. As evidence, Baker Book House saw fit to follow their *Evangelical Dictionary of Theology* (1984) with *Evangelical Dictionary of Biblical Theology* (1996).
6. See note 15 in Dr. Yarbrough's article (footnote 4 above).

Kant was responding to the empirical philosophy of John Locke (1602–1704), Bishop George Berkeley (1685–1753) and its consummate expression in David Hume (1711–1776). The agnosticism of some of these philosophers comes up later for attention in a later chapter.

The Special Vocabulary of Neo-orthodoxy.

Certain words and expressions are peculiar to a group of thinkers who have come to be called 'neo-orthodox'. The early advocates most influential in North America were Emil Brunner, Paul Tillich and Karl Barth. All three wrote in German but their writings were rather quickly translated into English and avidly read in liberal circles first, and later in all religious circles, Protestant, Orthodox and Catholic. Among these philosopher-theologians, a *proposition* is a statement of fact; a proposition employs language to pass on a datum of truth. Relying heavily (though not entirely) on the distinction between *phenomena* and *noumena* and the epistemology of empiricism it is held that all eternal, divine facts lie in the world of the *eschatological*. By this is meant supernatural (emphasis on *super*), though the word 'supernatural' is not often employed. The eschatological cannot enter the space-time world (Kant's *Phenomena*) without destroying itself, they say. Nevertheless, it can be known in the *event* or *Krisis* (=crisis) of *personal encounter* between God and men. These are always *I-thou* encounters (also called confrontations), never *I-He*. That is to say, the experiences are true confrontations with the person, God, not discourses about God by a third party, say an angel or a prophet. Though the encounters may be reported, there is no propositional content, there are no data to report about the eschatological. So the Bible may not be read to collect data about God. Let us pursue this matter briefly.

Emil Brunner wrote with disciplined brevity and readable clarity. Hence I cite his view of truth and the vocabulary of his theology of truth. He stated his developed views in a book translated into English as *Reason and Revelation*.[7] Shortly afterward, he summarized that book in the first chapter of the first volume of his *Dogmatics*. I cite the chapter. Biblical revelation – truth about God – cannot be expressed as an abstract idea. Even in the *revelations witnessed* to by (and in) the Bible God is both concealed and *disclosed*. *Truth* about God is always *personal*, *experienced* as an *encounter*. The abstract concepts in traditional theology – with an infallible Bible for Protestants and an infallible pope for Roman Catholics – are equally reliant on Greek ideas imposed by the framers of the early creeds. After asserting at length the Bible itself contains no revelation, only several sorts of *witness to revelation(s)* about *primal history*, The incarnation is a major example, apostolic and prophetic experiences are other such *events*. Dr Brunner summarizes:

> [R]evelation is certainly not a 'Something', a 'thing'; but a *process*, an *event* which *happens to us* and *in us*. Neither the prophetic word of the Old Testament, nor Jesus Christ, nor the witness of the Apostles, nor of the preachers of the Church who proclaim Him, 'is' the *revelation*; the reality of the revelation culminates in the 'subject' who receives it... If there is no faith, then the revelation has not been consummated: it has not actually happened... but is only at the first stage. All objective forms of revelation need the 'subject' in whom they become revelation. The Bible itself calls this inward process [not the matter made a matter of record] 'revelation'.[8]

What Brunner denominates 'revelation', the Bible really calls enlightenment or illumination and theology 'the inward testimony of the Holy Spirit'. All italicized words in the above quotation are my emphasis as characteristic ideas and terms of neo-orthodoxy which have passed into almost all recent theological discourse. Barth used most of them, though he likes the word *Krisis* (= crisis) for the event of 'revelation'.

Every Bible reader knows that there are indeed reports of personal meetings with God in the Bible. But contrary to the above notions, while the element of the unreportable and incommunicable is often present (Isa. 6; Ezek. 1–3; Acts 7; Rev. 1–22; and especially 2 Cor. 12:1-4 are examples), the people who had these experiences frequently report words heard and sights seen. These words and sights (visions) are not presented as a meeting of God 'in Himself' or of 'reality in itself' (*der Ding am sich* of Kant) or of the eternal heavenly world, but they are represented as valid, true (though partial) insights. They pass on to us, through the Bible, true knowledge of eternal things. Where some of the experience is incommunicable, the Scripture author plainly says so (see 2 Cor. 12:1-4 ASV, NASB, RSV). The later Bible authors plainly obtained their basic knowledge of divine things from the earlier writers of Scripture and sometimes plainly say so. Some of their knowledge obtained by reading Scripture already in existence

---

7. *Reason and Revelation*, trans. Olive Wyon, (Philadelphia: Westminster Press, 1946).
8. Emil Brunner, The Christian Doctrine of God, vol. I (Philadelphia: Westminster Press, 1974), p. 19. Note: he is summarizing Offenbarung and Vernurft, pp. 134–161.

was measurable – or quantifiable, as the current idiom has it – information. Daniel, for example, knew what the length of the servitude of the Jews to the king of Babylon was to be by reading the prophetic writings of Jeremiah (Dan. 9:2; cf. Jer. 29:10; 2 Chr. 36:20-23; Ezra 1:1, 2).

Even the neo-orthodox theologians, whose ideas we have just reported, like to use the Bible to support their teachings. Some even try to discover their teachings in the Bible. Therefore, despite their special views, they seem often to use the Bible the same way the rest of us do.

Another group of terms, often quite helpful in stripping down a problem to its true dimensions, derives from the writings of the late Paul Tillich, a philosopher-theologian, though hardly a biblical one. His definition of religion and the religious as a matter of *ultimate concern* is perceptive and once a Christian thinker gets a hold on the term he will almost inevitably begin to use it. Tillich's ideas about God and revelation, that God is *being in itself,* and of *being* as essentially unknowable are variant names for another variety of *Krisis* theology (another name for neo-orthodoxy) and of Kantian philosophy just stated above. We shall have opportunity to meet Tillich's philosophy of religion later.

Apologetics.

Apologetics designates a certain area of study associated with systematic theology. Specifically, apologetics is the division of theology that rationally answers attacks upon Christianity. In doing so, it seeks to establish the truth of the Christian faith by various forensic methods and evidences. There is some intramural debate among apologists as to the usefulness of evidences and arguments. Not all scholars will agree on a definition, but it is important to know that when the word 'apologetic' or 'apologetics' appears in theological writing it designates positive, aggressive action. Apologetics seeks to meet the enemy and to defeat him at his point of attack. This is apology in the original sense, not an admission of fault with a request for pardon as now, in common speech. The Greek word is translated 'an answer' (Gr. *apologian*) at 1 Peter 3:15 NIV.

In a broad sense 'apologetics' is sometimes (confusingly) applied to all the philosophical extensions of theology (philosophy of religion, or philosophy of Christianity): also to the study of evidences of Christianity and the way Christian truth may relate to Christian culture.

Special Questions in Talk about God.

(1) Faith and Reason.

These are terms we shall meet, sometimes in association. Are they friends or enemies? Fortunately, these words should mean about the same in religious discussion as in any other. They are often introduced as if they were incompatible. It is commonly supposed that faith represents one way of knowing God and reason another. In such a case, the former is biblical and Christian while the latter is Greek and pagan. But this is to have a defective understanding both of reason and faith. Actually, in biblical thought, each has to do with *response* to knowledge, whether imparted by divine revelation or otherwise. Some authors have even juxtaposed *reason* and *revelation* as competitors, as if the former were allied with false religion and the latter with true biblical religion. Again, faulty understanding of biblical ways of looking at things is the root of difficulty. In Scripture, faith is not the source of our knowledge of things of God or of anything else. 'Natural light' (see below) and divine revelation are the sources. Reason (rational faculties, processes, categories, terms) furnishes the organization of those truths too. Nothing else can associate the revealed data (God is all-powerful and is all-knowing, are examples) and the experimental facts reported (Christ arose) into knowing relation. Therefore, faith and reason are twins, not enemies. Of course, if one does not use faith in response to God's Word, then our reason will oppose both God and His Word. That, however, is non-faith and reason falsely employed. True faith and sound reason are still steadfast friends. The Bible does not even hint that one must be unreasonable in order to believe God's Word.

This matter requires some enlargement. Systematic theology is a scientific enterprise. The Bible presents truths in the form of facts and ideas, but it does not follow any historical system of logic. Although there is progress in divine revelation there is also unity of truth; it is a system of truth even though a growing system of which the several parts are always organically connected. Those who know the Bible and believe it to be true will inevitably seek to bring these truths into systematic logical relation with one another. This is both necessary and feasible, for truth is in harmony with itself. Again, to cite Robert Yarbrough:

While contrasts and tensions exist within the biblical corpus due to the local and temporal soil from which its components first sprang, a solidarity underlies them. This solidarity is grounded in the oneness of God's identity and redemptive plan. It is also rooted in humankind's sinful solidarity in the wake of Adam's fall. Scripture's undeniable diversity, commonly overplayed in current critical discussion, complements rather than obliterates its profound unity. Scripture is its own best interpreter, and uncertainties raised by one portion are often legitimately settled by appeal to another.[9]

The theologians' task is therefore, 'to think God's thoughts after him under the guidance of the Holy Spirit, to assimilate comprehensively the truth revealed in the word of God and to reproduce it logically in systematic form'. Speculative reason is not a source or norm of theological truth. Rather the rational faculties of the theologian function to unite 'particular ideas and facts contained in the Word of God' and to organize them into a coherent system of truth. Reason should not be committed to function independent of faith. In theology faith corresponds with the revealed knowledge of God and serves as a necessary instrument for appropriating divine truth. To summarize: faith appropriates revealed truth, reason organizes and systematizes it.[10]

(2) Can Mere Men Truly Know God?

The *knowledge of God* is another idea that needs explanation before extended study of God's being, attributes, works and relations. If by knowledge of God one means exact information about measurable data relating to the wholly spiritual being of eternal, infinite God, no one can possess it. Yet we observe, upon reflection, that in a measure the same is true of one's knowledge of all persons. I scarcely know my own wife or my children in this way. Our bodies, our voices, our tastes vary from day to day and they change permanently with age. Yet we know the persons we meet. We have acquaintance with the ones we 'know' intimately. It is instructive to observe that the first reported act of sexual intercourse in Scripture – about as intimate a form of acquaintance between persons as it is humanly possible – is reported as a knowing: 'And Adam knew Eve his wife, and she conceived, and bare Cain' (Gen 4:1 KJV). Of course we never tangibly encounter God's being any more than we touch one another's being, but we can have acquaintance with them as they manifest themselves.

The division of philosophy known as epistemology would like to claim jurisdiction over the subject of knowing other persons. In real life, however, we yield neither to philosophy nor science. If life is to go on we must assume that on the level of our present earthly existence the way most things appear to be has essential correspondence to the way they really are. Neither science nor philosophy interferes with the kind of knowing involved in a lover's kiss. Science might propose some ingenious contraption to gauge temperature of skin surfaces, others to measure fluctuation in heartbeat, blood pressure, and skin surface pressure; but all to no avail if the goal is to know what a lover's kiss really is. This is known only by lovers who kiss – and they (one must acknowledge) only experientially. They throw themselves into the action heartily and learn what they need to know. They may have had wise guidance beforehand and (we hope) carry that successfully into the embrace, but they will not have any help from the science and philosophy professors. (My students in college courses in philosophy of religion always listened raptly to this illustrative example.)

(3) How Do We Learn about God?

The answer is, by *'natural light'* and by *revelation*. I put one of the terms in quotation marks because almost no one uses it any longer. Recent writers like to refer to the knowledge of God gained through the things which He has made – particularly the material creation and the nature of humanity – as general revelation. This sort of information used to be called 'natural light' and sometimes 'the light of reason'. The latter is a good descriptive term since our rational powers, reflecting upon experiential information, are a way of gaining this knowledge of God. *Revelation*, in this older manner of speaking, refers to the act of God in making Himself known in some supernatural way. In recent times, however – and the result is partial confusion – both methods have been called revelation. The former, as we have observed, then is called *general* revelation and the latter *special* revelation. We must of course come to terms with the newer way of speaking. There is less confusion in the older works wherein

---

9. Yarbrough, *op. cit.*, p. 62.
10. This paragraph is part quotation and part paraphrase of the article on Louis Berkhof by Henry Zwaanstra in *Reformed Theology in America: A History of Its Modern Development*, ed. David F. Wells (Grand Rapids: Baker Books, 1997), p. 147.

revelation was usually reserved for what people know of God by His gracious supernatural acts of self-disclosure, and another designation was used for what people know apart from God's special gracious supernatural acts. In a later chapter we discuss the several ways by which God has made Himself known to us.

Anthropomorphism.

This word, from Gr. *anthrōpos*, mankind, a man, and *morphē*, a form, means literally, man-form-ism and signifies the representation of God in speech, or writing in the form of a human being. Under this general heading three different, but related, features of human efforts to represent deity may be distinguished: (1) When God's activity is expressed in the form of analogy with human activity this might properly be called *an-thro-po-poi-ē-sis* (man-action). 'All the ways of a man are pure in his own eyes, but the LORD weighs the spirit' (Prov. 16:2) is an example. God's act of distinguishing good and evil in human beings is said to be *weighing*, as in a pharmacist's scale. (2) When the impassible God, whose Spirit cannot be disturbed by anything, responds to events in a manner comparable to human passion and He is said to be glad, sad, angry, etc., the figure of speech is properly called *an-thro-po-path-ism* (man-passion). 'And the LORD was sorry that he had made man on the earth, and it grieved him to his heart' (Gen. 6:6) is a clear example. (3) When God is represented as having bodily parts like ours – eyes, ears, nostrils, arms, hands – the literary device is called *an-thro-po-morph-ism*. So in the broad sense anthropomorphism includes anthropopoiesis and anthropopathism as well as anthropomorphism proper.

'Anthropomorhism' has been used to designate a proper, biblical representation of God and also a wholly improper, even corrupt, manner of representing deity. So some further distinctions must carefully be made.

The Proper Employment of Anthropomorphism.

There have been (and no doubt are) philosophers and theologians who deny it, but most have agreed that all formulated knowledge about God is analogical. This is to say that when one makes a declarative statement about God's person, essence or nature – such as 'you hate all evildoers' (Ps. 5:5) or 'The Lord is compassionate and merciful' (Jas. 5:11) – these statements are meaningful only because we know something of what hate and mercy are in ourselves and other people. Even when speaking of hate and mercy in other people or in hearing about them, one automatically imputes to the other person, in some degree or an other, what we know to be hate and mercy in ourselves. This is to say that all knowledge, thoughts, emotions and character of other persons are analogical. There is no possibility of direct sensation of personality in others. I, for example, hear my secretary laugh, but I have no direct sensation of her joy. Yet, I know how I feel when I want to laugh joyfully and assume analogically that the same sort of thing produces her laughter. It must be acknowledged, however, that *analogically* perceived knowledge is not perfect. It may, for example, be distorted by distorted self-knowledge. The Psalmists frequently prayed for clearer vision of the self (e.g. Ps. 19:12, 'Who can discern his errors? Declare me innocent from hidden faults'). We all make serious mistakes in judging the motives (character, person, self-hood) which produce what other people do and say. We even misjudge our own motives sometimes. So the existentialist theologians (especially Paul Tillich) are not entirely wrong in their ideas regarding revelation about God; they only carry too far what the Bible itself and all the orthodox theologians have affirmed. We do have knowledge of God which is true; it is possible correctly to formulate it in declarative sentences; it is proper to memorize affirmations such as, 'God is that infinite and perfect spirit in whom all things have their source, support and end', or 'There is but one only living and true God, who is infinite in being and perfection, a most pure spirit, invisible... almighty; most wise, most holy, most free'.[11] Yet we must constantly remind ourselves that all these words have their meaning shaped by our own inner and outer experience and that the gulf between Creator and creature separates us from Him who alone is true God. Except for the dim light of nature, which tells all people that God is mighty, glorious (Ps. 19:1-5; Rom. 1:20) and that we are responsible to Him for what we do of right or wrong (Rom. 2:14, 15), natural men know very little of God. Our proposed analogies lead us astray. We suppose God's justice is feeble like our own, that God's love is sentimental like our own.

Thus we understand that the image of God in mankind (Gen. 1:26-27) makes a degree of analogy (anthropomorphism) in our thoughts about God as man-like quite proper. However, until the moral likeness is restored in regeneration, such analogies may lead to grievous error – as in all representation of the invisible God by

---

11. *The Westminster Confession of Faith*, Chap. II, 'Of God, and of the Holy Trinity'.

images to be worshipped. Our understanding will be undistorted fully, only when sanctification and glorification are complete, whereupon we shall enjoy some degree of direct vision, the *beatific* vision contemplated by the medieval mystics, for 'we shall see him as he is' (1 John 3:2).

Meanwhile, in the very broadest sense, all affirmations about God are anthropomorphic.

More specifically, the Bible employs the three figures of speech, previously noted, all falling under the common category of anthropomorphism in speaking of God. Let us enlarge on this matter.

1. Anthropopoiesis.

This concerns divine actions analogous to human actions, as in 'God said, "Let there be light"' (Gen. 1:3). That sentence is in Hebrew, a language that came into existence ages after the initial creation on the first day of the creative week. Did the pre-incarnate Logos communicate with the Father in audible speech? If so, how, for God has none of the bodily parts (lips, teeth, tongue, palate, etc. employed in human speech)? This declaration is anthropomorphic. God decreed the existence of light but did not speak the Hebrew words, *ye-hi* (let there be) *'or* (light). (The Hebrew language in which the first chapter of Genesis was written did not exist at the creation.) 'God… breathed into his nostrils the breath of life, and the man became a living creature' (Gen. 2:7). God, of course, conferred life upon human beings, life of a special sort like His own divine life in some important respect (personal, self-conscious), but God has no lungs, ribcage or nasal passages for breathing. The statement of what God did is *anthropopoietic*. 'And the LORD came down to see the city and the tower' (Gen. 11:5). The omnipresent Creator and imminent Sustainer of the heaven and earth made no intergalactic journey. He did devote, however, some special attention (another anthropomorphic statement) to what was happening on the plains of Shinar (Gen. 11:2). There are many examples of this throughout the Bible.

A special class of events called *theophany*, by theological writers, must not be placed in the category of anthropomorphism. The divine spirit, usually interpreted as the pre-incarnate *Logos* (John 1:1-3), sometimes assumed a *temporary* human form, visible to people, and held converse and social intercourse with them. Examples are the three men who visited Abraham in the plains of Mamre (Gen. 18:1-33) and the 'man of God' (Judg. 13:6) who appeared to Manoah and his wife, parents of Samson (Judg. 13:2-25). The record even quotes Samson's mother as saying, 'we have seen God' (v. 22). These theophanies seem all to have been appearances of the Second Person of the Trinity.[12] R. Laird Harris is therefore correct when he affirms: 'Such anthropomorphisms are to be distinguished from the appearance of God in human form to Abraham as he sat at his tent door in Mamre. The divine appearance in human form is called a theophany and is not a figure of speech.'[13]

2. Anthropopathism.

Not all theologians have consented to say God is impassible, i.e, 'incapable of suffering; inaccessible to harm' (*Webster's Unabridged Dictionary*), but it must surely be affirmed that God's inner, conscious essence is always undisturbed and unruffled by anything He has created.[14] Yet the Scriptures find in the Godhead that which is called emotion in human beings – love, hate, joy, grief, repentance and the like.

> Such [passages] as speak of his repenting and grieving, Gen. 6:6, 7; Jer. 15:6; Ps. 95:10; of his being jealous, Deut. 19:20, etc. represent the truth with respect to God only analogically, and as seen from our point of view… When he is said to repent, or to be grieved, or to be jealous, it is only meant that *he acts toward us as a man would when agitated by such passions* [emphasis added]. These metaphors occur principally in the OT, and in highly rhetorical passages of the poetical and prophetical books.[15]

Many of these anthropopathisms seemed crude to the translators of the Septuagint (ancient Greek translation from about the fourth to second centuries BC) and were rendered by expressions they thought more elegant. Many modern vernacular Versions likewise remove these 'crude' expressions. For example, 'the anger of the LORD was kindled against Moses' (Exod. 4:14) is in Hebrew, 'the nostrils of the LORD burned'. A word for heat, poison, fury, rage is used by Moses in Psalm 90:7 of the *feelings* of God in inflicting death on all the 'children of man'. The picture conveyed in Hebrew is of virulent, passionate temper out of control. 'And the LORD was sorry that he had

---

12. See summary of evidences, A. A. Hodge, *Outlines of Theology* (Grand Rapids: Eerdmans, 1860, 1957), pp. 169–172,
13. R. Laird Harris in *Zondervan Pictorial Encyclopedia of the Bible*, vol. i (Grand Rapids: Eerdmans, 1975), p. 177.
14. See A. H. Strong's discussion in *Systematic Theology* (Old Tappan, NJ: Revell, 1907), pp. 266–268.
15. A. A. Hodge, *op. cit.* p. 132.

made man on the earth, and it grieved him to his heart' (Gen. 6:6) furnishes two vivid examples of the metaphor, anthropopathism. 'Was sorry' ('repented' KJV) is *naḥam*, frequently used in the sense of being sorry for something one has done and has that meaning here. This cannot be literally true of God, who makes no mistakes, works all things after the counsel of His own will and 'doeth all things well'. God knew exactly what He was doing when in His eternal counsels He decreed the permission of sin. But the metaphor helps us understand what God *did* when He brought the Flood. Similarly 'grieved' is a word which in simple degree (*qal*) means to hurt someone or to cause pain, but here, in intensive reflexive degree (*hithpael*), means to have vexation, as in the case of the sons of Jacob, when they learned that Shechem had seduced or raped their sister, Dinah (Gen. 34:7). Again, God has no inner disturbances of spirit, such as those none-too-innocent brothers experienced, but the metaphor helps us understand God's action in saving Noah's clan and destroying all of mankind in the Flood (Gen. 6:6). When God became incarnate in Jesus of Nazareth (the divine nature being joined in indissoluble union with the human nature), affirmations about divine suffering, rejoicing, grieving, hating, etc., all became less metaphorical. Though one of the lesser benefits of the incarnation (Heb. 2:9-18; 4:14-16), it is very comforting to believers as we face the crisis of physical death. Yet let us not forget that Patripassionism, the doctrine that the Father lived, suffered and died in Jesus Christ (Modalistic Monarchianism), was one of the earliest Christian heresies to be condemned by the church.

3. Anthropomorphism Proper.

Anthropomorphism proper assigns God the bodily parts and organs of a man in order to convey ideas of His person and action. These are numerous in all parts of the Bible, but like anthropopathism, especially numerous in Old Testament poetry and prophecy. God's power is referred to analogically as His arms or hands, His knowledge as His eyes, His response to prayer as His ear, His pleasure (an anthropopathetic term) as His nostrils. This metaphorical manner of speech is prevalent in Hebrew sentences about almost any subject – the power of the patriarch Joseph's tribe in war, for example, is said to be 'the arms of his hands' (Gen. 49:24 KJV). Every reader of the Bible in the Authorized Version of 1611 is familiar with this kind of anthropomorphism, because a large number of figures of all kinds are literally rendered into plain English. God's eyes thus stand for sympathetic acceptance (Gen. 6:8; 34:11), His supportive attention (Deut. 11:12), God's moral judgment (Deut. 32:10), His omniscience and benevolence (2 Chr. 16:9). God's ear as a metaphor for His response to all genuine human prayers is found at least a dozen times in the Psalms (10:17; 17:6; 18:6; etc.). Several very meaningful anthropomorphisms appear in Isaiah's memorable appeal to backslidden Israel: 'Behold, the LORD's *hand* is not shortened, that it cannot save, or his *ear* dull, that it cannot hear; but your iniquities have made a separation between you and your God, and your sins have hidden his *face* from you' (Isa. 59:1, 2 emphasis added).

It is instructive, to some amusing, that the bodily-parts metaphor sometimes is carried to the point of sub-human creatures. Thus Boaz spoke of Ruth the Moabitess as now trusting under *the wings* of the LORD God of Israel (Ruth 2:12); and a Psalm naively asserts that God 'will cover thee with his *feathers*' (Ps. 91:4 KJV); and once God, Himself, speaks of bearing the Israelites on 'eagles' wings' (Exod. 19:4). Yet these *metaphors* must be understood no less purely symbolically than the *simile* of Deuteronomy 32:11, 12: 'Like an eagle stirs up its nest, that flutters over its young, spreading out its wings, catching them, bearing them on its pinions, the LORD alone guided him [Jacob]'.

4. The Names of God.

Scripture uses few generic words for deity. In the Old Testament there are ten names traditionally considered as the chief ones. There are also numerous adjectives, such as 'The Merciful' or The One who does this or that. Upon reflection; every one of these names is an anthropomorphism – God seen man-wise. How else could we mere people talk about Him? This is most obvious in names such as Father, or Rock. Yet as we shall see even 'the most High' and *Adonai* (Lord) are anthropomorphic.

5. The Attributes of God.

Man was made the image and likeness of God. Scripture not only says man is in that image, it says also man *is* the image of God. The moral attributes scripture ascribes to God are without exception such excellencies as we have, partial and limited as creatures, defaced and spoiled as sinners. This will be discussed again in connection with the names of God and the attributes of God.

The Improper Employment of Anthropomorphisms.

Certain modern philosophers have asserted that none of our statements about God as a person or spirit, and as having personal, spiritual attributes is even analogically correct. They claim that such statements do not in any sense conform to objective fact. Hence, when in pantheistic (all is God/God is all) expressions of opinion, all affirmations about God are said to be anthropomorphic, it is meant that, failing even of analogical correctness, they are wholly without validity. Of course, when pagans construct images and other likenesses of God as true representations, they are creating a god in their own image and likenesses and, hence, not only false in message but also blatantly illogical. Paul so reminded the pagan philosophers of Athens (Acts 17:18-31). Such idolatry is also a corrupt practice, as the Old Testament prophets sarcastically asserted (e.g. Elijah, 1 Kings 18:20-40).

A group of ancient Christians who took the anthropomorphic language of scripture literally are known to history as anthropomorphites and were regarded as heretics. This bit of simplistic naivety has been revived in modern times by self-designated Latter Day Saints (Mormons).

4
Why People do Believe in God

A few years ago, on a return flight from the Holy Land I sat in an aisle seat, my wife in the seat to my left. Members of our tour group frequently passed questions to me or stepped down the aisle to talk. God's name was spoken frequently in our conversations. Near the end of our journey (Kennedy Airport) an angry-looking small man across the aisle first made a very disparaging remark about my voice and then sarcastically asked, 'What gives you the idea that the person [God] you keep referring to even exists?' I first attempted a courteous acknowledgment of his presence and then replied, 'I have been explaining just that to about 500 students in a series of thirty lectures. Do you want the whole course or just a summary?' Obviously already regretting his antagonistic sally he mumbled, 'Just the summary.' So I did give him a twenty-minute summary. I led off with the same sentence I had used to students at Campus Crusades summer school: 'I believe in God because, like most people before they invent reasons for disbelieving, I find it much more reasonable to believe than not to believe.' The statement answered the man's question directly and affirms the ancient order–faith in search of understanding.

Authentic Christian apologetics does not pursue the goal of faith-compelling reasons for believing but frankly the aim of removing some obstacles to listening to the Word and of encouraging the perservance of believers. Faith comes by hearing the Word of God, not in response to arguments. To convince atheists, however, that belief in God is supported both by factual evidence and rational arguments might very well humble their pride to the point they will listen to the Word. In this respect 'Evidences' may be and frequently have been useful to the Spirit of God in producing repentance and faith.

'Belief', 'believing' and various synonyms are used in this chapter to mean simple acknowledgment of the existence of something. This is only a small part of the full Christian meaning. This distinction between this simple acknowledgment and the full meaning needs illumination.

In sermons and lectures I have got the distinction across to a group by requesting: 'Everyone who believes in a personal devil please raise his hand.' When everyone else (usually) has his or her hand up I said, 'Please put your hands down', and add, 'I do not believe in the devil because I believe in the living God.' As the effect was sometimes more devastating than is desirable I quit doing this! But the point is that we may accept something as a fact which we may wish were not a fact. Our language permits me to say in such a case, 'I believe in a personal devil.'

Belief in God Is Universal.

In exactly this simple sense people everywhere do believe in God. This is not to say that their ideas about God correspond to biblical teaching about 'the God and Father of our Lord Jesus Christ', the God of Abraham, Isaac and Jacob, nor that their ideas about Him are well defined at all. Yet, as we saw in chapter 1, the idea is sufficiently definite that several Scripture writers do refer to the fact that the Gentiles (heathen, nations), people without direct knowledge of the biblical revelation, are aware of God's existence. In speaking or writing to pagans, Scripture authors refer to God, employing common names for deity, expecting their readers or auditors to recognize whom they mean. There is a limited community of understanding and of agreement.

For example, when Jonah addressed Nineveh with the abrupt warning, 'Yet forty days and Nineveh shall be overthrown' (Jonah 3:4), the inhabitants knew who had sent the prophet to preach that warning. In whatever language Jonah preached (Babylonian-Assyrian? Aramaic?) and by whatever name for God, 'the people of Nineveh believed God ['*elohim*, a name of the Hebrew deity as well as a generic term]. They called for a fast and put on sackcloth, from the greatest of them to the least of them (Jonah 3:5). By whatever name or designation they used for God, they identified him with the one God of the Hebrews – however incomplete their knowledge of Him.

Similarly, Genesis tells us how the patriarch Abraham, who had been residing in the South of Canaan, took up an unexpectedly brief residence in nearby Gerar, known (later perhaps) as the Land of the Philistines. In order to avoid possible trouble over his beautiful wife Sarah he foolishly, it turned out, gave out the report that Sarah was his sister. 'And Abimelech king of Gerar sent and took Sarah. But God (*'elohim*) came to Abimelech in a dream by night and said to him, 'Behold you are a dead man because of the woman you have taken, for she is a man's wife' (Gen. 20:3). The rest of the story sustains the point that there was continuity and partial identity of the pagan king's notion of deity and the Hebrew knowledge of God. Abimelech knew who was addressing him in the dream and that pagan king called God *'Adonai* (Lord), just as Abraham did on occasion. The narrative demonstrates that their respective communities identified deity – probably in each case the supreme deity – with Abraham's God, *'elohim*, even though the Hebrew patriarch had thought there was 'no fear of God in this place' (Gen. 20:11). But he was mistaken.

Once Paul spoke of how the Athenians ignorantly worshipped God (Acts 17:22-28). There is a certain irony about this, captured well in this famous sentence: 'You believe that God is one; you do well. Even the demons believe – and shudder' (James 2:19).

Not everyone *seems* to believe in God. This is, in part, because of our ability to put unwelcome knowledge out of our conscious thoughts. Just as some people put their illnesses or serious problems aside as if they did not exist, living in a fool's paradise, so human beings do not glorify Him as God (Rom. 1:21) and their Creator is not even in their thinking. As Gerald Bray suggests, their belief in God is about as life-affecting as their belief that the world is round.[1]

Some people affirm belief in God but are dissatisfied with Him. They suppose they know more of justice, morality, goodness, beauty and truth than He. They weary the LORD with their words (Mal. 2:17), and sometimes long treatises on philosophical themes.

A few participate in religious forms but in the heart, centre of affection and interest, they live without Him. 'The fool says in his heart, "There is no God"' (Ps. 14:1). This sort of fool is not a dogmatic atheist but a practical one. The fool may be a church elder or the village priest, but he is a hypocrite, for 'in his heart' life goes on as though God does not exist.

There are, of course, avowed atheists; yet, as we shall see, they may not truly be atheists but 'believers' too, in the simple sense we are employing the word here.

We shall now address three questions: (1) Why do people universally (or nearly so) 'believe' in God? (2) Why should people believe in God? That is, what reasons may be cited for belief in God? And, though we shall not provide a special section on the subject, we shall observe in passing some answers to the question. (3) What do people in general know and believe *about* God?

Why People Do Believe in God.

Why do people universally 'believe' in God? Many have commented on the fact and some impressive theories have been proposed as to why this *consensus gentium* prevails. Some have argued that the common belief is a remnant of primitive truth. By this, they mean truth known in the early generations of the human race when God had

---

1. Gerald Bray, *The Doctrine of God* (Downer's Grove, IL: InterVarsity Press, 1993), p. 14.

daily intercourse with us, as Genesis 2 and 3 report. It is thought to have endured in garbled form through all the generations to the present. There may be something to this, but it seems likely that some sections of the human race would have failed to pass the knowledge on. Yet the conviction appears to be well nigh universal. It seems more in harmony with the Bible, which does throughout address mankind as aware of God, to find the source on some deeper level.

Others have suggested that the common belief in God is based on inferences from the observed phenomena of nature. Maybe all of us make this inference – invariably if not necessarily. But if so, there seem to be no parallels. Inductively acquired notions are seldom so uniformly held.

Is then this common belief in God a spontaneous development? George Park Fisher, an American Presbyterian theologian of a century ago, thought so. He said the conviction arises in quite another way:

> Belief in God is not ultimately founded on processes of argument. His presence is more immediately disclosed. There is a native [i.e. born-in] and universal belief, emerging spontaneously in connection with the feeling of dependence and the phenomena of conscience, however obscure, inconstant, and perverted that faith may be.[2]

The 'feeling of dependence', in the above quotation, prevailed in the atmosphere of academic theology when Fisher wrote in the early 1880s, in the same way 'demythologize', 'process', and 'existential' have been in recent decades. F. D. E. Schleiermacher (1768–1834) gave this expression to theology in many writings. He built a whole dogmatic system in his two-volume work, *The Christian Faith*, 1821, 1831, on the foundation of the 'religious consciousness' which all people have. We each become aware early in childhood that we are not independent but dependent beings. The dependence we feel is of *absolute* dependence. The essence of this consciousness is not knowledge or action, but a feeling different from all others, being a direct consciousness of 'the absolute', another nineteenth-century philosophical preoccupation. George W. F. Hegel (1770–1831) who wrote more than many scholars ever read in a year, impressed many and convinced more (Karl Marx, for example) of 'process' or 'dialectical movement'. This theme 'runs through everything Hegel wrote' (Will Durant). This movement (process, becoming) is identical with 'the absolute', the supreme Reality. The world process – as in all pantheistic idealism – is its own cause and goal. Somehow Hegel's notion stuck and has not disappeared.

Hence people everywhere believe in God as the Absolute on whom they have 'feeling of dependence' or 'the religious consciousness'. There is something of the ring of truth in this theory.

In other words, God made each person – the first man and all his descendants – with such nature and characteristics that when we come to full conscious awareness of the external world and our inner thoughts and feelings, an awareness of God appears. The awareness is dim and only partly formulated in some, for many of us are neither very reflective nor especially alert to ideas. Additionally, some of us are not very sensitive to other persons. In others the awareness of God is clear and well formed. Among at least a few the voice of conscience speaks 'loud and clear', while in others that pointer toward the moral Governor of this world seems hardly to exist. Pilate's wife might serve as an example of the former (Matt. 27:19), Pilate of the latter (John 18:38).

Is God a first truth? Since very ancient times, at least as early as the Greek philosophers of the fourth century BC, many learned men have said that God is immediately present in people's minds as one of several 'first truths'.

A. H. Strong, author of the most enduring and widely read book of Baptist theology, taking a hint from this, puts this universal awareness of God in the category of 'first truths'. Orthodox Protestant theological writers from Calvin onward have taught, on the basis both of Scripture and 'natural light', that this awareness exists. Not all provide the same list of first truths or explain the awareness of God in this way.

By this pregnant expression writers mean truths existing in the mind previous to thought or reflection. They are truths the mind unconsciously presupposes in order to think about any subject whatsoever. Sometimes they are called (not very aptly, for a false impression is conveyed thereby) innate ideas, that is, ideas we are born with. Such ideas are not thought to be consciously present at birth or even when first used. Yet when experiences through the senses (percepts) furnish data for the mind to reflect upon and shape into concepts, the mind is already furnished with 'categories' into which to arrange and file them, plus techniques for so employing the data. Thus when the distance between A and B is perceived, the idea of *space* or *distance* immediately moves from *latent* existence to *patent* existence in the mind. A person employs the idea of space without ever being taught it by someone else or by

---

2. George P. Fisher, *Grounds of Theistic and Christian Belief* (New York: Charles Scribner's Sons, 1888), p.37.

experiencing it through the senses. Similarly, when events transpire within an infant's sphere of observation (a loud noise, movement, change of any sort) the child looks for a *cause*. Cause is another first truth, innate, not produced by experience, but latently present and becoming patent in first experience. Kant taught a similar doctrine of knowledge. Although there are certain similarities to Plato's thought about the question of how we know things, there is no connection really with his doctrine of pre-existing 'forms'.

Now, says this line of approach, God is one of these first truths. The *latent* idea springs up into conscious presence in the mind at a certain point in every person's conscious life. It may be at first awareness of wrongdoing, or a first interest in cause-effect relationships, or some other occasion.

Is God discovered by the correspondence of two worlds? One may defend this view of things (Fisher and Strong were only two of many who do) by a slightly different approach. There is an external world (sea and land, clouds and sky, people and things) to be observed. I observe it; you observe it; almost everyone does. We each enter into knowing relationship with it, for we find in our minds mental shelves, bags, hooks, slots and drawers (so to speak) into which, tentatively at least, we arrange these numerous bits of information. Colours go in certain shaped bags, distances on shelves, values in drawers, pleasures in slots, and pains on hooks, so to speak. So my inner mental world, in a general way, corresponds *genuinely* with the external world. When I talk with you I discover that you have done the same in similar, if not identical, ways. We both *know* the external world and can actually have discourse about it. How? And Why? Because Someone greater than all reality has put all parts of all the observable reality of our world in these commensurable relationships. I must assume Him in order even to think about *me, you* or *it*.

You might say simply that the external world that we see, feel, touch, hear and taste corresponds with our inner world that knows the outer one. Everyone who thinks about it must ask, Why? A power to whom our language gives the name God seems to be the only answer the mind can readily supply.

Is conscience the source of our knowledge of God? As G. P. Fisher's statement quoted earlier suggests, conscience may be a source of the universal notion of God. Conscience, Paul says, either accuses or excuses (blames or praises) us (Rom. 2:15). It must exist in us all because all people do make moral judgments. The human mind has a way of skipping all the steps of logic and apparently, by intuition, coming to a sound conclusion. We have to do this in a split second to stay alive sometimes. Perhaps we all do this in reasoning from conscience to God. Maybe this explains the universal awareness of God. To be the God whom conscience fears, God must be exceedingly great in wisdom and power. He must also be holy and just. Whether He be also gracious or not is a question conscience does not answer, for conscience gives the soul of a person small comfort and ultimately no mercy at all. The sinner receives assurance of forgiveness after he repents and confesses, all right, but even then, he may find conscience hard to mollify. Assurance of forgiveness comes rather from the revealed Word of God which tells him what God has done to remove transgressions, to cover sin and to cancel guilt (see Ps. 32:1-5 and compare 2 Sam. 12:1-13; see also 1 John 1:8, 9).

These reflections on the question of why people everywhere have an awareness of God are of at least provisional value. That is, they will do until some better answer to a persistent question is proposed. At any rate, we have every reason to make the same assumption that the Bible makes: people do not need to be introduced to the idea of God. They already know about Him.

The Bible does assume that people believe in the existence of God. The Bible also assumes that people's ideas about Him are sufficiently correct to make conversation about Him possible. We must accept this if we are going to address people's minds as Paul did at Athens (Acts 17:16-34) or as John Bunyan, for that matter, did in the Bedford Gaol.

Not only so, having accepted this universal awareness as a fact, on the basis of it we have the privilege and duty of initiating Christian witness to anyone on earth.

Is our knowledge of God an intuition from the contingency of all things? Is it obvious that the innumerable things we learn about, beginning with our first day of conscious existence, are necessarily here in the world, not somewhere else. Do you remember the surprise you felt the first time you touched a kitten, a stone, a piece of ice, a fly? Or the first time you heard a meadow lark sing or first heard a symphony orchestra? Later you learned the connections between some or all of these things. You know there is regularity in the relations of all these things – we call the regularity, laws.

About these 'things' and the 'laws' Rudolph Otto asked some questions:

> Whence have both these come? Is it a matter of course, is it quite obvious that they should exist at all, and that they should be exactly as they are?... if the world were so constituted that it would be impossible for it not to exist, that the necessity for its existence and the inconceivability of its non-existence were at once explicit and obvious, then there would be no sense in inquiring after a cause. In regard to a 'necessary' thing, if there were such, we cannot ask, 'why, and from what cause does it exist?' If it was necessary, that implies that to think of it as not existing would be ridiculous... and impossible. Unfortunately there are no 'necessary' *things* [emphasis added], so that we cannot illustrate the case by examples. But there are at least necessary *truths* [emphasis added] as distinguished from contingent truths... For instance, a necessary truth is contained in the sentence, 'Everything is equal to itself', or, 'The shortest distance between two points [on a plane surface] is a straight line.' We cannot even conceive of the contrary.[3]

'It rained yesterday' is a contingent truth. 'It all depends', we say. Now it seems entirely possible that in an informal manner people of all times and places find it necessary to accept a cause of all contingent things. The cause is axiomatic, not something to be proved. Perhaps for most of us 'proof' in the sense of absolute demonstration is neither desired nor necessary. We look at the 'things' that are made (Rom. 1:20) and unconsciously accept God as the Maker without the slightest effort at a syllogism. We do so in the same unreflective but valid way we cut across the backyard to get to the neighbour's back door rather than taking to the street and walking around the block.

This intuition, formalized, is the rational basis of the causal or cosmological argument, to be treated in the next chapter.

Is Belief in God a Practical Necessity to Meet the Needs of Human Life? It is a generally acknowledged fact that religion is a universal phenomenon. Some authors account for it as arising out of some spontaneous impulse that is as natural as breathing or eating food. Augustine phrased the thought memorably in the language of Christian theism: 'Thou has made us for thyself and our heart is restless till it rest in thee'. Others have described the impulse to worship some unseen 'higher power' as 'felt need'.

Through several generations Boston University has been favored by a succession of brilliant exponents of a theistic world view. Among these, one who after a hundred years is still widely quoted and whose arguments and exposition still speak is Borden P. Bowne. I will call upon the closing chapter of his *Theism, Comprising the Deems Lectures for 1902* at New York University. At that time NYU was a Christian institution. He introduces the chapter 'Theism and Life' as no proof of God's existence but to introduce belief in the God of theism as needful for human happiness as follows:

> [M]an is not merely nor mainly contemplation; he is also will and action. He must, then, have something to work for, aims to realize, and ideas by which to live. In real life the center of gravity of theistic faith lies in its relation to these aims and ideals. God is seen to be that without which our ideals collapse or are made unattainable, and the springs of action are broken. Hence the existence of God is affirmed not on speculation or theoretical grounds, but because of the needs of practical life.[4]

One Hebrew poet exclaimed, 'My soul longeth... my heart and my flesh crieth out for the living God' and another 'My flesh longeth for thee in a dry and thirsty land' and still another, 'God is the strength of my heart, and my portion forever' (Psa. 84:2; 63:1; 73:26 KJV).

Bowne concludes on the point: 'All that can be done... is to show that theism is a demand of our moral nature, a necessity of practical life. Whether to accept this subjective necessity as the warrant for the objective fact every one must decide for himself... our human interests can be conserved, and our highest life maintained, only on a theistic basis'.[5] Universally felt needs for a meaningful happy life may also explain why people of all ages and in every place believe in a god.

Why Should People Believe in God?

It is a fact that sizeable numbers of people have, like the man in my story at the beginning of this chapter, rejected their 'belief' in God. They 'by their unrighteousness suppress the truth... For although they knew God, they did not honour him as God or give thanks to him, but they became futile in their thinking, and their foolish hearts were

---

3. Rudolph Otto, *Naturalism and Religion*, trans. J. A. Thomson & Margaret R. Thomson (New York: 1913), pp. 61, 62. This sort of truth – necessary truth – is called an axiom. We do not ever prove axioms for we cannot even think without them. They can, however, be suppressed.
4. Borden P. Bowne, *Theism* (New York: American Book Co., 1902), p. 291.
5. ibid., p. 292.

darkened. Claiming to be wise, they became fools' (Rom. 1:18, 21-22). Scripture holds these folk – idolaters all – wickedly responsible for denying and perverting their knowledge. Yet, they are not only to be loved as God loves them (John 3:16; Rom. 5:8) but also to be hated as God hates them (Pss. 97:10; 139:21). Wherever he went, Paul got into trouble because he rebuked idolatries of all kinds and successfully overthrew them.

What shall we do when we meet the wholly secular mind? We, of course, shall declare the gospel. If I understand what the 'presuppositional' disciples of Cornelius Van Til aright, they hold this to be the only 'apologetic', i.e. proof of the truth of 'the Faith' available to us. There is, they say, no common ground of agreement we can find to mount a programme of evangelistic or pre-evangelistic encounter with unbelievers. The effect of the fall has rendered their minds incapable of considering the saving truth of the gospel. Arguments are unavailing. We must simply proclaim the truth and leave the rest to the sovereign work of the Holy Spirit.

If, however, secular-minded unbelievers will not consent to hear the gospel, is there anything else one can do? Certainly. If we can at least get their attention (as Jesus did in His interesting parables and as Paul did at Athens) by speaking first of matters not apparently part of a distinctly Christian doctrinal system, we may cause them to listen to some gospel too.

The classical arguments for the existence of God are latently in the Scriptures, sometimes almost explicitly stated. Therefore, to present them is really to speak from logical-spiritual ground that is uncompromised. As the witness speaks, and if his homework has been done well, several good things may happen to the unbeliever also.

In the first place the garden-variety secular listener will likely come to see for the first time in his life that evangelical Christianity is not what he thought it to be—a superstition or a device for gaining social benefits or a spooky bit of a magic for small-minded fanatics. This may come as quite a shock to him, sufficient shock either to anger or humble him. The listener may at least begin to doubt the certainty of his smug atheism and to feel a bit foolish. Carl Sagan might possibly have had a bad night had he encountered John Gerstner (who was an aggressive Christian apologist) in the next seat of a trans-Atlantic flight to Paris. In other words, sound arguments can teach unbelievers a bit of respect, even if they do not initially convince. St Augustine, himself, says his *mind* was turned toward Christianity by meeting a persuasive argument for the existence of souls, and it did not even come from a Christian source, but from pagan Platonic philosophers.

Unbelievers may have more than one kind of obstacle to belief, susceptible to more than one kind of help from those who sincerely desire to win them over. Some years ago, a practicing Christian psychologist addressed the students and faculty of Wheaton College on the question of whether or not psychology can be used to convert unbelievers to Christ. He said, in sum, no, not as such. However, many people are not fully sane and some are not sane at all. The gospel addresses a person's rational understanding. He will therefore remain lost until some degree of sanity is restored. Otherwise he cannot even discern the gospel when he hears it. If psychological counselling or psychiatric treatment can return him to sanity, then the gospel power can operate in him and he may be saved.

In a similar way, if a 'professing-himself-to-be-wise' person, who has rejected native belief in God, will stand still long enough while I present some arguments for God's existence, good things may happen to him. Firstly, he may open his mind just a little to the idea that God is. The moment he does so, his conscience will again operate to produce shame for his guilty unbelief. In the second place, while the unbeliever listens to my arguments, I shall also be declaring some of my own faith and reporting some of God's Word. Logical arguments need not be separated from scriptural truth and Christian testimony. The listening unbeliever therefore is 'dangerously' close already to being under gospel power. 'Faith comes from hearing, and hearing through the word of Christ' (Rom. 10:17).

A third thing will occur too. I shall be strengthening my own faith if I have troubled to make myself 'ready' (1 Peter 3:15) to give answer to those who inquire. G. P. Fisher, quoted above, goes on to say: 'The arguments for the being of God do not originate this faith; they justify at the same time that they elucidate and define it. They are so many different points of view from which we contemplate the object of faith. Each one of them tends to show, not simply *that* God is, but *what* He is. They complete the conception by pointing out particular predicates brought to light in the manifestation which God has made of himself.'[6]

---

6. G. P. Fisher, *op. cit.*, p. 37.

The arguments we are about to examine are all ancient; as asserted earlier, some even appear in the Bible. Modern theologians are not in full agreement as to their value. This I judge to be because we bring a recent world-view to the problem. As these arguments were developed over the years, say from Anselm (eleventh century) to Calvin (sixteen thcentury), they were not employed by themselves to convert non-theists to belief in one true God. Rather, everyone in Christendom endorsed the creeds: 'I believe in God the Father Almighty, Maker of heaven and earth.' This sort of 'pre-evangelism' was not particularly needed. The arguments were not formulated as demonstrations or proofs for some unprejudiced, critical court of review. Rather, St Thomas and the others held, there was cause for affirming the existence of God quite independently of creed or Bible. God is *knowable* in the sense of knowing that He *is*, by virtue of information drawn from the world that God made. The tool for mining the treasure, it was held, is natural reason. Until recently, however, 'reason' included much more than what we usually call 'reason' today. Our very word *logic* is an old Greek word meaning *word* in the first place. In these authors, still read today, reason includes about all the arts of persuasion, including deductive and inductive processes and much more besides. In the KJV New Testament of 400 years ago 'reason', 'reasoning', and the like, still translate words meaning to discuss, to dispute, to argue, give exposition, build a case, and similar. Neither Anselm nor Thomas supposed that pure logic, as we conceive it today, would convince people indisposed to believe. There were not then or now any faith-compelling syllogisms—not even faith-compelling miracles (John 12:37-41).

The most we can claim for these arguments is, given the kind of beings people ought to be, the evidences of natural light are such that people ought to give assent to the fact that God is. We will assess how much more the arguments tell us about God as we treat them.

The church Fathers took over these proofs from ancient philosophers, and some proceeded to set too much value on them. The age of scholasticism (tenth to fifteenth centuries) similarly made too much of them. The Reformers received this natural theology also, but following the Scriptures, they incorporated it into Christian doctrine, rather than treating it as something merely preliminary to or in addition to scriptural revelation. It is something for Christians to employ as Christians, not merely as fodder for dialogue or debate with unbelievers.

In a well-known passage Calvin says:

> The final goal of the blessed life... rests in the knowledge of God. Lest anyone... be excluded... he not only sowed in men's minds that seed of religion [awareness of God]... but revealed himself and daily discloses himself in the whole workmanship of the universe. As a consequence, men cannot open their eyes without being compelled to see him. Indeed, his essence is incomprehensible; hence, his divineness far escapes all human perception. But upon his individual works he has engraved unmistakable marks of his glory, so clear and so prominent that even unlettered and stupid folk cannot plead the excuse of ignorance.[7]

Calvin then devotes a page to exposition of Psalm 104, Hebrews 11:3, Psalm 19 and Romans 1:19, 20 and adds:

> There are innumerable evidences both in heaven and on earth that declare his wonderful wisdom; not only those more recondite matters for closer observation of which astronomy, medicine, and all natural science are intended, but also those which thrust themselves upon the sight of even the most untutored and ignorant person, so that they cannot open their eyes without being compelled to witness them.[8]

It is clear that while Calvin thought education might help one to see God's message in the natural world, no one is so bereft of 'reason' as to be unable to read the essentials of the message.

For any theologians who may read these lines, I cannot but express the opinion that Calvin would have been both puzzled and angered by the odd reluctance of some Calvinistic presuppositionalists in apologetics to see value in employing natural 'revelation' in evangelism, granting its limitations. After all, every truth as well as *the Truth* has power. And some truths of 'natural light' are also *the Truth* of God's revealed Word.

---

7. John Calvin, *Institutes of the Christian Religion* (Philadelphia: Westminster Press, 1960), I, v, 1.
8. ibid., I, v, 2.

5
Reasons for Believing in God

We proceed to see how the chief classical theistic arguments have been formulated and to evaluate them.

The Causal Argument. This argues from the present existence of the universe. This argument is also called the Argument from the Idea of First Cause and the Cosmological Argument. It begins with the fact of the universe and asks the question, How did it get here? Then it answers that the universe was created by an Adequate Cause. The name given to Adequate or First Cause is God.

In spite of certain objections, it is properly called an argument from effect to cause (*a posteriori*, from here *back* to there). Unless one is willing to affirm, as certain people do, that the universe is self-caused and eternal, one must admit that the 'heavens and the earth' is a universe begun at some point. So we state the argument, 'Everything begun, whether substance or phenomenon, owes its existence to some producing cause. The universe at least so far as its present form is concerned, is a thing begun, and owes its existence to a cause which is equal to its production. This cause must be indefinitely great.'[1] Objections have been raised and weaknesses cited. Someone wants to know if instead of *first* cause where 'the buck stops', perhaps an infinite regress of causes may be just as adequate. According to a Hindu myth, the world rests on the back of a gigantic elephant, the elephant's feet rest on the back of a gigantic turtle. Sometimes the turtle is said to be swimming in a great sea. Ask the Hindu what contains the great sea and all he can do is shrug his shoulders or change the subject. Is this just as reasonable and believable as the argument for First Cause?

Someone else wonders if we must find the cause of the heavens and the earth outside the universe, both anterior (before it) and exterior. Perhaps the cause is coeval (of the same age) with the universe and interior, i.e. immanent (dwelling in the world) and not transcendent (above the world). If so, then maybe the universe itself is the cause and you have invented pantheism all over again. All that exists is God in various expressions and emanations. This is the philosophy underlying several oriental religions. When idolatrous paganism turns sophisticated or when biblical religion turns to excessive ritual and becomes intellectualized, as in eighteenth-century continental Europe, pantheism is the form religion takes. Several pantheistic sects are currently in vogue in America, among them Rosicrucianism, theosophy, transcendental meditation and several varieties of New Ageism.

---

1. A. H. Strong, Systematic Theology (Valley Forge, PA: Judson Press, 1907), p. 73.

Another objection takes the shape of frontal attack. An aged professor challenged my faith in college days by sarcastically asserting: 'I can as justifiably posit an eternally existing, self-sustaining universe as you can an eternal, all wise, all powerful creator-God.' Such a world must run on eternal, immutable laws.

What shall we say? In the first place, an infinite regress of causes is generally unsatisfying to thoughtful people. It is a solution undesirable for almost any problem we can think of. The mind seeks a resting place. Furthermore, there is clear evidence of a master design through all the parts of the universe. There must have been a beginning at some point when the design was made by an intelligent being. We shall say more about this shortly. So the idea of infinite regression is seen to be a very weak explanation. It is really to give up making any explanation. The same objections prevail against both pantheism and the notion of an eternal, uncaused universe.

Furthermore, the evidence of observation, both of causal, unlearned observations and of technical, scientific research, clearly indicate that the universe is neither self-sustained nor eternal. It had a beginning.

Poetically stated we observe to our distress:

> Swift to its close ebbs out life's little day.
> Earth's joys grow dim, its glories fade away.
> Change and decay in all around I see.

Everything we see is temporary and dependent on something else. This includes that portion of our own beings that we know to be part of the natural order (our physical bodies). Everyone knows this. Likewise scientists who search the skies with several kinds of instruments and several kinds of research have established that our universe is moving toward infinite dispersion at a regular rate. Analysis of light from the stars with an instrument called a spectroscope, shows that like painted dots on the surface of a toy balloon being blown up, each spot in the universe is moving farther from every other spot. Names given to the observance of this phenomenon are Red Shift, Doppler Effect and 'expanding universe'. The farther the objects in space are from one another the faster they accelerate toward infinite velocity. Though evidence has been sought for a slowing down at the borders of the universe none has yet been established. The universe could not have been operating in such a way from eternity past. It would now be infinitely dispersed. Certain theorists have invented a doctrine of continuous creation of matter. If matter is being created as fast as it disappears, than the cosmos is in a state of equilibrium. It is an interesting idea, but such a dynamic engine for maintenance of our world is without evidence and would need to be explained by some First Cause.

Another fact of common observation, formalized by science, is that the world is running out of available energy. The world is running down. There will be as much matter and energy in aggregate at the end of time as now, but energy will be locked up in ways it cannot be used. When the sun has dissipated all its matter and energy to the extremities of the solar system our world will be at an end. The law of entropy (i.e. of unavailable energy) will have had its say. What if the sun had started giving off its energy an eternity ago? The solar system would have disappeared, along with our earth, long ago.

The Bible, moreover, contains several extended sections on the created heavens and earth as constituting a message about God to His rational creatures everywhere. It was not a philosopher, but a sensitive shepherd boy grown up, who wrote of this in poetry both pleasant to the ear and a pleasure to read:

> The heavens declare the glory of God,
> and the sky above proclaims his handiwork.
> Day to day pours out speech,
> and night to night reveals knowledge.
> There is no speech, nor are there words,
> whose voice is not heard.
> Their measuring line goes out through all the earth,
> and their words to the end of the world.
> In them he has set a tent for the sun,
> which comes out like a bridegroom leaving his chamber,
> and, like a strong man, runs its course with joy.
> Its rising is from the end of the heavens,
> and its circuit to the end of them,
> and there is nothing hidden from its heat.[2]

---

2. Ps. 19:1-6.

Full exposition of these verses would require space at least as long as this chapter, but several matters are clear. God has placed a message about Himself in the created heavens of the sun, moon and stars. There His majesty and power may be seen (v. 1). The message is 'round the clock' (v. 2) and it is silent testimony (v. 3), hence peculiarly susceptible of being ignored. The messengers are beautiful and vigorous (v. 5) and they deliver their message everywhere and to all people (vv. 4 and 6). The Bible is squarely behind the argument that God's existence is manifestly declared in nature.

Romans 1:18-32 is not poetry and it is not pleasant to hear – nor did its author intend it to be reading for relaxation. The passage contains what may be the bitterest, most judgmental sentences in human speech. Here the Bible declares that nature provides such strong testimony to God's existence, character and attributes that human beings are universally and severally rendered guilty and wrath-deserving, under the righteous judgment of God. The divine treatment of the heathen – both in judgment and grace – is sufficiently grounded on this passage alone. It is the clearest biblical statement of the reason for pagan guilt, thus the justification for Christian missions. It is hard to imagine a higher evaluation of the causal argument than that which Paul has provided in this passage.

Even apart from the other theistic arguments and evidences this evidence ought to make people ask questions about God. It has always had an important place in preparing the hearts of many to believe the gospel, perhaps even to seek to hear it. David assumes the causal argument in poetic logic when he asks, 'He who planted the ear, does he not hear? He who formed the eye, does he not see? He who disciplines the nations, does he not rebuke? He who teaches man knowledge ... knows the thoughts of mans' (Ps. 94:9-11).

One of the great names of British science, mathematics and philosophy is Sir Isaac Newton (1642–1727). Sir Isaac had a miniature model of the solar system made. A large golden ball representing the sun was at its centre and around it revolved smaller spheres, representing the planets – Mercury, Venus, Earth, Mars, Jupiter and the others. They were each kept in an orbit relatively the same as in the real solar system. By means of rods, cogwheels and belts they all moved around the centre gold ball in exact precision. A friend called on the noted man one day while he was studying the model. The friend was not a believer in the biblical doctrine of creation.

Their conversation has been reported as follows: *Friend*: 'My Newton, what an exquisite thing! Who made it for you?' *Newton*: 'Nobody.' *Friend*: 'Nobody?' *Newton*: 'That's right! I said nobody! All of these balls and cogs and belts and gears just happened to come together, and wonder of wonders, by chance they began revolving in their set orbits with perfect timing.'[3] Of course the visitor understood the unstated argument that, 'In the beginning, God created the heavens and the earth.'

The two arguments for the existence of God, now to be presented, likewise rest upon the principle that there must be a cause for every effect. The cosmological argument applies the law of cause to the universe as a whole. The two now to follow apply it, firstly, to the evidence of design in the natural order, including the human body (the teleological argument), and secondly, to the mental and moral side of human nature (the anthropological argument, also called the moral argument).

Argument from Design. This is the argument from the presence of order and mutually useful common relationships in nature. This is called the *teleological* (from Greek *telos*, end, goal) *argument*. There is a major premise: when an observed orderly arrangement, coupled with useful common relationship, pervades a system it implies intelligence and purpose in the cause of the system. Both order and useful common relationship can be seen pervading all that we can observe in the universe. There must therefore have been, at the beginning, an intelligence sufficient to design that order and to conceive the purpose. There must also have been power to direct the natural order toward these ends. Though he did not state it just this way, the eminent philosopher Emmanuel Kant (1724–1804) was convinced that this argument, though not 'apodictic', is the highest 'proof' of a Designer, though not necessarily of a Creator.

The major premise expresses a primitive and universal conviction. When, for example, we find a material object apparently made to be used for some purpose, say a stone axe, we feel certain that some person (intelligence) made it to cut wood (purpose). Both the intelligence and the purpose lie in the maker. We see unmistakable order all about us in nature. We see mutual dependence and relationship in all of it. We know people did not make these features of our world. We know that only a Being with adequate intelligence to plan this system and with power to create it could cause it and did indeed cause it.

---

3. Reported in *The Daily Bread* devotional.

The major premise is a conviction shared by all mankind. We cannot conceive of a universe (that is, a world of many things harmonized in working unity) of weather, soil, water, temperature, a world animate and inanimate, evidently unique to our planet, as existing without One who designed it for these ends. We find our innate feelings and primitive convictions that such a power does exist all confirmed. Why not call Him God?

Volumes have been written showing how the immense complexity of all creation, all operating in a system, manifests design, that is, purpose, in the structure of reality. The most famous statement is that of William Paley (1743 – 1805). He articulated the argument in his *Natural Theology, or Evidences of the Existence and Attributes of the Deity Collected from the Appearances of Nature* (1802). It may be found in back shelves of college libraries even today. The book's title speaks for itself. A more recent small book made a whole generation aware of these evidences in a forceful, popular way – *Man Does Not Stand Alone* by A. Cressy Morrison (Revell, 1944). This book was published in digest form by Reader's Digest two years later and it is still widely read.

The argument from design has impressed reflective people throughout the generations – 'You cause the grass to grow for the livestock and plants for man to cultivate, that he may bring forth food from the earth and wine to gladden the heart of man, oil to make his face shine and bread to strengthen man's heart.' This verse from Psalm 104:14 and 15 is early, but not unique. Plato in the dialogue *Philebus* drew an analogy that puts it like this: all the elements in the human body are derived from the great mass of elements in the cosmos. Hence the mind of man must be derived from 'a royal soul and mind in the nature of Zeus'. In fact, Anaxagoras, Socrates, Plato and Aristotle all honored a teleological explanation of the universe. It was a favourite of the scholastic theologians and even impressed Emmanuel Kant as deserving most respect of the usual theistic 'proofs', though he rejected them all.

David Hume (1711–1776) wrote a devastating critique of the teleological argument (*Dialogues Concerning Natural Religion*) twenty-three years before Paley produced his famous work advocating it. Perhaps Paley never read it. In the dialogue, speakers discuss the pros and cons of basing any religious belief on nature (miracles he excluded altogether).

The impression most students derive from Hume's book is that he believed the existence of 'God is assured by reason of the amount of order discoverable in the universe, but that the evidence is insufficient to warrant many conclusions about his nature and attributes.'[4]

A number of religious philosophers have incorporated these evidences for God's existence into essentially non-theistic explanations, arguing for an '*elan vital*' or 'vitalism' or any one of a number of impersonal powers as cause of design and apparent purpose.

Evolutionary theory substitutes the idea of *cause* – natural selection, survival of the fittest, and similar – for the idea of *purpose*. The evolutionary theory was at least 2,200 years old when Darwin was born. Empedocles (494–434 BC) taught that the primal elements came together by *chance* and produced fragmentary structures (such as arms, necks, horns, sex organs). The fragmentary structures then met casually and those *adapted* to each other survived while the others disappeared. Simple structures came first and when several structures joined more complex were formed. Thus from spontaneous aggregations of casual aggregates 'which suited one another *as if this had been intended* [emphasis added] did the organic universe spring… It is impossible not to see in this theory a crude anticipation of the "survival of the fittest" theory of modern evolutionists.'[5] Democritus (460 – 362 BC) had another evolutionary, mechanistic, tychistic (chance) system. To the present moment no one has produced a feasible explanation of *how*, that is, the *mechanism* by which intelligent purpose can be replaced by chance. Evolution has no explanation of *arrival* much less of *survival* of the fittest.

Someone wants to know if maybe the intelligence implied in design may be within the system of nature – and it is theoretically possible.

It must be acknowledged that formally there is no *proof* of a personal Creator in the bare appearance of design. True, it *formally* 'proves' the existence of an Architect or Designer only. Yet when people reflect on the evidence of design in nature their intuitive logic quickly arrives at an intelligent, all-powerful person, rather than impersonal force as the cause of it.

It has been objected that the widespread presence of evil indicates the absence of beneficent design in nature. Can God be the author of a universe where pain and calamity are as prevalent as they are in our universe?

---

4. William K. Wright, *A History of Modern Philosophy* (New York: Macmillan, 1941), p. 211.
5. William Wallace, art. 'Empedocles', *Encyclopaedia Britannica*, 11th ed., 1911, vol. 9, p. 345.

The seriousness of the objection must be acknowledged. Perhaps the most important answer is simply that while the evidence for 'intelligent design' (as a burgeoning current revival of this argument aptly phrases) is clear, the evidences for lack of it are ambiguous. True, we do not know why there are disasters of all kinds, tremendous waste and seeming meaninglessness, but that does not mean there are no purposes being served. We just do not know what they are. We know that in certain cases of moral evil, at least, God had a purpose in allowing each.

The argument from design is often poetically framed in hymns of Christian worship. One of the finest, not frequently sung anymore, is Addison's.

> The spacious firmament on high
> With all the blue ethereal sky,
> And spangled heavens, a shining frame,
> Their great Original proclaim.
> The unwearied sun from day to day
> Does his creator's power display,
> And publishes to every land
> The works of an almighty hand.'[6]

The Bible declares that evil does indeed have a place in the world of God's providence (see Gen. 50:5-21; Acts 2:22-24). It is not unavoidable by God and undesigned by Him but something designed for human discipline. Evil, especially moral evil, remains a problem of thought, but it is not a barrier to faith. See a later chapter for discussion of the problem of evil.

Argument from Human Nature. The argument from the nature of mankind is also called the moral argument, or the anthropological argument. As soon will become apparent, this, like the teleological arguement, is a special form of the argument from cause.

We cannot avoid observing that people of all races, in all places and of every social condition have a sense of right and wrong. They make moral judgments. If someone says it is wrong for people to have a sense of right and wrong, then he has made a judgment of right and wrong and seems inconsistent. If reminded of this he may assert that he has only made an intellectual judgment. If I tell him I think he has made a moral judgment and that it is wrong for him to deny it he ought to say nothing, for if he says (as almost certainly he will) that it is wrong for me to say a non-fact is a fact, he has made a *moral* judgment. John Gerstner has written of this that 'As intellectual beings we judge that certain things are right or wrong, but with that judgment always comes the notion that what we judge to be right, we *ought* to judge to be right; and what we judge to be wrong we *ought* [emphasis added] to judge to be wrong.'[7] People everywhere agree that it is wrong to oppose a correct judgment of fact and conversely it is right to support it. If we do otherwise we feel an inner sense of wrongdoing. Something within accuses and threatens us.

Though it is now commonly attributed solely to social conditioning, Paul says our conscience accuses and threatens us when we offend our own standards of right and wrong and excuses (approves) us when we please our own sense of right and wrong (Rom. 2:12-16). Conscience does not tell us what is right. Our training, perhaps some innate sense of right and wrong, and perhaps much else, informs us of what is right (correctly or incorrectly). The conscience only judges how well we are doing. It does not furnish the standard.

The 'something' which judges our own and others' actions we call *conscience*. The word, however, and many of the ideas that go with it are not an original part of divine revelation. The word does not even appear in either Testament of the English Bible until John 8:9 – a non-genuine text – and next at Acts 23:1, where the Greek word is *suneidēsis*, *sun* (plus), with *eidēsis* (knowledge): hence, Latin *con* (with), and *science* (knowledge). Perhaps Zeno of Citium (founder of Stoics, fourth and third century BC) first postulated a 'human nature' and invented the word, though Bias and Periander, both more ancient, are said to have employed the word 'conscience'.[8] At any rate, this moral sense of what is right and our duty to do it, though it accuses and excuses, may be weak (1 Cor. 8:12), good (1 Peter 3:16), defiled (1 Cor. 8:7), seared (1 Tim. 4:2), strong or pure (1 Cor. 8:7, 9). But it is never fully absent.

---

6. Joseph Addison, 1627 – 1719, son of an Anglican dean, composer of this hymn, published a series of papers on the subject of this section, entitled 'Evidences of the Christian Religion'.
7. John Gerstner, *Reasons for Faith* (New York: Harper & Brothers, 1960), p. 39.
8. Liddel & Scott, *Lexicon*.

The only adequate explanation is that the great Moral Being, who created us all, planted the moral sense in us. Training or conditioning (certainly not material nature) can hardly be the cause. They may affect it by influence bad or good but not originate it.

There are many other approaches to the moral argument. It was this 'practical reason' as opposed to ordinary or 'theoretical reason' that compelled even the sceptical philosopher Emmanuel Kant to postulate the existence of God and immortality of the soul. However stated, it comes closest to rational 'proof' of Christian theism of all the theistic arguments. C. S. Lewis has popularized this argument in a convincing way in several of his earlier apologetical works.

When, therefore, this argument is treated with so much respect by Kant and by many others

> after him that the other proofs are made to recede entirely in the background, this is not due to its logical force, but to the irresistible testimony of man's moral consciousness. Even though it may be ever so difficult for anyone to detect a moral order in the world round about him, in his *conscience* every one, whether he wills it or not, feels that he is as much bound to this order as his mind and reason are to the laws of thought... He will persevere... and this conviction will... involuntarily result in recognition of a... holy God, who exercises sovereign power over all creatures.[9]

Argument from the Idea of Being. The common name for this argument from the idea of being is the Ontological Argument.

In the last previous chapter I have already presented several forms of this argument under the heading, 'Why People Do Believe in God.' These forms of the argument are judged sound by many good scholars. The classical form of the Ontological Argument was originated by the Father of medieval scholasticism, Anselm of Canterbury (1033–1109), in a skilfully articulated treatise called *Monologion* (monologue). In it the author thinks reflectively on himself and is convinced he has found God, at least an absolutely irrefutable proof of His existence.

In seeking over the years to explain the *Monologion* to students I have summarized Anselm's argument in the following syllogism – major premise, minor premise, conclusion – both fair to Anselm and understandable to students. A syllogism works this way: *major premise*: 'All men are liars.' *Minor premise*, 'Harold is a man.' *Conclusion*, 'Harold is a liar.' So Anselm seems to say: *major premise*, 'I have the distinct idea of an infinite, perfect spirit whom I call God.' *Minor premise*, 'A distinct aspect of perfection is existence [a non-existent spirit would hardly be perfect].' *Conclusion*, 'God exists.'

I think there is a serious fallacy here. If we keep the premises and conclusion in the realm of thought, of course, the reasoning is perfect. God exists – in the thinker's mind. But transfer the subject to apples. I start with two apples in my pocket. They are real in the realm of existent, objective things – whether I think about them or not. For awhile I forget about them and think about two perfect apples in my mind. It is correct to say two apples 'exist' as *ideas* in my mind. But when I go to eating apples, I only have the original two in my pocket. I cannot eat two apples whose existence is solely in my mind. Nor can I add two mental apples to two real ones in my pocket for a sum of four apples in the realm of real, objective things.

So much for this part of Anselm's argument. Early in this chapter we discussed reasons why people do believe in God. Much of this material will be found also in Anselm's argument. In that I judge him to be mainly correct.

All of Anselm's writings have been competently translated into English and published. Read for yourself: *Anselm of Canterbury*, writings edited and translated by Jasper Hopkins and Herbert Richardson.[10]

Argument from Universal Consensus (*ex consensu gentium*). We have already taken note that there is a universal awareness of God. No section of the human race has been able to shake the notion, 'He is there.' The polytheists of old were convinced of a power above the gods and goddesses of whom they made images and carried in their processions. Some pre-Socratic philosophers spoke of 'God', singular number as in monotheism. From the age of Plato onward Greek literature speaks as easily of *ho theos* (God) as *hoi theoi* (gods). Cicero and Seneca assumed a sort of monotheism. Even in the gross animal-worship of Egypt 1,000 years before an henotheism which acknowledged one high god prevailed in court for awhile (thirteenth century BC, Amenhotep IV). In a sense, the very fury of modern atheists (Feuerbach, Lenin, Nietzsche, *et al*) indicates not so much that there is no God but that many sinful men do not like Him very well.

God as Necessary Postulate (*Kant's Argument*). A postulate is a necessary assumption demanded by something else that is true. Kant (as do most people if they think about it) held that there is not simply one *summum bonum* (highest good). Every human being is taught by the moral conscience (1) the fulfilment of duty, and (2) that happiness *bonum*

---

9. Herman Bavinck, *The Doctrine of God* (Grand Rapids: Eerdmans, 1951, 1983), pp. 75, 76.
10. *Anselm of Canterbury*, four volumes (Toronto and New York: The Edwin Mellen Press, 1974 – 1976).

consummatum (consummate good) is the result of doing the first.

Morality, he agreed, is against human tendency. Morality must often proceed against pleasure. To be honest one must often suffer material loss. Yet my moral sense insists that honesty must be pursued. This requires that a Regulator stand behind the moral sense, one who will make happiness a necessary ultimate concomitant of morality.

Morality is valid for this life. Civilization and personal happiness require it to be so. Therefore, there must be a God who reigns over this state of affairs or else there is no morality in this life. Not that we do good for reward, as such, but we should seek *balance* between present good and future happiness. No one ever does his duty fully in this life. His impulses and circumstances forbid. Yet he ought to do his duty and for this, besides the existence of God, the moral regulator, two other postulates are necessary; freedom of the human will and immortality.

At this point a digression into the metaphysics, ethics and epistemology of Kant and his post-Kantian successors in the German universities is tempting (Fichte, Schelling, Hegel and Schopenhauer) but unnecessary for present purposes. A consensus prevails among philosophers that Kant redirected philosophy. In some respects he still dominates the field. The late Carl F. H. Henry, for example frequently raised the spectre of Kantian metaphysics and theory of knowledge.

At the age of 57 Emmanuel Kant wrote his first book of world importance, the *Critique of Pure Reason* in 1781. The *Critique of Practical Reason* followed in 1788 and the *Critique of Judgment* in 1790. These volumes are currently available in English translations though few ever aspire to digest their cumbersome content. Their contents however are widely known. My professor of philosophy, the late Allen Miller of Heidelberg College and Edens Seminary devoted considerable class time to Kant's Critiques.

In the first Critique Kant devoted attention to the theistic arguments, which he held to be three, not the usual four, and found them inadequate to prove God's existence. He did express great respect for the argument from design (teleological), for he took notice in the world of signs of order, design and purposiveness. Yet he found these evidences 'insufficient to establish the existence of an infinite Being, i.e. the most real being (*ens realissimum*).[11]

In the *Critique of Practical Reason*, however, Kant thought he established necessity for belief in God on the basis of what he called the *categorical imperative*. By categorical he meant an unqualified command, morally obligatory upon all whether they obeyed it or not. People everywhere in every age are consciously aware of this imperative. Hence, Kant intended to show that one is justified in postulating God upon the grounds of faith. This 'ideal' is never a part of experienced reality, he asserted, but because the imperative demands our compliance it must be regarded as regulative.

The *Critique of Judgment* furnishes further reasons to postulate God. Just as the universal feeling of respect for *moral law* (the Categorical Imperative) so the feeling of respect for *beauty*, and for the *sublime* and for *design* in nature suggest an *a priori* element in nature. By *a priori* Kant means present before we mortals experience (see, hear, taste, touch) them. When we do experience (sense) the beauty of an object (though we know not how or why) or stand in awe of the starry sky or reflect on the apparent adaptation of the innumerable parts of nature to some common purpose we are justified in drawing the conclusion (i.e. critique of judgment) that 'my own mind is greater then the universe [within] which it has made in terms of its own perceptual forms… Likewise the moral law with its postulate of immortality… suggests I am a being superior to the mechanical world'.[12] Further, 'The beauty and sublimity of nature and the purposiveness of organisms indeed suggest to us that the world may be the production of an infinite Artist, of a genius who has produced it as human artists produce their creations. We may hope that this is true, but we do not know'.[13]

The post-Kantians and philosophers to the present day have worked his system over both with refutation and refinements – but always with respect. His postulate of freedom has taken heavy hits from the materialistic naturalism which has grown in strength since the Enlightenment.[14]

Let us close this chapter with an evaluation of the exercises of the mind that we call theistic arguments, or somewhat less accurately, natural theology. Let us acknowledge they are not *apodictic*, that is, absolute demonstration to every mind as proving 'God is', certainly not 'the God and Father of our LORD Jesus Christ'. To reflective minds

---

11. W. K. Wright, *The History of Modern Philosophy* (New York: Macmillan Co., 1941), p.281.
12. ibid., p. 291.
13. ibid., p. 292.
14. The most thorough discussion of moral freedom I am aware of is, *Moral Freedom* vol. iii of his 3 volume *Ethics* by Nicolai Hartmann (New York: Macmillan Co., 1932, 1962). He holds 'morality is possible only in a world determined throughout, mentally as well as physically, by the law of cause and effect'.

these evidences provide material for meditation and contemplation, and in the hands of skilful exponents can serve to make the dogmatic atheist appear a bit foolish. So while there is no clear, unambiguous content of saving truth in the theistic arguments, it is proper to exercise the mind in these matters. Orthodox, classical Christian theology says natural theology is profitable in three ways.

(1) The *usus paedagogicus*, or preparatory value. It is pointed out that these mental exercises help us distinguish God's qualities and attributes. They raise our sense of need for revelation and desire for it. The pagan philosophers unknowingly brought some awareness of need for the God of the Bible and longing for something better than the official religion and the cults provided. (See chapter on preparation for Christ in Part 4: Christology.) Justin Martyr, Origen and Augustine thought so. It is, of course, true that some ancient pagan writers who were touched by Christianity did not see anything they wanted in genuine Christianity (Marcus Aurelius, Julian the Apostate).

(2) The *usus didacticus*, or teaching use. Good teachers employ thoughts, terms, techniques of non-revelational theology in every age. Even the writers of the New Testament employed (usually with modification and adaptation) ideas and words from philosophical and religious discourse of the world they lived in to teach a revealed theology. Light and darkness, the *logos* (word) idea, *pleroma* (fullness) are examples. Even the name *kurios* (Lord) for *Yahweh* in the Old Testament and for Jesus in the New Testament is derived from the civil and religious vocabulary of Greek society. The philosophers furnished many categories of thought and logical framework for organizing ideas. Think of Aristotle's formal, efficient and final causes, for example, and such useful tools for analysis as nature, cause, proximate, postulate, axiom, syllogism and the like. Nevertheless, the philosophers could not furnish much valid content, though the framework for organizing thought to which they gave early expression is still with us and every theologian, lay or professional, uses them. In a more special way the Greek philosophers furnished many of the basic canons both of art and music. It has been said, Aristotle cannot be baptized by Christ; i.e. the content of Aristotle's thoughts on metaphysics and ethics cannot be transplanted to Christianity. But insofar as his discoveries in logical methods conformed to reality as God created it, they are useful. In fact those Christian philosophers who reject most of this paragraph use them – knowingly or unknowingly. Barth and Van Til must speak of *physis* (nature), *hypostasis* (substance) and *ousia* (being), terms of natural theology, along with the rest of us.

(3) The *usus paedeuticus*, or educational value. In a time when preparation for the ministry included education in the Greek and Latin writings of classical antiquity, such authors as Seneca and Marcus Aurelius were read for profit. Even such adherents to the *sola scriptura* formulas as Luther and Calvin quote them at length. Calvin's first major work was a commentary on Seneca's *De Clementia* (concerning mercy), published in 1532. The expository method he employed in his pre-conversion days was employed throughout his life in composing the forty-five lengthy books of *Commentary* which sit on a shelf near my desk. He commented on the *De Clementia* as a Christian humanist and never repudiated what he said there as far as I know. Though the users may not be aware of it, the commentaries which line the shelves of pastors and professors today perpetuate as well as assimilate both the content and method of Calvin learned from the classical authors – to the immense benefit of the church ever since. Calvin was the first extensive modern commentator on the Bible.

Marcus Aurelius (*Meditations*)[15] and Seneca (*De Clementia*) and numerous other classical authors of late antiquity believed in a moral God and insisted on obligation to moral duty. This, while valuable to the soil in which Christian evangelism was planted, could also issue in superstitious thinking and ascetic practices. Apart from the clear light of revelation we may theologize and speak in superstitious patterns and act in a fashion far below revealed patterns of morality. As a religious person I may be a Pharisee, yet even natural theology condemns hypocrisy.

It is evident that, though 'natural light' (let us not call it revelation, general or otherwise) has some uses, it is dangerous if pressed to the point of equality with biblical revelation. There is a place in a good housekeeper's cleaning closet for astringents, powerful soaps and solvents. There is no place for them in the pantry where wholesome foods and seasonings are stored. 'He that is spiritual' may use the information and tools supplied by nature (human and otherwise) to explain and organize the truth of the Word of God. Paul, for example, in his famous disquisition on the foolishness of the gospel (1 Cor. 1 and 2) employed the categories of Greek thought furnished by the academy and the *stoa* to make his points.

---

15. Marcus Aurelius, Roman Emperor AD 161 – 180 was one of the few emperors whose writing had permanent value. In his twelve books of *Meditations* 'he restated the old doctrines with a new intensity of religious and moral feeling, and in a lapidary style which is all his own; this has made his meditations a breviary for contemplatives throughout the centuries'. 'Aurelius', *The Oxford Classical Dictionary* 2nd ed. edit. N. G. L. Hammon & H. H. Scullard (Oxford: Clarendon Press, 1970), pp. 152, 153.

6
How God has Revealed Himself to Mankind

The title of this chapter has to do with the Bible, as such, only in a fractional way. True, God has told us of Himself through the Scriptures and the Scriptures have a unique place in the history of revelation. Yet there were many people who received a saving knowledge of God before there was a syllable of written Holy Scripture (Abel, Enoch, Noah, Abram). Even at the present time there are whole communities of Christian believers wherein only a small minority can read. Yet they have received saving knowledge of God from missionaries and others who have preached the Word to them. Granting that the Bible is now our chief source of knowledge of God, our purpose is to set forth by what variety of means God has made Himself known to people in times past and perhaps presently. To put the matter another way, granting the Bible conveys all the perfect information we have about God, where did the writers learn these things? Further, we are interested in the clarification of the connection of such matters with our belief in God.

Already the language of this chapter has brought us into collision with several theological opinions, for there are many varieties of modern theology which say that even though there must be divine *revelation* if there is to be salvation, this has nothing at all to do with information about God. The recent books on my shelves specifically treating the problem of the relation of knowledge *of* or *about* God to revelation and to the Bible fill several feet of shelf space. I have read most of them and have learned that the majority of these theories assert in one way or another that revelation is an event or 'constellation' of events wherein God meets (as event) or speaks directly as Person to person or a group of people. No information is imparted. The Bible is the witness of the people who experienced these 'revelatory events'. Lectures and books on doctrine from this perspective provide very little information about God, though there are thousands of words. One of the authors says we learn from the Bible mainly in that we must listen carefully as we read Scripture and obey – that is all. Yet he says nothing specific about what one learns therein about God.

The niceties of this argument promise to occupy nimble wits in a rather fruitless debate for another generation, for after more than fifty years of it, the sometimes fierce exchanges seem unabated. This philosophers' game has given us the 'God-is-Dead' movement (of late unlamented memory) and confusing theology in both liberal and conservative churches. As believers in the full trustworthiness of Scripture, should we then take up again where we were before our generation entered this cul-du-sac? I think so.

When I was in college this view was convincingly purveyed to us as *krisis* theology, also called *existential* and *dialectical* theology. In the process of time it was named neo-orthodoxy. It all seemed very reasonable at the time and we learned the key words: eschatological, infinite-qualitative gulf, confrontation, encounter, witness to revelation and at least a dozen more. Then we heard of philosophers named Jaspers and Heidegger and theologians Barth and Brunner, then Tillich, all Europeans. The American teachers who followed them, at least in part, were credible and serious social-theological thinkers – most importantly, Reinhold Niebuhr, a truly original thinker. More recently we have John Macquarrie and many more to read.

These men and their very numerous disciples differ in many and important ways. Several appear to have orthodox views of the Trinity and the Person of Christ, though I have not found one who teaches a doctrine of atonement which regards Christ's work as a propitiation of divine wrath or even centers redemption in the cross as objective reconciliation, much less propitiation of divine law or wrath.

They seem all to agree that there are no objective, factual, revelatory data (propositions) about truth in the Bible... – even though when it suits their purpose they use the Bible the same way the rest of us do.[1] It has not lost its appeal to many.

At the twentieth century John Baillie, Dean of the faculty of Divinity at the University of Edinburgh, admirer of Brunner, authored a survey of recent views of revelation in which he said:

> Throughout the greater part of Christian history... the distinction between revealed and natural or rational knowledge [was commonly made] and an intelligent schoolboy could have told you what the distinction was. He would have explained to you that there are two sharply contrasted ways in which men have gained knowledge of God and things divine – by the unaided exercise of their own powers of thinking, and by direct communication from God Himself. If instead of the schoolboy you had consulted a learned theologian, you would have received very much the same answer.[2]

After going on to show that even rationalist philosophers took this view of the matter, Baillie pointed out that the Reformers maintained that on account of 'the corruption of human nature. . . human reason was now so damaged an instrument as to yield little or no reliable knowledge of things divine'.[3]

The same distinction held generally (with exceptions) through the nineteenth century.[4] Presently almost all theologians refer to any knowledge of God among mankind, whether derived from 'natural' sources, and apprehended by innate human powers (natural light), or knowledge of God derived from supernatural sources (revelation) as revelation. The former is designated general revelation and the latter special revelation.[5] Though one might wish the older, more precise distinction was preserved in present-day theological discourse, the newer is frequently employed in the pages to follow.

To say that God has *revealed* Himself is not to say that He has *exposed* Himself. We do not mean that any man, or angel with eyes which transfer impulses from fleshly organs to a fleshy brain, ever has seen that infinite and eternal Spirit whom we call God. '[Y]ou cannot see my face, for man shall not see me and live' (Exod. 33:20) and 'No one has ever seen God' (John 1:18). Granting that certain biblical persons had very special meetings with God (Isaiah, Moses and Paul, among others) and that these disclosures of God are rightly called revelations of a special sort, it is in full keeping with the usage of language and a sound theology to employ *reveal* and *revelation* of the making known of truth, fact and information. Revelation in this sense of the word may be a statement of a fact ('In the beginning, God created the heavens and the earth') or announcement of abstract truth ('Righteousness exalts a nation'). It may take the form of a command ('Thou shalt not commit adultery'), or of a narrative of past events (the book of Chronicles), or a prediction ('Your God shall come'). Sometimes it is reflection of the human author on spiritual experiences ('The LORD is my shepherd; I shall not want').

That God should make Himself known to mankind is antecedently probable. More than one version of the following story illustrates the intrinsic probability of revelation by such a God as the Bible describes. A certain woman from a tribe that had never heard the gospel before listened as the missionary told the grand story. Afterwards she

---

1. This prevalent brand of theology was thoroughly explained to evangelical readers in a book sponsored by The Evangelical Theological Society by Paul King Jewett, *Emil Brunner's Concept of Revelation* (London: James Clark & Co.,1954).
2. John Baillie, *The Idea of Revelation in Recent Thought* (New York: Columbia Univ. Press, 1956, 1958), pp. 3, 4.
3. ibid., p. 8.
4. A. A. Hodge, *Outlines of Theology* (Grand Rapids: Eerdmans, 1957, reprint of 1878 ed.), pp. 53–64 and article 'Natural Theology' in *McClintock & Strong Cyclopaedea*, vol. vi (Grand Rapids: Baker Books, 1968–70), pp. 862–864.
5. G. C. H. Berkouwer, *General Revelation* (Grand Rapids: Eerdmans, 1955, 1971) pursues this matter through debates of modern times. Excellent articles are 'General Revelation', by B. A. Demarest and 'Special Revelation', by Carl F. H. Henry, both in the *Evangelical Dictionary of Theology*.

was heard to say: 'I always thought there ought to be a God like that.' The felt need of people everywhere witnesses to the need for a divine revelation.

That there is something in a person which renders revelation not only helpful, appropriate and possible but also *necessary*, if we are to be fully happy, is illustrated by a story. Helen Keller was blind and deaf and without the sense of smell from the age of two years. In the process of her training she came to the place where she could receive messages and respond with words. After this point in her training (it has been reported) she was told of God, the Father of the Lord Jesus Christ. Her immediate response was, 'I always knew He was there but I didn't know His name.' As is generally known, while Miss Keller never became a particularly devout Christian, she was a believer.

According to the Bible, from the time of the fall in Paradise, and ever after, God has sought to make Himself known. The very framework of the Bible, from the story of the dispersion of the human race at Babel, after the Flood, through the story of Abraham and on to the end, is the theme of God's providing both redemption and revelation for mankind. Let us look to the story of the means and modes God employed, together with an estimate in each case of the content, distribution and values of each.

Let us try to think of ourselves as living in a time before a word of the Bible had been written. Let us agree, since God is the kind of Person He is, that it would be entirely in keeping with His character to communicate with the creatures whom He made to be like Himself in some important way. Let us also agree that as sinners we would be utterly hopeless of eternal felicity unless He had provided both knowledge of Himself and redemption. How would God have gone about it?

There is a summary sentence in the New Testament that partially answers this. The passage grandly states that in Old Testament times God spoke through prophets and since then He has spoken by a Son (Heb. 1:1, 2). But how did He speak to the prophets? The text simply says, 'in many ways'. All right then, what were some of these 'many ways'? Also, what sort of information or communication was conveyed? By what means did Cain and Abel learn that God requires sacrifice, or for that matter, requires worship at all? If Enoch walked with God and pleased Him, how did Enoch know what God wanted from him in the first place? If, as Paul says, the heathen suppress certain known truths about God before any missionary even finds them (Rom. 1:18), what is the content of their knowledge of God and how do they apprehend it? There are further questions such as: Are the heathen who never hear the gospel truly lost? How shall we discover a true answer to the question? We shall take the Bible as our guide, as usual in all matters of religious belief, but if so, then the Bible must point beyond itself to certain other sources of information.

1. The Inward Prompting by the Holy Spirit.

In the first place, there is strong evidence in the Bible that the Holy Spirit, who does now in a very special way convince people's hearts of sin, has always striven with those hearts. He has used such influences as we can only surmise to prompt members of our fallen race 'that they should seek God, in the hope that they might feel their way toward him and find him' (Acts 17:27, see the context; compare Gen. 6:3). This admirable impulse has not often led to true religion but rather to idolatry and polytheism as well as even baser forms of worship. May it not be said that all the multitude of expressions of worship in false religions in the world has at least this much realized truth at its root?

The papal Roman Church since Vatican II continues to make her exclusive claims as sole sphere of salvation and custodian of divine revelation.[6] Yet she, consistent with her insistence that human reasoning faculties remain unimpaired by the fall, allows – or at least seems to allow – that without benefit of special revelation human beings can and do know God in a saving way. I quote:

> The sacred Synod professes that 'God, the first principle and last end of all things, can be known with certainty from the created world by the natural light of human reason' (cf. Rom. 1:20). It teaches that it is to his Revelation that we must attribute the fact that those things, which in themselves are not beyond the grasp of human reason, can, in the present condition of the human race, be known by all men with ease, with firm certainty, and without the contamination of error.[7]

This is quite in keeping with the latent doctrine of universal salvation prevalent in many Vatican II pronouncements

---

6. *Dogmatic Constitution on Divine Revelation*, Vatican II, Dei Verbum, 18 November, 1965 (Vatican Collection, Vatican Counsel II, 1975, 1996), vol.ii, chapters I – III.
7. See *Dogmatic Constitution on Divine Revelation*, Vat. II, Dei Verbum, 18 November, 1965, VCVC vol i, p. 752.

and in the *Church Dogmatics* of Karl Barth. Several Roman Catholic theologians of world-wide reputation prepared the way for the Vatican II pronouncements and various subsequent official statements.

In any case, if God *is*, He must not be ignored but worshiped! Jesus spoke of how the Comforter (Holy Spirit) would be sent to convict the world of sin (John 16:7-10), but it is doubtful if Jesus' promise relates to the Spirit's work apart from the preaching of the Word. Aside from that promise, it has been argued from John 1:9 that Christ the eternal Logos (Word) has always been lighting every person 'coming into the world' and that such is the meaning of Micah 5:2, 'one… whose origin is from old, from ancient days'. Whether or not these texts teach such a doctrine, which is doubtful, the presence of God's Spirit in the world has always been, through what some teachers call God's 'common grace', an influence for good and a restraint on evil. In this way God tells the heathen mother, for example, to care for her helpless infant and not only instructs the civil magistrate to restrain violent men but moves the common man to obey the magistrate, at least most of the time.

J.O. Buswell, a trusted writer, says,

> In my opinion the convicting work of the Holy Spirit in the world in general, is a work upon the hearts of all men prior to either faith or regeneration, a work wherein not only is the gospel freely offered to all, but all are brought to a point of enablement to such a degree that, if having been convicted, they reject the Grace of God thus offered to them, but they are subject to the eternal wrath and curse of God *because* they have not believed (John 3:18), and because they 'have not received the knowledge of the truth … but have taken pleasure in unrighteousness' (2 Thess. 2:10-12).[8]

Dr Buswell admits that his idea, rather timidly advanced, lacks clear scriptural support.

This teaching seems to carry the matter too far. I find it hard to adjust to the clear teaching of Romans 10:11-17, that preaching of the Word is necessary for people to know anything at all of a saving gospel and, elsewhere, Dr Buswell grants this.

2. God Reveals Himself Through what He has made.

God has certainly revealed Himself through the material 'heavens and earth' which He has made. As noted earlier, older theologians call this 'the light of nature'.

The Bible is very clear as to the fact that nature does have something to say to people about their Creator. Some of the affirmations are clothed in the beautiful poetry of the Psalms. Psalm 104 speaks of the clouds as God's garments (v. 2), and of beams of light shining through them as beams of His chamber (v. 3). The rest of the Psalm declares how, in detail, all aspects of nature are God's work in creation, preservation and government. They are *all*, including mankind and human works, God's works (vv. 24, 31). The Psalmist's reflections on nature call attention to God's greatness, His honor and majesty (v. 1; cf. 86:8); God's manifold wisdom and great riches (v. 24); His eternal glory (v. 31); and God's joy in His works in nature. Just as a man, made in God's likeness, rejoices in doing and making things, so the Creator rejoices eternally in His works. The discerning believer, by means of this revelation, understands his dependence on God and the importance of praiseful worship of God while life shall last (v. 33). He also understands the *unnaturalness* of the presence of sin and of sinners in God's perfect creation (v. 35a).

Several ancient manuscripts make the anonymous Psalm 104 a continuation of Psalm 103, thus like 104 a Psalm of David. David the shepherd and king, sweet psalmist of Israel, was keenly appreciative of the lineaments of God visible in nature. He lived in primary relation with nature. He fed sheep; he saw stars at night; he planted his feet in the rocky soil whenever he went some place. Few people today live close to nature. Even farmers nowadays are only slightly in this primary relation to nature – many care for no animals, the mercury lamp steals their view of stars at night and protected both from cold and heat in the cab of their farm tractors, they seldom walk very far on their acres. But David considered (Ps. 8:3) the daily and nightly parade of God's material accomplishments in earth and sky and wrote the nineteenth Psalm:

> The heavens declare the glory of God;
> and the firmament sheweth his handywork.
> Day unto day uttereth speech,
> and night unto night sheweth knowledge.
> no speech nor language,
> their voice is not heard.[9]

---

8. J. O. Buswell, *A Systematic Theology of the Christian Religion* vol. iii (Grand Rapids: Zondervan, 1971), p. 157.

The message from and about God is the same as that of Psalm 104, but we learn also that the message goes forth constantly, day and night (v. 2). Significantly, the point is made that since nature's testimony is a silent one (v. 3, see asv, NASB, RSV) people may ignore it and do ignore it, even though God holds them responsible to heed it.

That God holds people thereby responsible for their unbelief and disobedience is the important addition to these truths made by Paul's Epistle to the Romans:

> For the wrath of God is revealed from heaven against all ungodliness and unrighteousness of men, who by their unrighteousness suppress the truth. For what can be known about God is plain to them, because God has shown it to them. For his invisible attributes, namely, his eternal power and divine nature, have been clearly perceived, ever since the creation of the world, in the things that have been made. So they are without excuse. For although they knew God, they did not honour him as God or give thanks to him, but they became futile in their thinking, and their foolish hearts were darkened. Claiming to be wise, they became fools, and exchanged the glory of the immortal God for images resembling mortal man and birds and animals and reptiles (Rom. 1:18-23).

All the truth about the light of nature pointed out in Psalms 104 and 19 (Ps. 8 and others could be read also) is here in Paul's Epistle. The frightening addition is that human beings, as rational, responsible persons, must bear the full weight of responsibility for responding righteously to the knowledge which God has imparted. However, they do not do so. They, in fact, without exception, have suppressed the truth (v. 18) and in spite of the truth of God's invisible, immortal nature, have practiced idolatry. They are therefore 'without excuse' (v. 20) and 'the wrath of God is revealed' in Scripture and conscience, as we shall see, against them. They have presently been abandoned to follow out their unrighteous decisions: 'God gave them up' (v. 24); 'For this reason God gave them up to dishonourable passions' (v. 26); 'And since they did not see fit to acknowledge God, God gave them up to a debased mind to do what ought not to be done' (v. 28).

What then is the content of nature's message about God? It tells of His greatness, His honour and majesty. It displays the riches of His wisdom, and great glory together with His joy in creating such wonders. Such revelations teach also the utter inappropriateness of sin and of the presence of sinners in God's world. They have no rightful place here. Practically speaking, though a source of great pleasure for redeemed people, nature's message to sinners is, in part, one of damnation – though one shrinks from saying it.

There is a message of God's goodness (benevolence) in nature, as Psalm 104 hinted. It is muted, however, for nature provides earthquakes, tornadoes, pestilences and floods, too. The gifts of sun, wind, rain, fertile soil, fruitful seasons fill people's 'hearts with food and gladness', as Paul says elsewhere (Acts 14:17). The goodness of God ought to bring me to repentance (Rom. 2:4), but sadly it rarely does so (Rom. 2:5).

3. God employs Mankind's Own Personal, Moral and Rational Nature.

A further mode God has employed in speaking to the sinful race in all ages is to employ mankind's own personal, moral and rational nature.

Certain philosophers, from ancient times, have sought to begin their search for ultimate truths by searching their own hearts and minds. 'Know thyself' and 'I think, therefore I am' are famed expressions of this method. John Calvin wrote at the opening of his great work of doctrine,

> No one can look upon himself without immediately turning his thoughts to contemplation of God in whom he 'lives and moves' [Acts 17:28]. For, quite clearly, the mighty gifts with which we are endowed are hardly from ourselves; indeed, our very being is nothing but subsistence in the one God. Then by these benefits shed like dew from heaven upon us, we are led as by rivulets to the spring itself.[10]

Calvin's logic is correct, but it is regenerate, sanctified logic. Only Scripture and agencies derived from Scripture speak plainly of mankind's being, specifically of this rational and moral nature, as being a source of common knowledge of God.

We must start with the fact that mankind was created originally in God's likeness. The likeness is chiefly, though certainly not exclusively, our personal, rational and moral nature. Though marred by the fall and as to

---

9. Psalm 19:1-3 KJV with italized words of v. 3 removed.
10. John Calvin, *Institutes of the Christian Religion*, Vol. I (Philadelphia: Westminster Press, 1960), I, 1. 1.

holiness and love for God, wholly spoiled, the image remains. It is mankind's present possession of that likeness which renders murder a heinous crime (Gen. 9:6) and slander or malicious cursing of other people a vicious iniquity (James 3:8-10). People do legitimately reason of God's nature from their own. Their common mistake has been to impute God-likeness to their corruptible bodies and to make a visible, physical, corrupt God in their own physical image.

Others (we think of some of the best representatives of ancient Greek philosophy) knew God to be a universal, free spirit, and cautiously said so, even though it was dangerous to deny the prevailing idolatry. Socrates, for example, was executed for atheism. Paul was understood when he appealed to the Greeks on the basis of their God-likeness to see the stupidity of their idolatry (Acts 17:22-34, especially verses 28 and 29). Idol worship turns God into the image of mankind and others of God's creatures.

So we may be sure that Paul was understood also when he wrote: 'when Gentiles, who do not have the law, by nature do what the law [Moses' law] requires…They show that the work of the law is written on their hearts, while their conscience also bears witness, and their conflicting thoughts accuse or even excuse them on that day when … God judges the secrets of men by Christ Jesus' (Rom. 2:14-16). Some moral standards are written on people's hearts. They know that right and wrong exist; they know what some of the standards are and they know they ought to do right. When they act in a manner that their own standards approve they have good conscience – one that is painless, non accusing – and conversely when they violate their own standards they feel accused by painful conscience. They sense the sanctions of a righteous God threatening them on the Judgment Day.

Thus people everywhere can know and we may presume generally *do* know that God is, like themselves, a moral being; also that, unlike themselves, He is entirely righteous. On other grounds, they know Him to be Creator and hence moral Governor of all people. Therefore, they expect a judgment day when they must face God, even though they are afraid of Him. 'It is appointed for man to die once, and after that comes judgment', though a biblical quotation has been written in the sub-consciousness, if not the consciousness, of every human being. The whole existence of ancient Egypt's reigning elite, no less, was self-regulated in order to come off well in that judgment. Hence, the national wealth came to be devoted to funeral arrangements and memorials.

It is now time to pause for certain reflections. Nothing we have turned up thus far informs people that God is gracious, that He has redeemed them or that He loves them. The promptings of the Spirit in His works of common grace, whereby He preserves human society from utter corruption and self-destruction, perhaps hint at His love. However, nature frowns about as much as she smiles and no prosecutor or judge can be more unrelentingly antagonistic than 'guilty' conscience. We turn now to some of the modes of information whereby God conveys His message of love, of grace and of redemption.

4. God's Original and Direct Revelation.

God made Himself known to all subsequent generations of mankind when He spoke to our first parents through original and direct revelation. This may have continued awhile, for some people still 'walked with God' (Gen. 5:22; 6:9) and conversed with Him (Gen. 3:8 – 4:15) through the antediluvian epoch. Here is how one orthodox writer presents this information and supports it.

> The Bible indicates that God revealed Himself to mankind at the beginning of human history, and that He hath not left Himself [in any age or place] without a witness (Acts 14:16, 17). There is corroborative data in the study of comparative religious and cultural anthropology, indicating that the oldest religious traditions are the nearest to biblical theism. The scriptural teaching on primitive revelation [i.e. original and direct] must be considered…There is generally among primitive peoples some trace or tradition of knowledge of the true God.[11]

A century ago there was considerable emphasis on primitive revelation as enduring through time. One of the most cogent and balanced of the era, W. G. T. Shedd (1820–1894), devoted eight pages of his *Dogmatic Theology* (I, 201-208) to survival of primitive revelation in the universal consciousness of mankind. All sound theology must deal with Paul's clear doctrine of apostasy from primitive revelation (Rom. 1:18-32). A text prescribed

---

11. J. O. Buswell, op. cit., p. 159.

for my college course in apologetics by Fr. W. Schmidt of Vienna summarized evidence derived from researches among every known kind of primitive society for existence of the 'highest God' of monotheism in their religious heritage. No society apparently – or at least no known societies – are without it. Monotheism might be a universal inference; it might also be an inheritance from the beginning of the race.[12] Schmidt's book is a very impressive work, not superseded, as far as I can determine.

Some modern psychological theory makes much of alleged innate memory of race experience. Sometimes this is called primal history, or *Urgeschichte*. The Bible does not either affirm or deny this but the unity of humankind in being essentially one biological family suggests that certain traditions would be passed down to us all – or nearly all. I cite a striking personal example. There is in the Culver family an interesting tradition at least 1,300 years old, though I discovered it only recently. My father's given name was Cyniard. He never liked the name and always wondered where it came from. He knew only that he was named for a distant relative of his grandfather's generation, but he did not know that he, himself, was of English descent, a tenth generation American of the Culver family, likely through Governor John Winthrop, the elder, and that Culver is an old Saxon name. In 1973, in reading the first volume of Trevelyan's *History of England*, I found my father's given name, Cyniard, attached to a young king of the Saxon kingdom of Mercia, in Great Britain. The mystery was solved – at least for me. A fragment of culture from our ancestors in continental Saxon Germany still survives, for a grandson and a great-grandson bear my father's first name. We can pass tradition on for thousands of years without knowing we do. Some words of common English speech, for example, can be traced to sources thousands of years removed. All language is populated with verbal fossils of remote antiquity.

Perhaps most of the best ideas people have about God have come to us in this manner. My own teacher of theology thought that 'most of what men believe about God has come to us in this way'. He thought it accounts for the truths in ethnic religions, though garbled, misunderstood and corrupted.

There is no evidence that God communicates with people today in any reportable manner. For good reasons we live under a 'silent heaven', walking wholly by 'faith and not by sight'.[13]

Later we shall study God's providence. Providence is God's general direction of history and there is also His special control, which we call the miraculous.

5. God Reveals Himself in Special Works.

Hence we may speak of how God has revealed Himself in special providential and miraculous works. Sometimes we do not know if some extraordinary event falls in the category of God's ordinary working (the 'laws' of nature) or His special working (miracles). The distinction, however, is valid and, in either case, what God does says something about Him. If, as some claim, it was a landslide that cut off the waters of Jordan when the Israelites passed through, or a natural wind which parted the Red Sea, it was God's omniscient, omnipotent working in a special providence. We truly do not know *how* He works in either creation or providence, as the Almighty overwhelmingly reminded Job (Job 38, 39). We know no more about how God performs miracles.

We do not know whether the first plagues of Egypt came of natural causes or not; their timing certainly did not. God's power operated in either case for special reasons. One of them was to teach Pharaoh and all the nations who heard the report of them. Pharaoh had said, 'Who is the Lord, that I should obey his voice' (Exod. 5:2). But the Lord said, 'I will ... multiply my signs and wonders in the land of Egypt ... The Egyptians shall know that I am the Lord, when I stretch out my hand against Egypt' (Exod. 7:3-5, see also verse 17). God purposed that Pharaoh and all of his people would learn some things about the Lord God of the Hebrews. Moses said to the Egyptian king during one of the plagues, 'I will stretch out my hands to the Lord. The thunder will cease, and there will be no more hail, so *that you may know* that the earth is the Lord's' (Exod. 9:29 emphasis added).

Not only so, by those events the people of God of that generation and all later generations were to be taught (as we now are being taught) about God: 'Then the Lord said to Moses, "Go in to Pharaoh, for I have hardened his heart and the heart of his servants, that I may show these signs of mine among them, and that you may tell in the hearing

---

12. W. Schmidt, *The Origin and Growth of Religion, Facts and Theories*, trans. H. F. Rose (New York: Dial Press, 1935), 302 pages.
13. *The Silence of God* is the title of a very influential book, reprinted through most of the twentieth century. 'God is silent now because He has spoken his last word of mercy and love in Christ' says the author. Reprint: Sir Robert Anderson, *The Silence of God* (Grand Rapids: Kregel Publications, n.d.), 215 pages.

of your son and of your grandson how I have dealt harshly with the Egyptians and what signs [miracles] I have done among them, *that you may know that* I am the LORD' (Exod. 10:1-2 emphasis added).

Throughout biblical and Christian history God's people have learned many things about their God through the biblical miracles and providences of God. The prophets frequently rebuked Israel of old for forgetting about God's miracles of deliverance or for misinterpreting them.[14]

From these texts and others the reader of the Bible will learn or have confirmed several things about God. Israel discovered that their God never fails to keep a promise. They came to understand, as David (quoted by Lincoln with reference to divine providences in the American Civil War): 'the judgments of the LORD are true and righteous altogether' (Ps. 19:9 KJV). We may be sure that God still reigns. By His reign He taught England and Wellington on the one hand and France and Bonaparte on the other by the battle of Waterloo, as later all the nations in the great wars of the twentieth century. God speaks to us also through raindrops and wild flowers, and all the true discoveries of science, as Tennyson wrote in 1869:

> Flower in the crannied wall,
> I pluck you out of the crannies,
> I hold you here, root in all, in my hand,
> Little flower – but *if* I could understand
> What you are, root and all, and all in all,
> I should know what God and man is.

6. The Message that Comes from God Through Scripture.

In a special category, because it is a perfect revelation and includes all the others, is the message from God that comes to people through the Holy Scriptures. Extended discussion of this belongs to another locus of doctrine, but several observations about the Bible as a source of truth about God are appropriate here.

The Bible claims to be not one but a series of messages about God, beginning with the earliest prophetic deliverances of the Old Testament through the last of our Lord's apostolic witnesses (Heb. 1:1, 2; 2:1-4). The gospel of Christ was promised in the Old Testament (John 5:39; Rom. 1:1-3), and fulfilled and spelled out plainly in the New Testament (Rom. 1:15-17; cf. Luke 24:25-27, 44-47). The Scriptures are a *complete* guide to what we must believe as well as all the information we need for service and holy living (2 Tim. 3:16, 17). There is also imponderable, mysterious power in the Scriptures, when read in the vernacular language of any people, and made known by preaching and teaching. That power will convert and reform individuals while also improving and refining their morals, manners, economy and material culture. Such is the power in the Bible, the written Word of God (see Rom. 10:9-17; Heb. 4:12; 1 Peter 1:23-25).

7. God's Unique Revelation in His Son.

God has revealed Himself uniquely in His Son, the Second Person of the Godhead, our Lord Jesus Christ: 'God who in many parts and many manners spake in time past to the fathers by the prophets has at the last spoken to us by a son' (Heb 1:1, 2 literal translation). The Greek text does not furnish 'The' or 'His' before *huiō*, son. The point of emphasis is that though revelation in the old dispensation had been through authentic prophets, in the new dispensation revelation came through one of a superior order, that is *a* Son of God not *a* son of man. (It is a subtle point not missed by commentators on the Greek text even though suspect by some not competent in such matters.) His very name, Immanuel, means 'God with us' (Isa. 7:14). John wrote: 'the Word became flesh and dwelt among us, and we have seen his glory, glory as of the only Son from the Father... No one has ever seen God; the only God [the only begotten Son (KJV)], who is at the Father's side, he has made him known' (John 1:14, 18).

This revelation stands apart from all the others, the end of all searching, the consummation of all hope for finding God or of His finding us. Jesus Christ provides a *perfect* revelation in that it is *complete* and *final*. When God had finished speaking through our LORD there was nothing more to say; so the risen, ascended Christ 'sat down on the right hand of the Majesty on high' (Heb. 1:3; cf. Col. 2:9; John 14:8-19; 16:12-15). His work as revelator was essentially finished.

We shall yet learn more of our Lord when we see Him face to face, for there is more of His 'grace ready to be revealed' (1 Peter 1:5 RSV). However, God presently has no new avenues of revelation to open. In a certain way, this is

---

14. Some other Scripture passages that discuss this matter are Deut. 4:33-35; 7:8, 9; Josh. 4:23, 24; Isa. 45:1-6; Ezek. 11:9, 10; and John 10:38.

true of the Scriptures. There are no new verses or chapters to be written, but it is possible every time we read the Bible or hear it expounded we may notice a new-to-me fact or gain new insight into truth only dimly perceived before.

As we reflect on the variety of modes of acquiring knowledge of God discussed in this chapter, it becomes apparent that very little of God's grace and redemption are known to us apart from the three last mentioned: God's providential and miraculous works, the Scriptures, and the Lord Jesus Christ. The other sorts of revelation, each valid in some circumscribed way, are inadequate, being both partial and obscure. All of them must be tested and judged by Scripture. Each achieves a normative, dependable status only as interpreted by Scripture. The Bible and Christ alone are complete and perfect while only Christ speaks about God (or anything else, for that matter) in a final way.

In an important sense, all revelation is by Jesus Christ, the 'founder and perfecter of our faith', for He provided all the others, being the Creator of both universe and mankind (John 1:1-3). He was the Giver of that original revelation, and the experiences of Israel whereby they through providence learned of God (see 1 Cor. 10:1-3). His Spirit also gave us the Holy Scriptures (1 Peter 1:10, 11).

The Bible also obviously occupies a unique place in revelation. Its report of primeval, original revelation, while incomplete, is sufficient for all the information we need to have and the only dependable one we have. The Bible includes some of each of the others. The Bible bears to us all we need for life and godliness (2 Tim. 3:16, 17; cf. 2 Peter 1:3), and it interprets them properly. Christian understanding of the Bible grows in individual lives and through the generations of readers and scholars in the history of the church. Furthermore, the only truly *authentic* report we have of the person and redeeming work of Christ is found in the Bible. Without the Holy Scriptures we could not know truth about Him unmixed with error. So, even though our faith for salvation is wholly on Christ, we learn of Him in the Bible:

> Jesus loves me this I know
> For the Bible tells me so!

And, though 'If anyone hears my voice', said the risen Christ to John the Revelator, 'and opens the door, I will come in to him' (Rev. 3:20), the voice with which he speaks always expresses the truths of the words of Holy Scripture. In addition, amazingly throughout our lives the Bible seems to speak in the language of the particular translation in which we first heard and read the Bible.

7
The Names of God

We do not read far in the Old Testament until we learn that personal names and many other proper names are important. They are important because they have meaning. Each name has some special meaning obvious to the ancient Hebrews who read the Bible in its original language. For example, the first human name, Adam, is the word for 'ground', 'soil', 'earth', signifying that the human body is taken from natural elements in the soil. Eve (Ava) means 'life', signifying she is mother of all the people who ever lived. Cain means 'smith' (metal-worker), indicating the origin of metallurgy among his progeny. David means 'beloved', Solomon, 'peace', and so on. Some names indicate something the one who bestowed it hoped would develop in the character or history of the person designated. Since many of our personal names have their meanings in forgotten stages of our own language, dead languages or foreign languages, we do not know the meaning of the names we bear, though they do designate their bearers. George, for example, designates my friend the Culligan man. But hardly anybody knows that George (every consonant and vowel pronounced) is a Greek word for 'farmer', rendered 'husbandman' in KJV. A number would do almost as well. Gail and Charis mean 'Joy' in Hebrew and 'Grace' in Greek. But while my friends Joy and Grace know the meanings of their names, Gail and Charis do not.

When we speak or write about God and when we address Him, we must employ some name or name-like term. God, *Elohim* and *Jehovah* have already appeared above. Surely we ought to learn the names by which God prefers to be known and addressed – His own self-designated names. These will be found in each case to indicate some important characteristic of God or information about Him.

Several of God's names arose out of believers' experiences with Him. They give insights to God's ways of dealing with us. All of this class of names are compound, such as *Jehovah-Jireh* (the LORD will provide) and *Jehovah-Tsidkenu* (the LORD our righteousness). Theological writers emphasize that these are the ones that most distinctly draw *analogies* between human beings and the creator-God, i.e. they are most distinctly *anthropomorphic*. Space does not allow us to treat them here.

The origin of the commonest of God's names is now lost, for the most part. Where the names came from is less important than what they mean. The meaning of some is a matter of special revelation. Some appear to have been long employed before Abraham and Moses. All of them interest us as preliminary statements of God's attributes.

St Jerome, following Jewish custom of the time, said there were properly ten biblical names of God.[1] Jerome listed them as *El, Elohim, Eloha, Sabaoth, Elyon, Esher Ehye, Adonai, Yah, Yhwh* (Jehovah, Yahweh), *Shaddai*. These are indeed some important Old Testament names. This variety does not carry over to the New Testament except as the writers reflect the Old Testament. Several adjectives, such as *almighty*, and metaphors, such as *shepherd*, appear.

There is, however, a poetic chapter of the Bible that, in a beautiful way, uses almost all the most important Old Testament names. In this chapter Moses employs names for God which arose among people who had learned about God as He 'walks in the midst of your camp' (Deut. 23:14). These names we may suppose as arising somewhat as nicknames are invented spontaneously by the common people – 'Old Hickory' (Andrew Jackson), 'Honest Abe' (Abraham Lincoln), 'Slick Willy'. In our high school the principal was a prim lady of near retirement age who was regularly to be seen padding about halls and rooms in soft-soled shoes. Though we called her 'Mrs Hathaway' when brought to her presence, her name among all students was 'Old Pussy Foot'. She never heard it, but from the standpoint of those beneath her authority, it fit exactly.

We shall treat most of the names within the framework of that chapter. Two current, readily accessible treatments, each entitled 'The Names of God', are recommended as guides to the subject and relevant literature.[2]

The Song of Moses – a Mine of Information About God's Names.

Near the end of his life, Moses, the great lawgiver, delivered a series of sermons to his people, the children of Israel. They had conquered Trans-Jordan. They were poised to invade Canaan under fresh leadership. Before taking leave to die and go home to God, Moses composed a song which he recited before the assembled tribes. We have it in Deuteronomy 32:1-43. Most of the common Old Testament names of God appear in the first fifteen verses.

1. *YHWH* (Deut. 32:3, 6, 9, 12, 19, 27, 30, 36 KJV usually LORD), from the Old Testament point of view, is the only *proper* name of the national God of Israel. Therefore, it is not surprising it appears most frequently – nearly 7,000 times and almost 1,000 times in Psalms alone. Yah (Jah KJV) is an abbreviated form of this name. The Tetragrammaton (YHWH) is the focal point on which the document-development theory of the authorship of the Pentateuch (Graf-Wellhausen) developed over the eighteenth and nineteenth centuries.

In abbreviated form (iah, Je, Jeho, jah), this name is very common in theophoric Old Testament names. Aha*ziah* suffixes the name to A*haz* whereas *Jeho*ahaz prefixes the name. El*ijah* joins two names for God ('my God is jah').

'For I will proclaim the name of [Jehovah]' (Deut. 32:3). This is the personal, proper name Israel had for their God. Later in the song, Moses says, 'For [Jehovah]… shall judge his people' (v. 36 KJV), showing again the special character of the name as personal and as of meaning to His people. The word *judge* here means mainly 'to rule as a magistrate'. See also verses 12 and 19. After the exile this came to be regarded with such a nearly superstitious reverence it was thought to be dangerous even to pronounce it ('for the LORD will not hold him guiltless that takes his name in vain', Exod. 20:7). Therefore, the correct pronunciation of YHWH, God's personal and covenant name, was lost forever. Ancient Hebrew was spelled without vowels. In medieval times Jewish scholars supplied the vowels to the text and for YHWH supplied the vowels of *Adonai* (LORD), which they read to the present day. When these vowels are read with YHWH an approximation of 'Jehovah' comes out. This word, now for centuries firmly in the idiom, is not likely to be replaced in Bible-related speech. Scholars suppose *Yahweh* to be nearer the original pronunciation, and is now commonly used in scholarly literature, though this is far from certain. What is called *Sephardic* (similar to Arabic) pronunciation of Hebrew was followed by most Christian scholars until the influence of Yiddish on modern Israeli Hebrew caused *Ashkenazic* pronunciation to prevail in scholarly circles. So there are variant pronunciations of the transliterated (supposed) original. While 'Jehovah' is certainly incorrect it does have the advantage of long established use.

When God explained the meaning of the name to Israel He emphasized connection with: (1) God's *promises* – He has come to fulfill the promises made to Abraham, Isaac and Jacob, the national patriarch; (2) God's *presence* – God said He would be with Moses and His people, Israel; (3) God's *salvation* (deliverance) – the Israelites were to be rescued from the bondage in Egypt; and (4) God's *provision* for every one of their needs. See Exodus 3:1-22 and 6:1-8.

---

1. 'Epistle to Marcellus' as cited by Francis Pieper, *Christian Dogmatics* (St. Louis: Concordia Publ., vol. i, 1950), pp. 432, 433.
2. Thomas McComiskey, *Evangelical Dictionary of Theology*, Walter Elwell, ed. (Grand Rapids: Baker Books, 1984). Elmer Martens, *Evangelical Dictionary of Biblical Theology*, Walter Elwell, ed. (Grand Rapids: Baker Books, 1996).

It is not surprising, then, that when Moses got around to writing the first books of our Bible, the name YHWH was employed most frequently of God when reporting His saving work on behalf of His people. This name is in the Hebrew name 'Joshua' (*Jehoshua'*, Greek, Jesus), which means, 'Jehovah saves' (see Matt. 1:21).[3]

2. *Elohim* (*'Elo-him*) (Deut 32:3, 15, 17) is pronounced *El-o-heem*. In 'Ascribe greatness to our *God!*' (verse 3 emphasis added) 'God' is 'Elohim'. From the biblical point of view, 'This name properly represented One only Being, who revealed Himself to man as creator, ruler, and LORD. It was His own peculiar title, and ought to have been confined to Him.'[4] We do not know what language was spoken in Eden, but Elohim, or its equivalent in that language, is represented as the proper designation of the Creator. It is the only one used in the first chapter of Genesis. An older standard work on the name states:

> In after ages the worship of the Creator as Elohim began to be corrupted. The Name, indeed was retained, but the nature of Him who bore it was well-nigh forgotten. When men were divided into different nations, and spoke various dialects and languages, they must have carried with them those notions of Elohim which they had inherited from their fathers, but the worship which was due to Him alone was in the lapse of ages transferred to the souls of the departed, to the sun, moon, and stars, and even idols made by men's hands.[5]

Recent researches of critical scholars neither confirm nor dislodge Girdlestone's dictum. Some authorities, however, suggest that Elohim, its singular form *Eloah*, and the elemental form *El*, are simply generic words for deity as our English word, 'god'. When used by Christians and in Scripture translation it is capitalized *God* only when referring to the one true God. It is doubtful if the Northwest Semitic word for deity was employed in Eden. At any rate we learn of 'strange' *'elohim* (Gen. 35:1-4). When Rachel ran away with her father Laban's images he demanded his *'elohim* back (Gen. 31:19, 30). Jacob, who did not regard them as genuine deities, nevertheless, for purposes of communication, used Laban's word (v. 32). The case is about the same with the word 'prophet'. There were genuine prophets in Old Testament times, men who spoke for God authentically. Hundreds who were inauthentic claimed to be God's prophets. So even the true prophets, for purposes of communication, called the false prophets by the same name (Hebrew *navi'*) as the genuine (see 1 Kings 18:19; Jer. 28:1-6, 16, 17).

Elohim is God's title, meaning deity. Jehovah is His personal name. In keeping with this, people in the Scriptures say, 'my Elohim', but never 'my Jehovah'. He is 'the Elohim of Israel', but never 'the Jehovah of Israel'.

Later on in Moses' song there are examples of the use of this word *'elohim* as a 'courtesy title' for heathen deities (non-deities) while in fact reserving the title for the God of heaven and earth whose name is Jehovah:

> Then he [Jehovah] will say, 'Where are their gods ['elohim],
> the rock in which they took refuge...
> Let them rise up and help you;
> let them be your protection!
> See now that I, even I, am he,
> and there is no god [elohim] beside me;
> I kill and I make alive;
> I wound and I heal;
> and there is none that can deliver out of my hand' (Deut. 32:37-39).

There is a singular form of this name for God, *'Eloah*. It appears for the first time in Scripture in this chapter (v. 15) and about fifty other times in the entire Old Testament, usually in poetry. Elohim occurs hundreds of times, being the commonest word for deity.

3. *Hats-tsur*, the Rock. *Rock* is a transparent figure employed as a name of God (Deut. 32:4, 15, 18, 30, 31), as in 'The Rock, his work is perfect' (v. 4). That this is a name for Israel's God and ours ought to be acknowledged. Various translations (KJV, RSV, ASV and others) capitalize the first letter, as in all proper nouns. The word means rock, cliff or bedrock, such as is a quarry site (see Isa. 51:1). Throughout this song *hats-tsur*, the Rock, stands for the great stability of God, His sole reality as God. It is used in apposition with Jehovah, Elohim and El (vv. 3, 4, 17-19, 30, 31). He is the only One who is real and therefore the only sound foundation for the life of a person or a nation. His work is perfect (v. 4).

---

3. This name is treated further in connection with God's attributes.
4. Robert B. Girdlestone, *Synonyms of the Old Testament*, 2nd ed. (Grand Rapids: Eerdmans, n.d.), p. 19.
5. ibid., p. 20.

He is, as the Rock, the source of salvation for sinful people, 'the Rock of his salvation' (v. 15). David prayed to the Rock in Ps. 19:14: 'Let the words of my mouth and the meditation of my heart be acceptable in your sight, O LORD, my rock (*tsur*) and my redeemer.' The word for 'rock' is exactly the same as in Deuteronomy 32 and the word for redeemer is the same in every way as in Job 19:25, in each case receiving an initial capital letter as a proper noun. It should be the same in Psalm 19:14 – 'LORD, my *rock* and my *redeemer*' (emphasis added).

This name is specially connected with our LORD in His pre-incarnate capacity as the Jehovah, the God of Israel. Referring to the wilderness journeys of Israel, Paul says: 'our fathers… all ate the same spiritual food, and all drank the same spiritual drink. For they drank from the spiritual Rock that followed them, and the Rock was Christ' (1 Cor. 10:1, 3, 4). Moses spoke to one earthly rock and struck another in frustrated anger. In each case water came out. But neither was a 'Rock that followed them'. That Rock was the Rock, Jehovah-Jesus, of Deuteronomy 32! Paul is affirming not the *typical* presence of Christ, but the *real* presence of Christ with Old Testament believers as He is today with us. There ever has been only one Mediator of salvation: 'For no one can lay a foundation other than that which is laid, which is Jesus Christ' (1 Cor. 3:11). In the words of William O. Cushing's hymn,

> Oh safe to the Rock that is higher than I,
> My soul in its conflicts and sorrows would fly;
> So sinful, so weary, Thine, Thine would I be;
> Thou blest Rock of Ages, I'm hiding in Thee.

'Rock' as a name for God is the most prominent of several inanimate objects of God's creation, which, by analogy, are employed as name or name-like designations for Him. They are all metaphors. Some of them are the sun (Ps. 14:11), a light (Ps. 27:1), a lamp (Rev. 21:23), a fire (Heb. 12:29), a tower (Prov. 18:10), a shadow (Ps. 91:1; 121:5). There are many more.

4. *'El*, the Mighty One. This name (with or without the definite article), and found in Deuteronomy 32:4, 18, 21, usually designates the true God, as in verse 4: 'A God [*'El*] of faithfulness and without iniquity, just and upright is he.' Sometimes as in verse 12, 'no foreign god [*'El*] was with him', the word is used of the non-gods of the heathen. This word is likely derived from a verb meaning to be strong, to be in front of, hence 'the mighty One'.

Unlike the similar word, *'Elohim*, this name is often joined with a separate word, '*Elyon*, another name of God. So we read of 'God Most High' (Gen. 14:18, and frequently elsewhere), 'God Almighty' (*'El Shaddai*, Gen. 17:1), 'the God of Bethel' (*'El Beth 'El*, Gen. 31:13), 'the God of your father' (*'El-'Abikha*, Gen. 49:25).

In Exodus 34:6, 7 *'El* is used with a whole constellation of names for God and name-like adjectives: 'The LORD, a God [*'El*, a Mighty One] merciful and gracious, slow to anger, and abounding in steadfast love and faithfulness, keeping steadfast love for thousands, forgiving iniquity and transgression and sin, but who will by no means clear the guilty, visiting the iniquity of the fathers on the children and the children's children, to the third and fourth generation.' This statement is without parallel in Scripture.

5. *Father*. '[I]s not he thy father that hath bought thee' (Deut 32:6 KJV)? Only NASB of standard English Versions capitalizes 'father' here. Keil's translation in his commentary does so also. Moses is referring to the fact that their God, like a father who begets a child, had brought them into existence as a people, thus calling to remembrance all their past history from Abraham onward. The conservative scholars who gave us NASB have no objection to a doctrine of divine fatherhood as early as Moses. Isaiah 63:16 twice calls God Father – one more loyal than Father Abraham – and Redeemer. Even RSV is willing to have 'Father' be a name for God by Isaiah's time, but strangely not NEB. See also Isaiah 64:8 and Malachi 2:10. God is Father in the thinking and affection of Christians because we learn from the example of Jesus (Luke 23:34; John 17:1, 5), His instruction for prayer (Matt. 6:6, 8, 9) and His regular references to God in this way. The opening verses of nineteen of the Epistles of the New Testament refer trustingly to God in this way.

Some of the latest generations of scholars and their students have difficulty accepting the 'fatherhood of God', regarding it as a sexist anthropomorphism. Earlier Modernists promoted the idea as the very crowning contribution of Christianity. A brief comment on the subject at this point is appropriate, where the idea is put by scholars in its clearest and most favourable light. Obviously God is not a literal father. He does not literally impregnate females as human males do. Yet the word 'father' conveys knowledge of God to us sinners which, though partial and inadequate as such, is nevertheless true, dependable, useful, sufficient for our present state and satisfying to our hearts.

Anything which God has made has pertinence to Him. Anthropomorphisms and other metaphors employ that truth. Scripture never attributes a body, as such, to God but just about every human bodily member or part is applied in figure of speech to God. Yet God is pure spirit (John 4:24). Some of the physical features of human constitution applied to Him are face, eyes, eyelids, ears, mouth, tongue, lips and bosom. So also are human emotions such as grief, regret, anger, fear, compassion, mercy, grace, jealousy, hatred, love and wrath. All imply change and some even misery in the Godhead, yet we know that God does not change (James 1:17) and that He is always perfectly blessed (Rom. 9:5; 1 Tim. 6:15).

Furthermore, in the pictorial language of scripture, God acts like a human being: speaking, resting, working, smelling, visiting, coming down, passing by etc. He wipes away tears like a tender mother and is even compared to animals such as an eagle, a lion, a hen and a lamb. God has wings in one striking passage. Jesus is a lamb throughout the Apocalypse.

Considering all this, attractive as it is to find 'Father' as a name for God in Deuteronomy 32, it probably lacks the naming function of denoting or designating in a particular way. After all, in the Bible, God is also a physician, a shepherd, a farmer, a carpenter, an architect and a soldier. Yet we do not say 'Farmer' (KJV husbandman) is a name for God. We do sometimes see 'Shepherd' capitalized as a proper name for God in popular literature.

Though all biblical names for God are to a degree metaphorical, Scripture does not treat all the metaphors as names. Neither should we. 'Father' and 'Rock' partake of the metaphorical more than the other names in this treatment.

6. *'Elyon*, The Most High.

> When the Most High gave to the nations their inheritance,
> when he divided mankind,
> he fixed the borders of the peoples
> according to the number of the sons of God (Deut 32:8).[6]

This verse means that God as 'Most High' has apportioned each nation, throughout history, its lands, just as He did Israel. When one considers how much of that took place by conquest it seems a truly remarkable statement, and places wars within God's rule over the affairs of nations (Dan. 3:26; 4:17, 24, 25, 32, 34; 5:18, 21; 7:25) and in the expressions of divine worship in the Psalms (examples are Pss. 7:17; 91:1, 9) – eighteen times in all. The New Testament equivalent corresponds with the Psalms usage (examples, Luke 1:32, 35, 76; 2:14).

The name *'Elyon* is a verbal adjective, formed from *'alah*, to ascend. The ascended, the highest (being), is the self-evident meaning. This concept of God is one that peoples who have not yet heard of the true God of Scripture readily accept. When one has thought above and beyond all created beings and things, there is still 'something more beyond'. After that *ne plus ultra*: nothing more beyond. This is close to the God-idea which Paul assumed his hearers at Athens already had before they heard the gospel. It is the assumption likewise of all the many Old Testament prophecies addressed to the nations. Examples are Isaiah 13–24; Jeremiah 46–51; Ezekiel 24–32 and Amos 1:3; 2:3; Obadiah; Nahum; and parts of the book of Jonah, chapter 2. Each of these prophetic messages calls heathen peoples to account before a God – *'Elyon*, the Highest, whom they already know about.

There are two other important names of God found in the Bible that do not appear in Deuteronomy 32. They are *Shaddai* and *'Adonai*.

7. *Shaddai*, Almighty. 'I am God *Almighty*; walk before me, and be blameless' (Gen. 17:1 emphasis added). The word is plural in form, usually held to be a plural of majesty.

This title indicates the fullness and richness of God's grace. It reminded the Hebrew reader in a graphic way that every good gift comes from God, and that we have not because we ask not. We shall confine the examples cited to Genesis and begin with the last example in the book (Genesis 49:25). This one shows how graphic a term it is. There is a Hebrew word for a mother's breasts, *shad*, usually (and understandably) dual, a pair (see Song of Solomon 8:1; Hos. 2:4; 9:14). This word seems to be the source of *Shaddai*, hence the meaning is close to our word 'exuberance'. This connection seems explicit in the last appearance of the word in Genesis. Jacob is blessing Joseph and says, 'From the *'El* of thy father, there shall be help to thee and with *Shaddai*, there shall be blessings to thee, blessings of heaven above... blessings of the breasts [*shadayim*, the two breasts], and blessings of the womb' (Gen. 49:25, my rendering).

An examination of the other occurrences in Genesis shows that each one has to do with God's conferral of the blessing of fruitful life (Gen. 17:1-8; 35:11; and 43:14).

8. *'Adonai*, Lord. This is a special plural form of the normal word of respectful address to another male, especially a superior – Master, Lord, Sir. It receives all these translations (Gen. 43:20; 1 Kings 16:24; Gen. 18:12; Gen 24:9).

---

6. This very ancient reading, also followed by RSV, has 'according to the number of *the sons of God*', that is, the angels.

As used of God it means the same thing except that being, like *Shaddai*, a plural, the aspect of respect is heightened.

This term of respectful address reminds us that God is a great King. We may come boldly to His throne of grace (Heb. 4:16). Yet we must at the same time 'offer to God acceptable worship, with reverence and awe, for our God is a consuming fire' (Heb. 12:28, 29).

Theological Significance of Names.

Biblical names have far more theological significance than our supposedly rational epoch usually allows.[7] Notwithstanding modern reluctance about philology and history of usage, the Bible, in innumerable cases, compels the reader to pause to learn the etymology of a name or the historical reason why such and such a place or person has the name it bears or used to bear. Some explanations are given twice, as with Beer-sheba (Gen. 21:31; 16:33). The naming of Jacob's thirteen children illustrates the importance Bible people put on the meaning of human names (see Gen. 29:32-35; 30:6, 8, 11, 13, 20-24; 35:18). Each name expresses a hope, a prayer, a circumstance in the heart of the parent, usually the mother. The prophetic blessings on these offspring by the dying Jacob (Gen. 49) is related to the meaning of their names, again illustrating the principle. Even the name conferred on Jesus (Matt. 1:21) is specifically related to its meaning in Hebrew, a language little used by Jesus or His parents.

We may be sure the biblical names of the supreme Being are meaningful to the doctrine of God. They tell us much about who He is, what He is like and what He has done, as well as what He now does and shall yet do. 'Taking the Books as they stand, the important point to notice is that the various names are used by the sacred writers advisedly, so as to bring out the various aspects of His character and dealings.'[8] God the Creator is therefore *Elohim* in Genesis 1, but in chapter 2, where Elohim communes with mankind, He is called *Jehovah-Elohim*. The serpent (chapter 3) avoids the name Jehovah, but 'In the fourth chapter the offerings of Cain and Abel are made to Jehovah, and this is the case with the whole sacrificial system [of God in covenant with man] of later Old Testament story.'[9]

These things give color and power to the many promises and warnings involving God's name or names. 'The name of the Lord is a strong tower; the righteous man runs into it and is safe' (Prov. 18:10) – a saying of the wise. 'And those who know your name put their trust in you' (Ps. 9:10). The more we know of the meanings of His name(s) the greater our information about God will be and the stronger our faith will be.

Isaiah, after, as we have seen, calling His God *Father*, *Jehovah* and *Redeemer*, adds 'from everlasting is thy name'. God's name is Eternal. He is endlessly the same.

The Practical Necessity of Names and Metaphors of God.

The Bible brings every sphere of nature to make its contribution to its description of God. There are few limits (with the exception of evil things). Names, comparisons and figures are drawn from human, organic and inorganic spheres. Augustine put it like this: though God is without name as to His essential nature, in His revelation (Scripture) He possesses many names. Everything positive can be said of Him, but nothing said is fully worthy of Him. He goes on – Why are so many names, anthropomorphisms, comparisons and symbols necessary for us? God does not need them. Why do we need them? Augustine compares soul needs with bodily needs. The body needs a place to dwell, clothing to wear, food to eat, water to drink, air, light and the like. The natural world fills the needs.

The soul's needs are just as various, but instead of a world providing the supply, God Himself supplies them all. You go to a fountain when you need water; but to find the fountain you need light, and other things. One must go to a thousand places to meet natural needs. All the soul's needs are met in God Himself, and nowhere else, hence He is *bread* of life, *water* of life, Lord, Most High, Rock and Shepherd. Bread cannot meet your Shepherd need nor water your Master needs, and so on. Spiritually, however, God meets every need.

Thomas Aquinas looked at the same facts in a slightly different way. If believers wish to glorify God and if they wish to come to full knowledge of Him, they must think of Him in terms of His creatures and they must use anthropomorphic names and adjectives, metaphors and similes drawn from the Creator's creation. Otherwise they

---

7. The names of God appear thousands of times in the Old Testament and have therefore both attracted and challenged critics and commentators over the centuries. Journal articles on one or more of all the names appear frequently. I recommend J. Barton Payne's brief chapter, 'The Names of God' (*The Theology of the Old Testment*, Grand Rapids, Eerdmans, 1962, pp. 144–150) and the articles in *Theological Wordbook of the Old Testament* on all the names as well as the Old Testament Theologies of W. Eichrodt, G. Oehler and especially Hermann Schultz, trans. of the German ed. by J. A. Patterson, vol. ii, Edinburgh, 1892, pp. 116–146. He provides details I have found in no other source.
8. ibid., p. 38.
9. ibid., p. 38.

know nothing of Him and cannot speak a single word about Him.[10] John Calvin, who certainly was fully aware of the limitations of natural revelation and the danger of confusing the creature with the creator, nevertheless wrote most eloquently of the importance, necessity and propriety of seeing the lineaments of God in creation. An entire chapter of Calvin's *Institutes* is devoted to the subject.[11] This, he goes on to say, is a secure basis for the way God in Scripture 'babbles' to us in our own creaturely realm in creaturely terms – anthropomorphic names, metaphors, similes and the like.

How infinite God accommodates His manner of 'speaking' to finite people like ourselves is a frequent theme in the *Institutes*. Two of Calvin's sentences summarize his thought on the subject:

> [W]ho even of slight intelligence does not understand that as nurses commonly do with infants, God is wont in a measure to 'lisp' in speaking to us? Thus such forms of speaking do not so much express what God is like as accommodate the knowledge of him to our slight capacity. To do this he must descend far beneath his loftiness.[12]

An Important Practical Value.

Only man is the *image* of God among God's creatures. Yet since like all of nature he is a creature he has a place in nature that he cannot fully escape. He alone among earthbound creatures is the 'offspring' of God (Acts 17:28). God, however, so created the natural realm, as we have seen, that His marks are everywhere in it. He is immanent in it as Sustainer and providential Ruler (see Ps. 104). In this sense, apart from God there is nothing at all, even though He created it *ad extra*, not out from Him, but *de novo*, as the uniquely fresh, new.

Many ancient and modern philosophies and heresies have represented nature as something independent and hostile, even prior, to God (Gnosticism, Neoplatonism and Manichaeism of early Christian centuries and 'Christian science', various ascetical and mystical moods and movements of today). Nineteenth-century idealism, still with us in mutated forms today, is another.

God, however, will not be excluded from anything He has made – our bodies and our lands, our houses and other possessions. Nor will He be excluded from our scientific projects either. He demands Lordship in them and will ultimately secure it.

Unless we accept the propriety of God's presence in the world of nature our work in the world will always be thought of as 'dirty business'. Though of a different sort, it is as much God's business as the mission agency and the theological college. The Bible has a message for every worldly department of private and public life. The Christian revelation will not be restricted to the private, religious sphere.

An important Dutch theologian speaks eloquently of the consequences of effort to exclude God and revelation from worldly life:

> In this way the realm of nature with its forces and energies, man in his social and political life, and also science and art, are given a sphere outside the sphere of God's revelation. They become neutral spheres, and are viewed as existing apart from God. Of course, a proper appreciation of the OT and of a large part of the NT is impossible on this basis. Nature is deprived of its message for the believer. The revelation of God loses all its influence on outward life. Religion, altogether confined to the inner chamber… forfeits every claim to respect. Dogmatics [Systematic Theology], and in particular the 'doctrine of God' is reduced to a minimum; and theology is no longer able to maintain its proper and important position; it is no longer able to speak about God, because it no longer recognizes him as its source and goal. *It has no names for God*. He becomes the Great Unknowable; and the universe becomes first a sphere without God, later on 'an antigod.'[13]

How comforting to faith! How inspiring to worship!

> Come, thou Almighty King,
> Help us Thy name to sing,
> Help us to praise;
> Father, all glorious,
> O'er all victorious,
> Come and reign over us,
> Ancient of Days.

---

10. See Aquinas *Summa Theologica*, First Part, Question 12, articles 3 & 4.
11. John Calvin, *Institutes* I, i, 5.
12. ibid., I, i.13.
13. Herman Bavinck, *The Doctrine of God*, Tran. Wm. Hendrickson (Grand Rapids: Baker Books, 1951, 1983), p. 90.

8
The Attributes of God

We shall introduce this important subject by a simple mental exercise. Let us go back to Junior High School science class for a few moments. The teacher brings a beaker three-fourths full of an unknown substance to the desk. He holds it up so that all in the room can see. It is seen to be a liquid, a clear liquid. Is it methyl alcohol? No, for it has no odour at room temperature. So now we know it is an odourless, clear liquid. Does it taste like any known clear liquid? No, it is tasteless as well as odourless. Further testing over the Bunsen burner shows that it boils at +212°F, and it is said, by the teacher, to turn to solid state at +32°F. The teacher also tells the class that it has been shown to be composed, by weight, of 11.188 per cent hydrogen and 88.812 per cent oxygen and nothing more. By now, every child in the class knows for sure what the substance is: water. How is water defined? By its attributes (characteristics).

Something like this simple mental exercise is now necessary to this study. We have now reached a point where it is appropriate to discuss God's characteristics, or as theology now calls them, His attributes.

Some of the medieval scholastics call them 'properties', as Anselm in *The Monologion* does. Science likes this word to describe distinctive features about the way a thing appears or acts, e.g. *bitterness* is a property of chokecherry fruit; vapourizing at 212°F is a property of water. Attributes is a better term in theology to indicate what an object of thought is as well as what it *does* or what its *effects* are.

The Bible says in a thousand ways that God is gracious, angry, true, faithful, merciful, righteous and so on. At first, the reader does not think of classifying and organizing these statements. Yet, as we read the Bible through, if we were to make a list of them, without arranging the statements in some systematic way, it would be impossible meaningfully to report the information to another person, or to understand it as we understand all organized knowledge.

Theology must put these important facts about God in some sort of system. We must consider how earlier saints and scholars organized this data and we must relate the same to current thinking.

Certain initial questions must be addressed.

1. Can God Be Defined?

Is it possible to define God at all, and if so, how should one proceed? Good theology has always been cautious about attempting to define God. Recently, exponents of dialectical-existential theology have been insisting it is impious even to try. God can only confront us in personal encounter. When we define or state propositions about these essentially unreportable confrontations, they say, we compose a God to suit ourselves. Some cold statement that God is 'the ground of being' may be allowed.

Christian theology had been aware of this difficulty from the very beginning. The first extensive and successful efforts at systematic statement of a theology about the God of Christianity were by Gregory Nazianzen (c.325 – c.389) called 'the Theologian' and 'The Great'. He opposed those in his time who thought they knew everything about God. As he began his own more modest effort to 'define God' he wrote:

> [W]e must begin thus. It is difficult to conceive God but to define Him in words is an impossibility… to comprehend the whole of so great a subject as this is quite impossible and impractical, not merely to the utterly careless and ignorant, but even to those who are highly exalted, and who love God.[1]

He adds:

> For it is one thing to be persuaded of the existence of a thing, and quite another to know what it is.[2]

C. A. Hodge sensibly anticipated the current endless verbosity on this subject by pointing out that though a definition may not tell what a thing is in itself, it can do it no harm or despite. For 'to define is… simply to… distinguish; so that the thing defined may be discriminated from all other things. This may be done (1) by stating its characteristics. (2) By stating its genus and its specific difference. (3) By analyzing the idea as it lies in our minds. (4) By explanation of the term or name by which it is denoted.'[3] We must define God by some sort of descriptive statements about Him if we are to discuss theology at all. Even the dialectical and existential theologians do. Neither they nor we can avoid it. The Bible not only reports 'the mighty acts of God' allowed by the neo-orthodox and other objectors to propositional statements, but also makes factual statements about God on about every page. We must affirm some statement that begins 'God is…' to have orderly discourse about Him.

Perhaps the most respected definition in Protestant Christian history is the Westminster Confession's definition. It begins, 'There is but one only living and true God, who is infinite in being' and goes on to mention about twenty-five characteristics (attributes) with scriptural 'proofs' for each one – thus committing several 'sins' against current liberal theological thinking. Among such offences to liberal theology are proof-texting and factual statements about divine things and speaking without reservations in both respects. This respected creed is similar, in its forthright statements about God, to several old, respected catechisms, each of which has instructed many generations of Christian children. Each is composed of crisp statements about God, mankind and things, each with Scripture 'proof'. This contrasts sharply with the ponderous and extensive volumes of existential-dialectical theology (cf. Barth's thirteen volumes) and claims to make no such statements (though they do). God cannot even state facts about Himself in the neo-orthodox Bible.

2. Can God's Essence be made known?

Can the essence, or being, of God be made known to us at all? As already discussed in earlier chapters, God, of course, is not knowable in His essence except as He has seen fit to reveal Himself in various ways. Kant and his disciples would have every essence, or thing in itself (*der Ding am sich*), forever out of reach of human knowledge, as would Hume, Feuerbach and others who would restrict all valid knowledge to that derived from sensory experience. In a measure, they are correct, especially of other intelligences or persons – but only in the sense of direct sensory (empirical) information. A man may live with his wife for fifty years and never have direct sensory experience of her inner spiritual being. Yet he gains immense knowledge-by-acquaintance with her inner spiritual being through her manifest attributes (characteristics). These attributes all come to his attention and awareness in bits and pieces in one way or another, through sensory experience of what she says and does. By means of his rational faculties, he will inevitably – consciously or unconsciously – make generalizations about his wife's inner character. She may also deliberately speak to him about her inner self. Knowledge of God comes in a similar manner. It is twofold.

---

1. Gregory Nazianzen, *Oration XXVIII*, iv, NPNF, pp. 289 – 290.
2. ibid., v, p. 290.
3. Charles Hodge, *Systematic Theology I* (Grand Rapids: Eerdmans, 1970), p. 366.

(1) We know God's attributes through His creation. People do have such awareness – however it be accounted for. There is general awareness that God is great, good, wise – otherwise why the fear of meeting Him in the Judgment? This awareness takes different forms of expression in different cultures. Creation did not emerge out of God by emanation. Yet He made it and left marks of His character throughout – even though not without some ambiguity, owing to sin presently in us and sin's curse on creation.

(2) We also know God's attributes as they are stated and described in Scripture. This knowledge is not complete, but it is sufficient for orderly human life on this earth if not perverted or denied. The attributes of God, as explained and fulfilled in creation and redemption, are all we need to know of His essence. 'And we know that the Son of God has come and has given us understanding, so that we may know him who is true; and we are in him who is true, in his Son Jesus Christ. He is the true [*alēthinos*, genuine, real] God and eternal life' (1 John 5:20; cf. John 17:3).

The attributes are not parts of the essence, of which this latter is composed. The whole

> essence is in each attribute and the attribute in the essence. We must not conceive of the essence as existing by itself, and prior to the attributes, and of the attributes as an addition to it. God is not essence *and* attributes, but in attributes.[4]

3. How Are God's Attributes Related to Him?

Another problem, frequently discussed from earliest Christian times, has been, how are the attributes related to God? They are not related to God's essence as *major genus* and *differentia*, as every other entity is, for God is the sole member of His genus or class. 'Besides me there is no other.' A chair may be said to be a piece of furniture (*major genus*) composed of a seat, back, four legs and designed for sitting (*differentia* from other kinds of furniture). But God may not be described in such a way. Furthermore, the attributes of God cannot be regarded as symbolical representations, as say crown and scepter for a king, or a fish for the church. In these cases, the symbols have no necessary similarity to or identity with a king or the church; they are, in fact, dissimilar. They only represent a king or a church, both of which are wholly other than the symbol. In contrast, the attributes of God are like Him. In fact, they are more than *like* Him because they are identical with His being. They do not *conceal* what and who He is but rather reveal Him. The attributes *are* what God is, in some meaningful way. They are identical with God's essence, and are not hypostases (personifications), as in polytheism and medieval Jewish speculation. Nor are they independent archetypes of love, beauty and the like, as in Platonic philosophy. Nor are they emanations out of God (eons), as in Gnosticism and other pantheistic systems ancient and modern. When the Bible says God is righteous, it means that righteousness is an aspect of God's being, God seen from a certain perspective – all of God in that aspect or perspective – and so on for every biblical statement about God. When the Bible says that God is righteous it means all of God – God in every respect – is righteous. Every positive attribute of God inheres in all of them.

4. Do Words Applied to God Mean the Same as when Applied to Human Beings?

Do words such as love, mercy, good, gracious, Lord and the like mean the same when applied to God as when applied to mankind? They do only to a degree. When a wife says, My husband is kind, or addresses her neighbour's husband as 'Sir' (in older usage, 'Lord') she does not mean exactly the same as Scripture does when it employs the same terms in speaking to or about God.

Dispute over this problem in ancient times set the terms of the discussion and we still must employ them today. There are three possible views with respect to possible equivalence between the meaning of these terms as used for human beings and things on the one hand and as applied to God on the other. Every Sunday School teacher or serious Bible student must decide. It is not an unimportant matter.

One view affirms that these words mean the same whether used of God or mankind: the *sound* is the same; *spelling* is the same; *meaning* is the same. The sense is said to be *univocal* (=Latin, 'one voice'). When we say that God is good we mean the same as when we say that Margaret is good.

A second possible view says, No. The sound is the same; *spelling* is the same; but the meaning is *different*. The Latin word is *equivocal* (=Latin, 'equal voice'), that is, though the sound is the same the meaning is different. Hence, to equivocate means to speak ambiguously or to lie. When a person only *seems* to say what we think he says, he equivocates.

---

4. W. G. T. Shedd, *Dogmatic Theology* I (Grand Rapids: Zondervan, 1969), p. 134.

A third possible view is that when the Bible applies to God words commonly used of human beings there is a partial correspondence, a correspondence which, though partial and even fragmentary (1 Cor. 13:9), nevertheless conveys true and reliable information. This sense is called *analogical*. Analogy affirms correspondence or similarity, in some important respect, but not strict identity. In this case God possesses the matter in a primary, perfect and absolute way; people have it only in a secondary or derived manner.

5. How Do the Attributes of God Relate to Each Other?

How are the attributes related to one another, holiness to love and mercy, omnipotence to infinity in time and place, and so on? Is one attribute more important to sound theology, that is, to a correct understanding of God and His ways, than another? There is considerable variance of views. It can scarcely be doubted that some attributes receive more emphasis in Scripture than others do. No one can read Leviticus and Isaiah (or Ezekiel) without observing emphasis on holiness. Let us leave this question open at this stage.

6. What Is the Meaning of the Simplicity of God's Being?

Orthodox theologians generally affirm that the being or substance of God is simple. Then they try to explain and offer cautions. By simple or simplicity, we mean without parts. 'Every attribute is identical with God's being by reason of the fact that everyone of God's virtues is absolutely perfect in God' (Bavinck, p. 168). There is no variance in any one or all the attributes, for they are steadily the same, as we shall consider later in connection with God's immutability (changelessness) and impassibility. Any who doubt these affirmations (and in view of present mutterings of some writers on the fringe of orthodoxy there may be readers who do doubt) should be made aware of the uniform conviction of divine immutability among the ancient Fathers – notably Augustine – medieval school men, both Reformers and Roman Catholics, and on to present orthodox writers. In a later chapter, we shall consider the simplicity of the divine nature as it relates to the blessedness or impassibility of God.

Father, Son and Holy Spirit are not three parts of God. They are three 'modes of subsistence', to use one of the phrases of the older Protestant dogmaticians. There is one mode of subsistence called Father, another called Son and another Holy Spirit. However, there is one simple undivided substance. The word 'mode' is employed not only by the post-Reformation Protestant scholastic theologians in this way but it is to be found in authors such as C. A. Hodge, Shedd, Strong and Pieper as well as the ancient Christian orthodox writers. Barth uses the word 'mode' in this same connection. In connection with God's perfection, Karl Barth writes: 'It should be noted that in this matter we have an exact parallel to the concern of the doctrine of the Holy Trinity. In this doctrine the one God in his three modes of being corresponds to the Lord of glory, etc.'[5] He goes on to say these modes are internal and prior to external modes, amongst other things. He seems to reject Sabellian heresy of modalism. The point I make here is that three Persons of the one, simple essence of God do not 'divide the substance'.

> This nature is common to the three Persons in God, but not communicated from one to the other; they each of them partake of it, and possess it as one undivided nature... 'as all the fulness of the Godhead dwells in Christ', so in the Holy Spirit; and of the Father, there will be no doubt.[6]

The attributes, of course, are each the whole, undivided divine essence viewed in a particular way or in relation to different objects.

7. Why Classify the Divine Attributes?

'On few subjects have greater thought and labor been expended than this.'[7] The goal of classification is to make the total number clearly comprehensible.

Among the 'bipolar' classifications that are proposed are: negative and positive attributes, quiescent and operative; internal and external, absolute and relative; immanent and transcendent; metaphysical and moral; primitive and derived.[8]

---

5. Karl Barth, *Church Dogmatics I*, trans. G. W. Bromiley (Edinburgh: T. & T. Clark, 1975), p. 327.
6. John Gill, *Body of Divinity I* (Grand Rapids: Baker Books, 1978), p. 44.
7. C. A. Hodge, *op. cit.*, p. 327.
8. Karl Barth, *Christian Dogmatics II*, Part I (Edinburgh: T. and T. Clark, 1975), chapter VI, pp. 340, 341.

The Reformers were disgusted with the fruitless efforts of late medieval scholastics to explain essence and attributes, and sterile controversies about them. Hence, Calvin has a single chapter on the Trinity,[9] three on God's unity and spirituality,[10] but there is nothing like any effort to organize the biblical references to attributes. Melanchthon's *Loci Communes*, the first Lutheran handbook of doctrines, discusses the trinity and unity of the Godhead but has nothing specifically on attributes. Gordon Clark seems excessively harsh in calling later efforts at definition and classification 'rubbish' that has 'been dug up'.[11]

Karl Barth, who liked to think of himself as an authentic successor to the Reformers, has an extensive discussion of what he terms 'God's being'[12] and 'God's perfections.'[13] In this treatment, he has a section of criticism of the various systems of defining and arranging the attributes of God and comes to this interesting summary, in which I concur.

> In this matter the chaos of opinion is not so great as perhaps at first sight appears, and it should be clear that in accordance with the presuppositions [his] we have no need to look around for a radically new solution. Indeed, we have absolutely no other choice but to adopt basically – reserving the right of more detailed elucidation and purification – this fourth and, as we may call it, classical approach.[14]

One searches almost in vain for a satisfactory history of classifications. An adequate history is very competently supplied by Herman Bavinck's thirty pages in his *The Doctrine of God*. Bavinck, in common with most orthodox authors, places the *aseity* (Latin, 'out-of-self', or self-existence) of God's being as primary. Though he calls *aseity* (absolute- or self-existence) an attribute, he means to say that it is in a class by itself, prior to the other attributes. I give assent to Bavinck's summary:

> [I]t is only because these attributes pertain to God in an *absolute*, altogether unique sense, that they are *divine* attributes. Hence, in that respect *aseity* (absolute essence) may be called the primary attribute of God's being.[15]

Bavinck adds: 'We must, therefore affirm God's aseity: that there is nothing above him; hence, wisdom, grace, love, etc. are identical with his being.'[16] Bavinck is saying attributes are attributes of *something*. In this case, the something is absolute essence (being), God's being. Obviously, attributes inhere in God's being.

Theologians – Reformed, Lutheran and Roman Catholic – have followed an essentially identical method with near identical results. About the only variety is that some writers siphon off attributes of the *being* of God and call them aspects of the essence. H. C. Thiessen lists spirituality, self-existence, immensity and eternity as 'not attributes at all but different aspects of the divine substance.'[17] It is the judgment of most theologians that all the attributes are 'different aspects of the divine substance'. Thiessen and H. B. Smith, whom he follows, are reviving the views of medieval realists. This opinion was condemned by the Council of Reims (1148).[18]

In these studies, the attributes will be presented mainly as derived from Scripture. We must acknowledge, however, that several traditional modes of deriving our ideas about God have their place. They are three converging lines which theology has employed for centuries in elaborating what the Scriptures have to say about God's attributes.

Wolfhart Pannenberg summarizes:

> Pseudo-Dionysius... worked out the three-fold method of knowing God that achieved such fame and was normative until well into the 19th century, the *via negationis* (*aphaireseos*), the *via eminentiae* (*hyperoches*) and the *via causatitatis* (*aitias*) [these are the Latin and Greek equivalents].[19]

(1) The Way of Affirmation (Positive).

We see perfections (excellencies) in nature and in ourselves – intelligence, for example. Hence, we infer intelligence in the Creator. We cannot conceive of God otherwise and if there were not a single, specific Bible verse affirming 'God is intelligent', we would affirm it as Christians. As a teacher of theology I sometimes sense some futility in citing 'proof texts' on points like this – as though trying to clarify the perfectly obvious.

---

9. Calvin, *Institutes I*, 13.
10. ibid., x–xii.
11. Gordon Clark, 'The Divine Attributes' in *Baker's Dictionary of Theology*, ed. by E. F. Harrison (Grand Rapids: Baker Books, 1960), p. 78.
12. Barth, *op. cit.*, pp. 257–321.
13. Barth, *op. cit.*, pp. 322–350.
14. Barth, *op. cit.*, p. 341.
15. Herman Bavinck, *The Doctrine of God*, trans. Wm. Hendriksen (Grand Rapids: Eerdmans, 1951, 1983), pp. 113–142.
16. ibid., p. 170.
17. H. C. Thiessen, *Introductory Lectures in Systematic Theology* (Grand Rapids: Eerdmans, 1949, 1966), pp. 119–123.
18. *The Catholic Encyclopedia II* (New York: Catholic Encyclopedia Press, 1907–1922), pp. 63–65.
19. Wolfhart Pannenburg, *Systematic Theology*, vol. ii, pp. 343, 344.

(2) The Way of Negation (Negative).

We concentrate our minds on God's greatness and His oceanic abundance of perfections. We reflect on the finiteness and imperfections of all creation. Hence we infer immensity (Latin *in-*, 'not', plus *mensus*, 'measure'), infinity (no limit), immutability (no change) and the like. These verbal negatives may rightly be viewed as positives, affirming – by contrast – the absolute fullness of God's being and perfections. The negative form of statement, however, is accurate and impressive. Most Christians have at least some inchoate awareness of these attributes of God and bring them to the Scriptures, even as they refine their convictions by the Scripture 'proofs'.

The Bible sets a standard for negative statements about God, such as those that relate to attributes and essence, for example: 'with whom there is no variation or shadow due to change' (God's immutability, James 1:17); a negative statement of truthfulness ('it is impossible for God to lie', Heb. 6:18; and deathlessness ('who alone has immortality', 1 Tim. 6:16).

(3) The Way of Eminence (Supreme Degree).

Those perfections we see about us, especially in human beings, we infer to be subsisting in infinite degree in God. We infer this as in God's image and as His creatures. We see power about us, we know something of love, mercy and the like in ourselves, and quite easily assign the same to God in infinite degree. We also bring these ideas with us to the reading of biblical statements about God's attributes.

Calvin, after asserting that 'in his essence God is incomprehensible', went on to say: 'But upon his individual works, he has engraved unmistakable marks of his glory... Therefore the prophet very aptly exclaims that he is "clad with light as with a garment".' He cites a catena of passages of Scripture, chiefly from Psalm 104.[20]

Thomas Aquinas put the matter thus: 'God is the supreme good simply, and not as existing in any genus or order of things... Therefore as good is in God as in the first... cause of all things, it must be in Him in a most excellent way; and therefore He is called the supreme good.'[21]

As stated earlier, the attributes of God have been classified as (1) *positive* and *negative*, (2) *communicable* and *incommunicable* (what God is in and of Himself), (3) *quiescent* (static) and *active*, (4) *relative* (to creation) and *absolute*, (5) *transitive* and *intransitive*, and (6) *metaphysical* and *moral*. Though God has always been known to be both great and good, no one, as far as I know, thought of classifying the attributes in this a seventh way, *great* and *good*, until Alva J. McClain did so about 1930. Following McClain, who taught me this classification, which is appealing as well as accurate and simple, I have employed it through several decades of lectures and I now find it in recent widely published textbooks, though whence derived it is hard to say.

By whatever terms they are designated, all of the attributes of God fall into these two classes of great and good in theological writing, whether the theological writer be Roman Catholic, Reformed, Lutheran or other orthodox writer. This arrangement seems to be a kind of ecumenical consensus, fruit of 1,500 years of thinking about the subject by Christian scholars.

Some employ this basic scheme but introduce a pedagogical principle – introducing the pervasive biblical emphasis on the spirituality of the God of Scripture first, then the unity (sole existence) of the Godhead as a parallel whole-Bible emphasis, then the usual twofold divisions, closing with the most difficult, the doctrine of the Trinity. My own approach will be like this.

For the sake of interest and simplicity, I gather the subject of the attributes under five biblical captions or affirmations. There is the added advantage of making biblical authority more apparent. It is, of course, perfectly obvious that to understand these difficult ideas every aid that can be borrowed from any legitimate source whatsoever is brought to the exposition. Systematic theology can never be simple proof-texting, however important biblical documentation of beliefs in religion must always be for Christians.

These affirmations and phrases are: *firstly*, 'God is spirit' (John 4:24); *secondly*, 'the LORD is God in heaven above and on the earth beneath; there is no other' (Deut. 4:39); *thirdly*, 'our God is greater than all gods' (2 Chr. 2:5); *fourthly*, 'Oh give thanks to the LORD, for he is good' (Ps. 107:1); *fifthly*, 'the name of the Father and of the Son and of the Holy Spirit' (Matt. 28:19).

Each of these scriptural captions are used as headings for each of the chapters immediately to follow.[22]

---

20. Calvin, *op. cit.*, v.1.
21. Thomas Aquinas, *Summa Theologica*, First Part, Question 6, art.2.
22. I acknowledge my debt to the esteemed late President of Grace Theological Seminary for the essentials of this arrangement which he taught in his course called 'God and Revelation'.

9
The Spirituality of the Godhead

'God is spirit'(John 4:24)

'God is spirit', a saying of Jesus (John 4:24), was spoken for practical reasons. Jesus was introducing an age wherein the geographical location and physical implements of worship are no longer of great importance. Whatever temporary value the Old Testament ritual actions and materials may have had, they are worthless now. They may teach us but we dare not perpetuate them. God is Spirit and they that worship Him must worship in spirit and in truth (John 4:24). It is all in the spiritual realm, however much mankind's unity of body and spirit and residence in a material world require such things as buildings, music, hymn books, Bibles, pews and central heating as well as convenient location and accessible premises. Ceremonies, religious buildings and objects are now secondary to the purely spiritual. (It has not yet been demonstrated that electronic implementation of sounds, and projection machinery as 'aids to worship', are very helpful.) We are free from an elaborate ceremonial system which would be 'a yoke on the neck of the disciples that neither our fathers nor we have been able to bear' (Acts 15:10). We put ourselves on notice that so-called 'holism' in worship, if not severely restrained, may lead to overt idolatry of sensible leaders, forms, objects, sounds and rituals.

No one has ever framed a definition of spirit that fully satisfies everyone. Commitments about reality in general are involved. For those who believe matter and the chemistry of it to be only *part* of reality, holding that there is non-material reality, incommensurable with all measurements of length, breadth, height, weight and similar, the following definition may suffice. Spirit is a non-material, personal, reality. Why not say that spirit is a non-material, personal substance?

Is the Divine Spirit a Substance?

There is a certain reluctance to speak of the divine Spirit as a substance. This is because our minds can scarcely conceive of a substance without the quality of materiality. Yet we know God is not a mere idea (unless we adopt the unbiblical philosophy of metaphysical idealism). God is not a *thing*, however, but the most real object or subject. The truth is, God is a spiritual substance. Our souls or spirits are spiritual substances too. We can think of deceased parents or children as spirits without material bodies and we can think of God in a similar manner, even granted there is a certain awkwardness about it.

Augustine relates in the *Confessions* his intellectual journey from materialism (where nothing is real but matter) to the biblical view of God and of reality as a problem of conceiving of a spiritual substance. At first 'the more defiled by vain things as I grew in years, who could not imagine say substance but such as is wont to be seen with these eyes... Whatsoever was not extended over certain spaces, nor diffused, nor condensed, nor swelled out, or did not receive some of these dimensions, I thought to be altogether nothing' (VII). 'Could I have conceived of a spiritual substance, all their strongholds [Manichaeism] had been... cast utterly out of my mind; but I could not.'[1] Augustine's ability to think of God as spiritual substance, in whom all the biblical divine attributes inhere, resulted from the prayers of believers, the preaching of Ambrose and especially his reading of Paul's Epistles, but philosophy had something to do with it also.

Augustine possibly might never have considered the Epistles of Paul seriously except through the reading of certain 'Platonist' philosophers – now called Neoplatonists. It was their service, in God's providence, to enable 'Augustine to bridge the gap between Manichaean materialism and the Christian understanding of a purely immaterial substance'.[2] Augustine puts it this way: 'And thus gradually, [I progressed] from bodies to the soul which senses through the body, and thence to that internal power, to which the bodily senses bring information about external things'. He goes on to say that seeing his judgments are changeable his 'soul' turned to his soul's intelligence to find what the light was which irradiated his soul. From this, he reasoned to invisible reality wherein is 'the unchangeable', whereupon his reason 'arrived in the flash of an anxious glance, at that which is. Then... I saw intellectually Thy [God's] invisible things through those things which are made.'[3] He had employed some of the logic of Romans 1:19, 20 without yet being aware of the scriptural guarantee of the validity of his now Spirit-enlightened logical processes. Augustine only gradually fully accepted this new way of thinking.

God, as pure spirit, is as substantial as are our own spirits, though His spirit is not spatially enclosed in a body as ours are. God's self-conscious spirit cannot be a mere 'stream of consciousness', as in positivist psychology (Watson, Skinner), any more than ours are:

> We cannot conceive of the soul as only a series of exercises. There must be an agent in order to agency; a substantial being in order to exercises. To ask us to think away the substance of the soul, and then to conceive of its exercises is like asking us to think away the earth around a hole, and then to conceive of the hole.[4]

The Bible presents God as self-conscious personal spirit. He is the living God, active and intelligent. He is not only a God who acts freely (self-determination) but also with sovereign purpose. We must think of this group of ideas in connection with the statement: God is spirit.

We are not to completely isolate these elements, even for purposes of discussion. It is impossible. Some of the ideas group themselves together more closely than others. The first group includes personality, self-consciousness and freedom, or self-determination.

1. Personality.

A person is a subject who thinks. A person is also an object of thought. By this, we mean that there is a kind of relationship of persons to persons that is unique to persons. I address *thee* (to employ the old second person singular form). I am *thou* to *thee* and *thou* art *thou* to *me*. This again is unique to persons. Anything other than a person with whom I relate myself as a person is an 'it'. Of course, when I discourse about *thee* with another *thou*, then *thou* art a *he* or *she*, for purposes of discourse. In a definite manner, we have just now seen practical demonstration of how personality works rather than of what '*it*' is. We know ourselves to be persons. From the way the Bible speaks of God and from the way God speaks therein, always an 'I' addressing a 'thee' or 'ye' (plural) and referring to 'him', 'her' or 'them,' we know God to be a person.

Most readers will need to trace these matters through only a fragment of the biblical evidence to be convinced. God is never a distant impersonal spook that sounds itself impersonally through some occultist medium, nor is He an eternal force impersonally regulating the fall of dice from some priest's hands. He is always a great person. The personal character of God is as plain in His conversations with Adam and Eve in Genesis 3:9-23 as it is with Abraham and his wife Sarah later in Genesis. The meeting of Moses with God at the burning bush (Exod. 3:3-6) is no mere meditation of some pious sheep-herder (as some say) upon the magnificence of a storm or a sunrise or sunset over Mount Horeb, but a sustained, sometimes fierce, conversation (Exod. 3:1–4:17) between persons. The events

---

1. St. Augustine, *Confessions VII*. (Middlesex, England: Penguin Books, 1973), p. 104 ff.
2. V. J. Bourke, *Augustine's Quest of Wisdom* (Milwaukee: Bruce Publ., 1945), p. 57.
3. Augustine, *op. cit.*, pp. 17, 23.
4. W. G. T. Shedd, *Dogmatic Theology I* (Grand Rapids: Zondervan, 1969), p. 166.

at Sinai, when the voice of God spoke persuasively to a whole nation, came in personal modes (Exod. 19:9-19; Deut. 4:8-13; cf. 18:16). Those were not, as misbelief and unbelief sometimes make them out, some sort of natural phenomenon such as a volcanic eruption. Nor were they the creation of subsequent myth-making.

We must remind ourselves, however, that in declaring God a 'person' we are doing something Scripture never does. We must think of Him only as our excellent, but limited, human powers allow. We are merely the humble beings whom God created 'male and female' and 'named them Man when they were created' (Gen. 5:1,2), not gods. 'Person' is really a quite modern word in the sense we now use it. Personhood in God is much more than personhood in mankind. How much more, we shall never know, for the 'true God... is infinite in being and perfection, a most pure spirit...'[5]

When we say that God is a person we mean, before all else, that He is the God of Holy Scripture, One who addresses us in Scripture and sermon, One who sometimes during the epochs of revelation spoke in audible verbal modes to other persons such as apostles and prophets. He is One to whom people respond – Adam and Eve, Abraham, Moses, Samuel, Isaiah, and many others. In a less distinct, but equally important manner, we respond in love, obedience, devotion, worship, prayer and service. He is One with whom men of old had conversation (see Gen. 18:33). One of them, in fact, became so intimate with God that the man's name became 'the Friend of God'.

Once in Scripture God, Himself, calls Abraham 'my friend' (Isa. 41:8). King Jehoshaphat, in addressing God, refers to Abraham as 'your friend' (2 Chr. 20:7) and James states that Abraham was called 'a friend of God' (Jas. 2:23). To this day, the Muslim Arabs frequently refer to that patriarch as '*el Khalil*' – the friend.

This relationship between God and Abraham grew as all friendships – between persons who shared their interests. God was on His way to destroy Sodom and Gomorrah. En route, He stopped by Abraham's tent to talk business, urgent business, with him. There was food (Gen. 18:18) and conversation as is quite usual when friends are entertained (Gen. 18:9-18) during which the present business was cared for. There was chiefly a final announcement of fulfillment of the promise of birth of a child by Sarah, through whom blessing would come to the whole world (Gen. 12:1 ff.). Isaac would be born within a year.

After business matters had been cared for, before 'the men' (i.e. the angels of the LORD, addressed by Abraham as 'my LORD'), went on to destroy the cities of the plain, 'The LORD said, "Shall I hide from Abraham what I am about to do"' (Gen. 18:17). God went on to affirm His abiding confidence in Abraham and then bared His heart of what was now uppermost in His mind. God was treating Abraham as an intimate friend. The rest of the chapter narrates their conversation, very significantly closing: 'And the LORD went his way, when he had finished speaking to Abraham, and Abraham returned to his place' (Gen. 18:33). These conversations are as real as a conversation between Jacob and Rachel or David and Jonathan or of Jesus with the woman at the well of Sychar. The God of the Bible is a person, so much a person that one man of history became His confidant – Abraham, the friend of God.[6]

A first caution should be observed in saying God is a person, or God is a personal spirit. The meaning is not exactly the same as when the three members of the triune God are called persons. The three 'Persons' are three 'properties' of the one God. *Person* (Lat. *persona*, mask used by a dramatic actor) indicates the sense in which God is three. But there is only one God. Peter, James and John are three separate persons, yet share a generic unity of nature – humanity. Humanity exists separately from them in billions of other people also. Contrariwise, Father, Son and Holy Ghost are three 'persons' each of whom posesses *numerically* and *totally* all the divine nature (Godhead, divinity) there is. There are not three gods, each of whom shares in a generic something called divinity, 'Godness' or Godhead. Where the Father is, there also are the Son and the Spirit.

A second caution also should be observed. Our personal nature is analogical to God's nature (essence, being) in some important ways. Yet God is an infinite and self-existent person while we are limited and dependent wholly on Him. Christian theology took centuries to decide to use 'person' of the Godhead and we need to be cautious how we understand it. The analogy is not complete. There is a regrettable but significant incubus of tri-theism in much popular Christian devotion.

2. Self-consciousness.

Self-consciousness is part of what it means to be a person. Sometimes, by a freak-of-language figure of speech, we refer to animals as though they were persons. We may even address them as persons and fondly imagine that they so respond. However, in a fully lucid moment no one believes an animal to be reflectively self-conscious. Our pets

---

5. *Westminster Confession*, Chapter II, par. 1.
6. The Muslim Arabs refer to the great building over the cave of Machpelah near Hebron (Gen. 23) as *el Kahlil*, the Friend, in reverence for Abraham's connection with the place.

and domestic beasts are conscious, of course. They go to sleep and awaken. They receive stimuli, have sensations and respond to them. But only human beings among God's earthly creatures have the ability to think of themselves objectively, engaging in introspection as we do. We are aware of our own actions and states of mind and we can rationally distinguish the self which is the subject of those states of mind and which initiates the actions. Brutes cannot accomplish these feats of personal beings. 'In consciousness the object is another substance than the subject; but in self-consciousness the object is the same substance as the subject.'[7]

This patent truth is one aspect of the famous declaration of God to Moses as he responded to Moses' question, 'What is his name?' 'I AM WHO I AM... Say this to the people of Israel, "I AM has sent me to you"' (Exod. 3:14). This is self-conscious person in ultimate verbal self-disclosure.

God's self-consciousness, like all other features of His being, is His in perfection. In this respect, our Creator is both like and unlike the most excellent crown of His creative art. There are innumerable crannies of my personality of which I am unconscious. Some I do not wish to acknowledge even when others who see them clearly point them out to me. 'Who can discern his errors?' David wanted to know. 'Declare me innocent from hidden [i.e. hidden from myself] faults', was his prayer (Ps. 19:12) and more at length, 'Search me, O God, and know my heart! Try me and know my thoughts!' (Ps. 139:23). God knows Himself completely. He is never surprised at what He says or does. So it was with our Savior in the days of His flesh (John 6:6). Because this is so, we may ask our God to help us discover ourselves, and some of the deep things of God Himself. We need His Spirit to give meaningful effect to the very words about Him on this page. So, though no merely natural eye can see nor ear hear the 'things' of redemption which God has done for us, His Spirit can help us. He knows the deep things (1 Cor. 2:9, 10). 'So also no one comprehends the thoughts of God except the Spirit of God. Now we have received not the spirit of the world, but the Spirit who is from God, that we might understand the things freely given us by God' (1 Cor. 2:11, 12).

3. Freedom, or Self-determination.

This idea, though somewhat self-explanatory, needs some limitation, if not clarification. All things we can think of are determined in some way, certainly by the characteristics of their own natures. The forces that shaped them to be what they are put these characteristics into them. Material elements are so determined by their inherent nature that science can discover what they will invariably do under controlled conditions. To an almost equal degree the same is true of brutes. All animal training is based on this. To a limited degree human beings are thus determined and much of our societal behaviour (eating requirements, recreation and the like) is to a degree predictable. In so far as politicians, social planners, technocrats and similar, can manipulate us individually and collectively we are beings determined by what we collectively are. However, people's responses can neither be wholly conditioned nor directed by external management. We are truly, within limits, self-determined. To date, every totalitarian political regime has run aground on people's unwillingness to yield determination of their behaviour to someone else for a very long time, except within the legitimate parameters of limited government. The bad side of this is recurrent lawlessness. But on the good side, it is precisely their God-likeness as free persons which makes people this way. At best, however, our self-determination is limited and at worst, dreadfully misused. We are, after all, a sinful race.

Mankind's self-determination is under *Almighty* God. Humanity has faculties (or if you prefer, functions) for self-determination. They were great before man fell and thereby ceased to operate wholly in God's moral will. God only is fully self-determined. No one tells Him what to do. Yet even He takes counsel with Himself (Gen. 1:26).

The first chapter of Isaiah's famous 'Book of Consolation' (Isa. 40–66) is heavily laden with this doctrine of divine self-determination. First, the prophet promises his downtrodden people, 'Behold, the Lord GOD [*'Adhonai-Jehovah*] comes' as deliverer (Isa. 40:10). God's utterly independent self-determination is then set forth in several questions: 'Who [else] has measured the waters in the hollow of his hand and marked off the heavens with a span, enclosed the dust of the earth in a measure and weighed the mountains in scales and the hills in a balance? Who [else] has measured the Spirit of the LORD, or what man shows him his counsel? Whom did he consult, and who made him understand? Who ... showed him the way of understanding?' (Isa. 40:12-14). In each case the answer is, no one but God – *'Adhonai-Jehovah*.

---

7. Shedd, *op. cit.*, p. 179.

Later we shall discuss life and activity as aspects of God's personality. They are prerequisites of self-consciousness and self-determination. In this respect, the Christian God is wholly different from the gods of the great oriental religions, i.e. Hinduism, Buddhism, Parseeism and others. There is no personal, self-conscious, self-determining, active, self-moving, living centre in these gods. The centre of reality is impersonal, unconscious, unmoving and certainly not alive. These religions are pantheistic at heart, God – in so far as it is correct to speak of the central fact of their religion as God – is personal only in mankind or other spirits. Although the notion is not entirely consistent with Hindu doctrines about escape from the wheel of finite existence, all (=God) is under the control of eternal, immutable laws. There is no rightful place for personality, freedom and consciousness in God Himself, for there is no Self. These attributes are held to be a defective condition wherever they appear.

These aspects of the God of the Bible have imparted a certain vibrant, joyous tone to biblical religion wherever and whenever it appears. It enables us to rejoice in our humanity and has inspired us to improve ourselves as redeemed in Christ. Awareness of these personal attributes in our God engenders a certain godly pride in being human and numbered among the people of such a God.

The Bible speaks frequently of the will of God in such a way as to show that just as there is a 'human will' as a person so there is a 'will of God' as a person. Classical theologians of great repute (Augustine, Aquinas, Turretin, Strong, *et al*) warn us against carrying the parallel too far. Calvin makes the point at the very beginning of the *Institutes*, that to know one's genuine human self-will is to know something of the Creator in whose image we are made.[8] He immediately follows with warnings against carrying the simile too far, because of the sin in our hearts which distorts the image and leads to warped opinion, ignorance and even malice.[9]

It is apparent that freedom, or self-determination, in all wise, all holy, omniscient God has none of the strictures we must ascribe to ourselves, His finite creatures. Louis Berkhof discusses the will of God, as does this brief excursus, primarily 'in relation to the faculty of self determination'. Though the will of God *necessarily* exhibits His nature (being, essence), His will is the free expression of the person who 'is Who He is'. As others put it:

> We must hold that the will of God is the cause of all things; and that He acts by the will, and not, as some have supposed, by a necessity of His nature.[10]

> I say that God wills himself necessarily... by an absolute necessity. He is the ultimate and the highest good. He is the ultimate end and highest good which cannot but will and love... for he cannot nil his own glory or deny himself. But other things he wills freely because, since no created thing is necessary with respect to God but contingent (as he could do without them), so he wills all things... (i.e. by the liberty not only of spontaneity, but also of indifference).[11]

The will of God is the ultimate cause of all things. To join God's will of this or that to His nature, without notice that God is a spirit who performs free acts of personal expression, leads to pantheism, not to the biblical God. Freedom is part of the law of His being.

The many biblical terms employed for God's will presuppose God's permanent character (nature), yet represent a variety of meanings, rendering it necessary to distinguish a range of meanings to 'the will of God'. The three commonest of these words are employed in Ephesians 1: 5, 9 and 11. Verse 5, in KJV, speaks of 'the good pleasure [*eudokia*] of his will' (*thelēma*); verse 9 repeats these words; while verse 11 has 'the counsel [*boulē*] of his own will' (*thelēma*). Though there is some overlapping of meaning in general use, the core thought of each suggests an important distinction. The third, *boulē* (pronounced *boo-lay*), lays emphasis on God's will as purpose, plan, especially the decision of a divine consultation within the Godhead. The second, *thelēma*, is the more general term for what one wishes to happen. The first signifies what gives pleasure. So these terms distinguish God's will as sometimes (1) what He has planned (decrees, predestination, election, the course of history, including the permission of sin and evil); (2) what God wishes or prefers (righteousness, obedience, that none shall perish); and (3) what gives God pleasure (fulfillment of His moral government, the repentance of sinners). Since, however, the New Testament does not strictly observe these apparent distinctions, further refinement is called for.

---

8. Calvin, *Institutes I*, 1–3.
9. ibid., iv.
10. Thomas Aquinas, *Summa Theologica*, Part One, Q 19, art. 5.
11. Francis Turretin, *Institutes of Elenctic Theology* 3rd Topic, 14th Question, paragraph 5.

Classical theology has proposed the following. God's will in all its aspects is rightly said to be both *necessary* and *free*. It is necessary in regard to Himself; that is, what He wills is true to who and what God is in Himself. However, 'God's will is free with respect to creation. He did not have to make the world... Creation, preservation and salvation are free acts of God.'[12] Some distinguish between the *decretive* and *preceptive* will of God. The former refers to God's decrees or plan, by which from eternity He has determined all that shall come to pass, and the latter to rules for the life of moral beings. 'The former is always accomplished while the latter is often disobeyed.'[13] This is to explain God's general call (invitation) to all people everywhere to repent and believe (which many reject), and the special call which, by Word and Spirit, brings some people to Christ.

God's desire for 'all people to be saved' may not be accompanied by His will to extend special influences to save them. These desires are meant by the phrase '*revealed*' will' in the old theologians: His purposes to bestow special grace by the phrase, '*secret* will'.[14]

The secret will may also be said to refer to God's decrees, which are known only as He chooses to make them known to us. 'The secret things belong to the LORD our God, but the things that are revealed belong to us and to our children forever' (Deut. 29:29). This is the commonest and most important distinction. Everything God has not yet made known to us of the destiny of mankind and of things – His unrevealed counsels (Ps. 115:3; Dan. 4:17, 25, 32, 35; Rom. 8:18, 19; 11:33, 34; Eph. 1:5, 9, 11) – constitutes His *secret* will and is not accessible to us. However, the *revealed* will of God, that is His own word, 'is very near you. It is in your mouth and in your heart, so that you can do it' (Deut. 30:14 cf. Rom. 10: 5–10). It is mainly the same as the above preceptive will of God.

The second group of attributes involved in the spiritual nature of God are life, activity and intelligence including purpose.

4. Life.

Our God is the living God. The Bible is very explicit on this point. Perhaps the reader has noticed the rather frequent recurrence in Scripture of the phrase, 'the living God'. A few moments with a concordance will locate it in every section of the Bible from the Pentateuch – where Israel is reported to have 'heard the voice of the living God' speaking from Mount Horeb (Deut. 5:26) – to the book of Revelation, wherein a flying angel has 'the seal of the living God', and God is said to be 'him who is seated on the throne, who lives forever and ever' (Rev. 4:9).

As one examines the texts, it becomes apparent that 'the living God' is associated with all of God's attributes and works. These acquire new lustre from the association, while they in turn reflect light upon the meaning of the phrase, 'The Living God'.[15] One of these many texts (Jer. 10:10, 11) explains why: 'But the LORD is the true God; he is the living God and the everlasting King. At his wrath the earth quakes, and the nations cannot endure his indignation. Thus shall you say to them: "The gods who did not make the heavens and the earth shall perish from the earth and from under the heavens."' God is angry with the nations because they have given worship to idols, idols supposedly indwelt by deities who, the prophecy goes on to say, are empty and vain, non-existent (vv. 14, 15). '[T]here is no breath in them' (v. 14). God the Creator, on the other hand (v. 12), continues to show Himself to be the living God by preserving the world that He created and by controlling it (His providence, v. 13).

Scripture indicates clearly how important it is that Jehovah is 'the living God' and why.

(1) God is greatly to be feared, because except for the elect people of God, who were prepared for the event at Sinai, no other can even hear God's audible voice and live (Deut. 5:26). 'It is a fearful thing to fall into the hands of the living God' (Heb. 10:31). This, again, is in contrast to the idols of the heathen for whom the biblical believer should have nothing but contempt (Jer. 10:1-15 above). This must surely have been in Paul's mind when he wrote to the Thessalonians of how they 'turned to God from idols to serve the living and true God' (1 Thess. 1:9). As the living God, He will show Himself powerful on behalf of His people, if they obey Him.

(2) Since He is the living God, His people may safely go on the offensive in pursuit of the goals of His kingdom: 'the living God is among you and... he will without fail drive out from before you the Canaanites...' (Josh. 3:10; cf. 11-17). The living God also rescues His own from physical threats to their lives when His purpose and will are served thereby. To his great surprise, Nebuchadnezzar discovered this (Dan. 6, esp. vv. 25-27). The

---

12. M. E. Osterhaven, 'Will of God' in *Evangelical Dictionary of Theology* (Grand Rapids: Baker Books, 1984, 1991), p. 1172.
13. Louis Berkhof, *Systematic Theology* (Grand Rapids: Eerdmans, 1941, 1979), p. 11.
14. A. H. Strong, *Systematic Theology* (Valley Forge, PA: Judson Press, 1907), p. 791.
15. A. H. Strong, *Philosophy and Religion* (New York: A. C. Armstrong & Son, 1888), pp. 180–188.

intrepid missionary preacher may safely pass by various promising exercises leading to fame and wealth, in favour of missionary life full of privations (1 Thess. 4:8) 'because we have our hope set on the living God' who has given 'promise for the present life and also for the life to come' (1 Tim. 4:8, 10).

(3) God's eternal life is the ground of assurance of our future 'resurrection of life' (John 5:29), eternal life for His people. Jesus is the Mediator of that life of God to us, being Himself made after 'the power of an indestructible life' (Heb. 7:16) 'As the living Father sent me' (John 6:57). Moreover, having life in Himself (John 14:6), He said, 'Because I live, you also will live' (John 14:19). In heaven, where vision of His beatitude is plain, the 'living creatures give glory and honour and thanks to him who is seated on the throne, who lives forever and ever' (Rev 4:9).

5. Activity.

This idea is scarcely separable from the idea of life. It is nevertheless a distinct feature of the biblical God, who can act. The prophets of the Old Testament pour scorn on the gods of the heathen (idols) which never move unless their devotees move them. Elaborate ceremonies – dressing, going to dinner, retiring for the night and similar – were conducted for the gods and goddesses of Mesopotamia. Their priests actually clothed, unclothed, fed and gave them such care. A recent lead article in *The Biblical Archaeologist* (now with a new name) describing in detail these fruitless processes would be hilariously funny if not so tragically unreal – utterly offensive to the God of Abraham, Issac and Jacob.

People intuitively discern action or possible action as an integral aspect of life, even though much that moves (acts) is not alive. It is *self*-movement which is a sign of life. The flicker of an eyelid restores hope of life for an unconscious person not known to be dead or alive, even though the movement (falling) of a long-dead tree is precisely a sign of death. There are passages of Scripture which employ 'dead' in the sense of absence of moving spirit (Jas. 2:26) and idols are said to be dead because they do nothing (Isa. 44:9-20; Jer. 10:1-11; see also Isa. 8:19).

These passages lay emphasis on the divine efficacy – not just activity. God acts *effectually*. As we shall see, when He acts, He does so omnipotently. The infinitely great, eternal Spirit, whom Christians worship as the one, true and living God, is willing and able to work. He who planned the heavens and earth and created them now sustains and rules them. As He wills, He may step into the orderly process of nature with mighty miracles as He did when He raised up Christ from the dead.

It is such a God as this whom the healthy heart seeks out in prayer and in other forms of worship declares: 'How lovely is your dwelling place, O LORD of hosts! My soul longs, yes, faints for the courts of the LORD; my heart and flesh sing for joy to the living God' (Ps. 84:1, 2).

God always has been an active being. Unitarianism, by depriving God of inner Trinitarian communion, would give Him nothing to do before creation and deism, by withdrawing God from His world, nothing since. In Christianity God is eternally the God who 'has something to do'. The triune God stood in no need of creating in order to have something to love. Before the world was there was in the Godhead no less to contemplate than after creation. Creation, providence and redemption were not dictated by necessity. The Trinity is the most rational of all doctrines, because only by it can God's eternal independence, as the living God who acts, be maintained. The alternative of a Unitarian doctrine of God proposes a desolate God who comes to limited blessedness only in creation of finite conscious life. In current 'process theology' God has not even yet discovered what He is going to be. He is growing with the world and apparently limited to that.

There are further practical benefits. I suggest two. (1) We are delivered from the hopelessness of human life in a world with only natural laws in control. The Maker of the laws of nature and of destiny is a person. People cannot in any absolute manner override or direct nature's caprices and their own destiny; but for His mercy's sake God can and did (at Calvary) and does so every day in response to prayers. (2) Moral living has sufficient motive. We are not just getting in harmony with 'nature's laws' but we 'serve the living and true God' (1 Thess. 1:9) who 'will bring every deed into judgment, with every secret thing, whether good or evil' (Eccles. 12:14). Also, one can revel in Jesus' comforting assurance that 'whoever gives you a cup of water to drink because you belong to Christ will by no means lose his reward' (Mark 9:41).

6. Intelligence.

This word means true perception of facts as they are (knowledge), genuine awareness of the meaning of those facts (understanding) and ability to put all those facts in proper relation (wisdom). This aspect of the divine Spirit whom Christians call God must be noted and explained to protect ourselves against ideas fatal to biblical faith. These ideas are mainly of two kinds. On the one hand there is the doctrine that the world has no personal centre, creator or control, called God, only a certain substance, an 'it', in which inhere eternal 'principles' or 'laws'. In secularized Western lands, where Christianity has long held nominal allegiance of the majority, this doctrine usually appears in supposedly harmless guise. 'It' is called 'Nature', 'Mother Nature' or 'Mother Earth'. In German idealistic philosophy of the late eighteenth and nineteenth centuries, God was homogenized with nature as 'the Absolute'.

On the other hand, in pantheistic (all-is-God) religion, distinct knowledge of particular things is disparaged completely. Personal being is esteemed to be retrogression from the utter non-particularity of ultimate reality. Inasmuch as particular knowledge is denial of this ultimate, it is affirmed (in Hinduism, Buddhism, Theosophy, Rosacrucianism) that a God who knows is closer to the Christian idea of Satan than our LORD Jesus' holy Father. No pantheist can find the comfort of David's assuring words, 'As a father shows compassion to his children, so the LORD shows compassion to those who fear him. For he knows our frame; he remembers that we are dust' (Ps. 103:13, 14). A Hindu can find some comfort from the 'lesser' spirits and gods of his religion. In this respect Hinduism is polytheistic.

The same is true of the cosmic evolutionism of Pierre Teihard de Chardin. He would transform the Christian doctrine of the personal, living, acting triune God into a cosmic mechanism wherein every life is organically hooked to every other living thing – all in motion toward an omega point, the consummation of the cosmic evolutionary process. This point he calls Christ. Life runs according to an anatomy of fixed laws.

There is something similar in the *panentheism* of process theology. It's god is growing with the cosmos, scarcely distinguishable from it. One of the leading advocates in America, John B. Cobb, Jr, identifies Christ with the process of universal change. Though he claims to have constructed a synthesis of traditional orthodoxy and Modernism, he has conformed this theology to a congeries of current and discarded pantheisms. As Teihard, Cobb has joined his pantheism to evolutionism.

C. S. Lewis has deftly removed the mask of modernity and of scholarship from the ancient delusion of pantheism and lines that contrast well:

> Pantheism certainly is… congenial to the modern mind; but the fact that a shoe slips on easily does not prove that it is a new shoe – much less that it will keep your feet dry… it is almost as old as we are. It may even be the most primitive of all religions… It is immemorial in India. The Greeks rose above it only at their peak, in the thought of Plato and Aristotle; their successors relapsed into the great Pantheistic system of the Stoics. Modern Europe escaped it only while she remained predominently Christian… Pantheism is in fact the permanent natural bent of the human mind… Pantheism… has only one really formidable opponent – namely Christianity… Yet, by a strange irony, each new relapse into this immemorial 'religion' is hailed as the last word in novelty and emancipation.[16]

The human mind has an apparent universal impulse toward pantheism.

'Nature knows', or 'Mother Nature' teaches the birds where to make their nests, are forms of statements utterly out of place in a Christian setting. For Christians, the personal Creator remains in personal support and government of the whole order of nature. Psalm 104 is instructive in this regard. The clouds, with shafts of light beaming through, are like garments and chambers for Him, since He makes them (vv. 1-3). The winds and lightnings are His messengers (vv. 3, 4). He holds earth steady (v. 5) and God covered the oceanic mountains with water (v. 6). The thunder is His voice (v. 7). Streams, springs, wild animals, plants and the like, are directly dependent on Him. Our daily cycle of life is God's order for us. Many of God's works are involved in this justly famous literary display of the personal Creator's personal involvement in all of material nature – for our benefit and ultimately for God's own glory.

The present reason for citing these matters is that it is God's personal *knowledge* that insures nature's practicality, its success, its magnificent rhythms and cycles. This point is made by the anonymous Psalmist, himself: 'O LORD, how manifold are your works', he says (Ps. 104:24a), and we think of 'the living God' and of His activity noted earlier. Then the Psalm continues, 'In wisdom have you made them all' (v. 24b).

All the wisdom of the creatures of nature in their manifold life-processes, all operating to preserve the order of nature in what we have come to call 'ecological balance', has been planted there by God. Nature 'knows' nothing in the sense of rational knowledge.

---

16. C. S. Lewis, *Miracles* (New York: Macmillan, 1945), pp. 84, 85.

The tilled acres of the farm where Mrs Culver and I live has recently been turned into three pasture fields where thirteen of a distant neighbour's cows and their calves grow fat. Four days ago they escaped into the surrounding forest through a gate thoughtlessly left open by a turkey hunter and disappeared for two days. Then yesterday they reappeared in a nearer neighbour's 'new seeding' of alfalfa a mile from where they left the open gate. The owner of the animals and his son-in-law came and as savvy operators gently started the anxious mothers moving back toward the forest and the distant gate. They 'remembered' each twist and turn through the gulches and ridges, even an abrupt 120 degree hillside turn, re-entering the pasture through the open gate that had enabled their wandering adventures two days before. There was no intellectual content in this bovine 'knowledge' of 'the way home', only some genetically derived instinct implanted not by impersonal nature but by the living God. In this way animals sometimes 'know' what people ought to know, but do not: 'The ox knows its owner, and the donkey its master's crib, but Israel does not know, my people do not understand' (Isa. 1:3). This is one of the 'facts of nature' placed in contrast to the ignorance of Job and his friends by the LORD in the argument of the book of Job (Job 38–41).

We often speak of birds or fish as if they were knowing subjects, as when we say the migratory salmon *know* how to return to the place of their hatching in order to lay and fertilize their own eggs. But this is anthropomorphism – transferring of human characteristics to subhuman. 'The LORD by wisdom founded the earth; by understanding he established the heavens; by his knowledge the deeps broke open, and the clouds drop down the dew' (Prov. 3:19, 20).

God is characterized in Scripture as 'a God of knowledge' (1 Sam. 1:3); His Spirit is 'the Spirit of wisdom and understanding, the Spirit of counsel… the Spirit of knowledge' (Isa. 11:2). A person, when he impudently speaks of God's character and ways, without consulting what God has said about the subject first, is one who 'darkens counsel by words without knowledge' (Job 38:2). God challenges: 'Shall a faultfinder contend with the Almighty?' (Job 40:2). The end of Job's debate came when the free, living, acting, personal, knowing God simply overwhelmed him by His knowledge of nature and mankind's ignorance of it (Job 38–41). The only proper response was the one Job made – he repented in dust and ashes (Job 42:6). So it should be with today's scientists (Latin for 'knowledge-ists') who challenge God's rightful place in nature, beneath nature and above it. 'Shall… the thing made… say of its maker, "He did not make me"; or the thing formed say of him who formed it, "He has no understanding"?' (Isa. 29:16).

It is not in nature, however, that God's wisdom shall be most fully revealed. The church of Christ, the household of belief in the one true living God, is yet to be the scene of the manifestation of that wisdom, in spite of all her failures here below and in spite of all her detractors (Eph. 3:10, 11).

Earlier comments in this chapter on the will of God spoke of God's purpose and purposes as later chapters will speak of His plan (decree) for all creation. That the living God, who is a person, should have purpose in being alive is not a mere anthropomorphism. Yet as human beings we cannot think of God apart from His having plans deep in the center of His being. Living is not a mere anthropomorphism. Yet as human beings we cannot think of God apart from His having plans deep in the center of His being. We know in ourselves that life without purpose is life without meaning, even if we do not reflect on our goals or if we do not clearly formulate them. We have already taken notice of passages relating to God's eternal purposes. Isaiah speaks of God's 'purpose that is purposed concerning the whole earth' and adds, 'For the LORD of hosts has purposed, and who will annul it?' (Isa. 14:26, 27). Paul's most exalted prose reflects on God's attribute of purposiveness.

Let us close this consideration of features of the spiritual nature of God with Paul's ecstatic exclamation: 'God… created all things, so that through the church the manifold wisdom of God might now be made known to the rulers and authorities in the heavenly places. This was according to the eternal purpose that he has realized in Christ Jesus our Lord' (Eph. 3:9b-11).

10
The Unity of the Godhead

'[T]he LORD is God in heaven above and on the earth beneath; there is no other' (Deut. 4:39)

One might suppose the trinity of the Godhead to be more difficult to explain than God's unity. Moreover, it is correct to say that the Trinity, like the two natures of Christ, posed a severe problem for the early Christians to formulate in a manner true to Scripture and at least amenable to reason even if not fully explicable. Yet such is not entirely correct. Wolfhart Pannenberg, for one, has delineated how the New Testament clearly represents God, the forever invisible, dwelling in inaccessible light (1 Tim. 6:16), made known by the Son who is visible in the flesh (Matt. 11:27), citing Luther's famous formulae, God is both *deus revelatus* (God revealed) and *deus absconditus* (God concealed, unknown). Even in Christ (says Luther) God is revealed as still concealed. In other words, God 'whom no one has ever seen or can see' (1 Tim. 6:16) is still true God even though revealed in the life, words and work of Jesus. After all, Paul wrote these words long after the incarnation had occurred. Our problem is how are we to affirm God's essence as one possessed fully by each 'person' – Father, Son and Holy Spirit?[1]

Christians have had difficulty explaining the oneness of their Trinitarian God to adamantly monotheistic Jews from the beginning, and forever afterward to Muslims. Pannenberg comments:

> The theology of the early church realized that the incomprehensibility of God applies to the essence and qualities of the living God and not merely to the statements of the doctrine of the Trinity.[2]

Christians then, as now, needed to affirm to themselves that their God is one, identical with the Jehovah of the Old Testament, even though in that divine essence there are three who possess the infinite essence entire without division.

Interestingly, Eastern scholars – the three Cappadocians, Basil, and the two Gregories of Nyssa and Nazianzus – went to work seriously on the problem of the one and the three only after the First Ecumenical Council (AD 325) had spelled out the full deity of the Second Person. Though orthodox Trinitarians contended with unitarian Arianism for a long time, these three Fathers sought with acknowledged success to state the unity and the Trinity in a way true both to sound reason and the Scriptures. They were pressed to do so not only to clarify their orthodoxy to

---

1. Wolfhart Pannenberg, *Systematic Theology vol. i* (Grand Rapids: Eerdmans, 1991), chapter. 6, 'The Unity and Attributes of God'. I have paraphrased Pannenberg.
2. ibid., p. 342.

themselves but also to defend it from the Arians. Further, others were mounting seriously flawed explanations that they felt required to resist. The writings of one, Eunomius, Arian bishop of Cyzicus (d. 394), were the trigger for some of the most definitive works of the Cappadocians.[3]

First, there was the lesser task of repudiating 'the superstition of polytheism'.[4]

> [T]he God of Abraham, Isaac and Jacob was one God; and the God of the [more advanced] philosophers [of the day], rightly understood was one God. But was the God confessed as Father, Son, and Holy Spirit by Christians, both orthodox and heretical, still one God, and one in the same sense? It was the fundamental argument of the Cappadocian case for Nicene trinitarianism that authenic monotheism was the rejection of the many [of polytheism] for the sake of the One. The ground of that argument was formulated by Basil: 'The terms 'one' and 'only' are predicated of God not to mark a distinction from the Son and the unreal gods falsely so called.[5]

As to the Trinity of Persons, the Cappadocians were the first to explain and defend at length that every attribute properly assigned by Scripture or sanctified reason to God was fully shared qualitatively and infinitely by the Son and the Spirit no less than the Father. This is an emphasis of their doctrine and ours today as believing, orthodox Christians, when we affirm the unity of God. I know of no historical resource more complete, learned and faithful to history, Scripture and orthodox theology than Pelikan's entire work *Christianity and Classical Culture* cited above.

The scientific study of religions practised around the world has produced a large number of special terms helpful in any study of the subject. These terms are often employed in such a manner as to indicate stages in a supposed evolutionary development of religion. Such, however, is not necessarily the case, any more than a classification of forms of life, past and present, on this earth necessarily implies organic evolution. Any classification inevitably moves from simplicity to complexity or the reverse. Single-celled animals (or plants) may be at the lower end of the scale of classification and vertebrate mammals at the other, but no organic development from one level of the scale to another is necessarily inherent in the scheme. Evolution may be in some scientists' scheme of classification, but not necessarily in the specimens classified. So it is with a scientific classification of religions. The informed Christian student of his own faith will be well advised to get acquainted with some of the special terms of formal discussion of religions and of ideas about God.

Special Vocabulary of Study of Religions.

Several terms are employed to describe what is usually thought to be the lowest forms of religion.

There are people who wear charms, amulets – objects to bring good luck to the bearer and to ward off bad luck. The belief prompting the practice is known as *dynamism* (from Greek *dynamis*, power). Some sort of non-material (spiritual is hardly the word), but impersonal, power is thought to pervade everything, but especially the material object worn. This form of belief may be held in common with other ideas about religion.

Fetishism is a refinement of dynamism: a particular, powerful spirit is thought to inhabit some material object. Perhaps some beneficial incident seemed to take place in connection with a man-made object or some portable natural object. Afterward a man or his tribe adopts the object and venerates it, even carrying it along in migration or warfare.

Animism is a belief in nature spirits – many of them. They are thought to inhabit streams, springs, trees, waterfalls, mountains and so on. The phenomena of nature are thought to be caused by them.

Totemim is a system wherein a family, clan or tribe is grouped according to totems. Totems are usually animals to which the family, clan or tribe considers itself related by blood and which affect affairs of life, death and the hereafter. Totemism, as a form of worship, is very common among primitive peoples living close to nature.

Taboo is a group prohibition placed on certain people, places and things, rendering them untouchable and sometimes even unmentionable, not even to be looked at. It is an accompaniment of dynamism.

All of these beliefs exist, sometimes coexist, in very low levels of culture.

Ancestor-worship is a self-explanatory feature of worship even among some cultivated peoples, eminently the Chinese.

---

3. Somewhat later Augustine was working out the Christian repudiation of polytheism in his *The Kingdom of God*.
4. Gregory of Nyssa, *Against Eunomius* 3.2.94, cited by Pelikan (see footnote 5).
5. Jaroslav Pelikan, *Christianity and Classical Culture* (New Haven: Yale Univ. Press, 1993). p. 232.

On a more 'advanced' level of culture and presumably, therefore, one in which people are more reflective, there is a tendency 'to universalize various types of phenomena and identify each with a particular deity such as a god of storms, another of harvest and another of procreation'.[6] We are familiar with this in the classical *polytheism* of Greeks and Romans and in the less-publicized, pre-literate worship of the nations of western and northern Europe. This form of worship of 'many gods' is memorialized in several of the days of our week – Thor in Thursday, Wotan in Wednesday and in June (for Juno), January (for Janus), March (for Mars), and so on, among the months of the year. The Old Testament preserves fragments of ancient Near-Eastern polytheism in the names of several gods and goddesses (Baal, Hadad, Moloch, Ashtoreth, etc.). Scholars disagree as to whether these deities represent a breaking up of the functions of nature from some more unified way of looking at things or the personification of the multifarious powers of nature.

An invariable accompaniment of polytheism is *idolatry*, wherein an image of the god, thought to be the actual local seat of the god's person (these gods are human beings writ large), is worshiped. The idol and the god are identified in the worshiper's thought, however stupid that might appear to a man of Elijah's, Jeremiah's, Isaiah's or Paul's insights.

The association between idol and its distinct god or goddess is thought to be permanent. No informed Israelite, on the contrary, supposed that the Philistines had captured Jehovah when the Philistines took away the ark of testimony, but when the idol Dagon fell off his pedestal in the presence of the ark, the Philistines 'took Dagon and put him back in his place' (see 1 Sam. 5:1-3).

There are examples of *monolatry* wherein one of the many gods is chosen for a special place and afterward worshiped as sole practising deity. On a somewhat more sophisticated level there have been cases wherein a king would designate a certain single god as the only one worthy of worship, meanwhile regarding the other deities of the nation and its neighbours as real. The worship of the sun-god at Thebes at a certain stage of Egypt's history (fourteenth century BC) was this sort of *henotheism* (worship of only one god among many acknowledged to exist).

Dualism regards matter and spirit (or mind) as each an eternally real principle and orders life in relation to these two principles. In such a case, matter is held to be evil, spirit good. Parseeism, the modern form of ancient Zoroastrianism, is a contemporary, overtly dualistic religion.

Pantheism regards all that exists as manifestation of a single impersonal substance or principle. Hinduism, Buddhism and several cults of oriental origin – theosophy, Rosicrucianism and transcendental meditation – are pantheistic. *Deism* affirms the sole existence of one creator-God, wholly transcendent, having no present relation with creation. It is often a phenomenon of advanced civilizations. There have been, however, few fully consistent deists.

Monotheism is the worship of one Supreme Being, personal and ethical, transcendent above the world as creator, yet immanent in the world as its preserver and ruler. Judaism and Islam are, besides Christianity, the only historic monotheistic faiths. *Theism* is a form of monotheism. As understood by Christian writers, theism includes the idea that God is self-revealing as in miracles and prophecy and (in the case of Christian theism) in Jesus Christ our Lord. Usually, whether stated or not, Christian theism is the view of deity which the author employing the term 'theism' thinks it means.

Scholars inclined toward naturalistic interpretations of all faiths like to find examples of all these forms of religion in the growth of Israel's religion. They draw no distinction, for example, between Rachel's evident reverence for the portable family idols and Israel's use of the portable Ark of the Covenant, or between Nebuchadnezzar's evident henotheism and Abram's worship of the Most High God. Whatever may be said for the low level of perception of true worship among the Hebrews when God first delivered them from the pagan atmosphere of Ur and Haran (see Josh. 24:2), the *revealed* faith, that worship which the Bible from beginning to end inculcates, is monotheism and theism. It must be acknowledged, that far from manifesting any 'genius for religion', as some Jewish writers like to say, the Hebrews certainly were tardy in understanding their own religion. The history and prophecy of their Scriptures painfully relate this sad story. It was consummated at the rejection of their Messiah.

It remains to be added that outside of Christianity and Judaism, and to a lesser degree Islam, peoples of the world have generally been aware of no inconsistency in holding several religious views at the same time. Polytheists, for example, may also be animists and fetish-worshipers in addition to their idolatry, the twin of polytheism everywhere. Polytheism, idolatry and animism flourish in Hindu pantheism.

---

6. L. Harold DeWolf, *A Theology of the Living Church* (New York: Harper & Brothers, 1953), p. 89.

Why Believe in One God?

In chapter 2, some of the reasons why people do believe in God were introduced, but little was said about *why* we should believe in only *one* God, even though monotheism was the assumption upon which we proceeded. It must be admitted, however, that approaching the subject from a rational standpoint, more must be said before those evidences point unmistakably toward the monotheistic ideal of all Christians.

1. It is interesting that antiquity provides *many examples of monotheistic conceptions*, if not of monotheistic *faith*. One of the pharaohs of Egypt led his people temporarily as far as henotheism when he proclaimed and enforced the worship of the sun-god alone. *Theos*, the commonest abstract Greek word for God, appears often in the singular number among the later Greek writers. Several philosophers expressed theoretical (hardly religious) ideas close to monotheism: Xenophanes, Heraclitus, Anaxagoras, in addition to Socrates, Plato and Aristotle. After Alexander (fourth century BC) the Greek civilizing influence grew strong everywhere and the Roman Empire brought stability. The upper classes of literate people were particularly exposed to the new conditions. Among them, faith in the polytheistic deities declined. Many people pondered the possibility of one single, personal, creator-God. All the rational proofs available to us were available to them also. The Greeks and Romans pondered them. It is true that, 'In the historic development of religion there is a tendency for thought to move in the direction of monotheism... It is no accident that as a religious people increase in knowledge, in powers of discipline, in systematic thought and depth of cultural experience they tend to move toward monotheism.'[7] Is not this fact in itself strong evidence for the sole existence of one creator-God, Lord of history? Consider the unlikelihood of the contrary development of history. The growth of civilization, education and mental culture toward a climax in polytheism or animism is very unlikely and, as far as I know, without historical precedent.

2. *The coherence of the material universe into a single system of cause and effect* suggests rather forcefully that there is a *single* all-wise, all-powerful, everywhere-present, personal power behind it. The more science probes the minute and infinitesimally small, the more it appears that all matter and energy are aspects of a cosmic system. The same system of causes and effects seems to prevail in the farthest reaches of space. We, then, live truly in a universe not a 'pluriverse' or 'multiverse'. People can rationally formulate laws of cause and effect which are valid everywhere. This makes it more reasonable to believe in one 'prime mover' or 'first cause' rather than several.

3. *The coherence of all authentic abstract truths* in a single system is further evidence that the God of creation is one. These abstract data exist quite apart from the people who discover them. In the small business houses of all China, people figure the bills of customers on a frame of parallel spokes on which wooden rings are moved, called an abacus. The nearby grocery has replaced the mechanical cash register with a computerized machine. Our paint merchant uses a hand-held electric calculator. My mother uses pencilled figures on paper to add up her bills. (I let my wife figure them out!) The data and results of all mathematics, however, (4 multiplied by 3; 10 plus 2; 20 minus 8; 72 divided by 6: all yield the number 12) are invariable and universal.

The same is true of formal logic as taught in the schools of philosophy, whether the classical system of Aristotle's or modern symbolic logic. These are true laws of reality. They can be discovered and formulated but never invented. Deduction and induction are nothing but aspects of one all-inclusive system of abstract truth. Abstract truth underlying or accompanying all other truths is a universal network, existing in perfection. This system sets bounds and binds us all. There is no rational existence as mankind without submitting to it. We call people crazy who do not. If this system of universal abstract truth is attributable to the mind(s) that created us, not to the rational discoverers of it, is it not rational, within the system of rational truth, to attribute it to One rather than to many?

4. Another argument is an extension of the anthropological or moral argument for the existence of God: *there is a system of ethical ideals*, adherence to which is necessary for any sort of order in any community, from a simple partnership to a civilized world order. Loyalty to ideals and to legitimate human leaders is necessary to civil order; honesty, to the flow of trade; truthfulness, equally necessary to science or business; discipline of children, to family, school, civil commonweal. The Old Testament Decalogue, though given by God at Sinai, is a kind of moral consensus, necessary to 'the greatest happiness for the greatest number'. Generally speaking, except perhaps for the prohibition of images in worship, the Ten Commandments are praised around the whole world. There is, indeed, beneath the

---

7. ibid., pp. 89, 91.

multiplicity of rules concerning social life (sumptuary laws) and rules of custom (consuetudinary laws) a single system of moral law. These ideal norms are objective and real, even though stated in different ways. The 'Golden Rule' of Jesus, for example, can also be found in the teachings of several moral philosophers (Confucius, Socrates, Buddha, Santayana) of widely separated epochs and places. Does not this single, universal, accepted standard of human behavior argue forcefully for a single moral Mind, rather than several, for its cause?

5. There is also *a certain logic from the nature of religious devotion* which impels toward the conviction that God is one. We are told in the Bible, of course, that we must love the LORD our God with the whole of our being. The God of Abraham, Isaac and Jacob allows no competitors. He is a 'jealous God'. Let us turn this fact upside-down. Thoughtful, cultivated worshipers of deity, in any religion, are apt to assume that their god desires single-minded, whole-souled worship. They tend to become devotees of a single deity, even while appeasing competing deities. Schleiermacher (1768–1834), a most influential theologian, insisted that religious experience has an inner logic which, when developed, impels toward faith in a single divine Being. In this respect, he seems to have been right. There is, in this way, an argument from the very nature of religious devotion for a single object of worship.

The teaching of Scripture is on a totally different level. The sole existence of one, authentic, creator-God is assumed from the opening statement, 'In the beginning God created the heavens and the earth' to the claim of the last chapter, 'I am the Alpha and the Omega, the first and the last, the beginning and the end.' Let us see how the biblical evidence stands, what it means, and what the consequences for our thinking and action are.

Evolution Toward Monotheism in the Bible?

Someone, however, wants to know if there is not to be discerned in the Bible a beginning in low forms of religion and a subsequent evolution toward monotheism, triumphant at last. Is there not even evidence that some of the heroes and heroines of the early narratives, such as Abraham and Sarah, Isaac and Rebekah, Jacob and Rachel, Moses and his family, and others, practiced lower forms of religion such as animism and fetishism? Did they not really slowly move from acknowledgment of the existence of lesser gods, that is, polytheism, through henotheism to the true monotheism of the great prophets of Israel?

An affirmative answer to this question, it is said, is found in many features of the Old Testament. Abraham's attraction to the oaks of Mamre as a place to live implies belief that favourable spirits dwelt in those trees (animism), we are told. Isaac's well-known interest in certain springs and wells is evidence of the same. When Jacob returned to the environs of Bethel where his grandfather had spent some time, and rested his head on a stone for a pillow, he demonstrated an animism or even fetishism which believes in the good influence of the spirits in portable objects. The story of angels descending and ascending, though told in good monotheistic framework, is said to rest upon the animism and fetishism of Jacob's time.

When 'the Lord… sought to put him [Moses] to death' at an inn in the desert (Exod. 4:24-26) on account of the neglect of circumcision of his son, Jehovah, Himself, is said to behave like a demon of the wilderness, showing the superstition of the time and low views of God. The Ark of the Covenant – just a gold-cased wooden box – is evidence of fetish-like beliefs. In addition, the many references to the object of Abraham's worship, as well as of his later progeny, as 'the Most High God', imply acknowledgment of lesser deities. The language of the historical sections of the Old Testament, we are assured, in no wise denies the existence of the gods of fertility and of weather (Baal, Moloch, Hadad and the like) of Israel's neighbours. It only marks their rejection by Israel's best leaders as proper objects of Israel's devotion, we are told. Much of what goes for Old Testament theology and the history of Israel in current liberal literature follows this line of thinking – of which a leading example is Gerhard von Rad's *Old Testament Theology*.

In response, several things can be said to relieve the Bible-reader from acceptance of any such inferences as these. First of all, the claims rest on no straightforward declarations of the Bible. That is to say, the Bible *teaches* none of these things. They are all inferences drawn from a so-called history of Israel reconstructed upon evolutionary principles and literary analysis of the nineteenth-century type. Both the historical reconstruction and the literary analysis are now somewhat out of style and have been rendered doubtful by twentieth-century findings of archaeology. Yet recent 'liberal' scholars seem to have dropped few of the types of pejorative estimates of Old Testament religion just cited. A representative 'modernist' writer speaks of the 'intermittent monotheism' of the earlier writers while insisting on a final triumph of monotheism.[8]

---

8. ibid., p. 94.

That many of the Israelites were more henotheistic than monotheistic may readily be granted. We know that some of Abram's ancestral family practised polytheism, as did many of the children of Israel during their sojourn in Egypt (Josh. 24:3). We cannot explore Abram's mind, but God's self-revelation as Almighty God (Gen. 17:2) and Abram's assurance that his God was 'Judge of all the earth' (Gen. 18:25) are quite inconsistent with henotheism. Furthermore, 'the Most High God' of Melchizedek and of Abram (Gen. 14:18, 19) was 'Possessor of heaven and earth'. Thus, the alleged henotheism turns out on examination of the actual text of scripture to be full-blown ethical theism, or monotheism.

The inferences about Abram's trees, Jacob's stone pillow, the ark of Testimony and such like are not necessary inferences, but tendentious assertions resting on the slender evidence of higher-critical orthodoxy, not sound history and literary study. This orthodoxy shoots its bullet into the barn door, then draws circles around the hole made by their projectile and proclaims: 'Bull's Eye'!

It may be freely acknowledged that many of the good people of Old Testament times partially misunderstood their own religion. Apostasy to idols and polytheism, as is plain to be read, was a constant threat. Certain elements of the Israelite population were drawn to occult practices and raw heathenism (2 Kings 17:6-23; cf. Deut. 18:9-14). It was for their backslidings that the two Israelite nations came to an end. Nevertheless, in no case does the Scripture for a moment even hint that the God of its pages is less than personal Creator, Sustainer, Governor and moral Judge of all the earth and heaven.

Direct Biblical Affirmations of Monotheism.

The statements of this doctrine, as with most Bible truths, are generally in connection with some command or duty, the doctrine furnishing the motive power for obedience.

Never mind that some of the strongest statements of all, from Deuteronomy, are said by the reigning liberal orthodoxy to come from the late kingdom epoch rather than the Mosaic. There is no doubt that on the Bible's own ground the first testimonies in the literary order of the Bible are also the earliest. Only by rejecting the Bible's own testimony to Moses' monotheism can an Amos have been the inventor of Old Testament monotheism, or, as some say, if not Amos, an anonymous prophet in the time of the Babylonian exile, author of Second Isaiah (Isa. 40–66). Observe that these early statements from Deuteronomy constitute a full, vigorous, uncompromising affirmation of the substantial unity of the Godhead. They have never been superseded.

In Deuteronomy Moses reminded Israel that God showed to them the miracles of deliverance from Egypt and the theophany at Sinai, 'that you might know that the LORD is God; there is no other besides him' (Deut. 4:35). These words were spoken in the context of Moses' dying exhortation to unswerving loyalty to Jehovah and to His revealed faith. Moses went on to say: 'Hear [Hebrew *shema'*, hence, the Shema'], O Israel: The LORD our God, the LORD is one. You shall love the LORD your God with all your heart and with all your soul and with all your might' (Deut. 6:4, 5). There is only one God, hence all worshipful love anywhere by anyone is due Him.

The theology of the poetical books of the Old Testament is profoundly and exclusively an ethical monotheism. Occasional reference to other deities (as for example, 'Who is like thee among the gods?') must be interpreted in view of the uniform monotheism. We should understand them as referring to *alleged* gods, as did Elijah, who, while ridiculing the non-god Baal, spoke of him in taunting the Baalish prophets as though existent (1 Kings 18:17-29, esp. v. 27).

The prophets of the Old Testament, Isaiah in particular, had a striking way of asserting the sole existence of the God of Israel. With their assertions, they provided proofs derived from His knowledge of the future and power to communicate it to His servants, the prophets. Let us note some powerful examples.

'Thus says the LORD, the King of Israel and his Redeemer, the LORD of hosts: "I am the first and I am the last; besides me there is no god. Who is like me? Let him proclaim it."' (Isa. 44:6, 7). Verse 6 makes fulfillment of prophetic predictions a solid proof of God's sole existence as LORD of time. Is He not 'the Father of Eternity' (Isa. 9:6 ASV marg.)? The passage continues this theme through 45:1-6. In it, the coming of the Persian King Cyrus, 150 years later, in fulfillment of Isaiah's predictions of him, is said to prove 'I am the LORD, and there is no other, besides me there is no God; I equip you [Cyrus], though you do not know me, that people [on earth] may know, from the rising of the sun and from the west, that there is none besides me; I am the LORD, and there is no other' (Isa. 45:5, 6). The ethical teaching (i.e. duty) is to believe God's prophetic messengers and their message of Jehovah's sole existence as God.

Mark 12:28-34 tells how Jesus employed the *Shema'* (Deut. 6:4) to instruct a somewhat hypocritical, but inquiring, scribe in the duty of undivided love for God. In John 5:44, Jesus refers to deity as 'the only God' and in His high priestly prayer as 'the only true God' (John 17:3). In the former case, Jesus is teaching the importance of seeking God's approval rather than man's and in the latter Jesus asserts the high privilege of true Christian worship.

Four citations from Paul display much of the religious and moral meaning of the sole existence of one God. Since God is 'one God', there is only one way of salvation for all classes of people (Rom. 3:19, 30). Since there is only one God, the idols of the heathen are bogus deities (1 Cor. 8:4, 5). In an oft-recited benediction Paul invokes 'the only God' (1 Tim. 1:17) as the only source of human happiness and as the end of all praise and honour. He employs the same doctrine to appeal for steadfastness in Christian duties (1 Tim. 6:16).

James cites the 'one God' as worthy of faith (James 2:19) and Jude 4 speaks of denial of the same as most reprehensible.

These are only a few selected texts that speak specifically to the point. The whole Bible breaths the atmosphere of worship and love for that 'blessed and only Sovereign, the King of kings and Lord of lords, who alone has immortality, who dwells in unapproachable light, whom no one has ever seen or can see. To him be honour and eternal dominion. Amen' (1 Tim. 6:15, 16).

Let us guard against several common misunderstandings of the biblical statements.

(1) God is one, not in the sense of a generic name, as *equus* for all horses or *homo* for all members of the human race.

(2) Nor do the biblical declarations of the essential unity of God mean that there is merely a moral or intellectual agreement of entities in one.

(3) Nor does the affirmation mean unity in the sense of union. Certain Trinitarian expositors of the *Shema'* have seemed to err in this direction. The affirmation univocally designates *singularity*. There is numerically one indivisible, undistributed, living God. It is God's inherent nature to be one.

(4) The doctrine of biblical monotheism (as previously suggested) does not exclude the possibility that certain other objects of human discourse, real or supposed, may be 'called gods'. Idols worshipped as gods are called gods in the Bible and the supposed, but unreal, unseen deities of polytheism are also called gods (see 1 Cor. 8:4, 5). If we understand Paul correctly, even though the supposed divine objects of the Greek-Roman Pantheon have never existed, there are certain divinely created, but fallen, corrupt, evil, unseen spirits, called demons, who sometimes appropriate the service offered to idols by corrupt worship. In chapter 8 of 1 Corinthians Paul specifically brands the gods and lords of heathenism as being quite as unreal as their idol effigies. Yet, he enlarges on the subject in chapter 10 by saying, 'Consider the people of Israel: are not those who eat the sacrifices participants in the altar? What do I imply then? That food offered to idols is anything, or that an idol is anything? No, I imply that what pagans sacrifice they offer to demons and not to God. I do not want you to be participants with demons. You cannot drink the cup of the Lord and the cup of demons' (1 Cor. 10:18-21). In this text the apostle dearly distinguishes between malevolent spirits, i.e. *daimonioi* (demons) and *theoi* (gods). The pagan thinks he worships gods but they really are not in that class where only One exists. Created evil spirits do exist and may be associated with the pagan idols.

(5) The doctrine of monotheism does not forbid the possibility of more than one person in the Godhead, for Jesus Himself affirmed, 'I and the Father are one' (John 10:30). How this can be true will be treated more at length in the chapter, 'The Triunity of the Godhead'.

Biblical Proofs of Monotheism.

The Bible has its own methods of proof of this teaching. As we have seen, certain events were employed at the time of the Exodus to establish Israel in monotheism and to insure their perseverance in worship of only one God throughout the future.

First, there were the mighty works of God, properly called miracles, associated with Israel's deliverance from Egypt. Moses was to identify himself and also to verify (certify) himself as a true messenger of the God of Abraham, of Isaac and of Jacob by three remarkable *signs* (miracles). These are mentioned specifically in Exodus 4:1-9: the changing of his inert rod into a serpent; the changing of Moses' normal hand to a white leprous one, at his will, and the reversal of the same back to normal again; and the taking of water from the Nile which, as Moses poured it on the dry ground, became blood. Verses 28-31 tell how Moses, ably seconded by his brother Aaron, performed the miracles, with the result that 'the people believed'. Later a series of even greater miracles, which we call the ten plagues, convinced Israel even more deeply and made a similar impression even on the magicians of Egypt (see Exod. 8:19). The stubbornness of Pharaoh was God's way of rendering necessary all the miracles and in doing so strengthened conviction among the Israelites (Exod. 14:30, 31). This unique method was God's way of certifying the messengers who announced the truth of the sole existence of the God of Israel. In this case, God authenticated Himself as sole God by the inauthenticity of all the gods of Egypt.

Moses and Aaron also relied on prediction and its fulfillment to authenticate themselves and their message. We have already noted this in connection with biblical testimony to monotheism in an earlier chapter. Each of the miracles called the ten plagues involved prediction and fulfillment in the near future. Even the Son of God, Second Person of the triune God, employed these proofs.[9]

Religious Values of Monotheism.

There are many religious values derived specifically out of monotheism. Believers are delivered from the frustration of not knowing whom to try to please, as in all non-monotheist systems. As the clear biblical truth is blurred or perverted in Christendom, the confusion returns. We now notice this confusion in current efforts to placate the demi gods of occultism. An over emphasis on the personality and alleged powers of Satan and his minions has produced superstitious fears even among some uninformed orthodox Christians. They come to fear the strange, the dimly lighted and the weird as though the only omnipotent God were not in control of mankind and nature. 'They sacrificed to demons that were no gods, to gods they had never known, to new gods that had come recently, whom your fathers had never dreaded. You were unmindful of the Rock that bore you, and you forgot the God who gave you birth' (Deut. 32:17, 18). The worship-like veneration that multitudes of modern, secularized, de-Christianized people pay to science, government, 'the environment' and even to education is a servitude to new gods. Some, having abandoned belief in their fathers' God, pay their offerings in taxes to support the bloated budgets of contemporary civil government on its several levels.

The Bible assures us that there is a single God for the entire human race. Therefore, even though there may be a 'chosen people', God's ultimate goal is a blessing of 'all the nations' (Gen. 12:1-4). The sinner in Russia or Albania is quite as loved by God as the sinner in Britain, the Netherlands or Canada. The doctrine of racial equality before God rests in part on this ethical monotheism no less than on the image of the one, true God that every child of Adam bears.

The principle of the uniformity of nature, which makes true science possible, rests upon the same truth. It is no accident that the age of science (not to neglect scientific achievements elsewhere) had its origin and greatest development in Christian lands. Though theoretical scientists, as a group, do not seem especially prone to devotion, and lamentably have their share of aggressive, self-proclaimed atheists, denial of the existence of the one God of Christian theism is by no means universal among competent scientists.

---

9. Note His response to John's questions about 'he that should come', Matt. 11:2-5; cf. Isa 35:5, 6; 61:1. See further Peter's reliance on these proofs, in Jesus' case, Acts 2:22-40 and the Mosaic basis of this method of certification (Deut. 13:1 to end; 18:9-22 and compare 1 Kings 18:36-39).

11
The Greatness of the Godhead

'Great is our God above all gods' (2 Chr. 2:5 KJV)

The Swedish hymn, 'How Great Thou Art', translated by Stuart K. Kline and popularized by George Beverly Shea, finds an answering chord in most Christian believers. However, God is great in ways that far outstrip worlds, stars, thunder and power 'throughout the universe displayed' of which the hymn speaks.

The historic creeds have distilled the Scripture statements and in timeless words have captured the greatness of God that even the hymns do not match. One of them speaks of God as 'a Spirit infinite, eternal and unchangeable in his being, wisdom, power, holiness, justice, goodness and truth'.[1] These are cool, abstract words of logical analysis. That is something we must all develop some appreciation for, if our understanding of God's greatness is to go as deep as in our better moments we wish.

Nothing is of greater importance to sound faith and life than *understanding* of several of God's attributes of greatness. It is not enough to have a feeling for God or even a love for Him. We need an intellectual apprehension of His characteristics – attributes as they are usually called. Israel of old was impressed by God's power. They trembled at God's thundering, trumpet-like voice and His fire at Sinai. But after a few months of camping on the spot, in a mass act of apostasy hard for us to understand after generations of inherited Trinitarian monotheism, they made an image of God which looked like a calf; then they worshiped it. The problem was they simply did not understand who God is or what He is like.

God's greatness stretches the thinking both of gifted poets (Ps. 8) and of learned theologians (Anselm's *Proslogion*). As we come to know more of what God is like we will be able to serve Him better.[2]

We shall only touch the hem of the outskirts of His garment in this short chapter: God's self-existence (aseity), His eternity, immensity, omnipresence, omniscience, omnipotence and His incomprehensibility.

Self-existence of God (or Aseity).

God is the ground of His own existence. His only necessity is the necessity of His own being. It is God's nature *to be*. Nothing else we can observe or rationally conceive of exists apart from some chain of causes. The more we learn of mankind, the crowning excellency on earth of God's creative art, the more we are made aware of the frailty

---
1. Westminster, *The Shorter Catechism*, Q. 4, 'What is God?'
2. At the end of this chapter there is a discussion of some additional terms and ideas which help us talk about His greatness.

of our dependent being. All beings, heavenly and earthly, except God Himself, both the first and the final cause, are dependent beings. An endless succession of causes for the world is unacceptable to the human mind. Like the Psalmist, our heart and flesh cry out for the living God.

Scripture Statements.

In the statements 'I AM WHO I AM' (Exod. 3:14) and 'my name the LORD' (Exod. 6:3) YHWH, or Jehovah, the name which Jews will not speak, is God's self-affirmation. The Hebrew word – in what scholars presume to have been an early form – for 'I am' is *'ehweh*. Changed to third person singular masculine, the same word (in an assumed archaic form of Hebrew) becomes *Yahweh*: 'he is' or 'he will be'. Ancient Hebrew writing was spelled without vowels. Hence, modern scholars sometimes refer to this name simply as the 'quadriliteral' (four letters, YHWH). The word translated 'I am' is not meant merely to connect the two parts of a nominal sentence (as in, 'Mary *is* a girl'), but is a statement about existence. In his book on this subject (*The Trinity* I.1, 2), Augustine said that God alone is the one of whom it can be unequivocally and unconditionally said, 'He is'. '[T]he Father has life in himself' (John 5:26). He is 'the fountain of living waters' (Jer. 2:13), 'the fountain of life; in your light do we see light' (Ps. 36:9).

The Practical Benefits.

Believers are assured that they truly have an eternal life. '[W]hoever hears my word', we read, 'and believes him who sent me has eternal life. He does not come into judgment, but has passed from death [our condition by nature] to life [our condition in Christ]… For as the Father has life in himself, so he has granted the Son also to have life in himself' (John 5:24, 26). God's being is the ground of our being. His power to create and sustain being ensures the stability of the world. It is His will to preserve it: 'While the earth remains, seedtime and harvest, cold and heat, summer and winter, day and night, shall not cease' (Gen. 8:22). The garish threats of extinction proposed in the pages of the Sunday newspapers may safely be ignored, as also some of the less rational predictions of the environmentalists.

Eternity of God.

To speak of eternity necessarily involves the concept of time, a concept no one in the history either of philosophy or theology has defined in a manner fully satisfactory even to himself. Even Augustine almost gave up on the task, writing: 'What, then, is time? If no one asks me, I know; if I wish to explain to one who asks, I do not know. Nevertheless, I confidently affirm that I know that if nothing passed away, there would not be past time; and if nothing were coming, there would not be a future time; and if nothing were, there would not be present time.'[3] For purposes of present discussion, our minds can settle for the idea of *duration*. There is a certain arbitrariness about this approach, for the past no longer exists, as such, and the present strictly is only a 'line' through which duration passes to become the future, which as yet does not exist.

Since God deals with the world He has relation with time, yet He cannot be measured by time, since He has no beginning or ending and is Himself the cause of other existent things which have duration. Thus it can be said that time is real because it is in God. Another way of speaking of God's relation to time is, that He is *above* time. It does not seem quite correct to say He lives in an eternal now, as we do occasionally read, for the past and future are present in God's mind as truly as the present. As just noted above, there is a sense in which 'now' is never anything more than a point or line which the future passes in becoming past time. Hence God lives in eternity, not in a line separating past from future. There is logical succession in God's thoughts, but no chronological succession; since, however, creation does now exist in succession of events, God sees them and knows them. Time is therefore as *real* for God as it is for us.

To illustrate: when the neighbouring village deploys the annual Pioneer Day's parade, the various vehicles, clowns, horsemen, floats and so on may extend for a mile among the streets and highways below Magelson's Bluff. From a stand at the centre of town (the only traffic signal), when half the train of parade has passed by, I may see the horsemen before me and a bit more coming on and a bit more already passed by. In a manner of speaking I see 'the present' part of the parade. If, however, someone else, say, the town safety commissioner, were to take his stand on the water tower high on the bluff overlooking the town, he could see the whole parade from *before* the beginning, the whole length of it, and beyond the end, the last passing vehicle. God's relation to time may be said to be like the view from the height.

3. Herman Bavinck, *The Doctrine of God*, trans. Wm. Hendriksen (Grand Rapids: Baker Books, 1977), p. 154.

Human beings may live above time, in a measure. By reflecting on remembered things, we are able to 'live in the past' and by projecting present tendencies, causes, movements and the like, we can 'live in the future'. 'Believers' are by the very definition of that word 'past oriented' as regards redemption and 'future oriented' as regards the consummation. Our religion as evangelical Christian believers, therefore, will be attacked by some, as being hopelessly detached from present problems into delusions about the future life, and by others as too conservative, mindlessly mired in the past. They are right to say of themselves they are anchored safely in present reality because of being adequately related both to the past and the future and therefore free to engage the present vigorously.

Scripture Statements.

'Before... ever thou hadst formed the earth and the world, even from everlasting to everlasting thou art God' (Ps. 90:2 KJV). The LORD describes Himself as 'the One who is high and lifted up [transcendent], who inhabits eternity' (Isa. 57:15). Christ is the one by whom God 'made the ages' (Heb. 1:2, Greek) and God is 'the King of ages' (1 Tim. 1:17).[4]

Practical Benefits.

God is as youthful and strong today as when Abel was born. '[Y]our years will have no end'. '[Y]ou are the same'. There is a place of quiet rest, near to the heart of God precisely because 'The eternal God is your dwelling place, and underneath are the everlasting arms' (Deut. 33:27; see also Ps. 102:1-13; Heb. 1:5-12).

> Swift to its close ebbs out life's little day,
> Earth's joys grow dim, its glories pass away;
> Change and decay in all around I see –
> O thou who changest not, abide with me.

Skeptical poets have sought to deal with their anxiety in a world without an eternal God in charge. Long ago this freshman's heart trembled, even though attracted, by Percy Byshe Shelley's pensive short poem:

> Unfathomable Sea! whose waves are years,
> Ocean of Time, whose waters of deep woe
> Are brackish with the salt of human tears!
> Thou shoreless flood, which in thine ebb and flow
> Claspest the limits of mortality,
> And sick of prey, yet howling on for more,
> Vomitest thy wrecks on its inhospitable shore;
> Treacherous in calm, terrible in storm
> Who shall put forth on thee, Unfathomable sea?[5]

Immensity of God.

God's nature is not extended in space; He is without spatial dimension and yet in Him all things consist, being Himself the Creator of space. It will readily be seen that as 'eternity' designates God's infinity in relation to time, 'immensity' is God's infinity in relation to space (this is how it is treated here, at least). This agrees with the dictum of the Roman Catholic theology of Ludwig Ott, '*Immensity* or spacelessness connotes the negation of spatial limitation; omnipresence expresses the relation of God to real space. *Immeasurability* [emphasis added] is a negative attribute; omnipresence is a positive and relative one.'[6] Further, as in the case of time, God having created space has relation to it.

Scripture Statements.

Solomon prays, 'But will God indeed dwell on the earth? Behold, heaven and the highest heaven cannot contain you; how much less this house that I have built!' (1 Kings 8:27). Was Solomon thinking of Genesis 1:1? We do not know, but it is clear that Paul put 'things present' and 'things to come' (aspects of time) along with 'height' and 'depth' (aspects of space) among the creatures of God (Rom. 8:38, 39).

---

4. See also Gen. 21:33; Deut. 33:27; Ps. 102:12; Isa. 41:4; Rom. 1:20; 1 Cor. 2:7; Rev. 1:8; 4:10.
5. Percy Bysshe Shelley, 1821; 1824.
6. Ludwig Ott, *Fundamentals of Catholic Dogma*, L. trans. P. Lynch (Rockford, IL: TAN Books and Publ., 1974), p. 37.

Omnipresence, omnipotence and omniscience are aspects of God's immensity too, even though the outline here presents them co-ordinately with it. No division of the attributes can fully separate them one from another logically, and certainly not metaphysically or substantially.

Omnipresence of God.

'God', a famous Baptist theologian once wrote, 'in the totality of his essence, without diffusion or expansion, multiplication or diffusion, penetrates the universe in all its parts'.[7] We have already met this idea, less critically defined, under the immanence of God. The idea is hard to grasp because the mind finds difficulty in conceiving of ideas without images, either material (God looks like my grandfather) or represented by an imagined figure (like lined structural designs on drafting paper). Even though God is pure spirit, children and naive adults almost necessarily think of God in corporeal images. When as a small child I first read in the Bible, 'God created man in his own image' (Gen. 1:27 KJV), it never occurred to me to doubt that God looks something like my father. 'It must be said… that it is better for children and the unlearned to think of God corporeally rather than to think of Him as unreal. Yet it is remarkable with what steadfastness the main stream of Christian thought has kept within the bounds of spiritual conceptions' (DeWolf, *Theology of the Living Church*, p. 98). Bodies are bound to locality in space. We do not know if spirits are *transpatial* or not, i.e. whether or not they have spatial relations. Primitive belief has always thought so. 'How many angels can stand on the head of a pin?' the famous scholastic inquiry, was not really frivolous. Angels evidently are not trans-spatial (Dan. 10:12, 13). But God's Spirit is not so bound.

Theologians have always found God's omnipresence, though widely witnessed to in the Bible, hard to formulate as a doctrine. They tend to both affirm and correct one another's statements on the subject. Some refinements supplied by writers old and new follow, first Wolfhart Pannenberg:

> [W]here as God's eternity means that all things are always present *to him*, the stress in his omnipresence is that he is present *to all things at the place of their existence*. God's presence fills heaven and earth (Jer. 23:24)… The presence of God that fills all things does not mean that we are to think of the divine essence as extended across the whole world… if God had had extension he would necessarily exist as a body… He is present to his creatures by his eternal power and duty, and his presence, unlike that of a body does not exclude the simultaneous presence of other things in the same place.[8]

Karl Barth, not atypically, thinks everyone else has it wrong and that omnipresence does not belong to God's infinity but to the attribute of love and freedom. He promises to give God's 'unity and omnipresence' a more biblical and therefore Christian basis than it had in the early church, the Middle Ages and Protestant orthodoxy.[9] He ends fifty pages later having discussed God's simplicity, faithfulness, and so on, but leaving omnipresence more mysterious – to this reader at least – than before.[10]

In Lutheran-Calvinist polemics, the topic of divine omnipresence becomes lodged in the manner of the presence of the body and blood of Christ 'in' and 'with' the 'sacrament' and has never yet been dislodged.

John T. McNeill observes 'a systematically presented list of divine attributes… characteristic of both medieval theologians and Reformed orthodoxy, is notably absent from Calvin.'[11]

Ludwig Ott states: 'The first monograph on the substantial presence of God in the whole world and in all the parts thereof and on the indwelling of God in the just, was written by St. Augustine in his, *Liber de praesentia Dei ad Davidanum* (Ep.[istle] 187).'[12]

Scripture Statements.

'Where shall I go from your Spirit?' inquired the Psalmist, 'Or where shall I flee from your presence? If I ascend to heaven, you are there!… If I take the wings of the morning and dwell in the uttermost parts of the sea, even there your hand shall lead me, and your right hand shall hold me' (Ps. 139:7-10). This is the divine omnipresence from

---

7. A. H. Strong, *Systematic Theology*, p. 279.
8. Wolfhart Pannenberg, *Systematic Theology*, vol. i, pp. 410, 411.
9. Karl Barth, *Church Dogmatics II*, Part I (Edinburgh: T. and T. Clark, 1936) p. 466.
10. ibid., p. 490.
11. Calvin, *Institutes*, Westminster Ed. of 1960, note #1, I, 120.
12. Ludwig Ott, *Fundamentals of Catholic Dogma*, p. 38.

the viewpoint of a godly believer endowed with a delightfully vigorous poetic imagination. Another passage presents the mysterious doctrine from the divine point of view: 'Am I a God at hand, declares the LORD, and not a God afar off? Can a man hide himself in secret places so that I cannot see him? declares the LORD' (Jer. 23:23, 24). This is the immensity of God stated in relation to the created, material universe – God fills it.

Christians must be on guard not to think of God's omnipresence in any material, tangible sense whatsoever. A youthful 'hippie' known to me, converted to Christ at a charismatic retreat, thought the rising mists of early morning must be 'the presence of the Holy Spirit'. The young woman later learned better. As to His essential being, it is false and fatal to any true religious spirituality to think of God as materially sensible in any manner whatsoever. All sorts of crass forms of mysticism grow in the soil of material conceptions of God's omnipresence. A college chapel speaker, later a well-known novelist (the late Eugenia Price), even spoke of feeling God in her bath water! Another mystical enthusiast knew the Spirit was in a meeting because, he said, he felt the pressure of His power under his fifth rib! Right? Left? Counting from the top? Bottom?[13]

Practical Benefits.

The presence of God is beneficial for *devotion* – we can never be in any place where God is not present to hear our prayer and ready to receive our worship (Ps. 139:7-10). It is also beneficial for *assurance* – we can never be physically or geographically beyond God's help, for He is present whether in a prison (as with Joseph, Gen. 39, 40), in a den of lions (as with Daniel, Dan. 6) or in the emperor's presence (as with Nehemiah, Neh. 1). According to Psalm 107, God is present to help when lost in the desert (4-9), when in prison (10-16), when on a sickbed (17-22) and when in storms at sea (24-30). The presence of God is also beneficial as *warning* against disobedience to God and attempted flight from Him, both to the believer (the book of Jonah, esp. 1:1-3) and to the unbeliever (Amos 9:1-4).

A Problem.

How can an omnipresent God be said to dwell in heaven (Matt. 6:9; 1 Kings 8:30) and to come (travel?) to earth from heaven (Gen. 11:5)? The Bible writers saw no contradiction. Compare 1 Kings 8:30 with 8:27. The particular notion in most of such texts is God's manifestation, not the spatial location of His Spirit. He is permanently manifest in a special way in heaven, hence is said to dwell there. He also, as He chooses, specially manifests Himself on earth at various times and places, hence he is said to come to those places. Even the Tabernacle in the wilderness and the first temple (built by King Solomon) are said to be God's *mishkan*, dwelling (house). His *shekinah*, dwelling (presence) was there also. His actions in providence and miracles are represented to human minds in this manner.

Omniscience of God.

This term designates God's cognitive awareness. He has perfect, immediate, knowledge of all events and things, whether actual or conditional upon the acts of 'free' beings; whether the events or things are only possible or actual; and whether they are past, present or future.

Inasmuch as the scriptural statements are overwhelming in detail, let us give them full opportunity to speak. God has *perfect knowledge*: 'no creature is hidden from his sight, but all are naked and exposed [laid bare, RSV] to the eyes of him to whom we must give account' (Heb. 4:13). Also, 'the eyes of the LORD run to and fro throughout the whole earth, to give strong support to those whose heart is blameless toward him' (2 Chron. 16:9). God's knowledge is immediate awareness, not based on experience, deductions or inductions of fact or truth. His knowledge is not acquired knowledge, for God's knowledge of all things is eternal, present always in His mind.[14]

God has knowledge of all time: past and future (Isa. 46:9-11). Does God know therefore conditional events of the future, even events dependent on the future acts of 'free beings'? Modern liberal writers of theology quite uniformly deny this, e.g.

---

13. See also Acts 17:27, 28; Isa. 57:15.
14. In detail: of material creation (see Ps. 147:4; Job 28:24; Ps. 139:15); animate creatures (Matt. 10:29); men and their deeds (Ps. 33:13-15); human thoughts (Acts 15:8; even before we think them, Ps. 139:2); small details of our lives (Jer. 1:15; Ps. 139:1-4; and many more).

> The knowledge of God… must be limited by His own nature and purpose… if He has put a check on His power to give man freedom of will, then He must have limited somewhat His knowledge of the future… If God knows now every choice any man will ever make, then every choice is already determined and freedom is a delusion… if men have any margin of free will whatever, then God's foreknowledge of some of their choices must be a knowledge of probabilities, not of certainties.[15]

This author is saying that God purposely limited His knowledge of the future by creating agents who have 'freedom of the will': that complete knowledge of the future by God would destroy freedom of the will.

But this seems contrary to the view which the same author takes of 'the super-temporal eternity of God' (p. 102) and it is certainly contrary to the plain truth of the Scriptures. Old Testament prophecy of the career of Christ specified many details utterly conditional upon the future acts of yet unborn people. All predictive prophecy, of any meaningful sort, depends upon God's detailed foreknowledge. Precisely for this reason, modernist or 'liberal' theologians quite uniformly deny the possibility of detailed prediction of the future in the Bible. The result has been a revolution against historical, orthodox faith in the trustworthiness of the testimony of the Bible itself as to the date and authorship of every portion which predicts identifiable events such as the destruction of Jerusalem (586 BC) or the desecration of the temple (165 BC). Therefore, there is now for such scholars a Second Isaiah (chaps. 40–66), composed after and during the exile, and a second century BC date for Daniel. However, Peter says that Christ was 'delivered up [crucified] according to the definite plan and foreknowledge of God' (Acts 2:23) and Jesus was able to show His disciples His whole career predicted in the Old Testament (Luke 24:25-27, 44-47).

There is a story in 1 Samuel of how God made known the ideal, contingent future, e.g. He answered a 'what if' question about an event that never really occurred (see 1 Sam. 23:12 and context). Even events which people attribute to chance are said to be known because they are under God's control (Prov. 16:33, RSV). Such knowledge is 'wonderful' (Ps. 139:6), deep and incomprehensible (Rom. 11:33) to the truly devout. It is eminently wise as well (Ps. 104:24; Eph. 3:10). Denial that God has certain knowledge of the contingent future is too much of a concession to make to a prejudice against predestination.

Free will and predestination present a great mystery, but true Christian piety should not deny anything God reveals about either of them.

It seems every so many generations of scholars must go over the well-canvassed objections to God's prescience of events of the future conditional upon the choices and acts of free personal beings. At present, under the rather ambiguous guise of 'the openness of God', (openness to what?) it is being fiercely debated in several theological journals and promises to go on for some time.

Over the generations, the argument of those who deny God's foreknowledge of events conditional upon the future acts of free beings goes about as follows. It is agreed God foreknows all things which are objects of knowledge. Excluded from the number of such objects are those events that depend on the 'unpredictable' choices and acts of free beings such as men and angels. It is contended that God limited His sovereign control of the course of the future in the act of creating the human race and angels. Hence, He can be surprised by developments. I shall not here attempt to record the present on-going debate. It bears some relation to the debate between Arminian-Wesleyan theology and Calvinist theology, but Wesleyan theologians usually do not demur on the assertion that God knows the future in detail, although they do not relate the divine foreknowledge to divine decrees in the same way Calvinists do.

Jesuit theologians of the Roman Church (notably Luis DeMolina, 1535–1600) developed a doctrine of 'middle knowledge' – an area of divine knowledge dependent upon His foreknowledge of the acts and decisions of free creatures rather than upon His decree. The purpose of the Jesuits was to defend the Semi-Pelagian teaching (later Socinian, and Wesleyan) that election is based on foreseen faith. Middle knowledge was rejected by theologians of the Dominican order, notably refuted by Cornelius Jansen (1585–1638), and Jansenist successors to the controversy.

In Scripture God has no 'middle knowledge'. There is no created thing hidden 'from the sight' of Him with whom we have to do, 'but all [things past or future] are naked and exposed to the eyes of him to whom we must give account' (Heb. 4:13). Francis Turretin furnishes a discussion of the middle knowledge theory.[16]

Theologians as diverse as A. H. Strong (Baptist) and Ludwig Ott (Roman Catholic) remain convinced that

---

15. L. Harold DeWolf, *A Theology of the Living Church* (New York: Harper & Brothers, 1953), p. 109.
16. Francis Turretin, *Institutes of Elenctic Theology vol i*, trans. G. M. Geger (Phillipsburg, NJ: PR Publishing, reprint 1992), pp. 212 – 218. See also articles on 'Luis DeMolina' and 'Jansenius and Jansenism' in the *Catholic Encyclopedia*.

God knows the future, and that the divine decree precedes the knowledge, but regard the mode or medium as unexplained and inexplicable.[17]

Let us be reminded that although the 'faculty of volition' – the power to choose – is present in us all, our freedom in the exercise of it in loving obedience to the will of God has now been greatly damaged by the fact that we are all now sinners; we are 'children of disobedience', and that without exception. Furthermore, the biblical doctrine of divine decrees (i.e. God's sovereignty over all history) has important bearing on this subject.[18]

Two related groups of theologians have attacked the doctrine of divine omniscience in the recent past. The earlier calls itself process theology. These theologians have been influenced not only by the liberalism that has devalued orthodox doctrines and scriptural authority but also by a vigorous philosophy known as panentheism. Panentheism maintains that God exists but not previous to or apart from the universe. He is not its Creator but exists contemporarily as a 'pole' exterior to it and also within all the universe, which is God's other 'pole'. Though God is ubiquitous in the universe, He is neither omnipotent nor omniscient, for, like the world, God Himself is evolving, *in process*, hence the name, 'process theology'. As advocates acknowledge, those without 'academic preparation' – i.e. without twentieth century, non-biblically rooted 'philosophical theology' – will 'find it demanding' to understand what these theologians mean.[19] Though these theologians employ many Christian categories of thought (e.g. incarnation,[20] body of Christ[21]) and the language traditional to Christian discourse, they claim as much affinity with atheistic existentialism[22] and even pagan religion[23] as with orthodox Christian theology. Philosophically, the ancient roots of this system lie in the pre-Socratic Greek philosophers whose world, including their gods, was evolving forever in the void with no superintending wise and powerful supervision. This theology builds mainly on the work of Alfred N. Whitehead (1861 – 1947), a mathematician turned logician and philosopher, and to a lesser extent the thought of Bertrand Russell (1872 – 1970). Whitehead, incorporating relativity theory, postulated that the stuff that we experience in our sensorium consists of *point-events* in *space-time*. These occur and exist independently of our perceiving them. The occurrences he calls *occasions*. Over and above them, there exists a world of essences or *eternal objects* – not unlike the 'pole' outside the universe which the process theologians call God. These eternal objects collide (intersect) with one another in any given *occasion* or *actual event* and thus produce *this* rather than *that* or *those*. From this matrix of reality proceeds all that is. Process theologians buy into as much of this as suits their scheme of a somewhat Christian-sounding scheme of religious philosophy.

I have presented this perhaps over-simple summary of process theology and its roots to suggest strongly it is quite inconsistent with the unmistakable biblical doctrine of divine omniscience. Process theology has no personal centre such as the triune God who might know, much less predestinate or plan anything. Yet from within evangelical circles have emerged several academicians who borrow as much 'process theology' as they think can be brought 'into sync' with an orthodox doctrine of God. But this god of process theology is a greatly diminished Lord, a diminutive shadow of the Lord God Omnipotent, 'pavilioned in splendour and girded with praise' of true Christian worship and biblical story. The God of the Bible declares the end from the beginning, both because He planned it that way and because He has power to bring it to conclusion just as He planned it; and therefore knows all about it, down to the minutest detail.

John Wesley and his authentic interpreters have had great reservations about the doctrine of individual personal election to salvation, but this has not impaired or diminished their proclamation of an orthodox doctrine of divine omniscience. Richard Watson, first and still major interpreter of Wesley, in my judgment, supported God's knowledge of the future (prescience) as included in His omniscience. In fact, in responding to the detractors of God's perfect foreknowledge of the day (1823), Watson anticipated the current detractors (process theology, and 'openness of God' advocates). After presenting the plain biblical 'proofs' of omniscience from Scripture, he says it has 'unquestionably the authority of the Holy Scriptures'.[24] He proceeds at length (about 8,500 words) to meet the objections, especially objections to God's perfect foreknowledge of future events conditional upon uncoerced choices made by 'free' beings.

---

17. A. H. Strong, *Systematic Theology* (Valley Forge, PA: Judson Press, 1907), pp. 284 – 286. Ott, *op. cit.*, pp. 40 – 43.
18. See chapter 10, 'God's Final Plan for The Heavens and The Earth'.
19. John B. Cobb, Jr, and David Ray Griffin, *Process Theology* (Philadelphia: Westminster Press, 1976), p. 10.
20. ibid., p. 22.
21. ibid., p. 107.
22. ibid., pp. 89, 80 – 82.
23. ibid., p. 62.
24. Richard Watson, *Theological Institutes, vol. i*, ed. J. McClintock (New York: Nelson & Phillips, 1850), p. 375.

Omnipotence of God.

The word omnipotent means, having all power. A sonorous biblical synonym is 'Almighty' (Greek, *pantokrator*), appearing nine times in the New Testament, usually in an eschatological context of the final Judgment (eight of the nine occurances are in Revelation). In the Old Testament (KJV) it is a translation of *Shaddai*, a name of God appearing often in the earliest parts of the Old Testament (see Exod. 6:3; cf. Gen. 17:1; 35:11; 48:3). The theological doctrine is simply that God is able to do all things that are objects of power and that He is able to do so without diminution of His infinite strength. In a later part of this book not only God's power but also His wisdom in His decrees and works of creation, preservation and providence come in for treatment.

We say that God is able to do all things that are 'objects of power', inasmuch as such things as the multiplication table, the law of non-contradiction and such other abstractions are not objects amenable to or commensurate with power. Power has nothing to do with them. Legislators and kings neither originated them nor control them. God created the world in harmony with His own reasonable nature. A world where there were several contradictory multiplication tables would not be 'heaven and earth' but hell – not universe, but chaos. A theologian's professional joke runs: 'If ever you should meet an angel who tells you 3+4=8, he will certainly have soot on his wings!' *Per contra*, in my files is a pastor's Christmas letter in which he asserts that the Trinity is an example of God's ability to break mathematical laws, because He is both one and three!

A better theology affirms that God is not three in the same respect He is one. Further, God exercises His power according to His own will. He never acts in power apart from wisdom. God is not the servant of His own unlimited energy. A scriptural way of saying this is, 'he cannot deny himself' (2 Tim. 2:13). Therefore God 'cannot be tempted with evil' (James 1:13) and He 'cannot lie' (Titus 1:2, KJV).

Scripture Statements.

Jesus said, 'with God all things are possible' (Matt. 19:26, see the context and note the contrast in meaning with the similar saying, 'Anything can happen'). Texts are numerous which trace everything, both specifically and in general, to God's creative, sustaining and governing power (Gen. 17:1; 18:14; Jer. 32:17; Job 42:1, 2; Isa. 40:28; Eph. 1:11; Rev. 19:6). (Other texts speak more specifically, among them are Gen. 1:1-3; Isa. 44:22; Heb. 1:3; 2 Cor. 4:6; Eph. 1:19; 3:20; Matt. 3:9; Rom. 4:17.)

Practical Benefits.

If God hears prayers, He is able to answer, 'our God whom we serve is able… and he will' (Dan. 3:17). If we are sent to be evangelists, there is power available to secure results, as God pleases, 'Who then can be saved?… With God all things are possible' (Matt. 19:25, 26). Should the course of the world seem perverse and threatening, God has power to change it if He wills; He has power to judge and replace it with a better one, as He certainly will! Things will be looking up in due time (Rev. 11:17-18; 19:6). This doctrine is a deep well from which to draw abundance of comfort.

Some theological teachers introduce the perfection of God as an attribute, at some stage in the treatment of His greatness. There is something commendable about this, for perfection, in the sense of completeness (where nothing is lacking which ought to be), pertains to all His attributes of greatness. It seems better therefore to some other writers to consider perfection simply as a feature of all the attributes of greatness. It is true that the Father is said by Jesus to be perfect (Matt. 5:48). God's gifts (James 1:17), His work (Deut. 3:24), His ways (Ps. 18:30), His law (Ps. 19:7), His will (Rom. 12:2), His knowledge (Job 37:16) and similar, are said in Scripture to be perfect. We shall follow the lead of the writers who prefer to discuss God's perfection later, as a feature of God's moral nature and in connection with attributes of goodness such as love, holiness and truth.

Incomprehensibility of God.

This somewhat misleading term indicates simply that no one except the triune God fully comprehends God. People should not find this difficult to accept, for we do not quite understand ourselves or our fellows. '[T]he heart of kings is unsearchable' (Prov. 25:3). This, however, is not because either kings or lesser people are impossible to comprehend. Rather we do not *fully* understand because we lack opportunity completely to observe. We cannot fully comprehend God because we are finite, whether in the sinlessness of Eden or in the presence of angels in heaven. Hence, we cannot now, and never shall, fully understand all that an infinite God is and does.

Scriptural Statements.

Perhaps nothing will impress the student more than to place David's poetic statement that follows along with that magnificent expression of St Paul which David's statement inspired. Psalm 36:5-6 states, 'Your steadfast love, O Lord, extends to the heavens, your faithfulness to the clouds. Your righteousness is like the mountains of God; your judgments are like the great deep.' Paul says: 'Oh, the depth of the riches and wisdom and knowledge of God! How unsearchable are his judgments and how inscrutable his ways' (Rom. 11:33, cf. 34-35). God's mercy, faithfulness, righteousness and His judgments, David says in the foregoing imaginative language, exceed human comprehension. Paul, in the above quotation, adds God's wisdom, knowledge and ways. Every aspect (attribute) of the nature of our infinite God exceeds our limited comprehension as even Job's 'comforters' understood: 'who does great things and unsearchable, marvellous things without number' (Eliphaz, Job 5:9); 'Can you find out the deep things of God? Can you find out the limit of the Almighty' (Zophar, Job 11:7).

Practical Benefits.

Each of the texts quoted above represents saintly folk's worshipful wonder at the surpassing greatness of God. These things do not inspire long speeches, rather stumbling words of repentance and silence, as illustrated by Job's excellent example (Job 38 – 40). They also lend great support to two admirable human impulses and enterprises – artistic expression and the pursuit of knowledge. No painter will ever exhaust the beauty of God's own workmanship; nor will any oratorio attain the heights and depths of the Lord God Omnipotent whom the composer seeks to praise. As for learning – the researches of the academic disciplines – as one of Job's 'friends' declared, we will never know more than the outskirts of His ways. There will always be immensely more to challenge the researcher.

An Additional Glossary.

Precise, special terms help us understand truths of great depth. The student of God's truth who masters some of the terms of the doctrine of God greatly benefits. Whether we try to present God's greatness in the simplest way or try for comprehensive depth, we cannot seem to dispense with some abstract terms such as eternal, absolute, transcendent, immanent, timeless, above time and time-space. We seem unable to speak exactly about God's greatness without them, even though none of them appears in the Bible and almost none in the great theological confessions. For that matter, very few of the names that theologians necessarily give to the characteristics (attributes) of God's greatness appear in Scripture. Yet it would be hard to get along without them, because they help us formulate answers to our own and others' questions.

1. The Absolute Being of God.

The word absolute in common speech seems to mean 'without qualification', and usually is part of a vigorous affirmation or denial. In pantheistic idealism the absolute is the all: the substratum of the universe of which all things particular are emanations. Sometimes 'absolute' seems to designate ultimate authority, or court of final appeal, as when used of dictators, headmasters and supreme courts. As used of God, Christian theologians mean to say that God has independent existence, being utterly without need, without external sustenance or support or stimulation either to exist or to be happy. We know, for example, that God did not create the world in order to supply some need of His. God has always been the 'blessed and only Sovereign' (1 Tim. 6:15) and 'blessed forever' (Rom. 1:25).

2. The Infinity of God.

This does not mean no known bounds (which would only be indefiniteness), but no bounds at all. His being is not limited by any other being or by what He has created. The idea is positive even though 'infinite' (*lit.*, no end) seems like a negative expression. This does not mean God can make a weight so heavy it cannot be lifted or create a world wherein 3+4 could equal 9 or 11. These and various other nonsense suggestions need not detain us. God, of course, may limit Himself, but that is a function of His boundless will. None of the attributes of God, being grounded in His infinite person, is willed by God, for they are aspects of who and what He is, not of what He does or where He is. They therefore are infinite also. Infinite does not mean quite the same as 'without qualification'. To say, for example, that God's mercy is limitless does not mean that it is not qualified in some way. God's mercy will end for those sinners who never repent.

3. Transcendence and Immanence of God.

These words have to do with God's relation to the whole of His creation. In all ages, among both Christians and others, some thinkers have stressed the distance that separates the world and mankind, as creatures, from the Creator. This distance is what is meant by transcendence, and it is clearly taught in Scripture. The distance is both physical and metaphysical (i.e. on a different level of being) as well as moral. This distance, however, can be stressed to such extremes, and with such persuasive force, that in the recent but now past heyday of Barth and Brunner (neo-orthodoxy) an 'infinite qualitative gulf' was widely accepted. In *deism* this becomes dogmatic assertion (God made the world, set it going and has withdrawn from it). In Christendom, this view is seldom thoroughly consistent. The so-called deists among the 'founding Fathers' of eighteenth-century America believed in prayer and otherwise showed their theistic convictions. Moreover, God 'crashes the barrier' once in a while even in neo-orthodox doctrine.

Others have stressed immanence, the presence of God in the creation, i.e. His in-man-ence, from Latin words meaning *to dwell in*. This is also biblical truth. The tendency of many people to rely greatly on feelings in religious matters strengthens acceptance of the immanence of God, as much private devotion and public worship show. Harriet Beecher Stowe wrote:

> Still, still with Thee...
> Alone with Thee amid the mystic shadows –
> The solemn hush of nature newly born;
> Alone with Thee of breathless adoration,
>   in the calm dew and freshness of the morn!

In the excesses of Christian mysticism, and in all pantheistic religions (Hinduism, Buddhism, Parseeism) and in several sects now growing (theosophy, Rosicrucianism, several varieties of 'New-Ageism') this aspect of the immensity of the Godhead becomes exclusive of His transcendence and thereby fatally erroneous. The popular 'prophet', Khalil Gibran, passes pantheistic mysticism to credulous public readers. Pantheism, discussed in an earlier chapter, affirms God's immanence but denies His transcendence. Deism does the reverse.

4. Time and Space, Space-Time, and God.

We think of time as duration, succession of events, in some measurable way: of space as extension within the created universe. There are texts of Scripture (e.g. Ps. 90:1, 2; 1 Cor. 2:7) which tell us that God is greater than time. Does this mean that He has no temporal relations at all? Similarly, God is without extension in space. However, both 'height and depth' are His creatures (Rom. 8:39), not His dimensions or extensions, and heaven cannot contain Him (1 Kings 8:27).

Does this mean that space is without meaning for God? Space and time are related together in recent scientific theory. Science also uses time as a fourth dimension analagous to the three dimensions of space. Does this do away with the validity of these dimensions? Of course not. Science has found the abstractions – space-time and time as fourth dimension – useful for formulating the behaviour of the universe into laws. These abstractions help solve problems of mechanics, as any one who ever tried to describe what it would be like to trace the 'absolute' trajectory of a tossed coin on a rising elevator knows, but they cannot be employed to deny the testimony of our senses. Our senses tell us that both space and time are quite real. Space-time and fourth dimension are useful abstractions. They are ludicrously false in the world of living people. To say, therefore, that God is eternal and that He is omnipresent in all creation are meaningful statements. Now that God has created a world of clocks and yardsticks, time and space are both meaningful. God even enters into relationships with them.

12
The Goodness of the Godhead

'Oh give thanks to the L<small>ORD</small>*, for he is good' (Ps. 107:1)*
'No one is good except God alone' (Mark 10:18)

'Moral' is a neutral word. Both sin and its opposite, righteousness, are moral concepts. Good and goodness also are moral concepts. 'Good', however, has a much narrower field of reference than does 'moral' and it is this narrow sense, later to be explained, which is the subject of the present chapter. This is not to deny that we shall be considering what are sometimes called 'the moral attributes' of God. Yet it is the focused idea of goodness rather than morality, as such, that is under consideration.

What is 'the good' – how shall we define it? Ethics is the division of philosophy that for 2,500 years has sought to define 'the good'. For Socrates the good is the useful. For his disciple, Plato, the good is whatever on earth conforms to the eternal transcendent form (idea) of what *ought* to be. Aristotle, whose ethical thought seems to have been revived today, thought *the actual*, what *is*, is good. Augustine came close to welding Plato and Aristotle together by regarding good and being in God (the transcendent) as fundamentally identical. The mood of our times is to do away with the whole idea of good in favour of consensus or social utility, and such like, including eudemonism (or happiness), the greatest happiness to the greater number. James J. Fox was undoubtedly correct in saying: 'Good is one of those primary ideas which cannot be defined.'[1]

Let us then employ an approach not *to* the Scriptures but *from* the Scriptures and *with* a common-sense understanding of the good.

The book of Job opens by telling the reader that Job was a good man. Then it goes on to say that he had a family of ten children, and immense wealth in livestock, and adds that 'this man was the greatest of all the people of the east' (Job 1:3). Ownership of 7,000 sheep, 3,000 camels, 1,000 oxen, 500 ass-mares and employment of hundreds of servants made him *great* in people's eyes. What made him *good*? The fact that he 'was blameless and upright, one who feared God and turned away from evil'. This made him good in God's eyes (Job 1:1; cf. v. 8). There are other people who are great in wealth or intellectual power or fame but who are small in goodness, that is, in character and wisdom. In addition, some are little in fame, in 'good' and physical power and also very bad people.

Sometimes, good means about the same as perfection of character. So, when we say of a person that he is a good man, we intend to say that he has those traits of character that constitute what a man ought to be. In this sense, the Bible says that God is holy, 'of purer eyes than to see evil' (Hab. 1:13).

---

1. James J. Fox, 'Good' in *The Catholic Encyclopedia*, vi, p. 636.

On the other hand, we may be thinking of God's good treatment of His creatures, that is, benevolent and beneficent, when we refer to God's goodness: 'God is good to Israel' (Ps. 73:1); and, 'Oh, taste and see that the LORD is good!' (Ps. 34:8).

We are now interested in the goodness of God in both of these senses: (1) what He is as to inward goodness of character (immanent goodness), namely, *holiness, truth* and *love*; (2) what He is in manifestation of that good character (emanative, or transitive goodness), namely, *righteous, faithful* and *merciful*.

This analysis and other similar ones are not very pleasing to most 'modern' theologians. The headings and divisions are said to 'lack religious value, and are contrary to the findings of modern psychology and religious experience'. This judgment need not surprise us, for 'modern theology is in disagreement with the theological method of the old theologians who describe the divine attributes on the basis of, and according to, Scripture' according to Pieper.[2] We hope now to show that this way of teaching people about the good character of God and its manifestation among His creatures, however lacking in absolute precision and completeness, is according to the Bible.

No classification or list of the divine attributes is fully satisfactory, for overlapping and repetition cannot be avoided. In so far as the terms are psychological in flavour, they have the same lack of precision characteristic of all human language which attempts psychological analysis. Yet the mind calls for 'rhyme and reason' in the relationship of things. So, if we are going to discuss the features of good character at all, God's or any others', analysis is both helpful and necessary. The fact that the Bible makes numerous analytical statements about God's moral character would justify theological analysis.

1. Holiness: God is Holy.

God's character is holy. Biblical testimony to His holiness is very extensive and is mainly in the Old Testament. In a unique sense, holiness is basic to every aspect of God's goodness. Therefore, we might expect it to be highlighted in the early portions of the Bible.

At this point we interrupt development of the theme to take note of modern critical treatment of the 'development of Israel's religion'.

W. Robertson Smith crystallized a century of Enlightenment thought about how ethical monotheism and its high view of the holiness of God and of His people, Israel, came to be. Smith did not find a place for a high concept of ethical holiness in Israel's history until the time of the writing prophets. After a quite correct statement of biblical holiness, he writes: 'This conception of holiness goes back to the Hebrew prophets, especially to Isaiah.'[3]

A generation later many of Smith's ideas as to what constitutes 'The Idea of The Holy' were modified in a book of that title by Rudolph Otto. Both of these quite original works supplied useful information and Otto furnished a vocabulary (numinous, fascinans, tremendum, etc.) which now all writers of every school find useful. The notion that Abraham, Isaac and Jacob, Joseph and his brethren had no concept of holiness; that Moses, Miriam and Aaron, Joshua, Samuel, and David knew nothing of a high ethical holiness in connection with Jehovah and Israel has not even held the field among later critics. The idea is said to have been known from the Exodus onward in some recent critical discussion, though the pentateuchal legislation regarding holiness (the so-called Holiness Code, Lev. 17–26) is said likely to have been composed after the book of Ezekiel. R. H. Pfeiffer of Harvard spoke for Graf-Wellhausen criticism before his time, giving what is still the prevailing critical opinion: 'While it seems certain to most critics that the compiler of H [Holiness Code in the Pentateuch] and Ezekiel wrote in the sixth century, they do not agree which one of the two is earlier.'[4] A year 2000 paper, *Holy Fathers?: Holiness in the Era of the Patriarchs*, read by William D. Barrick at the annual meeting of the Evangelical Theological Society, reported recent critical opinions. Barrick cites several. '[T]he notion of holiness, which from the Exodus onward is a basic characteristic of God and a major requirement for Israel, is entirely lacking in the patriarchal traditions.'[5] '[T]raits peculiar to patriarchal religion' include 'the lack of the concepts of sin and judgment'.[6] Barrick acknowledges: 'Prior to the book of Exodus… the… *qdsh* word group [holy, holiness, etc] is found only once in the early narratives. Indeed it is found only in the primeval history at Genesis 2:3. Then God blessed the seventh day and declared it holy.'

---

2. Francis Pieper, *Christian Dogmatics, i*, (St. Louis: Concordia Publ., 1950), p. 435.
3. W. Robertson Smith, *The Religion of the Semites* (Edinburgh: 1889; 3rd ed. New York: Ktav Publ., 1969), p. 132.
4. Robert H. Pfeiffer, *Introduction to the Old Testament* (New York: Harper & Bros., 1941), p. 242.
5. R. W. L. Moberly, *The Old Testament of the Old Testament* (Minneapolis: Fortress Press, 1992), p. 99.
6. Barrick cites Augustine Pagolu, *The Religion of the Patriarchs*, JSOTSS 277 (Sheffield, England: Sheffield Academic Press, n.d.), p. 23.

It will be sufficient here to remark, first, these critical opinions are simple extensions of two secularist procedural opinions: (1) ethical concepts in early peoples developed in an evolutionary manner, and (2) Israel's religion developed in a manner parallel to the religion of other ancient peoples in their area. Taking Genesis at its face value as a genuinely Mosaic, truthful document, I remark, secondly, that though the words 'holy' and 'holiness' and synonyms do not appear often in Genesis, the idea of ethical holiness and its practical expression in righteousness saturate the book. Examples abound. Sin crouches at Cain's door and his sentence is punishment for guilt incurred (Gen. 4:7, 13). Stories of the Flood, destruction of Sodom and Gomorrah, are wholly about the righteousness of people that is demanded by an ethically pure (holy) God. Holiness underlies Abraham's world-view in his questions: 'Will you [God] indeed sweep away the righteous with the wicked?' (Gen. 18:23), and 'Shall not the Judge of all the earth do what is just?' (Gen. 18:25). Third, many New Testament references to godly people of the patriarchal age impute holiness to them. The aged Zacharias spoke of the 'holy covenant' with Abraham (Luke 1:72, 73), as Psalm 105:42 does of 'his holy promise', and Sarah is introduced as a 'holy woman' (1 Pet. 3:5). Hence, we may assert that the New Testament assumes the patriarchs 'understood the concept of holiness' (Barrick, p. 2).

No one should dispute that in 'the progress of dogma',[7] there is rising clarity of vision of the idea of holiness in the Bible. Unless we wish to abandon or confuse the Bible's own evidence, we must begin study of the subject on the first page.

The gods and other objects worshipped by the ancients were not holy in an ethical sense. We must agree with Rudolph Otto, who said of the worship of 'spirits, magic, fairy tales' and the like: 'Different as these things are, [they are] haunted by a common — and that a numinous element.'[8] The numinous, or supernatural, approximates one aspect of holiness, as we shall see. Though properly to be treated with respect, the gods of the ethnic pantheons behaved much as their human counterparts did. However, the same as people, they were rewarded or punished for breaking an implicitly assumed moral code. There was an awareness in their human worshipers of an ethical Power to which 'the gods, whose dwelling is not with flesh' (Dan. 2:11) were as responsible as the flesh-and-blood people on earth. It seems apparent in the story of Abraham, Sarah and Abimelech, king of Gerar, that even the pagan king (who probably worshiped the god Dagon) was aware of a one '*Elohim* before whom all three of them — Abram, Sarah and Abimelech — would appear in righteous judgment at a future time. So, though the supposed gods of ancient heathenism were as immoral as their worshipers, the idea of moral purity was understood, even though it was hardly the precise equivalent of biblical holiness. We forego to introduce the mountain of controversial critical literature created over the past two centuries relating to this subject. The articles by O. Procksh[9] and William Ury[10] are reliable introductions.

To resume treatment of the holiness of God's character, we can state: in a unique sense, holiness is basic to everything about God, not merely one among many moral attributes of goodness. Not without reason did A. H. Strong frame and persuasively defend the proposition, *Holiness is the fundamental attribute of God*. We might well expect it to have been highlighted in the initial encounter of the great legislator and revelator Moses with God on the occasion of his call and commission to lay the groundwork of biblical revelation and revealed religion at the first appropriate occasion (Exod. 3:1-5). The same unrelieved glare of manifest holiness accompanies every subsequent, direct, personal encounter of divine and human in the Bible.

Some of the pervasiveness of this truth is made plain by perusing the following.

- God's *person* is holy: 'for the LORD our God is holy!' (Ps. 99:9; see also 1-8).
- God's *spirit* is holy: 'take not your Holy Spirit from me' (Ps. 51:11).
- God's *name* is holy: 'thus says the One who is high and lifted up, who inhabits eternity, whose name is Holy' (Isa. 57:15).
- God's *word* of promise is holy: 'For he remembered his holy promise' (Ps. 105:42).
- God's *oath* is holy: 'Once for all I have sworn by my holiness' (Ps. 89:35).

---

7. To borrow James Orr's felicitous title, *The Progress of Dogma*, 1901.
8. Rudolph Otto, *The Idea of the Holy*, trans. J. W. Harvey (New York: Oxford Univ. Press, 1958), p. 117. See all of Chapter. XV, pp. 115–131.
9. O. Procksh, *TDNT* I:88–110.
10. M. William Ury, 'Holy, Holiness' *Evangelical Dictionary of Biblical Theology*, ed. Walter A. Elwell (Grand Rapids: Baker Books, 1996), pp. 341–344.

- God's *dwelling* is holy: God's *habitation* in heaven (Deut. 26:15) and the *heavenly throne* from which He reigns (Ps. 47:8), as well as His *temple* at Jerusalem (Hab. 2:20) and objects there devoted to Him (Lev. 27:28; see also Zech. 14:20, 21), are holy.

Texts could be multiplied indefinitely.

The Meaning of 'Holy' and 'Holiness'.

What is the meaning of holy and holiness? As these are common words of religious conversation among common people in the Bible, the meaning should not be obscure (even though some careful distinctions should be noticed) and it is not obscure. Our English word is related in origin and meaning to *hale* and *whole*, that is, in one piece, sound, healthy. The common meanings are (1) belonging to or coming from God; (2) untainted by evil or sin; and (3) deserving of reverence.[11]

This group of ideas is essentially what one finds in the Bible. If we refine our definition with more extensive consideration of biblical use, the following emerges: (1) whatever people set apart for any special purpose is 'holy', about the same as *dedicated*. This is essentially a non-religious notion. In English we would not use 'holy' of a plot of ground 'dedicated' to be used as a 'Farmers' Market' because that word is uniformly a religious term and there is nothing distinctly religious about a marketplace. (2) That which is set apart from common use and devoted entirely to God is holy, whether persons, places or things. (3) Moral purity, i.e. apartness from evil of any sort: this last, absence of evil (always spoiling and harmful to its subject) is why holy, meaning hale, whole, sound, was used by early translators of the Bible into English, for this most often mentioned feature of God's character. To be less than holy is not only to be unsound (unhealthy, less than whole), but also unclean, defiled, corrupt.

God is said to be *holy* in that He exists on a level of being entirely apart from all that is creaturely, earthly or human: 'The LORD reigns; let the peoples tremble! He sits enthroned upon the cherubim; let the earth quake! The LORD is great in Zion; he is exalted over all the peoples. Let them praise your great and awesome name! Holy is he!... worship at his footstool! Holy is he!' (Ps. 99:1-3, 5b). He is 'the One who is high and lifted up, who inhabits eternity, whose name is Holy: "I dwell in the high and holy place"' (Isa. 57:15).

If God is the high, exalted One, above all people, as these Scripture texts say, He is also far removed from all that is sinful.[12] In Old Testament religion, especially the prophets, holiness, as ethical purity, becomes the most prevalent and important affirmation God has to make about Himself. In the New Testament God's ethical purity is almost the exclusive sense of His holiness.

Modern theologians sometimes refer to God's holiness, in the sense of separateness or transcendence, as the 'movement of withdrawal'.[13] There is an opposite 'movement of inclusion'. In this sense, anything especially close to God, or that to which He lays *exclusive* claim for His own service, is holy. So Scripture extends 'holy' and 'holiness' to many of His creatures: holy ground, holy place (sanctuary), holy Sabbath, holy nation, holy oil, holy water, holy garments (priests' vestments) – and holy jubilee, house, city, bread, altar, first-born. A page-full could be added of holy persons and things supported by innumerable citations of Old Testament Scripture. In the coming kingdom of God even the bells of the horses will be 'Holy to the LORD' (Zec. 14:20).

All the holiness that exists, therefore, is God's. He alone is the fount of holiness and He alone confers it on others. The holiness of the nation of Israel, for example, was not something the people attained by choice or self-improvement. God made them his own (holiness) by sovereign choice and redemption. They were to sanctify themselves only because God had already sanctified them for Himself. This sanctification of self may initially have been little understood. The ceremonial washings and ritual offerings involved, together with their awareness of being a 'chosen people', may well have been the upper limit of the perception of many. However, before long there were apparent implications of moral purity and of righteousness in the thought-life, in relations with other people – specified in a thousand ways from Exodus on to the close of the Old Testament. In the whole of the life of God's people, transitive holiness in righteous action is required by the Old Testament as well as the New – personal, domestic, political, civil and religious as well as the ritual of religious observance.

---

11. *Webster's New World Dictionary of the American Language.*
12. The word *qadosh*, meaning holy, was a Canaanite word before it became a Hebrew word. In Canaanite religion it had no special ethical sense – priests and priestesses were called *qadosh* in the sense of being devoted to the god or goddess, but not in the sense of ethical purity. They were impure, in fact, as were the deities. Sacred prostitution was part of their religious exercises.
13. H. Emil Brunner, *The Christian Doctrine of God, Dogmatics, vol i* (Philadelphia: Westminster Press, 1950, 1974), p. 162.

Both ideas – God's transcendence as Creator and His purity as moral-ethical Governor – appear together (in this order) frequently. Psalm 99:1-5, cited above, speaks of His loftiness but the remaining verses (6-9) relate to His purity. In the ecstasy of beatific vision, Isaiah first saw the LORD, 'high and lifted up... Holy, holy, holy' (Isa. 6:1-4). However, the vision immediately made the prophet aware not so much of his 'creatureliness' as of his sinfulness (vv. 5-7). Therefore, later, Isaiah reports God's hatred of all that is morally impure (Isa. 57:15-17). In the language of worship, the same joining of ideas (God's distance from us as Creator and His moral purity) occurs: 'Who shall ascend the hill of the LORD? And who shall stand in his holy place? He who has clean hands and a pure heart, who does not lift up his soul to what is false and does not swear deceitfully' (Ps. 24:3, 4).

Such passages as Isaiah 6:1-3 and Isaiah 57:15 seem clearly to treat holiness as something *fundamental* to God's character, whether the transcendence of His being, or the purity of His character, or both, it is hard to say.

God's laws, including the punishment of death for sin – any sin at all[14] – are an extension of His holiness. It would be tedious to quote the innumerable times every distinct feature of Old Testament worship is related specifically to God's holiness. It is everywhere in the 'worship manuals', that is, Exodus, Leviticus and Numbers, so also Psalms, Isaiah and Ezekiel.

This biblical emphasis has consequences. We may, for example, therefore be certain that however much wickedness may seem to prosper more than righteousness, it is better to do right; we ought to do right simply because it is right. 'Children, obey your parents... for this is right' (Eph. 6:1). Paul could cite no greater sanction.

The holy God our Creator is our Governor He 'will judge the world in righteousness by a man whom he has appointed' (Acts 17:31). Our conscience assures us of God's holiness, though it tells us nothing at all of God's love and mercy. As James Russell Lowell puts it:

> Careless seems the great Avenger;
> history's pages but record
> One death – grapple in the darkness
> 'twixt old systems and the Word;
> Truth forever on the scaffold,
> wrong forever on the throne[15]

The practical importance of God's holiness extends to everything about Christian character, action and hope for the future. As we have noted above, God's holiness exposes our sins and need for cleansing as well as forgiveness (Isa. 6:1, 5). His holiness assures us that God will not go back on anything He has said, either of warning or of promise. 'I will not violate my covenant... I have sworn by my holiness; I will not lie' (Ps. 89:34, 35). The sphere of salvation will always be one of orderly morality, for His 'holy arm' brings it to pass (Ps. 98:1) and with righteousness He reigns (vv. 2-9). His invisible kingdom now and His manifest kingdom of the future are holy, too (Ps. 47 esp. vv. 7 and 8; Isa. 11). Finally, God's holiness both demands and moves the practical holiness of His people: 'For I am the LORD your God: ye shall therefore sanctify yourselves, and ye shall be holy; for I am holy' (Lev. 11:44 KJV; compare 1 Peter 1:15, 16; Heb. 12:10).

Further Theology of Divine Holiness.

The Israelites and the Canaanites of old employed essentially the same language. In the religion of Canaan, the holy was simply that which was dedicated to the gods. Therefore, the vile male and female prostitutes of their shrines could be called holy. 'Sodomite' is how the Hebrew word for 'holy' comes out in the King James Version, when used of the male homosexual prostitute of a Baal shrine, and 'harlot' of female temple prostitutes. There was no ethical sense at all.

In biblical religion and most of biblical literature, however, holiness as ethical and moral purity is the most prevalent and important affirmation God has to make about Himself. In the New Testament, when used of God, moral purity is almost the exclusive sense of holiness.

Theologians have struggled to define the holiness of God and many consequently have neglected to say much about it. We attempt a brief summary of important discussions. The medieval theologians, Peter Lombard (*The Sentences*) and Thomas Aquinas (*Summa Theologica*, 5,750 columns of dense print in English translation), do not discuss it; nor

---

14. Gen. 2:17; Rom. 6:23; Ezek. 18:4, 20.
15. James Russell Lowell, *The Present Crisis*.

does Philipp Melanchthon's *Loci Communes* (the first Lutheran systematic theology). Calvin, though it is clear that he thinks holiness undergirds God's law and our sanctification, says little that is specifically on God's holiness.[16] Luther's profound awareness of God's holiness does not provide in all his writings any systematic treatment of what constitutes God's holiness, as far as I can determine. John Gill (Baptist, eighteenth century) gives God's holiness due attention but no definition, except to say holiness 'gives a lustre to all [God's] perfections, and is the glory of them'.[17]

For many modern existential and dialectical theologians holiness is a phenomenon of human experience only, not something that belongs to God in and of Himself. For Paul Tillich, religious feeling of 'the numinous' – the sphere of the gods in contrast with the secular – is sufficient explanation.[18]

For Barth and Brunner, however, emphasis on divine transcendence leads them to a somewhat better view. They see God's holiness as His transcendence, the 'wholly other' – a term met endlessly in their writings. The truly path-breaking work, *The Idea of the Holy* by Rudolph Otto, informs them, as us all, at least as to terminology for discussing holiness. There is validity, but nothing distinctively biblical or Christian, to Otto's analysis, yet Brunner's summary is worthy of attention:

> Modern students of religion have come to the unanimous conclusion that the fundamental act of all religion is the worship of the Holy. 'The Holy' as Rudolf Otto's beautiful book has shown us in an impressive and beautiful manner, is that to which the religious act is directed. Holiness is the very nature of the Numinous, of that which is divine, thus of that of which characterizes 'the Deity', 'the gods', or the *mysterium tremendum* [also in Otto, *mysterium, tremendum, fascinans*], towards which man, as a religious being, turns. Just as from subjective standpoint the chief word in all religion is reverence or the fear of God, so from the objective point of view, the Holy is the chief word in all religion, the word which alone describes the dimension in which all that is religious is found. In the Biblical revelation, however, we are concerned not with 'the Holy' (as an abstract conception), but with the Holy One (as personal).[19]

In the sense that awe is inspired by the presence of the numinous (*mysterium, tremendum, fascinans*) of sacred sites and settings even MacQuarrie's existential theology allows primacy to holiness among God's attributes. There have been sincere but misdirected efforts to resolve holiness simply into the perfection of all the divine attributes or into another name for divine love – both love of Himself and benevolence toward His creatures. I have read nothing that faces these issues adequately as the writings of A. H. Strong. Strong devoted careful (and passionate) attention to refuting these erroneous views because of the persuasive advocacy of 'moral influence' theories of the atonement (Horace Bushnell) and 'the social gospel' (Walter Rauschenbusch) in his time and in his own denomination (Baptist).

God's holiness cannot be dissolved into God's self-love, even though as generally orthodox a theologian as Jonathan Edwards in his *Essay on the Trinity* affirmed the holiness of God consists in infinite love to Himself. If he had said self-affirmation or regard for His own integrity, Edwards would have been closer to the truth. 'Enlightenment' and 'modernist' or 'liberal' theology almost uniformly puts love ahead of God's holiness in the divine attributes or mixes the two in such a manner as to deny both. I quote A. H. Strong once more and somewhat at length regarding the importance of seeing that holiness controls divine love rather than the other way around or some form of co-ordinate standing.

> Our conclusion at this point in our theology will… determine what our future system will be. The principle that holiness is a manifestation of love, or a form of benevolence, leads to the conclusions that happiness is the only good, and the only end; that law is a mere expedient for securing of happiness; that penalty is simply deterrent or reformatory in its aim; that no atonement needs to be offered to God for human sin; that eternal retribution cannot be vindicated, since there is no hope of reform. This view ignores the testimony of conscience and of Scripture that sin is intrinsically ill-deserving, and must be punished on that account, not because punishment will work good to the universe, – indeed, it could not work good to the universe unless it were just and right in itself. It [holiness, defined as a manifestation of love] ignores the fact that mercy is optional with God, while holiness is invariable; that punishment is many times traced to God's holiness, but never to God's love; that God is not simply love but light – moral light – and therefore is 'a consuming fire' (Heb. 12:29) to all iniquity. Love chastens… but only holiness punishes.[20]

---

16. John Calvin, *Institutes V*, iii – v.
17. John Gill, *Body of Divinity I* (Grand Rapids: Baker Books, 1978), p. 149.
18. Paul Tillich, *Systematic Theology I* (Chicago: Univ. of Chicago Press, 1951), pp. 215 – 218.
19. Brunner, *op. cit.*, p. 157.

His holiness accounts for God's absolute intolerance of any competing object of worship, especially idolatry. He is a 'jealous God' and a 'consuming fire' toward those who commit *lese majesty* against Him. Holiness explains why divine law is on every occasion an expression of what God is: 'Be ye holy for I am holy.' Consequently, God's glory is the only proper end of creaturely action and the 'fear of God' is the normal response to Him.

Scripture not only teaches these attitudes toward God and His demands, but conscience accuses us and threatens us for non-compliance. God's absolute holiness is the standard of enlightened conscience also. Rationalistic liberal religion replaces holiness with the amorphous notion of 'unconditional love'. Of a truth, God does not love any sinner unconditionally any more than He also 'hates all evildoers' unconditionally (Ps. 5:5) and precisely because of His holiness. That is, for the sake of His own integrity He will require the uttermost farthing in the judgment for every unrepented and unrequited sin. Sin's dimension of magnitude is measured by divine holiness, and that is without limit. It was divine holiness, not love, which was basic to the *requirement* of death when the God-man became sin for us at Calvary.

2. Righteousness: God Is Righteous.

Since God is holy in character, all manifestation of that character will be righteous. The Bible therefore speaks frequently of the righteousness of God.

The divine attribute of righteousness may be thought of in a twofold way. Firstly, God always acts in harmony with His own holy nature. He loves righteousness (Ps. 11:7) therefore He cannot lie (Titus 1:2); He will never deny Himself (2 Tim. 2:13) or fail to keep one of His covenant promises. If He saves a sinner, it will be in a manner consistent with His own holy nature. If He announces a moral law it will be righteous precisely because it will be an expression of His holy will.[21]

Because God is sovereign, He does not therefore have to answer the question, Why? Moreover, we have no right to ask it. Nevertheless, for Himself, His laws are right because they express His holiness. God's laws are expressions of a holy will that in turn is expression of a holy character. The righteousness by which God orders His world is neither something created, external to Himself, nor something other than God Himself in any manner whatsoever. His righteous acts are His character in action; God is law unto Himself.

Secondly, God deals with His creatures in justice (righteous treatment). The classical theologians call this *rectoral* justice when viewed as administration of His universal government. 'Rightousness and justice are the foundation of your throne' (Ps. 89:14). It is called *distributive* justice in regard to His extending to each of His rational creatures his due reward or punishment. It is worth noting that distributive justice is not to be confused with equality of treatment of people by God or equal status in the world. This is because God creates both the blind and the seeing, both rich and poor, both wise and the foolish: some to be born in a clean bed to be reared in piety and plenty, some in filth to be raised in a morally polluted atmosphere, and so on. Distributive justice is not properly a code name for 'equal opportunity', as nowadays in social history, or for equality of goods and wealth as in socialistic economics. When viewed as giving each of His creatures his due reward or punishment, Scripture says: 'Righteous are you, O LORD, and right are your rules' (Ps. 119:137). God's justice is *punitive* or *vindicatory* (not vindictive) justice in connection with punishing of all sin, because of sin's intrinsic ill desert, for the sceptre of God's kingdom is a sceptre of equity (see Ps. 45:3-7).

There is a further very important sense in which we must think of God's righteousness. It is the imputed righteousness of God, first mentioned at Genesis 15:6 in connection with Abraham's faith. This is the righteousness or acquittal called justification. Christ's righteousness becomes vicariously ours, imputed to us by God when we believe on His Son. This amazing doctrine is taught throughout the Scriptures (see Rom. 3:21) but treated at length especially by Paul (see Rom. 3:21-5:21, especially 3:21-28; Gal. 1–4). Imputed righteousness is not one of God's attributes, even though the fact that God declares ungodly sinners, who are not righteous, to be righteous, must be squared with God's truthfulness and justice. God is both 'just and the justifier of the one who has faith in Jesus' (Rom. 3:26).

God's righteousness will be manifest at last on the Judgment Day (see Rev. 16:4-7) just as long ago it was manifest when 'it was the will of the LORD to crush' His Son at Calvary, once He took our place as sinners (Rom. 3:25). If we are wise we will see God as righteous in His treatment of us as believers, not only in forgiving our sins (1 John 1:9)

---

20. A. H. Strong, *Systematic Theology* (Valley Forge, PA: Judson Press, 1907), p. 272 and pp. 268–275; see also Strong, 'The Holiness of God' in *Philosophy and Religion*, pp. 188–200.
21. This does not mean that God's will is arbitrary, ignoring the 'fitness of things'. The scholastic followers of Duns Scotus exaggerated the dependence of divine righteousness on divine will.

but also in chastening us His people (Dan. 9:14) and making the demand of a righteous life (see Jer. 7:8-11). If at times we have difficulty in seeing the justice of God in the way He temporarily allows evil to prosper, we may nevertheless trust His justice to triumph at last (Ps. 73; Hab. 2; Jer. 12:1-4).

> Though the cause of Evil prosper,
> yet 'tis Truth alone is strong,
> And, albeit, she wander outcast now.
> I see around her throng
> Troops of beautiful, tall angels,
> to enshield her from all wrong.[22]

3. Truth: God is True.

It will help us to quote several leading statements of Scripture in order to understand this attribute of the Godhead before a definition is attempted. Jesus prayed to His Father as 'the only true God' (John 17:3) and Paul spoke of Christian conversion as a turning 'to God from idols to serve the living and true God' (1 Thess. 1:9). In these passages, 'true' means genuine, the real and the valid. In contrast to idols, demon spirits and all false objects of veneration or worship, God is authentic God. Paul says 'we know that "an idol has no real existence", and that "there is no God but one"… although there may be so-called gods' (1 Cor. 8:4, 5; cf. 1-6). Of all the alleged objects of discourse called 'god', the God of the Bible is the only true God. He is *veritable* (to use the old ecclesiastical term) God. God's attributes and ways of doing are true in this same sense of being genuine. God's peace, for example, is true peace (Jer. 33:6), likewise His kindness is true kindness (2 Sam. 2:6), His goodness, authentic goodness (Exod. 34:6), and His grace, genuine grace (John 1:17), whereas 'the mercy of the wicked is cruel' (Prov. 12:10).

In a different but related sense, He is also the *veracious*, truth-speaking, truth-communicating God: 'Let God be [found] true though every one were a liar' (Rom. 3:4); 'I… give thanks to your name for your steadfast love and your faithfulness, for you have exalted above all things your name and your word' (Ps. 138:2; see also John 3:33; Rom. 1:25; John 14:17; 1 John 5:7).

Since the veritable (true) and veracious (truthful) God is the Creator and Governor of heaven and earth, a third sense appears: He is the ground of all truth. Scripture thus addresses Him as 'LORD God of truth' (Ps. 31:5 KJV). This is asserted directly in passages such as Psalm 111, which discuss God's works. The works of God are first said to be great, honourable and wonderful. Then 'The works of his hands are faithful and just; all his precepts are trustworthy; they are established forever and ever, to be performed with faithfulness and uprightness' (Ps. 111:7, 8).

A diversion into recent theories of language analysis and of hermeneutics at this point would show how scepticism, denial that anything anyone speaks or writes is true in any important sense, has imported Pilate's skeptical question wholesale to the academy. Recently these theories have invaded all university departments except the hard sciences. The public has been made aware of this disastrous development as 'deconstructionism'.

Deconstruction uses figures, tropes, neologisms, irony and philosophy to sever any connection between an author's true self and what he has written. The motives of these literary dogmatists apparently are chiefly to create an elite of critics who have their own club. The strength of this syndrome is an informal connection of ambitious professors and their admirers, supported by tenure rules that deliver the star performers from necessity of constructive labour.

Though still present, more subtle but equally destructive of trust of a neighbour's words, written or spoken, are other newly minted theories – all the more subtle because there is a germ of truth to ensnare new students in each one of them. The inquirer will see how this is related to biblical interpretation and theology by examining the book *Introduction to Biblical Interpretation* by Klein, Craig and Hubbard.[23]

Christians therefore should never be either cynics or skeptics. The cynical temper, doubting everything and everybody, challenging every statement as if there were no true statements, has only the appearance of the love of truth. The 'adversarial spirit' in theological schools and faculties, debating all doctrine, challenging every tradition, has harmfully contributed to the cynical spirit so prevalent in church life of recent times. We know that God is truthful, that He made our organs of sense and powers of reason not to mock us but to bring us in valid, cognitive touch with a created universe that is genuine. Skeptics and cynics are out of touch with God's world.

---

22. From James Russell Lowell, *'The Present Crisis'*.
23. Wm. W. Klein, C. L. Craig, R. L. Hubbard, Jr., 'Modern Approaches to Interpretation,' *Introduction to Biblical Interpretation* (Dallas: Word Publishing, 1993) pp. 427-457.

Christians, as lovers of God, are not only lovers of truth considered abstractly, but of every truth individually, because we know Him who is true (John 8:13, 14, 16, 18, 28). Our God is the author of truth. His children, therefore, should not be obscurantists afraid to embrace any truth newly presented. They will be lovers of true chemistry and geology, astronomy, farming and industry, as well as true love, true Christian doctrine and true Bible interpretation.

4. Faithfulness: God is Faithful.

Since God is true He will not change His character. He will be true to Himself. To us, His creatures, He will remain the same as He has always been.

A number of important texts declare this to be a fact, but Deuteronomy 7:9-11 is outstanding:

> Know therefore that the LORD your God is God, the faithful God who keeps covenant and steadfast love with those who love him and keep his commandments, to a thousand generations, and repays to their face those who hate him, by destroying them. He will not be slack with one who hates him. He will repay him to his face. You shall therefore be careful to do the commandment and the statutes and the rules that I command you today.

In keeping with this trait of character He is called a Rock (Deut. 32:4, 15, 18; Ps. 19:14), a Fortress (Jer. 16:19), a Defence (Ps. 89:18); His word is said to be sure (Ps. 19:7) and steadfast forever (Dan. 6:26). As Frederick M. Lehman writes:

> When hoary time shall pass away,
> and earthly thrones and kingdoms fall;
> When men who here refuse to pray,
> On rocks and hills and mountains call;
> God's love, so sure, shall still endure,
> All measureless and strong;
> Redeeming grace to Adam's race –
> The saints' and angels' song.

Because God is steadfast, the world of nature, the sphere of His creation, preservation and providence will remain steadfast. 'While the earth remains, seedtime and harvest, cold and heat, summer and winter, day and night, shall not cease' (Gen. 8:22). The farmer may plant his crops knowing that within the variety of climate and rainfall he can count on a crop if he tends his fields. The scientist may rely on what he calls the uniformity of nature. Gravity, the rates of expansion of gases, the velocities of electrons and light waves, and the like, will, under constant conditions, be everywhere the same. Natural events can be explained by natural causes. Superstitions, 'old wives fables', astrology and similar, may be ignored, as far as practical action is concerned. God's faithfulness is thus the solid foundation of reality, of a life of intelligent action.

In the spiritual realm, God's promises may be counted upon: His covenants are unbreakable. Ethan the Ezrahite sings of this in Psalm 89: 'with my mouth I will make known your faithfulness to all generations… in the heavens you will establish your faithfulness' (vv. 1-2). He says the heavens shall praise God's faithfulness, as well as the congregation of believers on earth (v. 5), and shall proclaim it to be unique (v. 8). God is faithful in His rule of nature (vv. 9-13). God's faithfulness is associated with His justice and judgment, mercy and truth (v. 14). Faithfulness has been singularly prominent in God's dealing with the house of David, defending the anointed sons when they kept covenant, faithfully chastening them for their own good when they did not faithfully follow his laws and ordinances (vv. 20-32). David's seed (v. 36) 'shall endure forever', a promise having connection with the endless resurrection life of our Lord Jesus Christ, 'Like… a faithful witness in the skies' (v. 37).

The truth has an obverse side too. If God will fulfill His promises faithfully, so will He carry through on His threats. This is concomitant with being Himself, for He 'cannot deny himself' (2 Tim. 2:13). Furthermore, 'Do not be deceived: God is not mocked, for whatever one sows, that will he also reap' (Gal. 6:7).

> Great is Thy faithfulness, O God my Father,
> There is no shadow of turning with thee;
> Thou changest not, Thy compassions they fail not;
> As thou hast been Thou forever wilt be (Thomas O. Chisholm).

5. Love: God is Love.

Another of God's attributes of goodness is love. We shall here make a distinction between love and mercy. Mercy is a manifestation of God's love just as faithfulness is a manifestation of His truth, and His righteousness of His holiness.

Love is exceedingly difficult to mention, in times like ours, without danger of misinterpretation. The physical passion of the mutual attraction of the sexes seems to be such an absorbing interest of our times that this universally experienced and fascinating form of love tends to exclude all other forms of love whenever the word is spoken.

The distinctive element in the love of God is self-communication. This is different from either holiness or truth and we must not think of it as including them. If these three are confused in any way whatsoever, serious harmful theological errors are bound to follow. The Bible neither identifies one with another nor confounds them. If holiness and love are equated, then sin may be overlooked, for then holiness poses no barrier to acceptance of sin. Justice is made maudlin. Final judgment and punishment are thereby rendered unnecessary. If love and truth are equated, then untruth may be tolerated. True, 'God is love' (John 4:8), but that must be understood as meaning that God is a loving being, just as He is also a holy being and true being. Writers sometimes assert that holiness is not a distinct attribute but the perfection of all of them. Others assert that holiness is a form of love, i.e. self-love. As we have tried to demonstrate earlier in this chapter, both of these assertions are incorrect, misleading and dangerous. It is indeed correct to say that God's holiness is self-affirming, but love as a communication of the self is hardly the same as maintenance of the self.

As any one who has read the stories of God's chastening of the Israelites (Exodus to Malachi) ought to know, God's love for them was at every point directed and bounded by His holiness. There is nothing maudlin about the love of God. 'You hate all evildoers.'

God 'did not spare his own Son',[24] therefore, when His son 'became sin for us' at Calvary;[25] God caused Him to be 'wounded for our transgressions… it was the will of the LORD to crush him'.[26] Thus, we see in what poignant ways holiness and love meet, 'For God so loved the world, that he gave his only Son'.[27] In this verse 'so' does not mean 'so much' but 'thus' or 'in this manner'.

A well-known hymn says of God that His 'Love found a way to redeem my soul! Love found a way that could make me whole.' And, indeed, God's love did. Not, however, at the expense of His truth and holiness. The 'expense' was the life of God's only begotten Son, not at the expense of God's holiness, justice and truth.

Neither is God's love a mere 'positive attitude' toward all created beings. Quite to the contrary, He hates not only 'wickedness' (Ps. 45:7), but also 'all evildoers' (Ps. 5:5; cf. 11:5). If we who are forgiven sinners want a formula for our attitude toward sinners that shares God's attitude, then we must put something together better than 'Hate the sin but love the sinner'. It sounds right but does not quite match what we know of God and His ways. The Almighty Creator of this now fallen world has no love for it, nor should we, except with the ethical goal of bringing people to conformity with His holiness.

God's love is holy. As a holy being, His love is directed knowledgebly and voluntarily in ways harmonious with truth. He will not propagate a lie or perpetuate one. Paul prays that our Christian 'love may abound more and more, with knowledge and all discernment' (Phil. 1:9). It is incorrect to say that God's love is unconditional, for it is conditioned by His holiness of being and His love of Himself – i.e. by truth. He did not need a world to have a sufficient object of love. God loves the world of mankind because we bear His image. His love is *holy*, designed fully to restore that image but also *true*, in that our sinfulness is taken into account.

God's love is of course an attribute of God cherished much by all systems of theology. In soundly biblical theology, God's love is never at the sacrifice of His holiness. Perhaps the most complete and convincing statement of this fact is by A. H. Strong, whose exposition explores the relation of divine love to other attributes, especially His holiness.[28] G. C. H. Berkouwer summarizes the failure of the neo-orthodoxy of Karl Barth in this regard:

> In Barth's doctrine of the divine attributes, the love of God dominates over His righteousness, His grace over His wrath. It would seem that he thus allows the gospel of grace, the Scriptural message of the love of God

---

24. Rom. 8:32.
25. 2 Cor. 5:21, KJV
26. Isa. 53:5, 10.
27. John 3:16.

unto the salvation of the world, to come to its full expression. But the manner in which Barth speaks of God's *yes* and *no* reveals a concept of grace different from that of the Biblical message. Barth conceives of a new order of grace, established in redemption and in the election in Christ, in which all now share [universal salvation]. Unbelief is nothing but the nonsense of rejecting this irrefutable fact: the universal love of God.[29]

If God was to love us sinners, then there was a cost to Him – as inharmonious with His perfect blessedness of being as that seems. Atonement through the passion and death of the Son of God was the fruit of that love, for Christ is 'the Lamb slain from the foundation of the world' (Rev. 13:8, KJV; cf. 1 Peter 1:19, 20). Therefore, the permission of sin in God's eternal counsels was at great cost to Him. Early in the scriptural record, it is said of sin that 'it grieved him to his heart' (Gen. 6:6). Ephesians 4:30 speaks of grieving the Holy Spirit. He is said to share in the afflictions of His people (Isa. 63:9). Abraham's grief over his 'not withheld' son (Gen. 22:16) is a picture of the grief of God when 'He… did not spare his own Son' (Rom. 8:32).[30]

The Bible makes God's love not only the ground of proper human love (1 John 4:11) but also the effective cause of it, for 'We love because he first loved us' (1 John 4:19). Our love for God and other people is both evidence and fruit of God's indwelling presence in us and is the means God uses to reveal His holiness and love to the world, for 'No one has ever seen God; if we love one another, God abides in us and his love is perfected in us' (1 John 4:12).

6. Mercy: God is Merciful.

The attribute of mercy is often called 'transitive love', and such it is. It is love in action for those who do not deserve the blessed provisions of God's love but do desperately need His love. The word 'mercy' (almost always God's mercy) occurs much more frequently in the King James Version than the word 'love'. The Revised Standard Version, and the English Standard Version, change many of these to 'steadfast love' and New International Version to 'love'. The Hebrew and Greek words involved show some variety. The emphasis in the King James Version, however, lays legitimate emphasis on the action of God's love.

Eddie Arnold (a retired ikon of country music) sings a song about a lover who reflects sadly that the great love of his life, one who married another, never knew he loved her because he never told her! This is not true of God's love, for His mercies on the undeserving have been showered upon them. He has shown it in His care for all His creatures (Ps. 145:15, 16), and in His allowing His enemies and blasphemers to live, while helping all undeserving in one way or another (Neh. 9:17-21, 27-32). A Psalm exclaims, 'The earth, O LORD, is full of your steadfast love' (Ps. 119:64). Another Psalm exclaims, 'Oh give thanks to the LORD, for he is good, for his mercy endureth for ever!' (Ps. 106:1 KJV). Psalm 136:11 (KJV) repeats the very same words and adds, 'for his mercy endureth forever' twenty-five times. Certainly, God's mercy is an emphasized aspect of God's goodness in the Bible.

The goodness (benevolence) of God toward all His creatures, especially sinful men, is a special feature of God's mercy. Paul declares that it is a witness to God even among the heathen (Acts 14:17). In another text he joins God's holiness, truth, love and mercy, appealing to sinful men in a special way (Rom. 2:1-5), focusing on God's goodness (i.e. benevolence or mercy): 'Or do you presume on the riches of his kindness and forbearance and patience, not knowing that God's kindness is meant to lead you to repentance?' (Rom. 2:4).

These three pairs of attributes of God's goodness – *holiness* manifest in *righteousness*; *truth* in *faithfulness*; and *love* in *mercy* – do not exhaust the number of such attributes mentioned in Scripture. There is no prescribed list. Yet I think a little reflection on others – compassion, loving kindness, pity, tender mercies and the like – will show they are subsumed by, or are refinements of, these six.

---

28. Strong, *op. cit.*, pp. 269 – 275.
29. G. C. H. Berkouwer, *The Providence of God*, trans. L. B. Smedes (Grand Rapids: Eerdmans, 1972), pp. 264, 265.
30. How Scripture may properly portray God as 'blessed forever', and 'with whom there is no variation or shadow due to change' (according to immemorial theological tradition, 'impassible'), will be the subject of a later extensive excursus.

13
The Triunity of the Godhead in Biblical and Christian History

'the name of the Father and of the Son and of the Holy Spirit' (Matt. 28:19)

The Trinity in Ancient Formal Statements.

Three hundred and seventy-five pastors, or bishops, of churches throughout Christendom (the Roman world) assembled at Nicea, not far eastward from Constantinople in what is now Asiatic Turkey, in AD 325. The purpose of this conference (First Ecumenical Council), called together by the Constantine I, Emperor of the Roman Empire, was to formulate a clear, summary statement of what the Scriptures teach about the relation of the Son of God to God the Father. The Holy Spirit was not yet a focus of intense and prolonged study or of controversy. A modern author has rightly commented, '[It is] readily apparent that the Nicene Creed is an expansion of the Apostles' Creed and a defense of [it] from misuse by reinterpretation.'[1]

Let us emphasize that both the Apostles' Creed and the Nicene Creed, which follows it and enlarges it, are essentially statements about events in history. They do not, like the creeds of most other religions, make claims about ultimate reality or seek to sort out ideas of mind and matter, space and time, and the like. These two creeds read much more like Peter's simple recital of the faith, as history, to spiritually anxious seekers of the household of Cornelius (Acts 10:34-43) than any ancient Hellenist or Gnostic statement of how the world operates. In this, they are much more like the Bible itself than books of theology – so much for charges of spoiling the plain Bible message with infusions of pagan philosophical vocabulary and patterns of thought. What Christians now call the Holy Trinity doctrine is latent in the New Testament beginnings and had been taught from the earliest Christian times. The Council of Nicea was the first, focused, common effort to define the doctrine against the errors of several divisive teachers and sects that were undercutting the very heart of Christian truth. The Nicene Fathers' effort was never conceived as one to dissolve the essential mystery of the Godhead, for they recognized such could not be done. Their intention, successfully achieved, was precisely to *preserve* the mystery. Nor was theirs an effort to frame a 'metaphysical' definition of God. Rather it was to state intelligibly that God the Father, Son and Holy Spirit are three without denying in any fashion that God is one Lord.

The result was a brief statement of belief affirming that the oneness of the Godhead is in respect to being (Latin *substantia*, substance; Greek *ousia*). The Son is *homoousios* (same substance) with the Father. The Spirit is to be

---

1. R. J. Rushdoony, *The Foundation of Social Order* (Philadelphia: Presby. & Reformed Publ., 1968), p. 16.

worshiped together with Father and Son. Those who, like the present author, believe that civilizations are but the expressions of beliefs about ultimate matters (that is, religious beliefs) will agree with Philip Schaff:

> The Council of Nicea is the most important event of the fourth century, and its bloodless intellectual victory over a dangerous error [Arianism] is of far greater consequence to the progress of true civilization than all the bloody victories of Constantine and his successors.[2]

About 125 years later, an ecumenical council at a place not far from Nicea, called Chalcedon (AD 451), the Latin word *persona* (person) and the Greek word *hypostasis*, though previously often translated in Latin as *substantia* (English, substance), came to be adopted as the accepted term for the sense in which the members of the Trinity are three. There was no effort to phrase the biblical revelation in the thought-patterns of Greek philosophy, as antagonists of orthodoxy frequently assert today. The contrary was the case. The simple doctrines of Scripture – the Father is God; the Son is God; the Holy Spirit is God; there is only one God – were retained in resistance to the efforts of errorists of the time to dissolve the palpable paradox, or mystery, in some philosophic formula. The full humanity of the Son and His full deity, two natures in one 'person and subsistence', is spelled out plainly. The great creed of Nicea (as given final form at the Second Ecumenical Council, Constantinople, AD 381) and the Definition of Chalcedon are with us still as standards precisely because they leave the mysteries of Scripture intact.[3]

The reader may wonder if all this precision ('getting technical') is necessary. Yes, it is, if one is going to meet the challenges to the deity of our Lord mounting higher in our time, as they did in that of the Nicean Council. Arius advocated the very same reasonable-sounding, fatal denials that we hear both from learned 'modernists' and the unlearned cultists today. Arius and his partisans proposed to worship Christ as a great angel, of *similar substance* (Greek, *homoi-ousios*), with the Father, while Athanasius and those in agreement insisted, on scriptural grounds, Christ the Son is no created being, but like the Father, He is an eternal being, consubstantial (same substance, Greek, *homoousios*) with the Father. There is only an *iota* (Gr. *i*) of difference, but the difference involves the very heartbeat of our faith.[4]

There is some merit to Hendrikus Berkhof's cautions against supposing any pronouncements, dogmatical or speculative, have succeeded in explaining the mystery of the triunity of God. Of 'traditional' and 'speculative theology' he wrote:

> [W]e must not forget that we (Protestants) have no 'dogma of the Trinity' inherited from the ancient church, only some pronouncements of Councils about the divine character of Christ and the Spirit. The formula 'one being, three persons' from the very first moment left open several interpretations; even today it veils the problems instead of solving them.[5]

The Reformation and the Trinity.

Nearly 500 years ago Arianism (Socinianism, Unitarianism) again challenged the orthodox faith. The Protestant Reformation responded valiantly and successfully. Luther accepted the orthodox doctrine because he knew it was scriptural. He placed equal emphasis on both the oneness and the *Dreifaltigkeit* (threefoldness). Luther taught, 'One God in three persons – every person is the entire deity and yet no person exists as the deity for itself without the other two.'[6] I am aware of no record of any extended treatment of the Trinity by Luther, but he discussed it in his Bible expositions, theses and debates and especially in Advent sermons. He thought, as did all the leading Reformers, that the medieval schoolmen had erred greatly in supposing they could derive the Trinity from the nature of God and render the doctrine *fully* amenable to reason. He said, 'The scholastic teachers have attempted to make this understandable with very great subtleties.' A Luther scholar explains, 'Instead of this, one should stick to the simple, clear, powerful words of Scripture.'[7] Luther held no brief for the traditional Trinitarian vocabulary (nature, essence, *ousia*, *hypostasis*, and the like). One uses the vocabulary as convenient, though inadequate to express the mystery. One is free to use other language, but at the peril of misrepresenting the biblical revelation.

---

2. Philip Schaff, *History of the Christian Church*, vol. iii (Grand Rapids: Eerdmans, 1960, based on ed. publ. in 1910), p. 631. See 'The Nicene Creed' at end of this chapter.
3. See 'The Definition of Chalcedon' (Chap.14, p. 118).
4. The idiom, 'not an iota of difference' originates in the *homo-homoi* disjunction.
5. Hendrikus Berkhof, *The Doctrine of the Holy Spirit*, Chap. VI 'The Spirit & The Triune God' (Atlanta: John Knox Press, 1977), pp. 109, 110.
6. Paul Althaus, *The Theology of Martin Luther* (Philadelphia: Fortress Press, 1966), p. 199.
7. ibid., p. 200.

At first, Calvin seemed to avoid traditional formulations of the Trinity doctrine. This brought on criticism by a jealous colleague. Later on, without mentioning the colleagues or the names of the contemporary sixteenth-century Arians, Calvin refuted their views and stated well why Christian people of all ages must get this matter straight in their thinking, and in doing so must also learn a few new words. This Reformer, whose own language was studiedly direct and simple, points out that for ages past learned Christians (Hilary, Jerome, Augustine) had protested the use of the technical words for the distinctions, but had nevertheless been compelled to employ them. Then he wisely adds, 'And this modesty of saintly men ought to warn us against forthwith… taking to task those who do not wish to swear by the words conceived by us.' Thus he sympathizes with the simple man's impatience. Nevertheless, he goes on to say why the simple man also must have some patience, to learn a few useful new words.

Without these terms, we cannot clarify issues and distinguish a teacher who is a willful, dangerous heretic from one who is mildly erroneous or entirely orthodox. Calvin observes:

> Arius, says that Christ is God, but mutters that he was made and had a beginning. He says that Christ is one with the Father, but secretly whispers in the ears of his own partisans that He is united to the Father like other believers, although by a singular priviledge. Say 'consubstantial' and you will tear off the mask of this turncoat, and yet you add nothing to Scripture.[8]

Every stream of orthodox Christianity derived from the sixteenth-century Reformation preserved the heritage of the ancient church in regard to the triunity of the Godhead.

The late Kenneth S. Kantzer of Trinity Evangelical Divinity School has said that though 'the major doctrines were worked out in the very ancient church,'

> Evangelicals look back with deep gratitude to their Reformation heritage. To Luther, Calvin, Cranmer, and their associates they acknowledge an immeasurable debt – particularly for their insights into justification by faith alone as the very heart of the gospel and for their loyal defense of the final authority of the Bible as the inerrant written Word of God. Less clearly recognized is the Reformation contribution to the doctrine of the Trinity.[9]

Kantzer goes on to explain how 'the Genevan reformer, following guidelines laid down by Augustine, worked out the details of the doctrine more fully than any of the other reformers'.

Why Christians believe in the Trinity of the Godhead.

Why do Christians always everywhere uniformly insist on this doctrine? No text of Scripture says specifically that God eternally exists as one being (ousia, substance) in three persons, each of whom fully and perfectly possesses that substance. The orthodox doctrine is that each of the persons is God in a *quantitative* sense – all the God-ness there is – not in any mere *generic* sense, as when we say all men are human, as a class or category of being. Christians insist that it is necessary to believe this. Again. Why?

The answer has to do with history; not church history, but biblical history. The Old Testament tells of how God called a man named Abram out of a culture where many gods were worshipped (Josh. 24:2) in order to make known to him the one, true God. Abram came to see that *Yahweh-'Elohim* is 'the Judge of all the earth' (Gen. 18:25). He would use Abram to create a people through whom that message would be conveyed to other families of earth. God enforced the truth of monotheism to the Israelite descendents of Abram at the time of Moses. The historical books tell of the frequent apostasies of the Israelites from this truth and of their permanent acceptance of it through the sufferings of the Babylonian exile. Israel's apostasies from monotheism were never again repeated on a general scale.

The first disciples of Jesus were Jews (Israelites). As time passed these incurable monotheists recognized that Jesus of Nazareth was God, the same God as He whom their Fathers had worshipped under the Mosaic economy. They said so in their sermons and writings[10]

Jesus told them shortly before his crucifixion (John 14–16) and afterward that the Father would send to them another Comforter, the Spirit of Truth, 'to be with you forever'. He was to be another (*allos*) of the same, not a different (*heteros*) kind. When He, the Holy Spirit, came in the special way described in the second chapter of Acts,

---

8. John Calvin, *Institutes of the Christian Religion* (Philadelphia: Westminster Press, 1960), I, 15. 5.
9. Kenneth S. Kantzer, 'John Calvin & the Mystery of the Trinity,' *Voices*, a publication of Trinity Evangelical Divinity School, n.d., p. 10.
10. It should not be necessary at this point to demonstrate that the New Testament teaches the deity of the Lord Jesus Christ, nor that the disciples believed it. Peter's confession and Thomas' exclamation are enough for now. A later section of systematic theology, 'Part 4: Christology: Person and Work of Christ'.

the disciples immediately recognized the Holy Spirit also as God. They formed no doctrinal statement about the Holy Spirit for several centuries but, following apostolic usage, joined His name with the Father and/or the Son in proclamation, prayers, benedictions and blessings. Moreover, while steadfastly acknowledging that there is only one God (as all Jews affirmed), they also affirmed that the Father is God, the Son is God and Spirit is God.

With new insights provided by fulfillment of 'the promise of the Father' which (they) heard from Christ Himself (Acts 1:4, 5; cf. 2:33; 11:16; and Matt. 3:11), the apostles were able to identify the Holy Spirit with the Spirit of God in the Old Testament. Beginning with the New Testament record itself, they quoted and cited Old Testament references to God's Spirit as identical with the Holy Spirit.

Their example bids us to make (with attention to controls) the same equation. They attributed everything the Old Testament said about the Spirit of God to the now arrived, personal, Holy Spirit. He was 'another of the same kind' as Christ Himself (see John 14:10). In such case, asserts B. B. Warfield:

> It was their own Holy Ghost who was Israel's guide... whom Israel rejected when they resisted the leading of God (Acts 7:51)... In him... Christ... preached to the antediluvians (1 Peter 3:18)... He... was the author of faith of old as well as now (2 Cor. 4:13)... He... gave Israel its ritual service. It was He who spoke in and through David and Isaiah and all the prophets (Matt. 22:43; Mark 12:36; Acts 1:16; 28:25; Heb. 3:7; 10:15).[11]

Peter's oft-quoted declaration about the prophetic origin of Old Testament Scriptures (2 Peter 1:21) maintains that it was the Spirit of Christ who moved the writing prophets – as Zechariah (7:12) and Nehemiah (9:20) were aware. Again, Peter claimed the prophecies of Christ written by such men as Daniel, Isaiah, Jeremiah, Ezekiel and the other Twelve were taught what to say by the 'Spirit of Christ' (1 Peter 1:11). The promised Spirit of God of Joel (2:27, 28) is the same Holy Spirit who descended at Pentecost (Acts 2:16). Isaiah's predictions of the special presence of the Spirit of the Lord with and on the righteous Servant (Son, Messiah)[12] were fulfilled, says the New Testament writers, in Christ.[13]

It is instinct with vital Christians, when they read the Bible, to understand Old Testament references to the Spirit of God along with the Holy Spirit revealed in the New Testament. No rigid hermeneutics, which in every case severely limits the reference of an Old Testament text to the intellectual and historical horizon of the original writer or of the first readers, is likely to talk the present Christian heirs of sixty generations of Christian Bible readers out of this conviction. Not only so, New Testament believers prayed in the Spirit *to* the Father *in the name* of the Son. In their benedictions they pronounced the grace of our Lord Jesus Christ, and the *love* of God the Father, and the *communion* of the Holy Spirit upon their departing assemblies (2 Cor. 13:14). Baptism, by the Lord's command, was in the name of the Father and of the Son and of the Holy Ghost (Matt. 28:19).

Every element mentioned in the previous paragraph is thoroughly imbedded in the fabric of the New Testament. The putting of all these elements together in a formal statement was bound to come. Significantly, the very oldest surviving post-New Testament Christian creed is essentially a confession of faith in 'God the Father Almighty... and in Jesus Christ, His only son... and in the Holy Ghost.'[14]

When in later times, church councils (i.e. as we now say, conferences) hammered out formal statements of the doctrine of the Holy Trinity, they were doing in a co-operative capacity what every biblical pastor does when he prepares his Sunday morning sermon and delivers it to his people. They were doing what they had to do in the face of problems and divisions. These threats to unity of the faith were brought on by attacks from sophisticated, learned, aggressive errorists within the professing church. The church today is by no means bound unquestioningly to follow ancient traditions. Yet we may rightly thank God for what previous generations of devout Christian scholars and teachers have done to formulate the Christian doctrine of the triune God and other doctrines. This is the true apostolic succession, spoken of as guarding a deposit, or committing to a rising generation of believers what has been passed down (the true Christian meaning of tradition) by earlier generations of believers (2 Tim. 2:1, 2).

Edward Bickersteth (1786–1850), lawyer, Anglican clergyman, promoter of missionary evangelism, evangelist and one of the founders of the Evangelical Alliance, summarizes our answer to the question, 'Why do Christians believe in the triune Godhead?' Because, he says,

---

11. B. B. Warfield, 'The Spirit of God in the Old Testament' ed. Samuel Craig, *Biblical and Theological Studies* (Philadelphia: Presbyterian & Reformed Publ., 1952), pp. 129, 130.
12. Isa. 11:1 ff.; 42:1; 61:1.
13. John 1:29-34; Matt. 3:13-17; Mark 1:1-12; Luke 3:15-17; 4:16-21.
14. Henry S. Bettenson, 'The Old Roman Creed' *Documents of the Christian Church* (New York: Oxford Univ. Press, 1963), p. 33.

> He reveals himself by his names, his attributes, and his acts. And, therefore, if, combined with assertions that God is one, we find three revealed in Scripture to whom the same names, attributes, and acts are ascribed, the same so far as a personal distinction allows; if we look vainly for any fourth Divine one, or any intimation of more than three; if we connect with this the intimate and necessary union affirmed to exist betwixt the Father, and the Son, and the Spirit, as when the Lord Jesus says, 'I and my Father are one,' and when Paul says, 'The Spirit searches the depths of God'; if, then, we find that every Christian is baptized into one Name, – the Name of the Father, and of the Son, and of the Holy Ghost, – we are led swiftly and irresistibly up to the doctrine (call it by what name you will) of the Trinity in Unity.[15]

A summary follows of Bickersteth's summary-propositions and Scripture proof texts. This is useful in showing that the Father is God, the Son is God, the Spirit is God; and yet there is only one God.

(1) The Father, the Son and the Holy Ghost are eternal (Rom. 16:26; Rev. 1:17; Mic. 5:2; Heb. 9:14; Deut. 33:27).
(2) The Father, the Son and the Spirit created all things (1 Cor. 8:6; Ps. 100:3; Col. 1:16; Job 33:4; 1 Peter 4:9).
(3) The Three are each omnipresent (Jer. 23:24; Matt. 28:20; Ps. 139:7; Acts 17:28, 29).
(4) The Three are each omniscient (Matt. 11:27; Acts 15:18; John 21:17; Isa. 40:13; 1 Cor. 2:10; Heb. 4:13).
(5) The Three are each true and good (John 7:28; 17:17, 25; Ps. 34:8; John 10:11; 14:6; Acts 3:14; 1 John 5:6; John 14:26; Ps. 143:10; Rev. 15:4).
(6) They each have a self-regulating will (Eph. 1:11; Matt. 11:27; John 17:24; 1 Cor 12:11; Acts 21:14).
(7) They are each the fountain of life (Ps. 36:9; Eph. 2:4, 5; John 5:21; John 3:8; Deut. 30:20).
(8) They each sanctify us (Ps. 138:3; Isa. 66:13; Jude 1; Phil. 4:13; 1 Cor. 1:2; Eph. 3:16; John 14:26; Rom. 15:6).
(9) Each fills our souls with divine love (1 John 5:1; 2:15; 2 Cor. 5:14; 1 Cor. 16:22; Rom. 15:30; Col. 1:8; Deut. 6:5).
(10) Each gives divine law (Ps. 19:7; Isa. 11:8; Ezek. 2:4; Gal. 6:2; Col. 3:16; Rev. 2:18; Rom. 8:2; 2 Peter 1:21; Acts 13:2; James 4:12).
(11) Each dwells in believers' hearts (1 Cor. 14:25; John 1:3; Eph. 3:17; Col. 1:27; 1 John 1:3; John 14:17; 2 Cor. 13:14; Isa. 57:15).
(12) The Father, the Son and the Holy Spirit are, each by Himself, the supreme Jehovah and God: (a) 'I am Jehovah thy God' (Exod. 20:2); (b) 'Jehovah our God' (Isa. 4:3; cf. Matt. 3:3) and 'the Highest' (Luke 1:76; and Matt. 10:11); (c) 'Jehovah God' (Ezek. 8:1, 3) and 'the Highest' (Luke 1:35). Yet God is one (Deut. 6:4).

To summarize Bickersteth: each Person, has the same *attributes*. The persons concur in *mind, will and heart, personally distinct* yet harmonious, and performing the same *works*. They have some of the same *names*. They are to be *worshiped* equally.

Explicit Trinitarian Belief, Confession and Proclamation before Nicea AD 325.

There is, of course, no formal theological dogma of the Trinity in the New Testament. As we have already seen, however, the history recorded there of Jesus' words, promises and fulfillments about the Holy Spirit, and His own names, words, works and claims about and for Himself, created the atmosphere in which the primitive Christian teachers thought. In this climate of reflection, Father, Son and Holy Spirit were regarded – in the very texts of the Gospels and Epistles – as together constituting the one God. Did the Christians who lived in the second and third centuries, however, see these connections and believe, confess and proclaim a triune God – either implicitly or explicitly?

The writers immediately after the apostles, and for several generations, were so pressed by other concerns that they did not engage in doctrinal speculations about the Trinitarian formula of baptism and Trinitarian benediction in the New Testament. Neve says:

> [T]hey used the Trinitarian formula; but this formula did not provoke them to discussion of the relation of the three to each other. Concerning Christ's relation to the Father we can only say that they regarded Christ as the Son of God, and ascribed to Him those attributes which can be predicated of God alone. And with Father and Son, the Holy Spirit is mentioned in so many cases.[16]

---

15. Edward Bickersteth, *The Trinity* (Grand Rapids: Kregel Publ., 3rd Printing, 1965), pp. 150.
16. J. L. Neve, *A History of Christian Thought*, vol. i (Philadelphia: Muhlenberg Press, 1946), p. 106ff.

He adds: 'It must be admitted that the language of the Post-Apostolic Fathers was frequently binitarian [i.e. Father and Son are God]. The Spirit was taken as the Spirit of Christ as in 2 Corinthians 3:17. But with this they did not mean an actual identification of the Spirit with the Son. It was simply an abbreviation in expression. There was the natural difficulty of speaking of the Holy Spirit in hypostatic [personal] terms' (heightened by the fact that *pneuma*, spirit in Greek, is a neuter noun).[17]

Neve is correct in saying that, within the Godhead, the presence of the Son is more easily found than the Holy Spirit in Christian literature coming from those centuries; there is an explicit 'binitarianism' and an implicit 'trinitarianism'. The equality of the Spirit with the Son and the Father is present but not advertized, so to speak.

The earliest post-New Testament Christian writing, the *Epistle of Clement* to the Corinthians (about AD 95), closes with a benediction similar to Paul's, and like some of Paul's, omits the Holy Spirit: 'The grace of our LORD Jesus Christ be with you and with all men who have been called by God', and so on.[18]

Justo L. Gonzalez, in his justly acclaimed *History of Christian Thought*, says: 'Clement's doctrine of God is clearly Trinitarian, in the sense that several Trinitarian formulas appear in the Epistle.'[19]

Shortly thereafter Polycarp of Smyrna,[20] just before his execution by fire, prayed: 'I glorify thee, through the eternal and heavenly high priest, Jesus Christ, thy beloved Servant, through whom be glory to thee through him and the Holy Spirit both now and unto the ages to come.'[21]

Perhaps the most explicitly Trinitarian statement from the Fathers of the earliest epoch is that of Athenagoras. He was an Athenian philosopher who had embraced Christianity and wrote *A Plea For The Christians* which was presented to the Emperors Aurelius and Commodus about AD 177. He is competently judged 'one of the ablest of the early Christian Apologists'. The editor of the *Plea for the Christians*, in the second volume of *Ante-Nicene Fathers*, heads the tenth chapter, 'The Christians Worship the Father, Son and Holy Ghost'. In this chapter of less than 300 words, Athenagoras confesses and teaches both a biblically informed and sophisticated monotheism and doctrine of a triune God approaching the quality of the fourth and fifth century creeds. I quote the short chapter in full, as both interesting and instructive, and decisive on the question raised in this part of the present chapter.

> That we are not atheists, therefore, seeing that we acknowledge one God, uncreated, eternal, invisible, impassible, incomprehensible, illimitable, who is apprehended by the understanding only and the reason, who is encompassed by light, and beauty, and spirit, and power ineffable, by whom the universe has been created through His Logos, and set in order, and is kept in being – I have sufficiently demonstrated. [I say 'His Logos'], for we acknowledge also a Son of God. Nor let any one think it ridiculous that God should have a Son. For though the poets, in their fictions, represent the gods as no better than men, our mode of thinking is not the same as theirs, concerning either God the Father or the Son. But the Son of God is the Logos of the Father, in idea and in operation; for after the pattern of Him and by Him were all things made, the Father and the Son being one. And, the Son being in the Father and the Father in the Son, in oneness and power of spirit, the understanding and reason [*nous kai logos*] of the Father is the Son of God. But if, in your surpassing intelligence, it occurs to you to inquire what is meant by the Son, I will state briefly that He is the first product of the Father, not as having been brought into existence (for from the beginning, God, who is the eternal mind [*nous*], had the Logos in Himself, being from eternity instinct with Logos [*logikos*]; but inasmuch as He came forth to be the idea and energizing power of all material things, which lay like a nature without attributes, and an inactive earth, the grosser particles being mixed up with the lighter. The prophetic Spirit also agrees with our statements. 'The LORD,' it says, 'made me, the beginning of His ways to His works.' The Holy Spirit Himself also which operates in the prophets, we assert to be an effluence of God, flowing from Him, and returning back again like a beam of the sun. Who, then, would not be astonished to hear men who speak of God the Father, and of God the Son, and of the Holy Spirit, and who declare both their power in union and their distinction in order, called atheists? Nor is our teaching in what relates to the divine nature confined to these points; but we recognise also a multitude of angels and ministers, whom God the Maker and Framer of the world distributed and pointed to their several posts by His Logos, to occupy themselves about the elements, and the heavens, and the world, and the things in it, and the goodly ordering of them all.[22]

17. ibid., p. 107.
18. Clement of Rome to the Corinthians, from *The Apostle Fathers* by J. B. Lightfoot, 1898, p. 85.
19. Justo L. Gonzalez, *A History of Christian Thought I* (Nashville: Abington Press, 1970), p. 64.
20. Died AD 155 in very old age.
21. From *The Martyrdom of Polycarp*, as cited by Thomas Oden, *The Living God, Systematic Theology I* (San Francisco: Harper Collins, 1992), p. 210.
22. Athenagoras, *A Plea for the Christians*, ANF vol. ii, pp. 133, 134.

There should be no doubt, therefore, that, from the very first, Christianity has affirmed the 'essential' unity of Father, Son and Holy Spirit on the level of 'being' (to use an English word) though also in some mysterious sense also three. As good a brief guide to early patristic thought on the subject as I know of is fourteen pages on 'The Three and the One' by Jaroslav Pelikan.[23]

Old Testament Preparation for Revelation of 'God in Three Persons, Blessed Trinity'.

The Old Testament prepared for revelation of the triunity of the Godhead by dropping hints, raising questions and posing problems, which suggest or point up the need for the New Testament revelation. The commonest name for God' (*'elohim*), appearing in the first sentence in the Bible, is a plural form. The sense, however, is almost always singular, when used of the God of the Bible. Once (Gen. 35:7), however, the Hebrew would normally be translated, apart from the context, 'the gods were revealed to him', even though the one true God is meant. Also, several times God refers to Himself as 'us' (Gen. 1:26; 3:22; 11:7; Isa. 6:8) and there are contexts wherein God, in a puzzling manner, seems to be more than one person (see Gen. 18:2, 16; 19:2; Isa. 44:6). Psalm 110:1 is a special case, because Jesus commented on the verse to prove that it is not improper for people to call Him the Son of God (Matt. 22:41-46). None of these passages explicitly teaches a plurality of persons in the Godhead, but it is not far-fetched (as Jesus' use of Psalm 110:1 shows) to challenge teachers, who reject the Trinity, to provide a better explanation of the verses.

A startling, impressive passage, (Isa. 63:7-10), brings the LORD (Jehovah), 'the angel of his presence' and 'his Holy Spirit' together. And in another passage, we read, '"I have been there". And now the Lord GOD has sent me, and his Spirit' (Isa. 48:16). If the One who refers to Himself as 'I' and 'me' is the Servant of Isaiah (52:12–53:13), this text does indeed have a Trinitarian ring.

Modern 'scientific' exegesis, whether liberal or conservative, has a hard time following apostolic practice in interpreting many Old Testament references to 'the spirit' or 'the spirit of God' as designating the Holy Spirit, Third Person of the Godhead. The apostles do not hesitate in bringing New Testament history and revelation to Old Testament interpretation of this particular doctrine. They do not 'read the New Testament into the Old', but they do bring light shed by that history when 'the fullness of time had come, God sent forth his Son' (Gal. 4:4) to be 'the Savior of the world', (John 4:42; 1 John 4:14) and the Son promised the coming of 'the Spirit' who would proceed from the Father and the Son. By this means, the Old Testament is held to say much about the Holy Spirit.

None of these Old Testament literary phenomena is sufficient ground for a doctrine of three persons in the Godhead. No Jew was looking for the God-man at Bethlehem, as far as we know, on the basis of any of these and similar passages. Yet the revelation of the Trinity furnishes a basis for a better understanding of these texts of the Old Testament than was possible before the incarnation of the Second Person of the Trinity and the special sending of the Holy Spirit at Pentecost. [Necessary limitation of the size of this book prevents incorporating lectures delivered in a seminary course in the Doctrine of the Holy Spirit at this point.]

The New Testament Doctrine.

The Pole Star of all biblical teaching is the unity of God. Our Lord commented favourably on the Mosaic formula, 'The LORD our God, the LORD is one' (Deut. 6:4; cf. Mark 12:28, 29), and His disciples, reared in the Mosaic Torah, never doubted it. They would never have followed a Messiah who announced a doctrine of tritheism (three gods) and neither they nor Jesus ever entertained such a repugnant pagan thought.

As we have seen, recognition of three members of one Godhead was pressed upon the consciousness of the first Christians by events of salvation history. The New Testament, we should observe, was written some time after the deity of the Lord Jesus Christ and of 'another Helper' had been thoroughly accepted. Thus numerous expressions occur on its pages which should be interpreted as referring to 'persons' recognized by the early believers as God. These three 'persons' are 'God the Father', 'Christ who is God over all' and 'the Holy Spirit… God' (see John 6:27; Rom. 9:5; Acts 5:3, 4). Of these 'persons' there are three, no more, no less.[24]

---

23. Jaroslav Pelikan, *The Emergence of the Christian Tradition vol. i* (Chicago: Univ. of Chicago Press, 1971), pp. 211 – 225.
24. I put 'persons' in quote marks because that particular designation did not arise for several generations thereafter.

The distinction between the three members, each clearly regarded as God, can be demonstrated in several lengthy passages, Ephesians 1:3-14, for example. The most important of these lengthy passages is John 14, where the distinction between the three Persons is particularly apparent.

Jesus, Himself, in speaking to the twelve apostles, after Judas' departure from the Upper Room, said, 'I will ask the Father, and he will give you another Helper' (John 14:16, Comforter KJV). Then, after discussing the Spirit's coming and future relationship to believers, Jesus added, 'the Helper, the Holy Spirit, whom the Father will send in my name' (v. 26). The unity of the Godhead is also there, for the coming of the Spirit is a spiritual coming of Christ (v. 18). Yet no discerning Bible reader will ever confuse the Persons of the Godhead on the ground of John 14:18, however difficult of explication the doctrine of the spiritual presence of Christ may be.[25]

There is one occasion, the baptism of Jesus, which provides all the most penetrating Unitarian critic could demand, by way of clear distinction between the three Persons (Luke 3:21, 22; John 1:32-34; Matt. 3:16, 17; Mark 1:9-11). The incident must have importance to the Providence that inspired the Bible, for all four Gospels report it. We do not know how many people were present, but John the Baptizer was there and reported what he did, what he saw and what he heard (John 1:32-34). The two men entered the water and John baptized Jesus. (The mode of applying water to the subject is not relevant to the present discussion.) Then John saw the Spirit descending in the form of a dove and the voice of the Father was heard saying, 'This is my beloved Son, with whom I am well pleased' (Matt. 3:17).

The essential, substantial unity of the Godhead is preserved in the New Testament, as well. There is only one God, not three gods. John 14:23, for example, states that when believers love Christ and keep His words, the Son and the Father come in the Spirit. In the same context, the coming of the Spirit is a coming of Christ (v. 18). Certain statements affirm the unity in even more specific language. The indwelling of 'the Spirit of God' is the indwelling of 'the Spirit of Christ' (Rom. 8:9). The argument of 1 Corinthians 3:16 draws a parallel between the indwelling of the Spirit in the church and the indwelling of the Old Testament temple by the God of the Old Testament, i.e. Jehovah. In John 10:30 Jesus says, 'I and the Father are one'. Therefore, the unity of the Godhead, presented in the New Testament, is something far deeper than emotion, sentiment, policy or opinion as when we speak of unity of feeling, thinking, plans, action or purpose among people. It is a unity in respect of *being*. The Father, the Son and the Holy Spirit are not mere sharers of a *category* of being, as when we say each of three brothers is a man. They are one in *being*.

There is no regular order employed in association of the names of the three. Because of our familiarity with the three names in the baptismal formula at Matthew 28:19 we do naturally think of the three as Father, Son and Holy Spirit, in that order. However, in the familiar benedictions of 2 Corinthians 13:14 the order is Christ, God (Father), Spirit. In Ephesians 4:4-6 the order is Spirit, Lord (Christ), Father.[26]

Nor do the relationships indicated by 'Son of' and 'Spirit of' indicate inferiority of being. The Son has the same *power* that the Father has, 'For as the Father raises the dead and gives them life, so also the Son gives life to whom he will' (John 5:21). He also deserves the same *honor*: 'that all may honour the Son, just as they honour the Father' (John 5:23).

It is greatly to be regretted that some famous and influential theologians of our time apparently affirm the triune God but explain their doctrine in ways that deny the distinctness of the three Persons. They may endorse ancient creeds, but their 'recitals' are doxological – a mode of religious confession made without actually intending exactly what one says. They bear no clear witness to the doctrine of 'one substance but three persons', appearing to favour one substance, one person, three modes of working or some kind of 'adoptionism'. One of my best college professors thought he was orthodox, but confessed to me personally that the Father adopted the Son at His baptism.

We must not be so cautious, however, that, while affirming the sameness of the three persons we fail to distinguish the differences of who they are and what they do within the Holy Trinity as persons. Many passages affirm that the Father sent or gave the Son (John 3:16; 1 John 4:10 for examples). No text says the Son sent the Father. Jesus said the Father would send the Spirit (John 14:26) yet Jesus also said that He Himself would send the Spirit from the Father (John 16:7). Since AD 876 initially, and permanently since AD 1054, Christendom has been divided into East and West over 'filioque' (and the Son), which the Westerners, in harmony with John 14:26, added to the ancient Nicene Creed.[27]

---

25. See also John 15:26 and compare Luke 1:35.
26. See also 1 Cor. 12:4-6; Jude 20, 21; Eph. 5:18-20; 2 Thess. 2;13, 14.
27. Henry Bettenson, *op. cit.*, note #3, pp. 36, 37.

Certain texts of the New Testament seem to provide a formula for at least a glimpse into the relations, both functional and immanent, of the three Persons. In explaining the meaningless vanity of idols Paul wrote, 'yet to us there is one God, the Father, of [*ek*, out of] whom are all things, and we unto him; and one Lord, Jesus Christ, through whom are all things, and we through him' (1 Cor. 8:6 ASV). The passage has the ring of a familiar formula of some kind. In this affirmation of monotheistic faith, there is no mention of the Holy Spirit. Paul completes the idea when he elsewhere writes, 'through him [Christ] we... have our access in one Spirit unto [*pros*, to, toward] the Father' (Eph. 2:18 ASV). This suggests that the Father is the source in creation and redemption, the *planner*; the Son is channel or means, the *mediator*; the Spirit is agent, the *applier*.

An examination of the doctrine of the triune God in Ephesians 1 yields similar results as regards the work of the Trinity in redemption. Here the Father, as source, is said to have *chosen* us, He being the One who planned redemption (Eph. 1:3-6); Christ the Son *provides* our redemption (vv. 7-13a); and the Spirit is the seal and earnest of fully *applied* redemption (vv. 13b and 14). The correspondence with 1 Corinthians 8:6 and Ephesians 2:18 is not exact, but nearly so.

These distinctions in the work of the Trinity are not absolute. John 3:16, for example, says God gave His Son, while Titus 2:14 says the Son gave Himself.

We are also taught by New Testament examples to pray *to* the Father, *in* the Spirit, *in the name* of Jesus, the Son. This shows that, in our approach to the Godhead in worship and prayer, the distinct relationships of the three members should be acknowledged.

At this point, our sketch of the New Testament teaching of a triunity, one God (one essence) and three Persons might have continued with a survey of proposals set forth by orthodox theologians to explain it. Some have been alluded to and more will yet appear in this study, but with no attempt on my part to do so. Instead, I submit the opinion of several learned, orthodox scholars as to why the effort is largely unfruitful. First, after a rather complete survey of such efforts ancient and modern, George Christian Knapp (1770–1825) asserted:

> The conclusion is obvious that, while we are taught by the Scriptures to believe in three equal subjects in the Godhead, who are described as persons, we are still unable to determine in what manner or in what sense these three have the divine nature so in common that there is only one God.[28]

A. H. Strong, perhaps the most influential Baptist theologian, devoted eight final pages of his lengthy treatment to develop the theme: 'Inscrutable, yet not self-contradictory, this Doctrine furnishes the key to all other doctrines.'[29] Jonathan Edwards (1703–1758), in a celebrated essay on the Trinity, wrote:

> When we tell a child a little concerning God he has not an hundredth part so many mysteries in view on the nature and attributes of God and His works of creation and Providence as one that is told much concerning God in a divinity school; and yet he knows much more about God and has a much clearer understanding of Divinity and is able more clearly to explicate some things that were very dark and very unintelligible to him.[30]

Gregory Nazianzen (cited earlier), in one of his orations, declared that simple Christian believers were orthodox, even though not fully informed, often more so than speculative thinkers.[31] Augustine did not write his fifteen books on the Trinity to *explain* it rationally. On the one hand, he wrote them to show scoffing rationalists that it is not an irrational teaching, incapable of acceptance by 'scientific' minds. On the other, he wrote to lead believers *part way only* to understand what they were being taught *by the church*, and further to follow the apostle Paul in his method of humble submission to Christ (he cites Col. 2:3; 1 Cor. 2:2, 3; 1 Cor. 3:1, 2).

Jeremy Taylor (1613–1667), a noted English scholar in his day, wrote:

> He [who] goes about to speak of the mystery of the Trinity, and does it by words and names of man's invention, talking of essence and existence, hypostases and personalities, priority in coequality, and unity in pluralities, may amuse himself and build a tabernacle in his head, and talk something – he knows not what; but the renewed man, that feels the power of the Father, to whom the Son is become wisdom, sanctification, and redemption, in whose heart the love of the Spirit of God is shed abroad – this man, though he understand nothing of what is unintelligible, yet he alone truly understands the Christian doctrine of the Trinity.[32]

---

28. George Christian Knapp, *McClintock & Strong Cyclopedia vol. x* (Grand Rapids: Baker Books, 1970), p. 555.
29. A. H. Strong, *Systematic Theology* (Valley Forge, PA: Judson Press, 1907), pp. 344-352.
30. As cited by Strong, *ibid.*, pp. 344-352.
31. Jaroslav Pelikan, *Christianity & Classical Culture* (New Haven: Yale Univ. Press, 1993), p. 175.
32. Cited by A. H. Strong, *op. cit.*, p. 352, as the closing of his lengthy section on the Trinity.

14
The Triunity of the Godhead: Questions, Traditional Expressions, Illustrations, Values, Refinements, Cautions

Questions.

How shall we interpret certain puzzling statements in the Bible about the Persons of the triune God?

1. Why, if the Second Person is equal and co-eternal with the Father, is He very frequently called the 'Son of God'?

To many Christian people, especially new believers and the young, this seems to indicate that the Son had a beginning in time. It seems to them to say the Son is derived somehow from the Father. On the contrary, in Hebrew usage, 'son of', is used metaphorically, as often as not, to indicate something about the position, condition or nature of an object of discussion rather than its origin.

Hebrew and Arabic are related Semitic languages and express similar outlooks. In Arabic *abu* (father) and *bin* (son) and *um* (mother) are almost identical with Hebrew for father, son and mother. In modern Arabic these words are used daily for relationships which may have nothing to do with derivation, physical or otherwise, but describe a whole range of relationships. The Hebraic use of the Bible is similar.

Thus a literal rendering of the Hebrew of Genesis 7:6 says, 'Noah was a son of six hundred years', i.e. 600 years old. Similarly, James and John were 'Sons of Thunder', i.e. forceful in speech (though perhaps Jesus meant this facetiously), and so on. The people of Jesus' time understood Son of God to mean a divine person, not the offspring of God. So when Jesus accepted the accolade the Jew took up stones to stone Him for blasphemy (John 5:18), since they understood His claim but rejected it. 'Son of God' in such a context means simply, divine person, a person who is God. Of course, when Luke, in a different context of discourse, says 'Adam, the son of God' (Luke 3:38) or the book of Job that Satan came among the 'sons of God' (Job 1:6), something quite different is indicated.

2. What does *monogenēs* ('only begotten' in older Versions) mean when used of Christ's relation to the Father (John 1:14, 18; 3:16, 18 KJV; 1 John 4:9 KJV)?

'Only begotten' is a favourite expression of John, and only John with reference to Jesus. In English, 'begotten' appears to be related to the word 'beget', the function of a male parent in the conception of a child. The Greek word 'begotten' also is similar in form to the word 'beget'. A majority of recent scholars regard it as firmly established, however, that the Greek word *mono-gen-es* ('only begotten') is not directly related to the word *gennao*, 'to beget', but to *gen-ēs*, family, kind or class. *Monogenēs*, the word translated in older Versions 'only begotten', means only-one-of-its-kind. So at John 3:16 and the other texts cited above, 'only', or 'unique', is the true sense. NASB margin renders, 'unique, only one of His kind'; NIV has 'one and only'; and ESV, RSV and NEB 'only Son'. This is how I was taught to believe by professors strongly under the influence of B. F. Wescott.[1]

The teaching that the Son is eternally being begotten, that is, in some sense drawing his divine being from the Father's divine being, is therefore not necessarily correct, say advocates of the modern view, though many notable orthodox writers have affirmed it.

There has been a steady and, it seems, growing group of scholars who contend the old understanding of *monogenēs* as only begotten in the straightforward sense of the word is correct.[2] Buechsel shows the classical sense meant of sole descent, i.e. without brothers or sisters, and this is apparently how early Greek-speaking Christians interpreted the word, hence 'only begotten Son'. Buechsel affirms 'the word can also be used more generally without reference to derivation in the sense of "unique", "unparalleled", "incomparable"'.[3] In the New Testament, he says, 'it means "only begotten"' (no brothers or sisters) even in Hebrew 11:17, Luke 7:12 and Luke 8:42. Buechsel's evidences and arguments are quite convincing. David J. MacLeod[4] devotes twelve pages to comparing the views, leading one to think that the ancient Fathers, who surely understood their own language as well as nineteenth- and twentieth-century scholars with their grammar books and concordances, were probably correct – that Jesus is eternally the *monogenēs* (only begotten) Son of the Father, and that a distinction between filiation (see below) and paternity in the Godhead is justified.

3. In what sense is Christ the 'Firstborn' or 'first begotten' in Romans 8:29 and Hebrews 1:6?[5]

Again, Jewish custom and word-usage supply adequate answer. The first male child of a married couple was normally the heir. He had pre-eminent position and rights of primo-geniture in the family. So Christ is, of all God's creation, the one having pre-eminence. The term has nothing to say about the time of His origin. Note that 'This day have I begotten thee' (Acts 13:32, 33; cf. Ps. 2:7 KJV) is usually understood as referring to the resurrection of Christ, and as demonstrating, or publicly declaring, His Sonship to the Father. Another interpretation of Acts 13:32, 33 applies 'raised up' (KJV) to bringing the Messiah 'up', i.e. birth, life and the like.

Some Traditional Expressions.

Several expressions have been traditionally employed to designate certain inner relations between the Father and the Son, and the Father and Son with the Spirit. These expressions are the *eternal generation* of the Son by the Father and the *eternal spiration* (or *procession*) of the Spirit from the Father and the Son. They began to be employed about the time of the Council of Nicea (AD 325). They expressed in scriptural language the idea that the Son and the Spirit were eternally with the Godhead. John 1:14 (KJV) refers to our LORD as the 'only begotten' of the Father. John 14:16, 26 and 15:26 speak of the Spirit as proceeding from the Father and the Son; likewise He is called the Spirit of the Father (Matt. 10:20) as well.

According to the noted theologian of the Lutheran Church (Missouri Synod), Francis Pieper, these internal actions:

> are not common to all three Persons... but are ascribed only to one or two Persons. The generation of the Son is ascribed only to the Father, the spiration of the Holy Ghost only to the Father and the Son, and thereby the Father is revealed as a person distinct from the Son and the Holy Spirit as distinct from the Father and the Son... This terminology is not meaningless jargon, but necessary theological apparatus. Of course, Christians might wish that the Church would never have been troubled by Unitarians and therefore would have had no occasion to formulate this terminology [He mentions several very technical Latin terms]. Christians say with St. Paul: 'I would they were even cut off which trouble you' (Gal. 5:12). But... this terminology became necessary on account of the errors and the treachery of the heretics.[6]

1. *The Gospel According to St. John* and *The Epistles of St. John*.
2. *TWNT*, iv, 738.
3. ibid.
4. Art., 'The Trinity and Scripture' in *The Emmaus Journal*, 11, 2, Winter 2002, pp. 127 – 129.
5. Luke 2:7; Col. 1:5 and Rev. 1:5 present no problem.
6. Francis Pieper, *Church Dogmatics, i* (St. Louis: Concordia Publ., 1950), p. 416, 417.

Erroneous Views and Denials of the Trinity.

Since the second century, the usual way of introducing error into the church, in regard to the Trinity, has been openly to confess the Father, Son and Holy Spirit but to explain the confession in such a way as virtually to deny the orthodox doctrine. This most frequently has been done by affirming that the Three are manifestations *in time* of one Person who alone is God. God as united to and working through Jesus of Nazareth is Son; God as united to and working in the church is Spirit; in creating the heavens and earth He is Father. This was the 'modalism' or 'economic trinity' of Sabellius (fl. AD 250). Somewhat earlier a simpler modalism was called *monarchianism* (i.e. only one ruler or God) because it held that the one God-Father suffered in Christ in human form. This was also known as *patripassionism*.

Modalism, as discussed earlier, is still with us today. The notion that when God is creating He is called Father, when redeeming, Son, when comforting, Spirit, sounds so obviously correct that active-minded, intelligent people may even think of it without prompting — if they do not read *all* Scripture says about God, and forget what they learned in catechism or pastor's instruction class. This doctrine is patently unscriptural, rendering Jesus' many prayers to the Father ridiculous soliloquies and such scenes as the baptism of Jesus, with the descent of the dove and voice from heaven, impossible.

The more forthright error is that of Arius of Alexandria, condemned at the Council of Nicea AD 325. He held that both the Son and the Spirit were themselves created by the Father, who only is an eternal being. Revived in Reformation times, the Socinians of that period, like Arius, held that Christ should be worshiped. Servitus, an anti-Trinitarian of the epoch, was unfortunate enough to be burned at the stake for his views, even though he died with words of worship for Jesus on his lips. Unitarians of recent times have honoured Jesus but neither worship Him nor pray to or through Him. The so-called 'Jehovah's Witnesses' of our time aggressively distribute less-learned forms of Arianism to the doorsteps of millions around the world.

The intransigence of orthodox people on this teaching may seem strange in our extremely accommodating and compromising, undogmatic times. It may seem excessive, and the language of the creeds and confessions may seem unnecessarily harsh in condemnation. If so, the words of Galatians 5:12, quoted above, may be recalled in defence of the intransigence and the severity, likewise the following. 'No one who denies the Son has the Father' (1 John 2:23). '[E]very spirit that does not confess Jesus is not from God. This is the spirit of the antichrist' (1 John 4:3). 'If anyone has no love for the Lord, let him be accursed' (1 Cor. 16:22). Twice Paul pronounces the anathema on any who preach either a perverted or a contrary message as 'gospel' (Gal. 1:8, 9). These scriptural pronouncements are at least as severe as the creed of Nicea, which closes: 'And those that say "There was when he was not," and, "Before he was begotten he was not," and that, "He came into being from what-is-not," or those that allege, that the Son is "of another substance or essence" or "created", or "changeable" or "alterable", these the Catholic and Apostolic Church anathematizes.'[7]

We have a Christian duty to shun professed Christians who reject the human incarnation of true God in our Lord Jesus Christ. Second John 1:7-11 teaches this. Verses 10 and 11 are particularly demanding of us: 'If anyone comes to you and does not bring this teaching, do not receive him into your house or give him any greeting, for whoever greets him takes part in his wicked works.'

Illustrations and Analogies of the Trinity.

Illustrations of the Trinity, however helpful, are inevitably dangerous, for if carried beyond some very narrow area of the subject, they introduce denials of what must necessarily always remain a mystery. God cannot, of course, be one and three in the same sense. This is not the hard part. How can each person possess the whole being-essence-substance without dividing it or confusing themselves with one another? A friend of mine, and fellow Wheaton College professor, examined St Augustine's illustrations in *de Trinitate* (on the Trinity) and thought he found thirteen of them, all psychological and resting on the fact of mankind's bearing the image of God, which Augustine limited mainly to man's rational nature. His best one is the power of the soul to dialogue with itself.[8] 'I' ponder 'me' when I inwardly reflect on any question, then objectively in a kind of third capacity — the neutral spectator — I render a decision. This is a 'safe' illustration but the yield of understanding is small.

---

7. Henry Bettenson, *Documents of the Christian Church* (New York: Oxford Univ. Press, 1963), p. 36.
8. James Orr, *The Christian View of God and the World* (Grand Rapids: Eerdmans, 1947), pp. 217, 272.

Augustine was forty-six years old when he began to write *De Trimitate*, fifteen books[9], and he worked on it sporadically for sixteen years – some of his best mature years. Before his time many had addressed the subject and he read everything he could lay his hands on in Latin. Early in the treatise he offered a clear summary of the Catholic (everywhere, always, by all) doctrine of the Trinity. It is compact and so well expressed that it deserves quoting in full. This translation is not that in *NPNF* but by Vernon J. Bourke, a Roman Catholic scholar.

> All those Catholic interpreters of the Holy Scriptures, Old and New, whom I have been able to read, and who have written before me about the Trinity, Who is God, have agreed in the following teaching which is in accord with the Scriptures. The Father and the Son and the Holy Spirit, of one and the same substance, in an inseparable equality, constitute (*insinuent*) a divine unity. Therefore they are not three Gods, but one God; although the Father has generated the Son, and so He, Who is the Father, is not the Son. And the Son is generated by the Father, and so He, Who is the Son, is not the Father. And the Holy Spirit is neither the Father nor the Son, but the Spirit of the Father and the Son, yet Himself co-equal with the Father and Son and belonging to the unity of the Trinity. Not that this same Trinity was born of the Virgin Mary, and was crucified and buried, under Pontius Pilate, rose again on the third day, and ascended into Heaven – but only the Son. Nor did this same Trinity descend in the form of a dove, upon Jesus when He was baptized (*Matt. 3:16*); or, on Pentecost, after the ascension of the Lord, when there came a sound from Heaven, as of a violent wind coming, and they were each of the settled upon with parted tongues as of fire – this was solely the Holy Spirit (*Acts 2:2-4*). Nor did this same Trinity say from the Heavens, 'Thou art my Son,' either when He was baptized by John, or when the three disciples were with Him on the Mount (*Matt. 17:5*), or, when the voice sounded, saying, 'I have both glorified it, and I will glorify it again' (*John 12:28*); but that was only the voice of the Father, spoken to the Son; although the Father and the Son and the Holy Spirit, just as They exist inseparably, work inseparably. This is my faith, too, because this is the Catholic faith.[10]

This statement does not reflect cogitation of a philosopher but of a philosophically minded theologian,[11] one who proceeded to write seven 'books' on the scriptural basis for the Trinity doctrine before eight 'books' of speculative reflection. He spoke from the ground of Scripture to correct merely speculative, reason-based theology. In his opening sentence, Augustine says:

> The following dissertation concerning the Trinity, as the reader ought to be informed, has been written in order to guard against the sophistries of those who disdain to begin with faith, and are deceived by a crude and perverse love of reason.[12]

A favourite illustration (or analogy) of the Trinity since the Middle Ages is water (one *substance*), present somewhere on earth in purity but in three forms at all times; that is to say, it exists in three *modes*, liquid, solid (ice) and gas (vapour). This illustration, which seems to clarify everything, quickly leads to denial of any Trinity at all in favour of Sabellian modalism.

The favourite source for analysis as to the Trinity has been the nature of mankind. As frequently noted before in this chapter, Calvin began his *Institutes* with analogies between mankind and God, though mainly with reference to the single being of God not His threefoldness (*Dreifaltegkeit*, as the German ponderously expresses it). However, from Augustine onward to Edwards (who wrote an essay from the same outlook), man himself, in his non-physical side usually, but sometimes including his body, has seemed to some the probable key to understanding the mystery. Even the gifted English playwright and author of detective stories, Dorothy L. Sayers, tried her hand at this approach (*The Mind of the Maker*). Perhaps there is something to taunt the curious here in the rebellious youth both of Sayers and Augustine. At any rate Sayers's effort prompted one of her youthful neighbours, after he became an Anglican prelate, to carry her argument into scholarly parlance with a bit of verve.[13]

Nature pretty well fails to provide an illustration of the Trinity that does not also lead to error if followed seriously. Two diagrams have been widely accepted. The equilateral triangle, each side equal (Father, Son, Holy Spirit), each 'containing' the triangle (God), is as good as any common figure. But do the sides each contain the whole? The 'Shield of the Trinity' is the best diagram so far proposed. The ancient form of it, in which the writing, all in Latin, is here translated. It merits study.

---

9. 424 columns in *NPNF* 3.
10. Vernon J. Bourke, *Augustine's Quest of Wisdom* (Milwaukee: Bruce Publ., 1947), p. 204.
11. ibid., p. 203.
12. Augustine, *On the Trinity* i.1.1, *NPNF* 3.17.
13. John Thurmer, Chancelor of Exeter Cathedral, *A Detection of the Trinity* (Exeter: The Paternoster Press, 1984), 93 pages.

The Shield of the Trinity.

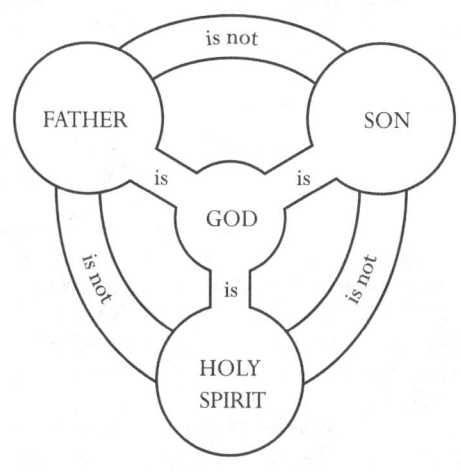

(Diagram: Father — is not — Son; Father — is — God; Son — is — God; Father — is not — Holy Spirit; Son — is not — Holy Spirit; Holy Spirit — is — God.)

There are many other illustrations. The inadequacies and dangers in them all underscore the essential, necessary, ineluctable mystery of the Trinity. It is a revelation. Like all revelations of God, Himself and His miraculous works – His eternity, omniscience, omnipotence, the creation of the world, future resurrection and judgment of all humanity – we know they are true, because God has told us about them. We carry rational understanding as far as our powers of thought and limitations of information take us, but ultimately we must stop in the presence of inscrutable mystery.

Values of the Doctrine.

1. The triunity of God suggests an answer to the ancient question, 'What was God doing before He created the world?' He was not preparing hell, as one facetious wag in Augustine's time suggested, for the over-curious, but engaged in loving, interpersonal intercourse within the Godhead. This may carry anthropopathism too far. It is a suggestion, not dogma.

2. 'It would be impossible', writes Buswell, 'for our minds to grasp all of these facts centering in the atoning work of Christ, except in terms of the Triune Godhead. "For God [the Father] so loved the world that he gave his only begotten Son… that whosoever believeth in him [through the conviction and enabling of the Holy Spirit] should not perish"', etc. (John 3:16).

3. In an age of social emphasis in all realms of learning and action, a triad of persons rather than a monad gives greater appeal to the Christian faith.

The value really cannot be overestimated. Christianity is in every way a Trinitarian faith.

Definitions.

The Nicene Creed.

Many readers of this book do not attend churches where formal, explicit creeds are employed in instruction and worship. The Nicene Creed, as enlarged at Constantinople (381) and approved at Chalcedon (451) and as it is usually employed in Protestant churches, is therefore supplied as follows:

> I believe in one God the Father Almighty; Maker of heaven and earth, and of all things visible and invisible.
> And in one Lord Jesus Christ, the only-begotten son of God, begotten of the Father before all worlds, God of God, Light of Light, very God of very God, begotten, not made, being of one substance with the Father; by whom all things were made; who, for us men and for our salvation, came down from heaven and was incarnate by the Holy Ghost of the Virgin Mary, and was made man; and was crucified also for us under Pontius Pilate; he suffered and was buried; and the third day he rose again, according to the Scriptures; and ascended into heaven, and sitteth on the right hand of the Father; and he shall come again, with glory, to judge both the quick and the dead; whose kingdom shall have no end.

And I believe in the Holy Ghost, the LORD and Giver of Life; who proceedeth from the Father and the Son; who with the Father and the Son together is worshiped and glorified, who spoke by the prophets. And I believe in one Holy Catholic and Apostolic Church. I acknowledge one baptism for the remission of sins; and I look for the resurrection of the dead, and the life of the world to come. Amen.

The Definition of Chalcedon.

The Definition of Chalcedon, in recent translation, as it appears in *Documents of the Christian Church*, Henry Bettenson now follows:

> Therefore, following the holy Fathers [of AD 381 and 325], we all with one accord teach men to acknowledge one and the same Son, our Lord Jesus Christ, at once complete in Godhead and complete in manhood, truly God and truly man, consisting also of a reasonable soul and body; of one substance [*homoousios*] with the Father as regards his Godhead, and at the same time of one substance with us as regards his manhood; like us in all respects, apart from sin; as regards his Godhead, begotten of the Father before the ages, yet as regards his manhood begotten, for us men and for our salvation, of Mary the Virgin, the God-bearer [*theotokos*]; one and the same Christ, Son, Lord, Only-begotten, recognized in two natures, without confusion, without change, without division, without separation; the distinction of natures being in no way annulled by the union, but rather the characteristics of each nature being preserved and coming together to form one person and subsistence [*hypostasis*], not as parted or separated into two persons, but one and the same Son and Only-begotten God the Word, Lord Jesus Christ; even as the prophets from earliest times spoke of him, and our Lord Jesus Christ himself taught us, and the creed of the Fathers has handed down to us.[14]

An important and influential book by R. J. Rushdoony,[15] shows how this definition of the Trinity is the philosophical-theological-practical foundation of Western civilization.

Inner Ontic Relations of the Triune God.

We understand that God is eternal, existing always before He created the universe, now and ever into the future. Time exists in Him, not the other way around. Furthermore, God is 'blessed forever', 'blessed and only Potentate' with or without a creation, being under no necessity to do anything external to Himself – ever the only living and loving, active and knowing God, subsisting in three modes known in Scripture as Father, Son and Holy Spirit. Thoughtful Christians must ask, 'What was God doing eternally? What is the inner relation of Father, Son and Holy Spirit?'

I fear that popular thinking about this question runs somewhat to the notion of a happy family, father, mother and offspring, as an answer. In post-Reformation times Jacob Boehme, Count Zinzendorf and Emmanuel Swedenborg put it just that way. The error is not quite innocent, but a harmful distortion, leading easily to merely sentimental, maudlin expressions of devotion and worship. The church seems always supplied with simple-minded, over-helpful, self-appointed teachers who furnish easily understood, cozy formulas to replace necessarily severe, distinct definitions. Some of these people organize themselves into translation committees that produce paraphrases masquerading as faithful translations. Thus, the doctrine of election has been expunged from one so-called Version.

After all, not quite everything in theology and the Bible can be made perfectly simple; the Trinity of God is a great biblical mystery, utterly incommensurable with the created social setting whereby God chose for the human race to live together in small family units, to be fruitful, multiply and nourish itself. Late patristic theology employed the Latin word *circumcessio*, Greek, *perichorēsis*, meaning mutual interpenetration, for mutual relations of the Trinity of Father, Son and Holy Spirit. The main idea in this construction is that each 'person', while retaining its own special identity, is mutually 'penetrated' (for want of a better term) by the other two. Several Roman Catholic theologians argue from these notions that the Trinity is a model for good family life and other social and political relationships. I have already expressed disapproval of all such efforts as pressing analogies and likenesses too far. In truth, all the terms *perechorēsis* and *circumcessio* provide is names for our ignorance (hardly biblical mystery) in an exalted area of reality too high for us likely ever to learn anything about.

---

14. Bettenson, *op. cit.*, p. 73.
15. R. J. Rushdoony, *Foundations of Social Order*, (P and R Publ. Co., 1968.)

Heroes of Trinitarian Theology.

The churches of the East (Greek-speaking) and of the West (Latin-speaking) after Nicea (AD 325), and for several generations, refined a set of terms and understanding of them that defined orthodox belief regarding the internal, eternal relations of the triune God. This, as we have noted in earlier pages, passed on through medieval times, was accepted by the Reformers, both Lutheran and Reformed, as well as by Roman Catholic scholars of the time. That same orthodoxy was passed on to the Protestant denominations of America and is standard for all today. The Trinity is still (with the incarnation) the central mystery of Christianity. Though we do not end statements of doctrines with, 'Let him be anathema', any longer, it is true that no one has a right to claim the name Christian who varies in any serious way from these definitions. This is true because they are firstly, biblical; secondly, they spell out in necessary rational ways how the Bible ought to be understood; and thirdly, they represent what the church through the ages has believed, taught, confessed and expressed in hymn and liturgy. The theology of orthodoxy is the doctrine of the churches' hymnbooks, lectionaries, printed liturgies, sermons and manuals for instruction.

We ought to honour the saintly, thoughtful and courageous men of God who pounded out those expositions which led to the Athanasian (so-called) and Chalcedonian reformulations of Nicea. Precedence of honour should go to Athanasius (died AD 373), whose chequered career at Alexandria was a life of sharp conflict with errors. 'Athanasius against the world' is a proverbial expression. Athanasius was a fervent and consistent advocate of the Nicene theology during the critical first forty years when there was great opposition – even among some dissembling clergy who had voted for it in AD 325. We have already devoted some attention to Augustine of Hippo, whose long life ended in AD 430, shortly before the Council of Chalcedon. He benefited from predecessors whose work he consciously summarized and perfected for the Western church all that preceded in his great work, *De Trinitate* (concerning the Trinity), composed in the years 400–418/19.

Special honour goes to three contemporary clergymen of Cappadocia. They are Gregory of Nazianzus (died AD 389), Basil the Great, bishop of Caesarea in Cappadocia (died AD 389), and Basil's brother Gregory, bishop of Nyssa (died 395). Recent studies point out how the latter two were influenced and instructed by their oldest sister, Macrina.

> To the three Cappadocians should be added as 'the Fourth Cappadocian', Macrina (the younger)... named for their grandmother... Not only was she, according to Gregory's accounts, a Christian model for both of them by her profound and ascetic spirituality, but at the death of their parents she became the educator of the entire family, and that in both Christianity and Classical culture. Through her philosophy and theology, Macrina was even the teacher of both of her brothers, who were bishops and theologians, 'sister and teacher at the same time' [*he adelphe kai didaskalos*], as Gregory calls her... Adolph von Harnack once characterized *The Life of Macrina* by Gregory of Nyssa as 'perhaps the dearest and purest expression of the spirituality of the Greek Church'.[16]

The three Cappadocians are remembered particularly for defining the relation of the Holy Spirit to the Godhead. They are commonly regarded as being among the chief artisans of terms and architects of the final form of the doctrine of the Trinity, especially as regards the relations of the three 'subsistences' to one another within the one 'essence' of God as well as external relations. It is customary to call the former the *immanent* or *ontological* relations of the Trinity and the latter *external*, *emanent* or *economic* relations.

Jaroslav Pelikan pays special honour to Bernard of Clairvaux in defining the mysteries of the incarnation and the Holy Trinity.[17] For Bernard, says Pelikan, 'The Trinitarian confession was fundamental not only to Christian faith, but also to Christian life, for each person of the Trinity has a special relation to the disciple of Christ'.[18] Further, for Bernard, 'The doctrine of the Trinity was not a speculative construct, or an exercise in dialectical subtlety, but a soteriological necessity'.[19]

Final Words of Caution About the Vocabulary of Trinitarian Theology.

The distinctive 'personal' features of each of the three are best not called attributes, but *properties*. The three 'persons' are said to be 'three modes of subsistence' or 'of existence' of the Godhead. The word *mode* here has no reference to the false notion that Father, Son and Holy Spirit are three modes by which a 'unitarian' God makes Himself known

---

16. Jaroslav Pelikan, *Christianity and Classical Culture* (New Haven: Yale Univ. Press, 1993), p. 8.
17. *The Growth of Medieval Theology 600 – 1300, vol. ii* of *The Christian Tradition*, pp. 144 – 151.
18. ibid., p. 145.
19. ibid., p. 146.

or acts in creation and redemption. *Mode* in the sense approved here has continuous precedents going clear back to the immediate post-Nicene period.

Latin terms employed for the sense in which God is one, anglicized or translated, are *essence*, *substance*, *nature* and our word *being*. In the East, the Greeks preferred the word *ousia* that means being and *physis*, which is translated *nature*. Each of these words is necessary in precise discussion of the doctrine of God to the present day. Otherwise, we have no clear language to answer the current heresies such as denial of the Trinity in 'Jehovah's Witnesses' and perversion of it in Mormonism – to say nothing of liberalism.

Terms for the sense in which the Godhead is three were, in the West, mainly *persona* or person and *subsistence*. Though the word came to mean role or part played in a drama, *persona* is literally the Latin word for a mask representing an individual played by an actor. Later *subsistence* was used in the same sense as person or even 'mode of subsistence' by orthodox authors.

On 'Person' in Trinitarian Definition.

It is to stand history of language on its head, however, to begin our understanding of the three divine 'persons' with contemporary understanding of what a person or personality is. In veritable fact the word entered the English language from the ancient Christian use of the Latin word *persona*, meaning the mask which actors (always male) in Roman dramatic plays put over their faces to represent the individual man or woman or other being portrayed by the actor. *Persona* in Latin translates Greek *prosopon* (face), the idea being that the *face* or similitude of a priest, a farmer, a beautiful maiden, or a dog or donkey indicated the part being played by the actor who played it.

The idea that certain 'attributes of personality' (emotion, intellect, will or whatever) or 'centre of consciousness' as we think of today as constituting a person or personality did not belong to the word originally at all.

So the creedal formula 'one nature, or substance; three persons or hypostases' does not, in first instance, mean three centres of individual consciousness such as father, mother and child in a family of three.

According to the *Oxford English Dictionary* person was 'in earliest use, the human being acting in some capacity, personal agent or actor, person concerned' (Compact Ed., p. 2140). The first occurrence cited by the *Oxford English Dictionary* dates to AD 1225 in which it indicated 'an individual human being, a man, woman or child', as distinguished from a thing or animal: that is, a man or woman of distinction. Apparently the latter is about the sense of James (with respect of persons, *en prosopolempsiais*, James 2:21 KJV) and Peter (1 Peter 1:17) 'without respect of persons'. The Greek elements mean, 'to receive the face (*prosopon*) of someone', and so in the Old Testament, where often the word 'person' translates the Hebrew word for face (Lev. 19:15; Deut. 1:17; Ps. 82:2).

The *Oxford English Dictionary* also, very briefly, defines person 'in general philosophical sense; a self-conscious or rational being' and the only quotations are from Christian theological discourse, specifically creeds and dogma.

So, let us heartily sympathize with Augustine in his dilemma. One of the finest American authors of the history of doctrine said:

> Respecting the Trinity, Augustine insists on the divine unity. His mode of presenting this doctrine is in contrast with that of Gregory of Nyssa and the later Nicaeans, and is akin to that adopted by Athanasius. The distinction of persons is limited to their relation to one another. There is but one substance or essence, and when we speak of 'three persons', it is only because we lack words to express the distinction between the Father and the Son, and between the Holy Ghost and the Father and the Son. 'Certainly there are Three'... Yet when it is asked, what Three, human language labors from great poverty of speech. We say 'three persons', not that it may be so said, but that we may not keep silence.[20]

'Person' had none of the psychological overtones it now has – a cause of considerable misunderstanding among uninstructed Christians who want to think of the Godhead as three members of a cozy family. In the Greek East the word was *hypostasis*. Unhappily that word would normally be rendered *substance* (what stands under), the Latin word for the one nature of the one God. It is no wonder it took half a century to clear up communication between East and West after Nicea.

The distinctive personal *property* (not attribute) of the Father is said to be, of course, *paternity*. This has reference negatively to the fact that He has 'unbegottenness,' (Gr. *agennēsia*, not to be confused with *agenēsia*, which means without beginning, possessed by each member of the Trinity). Therefore, there was confusion over that too. It was held that His relation to the Son is eternally that of Father. The Son has been eternally begotten by the Father – no

---

20. George Park Fisher, *History of Christian Doctrine*, 2nd ed. (Edinburgh: T. & T. Clark, 1896, 1927), p. 178. The quote from Augustine in *De Trin* V. i. 9.

reference to the incarnation. Moreover, begotten does not mean 'created', for the Son has the same eternal nature as the Father.

The distinctive property of the Son is said to be filiation, from Latin *filius*, son, hence being a Son. This indicates a precedence of the Father to the Son in their eternal relation.[21] The Father-Son relation (1) is an act of divine spirit; (2) implies the Father and the Son are of the same essence; and (3) is an eternal generation.

Since the Holy Spirit is said in Scripture to proceed from the Father (John 15:26) and the Son (John 14:26), His distinct property is eternal *procession*. Sometimes the word *spiration* is used. Procession from the Father and the Son is His distinctive property, though there is not unbroken assent to the Spirit's *procession* from 'the Son'.

These terms will not appeal to everyone. We do not live in a very reflective age. Even the ancient Christian scholars who first employed them in theology had difficulty at first in explaining them fully to one another and in keeping them straight. The special vocabulary was nevertheless necessary to keep the church from returning to polytheism, pantheism, dualism and Judaism in its doctrines, even while using scriptural words and phrases in sermons, hymns and prayers. They are no less necessary in our age of impatience.

---

21. 'A Defence of the Doctrine of the Eternal Subordination of the Son', by Stephen D. Dovach and Peter R. Schemm, Jr, *Journal of the Evangelical Theological Society*, vol. 42, no. 3, pp. 461–476, traces the rather steady support of this variety of 'subordinationism' in the imminent Trinity – as opposed to the economic Trinity – from earliest times to the present. Feminist theologians dislike it because they think it supports the principle of subordination of authority of wives to husbands. Millard Erickson and J. O. Buswell are recent theologians who quite exceptionally reject any precedence of the Father to the Son.

15
Predestination or the Decrees of God: God's Eternal Plan for the Heavens and the Earth, Part I

Introduction.

Let us begin this most difficult section where W. G. T. Shedd, one of the most skilled and devout exponents of Augustinian theology, ended: with a caution against exposure to the doctrine of predestination, or the decrees of God.[1] As every theologian ought to know, after Jesus Himself Paul made the strongest statements on the subject of predestination in the New Testament. Hence, we understand Peter's remarks:

> Our beloved brother Paul, according to the wisdom given him, wrote to you [think here of Romans 9–11], as also in all his letters, speaking in them of these things, in which are some things hard to understand, which the untaught and unstable distort, as they do also the rest of the Scriptures, to their own destruction (2 Peter 3:15, 16 NASB).

Nothing among the 'things hard to understand' of Paul's letters presents more difficulty to the 'untaught and unstable' than his remarks about God's sovereign government of people, plans and things in Romans 9–11 and Ephesians 1–3. The same spiritually untutored folk of rural Palestine had similar difficulties with Jesus' parables (Matt. 13:14, 15), as he explained: 'To you it has been given to know the secrets of the kingdom of heaven, but to them it has not been given' (Matt. 13:11).

Nothing in the scheme of Christian doctrine is so offensive to the secular spirit or so preposterous to the unbelieving mind as to propose that God has a plan for the whole universe down to such minute details as the hairs on one's head or the death of a sparrow (Matt. 10:29, 30) and is unfailingly executing the same.

Yet the fact that God 'worketh all things according to the counsel of his will' is an important article of 'the whole counsel of God' and of great 'consolation and satisfaction... to believers... properly understood... Hence we think that this doctrine should be neither suppressed from a preposterous modesty nor curiously pried into by rash presumption.'[2] It was Albrecht Bengel, no less, who cautioned, 'Man must not attempt to look at God behind the scenes.'[3]

As this study develops it will become clear that God's government of the world is controlled by a plan. God's government of His creation is what theologians call *providence* and the plan that providence executes is called *predestination*, or the doctrine of the *decrees* of God.

---

1. W. G. T. Shedd, *Dogmatic Theology I* (Grand Rapids: Zonderdan, 1969), pp. 459–461.
2. Francis Turretin, *Institutes of Elenctic Theology I*, trans. G. M. Geger (Phillipsburg, NJ: PR Publ., reprint 1992), p. 329.
3. Cited by Shedd, *op. cit.*, p. 461.

These doctrines are the first and last elements of 'the Christian View of God and the World', to borrow the title of an important book.[4] Simply put: (1) God *planned* the world, (2) God *created* the world, (3) God *sustains* the world and (4) God *governs* the world. These four propositions constitute the primary elements of the biblical world-view, or *Weltanschauung* of German academic idiom.

Theologians have long wished they could dispense with the words 'decrees' and 'predestination' in connection with the divine plan because of their offence to the post-enlightenment outlook that thinks the world runs (whether well or badly) quite without God. As for origin (or first cause) in an intelligent design, though obvious to many, is quite unacceptable to the academic elite of today; it is certainly very controversial. However, controversy seems forever to have been the seedbed of progress in Christian thought and no generation where Christian zeal flourishes has ever been without it.[5] Controversy need not be vituperative. Among believing scholars it can be both genial and vigorous.

Further, as we shall see, nothing is more assuring for believers, in a dangerous world where earthly hope is sure to run out, than certainty God's determinate will is being done. In the natural order 'seedtime and harvest, cold and heat, summer and winter, day and night' will not be interrupted 'While the earth remains' (Gen. 8:22). 'You [God] rule the raging of the sea' (Ps. 89:9). God 'shut in the sea... and said ,"Thus far shall you come, and no farther"' (Job 38:8-11). As for 'the slings and arrows of outrageous fortune' – Hamlet spoke as a suicidal weakling, not with the calm assurance of Moses 'the man of God' (Josh. 14:6). 'The eternal God is your dwelling place, and underneath are the everlasting arms' (Deut. 33:27).

The biblical-theological basis of the *Weltanschauung* (world-view) we are introducing has been neglected, hence not fully understood by the mass of believers in our time. People in the grip of the *Zeitgeist* (spirit of the age, to employ another useful term of German academics) do not know about the doctrine and would reject it if they did. How can the moguls of the media, the wiseacres of the university chairs and the denizens of our courts, get this matter straight if we ourselves do not know of 'the decrees of God', meaning 'that eternal plan by which God has rendered certain all the events of the universe, past, present and future'?[6] Every person on this planet should know about God's purpose and plan.

Refinements and Limitations.

Still preliminary to development of God's decrees, creation, preservation and providence, several refinements and limitations of relevance must enter the record.

1. 'The sovereignty of God' may be said to include both decrees and providence, for it is 'the biblical teaching that God is king, supreme ruler, and lawgiver of the entire universe'.[7] 'The LORD has established his throne in the heavens, and his kingdom rules over all' (Ps. 103:19). Some of God's names considered earlier express that sovereign rule – God Almighty, LORD God Almighty, *et al*.

2. Several of God's attributes of immensity, viz., omnipotence, omnipresence, and, especially, omniscience, imply that God planned the heavens and earth which He then created and now sustains and will guide to their predestined goal. As omniscient, God is fully aware of all that goes on, precisely because He is present everywhere in creation (omnipresence) and has potency (omnipotence) to direct it all to the consummation.

3. Though the decrees of God are matters internal to the Godhead, they have reference to things *external* to God, in no wise emerging or emanating from His essence (being). *Internally*, as we have already seen, theologians say the Father is distinct in the sense of *paternity*; the Son in the sense of *filiation* (being a son); the Spirit in the sense of *spiration*. These terms are names theology has used for mysteries no one really understands. The ideas of the Son as being begotten (eternally), and the Spirit as proceeding (eternally) from the Father and the Son, have the benefit of scriptural phraseology, but probably apply not to inner (imminent), Trinitarian relations but to *economic* (i.e. *ad extra*, outside the being of God) relations to the world of creation and redemption. The creedal phrase 'very God of [*ek*, out of] very God', was employed by the Fathers of Nicea and Constantinople (AD 325, 381) to mean an eternal begetting of the Son by the Father; it was to stem the challenge of Sabellianism – that the Trinity is only three modes of acting by the one divine person.[8]

---

4. James Orr, *The Christian View of God and the World*.
5. See the article 'Controversy' in *Baker's Dictionary of Theology* (Grand Rapids: Baker Books, 1960).
6. A. H. Strong, *Systematic Theology* (Old Tappen, NJ: Revell, 1907), p. 353.
7. 'Sovereignty of God' *Evangelical Dictionary of Theology*, ed. Walter Elwell (Grand Rapids: Baker books, 1984), p. 1038.
8. Robert L. Reymond, *A New Systematic Theology of the Christian Faith* (Nashville: Thos. Nelson, 1998), pp. 321–341.

4. After reading again many treatments of the subject in revising the manuscript for this chapter, it became apparent that theologians of Arminian persuasion speak approvingly of providence, God's control and government of the world, but refer to His plan only obliquely. Thomas Oden, a Methodist scholar, plainly believes God planned the world He created, though he furnishes no category such as predestination or decrees. He is aware of the vast body of Old Testament Scripture that grounds 'the Reformed Doctrine of Predestination' (the title of L. Boettner's book). Yet Oden writes extensively of Providence as executing such a plan. I furnish some quotations from his book, *The Living God*. Throughout this whole historical process is God's own guiding directing activity. Each of billions of events has its own *telos*, or 'purpose', at any given moment. *Seen in the light of the scriptural revelation of God's providential activity* [emphasis added], all of this is moving toward a plausible, trustable end: the fulfilment of God's purpose in creation'.[9]

The great value of Oden's work is the introduction he lavishly provides to theology of the past. He aims, however, at a 'consensus' theology, which perhaps explains why the best supporting writings for a detailed divine plan for the universe (decrees) never appear.

> On those particular points on which otherwise highly respected patristic writers tend to diverge from the more central ancient ecumenical consensus (e.g. Origenist views that the power of God is limited or that the stars have souls, or Novatian's view of the exclusion of the lapsed, or Gregory of Nyssa's universalism, or some of Augustine's views of election and reprobation), I will be less prone to quote them, but I will quote freely from their writings that have been widely received.[10]

As one reads Oden at length it is clear that he believes God has a detailed plan, much as Calvin explained it, but cannot bring himself to say so plainly, preferring rather for the reader to infer it from the doctrine of providence. In elaborating the truth that God as Creator 'remains the one source and end of time' he comes close to articulating a doctrine of 'the decrees of God' worthy of any Calvinist. Oden goes on:

> One might say that something 'occurred' in the mind of God before creation – namely, God chose to love the world and *decreed that a world should be* [emphasis added]. God had eternity in which many different creations would have been conceived.[11]

Richard Watson, first systematic theologicial interpreter of Wesley's form of Arminian theology, published his massive *Theological Institutes* 'neither Calvinistic on the one hand, nor Pelagian on the other' (from the 'Advertisement to the London Edition' of 1823). A sympathetic assessment would describe Watson's position as semi-Augustinian rather than (as unfortunately some say) 'semi-Pelagian'. While specifically rejecting the doctrine of decrees and the reigning Calvinistic scheme of his day, Watson made a strong affirmation of 'total inability' but also held that God had *graciously*, through Christ's universally effective atonement, restored to every human being both the ability and the obligation to believe unto salvation.[12] Watson does not seem to distinguish between the doctrine of decrees and the doctrine of election, which is a *soteriological* doctrine not to be confused with God's decrees concerning the whole creation.

5. Discussion of predestination usually tends quickly to the topic of divine election, a subject related to the redeemed alone. For reasons that shall appear later, let us not mix *soteriology* (the topic of salvation) with the doctrine of God, theology proper. At present, our focus is on God, not mankind. Election deals with mankind as fallen, not as created (Sublapsarian not Supralapsarian). In the decrees, our thoughts are directed to God's created, sustained and governed uinverse wherein nothing is strange to God's eternal plan and purpose. A. H. Strong is almost alone among American theologians in seeing the pedagogical importance of the order of treatment.[13]

As predestination relates to salvation of individuals the problems discussed have ever been the same. In periods when the arguments are discussed controversially by *genuine evangelicals* they usually have led through the following steps.

All agree that in the fall of Adam human nature had lost its normal spiritual powers and could regain them only by grace. To Augustinians it seems incongruous therefore 'at one and the same time to assert that grace was necessary because of original sin and yet to reject the corollary doctrine of predestination' – i.e. that we have no power to choose Christ until imparted sufficient spiritual power to do so (1 Cor. 2:14).[14] The evangelical opponents

---

9. Thomas Oden, *The Living God* (San Francisco: Harper Collins, 1992), p. 287.
10. ibid., p. xii.
11. ibid., pp. 261, 262.
12. Richard Watson, *Theological Institutes vol. ii* (New York: G. Lane & P. B. Sanford, 1843) pp. 381 – 448.
13. A. H. Strong, *op. cit.*, pp. 355, 779 – 790.
14. Jaroslav Pelikan, *The Christian Tradition, i* (Chicago: Univ. Of Chicago Press, 1971), p. 319 also pp. 297, 298, 302, 303, 215 – 218, 327 – 330.

of Augustinian thought, while acknowledging inability, might propose a sufficient remnant of ability to co-operate or at least not resist, or sufficient power of reason and will remaining to turn to God. Others posit, as a matter of divine justice, a *universal restoration* of power to believe if one wills to do so. Arminius did that. Wesley and his followers derive from Arminius the doctrine of universal restoration of power to repent and believe, but say it is by God's grace (not as with Arminius a matter of justice) effected by Christ's atonement, He being 'the true light… coming into the world… which enlightens everyone'.[15]

6. No personality of Scripture narrative and authorship is more decisively articulate on the subject than Paul. I think we may assign two causes as to why. The first is the manner of his conversion. He had execrated the very name of Jesus while vigorously persecuting, even murdering, those who dared to believe on His name. However, God stopped him abruptly in his tracks, instantly changing the hardened heart of the grand inquisitor to the suppliant believer. This his friend Luke faithfully, and in detail, reported. The initiative to save Paul's soul and make an apostle of him did not originate in Saul of Tarsus. If ever there was a clear case of *pre*-destination, divine choosing, it was his, and Paul never tired of testifying to that fact and applying the principle of predestination onward from the personal to everything else under the highest heaven.

The second reason was vividly set forth by Francis Davidson, a Scottish professor in a lecture to the InterVarsity Fellowship:

> The doctrine of predestination is Pauline only in the sense that it fell to the lot of the great apostle to the Gentiles to develop it to its height. It is a mistake to think that Paul originated the doctrine, or wandered into a bypath of revelation as he matured its truth. The Rabbi of Tarsus inherited the very spirit of the doctrine from the teaching of his race. The Old Testament Scriptures are infused with the breath of the sovereignty of almighty God, who is so exalted as first cause in his own universe, that second causes are of immaterial account. God is in intimate contact with all events, and nothing lies outside His holy and wise control. Every happening is the expression of the divine will. The voice of the Lord is heard on land and sea and in the sky, 'the Lord sitteth king forever' (Ps. 29). The prophet, like the psalmist, is equally God-conscious and even dares to postulate the emergence of evil to the all-embracing and absolute will of God. 'Shall there be evil in a city, and the Lord hath not done it'? (Amos 3:6). It is so in the warp and woof of the Old Testament writings, all of which were in the heritage of the apostle Paul.[16]

When this study takes up election as an aspect of soteriology (the doctrine of salvation) we shall devote further attention to Paul's theology of predestination.

7. Our procedure at this point might trace the notion of divine predestination through the two Testaments and conclude with summaries in the inductive manner of some 'biblical theology'. In order, however, to be as brief as possible within bounds of adequacy of treatment, I shall bring the fruits of inductive biblical studies to a structural form of statement. The subject of predestination had already been widely discussed by Christian teachers before Augustine gave the subject extended statement – both as positive doctrine and in polemical writings against Pelagius and his disciples.

8. As handled by skilful advocates, providence is the companion of predestination. It is addressed *first to believers* as supreme comfort in and among the unavoidable difficulties of life and, *secondly to others*, simply as a wonderful fact of existence. John Flavel, a Puritan preacher who survived the Stuart 'Restoration' of 1660, published *The Mystery of Providence* in 1678 as a sort of manual of Christian discipline in holiness and comfort in tribulation. He lived on until 'the Glorious Revolution' of 1688 bestowed the crown on William and Mary, February 13, 1688 (in time to have a college in Virginia named for them). Preaching at the national celebration of this victory over the papal forces of Europe and Britain, John Flavel (one of the few surviving Puritan preachers) observed what he called, 'a remarkable coincidence'.

He said that in 1588 England had experienced a signal deliverance from Roman Catholicism.

> The mighty armada of Spain, sent to dethrone the Protestant Elizabeth and restore her people to the 'old faith', had been blasted by the winds and waves. A hundred years had passed, Flavel reminded his hearers, 'Yet behold another Eighty-eight [1688] crowned and enriched with mercies, no less admirable and glorious than the former.' Another attempt to subjugate England to the yoke of Rome had been thwarted by the Providence of God.[17]

---

15. This matter will be given fuller treatment in 'Part 5: Soteriology: Salvation Applied'.
16. Francis Davidson, *Pauline Predestination* (London: The Tyndale Press, 1946, 1964), p. 3.
17. Michael Boland in 'Publisher's Introduction' to John Flavel's, *The Mystery of Providence* (London: Banner of Truth Trust, republished 1963), p. 7.

It is important to note that decrees and providence must be present in any thinking about ultimate questions by orthodox theologians. As noted earlier, Thomas Oden, a Methodist theologian, makes no formal place for 'decrees' or 'predestination' in his construal of 'the Works of God'.[18] Yet he felt compelled several times almost subliminally to introduce the subject of decrees. I quote the first.

> If theology is to speak of the God of history, there must be a stage on which history is played out. There is redemptive *intent* from the beginning in creation, so there is a subtle sense in which God's redemptive *purpose* is prior to God's creative *purpose* [emphasis added] (1 Cor. 2:7; 2 Tim. 1:9; Titus 1:2; Rev. 13:8; John 1:1-20; Eph. 1:5-11; Barth, *CD 2/2*). But there is a less subtle sense in which creation is prior to redemption, for how could one have something to redeem if something does not exist.[19]

Though as a presumed Wesleyan he carefully avoids the traditional terms 'predestination' and 'decrees', he employs the terms *intent* and *purpose*, thus introducing the ideas of predestination and decrees and even the question of the order of the decrees – whether Supralapsarian or Infralapsarian. Further he makes reference to Barth's volume (*Church Dogmatics 2/2*) wherein 'Barth emphasizes the freedom, mystery and righteousness of God's predestinating will', etc. – showing that Dr Oden is fully aware of the subtlety.[20]

The Biblical Doctrine of Predestination.

In this and the next chapter, let us try to subsume the biblical teaching of divine decrees, or predestination, under a series of propositions.

The Bible Teaches that God Planned the World.

The word 'plan' presents a better face to the reader because the singular number (decree, not decrees) excludes the implication of possible alternate courses for the world in God's mind and it neither suggests nor implies arbitrariness or hesitancy on God's part. God was and is in charge and knows exactly what course the cosmos He made should and will take. Let us observe several realities.

The Bible Employs Many Direct Statements about God's Plan.

The Bible furnishes many direct statements that *in context* as well as form of statement teach that God has a fixed plan for all creation. The notion that assumes 'the serious intentions of God may in some cases be defeated, and that man, who is not only a creature but a sinful creature, can exercise veto power over the plans of Almighty God' contrasts starkly with all these texts, which I shall now enter as they appeared in the first book I ever read on the subject of systematic theology.[21]

> [H]e does according to his will among the host of heaven and among the inhabitants of the earth; and none can stay his hand or say to him, 'What have you done?' (Dan. 4:35).
> Ah, Lord GOD! It is you who has made the heavens and the earth by your great power and by your outstretched arm! Nothing is too hard for you (Jer. 32:17).
> All authority in heaven and on earth has been given to me [Christ] (Matt. 28:18).
> And he put all things under his feet and gave him as head over all things to the church (Eph. 1:22).
> In him we have obtained an inheritance, having been predestined according to the purpose of him who works all things according to the counsel of his will (Eph. 1:11).
> The LORD of hosts has sworn: saying, 'As I have planned, so shall it be…' For the LORD of hosts has purposed, and who will annul it? His hand is stretched out, and who will turn it back? (Isa. 14:24, 27).
> Remember the former things of old; for I am God, and there is no other; I am God, and there is none like me, declaring the end from the beginning and from ancient times things not yet done, saying, 'My counsel shall stand, and I will accomplish all my purpose'… I have spoken, and I will bring it to pass; I have purposed, and I will do it (Isa. 46:9, 10, 11).
> Is anything too hard for the LORD? (Gen. 18:14).

---

18. Oden, *op. cit.*, pp. 223–315.
19. Oden, *op. cit.*, p. 229.
20. Oden, *op. cit.*, p. vii.
21. Lorraine Boettner, *The Reformed Doctrine of Predestination* (Grand Rapids: Eerdmans, 1932 and continuously through many printings), pp. 33, 34; pp. 26–29 quotes and cites dozens of other specifically relevant passages.

> I know that you can do all things, and that no purpose of yours can be thwarted (Job 42:2).
> God is in the heavens; he does all that he pleases (Ps. 115:3).
> Whatever the LORD pleases, he does, in heaven and on earth, in the seas and all deeps (Ps. 135:6).
> So shall my word be that goes out from my mouth; it shall not return to me empty, but shall accomplish that which I purpose, and shall succeed in the thing for which I sent it (Isa. 55:11).
> But who are you, O man, to answer back to God? Will what is moulded say to its moulder, 'Why have you made me like this?' Has the potter no right over the clay, to make out of the same lump one vessel for honoured use and another for dishonourable use? (Rom. 9:20, 21).

Many further plain texts and narrative incidents will be added to these uncontestable biblical declarations that there is indeed an 'eternal plan by which God has rendered certain all the events of the universe, past, present, and future'.[22]

The universe is the largest conceivable project. It seems preposterous to suppose a project including the galaxies in their motion and orbits, as well as the life-processes of a microbe; including objects as complicated as the solar system and as mysterious as light and human consciousness; including processes as closely harmonized as the electrical hook-up between the human brain and hands playing a violin could simply have occurred without an intelligent design formed by an intelligent designer. The larger the enterprise the more important is the plan. If the Sears Tower of Chicago or the Metro system of Paris required detailed blueprints before construction could begin how much more the cosmos of which even man himself is a very complicated part? Darwinism of the sort that excludes intelligent design from its dogma has recently been challenged by some of its own evolutionary thinkers. How much less can a strong doctrine of divine planning, or predestination, be expunged from a sound theology of the Christian religion.

The Bible uses a Variety of Terms to teach Predestination.

The Bible employs a vocabulary of semi-technical terms to teach the doctrine of predestination. We shall enter some of the Hebrew and Greek terms in due time but the terms employed in standard translation are clear enough. As, historically, the discussion has been framed in the idiom of the Authorized Version (KJV) we shall employ the same and quote here from that Version. Let us see some of these words in contexts that both illustrate the doctrine and give a sense of the meaning of these English words. Some are groups of related words.

1. *Know* in various verbal tenses and *knowledge*. 'Before I formed thee in the belly I *knew* thee' (Jer. 1:5) 'You only have I *known* of all the families of the earth' (Amos 3:2). '[S]eeing I *know* not a man' (Luke 1:34). 'And Adam *knew* Eve his wife; and she conceived' (Gen. 4:1). '[B]eing delivered by the… *foreknowledge* of God' (Acts 2:23; 1 Peter 1:2). '[W]hom he did *foreknow*, he also did predestinate' (Rom. 8:29 [emphasis added]).

These words in context show that God, in the case of two men (Jeremiah and Paul, cf. also David, Ps. 139) were 'known' by God in a special way before they were even conceived and had their lives planned out for them. In each case *to know* designates a relationship with God, with the individual person and, in the case of Amos 3:2, with a whole nation. These words usually apply to 'God's elect' in some specific sense.

2. *Choose, chosen*. 'The LORD did not… choose you, because ye were more in number than any people', etc. (Deut. 7:7). 'I know whom I have chosen' (John 13:18; cf. 15:16, 19).

These words are very frequently used in connection with sovereign divine choice of persons or nations for reasons God is not obligated to give; nor does He give reasons. 'Jacob have I loved, Esau have I hated' before either had been born (Rom. 11:10-13). In a theological sense, the Bible uses these words usually only of God's relation to 'the elect'.

3. *Elect, elected, election*. These words are never used in the Bible except in relation to Christ (Isa. 42:1), good angels (1 Tim. 5:21), God's chosen people (Isa. 65:9, 22) and those whom divine grace has brought from death to life, from the power of sin into the liberty of full salvation. They appear twenty-seven times, sixteen of them in New Testament Epistles. The terms are never used of the unsaved as such.

4. Other expressions such as refer to God's *counsel*, *determinate counsel* and *will* are used in Scripture to express not only God's control of the universe He created but also that it exists as He planned it.

Already questions and problems arise in the reader's mind. While these ought to be recognized in such a treatment as this. C. A. Hodge cautions:

---

22. A. H. Strong, *op. cit.*, p. 353.

> It must be remembered that theology is not philosophy. It does not assume to discover truth, or to reconcile what it teaches as true with all other truths. Its province is simply to state what God has revealed in his Word, and to vindicate those statements as far as possible from misconceptions and objections.[23]

Hence, when we write about the eternal counsels and purposes of the Almighty we must stand in awe and speak with reserve for 'no one comprehends [knows KJV] the thoughts of God except the Spirit of God' (1 Cor. 2:11) and that which the Spirit has made known in the Scriptures. That which Scripture says, we must state as clearly as we can, without reserve, and leave it to the reader to ponder and receive if he will.

The Place of Predictive Prophecy.

There is still another way in which the Creator of the world has made known that he created it according to a plan and is directing it toward a certain consummation – by predictive prophecy. The reader should not form an opinion of biblical prediction based on some distortions advertized in sensational preaching and imaginative movies and books of fiction. Rather let the LORD God speak for Himself.

Beginning at Isaiah 40:25 and on through 42:9 the prophet presents 'God', 'the LORD', 'the Spirit of the LORD', 'the Holy One' (Isa. 40:13, 18, 25, 27) in verbal discourse with His contrite people and idolaters, they who challenge the existence of the invisible 'Spirit in whom all things have their source, support and end' (Strong). It is partly in the form of challenge to debate. After representing God as the incomparable Planner, Creator, Sustainer and Governor of the world (40:12-24), the Incomparable (40:18, 22) Himself enters a challenge: 'To whom then will you compare me, that I should be like him?' (40:25). Onward through the seven remaining verses of chapter 40 and 41:1-20, God, the LORD, displays His creative omnipotence, sovereignty and grace, finally issuing a challenge to any detractors from His creative power and sovereign control of history as it unfolds:

> Set forth your case, says the LORD;
> bring your proofs, says the King of Jacob.
> Let them bring them, and tell us what is to happen.
> Tell us the former things, what they are,
> that we may consider them,
> that we may know their outcome;
> or declare to us the things to come.
> Tell us what is to come hereafter,
> that we may know that you are gods;
> do good, or do harm,
> that we may be dismayed and terrified.
> Behold, you are nothing,
> and your work is less than nothing;
> an abomination is he who chooses you.[24]

So much for the impotence of heathen gods to control ongoing history. God goes on to speak of the far-future rise of one known already to God and revealed to Isaiah in the eighth century BC and his God as 'his anointed ...Cyrus' (Isa. 45:1) who did not appear on the plane of history until the sixth century BC, as follows:

> I stirred up one from the north, and he has come,
> from the rising of the sun, and he shall call upon my name;
> he shall trample on rulers as on mortar,
> as the potter treads clay.
> Who declared it from the beginning, that we might know,
> and beforehand, that we might say, 'He is right'? (Isa. 41:25, 26. See on to v. 29.)

Soon God, the LORD, sums up his argument based on His planned knowledge of the future and control of it:

> I am the LORD; that is my name;
> my glory will I give to no other,
> nor my praise to carved idols.

---

23. Charles A. Hodge, *Systematic Theology, Vol.* I (Grand Rapids: Eerdmans, 1970), p. 535.
24. Isa. 41:21-24.

> Behold, the former things have come to pass,
> and new things I now declare;
> before they spring forth
> I tell you of them. (Isa. 42:8, 9).

The strongest statement, in the book of Isaiah, by God Himself of His power to predict the future, to tell it to His prophets, and to guarantee the future by His own 'counsel' and 'pleasure', has just been quoted. However, Isaiah's prophecy goes on to say the future will unfold as determined by God. Everything in God's world proceeds according to plan – no emergencies, no surprises. Hear Isaiah again [all emphasis added]:

> [R]emember the former things of old;
> for I am God, and there is no other;
> I am God, and there is none like me,
> declaring the end from the beginning
> and from ancient times things not yet done,
> saying, 'My counsel shall stand,
> and I will accomplish all *my purpose*',
> calling a bird of prey from the east,
> the man of *my counsel* [Cyrus] from a far country.
> I have spoken, and I will bring it to pass;
> I have purposed, and I will do it.[25]

Perhaps the single greatest scriptural witness to divine predestination is in the widespread predictive prophecies of the Bible. Christ and the apostles certainly thought fulfilled prophecy to be the greatest scriptural witness to their own authenticity as divine spokesmen. The prophets told of coming events in Jewish history long before they came to pass. One, for example, was that the Jews would be made servants to the king of Babylon and after seventy years would be made free to return to their native land from the place where that king had transported them. Part of this is in Jeremiah's prophecy: 'behold, I will send for all the tribes of the north, declares the Lord, and for Nebuchadnezzar the king of Babylon, my servant, and I will bring them against this land… This whole land shall become a ruin and a waste, and these nations shall serve the king of Babylon seventy years. Then after seventy years are completed, I will punish the king of Babylon…' (Jer. 25:9, 11, 12).

About seventy years later (Jeremiah spoke at the beginning of the seventy years) another prophet, in Babylon, read Jeremiah and waited expectantly to see what the older prophet had announced come to pass. And it did.[26]

Now some might suppose God merely noted what 'natural laws' or some such thing would bring to pass and by this 'foreknowledge' told Isaiah, Jeremiah and Daniel about it. However, the Governor of the world is no such second guesser as that. Rather, after a lengthy oracle on the future of two ancient kingdoms, Babylon and Assyria, Isaiah writes:

> The Lord of hosts has sworn:
> 'As I have planned,
> so shall it be,
> and as I have purposed,
> so shall it stand,
> that I will break the Assyrian in my land…'[27]
> This is the purpose that is purposed
> concerning the whole earth,
> and this is the hand that is stretched out
> over all the nations.
> For the Lord of hosts has purposed,

---

25. Isa 46:9-11, emphasis added. Those who believe not only what the Bible says, but what the Bible claims to be – in this case Isaiah 40–66, a composition by a prophet who wrote near the hinge between the 700s and the 600s BC and prophesied of Cyrus, whose career as king of Medes and Persians was in the middle third of the 500s – will defend the genuineness of this part of Isaiah. Otherwise the claims of God to control the future and thereby to know it and predict it through His servants the prophets are false.
26. See Dan. 9:1-3; Isa. 44:21-45; 2 Chron. 36:19-23; and Ezra, chapter 1.
27. See Isaiah 36 and 37 for the fulfilment.

  and who will annul it?
  His hand is stretched out,
  and who will turn it back?[28]

Consider also Isaiah 46:9, 10: 'I am God, and there is none like me, declaring the end from the beginning and from ancient times things not yet done, saying, "My counsel shall stand, and I will accomplish all my purpose"'.

People 'whose God is not in their thinking' usually do not realize they are carrying out God's plan. As they do their wicked deeds they think like W. E. Henley, in his well-known poem, *Invictus*: I am the master of my fate;/I am the captain of my soul!

The wicked Assyrian king, furious against the kingdom of Israel, had no awareness that he was a simple instrument of God's fury – 'Ah, Assyria, the rod of my anger… I send him… against the people of my wrath… But he does not so intend, and his heart does not so think; but it is in his heart to destroy…' (Isa. 10:5-7).

These passages are only a fraction of the biblical evidence that there is an 'eternal plan by which God has rendered certain all the events of the universe, past, present, and future'.[29] Some of the specific aspects of this plan will be noticed in the next paragraphs, but still with regard to the general proposition that there is such an all-inclusive plan, attention is called to the following: 'Known unto God are all his works from the beginning of the world' (Acts 15:18 KJV, note the context of world evangelism); 'having been predestined according to the purpose of him who works all things according to the counsel of his will' (Eph. 1:11).

The previous chapter introduced the biblical teaching that God made a plan for the world before He created it. This feature of divine sovereignty includes everything that should come to pass. The first proposition was 'The Bible Teaches that God Planned the World.' We proceed with a second.

---

28. Isa. 14:24-27.
29. A. H. Strong, *op. cit.*, p. 353..

16
Predestination or the Decrees of God: God's Eternal Plan for the Heavens and the Earth, Part II

The Bible Teaches that all of God's Purposes and Decrees for the World are Parts of a Comprehensive Single Plan.

Paul referred to the plan in this way, speaking of God's 'eternal purpose' (Eph. 3:11) and 'the purpose of him who works all things according to the counsel of his will' (Eph. 1:11). Notice the singular number of purpose, counsel and will in these texts. The same is true of Romans 8:28, which begins with 'all things' but ends with 'according to his purpose'.

Among the many attempts to explain 'the one and the many' in simple language, A. A. Hodge may have produced the best:

> The cause of one event is the effect of another and every event in the universe is more immediately or remotely the condition of every other so that an eternal purpose on the part of God must be one all-comprehensive act.[1]

Later he says:

> All the speculative errors… on this subject [either toward fatalism and determinism on the one hand or to tychism, i.e. chance, luck, absolute free – will of mankind on the other], spring from the tendency of the human mind to confine attention to one fragment of God, eternal purpose, and to regard it as isolated from the rest.[2]

He goes on to say that though we must separate the many works of God in thought, they are all connected just as all of nature is connected. Innumerable inseparable parts of a great painting are in the mind of a major painter before he applies brush and paint to a surface. In the artist's mind, the work is totally present at once even though all of it may come to conscious awareness and visibility only as he paints one tiny detail after another. Alternatively, consider a great sculptural piece like the Pieta at the Vatican, all contained at once in the great sculptor's mind as he attacks the great chunk of marble, hammer and chisel in his hands. He, however, focuses on one chip at a time as the work comes forth and finally dazzles its viewers by its perfection while redounding to the reputation of its creator.

---

1. A. A. Hodge, *Outlines of Theology* (Grand Rapids: Eerdmans, 1957), p. 204.
2. ibid., p. 204.

The Christian thinker must be careful at this point lest he himself fall into a serious error, the error that denies to us the freedom (albeit not absolute) which the Bible and our own consciousness tell us we have. He must also be prepared to refute the learned deterministic errors proposed by modern philosophy without assimilating them.

G. W. F. Hegel (1770–1831) is in a class by himself. His metaphysics has affected about everything written in philosophy since his times. He thought 'we must conceive of all facts as *necessary*. Given all the possibilities, the fact *must* emerge. *What is, must be*, because the conditions which enable it to exist *could not* produce any other fact' (emphasis added).[3] The academic spectrum furnishes (or has until recently) many leaders in every field who assume some sort of cause-effect determinism derived from the interconnectedness of all things.

Bible Names for God's Plan.

God's plan goes by several biblical names and designations. Each of the technical and semi-technical terms emphasizes some aspect of the doctrine and is therefore helpful in understanding it. The industrious reader will do well to read from the Bible itself the context of each of the passages about to be quoted here and to ponder the words emphasized. Each passage presents a different, but obvious, designation of God's plan for His creation: 'My *counsel* shall stand, and I will do all my *pleasure*' (Isa. 46:10 KJV); those he has '*called* according to his *purpose*' (Rom. 8:28); He 'works all things according to the *counsel* of his *will*' (Eph. 1:11; cf. Dan. 4:35); God 'having *determined allotted* periods' (Acts 17:26); Christ was '*foreordained*' (1 Peter 1:20 KJV); we 'having been *predestined*' (Eph. 1:11; cf. Rom. 8:30) (emphasis added)).

A Single, Comprehensive Plan.

There are about three varieties of determinism advocated in the world. This is to say, those who think we have no freedom at all, propose one or all of three causes for this lack of freedom. One is a sort of impersonal, materialistic fate thought to be built into the very fabric of the universe. This is the *moira*, *aisa* or *fatum* (fate or the fates) of Greek and Roman antiquity. The gods were 'born' into a world already existing, a world sometimes thought of as directed by fate, rather naively considered. As the ancients became scientific, a second form of determinism – cause-effect in an eternal chain – arose and is still with us as 'scientific or naturalistic determinism', either environmental or hereditary or both. Astrology, which assumes the stars of the sky determine destiny ('your lucky stars') arose very early in human history. It was drawn upon to support the first form of determinism, that is, fate. Both have had revivals in modern times and together reign on most university campuses today. A third form is religious determinism, a major feature of Islam, a non-Trinitarian monotheism. Any strongly held monotheism that has no Savior-God, no wise, loving, holy Father, quickly becomes a hard fatalism, as in the whole Muslim world. The same views develop in forms of Christianity where awareness of God's sovereignty is not matched with awareness of His love, mercy and holiness and does not give sufficient emphasis to that freedom *under* God that all human beings have as being, by creation, God's image.

God's Plan Is Eternal and Therefore Changeless.

The Bible teaches this single, comprehensive plan of God is an eternal plan and therefore unchangeable. This declaration rests on many plain statements of simple, but profound, facts.

God's Purposes Are Formed in Eternity.

Paul grandly proclaims his duty to 'bring to light for everyone what is the *plan* of the mystery hidden for ages in God *who created all things*' and that 'This was according to the *eternal purpose*', etc. (Eph. 3:9-11 (emphasis added)). In context, God's plan for the church is the centre of interest, but Paul – in declaring divine purpose in unmatched, exalted language – informs the church that it is part of an eternal purpose, along with 'all things' He has 'created'. As Peter says, Christ the Lamb of God 'was *foreordained* before the foundation of the world, but was *manifest* in these last times', etc. (1 Peter 1:20 KJV).

> The divine decree is formed in eternity, but executed in time. There are sequences in the execution, but not in the formation of God's purpose... There were thirty-three years between the actual incarnation and the crucifixion, but not between the decree that the Logos should be incarnate and the decree that he should be crucified... 'The Lamb was slain from the foundation of the world' (Rev. 14:8).[4]

---

3. B. A. G. Fuller, *History of Philosophy*, II, rev. ed. (New York: Henry Holt & Co. 1945), p. 315.
4. W. G. T. Shedd, *Dogmatic Theology I* (Grand Rapids: Zondervan, 1969), p. 394.

God Is Changeless.

God is immutable; there are no sequences or changes in him. As the Psalmist declares, though all else change, 'you are the same' (Ps. 102:27), and the prophet, 'I the LORD do not change' (Mal. 3:6), and the LORD's brother, about 'the Father of lights with whom there is no variation or shadow due to change' (James 1:17). He can neither decrease nor increase (as 'process theology' asserts), improve nor deteriorate, nor does He change plans in case of emergencies – because there are no unforeseen emergencies for Him who not only forecast the end from the beginning but decreed it so.

Recent advocates of a theory self-designated as 'the openness of God' argue that God cannot know contingent future events and think they find support in certain passages of Scripture, especially those which speak of God as repenting. Orthodox theology replies as follows.

1. Some passages (such as Abraham's wheedling God to make concessions in His plans to destroy Sodom and Gomorrah) illustrate only how God deals with us creatures, meeting us where we are, taking events where He plans for them to go by stages of experience and of discipline. Parents do the same with their children.

2. Some passages are 'anthropomorphic representations of the revelation of God's unchanging attributes in the changing circumstances and varying moral conditions of creatures'.[5] We should interpret Genesis 6:6 in the light of Numbers 23:19 ('the LORD was sorry that he had made man', 'God is not man, that he should lie, or a son of man, that he should change his mind') and 1 Samuel 15:11 with verse 29 ('I regret that I have made Saul king', 'the Glory of Israel will not lie or have regret, for he is not a man, that he should have regret'). If we do so we can understand that from a human standpoint God seems to change His mind about people and things, but really He is represented to us that way. His treatment of us was and is always the same – a holy response to our good or evil actions and intent. Divine predictions Jonah made of Nineveh's destruction were conditional upon the city's response to the threats (of resistance or repentance). The mass and composition of a column of mercury in a thermometer remains exactly the same twenty-four hours of the day yet rises every time temperatures outside rise and falls every time temperatures fall.

The Decrees of the Unchanging God Determine Actions Set in Time.

Though there is no change in God or even temporal succession His decrees made in eternity terminate on works set in time. The Scriptures report His past immediate work of creation (now finished), His present works of preservation and providence mainly through second causes, and immediate works such as miracles and regeneration of sinners and acts such as justifying believers by faith. 'My Father is working until now, and I am working' (John 5:17). Immutability is not immobility in God any more than God's impassibility, or perfect blessedness, is to be confused with impassivity. God does not suffer (impassibility) though, in His human nature, the Theanthropos [Gr. for Godman] did both suffer and die. Nevertheless, God is as immutable and impassible as He is also immortal ('who alone has immortality'). Some immense mystery is present in these truths. Immutability (in God) is fully consistent with unrelenting activity (even 'work') and perfect freedom, for 'he does according to his will among the host of heaven and among the inhabitants of the earth' (Dan. 4:35).

God's Decrees Are Certain of Fulfillment.

Predestination is certain of fulfillment. Human programmes, schedules and budgets are prone to failure in execution, but not God's decrees made in eternity.

If Christ is the Lamb slain from before the foundation of the world, the creation of mankind, mankind's fall and need for the atoning blood were in the plan too. There were no glitches in execution of the parts of the plan. The first church prayerfully responding to the jailing of their pastor acknowledged that all Herod, Pilate, the soldiers and 'the people of Israel' (Acts. 2:27 KJV) had conspired to do was only 'whatever your hand and your plan had predestined to take place' (Acts 4:28). Peter's rescue from jail by an angel (Acts 12:7, 8) and Paul's deliverance from shipwreck were not improvised 'in the nick of time' – *ad hoc* or as an expedient. God's manoeuvres sometimes surprise *us*, but He is never surprised by anything. His eternal plan, according to several passages, is one which cannot be changed (eg. Eph. 3:11; James 1:17). True, 'The LORD brings the counsel of the nations to nothing; he frustrates the plans of the peoples', but

---

5. A. H. Strong, *Systematic Theology* (Valley Forge, PA: Judson Press, 1907), p. 258.

not so His own plan, for 'The counsel of the LORD stands forever, the plans of his heart to all generations' (Ps. 33:10, 11; cf. 89:1). And what a marvellous thing it is to be one of the Lord's people, knowing about His purpose: 'Blessed is the nation whose God is the LORD, the people whom he has chosen as his heritage!' (Ps. 33:10-13).

This single, eternal, all-inclusive plan becomes precious and meaningful to believers as they consider the detail with which it is described in Scripture. Most of these details accompany some message of duty, of comfort or of further enlightenment.

God's plan is never presented in the Bible in such a way as to relieve believers either of hope or responsibility, or to discourage effort, in the slightest way. We should not be dismayed by objections and questions. Some people will say, 'I don't see how you can believe this doctrine and still believe that moral effort will get you anywhere.' Others will ask, 'If God has everything planned out how can He hold us responsible for either good or evil actions?' These questions arise out of incomplete understanding, that is, seeing only part of the Scripture teaching on the subject. Sometimes some detail of revelation, which seems to present a problem, keeps one from believing the whole of what the Scriptures plainly say. In addition, sometimes people reject the teaching because they do not like it. This teaching is either comfort or warning, depending on which one needs.

Details of God's Single Plan.

Some of the many details of the plan the Bible associates together in His 'eternal purpose' follow.

1. God's Plan includes the Permanence and Stability of the Material Universe.

God's plan includes the permanence and stability of the material universe, what scientists call the uniformity of nature. 'Your faithfulness endures to all generations; you have established the earth, and it stands fast. By your appointment they stand this day, for all things are your servants' (Ps. 119:90, 91).

It is this guaranteed uniformity of nature – the same in every corner of the world – that caused science to arise first in Christian lands and to surpass all peoples outside Christendom in material culture. There could be no scientific research if nature were not uniform everywhere.

About AD 72, Pliny the Elder compiled his *Historia Naturalis* (Natural History) from some 327 Greek and 146 Latin authors. Though popular until the rise of modern science, Pliny's uncritical and credulous outlook prevents anyone today from finding any important information about the origins of metallurgy, chemistry, weather-forecasting and the like in his work. Reflection on the origins of science have come relatively late but many have sought to explain how and when science arose. There is a tradition among some writers opposing Christianity to the origin and progress of science. One famous book calls it a 'warfare'.[6]

R. Hooykaas' book, *Religion and the Rise of Modern Science,* has shown how in late Renaissance and Reformation times it was Christian thinkers with their roots in biblical revelation who gave science its theoretical support.[7]

Perhaps the person who has done the most to give the Christian doctrine of God and His providence its fair place in the rise of science is the realist philosopher and Roman Catholic priest, Stanley L. Jaki. Bernard Ramm's book, *The Christian View of Science and Scripture* came to my aid when I was teaching about this subject at Wheaton College (in Apologetics)[8] but Jaki has covered the field of science and Christianity in a whole series of books, most specifically on the modern origins of science in *The Origin of Science and the Science of Origins*. An excerpt explains why science never took hold in any civilization except Christendom.

> That in all those cultures – Chinese, Hindu, Maya, Egyptian, Babylonian, to mention only the most significant ones – science suffered a still birth, can be traced to that mesmerizing impact which the notion of eternal returns exercised on them. It was a mesmerism fomented by the lack of a firm foothold, which in turn could only be provided by the perspective of absolute origin, an origin inconceivable without belief in creation out of nothing, implying a Creator.[9]

---

6. A. D. White, *A History of the Warfare of Science with Theology In Christendom* (London: 1896).
7. R. Hooykaas, *Religion and the Rise of Modern Science* (Grand Rapids: Eerdmans, 1972). See especially his chapter 'Sceince and the Reformation', pp. 98–144, about one-third of his book.
8. Bernard L. Ramm, The *Christian View of Science and Scripture* (Grand Rapids: Eerdmans, 1954).
9. Stanley L. Jaki, *The Origin of Science and the Science of Origins* (South Bend, IN: Regnery Gateway by arrangement with Scottish Academic Press, 1979), p. 93.

Jaki shows how the linear view of history found in the Christian doctrine of redemption also supported the rise of science. He goes on to say:

> [I]t was the Gospel that turned into a widely shared conviction, the belief in the Father, maker of all things visible and invisible who… disposed everything in measure, number and weight, that is, with rigorous consistency and rationality.[10]

This is to say God created the world and set it operating according to regular laws which He Himself sustains and is governing it to attain the goals He set (His decrees) before the beginning.

In agreement with this is Jaroslav Pelikan, who says the early Christian apologists were compelled to attack the Greek interpretation of history as 'recurring cycles'. He adds: 'In declaring loyalty of the Christians to the [Roman] empire [and emperor] while repudiating the deification of the emperor, apologetic theologians were compelled to clarify their reasons for differing from [Greek-Roman] theories of history.[11]

God's certain and settled decree is such a sure matter that the Bible compares the certainty of God's promises to His people to the certain regularity and permanence of God's ways in nature. God's invisible gracious plan in redemption is parallel with His inescapably apparent works in nature. The two paradigms are graphically displayed in Jeremiah 31:35-37: 'Thus says the LORD, who gives the sun for a light by day and the fixed order of the moon and the stars for light by night, who stirs up the sea so that its waves roar – the LORD of hosts is his name: "If this fixed order departs from before me, declares the LORD, then shall the offspring of Israel cease from being a nation before me for ever." Thus says the LORD: "If the heavens above can be measured, and the foundations of the earth below can be explored, then I will cast off all the offspring of Israel for all that they have done, declares the LORD."' In this case it should be noticed that human failures and sins do not obstruct the certain fulfillment of divine plans and purpose. A current comprehensive and convincing development of this theme is found in H. L. Poe and I. H. Davis, *Science and Faith: An Evangelical Dialogue,* Nashville, TN, 2000, 259 pages.

2. The Plan of God Specifically Relates to the Nations of Earth.

The plan of God also specifically relates to the nations of earth – their boundaries, governments, resources, history and condition. We accept this rather easily of Israel, well known to have been an object of special divine attention. However, according to Scripture, God gives every nation its territory. The Horites and the Edomites ('children of Esau') were given their land as God gave Israel theirs (Deut. 2:12). Furthermore, 'When the Most High gave to the nations their inheritance, when he divided mankind [cf. Gen 10:32], he fixed the borders of the peoples' (Deut. 32:8). Paul is direct to the point, saying to a Gentile audience, 'The God who made the world… made from one man every nation of mankind to live on all the face of the earth, having determined allotted periods and the boundaries of their dwelling place' (Acts 17:24, 26). Therefore, though both Kaiser Wilhelm and Adolph Hitler thought the German people needed more *Lebensraum* (room to live), God saw to it that, for a time at least, they were not to get it. These passages invite further study of the decrees of God regarding the history of nations.

3. God has no Known Preference for Any Particular Kind of Government or Sovereignty.

It may come as a shock to learn that God has no known preference for any particular kind of government or 'theory' of sovereignty for rulers. Scripture favours no particular doctrine of the human authority by which magistrates rule – whether dictatorship, empire, monarchy, aristocracy, plutocracy, military, pure democracy, party dictatorship or republic. The Bible is equally for and against them all. 'The sentence is by the decree of the watchers, the decision by the word of the holy ones, to the end that the living may know that the Most High rules the kingdom of men and gives it to whom he will and sets over it the lowliest of men' (Dan. 4:17). '[T]here is no authority except from God, and those that exist have been instituted by God' (Rom. 13:1). On every occasion the Bible raises the subject it emphatically declares that God reigns over the nations, that events express His sovereign decree. If the reader has any doubt of this, do read Psalms 93–99. A summary of sorts is Psalm 96:10, 'Say among the nations, "The LORD

---

10. ibid., p. 93.
11. Jaroslav Pelikan, *The Christian Tradition I,* 'The Emergence of the Christian Tradition' (Chicago: Univ. of Chicago Press, 1971), p. 37.

reigns! Yes, the world is established; it shall never be moved; he will judge the peoples with equity.'" This is not to say that some systems of government are not more friendly to the Christian ideals of society than others. I have dealt at length with the subject of this paragraph in *Civil Government, A Biblical View*.[12]

4. God's Plan includes the Precise Length of Each Person's Life.

Also included in God's plan is the precise length of each person's life. This is not a philosophy of 'when your number is up' – far from it. Rather it is a truth designed to inculcate an attitude of peaceful confidence among God's children, delivering them from bondage to fear of death all their lifetime (see Heb. 2:15). Job was aware of this, declaring a person's 'days are determined, and the number of his months is with you [God], and you have appointed his limits that he cannot pass' (Job 14:5). This implies certain responsibilities at the opposite pole from what is popularly called fatalism. Moses said that since God has numbered our days in His wisdom (Ps. 90:3-12) we also should 'number' them. 'So teach us', he prays, 'to number our days that we may get a heart of wisdom' (Ps. 90:12).

I once heard a Free Methodist evangelist say in a sermon, 'Every man is immortal until his work is done', and he was undoubtedly correct. This, in part, accounts for the cheerful, good hope of the apostle Paul throughout the New Testament reports of his ministry, even when in prison, for alleged capital crimes (Philippians). It accounts also for his quiet resignation to the rigours of imprisonment and the end of life, soon to come, knowing he had finished his divinely charted course and kept the faith (2 Tim. 4:6-8). This outlook lies behind the many scriptural spurs to effective effort in accomplishing goals of life in a systematic and timely manner. Of the 'blessed man' Scripture says: 'He is like a tree planted by streams of water that yields its fruit in its season, and its leaf does not wither. All he does, he *brings to completion*' (Ps. 1:3, words in italics my translation of the last clause; compare also Jesus' own dying exclamation, 'It is finished!').

5. God's Plan includes the Circumstances Under Which We Live.

God's sovereign plan includes the circumstances under which we live – poverty or riches, labor or leisure, sickness or health, bad times or good, and the circumstances in which we die. So it is right for believers to learn to say, from the heart, 'If the Lord wills' about all plans for their future (see James 4:13-15). As great a man as the apostle Paul found it right to submit his missionary plans to God, even when he might have planned otherwise (Rom. 1:10-13).

Modern people with their ideas about equality are frequently out of patience with any God who sanctions social and economic classes. Other generations have not felt this way. John Calvin, for example, already in middle age when he accepted his counsellors' advice to take a wife, disapproved of their first candidate, owing to her higher social standing than his. In any case no aspect of this subject is sketched more sharply than that God designs some to be rich and others poor, some to lead and others to follow, some to command and others to obey, some to be prominent celebrities, others to live out energetic constructive, but plain lives in obscurity (Ps. 73). It is also apparent that if one's efforts to break out of such categories do fail, God is not to be charged with cruelty or unfairness (Rom. 9:19-21).

It is also hard for us to accept either ill health or poverty as the will of God for anybody. Let those who think this way read what Paul had to say about slaves (1 Cor. 7:20-24), unmarried people (vv. 25-26), the married who might wish not to be (v. 27), the divorced (v. 27, see also verses 28-31). Even certain preachers can be heard to say that it is not God's will for any one to be sick. If you think this way read Paul's words about sickness as sometimes God's will (2 Tim. 4:20; 2 Cor. 12:7-10). Poverty can be God's will for us too. Other generations have understood this also better than ours. The young prophet, Jeremiah, for example, though he found it painful, accepted the LORD's command not to take a wife, establish a home and beget children owing to the rigours of his office in a time when genuine prophets were unwelcome in court and out of favour with the Jewish population. The young prophet bewailed his limitation in this regard but like Job 'in all this' he 'did not sin or charge God with wrong' (see Jer. 16:1–9). This was in order to carry out God's plans for Jeremiah's life work as a rejected prophet, to be crowned with a martyr's death; and his part to play in the last, steeply declining days of his country's slide to doom and judgment.

---

12. Robert Culver, *Civil Government, A Biblical View* (Edmonton, Alberta: Canadian Institute for Law, Theology and Public Policy, 1999), 308 pages.

There are several specific examples of how God had predetermined how and when certain men, at least, would die (Abraham, Gen. 15:15; Jesus, John 2:19). We cannot doubt that the same is true of us all. One Psalm says, apparently of all, both beasts and people, 'These all look to you... When you give it to them, they gather it up... When you hide your face, they are dismayed; when you take away their breath, they die and return to their dust' (Ps. 104:27-29). This is the theology, both theoretical and practical, of the 'Prayer of Moses, the Man of God' (Ps. 90).

6. God's Plan includes People's Evil Acts as well as Good Ones.

God's plan includes evil acts of people as well as their good ones. The Bible specifically says of the wicked deeds of Joseph's brothers, in selling Joseph to travelling merchants (Gen. 37:23-28), that though they did intend evil 'God meant it for good' (Gen. 50:20; cf. Ps. 105:17; and Gen. 45:4-8). Similar interpretations are given by the Bible to the hardening of Pharaoh's heart and even to the betrayal and shameful execution of Jesus. As the Apostle Peter explained under the difficult circumstances of his second Christian sermon: 'And now, brothers [the crowd who demanded Jesus be crucified], I know that you acted in ignorance, as did also your rulers. But what God foretold by the mouth of all the prophets, that his Christ would suffer, he thus fulfilled' (Acts 3:17, 18). Judas had a part in God's plan (see Jesus' comments, John 17:12; Mark 14:18-21). Christ's suffering was even prophesied in the Old Testament.

The jealous Jewish leaders, who were responsible, played a part in God's plan too. Peter told them this plainly: 'Men of Israel... Jesus of Nazareth, a man attested to you by God... delivered up according to the definite plan and foreknowledge of God, you crucified and killed by the hands of lawless men' (Acts 2:22, 23). The fact that the wicked deeds of these parties to crime were all in God's plan, some even predicted in Scripture, in no wise relieved the men who did those things from guilt and punishment for them. This is plain in each case, especially Judas – 'It would have been better for that man if he had never been born' (Mark 14:21). We saw in connection with God's omniscience that He even foresees events which are conditional upon future acts of free beings (we cited 1 Sam. 23:11-14). If He foreknows such things, it is because He has predestined them as well.

7. Both the Judgment of the Impenitent and the Salvation of the Believing are in the Plan of God.

We must understand then that, though the decrees are different, some causative and gracious, others permissive and just, both the judgment of the impenitent and the salvation of the believing are in the plan of God. '[F]or those who do not believe, "The stone that the builders rejected has become the cornerstone", and "A stone of stumbling, and a rock of offence." They stumble because they disobey the word, as they were destined to do' (1 Peter 2:7, 8).

Questions and Problems.

Now, granting that the biblical teaching has been fairly presented, some questions and problems arise which should, if possible, be answered. This does not mean that merely because a question can be asked, it ought to be asked. Mere men cannot answer all the possible questions that the mind can raise. God's ways are not our ways or His thoughts ours. Our part is to believe what God says to be true is true. Only after that do we attack the problems.

The most serious question relates to freedom. How can there be freedom of choice if God has decreed all that shall happen, from the fall of raindrops and sparrows to the rise of stars and empires? The following comments may be helpful to honestly perplexed readers. The problems are not insuperable.

1. The Bible speakers and writers are usually conscious of no difficulty. Although Jesus, in speaking of Judas to the Father, called him 'son of perdition', it was only after Jesus had made the most touching appeal imaginable that He not go through with his appalling plot with the Sanhedrin (John 13:21-30). A few days later, Peter and assembled believers, in prayer to the same Father, and knowing that Judas' defection had been prophesied in the Old Testament, observed that Judas by his own transgression fell 'that he might go to his own place' (Acts 1:25 KJV). A person can be as free as the Bible says he is (not an absolute freedom by any means), and yet acting out God's decree, without introducing a conflict in the mind of a Jesus or a Peter. Who is he who supposes himself more rational or insightful or just than they?

2. Making a distinction between the decrees and their execution alleviates the seeming conflict with freedom. God made the decrees and in no wise externally compels anybody to do either right or wrong. In the cases being questioned, responsible people carry out the decrees, yet without coercion by God. They do so wholly voluntarily. If they are slaves to sin, as Jesus said, that is hardly God's fault. One thinks of the sons of Eli – 'worthless men. They

did not know the LORD' (1 Sam. 2:12). They were rebuked by their father for their gross sins. But, says the Scripture, most significantly, 'But they would not listen to the voice of their father, for it was the will of the LORD to put them to death' (1 Sam. 2:25). Thus the doctrine is confirmed and it is clear that without any compulsion from God or men (quite to the contrary, the whole nation was opposed to what the two young men were doing) they freely chose to do the evil which destroyed them (see 1 Sam. 4:17).

3. The idea of freedom must be clarified. Though 'freedom', 'freedom of choice' and 'freedom of the will' appear often in discussion of this subject there is considerable difference of opinion as to what 'freedom' is. There are different kinds and degrees of freedom. As we shall see later in the doctrines of grace and of sin, there is no absolute freedom. Discussion of predestination and how it relates to freedom did not originate in jam sessions at a theological seminary students' dormitory. Argument over the subject is recognized in Romans 9:11-29. In the early church, division arose to a peak in fifth-century controversy. Pelagius, a British monk, sought to deny divine sovereignty and predestination and, along with that, the biblical teaching of original sin and of depravity. Augustine defended predestination and the corollaries – depravity and atonement. Gottschalk, a learned Benedictine monk (died AD 867), read Augustine, was convinced, and got in trouble with his bishop, who imprisoned him for speaking against the prevailing crypto-Pelagianism. Deprived of last rites and Christian burial, he died in his Augustinian evangelical faith, 30 October 867, disgraced but admired and defended by many supportive clergymen. Over 600 years later, the same set of doctrines revived the church in what we now call the Protestant Reformation.

Party Strife Over Freedom.

Discussions of this subject have been fruitful, but not all of the party strife. I am indebted to *Our Daily Bread*, published by Radio Bible Class, for a very helpful tale in this regard.

> The story is told about the members of a congregation who got into a squabble one day over the issue of predestination and free will. While the controversy raged, the people separated, going to opposite sides of the auditorium. One man, not knowing which group to join, slipped into the predestination crowd. But he didn't stay long. Someone asked him, 'Who sent you here?' He replied, 'No one, I came of my own free will.' This brought the angry response, 'What? You can't be one of us and talk that way.' Quickly he was shoved across the aisle. But now he was questioned about his reasons for joining the free-will group. When he said, 'I was forced over here,' they indignantly shouted, 'Get out! You can't join us unless you choose to do so.' This poor believer was shut out from his brothers and sisters because they were fighting over a problem that's beyond the full grasp of man's puny little mind.

Contradictions, Disputes: Decrees and Foreknowledge.

The reader interested in further discussion of the alleged contradictions and problems is referred to the classical theological works. Lutheran, Reformed, Baptist and many other theologians, including Thomas Aquinas, generally define and defend the teaching as set forth here. Some orthodox Methodist, Episcopalian and other writers, including dispensationalist H. C. Thiessen, while not rejecting the teaching of the decrees in the Bible, seek to modify the doctrine by asserting that God decreed only what His omniscience (knowledge of future events) informed Him would happen anyway. H. C. Thiessen asserts 'God foreknew what men would be in response to common grace; and He elected those whom He foresaw would respond positively.'[13]

This really is not to modify the biblical doctrine (decrees, counsel, plan of God, predestination) but to subvert it. It seems like common sense, the same as works-righteousness does. Yet it is denial of clear biblical truth, in my judgment.

That God's foreknowledge in the sense of foresight may have a place in our understanding of the decrees cannot be doubted. Yet if foresight is made dependent on God's knowledge of the forces prevailing among 'men and things' (as it sometimes is thought to be) let us remember that God made the laws, thus insuring the results. Moreover, there is something else very important to understanding God's 'foreknowledge'. 'Foreknew' and 'foreknow' appear only once each in the KJV (Rom. 8:28 and 11:2), Gr. *proginoskō* in the second aorist tense each time; in each case the people of God is the object of God's foreknowledge. The meaning in each case, in context, and indicated even by the *Lexicon* of Bauer, Arndt, Gingrich, is to 'Choose beforehand... someone'. 'Foreknowledge' in KJV appears

---

13. H. C. Thiessen, *Introductory Lectures in Systematic Theology* (Grand Rapids, MI: Eerdmans, 1949, 1966), p.157.

only twice. In the former case, Peter addressing the Pentecost crowd said Jesus was 'delivered by the determined purpose and *foreknowledge* of God' (Acts 2:23 NKJV). Foreknowledge here is the Greek word *prognosis*, the noun corresponding to *proginoskō*. Peter is saying that God delivered Jesus over to judicial execution. It was something God *determined* in His own *counsel* and *foreknowledge*. In such case foreknowledge is not mere previous information of what would happen but actual direction (if not implementation) of the future event. The certainty of the future event was decreed by God, and in this case not by any entirely *secret* counsel, for Psalm 22 and Isaiah 52:13–53:12 predicted the event and attending circumstances in detail. Further, knowledge in Scripture frequently has reference to establishment of a relationship rather than information possessed, as in 'Now Adam knew Eve his wife, and she conceived' (Gen. 4:1 NKJV). Here 'to know' is to establish the most intimate of all human relationships. So when Peter used the word again (1 Peter 1:1, 2) he was thinking not that some certain people in time to come would be saved, but that they had always been 'elect… according to the foreknowledge', i.e. according to an eternally established relationship.

Is God the Author of Sin and of Evil?

Someone wants to know if this understanding of predestination does not make God the author of sin. By no means. Sinners are the authors of sin. They are not coerced to sin, but do so voluntarily. God even preserves them in life while they commit their sins of disposition, thought and deed. They follow self-chosen paths. God overrules evil for good, as we have seen. It is also true that He holds the evil-doers guilty. A distinction may be made between efficient decrees of God and permissive ones. If this be allowed, then the divine decree of sin is not *efficient*; it is only *permissive*. Though some Supralapsarians and other followers of scholastic hyper Calvinism reject these distinctions, some of the best theologians, Roman Catholic, Calvinist and Arminian find them both biblical and helpful. Why God permitted Satan to tempt Eve, why He allowed evil at all is, of course, never explained in the Bible, though the plain fact is that God not only did not prevent it, He put it in His plan. To allow sin *now* is only an extension of the decree to allow sin in the first place. With all its mystery, the biblical narrative still provides the best answer ever propounded.[14]

W. G. T. Shedd wrestled the problem to the ground as well as any modern writer. I cite some of his lines on the 'principal practical value of the doctrine that God decreed [planned in] sin'.

> It establishes the Divine sovereignty over the entire universe. By reason of his permissive decrees, God has absolute control over moral evil, while yet he is not the author of it, and forbids it. Unless he permitted sin, it could not come to pass. [Let the reader think of the situation in Gen. 2.]… Sin is preventable by almighty God, and therefore he is sovereign over sin and hell as well as over holiness and heaven. This is the truth he taught to Cyrus, to contradict the Persian dualism [God and evil are equally powerful and real]: 'I form the light, and create darkness; I make peace and create evil. [Let the reader ponder!] I, the LORD, do all these things,' Isa. 45:7. Compare Amos 3:6, 'Shall there be evil in a city, and the LORD hath not done it?' Gen. 20:6, 'I withheld thee [Abimelech] from sinning against me.' To deny this truth, logically leads to the doctrine of the independence of evil and the doctrine of independence of evil is dualism, and irreconcilable with monotheism.[15]

Shedd goes on to say, God purposes ultimately to overrule evil for good and cites Psalm 76:10 and other texts I have cited in this chapter.

Anselm of Canterbury (1033–1109), the first 'great' of the medieval scholastics, illustrated the truth of God's providential control of sin this way:

> If those things which are encircled by the heavens wished not to continue to exist beneath the heavens, or wished to get away from the heavens, they would nonetheless be able to exist only beneath the heavens and able to go away from the heavens only by coming toward them. For no matter from what place or to what place they would go they will still be circumscribed by the heavens. And the farther they would get from any one part of the heavens, the closer they would get to the opposite part. Similarly, even though men and evil angels do not want to submit to the divine will and ordinance, they are unable to escape from it. For if they want to get out

---

14. See my essay, Robert D. Culver, 'The Nature and Origin of Evil' in *Vital Apologetical Issues*, ed. Roy B. Zuck (Grand Rapids: Kregel Publ., 1995), pp. 10–18.
15. W.G. T. Shedd, *Dogmatic Theology I* (New York: Chas. Scribners Sons, 1888; Zondervan reprint 1953 and more recently, 1969), pp. 405–412.

from under God's directive will, they run beneath His punitive will. And – if you ask about the route they will traverse – they make their way only under His permissive will. And that which they perversely will or do is redirected by Supreme Wisdom towards the order and beauty of the aforementioned universe.[16]

Alternatives to the biblical doctrine are manifestly unacceptable, all without exception leading to theological errors. Of these the chief are denial of original sin and the consequent universally corrupt human nature (depravity) on the one hand and the doctrine of a limited God on the other.

Practical Reconciliation of Views.

Most orthodox Christian authors who support a 'free will' outlook readily – as opposed to 'depraved will' – acknowledge that God knows all future events before they happen, even those events contingent on decisions and acts of free beings. Hence, a practical reconciliation between parties in the strife over predestination has been possible. There has been sufficient agreement to secure mutual effort in evangelism, at a minimum.

Values.

This doctrine, rightly expounded, has had great influence for good in Christian communities which accept it.

1. As observed at the beginning of this chapter, the teaching of providence promotes a solemn but joyful confidence that with the future in God's hands, the story of the human race will indeed 'come out right' in the end. Romans 8:28 is truth, not just overheated enthusiasm. People who deeply believe this tend to be steady, productive citizens of the community. They know that 'in the Lord your labour is not in vain'.

2. Awareness of God's comprehensive plan inculcates humility in the face of God's complete sovereignty over the past, the present and future.

3. It should cause the unbelieving and impenitent to be aware that their sins too are in God's calculations. They will never 'get away with' a thing. He will bring every deed to judgment and thereby,

4. Through this awareness of judgment the sinner is pointed to the means of God's grace that he might learn of Him, believe and be among those whom God counts as His people – the redeemed of all the ages.

If God has decreed the course of our lives He will take charge of them too – call it 'providence'. A lovely parody of Henley's *Invictus*, entitled *My Captain*, by Dorothea Day, celebrates God's decrees and providence.

>Out of the light that dazzles me,
>Bright as the sun from pole to pole,
>I thank the God I know to be
>For Christ the conqueror of my soul.
>Since His the sway of circumstance
>I would not wince nor cry aloud.
>Under the rule which men call chance
>My head with joy is humbly bowed.
>Beyond this place of sin and tears –
>That life with Him! and His the aid,
>That spite the menace of the years,
>Keeps, and shall keep, me unafraid.
>I shall not fear, though straight the gate;
>He cleared from punishments the scroll.
>Christ is the Master of my fate;
>Christ is the Captain of my soul.

---

16. Anselm, *Cur Deus Homo* i,15. in *Anselm of Canterbury vol. III*, ed. & trans. by J. Hopkins & H. Richardson (Toronto & New York: The Edwin Mullen Press, 1976), p. 73.

17
God's Work of Creation, Part I

Sources for a Theology of Origins.

'In the beginning, God created the heavens and the earth.' There were no human observers about when God created the world. Our only source of authentic, first-hand information, then, is the creator-God, Himself. If He does not tell us about creation we shall never know about it – tenuous inferences derived from geology, astronomy, physics and biology notwithstanding. Inferences based on 'science', as to how and when the 'universe' came to be, have always changed with the times and the changing theories of science. Revelation, however, has not changed since God last spoke 'through a Son'. Christian interpretation of enscriptured revelation has made few changes as regards the main features of the doctrine of creation since earliest times. From the standpoint of eternity (*sub specie aeternitatis*) the changes have not been very important. Christians have believed from the beginning that in the early chapters of Genesis they have a God-given and therefore truthful account of the creation of the world. Such affirmations as 'All Scripture is breathed out by God' (2 Tim. 3:16) was Paul's conviction. Jesus said, 'Scripture cannot be broken' (John 10:35).

That Jesus meant to include the Genesis creation account is evident. At every point in His ministry He plainly employed Scripture as God's Word – factual and true. At several critical junctures of His ministry, He quoted Scripture in support of His own perseverance in the task God gave Him. This is seen especially at the temptation.[1] He also made several comprehensive statements about the Old Testament Scriptures.[2]

Our Lord never argued that the Bible, including the creation story, is true. Nor do we find such words as inerrant and synonyms in His estimate of Scripture. He did say that 'Scriptures cannot be broken'. He simply used the Scriptures as God's true Word. Two basic human institutions are marriage and the Sabbath. He traced the origin of both back to the Genesis creation story.[3] Followers of Jesus will therefore follow the Lord in trusting the Genesis account of creation as true. This, of course, is not to deny the same breadth of interpretation in the first chapters of the Bible which all claim for the last chapters of the Bible. No one I have heard or read has declared his group's understanding (whether literal or figurative) of Revelation 21, 22 as the only possible orthodox, believing

---
1. See Matt. 4:4, 7, 10; cf. Deut. 8:3; 6:13, 16; and 10:20.
2. See Matt. 5:17, 19; John 10:35; Luke 24:25-27, 44-47 for example.
3. See Matt. 19:3-6 and compare Gen. 1:27 and 2:24; also see Mark 2:27 and compare Gen. 2:1-4.

view possible. At present, however, we are afflicted by some writers and promoters who seem to think their view of the Creative week (of twenty-four hour days) and the Flood (that it created geological history) is the only view consistent with ortodoxy and possible to an honest reading of the text of the first nine chapters of Genesis.

The creation itself witnesses to its creation by God. Francis Pieper affirms: 'All creatures bear the divine stamp… But our knowledge of the particular circumstances of the creation… is derived solely from God's revelation in Scripture. Men who presume to correct God's record of the creation through conclusions drawn from the present condition of the world are playing the role of scientific wiseacres, a procedure unworthy of Christians.'[4] It is not wrong, however, for geologists, physicists, astronomers and other scientists reverently to seek better to understand the biblical revelation and to increase their knowledge of creation by their researches, provided always they do not put nature in a class with Scripture as revelation.

As noted elsewhere in this book, strictly speaking, nature gives information but is not revelation, even though for some time writers have been speaking of nature as a part of 'general revelation'. We are not quite ready to classify scientific orthodoxy and the geologic table with the first chapter of Genesis in degree of authority on earthly origins, even though some recent writers seem inclined to do so. Moreover, interpreting the fossil record is not quite parallel to interpreting the Bible as regards creation. The Bible is designed primarily as a *message* from God, while the earth was designed as a *habitation* for mankind, not a guide to the subject of its own origin. [Current writers on 'intelligent design' discuss this principle in nature as the 'anthropic principle'.]

All parties to the present debate over creation – theories of 'young earth', 'creation science' and 'progressive creation' – should acknowledge this. The Bible is a book intended to be an interpretation of our world from the standpoint of the divine mind for religious purposes, while the earth is a creation, designed by the same mind as a habitation for mankind. Information about origins is scanty and obscure in the creation. It is apparently not spiritually necessary for us to know anything at all about the physics and chemistry of creation. It is mixing things that are essentially different to speak of Scripture and earth as both revelations of God requiring interpretation. There is just enough truth in the statement to make it dangerous in the hands of some people.

References to God's acts in creation are made in many parts of the Bible, often with interpretation of the spiritual meaning thereof. In addition to Genesis 1 and 2, mention should be made of Psalms 8, 33 and 148; Job 38; Proverbs 8 and John 1:1-5. The texts outside of Genesis that interpret Genesis take on an importance for doctrine as great as the Genesis creation accounts and will be quoted and cited throughout the discussion now to follow.

The World's Beginning.

There was a time when there was no world. It did not exist. The Psalm of Moses puts it this way, 'Before the mountains were brought forth, or ever you had formed the earth and the world, from everlasting to everlasting you are God' (Ps. 90:2). Passages speak of time 'before the world existed' (John 17:5) and 'before the foundation of the world' (John 17:24).

That the world had a beginning is assumed in all the Scriptures teach concerning such doctrines as decrees (predestination) and preservation. It is a patent fact so obvious in the biblical world-and-life view that Bible-reading-and-loving people can scarcely think in any other way about the world. They know the world is not without beginning and not self-generated.

Simple observation teaches us that though the processes of regeneration and restoration are at work in nature, they do not quite restore nature. Most of the mountains are a little lower each year. The energy given off by the sun is never returned to it. The more sophisticated observations of science report that the universe is spreading out and running down. This, too, points to a beginning in finite time.

Wiseacres of our secularist age have nothing to say as to what the cause of beginning was. A few, contrary to the material evidences, speak vaguely of an eternally existing, uncaused world.

Followers of existentialist theology are told that God is *Being*, not another being, and that 'How did the world begin?' and 'Who made it?' are improper questions.[5] We must rather look at mankind 'in order to learn what the Creator-creature relationship is'.[6] God does not create, He only 'lets be' in this theology.

---

4. Francis Pieper, Christian Dogmatics I (St. Louis: Concordia Publ., 1950, 1957), p. 467.
5. John Macquarrie, *Principles of Christian Theology* (New York: Charles Scribner's Sons, 1966), p. 212.
6. ibid., p. 213, citing Rahner.

In Process Theology it is unimportant to ask how the world began. Rather we must seek to understand how God who is in the world (pantheism) is growing with it and we along with Him. There is no affirmation of God's omnipotence or omniscience in a traditional sense in either of these approaches to theology.

There have always been religious people who opposed the idea of a beginning of the world. This opposition has usually taken one of two forms. One is *emanation*. The world is identical in substance with God. It has been produced by successive emanations out of Him. The things we see are little pieces of God. Folk who identify God with what they see in nature, rather than seeing nature as His work, are taking this view of things whether they know it or not. There are many anti-biblical affirmations and implications involved. The doctrine of emanation virtually denies God's transcendence; it compromises God's holiness by making all that is evil a part of Him. Ancient Gnosticism, a system which sought to interpret Christianity in the forms of Eastern theosophy (such as Hinduism), taught emanationism. Emanationism has always been a temptation to the mystically inclined, that is, to people who seek direct routes to God through meditation and ascetic practices apart fom the historical Christ and a written revelation. Contemplate almost anything about yourself and you have a bit of God. Follow it back through prescribed exercises and you may get a clear vision or feeling of God. This is a simplified description of the mystical approach.

Another form of denial of a beginning (and of creation) is *dualism*. Dualism teaches that God (thought of as idea) and matter, though distinct from one another, have always existed and always shall. It is essentially an effort to explain the presence of evil by attaching it to material things.

Absolute Beginning.

The world was brought into existence by the one, true, eternal God out of no materials at all. There was an absolute beginning of things.

'In the beginning, God created the heavens and the earth' (Gen. 1:1). These words must be understood as taking the reader back to the time when, in the presence of nothing outside the Godhead, God brought the heaven and earth into existence. 'By faith we understand that the universe was created by the word of God, so that what is seen was not made out of things that are visible' (Heb. 11:3).

Sometimes this act or series of acts has been further defined as creation 'out of nothing' (*ex nihilo*). This is correct as long as a certain error is avoided. 'Nothing' must not be regarded as a 'something'. It is not a designation for primeval chaos. This error is found in classical Greek philosophy, frequently as formlessness, a source of evil, and in modern existentialism as the principle opposing authenticity. It might be better to say God created into nothing, that is, where nothing (non-existence) was, God created something. This involves ambiguities also, owing to the fact that we cannot conceive of nothingness apart from a mental image of a 'nothing', thereby confusing the idea. We are apt to end up being dualists.

Genesis 1:1 does not say that God used no materials in the creative work of that verse. But if it is absolute beginning to which Moses refers, then the situation requires it. The nature of the idea and its context must decide for us.

Very early, Christian theologians had to deal with the views of the origin of the world held by pagan authors and schools as well as heretical views among Christian teachers who were affected by the pagans. The Greek 'Apologists' of the second century and other early writers felt particularly obliged to clarify and to defend the absolute beginning of the world by an uncreated eternal divine being who brought the world into being by speaking it into existence. Of these Christian scholars (Marcianus, Aristides, Justin Martyr, Tatian, Athenagoras, Theophilus), and others shortly after them (Clement of Alexandria, Tertullian), Jaroslav Pelikan says:

> Apologists... recognized that the coeternity of God and matter was inconsistent with the sovereignty and freedom of God. In spite of the difficulties raised by the doctrine of creation *ex nihilo* for any attempt to cope with the problem of evil, the alternatives to this doctrine appeared to be a pantheism... or a dualism.[7]

Theophilus of Antioch found explicit Christian creationism in direct conflict with six philosophical theories among the Greeks.[8]

---

7. Jaroslav Pelikan, *The Emergence of the Christian Tradition* vol. I of *The Christian Tradition* (Chicago: Univ. of Chicago Press, 1971), p. 36.

8. To *Antolycus*, .4, *ANF*. 15 (London: publisher not provided)..

These theories Thomas Oden has parsed out as: (1) there is no God; (2) God cares for none but himself; (3) the world is uncreated and nature is eternal; (4) God exists only in each person's conscience; (5) God is a spirit which pervades all things; and (6) both God and matter are uncreated, i.e. coeval. Oden's grasp of both theology and modern philosophy led to this comment:

> All these views were late to appear and grow into major challenges to the Christian teaching of Creation and remain as modern challenges in the voices of 1) Nietzsche, 2) Freud, 3) Hume, 4) Kant, Schleiermacher, Feuerbach, 5) Wieman and 6) Schelling.[9]

Further Statements of Method and Scope of Treatment.

1. Though seldom first in any general treatment of Christian doctrine, and even found in a special development of the doctrine of God, 'God the creator of heaven and earth' is fundamental and primary to all Christian teaching and a Christian world-view. E. P. Siegfried, a Roman Catholic scholar, rightly said:

> [B]elief 'in God the Creator of heaven and earth' is the theoretical basis of all religious and theological truth, the real foundation underlying all other truths concerning God, and the objective principle whence all other truths proceed.[10]

2. The topic of this chapter is God as the originating cause of all that exists except God Himself. It is apparent that this title, the text (Gen. 1:1) and the opening sentences commit this study to classical, Christian theism, to a biblical theology of existence, and to a particular tradition of translation of the opening verse of the Bible, as shall appear as the discussion develops.

3. In previous chapters our discussion has not at every point related directly to science and philosophy. If, however, we claim that all that human perception experiences, or can imagine as existing in the universe of which we occupy a part, was brought into existence by the God of the Old and New Testaments, then we are already in territory claimed by every branch of science and philosophy. The treatment will necessarily respond to that fact.

4. The treatment to follow presupposes the God of Christian theism of the previous chapters, for whom 'the maker of heaven and earth' of the Creed is an appropriate title. Many have followed this route before and done so admirably well. Alternate explanations, both religious and philosophical, of the origin of the world in which we live were proposed at least as early as the Genesis account. In recent times science has been heard from in this regard also. Within limits of a chapter or two – not a whole book – I shall respond to these proposals. The creationist paradigm has undergone very serious attacks from many quarters. Problems, especially the presence of evil in a world created by an almighty, benevolent God, must be recognized and responded to.

5. What St Paul called 'the whole creation' or 'all things' (Gr. *ta panta*), Genesis 1:1[11] designates simply as 'the heavens and the earth', and the Prayer of Moses portrays as 'the earth and the world' (Ps. 90:2) teach no form of cosmology. Neither the Ptolemaic geocentric universe is propounded, nor the Copernican solar-centric systems, nor any other. '[T]he heavens and earth' to Moses and his first readers meant simply everything above our heads and everything beneath our feet as far as they extend in any direction. The world they meant was the one they saw, felt, heard, smelled and tasted, however constituted. But the modern term, universe, 'the world of existing things as constituting a systematic whole' (*Oxford English Dictionary*) is an interpretive term implying both variety and unity in a system – though not any particular sort of system. The one thing all these expressions share is reference to all created existences – whether a system or chaos. Whether God be the Creator or exists in some other relation to 'the world of existing things' is a major consideration of this chapter.

Our discussion will be arranged under a series of propositions to be understood as what 'The Bible teaches'. It might please lovers of the inductive method to cite all the supporting passages, in context, first, and then generalize in some conclusions, but that is inversion of the declarative, didactic approach the present task calls for.

---

9. Thomas Oden, *The Living God* (San Francisco: Harper Collins, 1992), p. 251.
10. E. P. Siegfried, art. 'Creation'. In *The Catholic Encyclopedia iv* (New York: 1908), p. 475.
11. Also 2:1; 14:19, 22 *et al*.

I. The World, including Heaven and Earth, all that exists, was Created by God.

Says Langdon Gilkey.

> Were one to ask 'What is the first thing Christians say when they begin to state their beliefs?', he might reasonably conclude this primary role was filled by the idea of creation. For when he opened the Scriptures, he would find the first line stating this belief: 'In the beginning God created the heavens and the earth.' And if he listened to the most universally repeated Christian creed, he would hear the opening words: 'I believe in God the Father Almighty, Maker of heaven and earth.'[12]

The Bible states this unequivocally from beginning to end, usually in support of or accompanying some related truth, derived benefit or duty. The first reference is connected with the privilege and duty of a weekly Sabbath rest (Gen. 1:1; 2:1-3 cf. Exod. 20:9-11) while among the last is the correlate duty and privilege of worship: 'Worthy are you, our Lord and God, to receive glory and honour and power, for you created all things, and by your will they existed and were created' (Rev. 4:11). In between, other biblical passages connect God the Creator with renewal of strength for those who wait on Him (Isa. 40:28-31; 43:1-13), and with assurance of the restoration of Jerusalem and the cities of Judah (Isa. 44:24-26). In the Psalms there is frequent conjunction of God's redemption, salvation, mercy and government with His being the universal 'Maker'.[13] In the New Testament, the Word made flesh is also the eternal 'God,' the 'life' and 'light of men' (John 1:1-12).

Indeed the fact that God created a world planned by Him, preserved and governed by Him, is the most fundamental affirmation of a Christian world-view, distinguishing biblical religion from all others as false. It separates biblical religion from every form of polytheistic worship, because 'the LORD is the true God; he is the living God... "The gods who did not make the heavens and the earth shall perish from the earth" (Jer. 10:10, 11, cf. whole context). The identity of the Maker of heaven and earth with 'God manifest in the flesh' distinguishes the New Testament faith from every other faith (see Rom. 11:25-36 and Eph. 3:9).

II. The World had Absolute Beginning when God created the Heavens and the Earth.

The world had absolute beginning when God created the heavens and the earth, at which moment (or epoch) both time and space came into existence. These are matters which have puzzled both philosophers and theologians as well as scientists since antiquity. Perhaps more than one complementary perspective appears in Scripture about time and space, but I think there are definitive statements and necessary inferences.

1. The world had a beginning. It has not always existed. There is a 'before the world began' (2 Tim. 1:9; Titus 1:2 KJV) 'before time began' (NKJV). Jesus spoke to His Father about 'the glory that I had [was having; *eichon*, first person imperfect] with you before the world existed' (John 17:5) and that 'you [the Father] loved me before the foundation of the world [*kosmos*]' (John 17:24). Before the world 'to be' or its 'foundation' the Son was loved by the Father and He had a glory with the Father. Paul says that the God and Father of our Lord Jesus Christ 'chose us in him before the foundation of the world' (Eph. 1:4) and Moses in praise to God rhapsodizes that 'you are God... Before the mountains were brought forth, or ever you had formed the earth and the world, from everlasting to everlasting' (Ps. 90:2).

2. It is noteworthy that in these passages no mention is made of a 'time' as such before creation; nor does any other passage, unless it be Romans 16:25. (There are similar statements at 2 Timothy 1:9 and Titus 1:2.) Paul speaks of a mystery kept silent *chronois aōniois*, in or through times eternal. *Chronos* signifies the durative not the seasonal aspect of time. Commentators are divided as to whether reference is to ages before or after creation, probably because of opinions brought to interpretation. Whether there was time before creation or not, however, there are two reasons for the judgment that the *chronoi* (times) are post-creation. The first is scriptural, the second rational. (1) The author of this statement (Rom. 16:25) put time in this *ktisis hetera* (any other created thing) a few columns earlier in the same autograph (Rom. 8:39). The times are '*enestōta... mellontai*' (things present or things to come). Scholastic theology may rightly speak of God's 'uncreated glory' but not of His 'uncreated time'. (2) Both time and space have to do with things, objects. Before creation there were no 'things', God alone is self-existent and all things

---

12. Langdon Gilkey, *Maker of Heaven and Earth: The Christian Doctrine of Creation in the Light of Modern Knowledge* (Garden City, NY: Doubleday & Co., 1965), p. 1.
13. Ps. 89:11-15; 90:1, 2; 146:5, 6; and all of Pss. 90, 104, 136, 139, 147, 148.

outside of Him are neither contemporaneous with His 'origin' (if we may so speak), nor with Him when He creates them. He has no reference to them nor He to them. It is customary and correct to say that time existed 'in God' from eternity, and so existed before creation. But that existence is not concrete, objective existence any more than are Plato's eternal forms or the monads of German philosophers or whatever is reckoned to be in the Absolute. My right hand and the Japanese mechanical pencil I hold in it existed in God's eternal counsels before the world began also, but not as real existence in a created world.

Commenting on eternity as an attribute of God, A. H. Strong observes:

> 'We must not make *Kronos* (time) and *Ouranos* (space) earlier divinities before God'. They are among the 'all things' that were 'made by him' (John 1:3) [quoting I. A. Dorner]. Yet time and space are not *substances*; neither are they *attributes* (qualities of substance); they are rather *relations* of finite existence... With finite existence they come into being; they are not mere regulative conceptions of our minds; they exist objectively, whether we perceive them or not... 'They furnish the conditions of our knowledge... Space and time are mental forms, but not only that. There is an extramental something in the case of space and time as in the case of sound' [quoting G. T. Ladd].[14]

This topic is among listings of about every encyclopedia.[15]

3. This biblical concept of time as created, linear durative has had a determinative influence on Christendom, where it has been nourished.

Carl F. H. Henry, in two dictionary articles, starts his development of time in history, theology, philosophy and the Bible with this fine statement, speaking of

> one of the most vexing problems of philosophy. The Bible presents a distinctive conception of time... Instead of viewing time abstractly as a problem, it regards time *as a created sphere* [emphasis added] in which God's redemptive plan is actualized.[16]

The importance of regarding time as a creature of God, not a condition within which He exists and works, has been seen clearly by most theologians – as opposed to the idealistic philosophers of the nineteenth-century (Hegel and disciples) who placed time and history in the *Absolute*, their God. Neo-orthodox writers credit the Hebrew people (not Old Testament Scripture as such) with correcting among the ancients the cyclical view of history. Early Christian theologians saw the cultural importance of doctrine long ago.[17] In a comprehensive treatment of the doctrine of divine creation Langdon Gilkey has this to say:

> One of the most significant and dramatic points in the development of Western culture was the victory over [the] deadly view of circular time achieved by the biblical understanding of history. As important culturally as the destruction of the pagan gods was the overthrowing of the endless cycles: for on nothing does the modern sense of life depend so directly as on the Christian view of time. The contrast between these two conceptions of time was absolute; and only a faith as virile and certain as that of early Christianity could have uprooted the ingrained sense of temporal meaninglessness that permeated and deadened the ancient world.[18]

Gilkey goes on to warn the Western world once transformed by the biblical view of time but now operating on a theory of evolutionary 'progress' (and, I would add, of 'cultural diversity'):

> Having dispensed... with its religious foundation on the rock of the divine eternity, the divine creation, and the divine providence, this edifice [belief in progress as norm] has proved too shaky. Based now solely on the sand of historical observation instead of the rock of faith, it has no deeper foundation on which to stand the recent storms of history, and threatens to collapse.[19]

Unfortunately Gilkey, who came to write theology after a short career in literature, accepted the disjunction between a factual revelation and a myth-but-true revelation of the then prevalent neo-orthodoxy. He has no assurance that the absolute beginning taught in Scripture and understood by numberless generations of Jews and

---

14. A. H. Strong, *Systematic Theology* (Valley Forge, PA: Judson Press, 1907), p. 275.
15. A contrary view is set forth by R. A. Killen. R. A. Killen, 'Time'. In *Wycliffe Bible Encyclopedia* vol. II, ed, Pfeiffer, Vos & Rea (Chicago: Moody Press, 1975), p. 1708.
16. Carl F. H. Henry, article 'Time' appears in both *Evangelical Dictionary of Theology* and the earlier *Baker Dictionary of Theology*.
17. See Augustine, *The City of God*, Book 12, chapters 13 and 14.
18. Gilkey, *op. cit.*, p. 301.
19. Gilkey, *op. cit.*, pp. 309, 310.

Christians is factually true. Thus the unstable tension between 'religion' and 'science' as he understood it is given the status of a learned form of enlightened 'orthodoxy'. Though he and others of similar persuasion keep the 'religious value' of absolute creation, they tie it to the idea of a continuation of divine creation in the evolutionary process. Hence, to borrow Browning's line, Gilkey's idea of creation 'That began best' did 'end worst', and what was 'once blessed' has indeed 'proved accurst'.[20]

III. Genesis 1:1-3 and the Doctrine of Creation.

The discussion of God's work of creation to this point has established that the Bible teaches (1) the world, including heaven and earth, all that exists, was created by God and (2) the world had a beginning when God created the heavens and the earth, at which moment (or epoch) both time and space came into existence.

Before proceeding to discuss the methods, means and purposes of the triune God in creation some problems and questions related to our discussion this far call for at least brief attention. They are as follows. First, is Genesis 1:1 a distinct, independent sentence or is it a subordinate clause qualifying the second verse? Second, is Genesis 1:1 a summary of the passage on to the end of the creation narrative or a statement of absolute origin of the matter and energy of the universe with the rest of the narrative relating what happened following? Third, how should the seven days of creation and of Sabbath rest be interpreted? The first two questions just proposed, as necessary preliminaries to further considertion of the doctrine of creation, will be answered together.

The first 'offical' translation of Genesis 1:1-3 is the Greek Septuagint of about 280 BC. It was made by Jewish scholars familiar with Hebrew as a second (perhaps first) language and probably used at home as well as synagogue. At any rate they were familiar with Hebrew syntax, grammar and idiom. They translated verse 1 as an independent statement of which verse 2 is an enlargement about the same as KJV, RV, RSV and, recently, ESV. Juxtaposed below are the RSV of 1952, the NRSV of 1989 and Spieser's translation in *Genesis* of *The Anchor Bible* of 1964. RSV retains the independence of verse 1 and represents the obvious, simple syntax of the Hebrew text and of previous versions. The other two introduce principles of modification that scarcely fit any category except adaptation to modern evolutionary, materialistic understanding of reality. That principle is evolutionary theory applied to translation and interpretation. Hold in mind that though some recent evangelical, orthodox scholars might accept one or the other of the 'new syntax' versions, it originated in liberal (if not post-modern) interpretation of the history of ideas.

RSV of 1952 '1. In the beginning God created the heavens and the earth. 2. ['and' omitted] The earth was without form and void, and darkness was upon the face of the deep; and the Spirit of God was moving upon the face of the waters. 3. And God said, "Let there be light", and there was light'. NRSV of 1989 '1. In the beginning when God created the heavens and the earth, 2. the earth was a formless void and darkness covered the face of the deep, while a wind from God swept over the face of the waters. 3. Then God said, "Let there be light"; and there was light.'

The Anchor Bible: Genesis of 1964 '1. When God set about to create heaven and earth – 2. the world being then a formless waste, with darkness over the seas and only an awesome wind sweeping over the water – 3. God said, 'Let there be light'. And there was light'.

Except for the omission of 'and' as the first word of verse 2 the RSV of 1952 has essentially the same sense as all translations from the Greek Septuagint of about 280 BC to Luther's Bible of four centuries ago and on to the ASV of 1901.

Thoroughly to report, discuss and document the reasons for the obvious changes in Spieser's translation in the *Anchor Bible* and the NRSV, now standard in liberal churches and used in some conservative evangelical ones, cannot be undertaken here. Having myself, over an initial period of ten years of teaching seminary courses, taken students painstakingly through the first twelve or fifteen chapters of Genesis annually, it is tempting to wade in more deeply than is prudent here.

Let us make one general observation and several specific ones. I shall try to avoid use of technical grammatical-syntactical jargon.

1. There is ongoing controversy over how much of the translator's interpretation of the text should be incorporated into translation from original languages of the Bible to current languages. The degree varies within the first known one, the Septuagint, but generally speaking the translators who issued the Authorized Version of 1611 held as close to

---

20. Robert Browning, *Apparent Failure*, lines 62 and 63.

literal rendering as possible for conveying meaning in language of minimally educated people. Yet they rendered the text as elegantly as possible. If slang existed then they did not use it but made few concessions to prissy sensibilities (as, for example, David's oath).[21] However, several of the new Versions, sometimes with reserve, sometimes blatantly, adjust the translation, against the long tradition of meaning and against the natural reading, to fit their opinions of what the ancient Hebrews really thought and said. This is clearly the case in these late twentieth-century translations.

2. Both NRSV and *Anchor Bible* say that when God 'created' heaven and earth 'the earth' (NRSV) or 'the world' (AB) was already in existence. The translators are assuming, in spite of the simple and plainest sense of this passage, that the cosmology and cosmogony (order and origin of the world) prevalent among ancient heathen nations of the Levant and Mesopotamia was shared by the author(s) of Genesis 1:1-3. It is true that the myths of the priests of Mesopotamia and Canaan presuppose the existence of formless matter previous even to the birth of their gods. So their 'creation' myths have the gods creating the heavens and earth (and underworld too) of pre-existing materials. About the standard Mesopotamian form of the myth, the *Enuma Elish* epic, Jack Finegan, in one of his many standard volumes says:

> The account begins with the time when only the two divine principles, the mythical personalities Apsu and Tiamat, were in existence. These two represented the living, uncreated world-matter, Apsu being the primeval sweet-water ocean and Tiamat the primeval salt-water ocean… Tiamat is explicitly called a woman in the myth… and she and Apsu become the mother and father of the gods.[22]

After awhile, in one of the myths, Marduk, one of the created gods, created the earth. Later on, one of the pantheon named Kingu 'was slain and when his arteries were cut open the gods fashioned mankind with his blood.'[23] Speiser points out (correctly) that in ancient Mesopotamia (whence Hebrew ancestors came) 'science often blended into religion' and claims 'that on the subject of creation, biblical tradition aligned itself with the traditional tenets of Babylonian "science"'.[24] He thinks (as about all who follow this line of thought) that the Hebrew account (Gen. 1) is the myths, purified by ethical monotheism.

Speiser marshalls his arguments from grammar-syntax for the new view on one and one-third pages.[25] They are not definitive, however, as even the scholars of NRSV acknowledge in their first footnote, which says: 'The traditional translation as an independent sentence, following the Greek Bible (Septuagint) of the 3rd century BC, is defensible', etc. In their notes NRSV proposes three defensible translations, of which the traditional is one. In any case they know the evidences are not compelling.

Franz Delitzsch (not in the Keil and Delitzsch series) brought his immense mastery of Hebrew and related studies to these three verses. He commits himself to the traditional translation, in the way he introduces comments on Genesis 1:1 – 'The Fact of creation in a universal statement: In the beginning Elohim created the heavens and the earth.' Yet he gave full range to contrary views and proposed contrary evidence, making this statement:

> Ancient translators all regard verse 1 as an independent proposition. Rashi [celebrated Jewish Scholar, 1040–1105], however, and among moderns Ewald, Bunson, Schraeder, Budde construe: In the beginning, when Elohim created heaven and earth – and the earth was waste and desert, etc. – then God said; otherwise Abenezra [1092–1167, one of the most distinguished Jewish scholars of the Middle Ages] and Grotius [Dutch savant]: In the beginning, when Elohim created the heaven and the earth, the earth was waste and desert.[26]

So the current departures from the traditional rendering of Genesis 1:1 have these precedents. Delitzsch, however, in a display of technical finesse hard either to report or to match, I think, demolished the notion of this supposed biblical ground for a world of chaotic mass of material in existence before God first moved to create the present world order. H. C. Leupold, in his justly praised work, declares:

> The phrase, 'In the beginning (*bereshith*) refers to the absolute beginning of created things… This fact is supported by the following arguments in the face of many and strong claims to the contrary.'[27]

---

21. 1 Sam. 25:22, 34; cf. 1 Kings 14:10; 16:11 *et al.*
22. Jack Finegan, *Light from the Ancient Past: The Archeological Background of Judaism and Christianity* (Princeton: Princeton Univ. Press, 1969), p. 63.
23. ibid., pp. 64, 65.
24. E. A. Speiser, *The Anchor Bible: Genesis* (Garden City, Doubleday, 1964), p. 11.
25. ibid., pp. 12, 13.
26. Franz Delitzsch, *New Commentary on Genesis* (Edinburgh: T. & T. Clark, 1888), pp. 74, 75.
27. H. C. Leupold, *Exposition of Genesis* (Columbus, OH: Wartburg Press, 1942), p. 39.

Leupold is an arch conservative, but Gerhard Von Rad, a celebrated recent Form-Critical Old Testament scholar, and convinced advocate of the documentary theory of pentateuchal origins, regards the view we are resisting here as impossible for theological reasons, precisely because the late priestly (post-exilic) author could not have assigned any truth at all to the Babylonians. This he emphatically renounces, holding as plain sense the demand for full rejection of the myths.[28] I must agree when he states, 'These sentences [Gen. 1:1-2, 4a] cannot be easily overinterpreted theologically' (p. 46)! I must quote somewhat at length. After his strong language in support of the ancient and traditional translation of Genesis 1:1-3, one reads:

> Syntactically perhaps both translations are possible, but not theologically. One must not deprive the declaration in v. 1 of the character of a theological principle. If one considers vs. 1-2 or 1-3 as the syntactical unit, then the word about chaos would stand logically and temporally before the word about creation. To be sure, the notion of a created chaos is itself a contradiction; nevertheless, one must remember that the text touches on things which in any case lie beyond human imagination. That does not mean, however, that one must renounce establishing quite definite and unrelinquishable theologumena. The first is that God, in the freedom of his will, creatively established for 'heaven and earth,' i.e. for absolutely everything, a beginning of its subsequent existence. The second is expressed in v. 2, for unless one speaks of chaos, creation cannot be sufficiently considered at all. To express divine creation, the Hebrew language already had a verb, which, as the Phoenician shows, could designate the artistic creation. But the Old Testament usage rejects even this comparison. The verb was retained exclusively to designate the divine creative activity. This effective theological constraint which extends even into the language is significant (cf. *salah*, 'to forgive,' alluding only to divine forgiving). It means a creative activity, which on principle is without analogy. It is correct to say that the verb *bara*, 'create', contains the idea both of complete effortlessness and *creatio ex nihilo*, since it is never connected with any statement of the material. The hidden pathos of this statement is that God is the Lord of the world. But not only in the sense that he subjected a pre-existing chaos to his ordering will! It is amazing to see how sharply little Israel demarcated herself from an apparently over-powering environment of cosmological and theogonic myths. Here the subject is not a primeval mystery of procreation from which the divinity arose, nor of a 'creative' struggle of mythically personified powers from which the cosmos arose, but rather the one who is neither warrior nor procreator, who alone is worthy of the predicate, Creator.[29]

Robert L. Reymond provides a valuable advocacy of the syntactical independence of Genesis 1:1, including the excellent contributions of Edward J. Young.[30]

I summarize reasons for continuing to treat Genesis 1:1 as an independent sentence, opening the Bible with the profound declaration of absolute origin of the world by God's act of creation 'in the beginning'.

1. *Bereshith* (in the beginning) as accented by the Massorites (standard in all Hebrew Bibles)[31] tends to support the independence of the sentence.

2. Though contested, as noted above, the Massoretic pointing (vowels) and accentuation, standard now for over 1,000 years, supports (if it does not demand) the independence of verse 1 from verses 2 and 3.[32]

In other words, the technical features in no wise require a change from the traditional rendering. This is convincingly supported by Delitzsch and Edward J. Young among many others. See also G. J. Spurrell.[33]

3. The proposal to unite verses 1-3 into one complex sentence 'is opposed… to the simplicity of style which pervades the whole chapter, and to which so involved a sentence would be intolerable, apart altogether from the fact that this construction is invented for the simple purpose of getting rid of the doctrine of *creatio ex nihilo*, which is so repulsive to modern pantheism.'[34] Though I cite the authority of Keil, thousands of readers of Genesis in the standard versions before the NRSV of 1989 would share Keil's opinion as well as the thousands of seminarians who have learned to read the verses in Hebrew. Speiser does not document his statement: 'the majority of medieval Hebrew commentators and grammarians… could see no objection to viewing Genesis 1:1 as a dependent clause.'[35] Are Rashi (1041–1105) and Aben Ezra (1092–1167) a 'majority' of Jewish scholars of the Middle Ages?

---

28. Gerhard Von Rad, *Genesis, A Commentary* (Philadelphia: Westminster Press, 1961), pp. 45, 46.
29. ibid., pp. 46, 47.
30. Robert L. Reymond, *A New Systematic Theology of the Christian Faith* (Nashville: Thomas Nelson, 1998), pp. 384–391.
31. See Delitzsch, pp. 74 – 78, also Young, as cited by Reymond.
32. See Appendix to this chapter, p. 151.
33. G. J. Spurrell, *Notes on the Hebrew Text of the Book of Genesis* (Oxford: Clarendon Press, 1887), pp. 1–3.
34. C. F. Keil, *Biblical Commentary on the Old Testament, vol. i*, Keil & Delitzsch (Edinburgh: T. & T. Clark, n.d.), p. 46.
35. Speiser, *op. cit.*, p. 12.

4. Liberal modern scholarship is opposed to the idea of revelation to divinely accredited messengers (Moses, apostles, prophets). This predisposes most of them to assume the author(s) of Genesis 1–3 shared the view of the ancient Near East that chaotic matter, not a self-existent Creator, was already present 'in the beginning'. Dr Reymond enlarges on this important point.[36] This explains why – although most of them acknowledge that verse one may properly be an independent sentence – they prefer to regard it as subordinate to verse 2. This supports their views of the evolutionary origin of cultural ideas.

5. John's Gospel, in obvious and usually uncontested reference to and dependence on Genesis 1:1, says: 'In the beginning was the Word... All things were made through him'. This depends entirely on understanding Genesis 1:1 as an independent sentence.

6. The Septuagint of Genesis 1:1, the most ancient extant translation, reads *en archē epoiēsen ho theos*, etc. (and there is no proof of modification of the text of this verse). This translates the Hebrew as an independent sentence. It is also the obvious source of the opening of John 1:1. In each case the phrase refers to absolute beginning.

7. The Jews in ancient times, when Hebrew was still a living language for some, and widely comprehended by others, understood Genesis 1:1 as teaching the absolute origin of all things in acts of God. This too is acknowledged by some of the scholars who think that a mistake. We have already noted the Septuagint rendering of about 280 BC.

8. Creation out of 'things that were not' was the common faith of ancient Jews throughout their history. This is apparent in the many references to creation in the Old Testament. Also, in the inter-testamental period we have the confession of the martyr mother of the seven martyr brothers who admonished her son: 'I beseech thee, my son, look upon the heaven and the earth, and all that is therein, and consider that God made them of things that were not' (2 Maccabees 7:28). A faithful regard for the Bible's own claim for the Mosaic antiquity of the first chapter of Genesis would insist, it seems to me, that these ancient people derived their view of creation from the first chapter of the Torah, not by inference from some experiences in the eighth to fifth centuries BC (as Von Rad supposes).

9. What has been said in the previous paragraph applies to statements of the New Testament, such as Hebrews 11:3 – 'the universe was created by the word of God, so that what is seen was not made out of things that are visible' – and Romans 4:17, which speaks of 'God in whom he [Abraham] believed, who gives life to the dead and calls into existence the things that do not exist', and much more.

A Final Comment.

Von Rad, as many who share his opinion, acknowledges that ancient Jews interpreted Genesis 1:1 as an independent sentence affirming 'creation out of nothing' by God, *yet* holds they were mistaken.

Arguments as to the grammar and syntax of Genesis 1–3, pro and con, have been vigorously pursued for about two centuries now in the scholarly literature. The reader should be aware that this is contemporary with the rise of evolutionary theories of development of all religions, including the religion of Israel. The same is true of most critical theories of the origin and growth of the literature of Israel which we call the Old Testament. This led negative critical scholarship away from any notion of supernatural (special) revelation. Hence the appearance of a strictly monotheistic religion and a doctrine of fiat 'by the word of God' creation in the fifteenth or fourteenth century BC and a prophet like Moses is unthinkable. So if feasible such critics will take fiat (*ex nihilo*) out of Genesis 1:1-3. They prefer a primeval, pre-existing chaos to be expressed in Genesis 1:1-3, such as was the view of second millennium BC Babylonians, Assyrians and Canaanites. Interestingly, however, Von Rad sees the logic of a late Priestly origin (P of the JEDP theory) for Genesis chapter 1 would require the doctrine of creation *ex nihilo*, then admittedly present in Jewish minds. He advocates the same documentary theory of origin held by those represented by Speiser but a better logic and, hence, a better syntax!

Appendix to Chapter 17.

No one brings better technical credentials to interpreting Hebrew texts than were brought by Umberto Cassuto, a Jewish scholar. In his commentary, he states the opposing view that in Genesis 1, verses 1 and 2 (or perhaps the first three verses) are parts of one sentence, then says:

---

36. Reymond, *op. cit.*, pp. 387–389.

[A] decisive objection can be raised on the basis of the syntactical construction of verse 2. If the first rendering ['at the beginning of the creation of the heavens and the earth, when the earth was without form and void'] were correct, the predicate in the second verse would precede the subject, *viz. wattehi ha'arets* ['and was the earth'], or *hayetha ha'arets* ['was the earth']; cf. Jer. 26:1, 'In the beginning of the reign of Jehoiakin... CAME THIS WORD, etc.; so too Jer. 27:1; 28:1 and Hos. 1:2: 'when the LORD first spoke to Hosea, SAID THE LORD to Hosea'. Had the second translation [verses 1-3 a single sentence, 'at the beginning... when the earth was... God said', etc.], been correct, the wording would have been: *weha'aretz tohu wabhohu* ['and the earth without form and void'] omitting *hayetha* ['was'].

Here Cassuto illustrates from the Hebrew text of 1 Samuel 3:2-4 and concludes: 'It follows, therefore, that the first verse is an independent sentence that constitutes a formal introduction to the entire section, and expresses at the outset, with majestic brevity, the main thought of the section: that in the beginning, that is at the commencement of time, in the remotest past, that the human mind can conceive, God created the heavens and the earth.'[37]

---

37. Umberto Cassuto, *A Commentary on the Book of Genesis, Part One*, trans. Israel Abrahams (Jerusalem: Magnes Press, The Hebrew University, 1944, 1978), pp. 19, 20.

18
God's Work of Creation, Part II

IV. The Divine Work of creating the Heavens and Earth was Completed.

The divine work of creating the heavens and earth and all that is in them had not only a time of beginning but a definite time of completion. This proposition must be qualified to point out that there is a 'heaven of heavens' above the material universe where angels 'behold the face' of Jesus' 'Father who is in heaven'. These angels were present when God 'laid the foundation of the earth… when the morning stars sang together and all the sons of God shouted for joy' (Job 38:4, 7). We do not know what worlds there may be besides the cosmos, of which is our galaxy, near the eye of which our solar system revolves, about whose center our earth, scene of important transactions, occupies a portion. This world, however, is no longer coming into existence. God began to create 'in the beginning' and completed the great work in six successive creative [not necessarily solar] days. After that 'on the seventh day God finished his work that he had done, and he rested on the seventh day from all his work that he had done' (Gen. 2:2).

Was there any continuing work of creation? Moses seems to answer with an emphatic *No*. 'Thus the heavens and the earth were finished, and all the host of them. And… God finished his work' (Gen 2:1, 2a).

The Bible occasionally describes some subsequent works of God as creating, making, forming, and the like. In each case there is no suggestion that God is adding materials to what He did in the biblical creative beginning. This world which God created and where redemption is in process is, as far as divine revelation is concerned, no smaller or larger than when on the seventh day 'he rested… from all his work that he had done'. There are continuing divine works in this world. Jesus said so, as we shall shortly attend to, but they involve preservation and providence, upkeep and governance, to employ non-theological language.

As we shall demonstrate shortly, the primary meaning of the Hebrew word *bara'*, create, is to bring into existence something new, having no inherent reference at all to whether pre-existing materials are used. It is the context of the statement, the syntax of the sentence and numerous later statements of Scripture that definitively show that 'the heavens and the earth' (our universe) had absolute beginning in God's creative act, and such is what the opening statement of the entire Bible means. When God says, 'behold, I create new heavens and a new earth' (Isa. 65:17) it is *re-newal*, as the next verse, in parallel use of *bara'*, shows. There God says 'behold I create Jerusalem to be a joy' – clearly a renewal, not something *ex nihilo*.[1] God is said to create the changes in the world of nature (Ps. 104:30) but that is equated with renewing 'the face of the ground' in parallel statement.

To sum up, in the many texts of Scripture which speak of God's creating something, never is any addition to the material creation intended. Procreation – as in the birth of babies and animals – is quite the same. In no case is new material brought into being, as in the sense of Genesis 1:1 and subsequent references to it.

To cite an admirer of Augustine who was also well acquainted with Aquinas, Calvin comments on Psalm 104:30:

> He [the Psalmist] again declares, that the world is daily *renewed*, because God *sendeth forth his spirit*. In the propagation of living creatures, we doubtless see continually a new creation of the world (emphasis added).[2]

Calvin plainly interprets the propagation of life, in what we now call nature, as *renewal* not *fiat* (or *de novo* or *ex nihilo* creation).

Jonathan Edwards and several New England theologians who followed, while not rejecting an original divine creation, asserted continuous moment-by-moment creation. Descartes, before Edwards, taught that preservation means ongoing creation at each moment.[3] Edwards' is more a theory of metaphysics than of theology and is of interest chiefly because it was famously advocated by a learned and godly man of historical importance. The central idea is that the same sort of divine action which began the world and all its parts is necessary continually to maintain it, else it would retreat to nothingness. A. H. Strong devotes about a page to the advocates and their arguments and two to his objections[4] and likewise C. A. Hodge.[5]

The doctrine of *continued creation* is rather conspicuously proposed by some recent authors. Thomas Oden – in a quite satisfactory discussion of the origin of time and space concurrently with creation of the cosmos – proposes this somewhat puzzling sentence:

> The very idea of creation implies this paradoxical conjunction: as divine activity, creation is eternally occurring, transcending all specific times and places; as temporal effect, creation has a beginning and end, however remote.[6]

Oden goes on to refer to Augustine (*Confessions* XI.10–13). But I think Oden has misread Augustine, for in the section cited the bishop of Hippo said: 'If we mean by the whole of creation when we speak of heaven and earth, I unreservedly say that before he made heaven and earth, God made nothing' (*Confessions* XI.12). He additionally makes clear that ideas in the mind of God have no concrete existence in the world of heaven and earth. Oden also cites Thomas Aquinas (*Summa Theologica* I.45.1). But in that article Aquinas says nothing remotely like Oden's opinion that 'creation is eternally occurring' in God's mind or anywhere or any other time than in the one creative epoch.

Dr Oden's enigmatic statement does not really endorse the notion the world we live in is either *continuously* being created or that in it God is occasionally creating new materials for the world He made 'in the beginning'.

What Thomas Oden seems merely to hint, perhaps as reflection of some unstated metaphysical speculation, Wolfhart Pannenberg states – not without reservations and concessions to what he acknowledges to be the contrary sense of 'the Old Testament stories', but plainly. Pannenberg is a learned writer, as much metaphysician as theologian. He brings the weight of the history of philosophical speculation to bear, and an apparent acceptance of the ancient creeds, but only as much authority of Scripture as passes the bar of the critical judgment of modern criticism. Let Pannenberg speak for himself:

> A trinitarian exposition of the concept of creation makes it possible, then, to relate what is said about creation to the totality of the world from the standpoint of its duration in time. It does not concern merely the world's beginning. To limit it [creation] to the beginning, as the Old Testament stories seem to do in accordance with Near Eastern myths of a primal era, is one sided. Yet what the two Genesis accounts are really seeking to describe is the normative and abiding basis of creaturely reality in the form of depiction of the initial event.

---

1. I sought to demonstrate that the eschatological 'new earth' of 2 Peter 3:10-13 and the last chapters of Revelation is re-pristination of the old one in a dissertation published as *Daniel and the Latter Days* and later in *The Earthly Reign of Our Lord With His People*. Robert D. Culver, *Daniel and the Latter Days* (Chicago: Moody Press, 1954, 1977), pp. 177–190. *The Earthly Reign of Our Lord With His People* (20508 County 26, Houston, MN 55943: Vinegar Hill Press, 1999), pp. 188-200.
2. John Calvin, *Commentary on the Psalms* vol. IV, trans. James Anderson (Edinburgh: Calvin Translation Society, 1847), p. 168.
3. Descartes, *Meditations III*, 36 cited by Pannenberg in *Systematic Theology II* (Grand Rapids: Eerdmans, 1994), p. 49.
4. A. H. Strong, *Systematic Theology* (Valley Forge, PA: Judson Press, 1907), pp. 415–419.
5. Charles A. Hodge, *Systematic Theology I*, (Grand Rapids: Eerdmans, 1960), pp. 577–581.
6. Thomas Oden, *The Living God, Systematic Theology I* (San Francisco: HarperCollins, 1992), p. 242.

> Thus preservation goes with creation. Nor are we to view preservation simply as an unchanging conservation of the forms of creaturely existence laid down at the first. *It is a living occurrence, continued creation* [emphasis added], a constantly new creative fashioning that goes beyond what was given existence originally. Creation, preservation, and overruling [providence] thus form a unity whose structural relation has yet to be defined more closely.[7]

Thus while quite traditionally recognizing the three distinct divine works of God toward the cosmos (creation, preservation and providence), he also blurs their distinctions and affirms 'continued creation'. He promises to define the 'relations' 'more closely' later. Which indeed he does through the following 128 pages. It includes a systematic survey of views of the cosmos; the nature of reality in philosophy from the pre-socratic Greek metaphysicians through Whitehead, Bergson and Bertrand Russell; the theologians, Jewish, Christian and Islamic, from Philo to Teilhard de Chardin and Karl Barth; and the scientists from feeble beginnings to the amazing discoverers and discoveries, Planck, Einstein, Heisenberg and the rest. Along the way several of Pannenberg's ideas regarding the doctrine of creation are clarified and supported.

1. Pannenberg's understanding of divine creation of the natural order by evolution requires that creation and preservation be one ongoing process. He appeals to scriptural statements about 'the creative nature of God's acts in history' and acknowledges 'this approach has its roots in the atomic theory of Democritus'. He asserts that 'the element of chance [as Democritus featured it]... is important for theological interpretation of the ongoing creative action of God'.[8]

2. Creation, preservation and providence must be united with the consummation.[9] This consummation is being progressively realized in an evolutionary process. He has fully absorbed evolutionary process as developed by Darwin and clarified by leaders of thought in recent times. That the universe is expanding indefinitely and gives added space for onward development.[10]

3. The resistance to evolutionary explanation of the world by Christians has been mistaken and futile.

> In the 19th and early 20th centuries Christian churches and theologians were painfully slow to recognize this opportunity that evolution had given theology relative to natural science. The fight against Darwinism was a momentous mistake in the relations between science and theology... We say this in spite of the hypothetical character of the theory of evolution.[11]

4. The Holy Spirit (whom he firmly sees as the *ruach*, spirit, not wind in Gen. 1:2) is the agent of creation in the evolutionary world process (76–115). He finds connection between the 'field of force' theories of recent physicists and the energy of the Spirit of God effecting the 'sequence of forms' and all else moving to the perfection and consummation (108–110 *et al*). In a manner he does not make clear, the Spirit of God is 'the dynamic of natural occurrence, which is in effect the evolution of earth and its living inhabitants'. He says: '[I]n the history of earth... the development of organized life... changed the face of the earth. Vegetables... molluscs... reptiles... mammals ... and then humans.' He sees in this 'higher structuring... from atoms and stars to humans, and especially the development of life... a kind of countertrend to the increase of entropy in natural processes... The evolution of life [is]... an upward movement toward increasingly higher and more complex forms of organization.'[12]

5. As far as the narrative account of creation and the flood is concerned, though there are good insights, it is based on an antiquated view of the world, hence not to be regarded as authoritative. He calls it 'time bound'. He writes:

> The story carries features of a view of nature that was widespread in the Near East in the first millennium [not second, Moses' time]... a particular example of a time bound insight that we have now.[13]

---

7. Wolfhart Pannenberg, *Systematic Theology II*, trans. G. W. Bromiley (Grand Rapids:, Eerdmans, 1994), p. 34.
8. I have already stated biblical reasons for rejecting the continued-acts of creation theory, which I shall not repeat. Pannenberg brings modern developmental theories of evolutionary development not only to his doctrine of creation but by way of the documentary-development theory of the composition of the Old Testament and to the formation and history of Israel's religion of faith in one God, the rituals, sacrificial and festival system, and the ethics of the Pentateuch and prophetic section of the Old Testament.
9. ibid., pp. 136 – 140.
10. ibid., p. 127.
11. ibid., p. 119 and note 310, p. 119.
12. ibid., p. 113.
13. ibid., pp. 116, 117.

6. Though the authors of Genesis 1 had an utterly mistaken word picture (*weltbild*) ('The story of the flood tells us what happens when leaks in the vault [firmament] occur and are not stopped') they were only 'bearing impressive testimony to the science of antiquity'. We should not follow their cosmology, but 'should follow where the biblical witness leads by claiming current knowledge of the world for a description of the divine work of creation... theologically appropriating contemporary knowledge'.[14]

I shall not repeat my reasons for rejecting the idea of continual creation complementing or completing at the beginning a cosmos, including all its living creatures. Whatever place there may be in real history for development in the variety of the earth's features – inert, chemical, topographical, geological and biological – there is no place in plain statements of theological fact in the Bible to support emergent evolution or equating a so-called *elan vital* with the Second and Third Persons of the Godhead in a continued creation.

V. God and Man in the Present Created Order.

I have in mind features of the world created in part by God, presently sustained and governed by Him, which are built into that *cosmos*. Cosmos is the Greek term (*kusmos*) usually behind 'world' in the English New Testament. We are thinking of the world, the creation, into which we, the descendants of Adam, the first man, are born and from which we view 'the heavens and the earth'. Let us look closely, briefly and naively, without bringing speculative, philosophical theories along with us.

1. God has left traces of Himself in the created material world. By means of these 'traces', as I have called them, people are able to draw inferences about their Creator. Just as the electric light tells us something (though only a little) about the genius of Thomas Edison, its inventor, and my sister-in-law's beautiful handmade quilts about Marie their maker, so 'The heavens declare the glory of God, and the sky above proclaims his handiwork' (Ps. 19:1). This is Hebrew idiom for majesty and power. Paul says that though God's attributes as such are 'invisible', 'since the creation of the world' (cosmos), God's 'power and divine nature' are 'clearly perceived' by the mind, by way of necessary inference (Rom. 1:20). Scripture also says the wisdom of God is manifest in His works, especially in the subtlety and variety of the creatures: 'In wisdom have you made them all' (Ps. 104:24). See Calvin's comments on Psalm 119:15.[15] Calvin said the knowledge of God shines forth in the fashioning of the universe and the continuing government of it, beginning his chapter on the subject with these eminently quotable sentences:

> The final goal of the blessed life... rests in the knowledge of God. Lest anyone then, be excluded from access to happiness, he not only sowed in men's minds that seed of religion of which we have spoken but revealed himself and daily discloses himself in the whole workmanship of the universe. As a consequence, men cannot open their eyes without being compelled to see him. Indeed, his essence is incomprehensible, hence, his divineness far escapes all human perception. But upon his individual works he has engraved unmistakable marks of his glory, so clear and so prominent that even unlettered and stupid folk cannot plead ignorance.[16]

Calvin, like good Bible expositors and theologians before and since, brought numerous texts of Scripture as unmistakable evidence, among them Psalm 19: 1-4, Hebrews 11:1-3 and Romans 1:19, 20.

Recent developments in Christian evidence (factual apologetics, some call it) have developed what used to be called 'the teleological argument' or 'argument from design' and 'intelligent design in nature' – the latter both by evolutionary and non-evolutionary theists. Except for technical features of recent science in these discussions all is anticipated in Calvin's treatment. From Butler's *Analogy* onward the teleological argument has varied only in the amount of supporting data supplied, the linguistic force of the argument and the way the conclusions are drawn.

As of this writing two recent books in particular have argued convincingly for the presence of 'intelligent design' in the natural order. Michael Behe, a Roman Catholic author who writes from his professional standpoint as a professor and researcher in one of the life sciences, suggests that perhaps organic evolution does prevail in the natural order and is thereby 'intelligent design' – hence a Creator-Designer. Evidences drawn for intelligent design seem decisive.[17]

---

14. ibid., pp. 116, 117.
15. John Calvin, *Institutes III*, 25.7 and I,15.3.
16. Calvin, *Institutes I*, 5.1.
17. Michael Behe, *Darwin's Black Box: The Biological Challenge to Evolution* (New York: Free Press, 1996).

Phillip E. Johnson, a lawyer, argues somewhat less technically to a conclusion of intelligent design.[18] A stream of new literature, videos, and similar, supporting this approach, is developing.[19]

Not only primal unfallen mankind but sinners such as we are do see these unmistakable evidences. It is only a mark of our depravity, according to Scripture (Rom. 1:19 ff.), that people refuse to retain God in their knowledge and are therefore 'without excuse'.

2. God has left far more than traces of Himself in the created constitution of human beings. That mankind is 'the image and likeness of God' says this in a general way. Mankind's nature, what and who we are, mirrors God's nature in some particulars – certainly not completely. Further, by creation and subsequent procreation, every child of Adam has the voice of God in his heart (conscience) telling everyone of us we *ought* to do right and 'accusing' or 'excusing' our thoughts, which says much more. This is taught specifically in Romans 1:19, where Paul says 'For what can be known about God is plain *to them*' (emphasis added), later expounded in Romans 2:14-15. Even the heathen have 'the work of the law... written on their hearts, while their conscience also bears witness, and their conflicting thoughts accuse or even excuse them' (Rom. 2:15). This expresses knowledge of God as lawmaker and judge is written in mankind's consciousness, suppressable but not expungeable.

Moreover, by looking carefully at other members of our race and by serious introspection – as being the image and likeness of God (Gen. 1:26, 27) and 'the image and glory of God' (1 Cor. 11:7) – we find not only our sinful self, but in our creaturely excellencies a 'clear mirror of God's works' (Calvin, *Institutes I*,1.3). Calvin again here has an excellent paragraph (*Institutes I*,5.3). I take the matter up more fully in treatment of the doctrine of mankind (see Part 2: Anthropology: Man as Created).

There is considerable difference of opinion as to whether so-called 'general revelation' in God's creatures, nature and human beings, is sufficient basis for a 'natural theology' parallel to 'revealed theology' or as preliminary to revealed theology. Neo-orthodox theologians Barth and Brunner debated this in terms no longer of much interest today. I shall here forebear entering that not very fruitful debate. It does seem to me that based only upon the limited content of natural (general) revelation there are important theological affirmations to be made: that God is; that God is an almighty, glorious person, creator of me and all I see, hear, feel, touch, taste; and that, if so, He must be worshiped. Further, though spoiled by sin and rendered spiritually dead thereby, people nevertheless have value to God because of our likeness to God and, hence, even in estrangement salvagable.

The literature of this subject was already very large in Martin Luther's time. In his paradoxical manner of teaching salvation wholly by grace through faith on the ground of Christ's work of redemption he characterized theology derived from creation (Rom. 1:20) as false theology when employed by the worldly wise, citing 1 Corinthians 1:21-25. Adam before the fall might have constructed a 'natural theology', but now it only makes those who construct a natural theology fools. What is available to us now is not God's invisible nature but only as much as was made visible in Christ's suffering on our behalf. Luther in this way was repudiating the speculations of medieval scholasticism. One wonders what he might have said of some of the speculations and refinements of the age of Protestant theological scholasticism which immediately followed.[20]

3. Certain creaturely privileges and duties of mankind as crown and climax of God's creative art are set forth in the creation narrative of Genesis. Among these are duties to propagate the race, to exercise dominion (i.e. rule and conservations) over the created environment which supports His existence, to observe a weekly Sabbath, to work as keeper of the garden of Paradise and subsequently elsewhere. These matters I reserve for extended treatment later in the doctrine of mankind.

VI. Social Order for Primal Mankind in a Created Order.

The subject of human society in the created order of things is a topic not always treated in connection with the doctrine of creation but which, in view of current social interests and radical differences of current thought, calls at least for brief attention. Whether viewed as a second creation account or as a fuller account of the sixth day of the creative week, Genesis 2 after verse 4 relates entirely to the creation of 'Man' (Gen. 5:2 ESV): male called *Adam* (earth) and female *Eve*, or more correctly *Ava* (life). The theological implications and consequences of the unity of

---

18. Phillip E. Johnson, *Darwin on Trial* (Downers Grove, IL: InterVarsity Press, 2nd Ed., 1993).
19. Stanley Grenz, *Renewing the Center* (Grand Rapids: Baker Books, 2000), p. 155.
20. See Paul Althaus' treatment of Luther's 'Theology of the Cross'. Paul Althaus, *The Theology of Martin Luther*, trans. R. C. Schultz (Philadelphia: Fortress Press, 1966), pp. 23–34.

the race in the first male, as related to the fall of chapter 3, belong in theological anthropology and I treat them there (in Part 2 of this book) at some length. There are enormous social implications and consequences of the fall as well. I have written a book on that subject.[21] Coercive civil government was not a part of the created human social order. Rather it is a late, post-diluvian development, an aspect of divine preservation and providence. Coercive rule of the mass of mankind by other men was devised by God to control the devastating social effects of the fall.[22] Each of us comes to full flower in society with other people but not necessarily in the state.

There is validity to the contention of some (as noted earlier in the chapter) that God is essentially 'creative' in the sense that in ordering of the world, in His power, wisdom and love, God produces 'new things' – but as an aspect of preservation and providence. The heavens and the earth, however, were finished from the standpoint of the creation narrative, at the end of the sixth day and, on the seventh day, evidently even terminated. As regards creation, God is now resting.

The earth was created in anticipation of mankind's residence there. This is a necessary inference from the Genesis record – mankind is the crown of creation, last created, only then is everything 'very good' (Gen. 1:31) – and it is specifically stated in Psalm 115:16: 'The heavens are the LORD's heavens, but the earth he has given to the children of man.' Karl Barth makes this fact the basis, in part, of the doctrine of angels – those messengers between heaven (the 'above') and earth (the 'beneath') – in *Church Dogmatics III*.[23]

The various spheres of human expression are rooted in created human nature and cannot be made to derive from any source other than what it is to be human. In other words, both personal expression of individuals and of society flow out from human nature. The state or some agency created by the state cannot successfully produce results foreign to the created nature of mankind.

The most obvious of these 'orders' or 'spheres' is marriage and family as the organ for propagation of the race and the primary sphere of social happiness. The philosophers of the French Revolution thought they could abolish it; the Soviets and Maoists and more recently the biological technocrats who wish to give us clone babies have tinkered with abolishing or modifying the family. Yet the formula of monogamous marriage initiated at creation (Gen. 2:21-25) may be corrupted by sinful people, attacked by ambitious technocrats, but hardly abolished. It will always be true that the LORD 'makes... families like flocks' (Ps. 107:41) and where social and civil *shalom* prevails God sets all the solitary 'in families' (Ps. 68:6). Even the numerous social engineers of the secular establishments are now beginning to acknowledge that good families are the only sound foundation of a sound social order.

Other spheres of human expression derive from the created order of things. Among them are the following.

1. The necessity of labour by the human male to support his wife and family. It was Adam not Eve of whom it is said 'The LORD God took the man and put him in the garden of Eden to work ["tend" KJV] it and keep it' (Gen. 2:15). 'Tend' translates Hebrew '*avadh*, meaning to do work, and in certain forms meaning servant and slave. Hard work is not absent from the meaning here. This is previous to the fall, hence in this prototype of the *normal* adult, he is to work vigorously at something as an engine of supply for family needs. The fall only rendered this 'natural' state of affairs more rigorous: 'in pain you shall eat... all the days of your life... By the sweat of your face you shall eat bread' (Gen. 3:17, 19). Like all the duties inherent in mankind by virtue of creation, this duty is also at its best both privilege and sphere of joyful personal fulfillment as well as the means whereby civilization is created.

2. Art, science, education, religion, music, medicine – indeed every form of social expression (of which no complete list has ever been attempted) – are not inventions created by human beings but modes of expression of what they already are. In such a case each such expression has duty and privilege to do and be what it is. They exist together in society and complement one another but are not controlled by one another. The same person may be interested and creative in both art and education, or science and religion, or even in all four and more besides (say architecture and farming). However, he does not learn how to worship God from art any more than he demands that as a builder (architecture) he consult the local pastor (religion) as to how to construct the court house. As Christians it is our duty to bring each of these spheres to the judgment and direction of God, the Creator, who has given freedom to each, conditioned by respect of every one of the other spheres.

---

21. Robert D. Culver, *Civil Government: A Biblical View* (Edmonton, Canada: Canadian Institute for Law, Theology and Public Policy, 1975, 2000) 308 pages.
22. ibid., pp. 64–80.
23. Karl Barth, *Church Dogmatics III*, trans. G. W. Bromiley (Edinburgh: T. & T. Clark, 1975), pp. 369–531.

A creation subjected to the vanity of sin both in mankind and all we survey is inevitably destined for conflict. Which of God's gifts have not we corrupted in some way? Nevertheless the church is not the 'guardian' either of art or science, like minor children *en route* to maturity, even though in our own time we have seen the world which lies in the wicked one take them over. Further, it is right that each of us engage our abilities and gifts in any of these areas of life which a kindly Providence opens up for us. Nor should the devout believer scorn the developments of the arts, sciences and the like among unbelievers, however cautious in embracing them. I cite a famous passage of John Calvin's commentary on Genesis 4:21, 22, which reports that art and science arose first among the descendants of Cain, the rebel, not of Seth whose sons called on the name of the LORD (Gen. 4:26).

> [T]he liberal arts and sciences have descended to us from the heathen [ancient Greeks and Romans]. We are, indeed, compelled to acknowledge that we have received astronomy, and the other parts of philosophy, medicine, and the order of civil government from them. Nor is it to be doubted, that God has thus liberally enriched them with excellent favours that their impiety might have the less excuse. We admire the riches of his favour.

Calvin goes on to say:

> [A]lthough the invention of the harp [by Cain's family], and of similar instruments of music, may minister to our pleasure, rather than to our necessity, still it is to be thought not altogether superfluous; much less does it deserve in itself to be condemned, unless it be combined with the fear of God, and with the common benefit of society. But such is the nature of music, that it can be adapted to the offices [service] of religion, and made profitable to men... Finally, Moses, in my opinion, intends to teach that the race flourished in various and pre-eminent endowments, which would both render it inexcusable, and would prove most evident testimonies of the divine goodness [in created endowments].[24]

As civilization has developed and channels of the expression of human creative ability have multiplied mankind has usually claimed credit for it. For 200 years random evolution by some material law of progress (or logic, as in the case of science) has been given credit for these advances. Deductivists, empiricists, behaviorists, idealists and similar have explained it all by their favorite theories, and after doing so have usually in recent times sought to make each a department of government. They have no better way to explain and to exploit the behavior of people in society.

To the contrary, Scripture traces these developments into the created nature of mankind and their environment. The Reformers and later Christian biblical theologians taught that God placed before man in the Genesis revelation and in his nature 'ordinances for practical societal institutions, such as the church as an institution, the state, the school, university and industry... there is no one social institution such as the state of which the others are merely parts'.[25]

This is close to Luther's teaching that all human activity 'is both established and limited by God's *creative* [emphasis added] will... [It is] nothing else than a form of readiness to receive God's gifts'.[26] Luther wrote:

> Man must and ought to work, ascribing his sustenance and the fulness of his house, however, not to his own labor but solely to the goodness and blessing of God... God wants the glory as the one who alone gives the growth... And so we find that all our labor is nothing more than the finding and collecting of God's gifts; it [our labour] is quite unable to create or preserve anything.[27]

I cited Calvin's comments on the independent authority of musicians to make music unfettered by rules supplied by science or 'religion', and the like, as exemplary, first, of his outlook on liberal arts (which he mentions) and, second, of his outlook on all human gifts, powers, 'talents' as we say today. All, however, was to be subject to all divinely revealed truth. He held that civil government should protect the church and (in a Christian commonwealth such as Geneva) should support it.[28]

Spiritually discerning Christians will be on guard not to follow the world's enticement into doubtful and

---

24. John Calvin, *Commentary Upon the Book of Genesis*, trans. John King (Edinburgh: Calvin Translation Society, 1847), pp. 218, 219.
25. E. L. Hebden Taylor, *Reformation or Revolution* (Chatley, NJ: Craig Press, 1970), p. 320.
26. Althaus, *op. cit.*, p. 106.
27. Althaus, *op. cit.*, p. 320.
28. The theology of 'sphere sovereignty' and endorsement of full participation in the created orders of human society introduced here with cautious approval is no new thought, not presently widely discussed in evangelical theological circles. The seed of these ideas is to be found in both Calvin and Luther. In slightly different language it was proposed by Helmut Thieleke and Werner Elert, both German Lutherans, and by Emil Brunner. It received fullest expression in the writings of Abraham Kuyper and Herman Dooyeweerd and has been taken up by R. J. Rushdoony and other 'Christian Reconstruction' theologians in America. Its most balanced and persuasive proponent has been E. L. Hebden Taylor.

unrighteous channels in these quite proper areas of human activity, especially as currently organized, sometimes under government sponsorship. I cite Abraham Kuyper's telling remarks about the membership in the social organizations (labor, political, etc.) which modern society creates to support their agenda.

> In mixing socially danger always lurks for Christians. One so easily allows the law to be laid down by society and its worldly forms. What society can get away with Christians too can so easily permit. One floats on a stream to which one can offer no resistance. And consciously one exchanges the principle of the Christian life for the unpurified principle of worldly society.[29]

Kuyper's concluding remarks stand as a stark rebuke to conducting any lawful enterprise according to corrupt worldly standards and against drifting with the currents in the worldly organizations we may be inclined to join.

> The spirit at work in such principally unbelieving social organizations is so alluring and contagious that almost none of us, once he enters into such company, can offer resistance to it. One absorbs this godless spirit without suspecting it. Especially so because one is a part of such organizations, one sees one's Christian principles doomed to silence.[30]

The Method of God in Creation.

We live in an age that likes to think of itself as scientific. Science is interested in methods, so people want to know *how* God created the world. Did He do it all at once? Once He created matter and energy did the rest develop by laws He created with the matter and energy? By virtue of the nature of the case these questions cannot be answered for certain.

Firstly, creation out of nothing was a supernatural event. Since there was as yet no order of nature it might be better to say, a non-natural event. Once all the 'natural' causes for an event are explained it ceases to be a supernatural event and loses its force as one.

Secondly, try as the astronomers, geologists and physicists may, they can never know how God created. There are several competing 'scientific' models of creation. However one decides to interpret the six days of the Genesis creation-narrative, it is very clear that God ended the work of creating things when the epoch was over. According to Genesis 2:1-3, God rested (ceased) from the now finished work of creation.

VII. What Revelation says about Method and Means, Purposes and Agencies in Creating.

Preservation continues, but God's methods are probably different in this present work. Hence, though the scientist may learn much about present-day natural processes, he can never be quite sure they prevailed in creation – whether it took a moment, six twenty-four-hour days, or several billion years. The processes he observes now relate to God's works of preservation and of providence, not of creation. By revelation we do know several things about the methods God used in creating our world, but even what revelation tells us relates more to things modern people are not particularly curious about, even though they ought to be. These constitute the matters Christian teachers ought to enforce in our churches, rather than (I judge) theories of *how* or *how long*. Here are several of them.

1. God employed His *wisdom* in creating. In Proverbs 8, Wisdom (represented as a female) stands forth (vv. 3, 4) and cries, 'The LORD possessed me at the beginning of his work, the first of his acts of old' (v. 22). Then Wisdom claims to have been present at the various stages of creation, assisting at each juncture (vv. 27-31). Elsewhere Scripture states, 'he… established the world by his wisdom… by his understanding' (Jer. 10:12b); 'O LORD, how manifold are your works! [creation and preservation] In wisdom have you made [creation] them all' (Ps. 104:24). These texts are telling us the functional efficiency of the creation, including that the starry heavens testify to God the Creator's intelligence.

2. God employed His *power* in creating. This seems so evident, even apart from texts which say it, that it scarcely can be doubted. David was impressed with the creative power of God, saying, 'the sky above [i.e. the expanse of space] proclaims his handiwork' (Ps. 19:1).

As a young pastor I personally built most of a church house with my own hands. The walls were of twelve-inch

---

29. Abraham Kuyper, *Pro Rege*, Vol III, pp. 189–191 as cited by E. L. Hebden Taylor in *The Christian Philosophy of Law, Politics and the State* (Nutley, NJ: Craig Press, 1966), p. 603.
30. op. cit., p. 191.

concrete blocks, each weighing in excess of sixty pounds. The size of the building was fifty-two feet by sixty-four feet. How my muscles hurt during those fourteen months! To the present day I never pass large masonry construction without silently calculating the power necessary to put the stones in place. The first time I saw the gigantic, dressed Herodian stones at Hebron – several feet in each dimension – I had to ponder them quietly for several minutes to estimate their weight. What power it took to emplace them! But God effortlessly put the lights in the expanse of heaven – the greater to rule the day, the lesser to rule the night. He made the stars also (Gen. 1:14-18) and has been, by preservation, keeping them in place ever since. 'He… hangs the earth on nothing' (Job 26:7). 'It is he who made the earth by his power' (Jer. 10:12).

3. God employed His *will* in creating. The four and twenty elders of John's vision say to God: 'for you created all things, and by your will they existed and were created' (Rev. 4:11). This means that the various aspects of creation are God's execution of His own eternal decree. Will is the nearest thing that we have to creative power, as God's only rational earth-creatures. We can create ideas in the mind without apparent reduction of energy. These ideas are, in the case of some of the more artistic of our number, the finest work we do, for the ideas are parent to works like Rembrandt's paintings or Gutzon Borglum's statuary or the Grand Coulee Dam.

4. God employed His word in creating. Many times the formula, 'And God said, "Let there be"… and there was', appears in the familiar narrative. The Bible reader naturally connects this with Hebrews 11:3 (KJV), 'the worlds were framed by the word of God'. Several other passages bear on the subject: 'By the word of the LORD the heavens were made, and by the breath of his mouth all their host… For he spoke, and it came to be; he commanded, and it stood firm' (Ps. 33:6, 9); 'For he commanded and they were created' (Ps. 148:5). The word of God may be written (the Scriptures), spoken (as at Jesus' baptism), personal (as the Son of God in John 1). There may be other senses. All derive from the familiar phenomenon of human language whereby ideas, commands, wishes and the like are communicated.

5. All three members of the Godhead co-operated in the work of creation. Some attention has already been given to the fact that the distinction between the Three Persons of the Godhead are in part with reference to functions outside the Trinity (*ad extra* is the Latin phrase) rather than immanent relations within the Godhead. We know that all three of the Persons participated in the creation of the heavens and the earth, just as also in the work of redemption. Sometimes Scripture speaks simply of God as the Creator. Sometimes this way of putting things draws redemption into the sphere of what the one true God has done, with the result that both creation and redemption appear together. One such text is 2 Corinthians 4:6. Paul has been speaking of the devil, 'the god of this world', and of how he 'has blinded the minds of the unbelievers' (v. 4). Then he shows how Christ is God's light and follows with a striking sentence joining creation and redemption to the individual persons: 'For God, who said, "Let light shine out of darkness", has shone in our hearts to give the light of the knowledge of the glory of God in the face of Jesus Christ' (2 Cor. 4:6).

The Scriptures, therefore, in creation as in redemption, preserve the formula 'of the Father', 'through the Son', 'by the Spirit'. The Father as Planner originates: 'there is one God, the Father, from whom are all things' (1 Cor. 8:6). The Son as Mediator effects the plan, 'For by him [the Son] all things were created… all things were created through him' (Col. 1:16[31]). The Spirit of God (in the Old Testament not always clearly the Third Person) completes and operates day to day (see Gen. 1:2; Job 26:13).

6. The Bible declares that God had certain *purposes* in creating the world. Why did God create the world? Secularist writers of today do not concern themselves with purposes. If, as they suppose, there is no reality outside the material world, locked up in cause-effect sequences, there is no goal of the world except just to be whatever it is. An important text of Scripture speaks to the contrary: 'The LORD has made everything for its purpose' (Prov. 16:4). The purpose in view in this verse may be an immediate functional one, as for example, the sun to shine, eyes to see, ears to hear, fins for swimming, legs for walking. But each immediate purpose was intended to serve one ultimate, divinely intended purpose for the whole of creation. That purpose may be summed up in three short statements, each scripturally derived.

i. The 'chief end' of creation is God Himself, 'For from him and through him and to him are all things. To him be glory for ever. Amen' (Rom. 11:36). God's design is, as Paul puts it, 'that God may be all in all' (1 Cor. 15:28; cf. Isa. 48:11). From what we know of creativity in ourselves, we should suppose that the Maker's own satisfaction is a primary goal in creativity, not that it is the only one.

ii. The goal of God for Himself, in creation, is the manifestation of His perfections. This is spoken of as His

---

31. See also John 1:3, 10; Heb. 1:2, 10.

will, or His pleasure. James Orr pointed out that the creation of mankind had a distinct place in God's scheme for displaying His own perfections:

> Till a mind of this kind appeared, capable of surveying the scene of its existence, of understanding the wisdom and beauty displayed in its [creation's] formations, and of utilizing for rational purposes the vast resources laid up in its treasuries, the very existence of such a world as this remained an inexplicable riddle: an adequate final cause… was not to be found in it.[32]

Orr goes on to say, 'There is a delight which creative wisdom has in its own productions, which is an end in itself. God saw the works that he had made, and behold they were good; though not until man appeared on the scene were they declared "very good" [Gen. 1:31].'[33]

iii. The above paragraph must be joined to another thought for proof and development – God created the world for His own glory. All of God's works are for this purpose. In the achievement of this goal all other goals are attained. That to achieve His own glory was God's goal in creation is the plain truth of Scripture and is demonstrable by reason as well.

In the first place, when God purposed to create He did so before any creature existed. It must be, therefore, that the reason lay in God Himself, not in the non-existing creature. The absolute cannot be subordinate to the finite.

Secondly, God is a more worthy being than the sum of all creation. His own excellence on display is therefore more worthy than the excellence or happiness of all or some of creation. Thirdly, even among ourselves as people, the excellency of our makings and doings – be it building a better mousetrap or running a faster mile – is rightly attributed to the maker and doer. The same is surely true of God, the master Maker and Doer, and His creation.

Finally, the securing of the Creator's glory as the 'chief end' not only of mankind but of all creatures, secures also their own highest good, happiness and excellence. A. H. Strong has written:

> His own glory is an end which comprehends and secures, as a subordinate end, every interest of the universe. The interests of the universe are bound up in the interests of God. There is no holiness or happiness for creatures except as God is absolute sovereign, and is recognized as such. It is therefore not selfishness, but benevolence, for God to make His own glory the supreme object of creation. Glory is not vain-glory, and in expressing this ideal, that is, in expressing Himself, in His creation, he communicates to His creatures the utmost possible good.[34]

A survey of selected Scripture passages shows that the chief end of God, not only in creation but also in His eternal decrees and government of the world, is His glory. As regards God's ends in creation, see Colossians 1:16, Revelation 4:11 and Romans 11:36. Compare Isaiah 43:7, Isaiah 60:21 and 61:3. As regards God's end in decrees (predestination) see Ephesians 1:5, 6, 12 and as to God's ends in providence (government) and gracious arrangements for His creatures, see Romans 9:17, 22, 23 and Ephesians 3:10.

It is the duty of mankind and angels to adopt God's goal as their own: 'So, whether you eat or drink, or whatever you do, do all to the glory of God' (1 Cor. 10:31; cf. 1 Peter 4:11).

VIII. Mediate or Immediate Creation and Science.

This leads to a current debate. Some very serious Christians think that when expressions like these concerning divine goals and actions are used, *immediate* application of divine power is always designated; secondary (as opposed to primary), mediate causes are thought to be eliminated. So the creation of the world had to be a succession of instantaneous divine 'fiats' – literal spoken commands which without passage of time, and without employment of means of any sort, material or otherwise, effected creation. There are several recent books employing considerable display of scholarship to prove that in the texts which speak of creation by God's word (mouth, breath, command), the Bible specifically means immediate (without means), instantaneous creation and nothing else. All this must have happened not very long ago, perhaps 10,000 or 15,000 years.

It should be pointed out, however, that such has not been the view of some first rank conservative scholars from

---

32. James Orr, *The Christian View of God and the World* (Grand Rapids: Eerdmans, 1947), p. 135.
33. ibid., p. 135.
34. A. H. Strong, *op. cit.*, p. 400.

early to recent times. Many of them have thought the opposite (use of means and extended time), if not specifically indicated, is at least allowed.

Insistence that the six days of creation in Genesis 1 must be interpreted as six literal, twenty-four-hour days as we know days and nights, evenings and mornings, has not by any means been characteristic of all the great teachers or of the church of the past. It seems rather to be the child of modern controversy. Says one respected and saintly modern writer:

> Respecting the length of the six creative days, speaking generally, for there was some difference of views, the patristic [church Fathers] and mediaeval exegesis makes them to be long periods of time, not days of twenty-four hours. The latter interpretaiton has prevailed *only in the modern church* [emphasis added]. Augustine teaches that the length of the six days is not to be determined by the length of our week-days. Our seven days, he says, resemble the seven days of the account in Genesis, in being in a series, and in having the vicissitudes of morning and evening... He calls attention to the fact that the 'six or seven days may be, and are called six days, God-divided days,' in distinction from 'sun-divided days.' Anselm remarks that there was a difference of opinion in his time.[35]

Shedd adds that there is merit in the suggestion that 'the seven days of the human week are copies of the Divine week. Thus "sun-divided days" are images of "God-divided days".'[36]

Let me try to convince the reluctant reader that God's word of creation does not necessarily mean immediate, instantaneous creation. One of the most important texts is 2 Timothy 3:16 which says all Scripture is *theopneustos*, literally, God-breathed. Conservative scholars everywhere accept the evidence adduced and summarized by B. B. Warfield, that the breath of God and similar expressions (command, mouth) refer simply to His creative acts. Warfield cites all the passages I have cited above and more. He also affirms that either mediate or immediate creation may be meant.[37]

In the case of Holy Scripture we know God took about 1,500 years and must therefore have used both time and human means in addition to writing materials. At least several dozen human authors produced the sixty-six books. God's breath, command, word, mouth and similar in such contexts indicate *God's creative power in action, by whatever means effected and taking as long a time as needed*. The Bible really says little specifically about the means employed. On the other hand, neither does the so-called geological or astronomical record. Theories about the means and time employed will always remain just that – theories. We do not have sufficient revelation as to the means of creation and the time of it to construct a dogma about the week. It was a God-divided week, whether a sun-divided week or not is not ours to say until God says so.[38]

It is presently the style to demonstrate this or that alleged truth by 'scientific' evidence. A system of thought called 'Creation Science' has been proposed. So efforts to prove how and when creation took place take the form of books, articles and debates on a scientific outlook on creation. But it has been futile as far as *proof* of how and when God did what He did. Thomas Aquinas' comment is apropos:

> The will of God cannot be investigated... But the divine will can be manifested by revelation, on which faith rests. Hence that the world began to be is an object of faith, not of demonstration or of science. And it is useful to consider this, lest anyone, presuming to demonstrate what is of faith, should bring forth reasons that are not cogent, so as to give occasion to unbelievers to laugh, thinking that on such grounds we believe things that are of faith.[39]

Questions About Creation.

There are several questions which almost must occur to those who become acquainted with the biblical view of creation. One is a philosophical question, the others a problem of Bible interpretation.

1. How can there be evil in a world which the holy God has made? The presence of sin in the world is never explained in the Bible. The serpent is there at a very early stage. We know how the human race fell into sin. It came through a wrong exercise of God-given freedom by our common father, Adam. '[S]in came into the world through one man... For as by the one man's disobedience the many were made sinners' (Rom. 5:12, 19). Sin therefore is present and prevalent in the race through an original sinner's sin. It is therefore here by God's permission. God placed the man

---

35. W. G. T. Shedd, *Dogmatic Theology I* (Grand Rapids: Zondervan, 1969), p. 475, 476.
36. ibid., p. 477.
37. B. B. Warfield, *The Inspiration and Authority of the Bible* (Philadelphia: Presbyterian & Reformed Publ., 1958), pp. 243–296.
38. See the section, 'Questions About Creation', below.
39. *Summa Theologica*, 46.2.1.

in the situation of trial by moral decision. But Genesis does not say a thing as to the ultimate source of sin, for though the serpent – or Satan the tempter (Rev. 12:9) – was there, he is left unexplained throughout the Bible. God himself only is uncreated. Satan exists. Therefore Satan is a created being. God's Creation is good, therefore Satan was not originally evil. Moral evil originates in a wrong exercise of freedom on the part of a moral being. So Satan is a fallen moral being. A comparison of Romans 8:20-22 with Genesis 3:16-19 shows that the physical evils of our world are related to the entrance of moral evil and both will be eradicated at the consummation. The present imperfect state is temporary.

2. How should certain details of the Genesis account be interpreted? Large volumes have been written in response to some of these questions. Some are piously speculative questions; some have to do with the literary form or forms of the several sections: Genesis 1:1, 2: 4a; Genesis 2:4b-25; Genesis 3. Others, related in part to the above, are concerned with interpretation of specific words, phrases, sentences and sections. These are some of these questions: Are the days of creation literal twenty-four-hour, earthly days? And if so, why this or that (e.g. why is vegetation, which requires sunlight, a day ahead of sun and sunlight)?

3. Is there unbroken continuity in the narrative, or is the creation of heaven and earth (Gen. 1:1) a separate event from the rest of chapter 1? An unmentioned judgment has been postulated as falling between verses 1 and 2. The rest of the chapter has then been interpreted as orderly restoration of a primeval condition.

4. Might the days be days wherein God revealed the creation to Moses according to topics: light and darkness, day and night, day one, and so on, to animals and mankind, day six?

5. Might the days be 'geological ages' or some other taxonomic arrangement?

6. Might the days be a 'revelatory device', something like a series of six slide-frames whereby God makes known *what* He has done and showing by arrangement mankind's importance as last, lord of earth under God and crown of God's creation?

7. How much is literal and how much figurative? Is it historical with symbolical elements? Is it symbolical with historical elements?

These are only a few of the questions. Each generation of readers and interpreters brings its own 'science' and philosophy to the questions and phrases them differently. Yet the doctrine of the Genesis account of creation remains essentially the same throughout Christian history. These questions and many more like them are beyond the scope of this chapter. Suggested answers will be found in later sections of this volume. Several old and new books of theology, as well as numerous controversial monographs, essays and journal articles, argue for this or that interpretation. Meanwhile we must keep right on employing the plain scriptural data for theology. We cannot wait for the inscrutable to be scrutinized, for the imponderable to be pondered. Revelation is a miracle and so is creation. Miracles cannot be fully explained. The revelation regarding creation in the Bible is addressed to our faith by way of our minds, but it is not addressed to curiosity.

Many an earnest *tour de force* is presently being mounted to win our minds to 'early earth', 'young earth', 'creation science' and other causes by people who wish to do good. Meanwhile, important truths of revelation regarding creation are not being taught our youth in church and school, truths such as that God is Creator of all except God, Himself. All other existences began not in Him but were created *ad extra* by Him. God created in His *wisdom*, by His *power*, by His *will*, by His *word*. The triune God, Father, Son and Holy Spirit, was active in bringing the world to existence. God created the world for Himself, to manifest His perfections for His own glory. These are some of the chief matters Scripture is concerned about. They are deeply religious truths and must be disseminated. These are the real alternatives to evolutionism, to scientism, pantheism, and indeed to humanism and secularism. These truths represent the proper arena of discussion if we are to win people's minds to God, revealed truth and morality.

Readers are well advised to commit themselves without reserve only to the clear theological truths of Scripture revelation, likewise to the truthfulness of the chapters of Genesis and other scriptural passages on creation. Beyond that they will be wise to listen to the voices of moderation. Those who insist that we simply must agree with them or else be somewhat sub-Christian or of questionable loyalty to biblical revelation are shouting too loudly to be obeyed. It will be wise to commit ourselves irrevocably to none of the theories. Creation was supernaturally brought to pass. As such it is a divine mystery. We can never penetrate it, though we may trust all that God has said about it.[40]

---

40. Since writing the above I have carefully read and added to a long shelf of my reading on this subject a very insightful book by Harry L. Poe, an evangelical theologian, and Jimmy H. Davis, an evangelical chemistry professor, *Science and Faith: An Evangelical Dialogue* (Nashville, TN: Broadman and Holman Publishers, 2000). Apparently quite independent of anything I have said or written about creation, the creative week and present processes of nature, they have reached conclusions similar to mine and have carried them further. Their relating the same to quantum theories, chaos theory, etc. is instructive. I disagree with their somewhat hesitant theory of continuous creation..

19
The World of Unseen Spirits: Their Place in Creation

'[B]y him all things were created... visible and invisible'
(Col. 1:16)

Interest in Angels and Demons.

In the recent past I made a special effort to gather a select, working library of worthwhile books on the subject of this chapter. I am still puzzled by something I found out rather quickly: the publishing lists are well supplied with books on demons, witches, Satan, and other real, or imagined personnel of the dark side of the unseen world, but only a very few currently on the subject of God's messengers, the angels. Yet the Bible mentions angels well over 250 times, over half in the New Testament.

Angels have not attracted much interest among many recent writers. For example, Lewis and Demarest in a sound work and generally thorough treatment[1] make only passing remarks about angels. Neither angels nor Satan appear in the index of A. E. McGrath's *Christian Theology*,[2] and R. L. Reymond's *A New Systematic Theology*[3] has only three or four paragraphs on Satan and no discussion of demons or angels at all. A few generations back it was thought necessary to devote a considerable amount of scripturally related discussion to this subject in an adequate textbook of theology. A. H. Strong devoted twenty-four densely packed pages[4] and H. C. Thiessen's lectures[5] have a fine discussion.

Peter L. Berger wrote at a time when general scholarly interest in the supernatural was nil and a fad prevailed among leftist theologians proclaiming 'God is Dead' (I shall not cite their dead books). Writing as a sociologist [6] he felt his intent might be misunderstood by readers, so he wrote a sequel of sorts: *A Rumor of Angels: Modern Society and the Rediscovery of the Supernatural*. He maintained that only through belief in the supernatural (including angels, perhaps) can mankind grasp 'the true proportions of his experience'. Berger is a sensitive and wise man – to a point. But his book did not presage a recovery of Christianity quite so much as of occultism. When I finished reading the book about 1968, I wrote on the dust cover: 'In this God equals transcendence: signals of transcendence [hence "rumor of angels"] replaces revelation; man discovers replaces God reveals. Worship is only a gesture of

---

1. Lewis and Demarest, *Integrative Theology* (Grand Rapids, MI: Zondervan, 1990).
2. A. E. McGrath, *Christian Theology* 2nd Ed. (Oxford: Blackwell, 1997).
3. R. L. Reymond, *A New Systematic Theology* (Nashville: Nelson, 1998).
4. A. H. Strong, *Systematic Theology* (Valley Forge, PA: Judson Press, 1907), pp. 443–464.
5. H. C. Thiessen, *Systematic Theology* (Grand Rapids, MI: Eerdmans, 1949).
6. *The Sacred Canopy: Elements of a Sociological Theory of Religion* (Garden City, NY: Doubleday, 1967).

hope toward transcendence. The historical Jesus is not the Christ in any unique sense, and the author puts his own amateur judgment far above either Scripture or theology. Even so his book is an excellent argument for the supernatural (including angels). Mortimer Adler would approve. It is an important book.'

Dialectical and existential theologians are an exception to the general neglect of angels and demons in theology. They do not, however, develop a theology of this subject from the Bible. John Macquarrie believes in a hierarchy of spiritual beings superior to mankind but the angels of traditional theology 'belong to the mythology and poetry of religion rather than theology'.[7] Karl Barth, for whom 'the reality of nothingness' explains demons and evil angels, strongly affirms the biblical idea of angels must be restricted simply to the 'existence' of messengers or ambassadors, plenipotentiaries of God. But we know no more about the subject than this. He does not hesitate to say 'myth' and 'saga' account for some Bible stories of angels. Whatever we do, we must not construct a *dogma* or *theology* of angels by synthesizing and organizing the data of Scripture about angels, as he acknowledges orthodoxy before him has always done.[8] In process of his negative dogmatics, however, Barth has produced valuable information on the history of the subject. Emil Brunner – as usual plain and to the point – assigns the biblical stories of angels to 'the outskirts of Biblical truth, e.g. in apocalyptic passages or in those which are evidently legendary in character'.[9] Like Barth, Brunner thinks there are good spiritual beings beyond our sight that mediate God's will and work on earth and affect human beings in unseen ways – and also evil powers, perhaps yet to be discovered by depth psychology. But as for a theology of angels derived from literal understanding of Scripture: '[W]e must be ready to admit that even the Biblical writers were children of their own day and that the world from which they derived their ideas has no authority for our faith.'[10] *Per contra*, here is a better respect for our predecessors' claims, in the language of A. H. Strong, a theologian at least as informed as Brunner:

> There is certainly the possibility that the ascending scale of created beings does not reach the highest point in man. As the distance between man and the lowest forms of life is filled with numberless gradations of being, so it is possible that between man and God there exist creatures of higher than human intelligence. The possibility is turned to certainty by the express declarations of Scripture.[11]

A fine fairly recent book on angels by Mortimer Adler, a famous scholar, has not sold very well though one by Billy Graham, a famous evangelist, is fairly widely read. On the other hand a rather sober book on Satan by a popular Christian writer[12] has been eagerly bought by many, I am told. Perhaps good news is less interesting than bad news. Similarly, a somewhat irresponsible and vagrant uncle will often be more colourful and hence more interesting to his nephews than his more upright and conventional brother. 'Demonology' has, however, been a vastly overworked and overwrought subject in a rash of popular books recently. More about this later.

The Importance of Angels in Scripture.

Though we live in a world of things seen and heard, there is about us another world of unseen spirits. When Elisha's fearful servant said, 'Alas, my master! What shall we do?' Elisha prayed, '"O LORD, please open his eyes that he may see." So the LORD opened the eyes of the young man… and behold, the mountain was full of horses and chariots of fire all round Elisha' (2 Kings 6:15, 16). Unseen to us are all these *benign* forces. Perhaps it would be better to say that in our world we are not able to observe all the many invisible personal beings who affect our lives. In several very exalted Pauline rhetorical flights in the New Testament, the world of *malign*, unseen, created spirits is squarely before the thoughtful Bible reader. One of these urges: 'Put on the whole armour of God, that you may be able to stand against the schemes of the devil. For we do not wrestle against flesh and blood, but against the rulers, against the authorities, against the cosmic powers over this present darkness, against the spiritual forces of evil in the heavenly places' (Eph. 6:11, 12).

Evidently to help his readers avoid any worship of these spirits, Paul wrote of Christ's victory at the cross

---

7. John Macquarrie, *Principles of Christian Theology* (New York: Charles Scribner's Sons, 1966), p. 234.
8. Karl Barth, *Church Dogmatics III*, trans. Bromiley (Edinburgh: T. & T. Clark, 1975), pp. 369–531.
9. Emil Brunner, *The Christian Doctrine of Creation and Redemption* (Philadelphia: Westminster Press, 1952), p. 133.
10. ibid., p. 147.
11. A. H. Strong, *Systematic Theology* (Valley Forge, PA: Judson Press, 1907), p. 444.
12. Hal Lindsey, *Satan is Alive and well on Planet Earth*.

as a triumph over certain of these spirits. He says Christ at Calvary not only rendered legalistic rules obsolete but 'He disarmed the rulers and authorities and put them to open shame, by triumphing over them in him' (Col. 2:15). Near the end of his great eighth chapter of Romans Paul mentions angels, principalities and powers as possible opponents (Rom. 8:38). They are not of the natural order (flesh and blood); they are spiritual and wicked; they rule the dark world; they are in high places; they are princes (principalities) and have great power. They have been conquered by Christ, but are nevertheless to be conquered by us only when we employ the whole panoply of spiritual armour – truth, righteousness, the gospel of peace, faith, salvation, the Spirit, the Word and prayer (Eph. 6:13-18). As for the holy angels – Jesus informed some of His disciples there are 'legions' of them.

The Pauline summaries all relate to evil spirit-beings. Paul's Epistles furnish no similar summaries regarding good unseen spirits, who aid rather than oppose the Christian. From Genesis to Revelation almost always they are incidental to the Bible narrative and doctrine. Perhaps Paul was relying on the prevalence of angels in the biblical narrative to inform his readers.

A Preliminary View.

All of these beings are represented as personal spirits. They frequently appear as men, apparently dressed according to the styles of the times. Apart from this, all visual representations of them in imagination, art and statuary are without foundation (except possibly the seraphs and cherubs). Though uniformly referred to in Scripture by pronouns in masculine gender, they are specifically said to be without sexual feature or function. The wings almost always appearing in pictures of angels are without scriptural foundation, except for a certain class of beings called seraphs (Isa. 6:1 ff.) who may or may not be angels. So it is wise to start with the Bible and engage in no discourse or speculation about angels until it has been pretty well canvassed.

Beliefs about Angels in Late Pre-Christian Judaism.

Raphael Patai, an eminent contemporary Jewish authority on the beliefs of ancient Jews has written:

> From the first century B.C.E. [BC] the Messiah was the central figure in the Jewish myth of the future. The Jewish messianic mythographers know and expound in minute detail the acts of all the protagonists of the great drama that will unfold in the End of the Days. And more than that; they present verbatim transcripts of the dialogues and discussions that will take place between and among God, the two Messiahs, the prophet Elijah, the people of Israel, the pious and the wicked, the nations of the world, God and Magog, the satanic Arimilus, the archangels Michael and Gabriel, the ministering angels, Samael the Satan, and even the earth, the mountains and the waters... They recount, not unlike the all-informed modern novelist, what the actors in the cosmic drama of the future will feel... all are presented in elaborate and often astounding detail.[13]

The first Book of Enoch, though known to the church Fathers, was lost to the world until restored to circulation in the nineteenth century. It is quoted in the New Testament (Jude 14). This was evidently current literature in the first century BC and not only contributed to unhealthy interest in unseen spirits but also contributed to fantastic elaboration of their activities among our LORD's immediate ancestors. In the history told by Emil Schürer we learn additional names of several angels: Raphael, Phanuel, Uriel and how with the aid of angels Enoch was transported throughout all time and through the whole universe.[14]

This unhealthy preoccupation with an occult doctrine of angels is not reflected in the New Testament, but rather corrected – as is fantastic interpretation of prophecy by Jewish non-biblical apocalypse.[15]

---

13. Raphael Patai, *The Messiah Texts* (Detroit: Wayne State Univ. Press, 1979) XXVII, XXVIII.
14. Emil Schürer, *History of the Jewish People in the Age of Jesus Christ* Vol. III (Edinburgh: T. & T. Clark, 1973), pp. 56–59.
15. Accurate, readable information regarding the beliefs about angels among Jews of Jesus' time will be found in Alfred Edersheim's old standard, *The Life and Times of Jesus the Messiah*. (Vol. II, Appendix XII, Grand Rapids: Eerdmans, 1962, pp. 748-766.) For readers of German an authoritative source is Herman Strack and Paul Billerbeck, *Kommentar zum Neven Testamentum aus Talmud und Niedrasch*, comments on Matthew 18:10 (Vol. I, 781 – 783); Matthew 25:31 (I, 973 – 975); Luke 16:22 (II, 223 – 225); and Ercursus 21, *The Ancient Jewish Demonology*. Edersheim points out how fully Jesus was free of the dogmas and superstitions of His contemporary Jewish 'angelologists' and 'demonologists' Jesus really was.

Angelology in Patristic and Medieval Times.

Already in New Testament times, for good reason, Paul warned both Jewish and Gentile readers against 'worship of angels' (Col. 2:18). Unlearned Jewish Christians no doubt brought with them some of the fantastic superstitions of low-grade Judaism of the time and converts from heathenism came with the baggage of superstition about unseen spirits, good and bad. That in the fourth century, worship of angels was practised by ignorant Christians is witnessed by a canon of a synod of Laodicea (sometime between 343 and 381) forbidding such as idolatrous, and that this persisted into the fifth century is revealed by a canon of the Fourth Ecumenical Council (Chalcedon 451) which 'declared ecumenical' the canons of Laodicea. I am indebted to Henry Alford[16] for the exact wording: 'It is not fitting that Christians should… call on angels, and make celebrations to them in unlawful ways. If therefore anyone be found employed in this covert idolatry, let him be accursed, insasmuch as he is a denier of Jesus Christ, the Son of God, and a pervert to idolatry.' The movement was not stifled for worship of angels and 'saints' was a corruption remaining to be corrected by the Reformation of the sixteenth century and has not even yet been fully removed from Roman Catholic popular religion. Even the Catechism of 1984 (paragraph 2502) preserves an official form of angel-worship (called 'adoration') in the following and other words about 'Sacred art', 'This spiritual beauty of God is reflected in the most holy Virgin Mother of God, the angels, and saints. Genuine sacred art draws man to adoration.'

As children of their times, some of the early Fathers blundered into some unbiblical angelology. With the best of intentions, for example Justin – martyr and apologist – thought he was silencing the pagan charges of 'atheism' by this atrocious statement: 'But both Him [Father God], and the Son (who came forth from Him… and the host of the other good angels)… and the prophetic Spirit, we worship and adore… as we have been taught' (*Apology I*, 6, ANF I, 164). On the other hand there was the clear condemnation of worship of angels by the local synod of Laodicea and the Ecumenical Council of Chalcedon.

This ambivalent attitude was nurtured by a spurious document known as *The Celestial Hierarchy* falsely attributed by its author to one of Paul's converts, Dionysius the Areopagite (Acts 17:34), about AD 500. This fraudulent work was not exposed until the Renaissance, and though despised as disgusting by the Reformers, was not acknowledged as fraudulent by the Roman Church for another century. At one time this 'Pseudo-Dionysius' was in the Roman calendar of saints.[17] This work both created and supported notions of a world of angelic hierarchy (nine orders of them), their powers and influences, though utterly without foundation, to be reflected in the *ecclesiastical hierarchy* of the Roman Church. What was really going on was a successful effort to incorporate certain features of Neoplatonism into Christianity, as was set forth in Dionysius' second book, *The Ecclesiastical Hierarchy*.[18]

The Scriptural Doctrine.

Angels are designated only part of the time by Hebrew *malakh*, and Greek *angelos* renders angel but meaning 'messenger' – whether of God or of other men. They are also called 'men' for they had the appearance of men (Gen. 18:12ff.); 'watchers' (Dan. 4:13), evidently because they observe human behaviour; 'holy ones' (Dan. 4:13; Jude 14), because of their ordinary presence near God (see Matt. 18:10); 'sons of God' (Job 38:7), perhaps because they are each God's immediate creation (not a race of beings genetically related) or because they are part of God's celestial retinue.[19] Delitzsch combines these explanations.[20]

Angels seem to be called 'sons of gods' (*bene 'elim*) in Psalm 89:6. The passage is obscure. Verses 6 and 7 are saying that God is reverenced in His heavenly court. Calvin says that the title is 'given to angels because neither have their origin from earth, nor are clothed with a corruptible body… a greater majesty shines forth in the angels than in other creatures' (*Commentary* on Ps. 89:6). '[A]ngels of God' are called 'God's camp' or 'army' in Genesis 32:1, 2 – a conception common to many passages of Scripture. In many other texts, the host (or army, in modern English) of Israel is the LORD's host (see Josh. 5:13-15, where a 'man' is a manifestation of Jehovah Himself).

Angels are once only said to be 'ministering spirits' for the heirs of salvation (Heb. 1:14) and because of the high position of some, called 'princes' (Dan. 10:13), and for a similar reason, some (apparently evil angelic spirits) are 'principalities and powers'.[21]

---

16. *New Testament for English Readers*, p. 1300.
17. See the lengthy article in McClintock and Strong *Encyclopedia ii*, 808–810.
18. See Calvin's justly sarcastic remarks in *Institutes I*, iv. 4.
19. Pope in *Anchor Bible xii*, p. 242.
20. F. Delitzsch, on Job 38:8 and referring to Job 1:1 and 2:1.
21. Eph. 1:21; 3:10; 6:12. See also Jude 6.

Only two angels of the Bible have 'personal' names—*Michael* (Dan. 10:13; Rev. 12:7, *who is like God?*) and *Gabriel* (Dan. 8:16; 9:21; Luke 1:19, *man of God*). This does not prove each angel has a name. The king over the apocalyptic 'locusts' from the abyss is said to be named 'Perdition' – to translate *abaddon* and *apollyon* – which seems to be an allegorical kind of name, not necessarily personal.

It should be noted that much of the above is extracted from apocalyptic passages where truth is prevalently conveyed by symbols. One is cautioned against extracting overmuch strict doctrinal theology from these names and other designations.

The Bible also mentions *cherubim* (plural of 'cherub') and *seraphim* (plural of 'seraph'), as well as demons, evil spirits and Satan (= the devil).

There is no clear information whether the single and most common generic name, angel (Heb. *mal'akh*, Gr. *angelos*), meaning 'messenger', applies to all of them or not. Several respected modern authorities treat all as angels (Strong, A. Hodge, C. Hodge, Pieper, Mueller). In fact, this is the general rule.

The Origin of Angels.

We are not left to general inferences as to the origin of these beings, for we read in Scriptures, 'by him [Christ, the Son of God] all things were created, in heaven and on earth, visible and invisible, whether thrones or dominions or rulers or authorities – all things were created through him and for him' (Col. 1:16; cf. 1 Peter 3:22). At least one other text is just as plain, 'Praise him, all his angels... For he commanded and they were created' (Ps. 148:2, 5). They were created previous to the creation of the universe, for they 'shouted for joy' when that happened (Job 38:7). Outside of areas where Christianity has long been prevalent, it is news to people that there is only one eternal, immortal Spirit (1 Tim. 3:16) and that all others have been created by Him and are under His control. It is for this reason that angels, demons and Satan usually appear under the rubric, 'the works of God: creation', in theological literature. Calvin's quaint comment on Psalm 34:7 ('The angel of the LORD encamps around those who fear him, and delivers them') is both relevant and comforting: 'However great the number of our enemies and the dangers by which we are surrounded may be, yet the angels of God, armed with invincible power, constantly watch over us, and array themselves on every side to aid and deliver us from all evil.'[22] While the Scriptures give no definite figures as to how many angels God created we are informed there were very many of them.[23]

The Nature of Angels.

It is equally certain that these beings (specifically angels) are intelligent, voluntary agents. They function as persons in the modern sense of that word. The angel who appeared to Peter (Acts 12:7-10) functioned in every way as a human person would, tapping him awake, raising him up, speaking instructions, leading him out of a building into a street. They are said to have wisdom (2 Sam. 14:20) and they have moral character, being either holy (Mark 8:28) or sinful (2 Peter 2:4). This does not mean they are a superior order of human beings, even though like us they are rational spirits. The Epistle to Hebrews, in describing the classes of residents of the heavenly Jerusalem, specifies 'innumerable angels... gathering' distinct from 'the spirits of the righteous [just men KJV] made perfect' (Heb. 12:22, 23).

There is disagreement as to whether or not angels are corporeal beings. They are called 'spirits', a word used sometimes to designate the souls of people after death (1 Peter 3:19). We also know that angels have no sexual parts or functions, for Jesus made this known in some comments about eunuchs and celibacy (Luke 20:34-36; Mark 12:25). They are therefore not a race propagated from a single original pair as the human race. They must have been created separately. They are also said to be deathless (Luke 20:36) even though God 'alone has immortality' in the highest sense (1 Tim. 6:16). They are not 'flesh and blood' (Eph. 6:12). When they appear in Scripture narrative they sometimes look like men and sometimes eat food, lodge and speak as men do, being mistaken for them (Gen. 18:8; 19:3).[24] Occasionally an angel appears as a man with frightening, glorious appearance (Dan. 10:5, 6; Judg. 13:3, 6, 10, 11) and performs in some amazing way (Judg. 13:19). Sometimes they come in 'swift flight' (Dan. 9:21) – by what means we do not know – and sometimes angels are tardy (Dan. 10:13).

---

22. John Calvin, *Commentary on the Psalms* vol. I, trans. James Anderson (Edinburgh: Calvin Translation Society, 1845), p. 563.
23. Dan. 7:10; Matt. 26:53; 2 Kings 6:17; Heb. 12:22.
24. But see the discussion of these passages and their context earlier. If, as seems likely, theophany is being described then the 'men' are not angels.

It seems clear that angels belong in a realm (call it spiritual, supernatural, eschatological) where body and form exist (witness Christ's glorified body) and truly exist, but not in the same mode as that in which we flesh-and-blood people do. In His resurrected body Jesus could masticate food (Luke 24:41, 42) and He had 'flesh and bones' (Luke 24:39). Yet it was a 'spiritual body' in which he ascended to heaven and will come again. Some of the finest theologians suggest that angels have bodies similar to the risen body of Jesus, others that they are pure spirits who assume bodies for specific reasons. The question arises later in this chapter in connection with 'the sons of God' of Genesis 6. The question should be left open.

The Relative Position of Angelic Beings.

As a class of intelligent, spirit-beings angels are different from either God or mankind. They are 'all ministering spirits' (Heb. 1:14; cf. v. 7; and Ps. 104:4). People are spiritual beings too, but angel spirits are inferior to mankind in order of being in some respects, since they have been designated by God for the service of the heirs of salvation, as Hebrews 1:14, cited above, goes on to say.

On the other hand they are in some other respect superior to mankind. Peter compares them with human beings – certain false teachers – and says, 'angels, though greater in might and power, do not pronounce a blasphemous judgment against them' (2 Peter 2:11; cf. v. 1). Evidently it is in knowledge and power that they are superior to us. Jesus spoke of them as having great knowledge – 'concerning that day and hour no one knows, not even the angels of heaven' (Matt. 24:36) – and Peter in a message just cited, speaks of their 'might and power'.

They are, however, of limited knowledge and power. They are not divine beings. In another place Peter speaks of them as seekers after information (1 Peter 1:12). Two passages inform us that they do not know as much as God knows (Matt. 24:36; Mark 13:32). These facts – that they are more powerful and of greater knowledge than mankind yet strictly limited in knowledge and power, incomparably inferior to God – explain both why some people have been tempted to worship them (see Col. 2:18) and why it is wrong to do so. This is enforced by still another revealed fact; people shall be their judges at some future time. Paul says, in a passage designed to convince believers of their competence to 'judge' matters of congregational controversy, 'Do you not know that we are to judge angels? How much more, then, matters pertaining to this life!' (1 Cor. 6:3).

Ranks, Organization and Dignity Among Angels.

While on the subject of their rank in relation to God and mankind it is appropriate to raise the question of ranks among themselves. Are there ranks and orders of angels?[25] The Reformers vociferously repudiated any elaborate hierarchy of angels (Calvin, *Institutes I*,1.4 and 8). In the democratic atmosphere of modern Western countries, wherein one president in recent history was an 'Ike' and another a 'Jimmy', and where manners, dress and language tell us very little about social position, this question may not occur without prompting. Yet democracy as it exists in America is almost without precedent and is of recent development there. As to angels – we read of an archangel (1 Thess. 4:16; Jude 9), and of thrones, dominions, principalities, powers and such like (Eph. 1:21; Col. 2:15). One of them is a chief prince (Dan. 9:21; Luke 1:19, 26; 1 Thess. 4:16). Some are said to stand in the presence of God (Luke 1:19). So, though we do not know exactly what their lines of authority and positions of honor are, we know there are such. We also know that angels pay respect to these positions of honor (see Jude 9).

We should add to this picture of rank (1) that however the notion of equality be interpreted ('self-evident that all men are created equal') it does not mean that all people are equal in authority in relation to one another. Society could not operate in such a case. (2) Neither should any elaborate structure of authority among a 'celestial hierarchy' be accepted except as directly derived from Scripture. Calvin, with some sarcasm, contrasted the garrulous nonsense of Dionysius 'whoever he was' with 'Paul, who had been caught up beyond the third heaven [2 Cor. 12:2], not only said nothing about it, but also testified that it is unlawful for any man to speak of the secret things he has seen [2 Cor 12:4]. Therefore, bidding farewell to that foolish wisdom, let us examine in the simple teaching of Scripture what the Lord would have us know of angels' (*Institutes I*, 14.4).

---

25. Medieval theology, stimulated by *The Celestial Hierarchy* of the pseudo-Dionysius, was greatly interested in this question. See Thomas Aquinas, *Summa Theologica* Part One, Quest. 106 – 114; *Summa Contra Gentiles*; also Calvin, *Institutes*.

Activities of Angels and Their Work.

We may be sure that in any God-ordered society (see 1 Cor. 11:2, 34; 14:33, 40) position and rank will serve useful purposes – the doing of work being one of them. What do angels do? (At this point we are thinking only of good angels.) A search of the Scriptures on this matter turns up a truly amazing mass of information. Angels are mentioned in about 275 passages of Scripture in at least seventeen Old Testament books and in seventeen of the New. One of my theology professors, the late Alva J. McClain, organized this material and found no less than thirty-four specific kinds of work in three special and several general categories.

Though long lists of Bible verses do not appeal to readers – it slows us down to look up the verses – the nature of this subject requires some such lists and I therefore submit some here, hoping that readers will not be daunted by them and will inform themselves by searching them out. In the texts we are about to cite the word 'angels' does not always appear, for these beings go by a number of names, descriptions, epithets and the like. Even 'angel' is not always the name of a class of beings, for, as we saw, the word simply means 'messenger' and is used of both 'men and things' (Mal. 3:1; Luke 7:24; 2 Cor. 12:7) as well as the beings we call angels. Other designations appear to be sons of God (Job 1:6; 38:1-7), men (Gen. 18:2), watcher and holy ones (Dan. 4:13, 17, 23; cf. Jude 14), God's host, or army (Josh. 5:14, 15), sons of the mighty (Ps. 89:6). They are also called spirits and ministers of God (Heb. 1:7; see Ps. 104:4 and Heb. 1:14). Also, they are designated by the ranks they hold – principalities, powers and such.

Regular Services of Angels.

We discover that in a general way angels occupy their time (Is there time in heaven?) in at least six kinds of service to God on a regular basis, perhaps constantly.

(1) Angels praise God (Ps. 148:1, 2).

(2) They worship Him (Ps. 29:1, 2; see p. 00).

Moreover, (3) they rejoice in His work (Job 38:6, 7).

Regrettably, these activities will neither please nor inspire many modern people accustomed to advertising 'hype' for various novel ways to be entertained. Yet all the great saints whose lives we know in detail, gloried in these activities. These three related activities are mentioned in various ways. John writes of seven spirits before God's throne (Rev. 1:4). Though these may symbolize the Third Person of the Godhead, we do know that certain angels do stand in God's presence (Luke 1:19). If the seraphs of Isaiah 6:1 ff. are considered angels, worship is clearly involved. Other passages are specific (Ps. 148:1, 2; Ps. 29:1, 2; Job 38:6, 7). The Job passage indicates that angels ('sons of God') were created long before mankind was and therefore were present to praise God and rejoice in God's creative activity.

(4) Psalm 103:19-22 says that God has a universal kingdom and broadly suggests that in this kingdom His messengers (the Hebrew word used is the standard one rendered 'angels') do His bidding as ministers of state, so to speak, executing God's commandments: 'ministers, who do his will… in all places of his dominion' (Ps. 103:20-22). All governments, both good and bad, require services of this kind.

(5) Paul once suggests that angels are spectators of earthly affairs, especially apostolic work (1 Cor. 4:9) and of human government, as the name 'watcher' (Dan. 4:13, 17, 23) clearly implies.

(6) Angels compose a heavenly court or council – sometimes portrayed also as a retinue. Scripture must not be bent to teach that the invisible things of God's immediate presence in the heaven of His special, permanent manifestation, is literally portrayed just as it actually appears in the several passages of Scripture which say such things. We do not know to what extent scriptural revelation accommodated heavenly things to the ideas of the proper structure of a monarchial court and government prevalent among Israel and their ancient neighbours.

John's vision of God's court in heaven is of a throne on which One sits on a magnificent throne, immediately surrounded by seven spirits and four cherub-like 'living creatures' and, more remotely, by many angels around the throne and, still more remotely, by 'every creature in heaven and on earth and under the earth and in the sea' (Rev. 4 and 5), which seems to represent the whole universe in worshipful attendance. Throughout the rest of the book all the dramatic action flows from that scene. It is not parable, allegory or even prophecy as ordinarily considered, but *apocalypse* – a way of representing literal truths but not every feature of which is literally intended.

The same may be true of other representations of an angelic heavenly 'host' or 'council' or 'entourage'.

How God's 'court' of angels fits in with a 'periodic' assembly of 'the sons of God' including at least one evil 'son of God', Satan – Job's adversary and ours – is hard to say. We will have to await better information.

Angels in Service of Christ.

Though Christ as God and Creator of angels (John 1:1-3) is above angels (Heb. 1) in His incarnation, He is 'for a little while' lower than angels. Angels are prominently mentioned in connection with the coming and career of Christ as assisting and attending Him. An angel predicted His birth (Matt. 1:20; Luke 1:26-38) as well as the birth of the forerunner, John (Luke 1:11-20). Later, angels announced Jesus' birth (Luke 2:8-14). Not long afterward an angel warned Jesus' parents of the evil intent of King Herod (Matt. 2:13).

Angels attended Christ to aid Him at the beginning of His ministry in order to minister to Him (Matt. 4:11) and again near the end (Luke 22:43) to strengthen Him. It may be significant that though He could have called upon 'legions of angels' to help at any time (Matt. 26:53), there is no mention in the Gospels of their giving Him aid during the period of public ministry, except at the end of the temptations by the devil and during the agony of Gethsemane. In the latter case it may have been to assist Him physically to survive until the trials and crucifixion could take place. Angels likewise had services to perform at the time of the resurrection (Matt. 28:2, 5, 6) and possibly at His ascension to heaven, for the 'cloud' which 'took him out of their sight' may have been a 'crowd' of angels. So contend some sober scholars. Angels are presently devoted to the praise and worship of our Lord (Rev. 5:11, 12). He will come again 'in the clouds,' attended by angels 'in the same way' as the apostles saw Him go (Matt. 25:31; 1 Thess. 4:16, 17; Acts 1:9-11; Jude 14).

His Second Advent will be accompanied by much angelic activity. In addition to the aforementioned attendance at His coming *parousia* (arrival), the establishment of His kingdom will be effected, in part, by angelic work. Specifically, angels shall, in a police-like action, gather unclean things and unclean, unqualified persons out of the world. In interpreting His own parable of the tares, Jesus stated, 'The Son of Man will send his angels, and they will gather out of his kingdom all causes of sin and all law-breakers, and throw them into the fiery furnace. In that place there will be weeping and gnashing of teeth' (Matt. 13:41, 42).

Angels in Executing Providence.

Angels have some kind of special place in God's providential rule over the nations. God has an interest in national fortunes. He has decreed the bounds of national habitation, the rise and fall of the rulers of nations and the course of their histories (Ps. 24:1; Isa. 40:15; Rom. 13:1). God uses angels in the execution of His will for them.

The great A. B. Davidson, one of the editors of the *Hastings Dictionary of the Bible*, wrote: 'The Old Testament assumes the existence of Jehovah's retinue. The God of Israel is above all things a living God, who influences the affairs of the world and men and rules them. If He uses agents they are supplied by the "ministers" that surround Him.'[26] He goes on to trace the 'heavenly host' or court through the whole Old Testament.[27] The book of Daniel is especially interesting in this regard. In a frightening dream Nebuchadnezzar (according to his own report) learned that God's watchers, or holy ones, decreed his (Nebuchadnezzar's) rise and fall and restoration (Dan. 4, esp. v. 17). In Daniel's vision, received during the third year of Cyrus the Great of Persia (Dan. 10:1), Daniel learned that there was an angelic prince designated for the kingdom of Persia (10:13), another for Greece (10:20) and still another for Israel (10:21; cf. 11:1). Some of these angels seem to be satanically assigned.

An age like ours vacillates between a strictly naturalistic, cause-effect, laws-of-nature outlook and a strange predilection for astrology, magic and the occult. These insights from Daniel, therefore, both repel and attract. In any case, Christians must accept them into their world-view, as did Elisha and his servant during the siege of Samaria. '[T]he servant said, "Alas, my master! What shall we do?" He [Elisha] said, "Do not be afraid, for those who are with us are more than those who are with them." Then Elisha prayed and said, "O LORD, please open his eyes"... So the LORD opened the eyes of the young man... and behold, the mountain was full of horses and chariots of fire all round Elisha' (2 Kings 6:15-17). God always has to 'babble' to us, as Calvin says; that is, He adapts His revelation to our level of understanding and perceptual modes of understanding. The supernatural protectors of Elisha were neither ancient war chariots nor twentieth-century artillery pieces. They were and are *real*, however, more real than any objects of natural sensation. We know God's angels are *there*. They are *for us*. Let us therefore 'look not to the things that are seen but to the things that are unseen'.

---

26. A. B. Davidson, 'Angel' in *Dictionary of the Bible, vol. i* (popularly Hastings Dictionary of the Bible), (New York: Charles Scribner's Sons, 1908).
27. He cites Gen. 28, 37; Josh. 5, 12; Isa. 6; 1 Kings 22:19; Ps. 148:2; Job 1:6; 2:1; 33:23; 5:1; 4:18; Ps. 103:20; Joel 3:11; Zec. 14:5; Ps. 68:17; 2 Kings 6:16, 17; Isa. 66:15; Deut. 33:2; Dan. 7:16; Judg. 5:20; Isa. 14:12; 24:10; 40:26; 2 Kings 17:16; 21:3; Jer. 19:13; Zeph. 1:3 and on to Matt. 25:31.

The first book of the Bible and the last represent angels as God's messengers and instruments of both providential judgments now and final judgment hereafter. Angels announced the destruction of Sodom both to Abraham (Gen. 18) and to Lot (Gen. 19). They shall pour out the bowls of God's judgment on mankind in the coming 'wrath of God... on the earth' (Rev. 16:1-12). They shall bind the devil and incarcerate him at the beginning of the millennium (Rev. 20:1-3).

The Ministry of Angels to God's People.

It is a matter of great importance to Christians to know that angels have a special function in God's care of believers. We have already noted how an angel rescued Peter from prison. 'Are they not all ministering spirits sent out to serve for the sake of those who are to inherit salvation?' (Heb. 1:14).

Whether each Christian has an angel assigned to him, or to each child, or to each church, as has been inferred from certain texts (Matt. 18:3, 10; Heb. 1:14; Rev. 1:20), is doubtful. Calvin devoted an interesting and instructive paragraph on the subject of guardian angels which set a standard for about all said since (*Institutes I*, 14.7). But we do know that all of God's angels are working for us.

They are interested in our efforts in missionary evangelism and aid in securing the physical safety of the messengers (Acts 5:19; 12:7-10). Calvin drew from the Old Testament a startling case wherein an angel defended a whole city to deliver its inhabitants from annihilation by the excellent military power of antiquity, saying: 'Thus to fulfill the task of protecting us the angels fight against the devil and all our enemies, and carry out God's vengeance against those who harm us. As we read, the angel of God, to lift the siege of Jerusalem, slew 185,000 in the camp of the king of Assyria in a single night [2 Kings 19:35; Isa. 37:36]' (*Institutes I*, 14.6).

Angels are present in some mysterious way, to help at the time of death, as may be inferred from the fact Michael would not let the devil disturb the grave of Moses, whom God Himself had buried (Deut. 34:6; Jude 9), and the soul of the godly beggar Lazarus was carried by angels to Abraham's bosom (Luke 16:22). The 'rich man' simply died, was buried and went to 'Hades' ('hell' KJV).

These remarks by no means exhaust the teachings of Scripture about the place of angels in the divine scheme of things. Is it possible that in our modernity we have escaped something here which ought to capture us again? There should be no place in the believer's view of reality for superstition of any kind. The steady course of nature may be trusted. Angels, good or evil, will not overturn the slightest aspect of that. But human minds are not strictly within the natural, cause-effect sequence of things (as the positivists, behaviorists, and other, modern-minded scientists seem to be telling us). God has said, 'The angel of the LORD encamps round those who fear him, and delivers them' (Ps. 34:7).

In the year 1943 a fine evangelist-pastor by the name of Bernard N. Schneider, now with the LORD, held a series of meetings in the church of which I was pastor. While there he told a story which he included in his book, *The World of Unseen Spirits*. I close this portion of the chapter with his striking story.

> During the years of World War II we lived in Washington, D. C… On a Monday afternoon in the spring of 1941 we took a drive toward the city of Baltimore… My wife and five-year-old daughter went along for the ride. There were no freeways and interstate roads in those days, and we drove out Blandensburg Road and old U. S. Highway 1, which was then the main road between Washington and Baltimore. When we arrived in the suburbs of Baltimore, we agreed we had gone far enough and decided to turn around. So I turned into a side street to my right at an intersection with a traffic light, turned around in the next block and came back to the intersection. The traffic light turned green for us just before we got to it, and I proceeded to make the left turn to get back on the highway toward home. Just at that moment a peculiar sensation gripped me which urged me to stop. I did not hear a voice audibly, but there was an inner voice which I can best describe as a compelling urge which said: 'Stop.' I did stop right in front of the green light which said: 'Go.' And just then a large truck came through the red light from our left at a very high rate of speed. Had I not stopped at the green light, we would likely have been three dead people in our car. What made me stop when the light said go? I do not remember of ever doing that deliberately, except on that day. I believe it was an angel from the Lord looking after us.[28]

Mr Schneider, whom I knew very well, was a highly intelligent man, not the least prompted by silly sentiments of any kind, as far as I know.

---

28. Bernard N. Schneider, *The World of Unseen Spirits* (Winona Lake, IN: Brethren Missionary Herald Books, 1975), p. 40.

Epochs of Manifest Angelic Activity.

A bit of reflection by a reader fully conversant with all parts of the Bible will conclude that miracles were completely absent from most periods of Bible history. Leave out the story of the Exodus from Egypt, of the prophets Elijah and Elisha, and the period of our Lord's ministry, and not many manifestly, belief-compelling supernatural events, public or private, occurred. God is always acting above, within and in spite of what people call 'natural laws', but in such a way that unbelief cannot or will not acknowledge it to be so. Events yet future, at the consummation of the age, will include many miraculous events. At present, however, 'we walk by faith, not by sight', though no believer doubts God is at work in, above and in spite of 'nature', whether in answer to prayer or in other ways we know not what. We endure 'as seeing him that is invisible', though having 'not seen him, [we] love him' and we acknowledge that 'faith is… the conviction of things not seen'.

The same is true of the *manifest* activity of angels. They sang at creation (Job 38:7), they appeared from time to time to the patriarchs Abraham and Jacob, and made very rare appearances at critical junctures of Israel's history. They were active at Christ's birth and through His passion and the early period of apostolic ministry. At the Second Advent they will be in *manifest* activity again.

Meanwhile, we may be sure that 'out of sight' they are busy today as God's messengers and agents throughout the universe, particularly on behalf of God's people, for 'The angel of the LORD encamps round those who fear him, and delivers them' (Ps. 34:7).

Satan and Evil Angels.

We have postponed until this point any specific discussion of *evil* angels.[29] The Bible never makes a point of it, but the record is clear that the issues of freedom and moral responsibility were worked out in this universe long before the present order of the cosmos began. Someone (or many) tested out the law of God about obedience on the one hand and confirmed depravity on the other, long before Eve and Adam did. The existence of that other world is here, like the cosmic dust of some long exploded and vanished star. Precisely where the Bible narrative of moral life begins, there is the first presence of moral evil in the Bible.

The serpent, later clearly identified as being (perhaps symbolizing or acting for) Satan (Rev. 12:9), was there (Gen. 3:1-15). His evil moral influence was brought to bear and he won his first encounter. Through five books of the Old Testament (Genesis, 1 Chronicles, Job, Psalms and Zechariah, perhaps also Isaiah 14 and Ezekiel 28) and nineteen books of the New Testament (including every writer) the doctrine of Satan is taught in the narrative fashion characteristic of the Bible. Twenty-five of the references to him in the Gospels are from the mouth of Jesus Himself.

Co-ordinate with this teaching, the Bible refers to other beings, evil angels; sometimes they appear to be associated with Satan as their leader. In other words there are not only the holy, elect angels (Mark 8:38; 1 Tim. 5:21) but 'angels [that]… sinned' (2 Peter 2:4). Michael and his angels are at war with 'the dragon and his angels' (Rev. 12:7).

There is an inference to be drawn. If Satan has an army of angels, presumably they were gathered to him as a rebellious host in some primeval event unreported in Scripture. Christians have always drawn this inference from the data, an inference exploited in classic beauty in Milton's *Paradise Lost*. These evil angels were still Satan's to muster, deploy and use in New Testament times.

Who can doubt they still are? Peter did not hesitate to find the power of one of them (Satan) to fill the heart of two early believers to 'lie to the Holy Spirit' (Acts 5:3) and later to say that the same 'adversary the devil prowls around like a roaring lion, seeking someone to devour' (1 Peter 5:8). Paul is apparently including wicked angels among 'the spiritual forces of evil in the heavenly places' (Eph. 6:12) against whom we must 'take up the whole armour [Gr. *panoply*] of God' in order successfully to 'withstand in the evil day' (Eph. 6:13). They are arrayed in strength in support of their leader, Satan, in war against 'Michael and his angels' (Rev. 12:7ff.; cf. Dan. 10:13).

The range of these evil beings is inexplicable to this Bible interpreter. They are presumably among the 'rulers and authorities in the heavenly places' openly shamed by Christ at the cross (Eph. 3:10; Col. 2:15). The 'heavenly places' of these passages is surely not the heaven called God's 'dwelling place' (2 Chr. 6:30, 33). Perhaps it is the

---

29. The 'evil spirit' (1 Sam. 16:14, 16) said to be from the LORD or a 'lying spirit' sent by God (see 1 Kings 22:22, 23; 2 Chr. 18:21, 22) should not be thought of as one of the devil's angels or a demon, but as one of God's holy messengers sent to perform a disagreeable task. Paul said, 'The Lord shall send them strong delusion that they should believe a lie' (2 Thess. 2:11).

'heaven' of 'the prince of the power of the air' (Eph. 2:2). At least 'four' of these 'angels' are 'bound at the great river Euphrates' (Rev. 9:14, 15) and Satan has free range on earth for now. Yet some have been 'cast… into hell' (Greek, *Tartarus*, 2 Peter 2:4) being 'kept until the judgment' and one other angel (presumably evil) is a 'king', 'the angel of the bottomless pit [abyss]' (Rev. 9:11).

I accept all these statements as I do flashes of light from distant sources and from the rim of solar eclipses, but feel no competence to put it all together. Further, I distrust the seemingly all-wise interpreters, numerous long ago when I was first learning about these things, from preachers on prophecy and their books and charts. I cite the 'faithful saying' of the first Protestant master of theology:

> Let us not indulge in curiosity or in the investigation of unprofitable things… The theologian's task is not to divert the ears with chatter, but to strengthen consciences by teaching things true, *sure* and profitable (*Calvin's Institutes* I.14.4, emphasis added).

But there are others, referred to in 2 Peter 2:4 and Jude 6, who apparently sinned at some specific time other than when Satan and his hosts fell, and were henceforth imprisoned by God, to be kept in custody until the Judgment Day. The two texts cited above are both very specific about this. Some interpreters regard these incarcerated beings as the same as 'the sons of God' of Genesis 6:4 who 'came in to the daughters of man'. Was there an incursion of superterrestrial persons into human affairs at that time? Most interpreters at present think not. Our culturally derived predilections are all against it. The minds of most educated people today recoil against such apparent 'superstition'. Yet the same is true of all the teachings of Scripture about angels and other important subjects – miracles, new birth, incarnation and Second Advent. Such an incursion cannot on principle be ruled out as preposterous. Some of the most sober writers in the history of biblical interpretation have thought Genesis 6:1-4 does describe such an incursion and that it was one of the causes of the judgment of the Flood. Josephus and the most ancient of the Christian Fathers supported it, among them Justin Martyr, Tatian, Athenagoras, Clement of Alexandria, Tertullian, Cyprian and Lactantius. Augustine mentions the view, but with most later Fathers, rejected it. Many liberal, rationalistic modern writers adopt it, for it is no concern of theirs to protect Scripture interpretation against 'mythology'. Perhaps the best known modern writers in favor of this view are Franz Delitzsch [30] and Henry Alford.[31] Most recent evangelical commentaries and theologies are against the 'fallen angel' view. But whatever view one takes, the fact remains that because of some special sin, some fallen angels are imprisoned while others are not. Second Peter and Jude are specific and plain.

Evil angels, in general, are not a major biblical theme, but the one called Satan, Devil, Serpent, Dragon, Tempter, Beelzebub, the god of this world and several other designations, is a major theme. The biblical names employed divulge his malevolent character.

The literature of the subject is vast. The reader is advised to be cautious in selecting doctrinal sources for reading. They tend to be either sceptical on the one hand or superstitious on the other. Among contemporary evangelical authors the subject is treated with considerable verve by those who regard Isaiah, chapter 14 (a prophecy about the king of Babylon) and Ezekiel chapter 28 (a prophecy about an ancient king of Tyre) as being in some important sense prophecies also about Satan, his primeval fall, his present state and activity, and future judgment. The standard theology books generally are much more reserved and tend to have little to say about Satan's origin. I shall be content here[32] to quote briefly a passage from A. A. Hodge, one of the old Standards.

> Satan, like other finite beings can only be in one place at a time; yet all that is done by his agents being attributed to him, he appears to be practically ubiquitous.
>
> It is certain that at times at least they [Satan's agents] have exercised an inexplicable influence over the bodies of men, yet that influence is entirely subject to God's control (Job 2:7; Luke 13:16; Acts 10:38). They have caused and aggravated diseases, and excited appetites and passions (1 Cor. 5:5). Satan, in some [restricted, undefined] sense, has the power of death (Heb. 2:14).

---

30. *New Commentary on Genesis*, vol. i, pp. 222–233.
31. *New Testament for English Readers*, Introduction to Jude.
32. I have published about Satan and his activity, 'The Nations of Earth and Their Governments as Part of a Satanic Kingdom,' and have an unpublished written theology lecture on the subject. See Robert D. Culver, *Civil Government: A Biblical View* (Alberta, AB, Canada: Canadian Institute for Law, Theology, and Public Policy, 2000), pp. 49–60.

With respect to the souls of men, Satan and his angels are utterly destitute of any power either to change the heart or to coerce the will, their influence being simply moral, and exercised in the way of deception, suggestion, and persuasion. The descriptive phrases applied by the Scriptures to their working are such as the deceivableness of unrighteousness, 'power, signs, lying wonders' (2 Thess. 2:9, 10); he 'transforms himself into an angel of light' (2 Cor. 11:14). If he can deceive or persuade he uses 'wiles' (Eph. 6:11); 'snares' (1 Tim. 3:7); 'depths' (Rev. 2:24); he 'blinds the mind' (2 Cor. 4:4); 'leads captive the will' (2 Tim. 2:26); and so 'deceives the whole world' (Rev. 12:9). If he cannot persuade he uses 'fiery darts' (Eph. 6:16) and 'buffetings' (2 Cor. 12:7).[33]

Demons.

There are certain unclean spirits called demons (kjv devils) mentioned in several parts of the Bible. They are particularly prominent in the Gospels in connection with the public ministry of Jesus. Outside of the Gospels these are, as we noted in the chapter on the unity of God, usually represented as appropriating the worship offered to idols. The word demon (from Gr. *daimon*) simply means a spirit. The Greeks thought of some demons as good, some as evil. They had a special word for each kind and gave respectful veneration to all of them. In his famous speech to the Athenians, Paul put this matter before them in a skilful manner. A literal translation might read, 'I see you all are very-much-demon-worshippers' (Acts 17:22). The four underlined and hyphenated words are all one long word in author Luke's Greek, *deisidaimonesterous*. The rsv and esv rendering, 'very religious', represents how the Greeks felt about it and 'too superstitious', the kjv rendering, how Paul and any Christians or Jews present felt. One of the historical Psalms says that the apostate, idolatrous worship of the children of Israel in Canaan was sacrifice to demons (Ps. 106:37). Moses said the same of the Israelite apostasy of his time (Deut. 32:17) and Paul of the heathen worship of Corinth (1 Cor. 10:20, 21).

It is likely that everything said earlier herein about wicked angels should be applied likewise to these demon-spirits. No one in Scripture is ever said to be possessed by an evil angel as such, but considering the essential 'messenger' nature of all angels, it is not difficult to identify demons with fallen angels, though specific proof is wanting.

The New Testament distinctly regards what is called 'demon possession' as reality. It is not the same as mental disease, though apparently some symptoms are similar. Jesus addressed the demons as distinct from the human persons possessed and the persons as distinct from the demons. There are reputable conservative theologians who think Jesus accommodated Himself to the then current opinion that insanity, epilepsy and the like are caused by demons. In such a case His words cannot be used for a theology about 'demonism'. It is notable that the New Testament provides no certified list of symptoms whereby to identify demon-caused mental disease. Let us be grateful for this silence. The various other ailments which Jesus healed, however, are not said to be caused by evil spirits – there is no 'evil spirit' theory of disease in the Gospels.

Demon possession is not the same as demonic influence. Demons use their influence through false teachers (1 John 4:1-3). Through the susceptibility of us all to mental suggestion, demons certainly have an open field for action, as the case of Peter's foolish acceptance of a satanic suggestion shows (Mark 8:33). Ananias, who allowed Satan to fill his heart with a bad motive, is another example of demon influence on the mind (Acts 5:2). Satanic (demonic) influence is all about us; we can and do resist it. But in demon possession the person is 'possessed' by the evil spirit and is apparently powerless against the demon.

No person on earth really has authority to pronounce a given case of irrational or malevolent behaviour as demon possession, though we may be sure it exists. As previously noted, there is no approved list of symptoms for certain diagnoses of cases. Exorcism is not a biblically authorized procedure for care of demon possession or demon oppression (whatever that may be), though prayer in Jesus' name is. Perhaps the rationalistic teachers and preachers who deny the true deity and Lordship of Jesus Christ are the demon-possessed of our time. If Satan is as cunning as represented, and if he has numerous invisible agents at his service, then in our age, surely his tactics will not deploy them primarily in physically and mentally tormenting folk, as in the Gospel narratives. How much more strategic to place them in university chairs, prominent pulpits, government bureaus, editorial offices, social service agencies and courts of law. Perhaps something like this is behind the progressive corruption and paganizing of the news-gathering and disseminating media and the entertainment industry. Could it explain the acceptance of Nazism and the so-called holocaust? The drift of the general population toward acceptance of homosexuality as a normal 'lifestyle' and of 'same-sex marriage' comes to mind. Many very respectable articles and books, not all by any means by orthodox Christian authors, written since World War II, have suggested as much.

---

33. A. A. Hodge, *Outlines of Theology* (Grand Rapids: Eerdmans, 1956), pp. 255, 256.

20
Satan and Demons: Fallen Created Spirits

I. The Doctrine of Satan.

1. For sufficient reasons the evil being called Satan is to be regarded as a fallen angel. Hence everything in the previous chapter relates to him. Michael, an archangel, and his holy angels are paired with their opposite 'the dragon and his angels' (Rev. 12:7). Hence also it is commonly and probably correctly thought that he began his career as an archangel.

2. The evil being introduced in Genesis 3 as the 'serpent' is the same as 'the dragon', 'the devil' and 'Satan' according to Revelation 12:7-9. So little is said of Satan in the Old Testament that it would be difficult certainly to identify the serpent with the one named 'Satan' and 'the devil' apart from Revelation 12:9.

In addition to these two names he is characterized twice as 'the tempter' (Matt. 4:3 and 1 Thess. 3:5) and 'the accuser of our brothers' (Rev. 12:10). Presumably when the Pharisees referred to 'Beelzebub, the prince of demons' (Matt. 12:24) they were thinking of Satan, though the name means 'Lord of flies', a Philistine god (see 2 Kgs. 1:2, 6). It is likely Jesus understood them as referring to 'Satan' (Matt. 12:26). Jesus called him also 'the ruler of this world' (John 12:31) and Paul 'the god of this world' (2 Cor. 4:4), 'the prince of the power of the air' (Eph. 2:2) and 'the spirit of the world' (1 Cor. 2:12).

The Existence of Satan and of Demons in Scripture.

More than is the case with good angels, many leading theologians outside evangelical circles have departed from a straightforward acceptance of the biblical witness about them. As for the biblical witness, however, 'It would be a waste of time to prove that, in various degees of clearness, the personal existence of a Spirit of Evil is revealed again and again in Scripture... It is obvious that the fact of his existence is of spiritual importance'.[1] We mentioned the less radical Barth and Brunner in the preceding chapter. Rudolf Bultmann set in motion a 'program of demythologization' which eliminates everything unverifiable by accepted scientific methods, so devil, demons and angels all must be regarded as unreal. In the widely influential – but hardly clear – language of Paul Tillich, demon and demonic have no reference to unseen evil spirits. Tillich would have us limit 'demonic' to 'the claim of

---

1. McClintock & Strong, *Cyclopedia, vol. ix*, p. 361, right column.

something finite to infinity or to divine greatness'.[2] Himself a victim of and observer of Nazi persecution close up, Tillich labeled Naziism 'demonic'. But Tillich's ideas seem to have strengthened occult movement while casting reproach on biblical teaching regarding the demonic and encouraging, if not prime cause of the widely advertized apostasy of Bishop Pike.[3]

So much superstition has been passed down from earlier times on the subject of demons that one is tempted to pass by the truly massive, sober literature by competent Christian scholars, and some hard-nosed secular scholars, to confirm the existence of evil spirits which, employing an old Greek word, are called demons. Two works by Merril F. Unger *Biblical Demonology* (Scripture Press) and *Demons in the World Today* (Tyndale House), an older work by John L. Nevius, *Demon Possession and Allied Themes* (Revell, 1894 and many reprints) find as much evidence in Scripture for the existence, nature and activities of demons as for good angels, and, for that matter, for good and bad kings. Nevius, an Anglican missionary to China, researched demon 'possession' as it was thought to exist by Chinese folk and found numerous examples of what the Bible describes, parallel to the cases in the Gospels.

Demon (Gr. *daimonion* or *daimon*) in pre-biblical, classical Greek designates supernatural personal spirits, not necessarily evil. They are sometimes the gods (*theoi*) themselves and sometimes their messengers or other spirits, good and bad. Although these notions and the names for them originated in the milieu of primitive Greek animism, by the time the authors of the Septuagint and the New Testament used the word, *daimonion* designated an evil, personal spirit, usually associated with idol worship, the equivalent of unclean spirit (*pneuma akatharton*).

Werner Foerster, in a thorough canvas of all New Testament passages referring to demons, observes that in the New Testament they are seldom referred to except in cases of demon possession, and they are never ghosts of the dead. Missionaries did not fear them as perils to travel, which is quite a contrast to some Jewish beliefs.

Foerster summarizes:

> [T]he fact that demons are mentioned only with relative infrequency in the New Testament does not mean that their existence and operation are contested or doubted. For Paul witchcraft is meddling with demons. But there can also be intercourse with demons in the normal [ordinary?] heathen culture [rituals, ceremonies, etc.] (1 Cor. 10:20 f.). While idols are nothing, and the Christian enjoys freedom, demons stand behind paganism… In Revelation too, we read of the worship of demons along side that of blind and deaf [idols] (9:20). In the last time both Paul and Revelation expect a particular activity of demonic powers [he quotes 1 Tim. 4:1 and Rev. 16:13 ff.]… The ascent of of locusts from the abyss [Rev. 9:1ff.] denotes an activity of demonic powers under the leadership of a single power [the angel of the abyss].[4]

So much for the existence of demons as far as the Bible itself is concerned, however unlikely to many moderns. Even as devout an evangelical writer as David Smith,[5] pressed by the humanistic optimism of the time, felt the affirmation of demons by Jesus was by way of accommodation to popular beliefs.

Though Satan appears by name in only four Old Testament passages he appears by many titles, adjectives and aliases on numerous occasions in the New Testament. Unless one wishes to reinterpret these references in the manner of Rudolf Bultmann, and some of his equally radical followers, his reality as far as the Bible is concerned may not be doubted. 'It would be a waste of time to prove that, in various degrees of clearness, the personal existence of a Spirit of evil is revealed again and again in Scripture'.[6] Yet the Old Testament says very little about Satan. It is reasonable to suppose the reason for this reserve was to be found in the inveterate tendency of the Israelites to idolatry. They already had an unhealthy regard for evil spirits associated with Canaanite religion and witchcraft. The desire of survivors of the Babylonian destruction of the country by Nebuchadnezzar's armies for worship of a better god than Jehovah, one able to save the idolater in his sin, would readily have found an object for worship in a Hebrew Satan (see Jer. 43).

---

2. Paul Tillich, *Systematic Theology III* (Chicago: U. of Chicago Press, 1963), p. 102.
3. I struggled through many lean years to finish a four-year college degree, completing my work while a mission pastor supporting a family. Without the sympathetic help of the kindly dean of the church-related college who also taught my course in English literature I might not have succeeded. That dear man, product of the liberal Protestantism of the time, was not so much repelled as amazed that I was the only student in his class who seemed to love the subject and catch the nuances of Spenser and Milton who also believed there really are angels, demons and a Satan. Satan has not been alive and well in the estimation of liberal religion for several centuries.
4. Werner Foerster, *TDNT II, daimon, daimonion*, p. 17.
5. David Smith, *The Days of His Flesh: The Earthly Life of Our Lord*, 8th ed. (London: Hodder & Stoughton, 1910).
6. Alfred Barry, *Smith's Dictionary of the Bible*, Hacket Edition IV, 'Satan' p. 2846.

The Origin and Fall of Satan and Demons.

It is a plain matter of fact that the Bible never plainly declares when, where or how these created beings came into existence or how they became evil. Down through the ages Jewish and Christian traditions have relied upon the prophecy of Isaiah 14, regarding the king of Babylon, and Ezekiel 28, regarding the king of Tyre, as telling us Satan began as an 'anointed guardian cherub' stationed highly in God's host of heaven near the throne of the Almighty. If these passages refer to Satan it must be assumed the two kings – of Tyre and of Babylon – are types or shadows of that familiar but unseen wicked spirit described as *hassatan*, 'the Adversary'. It is of course true these kings claimed superhuman origin and status. Hence one should not reject that view out of hand, knowing that great minds have endorsed it and the text itself hints of a kind of double-entendre. This interpretation is supported by suggestion in Paul's list of requirements for elders: 'he may become puffed up with conceit and fall into the condemnation of the devil' (1 Tim. 3:6). It is 'commonly understood to mean the condemnation which the devil incurs for the same sin.'[7] But as frequently as Satan is mentioned in Scripture, it is strange that no allusion whatsoever to a primeval fall ever appears, such as is thought to be described by Isaiah and Ezekiel. Persuasive Christian preaching and writing have been constructed on this interpretation by Donald G. Barnhouse,[8] Richard W. DeHaan,[9] and many others. Standard theology books have been generally much more reserved in this regard, grounding the doctrine in the plethora of materials elsewhere in Scripture. I shall follow that example, with some reluctance.

Truly, Satan scarcely figures at all in the Old Testament except as one of the 'sons of God' in Job, the adversary of the restoration priest Joshua (Zech. 3:1, 2), a single doubtful reference at Psalm 109:6 and as the serpent in Genesis 3. James Kallas, in a valuable small book, sums up:

> The whole of the Old Testament doctrine of Satan can be summed up in two words – insignificant and a servant. Mentioned only three times, only once at length, and in that one lengthy passage a loyal [in the Book of Job?] servant. That is all the Old Testament has to say about Satan! Anymore than that is untrue to the Old Testament.[10]

It is not improper to infer from what the New Testament says about 'the devil and his angels' that Satan deployed his servants, fallen angels, to resist Michael, as Daniel reports. Nor is it certain that however puzzling the presence of Satan (adversary) was in God's company (Job 1, 2) Satan was a 'loyal' servant. He just might have been present coercively.

We must assume that, however Satan became evil, it was through a fall from an original created state of moral good. This state included the power of free will and without external temptation by anything evil in itself, he aspired to be and to have what was not rightly his. He thereby fell and has not paused in descent. This, it must be acknowledged, is precisely the picture drawn by those who take the Satan interpretation of Isaiah 14 and Ezekiel 28.

The Character of Satan.

The Scriptures are explicit. The Hebrew name, 'Satan', means adversary. He is *against* all that is godly and good. The more common 'devil' (Gr. *diabolos*), 'accuser' or 'slanderer', amount to about the same. In fact the Septuagint frequently translates the Hebrew 'Satan' (whether of the great adversary or some other) by *diabolos* (Job 1:6; 2:1; Zech. 3:1 *et al*). He slandered God to Eve on his first appearance and mankind to God in the case of Job. He is a murderer (John 8:44), a liar (John 8:44), a thief (Matt. 13:19), and evil (Matt. 13:18). These evil traits derive from 'his own nature' and 'there is no truth in him' (as the RSV renders John 8:44). The believer is wise to take note that he is 'the god of this world' (2 Cor. 4:4), 'the spirit of the world' (1 Cor. 2:12), 'the deceiver of the whole world' (Rev. 12:9) and that 'the whole world lies in the power of the evil one' (1 John 5:19). It follows that the world – as *cosmos*, arranged in a certain way – will reflect the devil's policies and is therefore a very dangerous place in which to dwell (spiritually, morally, physically), especially to rear our children! (Should we expect their schooling under worldly government aegis to reflect godly principles?) The character of the devil and his powers explains the warnings against his 'schemes' (Gr. 'methods', Eph. 6:11), his 'designs' (2 Cor. 2:11) and the 'snare of the devil' (1 Tim. 3:7).

---

7. Charles A. Hodge, *Systematic Theology I* (Grand Rapids: Eerdmans, 1970), p. 643.
8. Donald G. Barnhouse, *The Invisible War* (Grand Rapids: Zondervan, 1965), pp. 28–51.
9. Richard W. DeHaan, *Satanism and Witchcraft* (Grand Rapids: Zondervan, 1972), pp. 9–20.
10. James Kallas, *The Real Satan* (Minneapolis: Augsburg Publ., 1975), p. 25.

Nearly thirty years passed by between the publication of the *Theological Dictionary of the New Testament* article *Diabolos* by Werner Foerster (Vol. II) and his article *Satan* (Vol. VII). In the interval the Dead Sea Scrolls brought many New Testament data into sharper focus, illuminating Jewish ideas about evil in the period shortly before Christ. Foerster points out that at Qumran there is little or no reference to *Satan*, usually called *Belial*, as a fallen creature, but rather as created *angel of darkness*, who has the world in his sway. Against Belial and his people God also employs the created angel of light. The two forces will be in contest till a last violent battle when Belial, his angels and his people will be judged and God will create something new, 'the return of Paradise and a life of men with angels'. 'The men of Qumran were concerned to solve the problem of evil by tracing back to God even that which he hates and rejects.'[11] He goes on to say, 'In the history of later Judaism this battle between light and darkness is the theme of world history... Thus a whole series of statements from the Old Testament and other sources is set aside. Nothing is said about Satan as the accuser before God, about the fall of Adam or his seduction by the serpent or Satan, about the fall of angels... or about Lucifer.'[12] There is no doctrine of original sin in Judaism. If Foerster is correct in assessment of the Qumran sect their view of sin and Satan is similar to Parseeism's doctrine of two eternal, uncreated principles of evil – Ormazd and Ahriman, a metaphysical-ethical dualism. Manichaeism – founded by a third century Persian prophet – made a religion of dualism and though it helped the youthful Augustine escape materialistic philosophy it also challenged the faith of Christians of the time.

Satan's Career and Destiny.

Whether or not one thinks Satan is the one of Ezekiel 28:14 who was 'on the holy mountain of God' or who in the language of Isaiah 14:13 sought to 'ascend to heaven above the stars of God', he began his career as a created mighty angel (one of the 'sons of God', Job 1:6, 7, 8, 12; 2:1-6), with access to God in the heavenly council. Though at present 'prince of the power of the air' (Eph. 6:11, 12; 2:2), it is doubtful he 'sees God's face' as holy angels do in the 'heavenly places' which are now his realm in the unseen world. He has some sort of access to God, perhaps. One hesitates to generalize from the picture drawn by the first two chapters of Job.

Jesus spoke of a fall of Satan when 'The seventy-two returned with joy, saying, "Lord, even the demons are subject to us in your name!"' after which He declared, 'I saw Satan fall like lightning from heaven' (Luke 10:17, 18). This has affinity of language with Revelation 12:7-12. Michael and his angels are fighting against the dragon (Satan) and his angels. Both 'the deceiver of the whole world' and his angels are cast down to the earth. A loud voice from heaven proclaims the arrival of the kingdom of God and with it the overthrow of 'the accuser of our brothers... who accuses them day and night before our God. And they have conquered him by the blood of the Lamb and by the word of their testimony, for they loved not their lives even unto death' (Rev. 12:7-12).

Surely these passages have more than mere verbal connection with Paul's doctrine that at the cross 'He [Christ] disarmed the rulers and authorities [the devil and all his host] and put them to open shame, by triumphing over them in him' (Col. 2:15).

What shall we make of these passages? Paul at Ephesians 2:2; 6:11, 12; Jesus speaking at Luke 10:17, 18; John at Revelation 12:7-12, each of which finds Satan in a heavenly place but cast out, whereupon (in Rev. 12:13) he persecutes 'the woman' (= God's people, perhaps Israel, perhaps the church).

I have great sympathy for the opinion of H. B. Swete: 'It is vain to attempt to grasp the nature of the spiritual fact which these visions symbolize, so far as it belongs to the celestial order.'[13] Over a period of a long life I have earnestly read dozens of serious books and articles by competent, devout scholars on these verses in Revelation chapter 12. After I had read the first commentary (Joseph Seiss, *The Apocalypse*) very long ago, I thought I knew – the Revelation passage applied strictly to an event after the rapture of the church in the closing months of the present age. I still share a general futurist interpretation of Revelation, but I have come to see that even so, I must merge all into what we see as the foreshortened view of the future of John who wrote, and the people who first read, his 'breaking news' from Patmos (Rev. 1:4). For them the document was 'The revelation of Jesus Christ, which God gave him to show to his servants the things that must soon take place' (Rev. 1:1), with a 'fall like lightning from heaven' (Luke 10:17, 18), and in the Roman persecutions the martyrs saw their picture in Revelation 12:11 – overcoming by the precious blood and the 'word of their testimony' sealed with their own blood. Yet, the 'short

---

11. Werner Foerster, 'Satan', *TDNT*, vol. vii, p. 153.
12. ibid., p. 156.
13. H. B. Swete, *The Apoclypse of John*. The Greek Text with Notes and Indices (New York: Macmillan, 1907), p. 154.

time' (Rev. 12:12) of Satan's remaining freedom to do his worst during the final period of 'the great tribulation' (Rev. 7:14) surely applies. This deliberate merging of near and far – prediction of a kind of events without full and limited specification of a particular event – is familiar to all believing interpreters of Old Testament prophetic books, including apocalypses.

So as to his power to accuse 'our brothers' (as in Job and Rev. 12:10), Satan was destroyed at Calvary. In this sense Satan fell from heaven as lightning – whatever real access he may or may not have had to the heaven of God's special manifestation (see 2 Chr. 6:18). This is what Paul is referring to in the Ephesians and Colossian passages (and other New Testament references to the same). The Revelation passage certainly includes this reference (after all, the martyrs of Revelation 12 overcome Satan by the blood of the Lamb) but there is also an eschatological reference. In that final conflict at the brink of the end of the age Satan will be removed from every realm except the earthly. The battle of Revelation 12 'is the cosmic prelude to the consummation. It explains the intense hostility to be poured out upon the church in the days of final tribulation... Satan and his forces are defeated in battle and must forfeit their place in heaven... and his angels are defeated in battle and cast down to earth. It is the beginning of the end.'[14]

Granting a lack of clear biblical revelation about the precise time and place of Satan's beginnings we can summarize the periods of Satan's career and his destiny as follows: (i) high position (Jude 8, 9; cf. Ezek. 28:14) among the heavenly host before the creation of the heavens and the earth (Job 38:7; cf Ezek. 28:14); (ii) 'in heavenly places' after a primeval fall (1 Tim. 3:6; Eph. 5:11, 12) but present on earth as god of the present evil world (most references throughout the New Testament); (iii) cast down to earth, where he has a little time to do his worst (Rev. 12:7-12) near the end of the present age; (iv) incarcerated in the abyss ('the bottomless pit') 'for a thousand years' (Rev. 20:1-3); (v) 'for a little while' back on earth again; and (vi) finally consigned to the 'lake of fire'. In all these matters the best informed theologians know no more than the least sophisticated, but informed Bible reader. Neither can penetrate beyond the present veil between the present order where we walk by faith and not by sight. Efforts to gain present access to that other world end only with spiritual and moral disaster (Isa. 8:19; Deut. 18:9-14; 1 Sam. 28:7-25).

Satan's Present Activities and Devices.

There is no place where a theology thorough in assessing what the biblical record displays meets us 'sinners by choice and aliens by birth' more fully than the devil's devices. Moreover, we need not be 'ignorant of his designs' (2 Cor. 2:11) or unable 'to stand against the schemes of the devil' (Eph. 6:11).

He begins his slithering course through the Bible by *slandering* God to Eve (Gen. 3:4, 5) and is next seen as *adversary* to God's high priest Joshua[15] (Zec. 3:1 ff.) and later to God's Messiah (Matt. 4:1-10). He counterfeits God's word and work (2 Cor. 11:14, 15; cf. Rev. 16:13) and in final opposition to God energizes the man of sin, the final Antichrist (Rev. 16:13 ff.; cf. 2 Thess. 2:7-12).

As to the present age (eon, *aiōn*) and world (cosmos, *kosmos*) Satan is its god (2 Cor. 4:4); he dictates its principles and strategies (Eph. 2:1, 2), and it lies in his embrace (1 John 5:19), for he is 'deceiver of the whole world' (Rev. 12:9). Within this organized world he deceives the nations. At the time of Jesus, Satan led them in the attacks which led to undeserved execution of the Savior. This is the gist of perennial Christian interpretation of the prayer of the first Christian assembly (Acts 4:23-31) and the plain sense of Revelation 12:1-4, 13. Satan's actions to destroy Jesus began with Herod and ended with the closing events of the 'last week'. The great red dragon will in the closing period of this age gather the nations to a last anti-Christian, anti-God convulsion at a place 'that in Hebrew is called Armageddon' (Rev. 16:12-16).

Among the unbelieving people of the world 'the god of this world has blinded the minds of the unbelievers, to keep them from seeing the light of the gospel of the glory of Christ' (2 Cor. 4:4); he 'takes away the word from their hearts, so that they may not believe and be saved' (Luke 8:12). He moves some of them both subtly and confrontationally to hinder success to God's witnesses in missionary work (as with Elymas the magician, Acts 13:4-12). He incites them to persecute, even to slay good people, from Cain's brother (1 John 3:12) to the last Christian martyr (Rev. 6:9-11; cf. Rev. 12:11). He promotes lies, deceit, treachery, disease and every evil, whether beautiful or ugly, and the final tragedy, death, for he is not only a liar and the father of lies but of death (John 8:44). 'Whoever desires to love life and see good days, let him keep his tongue from evil and his lips from speaking deceit' (1 Peter 3:10). 'Resist the devil, and

---

14. Robert H. Mounce, *The New International Commentary on the New Testament, The Book of Revelation* (Grand Rapids: Eerdmans, 1977), pp. 240, 241.
15. Joshua = Jesus.

he will flee from you' (James 4:7). 'Flee youthful passions' (2 Tim. 2:22). '[F]lee from sexual immorality' (1 Cor. 6:18).

As for believing children of God, their *external* 'enemy' is 'the devil' (Matt. 13:39) who promotes discord and distress in 'the field [which] is the world' (Matt. 13:38) by sowing weeds ('sons of the evil one') among the 'good seed', who are 'the children of the kingdom' (Matt. 13:38; cf. 18-23; and 36-41). He hinders missionary evangelists in their work, as when in the case of Paul and his party, he reported, 'Satan hindered us.' The devil stirs up persecution of believers – as predictive of the suffering church of Smyrna, 'the devil is about to throw some of you into prison' (Rev. 2:10). He is also the 'enemy' *within*, suggesting all the evil thoughts and all the wrong answers to the mind as he did to Peter in the famous episode at Caesarea Philippi (Matt. 16:21-23). This power of suggestion is especially operative in placing us in situations friendly more to immodest and immoral behaviour than to right conduct (see 1 Cor. 7:5 and context).

Against these attacks the apostolic exhortation is to 'Put on the whole armour [Gk. *Panoplia*, panoply] of God' (Eph. 6:11 ff.).

Reflections on the Devil and All His Works.

Ancient Christians at baptism (and later at confirmation) were required publicly to 'renounce the devil and all his works'. Sometimes a rather particular list of his 'works' was furnished for renunciation. Preaching has often sometimes for good reason, sometimes not, followed a similar route. The Bible does not tell everything about Satan's aspirations, but it is clear that he intends to subvert God's rule, to make the 'kingdom[s] of this world' of mankind his rather than 'of our Lord and of his Christ' (Rev. 11:15). The theatre of contest is the human race – from Genesis 3 to Revelation 20. We err if we suppose his goals are simply to promote crimes, civil disorder and immorality. Rather, Satan would have human beings – whether crude and primitive, or refined and sophisticated – worship any creature rather than the Creator, to follow their own wills to death and hell rather then God's will to life everlasting. To this end Satan is less the ruffian than an 'angel of light', as much at work in dignified courts of law, legislature, universities and schools of art – even theological seminaries and church conferences – as in bars, brothels and opium dens (2 Cor. 11:14 ff.)!

Encouragements and Cautions.

Scripture puts believers on notice that the devil is dangerous and the world he ranges about in is a perilous environment, as we have seen. Moreover, though Christian influence and acceptance has spread from Jerusalem to the ends of the earth, it has also died out in geographical areas where the salt had lost its savour and hence 'thrown out' as fit only to be 'trampled under people's feet' (Matt. 5:13). Satan has an ally in the sinful heart of every 'man born of woman', without exception. Yet as believers indwelt by the Spirit of God 'he who is in you is greater than he who is in the world' (1 John 4:4). So we best join Michael (Jude 8, 9) in respecting the devil, never speaking contemptuously to or of him, yet not estimating the devil and his minions too highly or thinking or talking of him overmuch. Throughout the book of Job, Job fights the devil through all those speeches without knowing about the contest in heaven of which he was centre or ever once referring to Satan in his speech. The action was all in Job's soul. We do know about Satan's part in Job's contest. Yet we need not live in superstitious fright of the Evil or his host. Observe the following.

1. Satan has already been judged and defeated at the cross. When he approached Christ at the beginning of His ministry he lost the contest (Matt. 4:1-11), and in the very shadow of the cross Jesus declared that Satan has been 'judged' (John 16:11). Paul explained that God through Christ at the cross 'disarmed the rulers and authorities [Satan and his host] and put them to open shame, by [with his resurrection] triumphing over them in him' (Col. 2:8, 14, 15). As Luther's great hymn has it, Satan's 'doom is sure' even though now free on temporary release, 'by exercise staying healthy for execution'!

2. We are assured of our Lord's intercessary prayers for us. As He prayed for Peter's victory over Satan's 'sifting' (Luke 22:31, 32) so He prays for us today (cf. John 17:15-26; Heb. 7:25).

3. In the midst of fiercest opposition we have been promised stress relief. 'But the Lord is faithful. He will establish you and guard you against the evil one. And we have confidence in the Lord…' (2 Thess. 3:3, 4).

4. Satan is a fellow creature after all, not omnipotent by any standard. We have the duty to resist him as we should any other evil creature (James 4:7; Eph. 4:27), putting on 'the whole armour of God' for defence and taking the offensive against him as well (Eph. 6:11-18). As we conquer his territory by the Word of God (which is a sword of the Spirit) he may be defeated (Rev. 12:11).

5. It was not without reason that through the ages of the church when the majority of Christians were illiterate,

unable to read the Scriptures, and pastors not much more learned, among the first duties of children and new believers was to learn 'the Lord's Prayer' (Matt. 6:9-13). The prayer has been variously expounded. (a) It has been seen as *eschatological* in perspective, in which case 'deliver us from evil' means from 'the Evil One', hence Paul's 'frequent warnings of heightened intensity of the Kingdom's inauguration'.[16] (b) The prayer relates to life in the present age, however long that may be, and the request 'deliver us from evil' means from evils in general. (c) As in (b), but deliverance from the Evil One is the petition. 'The whole weight of New Testament language is in favor of the latter meaning'.[17] In such a case, we are specifically taught by Jesus and catechizers of the church for ages ('Give us this day') to pray for deliverance from the devil. Prayer, with employment of the means of grace, will furnish daily victory over 'the world, the flesh, and the devil'.

II. The Doctrine of Demons.

The word demon (from Gr. *daimon* and *daimonion*) simply means a spirit. The Greeks thought of some demons as good, some as evil. They had a special word for each kind and gave respectful veneration to all of them. In his famous speech to the Athenians, Paul put this matter before them in a skillful manner. A literal translation might read, 'I see you all are *very-much-demon-worshippers*' (Acts 17:22). The four italicized and hyphenated words are all one long word in author Luke's Greek, *deisidaimonesterous*. The RSV and ESV rendering, 'very religious', represents how the Greeks felt about it and 'too superstitious', the KJV rendering, how Paul and any Christians or Jews present felt. One of the historical Psalms says that the apostate, idolatrous worship of the children of Israel in Canaan was sacrifice to *demons* (Ps. 106:37). Moses said the same of the Israelite apostasy of his time (Deut. 32:17) and Paul of the heathen worship of Corinth (1 Cor. 10:20, 21).

It is likely that everything said earlier herein about wicked angels should be applied likewise to these demon-spirits. No one in Scripture is ever said to be possessed by an evil angel as such, but considering the essential 'messenger' nature of all angels, it is not difficult to identify demons with fallen angels, though specific proof is wanting.

A distinction should be made between *demonology* (or demonolatry) and the biblical *doctrines of demons* (1 Tim. 4:1). Articles in general encyclopedias entitled 'Demonology' relate to spirits thought by primitive folk to inhabit objects of nature such as trees, rocks, wells and similar (animism) and roving spirits of deceased people, sprites, elves, fairies and the like (superstition).[18] The Bible, however, neither endorses superstitious beliefs nor advocates the 'demonology' of some low periods of Jewish and Christian beliefs. With the rise of evolutionary (developmental, Hegelian) theories of the origin of religion and of Scripture there has been much written, as well, to interpret the Old Testament as containing animist and even polytheistic elements.[19] Robert Pfeiffer thought that in Moses' experience of acute illness (Exod. 4:24-26) Jehovah is nothing more than 'a malignant demon of the wilderness'.[20] The foundations for such views were laid by several nineteenth-century biblical scholars – prominently Lenormant in *The Beginnings of History*[21] and W. Robertson Smith.[22] W. R. Smith's point is that the prevalent superstitions of all Semites – including Arabs – were present among all the Hebrews. He does not sufficiently point out how, if so, Scripture corrects those superstitions.[23] The article in the *Hastings Dictionary of the Bible* reflects this outlook. The article itself – Old Testament and New Testament – does not rise above animistic and totemistic beliefs, e.g. the serpent of Genesis 3 is a totem and even 'St. Paul... shared the conception of his contemporaries respecting devils.'[24] Any one who believes the Old Testament is as Jesus described it (John 10:35) and Paul declared (2 Tim. 3:16) will be assured that however much superstitious belief may have survived in the minds of biblical people, those beliefs are not endorsed by the Bible, but rather corrected by it. R. K. Harrison addresses this matter at length from this

---

16. W. F. Albright & C. S. Mann, *Matthew, The Anchor Bible* (Garden City, NY: Doubleday, 1981), p. 77
17. Ellicott. See Matt. 13:19, 38; John 17:15; Eph. 6:16; 2 Thess. 3:3; 1 John 2:13, 14; 3:12; 5:18, 19.
18. 'Demonology', *Encyclopedia Britannica*, 11th ed., vol. viii, pp. 5–8.
19. E.g., 'Remnants of Animism in Hebrew Religion: Sacred Stones, Rocks, and Mountains', W. O. E. Oesterley & T. H. Robinson, *Hebrew Religion, Its Origin and Development* (Chap. IV, 1937 and on to the present).
20. Robert Pfeiffer, *Introduction to the Old Testament* (New York: Harper, 1941), I have lost the page reference.
21. Francois Lenormant, *The Beginnings of History according to the Bible and the tradition of Oriental People* (New York: Charles Scribner's Sons, 1891).
22. W. Robertson Smith, *The Religion of the Semites* (Edinburgh: Adam & Slack, 1889 and New York: Ktav Publ., 1969, 3rd ed).
23. ibid., pp. 422–427.
24. *Hastings Dictionary of the Bible*, vol. i (New York: Scribners, 1898), p. 594.

outlook.[25] He reminds the reader that most of the references to the demons are in poetry and exalted prose, are employed metaphorically, and do not imply endorsement.

Granted, there are no specific declarations in Scripture from which to derive a 'doctrine of demons' and the mere opinions of biblical personages do not have doctrinal authority (after all, Peter at one time believed in ghosts, Luke 24:37). There is, however, sufficient information of a descriptive sort to derive some settled facts, some tentative judgments and some practical guidance on the matter.

I. The Real Existence of Demons.

As to the real existence of demons, Calvin's rather wry statement should suffice: 'It would be using quite improper forms of speech to say that the judgment of God will come upon the devils [Matt. 8:29], that the eternal fire is prepared for them [Matt. 25:11], that they are already in prison awaiting their last sentence [2 Peter 2:4], and that Jesus Christ tormented them at his coming [Matt. 8:29], if there are no devils at all' (*Institutes, I*, 14.19). Luther, most would agree, may have been over-convinced about the reality of devils (demons) in his *Commentary on Galatians*.[26]

Satan, demons and 'possession' have been an embarrassment to liberal biblical scholars. S. Vernon McCasland had this to say, 'In my own book, *By the Finger of God* (1951) I have interpreted demon possession as mental illness [hardly original]... and in *The Pioneer of Our Faith* (1964) I have presented the view that Satan as the Tempter should be interpreted as man's innate tendency to sin.'[27] Many liberal authors argue that though we must not take Satan and demons literally, the New Testament authors intended us to take them in this way. James Kallas developed the thesis that Jesus Himself was convinced of the reality of these invisible evil spirits and that all His teachings presuppose this belief. Kallas does not think Jesus was necessarily correct in His thinking, however.[28] For Wolfhart Pannenberg, angels and demons are more like 'a field of forces' than personal spirits, if I understand him correctly. He exclaims:

> To the astonishment of many observers... experience... [has] produced in 20th century theology a revival of the doctrine of angels and demons. Paul Tillich likened them to the archetypes of depth psychology and to a new awareness of the superhuman power of demonic in literature [*Mein Kampf* by Hitler!]. Gerhard Ebeling related them to the experience that forces are at work in our relation to God and the world that are hidden from us but nonetheless active. Paul Althaus said that the reality of angels [bad and good] was a matter not merely of faith but also of experience. Hans-George Fritzsche used the term 'field of force' in this connection... a field of force that embraces the ego, which is where angels and demons belong.[29]

These statements are suggesting invisible 'fields of force' – invisible like radio and sound waves and mass attraction – which impinge directly on the minds of people without employing physical means. A pastor-evangelist of my youth taught this doctrine about demons, basing his remarks on Revelation 16:13, 14: 'And I saw, coming out of the mouth of the dragon and out of the mouth of the beast and out of the mouth of the false prophet, three unclean spirits like frogs. For they are demonic spirits... who go abroad to the kings of the whole world...' The author found possible reference to demonic origins of socialism, communism and fascism in these 'three unclean spirits... of demons'.[30] Nazism was not yet prominently on the scene or Dr Bauman might have replaced socialism with Hitler's mantra. After World War II was over and until the present many philosophically inclined have wondered if the successive illusions sweeping the world since 1945 have not been demon-inspired and propagated (see 2 Thess. 2:11 and the context; cf. 1 Kings 22:22, 23).

Knowing how little all this tells us about the obscure and difficult subject of demons (also called 'devils' in English Bibles), evil spirits, familiar spirits and unclean spirits – perhaps also called (evil) angels – let us disclaim any of the exaggerated and morbid notions of witchcraft and medieval speculations and of recent hysterical popular literature.

II. What Are Demons and What Is Their Origin?

Whether or not 'fallen angels' are to be thought of as angels we cannot know for certain. They may be. We do know that they certainly are not, as some folks believe, the spirits of dead people. (I found this belief alive and well among

---

25. R. K. Harrison, 'Demon, Demoniac, Demonology,' *ZPEB*, vol. ii, pp. 92–101.
26. See Paul Althaus, *The Theology of Martin Luther* (Philadelphia: Fortress, 1966), pp. 208–211.
27. S. Vernon McCasland, *Journal Biblical Lituratue*, 1987, Part iv, 479.
28. James Kallas, *Jesus and the Power of Satan* (Philadelphia: Westminster, 1968).
29. Wolfhart Pannenberg, *Systematic Theology II*, trans. G. W. Bromiley (Grand Rapids: Eerdmans, 1994), pp. 105, 106.
30. Louis S. Bauman, *Three Unclean Spirits Like Frogs* (Long Beach: self-published, 1936).

Chinese theology students in Hong Kong in 1971.) The spirits of the deceased do not tarry near graveyards nor in haunted houses, for, according to Scripture, the spirits of the saved 'depart and be with Christ' (Phil. 1:23) while the lost go to a place of torment (Luke 16:22, 23). Moreover, a 'great chasm has been fixed' (Luke 16:26) between the two places, and from scenes of earth as well.

Unless Scripture is misleading us, demons are personal spirits which at present have no bodies of their own but seek to inhabit and control human bodies (see Mark 5:6-8; Matt. 12:43). As to personhood, they speak (Matt. 8:31), they have knowledge (Mark 1:24), they 'believe – and shudder' (James 2:19), and they seek 'rest' (Matt. 12:43) – all marks of intelligence and personhood. Though now without bodies of their own, it is thought that, in some remote past time, they may have become disembodied.

The Bible offers no direct clues as to their origin. One theory proposes they are disembodied spirits of sentient pre-Adamites, corporeal beings who inhabited the earth before the creative week of Genesis 1:3 and following. They sinned, were killed by a catastrophe like the Flood of Genesis and were condemned to permanent disembodiment. Another theory suggests that they are angels who followed Satan in a primeval rebellion against God and were cast out of heaven with him. They are thought to be the angels that 'sinned' (2 Peter 2:4) and 'the angels who did not stay within their own position of authority' (Jude 6). This view is at least as old as Origen, who set it forth in *De Principiis II.9.6*. It was favoured by Augustine and Peter Lombard. Thomas Aquinas argued at length for this view. He equates fallen angels with demons. He cites Augustine at length in support as well as John of Damascus, Origen, Gregory the Great and connects the usually cited texts from Isaiah 14, Ezekiel 28, John 8:44 and Revelation 12:4. His treatment is a fair index to patristic support of this view as well as of the scriptural support.[31]

Against this is the fact that these angels are presently confined 'in eternal chains' (Jude 6), awaiting judgment, where demons are 'wandering' spirits. It has been proposed that they are offspring of angelic 'sons of God' and the 'daughters of man' (Gen. 6:1-4). There are many obstacles to this view. This view is as old as the Apocrypha book, 1 Enoch 10:11-14, and found favour among some church Fathers. Ancient rabbis had many different views. We can state with absolute certainty only that they are fallen spirit beings who have committed themselves to Satan (i.e. the adversary) and that they hate God and seek to harm His people. 'No clear distinction can be made between fallen angels and demons, for they are all evil spirits... far too great and powerful for us to defeat in our own strength.'[32]

The Evil Character of Demons.

Every expression in the New Testament of the point of view of the authors regards demons as wholly evil. True, the pagan Greeks imagined there were both good and bad demons (the words *daimon* and *daimonion* have a very interesting history in the classical language). Even learned Pharisees of Paul's time had accepted superstitious ideas about 'good demons' (see Acts 23:9). But their opinions are not presented as New Testament teaching. Satan is a murderer and a liar, but also may act like an angel of light. These beings seem to be uniformly malignant. They are usually, in the Gospels, specifically designated as *unclean* spirits, evil spirits, elsewhere in the New Testament as seducing spirits (1 Tim. 4:1), and in Revelation as horrible, monstrous creatures (Rev. 9). Some, however, are worse than others (Mark 9:17, 18), and some more powerful (Mark 9:17, 18). They find fulfillment in tormenting anybody or destroying anything. Satan is their leader and they are agents of his kingdom (Matt. 12:24-27).

The Powers and Acts of Demons.

In Old Testament Times.

It will be convenient here to observe that the Old Testament furnishes few references to demons. Some references say God sent 'an evil spirit' to do this or that (Judg. 9:23, 24; 1 Sam. 16:14-16; 18:10, 11; 19:9, 10). R. K. Harrison suggests these are called 'evil' only as producing evil effects – as a storm, or a disease, or a bad mood, etc.[33] It seems likely they are to be regarded as good messengers (angels) to produce certain distressing results (1 Kings 22:19-23; 2 Chr. 18:18-22). There are also angels of evil character from Satan's organization (Dan. 10:13). Questionable Old Testament references to demons are Leviticus 17:7; 2 Chronicles 11:15; Isaiah 13:21; 34:14.

---

31. *Summa Theologica*, Question 63, arts. 1–9.
32. Richard W. DeHaan, *op. cit.*, p. 25.
33. R. K. Harrison, 'Demons, Demoniac, Demonology', *op. cit.*, vol. ii, pp. 92-101.

In the Career of the Messiah.

The most pronounced demonstrations of demon power and activity are during the life of Jesus after His official entrance on His career as Messiah. Satan mounted his first attack on Jesus with the goal of killing Him as an infant, and seems to have withdrawn until Jesus opened His career at the baptism. The Spirit led Jesus 'into the wilderness' but while there forty days He was intensely tested by the devil, unsuccessfully. After that Jesus carried the battle into the devil's territory, emerging victorious (to Satan's discomfort) through death, burial, resurrection, ascension and enthronement at God's right hand. As He and His apostles battled for the hearts of the people of Israel (Matt. 10:5, 6) Jesus said, 'as you go... Heal the sick, raise the dead, cleanse lepers, cast out demons' (Matt. 10:7, 8). This both He and they did from the first encounter on that Sabbath at the synagogue of Capernaum (Mark 1:21-28) on till late in His public ministry He sent out 'The seventy-two' (Luke 10:1-24). The record says, 'The seventy-two returned... saying, "Lord, even the demons are subject to us in your name!"' (Luke 10:17) – which evoked Jesus' response: 'I saw Satan fall like lightning from heaven' (Luke 10:18). Did our Lord see in the spectacular defeats of demons by the kingdom message (Luke 10:19) conveyed by seventy-two common 'Christians' the effective defeat of Satan at Golgotha a few weeks later (John 12:31; 14:30; 16:11)? It is in this campaign of attack against the province of Satan and his demons that some of the powers and activities of demons are demonstrated. There were about eight or nine specific reported encounters between Jesus and the demons, though some of the seemingly parallel accounts may really be of separate incidents. We cannot be sure of the order of the incidents. Furthermore, we do not know in each case what the symptoms were of demon afflictions – or why the afflicted sufferer, his family and friends, thought he was afflicted by demons.

The devil no doubt had his greatest success in leading those Jews of Judea, Samaria, Galilee, the Decapolis and Perea into unbelief and sin. Their leaders were thoroughly apostate and the people were like them: 'like people, like priest' as in Hosea's time (Hos. 4:9; see Jer. 6). In such a case the evidence of the victory of demonic powers is simply sins of every kind and spiritual apathy. The powers of darkness have 'blinded the minds of the unbelievers' to the 'gospel' (2 Cor. 4:4).

The narratives of Jesus' ministry report that demons had caused various ailments, most of them related to mental and nervous disorders – muteness (Matt. 9:32, 33; Mark 9:17; Luke 11:14), blindness (Matt. 12:22), screaming (Mark 1:26; 5:7; 9:26), crying (Mark 5:4), convulsions (Mark 1:26), apparent epilepsy (Mark 9:18-21), self-infliction of wounds (Mark 5:5; 9:22) accompanied by incessant active wakefulness (Mark 5:5), and demonstrations of unusual physical strength (Mark 5:4) and insanity (Mark 5:1-5, 15).

Demons in Acts, the Epistles, the Revelation.

There is the story of a certain 'slave girl who had a spirit of divination' and followed Paul's party about announcing, 'These men are servants of the Most High God, who proclaim to you the way of salvation' (Acts 16:16-18). After some days Paul exorcised the 'spirit' (or demon), which brought the wrath of the girl's owners on him and resulted in his being driven out of town. In this case the demon prompted harassment of God's evangelists by clever endorsement by the wrong people and in a wrong way. There was a similar incident at Ephesus some time later (Acts 19:13-17). Demons also instigate moral and spiritual disorder among believers, including to 'be false to the truth' (James 3:14). Considering the frequency of this sort of trouble in churches this may be a preoccupation of demons.

In demonic attacks against the LORD's people, the enemy has employed tactics different from those in the cases of exorcisms by Jesus and His disciples. They now attack the truth of the Christian gospel, deceiving some (2 Cor. 11:12-15); blinding others to truth (2 Cor. 4:3, 4); and misleading from truth (2 Tim. 3:13; 1 John 2:26; 3:7), and toward sensual pleasures (Eph. 5:6; Col. 2:8; 2 Thess. 2:3). They also propose appealing falsehoods (1 Tim. 4:1; 1 John 4:1-4).

We do not know exactly how 'Satan hindered' in the case of Paul's desire to visit the believers at Thessalonica (1 Thess. 2:18) nor the nature of Paul's 'thorn... in the flesh... a messenger of Satan to harass me' (2 Cor. 12:7). The following context rather indicates a physical defect or illness. No doubt from one point of view it was also God's 'messenger' (2 Cor. 12:8-10), as was the case with Job's well-known afflictions.

Evaluations and Conclusions.

Our limited survey does not include reference to the perennial claims of mediums, fortune-tellers, astrologers, witches, seers, ESP, to be in contact with spirits, either of dead people or of other spirits, evil or good. It is of course impossible for the living to communicate with the dead. Their spirits are far away and 'they shall not return'. Job's complaint is true: 'he who goes down to Sheol [the grave KJV] does not come up; he returns no more to his house, nor does his place know him any more' (Job 7:9, 10). Job had hope yet to 'see God' and that as a friend, but not here and now (see 19:25, 26 and context). The same hope is shared by all Christians on well-known scriptural grounds. But the efforts of the living to communicate with the dead or vice versa are condemned in many parts of the Bible, and for good reason. The single case of Saul and the witch of Endor and the encounter with Samuel (probably a case of a miracle, quite as surprising to the witch as devastating to Saul) does not change the general teaching of the whole Bible: the dead do not communicate with the living.

That there may be real contact with evil spirits (demons) in some forms of spiritualism, parapsychology, psychic prophecy and other occult practices may not be denied. It is also certain that much, if not most, is quackery, deceiving people by trickery – in either case to be strictly avoided.[34]

In my opinion demon possession is not the best designation of the demon phenomena of the New Testament. 'Possessed' in 'the demon-possessed man' (Luke 8:36) renders *daimonistheis*, an aorist participle of *daimonidzō* (demonize), which indicates more infestation, affliction and being harrassed by demons than being possessed (or owned) by them. In the only other New Testament use of 'possessed' with reference to demons (in the KJV, Acts 16:16) a girl is said to be 'possessed with a spirit of divination', which translates *echousan pneuma puthona*, literally 'having a spirit of python' – *python* refers to the ability to prophesy, according to common belief in Greek civilization; the verb is a present active feminine participle of *echō*. In this case the girl possesses the spirit, not the other way around. She seems to be a willing partner in the practice of 'divination'. The sense seems not to be negative, as in 'Susan has chicken pox'. It is significant that when the scribes said of Jesus, 'He is possessed by Beelzebub,' and 'by the prince of demons he casts out the demons' (Mark 3:22) this same Greek verb *echō*, present active sense as in Acts 16:16, is employed ('he has Beelzebub').[35] Jesus performed (they said) His exorcisms by Satan's power. They seem to say that Jesus was the manipulator, using the devil (= chief demon) to work His miracles of exorcism. Is Luke then saying the slave girl used the demon to tell fortunes and by the demon's power she recognized the true identity of the missionaries, amongst other things? I think so. In such a case it might be quite as correct to say the girl possessed the demon as that the demon possessed the girl. We do not know if the girl desired to be rid of the demon and we do not know what happened to her after she was no longer useful to her owners as a prophetess (Gr. *python*). Similarly, the beast of Revelation is willing host of the dragon (Satan), who gives him his supernatural powers (Rev. 13:2).

There is no question that Satan and his demons do in a real sense 'possess' the world and its inhabitants, except those who have been saved out of it. I have developed that proposition somewhat at length in three chapters of another book, *Civil Goverment: A Biblical View*.[36] That does not mean that everyone who manifest the pathological behaviour of the demoniac of Gadara or of the lad of Luke 9:37-42 is 'demonized'. Rather, for causes we do not know, some people of Jesus' time were so demonized.

No trustworthy list of verifiable symptoms of demon 'possession' is provided by Scripture. The opinion of unqualified observers is not to be relied upon. Hence I know of no way to verify abnormal conduct such as we find in the Gospels as a case of being demonized. We may be sure no one, including believers, is immune from demonic attack, if not 'possession'. Satan attacks us largely through weakening our faith in God and His truth (see 1 Tim 4:1; 1 John 4:1-4). Demons shall some day employ pseudo-miracles ('lying wonders') to deceive (2 Thess. 2:7-11; Rev. 16:14). A. Scott Molteau says:

> Demons do not own or possess any Christians, who are God's sole possession (as are the demons themselves)… This does not mean that they cannot be demonized or temporarily controlled by demons or have demons temporarily indwell them… Evidence in favor of the demonization of believers includes the statement of our need to know Satan's schemes (2 Cor. 2:11) so that he will not gain a foothold on us (Eph. 4:26-27).[37]

Paul's remarks about a 'thorn in the flesh… the messenger of Satan to buffet me' (2 Cor. 12:7 KJV) directs our attention to the possibility of demon activity, whether as ordinary or sometimes causal agent in disease.

---

34. See Richard DeHaan, *op. cit.*; Walker I. Knight, *Weird World of the Occult* (Wheaton, IL: Tyndale, 1972); Victor H. Ernest, *I Talked with Spirits* (Wheaton, IL: Tyndale, 1972 – a tale told by a convert from lifelong 'spiritualism' to evangelical faith).
35. The article 'Echo' by Hanse in *TDNT II*, 'Demonic Possession' pp. 821, 822 is helpful at this point.
36. Robert D. Culver, *Civil Government: A Biblical View* (Edmonton, AB, Canada: 1974, 2000), pp. 30–57.
37. A. Scott Molteau, 'Demons' in *Evangelical Dictionary of Biblical Theology* (Grand Rapids: Baker Books, 1996), p. 165.

Recent and Current Interest in Demons.

Flurries of interest in demons and popular level publishing about demons have occurred through the last 150 years. David F. Strauss (1808–1874), a disciple both of Hegel and Schleiermacher, published *Leben Jesu* (Life of Jesus) in 1835. It was an immediate sensation and created a new epoch in treatment of the rise of Christianity. His 'mythical theory' of Christian and New Testament origins held that most of the history of Christ, including Jesus' miracles of healing and casting out of demons, was the result of unconscious exaggeration by devoted, immediate disciples that the credulous authors of the Gospels put into writing some generations later. Demon possession is therefore to be regarded by enlightened moderns as a vivid symbol of evil in the world and the 'miracles' of casting out demons as an equally vivid symbol of the conquest of evil by Christ's example and teaching. This became the prevailing opinion of modernism – liberalism in Christian theology. Though the debate launched by Strauss' book has not quite ebbed even today, a survey of the literature would be both daunting and of little profit.

There has also been sober study of the Scriptures by scholarly evangelicals. I close this section by extracting the views of several of them as to the relation of demon possession to disease – then (New Testament times) and now.

1. *Demon 'possession' was a popular fallacy to which Jesus accommodated himself without endorsing it. He healed by restoring health to souls.*

One could cite almost every liberal-Christian scholar of the nineteenth and twentieth century as supporting this view, including also many neo-orthodox writers. What may be surprising to most readers is that David Smith, thoroughly evangelical author of a magnificent book on *The Earthly Life of Our Lord and Savior Jesus Christ*, took this view.[38] This book of amazing breadth of scholarly detail, fully abreast of all relevant literature of the day in both ancient and modern European languages, interprets demon possession of the Gospel records as 'a fantastic notion of a dark age unskilled in natural science' and opined that 'it was nothing strange that the people of the New Testament believed it'.[39] He finds no evidence of general belief in demonic causes of sicknesses and manic disorders in Old Testament times. Rather 'the idea of demoniacal possession originated in Persia, and by the time of our Lord it had rooted itself not only in popular belief but in science and philosophy, despite the protests of certain physicians who assigned diseases to natural causes'.[40] Smith points to 'Jesus' singular detachment from current theories. He never entangled his teaching with contemporary ideas'.[41] Jesus utterly rejected both the methods and doctrines of the exorcists of His time. 'Jesus dealt with the demoniacs after the manner of a wise physician. He did not seek to dispel their hallucination.' Once He had their trust, then He could deal with their problem by dealing with their *real* problem. 'Where faith was lacking he could perform no mighty work.'[42] He argues that Jesus never did endorse the idea of demonic causes of the various physical and mental torments presented to Him for help. The demonism lies wholly in the opinion of the populace, including the authors of the Gospels.

Smith is convincing until one checks to notice, first, that Jesus thought demon 'possession' a real enough phenomenon to produce a short discourse on the subject (Luke 11:17-26). Second, over and over the narrative record distinguishes between diseases and affliction by demons. Third, this distinction appears in Jesus' own words in the commission of the apostles in their first mission: 'as you go… Heal the sick, raise the dead, cleanse lepers, cast out demons' (Matt. 10:7, 8).

2. *According to a more prevalent view demon-caused psychological distresses and physical ailments cured by Jesus and His disciples were hardly more than acute cases of the same influences Satan and his minions inflict on the entire race of sinful people.*

The ailments, in most if not all cases, might be described accurately in 'clinical' terms by modern physical specialists in neurology and other medical specialities as to etiology and symptoms. I do not think R. K. Harrison is entirely clear in his wide-ranging article, 'Demon, Demoniac, Demonology' but this seems to be his conclusion.[43] He never quite states such a conclusion. I cite important lines leading me to state his conclusion in this way.

---

38. David Smith, *The Days of His Flesh: The Earthly Life of our Lord and Savior Jesus Christ*, 8th ed. (London: Hodder & Stoughton, 1910) pp. 105–109.
39. ibid., p. 105.
40. ibid., p. 105.
41. ibid., p. 106.
42. ibid., p. 108.
43. R. K. Harrison, 'Demon, Demoniac, Demonology' in *ZDEB II*, pp. 92–101.

> Indeed, in so far as specific clinical conditions can be identified as emotogenic, the same consideration could apply to a significantly wider range of human afflictions. Because modern psychosomatic medical research has shown that attestable clinical disease can result from such metaphysical [by which Harrison seems to mean non-material, i.e. demonic] entities as suggestion, emotional conflicts, fear, and the like, it is no longer possible to dismiss as implausible the noxious effects which the various forms of evil, working through the personality of fallen man, can have upon individual and mental well-being. Indeed, Jesus viewed all disease in these general terms... He frequently saw the incidence of disease as the result of evil producing an inbalance within the personality.[44]

He goes on to say:

> The soundest approach to the situation is ultimately a theological one, which recognizes that because of depravity of human nature the mind is peculiarly liable to the influence of evil. In inbalance this constitutes a form of possession, however mild, since the personality is then at the disposal of darkness to some extent.[45]

A similar outlook was tentatively set forth by J. H. A. Ebhard in the *Schaff-Herzog Encyclopedia of Religious Knowledge*.[46]

3. *Passages such as the healing of the demoniac of Gadara (Luke 8:26-39) and the epileptic boy harassed by a demon (Luke 9:37-42) should be treated with 'ordinary and literal interpretation'.*

> [T]hese are evil spirits, subjects of the Evil one, who in the days of the Lord himself and his apostles, especially, were permitted by God to exercise a direct influence over the souls and bodies of certain [people]. This influence is to be distinguished sharply from the ordinary power of corruption and temptation wielded by Satan.[47]

Such 'possession' is not a part of God's general providence, but special supernatural manifestations of Satanic power. It might be said that the healings were divine miracles overcoming satanic miracles. Advocates of this approach usually affirm the following.

(a) Neither all deranged minds and erratic conduct nor diseases of the types reported as being corrected by deliverance from demons are caused by demons. Neither in the Gospels nor elsewhere in Scripture is demonizing distinguished from sickness from natural causes.

(b) It may be that the demon infestations of Palestine of Jesus' time were peculiar to that time and place. Just as Satan himself attacks Jesus Himself in a special way several times in His career (at the temptation, at Caesarea Philippi, at Gethsemane) so his minions were deployed in a more open and direct hostility in periods of Jesus' ministry, knowing that their time was short (John 12:27-33).

(c) Far from sanctioning the superstitious belief of either ancient Jews or Gentiles[48] Scripture only acknowledges such things by condemning them (Lev. 19:31; 1 Sam. 28:7; 2 Kings 21:6; 23:24).

(d) The devil uses every form of mental defect or derangement of God's people in particular and everyone in general to defeat God's purpose, which is that they, under the conditions of the fall, be like the 'blessed man' of Psalm 1:3:

> He is like a tree
> planted by streams of water
> that yields its fruit in its season,
> and its leaf does not wither.
> In all that he does, he prospers.

I can claim no special competence in dealing with perils from demons. I have never felt directly attacked by them and am convinced that they have no supernatural physical powers. I do not have a clue as to how some people of Jesus' time – when demons were conspicuously active – became 'demonized', producing the symptoms described in the Gospels, nor do I know how anyone's physical or mental disorders were recognized as demonic directly in origin. Nor do I have any information as to how 'familiar spirits' come to be used by mediums (witches, and similar) or possibly the other way around. Nor is it certain that in every place in the Gospels where the word demon,

---

44. ibid., p. 100.
45. ibid., p. 100.
46. J. H. A. Ebhard, *Schaff-Herzog Encyclopedia of Religious Knowledge, vol. I*, pp. 624, 625.
47. 'Demoniac' *McClintock-Strong Encyclopedia of Religious Knowledge*, vol. ii, p. 642.
48. Tobit 8:1-3, Josephus, *Antiquities* viii.2,5; Acts 19:13.

devil, familiar spirit and the like is mentioned this is a genuine case of supernatural, demonic activity. I wonder, for example, if Mark's account of the healing of the Syrophoenician woman's daughter is not to be interpreted by Matthew's comments on the incident. Mark says, 'whose little daughter was possessed by an unclean spirit'. Matthew says that the woman *said*, 'my daughter is severely oppressed by a demon' (Matt. 15:22). Later Matthew reports simply, 'her daughter was healed instantly' (Matt. 15:28). Why did the woman think her daughter was afflicted by an unclean spirit (or 'demon')? How could she know? Jesus does not say, 'your diagnosis is correct'. What was her competence to diagnose her daughter's condition? She was witty, but not a skilled diagnostician. And who can say what the infallible signs of the presence of demons are?

In the case of the demoniac(s) of Gerasa (Gadara), unclean spirits inhabited the bodies of the victims. There are three accounts, each affirming the afflicted person(s) was 'demon-possessed' or 'with an unclean spirit' or 'had demons'. Further the rest of the story makes clear that the distress of the afflicted was caused by infestation by many wicked personal spirits (demons) whom Jesus addressed as such and who responded as such. The same is true of the demoniac boy (Mark 9:14-29; Matt. 17:14-20; Luke 9:37-43).

So today credence is not to be given to every supposed case of 'demon possession'. There are many credulous people whose claims to 'spiritual discernment' in such matters lacks authentication and some of them quite honorable folk. I observe that sober, competent, evangelical authors show great reserve in commenting on the signs or symptoms of 'demon possession' today.

(1) I propose that we do not need to know. It is enough to be informed that all our 'wrestling' is against 'spiritual forces of evil', as Paul says, and to be assured our defence is to harness ourselves with the *panoply* (full armour) of God, all the parts being effective and universally available to believers (Eph. 6:12-19).

(2) I find no specific instruction for believers at the present time to engage in formal exorcisms of demons. I have seen such exorcisms tried by sincere Christian 'practitioners' who apparently claim the same insights and powers granted the Twelve (Matt. 10:8), the seventy-two (Luke 10:17) and which we see rarely (Acts 16:18 for example) granted to others. The exorcisms of demons by Jesus and His authorized messengers around the Palestinian countryside were specific proof that 'the kingdom of God has come upon you' (Matt. 12:28; and cf. 11:1-6). They were a specific sign to that people (Israel) and that generation.

(3) If one should be presented with a situation where one feels 'demonizing' (oppression, possession, affliction) is present, the resource of *prayer* in the name of Jesus surely will be as effective as a *command* (exorcism) addressed to the 'resident' demon. One of the most biblically informed and spiritually discerning ministers I have ever known reports his efforts at an 'exorcism' with *apparent* success at first but with equally apparent failure ultimately.[49] There is a spectacular incident reported in Acts of how presumptuous attempts at exorcism in Jesus' name by unqualified persons backfired with harmful results to the would-be exorcists (Acts 19:13-16). We read in the story that Paul, an apostle, performed genuine miracles of demon-cleansing (Acts 19:11, 12). We read of no exorcisms by Paul's assistants or converts.

(4) We are told to 'resist the devil, and he will flee from you' even if he does roar and threaten. Try on the theology of Luther's hymn, 'A Mighty Fortress'. We are apprized of dangers to our souls *via* the temptation of the world, the flesh and the devil, but nowhere in the New Testament are we told to wander through life in fear of demons. It is to revert to heathenism and foolish superstition to live in such fear. The agents of Beelzebub were opposed to the apostles on mission, but Jesus twice told the Twelve: 'have no fear of them' (Matt. 10:26, 28) and 'we can confidently say, "The Lord is my helper; I will not fear; what can man [or demon] do to me?"' (Heb. 13:6).

(5) On the other hand there is terrible liability to both spiritual and moral as well as physical danger in dabbling in any form of occult practice. If there is 'demonizing' today similar to that reported in the Gospels it lies in this quarter. The law of Moses strictly forbids consulting any person who claims powers supernatural or occult – 'alleged mystic arts, such as magic, alchemy, astrology, etc.' (*Webster's New World Dictionary*). '[W]hoever does these things is an abomination to the LORD' (Deut. 18:12).[50] Most of these supposed occultists are imposters, really practicing deception by some of the same tricks magicians use and by the techniques of hypnotism.

(6) There is no special information about the present, much less the future, available to these practitioners of

---

49. Bernard Schneider, *The World of Unseen Spirits* (Winona Lake, IN: BMH Books, 1975), pp. 120–122.
50. See Deut. 18:9-14; Isa. 47:12-14; Acts 19:19, 20.

the occult. Said Isaiah: 'And when they say unto you, "Enquire of the mediums and the necromancers who chirp and mutter," should not a people enquire of their God? Should they enquire of the dead on behalf of the living? To the teaching and to the testimony! If they will not speak according to this word, it is because they have no dawn' (Isa. 8:19, 20). Isaiah presents the LORD as repeatedly challenging the ability of so-called diviners (mediums, 'futurists' and similar) and denouncing them as both failures and wicked (Isa. 41:21-24), concluding: 'Behold, you are nothing, and your work is less than nothing; an abomination is he who chooses you' (Isa. 41:24).

As footnotes to this chapter, first, I suggest even though I have not referred to Alfred Edersheim's work in the body of this chapter, his evaluation of the materials on demon activities in the Gospels is excellent and I find myself in agreement. His comments regarding angels, Satan, demons and magical practices occur in his expositions of outstanding examples in the Gospels.[51] Second, the state of informed, evangelical study and practice in regard to demonism as well as introduction to the literature, was sketched by seventeen pages in *Christianity Today* magazine in 2001.[52]

51. Alfred Edersheim, *The Life and Times of Jesus the Messiah* (Grand Rapids: Eerdmans, 1962), vol. i, pp. 479–485, 607–612; vol. ii, pp. 748–763, 770–776.
52. *Christianity Today*, 45.1, September 3, 2001, pp. 46 – 62, 'Possessed or Obsessed?' by Agnicszka Tennant and 'Exorcism 101' by Clinton E. Arnold.

21
God's Work of Preservation and Providence

'My Father is working until now, and I am working'
(John 5:17)

How God keeps the World Operating and Governs it.

Ours must surely be one of the most anxious generations in the entire history of Western civilization. The community in the rural south-east corner of Minnesota where I live exposes to the eye few signs of severe poverty. There are sufficient hospital rooms at the county seat for two counties; Mayo Clinic is an hour away. Everything is here to make its well-fed citizens happy, including some of the most graceful hills, interesting river bluffs, valleys, forests and farms one would ever care to see. Yet, the mood in the places where people meet – small cafes, bars, bank vestibules and church foyers, even farm auctions and sale barns – though it ranges from grief to joyous laughter, seems to be characteristically a sigh.

The national anxieties have been institutionalized and professionalized in many medical and quasi-medical centers. There are several related professions which minister to our fractured psyches. Anxiety is the engine for human behavior in the most accepted post World War II philosophy, existentialism. Have you heard of 'metaphysical *angst*', 'the concept of dread', 'the threat of nothingness'? A segment of our youth of decades past must have heard about all this, judging from their sad, pouting faces, though the fad passed away before the sad but spectacular decease of Elvis Presley and several other of their well-paid, popular models.

Contrast with this the ideal of Christian joy in the book of Philippians, 'Rejoice in the Lord always; again I will say, Rejoice' (Phil. 4:4); 'The Lord is at hand; do not be anxious about anything' (Phil. 4:5, 6). Jesus' own prevailing good humour sets the pace expressed in His famous advice against anxiety (Matt. 6:25-34), concluding, 'Therefore do not be anxious about tomorrow, for tomorrow will be anxious for itself. Sufficient for the day is its own trouble' (Matt. 6:34).

The support for this cheerful optimism is the biblical world-and-life view. Specifically, we understand firstly, that God made the world 'good... very good', (Gen. 1:10, 31) 'He has made everything beautiful in its time' (Eccles. 3:11) (*Creation*); secondly, that this was according to a plan which he formed in eternity (*Decrees,* or *Predestination*) so that no emergencies would ever arise requiring patchwork maintenance; thirdly, that when He finished creating the world He immediately set about maintaining it in good order (*Preservation*); and fourthly, that He is governing it in such a way as to accomplish His good goals (*Providence*). These four aspects of God's permanent relation to the world are clearly taught in the Bible. They have been almost unconsciously absorbed by people exposed to the whole Bible over any lengthy period of time. Together, these few profound truths are the prescription for human happiness (joy) in spite of pain, illness, disappointment, decrepitude, and, ultimately, death. We have already considered the first two, now let us attend to the third.

The Doctrine of Preservation.

As we have seen (under creation above, chapters 16, 17), God ceased from creating the natural order and mankind and has not resumed that kind of creative work (Gen. 2:2). That sabbath of rest still endures, but God is still working. Not so evident in English as in Hebrew, a servant is one who works (*obhedh*); so the incarnate Second Person of the Trinity, 'the Servant of the LORD', said of the Father and of His incarnate self: 'My Father is working until now, and I am working' (John 5:17). This was the high point of an argument about working on the weekly Sabbath. Jesus is saying in effect that not every kind of work is unlawful on Sabbath; God has a permanent sabbath from creating the world but He is nevertheless working still at other projects.

That project of working still, at least as regards the created universe, is maintenance, or preservation. It is important that theology recognize this logically and scripturally necessary work and to distinguish it from both creation and providence. The distinction is clearly made in Ezra's ascription of praise to God, showing how Ezra, the paramount theologian of late biblical Judaism, interpreted the Mosaic revelation, and Ezra said: 'You are the LORD, you alone. You have made heaven, the heaven of heavens, with all their host, the earth and all that is on it, the seas and all that is in them [what God did in the distant past]; and you preserve all of them' (what God is doing now) (Neh. 9:6). One of David's temple hymns proclaims, 'O LORD, You preserve [save ESV] man and beast' (Ps. 36:6 NKJV) – *preserve* renders the Hebrew root *yasha*, hence *Jeshuaʻ* or Jesus). Job, a Gentile saint, addressed God as 'thou preserver [*notser*, one who guards or looks after another] of men' (Job 7:20 KJV).

So plainly it is fully scriptural to say that both with regard to the whole and to its individual atoms, the Creator is, in the present, actively, immediately, and continually preserving and maintaining creation, and that this is to be distinguished from a forever finished work of creating this particular heaven and earth. Providence is not so distinct from preservation, for it also is a continuing work of the triune God. Some theologians speak of sustaining providence (preservation) and governing providence. There appears to be no serious error in thinking this way, but to make preservation a species of creation is false and misleading, as we shall note in the case of Jonathan Edwards, theologian, and René Descartes, philosopher.

As in most aspects of divine activity each person of the triune God participates, yet as with creation (John 1:2) preservation is the peculiar work of the Son as well. There are two plain statements, both relating the work of preservation to the Son: 'And he is before all things, and in him all things hold together' (Col. 1:17); 'He is the radiance of the glory of God… and he upholds the universe by the word of his power' (Heb. 1:3). Paul told a pagan audience that the God 'unknown' but worshipped in ignorance by them, not only gave all their life and breath to every nation of earth but is also the one in whom 'we [all mankind] live and move and have our being' (Acts 17:23, 28).

Preservation, therefore, implies the immanent presence of God in the remotest star as well as the nearest object, in the functions of mass attraction as well as the movement of my pen and in the largest galaxy as well as in the smallest subatomic particle. Nothing would operate except by what theologians call divine *concurrence* in all operations of matter and mind – in every movement as well as all properties, powers and processes. Though we as personal beings have permanent existence and God's immediate power is not a force of which we are immediately aware, it is nevertheless true that apart from divine concurrence we would cease to exist – and that will be forever true whether in hell or heaven. In direct support of such a statement, in addition to passages already cited, Job said rightly that in the 'hand of the LORD… is the life of every living thing and the breath of all mankind' (Job 12:9, 10). Daniel reminded the cowering Belshazzar, 'God' is the One 'in whose hand is your breath' (Dan. 5:23) – as many other passages state or imply. Psalm 104 ought to be read to show how this upholding maintenance (concurrence) by renewal extends to all the natural order – the heavens, weather, soil, plants and mankind – in politically correct language, to the *environment*.

Hollywood has not yet found a way to produce the illusion of a realistic decapitation. If they do the viewer will see a gush of blood spouting several feet. The heart never rests except between beats and all the blood in the body passes through it hundreds of times every day, pumping plus or minus 2,500 pounds every hour. It beats about seventy-two times a minute. Yet I am scarcely aware of this amazing organ except after vigorous physical exertion, illness or when I lie awake with my ear on a pillow. Yet it has been serving me without interruption for three-quarters of a century with scarcely a flutter. It will continue to do so with God's concurring operation, called *preservation* by well-taught believers and by good theologians. Whether one knows a name for this concurrence or not it is understood by every Bible reader who has absorbed the sense of the whole Bible. Let us continue with more detail.

The Integrity of Creation Preserved by God.

The doctrine of preservation teaches that God maintains the integrity of things, both simple (the periodic table of elements, the key of 'C') and complex (H_2O, the solar system, laws of musical harmony). One author speaks of the 'existence of the whole created universe' and its 'laws, properties, powers and processes'. Another asserts that preservation is that continued exercise of divine energy whereby the Creator upholds all his creatures in being, and in the possession of all those inherent properties and qualities with which he endowed them at their creation. That is, both the being, the attributes of every species, and the form and faculties of every individual are constantly preserved in being by God.

It is easy to see how science, and industry dependent on the discoveries science makes, could develop in a civilization committed to this sort of world-view. And it is precisely in such a place, Christian Europe, where it did marvellously emerge in the period of the Renaissance and the Reformation.

Amazing Detail.

The scriptural detail is truly amazing. Let us start with the sky above: 'Lift up your eyes on high and see: who created [past tense] these? He who brings out [present tense] their host by number... by the greatness of his might, and because he is strong in power not one is missing' (Isa. 40:26). Job and his friends understood, 'In his [God's] hand is the life of every living thing' (Job 12:10).

Psalm 104 starts off with a present-tense, pictorial representation of God as presiding over the weather (vv. 1-4). Then after a past tense 'frame' about the creation (its terms suggest geological history, vv. 5-9), the Psalm continues with a presentation of God's gracious care for all His earthly creatures. He provides water for all beasts (vv. 10-13), then provides for the growth of animals and plants (wind, oil, bread and trees for birds). He causes mountains and crags to rise up for exotics like wild goats and badgers (vv. 14-18). The heavenly bodies mark the seasons: night is for wild beasts to stalk prey; day for their sleep and for mankind's work (vv. 19-23). Birth and death are within God's power as well as the sequence of day and night and of the seasons.

> Full many a gem of purest ray serene
> The dark unfathomed caves of ocean bear;
> Full many a flower is born to blush unseen
> And waste its sweetness on the desert air.

These lines from Gray's *Elegy* are not strictly true, however sadly evident they seem, because God has a place for all good things and employs them to support that plan wherever and whenever they are. Furthermore, even if no human being sees a pearl hidden in an oceanic crevice and most wild flowers grow where no human eye observes, the heavenly Father does see and for His pleasure 'they are and were created'.

A Continuous Work.

The divine work of preservation is never represented in Scripture as simply the running down of a clock-like cosmos, wound up at creation and now unwinding. Some theological writers assert that it is unreasonable to suppose that God could or would or should be personally concerned with the innumerable details of millions of human lives, to say nothing of all existing things. It is, however, precisely God's present sustaining of us, His people, which imparts much of the 'religious' value to the Christian idea of God. 'I can do all things through him who strengthens me' (Phil. 4:13); 'The eternal God is your dwelling place, and underneath are the everlasting arms' (Deut. 33:27).

Jesus taught His disciples to rely on this truth. '[D]o not be anxious about your life, what you will eat or what you will drink, nor about your body, what you will put on... Look at the birds of the air: they neither sow nor reap nor gather into barns, and yet your heavenly Father feeds them. Are you not of more value than they?' (Matt. 6:25, 26) and 'Are not two sparrows sold for a penny? And not one of them will fall to the ground apart from your Father... Fear not, therefore; you are of more value than many sparrows' (Matt. 10:29, 31). Comforting, quotable, reliable, psychic medicine such as these passages is not available in any religion wherein God is Creator only. He must act concurrently with us as well.

We know that God sustains evil people in their ways too – not because they are evil, but because they are His creatures. 'God concurs with the evil acts of his creatures only as they are natural acts, not as they are evil.' The sense of this statement by A. H. Strong, appears frequently in orthodox theologies of every denominational persuasion.[1]

A Gracious Work.

The gracious work of God in preservation may be regarded as an aspect of His faithfulness, love and mercy for all, for the human race in particular. The sun, moon and stars go through their motions at the right times. Spring ever returns after winter. 'While the earth remains' (Gen. 8:22) lovers marry, families are born, science and industry operate, indeed life goes on, because God is faithful to maintain His creation. David summed it up: 'Your steadfast love, O LORD, extends to the heavens, your faithfulness to the clouds. Your righeousness is like the mountains of God; your judgments are like the great deep; man and beast you save, O LORD. How precious is your steadfast love, O God! The children of mankind take refuge in the shadow of your wings' (Ps. 36:5-7).

The Doctrine of Providence.

Providence is the theological term for the continuous going forth of God's power whereby He causes all features of the created universe to fulfil the design for which He created them.

Creation explains how there happens to be a world at all; *preservation* explains why it still exists in good order; and *providence* explains how it will develop toward God's eternally planned goal. It is the consummation in time of the plan of God made in eternity.

'General' and 'special' providence are terms without a fixed meaning used by theologians. For some, e.g. Louis Berkhof, the former denotes 'God's control of the universe as a whole' and the latter 'his care for each part of it in relation to the whole'.[2] Calvin reserves 'providence' as a term for the 'especial care over each of his works'. 'Yet', says he, 'I do not wholly repudiate what is said concerning universal providence', though he regards it as 'some kind of blind and ambiguous notion'.[3]

There are also theologians who restrict 'special' or 'particular' providence to 'such particular exhibitions of [God's] wisdom and power in emergencies... to awaken conviction of his interest in and guardianship over his creatures'.[4] These instances are usually restricted to miracles, fulfillment of prophecy, special acts of God in redemption and answers to prayer.

As applied to any specific event, the Bible seems to suggest that providence originates with God's *foreknowledge*. In the Bible, foreknowledge is not mere information in the sense of God's mind knowing what He prefers to do. Foreknowledge is God's act of informing His will. Although there is no temporal 'process' in God's mind, we may think of a logical order in God's mind and action. So in this manner of speaking we may think of God in the 'process' of *planning* (decreeing) to do what He knows His will is; then through *creation*, next *preservation* and finally *providence*, events come to pass.

Examples of Providence.

Let a biblical, historical incident furnish an example of providence (2 Sam. 15-18). We know from many texts that God planned to rule Israel through David for a while and, more importantly, to bring Christ into the world through David. There was a plot by a rebellious son, Absalom, to destroy David. Ahithophel and Hushai were King David's counsellors. When David fled Jerusalem both advisors stayed behind: Ahithophel voluntarily, for he joined Absalom's rebellion; Hushai at David's request. Not long afterward Ahithophel gave Absalom *good* advice, if Absalom was to destroy his father; while at about the same time Hushai gave him *bad* advice, knowing it was bad and hoping thereby to destroy Absalom and to save David. Absalom followed the bad advice of Husahai, lost the battle, lost his kingdom, lost his life, while Ahithophel went to his home city, put his business affairs in order and hanged himself.

---

1. A. H. Strong, *Systematic Theology* (Valley Forge, PA: Judson Press, 1907), p. 418.
2. Louis Berkhof, *Systematic Theology*, 2nd rev. ed. (Grand Rapids: Eerdmans, 1941), p. 168.
3. John Calvin, *Institutes I*, 16.4
4. S. H. Platt, 'Providence' in *McClintock and Strong Cyclopedia VIII*, pp. 710, 711.

Now God was not far away in heaven simply letting history unwind in the grip of immutable laws of men and things. No person's freedom was limited by God. Many individuals – Joab, Ahithophel, Hushai, the elders and the men of Absalom's partisans – each did what he voluntarily decided to do. Yet, says the Scripture, 'And Absalom and all the men of Israel said, "The counsel of Hushai the Archite is better than the counsel of Ahithophel." For the Lord had ordained to defeat the good counsel of Ahithophel, so that the Lord might bring harm [a disastrous defeat] upon Absalom' (2 Sam. 17:14). If biblical narrative is authority for doctrine, and it is, this narrative teaches a strong doctrine of particular providence. I do not think any Christian is at liberty to disbelieve it.

The Bible itself employs the story of Joseph and his brothers as an illustrative example of divine providence. The force is of such magnitude to warrant including all the texts. I assume the reader knows the story (Gen. 37–45). At the denouement when Joseph, last seen by his family as a boy, and now middle-aged, is unveiled to their eyes as their betrayed brother Joseph, he reassured them with these words:

> And now do not be distressed or angry with yourselves because you sold me here, for God sent me before you to preserve life [in Egypt as well as in Jacob's family]... God sent me before you to preserve for you a remnant on earth, and to keep alive for you many survivors. So it was not you who sent me here, but God (Gen. 45:5, 7, 8).

Much later Joseph reassured the brothers, when after their father's death they feared Joseph might take vengeance on them, with this affirmation of providence:

> Joseph said to them, 'Do not fear, for am I in the place of God? As for you, you meant evil against me, but God meant it for good, to bring it about that many people should be kept alive, as they are today' (Gen. 50:19, 20).

The thought of Psalm 105 is wholly occupied with divine preservation and providence and takes up the story of Joseph and his brothers as an example of the same (Ps. 105:16-23). In the recital, amongst other things, God 'summoned a famine' and 'he sent a man ahead of them, Joseph, who was sold as a slave... until what he had said came to pass... to bind his princes at his pleasure'.

Finally, Stephen in his address to the mob who killed him recited the same story as part of his narrative of God's providential and preserving care of the Hebrew people from Abraham onward (Acts 7:9-16).

Regular Methods and Means of Providence.

The Bible informs us of at least three ways through which God regularly executes His work of providential control.

(1) The most obvious is through supernatural miracles and 'special' uses of natural forces. God saved Jerusalem during Hezekiah's reign through a supernatural plague (Isa. 37:36-38); He got the Israelites out of Egypt through a succession of eleven wonders (ten plagues and the parting of the Red Sea); He secured their entrance into Canaan by stopping the waters of Jordan, then by shaking down the walls of Jericho and causing the sun to 'stand still' for several hours. That some of these wonders were accomplished by uses of natural forces is certain – an east wind, for example, helped at the Red Sea (Exod. 14:21). Yet each was specially God's act in an extraordinary way.

It is hard to find absolute, unlimited human free will in these cases. On closer look it cannot be denied that some people's wills were indeed manipulated by circumstances controlled by God. The Egyptians were made willing to give abundance of goods, silver, precious stones and costly textiles by the ten divinely inflicted plagues. We cannot imagine love or generous feelings promoting such generosity for a despised lower class. Pharaoh and his army, for another example, were deliberately baited to follow the Israelites, yet as soon as they got into the trap of the seabed, God sent the waters back to destroy them.

These stories of divine providence in action are not shaded by the writers of Scripture to let God off from being in charge even of the uncoerced actions of free people. Mankind's power of voluntary choice is unimpeded by God in each case. Yet on closer examination it is also plain enough that God directed (if 'manipulated' be too strong a term for the reader's taste) people's choices by His control of the circumstances. Paul dealt with objectors who complained, 'Who can resist his will?' by a sort of 'so what' response: 'But who are you, O man, to answer back to God? Will what is moulded say to its moulder, "Why have you made me like this?"' If anyone can think of a better response to objections to a God who is in charge, let us hear it!

The miracles of the virgin birth of Jesus and His resurrection, like His death in our place, were planned in eternity and executed in time. If, however, Augustus had not decreed his census (Luke 2:1-5) and if Herod had not sought the young child's life, Jesus would never have fulfilled the prophecies involving both Bethlehem and Egypt (Matt. 2:19-23). We may be sure that neither Augustus nor Herod was coerced in any way to do what he did. Herod was no poor king – certainly no victim or object of sympathy. He was a monster who did exactly what his inclination, already bond-slave to sin, inclined his will to decide. Similarly, if Bethlehem (Mic. 5:2) was to be the scene of the Savior's birth, then God sent Naomi and Ruth back home to Bethlehem, and Jesse did business there. Fulfillment of prophecy requires divine governance in detail of everything that exists.

It is important to observe that in no case did God coerce anyone's will. Providence operated effectively and people acted without coercion. I am not quite sure we should say they acted 'freely' for they were 'slaves' to sin, as Jesus affirmed (John 8:34). The usual disjunction between the 'free will' of mankind and the sovereignty of God is incorrect. Mankind does have the unimpeded power of voluntary choice and we are not coerced by God. But we are slaves to sin and so not entirely free. Jesus, as cited above, says everyone who sins (and there are no exceptions) is a slave of sin. The disjunction is between the free will of mankind and the sovereignty of God only if by free will one understands *uncoerced* will. The power to choose is there, but not apart from predisposition to choose in a certain way. It helps in thinking about this problem to propose that every man or woman is a self-determined free agent (as all parties do agree) whose choices (will) are determined by what the person already is – a natural-born sinner.

Calvin, who canvassed the dimensions of the problem, liked to compare a healthy free will to a person with good legs but the will of a sinner to a person with two complete legs, both broken. The sinner has the right equipment for walking but it is out of order.[5]

(2) A second area of providence is the regular processes of nature. Psalm 148:8 speaks of fire and hail, snow, vapor, and stormy winds fulfilling God's word. Again people find little to offend them in this – unless they think deeply. It is easy to say that God sent a snow flurry to Waterloo in Belgium, two centuries ago, to defeat Napoleon, or to say that God kept the English Channel calm for several days to allow the defeated British army at the Dunkirk beachhead to escape Hitler's forces in the early days of World War II. Yet, few approve the suggestion that a Chicago fire may have been caused by God, especially when the cow of a careless Irish housewife can be blamed. What about the San Francisco earthquake, and floods and quakes in China? A few years ago the television news showed a Turkish woman renouncing Allah because her grandchild had been killed in a terrible earthquake a few hours before. People find it easier to say Hitler unnecessarily destroyed the heart of Britain's cities than that God rained bombs on them as He did fire on Sodom. Is it that Sodom deserved judgment while London did not? Or is it that the fires that rained down on Sodom may have been natural and volcanic while the bombs which fell on London were manufactured in Munich or Stuttgart? Let us defer answering to the next few paragraphs.

(3) A third area of providence is the acts of moral beings, both angels and people, both good and bad. In the course of recent chapters we have cited certain examples of how God accomplishes His will through the acts of 'free' beings. Joseph and his coming to Egypt through the evil deeds of his brothers has been cited, as also the rejection of Jesus by the leaders of the Jews, which rejection brought Jesus to Calvary (Acts 2:23). Judas' treachery is another example often cited – he fulfilled a prophecy. Paul cites the rejection of Jesus by the nation of Israel in a similar way (Rom. 11). Shortly we shall try to provide further suggestions to alleviate any distress from our natural sense of justice or from our intuitions of 'freedom'.

God's Providence is All-inclusive.

The Bible is clear that nothing at all in this entire universe is outside the Creator's providential control. The evidence is varied. The teaching is in all parts of the Bible and it is overwhelming. The article on providence in the *McClintock and Strong Cyclopedia*, after an extensive citation of passages, adds, 'The teaching of the more than five hundred passages might be confirmed, were it necessary, by nearly as many thousands more, showing with what emphasis the Scriptures proclaim the doctrine of divine providence.'[6] So comprehensive is this that it is said, 'his kingdom rules over all' (Ps. 103:19); He 'does according to his will among the host of heaven and among the

---

5. Calvin, *Institutes II*, chapters. 2 – 5.
6. *McClintock & Strong Cyclopedia, viii*, p. 708.

inhabitants of the earth' (Dan. 4:35); and He 'works all things according to the counsel of his will' (Eph. 1:11).

It will be impressive to examine a few of the more comprehensive categories of things wherein divine providence works. We will cite only a few passages, though in most cases there are dozens of other passages which might also be cited. God's providence rules over the following.

(1) The *physical world*. 'Whatever the LORD pleases, he does, in heaven and on earth, in the seas and all deeps. He it is who makes the clouds rise at the end of the earth, who makes lightnings for the rain and brings forth the wind from his storehouses' (Ps. 135:6, 7).[7]

(2) *Plant life*. 'The trees of the LORD are watered abundantly, the cedars of Lebanon that he planted' (Ps. 104:16). Psalm 104:21, 28 says that the lions are fed by God, Matthew 6:26 that He feeds the birds, and Jesus said of the sparrows, 'not one of them will fall to the ground apart from your Father' (Matt. 10:29). God 'appointed' the great fish which featured in Jonah's experiences (Jonah 1:17), as also the worm (Jonah 4:7).

(3) *People's social position*. God rules over people's birth, and place in life. David (Ps. 139:16), Jeremiah (Jer. 1:5) and Paul (Gal. 1:15, 16) were aware of this. There were many fine families in Israel but the one to provide the new king was prepared by God (1 Sam. 16:1).

(4) *People's successes and failures* are brought to pass by God, 'For not from the east or from the west and not from the wilderness comes lifting up, but it is God who executes judgment, putting down one and lifting up another' (Ps. 75:6, 7). Furthermore, 'he has brought down the mighty from their thrones and exalted those of humble estate' (Luke 1:52).

(5) *The time and circumstances of a person's death* are under God's government. Such was the case with Moses (Deut. 32:48-50), as well as all the adult Israelites who came out of Egypt (Num. 14:29). But the same was true of Peter (John 21:18, 19). And Job was not mistaken when he said, 'In his hand is the life of every living thing and the breath of all mankind' (Job 12:10; cf. Ps. 104:29).

(6) *Guidance and spiritual needs*. God supplies the material needs of His people (Matt. 5:45; 6:8, 11, 26; Phil. 4:19) and their spiritual guidance. Paul knew when 'Satan hindered us' (1 Thess. 2:18) and when he was 'forbidden by the Holy Spirit' (Acts 16:6). While we do not have quite the same insights as a prophet or an apostle, we have assurance of His superintendence over our lives.

(7) *His people*. God's care for His people is so complete that seeming calamities are blessings in disguise (Phil. 1:12-14; cf. Eph. 3:1).

(8) *Apparent calamities*. These may even be the very means of God's grace to others (Phil. 1:12-14; Philem. 15).

(9) *Temptations, trials, persecutions*. Deliverance from temptations, trials, persecutions have all been provided for (1 Cor. 10:13; cf. Dan. 3:17, 18). The Christian outlook thus permits me to see national events of great moment as developing out of seeming trivial, chance events – a sleepless night (Esther 6:1) or a sad countenance (Neh. 2:1, 2). These seeming trivialities are often more decisive than the decisions of judicial and legislative assemblies or executive decisions of national leaders.

There is no doctrine about God more resoundingly proclaimed throughout the Bible than that of providence. In addition to the selections already cited here, there are dozens of texts which assert God's direct control over nature, birth, disease, death, afflictions, adversity, prosperity, rewards, punishments, deliverances, disasters, bad laws and good ones. 'The teaching of more than five hundred passages [cited in the article] might be confirmed, were it necessary, by as many thousands more, showing with what emphasis the Scriptures proclaim the doctrine of divine Providence.'[8]

Providence and Chance.

Does God's providence extend to chance – to what is sometimes called statistical probability? The answer is affirmative, with qualification. 'The lot is cast into the lap, but its every decision is from the LORD' (Prov. 16:33). This bit of proverbial wisdom assumes that God is in charge even of card games and roulette wheels. No Christian can accept chance as an 'undesigned cause' of reality in general. The regularity and uniformity of the sequences of nature are not assigned to chance in the Bible, even though some scientists base their logic for the theory of evolution on chance and explain origins that way. The Bible traces the origin and present integrity of every existing thing to God, the Creator.

---

7. See also Job 37:5, 10; Matt. 5:45; Matt. 6:30.
8. S. H. Platt, *op. cit.*, viii p. 708.

> Chance had a name among the ancient Greeks, *Tyche*. She became an important goddess, in Latin *Fortuna* (hence our words, fortune and fortunate). She was not above control by some other deities – the fates, hence our words fate and fatal. As Douglas Spanner writes:

> > [Man] cannot help being a religious animal; so what does he do? He makes his own gods, of a sort which won't impose unacceptable demands on him and which he can manipulate. The mysterious and unknown, of course, must enter into their constitution, or they could hardly be gods. So he looks around for suitable material, and Chance [luck] suggests itself as an eligible candidate. It accordingly becomes deified, an active agency in its own right.[9]

Tyche, chance, fortune, fate are all of the 'nothing' variety of whom Paul wrote (1 Cor. 8:1-4). Chance turns out to be a name of what God knows but we do not (Ps. 139:1-5; Isa. 40:27, 28; Jer. 23:24; Luke 12:6, 7). Because God controls even the casting of lots it could be said[10] both that it was by lot and that it was proportioned to the size and need of each tribe and according to divine plan.

There is a class of Scripture passages which assert God's government of what people call chance and accident. Among the 'statutes' accompanying the decalogue, for example, is this: 'Whoever strikes a man so that he dies shall be put to death. But if he did not lie in wait for him, but God let him fall into his hand, then I will appoint for you a place to which he may flee', and similar (Exod. 21:12, 13; cf. Deut. 19:45). Elijah predicted, 'In the place where dogs licked up the blood of Naboth shall dogs lick your [Ahab's] own blood' (1 Kings 21:19). Later in the battle of the allied kings (Ahab and Jehoshaphat) against the Syrians, 'a certain man drew his bow at random and struck the king of Israel between the scale armour and the breastplate... So the king died.' They brought the king's body back to Samaria in his blood-soaked chariot, which they washed by 'the pool of Samaria, and the [prophesied] dogs licked up his blood... according to the word of the LORD that he had spoken' (1 Kings 22:34-38).

Occasionally the Scriptures call an event 'chance'. These are events *unpurposed by human beings*. Even Jesus spoke of chance in this way (Luke 10:31). The Hebrew word for 'chance' or 'hap' (literally, a meeting) is used of Ruth's undesigned (as far as she was concerned) gleaning in the field of Boaz (Ruth 2:3). It is therefore correct to think of unpurposed human events as occurring by chance. But God has a purpose in every event. Chance is simply our name for certain things, not God's. He merely deigns occasionally to use our term instead of His.

A paragraph from A. H. Strong gives sensible advice:

> Not all chances are of equal importance. The casual meeting of a stranger in the street need not bring God's providence before me, although I know that God arranges it. Yet I can conceive of that meeting as leading to religious conversation and to the stranger's conversion. When we are prepared for them, we shall see many opportunities which are now as unmeaning to us as the gold in the river beds was to the early Indians in California.[11]

Paul calls such occasions 'Redeeming the time', i.e. making use of every opportunity (Eph. 5:16 KJV).

Chance therefore is a valid notion in the context of human ignorance of what God's plans and actions are. It has a place in the science of physics and statistics, and the like. Whether the idea is sound of chance mutation as sufficient mechanism for evolution in the history of organic life is a thought for another occasion.

Providence and the Evil Acts of 'Free' People.

Everything said earlier about divine concursus in all acts of people and freedom of the will as non-coercion of people's wills and acts is relevant to evil acts as well as good ones. In addition, it has seemed that when God's government of His world includes evil acts of His creatures, providence may be explained as of four kinds: (1) *permissive*, (2) *preventive*, (3) *directive* and (4) *limiting*. The terms have been supplied by generations of theologians but the ideas are biblical, even though some Supralapsarian 'super' Calvinists are rather scornful of these distinctions. It seems such an analysis of the scriptural evidence is valid, as can be seen.

1. *Permissive providence.* Though God might have restrained them, Paul declared 'In past generations he allowed all the nations to walk in their own ways' (Acts 14:16), and regarding the heathen, 'God gave them up in the lusts of their hearts... God gave them up to dishonourable passions' (Rom. 1:24, 26). Paul explains that, previous to

---

9. Douglas Spanner, *Biblical Creation and the Theory of Evolution* (Exeter: Paternoster Press, 1987), pp. 47, 48.
10. See Josh. 18:10; Ps. 47:4; Acts 1:24-26.
11. A. H. Strong, *op. cit.*, p. 428.

the propitiation wrought by Christ, 'in his divine forbearance he had passed over former sins' (Rom. 3:25). God simply withheld impediments to their wickedness.[12]

2. *Preventive providence*. In Abimelech's dream God explained, 'It was I who kept you from sinning against me. Therefore I did not let you touch her [Sarah]' (Gen. 20:6). This is one of many similar passages. Hosea's immoral wife could not be restrained as far as her husband's power went, but Israel could be restrained. Therefore God addressed a poignant appeal to the nation, in the midst of which he said, 'I will hedge up her way with thorns, and I will build a wall against her, so that she cannot find her [wicked] paths' (Hos. 2:6). Thus God prevents sins which might otherwise be committed. The 'hedge' and 'thorns' may be age, disease, enlivened conscience, memory of neglected lessons and so on. There are many such scriptural texts and illustrative passages.

3. *Directive (or redirective) providence*. Here we recall the earlier example in the life of Joseph (Gen. 45:7, 8; 50:20, 21). Similarly, the Assyrians served God's good purpose though they intended evil. Assyria was 'the rod' of God's anger in judging many wicked nations. 'But he does not so intend, and his heart does not so think' (Isa. 10:5, 7). '[Y]ou meant evil… but God meant it for good'.

4. *Limiting or determinative providence*. In a sense this is an aspect of common grace whereby God keeps evil movements in society, evil people in our company and evil impulses in individuals from full development. Otherwise life on this planet would cease. There are many passages in which God places severe restraints on intended evils in order to spare His people (Ps. 124:2; Job 1:12; 2:6). He thus shields each saint from overmuch trials (1 Cor. 10:3). Finally, God will put such immediate restraints on 'that ancient serpent' (Rev. 20:2, 3). Except for this extension of God's gracious providence, the race would have come to oblivion long ago.

Providence and 'Hypothetical Contingency'.

What will Mr X do if he discovers Mrs X is lying about where she spends her Saturdays? If Grandfather gets well by Christmas will he really take me skiing? Can God predict and control such things? Actually, God's knowledge is specfically involved in such cases more directly than His government. There is a passage where just such a hypothetical situation is proposed. Would the citizens of a certain town betray David if they had opportunity? David inquired of God and got the answer, Yes they would. So David acted accordingly and left town (see 1 Sam. 23:1-2). A little reflection will convince one that if we accept the other areas of God's providence, then hypothetical contingency is as much an area of His government as any other.

The relation of predestination and providence is closely related to the topic of divine omniscience. The 'openness of God' sect of theology and 'process theology' deny God's omniscience and with it His complete control (providence, government) of the world He created and sustains.[13]

Providence and Prayer.

Does God's plan and its certain fulfillment leave room for prayer by believers and answer by God? We are told by Jesus (Luke 18:1) that we ought always to pray and by the great Apostle to pray without ceasing (1 Thess. 5:17). Paul, who wrote more about God's decrees and providence than any other writer of Scripture, not only commanded Christians to pray but showed great confidence that God does answer prayer. Thus, the answer to our question is 'Yes'. Providence not only leaves room for prayer – it requires prayer.

We do not answer, 'Yes', but mean only that prayer has reflex action on the one who prays. This would be merely a religious athletical exercise. Subjective effects from prayer may or may not be good. Daniel was exhausted by his prayers and would not have engaged in prayer except that he expected objective results from God (Dan. 7:28; 8:27). Nor do we mean that prayer is a precondition to spiritual blessing, though that is true in some cases.

The Christian God is the God of all creation. He has known all along about our prayers. 'Before they call I will answer; while they are yet speaking I will hear' (Isa. 65:24); 'Then you shall call, and the LORD will answer; you shall cry, and he will say, "Here I am"' (Isa. 58:9). God's plans included the prayers. God not only

---

12. See also 2 Chr. 32:21; Deut. 8:2; Ps. 81:12, 13; Hos. 4:17.
13. See the earlier section on God's attribute of omniscience, and discussion of 'middle knowledge' (Chapter 10, The Greatness of the Godhead).

recommends prayer, He commands prayer and moves our hearts to seek Him out in prayer. This should be kept in mind in reading how that 'The eyes of the LORD are towards the righteous and his ears towards their cry' (Ps. 34:15).

Let us boldly assert that God's plans are all-important in prayer. Three times in one terrible night Jesus asked God to let the cup of Calvary's suffering pass from Him, yet added, 'Nevertheless, not my will, but yours, be done.' He acknowledged that His death for sinners was planned from eternity and that Scripture predicted it (see John 1:29, 36; Rev. 13:8). Christ was and is the 'lamb... foreordained before the foundation of the world, but was manifest in these last times' (1 Peter 1:19, 20 KJV).

We may be sure that the will of God *ought* to condition all our requests in prayer. We cannot command God, nor is strong faith always necessary; Jesus responded favourably to hesitant faith more than once.

At first glance James 1:6-8 seems to demand very vigorous faith as prerequisite for prevailing prayer – 'the one who doubts... will [not] receive anything from the Lord'. In view, however, of what Jesus said about faith being 'like a grain of mustard seed' (Luke 13:19) and instances of amazing answers to hesitant prayers the wavering of James is not hesitancy between strong faith and weak faith but between unbelief and genuine belief. Tennyson's lines come to mind: 'There's more faith, I tell you, in honest doubt, than in half the [recitals of] creeds.'

If, in prayer, we 'ask anything according to his will' (1 John 5:14), we ought to devote ourselves to diligent Bible study and reflection on Scripture, consulting also with Christians wiser than we are. These are part of genuine faith. Let us seek to learn what God wants and wish for the same, even if personal loss, suffering or even death are necessary to bring it to pass. It is not wrong to pray for one's self. The Psalmists did and so did our LORD. But effective prayer will certainly focus on God and His plans. Our plans will be adjusted to His.

There can be no *physical* demonstration that God answers prayers. There are moral preconditions which forbid a scientifically controlled situation. God's will is not subject to scientific analysis and His sovereign power cannot be brought to the laboratory. 'You shall not put the Lord your God to the test.' Faith-compelling answers even to saintly prayers are rare. God answered Elijah's prayer for such a demonstration for good reasons, and we know what they were (see 1 Kings 18:36-39). But when the Pharisees said to Jesus, 'Master, we would see a sign from thee', Jesus responded, 'An evil and adulterous generation seeketh after a sign; and no sign there shall be given to it' (Matt. 12:38, 39 KJV).

Providence and Christian Effort.

Does belief in providence hinder Christian effort? Hardly! Some of the most active evangelists and pastors, philanthropists and missionaries have had great confidence in God's providence. Again Paul may be cited[14] and he is typical.

Quietism counsels self-abnegation, abandonment of effort, quiet yielding. Extremists of this persuasion advocate the giving up even of will and reason as demanded by the will and wisdom of God. Contrariwise, naturalistic or sceptical advice leaves no place to trust anything but self-help and human effort. But both trust and effort are parts of God's will for us. We know that God uses means for almost everything He does. We are His means to accomplish many things.

> You are the only Bible
> The careless world will read.
> You are the sinner's Gospel,
> You are the scoffer's creed.

Prayer without employment of God's means is an insult to Him. If the house catches on fire, call on God to put it out but also call the fire department and get busy with a water bucket. 'When God gets ready to save the heathen He will save them', all right, but don't be surprised, if you are interested in *when* He does it, that He tells you to help in the project now!

Providence and the Will of God.

George Mueller of Bristol, one of the most active Christians who ever lived, had some fine things to say on this subject.

> I seek at the beginning to get my heart into such a state that it has no will of its own in regard to a given matter. Nine-tenths of the difficulties are overcome when our hearts are ready to do the Lord's will, whatever it may

---

14. See Rom. 9:1-3, 15-18; 10:1-3, 12-15.

be. Having done this, I do not leave the result to feeling or simple impression. If I do so, I make myself liable to a great delusion. I seek the will of the Spirit of God through, or in connection with, the Word of God. The Spirit and the Word must be combined. If I look to the Spirit alone, without the Word, I lay myself open to great delusions also. If the Holy Spirit guides us at all, He will do it according to the Scriptures, and never contrary to them. Next I take into account providential circumstances. These often plainly indicate God's will in connection with His Word and His Spirit. I ask God in prayer to reveal to me His will aright. Thus through prayer to God, the study of His Word, and reflection, I come to a deliberate judgment according to the best of my knowledge and ability, and if my mind is thus at peace, I proceed accordingly.

Thus the great founder of Christian orphanages brought prayer, God's will (decrees) and His providence to focus in a marvellously useful life.

'Application of the Doctrine of Providence.'

I have borrowed the heading from John Flavel, whose book, *The Mystery of Providence,* first saw the light of day in print in 1687, over 300 years ago. The last forty-one pages of his 221-page book are devoted to practical application of providence to Christian life.

I select a few lines:

> If God performs all things for us, then it is our great interest and concern in all things to study to please him upon whom we depend for all things... Fear nothing but sin. Study nothing so much as how to please God. Do not turn from your own integrity under temptation. Trust God in the way of your duty. These are sure rules to secure yourselves and your interests in all the vicissitudes of life.[15]

The whole book is a treasure very productive of 'righteousness and peace and joy, in the Holy Ghost'.[16]

---

15. John Flavel, *The Mystery of Providence* (London: Banner of Truth Trust, 1963) from last paragraph of chapter 11.
16. Available from Banner of Truth Trust.

22
Appendices on God's Preservation and Providence (Chapter 21)

Appendix I.

Creation, Preservation, Providence, and the Rise of Experimental and Applied Science.

As long ago as the late third century BC, Aristarchus of Samosa, a Greek astronomer, was convinced by his observations and calculus that in spite of appearances the sun is larger than the earth, hence not likely to be revolving around the earth as it seems, but the other way around. He even anticipated the modern methods of employing trigonometry to calculate the distances of sun and moon from our earth.[1] But the time was not ripe, so in want of undisputable evidence, these ideas gained no general acceptance until the age of discovery (1400s AD) and the development shortly thereafter of an experimental, then fully inductive, study of nature.

Why did it take so long? The wisdom of the Greek philosophers never seriously engaged the material world. They had 'little sympathy for a disinterested science of nature'.[2] Greek 'intellectuals (Plato and Aristotle, for example) held manual labor in low esteem'. The philosopher considered it beneath his dignity to engage in manual work or to use working methods of mechanics to solve his scientific problems. The age of science had to wait until there was social acceptance for putting head and hands together.

There is a catch, however, as anyone knows who has read of Adam's duty to dress and guard his garden and to earn his bread by the sweat of his brow, or of Jesus' dictum, 'My Father is working until now, and I am working', or Paul's stern sentence, 'If anyone is not willing to work, let him not eat' – the Bible from beginning to end sets a high social value on work. Why then did not an intellectual and social climate conducive to manual work, and material experimentation essential to applied science (industry), develop in the lands of Christendom? I think R. Hooykaas has the right answer. He asserts:

> For the building materials of Science (logic, mathematics, the beginning of a rational interpretation of the world) we have to look to the Greeks; but the vitamins indispensable for a healthy growth came from the biblical concept of creation [also preservation and providence, guaranteeing the uniformity of nature]. The fact that the victory of

---
1. *The Harper Encyclopedia of Science, vol. i*, p. 88.
2. R. Hooykaas, *Religion and the Rise of Science* (Grand Rapids: Eerdmans, 1972), pp. 78, 79.

Christianity did not bring an immediate liberation from the bonds of Greek metaphysics [where either fate and chance rule over falling atoms of air, earth, fire and water falling in a void] in no way disproves this statement. The compromise of Christian religion, first with Platonism, then with Aristotelianism, strongly influenced not only secular learning but also theology. Even the positive biblical appreciation of the crafts hardly overcame the traditional attitudes of Graeco-Roman (and perhaps also autochthonous [indigenous]) social conception, especially after the first force of love had spent itself and Christianity had become a firmly established world religion.[3]

In the changing atmosphere of the Renaissance, the Reformation reintroduced the biblical view of nature in a time when religious convictions of the general culture had to be accommodated by the movers and shakers of society.

Augustine may have come close. He certainly had a strong doctrine of providence. He interpreted history in terms of providence but focused on the spiritual side as a long 'drama of sin and redemption [which] philosophy dominated the Middle Ages'.[4] Some of the scholastics of a nominalist trend may have come close to escaping the closed system of medieval thinking. God's world was still full of superstitious fears of the unknown (causes of disease, spooks, demons out of control), and in Roman theology, at the local level, miracles occupied the minds of priests and laymen much more than a benign providence.

The Reformation changed that wherever its thought-patterns prevailed. All the Reformers deprecated the popular beliefs in the power of relics, amulets, priestly blessings, apparitions of saints and similar to interfere with the normal 'order of nature', as Calvin called it. After citing several passages of Scripture he summarizes: 'From this we gather that his general providence not only flourishes among creatures so as to continue the *order of nature* [emphasis added] but is by his wonderful plan adapted to a definite end.'[5] Rejecting confused ancient semi-pantheistic or vitalistic notions of God's presence in nature, which made 'a shadow deity to drive away the true God, whom we should fear and adore', he goes on to say:

> I confess... that it can be said reverently, provided it proceeds from a reverent mind, that nature is God; but because it is a harsh and improper saying, since *nature is rather the order prescribed by God* [emphasis added], it is harmful in such weighty matters, in which special devotion is due, to involve God confusedly in the inferior course of his works.[6]

It is the same Calvin who a few pages later affirmed of the special 'nature' of things:

> [T]he depravity and malice both of man and the devil or the sins that arise therefrom, do not spring from nature, but rather from the corruption of nature. And from the beginning nothing at all has existed in which God has not put forth an example both of his wisdom and of his righteousness.[7]

In this way this Reformer soundly rejected the false basis of asceticism – that there is something evil in the fleshly-material side of ourselves and the world about us – opening up for investigation and practical use the vast world which experimenters and synthesizers have explored since that time.

Calvin found this new outlook in the biblical teachings of creation and providence. In this world, speaking strictly, 'God's providence, as it is taught in Scripture, is opposed to fortune and fortuitous happenings... And concerning inanimate objects we ought to hold that, although each one has by nature been endowed with its own property, yet it is directed by God's ever present hand... Nothing is more natural than for spring to follow winter; summer, spring; and fall, summer – each in turn. Yet in this series one sees such great and uneven diversity that it readily appears each year, month, and day is governed by a new, a special, providence of God.'[8]

In another Appendix we shall see that for this Reformer the steady maintenance and control of nature by God condemns the flourishing of the miracle business rampant in the medieval church, resulting in further corruption of an ignorant population of Christendom.

Luther did not develop a systematic doctrine of providence. Rather, thougout his reforming career he wrote and spoke of God's power and will by which He energizes and controls everything which exists. Among hundreds

---

3. ibid., p. 85.
4. Dagobert D. Runes, *Twentieth Century Philosophy* (New York: Philosophical Library, 1943), p. 97.
5. Calvin, *Institutes I*,16.7.
6. ibid., 5.5.
7. ibid., 14.3.
8. ibid., 16.2.

of possible quotations I cite one. Luther does not distinguish sharply between God's creating, preserving and providential works.

> It is God who created, effects, and preserves all things through his almighty power and right hand, as our Creed confesses. For he dispatches no officials or angels when he creates or preserves something, but all this is the work of his divine powers itself. If he is to create or preserve it, however, he must be present and must make and preserve his creation both in its innermost and outermost aspects. Therefore, indeed, he himself must be present in every single creature in its innermost and outermost being, on all sides, through and through, below and above, before and behind, so that nothing can be more truly present and within all creatures than God himself with his power.[9]

Luther thought of this work as an aspect of sovereign divine omnipotence and carried that outlook into the doctrine of justification as a matter of divine creativity.[10]

It was Melanchthon who sorted out Luther's teachings in this regard and gave them 'scientific' statement in the *Loci Communes* (common topics of theology) of 1555, citing the same texts of Scripture I have employed in demonstration of creation, perservation and providence. The fourth of his five main affirmations in connection with this article says:

> Human blindness thinks that God is like a carpenter who, having built a ship, departs and abandons it to water and weather, and has nothing further to do with it. Men imagine that after creating this earth and mankind, God departed, and now has nothing to do with this realm of created things. We must root these false thoughts out of our hearts with God's work, and we must learn the solace of true doctrine and believe that God is truly present in all places, that he sustains the being of all things, and that everything that has being or life [*Wesen* or *Leben*], so long as it remains in being or life, is sustained by God. So the heavens, the sun, and moon remain in being and have their ordered courses; the earth annually yields fruit; angels, men, and animals live; and all this happens through the concurring activity [*Mitwirkung*] of God.[11]

Of course some Roman Church theologians understood the biblical teaching of creation, preservation and providence. There are passages in Thomas Aquinas similar to these quotes. They did not, however, disseminate, much less convince, the priests and laymen of Europe. The Roman Catholic parts of Europe lagged far behind the Protestant parts for generations in developing the experimental and applied science which broke out rather quickly in the Netherlands and Britain. Many streams of change were in the air in the sixteenth and seventeenth centuries, slowly overcoming the stagnation of medieval ages. The most effective impulse toward what we now call science, reflecting a correct biblical view of the world of nature, came from Francis Bacon (1561–1626) who had studied the matter deeply. In his *Novum Organum* and other works he explained the sad situation of 'the sciences', where the best effort of the best minds was expended on fruitless 'wars of words' (*logomachies*). This inevitably led, Bacon said, to separation of the best thought from nature and experience to 'superstition and blind religious zeal', excessive reverence for antiquity (the error of the new humanism), reliance on abstract theories and traditional prejudices. In other words Christendom had neglected the world-view of the Bible. When in Europe, particularly the Netherlands and Britain where the Calvinists' form of the Reformation prevailed, science flowered, slowly at first. I shall leave to others the development of the story. I refer the reader to Hooykaas' two chapters, 'The Rise of Experimental Science' and 'Science and the Reformation'[12] and his extensive bibliography.

'It is interesting to note', says Garret Vanderkooi, 'that natural science developed and flourished in the Western Hemisphere (*sic*) during a time when belief in a supreme creator God was widespread. No comparable development took place in Eastern animistic or Hindu cultures where natural events are often given magical explanations.'[13]

---

9. Paul Althaus, *The Theology of Martin Luther*, trans. R. C. Schultz (Philadelphia: Fortress Press, 1966), p. 106.
10. ibid., pp. 118–129.
11. Philipp Melanchthon, *Loci Communes*, trans. C. L. Manschreck (Grand Rapids: Baker Books, 1982), p. 41.
12. R. Hooykaas, *op. cit.*, pp. 75 – 144. Professor Hooykaas' book is based on The Gunning Lectures delivered by him under the auspices of the University of Edinburgh in February, 1969.
13. Garret Vanderkooi, 'A Theistic Approach to Science' in John Warwick Montgomery's book, *Evidence for Faith* (Dallas: Word Publ., 1991) p. 45. Since writing the above, the year 2000 recent work of H. L. Poe and J. H. Davis (*Science and Faith: An Evangelical Dialogue*) likewise sets the matter straight and encourages Christians to claim their intellectual inheritance in the confluence and mutual support of a sound science and a sound interpretation of Scripture.
14. A. D. White, *A History of the Warfare of Science with Theology in Christendom*, two volumes, (NY: Appleton & Co., 1876).

A. D. White contended that liberal 'religion' fostered science but orthodox theology smothered it.[14] As late as 1965 Bruce Mazlisch, in the introduction to an abridged edition, expressed the opinion that White had established his thesis. But say D. C. Lindberg and R. L. Numbers:

> Such judgments... overlook mounting evidence that White read the past through battle-scarred glasses. A number of scholars, including Alfred North Whitehead and Michael B. Forster, had begun to downplay the conflict between science and Christianity as early as the 1920s and 1930s. Indeed, Whitehead and Forster became convinced that Christianity, rather than impeding science, had actually encouraged it by establishing that nature behaves in a regular and orderly fashion – a basic promise of modern science.[15]

In an earlier chapter I cited Stanley Jaki and R. Hooykaas in support of this theme. Lindberg and Numbers are citing Whitehead and Forster to the same effect.[16]

Appendix II.
Providence and Miracles.

As we have seen, there is basis for the regularity of nature including systematic sequences of seasons, chemical reactions, verifiable causes and effects, and the like, in the divine government by God's law and will. Without this there would be chaos rather than cosmos. Life could not continue. In such case, how do miracles, both biblically reported and others, which seem to violate this regularity, fit into the scheme of things?

The Bible of course reports many unusual occurrences, such as Jesus turning water into wine and the feeding of the 5,000, the parting of the waters of the Jordan by Joshua, and Elijah's calling down fire to consume water-soaked sacrifice on Mount Carmel. Some of these 'miracles' might seem like circus stunts to some but others are of acknowledged timeless significance, as for example the crossing of the Red Sea on dry ground at Moses' word. It is celebrated throughout the rest of Scripture as an important work of God of timeless significance. Let us consider as briefly as possible how this variation from the ordinary laws and course of nature, secured by divine providence, should be regarded.

1. Let us observe first off that in Scripture everything that occurs on earth or in heaven is within God's plan, is sustained and ruled by Him. In biblical thought, the explosion of a distant star is no less the work of God than the raising of Lazarus, the emergence of a duckling from an egg no more or less than the healing of the demoniacs of Gadara. God is immanent in all creation as well as transcendent above it. He made it and though God uses 'second causes' such as mass attraction, Boyle's Law and Charles' Law for expansion and contraction of gasses, these forces and 'laws' have been aptly characterized as God's habits of operation. They are under His control and, like the world picture of Psalm 104, ordinarily can be counted on by mankind for 'service... food... wine... oil... and bread' (Ps. 104:14, 15 KJV), though not without interruption. The weather may not be quite as regular as mass attraction, yet the laws that control the weather are as regular as mass attraction.

The immediate power of God can operate either in nature or in mankind, as in the case of that special calling or prevenient enlightenment (some call it regeneration) which God effects in every person who comes to Christ in faith.

2. From this point of view some theologians have aptly placed miracles *within* providence. The ordinary habits of God in the world are *general* providence, while the unusual works of God that seem to interrupt the ordinary course of nature are a species of *special* providence. In special providences God concerns Himself with *particular* events of history (say the calling of Isaiah to be a prophet) or with answers to prayer and particular needs of His people. To coin a term, miracles might be termed *extra-special* or extraordinary providences.[17]

3. In coming to an exact definition of a miracle (as opposed simply to the supernatural) the special vocabulary of Scripture will help us. These special events of divine activity which we sometimes call miracles have several semi-technical designations in the Bible.

---

15. D. C. Lindberg and R. L. Numbers, *God and Nature: Historical Essays on the Encounter Between Christianity and Science* (Berkeley, CA: Univ. of Calif. Press, 1986) pp. 2-4.
16. Alfred N. Whitehead, *Science and the Modern World* (New York: Macmillan, 1925) and Forster, 'The Christian Doctrine of Creation and the Rise of Modern Science' in *Mind* magazine, 43, 1934), pp. 446-468; also 'Christian Theology and the Modern Science of Nature' in *Mind* magazine, 44, 1935), pp. 439-466 and *Mind* 45, 1936), pp. 1-27. More recently M. Klaren, *Religious Origins of Modern Science, Belief in Creation in Seventeenth Century Thought* (Grand Rapids: Eerdmans, 1977).
17. Louis Berkhof, *Systematic Theology* (Valley Forge, PA: Judson Press, 1907) pp. 168, 169.

In the Old Testament the chief term is *'oth*. 'Most of the eighty occurrences... refer to miraculous signs: all the plagues on the Egyptians are called "signs". In these contexts the complementary word *mopeth* meaning "wonders" often occur.'[18] Throughout the Old Testament the special, distinct character of a miracle is not so much in its departing from the ordinary course of nature, as the divinely intended meaning usually supplied by a prophet. They are both signs (of meaning) and wonders.

In the New Testament four Greek words designate these extraordinary events of God's providential government of the heavens and earth He created. Of these one is *sēmeion*, 'a sign consisting of a wonder or miracle, an event that is contrary to the usual course of nature',[19] which answers precisely to the Hebrew *'oth*, both translated in the plural 'signs'.

A second Greek word *teras*, usually plural, meaning 'a prodigy, portent, omen, wonder',[20] is usually coupled in plural form with *sēmeion* ('signs and wonders'). This word has more reference to the effect on observers. A verb of similar meaning (*thaumadzō*, to marvel or wonder) describes this effect. This is what modern secularist people really mean by the overworked term, 'miraculous' or 'a miracle' – simply something to impress as exceptional, amazing, marvellous. The effect on viewers of such events depends much on what they bring to it – as seen in the case of Jesus' miracle of healing on the Sabbath (Matt. 12:9-45).

A third word is *dunamis*, rendered as might, power, authority. In Acts 2:22 it is parallel with signs and wonders 'that God did', referring to the miracles which Jesus performed publicly among the Jews of His time. This word points to God's special activity in 'miracles'. This word is occasionally rendered 'miracle' in KJV and does particularly indicate the divine power which God employed in performing signs and wonders.

A fourth word is *ergon*, which simply means a work, in this case a work of God. It designates the fact – healing a leper, a pot of oil that never runs empty, a Lazarus coming forth, fire called down from heaven.

4. These original words of the Scripture language provide a guide to defining what miracles are, their effects on observers and others who learn of them, their function as signigicant events of special meaning and their cause in God. Biblical miracles are extraordinary events (*ergon*) which capture public notice, producing amazement (*mopeth, teras, thaumadzō*) and which have meaning (*'oth, sēmeion*). This meaning is the special presence of God in some special way usually declared by a prophet (Aaron, Elijah, Moses, Jeremiah). Finally a biblical miracle is *dunamis*, the product of and evidence of divine power and authority, not only in the event itself but of delegated power in the divinely authorized person at whose word the miracle took place.

5. As 'wonders', the miracles of the Bible are publicly observed events connected with revelation and redemption. By the ten plagues of Egypt, and the miraculous crossing of the Red Sea, Israel was redeemed from Egypt and by them God made His love, wisdom, judgment, power and glory known. By these same miracles Moses was certified and magnified before Israel as leader, revelator and governor. Without the miracles Moses would have been no more convincing or effective as liberator than he was to the Hebrew who saw him kill an Egyptian taskmaster. Jesus of Nazareth became 'a Man attested by God to you [Jews] by miracles [*dunameis*], wonders [*terasi*] and signs [*sēmeiois*], which God did through Him in your midst' (Acts 2:22 NKJV). And He was 'declared to be the Son of God in power' before all by 'his resurrection from the dead' (Rom. 1:4).

Jesus held the Jews of His time to be hardened sinners precisely because His person and message had been accompanied by authenticating 'works', saying: 'If I had not come and spoken to them, they would not have been guilty of sin, but now they have no excuse for their sin... If I had not done among them the works that no one else did, they would not be guilty of sin [that of rejecting Jesus], but now they have seen and hated both me and my Father... "They hated me without a cause"' (John 15:22-25; cf. John 10:25, 37, 38). The same method of accrediting divine messengers identified and magnified the prophets before Israel, and the apostles before the church (Heb. 2:1-4). Predictive prophecy is a special form of miracle, of the same effect in revelation and redemption. Revelation and redemption are truly aspects of divine providence. Extraordinary works, signs, wonders and powers (miracles) were employed by God in effecting revelation. Where the extraordinary is useful to revelation and redemption, God is free to use it. He is not bound to the ordinary.

In Scripture, miracles and successful predictive prophecy, as proof of the authenticity of divine spokesmen, loom large. These spectacular accomplishments did not however *per se* authenticate prophets and apostles. Two passages of Deuteronomy set the standards – chapters 13 and 18. The prophet must also be of the nation of Israel (cf. Rom. 3:1),

---

18. Robert L. Alden, *Theological Wordbook of the Old Testament, i* (Chicago: Moody Press, 1980), p. 18.
19. Bauer, Arndt & Gingrich, *Lexicon*, p. 755.
20. ibid., p. 820.

he must speak in the name of the God of Abraham, Isaac and Jacob, and his message must conform to the Mosaic revelation, including moral and spiritual elements. The tests on Mt Carmel (Elijah and prophets of Baal, 1 Kings 18), and Jeremiah against Hananiah (Jer. 28), are illustrative examples. The Eleven against Judas (Acts 1) is another example. Careful perusal of the above extended texts will amply demonsrate these assertions.

The amount of literature on miracles as attesting divine revelation and its revelators, produced in the past three centuries, is baffling to the mind of anyone who attempts to list it, much less to master it. I excerpt a few related remarks from the superb article in McClintock and Strong.

> The Universal instincts of men prove the necessity of religion… [A] revealed religion [as opposed to natural religions] can be proved only by that which involves the supernatural. What our Lord says to the Jews, that 'they would not have sinned in rejecting him but for his works' (John 15:24), commends itself at once to our reason… In order to its being revealed, God must be the giver of it. And how are we to know it is to he who speaks? Its strength, its value, its authority, all depend on its being the voice of God… We must have direct evidence – something pledging God himself – before we can accept religion as revealed.[21]

There really isn't much to say on the subject of miracles not covered directly or indirectly in the forty densely printed columns in the volume, under 'Miracles' and 'Ecclesiastical Miracles'.

Jesus said once, 'no one who does a mighty work in my name will be able soon afterward to speak evil of me' (Mark 9:39), but on another occasion remarked, 'On that day many will say to me, "Lord, Lord, did we not prophesy in your name, and cast out demons in your name, and do many mighty works in your name?" And then will I declare to them, "I never knew you; depart from me, you workers of lawlessness"' (Matt. 7:22, 23). Luther used Balaam (Num. 24) as an example of one who fits the seeming contradiction. All his motives were false even though his miracle was authentic. Absent was the moral characteristic of love – Luther cited 1 Corinthians 13:2, 'And if I have prophetic powers, and understand all mysteries and all knowledge, and if I have all faith, so as to remove mountains, but have not love, I am nothing.' Luther often discussed this verse in controversy with the Roman Church. His latest thought on it was that the statement was 'aimed at people who called themselves Christians and who did great things with their faith but had no love'.[22]

6. We have no way of knowing how many times each day in answers to prayers or for other reasons, Providence directs second causes in a 'supernatural' way. The conversion of every sinner is a supernatural event in that the Spirit of the Father in concert with the Word of God plants spiritual life in a soul in a way that is contrary to the workings of 'nature' – human or otherwise. But such events are short of *public* demonstration of the significant, amazing working of divine power. Secular scientists will explain such conversion experiences as wholly resulting from natural causes, including *The Will to Believe* (William James' famous thesis, 1897). Public miracles, openly demonstrating the presence of supernatural power, are quite rare in the Bible.

Note for one thing that miracles occurred almost exclusively in brief epochs: the time of the Exodus from Egypt and entering Canaan, the crisis of apostasy among the northern tribes in the time of Elijah and Elisha, the birth of Jesus, again during His ministry and of course His resurrection, and the early period of the book of Acts and the ministry of Paul (Rom. 15:18, 19).

Note also that a comparison of Deuteronomy 18:9-22, with Deuteronomy 13, shows that miracles served to authenticate Moses as God's appointed teacher, legislator and revelator – the burning bush of Exodus 3, the miracles of the rod, the leprous hand and turning water to blood (Exod. 4:1-9). Just so many, if not all, succeeding prophets to Israel, and God's authentic mouthpieces and writers of Scripture, whether prophets or apostles, were similarly authenticated.[23]

7. Evidence is far from certain that supernatural signs, that is miracles, continued in any general sense after the apostolic age. Like the 400 plus silent years in Egypt (Exod. 12:40, 41) and the 400 plus years after the prophet Malachi – when prophecy was silent and miracles ceased – the present age is a similar time. There is to be a time of renewed miracles at the Second Advent. Even during times of prophets and apostles miracles were not daily affairs. General providence held sway, when laws of nature's cycles, of morals and economics, sowing and reaping, were not repealed or superseded by a wholesale relaxation of the order of nature.

---

21. McClintock & Strong, sentences from 'Miracles' in *Cyclopedia of Biblical Theological and Ecclesiastical Literature* (New York: Harper & Brothers, 1876, reprinted Grand Rapids: Baker Books, VI, 1969), p. 308.
22. Paul Althaus, *op. cit.*, p. 436.
23. See for example 1 Kings 18:36-39 and Jer. 28; Heb. 2:1-4; 2 Cor. 12:12.

Even in apostolic times, after the apostles and prophets who founded the church and produced revelation had been thoroughly accredited by 'signs and wonders', the supernatural sign gifts fade from the New Testament record. Norman Geisler points out that in the period of the book of Acts (AD 30–60) 'tongues', healings, exorcisms, even raising from the dead occurred, but in the later period – the period say AD 60 onward – tongues are never mentioned, nor healings, exorcisms or raising the dead. Geisler (as many good writers before him) points out:

> [A]s soon as we arrive at the time of Paul's imprisonments (around AD 60–70) there is not only a complete absence of reference to any of these special apostolic gifts... there is strong evidence that they no longer possessed these abilities. For example, the same apostle who could heal everyone on an island (Acts 28:9) could no longer even heal his coworkers in the ministry. The apostles could heal a person born lame (Acts 3), but Paul could not give Timothy relief from a simple stomach ailment and had to recommend that he take medicine for it (1 Tim. 5:23). The same apostle who exorcised a demon on command (Acts 15) could only hope for repentance that Hymenaeus and Philetus would 'escape from the snare of the devil' (2 Tim. 2:26). And the same apostle who once had the power to raise the dead (Acts 20) now cannot even raise his needed friend Trophimus from a sick bed (2 Tim. 4:20). And when we reach Hebrews (AD 68–69) the sign gifts are referred to as a past event (Heb. 2:3-4). The writer says that what Jesus announced '*was confirmed* to us by those who heard him [apostles]. God also testified to it by signs, wonders and various miracles'.[24]

Geisler goes on to say: 'the sign gifts have ceased, just as Paul predicted they would (1 Cor. 3:8). Although Paul does not specify when these gifts would cease, he does say they will. Furthermore, he hints that this would occur as the church progressed toward "maturity" (1 Cor. 13:10; cf. Eph. 4:12) although this will not be complete till the Second Coming (v. 12), he does not say that all the gifts will last until then. Indeed, it is obvious from the contrasts above that the miraculous gifts petered out as the early church matured.'[25]

8. From two sides evangelical Protestant religion has had to defend itself from a demand that the movement produce miracles. The first was from the side of the Roman Church in early Reformation times. The credulous, illiterate populace of Christian Europe had developed an appetite for miracles – of which the 'miracle of the altar', transubstantiation, was only a tame sample. Superstitious expectations increased and have not ceased in many Roman Catholic countries even today. (In Reformation times Belarmine, official Roman apologist, sought to prove 'the continuity of the miraculous power of the Church of Rome [and] the Protestant Church lacking this [power] is manifestly not of God.'[26] In an endeavour to embarrass the evangelical leaders of Geneva and win back the Reformed community there, Bishop Sadolet of that jurisdiction had written a letter to the Genevans charging among other things that the 'new' religion lacked the 'miracles' which were still being produced in the mother church. To this Calvin replied, in his Prefatory address to King Francis I:

> In demanding miracles of us, they act dishonestly. For we are not forging some new gospel, but are retaining that very gospel whose truth all the miracles that Jesus Christ and his disciples ever wrought serve to confirm. But, compared with us, they have a strange [i.e. inauthentic] power; even to this day they can confirm their faith by continual miracles! [So they say.] Instead they allege miracles which can disturb a mind otherwise at rest – they are so foolish and ridiculous, so vain and false... God's name ought to be always and everywhere hallowed, whether by miracles or the natural order of things.[27]

Calvin goes on to show how the apostles were authenticated by signs and wonders (citing Acts 14:3; Heb. 2:4) but miracles were not sufficient 'to confirm falsehoods'. One must 'examine that doctrine which the Evangelist says is superior to miracles' (John 7:17, 18) and see if it tends to God's glory (John 8:50; Deut. 13:2 ff.). Calvin goes on to warn against the tricks of magicians (Pharaoh's magicians) and of Antichrist (2 Thess. 2:9, 10).

There are still elements in the Roman Church which would derive authentication – say of elegibility for beatification – from miracles. This is presently an embarrassment, hence Vatican II said,

> Let us teach the faithful, therefore, that the authentic cult of the saints does not consist so much in a multiplicity of external acts [miracles], but rather in a more intense practice of our love, whereby, for our own greater good and that of the Church, we seek from the saints [i.e. the officially beatified] example in their way of life,

---

24. Norman Geisler, *Signs and Wonders* (Wheaton, IL: Tyndale House, 1988), p. 137.
25. ibid., p. 137.
26. McClintock & Strong, *op. cit.*, pp. 320 – 326.
27. Calvin, *Institutes, vi*, Prefatory Address to King Francis, Westminster Ed., vol. i, p. 16.

fellowship in their communion, and the help of their intercession [as deceased, now in heaven with direct access to Jesus, etc.] [28]

From another quarter, time to time throughout church history, from the Montanists onward through 'enthusiasts' of Reformation times and 'pentecostalists' of recent decades, groups of folk have arisen within the church demanding the church produce all the supernatural gifts present in the apostolic church, including the performance of miracles – duplicating all the miracles of Jesus, the Twelve and the Seventy. I am of the opinion the vast majority of Protestant theologians (and denominations) still hold, as Dr Charles Hodge wrote:

> [W]hile there is nothing in the New Testament inconsistent with the occurrence of miracles in the post-apostolic age of the church… when the apostles had finished their work, the necessity of miracles, so far as the great end they were intended to accomplish was concerned ceased. This, however, does not preclude the possibility of their occurrence, on suitable occasions, in after ages. It is a mere question of fact to be decided on historical evidence.[29]

The above statement by Dr Hodge states the matter precisely. From long, often unpleasant experience, including pastoral survival through the waves of television healing (Kathryn Kuhlman, Oral Roberts and similar) and before them neo-Pentecostalist invasions of post-Depression congregations of anxious people I have learned that good people of this persuasion must be left to discover what someone has called 'the unerring verdict of history'.[30] A current scholarly opinion by C.L. Blomberg somewhat generous toward assertions of need for contemporary miracles will conclude this discussion:

> Throughout the Bible, miracles consistently serve to point people to the one true God, ultimately revealed in Jesus Christ. Their primary purpose is not to meet human need [Jesus did not heal all the sick in Palestine], although that is an important spin off blessing. But they are first of all theocentric and Christocentric, demonstrating the God of Israel and of Jesus to be supreme over all rivals. Contemporary experience suggests that this pattern continue; miracles today seem most frequent in regions where Satan has long held sway and where people require 'power evangelism' to be converted. But God's sovereignty warns against trying to predict when they may occur and refutes the 'name it and claim it' heresy that tries to force God to work miracles upon demand, if one exercises adequate faith.[31]

Per contra, veteran China missionary Doris Ekblad writes me that her father, a pioneer missionary to north central China about sixty-five years ago, had a standard formula for people who came from distances to have him deliver someone from demon 'possession'. She says, 'My father would cleanse them both spiritually by prayer and physically – with a big spoon of caster oil. I expect they never came back!'

Appendix III.

The Problem of Evil, Theodicy, Protest Atheism and the Structure of Barthian Theology.

The Problem of Evil.

It is true that when seemingly random tragedy strikes the 'undeserving', reflective people wonder if a wise, just and omnipotent good God is really in charge, governing the whole creation. Likewise when monstrous catastrophes strike large numbers of people, violently carrying away thousands at once, waves of doubt of God's goodness or of His power distress many of the faithful and give strength to avowed sceptics. This was true when the world heard the news of the terrible earthquake which struck the great city of Lisbon, the port from which the Spanish Armada sailed to attack Britain in 1688. On the first of November, 1755, the city was reduced almost in an instant to a heap of ruins. At the same time a tidal wave broke over the docks and warehouses followed by fires. About 40,000 people lost their lives. Good and bad, young and old, believers and unbelievers died together.

---

28. *Vatican Council II*, vol. i, *The Conciliar and Postconciliar Documents*, New Revised Ed., 1996, p. 412.
29. Charles Hodge, *Systematic Theology, iii* (Grand Rapids: Eerdmans, 1960), p. 452.
30. For any earnest and ambitious enough to seek guidance I suggest two old reliable sources: the lengthy article 'Miracles' and 'Ecclesiastical Miracles' in McClintock and Strong's *Cyclopedia* and Hodge's chapter on 'The Ninth Commandment' (appropriately entitled 'Thou Shalt Not Bear False Witness'), pages 437 – 463 in the work cited above. After these sources *The Silence of God* by Sir Robert Anderson and perhaps *Miracles* by B. B. Warfield and *Signs and Wonders* by Norman Geisler brings the matter up to date.
31. C. L. Blomberg, art. 'Miracles' in *Evangelical Dictionary of Biblical Theology* (Grand Rapids: Baker Books, 1984), p.534.

This was during the 'age of reason' among Europe's intelligencia and, though more severe catastrophes have occurred since, the professional sceptics of that time (David Hume in particular) found in Lisbon the proof of the non-existence of the good God of Christianity. In the twentieth century what is called 'protest atheism' took over their arguments and added more.

From ancient times philosophers have sought to define 'the good' along with 'the beautiful and the true' without ever coming to a settled opinion. But to judge whether or not the presence of physical evils in the world such as pain and 'premature death' (as it is now said) are irrational, purposeless evils or not, there must be a standard of the good by which to judge. Several recent Christian philosophers have challenged sceptics and atheists at this point to present a universal standard of the good which is a manifest improvement on the will and love of God.

As observed previously in the chapter on providence, the Bible represents evil, whether moral or physical, as a real problem in the world. It does not trace its origin or cause to the basic structure of the universe, nor to any element of nature or mankind, nor to God as its Creator. Evil is here by God's permission. Why God has permitted evil, we have not been told. The Bible nowhere directly addresses the question, even though both David and Habakkuk directly asked the question (Ps. 73; Hab. 1:1-11).

Extensive treatment of theories proposed by philosophers as to the nature and origin of evil would divert us into something far different from a biblically based theology. Several hours reviewing my files, scanning long-shelved books on ethics, meta-ethics, philosophy of religion and the like, have reawakened my awareness of at least a dozen indecisive philosophical kinds of ethical systems defining good and evil and explaining its origin. It will be pertinent here only to take note of some of the theories which have taken root on Christian soil and which have had important bearing on secular attitudes and theologies of our own time. Alvin Plantinga has addressed the problem of evil in several works.[32] His first burden is to show that the certain existence of evil is no proof of the non-existence of God. John E. Hare evaluates Plantinga's contribution at length.

> I think Plantinga is largely successful in what I shall call the *negative project*. This is the project of showing that there is no demonstrative or conclusive proof from the existence of evil to the non-existence of God. This leaves, however, the most important positive project untouched. Plantinga is himself completely pessimistic about the success of any positive project. Numerous discussions of this problem have appeared since the 1970s, though probably little new can be said.[33]

Probably no one has contributed a more comprehensive, readable and convincing report of the unsuccessful philosophical literary effort to explain the presence of evil in society while maintaining mankind as essentially the good victim than Reinhold Niebuhr. His brilliant summary, to which I am indebted, is chapter 4, 'The Easy Conscience of Modern Man'.[34] P. H. T. Holbach (1723–1789) of the German *Aufklärung*[35] and C. A. Helvetius (1715–1771), a Frenchman of the so-called Enlightenment, in common with many *literati* of their age, felt entrenched religious and political conservatism of their own and previous times was the cause of social evil.[36] A return to a state of nature would cure it. This was the naturalism of Epicurus brought up to date. In such a case, these 'enlightened' philosophers seemed quite unaware that if mankind are bond slaves of history they are hardly capable of writing books on politics and philosophy.

Only a little earlier Thomas Hobbes (1588–1679) held a nearly reverse view (*The Leviathan* 1:13-14 and 2:1-21): regarding evil as a primeval peril from nature. Two centuries later this theory merged with Darwinian evolutionary doctrine, teaching that moral evil is a hangover from mankind's brute ancestors and a stage toward good – in some writers *en route* to attainment of Christian character.[37] Hobbes thought civil government, preferably absolute monarchy, the best restraint of evil.

John Locke (1632–1704) was another who supposed moral evil rises out of mankind's condition in a state of nature, though he retained what he believed was biblical orthodoxy. He thought that a social contract establishing

---

32. Alvin Plantinga, *The Nature of Necessity* (Oxford: Oxford Univ. Press, 1974), chapter 9; *God, Freedom and Evil* (New York: Harper Torchbook, 1974), and journal articles.
33. John E. Hare, 'The Problem of Evil' in *Evidence of Faith*, ed. J. W. Montgomery (Dallas: Word Publ., 1991).
34. Reinhold Niebuhr, *The Nature and Destiny of Man: A Christian Interpretation, vol. i, Human Nature* (New York: Scribners, 1943).
35. ibid., p. 197.
36. ibid.; also McClintock & Strong, *Cyclopaedia of Biblical, Theological and Eccleseastical Literature* (1969 ed.), 4:179, 180.
37. John Fiske, *Through Nature to God*, (Boston and New York: Houghton, Mifflin & Co., 1899), a book dedicated to T. H. Huxley.

democratic government, wherein 'freedom' could be exercised, would be a sounder basis of (social) deliverance from the state of nature.

David Hume (1711–1776), if I understand his remarks correctly, thought that the presence of evil was everywhere, and so, acknowledged and experienced by everyone, might be the very spring from which the idea of God arises in all people.[38]

A lineal descendant of such thinking was the *laissez-faire* economic-philosophical-ethical philosophy of Adam Smith (1723–1790), Scottish economist. Though Smith had much to say which harmonizes with the biblical doctrines of mankind and sin, yet he taught that there is a pre-established harmony in 'nature' which if interfered with will produce economic injustice. When Smith's 'let nature take its course' in economics was joined to Darwinian evolutionary theory the result was social Darwinism and some of the economic-social disorders of the late nineteenth century.

All these physiocrats and democrats, and similar, in finding the causal source of moral and physical evil in social institutions of one sort or another were equally in error. For if moral evil (and physical evils to an important degree, according to the biblical narrative and interpretation thereof) lies anywhere in mankind, it is in their perilous, but God-given, moral capacity, involving voluntary use of uncoerced freedom of choice.

I defer to the plentious literature of Karl Marx (1818–83) and Friedrich Engels (1820–95) and their theory of evil and good (dialectical materialism), similarly the 'positive' theories of the founder of sociology, Auguste Comte (1798–1857). With Comte's Marx-like views of mankind and nature both sin and crime are thought of as 'anti-social conduct'. This term has passed into modern language along with many other terms and ideas more subversive, in my opinion, of the moral realm of Scripture and authentic ethical-social analysis than is commonly recognized even in centres of evangelical learning.

Theodicy.

The Bible never mounts an effort at *theodicy*, an effort to save the character of God from harmful inferences derived from the presence of evil. Evil is allowed in the world for reasons God has never seen fit fully to disclose and which no human wisdom, Christian or otherwise, has been able fully to discover or to explain. As we have seen, evil is not beyond His control. This has prompted such biblical sayings as, 'Surely the wrath of man shall praise you' (Ps. 76:10). It also has resulted in reports of how God raised up wicked tyrants 'that my name may be proclaimed in all the earth, (Exod. 9:16; cf. Rom. 9:17) and in prophetic declarations wherein God called an oppressive and destructive emperor 'my servant' (Jer. 25:9).

This does not mean that it is wrong to wonder if God was obligated to create the 'best possible of all worlds' or if the best possible is one where there would have been no freedom to sin, or if there really is something rightly called 'free will' without qualifications. These and other musings have been canvassed enough. There has been great difference of opinion among theologians on these questions. Gordon Clark's chapter 'God and Evil' treats the problem of theodicy in a manner deserving respect.[39] Anyone interested might start his research by examining the articles by John Feinberg on 'Theodicy', 'Problem of Sin' and 'Pain' in his 2001 volume on the doctrine of God, *No One Like Him* and pursue the bibliographical suggestions. These topics are of more legitmate interest in the philosophical disciplines of ethics and its recent twin *axiology* (values), and the theological disciplines of philosophy of religion and apologetics. [Dr Feinberg has also published a book in which he addresses the problem of evil.]

Before we move on let us note that both the musings and the severest rational reflections of theists – whether devoutly orthodox Christians or not – have usually come to the conclusion that God willed that moral evil (sin) should enter the world, but did so not *antecedently* but *consequentially*. This means that He planned for good *ultimately* (beyond the detailed history of creation) as fruit of history, that the presence of temptation to moral evil was necessary to the good of fixed moral character, that sin came to be as a *consequence*. This helps with the narrative of Genesis 3 but does not explain how the serpent (= Satan) came to be morally evil. Who tempted him? Was the temptation simply God's exalted position and glory? If created wholly good, what inner movement of will caused him to envy God and desire to be his own god, to seek other than God's proper glory as Creator?

---

38. David Hume, Remarks of Demea in *Dialogues Concerning Natural Religion*, Part X, reprinted in *God and Evil*, ed. Nelson Pike (Englewood Cliffs, NJ: Prentice Hall, 1964), p. 17.
39. Gordon Clark, *Reason, Religion and Revelation* (Philadelphia: Presbyterian & Reformed Publ., 1961, republished by Trinity Foundation in 1995), pp. 194–242.

As to physical evil, why do we have plagues, tornadoes and earthquakes which are purely natural, and why does God allow humanly caused harm to others: whether small, such as the proverbial family starving because the father spends his earnings on alcoholic drink, or large, such as the attempted extinction of Jews by Hitler and the killing of 100,000,000 people in the twentieth century by the communisms of Russia, China, Cambodia, Yugoslavia and others. Again, theistic efforts at theodicy in one way or another suppose that natural perils to life and health on small or large scale are necessary parts of reality, aspects not subject to 'power', whether limited or unlimited.

F. R. Tennant, Anglican clergyman and Cambridge Professor, put it well:

> That painful events occur in the causal chain is a fact, but, that there could be a determinate... world of unalloyed comfort, yet adapted by its law-abidingness to the development of rationality and morality, is a proposition the burden of proving which must be allotted to the opponent of theism. One can only add that, so far as experience in this world enables us to judge, such proof seems impossible. To illustrate what is here meant: if water is to have the various properties in virtue of which it plays its beneficial part in the economy of the physical world and the life of mankind, it cannot at the same time lack its obnoxious capacity to drown us... There cannot be assigned to any substance an arbitrarily selected group of qualities from which all that ever may prove unfortunate to any sentient organism can be eliminated, especially if one organism's meat is to be another's poison.[40]

Tennant goes on to observe that the order of nature, the regularity of nature as part of the divine world plan, insures the conditions of life.

> Thus physical ills follow with the same necessity as physical goods from the determinate 'world plan' which secures that the world be a suitable stage for intelligent and ethical life.[41]

Like every attempt at a Christian theodicy ever proposed – from Irenaeus and Augustine onward – Tennant's essay is not unchallengeable. Already pagan ethical philosophers of late antiquity such as Seneca and Cicero attempted to justify the god of their incipient monotheism. But it probably is as good as any proposed. All are musings, reflections in effort to satisfy the demand of human minds for rational consistency. President Lincoln tried to think through to God's honour and righteousness in bringing the United States to a great Civil War, but like us all had simply to acknowledge without emperical proof, that (citing Psalm 19:9 KJV) David was right when he confessed, 'the judgments of the LORD are true, and righteous altogether.'

Protest Atheism and Barth's Theology.

As, however, Paul reminds us, 'yet for us there is one God... from whom are all things... However, not all possess this knowledge' (1 Cor. 8:6, 7). Paul was speaking of the lack of knowledge of *only* one God in an age of prevalent polytheism. The same lack of knowledge (or rejection of the same) in Enlightenment and now post-Enlightenment times takes the form of atheism (no-god-ism), the extreme opposite of polytheism (many-gods-ism).

The term atheism is not without ambiguities. Its meaning varies (1) according to how the one who uses it defines 'god', (2) whether deliberately adopted by someone as a name for his own theological view, or (3) as applied by opponents for some other view. In our case it is the second – how certain writers describe their own religious outlook. It is worth remembering that Socrates, a monotheist of sorts, was called an atheist by Athenians because his god was not one of their family of deities who lived up on Mt Olympus. The Christians among the heathen populace of Rome were called atheists for similar reasons.

Further, since Enlightenment times, in some religious writing there is dogmatic rejection of the 'theistic arguments' for the existence of God (i.e. in this narrow sense of theism). Some of these opponents of 'theism' are designated *critical* atheists. If there is a god, they say, you theists have not proved it so, these critical atheists say. These same thinkers and others from another epistemological slant simply distrust or deny the capacity of finite minds to say anything at all about an infinite God, if He exists, hence are distinguished as *sceptical atheists* or perhaps *agnostics*. Finally there are the *dogmatic atheists* who outrightly deny the existence of any being answering to the biblical Jewish or Christian God.

---

40. F. R. Tennant, *Philosophical Theology II* (Cambridge: Cambridge Univ. Press, 1930), pp. 197 – 205, as reprinted by G. L. Abernathy and T. A. Langford, *Philosophy of Religion* (New York: Macmillan, 1962), p. 441.
41. ibid.

In the eighteenth century several widely influential writers in the several languages of Europe were sceptical or dogmatic atheists in the sense that the God of the Bible does not exist. They lived in a time when inherited belief in God was shared by nearly 100 per cent of the population of Europe and America. David Hume (1711–76), for example, was the ultimate empiricist, insisting that all knowledge is based on sense experience. He was consistent therefore in asserting that given the universal absence of sensory experience of a god, and therefore also the incapacity of reason to inform us about a god, there can be no proof of God's existence. Miracles cannot certify any message or messenger of God because miracles never occur. In his best-known essay he summarized:

> There must, therefore, be a uniform experience against every miraculous act, otherwise the event would not merit that appellation. And as a uniform experience amounts to a proof, there is here a direct and full *proof*, from the nature of the fact, against the existence of any miracle.[42]

Hume concluded his *Essay* with this challenge:

> If we take in our hand any volume of divinity or school metaphysics let us ask, *Does it contain any abstract reasoning or number?* No. *Does it contain any experimental reasoning concerning matter of fact or existence?* No. Commit it then to the flames for it can contain nothing but sophistry and illusion.[43]

Hume relates to the subject of this Appendix primarily in that he consistently insisted that the presence of evil in the world absolutely forbids that theism could prove the existence of the same God more fully described in 'revealed religion'. He sought to demonstrate that, in want of sense experience of God, 'reason is impotent either to establish or falsify religious beliefs'. In *The Dialogues Concerning Natural Religion* he has one of his debaters say sarcastically: 'This world for aught (any man) knows, is very faulty and imperfect compared to a superior standard; and was only the first rude essay of some infant deity, who afterward abandoned it, ashamed of its lame performance.'[44]

In Hume's world there is no guiding Providence bringing history to happy consummation, much less working all things together for good for any particular lover of God. Also, sad to say, to venture however briefly into Hume's thought where empiricism reigns (all we know is via sensory experience) is to feel a profound sense of uneasiness. John Stuart Mill and Ludwig Feuerbach drew out some consequences less considerate of the tender feelings of theists in general and Christians in particular but hardly moved beyond Hume.

Ludwig Feuerbach (1804–77) 'saw himself as giving birth to a new religion of man'. He saw the Christian God as nothing more than 'projection of finite human attributes to an imagined transcendent being called God'. He rejected the speculative idealism of Hegel, his teacher. Reality is not the subjective idea in my head but is received through the organs of sense, especially sight. Reality is in the material objects of sense.

N. Waite Willis, Jr. relates this central fact of Feuerbach's philosophy of knowledge to our present purpose well.

> If objectivity of thought and truth are to be achieved, the objects of our thoughts must be primary, must control our knowledge of them. *Sensual experience must take precedence* [emphasis added]: thinking must follow sensation of the concrete object. 'In sensation,' Feuerbach declares, 'I am determined by objects. In thought I determine the object' [Feuerbach, *Preliminary Theses Concerning the Reform of Philosophy*, as cited by Willis, p. 29]. Therefore according to Feuerbach to arrive at truth… thought must give up control of its objects and allow to objects [of sensation only] their proper autonomy as independent subjects [Feuerbach, *Principles of the Philosophy of the Future*, Trans. Manfred Vogel, Indianapolis: Bobbs-Merrill Co., 1966, p. 54 as cited by Willis].[45]

In another lecture Feuerbach laid out the principle which later Barth took up as the structural 'omega point' of his *Dogmatics*:

> In thought, I am absolute subject… I am intolerant. In the activity of the senses, on the other hand I am liberal; I let the object be what I myself am – a subject, a real and self-actualizing being. Only sense and perception give me something as subject.[46]

On such principles Feuerbach determined that Christian theism, since it starts with thought not sensible objects, is nothing more than projection of what the theologian *sees* in himself and other people.

---

42. David Hume, *An Inquiry Concerning Human Understanding* (New York: C. H. Hendel, 1955), p. 120 as cited by J. C. Livingston, *Modern Christian Thought* (New York: Macmillan, 1971), p. 54.
43. ibid., p. 173.
44. G. L. Abernathy & T. A. Langford, *Philosophy of Religion: A Book of Readings* (New York: Macmillan, 1962), p. 141 note.
45. W. Waite Willis, Jr., *Theism, Atheism and The Doctrine of the Trinity* (Atlanta, GA: Scholars Press, 1987), p. 29.

If Barth is important to recent theology, Feuerbach, the idealists (Hegel and disciples) against whom he reacted, and the empiricists (Locke, Berkeley and especially Hume), whom he duplicated, are important for understanding Barth. Barth wrote the essay which serves as introduction to my thumb-worn (by my students) copy of the English translation of Feuerbach's *The Essence of Christianity*.

Barth's efforts to withdraw from the 'modernism' of his day seemed to be supported by Feuerbach's essay. He too rejected the god of the 'theism' of the nineteenth century, that of idealistic philosophers and their theological counterparts. He felt that by accepting the empirical epistemology of Feuerbach he could start theological construction with the concrete Jesus of Nazareth as God in the flesh. Jesus as God-man gave God concrete visibility. This in turn gave the New Testament reports of Jesus' life, death and resurrection great importance. All the literary production of Barth seems to be built on this approach to a system of theology. So the visible Jesus, and with Him as also Son of God and Second Person of the one triune God, become for the multi-volume *Church Dogmatics* the organizing structure and, by variegated lines of reasoning, the substance of all else.

The three Persons of the Godhead have served a few theologians as rubrics for arranging the topics of a theological system. Melchior Leydecker, professor of theology at Utrecht (b. 1679) and an ardent champion of the Reformed system and Hans L. Martensen, professor of theology at Copenhagen (1808–1884) and a somewhat mystical theologian, employed this arrangement. Barth not only makes a 'big deal' of putting the Trinity first in his order of treatment but as such carries his own construction of Trinitarian Christology throughout his system.

This God-as-Trinity meets individuals in an 'I-Thou confrontation' (also a Feuerbach notion) and these confrontations are revelation, personal events, from which theology is built. The Bible may be read as a somewhat factual report (if guided by sound critical procedures) of these confrontational revelatory events, hence of use for systematic theology.

But more: Feuerbach asserted that the presence of evil in the world, especially the extreme suffering of human beings, renders ridiculous the belief in a benevolent God of either theism or Scripture. Barth has deemed Feuerbach correct in this except that all three Persons of the immanent Trinity actually took human sufferings into themselves. Thus Barth thinks he captures Feuerbach's empiricism for Christian theology.

Twentieth-century Atheistic Pessimism.

At this point the reader should know that throughout the early and middle years of the twentieth century – especially after World War I – several forms of utterly pessimistic, atheistic philosophy gained great notice in intellectual circles. These entered university classrooms and the liberal seminaries as feasible outlooks on life. The 'beat generation' and the 'hippies' and other sad-faced subcultures of young people were only a few of the outrageous later outcomes.

The evils of the first half of the twentieth century seemed to highlight the perennial challenge pain and death make to the very existence of God on the one hand and to His benevolence and power on the other. A 'creation which includes such conditions is incomprehensible, but that there is a just God who would allow them to persist is a contradiction. For the sake of the human feeling for God, God must be rejected.'[47] This is the 'protest atheism' of F. W. Nietzsche (1844 – 1900) risen again in the writings of Ernst Block, Albert Camus and Max Horkheimer; of Karl Jaspers and Jean-Paul Sartre and the schools of existentialism they founded.

The niceties of thought in these authors and the volume of literature they generated among themselves and inspired in others is unimportant here. It is important to know that Barth's Christological and Trinitarian theology was developed in the atmosphere of the challenges of 'protest atheism' and that he thought he provided an adequate 'dialectical' (which means a 'yes' and a 'no') answer in his doctrine of Christ, Trinity, covenant and incarnation.

Karl Barth closed his treatment of the incarnation and what is usually called the *Work of Christ* in 1955,[48] thirty-five years after he wrote his essay on Feuerbach. He is still concerned there with failures of the God of theism and the enigma of sin and suffering in God's world. He acknowledges still that 'we have been speaking in riddles' and though 'Paradox cannot be our final word in relation to Jesus Christ' he must retain, to the glory of God, this obscurity because he thinks the New Testament does so.[49] The whole Trinity is in the man Jesus, 'the elect' man in whom also is the entire human race, elect in Him in what appears to this reader a 'covenant of salvation' (Barth does

---

46. ibid., p. 29.
47. ibid., p. 80.
48. Karl Barth, *Church Dogmatics, iv*, ed. G. W. Bromiley & T. F. Torrance (Edinburgh: T. & T. Clark, 1936), /2, p. xiii.
49. ibid., p. 348.

not claim to speak perspicuously). He comes as near to clarity as anywhere in a passage in this section where he explains to his own satisfaction that the ancient Patripassians just might have had it right.[50]

> For what is represented and reflected in the humiliation of God is the mercy of the Father in which He too is not merely exalted but lowly with His Son, allowing Himself to be so affected by the misery of the creature, of man, that to save it, endow it with eternal life, He does not count it too high a cost to give and send His Son, to elect Him to take our place as the Rejected, and therefore to abase Him. It is not at all the case that God has no part in the suffering of Jesus Christ even in His mode of being [Barth prefers this expression to hypostasis, or person] as Father. No, there is a *particula veri* [a particle of truth] in the teaching of the early Patripassians. This is that primarily it is God the Father who suffers in the offering and sending of His Son, in His abasement. The suffering is not His own, but the alien suffering of the creature, of man, which He takes to Himself in Him. But He does suffer it in the humiliation of His Son with a depth with which it never was or will be suffered by any man – apart from the One who is His Son. And He does it so in order that, having been born by Him in the offering and sending of His Son, it should not have to be suffered in this way by man. This fatherly fellow-suffering of God is the mystery, the basis, of the humiliation of His Son; the truth of that which takes place historically is His crucifixion.[51]

In this way the Father of neo-orthodoxy and the most dominant figure of left-of-centre Protestant theology of the twentieth century worked around simple acceptance of plain biblical facts. God planned a world in which He determined to permit the presence of moral evils and consequent physical evils. His reasons God has not seen fit to reveal. Faith is assured that God's reasons are sufficient and wise and good. Most Christian theologians have not thought it necessary to write twelve enormous volumes of theological literature to justify God in His decision, nor to torture Scripture as Barth does in the process of creating his system. Several recent theologians, Protestant and Roman Catholic, have modified or rejected classical theism in the direction of divine participation in all the suffering, affecting the origins and form of the theology of the very influential Karl Barth, whose twelve volumes of *Church Dogmatics* still seem to demand attention.[52]

---

50. In context Barth seeks to demonstrate the Holy Spirit also was involved in suffering.
51. ibid., /2, p. 357.
52. Thirty years ago I wrote an essay on the problem of evil which appeared in *Bibliotheca Sacra* ('The Nature and Origin of Evil') and later under the same title in *Vital Apologetic Issues*, ed., Roy Zuck (Grand Rapids: Kregel, 1995), pp. 10–18. Much of that essay is incorporated into this chapter.

23
God's Blessedness, or Impassibility

In a familiar passage wherein Paul speaks of how God 'gave them up to dishonourable passions' (Rom. 1:26) he prefaces the remark by referring to God 'the Creator, who is blessed forever' (Rom 1:25). There is an apparent contrast between people who have 'dishonourable passions' and the Creator, who as 'blessed', has no passion at all. 'In the New Testament *eulogētos* (blessed) is never used of men. It is exclusively doxological'.[1] When the ancient rabbis contemporary with the New Testament, and the people who emulated them, used this word for God (or its Hebrew-Aramaic equivalent) it was as '*Ersatz des Gottesnamens*' (substitute for God's name).[2]

Though throughout the Bible God is anthropopathically represented as hating, repenting, grieved, loving and similar, these terms were not (or should not be) understood literally any more than references to God's eyes, nostrils, wings, feathers, hands and the like.

God is 'blessed forever' (Rom. 1:25; 9:5), never before time began, nor since, in need of anything to be supremely 'happy'. He created the world sovereignly by will and word, but not out of any inner or outer necessity, nor swayed by emotion.

That there is something in God which is commensurable by analogy with human emotions (as we shall say more about) cannot be doubted. But it is not *per se* passion, pain, feeling in any ordinary sense.

At the present time, social and intellectual forces, both within and without orthodox theology, are very unfriendly to the consistently-held orthodox doctrine of the divine blessedness, or impassibility: hence this chapter, which is a condensation of my own research on the subject.

I. Definitions.

Impassibility comes into our language as translation of the Greek word *apatheia* in the writings of church Fathers, according to the Oxford English Dictionary. *Apatheia*, despite the obvious etymological connection with apathy and apathetic in modern English (Pelikan), started out as meaning 'the state of an *apathēs* (alpha privative, plus *pathos*) without *pathos* or suffering'.[3] Among the Greek Fathers *pathos* or passion was the right word for the

---

1. *TDNT*, ii, 764, sub *eulogetos*.
2. *Strack-Billerbeck, ii*, sub Mark 14:61, p. 51.
3. Liddell and Scott, *Lexicon*.

suffering of Christ, as it still is. So in theology, to be impassible means primarily to be incapable of suffering. Early theology affirmed that in heaven our resurrected bodies will be *apathēs* in this sense. The word came to be extended to mean incapable of emotion of any kind and beyond that, *apathēs* (impassible) in important theological discourse meant without sexual desire.[4] As applied to God, incapacity for any emotions sometimes is meant. We will return to this. The twelfth canon of the Second Council of Constantinople (AD 553, Fifth Ecumenical) seems to say that Christ on earth was impassible in the sense of 'longings (passions, presumably sexual) of the flesh'.[5]

In this chapter I am interested mainly in the question of whether or not the divine nature is capable of emotion, including, in a secondary way, the experience of suffering.

II. Impassibility in the Ancient Church.

There was no difference of opinion on this subject among orthodox theologians of the ancient church. Even Tertullian (c. 160–240), perhaps the most anti-philosophy theologian among important early writers, vehemently opposed the notion that God could suffer pain.

This appears prominently in the first line of Tertullian's five books *Against Marcion*. Arguing that since goodness is the most central attribute of God, this center never wavers for any cause. The *expression* of this goodness as it occurs in what God does in His creation varies. 'The differing expressions', says Tertullian 'are but the expressions of the one constitutive attribute of God – his unchanging and perfect goodness. Thus while God himself does not change... yet the mode of expressing his goodness changes in accordance with the change in the human situation and circumstance.'[6]

Reading of the Cappadocian Fathers (Gregory Nazianzus, Gregory of Nyssa and Basil the Great) in preparation for a paper on the post-Nicea apologetics of orthodoxy sparked my notice of uniform and vehement agreement of Christians on God's impassibility. A careful rereading of J. N. D. Kelly's *Early Christian Doctrines* confirms that all the Fathers, including even most heretics, strongly believed the divine Being is impassible.[7] Jaroslav Pelikan shows at length and in detail that belief in divine impassibility was firmly asserted by all the orthodox Fathers.[8]

This issue colored every aspect of efforts to clarify Christology at the first four ecumenical councils (Nicea 325, Constantinople 381, Ephesus 431, Chalcedon 451). Nobody orthodox denied impassibility and even the heterodox acknowledged it. They did not separate impassibility from divine simplicity (mentioned more frequently) but regarded it as a necessary aspect of simplicity. They did not cite Aristotle's unmoved mover, Plato's eternal forms or anything of the sort. Their arguments were based mainly on the usual biblical texts we still today cite to teach God's immutability.[9] Simplicity, that is, God is not composed of parts, was then as now, established logically. Anything composed of parts is the sum of the parts, each of course less than infinite. Any number of finite parts do not add up to infinity. Since God is infinite, as established by Scripture and demonstrated by reason, God is simple, not compound or complex. The three members of the Trinity each possess the Godhead fully. They are not three thirds: a trinity of God, not three gods.

At this point I want to anticipate charges that the early church Fathers corrupted a pure biblical doctrine of a loving, personal God through introduction of Greek speculative philosophy. Let us hear what they said about this charge.

Thomas Weinandy in concluding his chapter on 'The Patristic Doctrine of God' observes:

> What the Fathers brought to the philosophical conversation, a conversation that had been in progress for centuries was precisely the new data of the Christian faith – the revelation of the Hebrew and Christian scriptures. Whatever they said that was new was not due to their faithfulness to some philosophical innovators. They were theological innovators and their innovation was founded on the Bible.[10]

---

4. Gregory of Nyssa, *The Great Catechism*, chap. xxxv in *NPNF*, II, 5, pp. 502–504.
5. Henry Denzinger, *The Sources of Catholic Dogma*, trans. R. J. Deferrari (St. Louis: Herder & Herder, 1954), p. 224.
6. Thomas G. Weinandy, *Does God Suffer?* (Edinburgh: T & T Clark, 2000), p. 101
7. J. N. D. Kelly, *Early Christian Doctrines*, Revised ed. (New York: Harper Collins, 1978). See pages 84, 120, 122, 142, 143, 169, 291, 299, 372, 314, 317, 322, 325, 476, 488.
8. Jaroslav Pelikan, *The Christian Tradition, vol. I The Emergence of the Catholic Tradition (100 – 600)* (Chicago: Univ. of Chicago Press, 1971), pp. 52 – 55.
9. Ps. 102:27; Isa. 40:10; Mal. 3:6; James 1:17.
10. Thomas Weinandy, op. cit., p. 108.

A sophisticated Christian theology which employs formal logic, precise definitions and elegant literary techniques, as some of the ancient theologians did, does not constitute betrayal of the gospel treasure. The early theologians nevertheless had to defend their doctrine against detractors and opponents. Irenaeus, while insisting 'the faith' is 'one', yet explained that theological refinements were of value. In *Against Heresies* he says, 'Inasmuch as certain men have set the truth aside... by means of their craftily constructed plausibilities draw away minds of the inexperienced... I have felt constrained to compose the following treatise in order to expose their machinations'.[11] These 'certain men' are later named. Most of them were highly educated scholastics, wise in their own eyes, whom Irenaeus felt he had to meet, not entirely on their own ground, but in such a way as to provide his readers sufficient skill and knowledge to rescue themselves from these so called 'gnostics' – not a term of derision then, but more equivalent to our 'experts' or 'intelligensia'. His book is strewn with the language of these people. So to answer these errorists some skill (he does not call it philosophy) is helpful. They should not be allowed to get away with doctrinal murder, so to speak, just because they are cunning and eloquent.[12] More importantly, by such skill 'one may [more accurately than another] bring out the meaning of those things which have been spoken in parables, and accommodate them to the general scheme of the faith; and explain [with special clearness] the operation and dispensation of God connected with human salvation...'[13]

Christian theology was not 'as Harnak tried to maintain, the product of encounter between Gospel and Hellenism. It is not the Hellenisation of Christianity. It was not the fruit of speculation but sincere effort to use the techniques of the learning of the day to elaborate Christian truth.'[14]

Clement of Alexandria had to face opposition from those who opposed any employment of philosophical learning. He said they 'prefer to block their ears in order not to hear the sirens' and that Christians as a whole 'fear Greek philosophy as children fear ogres – they are frightened of being carried off by them. If our faith (I will not say our gnosis [knowledge]) is such that it is destroyed by force of argument, then let it be destroyed; for it will have been proved that we do not possess the truth.'[15]

Clement asserted that philosophic learning has many positive uses. He really means theology which employs the techniques of learning, which we would now call systematic theology.[16]

The climax of ancient consolidation of orthodoxy was in AD 451, at Chalcedon, the Fourth Ecumenical Council. Jaroslav Pelikan devotes several pages merely to summarize the impassibility doctrine as expressed in the Fathers before the Fourth Ecumenical Council.[17] Rather, since the climax of consolidation of orthodoxy came at Chalcedon 451, the Fourth Council, let me cite two learned Fathers whose views on impassibility coincided quite exactly and whose views were specifically endorsed and incorporated in the Definition and Canons of that Council. The letters of each were read at the Council and essentially adopted as the doctrine of the Council: hence passed into received orthodoxy of the church from that day to this.

Neither was present and neither expressly addressed the Council. Cyril's 'Dogmatic Letter' addressed the heresy of Nestorius and had been written to him twenty years earlier. The letter by Leo, Bishop of Rome *(The Tome of Leo)*, had been first addressed to Flavian, Bishop of Constantinople, two years before the Council. Both Epistles were read, weighed and vigourously endorsed at Chalcedon.

Cyril's letter had been first addressed directly to Nestorius just before the Third Council (Ephesus 431) because it was he who was deemed to be dividing the church through denial that Mary gave birth to incarnate deity. Cyril's Epistle to Nestorius was then read at the Third Council. It had a positive effect in winning that Council to the orthodoxy of 325 (Nicaea) and 381 (Constantinople). But shortly trouble arose from another quarter. Eutyches, an old archimandrite at Constantinople, promoted the doctrine 'not only that after his incarnation Christ had only one nature but also that the body of Christ is not of like substance with our own'.[18] This and other problems made a Fourth Council (Chalcedon 451) necessary.

---

11. *ANF*, I,1.
12. *ANF* I, x. 2, 3.
13. *ANF* I, x. 3. Above citations are all from *Antenicene Fathers*, I, pp. 315–331.
14. Jean Danielou, *Gospel Message and Hellenistic Culture: A History of Early Christian Doctrine Before the Council of Nicaea*, trans. J. A. Baker (Philadelphia: Westminster Press, 1973), p. 303.
15. Danielou, *op. cit.*, pp. 304, 305.
16. Danielou, *op. cit.*, pp. 306–322.
17. Pelikan, *op. cit.*, pp. 52–55.
18. J. H. Kurtz, *Church History I*, trans. John MacPherson (New York: Funk & Wagner, n.d.), p. 334.

So Cyril's letter was read again at the later Council.[19] Some revelant portions of Cyril's letter now follow:

> We say that he 'suffered and rose again'. We do not mean that God the Word suffered in his Deity... for the Deity is impassible because it is incorporeal. But the body which had become his own body suffered these things, and therefore he himself is said to have suffered them for us. The impassible [God] was in the body which suffered.[20]

The *Tome of Leo* was read by his representative. Hold in mind that the doctrinal problem being addressed was to define the incarnation of the Son of God. As Cyril's letter was intended to correct Nestorius, so Leo's *Tome* was to correct Eutyches. I cite several portions related to impassibility.

> While the distinctiveness of both natures was preserved, and both met in one Person... the inviolable [divine and impassible] was united to the passible, so that... the same 'Mediator'... might from the one element be capable of dying and also from the other be incapable [of dying].[21]

> The Lord of the universe allowed his infinite majesty to be overshadowed, and took upon him the form of a servant; the impassible God did not disdain to be passible Man, and the immortal to be subject to the laws of death.[22]

> To pass by many points – it does not belong to the same nature to weep with feelings of pity over a dead friend [Jesus over Lazarus] and, after the mass of stone had been removed from the grave where he had lain four days, by a voice of command to raise him up to life again.[23]

In the first excerpt passibility is said to be part of human nature but not of God's. In the second the same idea is enlarged in elegant language which says that God was impassible and immortal, hence incapable of suffering as of dying. In the third, as God the Son our Lord was 'incapable of feelings of pity', such as He expressed when He wept at Lazarus' tomb. 'Incapable of feelings of pity' means impassible in the sense of incapable of emotion.

At this climax in the doctrinal consolidation of Christian antiquity, the report of Session II goes on to say that 'after the reading of the foregoing epistle' the most reverend bishops cried out: 'This is the faith of the fathers, this is the faith of the Apostles... Piously and truly did Leo teach, so taught Cyril. Everlasting be the memory of Cyril... This is the true faith.'[24]

In all of Christian antiquity I was able to find only Origen (AD 185–254) among the learned, orthodox writers (later declared heterodox) who dissented from this view. In a book on early Christian doctrine, *Gods and the One God* by R. M. Grant, the author shows that Origen's early views promoted the Christian consensus that God is impassible but late in life, when of about sixty-nine years, he taught that God is passible. Grant comments, 'Apparently the threat of Patripassianism did not bother Origen, at least at this point.'[25]

[My pursuit of the subject of this chapter has not, of course, included reading even in translation of all of Origen's extant writings. Others have, among them Thomas Weinandy, cited frequently in this chapter. He contends that Origen, in an anthropopathic sense, meant that the transitive attributes (my term) of God set forth in Scripture mean to say God has steady unwavering love, hate, grief, etc. Yet, as a metaphysician trying to affirm absolutes, even Origen held God to be impassible. This is to say, 'Origen upholds both the impassibility of God and the passion of God. To say that god is impassible is to deny emotional (i.e. to speak with anthropopathism) changes of states with God. It is a negative way of upholding the absolute otherness of God and of His radical perfection'. [Thomas Weinandy, *Does God Suffer?* (Edinburgh: T. & T. Clark, 2000), p. 99]

III. Why the Patristic Consensus on God's Impassibility?

Enlightenment and liberal critics and historians blame the influence of Plato and other Greek philosophers, but I propose to the contrary a compelling reason in the fact that in Scripture God is most forcefully and grandly said to be supremely 'blessed'.

---

19. The article on Cyril in William Smith's six-volume *Greek and Roman Biography, Mythology and Geography*, vol 1, p. 918, right column, says Ephrem of Antioch speaks of a now lost treatise by Cyril on impassibility and another on suffering.
20. Henry S. Bettenson, *Documents of the Christian Church*, 2nd ed. (New York: Oxford Univ. Press, 1963), p. 67.
21. *NPNF, vol. 14*, p. 255.
22. ibid., p. 256.
23. ibid., p. 256.
24. ibid., p. 253.
25. R. M. Grant, *Gods and the One God* (Philadelphia: Westminster Press, 1986), pp. 91–93.

This occurs ten times in the New Testament, eight times employing *eulogētos*, used only of God in the New Testament. I cite two of these, Romans 1:25 and 9:5. The first refers to 'God... the creator, who is blessed [*eulogētos*] forever! Amen.' The second speaks of 'Christ who is God over all, blessed forever. Amen.'[26] The first two refer to Jehovah God, the others to the 'Father of the Lord Jesus Christ'. In Mark 14:61 the high priest is employing 'the Blessed' as a very old circumlocution for Jehovah and in 2 Corinthians 11:31, 'he *who is* blessed [*eulogētos*] forever' [emphasis added] is undoubtedly the familiar Septuagint rendering of Exodus 3:14 'I am *ho On*' (I Am The One Who Is). It seems to me relevant to the 'impassibility' of God that *eulogētos* means 'blessed', that it renders *baruk* (blessed) throughout the Septuagint and seems to refer to the joy of God in heaven and of those whom God has blessed there. In standard Christian theology and hymnody 'blessed' and 'blessedness' is the standard word for the joys of heaven, unmixed with pain or sorrow (Rev. 21:4).

Twice in the New Testament, the word *makarios* is used of God, both times by Paul (*viz*. 'the gospel of the blessed God', see 1 Tim. 1:11 and 6:15,16). It is a peroration of Paul: 'the blessed [*ho Makarios*] and only Sovereign, the King of kings and Lord of lords, who alone has immortality dwelling in unapproachable light.' In this passage Paul seems to exhaust the powers of the Greek language to proclaim what recent scholars (neo-orthodox, orthodox, Roman Catholic and even some evangelicals) phrase as 'the Wholly Other', still 'dwelling in unapproachable [uncreated] light' even as incarnate in Christ on the cross. I think *ho apathētos* (impassible) if it had then been in current use for precise theological statement, Paul might have put it in in apposition to *ho makarios*, the blessed.'.

Though I shall not here carry this argument further, the biblical evidence from *eulogētos* and *makarios* has impressed me that we need not give up the impassibility of God. God transcendent in heaven and immanent in all creation is supremely happy (a synonym of blessed), always has been so, and forever will be.

IV. Impassibility to the Reformation.

As an aspect of the simplicity of God, impassibility continued to be a seldom contested assumption of orthodox theology. It shall be sufficient for present purposes to cite the scholastic work of Anselm that evangicals love most to cite – *Cur Deus Homo* (Why the God-man). 'The doctrine of the atonement in Anselm of Canterbury was based on the axiom that the divine nature is impassible, and that it can in no sense be brought down from its loftiness or toil in what it wills to do.' I quote one of Anselm's responses in his dialogue with Boso in *Cur Deus Homo*:

> For without doubt we maintain that the divine nature is impassible – that it cannot at all be brought down from its exaltation... And we affirm that the Lord Jesus Christ is true God and true man – one person in two natures, and two natures in one person. Therefore when we state that God undergoes some lowliness or weakness, we understand this to be in accordance with the weakness of the human substance which he assumed, not in accordance with the sublimity of his impassible [divine] nature.[27]

V. Impassibility among the Reformers of the Sixteenth and Seventeenth Centuries.

It is frequently remarked that Martin Luther was unconcerned about consistency in doctrines. Neo-orthodox writers are pleased with his alleged paradoxes. And we must acknowledge that his kerygmatic theology (doctrinal preaching) was at certain points in tension with his dogmatics, if it is correct to use that word in its proper sense. At the close of Althaus's treatment of Luther's 'Two-nature Christology' he remarks that it was not 'unified within itself but displays contradictions'.[28] In one place Luther could say 'Christ on the cross did not feel his deity but suffered purely as a man'.[29] Yet he could also say that 'the deity of Christ, because of the incarnation and of its personal unity with the humanity, enters into the uttermost depths of its suffering. God suffers in Christ. However Luther did not teach patripassianism... He always regarded God's suffering as an incomprehensible mystery.'[30]

Calvin was more explicit about employing two manners of speaking about God. On the one hand he insisted that we must employ the *ad hominem*, metaphoric language of biblical revelation, and on the other hand we must employ some technical language in dogmatics because it is necessary to define truth and to expose heresy. In this

---

26. See also Mark 14:61; Luke 1:68; 2 Cor. 1:3; 11:31; Eph. 1:3; 1 Peter 1:3.
27. *Anselm of Canterbury, vol. iii*, ed. and trans. by J. Hopkins & H. Richardson (Toronto & New York: Edwin Mellen Press, 1976), pp. 58, 59.
28. Paul Althaus, *The Theology of Martin Luther*, trans. R. C. Schultz (Philadelphia: Fortress Press, 1966), p. 196.
29. ibid., p. 198.
30. ibid., p. 197.

I think Calvin had as great a debt to Hilary of Poitiers as to any other theologian. He does not quote Hilary but acknowledges admiration for him, especially Hilary's idea about how to interpret the Bible's way of communicating truth about God. I cite a sentence in comment on Psalm 110:3, 'I have begotten thee from the womb before the morning' (LXX). God's 'purpose is to educate the faculties of men up to the knowledge of the faith by clothing Divine verities in words descriptive of human circumstances'[31] and similarly through several paragraphs.

Calvin puts it this way: 'Let us then leave to God the knowledge of himself... But we shall be "leaving it to him" if we conceive him to be as he reveals himself to us, without inquiring about him elsewhere than from his word.'[32] Many times in his writings Calvin discourages all speculation about God's essence. Rather, says he, we should contemplate God in His works as guided by the Bible.[33] Yet that did not prevent Calvin from employing the somewhat speculative categories of the 'way of negation' ultimately derived from ancient 'enlightened' Greek speculations about Zeus or Theos conceived in a monotheistic manner (immutability, infinity and similar). Among these Calvin rather incidentally lets out his acceptance of the patristic consensus on divine impassibility. Once in comment on God's 'repentance' he says the description of the deity is 'accommodated to our capacity so that we may understand it. Now the mode of accommodation is for him to represent himself to us not as he is in himself, but as he seems to us. "Although he is beyond all disturbance of mind... whenever we hear that God is angered, we ought not to imagine any emotion [i.e. passion] in him, but rather to consider that this expression has been taken from our own human experience" [emphasis added].'[34] A sifting of the Institutes turned up several passages wherein Calvin accepts it as axiomatic that the divine nature in itself is impassible.

Impassibility was not in itself an important issue in the sixteenth century. However, it is clear that the patristic axiom was not rejected. Theologians continued to affirm the immanent attributes of God such as simplicity, immutability, infinity and the rest. In that context of *a priori* thought about God, impassibility really does not need to be mentioned, for it is a near necessary inference.

Quite early in the Reformation Era the Anglican Articles of 1553 (Art. #1) affirmed that, 'God is without bodily parts or passions.' This is usually understood to mean that in His incorporeal essence God has no passions, for He is forever 'blessed and only potentate', and so on. The first paragraph of the Augsburg Confession says that evangelical churches confess 'that the decree of the Nicene Synod concerning the unity of the divine essence... to wit, that there is one divine essence... eternal, incorporeal [*incorporeus*], without parts'. The word impassible is pointedly omitted, though the Nicene Creed as understood by the framers of it (AD 324, 381) unquestionably meant that too.[35] Charles P. Krauth, the greatest of Lutheran historians of *The Conservative* (Lutheran) *Reformation*, evidently thinks that the divine nature was impassible before incarnation but by virtue of communication of attributes (*Communicatio Idiomatum*) the divine nature became passible. So before the incarnation God was impassible but now is passible. He argues this at length.[36] If Krauth is right, then after the incarnation the divine nature – Father, Son and Holy Ghost – is passible.

The Roman Church, following the ancients, continued to affirm God the Father is 'invisible, incapable of suffering, immortal, incomprehensible, immutable'[37] though the Son incarnate was impassible, untroubled 'by the sufferings of the soul and the longings of the flesh' (cites Canon 12 of Second Council of Constantinople [Fifth Ecumenical]).[38]

VI. Among the Immediate Heirs of the Reformation (1600s, 1700s).

Through the scholastic period of Protestant theology I detect no variation from the patristic consensus. The Westminster Confession I, iv, approved by the Long Parliament 1647, says 'God... is... a most pure spirit, invisible, without body, parts, or passions'. I think that clearly says that God's 'infinite being' is 'without parts or passions' as in similar way theology of the day affirmed, though Buswell does not think so[39] and A. A. Hodge is obscure on the

---

31. *On the Trinity*, vi, 16 *NPNF, II*, 9, p. 103.
32. Calvin, *Institutes, I*, xiii, 21.
33. ibid., V, 6, 1.
34. ibid., V, 17. 13.
35. Lutherans, at least some of the time, think they should stick by strict biblical language more than Calvinists do.
36. Charles P. Krauth, *The Conversative Reformation and Its Theology* (Philadelphia: Lippincott, 1875), pp. 316-320.
37. Denzinger, *op. cit.*, Index 18, right column.
38. ibid., Index 8 f and #224, pp. 88, 89.
39. James O. Buswell, *A Systematic Theology of the Christian Religion, i* (Grand Rapids: Zondervan, 1971), pp. 56, 57.

matter.[40] Buswell seems to say that it means God has no body which has parts. I think it says God's *infinite being* has no body, no parts and no passions, and so agree all the usual readers of the confession.

For present purposes I shall quote only one further representative of the period, the most learned and voluminous of England's dissenting (Baptist) theologians, John Gill (1697–1771). His two great volumes (*A Body of Doctrinal Divinity*) are the very embodiment of a systematic theology bound to the Scriptures. Even present-day publishers of new editions of Gill's *Divinity* emphasize that his discussions are in the very language of Scripture. He wrote:

> ...for as it has been commonly said, 'Christ remained what he was, and assumed what he was not'; and what he assumed added nothing to his divine person; he was only manifest in the flesh; he neither received any perfection or inperfection, from the human nature; though that received dignity and honour by its union to him and was adorned with the gifts and graces of the Spirit without measure... Nor was any change made in the divine nature by the sufferings of Christ; the divine nature is impassible, and is one reason why Christ assumed the human nature, that he might be capable of suffering and dying... Yet he was crucified in the human nature only, and his blood was shed in that, to which the divine person gave virtue and efficacy, through its union to it; but received no change at all by this.[41]

If you have followed the progress of this chapter you will recognize this extract as a near republication of Cyril's *Epistle to Nestorius* and Leo's *Tome* at the Council of Chalcedon (AD 451).

Both Lutheran and Reformed theology went through a stage of 'scholastic fortification' of the early evangelical symbols and other Reformation formulas: to be followed by a rationalistic reaction in the 'Age of Reason'. In the scholastic period, speculative writing about the simplicity and immutability of God rendered Him not just immutable but almost immobile, hence of course impassible.[42]

VII. In the Late Protestant Era.

In Britain and America, the immutability of God came to be a matter of dispute between orthodox writers of Calvinistic persuasion and Wesleyan theologians. I suppose it was a spin-off from the debated question of free will. This is explained clearly in the article on 'Immutability' in the McClintock and Strong *Cyclopaedea* (IV, 20). This truly great work of the nineteenth century, though of Arminian-Wesleyan aegis, is always scrupulously fair.

The article first quotes the work of Stephen Charnock (1628–75), *On the Divine Attributes*, on immutability, a decidedly Calvinistic work. The excerpt was well chosen by the editors. Charnock is still in print and read today as he was when I was in seminary, and for about 300 years now. For Charnock, God is a 'Being, whom nothing from without can affect or alter... an eternal Being, who always has and always will go on in the same tenor of existence'. The word impassibility is not there, but the idea is clearly affirmed in other words.

Then the *Cyclopaedea* assigns equal space to Richard Watson (1781–1833), the classic interpreter of Wesley in theological terms and most eminent Wesleyan theologian (and perhaps still ought to be).[43] After gentle warning to take the Calvinists cautiously Watson (who always wrote in the style of educated English Calvinists) defends the view that God's immutability consists not in his essential nature or even adherence to his '*purposes*' (which in Arminian theology are subject to change) 'but in his never changing the *principles* of his administration'.[44] In favour of this Watson (whom I checked out at length in the two tattered volumes of his *Institutes* that I am privileged to own) writes at considerable length. I suppose this divergence prevails to the present. Interest in such matters has waned in modern Methodism, though not in some related evangelical Wesleyan groups.

VIII. The Impassibility of God in Recent and Contemporary Theology.

With the coming of the Age of Reason (the eighteenth century onward), theologians outside the stream of rather strict Augustinian orthodoxy (Calvinist and Roman Catholic) have veered sharply away from views of God which could entertain simplicity (no parts), and hence immutability and consequent impassibility. Orthodox Wesleyan

---

40. A. A. Hodge, *The Confession of Faith* (London: Banner of Truth Trust ed., 1964), pp. 48, 49.
41. John Gill, Complete *Body of Divinity*, vol. i (Grand Rapids: Baker Books, 1978), p. 54. 1767 is the original publishing date of *A Body of Doctrinal Divinity* quoted here.
42. J. A. Dorner, *History of Protestant Theology II* (Edinburgh: T. & T. Clark, 1871), pp. 120 ff.
43. Richard Watson, *Theological Institutes II* 29th ed., ed. J. McClintock (New York: Nelson & Phillips, 1850), p. 401.
44. ibid., p. 492.

Arminianism, early in the epoch, has already been noted. Philosophical-theological development (Schleiermacher and his emphasis on feeling, Kierkegaard and his anti-metaphysical subjectivism, and the like) began the mood that welcomed departure from classical theistic-Trinitarian assumptions. Then came Ludwig Feuerbach (1808–1872). In his books *The Essence of Religion* and *The Essence of Christianity*, Feuerbach made two points of interest to the present subject. In the *first place*, theological dogma is purely subjective in origin and crystallizes the inner aspirations, hopes and fears of people. Their inner yearnings create pictures of what they seek. The mental pictures are projected by creating gods which embody what they seek. In the *second place*, the pervasiveness of evil in the sense of human suffering proves that an omnipotent, holy and loving God does not exist. He is only the creation of religious people, by projection of what they desperately wish to be true. Feuerbach also had a socialist-political agenda to promote with his 'protest atheism'. He rightly discerned that the God of the Bible and Christian creeds could hardly be enlisted to support Feuerbach's political-social programme.

Then also came Adolph von Harnak (1851–1936). In his view Christian theology got off to a bad start by pollution with classical Greek ideas of God, derived mainly from Plato. His seven volumes of *History of Dogma* (1886–1890) trace what he thought was a true history of a false orthodox theology which 'jumped the track' of ethical religion in the first apologists of the second century and never got back. Christian theology until the rise of liberalism has been simple faith in a God of love taught and exemplified by Jesus, but transformed by the influence of Greek philosophy into cold-blooded dogma.

Several recent and contemporary figures including Karl Barth, John Macquarrie and Jürgen Moltmann, all theologically somewhere between historic orthodoxy and modern liberalism, have sought to answer the protest atheism of Feuerbach, the pure ethicism of Harnak, and liberalism in general by resort to a redefinition of our Lord's incarnation and the holy Trinity. By resort to a redefinition of Trinitarianism these authors have sought to rescue God from the charge of impassibility, which they equate to impassivity and immobility. Jürgen Moltmann, in a manner quite consistent with ancient Patripassianism, has opposed the historic orthodoxy. Recent Roman Catholic theology (not all of it orthodox in any historic sense) is on both sides of the issue.

They have influenced many in the same direction, some of them evangelicals. Among those who now rather thoroughly reject impassibility and regularly participate in programmes of the Evangelical Theological Society are Gordon Lewis and Millard Erickson. One of the founding members of ETS, J. O. Buswell rejected it also.

A rather dispassionate survey of the present situation will be found in Alister E. McGrath's *Christian Theology*.[45] McGrath, who seems to be writing for secular university classes, presents the matter rather clearly but characteristically, without making any commitment of his own. Perhaps it's the current British style, though if so there are exceptions.[46]

Process Theology, as a matter of principle, rejects the impassibility of God. Tracing their theology to the philosophy of Hartshorne and before him of Whitehead, they say that 'this concept derives from the Greeks'. Since the world is part of God's 'constitutive reality', the future of the world is not foreseen to God. Self-determining acts of free, worldly beings like human beings contribute to His being. Hence 'These three terms – unchangeable, passionless, and absolute – finally say the same thing, that the world contributes nothing to God and that God's influence upon the world is in no way conditioned by unforeseen, self-determining activities of us worldly beings. Process Theology denies the existence of this God.'

W. Waite Willis, Jr claims the Trinitarian theologies of K. Barth and J. Moltmann as his own and claims Karl Rahner also as a fellow traveller. He asserts that this theology answers the atheistic critics of Christianity of modern times, especially Feuerbach. The God of speculative theology, says Willis, is the one against whom 'protest atheism' succeeds. The Trinitarian God of the Bible has no problem of unexplained suffering. He's against it and suffers from it along with us and will continue to do so until in the consummation, God, we may suppose, becomes completely God. Is this a union of *krisis* theology with process theology and with liberation theology?[47] As related specifically to impassibility, I cite the following assertions of Willis regarding theodicy and the Trinity:

---

45. *Christian Theology, An Introduction*, p. 250–254.
46. Alister E. McGrath, *Christian Theology, An Introduction* 2nd ed. (Oxford: Blackwell Publ., 1997), pp. 248–54.
47. W. Waite Willis, Jr, *Theism, Atheism and The Doctrine of the Trinity: The Trinitarian Theologies of Karl Barth and Juergen Moltmann in Response to Protest Atheism* (Atlanta, GA: Scholars Press, 1987), pp. 106–107 and chapter vi 'The Exchaological Trinity'.

God... has become concrete and sensuous... [T]he Trinity comprehends the Christian God's concrete, sensuous, praxis on behalf of human suffering... God... joins the protest... against human suffering... works in suffering love and... will not be fully God while suffering persists... surrenders his impassibility.[48]

Conclusions and Proposals.

But we really cannot give up the doctrine of divine impassibility. Recent movement to demolish it takes away too much. I see no mightier than Cyril, Leo, Augustine, the three Cappadocians, Anselm, Aquinas, Calvin, Edwards, Gill and Shedd on the present scene or the future horizon. It may be that chucking the ancient faith in this regard is a concession to the *Zeitgeist*, particularly to the subjectivism at all levels in popular thought today.

When the language of biblical revelation speaks of a wide range of God's emotions it is speaking analogically. Perhaps Thomas Aquinas can help us.

Thomas pointed out that when an adjective (attribute) is ascribed to God, 'wise', for example, it must be understood to apply to God's very being (essence), an aspect of His indivisible simplicity. But when applied to mankind, 'wise' does not apply to our essence, for sometimes we are unwise. So there is analogy between God's 'wise' and mankind's 'wise', but only of *proportionality*. In an analogy of proportion, 'Two things are related by a direct proportion of degree, distance, or measure: e.g. 6 is in direct proportion to 3, of which it is the double... This analogy is called analogy of proportion.'[49] But when 'two objects are related one to the other by means of another and intermediary relation; for instance, 6 and 4 are analogous in this sense that 6 is the double of 3 as 4 is of 2, or [in mathematical procedure] 6:4::3:2... this kind of analogy is based on the proportion of properties; it is called analogy of proportionality.'[50] G.M. Sauvage cites Thomas' treatise, '*De veritate*' (Concerning Truth), not in either *Summa Theologica* or *Summa Contra Gentiles*. Thomas does not describe analogy of proportionality in the articles on analogy in the two *Summas* (*Theologica i, 13* and *Contra Gentiles i, 34*).

I think analogy is still the route to go, especially what Thomas Aquinas called the analogy of proportionality, or, as I prefer, of 'commensurability'. Because mankind is commensurable with the divine essence, God could become a member of our race, but never an ape, a camel, an insect or a fish.

Yet we cannot leave the matter there even today. Like us, the believers of old said, 'Jesus loves me, this I know, for the Bible tells me so', and 'the Father loves me too, or He would not have given his only begotten Son to save us from our sins'. The pastors of ancient times also read their Bibles – more than we, for they didn't have all the 'how to' courses in seminary to teach and to master! So they also knew of God's love for His people in every age, however explained.

Final Proposals.

To bring this matter to at least a tentative conclusion, it seems to me we must affirm that we know as much of God as He has seen fit to reveal. The way of negation (incomprehensibility, immutability and similar) in theology is a way of confessing this in part. The simplicity and immutability of God are, however, not merely speculation, Greek or otherwise. Sound Trinitarian teaching affirms not a tripartite God but one God – a God who has no parts at all. In the plurality of *personae, prosopa, hypostases*, persons is a plurality-in-unity that cannot quite fully be explained, but only affirmed and believed. Like Augustine we affirm, 'Certainly there are three... Yet when it is asked, what three, human language labors from great poverty of speech. We say "three persons", not that it may [rightly] so be said, but that we may not say nothing at all'.[51]

Similarly, it seems to me, to reject the impassibility of the Godhead is to dissipate the unity (simplicity and immutability) of God in accommodation to a modern understanding of what constitutes personality that is unknown to the people who gave us not only the doctrine but the terminology of a Trinitarian theology. The creeds do not teach three distinct centres of consciousness in the Godhead, as is popularly supposed. Where we say *person* the ancients said *soul*. They did not say there are three souls in the Godhead; but that seems to be what many mean by three persons.

---

48. ibid., pp. 105, 106.
49. G. M. Sauvage, 'Analogy' in *The Catholic Encyclopedia*, vol. I, p.449.
50. ibid.
51. *de Trinitate*, V, 9; see *Nicene and Post-Nicene Fathers*, Vol III, p. 92.
52. G. P. Fisher, *History of Christian Doctrine* (Edinburgh: T. & T. Clark, 1949, 2nd ed.), p. 406.

Jonathan Edwards rejected every notion of an indigent, insufficient or mutable God 'or any dependence of the creator on the creature for any part of His perfections or happiness'.[52] In such a case God did not plan, create and control a world with a man in it who would breed a fallen race so God could either be happy or unhappy. God did not need mankind either then or now in order to be 'God blessed forever'.

The anthropopathisms of the biblical revelations are all true on the basis of analogy. Analogy means similarity of some sort, but not equivalence; otherwise it is not analogy but definition. Ancient theologians figured out right away that God's 'repentance' is not an emotion of His being but a change of treatment of mankind or some other part of the creation. Their writings employ the very illustrations (sun's actions on clay or wax, and so on) that we use today. The analogy is a bit crippled but about the best 1,900 years of thinking has produced. As to God's love and all other emotions – fear, hate, jealousy and the like – we then must say that just as there is analogy between mankind's repentance and God's change of treating us so there is analogy between our emotions (or passibility) and something about God's treatment of us. We just have not found a good name for it – yet. There is no consistency in regarding God's hate, repentance and wrath as only analogically true while making out love and suffering to be non-analogical. We cannot, in my judgment, have it both ways, and this is what those theologians – evangelical or otherwise – are asking us to do in saying God is passible, that is, subject to emotions, either of suffering or its opposite. Prayer is only one aspect of worship which depends on the validity of analogy. In prayer we say, 'Our Father'. Yet father is a human word indicating a human function of begetting with a whole plethora of accompanying ideas. Some of this is like God. Some is not. It does not fit God perfectly at all, but whether in the prayer of a small child or the dying words of his grandmother, 'Father' is a right name for the God of revelation and the vocabulary of prayer.

Conclusion: Minding our Language and Mending it.

Though we affirm the limitations and values of analogical language, let us not read into God's being any human ideal having its origin in the spirit of the present world. The spirit of our epoch is not the Spirit of God, but the sullen mood of this present evil age. There may be something analogous to sexuality in God – the doctrine of the image of God may imply such – but no sexuality. So there is something in God by way of a certain analogy called love and/or hate, but no emotion.

I think we may greatly exaggerate correspondences of analogy in talk about God. There may be analogy of proportionality rather than of strict proportion, to employ the language of medieval, scholastic discourse. But the distinction between analogy of proportion and analogy of proportionality drawn from Thomas Aquinas is a subject for another day. Something about mankind is analogous to something in God. But that scarcely gives us leave to define God as simply a human being on infinite scale, as has been done in polytheism and some Christian writing. The other extreme is so to emphasize the immutability of the divine Being as to render Him immobile, not free even to answer our prayers. This was characteristic of some theology of the age of Protestant scholasticism.[53]

The language of technical theological discourse has its place, and that is what I am defending. I must, however, live and die with the language of revelation as expressed best in the perennial hymns. In this too God's lack of change of any kind, dare I say, impassibility, has a prominent place. A stanza from Henry F. Lyte's hymn lyric, *Abide With Me*, is a noble example:

> Swift to its close ebbs out life's little day;
> Earth's joys grow dim, its glories pass away;
> Change and decay in all around I see;
> O thou who changest not, abide with me.

---

53. Dorner, *op. cit.*, p. 142 ff.

PART 1
THEOLOGY PROPER
Introduction and Doctrine of God

PART 2
ANTHROPOLOGY
Man as Created

PART 3
HAMARTIOLOGY
Man as Sinner

PART 4
CHRISTOLOGY
Person and Work of Christ

PART 5
SOTERIOLOGY
Salvation Applied

PART 6
ECCLESIOLOGY
Church Local and Universal

PART 7
ESCHATOLOGY
Last Things, Personal and Universal

BIBLIOGRAPHY

SCRIPTURE INDEX

GENERAL INDEX

1
Introduction to Anthropology

Two appealing preliminaries tempt us away from direct engagement with the Scriptural doctrine of mankind. Neither can be fully avoided but attention to each must be limited. One is the abundant literature of the world, all of which in one way or another celebrates mankind's excellencies or failings; ecstasies and despairs; accomplishments and 'affairs' in prose, poetry, art and drama. But the 'world itself could not contain the books' (John 21:25) if that route were to engage major attention. A second temptation is to join battle with the 'rational-animal-nothing-more' view of mankind which permeates both the social life and intellectual atmosphere of our time.

These variegated areas are both interesting and of some importance to the study of our race. They should claim some attention in every offering in the liberal arts division of a university. For, a Christian doctrine of mankind ought to condition all our thoughts about the liberal arts we study and enjoy as well as about how we live. Our present duty, however, focuses primarily on *humanitas*, humanness in and of itself, and not in the various special creations, accomplishments and failures of the members of our race. It is our duty to release these topics to other venues.

A Major Topic of Theology.

As the study develops it will become clear *why* theological *anthropology* is a major consideration of most books of systematic theology. Why should it not be? There are members of our race on every page of the Bible: the story of our origin on the first page and of our destiny on the last with the story of our fall and redemption traced through all the pages in between.

Christian anthropology is not founded on empirical study of mankind in their physical and cultural variety. Christian, theological anthropology derives most of its biblical data from the accounts in Scripture (mainly the first two chapters) of the creation of *primal* mankind. These two chapters, together with the many interpretative statements elsewhere in the Bible, especially Psalm 8, constitute the major sources of our doctrine. John Murray's opening sentence in treatment of the doctrine of man declares: 'For our knowledge of man's origin we are mainly dependent upon the first two chapters of Genesis (cf. also Matt. 19:4, 5; Mark 10:6, 7; Luke 3:38; 1 Cor. 11:8, 9; 1 Tim. 2:13).'[1] The doctrine of sin, or mankind as they now are, fallen from their original state, is the next *locus* of theology, usually entitled hamartiology, or the doctrine of sin.

---

1. John Murray, *Collected Writings*, Selected Lectures in Systematic Theology, Vol. II (Edinburgh: Banner of Truth Trust, 1977) p. 3.

This introductory chapter addresses those first two chapters of Genesis, summarizing what we deem to be the most relevant information and stating some necessary inferences, some primarily historical, others theological and practical. In later chapters we return to relate the whole of scriptural information to the question of the Hebrew shepherd-poet: 'what is man that you are mindful of him, and the son of man that you care for him?' (Ps. 8:4).

The Lost Image of Mankind.

If a human being were a mere 'sac of water' with an interesting 'variety of chemicals reacting with one another therein,' as in some current materialistic philosophy, then a book on physics and chemistry might explain him sufficiently, though no such being, in my judgment, could possibly either write or read such a book. If he were also 'a fantastic piece of workmanship in bone, muscle, and nerve – a high point of evolution in the animal kingdom,' a biological approach might suffice. If he be only a 'busy hedonist' prowling for pleasure until jaded and exhausted he covers his disillusionment in the night of death, then something on psychology might help explain mankind. If, Gnostic, New-Age style mankind is a misplaced piece of divine mind, temporarily dislodged and longing for home back in the cosmic flux, then a dash of metaphysics is in order. (The quotes are from F. I. Collingwood.[2])

But, if mankind is as significant and magnificent as his aspirations (freedom, fulfillment, immortality) and ideals (goodness, beauty, truth) suggest, then the religious dimension must be brought to the Hebrew poet's question. Only the illogic of special interest, or of intellectual myopia, could lead one to accept any one of these partial views just suggested. Yet there are contemporary 'intellectuals' committed to each one of them.

There is nothing to inspire art, poetry and song in these current departures from belief in God and mankind's greatness as His special creation. It should be no surprise that increasing numbers of all social classes have taken up a style of life commensurate with their *Lost Image of Man*, the title of a book by Julian N. Hartt.[3]

The Specifically Revelant Texts.

As already observed, three portions of the Old Testament form the initial ground of biblical anthropology. They are Genesis 1:1–2:4a; Genesis 2:4b *ad fin*; and Psalm 8. Poe and Davis say of the origin of individuals, 'all people are made of clay by God (Job 4:19; 10:8-12; Isa. 29:16, 64:8; 45:9, 64:8; Lam. 4:2; Rom. 9:20, 23; 2 Cor. 4:7), yet the Bible just as steadfastly asserts that God made each person within each of his or her mother's womb (Job 10:18; Ps. 139:13-16; Isa. 44:2; Jer. 1:5).'[4] Many have noticed the three Scripture passages do not appear to be of exactly the same literary genre, or, if the same then with markedly individual features. One like the present writer, a professional theologian, scarcely dares express a view on the subject lest he alienate a major portion of the readership, for opinions are strong and often associated with deep emotions. Yet whether strict historical narrative, parable, pictorial summary or whatever, the apparent meanings and the plain inferences are the true ones. The part of the first passage (Gen. 1:1–2:4a) which bears directly on anthropology is contained in verses 26-29 of chapter 1.

The Question of Literary Genre.

A full discussion of the literary genus of Genesis 1 and 2 is too large a project for now. I have already argued for the presence of symbolical as opposed to strictly a historical-literal interpretation of every sentence. I shall get back to that, but at this point it must be said that whatever the genus (genre) or literary vehicle we decide the author of Genesis 1 and 2 employed, the weight of later biblical references requires the believing interpreter to insist on the basic historical nature of the narrative itself and factual referrents for every symbol. Authentic symbols represent *something* and in the Bible that something is true. Jesus treated the narrative of Genesis 1 to 3 as factual and founded a theology of marriage as it ought to be upon it (Matt. 19:3-8). Paul constructed his arguments regarding the ministry of women and the relation of the sexes squarely on the creation accounts not only as true but essentially historical (1 Tim. 2:9-15; Eph. 5:28-31). Isaiah's challenges to the encroaching idolatry of his day were based largely on the Genesis creation account (Isa. 40:21; 42:5; 45:18 *et al*). Jeremiah alludes to the story (Jer. 4:23) and many Psalms reflect not only awareness of the account but full acceptance of it – especially Psalm 33:6-8.

---

2. F. I. Collingwood, *Man's Physical and Spiritual Nature* (New York: Rinehart & Winston, 1963), p. 1.
3. Julian N. Hartt, *The Lost Image of Man* (Louisiana State University Press, 1963).
4. H. L. Poe and J. H. Davis, *Science and Faith: An Evangelical Dialogue* (Nashville, TN: Broadman & Holman, 2000), p. 131.

Ten Preliminary Propositions.

It will be convenient in this preliminary assessment to group teaching regarding mankind's original constitution and situation under seven propositions.

1. Man is the crown of God's creative art, the *piece de resistance*, and best in an ascending scale. Beginning with an inchoate 'heavens and the earth' the narrative proceeds through the ordering of earth for various living genera – of plants, aquatic life, birds, animals – and finally of mankind, male and female. The language moves from the inanimate through vegetable life and then increasingly complex forms of animal life to human beings. It is the honest prose of common people, direct and plain – not unscientific but pre-scientific and non-technical. That the ascending scale is intended to show mankind's superior excellence cannot seriously be doubted.

There is further basis in the dominion of mankind over all living creatures on earth proclaimed in Genesis 1:26. H. C. Leupold concludes a long discussion this way:

> Taking the verse as a whole, we cannot but notice that it sets forth a picture of a being that stands on a very high level... of singular nobility and endowed with phenomenal powers and attributes, not a type of being that by its brute imperfections is seen to be on the same level with the animal world, but a being that towers high above all other creatures, their king and their crown. [5]

2. Mankind is like God – or perhaps better, simply God's image – in a unique, but unspecified manner. This apparent grounding of his excellencies, privileges and duties will call for extensive elaboration in later chapters.

3. Mankind was created male and female, with no distinction being drawn between the degree to which each sex shares in the excellencies, privileges and duties involved; perhaps the two in *aggregate* rather than each *in toto* is 'in the image and likeness of God.' This also will be treated at length later.

4. Human beings have the privilege and duty of dominion over the rest of God's earthly creatures (Gen. 1:26). Already at this pristine state of revelatory history, mankind's rule over terrestrial creation is not a goal to be attained but an announced fact. People will fulfill the mandate whether aware of the 'command' or not. It is a part of human nature to do so as the progressive dominion of the race over surrounding nature, even under the misdirection caused by sin, demonstrates. It is worthy of note that the heavens are not included in the mandate, a matter of fact reflected in Psalm 115:16, 'The heavens are the LORD's heavens, but the earth he has given to the children of man.' This announcement is reaffirmed as well as explained and enlarged for postdiluvian mankind: 'The fear of you and the dread of you shall be upon every beast of the earth,' etc. (Gen. 9:1-3). Some exegetes call attention to the plural, 'let their,' and similar, suggesting that this authority was intended for all Adam's posterity, 'hence we infer that none of the conveniences and necessities of life might be wanting to men.'[6] Others note the high status of human beings here.

5. Related but added is the privilege and duty to subdue the earth. This may be presumed (in parallel with what has actually happened throughout history) to mean that we human beings are supposed to employ earth's resources (exploit is not too strong a word) for our own service. If, as an older commentator wrote, the former privilege, 'have dominion,' is 'the colonist's charter,' then 'subdue it' is the farmer's, the scientist's and the industrialist's charter. Contemporary environmentalist criticism of these provisions will be treated later.

6. Human beings have the duty to multiply their species by natural reproduction. It is apparent that though stated in what seems like an imperative mode, it is grammatically in Hebrew (as English) a declarative. It is our nature (as we sometimes as sinners have reason to regret) at a certain age to take conjugal action to reproduce our kind. There was first a single act of divine creation, producing an original male. Then out of the male the first female (Gen. 2). After that, procreation was to be the method of enlarging the numbers of our race. That this was to be only within monogamous marriage is later specified (Gen. 2:23-25; 4:1ff.). Given the full integrity of human nature before sin and consequent loss of the generations by death, the duty to 'replenish' (Heb. 'fill') the earth would have been accomplished after many generations by very small families. This is only an inference, but a necessary, interesting and important inference. Imagine fifty generations living contemporaneously! This also calls for later exploration.

7. A special point is made of the privilege of mankind to use the fruit of the earth (as do animals also Gen. 1:29, 30) for food. This privilege is not an aspect of *dominion* and *subduing* set forth earlier in Genesis 1, even though perhaps intended as enlargement. The ground from which the human body was taken is to furnish his bodily nourishment. This will appear again in chapter 2 of Genesis.

---

5. H. C. Leupold, *Exposition of Genesis* (Columbus, OH: The Wartburg Press, 1942), pp. 92, 93.
6. John Calvin, *Calvin's Commentaries, Genesis i* (Edinburgh: Calvin Translation Society, 1847).

8. Mankind has affinities with 'the earth,' the inanimate creation of the ninety-plus elements. God 'formed' us not by simple fiat, *ex nihilo*. Genesis 2:7 explains Genesis 1:26, 27. Hence Paul could say, we are 'from the earth, a man of dust' (1 Cor. 15:47). Though this affinity resulted in a return to dust in death after man became the sinner, his affinity with the natural world was necessary. From the beginning he gained sustenance from the fruits of the ground, walked on it, breathed its atmosphere. John Murray comments:

> There is congruity between man and his environment. And for this there is a necessity. If it were not so there would be a discrepancy between man and his habitat, between man and his task, in incompatibility that would have negated the verdict... 'very good.'[7]

9. Though by virtue of unique likeness to God, there is no personal, spiritual, rational correspondence with other earthly animate creatures, we have affinities with other living creatures (2:7, 19). They, like our first male parent, were formed from earthy substance: mankind 'of dust from the ground' (Gen 2:7); they from 'the earth.' They, like mankind, have animate life for which every person should have a care, hence 'Whoever is righteous has regard for the life of his beast' (Prov. 12:10; cf. Deut. 25:4; 1 Cor. 9:9; 1 Tim. 5:18).

10. Finally, it should appear that God had His highest purposes for mankind. His place as the crown and climax of creation as well as several of the privileges granted and duties imposed suggest that God intended earth to be an orderly and cultivated planet, and a 'developed' one (in the current social-economic sense). The story of Genesis 3 shows that mankind was made in God's image to have fellowship with Him in a happy situation within and without. Recent writers of Christian apologetics have turned mankind's eminence in the natural order into what they call 'the anthropic principle' – as evidence of intelligent design in the whole natural order.

If the revelation in Genesis 1 were all we knew of mankind, we would still possess much important and precious information – sufficient to encourage us to believe it is a marvelous thing to be born a member of the human race.

The Two Accounts.

In the next section of the Genesis account of creation a somewhat different literary mode is employed, as we shall see. Whether the second section begins at the end of Genesis 2:4 or in the midst of it is a matter of minor exegetical difficulty. There is an important tradition of exegesis (I think the correct one) which holds that the first part of Genesis 2:4 ('These are the generations of the heavens and the earth when they were created') is the end of the first account, a kind of colophon or signature. See for summary evidences G. P. Spurrell and P. J. Wiseman.[8] In this case, starting mid-verse for the second section, the section begins: 'in the day that the LORD God made the earth and the heavens. When no bush of the field was yet in the land,' etc.

Editors and translators are rightfully cautious about introducing new features of format in Bible Versions that affect interpretation. Topical headings are important always. Just where the first 'account' ends and the second begins is of great importance to interpretation here. The New International Version and the English Standard Version puts all of Genesis 2:4 in the account of Adam and Eve's creation. The New English Bible, with which I concur in this case, divides the verse in the midst, viz.: 'This is the story of the making of heaven and earth when they were created' ends the narrative which began at 1:1, 'In the beginning,' etc. Then NEB inserts the topical heading, 'The beginnings of history' and continues with the translation: 'When the LORD God made earth and heaven, there was neither shrub nor plant growing wild upon the earth... nor was there any man to till the ground.' Then after one short verse (6) comes the statement about the creation of mankind in verse 7, 'Then the LORD God formed a man,' etc. Commentators are divided.

Even if the second section now before us is given less of an independent relation to the first than this explanation suggests, the emphasis of the second section (Gen. 2:4b-25) is different in a supplemental sense, from Genesis 1. In chapter 1 mankind is culmination; in chapter 2 mankind is center.

Literal – Figurative – Factual.

Let us not rush to judgment as to how much of the Mosaic account of creation is literally intended and to what extent figurative. Meanwhile let us assume that historical facts are conveyed to us (as shall be defended later). Many uncontestable contrary realities place severe restraint on efforts to make these two chapters read like the historical accounts in Exodus or Samuel and Kings.

---

7. Murray, op. cit., pp. 6, 7.
8. G. P. Spurrell, *Notes on the Hebrew Text of the Book of Genesis* (Oxford: The Clarendon Press, 1887), pp. 20, 21. P. J. Wiseman, *New Discoveries in Babylonia About Genesis* (London: Marshall, Morgan & Scott, Ltd., 1946), pp. 45-47.

In the first place, the nature of the creative events is all supernatural, even in minor detail. Consider even the food eaten by Adam and Eve on the sixth day of creation. If grain, was it miraculously created? Or did it have a year's history as grain today. If it had a history, when? Similarly, no one knows the precise source of the barley loaves and Galilee fish miraculously supplied for the 5000 at the time of the famous miracle. Claims are made that they were all specially and instantaneously created de novo in the hands of Jesus. Yet no one can know for sure that such was the case. Or the bread and fish on the coals which the risen Christ fed seven astonished disciples (John 21:9). Did a fishmonger and an early-rising baker sell them to an unrecognized, risen Jesus? Who gathered the sticks for the early morning fire? Did Jesus 'create' the fire, the sticks, the fish, the bread ex nihilo? Anyone who says he knows is pretending.

Some advocates of 'creation science' and of young earth theories claim the bread had a created history of seed, germination, growth, ripening, harvest, milling and baking all compressed into a moment of creation. That certainly may be true, but though suggestive, hardly demonstrates the theories of 'creation science' regarding geological history. Neither can the theory be arbitrarily discounted.

I have no purpose either to encourage or discourage the efforts of advocates of recent creation and a 'young earth.' *The Genesis Flood*[9] has now been read widely for several decades. Subsequent volumes, such as *The Early Earth*, 1972 (by Whitcomb), continue to convince some. I suspect that contrary views by evangelical scholars that give the geologists free range to attempt a history of earth to beginnings billions of years ago have been equally persuasive. They have been less persuasive in making a case for remote antiquity of mankind. It seems to me the early earth advocates err for sure in only one respect – their regular disparagement of the integrity of the faith of evangelicals who disagree with them. This is evident throughout Whitcomb's books. The following is typical. Having asserted sudden creation with a 'superficial appearance of age,' John Whitcomb adds:

> Few doctrines of Scripture have met with such misrepresentation and ridicule as this, not only by secular writers but also by some who claim to be evangelical Christians.[10]

This is a put-down for such evangelical stalwarts as J. Oliver Buswell, author of extensive arguments for a great antiquity of human origins.[11] As for the requirements of Scripture, Buswell wrote: 'as for the antiquity of man on the earth, we must bluntly say that the Bible gives us no data on which to base any conclusion, or even any estimate.'[12]

Dr Whitcomb had all his seminary courses in Old Testament from me quite a few years ago. We have been friends – engaging in correspondence- – throughout the years. This is only the latest in my so far unsuccessful efforts to convince his sharp mind he cannot be absolutely sure he's right on this matter and ought not to make his view a test of the integrity of the faith or scholarship of others.

Secondly, the entire narrative of Genesis 1 and 2 was revealed to Moses (I know no better name for the author). Whether God spoke to Moses 'face to face, as a man speaks to his friend' (Exod. 33:11), or some other way, there is little likelihood that 'all the wisdom of the Egyptians' (Acts 7:22) educated Moses to the level he would have understood the technical data of creative events any more than, without an engineer's training, I will ever be able to understand the mysteries of a funny-looking box with typewriter keys and a video screen that sits in my study cabin. For example, it seems very likely (if less than absolutely certain) that in the momentous announcement of Genesis 1:1 and the record of the Flood 'the earth' (Heb. *ha'aretz*) meant anything more definite than the firm ground beneath Moses' feet as far as one can see and perhaps wherever it extended. Such ideas as 'sphere,' 'planet,' 'orbit,' 'circumference' and the like were still far in the future and no matter of concern to readers of the Pentateuch for many generations.

Stated otherwise, everything about the narrative must be interpreted first within the limits of the meanings of the words employed and in a manner compatible with the understanding of the first human author and his readers. Some of the questions addressed to the story today are not relevant to the text, because the text was addressed to different questions. In the section of this systematic theology treating God's work of creation,[13] I have argued that these chapters supply not one scintilla of proof for evolutionary origins. Nor can all the assertions about the 'young earth' of current 'creation science' be based strictly on the language of this chapter.

---

9. J. C. Whitcomb and H. M. Morris, *The Genesis Flood* (Philadelphia, PA: Presbyterian Reformed Publ., 1961).
10. John Whitcomb, *The Early Earth*, rev. ed. (Grand Rapids: Baker Books, 1972, 1986), p. 40.
11. James O. Buswell, Jr, Systematic Theology of the Christian Religion I (Grand Rapids: Zondervan, 1971), pp. 321-343.
12. Buswell, ibid., p. 325.
13. Part I, chaps. 17, 18.

In the third place, it seems utterly reasonable that if signs and symbols, unchronological parentheses and foreshortening of perspective are employed in Scripture to represent future eschatological events beyond strictly human ken, then the same would apply to the remote past beyond human ken. Creation was a supernatural event, by definition, inexplicable. It is a severe challenge for the super-literalist to interpret even the first three verses of Revelation 20 in strict, literal fashion. Keys we know are made of hard materials like iron and brass. Chains are likewise composed of many links and hooks. Does my hypothetical strict literalist think that the great evil spirit, 'that ancient serpent… the devil and Satan,' will be kept in restraint for a millennium by such means? So most convinced advocates of literal interpretation acknowledge, upon reflection, that many of the terms in this very important text have to be interpreted symbolically and that one really does not know the supernatural means by which Satan will be put under 'absolute restraint.' The theology of the passage is no less true if premillennialists are right and they are no less dependent on common-sense, figurative hermeneutics than the most ardent non-millennialist. One therefore should not hesitate in applying similar common sense to the situation in the early chapters of Genesis. In regard to mode of revelation, these chapters are not unlike the predictive sections of the Bible.

Let us therefore think of Genesis 1 and 2 as theological summaries rather than strictly chronological registers. Recent theology has rightly pointed out that the Mosaic account must be set against the contemporary polytheism, idolatry and animism in ancient culture – all shot through with an undefined but latent pantheism. Viewed as theology (orthodox and restrained), whatever else these chapters at the beginning of our Bible may be, as we have already observed from Genesis 1, a beautiful and utterly practical doctrine of mankind emerges.

The talk is in the language of appearances, not of science, or no one would have understood it for thousands of years. Think of Genesis 1 as a literary pyramidal structure with mankind at the pinnacle, and chapter 2 as a spiral of concentric circles with man, male, at the center, woman his mate being nearest.

The Supplementary Account.

The scene at the beginning of movement is an earth in whose field there is no 'bush of the field.' Thereupon, 'the LORD God formed the man of dust from the ground and breathed into his nostrils the breath of life, and the man became a living creature' (Gen. 2:7). Then God planted a garden, 'and there he put the man [male only] whom he had formed' (v. 8), with fruitbearing trees for food – all produced from the same ground out of which he had been taken. The man's task was to till the garden. Next God created useful beasts and birds (fish not being mentioned) which the man named but among whom there was found no companion for him (vv. 18-20). Lastly, out of the flesh and bone of the man God makes a woman, bone of his bone, flesh of his flesh, and presents her to the man who acknowledges her as his mate (vv. 21, 22). The author of Genesis indicates that this is the foundation of the human family in the monogamous union of man male and man female (v. 24). Thus man, male, is joined by female at last at the center with earth's animate members gathered about them to serve and help them.

The doctrine of mankind here gains very important truth, supplemental to the revelations of Genesis 1, regarding his original constitution, his duties and his privileges.

1. The creatures of earth are for mankind – for their use and pleasure. As just noted, the frame of the narrative (the circles with mankind at center) and the interpretive comments within Genesis chapter 2 (see vv. 18-20) clearly indicate this. While this element is not quite absent from Genesis 1 it does not receive emphasis there. The *Weltbild* of Genesis 2 is definitely anthropocentric.

2. Nevertheless, as God made him, man is also earthbound. He can never (space travelers not excepted) quite see the earth-system as a spectator. Mankind is 'of the earth, earthy' (1 Cor. 15:47 KJV). He is now always physically and emotionally a participant in the earthly scene however high he may think he rises above it and even though destined for heaven later. He is fit by original constitution for earth only – an earthling. The Bible makes few statements in these chapters which can be construed to describe the literal mechanical, physical connections of the various parts of God's creation, but as to scales of value and spheres of interest or importance to God's revelation, the Bible is clearly geocentric – earth-centered. And in the same respect, as just noted, the earth-system is anthropocentric. Thus Psalm 115 assures us that 'Our God is in the heavens' – that He alone is to be trusted rather than mere idols that are but human artifacts. As Maker of all that exists, 'The heavens are the LORD's heavens, but the earth he has given to the children of man' (Ps. 115:16). The race of mankind are earthlings. They are crown and center of

creation, but they belong here on earth. Exploration of the moon in a spacesuit tends only to render that more emphatic. To live elsewhere mankind must reproduce earth's conditions and take them along. Wherever they may travel, they will never cease to be earthlings. John Murray writes:

> There is congruity between man and his environment. And for this there is a necessity. If it were not so there would be discrepancy between man and his habitat, between man and his task, an incompatibility that would have negated the verdict: 'God saw everything that he had made, and behold, it was very good' (Gen. 1:31).[14]

3. Another emphasis of Genesis chapter 2 is that man's nature is in part on the level of other creatures and in part on the level of his Creator, i.e. some things he shares with all else formed from 'the earth' but others he alone shares with God who breathed something special into him. That is to say, man is only in certain respects a part of 'nature,' i.e. the world of determined things, ruled by what people call 'natural laws.' He is in other respects not a part of the natural order at all. This will, of course, be denied by the positivists and the naturalistic materialists. It is not the present purpose to defend the idea. We wish only to show that the Scriptures teach it.

This is the meaning of Genesis 2:7. Those interpreters (and they are legion) who see in the act of God in breathing into man's nostrils the breath of life (whereupon he became a 'living soul,' KJV) the creation of mankind's rational and spiritual faculties and his spirit (soul) are surely correct. This may be established not strictly on the meaning of the Hebrew words rendered 'breath... soul... life [living]' but upon the consistent teaching of the Scripture (taken on its own terms rather than the terms of the 'reconstructing critics') that man is a spiritual being, that while a person's spirit may die towards God, it is essentially indestructible. This indestructibility is not immortality, for by biblical definition alienation from God is death. Nor does 'essentially indestructible' mean that the spirit (soul) has existence then, now or ever apart from the continuing divine work of preservation. True, in the milieu of philosophical discourse one may speak properly of the 'immortality of the soul.' But then immortality simply means the same as durability or indestructibility. In biblical language God 'alone has immortality.' Genesis 2:7 in graphic pictorial language presents this truth of mankind's spiritual nature.

4. A fourth and very important emphasis is the organic vital unity of the human race. '[T]he LORD God caused a deep sleep to fall upon the man, and while he slept took one of his ribs and closed up its place with flesh. And the rib that the LORD God had taken from the man he made into a woman and brought her to the man. Then the man said, "This at last is bone of my bones and flesh of my flesh; she shall be called Woman, because she was taken out of Man' (Gen. 2:21-23). The narrative proceeds to trace the life of every human being back to this pair (Eve is called 'the mother of all living,' Gen. 3:20), as a comparison of Genesis 5:3-32 with 9:18, 19 shows. This unity provides the key to the possibility of redemption through the 'last Adam' (Rom. 5:12; 1 Cor. 15:45).

5. The first man, while as far as we know not highly informed, possessed great native intellectual ability such as enabled him to assess the quality of all the animals brought before him by the Creator and to give them names. In the later culture of the Bible, as well as in scientific nomenclature, names usually suggested something important about the one on whom they were conferred. Presumably that would be true of the case here in Genesis 2:19. We should not be surprised by reports later (Gen. 4) of the early, and possibly sudden, development of many of the chief aspects of culture with us today. There are no pre-humans or hominids in the Bible, only *Homo sapiens*.

Lutheran theology preserves a persistent tradition going back to Luther himself that Adam and Eve both had great scientific and philosophic knowledge that did not persist through the fall: 'man... had such a grasp of natural science such as unattainable today even by diligent study.'[15] This knowledge, according to John Theodore Mueller, Francis Pieper's summarizer, was 'intuitive knowledge of God's creatures (science) such as no scientist after the Fall has ever attained.'[16] Both Pieper and Mueller cite Luther. This carries a legitimate *apriorism* in epistemology a bit too far. Dorner, a great Lutheran scholar of the nineteenth century, while rejecting pure empiricism (all knowledge comes from sensory experience) asserted,

> The soul is never a mere *tabula rosa*... there is a world of the unconscious. If in our knowledge there is already inherent no innate relation to what is rational and good – a relation that is an original dowry of our nature and not our own work – then knowledge of truth and goodness is out of the question.[17]

---

14. Murray, op. cit., p. 6.
15. Francis Pieper, *Christian Dogmatics I* (St Louis: Concordia Publ., 1950), p. 517.
16. John T. Mueller, *Christian Dogmatics* (St Louis: Concordia Publ., 1955), p. 206.
17. J. A. Dorner, *History of Protestant Theology* (Edinburgh: T. & T. Clark, 1871), p. 82, as cited by Gordon Clark, *The Biblical Doctrine of Man* (Jefferson, MD: Trinity Foundation, 1984), p. 20.

A. H. Strong also strongly supported an *apriorism* in human knowing but rejected the extreme of Luther and some of his later disciples. He spoke of

> first truth... a knowledge which, though developed upon occasion of reflection, is not derived from observation and reflection – a knowledge on the contrary supposed, in order to make any observation or reflection possible.[18]

6. The joyful, relaxed relation of the sexes is given emphasis, as is their freedom from onerous restraints. They do not even wear clothing. In that connection it is announced that the procreation of children is to occur only within monogamous marriage. This is a distinct advance from Genesis chapter 1, where the command to multiply is without this condition. This should be acknowledged as evidence that even on the natural physical side of mankind's nature he is not at the level of the brute creation. That the passage (2:23-25) is intended to teach monogamy is decisively supported by Matthew 19:3-8. In this connection it is well to note the dignity of womanhood found in the passage. Many find here essential equality with the man hinted by the fact that she was taken not from the man's feet (to suggest inferiority), nor from his head (to suggest superiority), but from his side (suggesting equality).

7. A duty barely suggested in Genesis 1 (v. 28) is rendered explicit herein – the duty of labor. God 'put him in the garden of Eden to work it and keep it' (2:15). Many inferences may be drawn: mankind is *homo faciens*, toolmaker and user from the beginning. The ethic of work is not a 'Calvinist ethic' but a clear biblical teaching. Not only so, mankind the laborer, given the normal condition of non-sin, is fully capable of developing the arts – in the absence of abundant leisure time. Sad is the fact that a low level of moral attainment has all too frequently accompanied artistic excellence. Does this suggest why? In his excellent discussion of the creation ordinances John Murray has well stated the connection between manual labor and true high culture – a connection at present largely unnoticed. A few lines will impart a bit of the flavor of his remarks.

> There is warrant for the judgment that economics, culture, morality and piety have suffered grave havoc by failure to appreciate the nobility of manual labor. Multitudes of men and women, if they had thought in terms of this principle and had been taught in the home, in the church, and in the school to think in these terms, would have been saved from the catastrophe of economic, moral, and religious ruin because they would have been preserved from the vain ambition of pursuing vocations for which they were not equipped and which, on sober and enlightened reflection, they would not have sought. It is a fallacy to think, and it is one that has greatly impoverished the life of society that culture cannot exist and flourish among manual toilers.[19]

After the fall of man the duty of labor is made even more explicit (see later in this chapter). The New Testament treats voluntary idleness as sin serious enough to be rebuked with the kind of strong language often directed toward fornication, idolatry, drunkenness and other coarse sins. Said Paul, 'If anyone is not willing to work, let him not eat' (2 Thess. 3:10; cf. 6-10; 1 Tim. 5:8-16; 2 John 10, 11).

8. Without laboring the point, it seems to me that those who find a command for man to observe the Sabbath of God in connection with his work, here in Eden, are correct. Does Jesus' remark, 'The Sabbath was made for man' have reference to Exodus 20 or to Genesis chapter 2? See also Exodus 16:22-30 and Nehemiah 9:13, both of which indicate that the Sabbath long antedated the Mosaic ordinance.

The third great biblical passage treating the state of mankind at creation is Psalm 8. Actually the passage does not contemplate 'the fall' at all. It treats the Genesis revelation as though the facts about mankind's creation reported there, in the main, relate to postlapsarian quite as much as prelapsarian humanity. Such is indeed the case, in general. Yet adjustments had to be made, as we shall soon observe in later chapters. However, mankind remained mankind. Only such adjustments as sin made necessary were introduced.

Some Questions.

There are several questions about mankind's nature and original state that reflection on these revelations in the light of later biblical statements inevitably arouses. People want to know if man's nature was morally free or determined; if he was able not to sin or not able not to sin; if soul is the same as spirit in mankind, or if they are different; and if

---

18. A. H. Strong, *Systematic Theology* (Valley Forge, PA: Judson Press, 1907), pp. 52-56.
19. John Murray, *Principles of Conduct* (Grand Rapids: Eerdmans, 1957, 1971), p. 36.

the souls of human offspring are procreated by parents, as are their bodies, or if God creates the souls in some other manner and infuses them into the bodies, and, in either case, when? and how? A further question is: What constitutes 'the image of God' in which God created 'them' (i.e. the first pair)?

The significance, difficulty and importance of these questions is indicated by the size of the books theologians write, sometimes on only one of the above questions. An older work, Hurd's, *The Tripartite Nature of Man* for example, on the question of whether soul and spirit are the same, runs to nearly 400 pages. Volume one ('Human Nature') of Reinhold Niebuhr's *The Nature and Destiny of Man* runs to over 300 pages, while G. C. Berkouwer's *Man: The Image of God* runs to 375 pages. The anthropology sections of standard works of Systematic or Dogmatic Theology for over fifteen centuries (if we include Augustine's *Anti-Pelagian Writings*) have been about the most ponderous of all sections of those works.

These questions of interpretation must not obscure what ought to be plain as day: mankind's original state was one of happiness wherein personal and community fulfillment were possible. This is the *normal* state of mankind. It was sadly not to be a permanent state. As to why God allowed sin to enter we can speculate but our best answers fall short of certainty. This is true not only because God has not revealed why, but also because the reasoning powers of fallen people such as we, in such an area of investigation, are not fully to be trusted. It is too easy to let erroneous or sinful presuppositions get in the way.

Some Conclusions.

If human beings were today such as mankind then was, social organization could be completely effective for beauty, truth, happiness, fulfillment, freedom and all other possible goods. Such social organization would not need to be coercive, for people would respond joyfully to such organization without constraint. What we call coercive civil government or social 'control' would not exist. Not only is the man of paradise normal man, but he is essential man. That is to say, just to the degree that mankind is perverted, degraded or alienated from his original nature he is variant from *essential* humanity. The proverb 'To err is human' could not be further from reality. The truth is 'To err [i.e. to sin] is inhuman.'

None has ever seen this more plainly nor put it more vividly in words than Blaise Pascal, French mathematician, philosopher and Christian apologist (1623–1662). He wrote:

> The greatness of man is so evident that it is even proved by his wretchedness. For what in animals is called nature we call wretchedness in man; by which we recognize that, his nature now being like that of animals, he has fallen from a better nature which once was his. For who is unhappy at not being a king except a deposed king? ... Who is unhappy at having one mouth? And who is not unhappy at having only one eye? Probably no man ever ventured to mourn at not having three eyes. But anyone is inconsolable at having none.[20]

Few have been more precise in addressing this truth to the present world than Reinhold Niebuhr. Though not quite the sensation today that they were when he published them first in 1941, the words of his chapter 'Justitia Originalis' are still impressive:

> No man, however deeply involved in sin, is able to regard the misery of sin as normal. Some memory of a previous condition of blessedness seems to linger in his soul; some echo of the law which he has violated seems to resound in his conscience. Every effort to give the habits of sin the appearance of normality betrays something of the frenzy of an uneasy consience. The contrast between what man is truly and essentially and what he has become is apparent...[21]

Though Niebuhr's views of the 'previous condition of blessedness' take some liberty with the proper sense of Scripture, for he rejects out of hand the idea of a historical fall of man, he is right again when he writes:

> The reason why there is a heightened sense of sin in Christianity is that the vision of Christ heightens the contrast between what man is truly and what he has become; and destroys the prestige of normality which sinful forms of life periodically achieve in the world.[22]

---

20. Blaise Pascal, *Pensees (Meditations)*, para. 409.
21. Reinhold Niebuhr, *The Nature and Destiny of Man, A Christian Interpretation*, Vol. I (New York: Chas. Scribner's Sons, 1941, 1964), p. 265.
22. ibid., p. 266.

A man born blind and deaf would naturally suppose that all people, known to him only by the other three senses, were blind and deaf, except that he would have no concept of blindness or deafness. Sin, disorder and violence, manifest signs of human moral squalor, everywhere appear among the manifest signs of mankind's magnificence. Mankind viewed either as an individual person or as a society is magnificent – a magnificent ruin! Seen in full perspective he is more similar to the ruined Parthenon atop the Acropolis of Athens than the Washington monument or the Taj Mahal.

Excursus 1. The Gender Problem of 'Man' and Generic Pronouns.

I have deliberately waited till well into the discussion of theological anthropology to introduce the meaning of the word, 'anthropology,' and a problem related to it. The problem is 'inclusive language' or the so-called 'gender neutral' use of language being demanded of us, not only by feminists but by some editors and publishers in deference to the sensibilities of some prospective readers.

Anthropology is of course derived from a masculine gender noun, *anthropos*, man or mankind, used as a term for individuals *of either sex* or as a generic term for the human race, rarely with the feminine article, sometimes employed of a woman (with the masculine gender endings).[23] Greek has another term, *anēr*, which refers always to a human being of the male sex (a significant case in 1 Tim. 2:8).

German (to which our 'Anglisch' is related) has *Mensch*, used about as the Greek *anthropos* above. German also has our word 'man' (with two 'n's), man, male, husband, but in compounds sometimes refers to females too (*Mannbarkeit*, fem. gender, womanhood).

In English, except by borrowing the adjective *human* from Latin, and lately, turning it into a noun, we have only the word *man*, sometimes a generic name for the race of man, sometimes referring to an individual male, and in compounds such as man-child and manly; in other compounds generic, i.e. mankind – as in Tennyson, 'The parliament of man, the federation of the world' (Locksley Hall). In common speech as well as literature of all sorts, *man* has always been employed either to designate an adult male of our race or in a generic sense to designate the human race. He, his, him, ordinarily are understood as pronouns (stand-ins for nouns) whose antecedents are masculine gender or, generically, for either sex. Examples: 'When somebody gets sick *he* goes to a doctor.' 'When a criminal is about, we hope the police arrest *him*.' 'Somebody drove *his* car off the road here.' Some legal documents carefully point out that throughout, 'he, him, his, they, them' refer to either or both sexes. My thoughts coincide with Michael Novak's, viz.:

> That certain words have more than one sense, covering varying ranges of cases, is true of all languages and of the nature of language itself, if not indeed, the workings of the human mind. The Latin word *homo* may be used of a male alone (as in 'Ecce homo' [Behold the man]) or by contrast that includes *vir* (male [virility]), *mulier* (woman), *infans* (infant), *puer* (boy), and *puella* (girl). *Intelligent* people ought to be able to follow basic laws of language without artificial crutches, and to judge from context how broad a range of applications is intended, without turning linguistic somersaults.[24]

Hence we employ the doctrine of 'mankind' or 'man' interchangeably with 'anthropology' in deference to immemorial use but without intent to bruise the feelings of any who are sensitive about the matter. I think when 'the moon is old and stars are cold' the created nature of the world, including mankind, will then be as it has been for time out of mind in this regard – including generic pronouns he, him, his and the masculine gender of all nouns and pronouns referring to God. I note that technical and scientific discourse, including television, has remained pretty much unaffected by feminist sensitivities and agenda in regard to masculine generic nouns and pronouns.

I regret that the subject (*anthropology*) of this part of my book seems to have required this diversion. I hope that readers of different sensibilities who have read through the first chapter with some sense of pleasure and profit will not be now alienated by this forthright explanation.

It remains to be said about the word 'anthropology,' that the Greek term meaning 'the science of mankind in the widest sense' (*Oxford English Dictionary*) in philosophical and religious context, is at least as old as Aristotle (384–322 BC), ages before a branch of modern science co-opted the word.

---

23. Liddell and Scott, *Lexicon*.
24. Michael Novak, 'Women, Ordination, and Angels,' *First Things* magazine #32, April, 1993, p. 26.

Excursus 2. The Schema of the Doctrine of Primal Mankind.

No faithful, informed treatise on systematic theology ever becomes quite irrelevant or out of date. Insofar as authors relate Scripture truly to the study of theology and to the current human scene, they remain perennially pertinent to a Christian understanding of divine things and to life in this world where divine providence reigns. Human nature has not changed at all; God is ever immutable and 'the present evil world' as well as the natural order only go through many phases. I think, for example, in his prime, Julius Caesar or Marcus Aurelius or Niccolo Machiavelli would make himself at home in the political swirl of the Washington Beltway in a fortnight.

The ancient Christian anthropology of Augustine – really the first after Paul to put this theme together – was rightfully preoccupied with man's cognitive powers, his moral constitution and body-soul questions. In medieval times Thomas Aquinas anticipated later Christian anthropologies in treating the doctrine of mankind – after God and creation – and like Augustine in psychological emphases in his main topics (free choice of the will, and the like). These were topics reflective folk and the learned of his times talked and wrote about.

The anthropologies of Charles Hodge and Robert Dabney, both nineteenth-century Presbyterians, in addition to the usual attention to mankind's spiritual and moral constitution, lay emphasis on his probation and fall in relation to his covenant relation to God, while contemporary W.G.T. Shedd was concerned much about the race's physical and spiritual connection with the Adam in our probationary test in Eden. Shedd produced the most extensive (and I think decisive) advocacy of traducianism in the history of Christianity. All three were responding to the rising popularity of evolutionary theories. A. H. Strong's massive volume devotes unwonted large space to evolution, by way of accommodation to the spirit of the age, in a superb treatment of anthropology otherwise acceptable to historic British-American, Baptist Calvinism. Recently Charles Ryries' popular survey likewise devotes major space to evolution in connection with creation and anthropology, but by way of rebuttal. The positive doctrine of mankind is treated very briefly, almost summarily. Millard Erickson, to conclude with a contemporary, prominent Baptist writer, takes special care (perhaps with good reason) to relate his 'doctrine of humanity' (without endorsing feminism, he is accommodating toward feminist concerns and fights shy of the generic term *man*) to a theology of society, a consuming interest of the last half of the twentieth century. He devotes this last of his five chapters to the races, the sexes, the poor, the aged and the unmarried.

Each had his own good reasons. In my judgment, 'the present distress' calls for emphasis simply on the elements of a theological doctrine of mankind as directly derived from Scripture as possible, but in continuation of the Augustinian anthropology of the great Reformation theologians. This, I hope to show, is what the present world of intellectual discourse among Christians desperately needs. Psychological theories come into style and go out of style several times in each generation. Our anthropology should not therefore be couched in terms fully acceptable to ephemeral theories of psychology. The same can be said of social theories and current perceptions of the social order. The same must apply to our theories of church growth and Christian nurture. These too are part of the very unprecedented preoccupation of recent decades with human feelings and perceived needs. If the church is to recover its own character as the body of people where truth is sacred and Holy Scripture reigns supreme over our religious convictions – where Christ is LORD – then we must come to understand ourselves both as we are, might have been and by grace yet shall be. We must return to a primary concern with truth, that is, a doctrine of mankind as revealed by the LORD of truth and with a decent respect for the shape of anthropology as delivered to us by the Reformation theologians who paid great price for their convictions.

I intend to merge my hermeneutical 'horizon' with that of Moses as Anthony Thistleton[25] admonishes and I do acknowledge, as Professor Stanley Grenz proposes, that I am consciously constructing theology in this sensitive area for 'post-moderns' within the paradigm of plausibility supplied by my own conservative evangelical 'community of faith.'[26] How do we reach the ear and keep the steady attention of the post-moderns out there, as Stanley Grenz describes them? He has not provided a solution to the problem these post-moderns create for us who write theology, but I can't wait to learn. Maybe I already know. I will try.

A proper approach to a scriptural doctrine of mankind necessarily has two parts, based on the fact that we are not today *normal* in the best sense of that word. A fall from our primal, created condition took place at the beginning

---

25. Anthony Thistleton, *The Two Horizons* (Grand Rapids: Eerdmans, 1980).
26. Stanley Grenz, *Renewing the Center* (Grand Rapids: Baker, 2000).

of human history. To understand our present fallen condition we must understand what God has revealed of our former condition. Hence we must first consider man as created by God. This will entail attention to many facets of revelation, but they will all be subsumed under rubics which appear as chapter titles to follow.

2
The Origin and Unity of Mankind by Creation

In systematic theology, logically everything that *follows* anthropology grows like a many-branched tree *out of* anthropology. The views one takes of mankind's original constitution and primal history determine in a direct way views one takes of Christ, His work of redemption, the doctrine of salvation and even of final destiny (in heaven or hell). It is therefore important that we seek to understand the first part of the Bible about human origins in the light of how the rest of the Bible understands it. There is a unity of teaching. Stanley Grenz in a provocative book proposes that evangelical theology is more a mosaic of beliefs than a system of doctrines.[1] He may be correct, but he does not (nor does any competent theologian) say this is how Christian doctrines *should* be arranged. A preacher's beliefs may even resemble a *montage* or simply a *collection*. But if there is no system (logical order) he ought not to mount a pulpit. There is a matrix, and a growth out of it. A sound theology must look at all of it.

I. The Human Race Began in a Single First Man.

The Scriptures teach that the human race began in a single first man, male, who was brought into existence by creative acts of God.

No Pre-Adamites and No Non-Adamites.

That there was an original, single, first male is a revelation of the familiar narrative of Genesis. There were no pre-Adamite human predecessors. What puts this out of all question, with those who believe the divine revelation, is, that it is expressly said, that before Adam was formed, 'there was not a man to till the ground,' (Gen 2:5).[2] 'And the LORD God formed man of the dust of the ground, and breathed into his nostrils the breath of life; and man became a living soul' (Gen 2:7 KJV).[3] All we really know about the origin of mankind is furnished by the accounts of Genesis 1 and 2.

Every aspect of the New Testament doctrine of mankind as expressed by the LORD and the apostolic authors is plainly derived from the account of Genesis. Matthew 19:4 and Mark 10:6 ('God made them male and female') refer to Genesis 1:24 and 5:2. Mark 10:7, 'Therefore a man shall leave,' etc. directly quotes Genesis 2:24. When

---

1. Stanley J. Grenz, *Renewing the Center* (Grand Rapids: Baker Books, 2000).
2. John Gill, *Complete Body of Doctrinal and Practical Divinity I* (Grand Rapids: Baker Books, repr. 1978), p. 5.
3. Because discussion continues to move in the language of the King James Version, we will employ it fairly frequently in this chapter.

Paul wrote as his doctrine, 'Adam was made a living soul' (1 Cor. 15:45 KJV) he is employing the language of Genesis 2:7. His argument for the oneness of the race both in sin and reconciliation builds his case on the Genesis story of human origin (Rom. 5:12-19). He employs the same method in teaching the proper relations and functions of male and female in the Christian assembly (1 Cor. 11:9, 10; 1 Tim. 2:12-14).

This verse (Gen. 2:7) is not an enlargement, but a narrowing focus of the thought of Genesis 1:26, 27, upon the separate, single creation of the man, male, previous to the existence of the female. 'Then God said, "Let us make man in our image,"' etc., (v. 26) and 'So God created man in his own image' (v. 27). That in Genesis 1:26 the race as a unit was in God's mind ('Let us make man' etc.) is indicated by absence of the usual Hebrew article *ha* before *'adham* (man). That the race is indicated, not an individual, is borne out by the further statement 'male and female he created them.' *'Adham* is singular, 'man' not 'sons of men,' *bene 'adham* (a circumlocution for the plural, 2 Sam. 7:14). Mankind is an excellent translation. At Genesis 2:7 the word *'adham* ('the LORD God formed the man' bears the article *ha* prefixed, viz. *ha-'adham*. '[T]he man' (NIV, ESV) is grammatically correct, but the true sense is better conveyed by ' ...the LORD God formed *a* man' (NEB), i.e. a single specimen. A later section of this chapter will give attention to the significance for all *loci* of theology, of the fact there was a single human, male being before there was a pair, male and female.

Adam, Something New, Without Precedent.

We are still considering the proposition stated above: '...the human race began in a single first man, male, who was brought into existence by creative acts of God.' There is an extensive variety of verbs for God's 'creative' acts, viz.: 'Let us *make* man' (1:26); '*created*... created... created' (1:27); 'God *formed* a man' (2:7 NEB). 'Make,' 'created,' 'formed' – just what is indicated by these expressions? Each English word translates a different Hebrew word.

It must regretfully be acknowledged that most scholarly interpretation has paid scant attention to the Old Testament usage of these terms. A majority of orthodox writers acknowledge that 'made' and 'formed' allow the employment of existing materials and then make the claim that 'create' means to bring into existence without employment of existing materials. Hence Genesis 1:1, 'God created,' is said to mean God brought the world into existence *ex nihilo*, out of nothing. In the case of the creation of mankind, likewise some aspect (the soul) was created *ex nihilo*. It is true that logic and context require absolute beginning of 'the universe,' hence *ex nihilo* creation somewhere in a Christian doctrine of origins.

But such doctrine is not inherent in the meaning of the words used. It is true, as frequently observed, in the simplest verb *stem* (Kal) of the Hebrew, *bara'*, God is always the subject of the verb. This does not however imply *ex nihilo* either. It is *not* correct to say, as do many writers, 'the verb *bara'* [in the Kal]... signifies an effect for which no natural antecedent existed before, and which can be only the result of divine agency,'[4] for it is not supported by examination of the way the Hebrew Bible uses the word.

It is quite demonstrable that such qualifications as 'out of nothing' (*ex nihilo*), 'no natural antecedent,' 'immediate,' 'no pre-existing material' have no relation at all to the essential meaning of *bara'*, usually rendered, 'create.' This becomes evident in certain definitive occurrences wherein we learn what Moses and the Hebrews understood by *bara'*, 'he created.' Unlike other Hebrew words for doing, making, forming, of which there are several, when *bara'* is used the product is always something new. The product, not the materials employed, is new. When God creates something in the sense of *bara'* the product is fresh, new, unique, even unprecedented – something that has not happened before. Materials employed are irrelevant.

The clearest demonstration of this fact is in the story of Korah's rebellion of Numbers 16:1-50. The rebellion threatened the very existence of the covenant nation, especially the integrity of Moses and the Mosaic covenant. Decisive action was called for. At the critical moment (see vv. 1-30) 'Moses said... "If these men die as all men die, ...then the LORD has not sent me. But if the LORD *creates something new* [emphasis added], and the ground opens its mouth and swallows them up, ...and they go down alive into Sheol [grave?], then you shall know that these men have despised the LORD' (vv. 28-30). The sequel was immediate and exceeds in terror the laconic manner of reporting.

To further demonstrate this distinctive of *bara'*, observe the root word appears twice in series, viz.: 'creates' and 'something new.'[5] It appears here as an 'imperfect' form of the word, *bara'* Kal, masculine, singular following *'im*, 'if.' Then follows the noun feminine, singular, *beri'ah*, derived directly from *bara'*, and aptly rendered 'something new,'

---

4. A. H. Strong, *Systematic Theology* (Valley Forge, PA: Judson Press, 1907), p. 375.
5. 'Make' in the KJV is an exceptional translation. It is usually 'create.'

'something totally new' (NIV), 'an entirely new thing' (NASB). The Brown, Driver and Briggs *Lexicon* aptly supplies, 'unparalleled,' and tells us *Beri'ah* is a 'cognate accusative.' This is a characteristic Hebraic device whereby the verb gives its own meaning to its object or vice versa, as Luke 8:5, 'a *seeder* went out to sow *seed* his *seed* and as he *seeded*,' etc. (Gr.). Thomas McComiskey asserts, the root *bara'* has the basic meaning, 'to create.'[6] It seems clear the basic meaning is 'to bring into existence something new.' Newness is always present where *bara'* appears in the Hebrew text.

Never in earth's history had a chasm opened up to swallow alive a previously designated group of people. When it did God acted in the special sense of *bara'*. The event was then properly called a *beri'ah*, an unparalleled, unique, totally new thing. This distinct sense of *bara'* is present in every use in the simple (Kal) stem and is possible in other stems. See especially Jeremiah 31:22 (v. 21 Heb.) where *ḥadash*, new, is used with *bara'* in the exact sense of *beriah*: also Psalm 51:10 and Isaiah 65:17. In Exodus 34:10 the niphal (simple, passive stem) of *bara'* is rendered, 'I will do wonders *never before done* [emphasis added] in any nation in all the world' (NIV). '[N]ever before done' translates only one word, an inflected form of *bara'*. Again this shows how the idea of newness, something unprecedented, is inherent (i.e. not derived from the context) in the word.

Hence both in the case of mankind and of other instances where *bara'* is employed (Gen. 1:1, 21) God brought into existence something new, not seen before. If Latin is desired, then *de novo* is perhaps the right phrase, 'toward something new.'

Whether God, therefore, used materials previously brought into existence by Him or by simply speaking them into existence is not conveyed by the word *bara'*, create.

If the words for 'create' and other synonyms employed (make, form) do not require creation out of nothing, neither do they specify any other manner or means. For over a century now, a few evangelical theologians have conceded a possible evolutionary origin of mankind from lower animals. In my judgment, though seemingly necessary, the lopsided attention to evolution draws attention away from the strict silence of Scripture as to how God's power, wisdom and plan really worked. The Bible really says nothing about evolution or any other supposed manner or means, except at Genesis 2:7 where divine breath and dust of the ground are mentioned. The many later references in the Bible say little more.

Commenting on the sharp shift of narrative of the creation at Genesis 2:7, Allan MacRae, a quite strict 'fundamentalist,' wrote:

> Here God made something that was sharply *differentiated from anything that had existed before*. Patterns of similarity might have been used, but a distinct divine act is described, and *man becomes animate* only *after* he becomes man [emphasis added].[7]

We observe further that after the man is 'formed… of dust from the ground' (Gen. 2:7), the next time dust appears in the record is in the pronouncement, 'you are dust, and to dust you shall return' (Gen. 3:19) – dust, that is, of the grave, not of some beast ancestral to the first man.

Unnecessary Concessions to Evolutionism.

Roman Catholic concessions to the evolutionary-favorable atmosphere in both science and theology have been considerable, though cautious. Regarding human origin, Pius XII[8] declared the question of origin of the body, though not the soul, open to unrestricted research by scientists and theologians, but warned that the origin of the human body from organic (animal) material was unproved.[9] Ludwig Ott in his authoritative volume, *Fundamentals of Catholic Dogma*, says: 'According to the Bible Commission the literal historical sense is to be adhered to in regard to the formation of the first woman out of the man… 1 Cor. 11:8: "The woman is of the man." However, the saying is and remains mysterious.'[10]

If somehow we can order our minds so that Darwin and his disciples slip below the view of our mental and theological horizon, perhaps the profound simplicity of the doctrinal materials will make a proper impact.

---

6. Thomas McComiskey in *Theological Wordbook of the Old Testament*, ed. Harris, Archer and Waltke (Chicago: Moody Press, 1980), I, 127.
7. Allan MacRae, 'The Principles of Interpretation of Genesis 1 and 2', *Bulletin of the Evangelical Society, II*, 4, 1959, p. 5.
8. Encyclical *Humani generis*, 1950.
9. Denzinger, Henry, *The Sources of Catholic Dogma*, trans. R. J. Deferrari (St. Louis: Herder & Herder, 1954, 1957), paras. 3027 and 2286.
10. Ludwig Ott, *Fundamentals of Catholic Dogma* (Rockford, IL: TAN BOOKS, 1960, 1974), p. 95.

We have already observed that the critical word *bara'* is irrelevant to this matter. The context only *seems* to have the *earth* 'bring forth' bird and 'the waters bring forth' the denizens of the waters, presumably fish (Gen. 1:20, 24 KJV). The Hebrew text does not have the waters or the earth as such *producing* either fish or animals, and not birds of the air. The language only indicates that God said there should be swarms of life in the waters and that birds should fly over the earth. It is impossible to tease any material source for these living things out of the text. Once (v. 21) *bara'* is used of God's action in 'creating' whales, other water life and birds. True, on the sixth day 'God said, "Let the earth bring forth"', of the creations of larger land animals – Hebrew *totse'*, 'cause to come forth' (v. 24). This indicates a mediate creation. Appropriately they came from the earth and all return to it. Verse 25, however, traces the result to God's action not some dynamic of the earth: 'and God made... according to their kinds.' I have abbreviated H. C. Leupold's comments.[11] The meaning in each case has reference only to *what* God produced not *how* (method) or by what means. It is bad exegesis even to introduce such issues into interpretation of the text of the first chapter of Genesis.

Except for Genesis 2:7 nothing is said of what method or materials God did or did not use in creation of anything. For those whose minds crave some assurance at this point I make two suggestions. The first is that there is not a positive suggestion or hint in the early chapters of Genesis or elsewhere in the Bible that evolution of any sort had any part in the creation of the universe and the natural order. People already convinced of evolutionary origins have managed to adapt the Genesis narrative to their version of evolution, but not one ever derived his theory from the Bible.

Creation Language.

My second suggestion is that the narrative language can be interpreted, but not necessarily so, to support the immediate creation of mankind by God. It is said that since context and logic imply absolute beginning in *bara'*, 'create,' in Genesis 1:1 the same may be true when the same word ('Let us create,' etc.) is used of the origin of mankind (Gen. 1:26, 27). If so, only the soul was immediately created for at 2:7 God 'formed man of the dust of the ground' (KJV). The earth 'brought forth' the animals (1:24) in some unspecified way. The language of 2:7 suggests a more direct act of God, viz.: He 'formed man' (Heb. *yatsar*, used of what potters do with clay, many times in Jer. 18; used of divine shaping of the fetus in his mother's womb in Jer. 1:5; and twice used of a sculptor shaping an image in Hab. 2:18). The origin of the human soul, not only in the first man, but in all mankind, will soon be treated at length.

Let us seek to dissociate the question of evolution from other possible employment of means or material. The divine breath (2:7) is an obvious figure of speech. Whether a figure for creativity itself or of some imparting of divine nature or likeness cannot be settled apart from general doctrinal considerations. God certainly does not breathe air into nostrils in the manner of resuscitation procedures.

The 'Creation' of the Bible Over 1,500 Years.

It is easily (though not frequently occurring in the polemical atmosphere of inter-creationist controversy) demonstrated that means or materials are employed even when Scripture language seems to imply immediacy.

Let us start the demonstration with a familiar proof text of the divine origin of Holy Scripture, 2 Timothy 3:16, 'All scripture is given by inspiration of God' (KJV). This verse in the King James Version has given English-speaking Christian peoples the name 'inspiration' for the doctrine of Holy Scripture. It has become well known to students everywhere that the single Greek word, *theopneustos*, is here rendered 'given by inspiration of God,' five words, and that the literal rendering would be 'God-breathed-out' not 'God-breathed-into.' How do we know that? Quite apart from grammatical considerations, we know because Paul was employing a very prevalent biblical figure of speech for the divine activity of creating things. Human breath over vocal cords through throat, tongue, teeth and lips creates words of human speech. Thus the repeated, transparent 'God said,' 'Let there be,' etc. of Genesis 1 means simply 'God created.' God, of course, does not have physical organs to produce the vibrations of air we call speech. This figure for divine creativity is vigorously employed in the Psalms, viz.: 'By the word of the LORD the heavens were made, and by the breath of his mouth all their host.... For he spoke, and it came to be; he commanded, and it stood firm' (Ps. 33:6, 9). Hebrews 11:3 reflects these verses in the Psalms and in Genesis. This interpretation of the anthropomorphism of the divine speech or breath is based on uniform analogy of Scripture from Genesis 1:3 to Revelation 19:15.

---

11. Herbert C. Leupold, *Exposition of Genesis* (Columbus, OH: Wartburg Press, 1992), pp. 82–85.

So Paul says Scripture, like the universe, was spoken or breathed into existence by God. Yet (and here's the nub of the evidence) God used forty or so human authors who employed parchment or paper and ink, plus several secretaries whose names we know (Baruch, Tertius) to 'breathe'… 'speak'… 'command' 'all scripture' into existence, and required from about 1,400 years BC to AD 100 – roughly 1,500 years – to do so!

The Bible Does Not Affirm Either Mediate or Immediate Creation.

Hence if Bible language regarding the divine creation of Scripture by command, breath and speaking, when many years, human agents and material means were required, then when the same sort of language is used of creation of people and things it is illogical in the extreme to exclude the possibility of agents, materials and time. It may all have occurred by instantaneous events of coming into existence but the language of Scripture cannot be compelled to convey that meaning. These details are God's business. He has seen fit not to reveal a smidgen of information about it. Certain scientists may suppose a big bang origin of matter and certain Bible interpreters may suppose a similar big bang origin for everything created by God, but the language of Scripture, understood in the *Sitz im leben* of Bible times and peoples does not support them. The creation of mankind is, like the feeding of the 5,000, the parting of the Jordan and the widow's flour bin, a miracle. We know nothing for certain now about how God did it. It is unlikely either the 'creation scientists' or the scientism of the universities of today will ever tell us.

II. The Organic Unity of the Human Race.

The Scriptures teach the organic unity of the human race in an original, single, human, male specimen out of whom all others, including the first female, were formed.

The language of Genesis 1:26, 27 plainly indicates that 'man' includes not the 'male' only but also the 'female,' viz.: '*man* in our image… male and female he created *them*.' Throughout Genesis down to 4:1 the word *'adham* has the article (*ha'adham*), indicating either the male or mankind, not an individual *person's* name. Beginning at 4:25 the prefixed article *ha* (the) is dropped. *'Adham* (English Adam) is the proper name of the first male, human specimen. Hebrew proper names do not normally take the definite article, as the Greek language of the New Testament does. The distinction is not always plain, for the summary of previous race history at 5:1, 2 employs *'adham* without the article, perhaps because Adam's personal history was essentially the race history in creation and fall. His name is personal at 4:25.

The narrative of the forming of the first female, Eve, mate of the first man and 'mother' thereby 'of all living,' out of Adam's side is too familiar to require repetition here, though later it will call for special attention.

Whatever the female was, was completely derived from the male. A whole traducian event. As Paul says, 'For man did not come from [*ex*, out of] woman, but woman from man' (1 Cor. 11:8 NIV). Discussion of the origin of souls will soon occur herein, but at this point it must be emphasized the narrative drops no hint that God specially created a soul for Eve. Paul distinctly writes that the entire woman came out of the man. His subject at 1 Corinthians 11:8 is not precisely the organic unity of the race but that doctrine is certainly consistent with Paul's argument. Let us develop the subject further.

III. Organic Unity Before Forensic Unity.

The human race is an organic unity by natural generation from a single pair who in turn began in the single male from whom the female was taken.

1. This is firmly established not only by the narrative features of the first chapters (1:27,28; 2:7; 2:22) but also by two summary statements, viz.: before Adam was created, 'there was no man to work the ground' (2:5) and of Eve that 'she was the mother of all living' (3:20). These texts plainly trace the origin of every human being, including Eve herself, back to Adam. The line of physical descent from this pair, through their son, Seth, leads to Noah's three sons 'Shem, Ham, and Japheth… and from these the people of the whole earth were dispersed' (Gen. 9:18, 19). It is the clear intention of the author of Genesis to teach that the entire human race, without exception, is derived from the first man, Adam.

> Jesus did not comment on the unity of the human race but he did evidently accept the story of human origins in Genesis as true (Matt. 19:4-6) and related it to the subject of marriage. Paul developed several teachings on the basis of the unity of the race in a first man through a primal pair, male and female.[12]

---

12. John Murray, Collected Writings, *Selected Writings in Systematic Theology*, vol. II (Edinburgh: Banner of Truth Trust, 1977), pp. 10, 11.

2. The doctrine of universal prevalence of guilt, corruption and culpability of the human race, through Adam's first transgression, is built squarely upon the unity of the race in Adam. 'Therefore, just as sin came into the world through one man, and death through sin, and so death spread to all men because all sinned' (Rom. 5:12). Paul does not tell the story, but he assumes the readers are acquainted with it, refers to it, believes it and employs it. Sin and all its consequences were passed on from and through Adam to all his progeny throughout their generations. Adam was not merely archetypal man, he was *man*, the race, in a way that cannot be explained to Paul's satisfaction apart from the organic oneness of the race in Adam. If, as shall be treated later in connection with the doctrine of sin, we hold that Adam was the *representative* head of the race (C. A. Hodge and many Reformed theologians), then it is proper to remind ourselves that the seminal, organic connection of Adam with the race explains why God chose to regard him as our federal representative head. This also calls for extended treatment later.

3. Paul grounds the provision of salvation for all mankind in the unity of the human race, with which our LORD became united by incarnation: 'by the one man's obedience the many will be made righteous' (Rom. 5:19). The Epistle to Hebrews completes the connection: 'Since then the children have flesh and blood, he too shared in their humanity so that by his death he might destroy him who holds the power of death' (2:14 NIV) and 'he took on him the seed of Abraham' (2:16 KJV). This also must receive much fuller consideration.

4. Paul, like Isaiah and Jeremiah, employed the fact of the divine creation of mankind to refute the practice of idolatry, first among unlettered heathen (Acts 14:15-18) and later among the literate and sophisticated idolaters of Athens. He appealed both to the fact of divine creation (Acts 17:22-25, 28, 29) and, more pointedly, to the unity of all mankind in a single common ancestor, viz. 'From one man [*ex henos*, out of one; msc. sing.] he made every nation of men... Therefore... we should not think that the divine being is like... an image made by man's design and skill' (Acts 17:26, 29 NIV).

Races Within the Unity of Race.

This is an appropriate juncture to consider what guidance the Scriptures might supply to the fact of *races* of people ('Red and yellow, black and white/All are precious in His sight') and of the apparent 'natural' tendency of peoples and races to separate themselves into continents ('black Africa'); into regions, as eastern Asia (the so-called 'yellow' races); the white people in Europe and other rather definite regions; into nations (Arabia, Serbia, Armenia, etc.); and into communities, cities, clubs and churches, even racially distinct tables in college commons and benches in the park.

There is no general teaching in Scripture this writer knows of why people come in genetically perpetuated colors. The history of population growth and of culture, including religion, may help explain national and regional groupings (see Gen. 10), but they tell nothing of the origin of skin pigmentation and other 'racial' features. The Scriptures do provide doctrines, hints and inadvertent data which bear upon the question.

In about the year 1968 when race and civil rights were pressing issues I participated in a public forum on the subject of racial problems in America. I was expected to speak in summary of the bearing of Christian theology on the topic. What follows is a condensation of what I said.

1. The distribution of mankind into national groups and permanent people-associations is a matter of *special* divine providence. The ancient Song of Moses has this striking stanza,

> When the most High gave the nations their inheritance,
> When He separated the sons of man [or Adam],
> He set the boundaries of the peoples
> According to the numbering of the sons of Israel.
> For the LORD's portion is His people;
> Jacob is the allotment of His heritage (Deut. 32:8, 9 NASB).

Three technical matters require notice. 1) There is an obvious connection, intended by the author, between 'the sons of men' (whole human race) and 'the sons of Israel.' 2) There is no weighty evidence for the Septuagint and Qumran reading, 'the angels of God' instead of 'the sons of Israel.' 3) Verse 9 is intended to explain and enlarge verse 8, *viz.* 'For' or 'Because' (*ki*, Heb.) makes the connection. Hence the special providence for 'the sons of Israel' (God's elect nation) was because they were the LORD's 'portion' or 'inheritance' (v. 8, cf. Deut. 7:6; 10:15; Exod. 19:5).

In context (v. 7) this means all previous distribution of mankind ('the sons of man') from the earliest (Gen. 10) onward was directed by God for the benefit (in part, at least) of God's own special people ('portion' 'inheritance').

There must always be room for them. It is the 'land of Israel,' ''the holy land.' As we shall see, Paul explained these territorial arrangements as for the benefit also of all mankind – 'nations,' 'peoples,' 'sons of Adam.' This special divine concern for land-space for God's special people, of course, does not fit the present *zeitgeist* (spirit of the time) nor is it pleasing to the wise of this present world. It will not fly well either in the *Village Voice* or the *New York Times*, much less the U. S. Congress. Wherever the races of mankind dwell, God's providence was not absent in arranging it, whether by means of peaceful settlement, war or even unlawful infiltration. History goes on as history does and God is never surprised.

2. The providential movements of nations and races of mankind, including permanent settlements, are designed for their spiritual opportunity and possible salvation. Near the conclusion and application of his Areopagus sermon the great Apostle of the Gentiles made this point: 'From one man he [the God who made the world and rules it] made every nation of men, that they should inhabit the whole earth; and he determined the times set for them and the exact places where they should live. God did this so that men would seek him and perhaps reach out for him and find him' (Acts 17:24-28 NIV). The lands of earth provide sufficient for everyone to have enough to eat, wherewithal to be clothed and to dwell, not necessarily economic superfluity as people now demand, but enough advantage that if they pursue it they find God. Of course most of them do not. This is not the place to pursue the questions of natural light and general 'revelation.'

These two texts, Deuteronomy 32:8 and Acts 17:24-28, balance one another. The former states God's special concerns for the elect nation, the children of Israel (and as the New Testament elaborates the Old Testament types, His 'elect [are to be taken] from every nation'), the latter His love and concern for all mankind – this in regard to the races, nations and peoples of the whole earth.

3. Beyond these two principles, the Bible barely recognizes the existence of distinctly colored (pigmented) races of mankind. It is difficult to find a biblical Hebrew or Greek word which unambiguously designates any group of human beings by color of skin or any other physical feature, except greatness of size – there are *anakim* (giants) as well as *gibborim* (heroes). The one exception seems to be the *Cushite*, or Ethiopian, as we note in the following point.

4. There is only a trace of the presence of race antagonism (or prejudice) in Scripture. I know only of two references. The KJV very literally and accurately translates the relevant passages and is to be preferred.

'And Miriam and Aaron spake against Moses because of the Ethiopian [Heb. *Kushith,* i.e. Cushite] woman whom he had married' (Num. 12:1). The word itself is the word for Cush, in Moses' time a region above upper (southern) Egypt, with a feminine gentilic suffix, a woman of Cush. Unless this be an exception, Cushite *always* refers to people from Nubia, a region in the area of the Upper Nile River. Archaeological and documentary evidence is interpreted by some to mean Cushites were dark-skinned, *probably* Negroes, by others certainly black Africans (Negroes). My opinion rests partly on Jeremiah 13:23 (NIV): 'Can the Ethiopian [*kushi* = Cushite] change his skin or the leopard its spots? Neither can you do good who are accustomed to doing evil.' The translation is accurate. The implication is that changing (from black to white) would be something an Ethiopian might wish to do. Further, during the twenty-fifth dynasty of Egypt that land was ruled by Kushite (= Ethiopian) kings. The 'Tirhakah' king of Ethiopia (2 Kgs. 19:9) was one of them.[13] These conquerors, whom the Egyptians called Kushites, are represented sometimes in Egyptian art as black Africans. At an earlier time a schoolboy copied a royal inscription (the documentation is in J. A. Wilson, *The Culture of Ancient Egypt*) as follows: '…one prince is in Avaris [eastern delta, near Asia], another is in Ethiopia, and (here) I sit associated with an Asiatic and a Negro…'[14] Obviously the Ethiopian prince was a Negro.

So, despite many demurrals by writers who wish to escape the obvious, it seems clear that Miriam's and Aaron's displeasure with Moses' new wife was based on offense at her skin color! (Num 12:1). And some people of Jeremiah's time who were black wished they were white (Jer. 3:23). None of this approves of racial pride or prejudice. The first reference, however, as any one ought to know, shows that miscegenation may be a cause of family tensions and inter-alienation when it occurs. Those contemplating marriage outside their own 'race' will be wise to think about that. Miriam and Aaron were punished by God for their public rebellion, not for their feelings about their sister-in-law. In the aphorism of Jeremiah, perhaps we may conclude only that when surrounded by white people and a white man's culture, black people might wish they were white [not black]. Similarly, we may suppose a white man might profoundly wish he were black if surrounded only by black people.

13. Jack Finegan, *Light From the Ancient Past*, 2nd ed. (Princeton: Princeton Univ. Press, 1959), p. 127.
14. J. A. Wilson, *The Culture of Ancient Egypt* (Chicago: Univ. of Chicago Press, Phoenix Books, 1951, 1960), p. 164.

5. There are many restrictions against social intercourse, including marriage, between the ancient people of God and neighboring heathen people. It was the idolatry and immorality of the 'nations round about' that was objectionable, not their color or ancestry. There are many reasons for assuming that the Canaanites were not racially different from Israelites and we know from the records of Genesis that Ishmaelites, one of many Arab peoples, the Moabites and Amalekites (Gen. 19), also the Edomites, people of Esau, Jacob's twin, were not of a different race or shade of skin.

Further Aspects of Racial Unity.

6. The general tenor of the whole Bible is to emphasize that mankind is one, the human race. Cultural differences there were and are – all to the good. It was more interesting to travel before world commerce, cinema, TV and radio homogenized most outward aspects of cultures, or at least brushed over the surface of the world's cultures. Of whatever level of culture, race or education, people vary greatly in size, health, worldly goods and in many other ways, but on the deepest levels we are all the same.

We are one in many ways. Let us take note of some of them.

• In a common created human nature, both physical and psychical. Each branch of mankind is cross-fertile with every other. Given similar nurture in similar physical and social environment we develop much the same excellencies, display much the same weaknesses and tend to commit the same sins. There are prominent national traits (see Paul's comments on the Cretians, Titus 1:12) and special gifts and tendencies, but only within narrow limits.

• In guilt, corruption and punishment for original sin. 'Therefore, just as sin entered the world through one man, and death through sin, and in this way death came to all men, because all sinned' (Rom. 5:12 NIV), including even infants ('all sinned... even... those who did not sin by breaking a command,' Rom. 5:12, 14 NIV). Rich and poor, great and small, male and female, Greek philosopher or barbarian, all are 'under sin.'

• The work of Christ in life, Passion, death and resurrection has made eternal life applicable and available as far as sin has gone. In the language of Romans 5:18, 'so one act of righteousness leads to justification and life for all men.'

• The gospel of grace is for all people, without distinction, viz.: 'For everyone who calls on the name of the LORD will be saved' (Rom. 10:13).

• Finally, the body of Christ on earth and the 'assembly of the firstborn who are enrolled in heaven' (Heb. 12:23) will be composed ultimately 'from every tribe and language and people and nation' (Rev. 5:9).

3
Mankind the Image of God

Specific and Indirect Biblical References.

'Then God said, "Let us make man in our image, after our likeness.... So God created man in his own image, in the image of God he created him' (Gen. 1:26, 27). Everyone who has even begun to read the Bible knows about the doctrine of the divine image in mankind, for these redundant expressions (four times) meet the reader the first time human beings are mentioned. That is half the number in the entire Bible of sentences saying God made man in His image or likeness. The others are at Genesis 5:1; 9:6; 1 Corinthians 11:7; and James 3:9. In these seven verses mankind in the image of God is announced eight times. There are no other *direct* references to God's image in mankind in the Bible.

Language suggestive of the idea turns up in two New Testament verses (Col. 1:15 and Eph. 4:24) where Christ is said to be the perfect image of God. Similarly, three brief passages refer to the new, regenerate mankind as an *eikon* (image) of Christ, who in turn is understood to be the image of God (Rom. 8:29; 2 Cor. 3:18; Col. 1:10). These five texts clearly allude to the Genesis passages. Though these texts do not directly restate the doctrine they may be understood as amplifying the doctrine of mankind, the image of God. It is clear, therefore, that though a person's relation to God, to himself, to the created order and to other people is the very stuff of every page of the Bible even though Scripture does not directly employ the doctrine of the divine image as a framework of any subject of doctrine.

The Theological and Exegetical Tasks.

In our time the worlds of science, philosophy and public education labor mightily to relate mankind totally to the order of nature. The world of 'socially correct' discourse is as Abraham said of ancient Gerar: 'There is no fear of God at all in this place' (Gen. 20:11). Diane Sawyer on ABC television network omitted 'by their Creator' in citing the *Declaration of Independence* – 'all men are endowed by their creator,' etc. Perhaps in reaction some have been understandably tempted to outdo the scriptural dimensions of the biblical teaching that all mankind are the image of the Creator. Let us try to treat the doctrine in biblical, historical and traditional context meeting the challenges of unbelief as well as avoiding exaggerations of overzealous advocates of 'fulfillment' ideals among certain Christian psychological and sociological movements.

We want to know as precisely as possible what the Scripture phrases meant at the time they were written: 'in our image, after our likeness... in the image of God' (Gen. 1:26, 27). What do the later uses of similar phrases – 'in the likeness of God' – mean (Gen. 5:1; Col. 1:15; Eph. 4:24)? What is the connection of the divine image with the dominion of mankind over the animals and his commission to subdue the earth and to exploit it? Is God's creativity in Genesis 1:1-25 the original of which mankind's creativity is the image? How are image and likeness related? What precisely in each man and woman constitutes the image? Such questions are primary and must be addressed.

Most of these questions might not need to be raised if the Hebrew language were furnished with the fine set of precise terms for every sort of grammatical connection, which New Testament Greek and our own English language have. But Hebrew does not have them and Moses did not invent any such linguistic refinements. Obviously, the passages are as plain as God intended them to be, so eschewing the eager help of overly interpretive translations and paraphrases we do the best we can. I shall not attempt to take the reader through all the technical linguistic data and arguments, but will in a series of statements lay out the subject as clearly as I can make it.

1. Mankind was created 'in the *image*' of God. This is stated three times in Genesis 1:26 and 27. Though 'likeness' is also employed once here and again at Genesis 5:1, 'It is clear that the key term is *tselem*, image.'[1] What is a *tselem* or 'image' as understood in Old Testament times? It is derived from a root meaning to cut, as of a statue or chiseled likeness (1 Sam. 6:5, 11) in two or three dimensions as of heathen gods (Amos 5:26) or even of pictures (Ezek. 23:14).[2] A chiseled, three-dimensional statue is the primary sense, though a molded image also could be a *tselem* (Num. 33:52). Beginning my reading of the Bible at Genesis at age twelve it was natural to assume that God looked something like my father. That impression of course was spiked long before I reached John 4:24, but the Old Testament nevertheless several times gives us leave to believe that the divine Spirit sometimes may properly be *represented* as having form, even if He does not *have* a two or three-dimensional form (Dan. 7:9, 10; Rev. 4:2; 5:1, 8). Even though Israel heard the sound of words of God at Sinai and 'saw no form' of Him (Deut. 4:12), and Isaiah 40:18 denies any comparison or 'likeness' of Him, nevertheless Ezekiel says that he saw the 'likeness' (the same word as in Gen 1:27) of a man – 'a likeness with a human appearance [from the Hebrew word to see]' – in his vision of the heavenly throne and its occupant (Ezek. 1:26). He goes on to say he saw not a likeness of God, but 'likeness of the glory of the LORD' (Ezek. 1:28). *Something therefore about God or His glory may at least be represented to people as manlike in form.* Or one might say, when the LORD God of the Old Testament assumed a form (as in Ezekiel's visions and in theophanies) it was appropriate that the form should always be a human form.

2. The image or representation of God in mankind is similar to God in some unspecified manner, that is to say, the *tselem*, image of God, is more than a mere sign or symbol such as a national flag or representation, viz.: 'man in our image, *after our likeness*' (Gen. 1:26); 'he made him in the *likeness* of God' (Gen. 5:1). It has been asserted that 'image' (*tselem*) and 'likeness' (*demuth*) are simple Hebrew parallels or *hendiadys*, a grammatical term meaning *one through two*. In such a case the two words would express only one idea. This however is by no means certain, and the words are not strictly synonymous any more than 'instruction' (*musar*) and 'law' (*torah*) are, though they frequently appear in so-called synonymous parallel (Prov. 1:8).

In this case likeness (*demuth*) following image (*tselem*) certainly explains, enlarges, specifies *tselem* as an image that is not merely representative of God, but actually like Him. The flag of fifty stars and thirteen stripes only *represents* the U.S.A. but is not like the U.S.A. at all. A two-dimensional map, however, is somewhat like the country, a three-dimensional raised map even more so. Although both mainly represent, there is real similarity. From the whole Bible context of Genesis 1 we are assured that important, perhaps even structural, similarity is intended (see Gen. 9:6 and James 3:9).

3. We must consider whether mankind *is* the image of God, not merely *in* the image of God. Paul says 'man... is the image (*eikon*) and glory of God,' thus giving biblical legitimacy to the notion. There is also a possibility that Genesis 1:26 should be rendered, 'Let us make man *as* our image,' so also in verse 27.

There are three Hebrew prepositions called 'inseparable prepositions' – joined in *pre*-position directly to the following word. They are *b* (in, by, with), *k* (as, like, according to, a word of comparison) and *l* (to, for, at, frequently like 'to,' in English, a prefixed part of an infinitive as in 'to read,' and similar).

---

1. J. A. Clines, 'The Image of God in Man,' *Tyndale Bulletin*, 1967, p. 70.
2. Brown, Driver & Briggs, *Hebrew and English Lexicon of the Old Testament*.

Since Hebrew is exceedingly poor in logical connectives of all kinds, the Bible employs these three tiny words, plus *and*, another single consonant (our double U).[3] Translators know these four words fill in for many transitional and relational thoughts for which Hebrew has few strictly equivalent terms. A full listing, therefore, of the renderings of *b* (primarily meaning 'in,' as Greek '*en*' and Latin '*in*') in the several Versions and the renderings proposed by commentaries, would extend to several pages.

There is precedent in the Old Testament for rendering the *b* before *tselem*, '*as* the image.' The Brown, Driver and Briggs *Hebrew and English Lexicon of the Old Testament* finds about forty shades of meaning in five categories – demonstrating how poor Hebrew is in special transitional and relational connectives and conjunctions of distinct meanings. Among these is *b essentiae* of the grammarians. In such cases *as* is a proper translation. Among examples cited in *Gesenius' Hebrew Grammar* the most convincing are Isaiah 28:16, which might be rightly translated, 'I make Zion a foundation' and Ezekiel 20:41, 'As a pleasing aroma I will accept you.' In the latter case the grammatical structure is somewhat similar to '…make… in our image.'[4] J. A. Clines, in a well-documented article, has sought to show that *b* here is *b essentiae* (as the image).[5] I do not think Clines has *proved* his case, but he has made it not unreasonable to accept it. His summary statement says that

> mankind is created not *in* God's image… but *as* God's image, or rather *to be* God's image, that is to deputise in the created world for the transcendent God who remains outside the world order. That man is God's image means that he is the visible corporeal representative of the invisible, bodiless God; he is representative rather than representation..... However, the term 'likeness' is an assurance that man is an adequate and faithful representative of God on earth.[6]

Note that Clines says image means *representative*. He does not mean *representation*. If so, 'in the image' means mankind is God's vicegerent, minister-in-place-of on earth. I have written above that an image is sometimes a representation. As for example, the figure of a pine tree on a tourist map of America's Northwest represents the lumber industry. In the case of mankind, however, the representation (*tselem*) is truly similar (*demuth*) . This view is similar to Clines' but differs in that Clines then affirms that mankind's rule over earth is the central affirmation of God's *tselem* (image) in mankind. This remains to be proved. In my judgment, to render 'as the image of God' or to say 'mankind is the image of God' does not settle other related questions, though it has an important bearing on them, as we shall see. How much difference does it make whether one says John Jr. 'is spat *in* the image of his father,' as the proverbial saying has it (corrupted to 'the spittin' image of'), or 'Johnny is the image of John Sr.'?

Whatever the narrowest possible significance of God's making man *betselem* (in the image, or, perhaps, as the image) it has always been plain (*ubique, semper, ab ommnibus*) to believing Christians, lay or scholars, that man is different in kind, not mere degree from the rest of creation, that this difference consists in a likeness to God, and that competence to be and do what God commands flow from these facts. The question of Psalm 8, 'what is man?' does not refer specifically to the divine image, nor does it say or imply that in crowning him with 'glory and honor' as well as making him to have 'dominion' over God's other works the image consists of these. The thrust of Psalm 8 it not to indicate man's likeness to God, or to call attention to the image; rather it is to give worshipful expression to man's *essential* distance from and humble inferiority to Him, even though graciously exalted by God in several marvelous ways. This is the tenor of the whole Psalm. It exalts God, not man.

4. The *whole* of man, soul and body, is 'in the image of God' and 'according to his likeness,' or to quote James, 'after the similitude of God' (James 3:9 KJV), yet not every aspect or part of the human being in the same manner or to the same degree.

One of the early false starts in explaining the image of God in mankind was Augustine's effort to show how the pattern of his constitution is found in the Trinity. Calvin, who truly respected Augustine's insights, nevertheless said: 'Augustine, beyond all others, speculates with excessive refinement, for the purpose of fabricating a Trinity in man.' He goes on to acknowledge that Augustine, in accepting Aristotle's ennumeration of 'three faculties of the

---

3. Richard C. Steiner, 'Does the Biblical Hebrew Conjunction Have Meanings, One Meaning or No Meaning at All?' *Journal of Biblical Literature*, Summer of 2000, pp. 249–267.
4. A. E. Crowley, ed. 2nd English ed., *Gesenius'* Hebrew Grammar (Oxford: Clarendon Press, 1910, 1963), p. 119, para. 5.
5. Clines, op. cit., pp. 53–103.
6. Clines, op. cit., p. 101.

soul' – intellect, memory and will – might be right. He himself prefers the simpler 'two parts, which is more used in scripture.' [7]

The whole creation reveals God's glory and His attributes of wisdom and power. So it should not be thought improper to find in man's nature certain likenesses to deity, even though the likeness be only by some sort of analogy. Since God is Spirit and Scripture fiercely guards against any idea of physical form or feature in God, theology must be on guard against ancient errors of literal idolatry in efforts to 'explain' this mystery.

Among the dozens of theologians who comment on the question I have never found one who would say the human body is like (or an image of) God's body. Yet there seems to me full warrant to say that there is something about the human body which is analogus to something in the Godhead. In the process of time God took 'the form of a man,' including a man's body. It was appropriate that God should do so or there would have been no 'Lamb slain from the foundation of the world.' It is unthinkable that the permanent incarnation (enfleshment) of the Second Person of the Godhead should have been in 'the form of' a snail or even a lion or a sheep – both of which serve as metaphors ('Lion of the tribe of Judah,' and 'Behold, the Lamb of God'). Calvin might agree, though he argued from 'renewal' of the image 'through Christ,' citing Ephesians 4:24 and Colossians 3:10 that the image consisted in knowledge of God, 'true righteousness and holiness.'[8] Yet even he elsewhere makes remarks in agreement with what I have said above. Most Calvinist writers do not depart far from their master teacher. Even Gordon Clark, who restricts the image to mankind's rational faculties might acknowledge that human bodies are more 'commensurable' to the form of God (Phil. 2:6) than the bodies of four-footed beasts and creeping things.[9]

Perhaps, some say, this is the form (Gr. *morphē*) Paul had in mind when he wrote of the pre-existent Christ; He existed *en morphē theou* (Phil. 2:6). Though *morphē*, form, almost always indicates outward appearance or shape in the *koinē* (common spoken and written Greek of New Testament times) literature, theologians have insisted that here it refers to the dignity and prerogatives of deity, and not a structure (1), since God as pure Spirit has no 'form' in the ordinary sense and (2) in context the 'form of God' is contrasted with 'the form [*morphē*] of a slave' (*doulos*) not the form of a man (*anthrōpos*). Yet in context God the Son becomes (*ginomai*) in 'the likeness of' generic mankind (*anthrōpos*). Though reminiscent of Genesis 1:26, 'after our likeness,' this expression, so far from indicating, in context, only similarity, means 'in every respect he was a man.' So, whatever the analogy, mankind's physical form is not like any physical 'form' in God.

It is important that the superlative 'very good' was pronounced upon the created world only after mankind was created (Gen. 1:31). The supreme goodness and beauty in the mind and Person of the Creator when He created mankind are mirrored (a word often used by theologians in this connection) in the human body. I am certain brides and grooms through the ages would all agree that the human body, male and female, is the highest of earthly beauties. Romantic verse, crude or elegant, supports the allegation.

Whether or not the Mosaic level (Genesis) of revelation conceived of human nature as composed of body and soul may be moot. It is certain from later texts that God knew about this distinction. In such a case, if (as agreed) the non-material aspects of mankind (call it soul or spirit) are in God's image it is fitting that the house (body) should also be in God's image, granted that it is more difficult to conceive. We should be on cautious notice that throughout the Bible the soul is frequently put for the individual – whether animal or human.

In forming the body of man from material creation, which already bears the impress of God's power and glory (Ps. 19:1, 2), God went a step further. The language of Genesis 2:7 requires a special house for whatever was uniquely conveyed by the very breath of God.

Some recent theology likes to carry this line of reasoning a step further, finding the divine image in the distinction of male and female and in their conjugal relation. The texts of Scripture nowhere say so. It may well be that even though not aspects of the image, the image makes possible unique physical, psychical, emotional, and social beauties and benefits to mankind through the distinction of male and female. Sex differences are basic to the distinct psychical and emotional (perhaps also intellectual) inclinations and powers manifest in men on the one hand and in women on the other. I shall not in the present charged atmosphere pursue that thought very far. Of course there are mother-like as well as father-like qualities in God (even Moses called himself a 'nursing father'). The very form of

---

7. Calvin, *Commentary on Genesis I*, Edinburgh: Translation Society, p. 93.
8. Calvin, *Institutes I*.15.4.
9. Gordon Clark, *The Biblical Doctrine of Man* (Jefferson, Maryland: The Trinity Foundation, 2nd ed., 1992), pp. 14–19.

embrace in sexual coition appears to be a part of the plan of God to make deep spiritual community a part of the physical act. Is this why *only* fornication is said in Scripture to be a sin against the body (1 Cor. 6:18)?

Dietrich Bonhoeffer, evidently taking a cue from the 'male and female' shortly following 'in his own image' (Gen. 1:27), declared therefore, 'Man duality – man and woman – is brought into the world of the fixed and the living in his likeness to God,' and 'The likeness, of man to God, is not *analogia entis* [analogy of being] but *analogia relationis* [analogy of relation].' Though Bonhoeffer drew some nice thoughts about social relations and God-man connections this is not one of his better ideas.[10]

Karl Barth promoted a similar notion of the image being relational, connecting 'Let us' with various dualities (soul-body) in the human constitution as well as the male-female and man-fellowman. He never, in many pages, gets around to summarizing the notion.[11] Wolfhart Pannenberg comments on this theology and the connection of 'male and female' with 'Let us' and 'in his own image': 'It allows us to conclude that both man and woman are created equally in the divine image but not that the likeness consists of the relation between the sexes.' He rightly rejects flat out Barth's notion that 'the sexual relation corresponds to the trinitarian relation.'[12]

Of course the truth of John 4:24, 'God is a spirit,' and of the numberless warnings of the Old Testament against any thought of a material substance in God, whether visible or invisible, prevent us from considering that the physical aspect of mankind is the image of a physical aspect of God. It is apparent that while the human body, *per se*, is in no respect an image of the God of the Bible, all of man's physical nature was originally created to bear that image. This may seem to be an excessively fine distinction, but it is a necessary one.

Some theologians see a humanity of God suggested by the prevalent anthropomorphism of the Old Testament. Yet this road does not lead far, because God in the metaphorical language of the Bible has wings and feathers too, as well as hands and arms. The profusion of anthropomorphism in Scripture yields no evidence for a divine image in the human body, for there is 'zoomorphism' as well. God is not like a beast.

The Bible says nothing specifically to the effect that the divine image resides only in our 'higher powers' – spirit, intelligence and the like. Yet this also must be said: there are two aspects of man's nature – as will be shown in a later chapter – soul/spirit and body. This is suggested by the creation event as described in Genesis 2:7. Like the beasts, mankind's body is from the earth. That which distinguishes him from beasts is not derived from earth but from the creative 'breath of God.' The earthy side of mankind is visible. Our outward, physical likeness to beasts (though superior in many ways) may indeed in some way mirror something about God as well as our spirit and personality. The implication has been stated well by Norman Shepherd:

> However as man's kinship with the earth is most clearly visible in the body, so the image of God is best seen when man is viewed from the perspective of his spirituality. Theologians [the present writer among them] have sought at this point to enumerate those aspects of man's spirituality that define his humanity and set him apart from the animal creation.... It is the personality of man which separates him from the animals and is a reflection of the personality of God. The animals have their existence *from* God, but man has his being *in* God, and is his offspring, Acts 17:28, 29.[13]

This outlook is not out of step with Aquinas, who held the image to be present in the human body as 'traces' and with Calvin who asserts in a summary, 'although the primary seat of the divine image was in the mind and heart, or in the soul and its powers, yet there was not part of man, not even the body itself, in which some sparks did not glow.'[14]

5. Being a creature in God's own image means people are distinct from animals in an *absolute* manner, notwithstanding our having, as animals also do, a physical body. The Bible furnishes no ground whatsoever for any *genetic* connection between the 'lower' species (animals) and the 'higher,' mankind. Mankind is the crown of creation but not of evolution as far as Scripture is concerned. Genesis 2:7 states simply and clearly, 'man became a living being' (NIV, NEB), not the other way around. Whatever may be said for possible mediate creation of mankind, this verse cannot be stretched to say any living creature or 'soul' became a 'man.' Hence, 'The Bible does not

---

10. Dietrich Bonhoeffer, *Creation and Fall* (New York: Macmillan, 1959), pp. 36–38.
11. Karl Barth, *Church Dogmatics III* ed. G. W. Bromiley & T. F. Torrance (Edinburgh: T. and T. Clark, 1936, 1975), pp. 1. 190 ff. and II. 323, 324.
12. Wolfhart Pannenberg, *Systematic Theology II*, trans. G. W. Bromiley (Grand Rapids: Eerdmans, 1994), pp. 205, 206.
13. Norman Shepherd, 'Image of God' in *Baker Encyclopedia of the Bible* (Grand Rapids: Zondervan, 1988), p. 1018, col. 1.
14. John Calvin, Institutes I, 15. 3.

countenance the view that a previously living creature developed into a man, nor... that the image of God evolved from a lower form of life. The moment man became a living creature, he was in the image of God.'[15]

Those who understand that the Bible is what it claims to be in all its parts, including a Mosaic Pentateuch, the very opposite of an animal ancestry is how they understand the record. Yet there have been exceptions – i.e. advocates of 'mediate' creation of mankind, the 'dust of the ground' (Gen 2:7) being understood as animate dust. It is apparent, for example, that A. H. Strong, premier Baptist theologian of the past 125 years, very reluctantly adopted theistic evolution.[16] He sought to harmonize this view of mankind's origin with the dominant Darwinism of his day. Yet, no one ever labored more earnestly to show the utter contrast between animal nature and human nature than he. He restricted the possible evolutionary origin of man to the body alone, summarizing:

> The radical differences between man's soul and the principle of intelligence in lower animals, especially man's possession of self consciousness, general ideas, the moral sense, and the power of self-determination, show that that which chiefly constitutes him man could not have been derived, by any natural process of development, from inferior creatures. We are compelled, then, to believe that God's 'breathing into man's nostrils the breath of life' (Gen. 2:7), though it was a mediate creation as presupposing existing material in the shape of animal forms, was yet an immediate creation in the sense that only a divine reinforcement of the process of life turned the animal into man. In other words, man came not *from* the brute, but *through* the brute, etc.[17]

Strong then goes on to argue so strenuously against any *natural* evolutionary origin even of animals apart from the immediate and imminent power of God that one wonders truly *if* and *how* he ever even tentatively adopted an evolutionary origin of any living form in the first place.[18] It is, of course, of a piece with his doctrine of the imminent Logos, which he adopted in late career and never succeeded quite in merging into his previously composed, thoroughly orthodox, Calvinist systematic theology. Yet the importance and value of Strong's work is witnessed that through various editions it remained in print from the first printed 'Lectures in Theology' (1876) up to the present. It was for generations a widely prescribed textbook in fundamentalist and evangelical schools for ministers. A friendly but critical assessment of these and other developments within Strong's theology will be found in Carl F. H. Henry's Ph.D. dissertation *Personal Idealism and Strong's Theology*.[19] Strong's contemporaries, B. B. Warfield and several other orthodox Protestants of the epoch, adopted theistic evolution. See article 'Evolution' in *Evangelical Dictionary of Theology*.

As we move away from the primal narrative in Genesis 1 and 2 to bring the rest of Scripture to bear on the doctrine of the *imago dei* it appears that the doctrine is assumed throughout but never defined. Questions arise to which answers, however tentative or limited, must be given. I shall continue the propositional approach.

6. The fall of man marred the image of God, but did not remove it. Let us consider some of the scriptural evidence. There are only three passages which bear directly on the matter and they seem to me decisive.

'*Whoever sheds the blood of man, by man shall his blood be shed, for God made man in his own image*' (Gen. 9:6). This is the definitive text on the punishment of the crime of murder. It is postlapsarian and pre-Sinaitic law, i.e. it relates to divine law for the human race under the condition of race-wide depravity through all ages and 'dispensations.' It relates to mankind whom Paul describes as 'by nature children of wrath' (Eph. 2:3) and 'alienated from the life of God' (Eph. 4:18). It seems utterly lame logic to say, as some do, that this drastic punishment of murder by the death of the murderer is only out of respect for what man once was but no longer is, similar to Jehu's concern that the remnants of Jezebel's corpse be given decent burial because she was once a princess. See John Murray's excellent discussion in *Principles of Conduct*[20] and *Collected Writings*.[21]

'*With it [the tongue] we bless our* LORD *and Father, and with it we curse people who are made in the likeness of God*' (Jas. 3:9). This statement plainly refers to people in general: not specifically before the fall or after regeneration. It is not with reference to what mankind once was, but to the divine likeness, which all people of every age bear,

---

15. Shepherd, op. cit., p. 1018.
16. Strong's contemporaries B. B. Warfield and several other orthodox Protestants of the epoch adopted theistic evolution. See article "Evolution" in *Evangelical Dictionary of Theology*.
17. A. H. Strong, *Systematic Theology* (Valley Forge, PA: Judson Press, 1907), pp. 466, 467.
18. ibid., pp. 467–474.
19. Carl F. H. Henry, *Personal Idealism and Strong's Theology* (Wheaton, IL: Van Kampen, 1951) (a very rare book).
20. John Murray, *Principles of Conduct* (Grand Rapids: Eerdmans, 1957, 1971), pp. 112, 113.
21. ibid., pp. 35, 36.

imparting a supreme dignity. To curse with the tongue is to commit a form of *lese-majesty*, the majesty of the divine image present in every human being.

'*For a man* [anēr, *male of our race*] *ought not to cover his head, since he is the image and glory of God, but* [de, *on the other hand*] *woman is the glory of man*' (1 Cor. 11:7). Paul is treating proper decorum in dress for group worship. He is making a specialized use of the doctrine of the divine image, not denying the woman is also in God's image. Its relevance to the present discussion is simply that the divine image is still present in mankind. (See Murray's discussion in his *CollectedWritings*.[22]) Other passages presuppose a special analogy, likeness, correspondence between God and human beings (Ps. 94:7-10; Prov. 20:12; Exod. 4:11; Luke 11:9-13). The assertion that the image of God is permanent in mankind, is enlarged and supported by the following.

7. The image of God in the creation narrative in Genesis and in the other references cited above, appears to be what distinguishes mankind from the rest of animate creation. Our first parents, as created, undoubtedly possessed human nature in its full integrity including knowledge of God, true righteousness and holiness. Though they lost that integrity in the fall, it does not follow that knowledge, righteousness and holiness constitute *per se* the divine image. If defined in these terms, as Calvin observed, then of course the divine image was lost in the fall. However, the Genesis narrative (Gen. 1:26, 27; 5:1) and other specific references (Gen. 9:6; 1 Cor. 11:7; James 3:9) do not affirm that moral integrity constitutes the image, even though before their fall our first parents possessed moral integrity. It may be much better to say that possession of the image and the gift of freedom that accompanied it precisely rendered mankind capable of sin. Animals are not capable of sin. They do not and cannot sin. It is possession of the image which renders mankind in fallen condition not merely unhappy and miserable but a sinner, a rebel against God.

The image of God therefore constitutes mankind as mankind. It still today renders sin the atrocity that it is, worthy of divine wrath forever.

8. The question of how the race, after loss of moral integrity and in a fallen condition, could continue to possess the image of its Maker as in its first integrity, has been commonly addressed by distinguishing between the image in a *broad sense* from a *narrow sense*, the latter being lost in the fall, the former being retained. The broad sense (sometimes called *natural* likeness) includes such elements as personality, rationality, moral sense and capacity, aesthetic sense, and perhaps sense of humor and love of play. These are aspects of spiritual being: the narrow sense being moral likeness (righteousness and holiness) and true knowledge of God. In the broad sense then, mankind is still mankind though greatly marred, while in the narrow sense the image is gone. This latter is what is involved in being 'dead in trespasses and sins,' 'the natural man,' who cannot even desire to know the 'things of the Spirit of God.' Though held by far the majority of Protestant, especially Reformed, theologians, few propose it as more than theory. On Protestant principles these proposals (especially 6 and 7) are almost a necessity. Not so the Roman Catholic teaching as we now proceed to show.

9. In usual Roman Catholic doctrine, the 'image of God' consists of our powers of reason and free will. These constitute mankind as mankind. Though not totally unaffected by the fall they survive intact. Thus by use of reason, man can know much of God by reasoning from the facts of the created world, including himself.

In Tridentine Roman Catholic religion the 'likeness' of God is something different from the image of God. It refers to the moral and ethical integrity of primal mankind. This likeness is not a part of basic human nature (= image of God) but something imparted (*donum superadditum*) by God to Adam in addition to the complete humanity (*humanitas*) or image of God. In the Fall mankind lost this likeness but not the image.

Seeds of this view are to be found in Origen and Irenaeus.[23] The doctors of the Western church through the ages have not been in agreement as to when, to what degree and at what time the 'image' was conferred and whether contemporaneously with or later than the 'likeness' (superadded gifts). Since Trent and the defender of Trent, Robert Bellarmine, official dogma has been quite clear. In the fall, Adam lost such added 'graces' as holiness, righteousness and immortality and we do not have them in 'the state of nature.' 'Since the Fall of Adam' the condition of mankind 'is only different from Adam's condition before the Fall in the sense that Adam has been bereft of his clothes [superadded holiness, righteousness, etc.]' whereas 'man since the Fall' has not yet put them on. 'Human nature is no more afflicted with ignorance and weakness, than if it were in a state of [pre-fall] pure nature.'[24] The mischief this doctrine has introduced into the Roman view of sin and salvation is incalculable.

---

22. ibid., pp. 36, 37.
23. Irenaeus, *Against Heresies* 5.6.1.

Commenting on this point Gordon Clark says:

> Even though the neutral state [immediately after the fall] was soon defaced by voluntary sin, man without saving grace could still obey God's commands upon occasion. After regeneration a man could do even more than God requires. This then becomes the foundation of the Roman Catholic doctrine of the treasury [of merit] of the saints. If a particular man does not himself earn enough merit, the Pope can transfer from the saints' accounts as many more merits as are necessary for entrance into heaven. One horrendous implication of all this is that although Christ's death remains necessary to salvation, it is not sufficient. Human merit is indispensable.[25]

Yet even orthodox Romanism at its best grants in its own way that sinners are unable to come to faith by reason alone apart from grace and special divine enablement. Readers may be both encouraged that there are soundly 'saved' Roman Catholics as well as surprised by the comments of the premier Roman Catholic theologian, Thomas Aquinas. Commenting on Philippians 2:8-10 he says: 'But this salvation of grace is *by faith* in Christ. In the justification of an adult who has sinned, the movement of faith towards God, coincides with the infusion of grace.' The 'infusion' of grace is not what Paul meant, as our Reformers insisted, but at least Aquinas did not believe in 'total ability' of unaided, fallen, human nature to seek and find God. He goes on to say that faith does not originate within ourselves, that 'free will is inadequate for the act of faith since the contents of faith are above human reason.' Faith must be taught by the Spirit of God. Then arguing from Romans 11:6 ('by grace... no longer on the basis of works') and 1 Corinthians 1:29-30 ('no human being might boast in the presence of God') he even argues for particular divine election, citing the same texts the Reformers used against Catholics of their day, concluding on the basis of Romans 8:30: 'For predestination is nothing else than the pre-arrangement of God's blessings, among which blessings our good works themselves are numbered.'[26] In this exposition the Angelic Doctor turns in altogether a better exposition than many of the deliverances we hear from pulpits and broadcasts of supposedly sound evangelical preachers today.

10. Paul does not specifically claim to be interpreting the references to the divine image of God, but in several places he alludes to the Genesis texts in such a manner as to demonstrate that restoration of the moral image of God, considered as righteousness and holiness, is the goal of the sending of the Messiah into the world. Christ as Last Adam bears the true image of God (not merely an *eikon* or *tselem* or image). Christ is the image of God (*eikon tou theou*, 2 Cor. 4:4; Col. 1:15). He is not image in a derived sense, but according to Hebrews 1:3(ASV) 'the very image [*character*] of his substance [*hupostasis*].' Though *hupostasis* in course of theological statements in the Greek language came to be used alternately for Latin *persona*, a theatrical mask or impersonation, the common meaning when Hebrews 1:3 was written was substance, being, or essence. This is reflected rightly in the NIV translation as 'being.' Hence, whatever the *being* of God is, the Son of God is – not by derivation or creation but by nature. Christ came into the world not to demonstrate what God's *body* is like, but to demonstrate fully what God's holy character is. In His redemptive work as Last Adam He has made it possible for human beings to recover the lost moral likeness which was possessed by the man of paradise but lost wholly in the fall.[27]

I do not think this line of argument, exploited in an impressive way by Calvin, leads to Calvin's conclusion that the divine image of Genesis 1:26, 27 is precisely 'knowledge, then pure righteousness and holiness.' It seems to me it is rather that the divine image, constituted in mankind's spiritual nature, as a personal being, enables mankind to have true 'knowledge... pure righteousness and holiness' and then by disobedience to lose them.[28]

No doubt Calvin as well as Aquinas [29] before him and texts of other authors (C. Hodge, J. O. Buswell) follow that line of argument I have reported as being drawn from Paul's teachings (2 Cor. 4:4; Col. 1:15) and Hebrews 1:3 (I have not produced all the texts) are right in finding Christ's holy character an example of the divine image undistorted by sin. Historically, as early as Athanasius,[30] a similar line of argument was proposed and related to the

---

24. Robert Bellarmine, *Disputations Tom.*, 4, p. 11, col. 2. Also as cited by A. A. Hodge, *Outlines of Theology* (Grand Rapids: Eerdmans, 1860, 1957), p. 336. *The Catechism of the Catholic Church of 1994* does not quite agree: 'Human nature has not been totally corrupted: it is wounded in the natural powers proper to it; subject to ignorance, suffering, and the dominion of death; and inclined to sin.' Para. 405, p. 102. English ed.
25. Gordon Clark, op. cit., p. 13.
26. Thomas Aquinas, *Commentary on Saint Paul's Epistle to the Ephesians*, trans. M. L. Lamb (Albany, NY: Magi Books, 1966), pp. 94–97.
27. He did not lose what may be called *moral capacity* or he could not be morally responsible and a sinner.
28. Calvin, *Institutes I*, XV, 4.
29. Aquinas, *Summa Theologica i*, 93,6.
30. Jaroslav Pelikan, *The Christian Tradition, 5 Christian Doctrine and Modern Culture (since 1700)* (Chicago: Univ. of Chicago Press, 1989), p. 203.

Logos doctrine. John of Damascus taught that the components of the image in the man of paradise were intelligence, free will and virtue, which had their seat in the human reason and spirit, 'But all of these qualities found their fullest expression in the Logos as "the substantial image of God," through whom the image of archetypical humanity could be said to have its reality.'[31] Damascus' view leads to a further development (which Calvin did not endorse) that Adam was created in the image of the humanity of Christ that in eternity was foreknown (determined) in the mind of God. This early, but somewhat bizarre variation, has never disappeared. Though Calvin's view is similar in many ways to Aquinas',[32] I do not recall that Calvin ever cites Aquinas in this connection.

11. It seems correct to say that the story of redemption which occupies every page of Scripture is tracing what God has done, is doing and shall do to restore the holy character of mankind's being, which whether constituting the image as many hold, or as lost to the image as I and many others prefer to think. Hence it is correct to speak of the restoration of the image of God in redeemed humanity by the Last Adam (Scripture does not speak of a 'second' Adam, as if there might be several; see 1 Cor. 15:45).

It is objected that anything unholy cannot bear God's image (Hodge). This is like saying that John, Jr., who looks exactly like his father, cannot be 'spat in the image' because he is a bad boy.

12. The fellowship of mankind with God in paradise is not featured in the Genesis account, but it reports that God sought Adam (3:7-10) in the Garden. The context clearly implies previous communion between the Creator and the pair created in His image with instructions to fill the earth with their progeny. The conclusion, therefore, cannot be avoided that in the Hebraic way of simply juxtaposing ideas that belong together in causal or purposive context without stating the connection, God created mankind for fellowship. This theme is capable of expository development with reference to Israel at Sinai that God might 'dwell with you' and of the *mishkan*, tabernacle or 'dwelling' 'in the midst' of the camp; further, of the sad movement of the *shekinah* or glory presence out of Jerusalem in Ezekiel and of His return at the Second Advent (Zech. 14:1 ff.). The doctrine of the church in its own oneness and with Christ falls in line. 'Yet she on earth has union with God the Three in One and mystic, sweet communion with those whose rest is won.' With the image restored and perfected in the redeemed, worship of the Godhead and fellowship with Him is our prospect for eternity (Rev. 21:22).

From a somewhat similar point of view this aspect of the doctrine of the divine image in mankind is movingly expounded in relation to the latter chapters of John's Gospel by Cornelius Plantinga, Jr., in 'Images of God.'[33]

13. It has been argued cogently by many through the centuries and fervently in the twentieth century (by Dorothy L. Sayers in *The Mind of the Maker*) that mankind's creativity in fulfilling the command to 'work, till the garden,' and the like is the essence of the image. More theologians have been attracted to the interpretation that mankind's capacity as vicegerent (or vice-king) of the earth implied in 'have dominion, fill the earth and subdue it,' constitutes the divine image. In my judgment it is more consistent with the text of Genesis 1:26-30 to regard the image of God as *qualifying* mankind to rule and subdue the earth and as enabling him through the rationality-aspect of the image to use his latent physical powers creatively. In other words, fellowship with God is a *goal* or *purpose* of God in making mankind in His image, not an aspect of it; dominion is *made right* and *possible* by the image, not of its essence; and conquest ('subdue it') or exploitation, in a reasonable and fruitful way, the *privilege*, not the image, as such.

14. I cautiously raise the matter of the practical bearing of the image of God in mankind on arts, scientific disciplines, social projects and similar in Christian perspective. I commend the measured comments of M. J. Erickson in his *Christian Theology* under the heading of 'Implications of the Doctrine.'[34] The older works in my library I regard highly say nothing about it. Even L. Berkhof who published a *Systematic Theology* in 1949, says nothing directly about this.

A. J. McClain, my very practically oriented professor of theology, made remarks that survive in my notes on his lecture: (1) 'It is the likeness to God which gives man his peculiar dignity and worth even as a fallen being.' I later heard him apply this insight to the importance of care for human need, respect for people's rights, and the like. (2) It justifies capital punishment for murder, quoting Genesis 9:6. (3) Cursing anybody is evil because every person is in the image of God, hence directed against the Creator, citing James 3:9 in ASV. (4) Human life is sacred.

---

31. ibid., p. 203.
32. Aquinas, op. cit., Q93, 6–8.
33. Cornelius Plantinga, Jr., 'Images of God,' *Christian Faith and Practice in the Modern World*, ed. M. A. Noll & D. F. Wells (Grand Rapids: Eerdmans, 1988), pp. 51–67.
34. Millard J. Erickson, *Christian Theology* (Grand Rapids: Baker Books, 1985), pp. 515–517.

As I reflect on the matter it seems to me McClain covered the ground in a seminal but comprehensive manner. If Job had thought of these things he might not have cursed the night he was conceived and surely would not have been so displeased with his birthday as the third chapter of Job famously declares!

Yet the doctrine is capable of being pressed too far. It does not justify every human impulse, now stimulated and titillated from every quarter, toward self-fulfillment. Not quite every natural or induced longing of the heart is either holy or wholesome. Christian 'counsellors,' as the current jargon has it, need be cautious in this regard. Christian psychology and sociology as well as 'Christian Education' are businesses nowadays, as well as fields of enterprise and, we hope, of service. Let this caveat be the last word in the present chapter: every Christian professional discipline would like to find a biblical authority for its enterprise. This is especially desirable for innovations, without traditional precedent and clear texts in the Bible to support them (as with pastor, evangelist and the like). Many seek to find root and authority in human need, interpreted in light of the divine image of God in mankind. Let us beware that we do not judge the needs under the influence of the spirit of the age rather than the doctrines of creation, fall and redemption. The Scriptures interpret the *Zeitgeist*, not the other way around. Let us not decide independently of Scripture what we think mankind is and needs and then seek scriptural authority to justify our procedures.

4
The Non-physical Aspects of Human Nature

The absence of a chapter on the human body, the physical aspect of mankind, does not mean that we do not regard it as important, for it is. There is sufficient reason for absence of a separate chapter. The body can be perceived by our senses. No one in his right mind forthrightly denies its existence. The same is not true of the soul.

The Soul, Its Distinct Features and Functions.

God did not first create the soul and put it in a body but the other way around (Gen 2:7). John Murray, revered professor of theology at Westminster Seminary said:

> The notion that the body is the prison-house of the soul is pagan in origin and anti-biblical; it is Platonic, and has no resemblance to the biblical conception. The Bible throughout represents the dissolution of body and spirit as an evil, as the retribution and wages of sin, and, therefore, as a disruptions of that integrity which God established at creation. If [Adam] were not dust, he could not return to dust. But the reason for return to dust is not that he is dust, but that he has sinned (Gen. 2:17; 3:17).[1]

In Funeral Liturgy.

In the graveside liturgy of Christian committal, Protestant ministers usually intone the following from *The Book of Common Prayer*: 'Unto Almighty God we commend the soul of our brother [or sister] departed, and we commit his [or her] body to the ground,' etc. The Westminster Confession of 1647, normative for Presbyterians, Congregationalists and (until recent decades) for most Baptists, states: 'After God had made all other creatures, he created man, male and female, with reasonable and immortal souls.' The Westminster Assembly mandated Scripture 'proof' for 'male and female' is of course Genesis 1:27; for 'immortal souls' it is Genesis 2:7 (KJV) – 'God… breathed into his nostrils the breath of life, and the man became a living soul.' They included Ecclesiastes 12:7, 'and the dust returns to the earth as it was, and the spirit returns to God who gave it.' Other 'proofs' include Luke 23:43, recording the dying pronouncement of Jesus upon the repentant thief, 'Truly, I say to you, today you will be with me in Paradise,' and Jesus' warning in Matthew 10:28: 'And do not fear those who kill the body but cannot kill the soul. Rather fear him who can destroy both soul and body in hell.'[2]

---

1. John Murray, *Collected Writings ii* (Edinburgh: Banner of Truth Trust, 1977), pp. 14, 15.

In the above quotations from the Anglican service book and the Westminster confession, 'soul' is being used in a sense common to English-speaking people for centuries, referring to the immaterial part of mankind, seat of consciousness, thinking, feeling, of personal being and which endures ('survives' death is an oxymoron) beyond death. Peoples everywhere in every age of whom there are written records, even archaeological remains, are known to have assumed this personal center = soul. Even when 'soul' is used for the sense of individual person ('She was a cheerful soul') the body is not the focus of meaning but the *person*, the word the present generation prefers to employ.

A Cautious Statement.

Under the heading, 'Man's two-fold Being,' J. O. Buswell provides a cautiously-stated definition of age-long Christian doctrine, relating anthropology of 'the soul' to an eschatology of the same – as must be done. Orthodox doctrine employs sayings of Jesus and of the New Testament to explain or enlarge what Genesis says of the 'living being' brought to existence by divine breath after God formed mankind of the dust of the ground. He says it is obvious (and wearisome volumes and columns of so-called biblical theology to the contrary of recent generations will never erase the obvious)

> That according to the Bible man is both a material and a non-material substantive entity, both body and soul, and that these two aspects of man are not only logically distinguishable, but separable, so that at death the non-material man goes into the realm of the unseen [either], heaven or the place of the wicked dead, to be reunited with his body at the resurrection, and that the body returns to the dust, awaiting the resurrection – that there is this two-fold division in the being of man as presented in the Scripture is most obvious.[3]

People have always thought this way. The slightest acquaintance with the religion and mythology of ancient Egypt, Mesopotamia, Greece and Rome and any other large group known to man, demonstrates that belief in the existence and 'immortality' of the soul is a universal human orthodoxy produced and enforced by conscience, *Ubique, semper, ab omnibus*.

Many modern writers of 'Old Testament theology' try to explain it away. Yet the temptation of 'necromancy' or communication with the dead prohibited specifically in Deuteronomy 18:11 – the practicers were said to be 'an abomination to the Lord' – shows that belief in separability of body and soul, with the soul enduring intact, was assumed by ancient Israelites. Not that some ancient people did not deny it. In several of Socrates' monologues in the dialogues of Plato, the famous philosopher refers to these skeptics – ancient counterparts of the positivists and behaviorists and other infidels and atheists of our time.

The Bible sometimes uses our word 'soul' as name for the immortal non-material aspect of man's nature, but not often. When these studies reach Eschatology (Part 7), in connection with the doctrine of death and the intermediate state, a fuller account must be given. For now it needs to be said that contrary to the frequent assertions that belief in the 'immortality of the soul' or 'life after death' is absent from the Old Testament, there is strong evidence for such belief. (1) The Hebrews would hardly have avoided being quite saturated with that belief, recalling their origin in Mesopotamia, sojourn in Canaan and long residence in Egypt, countries where there was profound acceptance of such belief. (2) The New Testament comments on the Old Testament and interpretations of it, especially the faith of Old Testament believers and saints, makes plain they cherished the blessed hope of eternal life with God, that death does not end all. Though most of the evidence (in both Testaments) relates to the resurrection of the body in an eschatological setting, there is evidence of belief in 'immortality of the soul' also, though that phrase must be severely qualified, as we shall see.

How the New Testament Interprets the Old Testament.

The chief evidence is the New Testament interpretation of Old Testament faith and hope found in certain outstanding passages of the New Testament. A passage in Hebrews is especially plain. After surveying the life of faith *on earth* of Abel, Enoch, Noah, Abraham, Isaac and Jacob, Scripture says: 'All these people were still living by faith when they

---

2. The 'scripture proofs' incorporated into the Westminster Confession were added by parliamentary directive after the Westminster Divines submitted it. This does not mean those truly consciencious biblicists had not considered the Scripture evidences first in composing the document. The initial parliamentary mandate had not clearly specified Scripture 'proof texts.'
3. J. O. Buswell, *Systematic Theology of the Christian Religion I* (Grand Rapids: Zondervan, 1962), p. 237.

died. They did not receive the things promised [land in Syria, numerous offspring on earth]; they only saw them and welcomed them from a distance. And they admitted that they were aliens [pilgrims] and strangers on earth. People who say such things show that they are looking for a country of their own... they were looking for a better country [home] – a heavenly one' (Heb. 11:13-16 NIV). Obviously these folk did not expect to take their bodies along to their 'better country' in heaven.

It must be admitted that this hope for a home of the soul in heaven is not plain in the narrative of the Old Testament. The writer of Hebrews is plainly thinking of what certain patriarchs and others *said* ('People who say such things'). Jacob, speaking to Pharaoh, referred to his 130 years and the long lives of Abraham and Isaac as a 'pilgrimage' or 'sojourning' (Gen. 47:9). In the closing hour of Jacob's life he declared, 'I wait for your salvation, O LORD' (Gen. 49:18). At such a moment an earthly salvation would not have been on Jacob's mind.

The author of Ecclesiastes, a preacher, declared expectation of a coming time (Eccles. 12:13,14) when the deeds of earthly life would be brought to judgment – a near universal faith. '[T]he Preacher' says nothing here of a resurrection of the body. The author of Psalm 119:19, in praise of 'the Law,' which Paul pronounced 'spiritual,' exclaims, 'I am a sojourner on the earth; hide not your commandments from me.' These and who knows what other Old Testament sayings were in the mind of the Apostle who wrote Hebrews 11:13. Charles Bridges, in an old but very valuable commentary on Psalm 119, says: 'this has been the character, confession, and glory of the LORD's people.' Bridges cites in addition to the above texts Genesis 23:4, wherein Abraham declares to the Hittites of Hebron, 'I am a sojourner and foreigner among you' and Psalm 39:12, in which David worships saying, 'O LORD... I am a sojourner with you, a guest, like all my [pious] fathers.'[4] It appears David felt that all his godly ancestors thought their natural home to be with God in the unseen world, and were only pilgrims and foreigners on earth. John Murray concludes:

> The highest exercises of man as a rational, moral, religious being are predicable of men by this aspect [the soul retains identity and character after death]. All that we are most characteristically as beings created in the image of God, has its seat, unity and abiding meaning in the entity. There is an 'ego,' spiritual in nature, indivisible and indestructible continuously subsistent and active through all the changes in this world, in the disembodied state, and in the resurrected life in the age to come.[5]

An Old Testament Theology of the Soul.

In the section concerned with eschatology, the last part of this book, detailed attention will be directed toward important Old Testament features expressing belief in 'souls' as distinct from 'bodies' and the destiny of souls. I therefore find it interesting that one finds Herman Schultz, a critical and sometimes rather skeptical Old Testament theologian, making remarks like these about Old Testament teaching:

> There is a possibility of man "living forever" should he eat of the tree of life[6].... Man is capable of holding personal communion with God, and of living a life that reaches out beyond space and time.... As a spiritual and personal being, man is the goal of creation.[7]

On the creation of mankind in the image of Elohim, though acknowledging possible reference to the body, it is the body

> as expressing the self-manifesting personality [which] must have seemed to this narrator [the P of the Wellhausian scheme] to have the likeness of God, and to bear the stamp of dignity characteristic of human nature[8].... On the basis of impersonal life [body], man is to be personal; on the basis of transitory life, spiritual; on the basis of limited, sensuous life, morally free.[9]

Whether or not in the Old Testament 'the belief that eternal life also belongs to the idea of man,' the idea starts 'as far back as we can go.' On the basis of Genesis 6:3, if 'mankind' had not sinned as Genesis 6 says they did, 'they would have had the Spirit of God "ruling in them forever" – in other words, they would have been immortal.'[10]

---

4. Charles Bridges, *Exposition of Psalm CXIX*, 17th ed., 1861, p. 33.
5. Murray, op. cit., p. 21.
6. Herman Schultz, Old Testament Theology II (Edinburgh: T. and T. Clark, 1892), p. 254.
7. ibid., p. 256.
8. ibid., p. 257.
9. ibid., p. 258.
10. ibid., p. 264.

Then arguing from 2 Kings 2:1-11 (the translation of Elijah) and Genesis 5:21-24 (the translation of Enoch) Schultz draws the conclusion: 'without dying' they are 'taken up to fellowship with God. Consequently, when man raises himself [where is the grave here?] into a true union with God, he is represented as fit for an everlasting life with God.'[11]

The Bible devotes little attention either to the existence of the non-material part of human nature which we call the soul, or to the *existence per se* of unembodied created spirits (demons, angels). Both are assumed. When a saint dies he goes to Abraham's bosom or the paradise of 'the house of the LORD for ever' or 'my Father's house.' It is assumed that readers will understand these expressions as referring to a disembodied state of undying souls of people.[12]

Little is to be gained by study of the Hebrew and Greek terms for mankind's psychic side (heart, mind, bowels and the like). They turn out to be popular terms occasionally used in a simple primary sense but usually in the same general, inexact, frequently metaphorical senses people do today in speaking of the same things. Literary efforts toward a psychology of the Bible based on study of language and words have been of very limited success. Hebrew and Greek words for soul, spirit, affections, hates, mind, evil and the like are usually names for some part or function of the physical body, as for example, heart, bowels, breath, but have come to be attached to some aspect or function of the psyche or soul. Then that aspect or function is frequently, by a figure of speech (*synecdoche, metonymy*), put for one's whole being as when David cries, 'my heart and my flesh sing for joy to the living God' (Ps. 84:2).

Theology must concern itself with those features of mankind's constitutional nature that provide capacity for right and wrong action, with consequent effects on communion with God and eternal life with God, in the New Testament sense (John 3:16; 5:24; 10:25, 26). Like God and other created spirits, man is a moral being. This means he must be able to think in order to weigh actions and consequences, to feel emotions of sorrow, joy, despair, and exultation, and the like. And he must be able to make choices. Theology summarizes these capacities and refers to them as *emotion* (feelings, desires, affections), *intellect* and *will*. This threefold analysis of mankind's rational-moral constitution should be conditioned by two cautions. (1) The analysis into three is not uniformly accepted – it is only convenient. (2) Since body and soul *in this life* are united it is correct to say that emotion is the whole person feeling; intellect, the whole person thinking; will, the whole person choosing – even though these are transacted in the center which we call the soul. Somewhere in this complex of capacities, not the same as any of them but related to all of them, is that activity of the soul called conscience.

Since God has thoughts, loves and hates, wills and chooses, mankind in His image has the same. Since the soul is immortal, even death cannot end these activities (see Luke 16; Rev. 6; and similar).

Theology is specially concerned with those activities of the soul called *will* and *conscience* – in the case of the former, with a proper definition and whether it is free or determined; in the case of conscience, with proper definition, its competence and its relation to the moral life of mankind.

The Will and Its Freedom.

A wise theologian once said: 'In every system of theology... there is a chapter *De Libero Arbitrio* [concerning free choice]. This is a question which every theologian finds in his path, and on the manner in which it is determined depends his theology, and of course his religion.'[13] Hodge is thinking of mankind's will under the condition of sin. No one doubts everybody has the faculty of making choices and that we feel no external coercion in choosing. But whether those choices are made apart from a permanent inner disposition away from right choice is another matter.

Theologians have learned to be cautious in defining aspects, functions and powers of the soul, even as they must be careful to have regard to the normal (i.e. in living people) unity of a person's nature. Intellect, emotion and will are not faculties or organs like eyes as organs of sight or ears as organs of hearing, but activities of the whole of a person thinking (learning, knowing), feeling and choosing. Of course, we think with the mind (or soul) not our feet

---

11. ibid., p. 264.
12. Recent controversies with monism of mankind's nature as advocated by Murray Harris will be reported later in this book, in connection with Eschatology (Part 7).
13. Charles A. Hodge, *Systematic Theology II* (Grand Rapids: Eerdmans, 1970), p. 278.

or hands, but there are consequences for the hands and feet. The adjective *psychosomatic* conveys the idea of this unity. Nevertheless the act of a person in thinking and feeling consummates in decisions resulting in actions. It is the power of the soul to decide, the 'executive faculty' of the soul which must be considered.

Some Christian Philosophical Failures.

Augustine, adjusting his thoughts in relation to the pagan philosophers of his time, wrote a fair-sized book, *De Libero Arbitrio Voluntatis* (Concerning Free Choice of the Will). I once taught a college course in which we spent days trying to master it. Aquinas has nine articles on the will.[14] Both seem quaint and strange today. Neither I nor my students felt particularly persuaded of anything. I fear our benefits were chiefly antiquarian. Neither Augustine nor Aquinas got around to an adequate definition of the problem.

Calvin's modest approach to this subject, after reading Augustine and Thomas, comes as a great relief. In raising the subject of the soul and its faculties he remarks, 'It would be foolish to seek a definition of "soul" from the philosophers' and 'I leave it to the philosophers to discuss these faculties in their subtle way.'[15] He felt they all failed to give sufficient notice to effects of the fall on all the soul's 'faculties.' Then after noting Plato's thoughts on the five senses and Themistius's three appetitive faculties – will, anger and desire – he comments: 'Since I fear that they may involve us in their own obscurity rather than help us, I think they ought to be passed over.'[16] I shall recommend the same for my readers and suggest 'passing over' the strange views of America's foremost theologian, Jonathan Edwards, in his *Essay On the Freedom of the Will* (1754) and the volumes of response it generated. His *Treatise Concerning Religious Affections* directly and plainly supports the views advocated here.[17]

A Modest Proposal.

Calvin reduced the number of aspects of the soul of concern to theology to two – understanding (or intellect) and will. Of these he dealt only with will, and there only with the question of freedom of the will in a preliminary way, viz.:

> Let us, therefore, hold – as indeed is suitable to our present purpose – that the human soul consists of two faculties, understanding and will. Let the office, moreover, of understanding be to distinguish between objects, as each seems worthy of approval or disapproval; while that of the will, to choose and follow what the understanding pronounces good, but to reject and flee what it disapproves[18].... Choice [was] added, to direct the appetites and control the organic motions, and this makes the will completely amenable to the guidance of reason.[19]

He is, of course, speaking of mankind as created, not as fallen. Attention to the state of the corrupted will comes later in his treatment.

Calvinists, Arminians, and any other serious, orthodox theologians including Roman Catholics, have no necessary disagreement on the above limitation of the question, even though they disagree on the answer.

Theology is not concerned greatly with psychological processes as presently conceived. Materialistic schemes such as Watson's and Skinner's behaviorisms, which deny the existence of a 'psyche,' i.e. a soul, immortal or otherwise, have nothing really to talk about that theology has any interest in and *vice versa*. Psychology today, except under Christian aegis, regards people as we find them as normal mankind. The idea of the predisposition of the will to evil, by having been corrupted by a primeval fall – a depraved will, in theological language – is foreign to the 'natural man,' of any occupation or profession.

Was it possible for Adam not to sin (*possere non pecare*) and thereby continue in that original righteousness until confirmed and permanent? Might Adam have attained some heavenly bliss such as Enoch (Gen. 5:21-24) attained by translation and which is the prospect of all the redeemed, without sin and death? Most theologians have thought so. Calvin says it well:

> In his integrity man by free will had the power, if he so willed, to attain eternal life. Here it would be out of place to raise the question of God's secret predestination because our present subject is not what can happen or not, but what man's nature was like. Therefore Adam could have stood if he wished, seeing he fell solely by his

---

14. Aquinas, *Summa Theologica I*, Q82, 83.
15. Calvin, Institutes I, 15. 6.
16. ibid.
17. I am following Gordon Clark, *The Biblical Doctrine of Man* 2nd ed.(Jefferson, Maryland: The Trinity Foundation, 1992), pp. 79–81.
18. Calvin, op. cit., 7.
19. Calvin, op. cit., 8.

own will. But it was because his will was capable of being bent to one side or the other, and was not given the constancy to persevere [why God did not give us this constancy is not ours to inquire] that he fell so easily. Yet his choice of good and evil was free, and not that alone, but the highest rectitude was in his mind and will, and all the organic parts rightly composed to obedience, until in destroying himself he corrupted his blessings.[20]

Later we will show that even after the fall mankind is still no automaton, acting like the beasts in response to instinct and external stimulus. People still make decisions informed by intellect and moved by feeling; they act freely in the sense of being uncoerced by God, destiny or any other necessity than their own being, which has been affected by sin in all its parts and aspects.

The ruin caused by the fall, says Gordon Clark,

> did not reduce [man] to the status of an irrational animal. Man is still man after the fall... still a person... still rational. To be sure, he acts irrationally. Yet his life is not one of instinct as is the case with animals. Sin does not eradicate the image, but it certainly causes a malfunctioning.[21]

That ruin put man's heart, the spiritual, mental, cognitive center of his being, in a perverse mode which is called depravity. He cannot be rescued except the LORD reach into his heart and turn him around. '[N]o one understands; no one seeks for God' (Rom. 3:11). Jesus said, 'No one can come to me unless the Father who sent me draws him' (John 6:44). Fuller development of this sad theme will come shortly in connection with the doctrine of sin (Part 3 of this book).

Statements of Scripture about mankind's depraved heart refer to ordinary, garden-variety people – all of us – not to some extraordinarily degraded specimens. The following selected passages apply universally: 'Out of the heart come evil thoughts, murder, adultery,' etc. (Matt. 15:19); 'The heart is deceitful above all things, and desperately wicked (Jer. 17:9 KJV); 'The LORD saw that the wickedness of man was great... and that every intention of the thoughts [not feelings] of his heart was only evil continually' (Gen. 6:5). Paul says of this 'generic' common man that he 'does not accept [they are distasteful] the things of the Spirit of God, for they are folly to him, and *he is not able* [emphasis added] to understand them because they are spiritually discerned' (1 Cor. 2:14). His receiving apparatus was 'fried' in Eden long ago.[22]

The Conscience.

Conscience[23] is a universally observed fact of human nature. All people are aware of a sense of right and wrong. They know they *ought* to think and do certain things and *ought not* to think and do others. Very early in life everyone experiences a *sense of duty*. This 'sense' (inaccurate inasmuch as no sensation occurs) is never given a name in the Old Testament, though, without a name, the idea occurs frequently. When one thinks or does what his 'heart' tells him is wrong, feelings of self-accusation and ill desert arise coupled with fear of retribution; or if one does right, opposite feelings arise.

Biblical Examples of Conscience Working.

The Old Testament furnishes many examples of the operation of moral sense (for want of a better name) informing the heart, with resulting self-condemnation or self-approval. Abimelech, king of Gerar, was not in fear of mere social convention when, deceived by Isaac into thinking beautiful Rebekah was unmarried, he complained, 'One of the people might easily have lain with your wife, and you would have brought guilt upon us' (Gen. 26:10). He is speaking of objective guilt, of doing wrong deserving of punishment. This untaught awareness of right and wrong, a 'sense' that one *ought* to do right and that punishment will follow doing wrong (cf. Gen. 12:7 and context), was at least as strong in the pagan Abimelech as in either Isaac or Rebekah. We might say that he had 'a sense of decency.' Abraham, earlier, had been mistaken when in an amazingly near-identical situation he shamefaced apologized saying, 'I thought, There is no fear of God at all in this place' (Gen. 20:11). In the same early epoch Joseph made an appeal to the law of God written in the heart, in appealing to the wife of Potiphar (Gen. 39:9).

---

20. ibid., i. 15. 8.
21. Clark, op. cit., p. 73.
22. See Bruce K. Waltke's article 'Heart' in EDBT, '[T]he heart plans, makes commitments, and decides. It is the inner forum where decisions are made after deliberation; here a person engages in self-talk.' See also Gordon Clark, op. cit., pp. 78–88.
23. See Calvin, *Institutes, IV*, 10.3-8; Erickson 583–5; J. Rickaby, 'Conscience,' Catholic Ency. IV, 268–273.

These cases point to several facts of human nature: first, deep conviction that some things are right, others wrong; second, a common universal awareness of what some of those rights and wrongs are; third, feelings of self-accusation when wrong is done; fourth, and conversely, of self-congratulation when right is done; and fifth, apprehension of future punishment by God when wrong is done. The worshippers of the LORD God of Israel were apparently no more in fear of an eschatological 'judgment' than Philistines, Egyptians, Greeks or Romans.

Writers on conscience sometimes say that the Old Testament makes nothing of this 'innate' conscience, but speaks only of obedience or disobedience of God who makes himself known in the written Torah.[24] It is of course evident to any one who has read the Old Testament that obedience and disobedience to the revealed will of God is a ruling theme. Nevertheless at the beginning of our human story both our first parents had an inner sense that they ought to obey and ought not to disobey. Furthermore, Adam and Eve sought to hide from God because they had broken His commandment and knew the consequences. This does not however explain why they felt shame at their nakedness. Here we have the first case of fallen moral being, the self, being accused by that other thing, the conscious self, hence the word *con* (with) *science* (knowledge).

Two Elements in Conscience.

Two elements are involved in conscience, the 'I' or self which is aware of itself and that other something, indefinable, which accuses or excuses the I-self. This understanding of the subject – the I-self which has knowledge of a standard of right, which does or does not do right, in parallel with an internal witness and tribunal which truly judges – is patent in Romans 2:12-16. I quote part of the passage:

> For when the Gentiles [*ethnoi*, heathen, nations], who do not have the law [written biblical law, or *Torah*], by nature do what the law requires, they are a law to themselves, even though they do not have the law. They show that the work of the law is written in their hearts, while their conscience also bears witness, and their conflicting thoughts accuse or even excuse them (Rom. 2:14-15).

Paul is not commenting on what *some* few extraordinarily depraved of the common run of mankind are or are not, do or not do, rather as C. A. Hodge says:

> It is evident from the context… His object is to show that the heathen world have *a rule of duty* [another name for conscience] written on their hearts; a fact which is not proved by some heathen obeying the law, but which is proved by the moral conduct of all men…. Men generally …all men, show… they have a knowledge of right and wrong.[25]

Conscience Is Constitutional in Mankind.

This knowledge, which mankind in general has, is not an induced condition but a constitutional one of what we are 'by nature' (Gr. *physis*) (Rom. 2:14). 'The *physis* of anything,' Hodge goes on to say, 'is the peculiarity of its being, that in virtue of which it is what it is; it is that which belongs to its original constitution, and is opposed to what is taught, acquired, or made.'[26]

Paul here introduces the word *suneidesis* (Rom. 2:15), the exact Greek equivalent of our Latin-derived word, conscience. We shall later see how this word and its central meaning are employed in Scripture. Of it Hodge adds, '*Suneidēsis* is… the inward judge, whose acts are described in the following clause: "their thoughts alternately accusing or even excusing"…. The inward monitor [= conscience] acquits or condemns, as the case demands.'[27] There is among all people a 'present operation of conscience, which approves or condemns their conduct.'[28]

All up to now has been related to what conscience is. We have noticed appearances of something like conscience in the stories of Adam, Abraham, Isaac and Joseph. We took note of awareness of a universal divine law in the souls of men, together with that monitor within the heart which brings one's own deeds to judgment and threatens punishment. Though technically only the monitor is conscience, it is a common thing to speak of the whole of these matters as conscience.

---

24. The well-researched article in *Zondervan Pictorial Encyclopedia of the Bible* on 'Conscience' (I, pp. 941–949), by L. I. Grandberg and G. E. Farley should be corrected in this regard by the brief summary in A. M. Rehwinkel's article 'Conscience' in *EDT*.
25. Charles A. Hodge, *Commentary on the Epistle to the Romans* (Grand Rapids: Eerdmans, reprint 1947, 1993), pp. 54, 55.
26. ibid., p. 55.
27. ibid., p. 56.
28. ibid., p. 57.

In his book, *The Voice of Conscience*, A. M. Rehwinkel has written at length and well on conscience. He summarizes, in an encyclopaedia article, as follows:

> Conscience is innate... not the product of environment, training, habit or education, though it is influenced by all of these factors. As to function, conscience is threefold. (1) Obligatory. It urges man to do that which he regards as right and restrains him from doing that which he regards as wrong. (2) Judicial. Conscience passes judgment upon man's decisions and acts. (3) Executive. Conscience executes its judgment in the heart of man. It condemns his action when, in conflict with his conviction by causing an inward disquietude, distress, shame, or remorse. It commends when man has acted in conformity with his convictions.[29]

Professor Rehwinkel shows that Paul was perhaps more accurate even than he knew when he spoke of the natural knowledge of right and wrong and of an inward voice that approves or disapproves. He writes 'that man by nature... has an awareness of sin and consciousness of guilt when he violates this natural law is confirmed in an extraordinary manner in the literature of pagan nations of old.'[30] He then quotes at length from the *Book of the Dead* of ancient Egypt the confession before the god Osiris of a man at the approach of death. It goes on for thirty-five lines. Rehwinkel then moves on to ancient Babylon, quoting a 'penitential hymn' of similar length which reveals, he says, 'a most remarkable knowledge of basic requirements of the universal moral law referred to by Paul, and a deep sense of guilt for having transgressed that law, not because they had offended society, but because they had sinned against God.'[31] Then Rehwinkel turns to ancient Persia and the Vedas of ancient Hindus, where words similar to David's penitential Psalm 51 are quoted,[32] and finally to classical Greeks and Romans.[33]

Near the close of this section our author summarizes with a quote from Sir William Blackstone, the eminent English jurist.

> The Law of Nature, being co-equal with mankind and dictated by God Himself, is of course superior in obligation to any other. It is binding over all the globe, in all countries and at all times. No human laws are of any validity if contrary to this.[34]

But to speak precisely as 'teachers of the Law' and in order to understand what we do in our calling to 'cure' or 'care for' souls, let us propose the following.

How Conscience Works.

A *sound* conscience does not legislate or discover laws for the soul. It is neither teacher nor comforter. Conscience is the monitor or judge – either of one's own acts and thoughts, or those of others when we say their conduct offends one's conscience.

The conscience judges on the basis of opinions, laws, norms supplied by all one's sources throughout previous life, perhaps even innate knowledge. This explains why all people feel obligated to follow their conscience's directives, yet one man's conscience may direct differently from another's in many areas. Reason and experience plus nurture have created these differences.

Yet conscience is steady and infallible in that it, with sternness, inwardly commands every person on earth to do what one is convinced is right. It is at this point that evolutionary naturalism, as in non-theistic ethics, loses its argument that conscience is wholly acquired, like the conditioned reactions and behavior of animals. No animal ever thought he ought not to steal his neighbor's food out of bad conscience.

The idea of conscience as set forth in this chapter is deep in many narratives and moral instructions in the Old Testament, even though no word for conscience, as such, exists in biblical Hebrew. Usually the Hebrew word employed for conscience is *lev*, or *levav* (heart), as when 'David's heart smote him.'[35] The *heart*, or mind, or soul in which moral sensibilities reside is designated.

---

29. A. M. Rehwinkel, 'Conscience' in *Evangelical Dictionary of Theology*, ed. Walter Elwell (Grand Rapids: Baker, 1984), pp. 267, 268.
30. A. M. Rehwinkel, *The Voice of Conscience* (St Louis: Concordia Publ., 1956), p. 34.
31. ibid., pp. 36-38.
32. ibid., pp. 37-40,
33. ibid., pp. 40-45.
34. ibid., pp. 47, 48.
35. 1 Sam. 24:5; cf 2 Sam. 24:10; 1 Sam. 25:31; 1 Kgs. 8:38.

The word is employed thirty-three times in the New Testament and in such a way as to insure it reflects a common understanding of *suneidēsis* in the Greek-speaking world. Though biblical religion puts a special 'spin' on the word, the restraints of common grace on mankind have insured survival of the moral monitor everywhere in the Greek literature of which the New Testament is a part.[36] Without further effort at precise definition I offer the following as important biblical teachings about conscience.

The Conditions of the Conscience.

1. Conscience is intact and operative in the unbelieving heart as well as the believing heart. The scribes and Pharisees slunk away from their encounter with the penetrating insight of Jesus, in the episode of the adulterous woman, 'being convicted by their own conscience' (John 8:9 KJV). And, the 'conscience' of the heathen 'bears witness… their conflicting thoughts accuse or even excuse them' (Rom. 2:15).

2. Christian conscience should be to some degree informed and regulated by purely human ordinances. In as much as a magistrate is a 'minister of God… ye must needs be subject, not only for wrath [i.e. wrath of human law and civil magistrates], *but also for conscience sake*' (Rom. 13:4,5 KJV). We all live in a world where government frequently exceeds its divinely given limits by meddling with matters properly none of its business, and where (as in Europe's Middle Ages) the rules of an established church are enforced by civil power. This chronic condition has always been and remains a source of acute distress for *conscientious* Christians.

At the time of the Reformation, Protestant leaders had to think through the question of what limits, if any, the Scriptures place on the submission of Christians to unrighteous demands of civil government and of church demands enforced by civil law. The most important for developments within western Europe and English-speaking America were the careful writings of John Calvin. This issue is the declared topic of a chapter of the *Institutes*[37] and is never quite out of sight in the entire Fourth Book of 510 pages.

Calvin's definition is brief.[38] Previous discussion in the present chapter is quite compatible with it, as are most Protestant treatments. Calvin's concern was to decide to what extent people of Christian Europe were bound 'for conscience sake' to obey the dictates of rulers, civil and ecclesiastical. He denies, however, that bad laws of rulers and ecclesiastics bind Christian conscience. Rulers have authority over conscience only in matters of proper jurisdiction.[39] 'Human laws, whether, by magistrate or by church, even though they have to be observed (I speak of good and just laws), still do not of themselves bind the conscience. For all obligation to observe laws looks to the general purpose ['genus'], but does not consist of the things enjoined ['species'].'[40]

This bit of Protestant scholastic casuistry has had enormous consequences in the religious and political life of Europe and America. These convictions led to the exasperated, reluctant resistance of Reformed, Presbyterian, Baptist, Quaker and other denominations *against* the laws of the nations of Europe and thereby to fierce wars in what was thought to be defense of liberty of conscience and of political freedom. These words were echoed in thousands of sermons in the pulpits of the thirteen U.S. colonies in the decades before July 4, 1776.[41] This Protestant understanding of conscience has had and continues to have enormous consequences. How this could have happened in the supremely conservative thinking of Calvin, his disciples and successors is the story of Western history since 1536 when the Basle printers, T. Platter and B. Lasins, issued Chapter Six of the first edition of Calvin's *Institutes of the Christian Religion*. In this chapter Calvin expounded not only a biblical conception of Christian freedom of conscience but also set forth a coherent conception of 'what the relation between Church and State would be in a society inspired by the Gospel.'[42]

This brief treatment of Calvin's thought about conscience is designed to show that a biblical conception of conscience has been and remains of inestimable import and consequences not only for both personal Christian conduct but also for community and national life wherever biblical religion is a significant factor in society.

---

36. Maurers' article in *Theological Wordbook of the New Testament VI*, sunoida, suneidēsis, pp. 899-919.
37. Chapter X of Book IV, pp. 1179–1210.
38. Calvin, *Institutes IV*, 10. 3.
39. ibid., IV, 10. 5.
40. ibid., IV, 10. 5.
41. Alan Heimert, *Religion and the American Mind From the Great Awakening to the Revolution* (Cambridge: Harvard Univ. Press, 1966), p. 668.
42. Francois Wendel, *Calvin: The Origins and Development of His Religious Thought* (New York: Harper & Row, 1950, 1963), p. 112.

3. A 'good conscience' (Acts 23:1) and 'pure conscience' (2 Tim. 1:3 KJV) may be defined in the words of Paul, who furnishes two-thirds of the thirty-three occurrences in the New Testament, as a conscience 'void of offense toward God' (Acts 24:16 KJV) which 'bears' one 'witness' (Rom. 9:1) as truthful and is supported by 'everyone's' conscience and even before God (2 Cor. 4:2). This was a very great comfort for the Apostle Paul, much maligned by outraged legalistic countrymen and jealous religionists. Everyone who has been falsely charged of wrong by family, friends or foes knows how comforting such a conscience is and how difficult to obtain apart from the grace of redemption.

4. A 'weak conscience' (1 Cor. 8:7,10,12) is unjustifiably scrupulous about matters indifferent (*adiaphora*), and tends to be unnecessarily offended by others who exercise Christian liberty in good conscience. This has always been a problem, especially in multicultural societies like that in ancient Corinth (see 1 Cor. 8) and Rome (see Rom. 14:1-23). It is difficult for folk truly to accept the words of Jesus, oft repeated to His disciples, that there is nothing entering into the body which defiles it, that evil has its origin in the heart not in substances. Weak consciences abound in every corner of Christendom and perhaps in some corner of every Christian soul.

5. The 'seared conscience' (1 Tim. 4:2) belongs to the person who has sinned so often and so seriously that conscience ceases to speak very loudly. The sinner sins largely undisturbed by self-accusation. He sleeps well at night after committing all his favorite sins.

6. A 'defiled conscience' (Titus 1:15) is the opposite of a pure conscience. This conscience calls good evil and evil good (Isa. 5:20, 21).

7. An 'evil conscience' in context (Heb. 10:22) appears to be simply the heart of natural man who 'does not accept the things of the Spirit of God,' to whom such things are a 'folly' (1 Cor. 2:14), 'dead in ... trespasses and sins' (Eph. 2:1), 'darkened in their understanding... alienated... because of... ignorance... hard... of heart... callous' (Eph. 4:18,19).

8. The 'purged conscience' (Heb. 9:14 KJV; cf. 10:2) has been delivered by grace through justifying faith from 'evil' and 'defiled' conscience. It is the ideal of the Christian heart.

9. The Christian may expect faithfulness to God's revealed will in good 'conscience toward God' (1 Peter 2:19 KJV) will get him into trouble, in which case Christ, Himself, is his example (1 Peter 2:17-25).[43]

10. Inconvenient and limiting in some ways as it is, true love for one's brother will direct us to limit the liberty we have in Christ out of deference to the brother (1 Cor. 10:28-33) – though we may also use our liberty to instruct the 'weaker brother.' He really needs to learn who is strong and who is weak. Choose the occasion carefully!

---

43. Christians may protect good conscience in many social situations by not asking too many questions before responding to invitations to social gatherings (1 Cor. 10:27).

5
The Elements of Human Nature

Introduction to the Problem.

Before setting out on a quest for the origin of souls, another question must be raised, and at least tentatively resolved, whether or not 'soul' is a designation of all of mankind's non-material nature: specifically whether the invisible inner man, director of the visible outer is *one* aspect or *two* aspects, one 'substance,' if we may allow the word, or two. Is mankind body and soul-spirit (bipartite), or body, soul and spirit (tripartite)? This is the way the question has been put since the very beginning of reflection on a Christian doctrine of mankind.

Karl Barth has said man *is* body and soul, in common with all independent living creatures of earth (i.e. animals but not plants), but he *has* spirit also by virtue of the coming of God's Spirit into vital union with the soul, rendering him thus a person, ego, self-conscious being. This is something more than dichotomy, something less than trichotomy. It is indeed a mixed view. Mankind *is* body and soul but he *has* spirit (not a spirit) or Spirit depending on what point of anthropology Barth is making. Paul's dictum, 'In him we live and move and have our being' (Acts 17:28), together with the many texts which associate beginning and support of life with the entrance of God's Spirit as in Psalm 104:30, are Barth's scriptural support for this doctrine. This presence of Spirit/spirit is what renders each member of the human race different from 'the beasts which perish'; it is the unique *humanity* of every human being.

One is never quite certain Barth himself would agree with this or any other summary of his doctrine, but this is how I understand his very extended statements, restatements, summaries, cautions and distinctions over the 100 plus pages of his treatment of the elements of human nature.[1]

The theory meshes with Barth's soteriology and eschatology. For him, God has graciously taken the human race into a covenant of salvation whereby all ultimately will be saved. Therefore he has no problem with the presence of God in the 'mode' (Barth's word) of Spirit residing permanently in union with every soul of man. I shall regard this view, in my further discussion, as a variety of dichotomy view, to be treated shortly, as Barth indeed shows without employing the word 'dichotomy.'

---

1. Karl Barth, *Church Dogmatics iv* (Edinburgh: T. & T. Clark, 1936, 1975), pp. 344–436.

Anthropological Monism.

There are many monisms in philosophy – idealism and materialism in metaphysics as well as pantheisms of various sorts. All regard ultimate reality, the basic building blocks of the universe, as a single essence or substance. In theological anthropology this not very apt name is employed for the view that what others call soul does not and cannot exist apart from the body. Hence when the body dies the soul ceases to exist. By some it is said to sleep. This is not the same figure of speech which the Bible employs where the sleep-like posture and appearance of a corpse suggests 'sleep.' Jesus and Paul both employ it (John 11:11; 1 Thess. 4:13,14).

Monism can lead to other results than soul-sleep, in older literature called *psychopannychia*.[2] The error often arises among folk who begin by fixing attention on the many texts of Scripture which do indeed speak of the *normal* unity of each "specimen" of our kind, then proceed by reinterpreting the doctrine of death as annihilation and non-existence or sleep until a future resurrection, a resurrection which would really be a re-creation. Passages which speak clearly of the conscious existence of the soul 'whether in the body or out of the body' are then wrested to support their case.

Dr. Murray Harris, in two books, *Raised Immortal* (Eerdmans, 1985) and *From Grave to Glory* (Baker, 1990), insisted on a 'basic monism of the New Testament' and managed the New Testament texts to teach that each believer at death immediately receives a permanent resurrection body. So there is no period of disembodiment between death and resurrection. According to this scheme apparently our earthly bodies remain in their graves forever. He supposes that after teaching a physical resurrection of believers at the future Second Advent in a very early Epistle (Gal. 4:13 ff.) Paul changed his mind and taught reception of a spiritual body, freshly created at the moment of one's death in the later Epistle (2 Cor. 5:1 ff.).[3]

Dr. Harris claims the names of thirty-eight modern scholars as supporting this change in Paul's teaching.[4] I noticed few conservative scholars' names in his list. It has been reported that Dr. Harris may have reversed his opinion. He has done so on other matters of doctrine.

As we shall see, monism (the doctrine that the human soul has no existence apart from a body) is unbiblical and, if strictly adhered to, is incompatible with orthodox Christianity. Yet it can be innocently stated in connection with an undoubted truth: each individual man is truly a psychosomatic unity. If one adds the word indissoluble as in, 'Each human being is an indissoluble psychosomatic unity,' then monism is being affirmed, that is, the soul does not exist apart from the body. What is frequently meant is, each human being is *normally* (that is if sin and death had never introduced an abnormality into the human situation) a psycho-somatic unity. At death body and soul are rent apart. The unity is broken, the body going to death and dissolution, the soul to be in heaven or hell!

The doctrine of monism is prevalent today in liberal theologies of the Old Testament as well as in Reformation times among certain radical Anabaptists. Soul-sleep, corollary of monism among religious people, is official teaching of several Adventists sects, notably Seventh Day Adventists. An offical publication sets forth the teaching in detail.[5] The book states, 'The dust of the ground minus the breath of life yields a dead person or dead soul without any consciousness.... The elements that made up the body return to the earth from which they came.... The soul has no conscious existence apart from the body, and no Scripture indicates that at death the soul survives as a conscious entity.'[6] I have already addressed this ancient error in a previous chapter. It is introduced here simply as one of the views of the non-material side of mankind. It has never been held by any large number of otherwise orthodox believers.

It would be a distraction from Christian theology at this point to go deeply into the question of mind-body relationships as treated in philosophy and psychology. The following summarizes what you might learn about mind-brain (body-mind) connections in a college course in Introduction to Philosophy. For strict *materialists* there is no problem. We are our bodies, our thoughts are electrical brain waves, energy passing through nerve cells, or like the morning star and the evening star, two ways of viewing the planet Venus. For pure *idealists* we and everything else in the world are pure ideas, hence no problem. The idealists and materialists think reality is of one kind of 'substance' – they are called *monists*. Granting the soul and body are not the same, philosophers have proposed that mind

---

2. The young Calvin wrote a book in refutation of 'soul sleep,' *Psychopannychia*, available in English (*Calvin Trails*, trans. H. Beveridge, Edinburgh: Calvin Translation Society, 1851, which I found valuable in refuting the error in present forms of what in the sixteenth century was regarded as an 'Anabaptist error').
3. Murray Harris, *Raised Immortal* (Grand Rapids: Eerdmans, 1985) p. 98.
4. ibid., p. 255, note 2.
5. *Seventh-Day Adventists Believe* (Hagerstown, MD: Review & Herald, 3rd printing, 1989), chap. 7, 'The Nature of Man.'
6. ibid., pp. 352, 353.

and body interact causally on one another producing both mental events and events in our bodies (*Interactionism*). *Parallelism* holds minds and bodies are not causally connected but even so are correlated in some mysterious way, running side by side. Nicholas Malebranche (1638–1715), a Catholic philosopher, proposed God Himself is the causal connection between body and mind (soul). God produces corresponding mental and physical events. When the mind wills the body to do something, on that occasion God causes the body to do it (hence *occasionalism*). This is not a widely held view in today's secular climate. A more popular theory today holds that while body and mind (whatever it is) are not the same, two kinds of entity, all mental occurrences have physical causes. There is no reciprocal effect. Conscious, mental processes simply accompany certain events (processes) in the neural (nerve) system – hence *epiphenomenal*, like the fever which accompanies an infection, the mental effects are not the *main* event. So this primarily medical term enters philosophy. The theologian is under no biblical obligation to adopt any of these theories, though it is useful to know about them.

Evidences of Dichotomy.

Some such theories seem amenable to Christian teachings about the soul and body of mankind. The Bible says much of flesh and spirit as ethical terms, but nothing of a mode of brain-mind connections. Barth reluctantly addresses the subject of the soul's relation to the body and brain.

In one of his better passages (he says he will be brief and in a measure succeeds) Barth points out that 'the Bible actually describes the activity of the body and its organs wholly as that of the soul, or conversely, and in the same terms, the activity of its soul wholly as that of its body.'[7] He has already made four summary points explaining how 'The human existence of the one man is that he [the man] is the soul of his body and then also the body of his soul.'[8]

In the Old Testament, Barth points out, the flesh cries out for the living God (Ps. 84:2) and that flesh does so in a dry and thirsty land (Ps. 63:1). Sometimes a person's 'bones are troubled' (Ps. 6:2), or strengthened by God (Isa. 58:11) or waste away when a person keeps silent before God (Ps. 32:3), or the bones may even rejoice (Ps. 51:8). Other parts of the individual human being stand for the whole man, body and soul. He cites bowels (Jer. 4:19; Job 30:27; Lam. 1:20) the reins (kidneys) (Jer. 11:20 KJV; Ps. 7:9 KJV; Prov. 23:16 KJV). 'More frequent and emphatic... is the heart.'[9] Barth thinks that these expressions are poetic, but not purely figurative. They must be understood as referring to both body and soul 'or they cannot be understood at all.'[10]

Barth has put his own mark here upon what is a near consensual interpretation of the biblical information. An article by V. E. Anderson and B. R. Reichenbach on the contributions of modern science to understanding human nature ends: 'One might wish that from this discussion a definitive picture of the human person might arise.' They admit failure on this point but claim their study 'does point to a number of important conclusions.' If I may be permitted to summarize: (1) both brain and genetic research have enlarged our knowledge of important formative roles played by our biological heritage; (2) this 'bottom up' approach, though somewhat fruitful, cannot give a 'complete account' of mankind without learning from a 'social science', which they characterize as top down; (3) hence, practice of medicine and other health care must be 'holistic'; (4) the scientific account of the human person is from the Christian perspective incomplete, for it fails to take account of our relatedness to God. They appeal for an approach to study of mankind which employs 'both the lenses.' The cautious authors do not seem hopeful. Agreed. We will wait and see where science leads.[11]

Dichotomy and Trichotomy.

Monism is essentially an unbiblical and un-Christian teaching. Even as explained by some early Anabaptist and presently by Seventh Day Adventist believers, it must be labeled error. H. C. Thiessen says, 'All are agreed that man has both a material and an immaterial nature. His material nature is body; his immaterial nature is his soul and spirit.'[12] Most

---

7. Barth, *Church Dogmatics iii*, 2, p. 435.
8. ibid., p. 432.
9. ibid., p. 435.
10. ibid., p. 435.
11. Anderson and Reichenbach, 'Imagined through the Lens Darkly: Human Personhood and the Sciences' in *Journal of the Evangelical Theological Society*, 33,2, June, 1990, pp. 197-213.
12. H. C. Thiessen, *Introductory Lectures in Systematic Theology* (Grand Rapids: Eerdmans, 1949), p. 225.

theologians hold that soul and spirit are not two 'parts' but alternate names for the same, sometimes with different emphasis. This view is called *dichotomy*. A smaller number hold soul and spirit are not the same, i.e. distinct parts of mankind's threefold nature. This view is called *trichotomy*.

Anthropological Dichotomy.

The word 'dichotomy' is derived from the Greek word for two and the word for part. In theology it refers to the theory that complete human nature (the whole man) is composed of two and only two elements. In contrast to monists, dichotomists hold that soul or mind is not *per se* a function of body (brain), nor is its existence dependent on the body. In contrast to the trichotomy theory, anthropological dichotomy holds that the soul (= spirit) includes all our non-material features and qualities – emotions, intellect, i.e. both feeling and thinking, as well as choosing.

Dichotomy does not deny that human nature is normally a unity. 'The Bible teaches us to view the nature of man as a unity, and not as a duality.'[13] During life on this earth each person exists as a unit, not two elements, body and soul in parallel. It is the whole man who is well or sick, who is innocent or guilty, and who is alive or dead. When God created mankind, admittedly the body is represented as formed first, into which God breathed the breath of life (Gen. 2:7). When the text adds that the man 'became a living soul' the meaning is that man was now a living being, an animated being. That animation in his case came as a special act of his Creator so his life was not the same as other animate things (animals). The text does not mean that man is a soul which inhabits a body. True, Scripture plainly teaches that the conscious soul endures in a disembodied state after the man dies, but Jesus did not say (Luke 16:22) that the body of the beggar died and the soul lived on. He said 'The poor man died' – the *whole man* died. Of course his body went to dissolution, but the LORD went on to say the beggar 'was carried by the angels to Abraham's bosom'(KJV).

Jesus speaks of Lazarus in Paradise and of the rich man in Hades, each a soul without the natural body, as a person – a man, a human being. I say that my father and mother, both as persons (if not quite whole until the resurrection), are present with the Lord in heaven. But I mean something quite different when I say my parents sleep side by side in their graves in a graveyard in Yakima County, Washington.

Though it is natural to say that the body is dead while the soul lives on in heaven, of Lazarus the beggar's case, it is more correct to say, 'Jane Doe is dead,' as when Jesus Himself declared of another man with the same name: 'Lazarus has died.' The body of Lazarus of Bethany has now long since dissolved to physical elements (for after awhile Lazarus died again); his soul endures in heaven with Christ. As long as we understand this we will not be greatly in error when we inexactly say the soul lives on after death, or even that it *survives* death. Jesus, Himself, seems to have suggested such (Matt. 22:33) and perhaps also Peter (1 Peter 3:18 'made alive in the spirit'; also RSV, ASV, cf. NEB).

Both dichotomists and trichotomists agree in what has just been said. Their differences are not critical, except that some have used trichotomy to support erroneous theories of original sin, of sanctification and of the two natures of Christ. These errors are not, however, inherent in trichotomism and are equally rejected by both orthodox parties.

The real enemies of trichotomy are enemies likewise of dichotomy – the anthropological monists in psychology who see nothing but a material organism in mankind, in whom all intellectual, affective and volitional elements are functions of the body (brain, neurons and the like). Gordon H. Clark has provided a succinct epitome of mind-body theories from ancient to modern times.[14]

It is probably impossible for faith-compelling 'scientific' proof ever to be produced for the existence of the human soul apart from the body. Maybe 'honest unbelief' is possible, but research since about 1950 may have made it less respectable. A long article in *Coronet* magazine (3/51) began, 'Startling experiments are lifting a mysterious veil and confounding the skeptics.' The experiments were by doctors treating brain-damaged or epileptic patients at the Neurological Institute in Montreal. The article summarized: 'When everything about the brain (including all its physical and mental associations) has been explained and explored, something inexplicable remains. The surgeon can make the patient move, hear, see, have sensations and even dream dreams. But the patient never believes that he does these things of his own accord.' By stimulating the appropriate region of the portion of the brain, exposed by surgery, with an electrode 'The doctor can force the patient to lift his arm but he cannot make the patient *will* to do

---

13. G. C. H. Berkouwer, *Man: The Image of God* (Grand Rapids: Eerdmans, 1962), p. 192.
14. In 'A Philosophical Appendix,' Gordon H. Clark, *The Biblical Doctrine of Man*, 2nd ed. (The Trinity Foundation, 1992), pp. 88–95.

it... although [the surgeon] now can probe into the brain's deepest recesses [he], still cannot manipulate the human mind... Scientists have begun discovery of the physical basis [intrument?] of the mind – the "seat of the soul"... but their work does not explain the nature of the elusive spirit who seems to dwell there.' The scientists have discovered the switchboard but the operator, who is apparently there, is still beyond their reach.

This and much further research is fully reported, along with names of the scientists and their reports, in *The Mysterious Matter of the Mind* by the late A. C. Custance, M.D.[15] The book is very encouraging reading.

Again, dichotomy asserts that mankind's nature is in one respect material, called *body* or *flesh,* and in another respect immaterial, called *spirit* or *soul*. Further, the immaterial aspect of mankind is one element of our being, not two.

Trichotomy as noted above holds that there are two distinct elements in our immaterial nature, *soul* and *spirit*. The soul (*psuche*) is the principle of our animal life, perhaps seat of the emotions, and the spirit (*pneuma*) is the principle of our rational life – intellect, conscience, will and similar.

As evidence that dichotomy is the better theory, I cite the following:

1. Reflection on human conscious awareness can distinguish an immaterial element and a material element in my being but not two immaterial ones. The material (body) and immaterial (soul) are always associated and interactive in this present life. I can discern that some pleasures (taste of candy) and pains (a sore throat) are more directly concerned with the material, and others with my emotional life (the pleasures of sight and sound, enjoyment of baseball), and still others with intellectual accomplishment (winning at checkers, understanding quadratic equations); but I am not aware that there is one seat of enjoyment of sight and sound and another of winning at checkers.

2. There is no two-stage in-breathing of the divine Spirit at creation, but one action (Gen. 2:7) whereby the clayish body was made a whole human being. Life from God gave the body a single added principle. Together they constitute mankind a living being. In the language of the Old Testament life and soul exchange (Job 27:33; 32:8; 33:4 and 18), indicating a possible identity intended by the language.

3. The words 'soul' and 'spirit,' not only in the English Bible but in the original texts, are frequently used interchangeably, that is, 'so far from the *nephesh* [Heb.], *psychē* [Gr.], *anima* [Lat.] or soul, being distinguished from *ruah* [Heb.], *pneuma* [Gr.], *animus* [Lat.], or mind [or spirit]... these words all designate one and the same thing. They are constantly interchanged... [or] substituted... and all that is predicated of the one... is predicated of the other.'[16] Many passages support these statements.[17]

4. The soul is assigned the very highest place in man's nature, in no wise less capable of personal relation to God than the spirit, contrary to the trichotomist view. The Bible refers to the soul (*nephesh, psyche*) as the principle of life; it can be saved or lost; it goes to meet God when we die; 'The soul is the man himself.'[18] Leviticus 4:2, quoted elsewhere in Scripture, says it is the soul that sins. Everywhere in Leviticus this is so. It is for the soul that atonement is made. The soul loves God. 1 Peter 1:9, as other texts, says that the end of faith is the soul's salvation. The list could go on. There is nothing in human nature higher, more capable of fellowship with other persons or even God than our soul.

5. To the same effect, the Bible represents body and soul, or body and spirit, or body, soul and spirit as constituting the whole person. Such is the force of Jesus' remark regarding body and soul (Matt. 10:28), of Paul's regarding body and spirit (1 Cor. 5:3), and again of Paul's regarding 'your whole spirit and soul and body' (1 Thess. 5:23). In the last case Paul seems to be speaking non-technically, indicating the whole of each and every man, woman and child, and emphasizing the idea by repeating the idea with a different term – as Jesus did (Mark 12:30, 33).

6. A. H. Strong calls attention to passages of Scripture in which the *soul* is distinguished not from the *human* spirit but from the divine Spirit from whom the human spirit proceeded originally (to Adam) and from the body. Numbers 16:22; Zechariah 12:1; 1 Corinthians 2:11; and Hebrews 12:9 distinguish the Spirit of God from other spirits whom He has created and thereby refute emanationism or pantheism. Genesis 35:18, 1 Kings 17:21, Ecclesiastes 12:7 and James 2:26 distinguish the soul, or spirit, of man from his body and refute monism and materialism.

---

15. A. C. Custance, *The Mysterious Matter of the Mind* (Grand Rapids: Zondervan and Probe Ministries, Int'l, Richardson, TX 75080, 1980), p. 105.
16. Charles A. Hodge, *Systematic Theology II* (Grand Rapids: Eerdmans, 1970), p. 48.
17. Examples are Gen. 41:8; cf. Ps. 42:6; John 12:27; cf. 13:21; Matt. 2:28; cf. 27:50; Heb. 12:23; cf. Rev. 6:9.
18. op. cit., p. 48.

7. In a class by itself are references to the soul (*psychē*) and spirit (*pneuma*) of Jesus. In one of the seven sayings of Christ on the cross he cried, 'Father, into your hands I commit my spirit [*pneuma*]' (Luke 23:46) and it is said that 'he bowed his head and gave up his spirit [*pneuma*]' (John 19:30). Yet in other texts it is said he gave 'his life [*psyche*] as a ransom' (Matt. 20:28) and 'I lay down my life [*psyche*] for the sheep' (John 10:15).

Anthropological Trichotomy.

Anthropological trichotomy is the view that human nature has three distinct elements or aspects: body, soul and spirit.

The view took form very early as part of efforts by the Fathers Clement of Alexandria and Origen to harmonize original sin with free will and regeneration. Clement taught that the initiative in renewal of the sinful human heart is taken by the free will of the sinner himself. Fallen man still has power to turn toward God and holiness, after which God will help him. Origen said that though God gives the faculty to will righteousness, mankind's power to use it is wholly his own, with God's help. W. G. T. Shedd comments:

> To understand their theory of original sin it will be necessary first to exhibit their psychology. They subdivided the constitution of man into *soma*, *psuche* and *pneuma*. The first was the material part; the second included the principle of animal life, together with the sensuous appetites and passions that relate to the physical world; while the third was the rational and spiritual principle, including the will and the moral affections of human nature.[19]

According to these two teachers at Alexandria, the corruption of original sin inheres only in the body and sensuous parts (soul = *psychē*) of mankind but not his spirit (*pneuma*). But they thought that each spirit pre-existed from an earlier epoch and since it entered the body after conception it did not directly participate in the corruption inherent in soul and body by generation of parents. Will is seated only in the *pneuma* (= spirit), the *psychē* (= soul) and is free to do as corrupt body and soul incline to or not to do so. Hence, though caused to sin by corrupt body and soul, the spirit does so by free will![20]

Another ancient error found support in trichotomy. According to Apollinaris, Bishop of Laodicea (died about 390), Christ derived only a human body and soul (*psyche*) from the Virgin Mary. However, the spirit (*pneuma*) of Christ was not a human spirit but the eternal Word. Jesus had no human *nous* (mind), or *pneuma* (spirit), in which case our LORD was two-thirds man and one-third God – a *tertium quid* (a third kind of entity, neither human nor divine). Apollinaris' proposal seemed reasonable to many in a time when the 'Christological problem' occupied the attention of all the best minds in Christendom, that is, from the First Ecumenical Council (Nicea 325) to the Fourth (Chalcedon 451). Trichotomy is not rendered false because it became the vehicle for a seriously defective Christology, of course. Though regarded then and now as a 'capable and enthusiastic defender of the Nicene orthodoxy... Apollinaris, his teachings and his followers, were condemned at Rome in 377, at Antioch in 378, by the... Second Ecumenical Council at Constantinople in 381, and by Rome again in 382.... The Decree of Chalcedon (451) was very explicit in its rejection of Apollinarinism.'[21]

More recently, uncritical, popular anthropology has been heard to say that unsaved people have intact a living body and soul but are without a living spirit, hence incomplete until at regeneration the Holy Spirit makes the spirit alive. Ephesians 2:1, of course, is cited.

Most trichotomists of today, however, are not errorists or heretics. On the basis of Paul's references to *natural* man (*psychikos*), *carnal* man (*sarkikos*) and *spiritual* man (*pneumatikos*) in 2 Corinthians 2:14–3:4 and 1 Thessalonians 5:23 (which says, may 'your whole spirit and soul and body be preserved blameless' KJV) a threefold nature of mankind is posited. A supporting text is Hebrews 4:12 which speaks of God's word as 'piercing to the division of soul and spirit' (RSV). Yet, the verse does not say soul and spirit are separated, but penetrated. Soul and spirit are in apposition here. Mark 12:30, where heart, soul and mind indicate not three immaterial parts of human nature but simply one's innermost being, is cited by opponents of such an interpretation of these texts.

Most theologians agree that there is a higher *aspect* or *activity* of mankind's immaterial, invisible nature, the rational aspect which is 'receptive of the Spirit of God' (Alford on Heb. 4:12), and lower aspect which he has in common with animals. Like animals, which also are conscious, though not self-conscious, man has many

---

19. W. G. T. Shedd, *A History of Christian Doctrine II* (Minneapolis: Klock & Klock Christian Publ., reprint 1978), pp. 34, 35.
20. ibid., p. 34.
21. J. L. Neve, *A History of Christian Thought*, vol. I (Philadelphia: The Muhlenburg Press, 1946), pp. 126, 127.

appetites for which the organ of expression is the body. Unlike animals he is a self-conscious person, is attracted to 'goodness, beauty and truth,' and has personal attributes and functions by virtue of being in the image of the Person who created him. It is not unbiblical to call the lower 'part' soul or soulish (*psychikos*) and the higher, spirit or spiritual (*pneumatikos*). Yet soul and spirit, as frequently used interchangeably, do not designate two parts of mankind's invisible nature.

I am partially obliged to A. H. Strong for suggesting six reasons, aside from the main theological considerations, for regarding trichotomy as untenable.

- *Pneuma* as well as *psychē* is used of the brute creation, even of fish (Rev. 3:21; 16:3).
- *Psychē* is ascribed to Jehovah (Amos 6:8, Heb. 'by his soul'; Isa. 42:1; Jer. 9:9; Heb. 10:38).
- The disembodied (righteous) dead are called *psychae*, souls (Rev. 6:9; 20:4).
- The highest exercises of religion are attributed to the *psychē* (Mark 12:30; Luke 1:46; Heb. 6:18,19; James 1:21).
- To lose the *psychē* is to lose all (Mark 8:36, 37).
- Passages relied on to support that soul and spirit are two parts of our immaterial aspect may be better explained not to indicate that the soul and spirit are two distinct substances or parts, but to designate the immaterial aspect of mankind's being from different points of view.

6
The Origin of the Soul

There is a certain irony in the appearance of this topic in a book of systematic theology, for all theologians agree the Bible says little or nothing direct and specific about how human beings acquire their souls. Yet a quick check of some seventy volumes of systematic and biblical theology within reach shows that most who treat biblical anthropology have a section on this subtopic and several have extensive discourses on 'the origin of the soul'! An interesting major exception is John Calvin, who was somewhat impatient of any discussion of the subject of the origin of souls (see below).

Shedd (1888) devotes 132 pages advocating Traducianism; Barth (1951) has hundreds of pages, expounding an existentialist metaphysic with an act-of-God formula for body-soul-spirit connection; Aquinas (thirteenth century) devotes 142 pages of the *Summa Theologica* anthropology and later six pages to a creationist doctrine of the origin of human souls since Adam – and so on.[1] Thomas Aquinas is the only theological writer I have encountered who labeled 'heretical' the view that human souls are derived from human parents. Granted his premises, of course, he was correct.

The subject can be slighted but not quite ignored. Why? Because of the inextricable connection of the origin of the soul with the doctrines of inborn, or original sin, together with a proper understanding of imputation of Adam's guilt for sin to all people and the imputation of Christ's righteousness to all who believe, i.e. to the elect. The precise connections will appear more plainly when those topics are discussed later.

In previous chapters we have treated the existence of the human soul as a distinct, identifiable immaterial substance normally joined to the body, but the origin of souls, whether by natural generation (procreation) by the parents from generation to generation or by special divine creation, the only proposals compatible with biblical Christianity, is quite another question, yet to be addressed. It must be addressed before the question of imputation of sin may be logically addressed.

If the substance of my soul was present in Adam, if the substance of Adam's soul was passed on to me by natural generation, then I participated in Adam's fall and all the results of it *really* and therefore I am guilty of his sin by participation in it. When theologians use 'really' and 'real' of our presence in Adam's nature and participation in his probation and fall they are not thereby pledged to philosophical realism in the question of the status of universals.

---

1. Aquinas, *Summa Theologica*, trans. by the English Dominican Province (Westminster, MD: Christian *Classics*, 1911, 1981), Q 118, art. 2.

One can take any view of that and still affirm *natural*, *seminal* or *real* existence of the human nature we each possess in Adam.

On the other hand, if God creates each soul individually at natural conception or birth it apparently becomes sinful by the effect of union with a corrupt (depraved) body not by immediate participation in Adam's sin. In such a case the guilt of Adam's sin is imputed to me because God counted the whole race in Adam and therefore God imputes Adam's sin with all its results to me. I was not there except by representation. In the first view (Traducianism) Adam was my *seminal* or *natural* 'head'; in the second (creationism) my *federal* or *covenant* head (representative or federal view).

Views of the Origin of Individual Human Souls.

Roman Catholic theologians, who always like to start with the patristic age, have slightly different names for the views, providing a somewhat more specific analysis than the Protestant nomenclature does. Ludwig Ott speaks of (1) *Pre-existentialism*, (2) *Emanationism*, (3) *Creationism* and (4) *Traducianism*.

1. Pre-existentialism.

Pre-existentialism teaches that souls exist even before connection with physical bodies – according to Plato and Origen, from all eternity – and are exiled in bodies, as a punishment for moral defect.[2] He points out it was condemned by synods in 543 and 561. See Denzinger in *Sources of Catholic Dogma*.[3] Orthodox Christianity in all its branches shook off this pagan outlook in the fourth century and has never again been overcome by it. Passages of Scripture which specifically renounce such a view are Genesis 1:31, which pronounces the first man 'good' – in soul and body; Romans 5:12, which says sin entered the world through the disobedient act of our first parents; and Romans 9:11, which says of Jacob and Esau that while in their mother's womb they had not yet done either good or evil. For biblically oriented Christians this idea is scarcely more than a curiosity – more related to the pagan Greek *metempsychosis* and Hindu *samsara* (reincarnation) than Christian revelation.

2. Emanationism.

Emanationism is Ott's word. Protestants know of it but usually make no mention of it. Barth is an exception. He says: 'According to this doctrine the human soul is an efflux or emanation of the divine substance. It is not a creature, but of divine substance.'[4] In the present time, when Eastern pantheistic religions are competing for the minds of Christians, it is important to know that there were ancient Gnostic and Manichaean sects, renounced by the undivided church, which taught that every human being is an emanation *out of* God (not a creation by God). Mystical extremes among Christians throughout our history have veered toward that error. Catholic mystics seeking the 'beatific vision' of God have yielded ground toward it. Modern 'New Age' religion revels in it.[5]

3. Creationism.

According to this view 'the soul of the child is created by the immediate agency of God.'[6] The important word is 'immediate,' for Traducianists hold that God creates children mediately through human parents by *procreation*. Though a leading contender for this view, Hodge closes his remarks in a way quite amenable to Traducianism: 'Creationism does not necessarily suppose that there is any other exercise of the immediate power of God in production of the soul, than such as takes place in the production of life in other cases.'[7] He admits that 'since the origin of souls is not clearly revealed in Scripture' certainty cannot be attained. Yet creationism becomes pivotal to much Hodge later has to say about imputation of Adam's sin to the race in a succeeding chapter. His Scripture

---

2. Ludwig Ott, *Fundamentals of Catholic Dogma*, 4th edition (Rockford, IL: TAN Books, 1954, 1974), p. 99.
3. Henry Denzinger, *The Sources of Catholic Dogma* (St. Louis: Herder & Herder, 1954, 1957), pp. 203, 236.
4. Karl Barth, *Church Dogmatics III* (Edinburgh: T. & T. Clark, 1936), pp. 572, 573.
5. A footnote in the Westminster ed. of Calvin's *Institutes* (Calvin, *Institutes I*, p. 249, note 10) calls this view '*Traducianism*, by which Adam's soul is regarded as bearing an element transmitted from the divine essence and as the source of all human souls.' Such use of 'Traducianism' can be defended etymologically, but in ordinary theological discourse emanationism and Traducianism are poles apart in meaning. Perhaps the note itself is in error. I know of no confirmation of such employment of 'Traducianism' except in this note.
6. Charles Hodge, *Systematic Theology ii* (Grand Rapids: Eerdmans, repr. 1970), p. 70.
7. ibid., p. 76.

'proofs' of creationism are brief and inconclusive though he thinks their trend is 'against traducianism and in favor of creationism.'[8]

Though many Reformed theologians tend to favor creationism (as more amenable to an emphasis on the idea of covenant of grace and the 'federal headship' of Adam) Calvin himself seems less than decisive. His comments are very precise in his discussion of the seat of original sin and its transmission.[9] He is somewhat impatient with emphasis on the problem: 'Who should worry about the derivation of the soul when he hears that Adam had received for us no less than for himself those gifts which he lost.' Though not all agree in my opinion, it seems to me that the rest of the section leaves Calvin uncommitted to any theory of the origin of the soul.[10] The older Augustine ended up the same way, even though the younger Augustine was Traducianist. Luther was aware of the state of the problem though ultimately inclined to 'Augustine's theory of Traducianism.'[11] Lutheran theologians generally are Traducianists. F. Pieper lists the subject of the soul's origin among 'open questions.'[12] Theologians who distinguish very severely between God's acts of *creation* (which ended on the seventh day of the creative week) and His continuing work of providence, tend to be Traducianists, as, e.g. A. H. Strong[13] and, very interestingly, Gordon Clark, who says, 'Traducianism is well nigh inescapable.'[14] Clark digests Shedd's overwhelming biblical argument for Traducianism and declares it a winner over C. A. Hodge's 'poor showing.'[15] But Luther does not make that strong a distinction, hence, 'He who made man out of the ground also creates men to this day from the blood of the parents.'[16] This is Traducianism.

Arguments for creationism are not complicated.

1. Ott (Roman Catholic) says creationism 'is intimated in Ecclesiastes 12:7: "The spirit returns to God who gave it,"... and Hebrews 12:9 (distinction between fathers of the flesh and the Father of Spirits = God).' In *Fundamentals of Catholic Dogma* Ott also cites the apocryphal Wisdom 15:11. C. Hodge would add Zechariah 12:1, God forms 'the spirit of man within him'; Isaiah 42:5, 'God... giveth breath to the people... and spirit'; Numbers 16:22, 'God of the spirits of all flesh,' i.e. spirits of people's bodies.[17] Berkhof and other creationists rely on the same texts, of which Hebrews 12:9 is by far the strongest as F. Delitzch, a Traducianist, asserts in his *Commentary on Hebrews* (loc. cit.).

2. Creationism 'is clearly far more consistent with the nature of the human soul than Traducianism.'[18] Creationists claim that the soul, being immaterial, is also simple and indivisible (Hodge and Berkhof). God can create such new souls, but Traducianists must, according to Hodge and Berkhof, admit separation out from the substance of Adam's soul if their spirits are generated (procreated) by parents. Aquinas agrees similarly.[19] Shedd, who has produced perhaps the most persuasive and voluminous arguments for Traducianism, agrees as to the fact: 'Generation in the Godhead admits no abscission or division of substance; but generation in the instance of the creature implies separation of essence. A human person is an individualized *portion* of humanity.'[20] He obviously thinks this is no obstacle to Traducianism. No one knows precisely how our bodies (complex) are separated out in seminal substance from the substance of our parent's bodies. Recent discoveries about cells, genes and DNA, and the like still do not tell us how, hence they provide no advance useful to a theology of the origin of souls.

3. Creationists point out that they have no problem explaining our LORD's sinless human nature, for sin of nature belongs to soul not body. If God created the human soul of Jesus *de novo*, it was obviously sinless and remained so, but creationists must be embarrassed by the fact that they cannot explain how immediately created souls of the rest of the human race are invariably sinful. Both Hodge and Berkhof (I cite them as representative evangelical creationists) both acknowledge the difficulty. Traducianists almost invariably account for our LORD's sinless soul and uncorrupt body by the miraculous conception in the virgin, without a human male parent, by a sancification of the

---

8. ibid., p. 71.
9. Calvin, *Institutes II*, 1. 7.
10. ibid.
11. Paul Althaus, *The Theology of Martin Luther* (Phladelphia: Fortress Press, 1966), p. 160.
12. Francis Pieper, *Church Dogmatics i* (St. Louis: Concordia Publ., 1950), p. 94.
13. A. H. Strong, *Systematic Theology* (Valley Forge, PA: Judson Press, 1907), pp. 493-497.
14. Gordon Clark, *The Biblical Doctrine of Man* (The Trinity Foundation, 1992), p. 53.
15. ibid., pp. 45-52.
16. ibid., p. 88.
17. C. Hodge, op. cit., pp. 70, 71.
18. Louis Berkhof, *Systematic Theology* (Grand Rapids: Eerdmans, reprint 1979), p. 199.
19. Aquinas, *Summa Theologica I*, Q 118, art. 2.
20. W. G. T. Shedd, *A History of Christian Doctrine ii* (Minneapolis: Klock & Klock Christian Publ., 1978), p. 434 footnote.

human nature of Christ in the womb. Further, if, as creationists must say, all human souls invariably become sinful as result of union with bodies generated by Adam's fallen physical nature, why was not the same true in Christ's case? A miracle must be assumed in the case either of Traducianism or creationism.

4. Thomas Aquinas is the only author ancient, medieval or modern known to me, who declares Traducianism heretical. The heart of his reasoning is this: 'Since it [intellectual soul] is an immaterial substance it cannot be caused through generation, but only through creation by God. Therefore to hold that the intellectual soul is caused by the begetter, is nothing else than to hold the soul to be non-subsistent [i.e. not independently existent], and consequently to perish with the body. It is therefore heretical to say that the intellectual soul is transmitted with the semen.'[21] So, the Angelic Doctor thought 'generationism' (his name for Traducianism) no possible orthodox alternative because it led to what we might today call behaviorism, the psychological theory of Watson and Skinner. Of course, neither the ancient Traducianism of Tertullian and the early Augustine nor that more recently held by Shedd and Strong and others even remotely endorsed anything like the materialism Aquinas feared. Science can now describe the development of infant bodies in the womb but has no information as to ultimate causes, much less their souls! 'As you do not know the way the spirit comes to the bones in the womb of a woman with child, so you do not know the work of God who makes everything' (Eccles. 11:5).

4. Traducianism.

All human beings are in every respect a 'kind' or 'species' of living being and like every other sort of species of sexually-propagated living beings, the species was created whole in its first pair and propagated by them and successively by their progeny. Traducianism affirms that every human being is a divinely created being in the sense of mediate creation – God creating through human parents. God's creative power is employed in the beginnings of all life in nature, as Psalm 104:14-30 proclaims, climaxing in the words, 'When you send forth your Spirit, they are created.' When God hides His face, 'they are dismayed; when you take away their breath, they die and return to their dust' (v. 29). But in every case of such beginning of life in 'man or beast' God's power is effected in the parent-medium. We do not know how God's power is extended to or effected in the parent, to produce offspring any more than we know how, having created the worlds, His power now sustains them in their places by His invisible forces. 'The laws of nature are the habits of God.' Throughout human history and to the present moment no one has yet quite figured out what any kind of natural life is, much less exactly how living human souls originate.

Traducianism need not affirm that either the body or the soul of the parents or body and soul together generate the child's soul. It seems almost impious to ask. It seems to be true that while every human body has parts, the soul is simple, having no parts. In such a case no one can know how separation of a part could take place. On the other hand neither do we know how generation of the body of a child takes place. We know about sperms, ova, gonads, wombs, birth canals and similar but no one has a clue as to what the life is which is previous to conception or afterward. Generation of souls is scarcely more mysterious. Perhaps human 'life' is the soul. If so, the biblical terms would harmonize perfectly, as any one familiar with the Hebrew and Greek vocabulary of human nature knows. The translations reflect it.

Biblical evidences supporting this view of the matter will be presented here: first, as the *natural sense* of the Genesis narrative; secondly, as indicated by the use of the *words for man*; thirdly, as indicated by the 'building' of woman *out of man*; fourthly, taking account of texts which seem to *forbid creation ex nihilo* of human souls; and fifthly, considering other texts that relate to the origin of human souls and that can be explained best by mediate creation, that is Traducianism.

1. *Supported by the natural sense of the Genesis narrative.* The creation of mankind climaxes a narrative wherein every living thing in the waters was to reproduce 'after their kind,' likewise every 'winged fowl' and every beast of the land and domestic animal 'after their kind.' In each case no one doubts the whole living creature in each offspring was to be *completely* the procreated offspring of its parents. Creation first of man, male, then of man, female comes precisely at the climax of that movement of the narrative, with the command to 'be fruitful and multiply.' It would be assumed by any one who reads on that the same would be the case, notice to the contrary lacking. The same fully 'after their kind' in every respect would be assumed to be the case when in obedience to the command to be fruitful, it is said 'And [connecting with previous narrative] Adam knew Eve his wife; and she conceived, and bare Cain' (Gen. 4:1 KJV). It is plain Eve was aware that God was the effecting power of the procreation (mediate creation), for she said, 'I have gotten a man from the LORD' (KJV). Genesis 5:1-3 carries the plain fact further when it says that God created man (generic, *adham*) 'in the likeness of God,' and that they, male and female, were called man (*adham*,

---

21. Aquinas, op. cit., 118.2.

generic man), and then that 'When Adam had lived for 130 years, he fathered a son in his own likeness.' Should we suppose that what Adam and Eve brought forth was half created *de novo* by God, utterly apart from their own procreative powers implanted in the first place by their Creator, God? I think not.

2. *That man was created a species*, that the species included the male and the female and was commanded as a species to be fruitful and multiply (Gen. 1:26-28), indicates clearly (the contrary absent) that every aspect of the species in the two parents would be replicated in the offspring, both body and soul. As already noted, *adham*, man in Genesis 1:26 ('Let us make man') and Genesis 1:27 ('So God created man') is without the article, indicating not a specific individual named Adam, but the race of mankind. When God 'formed' man of the dust (2:7) it is the same.

3. The species was in the first male (not yet called Adam). The woman (in Hebrew, 'female man') is drawn completely from the man. It is 'the man,' *adham* without the article (2:22), from whom a rib was taken and from whom the LORD God made a woman (2:22). Then 'the man' said 'she was taken out of Man' (2:23).

The Hebrew word for 'made' is *bana,* occuring over 300 times in the Old Testament and is almost invariably rendered build, built, building and the like, usually with employment of appropriate materials – wood, stone, brick and similar. Here God took the materials from the human specimen already created and this time *built* (not created) another specimen. I shall not here address the question if the female element of the species was present in Adam previous to the forming of Eve.

We must emphasize that the Greek New Testament even more distinctly affirms that man is a species, and that the common designation, *anthrōpos*, designates the race, composed of both males and females. And, further, it must be acknowledged that the most primitive and pervasive designation of that in all Germanic languages, including English, is simply man(n).

It seems to this writer that it takes some shading of evidence from sincere convictions drawn from another quarter of doctrine to suppose that *adham* and *anthrōpos* (whence 'anthropology') ever means just man's body to the exclusion of his soul.

4. We may grant to creationism that a creationist interpretation might be placed on the passages cited above where begetting, conceiving and bearing children are the subject. I do not know any evangelical creationists whom one would accuse of wresting Scripture in this connection. Is it possible that when it is said that Eve became 'the mother of all living' and that Adam 'fathered a son in his own likeness' the natural propagation was only of the bodies of offspring? That such is *not* the case is contrary, we think, the following texts of Scripture show.

Romans 1:3 (KJV) states that our LORD 'was made of the seed of David according to the flesh.' In this case, as in John 1:14, 'the Word became flesh,' flesh designates the whole human nature of Christ, body and soul. He 'was made' renders the verb *ginomai*, meaning 'to become.' It refers not to *ex nihilo* creation but in this case to conception and birth as in the nativity stories. Jesus' entire human nature therefore, body and soul, 'became,' through the virgin mother, seed of David. The passage does not even hint that His human soul was created *ex nihilo* by God.

Hebrews 12:9, often claimed in support of immediate creation of the soul. really supports Traducianism. The verse reads, 'we have had fathers of our flesh... and we gave them reverence: shall we not much rather be in subjection unto the Father of spirits, and live?' (KJV). Is this contrasting human males as fathers of our material nature and God as Father of our immaterial nature? Quite to the contrary. Note it is not said God is Father of *our* spirits, but simply of spirits. The argument is from the less to the greater to encourage reverence toward God. So the author is arguing that if we revere the lesser earthly parents of our humanity we surely should revere the greater universal heavenly Father-God of all spirits. The manner of generating parts of human nature is not even under consideration.

Other passages seem to imply quite direct, human, parental generation of the complete human nature of all offspring, i.e. Traducianism.

Genesis 46:26 (KJV) refers to the 'sons of Jacob' who migrated to Egypt as 'All the souls that came with Jacob into Egypt, that came out of his loins.' '[S]ouls' is plural (here) of *nephesh* with *kol*, 'All,' and means not soul in any narrow sense, as all agree, but is about equivalent to 'the whole people' – seventy plus or minus of them. The passage simply and without sophistication means that these people as such (the wives are not included) came out of Jacob's genital organs – not by Jacob's soul. No metonymy seems intended, though of course it is possible.

Hebrews 7:10 (KJV) and context argues for the superiority of Melchisedec's priesthood over that of the sons of Aaron by pointing out that Aaron's tribal eponym, Levi, was 'yet in the loins of his father [Levi], when Melchisedec met him [Abraham].' That reverence which Abraham (Levi and Aaron being in his generative organs) paid with 'tithes of all' (Gen. 14:20) to Melchisedec was not of mere physical posture (bowing or prostrating the body) but an act of spiritual worship of 'God Most High, Possessor of heaven and earth' (Gen. 14:19). One may scoff at the logic, if he wishes, of the notion that Aaron and his sons were, as to their souls, seminally present in Abraham's genital apparatus, but it is nevertheless the argument of the passage.

In Jeremiah 1:5 the initial divine summons of the prophet announces, 'Before I formed you in the womb I knew you, and before you were born I consecrated you; I appointed you a prophet.' Almost every devout scholar on record says this means that Jeremiah's tender heart impelled him to plead with his people with earnest tears; likewise his steadiness of purpose and courage, which enabled him to denounce kings, and generals, and priests and scholars, were formed by God in Jeremiah's soul in the gestation process in his mother. God knew him and consecrated him, but his parents procreated him, body and soul. All his ancestors had a part in generating the soul of the weeping prophet. Similar remarks could be made regarding Paul's birth. God, says Paul, 'set me apart before I was born, and… called me by his grace' (Gal. 1:15). Those qualities, which by heredity were part of Paul's nature, equipping him for apostolic missionary evangelism, were apparently not created *ex nihilo* but passed on to him from all his ancestors. Characteristics dominant or recessive from each mother and father back through the countless generations to our first parents came to manifestation again in the lively hearts, minds, souls and spirits of Jeremiah of Anathoth and Saul of Tarsus. Divine power working in providence 'created' the souls of the prophet and the Apostle as the same providence does for us all. These usual inferences were heard often of old from expository pulpits, no less from creationist pulpits than Traducianist, but more consistently, I think, from the latter.

I will close this treatment of the origin of human souls with some general remarks.

1. The origin of the soul became important to Calvinists persuaded of 'covenant theology.' In this system the ground of imputing Adam's sin to us is usually explained as the same as ground of imputing our sins to Christ – by the representative principle. Christ, though without sin, became our *representative* in bearing guilt and punishment as our representative in our place. So the sin of Adam our representative is imputed to us. Even though we were not in Eden we were there in the divine mind. We stood or fell with our 'federal head,' not because we were really there but because our representative was.

In this system the natural (seminal) presence of us all in Adam may be acknowledged, but if important, it is so only as making representation more appropriate. If our souls are drawn from Adam by genetic connection through the 'nature' then we were really present in Adam not merely representatively. Our soul-substance is then 'condemned already' naturally from the moment of conception. In federal-creationist theory the soul is not derived from Adam's substance, but created by God at conception. How souls become corrupt is therefore something of a mystery. In any case, say the federal theologians, they are culpable and guilty because they are counted so in their representative. So the parallel of covenant theology is preserved: the soul is guilty of sin the same way Christ on the cross was – by representation. Christ for us, Adam for us.

Calvin, himself, remained purposely naive on this subject. He roundly condemned the notion that human creation was by emanation out of God (a view by some called *Traduction*).[22] But Calvin also clearly implies a Traducian origin of our souls in an important passage. I refer to his discussion of what the editor of the Westminster Edition of the *Institutes* captions, 'Original Sin defined as depravity of nature which deserves punishment.'[23] He modestly declines a judgment on previous writers and says that 'it appears' to him 'originial sin is a hereditary depravity and corruption of nature, diffused into all parts of the soul.' Calvin goes on to 'note,' and I quote:

> First, we are so vitiated and perverted in every part of our nature that by this great corruption we stand justly condemned and convicted before God, to whom nothing is acceptable but righteousness, innocence, and purity. And this is not liability for another's transgression. For, since it is said that we became subject to God's judgment through Adam's sin, we are to understand it not as if we, guiltless and undeserving, bore the guilt of his offense but in the sense that, since we through his transgression have become entangled in the curse, he is said to have made us guilty. Yet not only has punishment fallen upon us from Adam, but a contagion imparted by him resides in us, which justly deserves punishment. For this reason, Augustine, though he often calls sin 'another's' to show more clearly that it is distributed among us through propagation, nevertheless declares at the same time that it is peculiar to each. And the apostle himself most eloquently testifies that 'death has spread to all because all have sinned' (Rom. 5:12). That is, they have been enveloped in original sin and defiled by its stains. For that reason, even infants themselves, while they carry their condemnation along with them from the mother's womb, are guilty not of another's fault but of their own. For, even though the fruits of their iniquity

---

22. Calvin, *Institutes I*, 15.5, note 15, Westminster Ed., 1960, p. 191.
23. ibid., ii, 1.7, p. 250.

have not yet come forth, they have the seed enclosed within them. Indeed, their whole nature is a seed of sin; hence it can be only hateful and abhorrent to God. From this it follows that it is rightly considered sin in God's sight, for without guilt there would be no accusation.[24]

Calvin herein affirms the essential feature of Traducianism: that a 'contagion imparted from him [Adam] resides in us, which justly deserves punishment.' This is not representation but participation, not federal headship and not quite affirmation of 'real presence' but certainly 'seminal presence.'

The great systematizer of scholastic Calvinism was Francis Turretin (1623–1687).[25] Turretin hedged on the subject. Though immediate creation of souls favored his system, as Shedd points out he 'vibrates' from preference for creationism to grudging acknowldgement of Traducianism: 'Both theories are in his system, and are found in conflict.' 'Turretin defines Adam as the "stem, root, and head of the human race"… (IX. ix. 23) but qualifies this by saying he was so "not only physically and seminally, but morally and representatively." But a representative proper could not be denominated the stem, root, and head of his constitutents.'[26]

Dr. J. O. Buswell was a late twentieth-century evangelical Presbyterian and admirer of the Hodges. In his survey of teaching on the origin of the soul in the theology of his Calvinist Augustinian antecedents (Augustine, the Hodges, Warfield – he seldom mentions Shedd in his writing) and relating the same to the birth of Christ, he pushes all supposed arguments aside and concludes by taking note of 'the perfect uniformity and regularity of the arrival of a soul whenever a human life begins to be.' He then observes, '[W]e usually ascribe the results [in other matters] to the secondary forces which God has created and which He maintains by His providence. For this reason only, I am inclined toward the traducian view.'[27] Gordon Clark digests Shedd's overwhelming biblical argument for Traducianism and declares it a winner over C. A. Hodge's poor showing.[28]

G. C. H. Berkouwer's treatment (the latest prominent European Dutch Reformed theologian to publish his views extensively) comprises a lengthy chapter. He concludes that we should simply reject the dilemma. I finished this part of his book, *Man, The Image of God*,[29] with disgust and I wrote, 'This chapter as many previous in this book leads nowhere. Problems are stated, views presented, some biblical evidence set forth but no attempt at synthesis. Shall we just give up on theology and write *mystery* or *enigma* after the title to each division. The mind of thoughtful people will not rest where Berkouwer leaves him.'

Finally, in his recent, quality systematic theology text, Robert Reymond is equally disaffected by Berkouwer's cop-out, denouncing it as 'reductionist… unscriptual and cannot be safely followed.'[30] Reymond's reasons for favoring the Traducianist view are, like Buswell's, not complicated: (1) the Bible throughout 'appears' to assume it; and (2) it solves the problem best.[31]

In concluding this chapter, I add (among other reasons for committment to the tradutionary origin of souls): it satisfies the requirements of Romans 5:12-19, where the problem of original sin comes to focus. This will be discussed in the next section of this book, concerning hamartiology, or, the doctrine of sin.

---

24. ibid., p. 251.
25. Francis Turretin, *Institutes of Elenctic Theology*, 3 vols. trans. G. M. Geiger (Phillipsburg, NJ: Presbyterian & Reformed Publ., 1991).
26. W. G. T. Shedd, *Dogmatic Theology II* (Grand Rapids: Eerdmans, 1969), pp. 36, 37.
27. J. O. Buswell, *A Systematic Theology of the Christian Religion i* (Grand Rapids: Zondervan, 1962, 1971), p. 252.
28. Gordon Clark, *The Biblical Doctrine of Man*, pp. 45-52.
29. G. C. H. Berkouwer, *Man: The Image of God* (Grand Rapids: Eerdmans, 1962).
30. Robert L. Reymond, *A New Systematic Theology of the Christian Faith* (Nashville, TN: Thomas Nelson, 1998), p. 425.
31. ibid., pp. 424, 425.

7
Mankind's Original Environment, Circumstances and Capacities

In this chapter our inquiry relates to the external situation into which God placed the first human pair, what their capacities were for coping with that situation (call it *environment*, if you will, without current distortions of meaning) as given by their Creator. Again, to borrow from the current jargon, we mean original human *ecology*.

I had been thumbing English dictionaries and the lexicons of three or four foreign languages for twenty-five years, when in about 1964 my youngest brother told me his MSc degree at Oregon State University was to be in *ecology* – plant ecology, yet I had to ask him what the word meant. Older theology texts do not use the expression 'human ecology,' but as of now, original human *ecology* is precisely the subject of much of this chapter if not quite the name for it.

The Literary Genus of the Source.

We must begin with a few sentences about how the narrative of the first three chapters of Genesis should be understood. What kind of literature is it? This has always been a matter of minor difference of opinion among those who profess biblical religion, whether as in ancient Judaism or in Christianity. Most believers have understood the early chapters of Genesis in a straightforward manner right up to the present moment. This allows for the presence of undefined figurative elements, as in all normal verbal intercourse, but within a literal, factual framework.

The Hermeneutical Approach.

Briefly I hold that the literary form (Lat. *genus*; French *genre*) of the biblical creation account would have been one that those of the time who heard it read would have recognized as existing in the polytheistic culture of their time. The beliefs about origins in the pagan religions of Syria and Assyria-Babylonia were couched in narratives about the crude and licentious escapades of their supposed gods and goddesses. These tales came to clear light only in the nineteenth and twentieth centuries. It is to be expected that these forms of literature, some of the literary devices, forms and motifs, would be employed in the Hebrews' account.

Let me support that statement with analogy from the rest of the Bible. Those versed in the Greek literature of the Apostles' time point out that the forms of Epistles (Romans to Jude) follow the forms of epistolary literature of the time, whereas the Gospels, though unique, teach 'religion' through narrative, as many other religions did. The

Psalms are now known to employ poetic forms, devices and vocabulary that are identical in detail with religious poetry of the ancient Phoenicians. Exploration of the Ras Shamra literature of the official religion of Ugarit in coastal Syria has vastly enriched our understanding of the book of Psalms. Psalm study will never be the same again since the publication of Mitchell Dahood's three volumes (*Anchor Bible*) wherein every page brings to bear some linguistic or structural light from Ugaritic poetry and psalmody. Nineteenth-century translation of Egypt's hieroglyphs turned up the striking fact that the some of the proverbs of the Old Testament were similar in form and in content – except for the Yahwist monotheism. It came as a surprise to learn that the various sacrifices prescribed by Leviticus are matched by similar forms of sacrifice in surrounding religion and similarly some of the functions of priests and prophets and kings. *The Life and Times Historical Reference Bible*, annotated by thirteen competent and believing historical and linguistic scholars, helps the reader understand the Bible in its historical setting by pointing out innumerable instances – not borrowing from heathen religious writing *as such* but simply employing the language, its idioms and the culture, in which writers, readers and 'those who hear' (Rev. 1:3) were at home.[1] If we call the heathen stories myths, says Gordon J. Wenham,

> In all these cases there is no simple borrowing by the Hebrew writer. It would be better to suppose that he has borrowed [employed] various familiar mythological motifs, transformed them, and integrated them into a fresh and original story of his own.[2]

Finally, W. H. Griffith-Thomas comments: '[I]f by myth is meant a form of picturesque teaching suited to the childhood of the world, it may be said that even if myth in *form*, its underlying teaching and details must be true to *fact*. Even parabolic teaching pre-supposes facts which correspond to the symbol used.'[3]

The scope of the present book does not entertain extended debate on the subject. This author's views have been presented earlier. It is, however, necessary to make clear how much we do *not* share with what goes for systematic theology in writings currently popular. The following quotation from Robert C. Denton, a plain-spoken source puts in simple language what writers such as Brunner, Tillich, Reinhold Niebuhr, MacQuarrie, Norman Pittenger and their recent successors say extensively and obscurely.

> The story of the garden is, in reality, the story of Everyman. It is not concerned with events which happened once for all in a far-off mythical time, but with what had happened, and is happening, in the lives of all men everywhere. The very name Adam suggests that this is the proper interpretation of the story, since in Hebrew it means simply 'man.' This account of man's defection from his Maker is not placed at the beginning of Bible history because there really was a time when snakes could speak and trees bore fruit capable of conferring immortality or secret knowledge, but because there is no other story in the world's literature which pictures so clearly the essential human situation. Here we see mankind both in its high dignity and pitiful distress. We see man created for the noblest of destinies, called to serve God and live in fellowship with Him, but reduced instead to the status of an outcast, a sinner and a slave to sin, in desperate need of redemption from bondage to his sins and to his own corrupt self-centeredness.[4]

This is typical of the views of current liberal authors, who wish to be regarded as Christian theologians, yet contemporary and educated. Hence, though presented in the manner of a factual narrative, these early chapters are really mythological, or allegorical. Truth conveyed as myth or allegory or fiction is more truthful than history, they commonly affirm.

If, however, we follow the example of Jesus (if unacquainted read Matt. 19:4-6 for one example), and Paul (1 Tim. 2:13,14), as well as the underlying hermeneutical assumptions of the most serious anthropological reasoning in the whole New Testament (Rom. 5:12-21), we shall be compelled to interpret these chapters, with due allowance for figurative features (as in all language), in a literal way. A common designation is 'grammatical-historical.'[5]

A recent valuable textbook for biblical hermeneutics by Wm. Klein, Craig Blomberg and Robert L. Hubbard, Jr. observes:

---

1. *The Life and Times Historical Reference Bible: A Chronological Journey Through the Bible, Culture and History.* New King James Version (Nashville: Thomas Nelson, 1997).
2. Gordon J. Wenham, *Word Biblical Commentary: Genesis 1–15* (Waco, TX: Word Books, 1987), p. 33.
3. W. H. Griffith-Thomas, *Genesis: A Devotional Commentary* (Grand Rapids: Eerdmans, 1946), p. 25.
4. Robert C. Denton, *A First Reader in Biblical Theology* (New York: Seabury, 1961), p. 3.
5. See Bernard Ramm's extensive, now almost classical, discussion in his *Protestant Biblical Interpretation*, 3rd rev. ed. (Grand Rapids: Baker Books, 1970, 1990), pp. 113-127.

A second apostolic approach was that of *literal-contextual* interpretation. This approach interpreted Old Testament Scriptures according to their normal meaning. Here again, their method followed Jesus' example. Jesus rebutted Satan's clever but twisted use of Old Testament passages with straightforward Old Testament quotations (Deut. 6:16 in answer to Ps. 91:11-12; cf. Matt. 4:4, 7). Twice Jesus invoked the normal sense of Hos. 6:6 ('I want faithful love more than I want animal sacrifices' NCV) to answer the Pharisees' criticism of him or his disciples (Matt. 9:13; 12:8).[6]

However much symbolism may occur in the passage, the author intended to report real events which took place at the beginning of our race, just as the book of Revelation, with even more symbolism, predicts real events of the *eschaton*.

There is a further caution. Admittedly, in the matter of miracles, whether at the time of creation in the remote past or of the consummation (eschatology) in the remote future, divine revelation employs symbolism and the 'prophet,' in this case, Moses, functions as receptor and reporter of 'revelation' (Gr. *apocalypsis*) not as reporter of witnessed or researched history. Yet, we know Moses as agent of revelation was unique in more than one way. His intimate discourse with the deity (Num. 12:6-8) was 'mouth to mouth, clearly,' not in 'vision... dream... riddles.' In this respect the mode of revelation is much more plain and direct, with less necessity of decoding or interpretation, than is the case with the predictive portions of the great Old Testament prophets and John the Revelator of the book of Revelation. Yet it may be significant, as many commentators point out, that many features of the 'garden eastward in Eden' reappear in John's visions of the millennial earth (Rev. 20–22).

I. Eden, the Land of Mankind's Beginning.

The human race began its history in a circumscribed area of this planet in conditions partially unique to that time and place.[7] It was in a 'garden in Eden, in the east' (Heb. *gan-be-edhen miqqedhem*). Eden was eastward from the viewpoint of the author, as likewise we may suppose from all Scripture (see Matt. 2:1), actually the Tigris-Euphrates valleys and adjacent lands. This is the most natural sense.

The precise location of Eden with its pleasant garden, while not of primary importance, has captured the interest of countless generations and has generated some serious research, linguistic and geographical, as well as speculation. I remember being fascinated by the question about the same time I studied geography in the fourth grade.

The word garden (Heb. *gan*) is clear enough. An examination of biblical texts and language authorities yields an enclosed, well-watered, protected area where plants may grow and sometimes where animals range in a controlled situation, where birds nest, fly, etc., and where people can find both employment and enjoyment as well as sustenance. In the Septuagint (the ancient Greek Version) *gan* is rendered by *paradeisos*, in English modified to 'paradise.' The earliest extant uses of the word are by Xenophon (430–355 BC), who borrowed the word from Persian (his famous *Anabasis*, or Retreat, where he many times used the word, was in Persian territory at the time). The word is also in Hebrew as *Pardes*, three times in the Old Testament (Neh. 2:8, Eccles. 2:5, Song. 4:13).

There are good reasons for receiving the brief description in Genesis 2:10-14 as being factually intended. Let us proceed in a manner consistent with the rest of Genesis, subsequent Scripture and other acknowledged facts.

1. When mankind left Eden they located immediately in the region between and beside the two great rivers Tigris (Heb. *Hiddekel*) and Euphrates. These rivers have been known throughout historical times and to the present. They are not mythical like the River Styx.

2. After the Great Flood, the ark of Noah settled in 'the mountains of Ararat,' i.e. of Armenia (Gen. 8:4, not 'Mt. Ararat'). The highlands of ancient Armenia is precisely the area where, very close together, the headwaters of the two clearly identifiable rivers, the Tigris and Euphrates, are to be found – identifiable in Moses' time and ours.

3. The geography and location of the lands and rivers was still that of the time Genesis was written (observe the present tense in KJV of 'compasseth' [Heb. *Sovev*, v. 11], 'goeth' [Heb. *holekh* v. 14]). It should not be said, therefore, it seems to me, that the Flood 'drastically altered' the topography of the area as some advocates of 'flood geology' are wont to say.

4. 'A river flowed out of Eden to water the garden' must not be understood of a single stream that went *away* from Eden to water the garden, for the garden was within the borders of Eden (v. 8). That the Hebrew term *yatsa'*,

---

[6]. Wm. Klein, Craig Blomberg, Robert L. Hubbard, Jr., *Introduction to Biblical Interpretation* (Dallas, TX: Word Publ., 1993), p. 30.

[7]. At this point the reader who is not well acquainted with Genesis 2:8-17 should read it carefully.

to go forth, is used in the sense of issuing or springing forth from the earth (within Eden), especially as applied to plants and streams of water, is unquestionable.'[8] Such is the case here. 'Out of Eden,' is indication of source *in* Eden. The preposition *min* employed like the Greek *ex* and English 'out from' indicates *source from which* quite as well as the partitive (or separative) idea of *away from*. I cite the other instance wherein the same Hebrew *Kal* participle of *yatsa'* indicates water or plants *springing up in* a certain place, rather than departing from it. This is Deuteronomy 8:7 – 'fountains and springs, *flowing out* in [lit. springing up in] the valleys and hills'; Deuteronomy 14:22 – the seed that *comes from* the field year by year'; Ezekiel 47:1 – 'water was *issuing from* below the threshold'; Ezekiel 47:8 (KJV) – 'waters issue out'; Ezekiel 47:12 – 'water… flows from', etc.

Revelant and true also are these comments: '*Nahar* [river], is a stream, or used collectively, streams [as English 'fish' serves both for singular and plural], the river systems… a similar use is found in Jonah 2:4, where the same word in the singular and connected with a singular verb, denotes the ocean streams [currents] that surrounded Jonah.'[9]

5. There are several other large rivers which have their sources within a few miles of the sources of the Tigris and Euphrates. If any of these are Pison and Gihon cannot be known because these names, known when Genesis was written, have been lost entirely. There really is no scholarly consensus about the rivers Pison and Gihon.

6. Of the precise location of Havilah (v. 11), downstream from Eden, nothing can be ascertained as likewise the 'land of Ethiopia (Cush)'. This text is cited as evidence of a Cush in the East as well as the better known Cush south of Egypt.

These and other considerations far too lengthy to treat here lead this author to locate Eden in the area of the pre-diluvian headwaters of the Rivers Tigris and Euphrates. There is no important reason to think those rivers were in a different area of earth in either Moses' time or ours.

That Eden was a real place located in a definite place on this earth is helpful, if not essential, to a sound theology of mankind. If that place can be given some bearings of longitude and latitude so much the better. The Last Adam, 'the Savior of the World,' is a Man who lived out His earthly days in a defined area of this planet among a limited society of people. This fact is important to all aspects of Christian doctrine. The story of the Last Adam's career as Savior of the world has force and influence because He is no mythical 'voice' from Never-Never Land but from an area 75 by 150 miles in ancient Syria. The case is the same with the first man in Eden.[10]

Lamentably, once we set the narrative of human origins free of some definite space in finite time on earth we weaken the strength of reality for any biblical doctrine of 'normal' mankind. So enter the mythological interpretations (and worse) we have already rejected. Or, if from the standpoint of literary and form criticism, Genesis 2:8-15 is declared of 'no significance,' a discordant, interpolated 'independent element' is introduced in the form of myth in an otherwise fairly coherent theology of mankind.[11]

Those who think the story is borrowed myth scrubbed clean of polytheism find all sorts of inner incoherence. There is another outlook among many scholars who specialize in Near-Eastern studies for example, E. A. Speiser.[12] They regard the story as truly reflecting ancient Akkadian and Sumerian traditions, locating Eden near the head of the Persian Gulf, where the Tigris and Euphrates converge. This, they claim, is not revealed truth but simply very early tradition.

Some modern discoveries support the antiquity of the main elements of the story, locating it all in Mesopotamia, and lend some support to the view that a specific location there is meant. On Eden, E. A. Speiser has written,

> Heb. *eden*, Akk[adian], *edines* [is], based on Sum[erian] *eden* 'plain, steppe.' The term is used here clearly as a geographical designation, naturally enough, with the homonymous but unrelated Heb. noun for 'enjoyment.'[13]
>
> …[T]he geographical term 'Eden'… is especially significant in that this word is rare in Akk[adian] but exceedingly common in Sum[erian], thus certifying the ultimate source as very ancient indeed.[14]

---

8. George Bush, *Notes on Genesis* (Minneapolis: Klock & Klock Christian Publ., repr. 1976), p. 57.
9. S. C. Bartlett in the *Smith-Hacket Dictionary of the Bible i* (New York: Hurd & Houghton, 1875), p. 660.
10. Robert D. Culver, *The Life of Christ* (Grand Rapids: Baker Books, 1976, 1993), pp. 213–214.
11. See G. von Rad, *Genesis, A Commentary* (Philadelphia: Westminster, 1961), pp. 77, 78.
12. E. A. Speiser, *The Anchor Bible, Genesis* (Garden City, NY: Doubleday, 1964), pp. 14-20.
13. ibid., p. 16.
14. ibid., p. 19.

Speiser's comment rests on the fact that Akkadian culture (Assyro-Babylonian) was a relatively late arrival, one which took over the culture and language of Sumeria in that part of the world.

These evidencess do not prove Moses or any other writer of Holy Scripture 'borrowed' his 'facts' from Mesopotamian mythical lore, any more than John borrowed the doctrine of the *Logos* from Philo. They do suggest that what Moses knew by revelation, Mesopotamia, cradle of the human race, had not quite forgotten.

Theologically, to give up the literal, historical-geographical quality of the place called Eden is part and parcel of retreat to some form of mythological interpretation. I am, of course, employing 'myth' in its normal sense of fictitious, fanciful, imaginary. That 'myth' in another sense may sometimes be a powerful vehicle for teaching truth I do not deny.

II. Paradise the Scene of Mankind's Probation.

Paradise is simply the Greek word for a pleasant garden, modified slightly for English, employed long before Christ to translate the Hebrew word *gan* in Genesis 2 and 3. *Eden* as in 'garden in Eden' was a place name in ancient Sumerian at least a millennium before it entered the Torah of Israel. That in Hebrew the homonym means 'delight' is the probable reason why both words, paradise and Eden, have had such a marvelous history. Paradise was used by Jews from intertestamental times as a name for the destination of the righteous in Abraham's bosom – Jesus addressed the dying thief's understanding when He said, 'Today you will be with me in Paradise.' Paul says he was caught up to 'heaven,' also in context (2 Cor. 12:1-4) 'caught up into paradise.' In the Septuagint, 'a garden in Eden' (Gen. 2:8) becomes 'the garden of delight' (*to paradeisō tōs truphōs*) only seven verses further along (2:15), as also in Genesis 3:24, and echoed in Joel 2:3. So, though none of the prophets uses the word 'paradise' of the coming kingdom of Messiah (or of God) on earth, conditions characteristic of the paradise at the beginning (Gen. 2, 3) are predicted in great detail about a new earth in that coming kingdom (or city), where God's will is to be done on earth as presently it is in heaven (Isa. 11, 35, 65, 66 are examples). The visions of John the Revelator promise the same (Rev. 21; 22). Jesus refers to a future 'paradise of God' and even places 'the tree of life' in it (Rev. 3:7). He further connects paradise of old with the coming city by placing 'the tree of life' in its midst (Rev. 22:2). In this coming kingdom, or city, just as God walked and talked with mankind in the paradise of Eden so the Tabernacle of God shall be with human beings – He shall be their God and they shall be His people.

Hence, little as systematic theology of past and present has made of the paradise of Eden in anthropology, much has been made of it by the *narrative theology* of biblical prophets and apocalyptists. Paradise has captured the imagination and interest of expository and speculative preaching through the ages and to the present hour. It is too important to leave to the occultists, cultists, and sensationalists, and their followers. The ecology of mankind in paradise, in Eden, is adumbrative of mankind in heaven now and in the coming kingdom of God, and should not be left out of formal anthropology.

At this point, if limitations of time and space allowed, a full discussion of such questions as the antiquity of mankind, possible pre-Adamite, prehistoric man, theories of the origin and growth of culture, would be appropriate and profitable. I have been both observer and participant in the discussion and have modified my views of many aspects of this important subject over the years. In my judgment, however, a theology which deals in anything like doctrinal certainties will stay close to the strictly revelational element, i.e. scriptural sources, remaining open to any facts scientific research may discover. It was my assigned duty for several academic seasons to teach courses called Christian Evidences, Factual Apologetics, Philosophy of Religion, Philosophical Apologetics and the like in the academic atmosphere of informed and current evangelical commitment. I do not denigrate the value of those courses for young adults about to launch out either into the tempestuous seas of contemporary secularism and unbelief disguised as modern Christianity on the one hand or into reactionary religious conservatism on the other.

Experience teaches one to be cautious about making statements about earthly (and specifically human) origins not strictly warranted by Scripture on the one hand. On the other hand, unwarranted assertions of science 'falsely so-called' need not frighten us into sub-Christian, unbiblical dogmatisms about an evolutionary 'ascent of man.' We stand on essentially the same ground as far as *ultimate* questions about how the world began, human origins and mankind's first earthly 'ecology' as thoughtful Christian scholars before the rise of the modern sciences. Science has nothing to tell us about mankind before sin entered the family. Only God has immediate knowledge of it. We know only as much as the Scriptures tell us. Some learned folk think (possibly correctly) that 'original sin' may also be inductively established from data gathered from the history of the twentieth century – collectively in wars, holocausts, economic depressions brought on by cupidity and stupidity on the one hand; on the other, crime, the sexual revolution, and declining morals individually – in such a case 'unrelieved depravity' might be a more modest induction than original sin. Yet no amount of reasoning can establish an original righteousness nor can research establish that mankind ever existed in such a state or even if so, what the circumstances might have been. (A full discussion of theories and schemes of pre-history of the human race and earth in the literature and preaching of the last several generations, interesting as it might be, must find another venue. Research has not demonstrated any of the theories to be true. Furthermore, the theology of mankind, anthropology, is not furthered by digression from the spare but clear statements of the Bible itself.)

'The highest heavens belong to the LORD, but the earth he has given to man' (Ps. 115:16 NIV). Like 'The first man' we are all 'of the earth, earthy' (1 Cor. 15:47 KJV). These words indicate that though God placed the first pair initially within a limited space it was God's intention that later they were to inhabit any spot on earth they could subdue and have dominion over. Every 'seed' and 'fruit,' it is said, 'you shall have... for food' and they were to have dominion over every fish, bird, and animal – wild or domestic – of 'all the earth' (Gen. 1:26, 29).

Search for some reasonable extended exposition of the texts relating to the natural, physical aspects of the Garden of Eden has turned up nothing of consequence. My own reflections have proved likewise quite without extensive, reportable positive results. We can affirm the following:

1. It was a delightful place, if we may accept the normal meaning of Hebrew *edhen* (delight) as applicable. In any case sensuous delight is clearly indicated by the latent allusion to the paradise of Eden in the Song of Solomon 4:12,13 – a trysting spot for lovers. 'Your shoots are an orchard [Heb. *Pardes* = paradise]' and similar (v. 13). Indeed the whole section has a sensuous tone. Artists – painters and sculptors – through the ages have sought to give this visual expression. Our own over-stimulated and underdisciplined generation, believers and unbelievers alike, are well advised to check their imagination at this point (as well as their sensual fantasies). However, the race's beginning in nuptial purity in the midst of natural beauty ought not to be overlooked. Beauty as we know it in nature at its best – without thorns and thistles, blights, perhaps also droughts, storms, and other threatening disasters – was everywhere to behold and to enjoy.

Philosophers with too much time on their hands and too little to do will continue unsuccessfully to fabricate an answer to the question, What is beauty? Yet our first parents had knowledge of *true* beauty through the immediate sensations of their healthy bodies, and without a name for it recognized it intuitively.

2. The 'garden [paradise] in Eden' was an orderly, planned place – planted, cultivated, trimmed and harvested. It evidently was that way when God 'put the man' there (Gen. 2:8). It was already a *gan*, for which the lexicons give *enclosure* as first meaning, translated 'garden' always in KJV, where are waters, trees, herbs – and even a 'house' (2 Kgs. 9:27), or else attached to a house (2 Kgs. 21:18), usually enclosed (Song. 4:12). Sometimes it is artifically irrigated (Isa. 58:11; Jer. 31:12) as the one in Eden seems to have been. 'This accords with the statement... (v. 10): A river flowed out of Eden to water the garden emanating from a spring, and not by rain.'[15] In the case of the garden in Eden, it is so perfect a spot as to be a veritable 'garden of God' where there is nothing better (Ezek. 28:13; 31:8, 9) – more like Morton Arboretum or a model farm than Walden Pond or an environmentalist's favorite primitive 'unspoiled wilderness.' Eden was a place for people of some culture and taste. Such we must suppose our first parents to have been, poles removed from barbarism. Provision for all human physical wants and needs, anything conducive to health of body and mind, was there.

3. Relief from malaise or boredom was provided in the work of tilling and taking care of it ('keep it,' KJV). Just what this involved must be left to speculation. We are not told. It is enough to know that work, for which the physical and psychological nature of mankind, both male and female, is designed and necessary, was a part of the regular regimen. I will say more of the duty of labor. For now, 'to dress it' (Heb. *bhadh*) means to work it (with a hoe?), and to 'keep it' (Heb. *shamar*) often means to guard. Gardens must be protected then and now from the 'little foxes that spoil the vineyards' (Song. 2:15) and, in Minnesota, from the raiding racoons. Did Adam build a garden wall or fence to keep out herbivorous animals? There is more we do not know about 'the garden in Eden' than we know. The first inhabitants found it a cultivated garden of delight and were expected to keep it that way.

---

15. Umberto Cassuto, *A Commentary on the Book of Genesis*, Part One, trans. Israel Abrahams (Jerusalem: The Hebrew University, Magnes Press, 1944, 1978).

The weekly Sabbath rest is counterpoint to the duty of work.

4. Worship of God is both informal communion and formal recurring 'liturgical' event (if we may use the word). These ideas will be expanded shortly.

5. The garden was *botanical*, not zoological. 'Every green plant' God gave for food at this stage. How soon after the fall mankind began to eat the flesh of animals is not quite certain. God specifically authorized slaughter of animals for food after the Flood (Gen. 9:3), but immediately prior to that, Noah built an altar and offered 'clean' beasts and fowl as burnt sacrifice thereon. In later ritual 'clean' meant proper for either *food* for man or *sacrifice* to God. Much before that, in the first generation after the fall, righteous Abel was a keeper of sheep. One might ask, For what purpose? The words for offer (Hiphil of *bo'*) and offering (*minḥah*) in Genesis 4:2-4 are not decisive on the question, but by later prescribed Mosaic ritual a *minḥah* of grain such as Cain's would ordinarily be cooked in some way. An animal for sacrifice would be slain. Then the properly prepared carcases would in some cases be wholly burnt on an altar, in others shared between offerer, priest and the altar. Whether therefore Abel, Seth and Seth's progeny ate animal flesh should be left an open question.

The geological record, with its layers of fossil-bearing rock as well as the teeth and bones of fish and animals of ages past, shows no epoch when lions and leopards had teeth and digestive systems designed for consuming only plants – unlike bovines, sheep and deer. As far as the same record shows, there never was a time when most fish of the sea had anything to eat other than other fish! The best evidence produced solely from Scripture argues from prophecies of the coming kingdom of God on earth (Isa. 35; 65; 66; Rev. 21; 22) that in the world of Adam's innocence they did not 'hurt nor destroy' as in all God's coming 'holy mountain.' Death in the human race is the wages of sin, but not necessarily in the plant and animal kingdoms. If outside the garden in Eden nature behaved as today, then we have a clue as to why Adam's commission was literally 'to work it and keep [or guard] it'. He was evidently required to cultivate plants, even if there were as yet no thorns and thistles. Raccoons a menace to Adam's sweet corn?

Umberto Cassuto, who systematically and somewhat contemptuously rejects the critical documentary-development (JEDP) orthodoxy, translates v. 5, 'Now no *thorns* of the field were yet in the earth and no *grain* of the field had yet sprung up.'[16] Whereas the critics usually accept the KJV 'plant' and 'herb,' Cassuto, whose thorough competence cannot be discounted, turns the critics on their heads, saying: 'What is meant by the *siah* of the field and the *esebh* of the field mentioned here? Modern commentators usually concede the terms to connote the *vegetable kingdom as a whole*; thence it follows that our section contradicts the preceding chapter, according to which the vegetation came into existence on the third day. Dillman, for example, states that *siah* and *esebh*, the most important categories of the vegetable world, represent the latter in its entirety.'[17] He cites others who interpret the text as saying: 'even' such unimportant plants as these were missing. Cassuto comments: 'But there is nothing in the text corresponding to the all-important word *even*. All interpretations of this kind introduce something into the text that is not there, in order to create the inconsistency. When the verse declares that these species were missing, the meaning is simply that *these* kinds were wanting, but *no others*. If we wish to understand the significance of the *siah* of the field and the *esebh* of the field… we must take a glance at the end of the story.' He holds the 'thorns and thistles' (3:18) simply expand on *siah* (plant, KJV 2:5) and Adam will 'till the ground' to obtain *grain* (*esebh*) 'in order to eat bread' (3:23). Further, Cassuto reminds us that in that part of the world (and largely so elsewhere) thorns and thistles come up in tilled ground after rain soaks the field. So since rain had not yet fallen there were no thistles in the garden. He explains finally that Genesis 2 says plants that multiplied by seed alone (no cultivation) appeared on the third day. Thorns and thistles accompany cultivation of the soil, as Genesis 3 explains, even though a very few are in natural prairies and woods and 'corn' (in U.S., 'grain'), though in patches around the planet they have to be cultivated to grow in amounts to sustain the 'daily bread.'[18] Cassuto's evidences (abbreviated here) convinced me and modified my understanding of the relation of Genesis 1:1-2 and 2:4 *ad fin*.

If paradise had a wall or fence, as most Eastern gardens from time immemorial, then perhaps it would have required maintenance. Beyond this, if we have not already gone too far, it seems unfruitful to speculate.

How unfallen mankind would have gone about it to subdue the earth and rule it we do not presently know. One can only imagine. We should think of this 'cultural mandate' not so much as a command to be obeyed as an inner impulse deep within human nature to pioneer the vast expanse of the earth's surface as settler and farmer, and to

---

16. ibid., p. 100.
17. ibid., p. 101.
18. ibid., pp. 102, 103.

develop the resources, both those exposed to view and those hidden beneath the ground. The course these impulses took as civilization developed after mankind fell, leading to 'the end of all flesh' in the judgment of the Noahic Flood, was different from the course a race of holy people would have taken.

III. The Capacities of Mankind in Their Original Integrity.

1. *For dominion over the whole earth*. Some highly esteemed and competent biblical theologians have understood that 'have dominion… over all the earth' (Gen. 1:26) was an immediate state of mankind's relation to nature and that to 'subdue it' was an effortless enterprise at the beginning – a state of affairs rather than a future project. Francis Pieper, a leading orthodox, American Lutheran held that exercise of 'dominion over the creatures… was an immediate consequence of possessing the divine image… [W]illingly all creatures rendered man service. After the Fall, man retained only a caricature of his original dominion; he must now employ cunning and force to assert some kind of mastery over the animals.'[19]

> Then citing Luther as source, Pieper goes on to say:

> All that is left of this dominion, Luther calls a 'mock sovereignty'… It is true that man succeeds by cunning and coercion in subduing the creatures partially. But in spite of all the creature remains in revolt against its sinful master. The beasts harass, harm, kill, and eat their former LORD; in the air he breaks his neck; the water drowns him; the earth becomes his tomb, etc. Such considerations, says Luther, serve a useful purpose. They teach us what an abomination before God sin must be, since it has so thoroughly deranged the relationship between man and the rest of his creatures.[20]

J. T. Mueller, wrote in agreement:

> Man's dominion over the creatures, according to the Scripture was an immediate result of his possession of the divine image… The dominion of man, must be regarded as real sovereignty, so that all the other creatures willingly rendered him service. After the Fall man possesses only a faint vestige of this absolute dominion… The rebellion of the creatures against man is the direct consequence of his own rebellion against God.'[21]

Though the Lutheran theologians just cited regard the dominion of mankind over the creatures as a consequence of the divine image, their Reformed counterparts bring other passages of Scripture to suggest the dominion was to be progressively attained. Dominion was something 'to which our race was destined,' not to be immediately exercised.[22] Psalm 8 avers that God has placed all things under our feet. And 1 Corinthians 11:7 with reference to man, male, what the Apostle says about woman's subordination to man indicates that he 'should do nothing which implied the denial of his right to rule.' Hodge claims, however, that according to Paul, much more than authority over animals was intended by the Psalmist.

In 1 Corinthians 15:27, Paul says, 'when it [Psalm 8] says, "all things are put in subjection," it is plain that he is excepted who [i.e. God, Himself] put all things in subjection under him.' And Hebrews 2:8 says, 'Now in putting everything in subjection to him, he left nothing outside his control.' It was therefore an absolutely universal dominion, so far as creatures are concerned.

> This… has been realized and attained only by the incarnation and exaltation of the Son of God. But as God sees the end from the beginning, as his plan is immutable and all comprehending, this supreme exaltation of humanity was designed from the beginning, and included in the dominion with which man was invested.[23]

This latter view is far superior to the speculative, albeit evangelical views of Pieper and Mueller. Luther's picturesque exposition (*vid*. Pieper, op. cit.) failed to regard what Psalm 8 and the above-cited passages have to say by way of inspired comment on mankind's dominion. It is not something rendered void by sin, however difficult of attainment. Reinforced to the sons of Noah (Gen. 7:2, 3) it remains God's purpose for mankind as God's vicegerent on earth, to be consummated in and through the incarnate Son, the Last Adam. The grant to mankind in paradise of vicegerency over the creatures makes it right today for mankind everywhere to colonize, utilize and employ all things God has

---

19. Francis Pieper, *Church Dogmatics i* (St. Louis: Concordia Publ., 1950), p. 522.
20. ibid., p. 522.
21. J. T. Mueller, *Christian Dogmatics* (St. Louis: Concordia Publ., 1934, 1955), pp. 208, 209.
22. Charles Hodge, *Systematic Theology i* (Grand Rapids: Eerdmans, 1960), p. 102.
23. ibid., p. 103.

made and placed on this planet, but only in subjection to and direction by the laws of God, whether of what some call natural revelation or the teachings of Scripture. There is a basis here for a theology of conservation of natural resources, of environmental protection as well as of proper development and exploitation. It would be speculative and subject to contrary argument to theorize how civilization would have developed if the fall had not taken place, for Scripture has nothing to say about it. Eschatology must be brought to bear and from that direction it is well to remember the present world of mankind is under sentence of judgment, doomed to pass away and destined to be replaced by a genuine 'new world order.' It will be a new earth 'wherein dwelleth righteousness' and 'there shall be no more curse' and 'They shall not hurt or destroy in all' God's 'holy mountain' (Isa. 11:9). Meanwhile we had better respect the powers of God in what people call 'nature' and practice conservation of needed natural resources. As for the current 'save the environment' debates – may the wisest win!

2. *Powers inherent to achieve the divinely given mission to populate, subdue and rule the earth*. It would be difficult to say anything new on this subject. Rather clear inferences are to be made from the Genesis narrative and in a few instances what later relevant Scripture has to say.

In a general way we observe that Scripture doctrine clearly asserts or implies the following.

a. Mankind was created in a state of *maturity*. That is, Adam was a full-grown man, not an infant. If either he or Eve possessed a navel it was an unnecessary physical feature, for neither was ever in a mother's womb or had an umbilical cord attached. Nor was either of them ever a savage or barbarian – Scripture knows of no evolutionary 'ascent of man' from brute via savage and barbarian to civilized *Homo sapiens*. Homonids and humanoids of modern 'scientific' imagination are 'nothing in this world', as Paul declared of the gods and godesses of ancient heathen imagination.

b. Mankind was created in a state of *perfect adaptation* to the environment in which they were placed. It is impossible on the basis of Scripture to suppose the first people suffered a shivering, diseased, fugitive existence in caves, forests and marshes, pursued by cold and disease and threatened by beasts. During certain periods of history and prehistory in certain parts of the world genuine specimens of *homo sapiens* have existed under such conditions, but there is no proof at all that human life began that way. Such conditions have existed in many parts of the world throughout history and still exist. Our first parents did not do well with their fine natural gifts in a perfect environment but that was not on account of any defect of mind or body.

c. Primal mankind was endowed with full capacity for reflective thought and thereby the creative powers necessary for the divinely given mission on earth. Adam probably knew no algebra or calculus but neither was his mind a *tabula rosa* of the philosophy of empiricism. Adam would never have attempted to create a four-sided triangle nor Eve have added three cups of sugar to two gallons of vinegar for a sum of seven oranges.

d. Mankind initially had a language and was able to use it. They conversed with God. The first pair conversed with one another and Eve with the serpent. It is a singular fact that specific languages in their most primitive-known stages are very much more precise and fully inflected for every possible shade of meaning than in their later stages. They do develop increased vocabulary and multiply idioms. Adam must have begun the process, though at the Tower of Babel language took a new turn.

e. Capacity for reflective thought combined with rational use of verbal symbols enabled the man to name the animals of Eden. This involves both percepts and concepts as well as memory. Though there is no evidence Hebrew was the language of paradise, the language of the narrative and the conceptual framework is Hebraic. In that setting names are never simple arbitrary symbols like numbers and numerals on automobile license plates or serial numbers on mass-produced machine parts. Names signified perceived character or some important feature conceptualized. Adam was not nonplussed about the animals of Edenic paradise as St Paul was about what he saw in the paradise of the third heaven (2 Cor. 12:2-4).

f. Mankind was directed to subdue the earth. If we think of that even in the most limited sense of soil, rock and water, imagine what innate powers of invention were involved!

g. He was put in the Garden 'to work it and keep it.' Did Adam invent the first hoe? The first shears? What did the two use to sew 'fig leaves together' (Gen. 3:7)? Obviously they invented and used tools.

h. They could understand rules and foresee consequences or the terms of the 'contingent situation' of the 'Adamic Administration' (John Murray) which some Reformed theologians like to call 'the Covenant of Works.' Without this understanding their work would have been senseless exercise. This is another way of saying – as we have dwelt upon at length earlier – that they were moral beings.

Innate Human Rational, Ethical and Aesthetic Capacities.

Our first parents did not have to fall into sin to be philosophers. Eve had the concepts of 'goodness, beauty and truth,' or the conversations between the serpent and Eve, between Eve and God and between Adam and God would have been meaningless. The aesthetic sense was especially prominent in Eve, for the tree 'pleasant to the sight' (Gen. 2:9) became 'a delight to the eyes' (Gen. 3:6). Her sense of objective beauty was obviously intuitive. Beauty for Eve was recognized by her mind, not created by it. As everyone knows who has watched children grow up, their appreciation of music and ability to produce it start very early. People do not need to be taught notes and scales or learn about octaves to enjoy music. We apparently distinguish good and evil by the voice of conscience as soon as we can think. Eve knew about the distinction between truth and lie or the warnings about the tree in the midst of the Garden would mean nothing.

The Gulf Between Brutes and Human Beings.

The distance of 'man,' 'made him a little lower than the angels' (Ps. 8:5 KJV) from every animal is not merely a step upward on a gradual, evolutionary scale but a yawning gulf. Three centuries of effort by generations of scholars under the pervasive demands of Enlightenment and post-enlightenment atmosphere of discourse have failed utterly even to throw a line across that gulf.

The radical differences between the human soul and the principle of intelligence in the lower animals, especially our possession of self-consciousness, general ideas, the moral sense and the power of self-determination, show that which chiefly constitutes us humans could not have been derived, by any natural process of development from the inferior creatures.[24]

Though marred by too many concessions to the reigning Darwinism, Strong erected a formidable summary of evidence against any psychological-intellectual kinship with brutes. Man, said David in Psalm 8:4 and 5, is only a little lower than angels in this regard but infinitely above animals. Animal-rights folk and lovers of pets may impute human qualities to the behavior or responses of dogs or porpoises but here the desideratum is in the eyes of the viewer rather than in the nervous system of the animal. Strong points out the following:

> 1. The brute is conscious, but man is self-conscious… The brute does not objectify self… does not distinguish itself from its sensations… has percepts [but not] apperception, i.e. perception accompanied by reference of it to the self.
> 2. [The brute] has only percepts; man has also concepts… [no] power of abstraction… of deriving abstract ideas from particular things or… experiences.
> 3. [The brute] has no language… why… not? Because they have nothing to say, i.e. have no general ideas which words might express.
> 4. [The brute] forms no judgments, e.g. that *this* is like *that*… Hence no sense of the ridiculous [humor], and no laughter.
> 5. [The brute] has no reasoning… that this follows from that… a feeling that the sequence is necessary. Association of ideas [events] without judgment is the typical process of the brute mind.[25]
> 6. [The brute] has no general ideas or intuitions as of space, time substance, cause.[26] The physical in man, on the contrary is only an aid to the spiritual.
> 7. [The brute] has determination but not self-determination [that is, it is wholly determined by heredity and environment]. Even [Thomas] Huxley[27] has said that taking mind into account, there is between man and the highest beasts an 'enormous gulf,' a 'divergence immeasurable' and 'practically infinite.'
> 8. [The brute] has no conscience[28] and no religious nature.[29]

I close this section with the words of the eminent naturalist, John Burroughs – employing language both forceful and elegant.

> Animal life parallels human life at many points, but it is in another plane. Something guides the lower animals but it is not thought; something restrains them, but it is not judgment; they are provident without prudence;

---

24. A. H. Strong, *Systematic Theology* (Valley Forge, PA: Judson Press, 1907), p. 466.
25. Feed grain regularly to a horse or cow two or three times out of a white bucket and it will henceforth approach eagerly expecting a treat. In fact it will start moving when you slam the back door *en route* to the granary! This is known as the power of association – not knowledge of cause-effect sequence.
26. Hence no generalizing, no progress except physical, no power of association of ideas – only of events, no tool-making. The physical never serves intellectual or spiritual.
27. Still the famous skeptic 100 years after his death.
28. Aspen trees quake but are not afraid of anything, just as dogs skulk but feel no guilt. They only act out the ritual-like submission of canines to the dominant member of the pack, in this case a substitute in the form of a human master.
29. op. cit., pp. 467-469,

they are active without industry, they are skillful without practice... wise without knowledge... deceptive without guile... When they are joyful, they sing or they play [or appear to]; when they are distressed, they moan or they cry... and yet I do not suppose they experience the emotion of joy or sorrow, or anger or love as we do, because these feelings in them do not involve reflection, memory, and what we call the higher nature.[30]

That these capacities of the soul, present in primal mankind, are present, however diminished, in fallen mankind is demonstrable. They are not induced by nurturing in culture. They are born within. I frequently conduct graveside services and when I do almost without exception, along with the reading of appropriate Scripture, quote several moving lines from Tennyson's *Crossing the Bar* and Bryant's *Thanatopsis*. Recently, after reciting the lines over the grave of a pastor who died, as we say, an untimely death, a man who went to school only a little and never really learned to read, approached me. With tears and halting voice this supposedly crude man stammered, 'Pastor, that was beautiful.' Nobody had taught this dear man rhyme and rhythm, simile and metaphor. His own speech is of iron horse shoes; he lives the sights and scents of the livestock sale barn. Yet he understands the meaning of great poetry and responds to it – more truly and deeply than some of the so-called doctors in literature presently standing before many uncivilized denizens of our university classes.

'Down in the human heart, crushed by the tempter, feelings lie buried that grace can restore.' If these capacities for appreciation of goodness, beauty and truth are present in mankind's fallen state how much more so in the primal purity of the race, the image of God still fully intact in moral dimension!

---

30. 'Ways of Nature' as cited by Strong, op. cit., p. 469.

8
The Divine Purpose In and For Mankind

H. D. McDonald has pointed out in clear language the exegetical ground for a proper attention to the subject of this chapter.

> The impression... the Genesis account gives is that man was the special focus of God's creative purpose. It is not so much that man was the crown of God's creative acts, or the climax of the process, for although last in the ascending scale, he is first in the divine intention. All the previous acts of God are presented more in a continuous series by the recurring use of the conjunction 'and' (Gen. 1:3, 6, 9, 14, 20, 24). 'Then God said, "Let us make man"'. 'Then' – when? When the cosmic order was finished, when the earth was ready to sustain man. Thus while man stands before God in a relationship of created dependence, he has also the status of a unique and special personhood in relation to God.[1]

The personal, even naive sermonic manner of Calvin in commenting on the creation of mankind points with deep feeling to the pedagogical motive behind the very narrative in Genesis.[2] It was to tell us that the creation was made for mankind and mankind for God. I quote somewhat at length to give the reader a sample of the depth of insight. The narrative was not intended to satisfy cravings for information about origin. Rather

> Moses relates that God's work was completed not in a moment but in six days... [B]y this... we are drawn away from all fictions to the one God who distributed his work into six days that we might not find it irksome to occupy our whole life in contemplating it... [W]e ought in the very order of things diligently to contemplate God's fatherly love toward mankind, in that he did not create Adam until he had lavished upon the universe all manner of good things.[3]

The idea was so important to the sage of Geneva that he shortly repeated the idea in even more vigorous language and declared the special purpose of God in preparing a whole world for mankind's happiness. We must not only

> recognize that God has destined all things for our good and salvation but at the same time to feel his power and grace in ourselves [i.e. in God's image], and so bestir ourselves to trust, invoke, praise and love him.... [W]henever we call God the Creator of heaven and earth [reciting the Creed], let us at the same time bear in

---

1. H. D. McDonald, 'Doctrine of Man' in *Evangelical Dictionary of Theology* (Grand Rapids: Baker Books, 1984).
2. Francois Wendel, *Calvin: The Origins and Development of His Religious Thought* (New York: Harper & Row, 1950, 1963), p. 171.
3. Calvin, *Institutes, I*, 14.2.

> mind that the dispensation of all those things which he has made is in his own hand and power and that we are indeed his children.... So, invited by the great sweetness of his beneficence and goodness, let us study to love and serve him with all our heart.[4]

Probably no man who ever lived better mastered the grand scheme of God's plan expressed in Scripture – God's eternal purposes in creation, preservation, providence; mankind's fall, redemption and history's consummation in the *eschaton*. He would therefore have pondered and searched for God's purposes in the human race. They are to trust God, pray to Him, love Him and to serve Him.

Granted that God created mankind for Himself in some important way, the larger questions relate to the way in which this purpose was to be fulfilled. I have searched the literature for an answer – finding almost nothing. Exceptions are one nineteenth-century work of Old Testament theology and that of a recent Roman Catholic scholar. In the midst of a wonderful passage too long to include, G. F. Oehler relates the creation of mankind to 'the design of creation.'

> [I]n all His creating God approves the work of His hands; but still the creating God does not reach the goal of His creation until He has set over against Him His image in man. From this last plain fact it is plain that the self-revelation of God, the unveiling of His being, is the final end of the creation of the world; or to express it more generally, that the whole world serves to reveal the divine glory (*kabhodh*), and it thereby the object of the divine joy, Psalm 104:31.[5]

Psalm 104:31 reads, 'May the glory of the LORD endure for ever; may the LORD rejoice in his works.' Oehler thinks the final verse, 'Let sinners be consumed from the earth,' (v. 35) shows that God's glory is not fully revealed in the earth until there are no sinful men remaining in it.

This suggests that people – a term which includes both sexes without ambiguity – absent tarnishing of the divine image by sin – are the highest object of God the Creator's love and par excellence the manifestation of the created glory of God. This is not to detract from the uncreated glory of God to which Jesus referred as 'the glory which I had with thee before the world was' (John 17:5 KJV). This may account for the command to increase and multiply until the earth be filled with parents and children (Gen. 1:28) and the several predictions that when King Messiah has renovated the kingdoms of the world, 'they of the city shall flourish like grass of the earth' (Ps. 72:16 KJV), and our LORD's redemptive work is not for the few but for the many (Isa. 53:12). Further the Old Testament prophets predict an eschaton wherein multitudes of children romp in populous cities and John the Revelator saw multitudes of the redeemed around the throne of God and the eternal home of those 'saved out of the earth' as an immense city coming down from God out of heaven to earth where He put our first parents in a garden. Theologians may muse even if not allowed to predict, may they not?

Joseph Fichter, a pious Roman Catholic scholar, understood the difficulty, commenting: 'Let us admit... that a definitive study of man will always be in the making. Creation itself is mysterious, and man and his relationship to God are doubly so. Man's role in creation is one of ever active and dynamic response and surrender, set as it is in a situation where man can enter into dialogue with a transcendent Person.'[6] We should point out that in spite of restraint of men's sins by God's Spirit and dimming of His created glory by the sin of mankind (Gen. 6:3), and the decimation of earth's non-human inhabitants in the judgment of the Deluge, along with most of the human race, the continuance of the world order is assured – there will be no such future world-wide judgment 'While the earth remains' (Gen. 8:21, 22; 9:11).[7]

Divine providence has guaranteed that the divine image of God in mankind will be manifest supremely and for-ever, through the gracious plan of salvation, including the forming of a people for His name and glory, the church.

At this point let us recall that Psalm 8:5 literally reads of 'man' (v. 4 RSV), 'Yet thou hast made him little less than God [*Elohim*].' The Septuagint, perhaps following the weekly synagogue Targum, renders it 'angels' who are also called 'sons of God.' The idea is that we here on earth, in plain view to the universe, are only slightly below (in rank and capacity?) beings who 'do behold the face' of the Father. Verses 7-10 of Psalm 8 go on to relate this to LORDship of earth and her creatures. The Genesis 2 account, in a burst of 'narrative theology shows in the clearest manner possible, this unique position of man in the category of created beings.'[8]

---

4. ibid., 14.22.
5. G. F. Oehler, *Theology of the Old Testament* (New York: Funk & Wagnalls, 1883), p. 121.
6. Joseph Fichter, *Theological Anthropology: The Science of Man in His Relation with God* (South Bend, IN: Notre Dame Univ. Press, 1963), p. 37.
7. ibid., p. 121.
8. Hermann Schultz, *Old Testament Theology ii*, trans. J. A. Patterson (Edinburgh: T. & T. Clark, 1892), p. 255.

Thus Hermann Schultz, the learned and devout Goettingen professor, enlarged in beautiful prose, of which I quote only a few lines:

> [T]he body of man is formed by a special exercise of God's artistic power, as is the body of woman afterwards [Gen 2:7, 21, 22 *yatsar*, to mold as a potter would, *bana'*, to build as a master-carpenter]. The Spirit of God is communicated to the man by an operation which God personally performs on him. Human life is therefore regarded as in a definite personal relation to the divine life. Man does not merely reveal this divine life as a natural life, the way it is revealed by other forms of individual life in nature; he reveals it as a life personally active, self-conscious. Hence the other terrestrial creatures are created with express reference to man (Gen. 2:19).[9]

This sublime, and I judge correct, insight of God's purpose to make mankind *revelator* of the divine excellencies, came from one who thought there to be no history at all in Genesis 2, but a distillation of what 'saintly' Hebrews later thought of mankind in contrast to the gross conceptions of their heathen neighbors. In a measure Schultz's insight, with which I heartily concur, having met it first in his writing, suggests the purpose of the Christian faith also, as Peter says of New Testament saints, God's 'new creation': 'you are... a people for his own possession, that you may proclaim the excellencies of him who called you out of darkness into his marvelous light' (1 Peter 2:9).

William Shakespeare may have captured the creative sublimity of this insight in Hamlet's sarcastic response to Guilderstern: 'What a piece of work is man! how noble in reason! How infinite in faculty! in form and moving how express and admirable! in action how like an angel! in apprehension how like a god! the beauty of the world! the paragon of animals.'[10]

Many later theologians in their preoccupation with the 'hard questions' of mankind's origin and nature give spare attention to the divine purposes of God *in* and *for* mankind in creating him. Some standard works provide only incidental remarks, rarely a rubric or chapter. The evangelical creeds furnish only a little more. I have chosen to employ Question 6 and its answer in the most evangelical *Heidelberg Catechism* to organize my further treatment of the topic of this chapter, 'The divine purpose in and for mankind.' I quote here the translation from Schaff's *The Creeds of Christendom*. The sense is not changed in the translation of my philosophy professor, Allen O. Miller, published by United Church Press on the 400th anniversary of the original (1963).

> Q. 6. Did God then create man so wicked and perverse?
> A. By no means; but God created man good and after his own image, in true righteousness and holiness, that he might rightly know God his creator, heartily love him and live with him in eternal happiness to glorify and praise him.

A Significant Omission.

This primitive evangelical statement (1563) of God's purposes in the creation of mankind says nothing about a 'covenant of works.' Two generations later, early in the scholastic age of Protestant theology, the covenant idea became pervasively imbedded in Protestant creeds and theologies especially of the Reformed. The *Irish Articles of Religion* (1615) speaks of 'the covenant of the law' and the *Westminster Confession* after another generation expresses itself (VII, 2) thus: 'the first covenant made with man was a covenant of works,' etc.

As a consequence very little is said in much Reformed literature about the divine purposes in and for mankind, even though God's noble purposes for us is a truly appealing subject. Many others find the dour prospect of rigid covenantal language a poor introduction to theological anthropology. Perhaps that is why at least two representatives of recent generations (James Orr and John Murray, both Presbyterians) abandoned the idea at least as regards God's purposes and mankind's duties in paradise.

James Orr saw the values in this 'federalism' at the time in the seventeenth century when it arose but pointed out the greater deficiencies as the church entered 'the age of reason.' For the benefit of those who might otherwise never become acquainted with Orr's corrective comments, I cite at length.

> No doubt there is a Scriptural idea at the heart of the conception, and it had the conspicuous merit of introducing the idea of historical progress into the study of Biblical revelation [precious to Orr whose great work, *The Progress of Dogma*, is justly famous]. It brought the divine purposes into connection with time, and gave it something of that flexibility and movement – that *dynamical* character – which we have described as

---

9. ibid., p. 255.
10. Shakespeare, *Hamlet*. Act II, Scene II.

the corrective to the static conceptions of the eternal decree. At the same time it failed to seize the true idea of development, and by an artificial system of typology, and allegorizing interpretation, sought to read back practically the whole of the New Testament into the Old. But its most obvious defect was that, in using the idea of the Covenant as an exhaustive category, and attempting to force into it the whole material of theology, it created an artificial scheme which could only repel minds desirous of simple and natural notions. *It is impossible, e.g. to justify by Scriptural proof the detailed elaboration of the idea of a covenant of works in Eden* [emphasis added], with its parties, conditions, promises, threatenings, sacraments, etc. Thus also the Reformed theology – the more it had assumed this stiff and artificial shape – failed to satisfy the advancing intellect of the Age [of Reason], which, under the influence of new philosophical conditions, had already acquired a rationalistic bent.[11]

John Murray, late Professor of Theology at Westminster Seminary, was equally blunt. After laying out the divine arrangements for mankind in Eden, he refers to the same as 'the Adamic administration' and goes on to say:

> This administration has often been denoted 'The Covenant of Works.' There are two observations. (1) The term is not felicitous, for the reason that the elements of grace entering into the administration are not properly provided for by the term 'works.' (2) It is not designated a covenant in Scripture. Hosea 6:7 may be interpreted otherwise and does not provide the basis for such a construction of the Adamic economy. Besides (3), Scripture always uses the term covenant, when applied to God's administration to men, in reference to a provision that is redemptive or closely related to the confirmation of promise and involves a security which the Adamic economy did not bestow.[12]

Several popular, strident promoters of the notion of human history governed by a series of covenants (the federal idea) might not be taking the damage current polemics is dealing them if they had noticed the absence of this system in their rightful hero, John Calvin, the rejection of the same in their most outstanding twentieth-century transatlantic scholar, James Orr, and the good counsel of John Murray at their premier school in the U. S. A. I have no quarrel of a general sort with these fellow soldiers, numerous among conservative Reformed and Presbyterians. Yet they will not win on a non sequitur. They have all those in every age saved by an Abrahamic covenant, which for some is an everlasting covenant with two adminstrations – Old Testament and New. But as Murray reminds us, 'The first or old covenant is the Sinaitic [Mosaic, not Adamic or a former 'older' Abrahamic covenant]... The view that in the Mosaic covenant there is a repetition of the so-called covenant of works, current among covenant theologians, is a grave misconception and involves an erroneous construction of the Mosaic covenant as well as failing to assess the uniqueness of the Adamic administration.'[13]

For a quite contrary view of 'the Covenant of Works' in particular and the Federal theology in general see Dr. Robert L. Reymond's book, *A New Systematic Theology of the Christian Faith*.[14] For what some regard as a *coup de mort* of that theology, see *Abraham's Four Seeds* by John G. Reisinger, subtitled, 'An Examination of the Basic Presuppositions of Covenant Theology and Dispensationalism as They each Relate to the Promise of God to Abraham and His Seed.'[15] Several new authors, apparently in contact with Reisinger, are seeking to save what they can of the Federal system in a 'New Covenant Theology.'[16]

Some of those who prefer the 'covenant of works' framework do acknowledge that the Genesis record does not present the subject of God's purposes in and for mankind in the framework of a covenant. Herman Hoekema has no direct comment at all on the last half of Answer 6, rather a long chapter on a so-called Covenant of Works, of which the *Catechism* says nothing.[17] He admits the Covenant of Works framework to be an innovation of post-Reformation scholastic theology, making no effort to trace the innovation back to the prime Reformers.

There is great merit to the framework of covenants in many loci of theology. In fact the Scriptures frequently trace the benefits of salvation back to covenants of promise. This of course is mandatory Christian truth. Yet, I think we do well to think of God's purposes for mankind in paradise and in His eternal counsels under other biblical categories.

---

11. James Orr, *The Progress of Dogma* (Grand Rapids: Eerdmans, 1901, 1952), pp. 303, 304.
12. John Murray, *Collected Writings ii* (Edinburgh: Banner of Truth Trust, 1977), p. 49.
13. ibid., p. 51.
14. Robert L. Reymond, *A New Systematic Theology of the Christian Faith* (Nashville, TN: Thomas Nelson Publ., 1998), pp. 503-537.
15. Available at Sound of Grace, 5317 Wye Creek Dr., Frederick, MD 21705. John Reisinger is a Reformed Baptist pastor, author, lecturer of keen insight and rhetorical skill.
16. Tom Wells and Fred G. Zaspel, *New Covenant Theology*, 5317 Wye Creek Dr., Frederick, MD 21703: New Covenant Media, 2002.
17. Herman Hoekema, *The Triple Knowledge: An Exposition of the Heidelberg Catechism* (Grand Rapids: Eerdmans, Kregel, 1943), p. 1070.

Six Affirmations of Ursinus and Olevianus in the Heidelberg Confession.

Let us follow the language of Zacharius Ursinus and Caspar Olevianus, authors of the Heidelberg Confession. In their words God created mankind

> (1) that he might rightly *know* God his Creator, (2) heartily *love* him, (3) and *live* with him (4) in eternal *happiness* (5) to *glorify* [Him] (6) and *praise* him.

These six affirmations all terminate on God, Himself, as the end of mankind's created being. In this, of course, there is only a constriction of focus within the grand purpose of the whole created heavens and earth. The 'twenty-four elders' of John's vision express the broader theme. In heaven they worship God saying: 'Worthy are you, our LORD and God, to receive glory and honor and power, for you created all things, and by your will they existed and were created' (Rev. 4:10, 11). Christians acknowledge this in the hymns they sing, as do many of the biblical Psalms.

Man in paradise, however, was equipped to return intelligent worship to God by virtue of the undiminished divine image he bore, as crown of creation. As Psalm 104 says, the non-human, animate creatures dumbly and unknowingly wait on God that He may give them their meat in due season, but sub-human creatures do not know God and do not really praise Him – in spite of hymnic metaphors to the contrary. It is mankind's honor alone to express natures's praise to God. Only we, a little lower than the angels, can bring voiced, intelligent worship that is creation's debt to its Creator.

1. That He Might Rightly Know His Creator.

'God created man good and after his own image in righteousness and holiness, that he might rightly know his creator.'

This is to say that in mankind's original integrity he possessed the moral likeness to God, defined as righteousness and holiness. Ursinus and Olevianus, following good precedent, cite Ephesians 4:24 as proof of this aspect of the likeness, viz.: 'put on the new self, created after the likeness of God in true righteousness and holiness.' Colossians 3:10, cited without quoting, says: 'You ... have put on the new self, which is being renewed in knowledge after the image of its creator.' (In both these passages where ESV has 'self' the Greek word is *anthrōpos*, uniformly 'man' in older Versions. Some recent scholarship likes to understand the sense as *humanity*. This does rightly greatly expand the meaning.)

Considering how much the modern world thinks it knows, meanwhile devoting headlong effort to escape having anything whatsoever to do with God, it is necessary to label the world's knowledge not only defective but also false. Only '[we] know him who is true' and that because 'we are in him who is true'(1 John 5:20 RSV). The passages cited above imply that holiness, i.e. transparent moral purity of character, issues in and becomes manifest in knowledge of God. This knowledge results in faith, hope and love, in James' phrase: 'Religion that is pure and undefiled before God' (James 1:27). James H. Thornwell has said:

> Adam, as endowed with this knowledge, looked abroad upon creation and saw what science with all its discoveries so often fails to discern – the traces of the Divine glory.... Nature was a vast mirror, reflecting beauty, and as he saw he loved and adored.... [T]he whole universe was full of his name... written upon the starry vault, the extended plain, the lofty mountain, the boundless sea; upon every living thing.[18]

2. That He Might Heartily Love God.

For mankind in Edenic integrity truly to know God was sincerely to love God. This duty and privilege for the man of paradise arose spontaneously in him. In the history of salvation the same came to be incorporated in the 'great and first commandment': 'The LORD our God, the LORD is one. You shall love the LORD your God with all your heart and with all your soul and with all your might' (Deut. 6:4, 5; cf. Matt. 22:37). God intended the entire human race to serve Him in love. If to know God truly is to love Him, then to love God is to serve Him. As God's only knowing creatures here below and as God's servants, it is our duty in love to make God's will our law. 'Our wills are ours, We know not how; / Our wills are ours, to make them thine' (Tennyson, *In Memoriam*).

---

18. James H. Thornwell, *Collected Writings i* (Edinburgh: Banner of Truth Trust, 1875, 1986), p. 237.

3. That He Might Live with God.

The emphasis is on '*with* God.' The life mankind had in paradise was to be one of communion (fellowship, conversation, social intercourse) with the Creator.

We have little or no information as to how the LORD made Himself audible and visible to Adam. '[T]he LORD God commanded the man, saying' (Gen. 2:16), indicates speech and language. Most recent translations correctly, I think, use 'sound' (not 'voice'), i.e. of footsteps of God 'walking' in the Garden at evenfall. This indicates form and mass – perhaps a theophany like the many in the case of patriarchs, prophets and leaders in later Old Testament times. Or is this a profound anthropomorphism for something now lost to us and incapable of being fully communicated to us under the condition of sin? In either case the meaning is the same. We who presently walk by faith not by sight can only congratulate (envy?) the privilege of our first parents. Like the David of Robert Browning's *Saul*, 'My flesh in the Godhead I seek... see the Christ stand.' Throughout the Bible God declares His purpose to be with His people. Paul reminded an erring people of this to encourage holiness, saying, '...ye are the temple of the living God; as God hath said, I will dwell in them, and walk in them; and I will be their God, and they shall be my people' (2 Cor. 6:16 KJV). This purpose, interrupted at the gate of Eden long ago, was fulfilled penultimately 'in the days of his flesh' and ultimately in the restored paradise of a 'new earth' when 'now at last God has his dwelling among men! He will dwell among them and they shall be his people, and God himself [Gr. *autos ho theos*] will be with them' (Rev. 21:3 NEB). Restoration of this state is the major theme of the history of salvation from one end of the Bible and on through it to the very end. The Old Testament Tabernacle in the midst of the camp, the temple in the midst of the land, preserved the idea and pointed back to the paradise of Eden and forward to the future paradise of the new earth.

4. That He Might Live with God in Eternal Happiness.

'And enjoy him forever,' is how the Westminster Catechism puts it. God's purposed happiness for Adam cannot be separated from God's purposes of grace for the saved of all ages. The idea of an elect nation, church of the living God, whose names are written in heaven, was not an afterthought of the Godhead when He discovered a palpable mistake in exposing free beings to temptation. No, it was according to plan (Eph. 1:10, 11) and they were all individually chosen in Christ before the foundation of the world.

'Live with God in eternal happiness' – 'enjoy him forever.' This is nuptial language. Married couples are supposed to enjoy one another. 'Bliss,' a rather hyperbolical word for any earthly joy, is often predicated of some marriages. We should not therefore be surprised or shocked that the language of enjoyment or happiness of the ideal human marriage is directly applied to God and His redeemed people in the paradise of the new heaven and the new earth. Nor is it any wonder that much devout interpretation of the Song of Solomon has related the book to believers' communion with Christ or God. It is entirely proper, in light of amazingly vivid scriptural descriptions of the future estate of the redeemed, to apply the word *nuptial* to life in a paradisiacal future with God. The passages are familiar. The new Jerusalem is prepared as a bride adorned for her husband and even called 'the bride, the Lamb's wife' (Rev. 21:9; cf. v. 2) simply because God's redeemed people will live there. Nearly a hundred generations past – all much less conditioned than we against poetic figures and typological interpretation – have found the bride- or wife-husband imagery of the Song of Solomon typical of a God-Israel relation in the past and a Christ-church in the present or God-redeemed people of the future paradise. Sensual figures of marriage intimacies in mystical literature regarding communion with God are well known – even if not presently widely read.

The restoration of paradise up ahead tells us therefore what God intended for the Edenic paradise of old in respect to His happy enjoyment of a holy people and in respect to their's of Him.

5. That He Might Glorify God.

Few Christians will doubt or deny this truth encapsuled for us by the Westminster divines: 'Man's chief end is to glorify God, and to enjoy him forever' (*Shorter Catechism*, Question 1). No matter that 'although they knew God, they did not honor him as God' (Rom. 1:21). This purpose of God for mankind in paradise includes all the other subordinate purposes and includes all the good (blessedness, happiness) the Creator designed for our race, under Him. If God is all-wise, we may be sure His purpose was most comprehensive. Only in making Himself, the infinitely good and great, the end for which every 'creature under heaven' exists, could infinite wisdom be served. Further, we shall see mankind had and still has a central place in that order designed for God's glory. Human beings were in a special way to glorify God and to be the instrument for bringing glory from all earth's creatures to God.

The reader of this page could be overwhelmed with a list of readings from the Bible affirming in one way or another, explicitly or implicitly, directly or indirectly, that all of God's acts of creation were designed specifically that His glory – innate, inherent in God as God – be made manifest to intelligent beings – viz.: men and angels. Let me only list some of them in literary order: Numbers 14:26; Proverbs 16:4; Isaiah 43:7; 48:11; 60:21; 61:3; Ezekiel 20:9; 36:21, 22; 39:7; Romans 9:17; 11:36; 1 Corinthians 1:26-31; 10:31; 15:28; Ephesians 1:5, 6, 9; 2:8-10; 3:9, 10; Revelation 4:10, 11. The last reference perhaps captures the main thrust of all. Twenty-four heavenly elders in the presence of myriads of angels, and experiencing special manifestations of the three members of the Godhead, cry with faces downward in reverence, 'Worthy are you, our LORD and God, to receive glory and honor and power, for you created all things, and by your will they existed and were created.' [19]

Some cautions are in order:

a) When Scripture directs us to 'give God the glory' it does not mean He has no glory until we give it. Here language misleads us. Christian theology knows of God's 'uncreated glory' to which Jesus once referred (John 17:5). God is inherently glorious and perfectly happy. We only have the privilege and duty to acknowledge His glory, without resentment in our hearts and to express that privately or in public worship.

b) When God had created mankind He gave him three natural impulses (all three represented as commands). The first was to 'fill' the earth with his progeny, i.e. to populate it. Contrary to many misguided voices of recent times, it must then be that God wants mankind to dwell in all areas of the surface of this planet fit for habitation. The second was to subdue the earth. The one was 'the colonists charter.' One thinks of the royal charters of several British kings and queens resulting in a Virginia, a Carolina, a Georgia, and similar. The other was the royal charters, so to speak, of the guild of the smiths, who subdue the metals, and the hydrologists, who subdue the rivers, and so on. The third was to take dominion over the earth and all the living creatures, every living thing that moves (Gen. 1:28). The Hebrew *radhah* (here masculine, plural, imperative) means to 'have dominion,' and followed by an object with the Hebrew preposition, has the sense of 'rule over' (Brown, Driver and Briggs, Hebrew and English Lexicon of the Old Testament) . It is a 'take charge' word. Under the condition of sin many people instinctively resent the rule of others. Many others aspire to dominate other people and things.

c) There is no command for establishment of civil government – of some people by other people – in the Edenic arrangement. This came after the utter violence of antediluvian society brought on the divine judgment of the Great Flood.[20]

d) How God intended the dominion of mankind of paradise over beasts, fish, birds and 'every living thing that moveth' (including himself) is attractively set in the context of the coming Messiah's reign, when our LORD shall sit on the throne of His glory.

> In his days shall the righteous flourish,
> And abundance of peace, till the moon be no more.
> He shall have dominion[21] also from sea to sea,
> And from the River unto the ends of the earth (Ps. 72:7, 8 ASV).

e) Such a scheme was intended (some radical anti-biblical 'environmental' and 'ecological' propaganda notwithstanding) to produce a balanced and perfectly functioning society in which 'the righteous' do not suffer resentment from their peers, but 'flourish' and there is abundance of *shalom* (peace), prosperity, well-being, good health. Was Tennyson inspired by this vision? He

> [D]ipped into the future, far as human eye could see,
> Saw the vision of the world, and all the wonder that would be;
> ...There the common sense of most shall hold a fretful realm in awe,
> And the kindly earth shall slumber, lapped in universal law.[22]

f) Therefore, since the Scriptures plainly say repeatedly and in various ways that the created order of this planet was designed to bring glory to God and to enhance His reputation, and since mankind was told to populate it, subdue it and rule it as God's vicegerent, each person is not merely personally responsible to express heartfelt acknowledgement of God's glory, but, as the next paragraph asserts:

---

19. I have treated 'The Purpose of Creation' in Chapter 14 of Part I: Theology Proper: Introduction and Doctrine of God, pp. 113-121.
20. Robert D. Culver, *Civil Government, a Biblical View* (Edmonton, Alberta: Canadian Institute for Law, Theology and Public Policy, 2000), p. 308.
21. *radah* as in Gen. 1:28.
22. *Locksley Hall*, lines 120, 129, 130.

g) They are collectively also to take charge of this world in such a manner that the earth demonstrates not only God's power as Creator but His glory and majesty, by this planet's well-governed productivity, harnessed possibilities and the like. A world civilization of a type envisioned in Psalm 72:1-17 is required by the scriptural language everywhere.

6. That He Might Praise God.

Although the Scriptures amply support the proposition that God created the man of paradise in order that He should be praised by all creation, there appears to be no verse which specifically affirms this. The Psalter everywhere both expresses praise of God and enjoins it of godly people. For example, Psalm 107 begins, 'Let the redeemed of the LORD say so' (v. 2). Four times later (vv. 8, 15, 21, 31) comes this exclamation: 'Let them thank the LORD for his steadfast love, for his wondrous works to the children of men!' The final Psalm (150), a summary of all five books of the Psalter, begins and ends with 'Praise ye the LORD' (KJV) – in Hebrew either two words, *halelu Jah*, or joined as one, and in every language the familiar *Hallelujah*. There are thirteen clauses in Psalm 150. The verb for each one is the imperative verb, praise! The last verse says: 'Let everything that has breath praise the LORD!'

Every New Testament reader knows the recurring emphasis on praise as expression of Christian existence in God. In the Apocalypse, John the Revelator reports the final purpose of our race and of every created being, as announced in heaven, by angels, cherubim and myriads of redeemed men. 'These were all round the throne… Myriads upon myriads were there, thousands upon thousands upon thousands, and they cried aloud: "Worthy is the Lamb, the Lamb that was slain, to receive all power and wealth, wisdom and might, honor and glory and praise!" Then I heard every created thing in heaven and on earth and under the earth and in the sea, all that is in them, crying: "Praise and honor, glory and might, to him who sits on the throne and to the Lamb for ever and ever!" And the four living creatures said, "Amen," and the elders [perhaps representative of all the redeemed of ages now in heaven] fell down and worshiped' (Rev. 5:11-14 NEB).

This is how the story of creation, fall, redemption and consummation concludes. There can be no doubt God planned it that way from the beginning: for the worship of God by those *holy* people who *know* Him, *love* Him, *live with Him* in eternal *happiness*, to *glorify* Him and to *praise* Him. This was the purpose of God in and for the mankind of paradise and shall yet be accomplished at the end of the days. The 'mystery shall be finished'!

9
The Apostasy of Mankind: Probation, Temptation and Fall

Preliminary to Engagement with the Subject.

At this point in the structure of any system of Christian doctrines one must deal with a sad fact. No person such as the man of paradise exists on earth and, save for one, has never existed on earth, outside that primal period.

1. This chapter therefore treats the question of how it happens that people are universally sinful and every human life invariably ends in the tragedy of death. How and when did the change come? We already know from the last previous chapter that this was not God's declared intention. God created mankind holy, knowing God, living with God, loving Him, serving Him and in a happy state, and, as we shall see, with prospects of an eternal life of blessedness. When and how did the change come? Answers of course will be sought in the early chapters of Genesis.

Not every scholar agrees that the first three chapters of Genesis should be studied to find answers to questions about sin and death. John Skinner, author of the first volume of the *International Critical Commentary* says these chapters are 'aetiological or explanatory myths... of the most naïve and childlike description' explaining why a man should hold fast to his wife (Gen. 2:24), why a peasant must 'drudge' in the fields and the woman must endure the pangs of child-birth.' There is nothing of doctrinal value here at all.[1] Somewhat more on target, Umberto Cassuto, a learned, conservative Jewish commentator, says any doctrine of 'first causes' is absent; the message is related to practical uses.[2] If these authors are correct all Christian exegesis and biblical-systematic theology have been in error.

We affirm that both doctrine and practical moral guidance for godly folk in personal conduct and social relation are present in concentrated form here, as well as some of Skinner's 'aetiological' and Cassuto's practical uses. These chapters are the vestibule of the whole Bible, telling us by narrative and through archetypical authority exactly how life is and must be under the condition of sin. As we shall see, both Jesus and Paul employ the human actors (Adam and Eve) as being, in themselves and what happened to them and what God said to them, archetypes of all mankind. What they became, we are. What God said about them and to them is true of every one of us their offspring as well.

---

1. John Skinner, *Genesis, ICC.*, 2nd ed. (Edinburgh: T. & T. Clark, 1910, 1950), XII.
2. Umberto Cassuto, *Commentary on the Book of Genesis* (Jerusalem: Magnes Press, The Hebrew Univ., 1944, 1978), p. 139.

If any chapters in the Bible are profitable both for 'doctrine' on the one hand and practical for 'reproof, correction and instruction in righteousness' on the other, they are the first three chapters of Genesis.

A biblical-Christian view rejects all suggestions that mankind ever was a part of nature in the sense that death is a normal and necessary termination of all human existence on earth. The Scriptures nowhere indicate that Adam's sin had anything to do with the origin of death in the world of nature. Romans 5:12 relates to the origin of death in the human race, not among plants and animals, 'and so death spread to all men' (Rom. 5:12 RSV). The 'reign of tooth and claw' among all animals is supreme, invariable, and apparently always has been so. Plants die and by death serve the higher orders of life. The geological record, granting some validity to the geological table developed by specialists, gives us not a hint of any time, from Archaean to Pleistocene, when death was not normal and 'natural.' Though also 'of the earth, earthy,' the mankind of paradise was not merely a part of that order of nature. He was ruler-designate over it but not of it.

That mankind was in the created scheme the topmost 'specimen' is plain. Both in paradise and excluded from paradise mankind survives (lives on through) by exploiting nature and in the present is caught up in and by nature in its steady course (Gen. 8:22). In spite of nature's convulsions (plagues, floods, earthquakes, epidemics, droughts), whether we know about Noah and the Great Flood or not, we human mortals all depend on the Creator's post-diluvian promise: 'While the earth remains, seedtime and harvest, cold and heat, summer and winter, day and night, shall not cease' (Gen. 8:22 RSV). 'Nature' will continue to meet mankind's essential needs as a physical being. True, what has been called *natural theology* (doctrines derived from what God created, including the specific nature of man, rather than by special revelation) has some validity (though the older 'natural light' was more accurate. *revelation* used to be reserved for supernaturally supplied information). Yet, A. H. Strong was right in saying: 'The universal use of the phrase 'natural theology,' ...compels us... to employ the word "nature" in its broader sense as including man, although we do this under protest and with an explanation.'[3]

2. The object of our quest is not the origin of evil in the universe though it is appropriate now to set the record straight as to what Scripture says and does not say about it. An evil being, later referred to as the 'ancient serpent' (Rev. 12:9), 'who is called the devil and Satan [Adversary]' was already about and ready to exercise his poisonous presence in paradise of old. Neither he nor any of his minions or their principles will be allowed in the paradise to come (Rev. 21:27), which suggests that God designed for him to be present in the first paradise, and absent from the restored paradise. There is no passage of Scripture which speaks directly and clearly to the subject of the origin of evil and of Satan. It is a matter of considerable importance that the Bible nowhere attempts to justify God (theodicy) in allowing evil in the created world. The book of Job is sometimes supposed to explain its presence and to justify God. 'The denouement (chap. 38–42) shows God cannot be summoned like a defendant and forced to bear witness against Himself. No extreme of suffering gives mere man license to question God's wisdom or justice as Job had done. It is apparently on this very point that Job repents and recants.'[4] Yet, however much Job may tell the devout believer about right reactions to those 'natural' evils (loss of property, family, health and the like), which a pagan cosmology calls 'misfortune' or 'bad luck,' the book never once attempts either to blame God or to justify Him in letting it all happen. Rather God, who all the time is known (by the reader, who is let in on the conspiracy, so to speak) to be benevolent, omnipotent and omniscient, is acknowledged by a believing, but most fractious patriarch, to be so. The focus of interest is not the presence of evil in the world, but a good man's response to evil.

Furthermore, the Bible makes no bones about assigning the existence of evil to the permission of God's government (providence). Amos asks, 'Does disaster come to a city, unless the LORD has done it?' (Amos 3:6). Isaiah reports the LORD's words to Cyrus, 'I am the LORD, and there is no other, besides me there is no God.... I am the LORD, and there is no other. I form light and create darkness, I make well-being and create calamity, I am the LORD, who does all these things' (Isa. 45:5-7). This language seems to assign the natural evils mentioned to God's direct agency. It is, however, only a manner of speaking. It was clearly understood by the ones for whom the Bible was first written to apply to God's permissive providence operating through second causes toward certain ends which God's wisdom appoints. An example will help. 2 Samuel 24:1 reports an act of human disobedience to God as if it were brought about by direct divine agency: 'the anger of the LORD was kindled against Israel, and he [the LORD] incited David against them, saying, "Go, number Israel and Judah."' It shortly turns out that the taking of a census

---

3. A. H. Strong, *Systematic Theology* (Valley Forge, PA: Judson Press, 1907), p. 26.
4. Marvin H. Hope, *Job, The Anchor Bible* (New York: Doubleday & Co., 1965, 1980), p. lxxx.

was contrary to the moral will of God. It is also apparent that in both David's case and the nation's case, previous sins had brought each to a stage where judgment was necessary. Thus, the passage conveys the message that God set up this as occasion to bring matters to a head. Nevertheless, this is not the end of the matter. 1 Chronicles 21:1 indicates Satan's place in the affair as immediate, proximate cause of David's temptation to sin: 'Then Satan stood against Israel and incited David to number Israel.'[5]

This latter text (1 Chr. 21:1) is not an effort to save the character of God. The texts simply present two aspects of one truth. Evil is allowed in the world for reasons God has never seen fit fully to disclose and which human wisdom has not discovered. Yet evil is not beyond God's control. It is this fact of providence that prompts such a biblical saying as 'Surely the wrath of man shall praise you' (Ps. 76:10) or 'Ah, Assyria, the rod of my anger' (Isa. 10:5). God raised up wicked tyrants such as the Pharaohs of the oppression and Exodus so that God's name 'may be proclaimed in all the earth' (Exod. 9:16, cf. Rom. 9:17). In a prophetic declaration an oppressive and destructive Nebuchadnezzar is called 'my servant' by God (Jer. 25:9).

There are two prominent cases reported in Scripture wherein divinely permitted evil was overruled for great good – both inevitably cited when this subject comes up. The first is the villainy of Joseph's brothers in kidnapping him and selling him as a slave, thus leading to his enforced residence in Egypt – where he rose to high political office, whereby he saved from starvation not only many Egyptians but his own lately repentant brothers (Gen. 50:15-21; cf. 45:1-15). Joseph's words, 'you meant evil against me, but God meant it for good' (Gen. 50:20), can hardly be improved upon as statement of the distinction between divine agency and human agency – both divine providence and human action – in causation. The other case is the crucifixion of Jesus. (See Acts 2:23; 3:13-18; 4:27, 28.) When moral agents go too far in dallying with evil, God can so move in their own activity that even demonic acts fall in line to promote God's ultimate purposes. God sets limits on evil and even uses it, but He is not complicit in it.

3. Nor is our quest specifically the origin of moral evil, that is, of sin, in the sense of sin's cause either in the case of our first parents in paradise or of any one else. Origin as commonly understood involves cause. What caused something to begin is the goal of the search for origins, as usually understood.

In the biblical-Christian outlook, sin is an enigma, a fact incapable of explanation. We know, as all evangelical and orthodox maintain, that God is not the author of sin. We simply do not accept it as a possibility. This matter became important at the time of the Reformation and on that account found a place in several creedal documents. The chief Lutheran statement [6] cites Romans 9:22 and interprets Paul as teaching that God endured the human instruments of sin without making them what they are. God is not to blame. Our own human choices are to blame. God is neither the author nor the cause of sin. The Heidelberg Catechism asks (Q.7) 'Whence then proceeds this depravity of human nature?' and making no effort at ultimate cause of sin simply answers (A.7): 'From the fall and disobedience of our first parents.' The Westminster Confession (chap. VI, art. 1) says that God 'pleased' to 'permit' human sin but affirms nothing about cause. All the evangelical creeds of the sixteenth and seventeenth centuries are in agreement. The Roman Church is no less insistent on the matter, tracing sin only to its beginning not to some first cause. Its official dogmatic statements trace the beginning of sin in our race, and thereby of death, directly and solely to Adam's first sin. They rely, as we all must, on the plain statement of Romans 5:12: 'Therefore, just as sin came into the world through one man, and death through sin, and so death spread to all men because all sinned.' (It does not say 'death passed upon all created life – animal or otherwise – through Adam's sin.') Theologians of an exceedingly philosophical and speculative bent are here required to be simply biblical. There is nowhere else to go but to the Bible. The Second Council of Orange (529), assembled to combat Semi-Pelagian errors, issued this statement which is essentially Paul's interpretation of the story (Gen. 3; Rom. 5):

> If anyone asserts that Adam's sin was injurious only to Adam and not to his descendants, or if he declares that it was only the death of the body which is punishment for sin, and not the sin, the death of the soul, that passed from one man to all the human race, he attributes an injustice to God and contradicts the words of the Apostle: 'Through one man sin entered into the world and through sin death, and thus death has passed to all men because all have sinned.' [7]

---

5. A comparison of Revelation 13:2, 7 and 8 with 17:17 or reading of 2 Thessalonians 2:7-12 reveals similar instances.
6. *The Formula of Concord*, art. 19.
7. Gerald Van Ackeren, Editor, *The Church Teaches, Documents of the Church in English Translation* (Rockford, IL: Tan Books Publ., 1973), p. 157. A better rendering than Deferrari-Denzinger translation.

4. The Bible's explanation of the beginning of sin is a story – a true story. How could it be otherwise? As the great conservative volume of G. F. Oehler truly says:

> Genesis gives no theory of creation, no thesis on the essence of sin, no theory of its origin; but it sets forth, in the form of a story, a sin from which each one can easily for himself develop the theory, and the thoughts involved in the narrative – thoughts which are decisive for the whole course of revelation. A definition of *religion* is not given; but the way in which it came about that man feels a dread and fear of God... dominated... by the feeling of guilt, is exhibited in a statement of facts.[8]

As implied above, the beginning of sin is no more a legitimate subject of philosophical or speculative inquiry than the arrival of the first robin or the first runner past a finish line. The Bible simply reports the beginning (*entrance* would rather imply a previous train of causes) in the first three chapters. Those plain but profound chapters tell a story which countless generations have regarded as a sober history. Whatever there may be of what Calvin calls God's baby talk to us, condescending to our world-picture – call it time-space-bound frame of reference or cultural paradigm – it has every mark of being a sober history, to be taken in utter seriousness. Mythological and allegorical interpretations appeared very early among those predisposed already to that approach to much of the Old Testament – the school of Alexandria. As we have contended earlier in this book, the New Testament affirms the events of Adam's fall really happened. (I have already cited 2 Corinthians 11:3; 1 Timothy 2:14; Romans 5:12-19. Add Jesus' connecting the devil in John 8:44 with Genesis 3). Jews in the last epoch before the New Testament period accepted the story simply as it reads, as shown by the Wisdom of Solomon 2:24: 'Through the envy of the devil came death into the world.' Also Ecclesiasticus (Wisdom of Sirach) 25:24, 'Of the woman came the beginning [Gr. *archē*, as in John 1:1] of sin, and through her we all die.'

5. Even though the beginning of sin is reported in Scripture, a general ignorance of what sin is prevails among the masses of mankind. It is guilty ignorance. 'They did not like to retain God in their knowledge,' (Rom. 1:28) 'therefore their foolish heart was darkened' (Rom. 1:21). Jesus severely rebuked this guilty ignorance, even among disciples (Luke 24:25; Matt. 15:16,17; Mark 7:18; Mark 8:17,18). It accounts for the rejection of Jesus by the Jews (John 12:37-41). God has sent His Spirit into the world to convict it 'of guilt in regard to sin and righteousness and judgment' (John 16:8 NIV). As every converted sinner knows, the special work of awakening grace floods the darkened heart with the light, the light of truth. This light is unfiltered and unslanted by self-serving interest, rendering one aware that before God one is 'without excuse' (Rom. 1:20) and 'guilty before God' (Rom. 3:19 KJV). That sin, any sin at all, is gross – productive in every instance of pollution, culpability (blameworthiness) and guilt (deserving of punishment) – always comes to sinners as an overwhelming revelation if it is sufficiently vivid to lead to repentance and faith. Scripture and history provide outstanding examples – Saul of Tarsus (Acts 9), David (Ps. 32), Augustine (*Confessions*), Luther (in the tower of Wittenberg), John Newton (and Mr. Everyman).

6. In another respect sin is inexplicable nonsense. Words such as insane, senseless, pathological (i.e. mentally sick), terms often nowadays employed by otherwise blasé journalists to characterize especially repulsive crimes of violence, really apply to sin of any kind or degree. This idea is brilliantly developed by G. C. Berkouwer in his series of *Studies in Dogmatics*.[9] The riddle of sin bears no relation to biblical mysteries such as the Incarnation (1 Tim. 3:16) and the relation of Christ and the church (Eph. 5:32) known to mankind only because God has revealed them, even though still inexplicable to mere human intellect. Then there are things once unknown but later made known (Rev. 17:3-7). Sin is neither of these; it is a unique enigma, something insane, senseless and sick, out of step with the reality of the created scheme of things. 'One cannot find sense in the senseless or meaning in the meaningless.'[10] Those who approve of sin are fools. Such fools are the celebrated villains of the book of Proverbs. We shall return briefly to this theme in treatment of the doctrine of sin. For now, it is important to realize sin had a beginning in history, known to us only by biblical revelation, but there is absolutely no explanation of *why* or even *how*. See J. D. Godsey's *The Theology of Dietrich Bonhoeffer*.[11] Bonhoeffer writes: 'The fall of man... is both inconceivable [Godsey, Bonhoeffer's interpreter, uses *incomprehensible*] and unalterably inexcusable, and therefore... disobedience does not exhaust the facts. It is revolt... departure... defection.'[12]

---

8. G. F. Oehler, *Theology of the Old Testament*, rev. G. E. Day (New York: Funk and Wagnalls, 1883), p. 53.
9. G. C. Berkouwer, *Studies in Dogmatics: Sin*, chap. 5, 'The Riddle of Sin' (Grand Rapids: Eerdmans, 1971), pp. 130-148.
10. ibid., p. 134.
11. J. D. Godsey, *The Theology of Dietrich Bonhoeffer* (Philadelphia: Westminster Press, 1960), p. 137 ff.
12. Dietrich Bonhoeffer, *Creation and Fall* (New York: Macmillan, 1937, 1959), p. 77.

It does not occur to Christian believers who start their journey of Bible interpretation of Genesis with the dictum of Jesus ('it is they that bear witness about me,' John 5:39; Luke 24:24-27) to doubt that the first prophecy of Jesus is Genesis 3:15. So also they who let the New Testament interpret the Old Testament draw from Paul's remarks about parallels (negative and positive) between Adam and Christ (Rom. 5:12-19) know that Genesis 3 describes 'the Fall' of our race at the beginning of its history. We shall reserve most details for the next *locus* of theology, *hamartiology*, or the doctrine of sin (Part 3). Likewise many agree who come with 'critical' naturalistic assumptions, as for example John Skinner, who forthrightly refers consistently to 'The Creation and Fall of Man.'[13] Victor P. Hamilton notes 'not all… agree' (Claus Westerman, for example). He goes on to say, 'Kant praises Adam for his willingness to make his own moral judgment… the biblical scholar D. R. G. Beattie takes a similar approach in "What is Genesis 2 – 3 About" (*Expository Times* 92)… Similarly J. Bahr "The Myth of Man's Fall" (*Expository Times* 92, pp. 235-237).[14]

Although, as we have already noted, Judaism has no firm doctrine of 'original sin,' i.e. of a primeval fall, yet in the apocryphal book of *Ecclesiasticus*, Ben Sirach says: 'Of the woman came the beginning of sin, and through her we all die' (*Ecclesiasticus* 25:24). 2 *Esdras* says: 'O Adam, what have you done? Though sin was yours, the fall was not yours alone; it was ours also, the fall of all your descendants' (2 *Esdras* 7:119, Revised English Bible). These Jewish sources suggest rather firmly that when Paul wrote Romans 5:12-19 he was not creating a new theological idea. Yet most Jewish comments on the story of 'the fall', fall in line with the heresy of Pelagius that Adam and Eve only provide a paradigm of how everyone 'falls' into sin. Adam lost nothing for us all, he only set a bad example.

The Narrative of the Fall.

Rightly to interpret as an historical account the story of creation, temptation and fall, one must humble oneself. Where human learning would propose an erudite discourse on principles, the scribe of the kingdom of God will sit like the naive child, believing because God is speaking. Inductive treatment of the whole scope of probation and fall with comment on each detail as it appears is useful, but it is not the method of systematic theology. Dietrich Bonhoeffer's *Creation and Fall*[15] and Franz Delitzsch's *New Commentary on Genesis*[16] are two very different types of approach, but I have found them most interesting and suggestive. Of the systematicians, I have found the treatment by the Baptist John Gill, perhaps the greatest of eighteenth-century evangelical Old Testament scholars and theologians, the most helpful.[17] Over a long period of time I have found my own research in this crucial passage forwarded much by Gill's rather brief but clear treatment, though I follow my own plan not his. It would be unfruitful and confusing to attempt to document many years of reading on the subject of the fall and the exegesis of this passage.

Bare recitation of the momentous story of the fall of mankind and the attending results requires little time and effort; nor is there anything complicated – only twenty-four verses are devoted to it. Like a head-on collision of two automobiles on a two-lane road the event can be described quite briefly. However, the aftermath in human suffering as result of such an 'accident' will inevitably be enormous and the written record of the litigation might fill a file drawer. So it is with the most utterly disastrous events of the fall of mankind so very early in our history. The results do go on forever and the literature of the world – all of it in one way or another related to that fall – keeps growing and, to borrow John the Beloved's vivid language, 'I suppose that the world itself could not contain the books.'

We shall discuss as briefly as is consistent with our purposes, the scriptural narrative of the apostasy of mankind under the rubrics of (1) probation (Gen. 2:16, 17); (2) temptation (Gen. 3:1-5); (3) fall (Gen. 3:6); and (4) consequences.

I. The Probation of Mankind (Genesis 2:16, 17).

'And the LORD God commanded the man, saying, Of every tree of the garden thou mayest freely eat: But of the tree of the knowledge of good and evil, thou shalt not eat of it: for in the day that thou eatest thereof thou shalt surely die' (KJV).

---

13. John Skinner, *Genesis, ICC* (Edinburgh: T. & T. Clark, 1910, 1960, 1980), pp. 51-89.
14. Victor P. Hamilton, *The Book of Genesis* (Grand Rapids: Eerdmans, 1990), pp. 211, 212.
15. Bonhoeffer, op. cit., pp. 64-94, musing during a critical period in the author's life.
16. Franz Delitzsch, *New Commentary on Genesis*, vol. i, trans. Sophia Taylor (Edinburgh: T. & T. Clark, 1888), pp. 146-176.
17. John Gill, *Body of Divinity*, 2 Vols., first published 1795; rep. Grand Rapids: Baker Books, 1978. Vol. I, pp. 451-462, 'Of the Sin and Fall of Man' and 'Of the Nature of the Sin of Man.'

The Authorized Version (KJV) is to be preferred here because this is one of those texts where it is important to know if only one person, 'thou' (2nd singular), is addressed or more than one, 'ye.' The Hebrew clearly indicates that only Adam himself, responsible head of the human race, is addressed by God's commands in these two verses, prior to the creation of Eve. The narrative of Eve's creation immediately follows (2:18-25). We know that Adam must have conveyed the command to Eve from her response to the serpent (Gen. 3:2, 3).

Much theological writing misses the especially sharp, intensive, grammatical modes and fierce tone of these two verses (Gen. 2:16, 17), viz.: (1) of all the words for God's instructions to human beings, the word 'commanded' (Heb. *tsawah*) is the strongest. It never occurs except in the intensive stem, either *piel* (act.) or *pual* (pass.). When, as here, followed by the preposition '*al*, above, over, upon, against, the phrase means to command strictly. We can almost visualize Elohim shaking the finger at Adam and saying 'Do not!' In the case of permission 'thou mayest *freely* eat,' 'freely' translates the absolute or intensive infinitive of eat – 'eating thou shalt eat' – so 'freely' does partly capture the idea. But in the case of prohibition from eating the tree of knowledge of good and evil the LORD God's 'Thou shalt not' employs the very same mode. In English, the simple indicative future with the usual Hebrew negative *lo*', means 'no' or 'not.' It is used in eight of the Ten Commandments of Exodus 20 – 'Thou shalt not' – fourteen times in the passage. We can imagine a mild fatherly tone as the LORD God gave Adam custody of the Garden, but such a relaxed ambience is utterly foreign to the instructions about eating and not eating. The intensive (absolute) infinitive is used again to raise the emphasis on the certainty of death as penalty for breaking the *commandment*, viz. 'thou shalt surely die,' literally 'dying thou shalt die.'

'Of every tree… the tree of life in the midst of the garden… the tree of the knowledge of good and evil.' Each tree had a place in mankind's future. We know the tree of life was designed for life not death, as Revelation 22:1, 2 explains. We cannot doubt that had our first parents passed their probation – for how long a time we cannot now know – they would have been granted that access to life 'for ever' (Gen. 3:22) and not have had 'the way to the tree of life' (3:24) barred by God's cherubim. God wants everyone to have the same knowledge of good and evil – i.e. passage from righteous innocence to intellectual and moral maturity. This was to be attained by a right use of the freedom they enjoyed as created in God's image. They traded, so to speak, the possibility of a knowledge of good and evil such as God has for the kind the devil has.

The story does not tell all. One wonders why Adam and Eve had not already eaten of the tree of life. It was not prohibited (2:9). The answer probably is that the presence of the trees in paradise is only indicated at Genesis 2:9 as narrative setting for the action of chapter 3. There were many other trees in the Garden, but God called special attention only to the *tree of testing* – the tree of the knowledge of good and evil. Though we know there was a tree of life in the Garden, Adam may not have known about that until after the fall. The tree of testing was prominently set 'in the midst of the Garden.' The tree of life may have been set remotely in an obscure place. At any rate they were not attracted to it. Apparently Eve had no interest in the tree of knowledge until the tempter called attention to it by his suggestive question. Only then (3:6) did, 'the woman' see 'that the tree was good for food… delight to the eyes, and… to be desired to make one wise.'

The Ancient Snake.

The narrative does not say whence came this evil person. Evil evidently originated in another probation and fall in which there was no tempter, hence no redemption. The ancient snake, the devil, Satan (Rev. 20:2), then became the tempter of this probation. There have not been wanting critics and commentators to suggest that the tempter seems to have been necessary for the trial to take place. Necessary or not, he was there, and any doctrine of providence will find itself obligated to insist that the serpent was there quite as much by divine intent as the two trees which figure so prominently. The serpent was as certainly present in the Garden of Eden by divine design as Judas Iscariot was present among the LORD's apostolic group.

The foregoing remarks on exegetical details and their meaning, however, do not explain fully the significance of the trees and the command concerning them as a probation. The scope of this book does not allow a survey of (the several interpretations of these verses, and of) the narrative to follow, as myth. There are theories that regard it as an adapted oriental myth of the gods' jealousy to keep mankind from knowing their secret divine privileges, or a myth to explain the awakening of mankind to the pleasures and pains of sexuality. There is also the Story-of-Everyman theory which makes the narrative a moral lesson regarding how everyone meets moral temptation. And there are others.

Details of Interpretation.

Christians have always, with some minor variations, interpreted Genesis 2:16, 17 as setting out the basic details of a probation which our first parents failed utterly, with tragic consequences for us all. Probation designates a period of time during which certain subjects are placed under a set of rules requiring specified good behavior, at the successful termination of which they will receive or retain certain rewards, privileges and the like.

What was the promise on condition of obedience, presumably for a period of time? The threat contingent on disobedience was death. From this we may legitimately infer the converse promise was life everlasting in a growing continuation of the life already enjoyed with God and with one another in the Garden. Each of the negative commands of the Decalogue implies a positive. This same principle seems to apply here. This inference is supported by a number of data in the text and later biblical references to the probationary experiences. We observe the following.

1. The tree of life represented everlasting life in some unspecified symbolical or 'sacramental' way. God had some provision in mind in deliberately exposing this significance *after* the probation failed: 'Then the LORD God said, "Behold, the man has become like one of us in knowing good and evil. Now, lest he reach out his hand and take also of the tree of life and eat, and live for ever – "' (Gen. 3:22-24). To us later 'probationers' (of sorts) the Son of Man promises, 'I will grant to eat of the tree of life, which is in the paradise of God' (Rev. 2:7; cf. 22:2). This mystical language of the Revelation does not resolve all of the obscurity, but certainly 'leaks' the information that eternal life was God's design for a successful probation of the 'First Adam.'

2. Our LORD lived and died, rose and ascended, to provide or restore, what Adam lost. Adam had life which might have become elevated and made eternal *had he passed the probation*. Jesus passed the test and won for us God's gift of eternal life:

> If, because of one man's trespass, death reigned through that one man, much more will those who receive the abundance of grace and the free gift of righteousness reign in life through the one man Jesus Christ.... For the wages of sin is death, but the free gift of God is eternal life in Christ Jesus our LORD (Rom. 5:17; 6:23).

3. Paradise in which Adam was placed was suited by God to promote growth and development both in holy character and in happiness, that is, to pass successfully. Adam had the *society* of both a beautiful wife specially made for him to meet his social needs (Gen. 2:18 ff.), and a gracious heavenly Father who created him for His own fellowship, and a natural environment lacking no spiritual, material or aesthetic need or lawful desire.

4. There was the possible opportunity of attaining physical immortality (rather than the dread and pain of death before resurrection and translation which come to pass for us all). The means was the fruit of the tree of life (Gen. 3:24).

I have already suggested as much, but there is more that ought to be said. The Bible nowhere affirms 'natural immortality' of any created being. 1 Corinthians 15:45-50 contrasts the Last Adam and the First Adam, not as Adam was after his apostasy, but as 'made.' The phrase, 'was made a living soul' is quoted directly from the Septuagint of Genesis 2:7. As thus made he was – 'from the earth, a man of dust' (1 Cor. 15:47) and as only 'flesh and blood,' like the rest of us, could not in that state inherit (enter actual possession of) the kingdom of God (1 Cor. 15:50). He, like us, would have had to be changed. The means of change was the fruit of the tree of life apparently provided for checking decay and preserving youth. 'If Adam had maintained his integrity, the body might have been developed and transfigured, without intervention of death' – *able not to die* would have become *not able to die*.[18]

If Adam had improved on his opportunities for development of a confirmed, permanent holiness by passing his probation he would have been granted access to the tree. As to this possibility, Strong remarks:

> The tree of life was symbolic of communion with God and of man's dependence on him... because it had a physical efficacy. It was sacramental and memorial to the soul, because it sustained the life of the body [that is, it did not convey eternal spiritual life]. Natural immortality without holiness would have been unending misery. Sinful man was therefore shut out from the tree of life, till he could be prepared for it by God's righteousness. Redemption and resurrection not only restore that which was lost, but give what man was originally created to attain... Rev 22:14 'Blessed are they that wash their robes, that they may have the right to come to the tree of life.'[19]

5. The temptation, including both the tree of knowledge and the serpent, were the very arrangements designed by God to improve Adam's character, that is, not only to demonstrate holiness of character but by obedience to God to grow into confirmed holiness. In the language of Latin theology, Adam, who by free will, rightly used, was already

---
18. Strong, op. cit., p. 527.
19. Strong, op. cit., p. 527.

posse non peccare, able not to sin, would have become *non posse peccare*, not able to sin. Our LORD increased in wisdom and stature, in favor with God and man (Luke 2:15), proving Himself the competent, holy Last Adam. Even He had to be tempted, as is well known. Whereas the First Adam used his freedom to learn disobedience, the Last Adam 'Although he was a son, he learned obedience through what he suffered. And being made perfect, he became the source of eternal salvation to all who obey him' (Heb. 5:8,9).

In this section on the probation I have ventured into some details that might seem more speculative then exegetically derived. Yet precisely because Christians ask questions about these matters and try to offer answers to one another these comments seem necessary.[20]

II. The Tempter of Mankind (Gen. 3:1-5).

'Now the serpent was more crafty than any other beast of the field that the LORD God had made' (1a).

His Identity.

The tempter was ostensibly a creature of the 'field' – i.e. a wild animal – yet Scripture is plain that 'the serpent' was a great evil being in existence ages before paradise was planted. Whether the devil employed the organs of the snake to talk we cannot discover. The mystery is no less than the ass that reproved the prophet Balaam (in which case 'the LORD opened the mouth of the donkey' [Num 22:28]). Ordinarily neither snakes nor donkeys make speech in human languages except in Greek and German fables. We know the devil or Satan – to give him a proper name – was the one who supplied the snake's words. See Revelation 12:9 which identifies 'that ancient serpent' with the dragon, the devil and Satan (see also John 8:44; 1 John 3:8; 1 Tim. 2:11). We do not know how he became evil, or by what manner, means or process he fell from created holiness, but that pride was the root of his primeval fall we properly infer from 1 Timothy 3:6. Christian tradition takes that hint straight to Isaiah 14:12-14 and following ('Lucifer, son of the morning' KJV) and Ezekiel 28:10-19 ('in Eden, the garden of God'). A very impressive 'conflict of the ages' theology of universal history by the late pastor of Tenth Presbyterian Church of Philadelphia connects the Isaiah 14 and Ezekiel 28 passages with the serpent of Genesis 3 and the dragon of Revelation – to the edification of multitudes who heard him speak or who read his book.[21] John Milton, greatest of the Puritan literati, created two great epic poems around the same theme: *Paradise Lost* and *Paradise Regained*. Lacking absolute 'proof,' the consensus is nevertheless very impressive. Lucifer, light-bearer, as a name for Satan in Christian history, is supplied by the Latin Vulgate Version of Isaiah 14:12.

His Character and Methods.

He is wicked, threatening and dangerous, for he is likened to a roaring lion (1 Peter 5:8) and said to be a murderer and liar (John 8:44). Believers are told to beware of him, and to be sober and vigilant against him. This is because he is 'subtle,' that is, cunning, deceitful, everything a successful tempter needs to be. This, of course, Eve did not know. One wonders why the LORD God had not warned her of him. At any rate it was precisely the serpent's deceit, making evil appear good, desirable, and beautiful, that gave him victory over Eve. And the Bible does not fail to make that point for our benefit. Deceit is his *modus operandi* (Eph. 6:11; 2 Cor. 11:3; 1 Tim. 2:14). To discuss the Hebrew and Greek names of this being who first steps on stage here before the curtain of primeval mystery would be interesting and instructive, but distracting at this stage of present inquiry.

Steps Leading to the Fall: the Serpent's attack on Eve's Innocence (Gen. 3:1-5).

Minor problems of interpretation occur, but nothing that obscures the stages of swift collapse of human integrity brought on by the subtlety of the tempter. Let us supply a brief analysis of steps emanating from the serpent's subtle suggestion.

1. The serpent first insinuated doubt of the benevolence and veracity of God with a question: 'Did God actually say, "You shall not eat of any tree in the garden"?' (v. 1). It is to be supposed that the stealthy snake was lurking

---

20. My approach to these verses is traditional in the main, yet based on my own studies of the Hebrew text over a period of about 10 years when I taught first and second year Hebrew, never failing carefully to work through these verses. The interest of liberal critical scholars is keen but antiquarian, not theological. For them this is ancient ethnic saga filtered through Hebrew monotheism. Skinner, however, has witty outline captions: *The Temptation* (1–5); The Inquest (8–13), etc. Cassuto's Jewish interpretation makes verses 1-5 a parable that went on in Eve's mind!
21. Donald Grey Barnhouse, *The Invisible War* (Grand Rapids: Zondervan, 1965), p. 288.

somewhere nearby when God initially instructed Adam (2:16, 17) or when Adam passed along the word to Eve. Satan is not omniscient.

2. A parley with the devil on the subject of forbidden fruit then took place (vv. 1b-3). This was Eve's first step downward. 'She might have suspected... some design upon her, by introducing such a subject... by so extraordinary a creature; and therefore should have broken off at once.'[22] Eve's answer was truthful. '[N]either shall you touch it' seems to be an innocent comment, implicit in the command. She should not be charged with 'adding to the Word of God.' She surely understood fondling the fruit would be wrong, leading almost inevitably to eating it. Except for the mistake of even conversing with a disreputable character, Eve is still on safe, if risky, ground.

3. Then the serpent outrightly charged God with falsehood (vv. 4, 5). He did not, like the modernist or infidel, deny that God has spoken through prophet, apostle or Messiah, but acknowledged that God indeed *had* spoken and that what God had said was false. Like most audacious disturbers of the peace of the righteous, the devil really was and continues to be a garrulous windbag, guilty of the very trespasses against truth and domestic tranquillity he charges to others.

The attack was successful: 'the woman being deceived was in the transgression' (1 Tim. 2:14 KJV); '[T]he serpent beguiled Eve through his subtilty' (2 Cor 11:3 KJV).

Elements in the Temptation (Gen 3:6a).

The devil played his hand just right to remove obstacles placed by God's direct command. Now the interplay of the inner world of human nature with the external world led to the woman's swift slide to utter moral defeat. The tree and its fruit appealed to physical appetite for tasty food, 'good for food'; it appealed to her con-created feminine appreciation of beauty ('a delight to the eyes') and to that supremely blessed human capacity, curiosity (desire for knowledge of the novel) – 'the tree was to be desired to make one wise.' The last is closely related to the social impulse, to meet, associate with and converse with other people.

The same triad of channels to the will were employed ages later when the devil proposed three temptations of Jesus (Matt. 4), but with notable lack of success.

John says, if I interpret him correctly, that these three types of temptation (or channels of appeal) exhaust the possibilities – that there are no more. Having instructed, 'Love not the world' or anything in it he goes on to say: 'For everything in the world' (NIV) (which means all *without exception* here), viz.: 'the cravings of the flesh' (which certainly includes hunger, sexual pleasure, and similar), 'the lust of the eyes' and 'the pride of life.' The last employs *bios* for 'of life.' It is the word employed when Jesus said the father 'divided unto' his sons 'his living' (Luke 15:12 KJV), i.e. money, wealth, materials contributing to support of natural life. When later (15:13 KJV) the younger son 'wasted his substance [i.e. the 'living' given earlier] with riotous living' a wholly different word is used (*dzaō*), a verb meaning to be *alive* as opposed to *dead*. So John's expression, 'the pride of life,' means pride of owning or having something – anything from a kiddie car to a pretty face, to an unshared secret, to a university degree, to the secret of how to earn a million dollars.

These appeals of the world are neither good nor bad in themselves – certainly not before the fall. '[T]he whole world [*kosmos*, the world as managed by the devil] lies in the power of the evil one' (1 John 5:19), but everything in the world is still the good creature of God. In Eve's case the appeal was simple and direct.

III. The Act of Apostasy or the Fall (Gen. 3:6b).

The culmination of the act was in the eating of the fruit, first by Eve and then by Adam. '[S]he took of its fruit and ate, and she also gave some to her husband who was with her, and he ate' (Gen. 3:6b).

James 1:14 and 15 tell precisely what took place. I furnish my own translation to avoid the unnecessarily pejorative sense of 'lust' in KJV, and 'evil desire' of NIV, and others.

'But every man is tempted when he is drawn away by his own desire [neutral, neither good or bad] and enticed. After that when the desire has conceived it gives birth to sin' (James 1:14,15).

The heart had been corrupted before the hand plucked the fruit or ever it passed Eve's lips and passed on to Adam's hand and mouth. 'Thus man fell inwardly, before the outward act of eating the forbidden fruit... fell in that

---

22. John Gill, *Complete Body of Doctrinal and Practical Divinty* (Grand Rapids: Baker Books, 1978), p. 451.
23. Strong, op. cit., p. 584.
24. Gill, *Body of Divinity I*, p. 452.

one fundamental determination whereby he made supreme choice of self instead of God.'[23] '[H]ence she inwardly sinned before she ate of the forbidden fruit.'[24]

In our time of strange public bickering about 'victimization' of women and shrill counter-accusations, it might be well to know how esteemed authors of yesteryear regarded the relations of the sexes in this tragic affair. I cite one.

> That Adam sinned as well as Eve, is most certain; for though it is said 'Adam was not deceived' [1 Tim. 2:14]; the meaning is, that he was not first deceived, that he was not deceived by the serpent but by his wife [I wonder about this last]; and when she is said to be in the transgression [1 Tim. 2:14], the sense is, that she was in the transgression first; but not only [alone]; for Adam was also; hence we read of Adam's transgression, Rom. 5:14. And if he was with his wife when she ate of the fruit… he sinned in not attempting to detect the sophistry of the serpent; in not defending his wife from his assaults; in not persuading her not to eat of the fruit; in not warning her of the danger; yea in not using his conjugal authority [after all was she not supposed to be Adam's 'helper'?] and laying his commands upon her not to eat; for if he was present and silent, he must be criminal and accessory to her sin.[25]

These remarks, however trivial and a bit passé they may seem to a 'progressive' reader, do not seem so to most earnest people who give careful, knowledgable thought to the text and the doctrine of 'first sin.' Over the years I have presented these matters to graduate classes in theology and in Old Testament. These are precisely the questions people – lay and learned – ask and the sort of answers given. Gill is so very succinct I have cited his remarks almost as my own, even though now almost 200 years old. They were already old when Augustine discussed them, yet still new to each generation.

Over the generations Christians less prone to 'demythologize' than ours and, taking the narrative as true – what it says as well as what it does *not* say – have wondered, what if Eve had sinned in Adam's absence and then later 'gave to her husband' and if so with what persuasion, and he with what motives joined with her? Assuming Adam was not deceived *by Eve* (1 Tim. 2:14), it has been argued that he ate the fruit out of immense love for her, being unable to think of going on in integrity without her. Many sermons have argued thus and compared Adam's love for lost Eve with God's (Christ's) love for lost humanity even to the point of death in each case – all on the slim scriptural basis of 'Adam… who is the figure of him that was to come' (Rom. 5:14 KJV).

At any rate, Adam alone was the natural, or seminal, or organic head of the race of mankind and of Eve, as well, for she was taken out of his side. It has been conjectured that if Eve alone had sinned, the guilt would have been personal only. Since, however, she could not be mother of sinless generations to follow, God would then have produced another mate for Adam.

The persistence of these and related questions and proposals – some reasonable and some not – forbids that we ignore the speculations. Pastors and teachers as well as parents who do serious Bible reading with their children need to be aware; not surprised when questions arise about this very critical event in our history. We will continue to interpret the narrative of the fall in the next chapter.

---

25. ibid., pp. 452, 453.

10
Consequences of the Fall of Mankind

In the chapter just ended we were considering the narrative of the primeval tragedy which theology and preaching usually describe as 'The Fall of man.' The probationary arrangement, the temptation to violate the arrangement and the act of apostasy came before our attention. Now in this chapter we consider the consequences for mankind (personal, spiritual and moral), also judgment and grace for mankind, and the beginnings of civilization.

IV. The Immediate Personal, Spiritual and Moral Consequences of the Fall.

The consequences, of course, were precisely what God had said they would be, viz.: 'in the day that thou eatest thereof thou shalt surely die' (Gen. 2:17 KJV). There was to be grace in divine alleviation of the tragic sentence of death, yet not remission of the sentence.

There are three aspects of human death in Scripture. In that revelatory light the two aspects currently in effect are firstly, *spiritual*, that is, alienation from God. It is to be 'dead in [trespasses and] sins' (Eph. 2:5 KJV), 'alienated from the life of God' (Eph. 4:18). Secondly, death is *physical*, separation of the soul from the body. Physical death is more familiar to us since we see physical death in others and in the recurring biblical references to the departure of the spirit at death. The third aspect, 'second death' (Rev. 20:14) belongs to the eschaton, not a consideration in Genesis 2.

This understanding is enforced without question in the physical death of the Savior: 'Father, into thy hands I commend my spirit: and having said thus, he gave up the ghost' (Luke 23:46 KJV). Recent Bible Versions which change the recurrent 'gave up the ghost [or spirit]' of the King James and other older Versions to 'breathed his last' or some similar expression are yielding far too much to current culture and modes of speech.

Physical death follows spiritual death, being its consequence – sometimes occurring in the womb, sometimes being delayed 969 years (Gen. 5:27).

The alienation of Adam and Eve from the LORD God and loss of holiness is manifest in their hiding from Him and their efforts to conceal their nakedness. Their feelings of guilt come forth in their new sense of shame, and evasive response to God's questions (Gen. 3:7-12). These facts require no expert exegesis. They are readily understood in early childhood. Children are easily taught modesty about nakedness and early know both shame and guilty feelings.

In due time physical death came also. Of course if God ever planned a heaven and earth to be populated by the myriads of Psalm 72:16 and Revelation 5:11; 7:9, then the lengthened physical lives of Adam and Eve were in the plan. God did not simply and graciously decide to remit the words 'in the day… you shall surely die.' It is, was and always has been usual ('normal' is the wrong word) for physical death to come after an extended period of physical life, even for fallen mankind (Heb. 9:27). How could it be otherwise if the human race was to survive? These obvious facts must occupy our attention, however briefly, because it is being said by some that God did not carry out His threat of immediate death. (R. C. Sproul, among others, asserts this in a video lecture.)

There is no reason why the physical regenerative processes inherent in human physical nature could not continue to perpetuate life indefinitely. Death is not per se a physical necessity. Yet God set a schedule in mankind so that in each of us, at a certain point, the forces of dissolution become greater than the forces of growth and regeneration. Put another way, life is like a fire, not the fuel and oxygen that maintain it. The fire weakens and goes out when the supplies give out. A. H. Strong proposed still another way of approaching the difficulty, a law of grace to resist the 'law of sin and death':

> In a true sense death began at once. To it belonged all the pains which both man and woman should suffer in their appointed callings... [T]hat man's earthly existence did not at once end, was due to God's counsel of redemption. 'The law of the Spirit of life' (Rom. 8:2) began to work even then, and grace began to counteract the effects of the Fall. Christ has now 'abolished death' (2 Tim. 2:10) by taking its terrors away, and by turning it into the portal of heaven. He will destroy it utterly (1 Cor. 15:26) when by resurrection from the dead, the saints shall be made immortal.[1]

The Sanctions of the Law of God.

The state of death into which Adam fell by sin involved the sanctions of that moral order of the universe which may rightly be called divine law. Whether, and by what means, the entire human race fell with Adam, and is affected by those sanctions of the law of God, also are matters which urgently call for attention later. The sanctions of God's law were three: (1) *depravity*, or corruption of nature; (2) *guilt*, or blameworthiness, deserving of punishment (Latin *reatus culpae* – hence our word culpable – meaning accused state of blameworthiness); and (3) *penalty* (Latin *reatus poenae*, hence such words as penal, penology) meaning an accused state of deserving punishment, viz. punishment by the author of the moral law, to whom all rational creatures are responsible. This is called 'the wrath of God' in Scripture. Sometimes writers speak of only two sanctions imposed by God as consequences of the first sin of mankind – *depravity* (or corruption of nature) and *guilt*. In such a case, guilt is understood to include not only the fact of *blameworthiness*, as in courtroom language, when a jury reports, 'we find the defendant guilty as charged' but also *obligation to suffer punishment*, as when a judge announces 'I sentence you to be hanged by the neck until dead.' In the narrower sense *guilty* defines what the offender's state is, and penalty defines the consequence as a debt owed to justice. The former cannot be changed by anything at all; the latter can be removed by suffering the penalty, i.e. the punishment due in exact proportion to the offense committed – hence 'An eye for an eye... burn for burn' (Matt. 5:38, 39; Exod. 21:24, 25; Lev. 24:20; Deut. 19:21). Not vindictive, but vindicative punishment, serving divine justice, rendering service to what is right.

I conclude this necessarily brief summary on the subject of the theological meaning of Genesis 3:1-6 with a pronouncement of Wolfhart Pannenberg, sometimes cited as a guide to conservative theological renewal:

> We engage in sin because of the deception. Our voluntary committing of it is enough to make us guilty [we don't need original sin!]. There does not have to be a primal and one-for-all event of a fall for which Adam was guilty quite apart from all entanglement in sin. Paul certainly follows the paradise story when he says that 'one man's trespass led to condemnation for all men' (Rom. 5:18). But this was because 'all men sinned as Adam did' (Rom. 5:12). Adam was simply the first sinner. In him began the temptation by the power of sin that still seduces us all today. All of us sin because we think we can attain a full and true life thereby. In this sense the story of Adam's sin is the story if the whole race. It is repeated in each individual.[2]

This is the error preached by Pelagius and his disciples which called forth from Augustine of Hippo his most earnest and perennially applicable polemical and apologetical writings – called 'Anti-Pelagian' writings. Augustine saw in this theology the very spear-point of the devil's strategy to empty the Christian message of the pure grace of God.[3] So much for one of the lions of the supposed revived Protestant orthodoxy in late twentieth-century Europe. He teaches the heresy of Pelagius, condemned by every orthodox body of Christians.

---

1. A. H. Strong, *Systematic Theology* (Valley Forge, PA: Judson Press, 1907), p. 590.
2. Wolfhart Pannenberg, *Systematic Theology ii*, trans. G. W. Bromiely (Grand Rapids: Eerdmans, 1994), p. 263.
3. These writings have been sifted out of the immense number of surviving writings of Augustine and published as Volume 5 of *NANF*. Let the interested reader begin with 'A Treatise on Nature and Grace' (*NANF*, pp. 115-151).

V. Judgment, and Grace for Perpetuation of Mankind.

Such were the immediate personal, spiritual and moral consequences of Adam's sin. These, however, were not the only consequences, for life would now be different for the race from what they might have been if the probation had succeeded. 'Of all the sad words of tongue or pen,/The saddest are these: It might have been.' There would be changes in their bodies, for 'the law of sin and death' had now taken effect. The mutual relation of man and wife and man with man will now be vitiated by selfishness, pride and all the other fruits of concupiscence, i.e. natural desires gone wrong. And, if life and the generations were to go on to consummation in that restored paradise of a new heaven and a new earth, then a working world-order of human life, under divine providence, yet under the dominion of sin and the devil, would have to be established.

The third chapter of Genesis, with parts of chapter four, reinforced by the whole of sacred Scripture, specifies, reports, hints at what the newly adjusted world-order would be. To treat this fully requires a fair-sized book. I have written (but not yet published) such a book: *Human Life After the Fall: A Sociology for Sinners*. For present purposes some observations on Genesis 3:14-24 will set the stage for the doctrine of sin (hamartiology) to follow.

The form of Genesis 3:14-19 is a series of judicial sentences, first upon the serpent, then upon the woman and last upon the man. Yet in each case, even of 'the serpent,' there is a bit of grace.

1. The Serpent (vv. 14 and 15).

Our discussion must be limited. The first promise of redemption of the fallen race is here, as asserted in every age of the church and in the ancient Jewish synagogue as well.[4] No one should read these verses as applying solely to an animal (snake) which, because it must crawl on its belly, will swallow much dust. The curse is on the devil (see Rev. 12:9 for the identification). Satan's time is now limited. Though he shall afflict the race he shall be crushed ultimately by the seed of the woman (seed may be singular or plural; here it is singular as in Gal. 3:16), the Last Adam, even though Satan will inflict great injury on Him. What is only hinted here becomes explicit in the whole of the Bible, especially Isaiah 53. (Delitzsch's learned comments, being those of a Christian Jew, are recommended.[5] For the opposite extreme of critical liberalism see John Skinner).[6]

2. The Woman (v. 16).

Though addressed to Eve personally, the sentence is for her as archetypal woman, womanhood throughout the ages. There is infinite mercy and grace in the sentence. It is here that we begin to see the adjustments the fall made necessary in certain aspects of human behavior. These are chiefly in the conditions of family life. Here we are enlightened as to how the race can continue through stresses and tensions in relative domestic peace and social common weal – how among a race of corrupted, guilty sinners under the sentence of death (Heb. 9:27) the domestic virtues of home and family can even exist. What life might have been if our first parents had successfully passed their probation, and a holy society had developed, we cannot know. It certainly would have been different.

1. A very important facet of the new situation for womanhood is multiplied conception: 'I will greatly multiply thy sorrow *and thy conception.*'

Before proceeding, a matter of translation must be addressed. A literal rendering of the Hebrew results in the above (essentially the same in KJV, ASV, RV and NASV marg.). Eve will now have both more pains and more pregnancies. Several recent Versions, beginning with RSV (and now even ESV), change the sense from two things to one thing. The two things of the Hebrew text and of the 1611 Version are an increase in pains (sorrows) for woman (again Eve is an archetype) and an increase in the number of children she will conceive and bear. The one thing of the new translations is neither of the two but something else, namely, 'I will greatly increase your pains in childbearing.'

The two are said to be an *hendiadys*, a Greek word which means one-through-two. As nearly as I can trace it, E. A. Speiser spread this notion many years ago through his influence on a now older generation of scholars. For reasons I find utterly unconvincing, Speiser insisted on *hendiadys* as a strong feature of Genesis. No other author in the Anchor Bible series whom I have read makes such a big deal of *hendiadys*.[7]

---

4. Franz Delitzsch, *New Commentary on Genesis* (Edinburgh: T. & T. Clark, 1888), p. 164, note 2.
5. ibid., pp. 160-165.
6. John Skinner, *Genesis (ICC* Edinburgh: T. & T. Clark, 1910, 1950), pp. 71, 72.
7. E. A. Speiser, *Genesis: Introduction, Translation and Notes, Anchor Bible* (Garden City, NY: Doubleday & Co., 1964), p. 24.

Hendiadys does exist in the Hebrew Bible, but Genesis 3:16 is not an example of it. Sorrow and conception are not two phases or expressions of one idea. Quite the contrary. The whole human race seems quite agreed that there is much pleasure in connection with conception of babies (and far too much preoccupied). The sorrow comes later and lasts for years. As a matter of fact 'sorrow' or 'pain' appears later in the verse and as a separate member of the four-member address to the woman. Is the whole verse about sorrows for females? I think not! Bible translations are like many other things; improvements may be irregular; and not every new rendering is better than the old. Translators, like department stores, do follow fads. The coming of death for every person ('It is appointed unto man once to die') required 'a quantum leap' in the number of conceptions and births if the race were not to end soon. Each married couple must produce more than one or two offspring, or instead of 'increase and multiply' we have 'decrease and disappear' – as the Swedes are now grudgingly acknowledging of their new contraceptive society.

Women must now bear more children to perpetuate the race, since death has modified the social equation. If death had not entered, every baby born would have become a permanent inhabitant of earth. Countless generations would have become contemporary. Now, on the contrary, since death soon removes each generation within a few decades, every couple *on the average* must produce at least three offspring who survive to procreate children of their own, to fulfill the command to 'multiply and replenish the earth' – two to replace themselves; one for minimal increase.

2. Closely related but of wider reference than to the mere act of motherhood is, 'I will surely multiply your pain.' The word '*tsabbon* is used only three times in the Old Testament: once of the pains of the male earning a living from the soil (Gen. 3:17), once of the tragic sorrow of all human kind (Gen. 5:29); and here of female pains through the whole of life. Woman (man, female) surely does experience more sorrow and pain than man, male, does. From adolescence onward there is the recurring menstrual cycle with all its familiar complications, disorders and inconveniences. Motherhood is her normal *vocation* while fatherhood (i.e. siring offspring) can be, and nowadays frequently is, only an *avocation*. No loving husband who has stood by her side and listened to her cries in travail of childbirth can doubt that God did greatly increase her pain. One cannot suppose childbirth would have been like this in paradise.

Happily God made some more necessary adjustments to 'fine tune' the social machine. Otherwise the human race would have died out at the beginning. Why would any mentally balanced woman desire marriage under the conditions of increased conception and increase of severe pains of life (as well as the perils to life in childbirth itself) – given also a fallen, self-serving disposition (depravity) as well? And granting she did marry, why should she continue to sleep with her husband when childbirth has become a burden? This question is answered next.

3. There comes, then, a third adjustment in human nature, an inherent attraction to her husband: 'Your desire shall be for your husband' (v. 16). This means *she* desires her *husband* and not the other way around. The whole world is familiar with the pervasive, aggressive male desire for and interest in the female. Because men know this passion so well in themselves, many of them suppose they understand it in their women. However, understanding of the mystery of womanhood on this score will not come to a man by projecting his own feelings. Woman is dispositioned to desire and need a husband along the whole range of life together – though this is not to say women do not cope with widowhood better than most men do. Desire (I am told by good authority) is not initially focused on coitus as in the male. Adult maidenhood has well-known drawbacks; it is seldom deliberately chosen as a way of life.

The interpretation I have just given of 'Your desire shall be for your husband' is the common one among many conservative Protestants (e.g. G. J. Wenham),[8] as well as some liberal critics (e.g. John Skinner)[9] and Jewish scholars, e.g. U. Cassuto[10], who puts his learning into practical aphorism: 'Measure for measure, you influenced your husband and caused him to do what you wished; henceforth, you and your female descendants will be subservient to your husbands. You will yearn for them, but they will be the heads of the families, and will rule over you.'[11]

Susan Foh in the *Westminster Theological Journal* (37, 1974/75, pp. 376-383), and later in a book of which she alone was author, and finally in a symposium,[12] set forth the view – quite insistently – that the woman's urge (or desire) toward her husband (Gen. 3:16) is not a sexual craving or general interest in meeting his demands and

---

8. G. J. Wenham, *Word Biblical Commentary: Genesis 1-15* (Waco, TX: Word Books, 1987), pp. 81, 82.
9. John Skinner, op. cit., pp. 82, 83.
10. U. Cassuto, *A Commentary on the Book of Genesis* (Jerusalem: The Magnes Press, The Hebrew Univ., 1944, 1978).
11. ibid., pp. 165, 166.
12. Robert & Bonnidell Clouse, ed., *Women In Ministry, Four Views* (Downers Grove, IL: InterVarsity Press, 1989).

needs but a desire, said to be universal among wives, to dominate their husbands. Exegetical support is thought to be found in use of the same word, desire (*teshuqah*), for sin's 'desire' to dominate Cain (Gen. 4:7). I do not know if this interpretation originated with Mrs. Foh. (Her views on the subject of the scriptural position of women in home and church are traditional, with which I concur. I simply do not support her view of the clause 'your desire shall be to [dominate] your husband.') The third and only other occurrence of *teshuqah* in the Hebrew Bible is in Song of Solomon (7:10) where erotic love is the subject. So why not here in Gen. 3:16? Mrs. Foh cites no supporting scholars, ancient or modern. In a debate with her in the symposium (*Women in Ministry*) cited above I concluded with the following:

> There are enough agreed consequences of the sin of our first parents... we struggle with these grim theological and personal realities every day. We do not need another one – a putative, inevitable husband-wife contest for power. Let us be spared this till-now-undiscovered consequence of the Fall.[13]

Interest in a husband first appears in a young girl toward her father. (The words for man, male, and for husband are the same both in Hebrew and Greek.) It expands, changes direction and grows in adolescence; flowers in courtship and wedding; bears fruit and matures in the marriage-relation, children, home and extended family. It is perverted thinking to deny these things and futile as well as harmful to oppose them. This interest lasts as long as life. God has blessed it (Ps. 127, 128), yet it has its drawbacks, as every wife knows. Great harm has been done through unhistorical, unrealistic, unbiblical expectations. It is cruel to romanticize marriage out of the true shape of reality. Nothing causes quite such bitter disappointment and resultant frustration as failure of unjustified expectation. Marriage, as it took shape under the conditions of sin, was not designed by Him who blessed it, to be blissful. Bliss is reserved for heaven. Its very perpetuation requires built-in tensions – a yin and a yang. The racial dynamic is partly built upon them.

4. This leads to the fourth and last of the adjustments in the female role in life, like the other three, written more in female human constitution than in new laws of behavior: 'and he [husband] shall rule over you' (3:16).

That there should be a precedence of authority of the man in marriage is not the result of the Fall according to F. Delitzsch. 'The subordination of the woman to the man was intended from the beginning; but now the harmony of their mutual wills in God is destroyed, this subordination becomes subjection.... That slavish subjection of the woman to the man which was customary in the ancient world, and still is so in the East, and which revealed religion made more tolerable and consistent with her human dignity, is the result of sin.'[14]

That there should be a precedence of authority of the husband in marriage is not the result of the fall. Jesus gives us the example of returning to prelapsarian precedent in such matters, saying in regard to the lamentable prevalence of divorce in His day and the Mosaic concession, 'from the beginning it was not so,' referring to the initial establishment of marriage in Eden (Matt. 19:8) and, drawing His doctrine from Genesis 2:24, 25, made the original marriage mandates still valid (Matt. 19:3-6). So it is of greatest significance that of the archetypal pair in Eden that the woman was taken out of Adam's side and created, made for the man and not the other way around. We will suspend treatment for present purposes of 'I will make him a helper fit for him' (Gen. 2:18).

There is a rather large current literature on husband-wife relations in Bible times. The Bible itself provides some extended vignettes – the homes of the folk in the book of Ruth, the parents of Samuel, of Samson, of the virtuous woman of Proverbs 31. Zacharias and Elizabeth, Joseph and Mary demonstrate the godly *shalom* – 'Peace be upon this house' – that actually prevailed. This contrasts sharply with the degradation of women throughout most of the pagan societies of old.[15] Paul tells us plainly what this means in 1 Corinthians 11:3-12.

One hesitates to comment on account of heated controversy over the role of women. It is my opinion if the *plain* teachings of this and *all relevant texts* were better known and accepted as normative much of the debate among believers, at least, would soon subside. Let this much be said:

Viewed as a whole, the Bible explains and amplifies what is called the 'submission' of wives to husbands and the leadership of men in the church's congregational life, chiefly to demonstrate that it is not repressive for those

---

13. Clouse, ibid., p. 109.
14. Delitzsch, op. cit., p. 166.
15. Consult books on manners and customs and biblical antiquities. One of the best is an old one in *Biblical Archaeology* [Antiquities] by F. C. Keil, vol. i, pp. 150-202. Roland deVaux's, *Ancient Israel, Its Life and Institutions* (New York: McGraw Hill), Part I is helpful. Also articles on marriage, children, etc. especially P. Trutze, "Marriage" in ZPEB, vol. iv.

whom Peter – to the disgust of some feminists – calls 'the weaker vessel.' This will be the case, however, only under the condition of a civilization whose basic ethic is of biblical origin. The universal effect of paganism has been the degrading of womanhood, while the effect of Christianity on pagan culture has been uniformly a proper emancipation of women. There is a whole literature on the history of how Christianity purified the ancient Roman world of heathen practice regarding abortion, exposure of infants, divorce, both oppression and false elevation of women, and sanctifying family *contra* pagan practices, whether savage, barbarian or 'civilized.'

In the present apparent progressive paganizing of Western culture it is not hard to discern the regression of our women, both single, adult women (of whom there is a growing ratio) and the married, to drudgery and oppressive time-schedules under harsh conditions of marketplace and business office for which they were never intended by the God of Abraham, Isaac and Jacob, the Father of all mercies. The so-called post-Christian era, now in mid-stage, seems already to be regressing backward rapidly as the enslavement of women to men's work, with frantic encouragement from many quarters, progresses. The fearful cost in the lives of unhappy, dysfunctional families, broken homes, social disorder is frightful and the end, though easy to predict, not pleasant to contemplate.

3. The Man (vv. 3:17-19).

The divine sentences on the woman relate primarily to the future of home and family life. Those directed toward the man relate more to the human race in the total natural environment in which the history of human civilization would develop over the tempestuous millennia until 'the kingdoms of this world become the kingdoms of our Lord and his Christ and he shall reign forever.' They are threefold: the ground was cursed 'because of you,' he was condemned to hard labor and he would ultimately have to die. While we must think of these as punishments, as in the case of many divine punishments short of the final one, the punishments are also preservative and pedagogic, i.e. designed to keep the race alive through the generations, and representing God's gracious means of directing the thoughts of men toward better eternal things.

1. Cursing of the Ground.

'[C]ursed is the ground for thy sake' (KJV v. 17). Notice of this is significantly repeated later in connection with the birth of Noah (meaning 'comfort'): 'Out of the ground that the Lord has cursed this one shall bring us relief from our work and from the painful toil of our hands' (Gen. 5:29) – showing that many generations later mankind were suffering under the curse and understood why. Paul refers to the curse in Romans 8:20, 21, 'For the creation was subjected to vanity, not of its own will, but by reason of him who subjected it, in hope that the creation itself also shall be delivered from the bondage of corruption into the liberty of the glory of the children of God' (ASV) and adds that the present creation is groaning and travailing in pain. This curse may not mean that any important change in what we call *nature* occurred outside Eden. The very presence of sin and death in the earthly lord of creation, who was charged to 'subdue' the earth, was in itself to be in bondage to corruption. In such a case the blood of Abel (the first human death and first murder) brought forth from earth (in a figurative manner of speaking) a groan of protest (Gen. 4:10, 11) and a severe resistance to Cain's tilling of the ground as well (Gen. 4:12), as any one who has fought weeds with a hoe understands very well. No generation of the sons of Adam and Eve has escaped these consequences of the curse upon the very ground upon which we walk and which produces either immediately or mediately all our food, clothing and shelter.

2. Condemnation to Hard Labor (vv. 17b-19a).

Very severe labor is specified, for 'by the sweat of thy nose thou shalt eat bread' (v. 18, my translation). The standard Versions all miss this, avoiding, I suppose, the displeasing image of a bent figure in a hot field, hands gripping weeds or hoe or plough, with a stream of sweat falling off the end of the nose. The nose is used instead of face because the author intends to represent a worker bent over, breathless and panting from vigorous exertion. Sorrow (pain) shall always accompany his work to earn a living from earth – whether in primary contact as a farmer or several stages removed as in the case of a physician or salesman. Even old age will not end that ('all the days of your life… till you return to the ground'), as everyone who has lived into old age knows only too well. If there were no pain of hard labor in life there would be no 'Lord, How long?' If no affliction there would be less longing for heaven. Redemption already promised (Gen. 3:15) does not mean we are not 'by nature children of wrath' (Eph. 2:3), but it is not necessary to remain 'Accursed children' (2 Peter 2:14).

3. Death and the Return of the Body to the Ground (v. 19).

'[T]ill you return to the ground... to dust you shall return.' Adam was made from dust ('*aphar*) of the ground (*adhamah*) (Gen. 2:7). There is more than a mere play on words. Even mankind in paradise had no reason to put on airs, for he was of common clay, albeit capable of endless life. Now his life-term is limited. Let us observe the following.

Firstly, Eve shared in this severe sentence, being taken 'out of man' and, being also disobedient to the command, she was subject to the threat (2:17).

Secondly, it is perfectly natural in Hebrew idiom to understand that the threat of physical death, following spiritual apostasy and death, should not take place immediately. Hosea 13:1 states, 'Ephraim... incurred guilt through Baal and died.' Spoken not long before Ephraim, i.e. the northern kingdom of Israel, came to an end by military defeat. It was in consequence of a previous apostasy long before, when Ephraim rejected a pure worship of the one true God. Designed by his creator to walk the path of the righteous that shines brighter and brighter until full day (Prov. 4:18), by reason of his apostasy Adam came instead to judgment, death and the grave. Yet, by redemption and restoration to God's fellowship, life was possible. Thus Adam, by the name he gave his wife, 'Mother of All Living,' expressed faith in the offered redemption, as did their son Abel (Gen. 4:4; Heb. 11:4). There was still strong faith in the future. Hope had not been abandoned.

Thirdly, Old Testament religion, from these verses on to the end, was aware of the connection of death as a returning to the ground. I do not think it too much to say that believers throughout biblical history knew the story of Genesis 1–3, of death and the grave as penalty for sin, and of promised redemption.[16] References to the subject in later stages of the biblical story reflect the very language of Genesis 3. 'You return man to dust and say, "Return, O children of man!"' (The Prayer of Moses, Ps. 90:3). '[W]hen you take away their breath [man and beast], they die and return to their dust' (Ps. 104:29). Elihu proclaims, '[A]ll flesh would perish together, and man would return to dust' (Job 34:15). 'All are from the dust, and to dust all return,' says the Preacher (Eccles. 3:20) and 'The dust returns to the earth as it was' (Eccles. 12:7). 'So and So died and was buried' is standard biblical formula, expressing the same in different words. The preference for burial over cremation or other disposal of the bodies of the dead throughout the Christian era is in part a continuation of the same biblical awareness – 'We have borne the image of the earthy but shall bear the image of the heavenly!' 'Massa's in the cold, cold ground' (Stephen Foster), 'All valiant dust that builds on dust' (Recessional, R. Kipling) and hundreds of other hymns and poems perpetuate the repulsive but fascinating mystery of universal, inevitable – no exceptions – return to the ground of every child of Eve.

These are the three aspects of change for man, *male*, thrust out of paradise: (1) the very ground cursed; (2) universal condemnation to hard labor; and (3) the humiliation of death and return to the ground. They are of supreme significance in explaining life *in all ages* under the condition of sin. All three are heavy restraints upon the excesses of that ambitious aggressor, the untamed male of our species. Though earth challenges his effort and may even inspire him to work, she very reluctantly, in most cases, yields her fruits. He must toil to exhaustion to gather them (from a crop of peanuts to an ounce of uranium). Ultimately he must give them all back to the earth and return to her himself. There are no exceptions among either the rich and famous, the poor and lowly, both saints and sinners.

> The boast of heraldry, the pomp of power
> All that beauty, All the wealth e'er gave
> Await alike the inevitable hour;
> The paths of glory lead but to the grave.[17]

'You return man to dust and say, "Return, O children of man!"' – spoken by one who lived to 120 years of age, whose eye was not dim nor his natural force abated, Moses, the man of God (Ps. 90:3; cf. Deut. 34:7).

Yet in a society of sinners, this is how life is and must be if man, male, is to be the breadwinner, faithful husband and loving father. His wife is relieved of the excesses of his pursuit of his passions simply because toil has stolen from him the inclination to pursue them. If he is to be fit to live with, let him not have too many days off!

---

16. Under the rubric, 'Sin, Death and Life' Pannenberg furnishes a useful guide to modern ideas in liberal theology about death as a consequence (divine penalty) of, or as a normal consequence of, finitude and other views. He also brings Jewish views – ancient and later – to the subject. He says the resurrection of Christ puts the subject in a 'new light' but as near to an orthodox statement as he comes is the closing sentence: 'We achieve liberation from sin and death only when the image of the Son takes place through the operation of the Spirit of God'. op. cit., pp. 267-275.
17. Thomas Gray's *Elegy Written in a Country Churchyard*, lines 33-36.

VI. The Beginnings of Civilization in the Fallen Race (Gen. 4).

Civilization never had a chance to develop in a society of sinless people. So no one knows what customs and institutions, aside from family, might have developed. So the narrative continues immediately with initial developments of civilization among the growing population of sinful bearers of the noble image of God.

At this point some theological schools of thought begin to talk about covenants – of works and grace, or of nature and grace – as a category of thought for developing a theology of God's dealing with the human race through ensuing ages. The Reformers frequently spoke of the covenant of salvation by grace through faith on the ground of 'the redemption which is in Christ Jesus.' But the invention of what came to be called Federal, or Covenant Theology, was largely a seventeenth-century development, even though Calvin and immediate successors spoke of the covenant of salvation and similar expressions. This is acknowledged by its best representatives.[18] Though by no means uniformly adopted, it is common among Presbyterian, Reformed, a few Lutheran and even some leading Baptists, as Gill and Spurgeon.

More recently many other theologians have spoken of developments in God's management of the ages of sinful humanity under the category of 'dispensations.' This nineteenth-century development was crystallized in the Scofield Bible of 1909. It was a very popular Bible until about 1960. The notes became a systematic theology of sorts for multitudes, after liberalism took over the seminaries where pastors had formerly received their education. Such was my first personal Bible – in an epoch when many families could afford only one Bible. The Scofield Bible was modified in interaction with covenant theologians and others in the New Scofield Bible of 1967 and is being modified further among representatives in several different schools and denominations.

One should be aware of these presently vigorously debated approaches to understanding what has been called 'God's plan of the ages.' Each has a certain limited validity and should not be discouraged except to observe that each may be too rigorously applied. Then they fall into conflict.

Dr. Buswell presents an extensive discussion on human life in this age,[19] prefacing it with an extensive comparison of covenantal and dispensational approaches.[20] In this he is unique and, for those unacquainted with this subject, quite informative. Yet, as he proceeds, his commitment to covenant thinking does not seem to reduce his valuable remarks for readers not persuaded of his Federalism. Which leads me to say that the biblical record furnishes no comprehensive category under which to subsume these developments. What we do see in Genesis 4, in my judgment, is the beginnings of civilization, i.e. the activities and institutions of mankind, informally defined, in a society as they prevail to the present.

1. The Human Family.

One of the first activities (and perhaps institutions) of the family is the exercise of religion, each of the two sons engaging in *formal* worship of God the Creator. Some, especially those who like to employ the rubric of 'covenants,' call this 'institution' the *church*. Yet, however much validity the concept of covenant has in this connection, it seems unhistorical to use either word for this activity, for which no English words except religion and worship seem to fit.

2. Religious Worship.

One brother's worship was true worship as it was ever intended to be among a race of believing sinners, 'By faith Abel offered to God a more acceptable sacrifice' (Heb. 11:4), the other's false, essentially an anti-worship form of religion, 'Cain … was of the evil one and murdered his brother' (1 John 3:11, 12). It was a 'way' rather than a worship – 'they walked in the way of Cain' (Jude 11). Civilized life has supported both religions ever since, both competing for mankind's allegiance throughout our lifelong journey through the valley of the shadow – the one a vivifying hope, the other a hopeless ministry of death unto death. Here is the true answer to the philosophers' quest for the origin of religion. Generic religion does not exist. There are really only *religions*, and basically only two of them, both arising out of our need to return to God from alienation brought by sin – one a revealed religion of grace and another that pervasive, false, natural religion of human merit.

---

18. A. A. Hodge, *Outlines of Theology* (Grand Rapids: Eerdmans, 1860, 1957), pp. 362, 363. J. O. Buswell, *A Systematic Theology of the Christian Religion I* (Grand Rapids: Zondervan, 1962, 1971), p. 308. B. B. Warfield, *Biblical & Theological Studies* (Philadelphia: Presbyteran & Reformed Publ., 1952), pp. 268, 269.
19. op. cit., pp. 344-428.
20. op. cit., pp. 307-320.

Forms and Observances (Liturgy?).

There is a hint of an *appointed time* in the Hebrew, i.e. 'at the end of days' ('In the course of time,' v. 3). The idiom is not clear. It might have been seven days and related to a Sabbath command (Gen. 2:3; Exod. 20:11; Neh. 9:14). Perhaps there was also an *appointed place* known as 'the LORD's presence' (4:3 , 'to the LORD;' 4:16, 'the presence of the LORD').

The exegetical base of this distinction is less than definitive, yet it seems proper to note that both men seem aware of the *importance of sacrifice*. The Levitical language of slaughtered sacrifice is not used of either son's offering (Gen. 4:2, 3). The flesh of animals may not yet have been used for food. Presumably the fleece and skin of sheep and goats were used for clothing and other purposes. Perhaps Abel kept a diary! Each brought to God what his life-work produced, though Cain brought only a portion of grain and Abel from the choicest of his flock. It is not without significance, however, that these two members of the first generation born in our race were aware of the appropriateness of a 'gift' (Heb. *minḥah*) to be formally presented to God as an act of worship. One cannot avoid thinking of 'without the shedding of blood there is no remission' and applying the atonement theology of John 1:29 and Isaiah 53. There was excellence of some sort, for Hebrews 11:4 calls Abel's 'a better sacrifice' (NIV). Though perhaps it was wholly Abel's faith which rendered it so.

We are on solid ground in asserting that Abel's worship was accepted as pleasing to God because he had a heart of faith. H. C. Leupold remarks:

> But the significant thing, noticed by Luther and most commentators since, is that this regarding with favor directs itself first to the person, then to the offering; so in the case of both the brothers. This fact very significantly shows that the determining factor in worship is the attitude of the individual. Him or his heart, God weighs. If he is not found wanting, the gift is acceptable. If he fails to please the Almighty, his gift is reprobate. This fact is so important that it alone is stated.[21]

Hebrews 11:4 plainly says faith – the indispensable condition of salvation – was present in Abel and, if so, then based on some word from God to be believed and obeyed (Rom. 10:17). It is, of course, not unlikely that the 'word' from God was an impulse silently placed there by the Spirit of God. These remarks are in agreement with Delitzsch,[22] Keil[23] and Oehler.[24] Gerhard Von Rad, to the contrary, if I understand his terse remarks correctly, thinks the narrative means God was more pleased with 'the sacrifice of blood' because 'the narrator wants to remove the acceptance of the sacrifice from man and place it completely within God's free will.'[25]

These forms and truths were ever destined to be the heart of true worship of God, of true religion: (1) a place of recurring assembly; (2) 'the presence of the LORD' (cf. Heb. 10:25, not neglecting John 4:24); (3) a recurring time of assembly (whether on a first or seventh day of the week); (4) a basis in required *sacrifice*; and (5) a faithful heart.

Natural folk religion is 'the way of Cain.' The unbelief of Cain and the faith of Abel cannot humanly speaking be explained at all, except for what theology calls special grace. Perhaps Cain was not a bad boy and Abel a good boy. Apart from this work of the Spirit in Abel's heart there would have been no faith. Abel would have been another Cain. Cain observed good religious forms, perhaps about the same as Abel's, but just that – forms without heart faith. He came trusting the fruit of his own best effort, singing, so to speak, the very denial of 'Nothing in my hand I bring, simply to thy cross I cling.' His religion turned out to be vicious hate both for the true worshipper and his faith. The results, as for all 'will worship' and unbelief were disastrous: disappointment (vv. 5, 6), slavery to sin (v. 7), deeper depravity (vv. 8, 9), further disapproval by God (vv. 10-12), misery in this life (vv. 13, 14) and ultimately alienation from God forever. There is nevertheless a possibility for a better ending. God's last act on Cain's behalf was one of grace, a mark on Cain to lengthen his life and give space to repent. We shall have to wait for the rest of the story.

3. Two Lines of Family Descent.

Let us observe that civilization developed in two lines of family descent. The majority population were of the lineage of Cain the apostate, both genetic and spiritual; the minority – a remnant group it finally turned out to be – the genetic and spiritual lineage of Seth, who replaced Abel in the succession of righteous offspring of our first parents. This is only obliquely reported in the statement of verse 26: 'To Seth also a son was born, and he called his name Enosh. At that time people began to call upon the name of the LORD.' It has ever been so from that day to this.

---

21. H. C. Leupold, *Exposition of Genesis i* (Columbus, OH: The Wartburg Press, 1942), pp. 196, 197.
22. Delitzsch, op. cit., pp. 129-131.
23. J. K. F. Keil, *Biblical Commentary on the Old Testament, vol. i Pentateuch* (Edinburgh: T. & T. Clark, n.d.), pp. 109-111.
24. G. F. Oehler, *Old Testament Theology* (New York: Funk & Wagnalls Publ., 1883), pp. 54, 55.
25. Gerhard Von Rad, *Genesis: A Commentary*, trans. J. H. Marks (Philadelphia: The Westminster Press, 1961), p. 101.

4. Horticulture and Husbandry.

We are made aware of the immediate development of horticulture in Cain, who brought to God the fruits of his farm, and of animal husbandry in Abel, who brought the best of his flock and the fat of a slaughtered specimen of the flock. Again, it seems doubtful that flocks were kept solely for wool and hide and for sacrifice to God. Surely they served for food as well. A major portion of the diet of many bedouin to this day is milk, butter and cheese from flocks of sheep and goats.

5. Arts, Industry and Philosophy.

Arts were quick to follow, for in a few generations there were those who 'play the lyre and pipe' (v. 21), also metallurgical industry, forging 'all instruments of bronze and iron' (v. 22). Such developments require the gathering of population into centers, hence early in the history there was at least one city (v. 17).

The several sciences dealing with human antiquity do not help to sort out details of the springing up of culture in the early generations of mankind – urban development (vv. 16, 17), industry (vv. 20-22), philosophical and artistic expression (vv. 19, 23, 24). Modern science does not think these arose quickly. I have no desire to demean either Genesis or the labors of earnest scientists. Perhaps there is some foreshortening of perspective in verses 16-24: by omission of intervening generations. For our purposes, the important truth is that it all happened in a society of mankind impaired by the loss of moral integrity and in a climate of spiritual apostasy. There was as yet no coercive government to require civil order. Nothing was guaranteed. A steady decline toward a universal divine judgment (the Deluge), followed by a new world-order among fallen humanity, is not surprising at all. I have written at length of these matters elsewhere.[26]

---

26. Robert D. Culver, *Civil Government: A Biblical View* (Edmonton, Alberta: Canadian Institute for Law, Theology, and Public Policy, 2000), p. 208.

11
Fallen Mankind in the Order of Nature

Nature, in the sense of the earth, all in it and all that pertains to it, is intended by 'order of nature' in this chapter. It is the subject of the study of what used to be called natural history, by definition 'the study of zoology, botany, mineralogy, geology, and other subjects dealing with the physical world.'[1]

We have already taken note of the fact that in consequence of Adam's fall, there was a change in his relation to the earth from which he was formed and from whose soils he must draw his living – no longer by dressing and keeping a Garden (or paradise), but by working till the sweat drips from his nose! In that connection God's sentence on Adam includes the striking sentence, 'cursed is the ground because of you' (Gen. 3:17).

An important fine point connected with a play on words and derivation is present in the Hebrew. Among the several available terms for 'man' the one used in verse 7 (rendered Adam but meaning 'man') is *'adham*. Now, the word for ground used later in the verse is *'adhamah*, the same as the word for 'man' except that ground is feminine gender. Hence we understand that in calling him 'Adam' (*'adham*) God is calling attention to his physical origin from the ground – 'the LORD God formed the man [*'adham*] of dust from the ground [*'adhamah*]' (Gen. 2:7). Thus the derivation of the generic name and the first man's personal name designates our 'groundly' origin and provides a key to why, once he was cursed for sinning, the 'blessed ground' from which he was taken had to be cursed also. It is apparently neither possible nor proper for a cursed man to gain his living from blessed ground!

The Goodness of Nature.

Yet there is unquestionable evidence of Scripture that God's original pronouncement of 'good... very good' on all He had made has never been revoked. Six times in all, in connection with each creative day except the second, it is said, 'God saw that it was good' and finally, 'God saw everything that he had made, and behold, it was very good' (Gen. 1:31) – including mankind, male and female in that omnibus. Let us dispense for now with further examination of Hebrew words, for they add little or nothing by way of qualifications of what we intuitively understand by 'good' in the contexts of God's creative acts. Nor will we presently be diverted by disquisitions to define 'the good, the beautiful and the true.'

1. *Webster's New World Dictionary*, 3rd college ed., 1988.

The Bible throughout, especially Psalm 104, joyfully proclaims the goodness of creation and the benevolence of the Creator, for the happiness of the human race and all God's lesser creatures.

Psalm 104, the marvelous hymn of creation, rhapsodizes:

> You make springs gush forth in the valleys;
> they flow between the hills;
> they give drink to every beast of the field;
> the wild donkeys quench their thirst.
> Beside them the birds of the heavens dwell;
> they sing among the branches.
> From your lofty abode you water the mountains;
> the earth is satisfied with the fruit of your work.
> You cause the grass to grow for the livestock
> and plants for man to cultivate,
> that he may bring forth food from the earth
> and wine to gladden the heart of man,
> oil to make his face shine
> and bread to strengthen man's heart (Ps. 104:10-15).

The poem continues in this pleasant joyful train until near the end, after an address of praise to the LORD, a strange reversal of tone takes place with these harsh sounding words: 'Let sinners be consumed from the earth, and let the wicked be no more' (v. 35). Only two lines later, after another very brief address of praise, the poem abruptly ends. It is almost as if the poet had forgotten about sin and disorder as he contemplated the goodness of the natural order. When consciousness of evil deeds and evil men returned, he declared them to be out of place in God's earth and destined ultimately to be eliminated.

In What Consists the Curse of God on 'the Ground'?

This subject, introduced earlier, must now be more thoroughly considered. What then are we to say of 'cursed is the ground' and of thorns and thistles, also of tornadoes, earthquakes, floods, and other natural events disastrous to mankind and, at least at first glance, certainly not good?

Post-lapsarian mankind was to find nature perverse, unresponsive and only reluctantly fruitful. This was to be true of nature in her 'natural' state, as the roving Bedouin finds her, and likewise as modified by the efforts of the agriculturalist (i.e. the 'dirt farmer'). In the former case she gives not only grass, but also 'thorns and thistles' in the field; in the latter the hard ground compels endless grinding toil.

The New Testament explains the connection of the fall of mankind with the present condition of the order of nature as follows, 'For the creation waits with eager longing for the revealing of the sons of God. For the creation was subjected to futility [i.e. fruitlessness, failure of effort], not willingly [creation is unconscious and non-rational as such], but because of him [i.e. God] who subjected it, in hope that the creation itself will be set free from its bondage to decay [whether this be death in nature or perhaps defilement by mankind's sin and death is debatable] and obtain the freedom of the glory of the children of God. For we know that the whole creation has been groaning together in the pains of childbirth until now' (Rom. 8:19-22).

The curse may not consist solely in any divinely effected change in the material world *per se*. The man designated by his Creator to fill the earth with offspring and to 'have dominion over... every living thing' animate and inanimate in or on it (Gen. 3:27) became a sinful creature capable of rapacious exploitation and perverted use of God's good earth and its treasures.

This view is skillfully stated by Robert Haldane, author of a renowned commentary on Romans. He comments:

> What is called vanity in the twentieth verse is in the twenty-first denominated bondage of corruption. When the creation was brought into existence, God bestowed on it his blessing, and pronounced everything that he had made very good. Viewing that admirable palace which he had provided, he appointed man to reign in it, commanding all creation to be subject to him whom he had made in his own image. But when sin entered, then in a certain sense, it may be said that all things had become evil, and were diverted from their proper end. The

creatures by their nature were appointed for the service of the friends of their Creator, but since the entrance of sin they have become subservient to his enemies. Instead of the sun and the heavens being honored to give light to those who obey God, and the earth to support the righteous, they now minister to rebels. The sun shines upon the wicked; the earth nourishes those who blaspheme their Maker, while its various products, instead of being employed for the glory of God, are used as instruments of ambition, of avarice, of intemperance, of cruelty, of idolatry, and are often employed for the destruction of his children. All these are subjected to vanity when applied by men for vain purposes.[2]

This view of 'bondage to corruption' and 'cursed is the ground on your account' is supported by certain Old Testament prophets:

> Therefore I will take back
> my grain in its time,
> and my wine in its season,
> and I will take away my wool and my flax,
> which were to cover her nakedness (Hos. 2:9).

Sometimes the creatures are represented as protesting against the wickedness and venality of mankind: 'For the stone will cry out from the wall, and the beam from the woodwork respond' (Hab. 2:11).

Human evil has, in this sense, polluted the whole natural order simply by being present, the malodorous, garrulous, disruptive guest at the party. The prevalence of evil and misery witness to the dishonor done to creation's Author. It would be degrading the name of God to suppose that the present state of some of His works – wherein disorder and destruction are prevalent – is the same as that in which they were originally made or that they shall continue forever as they now are.

Dr. Franz Delitzsch interpreted the two passages just cited (Gen. 3:17, 18 and Rom. 8:19-22) in a similar fashion:

> All nature stands… in the closest actual relation to man, who is, in virtue of his personality, which is at once spiritual and material, the link between it and God. All that affects man affects at the same time that world of nature which was ordained for common development with himself. Man having fallen from communion with God, the world of nature became like him, its appointed head, subject to vanity, and needed as he did, redemption and restoration to recover its lost condition and high destination. Man, and with him nature, will, though by a long and indirect path at length attain to the 'liberty of the glory' (Romans 8:21), i.e. be free and glorified. Meanwhile the curse which has fallen upon the world has a reverse side of blessing for man. The curse is not peremptory, but pedagogic.[3]

Dr. Delitzsch goes on to affirm that nature in her resistance to mankind not only carries out God's judgment on him, but in the discipline of the sweat of his brow opposes his pretensions to usurp God's place and 'awakens aspirations for heaven.'[4]

Because of the importance of his remarks I quote Oscar Cullmann somewhat at length:

> We are… concerned with a particular aspect of the more comprehensive relationship between redemption and creation. The creation is discussed not only on the first page of the Old Testament but throughout the Bible, right up to the very last page of the New Testament.
>
> The fact that he is created in the image of God raises man, whom God created in the beginning, above all other creatures; but it also means that the whole creation has been drawn into the drama occasioned by man's sin. The earth is cursed for the sake of Adam. This is stated not only in the book of Genesis but also in the book of Romans (8:20). But for the same reason the redemption of man by Christ's death on the cross also affects the whole creation. According to the Synoptic Gospels the earth grew dark when Christ's sufferings reached their climax, and according to the Gospel of Matthew (27:51) the earth shook at the moment of his death, in which all things are reconciled to God through the blood of his cross (Col. 1:20).[5]

---

2. Robert Haldane, *Expositions of the Epistle to the Romans* (New York: Robert Carter, 1847 and reprints up to 1970), p. 378.
3. Franz Delitzsch, *New Commentary on Genesis I* (Edinburgh: T. & T. Clark, 1888), p. 168.
4. ibid., p. 168.
5. Oscar Cullmann, *The Early Church* (London: SCM Press, Ltd., 1956, 1966), p. 108.

Dr. Cullmann further explains that the creation shares in the waiting and 'groaning' of mankind (Rom. 8:21, 22) in a hope based on the 'all important event' which 'took place on the cross.'[6]

Death in Nature.

To raise momentarily one of the problems raised, did death in nature originate at the time of mankind's fall? The existence of fossils deep in the earth's crust, as many writers have noted, suggests a negative answer.

It is to be regretted that this has become a matter of severe difference among some evangelical writers. Over the past 100 years most learned evangelical authors who treat the subject accept as true the verdict of geology that the earth has been here for a very long time. They tend neither to be skeptical of the results supplied by the various 'scientific' time clocks nor outrightly reject them. I cite a wise and respected author whose helpful writings have been and continue to be read widely. Of 'the earth' Erich Sauer says:

> [The earth's] history reaches back to a more remote period than the beginning of the human race... the following case will be noted.
> The present condition of the world of nature on earth shows a fateful disharmony of splendour and terror, communion and confusion, life and death... and permit us to perceive that behind this discord in nature lies discord in the kingdom of the spirit. But this cannot have first entered with the history of man; *for the stratified rocks, showing the history of the earth, prove beyond doubt that death and destruction existed in unthinkable ages before the history of the human race begins* [emphasis added]. The Bible itself allows us to see that before the fall of man there existed an adverse kingdom of evil, and in some way it was clearly interested in the earth and in man. Therefore also, the command given in Paradise itself that the man should not only cultivate the garden but 'guard' it (Gen. 2:15).[7]

Mr. Sauer theorizes that this might be associated with Satan's fall and adds: 'In any case it is proved by the rocky strata of the earth that ancient destructions by death, with beasts and catastrophes were connected.' He wisely concludes: 'Closer investigation here is not the task of a history of salvation but of natural science.'[8]

My own view is, let the geologists and paleontologists 'do their thing.' We will judge their 'discoveries' and theories and form our own conclusions, not ignoring their advice.

I acknowledge a rather large literature defending the theory that the universe, including earth, is of recent creation – a few thousand years ago at most – and that the fossil record cannot be interpreted as geologists do to establish any systematic arrangement into eras and periods of time. It is asserted that the Noahic Flood killed all these fossil forms (vegetables, as coal and animal) and deposited them as they now are found. To the current leading advocates of this theory, it is therefore unthinkable that there should have been death in the world of plants and animals before the fall of mankind or that he ate the flesh of animals before the Deluge.[9]

Though asserted and defended with great vigor, and convincing to many, this outlook is not widely held among evangelical scholars, whether in the sciences or in the Bible and theology. I have read their literature, some of it by some of my best former students and (I say regretfully and with respect) without being convinced that their assessment of the facts, either of biblical revelation or of natural history, is correct. I find nothing in Scripture which demands that the earth's evident great age is a false impression. I find no compelling scriptural reason to affirm positively that human beings did not eat the flesh of animals before the Flood.

It is by no means certain that the death of living forms in nature is evil in any pronounced sense. Nor is it certain in what sense nature 'travails in pain' to be delivered. It is sufficient for the present study simply to know that it does.

A Note on Interpreting the Genesis Timescale.

I taught Old Testament, then Apologetics, for a period of several years before moving into Systematic Theology. In each discipline it seemed important and necessary to devote extended attention to interpretations of the creative week, the age of the earth, the antiquity of the human race and kindred questions. We have already devoted some attention to these questions herein.

---

6. ibid., p. 108.
7. Erich Sauer, *From Eternity to Eternity* (Grand Rapids: Eerdmans, 1957), p. 17.
8. ibid., p. 18.
9. See John Whitcomb and Henry Morris, *The Genesis Flood* (Philadelphia: Presbyterian & Reformed Publ. Co., 1961); John C. Whitcomb, *The World That Perished* (Grand Rapids: Baker, 1988); John C. Whitcomb, *The Early Earth*, rev. ed., (Grand Rapids: Baker, 1972, 1986).

The footnotes of my first Bible, my only Bible until I entered Seminary, offered the theory that the geological ages fall in a 'gap' between Genesis 1:1 and 1:2 on one page and that the six days might be the geological ages on another page. I rather quickly decided not to endorse or commit myself to either of these proposals. When I came to teach the subject to college and seminary students and necessarily read everything I could lay my hands on concerning this subject it became apparent to me that there is neither sufficient information available nor biblical mandate to require commitment to any theory of interpretation of the creative days. Reasons for not interpreting the six days as six solar days of twenty-four hours each follow in the order of importance in convincing me and my classes, (1) Plants were created on the third day before the sun – which causes plants to grow and nourishes them – was created on the fourth day. (2) The crowded schedule of the sixth day, during which God created all the animals, man, male and female, including surgery on Adam's side, formed of Eve, brought all the animals before Adam, and which included Adam's naming of these myriads of creatures. It seems obvious that this was not done on any ordinary Friday afternoon. (3) Genesis 1 and 2 approach the subject of creation with entirely different literary techniques, which I have explained earlier. While the second account is indeed somewhat supplementary, it is of somewhat different literary genre. (4) The number seven has a unique non-literal meaning in all ancient Near-Eastern literature, not the least the Old Testament. Take the number seven out of the Gilgamish Epic and you would modify the story. Moses appears to employ the number seven in similar manner. The evidence on this score is simply overwhelming. (5) As indicated earlier, God informed His prophets about the remote future in highly figurative language even though it appears to be literal on the first reading – see for example the last chapters of the book of Ezekiel, and the last two chapters of the book of Revelation. God used similar modes in revealing the unknown past. (6) Young earth theorists insist not only on six literal twenty-four-hour days of creation but that the Flood not only covered all the planet and that violent eruptions of the earth's crust and crashing mountains of water changed the configuration of the earth's surface – to form the various strata of rock, coal beds, etc. Yet the Bible plainly says that the Rivers Tigris and Euphrates were apparently still in the same places after the Flood as they were before, employed by Genesis to define the location of Eden (pre-Flood), and the route of Abraham to Canaan, as well as the northern border of the land of promise. (7) Finally, the suggestion of several towering figures in systematic theology, including W. G. T. Shedd and Aurelius Augustine, that the days of Genesis 1 and 2 are really heavenly days not days on earth at all. In such a case they are also days of revelation no more related to solar days than the wheels of Ezekiel's vision of deity are to a wagon wheel.

My opinion is, however, that further treatment of these extremely controversial questions would unnecessarily complicate this particular study of theological anthropology.

Moral Agents Not a Part of Nature.

Nature includes no moral agents. God stands above nature. Man also, though he shares biological life with nature, is, in the biblical perspective, and in very truth, above nature. This is, of course, commonly denied today. Yet biblically informed people, and even many others not convinced of materialistic humanism, insist that we are not really, at the deepest level of our existence, a part of nature. The God of nature is no God. Nature is God's creation, but He is beyond it, as the Hebrews had been taught. Nature is the kingdom of necessity, bound to unvarying laws, but God is eternally free. God exists outside nature and so does mankind, for although man is a child of nature, he is also a child of God. If he does not know himself as a child of God, he must eventually consider himself merely an animal, and has no rights except those that he says he has.

Modern Theories of Nature.

Came the theories of *Relativity* in physics, astronomy and related fields and with them a new concept of what 'nature' is. In a book first orally addressed to members of a chemical society (not mathematicians or physicists) Alfred North Whitehead explained the *new concept of nature*. The structure of material reality in this new physics/metaphysics is four-dimensional (in some very recent theory, multidimensional). The abstractions of science in the new concept of nature have made reality in nature to consist of 'the relations of events which arise from their spatio-temporal structure'. These 'abstractions of science are entities which are truly in nature.... These event-particles are the ultimate elements of the four-dimensional space-time manifold.'[10]

---

10. Alfred N. Whitehead, *The Concept of Nature*, MI: (Univ. of Michigan Press, Ann Arbor, 1959, repr. of the book first published by Cambridge Univ. Press, 1920), pp. 172, 173.

Most people who think they understand Einstein and Whitehead agree they are on to something – convinced, as I was when as a sophomore, I picked up and read in our high school library a new small book, *Space, Time and Relativity*.

'Man's Place in Nature' is more than a topic of theology, it is the title of another important small book. 'On November 29, 1859, Charles Darwin's *On the Origin of Species* was published... A pre-publication copy had been sent by Darwin to [Thomas H.] Huxley [grandfather of Aldous, Julian and Andrew], who on November 23 wrote an enthusiastic letter to Darwin... promising to stand by him' against inevitable 'abuse and misrepresentation.'[11] Huxley's book published in 1863, and afterward on into the twentieth century, is described as a 'classic' and 'a landmark in the history of science.'[12] Huxley was a self-confessed philosophical agnostic and skeptic. 'The only approach to certainty which he admitted lay in the order of nature.'[13] He had rejected previous evolutionary proposals but found in Darwin a 'consistent uniformitarianism' which postulated organic evolution. So he accepted it as an intelligible hypothesis good enough as a working basis.[14]

Huxley argued that mankind is a part of nature, organically in an evolutionary continuum with the genus of apes (not directly with extant apes). But he also recognized there is a 'gulf' (his word) between the physical and intellectual level of the highest animal and mankind. Further, he rightly observed the complete absence of transitional forms (living or fossil) between man-like animals and man: '[N]o one is more strongly convinced than I of the vastness of the gulf between civilized man and the brutes; or is more certain that whether *from* them or not he is assuredly not of them.'[15] So this skillful writer left the subject.

In the optimistic atmosphere of the times strong efforts were made to incorporate the doctrine of Darwinian evolution into Christian theology – and out came theories of theistic evolution as well as efforts to unite evolution with pantheism.

Since then the theory of evolution has become a 'fact' in the mind of millions, propagated vigorously in university textbooks and lectures, public schools, and the secular press generally. I have shown that God has 'created' some things mediately over time, but I see not the slightest hint that such was the case in the creation of mankind. Biblically, mankind's 'place in nature' in any case forbids that his spirit is derived from earth (Gen. 2:7).

It is therefore entirely in harmony with the Scriptures that in modern times those areas of mankind's habitation where his likeness to the living God is officially and dogmatically denied have been the precise areas (i.e. where Marxist, materialistic socialism prevails) wherein human rights and freedom have been most systematically suppressed and, significantly, where what we now call 'the natural environment' has been most severely neglected, raped and even destroyed.

Perhaps if the life of mankind was to continue at all on earth after his failure in his first probation, the world of nature in which his life must be set had to be adjusted appropriately. What those adjustments may have been we do not know. Mankind's connection with nature made this a necessity, as did also his subjection to God's judgment.

Ascetic and Legalistic Errors About Nature.

Care must be taken to keep strictly before one's attention that there is no moral quality whatsoever in inanimate and irrational things. Jesus took considerable pains to correct a contrary opinion which His disciples had derived from contemporary Judaism. Paul likewise emphasized that there is nothing unclean of itself, as the most influential and most deeply morally earnest of the Protestant Reformers likewise insisted. Yet precisely because some of Christ's most devoted followers today do not see this clearly the following testimonies are here presented.

There were 'traditions of the elders' of Jesus' day to the effect that the eating of food under certain conditions would defile the bodies of otherwise godly men.[16] It was thought likewise that there was moral defilement from eating from dishes not properly washed (Mark 7:1-4; cf. Matt. 15:1-3, 8). Unlike dualistic Manicheans and

---

11. Ashley Montagu in 'Introduction' to the Ann Arbor Paperback Edition of Thomas H. Huxley's *Man's Place in Nature* (Univ. of Michigan, Ann Arbor Paperback, 1959), pp. 1, 2.
12. ibid., p. 1.
13. W. T. Thiselton Dyer, *11th Edition Encyclopedia Britannica*, XIV, p. 19.
14. Huxley, op. cit., p. 18.
15. Huxley, op. cit., pp. 129, 130.
16. A reliable source of information regarding the prevalent legalistic and external formalism among the Jews of Jesus' time is the standard work of Emil Schürer, *The History of the Jewish People in the Time of Jesus Christ*, rev. (Edinburgh: T. & T. Clark, 1890; 3rd reprinting by Hendrichson Publishers, Peabody, MA, 1998), See especially Second Div., Vol. I, 'Halacha and Haggah' pp. 329-350 and Second Div., vol. ii, 'Life Under the Law,' pp. 90-125.

Zoroastrians, the pharisaic Jews did not, so far as is now known, hold matter to be evil and spirit to be good, but in practice they veered in the direction of such opinions. They obviously did not discern the mainly religious and ceremonial significance of the laws of ritual purity in the Pentateuch. To correct this Jesus said: 'Hear me, all of you [including all present-day legalistic pietists], and understand: There is nothing outside a person that by going into him can defile him, but the things that come out of a person are what defile him' (Mark 7:14-15). Observe the imperative mode of address. Jesus well understood the perverse tendency of religious people to put religiosity in place of true piety; to apportion the blame for one's personal inner corruption on things of environment, diet, amusement, and the like. Jesus did not say tobacco smoke would not induce cancer or that it is not physically a dirty habit. But inhaled tobacco smoke is not a moral or spiritual defilement of the 'temple of the body' – many sermons to the contrary notwithstanding. Jesus said 'There is nothing outside a person that by going into him can defile him.' In a case of disagreement between Jesus and clergy, let us always follow Jesus!

So Paul could circumcise Timothy for practical missionary reasons (Acts 16:3), but could leave another helper uncircumcised (Titus, Gal. 2:3) for other practical missionary reasons. In neither case was there anything bad or good, as such, about possession or non-possession of a foreskin. He could warn against excessive use of wine by bishops, deacons, and aged folk (for whom in days before Digitalis, Excedrin, Aspirin and Geritol, excessive intake of wine was a great temptation), yet he could also recommend wine for the 'stomach's sake' (1 Tim. 5:23) in the case of an ailing evangelist. To the Romans he wrote: 'One person believes he may eat anything, while the weak person eats only vegetables [so vegetarianism is no sign of robust spirituality]. Let not the one who eats despise the one who abstains, and let not the one who abstains pass judgment on the one who eats, for God has welcomed him' (Rom. 14:2, 3). How many there are who claim the Bible as their final authority, yet respond to Jesus and Paul on these matters with a 'Yes, but,' and continue to follow their own inherited prejudices! The human spirit is startlingly obstinate in such matters.

John Calvin, whom many think they can cite as a classical killjoy, really saw this subject in a biblical fashion. Dozens of passages in which he proposes moderate, temperate use of all earth's good gifts from God as part of God's will might be cited. In a famous essay on Christian liberty he inveighs against the abuse of Christian freedom for gluttony and luxury, but affirms: 'Surely ivory and gold and riches are good creations of God, permitted, indeed, appointed for men's use by God's providence. And we have never been forbidden to laugh, or to be filled, or to join new possessions to old or ancestral ones, or to delight in musical harmony, or to drink wine [we might add coca cola, coffee, tea or milk].'[17] Then he goes on to condemn intemperance, saying 'Away then, with uncontrolled desire, away with immoderate prodigality, away with vanity and arrogance – in order that men may with good conscience cleanly use God's gifts.'[18]

Any believer with doubts as to whether or not good Christians should enjoy the 'good things as gifts of God' should read Book III, chapter 10 of the *Institutes*.[19]

So we are taught by Scripture and the best of its expositors that even though in some not quite clear sense, the world of things is a 'fallen' world and 'in bondage to corruption,' it is not defiling as such. It is all to be used and received with thanks (1 Tim. 4:3). Defilement proceeds from within ('uncontrolled desire... immoderate prodigality... vanity... arrogance,' says Calvin in the paragraph above). Jesus' words to this effect call for no comment: 'Are you also still without understanding? Do you not see that whatever goes into the mouth passes into the stomach and is expelled? But what comes out of the mouth proceeds from the heart, and this defiles a person. For out of the heart come evil thoughts, murder, adultery, sexual immorality, theft, false witness, slander. These are what defile a person. But to eat with unwashed hands does not defile anyone' (Matt. 15:16-20). Having said this, we must observe further that we should not eliminate the possibility that the life of fallen but moral man will be something less than ideal – as it develops in the world of nature, which produces thorns, thistles and clods as well as fruits, vegetables and flowers; tornadoes and floods as well as gentle breezes and nourishing showers. The society of mankind will be a scene of both joy and despair.

These important facts have serious consequences for mankind in relation to the natural order. A rigorous realism will be necessary, together with a vivid idealism, to attain a proper balance of view. The magnificence of mankind by creation, and the goodness of earth by virtue of the same creation, render praiseworthy every effort of agriculture,

---

17. Calvin, *Institutes III*.19.9.
18. ibid.
19. Westminster ed. of 1960, Vol. I, pp. 719-725.

science, government and industry to promote order and harmony in lawful efforts to utilize the bounties of earth. Yet, on the contrary, there must be limits of expectation. Man will not cease to be the sinner and the soil will not cease to produce thorns and thistles to keep him toiling. This is for our own good. To date, all the efforts of science and industry have failed to deliver mankind from the dark side of nature. For example, the goals of added leisure for overworked toilers in the early decades of the industrial revolution, advocated by reformers and secured by civil laws, are desirable. But free a man from the divine decree of toil entirely and you attack both his moral character and his essential manhood. The present state of affairs in many departments of civil life manifests ignorance of the realism of the biblical record.

There should be no doubt that God has a purpose for the presence of evil, with consequent suffering and death, in the world. He planned, created, sustains and governs the world and He presently 'works all things according to the counsel of his will' (Eph. 4:11). There are hundreds of articles and whole books in print which wrestle with the problem of why God allowed moral evil in the first place, and still divine providence introduces calamities of every kind.[20] As to the specific question – Why, to what purpose, did God include sin and suffering in His plan (decree)? – Douglas Spanner's proposal is appealing. He proposes that God's plan 'envisages' a glorious consummation which required suffering and evil. He writes:

> [H]ow could God commend his love so powerfully to us if we had not been sinners? How could our Lord have manifested the 'greater love' to us if we had not been in mortal need?.... This line of thought, stemming from the suggestion that the primal creation contained elements of pain, may provide a clue to why the Creator has allowed evil in all his world.[21]

Not uncommonly non-theists, and even some non-Christian theists, have represented evil as merely limitation or creatureliness, or even as good in the process of becoming. And there are many other views of evil. But whether he knows the name for his view or not, every biblically informed Christian takes a theistic view – i.e. we know the world to be created, sustained and controlled by a personal God who is holy, wise and powerful in infinite degree. We may have moments of doubt when, like the patriarch Job, we may be tempted to reproach God for allowing pain or sin; we may reflect upon the hypothetical possibility that God cannot do better; and one may even question God's benevolence, asking, 'Does Jesus care?' Yet, faith always recovers, as Job's did, for our basic convictions, drawn from Scripture and experience, by the Spirit of God, allow us no recourse but to leave the questions with God, whom we know we can personally trust. We accept the partial answers we have, with faith, and await impartation of further knowledge in the day when the believer no longer walks by faith alone, but by immediate vision of God. It is not quite exact to say we suspend judgment on the question, for one makes a judgment on what one already knows of God, postponing rational explanations for the time when there is sufficient information, perhaps for ever.

---

20. Some of my own effort in this direction came out in an article, 'The Nature and Origin of Evil' in *Vital Apologetical Issues*, A Symposium, ed. Roy B. Zuck (Grand Rapids: Kregel, 1995), pp. 10-18.
21. Douglas Spanner, *Biblical Creation and the Theory of Evolution* (Exeter: Paternoster Press, 1987), pp. 148, 149.

12
Fallen Mankind, in their World

Our examination of mankind's relation to the order of nature after the fall and exclusion from paradise did not discover any complete disruptions. Properly treated, the environment furnished by the physical world is still friendly toward its human inhabitants, even though because of sin we must walk always through a valley of the shadow of death during three score years and ten, more or less. Spiritually and morally, however, the change from the happy existence of paradise is thoroughgoing and threatening.

There was a tempter even in paradise and Adam was required to 'work' and 'guard' his 'garden.' Two holy beings possessing holy nature, who were *possere non pecare* (able not to sin), did nevertheless yield to the serpent's enticement. The society of mankind known in the New Testament as 'the world' (*oikoumene*, inhabited earth; *aion*, present age; *kosmos*, the presently prevailing order of all human societies) would inevitably develop in a perverse and wicked manner.

'The Present Evil Age.'

Some striking New Testament references set out the sad state of affairs in this age of the world wherein after Adam's fall we all must live out our days.

'[Christ] gave himself for our sins to deliver us from *the present evil age*' (Gal. 1:4).

'...the *god of this world* [Satan]' (2 Cor. 4:4).

'...I testify about it,' said Jesus of '*[t]he world,*' 'that its *works are evil*' (John 7:7).

'[T]he *whole world lies in the power of the evil one*' (1 John 5:19).

'And the great dragon was thrown down, that ancient serpent, who is called the devil and Satan, the *deceiver of the whole world*' (Rev. 12:9).

To summarize: the world in which the sons of Adam dwell is *a present evil age*, its *works are evil*, its *god is the devil*, it *lies in the power of the evil one* and the *ancient snake of paradise who deceived Eve deceives it wholly*.

The world of nature is still relatively 'good,' certainly without moral taint. But the human race and all our systems of power, however necessary, are morally tainted, sinful and threatened ultimately with the judgment of God. As civilization increases in refinement and complexity, sins seem to multiply and intensify in proportion to the square of that increase. Western civilization, as everyone knows, seems to be on the brink of a crisis of that development. We have now lived a long time under the threatening shadow of 'the bomb.' Civlization could invent it but does not know how to control it. Cain killed Abel with a stone or perhaps his fist; Brutus used a knife to assassinate Caesar; while by Aaron Burr's time, human genius had provided a pistol to do in Hamilton. Present engines of mass murder stifle the imagination, however much the television producers try.

World-wide Social Crisis.

No innate human impulses nor divine mandate placed any coercive control on our race during the antediluvian epoch. Acutely aware, as we are, of withering of restraints on barbarism in the Christendom of our day it should come as no surprise that before long in the antediluvian age 'the wickedness of man was great in the earth, and... every intention of the thoughts of his heart was only evil continually.... Now the earth was corrupt... and... filled with violence' (Gen. 6:5, 11).

Institution of Coercive Social Controls in the World.

The Great Flood of Genesis 6–8 put an end to unrestrained corruption and violence generated by the imagination of human hearts 'only evil continually.' To insure that such drastic measures as the Flood would not need to be repeated to preserve the race from self-destruction God instituted coercive social control, placing the coercive power of the sword in the hands of *man* to punish and restrain the violent deeds of *men*.

> And for your lifeblood I will require a reckoning: from every beast I will require it and from man. From his fellow man I will require a reckoning for the life of man. 'Whoever sheds the blood of man, by man shall his blood be shed, for God made man in his own image. And you, be fruitful and multiply, teem on the earth and multiply in it' (Gen. 9:5-7).

Although most works of systematic theology make little or no reference to civil government as an aspect of the order of divine preservation, consequent to the fall, it is the most prevalent Protestant interpretation of the Scripture data. Luther set the pace. He became aware he had set loose social forces which were incompatible with the papal-Thomist theory that civil government proceeds necessarily from human nature as created. His approach to politics was theological. 'As a pastor he conceived it to be as much a part of his duty to instruct his flock on their temporal responsibilities as to prepare them for the spiritual life of the world to come.'[1] Luther's comments exegetical and expository on Genesis fill eight volumes of over 400 pages each.[2] His teachings regarding civil government are in comments on Genesis 9:5, pages 139–142 of Volume Two, Lectures on Genesis 6–14.

In Luther's *Commentary on Genesis*, Luther expressly contrasts the state with the original state of the world by saying that in the original state of mankind before it had fallen, God ruled men *uno notu digito* (with one movement of His finger).[3] When sin came, inner rebellion came into the world – and with it the threat of chaos. Then God was obliged to institute orders of force which would hold the menacing chaos in check. These orders of force are represented by the state. And thus the state iself becomes a representative of this aeon, which, precisely because it is a *fallen* aeon, requires force. And thus we may assume that, insofar as the demonic power is really the 'ruler of this world,' this dominion will find expression particularly in the area of the state.[4]

Augustine also found the basis for a doctrine of coercive, civil control of society (government) not in the created order, but in the presence of sin in every man[5] as did also most of the early Protestant writers.[6]

Believers in and into the World but Not of it.

Because the Christian knows that God loved the world and in Christ reconciled the world to Himself (2 Cor. 5:17) godly people can live peacefully in it. Since Christ is 'the propitiation' for the sins of 'the whole world' (1 John 2:2) believers must be actively in the world proclaiming peace to those both 'near' and 'far off' (Eph. 2:11-18). Yet, while they must go 'into the world' they are not 'of the world' (John 17:16-18).

---

1. Cargill Thompson, 'Martin Luther and the Two Kingdoms' in *Political Ideas*, ed., D. Thompson (New York: Basic Books, 1966), p. 27.
2. *Luther's Works*, 55 vol. ed. Jaroslaw Pelikan & Helmut Lehmann (Philadelphia, PA: Fortress Press, 1955).
3. Martin Luther, *Commentary on Genesis*, Weimar Ausgabe, vol. 42, 1-19.
4. Helmut Thielicke, *Man in God's World*, ed. and trans. John W. Doberstein (New York: Harper & Row, 1963), p. 181.
5. Aurelius Augustine, *The City of God*, trans.
6. I pursued this matter at length in a paper, 'Civil Government with Coercive Power of Special Divine Origin or Simply a Development in History.' 22 pages, read at the Evangelical Theological Society annual meeting in Washington, D.C., November 19, 1993.

This then means that though he lives on a cursed earth and in the midst of a fallen race, being himself only a sinner saved by grace, the Christian can view the world with compassion. However offended by what falls in the line of his spiritual vision, he can ever see, as God sees, a world doomed but presently approachable. Rescue of individuals is possible. Wider social influence is possible. It also means that he may feel admitted to the company of the world, if not quite at home in it. Though the world is still an enemy of God, a 'truce' has been effected.

Ambiguities in the Biblical World-picture.

So the world appears in Scripture somewhat ambiguously as created superlatively good, yet fallen on account of mankind's fall: in bondage to corruption; in moral perspective, a 'present evil age'; nevertheless reconciled to God by the death of His Son. As it is written, 'in Christ God was reconciling the world to himself, not counting their trespasses against them' (2 Cor. 5:19). If so, then the Christian believer has both rights and duties with respect to his human environment.

Origin of Civil Government.

These ambiguities of the biblical picture of the world – good but fallen, evil yet reconciled to God – present a pair of paradoxes. These in turn represent that condition of the world which the Reformers, especially Luther, saw as such that, except for the restraining presence of civil government, would have quickly destroyed itself. In the language of Luther, the state belongs to the order of preservation not of creation. According to the great Reformer, though, the fall set loose centrifugal forces that drive people apart and which send them toward destruction, through civil government inaugurated by the Noahic Covenant (Gen. 9) God gives an institutional instrument for preservation of the race from violent self-destruction.

As Helmut Thielicke has said, 'Hence the state is simply the institutional form of God's call to order.... for Luther the state is the gracious intervention of God which puts a stop to the self-destruction of the fallen world with a view to giving men a kairos [season] and bringing them to the last day.'[7]

Accordingly, the state must be seen as a work of God whereby some of the effects of redemption are distributed to the elect of all the nations and of all the ages. It is a force holding people in relatively peaceful check while the messengers of the gospel are free to preach and to persuade people to be reconciled to the God who has already provided the reconciliation by the death of His Son. Hence, though of the order of preservation, rather than of creation, practically speaking, in light of what we have seen of the present state of the world and the need for civil tranquillity as a condition of evangelism and Christian nurture, the state is important to the order of salvation. For that reason Christians should most certainly pray for their 'city' and their rulers. To 'all the people... taken into exile,' God commanded Jeremiah to write and 'seek the welfare of the city where I have sent you into exile, and pray to the LORD on its behalf, for in its welfare you will find your welfare' (Jer. 29:1, 7). Much later Paul would directly connect godly prayers for domestic tranquillity with the desire of God 'who desires all people to be saved and to come to the knowledge of the truth' (1 Tim. 2:1-5).

The World As Evil.

One New Testament text refers to it as 'this present evil world' or 'age' (*aion*) (Gal. 1:4). Jesus Himself, after being dared by the members of His own family to perform his 'works' openly in Jerusalem, to show Himself 'to the world' (*kosmos* John 7:3, 4), said to His unbelieving brothers: 'My time has not yet come, but your time is always here. The world cannot hate you, but it hates me because I testify about it that its works are evil' (John 7:6, 7). Jesus 'testifies' that the world's deeds (presumably all of the world's deeds) are evil. In Galatians 1:4 'world' is a Greek word which means age; the word in John 7:4, 7 has the essential meaning of world-system. Jesus' brothers, however, were not thinking of it in either of these senses, for they meant 'world' in the sense of public, and open as opposed to private. Nevertheless, Jesus' simple affirmation signifies that the present world-system ordinarily has no place for friendly reception of the Son of God, once He is recognized on the deeper levels of His being and significance.

---

7. I have tried desperately to recover the place of this quote in the many volumes of Thielicke in my library, without success. I vouch for its accuracy.

It is not important at this point further to elaborate or qualify the affirmation that the present world-system of mankind is evil. We cannot, indeed, dare not, forget that the present world-system occupies a world of nature created good by God. Even though fallen, it is without moral taint; it is still God's good gift, serving mankind in opposite ways. If its showers nourish, its floods chasten; if its zephyrs and breezes cool the land, its tornadoes and hurricanes rebuke us. This is the Christian and biblical point of view.

Progressive Deepening Evil.

But mankind and his man-created systems have been subverted to evil. The observed facts support the biblical assertions. As human civilization increases in refinement and complexity, its sins expand, multiply and intensify. A newspaper editorial brings out an aspect of this horrifying fact of existence:

> Mankind (as a wise member of the species once observed) hasn't learned yet how to use the wheel. Attached to multitudinous high-speed vehicles, it still kills thousands every year. How then can man be expected to be sage and undestructive in his use of such recent and overpowering creations as atomic power? That wisdom gap between technical brilliance and ethical stupidity has become a troubling concern of many scientists, and it was a subject of brooding concern at a recent meeting of geneticists... Geneticists have not only learned the code used in the transmission of characteristics from one generation to the next, they have reached a point where they will be able some day to direct the course of evolution [sic] by eliminating undesirable traits and creating desirable ones. Whither mankind?[8]

The editor goes on to say that so far mankind has already altered his environment by air and water pollution and may have scarred the race genetically by atomic radiation. Mankind who has extinguished so many other species may succeed only in extinguishing himself.

This editor is only saying on a popular level what scholars have been writing in their journals for years and what the Scriptures have taught for millenniums. Cain killed Abel with his fist or perhaps a stone. Brutus used a knife on Caesar while centuries later Burr shot Hamilton with a pistol. Presently we use flame-throwers, napalm, machine guns and many other garish horrors, but the root of it all is the same – fallen mankind operating in a present, evil, world-system. Both mankind and his world, viewed from the side of their own closed systems, are quite incorrigible. There is no hope for the future from this quarter.

This aspect of the doctrine of 'the world' comes in for extended treatment in a later section of this book.

The World As Reconciled to God by Christ.

Another ambiguity of the biblical depiction of the world is that the world already has been reconciled to God by Christ. This is not the place for extended discussion of the vexing theological question of the extent of the atonement. That subject will be examined more at length in Part 4: Christology, but I must relate it to the present topic.

This author is among the many who, holding that the Scriptures plainly teach a special reference of the redemptive ministry of our LORD to the elect, hold there is also a general reference of that work to all people, indeed to all creation. As is the case with many important Christian truths, though capable of being stated in self-consistent propositions, all of which, when viewed in full perspective, are also mutually consistent, there are refinements which at first seem paradoxical. All true biblical paradoxes, on full examination, in the light of completed revelation (some yet to come), are explicable.[9]

Since no one who has even a minimal knowledge and acceptance of biblical teaching doubts a particular value of the atonement for the elect (or if preferred, those who hear the gospel and believe it), that matter may be disposed of quickly. Jesus, as He paused momentarily before stepping out to meet Judas and the high priest's deputies that last night, distinctly indicated that His main interest was His chosen ones through the age to come after His death. 'I am praying for them,' said He, 'I am not praying for the world but for those whom you have given me' (John 17:9). And a bit later, 'I do not ask for these only, but also for those who will believe in me through their word' (John 17:20; *vide* v. 24). Other texts frequently cited in this connection are John 10:11 ('I am the good shepherd. The good shepherd

---

8. I have lost the source.
9. This does not apply to certain mysteries such as Christ's two natures or the Holy Trinity.

lays down his life for the sheep') and Matthew 1:21 ('...you shall call his name Jesus, for he will save his people from their sins'). So we know that in a strict sense Jesus, on these occasions at least, prayed only for those 'given' to Him; that He died in the stead of 'sheep' only; and that His whole coming was for the salvation of his 'people' only.[10]

Other texts of Scripture, however, speak of a work of reconciliation by Christ that went as far as sin has gone. The impact of these texts is cumulative and impressive. 'For God did not send his Son into the world to condemn the world, but in order that the world might be saved through him' (John 3:17). 'He is the propitiation for our sins, and not for ours only but also for the sins of the whole world' (1 John 2:2). 'And we have seen and testify that the Father has sent his Son to be the Savior of the world' (1 John 4:14). Paul's words are most explicit also – 'in Christ God was reconciling the world to himself, not counting their trespasses against them' (2 Cor. 5:19); 'Christ Jesus, who gave himself as a ransom for all' (1 Tim. 2:5, 6). These texts and several more have been the battleground for a long time between those who argue on the one hand that atonement is for the elect only and on the other that it is for every person in the entire world without distinction.

Many who wish to take all the Bible seriously and seek not to 'wrest... the... scriptures' (cf. 2 Peter 3:16 KJV) have sought a *via media*. It does not seem to be so hard to find as some think. Without pursuing the subject further at this point than is presently meet, observe that some of Paul's words seem almost to be a specific explanation of a *via media*. He affirms that all hope should be set on the 'living God, who,' he explains, 'is the Savior of all people, especially of those who believe' (1 Tim. 4:10). This seems clearly to say that though the Son of God is 'specially' the Savior of believers only, there is a broad sense in which He is the world's Savior too.

Those scholars appear to be on the right track who insist, then, that the redemptive work of Christ was not only personal and individual for each elect believer but also completely effective for them. This, of course, is overturned if the atonement is construed to be precisely the same for every human being who lives, has lived or ever shall live as for the elect. But I judge these same interpreters are clearly on the wrong track if and when they seek to empty the atonement in some sense of a clear biblical reference to all the world. Some weak arguments against any form of universal effect of the Savior's work, based on sickly irrelevancies such as 'all Judea' (Matt. 3:5) and other passages which do not bear on either the subject or the idiom, are really unworthy of serious notice.

Even as ardent a defender of 'limited atonement' as John Murray has written:

> Since all benefits and blessings are within the realm of Christ's dominion and since this dominion rests upon his finished work of atonement, the benefits innumerable which are enjoyed by all men indiscriminately are related to the death of Christ and may be said to accrue from it one way or another. If they thus flow from the death of Christ they were intended thus to flow. It is proper, therefore, to say that the enjoyment of certain benefits even by the non-elect and reprobate, falls within the design of the death of Christ. The denial of universal atonement does not carry with it the denial of any such relation that the benefits enjoyed by all men may sustain to Christ's death and finished work.[11]

Perhaps it is the difficulties of this subject that have been great enough to discourage even such a leading Calvinist as G. C. Berkouwer from discussing it. At any rate in his 350-page book on the work of Christ he discusses the topic hardly at all.

A comparison of Greek prepositions may render important assistance. Matthew reports the LORD's words: 'the Son of Man came... to give his life as a ransom for many' (Matt. 20:28). The 'many' are surely those who believe, not all men, but 'many' of them. The word rendered 'for' is *anti*, the Greek preposition which almost invariably in the New Testament carries the sense of 'in the place of.' In the strictest sense Christ's atonement was 'in the place of' only those for whom He prayed (John 17). Another text of similar sound reads: 'Christ Jesus... gave himself as a ransom for all' (1 Tim. 2:5, 6). Here the word 'ransom' (*antilutron*) combines the word *anti*, 'instead of,' with the usual word for 'ransom' (*lutron*) used in Matthew 20:28 quoted above. So the idea of substitutionary ransom is present. But the preposition 'for' renders a different word from that of Matthew 20:28. It is *hyper*. This word (though capable of bearing the sense of 'instead of') normally conveys either a 'locative' sense of over, above, beyond or a 'purposive' sense – for one's safety, for one's advantage or benefit. So Paul is saying that the ransom Jesus made was for the safety, advantage, benefit of all.

---

10. *Vide* also Ephesians 1:4-7; 2 Timothy 1:9, 10.
11. John Murray, *Redemption Accomplished and Applied*, rev. ed. (Grand Rapids, MI: Eerdmans, 1955, 1965), pp. 43-55.

A Truce Declared.

Paul is acutely aware of this fact of world-reconciliation, devoting an especially exalted peroration to it (Col. 1:19-23). He is deeply convinced of the special benefit for believers of Christ's work, as is indicated by the words 'in whom we have redemption, the forgiveness of sins' (Col. 1:14 *et al*). This is followed by declarations that nevertheless all that is, God excepted, was created by Jesus Christ and for Him, being Himself the very image of God. The church is His special body (v. 18). Then comes the great text:

> For in him all the fullness of God was pleased to dwell, and through him to reconcile to himself all things, whether on earth or in heaven, making peace by the blood of his cross. And you, who once were alienated and hostile in mind, doing evil deeds, he has now reconciled in his body of flesh by his death, in order to present you holy and blameless and above reproach before him, if indeed you continue in the faith, stable and steadfast, not shifting from the hope of the gospel that you heard, which has been proclaimed in all creation under heaven, and of which I, Paul, became a minister (Col. 1:19-23).

Our present interest focuses on verse 20, where reference is made to Christ's work 'to reconcile to himself all things... by the blood of his cross' and verse 23 which states that 'the gospel that you heard... has been proclaimed in all creation under heaven' (cf. vv. 5, 6: 'the gospel, which has come to you, as indeed in the whole world'). How has Christ reconciled 'all things' to Himself? In what sense has the gospel been 'proclaimed in all creation under heaven'?

'To Reconcile to Himself All Things.'

With regard to the first question, it must be stated initially that the doctrine of universal salvation, either of all creatures (including demons, fallen angels, and the devil) is eliminated as inconsistent with the doctrine of eternal punishment of the unrepentant distinctly sounded out elsewhere in the New Testament. It is also inconsistent with the fervent zeal of the early church and the apostolic witnesses to win people out of the world.

Limits on Reconciliation.

In addition to what has been presented above about limited redemption and unlimited reconciliation, we observe that here, though Paul uses the expression 'to reconcile all things,' employing *ta panta*, the ordinary expression for the whole of creation, when the writer particularizes he omits 'things under the earth.' The latter is the expression Paul uses elsewhere for the unseen evil powers in such enumerations, though he does mention 'things... on earth' and 'things... in heaven' (contr. Phil. 2:10, 11). So we need not suppose that Paul referred to any reconciliation with Satan and his hosts effected by Christ's redemption. Certain European authors (chiefly Oscar Cullmann and Karl Barth) have asserted and sought to prove that reference is here made to a victory by Christ in His redemption over the devil and his hosts which has compelled their obedient, if unwilling, service.

Oscar Cullmann has given wide advocacy to the notion that 'the powers that be' of Romans 13:1 are governmental officials backed by demonic powers – the real 'powers that be.' He constructs thereby a very interesting argument by connecting the same with the fact that Philippians 2:10 speaks of a conquest of the 'things under the earth', i.e. demon powers, by Christ. He does not seem to mean that Calvary atoned for them, but rather conquered them. In his book *The State in the New Testament* he notes that all the earliest Christian doctrinal formulae mention this conquest of the demon powers. Since these formulae collected 'only the most important points of their faith [this] proves how significant for them was this belief in the conquest of the powers.' Yet he notes that certain other texts (1 Cor. 15:25; Heb. 10:13) present the conquest as a future expectation. So the demon powers (within and above government), though conquered now, have a measure of freedom – they are bound with a rope that can be lengthened. He draws significant conclusions for governments and obedience to them by Christians. As long as government stays within limits imposed by God's past victory in Christ they are to be obeyed. When they make totalitarian demands, requiring for Caesar what is God's alone, they go too far and are to be resisted.[12] He does not use the word 'disobey.' He concludes:

> Against the background of this belief in the vanquished powers at work behind earthly happenings, it becomes especially clear that the State is now a temporary institution not of divine nature but nevertheless willed by God; that we must remain critical toward every State; that we must nonetheless obey every State as far as it remains within its bounds.

---

12. Oscar Cullmann, *The State in the New Testament*, rev. ed. (London: SCM Press LTD, 1963), pp. 43-55.

> But particularly, from this point of view, we shall understand how in the same New Testament in which we read the words from Romans 13:1: 'Let every person be subject,' and the rulers are 'God's servants'; we hear also about this same state – Nero's State (in Revelation 13) – that it is 'the beast from the abyss.' Now this is spoken from the point where the State is trying to free itself from its subordination and is becoming satanic, in that it is demanding what is God's. The state which makes itself independent, which absolutizes itself, deifies itself, is precisely the classic expression of the Antichrist.[13]

It seems to me more likely that Paul is thinking in the terms of ultimate restoration of the non-rational creation, which will take place with the glorification of God's regenerate sons (Rom. 8:19 ff.) at the consummation. Since mankind's fall brought the curse, their restoration and consummated glorification presages nature's 'redemption.' Thus a connection between the 'reconciliation' wrought through Christ's atonement and the 'reconciliation' and 'redemption' of 'all things' is established. The holy heavenly beings and things, since they have never been alienated from God, are not included in the reconciliation. This much only needs to be affirmed: *whatever the effects of human sin have been and wherever they have reached, there 'peace through the blood of His [Christ's] cross' has gone.* One may walk into a saloon, a brothel, a vice den, the godless emporiums of Wall Street or the financial districts of any city and say to the thoughtless and godless, 'God now holds nothing against you. The Spirit and the Bride say, Come, take of the water of life freely.'

'Preached in All Creation Under Heaven.'

In regard to the second problem, in what sense the gospel has been 'preached in all creation under heaven' it may be said that the gospel had already in Paul's time reached all areas of the Roman *oikoumenē*, the world civilization of the day. The meaning of 'all creation under heaven,' from the popular point of view Paul employs, is certainly nothing more inclusive than that, and needs no wider application than the command of Caesar that 'all the world should be enrolled' (Luke 2:1). 'The catholicity of the gospel is a token of its divine origin and power.'

This then means that though he lives on a cursed earth and in the midst of a fallen race, being himself only a sinner saved by grace, the Christian can view the world with compassion. However revolted by what falls in the line of his spiritual vision, he can ever see, as God sees, a world doomed but presently approachable. Rescue of individuals is possible. It also means that he may feel admitted to the company of the world, if not quite at home in it. Though the world is still an enemy of God, a 'truce' has been effected.

So the world appears in Scripture somewhat ambiguously as created superlatively good, yet fallen on account of man's fall and in bondage to corruption; thus in moral perspective, somewhat a 'present evil age'; nevertheless reconciled to God by the death of His Son.

(At this juncture, or as a supplement to the whole of systematic theology, it has seemed proper and necessary to many to expand greatly on the topic of this chapter – 'Fallen Man [Mankind] in His World.' As an example I cite the fourth and largest book of Calvin's *Institutes*, which significantly relates to this topic. John Gill's eighteenth-century, *Complete Body of Doctrinal and Practical Body of Divinity* is laced throughout with such matters, scarcely separating 'duties' from 'doctrines.' J. O. Buswell devotes more than a third of the 200 pages of anthropology to 'Human Life in this Age.' This chapter is drawn largely from a much larger section of my volume, *Civil Government: A Biblical View* [Edmonton: Alberta, Canada: Canadian Institute for Law, Theology, and Public Policy, 1975, 2000].

Beginning with the ninth chapter of Genesis on to the close of Revelation the fact of rule of men by man, i.e. civil government, pervades the holy Book. On the most basic level it is: 1) a fact of biblical history, a pervasive phenomenon under which people of all times, including ours, have lived. Civil government was 2) a frequent *topic of preaching and writing* by the prophets of Israel and Judah. On another level it is 3) a *subject of divine legislation* in four of the five Books of Moses and on still another level 4) a matter for much *reflection and practical advice* in the Old Testament Wisdom literature. In the New Testament human government is 5) a *subject of special instruction* – and example – by Jesus Himself and apostles and prophets, providing the ingredients of a Christian doctrine of civil government. Finally, there are 6) New Testament *exhortations and warnings* for believers with regard to their response both to just rulers and to unjust as well as proper attitudes toward their laws, courts, agencies and agents.)

---

13. ibid., pp. 55, 56.

PART 1
THEOLOGY PROPER
Introduction and Doctrine of God

PART 2
ANTHROPOLOGY
Man as Created

PART 3
HAMARTIOLOGY
Man as Sinner

PART 4
CHRISTOLOGY
Person and Work of Christ

PART 5
SOTERIOLOGY
Salvation Applied

PART 6
ECCLESIOLOGY
Church Local and Universal

PART 7
ESCHATOLOGY
Last Things, Personal and Universal

BIBLIOGRAPHY

SCRIPTURE INDEX

GENERAL INDEX

1
Introduction to Harmatiology

To present a comprehensive treatment of the doctrine of sin both focused and rationally organized is a difficult project. As we have seen earlier, sin is an irrational thing in itself and we scarcely understand it in ourselves. There is not complete agreement among theologians as to which aspects are comprehensive, which are essential or only tangential or even trivial. The Bible does not clearly reveal how moral evil originated in either earth or heaven, though we know how sin entered into the world of mankind. And this is not the only gap in our information, for the Scriptures do not categorically state how sin is passed down through the generations, even though we know it is, both from Scripture and experience.

In the face of such difficulties one must humbly recognize that the same Holy Scriptures which are sufficient for life and godliness also set limits to speculation on some doctrinal issues and bid us to come to terms with the facts of revelation we do have, whether pleasant or disagreeable.

No structure of the subject is immediately apparent. No outline that is specific in all its parts can include every feature. Hence this treatise is not alone in following an outline as much pedagogical as logical and packing unclassifiable material in an introduction and in more than one incursion of unclassified questions and problems.

Thinking man (homo sapiens) does try to make sense of his deepest convictions. We do not like to live with contradictory beliefs if we are aware of them. This is why decisions made about the innate conditions of human beings – such decisions as whether innately good or evil, whether innocent at birth or 'conceived in sin,' whether guilty of Adam's transgression or guilty only of personal transgressions consciously performed, whether culpable for a corrupt nature or only unfortunate, whether with a free will able to make choices for holiness or a child of wrath by nature – these decisions inexorably affect not only every subsequent division of systematic theology, but how we view salvation and the project of world evangelization.

The informed reader will recognize immediately by the way the last previous sentence is phrased that the present writer is in the tradition of orthodox Reformation theology, preceded by the evangelical thought of Anselm and Gottschalk to Augustine and ultimately to the emphasis of Paul in the Epistles of Romans, 1 Corinthians, Galatians and Ephesians.

In no area of theology, systematic as well as biblical, is the theologian more in debt to forebears in the discipline. One cannot escape them. They have furnished both the questions and the clues to answers. Yet the intellectual and social ferment of our times add color and poignancy, if not depth, to the discussion, as we shall see. The depths of the human heart, without acknowledged awareness of God and God-relatedness, have been plumbed by several depth psychologies and existentialisms. Yet they solve no important problem, only adding some color to David's cry: 'Who can discern his errors? Declare me innocent from hidden faults [hidden from myself]' (Ps. 19:12).

Decisions on certain aspects of sin have immediate effect on many problems of conduct, of course. What is not as well understood is how a doctrine of man that includes man as sinner affects many professional disciplines – psychological counseling and therapy for example. Though I taught the whole of systematic theology over a period of many years, for three or four years in the mid-1980s I was assigned annually classes of about twenty-five, most of whom were in a program leading to a degree in 'biblical counseling,' doing 'therapy' for emotionally and mentally distressed people. These earnest students were graduates of secular universities and being evangelical believers, had long been aware of sin but had never become fully aware of how blameworthy every child of Adam is for the corruption of human nature, each 'a sinner by choice and an alien by birth.' No one readily accepts this in the university-bred atmosphere of our time. Nevertheless, quickly and regretfully yet thankfully, every one of them accepted the truth of it when exposed in assigned readings and classroom discussion. The Christian revelation made sense in the nonsense of sin as they met it in their lives, in their world and in the Bible. Though the beginning of sin in the human race is narrated in grim detail in the third chapter of Genesis, as Paul assures us (Rom. 5:12), strangely, the word sin is not employed at all. 'Sin' first appears almost incidentally in the Bible at Genesis 4:7 in connection with the story of Cain, the first child of our race and the first act of murder. We do not know in what language God spoke to our first parents and their immediate offspring, but the report of the incident employs the most common word for sin in the Hebrew Bible, usually translated in the Greek Old Testament into the commonest New Testament term for sin.

If there is a generic term for sin in the Bible it is this word – *ḥaṭṭa'th* (and its verb equivalent *ḥaṭa'*). The Greek Old Testament (LXX) usually renders it by *hamartia* (238 times TDOT I, 268). *Hamartia* is the usual word in the New Testament for sin, following the Septuagint example.

The negative idea of missing, failing, neglecting is the primordial sense of both words and they are often used in that narrow sense, yet frequently also simply as designation of moral evil in responsible personal beings. Strangely, either as a noun or as a verb (*ḥaṭa'*) this word is not used at all in the narrative of the fall, not even once in the detailed report of moral corruptions culminating in the Flood. Paul, however, uses the 'generic' *hamartia* (noun) and *hamartanō* (verb) several times for Adam's sinning, as a comprehensive term. He uses several other terms, however, to designate the specific character of that event. Hence theologians have not been amiss in designating the doctrine of sin as *hamartiology*. Transgression, trespass, wickedness, etc., and their equivalent terms in the biblical languages are too specific to be used as the comprehensive name for moral evil.

There is no clear definition of sin in the Bible, though certain texts in the New Testament have been treated as definitions. Yet they are neither specific nor comprehensive. 'For whatever does not proceed from faith is sin' (Rom. 14:23) has only the appearance of a definition. In context it says only that when Christians parade their 'mature' faith by acting in such a way as unnecessarily to offend other believers they are not acting in faith, hence sinfully. However relevant to a full definition of sin, the verse is less than a definition. '[W]ithout faith it is impossible to please him [God]' (Heb. 11:6) is a near equivalent expression but has only the appearance of a definition of faith. The copula 'is' does not make a clause a definition except under specific conditions. First John 3:4 is in context closer to a definition: 'sin is lawlessness.' Yet it is more description than definition; for as we shall see, like the mystery of sin's origin, the very nature of sin is baffling. It is never the less fully apparent to human conscience. In due time we shall attempt a definition.

There are some distinctions intrinsic to the biblical doctrine of sin that must be considered.

1. Distinction Between Sin and Sins.

A careful reading of Scripture discovers a crucial distinction between *sin* and *sins*. This may be clearly perceived in connection with two similar sounding but subtly different passages, viz.: '...he will save his people from their *sins* [emphasis added]' (Matt. 1:21); 'Behold, the Lamb of God, who takes away the *sin* [emphasis added] of the world!' (John 1:29). The former, 'sins,' has obvious reference to the many evil deeds of 'people.' The latter reference, 'the sin of the world,' speaks of the world's guilt before God in which all men share. Romans 5:12 puts it this way: 'Therefore, just as sin came into the world through one man, and death through sin, and so death spread to all men because all sinned.' There is a 'sin of the world.' It 'came into the world' as a definite event at a particular past time. 'All' mankind 'sinned' in and with Adam in that event. Paul charged 'all the world... guilty before God' (Rom. 3:19 KJV). John declared 'the whole world lieth in wickedness' (1 John 5:19 KJV). James wrote: 'Do you not know that friendship with the world is enmity with God? Therefore whoever wishes to be a friend of the world makes himself an enemy of God' (James 4:4). All these texts find their unifying meaning in the fact that the world itself, in the sense of the spiritual principles upon which it is ruled (by Satan) and operates as a world, an organized *kosmos*, is itself presently destined to judgment. Many New Testament passages assume or state that the world itself is a single entity. From the time of Cain and Abel onward to the Last Judgment the world is *en bloc* simply sin. One cannot even live in the world as a Christian without being stained by it, hence Jesus' pronouncements on his last night: 'Peter said to him, "You shall never wash my feet." Jesus answered him, "If I do not wash you, you have no share with me"' (John 13:8). 'I am praying for them. I am not praying for the world... the world has hated them because they are not of the world' (John 17:9, 14) even though they are now sent into the world (John 17:18). Practically speaking, the world is a dangerous place, because *sin* is of its very essence, pervasive and powerful – as the whole narrative of Scripture bears witness and all human history and experience manifests. This was discussed in the last chapter of the previous section, 'The Doctrine of Man.'

2. Sin As a Principle.

In a related (but not identical) way *sin* (singular number again) is a principle. Or to use Paul's word, sin is a 'law' working in every man's 'members.' He discusses this in detail in Romans 7, vividly summarizing:

> ...but I see in my members another law waging war against the law of my mind and making me captive to the law of sin that dwells in my members.... So then, I myself serve the law of God with my mind, but with my flesh I serve the law of sin (Rom. 7:23, 25).

The Apostle uses the words 'flesh,' 'mind,' 'me' and 'I' as well as 'sin' and 'law' in varying senses in this chapter, yet his message is clear: there is a principle, law, or call it pervasive tendency or disposition, present even in regenerate people, which is properly called sin. The mere presence of this disposition toward doing evil is wrong. Even when the Apostle is 'wishing [*thelonti*] to do the good,' 'evil [*to katon*] is lying beside me' (*parakeitai moi*) (Rom. 7:21). This 'evil' is a law (*nomos*), the law of sin (Rom. 7:23). It takes advantage of the very law of God to work all sorts of sins and evil acts of thought, word and deed. The sins of 'saints' as well as of 'sinners' are many, but the root cause is a depravity deep in the heart, which Paul calls sin. Later we shall see this depravity is a punishment for Adam's original sin and that every human being bears deep-dyed guilt because of it.

3. Sin As Action of Personal Moral Beings.

Sins (plural) are evil events, actions, thoughts, deeds, states and intentions of personal moral beings. They are both simple and complicated, both devious and prevalent, and infinitely numerous.

Each of these three features – 1) sins and sin, 2) sin as a 'law' or principle, and 3) sin as a deed of moral beings – will be topics of discussion later in this book.

2
The Vocabulary, Common and Biblical, About Sin

As seen in the preceding pages, the Bible refers to sin and to sins. It does so in many ways. The English language employs hundreds of words for sin: verbs and adverbs, nouns and adjectives, some rude and plain, some delicate or even elegant. The English Versions employ a very large number of them and we know what the words mean: sin, wicked, wrong, lust, error, transgression, trespass, iniquity, fault, guilt, unrighteous, blame, vile, shameful and many more. They obviously share a common area of meaning, viz.: moral evil. The Hebrew and Greek originals of Scripture display a similar variety of expressions. 'Iniquity,' for example, appears about 250 times in the KJV but translates five different Greek words and at least ten different Hebrew words. 'Evil' is on the pages of the KJV about 500 times, but translates twenty or more different Hebrew and Greek words.

This is not as confusing as it seems, for usually the sense in context is plain. For a precise understanding of some of the variegated colors and various shapes of the sin and sins which are in the world some synthesis and organization of the materials is necessary. Many of the Hebrew and Greek words and expressions were drawn from commercial and legal discourse and the same is true of the English terms used to translate them. This serves to illustrate their meaning.

Three Comprehensive Aspects of Sin.

Beginning with the earliest pages of the Old Testament and on to the last page of Revelation three comprehensive aspects of this form of evil are always present, even if not always stated. Let us look at each in order and the relation between them. These three are: first, sin as *commission*, something positive; second, sin as *omission*, something negative; third, sin as *blameworthiness* for sins of commission and omission. Some of the words in English Versions of Scripture for the first are the nouns transgression, sin, trespass, rebellion, revolution, offense and related verbs. Common terms for the second are sins of ignorance, neglect, fault and missing. The commonest is simply sin. For the third, indicating sin as blameworthiness, the almost uniform KJV term is iniquity. However, at the first appearance of the Hebrew word commonly rendered 'iniquity' (*'awon*) in Cain's anguished complaint, it is there correctly rendered 'punishment' (Gen. 4:13 KJV, NIV, RSV, REB, NASB, ESV). Others are 'fault concerning' and 'mischief.' Significantly when divine forgiveness of 'sin' is stated, i.e. remission of guilt, this is the word (*'awon*) employed (e.g. Jer. 33:8 twice; Jer. 36:3).

1. Sin As Commission.

Two very frequently occurring Hebrew words in innumerable passages represent sin as doing something aggressive such as breaching of standards, passing a proper boundary, breaking a just law. The meaning of one of these, the verb (*'avar*), in a non-moral setting illustrates the sense, viz.: the children of Israel 'crossed [*'avar*] the brook Zered' (Deut. 2:14) and 'go over' the river Jordan (Deut. 12:10). Abraham is called an (*'ivri*), probably one who passed over, because he came across the Euphrates River into the Land of Canaan. Examples in moral life are, 'I have not transgressed [*'avar*] any of your commandments' (Deut. 26:13), 'All Israel has transgressed your law' (Dan. 9:11). The New Testament has the equivalent of this word (*parabasis* and *parabainō*) (Matt. 15:3 and Rom. 5:14) rendered transgression and transgress.

The second frequent Hebrew word also often rendered transgression (*pesha'*, noun or *pasha'*, verb) appears frequently in the context of civil life, and is there rendered appropriately rebel or revolt – in each case against some constituted authority, viz.: 'Moab rebelled [*pasha'*] against Israel' (2 Kgs. 1:1); 'Edom revolted [*pasha'*] from the rule of Judah' (2 Kgs. 8:22). Examples in reference to moral life are Isaiah 1:2, 'Children have I reared and brought up, but they have rebelled against me' and Psalm 51:3, 'I know my transgressions [*pesha'im*], and my sin is ever before me.'

2. Sin As Omission.

Several other words in the biblical vocabulary represent sin as something negative, something omitted: missing a target when one should hit it, failing when one should succeed, ignorance of what one should know, falling when one should stand, neglect of duty when one should attend to it, defaulting a debt when one should pay it.

This negative idea is the meaning of the commonest words for sin both in the Old Testament and the New Testament. The verb *hata* is rendered strikingly at Judges 20:16, 'every one could sling a stone at a hair and not miss' (*hata'*). Four other Hebrew words, all derived from this verb, mean essentially the same. These words appear hundreds of times. In usage usually rendered sin (noun) or 'to sin' (verb), they become almost a generic term for any sort of moral evil, yet also frequently in a way limited to the essential, original idea of missing or failing. Lexicons list to miss, fail, to go wrong and the like as first meanings and find the same root with the same meaning in ancient cognate languages (Aramaic, Assyrian, Sabean, Ethiopic). They point out that its New Testament equivalent is *hamartia* (noun), *hamartanō* (verb), discussed earlier herein. Illustrative passages usually cited are Judges 20:16, cited above, and Proverbs 19:2, (NIV) 'It is not good... to be hasty and *miss* [emphasis added] the way.'

In discussion of this word theological writers correctly point out that missing the mark or way in the biblical use of the two words suggests deliberate choice, hence culpable, blameworthy, not merely unfortunate. But this is not always the case. The book of Leviticus lists numerous 'sins of ignorance' for which sin offerings were required. One of the meanings of the Hebrew word is sin-offering, especially in Leviticus 4–23. In Leviticus 4 and 5 there are repeated references to sinning 'unintentionally.' In several of these cases (see Lev. 4:1, 22, 27) the word for sinning is *hata'*. Leviticus chapter 4 is very clear that one is rendered 'guilty' of breaking God's law even if done unintentionally. An even more convincing example is the case of any Nazirite who wholly unintentionally broke his vow of avoidance of anything ritually unclean. Numbers 6:1-21 gives details. He was not even to share in necessary preparation for burial of a next of kin: father, mother, brother, sister (v. 7). Verse 9 goes on to say: 'if any man dies very suddenly beside him and he defiles his consecrated head [of hair],' he becomes unclean. This canceled out his previous time under the regimen of his vow and required a 'sin offering' and 'burnt offering' and the priest was to 'make atonement for him, because he sinned [*hata'*] by reason of the dead body' (v. 11). In a system where all of life was regulated by very elaborate divine do's and don'ts plus even more elaborate and detailed ritual requirements, sins of failure were almost inevitable. Yet this is the doctrine of sin that is carried straight into the New Testament.

Paraptoma rendered trespass, offense, fall, sin, fault is employed twenty-two times in the New Testament: derived from *parapiptō*, fall beside the way or go astray. 'Fall' (Rom. 11:11, 12) and 'fault' (Gal. 6:1; James 5:16) convey the same negative idea of missing the mark present in the more common word *hamartanō*. In New Testament teaching, sin, therefore, is a fall beside the way when one should have stayed on the way. *Parakoē*, from *parakouō*, to hear casually or to overhear, conveys the idea of disobedience because of inattention.

Several recent writers rightly suggest that though 'missing the way,' 'failure and sins of ignorance' seem to indicate 'innocent ignorance,' the ignorance was willful 'due to their hardness of heart' (Eph. 4:18).[1] It is doubtful if all sins designated by these negative terms arise from *conscious* darkening of the mind. We are after all 'by nature children of wrath' (Eph. 2:3). David confesses for us all, 'I was shaped in guilt [*'awon*] and in sin [*heta'*] did my mother conceive me.' These expressions can hardly describe anything but inborn deficit of righteousness, innate guilt – more about this later. I was a sinner already before I was born. I do not need to premeditate my failure to perform duties or to neglect requirements. It comes quite without conscious deliberation – 'naturally.'

Isaiah 53:6, in the great prophecy of our Lord's atoning death for sin, employs another word and though seldom used elsewhere for sin, it provides what surely must be a defining metaphor for this negative aspect of sin: 'All we like sheep have gone astray' (*ta'ah*, to go astray, err, wander). The precise sense in a non-moral situation is in they 'wandered [*ta'ah*] in desert wastes, finding no way to a city to dwell in' (Ps. 107:4), 'your enemy's ox or his donkey going astray' (*ta'ah*) (Exod. 23:4). In most of the other occurrences moral lapse is involved: used about fifty times in *kal*; rendered, to err, go astray; in *hiphil* to cause to wander, cause to err, seduce. My comment in a lecture on exegesis of Isaiah 53 reads: 'This word does not seem to describe willful sin, so much as the result of innate weakness. [See Pss. 58:3; 107:4; Isa. 16:8; Isa. 28:7; etc.] Thus through no willful act [voluntary] of our own we enter into the sinful nature of the race. But as many point out, this sin is culpable... cause for personal guilt.' I do not think David was restricting his meaning to any special class of super-sinners when he said, 'The wicked are estranged from the womb; they go astray [*ta'ah*] from birth' (Ps. 58:3).

It is not generally understood quite how prevalent the distinction between sin as negative (missing, neglecting, failing) and as positive (trespassing, transgressing) is in passages which do not in translation obviously convey both aspects. The distinction has great importance, as shall appear shortly.

Illustrative Scripture and Historic Statements.

A quite faithful rendering of Psalm 32:1 and 2 might read: 'Oh the blessedness of him whose transgression (*pesha'*) is forgiven (literally, "lifted up"), whose sin (*hatta'th*) is covered. Oh the blessedness of the man (Heb. *'adham*) unto whom the Lord imputeth not iniquity' (*'awon*, guilt, punishment).' In this passage the positive offense against God's laws, passing of boundaries or transgression (*pesha'*) is taken away but the negative failures, flaws, etc., are covered. Transgressions are not coverable nor are defects capable of being taken away. In the case of the blessed man, taking away and covering have rendered the 'man' without guilt, i.e. justified. Paul takes these sentences to be comprehensive for the removal of sin in all its aspects (Rom. 4:5-8). A careful examination of other Old Testament texts, such as the scapegoat ceremony (Lev. 16) and the prophecy of our Lord's great act of atonement (Isa. 53), indicate that these two aspects – positive transgressions and negative failures to come up to standard (i.e. sins in the narrow sense) – include all the others. They provide scriptural precedent for the familiar liturgical lines from the General Confession of the *Book of Common Prayer*, 'We have left undone those things which we ought to have done; and we have done those things which we ought not to have done.' They also render support to Question 14 and Answer of the *Westminster Shorter Catechism*: 'Question. What is sin? Answer, Sin is any want of conformity to [negative], or transgression of the law [positive] of God.'

3. Sin As Guilt (Culpability, Blameworthiness, Deserving of Punishment).

These distinctions will be moved on to the next category: guilt or culpability involving deserved punishment, comprehending both sin as commission and as omission as one inevitable continuum. Guilt is of the very essence of sin.

The Hebrew word which most distinctly unites sins of all kinds with their penal consequences is *'awon*. The King James Version renderings are reflected in Brown, Driver and Briggs' *Lexicon*: 'iniquity, guilt or punishment.' Iniquity (I think not the best choice of word) is not a very specific word (the Latin negative, *in*, plus *aequus*, even, equal, just, fair), injustice or unfairness. But the Hebrew word always involves the legal sense of guilt as the invariable consequence of sin. Whatever personal moral evil happens to be the subject of discourse, personal guilt is its consequence. Illustrative passages are numerous. In the first appearance Cain complains, 'My punishment [*'awon*] is greater than I can bear' (Gen. 4:13). Job tells his accusatory friends that divine 'wrath brings the punishment [*'awon*] of the sword' (Job 19:29). The merging of wrong deed (iniquity) with guilt and punishment

---

1. Millard Erickson, *Christian Theology* (Grand Rapids: Baker Books, 1985), p. 565.

for the same is reflected in the alternation of translations in the common Versions. The subject of Numbers 5 is marital unfaithfulness, adultery, viz.: 'The man shall be free from iniquity, but the woman shall bear her iniquity' (Num. 5:31); 'Moreover, the man will be free from *guilt*, but that woman shall bear her *guilt* [emphasis added]' (NASB); 'The husband will be innocent of any *wrongdoing*, but the woman will bear the *consequences* [emphasis added] of her sin' (NIV). BDB *The Hebrew Lexicon* translates the first clause of Numbers 5:31 '[The man will be] freed from *punishment*' (emphasis added).[2]

Thus it is plain that though sin may be an act either of commission or of omission, in either case guilt for the same (blameworthiness) and deserved punishment are inevitable accompaniments. There are many other words for sin in the Bible. They fill out our understanding of causes for sins of omission and commission, varieties of the same, motives, etc., but we have before us the main content of biblical revelation on the subject. Enforcement and illustration of these broad assertions can be demonstrated for ancient Israel's sins in connection with *Yom Kippur* (Day of Atonement, Lev. 16) and the comprehensive, once-for-all act of 'propiation… for the sins of the whole world' (1 John 2:2) by the Servant of the Lord (Isa. 53, especially v. 6). Let us look carefully.

The first fifteen chapters of Leviticus constitute the whole complicated apparatus for ritual expiation and reconciliation for every aspect of Israel's sin and sins – for every class of people in the nation and for every situation. Every time one reads it one is impelled to wonder if any one ever completed one of the rituals exactly right.

The denouement took place annually on the tenth day of the seventh month (Lev. 16:29) in *Yom Kippur*, the Great Day of Atonement (Lev. 16). The tone and theme for this annual observance is set in Leviticus 23:26-32. Warnings were severe. All work was to cease. The whole nation went into solemn mourning from sundown on the ninth day till sundown on the tenth. During those hours the priest made ritual atonement for himself and his family (Lev. 16:11). Then he made ritual, sacrifical atonement 'for the Holy Place, because of the uncleannesses of the people of Israel' (Lev. 16:16). After that he made his once-a-year-only entrance to the holy place to make 'atonement for himself and for his house and for all the assembly of Israel' (Lev. 16:17).

Finally, the high priest climaxed the ritual removal of all Israel's sins in the ceremony of the scapegoat. During the previous preparatory ceremonies, an identical goat having been slain as 'the sin offering… for the people' (Lev. 16:15), another 'live goat' was kept ready. Then the 'live goat' was brought to the brazen altar. But it was not slain, rather:

> Aaron shall lay both his hands on the head of the live goat, and confess over it all the *iniquities* ['awon] of the people of Israel, and all their *transgressions* [pish'eyhem], all their *sins* [ḥaṭṭo'tham]. And he shall put them on the head of the goat and send it away into the wilderness by the hand of a man who is in readiness (Lev. 16:21).

Observe that the three words for sin as *commission*, as *omission* and comprehensively as *guilt*, are in this total confession of Israel's sins of the past year. In this case sin is last, and seems to be used in its non-specific sense as designating moral evils of all kinds. The next verse, however, makes it plain that '*awon* is the word which gathers up both aspects of sin, omission and commission, or whatever was blameworthy and deserving of punishment, for, 'The goat shall bear all their *iniquities* [emphasis added] on itself to a remote area, and he shall let the goat go free in the wilderness' (Lev. 16:22). In the final act of disposing of Israel's sins, now propitiated (Godward) and expiated (manward) by vicarious sacrifice the whole is removed comprehensively and completely as guilty, deserved punishment.

This sequence and relationship is even more precisely involved in the case of Isaiah's prophecy of our Lord's act as 'the Lamb of God who takes away the sin of the world' in Isaiah 53 (especially v. 6). The prophecy takes the form of a contrite sinner's confession. In order to highlight the three words for moral evil I cite my own translation. This is in my lectures on the exegesis of Isaiah and in my book, *The Sufferings and the Glory*.[3] 'All of us as the flock have gone astray; we have turned each one to his own way and the LORD has caused to strike on him the punishment due all of us.' There are intertwined here a fairly complete doctrine both of sin and of atonement for sin.

Conclusions in Isaiah 53:6.

1. *Man is collectively a sinner by nature*, i.e. born in Adam's sin. (a) This sin is universal: 'of us all.' This includes all who share in the confession. Though Delitzsch referred to it in context primarily to a repentant nation of Israel, Peter was not reluctant to apply it directly to Christian believers (1 Peter 2:22-25). That this is proper is further witnessed by the fervent manner in which Christians always enter personally and as a congregation into recitation

---

2. Brown, Driver & Briggs, *A Hebrew And English Lexicon of the Old Testament* (New York: Houghton, Mifflin & Co., 1906), p. 731.
3. Robert D. Culver, *The Sufferings and the Glory* (Eugene, OR: WIPF and Stock, 2001), pp. 6, 77–83.

of Isaiah 53:6. In this sin we have already moved 'as a flock' (Heb., *katson*).[4] The word is a figure drawn from the well-known movement of all gregarious herds of animals, especially the domestic flocks of the Near East (not just of sheep, but of sheep and goats mixed). '[L]ike sheep' in most Versions erroneously suggests individual movement rather than the collective motion of a mass as Romans 5:12 teaches.

More to the point, the *character* of the sin in which in Adam we *collectively* participated is not personal and not even consciously committed by the confessors, then or now. 'Have gone astray' might more exactly be translated 'went astray' (*taʿinu* Kal. perf. 1 c.plc. from [*taʿah*], go astray, wander, err). It all happened long ago, and still happens every day. The word characterizes not so much willful, rebellious 'sin with a high hand' as sins of innate weakness (see Isa. 16:8; 28:7; Pss. 58:3; 107:4; and 119:176), 'I have gone astray like a lost sheep.' Thus through no personal act of our own we participate in the sinful nature of our human kind. We are innately disposed to go astray. It is inherited sin whereby as one flock every human being has wandered away from God and become lost to Him except by rescue. This must receive special treatment later. It is 'not doing the things we ought to have done.'

2. *Men are individually sinners by choice*. The sequence of words of Isaiah 53:6 in Hebrew reads: 'Each to his own way has turned,' each (*'ish*, singular, distributive) is emphatic. The language is of the up to date, the here and now. Individual, personal sins are confessed. The sense of the word for each is rendered 'every man' (twice in Num. 16:17 KJV) and '*each* [emphasis added]... for himself' (Num. 31:53). And in this aspect, the character of sin is a personal act, 'every man for himself' deliberately chosen. This turning from the way of life, of obedience to divine commandment, contrary to the voice of conscience is, of course, what we have seen of sin as *commission* (rebellion, transgression, trespass, revolt and the like). This kind of moral offense in personal life is the fruit of Adamic sin (cf. Ps. 14:1 with Rom. 3:10 ff.).

3. *Sins of omission and commission are culpable*, that is, blameworthy, guilty, deserving of *punishment*, viz.: 'And the LORD caused to strike on him the punishment due all of us' (Isa. 53:6). It is of great importance that this clause lifts to highest prominence the word *ʿawon* (in the Versions, *iniquity*), as the precise burden our Lord bore at Calvary: that which in David's language is non-imputed to the contrite, believing and confessing sinner (Ps. 32:2), and which was imputed to the atoning Servant, viz.: 'the iniquities [guilt] of us all.' Cain said 'My *punishment* [emphasis added] [*ʿawon*] is greater than I can bear' (Gen 4:13). Through the prophet (Amos 3:2) God declares, 'Therefore, I will visit (*'ephqodh* from *paqadh*, to effect something upon, often rendered visit upon, in certain contexts) upon you all your punishments' (lit. trans.); this literal rendering gives the more precise sense of *ʿawon*, focusing on guilt and punishment, the results of transgression and sin.

A lengthy monograph would not exhaust the evidences for the above summary of the basic vocabulary about sin in Scripture.

Vocabulary of Sin in Common Speech of the Bible.

The very large number and variety of terms for moral evil is more a reflection of common speech about moral evil than a source for divine revelation on the subject. Bible dictionaries, which one might expect to go into some detail, do not do so. This I judge to be because the number and variety of biblical terms, aside from the more technical ones we have already discussed, are more a reflection of common speech about moral evil in ancient times than fruitful source for divine revelation on the subject. In agreement with this opinion I will present and discuss very briefly several of these words which in one way or another make us aware of how truly various are the manifestations and shades of moral evil and how great the dangers are from it.

Sin is an unpaid debt: we owe divine justice, or perhaps better, duty to God that we have not performed, as in the petition, 'forgive us our debts' (*opheilēma*, Matt. 6:12).[5] An examination of this word and related (*opheilē* and *opheilō*), owe, or be indebted, and *opheiletēs*, debtor (rendered 'offenders' at Luke 13:4, 'sinners' in KJV), shows we human beings enter this world to be God's servants and instead pay our debt of service to sin and the devil.

Agnoēma, 'errors' (KJV), 'sins... committed in ignorance' (NIV), appears only once in the Bible. It is used at Hebrews 9:7 in connection with the Old Testament sacrificial ritual for 'sins of ignorance' (cf. Heb. 5:1-3; and Lev. 4, 5, 22; and Num. 24–29). 'Folly is bound up in the heart of a child' (Prov. 22:15) and 'The devising of folly

---

4. (*ts'on*), means 'literally, small cattle [i.e. domestic animals], usually of sheep and goats in one flock' (*BDB*, p. 838).

5. Some incautious efforts to update scriptural language, such as to substitute 'debts' by 'sins' in the Lord's Prayer, are severely mistaken. *Opheilēma* means unpaid debt. Sin is the broader term, including unpaid obligations. The prayer is referring to our debt to love the Lord thy God with all thy heart, soul and mind, etc.

is sin' (Prov. 24:9). We are born with a wisdom deficit and never get over it, for as Peter says, men of every age are 'willingly... ignorant' (2 Peter 3:5 KJV), 'exchanged the truth about God for a lie' (Rom. 1:25) and 'did not like to retain God in their knowledge' (Rom 1:28 KJV).

Hēttēma, 'fault', appears only twice: of these only once as moral evil, in 1 Corinthians 6:7, 'there is utterly a fault [*hēttōn*] among you' (KJV); in Romans 11:12 rendered 'failure' (ESV) or 'diminishing' (KJV) and related to the verb *hēttaomai*, 'to be inferior,' and *hēttōn*, 'worse' or 'less,' this word for moral evil designates the condition of being less or worse than one ought to be – a failure to improve on opportunities. This, of course, as life goes on and one grows older bears fruit in envy and jealousy of others who are better and have more – particularly the poor man's sin. Material poverty is no sign of superior spirituality.

The atmosphere of Old Testament religion and conscience does not seem ever to sever guilt from threatened punishment (or possible atonement) from any aspect of sin or any word for the same. Existentialist philosophers often refer to the concept of dread or despair, which they hold to be an aspect of human finitude. Hence all people fear death and the unknown to follow. Paul Tillich, an existential theologian defined the task of theology as one of 'correlation,' 'namely the correlation between existential questions and theological answers.'[6] For Tillich, who rejected Scripture and the historical Christ Jesus as revelation, the question to be given an answer 'by correlation' is 'death, finitude and guilt.'[7] He really gives no answer other than the equivalent of Henley's *Invictus*, a counsel of despair:

> It matters not how strait the gate,
> How backed with punishments the scroll.
> I am the master of my fate.
> I am the captain of my soul.

The most specific biblical word for guilt as deserved punishment is *'asham*. The focus may be on some feature of omission or commission, but modern discovery and translation of ancient Near East literary remains shows the Hebrew people and their neighbors were unable to conceive of sins without devastating consequences – and God agreed. This the affair of Abraham's wife Sarah and Abimelech (Gen. 20:1-17, especially v. 9), and of Isaac's wife Rebekah and Abimilech (Gen. 26:6-11, especially v. 10) amply demonstrates. Pharaoh interpreted the 'great plagues' as punishment for taking away a man's wife (Gen. 12:17-19); Abimelech was warned that punishment would follow what the Philistine king himself called a 'great sin' (Gen. 26:9) with attending punishment, God being his informant (Gen. 26:6-7). In the incident of Genesis 26, after Isaac's affectionate display gave public lie to his claim Rebekah was only his sister, Abimelech complained: 'What is this you have done to us? One of the people might easily have lain with your wife, and you would have brought guilt [*'asham*] upon us' (Gen. 26:10). This word, and its derivatives, is the most comprehensive word for sin. 'The primary meaning of the word *'asham* seems to center on guilt, but moves from the act which brings guilt to the condition of guilt to the act of punishment.'[8] A learned article says, '...*'asham* varies in stress. It may denote acts of sin, responsibility for sin, punishment, and even the aftermath of punishment... the totality of alienation from God, including consequences.'[9]

The most specific New Testament word for sin as transgression of divine law is *parabainō* (transgress, break, deviate from the way, overstep) and its noun derivative, *parabatēs* (transgressor) and *parabasis* (transgression). This is normally used in the New Testament when sin is viewed in relation to God's will or law. Jesus said the Pharisees and scribes 'break [*parabainō*, "transgress" KJV] the commandment of God for the sake of your tradition' (Matt. 15:3); Paul, 'You who boast in the law dishonor God by breaking [*parabasis*] the law' (Rom. 2:23); and James, 'you are... convicted by the law as transgressors' (James 2:9).

Each of these words emphasizes some aspect of the biblical doctrine of sin, though no single one may be said either to define sin comprehensively or to designate the essence of sin.

Literature.

The literature of research into the biblical terms for and vocabulary for sin is endless. We have quoted and cited some of it already in the *Wycliffe Bible Encyclopedia*. A very superior article, remarkable for its brevity, is 'sin,' by C. C. Ryrie and R. A. Killen.[10]

---

6. Paul Tillich, *Systematic Theology I* (Chicago: Univ. of Chicago Press, 1957), p. 13.
7. ibid., pp. 66–68.
8. G. H. Livingston, art. in *TDOT I*, p. 78.
9. ibid., p. 79.
10. Ryrie and Killen, *Wycliffe Bible Encyclopedia II* (Chicago: Moody Press, 1975), pp. 1593–1595.

Sometimes the accomplishments even of prominent saints and scholars of previous generations are neglected simply because the welter of recent literature submerges it in obscurity. Even so an occasional accolade is paid to the superb chapters on sin in the *Old Testament Theology* of Herman Schultz. In his chapter XIV (Vol. II) 'Manifestation and Names of Sin in Israel,' in eleven pages, Schultz sets forth the data I have presented in classical elegant language of the nineteenth century with all the technical evidence in footnotes. If it were possible I would have inserted it into my book without modification instead of my less elegant, modest prose. I close this chapter with an exemplary quote from Schultz on 'the stages and climax of sin' from the above-mentioned chapter.

> Notwithstanding the variety of its forms, the sin of Israel is all of a piece. From comparatively small beginnings it advances step by step to its utmost height. From the most innocent forms, in which it still has a pleasing aspect, sin goes on growing till it openly boasts of its devilish hostility to God. It commences with sinful feelings in the heart, which even the good and pious still experience (e.g. Ps. 73:2; Prov. 4:23 ff.); with the sins of youth which are chargeable to human frailty – for 'stolen waters are sweet' (Job 13:26; Pss. 25:7; 19:13; Prov. 9:17). It commences with that rather innocent ignorance which God is still able to excuse. 'They are foolish, and know not what is right' (Pss. 19:13; 90:8; cf. Jer. 5:4). There is a sinful state in which the sinner still feels his sin a burden, a misery from which he seeks restoration and deliverance (Ps. 51:5; Prov. 9:4). But out of this rather animal state of nature, sin does its best to grow. It keeps firm hold of the will, until it ceases to struggle. It saturates with its poison the innermost parts of the Ego. It turns sinners into enemies of God, men who do evil habitually, and who yield themselves up wholly, with all their personal faculties and gifts (Pss. 6:9; 14:4; 37:1-7), as instruments of evil (Ps. 37:20; Deut. 5:9).
>
> The highest stage of sin is likewise shown by the shamelessness with which it flaunts itself openly. The fool, the scorner, despises rebuke; correction only makes him worse (Prov. 1:7; 9:7 ff.), he knoweth not shame (Zeph. 3:5). The boldness of its countenance testifies against God's people when, like Sodom, it openly proclaims its sin (Isa. 3:9; Hosea 5:5; Jer. 3:3; 6:15; 7:12). This is shown in wanton disregard of a neighbor's interests, when one considers everything allowable that one has the power to do (Micah 2:1). But the most terrible display of the real nature of sin is when a man delights in evil because it is evil, and loathes good because it is good (Micah 3:2, 9; Ps. 52:5). Then bitter is called sweet, and darkness light (Isa. 5:20; Amos 6:12; cf. Matt. 12:31). Then whosoever eschews evil is declared an outlaw (Isa. 5:15; cf. Prov. 29:27). Then men hate light and truth (Job 24:13), and rejoice over the misfortune of a neighbor (Ps. 35:11 ff.; 41:6 ff.). Nay more, they have no longer even the natural instinct of a brute beast for what is wholesome and good. They seek after their own hurt (Isa. 1:2 ff.; Jer. 8:4 ff.).
>
> At this stage, when a man takes delight in doing mischief, and cannot rest without doing it, when he is wise to do evil and 'exults the more, the greater the evil is' (Prov. 2:14; 4:16; Jer. 4:22; cf. Isa. 29:20), he is of course irretrievably lost. When one has grieved God's Holy Spirit (Isa. 63:10; 65:3), has, as it were, bidden God adieu (Job 1:11; 2:5, 9; 12:6; Ps. 10:3), the heart has then become insensible to every saving influence. Then it has to be said: 'As the Ethiopian cannot change his skin, nor the leopard his spots, so this people cannot do good, because it is accustomed to do evil' (Jer. 13:23; cf. 4:22; 7:24 ff.; 9:2, 4; Isa. 6). The soul of the wicked desires evil; he makes a jest of infamy (Prov. 9:23; 21:10; cf. Ps. 11:5).[11]

---

11. Hermann Schultz, *Old Testament Theology*, trans. J. A. Paterson (Edinburgh: T. & T. Clarke, 1892), pp. 289–291.

3
The Nature of Sin: Sin As Moral Evil

The Roman Church had already developed elaborate formulations of a doctrine of sin when the Reformation broke upon Europe. It was mainly a philosophical overlay of traditional and biblical concepts. The Reformers and immediate successors did not attempt a philosophical definition of sin. A Protestant perspective on sin began with Luther's acute consciousness of sin and from that day to this the progress of evangelistic, missionary, Protestant Christianity has begun its appeal to lost sinners with gospel preaching designed first to awaken sinners to their sad plight as condemned sinners (John 3:36). In preaching and missionary evangelism 'Law and Gospel' march together. Unless men's hearts are convinced and convicted of sin, grace has no meaning for them. Without necessarily defining law the preacher uses law. He seeks to bring truth to bear on conscience. He designs through Word and Spirit to make listening sinners aware of God, His will and law before whom they stand condemned. Like Paul, we expound divine law and human sin 'that every mouth may be stopped, and the whole world may be held accountable to God' (Rom. 3:19; see also Rom. 1:32; 2:12-14; 4:15; Heb. 10:26-31). The repentant thief (Luke 23:41), Isaiah in the temple (Isa. 6:5) and Peter in the presence of God manifest in flesh (Luke 5:8) needed no course in a theology of sin to know they were sinners under the judgment of divine law.

Sin Is Moral Evil.

There is still no agreed formal definition of sin. 'There is a variety of description in the Bible rather than formal definition, hence the various elements must be gathered together.'[1] G. C. Berkouwer rightly asserts:

> No one has ever defined sin in a way that embraces the multiplicity of the Biblical expressions. Such attempts have been made, of course, and have utilized a number of images to fill out our picture of 'sin'... That very multiplicity in expressions should caution us against a preference for any single term.[2]

In view of the way the Bible speaks about sin, however, there can be no doubt about its ethical character. It is not *mere* calamity that wreaks havoc among people. It is not merely social disruption. Contemporary loss of such words as fornication to 'sexually active,' 'adulterer and adulteress' to 'girl friend' and 'boy friend,' shows how far the

---

1. J. E. Kuizenga on 'Sin' in *International Standard Bible Encyclopedia IV*, p. 2798.
2. G. C. Berkouwer, *Studies in Dogmatics: Sin V* (Grand Rapids: Eerdmans, 1971), p. 255.

shapers of current thought and speech have moved public discourse from sound conscience and biblically shaped public awareness. In biblical teaching men are not mere victims of social evil. They are not mere passive captives of genetic misfortune. We are responsible for what we are and do. The Bible from Genesis chapter 3 onward to Revelation chapter 22 addresses us this way. Only personal moral beings can commit sins, and only they can be guilty of sin, and only they can understand what sin, i.e. moral evil, is. We are not under the control of irresistible forces or we would not be addressed by commands; nor would we be responsible for our behavior. A berserk elephant tramples its keeper and some spectators, but if blame is assigned it is likely to be laid on the keeper or the spectator. A panther attacked a San Diego jogger and even though the animal was shot later it was not because the animal was wicked. Animals can be dangerous but not sinful. Only personal moral beings can be instructed in moral good or evil. The immediate consciousness of moral beings may be addressed. The word 'ought' has meaning to them for the very center of being answers to it. 'He knows that when he is not what he *ought* to be; when he does what he *ought* not to do; or omits what he *ought* to do, he is chargeable with sin.'[3] Alfred M. Rehwinckel opens his book, *The Voice of Conscience,* with the following correct account of the universal awareness of 'I ought':

> When God created man, He did not make him only potentially a moral being: he was by his very essence a moral being. There was in him not only a knowledge of the will of God, but also a readiness to apply such knowledge as an ethical norm for his own will and his whole life. For God placed in him a natural aptitude, thereby his moral responsibility was spontaneously suggested to his consciousness and endowed him with the readiness and the power to respond accordingly. After the Fall this mysterious faculty in man is the most sublime… and most perplexing problem of human existence.[4]

Sin Is Primarily Against God.

The Bible represents sin as an attack against one or all of three parties. (1) Sin is an offense against the sinner himself. He is the first to suffer from it – in conscience. This is more than an inference drawn from the many stories of accusing conscience, which show this to be true. Numerous pieces of practical exhortation in the Proverbs expressly say so, viz.: 'he that sinneth against me wrongeth his own soul' (Prov. 8:36 KJV); 'He who commits adultery lacks sense; he who does it destroys himself' (Prov. 6:32; see also 18:6-8; 29:6). 'The coward dies a thousand deaths; a brave man dies but once' (old English proverb).

(2) Sin may be against other individuals and society as a whole. David's wicked decision to number all Israel was an offense against his kingdom (2 Sam. 24:1-10) resulting in the death of 70,000 people (2 Sam. 24:15). 'Bad company corrupts good character' (1 Cor. 15:33 NIV). Adam's sin brought disaster upon the whole human race (Rom. 5:12-19).

(3) Against God. Herman Schultz pointed out that from Amos onward Old Testament prophets were careful to show that 'manifold forms of sensuality and selfishness are at bottom a result of opposition to the will of God – that is, to God Himself, the whole of Israel's sin is really "a sin against God alone" (Ps. 2:6; cf. Jer. 8:7; 14:7, 20; 16:10; Isa. 42:24).'[5] The 'prodigal son' knew that he had harmed himself and had sinned against his father but when 'he came to himself' he determined to say, 'Father, I have sinned against heaven and before you' (Luke 15:18). Samuel was aware he would 'sin against the LORD by ceasing to pray' for Saul (1 Sam. 12:23). Disobedience to the law was seen by God's prophet to be sin against the LORD (Isa. 42:24). For Abimelech to take another man's wife was sin, not so much against Abraham and Sarah, who had brought their lying scheme down on their own heads, as against God the Creator and Lord of all His servants. '[I]t was I who kept you from sinning against me. Therefore I did not let you touch her' (Gen. 20:6).

David was aware he had done great harm to Bathsheba and Uriah her husband, to his family and kingdom as well as himself, yet in his conscience the offense of adultery was only against God. There had already been destructive personal and social consequences, but his agitated tongue could only say to Nathan 'I have sinned against the LORD' (2 Sam. 12:13) and his anxious pen could only write 'Against you, you only, have I sinned and done what is evil in your sight' (Ps. 51:4).

---

3. Charles A. Hodge, *Systematic Theology I* (Grand Rapids: Eerdmans, 1960), p. 181.
4. Alfred M. Rehwinckel, *The Voice of Conscience* (St Louis: Concordia Publ. Co., 1956), pp. 1, 2.
5. Herman Schultz, *Old Testament Theology*, trans. J. A. Paterson (Edinburgh: T. & T. Clarke, 1892), p. 288.

It may be that David's conscience was impressing on him the infinite wrong of sin against God in defiling God's image in himself and another man's wife and this moved him to say 'Against you only I have sinned' (*ḥaṭṭa'thi*). In the strictest sense it was not his own law he had broken or Bathsheba and Uriah's, but God's law. This gave his evil thought and acts a moral character. David goes on – 'and done that which is evil [*hara'*] in thy sight.' With reference to the affected people in such a case, the general term 'evil' would cover the material, physical, social harm. Bathsheba had conceived out of wedlock. She had been put to public shame and her husband was dead.

In its primary and distinctive character as sin, therefore, moral evil is only God-related. One may act wickedly so as to 'wrong his own soul' (Prov. 8:36) and do harm to others, but in its peculiar character as 'sin,' moral evil is specifically against God. '[T]he whole duty of man' is to 'Fear God and keep his commandments' (Eccles. 12:13). As Jesus Himself said: '[The] great and first commandment' is to 'love the Lord your God with all your heart and with all your soul and with all your mind' (Matt. 22:37). Conscience agrees with Scripture that offenses against self and neighbor are wrong because both are in the divine image. All belong to *Him*. All mankind are *His* servants.

The fields of psychology and sociology, even civil justice and penology, seem confused today in their operational philosophy by the lack of awareness of the God-relatedness of all human beings and of all human conduct. Without God-relatedness there can be social harm to be restrained, social utility to be promoted, but no moral evil to be reproved, punished or pardoned. 'Whatever is is right' (Alexander Pope) is 'enlightenment' philosophy, which has produced its own brand of denial of certainties of all kinds.

In eagerness, I suppose, to give a name to the burst of this confusion among people generally – at least the ones we professors meet – someone invented the term 'post-modern.' But it is also pre-modern, at least as old as the ancient Greek cynics and Pilate's cynical question, 'What is truth?'

Sin Is Moral Evil in Relation to God's Will and His Law.

In the context of this sentence 'will' means the general moral inclination of the Creator not any particular 'wish' or decree or plan. Law also in this connection is God's general standard for all moral beings. These do not change and there are no exceptions, whereas God's particular will and standard may vary. It was God's will for Jacob to move from Canaan to Egypt as it was also for Joseph and Mary to move from Egypt to Nazareth, but not law until they were informed about it. Earlier it was not the will of God for Abraham to go to Egypt; His orders (law) were to go as far as Canaan only. These are particular. The Decalogue is an expression of God's will in general, and expressed either on tablets of stone or written on the fleshy tablets of the heart is to be obeyed by all men everywhere and at all times.

Since God is holy, His will is holiness – perfect moral goodness – for every moral being. Lack of conformity to divine law, therefore, constitutes sin as sin. Its root is the very essence of uncongeniality of the creature's fallen nature with the Creator's perfectly holy nature. 'Be ye holy, for I am holy' is the permanent order of the created heaven and earth, but any man who glimpses that holiness becomes immediately aware he is not holy at all. Yet he knows he ought to be and must be.

For these reasons many good theologians have defined sin as lack of conformity to the character or will of God which, when expressed in any manner at all, is the law of God. This is not to say sin is *defined* as lawlessness in Scripture, though 'sin is lawlessness' (1 John 3:4) reads like a definition. Alford (also C. A. Hodge) is right in saying the sentence is convertible, viz.: lawlessness is sin. The sentence says something about sin and law but defines nothing any more than to say 'milk is a liquid' defines milk or 'trees are tall' defines trees. 'It is only one of many seeming definitions of sin.' G. C. H. Berkouwer is correct when he says:

> No one has ever defined our sin in a way that embraces the multiplicity of biblical expressions… That very multiplicity of expressions should caution us against a preference for any single term [i.e. one of the many Hebrew and Greek terms]….
>
> We agree that when scripture describes our sin we sometimes get the impression that it gives a 'definition.' Nonetheless its descriptions are never meant in an exclusive sense. 'Sin is lawlessness,' we read in 1 John 3:4, yet that same letter combines the terms *lawlessness* and *godlessness,* and both are viewed in close connection with *unrighteousness* and *wrongdoing* (1 John 5:17). It is incorrect to say that these biblical expressions 'complete' each other. At the same time they are mutually illuminating and ought to be seen as such.[6]

---

6. Berkouwer, *op. cit*, pp. 255, 256.

In a similar way, 'God is love' is not a definition of God any more than 'Our God is a consuming fire.' Some would make one or the other such, but only to produce an unbalanced and incorrect doctrine of God.

Sin in the members of our race is an internal *disorder*. Our nature made in the likeness of God with regard to moral disposition, thought-life and acts is now contrary to the divine will. A constitutional distortion of the moral nature has occurred. This unlikeness to God is sin. 'As the opposite of reason is unreason, and the opposite of good is evil; so the opposite of the divine holiness is sin. It is not mere negation or absence of the good (Augustine notwithstanding), for the positive aspect of sin is opposition to God's moral will and law' (C. A. Hodge). 'For the mind that is set on the flesh is hostile to God, for it does not submit to God's law; indeed, it cannot' (Rom. 8:7).

Faith in God involves acceptance of God's Person and Word and will. Hence 'whatever does not proceed from faith is sin' (Rom. 14:23). In context neither is this text a definition of sin. Rather, it states a principle of Christian morality, which is that for an act to be righteous it must be done in reverence of God. Otherwise it is sin. '[S]in is lawlessness,' i.e. *anomia*. It is sinful to do anything in disregard of divine law.

Every one of the words for sin in all its aspects in Scripture in one way or another has reference either to failure to come up to the standard of divine law or to breaking divine law. And throughout the Bible, as in human conscience everywhere, God 'the Judge of all the earth' (Gen. 18:25) sets the standard.

Sin Is Not Restricted to 'Voluntary Acts.'

To change the form of the statement: 'It is a grave error to say that only conscious and deliberate actions against God's will constitutes sin.'[7] Scripture says we are 'by nature children of wrath' (Eph. 2:3), i.e. we come into the world deserving God's wrath, long prior to conscious life and before we are capable of moral decisions. Sometimes, Paul says, when we want to do good, moral evil is already present in us, warring against any good impulses (Rom. 7:17-24). Many heinous crimes are committed entirely without previous reflective thought. They are sometimes produced by habits of response that in turn flow from the fallen, sinful condition of the soul.

Bondage of the Will or Freedom of the Will?

This question must be related to a proper understanding of what is meant by the word, will, and in what sense the will is free or in bondage. Reformation theology rejected the Roman theology on this point. According to many Roman scholastic theologians and even some official canons and decrees, only deliberate acts can be sins. The Council of Trent (assembled to answer the evangelical doctrines of the Reformation) was not entirely clear on the subject. We may safely take the citations by Henry Denzinger as sufficiently trustworthy. The official 'Systematic Index' of the volume summarizes Roman Catholic teaching regarding the relation of the knowledge and will of persons to sin. The Systematic Index summarizes numerous dogmatic sources throughout this famous book, viz.:

> To sin (actual) there is presupposed a knowledge of the law, whence it is not committed with invincible ignorance, but nevertheless with vincible; moreover, it ought to be a voluntary act, by a personal will; placed with true freedom, not only from coercion, but from necessity.[8]

The Papal Bull, '*Exsurge Domine*' of 15 June 1520, which condemned all the 'errors' of Martin Luther's earliest teaching, condemned Luther's denial of free will among sinful men.[9]

Papal anthropology teaches that the 'image of God' in man at creation (Gen. 1:26) consisted in his rational and spiritual faculties only. The 'image of God' is permanent and unaffected by the fall. The 'likeness' is not a natural endowment of Adam and his descendants, but a 'superadded' 'supernatural gift.' This likeness is said to be Adam's original righteousness (moral purity). As a consequence of the fall the superadded gift of righteousness was withdrawn. The rational, spiritual nature remained unaffected by the fall to the extent that man is fully able to perform acts of will (choice, etc.) freely.

W. G. T. Shedd said of the dogmatic teaching of the Council of Trent: 'Original righteousness being a supernatural gift, original sin is the loss of it, and in reality the restoration of man back again to the state in which he was created.'[10] In this, Trent differs from the main line of Augustinian anthropology in the earlier Catholic tradition. Bellarmine, semi-official expositor of Trent, remarks as follows:

---

7. Francis Pieper, *Christian Dogmatics I* (St Louis: Concordia Publ., 1950), p. 528.
8. Henry Denzinger, *The Sources of Catholic Dogma* (St Louis: B. Herder Co., 1957), 'Indexes,' p. 47.
9. ibid., pp. 775, 776.
10. William G. Shedd, *History of Christian Doctrine II* (2 Volumes, Grand Rapids, MI: Minneapolis, MN: Klock & Klock Christian Publ., 1978), p. 146.

> The state of man after the fall differs no more from the state of man as created... than a man originally naked differs from one who was once clothed... Hence, the corruption of nature results not from the subtraction of any gift belonging to [human] nature by *creation* nor from the addition of any evil quality, but solely from the loss of a supernatural gift which was over and above the gifts of nature.[11]

The Fifth Session of the Council of Trent declares:

> [C]oncupiscence, which at times the Apostle calls *sin* [Rom 6:12 ff.] [i.e. indwelling sin] the holy synod declares that the Catholic Church has never understood to be called sin, as truly and properly sin in those born again [i.e. by baptism], but because it is from sin and inclines to sin. But if anyone [Reformation theologians] is of the contrary opinion, let him be anathema.[12]

I quote these statements to assure the reader that even though some Roman Catholic theologians do not fully agree, church dogma rejects the teaching that man at heart is a sinner with a depraved will.

Three Senses of 'Will' and 'Voluntary'.

It will be helpful to point out there are different senses of 'will' and 'voluntary' in theological discourse. To be disposed by nature, or inclined by disposition, i.e. to be inherently and by habit disposed in the direction either of holiness or of sin is properly called will. To say truly as Paul, 'I delight in the law of God, in my inner being' (Rom. 7:22) [even when delight fails of accomplishment] or 'his delight is in the law of the LORD' spoken about the blessed man of Psalm 1:2, or the words of Psalm 40:8, referring to Messiah in His First Advent, quoted by Hebrews 10:7: 'I desire to do your will, O my God; your law is within my heart' (see also John 4:34 and 5:30) – all these designate the renewed will at the center of being, the heart.

Paul refers to the 'mind that is set on the flesh' ('carnal mind' KJV) which 'is hostile to God' (Rom. 8:7) and says, 'Those who are in the flesh cannot please God' (Rom. 8:8) and 'The natural person does not accept the things of the Spirit of God, for they are folly to him, and he is not able to understand them because they are spiritually discerned' (1 Cor. 2:14). This invariable inclination away from the holy creator-God, even though the heart be empty of all true joy without Him, is what Reformation theology calls 'the depraved will.' To it Jesus traced all sinful deeds and expressions. This sinful will He characterized as a sinful heart (Mark 7:20-23; Matt. 12:34, 35; Luke 6:45; Matt. 15:18). In all these texts 'heart' refers to the very center of our being, what the depth psychologists explore, discuss and ruminate about endlessly. They are on to something real, however, even though being without an adequate anthropology they cannot put an ethical value on their findings.

The Protestant doctrine of sin – both Lutheran and Reformed-Calvinist – as opposed to Roman and Arminian-Wesleyan, has consistently recognized three proper senses of the word 'will' in connection with the question of whether sin is confined to 1) deliberate, conscious choices of the will, but also 2) spontaneous actions rooted in affections or tastes, and 3) fixed habits or states of disposition.

As for the *first*, deliberate, conscious choices, one need not be an astute theologian to regard all acts of deliberate, conscious choice contrary to God's will and law as sin. That, however, is only the most obvious sense of the word 'will.'

A *second* sense of 'will' includes all spontaneous expressions of our feelings, loves and hates whether inherited or acquired. If these lead to evil actions, even if there is no reflective thought involved, the actions are sinful and are punishable, even in the civil laws of mankind.

As for the *third*, I shall seek to demonstrate that actions rooted in innate disposition or even acquired habits, if wrongful, are voluntary and properly classed as willful and sinful.

One of the most convincing treatments of this subject I know is by W. G. T. Shedd 'The Human Will.'[13] Other excellent treatments by writers of systematic theology are by Francis Pieper who cites the Lutheran confessional documents in support of the position taken here and writes, 'The Apology [to the *Augsburg Confession*] designates the teaching that only consciousness, deliberation, voluntariness belong to the essence of sin as a pagan error'[14] – see also C. A. Hodge,[15] and A. H. Strong, whose treatment is the best organized, focused and convincing on this point in print.[16] I am heavily indebted to his marshaling of the evidence.

---

11. Bellarmin, *De Gratia Primi Hominia* as cited by Shedd, ibid., pp. 148, 149.
12. Denzinger, *Sources of Catholic Dogma*, p. 792.
13. William Shedd, *History of Christian Doctrine* Chapter III, pp. 115–147.
14. Pieper, *Christian Dogmatics*, pp. 528, 529.

Is Sin to Be Defined As 'a Voluntary Transgression of Known Law'?

This question arises mainly because of John Wesley, the founder of the Methodist Church, the second largest denomination in English-speaking lands. Throughout most of his long ministry Wesley insisted on defining sin as voluntary transgression of known law. Wesley's definition was more often heard in discussions a couple of generations ago when Methodists in particular and other 'main line' denominations were more interested in personal salvation from sin than they have been through the recent social action epoch. In recent years, however, conservative evangelical Wesleyans have revived interest in Wesley's definition. New biographies of Wesley and new editions of his works are now being read. The Wesleyan holiness movements of say 1825 to 1950 in America have lost their aggressive force. Present-day 'holiness' preaching and literature seems to retreat from some nineteenth-century extremes and to seek to be more purely Wesleyan. Their scholars are expositors of the Wesley canon.

Albert C. Outler, who died in 1989, was perhaps the leading interpreter of Methodist doctrinal teaching in the twentieth century from his position at Perkins School of Theology. Outler was General Editor of *The Works of John Wesley*. In one of his latest works, Outler shows how Wesley's definition of sin is related to his doctrine of perfection. Outler affirms Wesley did not go so far as some later Methodist holiness movements with their doctrines of 'entire sanctification' 'as a second and separate work of grace.'[17] Yet many passages from Wesley biographies and even Wesley's works seem to teach something distinctly like that. I think Outler means Wesley did not think of entire sanctification as 'eradication of the old nature' – a phrase that seems to have passed out of 'holiness' vocabulary about 1965.

(In a class at Trinity Divinity School a few years ago I had just finished a lecture in which I identified the Mennonite Brethren in Christ [now United Missionary Church] as holding to eradication of the 'old nature.' At the end of class a student member of that group informed me the denomination had abandoned that doctrine. A few days later he brought a copy of their official statement of faith. It clearly affirmed progressive sanctification as in Reformation theology.)

As Wesley developed his doctrine of sin and sanctification in the face of criticism from other evangelicals of his day, it came to be taught that by employing some Wesleyan 'Methods' (hence Methodism) a state of perfection could be attained. Ogden says:

> In his view, 'perfection' may be 'realized' in a given moment (always a gift from God, received by trusting faith), yet never a finished state [one can lose it]. 'Perfection' connotes two conjoining 'powers': (1) the power to love God wholeheartedly, and (2) the power not to commit sin voluntarily ('sin properly so-called') which Wesley consistently defined as 'a violation of a known law of God.'[18]

Outler earlier affirms Wesley 'distinguished between voluntary sins (sin properly so-called) and our involuntary shortfallings (wandering thoughts, sin in believers, etc.),'[19] I do not find in Outler's remarks any clearer statements. Outler is more interested in showing development of Wesley's ideas than extended systematic display of them.

The same is not true of L. G. Cox, an outright evangelical scholar, which Outler was not. Cox's chapter on 'Sin and Grace' is plain.[20] Wesley had a grimly pessimistic view of fallen human nature. 'Man by nature is wholly corrupted, according to Wesley.'[21] Wesley said, 'Allow this, and you are so far a Christian. Deny it, and you are but a Heathen still.' Even though he defined sin as voluntary transgression of known law he believed all men are 'guilty of Adam's sin.'[22] Hence for Wesley, salvation is by grace alone (*sola gratia*). He did not however teach the usual Protestant doctrine of election. God does take the initiative. Wesley thus agreed *in part* with Calvinists. There is a 'common grace,' which God gives to all men. This grace, which Wesley called *prevenient* grace, makes orderly human life possible. In addition, according to Wesley (but not by either Lutheran or Calvinist theologians), by grace God has freed every man's will. He thought it better to call this extra benefit *preventing* grace. Unless one has quenched the

---

15. C. A. Hodge, *Systematic Theology II* (Grand Rapids: Eerdmans, 1960), pp. 186–188.
16. A. H. Strong, *Systematic Theology* (Valley Forge, PA: Judson Press, 1907), pp. 549–559.
17. Albert C. Outler, ed. T. C. Ogden and L. R. Longden, *The Wesleyan Theological Heritage* (Grand Rapids: Zondervan, 1991), p. 122.
18. ibid., pp. 121, 122.
19. ibid., p. 86.
20. L. G. Cox, *John Wesley's Concept of Perfection* (Kansas City, MO: Beacon Hill Press, 1964), pp. 27–67.
21. ibid., p. 28.
22. ibid., pp. 28, 29.

Spirit, every man is given 'conscience' and sooner or later has 'good desires.' These have been imparted (infused?) by grace (here defined not as unmerited favor as the Reformers did), 'So that no man sins because he has not grace, but because he does not use the grace he hath.'[23] God has restored to everyone the power to turn to God as an act of divine grace (not of justice as in Arminius).

So, we are on the way to understanding: 'a constant and clear teaching of Wesley and Wesleyans has been that the believer does not commit sin.'[24] From the Reformation point of view we are guilty for our sinful nature, under wrath as 'children of disobedience.' For Wesley, even though a Christian who has attained perfection still has remaining sin of nature (now thoroughly repressed), he bears a sort of 'guilt' for it but is not condemned for it. We are condemned only for personal acts of sin. These only are sin *proper*, 'voluntary transgression of known law.'[25] 'It is this willful sin that is pardoned because it alone can bring condemnation from God.... All this means... that the sin in an infant, or in a believer, is not that which makes one a sinner in the true sense of the word. It is his own personal turning to and choosing the sin as his own.'[26]

So Wesley and his true followers can define sin as voluntary transgression of known law and by this means say a sanctified believer may live without sin. I intend to show this is really declassifying much that the Bible calls sin. Wesley had no intention to deliver believers from adherence to every aspect of God's will and law, rather the opposite. He did, however, set the stage for later developments (antinomianism on the one hand, and the doctrine of entire sanctification (eradication of the fallen nature) on the other) among some of his followers. As one reads Wesley, his expositors and defenders, it becomes clear that Wesley never truly systematized his own views. As Cox, a spirited defender from the 'holiness' perspective, acknowledges, 'Wesley's opinions were too complex for many to follow him wholly.'[27]

As we shall show presently, whatever Wesley and others may have thought, the very worst forms of sin for which we are profoundly guilty are not voluntary in the sense of personal exercise of will at all, but rather in settled disposition of the heart.

> Dr. Warfield's ever present criticism of perfectionism is its inadequate notion of sin. Perfectionism is impossible, he claimed, in the presence of a profound sense of sin. The perfection of the Higher Life Movement is a subjective rather than an objective perfection, that is from 'known sin,' but not from the corruption of man's heart. And this because it ignores the fact that sin consists of any lack of conformity unto the law of God as well as transgression of that law.[28]

Is 'Concupiscence,' Even in the Regenerate, Sin?

Concupiscence, as all agree, remains even in the regenerate. Protestants, both Calvinists and Lutherans as well as others, have insisted that even before it breaks out in acts of sin, concupiscence (i.e. natural desires) is itself sinful. Catholics have said not. The confessional documents of Lutheran, Reformed and even the Anglican *Thirty-Nine Articles* say, 'Yes.' The same difference prevails to the present day among orthodox of each of these partisans. (Wesley must not have paid very close attention to this article.)

It will help us make up our minds to clarify the question and to set out the presuppositions upon which the Roman Catholics approach it from one side and all the original Protestants on the other.

Concupiscence is a very old term of theology, which now requires explanation for modern people. 'Concupiscence' (Gr. *epithumia*, literally 'on the mind') appears only three times in the Bible, 'But sin, taking occasion by the commandment, wrought in me all manner of *concupiscence* [emphasis added]' (*epithumia*) (Rom. 7:8 KJV; 'covetousness' ESV). Here it is something generated by the sin nature when stimulated by the commands of God, 'Mortify therefore your members which are upon the earth; fornication, uncleanness... evil concupiscence' (*epithumian kaken*) (Col. 3:5 KJV; 'evil desire' ESV). Concupiscence is one of several kinds of inordinate desire or sins related to uncontrolled desire. A believer is told to 'possess his vessel' (physical body) 'in sanctification and honor; Not in the lust [Gr. *pathos*, passion] of *concupiscence* [emphasis added]' (1 Thess. 4:4-5 KJV; '...not in the passion of lust' ESV). This seems to make concupiscence a source of lust, which in context is sexual desire, though perhaps pathos should be rendered as an adjective, 'lustful.'

---

23. ibid., p. 32.
24. ibid., p. 44.
25. ibid., p. 48.
26. ibid., p. 48.
27. ibid., p. 194.
28. S. C. Craig, in his *Preface* to B. B. Warfield's, *Perfectionism* (Philadelphia: Presbyterian & Reformed, 1967), p. XI.

In each case concupiscence translates *epithumia*, the Greek word for desire. Of course, in fallen man, none of our desires is pure – Adam lost that for all of us. But is desire *as such* impure? Is it sin?

In my judgment this question, which has been debated fiercely for centuries, suffers from lack of clarification of what the debate is all about. Bauer, Arndt and Gingrich supply the following information. In secular Greek the word *epithumia* is predominately employed as a morally neutral term and sometimes so in the *Septuagint*, for example, 'the desire [*epithumia*] of the righteous will be granted' (Prov. 10:24). It seems to be a neutral term in some New Testament passages, for example: Mark 4:19 ('desires for other things') and Revelation 18:14 ('fruit for which your soul *longed*' [emphasis added]). Of course, the Greek word is not rendered concupiscence in these biblical texts. The classical *Lexicon* of Liddell and Scott reports that in Herodutus and in Attic prose *epithumia* means 'longing after a thing, as water, bread, etc.' A look at the Latin dictionaries demonstrates that the primary meaning of *concupicentia* like the Greek it translates is 'an eager desire,' i.e. morally neutral.[29] The word also has a good sense, desire for ethical-spiritual, holy, pure things. In the New Testament Jesus said, 'With desire [*epithumia*] I have desired [*epithumeō*] to eat this passover with you' (Luke 22:15 KJV; 'earnestly desired' ESV) and Paul, 'I am hard pressed between the two. My desire [*epithumia*] is to depart and be with Christ' (Phil. 1:23).

There are, of course, numerous passages showing *epithumia* (concupiscence) has an evil sense, in which case in the New Testament it is the usual Greek word rendered lust.

When concupiscence was discussed by early theological writers (Tertullian, Augustine) they did not usually indicate whether they meant morally neutral desire (as for food and drink), or covetousness for riches, or the natural attraction men have to women and women to men, or inordinate lustful desire for any sort of thing.

The Fathers early got a perverted tilt toward the notion that even in marriage sexual desire is wrong. In these writers concupiscence, as a word, is almost always tilted toward a sexual frame of reference. The discussion was tainted with this misunderstanding down to the Reformation.

In Reformation times Lutherans and Calvinists asserted that righteousness (Lat. justice) was possessed by Adam as an aspect of the divine 'image' – for which 'our likeness' (Gen. 1:26) is simply a parallel term. Likeness and image are convertible terms. In such a case Adam's desires along the whole range of human interests were holy by nature. The Roman Church taught (and still teaches) that Adam's righteousness (*justitia*) was a superadded gift not an aspect of the image of God in man. So the desires of nature, inherent in the image of God, are morally neutral. If controlled by reason they issue in good, if not, then in evil. As such they are neither good nor bad.

Both the Lutherans and Calvinists and, somewhat later, Anglicans, were certain of two things: (1) separation of the image from the likeness is exegetically and theologically impossible, and (2) every part of man was vitiated by the sin of Adam. So, though desire of any kind in Adam would have been holy and good (proper for a creature in communion with his Creator), desire was not unaffected by the fall. Thus the very heart of man – his innermost being, where sin originates and from which every desire originates – is tainted, hence sinful: even so-called innocent desires for food and drink.

It has been rightly pointed out that the 'internal part' of the first sin 'was the originating and starting of a wrong inclination.' She 'desired' the fruit of a tree. Desire is what concupiscence means. 'This evil inclining and desiring is denominated "concupiscence" in theological nomenclature. In the Augustinian… anthropology [Calvinist and Lutheran and others] it includes mental as well as sensual desire; in the Pelagian anthropology, it is confined to sensual appetite.'[30]

Calvin said of Adam after he deserted his original righteousness: 'Not only did a lower appetite seduce him but… impiety occupied… his mind and pride penetrated to the depths of his heart.'[31]

Calvin rejected the medieval notion that impulses of the senses are the seat of concupiscence or the 'kindling wood' of sin and states:

> Paul removes all doubt when he teaches that corruption subsists not in one part only, but that none of the soul remains untouched by that mortal disease… the inordinate impulses of the appetites… especially the mind is given over to blindness and the heart to depravity.[32]

---

29. See the monumental *Latin-English Lexicon*, W. Freund and E. A. Andrews.
30. Shedd, *History of Christian Doctrine*, p. 179.
31. Calvin, *Institutes II*, i.,9.
32. ibid.

Shedd called attention to Luther's comments on Galatians 5:17:

> When Paul says that the flesh lusteth against the spirit, and the spirit against the flesh, he admonishes us that we must feel the concupiscence of the flesh, that is to say, not only carnal lust, but also pride, wrath, slothfulness, impatience, unbelief, and such like.[33]

In a relative sense, of course, many desires of our human nature are *as such* (if we were not fallen creatures) innocent. But we are not where Adam was before the fall. Desire is never '*as such,*' i.e. unaffected by our sinful nature. The sensations associated with appetite for food and consequent desire, for example, was probably the same in Edenic Adam as in us, but depravity at the center of fallen man today affects all our appetites. C. A. Hodge summarized the Romanist position this way:

> ...[T]he opposition between appetite [concupiscence] and reason is natural in man, and... though it be an imperfection it is not a corruption of nature. Nor have the inordinate desires [actual concupiscence] the nature of sin, being the free and deliberate transgression of the law of God [sic] can be only in the rational will [still unvitiated by the fall]; though it be true that they are temptations to sin, becoming the stronger and more frequent the oftener they have been indulged... they contract the malice of sin only when consent is given by the will... Hence the distinction of concupiscence antecedent and concupiscence consequent [note the persistent over refinement of scholastic distinctions such as antecedent and consequent] to the consent of the will; the latter is sinful, the former is not.[34]

These are not all the distinctions Romanist theology makes, but sufficient to clarify how they answer the question, 'Is concupiscence sin?' (I have not yet counted the number of kinds of 'grace' in Roman scholastic theology.)

The Council of Trent acknowledges, as we have seen earlier, that St Paul calls concupiscence antecedent to the will, sin, but asserts that he does so not because it *is* sin but because it can lead to sin.[35] The issue did not die, however, but continued to demand attention until the Bull of Pius VI, '*Auctorem fidei*' of 28 August 1794.

Let evangelical theology then stand where the sixteenth century Reformation stood: the bad news is that when mankind fell, everything about us became tainted with sin and corrupt, especially the heart. I was a pastor of a family where the godly wife and mother had a profane, raucous and promiscuous sister who visited frequently. This was a matter of grief to the husband and a strain on the family tie. Wife Zetta, who loved her wayward sister, once burst out to me as she, with tears, reported her sister's latest escapade: 'but Pastor, Lizzie is really good at heart.' Of course there was great value in the poor sister's soul, both for God and for Zetta. But the seat of the problem was precisely Lizzie's bad 'heart' where original sin remained, as in us all, and where the law of sin and death still prevailed.

It is very important to understand the basic difference between Lutheran and Reformed doctrine on the one hand and Arminian-Wesleyan and Catholic on the other to note a fact of history. The Lutheran position is clear in the *Formula of Concord*:

> ...[O]riginal sin is no trivial corruption, but so profound a corruption of human nature as to leave nothing sound, nothing uncorrupt in the body or soul of man.[36]

The concupiscence of original sin remains even in believers, according to Luther:

> ...[T]he believer... according to the flesh still has sin... There all manner of filth still clings to him, and evil concupiscence... always remains beside his faith.[37]

And according to the *Westminster Confession*, Chapter VI, 5:

> This corruption of nature, during this life, doth remain in those that are regenerated; and though it be through Christ pardoned and mortified, yet itself and all the motions thereof, are truly and properly sin.

The early Reformed leaders except for Zwingli were in complete agreement,[38] as also the official Confessions of the Reformed and Presbyterian churches. Generally so also were the many English-speaking denominations that developed out of Puritanism. Historically, the inclination to sin of our fallen nature which theologians call

---

33. Shedd, *Dogmatic Theology*, vol. 2, p. 180.
34. J. J. Ming in *Catholic Encyclopedia vol. IV* (New York: The Encyclopedia Press, 1913), p. 208.
35. Denzinger, *Sources of Catholic Dogma*, para. 792.
36. Formula of Concord, Art. I, iii, Philip Schaff, *Creeds of Christendom IV* (Grand Rapids: Baker Books, n.d.), p. 100.
37. Pieper, *Christian Dogmatics*, p. 236.
38. Pieper, *Christian Dogmatics*, p. 542, note 29.

concupiscence is sin whether or not it issues in acts of sin. They do not say hunger, thirst, social interest, the mating impulse, etc., per se, are sinful, but are seated in the fallen nature of man and therefore sinful, as is everything else about us, even after justification.[39] That concupiscence is sin was specifically rejected by John Wesley in some of his writings. Though Methodism adopted the *Thirty-Nine Articles* as its own it modified Article VII, 'Original Sin or Birth Sin' by omitting the part of Article VII which says original sin 'doth remain in them that are regenerated' and 'the apostle doth confess that concupiscence... hath of itself the nature of sin.'

---

39. See E. C. Gibson, *The Thirty-nine Articles of the Church of England*, 'Article IX, of Original Sin,' pp. 357–377, for further details of Reformation Theology of Concupiscence.

4
The Nature of Sin: Sin As Disposition

In this chapter we continue to define features of the nature of sin and to answer some related questions.

Sin Is a State or Disposition of Moral Evil (the Depths of Sin).

Among those for whom sin is esteemed to be the correct name for moral evil, who would deny that outward acts against moral standards are sin? Yet there is a common silent assumption of many that sin consists *only* in outward acts. Further, no one is so far advanced in holiness in this life as not to be reminded that 'as a man thinks in his heart so is he.'

In our time Christian doctrine no longer informs common opinion about what constitutes the soul of man. Many are not even sure there is such an entity as mankind or human nature, which might be either holy or corrupt. Behavior and 'relationships' are now the focus of attention even though motives, i.e. inner forces producing behavior, are the substance of what we now call psychological counseling. This movement calls what it tries earnestly to do, therapy. I presume there are schools of psychology which assign a moral quality to what their clients are 'at heart' when therapy starts, but we hear very little of moral judgments from psychologists. Such expressions as social harm, dysfunctional, sexually active, poorly adjusted personality, paranoid, etc., have no inherent moral content.

I have said earlier that for Christian counselors to be worthy of the name, and certainly to address the reality of their clients' condition they must come to realize that there is such a thing as a morally evil heart; further, that every human being, without exception, has such a heart. Partly because of my own experience in teaching classes of students already committed to Christian (called 'biblical') counseling, I feel it is important to point out what must be understood. This conviction has been deepened by literature on Jungian and other schools of psychology furnished to me by former students, now professors, by contacts with professors, and one of my children now a professional psychology clinician, Psy.D.

The following remarks are designed to remind believers that any departure from submission to God or lack of conformity to His law, in state or disposition – what the Bible calls the 'heart' – is sin. Perhaps some who are skeptical of the very categories of moral good and moral evil may even take notice.

Has 'Total Disability' Been Totally Annulled by Preventive (or Prevenient) Grace?

From a certain point of view, to say man is evil at heart is simply to affirm total depravity and original sin. Both of these expressions require considerable explanation if they are to be employed at all. 'Bad at heart... damned for original sin... totally depraved' are hard to accept. Such teachings seem to many to be contrary to experience. These charges seem to take too little account of the generous acts, noble aspirations and selfless charity of ancient and modern heathen – failure to notice, even among unregenerate men who never even heard of Christ, the goodness of mother love; filial piety; strivings after God; and admiration of the good, the beautiful and the true. Wesleyan theology claims that God has as an act of grace universally restored some of man's powers for good. Every man has the *restored* power under universal grace to choose Christ or to reject Him – without further divine aid. Wesley did not reject total depravity. He put it in a theoretical past, finding biblical support for his conviction in John 1:9: '[Christ]... the true light, which enlightens everyone, was coming into the world.' As previously noted herein, this is sometimes called prevenient (going before) grace or preventing (same essential meaning) grace. There are other refinements too detailed to report here. Augustinians respond that 'children of wrath' (Eph. 2:3) and 'not able to understand them' (1 Cor. 2:14) and similar texts tell us what we *actually* are – not what we would *theoretically* be apart from preventing grace.

Although L. C. Cox, Director of Ministerial Training at Marion College, of Wesleyan heritage, sets forth the Wesleyan outlook fairly,[1] for sake of brevity I quote the summary statement of another competent Wesleyan, R. G. Tuttle Jr, as follows:

> Prevenient or preventing grace for Wesley describes the universal work of the Holy Spirit in the hearts and lives of people between conception and conversion. Original sin... makes it necessary for the Holy Spirit to initiate the relationship between God and people... which prevents them from moving so far... that when they finally understand the claims of the gospel... he guarantees their freedom to say yes.[2]

A. H. Strong, while a rather strict Augustinian, was convinced that despite the utter blameworthiness of every fallen soul that fact does not mean 'the soul [is] wholly given over to the power of evil.' He says:

> While we maintain that this is true of man apart from God, we also insist side by side with the evil bent of the human will there is always an immanent divine power which greatly counteracts the force of evil, and if not resisted leads the individual soul – even when resisted leads the world at large – toward truth and salvation. This immanent power is none other than Christ, the eternal Word, the light which lighteth every man; see John 1:4, 9.[3]

Strong, however, was a believer in particular special grace and particular election, so he disagreed essentially with Wesley. His post-millennialism is evident in the above statement.

J. O. Buswell, a strict Calvinist, held to a doctrine somewhat like the 'universal enablement' of Wesley and the 'immanent divine power' suggested by Strong.[4]

> ...[A]lthough I cannot cogently prove it from the Scripture, I postulate that the convicting work of the Holy Spirit is absolutely universal to the entire human race in all ages and in all areas.[5]

Calvin went far toward what we have now seen in Wesley, Strong and prominently in Buswell, but with perhaps more precision. Having acknowledged the presence 'in every age [of those] who, guided by nature have striven toward virtue throughout life'[6] he affirms that 'amid... corruption of nature there is some place for God's grace; not such grace as to cleanse it, but to restrain it inwardly.'[7] Such uprightness and virtues as manifest in Camillus, a noble but unrewarded patriot, are 'not common gifts of nature, but special graces of God, which he bestows variously and in a certain measure.'[8] From this beginning set forth in the *Institutes II*, chap. iii, 1–14, developed the doctrine of common grace in H. Bavinck, C. Hodge and more recently in John Murray's 'Common Grace,' chap. 10.[9]

---

1. L. C. Cox, *John Wesley's Concept of Perfection* (Kansas City: Beacon Hill Press, 1964), pp. 38–44.
2. R. G. Tuttle, Jr, 'John Wesley' in *Evangelical Dictionary of Theology* (Grand Rapids: Baker Books, 1984), p. 1166.
3. A. H. Strong, *Systematic Theology* (Valley Forge, PA: Judson Press, 1907), p. 551.
4. J. O. Buswell, *A Systematic Theology of the Christian Religion II* (Grand Rapids: Zondervan, 1971), pp. 158–161, especially on the convicting work of the Holy Spirit.
5. ibid., p. 160.
6. Calvin, *Institutes II*, iii, 3.
7. ibid.
8. ibid., iii, 4.
9. John Murray, *Collected Writings II* (Edinburgh: Banner of Truth, 1977), pp. 93–119.

The Severe Blameworthiness of Innate Depravity of Heart.

These citations, of course, anticipate the doctrine of original sin later in this book. They are cited here to alleviate some of the grim, harsh impact on the reader of the certain fact that the evil habits of the heart, or the innate depraved disposition we all have as members of Adam's race, is sin and *more* blameworthy than the acts which proceed from it. I think a review of the evidence will convince the attentive mind, however reluctantly. I shall argue from (1) jurisprudence, (2) modern psychology and (3) the *consensus gentium* (the general opinion of the race), on the one hand, and (4) Scripture and (5) Christian experience on the other. The first three are suggestive, the fourth conclusive and the fifth supportive.

(1) The Principles of Jurisprudence.

Common knowledge available to any person aware of what goes on in our world is all we need for demonstration that every human heart is morally defective. It will not be necessary to cite particular parts of common law, or statutes of legislation, or cases to prove that in law a very clear distinction is made between unlawful acts performed 'with malice aforethought' and such acts of sudden response to circumstances (passion) and unlawful acts which are traceable to the offenders' prevailing disposition, constitutional avarice (nowadays called the criminal mind). There are other technical designations. Courts have always recognized these distinctions. We at present (the first decade of the twenty-first century) are seeing the reversal of a trend to be lenient toward the 'habitual' (dispositional) criminal on the supposition that environment and training had made him so. It seems more evident to jurists and laymen today that however and whatever the cause of such depravity, it deserves punishment as guilty and blameworthy. This is being forced upon very reluctant 'progressive' jurists and public. The law codes of antiquity, not least the Mosaic code, embody this principle. The *lex talionis* is the only just reason for punishment of crimes.

(2) Evidence of Modern Psychology.

As I have asserted, modern psychologists are not unanimous in rejecting moral judgments upon psychological states, though from what I read as a layman, it seems very many do. There seems to be agreement now and has been for over a century, that there is a vast area of the human psyche that lies below the level of awareness. Who can say for sure each man has an *id*, an *ego* and a *superego* or if in addition to the *conscious* there is an *unconscious* self and a *subconscious* self? I shall not pretend currency in the field by attempting to discuss important psychologists, their experiments and theories. They do all operate on the assumption that there is an area of great depth below consciousness.

Long ago Augustine, who certainly thought deeply and wisely on the subject, spoke of it many times as a 'vast court' (and as a 'vast field'). Therein 'great is the force of memory, excessive great O my God.'[10]

Out of this deep, below the level of ordinary awareness, proceed our dreams during slumber, and many of our thoughts in moments of reflection and suppressed lusts on occasion of temptation. We are disgusted with the coarseness of our own dreams, as well as the transgressions of our own moral sense in our fantasies. Whence comes all this? Sound theology joins some, at least, of modern psychology, in saying: from the self, which at the deepest level is still human nature, fallen human nature, and therefore corrupt and sinful.

(3) The *Consensus Gentium*, or the Common Opinion of the Human Race.

This is the larger datum of which the last previous point is a prominent aspect. I know of no essay or book that expands this matter, though theological textbooks do take note of it. People generally trace good deeds as well as bad ones, virtue as well as vice, to the more or less permanent moral disposition, i.e. the subconscious mind or soul, of the people who perform them. This is true of group behavior to a degree and strongly of individual behavior. This generally accepted outlook is manifest by such common expressions as 'terrible temper,' 'stinking pride,' 'insanely jealous,' 'criminal mind.' In recent political campaigns in the U.S. 'the character issue' has become important because many people feel what a man will do in office, how faithfully he will keep his promises, etc., can be known somewhat ahead of time if his character can be assessed accurately. He will be forgiven mistakes and even some sins, but not a markedly bad character. True or not, such labels as 'Tricky Dick' and 'Slick Willie' hung on a politician, and generally accepted as true, render him unelectable. (Sadly, some are tricky and slick enough to deceive both themselves and a majority of the electorate.) Further, people generally feel childhood

---

10. Augustine, Book 10 of *Confessions*, paras. 17–20.

is a time of character building; that bad impulses must be overcome, good ones strengthened in childhood and youth; that the more settled and permanent an evil disposition the worse it is – hence such proverbs as 'there's no fool like an old fool.' People condemn perceived bad character in any one, no matter how one comes by it – whether tendencies unrebuked by parents, hereditary family traits, or even sectional or group prejudices passed down through generations. The individual is blamed. 'We do not excuse arrogance or sensuality on the ground they are family traits' (Strong). Further, we know that the longer vicious tendencies are harbored and allowed to be acted out the worse the disposition becomes; till at last one is in the complete control of the vice. It is then most hateful and properly despised. Otherwise the most depraved man in the world would be the most innocent.

(4) The Proof from Scripture.

(a) As I write my mind is full of readings in the Pentateuch regarding the institution of atoning sacrifice in the Mosaic system (from some months of study and writing on the redemptive work of Christ). The most numerous scheduled offerings (daily evening and morning offerings, at Sabbaths, the seven feasts and festivals) were all for sins of ignorance, sins of failure, general sinfulness in Israel. To take only one of a multitude of examples, every woman who had 'conceived and borne a child' was required to offer specific sacrifice in a prescribed way for 'her purifying' (not physical, but spiritual). 'Atonement' was required. Even Mary, the mother of our Lord, was not exempt, no more free from inborn sin than the rest of us, the dogma of 'Immaculate conception of the Virgin' notwithstanding. (See Luke 2:22-24.) G. F. Oehler in *Theology of the Old Testament* explains:

> This sinful inclination is hereditary [and] is indirectly contained in the passages [Gen. 6:5; 8:21] cited, although it is not expressly said... Mosaism, although it derives the propagation of man's race from God's blessing, still regards all events and conditions which refer to birth and generation as requiring a purifying expiation; compare the Law, Leviticus 12:2-6 and 15:7 *ad fin* in which the thought lies that all these conditions are connected with the disturbance of sin.[11]

Further, in the Mosaic scheme of things every male infant was circumcised at eight days of age. J. Barton Payne has this to say about it:

> This early date possesses a two-fold significance. It demonstrates, on the one hand, man's need for redemption and regeneration, from the time of birth itself. David went even further and exclaimed, 'Behold I was brought forth in iniquity and in sin did my mother conceive me.'[12]

Circumcision is a minimal removal of the external male organ of reproduction. Of this Payne says (and several Old Testament theologians could be cited):

> As to the precise significance of this ceremonial action, it may be said negatively that uncircumcision expressed unfitness, and particularly that of the natural life (Exod. 6:12). When Moses referred to his 'uncircumcised lips' he meant he had poor native speaking ability. To specify therefore an uncircumcised heart (Jer. 4:4) was to picture a soul that was covered with its natural wickedness. In contrast, then, to circumcise meant to remove one's sin (Deut. 10:16).[13]

(b) In Pauline literature acts of sin proceed from a sinful heart. Paul's figures for this sin at the center are 'the sin,' 'the body of sin,' 'our old man,' 'this body of death,' 'flesh', 'the body of sin and death,' and 'the carnal mind.' All are figurative expressions for the sinful 'heart' which in turn is a figure for the center of man's rational being. From this fountain, says Paul, all our sinful deeds flow forth. In Galatians nearly a score of the 'works of the flesh' are mentioned, but the flesh itself is always only one, a unit, lying at the center of our being. 'Now the works of the flesh are evident...' (Gal. 5:19) and the names of seventeen of them follow.

(c) Jesus clearly taught the same, saying, 'But what comes out of the mouth proceeds from the heart, and this defiles a person' (Matt. 15:18). Then He mentioned seven of those things beginning with evil thoughts and murders, ending with false witness and blasphemies. He reproved the scribes and Pharisees, not for their outward works which were 'clean' like 'the outside of the cup and the plate' and white like the outside of sepulchers. Their fault lay in the fact that like sepulchers, they were 'within... full of dead people's bones and all uncleanness' (Matt. 23:25-27).

---

11. G. F. Oehler, trans. by George Day, *Theology of the Old Testament* (Grand Rapids: Zondervan, n.d. [originally publ. 1873], p. 162.
12. J. Barton Payne, *The Theology of the Older Testament* (Grand Rapids: Zondervan, 1962), p. 393.
13. ibid., p. 391.

(d) In Scripture sin as a state can even specially characterize certain tribal, family or national divisions of mankind so that they stand condemned as a group. They were to be under ban, to be excluded from any participation in the covenant of the Lord with Israel (except certain individual members after a 'third' or a 'tenth' generation) and deserving to be exterminated. Any 'heathen, dwelling as a stranger in the land, could by circumcision (or member of a circumcised man's household) [e.g. Ruth], become incorporated among the covenant people... (Exod. 12:48); with the exception, however of the *Canaanitish* tribes, which fell under the curse. To these the Moabites and Ammonites (Deut. 23:4ff.) were added as excluded persons.'[14] Later God's grace removed these bans, but the clear teaching is that the ban was justly imposed. This certainly was not in every case because of what these people did or might do, but because of extreme depravity of hearts. This is illustrated in the LORD's promise to Abram that only after several hundreds of years would his family return to the land of the Amorite kingdoms (Canaan) – 'for the iniquity of the Amorites is not yet complete' (Gen. 15:16).

(5) Support of Christian Experience.

An aphorism of Christian spirituality affirms 'the closer one is to the light the more plainly dark marks are seen.' Contrariwise, the less one has entered into a clear apprehension of the divine holiness, the more defensive of one's own character. Christians find this true whenever they undertake serious presentation of gospel and law to sinners. Frequently we find ourselves saying words, thinking thoughts, doing deeds on impulse, which we know to be expressions even, sadly, revelations of depravity of nature we are not ordinarily consciously aware of. It would burden these pages to quote them at length, but those very people of Christian history, famous for saintly lives, are the very ones who by their most earnest writings confess themselves still to have sin at heart, for which they grieve and make confession to God. Let us note several.

The longest chapter by far in St Augustine's *Confessions* is chapter 10. He declares his purpose 'to confess to men also in thy presence what I now am, not what I have been... what I am within.' Later, 'I... in thy sight I despise myself, and account myself dust and ashes.' He is, of course, thinking of an Old Testament saint who discovered his own heart (Job 42:6) saying, 'I... repent in dust and ashes.' Time would fail to tell of Luther, Edwards, Brainerd, King David (Pss. 51 and 32), Isaiah (Isa. 6:5), Daniel (Dan. 8, especially vv. 8-11), Peter (Luke 5:8) and Paul (Rom. 7; 1 Tim. 1:15).

'It may be doubted,' wrote A. H. Strong, 'whether any repentance is genuine which is not repentance for *sin* rather than for sins.'[15]

Sin Is Both Guilt and Corruption (Pollution).

Discussion of these two aspects of the doctrine is disagreeable, but both necessary and salutary: *necessary* because true and *salutary* because properly understood and accepted, they are seen to be part of the burden of the Savior when He became the Lamb of God, slain; *salutary* also because they remove the last supports of human pride. Both come in for larger treatment in connection with original sin. Our treatment here will be limited to definition and scriptural support. They were mentioned earlier as effects of the fall. Let us observe four points about sin as guilt.

(1) Guilt in the Bible, as in jurisprudence, is *never a subjective feeling* as in psychological literature today. It always refers to the objective state of one who has broken the law.

(2) In a popular, non-legal sense it means simply the state of being blameworthy, of inherent demerit. We speak this way all the time. When someone steals another's property (ball glove, doll, money, and hides it somewhere) that person is a thief. That person can never, never cease to be guilty of the theft till the end of time. It is true if no one else ever knows about it and till memory is dead it will always be a burden of conscience to be borne. Non-guilt can never be restored any more than a lost virginity.

(3) In a formal or legal sense, in human justice and in divine justice, guilt is an *obligation* to receive and pay the appropriate penalty, according to the common formula, 'the punishment should fit the crime,' and the biblical *lex talionis*, an eye for eye, a tooth for a tooth, burning for burning. Since sin of any degree or sort is against the majesty of God (*lese majestie*) it is deserving of the penalty for attacking all God is and stands for (i.e. death), as James says,

---

14. Oehler, *Theology of the Old Testament*, p. 180.
15. A. H. Strong, *Systematic Theology* (Valley Forge, PA: Judson Press, 1907), p. 556.

'For whoever keeps the whole law and yet stumbles at just one point is guilty of breaking all of it' (James 2:10 NIV). The law is as unforgiving as bungee jumping or hang-gliding – the punishment is as severe for one broken rope as for failure of every piece of the equipment!

Though what is usually called guilt, in the popular sense of blameworthiness or demerit, is permanent, formal or legal guilt on the other hand may be removed by meeting the just demands of God the Lawgiver in one's person or in Him who died for us all in our place – 'the LORD has laid on him the iniquity of us all' (Isa. 53:6).

That the whole world of mankind are guilty in both senses is taught expressly by Romans 3:19; 5:18; and Ephesians 2:3. In my judgment, R. L. Dabney was right in affirming that what I have called a 'popular' sense and he 'potential guilt,' the 'intrinsic moral ill-desert of an act or state… is of the essence of sin.' The legal sense (Dabney, 'actual guilt') is the 'penal sanction' and not of the essence of sin.[16]

It is, then, quite unreasonable to think of any personal being, infant or adult, who is morally corrupt (polluted, depraved) at heart as not being sinful and therefore not guilty.

In my judgment, however, this fact is not sufficient to render the pollution of nature by descent from Adam any sufficient basis for imputation of Adam's sin as in the theory of mediate imputation – to be treated later in these pages. We are guilty not only personally for sins expressing a sinful heart, but we enter *also* into guilt for Adam's sin, i.e. 'original sin,' and the latter more devastating (universal death sentence) than the former. In some important sense each of us was there in and with the head of our race when he took the awful plunge.

---

16. R. L. Dabney, *Lectures in Systematic Theology* (Grand Rapids: Zondervan, 1978), p. 310.

5
Sins As Acts Committed by Sinners

The preceding chapters have treated sin (singular) as a fact or phenomenon in the human race. Now the focus will be on particular sins committed by particular persons. Their number and variety are too numerous to count. One of the offenses of medieval theology against reality was the demand of the confessional for specific recounting of all sins — even the ones there was no name for. The Reformers protested that even King David, who certainly had occasion to reflect on the subject, exclaimed, 'Who can discern his errors? Declare me innocent from hidden faults' and 'my iniquities have gone over my head… they are too heavy for me' (Pss. 19:12; 38:4). Calvin remarks: 'Who would now think of reckoning up his sins when he sees David cannot begin to number his?'[1]

This does not mean a sound theology says nothing about sins. In fact *only* soundly religious people have anything substantial to say about their sins. And in so speaking they should wish to be biblically and doctrinally sound. The Bible furnishes many striking examples. Psalms 51 and 32, recited or read fervently at communion observances, are only sample texts. Not every pious Christian pursuit of perfection, i.e. of ceasing from committing sins, has had sound operating definitions.

The Bible from Genesis 3 through Revelation 22 is concerned with specific sins of sinful men. Earlier generations of believers were very concerned with knowing what the dangers were of temptation to particular *sins* as well as the call of God to particular virtues. There is great force to the stark simplicity of biblical warnings and exhortations in this regard (especially in the King James Version) of two verses in the last two chapters of the Bible:

> But the fearful, and unbelieving, and the abominable, and murderers, and whoremongers, and sorcerers, and idolaters, and all liars, shall have their part in the lake which burneth with fire and brimstone: which is the second death (Rev. 21:8 KJV). For without are dogs, and sorcerers, and whoremongers, and murderers, and idolaters, and whosoever loveth and maketh a lie (Rev. 22:15 KJV).

See also Proverbs 6:16-19 on seven things the Lord hates.

'Sin' and 'Sins' in our Language and Literature.

Every branch of the Teutonic group of languages has this word. Long before biblical virtues affected our ancestors' thought-patterns they made the moral distinction between what ought to be and what ought not to be. The *Oxford English Dictionary* traces the written employment of the word sin to AD 825 in a Psalter rendering of Psalms 4 and

---

1. Calvin, *Institutes III*, iv, 16.

108, and also a work of King Alfred (AD 897). 'As psychology recognizes a distinction of pleasure and pain, and metaphysics of good and evil, so morality assumes the difference between right and wrong in action.' The subject of this chapter is sin as action, hence the pertinence of these words of the famous Prof. Morris Jastrow of the University of Pennsylvania in the article on 'Sin.'[2] He goes on to say:

> As psychology recognizes a distinction of pleasure and pain, and metaphysics of good and evil, so morality assumes the difference between right and wrong in action, and good and bad in character, but the distinction in psychology and metaphysics applies to what is [whereas], the difference in morality is judged by what ought to be. When the act or the character does not correspond with the standard, this want of correspondence may in different relations be variously described. In relation to human society, and the rules it imposes on its members, action that ought not to be is *crime*; a habit which is injurious to a man's own moral nature, especially if it involves evil physical consequences is described as *vice*. If a man is thought of as under the authority of God, any transgression or want of conformity to the law of God is defined as sin. Crime is a legal, vice a moral, and sin a religious term... Sin is a term applied not only to actions, but also to dispositions and motives.[3]

The very word itself implies the existence of God, divine law and human responsibility to both; which fact explains why sin is a word not found frequently in current 'scientific' psychological literature. Happily there has been some success in restoring the word to popular use even among some psychologists.

'Sin' and 'Sins' in Ecclesiastical Tradition.

The medieval church, supported by scholastic theology, had an elaborate system of grading sins according to amount of demerit and necessary acts of contrition and penance. This system together with the confessional and the doctrine of purgatory was vigorously rejected by all the Protestant Reformers, mainly because it seemed to teach that some sins are undeserving of the full punishment of divine law and that their opposite virtues were somehow productive of earned merit toward eternal life. Whether these undoubted opinions of the laity then or now were official Roman doctrine or not is debatable. This system also tended to externalize sin whereas the biblical emphasis is on the heart attitude in 'acts' of sin. I am not sure what Rome today thinks of the 1966 Dutch Catechism. The Dutch Catechism does call attention to real dangers unnoticed by the more recent 'official' *Catechism of 1994*, viz.:

> The sharp distinction between 'mortal' and 'venial' sin contributed in no small measure to the education of the people.... It is a way of expressing the seriousness of sin – which is not concealed in Scripture.
> But a too precise juridical definition of the difference has also its disadvantages. One can be so preoccupied with it that the attention becomes exclusively fixed on the action while little heed is taken of the attitude of heart, which remains, however, as Jesus said, the real source of all evil (Mark 7:14-23).[4]

The Roman Church has preserved the system in the 1994 *Catechism of the Catholic Church* approved by Pope John Paul II, the present reigning pontiff. (Hereafter to be cited as 1994 *Catechism*.) The Roman teaching is summarized as follows:

> Sin is *mortal* or *venial*; it may be *actual, habitual, formal* or *material*...; of *ignorance* if the lack of knowledge is culpable, of *infirmity* if the result of sudden passion or a bad habit, and of *malice* if it is deliberate and calculated wickedness.[5]

In addition, Roman theology emphasizes the tenth commandment (which they divide into a ninth and tenth: coveting your neighbor's wife and coveting his property) as *internal sins*, 'more dangerous than sins which are openly committed.'[6]

There are further refinements. These are the leading points in Rome's efforts to inform her children and guide them to the sacramental removal of guilt. Some of the distinctions, at least, are derived from Scripture. A bit later I will treat some biblical categories of sins. For the present let us try to understand what the Roman preceptor means by these variations on the theme of sins as acts. I shall quote official sources.

---

2. Morris Jastrow, *Encyclopedia Britannica*, 11th ed., xxv, p. 137.
3. ibid.
4. *A New Catechism*, trans. of 'De Nieuw Katechismus' (New York: Herder & Herder, 1967), p. 452.
5. *The Catholic Encyclopaedic Dictionary*, 3rd ed. (New York: Macmillan, 1958), p. 463.
6. A. C. Neil, *Catholic Encyclopedia*, XIV, ii.

(1) *Mortal* and (2) *venial* sins. The 1994 *Catechism* on 'The Gravity of Sin; Mortal and Venial Sin' states:

> The distinction between mortal and venial sin, already evident in scripture [footnote to 1 John 5:16,17] became part of the tradition of the Church.... *Mortal sin* destroys charity in the heart of man by a grave violation of God's law; it turns man away from God, who is his ultimate end and his beatitude, by preferring an inferior good to him. *Venial sin* allows charity to subsist, even though it offends and wounds.... Mortal sin... necessitates... a conversion of the heart... normally accomplished within the sacrament of reconciliation [i.e. penance].[7]

The *Catechism* then quotes St Thomas Aquinas (*Summa Theologica*) to the effect that in the case of blasphemy, perjury, homicide, adultery, 'the sin is mortal but thoughtless offenses are venial.'[8] In my opinion a fair reading of St Thomas shows (in scholastic language) he really did not think there are categories of sins venial or mortal 'according to genus of the act,' but the gravity of it.[9]

'For a sin to be mortal,' according to St Thomas, it must be in 'a grave matter and which is committed with full knowledge and deliberate consent.'[10]

Protestant interpretation of Scripture insists that *all* sins of men are mortal in that they merit death of the sinner and venial in that they are remediable through the blood of Jesus Christ, which is sufficient atonement for any and every sin. *All* sins are likewise mortal in the sense that every sin proceeds from a fallen, sinful heart, which is in itself guilty and culpable. First John 5:16, 17 is the slender scriptural basis cited by the *Catechism*. With due respect to loyal lay and clerical Roman believers it must be said this distinction, which has been very productive for the confessional, has not created scrupulous moral concern in routine matters of commerce, politics, even of matrimonial faithfulness in lands where it has been widely adopted. It, of course, is incompatible with evangelical doctrines of salvation wholly by grace through faith.

(An extensive discussion of Rome's teachings on venial versus mortal sins and related sacrament of forgiveness by the church through the priest [confession, absolution, contrition, penance] would be relevant but a diversion at this point. A certain interpretation of 1 John 5:16, 17 and inferences drawn from it supply supposed support of the distinction between venial and mortal sins. Some medieval theology and the Council of Trent assert all 'grievous sins' [i.e. deadly] must be orally confessed to a priest in detail but confession of venial sins is not necessary, since sorrow for sins, prayer, good works, abstinence and Holy Communion are sufficient to expiate venial sins [see Ludwig Ott, *Fundamentals of Catholic Dogma*, pp. 432, 433 and Denzinger, paras. 899, 917].)

Raymond E. Brown, one of Rome's most generally trusted biblical scholars, expounds on 1 John 5:16, 17, citing other scholars, most of them Protestant, and says nary a word about 'venial' sins. Rather he thinks the passage is a warning against apostasy from faith in Christ (*Anchor Bible*, vol. 30, pp. 610–619). Some form of this view has the approval of scholars as early as Augustine. Alford lent his great name to this view and the *Expositor's Bible* gives it beautiful (if terrible) exposition. It seems Father Brown might even agree with Calvin's strong language: 'The Apostle... does not here distinguish between venial and mortal sin, as it was afterwards commonly done. For altogether foolish is that distinction which prevails under the Papacy' (*Commentary on the Catholic Epistles, en loc*). This difficult passage has at least fifteen somewhat overlapping but distinct interpretations.

My own judgment is that the sin unto death, or 'deadly' (= mortal) sin, is sin on account of which God calls some believers home early, i.e. the death in the aged Aposle's mind is natural or physical. Christian brothers and sisters should pray for one another, especially for victory over our manifold enticements to sin. He does not tell us how to recognize the exceptional kind of sin. Perhaps the formula 'according to the will of God' only two verses above is John's intention. '[A] sin unto death' (1 John 5:16 KJV) is too focused. There *is sin unto death* refers to many evil thoughts, words and deeds which in the wisdom and grace of God bring on early infliction of the universally applied sentence of physical death. Some of these sins are described in 1 Corinthians 5 and specifically at 1 Corinthians 11:30. There are several biblical parallels. Numbers 18:22 prohibited approach of non-Levites to the Tabernacle lest 'they bear sin and die' (lit. *sin of death*, ESV). A rapist was to be executed but the young woman raped was not to be punished because she has done no 'sin of death' (Deut. 22:25, 26). In Jubilees 33:12-18 incest is said to be 'a sin worthy of death.' In the New Testament Ananias and Sapphira committed sins the Apostle Peter deemed worthy of death, even though they were presumed true believers (Acts 5:1-11). Paul referred to such sins in 1 Corinthians 5:5 and 11:30. Finally,

---

7. Catechism of 1944, pp. 1854–1856.
8. ibid.
9. St Thomas Acquinas, *Summa Theologica I-II*, Q. 88, Art I.
10. ibid.

Jesus uses the phrase sickness 'unto death' of the physical death of Lazarus (John 11:4). As 1 John 5:16, 17 reads in the English Standard Version, the passage falls neatly into this understanding of John's meaning. 'If anyone sees his brother committing a sin not leading to death, he shall ask, and God will give him life – to those who commit sins that do not lead to death. There is sin that leads to death; I do not say that one should pray for that. All wrongdoing is sin, but there is sin that does not lead to death' (1 John 5:16, 17 ESV).

(3) Capital sins or (4) vices. Christian tradition recognizes 'four cardinal virtues': prudence, justice, fortitude and temperance. They were transferred to very early church tradition from ancient Greek philosophy. To these four traditions were added three 'theological virtues' (faith, hope and charity), which add up to seven. The capital sins 'are called "capital" because they engender other sins, other vices.' They are opposite the above-mentioned cardinal and theological virtues, and being seven in number are 'pride, avarice [greed], envy, wrath, lust, gluttony and sloth.'[11]

That there should be seven capital sins and seven cardinal virtues is not owed to Roman Catholic tradition, for the distinction long antedates the division of the church into eastern (Greek) and western (Roman, Latin). When Greek was still the language of popular discourse throughout most of the Roman world, young men destined to be scholars attended Greek academies, of which the most famous was at Athens, where Aristotle had taught his *Nicomachean Ethics*. Aristotle was still standard fare much later when the scholars and teachers of the churches of the first four centuries got their education. Paul, for example, who knew of the lesser lights of classical learning (he quoted Epimenides, Titus 1:12 and Aratus, Acts 17:28) would almost certainly have studied Aristotle.

From Aristotle all educated early Christians learned of four cardinal virtues: prudence (*phronēsis*), justice (*diakaiosunē*), temperance (*sōphrosunē*) and fortitude (*andreia*). From Paul they derived faith (*pistis*), hope (*elpis*) and charity (or 'love') (*agapē*) (1 Cor. 13:13). They had no trouble finding all the spiritually valid 'gentile' virtues of Aristotle in the formula of Philippians 4:8, 'Finally, brothers, whatever is true, whatever is honorable, whatever is just, whatever is pure, whatever is lovely, whatever is commendable, if there is any excellence' ('virtue' KJV, Gr. *aretē*), etc. Popular instruction simply matched these cardinal virtues with an equal number of capital sins. We might do well to remember all of both categories.

There is also the well-known biblical example of seven things especially abominable to the Lord (Prov. 6:16-19). Pride has first place in this 'Solomonic' list as well as the traditional Christian list. Several others coincide. Earlier generations more given to various mnemonic devices would have found both the Christian lists useful – along with the Ten Commandments, etc.

Following Thomas Aquinas in *Summa Theologica* I–II, Question 72, Answer 5, sins may be of (5) *commission* or (6) *omission*. This distinction is biblical and, of course, carried on into evangelical theology.

Another important distinction was between (7) *material* and (8) *formal* sins. (Calvin was contemptuous of this distinction.) Material sins turn out to be essentially sins of ignorance, what one does is wrong but he doesn't know it is wrong or steals another's property thinking it is his own. A formal sin would be one of doing right, but in bad conscience.

Sins are said to be (9) *internal* sins or (10) *external*. After the Reformation, Rome at the Council of Trent closely defined internal sins (Session XIV, c.v.) – partly, I think we may justly say – in shoring up the doctrines associated with Mass (Transubstantiation and the confessional). Roman moral theology distinguishes three kinds of internal sins: (a) *delictatio morosa*, i.e. the pleasure taken in sinful thought or imagination even when there is no intention to do what is imagined, (b) *gaudium*, i.e. ruminating without restraint on sins one has previously committed, and (c) *desirium*, desire (lust) for what is sinful.

Evangelical doctrine may judiciously employ some of these and other traditional distinctions and terms with approval. But we part company from Rome thoroughly because Rome insists there must be a conscious, willful component of 'sins' that are really sin.

Older Roman Church canonical literature is as plain on this point as is the 1994 *Catechism*. A. C. O'Neil, from the standpoint of Rome states:

> Luther and Calvin taught as their fundamental error that no free will properly so called remained after the fall of our first parents; that the fulfilment of God's precepts is impossible even with the assistance of grace, and that man in all his actions sins.[12]

Though O'Neil disapproves, he is, of course, correct as to these two Reformers and most Protestant theology.

---

11. *Catechism of 1994,* paras. 1805 and 1866.
12. op cit., p. 7.

In Rome's theology, grace is not as in Paul's doctrine a way God saves sinners apart from their lack of merit. Grace in salvation, for Rome, is something God imparts to sinners through sacraments by means of which, by works of righteousness, they come to merit salvation. Hence Rome calls evangelical teachings about grace in salvation 'Protestant Errors.' Though not so prominent in recent pronouncements, the liberal *Dutch Catechism* (pp. 287–289) and the conservative papal *1994 Catechism* practically equate grace with the saving activity of the Holy Spirit, helping us to be our most proper selves and to love God and man with our whole heart. I fear late twentieth-century Protestantism partially lost its roots at this same point. (See later pages in *Soteriology*, the Doctrine of Salvation.) Roman theology for all its sincere concern about sin and sins has not discerned the depths of fallen human nature. 'T'was grace that *saved* a wretch like me,' not by rendering assistance, but by reaching down and actually effecting deliverance. Jesus is *Savior* before He is Teacher. There is no point in theology where Rome and evangelical theology are both so near and so far apart. Rome teaches that salvation is all of grace – as a freely imparted divine enablement to merit salvation. Evangelical theology proclaims that grace is a name for God's method of saving sinners apart from their merit, hence *sola gratia*, by grace alone. See any Catholic encyclopaedia, theology or catechism on any entry containing the word, 'grace.'

Source and Causes of Sins.

The immediate source of all our sins is our corrupt nature: what Jesus referred to as the evil heart, the corrupt tree, and by other metaphors; Paul as the old man, the carnal mind, the flesh, sin, sin in the heart, sin that dwells in me, the law of sin (Rom. 7; Gal. 5).

This sinful, corrupt heart was received from immediate parents who received it from the generations of their ancestors. We Gentiles know our remote ancestors were all heathen, Gentiles who 'know not God' (Eph. 2:11-13; 4:5). They were children of disobedience (Eph. 2:3) and 'All of us also lived among them at one time' (Eph. 2:3 NIV).

That universal corruption arose from the corruption of nature brought upon them by their willful departure from holiness when our first parents failed their probation.

There are *internal* causes of sin and there are *external*. There would be no end to a pursuit of names and description of all such causes. The internal causes are as complicated as the human nature of which they are only aspects, while the external causes are as diverse as the wide world in which we live.

Let us restrict the discussion to some New Testament expressions that directly treat the causes of sin in a functional-analytical way. They are three: temptation, the world and desire, pungently captured in the proverbial expression, 'the world, the flesh and the devil.'

(1) *Temptation to Sin*. There is a large amount of literature on the subject, technical, devotional and sermonic. Earlier this book has treated the temptation of our first parents. Most of that previous discussion is apropos here.

Evolutionary theory, applying Darwinism to the realm of human moral development, finds impulses to what religion calls sin in surviving natural impulses from previous animal stages in human development.[13]

As a college student in philosophy from my young professor who was fresh from Reinhold Niebuhr's influence, I learned another theory: 'existential *angst*' or anxiety: 'Anxiety is the inevitable concomitant of the paradox of freedom and finiteness in which man is involved. Anxiety is the internal precondition of sin.... the internal description of the state of temptation.'[14] For Niebuhr an historical fall is not how sin began, but 'the temptation to sin lies in the human situation.'[15]

There are several economic theories to explain the causes of what Christians call temptation and resulting sin. Most of these have been influenced by Marxist views of mankind as essentially economic beings. Struggle between economic classes is as near as Marxism comes to a doctrine of sin. I leave to the department of Apologetics a thorough canvass of the several Marxist, essentially anti-Christian theories. Chief among them is liberation theology. Though it was primarily a movement among post-Vatican II Roman Catholics, students in undergraduate university classes in sociology met much of the same thought many long years ago when the now generally despised Stalin was still darling of many professors and Chairman Mao was soon to appear.

---

13. Millard Erickson, *Christian Theology* (Grand Rapids: Baker Books, 1983, 1985), pp. 581–585.
14. Reinhold Niebuhr, *The Nature and Destiny of Man I* (New York: Charles Scribner's Sons, 1949), p. 182.
15. ibid., p. 251.

There are various psychological interpretations of temptation. Some Christian psychologists see fallen human nature and temptation to sin in a biblical manner, but these professionals are a minority. I do not know to what extent professionals face the issue of whether or not man has an immortal soul; I do know that many operate as though he has none and reject even the idea of personal moral responsibility – with terrible consequences in our courts where victims of crime can now be made out to be the causes of it. I recently wrote the following response to solicitation from a graduate school of psychology where one of my family was a student.

> I am a regular reader of your bulletins and a 'careful reader.' Up to now I had seen little to indicate that your philosophy includes moral values in your approach. By warm welcome to 'Gay' (homosexual) and lesbian advocates and their so-called artists you take away (or at least, so it seems) the necessary frame of reference for human behavior. Normalcy does not exist in such a world. It is evident that sin has dropped out of your vocabulary. But the fact has not dropped out of human conscience and therefore not out of social standards and civil law.
>
> I beg you to reconsider this breach of decency and of common sense. You stand to lose much more than you gain.
>
> I wish to support your program. The recent announcement makes this difficult.
>
> Signed, Amicus

The factors in temptation consist simply in our being fallen physical, psychical and spiritual beings in a world created by God but presently dominated in certain ways by the evil 'prince of this world.'

(1) *Temptation* is an ethically neutral word, both in the original languages of Scripture and in English, though for sound reason it takes on the pejorative sense of enticement. *Nasah* to prove, or try, or tempt and *massah*, a trial or proof are the Hebrew words; *peiradzō* (verb) and *peirasmos* (noun) of similar meaning are the Greek words. These terms are of wide application – 'testing' Abraham's faith (Gen. 22:1); 'tempting God' (Exod. 17:2; Ps. 70:18; Acts 15:10; Heb. 3:19); Jesus 'tempted of the devil' (Matt. 4; Luke 4). The subjects tempted in each of these cases were morally upright and remained so. Typically, as when Jesus was 'tempted of the devil,' temptation takes the form of enticement. We are all familiar with the urgency of many enticements.

(2) The *World* (as we showed at length in treating the effects of the failure of Adam's probation) involves several polarities. The world is good as created, yet evil as employed by the devil: cursed yet redeemed. In relation to sinners, the subjects of temptation, it is evil or good as they respond to it. Psalm 104 which rightly revels in 'natural,' spiritual enjoyment of the world, ends miserably with sinister, almost spectral, notice that it is also evil (Ps. 104:35).

(3) *Desire* in man, at times seemingly in every fiber (as in our mating urges as well as hunger for food and thirst for drink) is directed toward that world. We have earlier treated *concupiscence* (Latin) and *epithumia* (Greek), the theological and New Testament words for ardent longing.

Temptation, i.e. desires within the man and the world without the man come together as they do in every human being who arrives at conscious awareness. Every infant is immediately invited to participation in life in the present world. It cannot be avoided. Yet this invitation, as enticement to sin, should be resisted at any cost.

Correlation Between Desire Within and the World Without.

The correlation between enticement and desire (what traditional theology called concupiscence) in temptation to sin is plainly set forth in 1 John 2:15-17. The King James Version is to be preferred as most literal here:

> Love not the world, neither the things that are in the world. If any man love the world the love of the Father is not in him. For all that is in the world, the lust [better, 'desire'] of the flesh, and the lust ['desire'] of the eyes, and the pride of life, is not of the Father, but is of the world. And the world passeth away, and the lust ['desire'] thereof: but he that doeth the will of God abideth forever.

Though the subject invites the writing of a book, let us be brief and to the point. John plainly intends to treat the temptations of the world completely and comprehensively: 'all that is in the world,' all its physical, economic, artistic features or whatever. He adds later, 'the whole world lieth in wickedness' (1 John 5:19 KJV; 'under the control of the evil one' NIV). This relates to all our eyes see, our bodies touch, our tongues taste, our nose smells, our ears hear: viewed as a *kosmos* or system it is geared by Satan to bring us down, even though we are bid to have 'dominion' over it, from one point of view, and to scratch out our living in it from another (Gen. 3).

The 'world' gets at us in three ways, and in only three ways in John's analysis. These three are by virtue of what we children of Adam are by created and fallen nature. We are drawn by three kinds of attraction in our 'environment' (i.e. 'the world'). It is difficult *not* to find this triad of enticements parallel to the three enticements and corresponding human desires in the temptation of Jesus. R. E. Brown (*Anchor Bible*), Augustine and others have related the Johannine triad to the three temptations of Jesus (Matt. 4:3-11; Luke 4:3-13): the temptation to turn stones to bread being related to 'the desire of the flesh'; the showing of all the kingdoms of the world to 'the desire of the eyes'; and the throwing of oneself from the pinnacle of the temple to 'the pride of life.'[16] The triad also parallels Eve's enticement: (1) 'good for food,' (2) 'delight to the eyes' and (3) 'desired to make one wise' (Gen. 3:6).

The first is literally 'the desire of the flesh.' Of the many metaphorical meanings of *sarx* (flesh) in the Bible – all living animals, the human race, wicked desires and impulses – none applies here. This is John writing, not Paul. Let us not read John's writings through Paul's spectacles. John is thinking of all possible human wants, needs and desires, not least those dictated by our hormones and enzymes – as R. E. Brown thoroughly demonstrates.[17]

If we indulge these appetites in unlawful and undisciplined ways, surrendering to physical and material pleasures, the devil's world has captured us.

The second is 'the desire of the eyes.' The eyes are the chief gate by which the world enters our soul's awareness. God planted our race in a garden of every sort of delight to the eyes, to be lawfully enjoyed. One cannot help but wish to walk in the beautiful world, travel about it, even make photographs of it. There are scriptural, ethical, disciplined, lawful ways at least to *attempt* 'possession' of the things our eyes see and souls desire. But several of the Decalogue's commands require that we earn (or inherit) what we own, and that we severely regulate our interest in the neighbor's ox, ass, wife, automobile or summer home.

The third is harder to define. John shifts from *epithumia* (desire) to *aladzonia* (pretension, arrogance; hence 'the pride of life' KJV). 'Life' is *bios* as in biology and biography. If we let John's own Epistle explain what kind or aspect of life he has in mind our clue is 1 John 3:17 where the literal rendering of KJV 'this world's [Gr. *kosmos*] good' (*bios*) (or goods) means worldly possessions which support life. The NIV interprets rather than translates, but does so correctly, 'material possessions.' Surely, then, this same author only a few verses earlier in chapter 2, verse 16, means pride of worldly goods or possessions by 'the pride of life.' There is much linguistic support for this, too extensive to burden these pages with it.[18] These possessions can be material, the possession of civil, ecclesiastical, political, economic power or even a record of recognized accomplishment. Everyone wants (and not necessarily unrighteously) a kingdom of one's own. A child's first word after 'Mamma' and 'No!' is likely to be 'Mine!'

So there is no limit on the external field of temptation by enticement: all that is in the world appeals to appetites of the flesh; the appreciation of beauty (and who knows what else) in what the eyes see; the pride of possessing things whether of goods or knowledge, position of honor and the like, or a record of doings. There apparently is nothing else. R. E. Brown suggests John 'does not state that these three factors are all that is in the world; they are examples of what is in the world.'[19] But this comment contradicts precisely what John says as an apparently all-inclusive statement: 'all that is in the world.' He did not say, 'samples of what is in the world.' As seen above, the world that offers these is in the lap of the devil.

The Occasion and Process of Temptation.

> Let no one say when he is tempted, 'I am being tempted by God,' for God cannot be tempted with evil, and he himself tempts no one. But each person is tempted when he is lured and enticed by his own desire. Then desire when it has conceived gives birth to sin, and sin when it is fully grown brings forth death (James 1:13-15).

In certain passages God is said to 'tempt' certain people, Abraham, for example (Gen. 22:1; see Deut. 4:34; 7:19; 29:3). And God's providence does place all of us in positions where our adherence to truth and righteousness are tested. Yet in such situations God's influence is always toward obedience to divine will and law. Believers are assured God is always on their side against enticement to sin (1 Cor. 10:13).

The occasion is always something 'out there' in the world: the world as remembered, as presently perceived or of future contemplation which draws one away by one's own inward impulses, thoughts and desires. In King David's case

---

16. R. E. Brown, *The Anchor Bible: The Gospel According to John* (New York: Doubleday, 1966,1970), p. 307.
17. ibid., pp. 306–308.
18. Brown, *The Anchor Bible*, John pp. 311, 312.

sexual desire was inflamed by sight of a beautiful woman bathing; Achan, sight of a wedge of gold and a Babylonish garment; Judas, mental contemplation of future monetary reward; Diotrephes, desire to possess preeminent honor in the church (3 John 9). The list could be as long as 'everything that is in the world,' to use John's words.

Each occasion for sin is also an opportunity for holy obedience as well. David could have gone downstairs and had a screen erected on either his own or Uriah's rooftop patio; Achan could have carried out the ban on Jericho and gone back to camp victorious; Judas could have become a 'hero in the strife' by remaining loyal; and Diotrephes might have promoted the apostolically chosen elder in his church rather than to attempt toppling him from pre-eminence. Jesus Himself is our example of holy resistance (Heb. 12:1-4) to temptation of whatever sort on whatever occasion.

The process of temptation is described in James 1:13-15 (RSV): 'Let no one say when he is tempted, "I am tempted by God," for God cannot be tempted with evil and he himself tempts no one; but each person is tempted when he is lured and enticed by his own desire. Then desire when it has conceived gives birth to sin; and sin when it is full-grown brings forth death.'

This brief but comprehensive passage by our Lord's brother is outstanding for accuracy, comprehensiveness, understandable simplicity and correspondence with universal experience.

(1) One is lured away by one's own desire. The word *exelko-ō*, 'lured,' means to lure away from hiding as in hunting or fishing, or 'to take something in tow' (Liddell & Scott, Thayer, Bauer). So the will allows desire to come out of disciplined control to become undisciplined desire, or lust. How easily and quickly this happens will be determined by previous moral and spiritual culture. Once the tiger is out of the cage, however, he is hard to recapture.

(2) Enticement (*deleadzō*), 'entice' (Bauer, Arndt & Gingrich, *Lexicon*; 'catch by bait,' used elsewhere only in 2 Peter 2:14, 18 – 'beguile,' 'allure,' Thayer, *Lexicon*). It is furnished by imagined pleasures in the world 'out there' – whatever captures the tempted person's attention. It is truly amazing with what dazzling glory one's imagination can supply as reward for breaking a commandment such as 'Thou shalt not steal' or 'Thou shalt not bear false witness.' We seem ready to be 'taken in tow,' to employ the suggested language of the lexicons.

(3) 'Then desire when it has conceived...' ('Then when lust hath conceived...' KJV). Lust, now no more disciplined desire, does 'conceive.' Steps are taken to act on impulses furnished by lust and the object of lust. The two are 'cast together' (as Gr. *sullambanō*, here rendered to conceive, suggests to conceive in the sexual sense) and now sooner, not later, the issue will come. The woman who has conceived a child in *utero* 'has to go through with it' one painful way or another.

(4) '...gives birth to sin.' Pregnancy is never partial, nor can it be terminated ordinarily apart from a birth. The seed planted, being what it is, determines what the result will be – horrible to contemplate by the remorseful conscience after the deed is done.

(5) '...and sin when it is fully grown.' Sin may be indulged for a long time, but not forever. It has to come to fruit.

(6) '...brings forth death.' 'The wages of sin is death.' The book of Proverbs is replete with warnings of this end and of the process leading to it.

> [T]emptation to sin cannot be from God, while trial is from him. The one, being our proof, works endurance and endurance, when she has a perfect work, life: the other, being bait and excitement arising from lust 'brings forth sin and sin being completed, brings forth death.'[20]

Satan As Adversary and Tempter.

The book of Job puts this on vivid display. One of Satan's names is 'The Tempter.' Long ago he set in motion the process by which fallen man is tempted by everything in his environment. This matter was treated earlier in this book as an aspect of the doctrine of creation and of the fall of man.

---

19. Brown, *The Anchor Bible*, John p. 306.
20. Henry Alford, *The New Testament for English Readers* (Chicago: Moody Press, n.d.), p. 1595.

6
Divine Control and Human Extremes

In this chapter we consider how God has made it possible for human families to exist and civilized life to go on in spite of the enormity of sins throughout human culture.

Divine Providence in Ruling and Overruling Sin.

Even though, as James insists (James 1:13), God tempts (i.e. entices) no one to sin, there are many texts which seem to say the opposite (e.g. 2 Sam. 16:10; 24:1; but cf. 1 Chron. 21:1). God sometimes severely judges those who will not welcome the truth, who prefer credulous acceptance of lies. In what may be the most pivotal chapter on eschatology in the Bible, Paul declared,

> ...because they refused to love the truth and so be saved. Therefore God sends them a strong delusion, so that they may believe what is false, in order that all may be condemned who did not believe the truth but had pleasure in unrighteousness (2 Thess. 2:10-12).

It is a terrible judgment. The scriptural doctrines of preservation and providence explain that in God's sovereign rule, sins are said to be divinely caused only in the sense of divine concurrence (or concursus) in all that happens, since He is not only Creator but Sustainer and Governor of the world. The Creator concurs in everything that happens in all creation in that He sustains all existing things, not because they are evil but simply as created existences. '[T]he universe was created *by the word of God*' (Heb. 11:3 emphasis added), so also is the world sustained for He 'upholds the universe [including wicked men and angels] *by the word of his power*' (Heb. 1:3 emphasis added). The wills of wicked men and angels are free, in the sense that they are not coerced by God. So God does concur in preserving them in existence though only they are responsible for what they do. God is still in sovereign control and uses even the acts of the wicked to procure His ultimate designs. The reflective sinner knows neither God nor the devil 'made me do it' when he sins. The prime impulse is from his own sinful heart, 'drawn away by his own lust,' as James said. Through sinful men only as proximate or second causes can God be said to 'tempt' and this is what the Bible itself assumes in the texts cited above. God has created those who choose their own course of sin and He preserves them in life. But in that course of sin even the reflective sinner attributes sin to himself, knowing God hates and will punish it.[1]

---

1. A. H. Strong, *Systematic Theology* (Valley Forge, PA: Judson Press, 1907), pp. 365, 411, 418, 419.

The doctrine of preservation implies a natural *concurrence* (mutual action of God and His creatures) in every occurrence either of mind or matter and whether good or evil. So there is a particular relevance to the doctrine of sin. Scripture says of political power, 'there is no power but of God' (Rom. 13:1 KJV) and the same is true of the physical power to press a computer key or to persuade an audience, and we all know that frequently these powers are by men directed toward morally evil ends.

(I have used concur, concurrence and concursus in two previous paragraphs. These terms have long been used by some theologians to signify the relation between God and all His finite creatures in effecting providential control of the world. Pulpit explanations frequently point out that ultimately divine power created and sustained the iron in the hammer that drove the nails into the hands of Christ and also sustained the arm and hand of the soldiers who swung the hammer. The Bible which insists on every page that God has complete sovereign rule over all that exists similarly insists that human decisions and acts are by truly responsible human beings. Augustine seems to have been first to speak of this as a divine *concursus*, the medieval scholastics perpetuated the term and the doctrine. Modern theology makes only a little of it, most subsuming all they have to say of preservation and providence without this refinement. C. A. Hodge explains the doctrine of *concursus* and evaluates it [*Systematic Theology*, pp. 598–605]. He does not condemn the teaching but raises three objections of which the most impressive is that it raises more questions than it answers: that it seeks to explain the inexplicable.)

Pelagians, Arminians and many others (who may have no consistent theology at all) object to the doctrine that God is in specific control (i.e. Providence) of everything that happens. They argue that specific concurrence previous to evil acts and in them makes God the author of sin. Augustinians (Calvinists and others who take the Bible seriously when it over and over affirms directly that God supplies concurrent power with every action, either of good or of evil) acknowledge the difficulty but do not think any one is free to deny God's absolute control even of 'free' actions of moral beings, angels or men, since the Bible clearly teaches it. The clearest texts which teach God's predestination and concurrence as cited in previous sections of this systematic theology are Genesis 45:5; 50:19, 20; and Acts 2:23; among many others are Exodus 14:17; Isaiah 66:4; Romans 9:22; and 2 Thessalonians 2:11.

We are staking out no new ground in pointing out that Scripture assigns four different kinds of divine control over men's sins.[2]

(1) Preventive Control. Some sins that would be destruction of the very order of the world or, if committed, would interfere with the divine plan, are prevented. God prevented Abimelech from committing adultery with Sarah (Gen. 20:6); Laban from doing harm to his son-in-law, Jacob (Gen. 31:24); David prayed for God to prevent him from deeper, presumptuous sins (Ps. 19:13) – to provide only a short list. God has used many means of preventive control, merciful checks on deadly courses of sin, viz.: fear of consequences, Sunday School, church, human laws, even ignorance, old age and weakness. To live a long life is to pass through stages where temptations to 'the sins of my youth' (Ps. 25:7) are replaced by that of middle age (Ps. 19:12, 13; the book of Job) and then of old age (Ps. 71:9). The unbidden voice of conscience, properly trained, has prevented innumerable sins. Sometimes God removes men from earth by death to prevent worse sins than they have committed already. Perhaps this is an aspect of the meaning of 1 Corinthians 11:30, 'That is why many of you are weak and ill, and some have died' and of 1 John 5:16, 'There is sin that leads to death.'

(2) Permissive Control. This is easier to understand and accept, since we are aware of no visible, identifiable obstacles placed by God against our sinful actions. God plainly left Hezekiah to his own impulses when he stupidly exposed the national treasures to ambassadors from Babylon (2 Chron. 32:31) and God gave His people over 'to their own stubborn heart, To walk in their own counsels' (Ps. 81:12 NKJV) and when they 'had a wanton craving in the wilderness… he gave them what they asked, but sent a wasting disease among them' (Ps. 106:14, 15). Many such statements are in Scripture (see Hos. 4:17; Acts 14:16; Rom. 1:24, 28; 3:25). God is not represented as either indifferent to sins or complicit in them. Rather the Old Testament sometimes speaks of God as doing what He only permitted to be done, to fulfil His own plan as in 'It pleased the Lord to bruise him'; to be sure God is even said to have 'put him to grief' (Isa. 53:10). Yet it was the work of several wicked men, whose names we know (Judas, Annas, Caiaphas, Pilate) and whose wicked acts are reported (Acts 2:23). God did not restrain them from planning the execution of the Savior and carrying it out, even though they might have been restrained by 'legions of angels' (Matt. 26:53).

---

2. Thiessen, *Lectures in Theology*, pp. 182, 183; Strong, *Systematic Theology*, pp. 423–425; Calvin, *Institutes I*, xvii, pp. 1–4; Wendell, *Calvin*, pp. 177–184; F. Pieper, *Christian Dogmatics I*, pp. 489, 490; L. Berkhof, *Systematic Theology* on 'Concurrence,' pp. 171–175.

(3) **Directive Control.** God guides the evil efforts of sinful men to ends of His own choosing rather than ends of their choosing, even though like the wicked brothers of Joseph and the betrayer of Jesus, they think they have secured their own goals. The classic sentence in this connection is from Psalm 76:10, 'the wrath of man shall praise you.' The King of Assyria did not know he was to be 'the rod of my [God's] anger.' He thought his own bloodlust to be the reason for his expedition against Zion, but God sent him 'Against a godless nation' (Isa. 10:5, 6), even though that 'godless nation' (Israel) was 'more righteous than he' (Hab. 1:13), and even though the Assyrian 'does not so intend, and his heart does not so think' (Isa. 10:7). God directed Joseph's brothers' wicked deeds. They 'meant evil... but God meant it for good,' that is, to spare many people from starvation (Gen. 50:20). Peter told the Pentecost crowd that when in the earlier Passover season they had by 'wicked hands' crucified and slain their properly accredited Messiah, it was by 'the definite plan and foreknowledge of God' (Acts 2:23).

We cannot doubt God is doing such things each day. Like the servant of Elisha, we do not see that 'the mountain was full of horses and chariots of fire all around Elisha' (2 Kgs. 6:17), even though Elisha saw it plainly. The secular spirit has so infiltrated thinking in our time that it is hard for us even to think in the category of divine providential control. How much more natural it is for us to say, 'It thundered' than 'the God of glory thunders' (Ps. 29:3)!

In God's directive control of the wicked acts of sinful men He in no way entices men to sin. The world and its god do that. Judas was moved by lust for money, Joseph's brothers by jealousy of his prominence. In each case God so directed the course of events that, though an undeserved execution (of Christ) took place, and some years of miserable servitude (for Joseph), great good came about.

(4) **Limiting Control.** Though the 'imagination of men's hearts is only evil continually' and the world offers vast opportunity to follow out those evil imaginations, God has set limits beyond which they cannot go. That a flood to destroy all mankind never be necessary again, God set limits on the extent to which violence and lust could lead (cf. Gen. 8:21, 22 with 9:5-7). Society nowhere exists in pure anarchy precisely because some undefined pervasive social 'instinct' for collective justice (civil control) became universally present in the post-diluvian race. Limitations in the unseen world of wicked spirits have been imposed by God (Job 1:12; 2:6). The 'mystery of iniquity' consummated in the man of sin has always been kept under control by some restraining power (2 Thess. 2:3-6 NIV), known to Paul's readers but unknown to us, and by some person ('one') as in 2 Thessalonians 2:7 NIV. In some mysterious manner this 'thing' and that 'person' assist believers in their efforts to resist temptation, either as *trial* or as enticement. David said that 'if it had not been the LORD who was on our side' our triers and tempters 'would have swallowed us up' (Ps. 124:2, 3).

Sins that Cry to Heaven for Vengeance and Sins of Outstanding Offense to God.

Some sins are worse than others because they are more productive of human misery or such perversion of divine order for the world that they threaten civilized social order or mount an assault against the majesty of God. It comes as a rebuke to socially complacent Christians and Christian groups that many of these sins occur in the manner of treatment we mete out to our neighbor – who may or may not be a fellow believer. I mention first those that are said to cry from earth to heaven to be set right or call for vengeance. The first four are part of what traditional theology calls 'the catechetical tradition', i.e. taught to children and others preparing for 'first communion.'[3]

(1) **Oppression of the poor or any socially disadvantaged group.** When the children of Israel were poor and oppressed in Egypt, 'the people of Israel groaned because of their slavery and cried out for help. Their cry... came up to God' (Exod. 2:23). 'Then the LORD said, "I have surely seen... and have heard their cry... and I have come down to deliver them"' (Exod. 3:7, 8). God took notice not only because of His covenant with their ancestors, for all sins of oppressing the poor on earth are particularly offensive to heaven, but because 'Whoever mocks the poor insults his Maker' (Prov. 17:5) and his sins will not go unpunished, for 'Whoever closes his ear to the cry of the poor will himself call out and not be answered' (Prov. 21:13). (2) A second sin that cries to heaven for vengeance is oppression of foreigners (refugees from oppression elsewhere), widows and orphans. The consequences of this sort of sin are harsh indeed. Among the 'judgments' associated with the giving of the two tablets of the law is one related to oppression of foreigners.

---

3. 1994 *Catechism*, para. 1867; Francis Pieper, *Christian Dogmatics*, p. 570.

> You shall neither mistreat a stranger nor oppress him, for you were strangers...You shall not afflict any widow or fatherless child... they [will] cry... to Me, I will surely hear their cry; and My wrath will become hot, and I will kill you with the sword; your wives shall be widows, and your children fatherless (Exod. 22:21-24 NKJV).

(3) Injustice to wage-earners who need their earnings to buy daily bread.

> You shall not oppress a hired servant who is poor and needy, whether he is one of your brothers or one of the sojourners [aliens, possibly refugees?] who are in your land within your towns. You shall give him his wages on the same day, before the sun sets (for he is poor and counts on it), lest he cry against you to the LORD, and you be guilty of sin (Deut. 24:14-15).

In addition to these sins that are said to 'cry out to God' there are others particularly offensive to the divine Spirit. One can almost say they trigger wrathful response like nothing else, as biblical history bears witness.

(4) Sins of sexual impurity and sexual perversion – specifically, fornication, adultery and homosexual acts are especially abominable to God. God loves mankind, He 'makes their families like flocks' (Ps. 107:41) and makes family life a picture of heaven. The Old Testament is a story of families. Therefore, sins against the propagation of and ordering of our race are hateful to God simply because God loves us. Hence, the expedition from heaven via Abraham's tent to Sodom and Gomorrah, whose 'sin is very grave,' and the heavenly messengers' grim word to Lot, 'we are about to destroy this place, because the outcry against its people has become great before the LORD, and the LORD has sent us to destroy it' (Gen. 18:20 and 19:13). The sin, laid bare in chapter 19 was plainly community-wide, unreproved and unrestrained homosexuality. This sin is an arrow aimed straight at the heart of marriage, home, personal and family discipline with terrible consequences in community and national life. No wonder the Torah calls homosexual practice an abomination, calling for the very most severe civil penalty. The eighteenth chapter of Leviticus goes into great detail on this matter. The very land is polluted when its inhabitants do such things. These sins brought on the divinely decreed annihilation of the Canaanites and later the land 'spewed out' the Israelites who took their place and repeated these sins. The language of Leviticus 18 (especially vv. 22-30) is sufficient to bring on a chill to any citizen of any corrupted country who takes these verses seriously.

(5) The sins of murder and failure of civil officers to discover, to convict and punish murderers. The first homicide called forth this reproof of the murderer from the victim's Creator: 'The voice of your brother's blood is crying to me from the ground' (Gen. 4:10). Cain was rightly convinced all men would regard his crime as deserving of death, with which the LORD agreed, but spared the miscreant by placing a special mark on him (Gen. 4:14, 15). The enormity of the crime of homicide offended heaven to the extent that when 'the earth was filled with violence' it was brought to a sudden end with the Great Flood and a true *novus ordo seculorum* (new order of the world, the inscription on all U.S. paper currency). (See Genesis 6:11, 17; 9:1 ff.)

The Noahic covenant, reinforced by the Mosaic code, requires that premeditated murder, like Cain's, be punished by death and made it a prime responsibility of civil rulers to see it is carried out. Failure to do so is very offensive to the divine Creator of human civil order. The importance of this matter is in full display in the thirty-fifth chapter of Numbers. After laying out a fair and thorough procedure for establishing guilt or innocence of murder, the severity of God's anger with murderers is plain, as also the civil punishment: '... he shall be put to death.' No monetary fine would substitute. Murder, as well as sexual pollution, '... pollute the land in which you live, for blood pollutes the land, and no atonement can be made for the land for the blood that is shed in it, except by the blood of the one who shed it' (Num. 35:31-33). God simply refuses to dwell 'in the midst' of any people who practise repugnant sexual license, sexual vice and avarice, no less where civil laws, officers and processes fail to discover, prosecute and punish murder. In comment on Deuteronomy 21:1-9, Gleason Archer writes:

> ...in the case of unsolved murders a public hearing had to be held in which the elders of the community in whose borders the crime had occurred would have to take an oath of innocence and then offer a sacrifice to God with an accompanying prayer for forgiveness, lest their land should remain polluted.[4]

(6) The sin of idolatry. The first and second commandments (Exod. 20:1-6) give this sin first place among all moral offenses. The worship of any material object makes a fool of man and dishonors God. 'I am the LORD... [and] my glory I give to no other, nor my praise to carved idols' (Isa. 42:8). There is only one God, by whom and for whom

---

4. Gleason Archer, 'Crime and Punishments' in *Zondervan Pictorial Encyclopedia of the Bible II* (Grand Rapids: Zondervan, 1975), p. 1032.

man was made in the beginning, hence, 'My glory I will not give to another' (Isa. 48:11). This sin, in literal sense of giving either veneration or obeisance to a material object, called forth the fury of divine wrath repeatedly in Old Testament history (see Ps. 78 and Judg. 2). It is condemned as the prime sin of the heathen world in Romans chapter 1, verses 19-25 and in Paul's sermon at Athens (Acts 17:22-31). The article 'Idolatry,' by F. B. Huey, Jr, gives a brief but thorough treatment, especially as to 'why idolatry is condemned in the Bible.'[5]

In ancient times astrology was a near invariable adjunct of idolatry and remains so in present-day New-Age religion. Astrology flourishes on the ashes of biblical religion produced by widespread apostasy into these delusions of our time. Abba Hillel Silver asserts:

> Under Canaanitish and Assyrian influence astral worship as well as astrology developed in Israel, for wherever there is worship of heavenly bodies there is also… astrology.… In the period of the prophets worship of the 'host of heaven' was prevalent in Isaiah, and the prophets… exerted themselves to the utmost to denounce it.[6]

(Rebuke of idolatry and its devastating effects occupies hundreds of pages of Old Testament law, narrative and prophetic writing. Its most ruinous form was sacrifice of infants to the Canaanite [Phoenician] god Moloch. The prevalence of the custom in the Semitic culture of Old Testament Israel is witnessed in the many acres of cemeteries for disposal of the bodies of the tiny unfortunate victims of this horrid practice. A classic book, *The Idea of the Holy* by Rudolph Otto [second edition of 1950], sets the background in human response to nature which gives rise to worship of unknown power; *The Religion of the Semites* by W. Robertson Smith [1927] is a second classic showing how the Semite, apart from a revealed and organized faith [or even in spite of it] responded with superstition and idolatry to the natural world in which Israel's history unfolded. F. B. Huey in a condensed article summed up the subject ['Idolatry,' *ZPEB III*, pp. 242–248].)

Idolatry was the prime sin of Canaanites leading to their expulsion. Associated with idolatry all sorts of wicked occult practices arose, all condemned by Moses (Deut. 18:9-14) and denounced by prophets.

Partaking of Other Men's Sins.

This phrase, taken from 1 Timothy 5:22, appears in a passage directly applicable only to Timothy and presumably pastors in positions like Timothy's as chief pastor at Ephesus. It has been variously interpreted. When in the twentieth century unbelief in the form of 'modernism' first arose among professors and seminaries, then among pastors, churches, and church literature and even whole denominations, problems of association were thrust upon many earnest believers. Sadly, the scourge of unbelief professing to be intelligent faith has gradually rendered much of Christendom apostate with the result that this admonition to avoid partaking of other men's sins has been difficult for pastors and members of those groups to obey. I will not attempt here to report the debate about the problem of ecclesiastical separation over the past century among American Protestants. The results of doing nothing decisive are manifest now in the sidetracking of 'mainstream' Protestantism in America. The natural tendency to be courteous sometimes even makes us complicit with outright heretical cults whose messengers call on us. John warns of the one who 'does not abide in the doctrine of Christ,' saying 'whoever greets him takes part in his wicked works' (2 John 11), and Paul says to 'avoid them' (Rom. 16:17; cf. 1:32).

Sin by Giving Unnecessary Offense.

To give offense in the sense of Romans 14:13 is to use one's Christian liberty in such a way as to offend the conscience of a brother who does not yet understand the liberty Christians rightly ought to enjoy. The teaching of the chapter is that we ought not to judge one another in things that God has blessed – food, drink, legitimate pleasures, things not wrong *as such*. Some believers, however, are not well informed about these *adiaphora*, or 'things indifferent.' Their feelings should be respected. The 'weak' (uninformed) ought not to judge his 'strong' brother (the informed about Christian liberty), yet consideration for the 'weak' should direct the 'strong' to respect the brother's conscience, lest he be induced to sin against his conscience (Rom. 14, especially vv. 21-23). To do otherwise is to put a stumbling-block (Gr. *skandalon*) in a brother's way (Rom. 14:13), an occasion for unnecessary distress or backsliding.

---

5. F. B. Huey, Jr, 'Idolatry' in *Zondervan Pictorial Encyclopedia of the Bible III* (Zondervan, 1975), pp. 242–248.
6. Abba Hillel Silver, *Messianic Speculation in Israel* (Boston: Beacon Hill Press, 1927, 1959), pp. 253–259.

A much more serious sin of offense (Gr. *skandalon*) is described in Romans 16:17. It is the offense of propagating false teaching within the church, viz.: 'I appeal to you, brothers, to watch out for those who cause divisions and create obstacles [Gr. *skandalon*] contrary to the doctrine that you have been taught; avoid them.' It is a sin to ignore the offense (false teaching) and neglect of duty not to bring the 'scandal' of false teachings and false teachers to the attention of the church. Much is said of this throughout the New Testament, especially Paul's Epistles. To fail to act is a form of partaking of other men's sins. I have written at length of it in my book of 1993, *A Wakeup Call*.[7]

Jesus denounced those who cause such scandal, viz.: 'Whoever causes one of these little ones who believe in me to sin, it would be better for him if a great millstone were hung round his neck and he were thrown into the sea' (Mark 9:42).

Our attention will now be directed to the question of how sin has been transmitted through the generations of man. This will require first, some further consideration of *original* sin, second, the imputation of sin, third, further exegesis of Romans 5:12-21, and finally the salvation of infants.

---

7. Robert D. Culver, *A Wakeup Call* (Clayton, CA: Witness, Inc., 1993).

7
The Transmission of Sin Through the Generations of Man

Importance and Difficulty of the Subject.

There is no theological system in Christendom with the slightest right to be called a system of orthodox Christian doctrine, which does not attribute immense importance to the probation and fall of Adam in explaining the spiritual ruin of our race. His sin somehow explains why we are sinful in thoughts, words and deeds and why we are aware of the fact, unless we suppress it. Yet the Bible says only a little about the connection. In fact the Old Testament says almost nothing about Adam after the fifth chapter of Genesis. We have the story of Adam's probation and fall in chapters 2 and 3, that he begat Cain, Abel and Seth in chapter 4, and he begat a son named Seth in his own likeness, as well as other sons and daughters, in chapter 5. 'But there is not a solitary passage in all the rest of the Old Testament which can… be made to suggest that the sin of Adam inflicted any injury of any kind upon his descendants.'[1] Job 31:33 and Hosea 6:7 refer to Adam's sin, but not to any effects on his sons and daughters of any generation.

In the New Testament, only Paul says very much about such a connection – not Jesus, not Peter or James or John or Jude – and he only in two texts. Each Pauline text proposes a parallel between a unity of men in Adam and a unity in Christ. In 1 Corinthians 15:22 it is said that just as all mankind are dying physically in Adam so all mankind will be resurrected physically in Christ. This text does not teach universal salvation in Christ; it teaches universal physical resurrection through the Logos (John 1:1-3) Creator of us all.

In the other text, Romans 5:12-21, Paul eight times and in as many ways declares that just as the one man Adam's offense brought the immeasurable evils of death and judgment, rendering all sinners, so our Lord's death in obedience to the Father's will brought the infinite blessings of life and righteousness, rendering many justified by the free gift of God's grace. R. W. Dale points out how even this passage introduces the subject as illustrative of something else.

> But even this passage – the critical passage on the doctrine – the account of the evil results of Adam's sin is incidental; Paul speaks of Adam's transgression and of the effects of it, not for the sake of giving an explanation of human sin, but for the sake of illustrating the greatness of Christian salvation.[2]

I shall discuss the passage in some detail later, but first let us see what doctrinal construction has been made of it.

---
1. R. W. Dale, *Christian Doctrine* (London, 1899), p. 214.
2. ibid., p. 215.

The Doctrine of Original Sin.

Through the first two and one-half chapters of the Epistle to the Romans, Paul establishes two facts related to the transmission of sin: (a) every man is a corrupt being at heart even before consciously committing sins. Not only so, we know at heart that this is true unless we suppress the knowledge. (b) We are also aware that we are guilty, under just condemnation by our Creator and deserving of punishment both for being sinners at heart and for transgressions we commit.

This is the main thrust of the first three chapters of Romans ending at chapter 3, verse 20. The evidence is summarized in verse 19, viz.: 'every mouth... stopped... all the world... guilty before God' (KJV). Calvin remarks, 'The whole third chapter of Romans [vv. 1-20] is nothing but a description of original sin.'[3]

Then through Romans 3:21-31, all of chapter 4 and through 5:11, the subject is justification – i.e. that God declares believing sinners righteous wholly of grace on the ground of Christ's finished work of redemption.

At this point comes Romans 5:12-21, both difficult in certain ways and yet marvellously plain. The unity of the race in Adam and his sin is presented as a parallel to and explanation for the oneness of the 'many' elect believers in Christ. It will call for later comment but for now, it seems that Paul felt his readers to be more thoroughly familiar with the harrowing of life and conscience by their sins than with the glories of divine grace. Experiential knowledge of the former (our thorough guilt for sin) would throw light on the latter (our full salvation in Christ), which must be first a matter of faith before it becomes a matter of growing experience.

Great as are the mysteries of justification 'in Christ' Paul is saying, they are not without parallel in something every competent sinner knows: that he and the race of which he is a member are guilty, deserving of punishment. The latter throws light on the former and Paul is bold, shocking as it may be, to let the fact of *damnation* in Adam throw light on *redemption* in Christ. Since very early in the patristic age these revealed truths about imputation of guilt of Adam's first transgression to his posterity and their depravity as basic to the imputation have been called 'Original Sin.'[4]

A. Original Sin As Understood in the Early Church.

Calvin sets the facts straight about how 'original sin' entered Christian theology. After noting that according to Romans 8:20-22 'all creatures... are groaning... subject to corruption, not of their own will... bearing part of the punishment deserved by man for whose use they were created,' he adds, 'therefore it is not unreasonable if it [corruption] is spread to all his offspring.' He then explains, 'This is the inherited corruption which the church fathers termed original sin.'[5]

The term 'original sin' was used somewhat diffidently by the Fathers – even obscurely. Historians agree the Latin Fathers were reluctant to articulate a doctrine of race sin in Adam lest they give Christians leave to blame their transgressions on someone else (Adam) and themselves fail to resist unto blood striving against sin.[6] This is why, after it had been fairly well articulated, Pelagius said he rejected the doctrine of original sin. Pelagius, a British monk of Irish origin came to Rome in AD 400 and was distressed at the low state of conduct there. Feeling that there was need of more moral effort he was shocked by the prayer in St Augustine's *Confessions*, 'Give what thou commandest and command what thou wilt.' His teachings seem to have aroused no stir until he went to Carthage (where Augustine was bishop) after the sack of Rome in AD 410.[7]

In the East before AD 200 opinions were not firmed up about individual moral depravity. The sin of every man, it was thought, had its *type* in Adam but the will was not clearly seen as impaired by Adam's fall.

> The moral depravity of every individual... appeared to be a repetition, rather than a consequence of the first sin... they had recourse to the influence of demons... rather than to a total bondage of the will as the result of original sin.[8]

---

3. Calvin, *Institutes II*, i,9.
4. A very competent introduction to this difficult subject will be found in Jaroslav Pelikan's *The Christian Tradition I, The Emergence of the Catholic Tradition* (Chicago: Univ. of Chicago Press, 1971), pp. 178-192.
5. Calvin, *Institutes II*, i,5.
6. J. L. Neve, *A History of Christian Thought I* (Philadelphia: Muhlenberg Press, 1946), p. 138.
7. Henry Bettenson, *Documents of the Christian Church*, 2nd ed. (New York: Oxford Univ. Press, 1963), pp. 73, 74.
8. Hagenbach, cited by Neve, *Christian Thought I*, p. 138.

J. L. Neve quotes J. H. Kurtz to the same effect:

> Opposition to Gnosticism and Manicheism led the elder fathers to emphasize as strongly as possible moral freedom of men and induced them to deny inborn sinfulness as well as the doctrine that sin was imprinted in men in creation, and to account for man's present condition by bad training, evil example, the agency of evil spirits, etc.[9]

Tertullian in his *De Anima* (Concerning the Soul) was the first clearly to teach original sin.[10] Yet a few years earlier Irenaus (died about AD 200) held the doctrine of original sin *in nuce*. He said:

> The first Adam misused his free will and disobeyed God, in consequence of which he fell, and with him all mankind. Through the fall man... lost the divine image and became the victim of death.[11]

Irenaeus followed with a soteriology derived in part, it would seem, from Romans 5:12-21.

B. Original Sin As Seen by Augustine and Later Augustinians.

Augustine had learned about original sin from his first Christian pastor and preceptor, Ambrose of Milan, but it was in response to a denial of any sort of effect of Adam's sin upon his descendants by the British monk, Pelagius, and his associate, Coelestius, that called forth his first extensive and fully coherent statement of our oneness with Adam in guilt, corruption and punishment (i.e. original sin). Augustine's writings on original sin and related matters are very extensive – many pages in *The City of God*, volumes of anti-Pelagian writings and at least seven letters to various parties.[12, 13]

Augustine said much on the subject and the English translations of his writings vary, but a comment on Psalm 119:119 in relation to the death of infants and the rite of circumcision is appropriate to quote here as bringing his argument to focus.

He has first asserted 'infants, not personally in their own life, but according to the common origin of the human race, have all broken God's covenant in that one in whom all have sinned [Rom. 5:12, 19].'[14] He goes on to argue from the practice of infant baptism for removal of guilt of original sin; a view common at that time, saying: 'If on this account, then, even the infants are, according to the true belief, born in sin, not actual [of act] but original, so that we confess they have need of grace for the remission of sins.' He argues from Psalm 119:119 which read in his Bible, 'I have counted all sinners on earth as lawbreakers' (*Septuagint*) that even infants have broken divine law and did so only in 'the law which was given in Paradise.'[15] In his lifetime Augustine was accused of inventing the notion of original sin by Julian of Eclanum (c. AD 418/419). See Vernon J. Bourke's *Augustine's Quest of Wisdom*.[16]

Contrary to claims of recent opponents to the Protestant-Augustinian view of imputation of original sin, Augustine does not make Romans 5:12 (Latin) pivotal to his view.

Anthropology and Hamartiology (man and sin) are the main foci of Shedd's great two-volume work, *History of Christian Doctrine*. To summarize Shedd's history: Augustine perceived that a biblical soteriology (doctrine of salvation) wholly by divine grace is required by biblical anthropology (doctrine of man) and of sin (doctrine of sin). Augustine's formulation of these doctrines rather quickly prevailed, particularly in the West. Lamentably, though honored in profession, these truths gradually were subverted to Semi-Pelagianism in actual practice during the Middle Ages. Augustine's theology of the fall of man and its permanent effects became the theology of the Protestant Reformation and, I think, correct to say, is still dominant in informed evangelical theology even today, at least ought to be. W. G. T. Shedd's important summary follows.

> 1. Man was created holy, and from this position originated sin *de nihilo* by a purely creative act. Original sin [as Adam enacted it] is voluntary in the sense of being self-will [not compelled by any external force], and is therefore a purely creative act.

---

9. Neve, *Christian Thought I*, p. 138.
10. ibid, p. 138.
11. Irenaus, *Against Heresies* 2,8, summarized by Neve, *Christian Thought I*, p. 80.
12. H. Pope, *St. Augustine of Hippo*, p. 180.
13. The core of the ancient literature of this controversy will be found in Henry Bettenson, *Documents of the Christian Church*, pp. 73–88 and passages in Augustine, *The Kingdom of God*, XII, 22; XIV, 11, 12; XIV, 11–15.
14. Augustine, *City of God Book XVI*, chap. XXIX, 27.
15. ibid.
16. Vernon J. Bourke, *Augustine's Quest of Wisdom* (Milwaukee: Bruce Publ. Co., 1945), p. 191.

2. Man was created as a species, in respect to both soul and body; and hence the Adamic connection relates to the entire man – to the voluntary and rational nature, equally with the corporeal and sensuous.

3. By the Adamic connection, the will, the *pneuma*, is corrupted as well as the *psyche* and *soma*.

4. Infants are guilty, because they possess a sinful bias of will, and not merely a corrupt sensuous nature.

5. The corruption of the sensuous nature is the (material) consequent, and not the antecedent of apostasy in the rational and voluntary.... The corruption of the flesh is not the cause, but the effect of the corruption of the reason and will.

6. The Holy Spirit takes the initiative in the change from sin to holiness, and there is no co-operation of the human with the Divine agency in the regenerating act. The efficiency or activity of the human will up to the point of regeneration is hostile to God, and therefore does not co-operate with him.[17]

C. Original Sin in the Protestant Reformation and Onward.

There is no aspect of doctrine unaffected by the decision one makes on the teaching of original sin. This effect is most profound in soteriology. I shall not here trace the history of the subject except to say, though the objections raised by Pelagius and Coelestius in the early fifth century have reappeared from time to time throughout Christian history, the main streams of orthodox Christian theology have preserved the main features of Augustine's construction (summarized above) intact. This is witnessed by the chief Reformation creeds and confessions, Calvin's *Institutes*, Melanchthon's *Loci Communes* of 1555 (Lutheran), and later standard works of theology. Luther himself, one may rightly say, in *The Bondage of the Will*, fully endorsed the doctrine of original sin (as James Packer's Introduction to the latest English edition avers vigorously).

Except for a rather subtle bent toward Traducianism in Shedd's summary (not incorrect, I think) what he writes is the confession of all Protestant orthodoxy today. Roman Catholic theology agrees with much of it, except that it regards man's rational faculties as not vitiated by the fall of Adam.

Groups of evangelical Christians who implicitly or explicitly reject systematic formulations of doctrines ('The Bible, the whole Bible, and nothing but the Bible') may not perceive the importance of original sin and its correlates, but join with confessional Christians in the hymns they sing – Reformed, Lutheran, Presbyterian, Congregational, Mennonite, Baptist, Independents, Pentecostal, and recently, Roman Catholics. Eastern Orthodox think somewhat differently, though there have been strong expressions of a similar synthesis even among them. See *Confession of Augsburg II* (1530) 'Of Original Sin' (Bettenson, 295); *The Formula of Concord*, Art. I 'Concerning Original Sin' (Schaff, *Creeds of Christendom*, 97–106); Calvin, *Institutes I*, i, 1–10; Anglican 'Articles of Religion,' art. IX 'Of Original or Birth-Sin'; *Westminster Confession* (1643) chap. VI 'Of the Fall of Man, of Sin, and of the Punishment thereof'; Methodist *The Articles of Religion* (1784), art. vii 'Of Original or Birth Sin' in *The Articles of Religion*, 1984, p. 57. *The Savoy Declaration* (1658) of Congregationalists embodies the *Westminster Confession* as does also *The Philadelphia Confession* (1685) of Baptists. This list could be extended at great length. I cite these to show that as unacceptable to unregenerate reason and the secular mind of every age as 'Original Sin' is, it is the confession of orthodox, evangelical Christianity as well as of the ancient church. With important modification it remains intact even in the Roman Church.

There is no more faithful exponent of historic Lutheranism than C. P. Krauth in his great work of 832 pages, *The Conservative Reformation*. He says of original sin and consequent universal necessity for regeneration:

> On this point, all sound theology of every part of our common Christianity is a unit.... The Romish and Greek Churches recognize the impossibility of the salvation of any human creature without change from that condition in which he was born.
>
> This great fact must not be forgotten that on the main difficulty of this part [necessity even for infants to be born again on account of original sin], all but Pelagians are in unity of faith with our church [Lutheran]. The testimony of the Church through all ages is most explicit on this point: That no unregenerate person, infant or adult, Pagan or nominal Christian, can be saved. Without holiness, no man shall see the Lord – but no man can be holy with his natural heart unchanged. Except we have the Spirit of Christ we are none of His; but this Spirit is given to us in and by the new birth alone.[18]

As for the recent past, neo-orthodoxy, flowering as it did (and does) after two World Wars, a terrible depression and concurrent with the revelation of the Nazi atrocities, used eloquent language in describing human depravity. I was a student, pastor, then professor while Barth, Brunner, Bonhoeffer, the Niebuhrs, Tillich and the rest discovered and

---

17. Wm. G. T. Shedd, *History of Christian Doctrine ii* (New York: Scribner, Armstrong & Co., 1863), pp. 91, 92.
18. C. P. Krauth, *The Conservative Reformation* (Philadelphia: J. B. Lippincott, 1875), p. 420.

expounded what the 'fundamentalists' knew all along. (I preached the community's 'Victory in Europe' Day sermon in 1945, taking Psalm 46 as my text.) I have long since destroyed my files on what I then read, though the memory lingers. In April of 1995 on the fiftieth anniversary, an article by Gerald Parshall in *U.S. News and World Report* makes the point with reference to how history has confirmed our orthodox faith in original sin, viz.:

> But the Holocaust was clearly more than a testament to the beastliness of Germans or the excesses of fascism. In an editorial called, Gazing into the Pit, the *Christian Century* wrote that the atrocities showed 'the horror of humanity itself when it has surrendered to its capacity for evil... Buchenwald and the other concentration camps spell doom. But it is not simply the doom of the Nazis; it is the doom of man unless he can be brought to worship at the feet of the living God.' Even for secular intellectuals, the Holocaust supplied the most powerful brief yet for the existence of original sin. Two centuries earlier, thinkers were asserting the perfectibility of man. Now, they were debating whether Germans were human. The answer, tragically was yes.[19]

Protestant evangelicals of today, largely through historical forgetfulness, are not aware fully of their spiritual ancestors' faith. In Reformation times the enormously learned linguist, Erasmus, published a 'Diatribe' expounding free will of man in the spirit of the Semi-Pelagianism of the Roman Church. Luther responded in *The Bondage of the Will*, 'The Masterwork of the Great Reformer,' of which a new translation by James I. Packer and O. R. Johnson was published in 1957. Near the end of their long Introduction these authors say:

'What is the modern reader to make of *The Bondage of the Will*? That it is a brilliant and exhilarating performance, a masterpiece of the controversialist's difficult art, he will no doubt readily admit; but now comes the question, is Luther's case any part of God's truth? And, if so, has it a message for Christians today? No doubt the reader will find the way by which Luther leads him to be a strange new road, an approach which in all probability he has never considered, a line of thought which he would normally label 'Calvinistic' and hastily pass by. This is what Lutheran orthodoxy itself has done; and the present-day evangelical Christian (who has Semi-Pelagianism in his blood) will be inclined to do the same. But both history and Scripture, if allowed to speak, counsel otherwise (reprint in 1994 by Baker Book House, Grand Rapids, Michigan, pp. 57, 58).'

The Problems of the Imputation of Adam's Sin to Succeeding Generations.

Earlier, in connection with the fall of Adam, we have seen that Adam's sin rendered him guilty, depraved and condemned to the punishment of death. Now we must consider *first* the question, put as poignantly as possible: Is each descendant of Adam truly guilty of that first sin? Put another way, are we guilty sinners in God's sight only because of our own personal transgressions or are we already born sinners under God's just sentence? In the language of John, are we truly 'condemned already' (John 3:18)? The question has become acute with seeming denials of the orthodox Protestant answer in recent evangelical publications. See David L. Smith's *With Willful Intent: A Theology of Sin*.[20] *Second*, assuming we are guilty of Adam's sin, how can this be? I remember nothing of any sin before my birth. I was not asked to join my ever-so-great grandfather in what he did wrong; how then can I share in his blame? It does not seem right, yet according to the Bible it is right. How? Why? The answers are found in Romans 5:12-19. We proceed here directly to the two questions. These two questions constitute the topic, imputation of Adam's sin.

(1) In answer to the first question, as to the fact, yes, the Scriptures clearly teach that: (a) 'by the one man's disobedience the many were made sinners' (Rom. 5:19). In the context of verse 12 the 'many' are 'all men.' 'Made' translates *kathistēmi* which in the New Testament never means to change the character of something: rather to establish, render, constitute (as a judge, or ruler, or the like; see Luke 12:14; Matt. 24:45) someone in a particular way. Hence, it is correct to say Adam's disobedience (transgression, sin) rendered all his descendants guilty by virtue of the first man's first sin.

(b) Adam's sin is charged to every member of the human race. This is only a different slant of the meaning of the point just made. Placing in parallel our justification in Christ but in contrast to it Paul says, 'the gift of God is not like the result of the one man's sin: The judgment followed one [man's] sin and brought condemnation' (Rom. 5:16 NIV). The KJV, 'by one that sinned,' renders *ex henos*, lit. 'out of one,' emphasizing one human actor or action. It could be either Adam himself or his first offense. 'Condemnation' renders *katakrima*, a judgment or sentence of condemnation by a judge. It was pronounced on 'all men' (vv. 12, 18, 19): plus 'many' (v. 15), not when each one sins, but on the occasion of Adam's transgression.

---

19. Gerald Parshall in *U.S. News & World Report* (April 3, 1995), p. 65.
20. David L. Smith, *With Willful Intent: A Theology of Sin* (Wheaton, IL: Victor Books, 1994), pp. 368–371.

(c) 'Death came to all men, because all sinned' (Rom. 5:12 NIV). Paul employs a tense of the verb for sin (*hamartanō*), the aorist tense, which in context places the action of 'all sinned' in one past act, not a succession of acts. The result was and is not merely that since Adam's transgression all his descendants are going to die (though 1 Cor. 15:22 does say so, 'in Adam all die' and human experience testifies that every man is indeed mortal); the sense is that *all* sinned in Adam and are from the first moment of natural life, dead already in trespasses and sins (Eph. 2:1; Col. 2:13). They are 'by nature children of wrath' – that is, divine wrath.

(2) In answer to the second question, assuming then the fact of original sin, guilt for Adam's act, how can it be? How can God justly hold each of us responsible for Adam's sin? (My professor of systematic theology did not presume to know how but simply accepted universal human guilt for Adam's sin as a biblical fact. Professor McClain may have felt the several theories as to *why* were too complex to explain adequately or inconclusive, and that there were better uses of time than to assess theories that go on forever.) Nevertheless, I propose the following as a probable solution to the problem.

(a) Because there is an organic, natural connection of Adam with each of his descendants. There is greater difficulty for the creationist, in whose view each human soul is directly created by God. But, on the basis of Traducianism, that each infant born was begotten and conceived entire, body and soul, in the womb of the mother, procreated by both parents, there is a lesser problem. All human nature, quantitatively and qualitatively, was in Adam when under the conditions of the probation he fell and thereby corrupted not only himself but the very nature of man. Nature is not a *material* substance as we ordinarily think of substance. One need not adopt the metaphysics of medieval 'realism' to adopt Traducianism and the idea that all mankind in that nature was *seminally* (i.e. in seed form) present in Adam and, as seed, fell with and in him. Robert Dabney well said:

> [I]n history, the *ex traduce* [Traducianism as defined above] theory has been thought more favorable to original sin, and has been usually connected with it, till modern times; while Creationism was strenuously advocated by Pelagians. If the Traducian theory can be substantiated it obviously presents the best explanation of the propagation of sin.[21]

I have observed that Calvin and Augustine, while never quite formally committing themselves to Traducianism, employ arguments for each individual's guilt for Adam's sin which plainly require both the body and soul be procreated by parents and their individual guilt for what he (Adam) did because he is seminally present in him. In one of several paragraphs against Pelagianism Calvin says,

> We must surely hold that Adam was not only the progenitor but, as it were, the root of human nature; and therefore in *his* corruption mankind deserved to be vitiated [i.e. mankind as nature in Adam deserved to be punished by being 'vitiated,' that is, corrupted].[22]

Calvin adds,

> Adam by sinning... plunged our nature into like destruction. This was not due to the guilt of himself alone, which would not pertain to us at all, but was because he infected all his posterity.[23]

Calvin's language on through several paragraphs of this section employs language implying that human nature fell in Adam – there was a nature including body and soul that fell in Adam and was propagated onward. Augustine makes many direct statements that come close to an endorsement of Traducianism. I cite only one of them which implies the seminal presence of every descendant in Adam and the corruption of human nature itself as grounds for guilt, condemnation and death of everyone.

> God created men aright, for God is the author of nature, though he is certainly not responsible for their defects. But man was willingly perverted and justly condemned, and so begot perverted and condemned offspring. For we were all in that one man, seeing we all *were* [emphasis added] that one man who fell into sin through the woman who was made from him before the first sin. We did not yet possess forms individually created and assigned for us to live in them as individuals; but there already existed the seminal nature from which we were to be begotten. And of course, when this was vitiated through sin, and bound with death's fetters in its just condemnation, man could not be born of man in any other condition... mankind is led from that... corruption at the root.[24]

---

21. Robert Dabney, *Lectures on Systematic Theology* (Grand Rapids, MI: Zondervan, 1972, first published in 1878), p. 317.
22. Calvin, *Institutes* II,i,6.
23. ibid.
24. Henry Bettenson translation, *Augustine City of God* (Baltimore, MD: Penguin, 1972), XIII.14.

This passage espouses the same justification for condemnation on account of original sin found in Shedd (*Dogmatic Theology*, 1888); Strong (*Systematic Theology*, 1907); H. C. Thiessen (*Lectures in Systematic Theology*, 1949); and in somewhat attenuated form in Erickson (*Christian Theology*, 1983); as well as Lewis and Demarest (*Integrative Theology*, 1990). Official statements among Protestants apparently grounded in the Traducian outlook begin with the Lutheran *Augsburg Confession* and the *Apology for the Confession*.

(b) The doctrine of race sin, hence universal guilty responsibility, is supported by the facts of human life. Think of what Hitler's depravity inflicted first on his own German people then on Jews and all the inhabited earth. Whether these effects are right, just, correct or not, they are true. (I refer the reader to a later section on 'the universality of sin.')

(c) We who lend at least tentative support to the above Traducianist theory agree at least this much with those who hold to Federal or covenant headship (see below) that Paul draws a parallel between race unity in Christ and in Adam. In Christ's case the unity was by forensic (legal) action of God (i.e. imputation). Imputation was made appropriate and possible, however, by Christ's natural (organic) connection with humanity in His incarnation. A careful reading of the chief modern advocates of *Federal* headship (including both the Hodges, C. A. and A. A., John Murray, Robert Dabney, James Thorwell, Louis Berkhof, and others) will show that in imputation of guilt for Adam's sin to posterity, the natural (or seminal) connection with Adam rendered the forensic appropriate and possible. Similarly, the imputation of Christ's righteousness to human beings was possible only by His becoming one of us by nature (incarnation) and likewise Adam's sin is ours and we are guilty in and with him only because we were truly, seminally, in him. The parallel is not exact. We cannot quite agree with those who, like A. H. Strong, hold that the race was created originally in Christ in any organic sense.

(d) Death among mankind is not in the true nature of things an inevitable event in normal course. It is abnormal, something inflicted on mankind as punishment for sin. The Bible is clear that death in human kind, at any age, is not merely the natural outcome of life, but the imposed penalty for sin. When infants die, it cannot be a penalty for consciously committed personal sins. The only proper explanation is that the infant shares in race guilt for Adam's sin. So Paul argues in Romans 5:14 and Augustine emphasizes. Adam had no built-in metabolic clock to tell his body when to grow old, but every one of his descendent children has one. Science has not found our 'life-maintenance clock' but it is there. It will neither be found nor reset – eager proponents of various kinds of life-science research notwithstanding.

(e) If the fruit (i.e. evil thoughts and deeds) of the fallen nature (the sinful heart) in each one of us deserves condemnation and punishment, then surely the evil root does also. Many texts throughout the Bible assert that both are evil, for example: Job 14:4; Genesis 6:5; Matthew 15:19.

(f) Further, everyone in possession of common sense knows he is individually responsible – whatever his nature and nurture – for his own offenses. He knows he ought to do right and knows he does much that is not right. Conscience tells him so. Conscience also threatens him with punishment. He knows his evil deeds are the fruit of evil in his heart and that he is guilty and punishable before the righteous Judge of all, if not before worldly tribunals, not only for the evil which he *does* but for the evil which he *is* in his heart. No man's conscience is quite at ease with a God who is 'a discerner of the thoughts and intents of the heart' before whom no creature is not manifest (Heb. 4:12, 13 KJV) until he has come to peace 'with God' through the blood of Christ and peace 'of God' through the life of the Spirit. He may not have the slightest idea where his bad heart came from but he knows it is deserving of punishment and he fears the judgment to come on account of that.

The Bible offers no palliatives for the clear teaching of original sin. The Bible plainly proclaims the bad news because until we not only know, but feel ourselves under the righteous judgment of God for what we are, we will never be in any mood to hear the good news or to have any inclination to respond to it. Like the prodigal son, we never say 'I will arise and go to my father' until we truly acknowledge, 'I have sinned against heaven… I am no longer worthy' (Luke 15:18, 19).

8
Theories of the Imputation of Sin

Up to this point the doctrine of original sin expounded and its corollary, imputation of Adam's sin to us all, has been the Augustinian view traceable through the Protestant churches of the Reformation and all the chief Protestant Reformers, back to Augustine. I do not mean to say we owe the doctrine of original sin to any theologian ancient or recent. It is spread throughout the New Testament. That the Christian message to mankind is called 'the good news' means it is to bring deliverance from the bad news. The structure of books like Romans and Ephesians is shaped on this premise. This view is essentially that also of Anselm and other defenders of Augustinian anthropology in the Middle Ages.

There are varieties of outlook on imputation by earnest theologians, but all the evangelical views are modifications of the primitive Augustinianism described above. These modifications inevitably led – and still lead – to variations from the Reformation Protestant doctrines of the decrees of God, atonement, election and especially the order of salvation (*ordo salutis*), viz.: if natural man is dead spiritually, then God must not only provide salvation in redemption but actually impart some spiritual life to the spiritually dead sinner, whose will is not free but enslaved and whose mind is darkened, before he can repent or believe. He must be made to want to believe before he chooses to do so.

The basic difference may be said to boil down to the question: Who determines who are to be saved? According to Semi-Pelagians, Arminians and Wesleyans, man determines. All hinges on human choice. In a strange way, so agrees Norman Geisler, who in an effort to avoid what he calls extreme Calvinism manages to become not a moderate Calvinist but a pretty good synergist, i.e. an Arminian.[1] According to the Augustinian scheme (including all the leading Reformers), God does. He not only provides the Savior but makes 'his people' desire to receive Him. And this modifies one way or another many other aspects of doctrine and of Christian life, personal and corporate.

Further implications are correctly pointed out by C. A. Hodge:

> Although this may be said to be the turning point [between systems of theology] which has divided the Church in all ages, yet this point, of necessity, involves all the other matters of difference: namely, the nature and design of the work of Christ; and the nature of divine grace, or the work of the Holy Spirit. Thus, in a great measure, the whole system of theology, and of necessity the character of our religion, depend upon the view taken of this particular question. It is, therefore, a question of highest practical importance, and not a matter of idle speculation.[2]

---

1. Norman Geisler, *Chosen But Free* (Minneapolis: Bethany House, 1999), pp. 232–234.
2. Charles Hodge, *Systematic Theology II* (Grand Rapids: Eerdmans, reprint 1970), pp. 330, 331.

These sentences significantly are from Hodge's remarks on 'The Plan of Salvation' not on his sections on original sin and imputation.

A satisfactory answer to this question (i.e. who determines who will be saved) has been confused historically by what look now to be overrefinement of issues and answers. No view is quite without problems. Yet some mention ought to be made of the way teachers of doctrine have phrased issues, evidence and answers. My procedure will be to present first historically important views orthodox Protestantism has regarded either as false or inadequate – even though some evangelical bodies hold to them. Then to discuss two views that merit being called orthodox Protestant or Augustinian, (both Calvinist and Lutheran) and a modification.

The Pelagian Theory.

Pelagius and Coelestius propounded their views in Rome, Carthage and elsewhere shortly after AD 400. Pelagius, whose views were condemned by the Council of Carthage (AD 418), denied the existence of any problem. Infants are born with souls immediately created by God, hence, innocent of any trace of sin, Adam's or otherwise. Their probation starts where Adam's did, in a state of innocency. Romans 5:12, 'death spread to all men because all sinned' means simply we all follow Adam's bad example and therefore die. God imputes guilt only for our own personal sins when we commit them. Pelagius is significant today chiefly because others, beginning with Augustine, have been stimulated by his attractive but unscriptural errors to formulate a coherent doctrine of sin. Later, Socinians (anti-Trinitarians of the Reformation epoch), Unitarians of the seventeenth and eighteenth centuries, and present-day 'liberal' theologians endorse teachings similar to Pelagius' views.

In an effort to prevent Coelestius from being ordained at Carthage, Paulinus, a deacon at Milan, sent a letter to the bishop charging him and Pelagius with six errors: (1) Adam was mortal and would have died whether he had sinned or not sinned; (2) the sin of Adam injured himself alone, and not the human race; (3) newborn children are in that state in which Adam was before his fall; (4) neither by the death and sin of Adam does the whole race die, nor by the resurrection of Christ does the whole race rise; (5) the law leads to the kingdom of heaven as well as the gospel; (6) even before the coming of the Lord there were men without sin.[3]

Bettenson provides a slightly fuller report.[4] The few original sources of information about Pelagius and brief explanation of his views are easily available in Bettenson.[5] Also A. H. Strong furnishes 'seven points of Pelagianism.'[6]

Every generation, however, has produced a few serious theologians whose reflections on the human condition would not allow them to accept the radical and universal sinfulness of man. There are not today, however, many theologians (or psychologists, for that matter) who think any human being has ever been innocent. The twentieth century, with its wars, economic depressions, social turbulence and crime, has not been conducive to optimism regarding human nature.

Semi-Pelagianism.

Both in origin and in history this view might perhaps better be designated semi-Augustinian. Augustine and his successors defined depravity as total: human will enslaved, salvation wholly of grace and wholly by God's initiative. These teachers, while not exactly in reaction to Pelagianism, were stimulated by it. Those who shortly after the Augustinian victory at the Council of Carthage (AD 418) and for the following century retreated somewhat from the decision of Carthage probably were not any kind of Pelagians – semi- or otherwise. They were semi-Augustinians.[7] They sought to define depravity, 'free will,' salvation by grace and faith in such a way as to leave man able to turn to God, to initiate repentance. The Semi-Pelagians agreed that all Adam's descendants received a fallen, corrupt human nature from Adam, but were only weakened by sin, not dead in sin. This appears in extracts from pertinent ancient reports.[8] These views were common among some 'Protestants' of Reformation times. The Lutheran *Formula*

---

3. J. C. Ayer, Jr, *A Source Book for Ancient Church History* (New York: 1913), p. 461; as reported by Williston Walker, *A History of the Christian Church* (New York: Charles Scribner's Sons, 1918), p. 186.
4. Henry Bettenson, *Documents of the Christian Church*, 2nd ed. (London and New York: Oxford Univ. Press, 1963), p. 76.
5. ibid., Section VI, pp. 73–88.
6. A. H. Strong, *Systematic Theology* (Valley Forge, PA: Judson Press, 1907), p. 597.
7. Henry Bettenson, *Documents*, note 1, p. 84; Richard Kyle in *Evangelical Dictionary of Theology*, p. 1000; Williston Walker, *History of the Christian Church*, p. 188.
8. Bettenson, *Documents*, pp. 84–88.

of Concord apparently first called this outlook 'semi-Pelagianism.'[9] It has affinities with Arminianism, Wesleyanism, some Southern Baptist theology, a good bit of Mennonite thinking and synergistic Lutheranism, as well as the Roman Tridentine theology. Even Zwingli has been accused of being 'semi-Pelagian' in his view of sin.[10] This outlook does not regard fallen man as quite dead in trespasses and sins, though he may be very sick. He has sufficient spiritual power to co-operate in conversion. As we turn to Arminianism and Wesleyanism (Methodist theology) it will be seen they partake of some main features of this semi-Augustinianism (named Semi-Pelagianism to condemn it).

Consistent Pelagianism is rightly called a heresy. It is an anti-Christian doctrine. Revived in Reformation times by Socinianism and in eighteenth-century American Unitarianism, it is still with us in apostate, that is to say, liberal religion, both Roman and Protestant, today as G. Gresham Machen proclaimed in his 1920 book, *Christianity vs. Liberalism*. As J. L. Neve comments in *A History of Christian Thought*, the Protestant Reformers and their orthodox successors were right in rejecting explicit synergism, the name then given to the notion fallen men have power, apart from enabling divine grace, to co-operate with God in coming to faith. Even the Canons of the Council of Trent agree on this point.

Semi-Pelagianism and its latent synergism rest on a defective understanding of what it means to be 'by nature children of wrath,' 'dead in trespasses and sins,' having no life because they are 'condemned already.' Still millions of thoroughly Christian people, if they think about the problem at all think of imputation of Adam's sin as Semi-Pelagians. Likewise they may think they came to Christ wholly by choice of their own 'free' will. In my judgment, they have, to that extent, a defective theology, but certainly not heretical. They still pray as though all depends on God and sing praise to the Holy Spirit in 'convicting me of sin' and at Christmas time, of how 'God imparts to human hearts/ The glories of his heaven.' The view of the Greek (Eastern Orthodox) churches of original sin and imputation of guilt for the sin of our first parents is to this day in all essentials the same as Semi-Pelagianism. For a description of Eastern Orthodox theology on these points by an Englishman who converted to orthodoxy and later wrote almost as spokesman to the English-speaking world see *The Orthodox Church* by Timothy Ware, on 'Grace and Free Will' and 'The Fall: Original Sin.'[11] For a fair presentation of 'The Greek Anthropology' see Shedd's *History of Christian Doctrine*.[12]

Arminius and Early Remonstrants.

After the death (AD 1564) of Calvin (whose expressions in the perspective of the history of scholastic Calvinism seem quite moderate) some of his immediate successors in Geneva and the Reformed leaders in the Netherlands stated the doctrines of depravity, grace and election in terms that then, as now, offended many sensitive believers and gifted scholars.

For Calvin, election (in distinction from the doctrine of decrees or predestination) is a soteriological doctrine: election is to eternal life from the mass of the unsaved. It presumes man as sinner already. Pressed on the point, Calvin acknowledged that if God has 'decreed all whatsoever comes to pass' that includes the damnation of the non-elect as well. As Paul, in Romans 11:33-36, both Luther and Calvin accepted this as a mystery of revelation. The logic is inescapable. If man is dead spiritually, then God, to save him, must find him, choose him, impart both spiritual enlightenment of mind and power of will to do so, in order to save him. The logic starts with the question of original sin and the corollary, imputation of guilt (death) for Adam's sin to all of Adam's progeny. In such a case regeneration is a 'monergism' – only God acts. Faith follows. Salvation by grace, means all of grace.[13] The beginning of faith is by divine power alone and by divine choice (election) alone. God foreknows because He elects, election being nowise dependent on 'foreseen faith.'

(I have already shown that by whatever name, the Scriptures teach the *total* absence of spiritual life in fallen men. In their natural fallen state, men do not love God and do not want to love Him. Wesleyans and Arminians are wont to diminish the total incapacity of the unregenerate in spiritual, God-related matters by diminishing the strength of the biblical language about it, saying for example, 'dead in…trespasses and sins' [Eph. 2:1; cf. Col. 2:13] is only a figure

---

9. Richard Kyle, 'Semi-Pelagianism' in *Evangelical Dictionary of Theology*, p. 1000.
10. Francis Pieper, *Christian Dogmatics II* (St Louis: Concordia Publ., 1950), see footnotes 28, 29, 30, pp. 542, 543.
11. Timothy Ware, *The Orthodox Church* (Middlesex, England: Penguin Books, 1963, 1972), pp. 226, 230.
12. W. G. T. Shedd, *History of Christian Doctrine II* (New York: Scribner, 1872), pp. 26–42, summarized pp. 41, 42.
13. So agree A. M. Hunter, *The Teaching of Calvin: A Modern Interpretation* (Westwood NJ: Revell, 2nd ed., 1950), pp. 93–134; Wilhelm Niesel, *The Theology of Calvin*, trans. H. Knight (Phila: Westminster, 1956), pp. 159–181; Francois Wendel, *Calvin: The Origins and Development of His Religious Thought* (New York: Harper & Row, 1950), pp. 263–284.

of speech. Man, they say, 'still has free will.' But Paul is using no mere figure. The total direction of the unrenewed will away from God is part of that spiritual death, which is not partial but total. This is the point Erasmus would not see and Luther stifled with an avalanche of Scripture truth in *The Bondage of the Will*.)

This teaching is capable of perversion and unbalanced advocacy as well as of caricature. In 'Supralapsarianism' (before-the-fall-ism), as it arose after AD 1563 (death of Calvin), God's way of manifesting His grace and justice was to select from hypothetically existing men (men to be created) a certain number to be vessels of mercy, and certain others to be vessels of wrath. In the order of thought of this scheme, election and reprobation precede the purpose to create and to permit the fall. Carried to a logically extreme conclusion, Christ's death was not 'for the sins of the whole world' (1 John 2:2). Infralapsarianism (below-the-fall-ism) as a more moderate Calvinism, holds, 'God, with the design to reveal his own glory... determined to create the world; secondly to permit the fall of man; thirdly, to elect from the mass of fallen men a multitude... as vessels of mercy,' etc.[14] There are sentences in Calvin's *Institutes* which some have interpreted as Supralapsarian. The *Institutes*, though revised several times by the author, remained essentially the same in doctrine as in his earliest work. His later comments on Scripture are clearly Infralapsarian and hardly favor the doctrine of limited atonement as stated by its most strident advocates. (See my comments later in Christology.) Calvin did not express himself precisely on this subject because severe controversy about the subject was not raised until he had passed off the scene. Most Protestants, including leading Calvinists, defend Infralapsarianism. (See, for example, A. H. Strong's citation of Calvin's comments on 1 John 2:2.)[15]

Soon a reaction against hyper-Calvinism set in, the chief spokesman being Jacob Arminius (or Hermansen) (AD 1560–1609), a professor at Leyden (Netherlands). He was a very learned man in a very learned age. The English edition of his collected works runs to 1771 pages. The controversy and its issue in the five 'Arminian articles of Remonstrance' and the contrary five points of the 'synod of Dort' (AD 1619) are beyond our present scope to report.[16] It is the teachings and assumptions of Arminius and followers regarding original sin and imputation of guilt for Adam's sin that interests us at this point.

Arminius did not hesitate to call Pelagianism a 'heresy'[17] and from his very learned and skillful writings enough moderate Calvinism can be extracted that Carl Bangs wrote an article entitled 'Arminius was a Calvinist' in *Christianity Today* magazine and Strong cites Moses Stuart in an article from *Biblical Repostory*, 1831, saying, it is 'possible to construct an argument to prove Arminius was not an Arminian.'[18]

His theology of sin is that of the ancient semi-Augustinians, whom modern church history calls Semi-Pelagian, and is very similar to the views of the Eastern Fathers before Augustine. A good many hours of examination of Arminius' writings confirms: 'It is plain that by inherited sin Arminius meant only inherited evil, and that it was not of a sort to justify God's condemnation.'[19] Though he makes many statements affirming Traducianism, 'He denied any being in Adam, such as made us justly chargeable with Adam's sin, except in that we are obliged to endure certain consequences of it.'[20] Arminius' statements regarding fallen man's ability to repent and believe are ambiguous. Sometimes Arminius seems to say fallen man has sufficient knowledge of God and residual freedom of will to turn to God for salvation even without God's special grace. He is concerned with God's justice in condemning sinners who have no power to repent and believe. So he posits grace sufficient to enable any one 'who wills' to believe and be saved, adding 'were the fact *otherwise, the justice of God could not be defended* [emphasis added] in condemning those who do not believe.'[21]

My own search of Arminius' works fully confirm the following assessment by W. G. T. Shedd:

> The Arminian theologians did not believe that the unity between Adam and his posterity... was of such a nature as to make the first sinful act of Adam a common act of mankind, and thereby justify the imputation of original sin as truly and properly sin... Their objection to the doctrine that original sin is guilt, proceeds on the assumption that Adam's act of apostasy was purely *individual*, and that the posterity were not in any such

---

14. C. Hodge, *Systematic Theology II*, p. 316.
15. Strong, *Systematic Theology*, pp. 772 and 778.
16. I devote an entire chapter to 'the Extent of the Atonement' in *Christology*.
17. James Arminius, *The Works of Arminius II*, trans. by James Nichols (Buffalo, NY: Derby, Miller and Orton 1853), p. 379.
18. Strong, *Systematic Theology*, p. 602.
19. Strong, *Systematic Theology*, p. 602.
20. Strong, *Systematic Theology*, p. 602.
21. Arminius, *Works II*, p. 498.

real sense as the phraseology of their own doctrinal statements, if taken in its strict and literal application, would imply.[22]

Socinianism, Unitarianism and Modernism.

The Socinians of the Reformation era in Europe, Unitarians of the eighteenth and nineteenth centuries in English-speaking lands, and Modernism of the twentieth-century era all departed from evangelical orthodoxy along the whole range of doctrines – though not always in the same way. They agreed, however, in repudiating any direct connection between the fall of Adam and the sinfulness of men.

All of early sixteenth-century Europe was influenced by the moralistic view of Christianity propounded by Erasmus. The presumption that his scholarship was unrivaled gave him and his views great prestige everywhere. 'His way of thinking was to have little influence on the Reformation as a whole, though much on Socinianism, and is that represented in a great deal of modern [i.e. Modernist] theology, of which he was thus the spiritual ancestor.'[23] The theology of Erasmus may be stated thus:

> To him Christianity was but the fullest expression through Christ, primarily in the Sermon on the Mount, of universal, essentially ethical religion, of which the philosophers of antiquity had also been bearers. He had little feeling for the sacramental or the deeply personal elements [repentance, faith, regeneration, etc.] in religion. A universal ethical theism [worship of one personal God], having its highest illustration in Christ, was his idea.[24]

Though the followers of Fausto Sozzini (Socinians) were concerned to be biblical, the following quotation applies equally to the theology of Socinianism, Unitarianism and the Modernism of the Protestant denominations between the two World Wars and through the Great Depression. 'Original justice meant for Socinus merely that Adam was free from sin as a fact, not that he was endowed with peculiar gifts; hence Socinus denied the doctrine of original sin entirely.'[25] Socinianism was an academic theology. Only what is provable by reason can be Christian truth (as in Kant's essay, *Religion Within the Bounds of Reason*).

In the sixteenth century, Poland became a refuge from the Inquisition for 'heretics,' including anti-Trinitarian theologians. The most influential of the anti-Trinitarians was the Italian, Fausto Sozzini (AD 1539–1604), nephew of Lelio Sozzini (d. AD 1562). The elder Sozzini trained the younger in his Unitarian views and left to his nephew his unpublished manuscripts. The Sozzinis were in opposition to the Roman Church and in Poland, F. Sozzini (Socinus) was influential in forming a body of Unitarian people whose doctrines are known as Socinianism.

The theology of the younger Sozzini was expounded in the Racovian Catechism in AD 1605 (so named for Racow, the Polish city where it was formulated). According to this theology, mankind was created in the condition of mortality. The first man possessed no high degree of wisdom or knowledge. Since his knowledge was imperfect and his will untried, desire (concupiscence) was stimulated by the command not to eat and being overpowered by it he yielded. It is almost as if God, Himself, were responsible for Adam's sin. The fall deprived neither Adam nor his descendants of the power of the will to good or evil. There is no inherited inclination to sin. Socinianism holds that scriptural commands to repent and believe show conclusively that ordinary people have inherent power to do either.

Socinianism, remarks Neve (and he could have said the same of later Unitarianism and Modernism), is not a theology of religious people. Neve quotes Harnak as saying 'The religious motive in the deepest sense is absent in these Italians' and then comments:

> Sin as a condition in man, irrespective of any special sinful act, the solidarity of our race coupled with the conviction of responsibility of the group for the individual and of the individual for the group, the whole matter of sin and grace as expressed in the language of piety, prayer, liturgy and song through the ages – out of this rings a testimony regarding sin as a natural depravity, involving a responsibility that cannot be ignored and a divine grace needed to meet this condition.[26]

---

22. Shedd, *History of Christian Doctrine*, pp. 186, 187.
23. Williston Walker, *History of the Christian Church*, p. 330.
24. Walker, *History of the Christian Church*, p. 330.
25. H. Pope, 'Socinianism' in *Catholic Encyclopedia XIV*, pp. 113-115.
26. Neve, *Christian Thought*, p. 85.

Renaissance rationalism produced Socinianism at the end of the sixteenth and early seventeenth centuries. The same views of Christianity, including doctrines of man and sin, arose in strength under the lengthening impulses of the Renaissance and the rising so-called 'enlightenment' of the eighteenth century and still later among the British and American Unitarians. Over the last 150 years, in Modernism, accelerated by recent scientific and philosophic forces, the heresies of Socinianism have been established first, in mainline Protestant colleges, seminaries and churches, and then in their Roman Catholic counterparts with even more drastic departures from orthodoxy.

Socinianism is, of course, with slight modification, the ancient heresy of Pelagianism *redivivus*.

Wesleyanism.

'Arminianism was to prove, in the person of John Wesley, its possibility of association with as warm-hearted and emotional a type of piety as any interpretation of Christian truth can exhibit.'[27]

The immediate followers of Arminius (Remonstrants) in the Netherlands quickly retreated from evangelical faith to views similar to Socinianism and practically disappeared from history. As imported to the Church of England, subsequently, Arminianism accompanied sharp spiritual decline; but Wesley and his followers favored what they called Evangelical Arminianism. The modification of Arminianism by Wesley and Wesleyans as well as the genuine revival of biblical religion in the masses, where Methodist preachers extended the revival, demonstrate the justice of the adjective, evangelical.

The Wesleys, John (AD 1703–1791) and Charles (AD 1707–1788), for a season allowed themselves to be yoked with evangelicals of fervent Calvinistic opinions. They were agreed fully in the main as to mankind's spiritual condition and the cure for it.

The language of Arminius over a century earlier had been so learned and so guarded that his yielding up of Augustinian views of original sin and imputation of Adam's guilt was not entirely plain. Wesleyanism, on the contrary, is forthright in its doctrinal outlook. I shall cite Richard Watson's *Theological Institutes II* for Wesleyan doctrine.

Richard Watson gave the first, and still preeminent systematic treatment of Wesley's theology. John Wesley never wrote a comprehensive detailed exposition of Christian doctrine. Watson's *Theological Institutes* follow the style and methodology of the Calvinist theologians of the time. Charles Hodge thought highly of Watson's work incidentally remarking 'the Rev. Richard Watson, whose excellent system of theology, or "Theological Institutes" is deservedly in high repute among Wesleyan Methodists, etc.'[28] In 1852 Dr John Brown of Edinburgh characterized Watson as 'a prince in theology, and the *Institutes* as the noblest work in Methodism.' J. W. Alexander compared him to Turretin in theology and Blackstone in law in eminence as the theologian of Methodism.

(At this point it is only fair to make the reader aware that learned and competent theologians of Wesleyan persuasion have carried Wesleyan doctrine of restored ability and Watson's careful formulations up to date. Among Wesleyan theologians who have addressed these problems are the following: John Miley [*Systematic Theology*, two vols. New York: Hunt and Eaton, 1892], Henry Orton Wiley [*Systematic Theology*, three vols. Kansas City: Nazarene Publishing House, 1940]. The three volumes of Thomas C. Oden's *Systematic Theology* [San Francisco: Harper Collins, 1920] avoid these problems. Dr Oden intends what he calls 'consensual theology.' Evidently he finds no consensus in these matters.)

He was learned, systematic and straightforward both in agreements with other orthodox and in the exposition of early Wesleyanism.

In Watson's understanding, all mankind were rendered corrupt at heart by the fall. The doctrine of total depravity is fully affirmed. Richard Watson is very explicit and emphatic.[29] But what formulations up to date Watson takes away with the left hand he takes back with the right, for the ability of fallen man exists only 'so far as they are left to themselves.'[30] He then asserts that by virtue of the 'Holy Spirit' who 'has been vouchsafed to "the world" through the atonement' the ability to repent and believe has been universally restored. He says commands imply ability to obey; invitations imply ability to respond favorably. He goes on to say:

---

27. Walker, *History of the Christian Church*, p. 456.
28. Charles Hodge, *Systematic Theology III* (Grand Rapids: Eerdmans, 1960), p. 190.
29. Richard Watson, *Theological Institutes II*, ed. J. M. McClintock, 29th ed. (New York: Nelson & Phillips, 1850), pp. 43–48.
30. ibid., p. 85.

It is thus that one part of Scripture is reconciled to another, and both to fact; the declaration of man's total corruption, with the presumption of his power to return to God, to repent, to break off his sins, which all the commands and invitations to him imply.[31]

Whether imputation of Adam's guilt to his descendants was *mediate* or *immediate* seems irrelevant to Wesley and his followers (though I may have missed something). Robert Dabney, one important Augustinian, thought the distinction seemed over-refined and unnecessary because it solves no problems.[32] The orthodox Protestant views begin by affirming universal human guilt for Adam's sin. This is their distinguishing feature.

Like Arminius, Wesley taught that God had restored to every man the ability to co-operate with God in responding favorably to the gospel, but with a very important difference. For Wesley this is due entirely to God's grace, hence his soteriology is soundly evangelical. In Arminius, restoration of plenary ability to repent and believe is a matter of justice, demanded *of God*. God owes it as a debt to justice. It is the same 'fairness doctrine' heard today in debate over many social issues and is implicitly a heresy.

If the Scriptures teach anything at all, salvation is not in any respect a matter that God owes sinners. Let us group together several theologians who agree we are sinners in need of grace, corrupt in heart by natural descent from Adam in one way or another, but not guilty and under sentence of death by any guilt for what Adam did.

A recent book by David L. Smith concludes:

> Adam's sin created a 'virus'... tending toward sin, which infects every human being coming into the world, being passed from parent to child in biological transmission. The guilt for sin however, is not imputed to an individual until he recognizes that he is a sinner by apprehending his or her guilt under the law. When that awareness of accountability as a lawbreaker occurs, the virus of sin becomes full-blown and guilt for transgression is then imputed and spiritual death occurs. Thus, those who do not reach a point of awareness and accountability are in a state of imputed innocence in which their sins [what sins?] are covered by the finished work of Christ on Calvary.[33]

In this view there is no imputation of guilt for Adam's sin at all. Our sinful tendency is a misfortune but there is no blame to be charged for it. Smith's view is not greatly different from that of the ancient Semi-Pelagians and modern Arminians and of LaPlace (AD 1596–1665) before he 'recanted.'[34]

Smith also shares essentially the same ground with what theologians call Mediate Imputation. Though the mediate imputation theory will be discussed later, Dr Smith's view merits attention here. The first articulate advocate among American Protestants was a thoroughly converted associate of Jonathan Edwards named Samuel Hopkins (AD 1721–1803), though he did not follow Edward's distinctive teachings. Bold to the point of rashness, he suddenly announced to his congregation (built by his own evangelistic efforts) of slave-traders and slave-owners at Newport, R.I. the demand 'in the name of the Highest' that they all manumit their slaves. 'Only one family left his church; the others freed their slaves,' is the historian's laconic summary of what happened. It was this energetic scholar-preacher who in Puritan New England, among other challenges to the current Calvinist consensus, propounded as his doctrine of 'original sin': 'Though men became sinners by Adam, according to a divine constitution, yet they have, and are accountable for no sins but personal.'[35]

This view is important because it was taught by prominent, influential, godly men, strategically placed. In addition to Hopkins, they were chiefly Nathaniel Emmons (AD 1745–1840) who thought himself to be neither a strict nor moderate Calvinist, but a consistent one; Timothy Dwight (AD 1752–1817) the preacher-president of Yale College whose faithful efforts delayed Yale College in its slide into unbelief; Nathaniel Taylor (AD 1786–1858, professor at Yale Theology Dept., 1822–1858) taught a near-Pelagian doctrine of sin, denying any connection with Adam's sin at all. Charles G. Finney is counted as among this group who while claiming to be Calvinists came in their latest representations to deny not only Calvinism but any Pauline theology of sin. For obvious reasons later theologians have called this line of development the New England or New School of Theology.

Dr David Smith rests his case on Ezekiel 18:1-20, especially v. 20, which he quotes in the NIV:

---

31. ibid., p. 86.
32. Robert Dabney, *Lectures in Systematic Theology* (Grand Rapids: Zondervan, first published in 1878, 1972), p. 339.
33. David L. Smith, *With Willful Intent: A Theology of Sin* (Wheaton, IL: Victor Books, 1994), p. 371.
34. Shedd, *History of Christian Doctrine*, p. 17 ff.
35. From *Memoir of Emmons*, See art. Samuel Hopkins in McClintock and Strong's *Cyclopedia IV*, p. 334.

> The soul who sins is the one who will die. The son will not share the guilt of the father, nor will the father share the guilt of the son. The righteousness of the righteous man will be credited to him, and the wickedness of the wicked will be charged against him (Ezek. 18:20).

He comments: 'Ezekiel is very clear, then, that the guilt of the fathers is not charged against their children. Thus we may be sure that Adam's guilt has not been passed on to us. The idea of inherited guilt contradicts the biblical teaching here.'[36] Earlier Smith writes, 'Augustine's doctrine that all human beings are made guilty because of Adam's sin is simply unbiblical. Ezekiel disposes of such a concept.'[37]

There are many false assumptions, errors of exegesis and misconstructions in those two sentences. One hesitates to oppose and forcibly reject sincerely held opinions of a fellow evangelical writer, but once noticed, the errors must be addressed. Anti-Augustinian writers for centuries who cite texts supposed to forbid any race guilt for Adam's disobedience usually also cite Deuteronomy 24:16: 'Fathers shall not be put to death because of their children, nor shall children be put to death because of their fathers. Each one shall be put to death for his own sin.' Let us attend to what these passages really say in the literary and historical context of each. They present no objection whatsoever to the immediate imputation of Adam's sin to each of his descendants. If they did the objection would apply as well to the imputation of Christ's righteousness to believers.

1. The precise question proposed by the exiles in Babylon whom Ezekiel was addressing related to the still recent destruction of Jerusalem by Babylonian forces, slaughter of many inhabitants, captivity of others to Babylon and break-up of the political commonwealth of Judah under the house of David. *The younger generation in Babylon were complaining that they in Babylon were suffering for the sins of their ancestors in 'the land of Israel'* (v. 2). There had indeed been a covenant between the LORD and their ancestors. The punishments by God on them and their offspring if they broke covenant are amply described in Deuteronomy 28. They are complaining about the alleged injustice of God in making them suffer for what their ancestors in 'the land of Israel' had done. Ezekiel is therefore setting the record straight that whatever Providence had done in the sad end of the Judean kingdom, His ways are 'equal.' Not one of them would die in punishment for his father's sins if he disapproved of those sins and did not repeat them.

2. This text has no reference at all to spiritual death and eternal life whatsoever. As far as our race of sinners is concerned, God kills millions of us every day. Some He takes to heaven and some to hell. We have no recourse. As for rewards and punishments on the human scale, no magistrate may justly set the children's teeth on edge (Jer. 31:29; Ezek. 18:2) for parental sins, and neither may he inflect the ultimate penalty on parents for the next generation's crimes, nor the converse. Neither Ezekiel 18 nor Deuteronomy 24 is relevant in the remotest manner to the subject of original sin.

3. If one were to allow that Ezekiel 18:23 applies somehow to some form of a doctrine of guilt or non-guilt for Adam's sin one runs into irreconcilable conflict with Exodus 20:5 which says, 'I the LORD your God am a jealous God, visiting the iniquity ['awon, guilt, punishment] of the fathers on the children to the third and the fourth generation of those who hate me.' God, it seems clear, can do as He pleases about such matters, whatever the magistrates and conquerors contemplated in Ezekiel 18 ought or ought not to do.

4. Furthermore, Dr Smith and others who deny we were born guilty sinners deny what Scripture specifically affirms, viz.: that we are all guilty before we come to consciousness, conceived in sin, children of wrath by nature and that Paul at least five times connects that wage of sin directly with what Adam did (Rom. 5:12-19). In the Bible, death, while not often inflicted on account of one's own sins or of one's parents (as Jesus was careful to say; see John 9; Luke 13), is without exception the penalty for sin of some kind by someone. In case of infants the death for *sin* is not their personal sins, for they have not personally committed any, but their first male ancestor's sin. The Bible is perfectly clear about this.

5. The probationary arrangement was with Adam not Adam and Eve. What is not plain with the dropping from the NIV of the singular *thee* and *thou* and even the plural *ye* (second person plural) of personal pronouns, is perfectly plain in the KJV and all older Versions. Those fateful words in Genesis 2:16, 17 were passed on to Eve by Adam, no doubt (Gen. 2:23), but the command was to the man and the issues lay with him and him alone. The effort of David

---

36. David L. Smith, *With Willful Intent*, p. 368.
37. Smith, *With Willful Intent*, p. 366.

Smith[38] and J. L. Garrett[39] to make Eve equally with Adam the bearer of the responsibility is negated not only by the narrative of Genesis but by every subsequent reference to the matter in the Bible. 'In Adam all die' 'through one man that sinned.'

Dr Smith's theory has much in common with the mediate imputation theory associated at the beginning with the name of LaPlace. Description and evaluation of that view follows shortly.

Under the rubric of 'original sin' we have already shown that the Bible clearly indicates that all mankind are corrupt at heart, under the just punishment of death and that this is because of shared guilt for Adam's first act of sin in his probationary state.

'[W]hile there has been difference of opinion and looseness of statement as to the grounds of our just accountability for Adam's first sin, the whole Church [including Roman Catholic] has always regarded our loss of original righteousness and innate moral corruption to be just.'[40]

Supplement on Romans 5:12-19.

Christian theology of every age has been driven to the doctrine of 'original sin' (to employ the usual term) by the plain sense of Romans 5:12-21. I shall presume the reader's acquaintance with the passage and beg the reader to open a standard translation to the passage before going on here. My statements will be brief and to the point. First let us look at the passage as a whole.

1. The theme of Romans 5:12-19 is righteousness and life through Christ, as it has been from Romans 3:21 onward to 5:11. The teaching of our unity with Adam in his sin and condemnation is introduced to serve as help to understand our oneness with Christ in righteousness and life.

2. The goal of Paul in the passage is to help sinners to understand forgiveness of sin and life in Christ by finding a reverse parallel of forgiveness of sin and life in Christ with sin and death in Adam 'who was a type [Gr. *tupos*] of the one who was to come' (Rom. 5:14, last clause).

3. As in all biblical types and parables the correspondences are not in *every* respect, but usually only *one*. So here the correspondence is only in respect of a certain oneness with Adam and oneness with Christ. Paul calls attention to differences between our oneness in and with Adam and our oneness in and with Christ by several negatives – 'the free gift is not like the trespass,' v. 15; again, 'the free gift is not like,' etc., v. 16; and several contrasts indicated by the adversative conjunction, 'but,' vv. 15, 16, 20.

4. Paul's emphasis and our interest here is in the first member of the comparison-contrast, i.e. what Adam gave us (what we have in him) in his fall, rather than what we have in Christ.

5. Let us note seven statements of the text as to what happened to us all (the human race) when Adam sinned, beginning with verse 12. Emphasis is added.

> (i) 'sin came into the world *through one man,* and death through sin' (v. 12)
> (ii) 'so death *spread to all men because all sinned*' (v. 12)
> (iii) 'many died through *one man's* trespass' (v. 15)
> (iv) 'the result of that *one man's sin*… the judgement following one trespass brought condemnation' (v. 16)
> (v) 'because of *one man's trespass,* death reigned through *that one man*' (v. 17)
> (vi) 'as *one trespass* led to condemnation for *all men*' (v. 18)
> (vii) 'by the *one man's* disobedience the *many* were *made sinners*' (v. 19)

6. The evidence is plain: in and through Adam's act of sin the human race *en toto*, as a whole, immediately (no lapse of time until we each could be born) became sinners.

7. The decisive terms are 'all sinned' (v. 12, past tense, aorist active) and 'made sinners' (v. 19, past tense, aorist active).

(a) As to the first, 'because all sinned' (*ef ho pantes hēmarton*) (v. 12); the usual aorist tense as used here indicates a 'punctiliar' act in the past. 'All sinned,' not 'have sinned' (which would normally require the Greek perfect tense), is the right translation as most recognize, even those who interpret the sense as the personal act of sinning which

---

38. Smith, *With Willful Intent*, p. 370, 371.
39. J. L. Garrett, *Systematic Theology: Biblical, Historical & Evangelical I* (Grand Rapids: Eerdmans, 1990), pp. 483–493.
40. A. A. Hodge, *Outlines of Theology* (Grand Rapids: Eerdmans, 1957), p. 353.

every human being of accountable age commits. The rest of the passage, which six times more connects our guilt and corruption to Adam's one act of disobedience tells us we should seek no other meaning. The comment of the learned Dean of Canterbury, commenting on 'all sinned' (*pantes hēmarton*), is on target:

> Observe how entirely this assertion of the Apostle contradicts the Pelagian or individualistic view of man, that each is a separate creation from God, existing solely on his exclusive responsibility – and affirms the Augustinian or traducian view, that all are involved by God's appointment from an original stock, and though individually responsible are generically in the corruption and *condemnation* [emphasis added] of their original.[41]

(b) A second decisive term, 'were made sinners' or simply 'became sinners,' falls in this sentence: 'For as by the one man's disobedience many were made [the verb is active, literally "many became sinners"] sinners, so by the one man's obedience many will be made righteous.' Paul is summarizing his doctrine of righteousness by our solidarity with Christ in His righteousness by paralleling it with our solidarity in Adam. The former is assumed as known to illustrate the latter. The way we become one with Christ is not the same as the way we became one with Adam but the onenesses do exist and are parallel. 'Were made' and 'will be made' are in each case one word, *kathistēmi*, which in these two cases means 'make, cause' (someone to become something) (Bauer, Gingrich, Danker, *Lexicon*). *TDNT* observes that the meaning of the Greek word in this context is about the same as *ginomai* (to become).

So we each became a sinner in Adam. When he sinned, we did. Paul does not explain the mode but simply that what he did constituted each of us a guilty sinner – 'condemned already' (John 3:18) 'by nature children of wrath' (Eph. 2:3).

The fact that death is the universal destiny of everyone conceived in the womb is a melancholy note pervasive through Scripture, human history and personal reflections. It is this that gives the good news both its urgency and glory: 'so that, as sin reigned in death, grace also might reign through righteousness leading to eternal life through Jesus Christ our Lord... For the wages of sin is death, but the free gift of God is eternal life in Christ Jesus our Lord' (Rom. 5:21; 6:23).

The literature on Romans 5:12-21 is extensive, much of it focusing on verse 12. Every form of orthodox theology has a special interest in it. I shall leave the matter where it stands here. Those equipped to examine the critical commentaries may do so. They are (in my opinion) apt to emerge from their efforts with the necessity to return to the rather stark facts in the above summary.

---

41. Henry Alford, *The New Testament for English Readers* (Chicago: Moody Press, repr., n.d.), p. 881.

9
Analysis of the Problem of Imputation of Sin and a Proposed Solution

Before attempting a brief summary of my own views of this particularly complicated subject we should bless the humility of the many truly devout scholars who have dared to explore this only partly revealed mystery of Scripture. In the heat of debate they may forget that we may not have sufficient capacity to understand all that God knows about it. The theologians — Roman, Orthodox, Calvinist, Lutheran, Wesleyan — try to be respectful of one another and the unknown, but no statement I have read puts the matter better than does O. W. Heick. Speaking of the reluctance of a certain cast of mind to accept either imputation of Adam's sin or Christ's righteousness, he says:

> Here all human analogies fail. To the replies which have been given concerning the position of the old Socinians we add this remark: there are certain mysterious truths which cannot and need not be proven by cold arguments. We all feel that death lies in sin (Rom. 6:23). If we could die not only the physical but also the eternal death of absolute separation from God and still live — then we could save ourselves. But we cannot, and therefore we need Christ as Savior. He, the God-man, was the only one who could die and still conquer death. It is in this consideration that we behold the mysterious philosophy of redemption. He who objects to this cannot be helped by rationalizing arguments; a capacity for the spiritual and for that which is truly religious is needed.[1]

Three Common Approaches.

No one can wonder why Adam, himself, should have been accounted guilty and worthy of punishment, but *how*, i.e. on what grounds in justice, all mankind since, as we have sufficiently noted, came justly to be accounted guilty is nowhere clearly stated in Scripture. This imputation of guilt for Adam's sin to us all has been explained in different ways by those whose thinking is strictly Protestant and orthodox and concerned to be faithful to Scripture. I am in debt to many good authors for much of the following analysis.

(1) A not uncommon approach is to accept the revealed facts without attempting to explain or integrate into a theology of imputation. Our just guilt for Adam's sin is accepted as truth revealed unmistakably by Scripture. No systematic attempt is made to explain it. Somehow we were all on probation in and with Adam. Just what the mode of union with him may be is not fully worked out. The fact that every human being including Eve (from Adam's flesh) was ancestrally 'in Adam' (1 Cor. 15:22; cf. Gen. 5:3) points to some substantial unity in him. We know nothing at

---

1. O. W. Heick and J. L. Neve, *History of Christian Thought II* (Philadelphia: Muhlenberg Press, 1946), p. 86.

all of how God created the worlds but 'by faith we understand' it was 'by the Word of God' and we understand that 'sin came into the world through one man... because all sinned' and 'so death spread to all' (Rom. 5:12-19). This is the reason why every descendant of Adam is by nature a child of wrath (Eph. 2:3). A preacher or theologian of this turn of mind trusts God's Word to tell the truth and since God sent His Son to die for us 'while we were yet sinners' he can proclaim that God Himself must believe it and so should we.

The great exponent of orthodox Lutheranism in America, C. P. Krauth, says regarding this problem:

> [O]ur Confession [at the Augsburg Diet]... does not define *how* [his emphasis] THEORETICALLY, the sin of Adam is related to us; does not touch the question of imputation at all... the doctrine of *imputation*, belongs to scientific theology... We cannot recall a single passage in any of our Confessions, in which the imputation of Adam's sin is alluded to... as an Article of Faith.... These expressions... do not exclude the doctrine of imputation.... It is a question of theology, as distinguished from the sphere of faith.[2]

J. A. Dorner traced the history of Lutheran views of original sin and its transmission. He showed that though discussed by earliest theologians there was no agreement beyond that having lost original righteousness, Adam 'could not bequeath it to his descendants; on the contrary, being himself corrupt, he could only transmit a corrupt nature.'[3] In the scholastic period of Protestant theology (1600s) both immediate imputation (i.e. we directly share) and mediate (we indirectly share) in a corrupt nature found advocates. Then by degrees (through Quenstedt, Hollatz and Gerhard) and others the Federal (or representative view) entered Lutheran theology as it did also in Reformed.[4]

(2) Many others no less convinced of the doctrine of original sin in Adam as well as our guilt and depravity on account of it find sufficient explanation in our natural union with Adam. They observe that Eve was taken out of Adam; that Adam begat Seth in his own image; that Seth and all other offspring of our first parents surviving the Flood and onward through the generations were *mediately* created by God in and through natural generation by male and female parents. The doctrine that body and soul of infants are procreated by parents (Traducianism) must be assumed. Stated in somewhat more sophisticated language: 'Seminally [as seed] all Adam's progeny were present in him.' Reference is made to parallels such as 'Levi... paid tithes through Abraham... [when] still in the loins of his ancestor' (Abraham) (Heb. 7:9, 10).

> The posterity were not vicariously represented... because representation implies absence of the party represented... and this first sin is deservedly imputed to them because in this generic [i.e. the whole human genus] manner it was committed by them.[5]

Guilt for Adam's sin, both in the sense of blameworthiness and of obligation to bear the punishment, is rightly deserved by all Adam's progeny inasmuch as in our common nature we were all actors. Shedd comments:

> The imputation of Adam's sin [to all the race] upon this theory, differs from the imputation of Christ's righteousness [to all the elect], in being deserved. In support it can be said the Bible consistently says fallen men *deserve* eternal death whereas in Christ the believer has imputed to him the righteousness of Another and receives the blessedness Another earned.[6]

This is essentially the Augustinian theory found implicitly in many passages of Calvin's writings and explicitly in the early literature of Lutheranism, including the Formula of Concord.

(3) There is a third approach in which as in the views above described, guilt for Adam's sin is accepted as a fact. An explanation is attempted by the theory of representative (or forensic or Federal) union with Adam. As reduced to a bare-bones description by a moderate but convinced advocate:

> The Federal View presupposes that natural relation. Adam stands before God [Eve is not involved]... as a free, responsible, fallible moral agent, with an animal body and a generative nature [i.e. living fleshly body and power to beget offspring; the soul is not generated by parents]. Without a miracle his children must be carried along with him in his destinies.... God, therefore... graciously constituted him the federal head and representative of

---

2. C. P. Krauth, *The Conservative Reformation* (Philadelphia: J. B. Lippincott, 1875), pp. 282, 283.
3. J. A. Dorner, *History of Protestant Theology* (Edinburgh: T. & T. Clark, 1871), p. 144.
4. ibid., pp. 144–146.
5. W. G. T. Shedd, *A History of Christian Doctrine II* (New York: Scribner, 1872), p. 14.
6. ibid., p. 3.

his race as a whole, and promised him for himself and for all, eternal life of confirmed holiness and happiness, on condition of temporary obedience under favorable conditions, with the penalty for him and for them of death, or condemnation and desertion, on condition of disobedience.[7, 8]

The development of this theory came to full development among Calvinists about a century after Calvin wrote the *Institutes*. Correct or not, it had the good effect of eliminating Supralapsarianism (i.e. hyper-Calvinism) among Calvinists. It came to be widely accepted among Lutherans, Arminian groups and even among some Roman Catholic theologians. As later formulated under the aegis of theologians who employ 'covenant' as their main motif in biblical interpretation, 'covenant' became another common name for the representative or Federal theory.[9] (John Murray is a model of scholarly reserve developing this theory in *Imputation of Adam's Sin*.[10]) Buswell seems unfair in calling the realism of Shedd and Strong the 'substantive view.'[11] It is very significant, I think, that the idea that God's probationary arrangement for Adam was a 'Covenant of Works' (as advocates of this view have been saying for 300 years) has now been reconsidered by prominent Reformed theologians. John Murray set the reconsideration in motion with the following, posthumously published in 1977. Significantly entitling his chapter, 'The Adamic Administration' he said:

> This administration has often been denoted 'The Covenant of Works.' There are two [really four] observations. (1) The term is not felicitous, for the reason that the elements of grace entering into the administration are not properly provided for by the term 'works.' (2) It is not designated a covenant in Scripture... Besides [3] Scripture always uses the term covenant, when applied to God's administration to men, in reference to a provision that is redemptive or closely related to redemptive design. Covenant in Scripture denotes the oath-bound confirmation of promise and involves a security the Adamic economy did not bestow. [4] It should never be confused with what Scripture calls the old covenant or first covenant... The view that in the Mosaic covenant there was a repetition of the so-called covenant of works, current among covenant theologians is a grave misconception and... fails to assess the uniqueness of the Adamic administration.[12]

Covenant and Covenants in the Westminster 'Standards'.

The Westminster Standards of the 1640s were composed at the very end of the 'Reformation Era' (Treaty of Westphalia AD 1648) when the theory of representative (Federal) headship had not yet been fully articulated. It was inevitable that in the heat of debate since that time between advocates of natural headship and advocates of representative headship, the support of the Standards should be claimed by each party, especially the party of covenant theology and the representative headship of Adam.

Perry Miller, a preeminent scholar of Puritan thought and author of many scholarly works on Puritanism (and English Calvinism) pointed out the greatly complicated theology of the Puritan Calvinism of the early 1600s as compared with the clear simplicity of Calvin's *Institutes*. Miller had in mind in part the elaborate theology of covenants and dispensations, which arose partly in conflict with Anabaptists in defense of the practice of infant baptism.[13] Both Luther and Zwingli *at first* thought they were 'obliged to demand faith *before* baptism as indispensable, in opposition to external magic' (i.e. baptismal regeneration).[14] Some of the language of covenants of works and of grace is embodied in the *Westminster Confession*. J. Pelikan says all writers of that time employed 'covenant' in setting forth Christian doctrines[15] much as today we throw around words formerly rare such as charismatic and existential. Sometimes they are employed in a specific sense, but more often in a broad general sense. It appears to many that the word 'covenant' is used in this broad sense in the *Westminster Confession* (chap. VII) and the Larger Catechism, viz.: 'the covenant being made with Adam, as a public person, not for himself only but for his posterity' (Q. 22). This language does not directly support 'covenant theology' with all its refinements; nor is it unacceptable for those who

---

7. A. A. Hodge, *Outlines of Theology* (Grand Rapids: Eerdmans, 1957), p. 362.
8. See B. B. Warfield, *Studies in Tertullian & Augustine*, pp. 289–412. What Buswell calls *substantive* views others call *realistic*.
9. J. O. Buswell, Jr, *A Systematic Theology of the Christian Religion I* (Grand Rapids: Zondervan, 1971), p. 307.
10. John Murray, *Imputation of Adam's Sin* (Grand Rapids: Eerdmans, 1959).
11. J. O. Buswell, Jr, *Systematic Theology of the Christian Religion I*, pp. 300–307.
12. John Murray, *Collected Writings II* (Carlisle, PA and Edinburgh: Banner of Truth Trust, 1977), pp. 49, 50.
13. Perry Miller, *Errand into the Wilderness* (Cambridge, Mass.: Belknap Press of Harvard Univ. Press, 1956), p. 53. See Pelikan, *The Christian Tradition V*, p. 372.
14. J. A. Dorner, *History of Protestant Theology I*, trans. Robson & Taylor (Edinburgh: T. & T. Clark, 1871), p. 300.
15. Jaroslav Pelikan, *The Christian Tradition IV* (Chicago: U. of Chicago Press, 1989), p. 372.

reject it. As for 'Adam as a public person,' etc., the Catechism goes on in a way fully acceptable to natural (seminal) headship, saying, '[A]ll mankind, descending from him by ordinary generation (Acts 17:26), sinned in him, and fell with him in that first transgression (Gen. 2:11; Rom. 5:12-20; 1 Cor. 15:21, 22).' Later it says 'Original sin is conveyed from our first parents unto their posterity by natural generation, so as all that proceed from them in that way, are conceived and born in sin' (Q. 26). This language with its near implicit Traducianism is far less amenable to representative headship than to natural (seminal) headship. It seems to me no zealous advocate of covenant theology and/or representative headship would have written such answers as these, so unfavorable to their position. Advocates of natural (seminal) headship could ask for no better support in such a document than the third article of chapter VI of the Confession: our first parents 'being the root of all mankind, the guilt of this sin was imputed, and the same death in sin and corrupted nature conveyed to all their posterity descending from them by ordinary generation.'

It seems to me therefore inaccurate to say, as it is frequently affirmed, that the Federal headship theory of Cocceius was espoused by the Westminster Standards.[16] Thousands of ministers who have sworn allegiance to the Standards have not thought so.

The language of Westminster is the language of Traducianism and the idea of 'undistributed humanity' in Adam (Shedd), very foreign to the doctrine that human bodies only are generated by human parents, the higher part, the soul, of each being created immediately by God.

Difficulties of Each View.

There are difficulties with each of the three chief views just described. The first suffers from indecisiveness. Inquiring minds will not rest there. Earnest and informed thinking Christians will seek some explanation of how it is that the guilt of Adam's sin is imputed to us. The theory of natural or seminal headship, sometimes called 'realism,' claiming a real seminal presence of us all in the total of human nature in Adam, is somewhat embarrassed by the question, asked even by Traducianists: How can a nature be guilty? Persons are guilty, not natures. And what is a nature?

The theory of representative, or Federal headship, especially as stated by Charles Hodge, its leading advocate, is embarrassed by different objections: 1) If our souls are not generated by our parents but directly created by God, how does it come that these souls are at no moment of their existence without evil tendency, i.e. depravity? It is unthinkable that God should create souls depraved from the first moment of existence. 2) One need not be a sophisticated scholar to sense intuitively that the Federal theory involving so-called covenants of this or of that is 'extra-scriptural' (A. H. Strong's term). The lay reader of the Genesis accounts of creation and fall and Paul's interpretation of the same (Rom. 5) finds nothing remotely like the word covenant and no one else seems to have done so until, as someone wrote, it was 'made in Holland.' Further, as good scholars point out, it seems to contradict the plain language of Romans 5:19 and 12. Verse 19 plainly says, '...by the one man's disobedience the many were made [constituted] sinners' and verse 12 declares death 'passed upon all men' (KJV) not because God imputed Adam's sin to them or regarded them as sinners but because 'all sinned.' The cause of their being sinners was something 'all' did, not something God did. The Federal view requires that just as the righteousness imputed to the saved and the sin imputed to Christ are *alien*, i.e. not properly belonging to the persons, so the guilt and corruption imputed to all mankind are alien, i.e. not deserved. Yet Paul distinctly places the ground of the one in contrast to the other (Rom. 5:15-19). The one point of comparison in the passage (Rom. 5:12-19) is unity of the race in Adam on the one hand and in Christ on the other. But, says Paul, otherwise all is different. Robert Dabney, who incorporated representation into his view said: 'The imputation of Adam's sin was a transaction of strict, judicial righteousness, the other transaction was one of glorious, grace.'

3) Another point of contrast between imputation of Adam's sin to us and of ours to Christ has to do with consent. As again Dabney pointed out, 'Adam's infant children receive the imputation, when they are incapable of a rational option or assent about it.' But 'Christ's bearing our imputed guilt was conditional on His own previous voluntary consent. See John 10:18. All theologians, so far as I know, regard this as essential to a just imputation of [alien] sin directly to Him.'[17] These are only the first and obvious questions.

---

16. Gordon Lewis & Bruce Demarest, *Integrative Theology II* (Grand Rapids: Zondervan, 1990), p. 193.
17. Robert L. Dabney, *Lectures in Systematic Theology* (Grand Rapids: Zondervan, 1878, 1972), p. 343.

Theories of 'Mediate Imputation'.

The Reformed churches of France in the sixteenth century had an important theological school in the university town of Saumur. At this school a Scottish professor named John Cameron in a brief tenure (AD 1618–1624) influenced three of his students toward considerable modification of Reformed (or Augustinian) doctrines. Among the most influential of his students were Moses Amyraut, Joshua LaPlace and Louis Cappel. Each of these earnest men contributed greatly to Christian scholarship in his day. They developed a theory of original sin and race guilt for Adam's sin (i.e. of imputation of Adam's sin) known to history as 'Mediate Imputation.' The apparent motive in this theory is to relieve God of the appearance of injustice in assigning guilt for an act we had no personal part in and certainly no previous agreement to be associated with and to avoid problems with what has come to be called 'immediate' imputation as in both the 'natural' headship and 'representative' headship forms of Reformation doctrine. LaPlace taught that every member of the race derives a corrupt (depraved) nature from Adam and that we are condemned because we are guilty of corruption, not for any identity with Adam in his probation and fall. Depravity was not and is not part of the penalty we receive for Adam's sin. We receive it by natural generation and are condemned because each of us is *personally* bad. Our 'legal' status as guilty is based on our condition, not the other way around.

Over a period of decades the churches wrestled with the learned arguments propounded. LaPlace finally was threatened with ecclesiastical censure for obviously denying what his peers saw as the plain teaching of Romans 5:12-21, whereupon he retracted sufficiently to acknowledge race-wide guilt of Adam's first sin but had meant to assert that though all are guilty of Adam's sin, the guilt is dependent on our sharing his corrupt nature, not the act of apostasy by which he failed probation.

This view, not surprisingly, has had great appeal to many. Yet when one accepts, as Scripture compels us to do, and indeed historically, as most official Protestantism does, that spiritual death is only a different name for depravity, or estrangement from God, and that the spiritual death we share from conception onward was and is God's just punishment for Adam's sin, mediate imputation becomes utterly unacceptable.

Furthermore, the Scripture plainly declares that God's sentence of condemnation was imposed on every man for the specific sin of one man. Mediate imputation denies this and moves the cause of the sentence of death to the depravity of each man. In Scripture Adam's guilt was and is the cause of depravity while mediate imputation makes depravity, inherited from Adam (not imputed), the cause of guilt of Adam's sin.

Mediate imputation in effect denies any imputation of *Adam's* sin at all. LaPlace was justly charged with this denial and, rather than accept discipline of the French church, inconsistently affirmed guilt for Adam's sin – but insisted still that it is mediately applied. In this system *Adam had probation but mankind did not*.

Mediate imputation denies the parallel between Adam and Christ so prominent in Romans 5:12-21. Advocates of mediate imputation (as does also Dr David Smith referred to earlier) argue it is unjust *ever*, under any circumstances, even by God, to be punished for the sins of another and that this is sufficient reason to reject immediate imputation of Adam's sin. It seems apparent that all theories of indirect (or mediate imputation of the original sin of Adam or Adam and Eve) rest on the feeling that it is wrong for God to punish one person for the sins of another person. Those who think this way (and who does not at least have the thought cross the mind?) should correct their thinking by reading such passages of Scripture as the following: 'I the LORD… am a jealous God, visiting the iniquity [punishment] of the fathers on the children to the third and the fourth generation' (Exod. 20:5). There were doubtless some believing Jews in Jerusalem in AD 70 but Jesus said 'all the righteous blood [of the prophets of the O.T.]… will come upon this generation' (Matt. 23:35, 36). Think of all the personally 'innocent' children who perished in the divine wrath of the Flood as also at Sodom and Gomorrah, the Midianite and Canaanite exterminations. It would be equally unjust for God to visit upon the Son the 'iniquity of us all' – to make 'him to be sin for us, who knew no sin; that we might be made the righteousness of God in him' (2 Cor. 5:21 KJV).

I share the impatience of many orthodox Protestant writers who regret the amount of attention that apparently must be paid to refutation of the theory of mediate imputation, a view attractive to some.

A Proposed Resolution: Probationary Unity Based on Natural (Seminal) Solidarity.

1. Let us make a fresh start by defining what imputation is and by clarifying what is meant by guilt for Adam's sin.

'Imputation' and 'impute' in legal, or forensic context, mean to assign responsibility for something, whether of evil to be punished or of good to be rewarded. Synonyms are reckon, think, regard, attribute, judge, charge. The

Protestant English Bible (KJV) for nearly four centuries has pretty well fixed the sense of the word in theological discussion from the thirteen occurrences in the Bible. The Hebrew and Greek words receive many other translations in KJV. The Hebrew word *ḥashav* is rendered impute in Psalm 32:2; 'Blessed is the man unto whom the LORD *imputeth* [emphasis added] not iniquity.' The Greek translation quoted by Paul at Romans 4:8 says 'Blessed is the man to whom the Lord will not *impute* [emphasis added] sin' employing *logidzomai*. Elsewhere in KJV and in more recent translations these words are rendered regard, account, esteem, reckon, think, suppose in both Testaments. The two words have a near equivalent range of meaning. The courtroom verdicts, 'guilty, as charged' and 'not guilty' convey the sense. When we read, 'He who justifies the wicked and he who condemns the righteous are both alike an abomination to the LORD' (Prov. 17:15), 'justifies' is imputation of innocence and 'condemns' is imputation of guilt, though in each case wrongfully.

Guilt has been defined earlier in these pages. (a) In a non-legal, personal sense guilt is inherent demerit, blameworthiness. Some older theologians call this 'potential guilt' – the intrinsic, moral evil and ill desert of anything one *is* or *does*. It is said to be of the essence of sin, the permanent character of its moral evil. When the sun is cold, the moon is old and the leaves of the judgment book unfold it will ever be true that so and so did such and such an evil deed and was such and such a man at a particular time. This kind of guilt was Adam's and his alone as regards his first sin of disobedience. Since I did not then exist *as a person*, except in God's foreknowledge, Adam's *personal guilt* cannot be mine.

(b) The legal or forensic sense is something else. Legal guilt is what the court says it is, in what after due deliberation, the judicial authority (judge or jury) declares to be the case. Courts cannot decree or determine ethical character but they can declare the accused *guilty* or *not guilty*.

Neither God nor man has declared any of Adam's progeny guilty for what he did in the sense of personal wrong-doing. It is the second that concerns us. We have before showed we are guilty of Adam's sin in God's court. We proceed assuming that we are guilty, that God has justly determined we are guilty, corrupt and punishable. The question being addressed is not if we are justly guilty of Adam's sin but upon what ground does God hold us guilty?

2. The imputation of Adam's sin to his progeny through the generations has been declared unjust by critics of the teaching. An answer on rational grounds would take us far aside from present goals, though there is much to cite from Scripture as to parallels and precedents in God's dealings with men to demonstrate that God acts justly in such matters, as Lincoln was pleased to quote: 'the judgments of the LORD are true and righteous altogether' (Ps. 19:9 KJV). This imputation has no strict parallels, being a unique event. We cannot be required to defend God's justice to unbelievers to their satisfaction at this juncture, though the effort has been made and is fruitful.[18]

We can, however, cite many biblical statements and precedents wherein God did hold family and others in solidarity with their progenitor or civil or legal head and thereby guilty and punishable.[19]

Let us look at some of them. One of the most impressive is Exodus 20:5 where in enforcing the command against idolatry God said He will visit 'the iniquity of the fathers on the children to the third and the fourth generation of those who hate me.' Similarly, Rahab's whole family was delivered by her own personal faith (Josh. 6:25); the utter destruction of the Amelekites in King Saul's time was on account of what their ancestors did centuries earlier (1 Sam. 15:2, 3 and following; cf. Exod. 17:8-16); the national judgment on the Israel of Jesus' time for the treatment of their Messiah by national leaders (Matt. 23:32-38; cf. 1 Thess. 2:14-16 'your house is left to you desolate' – Jesus; 'God's wrath has come upon them at last' – Paul). Theological writers cite many more with impressive comments in support of this principle, which they, I think somewhat inaccurately (and I shall explain), call 'representative.'

These citations, especially the last one, wherein Paul declares God's present judgment on the Jewish people, so offend current 'correct' sociological taste one hardly dare even mention them. Some who are a bit biblically literate cite Deuteronomy 24:16 against imputation of Adam's guilt to any one except Adam himself: 'Fathers shall not be put to death because of their children, nor shall children be put to death because of their fathers. Each one shall be put to death for his own sin.' The text is, however, part of a large section of Mosaic instruction and exhortation on the subject of the administration of human (albeit divinely given) civil law. It had to do with a political constitution. In such a setting there must be no imputation of guilt except to the person of the transgressor.

---

18. See Dabney, *Lectures*, pp. 338–340, 348–350; C. A. Hodge, *Systematic Theology II*, p. 221; Thornwell, *Collected Writings I*, pp. 334–344.
19. C. A. Hodge, *Systematic Theology II*, pp. 198–201.

The same must be said of Ezekiel 18:20, cited I think mindlessly through the generations by opponents of the clear biblical affirmation of universal guilt, punished by spiritual death, for Adam's sin, viz.: 'The soul who sins shall die. The son shall not suffer for the iniquity of the father, nor the father suffer for the iniquity [Heb. 'awon, guilt, punishment] of the son. The righteousness of the righteous shall be upon himself, and the wickedness of the wicked shall be upon himself.' As I pointed out earlier the audience in Babylon whom the prophet was addressing had been complaining that they were unjustly suffering in a foreign land for the sins of their immediate ancestors in Israel only a few years before. Ezekiel reminded them they also deserved to die for their own sins and would do so except they repent. This is the meaning of Ezekiel 18:20 and context – like Jesus' words to similar inquirers in the thirteenth chapter of Luke.

These texts are irrelevant to the subject of imputation of Adam's guilt to us. All of us are worthy of death and unless united with Christ in regeneration and justified by faith, already dead in trespasses and sins. So though God is not unjust to take the lives of infants and the unborn by the millions, every discerning Christian is horrified to contemplate this being done by mothers and fathers or abortionists. Yet God is inflicting punishment for Adam's sin (hardly their own personal sins) in each case. In the race of man, death at any age and by whatever cause or means is the curse put on Adam. If infants were not guilty in some true sense they would not die. God's providence is not absent from even senseless wars, massacres and murders.

3. The human race, dead, living and yet unborn, are not simply an aggregate of individuals. We are an organic, substantial unity by natural descent from one man whose very name was Adam, man, mankind – not simply the male but the species. Eve was also out of the man Adam (Gen. 2:23). True we are all descended from Eve 'the mother of all living' (Gen. 3:20), but that is unimportant to the *imputation* of the sin of the head of our race, as pointed out in an earlier chapter of this book, Part 2.1, 'The Origin and Unity of Man by Creation.' This is acknowledged by all party to the debate over the basis of imputation. Though some who endorse a purely representative headship of Adam declare each human soul is directly created by God, *de novo*, they still regard the above as correct – even C. A. Hodge who is almost unique in insistence that 'immediate imputation' excludes any *real* presence of our generic human essence in Adam. It is the burden of Genesis 1–5 to highlight this natural unity (1:26-28, 33; 3:20; 4:1-3; 4:26 and all of chap. 5; 9:19 and 32). J. H. Thornwell, though committed to the scheme of covenants of works and grace acknowledged: '... I am free to confess that I cannot escape from the doctrine, however mysterious, of a generic unity in man as the true basis of the representative economy in the covenant of works' and explains at length.[20]

The Genesis narrative is the obvious ground of Paul's summary statements of our unity in Adam's sin in Romans 5; Acts 17; and 1 Corinthians 15.

4. This substantial unity includes both body and soul of every one of Adam's progeny. I shall not here repeat arguments in the anthropology section of this book that are presupposed here.

5. The Genesis narrative theology is equally plain that Adam and his descendants with him formed a unity in the probation of Eden. This in my judgment is no less certain than the natural, organic unity of the human race. Probationary unity rather than 'covenant unity' or 'representation' is the preferable term for several reasons.

None of these terms – covenant or probation – appears expressly in the narrative. The extensive and ingenious efforts of C. A. Hodge, Louis Berkhof, Robert Reymond and others to find all the elements of a covenant, as they understand a covenant of works in Eden, are not without merit.[21] Yet the idea of covenant is not obvious in the passage. Proponents agree it is absent from pre-Reformation writings. It was a 'discovery' catalyzed by questions aroused by the immemorial, but hardly original practice of infant baptism. The Anabaptist martyrs made the problem acute.

Though I prefer not to call the probationary arrangement a covenant, I recognize one may call it a covenant in some general sense without adopting the system of 'covenant theology.' That this does not necessarily follow is evident in that Baptists such as John Gill – than whom no greater Baptist theologian ever lived, treated the probation as a 'covenant'[22] but rejected much of what goes for covenant theology. Gill rejected notions of correspondence between ordinance (i.e. sacraments) of Old Testament dispensation and New Testament dispensation while holding to salvation by grace and a consistent Calvinistic outlook. (Gill was pre-millennial in eschatological outlook.[23])

---

20. James H. Thornwell, *Collected Writings I* (Carlisle, PA and Edinburgh: Banner of Truth Trust, 1875, 1986), p. 349.
21. Hodge, *Systematic Theology II*, pp. 117–122; Dabney, *Lectures*, pp. 302–305; Gill, *Body of Divinity I*, pp. 444–451; Buswell, *Systematic Theology of the Christian Religion I*, pp. 307–320; Berkhof, *Systematic Theology*, pp. 211–218.
22. John Gill, *Body of Divinity I* (Grand Rapids: Baker Books, 1839, 1978), pp. 444–470.
23. Gill, *Body of Divinity II*, pp. 621–660.

The probationary arrangement was made specifically by God with Adam, not with Adam *and* Eve. This is clear in KJV of Genesis 2:15-17, 'the LORD God commanded the man' (v. 16). The verbs in Hebrew are all masculine, second person singular. The KJV preserves this distinction with 'thou [singular] mayest freely eat,' etc. (vv. 16, 17), obscured in NIV and other recent Versions which do not employ the second person singular pronouns. Eve's creation was subsequent. 'Probation' need not be defended here, for all agree it is accurate. A 'covenant' is not obviously present.

The evidence is plain that all Adam's descendants (including Eve, 'for she was taken out of man,' Gen. 2:23 NIV) were involved in the probation; that Adam acted as a public person, that the results were to apply to all, that what Adam won or lost for himself, he won or lost for us all. That all the human race through future history were in some manner parties to the probation in Adam is easily demonstrated by the very language of the narrative. Except that I would put 'probation' and 'probationary arrangement' for John Murray's 'Adamic Administration,' where Dabney employs 'federal' and 'covenant,' no one has put the matter more forcefully and succinctly than he. I quote at length. After citing Genesis 1:22, 28; 3:15-19; 9:3, Dabney states:

> In the dominion assigned over the beasts, in the injunction to multiply, in the privilege of eating the fruits of the earth, in hallowing of the sabbath, God spoke seemingly only to the first pair; but his words indisputably applied as well to their posterity. So we infer, they were included in the threat of death for disobedience, and the implied promise of 2:17 ['thou shalt surely die']. To see the force of this inference, remember that it is the established style of Genesis. See 9:25-27; 15:7; 16:12; and 17:20. In each case the patriarch stands for himself and his posterity, in the meaning of the promise. But this is more manifest in Genesis 3:15-19 where God proceeds to pass sentence according to the threat of the broken Covenant [better, the breached probation]. The serpent is to be at war with the woman's seed. The ground is cursed for Adam's sin. Does not this curse affect his posterity? The woman has her peculiar punishment, shared equally by all her daughters. And in the closing sentence, death to death, we all read the doom of our mortality. So plain is all this, that even Pelagians have allowed that God acted here judicially. But Adam's posterity [as Pelagians deny] is included in the judgment. No better description of imputation need be required.[24]

So it seems apparent that in addition to the damage (corruption, depravity) to human nature in Adam and ours in him, we were judged collectively in him as guilty of what he did. Granted in the first sense of guilt, actual personal responsibility as actor in what he did, Adam was alone, yet in the second sense, legal liability, we were accounted in him in the condemnation.

There is a residual mystery, as all must admit, but that does not relieve the theologian of expressing in words what evidently appears to be true, as far as we now can see.

6. I have contended earlier for a Traducian origin of every soul of man, not special creation by God but natural generation by human parents. The complete natural unity of the race depends on this, if we regard soul as part of human nature. All agree that imputation of Adam's guilt is more understandable and rationally defensible on the ground of Traducianism. It seems to me (and I shall not here repeat the scores of pages of Shedd's *Dogmatic Theology II*[25] and Strong's *Systematic Theology*[26] and many others, in support of Traducianism) Shedd was right in affirming: 'There are difficulties attending either theory of the origin of man [i.e. of the soul], but fewer connected with traducianism than with creationism.'[27] In my mind it is near unassailable that the Bible, read simply to form and inform our system of theology, makes no distinction in origin between human bodies and souls with regard to parents. Both are created by God through *second* causes (parents). The Bible thus makes all life on earth God's creations in this sense. But as far as *this earth* is concerned, as for primary and direct creation, God ceased from His labors on the seventh day and still completely enjoys His Sabbath. God is not presently creating new entities nor did He originally create a stockpile of souls to deliver as human parents procreated the physical bodies of babies.

7. Natural causes ('like begets like') do not account for our guilt and corruption. The special principle governing the probation accounts for the connection. God's sovereign government related particularly to Adam's probation and our connection with him in that probation alone. No parents since Adam have stood in probationary relation to

---

24. Dabney, *Lectures*, pp. 329, 330.
25. Shedd, *Dogmatic Theology II*, pp. 3–94.
26. Strong, *Systematic Theology*, pp. 492–497.
27. Shedd, *Dogmatic Theology II*, p. 19.

succeeding generations of offspring. God does not ordinarily visit death upon people today specifically for the sins of their parents. The probation ended with the fall. We inherit much from all our ancestors, of course, but that is not why we are 'dead in trespasses and sins.'

8. Adam was tempted in a way not unlike every temptation to sin. There are certain parallels between his temptation and ours. It begins with 'lust,' or 'concupiscence,' or 'inordinate desire,' viz. '…each person is tempted when he is lured and enticed by his own evil desire' (James 1:14). This must mean that evil desire (i.e. a corruption of heart) preceded the act of outward disobedience. How this could have happened in a holy being is unknown and cannot be known by us.

Logically, therefore, Adam became depraved before guilty, though it is not possible to affirm the presence of one without the other. In us, it is the other way around. Depravity as the corruption that is spiritual death (alienation from God, our wills captive to sin) follows the guilt. There is considerable confusion about this matter among authors owing to the fact that Jonathan Edwards asserted that depravity was before guilt without making clear he was referring to Adam himself rather than the human race, his progeny.

9. The guilt we share for Adam's sin is a forensic (or legal) matter. This is what is meant by the term 'imputation.' It relates not to who or what we are personally, morally, spiritually, but to where we stand in God's sight.

10. It is our natural solidarity with Adam in his sin that parallels our solidarity with Christ, but the ground of solidarity was different in each case. Paul goes to some length to make this plain. The fact that all of a certain group (all in Adam) are judged guilty in him, i.e. that guilt is *imputed* to them is the precise point of the parallel with the *imputation* of Christ's righteousness to all in Christ. Scarcely any other aspect of justification in Christ and condemnation in Christ parallel (Dr Hodge and his disciples notwithstanding).

We are regarded as guilty because we deserve to be so regarded. There is nothing vicarious about it. Adam did not sin vicariously in our stead. Not a sentence in Scripture affirms it. It is the exact opposite in the case of Christ and our justification. We do not deserve righteous standing at all. He took what we deserve that we might have what He deserves. To borrow the language of certain theologians, the righteousness imputed to us in justification is an *alien* righteousness whereas the condemnation and depravity imputed to us in original sin is not alien at all. It all comes quite naturally. We were never at any moment of our personal existence apart from it. Paul is very careful in Romans 5 to make clear that our relation to Adam is very different from our relation to Christ except for the principle of solidarity. 'But the gift is not like the trespass.… Again, the gift of God is not like the result of the one man's sin: The judgment followed one sin [back in Adam's time] and brought condemnation, but [in contrast] the gift followed many trespasses and brought justification' (Rom. 5:15-17 NIV).

It is important to note that *something* about Adam and those in solidarity with him is parallel to something about Christ and those in solidarity with Him, but not everything.

Further, Adam furnishes the illustration or analogy not the other way around. That in justification our solidarity with Christ is a forensic (legal) matter only, does not mean the same is true of our solidarity with Adam. It is correct to say Christ is our substitute; His punishment was *vicarious*, in our room, but it is grotesque to say Adam is our substitute, that he transgressed vicariously and was condemned vicariously for us.

11. Adam and Eve in Eden and in the probationary period – including pronouncements by God upon their apostasy – were archetypes of all male and female humanity since. This is not the same as saying God imputes everything about themselves and their acts of good or evil to the generations to follow, but it does serve to enforce our connection with them in God's plan and providence. An archetype is 'a primitive or standard pattern or a model' (*Britannica*) 'a model or first form' (*American College Dictionary*). To be an archetype is not the same as to be 'representative,' 'federal head' or in 'covenant relation' – which I find less than fully satisfactory ways of stating the relation.

But that Adam and Eve were 'primitive or standard patterns' of every man and woman in themselves is certain. God treated them that way from the beginning. Consider the command the pair received to multiply and fill the earth; the freedom to eat all the natural produce of earth (one tree excepted); the words about the nature of the conjugal married state, and so on similarly; after the fall the divine pronouncements about the serpent's seed and the woman's seed; the changes in Eve's relation to Adam (Gen. 3:16); the new relation of Adam to work, to nature, to Eve and to God. None of these, including the curse on the ground, was a state of affairs limited to their time only. What is said of Adam as man (that is, the race), of Adam as a man, of Eve as a woman, were and are to be true of mankind throughout all future generations. These arrangements were all wrought of God in His own mysterious way. They are not fully explicable on any purely rational or scientific ground. What God did to place us in solidarity with them besides (1) the declared probation and its results as above noted, and (2) the natural union by procreated descent from Adam we do not know for sure. But we ask questions about it and theologians do their best to avoid harmful wrong answers even while they acknowledge some reservations about answers that seem correct and wholesome.

12. Neither the representative (Federal, covenant) headship view nor the seminal (natural, real) headship view nor even both together is adequate fully to explain our acknowledged solidarity with Adam or how our relation to him furnishes adequate ground for imputation of Adam's sin. Both sustain the Augustinian (and Reformers') steadfast affirmation that we all do indeed stand guilty, corrupted in heart and condemned. Yet neither fully answers the objections of the other. The representative view acknowledges that the genetic connection is ground for representation.

We have already observed some partial analogies in Scripture. A thorough canvas of 'corporate personality' theories of recent decades would take us too far afield, but they would furnish many more evidences of group solidarities of various sorts in Scripture. But none I know of furnishes an exact parallel or analogy that would establish the ground of the imputation of Adam's sin to us.

My professor of theology, very well-read and articulate, systematic and logical almost to extremes, backed away from the question. My notes show he said 'Adam's fall brought condemnation upon all men,' and after citing Romans 5:16 and 18 added without further comment, 'The controversy is over *how* it did so.' That was all. Generally both Calvinistic and Baptist in outlook, he never raised the subject except in those two sentences. Another related question he asked was 'Does God really hold us responsible for Adam's sin? Yes, biblically we cannot deny it' and again cited Romans 5:16 and 18, but said no more.

Baptist scholars of yesterday tended to be forthright and positive in accepting the fact and explaining it, much as Luther, Calvin and Augustine long before. John Gill (AD 1697–1771) held that Adam's posterity, yet unborn, had a 'virtual and representative' being in Adam and were in him both seminally and Federally.[28] A. H. Strong rejecting representative headship, held firmly to seminal headship, or realistic connection. James Pedigru Boyce, long-time professor of theology at the Southern Baptist Seminary, was exceedingly clear on this matter.

'The Scriptures plainly assume and declare that God righteously punishes all men, not only for what they do, but for what they are. Men are indeed represented as more guilty and sinful than they know themselves to be... a corrupt nature makes a condition as truly sinful, and guilty, and liable to punishment as actual transgressions. Consequently at the very moment of birth, the presence and possession of such a nature shows that the infant sons of Adam are born under all the penalties which befell their ancestor in the day of his sin.' (James Pedigru Boyce, *Abstract of Systematic Theology*, Philadelphia, PA: American Baptist Publication Society, 1887, pp. 249, 250.)

Recently Baptists have tended to be less Augustinian and Calvinistic in the whole range of theology and no less here. David Smith, reported earlier in these pages, supports a non-Augustinian outlook with affinities both to Placean-Amyrauldian and Arminian teachings as do the several of his Baptist mentors whom he cites. Millard Erickson seems at first to adhere to an Augustinian view similar to Strong's, but J. L. Garrett, another Baptist author, comments, 'Millard Erickson has stated that he has "espoused" realism, or the theory of "natural headship, and… has attributed this view singularly to Augustine" but "in conclusion, abandoned realism and instead opted for what we will later identify as the Placean theory of the imputation of depravity." I do not find Dr Erickson, though somewhat indecisive, quite that confusing. In a different way I find Garrett's treatment quite unsatisfactory. Protestant theology has not, as Garrett does, sought to relate "the sin" of Adam *and Eve* to our sin.'[29] Scripture nowhere traces the cause of our guilt to Eve: rather to and through Adam alone. This confusion may be the influence of the current fads of feminism. Must Eve and her daughters have their due even in original sin? Further, Garrett is almost unique in first rather fully covering the theories and then concluding with no commitment at all to any theory of imputation. He ends by urging us to 'be aware of all that for which we are responsible' but gives no hint as to how we should interpret the relation of 'the sin of Adam and Eve to our sin.'[30] He needs, it seems to me, to review the Adamic connection, rather than the 'Adam *and Eve* relation.'

---

28. Gill, *Body of Divinity I*, p. 469.
29. J. L. Garrett, *Systematic Theology: Biblical, Historical and Evangelical I* (Grand Rapids: Eerdmans, 1990), p. 486.
30. Garrett, *op. cit.*, p. 493.

Lewis and Demarest of Denver Theological Seminary (Baptist) have produced competent and readable summaries of the views. There is a somewhat less than formal endorsement of seminal, substantial, natural headship, 'a realistic solidarity of the race' and, employing the NIV, interpret Acts 17:26 (*ex henos*) as 'from one man.' They also say: '[T]hese verses (Rom. 5:16, 17, 18) teach the transfer of the legal guilt of one person to others he represents.'[31] They report much that is true about suffering vicariously for sin and transfer of consequences. Yet, it seems to me, though endorsing a Calvinistic (or Augustinian) outlook in a general way, they decide not to recommend any of the competing views of Calvinists. They provide adequate analysis but less synthesis.

13. In my judgment there is a 'more excellent way.' 1) The human race was present in Adam in seminal substance. No one can deny it and all who believe the Scripture acknowledge it. Whatever human nature is, we are one in inheriting it from Adam. Adam had all the human nature there is and so does each of his progeny – call it 'flesh' (John 1:14) or 'human form' (Phil. 2:7) or 'flesh and blood' (Heb. 2:14) or whatever. 2) The probation of Adam was and is unique, never to be repeated. There are no very exact analogies or parallels, for there has been but one probation of all mankind in one man. That probation took place by virtue of God's sovereign rule. 'He doeth according to His will in the heavens and on the earth.' As earlier I have asserted, Adam was archetype of every man in everything about the probation. 3) Our *real presence* in him both as nature, or seminal substance, and *the forensic fact* that he was archetype on probation for us all are grounds for the divine imputation of his guilt and corruption to his progeny. The natural relation and the probationary archetypal relation in the case of Adam cannot be separated.

'Representative' is not quite an adequate or precise term for that forensic connection, because it implies designation by the ones represented. Further, to say Adam was our representative implies we were not there really in any sense. Our language means that. Mr Gutknecht is our Minnesota district representative in the lower house of Congress at Washington. He represents me but is not my probationary archetype. As my representative he is really there and he acts for me but I am not really there. The relations between me and Mr Gutknecht are purely formal, as represented and representative. This manner of speaking by C. A. Hodge and other like-minded Federalists is correct for what I think they mean to say, for they reject any real presence of Adam's progeny in the probation. By insisting all souls are immediately created by God, and likewise that the seat of depravity and prime bearer of guilt is not the body (for if any precedence in guilt exists it must be in the soul), these Federalists cut off any possibility at all of my or your real presence in Adam.

But in Adam my substance was indeed present – to what extent physical I do not know any more than of my immediate father, S. C. Culver, who begat me while the First World War was raging and who is now in heaven. In or by what mode my spiritual seed or substance was in him I do not know either, but as a convinced Traducianist I affirm, there it was. As certainly as God created Adam in His own image and that first archetypal man begat Seth and all his descendants on to Noah and his sons by whom the whole earth was overspread, I was generated by his seed in the image of his fallen nature. It does not seem to me my 'nature' *per se* albeit fallen was judged guilty, for only persons are guilty. But what Adam lost he, by divine arrangement, lost for all of us.

The difficulties with our solidarity with Adam in the fall are not as to the fact itself, but as to the how. 'Does not the remaining mystery lose itself in that abyss which is opened by the *fact of the permission of sin*, before which all theists on this side of the veil must bow in silence.'[32]

---

31. Lewis & Demarest, *Integrative Theology II*, p. 223.
32. A. A. Hodge in concluding his chapter on 'Imputation of Adam's First Sin,' *Outlines of Theology* (Grand Rapids: Eerdmans, 1860, 1957), p. 366.

10
The Worldwide Reign of Sin

The Prevalence of Sin in the World.

Sin in the person of 'the tempter' makes its first appearance in the first pages of the Bible and makes its departure ('exiunt *not* smiling') at the very end. ('The last enemy to be destroyed is death' and, of course, 'the sting of death is sin.') Every age between deals in one way or another, directly or indirectly, with sin, its prevalence, effects and salvation from it. Government by civil laws and authorities was ordained by God as only one of His measures for damage control of the devastation of society under the reign of sin. (If men were holy as are the angels we wouldn't need courts, police, governors and legislatures. *Toward a Biblical View of Civil Government*[1] took me many years to write and ran to hundreds of pages – to speak of only one little-noticed evidence of sin's universal domination.)

The Reign of Sin.

At this point to prolong this study by an excursion through the Scripture in the manner of current biblical theology is neither very interesting nor necessary, for a very important reason, viz. the Bible furnishes its own integration of all the evidence, both biblical and experimental. I refer to Paul's own 'systematic theology of the Christian religion' (Rom. 1:18–3:31; 5:12-21; and chap. 7). We do not need an inductive study of the prevalence of sin in the world through the whole Bible because Paul has provided the results of his own study for us.

Much of this section of Scripture has been cited and quoted at length previously in this book. Here our interest takes us to Paul's summary of all his previous argument. In doing so, with both scriptural and apostolic authority, he addresses and answers every important question ever raised about how far the sin introduced at the beginning of human history has prevailed and with what consequences both immediate and ultimate. The specifics are laid out in Romans chapter 3, beginning mid-verse 9 and on to the end of verse 20. The great spokesman for Christ (Rom. 1:1) was never shy of asserting his apostolic authority among Christians (albeit diplomatically), yet here he is at pains to reinforce his own authority with that of Moses, the poets and the prophets of the Old Testament. He is employing the power of recognized authority in the most bitter and devastating denunciation of the moral character of every member of the human race. There is probably nothing comparable in literature anywhere in any language except possibly Jesus' withering denunciations of official Jewry in Matthew 23.

---

1. Robert D. Culver, *Civil Government, A Biblical View* (Edmonton, Alberta: Canadian Institute for Law, Theology and Public Policy, 2000).

The Entire World of Humanity Brought to the Court of Divine Law.

The shadow of a court trial, almost subliminally, falls across the Epistle at this stage (Rom. 3:9-19). In one form or another, criminal court procedures are as old and as pervasive as society, already ancient then: in the litigious atmosphere of our times scarcely ever out of mind for a whole day. The tribunal has already heard opening charges, the prosecutor's statements and evidences. He is now drawing up his summary. I shall quote the NKJV.

In this climax of the prosecution we shall hear:

1. The Prosecutor's Statement (9b) 'all under sin.'
2. The Prosecutor's Summation (10-18) 'sinful in heart, speech, deeds.'
3. The Defense's Speechless Response (19b) 'every mouth... stopped.'
4. The Judge's Verdict (19b, 20) 'no flesh... justified.'

1. The Prosecutor's Statement:

'...we have previously charged both Jews and Greeks that they are all under sin' (Rom. 3:9b). This has reference to the prosecutor's case as previously developed (Rom. 1:18–3:8a). Having charged the entire race with *lese majestie* under divine wrath – ungodly, unrighteous, suppressing truth in unrighteousness (1:18) – he goes on (a) to show that the idolatrous, barbaric pagans suppress truth and insult the Creator. They do this by prostrating themselves before creatures far below their own dignity. They defile their own minds and bodies with grossest sins (1:19-32). Twice the prosecutor says God has given them up and concludes the bitter recital, saying, '[they] knowing the righteous judgment of God... are deserving of death' (1:32).

(b) Then the prosecutor turns his attention to the sophisticated heathen, the Greek and Roman legislators, moralists, and educators, and those who follow them (2:1-16). They have judged the unsophisticated pagan foolish in his brand of idolatry, but do the same things themselves, while claiming to know better. There is a law of God written on their hearts that they have knowingly and impenitently broken. They also are worthy of death according to four divine principles of judgment (2:2, 6, 11, 16). These principles, in the language of Paul (Greek text and KJV) are: i. 'according to truth', Gr., *Kata alētheion* (Rom. 2:2); ii. 'according to... deeds', Gr., *Kata ta erga* (Rom. 2:6); iii. 'no respect of persons,' lit., acceptance of faces, Gr., *ou... prosōpolēmpsia* (Rom. 3:11); iv. 'the secrets of men', Gr., *ta krupta tōn anthrōpon* (Rom. 3:16). A fifth might be added – all will be 'by Jesus Christ', Gr., *dia Iēsou Xristou* (Rom. 3:16). These principles come in for enlargement in the chapter on Judgment in the section on Eschatology.

(c) Next, the prosecutor files his indictment of the Jewish people (2:17–3:9a). As more enlightened than any other people, being custodians of the Holy Scriptures, they are guilty, more deserving of judgment, because of sinning against greater light than any others.

This is a sketch of what Paul means by the claim, 'we have previously charged both Jews and Greeks that they are all under sin' (Rom. 3:9).

If we may put this, if possible, in divine perspective, God's interest is to show that no matter what self-estimate we make of ourselves, whatever extenuations we claim, whatever excuses we offer, the fact of being guilty sinners under divine judgment remains. We are not to be let off for any excuse whatsoever. We may not plead innocent by reason of ignorance, insanity or lack of contrary choices.

Objections:

But objections have been raised against such an interpretation of Paul's language. Maybe, some say, Paul in saying 'all the world' is 'guilty before God' (v. 19) is only referring to some especially depraved section of society such as the male prostitutes of Corinth or the hypocritical scribes whom Jesus denounced (Matt. 23:15, etc.); or – as Moses Stuart, in his Commentary on Romans – perhaps Paul is thinking of groups such as Jews and Gentiles, among whom such sins occur, but not of every man. My memory is sharp of certain 'holiness' preachers who insisted no sanctified Christian ever does any of these things or has it in his heart to do them.

Let Jonathan Edwards, writing in the famous treatise, *The Great Christian Doctrine of Original Sin,* reply:

> If the words which the Apostle uses, do not most fully and determinately signify universality, no words ever used in the bible are sufficient to it. I might challenge any man to produce any one paragraph in the Scripture, from the beginning to the end, where there is such a repetition and accumulation of terms, so strongly and

emphatically, and carefully, to express the most perfect and absolute universality, or any place to be compared to it... *They are all – they are all – they are all – together – everyone – everyone*; joined to multiplied negative terms, to show the universality to be without exception; saying, *there is no flesh – there is none – there is none – there is none – there is none*, four times over; besides the addition of *no, not one – no, not one*.... When the Apostle says, *That every mouth may be stopped*, must we suppose that he speaks only of those two [Jews and Gentiles] great collective bodies, figuratively ascribing to each of them a mouth, and means that those two mouths are stopped?[2]

2. The Prosecutor's Summation (Rom. 3:10-18).

He employs the very language and text of Old Testament Scripture, lending scriptural weight to apostolic authority.

(a) A general charge of unrighteousness (v. 10). 'There is none righteous, no, not one' (quoting Ps. 14:1 and 3).

The skeptical reader should be reminded that these specific sentences are in the inspired text of Scripture three times and are echoed in many other passages. Examples are: 'for there is no one who does not sin' (1 Kgs. 8:46 NKJV); 'Who can say, "I have made my heart clean, I am pure from my sin"' (Ps. 20:9 NKJV).

(b) Men are sinful in their inmost part, the heart and mind, where are the springs of action (Rom. 3:11, 12). 'As a man thinketh in his heart, so is he.' 'There is none who understands' (Rom. 3:11a citing Ps. 14:2, 3).

The problem with us is at the deepest level. Theologians refer to this as the *noetic* effect of sin on the mind and heart. (See the very important condensed summary in Shedd's *Dogmatic Theology II*.[3]) The New Testament is very explicit, viz. 'the natural man does not receive the things of the Spirit of God, for they are foolishness to him' (1 Cor. 2:14 NKJV); 'having their understanding darkened' (Eph. 4:18, cf. v. 19 NKJV); 'the message of the cross is foolishness to those who are perishing' (1 Cor. 1:18 NKJV; see also Matt. 13:19-23). In each case the context relates these startling denigrations of fallen man's intellectual powers to spiritual and moral matters, though hardly without placing some doubt on the wholeness of all our noetic powers.

The possible impairment by sin of our powers to think straight has received much attention from apologists, philosophers and theologians, but the twentieth century with its unprecedented bloodlettings; 'holocausts'; and waves of gratuitous wanton vice, crime and violence have convinced even the liberal theologians (e.g. R. Bultmann, *The Presence of Eternity*) and especially the neo-orthodox, of the depravity of man's heart and consequent manifold impairment (see Reinhold Niebuhr, *The Nature and Destiny of Man* and E. Brunner, *Man in Revolt*).[4] Even secular journals have for fifty years, since the horrors of Nazi and Stalinist crimes against man came first to plain light, accepted the reality of universal moral impairment if not the biblical explanation of it.

'There is none who seeks after God' (Rom. 3:11b). From our first parents after the fall onward to the present we have been running away and except for persistent pursuit by The Hound of Heaven, would all be lost forever. God has done all the seeking. This is the message of prophets of the Old Testament, several parables of Jesus and special appeals throughout Scripture.

'They have all turned aside' (Rom. 3:12). Like sheep wandering or children lost in the rush of shopping mall traffic we are lost, irretrievably lost unless God's Spirit finds us and the Father brings us to Christ.

'They have together become unprofitable' (Rom. 3:12b). We are more trouble than we are worth and would have been blotted out as a bad bargain long ago at the beginning of human history, except for God's mercy, grace and love. We had become useless to God.

Before going on to particular supporting charges (vv. 13-18), Paul the prosecutor, still quoting Psalm 14:1-3, repeats the general charge.

'There is none who does good, no, not one' (Rom. 3:12c). Let us, following Paul's method, introduce further evidence of the general charge of universal sinfulness by further scriptural evidence and emphasis. In the light of God's holiness, and against the standard of totally pure motives as necessary quality of pure thought, word or deed, 'all our righteousnesses are as filthy rags.' The holiest of men have said of themselves as Isaiah 'I am a man of unclean lips and dwell in the midst of a people of unclean lips.'

Though many are by grace 'called... saints' (1 Cor. 1:2) and 'holy men' (1 Peter 1:21) the best of them are guilty of sin of nature and sins of thought, word and deed. Moses and Samuel (Jer. 15:1) and Noah, Daniel and Job (Ezek. 14:14) are cited as examples of unusual spiritual power of advocacy before God. Yet each one of these if not

---

2. Edwards, p. 425 as cited by Robert Haldane in *Exposition of the Epistle to the Romans*, 1847, pp. 116, 117.
3. W. G. T. Shedd, *Dogmatic Theology II* (New York: Charles Scribners Sons, 1888), pp. 196–198.
4. See especially R. Bultmann, *The Presence of Eternity*, p. 102.

convicted of sins on the pages of Scripture, at least confesses himself to be a sinner. Moses unrightously lost his temper and assumed honors – however briefly – that cost him dearly (Num. 20:10-12; 27:14). Samuel failed as a parent, sinning against God and his sons by indulging the sins of his boys, even with the horrible example of Eli and his wicked sons before him as he grew up in that great man's house (1 Sam. 8:1-5). Noah was guilty at least of careless indiscretion when he should have been discreet. Job, though commended in heaven as 'perfect and upright' (Job 1:1, 8; 2:3 KJV), confessed his sins and repented of them (Job 42:6).

Other famous holy people of the Bible are all really reclaimed backsliders, for example: Jacob, Abraham, Hezekiah and Peter. Ezra, of whom no faults are reported, joined himself with his people in confessing their enormous sins against light (Ezra 9:5-15) as is likewise true of Daniel (Dan. 9:1-18) signally addressed by Gabriel several times as 'greatly beloved' (of God) (Dan. 9:23; 10:11, 19 KJV).

The wisest people of Scripture, in their most solemn and reflective moments, say the same: Solomon at prayer, 'there is no man that sinneth not' (1 Kgs. 8:46; cf. Prov. 20:9), to which the greatest evangelical prophet agrees, 'All we like sheep have gone astray' (Isa. 53:6).

'There is none righteous... none who does good, no not, one' is assumed by Jesus. Without that fact His ministry and work of redemption have no meaning. 'Christ Jesus came into the world to save sinners.' 'God so loved the world that he gave his only begotten Son' because it was in need of saving. He addresses His circle of disciples as sinful men (Luke 11:13; cf. v.1). He announced the coming of the Holy Spirit as specially related to the world's sin (John 16:8-11). Every New Testament book and writer assumes or affirms that all are 'under sin.' John speaks for all of them and all of us when he writes: 'If we say that we have no sin, we deceive ourselves... If we say that we have not sinned, we make him [God] a liar' (1 John 1:8, 10 KJV).

Every generation has its share of men with seared consciences and hardened hearts who though deep in sinful thoughts and deeds seem unaware of it. To this non-professional observer it seems that the modern secular mind in university sociology, anthropology, psychology and related disciplines has about given up grounds for moral distinctions except for social utility and individual autonomy (called freedom). Thus average behavior becomes normal. Sin as a Godward aspect of 'anti-social' behavior is lost. This is not new, for it is to be found full-blown in some of the ancient Greek philosophers.

But the Bible assumes even saints may be unaware of some of their most egregious failures and transgressions. The ceremonial law provided special offerings for these unknown, unconscious sins (e.g. Num. 15:22-41; and Lev. 5:17-19). The prayers of the Psalter (Heb. *tehillim*, prayers) more than once express concern for this sort of thing (e.g. Ps. 19:11) where 'secret sins' or 'hidden' faults are those hidden even from the man at prayer and are in contrast with open 'presumptuous' sins (Ps.19:12). Psalm 90, the 'Prayer of Moses the man of God,' expresses the concern of 'the meekest man of all the earth' that God has 'set... our secret sins in the light of thy countenance' (Ps. 90:8 KJV).

Every faithful preacher knows that the very sinners who trumpet their moral innocence most loudly are the ones farthest from God, whose 'foolish hearts are darkened' most deeply. Some of the world's famous moral reprobates have been notoriously unconscious of any serious guilt feelings.[5] Perhaps the most impudent man of letters in the history of modern Europe was J. J. Rousseau (AD 1712–1778), one of the Fathers of the French Revolution – though he died too soon to know it. In his *Confessions* he 'confesses sin in a spirit that needs to be confessed' that he was a thief, advocated and practiced adultery, and sent his many illegitimate offspring to foundling asylums.[6] In elegant language he boasted, 'No man can come to the throne of God and say: I am a better man than Rousseau.' A few years ago Errol Flynn, one of Hollywood's leading male actors, was notorious in life for his marriages and adulteries and at his death left his teenaged concubine a delinquent ward of the state of California. Near the end he wrote an autobiography in devil-may-care style entitled, 'My Wicked, Wicked Ways.' The deficiency of such people in self-understanding is due evidence of the truth of all we have just reviewed of Paul's argument for universal sin.

(c) Men are especially sinful in speech, whereby their sinful hearts are given expression (Rom. 3:13, 14 NKJV). 'With their tongues they have practiced deceit' (quoting Ps. 5:9). 'The poison of asps is under their lips' (quoting Ps. 140:3). 'Whose mouth is full of cursing and bitterness' (quoting Ps. 18:7).

Paul takes note of all the organs of speech in man – throat, tongue, lips, mouth – and describes here the four principle vices of the tongue, viz.: *Firstly*, filthy language, the jargon of excited drunkards, cant of dregs of society

---

5. A. H. Strong, *Systematic Theology* (Valley Forge, PA: Judson Press, 1907), pp. 576, 577.
6. ibid., p. 576.

and the angry accusations of the best at their worst moments. 'Open tomb,' which portrays the stench of rotting human flesh from an exposed corpse, is the startling figure. *Secondly*, deceit, attempting to get others to believe what is not true, flattery, hypocrisy, dissimulation. 'With their tongues they have practiced deceit' characterizes flattery, dissimulation, what goes for diplomacy so common to all social, business and government discourse. The Psalms complain endlessly of this. We tend to speak deceit wherever our own special interests are concerned. There are even special words for such speech: dissimulation, dissembling and hypocrisy. 'The poison of asps is under their lips.' As venomous reptiles slay with their bites 'so… slanderers… destroy the character of their neighbors.'[7] Though 'A wholesome tongue is a tree of life' (Prov. 15:4 NKJV) both 'Death and life are in the power of the tongue' (Prov. 18:21; cf. James 3:3-12). 'Whose mouth is full of cursing and bitterness.' The name of Christ and of God may be used more frequently in the curses – both bitter and careless – of men (and increasingly women also) than in their prayers. All violent destructive language turns bitter and afflicting finally. The man after God's own heart feels, 'I lie among the sons of men Who are set on fire, Whose teeth are spears and arrows, And their tongue a sharp sword' (Ps. 57:4 NKJV), 'Who sharpen their tongue like a sword, And bend their bows to shoot their arrows – bitter words' (Ps. 64:3; cf. v. 4 NKJV), and Jeremiah's similar complaint, 'Their tongue is as an arrow shot out; it speaketh deceit: one speaketh peaceably to his neighbor… but in heart he layeth his wait' (Jer. 9:8 KJV).

(d) Men's violent deeds match their wicked speech, both of which proceed from the sinful heart (Rom. 3:15-17, all quoted from Isa. 59:7-8 and Prov 1:16). *Works* follow *words* and words come 'out of the abundance of the *heart.*'

'Their feet are swift to shed blood.' He who will curse his neighbor, lie to him and deceive him will kill him, given opportunity and the right circumstances. Except where suppressed by strong moral restraints based on sound faith in God and accompanied by proper civil restraint, injustice and violence prevail. The books of Samuel and Kings illustrate this truth as the prophets denounce it. The god of this world is 'a murderer from the beginning,' his policies as *anthrōpoktonos* (man-killer) is reflected in all world history, especially in killing 'the Lord of glory' (John 8:29-44; and 1 Cor. 2:6-8).

'Destruction and misery are in their ways.' This is meant to say that wherever mankind go they perpetrate violent destruction of others and consequent misery for all.

'And the way of peace they have not known.' The twentieth century bears out the charge. Never has peace received more official propaganda. Those old enough to remember the post-World War I promotions of 'peace among all nations' may recall, as I do, being told in church and school that there would be no more war. I could fill a small book with anecdotes of this well-meant but self-deceiving propaganda. Throughout the twentieth century the seeds of conflict were sown with every great and famous agreement or treaty. Witness Versailles, Yalta, Potsdam and Teheran, etc.

> Man's ferocity, which fills the world with animosities, quarrels, hatred in the private connexions of families and neighborhoods; and with revolutions, and wars, and murders among nations. The most savage animals do not destroy so many of their own species to appease their hunger, as man destroys of his fellow, to satiate his ambition, his revenge, or cupidity.[8]

(Violent force can, in a sinful world, only be restrained by force when other measures fail, hence the need for civil control of man by man, as first announced in the ninth chapter of Genesis.)

(e) The Proximate Cause, the source from which all this depravity of word, speech and work proceeds is stated: 'There is no fear of God before their eyes' (Rom. 3:18; Ps. 36:1).

The generation of the last quarter of the twentieth century may have been the one in which absence of reverential fear of God has been most fully absent from Western civilization. Some called it 'secularism.' In our own country all the vices of thought, word and deed described in these passages have inevitably followed. Whether there has been a formal human conspiracy of the university elite, the masters and servants of information and disinformation in news reporting and entertainment, the philosophy of courts and schools of law and public education is doubtful. Yet there is no doubt the devil and his minions are behind it. They have conspired. This world is indeed a *Kosmos* (cosmos), an arrangement.

Contrariwise, 'The fear of the Lord is the beginning of knowledge' (Prov. 1:7). The fear of God in a population is the ground of public social order, as Abraham observed to Abimelech (Gen. 20:11). When witnesses in courts of justice have 'no fear of God' neither do they fear to swear false oaths. Hence, oaths made in court are no guarantee of the truthfulness of witnesses. The Bible was written in a long epoch in which even the pagan neighbors of Israel

---

7. Haldane, *Exposition of the Epistle to the Romans*, p. 118.
8. Haldane, *Exposition of the Epistle to the Romans*, p. 119.

feared the oath as they feared their gods. This is one of the first impressions learned from study of the literature of ancient Canaan (Ugaritic) and Mesopotamia (Sumerian, Assyro-Babylonian). Cultivation of the fear of God is a precondition to the obedience of children, to the moral life, to sound social relationships. No wonder then that societies founded and developed on the ground of such fear of God are falling apart before our very eyes, now that the God of their Fathers has been renounced.

Paul moves on to the next theme of his greatest Epistle, justification by faith, at Romans 3:22. But before doing so he lightly touches, without further elaboration, two more features of the shadow trial. I have suggested as a structure of the passage the following: (1) the prosecutor's statement (3:9) that all are under sin and (2) the prosecutor's summation (3:10-18) that all are sinful in thought, word and deed. There now follows:

3. The Defense Speechless, Without Response.

'[T]hat every mouth may be stopped' (Rom. 3:19a KJV). The language seems to be drawn from Job who observed that when God decides to move in on man either in judgment or blessing 'iniquity stoppeth her mouth' (Job 5:16 KJV). That patriarch ill-advisedly decided to speak in the 'anguish' of his 'spirit' to 'complain' to God about the slings and arrows of outrageous Providence (Job 7:11), filling his mouth 'with arguments' (Job 23:4). When God did finally respond it was with mouth-shutting persuasion. Said the repentant patriarch: 'Behold, I am vile; what shall I answer thee? I will lay mine hand upon my mouth. Once have I spoken; but I will not answer: yea, twice; but I will proceed no further' (Job 40:4, 5 KJV). If such was the case with one whom God pronounced a blameless and upright man (Job 1:8; 2:3), what will the rest of mankind find to say to God?

'Sir, you did not make yourself plain,' Bertrand Russell claimed he would say if after death he should stand before God. What does he think about it now? Will not everyone stand before the great King, as the man without a proper garment in the Parable of the Wedding Feast? '[S]peechless' (Matt. 22:12).

4. The Judge's Verdict.

'[G]uilty before God' (Rom. 3:19b KJV). See passages of Scripture relating to the Last Judgment for elaboration or consult your own conscience in moments of remorse.

St Paul might have gathered pages of passages from the Law, the Prophets and the Psalms to enforce his argument in Romans 3:10-18 that the human race in entirety is sinful in heart, thought, word and deed and that the source lies in man's *real* (as opposed to professed religion) rejection of God's authority – true subversion of the majesty of God, Creator, Sustainer and Governor. Nothing is a more prevalent theme of the Old Testament than reproach of both Israelites and their pagan neighbors for their self-abandonment to sin. Men of every social and intellectual level and of material wealth are so reproved. But the great Apostle has cited sufficient to prove his point and I shall not burden this page with more than I have already cited.

It remains to be added that not every man, woman or child in one lifetime sinks to *all* the depths mentioned in Paul's summary or the preceding bill of particulars in 1:18–3:9. Nor have those who have been regenerated by the Word and Spirit and believe ever been so fully delivered, in this life, from the power of sin, that they have no remnant of it remaining in them. This Paul makes clear in subsequent chapters, as does the whole of the Bible and the record of even redeemed humanity in every age manifests. Sin, however, no longer 'reigns' in believer's lives.

Supposedly Contrary Scriptural Evidence.

Several passages of Scripture have been interpreted to exempt at least a few from the corruption and guilt of sin. They are not understood sufficiently in context. They only seem on a superficial level so to teach. Few serious scholars build any such doctrine on them. Yet because expressions appearing in these texts puzzle some sincere readers of the Bible and are occasionally misused in various ways, I present some of them and furnish some explanatory remarks. Most discussion has centered on the King James Version.

Matthew 9:12 and 13 (KJV): 'They that be whole need not a physician, but they that are sick.... I am not come to call the righteous but sinners to repentance.' Jesus was answering self-righteous Pharisees who had already rejected His message of salvation. They did not feel 'lost' so He would not offer what they felt sure they did not need anyway. The statements are ironic.

Luke 10:30-37: nothing in the story (parable) of the Good Samaritan suggests that because that 'good' man practiced a superior love of neighbor as compared with the self-justifying lawyer (vv. 25-29), that he was free of sin or even perfect in his love of God and one's neighbor. Jesus rebuked the lawyer by showing there was a righteousness of Gentile sinners superior to that of upper-class Jewish sinners. Jesus' statement to another Samaritan – the woman at the well – is apropos: 'Ye worship ye know not what: we [Jews] know what we worship: for salvation is of the Jews' (John 4:22 KJV).

Acts 10:35 (KJV): 'in every nation he that feareth him [God, cf. v. 34], and worketh righteousness, is accepted with him.' In the developing revelation, Cornelius, a man already justified by faith in the Word of God, though a Gentile, is seen by Peter (who up to now did not see it) to be as much welcome in God's family as any Jew. Cornelius, of course, needed to be enlightened to this fact also. There is no support here for salvation by divine worship (fear of God) or good works, for by nature 'There is no fear of God before their eyes' and '…we are all as an unclean thing, and all our righteousnesses are as filthy rags' (Isa. 64:6 KJV).

Romans 2:11-14 (KJV): 'For when the Gentiles, which have not the law, do by nature the things contained in the law,' etc., Paul is demonstrating the opposite of salvation or perfection by any inherent knowledge of God's law. He is showing that certain Gentiles do have a superior awareness of God's law and consciousness of keeping or breaking it. But he concludes with every mouth speechless in self-defense and all the world guilty (Rom. 3:19) and all under sin (3:9).

First Corinthians 2:6: Paul refers to mature Christians as 'them that are perfect' (KJV). ESV and NIV render this 'mature.' Paul – who was certainly a mature believer – thought of himself as chief of sinners (1 Tim. 1:15).

Philippians 3:15 (KJV): 'as many as be perfect.' In this context the same word (in the Greek text as well) appears and is apparently the same in sense as in 1 Corinthians 2:6 just cited. If, as is possible, ultimate sinless perfection is the Apostle's meaning, he has previously written (vv. 12-14) that such perfection is a goal he himself has not yet attained.

First John 3:6 and 9 present difficulties to Paul's insistence that no man alive is absolutely without sin – not even the Apostle himself (Rom. chap. 7; and 1 Tim. 1:15). Again because of the close adherence to the language of the Greek text I quote the two verses from KJV. 'Whosoever abideth in him sinneth not: whosoever sinneth hath not seen him, neither known him…. Whosoever is born of God doth not commit sin; for his seed [nature, RSV] remaineth in him: and he cannot sin, because he is born of God.' Whatever John means to say in these verses must be interpreted in light of what he had said earlier in the same Epistle: 'If we say that we have no sin, we deceive ourselves, and the truth is not in us…. If we say that we have not sinned, we make him a liar, and his word is not in us' (1 John 1:8, 10 KJV).

In a day when Greek was far more known by clergy and laymen than today Henry Alford (fl. 1850) was a pre-eminent exegete of the Greek New Testament. He vigorously rejected the then (and still) prevalent notions that John meant 'does not persist in sin' or 'does not allow sin to reign over him' – though either or both may be true. Alford, finding both Augustine and the Venerable Bede in agreement, asserted:

> Against all such the plain words of the Apostle must be held fast, and explained by the analogy of his way of speaking throughout the Epistle of the ideal reality of the life of God and the life of sin as absolutely excluding one another…The two are incompatible: and insofar as a man is found in the one, his is thereby separated from the other…. If the child of God falls into sin, it is an act against nature…. So that there is no real contradiction to chapter 1, verses 8-10, and chapter 2, verse 2, where this very falling into sin of the child of God is asserted and the remedy prescribed.[9]

Raymond Brown, whose massive volumes on the Johannine books enjoy the confidence of scholars far and wide, supplements the comments of Alford rather than disagreeing. He points out that in 1 John 3:6 John has been saying the adversaries whom he is resisting really never have 'seen' God; they are not even Christians because they have not seen that Jesus Christ is God. He is worried about propagandists who are attacking the assurance of the believers whom John addresses. John would have his readers know that the seed of God is in them permanently. Brown concludes: 'One is forced, then, to understand the claims to sinlessness and impeccability in 1 John 3:6, 9 in light of the statements in 3:1, 2.' He has much more to say, but he has led us back to the same point where Alford, 150 years earlier, led his readers.[10]

A. H. Strong, whose massive, condensed volume *Systematic Theology* has remained in print and wide use for a century, made lifelong research into non-specifically theological literature as it bears on Christian theology, publishing several volumes on the subject, in addition to remarks in the volume mentioned above. As examples of the truism that 'the common judgment of mankind declares… every man is prone to some form of sin and spontaneous "opposition to God and his law"', Strong quotes from such greats as Aristotle, Plato, Shakespeare, Pascal, and even Chinese and Hindu proverbs.[11]

---

9. Henry Alford, *The New Testament for English Readers* (Chicago: Moody Press, n.d.), p. 1724.
10. Raymond E. Brown, *The Epistles of John*, Anchor Bible, vol. 30 (Garden City, NY: Doubleday, 1982), pp. 429–431.
11. Strong, *Systematic Theology*, pp. 577–582.

11
The Personal Consequences of Sin

I will not repeat discussion of the effects of the first sin in Paradise on Adam, his spouse and all their descendants. Here our interest is more particular and personal. What does sin do to me and my fellow man? Let us observe, with as much regret and reserve of language as possible, several classes of effect. These are each enormously devastating, productive of infinite distress throughout the world through all time since the beginning. They should be observed humbly and with frank acknowledgment that, as Daniel said in his prayer of confession (Dan. 9:3-19): 'O Lord, to us belongs shame of face, to our kings, our princes, and our fathers, because we have sinned against You. To the Lord our God belong mercy and forgiveness, though we have rebelled against Him' (Dan. 9:8, 9 KJV). I shall be direct and as brief as possible in setting forth each of seven categories in a single word with discussion conducted mainly in the language of the Version of 1611 on account of its homely, simple force, superior in this area of unwelcome truth about ourselves.

1. *Defilement*. We have lost holiness and become 'unclean.' When the prophet awoke to reality in the presence of the holy he exclaimed, 'Woe is me... for I am a man of unclean lips, and I dwell in the midst of a people of unclean lips' (Isa. 6:5). There is graphic variety of description.

Certain texts speak of defilement of our *bodies*, e.g. 'There is no soundness in my *flesh*... neither... rest in my *bones* because of my sin... My *wounds stink* and are corrupt because of my foolishness' (Ps. 38:3-5 KJV, emphasis added). Others refer to defilement of *speech* (Ps. 58:3) and several others treated above in this chapter in connection with Romans 3:13, 14. Believers are admonished concerning 'filthiness of the *flesh* and *spirit*' while 'perfecting holiness in the fear of God' (2 Cor. 7:1 KJV, emphasis added). The '*mind* and *conscience*' of the 'unbelieving' is defiled (Titus 1:15 KJV, emphasis added). In sum, the whole of man, to the very center of being is defiled, for 'those things which proceed out of the mouth come forth from the heart; and they defile the man' (Matt. 15:17-20; cf. 7:17, 18 KJV).

2. *Perversion*. A perfectly normal man, acting out original concreated harmony of being, would regulate all his passions and acts according to the laws of God, freely submitting a holy nature to a holy God. But fallen man has lost full normalcy and in spiritual matters is not normal at all. Average man is not normal man.

Because it is not generally understood by Christian people that the character of their secular informers suffers from systemic defect, I will enlarge a bit. The verb *'awah* and its derivatives are used hundreds of times for sin in the Old Testament. It means 'bend, twist' (B.D.B. p. 730), to deviate.[1] Another word *'aqal*, 'to bend or twist,' and its derivatives appear only four times.[2] Significantly rendered 'wrong' (Hab. 1:4) is '*crooked* serpent' (Isa. 27:1). I comment in the words of another:

Another remarkable fact about sin is that it is *perversion* or distortion (*'awah*); it is a wrong or wrench, a *twist* to our nature (*'aqal*), destroying the balance of our faculties, and making us prone to evil. Man is thrown out of his center and cannot recover himself, the consequence of which is that there is a jarring of the elements of his nature. Sin is not a new faculty or a new element introduced, but it is the confusion of the existing elements – which confusion the Son of God came to take away, and lead him once more to a loving and self-sacrificing trust in God.[3]

Instead, however, a carnal (fleshy, Gr. *sarkikos*) nature and appetites expressing it dominate what he thinks and does. It is enmity against God, is not and cannot be subject to the law of God, and hence cannot please God (Rom. 8:7). The 'garden variety' of homo sapiens, the natural (Gr. *pseuchikos*) man, cannot even understand spiritual truth on this account (1 Cor. 2:14). 'By nature,' as we say, he does that which Paul says is 'against [created] nature' even in ways animals do not ordinarily attempt (Rom. 1:26, 27 KJV). It is properly denominated sexual perversion – not alternate healthy lifestyle. Our affections, as sinners, are not well ordered. The young, in any well-ordered society, will ordinarily be guided in this regard by adults who should at least have gained some balance (see 2 Tim. 3:3 and innumerable sayings of Proverbs). Leaders in education, law, and even science and apostate religion may even have their moral-ethical system turned upside-down as Isaiah warned, 'Woe unto them that call evil good, and good evil; that put darkness for light, and light for darkness; that put bitter for sweet, and sweet for bitter!' (Isa. 5:20 KJV).

3. *Paralysis*. We have lost spiritual and moral power and become impotent in those respects, 'when we were yet without strength, in due time Christ died for the ungodly' (Rom. 5:6 KJV). As the Bible and all its best interpreters take note, every man has the organs and natural facilities for genuine worship of God, love of neighbor and practice of holiness but they 'do not work.' Our spiritual and moral senses (and one wonders about recent developments in the aesthetical; witness what has happened to drama, literature and art) are only partially active at best until renewed by regeneration. Mankind are intellectually and morally 'darkened... hardened... past feeling' (Eph. 4:18, 19); 'sometimes darkness' (Eph. 5:8 KJV); their 'consciences' are 'seared' (1 Tim. 4:2). They are spiritually 'blind' and do not know it (Rev. 3:17) and 'deceived' by 'sin' (Heb. 3:13).

At this point the larger question arises: To what extent, if any, did the fall affect the intellectual faculties of mankind? – the 'noetic effect of sin.' We have already several times called attention to the doctrine of Rome that the 'image of God', man's rational faculties, were left fully intact, but the 'likeness,' a superadded gift of righteousness and holiness, was lost.

Luther and his theological disciples to the present contend otherwise. I will let Lutheran authority Dr Francis Pieper speak to the point.

> While natural man, after the Fall, still retains a certain amount of intelligence in natural things (Augustana, Art. XVII 1), he is utterly incapable of understanding spiritual matters... [then citing some of the texts I have cited on the paralysis of sin, he continues] Nor can any human schooling or culture remove this lack of intelligence.... The will of man gets the same rating. According to Scripture the will is not only opposed to the law of God, but cannot change its condition...The intelligence of Adam suffered an eclipse, and his will is changed into an evil will. [Luther]Taking issue with Rome's teaching to the loss of the divine image, merely a *donum superadditum* [superadded gift], left the natural powers of man essentially unimpaired... 'it is to be shunned as a deadly poison.'[4]

Similar quotations could be supplied from all the Reformers. The creeds of the time (including Trent) all demonstrate the same doctrine and emphasis.

Noetic Wisdom in Ordinary Matters.

Yet fierce as some of the denunciations of the position of Rome and however specific the portrayal of the spiritual darkness of the mind of natural man, it seems plain neither the Bible nor evangelical theology denigrate the powers of the human mind nor claims in ordinary worldly matters that regenerate people *per se* are 'wiser' than unregenerate. Did not Jesus Himself say: 'the children of this world are in their generation wiser than the children of light' (Luke 16:8), and the learning of Moses 'in all the wisdom of the Egyptians' is connected with being 'mighty in... words and in deeds' (Acts 7:22) and observed by Stephen with approval.

---

1. See Carl Schultz in *TWOT*, p. 652.
2. See Ronald Ballen in *TWOT*, p. 692.
3. McClintock and Strong, *Cyclopedia of Biblical, Theological and Ecclesiastical Literature Vol. IX*, p. 765.
4. Francis Pieper, *Christian Dogmatics I* (St Louis: Concordia Publ., 1950), pp. 543–545.

The problem of our logical competence or non-competence under the condition of sin arose early. Calvin commented that the Fathers before Augustine appeared to speak on both sides of the question because the issue had not yet been encountered squarely. 'Nevertheless,' said he, 'it is not difficult to demonstrate that they, in the ambiguity of their teaching, held every human virtue in no or very slight esteem, but ascribed every good thing to the Holy Spirit.'[5] Calvin assured his readers that his views are the same as Augustine's.[6] See Augustine on *Nature and Grace*.[7] Calvin set in motion the Reformed doctrine of common grace in many passages of the *Institutes*, but laid it out in some detail in *II*.2.12-17.[8]

A master of the revived 'humanities' (i.e. classical learning) of the time, vividly displayed in everything he wrote, Calvin had a deep appreciation of what God, by what he called 'general grace,' had bestowed on all mankind. So what loss of general competence Adam as archetype in the fall lost for us all has been partially, sometimes in 'special' grace, restored. To sum up, he concludes at the beginning of a last page on the subject:

> We see among all of mankind that reason is proper to our nature; it distinguishes us from brute beasts, just as they by possessing feeling, differ from inanimate things. Now, because some are born fools or stupid, that defect does not obscure the *general grace of God*. Rather, we are warmed by that spectacle that we ought to ascribe what is left in us to God's kindness. For if he had not spared us, our fall would have entailed the destruction of our whole nature.[9]

I shall not attempt to improve on what I have quoted and cited. The one who reads the whole passage in the *Institutes* will be both blessed and humiliated by the knowledge of what being human is.

God's Spirit continues to sustain us and prevent full paralysis; otherwise life in society would cease. Further, our faculties have not been equally affected. Those that have to do with man's relationship with his Maker are inoperative. '[T]he message of the cross is foolishness to those who are perishing' (1 Cor. 1:18 NIV) and 'The man without the Spirit does not accept the things that come from the Spirit of God, for they are foolishness to him, and he cannot understand them' (1 Cor. 2:14 NIV). 'Accept' ('receive' KJV) is Gr. *dekomai* to receive in sense of welcome (cf. Heb. 11:31). The disability is not merely that he cannot actively take – reach out and seize – but natural man does not leave the door of his heart open to God. He 'cannot understand them' because he lacks *operative* facility. He can understand worldly matters on an AM 'receiver' but he has no operative FM 'receiver,' so to speak, for spiritual matters. These facts have serious consequences for salvation. Clearly God must take the initiative in enlightening the mind before faith (to 'receive,' 'accept' Christ) can occur. Call it a special calling, illumination or regeneration; it has to come first. This, of course, leads to a strong doctrine of election (see 1 Cor. 12:3; Matt. 16:17; John 6:37, 39, 44, 45, 65). Nothing is more repulsive to unrenewed hearts and such an obstacle to worldly acceptance of Christianity and Christians. This theme is the burden of Martin Luther's great book, *The Bondage of the Will*.

4. *Bondage*. Sin took away our liberty and reduced us to slavery. Jesus insisted, against the Pharisaic advocates of 'free will' in his day, that inborn, active depravity has made every man a bond-slave of sin. To commit sin – any sin at all – is to become a 'bond-slave of sin' (John 8:31-36, especially v. 34). According to 'the Wise,' our sins, each one, through habit become cords that bring us into bondage – 'His own iniquities shall take the wicked himself, and he shall be holden with the cords of his sins' (Prov. 5:22 KJV). Even regenerate people (as Paul, himself, confesses) are, according to Romans 7:22-24, in such 'captivity to the law of sin' working in their bodily members that only Christ can save them from it. He asks, who 'shall deliver me from the body of this death?.... Jesus Christ our Lord' (Rom. 7:24, 25 KJV).

It is again precisely this fact that renders it important to distinguish between 'free agency' (i.e. self-determination of a sort), which without controversy every child of Adam has, and freedom of the human will, or even of human freedom of any kind in an absolute sense, which no one has. As indicated earlier, only the First Adam and the Last Adam had true moral freedom. The existentialist notion of authenticity as freedom (and of fulfillment) is really a hoax, no freedom at all but the nadir of despairing enslavement. Paul makes a strong point of being delivered into captivity to Christ, out of captivity to sin (2 Cor. 10:5).

---

5. Calvin, *Institutes II*, 2.9.
6. ibid., 2.12.
7. Augustine, *On Nature and Grace* iii.3; xix.21; xx.22 in NPNF vol V, pp. 122–127 ff.
8. See pp. 270–277 in Battles *Westminster Ed.* of 1960.
9. Calvin, *Institutes II*, 2.17, p. 276.

5. *Misery*. Sin took away the joy of living and replaced it with the furtive existence of the fugitive and the vagabond before history passed the mile post of the fourth chapter of Genesis (Gen. 4:12, 13). Because of sins the circle of activity which constitutes life on this planet, originally intended to be blessed and the source of true pleasures, has always overtones of regret, pain, boredom, ennui: finally exhaustion and death. 'You'll never get out of here alive.' Genesis 3 from verse 1 onward sets the archetypal tone. Sins undertaken in pursuit of pleasure unfailingly generate the opposite. '[Y]our sins have withheld good from you' (Jer. 5:25 NKJV). Three times the prophet Isaiah points to restlessness as characteristic of the wicked; 'no rest' becomes the literary device for setting off the sections of chapters 40–66 into three equal parts, the first nine ending with 'no rest' (48:22), the second with the same (57:20, 21) and the third with the whole of chapter 66. Thus the misery of sin is woven into the very fabric of Scripture. 'Even in laughter the heart may sorrow, And the end of mirth may be grief' (Prov. 14:13; cf. v. 12 NKJV).

6. *Guilt*. Sin took away innocency and replaced it with guilt and depravity. Treated at length earlier, we are 'by nature children of wrath' (Eph. 2:3; cf. Rom. 3:19).

7. *Death*. Sin took away life and replaced it with death (also treated at length earlier). '[T]he wages of sin is death' (Rom. 6:23) – death physical, spiritual and eternal.

Total Depravity?

Calvinistic theology, in controversy with Pelagians, Socinians, and some (not all) early followers of Arminius, called Remonstrants, employed the term 'total depravity.' By this they meant not that any person is as bad as he can be but that the perversion of normality and paralysis of spiritual powers consequent on original sin affect *every* aspect of every human being: (1) 'that the inherent corruption extends to every part of man's nature, to all the faculties and powers of both soul and body; and [2] that there is no spiritual good, that is in relation to God, in the sinner at all, but only perversion.'[10] I seldom use the term, because, unless explained carefully, it is thought to mean there are no admirable traits, no benevolence, disinterested works or kindly thoughts except among genuine Christians. Lewis and Demarest are aware of this problem and helpfully suggest 'holistic depravity.' This conveys better than 'total depravity' the fact that all our abilities and best achievements are tainted by evil without implying that we all are as bad as we could possibly be. 'No capacity of unrenewed nature escapes the taint of our sinful hearts.'[11] Quite to the contrary, the 'heathen' get some things right. As Paul says, the 'Gentiles, who do not have the law, by nature do the things in the law… who show the work of the law written in their hearts,' whose consciences give them fairly reliable 'witness' (Rom. 2:14, 15 NKJV). Luke, the author of two long books of the New Testament, was quite aware that kindness exists in many human hearts who have never heard of Christ and that they are sometimes rewarded for their kindness in this life, if not in the next. When Paul and his shipmates were wrecked on the Island of Malta, says Luke (who was along on the voyage), '[T]he natives showed us unusual kindness; for they kindled a fire and made us all welcome, because of the rain that was falling and because of the cold' (Acts 28:2 NKJV). They were shortly rewarded when 'the rest of those on the island who had diseases also came and were healed' (Acts 28:9 NKJV). Similarly, Publius: one 'of the leading citizen[s] of the island… received us and entertained us courteously for three days' and was rewarded when Paul visited Publius' sick father, prayed for him, laid his hands on him and healed him (Acts 28:7 NKJV).

Total Inability?

The same controversies of immediately post-Reformation times produced the term 'total inability' by which was meant (1) the unrenewed sinner cannot perform any work of righteousness that meets the standards that prevail in the kingdom of God. For example, even the upright Nicodemus, Jesus said, was not spiritually able even to see, much less enter the kingdom of God: 'I say unto thee, Except a man be born again, he cannot see the kingdom of God… Except a man be born of water and of the Spirit, he cannot enter into the kingdom of God' (John 3:3, 5 KJV). In failing to love God and to fear Him in every act there is nothing the unrenewed person can do to please God – 'they that are in the flesh cannot please God' (Rom. 8:8 KJV). (2) Further, the unrenewed sinner is without power to change his fundamental preference for self and sin to God and righteousness. The initiative for change must proceed from the Spirit of God (John 3:3, 5). The Bible provides no guide to procedures for obtaining this renewal,

---

10. Louis Berkhof, *Systematic Theology* (Grand Rapids: Eerdmans, reprint, 1979), p. 247.
11. Gordon R. Lewis and Bruce A. Demarest, *Integrative Theology II* (Grand Rapids: Zondervan, 1990), p. 211.

even though 'God… now commandeth all men every where to repent' (Acts 17:30 KJV). 'The wind bloweth where it listeth, and thou hearest the sound thereof, but canst not tell whence it cometh, and whither it goeth: so is every one that is born of the Spirit' (John 3:8 KJV). As Jesus also said, 'No man can come to me, except the Father which hath sent me draw him' (John 6:44 KJV). This does not mean the ordinary unrenewed sinner may not have many elevating aspirations and strive for better things. This plain fact of Scripture must not be separated from the further teaching that the Holy Spirit of God is in the world graciously 'striving' and 'convicting' or 'convincing' the world in respect of sin, righteousness and judgment (John 16:8-11). Many a boy or girl – by Whose promptings only eternity can reveal – has vowed:

> Build thee more stately mansions. O my soul,
> as the swift seasons roll!
> Leave thy low vaulted past!
> Let each new temple, nobler than the last,
> Shut thee from heaven with a dome more vast,
> Till thou at length art free,
> Leaving thine outgrown shell by life's unresting sea![12]

Any such strivings which are 'of faith' are induced by the special life-imparting action of the Spirit, normally employing the means of grace – someone's prayer, some communication of the gospel – for 'Whatsoever is not of faith is sin.' 'How then shall they call on him in whom they have not believed?… and how shall they hear without a preacher?… So then faith cometh by hearing, and hearing by the word of God' (Rom. 10:14, 17).

Concluding Reflections.

I close this section of the volume with some regretful reflections about sin's irrational presence in a world ordered by a God whose name is holy and the unwelcome necessity of discussing such a monstrous thing. Who, in writing a volume like this one, would not prefer to confine the subject to an obscure footnote or a brief appendix? I have indeed confined it to a condensed treatment in the shortest section. G. C. H. Berkouwer, who has written numerous large volumes of theology, produced his book on sin rather late in his career. It is the largest (599 pages in English translation) of the series, but with the shortest title, simply, '*Sin*'. On the surface it seems strange the great Dutch scholar could say sin is 'a riddle that is truly an "objective" and "essential" enigma… an "ineffableness" that has no analogue in the ineffableness of God's works (Berkouwer, *Sin*, p. 135) and then write 600 pages about it.

My choice has been to summarize what might be said. Almost every paragraph might be enlarged. Yet, it may rightly be claimed that from this point onward this entire volume focuses on the problem of sin. *Christology*, or the Provision of Salvation from Sin is next. Then comes *Soteriology*, or the Application of Redemption from Sin; after that *Ecclesiology*, or the Assembly of Redeemed Sinners saved from Sin and finally *Eschatology*, concerning the final destiny of Redeemed Sinners and the consummation in the City of God. Of that City it is said, 'They will bring into it the glory and honor of the nations. But nothing unclean will ever enter it, nor any one who does what is detestable or false, but only those who are written in the Lamb's book of life'.

---

12. Oliver Wendell Holmes, '*The Chambered Nautilus*', lines 30–35.

PART 1
THEOLOGY PROPER
Introduction and Doctrine of God

PART 2
ANTHROPOLOGY
Man as Created

PART 3
HAMARTIOLOGY
Man as Sinner

PART 4
CHRISTOLOGY
Person and Work of Christ

PART 5
SOTERIOLOGY
Salvation Applied

PART 6
ECCLESIOLOGY
Church, Local and Universal

PART 7
ESCHATOLOGY
Last Things, Personal and Universal

BIBLIOGRAPHY

SCRIPTURE INDEX

GENERAL INDEX

1
Introduction to Christology

An expression frequently encountered in Christian theology is 'the person and work of Christ.' It designates the subject matter of Christology, which might be stated as, Jesus Christ, who He was and what He came to do. It is to be observed that the frequency of occurrence of the full expression testifies that no understanding of the work of Jesus Christ is possible apart from an understanding of who He was and is.

The centrality of Jesus Christ's Person and work in Christian belief is indicated in the 'Apostles' Creed,' the earliest of the 'ecumenical' creeds, in continuous use in the church now for over 1,500 years. It is still today used in public worship, baptismal confession and instruction of the young in most of the branches of Christendom in all parts of the world. In the common English translation it reads:

> I believe in God the Father almighty, maker of heaven and earth; and in Jesus Christ his only Son, our Lord; who was conceived by the Holy Ghost; born of the virgin Mary; suffered under Pontius Pilate; was crucified, dead and buried; he descended into hell [a late addition]; the third day he rose again from the dead, he ascended into heaven, and sitteth on the right hand of God the Father almighty; from thence he shall come to judge the quick and the dead. I believe in the Holy Ghost, the holy catholic church, the communion of saints, the forgiveness of sins, the resurrection of the body, and the life everlasting. Amen.

There are 109 words in this creed: 69 of them relate to Jesus Christ directly and of these 21 relate to His Person while 48 relate to His work. This proportion is an accurate representation of the emphasis given in true Christianity.

The ancient creed cited is little more than a brief selection from and summary of the New Testament Scriptures. In these Scriptures there is constant focus on the fact that Jesus was destined, indeed, predestined, to accomplish His work by dying for the sins of men. Jesus did not say much about it, for He did not come to talk about dying, rather to die. Yet Jesus did make Himself plain, '…the Son of Man came not to be served but to serve, and to give his life as a ransom for many' (Matt. 20:28). Immediately after His announcement of purpose to build 'my church' (Matt. 16:13–18) it is reported, 'From that time Jesus began to show his disciples that he must go to Jerusalem and suffer many things from the elders and chief priests and scribes, and be killed, and on the third day be raised' (Matt. 16:21). To Peter, Jesus' crucifixion was by the 'definite plan and foreknowledge of God' (Acts 2:23) and His sacrifice was 'precious blood… of a lamb… foreknown before the foundation of the world' (1 Peter 1:19, 20) and to John the Revelator He is 'the Lamb slain from the foundation of the world' (Rev. 13:8 KJV). So central is a proper understanding of the death of Christ to biblical Christianity that the Apostle Paul could write to the churches where he preached, 'I decided [determined KJV] to know nothing among you except Jesus Christ and him crucified' (1 Cor. 2:2). In keeping with this emphasis the cross has been almost the only universal symbol of their faith employed by Christians.

Theologians differ as to the proper name for this division of systematic theology. To avoid confusion as much as possible let us try to sort out these names. Some of them are used for more than one aspect – *redemption* and *reconciliation* for example can designate the whole of Christ's Person and work, or His work only, or even a specific aspect of Jesus' sacrifice for sin. The context wherein the word appears will determine what the author means. *Salvation* and *soteriology* are employed by some for Christ's Person, work and the application of the same to sinners (election, justification, faith, etc.). *Objective soteriology* means the same as the Person and work of Christ while *subjective soteriology* means what happens in and for sinners who are 'saved' – such as election, regeneration and justification.

To amplify, soteriology has two parts. The first part is summarized in Ephesians 1:7, 'In him we have redemption through his blood' – Christ, His Person and work on our behalf – the second in Romans 8:28-30, viz. foreknowledge, predestination, calling, justification, sanctification and glorification, that is to say, application of His work to us sinners. Our interest now is in the first part only, Christ, His Person and work.

Some authors restrict *Christology* to the doctrine of Christ's Person and *soteriology* to His work.[1]

Throughout this book the plan of treatment stays as close as possible to the actual scriptural presentation of Jesus Christ but also with due respect to the immense amount of historical and traditional treatment of the Person of Jesus Christ and interpretation of His career of redemption. This approach incorporates the traditional 'person and work' but centers first on the Person of Christ *through* His redemptive career from beginning to consummation. In each stage of the study, facts, and interpretation of the facts, constitutes the doctrine. This, done in orderly fashion, constitutes systematic theology as opposed to speculative religious thought, which currently is in fashion, especially in liberal literature.

The first aspects of treatment relate to the *Person of Jesus Christ*, represented here by abbreviated chapter titles: 1) Preparation, 2) Preexistence, 3) Deity, Part One, 4) Deity, Part Two, 5) Humanity, 6) Virgin Birth, 7) Incarnation, 8) The *Theopneustos*. The eighth will of necessity make reference to the historical development of the Christology of orthodoxy and the Christological heresies that led to the formation of the ecumenical creeds.

All that follows, on to the end of the book relates to the redemptive work of Christ, what He came to do by virtue of what and who He is and was and ever shall be. These topics are 9) Topics, Terms, Issues, 10) Humiliation and Escaltation, 11) Sinless Life, 12) Passion and Death, 13) The Revealed Mystery, 14) Vocabulary of Atonement, 15) Vicarious Satisfaction, 16) Extent of Atonement, 17) Further Benefits, 18) Before Anselm, 19) Resurrection I, 20) Resurrection II, 21) Ascension, 22) Session, 23) Present Priestly Activity. Number 11, Sinless Life of Obedience, will include brief attention to the doctrine of the two *states* of humiliation and exaltation, as well as the offices of prophet, priest and king and number 12, the Death of Christ, of course, is where the doctrine of atonement will appear.

This scheme is not as different from traditional approaches as it might first appear. The nearest approach to a precedent for this structure of Christology is *Body of Divinity* by John Gill (first published 1769).[2] Though my emphasis on the declarative mode in teaching doctrine is more focused on meeting the student mind than Berkouwer's steady interaction with European theology, my ordering of the subject is similar to his as I found out when I was deep in a career of teaching theology. (See G. C. H. Berkouwer, *The Person of Christ*, 1954, 1973 and *The Work of Christ*, Eerdmans, 1965). The chief influences on my taking this route probably were Calvin (*Institutes*, Book II, 'The Knowledge of God the Redeemer in Christ, First Disclosed to the Fathers Under the Law, and Then to us In the Gospel') and A. J. McClain, my theology teacher during seminary training. His thought was in turn shaped by the orthodox faculty of theology at old Xenia (Presbyterian) Seminary in the days of its greatness, of which he often spoke.

The communicator's principle of selectivity in exposition must be rather severely applied. Christ is the theme of both Testaments, *latent* in the Old, *patent* in the New, but we must select and summarize. As to Christ in the Old

---

1. Philip Schaff, 'Christology,' in Schaff-Herzog, *Encyclopedia of Religious Knowledge*, or *A Religious Encyclopaedia*: or *Dictionary of Biblical, Historical, Doctrinal and Practical Theology i*, based on the *Real-Encyclopaedia* of Herzog, Plitt and Hauck, ed. Schaff (New York: Funk & Wagnalls Co., 1891), p. 451. See also R. A. Cole, 'Christology,' *Zondervan Pictorial Encyclopedia of the Bible i*, ed. Tenney (Grand Rapids, MI: Zondervan, 1975), p. 805.

2. John Gill, *Complete Body of Doctrinal and Practical Divinity i* (Grand Rapids, MI: Baker Books, 1978 repr. of 1839 edition), see the 'Contents of vol. i,' p. xxxiii and Book iv, 'Manifestation of the Covenant of Grace,' pp. 491–644.

Testament, E. W. A. Hengstenberg's still important *Christology of the Old Testament* runs to three large volumes. Yet, Oehler summarized 'Messiah, Messianic Prophecy' in five columns of the *Schaff-Herzog Encyclopedia* and Schaff entered only nine lines in his once famous article on 'Christology' in the same series. The same range of variety exists in recent volumes. Every decent volume of O.T. or N.T. theology treats Christology at some length and new volumes go to press on aspects of the subject every year. If someone desires to know everything in those books, let him read them. My treatment must be fiercely selective.

There are several questions, really more apologetical than strictly theological, that some think press for attention in introducing a book of Christology. *First*, shall we report the critical attacks on the truthfulness of the historic New Testament presentation of Jesus Christ onward from David Straus' book, *The Life of Jesus*, 1835, which used the new word 'myth' to characterize the Gospel reports of Jesus' supernatural character and miraculous works, to the 1977 symposium, *The Myth of God Incarnate* (ed. John Hick)? *Second*, shall we trace the search for the historical Jesus through its three main stages over the last 150 years? *Third*, shall we consider the question raised by Emil Brunner in *The Mediator* (1934) (my introduction to neo-orthodoxy in about 1943) whether Christology should start with the alleged *kerygma*,[3] especially Paul's proclamation (true or not) or, with Pannenberg, should we start with historical inquiry into critical events in the life and career of Jesus the so-called Christology from below? *Fourth*, shall we occupy ourselves with New Testament criticism to decide what the scholars (form critics; redaction critics; literary, text and audience critics; etc.) have decided is authentic? And *Fifth*, shall we pursue the ballooning chatter about hermeneutics before we interpret testimony of the Gospels and Epistles about the Person and work of Christ?

Frankly, I know no way to include *any* of this growing mountain of critical literature without attention to *all* of it. I am grateful to have had time and opportunity to read much of this literature and the responses in books and articles by conservative scholars. I have even taught seminary courses on several of these questions. But for the purposes of this treatise, pursuit of these avenues is neither possible nor fruitful.

W. G. Kümmel, one of the clearest and cleverest writers among recent generations of critical writers, said no one should try to form a Christology until the critics decide what Jesus really said and did. I cite from an earlier writing of my own.[4]

> Kümmel asserted... that the gospel accounts were tendentious, that is, they were twisted to prove a point. In Kümmel's opinion, the various critics should sort out the layers until they learn what Jesus *really* said. Only then would they be able to construct a theology on the basis of the *true* message of Jesus, relieved of the overlay that reflected the biases of the church about AD 60 and of the writers and their sources – Mark, Q, M, and L. Kümmel said: 'In the *oldest* tradition of Jesus' message, to be ascertained by critical methods, we meet with the Jesus whose *historical* message alone confirms the correctness of the apostolic message. To set forth this oldest message is therefore not only a historical task, but one that is theologically indispensable, and no hermeneutic mistake.'[5] In other words, we must all become committed adherents to and masters of Form Criticism before being qualified theologians.

Most debate on these questions continues quite apart from the churches, both laymen and pastors. Many participants are using academic clothing as a cloak for attack on historic Christianity. The discussion hardly illuminates divine revelation of God in Christ and it obscures the sublime simplicity of the eyewitnesses. The mighty volume of books, articles and seminars does provide a wonderful platform on which dilettantes may ply their trade, look and sound industrious and wise so as to maintain a respectable *modus vivendi*.

There are more practical questions to attend: How shall we package the biblical materials in manageable size? I follow four principles. *First*, keep the aspects of Christology distinct for discussion purposes one at a time and do not digress. *Second*, limit the discussion to what is necessary clearly to tie Christology in its every aspect to Scripture. *Third*, pay decent respect to the attainments of the first Christian centuries in formulating a doctrine in response to heresies and as light broke into their minds from individual study of Scripture, and to their ordering of logical statement and consensus in mutual counsel. I am referring to the writings of the church Fathers and the ancient creeds, confessions and definitions, especially the Nicene Creed and the Definition of Chalcedon. But let us not let the immensity of the history of doctrinal development distract from stating Christian doctrine for today's students,

---

3. Emil Brunner, *Jesus – God and Man* (1968) and *Dogmatics Theology ii* (1952).
4. R. D. Culver, *A Greater Commission* (Chicago: Moody Press, 1984), pp. 157, 158.
5. W. G. Küemmel, *Promise and Fulfillment: The Eschatological Message of Jesus* (Naperville: Alec R. Allenson, 1957), p. 105.

pastors, teachers and lay people. *Fourth* and perhaps definitively, Paul stated the sufficient rule in reflecting on his whole three-and-one-half years of indoctrinating the elders and people of the church at Ephesus, viz.: 'I did not shrink from declaring to you anything that was *profitable*, and teaching you... faith in our Lord Jesus Christ.' Then he adds, 'I did not shrink from declaring to you the *whole counsel of God* [emphasis added]' (Acts 20:20, 21, 27). So, introduce as much as is *profitable* for the intended readers (or listeners) and to do so in the context of the *whole* of that system of thought we receive as biblical and Christian.

On this point Christology is not primarily a voyage of discovery. Godly people of long ago have already found the Messiah. As Philip must have blurted to Nathanael, 'We have found him of whom Moses in the Law and also the prophets wrote, Jesus of Nazareth' (John 1:45). Most readers of books like this one have already made up their minds to 'follow Jesus' and expect the treatise to expound historic, orthodox Christology. I hope my readers will be like Paul's audience in Acts 20 above, who when Paul closed his remarks 'knelt down and prayed' together (Acts 20:36). One of their number was no doubt Timothy, who at Ephesus in Paul's absence had already been fulfilling his instruction: 'Till I come, give attendance to reading, to exhortation, to *doctrine* [emphasis added]' (1 Tim. 4:13 KJV). This 'profitable' doctrine of 'faith toward our Lord Jesus Christ,' which Paul 'received from the Lord Jesus' (Acts 20:21, 24) could be summarized, and adequately preached and mastered by teachers and their congregations. We are therefore not ploughing new ground here. We assume some degree of maturity in Christ among our readers as Paul did among the pastoral leadership of his time.

I cite the following to explain why our excursion into recent and contemporary Christologies will be a brief one.

> In the last analysis contemporary Christology has in many respects confused rather than clarified the extended revelation of the Word of God. It is, therefore, more important to discover what Paul or John says about Jesus Christ than to follow the latest learned theological pronouncement.[6]

The same goes for the philosopher-theologians since the time of David Strauss, referred to earlier. Yet, the Christologies of neo-orthodox and existentialist theologians of the epoch since World War II are still being expounded, hence, teachers of the church today need to know something about them. They prepared the way for the current situation among the so-called mainline theologians and the fringes of orthodoxy.

Wolfhart Pannenberg proposes a contrast between 'Christology from above' (traditional) and 'from below' (liberal since Schliermacher).[7] Regarding the 'from below' approach, David Wells has said:

> Christology from 'below' produces only a larger-than-life religious figure, the perfection of what many others already experience. The common assumption of these Christologies is that different theological workers can build a tower the point of which will pierce heaven itself, if only they sweat and toil over it long enough. They will not succeed. Their towers, their Christologies from 'below,' are never more than pictures of the ideal religious person, pictures which all too often merely personify their fabricators. Their Christs might be admired, but they cannot be worshiped.[8]

Of continuing importance to Christology is existentialism. Existentialism is a name for philosophy that distinguishes between what being or essence of someone or something is in and of itself and what it is or becomes in history. For example man lives in 'existence' not 'essence.' Essence is a name for what something is in and of itself apart from what it is or becomes in the world. So an orthodox theologian might say what Adam was before the 'fall' was essence. What he became afterward was and is existence. Only before the fall were essence and existence the same. Afterward essence became only a goal to attain, something like authenticity. Existential is the opposite of detachment. Existentialists are not interested in metaphysical analysis but in personal involvement.

The distinction is, of course, a bit like Plato's ideas that attain real form only partially in this world and Aristotle's potentiality (essence) and actuality (existence). Essence is the opposite of non-being, i.e. being. Authentic existence is attainment of authentic being.

We cannot present here a complete description of the several philosophies of existentialism.

I think of the writings of Paul Tillich[9] as the end point of any positive development of liberal (enlightenment) theology. Though more social philosopher than theologian, his work should be mentioned here for several

---

6. John Walvoord, *Jesus Christ our Lord* (Chicago: Moody Press, 1969), p. 9.
7. Wolfhart Pannenberg, *Systematic Theology vol. ii*, trans. G. W. Bromily (Grand Rapids, MI: Eerdmans, 1994), pp. 278 ff.
8. David F. Wells, *The Person of Christ: A Biblical and Historical Analysis of the Incarnation* (Westchester: Crossway Books, 1984), p. 172.
9. The summaries to follow are drawn mainly from Tillich's volume of 'Christology,' *Systematic Theology ii* (Chicago: University of Chicago Press, 1957).

reasons. *First*, he created an extensive vocabulary for dialectical (neo-orthodox, *krisis*) theology, a vocabulary which is now employed by many theological writers (ultimate concern, correlation, etc.). *Secondly*, he took existentialist theology as far as it could go in any positive direction. *Thirdly*, the seeds of the God-is-dead theology and subsequent post-modernism and even of New-Ageism (latent pantheism) are all in his writings, perhaps even process theology. *Finally*, in a positive way, many important social, historical and theological findings of Tillich's liberal predecessors (R. Otto, E. Troeltsch) were formative in his thought and passed on in his writings. Bibliographies of literature about him are of amazing length and continue to grow. There is even a Tillich Society, which meets regularly.

Our interest here must be limited to his Christology – the subject of the second of his three volumes.

Tillich erected a system of theology employing throughout the categories of existentialism. Though called neo-orthodox it is not really orthodox at all. Perhaps Barth and Brunner succeeded in attaching a semi-orthodoxy to a semi-existentialist framework but Tillich selectively preserved only the orthodox frame without any discernable orthodox content.

Other existentialists, with overtly humanistic, non-Christian outlooks, constructed respectable analyses of reality (Jaspers, Heidegger and Sartre). Dostoevski defined Greek orthodoxy in existentialist terms, Marcel with Roman Catholic-Thomist presuppositions, as Pascal with Augustinian, and Kierkegaard with Lutheran presuppositions. Each of these Christian existentialists had an approximately orthodox Christology but not Tillich. One can mouth his phrases and sound orthodox yet be as apostate as the atheist Marx himself. Tillich's theology is in part a grafting of the human-social analysis of depth psychology upon the skeleton frame of orthodox Christian theology. The *fall* and *sin* now reappear as ambiguity, abyss, estrangement, angst (anxiety), autonomy, etc.; justification and sanctification as authenticity, freedom, acceptance, theonomy and the like. God is ground of being, being in itself. Religion is simply a matter of 'ultimate concerns' and theology is statement of these concerns in whatever social, linguistic and philosophical climate the religious man finds himself in, whether third-century Hellenism or eighteenth-century Enlightenment. Tillich himself is a 'dialectical' theologian with 'yes and no' borrowings from an admirably wide reading from ancient to recent times.

Of importance to this book is his existential 'Christology.' We can be brief. Existentialist salvation is to rise from inauthentic existence to authentic existence, which may be defined as attainment of essence or essential being. Essential being is to participate in 'new being.' The New Being is Tillich's name for Christ.

Christology is defined in terms of depth psychology and social analysis, not in relation to Christian sources but to Tillich's own vocabulary of social-psychological analysis.

He led toward some 'norm'[10] – toward which to relate what he calls the 'symbols' (form) of revelatory events (material) in stating theology.

He said, '[T]oday man experiences his present situation in terms of description, conflict, self-destruction, meaninglessness, and despair in all realms of life.' His name for the 'tragic structures' that 'actualize' the tragedy of the human situation is 'demonic.' In this desperate situation we cannot any longer employ the Reformation recourse to a 'merciful God and the forgiveness of sins' or, as in the ancient Greek church, by adjustment to 'finitude, death and error' or as in more recent efforts at improvement of 'personal religious life' (evangelical puritanism, revivalism), or 'christianization of culture and society' (liberal religion). It is by overcoming self-estrangement, reconciliation, reunion, creativity, meaning and hope. 'We shall call such a reality the New Being.' 'Where is this New Being manifest'? Tillich asks. He responds, 'Systematic theology answers... "In Jesus the Christ!"'[11]

'The New Being in Jesus as the Christ' is our 'ultimate concern.'[12] How distant Tillich's conception is from an orthodox Christ is apparent throughout, never more clearly than in his 'Spirit Christology' where the New Being, he says, may be experienced in many religions. He was in many ways the forerunner of New Ageism quite as much as of the God-is-dead movement. 'The faith of the Christ is the state of being grasped unambiguously by the Spiritual presence.'[13] R. Allan Killen was correct in this disparaging comment after subjecting all Tillich's writings to a cool Calvinist critique: 'The Christ which Tillich produces is not the Christ of the Bible.'[14]

10. Tillich, *Systematic Theology i*, p. 28.
11. ibid., p. 49.
12. ibid., p. 50.
13. ibid., *iii*, p. 46.

The emptiness of Tillich's 'Christology' is plain in J. L. Adams' comment: 'Tillich says that the Christ symbol cannot be separated from the historical figure. But nothing concrete is taken up by the Christ symbol from the historical reality except the symbol of the cross, which, as he himself says, is a symbol of self-immolation before the unconditional transcendent.[15] A quote from C. J. Armbruster is interesting, 'Tillich... never uses 'Christ' as a personal name, but always as a title or symbol.'[16]

Even Reinhold Niebuhr criticized Tillich for his 'ontological speculations.' He went 'too far,' Niebuhr thought, in removing the 'Genesis myth' of man's creation and fall from the realm of real history. The story is about what man has always been from the moment he first evolved from irrational beast to rational man, interpreted in the new language of Tillichian speculative theology. It's really the story of man's existential estrangement from his essence and the ground of being as well as from other beings. It means that man as he *exists* is not what he *essentially* is and ought to be.[17] Niebuhr rightly rejected this Tillichian way of relieving us of responsibility for our evil hearts and making us instead victims of fate.[18]

This speculation is preparatory for speculation about the correction of estrangement by the New Being, wherever it happens, which in Tillichian phraseology is Jesus the Christ.

Niebuhr and Macquarrie and other dialectical (paradoxical) neo-orthodox theologians are rarely as transparently unbound by scriptural norms as Tillich, but they partake of the same freedom from what the Bible really says. Brunner and Barth feel somewhat more bound to some degree of literalism.

Let us spare ourselves the Christology of current process theology. This brief excursion should be enough to show that thorough examination of recent and current Christologies that depart from orthodox norms will not help us form a truly biblical Christology.

The method of this study is to look back on the whole Bible in all its parts and from that outlook give systematic statement about our Lord Jesus Christ. We will frequently need to trace how an idea or fact developed in the N.T., but only to clarify something or to define it, not merely to provide historical information. Most of the inductive processes of biblical theology should be finished before the systematic synthesis begins.

Christology may rightly begin with Jesus' question asked of the disciples in the region of Caesarea: 'whom say ye that I am' (KJV), still more literally, 'Ye say me to be whom?' (Matt.16:15). The question was addressed to all the disciples as the NIV modern English 'you' instead of 'ye' somewhat obscures. The question is a rather uncommon infinitive clause that in Greek as well as English requires both subject and object in accusative (objective) case, viz.: 'me to be whom?' hence the 'whom' of KJV.

But only one of the *ye* answered, Peter, whose answer was not the work of a council of 12 Apostles or 315 Nicenes, but as must always be the case in saving belief, the individual believer's heartfelt Latin, 'Credo' – I believe. The answer had to be a theological statement. Despite objections from some New Testament theologians, Jesus must be understood as referring to *Himself* as the Son of Man, not some other third party as is clear from parallel Mark 8:27 where *me* is parallel with *Son of Man* in Matthew 16:13.

The answer had to be a theological statement of what we now call orthodox Christology, including our Lord's (1) heavenly origin (Son of Man, Dan. 7:14; cf. Mark 14:61-64), (2) essential deity (Son of the Living God) as well as (3) essential humanity (Son of *Man*, and presupposed known human lineage) and (4) Messiahship ('the Christ'). Paul Tillich would have us believe, 'Without this reception the Christ would not have been the Christ' interpreted as 'the manifestation of the New Being in time and space,' in Tillichian theology as being neither alienated from self or from God.[19]

Peter had gained the right impressions and had come to a believing conviction over a period of time beginning with his call to discipleship. The culminating event was the miraculous feeding of the 5,000 shortly before Jesus resorted to regions about Philippi, according to Matthew. It was now time for the Twelve to decide the right answer to the Baptist's inquiry (Matt. 11:3).

There is no hint that any of the others yet fully shared Peter's conviction. Our Lord's 'Blessed art thou' was addressed to one only, Simon Bar Jonas. Why only Peter? The others saw the same things and heard the same

---

14. R. Allan Killen, *The Ontological Theology of Paul Tillich*, (Kampen: J. H. Kok, 1956), p. 240.
15. J. L. Adams, *Paul Tillich's Philosophy of Culture, Science and Religion* (New York: Harper & Row, 1965), p. 273.
16. C. J. Armbruster, *The Vision of Paul Tillich* (New York: Sheed & Ward, 1967), p. 290
17. Tillich, *Systematic Theology ii*, p. 45.
18. Reinhold Niebuhr, 'Biblical Thought and Ontological Speculation,' in *The Theology of Paul Tillich*, ed. Kegley and Bretall (New York: Charles Scribner's Sons, 1952, 1961), pp. 216, 217.
19. Tillich, *Systematic Theology ii*, pp. 97–99.

words over the same period of time. Some who heard and saw called Him a sinner, a blasphemer, an agent of Beelzebub. Their hearts were hardened, their eyes blinded (see Matt. 13:11-16; John 12:37-40). Peter's heart had been enlightened and softened by the Word and the Spirit of the Father. No human agency (v. 17), rather the Spirit, had brought him to that 'blessed' condition (1 Cor. 12:1-3) and the Spirit works sovereignly (John 3:8). (See Part 5: Soteriology: Salvation Applied).

Peter's confession, being a divinely inspired answer to 'Who is the Son of Man?' must be accepted as an adequate seminal statement of a true 'Christology.'

Though challenged by certain N.T. critics, there is no doubt that by 'Son of Man' Jesus was referring to Himself (cf. the parallel Mark 8:27). 'Son of Man' signifies many things. (1) His heavenly origin (Dan. 7:14; John 3:13), (2) His humanity (so the words mean when Ezekiel is called 'son of man') and so the expression is employed in the Old Testament and (3) our Lord's incarnation. The expression 'Son of Man' in contemporary Jewish understanding meant (4) deity as the high priest's reaction to Jesus' admission shows (Mark 14:61-64; cf. Dan. 7:14).[20]

'The Christ' refers to the promised messiah of O.T. expectation. This is not immediately clear because transmission of an idea through archaic custom and five languages is involved. The ancient Hebrews inducted their kings and priests (sometimes prophets also) to office by a ceremony of pouring oil on the head of the candidate (anointing). The Hebrew word for anoint is *mashaḥ* and *meshiaḥ* (Messiah) means anointed. The Aramaic of Palestine spoken by Peter was similar to the Hebrew. Hence by loose transliteration we have *messiah* in English. But Greek for anoint is *chrio;* for anointed, *christos* (of a male), in Latin the nominative masculine *us* ending for nouns gives *christus*. Our English word Christ is the Latin word with the case ending removed. (Greeks sometimes name children Christos. Our Greek lady guide in Corinth, calling *Christos*, our Greek bus driver, from a distance, shouted the vocative *CHRISTO-0-0-0*.)

'Son of the living God.' This means that Peter had already seen far more in Jesus than the usual Jewish expectation that their messiah would be merely one of their own selected by God for His eminent ability and devotion, as for example, David. Peter had seen Jesus in action, had taken note of His amazing claims and drew the proper inference that Jesus was divine in a sense no other being on earth could be. This is not the only hint of acknowledgment of deity in Peter's confession, but it is the plainest. (See John 5:18; 10:30-33.)

Though it is customary to call Peter's statement a confession, it really is more than that. It is a statement of faith more like a bit of dogma or doctrinal formula than a credo ('I believe'). It is quite proper to call it dogma or doctrine. Here is the beginning of Christology, not inductive 'biblical theology' as now understood, but systematic theology, informed by biblical theology.

Peter's confession is sufficient explanation why the first Christians were understood to be a people who worshipped a Person called 'Jesus' – and very soon 'Christ,' employed as a name more than a title. They actually prayed to Jesus. This is, of course, anticipating the doctrine of the triune God and of the two natures of Christ, the theanthropic Person.

> That Peter when he uttered the words, understood by them in detail all that we now understand, is not of course asserted; but that they were his testimony to the true Humanity and true Divinity of the Lord, in that sense of deep truth and reliance, out of which springs the Christian life of the Church.[21]

Further comment on Peter's discernment is appropriate. In saying 'Blessed art thou, Simon Barjona' (Matt. 16:17 KJV) on this occasion Jesus is not speaking casually but making a solemn pronouncement. Very clearly, in the language of Matthew 11:25-27, God had *revealed* Himself *in* the Son, the Son had willed to *reveal* the Father to Peter. This later occurred again when in a special manner, reserved for Paul, God in Christ chose to reveal Himself to the Apostle 'as to one untimely born' (1 Cor. 15:8).

This is not to say that the revelation to Peter in its seminal stage was clear in every respect. The full 'truth' became clear only with the completeness of 'all the truth' (John 16:13) that came to the Apostles, after the coming of the Holy Spirit and was enscripturated in the completed New Testament.

Over twenty-five times beginning with Matthew 13:11 and on to the book of Revelation 17:5 certain facts of revelation are called mysteries. Some of them are the kingdom of heaven (Matt. 13), the future salvation of natural Israel (Rom. 11:25), the openness of the church to Gentile and Jew (Eph. 3:3-9), of the union of the church with

---

20. C. W. Carter, 'The Son of Man,' in *Zondervan Pictorial Encyclopedia of the Bible* v, pp. 485–487.
21. Henry Alford, *The New Testament for English Readers*, repr. (Chicago: Moody Press, n.d.), p. 119.

Christ (Eph. 5:32), and of the theanthropic Person of Christ – the incarnation itself (1 Tim. 3:16). The last mystery is the one made known to Peter and 'confessed' by him at Caesarea Philippi.

A revealed mystery (*musterion*), being supernaturally made known, is not necessarily open to empirical investigation or capable of rational explanation. *Mystery* should be distinguished from *paradox* in its proper sense, which is seeming *contradiction* capable of being adjusted to univocal statement when all facts are known. Dialectical theology, which loves paradox, sometimes (especially Barth) seems to mean real *contradiction* by paradox and appears to ask us to believe real contradiction. Such might better be called *antinomy*. There are no antinomies, as such, in a real world, though there may seem to be. Paul's disparagement of worldly wisdom in the early chapters of 1 Corinthians did not prevent him from employing the law of non-contradiction in Romans 11:6. There are no Pauline oxymorons. God does not *equivocate*, which means to use the same word with shifted meaning without indicating the shift. It is to deceive. God's Word, however paradoxical (seemingly contradictory) it may be, is always univocal, never equivocal, for He is a 'God, that cannot lie' (Titus 1:2; cf. Heb. 6:18).

The divine mysteries are addressed to faith *before* understanding. Understanding can wait till God gives further information, which may be forever. Theology that tries to explore the mysteries without faith, as in this long extended 'age of reason,' or 'enlightenment,' has done little for real theology and much to harm it. Anselm of Canterbury's idea of 'faith in search of understanding' in his *Proslogion* gave classical expression to this outlook, now being recovered somewhat in liberal circles.[22] They also err who reject rational analysis and arrangement as in all who give little place to revelation as imparting facts, data, propositions of objective truth (neo-orthodoxy and post-modern theologies). The divinely revealed mysteries together with every datum of biblical historical truth can be placed in logically conceived order. The seemingly random facts of nature, whether of inorganic things (geology, chemistry, physics) or of organic (biology, botany, zoology), perhaps even of human thought-life and emotion (psychology, sociology), have been organized into learned disciplines. Otherwise we would have no civilization. The same is true of the Bible and its truths. Systematic theology, including Christology, is a necessary enterprise, someone has said, to keep thoughtful Christians from going crazy!

I must excuse myself and readers at this stage of our study from pursuing the negative course of that variety of New Testament 'research' which, coming to climax in W. Wrede and A. Schweitzer over a century ago, moved through their successors to the 'Jesus Seminar.' It has indirectly born some good fruit by stimulating careful re-examination of assumptions about the texts employed to support the church's creeds, confessions and orthodox Christology but little by way of direct contributions. The Christ who emerges from these authors looks more like themselves than the Christ of Gospels, Epistles and the Apocalypse. Who are they to tell us out of their own modern cultural prejudices how the only sources came to be or what they mean? I cite Anthony Bertocci, a competent contemporary orthodox writer to the same effect. After sketching these 'broad tendencies in New Testament scholarship' he asks:

> Why is it that only now, two thousand years after the event, we are at last beginning to understand what Christianity is all about? But, of course, by the word **we** what is in view is only an elite coterie of scholars. There are masses of Christians all over the world, who have no ability to pick their way through the layers of literary tradition in Scripture and are quite incapable of digressing on the differences between *Historie* and *Geschichte*. Are we to suppose that the real interpretation of Jesus is alone accessible only to a tiny minority in the church – its learned scholars – and that the remainder of Christian believers is excluded from such knowledge? To suppose such a thing is to subject the meaning of Scripture to a far more restrictive 'tradition' than anything proposed by Rome in the sixteenth century [Reformation era] and to invest our new magisterium [Roman Catholic teaching authority] – the coterie of learned scholars – with an authority more stifling and far-reaching than the Roman Catholic magisterium ever exercised… The Scriptures must be returned to the Church.[23]

---

22. J. C. Pugh, '*Fides Quaerens Intellectum: Anselm as Contemporary*,' in Theology Today, 55.1, pp. 35–45.
23. Documentation of this quotation has been lost and at publication time still unrecovered.

2

Preparation for the Coming of Christ

The distinct character of ordered providential history of mankind before the Advent of Christ as divine preparation for the Advent can be clearly seen in two biblical statements, each part of a verse. The one points to preparation for Christ in the history of Israel and says: 'in you all the families of the earth shall be blessed' (from Gen. 12:3, part of the initial form of the Abrahamic Covenant). The other is central to the New Testament – 'But when the fullness of time had come, God sent forth his Son' (Gal. 4:4).

The Old Testament tells of the preparation for the coming blessing in the history of Abram's descendants within a succession of covenants. It tells us that God ruled the nations by elevating certain rulers, and by chastisements of various sorts, but does not give details. Let us look first at the Old Testament, especially as the New Testament itself relates it to the Advent of the Savior.

Preparation Among the 'Chosen People'.

> The Jews prepared the way for Christianity by... expecting what Christianity offered, a divine Savior. The hope of a Messiah was cherished by all Jews as their dearest possession. To be sure it was held by them in gross and worldly forms. But in all its forms there was the essential thing, the ardent expectation of one sent of God to redeem his people... Christianity found all its first adherents among the Jews... and the one thing that qualified them to receive [Christianity] was the Jewish hope of a divine Savior.[1]

The Old Testament.[2]

Matthew's Gospel alone directly cites or alludes to the Old Testament at least 129 times, 89 of these references being preceded by the phrase, 'in order that it might be fulfilled which was spoken of the Lord by the prophet,' or some similar expression. There are approximately 63 such clear references in Mark and about 100 in Luke. As for the Fourth Gospel, scholars agree that it is an insoluble mystery without the Old Testament because it is saturated with Old Testament thoughts, imagery and language. More than 'literary dependence' is involved. An examination of the hundreds of references in the four Gospels will show that the four authors regarded the events of the New

---

1. R. Hastings Nichols, *The Growth of the Christian Church* (Philadelphia: Westminster Press, 1932), pp. 7, 8.
2. Much that appears under this heading here is drawn from my book, *The Life of Christ* (Grand Rapids, MI: Baker Books, 1976, 1991). It has been revised and re-issued as *The Earthly Career of Jesus, the Christ* (Ross-shire, Scotland: Christian Focus Publications, 2002).

Testament as the consummation of a redemptive history that began where the Old Testament narrative begins. Jesus Christ of the New Testament is indeed both the Messiah of Israel and the hope of the nations whom the Old Testament prophesies.

In addition to numerous brief statements in the Gospels connecting this or that item of Jesus' career with the Old Testament, there are comprehensive, definitive texts which do the same, especially in Luke and Acts, the two books written by Paul's physician-companion, Luke. He reports that on the very day of His resurrection Jesus joined two of the disconsolate disciples on the way to their home at Emmaus and upbraided them for failing to see His career predicted 'in all the Scriptures' (Luke 24:25-27). In the evening of the same day Jesus appeared to the same Cleopas and his friend, now at the meeting place of the Eleven at Jerusalem, and in different words connected His entire career, including even its issue in the church among all nations, with prophecies in the Law of Moses, the Psalms and the Prophets. To correct their misunderstandings He specially 'opened their minds to understand the Scriptures...' (Luke 24:45). Thus the Old Testament, on the authority of Jesus Himself, is a Christian book, no more distinctly Jewish than the church itself, even though both began among Jews. It was decades after Jesus had enlightened their understanding that the Gospels writers, by His enablement, drew those hundreds of connections between Old Testament preparation and prophecy and their fulfillment in Jesus. In the same spirit the sermons of the Apostles in Acts almost invariably demonstrate that Jesus is the Christ of God by resort to the prophecy-fulfillment technique. Evangelists and apologists still do the same today.

At this point an important matter must be clarified. Jesus and the Apostles regarded *all* the Old Testament as preparatory and predictive, not just a few selected 'messianic' (i.e. Christological) passages. This can be demonstrated beyond serious doubt. First observe the innumerable connections drawn by the Gospel writers. Then concentrate on Jesus' remarks cited above about 'Moses and all the Prophets... in all the Scriptures... everything written about me in the Law of Moses and the Prophets and the Psalms must be fulfilled... to understand the Scriptures' (Luke 24:24-27, 44-47). After that observe that all the Old Testament is regarded as written by prophets (Heb. 1:1, 2), and then turn to the four times that Peter, in sermons recorded in the book of Acts, claimed that prophecy of Christ and of the Apostles' gospel ministry is found in 'all the prophets' (Acts 3:18, 21, 24; 10:43). Paul charged that the Jerusalem Jews who condemned Jesus did so because 'they did not... understand the utterances of the prophets, which are read every Sabbath' and that they 'fulfilled them by condemning him' (Acts 13:27). A few minutes with the Bible, letting these texts, in context, speak their message, will deliver the reader from the much-abused approach to Old Testament Messianic prophecy of simple Old Testament 'proof-texting.' Paul felt that *any* day in which a Jew attended synagogue services he would hear prophecy of Messiah read (see also Acts 24:14). Thus any list of so-called Messianic texts out of the Old Testament, useful as it may be for certain purposes, may be misleading. The entire Old Testament is preparatory for Christ's coming and in many parts predictive. This accounts for the frequent N.T. references to Christ as 'the one who is to come' (Gr. *ho erchomenos*) as for example in Matthew 11:3.

How else can we who affirm our only *hope* is in Christ understand Paul's words at Romans 15:4? 'Whatever was written in former days (with obvious reference to the Hebrew Bible, the canonical OT) was written for our instruction, that we through endurance and through the encouragement of the Scriptures might have hope.' Perhaps the finest treatment on this subject in English is R. Payne Smith's Bampton Lectures of 1869.[3] The above quoted words are the text for the first of his nine lectures (nearly 400 pages!). Let his opening remarks open up the theme for us.

> St. Paul claims in these words for the Scriptures of the Old Testament a special quality distinct from... ordinary books... not for temporary use, ...for one age and one people, but for all time; and yet for a limited purpose... [T]hey were written 'that ye might have hope.'[4]

He calls attention to 'the hope' as better translation and calls attention to *Vaticanus* reading, 'the hope of the consolation' and comments:

> The added words are probably an explanatory gloss, but they give the right sense. 'The consolation of Israel' emphatically was the advent of Messiah; and what Paul affirms of the Old Testament Scriptures generally... is that directly or indirectly they were all prophetic [predictive], all looked forward to and prepared for Christ.[5]

---

3. R. Payne Smith, *Prophecy a Preparation for Christ* (Boston: Gould & Lincoln, 1870).
4. ibid., p. 29.
5. ibid., p. 30.

R. Payne Smith brought the sense of Romans 15:4 forward to the believers of this dispensation who find their 'hope' in the Scriptures of both Testaments, in words to be pondered.

> St. Paul's words are applicable to the Christian Scriptures [N.T.]... for they also are for our learning, that we by the exercise of patience, necessarily implied in the fact that we have not as yet the full possession of the promise, and by the comfort given us by the strong conviction that Christ will come again, we may have hope – the hope – that as Christ has come once to open the way of salvation for man, so he will come again to perfect His work.[6]

This understanding of the Old Testament, while not specifically rejected by evangelical scholars today has been submerged by interest in background studies, cultural history, archaeology and with the efforts of a certain number somehow to read New Testament revelation and the church back into the Old Testament. Delitzsch, Fairbairn, Edershein and other nineteenth-century giants of scholarship could be cited at length in harmony with Smith, above and my own vision; but one must search for such an outlook in current literature.

The Old Testament is not, however, all preparatory or predictive in exactly the same way. Discerning scholars have detected differing levels of precision in prediction. To these we now direct attention.

1. Every word of the Old Testament is certainly *Christological by way of preparation* for the coming of Christ. The first eleven chapters of the Old Testament tell of the need for a savior of men, while all the rest – Genesis 12 through Malachi 4 – traces the history of the chosen people who produced the Savior-Messiah. When He was born into the degraded and corrupt heathen world of antiquity, Jesus' childhood home was an island of relative purity produced by Old Testament religion. His parents were not defiled by any of 'the diseases of Egypt'. His mother was a pure Jewish virgin when she came to her husband; his earthly 'father', a true son of Abraham, understood righteous discretion; the cleanliness of the Jewish people, prescribed in the central part of the Pentateuch and famous then as now, guaranteed that clean food be placed on the family table and that He sleep in a clean bed. As Deuteronomy 23:13 required (when God walks the streets He wants human excreta underground) the community of Nazareth understood the value of a latrine (something missing in many country villages of the Near East today). This came about because God had taught a pagan named Abram to worship God Most High. Later that man's descendants, grown numerous in Egypt, learned law and discipline in the wilderness. They then as a nation lived out hundreds of years of history in the 'land of promise.' During those centuries (Joshua–Nehemiah) a righteous remnant of them lived out both the letter and the spirit of their divinely revealed religion. That remnant, encouraged by mutual support and nourished by the Scriptures, was on hand – as the early chapters of Matthew and Luke relate with great delicacy. (See especially in the reported character of Jesus' mother and earthly father [Matt. 1:18-25; Luke 1:26-56; 2:19-24], the parents of John the Baptist [Luke 1:3-80] and Simeon and Anna [Luke 2:25-38]. This small group (Mal. 4:5, 6; Isa. 6:13; Dan. 12:3, 10) produced, welcomed and nestled the Messiah when He came.

This readying of a society as home for Jesus during the 'days of His flesh' through Old Testament revelatory history constitutes that entire Book *Messianic by preparation* and justifies in part, at least, the frequent gospel formula, 'that the Scripture might be fulfilled,' and Paul's 'according to the Scriptures.' It is part of the function of the law as *paidagogos* (conductor of children) to lead the nation to Christ (Gal. 3:24 and 4:5).

2. Another way the Old Testament is both preparatory and Christological is in its prescription of moral perfection, that is, it is *Messianic by extension*. Let me explain. Jesus claimed to fulfill the Law and the Prophets – i.e. the entire Old Testament. One important way in which He did this was simply for the first time in history to exemplify every one of its moral excellencies. The Psalmist, for example, could pronounce blessed the man who neither walks nor stands nor sits with evil in any way (Ps. 1:1), and meditates on God's holy law day and night (Ps. 1:2). Yet these ideals were never truly realized until Jesus did so. By calling for human perfection the Old Testament calls for the Son of Man from heaven whose mission it was to produce just such human perfection. The practical wisdom of Proverbs, Job, Ecclesiastes, Song of Solomon and other practical-morality sections are in a clear and definite sense deposits of Messianic information and a call for Messiah's coming. In this way, Proverbs is quite as truly Messianic as some often cited verses about Immanuel (e.g. Isa. 7–9) or the Son of David (Isa. 11:15) in the great specific predictions of the Old Testament.

3. Another numerous class of texts are sometimes called *divine parousia* (personal presence) *prophecies*. Numerous texts connect the coming salvation with the coming of God Himself to deal in a direct and final way with the world's problems. 'For behold, the LORD is coming out of his place, and will come down...' (Micah 1:3;

---

6. ibid.

Pss. 93; 94; 50:3; cf. Mal. 3:1). These constitute predictions of the deity of the coming Christ, a fact which the Jews never fully understood and which renders a large part of the Old Testament distinctly Messianic and, in a certain sense, exclusively Christian.

4. What certain contemporary writers call *royal messianic prophecy* is by an older generation called *indirect messianic prophecy*. This important class of material in the Old Testament is chiefly 'Psalms in which in keeping with the circumstances of the time at which they were composed, Messianic hopes were centerd on a contemporary king, without, however, having been fulfilled in Him; so that in the mouth of the Church, which was still waiting for their fulfillment, they have become eschatological hymns, and we are perfectly justified in interpreting them *as such*, as well as in their bearing upon their own time.'[7] The royal Psalms have been the subject of quite a large body of literature, especially among Scandinavian writers.

5. Another variety of preparatory texts of the O.T. is sometimes called *indirectly Messianic*. Perhaps they might better be called *Messianic by hyperbole*, i.e. by literary exaggeration. Commentators often point out this feature of passages wherein a Psalmist, or other author, described his feelings and experiences in such a way that he was 'raised above his own individuality and time, and uses regarding himself hyperbolic [i.e. legitimately exaggerated] expressions, which were not to become full historical truth until they became so in Christ.'[8] Examples cited are usually related to persons who themselves are already typical of Christ (as David or Solomon). The 'why have you forsaken me?' of Psalm 22 is an example. David felt forsaken, even though elsewhere he wrote, 'Even though I walk through the valley of the shadow of death, I will fear no evil, for you are with me...' (Ps. 23:4). Yet, though David was never forsaken by his Creator and Redeemer, our Savior who made these His dying words was truly forsaken of God.

6. *Typical Messianic prophecy* is a valid traditional category with which most Bible readers are fairly familiar. A steady feature of Christian use of the Old Testament from the beginning, which has sometimes been overdone, has been the tracing of divinely intended typical connection (and, in that sense, *predictive* connection) between certain offices, institutions, persons, events, etc. in the Old Testament, and important features of the Lord's earthly career.

This feature of Old Testament history and the Mosaic institutions is fully validated by New Testament employment of typology, especially in the book of Hebrews, chapters 3 to 10. It is pervasively employed in veiled ways, as scholars of every shade of opinion recognize, even though they may not agree on the validity of it. It is not doubted by believing scholars. This feature of the Old Testament receives several different names in the New Testament – 'shadow,' *skia* (Heb. 10:1; Col. 2:16, 17); 'figure,' *parabole* (Heb. 9:9); 'type' or 'figure,' *typos* (Rom. 9:14); 'pattern,' *hypodeigma* (Heb. 9:23); 'pattern' or 'example,' *antitypon* (Heb. 9:24). On this account the book of Leviticus, large sections of Exodus and Numbers, even certain persons and events of Old Testament history (in the view of many) as well as portions of the books of poetry have specific Messianic (predictive of Christ) types. The literature of the subject is enormous. The 1852 edition of *The Typology of Scripture*, two volumes by Patrick Fairbairn (more than 900 pages), has left little for subsequent authors to say on the subject, though every text of biblical hermeneutics discusses it and most acknowledge debt to Fairbairn's exhaustive work.

John F. Walvoord's *Jesus Christ our Lord*, contains a much more complete discussion in chapter 4, 'Christ in Old Testament Typology.'[9] He discusses typical persons (e.g. Abel), events (e.g. the Exodus), things (e.g. brazen serpent), institutions and ceremonies (e.g. sacrifices and festivals).

7. On the very highest and most distinct level is *direct Messianic prophecy*. The traditional Christmas texts employed in the great oratorios fall in this category (Gen. 3:15; 12:1-3; 49:10; Micah 5:2; and many more). But so also does Isaiah 53, a chapter that so specifies the details of our Lord's Passion and death that even enemies of Christianity can scarcely miss it. It has even been claimed that Jesus read the passage and deliberately – if morbidly – planned His last days on the basis of it.

At the very opening of His ministry, Jesus could say, 'Do not think that I have come to abolish the Law or the Prophets; I have not come to abolish them but to fulfill them' (Matt. 5:17); and at the very end of His earthly career He could say with reference to that program of fulfillment, 'It is finished' (John 19:30).

---

7. F. Delitzsch, *Biblical Commentary on the Psalms*, 3 vols. (Edinburgh: Clarke, 1871, 1893), 1.
8. ibid.
9. John F. Walvoord, *Jesus Christ our Lord* (Chicago: Moody Press, 1969), pp. 62–79.

It is possible to treat these matters in a rigid, schematic, mechanical manner, as if Jesus, at every juncture from the dawn of human consciousness until death, consulted the Bible to see what move He should make next. A simple reading of the Gospels shows that, quite to the contrary, Jesus was the freest and most relaxed and natural of men. He was fully aware of the prophecies, but we are to understand that the same Providence which rules our lives ruled His and thereby brought 'prediction and fulfillment' together.

Above all, as observed earlier, Old Testament preparation and prediction explain the fervent expectation for the Messiah so prominent in the circle of devout persons at the time of His Advent – the quiet obedience of Joseph and Mary; the believing response of Zacharias and Elizabeth, parents of the forerunner, to the angelic announcements; the worship of the Magi, of shepherds, and of saints like Simeon and Anna. It also explains the frantic fears of the monstrous Herod.

The more we learn about the milieu of Palestine in the time of our Lord's first appearance at Bethlehem and Nazareth – as well as at His baptism and during His official ministry – the more important the prophecy becomes. The discoveries commonly associated together as 'the Dead Sea Scrolls,' considered against a deepening understanding of other extra-biblical and secular literature from early times, show there was great interest in Jewry and Judaism of all grades and varieties in the prophesies of Messiah at the time He did, in veritable flesh, appear upon the scene.

John J. Collin's studies of the Qumran and related literature demonstrate that expectations were not uniform; but he argues, 'however, that the variation was limited, and that some forms of messianic expectation were widely shared…. It is possible… to show that some ideas had wide distribution and were current across sectarian lines…. [T]he expectation of a Davidic Messiah was surely part of it.'[10] 'We shall find,' says Collins, 'four basic messianic paradigms (King, prophet, priest and heavenly Messiah).'[11] See also the same author's discussion of 'The Apocalyticism of the Scrolls in Context.'[12]

Not long after the early discoveries of the 'Dead Sea Scrolls' in the late 1940s reports began to appear in journals of archaeology. My early source was the *Biblical Archaeologist*, published by the American Schools of Oriental Research. Then translations, evaluations and interpretations came along. One enthusiastic Jewish Christian (Ph.D. under Albright) told our faculty (Wheaton College) we would now have to rewrite ecclesiology – which proved unnecessary. Many significant additions were, however, made to understanding of what we read in the New Testament relating to the first Christian community at Jerusalem and there are lesser connections with all the New Testament. Millar Burrows was among the first to bring balance to discussion of the meaning of the Dead Sea Scrolls for the New Testament and early Christianity. I read his works eagerly as a new professor of Old Testament.[13] I note that an eminent authority in these matters shares my high esteem for Burrows' early works. He quotes Burrows as follows:

> For myself I must… confess that, after studying the Dead Sea Scrolls for seven years, I do not find my understanding of the New Testament substantially affected. Its Jewish background is clearer and better understood, but its meaning has neither been changed nor significantly clarified.[14]

This flurry of effort produced a large and still growing literature. For present purposes the best non-technical summary for the subject as the 'scrolls' relate to the whole New Testament is by Jack Finegan, *Light From the Ancient Past*, ch. V, Part 4, 'The Dead Sea Scrolls and the Qumran Community,' especially pp. 288–293, 'Relations With Early Christianity.'[15] A larger semi-popular work by F. F. Bruce (*Biblical Exegesis in the Qumran Texts*) early on captured the light of the earliest finds edited and published on expectation of Messiah among Jews of the time.[16] This 1960 work is still valuable. Bruce shows in the very reserved manner of a polished, evangelical, British scholar that Jews of the holy land were excited about the expected soon-coming of Messiah. The much older work of R. Payne Smith, cited earlier, shows the same expectation of Messiah in rabbinical literature, apocrypha and pseudepigrapha, in possession of scholars for a long time.

10. John J. Collins, *The Scepter and the Star: The Messiahs of the Dead Sea Scrolls and Other Ancient Literature* (New York: Doubleday, 1995), p. 12.
11. ibid.
12. John J. Collins, *Apocalypticism In the Dead Sea Scrolls* (New York: Routledge, 1997), pp. 156–163.
13. Millar Burrows, *The Dead Sea Scrolls* (New York: Viking, 1955) and *More Light on the Dead Sea Scrolls* (New York: Viking, 1958).
14. James C. VanderKam, *The Dead Sea Scrolls Today* (Grand Rapids, MI: Eerdmans, 1994), p.162.
15. J. Finegan, *Light from the Ancient Past* (Princeton: Princeton University Press, 1969), pp. 288–293.
16. F. F. Bruce, *Biblical Exegesis in the Qumran Texts* (London: Tyndale Press, 1960).

More recent publication (1992) of text, translation and interpretation of fifty key documents, sequestered away from scholars for thirty-five years has served to show that interest in Messiah's coming (perhaps two or even more Messiahs) was intense among Palestinian Jews just before Jesus came and for a generation or two (up to the fall of Jerusalem and onward to the Jewish commonwealth) thereafter. Archaeological journals have reported this only in small part. I recommend chapter 1, 'Messianic and Visionary Recitals,' of *The Dead Sea Scrolls Uncovered* by Eisenman and Wise.[17]

Preparation Among the Nations of Antiquity.

'It has often been shown how politically, intellectually, morally, everything in the Graeco-Roman world was ready for such a universal religion as Jesus brought into it.'[18] The nineteenth century was very productive of such studies. Early in the twentieth century A. H. Strong provided a brief but very valuable treatment of the subject for theological students.[19]

The first words in my college text on church history, a book authorized by the Presbyterian Church U.S.A. that went through several editions, opened with these words:

> One of the things that make the study of church history inspiring is that by it we are made to realize that God is actually at work for the salvation of mankind in the world.... Nowhere do we see this working of God more clearly than in the strange and wonderful way in which the world was made ready for the coming of Jesus.[20]

The first chapter went on to speak of the 'contributions' (positive) of Romans, Greeks and Jews, then (negatively) of religious conditions, intellectual conditions and moral conditions.

Emil Brunner offers an excellent assessment near the end of an essay on this subject. He says:

> Jesus Christ cannot be understood from the point of view of world history, but world history is to be understood in the light of Jesus Christ.... But if [previous] world history is to be understood in the light of Jesus Christ, then it is understood as the time of promise and preparation... [and] specially in the history which is close to the Coming of Jesus in space and time, we can perceive something of this preparatory character, as we have tried to do.[21]

Brunner observes that not only Pharaoh and Cyrus 'but also Plato and Alexander, Cicero and Julius Caesar must serve God in order to prepare the way for Christ.'[22]

The kings of Assyria, Babylonia, Egypt, Greece and Rome, plus all the rulers of Israel's nearest neighbors did not know it, but they were subject to God's chastening hand for their own good until 'the desire of nations' should come. Though these rambunctious people and their kings were sent as 'rod of mine anger,' says Jehovah, to execute divine wrath on 'a hypocritical nation' they were totally unaware of it. ('Why doesn't God kill Hitler?' a 1943 sermon title read. Answer in Sunday sermon: 'God is letting Hitler exercise on a leash to keep him healthy for execution.')

Most recent and current treatises on Christology have paid less attention to preparation for Christ's coming in the developments in the ancient heathen world than the importance of the subject deserves. (Older works on almost any subject employed the words *Christendom* and *heathen*. Hymn books did so, especially missionary hymns and Christmas hymns – even Rudyard Kipling's and Whittier's poetry did so. Now multiculturalism has crowded these words out of common use. Lest readers be offended I also use them sparingly, 'until the time be changed.') God's providential rule over the nations is usually noted in detail in the doctrine of providence, but somehow that divine providence as leading up to the coming and career of the Jewish Messiah is not connected with His mission as the Savior of the world, just then ripe for it.

Consider what Paul told the idolatrous Athenians in Acts 17:22–31. He ends his message with announcement of the close of a long history of divine forbearance by the appearance of a Man who demonstrated divine authority to judge the world and to command 'all people everywhere to repent.' During previous ages He overlooked the

---

17. R. Eisenman and Michael Wise, *The Dead Sea Scrolls Uncovered* (New York: Penguin, 1993), pp. 17–50.
18. James Orr, art. *'Jesus Christ,' ISBE iii* (Grand Rapids, 1943), p. 1027.
19. A. H. Strong, *Systematic Theology* (Valley Forge, PA: Judson Press, 1907), pp. 665–668.
20. Nichols, *Growth of Christian Church*, p. 1.
21. Emil Brunner, *The Christian Doctrine of Creation and Redemption, Dogmatics: vol. ii* (Philadelphia: The Westminster Press, 1952), p. 337.
22. ibid., pp. 337, 338.

deepening depravity of the race even though 'he made... every nation of mankind' and determined the set time for them and exact places where they should live (Acts 17:26). This extended time of mercy, Paul declared, is now at an end (vv. 27, 30).

This does not mean that there were any saving revelations to the heathen even though we must credit them with many accomplishments and attainments in art, science, literature, and even ethics and religion. Their altars and sacrifices were rooted in normal instincts for religious expression even though their philosophy, art and science did not improve their morals as the depravity of the lives of the best examples (the homosexuality rampant among the philosophers of the greatest age of Greek philosophy) show. Their attainments aroused impulses and cravings that could not be supplied and raised standards they could not meet (Rom. 2:1-6).

The cross could not be set up at the gates of Eden (Strong) nor could Eve be the immaculate mother of the promised 'seed' that would crush the serpent's head. Ages must pass to prepare for the first *parousia* (arrival) of the promised seed 'in the fullness of time.'

I. In two ways the passing of time leading up to the Advent of Christ had demonstrated the need for a Savior rather than merely better sages, rulers and philosophers.

1. It showed the depth of human depravity – a depravity which, by the admission of friendly ancient and modern historians had sharply deepened in the Roman world immediately before the birth of Jesus. This may well be part of what Paul was denouncing in the brilliant summation of Romans 1:18–3:20. 'In past generations he allowed all the nations to walk in their own ways' even while God's goodness in sustaining their lives was a witness against them (Acts 14:16, 17). Long before Rome was more than a small muddy village on the banks of a small river, Isaiah pointed out that while the light of saving revelation was present in Zion and would someday result in the removal of 'the covering that is cast over all peoples.' In Isaiah's time there was a 'veil that is spread over all nations' (Isa. 25:6-8). The Apostle speaks of a similar veil of ignorance, blindness and hardness of heart which kept Jews from understanding the true sense of their own Scriptures (2 Cor. 3:13-15; John 9:39) making them no less than Gentiles in deep need of the 'light of the world' (John 1:4; 8:12; 9:5).

2. It showed the utter moral inability of human nature either to preserve or regain saving knowledge of God once it had been lost. We do not know much about the godly Gentiles who appear in Old Testament story. There is Melchizedek, the 'priest' and 'king of Salem' to whom Abram paid tithes and who 'blessed him,' and said, 'Blessed be Abram by God Most High, Possessor of heaven and earth' (Gen. 14:18-20; cf. Heb. 5:6, 10) and Jethro, Moses' father-in-law (Exod. 2:16-3:1; 18:1-27) and Job who was commended as 'blameless and upright,' one who 'feared God and turned away from evil' (Job 1:1, 3). Yes, we are sometimes amazed at the moral insights of the heathen, both the ones we know from ancient secular literature – Pythagoras, Pindar, Sophocles, Epinmenides, Plato, Socrates – and from biblical sources – Abimelech (Gen. 26), Pharaoh (Gen. 12), even Nebuchadnezzar (Dan. 4) and others. We do not know, however, that any were able to lead their contemporaries to 'the truth' and a genuine righteousness, nor so far as we know did any one ever claim they were.

One may think of the Graeco-Roman world of the time as inarticulately crying out for a Savior from the sin-burden of ages, much as Peter Anthony Bertocci describes individuals in utter soul need:

> [W]hen the doctor says he has done all he can or when one is forced to watch his loved ones make moves which will both decrease the good in their lives and increase his own sorrow, or,... when one sees the very meaning of his life in the balance, without his being able to do a solitary thing about the outcome, then he finds himself reaching spiritual arms out to the universe. Gone, in these circumstances, is the composed self-reliance; gone is the earlier determination to outgrow 'primitive' beliefs. Here one implores that something be done – yes, something that might be an exception to the rules.... We have all been in our psychological foxholes.... Having in all conscience done our best, we call to some agency beyond ourselves.... It is when the conceived good is at stake, when our towers of value seem to totter that we realize our lives and our values are without purpose if there is no aid beyond ourselves.[23]

II. Christ was first made known and widely received in the lands circling the Mediterranean Sea ruled by Rome, and thoroughly penetrated by Greek language and culture. The Empire was also host to numerous Jewish families and Jewish communities sprinkled throughout, with concentrations in several urban centers. Upper classes everywhere admired, absorbed and imitated the Greeks while Jewish enclaves in the cities made their own impression on many.

---

23. Peter Anthony Bertocci, *Introduction to the Philosophy of Religion* (Englewood Cliffs, NJ: Prentice-Hall, 1951, 1961), pp. 24, 25.

We cannot relate here how this came about but let us just trace some of the results of this *Diaspora* (dispersion) as they affected the appearance of Christ and the success of the early missionizing efforts.

1. A world civilization arose in place of the political and social fragmentation of previous epochs. This unprecedented development began with the conquests of Alexander in the second third of the fourth century BC, giving a large measure of political unity and a growing prevalence of the Greek language and culture. The 'world' (oikoumenē, Luke 2:1) was extended to the farthest points of northern Africa and western Europe by Rome, coming to a climax in the conquests and consolidation by Julius Caesar in the mid first century BC. Caesar also moved the political basis of Roman world rule from Republic to Empire. When about a century later the process of forming one Roman world was complete it could be said, as Edward Gibbon wrote:

> The empire of the Romans filled the world, and when that empire fell into the hands of a single person, the world became a safe and dreary prison for his enemies… To resist was fatal, and it was impossible to fly…. Beyond the frontiers, his anxious view could discover nothing, except the ocean, inhospitable deserts, hostile tribes of barbarians, of fierce manners and unknown language, or dependent kings, who would gladly purchase the emperor's protection by the sacrifice of an obnoxious fugitive. 'Wherever you are,' said Cicero to the exiled Marcellus, 'remember that you are equally within the power of the conqueror.'[24]

'[T]he Father sent his Son to be the Savior of the world.' (1 John 4:14; 1 Tim. 4:10). People were made aware of the existence of a 'world' by the development of the Roman Empire that included a large part of all mankind. Paul could appeal to this concept in his preaching (Acts 17:26) and Luke, the Greek-minded writer of New Testament histories, assumed it in reporting 'In those days a decree went out from Caesar Augustus that all the world should be registered' (Luke 2:1). The NIV 'Roman world' somewhat betrays the Gr. *oikoumenē*, inhabited or civilized world. For an acculturated Roman, the world ended at the borders of the Empire. Anything beyond did not count.

2. The messengers of the gospel were to take the message of salvation in Christ to the ends of the earth (Acts 1:8). The national governments before Alexander's conquests really enforced the natural prejudice of tribes and clans against foreigners. A foreigner could be suspected as an enemy. But the 'Peace of Rome' broke that down. Paul needed no passport to travel from Tarsus to Jerusalem or to Antioch or to Spain. As a free (non-slave) Roman citizen he could go anywhere. It is significant that Paul, who spoke to so many national groups, did not seem to have been even minimally aware of cultural bridges to cross or a new education for himself and party in order to proclaim the news 'from Jerusalem… to Illyricum' (Yugoslavia) and on to Rome and Spain (Rom. 15:19, 24). He could call upon Roman police to protect him from harm everywhere and did so more than once. A Jew in Corinth preaching a new religion in the days of Pericles five centuries earlier might have found those civilized Greeks quite unwilling to protect him, as the Roman Gallio, proconsul of Achaia did at the Greek city of Corinth (Acts 18:12-17).

3. Never before had the entire area had a common language understood by literate people everywhere. Alexander and his successors made their conquests as part of a larger mission to Hellenize the world, to spread the benefits, as Greeks understood them, of Greek language and culture everywhere. The wars of the Jewish Maccabees in the second century BC, came from the collision of that effort with Jewish resistance. The Romans themselves, not very literate or sophisticated, admired the Greek culture and adopted it unreservedly, even equating the Pantheon of Rome with that of the Greek classics. When Jesus was born, Greek was read and spoken, even by Jews, throughout the Empire. Hence the New Testament came to be composed in the Greek language mainly by Jews who had accepted that much of Hellenism. Greek was the language of the synagogue no less than of civil courts, marketplace and lecture hall. Thus was created, in the times immediately before Jesus, the linguistic vehicle that carried the gospel of Christ to the world of the first centuries of the Christian epoch.

4. Rome built the roads by which Christian disciples like the Ethiopian eunuch could take the message from Gaza to Ethiopia and Barnabas could fetch Saul from Tarsus. Later Paul and Silas could travel about Cilicia and the provinces of Asia, as well as Macedonia, Achaia and Illyria in Europe. The travels of Christians in commercial enterprises or about the business of living was then and for centuries the chief means of disseminating the message of Christ as He Himself had indicated in Acts 1:8. 'Sent' missionaries needed policed highways to get where the peoples of the world were. Rome made such unrestricted travel possible with roads to the very extremities of their world. Such access never existed until Rome created it.

---

24. Edward Gibbon, *The Decline and Fall of the Roman Empire*, abridged by F. C. Bourne (New York: Dell Publishing Co., 1963, 1970), pp. 74–75.

5. Recent changes of that day in the religious temper made the population ready to hear something new and better. Deep faith in the official gods had about perished. Strange exotic cults were sweeping in from the Orient (Cybele, Mithraism). Age-old pagan superstitions were gaining strength. Mystery religions – offering dramatic ceremonies for cleansing from sin, hope of eternal life and the joys of group fellowship – were enjoying growing popularity.

The Greco-Roman world was full of restless, discontented, spiritual yearning. In view of what Christianity brought, it should be noticed that three things were prominent (for the first time) in the prevailing religious temper: a growing belief in one universal God, a widespread sense of sin and desire for purification from it, and a great interest in the question of what comes after death.[25]

6. In many ways, though the great attainments of Greek philosophy had been achieved centuries before the Christian era, its lingering and growing effects were very helpful to acceptance of Christianity and to its later exposition. Acts chapter 17 brings together Athens, capital city of Greek higher education, Stoic and Epicurean philosophers (vv. 16, 17), and Paul, the chief exponent of Christianity of the time. Both of these Greek philosophies could rightly claim some success at analysis of the human condition (as also modern psychology and sociology) but were almost utterly impotent to do anything truly remedial about it. And for the same reasons they could not address ultimate problems like man's innate depravity, death and questions about *eternal* goodness, beauty and truth with certainty. In a few decades, however, real Christians who were as versed in the learning and jargon of the philosophies as any denizens of Athenian academia were preaching and writing persuasively in advocacy of faith in Christ. They showed Christ to be the answer to the philosophers' quest. They furnished what Socrates, Plato and Aristotle could not. They spoke with the authority of Christ Himself backed up by 'assurance to all' (Acts 17:31). And they supplied adequate answers rather than more insightful questions. One of the pagan elite, at the death of his daughter, wrote to a friend: 'Give me some fresh comfort, great and strong, such as I have never yet heard or read. Everything that I have read or heard comes back now to my memory, but my sorrow is too deep to be reached by it' (Pliny the Younger).

7. The dispersion of the Jews throughout the Roman world and beyond provided a core of listeners for the Christian witness far and wide. 'The preaching of the gospel was preceded and prepared for by the dispersion of the Jews.'[26] Josephus said 'the habitable earth is full of Jews' and quotes Strabo: 'these Jews… it is hard to find a place in the habitable earth that hath not admitted this tribe of men' (*Antiquities*, 14.7.2). ('Habitable earth' here translates *oikoumenē* rendered 'all the world' in Luke 2:1.) The sad exiles of Daniel's and Ezekiel's time could not have dreamed that the circumstances of the Jews' apostasy and resultant Diaspora – graphically exposed by the sermons and lessons of the prophets – would be a very valuable instrument for the growth of a body of Messiah's spiritual seed among the very Gentiles who were the means of divine chastisement. The story of Paul's missionary journeys, always beginning a new ministry at a local synagogue, illustrates this point.

8. To a limited degree the Judaism of the Diaspora was a missionary religion. The rabbis interpreted Old Testament prophecies of the extension of divine salvation to Gentiles as authority for proclaiming conversion to Judaism and even acceptance, as Jews, through instruction and certain initiatory rites. Those who went through circumcision and other prescribed rites were 'Proselytes.' Those who accepted Judaism but stopped short of the rites were called 'God-fearers.' The latter are the ones whom we meet in the book of Acts as 'men who feared God' (e.g. Cornelius) and those who 'gathered for prayer' such as Lydia and other God-fearing ladies at the river-side in Philippi to whom Paul witnessed. These God-fearers and proselytes were a fertile field in which to plant the gospel as it moved away from Jerusalem, for example the eunuch of Ethiopia (Acts 8:27), Cornelius and his household (Acts 10:1), Lydia and her friends (Acts 16:13, 14), and the proselytes of Antioch of Pisidea (Acts 13:16, 26, 50) and of Thessalonica (Acts 17:4, 17) and Justus, a Gentile worshipper of the true God in whose house the church at Corinth began (Acts 18:7). It is noticeable that the ones who stopped short of circumcision and other rites (baptism and offering sacrifice), the 'God-fearers,' were numerous – especially women – and the converts to Christianity came chiefly from these God-fearers. Perhaps the full proselytes were as fanatically anti-Christian as the born Jews.

---

25. Nichols, *Growth of Christian Church*, p. 11.
26. P. Levertoff, art. *'Proselyte,' ISBE. iv* (Grand Rapids, MI: Eerdmans, 1943), p. 2468.

9. May it not be true that when moral decline had bottomed out, or, to use another figure, when the pendulum had swung to the end of its arc toward the wrong, a turnaround toward the right was both likely and timely? I do not press the point, but many movements of the Spirit of God in Christian history support the notion. Then as now, the upper classes were no doubt horribly corrupt, the scandals reported by biographers of emperors and aristocracy abundantly show this. There were, of course, virtuous people also or orderly civilized life would have stopped. Yet until the spread of Christianity brought news of the Savior to that decadent age no strong force making for reformation and renewal existed – even though several emperors saw the need of it and sought to do something to enforce improvement.

3
The Preexistence of Christ

The word 'preexistence' summarizes the point of a question Jesus once asked His disciples, viz.: 'Then what if you were to see the Son of Man ascending to where he was before?' (John 6:62). Likewise Jesus' mysterious reference to Himself as 'he who descended from heaven' (John 3:13). There was a 'before' Jesus' conception in the virgin and a 'descended' when conception took place.

Theologians refer to this New Testament teaching as the preexistence of Christ. But the word 'does not fit comfortably in the vocabulary of Western man.... It seems a fugitive word escaped from a séance.'[1] Yet the idea has already met the minds of those who know about Plato's doctrine of preexistence of souls, echoed in Browning's 'Ode on Intimations of Immortality' where 'the Soul... hath had elsewhere its setting... trailing clouds of glory' as we 'come from God.' So though employed to name a false idea (preexistence of souls of mankind) in Platonic doctrine, the idea of preexistence (not necessarily the word) has an ancient and continuing home among informed Christians. The notion of the preexistence of souls also had a place in both ancient and medieval Judaism, though there is little evidence of it among biblically orthodox Jews of the time of our Lord.[2]

That Jesus was aware He had a preexistence 'with God' (John 1:1) is indicated by His favorite self-designation as 'the Son of Man.' The name borrows not from the prophet Ezekiel (who is addressed as 'son of man' throughout his book) but from Daniel 7:13, 14 where it is said 'with the clouds of heaven there came one like a son of man.' This Son of Man is a Being of heavenly origin, as distinguished from an earthly origin. That the Jews thought Daniel referred to a preexistent, divine Being comes out clearly when Jesus pointedly claimed the reference for Himself in the high priest's presence and was accused of blasphemy (Matt. 26:64, 65). Though as far as I know the Daniel passage was not used as support for expectation of a human messiah by the Jews of Jesus' time, we know that some Jews hoped for the coming of 'a preexistent, heavenly monarch who is to judge the world in righteousness.' B. B. Warfield documents this well.[3]

The deity of Christ is not necessary to His preexistence but preexistence is necessary to deity, one of whose attributes is eternity. It is therefore important to establish our Lord's preexistence in the mind before the deity of Christ, which we shall treat next. This was very important to the early church in firmly shaping what became the Christology of Nicea and Chalcedon. Further, inasmuch as most accounts of the life of Christ start the story with

---
1. F. B. Craddock, *The Preexistence of Christ* (Nashville, TN: Abington, 1968), p. 7.
2. See 'Preexistence of Souls,' article by J. M. Marshall, *Dictionary of the Bible iv*, ed. J. Hastings (New York: Charles Scribner & Sons, 1909), p. 63.
3. B. B. Warfield, *The Lord of Glory* (Grand Rapids, MI: Zondervan, n.d.), p. 38.

Bethlehem, wisdom dictates that we insist on special attention to our Lord's identity as 'the Lord from Heaven' (1 Cor. 15:47). Experience confirms the need. After one of my earliest Christmas sermons – the text being Philippians 2:5-8 – an aged lady shook my hand and thanked me for the sermon, earnestly declaring, 'I never knew till this morning that Joseph was not the father of Jesus.' Like many others, I suppose the word 'virgin' had meant no more to her than 'girl' or 'young woman.'

The New Testament Testimony to the Fact of the Preexistence of Jesus.

B. B. Warfield in his essay, 'The Person of Christ According to the New Testament' points out that the writings of the New Testament were completed within a very short period of time, most of them in a period of twenty years. It is 'all the product of a single movement, at a single stage of its development, and therefore presents *in its fundamental teaching* [emphasis added] a common character. There is small trace of developing ideas as much recent so-called biblical research seeks out. Of course Jesus, John the Baptist, the Synoptics, Paul, Peter and Hebrews do not present doctrine in exactly the same way, but they do support exactly the same set of historical and revealed truths.' I agree that, as Warfield goes on to say, 'In its fundamental teaching, the New Testament lends itself... more readily to what is called dogmatic [systematic] than to what is called genetic treatment.'[4]

Among these truths is the preexistence of the Son of God, our Lord Jesus Christ. Already in the New Testament, long before any counsel or synod formulated any formal, written creed or definition, the eternal preexistence of the Word made flesh (John 1:14) was a dogma (in the best sense of that word) in the church of the apostolic age. The teaching always appears incidentally 'as a thing understood by all, needing to be alluded to rather than formally expounded.'[5]

Some of Jesus' parables show that the preexistence of Christ is assumed by the text. In the parable (i.e. allegory) of the wicked husbandman, the owner of the vineyard (God), in addition to other servants (the O.T. prophets), 'had one more to send, a beloved son; he sent him last' (Mark 12:6 NASB). In the allegorical symbolism of the Parable of the Pounds (Luke 19:11-27) the nobleman '*went* [emphasis added] into a far country.' The nobleman of course is Jesus Himself and the kingdom He was to 'receive' is 'his own' (John 1:11), the Jewish people who 'did not receive him.' Afterward He was 'to return.' Whence He came and whither return are obviously heaven.

A. The greatest weight must be attached to Jesus' own awareness of preexistence and His testimony to that awareness. He is best qualified to speak, as He Himself claimed, 'Even if I do bear witness about myself, my testimony is true, for I know where I came from and where I am going' (John 8:14). This was His rebuff to the Pharisees' denying value to His testimony (v. 13). He laid claim to the fact that Bethlehem was a step down from previous existence when to Nicodemus He spoke of Himself as *Him* 'who descended from heaven' (John 3:13). Again the thought appears when He asked some defiant Jews, 'what if you were to see the Son of Man ascending to where he was before?' (John 6:62). Later as the mystery of His Passion was settling in, and in the solemn truthfulness of 'death-bed' prayer, He cried out, 'And now, Father, glorify me in your own presence with the glory that I had with you before the world existed' (John 17:5). About forty times in John's Gospel alone Jesus used expressions that, while not directly claiming preexistence, do imply it. I cite only one more example, from John 8:42 (KJV), 'I proceeded forth and came from God.'

B. Some of John's testimony to Christ's preexistence has already been cited, for he it is who was quoted in most of the above paragraphs. As the 'Beloved Disciple' his insights (perhaps John even shared some special revelation) gave him a special right to speak to this matter. The striking opening of John's Gospel (John 1:1-3) puts the Word at 'the beginning.' He carries the same dual witness (his own and Jesus' quoted words) on into 1 John where our Lord is 'that eternal life, which was with the Father, and was manifested unto us' (1 John 1:1, 2) and in the book of Revelation where Jesus speaks as 'the Alpha and the Omega,... who is and who was and who is to come, the Almighty' (Rev. 1:8 *et al*).

C. The forerunner, John the Baptist, more than hinted at preexistence when he said Jesus 'was before me' (John 1:15) and Paul, as usual, making doctrinal statements to support ethical-practical exhortation, places Christ, the 'Rock that followed them,' with Israel in the wilderness trek (1 Cor. 10:4-9) and preexisting 'in the form of God' (Phil. 2:6) and 'before all things' (Col. 1:17).

---

4. B. B. Warfield, art. *'The Person of Christ'* (1915), ISBE v (Grand Rapids, MI: Eerdmans, 1943), p. 2338.
5. ibid.

The liberal but honest presentation of Paul's affirmations by F. R. Craddock[6] required thirty-five pages for a mere survey of Paul's affirmations, allusions to and assumptions of this doctrine – already accepted among the readers of his Epistles.

Craddock shows how Paul relates the preexistent Christ to the original creation, to the incarnation and to history. The most pertinent is, of course, the preexistent Christ in creation as in two of the outstanding passages, 1 Corinthians 8:5, 6 and Colossians 1:15–20. In the first Paul says although there are 'so-called' gods on earth and in heaven 'for us there is one God, the Father, from whom are all things... and one Lord, Jesus Christ, through whom are all things and through whom we exist.' In the second, Christ is 'the image of the invisible God... all things were created through him and for him. And he is before all things, and in him all things hold together.'

The teaching of Christ's preexistence is not being *announced* in these great passages; rather it is *assumed* as an acknowledged fact, helpful for solving other theological and practical problems. In 1 Corinthians 8:5, 6 the problem is theological – monotheism *versus* polytheism. Paul directs their attention to the agreed fact that 'for us there is [only] one God... and one Lord, Jesus Christ.' The readers needed to be reminded of these accepted theological roots. In the Colossians passage the same polytheism ('thrones... dominions... principalities... authorities') needed to be dislodged from the minds of the former polytheists of the congregation not yet quite purged of pagan superstitions. In Corinth the worship of heathen gods was manifest in lingering attendance at the local pagan shrines and the meals served there (chap. 8), in Colosse the worship of angels, though we do not know what form it took.

Being now centuries removed from overt polytheism in our outlook it seems unnecessary to prove the nonexistence of supernatural spooks or spirits who must be honored or placated. But this was necessary then and in many parts of Christendom still is necessary. In theological parlance Paul is saying: the God and Christ of *redemption* is the God and Christ of *creation* and *providence* also. The so-called gods of heathenism have no more power to control crops, fortunes, health, winning or losing than power to save, which is none at all. The Redeemer and the providential Lord of creation are the same Lord Jesus.

The Apostle treats the preexistence theme as an aspect of incarnation. The goal is to inculcate moral and spiritual virtues. Among these virtues is *generosity*, 'For you know the grace of our Lord Jesus Christ, that *though he was rich* [emphasis added], yet for your sake he became poor,' etc. (2 Cor. 8:9), and *unselfishness*, 'Do nothing out of selfish ambition or vain conceit' (Phil. 2:3 NIV). The author is employing the moral leverage in the example of the preexistent Christ who in not hanging on to equality with God but humbling Himself, took our humanity to save us (Phil. 2:4-11).

He elsewhere employs the *dogma* of the preexistence as a rhetorical support in the perennial task, familiar to every pastor, of raising money for benevolent purposes. If they are to 'remember the poor' (Gal. 2:10) he reminds them they have Barnabas and Paul as models, but no less so the example of Jesus cited above (2 Cor. 8:9; Rom. 15:27). Thus not only are *creation* by the preexistent Christ and *redemption* by the same incarnate Lord twin doctrines, but the preexistence is also part and parcel of *salvation* doctrine too or Paul would not be coaching his 'second string' evangelists toward sanctification by appeals to it, as he does in these communications.

Let us take note of a final example. The new Christians at Corinth were prone to indulge their baser appetites by concessions to the immoral rites of idolatrous worship prevalent in this city. To encourage them toward better things he directed these former heathen to the direct spiritual assistance Christ gave to the Israelites at the time of the Exodus and wilderness wanderings, viz.: 'I want you to know, brothers, that our fathers were all under the cloud, and all passed through the sea, and all were baptized into Moses in the cloud and in the sea, and all ate the same spiritual food, and all drank the same spiritual drink. For they drank from the spiritual Rock that followed them, and the Rock was Christ' (1 Cor. 10:1-4). He then goes on to warn the new people of God at Corinth against similar sins of self-indulgence, idolatry, frivolity and fornication which brought about destruction of the Israelites of old. The point of the passage is that Christ was present as bread of life and water of life to ancient Israel and is still present now, faithful to provide strength to escape every temptation (1 Cor. 10:11-13). The rest of chapter 10 continues the lesson against self-indulgences of various kinds.

D. The Epistle to the Hebrews carries forward the same sequence of preexistence followed by incarnation. The opening paragraph says God who spoke in the Old Testament dispensation by prophets has spoken in the present dispensation finally by a son. This particular son, the Epistle goes on to say, happens to be *the Son*, the One by whom God made the worlds. '[B]eing... the express image' (KJV; 'exact imprint ESV; 'exact representation' NIV) of God's

---

6. F. R. Craddock, *op. cit.*

person, He is the One who purged our sins and then returning to heaven 'sat down at the right hand of the Majesty on high.' This with different emphasis and a different name ('my Son,' Heb.1:5), is the preexistence theology of John, chapter 1, where the One by whom God created the world is the Word.

Hebrews 2:9-18 is arguably the greatest Christological passage in the Bible. It is devoted to explaining the *nature* of the incarnation itself and the divine *purposes* for the event and its sequel in the life, death, resurrection and ascension of the Savior. The personal transaction of the preexistent Son is well put in verse 14, 'Forasmuch then as the children are partakers [i.e. by nature, conceived and born that way] of flesh and blood, he also himself likewise took part of the same.' The King James Version, just cited, cannot be much improved upon, except to note that like every Version I can recall consulting, for some strange reason it reverses 'blood and flesh' of the Greek, which is to be regretted. The author intended to emphasize not merely the humanity of incarnate deity but as Friederich Bleek explains: 'The whole sensuous corporeal nature of man, which he has in common with the brutes.'[7] The emphasis is on the 'infirmity, decay, and transitoriness' of being part of a material world. *Koinoneō* is the word rendered 'partakers' conveying what human beings naturally have in common by virtue of existence. *Metechō* is here rendered not partake which might have a passive meaning, not different especially from *koinoneō*. But the translators of 1611 rightly rendered it by an unmistakably active expression, 'took part.' The Son of God, so to speak, saw human kind in a material, physical world and *took part* in their humanity in order to die for them, as the last part of verse 14 says. He stepped up to the table, so to speak, and took part with them by means of the event of incarnation. A parallel of precise sense is the contrast of *forebear*, a passive notion, with *bear for*, an active idea.

The preexistent 'Jesus' (see Heb. 2:9) reached out and took our human nature. There is a realism here that has nothing at all in common with the mythical or occult mysticism to which some modern New Testament scholarship would assign this teaching. Nor is there the least maudlin sentimentality at Christmas often associated with popular folk-celebration about the manger scene of popular imagination and commercial exploitation. To those who would deny the propriety of such, F. F. Bruce replies:

> The man who says, 'I could not have a high opinion of a God who would (or would not) do this or that,' is not adding anything to our knowledge of God; he is simply telling us something about himself. We may be sure that all God does is worthy of Himself, but here our author singles out one of God's actions and tells us that 'it became him' – that it was a fitting thing for him to do.[8]

E. This theology is pervasive on through the book of Revelation – never introduced, as liberal religion would have it, as an interpretation of people's religious experiences, but report of what Jesus and the Apostles had said from the beginning. Nor is it the fruit of theological reflection by the Jewish or Jew-Gentile church, as liberal New Testament theology would have it, but as received truth addressed to Christians who already believed and had believed it for thirty years before Paul wrote Philippians 2:5-9.

The Preexistent Christ in Old Testament History and Prophecy.

A. As understood by the ancient church: No text of the Old Testament speaks with the clarity of John 1:1 or 17:5. Yet the Second Person of the Godhead, incarnate in Jesus, has a place in several aspects of Old Testament narrative.

The Eastern church Fathers read the Old Testament only in the Greek translation known as the Septuagint. The word for wisdom, *sophia*, has much overlapping of meaning with *logos*, quite as justifiably translated *reason* or *logic* as *word* even in the first chapter of John and elsewhere in the New Testament. So when the three Cappadocians – the two Gregories and Basil – in the late third century were sifting the Old Testament for evidence of Christ's preexistence and deity, Proverbs chapter 8 seemed like certain proof. It is a soliloquy by wisdom – Greek *sophia*, Hebrew *ḥokma*. Wisdom claims 'The LORD possessed me at the beginning of his work… Ages ago I was set up, at the first' (Prov. 8:22, 23) and similarly throughout the chapter. It is not surprising that before and after the Councils of Nicea (AD 325) and First Constantinople (AD 381) the supporters of orthodoxy quoted this chapter in support. By connecting Psalm 104:24 (LXX, 103:24) with 1 Corinthians 1:24 and John 1:1-3 they thought they had an airtight case and used it that way. J. Pelikan discusses this at length and with great profit for any reader.[9]

---

7. 'Lectures on Hebrews,' 1868, cited by Dean Henry Alford, *New Testament for English Readers* (Chicago: Moody Press, n.d.), p. 1465.
8. F. F. Bruce, *The Epistle to the Hebrews* (Grand Rapids, MI: Eerdmans, 1964), p. 41.
9. Jaroslav Pelikan, *Christianity and Classical Culture* (New Haven: Yale University Press, 1993), pp. 70, 71, 218 ff.

Yet suggestive as it is, the female *ḥakma-sophia-wisdom* of Proverbs is patently a personification of the ethical spiritual quality exalted from the first verses of the book onward (1:1-4) a synonym of the fear of God (1:7), similar to discretion, understanding, righteousness, judgment and equity (2:9-11). Wisdom in Proverbs 8 is not a hypostasis (person) but wisdom hypostatized (personified).

B. There is strong evidence from some early Jewish sources that one stream of thought among Jews, though not all, of two centuries before Christ and for several centuries afterward expected Messiah to be a preexistent person – not God Himself, but one created by God before the creation of sun and stars. There is a Jewish literature ('intertestamental'), sometimes called also Apocrypha and Pseudepigrapha, much of which has been known to Christian scholars for many centuries. Other ancient Jewish literature (e.g. the Book of Enoch in Etheopic translation) has turned up in modern times. Judaism also produced Mishna and Gemara (the Talmud), Midrashim (commentaries), and other writings emanating from the first to sixth centuries of our era. Then in 1947 and subsequently, the Qumran findings (Dead Sea Scrolls), have provided much information directly from a community of devout and zealous Jews who were intent upon being prepared spiritually to receive Messiah and to support what they expected would be Messiah's program of deliverances of 'the chosen people.'

Scholars, both Jewish and Christian, in modern times before the Qumran discoveries, canvassed that literature. One of the best was Joseph Klausner, who after a distinguished career in European universities became Professor of Hebrew Literature and Jewish History at the Hebrew University of Jerusalem. His book, *The Messianic Idea in Israel*, mostly written originally in German and published 1902–1921 was translated into Hebrew and then into English. In the second part, on the messianic idea in the Apocrypha and Pseudepigrapha, Klausner, commenting on the Etheopic Enoch states: 'The Messiah existed before the creation of the world – as in the later Baraithas of the Talmud... and in the Midrashim.' In a note he continues: 'To be sure only the *name* Messiah preceded the creation of the world' (p. 290). On a later section of *Enoch* he comments:

> The Son of man and his name are named before the Ancient of Days. 'Before the sun and the planets were created, before the stars in the heavens were made, his name was named before the God of Spirits' (48:2-3). Likewise even in the earlier Baraithas – Messiah's *Name* existed before the sun and stars: it is one of the seven things that preceded the creation of the world.[10]

The Messiah Texts by Raphael Patai treats the post-biblical literature of ancient Israel topically (logically, according to subject). Each chapter consists of an interpretive introduction and the texts in the author's translation. The second chapter is 'Preexistence and Names of the Messiah.' He says:

> Messiah first appears as preexistent in the apocryphal First Book of Enoch (180–150 BC).... From that period on the concept of the Messiah who was created in the six days of Creation, or even prior to them, or who was then hidden to await his time, became a standard feature of Jewish Messianic eschatology.[11]

I know of no reference to Messiah's preexistence in the Qumran literature or in the literature about it, nor any clear expectation of a purely non-human, divine Messiah. Michael (Who is like God?) and Gabriel (Man of God) do appear as accompanying Messiah in His coming. It would not be surprising if some text should turn up claiming a preexistent divine Person as Messiah on the basis of the Son of Man apocalypse of Daniel 7. The Sadducean priests were certainly conscious of such a connection, as Luke 22:71 shows. Sometimes Messiah is called 'Son of the Clouds' in the Talmud.[12] This suggests Daniel 7:13. The Talmud, Pirque Mashiah (chapters of Messiah) has a passage referring to King Messiah as coming 'as it is written, Behold, with the clouds of heaven came one like unto a son of man.'

In so far as the preexistence of Messiah appears in Jewish literature, it is not the eternal preexistence of God Himself but of One created in heaven before His coming to earth. A. H. Strong provides a valuable assessment of Christ as preexistent *Wisdom and Word*.[13]

C. The angel of the LORD (a subject better pursued at length in connection with the doctrine of the Trinity): The New Testament clearly identifies 'the angel of the LORD' of Old Testament theophanies with Christ, as a comparison of Malachi 3:1 with Mark 1:2 shows. This Person appeared to Hagar (Gen. 16), to Abram (Gen. 18), to Jacob (Gen. 32)

---

10. Joseph Klausner, *The Messianic Idea in Israel,* trans. W. F. Stinespring (New York: MacMillan, 1955), p. 292.
11. Raphael Patai, *The Messiah Texts* (Detroit: Wayne State U. Press, 1979), p. 16.
12. ibid. pp. 81–83.
13. A. H. Strong, *Systematic Theology* (Valley Forge, PA: Judson Press, 1907), pp. 320, 321.

and others and is called Jehovah (the Sacred Name; 'LORD' is used in most translations) in Genesis 18:18-21 and God in Exodus 3:2. 'Wonderful' is a 'name' for the predicted Christ in Isaiah 9:6 and 'wonderful' is also the name of 'the angel of the LORD' in the annunciation of the birth of Samson to his parents (Judg.13:18). This striking connection of the Angel of the LORD with the preexistent Christ has attracted the attention of scholars from ancient times. See Irenaeus,[14] A. A. Hodge,[15] A. H. Strong[16] and Pelikan.[17] It should be pointed out that 'the angel of the LORD' disappears with the Advent of Christ. 'The angel of the Lord' at Matthew 1:24 is not an exception. The article is by way of reference to 'an angel of the Lord' (v. 20), the particular one sent to announce the virginal conception.

D. Other suggestions: Though many Old Testament passages state, suggest or hint a future Advent of the LORD God of Israel, e.g. 'the Lord whom you seek will suddenly come to his temple' (Mal. 3:1), no one, it seems, identified these prophetic remarks as referring to Messiah. Yet certain rather well-known, acknowledged prophecies of Messiah suggest the Advent of an eternal personal Being. Micah 5:2, employed by the Jerusalem elders to guide the Magi to Bethlehem says 'whose goings forth have been… from everlasting' (KJV) and Isaiah 9:6 can best be explained from hindsight of the New Testament ('Mighty God, Everlasting Father') as implying the preexistence of the child born at Bethlehem. 'Everlasting Father,' Hebrew *'avi-'adh* means literally, Father of eternity in the sense of 'perpetuity' (Brown, Driver and Briggs) and puts our Lord before time, not in time, but time in Him.

The Scope of Christ's Preexistence and Activity Therein.

Once made thoroughly aware of the pre-incarnational Christ many scriptural statements take on a much larger meaning than otherwise. I shall attempt an outline of the subject.

A. As to the scope of His preexistence: as a very young man I remember reading of the birth of the present Dalai Lama, head of the Tibetan Buddhist religion. The announcement said (for I wrote this down) the newborn was 'preexistent, planfully incarnate, supernaturally conceived, and miraculously born.' This interesting refugee from communist China, even if one were to grant the claims made, is – if I understand the matter correctly – only supposed to be the re-embodiment of another religious leader who was born many centuries earlier. This Buddhist belief in metempsychosis, or transmigration of souls is itself a part of the general belief of millions of eastern and southern Asiatic peoples in the cyclic (repetitious) quality of the existence of all living beings (souls). Every soul embodied in some vital object is a re-embodiment of that soul in a chain of previous re-embodiments. There is no real beginning of things in this religious belief, for Hinduism and its offshoots (of which Buddhism is only one) have no substantive doctrine of original creation. In this regard Christ is unique in His claims. A sketch of the matter shows:

(1) He was present and active in the act of condescension by which the Son of God became incarnate in Mary's womb. '[T]aking the form of a servant,' 'he humbled himself' (Phil 2:7, 8).

(2) Some think He was present in the 'shekina' or glory-presence of the Mosaic Tabernacle and Solomonic and Restoration temples (though Jewish tradition claims no shekina for the restored temple). The story of the departure of the glory is told by Ezekiel who in a series of visions was privileged to see it happen. No one, in my opinion, can be sure how much of sheer symbolism is involved. The shekina, which was present in the Mosaic-Aaronic holy of holies, was present at least for awhile. '[F]ire came down from heaven and consumed the burnt offering and the sacrifices, and the glory of the LORD filled the temple' (2 Chr. 7:1) when Solomon completed the dedicatory prayer. Ezekiel's vision furnishes that temple with the 'glory' Presence (Ezek. 10:4) though whether or not it was anything merely mortal eyes could behold is doubtful. The date of the vision is about August–September 591 BC according to Ezekiel 8:1. As Ezekiel's vision presents it through the next four chapters the irremediable sins of the nation were driving the Presence away. The heart-rending spectacle, visible only to the prophet, shows the glory-Presence sorrowfully, heart-brokenly, reluctantly taking His leave – first from 'the cherub on which it rested to the threshold of the house' (Ezek. 9:3). Then he returned and did it again (10:4). Then as though taking a painful leave the glory 'went out from the threshold… and stood over the cherubim' (10:18). After that '…the glory of the LORD went up from the midst of the city and stood on the mountain [Olivet] that is on the east side of the city' (11:23) and

---

14. Irenaeus (in *Ante-Nicene Fathers*, ed. Roberts and Donaldson, 1885, repr. Peabody, Hendrickson Publ., 1994), *Against Heresies* 4.10.1.
15. A. A. Hodge, *Outlines of Theology* (New York: R. Carter and Brothers, 1860, repr. Grand Rapids: Eerdmans, 1957), pp. 170, 171.
16. Strong, *Systematic Theology*, pp. 319, 320.
17. J. Pelikan, *Christianity and Classical Culture*, pp. 210, 213.

presumably from that height departed for heaven – or at least disappeared. But Ezekiel was vouchsafed a promise of the return of the glory in the time of Israel's reformation and reconciliation when he beheld 'the glory of the God of Israel came from... the east: and his voice was like a noise of many waters' (Ezek. 43:2 KJV). Christians know that voice as that of the risen and glorified Jesus; 'his voice was like the sound of many waters' (Rev 1:15 RSV). Jesus likewise ascended from the Mount of Olives and, according to prophecy, there, according to respectable opinion, He shall return; 'On that day his feet shall stand on the Mount of Olives' (Zec. 14:4).

Interpreters will not all agree on the meaning of these very exciting prophetic revelations and I have no inspired insights. Yet they strongly suggest the presence of the Second Person of the Godhead in Israel's central sanctuary throughout its checkered history to the end of the first temple.

(3) He was present to David, who called Him 'Lord' (Ps. 110:1; cf. Matt. 22:41-5).

(4) He was 'with God' back in eternity 'past' (if we may use any word at all) through all duration (John 1:2) not only in co-existence but in the mutual Trinitarian fellowship throughout eternity.

B. As to His activity as the preexistent One: New Testament texts already cited as testimony to the fact all had something to say as to the activity of the preexistent Christ. It is no small matter that He was from the beginning 'with God.' He was a divine agent in creating the heavens and the earth, in preservation of the created universe, and in its providential governance.

Some more particular matters can create wonder in the pious heart as they receive attention. Moses' renunciation of the perquisites of a royal prince of Egypt is said to be a choice which esteemed 'the reproach of Christ greater wealth than the treasures of Egypt' (Heb. 11:26). What does this mean? F. Bleek in his *Lectures on Hebrews*, published in Berlin (1868), wrote: '[T]he reproach which Christ had to bear in his own person, and in his members.' Hence, comments Dean Alford:

> All Israel's reproach was Christ's reproach: Israel typified Christ... all Israel's sufferings as the people of God were Christ's... by that inclusion in Christ which they, his members before the Head was revealed; possessed... ever present in and among God's people.[18]

What did Jesus mean when He uttered the anguished appeal: 'O Jerusalem, Jerusalem, the city that kills the prophets and stones those who are sent to it! How often would I have gathered your children together as a hen gathers her brood under her wings, and you would not!' (Matt. 23:37)? The answer comes clear if we understand He was the One who inspired Jeremiah's urgent appeals and who sent the prophet 'Zechariah' (Matt. 23:35) to reprove the backslidden Joash, who then allowed the bold prophet to be stoned (2 Chr. 24:20), and He was the One who sent other prophets, likewise rejected (2 Chr. 24:19).

Not for proof as such, but to show how important the preexistence is to fully understand even some incidental features of Jesus' outlook on Himself, observe Jesus in verbal contest with the protesting Pharisees of Luke 15. They were offended that He received sinners and even ate with them. The crux of His defense was that there is joy *in heaven* when sinners repent and that, most significantly, before the throne of God. He is not really rebuking the Pharisees or vindicating Himself, rather Jesus is explaining how natural joy is and how normally business is carried on in heaven. To receive and rejoice over repentant sinners *as they had reproached Him for doing* is normal to heaven and its residents – of whom He has been one. This is simply heaven's normal operational procedure. And it is His also, because, as He said more than once, He was heaven come down to earth. He will ascend there later because He is the living bread that came down from heaven (John 6:41, 51).

---

18. Alford, *NT for English Readers* p. 1567.

4
The Deity of Christ, Part One: Introduction; Names and Attributes of Deity

The immensity of this subject requires some boundaries to the discussion in this chapter. A topic which fills about half the pages of the writings of the Fathers of the century before the Second Ecumenical Council (AD 381) obviously cannot be exhaustively treated here. Nor is it either desirable or necessary, as we shall see.

Principles and Approach to the Subject.

1. The deity of Christ is not an inference derived from cumulative evidence gained by inductive Bible research. Rather it is 'derived directly from statements concerning Him in the Bible. The references are so many and their meaning so plain that Christians of every shade of opinion have always regarded its affirmation as an absolute and indispensable requisite of their faith.'[1] For this subject recourse to the erudite tools that theologians and exegetes often deploy is neither necessary nor appropriate if the Bible is to control our thinking.

If arrangers of the New Testament canon had decided to put John's Gospel first instead of fourth, the New Testament would truly have opened at *the beginning* of Christology with these verses:

> In the beginning was the Word, and the Word was with God, and the Word was God. He was in the beginning with God. All things were made through him, and without him was not any thing made that was made.... And the Word became flesh and dwelt among us, and we have seen his glory, glory as of the only Son from the Father, full of grace and truth (John 1:1-3, 14).

Not that this is not plain enough, the same biblical author near the end of the *last* book of the New Testament says the One who ushers in the final judgment of this present order is One whose name is 'The Word of God' whose fierceness and wrath is the wrath of 'God the Almighty' and has the 'written' name of 'King of kings and Lord of lords' (Rev. 19:11-16). In another text the 'Christ Jesus' who stood 'before Pontius Pilate' is to have a second 'appearing' 'which he will display at the proper time – he who is the blessed and only Sovereign, the King of kings and Lord of lords, who alone has immortality, who dwells in unapproachable light, whom no one has ever seen or can see. To him be honor and eternal dominion' (1 Tim. 6:13-16). Such unmistakable assertions of the absolute deity of 'our Lord Jesus Christ' make it impossible knowingly to think the New Testament does not directly teach the deity of Christ.

---

1. 'Two Laymen on Christ's Deity,' *Christianity Today* (December 18, 1964), p. 11.

2. The New Testament nowhere goes out of the way to announce the deity of Christ, rather it is usually presented incidentally as something everybody on the inside of the Christian movement already understands. The deity of Christ was a matter of revelation not the fruit of reflection by Jesus' disciples as a liberal theory would have it. Nor is it the creation of a generation of Christians who created the 'myth' a generation or two after the Apostles died off, as skeptical scholars of our time would have it. And that revelation is primarily in the New Testament – all of it, really. It is true, of course, that there is some development in the way it is expressed. The manner of expression is related always to the purpose of introducing it. For example, the profound statement of condescension in incarnation at Philippians 2:5-9 is incidental to teaching unselfishness, humility and service to others. Paul is employing several features of the divine condescension for support of a moral lesson. In Romans 8:3 God 'sending his own Son in the likeness of sinful flesh' affirms Christ's deity (as eternal Son) only as part of a chain of argument for the doctrine of sanctification. It is assumed the Roman readers were already fully acquainted with Christ – as in Romans 9:5, 'God over all, blessed for ever' – and so on through all the Epistles and Revelation. B. B. Warfield developed this theme effectively in the article 'Person of Christ'[2] and in his article 'The Deity of Christ.'[3]

3. The exposition and arguments of this chapter are addressed primarily to those who have already acknowledged Jesus Christ as 'God and only Savior.' They may not yet be prepared to give a full account of why they believe Him to be so, but they know in their hearts who He is and, for deepening faith and strengthening assurance as well as resistance to erroneous views, they welcome evidence, proofs and analysis.

In most of the important matters of life fuller understanding comes after sufficient cause has produced knowledge and conviction. In the closing scene of Doctor Zhivago, the unhappy man sees the lady-love of his life fleetingly and only for a moment, through the window of his railway coach. She is walking slowly and the train is moving. He knows it is she and in the heightened excitement of the knowledge his weakened heart gives way and the poor doctor dies. Given a month to analyze how and why he knew it was she would have made him no more certain. His grounds were adequate. If granted time and opportunity we may suppose he could have written a book about her, for he 'knew' her much more intimately than he should have (cf. Gen. 4:1). So it is in recognizing one's signature on a check, or my father's picture in a photo of about 1915 – a smiling young man with mock ferocity swinging a double-bitted axe midair.

The church Fathers discussed the matter of Christ's deity and debated with errorists and heretics from the beginning. This was long before the strong affirmations of Christ's deity in the early creeds, confessions and definitions. If anything is plain about these orthodox writers it is their unanimous intention to teach, confess, affirm 1) nothing more or less than the apostolic Scriptures teach and 2) to preserve intact nothing more and nothing less than what the Apostles had taught in their churches. This explains the earnest vehemence of the writings of Athanasius, for example. It explains the careful brevity of the Nicene Creed and the Definition of Chalcedon as regards Christ's deity, humanity and the relation between them. They wished to preserve the first universal, if unsystematized consensus. Because of Paul's prominence in preserving that consensus in writing I cite the following rather lengthy passage:

> Written occasionally to one or another of the Christian communities... from twenty to forty years after the origin of Christianity, these letters reflect the conceptions which ruled in Christian communities of the time. Paul had known the Christian movement from its beginning; first from the outside... and then from the inside.... He was familiarly acquainted with the Apostles.... He explicitly declares the harmony of their teaching with his, and joins with his their testimony to the great facts which he proclaimed... The person of Jesus fills the whole horizon of his thought, and gathers to itself all his religious emotions. That Jesus was the Messiah [Gr. *Christos*] is the presupposition of all his speech of him and the Messianic title [English, *Christ*] has already become his proper name behind which his real personal name, Jesus, has retired. This Messiah is definitely represented as a divine being who has entered the world on a mission of mercy to sinful man... but... has ascended to the right hand of God, henceforth to rule as Lord of all.[4]

Hence, the present chapter is an effort in systematic form, and as succinctly as feasible, to set forth the faith of Christianity from remote antiquity to the present, for the living church today. 'All that Jesus is to the eye of faith'[5] is the adjusted focus of this chapter.

---

2. B.B. Warfield, art. 'Person of Christ' (1915), *ISBE v* (Grand Rapids, MI: Eerdmans, 1943), pp. 2338–2348.

3. B.B. Warfield, art. 'The Deity of Christ' *The Fundamentals: A Testimony to the Truth, ii*, chap. x (Los Angeles: The Bible Institute of Los Angeles, 1917), pp. 239–246.

4. B.B. Warfield, *The Person and Work of Christ* (Philadelphia: Presbyterian & Reformed, 1950), pp. 6, 7.

5. R. A. Cole, art. 'Christology,' *Zondervan Pictorial Encyclopedia of the Bible, i* ed. Merrill C. Tenney (Grand Rapids: Zondervan, 1975), p. 805.

4. This chapter, while not addressed directly to those who do not acknowledge Christ as Lord and God it is not without reference to them. After all, the very earliest theology, even in the New Testament was stimulated by the necessity of defining the faith against errors within and without the church. We must notice what the self-proclaimed Arians of old, Unitarians of yesterday and the liberal churchmen of today have to say about the texts of Scripture which they think show our Lord to be a mere man, even if an extraordinary one. To examine the academic Christology, prevailing in the university faculties of religion, where a third 'search for the historical Jesus' is now being vigorously pursued, would only be a barren waste of time for present purposes. The Jesus Seminar and writers of symposia like *The Myth of God Incarnate* may be safely ignored. They cannot be answered except for relatively brief periods, for in one lifetime the 'faith' of these self-appointed academic experts has changed its directions several times.

5. There are several types of evidence for the deity of Christ as the Bible presents Him: 1) the *names* He bears, 2) the *attributes* of deity He manifested, 3) the *works* of God He performed, 4) the *claims* He made for Himself, and 5) the *worship* which He received and accepted. These are the 'formal' proofs. While they are decisive as to the plain sense of the biblical texts, there are certain hermeneutical problems that require attention and the perversions of ignorance or of design by heretical groups call for response. These are the five consensual arguments, part of the legacy of centuries of Christian advocacy and apologetics. I suggest further 6) importance of the *cosmic functions* of Christ and 7) the underlying *assumptions* of all the New Testament literature.

Evidence of the Names He Bears.

The New Testament directly assigns names and titles for Christ, and name-like words, proper only for one who is God. Some very valuable treatments of the whole of Christology organize the data entirely about His names and titles.

1. *He is called God*. The most unambiguous possible designation of deity in the Greek New Testament is *theos* (God) with the article *ho* (the). Depending on the grammatical construction or emphasis, the same degree of clarity prevails without the article. In New Testament Greek, names usually have the definite article prefixed. When not accompanied by the article standard usage required a reason.

I shall rely heavily on the study of the late R. E. Brown, a renowned Roman Catholic scholar, for the technical dimensions of this matter.[6]

There are three passages which explicitly use *theos* of Jesus. I shall employ the KJV, precisely because it helpfully represents the distinction between second person singular (thee, thou) and plural (ye, you), which most recent Versions do not.

First is Hebrews 1:8, 9, which quotes the LXX of Psalm 45:6, 7. Our interest is in, 'But unto the Son he saith, Thy throne, O God, is for ever.' 'O God' translates *ho theos*, indicating deity in the most specific manner possible in Greek. It is clearly a vocative (mode of address) in the quoted LXX, parallel with the preceding verse where God is addressed 'O Mighty One.' Apparently the biases of some translators of the RSV New Testament 1952, emboldened them to turn the vocative noun into an attributive adjective ('thy divine throne'). But even the NEB perpetuated 'O God' and the same is still in the Revised English Bible and now the powers that be of publication have got religion and have restored an honest 'O God' in the New Revised Standard Version!

The second is John 20:28 where Thomas, face to face for the first time with the risen Christ, addresses Him, 'My Lord and my God!' Brown comments:

> This is the clearest example in the NT of the use of 'God' for Jesus... The scene is designed to serve as a climax to the Gospel... one at last gives expression to an adequate faith in Jesus... applying to Jesus the Greek equivalent of two terms applied to the God of the OT... in Psalm 35:23 where the Psalmist cries out: 'My God and my Lord [*Adonai*].' No devout Jew would have said it; or recorded it; nor would Jesus have approved it as he immediately did or have failed to rebuke it if not a true statement.[7]

The third is John 1:1, 'and the Word was God.' As we saw earlier John 1:14 and Revelation 19:11 ff. show exactly what the statement means. I quote the comment (probably by F. F. Bruce) in the *Christianity Today* article cited earlier.

---

6. R. E. Brown, 'Does the New Testament Call Jesus God,' *Theological Studies*, xxvi, 4, Dec., 1965. [I have not listed any journals or magazines in bibliography, RDC.]
7. Brown, ibid.

> Much is made by Arian amateur grammarians ['Jehovah's Witnesses'] of the omission of the definite article [here *theos* does not have it]. Such an omission is common with nouns in a precative [i.e. in a prayer] construction. To have used it would have equated the Word and the Word only with God, whereas without it the force is 'And the Word was Himself God'...[8]

There are several other texts which many scholars hold certainly employ *theos* or *ho theos* as designation for Jesus. Among these the strongest are Romans 9:5; Titus 2:13; 1 John 5:20, 21; Colossians 2:2; 2 Thessalonians 1:12; and 2 Peter 1:1. Also probably John 1:18 and more obscurely Galatians 2:20 (there is a textual difficulty) and Acts 20:28.

A problem arises. The word 'God' is occasionally used of some of God's creatures (angels and men) and occasionally in the Hebrew Old Testament as a kind of superlative, as in 'mountains of God' for high mountains (Ps. 36:6) or 'garden of God' (Ezek. 31:8, 9) for a fine garden, or a very strong man (Ezek. 31:11; 'mighty' in Hebrew is '*el*, God), etc. Does this weaken or invalidate the argument we propose? Jesus Himself seems to exacerbate the problem as reported in John 10:32-36 (though this is really *ad hominem*, debating the opponent on his own ground). He is alluding to the fact that in the Hebrew Bible local Israelite magistrates (judges), in several Old Testament passages, are called 'the gods' ('*elohim*) (Exod. 21:6; 22:8, 9, 28). The simple explanation is that the magistrate (Rom. 12:1) in civil government stands in God's place, viz.: Deuteronomy 19:17. In controversies 'both parties... shall appear before the LORD, before the priests and the judges who are in office in those days.' Judges (called '*elohim* in Exod. 21) 'judge not for man but for the LORD' (2 Chr. 19:6); 'the judgment is God's' (Deut. 1:17; cf. Isa. 3:13-15; Mic. 3:1-4; Jer. 22:1-4).

2. *Jesus is called the 'Son of God.'* This is common throughout the New Testament. That Jesus plainly approved of the name, exuberantly joyous that Peter confessed 'the name' (Matt. 16:16-19), makes Peter's 'confession' of high importance to the proper use of the name. On occasion Scripture refers to an ordinary human being as a son of God, or in plural as sons of God. Adam is listed in Jesus' genealogies as 'the son of God' (Luke 3:38; English only, not in Greek). There is no ambiguity about Luke's meaning – created by God. But as used in the Land of Israel in Jesus' time, 'the Son of God' or 'the Christ, the Son of God' meant 'God' as in Peter's confession. To use it of one's self was considered blasphemy (Matt. 26:63-66; John 5:18; 10:33-36; 19:6, 7). KJV is formally correct at Acts 4:30, 'thy holy *child* [emphasis added] Jesus' though NIV 'your holy *servant* [emphasis added] Jesus' helps the reader see the reference to Isaiah's prophecy of the *Servant of Jehovah* (Isa. 42–53, esp. 53:11, 'my righteous servant').

3. *Jesus is called 'only begotten Son* [emphasis added]' of God (mo-no-gen-ēs huios, John 1:18 – translated 'only begotten Son' in the KJV and most descended Versions). This familiar name, found also in John 3:16, has been the basis of some misunderstandings. Understood as though derived from *gennao*, to beget, the ancient church set forth the orthodox doctrine of the eternal begetting of the Son by the Father. This doctrine was formulated to protect the eternity of the Son of God. The Arians and their imitators through the centuries have used the phrase to prove the Son of God had a beginning in time. The Mormons have a doctrine that the Father in a literal physical way begat the Son. In recent times it has been proposed the word *monogenēs* is derived from *mono* (only, one, etc.) and *genos* (family, kind, kindred, race, etc.). Hence, 'only one of his kind,' i.e. unique. Thus the NIV has 'one and only' and the ESV 'only God' and 'only Son' in these passages. Jesus Christ then, according to this widely accepted view, is God's unique Son. Angels are His sons by creation, as is also Adam (Job 38:7; Luke 3:38). In the sense of mediate creation all men are God's *genos* (family, kindred, Acts 17:28). Jesus, however, is the Son of God in a sense that no other is. Not every conservative scholar agrees that unique or only is the precise sense of *monogenēs*. Yet this use of the word *monogenēs* in this sense is confirmed by Hebrews 11:17 where Isaac, brother of Ishmael, is called *monogenēs*. He was not an only begotten son, for Abraham begat Ishmael several years earlier and begat several more later (Gen. 25:1, 2; 1 Chr. 1:32), but he was a special son, enjoying a unique relationship to Abraham not shared by his older brother or his younger brothers.

4. *Jesus is called LORD (ku-ri-os).* The disciples customarily addressed Him this way, but perhaps only as a courtesy title like Sir or the German Herr so-and-so. The Hebrew word *Adhon*, translated lord, is such a title. Slightly modified in '*Adhonai*, it is an unmistakable title for the Almighty. And these words, through the Septuagint, come into the New Testament translated 'Lord.' The personal name of the God of Israel in written Hebrew is YHWH. We have no certain knowledge of the vowels because ancient Hebrews ceased to pronounce the name, substituting the name

---

8. 'Two Laymen on Christ's Deity.' *Christianity Today* (December 18, 1964), p. 16.

'*Adhonai* (Lord). The vowels of *Adhonai* were supplied to the Hebrew consonants in the written text; hence the word *Jehovah* of the English 'Authorized Version.' Yet no one can be sure *Yahweh* is correct either. The LXX uniformly renders the tetragrammeton (YHWH, Jehovah) by *kurios* and is therefore the prevalent referent. So it is in the New Testament. Unless there are clear contextual reasons, as in 1 Peter 3:6 ('Sara obeyed Abraham, calling him lord [*kurion*]'), New Testament use refers to the one true God of Abraham, Isaac and Jacob. (See Exodus 3:13-16.)

The prevalent use of *kurios* for Christ begins with the angel's announcement to the shepherds '…a Savior, who is Christ the Lord [*Christos kurios*]' (Luke 2:11). Jesus appropriated it (e.g. John 13:13), Paul employed it (Rom. 10:9) and prophesied universal acknowledgment of this name for Jesus Christ (Phil. 2:10).

Two important passages of Scripture enforce the certainty that the *kurios* of the New Testament is the Jehovah (YHWH) or Lord of the Old Testament. The first is probable; the second unmistakable. 1) The first is plain in the NIV rendering of Romans 10:9a, 'That if you confess with your mouth, "Jesus is Lord".' It does not say, 'address Jesus as Lord (sir)' but 'is Lord (*kurios*)' the uniform name for Israel's God, spelled all capitals in KJV, NIV, etc., LORD throughout the Old Testament. This name specifically designates the Jehovah (KJV) of the Old Testament. 2) The second is John 12:37-41. It comes at the very end of Jesus' public ministry, immediately before the Lord's Passion and death. John is summarizing all of Jesus' ministry of words and works. He says the rejection by the nation is fulfillment of Isaiah's prophecy (Isa. 53:1; cf. John 12:38). He says Israel's refusal to read the message of Jesus' many miracles is fulfillment of Isaiah 53:1. John attributes the cause to the hardening of the people's hearts rendering faith impossible and that this also was prophesied by the same Isaiah (Isa. 6:9,10) at the time of Isaiah's commissioning vision of Jehovah in the temple (See John 12:40, 41). Then the crux of the matter: John says in verse 41 the LORD (*Kurios*, YHWH) of Isaiah's vision (Isa. 6:1, 3, 8, 11, 12), before whom the seraphim cry 'Holy, holy, holy' is none other than Jesus: 'Isaiah said these things because he saw his glory and spoke of him' 'he saw Jesus' glory' NIV, (but the ESV and KJV are more exact).

The New Testament use of these four names, God, Son of God, only begotten Son, and Lord (*Kurios*) and supporting information are sufficient to establish beyond question that the names of Jesus Christ imply His full deity.

Scholarly criticism of recent generations, up to and including the authors of *The Myth of God Incarnate* and the *Jesus Seminar,* do not deny this. But this is the mythical Jesus, say the critics, produced by the 'creative reflections' of the first generations of Christians. I have read by now, I suppose, thousands of pages written by these busy denizens of apostate seminary faculties, religion departments of universities – and sadly – by some doubting Thomases in evangelical groups. I have followed the evolution of this debate through the last forty-some years in *Journal of Biblical Literature* articles and reviews, also in the literature of *Christology* and *The Life of Christ* without gaining many insights to the true meaning of Jesus. The arguments employed change every generation. For the past three or four decades they have changed as fast as graduate schools of religion could deposit new doctoral theses. To pursue these matters for purposes of professional scholarship, perhaps even apologetics, is of some value, but for theology Malcom Muggeridge's autobiography comes to mind: 'Chronicles of Wasted Time'.

Further New Testament evidence of the deity of Christ in His names is quite extensive. He is called *'the Lord of glory* [emphasis added]' (1 Cor. 2:8); in Psalm 24:1, 8-10 'the Lord of glory' is Jehovah. He is called *'the Holy One* [emphasis added]' (Acts 3:14 KJV), who in Hosea 11:9 is 'God and not a man, the Holy One.' Jesus is *'the first and the last* [emphasis added]' (Rev. 1:17, 18; 2:8), the 'LORD of hosts' in Isaiah 44:6. (Note a plurality in the Godhead in this verse, as also Isa. 48:12-16). Our Lord Jesus says, I am *'Alpha and Omega* [emphasis added]' (a Greek equivalent of A to Z in our alphabet, Rev 1:8 KJV; 22:13, 16). This is a cryptic way of saying, 'the first and the last.' The sonorous, rolling clauses of Psalm 90:1, 2 (KJV) may be applied directly to the Son of God, our Lord Jesus Christ: 'even from everlasting to everlasting, thou art God.'

Attributes of Deity Assigned to Christ.

The New Testament affirms attributes of Christ (directly and indirectly) that properly belong to God alone.

It is not appropriate to introduce here the problem of whether God's essence is knowable through divine attributes or not. Our only interest is to show that granting the theistic position, Christ is presented in the New Testament as possessing the attributes of the God of theism. If this is true, then we have a Christian theism. Since the attributes of personality, as such, are not in question – both God and man have them – we present discussion only of those attributes that are distinctive to God.

Jesus' several statements of His oneness with the Father bear upon this subject, especially John 16:15, 'All that the Father has is mine.' This is a stupendous claim. Nothing could be greater. This explains why in the previous verse (John 16:14) He could say that the work of the Holy Spirit is to glorify Christ: 'He will glorify me, for he will take what is mine and declare it to you.' Beyond Christ there is nothing to know about the character of God (John 14:9).

1. *Christ possessed the attribute of self-existence.* 'In him was life' (John 1:4) – in context this is a claim of divine life. 'I am ... the life' (John 14:6) does not say 'I have' but 'I am.' These verses must be understood against the background of the name Jehovah (*YaHWeH*) as explained in Exodus 3:13-15 and 6:2-9. 'Before Abraham was, I am' (John 8:58). The I Am of the burning bush is the same with the Lord Jesus Christ.

Peter informed the crowd at Pentecost, 'Ye killed the prince of life' – a paradoxical statement to be explained in relation to the divine purposes of the incarnation (see Matt. 20:28).

A problem is posed by Jesus' saying: 'For as the Father has life in himself, so he has granted the Son also to have life in himself' (John 5:26). Does this teach a doctrine of derived existence? Does it undercut the above statement of self-existence (aseity)?

There are two possible solutions to the problem. The more usual, and I think satisfactory, is that this describes the Father's act in giving life-in-Himself to Jesus *as man*. Self-existence could, by its very nature, be assigned only to One to whom it is germane, whose it properly is. This could never be a mere creature.

Another view holds that this and similar texts are referring to an *economic* (i.e. a matter of procedures) subordination of the Son to the Father which is eternal and is consistent with *substantial* equality as asserted in the great ecumenical creeds and definitions. (Dr Vincent Taylor devoted an immensely productive lifetime to this and other Christological doctrine. I furnish his very valuable discussion of this problem as an appendix to this chapter.)

2. *The New Testament affirms Christ possessed all God's attributes of immensity*. He is eternal, unchangeable, omnipresent, omniscient, omnipotent, perfect (nothing lacking) and incomprehensible.

a. Christ is *eternal*. Some of the passages which apply say: the Christ, as son of David, is to be called '*Everlasting Father* [emphasis added]' (Isa. 9:6); in God's house 'the son remains for ever' (John 8:35); eternal life is in God's Son (1 John 5:11; 1 John 1:2). Joined with texts affirming Christ's *eternal* preexistence the evidence is unmistakable. And it is interrelated to the doctrine of the Trinity (q.v.). 'Those who reject the one as speculation reject also the other.'[9] To refine the idea of eternal-eternity: as used of God it means without beginning or end, of created things, without end.

The early church debated this matter vigorously. I have discussed this matter somewhat in connection with the Trinity. New Testament Greek words for begotten, became, born, first born, first begotten seemed to indicate the Son of God had a beginning, some said, and had to be applied scripturally and understood Christologically when applied to One whom plain text said was an eternal Being, in the sense that God is eternal. I shall supply an appendix on this subject. Of these the most serious problem arises with first born (*prōtotokos*). Those which refer to Him as Mary's *prōtotokos* create no problem. The problem texts are: Rom. 8:29; Col. 1:15; Col. 1:18; cf. Ps. 89:27; Heb. 1:6; 12:23; Rev. 1:5. Colossians 1:15, the 'firstborn of all creation' is superficially the most likely to suggest Christ is a creature brought into existence before any other created beings. Several ancient heretical teachers and groups taught just that. Literally, first born of course means the first offspring produced by a male or female parent whether man or beast (Gen. 25:25 LXX; Luke 2:7, and several other examples). The literally 'born first' son was ordinarily heir of the family fortune and prior in position as well as order of birth. The sense of first in position is the sense in all the passages related to Christ, except the ones relating to birth by Mary. Even as first-born from the dead (Col. 1:18; and Rom. 1:5) this seems to be the case. In Colossians 1:15 and 18 Paul borrows the language of Psalm 89:27 (LXX) where the positional sense is indisputable.

b. Christ is *unchangeable*. In the familiar statement of Hebrews 13:8 ('Jesus Christ is the same yesterday and today and for ever'), though the name of the historic Jesus is used, it is clear the preexistent Person is meant. Similarly, Hebrews 1:10-12 shows the eternal Logos changed His position, but not His Person.

c. Christ is *omnipresent*. Jesus promised His disciples to be with them always (Matt. 18:20) and in the midst of every Christian gathering (Matt. 18:20); yet paradoxically, He has ascended to heaven to stay for awhile (Acts 3:21). He is 'all, and in all' (Col. 3:11). Since Jesus in His body ascended to heaven most Christians affirm that though He is 'really' present, especially in the memorial sacrament, He is so spiritually in the divine nature only.

---

9. G. C. H. Berkouwer, *The Person of Christ* (Grand Rapids, MI: Eerdmans, 1954), p. 184.

A body by reason of the permanent character of all bodies is always local and in one place at a time with limited spatial relationships. Jesus' body is now in heaven to stay for awhile (Acts 3:21; cf. 1:6-11). Yet He Himself is really present as a Person with His church and stands beside His missionaries, as the texts say. To support Luther's insistence on the material presence of Christ's body and blood 'in, with and under' the Eucharistic elements, many Lutherans have taught that while the body of Christ is not *omnipresent* (present everywhere), it is *ubiquitous* (present anywhere) when the Eucharist is enacted truly. Certain views of the church make more than our Lord intended by the vivid figure of the church as Christ's body, speaking of it very erroneously as a 'continuation of the incarnation.' Though widespread and persistent, both of these ideas lack the general endorsement of most orthodox theologians and I think are without any clear biblical support. A reading of reports of discussions between Lutherans and Calvinists of the Reformation era show, in my judgment, why no Lutherans have ever convinced any I know of except other Lutherans of the 'ubiquity' doctrine and I have personal knowledge of convinced Lutheran leaders who disagree with this teaching, opting for real, spiritual, *personal* presence in the elements of communion. Christ was with Israel personally and spiritually in the Exodus time, hence He is quite able to be with *us* in the same way today.

d. Christ was *Omniscient*. Though Colossians 2:3 says, 'in whom are hidden all the treasures... of... knowledge' and the disciples were convinced Jesus knew everything (John 16:30) and numerous New Testament reports illustrate His unusual knowledge (John 2:24, 25; 4:16-19; 6:4; 21:6; Rev. 2:2, 9, 13; 3:1, 8, 15; Matt. 17:24-7; Luke 5:22), a question arises: Are these passages sufficient to prove He was all-knowing in the state of humiliation?

There is a special mystery in this connection, for the Gospels seem to present Him as occasionally without information or seeking information. Certain of these cases involve no problem of omniscience, because a didactic purpose is involved. For example, His instruction to the Samaritan woman to call her non-existent husband (John 4:16) really demonstrates knowledge rather than ignorance, as well as a didactic purpose. See also John 6:5, 6. There may be texts that do demonstrate ignorance on some point, though all have been challenged by someone or other. If so, the explanation is to be found in the *kenosis* or humiliation of Christ, to be treated later in connection with the incarnation.

A special case is Mark 13:32: 'But concerning that day or that hour, no one knows, not even the angels in heaven, nor the Son, but only the Father.' Certain theologians, however, except this from 'kenosis' treatment in the following manner:

> Bengel, on Mark 13:32, adopts the explanation favored by Augustine, 'Christ's words may be understood to mean, that he does not know the time of the judgment day, because it was not among his instructions from the Father to *declare* the time. An apostle was able both to know and not to know one and the same thing, according to the different point of view ('I know that I shall abide,' Phil. 1:25): how much more Christ? [cf. Paul's 'I know not' in Phil. 1:22] 2 Cor. 2:2, to 'know' means to 'make known.' 'I determined to know nothing among you but Christ and him crucified.' The same is the meaning of 'know' in Gen. 22:12: 'Now I know that thou fearest God, seeing thou hast not withheld thy son from me.' God had made Abraham's faith to be known, by his trial.[10]

Some neo-orthodox writers today, while acknowledging His full deity, not infrequently assert that Jesus' omniscience was fully conditioned by His humanity in such a way as to be practically eliminated. In this way His authority on historical and literary questions is undermined.[11] The omniscience of the glorified Christ, as in Revelation 2:2, 9, 13; 3:1, 8, 15, etc., is acknowledged. It is the 'days of his flesh' on earth that are under question. These writers assert that His superior knowledge was only such as prophets have.

On purely doctrinal grounds it must be asserted on the contrary that if He was truth (John 14:6), then, as the perfect Savior, He never believed or taught error, or entered into complicity with it in any way ('If it were not so, would I have told you,' John 14:2). This is not to deny the mystery involved in Luke 2:52 ('increased in wisdom'). See later discussion of this question in connection with the incarnation.

e. Christ was *Omnipotent*. As in the case of omniscience, certain problems will be reserved for later discussion. If one accepts His essential deity on the grounds of direct statements, treated earlier, omnipotence logically follows. Yet as in the case of omniscience and omnipresence there are legitimate questions as to whether He employed these attributes of His divine nature in the state of humiliation. There is no doubt He claimed equality with God in power

---

10. W. G. T. Shedd, *Dogmatic Theology ii* (New York: Charles Scribner's Sons, 1894), p. 276 footnote.
11. Vincent Taylor, *The Person of Christ In New Testament Teaching* (London: Macmillan Co., 1958), pp. 104, 105.

(John 5:19). He is called *Pantokratōr*, Almighty, in Revelation (1:8; 22:12, 13). He demonstrated power such as only God has, over disease, death, the freaks of nature as the familiar Gospel stories illustrate. He even had full power, He said, over His own human existence (John 2:19, 20; 10:18).

f. The *Perfection* of Christ, without any conceivable shortcoming or limit is clearly taught, for example in Colossians 1:19 and 2:3, 9, 10 and Ephesians 3:8.

g. Finally Christ is said to possess the divine attribute of *incomprehensibility*. This is not to say Christ (or God) cannot be known adequately, by us sinners. It is to say that there is now and forever will be a *plus ultra*, more beyond. John 17:3 is clear that our possession of eternal life guarantees adequate knowledge of God and Christ. Christ claimed as Man fully to know the Father (Matt. 11:27) while Paul affirms the 'riches of Christ' are 'unsearchable' (Eph. 3:8) and the love of Christ for us 'surpasses' our 'knowledge' (Eph. 3:19).

3. *Christ possesses the moral attributes of God.* The Bible never makes a list of God's moral attributes. It does however, in our Lord's own words, affirm that only God is 'good' (Matt. 19:17, cf. Mark 10:18, Gr. *agathos* the opposite of evil, *ponēros*; Matt. 5:45). All the goodness of God is Christ's also – goodness in absolute degree. 'For in him the whole fullness of deity dwells bodily' (Col. 2:9 *en auto katoikei pan to plērōma tēs theotētos sōmatikōs*). In context this *plērōma* consists of those excellencies of God which an incipient 'gnosticism,' through false philosophy (v. 8) would affirm has nothing in common with men in bodies. But Christ Jesus has this fully as a human being with a body.

The way to see this perfect goodness is to read the Gospels. It is there seen in action.

It is proper also to note that moral excellencies can be analyzed and given names. Thus as God is holy, true, loving, righteous, faithful and merciful, so is Christ the Lord.

These virtues become in Him *practical* arguments for His Godhead of greater, *personal*, convincing weight to sinners whose hearts God has touched, than the proof texts for the metaphysical attributes. Like all truth of a basic sort, here truth is its own strongest argument: 'O, taste and see that the Lord is good!' (Ps. 34:8).

5
The Deity of Christ, Part Two: Works, Claims, Honors, Assumptions, Position of Deity

Christ's Works Exclusively and Uniquely of God Alone.

Christ performed *works* that are exclusively within God's power and privilege. This is related to the attributes of omniscience and omnipotence.

> We do not here speak of miracles which may be wrought by communicated power [such as the many miracles of Elijah and Elisha], but of such works as creation of the world, upholding of all things, the final raising of the dead, and the judging of all men. Power to perform these works cannot be delegated, for they are characteristic of omnipotence.[1]

Some of these works began in eternity past and are usually treated in connection with the doctrine of God's works and Christ's preexistence. 1) That He '*created* all things' has been noted (John 1:3; Col. 1:16; Heb. 1:10; 3:3, 4; cf. Rev. 3:14) as also that 2) 'in him all things hold together' (*preservation*) (Col. 1:17 RSV; see also Heb. 1:3). The forces of the world of space, time, energy and matter, such as mass attraction, centripetal and centrifugal force, which we call the laws of nature, 'are the habits of Christ, and nature is one organic whole, so that we can speak of a universe.'[2] 3) He also directs the course of history in what theology calls divine governance or *providence*. This is the sense of Hebrews 1:2, 'Through whom [Christ] he [God] made the ages' (NASV margin). 'Worlds' or 'ages' here is the plural of *aiōn*, which has been appropriated in English as 'eon.' So God through the Son made 'the eons' of geological time or of any other measurement. Thus the four works of God as regards the created universe except for decrees (predestination), which in Scripture is the distinct work of the Father, are all ascribed to Christ. In the symbolism of the Revelation it is the Lamb who has sole right to open the seven-sealed book of the consummation of history (Rev. 5:5) and whose agents say 'Come!' to the four horsemen of conquest, war, famine and death (Rev. 6:1, 5, 7, 9). The Lamb also comforts the martyrs in *heaven* (Rev. 6:9-17) and frightens 'those who dwell on the *earth* [emphasis added]' even while He seals the servants of God for their safety (Rev. 7:1-4).

Other distinctly divine prerogatives and powers assigned to Christ follow: 4) authority to forgive sin, a distinctly divine prerogative (Isa. 43:25), was manifest early in His public ministry in a very bold move (Mark 2:5-12), 5) power to bestow eternal life (John 10:28) and even to raise the dead – in the present age (Lazarus, John 11:25-44)

---

1. A. H. Strong, *Systematic Theology* (Valley Forge, PA: Judson Press, 1907), 319.
2. ibid., p. 311.

and at the 'last day' (John 5:21, 28, 29), a power inherently His according to John 5:21, not by delegated authority such as some clergy claim for the forgiving of sin. The New Testament makes a strong point of the fact that 6) Christ will be the presiding Judge in final judgment (John 5:22, 27; Acts 10:42; 17:31; and Matt. 25:31-46). Believers, who in some sense will share in this function (1 Cor. 6:3), are nevertheless to face Christ as their Judge after life on earth is over (2 Cor. 5:10).

Two other types of acts of omniscience and omnipotence are directed toward the aid of the believing church, namely 7) Jesus Himself builds and supports the church (Matt. 16:18; Eph. 4), and 8) He hears and answers prayer (John 14:14). All of these works of omnipotence and omniscience by nature belong to God alone as the LORD Himself argues at Isaiah 40:48.

The Claims, Honors, Assumptions and Deity of Christ Throughout the New Testament.

Christ made *claims* that clearly imply He thought of Himself as 'equal with the Father.'

This clear fact of Scripture is downplayed in the literature of current Gospels and New Testament criticism. Even some writers otherwise orthodox seem to fall over one another to deny He made any high claims for Himself. What did Jesus really think of Himself? The New Testament critics differ among themselves on many questions but most seem to agree on this matter. I cite the word of one reputed authority:

> The days are happily gone when that problem could be discussed in terms of 'the claims of Christ.' It is not only that the titles of dignity he used or accepted – Messiah, Son of Man, Son of God – are of doubtful meaning; the phrase itself is misleading, and even offensive. Jesus was not concerned to make 'claims' for himself. It was God and God's Kingdom that he preached. The Gospels have preserved for us a few intense utterances which give us passing glimpses into the mystery of his inner soul. We have to pass from the outer to the inner, and try to form some idea of how he judged his place and person from the total impress of his work and mission.[3]

It would be interesting to know by what name this author, whose own views are favorable to the doctrine of Christ's deity, would treat the following scriptural data if 'claims' are to be eschewed. Based on radical views of the origin of the Gospels this author and many others eliminate from the Gospels all direct claims or statements that Christ is God. This is supposed to have been an idea that only gradually dawned in the church's consciousness in later times – according to this class of interpreters.

The following remarks are directed to those who accept the Gospels as true and are acquainted with their contents, citing references but not quoting them. Any one who doubts may look up the verses in any standard Version and will find the assertions supported.

1. Jesus claimed authority over the laws of God and God's institutions on earth. Examples are the temple of God (Matt. 12:16), the holy Sabbath (Matt. 12:8), the law of God – think of His several 'Moses said, but I say' pronouncements (Matt. 5:31-34, 38, 39 with 7:28, 29) and even the kingdom of God (Matt. 16:19).

2. Jesus claimed to be the true object of saving faith. Men are to believe on Him just as they do the Father (John 14:1), as He said in a very solemn moment. Eternal life depends on knowing the Father and the Son of God (John 17:3) – the basis for Peter's claim, 'there is no other name under heaven given among men by which we must be saved' (Acts 4:12). Sometimes He points to Himself as the one true object of faith and devotion, saying, 'Come unto *me* [emphasis added]' (Matt. 11:28; John 3:36), 'love *me* [emphasis added]' (John 14:15). All other loyalties and ties of devotion on this earth are to yield to Him (Matt. 10:37-39) – no other gods on the shelf of idols. They must all come down and be trashed. God in Christ will not share His glory with another (Isa. 42:8; 48:11). These passages are conditioned by others wherein His power and glory are 'with the Father' (see John 17:5) where 'with' is Gr. *para*, alongside, i.e. equally. He Himself is the special Revealer of the Father, being the Author of each believer's faith, for He alone knows the Father and is the Way to Him (Matt. 11:25, 26; John 14:6).

3. He claimed to meet fully in Himself all the deepest needs of humanity. Not surprisingly most reports of these claims are in John's Gospel, designed to make believers of sinners (John 20:31). 'Come to me, all who labor and are heavy laden' (Matt. 11:28) says it all. In Christ those who come will find 'rest for your souls' (Matt. 11:28, 29). They will find the way to the Father God (John 14:19) and the 'way' to God (14:6), 'the light of the world' (8:12), 'the

---

3. S. Cave, *The Doctrine of the Person of Christ* (London: Gerald Duckworth, 1925), p. 11.

water' of 'life' (4:14; 7:37), 'the bread of life' (6:35, 51), 'the good shepherd' of souls (10:11) and the assurance of a voice they know (10:4-6), guidance (10:11; cf. Ps. 23), assurance of life forever (11:25, 26), fruitful living (15:5) and eternal safety in the 'Father's hand' (10:28, 29).

It has been said that Jesus really didn't make any claims for Himself (see earlier quotation from Cave). The exact contrary is true. If, of course, we eliminate the book of John as giving us the theological formulation of the second century (as in the Tübingen School) or as giving us the constructive theology of the Ephesian church in the late first century (cf. V. Taylor, *Person of Christ* and others), then the force of Jesus' claims is reduced. Even then it is not eliminated. See K. S. Latourette's treatment of Jesus and His effect on subsequent history.[4]

4. Christ received honor and worship due only to God. From a certain standpoint the whole Old Testament is designed to promote the idea that worship properly is directed only to the God of Abraham, Isaac and Jacob, the 'God, Most High' of Melchizedek and of all the cognomens of the Song of Moses (Deut. 32). The New Testament assumes that idea is correct and only occasionally reminds readers of it (Acts 10:25, 26; 12:21-23; 14:11-14; Matt. 4:8-10; Rev. 22:8, 9), but then directs that single eye of valid worship toward Christ. Sometimes He merely *accepted* worship (Matt. 14:31-33; 15:25-28; 28:9, 10, 16-18; John 19:35-39) but on others He *demanded* it (John 5:23) and the Father commanded even the angels to worship Christ (Heb. 1:6). The whole of creation will yet unite in worshipping Him (Phil. 2:10, 11; Rev. 5:9-14).

5. The deity of Christ is an assumption underlying every sentence in the New Testament. The abundance and prevalence of this assumption increases the difficulty of stating it. It is similar to the abundance and prevalence of salt in the seas of the world. Taste it, it is salty; weigh it in scales; test it by chemical analysis; bathe in it; boil a pot dry and perform these experiments in the Black Sea or the Gulf of Alaska; always, everywhere it contains salt and lots of it. To this point it is written in volume II of the famous *The Fundamentals*:

> The deity of Christ is in solution in every page of the New Testament. Every word that is spoken of Him, every word which He is reported to have spoken of Himself, is spoken on the assumption that He is God. And this is the reason why the 'criticism' which addresses itself to eliminating the testimony of the New Testament to the deity of our Lord has set itself a hopeless task. The New Testament itself would have to be eliminated. Nor can we get behind this testimony. Because the deity of Christ is the presupposition of every word of the New Testament, it is impossible to select words out of the New Testament from which to construct earlier documents in which the deity of Christ shall not be assumed.[5]

This has not kept the literary magicians of *Formegeschichte*, *Redactionsgeshischte*, the Bultmannians and their successors of the 'Jesus Seminar' from casting a 'trajectory' of Gospel fragments from Jesus and His friends through an assumed development from Jewish Christianity to Gentile Christianity to creation of a mythical divine messiah. At the present time, though many academics are consulting, competing for attention and publishing, not many Bible readers are listening. They have not erased the integrity of the New Testament. They have no evidence outside the New Testament and that is all against them. It cannot be suppressed in even the words of Jesus. His commonest self-designation is Son of Man. As such, Jesus' words, 'the Son of Man' sends out, not God's angels, but 'his angels,' any or all of them. At the Son of Man's behest the angels gather 'his elect' and 'all causes of sin and all law-breakers, and throw them into the fiery furnace' (Matt. 13:41, 42; 16:27; 24:31). This language cannot be expelled from the Jesus story nor explained by any theory except that He Himself said them. They have no appearance of being contrived to prove a point.

Dip into the waters of the New Testament ocean anywhere and this is what comes up in the bucket. The New Testament does not overtly prove the deity of its Subject, it presupposes it!

Even the National Council of Churches to date has not been inclined *officially* to deny the deity of Christ in its formal constitutional documents. The reason being, I suspect, that they have not found a way to do that without expelling both the New Testament and historic Christianity. As long as people read the New Testament, in or out of school, the conviction will remain with them that the New Testament is a gospel of Jesus Christ and a revelation of Him and that Jesus Christ is 'very God of very God' just as the creed affirms. Few will so decide on formally assembled inductive evidences or deductive syllogisms. To quote a wise author once more:

---

4. K. S. Latourette, *A History of the Expansion of Christianity, vol. i*, 'The First Five Centuries' (Grand Rapids, MI: Zondervan Publ., 1971), pp. 162–170.
5. B. B. Warfield, 'The Deity of Christ,' *The Fundamentals: A Testimony to the Truth, ii* (Los Angeles: The Bible Institute of L.A., 1917), p.243.

> We do not need to wait to analyse the ground of our convictions, any more than we need to analyse our food before it nourishes us; and we can soundly believe on evidence much mixed with error, just as we can thrive on food far from pure. The alchemy of the mind, as of the digestive tract, knows how to separate out from the mass what it requires for its support; and as we may live without any knowledge of chemistry so we may possess earnest convictions, without the slightest knowledge of logic.[6]

Hence the evidence one offers for belief in the deity of Christ may be inadequate and poorly stated, even though the evidence on which the faith rests may be irresistible.

6. The cosmic position and functions of the Christ of the New Testament testify to His Godhead. We may be brief. '[God] put all things (*ta panta*) under his feet, and gave him as head over all things [*ta panta*].' He is 'the fullness [to *plērōma*] of him [God] who fills all in all' (Eph. 1:22, 23). '[I]n him all things [*ta panta*] hold together' (Col. 1:17). 'For in him the whole fullness of deity dwells bodily' (Col. 2:9), and 'who is the head of all rule and authority' (Col. 2:10). Stephen sees him at the right hand of God (Acts 7:55). He is the 'brightness' (*apaugasma*) of God's glory and the 'express image' (*charactēr*) of God's 'person' (*hypostasis*) (Heb. 1:3 KJV). My mind cherishes the hours spent listening to lectures on those Greek words in seminary days and later acquainting myself with them in the Christian exegesis, theology and speculation through the ages. No one can acquaint himself with Christ's universal, cosmic position and function without knowing in his heart, such a Being is no less than God. Reject the conclusion if you wish, but in doing so also reject the New Testament.

Appendix I.

Vincent Taylor on the Economic Subordination of the Eternal Son.

After affirming that 'Christ is the divine Son of God in a relationship… of being and nature' Dr Taylor writes:

> Nevertheless, along with this exalted teaching, the same intractable element of subordination which we have already encountered in the Pauline Epistles and the Epistle to the Hebrews appears also in the Fourth Gospel. Indeed, it is present in a more emphatic form. Jesus is 'sanctified' and 'sent' into the world by the Father (John 10:36; cf. 17:18). His divine life, His authority to execute judgement, and His glory are all the Father's gifts (5:21f., 26f.; 17:22). The charge to lay down His life He has received from the Father (10:18). 'I can of myself do nothing' He says (5:30), and explicitly He declares, 'The Father is greater than I' (14:28). It is not possible to explain these sayings convincingly as reflecting the conditions of the incarnate life of Christ, for unlike St Paul the Evangelist does not think of that life as one of humiliation, except in so far as he thinks of the departure of the Son from the world as His glorifying (17:1, 5; 13:32). In the sayings quoted above, the context shows that in each case Christ is thinking of His glory as maintained during the conditions of His life on earth. In the same moment that He speaks of being consecrated and sent by the Father He asks if His claim to be the Son of God is regarded as blasphemy (10:36). His life-giving power, His authority to execute judgement, and His glory, although they are the Father's gifts, are divine aspects of the Son's incarnate life (cf. 5:21-27; 17:2). With reference to the Father's charge to lay down His life He says, 'I have power to lay it down, and I have power to take it again' (10:18). His statement that He can do nothing of Himself relates to His divine authority to execute judgement (5:30), and when He declares that the Father is greater than Himself, He is speaking of His going to Him (14:28). *The subordination, then, is not merely a temporary condition which obtains while He lives on earth, but an eternal relationship which is manifested amid the conditions of His human existence.*
>
> The eternal character of this relationship accentuates the subordination, but it also gives a clue to its true nature. It belongs to relationships of love which are interior to the life of the Godhead. It is as far as possible from the 'subordinationism' of the Arian controversies and the 'adoptionism' current in Spain and France towards the close of the eighth century. It is not a servant and master relationship, or that of an inferior and a superior, but that of two in perfect unity in an eternal fellowship of love. It is a state of being in which direction is the function of the one and obedience is that of the other in a relationship of love which robs direction of superiority and obedience of inferiority. It is our limited experience of such a unity which leads us to think of obedience as servility and of direction as lordship. And yet we are not without some knowledge of this unity. Even in military relationships in moments of extreme danger, and sometimes in industrial associations of long standing, it can be reflected; most of all in the highest expressions of human love in which service is perfect freedom.[7]

---

6. Warfield, ibid., pp. 240, 241.
7. Vincent Taylor, *The Person of Christ in New Testament Teaching* (London: Macmillan Co., 1958), pp. 104, 105.

Appendix II.
Principles for Writing About Christology.

By now readers know that this book of theology tries to get quickly to a positive presentation of a doctrine. Controversies over individual doctrines, history of the formation of individual loci and contemporary developments call for sufficient treatment to explain their part in the development of orthodox theology and to provide for systematic formulation of truth. What is true stands out for true in contrast to what is not true. We need to present as much as feasible about such matters but there are reasons why they are not major features here.

The best example in writing in this style may be John Calvin. Repeatedly he will obliquely or in summary fashion refer to some contemporary error, scholastic 'conceit' or ancient church Father's writing. Yet he rarely develops any false and inadequate views fully; only when it contributes *quickly* and *importantly* to his own theologizing. He says his task is to expound 'the whole sum of piety and whatever it is necessary to know in the doctrine of salvation.' The *Institutes* he called 'not a *summa of theology* but a *summa of piety*' – piety in the sense of praiseworthy devotion to God, a prerequisite for sound knowledge of God.[8] He cuts himself short repeatedly 'lest these remarks become unnecessarily prolix.'

We may emulate Paul's single-minded brevity. He would declare to the elders 'the whole counsel of God' not keeping back 'anything that was profitable.' He would warn of 'wolves' from outside who would threaten to devour the flock and teachers 'from among your own selves' who would try to divide the flock (Acts 20:20, 27, 29, 30). Yet in none of his Epistles do we learn more than the barest fragment of what these errorists taught or who they were. Neither Calvin nor Paul unnecessarily advertized heresies in their specifically theological writings. Calvin wrote at length in debates over doctrine and Scripture interpretation of his time. One may read more lengthy explanations of the errors and heresies he had to meet in his tracts and treatises and the like, published quite separate from his systematic theology, that is, *Institutes of the Christian Religion*. The errors of his own and earlier times are referred to but not discussed in detail in the *Institutes*. These tracts and polemical treatises were addressed to the people of his time in a direct manner both to friends and to adversaries. Practical apologetics is not absent, but scanty in the *Institutes*. I think Calvin shows an admirable impatience with perverse and stupid purveyors of error and heresies in the *Institutes*, though he is sometimes criticized nowadays for dismissing them briskly.

It is difficult to follow this course in Christology even after one decides where Christology belongs among the loci of theology.

The doctrine of the deity of Christ is almost a fugitive among the *loci* in books of systematic theology. Sometimes it is treated in connection with the Trinity as part of the doctrine of God, sometimes as a sub-point of the doctrine of the incarnation and sometimes nearly skipped altogether. Those who do not confess sincerely with Peter that he is 'the Christ, Son of the living God;' with Thomas that He is Lord and God, and with the creeds 'very God of very God' can be expected to marshal arguments against it. Over the past 200 years they have furnished a vastly complicated literature, designed to destroy. Any one who devotes less than an enormous amount of time quickly gets lost.

The literature of this 'Christology' whether believing and conservative or unbelieving and radical, as well as the ranges in-between, is amazingly enormous and growing by the day. In the process of writing a 300-page book on *The Life of Christ*,[9] an essay on Jesus' parables in a festschrift for Homer Kent and two on Gospels-criticism, several shelves of books on Christ and the Gospels have grown in my library. Not long ago I conducted a seminar course on contemporary 'Christologies.' Each of the class of thirty-one wrote on a different Christology. Now a few years later we might have found that many more! Most of the views we discussed then are now already out of date and unimportant even among the critical 'scholars' who keep the 'Jesus business' operating in universities and seminars, publishing and selling ephemeral books.

It is no wonder then, that teachers and writers of Christology can be tempted to slight the timeworn themes, evidences, arguments of our predecessors in order to keep up the 'exciting' developments in Gospels-criticism and new 'quests' for the historical Jesus and other projects unproductive of substantive Christian theology.

---

8. John Calvin, *Institutes of the Christian Religion*, ed. John i. McNeil, trans. and ed. Ford L. Battles (Philadelphia: Westminster Press, 1960), *Introduction*, pp. i, ii, iii.
9. R. D. Culver, *The Life of Christ* (Grand Rapids, MI: Baker Book House, 1976; enlarged edition with title, *The Earthly Career of Jesus, The Christ)*. See Bibiography.

Arguments against using the plain sense of the Bible, especially the New Testament, for the full deity of Christ as they have developed from the eighteenth-century Enlightenment to the present are chiefly five. 1) Jesus Himself did not make claims for Himself, even as reported in the Gospels, though some others in the story said He was God. 2) The parts of the Gospels in which the author or others in the story say He was God are mythological – fictitious, fabricated to support some religious opinion. 3) These mythological features are the creation of the early church after it became chiefly Hellenistic-Gentile in membership. The members brought the 'incarnation' myths of paganism with them into the church and Christianized them into the myths of God incarnate. 4) It is impossible for God to *become* a man. God and man are on incommensurable levels of being (the incarnation is defined erroneously and declared impossible thereby). 5) Modern people know what previous generations did not, that the supernatural does not exist, or even if it does cannot be empirically verified, hence it cannot be accepted by thinking, educated, modern people as true.

These and other arguments have been effectively answered by conservative New Testament scholars. I recommend the chapters and bibliography in G. E. Ladd's *A Theology of the New Testament*. Millard Erickson's (*Christian Theology*, chap. 31) is helpful in laying out the critical approaches and answering the currently reigning theories as of 1980. Lewis and Demarest (*Integrative Theology*, II, chaps. 5 and 6) traces the history of heresies and criticism in an orderly manner. Their principles of theologizing emphasize these matters.

There are precedents for coming immediately to a positively constructed spiritual doctrine of our Lord's deity. Long before the early church formulated a doctrine of the Trinity or phrased a careful statement of the incarnation (they came more or less together in the fourth and fifth centuries – AD 322–431) the deity of Christ was 'believed, taught and confessed' (J. Pelikan) every time Christians met together for worship. 'The most primitive confession had been Jesus Christ is Lord [cites Rom. 10:9; Phil. 2:11] and its import had been elaborated and deepened in the apostolic age.'[10] Of course they confessed His perfect manhood too. For the first confessors His humanity needed no proof, in fact that was all some of His enemies could see and it is still so today. It is no evidence of Ebionism to lay out clearly the scriptural evidences of His full deity, then move on to His humanity.

Our generation, largely without any veritable God 'in their thinking' worthy of worship but with multitudes of diminutive gods and goddesses of their own making, fleeting heroes and anti-heroes of sports and entertainment, need to meet the 'Alpha and Omega' whom John saw on Patmos. 'Jesus Christ… is Lord to Christians in the same sense Jehovah was Lord to the Hebrews… We have but one Lord: and Jesus Christ is Lord.'[11] The resurrection of the Lord assured their hearts He was 'the Son of God with power' (Rom. 1:3, 4). Said Bishop Charles Gore in the Bampton Lectures of 1891: 'The confession of Thomas after the resurrection… "my Lord and my God" is no less representative than the earlier confession of Peter… "Thou art the Christ of God," – the Christ, the Son of the living God.' Gore goes on to say Matthew's record of Jesus' last words 'gave permanence and security to their highest thoughts of Him as Son of God, by formulating the name, or revelation of God for all time as "the name of the Father and of the Son and of the Holy Ghost."' He says this persisted after Pentecost: 'The apostles had no doubt at all that Jesus Christ as Son of God was the summary object of faith and worship.'[12]

The following paragraph from a Christmas essay by an evangelical Christian philosopher (Ph.D.) errs in assuming the divine nature became *also* human nature: his philosophy is correct, but his definition of the incarnation incorrect. The divine Person, the *Logos*, added human nature to the Person. The natures are unmixed, though joined to the Person. I shall leave the author unidentified,

> Hardly any doctrine is more basic to biblical historic Christianity than the proposition that Jesus Christ was the God-man. When Jesus was born, God became incarnate. The Lord was still fully God and yet he became fully man. Philosophically, all this is utter nonsense and totally impossible. It isn't even conceivable. Historically, nonetheless, it is profoundly true and gloriously factual. Would it interest you to know that philosophically – more specifically, metaphysically or ontologically – this is utter nonsense? The fact of the matter is that according to all of which human reasoning is capable and according to all logical categories, it is impossible that the same being could be both God and also man. What philosophers have since the days of Aristotle called the basic laws of thought all contradict the idea. The law of identity says a thing is itself and nothing else. The law of contradiction asserts that a thing cannot be both itself and not itself. The law of excluded middle has it that a thing is either itself or not itself, but it cannot be something in the middle.

---

10. J. N. D. Kelly, *Early Christian Doctrines, Revised Edition* (San Francisco and New York, 1978), p. 138.
11. C. A. Hodge, *Systematic Theology i* (Grand Rapids, MI: Eerdmans, repr. 1970), p. 496.
12. Charles Gore, *The Incarnation of the Son of God* (London: John Murray, 1903), p. 15.

My treatment of the questions of Christology thus far has been frankly traditional, as systematic as I can make it and supportive of the creeds of the ancient church, that is, dogmatic in the proper sense. Thorough acquaintance with the doctrines of Christianity, biblically derived, historically shaped and systematically arranged is the very substance of systematic theology. Reference to contrary views of individual doctrines, how they are defended and how answered, should be employed to clarify sound doctrine not simply to inform. This is the way theology has been taught under church sponsorship (not university) for many generations. I was taught that way. Through the wilderness of competing Christologies since I finished seminary in the midst of the Second World War, the positive instruction of a master teacher of a sound Christology, 'biblically derived, historically shaped (respect for the creeds and definitions of ancient and Protestant orthodoxy) and systematically arranged' (Calvin to Thomas Oden) has been thoroughly adequate. Since then duty and inclination have driven me not only to read the competing literature but to teach in elective courses, also to write some about it. I emphasize, however, grounding in the truth should come first. One of the indirect benefits of this approach is the relatively smaller length of treatment. Multi-volume sets of theology cannot be read within the bounds of a seminary course. I think the 12 basic volumes of Barth's *Dogmatics*, some running to 900 pages, as a practical tool for ministers and missionaries, are an absurdity.

Further, through the ages, sound theology has sometimes been stimulated by doctrinal attacks from without the church and within it. This is observable in the New Testament itself. For example, Galatians was written to enlarge the doctrine of salvation by grace alone, through Christ alone, by faith alone. In the process Paul managed to address some of the points made by the Judaizing legalists, but we don't know the name of one of the false teachers in Galatia, where they came from for sure, or even the main points of their arguments, not even where the disputes took place, for certain. Colossians was in part composed to fortify the believers against what was likely an essentially pagan philosophy similar if not identical with Gnosticism. We infer (can't be sure) a mystical, somewhat pantheistic form of religion seeking to enforce another sort of legalism, was the foe. Again we have no names, no schools of thought or leaders of thought mentioned. Paul did not promote these errorists by advertizing their books and their scholastic lineage by leading off with pages about them. Imagine how famous these heretics might have become immediately if Paul, the consummate theologian, had conducted a seminar about them with the 'undergraduates' of Galatia and Colossae! Theology, however, would immediately have become a department of apologetics instead of the other way around!

Christology is the central area of Christian doctrine and of our religion as well. Hence in these last days it has become the focus of attention from those who would weaken the doctrine by revival of ancient errors or destroy it by erasing the time-honored orthodoxy of Nicea, Constantinople, Ephesus and Chalcedon, the Reformers and the faithful Protestant evangelical authors.

Adequately to trace the origins of these movements and to describe their teachings, furnishing proposed philosophical answers is not in my judgment the proper project of a book of basic theology.

Appendix III.

A Necessary Digression.

A soundly evangelical Christology rests on the reliability of the Gospels as truthful reports of the career, works and words of Jesus and the rest of the New Testament as dependable, authoritative (apostolic) interpretation of Christ, His works and words. Over the past century and more, a literature, too large to report here, has grown up which, denying the reliability of the Gospels and the Epistles as apostolic interpretation, has sought to disengage the Gospels' reports of Jesus' self-consciousness of Messiahship and divinity. Some of this literature would disconnect the high Christology of the rest of the New Testament from the first Jewish generation of believers and the leadership of the eyewitnesses as reported in Acts 1–12. The acknowledged high view of Jesus in the canonical writings was imported, they say, from various sources present in the Roman world into the belief system of the early church after it was no longer dominated by the beliefs of the Jewish church at Jerusalem and groups emanating from that matrix. We shall have occasion from time to time to call attention to these critical views and the conservative scholarship that has responded to them.

Competent conservative scholars have shown that quite to the contrary the pre-Pauline church (i.e. the first generation of believers, mainly Jewish) is the source of the testimonies to His Person given permanent form in the New Testament. It took several generations – down to the Ecumenical Council of Nicea (AD 325) and First

Constantinople (AD 381) and Chalcedon (AD 451) to work it out and give it permanent theological expression. Yet there is nothing in these creeds and definitions not assumed or implied or stated in the New Testament records. A condensed, relatively brief and thorough presentation of this matter, not superseded by any more recent work is *The Christology of Early Jewish Christianity* by Richard N. Longenecker (1970).

Longenecker concludes (in part):

> It has become popular of late to argue for the discontinuity of Christological conviction between Jesus, the Aramaic church in Palestine, and Hellenistic Christianity (whether Jewish, Gentile, or even Pauline). But our study has shown that while Christology of the earliest Jewish believers was primarily functional, it presupposed and carried in substratum ontological commitments; that while it received extensive development even within the Jewish Christian cycle of witness, that development was of the nature of explication and not deviation; that while it spoke mainly in terms understandable within a Jewish milieu, the proclamation of Christ in the Gentile mission in terms understandable in that context was in essentials not unfaithful to the earlier preaching; and that there is more than an implicit continuity existing between the self-consciousness of Jesus, the convictions of the earliest Jewish Christians regarding Jesus, and the affirmations of Paul in the Gospel mission.[13]

That long sentence might be compressed to assert: what we read in the Gospels and Epistles about Jesus is really what Jesus thought of Himself, what the first Christians accepted as true, and what the sermons in Acts and Paul's sermons truly mean to say.

---

13. R. N. Longenecker, *The Christology of Early Jewish Christianity*, (London: SCM Press, 1970) p.155

6
Anthropotēs, the Human Nature of Christ

Forty years after Jesus ascended to heaven Paul was appealing to the received consensus of believers everywhere when he addressed Timothy, his suffragan at Ephesus, about the human nature of Jesus in these words: 'For there is one God, and there is one mediator between God and man, Christ Jesus, himself man' (1 Tim. 2:5, NEB). Perhaps better than any other text of Scripture these words starkly isolate and emphasize the human nature of Jesus – His fully authentic membership in the human race. F. C. Baur (1792–1860) founder of the 'Tuebingen School of Theology' thought he found the Hegelian categories of thesis-antithesis-synthesis supported in this verse, excluding Jesus from the category of God. Ancient Monarchians and Socinians (the Unitarians of Reformation times) thought the text supported their opposition to the doctrine of the triune God. This, of course, is rejected with scorn by those who have read the whole chapter.

The verse is part of an exhortation to pray not only for kings and those in high places but for 'all men' (*pantōn anthrōpōn*, the generic noun for the human race, v. 1). Paul exhorts us to do this because God wishes 'all men' (*pantas anthrōpous*) to be saved (v. 4). There is a member of our race, 'himself man' (*anthrōpos*, singular, generic mankind) who became the 'go between' of God and men (*anthrōpon*, plural, generic, mankind). This Mediator, the passage goes on to say, 'gave himself a ransom for all [mankind]' (v. 6).

There is no possibility that Paul entertained any doubt of the Lord's full deity as well as humanity, for not many lines further on is one of the most outstanding statements of Christ's preexistence and deity (1 Tim. 3:16).

Jesus' maleness is not in view but His humanness, veritable human nature. Paul employs the Greek word for man as male often in his writings and does so three verses further on in specifying that prayer for all mankind is especially a *male* duty (1 Tim. 2:8). The NEB highlights this with a paraphrase, 'that everywhere prayers be said by the men [*andras*, genetive plural of *aner*] of the congregation' (1 Tim. 2:8) while the women (*gunaikas*, plural of *gunē*) have other duties (1 Tim. 2:9). This is a 'complementarian' text, assigning one spiritual duty for man, male and others for man, female.

So if any passage in the Bible lays out the fact of Jesus' complete, unimpaired humanity it is this one. We shall recur to it frequently.

The Earthly Jesus.

In the Epistles.

The Epistles of the New Testament assume the readers have knowledge of the earthly life and career of Jesus in the Land of Israel. It is not without significance that the first extensive report of the preached message, or *kērygma* (Acts 10:34-43), consisted chiefly of the story of who Jesus was; where He lived and worked; when He began His public ministry; His special relation to God; His mission of divine mercy in Galilee, Judaea and Jerusalem; His death 'in the country of the Jews' by crucifixion; His resurrection 'on the third day'; the apostolic witness; His command to preach 'to *the people*' (*tō laō*, in this case the Jewish people, not *tois laois*, to the peoples); the Old Testament prophecies; the remission of sins for 'everyone who believes in him.' There can be no doubt this outline, consisting largely of a sketch of Jesus' human, earthly career, was henceforth proclaimed, with enlargement by the apostolic witnesses wherever the gospel was preached and congregations of believers formed – and that was 'everywhere' (Mark 16:20).

The Epistles of Peter and the Epistle to the Hebrews show that both authors wrote with very full knowledge of Jesus' life on earth and of His career, though neither gives many details. The author of Hebrews knows of His suffering and death (2:9), that He was 'the seed of Abraham' (2:16), 'Jesus, the Son of God' (4:14), 'holy, harmless, undefiled, separate from sinners' (7:26 KJV); the body of Christ a sacrifice to God (10:5-10); Jesus' crucifixion and later exaltation (12:2). Peter gives a rather complete, brief summary of the events of the Lord's Passion (1 Peter 2:21-25).

All these messages of concern for moral and spiritual welfare assume the facts of the earthly life and career are about as familiar to the readers as to the writers.

B. B. Warfield pointed out Paul had no occasion to enter into the details of Christ's earthly life, 'But he shows himself fully familiar with them and incidentally conveys a vivid portrait of Christ's personality.' If one were to read all of Paul's Epistles one would learn Jesus was a descendant of David, born of a woman like everyone else, humbly lived out His life subject to the Mosaic law, as every other observant Jew, and died on a cross. Though Paul quotes only one of Jesus' sayings (and that in Luke's report of him, Acts 20:35) he is aware of many more, which he praises elsewhere as 'wholesome words' necessary for godliness (1 Tim. 6:3 KJV). Paul knows the details of the Last Supper of Jesus with his Apostles (1 Cor. 10, 11) and of water baptism. He never assays to inform about these details, rather he assumes they are already well known among Christians everywhere.

In the Gospels.

Luke, who probably wrote his Gospel sometime in the AD 60s before the execution of Paul, begins his narrative with a formal declaration that the story of Jesus' career from annunciation to Elizabeth and to Mary on to the ascension are matters already 'most surely believed among us' (Luke 1:1 KJV). Though Matthew and Mark (who may have written a bit earlier) do not say so, they certainly assumed the same narrative.

It is beyond the scope of this chapter to trace it all out, but the incidental references in all the Epistles are in full agreement with the formal treatises called Gospels. Only a few years at most after the bulk of the Epistles had appeared in places as far apart as Rome and Colosse, all this literature, except possibly the fourth Gospel and the other Johannine writings, came into existence in various places and from several authors writing independently except for casual contacts. *They were not collaborators.* There was, therefore, a commonly received knowledge of our Lord's person, words, works and career previous to the New Testament, made known throughout 'the world' (Mark 16:15, 16) through an acknowledged tradition. Oral transmission of the basic historical content of the Gospels and the doctrines of Christianity which interpret that history clearly preceded the written New Testament. There were indeed a primitive *kērygma* (preached gospel) and a confessed *didachē* (teaching, doctrine), both apostolic, previous in time to apostolic and prophetic New Testament Scripture.

The Gospels are not biographies, but regarding the period of His ministry they supply sufficient details of travels, discourse, miracles and conversations within sufficient chronological and geographical framework to make Jesus for all time the best-known figure of antiquity. It is important, for:

> [I]f the elements of time and space are stricken from the Gospels, the Lord's life ceases to be a truly human and intelligible one; He becomes only a wandering voice. The more fully we know the outward circumstances

of His life, and His relations to those around Him, the more do His words gain in significance and attest His discernment and wisdom. Thus it is of importance to know, so far as we are able, both the times and places of His utterances; and the labor spent in this study is not idle, but will yield rich reward.[1]

Emphasis on Jesus' Death.

One may speak of a 'Life of Jesus' only in a modified sense, however. The only sources available are the Gospels and though each contains some biographical information, only one incident from His life before opening His ministry is reported. For the rest we have the two birth narratives (Matthew and Luke) and the story of His public career. The latter concentrates on His Passion, death and resurrection. Taking the arrival at Bethany, less than a week before the crucifixion, as the beginning of the Passion narrative, John devotes the last ten of his twenty-one chapters to it, Matthew, chapters 21-28; Mark 11-16; and Luke 11:29 onward to chapter 24. About one-half of John and one-third of the Synoptics are devoted to Jesus' death on the cross and events immediately before and after. The writers report in detail how Jesus exerted Himself repeatedly during the last six months to prepare the Twelve for His inevitable death and resurrection.

The Gospels, though in a sense tragic narratives, have nothing at all characteristic of the dramatic tragedies of ancient writers. Plutarch's biographical *Lives* are quite unlike the four Gospels. They are *Gospels*, messages of good news for sinners everywhere on earth. The purposes of each writer – Matthew, Mark, Luke and John, whatever his emphasis, were subservient to the principle of salvation, viz.: 'you shall call his name Jesus, for he will save his people from their sins' (Matt. 1:21); 'to seek and to save that which was lost' (Luke 19:10); 'to give his life a ransom for many' (Matt. 20:28).

Redaction Criticism is an effort to get behind the Gospels to the true life and sayings of Jesus on the theory the authors slanted their writings *tendentiously*, to support what each thought would support views of Jesus current in their time but not necessarily original with Jesus and the circle of His first disciples. We agree each had different aspects to emphasize, but disagree they are tendentious (distorted details to prove a point) or are of late origin. And they are in complete agreement that the events of Passion Week, Jesus' death and resurrection are the climax and central meaning of each. That there is a distinct theological emphasis of each Gospel, each contributing something unique about the meaning of Jesus and His redemptive work, is a commonplace of New Testament scholarship from antiquity. See, for example, M. C. Tenney, *The Genius of The Gospels*.

Chronology of Jesus' Ministry.

Careful scholars have found sufficient information in the Gospels for dating His birth shortly before the death of Herod the Great (4 BC) and Jesus' death, probably at AD 30: and for a tentative framework of a ministry of three and a half years.

Except for the Gospel of John, almost nothing could be ascertained as to the precise length of our Lord's public career. On the basis of John's data, several chronologies of our Lord's ministry have been proposed.

There is an ancient one-year theory. A certain Ptolemy, disciple of the famous ancient Gnostic Valentinus, taught this theory, basing his argument probably on the silence of the three Synoptics and on a bizarre interpretation of Jesus' remark about 'the year of the Lord's favor' (Luke 4:19).

There is also an ancient ten-to twenty-year theory. Irenaeus (second century) refuted Ptolemy, arguing from 'about thirty years of age' (Luke 3:23) and 'not yet fifty years old' (John 8:57) that Jesus' ministry lasted between ten and twenty years.

On the basis of John's more complete data, in modern times the most generally accepted chronology takes as starting point Jesus' baptism by John a few months before Passover in March/April AD 27 and ends with His crucifixion on the day (by Jewish reckoning) of the 'last Passover' in AD 30.

It is safe to affirm that Jesus' baptism took place within a year of the opening of John's ministry. John began his ministry 'In the fifteenth year of the reign of Tiberius Caesar' (Luke 3:1). According to the method of counting employed in the eastern provinces of the Empire, reckoning would start with Tiberius's brief co-regency with Augustus, his fifteenth year being the calendar year (by modern reckoning) of AD 26. Jesus came for baptism some weeks, at least, before the next following Passover. If He was baptized earlier then it was in AD 26, if in the month

---

1. S. J. Andrews, *The Life of Our Lord Upon the Earth*, rev. ed. (New York: Scribner's Sons, 1891).

of January (as many scholars argue), then very early in AD 27. At this time He was 'about thirty years of age.' The December of His birth thirtysome years before would have been in 5 BC (from 1 BC to AD 1 is only one year). Passover falls in the Jewish month Nisan (Exod. 12:6) (formerly called Abib), our March/April.

This first Passover of His public career is mentioned only at John 2:13-23. The second is unmentioned by John, but Jesus' reference to 'four months' to 'harvest' in John 4:35 suggests that the narrative has moved on to the month Shebat (January/February) of AD 28. The next feast mentioned simply as 'a feast' (John 5:1) was almost surely (as idiom indicates) tabernacles, celebrated in autumn (Tishri, September/October). So though John does not mention the second Passover, he has rather clearly, if inadvertently, indicated its passing. Another close-to-certain indication of the passing of a second but (cf. Mark 2:23) unmentioned Passover is the incident of Luke 6, in which the disciples aroused the criticism of certain Pharisees by plucking ears of ripening grain. In the Holy Land small grains ripen shortly after a late Passover. The narrative does not appear to allow that Passover to be the one either of John 2 or of John 6:4. It has to fall between.

The third Passover (AD 29) is distinctly mentioned (John 6:4). The following context of John 6 treats incidents of His pilgrimage to Jerusalem to attend this Passover. Six months later He was again at Jerusalem for the feast of tabernacles (John 7:1, 14). Two months after that (Kislev, November/December) He was yet again in Jerusalem for the feast of dedication (John 10:22).

The narrative of events surrounding the last Passover, the fourth of His public career according to our reckoning, is the climax of each of the Gospels and provides the framework for the great bulk of the four accounts. They each trace the climactic development of events up to His death by crucifixion on the day before the evening when the whole of Jewry consumed their Paschal lambs 'without spot and without blemish.' This was in Nisan (March/April) AD 30.

The above is the most commonly received opinion – endorsed in a general way by the present author. It must be admitted, however, that even aside from emphasis in the Gospels on the last week, there seems to be a disproportionate amount of narrative, sermons, and discourses crowded into the last twelve months. But acknowledging the Gospels' emphasis on Jesus' death and associated happenings, this is quite to be expected. Some remove the difficulty by postulating still another Passover between the third and the final one, placing it shortly after the feeding of the 5,000 in Galilee. This requires a ministry of over four years. In support it is noted that John does not refer to the second Passover, though we know it took place before the third Passover of John 6:4, hence, no *a priori* objection to another un-noted Passover can be raised. In this way space is opened up for all the happenings from Mark 6:30; Luke 9:10; Matthew 14:13; and John 6:1 to the end of His ministry. Arguments are impressive but not compelling. Let us at least tentatively accept the traditional view that the Lord's public career lasted three years and three or four months, from His baptism to the crucifixion, meanwhile acknowledging that we are dealing with possibilities and probabilities rather than certainties.[2]

Authentic, Common Humanity on Display.

The genuine humanity of Jesus is displayed in fascinating though incidental detail in Luke, especially in the largest single block of His teaching activity in any of the Gospels, Luke 9:51–19:27. This falls chronologically in the last six months. We know most of this time was spent in Trans-Jordan (Peraea), though Luke's report is singularly free of geographical and chronological details. Luke is plainly interested in giving his readers extensive knowledge of typical, significant examples of Jesus' teaching.

Here as nowhere else we meet the human mind of Jesus, as well as the ancient, Palestinian, Jewish world in which His thoughts moved. These chapters furnish likewise the cultural patterns of the people, even for the casual reader.[3]

These chapters also show how fully Jesus was a part of that particular local human culture. When the woman at the well exclaimed 'How is it that you, a Jew…?', she too was thinking and speaking out of a very localized culture. She saw Him as the Gospels reveal Him and as we must see Him, not as a great cosmopolitan character, but as a Palestinian Jew. In fact, His culture may be described as that of a rural Galilean Jew. Jesus as seen by contemporaries was no cosmopolitan world-citizen. He had almost no intercourse with Gentiles. He never travelled more than a few miles from His childhood home. To summarize: Jesus participated in ordinary human nature the same way we all do. He was every inch a male, not androgynous (male-female).

---

2. I have discussed these matters more fully in *The Life of Christ* (Grand Rapids, MI: Baker Book House, 1976. See bibliography).
3. I discuss this in Excursus 10, 'Local Human Culture in Jesus' Discourses,' *The Life of Christ*, pp. 189–192.

That He was male rather than female or androgynous poses no problem for any one who takes Paul's teaching of the relation of female to male (1 Tim. 2:13; 1 Cor. 11:2-12) seriously as well as the narrative in Genesis 2 and 3.[4]

It is precisely because of these facts that His teachings are timeless. They are truly set in a single culture. The authors of the Gospels do not try to make of Jesus a sophisticated, urbane man of universal culture. There really can be no such person. Each of us also is a creature of a local culture. To the degree we are not, we tend to be disoriented, deracinated, without roots in any stable soil. By incarnation He became *man*, yet to do so He had to become an individual *man*. It is as such that He is the cosmic Christ, Savior of the world.

Across the distance of two millennia and the barriers between ancient oriental and modern Western culture, to say nothing of the distance between twenty-first-century urban life and ancient rural village life, the themes plainly come through.

The Theological Doctrine of the Humanity of Christ.

There is an historical dogma of the humanity of Christ. More will be said of this in connection with the incarnation. For the present let us examine relevant quotations from several creeds and other official Christian documents to show that the doctrine of Jesus' humanity has dogmatic standing. This may seem unnecessary since modern people are not generally aware that our Lord's humanity was ever in doubt. Our purpose is not so much to defend as to clarify.

After these official statements seven points should be made about the human nature of Jesus. It was and is: 1) genuine, 2) complete, 3) permanent, 4) sinless (impeccable), 5) from Mary alone, 6) always in perfect union with the divine nature, 7) a human personality which from the first moment developed in connection with the Person of the divine Son. The divine assumed the human. There was no duality of persons.

The dogmatic statements are all brief: 'Jesus Christ... was conceived by the Holy Ghost, born of the Virgin Mary' (the Apostles' Creed); 'was incarnate by the Holy Ghost of the Virgin Mary, and was made man' (Nicene Creed, AD 325, 381); 'We, then, following the holy Fathers, all with one consent teach men to confess... our Lord Jesus Christ... perfect in manhood... truly man, of a rational soul and body... consubstantial with us according to the Manhood' (*Anthrōpotēta*), in all things like unto us, without sin... born of the Virgin Mary, the *God Bearer* according to the Manhood (*anthrōpotēta*) (Symbol of Chalcedon, 22 October 451). '...it is necessary to... salvation: that one believe faithfully the Incarnation... that our Lord Jesus Christ... is God and Man... of the same substance of his Mother, born in the world... perfect Man, of a reasonable soul and human flesh subsisting... inferior to the Father as touching his Manhood... One Christ, One; not by conversion of the Godhead into flesh; but by taking [assumption] of the Manhood into God... by the unity of Person' (*The Athanasian Creed*, from arts. 28, 29, 30, 31, 32, 33, 35, 36). The first article of the *Profession of the Tridentine* (Council of Trent) *Faith*, 1654, reaffirms *en toto* the Nicene Creed. The evangelical (Protestant) Article viii of *The Thirty-Nine Articles of the Church of England* (1571) reaffirms the Nicene, Athanasian and Apostles' Creeds. The Heidelberg Catechism (1563) does the same. The Lutheran *Formula of Concord* (1576) affirms at length the same in detail (Art. I Affirmative) as does also the Westminster Confession (chap. viii, arts. 2, 3).

The fact that every one of these important dogmatic statements includes a strong and clear statement of our Lord's humanity (the standard English word is *Manhood*, i.e. 'Manness') shows two things: *first*, like every aspect of Christology, the fact of our Lord's normal humanness has been attacked or compromised in every age and, *second*, it must be clearly stated again for every age of the church. Each of the following seven affirmations has been occasioned by some fresh or renewed error or heresy regarding the true enfleshment of the Son of God. That is why the teaching, though explicit in the Bible, had to be formulated in many formal statements throughout Christian history.

1. The humanity (Latin, *humanitas*; Greek, *anthrōpotēs*, [Clement of Alexandria]) of Christ is *genuine*, or 'authentically human.' A rather special meaning has been placed on the latter term by the intrusion into theology of existentialist ideas and terms of neo-orthodox (dialectic, krisis) theology and, prominently, Paul Tillich. But in the proper sense of the word *authentic*, any one born of human parents, saint or sinner, sick or well, whole or maimed is authentically human – the presence of sin excepted, for sin is not essential to human nature. The archetypes, our first parents, gave up their full authenticity, or integrity when they sinned. In other words, before the fall our

---

4. See my essay in 'A Traditional View,' *Women in Ministry*, ed. by Clouse and Clouse (Downers Grove, IL: InterVarsity Press, 1989), pp. 25-27.

parents were *normal*. Afterward they and all their offspring have been *ab*normal. 'To err is human' is a misleading statement. 'To err' is only average, not normal.

So 'the holy one' who was born of a virgin and 'in whom was no sin' is more fully normal than any of us. The Bible is clear that Jesus was neither a monster nor a freak. After some of His exploits some might exclaim 'What manner of man is this?' But no one doubted He was truly one of mankind.

The writers of the New Testament almost inadvertently express this, as though the contrary did not occur to any one. Peter knew Jesus was the 'fruit of David's loins' which is certainly about as bluntly human as one can get in view of what we know about David; Paul, that Jesus was 'of Israel according to the flesh'; Matthew traced His ancestry through the generations back to Abraham; Luke to Adam; and Hebrews chapter 2 says He partook of 'flesh and blood' just as other people do. He had the apparent ethnic, physical characteristics of a Palestinian Jew and dressed Himself like one (John 4:9). He looked so unexceptionally the part of a Hebrew prophet some thought He might be John the Baptist or some ancient prophet risen from the dead (Matt.16:13, 14).

Insofar as we know the biographical details of His life until 'about thirty years of age' (and it seems to be about as much as we know of Julius Caesar or Plato to that age), Jesus' story reads like any one's story. He is first an unborn child in His mother's womb, known only to the mother and intimates with whom she shares the knowledge; then a newborn wrapped in standard infant wear, next a suckling babe in an itinerant carpenter's 'mobile home', after that in a house, later doted on by aged kinsmen and others, still later in a village-tradesman's shop assisting His human father, growing in wisdom, stature and good favor with neighbors and properly schooled in Jewish piety, then a confirmed son of the law (bar-mitzvah), an independent-minded juvenile and finally a mature adult about to embark on His life-calling.

2. From the standpoint of a biblical anthropology, whether one views it as a dichotomist (body and soul-spirit) or a trichotomist (body, soul and spirit) His humanity was *complete*, everything a normal specimen of humanity should have and be. One ancient error, proposed by someone who wished to rationalize the incarnation, had it that while His physical body and animal soul were those of man His spirit was not, being furnished by the eternal Word (*Logos*) (see later on the incarnation). The fact of His human body, which hungered and thirsted and became limp in sleep and bled when wounded is plain in the narratives. His soul is troubled at times or angered or grieved and He committed His human spirit to God when He died. Some of the ancient Gnostics and other Docetists (only *seemed* a man) thought the Jesus of Gospel story was a man possessed at a certain stage by the Son of God (of which more later) as does modern 'Christian Science,' but all the evidence is against the notion.

The fact Jesus was completely human can be verbalized simply as '*perfectly* human' – which raises the subject of His personal stature, physical type, and presence or absence of physical comeliness. It has been inferred from Isaiah 53:2 ('no form nor comeliness... no beauty that we should desire him' KJV) that Jesus was an ugly man. The passage means He had no *kingly* form or *regal* splendor or *worldly* majesty such as nationalistic Jews would look for in a claimant king. As to His physique, there is no scriptural attention to it at all. We know common people liked Him as did also children and many women. But great physical attractiveness is not required for that (Mother Teresa, for example). Physical details of Jesus' *persona* are obviously unimportant to the authors of the New Testament. The strange modern preoccupation of 'clinical' and analytical interest in every news event – giving in public such indiscreet morbidities as the length of Lyndon Johnson's abdominal incision and the precise location and direction of John Kennedy's fatal bullet wound – is absent from Luke's reporting of the baby Jesus. Two verses, no more, are devoted to the mother's delivery and the infant's first care. In place of statistics on length of time in labor, pounds and ounces, color of skin and eyes and hair, we know only that there was no public announcement of His birth emanating from the parents. We know the infant's bed was a manger and He was given careful infant attention and attracted a lot of attention from heaven and a few pious folk whom heaven touched in special ways.

3. The genuine, complete humanity of Jesus Christ is *permanent*. The ancient creeds stress this, for if there is anything made plain in the testimony of the Apostles and the words of Jesus plus angelic messengers, it is that when the 'Word became flesh' it was to be forever. In this case 'flesh,' as in John 1:14, is a term for both the material and immaterial part of man. His resurrection included body and spirit, He showed Himself alive in flesh and bones, demonstrated unmistakably in various ways (including eating in the Apostle's presence) and ascended before their eyes in that body, and according to the angels, will so come again.

4. The human nature of Christ was *derived entirely from His mother Mary*. As we shall treat more at length in connection with some thoughts on the virgin birth. He had no male parent, even though to show His full legal right to David's throne by male line of descent both the genealogies mention Joseph. There is an enormous modern literature on the subject. The Westminster Confession says the Son of God 'did take upon him man's nature... being conceived... in the womb of the Virgin Mary of her substance' (chap. viii).

Long ago, however, the ancient church learned how to state this matter. They phrased it well in more than one of the ancient confessional documents. Hold in mind that they wished to be faithful to the 'rule of faith' or 'desposit of truth,' received in the apostolic age, passed on faithfully in the churches, and loyal to the Holy Scriptures. 'The right faith is that the Lord Jesus Christ... is... Man, of the Substance of his Mother, born into the world' (*Quicunque* or, the Athanasian Creed, para. 31).

The last thing any of the orthodox fathers wished to be was an innovator of new doctrine. It is hard to say exactly when the books we now call the New Testament were in possession of all the churches, but we do know that the churches regarded apostolic authority equal with the authority of the Hebrew Scriptures and the authority of Scripture the same as the authority of God. This matter is made plain in the way they cite apostolic writings and the high regard that they held for the apostolic foundation of churches and teachings laid down in those churches. Tradition meant apostolic teaching preserved in apostolic writings and oral teaching as well.

Against the claims of supposed newly minted truths of Gnostic teaching, Irenaeus, bishop of Lyons, late in the second century called attention to the earlier authoritative teaching of the Apostle Peter. He cites at length Peter's sermon to Cornelius' household (Acts 10:37-44) and concludes:

> [I]t is evident from Peter's words that he did indeed still retain the God who was already known to them [i.e. the God-fearers of Cornelius' household]; but he also bare witness to them that Jesus Christ was the Son of God, the judge of the quick and the dead... Can it really be, that Peter was not at that time as yet in possession of the perfect knowledge which these men (gnostics) discovered afterwards?[5]

A few pages earlier he pointed out the Apostles did not preach or write until they were specially endowed with the gifts and power of the Holy Spirit (Pentecost).[6] After that they went about to the ends of the earth. He gives details of how the Gospels were apostolic.[7] Hence, 'If any one does not agree to these truths, he despises Christ Himself the Lord... opposing his own salvation.' He goes on to assert 'the tradition of the apostles remains in "the whole world" in the succession of bishops [that is, presbyter-pastors] in the Church... to our own times.'[8]

5. Christ was (is) a *sinless Man*. This means He was free both from original sin (hereditary depravity) and from any thought or act of sin. The New Testament is plain about this and other evidences support it. The traditional name is impeccability.

The New Testament says the child begotten of Mary would be 'the holy thing' (Luke 1:35, KJV). Jesus challenged His enemies to convict Him of sin (John 8:46) and claimed the devil 'has no claim on me' (John 14:30), i.e. no flaw in His character which would give the tempter any leverage for enticing to sin. He 'became flesh,' all right (John 1:14), but with the limitation that sin was not part of the 'likeness of sinful flesh' and it was 'for sin,' i.e. to deal with it in others, not to embrace it Himself (Rom. 1:3). Other texts affirm 'him... who knew no sin' (2 Cor. 5:21); 'in every respect tempted as we are, yet without sin' (Heb. 4:15); 'holy, innocent, unstained, separated from sinners' (Heb. 7:26). Jesus' sinlessness (impeccability) was by virtue of the miracle of 'immaculate conception', – not of the mother of Jesus, but of her child, without human male parentage. This is apparently the significance of the 'therefore' (KJV and ESV), 'for that reason' (NASB) in the angel's announcement: 'The Holy spirit will come upon you, and the power of the Most High will overshadow you, and for that reason the holy thing begotten shall be called the Son of God' (Luke 1:35, NASB margin).

Of the creeds of the Reformation era the statement of Westminster (1647) says the least about 'Man's nature' in Christ: He did 'take upon him man's nature and all common infirmatives thereof, yet without sin' (chap. VIII). The Thirty-Nine Articles of 1563, 1571 say the most, with good reason, according to E. C. S. Gibson.[9] Fanatics of the time

---

5. Irenaeus (in *Ante-Nicene Fathers*, vol. i, ed. Roberts and Donaldson, 1885, repr. Peabody, Hendrickson Publ., 1994), *Against Heresies*, 3.12.7, pp. 432, 433.
6. ibid., 3.1.1–3, pp. 314–316.
7. ibid., 3.1.1–2.
8. ibid., 3.1.3.
9. E. C. S. Gibson, *The Thirty-Nine Articles of the Church of England Explained with an Introduction*, 8th ed. (London: 1912).

'were some [Anabaptists] who revived docetic notions of our Lord's humanity, some who denied His atonement and asserted His sinfulness, and others who [maintained] the regenerate could not sin.'[10] Hence, article XV says, 'Christ in the truth of our nature was made like unto us in all things (sin only except), from which he was clearly void, both in his flesh and in His spirit. He came to be the Lamb without spot, Who by the sacrifice of Himself once made, should take away the sins of the world: and sin (as St John says) was not in Him. But all the rest (although baptized and born again in Christ) yet offend in many things, and if we say we have no sin, we deceive ourselves, and the truth is not in us.'[11]

There is a complete absence of tendentious reporting of Jesus' sinlessness. Mainly the matter is simply assumed. His mother observed the Mosaic rite for purification of herself, but not for her Son; He went frequently to the temple but never, we may assume, offered sacrifice for sins (as sin and trespass offerings of Lev. 5–7). He prayed 'Father forgive *them,*' but never 'forgive *me.*' His expressions of anger and irritation are obviously justified and never out of control. His prayers to the Father during the intense strain and suffering of the Passion, especially the last evening in Gethsemane, including the marvellous prayer of John 17, are in awareness of full fellowship with the Father unobstructed by the slightest taint of sin.

6. *The personality of His human nature existed only in union with the divine Second Person of the Godhead.* Many have sought to state and explain the absence of a human 'person' in a way fully intelligible and consistent with a genuine and complete human nature and we shall treat the matter further in discussing the incarnation, chapter 7. Berkouwer[12] is helpful; W. G. T. Shedd[13] is satisfying; H. M. Pelton[14] exhausts about all that can be said on the subject. Strong states it well:

> [T]he Logos did not take into union with himself an already developed human person, such as James, Peter or John, but human nature before it had become personal or was capable of receiving a name. It reached its personality only in union with his own divine nature. Therefore we see in Christ not two persons – a human person and a divine person – but one person, and that person possessed of a human nature as well as a divine.[15]

7. In His humanity ('Manhood' of the creeds) He constituted Himself the head of the new humanity. As Adam is the head of the fallen race of man Christ is the head of the race of redeemed mankind. He is the 'last Adam' (1 Cor. 15:45). What the First Adam was as head of a fallen race Christ is to the race of redeemed men (Rom. 5:12-19). This is a way of stating the prime purpose of 'God... sending his own Son in the likeness of sinful flesh' (Rom. 8:3). According to Hebrews 2:9-18 (NASB) God's Son became a brother to us, actively and voluntarily partook of the human nature (v.14) which we have involuntarily, to 'taste death for everyone' (v. 9), thereby begetting a new family of children (v. 13). This is the theology of further biblical statements. In Isaiah 9:6 our Lord is called 'Everlasting Father [emphasis added].' The saved are His 'offspring' in Isaiah 53:10. He is both 'the root' and 'the descendant of David' in Revelation 22:16 and 'the Son [who] gives life to whom he will' (John 5:21).

This concept of Christ as progenitor of a new spiritual race has intrigued many authors, and rightly so. The application of it is relevant to Scriptures that speak of Christ as 'head of the church' (Eph. 5:23), Christ as vine, of us as branches (John 15).

The importance of Christ's genuine, complete, permanent, sinless humanity joined, of course, to His deity, is so great that it is usually an adequate test for orthodoxy. According to 1 John 4:1-3 and 2 John 7, he who does not confess the genuine, permanent enfleshment of the Son of God is 'not from God,' 'of the antichrist,' a 'false prophet,' and 'a deceiver' and 'the antichrist.' What could be more emphatic?

The practical value is the subject of Hebrews 2:9-18 and 4:4-16. The present author's several sermons and essays on those texts will not be included here but the *humanitas* (Lat.), *anthrōpotēs* (Gr.) manhood of the Savior of the world will be an important substrate of all subsequent chapters of this book.

---

10. ibid, p. 441.
11. ibid, p. 439.
12. G. C. Berkouwer, *The Person of Christ*, trans. John Vriend (Grand Rapids, MI: Eerdmans, 1954), chap. 11.
13. W. G. T. Shedd, *Dogmatic Theology ii* (Grand Rapids, MI: Zondervan, 1969), pp. 298–308.
14. H. M. Pelton, A Study in Christology: The Problem of the Two Natures in the Person of Christ (New York: Macmillan, 1922).
15. A. H. Strong, *Systematic Theology* (Valley Forge, PA: Judson Press, 1907), p. 679.

7
The Virgin Birth of Jesus

The virgin birth of Jesus is important because it is the mode by which God deigned to enter earthly history as a member of the human race. On that account it became prominent in the theological reflections of the first Christians and has remained so to greater or lesser degree ever since. While we cannot know for certain that the incarnation could have occurred only by this very biological miracle we do know that the God of the canonical Scriptures is in charge of employment of miracles. It is reasonable to assume there were special reasons why this particular miracle took place – as we shall consider later in this chapter.

Definition and Designation.

As set forth in Scripture the birth of Jesus is not primarily a doctrine. It is a fact, event, occurrence, as is the worldly entrance of every other human being. In this case the conception took place in the womb of a human female without the then otherwise invariable act of previous sexual intercourse with a male. The entrance of our first parents is reported in the Bible as two dissimilar miraculous events, each a unique event, not to be repeated in the case of any others.

This raises the question of how rightly to name the event, and where to place the *locus* of the supernatural operation of God's Spirit (Luke 1:35; Matt. 1:20). The special 'power' 'of the Most High' (Luke 1:35) was specifically in the conception without a male parent (Matt. 1:20), not in the birth, which was quite ordinary as such. For this reason Bernard Weiss in his justly famous three-volume *Life of Christ* entitles the chapter on this subject 'The Immaculate Conception'[1] laying emphasis not so much on the virginity of the mother as on the absence of original sin in the offspring. '"Virgin conception", other things being equal, would be the most precise term to use. Even so, of the events of conception, gestation and birth, taken as a whole, custom and theology have agreed, "Virgin-birth" is the correct designation of the birth statement contained in the Gospels of Matthew and Luke.'[2] 'Supernatural conception' is too broad for there was a supernatural element in the conception of Isaac, Samson and John the Baptist. 'Immaculate conception' means non-contamination with a sinful nature and is really an interpretation of the event, not a proven feature of absence of a male parentage. Also, 'immaculate conception' tends to confuse unsophisticated people's minds with the alleged conception of Mary, herself, without a sinful nature – a Roman dogma not a scriptural teaching.

---

1. Bernhrd Weiss, *Life of Christ* trans. J. W. Hope, vol. i (Edinburgh: T. & T. Clark, 1883), p. 222.
2. L. M. Sweet, art. 'Virgin Birth of Jesus,' *ISBE*, ed. J. Orr (Grand Rapids, MI: Wm B. Eerdmans, 1939), p. 3052.

The Virgin Birth in the Ancient Church.

The ancient church, following Scripture, was uniform and consistent in holding to two important affirmations in connection with Jesus' birth. 1) He was conceived in Mary's womb by the power of God as says the Scripture (Matt.1:18; Luke 1:35) and 2) the mother was a virgin at the conception and remained so until after the birth of the child (Luke 1:27, 34; Matt. 1:18, 25). The alleged perpetual virginity of Mary is a dogma contradicted by Scripture.

With regard to the conception, the *Old Roman Creed*, of very great antiquity, says He 'was born of the Holy Spirit and the Virgin Mary.'[3] The Niceno-Constantinopolitan Creed (AD 325, 381) says He 'was made flesh of the Holy Spirit and the Virgin Mary, and became man.'[4] The Nicene Creed really carries over the affirmation of the Apostles' Creed of which the origins lie in the second century. Any one who doubts the church believed, confessed and taught this from the very earliest time should read the evidence cited by John G. Machen in *The Virgin Birth of Christ*.[5] One of the very earliest of the writing Fathers, Ignatius of Antioch (martyred not later than AD 117, perhaps as early as AD 107) mentions the virgin birth and miraculous conception. The writer's phrases appear as if not needing confirmation among his Christian readers, viz.: 'conceived in the womb of Mary... by the Holy Ghost' (both in *To Ephesians*, xviii). Twice in *To Ephesians* xix, he says 'the virginity of Mary was hidden from the prince of the world.'[6] Other similar statements showing acceptance of the virgin birth by Ignatius and his readers will be found in *To the Smyrnaeans* chapter I and other places.[7] Justin Martyr, who lived from about AD 110 to AD 165, is similarly at ease with the virgin birth, even devoting two chapters of his *Dialogue with Trypho* to prove from Old Testament prophecy that Christ was born of a virgin.[8] The matter was not seriously challenged so far as we know until post-Reformation times.

'It [the virgin birth] is a constant and... universally recognized element in the doctrinal tradition of the post-apostolic period, for of any important or fruitful opposition to it the history of doctrine knows nothing.'[9]

Yet there were mutterings of exception. Evidently some thought they found contradictions between the Matthew and Luke genealogies of Jesus. At any rate Julius Africanus, a Christian historian and friend of Origen and resident of Palestine who flourished about AD 220, wrote a letter to a certain Aristides, of which a fragment exists today in the *Church History* of Eusebius (AD 260?–340?). Eusebius comments that 'many suppose' the genealogies of Matthew and Luke 'are at variance with one another' (chap. vii, 1). He then goes on to cite at length Africanus' careful explanation of the alleged discrepancies.[10] This is the first hint I know of any Christian apologetics for the virgin birth. Yet even here it is treated more as a problem for reverent exegesis of a problem passage of the Bible than response to anti-Christian attack.

Objections Old and New.

Objections have not varied much through the centuries. Let us summarize some of them. In the interest of brevity I shall not try to trace the origin of the objections.

1. There are discrepancies between the details of the two genealogies of Matthew 1:2-17 and Luke 3:23-38. The history of this charge, as we have already noted, goes back to a time about 100 years after the two accounts were written. I shall not here enter far into the details of either of the alleged discrepancies or possible harmonizations. Julius Africanus tried to explain that both genealogies are of Joseph (Mary's husband), the legal father of Jesus, and that one traces the legal line by virtue of levirate marriage, and the other the actual biological line: 'Thus neither of the Gospels is in error, for one reckons by nature, the other by law.' Varieties of Africanus' view have many modern advocates.[11] A respectable modern attempt at harmonization, not very different from Africanus' theory, holds that

---

3. Henry S. Bettenson, ed., *Documents of the Christian Church* (New York: Oxford University Press, 1963), p. 33.
4. ibid., p. 37.
5. Machen, *The Virgin Birth of Christ*, 'The Virgin Birth in the Second Century' (Grand Rapids, MI: Baker Books, 1967), chap. 1, pp. 2–43.
6. Ignatius in *Ante-Nicene Fathers, i*, ed. Roberts and Donaldson, 1885, repr. (Peabody: Hendrickson Publ., 1994), p. 57.
7. ibid., p. 86.
8. Justin Martyr (in *Ante-Nicene Fathers, i*, ed. Roberts and Donaldson, 1885, repr. Peabody: Hendrickson Publ., 1994), chaps. xliii, p. 216 and lxvii, p. 231.
9. B. B. Warfield, *Biblical and Theological Studies* (Philadelphia: Presbyterian and Reformed, 1952), p. 158.
10. Eusebius in *Nicene and Post-Nicene Fathers*, Second Series i, ed P. Schaff, 1886, repr., Peabody (Hendrickson Publ., 1994), chap. 1, pp. 91–99.
11. Eusebius, *Church History, i*, trans. Isaac Boyle (Grand Rapids, MI: Baker Books, 1850, 1969), p. 7.

while Matthew's obviously somewhat artificially constructed plan is clearly Joseph's legal line of descent from David, stressing Jesus' legal right to David's throne, Luke's genealogy is of Mary. Alford summarizes this view in a kindly way but rejects it. The key idea is that in Luke 3:23 (KJV) the parenthesis should be enlarged to read, 'Jesus... being (as was supposed the son of Joseph), which [i.e. Jesus Himself] was the son [or, grandson *via* Mary] of Heli.' In such case the line of descent was Heli, Mary, Jesus. It is pointed out in support that every name in the genealogy is prefixed by the genitive article *tou*, whereas Joseph's name is not, thus putting Joseph outside the genealogy. This then would be Mary's line of biological descent from 'David's line.' This has always appealed to me as reasonable. Yet I share the rather reserved approval of this theory expressed by John Walvoord[12] and Alford's comment, 'Here as elsewhere... it is quite as presumptuous to pronounce the genealogies discrepant, as it is ever curious and uncritical to reconcile them.'[13] I was taught this view in seminary. Harold Lindsell presents this possible harmonization briefly and well in his note on Luke 3:23 in the *Harper Study Bible* RSV.[14] Perhaps the most readable and complete account of the views of the 'discrepancies' is by Samuel Andrews, *The Life of our Lord*.[15]

2. Many neo-orthodox writers think the virgin birth did not occur and that the doctrine subtracts from Jesus' true humanity while adding no support for Christ's full deity. Emil Brunner specifically acknowledges that he rejects the teaching, in the face of clear scriptural evidence to the contrary.[16]

Rudolph Bultmann and disciples treat the virgin birth in a similar way. The virgin birth did not occur but has worth as *myth* embodying value, amenable to the enlightened sensibilities of our age, which cannot believe in supernatural miracles. John Macquarrie, a dedicated Bultmannian, says the myth should be understood as pointing to Jesus 'as one who has come from God and in whom God's advent and epiphany... have taken place.'[17]

Macquarrie and the approach he represents need not be refuted, yet some further notice should be given. Rejection of the supernatural among professedly Christian scholars has nevertheless required of them some positive evaluation of Jesus as presented in the Gospels. Many of them have been clergymen – pastors, teachers – and some held chairs of theology in Christian schools. Through the nineteenth century the common approach of this sort of liberalism was to make of Jesus the highest ethical expression ever to appear on earth and Christian religion simply the promotion of Jesus' teachings and/or example. All we really know of Jesus and His teachings must be derived from the Bible, and since on principle the supernatural had been (wholly or partly) removed, what was left in this liberal treatment was a religious genius much like a cultivated European bachelor who was always a gentleman.

At the turn of the century this outlook lost much of its scholarly support, though it has never died out. Subsequent liberal movements in theology and New Testament studies have sought to discover 'the historical Jesus.' The new liberals still hold the supernatural in disdain in varying degrees. But the historical Jesus turned out to be no practicing gentleman but one who challenged people in a confrontational way and may even have been a political zealot.

The twentieth century was not twenty years old when a quite different reaction against easy-going liberalism set in. It came to be called neo-orthodoxy, also dialectical theology and crisis theology. Neo-orthodoxy embraces many of the elements of the old-but-continuing liberalism and 'the historical Jesus' thinking but fosters individual subjective religion – attainment of authentic existence, being or becoming one's real self. Crisis, confrontation, commitment, personal decision, etc. are the reigning ideas. These folk also have an interest in finding value in 'Jesus and His Story' in the Gospels.

Bultmann and his disciples in an eclectic manner embrace some of all of the movements of liberal theology just characterized. Hence Macquarrie, a *bona fide* Bultmannian rather encapsulates them all.

All these movements seem to be efforts to be both believing and unbelieving, rejecting the supernatural but trying to love Jesus.

Wolfhart Pannenberg is a prestigious contemporary writer somewhere on the scale of belief between nineteenth-century liberalism and orthodox acceptance of the factual truth of the New Testament documents. He does not receive the virgin birth narratives as historical truth, but like liberals as far back as David Strauss wants to find

---

12. John F. Walvoord, *Jesus Christ Our Lord* (Chicago: Moody Press, 1969), p. 104.
13. Henry Alford, *New Testament for English Readers* (Chicago: Moody Press, 1868), p. 314.
14. Harold Lindsell, Harper Study Bible *Revised Standard Version* (New York: Harper & Row, 1964), p. 1536.
15. Samuel Andrews, *The Life of Our Lord Upon the Earth* (New York: Scribners, 1891), pp. 58–68.
16. Emil Brunner, *The Mediator: A Study of the Central Doctrine of the Christian Faith*, trans. Olive Wyon (Philadelphia: Westminster Press, 1947), pp. 322, 323, 329, 361, 362.
17. John Macquarrie, *Principles of Christian Theology*, 2nd ed. (New York: Charles Scribner's Sons, 1977), pp. 280–282, 299, 395.

religious value in them. Even though his acceptance of the resurrection as reported is equivocal, for Pannenberg the resurrection has sufficient 'retroactive force' to validate Jesus as divine Son and sent by God.[18] He also speaks of the 'confirmatory force of the Easter event.'[19] Hence, he can dispose of any certainty in the virgin birth reports on the ground of 'the apparently legendary nature of the narrative.'[20] What is the religious value? Answer:

> Essentially this spiritual reality [Mary's humble receptivity] is not dependent on whether there was a male participation or not in the conception of the boy Jesus. It was enough on its own, however, to induce all Christians to show loving and reverent regard for Mary as the *theotokos* [God-bearer]. Christ is to achieve form in the life of every Christian as in that of her Jesus (Gal. 4:19).[21]

Having given some notice to these denials and weakenings of the Gospel reports of Jesus' virgin birth we must be quick to say refutation will not convince the gainsayers. They and we operate on different presuppositions. No amount of evidence *as such* will convince one who on philosophical grounds rejects the possibility (or at least the certainty) of a supernatural realm or a supernatural power capable of producing events in the natural order. We and they run on different epistemological tracks.

3. A related opinion held by liberal theologians for over a century and more recently by neo-orthodox and even a few conservative evangelicals is that whether true or not the virgin birth was unnecessary or unimportant. Whether deity could have assumed humanity in another way or the sinlessness of Jesus secured other than by absence of a male parent cannot be proved. Yet it can be truthfully said that if God, who does not appear to engage in miracle-mongering, could have accomplished these desiderata in another way, He would likely have done so.

Perhaps two important features of the incarnation would not have been possible except for the virginal conception of the baby Jesus. One is the sinlessness of Jesus, called 'impeccability' in formal theology and succinctly phrased, 'in all points tempted like as we are, yet without sin' (Heb. 4:15 KJV).

There is an enormous literature supporting this proposal. I shall not pursue it at length. The theme has attracted the interest of medical doctors M. R. Dehaan of *Radio Bible Class* fame and Arthur C. Custance whose 600-page book *The Seed of the Woman*[22] makes interesting and informative reading. Machen has something to say of this to which we shall return in a moment.

Another is the unity of the Person of the God-man, for which the ancient term was *anhypostasia*, or impersonality of the human nature, a later and better term is *enhypostasia* of the human person. The idea intended in the latter is the truth that the Person of the God-man was *one* and the One was and is the Second Person of the Godhead, further that the human *personality* was not a second self-consciousness or center of consciousness, but *a human consciousness or personal awareness that developed only in and with the divine Person*. The connection of this important ancient understanding of the unity of the Person (as in the Creed of Chalcedon and the Athanasian Creed) is this, viz.: the invariable consequent of the coming together of ovum and sperm in human conception is a new human person. In Jesus' case there was no *new* person but the eternal Person acquiring, by addition and union, a human nature without a new human person. The personality of Jesus developed in permanent union with the *Logos*, the Second Person of the Godhead. The preferred theological word for this is *enhypostasia* – meaning simply *in personality*, not non-personality.

Besides, as J. Gresham Machen reminds the learned rejecters, the virgin birth is (1) 'obviously important for the general question of the authority of the Bible.'[23] (2) It 'is important as a test for a man to apply to determine whether one holds a naturalistic or supernaturalistic view regarding Christ.'[24] The fact that many writers of various shades of departure from the authority of Scripture can think they believe in a genuine incarnation apart from the factual teachings of the Bible is irrational. How can we learn anything factual from the Bible if its 'witness to revelation' cannot be held to tell facts as they are?

I think we can follow Machen further. In the last three pages of his great book he makes several affirmations regarding the importance of the virgin birth, viz.: (1) as an event in history 'it fixes for us the time of the incarnation' (25 December may not be the day, but there was a day!). 'It is not strange that it has always given offense to the

---

18. Wolfhart Pannenberg, *Systematic Theology, vol. ii*, trans. G. W. Bromiley (Grand Rapids, MI: Eerdmans,1991-1994), pp. 303 (n. 92), 317-319.
19. ibid., p. 366.
20. ibid., p. 318.
21. ibid., p. 319.
22. A. C. Custance, *The Seed of the Woman* (Brockville, Ont.: Doorway Publications, 1980).
23. J. Gresham Machen, *The Virgin Birth of Christ* (Grand Rapids, MI: Baker Books, 1967), p.282 ff.
24. ibid., pp. 287 ff.

natural man.'[25] (2) The virgin birth erects a barrier against Pelagianism, which rejects 'the solidarity of the race in the guilt and power of sin,' In Pelagianism no man is a sinner by nature. Sinlessness is entirely possible to any one who has enough help. Even some orthodox writers make sport of any necessary connection between our doctrine and our Lord's sinless nature. Machen wants to know 'how except by the virgin birth, could our Savior have lived a complete human life from the mother's womb, and yet [be] from the beginning no product of what had gone before, but a supernatural Person [the *enhypastasia*, to be treated further in Chapter VI] come into this world from the outside to redeem the sinful race?'[26] (3) And maybe the virgin birth is sometimes part of the intellectual content of saving faith. 'Who can tell exactly how much? ...saving faith is acceptance of Jesus Christ "as he is offered to us in the gospel." Part of that gospel is which Jesus is offered to our souls in the blessed story of the miracle in the virgin's womb.'[27] (4) 'Even if the belief in the virgin birth is not necessary to every Christian, it is certainly necessary to Christianity... necessary to the corporate witness of the Church... and that... witness is strongest when taken as it stands.'[28]

4. It is charged the New Testament evidence for the virgin birth is weak. This is stated in different ways, viz.: only Matthew and Luke seem to know anything about it, or Jesus is completely unaware of it in Gospel reports, or there is no evidence in the Epistles that Paul or Peter and the other writers knew of any virgin birth. So perhaps it is a myth or legend that came to be incorporated in two Gospels. This in essence is to argue from silence. Because nothing is said about something by these writings does not demonstrate that Jesus was unaware and His disciples and Jewish contemporaries had heard no rumors of anything unusual about Jesus' manner of entrance into the world.

It is well to remember Matthew and Luke were likely written after most of the Epistles. For now, let us acknowledge that the conception of a baby is about as private a matter as this world knows. Even today in the sad lack of shame about sins and vulgar exposure of intimacy, orderly, common people don't talk or write about how and when a pregnancy began without some embarrassment. So we should not be surprised if the subject was not bruited about promiscuously by Jesus' immediate family. Evidence of the virgin birth in the rest of the Bible will be treated more at length shortly.

5. There is said to be such similarity between the legends and myths of the birth of the gods and heroes of paganism that the accounts of Jesus' supernatural conception and birth surely originated not in fact but legend or myth. A legend is an unverifiable or unhistorical story from earlier times handed down and accepted as true. Myth is sometimes used in the same sense as legend. David Strauss (1808–1874) proposed myth as the origin of all the miracles of the Gospels – meaning unconscious exaggerations of devoted first disciples put in writing a century or two later. R. Bultmann in the recent past employed myth as a hermeneutical principle, that is, the Bible must *today* be interpreted not as history but as imagery to express the otherworldly in terms of human life, the other side in terms of this side. He adopts this opinion frankly on the ground of plain and simple rejection of the supernatural. He writes, 'the idea of wonder as miracle has become almost impossible for us today because we understand the processes of nature as governed by law';[29] 'We recognize as real... only what can be set in this context of the rule of law; and we judge assertions which cannot be accommodated to this conception as fantasies';[30] '*The idea of miracle* has, therefore, become untenable and *it must be abandoned*'[31] (emphasis Bultmann's). Radical Gospels criticism recently has gone far beyond even this. Yet Bultmann wished to be regarded as a devout Lutheran.

With regard to the alleged myth-legend character of the virgin birth it will be sufficient for the believer to know that the classical myths of ancient heathendom (paganism or credulous rusticity, are not quite the words here for the sophisticated literature of these stories) have many stories of heroes and gods born to women who conceived by intercourse with supernatural beings in human form. Each one is an obscene tale. The Bible narratives are sober, chaste, transparently pure, sober reporting of what someone knew to be true. They are told as reports of miracles, usually known at least to two sane, surprised, overwhelmed but normal human beings in full possession of sound powers of sight, hearing, speech and of rational reflection.

---

25. ibid., p. 394.
26. ibid., p. 395.
27. ibid., p. 396.
28. ibid., p. 496.
29. Rudolph Bultmann, *Faith and Understanding* (London: SCM Press, 1969), p. 247.
30. ibid., p. 248.
31. ibid., p. 249.

Really this sort of rejection is based on presuppositions, prejudgment, one could say, prejudice. There can be no debate with this outlook. There is nothing compatible between belief and unbelief at this level. It is the *zeitgeist* of the world's intelligentsia today.

Through the rest of this chapter the goal is to consider the virgin birth of Jesus from the biblical perspective without intentional reference to apologetical questions. Let us now consider what the accounts say specifically about the conception and birth of the child, then move on to consider the nature and significance of the genealogies, next the background in the Old Testament, and after that the virgin birth in Jesus' own consciousness and in Mark and Luke as well as the New Testament outside the Gospels. The discussion will close with attention to problems and values and will be as succinct as the subject allows. There is an immense literature on almost every aspect of this outline in encyclopaedias, essays, monographs, commentaries and works of theology. I am indebted to all of them, particularly my own teachers, who had explored the subject at a time when it was the subject of much controversy. There is probably nothing original to be said about it but everything to affirm as to the facts and their meaning.

What the Accounts Affirm About Jesus' Conception and Birth and Surrounding Circumstances.

Let us consider the virgin birth rather narrowly at first, with attention to what chief points the two accounts *unite* in affirming.

They agree (1) the mother's name was Mary, in Greek, *Mariam*, more recognizable as the well-known name of the sister of Moses. Such a name suggests she was from an un-Hellenized peasant family (Matt. 1:18, 20; Luke 1:27, 30, *et passim*). The mother is declared to be (2) a virgin both at the time of conception (Luke 1:27, 34; Matt. 1:18, 23) and, as Matthew says, she remained so until after being delivered of her child (Matt.1:25; Luke 2:5). 3) She was betrothed to Joseph (Matt. 1:18; Luke 1:27), but 4) before consummation of the marriage she became with child (Matt. 1:18; Luke 1:34, 35) and 5) an angel made announcement of the fact (to Joseph, Matt. 1:20; to Mary, Luke 1:28-35). The accounts agree 6) the child was appropriately to be named Jesus (Greek equivalent of Hebrew, *Jehoshua*, the LORD saves) since he was to be Savior of His people (Matt. 1:21; Luke 1:31-33). 7) The name was commanded by an angel of God (Matt. 1:21, 25; Luke 1:31; 2:21). 8) The angel (or angels) explained to each parent that the conception would take place by the power of God – no hint of any carnal act by the deity (Matt. 1:18; Luke 1:35). Like all biblical miracles, the precise, invisible, intangible cause is left unidentified. It is important to note, that *pneuma hagion* (holy spirit) in the angel's announcement to Mary is without the article on either word. It probably should be read, 'Holy Spirit will come upon you,' not really identifying at this point the one who 'proceeds from the Father and the Son.' The doctrine of the holy Trinity did not exist as a formulated dogma when the angel spoke. The basis for it was to be laid in the New Testament yet to be written, but for a couple of centuries the church directed its best theological thought to clarifying and defending a doctrine of the Second Person of the Godhead. A formal doctrine of the Trinity and the deity of the Third Person of the Trinity came later. It seems probable a divine power, not a divine Person, is meant. Gabriel is thus emphasizing *special* divine agency working in a special supernatural way, not the work of God's Spirit in natural processes contemplated in such Old Testament passages as Psalm 104:30, where God's general preservation and providence in nature is designated. Albright and Freedman assert, 'In Aramaic at this time there was no differentiation between the definite and the indefinite article. The absence of the definite article in Greek at this point is therefore not significant.'[32] Perhaps so, but how can they be so sure? H. L. Strack and R. Billerbeck (warmly commended as indispensable to study of Matthew) say, 'the words signify the life-working creative power of God.'[33] This, of course, is not to say that the Third Person of the Godhead was not directly involved. Yet the emphasis of the passage is on the fact the virginal conception was by a creative act of God not that the Third Person of the Godhead begat Jesus the Son of Mary.

This view of the meaning of 'holy spirit' without the definite articles in the Greek text of Luke 1:35 (and the same in Luke 1:15; Matt. 1:18 and 20) is stated precisely by J. A. Fitzmeyer:

---

32. W. F. Albright and C.S.Mann, *Matthew vol. 26, The Anchor Bible* (Garden City, NY: Doubleday & Co., 1981), p. 8.
33. H. L. Strack and P. Billerbeck, *Kommentar Zum Neven Testamentum aus Talmud und Midrasch, i* (Munchen: C. H. Beck'sche, 1969), p. 48, 49.

The Greek text has no definite article. The parallelism of 'holy spirit' and 'power of the Most High' is intended to let the phrases explain each other. The latter phrase indicates that the Spirit is understood in the OT sense of God's creative and active power present to human beings.[34]

Fitzmeyer fully supports the doctrine of the Trinity but rightly finds here 'elements of the doctrine not the doctrine itself.'

Alford aptly refers *Pneuma hagion* to 'the creative Spirit of God,' Genesis 1:2. He goes on to say, 'But as the world was not created by the Holy Ghost, but by the Son [John 1:1, 2] so also the Lord was not begotten by the Holy Ghost, but by the Father; and that *before the worlds*' (Alford's emphasis).[35] So also Charles John Ellicott.[36]

9) Both accounts further report that the couple did not engage in conjugal intercourse until after the child was born (see above) and that there was no human fatherhood. In Matthew 1:16 (KJV), 'Jacob begat Joseph the husband of Mary, of whom was born Jesus,' 'whom' is *hēs* feminine gender, indicating Mary alone. Further, it seems quite feasible, as many scholars have proposed, that at Luke 3:33 the end of the parenthesis is properly not after 'supposed' but after 'Joseph' (see above) and that though Mary is not mentioned (there are no women's names anywhere in Luke's genealogy), Mary is the daughter of Heli and Jesus the *grandson* of Heli. It was quite usual to skip generations in using the word son in this way (again see above).

It is therefore quite unfair to assert, as one commonly reads in critical treatments, that the accounts are in disagreement as to the facts. They are different as being complementary, why should they not be? There is no contradiction.

The Nature and Significance of the Genealogies and the Nativity Narratives.

The only extended genealogy in the New Testament is of Jesus. Since His descent from Abraham and David was essential to His Messiahship, it was essential that an authentic line of descent should be known, especially considering that He was first manifest to Jews and that preaching the gospel during His ministry and for some years afterward ('Jerusalem and in all Judea' Acts 1:8) was only to 'the lost sheep of the house of Israel.' They were the first ones to be convinced the accounts of the virgin birth, oral or written, were authentic. We are certain that public records were kept of such matters at the time of Jesus' birth. This is not contested by modern Jewish authorities. Joseph and Mary returned to Bethlehem to satisfy legal requirements of enrolment. Josephus declares, in some detail, how the public records were kept at Jerusalem by the priests. He claims that even in foreign lands all Jews 'sent to Jerusalem the ancient names of their parents in writing, as well as those of their remote ancestors' (*Against Apion*, I, 6, 7).

Apologists and expositors have much to say about how the genealogies report different details, with different emphases and on different principles with different goals. It is amazing that with such differences (not discrepancies) the two narratives and genealogies come together on so many details indispensable to a consistent Christology. Matthew gives prominence to Joseph, in keeping with his purpose to show readers Jesus' right to David's throne through the line of David. It has been suggested that Matthew's division into three groups of fourteen generations each is based on a typically Jewish use of symbolical numbers, derived in the style of *gematria* from the numerical value of the three Hebrew letters (no vowels in written Hebrew) of David's name. David in Hebrew spelled DWD is the central member of the chain of ancestors (Matt. 1:6, 17 [twice], 20; cf. Luke 1:32). The numerical value is based on order in the alphabet, *daleth* D is fourth, hence value of four and *waw* W sixth, hence value of six. Four plus four plus six equals fourteen, the suggested basis of the three chains of fourteen. This may have meant little to Matthew, but likely would have impressed Jewish readers. (Douglas J. Culver, PhD in Hebraic Studies is the source of the above.)

Each genealogy has strong links with Old Testament Hebraic thought and culture, but Matthew's is especially so, in keeping with his apparent intention to address, instruct and convince Jewish readers. Matthew's genealogy therefore gives prominence to Joseph's lineal descent from David. We know not how many levirate marriages and other distinctly Mosaic or customary arrangements lie undisclosed or how many generations are skipped. Comparison with O.T. records suggests there are some. The genealogy at any rate emphasizes the Messianic line through David's royal family. The story of David's importance begins with 2 Samuel 7:12-13, where the throne is promised to David's

---

34. J. A. Fitzmeyer, *The Gospel According to Luke i–ix*, Anchor Bible (New York: Doubleday, 1981), p. 351.
35. Alford, *NT for English Readers*, p. 296.
36. Charles J. Ellicott, Editor, *Lllicott's Commentary on the Whole Bible*, vol. vi (Grand Rapids, MI: Zondervan, 1954), p. 247.

dynasty 'for ever' several times. Then the theme is carried on through the books of Kings and Chronicles, the Prophets (especially Isaiah 7-12; cf. Jer. 17:25), and many of the royal Messianic Psalms (see Pss. 72; 89:35, 49; 132:1, 11). Matthew is demonstrating Jesus' legal right by legal line of descent from David through Joseph His legal father.

Luke has the same interest in the Davidic connection, but he also shows our Lord's connection as Son of Man (our Lord's favorite title for Himself) with universal humanity by tracing His ancestry back to Adam the first man. And, many would say by giving biological descent through Mary (in a literal sense 'from David's loins' herself) Luke demonstrates that in a literal sense Jesus was 'the fruit of David's loins, according to the flesh' (Acts 2:29, 30). Jesus is frequently addressed in the Gospels, even by strangers, as the 'son of David' and Paul made a point of it (Rom. 1:3).

If there were human sources employed (Luke 1:1-4) they had to be primarily from Joseph and Mary. In such a case Matthew's account appears to come from Joseph. If church tradition had anything to do with it (which it is not necessary to suppose owing to the overlapping of the generation when the Gospel was written and the lives of Jesus' brothers and sisters, the offspring of Joseph and Mary) then Joseph could have been the only once removed source of Matthew's information. It is hard to imagine the development of such a sober statement of facts as folk tradition even among devout peasants, of whom Matthew, at least, certainly was not. He had been a hard-boiled tax farmer. Luke's more sophisticated Greek is interrupted by the large 'island' of Hebraic Greek in the birth narrative. The oracle-like, poetic expressions of Zechariah (Luke 1:67-79), Elizabeth (Luke 1:41-45), Simeon (Luke 2:28-32), and Mary (Luke 1:46-55), the lead personalities in the narrative, constitute this 'island' of Hebrew (Aramaic) thought in literal translation. This indicates Luke quoted unrevised sources leading back to these very people.

Critics almost invariably cite the absence of genealogies and virgin birth narrative in Mark and John as supposed evidence there is something doubtful about the two we do have. In response, let it first be said it suited Mark's purpose in developing his main theme of Jesus the Servant of God *not* to introduce the topic of origins. Slaves need no pedigree. Further, Mark clearly intended to be brief and to the point, to create an atmosphere of urgency throughout, as his employment of *eutheos* (straightaway, immediately, forthwith) over forty times demonstrates. No time for pedigrees! Throughout John's first chapter it is the full humanity of the incarnate Word which is emphasized, as we say now, incarnation. *Ginomai*, 'became' or 'was made' (John 1:14) has no reference to natural birth at all and should not be rendered 'born.' It is to be regretted that NIV translators at Galatians 4:4 ignore (or were ignorant of) the important point which the best ancient theologians made on the difference between *ginomai* and *gennao*, to bear, give birth, in reference to aspects of the incarnation. The very fact that Paul uses *ginomai,* 'made of a woman' rather than 'born of a woman' has suggested to generations of learned scholars that Paul was pointedly indicating something unusual about the birth of Jesus, even though he did enter the world through a birth canal, just as the rest of us do. Paul shifts to *gennao*, to bear, give birth, in the same chapter, three times later on (Gal. 4:22, 24, 29).

The Virgin Birth in the Other Gospels and in the Consciousness of Jesus Himself.

Mark and John, as noted earlier, say nothing directly about the virgin birth of Jesus. Negative criticism says this is because they knew nothing about it. The contrary is more likely. These books are not 'Lives of Christ' but summaries of His redemptive career and in John's case, a definition of who Jesus is. What book, for example, about Abraham Lincoln's presidency of a little more than four years would devote pages to his birth in Kentucky and boyhood in another state and early manhood in still another? A biography would do that. Yet such a book might provide indirect allusions or signs of generally understood awareness of his 'first estate.'

It is quite to be expected then, that given Mark's evident purpose (see above) he should come *immediately* (one of his pet words) to the ministry of the forerunner, John, which began only months before Jesus' baptism, temptation and the calling of the first disciples (Mark 1:1-20). Yet there is indirect evidence that even the common people of Nazareth and environs ('his own country,' Mark 6:1 KJV) may have been aware that Joseph was not His *sire* (to use the plain word), for they depart from the common form 'the son of so and so' (and the Aramaic *Bar Jonah* [Peter] *Bar Nabas* – Barnabas, Son of Consolation), rather saying, 'Is not this the carpenter, the son of Mary?' This is a very unusual mode of identifying a first-century Jew among his neighbors. When they follow with names of brothers and reference to sisters it appears from this side to reveal a very clear community consciousness of 'a story,' perhaps a scandal. Matthew's account in nearly the same words (Matt. 13:54-57) instead of 'Is not this the carpenter?' (Mark 6:3) has 'Is not this the carpenter's son?' and perhaps shows a similar diffidence about the matter for though Mary and her sons are named, Joseph, her husband, is not.

Only by prior rejection of the testimony of the early church as well as the claims of John's Gospel for itself (John 20:30, 31; cf. 1 John 1:1-3) can one insist the Gospel of John is a tendentious composition to support an elaborate Christology originating in an ethnic myth. This claim by Rudolph Bultmann and disciples is complicated and has been rebutted by believing scholars. Researches in history of the first centuries of our era do not support the Bultmannian frontal attack.

An alternate reading of the Greek text of John 1:13 would put a direct allusion to the virgin birth in the Prologue. 'Who,' the first word in the verse, in the Greek of the alternate reading is singular, referring to Christ, viz., ...his name, who (singular) was born, not of blood, nor of the will of the flesh, nor of the will of man but of God.' The textual evidence for this reading while not decisive is substantial, enough to convince a number of modern scholars.[37] Whether correct or not, the fact that very ancient readings of the text thus imply the virgin birth and that Tertullian, Origen, Ambrose and Augustine adopted the reading is further evidence of belief in the virgin birth from the beginning.

However we understand the details of Mary's pregnancy and Joseph's dilemma (Matt. 1:18, 19) we may surmise the village rumor and gossip mill of Nazareth was buzzing with it – for, even though the infant son was a legitimate son of Joseph, he was born less than six months after the mother 'was found with child' and began living with Joseph. (Strack and Billenbeck say according to rabbinic law a newly widowed woman could not marry until three months after the decease of her husband, because until then she could not know for sure she was not pregnant.)[38] Hence, though Joseph then 'took unto him his wife,' that is, she moved out of her parent's house and into his, it would have been common knowledge that 'the baby was three months early.' H. A. W. Meyer[39] and many others since his time have argued that the virgin birth has no connection at all with either the incarnation or His sinless nature. It is not uncommon to read a pronouncement like Meyer's that there is not 'the slightest whisper of so hostile a report' (p. 47) and apart from 'the preliminary history (Matt. 1; Luke 1) no glimpse of this doctrine appears anywhere in the N.T.'[40] But are these opinions fully justifiable?

Let us take note of two rather extended passages of the fourth Gospel. In the judgment of some competent believing scholars, properly to interpret chapter 6, one must hold in mind that Jesus Himself was fully aware of the unique manner of His conception and birth. Also, that the fickle crowd who followed from Tiberias to the Capernaum synagogue were quite aware of the 'scandal' of His birth. The second passage, chapter 8, is probably incapable of full explanation without His own awareness and at least some rumor of it among the temple crowd who listened to His great discourse on this occasion. This was so fierce an encounter that, as Westcott notes, it occasioned 'the first open assault upon the Lord with violence' (compare vv. 20 and 59).

After the crowd of 5,000 plus had pursued Jesus to the area of Capernaum synagogue He delivered a discourse (in the following I cite the RSV only) on the bread of life (John 6:22-40) that was interrupted frequently by murmuring of 'the Jews.' For true life, He said, they must eat of 'the bread of God' (v. 33) 'which comes down from heaven' (v. 33). He told them 'I have come down from heaven' (v. 38). That 'ticked them off,' as the saying goes (v. 41). He said much more about salvation and about faith, but what added puzzlement to anger among His listeners (v. 52) was the sentence 'the bread which I shall give for the life of the world is my flesh' (v. 51). The controversy, as it developed to this point, was simply about *His human origin*. This suggests at the very least that the question of His birth was already a live issue, especially among His fellow Galileans. If the crowd was not aware of the matter (and I cannot *prove* they were) the language Jesus used makes certain that the seed in Mary's womb which grew to an infant delivered on Christmas Day originated not in Joseph but in some sense 'came down from heaven.' The text is plain, it seems to me, that 'the bread' is 'my flesh' (not the eternal Son Himself in this text) 'which came down.' Is this not Jesus' language in John's Gospel for what the angel in Matthew and Luke referred to as 'that which is conceived in her is of the Holy Spirit,' i.e. of divine power (Matt. 1:20 and similar language in Luke 1:35)? The 'flesh,' or human nature of Christ did not 'come down from heaven' except that the divine power from heaven quickened the virgin's womb with the conception of the 'man, Christ Jesus.' Jesus was frequently quite oblique in speaking with His enemies and this is one occasion when He seemed purposely both pointed and vague.

---

37. Bruce M. Metzger, *A Textual Commentary on the Greek NT*, p. 196, 197 and the United Bible Societies ed. of the *Greek New Testament* of 1966, textual notes on John 1:13.
38. H. L. Strack and P. Billenbeck, *op. cit.*, pp. 47, 48.
39. H. A. W. Meyer, *Critical and Exegetical Commentary to the Gospel of Matthew*, trans. from the 6th ed. by F. Crombie and W. Stewart (New York: Funk & Wagnalle, 1884), pp. 45-48.
40. ibid. p. 48.

The eighth chapter of John focuses on His claim, 'I am the light of the world' (v. 12). This claim is connected with His further assertion, 'I know whence I have come and whither I am going' (v. 14). Then He added, 'the Father... sent me,' etc. (v. 18). At this point 'They [Pharisees, v. 13] said to him... "Where is your Father?"' (v. 19). The Versions generally capitalize the 'F' of Father in the Pharisee's question and most commentators defend it. But no less theologian than Augustine as well as Bede, the Venerable, and the scholars W. M. L. deWitte and Hermann Olshausen thought Pharisees meant a physical, human father[41] and some suppose, as I think possible, there may have been an allusion to the reputation of bastardy.

In the verses following Jesus makes further claims of His heavenly origin and of His soon return there, to which the Jews respond by 'Who are you?' (v. 25). Amid all the adjacent bitter words of 'the Jews' and Jesus' very severe responses, the issue of paternal origin becomes paramount: they say, 'We are descendants [seed KJV] of Abraham' (v. 33); 'Abraham is our father' (v. 39). Jesus says, 'I know that you are descendants of Abraham [physically, of course]' (v. 37) and 'If you were Abraham's children [spiritually], you would do what Abraham did' (v. 39). The Jews respond, 'We were not born of fornication; we have one Father, even God' (v.41).

It is difficult to know exactly what they meant by this denial. Are they speaking of true spiritual relation to God or have they descended to the insulting suggestion that Jesus was conceived out of wedlock? Passing over the next part of the dialogue, these particular Jews (who formerly had believed in Him, v. 31) tear into Him, saying, 'Are we not right in saying that you are a Samaritan and have a demon?' (v. 48). The Samaritans were 'half-breeds,' half Jew, half Gentile in origin, so they may be broadly hinting He had a Gentile father (a Roman soldier?).

One cannot erase from this passage the possibility that this group of bitter Jewish enemies of Jesus were throwing up more than a hint of bastardy and mixed ancestry – on account of the Nazareth rumors of His mother's pregnancy before full marriage to her husband.

The usual interpretation supposes that 'born of fornication' (v. 41) reflects the Old Testament, which frequently equates idolatry with fornication, and Jesus' Jewish attackers are protesting that He, having already acknowledged their physical descent from Abraham should acknowledge their spiritual sonship too. He had just accused them of being the devil's children. This may be true, but not necessarily.

I quote Raymond E. Brown whose three large volumes (*Anchor Bible*) on 'John' are as thorough a canvas of scholarship on the book as ever has appeared in English. After briefly taking note of the more common view that I have just described he says:

> But there is another possibility: the Jews may be turning to an *ad hominem* argument against Jesus. He has been talking about his heavenly Father and about their father, but were there not rumors about his own birth? Was there not some question of whether he was really the son of Joseph? The Jews may be saying, 'We were not born illegitimate [but you were].'[42]

When Philip referred to Jesus as 'Jesus of Nazareth, the son of Joseph' he was in a normal way distinguishing Him from others of the same name at Nazareth as we distinguish between Robert Smithwick, my brother-in-law, from Robert Hood who lives in the same neighborhood. But 'son of Mary' at Mark 6:3 is rather strange in the mouth of people of His home town and 'may be an insinuation of illegitimacy.'[43] Ethelbert Stauffer, *Jesus and His Story*, takes a similar view.[44] Origen. tells how a certain Jew claimed Mary was 'turned out of doors' by Joseph once he found he had married a pregnant girl. Later her son, Jesus, hired out as a servant in Egypt 'and having acquired some miraculous powers, on which the Egyptians pride themselves, returned to his own country... and by means of these proclaimed himself a God.'[45]

Convinced of this understanding by Professor A. J. McClain in my student days, I wavered on account of lack of support by many major scholars, Father Brown's sturdy Christological orthodoxy and support encouraged me to study further and to introduce it here. Brown's acceptance of the now widely spread view especially among Roman Catholic scholars, that John chapter 6 is a sort of misplaced Eucharistic liturgy or Last Supper discourse of course lends no support for my earlier remarks on John chapter 6.

---

41. ibid., vol. ii, p. 268.
42. Raymond E. Brown, *The Gospel According to John, i-xii, Anchor Bible* (Garden City, NY: Doubleday, 1966), p. 357.
43. ibid., on John 1:45, pp. 82–83.
44. Ethelbert Stauffer, *Jesus and His Story* (London: SCM, 1960), pp. 23–25.
45. Origen, *Against Celsus*, in *Ante-Nicene Fathers, i* (ed. Roberts and Donaldson, 1885, repr. Peabody: Hendrickson Publ., 1994), 1:28, p. 408.

We must not press the matter further. I add that all through John, especially chapter 17, Jesus addresses the Father God in a way that seems inexplicable apart from two assumptions. The *first*, that Jesus recognized no male being on earth, living or dead as His father.

To this point Warfield rightly wrote:

> It is just in proportion as men lost their sense of Divine personality of... Immanuel, God with us, that they are found to doubt the necessity of the virgin birth; while in proportion as... this fact remains vivid and vital with them, do they instinctively feel that it is alone consonant with that this Being should acknowledge none other father than that Father which is in heaven, from whom alone he came forth to save the world.[46]

Secondly, the absence of a direct statement about the virgin birth suggests the author of the fourth Gospel assumed that all his believing readers knew about the virgin birth of the main subject of his narrative. It is not possible adequately to answer Jesus' question, 'What do you think about the Christ? Whose son is he?' (Matt. 22:42) without reference to the virgin birth or at least to assume it – and it seems entirely reasonable, I think, that no writer of the New Testament attempted to do so.

The Virgin Birth in New Testament Doctrine.

In the fledgling journal, *Christianity Today* (vol. iv, 7 December 1959), most of the total of forty pages (about three and a half of advertisements, a little news) was devoted to four excellent articles on the virgin birth and an editorial by C. F. H. Henry on the same subject. Five years later (vol. ix, 18 December 1964, more news, fewer advertisements) the same journal again featured the virgin birth. In the earlier number an article by E. J. Carnell of Fuller Seminary claimed no connection at all between the virgin birth and '*Christ's incarnation*' or '*Christ's sinlessness.*' He said its significance was chiefly as a miraculous sign, like the smoking furnace and flaming torch to Abraham, Moses' rod and Gideon's fleece. I note the more recent work of Lewis and Demarest seems to endorse this.[47] Quite to the contrary, the earlier article in *Christianity Today* by James Taylor, then of Ayr Scotland, argued that the virgin birth is important both for our understanding of Christianity and the Person of Christ. The brief article finds in the virgin birth (1) attestation of predictive prophecy by fulfillment, (2) a miraculous sign of the presence of God's kingdom on earth in Christ, (3) 'the presence of mystery' as 'the footprint of the divine,' (4) 'unique attestation of the person of the Saviour,' and states, with support from Warfield[48] (5) 'the redemptive work of Christ depends on his supernatural birth to the virgin Mary.'

Warfield vigorously affirmed in the first place:

> His supernatural birth [in the sense of special miracle] is given already... in his supernatural life and his supernatural work, and forms an *indispensable* [emphasis added] element in the supernatural religion which he founded... the supernatural birth of Jesus is a necessity... not... unnatural or contra-natural, but distinctly supernatural.[49]

In this I concur.

Jesus said He was not 'out of this world' (*ek tou kosmou toutou*) indicating source, and that He came down from heaven. He was born into our race but His Person, the eternal Logos, was not of our race. He came down from heaven. Who is to say the Logos could have taken to Himself humanity without creating another human person, resulting in dual personality (an ancient heresy) apart from virgin birth? The incarnation was voluntary but not lawless. The invariable result of usual conception by a male and female coming together is a new person with a distinct, personal center of consciousness. The virgin birth was different. The incarnate Son was '*made* of a woman' (Gr. *ginomai*) according to Galatians 4:4 (KJV). This occurred in conception, gestation and birth when 'the Son' (Gr.) was 'sent forth' by God. It is a grievous error to mistranslate the verb *ginomai*, to become, as though it were *gennaō*, to be born or to bear a child, as the NIV does at Galatians 4:4. The whole process: virginal conception, the gestation *and* the birth 'of a woman' are in view.

Furthermore, to redeem sinners, the Savior must be without sins or sin nature. I do not know where Carnell got the notion '[T]he apostles trace Christ's sinlessness to his holy life.' But the rule of nature since Adam, whether

---

46. Warfield, *Biblical and Theological Studies*, p. 164.
47. Gordon Lewis and Bruce Demarest, *Integrative Theology ii* (Grand Rapids, MI: Zondervan, 1990), pp. 273 ff.
48. Warfield, 'The Supernatural Birth of Jesus,' in *Biblical and Theological Studies*, p. 161.
49. ibid., pp. 161, 163.

the soul be generated in the ordinary way by two parents or created specially by God is that ordinary procreation results in a sinful being who performs sinfully. Of course Mary was a sinner but the chain of cause-effect was broken in Jesus' case. The single case in all human history of birth of a sinless man came by virginal conception. Does not the angel's message strongly suggest so? Among theologians born of women 'there hath not risen a greater' lately than James Orr, author of a famous book[50] on the virgin birth of Jesus, editor of the *ISBE* and the major article therein on Jesus Christ. Orr wrote,

> The announcement itself was of the most amazing import… He would be 'holy' from the womb (Luke 1:35)… The holiness of Jesus is here put in connection with His miraculous conception, and surely rightly. In no case in the history of mankind has natural generation issued in a being who is sinless, not to say superhuman. The fact that Jesus, even in His human nature, was supernaturally begotten… does not exclude the higher and eternal Sonship according to the divine nature.[51]

The modern revised Greek text rightly excludes 'of the' after 'born.' A literal rendering will read, 'Holy spirit will come upon thee [sing.], and [the] Highest's power will shade upon thee [sing.]. Therefore also [*dio kai*] the [def. art.] thing born [neuter] shall be called God's son' (Luke 1:35). The words 'therefore also' (*dio kai*) join the 'inferential conjunction' with also, 'denoting that the inference is self evident' (Bauer *Lexicon*). Bauer lists Luke 1:35 among seven New Testament examples of this usage. Once the second 'of thee' has been properly eliminated it is clear that the begetting is by Holy Spirit and Highest power not Mary. Begetting is normally a male function not female (though sometimes the word is used otherwise in the New Testament). So, because begotten by divine potency not human male potency, 'the inference is self-evident' (Bauer) that the holy thing (neuter *grammatical* gender not *physical* gender) is called God's Son. That there is causal connection, therefore, between the virginal conception by divine power and the holiness of the One who after His birth was to be called God's Son seems to be affirmed (Meyer). There is no immaculate virgin here. But there is an immaculate 'thing born' and that because of a miraculous conception.

The Practical Importance and Values of the Virgin Birth.

Much has already appeared in this chapter on the matter of the practical importance and values of the fact of the virgin birth and of believing it to be a fact. It has been vigorously defended by exponents and apologists from the earliest times of which we have record – from Justin Martyr, Ignatius and Irenaeus, among others – on to the latest evangelical or Roman Catholic Bible dictionary. J. Gresham Machen, of Princeton, later one of the founding faculty of Westminster Theological Seminary and in some respects the leader of the American resurgence of Protestant orthodoxy, dedicated years of scholarly effort to the defense of this doctrine in *The Virgin Birth of Christ* (1932) already cited in this chapter as also did James Orr (*The Virgin Birth of Jesus*, 1907). The following remarks therefore draw from the veritable ocean of what has been said often before but needs to be said again. Like the gospel message itself, of which the virgin birth of Jesus is a part, related simply and earnestly in three chapters of two Gospels and assumed by all the rest of the New Testament, the importance and values of the virgin birth must be declared anew to every generation.

1. The virgin birth is essential to the trustworthiness of the Bible itself, not least the Gospels, the only source available as to how our Lord and Savior entered this world.

> It is perfectly clear that the New Testament teaches the virgin birth of Christ; about that there can be no manner of doubt. There is no serious question as to the interpretation of the Bible at this point. Everyone admits the Bible represents Jesus as having been conceived by the Holy Ghost and born of the Virgin Mary. The only question is whether in making that representation the Bible is true or false.[52]

Assertions like these will have little force with authors of the amazing volume of contemporary literature in 'search for the historical Jesus,' all of which disregards any possibility of the supernatural and rejects the claims of the Gospels themselves to authenticity. If, however, one wishes to read the Gospels with acceptance of what they really say he will find this doctrine spread across the first page of the first Gospel and the first chapter of the third. How can one believe much of anything *for sure* of the rest of the New Testament if he rejects the foundational message?

---

50. James Orr, *The Virgin Birth of Christ* (London: 1907).
51. James Orr, art 'Jesus Christ,' *ISBE* v, pp. 1631–1632.
52. Machen, *Virgin Birth*, p. 382.

2. Knowing as every Christian does, the importance of our Lord's holiness (impeccability, sinlessness), it is important that the record connects the fact of Jesus' holiness with miraculous conception by divine power (Luke 1:35) as also His being the Savior of His people (Matt. 1:21). We have reasoned earlier that the words 'Holy Spirit' being without the article ('Holy Spirit,' Luke 1:35, also Matt. 1:18 and 20) and joined in parallel with 'power of Highest' (again no article) signify simply the supernatural power of God rather than the Second Person of the Trinity. 'The parallel between the two expressions indicates that the one should be interpreted by the other' (Lange's *Commentary*, loc. cit.). James Orr, in the five-volume encyclopaedia of which he was general editor, comments on the above expressions:

> He would be 'holy' from the womb… His name was to be Jesus… denoting Him as Savior. The holiness of Jesus is here put in connection with His miraculous conception, and surely rightly. In no case in the history of mankind has natural generation issued in a being who is sinless, not to say superhuman.[53]

3. Even in our post-modern age of ethical relativism and the growing influence of evolutionary psychology of sex, it is of some importance that unless Mary was still a virgin, as Matthew and Luke say, when her first born was delivered she was the immoral, youthful mother of a bastard. This state of affairs would be disgraceful now even as then – the mother an object of rejection and pity rather than what she is in the Gospels, a pious, prayerful, devout and pure servant of God. The alternatives are simply unacceptable. Subsequent generations, just as she herself foresaw, have rightly risen to call Mary 'blessed' (Luke 1:48) and as the angel promised, she remains 'blessed… among women' (Luke 1:28 KJV). The Madonna of Hollywood and rock music is the parody: Mary the reality of pure motherhood.

4. The virgin birth provides a reasonable explanation for how a divine Being who is without beginning might take to Himself a human nature without the procreation of a new person. A. J. McClain, dean of Ashland Seminary and later first president of Grace Theological Seminary and long-time professor of theology said:

> The virgin birth gives the only *reasonable* explanation of the incarnation of God's Son in human flesh. The natural result of human procreation is ordinarily the beginning of a new person. But Christ did not get personhood through two parents. He was a person before he was born. There was therefore no need for the usual procreative process to bring into existence a new person. Such a process would have been out of the question. Employment of the ordinary procreation process would have required a special miracle to avoid a dual personality.[54]

The author of those sentences understood well the requirements of the creedal articles of *Chalcedon* and *Quicumque Volt*. The virgin birth was therefore both important and apparently necessary.

5. The foundation of the 'high Christology' of the creeds and of orthodox Christianity from that day to this came directly out of the virgin birth record of Matthew and Luke. This becomes evident first in the early second century in the writings of Justin Martyr and Ignatius, later in the century in those of Irenaeus. This doctrine was at the heart of discussion and debate of the idea of incarnation as well as the two natures of Christ. The manner of Jesus' birth was foundational in these discussions. Many modern writers have pointed out that in that early day when the chief antagonist was a corrupt but sophisticated heathenism the miracle of supernatural conception and virgin birth was set forth as the prime proof of Jesus' divinity and of the incarnation. This is easily demonstrated (Machen cites the literature fully in chap. 1, 'The Virgin Birth in the Second Century,' pp. 2-43) and the literature readily available in volume I of *The Antenicene Fathers and The Apostolic Fathers* by Lightfoot.

6. The virgin birth is a necessary, constituent part of an incarnation that was and is supernatural, as well as natural, through and through. One well said, '[I]t cannot be denied that the supernatural birth of Jesus enters constituously into the substance of that system which is taught in the New Testament as Christianity – that it is the expression of its supernaturalism, the safeguard of its doctrine of incarnation.'[55]

7. In a practical way the virgin birth tests whether a theologian or a theology is approaching Christianity with wholly naturalistic assumptions or is open to the supernatural. We live in an age of serial attacks on plain understanding of plain speech such as we find in the Bible. These have come from many quarters since the beginning of the Age of Reason, or the Enlightenment – none more persistent than in theology and hermeneutics (interpretation) of literature. It is not uncommon in liberal literature to read approving references to 'the Easter event' or 'resurrection faith' of the disciples or of the 'presence of the divine' in Jesus or even of 'the deity of Christ.' Yet the purpose of the

---

53. Orr, *ISBE iii*, pp. 1631, 1632.
54. McClain, from Robert D. Culver's handwritten record of the lecture.
55. Warfield, 'The Supernatural Birth of Jesus,' in *Biblical and Theological Studies*, p. 167.

author of the statements may be to deny or at least subvert the bodily resurrection of the flesh of Jesus and the 'very God of very God' of Jesus as is the plain sense of all the orthodox creeds and the Scripture passages underlying the creeds. The result has been an 'abysmal intellectual morass' in which it is hard to know who the confessors of Jesus really are.

The virgin birth furnishes a better test. As Machen stated the case: 'If a man affirms that Jesus was born without a human father, being conceived by the Holy Ghost in the virgin's womb, it is difficult to see how he can escape the plain meaning.'[56] This does not make the virgin birth central to the structure of Christian doctrine and the 'plan of salvation,' but it is a useful test. If, as Emil Brunner does say, the virgin birth is an unnecessary teaching, an incubus so to speak, that Christianity is better off without it, we know about where to place him in reference to orthodox Christianity.

8. On the contrary, the miraculous conception and virgin birth of Jesus have an importance all their own. Even children seem to understand this, perhaps better than their tutors. Christianity as we know it would be a different religion in its public expression in worship and in personal piety would not be the same.

It was a correct instinct which put the virgin birth – miraculous conception – in the 'rule of faith' expressed in the very earliest of post-apostolic confessions, catechisms and creeds. Some of these have been convincingly traced back to the first third of the second century.[57] These found permanent expression in the Old Roman Creed,[58] then 'the Apostles' Creed' so-called, then in the great ecumenical creeds and on to the present in almost every formal statement of church doctrine.

It was the same right impulse which made the virgin birth a major issue in the developing denial of historical Christianity in nineteenth-century liberalism and the response of alarmed believing scholars. James Orr, 'Defender of the Faith' as Peter Toon calls him in *The Gospel Magazine*[59] could produce his magnum opus, *The Christian View of God and the World* (1893), scarcely mentioning the virgin birth, but fourteen years later he produced a supplement, so to speak, *The Virgin Birth of Christ* (1907). This work, at a critical moment in the developing apologetics of orthodoxy, helped to cause the virgin birth to be understood by embattled defenders of orthodox faith of the time as a 'fundamental.' J. Gresham Machen in his 1930 book of similar title, affirming the same faith, but more from strict historical critical perspective, was as much as any man then alive the founder of the fundamentalist movement. These men, whom we should rise to call their names blessed, had the right instinct when, just as the framers of the ancient catholic *rule of faith* and later of the Apostles' Creed, they named 'the virgin birth' among 'the fundamentals' of the faith which call for special defense (not that they summarize all Christian beliefs). They meant to designate truths that cannot be abandoned without abandoning Christianity. It was the distinct privilege of The General Assembly of the Northern Presbyterian Church in 1910 to affirm 'five essential doctrines as under attack in the church: the inerrancy of Scripture, the virgin birth of Christ, the substitutionary atonement of Christ, Christ's bodily resurrection, and the historicity of the miracles.'[60] It was fitting that in *The fundamentals*, twelve volumes of articles published in Chicago between 1910 and 1915 as 'witness to the central doctrines of and experiences of Christianity, and as a defense against numerous... criticisms of orthodoxy'[61] one of the leading authors should be James Orr on the subject of 'The Virgin Birth of Christ.'

---

56. Machen, *Virgin Birth*, p. 390.
57. Machen, *Virgin Birth*, chap. 1, 'The Virgin Birth in the Second Century.'
58. Bettenson, *Docs of Christian Church*, p. 33.
59. *The Gospel Magazine*, August 1972, as cited in art. 'James Orr,' *Evangelical Dictionary of Theology*, ed. W. Elwell (Grand Rapids, Baker Books, 1984), p. 804.
60. Carl T. McIntyre, 'Fundamentalism,' *Evangelical Dictionary of Theology*, p. 435.
61. ibid., p. 436.

8
The Incarnation of the Son of God

This chapter concentrates attention to the meaning of the incarnation in Scripture and in the church.

The doctrine of the triune God is presupposed in the doctrine of the incarnation of the Son of God. In Scripture and history of doctrine the Father is distinguished from the Son and Spirit by *paternity*, the Son from the Father and Spirit by *filiation*, the Spirit from the Son and Father by *procession*. Now that we have considered our Lord's preexistence as eternal Son, His full deity and humanity in full integrity and supernatural entrance into the world we must pursue closer attention to what incarnation (Latin for enfleshment) involved. It is sometimes said to be an act of humiliation, condescension or *kenosis* in some recent theology. The characterization of the incarnation as a *kenosis* or self-emptying will be examined in chapter 10. Let us devote first attention to how the doctrinal expression developed in the church.

The Central Message from the Beginning.

We know when and where the followers of Jesus first came to be called Christians (Acts 11:26). The sermons of the first chapters of the book of Acts are evidence of why. They are about 'Jesus of Nazareth' at first, 'a *man* [emphasis added] attested... by God with mighty works and wonders and signs' (Acts 2:22), One who is nevertheless also 'Lord and Christ' (Acts 2:34-36). These were the first efforts, by a fisherman turned Apostle, to state a public, agreed Christology. The seeds of the highest whole-Bible, truly ecumenical theology are all there, viz.: Jesus is *man*, He is LORD, the Jehovah of the Old Testament, and He is Christ – the 'coming one' of prophecy – and Savior of men (cf. Matt.1:21). Some or all of these features of a doctrine of Christ's Person, nature and work prevail in every biblical expression of Christian witness: short and pithy (as Acts 16:30) or extended as Peter to Cornelius' household (Acts 10:34-43) and Paul's addresses from Acts chapter 13 onward. It is therefore clear *why* ancient believers were named 'Christians' by their neighbors in Antioch (Acts 11:26; cf. 26:28; and 1 Peter 4:16). These people knew nothing important to talk about save One who had by now come to be known as 'the Lord Jesus Christ' – not the name Jesus preceded by a modifier (Lord) and followed by the name of an office (Messiah-Christ) but now a compound name.

The Unique Apostolic Message and Claims.

This message and accompanying claims were unique. Though certain parallels have been alleged in pagan mythology of gods coming to earth as men and of men attaining deity by heroic deeds, it must be acknowledged that pagan antiquity quickly came to understand the uniqueness of Christian preachment of Jesus Christ, even though more than two centuries passed before the message received legal recognition as tolerable. It was shortly given permanent form in the apostolic and prophetic literary deposit we call the New Testament.

The Mystery and the Name.

We know of no apostolic writings to 'explain' the mystery of Christ (Eph. 3:4; Col. 4:3) to unbelievers – either Jewish or Gentile. Nor does any passage of the apostolic and prophetic Scripture really explain One who is Savior, Lord-God, Christ and Man of Nazareth. His grace and truth are proclaimed; his Person, divinity, humanity and career are stated and sometimes defended; but never is the slightest effort made to solve the unavoidable intellectual question of how one Person could honestly be the subject of all those momentous claims.

Later, when theology came to be a self-conscious effort of scholars, the word incarnation was coined as apparently a specifically Christian word for the event of 'Christ-came' and that aspect of Christology that relates to His nature and Person.[1]

The Classical Text.

John, the author of the fourth Gospel, says he wrote it in order to cause men to believe 'Jesus is the Christ' (John 20:30, 31). He therefore began with eighteen verses devoted exclusively to a theological statement of the incarnation, captured in a nutshell at verse 14: 'And the Word was made flesh, and dwelt among us, (and we beheld his glory, the glory as of the only begotten of the Father,) full of grace and truth' (in the KJV).

Later we shall return to this classical text to examine the precise meaning of every word and relation of each to the central affirmation of our religion, setting it so far apart from ethnic religious systems it scarcely fits the category of 'religion.'

Biblical Terms for the Incarnation.

There is considerable variety of expressing the incarnation in the New Testament. John states God sent 'his Son into the world' (John 3:17) and many times more in John's Gospel; John 3:13 that he 'descended from heaven' and 'came down from heaven' (John 6:51). The Baptist referred to Him as 'the one who is to come' (Matt. 11:3) and later Jesus says 'the Son of Man came' (Matt. 20:28). In the language of space and time these several expressions speak of a transfer from heaven of God to the world of men. *He came 'from there to here.'*

Sometimes the incarnation is said to mean that 'He' was '*manifested* [emphasis added]' (1 John 3:5 KJV) or 'grace... was... made *manifest* by the *appearing* [emphasis added] of our Savior Jesus Christ' (2 Tim. 1:9, 10 KJV) or 'God was *manifest* [emphasis added] in the flesh' (1 Tim. 3:16). These are telling us that 'a man called Jesus' and characterized by divine grace became visible as a normal human being, as well as manifest deity, on the face of this planet.

Some of the passages declare, hint or allude to the changes He made, the price He paid, the glory He laid aside, for 'he humbled himself' (Phil. 2:8), 'became poor' (2 Cor. 8:9) and 'was made lower than the angels' (Heb. 2:9).

Others emphasize the authenticity of His full humanity as 'the Word became flesh' (John 1:14), 'partook' of flesh and blood (Heb. 2:14) and was 'found in human form' (Phil. 2:8). Matthew and Luke describe the nativity of Jesus as entering this world the same way every human being does (Matt. 2:1; Luke 2:1-7) and, like every Jew of His time, as 'under the law' subject to the usual restrictions and duties of pious Jews (Gal. 4:4; cf. Heb. 2:17 KJV).

One text, however, carefully distinguishes the Lord's unfallen human nature as distinguished from our fallen nature, speaking of '[God] sending his own Son in the *likeness* [emphasis added] of sinful flesh' (Rom. 8:3). This distinction is preserved in the words, 'being found in human *form* [emphasis added]' ('found in *fashion* as a man' KJV) (Phil. 2:8), though here 'form' must not be carried to the later Docetics' conclusion that He only appeared to be (looked like) a man, masquerading deity as humanity.

His lowly state is emphasized in 'taking the form of a *servant* [emphasis added]' (Phil. 2:7).

---

1. 'Incarnation,' *Oxford English Dictionary*.

Theological Formulation in Christian Antiquity.

It should not then be surprising that *Christians* early in the era became deeply interested in combining all the biblical information available into some comprehensive statement or statements about the Person and nature of the Savior, Redeemer, Lord, King, Great High Priest, Captain of Salvation, Lamb of God, God, Man, Jesus, LORD and much more. This became a problem acutely necessary to address even before the Apostles were dead as is evident even on a few pages of the New Testament. The earliest heresies all related to the incarnation directly or indirectly and several arose in the apostolic age (1 Cor. 15:12; 1 John 4:2, 3; 2 John 7).

The story of how the ancient church tackled this project is fascinating for any one who bothers to search it out. Later in this series we shall address it. For now, let us pass on to the permanent results of it in the Creed of Nicea (AD 325) the enlargement of the same at Constantinople (Second Ecumenical Council of AD 381) and the Definition of Chalcedon (Fourth Ecumenical Council, 451). To the present no large group of Christians has permanently rejected the theology of these creedal monuments created by the 'Old Catholic' and pre-papal, undivided, ancient church. Though always subject to inspection and improvement by Scripture, they have stood the test of 1,500 years of Christian history. Any one who tries to rewrite ancient orthodoxy of the Incarnation does so to his own great peril. Menno Simons, for example, founder of Mennonites, is said to have rejected certain clauses, but orthodox Mennonite churches, even though they did not have formal creeds, soon had a Christology fully consistent with the ancient creeds. Further, many denominations, scarcely aware their evangelical heritage has a lineage directly leading to Chalcedon, Constantinople and Nicea, sometimes unknowingly reject all connection or dependence upon these ancient treasures of sound biblical religion. There is quite a literature of this sort among the 'free churches.' Titles such as *The Free Church Through the Ages* and *British and Foreign Baptists* and the like fill a section of my library and I was raised among some of that persuasion.

All orthodox, evangelical Christians should appreciate the contributions of the authors, chiefly British and American (many conservative Anglicans who had a special interest in the subject), who have defended and expounded orthodox Christology against the tide of perversions and denials of the past 200 years. A symposium, *The Myth of God Incarnate* (John Hick ed., 1976–1977), is a striking example.

The Central Affirmations.

Charles Gore (1853–1932), an Anglican bishop and scholar, was an outstanding defender of orthodox Christology in Britain in the late nineteenth century. In defense of orthodoxy he proposed a form of what has been called *kenotic* Christology. It was an effort to explain how Christ could apparently 'not know' certain things and yet be God, omniscient.[2]

Gore summarized the 'ancient venerable' definitions of the ancient creeds of Nicea (AD 325), Constantinople (AD 381), Chalcedon (451) and decisions of the general councils of the still undivided church in the Bampton Lectures at the University of Oxford (1891), published as *The Incarnation of the Son of God*. He wrote:

> These definitions consist in substance of four propositions:
> (1) that as Son of God, Jesus Christ is very God, of one substance with the Father;
> (2) that as Son of man, He is perfectly Man, in the completeness of human faculties and sympathies;
> (3) that though both God and Man, He is yet one person, namely the Son of God who has taken manhood into Himself;
> (4) that in this incarnation the manhood, though it is truly assumed into the divine person, still remains none the less truly human, so that Jesus Christ is of one substance with us men in respect of His manhood, as He is with the Father in respect of His godhead.[3]

To this Gore implicitly adds a (5), His complete manness, body and soul are His forever, i.e. the incarnation is permanent. Jesus, the Son of God, is still today a man in heaven. His exact words are:

> The humanity in Christ remains distinctively what it was: it is not transmuted out of its own proper character; the eternal person assumes the human nature, and acts through it, without its ceasing to be human. Christ, who is of one substance with the Father in respect of His Godhead, is of one substance with us in respect of our manhood, and that for ever.[4]

2. S. M. Smith, art. 'Kenosis, Kenotic Theology,' in *Evangelical Dictionary of Theology*, ed. W Elwell (Grand Rapids, MI: Baker Books, 1984), pp. 600–602.
3. Charles Gore, *The Incarnation of the Son of God* (London: John Murray, 1891), pp. 80, 81.
4. ibid., p. 95.

The Practical Connection of the Incarnation.

There are practical reasons set forth by Scripture, why some such understanding is mandatory for the purity and soundness, even survival of Christianity. Four profound major Scripture passages (John 1:1-14; Phil. 2:6-11; Heb. 2:9-18; 1 Tim. 3:16) give special treatment to the incarnation. Each is specifically introduced to enforce some moral or spiritual truth of the essence of our religion. If authentic Christianity is to survive it must adhere to what these and other passages plainly say and the ancient church clearly so understood. To think otherwise is to reject the first four and a half centuries of the church, which would be a bit of the arrogance of ignorance. Observe the connection of the incarnation with practical Christianity in these four majestic portions of the New Testament.

First, the Prologue of John's Gospel: 'The Word' who 'became [was made] flesh' is the One through whom 'all things *became* [were made, emphasis added]' and 'without him' *was made* not even one thing that was *made* (John 1:3). Not only so, even though 'the world *was made* [emphasis added] through him' this world did not receive him (v. 10), to those who 'believed in his name' he gives power 'to *become* [be made, emphasis added] children of God' (v. 12). This One in whose name we must believe, whose name we must know in some essential way, is He who '*became* [was made, emphasis added] flesh and dwelt among us' (v. 14). Each of these seven *becomes* or *becames* renders a form of *ginomai*. When we read 'there was man sent from God whose name was John' (John 1:6) 'was' might well be rendered 'came to be' or simply 'came,' for again the word is *ginomai*. Observe the new birth is connected with (not necessarily caused by) believing in the incarnate Word (John 1:12, 13). The force of these seven 'becames' leads to enormous practical consequences for us as well as for Him.

The classical definition of the incarnation at Philippians 2:6-11 is to teach us to look out for others' interests rather than our own (v. 4).

Hebrews 2:9-18, perhaps one of the most comforting passages in the Bible discusses the nature and purposes of the Incarnation in relation to our assurance of a sympathetic answer to the needs we express in our prayers.

First Timothy 3:16 ('[God] manifested in the flesh', etc.) is spliced in a niche between instruction on how a minister of the Word 'ought to behave' and a warning against being led astray by the deceiving spirits who propagate false doctrine and its accompanying false piety. 'Ideas have consequences' was known to Scripture long before Richard Weaver employed the sentence as title for a great book! In this case the idea is the complete and permanent manness of the Lord Jesus Christ.

Five Changes Involved in Incarnation.

Traditional exposition of the doctrine of the incarnation properly distinguished three 'states' of Christ, viz.: the state of pre-incarnate glory, the state of humiliation and the state of exaltation. We shall discuss these valid and useful distinctions a bit later. At this point let us note five changes for Him that the Bible indicates and seek somehow to understand as much as we can with our earthbound noetic powers and vocabulary.

1. There was *a change in His dwelling-place*. Jesus said, 'I am the living bread that came down from heaven' (John 6:51). A whole class of such New Testament texts speaks of the incarnation in similar language. These neither affirm nor deny that the pre-incarnate Logos was both immanent in the world and transcendent above it.

Nor is John, chapter 6 (as some falsely say) part of a late communion-table homily, dislocated from the first-century Jewish church to the pages of the New Testament. The sixth chapter of John, in context and taken at face value, has no more connection with the elements and ceremony of the Lord's Supper than do Jesus' several other 'I am' statements such as 'I am the vine,' 'I am the living water,' 'I am the light,' etc. Certain critics have tried to make it seem so. See the relevant discussion by R. E. Brown in the *Anchor Bible*.[5]

Quite the contrary, John 6:51 is a cryptic, personal statement by Jesus about His own origin to hard-hearted Jews who had already rejected Him. It employs symbolism drawn directly from the preceding day's miracle of the bread that fed 5,000 hungry men (cf. John 6:10; and 3:2-26). No cosmic geography of heaven and earth is intended when Jesus speaks of heaven as up and earth as down or 'lower parts of the earth.'

Modern science did not discover that 'up' is not literally the location of heaven. Solomon's prayer (2 Chr. 6:18, 30) shows he was aware that heaven is simply the 'place' of God's special permanent manifestation. He contrasts that heaven with the earthly temple building where He had chosen specially to manifest Himself on earth. When the Son of God became incarnate, Mary, Nazareth, Bethlehem, the Land of Israel became, until His ascension, the place of the Son's *temporary* special manifestation.

---

5. R. E. Brown, *Gospel according to John i-xii, Anchor Bible* (Garden City, NY: Doubleday & Co., 1966), pp. 268–294.

2. There was *a change in His possessions*. As *Logos-Creator*, of course, He is possessor of heaven and earth. But as the babe of Bethlehem and throughout His earthly career He laid that aside. Paul, writing to an ancient congregation, encouraged generosity by stating, 'For you know the grace of our Lord Jesus Christ, that though he was rich, yet for your sake he became poor' (2 Cor. 8:9). Jesus had 'food and clothing' and was no doubt 'with these... content' (1 Tim. 6:8) but He owned no real estate and none of this planet's 'worldly goods.' He was no Jewish Diogenes wandering about in a tub. Yet as pre-incarnate Word He was 'Possessor of heaven and earth' (Gen. 14:19, 22) and could say 'the world and its fullness are mine' (Ps. 50:12). But this lack of possessions was temporary. He will come again as King of kings and LORD of lords to take immediate possession (Rev. 19:16).

3. There was *a change as to His glory*. The Old Testament makes much of the 'weight' (Heb. *ḥavodh*) or glory of the God of Israel. This outward glory is even personalized in certain passages and represented as having something like a personal history in several chapters in Ezekiel. The heavens 'declare' His glory day and night. Yet, for thirty-some years on earth the Son of God was *incognito* in respect to His divine glory, even though muffled glory flashed forth on occasion, especially at the Transfiguration. Jesus made specific reference to this when He prayed, 'And now, Father, glorify me in your own presence with the glory that I had with you before the world existed' (John 17:5). At the end, of course, He was 'taken up in glory' (1 Tim. 3:16) and shall return 'with power and great glory' (Luke 21:27) and reign before His saints gloriously (Isa. 24:23). This absence of divine glory also was temporary.

4. There was *a change in position* in relation to the Father. This has always been very far from being fully understood. The eternal relation of the three Persons of the Trinity cannot change. He is eternally *Monogenēs Theos*, 'God... only begotten... which is in the bosom of the Father' (John 1:18 KJV). Yet in a way only God can fully understand, He, though 'he was in the form of God, did not count equality with God a thing to be grasped, but made himself nothing, taking the form of a servant' (Phil. 2:6, 7). The *form of God* is here in contrasting parallel with *form of a servant*, one whose will is constantly pliable, willingly agreeable to a master. 'Slave' in the American history of slavery is not the right word for the Old Testament ideal of voluntary obedience. 'I have come to do your will, O God,' He says, if we may borrow the language of Hebrews 10:7 which in turn quotes a Psalm. But, again, this is temporary. 'Wherefore... highly exalted': 'cross, then crown' is the triumphant verdict of Scripture. The state of humiliation ended with resurrection, ascension and session at the right hand of the Father. He is now *exalted* LORD and Christ (see Acts 2:33-36) and coming King.

5. There was *a change from form of God to fashion as a man*. (How can I characterize it with some logically appropriate word?) Paul's expression is 'being found in fashion as a man' (Phil. 2:8 KJV), a good literal translation. John says 'the Word became flesh' (John 1:14). By 'flesh' John means all that it means to be man, a member of the human race. We shall examine these two passages later.

This act of taking to Himself a complete human nature was far different from the other four changes. He came to earth, but returned to heaven; changed possessions for poverty, but gained back all He gave up plus a numerous posterity (Isa. 53:11; Pss. 22:30; 45:16); changed glory for humiliation, but He was received back to heaven in glory and shall so come again; equal with God He stooped to servanthood but is now LORD and Christ. His manhood, in contrast, is forever. When the moon is old, the stars are cold and the leaves of the judgment book unfold, the Judge of all the earth will be a man. When in the future all things will be subject to Him, it will be to the God-man.

When Jesus was on earth His favorite name for Himself was 'the Son of Man,' in Greek literally the son of the man, probably (in addition to other freight of meaning) indicating a particular man as repeatedly in Ezekiel a similar expression does. There is a slight but very significant departure from this at John 5:27, where the definite article is absent in the Greek: 'And he [the Father] has given him authority to execute judgement, because he is the Son of Man,' or 'a son of man,' i.e. a human being. His permanent humanity specially qualifies Him, as being Himself a descendant of Adam, to be a fully competent Judge of men, He will never cease to be a man. Hebrews 2:17, 18 and 4:14-16 make much of our Lord's present fully human nature as our Great High Priest in heaven.

They who witnessed Jesus' ascension 'as he went up' were told by two heavenly messengers that 'this *same* [emphasis added] Jesus ...shall so come' again (Acts 1:11 KJV).

When Stephen saw Jesus standing in heaven, it was 'Jesus' whom he saw standing (Acts 7:55), the man of Nazareth, not a spook or wraith. He is still *en sarki*, 'God manifested in flesh.'

The last page of the Bible, where our Lord reaffirms the whole of the book of Revelation as His own revelation, also affirms His own permanent full humanity as the 'descendant of David' (Rev. 22:16).

No Change of Personal Identity.

There was never any change of personal identity – being always from eternity to eternity God Only Begotten, Eternal Word of God. We put off development of this important fact to the next chapter and for now take note of the importance theology has always ascribed to the permanence of God manifest in human 'flesh' – after that first Easter in *resurrected flesh* and *bone*, but not less than full humanity. A doctrine of man is of course implicit. This also calls for further attention later.

The importance of the permanence of our Lord's incarnation as a complete man, body of flesh and soul (or spirit), has not been missed by good theologians nor has it been missed by historic creeds and confessions and works of theology. Let one outstanding example suffice for present purposes.

The Westminster Shorter Catechism, 'Q. 21... [the] Son of God became man, and so was and continueth to be, God and man, in two distinct natures, and one person, forever.'[6] The Confession states that as Mediator between God and man it was necessary that 'On the third day he arose from the dead, with *the same body in which he suffered; with which also he ascended into heaven*, and there sitteth at the right hand of the Father making intercession; and shall return to judge men and angels at the end of the world.'[7]

His office as Mediator required that the same baby's body that was conceived in and born of Mary, 'increased in stature,' in which He 'suffered and died' be the same (glorified to be sure, but not substituted) in which He ascended, now vehicle of mediatorial intercession and in which He shall return. L. Berkhof is accurate but unexceptional in heading a section of his fine work, *Systematic Theology*, 'The Physical Return of Christ.'

The success of the ancient undivided church in forming adequate statements of Christology, the Holy Spirit and the Trinity came only with protracted, exhaustive effort by several generations of saints and scholars – almost all of whom were pastors. This involved painful travel to four Ecumenical Councils all in the region of Constantinople the capital of the eastern (Greek speaking) part of the Roman world.

The Creed of the Undivided Ecumenical Church.

The Nicene Creed is the 'Creed of Nicea' of the 318 fathers who met at Nicea (AD 325) supplemented by the 150 who convened at Constantinople (AD 381), perhaps discussed at the Ephesus Council of 431, read and approved at Chalcedon (451). The Nicene Creed now follows in the translation of Henry Bettenson.

> We believe in one God the Father All-sovereign, maker of heaven and earth, and of all things visible and invisible;
> And in one Lord Jesus Christ, the only-begotten Son of God, Begotten of the Father before all the ages, Light of Light, true God of true God, begotten not made, of one substance with the Father, through whom all things were made; who for us men and for our salvation came down from the heavens, sitteth on the right hand of the Father, and cometh again with glory to judge living and dead, of whose kingdom there shall be no end:
> And in the Holy Spirit, the Lord and the Life-giver, that proceedeth from the Father, who with Father and Son is worshipped together and glorified together, who spake through the prophets:
> In one holy catholic and Apostolic Church:
> We acknowledge one baptism unto remission of sins. We look for a resurrection of the dead, and the life of the age to come.[8]

The Definition of Chalcedon.

The Definition of Chalcedon (451) is a refinement of some points of the Nicene Creed. It follows in Bettenson's translation.

> Therefore, following the holy Fathers, we all with one accord teach men to acknowledge one and the same Son, our Lord Jesus Christ, at once complete in Godhead and complete in manhood, truly God and truly man, consisting also of a reasonable soul and body; of one substance with the Father as regards his Godhead, and at the

---

6. *The Confession of Faith of the Presbyterian Church in the U.S.* together with *The Larger Catechism* and *The Shorter Catechism* (Richmond, VA: John Knox Press, n.d., but post-1944), p. 396.
7. ibid., chap. vii, sec. iv, pp. 55, 56.
8. Henry Bettenson, *Documents of the Christian Church* (New York: Oxford University Press, 1963), pp. 36, 37.

same time of one substance with us as regards his manhood; like us in all respects, apart from sin; as regards his Godhead, begotten of the Father before the ages, but yet as regards his manhood begotten, for us men and for our salvation, of Mary the Virgin, the God-bearer; one and the same Christ, Son, Lord, Only-begotten, recognized in *two natures, without confusion, without change, without division, without separation*; the distinction of natures being in no way annulled by the union, but rather the characteristics of each nature being preserved and coming together to form one person and subsistence, not as parted or separated into two persons, but one and the same Son and Only-begotten God the Word, Lord Jesus Christ; even as the prophets from earliest times spoke of him and our Lord Jesus Christ himself taught us, and the creed of the Fathers has handed down to us.[9]

It now is 'time to return to the LORD.' This Lord is the Christ of the Bible and of historic, orthodox, evangelical faith. The supine, somewhat effeminate *Doctor of Feelings* being featured in much popular 'evangelical' literature is not that Christ. He who claimed to be 'the descendant of David' (conqueror of Goliath) must be advertised anew. That Christ will produce a newly vigorous, truly righteous society of believers, only when our Sunday pulpits ring again with a sound of sound theology. Perhaps then the stacks of how-to-do-it books on marriage, sex, and other feel-good literature which flood both religious bookstores and our coffee tables will silently steal away.

The Personal (Theanthropic) Union.

Two terms not common to ordinary discussion but very important in any carefully defined Christology must be introduced at this point. Since most people educated in English are no longer taught Latin and Greek they seem strange to us, precisely because they were either invented or adapted by the Fathers of the church in a time when all of them spoke either Greek or Latin. Person (Latin *persona*, a mask) is one of those words. With reluctance it came into use in the Latin West to translate Greek *hypostasis* (what stands under) and *prosōpon* (face, front). Neither word meant an individual center of self-consciousness as we employ 'person' today. Another Latin word is *unio* taken over into English as union. From this welter comes out theanthropic and theanthropos (*theos*, God plus *anthrōpos*, man, mankind), both Greek words. So whenever we say theanthropic union or personal union we are talking in ancient Greek and Latin. The title of the next chapter, *The Incarnate Person of Christ*, except for 'the' and 'of,' is more Latin and Greek. I introduce these facts to promote acceptance by readers of some presently strange sounding words.

The New Testament represents Jesus Christ as a single undivided Person possessing a human nature and a divine nature. Each nature is unaltered in essence from its normal attributes and powers. The Person is the same divine Person who 'came down from heaven' and was joined to a complete human nature in the womb of Mary. Henceforth He is not properly God and man, but the God-man, in the ancient language of theology the *Theanthrōpos* or Theanthropic Person.

The bond which unites the divine and human in Jesus Christ is not physical, as between the mother and the unborn infant; or merely moral, as between parties in agreement; or fraternal as between brothers; or federal, as between parties to a covenant. It is a wholly personal (*hypostatic*) union of the divine nature with an *acquired* human nature. (Hypostatic is derived from Greek *hypostasis* a word that the church Fathers, after much discussion, accepted as equivalent to *persona*.)

For this reason, from very ancient times orthodoxy insists there is no human person in the *Theanthrōpos*, while there is a human personality, which developed from the first moment of incarnation in connection with the divine Person and nature.

So delicate is this matter one scarcely trusts his mind to furnish the words for his pen as he writes. Let me continue with the time-tested phraseology of Robert Dabney:

> *Hypostatic Union*. The doctrine of the constitution of Christ's person, is purely one of revelation and involves a mystery (1 Tim. 3:16) as great, perhaps, as that of the Trinity itself. But though inexplicable, it is not incredible. The scriptural argument by which this twofold nature in one person is established, is analogous to establishing a Trinity in unity. The text nowhere defines the doctrine in one passage as fully as we [i.e. orthodoxy theology] assert it. But our doctrine is a necessary deduction from three sets of scriptural assertions. First, Jesus Christ was properly and literally a man... Second, Christ is also literally and properly divine [in highest possible sense]... Yet [third] this Man-God [*Theanthrōpos*] is one and the same.[10]

---

9. ibid., p. 73.
10. Robert Dabney, *Lectures in Systematic Theology* (1878) (Grand Rapids, MI: Zondervan, 1972), pp. 466, 467.

The scriptural evidence for this perfect union is abundant in the New Testament and it is this which compelled not only the creedal agreement of antiquity but the sufficient rebuttal of the multitude of errorists and heretics through the ages of Christian history who in one way or another attempted to avoid, subvert, wrest and deny the massive force of the biblical evidence. The many writers who might be consulted on the scriptural proofs all say the same things in different or even similar words, differing mainly only in completeness and depth of coverage. It would be impossible to say anything new. In Scripture:

1. Our Lord always speaks of Himself as a single Person. The same prevails when He is spoken about or addressed by another. The human nature never addresses the divine or the divine the human, though the Father addresses the Son as a single Person (Heb. 5:5; 1:5; Acts 13:33) and the Son likewise the Father (John 17, *et passim*).

2. Though some attributes, powers and properties inhere in only one of the natures (e.g. omniscience in the divine; hunger and thirst in the human) yet the New Testament offers (ascribes, attributes) them to the one Jesus Christ. For example, the Jesus who became hungry in the wilderness and wept at Lazarus' grave is the same as He who stilled the waves and turned water into wine. Matthew does not say the divine nature stilled the waves or that the human nature grew hungry, but that Jesus did.[11] Admittedly some of this language is a manner of speaking, readily understood even without extended reflection. Wesley certainly knew that God is immortal, incapable of death, even though with poetic license he wrote 'God the mighty Maker died for man the creature's sin.'

3. No evidence of a dual personality in Jesus exists in Scripture. As discussed under the mediatorial office of Christ there is much emphasis on two natures, both united in one Person (hypostatic union above). Nothing comparable to Paul's two-part soliloquy (Rom. 7) appears in Jesus' words. In some passages one Person of the triune God addresses an other (Pss. 2:7; 40:7, 8; John 17:1, 4, 5, 21-24) but there is nothing of the sort in Jesus' reflexive language. In John 3:11 Jesus associates Himself with His disciples ('We speak that we do know' KJV) in distinction from Nicodemus, not His two natures speaking one to or with reference to the other.

A problem arises. Two Pauline texts speak of the death of Christ as though 'the Lord of glory' dies (1 Cor. 2:8) and of 'redemption' by the 'Son' who is 'the invisible God' (Col. 1:13-15). Acts 20:28 KJV speaks of the blood of God, recent Versions based on revised Greek text, of the blood of 'the Lord,' i.e. Lord Jesus. Conversely other texts seem to speak of the human nature as possessing divine attributes and powers (John 3:13; 6:62; Rom. 9:5).

These must be understood as a 'manner of speaking' for which there is no technical name I know of but similar to *prolepsis*, speaking of a future event or condition *as if* it had already happened. Examples are common in everyday occurrence: 'When President Eisenhower lived in Abilene, Kansas.' Or conversely 'the rail-splitter was commander in chief of the Union armies' – the reverse of *prolepsis*. Everyone ought to understand 'the manner of speaking' as truthful even if in manner of statement inexact. In each case the one Person, the *Theanthrōpos*, is simply being referred to by the title, name or attribute of one of the two natures.

Refinements of the doctrine of the two natures of Christ arise in part from the positive meaning of these and other passages. In a general way all orthodox Christians, except Lutherans, endorse the following doctrine of communication, or better, communion, of properties, operations and graces. The common understanding is:

a) A *communion of properties* of each of the two natures in the Person. The divine Person brought with Him, in His act of humiliation, all the attributes and properties of the divine nature. To the *Person*, but not to the divine nature, His human nature 'communicated' the properties of human nature. The Person Christ was hence united with the Father and the Spirit while on earth yet the God-man was local in Nazareth, Bethlehem, Egypt and Nazareth again. Lutheran theology insists the body of Christ is ubiquitous as sharing in the divine omnipresence. This doctrine is an aspect of the particularly Lutheran doctrine of the 'real presence' of the body and blood in the Eucharist as the very plain chapters in Pieper and Mueller amply show. Not every Lutheran, however, endorses this understanding of the *communicatio* and the real presence. Lutherans do not teach that human properties were imparted to the divine nature, because of God's immutability.

b) A *communication of operations* of each nature in producing the final results of redemption. Further accessible discussion of the *communicatio* for those interested will not be found in technical books of theology. Interest in these seemingly over-refinements arose in the scholastic period of Lutheran theology in support of Luther's rather

---

11. A. H. Strong, *Systematic Theology* (Old Tappan, Revell, 1907), pp. 684, 685; cf. H. Berkhof, *Systematic Theology* (Grand Rapids, MI: Eerdmans, repr. 1979), p. 383.

mystical theory of the real presence. The Reformed disagreed and then in the polemics with Lutherans introduced these terms to their own theology, though not with exactly the same meanings or consequences. Plain, yet irenic, brief treatments will be found in Strong and Berkhof from the Calvinist perspective.

The terms *perichōcēsis* (Greek) and *circuminsessio* (Latin) both meaning mutual indwelling or interpenetration, are usually employed rightly to describe the inner relations of the three Persons of the Godhead. Where the Person *is* or *works* the other two are also. This is a correlate of the *consubstantiality* of the three Persons. Some Lutherans (and no others I know of) say there is a *perichōrēsis* of the two natures of Christ. The importance of this matter to some orthodox Lutherans is shown by the fact that of the 340 pages of Francis Pieper's Christology, 162 pages are devoted to the communion of natures and of attributes as well as many pages in discussion of the distinctive Lutheran doctrine of the 'real presence' in the Lord's Supper.

It should be added that the mood, almost unprecedented, of current interest of Western people in social, experiential and psychological aspects of life is reflected in growing transfer of that interest to theology. Now some theologians try to find a social life in the Trinity and new experiences for God, especially for the Father. So the relation of deity to humanity in our Lord has grown exponentially.

Certain theologians (J. Moltmann, Hans Urs von Balthasar) recently have argued in support of this departure from the uniform and time-honored doctrines of God's immutability and impassibility from the standpoint of the doctrine of divine immanence. Though this has been called 'the new patripassionism' these authors have attempted to adhere to Christian orthodoxy. Certain others with a somewhat different outlook who claim to be evangelical and orthodox have accepted aspects of the doctrine of *panentheism*, a central feature of modern process theology. From this outlook they have sought to do what Norman Geisler calls 'Creating God in the Image of Man.' This outlook was proposed in a volume entitled *The Openness of God*.[12] I have defended the ancient orthodoxy in several papers delivered to the Evangelical Theological Society as has Dr Geisler in *Creating God in the Image of Man*.[13] The Journal of the Evangelical Theological Society has recently carried many articles in discussion of this subject. Rejection or modification of the doctrines of divine immutability, simplicity and impassibility accompanied some forms of the kenosis theories of mid-nineteenth century. The *new patripassionism* or *neotheism* has generated interest in the kenotic theology of 150 years ago, hence, recent translation into English of I. A. Dorner's 1956 essay and publication in America.[14]

---

12. Clark Pinnock, Richard Rice, John Sanders, William Hasker and David Basinger, *The Openness of God* (Downers Grove: InterVarsity Press, 1994).
13. Norman Geisler, *Creating God in the Image of Man* (Minneapolis: Bethany House Publ., 1997).
14. I. A. Dorner, *Divine Immutability, A Critical Reconsideration* (Minneapolis: Augsburg Fortress Press, 1994).

9
The Incarnate Person of Jesus Christ

This chapter relates to the doctrine of the personal union of a divine nature and a human nature in one Christ. The ancient Greek-speaking theologians were the first to adopt the word *hypostasis* for the idea of person, hence the term 'hypostatic union,' or personal union of the divine and the human nature in Christ. Though strange to our ears the expression defines and renders distinct and unique the idea it embodies as no other term does. Another useful term, as we have seen, is the adjective, *theanthropic* (from Gr. *theos*, God, and *anthrōpos*, man in generic sense, member of the human race). So theologians speak of 'the theanthropic person' of Christ and 'the Theanthropos,' the God-man.

It is not difficult to establish by Scripture that our Lord was God; nor that He was man. This is stated theologically as the doctrine of the two natures of Christ. But great problems inevitably arise. They arose in the first generations after the ascension. Peter delivered a very simple gospel – good news about Jesus – but identified Him only as 'of Nazareth,' 'anointed' by 'God' 'with the Holy Spirit' and that 'God was with him' (Acts 10:38). However, by the time the various Christological statements of Paul (Acts 17; Phil. 2; Col. 1, 2), of Hebrews 2, of John's Prologue and on throughout his Gospel and the Apocalypse were in circulation, a full understanding of the Person of God incarnate had become a contested and complicated matter.

One might rightly say the incarnation doctrine initially addresses the Christian's faith rather than his understanding. Yet if, as Augustine said, we believe in order to understand, all believing Christians, to say nothing of those who aspire to be teachers, have some refinement of thinking to do about the central, distinctive feature of our religion!

If Jesus was God *and* man, then apparently He must have been two Persons. Yet in Scripture He is invariably presented as only one single Person speaking, acting, reflecting on problems or making decisions, never two Persons as the ancient Nestorians taught (or at least were supposed by their opponents to have taught).

If He was only one Person, was the seat of the self-conscious Person in the human or the divine or both? If in one rather than the other, how could 'the other' exist in full integrity? Could He be two-thirds of a man and fully God as Apollinaris (condemned at Constantinople, AD 381) thought?

The Definition of Chalcedon (451) was intended to set the borders within which orthodox Christology could be expressed. Because it condenses the scriptural data it needs exposition. That exposition came and still comes in sermons, instruction of children, theology textbooks and courses. There had been intense study and conflicting opinions on some points among competent teachers and leaders before 451 and the same continued for awhile. It has been raised again in recent neo-orthodoxy and process theology among both Protestant and Catholic theologians as well as in nineteenth-century kenosis theology.[1] There is a further question: Is the incarnation permanent, that is, when the Son of God assumed a human nature, including a body of literal flesh, is that forever? Is he still today in heaven and indefinitely into eternity a man, 'my flesh in the Godhead' as Robert Browning puts in David's mouth in the poem, 'Saul'?

We must look into these questions and many more. The Definition of Chalcedon (451) dealt specifically with many of the main questions but not all derivative questions. The Fifth, Sixth and Seventh Ecumenical Councils further clarified and defined issues.

Sometime after Chalcedon the so-called Athanasian Creed appeared in western Europe. This really beautiful Latin composition (also called *Quicumque vult*) from the first two words, 'whosoever will' (be saved), in a thoroughly logical way addresses more questions. Some think it goes too far in solving indissoluble mysteries of the incarnation, but everyone should at least know what it says. The wide and prolonged use of this creed in Western Christendom bears witness to the felt need for the precision it supplied. It has been supposed Caesarius, Bishop of Arles (504–543), may have written the *Quicumque*. He is known to have used it as an elementary catechism. It is more likely he was taught it in his youth – he was not a creative writer. The earliest surviving evidence of its wide use is in surviving sermons in which clauses are quoted, as well as at the Fourth Council of Toledo (633). This Council (or synod) determined that the Christianity of Spain would be orthodox (i.e. Nicene, affirming Christ's deity) rather than Arian. The best guide to literature about *Quicumque* I have found is the excellent article 'Creeds' in the eleventh and fourteenth editions of *Britannica*. Denzinger's guide is less complete.

The relevant portions of *Quicumque vult* are articles 29 to 37. I furnish the numbers from Schaff[2] but the English translation is from Denzinger (the *Sources of Catholic Dogma*) for reference later in this chapter.

> 29. But it is necessary for eternal salvation that he faithfully believe also the incarnation of our Lord Jesus Christ.
> 30. Accordingly it is the right faith, that we believe and confess, that our Lord Jesus Christ, the Son of God, is God and man.
> 31. He is God begotten of the substance of the Father before time, and he is man born of the substance of his mother in time:
> 32. perfect God, perfect man, consisting of a rational soul and a human body [Lat. *carne*, flesh],
> 33. equal to the Father according to his Godhead, less than the Father according to humanity.
> 34. Although he is God and man, yet he is not two, but he is one Christ;
> 35. one, however, not by the conversion of the Divinity into a human body [Lat. *in carnem*, into flesh], but by the assumption of humanity [Lat. *humanitatis*, humanity] in the Godhead;
> 36. one absolutely [Lat. *unus omnino*, one wholly] not by confusion of substance, but by unity of person.
> 37. For just as the rational soul and body are one man, so God and man are one Christ.

Let us hold in mind that we are debtors to the ancient bishops (really local pastors) who at great personal cost and tremendous expenditure of time and treasure (travel was slow and expensive) came from far corners to Chalcedon, a town opposite Constantinople. There they wrestled with the question of the union of the two natures for weeks. It speaks eloquently of how important the truth was to them and how important to the public weal or woe. I personally am also indebted to all the faithful orthodox teachers who preached and have written on these questions, also to my immediate teachers and colleagues of yesteryear.

I am trying to make the point that every Christian preacher and teacher and serious Christian owes something to this subject in both time and attention in prayer and study. This is difficult in a generation when many Christians have not read the Bible very much and many of whose pastors care little about the injunctions to guard the deposit of truth handed down to them by Scripture and faithful shepherds. Saint Paul was determined, he said, not only to pray and sing 'with my mind' but also 'in church I would rather speak five words with my mind in order to instruct others,' etc. (1 Cor. 14:14, 15, 19). Let us have similar determination to understand all we can with the help of our predecessors in this profound matter.

---

1. David F. Wells, *The Person of Christ: A Biblical and Historical Analysis of the Incarnation* (Westchester, IL: Crossway Books, 1984), traces and summarizes these developments in accurate, readable prose. See pp. 148-170.
2. Philip Schaff, *Creeds of Christendom ii*, 1919 (Grand Rapids, MI: Baker Books, repr. n.d.), pp. 68, 69.

Without dependence on the ancient creeds, but not without their help and guidance, let us state in ten propositions what the agreed doctrine is.

(1) First Proposition. No informed theologian thinks the 'Great... mystery' of '[God] manifested in the flesh' (1 Tim. 3:16) has been fully illuminated. After all 'no one knows the Son except the Father' (Matt.11:27). If as Scripture says, 'the *love* of Christ... surpasses knowledge' (Eph. 3:19), the *Person* of Christ is no less surpassing. Yet the disciples (Philip in particular) were rebuked for not having at least rudimentary, correct, assured knowledge of Him and His relation to the Father (John 14:5). It is not that we cannot know enough for faith and godliness but that we do not know everything that can and ought to be known and certainly cannot explain everything we know. By definition, the New Testament mysteries are truths known to us only because they have been announced by God's emissaries (prophets, Apostles). However, Scripture encourages us to understand as much as humanly possible of 'all the riches of full assurance of understanding and the knowledge of God's mystery, which is Christ' (Col. 2:2), even though these 'treasures' 'are hidden' in Christ (Col. 2:3 NIV).

'[God] manifested in the flesh' is, exactly as Paul said (1 Tim. 3:16), a mystery. It is not fully comprehensible. The possibility for analysis is therefore limited. Empirical science can do nothing at all with it. Dissection is conducted on cadavers not living beings.

Perhaps the limitations for scientific study, which deals with lesser mysteries, are loosely parallel to this branch of theology. For example, a laboratory technician might surreptitiously mount some gadget to measure the temperature of the kisses of two lovers, perhaps also pressures and their fluctuations – even blood pressure, pulse rate and the like. Yet any freak who would try such an experiment might be the least capable of understanding the worldwide phenomenon of human love. Only lovers *know* such things, if any one does, and they do not fully understand or each pair of lovers would not seem to think they alone know what real love is. '[N]o one knows who the Son is except the Father' (Luke 10:22). To some the Father makes Christ known (Matt. 16:17) and they may not be able to tell us all they learn.

Which probably means that insofar as we are able to explore the mystery of incarnation it will be by divine gift and after that by contemplation, by prayer, and of course by consultation of Scripture, and the aid of previous godly scholars within the limits of received orthodoxy. The names of genuine innovators throughout church history have all turned out to be the names of heretics.

(2) Second Proposition. Without exception, when mentioned together, the deity (divine nature) and the humanity (human nature) are always assigned to the one Person.

One example is Romans 9:5 where Christ is 'God over all, blessed for ever,' yet also an Israelite descended from Hebrew patriarchs – 'and from their race... Christ' came (9:5). In Romans 1:3,4 one divine Person, called 'Jesus Christ our Lord' is 'descended from David according to the flesh' in which case, like John 1:14 'the... flesh' means complete humanity. The text (Rom. 1:3, 4) goes on to say He is 'declared to be the Son of God... according to the spirit of holiness,' designating His full deity. In the Old Testament the Immanuel, God-with-us of Isaiah 9:6, 7 is also 'a [human] child... born.'

(3) Third Proposition. Christ the Person expresses the one consciousness of the *one* Person who possesses both natures whenever He expresses Himself. 'I and the Father are one' (John 10:30) expresses one consciousness in awareness of His divinity, but 'I' in awareness of His human nature when He says 'I am thirsty' (John 19:28). The same single Person expressing Himself either as man or God can be seen in pairing John 17:5 with Matthew 17:46. In a similar way He asks Peter a question that draws out Peter's confession of Christ's deity but follows with very human exuberance when Peter gets it right (Matt. 16:15-17).[3]

There is a certain analogy to this fluctuation in ordinary people. When David said to his soldiers, 'Oh, that someone would give me water to drink from the well of Bethlehem' (2 Sam. 23:15), David's consciousness was formed by elements in his bodily (material) nature. When, later, elements in his mental and ethical nature, which no brute has, were shaping his consciousness he 'poured it out to the LORD,' aghast at the mortal risk taken by the two men who fetched the water. Yet this took place in the single ego of one man in each case. There is everything normal and not the least unusual about this. In Jesus there was one personal self-consciousness expressing a divine nature and a human nature and while unusual, even unique in all history, the hypostatic union was neither abnormal, nor weird and not freakish. Jesus was the most *normal* man who ever lived, albeit far above *average*.

---

3. A. H. Strong, *Systematic Theology* (Valley Forge, PA: Judson Press, 1907), pp. 232, 233; cf. W. G. T. Shedd, *Dogmatic Theology i* (Grand Rapids, MI: Zondervan, 1969), pp. 268–275.

Some very early theologians proposed that every human being furnishes an analogy to the one Christ, of two natures, divine and human. Man, created in God's image is body and soul. That is, there is a material, physical component 'of [the] dust from the ground' and a non-material, spiritual component, 'the breath of life' breathed into him by the Creator (Gen. 2:7). Article 37 of *Quicumque*, cited above, draws this analogy: viz.: 'For just as the rational soul and body are one man, so God and man are one Christ.'

Passages from the writings of Gregory of Nyssa and Augustine employ the analogy,[4] but perhaps Anglican Gilbert Burnet put it best in his *Exposition of the Thirty-Nine Articles*, 1699, commenting on Art. 2:

> [A]s a body is still a body, and operates as a body, though it subsists by the indwelling and actuation of the soul, so in the person of Jesus Christ the human nature [body and soul], was entire and still acting according to its own character, yet there was such an union and inhabitation of the Eternal Word in it, that there did arise out of that such a communication of names and characters as we find in the Scriptures. A man is called tall, fair, and healthy, from the state of his body; and learned, wise, and good, from the qualities of his mind; so Christ is called holy, harmless, and undefiled, is said to have died, risen, and ascended ... with relation to his human nature. He is also said to be in the form of God, to have created all things, to be the brightness of the Father's glory, with reference to the divine nature.[5]

The analogy has been carried even further (legitimately, I think). Every man has an 'animal consciousness,' as do brutes, in which one is aware of hunger, thirst, physical pain. Unlike brutes one can also experience rational, aesthetic and religious emotions ('joy in God,' Rom. 5:11 KJV, 'joy in the Holy Spirit,' Rom. 14:17, 'joy unspeakable,' 1 Peter 1:8 KJV). Yet he is one man. When one's tooth aches the source of that conscious awareness is the material. When one rejoices in solving a problem of geometry or figuring out how to put a new appliance together the source is in the rational capacities of the soul, as also when on a higher level one rejoices with joy unspeakable in Christ. Yet the soul of the same undifferentiated, undiffused, identical man is a 'person' with a center of conscious where all this is registered. So the Logos, joined with the human nature (John 1:14) was and is the personal center of everything the Gospels report of Jesus' life, sayings, experience and so forth.

(4) Fourth Proposition. When passages of the New Testament assign *human* actions, attributes and experiences to the Lord we must understand them of the Person of the Logos by virtue of His human nature and similarly divine attributes of the Person by virtue of His divine nature. Scripture thus may sometimes speak of the divine nature in a human way. Examples are the 'blood... of God' (Acts 20:28 KJV), '[T]hey... crucified the Lord of Glory' (1 Cor. 2:8) and the 'Son of the Most High' being conceived in Mary's womb (Luke 1:31, 32). In late antiquity some orthodox Christians began to call the virgin mother of Christ *theotokos*, God-bearer, against Arian and adoptionist heretics. In doing so they had a biblical, linguistic precedent. 'Mother of God' is a jolting expression for Protestants to hear, God-bearer less so.

More simply, Paul calls Jesus, 'man' (*anthrōpos*), 'the second man,' and 'the last Adam' in 1 Corinthians 15. This 'man' will raise the dead at the Last Day (1 Cor. 15:21, 45; John 5:28) and preside on the final Judgment Day (John 5:22). But in each case it is as incarnate God.

Calvin reassures us we are on the right track here, saying '[T]he most apposite parallel seems to be that of man, whom we see to consist of two substances. Yet neither is so mingled with the other as not to retain its own distinctive nature.'[6] In this he follows Augustine.[7]

In this, as in his whole discussion of the Person of Christ, Calvin 'adheres strictly to the line of Chalcedonian orthodoxy.'[8] Both W. Niesel[9] and F. Wendel[10] agree. Let Wendel speak for both authorities on Calvin's thought:

> Calvin had made the traditional trinitarian teaching his own, without the slightest reservation. The same attachment to the dogmatic tradition is prominent in his Christology... He adopts in full the dogma of the two natures and the current explanations of the relation between the two natures.[11]

---

4. Thomas Oden, *Systematic Theology ii* (San Francisco: Harper Collins, 1992), p. 172.
5. As cited by W. G. T. Shedd, *Dogmatic Theology ii* (Grand Rapids, MI: Zondervan, 1969), p. 318.
6. Calvin, *Institutes of the Christian Religion ii*, 14.1 (Philadelphia, PA: Westminster Press, 1960).
7. ibid., vol. ii, p. 482, n. 2.
8. J. T. McNeill (ed.), ibid.
9. Wilhelm Niesel, *The Theology of Calvin* (Philadelphia: Westminster Press, 1956), pp. 115–119.
10. Francois Wendel, *Calvin: The Origins and Development of His Religious Thought* (New York: Harper and Row, 1963), p. 215.
11. ibid.

Many sensitive souls will nevertheless wish Wesley had composed a less-jarring phrase than 'Christ the mighty Maker died for Man the creature's sin' and will prefer Mary the 'God-bearer' to 'Mother of God.' The point of the ancient Christians in insisting Mary was *theotokos*, God-bearer, was that Jesus was God incarnate from conception onward, not beginning at His baptism or some other time or manner.

Thus, in the Gospels, when Jesus speaks, it is always the Person talking though the words He says may express either a divine consciousness or a human consciousness. When the infant Christ cried out for a diaper change, it was not the Logos expressing Himself, it was infant humanity; likewise when on the cross He said, 'I thirst' (John 19:28) it was thirsty, adult humanity. Contrariwise, when on the previous evening He prayed, 'And now, Father, glorify me in your own presence with the glory that I had with you before the world existed' (John 17:5) it was the eternal Son expressing Himself, even though speaking through human lips.

(5) Fifth Proposition. On many occasions in the narrative of Jesus' life and ministry the attributes of each of the two natures appear side by side, very naturally expressing the single Person of the *Theanthrōpos*. Just to cite the more familiar ones: He sleeps from weariness yet arises to command a storm to cease (Matt. 8:24-26); He weeps at the grave of a friend yet raises the friend from the dead (John 11:35, 38, 43, 44); with only a look He strikes backward an arresting party of police yet is bound and flogged (John 19:1); He is hungry after forty days of fasting yet survives the devil's worst unscathed (Matt. 4).

In instructing disciples He promises his future eschatological arrival as heavenly Son of Man while predicting also an immediate future of abuse by priests and people. He bows His head in submission to baptismal identification with sin and sinners, yet challenges all comers to convict Him of any sin whatsoever.

In none of these cases, and they could be multiplied indefinitely, does the Scripture say His divine nature or His human nature did or said this or that but always Jesus, whom we know as the Logos who became flesh and camped (tabernacled, John 1:14) for awhile among us in our worldly realm.

(6) Sixth Proposition. In later theological reflection it is the same. Jesus is of the seed of David, yet declared to be the Son of God; He is 'the last Adam... the second man' yet also 'from heaven' (1 Cor. 15:45-47); Jesus is 'persecuted' by Saul of Tarsus, yet acknowledged Lord; He 'suffered when tempted' yet now 'is able to help [from heaven] those who are being tempted' (Heb. 2:18); He as man 'suffered once for sins' yet, ages before 'in the spirit... went and proclaimed... in the days of Noah' (1 Peter 3:18-20); He was heard, seen and handled; yet He is 'the eternal life,' which was with the Father, and was made manifest to us (1 John 1:2). In the Revelation He is the One who 'was dead' and 'pierced,' yet also Alpha and Omega, beginning and ending, who is, was and is yet to come, 'the *Pantokratōr*' (Rev. 1:8, 18). This pairing of New Testament references both to deity and humanity embodied in one Person, could go on to great length.

In all the Gospel records, Acts and Revelation, Jesus obviously speaks of Himself as one Person. Sometimes He distinguishes Himself from all other men, as whenever He refers to His being the bread or flesh from heaven in John 6 or from the Jews of His time, saying, 'You are from below; I am from above' (John 8:23).

He distinguishes His own divine personal self from the Father in many sayings, 'The Father who sent me bears witness about me' (John 8:18) and 'the Father is greater than I' (John 14:28); likewise from the Holy Spirit whom He calls the Spirit and *Paraclētos* (Comforter) many times in John 14:16–16:16.

The individual personality of Jesus is a point driven home in Jesus' bitter controversy with the Pharisees (John 8:23, 26, 28 and 58). Employing the emphatic personal pronoun *egō* (I, I myself), Jesus contrasts Himself with *humeis* (you, yourselves) in verse 23, 'You are... I am,' 'You are... I am not.' The meaning would have been the same (but in a weaker and less emphatic sense) if He had omitted *egō* (I, I myself) and simply used the verbs *este* (you are) and *eimi* (I am). This Jesus is emphatically 'I am' (*egō eimi*). This Person is the Son of Man from heaven (cf. v. 28 with 23) and yet He is 'a man' (*anthrōpos*) v. 40, with no implication of variation from the norm.[12] Yet in v. 58 this *anthrōpos* is the same Person who spoke to Moses at the burning bush, and called Himself 'I AM.'

This claim, 'before Abraham was, I am' (John 8:58) is unique in Scripture and calls for comment. '[W]as' renders *genesthai*, second aorist of *ginomai* (simple past, here) and means He became, He came to be. *Egō eimi* means I myself, am, present tense. This means Jesus a man (*anthrōpos*, v. 40), claimed personal existence even before Abraham came into existence. 'The phrase marks a timeless existence... "I was" would have expressed simple priority. Thus there

---

12. Raymond E. Brown, *Anchor Bible, The Gospel According to John* (Garden City, NY: Doubleday, 1966), p. 537.

is in the phrase the contrast between the created and the uncreated, and the temporal and the eternal.'[13] Raymond Brown says 'the climax of all that Jesus has said at that [Feast of] Tabernacles comes in the triumphant proclamation by Jesus of the divine name, I AM, which he bears,'[14] and devotes an extended Appendix IV to discuss and document proof of the same.[15]

(7) Seventh Proposition. Passages of Scripture which seem to interchange attributes between the divine and human natures should not be interpreted realistically but as figures of speech. We have already spoken of how Scripture language sometimes refers to the Person (Jesus) by one of His divine titles and assigns human characteristics to Him even though employing a divine title. The outstanding examples are 'crucified the Lord of glory' (1 Cor. 2:8) and 'killed the Prince of life' (Acts 3:15 KJV); and 'the church of God ['the Lord' RSV], which He obtained with his own blood' (Acts 20:28; see Col. 1:13, 14; Luke 1:31, 32). The reverse occurs when divine attributes are ascribed to the Person by one of His human designations. Examples usually cited are Revelation 5:12; Romans 9:5; and John 6:62 and 3:13. This is understood realistically only by a few modern writers – all I know of being strict Lutherans. Lutheran doctrine from the Formula of Concord onward holds (not always with equal explicitness) that the now ascended Christ is everywhere present according to His human nature and possesses the divine attributes of omniscience, omnipotence and omnipresence. Their chief interest is in omnipresence, to explain the '*real* presence' (by which they mean *entire* presence, including flesh and blood of Christ) with the elements of the Lord's Supper. This is called *ubiquity*, present anywhere.

Calvin, however, set the pace for most Protestants, saying,

> The Scriptures… sometimes attribute to him what belongs solely to his humanity, sometimes what belongs uniquely to his divinity; and sometimes what embraces both natures but fits neither alone. And they so earnestly express this union of the two natures that is in Christ as sometimes to interchange them.[16]

Then he adds, 'This *Figure of Speech* is called by the ancients *Communication of Properties*.'[17] Later in the *Institutes* his discourses on the sacraments discuss at length his views of the manner of the union of the human and divine natures in the Person.[18] He also produced numerous treatises some by way of instructing the church at Geneva and Reformed churches everywhere and some in debate with the disciples of Luther.[19]

The Second Helvetic Confession (1566) of Reformed Christians in Switzerland, chapter 11 typically teaches the local presence only of our Lord's body in heaven citing John 14:2 and especially Acts 3:21: 'Jesus, whom heaven must receive until the time for restoring all the things about which God spoke by the mouth of his holy prophets long ago.'[20]

In the Reformation era this matter was debated between Reformed and Lutherans. Calvin and Protestants generally since his day have been perfectly willing to confess the 'real presence' (Matt. 28:20; 18:20) of Christ in the church to the end of time, and even in a special mode, left undefined, in the Eucharist. But if definition be required the explanation is that by virtue of personal union with the divine nature, the human nature is exalted in many ways but cannot have any properties, as such, which are not human properties or give up any such properties, otherwise it would be a *tertium quid*, a third something else, somewhat similar to some expressions of the ancient Eutychians.

(8) Eighth Proposition. Relations between the three Persons of the triune God supply parallel to relationship of the divine nature and human nature of Christ. There is a serious flaw in applying terms which properly belong to the inner relation of the Trinity to the relations of the two natures of Christ – *circumincession* (Latin), *perichorēsis* (Greek), also *intercommunicatio, circulatio* and others. These terms were used by the ancient theologians to describe the inner relations of the three Persons of the triune God. As taught by Scripture, formulated by the creeds and confessed by orthodox believers ever since, there is one and only one divine nature possessed fully by each of three Persons,

---

13. Brook. F. Westcott, *The Bible with Commentary, New Testament, ii* (London: John Murray, 1899), p. 140; comment on John 8:5.
14. Brown, *Anchor Bible: John*, p. 367.
15. Brown, *Anchor Bible: John*, pp. 433–438.
16. Calvin, *Institutes*, ii, 14.1.
17. ibid.
18. Calvin, *Institutes*, iv, 17.
19. See the lengthy note, vol. ii, p. 483 of the Westminster Edition of the *Institutes* and the Second Volume of *Tracts and Treatises* by John Calvin, 592 pages in the English translation of Henry Beveridge, Edinburgh: 1849.
20. Schaff, *The Creeds of Christendom vol. iii*, 6th ed., p. 852.

Father, Son and Holy Spirit. The First is distinguished by *paternity*, the Second by *filiation*, the Third (the Holy Spirit) by *procession* from the First (Father) and the Second (Son). They, however, are present in one another in a manner not known to us. This *intercommunion* of the Persons (not of their distinctives) is what the theologians designated by *perichoresis* and *circumincession*.[21]

Somehow, unwisely, these two words came to be employed of the divine and human natures of Christ. It is certainly correct to say that all the attributes of deity, though employed under the conditions of voluntary humiliation (Phil. 2:5-9), were possessed by the Person of Christ: likewise all the attributes of created, unfallen human nature. But it is doubtful in the extreme if the deity assumed the attributes of flesh. ('Veiled in flesh the Godhead see, Hail the incarnate deity' is better.) Nor did the flesh assume the attributes of omnipotence, omniscience and omnipresence.

This issue was debated vigorously without meeting of minds in the Reformation epoch. The followers of Luther insisted upon the veritable *communication* of the divine attribute of omnipresence to the body of Christ in His risen and ascended state, thus literally, though invisibly and intangibly present in the Eucharist (Lord's Supper). No other branch of Christianity – Protestant, Roman Catholic or Eastern Orthodox – holds to this view. Luther's insistence on a supposed ubiquity of the body and blood of Christ in His risen and glorified state is consequential upon his doctrine of the 'real presence' of the body and blood in the 'sacrament of the Lord's Supper.' He rested his case on 'this is my body' in the words of institution. Paul Althaus shows how this doctrine, unique to Luther and his followers, grew in Luther's mind in the process of his controversies.[22] A. B. Bruce in the midst of the *Kenosis* debates of the nineteenth century showed how small was the basis of the enormous doctrinal weight – comparing it to a pyramid resting upside-down on a pebble.[23] See also David Wells' *The Person of Christ*, pp. 133-135. Philip Schaff points out how the *Kenosis* problem, on this account twice in Lutheran history led to internecine Lutheran controversy.[24]

The justly celebrated *Christian Dogmatics* of the late Francis Pieper of Concordia Theological Seminary devotes 150 pages in one section[25] to this *communication idiomata* and in dozens of other pages throughout the three volumes plus three and a half columns of index.[26] The Lutheran authorities back to Luther are cited at length. Pieper obviously thought this an important matter.

I have had some interesting experiences with my Lutheran neighbors and pastor-friends in this regard. The Formula of Concord statements of the Person of Christ (Article VIII) could be endorsed by any Protestant theologian. Calvin or Beza or even John Owen could have written them. The attributes are clearly not to be exchanged. The human attributes (including 'to be finite and circumscribed') 'neither are nor ever become attributes of the divine nature' (VIII.iv). The Epitome of the Formula of Concord says of the divine and human that 'each retains its essential properties and that they never become properties one of the other nature' (Art. VIII, affirmative 2). Yet 'Because of the sacramental union ['this is my body,' etc.] they [bread and wine] are truly the body and blood of Christ' (Epitome, VII, aff. 2). This to non-Lutherans seems to exclude the physical presence (visible, invisible, 'eucharistic,' 'non-spatial' or otherwise) in the ordinance. But the Formula and Epitome say the body and blood are 'really' there because of personal union in the Logos. The Formula clearly affirms that to deny the 'real' presence, as they understand it, of Christ's flesh and blood, *with* the sacrament is to deny the plain teaching of Scripture, viz.: 'God's right hand is everywhere' hence the flesh and blood may, like God in Christ be present in a 'mode' neither local nor spatial. Charles P. Krauth makes this point in his definitive work, *The Conservative Reformation and Its Theology*,[27] as does Francis Pieper, the major Lutheran Church-Missouri Synod theologian.[28]

Yet some Missouri Synod pastors have told me the presence of Christ's body and blood in the Supper is 'spiritual presence.' Others insist it is physical. In either case, it would seem that those who have difficulty accepting the strict Lutheran view ought to be admitted to communion, because the *Epitome* states,

---

21. Strong, *Systematic Theology*, pp. 332, 334; cf. Shedd, *Dogmatic Theology i*, pp. 194, 267–275, 300.
22. Paul Althause, *The Theology of Martin Luther*, trans. R. C. Schultz (Philadelphia, PA: Fortress Press, 1966), pp. 375–403, *et passim*.
23. Alexander Balmain Bruce, Cunningham Lecture 1876, published as *The Humiliation of Christ* and oft quoted, 2nd ed. (New York: George H. Doran, n.d.).
24. *Schaff-Herzog Encyclopedia of Religious Knowledge i*, based on the *Real-Encyclopaedia* of Herzog, Plitt and Hauck, ed. by Philip Schaff (New York: Funk & Wagnalls Co., 1891), pp. 461, 463.
25. Francis Pieper, *Christian Dogmatics ii* (St Louis: Concordia Publ., 1950–1957), pp. 129–279.
26. ibid., iv, pp. 147, 148.
27. Charles P. Krauth, *The Conservative Reformation and Its Theology* (Philadelphia, PA: Lippincott, 1875), chap. xiv, pp. 755–830.
28. Pieper, *Christian Dogmatics iii*, pp. 290–393.

We believe, teach and confess there is only one kind of unworthy guest, namely, those who do not believe... no genuine believer, no matter how weak he may be, as long as he retains a living faith, will receive the Holy Supper to his condemnation, for Christ instituted this Supper particularly for Christians who are weak in faith.... The entire worthiness of the guests at this heavenly feast consists solely and alone in the most holy obedience and complete merit of Christ, which we make our own through genuine faith (*Epitome* VII, affirmation, 8, 9, 10).

(9) Ninth Proposition. As asserted above, the human nature was made the vehicle of the use of certain powers of the divine nature, as for example the power to announce the forgiveness of sin (Luke 5:24) and to live a sinless human life. Throughout His earthly years Jesus was able not to sin (*potuit non peccare*). But good theology affirms this does not fully account for His sinlessness. Adam also was able not to sin, yet even though he was 'not deceived' (1 Tim. 2:14 KJV) by temptation, he did sin by free choice. He was not yet confirmed in righteous behavior. Jesus 'did no sin' (1 Peter 2:22). He was 'holy, harmless, undefiled' (Heb. 7:26 KJV). According to a persistent, but not invariable feature of orthodox theology, by virtue of the union of the divine and human, Jesus was not able to sin (*non potuit peccare*). Shedd defends this version of the impeccability doctrine.[29] C. Hodge rejects it.[30]

Strictly speaking, impeccability 'means not merely that Christ could avoid sinning, and did actually avoid it, but also that it was impossible for him to sin because of the essential bond between the human and divine natures.'[31]

The New Testament teaches that the human nature of Christ received a special conferral of the Holy Spirit enabling human nature to be a sufficient and holy vehicle of the divine works (miracles) and to endure 'the sufferings of Christ' after the beginning of His public ministry. This is the meaning of the descent of the Holy Spirit in the form of a dove, upon Jesus at His baptism by John.

The descent of the Spirit as a dove and the voice of the Father in approval after the baptism by John are without precedent in Jewish history.[32] Jesus and John were the only human witnesses. From the beginning His public career and redemptive work were specially guided and empowered by the Holy Spirit. The first effects were to support Jesus in the forty days of temptation immediately to follow and to assure Him anew that indeed in Him the work of the Servant-Son of Jehovah prophesied by Isaiah would be carried successfully to conclusion (Isa. 42:1-4; 53:10-12; 11:1 ff. with John 1:29-34; Matt. 3:13-17). Afterward Jesus was led into the wilderness by the Holy Spirit (Matt. 4:1) then out of it and on to the victory at Calvary. No miracles are reported in the New Testament to have been performed by Jesus before the descent of the Spirit; afterward only by His specially authorized messengers upon whom either He or His ministers *plenipotentiary* (Apostles) laid their hands. I find no exceptions to this in the New Testament.[33]

This enduement enabled the Apostles to perform the mighty works associated with the first stages of Christianity in the apostolic age (Heb. 2:1-4; Rom. 15:18, 19). Christ was guided by the same Spirit into reliance on the Holy Scriptures in resisting temptation (Matt. 4:4, 7, 10) as later every true believer would be: 'the sword of the Spirit which is the word of God' (Eph. 6:17). Through all ages except the epochs of Moses, Elijah and Elisha, the time of Jesus' ministry and of the Apostles, God's use of authentic miracles has been rare.

(10) Tenth Proposition. The union of the divine and human in Christ's Person are necessary to enable Him to be 'mediator between God and men,' being himself man (1 Tim. 2:5). Names and titles are found in Scripture designating His divine and human natures and His work. Some of these 'titles of office' are Alpha and Omega, Last Adam, Captain of Salvation, and several more; most in one way or another express His work as bringing God to man and man to God, in a word, *mediation*.[34] Hence, though Jesus is called Mediator (Gr. *mesitēs*) only four times (1 Tim. 2:5; Heb. 8:6; 9:15; 12:24), the idea is a comprehensive term for *all* He came to be and to do.

The idea of mediator in Scripture in reference to Christ's work has little to do with *arbitration* of disputes or *negotiation* of differences, which always imply compromise. Christ as Mediator in the offices of prophet, priest and king effected everything as the *Theanthropos*, God-man. He could answer Job's plaintive hope for an 'umpire' 'who might lay his hand on us both' (Job 9:33), where the LXX renders Heb. *Mokhi-aḥ* by *Mesitēs*, the New Testament term for mediator. As the ascended mediatorial intercessor in heaven He fulfills the human longing for the human face in God put so poignantly by Robert Browning cited earlier, 'my flesh in the Godhead! I seek and I find it... A Face like my face' (lines 307, 308 of *Saul*).

---

29. Shedd, *Dogmatic Theology ii*, pp. 330–349.
30. Charles Hodge, *Systematic Theology ii* (Grand Rapids, MI: Eerdmans, 1886, 1960), p. 457.
31. Louis Berkhof, *Systematic Theology*, 2nd ed. (Grand Rapids, MI: Eerdmans, 1941, 1979), p. 318.
32. R. D. Culver, *The Life of Christ* (Baker Books, 1976), pp. 60–73.
33. I have discussed this matter somewhat at length in 'Apostles and the Apostolate in the New Testament,' *Bibliotheca Sacra*, April–June 1977, pp. 131–143.
34. L. D. Bevan, art. 'Offices of Christ,' in *International Standard Bible Encyclopedia*, ed. J Orr (Grand Rapids, MI: Eerdmans, 1939, 1943), p. 616.

It is not too much to say that the idea of mediation, culminating in Christ, the Mediator, enabled to be such by incarnation of God in man is 'the key to the unity of the Bible.'[35] *The Mediator* is the title of the English translation of what is perhaps Emil Brunner's most faithful and enduring work of theology. When it appeared in 1947 it seemed to be pointing toward a return to orthodoxy among elite theologians. It remains a masterful 'Study of the Central Doctrine of the Christian Faith' (title page). Stripped of some lingering concessions to liberalism and *krisis* (or existential) presuppositions it remains today an excellent treatment, fully expounding the incarnation as the 'key to the unity of the Bible.'[36]

Conclusions and Reflections.

There never will be a complete resolution of all the questions and problems of thought which arise in contemplation of the 'mystery of godliness, God… manifested in the flesh.' I close this section by referring the inquirer to the *Quicumque Vult* (Athanasian Creed) and the Definition of Chalcedon, for in these formulas of the early church, orthodox Christianity has answered most of the questions raised by the mystery of the incarnation. I add some brief comments on certain questions that arise out of the ancient and persistent doctrine of the impassibility of God.

God, in Scripture, is said to be perfectly 'blessed' and changeless (immutable) as well. He did not create man in order for God either to be happy (blessed) or to suffer unhappiness. Though He is said frequently to be angry, repentant, sorry, have regret and the like, this must be assigned to His treatment of sinners and only by analogy, true of God Himself. These statements set forth something really present in God's being which is analogous or similar in some way to something in us (analogy of proportion) or perhaps only commensurable (analogy of proportionality, Thomas Aquinas' terms).[37] (Full discussion of Thomas' distinction would require a long detour.)

Theologians were quite uniform on this point until recently. Now several (notably Karl Barth and those influenced by him in this regard) wish to lead us to abandon the ancient doctrine of God's impassibility. Impassibility means incapable of the changes, which, in human beings, either accompany or constitute emotion or any kind of suffering.

Furthermore there has always been the question, granting the impassibility of the Godhead: Did not God the Father suffer when He abandoned the Son to suffering and death (Matt. 27:46)? A partial answer has been furnished in the assertion that Jesus suffered only in the human nature. Shedd put the matter this way:

> While… the acts and qualities of either nature may be attributed to the one theanthropic *person*, the acts and qualities of one *nature* may not be attributed to the other nature. It would be erroneous to say that the divine nature suffered, or that the human nature raised the dead; as it would be erroneous to say that the human body thinks, or that the human soul walks. The man, or 'person' whose is the body and whose is the soul, both thinks and walks; but the natures by whose instrumentality he performs those acts do not both of them think and walk. One thinks, and the other walks.[38]

This subject will come up for attention as we deal with the work of Christ.

The values for Christians of the fact that our Lord Jesus Christ was and is in heaven today, God incarnate, the *Theanthrōpos*, or God-man will be discussed in 'Our High Priest in Heaven,' the last chapter of Christology. His works as *prophet* (revealing God), *priest* (sacrifice, sacrificer, intercessor) and *king* (Lord) all hinge on the fact of the incarnate God in the Person of Christ. The fact of the incarnation also shows that man, the image of God, is in nature commensurable with God's nature. Though the gulf between Creator God and man, His creature, is immense it is not infinite, and contrary to some dialectical theology, is not exclusively qualitative. The incarnation proves it so or God could not be in personal union with one of our race as in Jesus. And similarly the incarnation proves sin not to be normal in human kind. Quite to the contrary, normal humanity (all it was created to be and was at the beginning) is sinless. He who is impeccable was made in the *likeness* of sinful flesh, but being in 'fashion as a man' still 'holy harmless and undefiled.' 'To err is human' is a false statement. 'Great indeed… is the mystery of godliness. He was manifested in the flesh' (1 Tim. 3:16). This mystery will remain just that for eternity for reverent contemplation.

---

35. D. M. Edwards, art. 'Mediation, Mediator,' in *ISBE*, p. 2025.
36. Emil Brunner, *The Mediator: A Study of the Central Doctrine of the Christian Faith*, trans. Olive Wyon (Philadelphia, PA: Westminster Press, 1947).
37. Aquinas, *Summa Contra Gentiles* (London: University of Notre Dame Press, 1975), Book One, chaps. 32-35; *Summa Theologica* (Westminster, Maryland: Christian Classics, 1911, 1981), Book i, Q. 13, arts. 5 and 6.
38. Shedd, *Dogmatic Theology i*, p. 323.

10
The Saving Work of the Incarnate Son of God: Topics, Terms, Issues, Development

This chapter is designed to introduce the saving *work* of the incarnate Son of God on earth. Previous chapters of this Christology have related to His Person, who and what He was and is. They answer Jesus' demand of Peter, 'who do you say I am?' in a fuller way than the dawning awareness of Peter would have understood or accepted at that time. We can now answer Jesus' question more fully in the full light of all subsequent written revelation and reverent reflection. It is a daunting project. In this and subsequent chapters we will be looking at our Lord's work on earth as the Theanthropos, the God-man. This chapter will try to lay out the ground to be covered in this challenging project.

Person and Work Distinguishable but Not Separable.

As asserted early in introducing Christology, the work of the Lord may not be separated from the God-man who performed it. Noteworthy also is the fact that not one word of any ecumenical creed suggests that the chief significance of Jesus was that of teacher of a new religion (or even the best teacher of an old one), nor example of ethical rectitude, nor revelation of the highest humanity, etc., as modern religionists frequently misrepresent His significance. Christians will readily acknowledge many of these compliments to their Lord, but will still insist that they are off target, for 'the Father has sent his Son to be the Savior of the world' (1 John 4:14). Thus the *doing* was part of the *being*; His work was not to tell us what to do but as the *Theanthropos* to do something for us.

We do not here attempt what some recent theology calls 'Christology from below.' The theory is that a theology of Jesus' Person and work should be composed of inferences, deductions and conclusions drawn from His actions, behavior and accomplishments. Rather, we start where John does: 'In the beginning was the Word.... And the Word became flesh and dwelt among us' (John 1:1, 14). Such reflection on His behavior as might theoretically be advisable or even necessary for Christology has already been done for us by that most reflective author of the latest Gospel (the fourth) and by the authors of the New Testament Epistles who intended precisely to interpret Jesus to the churches scattered about the Roman world of the middle decades of the first century. Only in this way can our theology possibly be rescued from the interminable fruitless excursions into the imaginative searches for the historical Jesus and critical reconstructions of the New Testament of recent decades. Let us give our reasons (in 'answer to every man,' 1 Peter 3:15 KJV) when asked but, for now, academic search for the 'historical Jesus' and Gospels criticism will have to wait in favor of attention to the Lord Jesus Christ of the Bible, who is both an historical Person and the object of our faith.

Jesus As Worker.

The work of Jesus Christ on earth was to accomplish the Father's purposes in sending Him. We now direct attention to what Jesus did to accomplish those purposes.

Jesus was a working Man from the beginning – not a nine-to-five denizen of the union halls but more like the blackened smithy of Longfellow's poem and the muscular farmers who, in the days of our great-grandfathers, scythed standing grain by hand – in midsummer heat – and cultivated endless rows of corn (maize) from dawn to dusk with a hoe. God Himself has set the example as Jesus reminds us: 'My Father is working still' and then added, 'and I am working' (John 5:17 RSV).

Jesus as 'worker' has direct connection with the Old Testament prophecies of 'the Servant of the LORD.' Throughout the Hebrew Bible the usual word for a servant is '*evadh*, a noun derived from the verb '*avadh*, which means to do work. Permanent Hebrew servants (or slaves) were by law always voluntary slaves. A man might pay off a debt by six years of servitude to another, but no more than six years according to the law of Exodus 21:1-4. Nevertheless 'if the slave plainly says, "I love my master... I will not go out free," then his master shall bring him to God, and he shall bring him to the door or the doorpost. And his master shall bore his ear through with an awl, and he shall be his slave ['*avadh*, do work for him] for ever' (Exod. 21:5, 6). This willing obedience is a prominently recurring motif in the Servant passages of Isaiah 40–53, especially 50:4-9 and 53:1-12 which applies to our Lord's Person and work and to no other.

Jesus was the disciples' 'Lord and Master,' and among them He was 'one that serves' and set the example in washing their feet (John 13). Yet the Scriptures plainly say He was *God's* willing servant, not mankind's. He bowed to God's will but stood up straight before Pilate, the high priest, and Herod. He was no sheep on the way to shearing in His fierce denunciation of 'scribes and Pharisees, hypocrites' on the last day of His public ministry (Matt. 23). In the Patmos vision He appears now not as servant of the churches but as their glorious Lord (Rev. 1–3). Such words as servile and subservient, though they contain 'serve' do not describe Jesus' temperament at all.

In this light we understand 'My food is to do the will of him who sent me *and to accomplish his work* [emphasis added]' (John 4:34). Jesus was on earth to work – about His 'Father's business' from His earliest years and onward.

His mission to do business, to perform God's holy will and purpose, at whatever price, gives great poignancy to His last words on the cross, just before committing His spirit to God: 'It is finished.'

The Nature of His Work.

What was to be the nature of His work? Four sayings from Jesus Himself provide some specifics of the work He came to perform.

> [T]he Son of Man came to seek and to save the lost (Luke 19:10).
>
> [T]he Son of Man came not to be served but to serve (Matt. 20:28).
>
> The Spirit of the Lord is upon me, because he has anointed me to proclaim good news to the poor. He has sent me to proclaim liberty to the captives and recovering of sight to the blind, to set at liberty those who are oppressed, to proclaim the year of the Lord's favor (Luke 4:18, 19).
>
> [T]he Son of Man came... to give his life as a ransom for many (Matt. 20:28).

1. To Seek and Save.

To seek and to save lost people was His work. And how He threw His heart into it! 'When he saw the crowds, he had compassion for them' (Matt. 9:36) and more than once figuratively described them as the plenteous harvest and called on His disciples to pray for 'laborers' to reap it (Matt. 9:38). Jesus considered 'The woman at the well' of Samaria and the crowd of her fellow villagers as a field 'already ripe for harvest' where godly men would labor to sow and reap (John 4:35-38).

2. To Serve or 'Minister'.

> [T]he Son of man came not to be ministered unto, but to minister (Matt. 20:28 KJV).

He came to be a minister in the sense of ministering to others. The *proximate* goal was to minister to His own nation. He made that very clear in the incident with the Canaanitish woman of Phoenicia (Matt. 15:21-28), saying as He refused her request for 'ministry' or 'service': 'I was sent only to the lost sheep of the house of Israel.' A bit earlier He had instructed the Apostles in their first itinerant mission to 'Go nowhere among the Gentiles, and enter no town of the Samaritans, but go rather to the lost sheep of the house of Israel' (Matt. 10:5, 6). Yet, as everyone should know, His ultimate goal was to provide a gospel of salvation to the whole world. Jesus explained this cryptically to the disciples in His last public discourse after certain Greeks requested an audience with Him (John 11:20-24). Jesus also used the occasion to emphasize again that those who would serve Him would, like Him, be servants, i.e. 'ministers' in the same sense Jesus came to do the work of ministering. 'He went about doing good' is how Peter explained His public service (ministry) to the Gentiles listening to Peter's first fully Christian sermon (Acts 10:38).

3. To Proclaim the Good News.

> The Spirit of the Lord is upon me, because he has anointed me to proclaim good news to the poor. He has sent me to proclaim liberty to the captives and recovering of sight to the blind, to set at liberty those who are oppressed, to proclaim the year of the Lord's favor (Luke 4:18, 19).

This public announcement of Jesus at His home synagogue in Nazareth explains more specifically what Peter meant when he told the household of Cornelius that Jesus 'went about doing good.' The mistake of the Jewish leaders and people of the time was to separate the material benefits, political and social improvement, from the spiritual requirements of the good news. The good news was designed for sinners only, but only *repentant* sinners. The 'social gospel' of yesterday and the liberation theology of today (and who knows what human betterment in Christ's name of tomorrow) seem rightly to find some grounding in Jesus' proclamation.

The Old Testament prophetic vision of a visible reign of Messiah over all the earth is implicitly present (Pss. 2 and 72; Isa. 2:1-4; Isa. 35; Ezek. 40-48; and similar passages). These projections see every human wrong righted, every yoke of oppression broken, every captive victim free, knowledge of God covering the earth as the waters cover the sea. And Jesus here claimed the whole program.

Viewed from the standpoint of our Lord's death, resurrection, ascension and session at God's right hand we know the passage must be interpreted eschatologically. It is not a complete formula for either Jesus' personal earthly work or ours as a church. Which brings us to the next point.

The Main Task.

4. A Ransom for Many.

'[T]he Son of Man came... to give his life as a ransom for many' (Matt. 20:28). This is our Lord's own explanation of what it would mean for Him 'to minister' (KJV), 'to serve' (ESV, RSV, NIV, *et al.*). The explanation of emphasis on the death of Christ in apostolic ministry is found, in part, in the leading place it has in the Christian gospel. Christianity is a missionary faith; it has a message of eternal salvation to proclaim. Those united with Christ are urged to set their hearts on heaven, not earth. Any program of human betterment is secondary. That message (gospel, preachment, Gr. *kerugma*) is what, when received by men, saves them: 'It was God's good pleasure through ... the thing preached to save them that believe' (1 Cor. 1:21 ASV marg). This gospel is 'of Christ' (Rom. 1:16 KJV), that is, His Person and work. Its content is (1 Cor. 15:1–3; Acts 10:36–43) Christ's Person and work, i.e. who He was and His redemptive career, especially His atoning death.

Old Testament Predictions of His 'Work'.

The distinctively Christian value of the Old Testament is found in the predictions therein of the Savior. This goes far beyond interesting details like the place of His birth, residence in Nazareth and the like, for the Old Testament also furnishes the vocabulary and categories for interpreting the Savior's career. At several junctures in the Gospel narratives of the Lord's last days before Calvary, the ruling force of Old Testament prophecies in shaping those events of Passion and death is introduced. When, at the time of His seizure by Jewish authorities, Peter thought to defend Jesus with a sword, 'Jesus said... "Do you think that I cannot appeal to my Father, and he will at once send me more than twelve legions of angels? But how then should the Scriptures be fulfilled, that it must be so?"' (Matt. 26:52-54). (See also Matt. 27:9; Mark 14:27, 49; Luke 22:37; John 12:37–41; 15:25; 17:12; 19:24, 28, 36, 37.) During the forty days before the ascension of Jesus He frequently interpreted the events just past as fulfillment of Scripture, even upbraiding His disciples for failing to see this (Luke 24:25-27, 44-46).

After the ascension, during the early period when the apostolic church remained near Jerusalem, Peter preached several sermons in which He connected the betrayal, Passion, death and resurrection with specific Old Testament prophecies (Acts 2:23-36) and even went so far as to say that 'all the prophets,' i.e. the whole Old Testament, was a foretelling of the death of Christ (Acts 3:17, 18, 24).

Many years later, addressing a synagogue, Paul startled his audience by declaring, 'For those who live in Jerusalem and their rulers, because they did not recognize him nor understand the utterances of the prophets which are read every Sabbath, fulfilled them by condemning him' (Acts 13:27; see also 28-41). In fact, invariably arguments used by the Apostles in appealing to Jews were based on the Old Testament prophecies of the Passion, death and resurrection of Jesus.

Furthermore, as indicated above, the Lord Himself and His Apostles held that Old Testament prophecy, ritual and history interpreted the meaning of the crucifixion and related events. Isaiah 52:13–53:12, a comprehensive prophecy of the Lord's suffering and dying Servant, lies in the background of interpretation of Jesus throughout the New Testament, from the words of the Father at the beginning of Jesus' ministry (Matt. 3:17; cf. Isa. 52:13; 53:4; Matt. 12:15-21; cf. Isa. 52:13; 42:1 ff.) to the apostolic interpretation of His suffering and death (1 Peter 2:22; cf. Isa. 53:9 and 2 Cor. 5:21; 1 Peter 2:23; cf. Isa. 53:7; Heb. 12:3; 1 Peter 2:25; cf. Isa. 53:6). Millions of Bible-reading Christians have read the Gospels and then later read Isaiah 53 only to say, Isaiah has drawn a picture of our Savior's death in our place. Literature on this subject on every level of scholarship and exposition and from many perspectives frequently appears. My own efforts in this direction, based on lectures I gave over several years to second-year Hebrew students in seminary are gathered together in my book, *The Sufferings and the Glory*.[1]

So merely 'doing good' (as Peter said in Acts 10:38) was a prelude to rejection, betrayal, denial, denunciation, condemnation and execution by crucifixion. A major part of each of the Gospel narratives relates the story. His death is clearly the main subject of 'the good news' or gospel. Repeatedly the Gospel writers report how Jesus punctuated His talks to the disciples during the final months with forecasts of this ghastly consummation. Let us take note of some of them.

Jesus' Steady Purpose.

Immediately after the climax of recognition as 'Son of the living God' which gave Jesus much joy (Matt. 16:16, 17) all three Synoptics say: 'From that time Jesus began to show his disciples that he must go to Jerusalem and suffer many things from the elders and the chief priests and scribes, and be killed, and on the third day be raised' (Matt. 16:21; cf. Mark 9:31; Luke 9:22). Any effort to deflect Him from this 'must go... and suffer' He regarded as from Satan. Shortly thereafter as the little party of four descended the Mount of Transfiguration He mentioned it again (Mark 9:9; Luke 9:44, 45). At the mountain top only minutes before, Moses and Elijah had discussed with Him His 'departure' ('decease' KJV, Gr *exodus*) which shortly would take place in Jerusalem (Luke 9:31). Later as they 'passed through Galilee' – evidently repeatedly and on different occasions – He taught His disciples and said to them, 'The Son of Man is going to be delivered into the hands of men, and they will kill him. And when he is killed, after three days he will rise' (Mark 9:31).

The same Gospel reports state that none of the disciples understood what Jesus was saying. Their minds could not countenance the notion that Jesus might fail in His mission as they understood it. Who in his right mind would join up with a leader who deliberately planned to fail? Each of the Gospels tells His story in such a way that the successful work of redemption by the blood of the cross is the denouement. When it was all over the Son and the Father each made an impressive announcement that it was so: 'Jesus uttered a loud cry,' 'It is finished' (Mark 15:37; John 19:30) – 'And behold, the curtain of the temple was torn in two, from top to bottom' (Matt. 27:51).

This steady purpose to accomplish the mission to give His life a ransom for many, to be the Lamb of God in a divine ritual of sacrifice of cosmic significance, is held to be the Christian's ideal example of steady purpose. We are exhorted to 'run with endurance the race that is set before us, looking to Jesus, the founder and perfecter of our faith' (Heb. 12:1, 2).

---

1. Robert D. Culver, *The Sufferings and the Glory* (Moline, IL: Christian Service Foundation, 1958, republished at Eugene, OR: Wipf and Stock, 2001). Based on this work I prepared the article on 'The Servant of the Lord' for the *Revised International Standard Bible Encyclopedia*, but on account of delays in publication and changes in editorial supervision my article was lost track of and another was used.

The Role (Function) of Mediator.

Though 'role' is derived from the French word for the roll of paper containing a dramatic actor's part and, in English, primarily means an actor's part in a play, we do now use the word role (or *role*) to specify the proper function of someone or something. The work of the Theanthropos (God-man) as Mediator was certainly no play-acting (even though a great spectacle to men and angels).

'For there is one God, and there is one mediator [Gr. *mesitēs*] between God and men, the man Christ Jesus' (1 Tim. 2:5 KJV, RSV and ESV).

Mediate, mediation and mediator are well-known words in common use, especially in labor-management disputes. Mediation is very difficult work in labor-management disputes, legal tangles in domestic quarrels and the like, and we all know about this. We know that truth and justice are frequently violated, perverted or at least slighted in mediation of human disputes. Compromises of principles seem necessary for perceived success. We are apt therefore to misunderstand the work of Christ as Mediator. Truth and righteousness are served perfectly in His mediatorial work. The work of the Theanthropos as Mediator was precisely to avoid compromise, viz.: 'to demonstrate his justice at the present time, so as to be just and the one who justifies those who have faith in Jesus' (Rom. 3:26 NIV).

The function of mediation between people frequently occurs in biblical narrative, though there is no special Hebrew word for it. Job (Job 9:33) expressed desire for a *mokiah*, 'one who could judge' (*hiph.* act. part of *yakah*) 'between us,' i.e. between Job and God. 'But even though the LXX renders *be-ne-nu* (lit. between us), by *mesitēs* ('mediator' in 1 Tim. 2:5) it is a tendentious mistake.'[2] Oepke insists it was employed to tickle the ears of educated Gentiles, not to give precise meaning to a Hebrew word. 'There is no single term for "mediator" in the Hebrew or Greek Old Testament.'[3] TDNT devotes twenty-six densely furnished pages to a faithful recital of the background of the word *mesitēs*, mediator. It is a legal term, the essential idea of the noun and corresponding verb *mesiteuo*, it being to achieve reconciliation between two alienated parties. The verb is used only once (Heb. 6:17) and not in the usual sense of 'act as mediator.'[4] But *mesitēs* (mediator) is none the less important in spite of its rare occurrence for two reasons. First, because it is the comprehensive word for all Christ has done and continues to do to bring lost men to God (1 Tim. 2:5). Second, because in Galatians Paul makes special use of it in two verses, showing what he means by the word. Theologians did not use the word *mesitēs* much in ancient times in Christology. In those days the Person of Christ loomed larger than any other question. It occupied the theologians until the close of the epoch of antiquity.

The *Mesitēs* in Paul's Theology of Redemption.

'[I]t [the law] was ordained by angels in the hand of a mediator [*mesitēs*]' (Gal. 3:19 KJV; 'intermediary' ESV). Moses, of course was the 'mediator.' And it was the hand of Moses which held the tablets of the 'law' (Decalogue) inscribed by God when, after forty days on 'the mount' with God, he descended to the people (Exod. 32:15, 18). Nearly forty years later Moses, describing the mighty events attending the giving of the law said, 'At that time I stood between the LORD and you.' So we know a *mesitēs* in Paul's thought was one who stood between the LORD and people in imparting revelation. Moses was a mediator in arranging the Sinai covenant ('negotiating' is the wrong word when one party is the divine Judge of the world) between God at the top of Mt. Horeb and Israel camped at the foot.

No doubt Moses is our prototypical, biblical *mesitēs* (mediator) and we know what he did. In the first place, he functioned as a *prophet*, mediating divine revelation, as the last four books of the Pentateuch abundantly relate. In the second place, as a priest, Moses occasionally offered sacrifice to God for the people (Heb. 9:19-22) and famously served as their successful priestly intercessor with God (Exod. 32:31-35). Thirdly, Moses was a ruler, in every respect as much as 'kings' such as Saul or David in the normal Hebraic sense. Stephen said, 'This Moses… God sent as both ruler and redeemer' (Acts 7:35). A. J. McClain comments:

---

2. Oepke, in Kittel, Gerhard and Friedrich, Gerhard, *Theological Dictionary of the New Testament iv*, trans. and ed. Geoffrey W. Bromiley (Grand Rapids, MI: Eerdmans, 1964–1976), p. 601.

3. ibid.

4. Arndt and Gingrich, *A Greek-English Lexicon of the New Testament & Other Early Christian Literature* (Chicago: University of Chicago Press, 1967).

It is true that Moses is never spoken of as a king. But that is true of more than one great figure in history who have ruled as absolute monarchs over various nations. The great difference between Moses and these other rulers is that in the case of the great law-giver, the regal authority was exercised under God and His direct control. Dr O. T. Allis is right in saying that 'Moses exercised the office of king; he represented the invisible King' (*Prophecy and the Church*, 1945, p. 59). The testimony of Acts 7:35 is decisive.[5]

'Now a mediator is not a *mediator* of one, but God is one' (Gal. 3:20 KJV). This verse has hundreds of variant interpretations. The English Standard and New International Versions' renderings suggest a partial answer: 'Now an intermediary implies more than one; but God is one.' The one God employed no *mesitēs* (mediator, intermediary) in announcing a covenant to Abraham (see preceding vv. 15 and 16). Abraham received divine promises also called a covenant. God (who is one, all in all) spoke directly to Abram without a mediator (Gen. 12, 13, 15, *et al*). The law associated with the name of Moses was by a *mediator* between two. Moses was the go-between. God gave the commands and conditions. Moses passed them on to the people. He didn't adjust differences he simply served as messenger – which in Greek usages was one of the connotations of *mesitēs* among Greek-speaking Jews. 'Angel' is the Greek word (*aggelos, pronounced angelos*) for messengers of God in mediation of the covenant.[6] So this verse rests on the concept of Moses' prophetic activity (organ of revelation) as *mesitēs*.

The Three Offices of the Mediator of Redemption.

The Old Testament is indispensable for a full understanding of the *work* of Christ. We refer to His threefold office of *prophet, priest* and *king*. It will help to understand this triplex office to observe several things. First, the comprehensive nature of His work as the God-man is indicated by a comprehensive term, 'mediator.' This word designates no single aspect of Christ's work of redemption but every aspect – 'For there is one God, and there is one mediator between God and men, the man Christ Jesus, who gave himself as a ransom for all' (1 Tim. 2:5, 6). Notice His mediatorial work is traced especially to His death as a 'ransom.' Second, 'Christ' is another comprehensive term for all He came to be and do. Though *Christ* came later to be used as a name for Jesus, it served first as His title as the predicted *Messiah* of the Old Testament. The nation of Israel observed the custom of inducting official men connected with their commonwealth into office by the ceremony of anointing with oil. This is first mentioned in Scripture in connection with the Aaronic priests (Exod. 28:41). It is mentioned also in connection with the induction into office of Israel's first king (1 Sam. 9:15; 10:1). Though the practice is seldom mentioned in that connection, prophets were also sometimes so inducted into office (1 Kgs. 19:16; cf. Gen. 20:7; Ps. 105:15).

Now, the Hebrew word 'to anoint with oil' is *mashah*; the derived adjective *mashiah*, anointed, becomes in the Greek translation of the Old Testament, *Messias*, whence the English word 'Messiah' comes. A step further, the Greek translation of this work is *Christos* (derived from *Chrio*, to pour oil). This is transferred to Latin as *Christus* and from Latin to English as *Christ*. Hence the title *Christ* points directly to the threefold office of Christ: prophet, priest and king.

Prophet.

The function of a prophet is to convey a written or spoken message from God to men: i.e. he was to teach with divine authority. Jesus did just that. In His Person, words and deeds He revealed the Father (John 8:26; 14:9; 17:8). And He taught the people (Matt. 5–7). He was declared to be a prophet and was said to have done a prophet's work (Deut. 18:15; cf. Acts 3:22; Matt. 13:57; Luke 13:33; John 6:14). In keeping with the requirements for a prophet (Deut.18:9 *ad fin;* and 13:1 ff.) He produced the signs of a prophet (He was a Hebrew, performed miracles, made near-term predictions which were fulfilled and fully honored the Mosaic covenant, Deut. 18:15-22). There can be no doubt that Jesus' work as Messiah, the Christ of God, included everything germane to His office of prophet.

Priest.

Jesus also fulfilled the office of anointed priest. O.T. priests had civil functions such as supervision of medical and sanitary affairs (Lev. 11–15; cf. Luke 5:14), on stated occasions taught the Law to the people (Lev. 10:11; Deut. 33:10; 2 Chr. 15:3) and pronounced blessings (Deut. 21:5; Num. 6:23-26). The chief biblical function of a

---

5. A. J. McClain, *The Greatness of the Kingdom* (Grand Rapids, MI: Zondervan, 1959), p. 59.
6. See *TDNT*, vol iv, p. 617 – Gal. 3:19.

priest was to mediate religiously between God and man in two ways: the offering of sacrifices (especially bloody sacrifices at the brazen altar) and to make intercession. Of these two, in the Mosaic ritual system, offering sacrifices was exclusively the priests' duty and right. The priest was mediator in a sense the prophet and the king were not, it being his function to represent God to the people in the functions at the altar and likewise to represent them to God in prayer.

That Jesus fulfilled both these functions and did so as divinely appointed priest is explicitly stated in Hebrews 7:24-28. In connection with a 'priesthood,' which He holds 'permanently,' He 'always lives to make intercession for them' and 'once for all... he offered up himself.' Jesus was both victim and sacrificing priest. *This is the work of redemption to which, in a sense, all other is ancillary and supplemental.* To it this study shall return.

King.

The third aspect of His office and work is that of king. So Nathanael could confess, 'You are the King of Israel!' (John 1:49); Jesus could speak of His kingdom (John 18:36), and when Pilate asked, 'You are a king, then' Jesus could answer, 'You are right in saying I am' (John 18:37 NIV). In the great prophecy of Psalm 2:6, the Lord God says of Him, 'I have set my King on Zion, my holy hill.'

Likewise, in Psalm 110, a prophecy Jesus appropriated for Himself as Messiah, God proclaims, 'Rule in the midst of your enemies' (v. 2). This Messianic rule, though it began before His ascension among His disciples, was formally inaugurated at the session at God's right hand (Eph. 1:19-23). That reign focuses, in the present age, on the church, a kingdom of grace and spiritual power. It shall expand to a visible kingdom, when at His Second Coming, He assumes the throne of David, over Israel (Ps. 72) and from that throne rules all the nations as King of kings and Lord of lords (Rev. 19).

This Old Testament background of the title of office, 'Christ,' explains the confession of Peter (Matt. 16:16) and of Mary (John 11:27). Both, 'You are the Christ, the Son of the living God' and 'you are the Christ, the Son of God, who is coming into the world' were spoken by pious Jews steeped in the Old Testament religious outlook. They could hardly have understood the title in any other way than that of designating one or all aspects of the threefold office of prophet, priest and king. The New Testament clearly indicates that Jesus fulfilled all three designations of the title, as we shall see. (See also Acts 4:26, 27.)

To summarize then, as Moses the great lawgiver and mediator of the 'old covenant' functioned in three offices of prophet, priest and king (as we have seen above) so Christ the Mediator of the 'new covenant' ('testament' KJV) (Heb. 8:6; 9:15; 12:24) functions in the same three mediatorial offices. In the work of salvation as *prophet* He is the Word of God to men, as *priest* He is offerer and offering at the sacrifice of Calvary, and as *king* He presently reigns at the right hand of the Father. This threefold characterization is more than a mere convenient way to arrange what Christ did, does and shall yet do for our salvation. It is the biblically furnished structure of biblical truth.[7]

The very title Christ (Anointed, Messiah) implies an authoritative structure. Jesus is 'the Anointed' prophet, priest and king, fulfilling the Old Testament promises and types, bringing the Mosaic institutions to consummation in Himself – thus furnishing authoritative structure for interpretation of the Person, life and work of the Mediator.

A Jewish author points out that 'the Anointed of the Lord' gives the proper bearer of the title a special sanctity, just as Christians find their New Testament says it should be with our Lord:

> [T]he person of 'the Anointed of the Lord' came to be considered sacrosanct; to harm him, or even to curse him, was a capital offense (2 Sam. 19:21). A further development of this concept can be seen in the belief that God provided special protection of His anointed king. The Psalms contain several references to the idea of divine intervention for 'the Anointed of the Lord,' the idealized Davidic king: 'Now I know that the Lord saveth His Anointed [*mashiaḥ*], He will answer him from His holy heaven with the mighty acts of His saving right hand' (Ps. 20:7). The Lord is a strength unto them, and he is a stronghold of salvation to His Anointed (Ps. 28:8).[8]
> [Patai might have added Ps. 105:14, 15.]

Eusebius, the most important historian of the pre-Nicene and Nicene age (fourth century) devoted chapter 3 of the first book of his *Church History* to elaboration of this point. After full elaboration of the Scripture precedents and types he summarizes:

---

7. Pieper, Francis, *Christian Dogmatics ii* (St. Louis: Concordia Publ., 1950–1957), p. 333.
8. Raphael Patai, *The Messiah Texts* (Detroit: Wayne State University Press, 1979), p. 22.

[A]ll these have reference to the true Christ, the divinely inspired and heavenly Word, who is the only high priest of all, and the only king of every creature and the Father's own supreme prophet of prophets.[9]

The expectations of godly folk at the Advent of Christ seems to evidence this same understanding of the three offices of 'the Coming One' (Gr. *ho erchomenos*). Even the Samaritan woman at the well of Sychar (John 4:19, 25, 26, 29) knew about the coming anointed Prophet and Jesus confirmed her information (John 4:26).

I can think of no such specific expression of expectation for a future anointed priest in the Gospels. The intertestamental literature, especially the Dead Sea literature, proves there was a lively expectation of a priest-Messiah, not necessarily however the same person as the prophet or king-Messiah.

Messiah [Anointed One] at Qumran and the Dead Sea Documents.

Several of the documents from Qumran refer to the lay messiah (Messiah of Israel, or anointed king) and the priestly messiah (Messiah of Aaron) and in one striking passage, they are mentioned together with 'the Prophet' (i.e. of Deut. 18:18; John 1:21). In apparent expectation of a soon arrival of all three *The Manual of Discipline* says of certain specially holy men (presbyters): 'Until the coming of *the Prophet* and of both the *priestly* and the *lay* [royal] messiah, these men are not to depart from the clear intent of the Law,' etc.[10]

The 'Amazing Dead Sea Scrolls' show just how fervently the Jewish people in the decades just before the Savior's birth – at least the most zealously religious of them – relished the coming of 'the Lord's Anointed' king, prophet and priest. They were not certain if one Messiah would hold all three offices, or two men or three. The subject is too large to enter these pages at length, for the scholarly literature of the subject is staggering in volume. (First came reports in *Biblical Archaeologist* and the Bulletin of the *American Schools of Oriental Research* as the early discoveries unfolded. Then came the journalistic literature of interpretation and something of a war of publication and custody of the delicate Qumran remains. It is a whole area of specialized study.) Two small books by F. F. Bruce will guide the inquiring reader to scholarly discussion of Messianic expectation of prophet, priest and king in the scrolls published before 1974.[11]

The long-sequestered but recently published (1991, 1992) literary remains of Qumran and its environs are available in text and translation in R. Eisenman and M. Wise. These documents portray vividly the ethical and spiritual character of the expected Messiah's coming work. Many of the texts which the Qumran community employed as prophecy of Messiah's prophetic, royal and priestly work are the same as those cited in the New Testament. These authors offer a chaste and reserved appraisal. They say:

> Interestingly, we do not have the two-Messiah doctrine in a few of the texts from the early days of Qumran research... but rather the more normative, single Messiah most Jews and Christians would find familiar.[12]

Simeon and Anna, Zechariah and Elizabeth, Joseph and Mary would have been quite at home in the Messianic discussions of their own time at Qumran.

Post-exilic Expectations Carried to Jesus' Time.

In the early years of the post-exilic Restoration, Ezra directed the people to postpone certain matters 'until a priest with Urim and Thummim should arise' (Ezra 2:63; Neh. 7:65). The Apostles expressed no surprise therefore when Jesus spoke of His 'flesh and blood' as spiritual life (John 6) and said in the Upper Room of the Eucharistic wine, 'This is my blood of the covenant, which is poured out for many' (Mark 14:24). Even the high priest was aware of this priestly aspect of Old Testament prediction of Messiah (John 11:47–50) and John confirms that Caiaphas spoke truly (John 11:52). Nathanael's exclamation, 'Rabbi, you are the Son of God! You are the King of Israel!'

---

9. Eusebius, in *Nicene and Post-Nicene Fathers i*, Second Series, ed. P. Schaff, 1886, repr. (Peabody, MA: Hendrickson Publ., 1994), p. 86.
10. T. H. Gaster, *The Dead Sea Scriptures*, rev. ed. (Garden City, NY: Doubleday & Co., 1964), p. 67.
11. F. F. Bruce, *Jesus and Christian Origins Outside the New Testament* (London: Hodder & Stoughton, 1974), p. 72; also Bruce, *Biblical Exegesis in the Qumran Texts* (London: Tyndale Press, 1960), pp. 46–55. Cf. also a more up-to-date opinion by James C. VanderKam, *The Dead Sea Scrolls Today* (Grand Rapids, MI: Eerdmans, 1994), pp. 161–162. Perhaps the most measured and competent brief assessment is Jack Finegan, 'Relationships with Early Christianity,' in *Light From the Ancient Past: The Archaeological Backgrounds of the Hebrew-Christian Religion vol. ii* (Princeton, NJ: Princeton University Press, 1969), pp. 288–293. There is an immense technical literature on this subject which cannot be entered here.
12. Robert Eisenman and Michael Wise, *The Dead Sea Scrolls Uncovered* (New York: Penguin, 1993), p.17.

(John 1:46) is sufficient to establish existence of a pious hope for a Messianic king. Hence, though many theologians have employed the division of the mediatorial offices into three – prophet, priest and king – it is much more than a convenient rhetorical flourish of theologians, rather it is a seldom stated but inherent feature of biblical teaching about the Messiah of Israel, Redeemer, Revealer, Lord of His people.

There is a reason, almost unnoticed, why the offices of prophet and king are usually lightly touched in writing Christology. That reason is, in first place, the Old Testament types (sacrifice and festival system) and prophecies lay clear emphasis on the Savior's atoning death for sin, His priestly work. Secondly, Jesus' prophetic ministry of revelation has been, as such, not a matter of as much controversy (liberals, for example, reduce Jesus' significance to being a prophet, that is a good teacher or example). Orthodoxy readily acknowledges Jesus as the last great prophet (Heb. 1:1 ff.) but does not exalt this above the priest who both offers sacrifice for sin and is Himself the sacrificial victim. Thirdly, His direct prophetic work in the sense of direct teaching was completed during His public ministry (Matt. 28:20; Luke 4:18; John 1:18; Heb. 1:1; Luke 13:33), while His present reign as 'King of the nations' (Rev. 15:3) is presently out of sight and the public rule and reign are in the future. His priestly work of atonement, to reconcile the world to God (2 Cor. 5:19; Matt. 20:28; Rom. 5:10; 1 John 2:2) is finished; yet it is that saving work He came most specifically to do. The Apostles made 'Jesus Christ and him crucified' (1 Cor. 2:2) the spear-point of everything they had to say. Atonement by the blood of the cross therefore always has been and always will be the theme of theology of sacraments (i.e. ordinances of the Lord's Supper and baptism), sermons and especially of worship on into the future when all the saints of all the ages gather about the throne of God with the 'four living creatures,' 'seven spirits' of God, 'twenty-four elders' and all the holy 'angels' to sing praise to the 'Lamb who was slain' (Rev. 4:1-11; 5:1-14). The same was glimpsed by Daniel the prophet (Dan. 7:13, 14), whose prophecy got Jesus in trouble with the Jewish Sanhedrin (Luke 22:66-71).

11
Humiliation and Exaltation: Two States of the Incarnate Life of the Son of God

Making this distinction is a return from the emphasis of nineteenth-century discourse about an alleged *kenosis* or self-emptying of the Son of God to the more biblical teaching of the two states of our incarnate Lord: humiliation and exaltation. Before going on to that let us take brief notice of the *kenosis doctrine* of Gottfried Thomasius (1802–1875) and his successors.

The complete story of the rise of the 'kenosis doctrine' cannot be told here. During the nineteenth century in Germany and somewhat later in Britain, several scholars attempted to bridge between rationalist criticism and an orthodox view of Christ as God incarnate. The several incidents and sayings of Jesus where He expressed lack of information (as of the time of His second advent and of what was going on about Him) or seemed to lack power (as when requiring the aid of angels and the like) were interpreted as loss of the divine attributes of omniscience and omnipotence. These scholars seized upon the word *ekenosen*, from *kenoō*, to empty, in Philippians 2:7, rendered 'made himself of no reputation' in the KJV, to support the idea of a Jesus limited essentially by the opinions of His time. Thus Jesus' testimony to the inerrant authority of the Old Testament and His belief in demons and the like is negated. He simply had given up divine omniscience and omnipotence and hence didn't know any better. The sincerity of many of the early advocates need not be doubted. Some of them earnestly desired a way to remain orthodox and to go with the flow of what was deemed to be scientific truth about nature and about the Bible as an inspired book not necessarily true in every respect.

D. Baillie, who was certainly no rigid fundamentalist as orthodox theologians go, pointed out that the *kenosis* (self-emptying idea) seems so very promising to many theologians today 'because it apparently enables them to combine full faith in the deity of Jesus Christ with a completely frank treatment of His life on earth as a human phenomenon, the life of a man.'[1] Baillie, in this famous book shows that the *kenosis* doctrine envisions a wholly humanized God without divine attributes. Louis Berkhof furnishes a guide to the subject from a wise orthodox perspective.[2]

The literature on this subject – almost all modern and recent – is amazingly large and keen minds have been devoted to it. I have read many books and articles about it, some very recently. Student papers in my classes have explored it as well as graduate theses I have had a part in directing. I do not hesitate to regard the 'kenosis theology' as a cul-de-sac, a wrong turn, one which we may now safely avoid though we shall make further notice of it in the following discussion.

---

1. Donald M. Baillie, *God was in Christ: An Essay on Incarnation and Atonement* (New York: Charles Scribner's Sons, 1948), p. 95.
2. Louis Berkhof, *Systematic Theology*, Fourth and Enlarged Edition (Grand Rapids, MI: Eerdmans, reprint 1979), pp. 327–329.

Let us come to the point immediately. The discussion begins with 'made himself of no reputation' (KJV), "made himself nothing" (ESV and NIV), 'emptied himself' (RSV) at Philippians 2:7. The word so rendered is *ekenōsen* (third person singular aorist one) from *keno-ō*. This verb is used only six times in the New Testament. A. H. Leitch put the term in right perspective in a brief article noting 'the fact that the other uses of the word *ekenōsen* (Rom. 4:14; 1 Cor. 1:17; 9:15; 2 Cor. 9:3) are uniformly figurative in their context and will not bear the weight of literal usage which the Kenoticists demand of the same word in Phillipians 2:7.'[3] Some English Versions and commentators have (unwisely, good authorities say) put He 'emptied himself' in the text of Philippians 2:7. The nineteenth-century orthodox Anglicans who struggled to explain our Lord's supposed (or real) ignorance were very competent scholars whom I admire greatly, but mistaken; present slight revivals are due to carelessness, in my opinion.

Usage of *keno-ō* in the New Testament so far from indicating the notion that the preexistent Logos gave up any attribute that constituted Him 'very God of very God' show exactly the opposite. Let us see.

If *keno-ō* sometimes means to empty or reflexively to empty oneself of some aspect or part of oneself, Philippians 2:7 is the only one of the six New Testament occurrences where it is so. (See Rom. 4:14; 1 Cor. 1:17; 9:15; 2 Cor. 9:3; Phil. 2:7). TDNT shows that in non-biblical Greek usage *keno-ō* means a) 'to deprive of content or possessions, to be desolate, etc., and b) to 'nullify' or 'destroy.'[4] TDNT says the first sense (giving up possessions) is the sense of Philippians 2:7 and in the others the sense is to nullify or invalidate something. Another standard authority says the idea in Philippians 2:7 is 'to divest himself of privileges.'[5]

If the translation He 'emptied himself' is allowed to stand it should be understood metaphorically, as the ancients for whom Greek was their native tongue did. In theology, as A. H. Leitch asserted, 'the term [*kenosis*] was used first in Patristic literature and... in Christian theology from about the first century, usually as a synonym for the incarnation itself. It is concerned with an emphasis on Christ's humiliation or condescension.'[6] Leitch goes on rightly to observe that Paul's teaching in Philippians 2:6-8 is parallel with the same author's comment 'that though he was rich... he became poor' (2 Cor. 8:9).

There is a minority opinion among scholars – I think likely the correct one – that the whole notion is that the pre-incarnate Son, 'existing in the form of God' is the subject of the clause *heauton ekenōsen* (*he emptied himself*, RSV and most recent translations). These words are immediately followed by *morphēn doulou labōn* rendered usually 'taking the form of a servant' (an aorist, active participle of *lambanō*, to take). The usual Versions, most commentators consenting, regard the taking of the form of a servant as following the act of emptying Himself. However, the participle, being aorist, may be rendered 'having [previously] taken the form of a servant,' etc. If so, then 'having taken the form of a servant', He emptied Himself. In such a case the incarnate Son, Jesus of Nazareth, is the subject of 'he emptied himself.' A note to myself in my file on this subject, quoting an article by Robert B. Strimple, reads: 'C. F. D. Moule... says he has found [now quoting Moule's *An Idiom Book of New Testament Greek*, 2nd ed.][7] in the New Testament [there is] no exception to the rule that an aorist participle denotes an action prior to that of the main verb, with the possible exception of two passages in Acts.'[8] Philip Schaff in an important article says, 'The *kenosis*, or self-humiliation cannot refer to the incarnate Logos, who never was *en morphē theou*, but must refer to the preexistent Logos...'[9] The matter deserves renewed study.

It does not seem profitable in this chapter to discuss modern ideas of kenosis further except to recommend some excellent treatments of the subject. Relatively recent and very helpful are: D. M. Baillie; Paul K. Jewett and A. H. Leitch. L. Berkhof and A. H. Strong[10] are very good guides to the subject as well as all of Vincent Taylor's

---

3. A. H. Leitch, art. 'Kenosis,' *Zondervan Pictorial Encyclopedia of the Bible iii* (Grand Rapids, MI: Zondervan, 1975), p. 784.
4. G. Kittel and G. Friedrich, *Theological Dictionary of the New Testament iii*, trans. and ed. G. W. Bromiley (Grand Rapids, MI: Eerdmans, 1964–1976), p. 661.
5. Bauer, Arndt, Gingrich, *Greek-English Lexicon* (Chicago: Chicago University Press, 1957), p. 429.
6. A. H. Leitch, *Kenosis*, ZPEB, iii, p. 784.
7. C. F. D. Moule, *An Idiom Book of New Testament Greek* (Cambridge: Cambridge University Press, 1959), p. 100.
8. Robert B. Strimple, 'Philippians 2:5-11 in Recent Studies, Some Exegetical conclusions,' *Westminster Theological Journal*, xvi, 2, Spring, 1979.
9. Philip Schaff, 'Christology', art in *A Religious Encyclopedia or Dictionary of Biblical, Historical, Doctrinal, And Practical Theology*, edit. Philip Schaff, New York: 1891, vol. i, p.460. This article, pages 453–467, surveys and summarizes the history of the subject from the apostolic age through the kenosis controversies of the nineteenth century in a manner that does great honor to its author.
10. Baillie, *God was in Christ* (New York, 1948), pp. 94–98; Jewett, 'Kenosis,' in *Wycliffe Bible Encyclopedia ii* (Chicago: Moody Press, 1975), pp. 986–988; Leitch, *Kenosis* (ZPEB, 1975), p. 784; Berkhof, *Systematic Theology* (1941), pp. 327–332; Strong, *Systematic Theology* (Valley Forge, PA: Judson Press, 1907), pp. 701–706.

writings. (Several recent academic theologians interested in some rapprochement with process theology – entailing that God is finite and changing – and ideas of the Trinity as a model of human society, community or family are reviving interest in the *kenosis* doctrine, leading to the translation of an 1856 essay of I. A. Dorner, leading German kenotic theologian: *Divine Immutability*.[11])

Doctrinal Development of Humiliation-Exaltation.

In Early Lutheran Theology.

The formal distinction between two 'states' of Christ dates back to Lutheran theology of the immediate post-Luther era. Lutherans taught the doctrine of the 'real presence' of the body and blood of Christ with the Eucharistic bread and wine. This was explained by asserting that the attributes of deity, including omnipresence, were communicated to the human nature and (rarely and with some hesitancy) the attributes of humanity to the divine nature, in the incarnation. This is a form of the doctrine of *communication* of attributes, unique to Lutherans. All orthodox theology holds to the *communion* of attributes in the Person of Christ. According to the Lutheran teaching, however, the risen Christ's body and blood are presented to communicants at the Lord's Supper in an *invisible mode* along with the visible elements of bread and wine. For example, hundreds of pages in the Lutheran book of *Systematic Theology* by F. Pieper are devoted to this doctrine.[12]

Francis Pieper states, 'The teaching of the Formula [of Concord] on the humiliation and exaltation affects only the human nature of Christ. It is blasphemous perversion to refer them to the divine nature.'[13] Most of the rest of orthodox Christendom – Protestant, Roman Catholic, Eastern Orthodox – would assert that on the contrary it was the divine Second Person of the Godhead, the *Logos* of John 1:14, the One who existing 'in the form of God... humbled himself' (Phil. 2:6-8), the One who 'was rich' and 'became poor' (2 Cor. 8:9), who experienced the humiliation and the glory.

I mean no lack of respect for historical Lutheranism in offering the opinion (widely held both in and out of Lutheranism) that the doctrine of *communication* (as opposed to *communion*) of attributes and the notion that the *humiliation* and *exaltation* of Christ relates to the *human nature* of Christ rather than the divine Person have always been tightly grasped only to defend the teaching, unique to Lutherans, that the 'real presence' (i.e. true body and blood) of Christ is in (or with) the material elements of the Lord's Supper. Reformed Christians, as well as some believing Lutherans, and Protestants in general, are convinced the real presence of Jesus is spiritual and the elements symbolical of the Lord's body and blood. The Roman Church teaches that the elements are in *essence* transubstantiated into body and blood though the *accidents* (taste, smell, texture, etc.) remain bread and wine. This subject must be refined further in connection with the doctrine of ordinances, or sacraments.

Lutheran-Reformed Debate.

The debates over this issue between Lutherans and Reformed in the Reformation Epoch became increasingly bitter. There was a great desire on the part of Melanchthon and sympathizers (Lutheran) and all the Reformed in Germany and Switzerland, represented by Calvin, to come to agreement and thereby present a united front to the dangerous force of the Roman Church as well as to promote a charitable Christian unity among all evangelicals. After Melanchthon's death Joachim Westphal (1510–1574), defender of the most extreme forms of Lutheran orthodoxy, fiercely opposed the Reformed. Calvin was discouraged beyond measure, greatly dismayed there was no longer an entreatable Melanchthon to address. (For the most important Reformed literature of that time on the matter see pp. 199–579 of volume II of *Calvin's Tracts*, Beveridge translation.[14]) This issue first arose in the decade following 1517 in what historians call 'The Sacramentarian Controversy' in which Luther and Zwingli were chief participants and Bucer the unsuccessful harmonizer. The controversy sadly simmered on until actual persecution of Calvinists in Mary's reign in England drove a group of Reformed Christians to northern Germany where they were treated almost as badly by the Lutheran magnates as by their Roman Catholic Queen 'Bloody Mary.' This is what called forth Calvin's bitter responses. The episode is one of the saddest in the history of 'evangelical' theology, necessary as it seemed to be to the participants at the time.

---

11. I. A. Dorner, *Divine Immutability: A Critical Reconsideration* (Minneapolis: Augsburg Fortress Press, 1994).
12. Francis Pieper, *Christian Dogmatics ii* (St Louis: Concordia Publ. House, 1950–1957), pp. 129–304 and elsewhere.
13. ibid., p. 282.
14. John Calvin, *Tracts Relating to the Reformation*, trans. H. Beveridge *et al* (Edinburgh: Calvin Translation Society, 1844 onward), II, pp.199–579.

Calvinists entered into debate in early attempts to resolve this difference and present a united face to Roman Catholic Europe. 'Real presence' could be accepted but not body and blood (or 'flesh and bones'), which ascended to heaven (Luke 24; Acts 1) and would remain there till 'the time for restoring all... things' (Acts 3:21).

Yet the distinction between the two states of Incarnate Son of God articulated by Lutherans was quickly adopted by leading Calvinists and on to the present. This is at least some positive fruit of the unhappy controversy.

The distinction between Christ's states of incarnate humiliation and incarnate glory became subject for careful definition and extended debate only in post-medieval, Reformation times, but it had been always believed by orthodox Christians because it is pervasive in Scriptures. Christ Himself sharply reproved some disciples on the first Easter as 'foolish ones' and 'slow of heart' to miss it in 'all that the prophets have spoken' about how it was 'necessary that the Christ should suffer... and enter into his glory' (Luke 24:25, 26; cf. 45, 46). Peter represents the humiliation-glory matter as a subject of both interest and puzzlement for those prophets of the Old Testament who made those predictions (1 Peter 1:10, 11). They knew of the contrasting suffering and glory and which came first but were mystified as to how to put the two together.

The States of Christ in Old Testament Prophecy.

Aspects of the humiliation and glory are, as Jesus said, to be found in 'the Scriptures' 'beginning with Moses and all the Prophets... all the Scriptures' (Luke 24:27). The Apostles using this sort of exegesis treated the whole Hebrew Bible as a Christian book – not just a few Messianic passages. I have presented the matter somewhat at length in other writings.[15]

Isaiah 52:13–53:12 is the most explicit and extensive of Old Testament passages pointing specifically to these two states of Christ's incarnate life. Franz Delitzsch points out how stages of Christ's humiliation and exaltation are somewhat cryptically prophesied. The LORD first exclaims 'Behold, my servant' (Isa. 52:13); then He details how 'my servant' is destined to succeed ('prosper') 'be exalted' (resurrection) 'and lifted up' (ascension) and 'shall be high' (the session or enthronement on high). Yet all this, as Delitzsch goes on to say, shall happen to a Servant whose 'appearance was so marred, beyond human semblance,' and His form so degraded in the Passion and crucifixion, that it no longer looked the part of a normal male of our species (Isa. 52:14).[16]

The Caesura – 'Wherefore... therefore... yet... but': several passages in each Testament strikingly emphasize the break between the state of humiliation and the state of exaltation by a 'wherefore,' 'therefore' or the like – similar to the pause or break in a poetic line which scholars of poesy call a caesura. Examples are the 'Therefore' after 'he shall bear their iniquities' and before 'I will divide him a portion with the great' (Isa. 53:11, 12 ESV margin). Similar are the 'Therefore' or 'Wherefore' (KJV) of Philippians 2:9, the 'it behoved' of Luke 24:46 (KJV) and the 'And now' of John 17:5 (see Berkouwer, *The Work of Christ*, chapter 3).

The stages of the humiliation and of the exaltation have been variously traced. Whether as various doctrinal-exegetical scholars propose there are four, five or eight stages downward and three or four or five upward, it seems to the present writer the burial marks the caesura or break between them, belonging to neither and yet to both. The ultimate stage of humiliation was death by Roman execution. After the thrust of the soldier's spear the Savior's body 'the hands of lawless men' ('wicked hands' KJV) (Acts 2:23) never touched Him again, inasmuch as His body was solely in the hands of loving friends and His human spirit had already taken flight to the Father in heaven into whose 'hands' He on the cross committed His spirit (Luke 23:46). Some suggest (perhaps with good reason) the several references to the 'hour' when He Himself was to be glorified is not the crucifixion but the 'glory' that was to follow. True, He embraced the coming agony with enthusiasm (Luke 12:40, 50), yet His exaltation was not in the shame of the cross but in 'the subsequent glories' (1 Peter 1:11). Perhaps Hebrews 12:1-3 should guide us here. There it is clear He 'endured the cross, despising the shame' because of 'the joy that was [still] set before him... and is seated at the right hand... of God.' Only in this view of the matter, it seems to me, can Jesus be our example: 'looking to Jesus, the founder and perfecter of our faith' of Hebrews 12:2.

Further, observe that the devil's last proposal (in Matthew's account) during the forty days of temptation was to bypass the suffering on the way to glory.

---

15. R. D. Culver, 'The Old Testament as Messianic Prophecy,' *Bulletin of the Evangelical Theological Society*, 1964, pp. 91–97; R. D. Culver, *The Life of Christ* (Grand Rapids, MI: Baker Books, 1976, 1991), pp. 19–24. There is however a focus on Isaiah 52:13-15; 53:1-12; and related prophecies of the Servant of the LORD in Isaiah 42–53 (treated at length in Culver, *The Sufferings and the Glory*, (see Bibliography).

16. Franz Delitzsch, *Biblical Commentary on the Prophecies of Isaiah vol. ii*, trans. James Martin (Edinburgh: T and T Clark, 1877), pp. 304–307.

Doctrinal Statement of the Humiliation.

We have already taken notice of the fact that some of the changes for the Son of God in assuming (adding) a human nature to the divine nature were temporary. However, assuming human nature is not one of the temporary aspects of incarnation. He is still a man at the right hand of God and exercises His priestly ministry in heaven as God *en sarki* ,– in flesh. Our Lord is a Man in the state of exaltation as well as the state of humiliation. Further, human nature by creation in God's image and by virtue of its being pronounced blessed (Gen. 1:28) and receiving the very breath of God (Gen. 2:7) cannot in itself be base or inestimable.

The event of 'humbled himself' (Phil. 2:8 ESV, KJV, RSV, NIV), the leading idea in 'The Humiliation,' is not therefore in becoming man (*anthropos*) or a man (*anēr*) but that 'as man' (*hos anthropos*) 'he humbled himself by becoming obedient to the point of death, even death on a cross' (Phil. 2:8). In a quite different sense Psalm 113:5, 6 (KJV) says that in His providential care of creation God 'humbleth himself.' In comment on God's care of even sparrows, Calvin comments, 'Surely if the flight of birds is governed by God's definite plan, we must confess with the prophet that he so dwells on high as to humble Himself to behold whatever happens in heaven and on earth' (*Institutes*, I, 16.5). It is true that He was 'for a little while... made lower than the angels' (Heb. 2:9) and if so, as Man, lower than God, but this is not what Paul means by 'he humbled himself.' Rather *as Man, already a little lower than the angels* 'he humbled himself,' becoming (*genomenos*) 'obedient to the point of death, even death on a cross' (Phil. 2:8).

Further, as we have earlier insisted, 'he made himself of no reputation' is approximately the right sense of *heauton ekenosen* in Philippians 2:7 (KJV). The clause has no reference whatever to self-emptying of the self. One's self cannot divest oneself of self. The act is set in contrast with self-aggrandizement, as the preceding context (Phil. 2:5, 6) makes perfectly clear.

No more should be put in the meaning of Philippians 2:4 ff., than the author put in. Paul is citing the ethical example of Jesus to enforce the duty to think and live for others rather than self. Ernst Lohmeyer introduced the idea that verses 5-11 were a pre-Pauline hymn incorporated into the text of Paul's letter (*Kyrios Jesus: Eine Untersuchung zu Phil. 2:5–11,* (Heidelberg, 1928). We need to remind ourselves that this notion, though widely accepted, is only a theory without any direct historical evidence. Rather, it seems to me, that Paul could find no greater example of such unselfishness than the incarnation and humiliation of Christ and employed the same not only here but also in 2 Corinthians 8:9. The exalted prose of both passages is quite characteristic of many of Paul's famously high rhetorical flights (e.g. Eph. 1:15-23; Rom. 8:31-39). There is no reason in the world why, if indeed Philippians 2:5-11 is a poem – and no one can be certain it is – Paul himself should not be regarded as the author. In my judgment the passage is simply exalted prose.

The incarnation as such does not therefore consist of a divine nature giving up something, but of adding something to a divine Person: that something being a human nature. We are to believe, therefore, that specifically the condition of the humiliation involved two matters only: surrender of visible divine glory, and obedience. Berkhof comments:

> On the basis of Phil. 2:7, 8 Reformed theology [and most orthodox theology except some Lutherans] distinguishes two elements [only] in the humiliation of Christ, namely, (1) the *kenosis*... consisting in this that he laid aside the divine majesty [or glory], the majesty of the sovereign Ruler of the universe, and assumed human nature in the form of a servant; and (2) the *tapeinosis* (humiliatio), consisting in that he became subject to the demands and to the curse of the law, and in his entire life became obedient in action [active obedience] and suffering to the very limit of a shameful death.[17]

That glory as God was laid aside is plain from the fact that people whom He met viewed Him as described in Isaiah 53:1-3, a rustic carpenter, a quite ordinary specimen of a town of bad reputation, nothing noble or regal about Him.[18] The moral glory of Christ was apparent only to those to whom God saw fit to reveal it (Luke 19:42; John 12:37-41). In Jesus' prayer of John 17, He prayerfully longed for the restoration of that pre-incarnate glory soon to be restored (John 17:5).

'[O]bedient to' (*hupeko-os mechri*) has reference to His life of submission to God's law and God's special will for Him throughout life, often designated 'active obedience' and second, obedience in accepting 'death, even death on a cross' (Phil. 2:8). The latter is sometimes called 'passive obedience,' though the distinction is not fully correct

---

17. Berkhof, *Systematic Theology*, p. 332.
18. Culver, *The Sufferings and the Glory*, pp. 39–59.

for the Gospels relate that He actively embraced the destiny of death and might have called upon legions of angels (Matt. 26:53) to deliver Him if He had so willed. There are active and passive elements in all His obedience, though we shall accept the distinction for purposes of having a commonly accepted verbal medium of reference.

Two More Questions.

It would greatly lengthen this chapter here to introduce the various views of the so-called *kenosis* and the history of the views from the Reformation to recent times. Let us limit remarks first to the question of how Christ can clearly appear *not* to be omnipotent, omniscient and omnipresent (divine attributes) in the Gospels and yet as God-man possess those attributes. Second, to the idea of humiliation as active and passive obedience.

Omniscience, Omnipotence and Omnipresence in the State of Humiliation.

The Gospel reports say that Jesus grew in wisdom as a child (Luke 2:52), yet during the 'last week' apparently expected a fig tree to have some fruit when it had none (Matt. 21:19, 20). Jesus sometimes appears to have asked questions to gain information (Luke 8:45, 46) and said He did not know the time of His second advent (Mark 13:32), information known only to the Father. The reports do not seem to represent Jesus as always on every occasion being consciously omniscient.

The same reports say that Jesus grew in physical stature, that He was wrapped in ordinary infant clothing, the cultural equivalent we may suppose, of diapers (Luke 2:7) – was weary (John 4:6), hungry (Matt. 4:4), thirsty (John 19:28), tempted by the devil (Matt. 4). The Gospels do not present Jesus as *manifesting* omnipotence on every occasion. We may be certain He slept regularly because He was weary and, on occasion, exhausted (Mark 4:38).

The same reports make plain Jesus was never in more than one place at the same time. His parents carried Him from Bethlehem to Egypt and thence to Nazareth. He made the thrice-yearly journeys afoot from the family home to the central sanctuary the same as every other Jewish male. The Jesus of the Gospels occasionally makes unusual movements – escaping crowds and attackers, walking on water, but no manifest omnipresence.

These observations really only emphasize the point the creeds make: that Jesus was *very man*. Not that in important ways He was not also a uniquely different Man (He was, for example, without sin). Nor do they show that He was a *mere* Man. They show that even though the Person was the Logos, the Second Person of the Godhead, as that Person, He did not employ all the powers of deity in the state of humiliation, and as regards the human nature, He renounced the use of the transient (or relative) attributes the divine nature possesses except as specially occasioned by the Father's will. We shall examine such occasions in the chapter on the deity of Christ.

This is not the way some of the *kenotic* theologians of the nineteenth century would interpret the renunciation of Philippians 2:7, 8, for they asserted that the Son of God either divested Himself of the relative attributes of omnipotence, omniscience and omnipresence (F. Delitzsch and Thomasius) or even gave up all the distinctly divine attributes and *became* man in the sense of metamorphosis (Godet and Mackintosh). Nor does this view even quite represent some orthodox writers who, at least on the matter of our Lord's omniscience, deny He knew less in the state of humiliation than in preexistence or exaltation.

Vincent Taylor's Contribution.

No writer has given more reverent attention to understanding the incarnation than Vincent Taylor. In contrast with much then current 'Jesus of History' speculation Taylor tried to interpret what the records (all the New Testament) really say. He found no contradiction in belief between the primitive church and the writing of the New Testament, observing: 'Primitive Christology… is not a stage merely antecedent to St Paul… it is the Christianity of the common man both before and after the time of the great writers.'[19] Taylor was convinced Jesus was conscious of His deity but stops short of trying either fully to understand or explain a mystery which transcends human categories. He observed rightly that no human being's personal consciousness is open to full understanding – even self-understanding. He thought many areas of Christology would remain mysteries, concluding with this:

---

19. Vincent Taylor, *The Person of Christ in New Testament Teaching* (London: Macmillan Co., 1958), p. 216.

> The NT writers do not solve the problems, as indeed theology has not solved them yet and will not solve them to its full satisfaction, but, in their thinking and teaching, they addressed themselves to the vital issues which are involved, and they did so in such a manner that what they... teach has proved to be inspiration of all subsequent Christian thought.[20]

Taylor seems to find Jesus' sayings about what He knew or did not know as conscious self-limitation to what the condition of life among men in the historic process involves. The God-man possessed the divine attributes (or would have ceased to be God) but did not employ them in any way to disturb the historic process. (I would add, that if Jesus said He did not know this or that, He certainly did not believe or teach any untruths. 'If it were not so I would have told you' is the rule.) Taylor heartily endorsed the historic creeds and states:

> The Christology which seems most in accord with the teaching of the NT is... that in becoming man, the Son of God willed to renounce the exercise of the divine prerogatives and powers, so that in the course of his earthly existence, he might live within the necessary limitations which belong to human finitude.[21]

I cite Taylor with the caution that some of his Christology makes concessions to kenoticism, the idea Son of God in humiliation did not *possess* all the attributes of deity in His humiliation. The late Dr Taylor's works on various topics related to the Person, life and work of Christ would fill a long shelf.

A. H. Strong's Admirable Summary.

A. H. Strong's treatment of 'the State of Humiliation' is correctly and admirably concise and has the virtue of brevity. It has been honored by wide adoption among evangelical teachers and writers. He added just enough (one word) to the usual orthodox statement to solve the problem of why sometimes Jesus seemed to be omniscient and omnipotent and sometimes did not. The word is 'independent.' Let me quote:

> Our doctrine of Christ's humiliation will be better understood if we put it midway between two pairs of erroneous views, making it the third of five...: (1) Gess: the Logos gave up all divine attributes; (2) Thomasius: the Logos gave up relative attributes only; (3) True view: the Logos gave up the *independent* [emphasis added] exercise of divine attributes; (4) Old Orthodoxy: Christ [i.e. the *theopneutos*] gave up the use of divine attributes; (5) Anselm: Christ acted as if he did not possess divine attributes.[22]

The views cited are views of theologians considered orthodox, not heretical as regarding an actual incarnation.

That in the state of humiliation the Lord surrendered the independent exercise of the attributes of the divine nature takes cognizance of His submission to the special divine will for the Mediator as well as divine law for all members of our race, also of His life of active and passive obedience.

Strong's formulation has been widely accepted among American evangelicals and adopted as almost standard evangelical orthodoxy. Though practically endorsing Strong's view, Lewis and Demarest rather sharply criticize Strong's phrasing of the doctrine. They say that since His use of divine power had always been in harmony with the Father and the Spirit, 'To say that Jesus gave up a *contrary* [their word, not Strong's] use of His powers seems like reporting that a husband quit beating his wife when in fact he had never beaten her.'[23] This seems capricious to me. Strong did not say 'contrary exercise of the divine attributes,' he said, 'independent.' He obviously did not mean *contrary* use by *independent* use. Jesus plainly spoke the language of *dependent* power and dependent will when He said, 'I can do nothing on my own... I seek not my own will, but the will of him who sent me' (John 5:30). Lewis and Demarest go on to say: '[T]he Son voluntarily gave up *the continuous use* of his divine powers and any *contrary uses of his human capabilities.*'[24] This is harmless, but did the Son 'give up contrary uses of... human capabilities' when 'existing in the form of God?' When He did not have any such capabilities as yet? Perhaps Strong got the message exactly right after all. (It is not without significance that recent orthodox Lutheran theologians of repute find frequent occasion to quote Strong's insightful formulation of Christological doctrine – e.g. F. Pieper and J. T. Mueller.[25])

---

20. ibid.
21. ibid., p. 287.
22. A. H. Strong, *Systematic Theology*, p. 704.
23. Gordon Lewis and Bruce Demarest, *Integrative Theology ii* (Grand Rapids, MI: Zondervan, 1990), p. 285.
24. ibid.
25. Pieper, *Christian Dogmatics*, iv, Index vol., p. 992; J. Th. Mueller, 'Have We Outmoded Chalcedon,' in *Christian Today* magazine, 7 December 1959, pp. 11, 12.

Christ's Active Obedience As an Aspect of Humiliation.

Both Calvin and Luther explained Christ's work of redemption as a work of obedience. Calvin did not separate active and passive obedience sharply in using these terms, but the distinctions are there.[26] I think he spoke most comprehensively as follows:

> How has Christ abolished sin, banished the separation between us and God, and acquired righteousness to render God favorable to us?... He has achieved this for us by the *whole course of his obedience* [emphasis added]... proved by Paul's testimony: As by one man's disobedience many were made sinners, so by one man's obedience we are made righteous [Rom. 5:19].... Paul extends the basis of the pardon that frees us from the curse of the law to the whole life of Christ [cites Gal. 4:4, 5]. Thus in his very baptism, also, he asserted that he fulfilled a part of righteousness in obediently carrying out his Father's commandment [Matt. 3:15]... from the time when he took the form of a servant, he began to pay the price of liberation in order to redeem us.[27]

In this and other passages Calvin relates Christ's obedience to God's law in Scripture as active obedience throughout life and obedience to God's special will for Him as passive obedience (though He actively embraced it) through Passion and death.

Luther commented on Galatians 4:4, 5 saying: 'In a twofold manner Christ put himself under the Law. First he put Himself under the works of the Law... circumcised, presented and purified in the temple... subject to father and mother...; yet... not obligated to do this for he was Lord of all laws. But he did so willingly.... In the second place, He also put himself under the penalty and punishment of the Law willingly' (Sermon on Galatians 4:1-7, cited by Thomas Oden).[28]

Some Details of the Humiliation in Active Obedience.

To describe in detail Jesus' unfailing obedience to the will of His Father would be to tell the story of the life of Christ. This is not the sphere of theological Christology. I have published a book of over 300 pages on that subject and will not repeat it here.[29]

It is the state of humiliation, the humbling aspect of that life, which pertains to the present discussion – 'no reputation... humbled himself... for your sakes became poor.' From the standpoint of the Bible God is so high He must humble Himself even to look down 'to behold the things that are in heaven' – much more the things 'in the earth!' (Ps. 113:6 KJV). It must therefore be proper to think of the *Creator* (John 1:1, 2) as humbled greatly to assume the *created* nature of man, even if in the normal condition of holiness rather than our abnormal condition of sin – starting right off associating Himself with sinners in the womb of a virgin, who like every other mother beginning with Eve, was a sinner. The doctrine of the virgin's immaculate conception is utterly without biblical support. Jesus' companying with sinners began early, in fact, before He was born.

(Some Protestant authorities claim there was a 'purification' of the human nature of Christ in the mother's womb. This seems to me about as unlikely as the 'immaculate conception' of the mother, Mary, and introduces a needless miracle. Let us use 'Occam's Razor' on this theological excess of refinement. The angel's '*therefore* [emphasis added] also that holy thing' (Luke 1:35 KJV) traces the holiness (sinlessness) of Christ to 'the power of the Most High' and the 'Holy Spirit,' i.e. the power of God Himself in the conception without a male parent, as we show in the chapter on the virgin birth of Christ.)

Though announced by angels He was delivered to a simple peasant maiden and her poor husband, visited first by rustic shepherds and cradled in a manger for animals. His first lengthy residence was in Egypt, symbol of corruption and disease throughout Scripture; boyhood in a disreputable town, growing up like a plant suckling from a root in very dry social and economic ground, without recognized nobility or stately accoutrements (Isa. 53:1, 2). Let us try to think of the Lord of Glory as weighing only six to ten pounds, crying for a diaper change, suckling at a woman's breast, babbling in His cradle, learning to talk, contending with neighborhood bullies, subject to unlettered parents (Luke 2:40, 52), known only in the neighborhood and that as son of a village tinker and taking his trade; and in our supposedly educated society let us try to understand the One called the very 'wisdom of God' (1 Cor. 3; Prov. 8) as arriving at maturity with less than a sixth-grade education (John 7:15).

---

26. John Calvin, *Institutes of the Christian Religion*, ed. J. T. McNeil, trans. and ed. F. L. Battles (Philadelphia, PA: Westminster Press, 1960), II, 12.7; II, 16.5; III, 11.12; 19.4; 8.5.
27. ibid., *II*, 16.5; see also *ii*, 12.7; *iii*, 11.12; 19.4; 8.5.
28. Thomas Oden, *Systematic Theology ii* (San Francisco: Harper, 1992), p. 359.
29. Culver, *The Life of Christ*, pp. 84, 91.

Once He said, 'My Father works and I do too.' Adam's work was to till the ground until sweat ran off his nose (Gen. 3:19) and until he would die and return to the ground. Like Adam, He labored, He sweated and He died.

'If it be possible, let this cup pass from me' was Jesus' prayer in the Garden. But Calvary was only the final and most bitter of cups in His public life of humiliation. He made Himself of no worldly reputation. He became obedient to rules made for the gainsaying and disobedient, for little minds and sinful people, until He had fulfilled every one of them. That was what it meant to be 'made' of a woman not only 'under the law' but subject to 'every ordinance of man.'

He was to be granted no exception from any humiliating legal requirement for good conduct. The law prescribed circumcision and participation in the whole ritual and sacrificial system, including three trips every year to the central sanctuary. Every one of these Mosaic requirements related to the Israelites as sinners. Jesus was innocent of any sin whatsoever, yet as 'under the law' He patiently went through all the motions without protest.

Dawn of Messianic Consciousness.

No one knows precisely when the human nature of Jesus became aware of His divine nature and mission of humble obedience. From the incident of being left behind by His parents (Luke 2:41-52) we have at least a *terminus ad quem*. I quote the following:

> We learn that by His twelfth year, for sure our Lord was aware of the nature of his mission. He knew that the temple was His Father's house and that the ritual there and the Law with its interpretation were His Father's business. We would like to know *if* and *when* Mary and Joseph told Him of the remarkable circumstances surrounding His birth, and if not, how and when He learned of His divine mission. When did the eternal *Logos*, eternal Son of the Father, become self-conscious in Jesus, the carpenter of Nazareth? People have always wondered. Many learned books have been written about it. Really no one can know for sure, but most readers will agree with James Stalker who wrote: 'With His reply to His mother ['Did you not know that I must be about my Father's business?'] before me I cannot trust myself to think of a time when He did not know what His work in this world was to be.'[30]

Christ's Passive Obedience in Passion and Death.

For reasons already given we turn quickly from the active obedience of Christ to the passive obedience, which will receive even briefer treatment, but as indicated earlier, for a different reason. His Passion is the closing part, especially the last week, of His life story. It is the subject of Matthew 21–26; Mark 11–15; Luke 19–22; and John 12–18 and so very productively considered in connection with exposition of those passages or in an organized way as the life of Christ.

The Passion and death of Christ are therefore the next major considerations. They were designated by Jesus as the chief reasons for the incarnation as we have already noted and shall see fully demonstrated later in this section.

His Passion and death are, as such, what theologians have designated His passive obedience. Recent popular theology and preaching have paid scant attention to (though not completely overlooked) the active obedience. Buswell explains that it was almost a discovery for him late in his theological exertions.[31] I myself never heard of it in the ordinary course of church attendance and it was omitted in my seminary education. It was a casualty of the intense effort of the loyal orthodox (now *disparagingly* called fundamentalists) a few decades ago, to rescue blood atonement, one of 'the five fundamentals' from the oblivion to which it was being assigned by the prevalent social gospel, theology of salvation-by-being-good propaganda in the historic Protestant churches. Even A. H. Strong, who was a Baptist and conservative in almost all his theology, fully competent and historically aware, mentions the distinction specifically on only two pages of his great work of systematic theology, as far as I can determine. Buswell provides an interesting discussion of 'active obedience of Christ' among the theologians.[32]

'Descended into Hell': Did it Happen?

Renewed use of the *Apostles' Creed* in worship has sprung up even among churches that traditionally eschewed anything like a traditional liturgy. I have witnessed it even in a Baptist church that did not use it in the previous ninety years of its history. This development makes appropriate some attention to the clause 'he descended into hell'

---

30. James Stalker, *The Life of Jesus Christ* (Westwood: Fleming H. Revell, Co., 1949), p. 22. The above paragraph is adapted from R. D. Culver, *The Life of Christ*, pp. 59, 60.
31. James O. Buswell, *Systematic Theology of the Christian Religion ii* (Grand Rapids, MI: Zondervan, 1962, 1971), p. 112.
32. ibid., pp. 110–113.

(Hades, spirit world) after 'was crucified dead, and buried.' The clause has been a problem for theologians as far back at least as Calvin. Recently there was a lively exchange of opinion in *Christianity Today* magazine about it – a 'free church' thorough condemnation of the clause and a Lutheran, Missouri Synod, defense of it. The clause has been and remains an obstacle to general use of the Apostles' Creed. Can we justify its presence in a confession which in public worship answers the question, 'Christians, what do you believe?'

Some Lutheran theologians have interpreted 1 Peter 3:18 ff. as meaning that immediately after being quickened in the tomb, therefore in 'soul and body,' the Lord went and preached a message of condemnation to the unsaved in Hades.[33] Lutherans are quite prudent to reject any notions of a preaching in Hades to offer a second chance to receive the gospel. The doctrine is officially affirmed in Article IX of the Formula of Concord. It is taught, these authorities say, 'by the clear teaching of 1 Peter 3:18-20.'

Roman Catholic doctrine, though acknowledging the clause to be a fifth-century addition to the Apostles' Creed[34] holds that 'after his death, Christ's soul, which was separated from his body [not in 'quickened body' and soul as in the Lutheran view], descended into the underworld and did so to proclaim the deliverance of the righteous dead from Limbo.'[35] Both the Lutheran and Roman Catholic views seem overrefined and unnecessary.

There is another understanding of 1 Peter 3:18-20 which commends itself to many, including this writer, as a preaching by Christ 'in the spirit' through Noah 'in the days... while the ark was being prepared' to 'spirits' *now* in prison (hell) but *then* alive and rejecting the preaching of 'the spirit' through Noah – an interpretation advocated by many commentators and fully compatible with the Greek text of 1 Peter 3:18-20.

If one wishes to recite the presently received form of the Creed including 'descended into hell' one may understand it of His burial – as with Bucer, Calvin's example and teacher at Strasburg and Beza, his successor at Geneva – or Calvin's own view that it refers to the Passion and pains He suffered (divine abandonment) on the cross. The latter is my preference.

Lutheran readers of this page can point out that Luther himself cannot be cited as clear authority for Article IX of the Formula of Concord. Paul Althaus shows that 'Christ suffers hell and wrath of God and overcomes them with the power of his love of God. This is how Luther understands the Article [pre Formula of Concord by several years] of Christ's descent to hell. It is part of Christ's death agony. Through it Christ gains the victory over hell. Luther took this position in all stages of his writing.'[36] Althaus notes that in what appears as self-contradiction 'Luther *also* teaches a descent of Christ into hell after his death' and observes it got him 'into difficulty.' Melanchthon took the view given confessional authority in the *Formula of Concord*. Althaus concludes this way: 'Lutherans for the most part opposed the Reformed understanding of the descent into hell as part of the humiliation without realizing that they were also polemicizing against Luther.'[37]

It is evident one may be a good Lutheran and still reject this view of Melanchthon and the Formula. This is one of the rare cases where Calvin is more similar to Martin Luther than to his esteemed friend Philip!

Now, having seen something of the full scope of Christ's work, let the field of inquiry focus on *the stages* of His work rather than the aspects of His work. These, as related to our subject, are Jesus' sinless life, His suffering (Passion), death for sinners, burial, resurrection and post-resurrection ministry (the forty days), His ascension, session at the Father's right hand, and His present ministry in heaven as our Great High Priest.

---

33. Pieper, *Christian Dogmatics*, pp. 314–320; John T. Mueller, *Christian Dogmatics* (St Louis: Concordia Publ. House, 1934), pp. 296–298.
34. Henry Denzinger, *The Sources of Catholic Dogma*, trans. R. J. Deferrari (St. Louis: Herder & Herder, 1954, 1957), nos.1–12; Ludwig Ott *Fundamentals of Catholic Dogma*, trans. L. P. Lynch (Rockford: TAN Books and Publ., 1954, 1974), no. 12, pp. 191, 192.
35. Denzinger, *SCD*, pp. 429, 385; Ott, *FCD*, no. 12, pp. 191, 192.
36. Paul Althaus, *The Theology of Martin Luther* (Philadelphia, PA: Fortress Press, 1966), p. 207.
37. ibid.

12
The Sinless Life of Jesus

In Europe, the Renaissance epoch (say 13th–15th centuries) merged into the 'age of discovery' (15th–16th centuries) in the midst of which came the Reformation. As the Reformers died off, their system of theology was refined about as far as it could go, by Protestant schoolmen (hence Protestant Scholasticism, so-called). This was followed by a time of somewhat anti-theological, anti-supernatural temper in Europe and Britain, called in Europe 'the Enlightenment' ('*Aufklärung*'), and in Britain, the 'Age of Reason.' For many of the intelligentsia of this latter age, Jesus was cherished as an example of human goodness and the religion He founded as valuable to promote the godly life as they conceived it. Already in Luther's time the outlook of Erasmus, whose *Diatribe* Luther answered in *The Bondage of the Will*, was a forerunner of the Enlightenment outlook. For these people, the special value of Jesus was not His work of atonement for sin but His marvellous example of a holy life. Hence the sinlessness of Jesus was no problem, at least not on the face of the issue. Thomas Jefferson in America is a shining example of this thinking (somewhat inaccurately also called deism). The very opposite of Marcion's canon which reduced the New Testament to a few of Paul's Epistles, his abridged New Testament gave full space to Jesus' good life and teaching as Jefferson understood them, but no place for His divine nature or miracles.

This religious outlook moved with the increasing anti-supernaturalistic temper of the nineteenth century to become liberal Protestantism. In Europe A. Harnack (1851–1930), in his *History of Dogma*, tried to demonstrate that Christian doctrinal formulation had been wrong from the beginning with its fixation on the Person of Christ (deity, incarnation, etc.) and the supposed atonement by vicarious sacrifice of Himself. The essence of Christianity is the founder's example of true goodness and His teachings. 'How often,' Harnack (1851–1930) asserted, 'theology is only the instrument by which religion is discarded' (in *What is Christianity?*).[1] Those teachings he was sure could be 'exhibited in entirety' under 'any one' of three heads: 'Firstly, the kingdom of God and its coming. Secondly, God the Father and the infinite value of the human soul. Thirdly, the higher righteousness and the commandment of love.'[2] Hence for the liberal Protestants, then and now, Jesus' importance for religion is the superb example of His life of genuine goodness and His teaching, with miracles and other supernatural elements removed. Not willing to give Jesus up as a moral teacher of the race, the vogue of writing lives of Jesus sprang up in the nineteenth century.

---

1. Adolf Harnack, *What is Christianity?*, 1900 (New York: Harper and Row, 1951).
2. Karl G. A. von Harnack, *History of Dogma* (New York: Dover Publications, 1961), p. 51.

Some, as for instance, Edersheim's *Life and Times of Jesus the Messiah* were thoroughly orthodox and of enduring value. Most of them, however, were laid to rest near the century's end by devastating criticism from their own ranks of liberalism. See David F. Well's remarks on *Kenoticism*.[3]

For the neo-orthodoxy which emerged from liberalism in this century (Barth, Brunner, Tillich, the Niebuhrs two, MacQuarrie, *et al.*), Jesus is valuable to us as One who is a shining example and teacher of *authentic existence* (with varying acceptance of some features of orthodox Christology).

For process theology of the contemporary scene, Jesus seems to have approached the Omega point of God's own development, hence His example of authentic being, His arrival at high degree of excellence, is of value.

Practical Urgency.

There is good reason for avoiding any unnecessary prolixity in dealing pastorally with this topic. As we shall see, the hearts of believing sinners cry out for assurance that when they need help in their own struggle with sin, a sinless Savior is there beside them to help. Yet they feel unable to lean heavily upon Him unless they also know in their hearts that He understands from experience something of the distress and grief of a desperate struggle. Many songs of Christian devotion, not the great doctrinal hymns, but the folk songs that sprang out of the struggles of common people, express this common feeling. A personal note: I lived with a dear wife and mother of my three children for thirty-seven years, who for various reasons related to early experiences and perhaps some physical defect, was never quite free of strange pains accompanied with feelings of despair – this coupled with love of God and trust in His saving grace. Though never an invalid, she never seemed fully well. She was often in doubt if I or any human being or even Jesus really understood. She asked me more than once how Jesus, a Man who was also God, however sympathetic, could really understand.

We are dealing here with a question both pervasive and perennial. Answers require some cogent understanding of Jesus' sinless life as taking place in conflict with genuine trial (or temptation) as the Son of God *and* a son of Man.

The sinlessness of Jesus is not introduced to the New Testament record just to show that His condemnation was unjust, or to explain problems of faith, but to show that He who was slain by 'wicked hands' was God's authentic sacrifice for sin – in the language of the sin-offering and the Passover sacrifice employed by John the Baptist, 'the Lamb of God, who takes away the sin of the world' (John 1:29). (The lamb of the Passover had to be without blemish: Exod. 12:5; Lev. 22:18-20; cf. 1 Peter 1:19; Heb. 9:14. The same was true of the sin-offering.) This, His *active obedience* to the law and will of God (as theologians say), qualified Him to be the perfect and sufficient sacrifice for all human sin. He being an infinite Person thus qualified Himself later, to use Paul's striking language, to be 'made . . . sin for us, who knew no sin; that we might be made the righteousness of God in him' (2 Cor. 5:21 KJV). This matter will call for attention in connection with discussion of Jesus' death.

The Fact of His Sinlessness.

Christians are so unanimously convinced of Jesus' sinlessness that it has never been a matter of serious controversy. Only a few early heretics and certain modern dabblers in the borderland of criticism and theology have questioned or denied it. Most believers think in terms of an unarticulated syllogism: God is sinless; Jesus Christ is God; therefore Jesus Christ is sinless.

This does not mean we do not wonder about certain verses in the Bible where at least the possible inference of some moral defect is present (harsh words to His mother, exasperation with His disciples, frustration over a barren fig tree, etc.). But we give Him the benefit of any doubt and suspend judgment as to the meaning of the text until we understand the passage better.

The sinlessness of Jesus is an emphatic affirmation of heaven on earth at the very moment of announcement by Gabriel who was 'sent from God… to a virgin' named 'Mary.' The messenger from heaven spoke to her of conception by 'the power of the Most High' of 'a son' and 'therefore the child to be born will be called *holy* [emphasis added]…' (Luke 1:26, 27, 31, 35). Two ideas present in the biblical concept of holiness are present in the word *holy* here: transcendence and ethical purity. As Son of God He is transcendent and as immaculately conceived by 'the power of the Most High' (Luke 1:35), ethically pure as God is pure.

---

3. David F. Wells, *The Person of Christ: A Biblical and Historical Analysis of the Incarnation* (Westchester: Crossway Books, 1984), pp. 133–141.

Christian reflection from earliest times has found the reason for the absence of the corruption of original sin in the fact of the 'immaculate conception' (of Jesus, of course, not the dogma of immaculate conception of the virgin mother).

Some argue there was a purification of the human nature of Jesus in the womb by 'proleptic' application of the benefits of Calvary, or by some other means. Though proposed by great theologians whom I greatly respect, I find these efforts unnecessary and merely scholastic, without basis in either Scripture or compelling reason and in neglect of Gabriel's 'therefore,' which connects Jesus' pure humanity directly with conception by 'the power of the Most High' not some post-conception purification. The usual method of conception by sexual insemination by a man is not, as such, either a cause of sin or sinful but, being polluted by Adam's sin, the seed of natural propagation cannot avoid the perpetuation of original sin – viewed as *corrupt* nature in the offspring. No further explanation seems necessary.

Tertullian (AD 145–220) pointed out that generation by a human father is not necessary to complete, perfect humanity, citing the case of Adam, as follows:

> [R]emember that Adam himself received this flesh of ours without the seed of a human father, so also was it quite possible for the Son of God to take to Himself the substance of the selfsame flesh, without a human father's agency.[4]

Augustine, who was a bit hung up on some supposed necessary connection between sexuality and sin said,

> Begotten and conceived... without any indulgence of carnal lust, and therefore bringing with him no original sin, and... united... in one person with the Word... a son by nature, not by grace, and therefore having no sin etc.[5]

Augustine is perhaps right about the hypostatic union but far off base on the other matter.

An early twentieth-century 'father of the church' put it better. Christ's sinlessness:

> can only be made credible by a creative miracle in Christ's origin... a sinless personality implies a miracle in its production. It is precisely because of this that the modern spirit feels bound to reject it. In the Gospels it is not the Virgin Birth by itself that is invoked to explain Christ's sinlessness but the supernatural conception by the Holy Spirit.[6]

New Testament Witnesses to Jesus' Sinlessness.

Jesus' Challenge to Accusers.

It is striking that men so intimately associated with Jesus would guilelessly, and without irony or embarrassment, pass on His seemingly extravagant claims of sinlessness. John, for example, reports a bitter controversy with the Jews over purity and fatherhood – possibly with undertones of gossip about His own mother's claims to have conceived her Son as a virgin (John 8:25, 33, 39, 41, 48) wherein Jesus pointedly accused His audience of various sins and challenged them with these words, 'Which one of you convicts me of sin?' (v. 46). He had already told them, 'I always do the things that are pleasing to him [the Father]' (v. 29). How fitting this should immediately follow the story of the woman taken in the 'very act' of adultery, which left Jesus alone with the woman after all her accusers had left!

Divine Approbation.

On three prominent occasions supernatural occurrences gave God's own verdict on the pure life and holiness of character of Jesus. On the very occasion of His baptism, when He formally associated Himself with sinners in public life and Passion and atoning death, the voice of God came from heaven saying, 'This is my beloved Son, with whom I am well pleased' (Matt. 3:17). Near the end, on Palm Sunday, as Jesus prayed, 'Father, glorify your name' there came a voice from heaven speaking in approval: 'I have glorified it and I will glorify it again'

---

4. Tertullian, *On the Flesh of Christ 16*, in *Ante-Nicene Fathers iii*, repr. of US edn. 1885, ed. A. Roberts and J. Donaldson (Peabody: Hendrickson Publ., 1994), p. 536.
5. Augustine, *The Enchiridion on Faith, Hope and Love*, ed. H. Paolucci with analysis by A. von Harack (Chicago: Henry Regnery Co., 1966), p. 51.
6. James Orr, 'Jesus Christ.' in *International Standard Bible Encyclopedia*, ed. J. Orr (Grand Rapids, MI: Eerdmans, 1939, 1943), p. 1636.

(John 12:28). 'I have glorified it' perhaps referring back to that earlier glorifying of Jesus on the Mount of Transfiguration when the Father spoke words of His unalloyed pleasure in the moral character and resolution to finish the course, at which time Moses and Elijah 'appeared in glory' with Him (Luke 9:31) and the three disciples 'saw his glory' (Luke 9:32). Many years later Peter spoke of this and the Father's attestation, claiming the disciples were 'eyewitnesses of his majesty' and His 'glory' that day and of the approving voice of God (2 Peter 1:16-18).

Apostolic Attestation.

Three features of the apostolic attestation of Jesus' sinlessness contribute to its convincing force. 1) These men were mostly peasant-class Jews, characteristically skeptical of uppity people who make large claims for themselves. Their high opinion of Jesus developed over a period of two to three years of intimate association with Him day and night and in a great variety of situations. As Peter said, 'the Lord Jesus went in and out among us, beginning from the baptism of John until the day when he was taken up from us' (Acts 1:21, 22).

2) The deep conviction of their Master's holy character and utter purity bears greater weight precisely because they never expressed their conviction as proof of something or as a proposition to be defended, rather simply as an unquestioned datum of observation cited for comfort or exhortation. 3) This conviction overcame the certain doubts of orthodox, practicing Jews versed in Old Testament certainty that no human being is sinless. Among the solemnities of Solomon's prayer of dedication for the new temple the king stated that there would be confessions of sin directed there in future days, saying, 'If they sin against you – for there is no one who does not sin...' (2 Chr. 6:36). Psalm 14:3 was quoted by an Apostle; 'no one does good, not even one' (Rom. 3:12). Let the several apostolic sentences speak for themselves. Of Peter: 'you denied the Holy and Righteous One, and asked for a murderer to be granted to you, and you killed the Author of life'; 'your holy servant Jesus, whom you [God] anointed'; redeemed '...with the precious blood of Christ, like that of a lamb without blemish or spot'; 'Christ... commited no sin' (Acts 3:14, 15; Acts 4:27; 1 Peter 1:19; 2:21, 22). Of Stephen, who was associated immediately with the Apostles: 'they killed those who announced beforehand the coming of the Righteous One' (Acts 7:52). Of the apostolically written or sponsored author of Hebrews, 'Jesus, the Son of God... one who in every respect has been tempted as we are, yet without sin' (Heb. 4:14, 15). Of Paul, Him 'who knew no sin... he hath made to be sin for us' (2 Cor. 5:21). Of John's vision of the Lamb in heaven (comparing John 1:29 and Peter's testimony above), the Lamb, who is also Lion of the tribe of Judah and the root of David (Rev. 5:6), is, like God, 'Worthy' (Rev. 5:12) and thereby adequate to purchase men of every tribe, tongue, people and nation (Rev. 5:9) and, like God Almighty, One who receives worship in heaven (Rev. 5:13).

Impressions of Enemies and Disinterested Observers.

The opinions expressed by Pilate (Luke 23:14, 15), Pilate's wife (Matt. 27:19), Herod (Luke 23:15), the centurion in charge of the crucifixion (Luke 23:47) and of the repentant thief (Luke 23:41) are well known. They are impressions only, and of differing levels of insight. Pilate knew that 'for envy' of excellence not on account of evil, leading Jews had denounced Him. So Pilate found no fault worthy of death. Pilate's wife was deeply impressed that He was a 'righteous man,' presumably before Roman law. Herod's opinion was similar to Pilate's. The centurion, being a superstitious pagan saw in Jesus virtues he could associate with his own deities, but hardly the ethical purity inherent in theology of biblical religion. We do not know how precise was the repentant thief's understanding. He knew Jesus had broken no law – 'nothing wrong' – and speaking the religious language of a Jew expressed new faith in the prophecies of a Messianic kingdom (Luke 23:42).

These testimonies and opinions lend more support to obviously correct public behavior and civic righteousness than sinlessness as such. The value of their testimonies is in the fact that as really disinterested observers they saw nothing to contradict the claims Jesus and His disciples made. The Pharisees, scribes, elders and priests accused Him of the crimes of Sabbath-breaking and blasphemy, but they were false accusations arising out of perverted understanding of the documents of their own religion and the true spirit of it, as expressed in the prophets (whom their ancestors slew) and out of complete incapacity to understand Jesus' Person and mission. Their accusations were and remain worthless.

No one did more to set the record straight regarding the Jesus of liberalism of a century ago (and in a measure still today) than James Orr. I refer to his great work on the incarnation.[7] He wrote concerning Jesus' sinlessness:

> The sinlessness of Jesus is a datum of the Gospels. Over against a sinful world He stands as a Savior who is without sin. He is the one life in humanity in which is presented a perfect knowledge and unbroken fellowship with the Father, undeviating obedience to His will, unswerving devotion under the severest strain of temptation and suffering to the highest ideal of goodness. The ethical ideal was never raised to so absolute a height as it is in the teaching of Jesus, and the miracle is that, high as it is in its unsullied purity, the character of Jesus corresponds to it and realizes it. Word and life for once in history agree. Jesus, with the keenest sensitiveness to sin in thought and feeling as in deed is *conscious of no sin in Himself, confesses no sin, disclaims the presence of it, speaks and acts continually on the assumption that He is without it* [emphasis added]. Those who knew Him best declared Him to be without sin. The Gospels must be rent in pieces before this image of a perfect holiness can be effaced from them.[8]

Critical Challenges to Christ's Sinlessness.

We are here not concerned to state and respond to the literature created by the several massive 'searches for the historical Jesus' of recent times. There have been three waves of this scholarly obsession – great talent devoted to fruitless endeavor. I was assigned to conduct a seminar course in 'Christologies' a few years ago in which thirty students each prepared a paper on one of about twenty different 'Christologies' by that many recent authors. I started them off with some guidance on the various theories of Gospels' origin, and then over two months they presented the papers and we discussed them. I closed with two or more weeks of lectures on historic orthodox Christology. We learned nothing from the new Christologies to contribute substantially to the historic orthodox understanding of the Person and work of Christ and no reason to abandon a straightforward acceptance of the Christology of Scripture, of the ancient undivided church, and, in the main, of Eastern Orthodoxy, of Roman Catholic, Calvinist and Lutheran churches today – as well as orthodox Baptists, Wesleyans, Quakers and Independents.

Philosophical objections have been raised, based on the notion that sinning is a necessary stage on the way to perfection for all moral beings, or that sin is a normal aspect of human life, not a departure from integrity of being. These are *a priori* judgments of people convinced on grounds that have nothing to do with Christian origins, theology or Bible interpretation and need not detain us.[9] Millard Erickson presents a good, brief but lively discussion of some of these objections.[10]

Yet history has furnished a few authors who at least have claimed to accept the New Testament at face value and tried to make a case against Jesus' perfect sinlessness with scriptural evidence. In most cases the supposed obstacle lies not in the biblical text but in the reader's misunderstanding either of the text or of Jesus Himself. Some of the claims may be rooted in the flawed character or logic of the objectors. The New Testament has something to say about wresting Scripture and unqualified aspirants to the teaching office. We will briefly address some of the alleged scriptural evidences against the sinlessness of Jesus. And following Berkouwer's example in *The Person of Christ*,[11] arrange them in three groups.

1. 'Why do you call me good? No one is good except God alone' (Luke 18:19). Mark 10:18 is identical in sense, though Matthew 19:17 renders the question in such a way as to make the question about the nature of goodness.

We may assume that originally Jesus spoke these two sentences in the Aramaic language of Palestine. In such a case each evangelist rendered his recollection or oral source into Greek as he thought best. We shall not consult the endlessly circuitous and imaginative ingenuity of the form critics and redaction critics to find out why, for none of them knows or has an opinion some equally qualified critic does not challenge. In any case the inspired text is in the Greek sentences of Matthew, Mark and Luke, not some real or imagined *Vorlage*.

---

7. James Orr, *The Christian View of God and the World* (Grand Rapids, MI: Eerdmans, 1947) and his eighty-eight column article 'Jesus Christ,' in *ISBE*, iii, pp. 1624–1688.
8. ibid., p. 1630.
9. G. C. Berkouwer, *The Person of Christ*, trans. J. Vriend (Grand Rapids, MI: Eerdmans, 1954). In the 365 pages of this large work, he disdains to discuss such objections, though some older writers do so at some length in response to Socinianism, Unitarianism, and the German and English rationalists. See J. McClintock and J. Strong, art. 'The Sinlessness of Jesus,' in *Encyclopedia of Biblical Theological and Ecclesiastical Literature II* (Grand Rapids, MI: Baker Books, 1968–1970), pp. 265–268.
10. Millard Erickson, *Christian Theology* (Grand Rapids, MI: Baker Books, 1989), pp. 718–721.
11. Berkouwer, *Person of Christ*, pp. 242–254.

The plain facts are that the 'Rich young Ruler' had addressed Jesus as 'Good Master.' The Greek word for good, *agathos*, has as broad a range of meaning as does English 'good,' but as an adjective with reference to God it means perfect.[12] Such is the case here in Jesus' answer to the young man. Used of a crowd of people gathered at random (Matt. 22:10), *agathos* means the opposite of *ponēros*, bad, but each only in a relative sense. The young man probably meant *estimable*, exactly as we still somewhat frivolously speak of a teacher as 'Good Doctor' or of a woman as 'Good Wife.' But Jesus chose to use the man's question as occasion to teach lessons that are of enduringly great importance, continuing His discourse on the subjects raised by the incident for some time (Matt. 19:16–20:16). So Jesus used the man's word 'good' in the absolute sense of moral perfection.

Berkouwer explains it well, pointing out that the Rich Young Ruler came with a 'plainly superficial view of the good. He believes he has fully accomplished' all the law requires of him yet 'cannot meet the demand which Christ makes upon him.... Whoever would deduce from this answer a denial by Jesus of his [own] sinlessness must... isolate it from the context... and from all those pronouncements of Christ in which he shows himself fully conscious that he is doing the will of his Father.'[13]

Plainly, the subject of this pericope has nothing at all to do with Jesus' relation to sin or to God but to the subject of human sin in general, particularly the superficial view of it held by the Jews of Jesus' time and by a 'certain ruler' (Luke 18:18 KJV) as well as by the rest of us who like to prop our egos with low views of God and His holiness. Objections to Jesus' sinlessness based on Jesus' immediate responses to the Rich Young Ruler flow from a superficial understanding of the texts of the three reports.

2. 'John appeared, baptizing in the wilderness and proclaiming a baptism of repentance for the forgiveness of sins' (Mark 1:4); 'Jesus came from Nazareth of Galilee and was baptized by John in the Jordan' (Mark 1:9). The juxtaposing of those two verses might seem to make apparent that Jesus needed repentance for forgiveness of sins and submitted to baptism in recognition of the same, *if* (a very big if) there were no New Testament context to show the exact opposite. As pointed out elsewhere in this volume, Jesus' baptism was an act of identification with sinners *ab extra*, from outside the realm of sin altogether. The devil had 'no claim on me [Jesus]' (John 14:30). His baptism signified full obedience to the Father's will and constituted public dedication to the course of active and passive obedience terminated at Calvary with the cry, 'It is finished.' Only by *a priori* rejection of any unifying integrity among the authors of each of the four reports of the life and career of Jesus, including the baptism, can any exception to their uniform testimony to Jesus' holy, sinless character be discovered in this initial event in Jesus' public career. It is of a piece with His circumcision, presentation at the temple – which involved sacrifices and His participation in the ritual sacrificial system all of which called for expiation for human sin. This of course is what called forth John the Baptist's initial objection to baptizing Jesus (Matt. 3:13-15).

3. '...he learned obedience through what he suffered' (Heb. 5:8). Is it possible that John 1:14 and Philippians 2:6-8, where Christ is presented as incarnate, holy God from the first are inconsistent with a Christ who had to learn obedience to the will of God as Hebrews 5:8, quoted above is thought to indicate? To settle such a question one would have to consider whether the author of Hebrews so understood the matter – which he evidently did not. For, later he says that from *before* the beginning of Jesus' earthly life His settled purpose was precisely to perform the will of God. Hebrews 10:5–7 reads, 'Consequently, when Christ came into the world, he said... Behold, I have come to do your will, O God, as it is written of me in the scroll of the book' (quoting Ps. 40).

This supposed problem involves the mystery of the incarnation, particularly the union of the two natures. In no case is it necessary to suppose that to 'learn obedience' to God is any more inconsistent with holiness than any other aspect of His humiliation. Speculations on this matter should not divert or confuse us in any manner. Those really are not inconsistencies between the clear New Testament affirmations of Christ's sinlessness and the equally clear presentations of God manifest in the flesh as a great mystery (1 Tim. 3:16).

Was Christ Impeccable?

Impeccabilitas is a Latin word literally saying no-sin-ability. The proposition that Christ was *able not to sin* (*possere non peccare*), His moral power being fully competent and successful in living a holy life without sin, was not seriously doubted at any stage of Christian doctrinal development. The related proposition that He was *not able to sin* (*non*

---

12. Bauer, Arndt, Gingrich, *Greek-English Lexicon* (Chicago: Chicago University Press, 1967), sub, agathos, p. 2.
13. Berkouwer, *Person of Christ*, p. 243.

possere peccare) was put before the Sixth Ecumenical Council (680–681) in the form of the question of one human will and one divine will (*ditheletism*) in the *Theanthropos* or only one (*monotheletism*). From the distance of thirteen centuries the problem may seem trivial and perhaps incapable of solution anyway. That the divine nature had a will was not a matter of dispute. Yet the Council did decide that the human nature also had a will. The decision is evidently correct, as Jesus' prayer in Gethsemane ('Nevertheless, not my will, but yours, be done,' Luke 22:42) seems to make plain.

In coming to decision on this matter the Sixth Ecumenical Council[14] referred to Augustine's comment on the passage:

> It shows truly that his will was subject to the Father... For that the Lord said this in his human nature, anyone will quickly see who studies attentively.... For therein he says, 'My soul is exceeding sorrowful even unto death.' Can this possibly be said of the nature of the One Word?[15]

Augustine (quoted by the Council) goes on to answer the objection that the nature of the Holy Ghost 'groans' (hence a divine nature could have a human-like will) and concludes:

> For had he not been made man, the Only Word could in no way have said to the Father, 'Not what I will.' For it could never be possible for that immutable nature to will anything different from what the Father willed. If you would make this distinction, O ye Arians, ye would not be heretics.[16]

Numerous N.T. passages relate that Jesus was steadily committed to doing the Father's will. He came into the world for that purpose (John 6:38; Heb. 10:7). The Third Council of Constantinople (680–681, Sixth Ecumenical) states the orthodox doctrine in this manner:

> And so we proclaim two natural wills in Him, and two natural operations indivisibly, inconvertibly, inseparably, unfusedly... but the human will following and not resisting or hesitating, but rather even submitting to His divine and omnipotent will. For it is necessary that the will of the flesh [i.e. human will] act, but that it be subject to the divine will according to the most wise Athanasius.[17]

At this late date let us not seek to correct the decree of the Council. Yet let us make the reservation that 'not resisting or hesitating' should not be understood as without struggle. Our Lord struggled mightily in the Garden or else the Agony (Matt. 26:36-44) is reduced to pantomime. '[H]is sweat became like great drops of blood falling down to the ground' (Luke 22:44) in the struggle. Further, so great were His struggles with the devil that angels sometimes came to His aid (Matt. 4:11; Mark 1:13).

Whatever may be the best way to think of the human will and the divine will in Christ, the Theanthropic union guaranteed the precedence of the divine will, hence the certainty of impeccability. There was never any contest of strength. In such a case it seems that it is correct to affirm with a respected Roman Catholic scholar, 'Christ has not merely not actually sinned, but also could not sin.'[18] A majority of leading Protestant theological scholars agree, including John Walvoord who devotes major space to the topic and makes a good case for impeccability.[19] Shedd wrote at length in support of impeccability,[20] though C. A. Hodge thought otherwise.[21] In my judgment Hodge meant to say Christ's soul had *capacity* for sin or righteousness as a human being. Such is my own modest opinion. Every man, whether John Doe, Jesus or Adam has moral *capacity*. It does not seem correct to say with J. O. Buswell that Jesus never 'felt inducement to evil.'[22] The story of the three temptations by the devil seems to be precisely

---

14. This was the Ecumenical Council that condemned as a heretic a previous occupant of 'St. Peter's' throne at Rome, Pope Honorius. This event, of course, has been a great embarrassment for the Roman Church's doctrines of an infallible church and an infallible pope. See H. R. Percival's pertinent remarks in *Nicene and Post-Nicene Fathers XIV*, ed. P. Schaff (repr., Peabody: Hendrickson Publ., 1994), pp. 351, 352. Also "The same council condemned Pope Honorius as a Monothelite heretic, and his successors confirmed it. This undeniable fact figured conspicuously in the Vatican Council (1870) as an unanswerable argument against papal infallibility, and was pressed by Bishop Hefele and other learned members of the council, although they afterwards submitted to an infalible modern pope and councils" (Philip Schaff, art. 'Christiology' cited earlier in this chapter).
15. *NPNF*, Second series, xiv, p. 334.
16. ibid.
17. Henry Denzinger, *The Sources of Catholic Dogma*, trans. R. Deferrari (St. Louis: B. Herder Book Co., 1957), para. 290, p. 114.
18. Ludwig Ott, *Fundamentals of Catholic Dogma*, trans. Patrich Lynch (New York: Herder & Herder, 1955, 1974), p. 169.
19. John F. Walvoord, *Jesus Christ our Lord* (Chicago: Moody Press, 1969), pp. 145–152.
20. W. G. T. Shedd, *Dogmatic Theology ii* (New York: Charles Scribner's Sons, 1888), pp. 330–349.
21. Charles Hodge, *Systematic Theology ii* (Grand Rapids, MI: Eerdmans, 1960), p. 457.
22. James O. Buswell, *A Systematic Theology of the Christian Religion ii* (Grand Rapids, MI: Zondervan, 1971), p. 61.

about inducements and how could He have a 'feeling of our infirmities' (Heb. 4:15 KJV) otherwise? In Adam's case he was holy but used the moral capacity wrongly in response to temptation, because he was not yet confirmed (as the theologians say) in holiness and in that condition employed moral capacity wrongly. Jesus as human had the same capacity, but by virtue of union with the divine nature, which always exercised *pre-cedence*, i.e. going before, could not ever sin.

F. Pieper (Lutheran) 'emphatically' denies it was possible for Jesus to commit a sin 'according to His huma nature,' relating his argument in a convincing way to the temptation and to the means Christ used in His 'freedom' to resist sin.

> Some object that impeccability would exclude temptability, would make of Christ's temptation a sham. However, Matthew 4:1 ff. does describe a real battle. Moreover, the objection is invalid even under purely human circumstances. One may be very sure of gaining the final victory and yet inflict hard blows upon one's opponent. [And receive hard blows as well.] Even so the temptation of Christ, although the outcome was never in doubt, was a real battle in which Satan attacked the soul of Christ with allurements and temptations [enticements] and in which Christ not seemingly, but actually fought; by grasping the Word ['it is written'] in faith. The assertion that 'freedom' must always involve the possibility of sinning operates with a false conception of freedom, etc.[23]

I personally have a certain uneasiness about the word *impeccability* as used of our Lord's human nature. I wonder if the question (was Jesus not able to sin or able not to sin?) is phrased rightly. The Bible is clear that Jesus did not sin. His holiness as man, joined in permanent union with the divine nature, could not be corrupted. His holiness as Man is traced to conception by 'holy Spirit' i.e. the divine Spirit of God in the O.T. sense, the One whom the seraphim proclaim to be 'Holy, holy, holy' (Isa. 6:3). '[T]herefore the child to be born will be called holy' (Luke 1:35).

I have set the arguments for impeccability before the reader, but would leave the subject with the more cautious language of number fifteen of the Thirty-Nine Articles of Religion:

> Christ is in the truth of our nature made like unto us in all things (sin only except), from which he was clearly void... He came to be the Lamb without spot, who by the sacrifice of Himself once made, should take away the sin of the world: and sin... was not in Him... and if we say we have no sin, we deceive ourselves and the truth is not in us.

See advice of the Wesleyans, McClintock and Strong (*Encyclopedia* IV, 561).

A related question: If Christ was a true man, descended from Adam, whose sin brought guilt, corruption and punishment on the whole race, was not Christ therefore a sinner like the rest of us and partaker of the common sinful nature (as Barth asserted)? In answer we may point to evidence cited earlier that the miracle of the immaculate conception of Christ *in* (not *of*) the Virgin Mary was the instrument used to exempt Christ from that connection; second, to the several passages of the Bible which specifically deny that He was in any sense whatsoever a sinner; and third, to Romans 5:12-21 where Christ, in several relevant ways, is declared to be different from Adam except in respect to the fact that each is a 'head' of the race, Adam by imputation and genetic connection; and Christ by imputation and, according to Philippians 2:7ff. and 2 Corinthians 8:9, by virtue of His willing and merciful act of incarnation whereby He joined our race.

Luther pointed out that Mary as well as every other member of our race had a sinful nature. He made a big point of her descent from Judah's incestuous intercourse with Tamar, his daughter-in-law (Gen. 38), to show Mary's natural 'flesh' was *extraordinarily* polluted. It was not virginal conception, as such, which stopped the passing down to her Son of the pollution of a very sinful branch of humanity, 'But in the moment of the virginal conception the Holy Spirit cleansed and sanctified the sinful substance' etc.[24] Though Luther as usual speaks as though he were certain of his view, other Lutheran theories have been propounded. Pieper is judiciously noncommittal: 'Leaving aside... the question of the how, the fact that Christ was exempt from original guilt is clearly revealed in Scripture' (Pieper, II, p. 75).

---

23. Francis Pieper, *Christian Dogmatics ii* (St Louis: Concordia Publ. House, 1950–1957), p. 76.
24. Luther's *Exegetical Works iv*, pp. 173 ff., cited by Pieper in *Christian Dogmatics ii*, pp.14, 15.

Further Questions and Issues About the Sinlessness of Jesus.

Does Sinlessness Exclude Physical Desire?

Ordinary Christians are quite ready to accept Jesus' sinlessness as a fact and the difficulties of His humiliation (active and passive obedience) as 'temptation' or trial in which He was 100 per cent victorious. But, along with the theologians they also ask (and that frequently) if in His inner life as a Man, male (*anēr*), He had the usual desires for the opposite sex we are all very familiar with. A passage everyone seems to know says He 'in every respect has been tempted as we are, yet without sin' (Heb. 4:15) and another, 'But each one is tempted when he is drawn away by his own desires and enticed' (James 1:14 NKJV). Both male and female understand those verses all too well *as regards sexual impulses*, even though perhaps in somewhat different ways. Did Jesus have those desires? Even if we oldsters do not ask the questions our sons and daughters and grandchildren do, we want to know: If He did, was that sinful? And what did He do about those desires? Take a cold shower or swallow some saltpeter? An answer is demanded and I propose the one given in this volume early in the section on the doctrine of sin. Let us extract some of that.

First, let us acknowledge that desires which are part of being normal 'man' (*anthrōpos*) are necessary to stay alive, from the moment an infant first nurses its mother's breast onward. But not everyone has quite every desire. '[T]he desires of the flesh,' or physical desire is normal to everyone, but not quite *every* physical object 'in the world' (see 1 John 2:15-17) is desirable to everyone. 'One man's meat is another man's poison.' Some people 'live to eat' but others only 'eat to live.' As for sexual desire, some perfectly normal people, as Jesus indicated, never develop the mating urge, but remain like pre-adolescents all life long (Matt. 19:12, 'eunuchs who have been so from birth'). A healthy, happy, successful, hard-working Christian bachelor now over ninety years of age whom I have known for over sixty years is such a person as Jesus described. This is not usual or average. But it is a narrow judgment of prejudice to say this is not normal or to be less than fully human. In this age of psychobabble it is very easy to throw around newly manufactured words and novel meanings for old expressions to hang on people whose standards, accomplishments or thoughts make us feel uncomfortable – maladjusted, out of sync, a little off, eccentric, deviant, etc. People who are 'born eunuchs' should not marry other people who were born with sexual desire, some so strong it is said to 'burn' (1 Cor. 7:9). That does not mean the unmarried state without the burning of sexual desire is not a superior or at least equal state with the married state. The Apostle Paul *may* have been in that class, though more likely he had 'the gift' of continence. In any case he recommended the unmarried state as Jesus did also (1 Cor. 7:7, 25-40; cf. Matt. 19:12).

Jesus therefore did not necessarily feel specifically sexual attraction to women. On the other hand perhaps He did. No text of Scripture says He did not. If He did it was as innocent, if controlled in harmony with 'the will of the Father,' as temperate indulgence in food and drink, non-covetous possession of his own (not another's) pocket knife or another's gift of expressing joy in song.

The record shows that many women, both 'good' and 'bad' were attracted to Jesus. We know the names of some of them. Yet there is no hint (prurient-minded commentators notwithstanding) there was anything specifically sexual about His attraction for them. They recognized Him as a Savior from their sins by most accounts, and admired the purity of His Person and teaching.

Christians of the early centuries had a very lopsided view of this matter, or at least so it seemed a generation ago to modern Christians. One famous ancient Christian scholar (Origen) even castrated himself to destroy desire (*epithumia*). After prolonged youthful sexual indulgence, the converted and saintly Augustine came to teach that even sexual intercourse in marriage was sinful – a large subject.

In the pagan 'soused-with-sex' atmosphere of today one can again understand the deep, moral concern of the first generations of Christians and sympathize.

(See the treatment of James 1:12-15 in *The Doctrine of Sin* for more extended discussion of desire [*epithumia*] as innocent in Adam and Eve before the fall and in the uncorrupted human nature of Jesus, but in our fallen race *always* tainted [hence called *concupiscence*].)

Jesus As Sinless Example.

The example of Jesus as a way to the Modernist version of salvation has turned out to be, as David said of God's attributes, 'too wonderful for me... I cannot attain it' (Ps. 139:6). 'What would Jesus do?' is not quite the appropriate model of behavior in every situation unless one is very selective among Jesus' words and deeds. Yet Paul did say, 'Be imitators of me, as I am of Christ' (1 Cor. 11:1) to give force to an exhortation to avoid unnecessary offense to other people and to bring glory to God. Peter cited the quiet, unprotesting behavior of Jesus in response to the wholly unjust treatment by Jewish and Roman courts on His last day, saying 'ye should follow his steps' (1 Peter 2:18-25 KJV). Jesus, however, overturned the tables of rapacious 'money changers' on at least one occasion and publicly pronounced 'woe to you, scribes and Pharisees, hypocrites' in the fiercest denunciation in any language (Matt. 23:13-36).

So as the ancient proverb wisely says, 'Circumstances alter cases.' The quiet, submissive Jesus is not the only Jesus in the N.T. Nor is 1 Peter 2:18-25 a blanket guide for response to persecution for righteousness' sake in every situation, for Jesus recommended flight in some circumstances (Matt. 10:23) and sometimes to 'talk back' before heathen 'governors and kings' (Matt. 10:18, 19) as Paul did many times and as Stephen paid with his life for so doing (Acts, chapter 7). Even Jesus Himself was not exactly supine and compliant always in response to false accusation. Yet He did not respond to vicious accusation in a vengeful way. His choice of submission and silence on some occasions and of denunciation and resistance, even aggressive physical action, on others depended on the situation and the purpose to be served. The mission of Calvary hung on His not calling the 'legions of angels' but adhering to the mission to die for sinners. When He comes again, as 'King of kings and Lord of lords,' He will be accompanied by an army of angels forcefully to execute judgment and to compel obedience (Matt. 13:40-43; Jude 14, 15 NIV 'holy ones,' i.e. angels; Rev. 19:11-21). So we, especially when any sort of physical resistance to evil persecutors would spell defeat for our effort to help or save others, should follow Jesus' example of silent submission as Peter states. Isaiah 53:7 says 'like a sheep that before its shearers is silent, so he opened not his mouth' and as Pilate observed with dismay (Matt. 27:12-14). I have dealt at length with the 'non-resistance' and pacifist doctrines and 'theology of the cross' issues in my book *The Peacemongers*[25] and in *Civil Government: A Biblical View*.[26] It is not always a sin to resist the devil when he stands before you as a violent robber or a wicked magistrate.

The Sinless Pathfinder Jesus As Model of Perseverance.

Let us take note that perseverance in faith – not sinless perfection – is necessary to salvation. '[T]he one who endures to the end will be saved' (Matt. 24:13) indirectly applies here. In this respect Jesus is our perfect model.

> Therefore, since we are surrounded by such a great cloud of witnesses, let us throw off everything that hinders and the sin that so easily entangles, and let us run with perseverance the race marked out for us. Let us fix our eyes on Jesus, the author [space forbids pursuit of the somewhat mysterious but meaningful word for Jesus' relation to us here – Greek *archēgos*, variously translated leader, ruler, pathfinder, originator, founder] and perfecter of our faith, who for the joy set before him endured the cross, scorning its shame, and sat down at the right hand of the throne of God. Consider him who endured such opposition from sinful men, so that you will not grow weary and lose heart. In your struggle against sin, you have not yet resisted to the point of shedding your blood (Heb. 12:1-4 NIV).

As the Sinless Victor Over Enticement to Sin Jesus Is Now Our Able Helper.

> For this reason he had to be made like his brothers in every way, in order that he might become a merciful and faithful high priest in service to God, and that he might make atonement for the sins of the people. Because he himself suffered when he was tempted, he is able to help those who are being tempted (Heb. 2:17, 18 NIV).

As the Enticed, Yet Sinless Great High Priest, Jesus Enables Us to Come in Prayer to a Throne Where Grace Reigns.

> Seeing then that we have a great high priest, that is passed into the heavens, Jesus the Son of God, let us hold fast *our* profession. For we have not an high priest which cannot be touched with the feeling of our infirmities; but was in all points tempted like as *we are, yet* without sin. Let us therefore come boldly unto the throne of grace, that we may obtain mercy, and find grace to help in time of need (Heb. 4:14-16 KJV).

---

25. R. D. Culver *The Peacemongers* (Wheaton, IL: Tyndale House, 1985).
26. R. D. Culver *Civil Government: A Biblical View* (Edmonton, AB: Canadian Institute for Law, Theology and Public Policy, 2000), p. 308.

13
The Passion and Death of Jesus

The Passion and Death Belong Together.

All Christians agree that the suffering (Passion) of Jesus and His death are together of central importance in definition of what we believe about Jesus. Among the earliest efforts to list distinctively Christian beliefs in a creed-like fashion is a passage in Irenaeus: 'The Church believes... in... the birth from a virgin, and the Passion, and the resurrection,' etc.[1] Here 'the Passion' (Gr. *to pathos*) obviously includes both the sufferings of His last day *and* the painful death under the words 'the Passion.' Later in the same book he enlarges only slightly: 'and having suffered (*passus*) under Pontius Pilate and rising again.'[2] In both cases 'the Passion' or 'suffered' includes His death on the cross.

Tertullian, at about the same time, lets 'crucified under Pontius Pilate' stand for His suffering *and* death; also in a similar list which he calls 'The Rule of Faith' concerning *Veiling of Virgins*.[3] The Apostles' Creed affirms that Jesus 'suffered under Pontius Pilate, was crucified, dead and buried.' Here the Passion and the death are distinguished. The Creed of Nicea (AD 325) subsumes Jesus' death under 'suffered' though the revision of AD 381 says 'was crucified... he suffered and was buried.' (The earlier [AD 325] creed is called the *The Creed of Nicea* to distinguish it from the revised and permanent form issued at Constantinople in AD 381. The latter is called either the *Niceno-Constaninopolitan Creed* or the *Nicene Creed*.) It is clear that in those times no important distinction, certainly no separation, between Jesus' suffering and death was made.

Religious custom in medieval times came to emphasize the sufferings of Christ on the last evening and day of crucifixion. Hence 'the Passion' came to refer to the events of the Last Supper, the institution of 'the Eucharist,' agony in the Garden, the trials, the *via dolorosa* to Golgotha, the crucifixion, the agonies on the cross and finally death.[4]

Evangelical theology, following the scriptural narrative, has tended to treat the Passion and death as essentially one subject, and not two. For some reason many Protestant works of doctrinal theology which treat the atonement at great length make no mention at all of 'the Passion' or 'the Great Passion' leading up to it. Reaction against the

---

1. Irenaeus, *Against Heresies I.x.1*, in *Ante-Nicene Fathers iii*, ed. A. Roberts and J. Donaldson, repr. of U.S. ed. 1885 (Peabody: Hendrickson Publ., 1994), p. 330.
2. ibid., iii, iv, e, p. 417.
3. ibid., iv, p. 39.
4. *The Catholic Encyclopedia: An International Work of References on Constitution, Doctrine, Discipline and History of the Catholic Church VIII* (New York: The Encyclopedia Press, 1907–1922), pp. 382, 383.

somewhat maudlin observances, lay and clerical, about the fourteen Stations of the Cross probably accounts for this. In Puritan and Reformed company, all ceremonies connected with the medieval Christian liturgy and calendar were either de-emphasized or rejected altogether. There is a precedent for treating Jesus' suffering and death as one subject in 1 Peter 1:11, which reads the prophetic 'Spirit of Christ' in the Prophets (Isa. 52:13–53:12 especially), testified beforehand 'the sufferings [including the death] of Christ and the subsequent glories.'

We proceed to consider first the sufferings, but by no means to separate them from the death, which consummated the sufferings and has enormous meaning in redemption all its own.

The Passion of Christ.

Question 37 of the Heidelberg Catechism (1563):

> What doest thou understand by the word suffered in the Apostles's Creed?
> Answer: That all the time he lived on earth, but especially at the end of his life, he bore in body and soul, the wrath of God against sin of the whole human race, in order that by his passion, as the only atoning sacrifice, he might redeem our body and soul from everlasting damnation, and obtain for us the grace of God, righteousness, and eternal life.[5]

This venerable affirmation, testifies that the Passion of Christ has no importance to Christians apart from its culmination in death. Christians witness to this by their frequent use of the expression, 'the suffering and death' of Jesus.

This suffering had its beginning in the treatment He received from His own household and neighbors. Long before 'Passion Week' his own brothers rejected Him (John 7:5). At a point very early in His ministry the men of His home village, when they heard Him speaking in the local synagogue, 'rose up and drove him out of the town,' and, except that He escaped them, would have killed Him by throwing Him over a nearby cliff (Luke 4:28-30).

For awhile He gained a sympathetic hearing among the common people, but for various reasons He lost their support. Before long 'he began to teach them that the Son of Man must suffer many things, and be rejected by the elders and the chief priests and the scribes and be killed' (Mark 8:31). And though all the elements of martyrdom-seeking were absent from Him, Jesus always understood that it was 'written of the Son of Man that he should suffer many things and be treated with contempt' (Mark 9:12). He explained to 'his disciples': 'The Son of Man is going to be delivered into the hands of men, and they will kill him' (Mark 9:31). While walking toward Jerusalem for the last time, 'taking the twelve again, he began to tell them what was going to happen to him, saying, "See, we are going up to Jerusalem, and the Son of Man will be delivered over to the chief priests and the scribes, and they will condemn him to death and deliver him over to the Gentiles. And they will mock him and spit on him, and flog him and kill him..."' (Mark 10:32-34).

Finally, even His disciples 'all left him and fled' (Mark 14:50) – only a few women supporters and a youth (the youngest Apostle) showed up for the crucifixion.

Three things made the suffering most acute: it was inflicted by those whom He loved and whom He had come to save; it was endured alone; the final blow was dealt by His Father – 'it was the LORD's will to crush him and cause him to suffer' (Isa. 53:10 NIV).

Now, all Christians accept a great deal of unfathomable mystery in this. The mystery is simply an intensified form of the mystery of the providential government of God over all things. They glory in it, knowing that existence would hold no depth of hope, only very obvious hopelessness, without this mystery. They see the power of God ruling and overruling, making the wrath of man to praise Him. They see Christ as 'The stone that the builders rejected' nevertheless by God's providence, 'become the cornerstone.' And though not excusing the hands of wicked men (Acts 2:23) for their violent deed, Christians nevertheless proclaim, 'This is the Lord's doing; it is marvellous in our eyes.' (1 Peter 2:7; cf. Ps. 118:22, 23).

The Death of Jesus: What Happened?

As indicated above, though the Gospels justify us in finding some distinction between the Lord's suffering and death, they lead us as they did the patristic authors and the Confessions cited, to discern the consummation of our Lord's suffering in His atoning death. In fact, though, all life long He was 'a man of sorrows and acquainted with grief.'

---

5. Philip Schaff, *The Creeds of Christendom vol. iii, The Evangelical Creeds*, repr. of 1877 ed. of Harper & Bros. (Grand Rapids, MI: Baker Books, 1966), p. 316.

When His cross was less than eighteen hours away He spoke of His suffering as still ahead – 'I have earnestly desired to eat this Passover with you *before I suffer* [emphasis added]' (Luke 22:15, 16). The suffering consummated in and found its meaning and purpose in His death.

The nature of the death Jesus experienced is no special problem to explain once a fully biblical view of His Person – incarnate God, fully God, fully Man, as the ecumenical creeds also state – is taken. Death has three aspects: physical death, spiritual death, and – yet ahead for lost humanity, that event utterly horrible to contemplate – 'second death' (Rev. 20:14), involving eternal exclusion from the presence of God. That physical death of the God-man took place has never been seriously doubted by Christians except for a few heretics ancient and modern – and of course, Islam. He bowed His head and commended His spirit to God (Luke 23:46). Shortly thereafter a spear was thrust in His side; whereupon gushed out blood and water, evidence that a separation of vital fluids in the heart region had taken place. The centurion testified to Pilate early in the evening that Jesus was 'already dead' (Mark 15:42-45; John 19:38-42).

Spiritual death, that alienation from God that is the invariable effect of sin, also took place. This alone, as has been generally understood, accounts for Jesus' agony in the Garden and His many remarks about revulsion from His 'cup' (Matt. 26:39, 42, 44; Mark 10:38). The misguided efforts of certain recent commentators (Oscar Cullmann and disciples) to show that Jesus' agony arose simply out of fear of non-existence (contrast with Socrates' last hours has been noted) is shortsighted, unbiblical and disrespectful of what the Bible says about the nature of man. The idea that the agony in the Garden was caused by resistance to efforts of Satan to kill Him prematurely then and there seems bizarre, even though sponsored by at least one reputable theologian.[6]

Spiritual death was the immediate consequence of sin in the first pair. It is the state into which all men are now naturally born (Eph. 2:1-3; 4:17-19). This alienation, which took place in those moments when the Lord took upon Himself our guilt and penalty, described in prophecy as making Himself 'an offering for sin' (Isa. 53:10) and in 2 Corinthians 5:21 (KJV) as becoming 'sin for us' is expressed in the Savior's heartbroken cry, 'My God, my God, why have you forsaken me?' (Matt. 27:46). No other godly man has ever been forsaken by God at the time of death (Ps. 23:4). 'Forsaken then, by God and men, alone his life he gave.' The precise nature of this alienation from the Father cannot be fully defined. It could not be metaphysical separation because the Trinity of the Godhead cannot be suspended; nor moral for nothing was more in harmony with goodness and righteousness; nor was the Son ever more loved by the Father than while He hung on the cross. Two scriptural phrases come as close as language can to definition: 'becoming a curse for us' (Gal. 3:13) and 'made him to be sin for us' (2 Cor. 5:21 KJV).

Heidelberg Catechism, Question 39: 'Is there something more in his having been crucified than if he had died some other death? Yes, for by this I am assured that he took upon himself the curse which lay upon me, because the death of the cross was cursed by God (Gal. 3:13). Christ redeemed us from the curse of the law, having become a curse for us – for it is written, Cursed is everyone who hangs on a tree' (cf. Deut. 21:23).

Did Jesus experience the 'second death' also? Was it 'eternal?' If it was a substitutionary death (and it was) and if second death is the destiny of unrepentant men (and according to the Bible it is Rev. 20:11-15) then His death was in some sense 'eternal' – or as might better be said – of infinite value in the remission of sin. As Anselm (*Cur Deus Homo*) argued and as orthodox interpreters usually agree, since He was an infinite Being as Second Person of the Godhead He could suffer eternal punishment in moments. We shall discuss this matter at length in the chapter immediately to follow. A certain amount of repetition in developing themes gathering around the death of the Savior cannot easily be avoided in these pages.

The Central Importance of the Death of Christ As Atonement for Sin in Biblical Religion.

Canon Dyson Hague said truly, 'The importance of this subject is obvious. The Atonement is Christianity in epitome. It is the heart of Christianity as a system; it is the distinguishing mark of the Christian religion.'[7] Leon Morris likewise: 'The atonement is the crucial doctrine of the faith. Unless we are right here it matters little, or so it seems to me, what we are like elsewhere.'[8]

---

6. James O. Buswell, Jr, *A Systematic Theology of the Christian Religion ii* (Grand Rapids, MI: Zondervan, 1962, 1971), pp. 61–65.
7. Canon Dyson Hague, 'At-One-Ment by Propitiation,' in *The Fundamentals* (Bible Institute of Los Angeles, 1917), p. 78.
8. Leon Morris, *The Cross in the New Testament* (Grand Rapids, MI: Eerdmans, 1965), p. 5.

In the Reports of Jesus' Career.

We have already had occasion to observe how Jesus announced that His mission on earth was to 'give his life a ransom' and tried over a period of several months without success to explain to the disciples and convince them of the necessity of His Passion and death. We have also noted how early the first Christians made His death, interpreted as a sacrifice for sin, a matter of public testimony even to an unbelieving world. The Gospel writers promote this theme steadfastly, sometimes subtly, sometimes explicitly and occasionally almost unconsciously, with gathering force. The specter of violent death appears in the earliest stage of the Gospels' narrative even in the literary neighborhood of the joyful announcements of the infant Jesus' birth. The aged Simeon is reported to tell the mother, '(and a sword will pierce through your own soul also), so that thoughts from many hearts may be revealed' (Luke 2:35). Is this not an intended broad hint of the career of a 'man of sorrows' ending in violent death in Mary's presence? Many careful exegetes and commentators have thought so, though Alford was a notable exception.

In Fulfillment of the Suffering Servant Prophecies of Isaiah 42–53.

The relationship of the Servant prophecies of Isaiah to Christ's suffering and death has been of great interest to scholars in modern times. 'At the outset we take the ground that no one can clearly apprehend this great theme who is not prepared to take Scripture as it stands, and to treat it as the final and authoritative source of Christian knowledge, and the test of every theory.'[9] This is the view taken by orthodox Christianity in general and will be pursued here. Some Christian scholars who do not concede real prediction of real events in Scripture nevertheless employ the prophecies to interpret Jesus' Person and death. H. Wheeler Robinson asserts that:

> The shadow of that Cross fell over His path long before he reached it, and was accepted by Him as part of the inscrutable will of God. But where did He gain His confidence that this was the will of God, so as to declare it beforehand to His disciples if not from the suffering of the Servant? Even if some of the references of this kind are due to the later attestation of the Gospel story from the Old Testament by the interpretive faith of the early Christians, yet we have still to account for the acceptance of death by Jesus as part of the Messianic mission, and there is no explanation so simple and direct, as that He was profoundly influenced by 'the Servant of Yahweh' before and in and after the baptismal hour.[10]

This author seems to say that while Isaiah (or 'II Isaiah') might not have been speaking of the personal Messiah in Isaiah 40–53, Jesus accepted the references to the Suffering Servant as prediction of Himself. Robinson seems to think the New Testament writers placed some of Isaiah's words in Jesus' mouth, so to speak. There are other scholars who reject predictive prophecy yet profess strong Christian belief and have a similar view. Among them are W. Zimmerli and J. Jeremias.[11] Literature of this sort is quite extensive. A common Jewish view is that 'the whole people of Israel in the form of the elect of the nation gradually became the Messiah of the World, the redeemer of mankind.'[12] Another Jewish author, Raphael Patai traces Jewish interpretation of 'The Suffering Messiah' citing many rabbis.[13] My own study of the subject is *The Sufferings and the Glory of the Lord's Righteous Servant*.[14]

The recurring connection of events in Jesus' career with prophecy of the Suffering Servant of Isaiah 42–53 shows that the death of Jesus was 'for the transgression of my people.'

This was never out of the Gospel writers' minds as they wrote. I submit the following list of references for those interested in examining the evidence in some detail. The references in the Gospels by allusion and quotation of the Servant prophecies of Isaiah show how extensive and pervasive the connection really is (Matt. 3:17; cf. Isa. 42:1; Matt. 5:18; cf. Isa. 53:4; Matt. 12:17-21; cf. Isa. 42:1-6; Matt. 20:22; cf. Isa. 51:17; Matt. 21:5; cf. Isa. 62:11; Matt. 21:13; cf. Isa. 56:7; Luke 2:30; cf. Isa. 53:10; Luke 2:31; cf. Isa. 42:6; 49:6; Luke 5:20; cf. Isa. 43:25; Luke 18:31 cites 'Isa. 53, Ps. 22, etc.' indicating these Old Testament chapters are prophecies of Passion Week; Luke 22:27; cf. Isa. 53:12; John 12:38; cf. Isa. 53:1; Matt. 26:38, 39; cf. Isa. 53:12; Mark 10:33, 34; cf. Isa. 52:3;

---

9. Hague, in *Fundamentals*, p. 78.
10. H. Wheeler Robinson, *The Cross of the Servant*, book 2 of *The Cross in the New Testament* (London: SCM Press, 1955, 1965), pp. 100, 101.
11. Walther Zimmerli and Joachim Jeremias, *The Servant of God* (London: 1941), pp. 98 ff., cited by Leon Morris, op.cit., p. 31.
12. Joseph Klausner, *The Messianic Idea in Israel*, trans. W. F. Stinespring (New York: Macmillan, 1955), p. 163.
13. Raphael Patai, *The Messiah Texts, Jewish Legends of Three Thousand Year* (Detroit: Wayne State University Press, 1979, 1988), pp. 104-116.
14. R. D. Culver, *The Sufferings and the Glory of the Lord's Righteous Servant* (Moline, IL: The Christian Service Foundation, 1958). Republished by Eugene, OR: Wipf & Stock, 2001.

John 1:10, 11; cf. Isa. 53:3; John 19:7; cf. Isa. 53:4; Matt. 26:63 and 27:11-14; cf. Isa. 53:7; Matt. 27:12, 14; and Mark 15:5;14:61; and Luke 23:9; and John 19:9; cf. Isa. 53:7; Matt. 27:57-60; cf. Isa. 53:9; John 1:23; cf. Isa. 40:3; John 1:29; cf. Isa. 53:10; John 10:14-18; cf. Isa. 53:11; Matt. 26:38, 39, 42; cf. Isa. 53:12).

The same is true of the rest of the New Testament, though more by way of reflection on the meaning of Jesus' death than on the event itself. See 2 Timothy 2:24 and compare the Servant of the Lord in Paul's thought with Isaiah 42:1 ff. and 52:13. (Likewise Rom. 15:21; cf. Isa. 52:15; Isa. 53:1; cf. Rom. 10:16; Isa. 53:5; cf. Rom. 4:25; 1 Cor. 15:3; and Heb. 5:8; cf. Isa. 53:5; Isa. 53:5, 6, 9; cf. 1 Peter 2:24, 25; Acts 8:32, 33; cf. Isa. 53:7; John 1:29; cf. Isa. 53:10; John 10:14-18; cf. Isa. 53:11; Phil. 2:9-11; cf. Isa. 52:13, 53:12; 2 Cor. 5:21; cf. Isa. 53:6, 11, 12.)

In the Structure of the Gospels' Story and Jesus' Warnings.

The Gospels each in some degree or other and by different literary devices early on show that the crucifixion and related events were to be the climax and denouement. Mark and Matthew do so in connection with Peter's great confession. This momentous declaration by Peter took place in the areas about Caesarea Philippi on the slopes of Mt. Herman, the highest mountain of the area (Mark 8:27-31; Matt. 16:13-21).

At the Transfiguration a week later, Moses and Elijah 'were talking with him... and spoke of his departure [Gr. *exodus*], which he was about to accomplish at Jerusalem' (Luke 9:30, 31). At about the same time He introduced the subject of His death and resurrection to the disciples (Mark 9:1-10; Matt. 17:1-9).

Luke places this great divide, so to speak, slightly later in the story and not in connection with the Petrine confession, but with a fearfully ominous sentence, 'And it came to pass, when the time was come that he should be received up, he steadfastly set his face to go to Jerusalem' (Luke 9:51 KJV). Uttered moments before His party headed southward through Samaria, presumably to attend one of the three mandatory Festival Feasts at Jerusalem (Luke 9:52). Jesus was looking past the *humiliation* to the *exaltation*, beyond the *suffering* to the *glory*, in this verse, the ascension. We are reminded that as Pioneer and Perfector of our faith He, for the joy that was set before Him, endured the cross, despising the shame (Heb. 12:1, 2); also reminded that in a prophecy of Isaiah 50:6, 7. He who would give His back to smiters and His cheeks to them that plucked off the hair and not hide His face from shame and spitting said also, 'But the Lord GOD helps me; therefore I have not been disgraced; therefore I have set my face like a flint, and I know that I shall not be put to shame' (Isa. 50:6, 7).

There is no such dividing point in John's Gospel – the movement toward Calvary is right up front from verse 11 of the first chapter: they that were 'his own received him not' (KJV) and moves right on to His baptismal dedication to die and the Baptist's proclamation, 'Behold, the Lamb of God, who takes away the sin of the world' (John 1:29).

As I researched, meditated and wrote in producing a *Life of Christ* I was gripped by the sudden gathering of the powers of darkness at the point of the Gospel narrative, especially as Luke gives it – made aware that 'it pleased the Lord to bruise him... to put him to grief.' It seemed wrong that it should be so. But inexorably the story picks up speed from this point on, hastening to the denouement.

Jesus is fully aware, even if the Twelve are not, of the growing power of darkness about to envelop them all and to kill Him; that as He now sets out for the Feast of Tabernacles, He will not even have a certain roof (Luke 9:58) or a pillow for His head, to sleep. The disciples who look back disqualify themselves for the kingdom of God (Luke 9:62). As He steadfastly set His face to go to Jerusalem to die, He must have felt too, now having put His hand to the plough, He must never look back. The purpose of Christ, formed in eternity, enforced and rendered explicit at the baptism and through temptation, would be sorely tested, but He would not fail nor be discouraged till He had set righteousness in the earth (Isa. 42:4).

The steady conviction that Jesus' death 'for our sins in accordance with the Scriptures' is fulfillment, in part of Isaiah 52:13–53:12 must reflect Jesus' attitude, no doubt communicated to the disciples at a time when they did not yet understand it but which struck with great force after His resurrection – along with much more that He said of His coming Passion, death and resurrection. (See, e.g. John 2:18-22: 'his disciples remembered that he had said this, and they believed the Scripture'; also Acts 8:31-35.)

It is not likely that Jesus entirely postponed informing the disciples of His violent death until after the incident near Caesarea Philippi. In the conversation with Nicodemus He referred to it obliquely in the saying, 'as Moses lifted up the serpent in the wilderness, so must the Son of Man be lifted up' (John 3:14), unless this is John's commentary rather than Jesus' express saying. The great discourse in or near a Capernaum synagogue falls earlier than Peter's confession (John 6:25-71). In that great discourse on the bread of life He said, 'the bread that I will give for the life of the world is my flesh.' The discourse at Jerusalem, about the Good Shepherd who 'gives his life for the sheep' (John 10:1-18) probably occurred later, when Jesus and His company attended the Feast of Tabernacles as indicated in Luke 9:51 ff. above.[15] If so, Jesus did not cease speaking of His approaching death in the ensuing months.

That Christ said much more about His death than is recorded cannot be doubted. Yet if He had said only a little or nothing at all to prepare the disciples for the seeming tragedy the reason is apparent – He came not to talk about death, His own or any others, but to 'give his life as a ransom for many.' After that the death of Christ came to be the heart of Gospel proclamation.

Other Old Testament Specific Predictions.

Other Old Testament passages which in 'so many words' say something directly about Jesus' death are few. Though not quoted in the New Testament as prediction, Isaiah 50:4-9 can hardly be given a reading friendly to belief in predictive prophecy without seeing therein a portrait of the Savior. Daniel 9:26, speaking of a Messiah (Anointed One), who shall be cut off after 483 years has always been regarded from earliest times as a specific prophecy of Christ's death by violent means. Psalm 22 is close to the same quality of specific prediction. 'They will look on him whom they have pierced' (John 19:37; see also Rev. 1:7) seems to take 'they look on me, on him whom they have pierced' (Zec. 12:10) as a prediction of what John 19:34 says really happened – 'one of the soldiers pierced his side with a spear.' John 19:37 says this fulfilled the prophecy of Zechariah 12:10. Whatever one may think of prediction and fulfillment in these passages, the impression of specific reference is hard to escape. See the cross-references between the Old Testament texts and New Testament texts noted above and in good cross-reference Bibles (ASV and NAB are especially helpful).

Importance in the Rites and Sacraments Prescribed by Christ for the Church.

Authority for baptism starts with the Lord Himself who made it the initiatory rite for every believer (Matt. 28:19). We have also the example of the complete apostolate in the Jerusalem church who baptized the first new believers on 'the same day' when the Spirit inaugurated the new age. Peter urged the anxious crowd on that first post-Easter Pentecost to be 'baptized... in the name of Jesus Christ for the forgiveness of your sins' (Acts 2:38). Because 'Christ Jesus died for our sins' making way for the baptism in the Spirit John had promised many months before (Matt. 3:11; Mark 1:8; Luke 3:16). This example (with modifications of time, mode, place) prevails to the present. The meaning of the rite (in part) is found in the way it represents the death, burial and resurrection of Christ, with which every genuine believer is now identified and united as says Romans 6:3, 4.

Authority for what Christians call the Eucharist, the Lord's Supper or Communion Service likewise was instituted by Jesus on the night of His betrayal (Matt. 26:26-29; Mark 14:22-25; Luke 22:15-20). It was explained by Jesus Himself as a perpetual observance to keep alive in Christian disciples' memory (see also 1 Cor. 11:25) their Savior's death for sins and to 'proclaim the Lord's death,' as Paul explains, until He comes again (1 Cor. 11:26). The rite may mean more than this, but whatever else it may signify, the heart of it is, as both Jesus and Paul say very clearly, 'remembrance' of the death of our Lord for our sins.

Importance As Fount of Every Blessing.

Jesus is 'fount of every blessing' because 'He... interposed His precious blood' as the hymn says (*Come Thou Fount*, R. Robinson). 'He who did not spare his own Son, but gave him up for us all, how will he not also with him graciously give us all things?' (Rom. 8:31, 32). Here in apostolic logic, all our blessings as believers are guaranteed by the death of Christ.

As Major Emphasis of New Testament Epistles and Revelation.

The major Epistles and Revelation as well give major emphasis to the death of Christ: it is more than just a keystone in the arch of Christian doctrine for all Paul's letters. It is in some paramount way his sole message (1 Cor. 2:1, 2). The atoning, propitiating, expiating, reconciling, justifying, sanctifying, work of Christ on the cross is suffused through all the other themes of Romans and Galatians, scarcely less Ephesians, Philippians, Colossians and Philemon. It supports the doctrine and exhortations of the Corinthian Letters and the Pastorals. Hebrews is

---

15. A. T. Robertson, *Harmony of the Gospels* (New York: Harper & Bros., 1950), pp. xxxiii, 119.

hardly about anything else in the central chapters, bringing all the Old Testament religious ritual and calendar to bear on the significance of the incarnation and death of the Son of God. The Epistles of John and Jude relate the death of Christ to Christian faith and obedience, while the Revelation presents the One who was 'pierced' as the main speaker through the first three chapters and as the slain 'Lamb of God' through all the rest.

Importance in the Interest of the Denizens of Heaven.

Scripture provides one glimpse of how even the angelic denizens of heaven, who no doubt have many interesting matters to think about, have special interest in the Passion of Christ as it relates to our salvation. According to the man who once tried to talk Jesus out of the whole idea of suffering, crucifixion and resurrection (Matt. 16:22, 23) the holy angels desire to 'look into' the sufferings and the glory (1 Peter 1:12 KJV). Angels of heaven need no salvation and would be ineligible if they did. Although the Son 'took not on him the nature of angels' (Heb. 2:16 KJV) the holy angels nevertheless, as spectators from 'outside the loop,' are fascinated with matters surrounding the salvation effected for the race of man through Jesus' humiliation, death and exaltation.

Importance in the World to Come.

Two permanent human residents of heaven, Moses and Elijah, each of whom had rather spectacular entrances to the celestial estate, came down to earth to discuss our Lord's coming 'exodus' *via* events at Jerusalem at the coming Passover season (Luke 9:31; cf. 28-32). This conference with the transfigured Jesus, on what may have been a slope of the same mountain where Peter sought to dissuade Jesus, shows the very supreme importance of the death of Jesus in the scheme of redemption by the 'Lamb slain from the foundations of the world.' Good scholars suggest the purpose of the Transfiguration and conference with Moses, the great messenger of the *law,* and Elijah, the greatest of the *prophets*, was to associate the work of Jesus with the meaning of Old Testament Scriptures and to encourage Him in facing the trials ahead. Yet others well observe that Moses and Elijah as representing the interests of saints of previous dispensations, all being saved 'on credit,' so to speak (Rom. 3:25, 26; Heb. 11:39, 40), were neither *un*interested nor *dis*interested observers of the coming enactment of 'eternal redemption' (Heb. 9:12) 'for us' – both those looking forward to Calvary and those looking back toward it.

In the heavenly world to come projected by *The Apocalypse,* the slain Lamb of God is a prevalent feature. The bride (the saved) will become 'the wife of the Lamb' (Rev. 21:9); the twelve foundations are 'the twelve apostles of the Lamb' (Rev. 21:14); together with the Lord God Almighty the Lamb is the temple of the city (Rev. 21:22), 'its lamp is the Lamb' (Rev. 21:23); all our names 'are written in the Lamb's book of life' (Rev. 21:27); and the 'throne of God and of the Lamb shall be in it, and [we] his servants will worship him' (Rev. 22:3).

Was the Death of Christ Necessary?

Let us approach this question with two truths about God and the world firmly established beyond question.

The first truth has regard to the fact that while God, Himself, is a necessary Being, He does nothing necessarily. 'Creation is a free act of God, not necessary on His part.'[16] Of the God of the Bible the record says 'Our God is in the heavens; he does whatever he pleases' (Ps. 115:3 RSV).

The second truth has regard to the fact that God having created the world sustains and rules it in perfect harmony with His counsel, His will and His character. God is perfectly free but 'he cannot deny himself' (2 Tim. 2:13).

These two principles will be of decisive force in answering the question,: Was the death of Christ necessary?

It is probably idle to speculate if God might have created a world in which a different set of circumstances would prevail. No one knows if God's character, will and counsel might have produced a world in which sin would not occur and redemption would therefore be unnecessary. An aspect of God's character is wisdom; so we may be sure that what He did create was 'only wise.' Yet, as Paul says, in God 'are hidden all the treasures of wisdom and knowledge' (Col. 2:3) – hidden except as He deigns to reveal them.

Logical Necessity?

Among God's creations are laws of logic. Philosophers speculate that logic is simply an aspect of reality for God, as well as for all His creatures. If so, logic is simply a name for God thinking. There is such a thing as logical

---

16. Francis Pieper, *Christian Dogmatics ii* (St Louis: Concordia Publ. House, 1950–1957), p. 480.

necessity. In this world of sinners do laws of logic render the death of Christ necessary? If so, the Bible does not trace any necessity of our Lord's death to anything like the product of a syllogism. As we shall see, Paul does not depart from logic in presenting the necessity of Jesus' death for sin, but he draws his arguments from other sources than logic.

Moral Necessity?

Philosophers and theologians distinguish between physical necessity, which belongs to the realm of nature and material things, and moral necessity, which applies to the actions of free beings who make choices. Material necessity, inasmuch as it operates in a world of many causes and effects, is also called contingent or consequent necessity. Example: a bullet from the barrel of a rifle necessarily goes in the precise direction the barrel is pointed, except as a crosswind or gravity affect (necessarily) its passage. People being free beings with moral capacity are under moral necessity always to do what is right, no exceptions. Was Jesus simply morally obligated to go to the cross? There are those (among them A. H. Strong) who have said once the Logos assumed our human nature He was under that obligation, that as Man He was obliged by unity with our race to pay our debt.[17] This, however, is only a fallible theologian's opinion, influenced by Strong's metaphysics of personal, idealistic pluralism. The Bible nowhere says the fact of incarnation *per se* placed Christ under moral necessity to die for the sinful race.

No Necessity?

The nominalists of the Middle Ages thought all generalizations of a universal sort were only mental constructs. So along with later Socinians they denied any necessity at all for the death of Christ. God did not need to demand satisfaction for sins. For modern liberal theology any satisfaction for sin is an error and even some Arminian-Wesleyan theologians, otherwise quite orthodox (Richard Watson, for example), think of the cross as a demonstration of God's government rather than strictly substitutionary satisfaction. However, Thomas Oden, a living Wesleyan, makes a strong case for substitutionary atonement.[18]

Absolute Necessity or Hypothetical Necessity?

In philosophy and theology 'a thing is said to be absolutely necessary when without it a certain end cannot possibly be reached' (G. M. Sauvage, 'Necessity,' *The Catholic Encyclopedia*, vol. x, p. 733). Hypothetical necessity, or relative necessity, is such as depends on an *a priori* matter of some sort.

As to the necessity for the death of Christ for our sin, whether absolutely necessary or relative (i.e. because God so decreed), theologians have differed and wavered.

No one can doubt that the 'moving cause'[19] is God's love (John 3:16; John 4:9, 10), grace (Rom. 5:6-10), mercy (Titus 3:5), wise purpose (Eph. 1:7, 8; 3:10).[20] 'The scheme of redemption, as formed in the eternal mind and council of God, is called 'the manifold wisdom of God.'[21] But this leaves unanswered whether there was or was not some other possible way for God to save lost mankind. If there is no other way the cross is an absolute necessity for man's salvation, if there are other possible ways ('God can do as He pleases') then the cross is a relative or hypothetical necessity. Calvin clearly opted for the latter,[22] as did Athanasius, Augustine and Aquinas.[23] Irenaeus of the ancient church, Anselm in *Cur Deus Homo* and most more recent Reformed writers opt for the former, absolute necessity.

A Proposed Resolution.

Jesus addressed the necessity of the cross. He told His disciples many times, beginning even before the Transfiguration 'that he must go... suffer... and be killed' (Matt. 16:21); 'The Son of man must suffer... be rejected... and be killed' (Luke 9:21, 22).

---

17. A. H. Strong, 'The Necessity of the Atonement,' *Philosophy and Religion* (collected addresses, essays and sermons) (New York: C. A. Armstrong & Son, 1888), pp. 213–219, and *Systematic Theology* (Valley Forge, PA: Judson Press, 1907), pp. 715, 716.
18. Thomas Oden, *Systematic Theology ii, The Word of Life* (San Francisco: Harper Collins, 1989), pp. 318, 373–379.
19. John Gill, *Complete Body of Doctrinal and Practical Divinity ii* (Grand Rapids, MI: Baker Books, 1978), p. 6.
20. ibid., p. 7.
21. ibid.
22. John Calvin, *Institutes of the Christian Religion ii*, ed. J. T. McNeil, trans. and ed. F. L. Battles (Philadelphia, PA: Westminster Press, 1960), 12.1.
23. Louis Berkhof, *Systematic Theology*, 4th rev. ed. (Grand Rapids, MI: Eerdmans, 1979), p. 369.

Jesus ascribed the necessity to several causes, *first* to divine foreordination (predestination in God's will and counsel). This is prominent in His Gethesemane prayers (Matt. 26:38, 39, 42, 44) to which Peter adds 'the lamb foreknown before the foundation of the world' (1 Peter 1:20). This is not different from tracing necessity to the 'command' of the Father to which Jesus referred more than once. *Secondly*, Jesus explained that His own purpose in coming into the world was to die precisely as He did: 'for this purpose I have come' into the world (John 12:27; cf. Matt. 20:28). By receiving baptism He submitted to the plan and dedicated Himself to this purpose. During the temptation in the wilderness He resisted the devil's effort to dissuade Him from His voluntarily assumed destiny. *Thirdly*, Jesus said He had to die to fulfil the manifold prophecies of the Old Testament (as has been noted earlier in this book). See especially Matt. 26:52-54 and Luke 24:26, 27, 44-46. And *fourthly* He had to die if He was to share His life with us. Like the brazen serpent He 'must' be lifted up to heal the deadly wounds of sin (John 3:14, 15) and like a seed of grain, 'except it' fall to the ground to die, it will never germinate, come to life and produce the fruit of multitudes of the redeemed (John 12:20-24).

However, none of this information about Jesus' understanding of necessity takes us logically prior to the divine decree. Left unanswered is the question: Was there no other way – i.e. absolute necessity?

Prior to all the subsequent and dependent reasons furnished by Christ for His own death for sin is God's purpose and will. Yet the will of God was not capricious or arbitrary in this or any other matter, but 'rooted in the very nature of God and is in harmony with [all] the divine perfections.'[24]

Christian orthodoxy has always affirmed that neither love nor holiness (justice, righteousness) is alone in this respect. As we hope to demonstrate, holiness is primary, but never alone in God.

According to Duns Scotus and the nominalist party in the late medieval debates, the atonement was not inherently necessary, only the way God sovereignly decided to secure salvation. God could have accomplished the result in any number of ways He might select.

To the contrary, in the wisdom of God, once His decree to create man and to permit the fall were in place, the decree to elect some fell in order; but to save the elect (or all who believe) it was absolutely necessary that the Lamb of God be slain to take away the sins of the world. *Within the created order* the death of Christ became an absolute necessity. That is to say, holiness required that if God was to be righteous in forgiving sins deserving punishment it was necessary for punishment to be executed.

This seems to be the argument of Romans 3:21-26, which says God set forth Christ Jesus to be a *propitiation* in order to show God's 'righteousness' (of character and deed) in 'passing over' sins of earlier ages of man and 'that he [God] might be [both] just, and the justifier of the one who has faith in Jesus' (Rom. 3:26 ESV, also compatible with KJV, ASV and NIV). 'There were two purposes to be answered; the vindication of the character [not the will] of God in passing by former sins, and in passing them now.... The death of Christ vindicated the justice of God in forgiving sin in all ages of the world [inasmuch] as those sins were by the righteous God, as Olshausen says, "punished in Christ."'[25]

A rather fierce debate in academic circles has sought to 'correct' the Reformation message of justification by faith alone, on the ground of Christ's propitiating work alone (by the blood). Space does not allow a full report of the debate.[26] Several articles in the *Journal of Biblical Literature* since 1985 have attacked the usual Protestant understanding of propitiation and justification in Romans. It has also broken out in literature from and critical of Westminster Theological Seminary.

The plain argument of Paul (Rom. 1:18–3:26) presents two truths within whose ambit the question of the necessity of Calvary must be placed: 1) the holy character of God made Calvary necessary if sinners were to be forgiven and 2) God's love made Calvary possible. No man can explain to another why God created a world in which sin could and would condemn creatures made in His image. And He has not deemed it wise to tell us. We do not need to know and it may be presumptuous to ask. It may well be that a sovereign God could have made a different kind of world if He chose. But He did not so choose. End of discussion.

The will of God (plan, purpose, decree) is of course an expression of His holy being. Hence both the will and the nature (character, essence, being) were involved in the permission of sin in our world and in the cure for it. (Passages affirming a connection of Calvary with both the *eternal plan* and the divine will are John 12:27; Matt. 26:38, 39, 42, 44; and Heb. 10:5-7).

---

24. ibid., p. 368.
25. Charles Hodge, *Commentary on the Epistle to the Romans* (Grand Rapids, MI: Eerdmans, repr. 1993), pp. 97, 98.
26. See *The Romans Debate*, ed. K. P. Donfried (Peabody: Hendrickson, 1991), note W. S. Campbell, 'Romans II As a Key to the Structure and Thought of the Letter,' pp. 251–264.

This is not all that needs to be understood about the necessity of the death of Christ. As far as Jesus Himself was concerned, the necessity was not simple fate, though He had said 'it is necessary' (Matt. 16:21 and parallels in Mark and Luke), using *de-i*, a very strong impersonal verb for absolute necessity. He as God had part in the divine foreordaining of 'the Lamb slain from the foundation of the world.' 'He humbled *himself*' to being 'found in human form.' His talks with the disciples were not just to prepare them (as a sickly parent would small children) for the parent's untimely death. Rather it was self-imposed acceptance of the necessary expense of a *lutrōsis*, ransom, of the world of mankind from the power of death and sin. He 'gave himself' a ransom (*lutron*, price paid for redemption). As the Good Shepherd He 'lays down his life for the sheep... No one takes it from me, but I lay it down of my own accord' (John 10:11, 18). Every recent generation has produced books and articles proposing some skeptical theory to explain how it happened, every one *imposed on* rather than *derived from* the only authentic reports available.

As we have already taken note in this digression on necessity, there are hints as to what both the remote and the proximate reasons were. Such sayings as 'in accordance with the Scriptures' (1 Cor. 15:3), 'how then would the Scriptures be fulfilled that say it must happen in this way?' (Matt. 26:54 NIV) and 'it behoved,' etc., of Luke 24:44-46 (KJV) suggest that the meaning of all previous revelation, the whole Old Testament, would have remained an unfinished book without the fulfillment of its types (about this more later) and prophecies in this true 'Omega Point' (to borrow a phrase from Pierre Teilhard de Chardin, an evolutionary Roman Catholic philosopher-theologian).

Further, if the Son of Man after a long life on earth had simply ascended to heaven alone, He would, in the language of John 12:23, 24 have dwelt there 'alone,' for the kernel of wheat must be planted and die to bear fruit. It was precisely to share His own eternal life with men that He 'descended into the lower parts of the earth' and to give 'gifts to men' (Eph. 4:8, 9).

We now turn to examine the meaning of the death of Christ, designated in preaching and theology as *The Atonement*.

14
The Meaning of the Death of Christ
Part One:
How to Explore the Revealed Mystery

A Christian Consensus.

There are some differences between the main branches of historic Christianity regarding the significance of Jesus' death, but the differences are tiny compared with the measure of agreement. This is a remarkable fact in view of severe differences in some other areas of doctrine. The ancient creeds define the Person of Christ and make statements about the main events in His career – birth, life, death, burial, resurrection, ascension, etc., but say almost nothing about their understanding of the permanent significance of Jesus' death – only 'and was crucified also for us under Pontius Pilate' (Nicene Creed of AD 381)[1] and 'who suffered for our salvation'[2] in *Quicunque Vult* (the Athanasian Creed),[3] nothing at all in the Definition of Chalcedon.

Yet the cross on which Jesus died early became the most widely employed symbol of Christianity, witnessing to His death as the most meaningful event in His career on earth.

The apparent reason no important creedal statement developed is that no widely spread heresy involving interpretation of the saving significance of the Savior's death arose prominently, as did arise in connection with His Person.

Such development of a doctrine of 'atonement' as took place up to the sixteenth-century Reformation did not lead to any rupture or serious controversy. At the time of the Reformation the death of our Lord, interpreted as atonement somewhat after the manner of Anselm and Aquinas, was as important in Rome and Paris as in Geneva and Wittenberg.

The following from an acknowledged Roman Catholic authority is correct.

> [T]he Atonement was not one of the subjects directly disputed between the Reformers and their Catholic opponents. But from its close connection with the cardinal question of justification, this doctrine assumed a very special prominence and importance in Protestant theology and practical preaching.… In their general

---

1. Henry Bettenson, ed., *Documents of the Christian Church*, 2nd ed. (London: Oxford University Press, 1963), p. 37.
2. Philip Schaff, *The Creeds of Christendom* vol. iii, The Evangelical Creeds (Grand Rapids, MI: Baker Books, 1966 repr. of 1877 ed. of Harper & Bros.), p. 69. Cf. The Catholic Encyclopedia: An International Work of References on Constitution, Doctrine, Discipline and History of the Catholic Church ii (New York: The Encyclopedia Press, 1907–1922), left col., p. 34, and Denzinger, *The Sources of Catholic Dogma*, trans. R. J. Deferrari (St Louis: Herder & Herder, 1954, 1957), para. 40, p. 16.
3. Bettenson, *Documents*, p. 73.

conception of the Atonement the Reformers and their followers happily preserved the Catholic doctrine, at least along its main lines. And in their explanation of the merit of Christ's sufferings and death we may see the influence of St Thomas and the other schoolmen.[4]

The Greek orthodox church from ancient times has delighted to speculate on mystical redemption by the incarnation and criticizes Western (both Roman and Protestant) theology for alleged legalism; yet underneath there appears to be much essential agreement with us. An important catechism of the Eastern church, after affirming Jesus Christ was crucified 'for us,' asks 'How does the death of Jesus Christ upon the cross deliver us from sin, the curse and death?' and answers, in part:

> ...as in Adam we had fallen under sin, the curse, and death, so we are delivered from sin, the curse and death in Jesus Christ. His voluntary suffering and death on the cross for us, being of infinite value and merit, as the death of one sinless, God and man in one person, is both a perfect satisfaction of the justice of God, which had condemned us for sin to death, and a friend of infinite merit, which has obtained him the right, without prejudice to justice, to give us sinners pardon of our sins, and grace to have victory over sin and death.[5]

With minor adjustments this speaks for Roman Catholics, Lutherans, Calvinists, Anglicans and Methodists, Baptists, Independents, and all the rest of orthodox believers. This would not be the case in many other areas of doctrine. In evaluating the Eastern Orthodox insistence on *theosis*, that is, deification, as salvation, and its seeming to slight the atonement in favor of the incarnation, this confession must be kept in mind. An Eastern Orthodox publication called *The Christian Activist*, in a polemical mood, liked to point to contrasts between evangelicals and orthodox. A recent article reads like Protestant liberalism, denying death is a punishment for sin and rejecting any penal aspect of Christ's death ('The River of Fire,' Dr Alexander Kalomiros, Winter–Spring 1997). But this is not quite typical.

According to the Scriptures.

Paul was quite representative of all writers of the New Testament Epistles when he said he would know nothing among the churches save 'Jesus Christ and him crucified.' The cross, as we saw earlier, was also the climax toward which each Gospel moved. 'The Lamb of God' has the same central place in the Apocalypse from chapter 5 onward. Paul interpreted the death of Christ for all Christians when he defined his gospel as 'first of all' 'that Christ died for our sins in accordance with the Scriptures' (1 Cor. 15:3). This is not the same 'spin,' as we say, on the crucifixion that Pilate or the high priest or Saul of Tarsus might have put on the crucifixion of Jesus. This sentence by which Paul introduces his great chapter on resurrection, Christ's and ours, is the matrix from which all discussion of the meaning of the death of Christ must spring. 1) What transaction took place? 2) How do the Scriptures define it? And 3) where in 'the Scriptures' is it so written? These are some of the questions we now address.

The chief biblical meaning of the death of Christ ('for sin' 'for our sins,' etc.) is defined by the need of every man for rescue from the condemnation of death for sin from which by ourselves we cannot escape. Those who, like the ancient Pelagians, sixteenth-century Socinians and modern 'Enlightenment' theologians deny the need, quite naturally find no cure. If there is no wrath of God and no created structure of justice and law in the universe neither is there place for a final judgment and forgiveness. Hence 'a survey of the theories which have proliferated across the centuries will show that the biblical data have been hammered into many conflicting shapes, often in forgetfulness of the mold which the word of God itself provides.'[6] The materials are immense both in Scripture and in theological literature. I propose some principles for correct understanding of biblical texts relating to the meaning of the death of Christ as reported in the New Testament and as interpreted therein.

Principles for Interpreting the Death of Christ.

1. The notion of slain sacrifice for forgiveness of sin, like every other major doctrine, has basic preparation in the Old Testament. The New Testament presumes throughout that a revelation perfect, sure, right, pure, clean, true and righteous exists already in the Scriptures of the Old Testament (Ps. 19:7-9). The teachings there are sufficient to convert sinners and make them to rejoice, be enlightened, to warn and to reward them (Ps. 19:7-11). This means

---

4. W. H. Kent, O.S.C., 'Atonement,' in *The Catholic Encyclopedia ii*, p. 58.
5. *The Longer Catechism* (Moscow of 1839, Q sections 206 and 208), in Schaff, *Creeds of Christendom ii*, pp. 475, 476.
6. Vernon Grounds, 'Atonement,' *Baker's Dictionary of Theology*, ed. E. F. Harrison (Grand Rapids, MI: Baker Books, 1960), p. 71.

that every Christian doctrine had its basic content laid out already, before a line of the New Testament was ever written, to complete the last chapter, so to speak (Heb. 1:1-2). Even in our Lord's own time He declared this to be so, frequently reproving purveyors of false views for not knowing the Scriptures or for misusing, misinterpreting or perverting what the Scriptures say. This aspect of Christian truth especially, being the major theme of the New Testament from beginning to end will never come to clear focus for any one who declines to become acquainted with the Old Testament. Its most forbidding passages – in Exodus, Leviticus and Numbers, which abound in tiresome details of Tabernacle and temple, their furniture, vessels, materials, priests and ministers, rituals and calendar – are the very portions which one entire New Testament book (Hebrews) employs to explain the meaning of the cross. Passages from Psalms and Prophets turn up in dozens of New Testament explanations of the meaning of Jesus' death. 'Christ died for our sins *in accordance with the Scriptures*' cannot be understood apart from those Scriptures that had been in existence centuries before a line of the New Testament was composed.

Certain recent and current writers on hermeneutics, including biblical hermeneutics, draw a distinction between the *horizon* (i.e. total personal and cultural background) which the present interpreter brings to the task of interpretation and the horizon of the writers, also to a distinction between intended *meaning* of the writer for his first readers (perhaps) and *significance* for us the current generation. Some authors assume great differences. Whatever validity these refinements of the task of Bible interpretation may have – and they are not without merit – it is my opinion we must regard it as the first task of the interpreter to seek to understand the writer's 'horizon' and to adjust our outlook, whatever our 'frame of plausibility,' to it. Borrowing the language of A. C. Thistelton,[7] joint authors W. W. Klein, C. L. Bomberg and R. L. Hubbard Jr rightly say: 'Genuine interpretation requires a fusing of the ancient and modern horizons where the meaning of the ancient text helps interpreters come to new understandings themselves.'[8] This volume (*An Introduction to Biblical Interpretation, Dallas, TX: Word, 1993*) provides an extensive bibliography of hermeneutics annotated from the standpoint of reverent, believing scholarship. The *significance* (practical or theoretical) for our time builds on and absorbs the *meaning* of the original author. The words *mean* and *signify*, *meaning* and *significance* will be used interchangeably in the following discussion.

(Strange as it seems to ordinary folk, there are now several schools of academic philosophy which contend hermeneutics has little to do with the intention of the author of a text. These authors start with some form of depth psychology to plumb the depths of human 'existence.' They seek to explain why the author wrote what he did rather than the strict meaning of what he intended to say and what the reader is in the depth of 'being' or 'existence' before extracting *significance* for the reader.

E. D. Hirsch has been the leading exponent of the common-sense view that it is the task of interpreters of a text to find and expound what the original author meant.[9]

There are now (or have been) several self-acknowledged schools of a 'new hermeneutic.' This means simply to interpret a text from the standpoint of the presuppositions of the reader – Marxist, Freudian, feminist, liberation, theology of revolution, etc. These interpreters often seek to explain the prejudices of the author – say patriarchalism or feudalism, etc. – to explain the errors of his writing as prior to finding any significance for the modern reader.

2. A second principle is related to the first. The thinking of the authors of the New Testament had already been shaped by the Old Testament. They were Jews steeped in the history, liturgy and doctrine, as well as the language of the Old Testament. Their lives had been shaped by the moral and religious outlook of orthodox Judaism. Such writers naturally expressed themselves in patterns and terms already imbedded in their minds. There was a time when Britain and America were populated by millions who in church, home, school and workplace were similarly shaped in the same by the Authorized Version of the Bible. This national treasure of moral and intellectual capital is even now not completely lost.

Such being the case, the diligent student of Christian doctrine aspiring to be fed on meat rather than milk and perhaps to be a teacher of the Word, must pause on the way long enough to attain more than cursory acquaintance with the Old Testament, 'beginning at Moses and all the prophets… in all the Scriptures.' To do otherwise would be like attempting calculus without knowing arithmetic. (To debate these matters with 'scholars' who have neither acquaintance with the Old Testament nor acceptance of its vocabulary of sacrifice is not very fruitful.)

---

7. A. C. Thistelton, *The Two Horizons: New Testament Hermeneutics and Philosophical Designation with Special Reference to Hiedeger, Bultmannm and Willgenstein* (Grand Rapids, MI: Eerdmans, 1980).
8. W. W. Klein, C. L. Bomberg and R. L. Hubbard Jr, *An Introduction to Biblical Interpretation* (Dallas: Word, 1993), p. 83.
9. E. D. Hirsch, *Validity in Interpretation* (New Haven: Yale University Press, 1967) and *The Aim of Interpretation* (Chicago: University of Chicago Press, 1976).

In such a case, wherever one wishes to enter the thought-world of the New Testament, acquaintance with the Old Testament background of the idea is a necessary consideration.

(Some scholars have determined that, for example, about three-fourths of the book of Revelation consists in ideas, words, phrases, sentences from the Old Testament and allusions in slightly different phraseology. A sizeable modern literature has grown up on this subject by some of the best scholars of our time. The article, 'How the New Testament uses the Old,' by E. Earle Ellis treats the subject thoroughly and in the notes provides an excellent bibliography.[10] See also *TDNT*; art. 'Tupos' ['type'] by L. Goppelt.)

3. In the New Testament, Jesus Himself in the Gospels and all the authors of the remaining books regard the coming and kingdom of Christ as completion of events, institutions, revelations and history reported in the Old Testament, as was discussed in some detail in chapter 1. This clear feature of the New Testament itself is quite removed from imposing the meaning of New Testament revelation upon Old Testament stories or statements of truth. But it does mean that in the unity of biblical truth *firstly*, Old Testament teaching (as opposed to mere reporting of beliefs and practices) will not contradict New Testament teaching; *secondly*, a Christological interpretation of the Old Testament is a natural thing, not a cramped, contrived process whereby a Christian orthodoxy is imposed upon the Old Testament. Jesus was very clear: '…beginning with Moses and all the Prophets, he interpreted to them in all the Scriptures the things concerning himself… "everything written about me in the Law of Moses and the Prophets and the Psalms must be fulfilled"… "Thus it is written, that the Christ should suffer and on the third day rise from the dead"' (Luke 24:27, 44-46). It is also written 'Christ died for our sins in accordance with the Scriptures' (1 Cor. 1:3). See further evidence cited in chapter 1.

Unity of the Two Testaments.

This unity of the Testaments is related to several matters of great importance to sound interpretation of the death of Christ.

The unity that believers and theologians have found in the facts and meaning of Scripture has been under serious attack since the beginning of the Christian era. These attacks have come for different reasons and in different ways too complicated to present fully here. Any one of them if successful would have destroyed Christianity as a system of beliefs and practices, hence no 'systematic theology' or systematic anything else. This, of course, is where the various recent fads of 'hermeneutics' (principles of interpretation) would take us – there is a new one every three or four years.

On the other hand some unquestionably competent scholars have lent important support to the unity of the Testaments and the progress of redemptive history.

A welcome scholarly acknowledgment of the divinely intended preparatory and participating connection of the Old Testament ritual sacrifices with the sacrifice of the cross comes sometimes from unexpected sources. An acknowledged, perhaps paramount, recent modern authority on Hebrew (Old Testament) antiquities was Roland De Vaux. In the preface to his treatise on sacrifice this renowned Roman Catholic priest-scholar says,

> The unique sacrifice of Christ has rendered obsolete the sacrificial rites of the Old Testament but these had played their part as an expression of the piety of our ancestors in faith and as a means of their sanctification. Moreover, the teaching of the Old Testament has not lost its value for Christians. By partaking in Christ's sacrifice they fulfil the fundamental obligation of worship, thanksgiving and expiation, which the Old Testament sacrifices were already intended to satisfy.[11]

The last four lines of the book comment on Isaiah 53:7. He concludes:

> Thus is a door opened upon the New Testament Jesus as the 'Lamb of God who takes away the sins of the world' (John 1:29), Christ knew not sin, God has made him a [sacrificial] victim for sin, *hattat*, so that in him we might become the justice of God (2 Cor. 5:21).[12]

---

10. E. Earle Ellis, 'How the New Testament Uses the Old,' in *New Testament Interpretation*, I. H. Marshall, ed. (Grand Rapids, MI: Eerdmans, 1977, 1991).
11. Roland De Vaux, *Studies in Old Testament Sacrifice* (Cardiff: University of Wales Press, 1964), p. vii.
12. ibid., p. 112.

Denials and Perversions of the Unity and Meaning.

From ancient times there has been a tendency among some to find the Old Testament antithetical to the gospel of salvation by grace through faith on the ground of a *bona fide* sacrifice of the body and blood of Christ – prominently: 1) the various Gnosticisms of the earliest generations; 2) the Socinians of the Reformation era; 3) transcendentalists, Unitarians and Hixite Quakers of the Enlightenment heyday; 4) liberalism of the past 150 years; 5) the doctrine of reconciliation by incarnation sometimes advocated in mystical theology and inherent in the existentialism of neo-orthodoxy; and 6) the evolutionary pantheism of current process theology (called *pan-en-theism*). The last three of these compete for acceptance today.

These denials and perversions have been proposed to explain away what the New Testament really says about atonement for sin, especially any traces of vicarious sacrifice or special saving value of 'the precious blood.' To do so one must reject or reduce any New Testament approval of or connection with the Old Testament bloody rites of sacrifice, its God-directed wars of conquest (book of Joshua) and portrayal of the one true God as a God of wrath who visits punishment either temporal (pestilence, fire from heaven and wars of annihilation) or eternal such as Jesus threatened (Gehenna, Hades, hell) or the Apocalypse (book of Revelation) promises (lake of fire, second death).

1. Denials and perversion since the beginning of the Reformation have taken the form *first*, of an effort to combine integrity and acceptance of the Bible as a report of honest men about real things as they saw them, with rejection of traditional interpretations (Socinianism of the sixteenth century and to a degree even the Unitarians of the nineteenth century).

2. *Then* an effort to accept Christianity and the civilization permeated by it, but to improve on it by rejecting any elements of the Bible unworthy of modern, enlightened civilized people (many Enlightenment-Age-of-Reason folk: an example is Thomas Jefferson).

3. *After that*, treating Christianity as something begun by Jesus, an ethical religion (reflecting nineteenth-century evolutionary, optimistic liberalism), to interpret Jesus as founder of Christianity not the object of Christian worship and trust as Savior; His death as something caused by His own mistaken ideas about the kingdom of God, etc. In this system there is no place for a Savior from sin. Early in the twentieth century an effort was launched mainly to place Jesus' death in the context of a tragic, failed effort. His movement nevertheless caught on with His friends, who for some reason supposed He was alive again. Their converts in the second and third generations afterward gave us first Epistles, then Gospels with a doctrine of vicarious sacrifice based on misguided interpretation of Isaiah 53 and similar texts.

These efforts have not been successful on the basis of exegesis of what the texts of Scripture really are and truly say. There have been enormous expenditures of energy, notwithstanding, to overturn the plain sense of the O.T. and N.T. in regard to the meaning of the cross.

4. The unbelieving higher criticism of the nineteenth century postulated an evolutionary history of Israel to make the sacrificial rituals a late addition against better ethical advice by the prophets. Criticism also postulated a pre-historic amalgamation of Canaanites and migratory tribes known as Hebrews instead of a conquest, etc., rejected Mosaic authorship of the Pentateuch and canonized a Documentary, layered analysis of the Pentateuch. In effect, all the rest of Hebrew history is reconstructed according to several evolutionary scenarios. This approach prevails in liberal seminaries and the literature of the world of so-called Old Testament theology. In this enormous literature there is no plan for such interpretation of the Old Testament as Jesus, Paul, Peter, Hebrews and John give. My inclinations as well as duties as a professor first of Old Testament, then of theology in theological schools and colleges, as well as writing over a good many years have made me rather acutely aware of the harm to authentic Christianity this sort of attack from the academic quarter has had. It strikes at the heart of all biblical historic, orthodox witness that Christ died for our sins in accordance with the Scriptures.

5. Add to the mix the confusion introduced by the extremes of literary (source) criticism of the Gospels, form criticism, redaction criticism, etc., the utter recklessness of the current search for 'the historical Jesus' and the reductionism of the 'Jesus Seminar' and its academic aftermath. As a result the Bible comes to mean nothing at all to those who are affected. I have lived with these developments as a scholar since before the present refinements of anti-orthodox and anti-supernatural biblical and theological teachings came to fruition in the moral and cultural calamities that overtook Christendom in the last several decades of the twentieth century, as well as general collapse of liberal denominations both in Europe and America.

We must do more than lament the collapse of liberal religion. Let us rather pursue the task mandated by Jesus Himself of finding the meaning of His Calvary work in the Scriptures.

(David F. Wells has provided a more extensive treatment of Christology in the hands of those who deny or pervert the New Testament message of 'Christ died for our sins in accordance with the Scriptures' in 'The Enlightenment and its aftermath' and 'Twentieth Century Turmoil,' chapters 7 and 8 in *The Person of Christ: A Biblical and Historical Analysis of the Incarnation*.[13] Though faithful to the 'Biblical' this excellent work is devoted mainly to the 'Historical.' Thereby it serves to supplement most evangelical readers' knowledge of the subject. Endnotes furnished by Dr Wells thoroughly document details of the report and analysis and are a guide to further study.)

Principles to Guide Interpretation of New Testament Doctrine of the Death of Christ.

Accepting both the truthfulness of the whole Bible, and interpreting with due attention to figurative elements and several *genera* (Fr. genre) of literature and the unity of the message of the Great Book, three principles of understanding the meaning of its central focus on the passion and death of Jesus will help us get it right. Though not always specifically stated (and of course with variety of expression) they have guided the best orthodox writers for 400 years. The group who translated the Authorized Version of 1611 numbered many godly classical scholars who were eminently successful in producing relative accuracy and consistency in the words relating to sacrifice in the Old Testament and the Christological language of the New Testament. The relevance of rabbinical studies and of the language of sacrifice in the Talmud came to be appreciated in the eighteenth century (John Gill in Britain) and growing appreciation of the importance of the Septuagint, linguistic bridge from Leviticus to Hebrews, so to speak, followed. And in connection with the Septuagint, archaeology (*papyri*) contributed greatly to knowledge of the sacrificial language both of the LXX and the New Testament.

These developments of the latest generations were not required to get at understanding of 'Jesus Christ and him crucified,' only to refine and to correct some minor false conceptions which it would take a rather full history of exegesis to trace out fully. I state the most controversial principle first.

A. There is a typical connection between central features of the Old Testament ritual system and the events of Jesus' redemptive career and the meaning of His life of obedience, Passion and death. This will be discussed at length later at an appropriate place.

B. The New Testament employs the very vocabulary of Old Testament ritual sacrifice to interpret the meaning of Jesus' life, Passion and death. This vocabulary was supplied by the Greek translation of New Testament times now known as the Septuagint, a translation used throughout the first-century Diaspora of Jews. This is the subject of the next chapter in this study.

C. The rabbinical writings of the Talmud and similar literature of orthodox Judaism preserve some of the religious ideas and language of sacrifice, prevalent in synagogue and synagogue schools of Jesus' time. The devout Jews of the apostolic circle would likely have employed some of this language, adapted to Christian understanding, in writing the New Testament. They could not easily avoid employing this treasury of vocabulary and patterns of thought in writing about a new covenant which they esteemed to be fulfillment of an old covenant. Aid from rabbinical Judaism is, however, seriously limited *first*, by reason of the fact there are almost no rabbinical writings of the first century now available. Furthermore, the teachings of the rabbis, except as preserved in the New Testament itself, were mainly preserved (fairly accurately, it is thought) orally. No one is certain when they were written in the Mishna, but it was several centuries later. *Secondly*, at the time of writing, the authors of Mishna had been reacting, for generations, against the claims of Christianity and its advocates. Hence there was reverse influence on rabbinical ideas and vocabulary from Christian sources as continues to the present.

I shall not refer often to the principles set forth in this chapter in the study to follow, but the reader should know that they are being employed.

---

13. D. F. Wells, *The Person of Christ: A Biblical and Historical Analysis of the Incarnation* (Westchester: Crossway Books, 1984), pp. 129–170.

15
The Meaning of the Death of Jesus Christ Part Two:
The Biblical Vocabulary of the Atonement

Earlier we have taken note of the *centrality* of the theme of atonement in the Bible and its steady presentation from Genesis 3 to Revelation 22. The *fullness* of scriptural representations of the meaning of the cross and *variety* of expression do not in any wise impair the *unity* of meaning everywhere in the Bible. The various expressions do not contradict one another. Rather they simply reflect the variegated, but comprehensive, organic unity of the biblical story of creation, fall and redemption. A sound understanding of God's nature and attributes (especially holiness and love in balance), His will and His law, man's nature as created and his condition vitiated by the fall must be brought to sound interpretation of the meaning of the cross, the central fact in the history of salvation.

By What Name?

It is no small matter to choose the right comprehensive name for the subject at hand. Many have struggled with it. The customary word in books, encyclopaedias, research articles, sermons and learned discourse is atonement. To atone originally in English meant to make or to be at-one: hence to reconcile and thereby at-one-ment, reconciliation.[1] And the one time 'atonement' appears in the English New Testament (KJV) (Rom. 5:11) it translates a Greek word which uniformly, in the rest of the New Testament Version of AD 1611, is rendered reconciliation. Reconciliation or at-one-ment, however, is only one of many aspects of the meaning of the cross as interpreted in the Bible.

Atone and atonement came to mean to make amends or reparations for wrongdoing, the satisfaction for wrongdoing – not unrelated to *some* reconciliations but not the same as reconciliation. There are at least a dozen other aspects of Calvary's meaning in Bible and theology, each designated by different words, so 'atonement,' the word as such, is not really a comprehensive term.

There is some law of language at work here. Scotland gets its name from a stray band of Irish Scots settled near the border with England; Greece gets its name from a small clan of Hellenes who happened to be near Italy; Asia, now the name for earth's largest continent, in Paul's time designated only a province in western Anatolia closest to 'civilized' Romans and Greeks – now called Asia Minor, and Africa was a tiny province directly opposite Sicily on the shore of a great unknown land mass now known in entirety as Africa.

---

1. *The Compact Edition of the Oxford English Dictionary* (Oxford University Press, 1971), p. 540.

So though it causes confusion we will go on speaking of the entire saving work effected by God in Christ at Calvary as the atonement, even though at-one-ment, or reconciliation, is only one of several aspects of that great accomplishment.

Devout Christians who get their theological vocabulary from familiarity with the sacred page know Jesus died, suffered, was obedient unto death, was slain, gave Himself, was a sacrifice for sin, was crucified, shed His blood and by many other turns of phrase know what happened. Each expression puts a slightly different slant on what the event was in and of itself and hence also some special meaning in the context of the citation.

Fulfillment of Divine Plan.

Some of the best-known texts emphasize the significance simply as fulfillment of divine plans, especially as expressed in Old Testament prophecy with which believers then and now should be familiar and should understand. Thus He is 'the Lamb slain from the foundation of the world. (Rev. 13:8 KJV); He 'Ought... to have suffered' (Luke 24:26 KJV); and 'it was necessary for the Christ to suffer' (Acts 17:3). The Old Testament prophets certainly, if dimly, 'predicted the sufferings of Christ' (1 Peter 1:11). It is asserted many times and at various junctures that no one who understood Scripture should have been surprised that Jesus was destined by God to die. Jesus even called disciples 'foolish ones, and slow of heart to believe all that the prophets have spoken' (Luke 24:25) for stupidity in this regard.

If 'Christ died for our sins in accordance with the Scriptures' and the Passion events were forecast 'in all the Scriptures,' a major feature of that forecast was in the sacrifices prescribed in Leviticus and Numbers. The very language of the four Evangelists, of Jesus Himself, of Paul, Peter, James and John is not only replete with references to the sacrificial system, but as we shall see, was shaped by its images. The New Testament language of atonement is almost totally obscure without knowledge of that system – in which our Lord fully participated, as did all the Apostles, including Paul.

> The very language of evangelists and apostles, which we now think so plain is all derived and moulded from these ancient rites... without [which] it would be exceedingly obscure.... These typical rites thus hold a place in the economy of revelation from which they cannot be spared.... The New Testament is necessary to a right understanding of them, but equally necessary are they to a right understanding of the New Testament.[2]

For Sin.

The death of Jesus was 'for sin' (Rom. 8:3), 'for sins' (1 Peter 3:18). He 'died for *our* [emphasis added] sins' (1 Cor. 15:3), and His death 'takes away the sin of the world' (John 1:29) and 'condemned sin' (Rom. 8:3). It was to 'put away sin by the sacrifice of himself' (Heb. 9:26). He was 'made... sin' 'For our sake' (2 Cor. 5:21). The death of Christ takes on great meaning as God's means to save us from our sins and explains really why God sent Him (Matt. 1:21). The shed blood of Christ (as a name for His death) is God's instrument not only to save us from the consequences of sins but to 'sanctify the people through his own blood' (Heb. 13:12) – not only 'forgiveness of sins' by His blood (Heb. 9:22) but the very purifying of conscience (Heb. 9:14).

This is the crux (another word for cross) of the matter. The death of Christ won salvation for *sinners*. In Pauline language 'saving grace' by definition has the meaning 'for sinners only.' He came to die for that purpose. If we do not get that straight nothing else will matter much.

> That does not mean that a carefully articulated doctrine of the atonement is necessary before a man can be called a Christian... But is does mean that, whether we can put it into words or not, our relationship to Christ and therefore to God depends on the way we view the Cross.[3]

The Biblical Expressions.

Theologians and exegetes have combed the New Testament for words and expressions that interpret (for sinners) the meaning of the cross. These New Testament terms are the vocabulary by which the Author of our salvation

---

2. J. A. Seiss, *Holy Types; The Gospel in Leviticus; A Series of Lectures on the Hebrew Ritual* (Philadelphia, PA: The United Lutheran Publication House, n.d.), pp. 23, 24.
3. Leon Morris, *The Cross in the New Testament* (Grand Rapids, MI: Eerdmans, 1965), pp. 5, 6.

deigned to convey to sinners the significance of the means He employed. They are not mere cultural expressions. A thoughtful review of New Testament terms declaring the meaning of our Lord's death renders the matter quite clear. My own rather informal survey turned up the following short list. It is both precise and plain. Christ's death is an offering, presented or offered up as a sacrifice, a vicarious sacrifice, precious, a price paid for redemption, a ransom, redemption from bondage, deliverance from curse, reconciliation and propitiation. It is obedience to God or unto death. It is justification or salvation. 'The Lamb' and 'the cross' also figure in the biblical interpretation. None of these is precisely equivalent to another. Some are used frequently, some only once or twice. Some are comprehensive as in themselves including most of the others.

There are two main reasons why these and some other interpretive, biblical expressions of the meaning of Calvary must be understood precisely. To gain a soundly Christian understanding of the central fact of our religion is of course the chief reason. The other is to defend against the fierce attack of modern liberal theologians and their allies among academic exegetes of the liberal establishment and their caricatures of the historic orthodox consensus referred to earlier. Orthodoxy has always found the necessity for atonement in human sin and divine wrath – both understood biblically; efficacy is grounded in substitutionary sacrifice; reconciliation in propitiation of God's wrath as well as expiation of sin's guilt. Liberalism finds all these teachings objectionable – even corrupt and hateful. For these reasons we now proceed to examine the material laid out. There is much at stake – the very nature of Christianity. Christianity and liberalism are not really forms of one religion but two very different religions, even though each in a different way is related to Christian history. (Note: unless noted otherwise biblical terms and passages cited in this section are from the Authorized or King James Version, mainly because the discussion was originally framed in those words and is still usually carried on in them.)

Sacrifice.

This is the most comprehensive term covering every aspect of meaning of our Lord's death. In connection with Jesus' death sacrifice invariably translates *thusia*. In the Greek Old Testament, however, *thusia* translates eight different Hebrew words for different kinds of ritual sacrifices. It occurs about 350 times. The corresponding verb, *thuō* is used once by Paul of Christ's death, saying, 'Christ, our Passover lamb, has been sacrificed [*thuō*]' for us (1 Cor. 5:7) and once, Christ has given Himself for an 'offering and sacrifice [*thusia*] to God' (Eph. 5:2). Hebrews employs *thusia* of Christ's death five times (5:1; 9:23, 26; 10:12, 26). Significantly the very same language is used frequently in the New Testament (e.g. Mark 9:13, 49) in reference to sacrifices of Old Testament times, even heathen sacrifices. The sacrifice offered to God by Jesus is said to be 'better' (Heb. 9:23), one and 'once for all', a sacrifice 'of himself' (Heb. 9:26), and that there can be no other sacrifice (Heb. 10:26).

If the meaning of 'the cross' is sacrifice we must establish the biblical meaning of sacrifice – *the* meaning of a meaning, so to speak. We will forbear entering the extensive old debates on that subject. A century and more of 'scientific' research and philosophical reflections on sacrifice and sacrificial customs among the world's peoples produced some very interesting literature, most of it no longer read (*The Golden Bough* by J. G. Frazer and *The Religion of the Semites* by W. R. Smith), and a whole school of writers on comparative religion. This 'scientific' research and philosophical reflection produced little specific to help us understand the idea of sacrifice in either Testament and is today mainly irrelevant to the meaning of Jesus' sacrifice. The recent past has been blessed with the extensive and more fruitful writings of men such as Leon Morris and Vincent Taylor employing historical and linguistic evidences from the standpoint of biblical theology. This present chapter is indebted to them (not to neglect the older work on *The Death of Christ* by James Denny and others).

Let me cite first some very helpful guides from a somewhat earlier time.

J. J. Reeve, after a careful survey of the Old Testament *phenomena* of sacrifice and nine competing theories of the idea and meaning of sacrifice wrote:

> The theory that the sacrifices were a vicarious expiation of sin and defilement, by a victim whose life was forfeited instead of the sinner's is the only one that will complete the Levitical idea of sacrifices.[4]

Similarly A. H. Strong in a vigorous summary said:

---

4. J. J. Reeve, 'Sacrifice, in the Old Testament' in *International Standard Bible Encyclopedia*, ed. J. Orr (Grand Rapids, MI: Eerdmans, 1939, 1943), p. 2650.

> The true import of sacrifice, as is abundantly evident from both heathen and Jewish sources, embraced three elements, first that of satisfaction to offended deity, or propitiation to violated holiness; secondly, that of substitution of suffering and death on the part of the innocent for the deserved punishment of the guilty; and, thirdly community of life between the offerer and the victim.[5]

Strong asserts 'We may classify Scripture representations of the atonement according as they conform to moral, commercial, legal or sacrificial analogies.'[6] Yet he goes on to devote only two pages to 'moral,' 'commercial' and 'legal' but eleven to 'sacrificial' analogies, demonstrating fully that the sacrificial aspect of Christ's work of atonement is most prominent in Scripture.[7]

Sacrifice and sacrificial customs among pagan peoples around the world has been studied extensively over the past 200 years. It has contributed little to understanding the meaning of the Levitical sacrifices and their antitype in Christ. Most of this literature, though very interesting (e.g. Frazer, *The Golden Bough*), is no longer read. It is largely irrelevant to our pursuit here.

There is, however, a large literature – much of it from a few generations back – which interprets the Levitical sacrifices, their meaning in relation to those who lived by them, their relation to Christ's sacrifice and of His to us. W. A. Van Germeren's article 'Sacrifices and Offerings in Bible Times' (*Evangelical Dictionary of Theology*, pp. 788–792) is a sound but very brief guide to study of current literature on the institution of sacrifice. Recent evangelical works of Systematic Theology characteristically say little about sacrifice as such.

Sacrifice enters biblical history ages before the time of Moses. The Mosaic system incorporated forms of sacrifice already employed both by Israelites and their heathen neighbors. Hence some remarks from excellent summaries of extensive studies by some of our theological forebears will serve to enlarge and support a sound doctrine of sacrifice – preliminary to understanding the doctrine of atonement by the death of Christ. I cite first a paragraph from McClintock and Strong, *Cyclopaedia*:

> [T]he idea of sacrifice is a complex idea, involving the propitiatory, the dedication, and the eucharistic elements. [*Propitiatory* has reference to appeasing the divine displeasure with sin. *Dedicatory* to presentation of the repentant offerer to God. *Eucharistic* refers to ceremonial action of religious value.] Any one of these, taken by itself, would lead to error and superstition. The propitiatory would tend to the idea of atonement by sacrifice for sin, as being effectual without any condition of repentance and faith; the self-dedicatory, taken alone, ignores the barrier of sin between men and God, and undermines the whole idea of atonement; the eucharistic, alone, leads to the notion that more gifts can satisfy God's service, and is easily perverted into the heathenish attempt to bribe God by vows and offerings. All three, probably, were more or less implied in each sacrifice, each element predominating in its turn; all must be kept in mind in considering the historical influence, the spiritual meaning, and the typical value of sacrifice.[8]

Excellent for comprehensive brevity and technical exactness as well as practical value is Calvin's explanation of 'what I have meant throughout the discussion by "sacrifice" and "priest."' He concludes:

> The sacrificial victims which were offered under the law to atone for sins [Exod. 39:36] were so called, not because they were capable of recovering God's favor or wiping out iniquity, but because they prefigured a true sacrifice such as was finally accomplished in reality by Christ alone; and by him alone because no other could have done it. And it was done but once, because the effectiveness and force of that one sacrifice accomplished by Christ are eternal, as he testified with his own voice when he said that it was done and fulfilled [John 19:30]; that is, whatever was necessary to recover the Father's favor, to obtain forgiveness of sins, righteousness and salvation – all this was performed and completed by that unique sacrifice of his. And so perfect was it that no place was left afterward for any other sacrificial victim.[9]

Perhaps the most respected and most quoted orthodox scholar of the early twentieth century on the subject of the meaning of the death of Christ was James Denney. In comment on the concept in Hebrews as the One sacrificed for sins forever he said:

5. A. H. Strong, *Systematic Theology* (Valley Forge, PA: Judson Press, 1907), p. 723.
6. ibid., pp. 716.
7. ibid., pp. 716–728.
8. John McClintock and James Strong, art. on 'Sacrifice,' in *Cyclopedia of Biblical, Theological and Ecclesiastical Literature vol. ix* (Grand Rapids, MI: Baker Books, 1968–1970), p. 227.
9. John Calvin, *Institutes of the Christian Religion ii*, ed. J. T. McNeil, trans. and ed. F. L. Battles (Philadelphia, PA: Westminster Press, 1960), p. 1442.

> There is the same sacrificial conception in all the references in the epistle to the blood of Christ.... In all these ways the death of Christ is defined as a sacrificial death, or as a death having relation to sin: the two things are one.[10]

After taking note of the variety of Old Testament sacrifices mentioned and the many details of 'sacrificial language,' he concludes:

> [N]o emphasis is laid on the distinguishing features of these various sacrifices, they are looked at simply in the expiatory or atoning significance which is common to them all. They represent a divinely appointed way of dealing with sin.[11]

These authorities, each from a slightly different but biblically informed evangelical point of view, affirms truly what is meant when the New Testament tells its readers the death of Jesus was a sacrifice paid to God for sin. Rather than parse the statements let us move on to examine the vocabulary of the Bible's own interpretation of the meaning of our Lord's sacrifice. In this examination the bearing of the Old Testament, directly through its prophecies, indirectly through its history and institutions, must have a part.

Scholars who take the Bible at face value generally agree. Writers who take the low view of Scripture characteristic of liberal Christian religion and overt opponents of Christianity have proposed many other interpretations of Jesus' death by crucifixion. The proposals of scholarly unbelievers have been as varied as ingenious: sincere martyr to a just cause, love of God, or love of man, crushed fanatical advocate of several lost causes, failed victim of a 'Passover plot' are some of the commonest.

An Offering, Something Presented to God.

This word as noun (*prosfora*) or as verb, to offer (*prosferō*), designates the death of Christ over twenty times in the New Testament. Sometimes it refers to Old Testament sacrifices (Acts 7:42; 21:26) but also figuratively as Christians employ 'offering' today, to prayers, acts of devotion such as giving money for Christian work or benevolences (Acts 24:17; Rom. 15:16). In the Septuagint (which furnished the New Testament vocabulary for such things) it often translates derivatives of *qarav*, to present something, usually a sacrifice, to God (though sometimes tribute or a gift to a human authority). This is the source of the word '*Corban*... a gift' (Mark 7:11) often used in reference to Levitical sacrifice in both Testaments. It adds to 'sacrifice' the factor of *presentation*, i.e. usually by *man* to God. Most of the New Testament occurrences of offer-offering are either to Old Testament ritual sacrifice or the sacrifice of Calvary.

Blood, Blood of the Covenant.

Six times Paul says salvation or redemption was secured for us by the blood of Christ (Rom. 3:25; 5:19; 1 Cor. 10:16; Eph. 1:7; 2:13; Col. 1:20), Peter, twice (1 Peter 1:2, 19). Peter's reference to the 'precious blood of Christ' suggests the special value of Christ's shed blood beyond the blood of other sacrifices. Hebrews affirms the same three times (9:12, 14; 10:19) as well as the Epistles of John and Revelation (1 John 1:7; twice in 1 John 5:6 and in v. 8; also Rev. 1:8). Hebrews 9:19-22 connects the shedding of Christ's blood with the bloody sacrifices of the Old Testament, connecting it with 'remission [or 'forgiveness' in many Versions] of sin.' In the Levitical sacrifices – especially the sin-offering and the trespass-offering – the *raison d'être* was remission of sin, not to deny worship and 'sacramental' obedience as aspects of the sacrificial offerings.

'[T]he blood of the covenant' (Exod. 24:8) or 'of thy covenant' (Zec. 9:11 KJV) or 'of the everlasting covenant' (Heb. 13:20 KJV) is a peculiar expression calling for some comment. Jesus' words of institution: 'this is my blood of the covenant ['new covenant' KJV], which is poured out for many unto remission of sins' (Matt. 26:28 ASV) is another similar expression seeming to connect all such references to the covenant of the Lord's sacrifice of expiation and propitiation at Calvary. Circumcision was accompanied by bloodletting, of course.

The covenant of circumcision admitted Jews to the Abrahamic covenant whereby they became part of a chosen people. This, however, can hardly be what Jesus, Paul, Peter and the author of Hebrews had in mind by the blood of the covenant, though Strack and Billerbeck (vol. I, pp. 991, 992) report such views in Jewish circles. Rather the

---

10. James Denney, *The Death of Christ*, rev. ed. (London: Hodder & Stoughton, 1911), p. 216.
11. ibid., p. 216.

expression reports (Exod. 24:8) and harks back (Heb. 10:29 and 13:8) to the parallel whereby just as the blood of animals was shed on the occasion of inaugurating the 'old' Mosaic covenant (or covenant of law, or of Sinai) and was applied, part to a special altar and part to the people (see Exod. 24:4-8), so the new covenant (or Testament) was inaugurated by Christ's shed blood. An entirely new epoch of God's dealing with the human race was inaugurated by the cross. God is not imputing trespasses just now, having reconciled the world to Himself – at least this seems to be the teaching of 2 Cor. 5:19. (See later chapter on 'The Extent of the Atonement.')

A Ransom, or Price Paid for Redemption.

Lutron (noun) and *lutroō* (verb) and the augmented forms, *apolutrōsis* and *antilutron* are the New Testament words. In each appearance the basic idea is a price paid (ransom) for a certain result (redemption).

Lutron appears only twice in the New Testament, sixteen times if the derived and augmented *lutrōsis* (three), *apolutrōsis* (ten), *antilutron* (once) are included.

The *tron* ending on nouns from the most ancient times 'denotes a means' usually with 'the sense of payment for something' (TDNT, IV, p. 340), especially the money to release prisoners of war or to release someone from a bond or to gain freedom for a slave. Liddell and Scott, *Lexicon* cites passages in Pindar, Aeschulus and Plato where it is *lutron haimatos* (ransom price of blood) 'in expiation, an atonement' (*sub lutron*).

The Old Testament backgound is to be found chiefly in the passages where payment of money takes place. Examples are releasing a Hebrew slave (Lev. 19:20), remission of the death penalty for capital crime in certain cases (Exod. 21:30), or restoration of alienated family property (Lev. 25:24, 26, 51, 52), or from bondage of various sorts, including the lifetime obligation of Levites (Num. 3:12, 46, 48, 49, 51).

The word *lutron* in the Gospels appears only twice, both times in the saying of Jesus: 'the Son of Man came not to be ministered unto, but to minister, and to give his life a ransom for many' (Mark 10:45 KJV; parallel Matt. 20:28). '[G]ive his life' (in death, of course) emphasizes voluntary self-presentation. 'For' is the Greek *anti*, meaning in the place of or instead of, in the room of – the strongest Greek preposition for substitution of one person or thing for another. Morris makes this point strongly, summarizing his ten pages of discussion of the evidences:

> The natural meaning of the ransom saying is that Jesus' death was in the stead of the many, He was to give His life instead of their lives.... It may or may not be easy to integrate this into some way the atonement works, but either way we are not justified in evading the plain sense of the Greek.[12]

Lutro-ō, cognate to *lutron*, though translated 'to redeem' in the three New Testament occurrences, means to redeem *in a certain way*, viz.: to 'free by paying a ransom' (Bauer, Arndt, Gingrich, *Lexicon*). The occurrence at Luke 24:21 is not directly relevant. At Titus 2:14, which says Christ 'gave himself [the ransom price] for us to redeem [*lutroō*] us' seems to refer to the saying of Mark 10:45. The third and only remaining verse puts the 'precious blood, as of a lamb' in contrasting parallel with 'gold or silver,' the usual price in human redemption of various sorts – either in Roman practice or Jewish Old Testament practice. This shows that providing payment by one for another, or others, is the governing idea.

Lutrōsis. The ending sis in Greek nouns often as here indicates the result of whatever the corresponding verb describes, hence, 'a ransoming,' 'being redeemed' (Liddell and Scott, *Lexicon*). In two New Testament cases it refers to the redemption that is awaited for by Israel or Jerusalem (Luke 1:66; 2:38) understood in context as 'salvation from [national] enemies' (Luke 1:71). The third and last time it is employed in the New Testament (Heb. 9:12) represents Christ as the Great High Priest who not through 'the blood of goats and calves, but by his own blood he entered in once [for all] into the holy place, having obtained eternal redemption [*lutrōsis*].' Redemption, or as noted earlier in this paragraph, *salvation*, is by the blood of Christ, the *lutron* presented as *sacrifice* in the sense of the Levitical sacrifices presented to God in the Mosaic system. The latter were typical (predictive) of the former. Hence the Levitical sacrifices had fulfilled their purpose when Christ was crucified. Therefore on the afternoon of that transaction at Calvary God Himself rent the old temple veil and thirty years later wrecked the temple that housed it, bringing the typical system to an end.

Apolutrōsis, an augmented form of *lutrōsis*, has been a subject of controversy among scholars, a controversy which for present purposes must be passed by. It is cogently argued that the idea of price paid for redemption inherent in

---

12. Leon Morris, *The Apostolic Preaching of the Cross* (Grand Rapids, MI: Eerdmans, 1965), p. 35.

lutron is brought into the word and the *apo* (away from) only augments the meaning. Whatever the case may be, in Romans 3:24, where it is rendered redemption ('through the redemption that is in Christ Jesus') *apolutrōsis* seems clearly to point to the result of ransom payment. John Chrysostom, for whom Greek was his first language and thus should have known what *apolutrōsis* means, commented, 'And he said not simple ransoming, but 'ransoming away,' so that we no more come into slavery' (comment on Romans 3:24, 25 in *Homilies on Romans*, no. vii).[13]

Antilutron. In the single New Testament occurrence of this rare word the text reads literally, 'who gave himself a substitutionary ransom [*antilutron*] on behalf of [*huper*] all' (1 Tim. 1:6). I shall reserve further discussion of this to later treatment of the *antilutron* of the benefits (i.e. for whom the price was paid) of the atonement in the chapter entitled 'The Extent of the Atonement.'

Purchase or Price Paid for Redemption.

Agorazō and *exagorazō*. The marketplace of a Greek city (as in Matt. 11:16; eleven times in New Testament) was called an *agora* (Latin, *forum*) from the earlier sense of a gathering of people (hence the medical term, *agoraphobia*, fear of crowds).

Though originally meaning to frequent the *agora* (*forum*), in New Testament times *agorazo* meant to buy, purchase, and is so uniformly translated. Twenty-four times it is employed in the New Testament in connection with purchase of a field (Matt. 27:7), grave wrappings (Mark 15:46), food (John 4:8). Six times believers are said to be 'bought,' in obvious reference to the atoning work of Christ in His death ('bought with a price,' 1 Cor. 6:20 and 7:23; the 'Lord who *bought* them,' 2 Peter 2:1 NIV; '*purchased* men for God,' Rev. 5:9 NIV; '*purchased* out of the earth,' Rev. 14:3 ASV; '*purchased* from among men,' Rev. 14:4 ASV [emphasis added]).

Exagorazō is used only twice. The prefix ex- conveys the sense of out from, hence 'bought out from,' or as in most Versions 'redeemed' *from under or from the curse* of the law. The legal-commercial figure is clearly understandable without elaboration. The analogy in these two words is drawn more from universal world culture than Old Testament Jewish culture.

Some writers take notice of *peripoieomai*, still another word for purchasing, used once with reference to the atonement, by Paul in his exhortation to the Ephesian elders, saying 'Take heed . . . to feed the church of the Lord, which he purchased with his own blood' (Acts 20:28 ASV; only one other occurrence, 1 Tim. 3:13). (There is disagreement as to the spelling of the verb in lexicons.) 'To make one's own, get for oneself' is the agreed sense.[14] This puts a unique slant on atonement – the price paid by the heavenly bridegroom to obtain a bride – comes to mind. See *peripoiēsis* and *peripoieō* in the lexicons and Leon Morris, *Apostolic Preaching of the Cross,* pp. 56, 57.

Reconcile, Reconciliation, Atone, Atonement.

The Greek terms are the verb *katallassō* and cognates including the noun *katallagē*, rendered in the Bible as reconcile, reconciliation, atone and atonement. It addresses the problem of our estrangement – alienation, enmity – toward God and His toward us as sinners.

The history of the words 'atone' and 'atonement' in English usage indicates that in the century before the 1611 Authorized Version of the Bible the words were usually understood as at-one and at-one-ment. Hence, the meaning of 'atone' and 'atonement' was precisely the same as reconcile and reconciliation. Atone and atonement in the sense of making amends to offended parties or appeasing someone's wrath was coming into use, however, as the marginal reading of the Authorized Version at Job 33:24 shows. By the time of Blackstone's *Commentaries on English Law* (1768) the sense of appease, propitiate was apparently the common one (*Oxford English Dictionary*).

It is therefore important to keep steadily before the mind that when atonement is met in the Authorized Version (KJV) of Romans 5:11 (a very important text) it means the same as reconciliation at 2 Corinthians 5:18 and *reconciling* at 2 Corinthians 5:19. (*Atonement* [KJV] in Old Testament sacrificial ritual texts will be treated shortly in connection with *propitiation*.)

Inaccurately, atonement has been widely adopted as the comprehensive name for all our Lord did in His Calvary work, thus making this diversion necessary.

---

13. John Chrysostom, in *Nicene and Post-Nicene Fathers xiv*, ed. P. Schaff (repr. Peabody: Hendrickson Publ., 1994), i, 11, p. 377.
14. Zerwick and Grosvenor, *Grammatical Analysis of the Greek New Testament* (Rome: Biblical Institute Press, 1981), p. 483.

Reconciliation (*Katallagē*) and reconcile (*Katallassō*) are from a Greek word-group rooted in *alassō*. This root and all related words have to do with change or exchange. They are words of relationship – of changed relationship. The previous existence of alienation, enmity, is presupposed.

Paul's use of these words evidently came over from his experience in Greek-speaking Judaism where 'If God renounces his wrath and is gracious again… this is called a *kattalagēnai* [reconciliation] of God' (F. Buechsel, *TDNT*, I, 254). So, Paul having spoken of God's wrath in Romans 5:9, declares we are 'now justified by his blood' (same verse) and goes on to say we 'were reconciled to God by the death of his Son' using the word *katallasso* for 'reconciled.' Divine wrath against us makes reconciliation necessary for salvation, a reconciliation effected by Christ's death.

Sin caused estrangement for us in many respects: primarily, of course from God, as David felt very deeply (Ps. 51:3, 4) and as Paul frequently lamented: 'alienated from the life of God' (Eph. 4:18), even become enemies of our Creator (Rom. 8:7), 'ungodly… sinners' under 'divine wrath' (Rom. 5:6, 8, 9). This is where we all were Paul says, before 'we were reconciled to God by the death of his Son' (Rom. 5:6-10).

We are, as born sinners, also alienated from our own primeval, created goodness, viz.: 'being dead in your trespasses and the uncircumcision of your flesh' (Col. 2:13; Eph. 2:1).

And being sinners at heart we are alienated in heart from other people, as manifest in envy, jealousy, malice, lust, slanderous talk, all graphically detailed in biblical history and law – nowhere more vigorously than in Jesus' oral denunciations of scribes and Pharisees (Matt. 15:1, 7, 19–20) and in Paul's Epistles (Rom. 1:28-32).

The biblical name for God's alienation from sinners is *wrath*. A teacher who would ignore this fact is not a good guide and any sinner who rejects it is beyond help, for until one knows in the heart through conscience that God's wrath leads to judgment and punishment he will not repent. This wrath toward sinners is the steady state of the same God who 'loved the world' in this manner, that 'he gave his only begotten Son' (John 3:16 KJV). John goes on to say, 'he that believeth not the Son shall not see life; but the wrath [Gr. *orgē*] of God abideth [remains] on him' (John 3:36 KJV).

If there is anything liberal theology is agreed upon it is that the frequent biblical references to God's wrath (anger, displeasure, indignation, rage, vengeance) must be interpreted down to mean something like frustrated love. Or failing in that, wrath is an automatic operation of impersonal forces a bit like Hindu karma.[15] Liberalism in all its varieties is sure there is no propitiation of divine wrath. Love and sovereignty cover all.[16] 'God is love' is the ruling idea in liberalism. Further history of theology to the present hour proves that often as not when any preacher or theologian announces doubt or rejection of the wrath of God and its correlates, final judgment and hell, he has started down the slippery slope.

> God is holy; he totally… distances himself from sin… corruption, and the resultant filth and guilt. He maintains his purity and rejects, fights against, and destroys that which would offend, attack or undo his holiness and love. God's anger and wrath must always be seen in relation to his maintaining and defending his attributes of love and holiness, as well as his righteousness and justice… A consequence of his wrath is vengeance, punishment, and death.[17]

Later I shall seek to show how 'in wrath' God 'remembers mercy.' It is true that He was loving and merciful to the human race long before the Son of God appeared to reveal the mercy of the Lawgiver as lawful. Whatever we say on this subject should in no wise weaken the force of the many warnings to 'fear him who has power to destroy both soul and body in hell' of which the most fierce is probably Hebrews 10:26-31. I have never read it publicly without an evident response of shock in the audience.

Wrath is God's reaction to the breaking of His law. 'The law was given by Moses but Grace and Truth came by Jesus Christ.' Law and gospel (i.e. grace in Christ) are in both Testaments and every dispensation, but God's wrath over broken law is a more explicit theme in the Old Testament than in the New Testament (see John 1:14-17; Titus 2:11; 1 Tim. 1:9, 10; Titus 3:3-6). Not strangely, God's warnings and judgments are mixed with grace and promise usually – like the rainbow after the Great Flood. But there will be no rainbow about God's throne (as in John's vision of Rev. 4 and 5) at the final judgment of the ungodly: 'And I saw a great white throne, and him that sat on it, from whose face the earth and the heaven fled away' (Rev. 20:11 KJV; cf. 12-15). The banishment of Adam

---

15. W. C. Robinson, 'Wrath of God,' in *Evangelical Dictionary of Theology*, ed. W. Elwell (Grand Rapids, MI: Baker Books, 1984), p. 1196.
16. D. M. Baillie, *God was in Christ: An Essay on Incarnation and Atonement* (New York: Charles Scriber's Sons, 1948), chap. vii.
17. G. Van Gronigen, 'Wrath of God,' *Evangelical Dictionary of Biblical Theology*, ed. W.Elwell (Grand Rapids, MI: Baker Books, 1996), p. 845.

and Eve from the Garden; the curse on Cain; the Great Flood; the awful judgments of the plagues of Egypt and the destruction of Pharaoh and his armies; the end of Belshazzar and his drunken lords; the names of Korah, Dathan and Abiran, Hophni and Phinehas, and Achan; the destruction of Jerusalem and captivities of both Samaritan and Judean kingdoms; the fiery judgment of Sodom and Gomorrah, and much more witness overwhelmingly to God's wrath. To the same may be referred the pronouncements of Jesus on the Jewish cities of the time; the terrible end of Judas; the deaths of Annanias and Sapphira, of Herod; and the threats of damnation by Jesus, Paul, Peter, Hebrews and John. The means by which God brings about a new relation of reconciliation is propitiation. We next attend to that matter.

Propitiation (Appeasement).

This important word is used only three times in the English Bible (KJV) and not at all in some recent Versions, viz.: 'Whom [Christ Jesus] God hath set forth to be a propitiation [*hilastērion*] through faith in his blood, to declare his [God's] righteousness for the remission of sins' (Rom. 3:25 KJV). The sense of 'propitiation' (*hilastērion*) here is propitiatory sacrifice. 'He [Jesus Christ] is the propitiation [*hilasmos*] for our sins, (1 John 2:2). 'God... loved us and sent his Son to be the propitiation [*hilasmon*] for our sins' (1 John 4:10).

If there is any word to focus the specific meaning of Jesus' death on the cross it is our word 'propitiate' (and propitiation) – as opposed say to a more general term such as sacrifice and a word of different specific meaning such as expiate. Propitiate means to cause someone unfavorably inclined to become favorably inclined. Synonyms are 'appease, conciliate (one offended) (Lat. *propitari*, render favourable).'[18]

Confusion between expiation and propitiation will be avoided as long as it is kept in mind that sins (offenses, trespasses, etc.) are expiated. Wrath, or the person who is wrathful is propitiated. One does not expiate God; one expiates sin. Nor does one propitiate sin; one propitiates God or His wrath. Since the same act of offering sacrifice viewed from the aspect of sin is expiation and, from the aspect of God, propitiation, confusion arises. Every successful propitiation therefore is also an expiation but propitiation and expiation are not the same. A pound of salt may be seasoning to a batch of my dill pickles but as regard the weeds in someone's asparagus bed it is a herbicide. It is not herbicide in pickles nor a seasoning in an asparagus bed. So in the passages that speak of Christ as 'propitiation for our sins' it is not the sins that are propitiated. Rather with reference to the wrath of God occasioned by the sins, God is propitiated.

It is no accident that the words expiate and expiation do not appear even once in the Authorized Version of 1611. The three occurrences of propitiation (Rom. 3:25; 1 John 2:2; 4:10) clearly refer to the death of Christ as having specific effect on God's attitude toward sinners – a change from disfavor to favor. In 1611 about everyone was able to accept that God is a just law-giver who has a care even for His creatures who do not love or obey Him. He could also hate both sin and sinner (e.g. Mal. 3:1; Rom. 9:13) yet love the same creatures supremely (John 3:16).

Liberal theology cannot accept that men are depraved through and through, deserving hell, or that God is absolutely holy, One who cannot break His own holy law by failing ultimately to enforce its penalties. Orthodox evangelical doctrine, anchored in *all* the Bible, proclaims all of a text like Exodus 34:5-7, 'the LORD, a God merciful and gracious... forgiving iniquity and transgression and sin, but who will by no means clear the guilty, visiting the iniquity of the fathers,' etc. (see Num. 14:18).

That expiation of sin is necessary to propitiation of divine wrath may not be denied. What we protest is the exclusion of propitiation (appeasement) of wrath in accomplishment of reconciliation of the world and in redemption.

In liberal thought (which tends also to reject divine immutability and impassibility) the redemptive suffering in atonement was not on the cross but 'the forgiveness of sins... implies a redemptive sin-bearing, a costly atonement, in the heart of God.'[19] Atonement is finished only in a sense of demonstration, in this thinking. A combination of covenant and incarnation is Karl Barth's notion of atonement,[20] incarnation and 'super-history' for Brunner.[21] Brunner denies that God is reconciled in the atonement.[22] In both Barth and Brunner the depravity of man and the

---

18. Oxford English Dictionary.
19. Baillie, *God in Christ*, p. 190.
20. Karl Barth, as set forth in the four volumes on 'The Doctrine of Reconciliation,' in his *Church Dogmatics*, trans. G. W. Bromily (Edinburgh: T & T Clark, 1956, 1974).
21. Emil Brunner, *The Mediator: A Study of the Central Doctrine of the Christian Faith*, trans. Olive Wyon (Philadelphia, PA: The Westminster Press, 1947), p. 504.
22. ibid., p. 519.

holiness of God seem to be more metaphysical distance than personal moral-spiritual alienation. Hence incarnation and covenant can secure reconciliation apart from satisfaction of the legal requirement and the propitiation of the wrath of a personal God.

Biblically speaking, this polarity within the divine Being can be accepted and explained on the basis of penal, vicarious propitiation and in no other way. So the liberal bias against the total depravity of man, the absolute holiness of God and penal-substitutionary atonement has also removed propitiation of the divine wrath from Romans 3:25; 1 John 2:2; and 4:10 where expiation replaces propitiation in the Revised Standard Version and NRSV as also the Revised English Bible. Even the New International Version (in an apparent mood of accommodation) has the non-specific 'sacrifice of atonement' at Romans 3:25 and 'atoning sacrifice' at 1 John 2:2 and 4:10.

The group of Greek words involved in the three texts and many more where the idea of propitiation is present includes *hilaskomai* (Luke 18:13), *hilasmos* (Heb. 2:17), *hilasterion*. Note the *hilas* element in each. *TDNT* has thirty-four pages on this word-group. L. Morris devotes 161 pages of the 280 pages of *The Apostolic Preaching of the Cross* to this word group, devoting extended proof of the prominence of 'The Wrath of God' in Scripture. Both these authorities demonstrate that the sense of appeasement, propitiation cannot be expelled from the word. C. H. Dodd agrees, but thinks nevertheless that when the New Testament says propitiate it means expiate.[23]

On the basis of Dodd's studies, D. M. Baillie acknowledges that these words mean appeasement and propitiation throughout Greek literature. Yet he flatly states that such cannot be the case in the New Testament.

> The rendering 'propitiation' is misleading, being in accord with pagan usage but foreign to Biblical usage.... [H]owever we translate those terms borrowed from the Jewish sacrificial system, it is quite plain (sic), they undergo a transformation of meaning because of the really extraordinary setting.[24]

Let us close on this point with Leon Morris' words in summarizing his lengthy study on propitiation:

> [T]he process of propitiation envisaged in the Bible is one which involves an element of substitution. In both the Old and New Testaments the means of propitiation is the offering up [as a sacrifice] of a gift, the gift of life yielded up to death by God's own appointment. The Scripture is clear that the wrath of God is visited upon sinners or else that the Son of God dies for them. Either sinners are punished for their misdoings or else there takes place... 'that self-punishment which combines the activities of punishing and forgiving.' Either we die or he dies. But 'God commendeth His own love toward us, in that while we were yet sinners, Christ died for us' (Rom. 5:8).[25]

A Penal, Substitutionary Sacrifice.

That death in the human race is the punishment for sin rather than simply the end of life in a natural process was treated at length and in detail in connection with hamartiology. That understanding is assumed here.

a) First, let us try to clarify the idea of penal substitution. We begin by taking notice of two clear Scripture texts affirming the vicariousness of Christ's death. They clearly assert or imply He received the *punishment* due us for our sin and sins. Isaiah 53:6 (KJV) says, 'the LORD hath laid on him the iniquity of us all.' As discussed in hamartiology, 'iniquity' (Heb. '*Awon*) is the specific Hebrew word for punishment or deserved punishment (guilt) for sin, so rendered, for example at Genesis 4:13, 'My punishment is greater than I can bear.' Galatians 3:13 says, 'Christ redeemed us from the curse of the law by becoming a curse for us.' The curse of the law was, of course, the punishment for breaking the law prescribed by the same law.

As we shall note again later, Anselm put a rather special slant on the doctrine of substitutionary-propitiatory atonement and sometimes it is supposed he was the first to phrase the doctrine in any form. But the doctrine, derived of course from Scripture, was stated by many of the Fathers and perhaps never better than by Augustine (d. 430) more than half a millennium before Anselm (d. 1109). Augustine's understanding of the vicarious sacrifice suits the modern mind better than Anselm's somewhat medieval appeal to the dignity of persons. In the *Enchiridion on Faith, Hope and Love*, written near the end of his life of seventy-six years he said:

> He was called sin [2 Cor. 5:21] that he might be sacrificed to wash away sin. For, under the Old Covenant, sacrifices for sin were called sins [i.e. the sin-offering of Leviticus (Hos. 4:8)]. And He, of whom all these

---

23. *Moffat New Testament Commentary, Romans,* on Romans 3:24, 25 and *The Bible and the Greeks* (London, 1935), p. 95 as cited by Baillie, see below and Morris, *The Apostolic Preaching of the Cross,* p. 178.
24. Baillie, *God in Christ,* p. 188.
25. Morris, *Apostolic Preaching of the Cross,* p. 185.

sacrifices were types and shadows, was Himself truly made sin. Hence the apostle, after saying, 'We pray you in Christ's stead be ye reconciled to God,' forthwith adds: 'for He hath made Him to be sin for us who knew no sin, that we might be made the righteousness of God in Him... That is, [God] hath made Him a sacrifice for our sins, by which we might be reconciled to God. He, then, being made sin, just as we are made righteousness (our righteousness being not our own, but God's, not in ourselves, but in Him); He being made sin, not His own, but ours, not in Himself, but in us, showed by the likeness of sinful flesh in which He was crucified, that though sin was not in Him, yet that in a certain sense He died to sin, by dying in the flesh which was the likeness of sin; and that although He Himself had never lived the old life of sin, yet by His resurrection He typified our new life springing up out of the old death in sin.[26]

These words on the subject by one of the greatest theologians between Paul and the Reformation show distinctly that the doctrine of justification as the imputed righteousness of Christ was no more 'invented' by Luther to explain his experience of forgiveness than substitutionary atonement was invented by Anselm or some other theologian. Both are necessarily derived from Scripture.

The aspect of substitution, 'the just [Christ] for the unjust [sinful people]' (1 Peter 3:18 KJV) is present in each of the previously treated seven aspects of the meaning of Christ's sufferings and death. Now, we direct attention to the chief biblical emphasis: Jesus the Son of God died on the cross in our place, being punished fully and exhaustively for our sins. I shall usually let the biblical statements stand by themselves, for quite apart from context or exegetical argument they speak plainly. Though neither the word substitutionary nor vicarious appears anywhere in our Bible, the idea of vicarious sacrifice fills its pages.

In the first place, direct, categorical statements of penal substitution (in KJV) of Old Testament prophecy, Isaiah 53, viz.:

'[H]e hath borne our griefs' (v. 4) 'and carried our sorrows' (v. 4), 'wounded for our transgressions' (v. 5), 'bruised for our iniquities' (v. 5), 'the chastisement of our peace was upon him' (v. 5), 'with his stripes we are healed' (v. 5). 'The LORD hath laid [heavily] on him the iniquity [punishment] of us all' (v. 6), 'for the transgression of my people was he stricken' (v. 8). 'Yet it pleased the LORD to bruise him' (v. 10), i.e. God's plan for redemption was to bruise the Lamb slain from the foundation of the world. God made 'his soul an offering' (v. 10), 'he was numbered with the transgressors' (v. 12). '[H]e bare the sin of many' (v. 12).

I once published a book of exposition of Isaiah 52:13–53:12 – fruit of several years of teaching exegesis of the Hebrew text.[27] As I wrote my heart was made full of thanks to God for its clear presentation of the saving work of our Lord in His suffering and death 'in my place.' The heart of the passage is Isaiah 53:5, which for exegetical purposes I translate 'And he was pierced for our transgressions; crushed for our punishment; the chastisement of our peace [reconciliation] was upon him, and by his welt healing is for us.' My closing remarks on the verse, citing two famous authors, were these: 'Dr. Albert Barnes... said concerning these words that if it is possible for human speech to describe substitutionary atonement, these words do so. Franz Delitzch – than whom few more learned scholars ever lived – said that such is the only possible construction to be placed on these words.'[28]

Five select categorical statements from the New Testament now follow. They are sufficient to make the point that the Bible categorically affirms that the Son of God was slain in the sinner's place. '[I]f one died for all, then were all dead' (2 Cor. 5:14 KJV). 'For... he made him to be sin who knew no sin, so that in him we might become the righteousness of God' (2 Cor. 5:21). 'Christ redeemed us from the curse of the law by becoming a curse for us' (Gal. 3:13). '[Christ] himself bore our sins in his body on the tree' (1 Peter 2:24). 'For Christ also suffered once for sins, the righteous for the unrighteous, that he might bring us to God' (1 Peter 3:18).

In each of these quotations 'for' is a rendering of *huper*, Gr. 'on behalf of.' The usual word for 'in the place of' is *anti*, which we will treat shortly. In later Greek authors *huper* often signified 'in place of, in the name of' (Euripides, Polybius, Josephus) and 'in papyri very often... to explain that the writer is writing as the representation of an illiterate person... Sometimes the meaning *in place of* merges with *on behalf of* ' – examples being Romans 9:3, 1 Corinthians 15:29, 2 Corinthians 5:14 (Bauer, Arndt and Gingrich, *Lexicon, sub huper*, p. 846). See Morris' one-page note presenting evidence for the substitutionary meaning.[29]

---

26. Augustine, *Enchiridion on Faith, Hope and Love*, trans. J. F. Shaw, ed. Henry Paolucci (Chicago: Regnery, 1961, 1966), pp. 51, 52.
27. Culver, *The Sufferings and the Glory of the* LORD*'s Righteous Servant* (1958, 2001). See bibliography.
28. ibid., p. 74.
29. Morris, *The Apostolic Preaching of the Cross*, p. 59.

b) In the second place is the employment of the preposition *anti* in our Lord's paramount declaration of the purpose of His earthly mission 'to give his life... for many' (Matt. 20:28; Mark 10:45). If there is any preposition whose normal and usual sense is 'to indicate that one person or thing is, or is to be, replaced by another *instead of, in place of*' it is *anti* (Bauer, Arndt and Gingrich, *Lexicon, sub anti*, p. 72). Bauer, Arndt and Gingrich go on to cite Matthew 2:22 and Luke 11:11 as defining texts, viz.: 'in place of [in the room of, KJV] his father Herod'; 'instead of a fish... a serpent.' Of course if Jesus died 'in the stead of [*anti*] many' it was also 'on behalf of them' as in 1 Timothy 2:5. But nothing should redirect the force of *anti* in the two reports (Matt. 20:28; Mark 10:45) of Jesus' express purpose of becoming a substitutionary sacrifice for sinners. We shall return to these two passages in connection with the extent of the atonement.

c) In the third place, the Old Testament sacrificial system clearly teaches the principle of atonement by substitution. No text categorically says animals were punished vicariously for the sinful men who brought them to the altar and slew them there. Rather, the principle was assumed in the language describing the events at the altar and their meaning. Furthermore, the New Testament assumes the same in employing various aspects of Old Testament ritual sacrifice in interpreting Christ's death.

Many times the Mosaic law states that any animal designated for sacrifice must have no physical defect (Lev. 22:21, for example; cf. 3:1, 6; 22:18–20; Exod. 12:5, *et al*). Peter relates this to the sinlessness of Jesus, divine-human sacrifice for our sin (1 Peter 1:19; cf. 1 Cor. 5:7, 8; Deut. 16:3, 4; Lev. 2:11). Professor W. G. Moorehead of United Presbyterian Seminary called attention to the fact 'the same word which the Septuagint translators used for "without blemish" is applied to Christ.'[30]

The offerer always laid his hands on the head of the sacrificial animal before slaying it, designating it as his ritual substitute in what followed in the shedding of the animal's blood, slaughter and burning some or all the flesh on the altar. This matter is discussed at great length in commentaries, biblical and systematic theological studies by scholars of every sort. Extreme liberals, who suppose religious practice in Israel must mean the same as similar practices in Canaan, Arabia or Mesopotamia, have said the whole affair was to supply food for the gods or, in Israel's case, for the LORD, or simply as a present. Others have said the animal was provided in this manner to furnish food for a communion meal with God – the LORD – eating His portion symbolically on the altar, the offerer, His family and the priests eating their portions in the vicinity of the altar. A festive, convivial, communion-with-God aspect of Old Testament sacrifice is prominent in the 'peace-offerings' (KJV), of course. There is scriptural support for the gift and communion aspects. Yet it is plain the main reason for animal sacrifice was atonement as the book of Leviticus says at least twenty-five times.

It seems necessary at this point to introduce the significance of the Old Testament sacrifices somewhat more fully and of their typical connection with Jesus' sacrifice in our place. I can do this best by adapting material from some unpublished lectures on the book of Leviticus.

The rites of the book must be explained as having at least a threefold significance. *First*, God designed to use them as a means of grace to mediate fellowship with Himself, i.e. personal salvation to all of Israel's commonwealth who accepted His revealed word by faith. Their first significance was as revelation of the designated saving means for the times. They remained so till Jesus rendered it all out of date by fulfilling their typical meaning. That salvation is by faith grounded in revelation needs no further proof here aside from a single text, Romans 10:17. That the sacrifices mediated forgiveness is stated over and over, as for example Numbers 15:27 and Leviticus 4:26. *Second*, they were intended as *predictive symbols*, that is, *types* of the perfect and final act of God whereby He provided redemption (salvation) for all who in faith receive it. The first (the type) was made possible because of the value of the second (antitype). *Third*, in a practical way the bloody sacrifices made known to human consciences of that age and ours, to heaven as well as earth, the absolute necessity of an act of redemption by 'the Mediator' – one both fully human and fully divine. As it is written: 'in these sacrifices there is a reminder of sin year after year. For it is impossible that the blood of bulls and goats should take away sins... offering repeatedly the same sacrifices, which can never take away sins. But... Christ had offered for all time a single sacrifice for sins' (Heb. 10:3, 4, 11, 12 RSV; see also Heb. 9:23-28).

This meaning of Old Testament Levitical ritual is advanced in the New Testament by five different terms. They refer to Mosaic ritual as: 1) 'a *shadow* [*skia*] [emphasis added] of the good things to come' (Heb. 10:1 RSV); 'only a

---

30. W. G. Moorehead, *Studies in Mosaic Institutions* (Dayton, OH: The Otterbein Publishing House, 1901), p. 140.

shadow [emphasis added] of what is to come; but the substance belongs to Christ' (Col. 2:17 RSV); 2) 'a *figure* [or parable] [*parabolē*] [emphasis added] for the time then present' (Heb. 9:9 KJV); 3) though employed of a person (Adam) not a ritual, Adam is said to be 'the figure [*tupos*] of him that was to come' (Rom. 5:14 KJV). Usually this Greek source of our word 'type' does not designate a predictive symbol such as theology means by 'type'. Of sixteen New Testament occurrences only possibly here does it do so. (See John 20:25; Heb. 8:5, where *tupos* means mark or copy, reversing type-antitype.) Hebrews 3–10 in various other ways draws parallels between Old Testament and New Testament, frequently pointing to typical connections. 4) Hebrews 9:24 says the Jewish holy places were a figure (KJV) (*antitupon*) of the heavenly sanctuary. But this does not relate to Old Testament typology and the same is the case with 5) Hebrews 9:23, in which temple and its furnishings are said to be 'copies' (RSV) (*hupodeigmata*) of 'heavenly things.'

Perhaps the most impressive statement is that Christ in heaven is now 'a minister of the true sanctuary, and of the true tabernacle, which the Lord pitched, and not man' (Heb. 8:2 KJV), showing an eternal *meaning*, as a copy of heavenly design, for the Old Testament ritual at the sanctuary, if not of its permanent existence. Still today we study the Tabernacle, its rituals, ministers and furnishings to understand spiritual truth of eternal value.

Much discussion of this large subject is not feasible here. Let us close on the matter by pointing out that as 'critical' and thoroughly competent an expert in such matters as Roland DeVaux argued that the laying on of the offerers' hands on the sacrificial victim indicated a representative connection [not his terms] if not identification or strict substitution (*Ancient Israel*, 1961, pp. 449, 433) and asserted, 'By sacrificial rites... the guilt of man is taken away' (p. 451).

The ideas of substitution and predictive symbolism present in the Old Testament ritual is treated in page after page by Patrick Fairbairn, perhaps the most authoritative writer on the typology of Scripture. I quote two brief passages. As one reads hold in mind that expiation of sin in Fairbairn's views also included propitiation of divine wrath, both ideas being present in the Hebrew word *Kaphar*, to cover, usually rendered 'to atone.' Patrick Fairbairn summarizes:

> To make our meaning perfectly understood... we shall go at once to... the very core of the religion of the Old Covenant – the rite of expiatory sacrifice. That this was typical, or prophetically symbolical of the death of Christ, is testified with much plainness and frequency in the New Testament.... Yet, independently of this connection with Christ's death, it had a meaning of its own, which it was possible for the ancient worshipper to understand, and, so understanding to present through it an acceptable service to God.... It was in its nature a symbolical transaction, embodying a threefold idea; first, that the worshipper having be.en guilty of sin, had forfeited his life to God; then, that life so forfeited must be surrendered to divine justice; and finally, that being surrendered in the way appointed, it was given back to him again by God, or he became re-established, as a justified person, in the divine favour and fellowship.[31]

Fairbairn also points out:

> For, in him alone was there real transference of man's guilt to one able and willing to bear it – in his death alone, the surrender of a life to God, such as could fitly stand in the room of that forfeited by the sinner – and in faith alone on his death, a full and conscious appropriation of the life of peace and blessing obtained by him for the justified. So that here only it is we perceive the idea of a true, sufficient, and perfect sacrifice converted into a living reality – such as the holy eye of God, and the troubled conscience of man, can alike rest on with perfect satisfaction. And while there appear precisely the same elements of truth in the ever recurring sacrifices of the Old Testament, and in the perfect sacrifice of the New, it is seen that what the one symbolically represented, the other actually possessed; what the one could only exhibit as a kind of acted lesson for the present relief of guilty consciences, the other makes known to us, as a work finally and for ever accomplished for all who believe in the propitiation of the cross.[32]

(For further study see C. F. Keil, *Manual of Biblical Archaeology* [Antiquities], sec. 43, I, 2750284; W. G. Moorehead, *Studies in Mosaic Institutions*, pp. 138-146; G. Vos, *Biblical Theology of Old & New Testaments*, pp. 172-189. All three are reverent evangelical scholars. Keil, however, seems to be in error on the meaning of the death of the sacrificial victims though he discusses the issues reverently and learnedly. Vos's treatment is brilliant, claiming no more or less than the Old Testament texts allow. Moorehead is succinct, readable, quotable and preachable. J. Barton Payne, *The Theology of the Old Testament* (pp. 380-394), I think claims too much support in Old Testament narrative and Law for

---

31. Patrick Fairbairn, *The Typology of Scripture i* (Smith and English: Philadelphia, PA: 1854), p. 68.
32. ibid., p. 69, see also ii, pp. 299–317.

the vicarious principle, but is helpful.[33] Vos, Moorehead and Payne lean heavily on the work of Fairbairn. In teaching biblical hermeneutics I found it necessary to collect and read a short shelf of books by recent and current authors. Every large treatment of biblical hermeneutics has a section on typology. Each has something to say about the typology of Old Testament sacrificial rituals – not greatly different from the older sources cited above, many cases citing the older works.)

---

33. J. Barton Payne, *The Theology of the Old Testament* (Grand Rapids, MI: Zondervan, 1962).

16
The Meaning of the Death of Christ
Part Three:
Atonement by Vicarious Satisfaction

Sophisticated Rejection.

At a certain stage of my education for the ministry I studied philosophy and religion for three years in classes under the very competent instruction of a recent Ph.D. from Yale Seminary and the University department of philosophy. By that time we held one another in some affection, so after class on the last day we spent some minutes in conversation. With my feelings (I suppose) exposed in body language and voice I asked this man a question designed to give me some assurance we were Christian brothers with common faith in the Savior: 'Dr Miller,' I inquired, 'Can we agree that everything we are and hope to be forever was secured for us by our Lord's death at Calvary?' The kind professor paused for several moments in deep thought, then gave this reply: 'It is true that the center of the Christian religion is the cross.' I went my way sorrowful, for he had evaded an opportunity to confess Jesus, as a believer in the saving power of the blood of Christ. He went on to spend the remaining years (he was not yet thirty) until retirement in one of the most 'liberal' seminaries in North America and finally in 'Seminex' the theological seminary established mainly with professors expelled from Concordia, Lutheran Church, Missouri Synod of St Louis because of their liberal theology. We corresponded annually with Christian greetings until his death.

Layman's Faith.

Many years later I used to buy eggs from an aged, neighboring farm wife, who with her husband were (and are) devout Roman Catholics. 'Ed' always used my incursion into the even tenor of their way to raise the subject of religion, eternal life, death and heaven. Of course, as frequent opportunities came, I quoted the Scriptures about salvation and as skilfully as I am capable, presented the gospel. Then, I proposed to this earnest seeker, 'Ed, will you agree with me that when you get safely to heaven you will not jump up and shout "I made it!" but you will think "I am here not by virtue of anything I have done for God but by what He has done for me. And He did it through my Savior Jesus Christ"? The old farmer soberly thought a moment and then with a bright smile softly spoke: 'That is right. That's the way it will be.'

    The first conversation illustrates the gulf between Christianity and apostate, liberal Protestant religion, the second the much obscured but essential agreement of historical orthodoxy, deeply felt, about the meaning and importance of what our Lord did for us. The Council of Trent did not quite destroy that faith in the hearts of many of the people over whom its dogmatic counsels have reigned these 400 years.

Atonement by vicarious satisfaction is present to some degree in all New Testament interpretation of Calvary's meaning even though there is great variety in the ways it is expressed. There are many passages in the Bible that in theological language define the doctrine *essentially*, but none *comprehensively*, as most theological writers agree. The Bible furnishes all the materials needed for theology, but it is a human task, under the Spirit's illumination to formulate doctrines and to relate them to the whole counsel of God and to our lives. So it must be with the critical matter of the meaning of the death (and life as well) of our Lord.

The Protestant Achievement.

We may perhaps regard the Protestant form of the doctrine of atonement as formulated early in the Reformation era and stated in several creeds, confessions and other summaries as the likely *ne plus ultra* of growth in the formulation of a thoroughly adequate statement of the doctrine. There is truly a consensus among evangelical Protestants, with some variations likely to remain moot. To parties in polemical debate no variation, of course, seems slight. The consensus is largely shared, as noted in chapter 11, with Roman Catholic and Eastern Orthodox theology. Though neither has uniform views held by all within the tradition, both tend to see the atonement as less than 'perfect.' It is the specific teaching of the Council of Trent 'that original sin is removed by the merits of Jesus Christ only, and that through baptism the merits of Christ are applied to adults and children.'[1] Further, '[E]ternal life is both a gift or grace promised by God and a reward for his own good works and merits.'[2] Among Calvinists there is some disagreement as to whether the vicarious satisfaction was for the elect only or for every man, woman and child in the human race, and if so, in what sense. We shall have more to say about this Calvinist controversy in a later chapter.

Reformation theology was mainly about soteriology – provision of salvation wholly by God in Christ, reception wholly by faith. The main issue was justification and all the blessings of salvation with it. The growing desire of the time was experience of salvation in the heart, an inward conscious assurance of salvation that the paraphernalia of the medieval Roman Church was not providing because it did not preach a finished work of Christ and the sufficiency of faith to appropriate it.

Though stated in the main in the eleventh century (Anselm) and somewhat improved in the thirteenth (Aquinas) it was not well understood or preached by the church to the masses who were spiritually famished for want of it.

Luther's Beginnings.

Luther's proclamation of justification by faith and faith alone, as far as man's receiving it is concerned, is well known. This justification by faith rests precisely on an atonement by vicarious satisfaction that is finished as to time and complete as to its provisions for all damage caused by the fall. Though Luther never wrote a treatise on atonement by satisfaction, he referred to it constantly. Paul Althaus in his fine work *The Theology of Martin Luther* has shown with dozens of fully documented citations from the *Weimar Edition* of Luther's Works and the English translation, *Luther's Works*, that Luther held firmly to the theory of atonement by substitutionary satisfaction as we know it today.[3] Martin Luther *wrote* more theology in his rather short life as an evangelical controversialist, preacher, pastor and professor than many in his profession today *read* in a lifetime. Yet, despite the wide range of his interest and variety of expression, his views can be summarized. Despite developmental stages there are constants in his doctrine of reconciliation and redemption.

He incorporates Anselm's doctrine of atonement but improves it. A holy God cannot simply forget about His law and wrath for broken law and forgive sinners unless His righteousness is satisfied. Christ is the One who by taking the sinner's place provides that satisfaction. As Althaus summarizes Luther:

> Christ makes satisfaction for sinners in a twofold way. He fulfils the will of God expressed in the law; he suffers the punishment of sin, the wrath of God. Both are done in our place and for our benefit.... Christ has not only

---

1. Ludwig Ott, *Fundamentals of Catholic Dogma*, trans. P. Lynch, 4th ed. (Rockford: TAN Books & Publishers, 1974), p. 189. See also Henry Denzinger, *The Sources of Catholic Dogma*, trans. R. J. Deferrari (St Louis: Herder & Herder, 1954, 1957), p. 790.
2. Ott, *Fundamentals*, p. 264. See Denzinger, *Sources*, par. 809.
3. Paul Althaus, *The Theology of Martin Luther*, trans. Robert C. Schultz (Philadelphia, PA: Fortress Press, 1966), chap. 17, pp. 201–211.

fulfilled the law, but he has suffered the punishment which the law pronounces over transgressors. Only this fully satisfies God's righteousness.[4]

In *Cur Deus Homo* Anselm had proposed only two possibilities for satisfying the requirements of a holy God's righteous law – either punishment for breaking it or satisfaction by keeping it.[5] Luther asserted that satisfaction took place through punishment – not of the sinner but of the sinner's substitute.

This is presented by Luther in a profusion of declarations of God's grace, mercy and compassion for the sinner's distress.

It has been pointed out that Luther took the position 'in all stages of his writing' that the article, 'descended into hell,' is part of the agony on the cross and that in this Calvin and most Reformed agreed.[6] Yet 'Luther also teaches a descent into hell after his death'[7] which brought him trouble later. 'In spite of this, there is no doubt that Luther's own personal understanding of Christ's descent into hell relates to his passion, Gethsemane and Golgotha.'[8]

Luther, like many pulpiteers before and since, sometimes portrayed the redemptive work of Christ as a battle against Satan and other demonic powers. Saint Paul, of course, does so also. God, he says, used these powers in His own service to bring about the events of Calvary – another ancient theme that we have already noticed. In Luther's large commentary on Galatians he expounds this understanding. Yet he does not advocate anything like a satanic ransom.

Luther also had very much to say about our being confronted with Christ's victory when we hear the Word preached; Christ meets the powers of evil in our hearts and we embrace Him by faith. Neo-orthodox writers refer to this as the 'contemporaneity' of Christ. They relish this aspect of Luther's teaching and employ it vigorously in promoting an existentialist interpretation of Christ's power to save us poor folk whose main problem is self-alienation. This of course is not what Luther intended.

This is the language of Lutheran orthodoxy to the present hour. As one who occasionally attends services in a congregation of the Lutheran Church Missouri Synod, I can assure the reader this theology is prominently proclaimed in the liturgy and enshrined in dozens of hymns (some singable!) and announced every month in the rite of the Lord's Supper. The well-marked pages of the orthodox Lutheran works in my library certify the continuing health of Luther's doctrine of atonement by vicarious sacrifice among orthodox Lutherans.

Melancthon's Common Places (*Loci Communes*) and the Lutheran Confessions.

Melanchthon, Luther's disciple and systematizer (d. 1560), in his summary of evangelical doctrines, *Loci Communes* (final ed. 1555),[9] added little to Luther but put Lutheran doctrines in rational order and succinct language as the *Augsburg Confession* (1530) did seminally in a brief article on justification (Part I, art. iv).[10]

The Lutheran Reformation developed the essential elements of the Protestant consensus on atonement a bit ahead of the Calvinistic developments at Geneva and other cities of the Reformed. It appears in the Augsburg Confession (1530) in a section on justification by faith, saying in part: 'Men... are justified by grace for Christ's sake through faith, when they believe that they are received into favor, and their sins forgiven for Christ's sake, who by his death made satisfaction for our transgressions. This faith God imputes for righteousness before him' (*Augsburg Confession*, Part I, art. iv). No mention is made here (or in Luther's Catechisms) of Christ's meriting eternal life for us vicariously by His doing God's will and keeping of His law (active obedience). Yet, Melanchthon in several sentences (no extended treatments) implies this in *Loci Communes*. The *Formula of Concord* (1576), last of the primary Lutheran creeds, expressly, but without employing the words vicarious or substitutionary, many times affirms the full doctrine of substitutionary satisfaction.

---

4. Althaus, *Theology of Luther*, p. 203.
5. A recent complete English translation of *Cur Deus Homo* (Why God Became Man) employed here is *Anselm of Canterbury III*, ed. and trans. J. Hopkins and H. Richardson (Toronto and New York: The Edward Mellen Press, 1976), pp. 43–137. Mr Hopkins taught philosophy at the University of Minnesota, Mr Richardson at the University of Toronto.
6. Althaus, *Theology of Luther*, p. 207.
7. ibid.
8. ibid.
9. Citations herein are from *Melanchthon on Christian Doctrine: Loci Communes*, 1555, trans. and ed. C. L Manschreck, intro. by H. Engelland (Oxford: Oxford University Press, 1965; paperback ed., Grand Rapids, MI: Baker Books, 1982). *Loci Communes* means Common Topics (of doctrine).
10. Philip Schaff, *The Creeds of Christendom vol. iii*, 1877 (Grand Rapids, MI: Baker Books, 1966), p. 10.

One example among many declares that 'Christ is truly our righteousness... the whole Christ according to both natures, to wit: in his sole, most absolute obedience which he rendered to the Father even unto death, as God and man, and thereby merited for us remission of all our sins and eternal life' and goes on to quote Romans 5:19 (*The Formula of Concord, Art. III, par. I*).[11]

All the salient features of the Reformation doctrine of atonement are present in the Formula. God became incarnate Jesus Christ to mediate our salvation. He did so as God-man, Mediator of God to man and man to God. As God, He had no obligation to the law to meet the ritual and ceremonial requirements of law but did voluntarily fulfill them actively as our Substitute.

This is often designated Christ's active obedience. He also vicariously assumed the penalties for man's breaking of God's law by suffering and dying in our stead. The Formula of Concord mentions the resurrection after the obedience and the Passion to affirm that the resurrection brought the work of atonement to successful conclusion. Nothing more needs to be done. It is finished. *Ne plus ultra*. There is no further sacrifice for sins (Heb. 10:26).

It has been objected frequently that Christ's life of active obedience was for *Himself* as a member of the race, and therefore only His 'obedience unto death,' passive obedience, was involved in satisfaction for sin. I shall not enlarge this already lengthy discussion save to point to the twenty-seven pages of Berkouwer's book.[12] He surveys the history of the discussion through Protestant dogmatics. I endorse his view that the Bible 'designates the work of Christ as obedience' both by His life (Heb. 5:8) and by His death (Phil. 2:8).

Much of this was shared by the Roman Church, but the Reformation applied the logic of the finished work of redemption in rejecting the notions of reiteration, repetition, reapplication, etc., brought out to defend the so-called 'sacrifice of the [Christian] altar,' or the Mass. Any place for merit for salvation from sin – pre-baptismal, post-baptismal or otherwise – was also thereby thrown out. 'Jesus paid it all' making satisfaction for our sins by taking the penalty in our place and providing title to eternal life by obeying the law of God *in our place*.

Anselm worked out most of these features in *Cur Deus Homo* (why the God-man) 400 years earlier, though he held it was God's majesty that rendered sin's debt infinite rather than God's justice and said nothing of the lifelong obedience of Christ as an aspect of vicarious satisfaction. The Reformers do not reject Anselm's thought on the subject; they complement it.

It would take us too far into historical theology to trace out the origins and later development of the active obedience doctrine. The active and passive obedience of Christ are treated in Calvin's *Institutes* as aspects of one obedience (II.121–123, especially see 12.3).

Roman Catholic Response.

In the Reformation era Rome responded to the Reformers' soteriology of atonement by making refinements of their doctrine of merit and of the sacrifice of the Mass. These developments effectively separated evangelical religion from Rome to the present – as far as formal theology is concerned. Four hundred years have found no *via media* or compromise and the future will likely find none, for the Reformation had rediscovered apostolic Christianity in a purer form.

Rome responded to the Reformers specifically at the Council of Trent (1545–1563). The severity of the language used does not detract from the great plainness of speech. Rome is as far as east is from west from the plain statements of Hebrews as to the perfection and once-for-all character of the atonement. The first three 'Canons on the Most Holy Sacrifice of the Mass' are herewith quoted from an authoritative source and speak for themselves.

> Can. 1. If anyone says that in the Mass a true and real sacrifice is not offered to God, or that the act of offering is nothing else than Christ given to us to eat: let him be anathema.
>
> Can. 2. If anyone says that by these words: 'Do this for a commemoration of me,' Christ did not make the apostles priests, or did not ordain that they and other priests might offer [in the Eucharist] His [Christ's] own body and blood: let him be anathema.
>
> Can. 3. If anyone says that the sacrifice of the Mass is only one of praise and thanksgiving, or that it is a mere commemoration of the sacrifice consummated on the Cross, but not one of propitiation; or that it is of profit

---

11. Philip Schaff, *The Creeds of Christendom*, vol. iii, p. 115.
12. G. C. H. Berkouwer, *The Work of Christ*, trans. C. Lambregtie (Grand Rapids, MI: Eerdmans, 1965), pp. 314–327.

to him alone [the priest, sometimes others] who receives; or that it ought not to be offered for the living and dead, for sins, punishments, satisfactions, and other necessities: let him be anathema.[13]

These canons are keyed to pronouncements of the Council, which purport to prove by arguments drawn from Scripture and tradition that the sacrifice of the Mass is 'a visible propitiation for the living and the dead.'

The chief text of Scripture relied upon by Roman theologians at that time was Malachi 1:10, 11, and more recently Hebrews 8:3. For the official pronouncements and arguments refer to Session xxii, 17 September 1562, chapters 1 and 2. For a recent pedagogical exposition in a text for instruction of priests see Ludwig Ott, *Fundamentals of Catholic Dogma*.[14]

Ott cites the canons and decrees of Trent along with other dogmatic pronouncements. The new *Catechism of the Catholic Church* sets forth these teachings so very objectionable to all evangelical believers but does so without any of the anathemas and much more subtly – even sweetly. But on these points Rome has not officially budged, however much rapprochement may be advocated or even achieved by individual theological writers.

Socinianism (Revived Pelagianism).

Opposition to both Reformation and Roman anthropology arose early in the epoch of Reformation in the form of Socinianism. Socinianism represents the renaissance rejection of Augustinian anthropology professed by the Roman Church and recovered fully by both Lutheran and Reformed (Calvinist) theology and preached in both communions. Socinianism was essentially a revival of ancient Pelagianism and forerunner of the optimistic view of modern liberalism which views man as morally good at heart, to be saved by good environment, teaching, example, etc. All God requires for forgiveness is repentance by the sinner. In such a case atonement is unnecessary, even immoral. The pattern for salvation (forgiveness) is the Parable of the Prodigal Son (Luke 15:11-32) not the cross of Christ. This is to be found in the literature of 'liberal' religion from Socinus to John Hick (who espouses it vigorously).

Defining Factors in a Biblically Controlled Doctrine of Atonement.

We are indebted to Jaroslav Pelikan for promoting the flash of insight that Christian tradition is essentially the history of exegesis of the Bible. We shall not seek to escape tradition in interpreting atonement in the New Testament. Vernon Grounds in an ingeniously structured and valuable article on 'Atonement' concludes with what he calls 'postulates of New Testament Soteriology' – meaning factors that must be dealt with in a sound theology of atonement.[15] These are all involved in the tradition Pelikan remembers[16] and which we have been expounding in these pages. Let us try to sort them out. I acknowledge they somewhat overlap one another.

1. In the first place the doctrine of atonement taught in the Bible will not be grasped unless one mentally and spiritually enters the thought-world of the whole Bible. The comprehensive term for the event of Calvary is sacrifice. The idea of sacrifice must be understood as the Messiah of Israel understood it. He was sent initially only 'to the lost sheep of the house of Israel' (Matt. 15:24). Twelve Jewish Apostles, steeped in Old Testament rituals and ideas, were the ones to whom Messiah explained the idea (Matt. 10:6). '[The] oracles of God' are 'entrusted' to 'the Jews' (Rom. 3:2) and we must learn from the Jewish Apostles who wrote our New Testament what the 'life' given 'as a ransom for many' (Matt. 20:28) truly means. Old Testament ritual religion was a religion which expressed itself in five kinds of ritual sacrifice, offered in elaborate ceremonies enacted every day at the national sanctuary and which consumed a very considerable portion of the 'gross national product' in required, stated, national assemblies three times a year, besides many other occasions.

2. In the second place to understand the doctrine of atonement scripturally one must bring to the project a 'framework of plausibility' which will admit the truth from whatever quarter and whoever speaks it – however previously unesteemed. All that Paul says about the foolishness of the cross to the worldly mind in the early chapters of 1 Corinthians is *apropos* Christ's atonement in particular. Vicarious sacrifice, the presence in God both of love

---

13. Denzinger, *Sources*, nos. 948, 949, 950.
14. Ott, *Fundamentals of Catholic Dogma*, 'The Eucharist as a Sacrifice,' pp. 402–415.
15. Vernon Grounds, 'Atonement,' in *Baker's Dictionary of Theology* (Grand Rapids, MI: Baker Books, 1960), pp. 75–78.
16. Jaroslav Pelikan, throughout the five volume series of *The Christian Tradition: A History of the Development of Doctrine* (Chicago: University of Chicago Press, 1971–1989).

for sinners and hate for sinners, absolute holiness with everlasting love in the God of redemption: all these must be admitted to the framework of reality which one regards as plausible. The literate Pharisee must somehow become willing to heed the language of rustic Galileans, One of whom reminded them that (Matt. 21:16 KJV) 'Out of the mouth of babes and sucklings thou [God] hast perfected praise.'

3. A sound soteriology (with atonement central to the project) must start with a sound anthropology, i.e. a doctrine of man and sin: created a holy being, in the image of God, but as fallen not only corrupt and guilty but under penalty of death, unable in any respect to save himself – not in a position to respond successfully to good example or good advice – utterly in need of a Savior not a self-improvement program. Rescue is necessary.

4. A sound soteriology (doctrine of atonement at center) will proceed with full acceptance of all the attributes of the divine nature, in particular not mitigating, reducing or slighting God's holiness and justice (call it personal integrity) on the one hand nor His love and mercy on the other. God's intrinsic nature both calls for an atonement by vicarious satisfaction and explains it. The necessity for such an atonement was frequently affirmed by Jesus. Matthew 16:21 explains why He set His face steadfastly to go to Jerusalem. 'Love found a way' but it was holiness demanded it.

A. H. Strong introduced the cosmic Christ, or immanent Logos idea into late revisions of his *Systematic Theology*. The result was some glaring inconsistencies which must be rejected. This was the judgment of C. F. H. Henry in his doctoral dissertation.[17] In spite of these elements in his discussion of atonement, Strong's presentation is of such excellence as to compel me to read it many times throughout the years I have taught Christology and soteriology. His way of stating atonement by vicarious satisfaction he called 'the Ethical Theory.' The following is the heart of it:

> The ethical theory holds that the necessity of the atonement is in the holiness of God, of which conscience in man is a finite reflection. There is an ethical principle in the divine nature, which demands that sin shall be punished. Aside from its results, sin is essentially ill-deserving... as there is an ethical demand in our natures that not only others' wickedness, but our own wickedness, be visited with punishment, and a keen conscience cannot rest till it has made satisfaction to justice for its misdeeds, so there is an ethical demand of God's nature that penalty follow sin.[18]

He goes on to cite Shakespeare's will and passages from seven of his dramas to demonstrate the commitment of that genius to salvation by Jesus' merit, not our own, and commends the excellent work of James Denney.[19] Then he concludes:

> In God this demand is devoid of all passion, and is consistent with infinite benevolence. It is a demand that cannot be evaded, since the holiness from which it springs is unchanging. The atonement is therefore a satisfaction of the ethical demand of the divine nature, by the substitution of Christ's penal sufferings for the punishment of the guilty.[20]

Strong elsewhere points out, as have many others and each believer's conscience confirms, that only this kind of atonement sets the conscience free from perpetual feelings of guilt and remorse. He goes on to say, 'This substitution is unknown to mere law, and above and beyond the powers of law. It is an operation of grace that does not suspend the law, but... fulfils it.'[21]

It is evident to me that this has been the understanding of the human predicament and what God has done to relieve it in every powerful revival, every vigorous missionary movement and successful Christian effort at moral improvement of individual people and of the mass of mankind.

5. Neglect no clear, specific biblical representation of the meaning of the cross of Christ. Some Scripture speaks of God as 'just and justifier' in achieving atonement for guilt or offenses or trespasses. These are juridical terms – i.e. related to law and jurisprudence. A large number suggest the condition of slavery and deliverance from it as ransom, purchase and redemption. A few speak of the work of atonement as conquest over the powers which oppress, corrupt, or suppress or terrify us – death, fear of death, the devil, etc. All of these modes of speaking accommodate eternal truths to the human scope of understanding, and when considered against the background of the whole of Scripture, convey plain truth.

---

17. Carl F. H. Henry, *Personal Idealism and Strong's Theology* (Wheaton: Van Kampen Press, 1951). See his conclusion, pp. 228, 229.
18. A. H. Strong, *Systematic Theology* (Valley Forge, PA: Judson Press, 1907), p. 751.
19. James Denney, *Studies in Theology* (Grand Rapids, MI: Baker Books, 1976, repr. of 1895 edition), pp. 100–124.
20. Strong, *Systematic Theology*, pp. 751, 752.
21. Strong, *Systematic Theology*, p. 752.

6. Perhaps the most important mode of New Testament representation, especially in the Epistles of Paul is that of a human court. The idea of God as Judge (or better, ruler) is prevalent in the whole Bible (Gen. 18:25; Judg. 2:18; 11:27; Pss. 50:6; 68:5; and on to James. 5:8 and the great scenes in Rev. 5, 6, 20). (The Hebrew words rendered 'judge' refer to all the functions of rulers – legislative and executive as well as judicial. We think of civil judges only as presiding officers in courts of law.) The Last Judgment up ahead is similarly witnessed to in many texts (such as Ps. 1:6; Eccles. 12:14, etc., in the Old Testament; and Rom. 14:10; 1 Cor. 3:13-15; Heb. 10:27). Paul in presenting 'the human predicament' vigorously pursues the fact of universal human sin, corruption of being and guilt throughout his first chapters in Romans. He brings every class of mankind before the judgment seat of God where the whole world is pronounced guilty (Rom. 3:19, 23). At this point, in the latent atmosphere of a court room, Paul introduces the means whereby God, 'who will by no means clear the guilty' (Exod. 34:7; Num. 14:18), brought divine holiness and perfect justice into harmony with His mercy and love through the work of Christ on the cross – Romans 3:24-26:

> ...and are justified by his grace as a gift, through the redemption that is in Christ Jesus, whom God put forward as a propitiation by his blood, to be received by faith. This was to show God's righteousness, because in his divine forbearance he had passed over former sins. It was to show his righteousness at the present time, so that he might be just and the justifier of the one who has faith in Jesus.

The salient terms are all directly drawn from or applicable to legal affairs and court proceedings – grace (*charis*); redemption (*apolutrōsis*), 'as a gift' ('freely' KJV), i.e. without cost (*doreān*); justified, i.e. declared innocent (*dikaio-ō*); justifier or 'one who pronounces innocent' (*dikaiounta*, present, active participle referring to God the Judge of all the earth). In this typically Pauline climactic, verbal crescendo the release from tension comes by announcement that God set forth Christ Jesus as a propitiation (propitiatory sacrifice, *hilastērion*). I have elsewhere in this section discussed what this word for atonement means. The point to be underlined here is that this paramount term in the New Testament interpretation of atonement falls in the context of a court of justice and is without a doubt the primary New Testament explanatory vehicle for atonement.

7. We must not fail to note that side by side with the legal representation of atonement Scripture also frequently represents the atonement as a change in personal relationships. In fact the very word 'atonement' – though now usually signifying making amends, making up for wrongs done, appeasement – in the single occurrence of the word atonement in the Authorized Version (1611) means at-one-ment, as in Middle English.[22] The same Greek word is elsewhere rightly rendered reconciliation. So, both propitiation of the wrath of the court and restoration of friendly relations with the Father God are proper to the atonement. Yet from Paul's representation in Romans (cf. 3:24-26 with 5:11 and the rest of chap. 5) truth requires that propitiation be understood as *cause* and reconciliation (at-one-ment) as *effect*. Even if propitiation of wrath be reduced to expiation of sin (the cause of wrath) the connection remains the same.

8. There can be no diminution or dilution of the wrath of God, the background against which atonement was effected. This is true whether God's wrath be considered in a legal sense (the wrath of the law of God) or personal (offended deity).

In the biblical proclamation love *springs forth* from the divine being spontaneously. 'God is love.' Wrath does not; it is called forth by the personal wickedness of His creatures. If there were no sin in the world there would be no divine wrath. Wrath is not an attribute of God but a name for the divine response to sin.

As reconciliation (at-one-ment) is on the personal level, so is the estrangement involved in the wrath pacified in propitiation. God is a truly offended party, even though he does not cease to love – yet. Divine wrath is a constant on sin and sinners, as John 3:36 says of those who disbelieve, 'the wrath of God remains on him' – this only a few lines removed from 'For God so loved the world, that he gave his only Son, that whoever believes in him should not perish but have eternal life.' 'The most poignant word about God's punishment is that it is the wrath of the Lamb who took upon himself and bore the sins of the world.'[23]

There are sixty-five pages on the concept of divine wrath (*orgē*) in TDNT, almost all of it supportive of the views expressed above.[24] It should be added that those features of human wrath, which are sinful ('Be angry and do not sin,' Eph. 4:26), are of course not present in divine wrath, any more than sinful features of some human love. The

---

22. *Oxford English Dictionary*, subject 'atonement.'
23. W. C. Robinson, 'Wrath,' in *Baker's Dictionary of Theology* (Grand Rapids, MI: Baker Books, 1960), p. 562.
24. Kittel, Gerhard and Friedrich, Gerhard, *Theological Dictionary of the New Testament v*, trans. and ed. G. W. Bromiley (Grand Rapids, MI: Eerdmans, 1964–1976), pp. 382–446.

steady age-long affirmation of 'the impassibility of God' is not likely to be reversed. God is always supremely 'God over all, blessed for ever' (Rom. 9:5). To speak either of the love or wrath (or hate) of God is to speak analogically. When the Bible says, 'The arm of the Lord is not short' the human analogy is called anthropomorphism; or 'The LORD was sorry that he had made man,' the analogy is called anthropopathism. Yet love and hate stand for that which is real and personal in a real and personal God.

Is it possible that the notion of divine wrath and propitiation of wrath are crude holdovers from Israel's beginnings or imported ideas from the heathenism of the ancient world? 'Wrathful deities are so vividly present in the consciousness of all peoples that attempts have been made to explain every cult as an effort to anticipate or soften the anger of the gods' (H. Kleinknecht, *TDNT*, '*orgē*,' V, p. 385). This was the case with the Greeks and Romans as any one who has read any of the classics knows. Augustine built his case for Christianity, in major part, on the foolish measures the pagans of ancient time took to appease the gods (*City of God*, Books I–VI). Augustine also took notice that several schools of philosophy, especially the Platonists, broke free of this superstition. Kleinknecht points out, however, the philosophers spoke only for themselves for 'not only in poetry but also in popular belief... the wrath of the gods demands expiation and expresses itself in punishments' (*TDNT*, V, p. 387). The O.T. from beginning to end balances God's wrath as response to sin with His readiness to forgive His people – even Ninevites – in response to repentance and obedience, always as a holy God. The New Testament vocabulary in discussing divine wrath pointedly avoids the words the Greek literature used for the wrath of pagan deities. G. Stahlin points out like the Septuagint 'the NT never uses the terms of Greek poetry for God's wrath' (*TDNT*, '*orgē*,' V, p. 422). The amazing coverage of this subject – sixty-five pages by six learned authors (*TDNT*, V, pp. 382–447) – shows that while divine wrath and propitiation of the same appear in all stages of biblical religion and in the polytheistic religions of antiquity, the wrath of Israel's God is offended holiness. The wrath of the gods of Greece and Rome was rooted in the reflected passions of the people who worshipped them. The wrath of a holy God is, however, plainly holy wrath and greatly to be feared.

The doctrine of sin furnishes the traditional (and biblical) category of 'sins that cry to heaven for vengeance.' These are chiefly: (1) oppression of the poor and disadvantaged (Prov. 17:5; 21:13); (2) oppression of defenseless foreigners, widows and orphans (Exod. 22:21-24); (3) injustice to wage-earners (withholding wages) who need their earnings to procure daily bread (Deut. 24:14, 15); (4) sins of sexual impurity and perversion (homosexuality, bestiality) (Lev. 18:24-30), (5) the failure of civil magistrates to punish murder (Num. 35:31-33; Deut. 21:1-9); and (6) idolatry. The LORD is fierce in declaring His supreme anger at all idolatry and severest punishment for those who pervert worship by this means. This sin is the subject of the first two of the Ten Commandments (Exod. 20:1-6). 'My glory I will not give to another' (Isa. 48:11) is terse language. Giving veneration or obeisance to any material object repeatedly draws forth the fury of divine wrath in Old Testament history (Ps. 78; Judg. 2). It is condemned as the prime sin of the heathen world (Rom. 1:19-25) because it not only insults God but also violates the divine image in man by accompanying sins of perversion. It was this combination of idolatry and immorality that brought on the annihilation of Canaanites and Midianites in Old Testament history. Even more severe is God's wrathful response to apostasy. (See Heb. 10:26–31 for a fearful example.)

It is the biblical teaching of 'the wrath of God' that renders reasonable the doctrine of propitiation as an aspect of atonement (see Walvoord, *Jesus Christ our Lord*, pp. 171-173).

9. Authors of good books and articles on atonement (J. Denney, V. Taylor, B. Warfield, L. Morris, A. Hodge, L. Boettner, G. Smeaton and others) all stress that the atoning work of Christ is something done, accomplished, finished. Another way of saying this is to say the atonement is *objective*. This is not to deny that contemplation of the atonement has subjective effects on elect believers – it melts their hearts and brings them to repentance and faith (Rom. 2:4). The opposite effect (as of all God's benevolence) takes place subjectively in unbelievers as Romans 2:4, 5, a very sobering passage, says: Do you not know 'that God's kindness is meant to lead you to repentance? But because of your hard and impenitent heart you are storing up wrath for yourself.' See 2 Corinthians 16, 17. '[W]hat an objective atonement means is that but for Christ and His Passion God would not be to us what He is.'[25]

A valiant effort was made by D. M. Baillie to provide a mediating explanation of the atonement as both objective and subjective. He asks the question:

---

25. James Denney, *The Christian Doctrine of Reconciliation*, 1918, p. 239; as cited by Vernon Grounds in *Baker's Dictionary of Theology*, p. 77.

What then, is the divine Atonement, which is... both historical and eternal? Is it an 'objective' reality, something done by Christ, something ordained and accepted by God, in 'expiation' of human sin, quite apart from our knowledge of it and its effects upon us? Or is a 'subjective' process, a reconciling of us to God through a persuasion in our hearts that there is no obstacle, a realization of His eternal love?[26]

Having asked his questions in a manner suitable for the answer the author wants to present, Baillie goes on to say, 'Surely these two aspects cannot be separated at all.... In theological argument on this subject we are apt to forget we are dealing with a realm of personal relationships and nothing else.'[27] But we must protest that Baillie is neglecting many features of the Scripture record. The Bible seldom if ever makes human response part of what happened at Calvary. He did it whether we respond or not. And more importantly, under number 6 above, the court of law where charges are made, forensic, legal processes, demands and judgments are carried through, is the paramount biblical representation of the atonement. There is of course a personal aspect in that as a result of the processes of justice personal reconciliation of God and man takes place.

Baillie goes on to destroy all vestiges of a distinct transactional event at Calvary, saying if Calvary was 'a sacrifice made by God Himself, then it is part of the sacrifice that God is continually making.'[28]

Thus the objectivity of Christ's atonement is really swallowed up in subjectivity – God's and ours, by the sort of theology of which, unfortunately, Baillie's is an example.

10. The vicarious aspect of atonement must be noticed here even though the exegetical basis in Scripture has been discussed earlier. Vicarious atonement has been attacked at several junctures of Christian history from four quarters, i.e. that it is (1) unnecessary, (2) impossible, (3) immoral and (4) a denial of forgiveness.

Vicarious Satisfaction Said to Be Unnecessary.

Ancient Socinians held vicarious atonement unnecessary because their view of man, sin and salvation was thoroughly moralistic. We are born into the world neutral regarding sin. Adam's fall brought neither corruption of mind nor guilt upon any of his generations of progeny. We are born mortal, but not as punishment for anyone's sin. Each of us forms his own character from 'ground zero' not in any manner affected by Adam's apostasy except his bad example.

Because much of Christendom today is ruled by Pelagian views let us see how this outlook views sin and salvation. I cite the excellent summary of W. G. T. Shedd:

> The general... prevalence of sin in the world is accounted for by the power of temptation and the influence of habit. It is possible for any man to be entirely sinless.... The grace of the Holy Spirit is... only relatively necessary in order to holiness; it renders its attainment easier.... Regeneration [is] the illumination of the intellect by the truth, the stimulation of the will by the threatenings of the law and promise of future rewards, and the remission of sins by the divine indulgence etc.[29]

Shedd fully documents this summary. Pelagius was contemporary with Augustine, yet this sort of thinking rules in liberal religion and 'newspaper religion' still today. It is, of course, directly contradictory to all orthodox, biblical Christianity. There are millions of lost folk counting on the divine indulgence rather than the grace of God in Christ's work at Calvary.

Vicarious Satisfaction Said to Be Immoral, Hence Impossible.

Some objectors claim vicarious suffering of the innocent for the guilty is not justice at all but injustice. A. H. Strong answered this charge by saying in ordinary cases the charge is true only on the supposition that the Son bears the penalty of our sins, not voluntarily, but compulsorily; or on the supposition that one who is personally innocent can in no way become involved in the guilt and penalty of others – both of them hypotheses contrary to Scripture and to fact.[30]

---

26. D. M. Baillie, *God Was in Christ: An Essay on Incarnation and Atonement* (New York: Charles Scribner's Sons, 1948), pp. 197, 198.
27. ibid.
28. ibid.
29. W. G. T. Shedd on 'Pelagianism' in *A History of Christian Doctrine ii* (New York: Scribner, Armstrong & Co., 1872; repr. Minneapolis: Klock & Klock, 1978), pp. 93, 94.
30. Strong, *Systematic Theology*, p. 738.

Granted there is mystery in how it could happen even with the best effort at logical explanation [of] the mystery of atonement. But an even greater mystery then follows as to how in justice a just God can grant unmerited pardon in a manner consistent with His holiness.

Granting then a strong element of mystery in atonement by substitutionary propitiation, apologetics does not refuse the task of defending it against attack. Nineteenth-century attacks on vicarious sacrifice by rationalistic and Unitarian writers evoked some strenuous responses. The orthodox did not attempt to prove what happened at Calvary for they accepted what Scripture says, only to explain how it was possible and morally right in light of the incarnation.

One of the most adept in such matters was Dr Shedd. He discusses divine justice at length in connection with the divine attributes.[31] Justice he defines as 'that phase of God's holiness which is seen in his treatment of the obedient and disobedient subjects of his government.'[32] At page 373 he begins discussion of 'the possibility of vicarious satisfaction of retributive justice' and continues through page 378. He proposes the relevance of Romans 1:18: 'the wrath of God is revealed from heaven against all *ungodliness* and *unrighteousness* of men' (Shedd's emphasis) and says, 'The divine displeasure expressed in punitive justice is not aimed against the *person* as such, and distinct from his sin.' He quotes Charnock: 'God is not displeased with the nature of man as man, for that is derived from him; but the nature of man as sinful, which is derived from the sinner himself. God hates only the sin not the sinner; he desires only the destruction of the one, not the misery of the other,' and Shedd adds, 'God loves the person as such.'[33] He relies on an affirmation of Scripture about God, viz.: 'As for God, his way is perfect' (Ps. 18:30 KJV). God cannot be false to Himself.

The section of Shedd's essay closes with a summary which states that, as in everything else, God is sovereign and free in respect to justice – yet not in relation 'to the *abolition*, nor to the *relaxation*, but to the *substitution* of punishment.'[34] He asserts God in His sovereignty can satisfy the claims of justice in more than one way. 'He has a choice of methods. He may inflict the full amount of suffering due to sin, either upon the sinner, or upon a proper substitute.... Divine justice... is free to do either; but one or the other it must do. God is not obliged either to accept or to provide a substituted penalty' but in either case 'it is grace and mercy towards the actual transgressor... permitting substitution and providing the substitute' are acts of mercy in harmony with justice. 'There is mercy in permitting another person to do for the sinner what the sinner is bound to do for himself; and still greater mercy in providing that person; and greater still, in becoming that person.'[35]

This all means simply that a sovereign holy God will by nature do what is right. It is right therefore for Him 1) to allow substitution and 2) to provide the substitute and 3) to be the substitute. I am not sure any theologian has with full success explained the divine justice in vicarious satisfaction. The explanation just reported is only the best I know of. We may be certain that Scripture teaches substitutionary satisfaction of the requirements of divine law at Calvary and that God is just.

In Volume II Shedd has 112 pages on 'Vicarious Atonement' and there develops the theme (pp. 450–463) that 'vicarious satisfaction of justice is the only mode of exercising mercy that is possible in a just Being' (pp. 377, 378). Quite to the contrary is the rather uniform opinion among liberal theologians who assert that:

Vicarious Satisfaction Is the Contrary of Forgiveness.

This is not unlike the Pelagianism that said satisfaction of divine justice is unnecessary. In recent times a Methodist bishop, echoing twentieth-century modernism in Protestant religion, laid the matter on the line so to speak, saying, 'If Jesus paid it all, or if He is the substitute for me, or if He is the sacrifice for all the sin of the world, then why discuss forgiveness? The books are closed. Another has paid the debt, borne the penalty. I owe nothing. I am absolved. I cannot see forgiveness as predicated upon the act of some one else. It is my sin. I must atone.'[36] This is theology, again as we have noticed before, grounded more on the Parable of the Prodigal Son and a form of salvation by self-effort, neglecting the careful, New Testament explanations of our identification first with Adam, then of Christ with us and we with Him. The whole Bible as well as Christian hymnody stands against this new Pelagianism.

---

31. W. G. T. Shedd, *Dogmatic Theology i* (Grand Rapids, MI: Zondervan, 1969), pp. 365–385.
32. ibid., p. 365.
33. ibid., p. 375.
34. ibid.
35. ibid., pp. 377, 378.
36. G. Bromley Oxnam, *A Testament of Faith* (Boston, 1958), p. 144 as quoted by Vernon Grounds in *Baker's Dictionary of Theology*, p. 76.

The faithful steward of the divine word of truth in the present epoch will be cautious about approving the doctrines of some very prominent recent theologians who adopt some of the language of atonement by vicarious satisfaction while really promoting another gospel. The theology I refer to here is often called neo-orthodoxy. It is part-way back from Pelagianism and liberalism to orthodoxy – close enough to make employment of orthodox language sound appropriate.

The teaching is not that the incarnate Son of God died in our place, rather that the Son of God became incarnate and by incarnation bridged the gulf between Creator and creature assuming thereby all our liabilities. Sometimes this is framed as a covenant of God with us. The innumerable, dense pages of Karl Barth[37] propose the covenant route and the eminently readable and persuasive pages of Emil Brunner's *The Mediator*,[38] the incarnation route, to bypass the genuine, historical, Protestant orthodox doctrine. I was a young professor when I first read Brunner's book, *The Mediator*, in a newly issued translation, about 1948 or 1949. As I read him then and as I read him now he seems to affirm expiation and propitiation, redemption, reconciliation, etc., and to relate their effectiveness for our salvation to a doctrine of real incarnation. He even affirms the obedience of Christ as an obedience of whole life in suffering and even says His death was 'vicarious.'[39] Due to his fondness for paradoxical statement and existential assumptions about the structure of divine-human relations no single paragraph says exactly what he (and his disciples) mean. The following selected from three paragraphs seems to say Christ's whole life of obedience made His death vicarious in the sense the whole human race was on the cross by virtue of the incarnation. There was no judicial action. It was *all* on the level of personal relations (as Baillie asserted above). The suffering was not penal. God was there and all of us were there getting our personal relationships (formerly alienated) straightened out.

> It is only [his whole life of obedience in suffering] which makes his death vicarious… the exact opposite of that which – not wholly wrongly – the doctrine of Anselm is taken to mean: an objective-personal [why not *and* personal?] substitutionary transaction. What we said above about sacrifice as an 'equivalent' is only protected from 'false objectivity' of this kind by means of vicarious offering. For vicarious offering (substitution) is something entirely personal; it is personal in that dual sense which characterizes the personality of the Mediator… acting vicariously for man and for God. For the people he acts as their high priest, who brings the expiatory sacrifice in the name of them all… Personal surrender can only be that wherein the personality is sacrificed.[40]

> His passion is not a transaction – as it certainly might seem to be in the doctrine of Anselm, a method of expiation ordained by God which gets its value from the costly nature of the sacrifice – it is a personal [only] act; …real, vicarious, etc.[41]

For Brunner, then, the atonement came by the incarnation without any specific reference to His death except that death is part of the experience of being human. Hence the caveat issued here against being deceived by orthodox-sounding language to suppose orthodox doctrine is being promoted.

Karl Barth's neo-orthodox interpretation of the work of Christ at Calvary is distributed through many of his books, including several of the 13 volumes of *Church Dogmatics*, some of which run to over 850 pages. When theologizing, Barth seldom states precisely what he means and does so garrulously. No one, I think, ever mastered his thought – perhaps not even Dr Barth himself, certainly not I, though I have tried. On the other hand his ventures into biblical exegesis and history of ideas is as competent, straightforward and precise as his long-winded theology is obscure. But again, let us not be affected seriously by much theological talk. His orthodox statements are seldom his final word on anything.

Let us take note of three brief portions of Barth's *Church Dogmatics* where he employs the orthodox language of vicarious satisfaction: 'In this one man, Jesus, God puts at the head of and in the place of all other men the One,' etc., 'and does it all for all who are elected in Him.'[42] Under the rubric 'the Judge Judged in our Place,' Barth speaks of penal suffering, and of propitiation:

---

37. Karl Barth, *Church Dogmatics*, vols. ii. 2 and iv.1, 2 (Edinburgh: T & T Clark, 1957, 1976).
38. Emil Brunner, *The Mediator: A Study of the Central Doctrine of the Christian Faith*, trans. Olive Wyon (Philadelphia, PA: Westminster Press, 1947).
39. ibid., p. 501.
40. ibid., p. 501.
41. ibid., p. 495.
42. Barth, *Church Dogmatics* ii.2.123.

Because He was the divine Judge come amongst us, He had the authority in this way – by this giving up of Himself to judgment in our place – to exercise the divine justice of grace, to pronounce us righteous on the ground of what happened to Him, to free us therefore from the accusation and condemnation and punishment.[43]

He even skillfully enters the intricacies of the New Testament Greek prepositions related to the subject, turning in a competent discussion of *anti*, *hyper* (or *huper*) and *peri* and says the passages which employ them 'speak of a place which ought to be ours, that we ought to have taken this place, that we have been taken from it… that we cannot add to anything he does there,' etc.[44]

Yet, there is no consistency in other sections where Barth teaches, like Brunner, 1) atonement, or reconciliation, by the incarnation itself not His sinless life of obedience and death in our place and 2) the election of every man who ever lived to salvation (more about these matters later).

While the Fathers of neo-orthodoxy were moving off stage their disciples and a new generation found leadership in Rudolph Bultmann and his disciples. They set in motion a new search for the historical Jesus, pretty much dissolving all the supernatural elements in Jesus' story into myths. Yet these authors also usually claim to be Christians. Bultmann himself was a lifelong churchman. Hence, they, like the earlier neo-orthodox, prefer to employ traditional theological language. John Macquarrie, who presents himself as a disciple of Bultmann, pointedly uses the terms of traditional orthodox Anglican religion and has a chapter on 'The Work of Christ.' There is less subterfuge in Bultmannians, however. Macquarrie, for example, says plainly that he is reinterpreting Christianity in non-traditional ways though using traditional terms. One who reads these authors *carefully* finds the self-contradictions of neo-orthodoxy prevalent, because they do not always explain they have a new set of meanings for old words.[45] I shall not here attempt to trace developments from neo-orthodoxy on to the present splintered character of what goes for academic theology in the universities and seminaries.

An important matter remains to be discussed before the work of Christ in atonement by vicarious satisfaction is laid aside. It has to do with the question, 'For whom did Christ die?' Was it for the elect only? Or, did He atone for the sins of every member of the human race? The answers given to the present time are so involved we shall have to limit the presentation severely.

---

43. Barth, *Church Dogmatics* iv, 1.223.
44. Barth, *Church Dogmatics* ii.1.230.
45. John Macquarrie, *Principles of Christian Theology*, chap. 13, 'The Work of Christ' (New York: Charles Scribner's Sons, 1966, 1967).

17
The Extent of the Atonement

The topic of this chapter is one 'over which theologians have sorely vexed themselves and each other.' The vexatious question (to which W. O. Carver refers in 'Atonement,' ISBE I, 324) is whether in His vicarious act of satisfaction of divine justice at Calvary Christ bore the sins of every human being of every generation or only the sins of the elect – the saved of all ages. What did God intend? A common-sense formula in Latin, coming down from the ancient church, has seemed adequate for most people, viz.: Christ died '*sufficienter pro omnibus, sed efficaciter tantum pro electis*' (sufficiently for all, but efficaciously only for the elect). It is very important to note that in this original form, 'for' (Lat. *pro*) means *in proportion to* or *in relation to*, not *in the stead of* as the Greek *anti* ('a ransom for many' Matt. 20:28; Mark 10:45) discussed at length earlier. The formula is saying simply the *benefits* of the atonement Christ made were sufficient for all, efficacious for only the elect. It says nothing specific about in whose place Christ died at Calvary.

Quite apart from the history of the question, once vicarious satisfaction of divine justice is accepted as the most adequate theory of 'the atonement' then a problem of right and wrong seems to intrude itself. If 'Jesus paid it all' at Calvary for every man, woman, child, ever conceived or born into the world, where is the rightness (justice) in a second punishment in hell? Stated otherwise, if the Son of God bore *all* the guilt and punishment, what is there left to pay? On the other hand if the sins of the non-elect, those who never hear or hearing never repent and believe, were not imputed to Christ at Calvary, there is no 'double jeopardy.' And when did the imputation of our sins to Him take place? Did it take place when Jesus suffered and died or does it take place at the moment of faith in connection with justification, the imputation of Christ's righteousness? Perhaps it is impious even to inquire. In any case, these are the questions that this chapter addresses.

How the Subject Arose As a Vexatious Problem.

General interest in the question of 'the extent of the atonement' did not arise among Protestants in Calvin's lifetime. After Calvin's death in 1564 leadership in the chief school for Reformed pastors (Geneva, Switzerland) passed to Theodore Beza, Calvin's protégé, successor as professor, and biographer. Beza, a learned and persuasive man, with less of the grace and scholarly reserve of his teacher, rigorously carried some of Calvin's teachings to lengths that invited reaction.

James Arminius (Jacobus van Hermann) (1560–1609) received his theological education under Beza but retreated from Beza's explanation of the logical relation of the decrees of God known as Supralapsarianism. In this word, *laps* has reference to the fall and *supra* means previous to. The decrees of election and reprobation are said to be logically prior to the decrees of creation, fall and redemption (not necessarily in that order).

Arminius reacted against this somewhat newfangled refinement of the biblical and Reformed teaching of election of *lost* men to salvation, advocating in his teaching and preaching a system which at several points differed not only from Beza's but the whole Augustinian tradition and Calvin as well. He disseminated his views from his position as professor at Leiden in the Netherlands – a land scarcely recovered from attempts by the Spanish Catholic government to exterminate the Reformed Christians.

The result was strife in the whole church in the Netherlands and in the national life as well. In 1610 the Arminians presented a petition called a remonstrance, to the States of Holland and West Friesland, which set forth the Arminian theory over against Reformed doctrine, in five articles. A national synod was called in response to deal with the acute problem raised.

This synod, held at Dort (Dordrecht) in 1618 and 1619, should best 'be conceived as a body of divines holding Calvinistic views, believing those views to be true, and called for the purpose of condemning and prohibiting the contrary opinions' in their country.[1] Delegates from several other countries, among them some from Britain, sent by James I, were seated. It was this conference in an exceedingly tense, controversial setting that set forth the famous five canons, of which: the first related to total depravity; the second to unconditional election, that is, not dependent on foreseen faith; the third to particular atonement; the fourth related to the effectual grace that brings the elect to faith; and the fifth to their unfailing perseverance. It is a logical construct throughout. And in my judgment quite correct if, as the Synod did, we define atonement as *particular*, rather than as *limited*, as I shall seek to explain.

Particular Atonement Connected with Election.

The subject of this chapter is of great interest mainly to those who are convinced of particular election or who are convinced to the contrary and wish to refute election of particular persons to receive the gift of faith (or the grace of regeneration). The doctrine of particular election is that out of the mass of lost humanity, before the creation of the world, God chose each individual person upon whom He would confer the benefit of salvation. This doctrine was taught by Augustine and true Augustinians (of whom there were few) through the middle ages and then by all the first rank of Protestant Reformers and the so-called pre-Reformers (Wycliffe, Hus).

Lutheran theology quickly dropped some of Luther's early passionate insistence on election in the controversies that arose with the Reformed (Presbyterians). So from then till now the doctrine of particular atonement has been discussed almost exclusively by Calvinists (Reformed, Presbyterians, Baptists, Congregationalists and others).

According to Arminians, God foreknew who would believe and persevere and, on the basis of that foreknowledge (prescience), elected them to salvation. Believers' self-election is hence logically prior to God's election.

Attempts to clear God of arbitrariness in electing some to salvation and 'passing by' others by interpreting election 'according to the foreknowledge of God' (1 Peter 1:2) as 'based upon foreknowledge' – (i.e. planning His own acts in conformity with what He knew men with 'free will' would do) are very old. Early on even Augustine succumbed to that rather 'weak line of thinking' (J. Pelikan). Commenting on 'Jacob I loved, but Esau I hated' (Mal. 1:2, 3; Rom. 9:13), 'he had suggested that the basis for the difference lay in the divine foreknowledge of the two.'[2] Later, having struggled through the Pelagian controversies, Augustine retracted that suggestion, 'because any such differentiation between the saved and the damned would be a negation of the priority of grace.'[3] See Jaroslav Pelikan.[4]

The Scripture says election is 'according to the foreknowledge' of God but never that election is based upon what God foresaw would happen anyway. In the treatment of election in the Soteriology section of this book I point out that

---

1. Article, 'Dort, Synod of' McClintock & Strong, *Cyclodedia*, vol. ii, p. 870.
2. Augustine, *Exposition of Certain Propositions from the Epistle to the Romans*, pp. 60, 61.
3. Augustine, *Retractions* 1.22.2.
4. Jaroslav Pelikan, *The Christian Tradition: A History of the Development of Doctrine iii* (Chicago: University of Chicago Press, 1971–1989), pp. 274, 275.

election is parallel (*kata*) to God's foreknowledge but neither foreknowledge nor election is based upon the other in Scripture. Augustinians insist that salvation from start to finish is all of grace. Even faith, 'the hand of the heart' which grasps the hand of the Savior, is 'the gift of God.' I discuss this matter at length in connection with soteriology.

Setting in 'The Plan of Salvation'.

Logically, the plan of salvation must be wholly related to the fact that every man is a sinner, dead in trespasses and sins. He is already perishing. He sees nothing interesting or desirable in the things of the Spirit of God because they are foolishness to him. Neither can he know them, they being discerned only when the Holy Spirit sovereignly and supernaturally enlightens him, being born again not by the corruptible seed of rational arguments (for which he has no adequate capacity in connection with spiritual matters), but 'through the living... word of God' (1 Cor. 1:18; 2:14; 1 Peter 1:23). The agency of the Holy Spirit in this new birth is wholly by the Spirit's sovereign, purposeful initiative (John 3:5-8). Faith does not induce new birth. It is the other way around. Apparently the Word accompanies new birth but the Spirit enables the understanding and reverses the will – again sovereignly. The soul is the receptor not the initiator of regeneration. As Jesus told Nicodemus, the Spirit moves where the Spirit 'listeth' (desires). Like the wind one can hear it but one cannot tell from whence it is coming or whither it is going. 'So is every one that is born of the Spirit of God.' 'How to be Born Again,' if Jesus is to be believed, is not the proper subject of a research project. 'Reasons for Faith' would be a more proper project.

The plan of salvation therefore is wholly about a rescue operation not a how-to-achieve-it project. The subject of the rescue, being 'dead in the trespasses and sins' (Eph. 2:1), does not know he is in need of rescue and resents the notion that he might need it until God restores real liberty of will, rescuing him from the bond-slavery of a depraved inclination away from God.

The Arminian Challenge.

Arminius' reflections led him to propose that indeed mankind are born dead in sins, as his Calvinist teachers said, but as a matter of *justice* (i.e. of fairness by a God who Arminius thought must not give less than equal treatment to everyone), God has restored to everyone power to believe in Christ and thereafter to be born again.[5] 'All unregenerate persons have freedom of will and a capacity of resisting the Holy Spirit, of rejecting the proffered grace of God... without any difference of *the elect and the reprobate*' (emphasis original).[6] This teaching in the Netherlands, where it began, quite logically rapidly moved toward the doctrine of universal salvation, and the followers, known as Remonstrants, ceasing to be a part of orthodoxy, simply died out. These ideas, with some modification, found a home in Britain among some Anglicans even though the Thirty-Nine Articles of Anglican beginnings is thoroughly Augustinian in this regard. Much later, John Wesley, while holding to many of the teachings of Calvinist orthodoxy, accepted Arminius' doctrine of universal restoration of fallen man's freedom of the will. Yet Wesley said God *out of pure grace* restored freedom of the will to every human being through the power of His death on the cross. The Arminians had said God must restore this ability or He would be unjust, Wesley, because God is gracious. The very slim basis of this amazingly bold assertion is said to be John 1:9, the Word 'was the true Light which gives light to every man coming into the world' (John 1:9 NKJV).

Restoration of 'Plenary Ability'.

This Arminian-Wesleyan teaching of universal restoration of a healthy will to all mankind assumes the universal application of the atoning work of Christ on the cross. This would mean not merely that the death of Christ made salvation possible for every human being but that it already has, in part, gone into effect in everyone. It should not therefore be surprising that this doctrine among the followers of Arminius (less so among Wesleyans) quickly turned into universal salvationism.

The Augustinian-Calvinist view of the matter is that this universal enablement of the will to respond favorably, whether of grace or out of justice, has never taken place. Paul says of the Ephesian believers that they were *all*

---

5. James Arminius, *The Works of Arminius ii*, trans. James Nichols (Auburn & Buffalo: Derby, Miller & Orton, recently repr. 1853), art. xvii. p. 497.
6. ibid., p. 497.

formerly dead in their trespasses and that they 'walked' in them; they were even 'past feeling.' In other words, something happened to some residents of Ephesus, now believers, when Paul first preached there, which did not happen to the other people of their city. This may be called enlightenment, special calling, even new birth (as narrowly defined). In other words, only those Ephesians in whom the atonement *went into effect* were the ones who became believers. None of the population of Ephesus had their darkened consciences enlightened except the elect, the believers.

A World Reconciled to God for Now.

But that is not the whole of the matter. Chapters 1 and 2 of 1 Corinthians must be read with chapter 5 of 2 Corinthians. The Corinthians believers were told the preaching of the cross, though it was foolishness to the perishing (1 Cor. 1:18), and the very power of God to those being saved (1 Cor. 1:18, 21), the cross nevertheless has some benefits for everyone in the world: '...in Christ God was reconciling the world to himself, not counting their trespasses against them' (2 Cor. 5:19). The world in this context means what we usually mean by the world (*kosmos*), this earth with all the people on it as presently organized and rationalized, 'the present evil age' (Gal. 1:4). The New Testament does not present a single clear case where 'the world' means only God's people, the saved, the elect or any similar designation.

It is very important to take note that John Calvin himself and B. B. Warfield – an outstanding Calvinist of the twentieth century – take this view of the meaning of world in 2 Corinthians 5:19 as well as in 1 John 2:2: 'He is the propitiation for [Gr. *peri*, about, concerning (not *anti*, in the stead of)] our sins; and not for ours only, but also for the sins of the whole world,' and several other related texts. Warfield wrote voluminously both on Calvin and Augustine as well as many books and articles on the work of Christ. Probably no man who ever lived was acquainted with these matters more thoroughly than he. In addition to these books and articles is his lengthy introduction and survey of the *Anti-Pelagian Writings* of Augustine in the Nicene and post-Nicene Fathers. I have read that lengthy introduction and spent some hours in Augustine's anti-Pelagian corpus. I have found no evidence in any of Warfield's writings or in Augustine or Calvin himself that they deny a distinct, divinely intended reference to the whole world in the work of Christ on the cross. Of course, I may have missed something.

Particular and General Aspects of 'Atonement'.

This suggests that we are here dealing with one of the many paradox-like aspects of the whole of revealed truth. There is a *particular* aspect of Christ's work on the cross and a *general* aspect. This is not to say this truth is one of the New Testament biblical mysteries. The kingdom of heaven is often called a 'mystery' in the Gospels. Paul uses the word mystery twenty-one times: of the hardening of Israel's hearts, of the change in our bodies in the resurrection (1 Cor. 15:50), of the incarnation (1 Tim. 3:16), of certain elements of his own preaching (1 Cor. 4:1), of the highest stage of doctrine (Eph. 2:7) and of the church (Eph. 5:32). Rather, there are truths that are in harmony as God sees them and may be partially understood by us, yet which we in our limited capacity cannot quite clarify. Much about the Calvary work of Christ falls into this category of the inexplicable, as Christian theology has always acknowledged, even though Scripture nowhere calls that work a *mysterion*.

Calvin's 'Paradoxical' Solutions.

How could the obedience and death of *one man* have such high value as to save multitudes? Luther answered, on the basis of the union with the divine nature, saying the divine participated in the sufferings of the human nature although 'in an inconceivable and inexplicable manner' as in sermons on 1 Peter 1:18 and other texts.[7] Calvin addressed the problem too, probably not fully satisfactorily.[8] There is no place in Calvin's theology for outright contradiction of one truth or fact by another. Yet Calvin often acknowledges limits to his and others' logic with a 'so to speak' or 'as though' indicating a breach between the divine and the human point of view. Calvin allowed many of these 'dialectical differences' in the final form of his writings.

---

7. Francois Wendel, *Calvin: The Origins and Development of His Religious Thought*, trans. Philip Mairet (New York: Harper & Row, 1963), p. 227.
8. John Calvin, *Institutes of the Christian ii*, ed. J. T. McNeil, trans. and ed. F. L. Battles (Philadelphia, PA: Westminster Press, 1960), ii.17.1–6.

In my judgment therefore one must not think of Calvinism as a theological extreme to be balanced by some other extreme, the truth lying somewhere in-between. He did not really build a tight system around some central ruling idea to which all else had to conform. I cite Wendel to show why Calvin must not be saddled with responsibility for some of the extreme views of some of the theological followers who claim his name for their work. In Wendel's summary conclusion, this very fair authority on Calvin's thought says:

> Calvin's is not a closed system elaborated around a central idea, it draws together, one after another, a whole series of biblical ideas, some of which can only with difficulty be reconciled.[9]

Calvin was only following sound precedent. He would have agreed with the opinion that if someone should hear an angel say 2 + 5 = 9 he would have soot on his wings. In other words, the law of non-contradiction is a fact both in heaven and on earth, even if omitted or denied in the devil's list of axioms. Yet, there is a history in sound theology of acceptance of certain truths that *seem* at odds with one another, because they are not understood fully as God understands them. Also there are truths (as Jesus' 'the last shall be first') that teach a single truth by a paradoxical form of statement. Among such 'paradoxes' we all accept are: the presence in God of both justice and mercy, of unrelenting hatred of sin and sinners with love for sinners (never quite adequately explained). Pelikan devotes ten pages to tracing the pervasive presence of paradoxes, as I have defined them, in Latin (Western) theology up to the end of the thirteenth century. He points out how many diverse and unsystematic elements there were in what he calls 'the plan of salvation' in that long period and, significantly for what I have written earlier in this paragraph about Calvin and Strong, Pelikan ends with this summary:

> [B]ut as this period set out to deal with 'the question of what that redemption of ours through the death of Christ may be and in what way the apostle declares that we are justified by his blood' (Peter Abelard), it worked with the presuppositions of its heritage about the being of God, about the nature of man, and about the mystery of the incarnation of the God-man.
>
> Each of these presuppositions [for a doctrine of redemption] had acquired definite form by this time [1300], so that there was no dogma of the atonement as such, no theory of redemption as such that overlooked any of these presupposition, or appeared to slight one or the other of them, would be deemed acceptable.[10]

Calvin on the Extent Of 'Atonement'.

One therefore should not be surprised to find that most of Calvin's discussion of atonement in the *Institutes* relates it to the elect – without commenting at length on how Christ's atonement relates to the world of mankind at large. In Calvin's commentaries on the Bible, however, he acknowledges a reconciliation (at-one-ment) of all mankind. Let us look at some of these passages.

On Matthew 26:28 and Mark 14:24: 'blood… poured out for many for the forgiveness of sins' Calvin explains, 'By the word many He means not a part of the world only, but the whole human race.'[11]

On John 1:29: 'the Lamb… who takes away the sin of the world' he comments, 'And when he says the sin of the world he extends his favor indiscriminately to the whole human race.'[12] On John 3:15, 16: 'whosoever' (KJV) etc., Calvin carefully explains:

> He has employed the universal term *whosoever*, both to invite all indiscriminately to partake of life, and to cut off every excuse from unbelievers. Such is the import of the term *world*; for though nothing will be found in the world that is worthy of the favour of God, yet He shows Himself to be reconciled to the whole world, when He invites all men without exception to the faith of Christ, which is nothing else than an entrance into life.[13]

Note that Calvin does not say more than that God was reconciled to the world at the cross. At-one-ment occurred, interruption of God's enmity in a reconciliation. A truce was effected.

---

9. Wendel, *Calvin*, pp. 358, 359.
10. Pelikan, *Christian Tradition*, 'The Growth of Medieval Theology 600–1300,' p. 118.
11. John Calvin, *Harmony of Matthew, Mark and Luke ii*, repr. (Grand Rapids, MI: Eerdmans, 1949), p. 214; new trans., iii, 1972, p. 139.
12. John Calvin, *Commentary on John's Gospel* (Grand Rapids, MI: Eerdmans, 1949), I, p. 64; new trans., iv, p. 32.
13. ibid., pp. 74, 75.

On John 3:17: 'not... to condemn the world, but in order that the world might be saved through him.' Here quite contrary to the sometimes strident insistence of some advocates of 'limited atonement' (for the elect only), Calvin comments on the presence of 'world' (*kosmos*) twice in the verse: 'the word *world* is again repeated, that no man may think of himself wholly excluded... showing that he here includes all men in the word 'world' instead of restricting it to comprise the elect alone.'[14] This is about as specific a rejection of 'limited atonement' as propounded by some 'high' Calvinists, by Calvin himself, as can be imagined.

On Romans 5:18: 'Therefore, as one trespass led to condemnation for all men, so one act of righteousness leads to justification and life for all men.' C. A. Hodge, a strong supporter of atonement limited to the elect only seeks to prove that the first 'all men' means the human race but the second only elect believers.[15] Hardly the best logic in a great book on Romans! Calvin, however, who did not find world-reconciliation to God objectionable, gave a quite contrary view, finding the whole world of mankind in 'all men' in both clauses of the sentence, saying God

> ...makes his favour common to all, because it is propounded to all, and not because it is in reality extended to all [i.e. through their hearing about it]; for though Christ suffered for the sins of the whole world, and is offered through God's benignity indiscriminately to all, yet all do not receive him.[16]

From this it should be apparent that Calvin held to a doctrine of universal *reconciliation*, if not universal *redemption* (as I shall explain shortly).

In comment on Colossians 1:14 Calvin asserts, 'by the sacrifice of His death all the sins of the world have been expiated.'[17]

A. H. Strong cites Calvin's apparent grounding of a message of salvation for the whole world in a 'propitiation' for the whole world.[18] The source, Strong says, is Calvin's '*Commentary* on 1 John 2:2...' as follows:

> Christ suffered for the sins of the whole world, and in the goodness of God is offered unto all men without distinction, his blood being shed not for a part of the world only, but for the whole human race; for although in the world is found nothing worthy of the favor of God, yet he holds out the propitiation to the whole world, since without distinction he summons all to the faith of Christ.[19]

I do not know the source of Strong's quotation of Calvin. It is not that of John Owen – perhaps the most strident defender of *limited* atonement ever – whose translation is The text of the Calvin Translation Society (Edinburgh, 1855). Owen has Calvin saying: 'Then under the word *all* or whole, he does not include the reprobate, but designates those who should believe as well as those scattered through various parts of the world.'[20]

Particular Atonement in the *Institutes*.

Calvin's systematic treatment of atonement in the *Institutes* is chiefly in Book II chapters 16 and 17 and the sections on election in Book III chapter 21, especially section 5 and his refutation of charges against election in III.23, sections 1–14, especially section 5. Here the focus of his discussion is not damnation of the reprobate but salvation of the elect. He focuses on the atonement of Christ as being God's loving work through Christ for the elect.

It is important here to note that in Calvin's zeal to show that atonement secured the salvation of all the elect he never denies that Christ's work on the cross had some reference also to those who would never even hear that Christ died. He does not deny universal reconciliation.

Any one who believes God chose him in Christ in eternity will not need to be convinced that atonement was specifically (particular atonement) for him – not just a provision made in the unlikely case he might hear the gospel and might believe.

---

14. ibid., p. 75.
15. C. A. Hodge, *Commentary on the Epistle to the Romans*, 1886 (Grand Rapids, MI: Eerdmans, 1947, 1993), pp. 171–173.
16. John Calvin, *Commentaries on the Epistle of Paul to The Romans*, trans. & ed. John Owen, (Edinburgh: Calvin Translation Society, 1849), p.211.
17. John Calvin, *Commentary on Philippians* (Grand Rapids, MI: Eerdmans, 1949), p. 148; new trans. xi, p. 308.
18. A. H. Strong, *Systematic Theology* (Valley Forge, PA: Judson Press, 1907), pp. 777, 778.
19. ibid., p. 778.
20. John Calvin, Commentaries *on the Catholic Epistles*, trans. & ed. John Owen, (Edinburgh: The Calvin Translation Society, 1855), p. 173.

Warfield Advocated a Form of General Reconciliation.

I have said the subject of atonement as limited to the elect in some important way is chiefly a Calvinist concern. Yet I know of no classic Calvinist who doubts Christ died 'sufficiently for all, but efficaciously *only* for the elect.' Calvin himself says so in comment on 1 John 2:2. Further, the outstanding Calvinist writer of the twentieth century, B. B. Warfield, specifically interprets the passages in the New Testament which speak of the world or all men as included in Christ's Calvary work of reconciliation (at-one-ment) as meaning just that. Yet he does so in such a way as not to deny particular redemption.

There is *something singularly important here*. Warfield wrote very extensively about Augustine and Calvin and the theology that the latter received from the former and passed down with both refinement and improvement to succeeding generations. Yet Warfield managed to do this without ever in any decisive way discussing the third point of the so-called 'five points' of Calvinism. Among Warfield's very latest works, revised not long before his death, is *The Plan of Salvation*.[21] He discusses the differences between all the major groups of Christendom and treats particular, unconditional election, of course. Yet for some reason in this small work Warfield never mentions atonement for the elect *only*. On the last page is this striking statement: 'There is no antinomy, therefore, in saying that Christ died for his people and that Christ died for the world.'[22] Nor do I find reconciliation for the elect only anywhere in the writings of Augustine. R. C. Sproul claims Augustine debated 'limited atonement' with Pelagius and C. A. Hodge asserts that it was periodically discussed through the Middle Ages. But the history of the period seems to furnish only Gottschalk of Orbais (805–868) and those immediately influenced by him. There may have been others.

One of the first scholastic systematizers of the results of the Synod of Dort was Francis Turretin (1623–1687). He says,

> Among the ancients, the Pelagians and semi-Pelagians contended that Christ died for all men; hence Prosper, in his letter to Augustine, concerning the remains of the Pelagian heresy, says, 'Those who embrace the Pelagian heresy, profess to believe that Christ died for all men universally, and that none are excluded from the atonement and redemption which the blood of Christ has effected.' Among those errors which they attribute to Augustine, they find this: 'the Savior was not crucified for the redemption of the whole world.' Faustus [presumably F. Socinius founder of the Unitarianism of the Reformation era] says, 'They wander far from the path of piety, who assert Christ did not die for all.'[23]

Turrettin goes on to refer to Gottschalk and the controversy of his time as mentioned elsewhere in this chapter. Turrettin, without documentation, says Augustine and his disciples Prosper and Fulgentius defended the doctrine that the non-elect were not included in Christ's work of atonement.[24]

The Ninth, Eleventh and Thirteenth Centuries and Late Reformation Periods.

The ninth century, beginning with the reign of Charlemagne, was a time of a modest revival of theological learning. The interested reader will find excellent history of the discussion of election in this period in Pelikan (vol. III, *The Growth of Medieval Theology 600–1300*, pp. 80-90) and of the corollary, redemption by Christ limited in some sense to the elect (pp. 90-95). Most of the issues raised later by Arminius and the Remonstrants and discussed at Dordrecht (1618, 1619) were raised there by Gottschalk and his detractors, including his insistence that our Lord made satisfaction only for the sins of the elect. This was centuries before the delegates at Dordrecht met to discuss the plan of salvation.

Anselm (eleventh century) and several others of his time echoed Augustine's thoughts on election and to a degree also on atonement. Thomas Aquinas (thirteenth century) took as strict an Augustinian view of election, free will and grace as Augustine, Luther or Calvin. A large section of *Summa Contra Gentiles*, might almost be transferred to the *Institutes* of Calvin or Luther's *Bondage of the Will* without seeming at all out of place (especially Book Three, chaps. 157–163). His views of atonement make some advance on Anselm, but I find nothing of 'particular atonement.'

---

21. B. B. Warfield, The Plan of Salvation, rev. ed. (Grand Rapids, MI: Eerdmans, 1973).
22. ibid., p. 104.
23. Francis Turretin, The Atonement of Christ, trans. J. R. Wilson, 1850, new ed. (Grand Rapids, MI: Baker, 1978), p. 115.
24. ibid., p. 116.

Hence, I think it proper to say that the doctrine of particular atonement, though a valid logical inference from the doctrine of election, was an inference seldom made in the history of Christian thought until the controversy among the Calvinists of the Netherlands in the last part of the sixteenth century over the whole plan of salvation.

R. C. Sproul asserts, 'Limited atonement was a major focus of debate between Augustine and Pelagius in the fourth century.' He does not document the claim. He also says limited atonement (as he defines it) is 'classical Augustinianism.' My limited investigation has not found it so. He insists, 'The Calvinist holds it [atonement] was only for the elect'.[25] C. A. Hodge makes similar broad statements.[26] I think both Hodge and Sproul may be in error on this particular point. There are many with perfectly sound Calvinist credentials who would say that while the work of Christ on the cross was *particular* in purpose and effect, securing the full redemption of all the elect (not merely making their salvation possible), it was also general, effecting reconciliation of God to mankind and of mankind to God – 'in Christ God was reconciling the world to himself.' Even Hodge acknowledges a 'special reference' to those 'elected to everlasting life,' I suppose parallel to a 'general reference' to the whole world. Perhaps it is only a slip of the pen.

I do not find Sproul's assertions supported by the literature. Perhaps I have missed something but I have found nothing about 'limited atonement' in Augustine's writings in the sense Sproul espouses and Calvin seems mainly to ignore the notion while affirming world reconciliation and even a propitiation *for* the world's sin if not specifically of it (see above).

Adherents to *Calvin's Calvinism* – of whom I generally admit to being one – can be cited on both sides of this subject. C. H. Spurgeon (who was a predestinarian Calvinist) as cited by Lewis and Demarest[27] held to general reconciliation and against limited reconciliation (at-one-ment), as also cited by N. F. Douty.[28] I have not been able to check their references. I think it is correct to say, as many Baptistic Calvinists, it was 'scholastic Calvinism' which 'narrowed the intent of the atonement and claimed that Christ died solely for the purpose of saving only the elect.'[29] In my judgment scholastic Calvinism in this matter goes beyond the relevant portion even of the Canons of the Synod of Dort, which wisely cautions against 'vainly attempting to investigate the secret ways of the Most High.'[30] Also A. H. Strong said, 'Much that is called Calvinism would have been repudiated by Calvin himself even at the beginning of his career, and is really the exaggeration of his teaching by more scholastic and less religious successors.'[31] John Gill – perhaps the most influential of all Baptist theologians – advocated a strict limited atonement doctrine.[32]

Why Not Before 1619?

Why did this almost unprecedented refinement of doctrine occur at the time and place it did, and not in the French-speaking world of Calvin but in the Netherlands where the Reformed church had become the state religion? *In the first place* the Dutch theologians were part of an embattled nation, recently delivered from threatened annihilation by Spain, the greatest Roman Catholic power in Europe. This had cost the Dutch people enormous national effort and loss both of civilian and military life. They rightly saw 'universal atonement' as *advocated by the Remonstrant party* as opening the door wide to a doctrinal enemy as dangerous as the Pope and his party. The rapid slide of the Remonstrants to the teaching of universal salvation justified their alarm.

Secondly, the enemy of orthodoxy in soteriology always is some form of self-salvation as in the unacknowledged Semi-Pelagianism of the Roman Church of the time and to a lesser degree in Arminius' doctrine. The Arminian form of the doctrine of plenary ability of fallen man was supported by a doctrine of universal atonement, as is also the case in Wesleyanism. Most Wesleyan theology to this day does not fully accept vicarious atonement but prefers a modification of the governmental theory. The Assembly at Dordrecht rightly saw that universal atonement was being employed to support a form of 'plenary ability' to the denial of a sound doctrine of sin (total depravity) as in all Augustinian theology. They were not mistaken in this and took what they deemed the proper step to correct it.

---

25. R. C. Sproul, *The Cross of Christ* (Orlando: Ligonier Ministries, 1989), pp. 68, 69.
26. C. A. Hodge, *Romans*, ii, p. 545.
27. Gordon Lewis and Bruce Demarest, *Integrative Theology ii* (Grand Rapids, MI: Zondervan, 1990), p. 381.
28. N. F. Douty, *The Death of Christ* (Swengel: Reiner, 1973), pp. 109, 110.
29. Lewis and Demarest, *Integrative Theology ii*, p. 381.
30. Philip Schaff, 'First Head of Doctrine,' in *The Creeds of Christendom iii*, 1919, repr. (Grand Rapids, MI: Baker Books, 1966), art. xiv, p. 584.
31. Strong, *Systematic Theology*, p. 778.
32. John Gill, *Complete Body of Doctrinal and Practical Divinity ii* (Grand Rapids, MI: Baker Books, 1978), pp. 11–32.

Thirdly, Lutheran theology had taken a turn away from Augustinian views of election. The Netherlanders and delegates from other lands wished to lift a standard of atonement to enforce the specificity and controlling force of election.

Fourthly, the evangelical revival that we call *The Reformation* was all about sound biblical, orthodox doctrine and all the evangelical part of Europe had paid an enormous price. (The French evangelicals were again at the time of the Synod of Dort in danger of life and limb and forbidden by their king to send delegates to the Synod.) Hence, no aspect of the doctrine of salvation seemed to be among 'the *adiaphora*' (non-essentials). These threatened Dutchmen and the other assembled delegates had the patience to sort through the problem and thereby to come to what they deemed to be logically sound, biblically correct and in step with the faith of the Apostles. It was not an epoch like our own of merely feel-good religion. They were of the conviction that universal redemption, as Arminians of the day (and some later Wesleyans) understood it, led to the doctrine of universal salvation, so they did not shrink from affirming that the specific, effective work of Calvary was for the elect alone. Let us see exactly what they said about it.

The Second Canon of the Synod of Dort.

The 'Second Head of Doctrine' treats 'Of the Death of Christ, and the Redemption of Men thereby' (not redemption 'of the elect,' but 'of men thereby'). First are several paragraphs on divine justice, grace, the perfect satisfaction in the sacrifice of Christ, its 'infinite value,' promise of the gospel, sufficiency of the 'sacrifice of Christ' even for those who do not repent or believe in Christ, and a sentence reaffirming salvation wholly by grace. Then the critical Article VIII follows.

> Art. VIII. For this was the sovereign counsel and most gracious will and purpose of God the Father, that the quickening and saving efficacy of the most precious death of his Son should extend to all the elect, for bestowing upon them alone the gift of justifying faith, thereby to bring them infallibly to salvation: that is, it was the will of God, that Christ by the blood of the cross, whereby he confirmed the new covenant, should *effectually redeem* [emphasis added] out of every people, tribe, nation, and language, all those, and those only, who were from eternity chosen to salvation, and given to him by the Father; that he should confer upon them faith, which, together with all the other saving gifts of the Holy Spirit, he purchased for them by his death; should purge them from all sin, both original and actual, whether committed before or after believing; and having faithfully preserved them even to the end, should at last bring them free from every spot and blemish to the enjoyment of glory in his own presence forever.

What Dort Did Not Say.

The critical words are, 'it was the will of God that Christ by the blood… should effectually redeem… all those, and those only, who were from eternity chosen to salvation.' The governing phrase is 'effectually redeem' and the decisive term is 'effectually.' This sentence moves in the previously announced territory of Articles III and IV which says Christ's death was of 'infinite worth… sufficient to expiate the sins of the whole world.' The sentence affirms nothing and denies nothing about the design of atonement as regards 'the whole world.' The sense is that Christ's blood effected salvation of the elect 'only' and was designed of God to do so. This was Dort's 1618 response to the second Arminian article of 1610 which asserts the 'Savior of the world… obtained for… all men and for every man, by his death on the cross, redemption and forgiveness of sins.'[33] It was evidently not of interest to the delegates at Dordrecht to specify further what God had done or had not done for the non-elect in the death of Christ. They were at pains to make plain that divine election was not conditioned by anything except God's sovereign will. They also made plain the salvation of these elect and accomplishment of salvation by particular atonement of particular people, the gift of faith to those same people, and their perseverance. This gift is a sovereign, gracious bestowal on the elect only.

In a series of 'articles' Arminius set forth the system of original 'Arminian' theology. In the fifteenth article Arminius constructed an order of the decrees of God.[34] In it election depends on foreseen faith. In the seventeenth article Arminius affirms, 'All unregenerate persons have freedom of will and capability of… rejecting the proffered

---

33. Schaff, *Creeds*, p. 546.
34. Arminius, art. XV, 'On the Decrees of God which Concern Salvation,' *Works, ii*, pp. 494, 495.

grace of God... without any difference of *the elect* and of *the reprobate*'[35] but they are condemned because God has given everyone 'sufficient grace' to believe, but the non-elect do not use it. This 'sufficient grace must necessarily be laid down [i.e. conferred by God]'. 'Were the fact otherwise, *the justice of God could not be defended* in his condemning those who do not believe.'[36] This is of course really a denial of by 'grace alone' in salvation. If to be fair (just) God 'must necessarily' do something for sinners condemned already (John 3:36) then it is not of grace at all. In Arminius' view 'restored ability' is a claim every sinner may justly demand of the Creator.

This was the kind of thinking Reformed Christianity had to expunge from its collective body or ultimately retreat to the Pelagianism from which by the Reformation it had escaped.

Yet in doing so the Canons of Dort do not deny general reconciliation (at-one-ment). They only proclaim 'particular redemption' as a necessary *logical* accompaniment of particular election, an election not based on the man's wise choice nor 'on human will or exertion, but on God, who has mercy' (Rom. 9:16).

In my judgment, the leading present advocates of a misapprehended *limited* atonement are correct in what they affirm but err only in what they deny. I think in the effort to deny any kind of reconciliation of the world to Christ in His Calvary work they err in explaining away plain texts, sometimes grotesquely.

W. G. T. Shedd's Suggestion.

W. G. T. Shedd was one of the most thoroughly, theologically, historically informed and biblically competent theological writers of modern times. Early in his treatment, Shedd explains the doctrine of particular atonement in a manner quite compatible with 'general reconciliation.' A. H. Strong, another competent Calvinist, seems to regard particular atonement in a manner consistent with his acceptance of an Augustinian form of election doctrine. Yet his brief defense of general reconciliation (at-one-ment) is convincing and, I think, correct.[37]

Let us look further at Shedd's contribution just noted. He points out that much disagreement is unfortunately caused by failure to agree on the words employed. Specifically, if applied to *intended application*, the extent of the atonement is limited to the elect, and there is no disagreement. 'If the word means value, then the atonement is unlimited.'[38]

Shedd goes on to make what I regard to be a correct and helpful distinction: 'Atonement must be distinguished from redemption. The latter term includes the application of the atonement.' Then turning to the 'statements that speak of the work of Christ as limited by... election' he points out the *Westminster Confession* (often held to teach limited *atonement*) really speaks of limited *redemption* (*Westminster Confession*, VIII.viii) and goes on to say, 'Accordingly the Scriptures limit redemption, as contradistinguished from atonement, to the Church [i.e. the elect].'[39] Then noting 'redemption includes reconciliation' he cites Bible passages which speak of Christ's work on the cross as effecting redemption specially for those who have faith, 'his people,' 'thy congregation,' 'the church of God,' etc.[40] He adds, 'Since redemption implies the application of Christ's atonement, universal or unlimited redemption cannot logically be affirmed by those who hold that faith is wholly the gift of God, and that saving grace is bestowed solely by election.'[41] So Shedd, along with many who claim to be Augustinian or Calvinist, affirms atonement (at-one-ment, reconciliation) is unlimited, and redemption is limited. Shedd goes on in his usual thoroughly biblical-exegetical manner to expound and to defend particular redemption.

This does not, however, quite close the discussion, for some will not accept the distinction and perhaps can point to difficult texts. More seriously, some who insist on unlimited redemption and deny particular, personal (not based on foreknowledge) election believe universal salvation is assured by universal atonement. This, of course, is thoroughly unbiblical and anti-Christian. Arminians (Wesleyans) hold that faith foreseen is really logically previous to election and therefore see no place for any real atonement that is not universal. Election is subsequent in logical order to 'deciding for Christ' and everyone has some power at least to *co-operate* with the Holy Spirit in making that 'step of faith.'

---

35. ibid., pp. 497, 498.
36. ibid., art. xvii, para. 12, p. 498.
37. Strong, *Systematic Theology*, pp. 771–773.
38. W. G. T. Shedd, *Dogmatic Theology ii* (Grand Rapids, MI: Zondervan, 1969), p. 464.
39. ibid., p. 469.
40. ibid., pp. 469, 470.
41. ibid., p. 470.

Richard Watson (1781–1833) systematized Wesley's thought and published it in two large volumes. A long section presents 'Redemption – Farther Benefits.'[42] Here he develops the doctrine that by virtue of universal redemption entire sanctification is attainable in the present life as a 'farther benefit' of Christ's work on the cross. This has been carried on by later theologians of Wesleyan persuasion in various holiness and 'entire sanctification' movements.

The Word of Life, volume two of *Systematic Theology*[43] by Thomas Oden, brings evangelical Methodist theology up to date. It is a major contribution to theology. The distinctives of Wesleyan thinking are not emphasized in Oden's book. Pages 390–392 treat 'The Extent of Beneficial Effects of His Death.' I have diligently read these pages several times to find what Oden's view might be. He quotes the *Russian Catechism*, *Church Dogmatics* by Barth and works of Bancroft, Gerhard and Schmidt, Aquinas, and cites Turrettin and Fuller. Yet he makes no clear statement of his own view of the controverted question of particular redemption. Perhaps this is not to be faulted in view of Oden's apparent intent throughout his three volumes of *Systematic Theology* to direct attention to the history of believing writing on theology rather than fine-tuned statements of his own on every question.

Agreement in Prayers and the Hymn Book.

It does seem, however, whatever the logic of the '*ordo salutis*,' all evangelical believers become Augustinians in prayer for the lost and in the hymn book.

The hymns and prayers of all evangelical parties to the debate imply not universally restored plenary ability but total inability of 'natural man,' most famously perhaps in Charles Wesley's line, 'hangs my helpless soul on thee' (from 'Jesus, Lover of My Soul'). Often on opposite page is arch-Calvinist Augustus Toplady's 'Rock of Ages' ('Thou must save, and thou alone'). Isaac Watts, third or fourth generation Calvinist preacher, appears in the Methodist Hymnal (1905) in hymns laced with the theology of Dort – 'How sad our state by nature is... Satan binds our captive souls... the voice of sovereign grace... the gracious call' (no. 668). In another by Charles Wesley he prays to the 'Son of God' to 'Speak with that voice that wakes the dead,/ And bids the sinner rise,/ and bids his guilty conscience dread/ The death that never dies.' This sounds much more like 'total depravity' and 'total inability' than universally restored freedom and power of the will to turn to God 'without further divine aid.' In the foxholes we all become believers that God *alone* can save.

A Note:

Some of the clearest statements of Reformation theology, including redemption and universal at-one-ment (reconciliation) current today are emanating from authors not associated with traditional 'Reformed' denominations. A. W. Pink (Baptist) in all his writings expounds these matters in full loyalty to biblical truth. Dr Curt Daniel, Ph.D., Edinburgh University (Reformed Bible Church) has produced a very helpful booklet *Biblical Calvinism: An Introduction to the Doctrines of Grace*.[44] These and many others are self-publishing some excellent literature for which the main-line presses have not found room. May their tribe increase! We seem to be returning to the most effective propaganda arm of the Reformation of the sixteenth and seventeenth centuries, pamphleteering on paper and in cyberspace.

---

42. Richard Watson, *Theological* Part ii, chap. xxix, vol. ii, pp. 450–469.
43. Thomas Oden, *Systematic Theology* (San Francisco: Harper Collins, 1992).
44. Contact P.O. Box 422, Mt Olive, MS 39119, USA.

18
Further Benefits and Accomplishments of the Death of Christ in our Place

The entrance of sin to the world in Satan and its extension to the human race whom God had created for His glory set loose a principle of disorder at the heart of the created order. The cross set things right, in principle, again. It is therefore to be expected that the cross which provided redemption for us poor, lost sinners should produce immense effects for good, setting things right again, throughout creation. Once the soul of the sinner, by the cross has been set free from bondage to fear death (Heb. 2:15) and the power of the devil, he is able unselfishly to contemplate the effects of redemption as far as the effects of sin had gone. Once set free from dread of the future the redeemed sinner is able to think of the cosmic environment in other ways than how it affects his health and his happiness. The entire created cosmos reaped a deliverance by Calvary. There were special gains for the Son of God as well as for the Father. The benefits of Calvary provide power for Christians to live victoriously and buoyancy to enjoy the victory.

These matters do not always gain the attention of theologians if their art is pursued only controversially, but ordinary devout believers relish the thoughts and blessings connected with our Lord's victory at the cross. Books of Christian devotion, like the New Testament itself, put the cross at the center of Christian piety.

The accomplishments of our Lord through the cross extended to the created cosmic order, to Christ Himself, to the Godhead and to the regenerate believer. They shall be discussed in that order.

Benefits for the Cosmic Order.

1. The atonement for sin wrought at Calvary reorganized the cosmos in some unexplained mysterious way – a manner that is reported in Scripture, but never explained. We know of it only by allusion. In Romans 8, one of Paul's great rhetorical flights, 'the whole creation' is said to have been unwillingly subject to 'futility... bondage... decay... groaning' (Rom. 8:18-23), to be fully delivered in the future at the time believers receive their resurrection bodies. No one knows exactly what this means, but evidently the fall of man harmfully affected 'the whole creation.' In his Epistle to the Colossians (1:19, 20) it is indicated that final deliverance of the whole creation is by a reconciliation which Christ has already effected 'by the blood of his cross,' 'through him to reconcile to himself all things, whether on earth or in heaven.'

Just how or why anything 'in heaven' should need to be 'reconciled' is not clear, yet Hebrews affirms that His 'better sacrifice... of himself' (9:23, 26) 'purified... heavenly things' in a manner analogous to the Old Testament priestly purification of things in an earthly sanctuary. Perhaps, as Calvin remarks about God's condescension in all biblical language, God is using baby talk here, accommodating to Jewish patterns of thought. Even so, the point is plain that Calvary's work left nothing in earth or heaven quite the same. The full integrity of the cosmic order of things was restored. He who 'inhabits eternity' had righted His time-bound world (Isa. 57:15; 66:1) in some way.

Older generations of believers, the ones who composed the lyrics for the hymn books most Christians still use, understood some of this. They were greatly interested in the subjective effects of 'the blood of Christ' on their character as we shall see, but they were fully aware of the universal effects of the transaction as well. Emphasis in recent religion has turned to how we feel about things rather than how matters really stand. Perception of reality not reality itself is the thing today! So the blood has been dropped from most recently composed religious music. Perceptions of reality rarely penetrate to the awful blot that called forth the wrath of God vented on the Son at Calvary.

2. Yet the New Testament emphasis, like our old hymns, is utterly unashamed of the bloody trace of redemption's story in personal salvation. The great C. H. Spurgeon in a sermon preached Sunday, 9 September 1888 met similar objections to the grim realities of what is derisively called 'slaughterhouse religion' with a warning:

> Remember, that Christ viewed as living, and not as having died, is not a saving Christ. He himself saith, 'I am he that liveth *and was* dead.' The moderns cry, 'Why not preach more about his life, and less about his death?' I reply, Preach his life as much as you will, but never apart from his death; for it is by his blood that we are redeemed.[1]

A partial list of the accomplishments specifically traceable to 'the precious blood' (1 Peter 1:19) will help to support the emphasis of this chapter: justification (Rom. 5:9), redemption (Rev. 5:9; Eph. 1:7; Col. 1:14), remission of sin (Heb. 9:22), forgiveness (Col. 1:14), loosing from our sins (Rev. 1:5), purging of conscience (Heb. 9:14), cleansing (1 John 1:7), sanctification (Heb. 13:12), reconciliation (Eph. 2:13), blotting out charges (Col. 2:14), Christian triumph over sin and Satan (Rev. 12:11; Col. 2:15), communion (1 Cor. 10:16). The blood has 'purchased' the church (Acts 20:28 KJV), it speaks 'a better word' (Heb. 12:24), it has been 'sprinkled' (Heb. 12:24). The blood of Christ is 'imperishable' (1 Peter 1:23), precious (1 Peter 1:19), supremely holy (sanctified) (Heb. 10:29) and innocent (Matt. 27:4).

'The blood of the Lamb' appeared almost as often in the hymn books of past generations as in the New Testament. Being 'washed in the blood,' however, falls offensively on the modern ear, now a generation or two removed from even dressing a chicken for Sunday dinner. So the hymns and the homiletical appeals made in connection with the hymns have fallen out of use. Let us take care the biblical doctrine which the blood signifies does not likewise disappear.

3. Closely allied with cosmic reconciliation, noted above, is the benefit, through Christ's death, for the whole human race, whether they ever hear of Christ or not or whether hearing the gospel they receive it in faith or not. Before we proceed I call attention to the fact that even some of the strongest advocates of 'limited atonement' agree with us on this matter, at least in part. Two strong, though reserved, advocates of 'limited atonement' are C. A. Hodge and John Murray. Hodge nevertheless acknowledges: 'Augustinians readily admit that the death of Christ had relation to man, to the whole human family, which it had not to the fallen angels... It... secures to the whole race at large, and to all classes of men, innumerable blessings, both providential and religious... There is a sense, therefore, in which He died for all.'[2] Further: 'He died for all, that He might... secure for men the innumerable blessings attending their state on earth.'

Likewise, J. Murray states:

> The unbelieving and reprobate in this world enjoy numerous benefits that flow from the fact that Christ died and rose again... The benefits innumerable which are enjoyed by all men indiscriminately are related to the death of Christ and may be said to accrue from it in one way or another.[3]

I shall not repeat what was stated in chapter 14 on the extent of the atonement, save to say the reconciliation of Calvary for 'the whole world' is based squarely on this text: '...that is, in Christ God was reconciling the world to himself, not counting their trespasses against them, and entrusting to us the message of reconciliation' (2 Cor. 5:19).

---

1. C. H. Spurgeon, *Metropolitan Tabernacle Pulpit* (London: Banner of Trust, 1965), vol. 34, no. 2043.
2. C. A. Hodge, *Systematic Theology ii* (Grand Rapids, MI: Eerdmans, 1960), pp. 545, 546.
3. John Murray, *Redemption Accomplished and Applied* (Grand Rapids, MI: Eerdmans, 1955), pp. 61, 62.

In my judgment this 'reconciliation,' in part, affects God's treatment of the sons of Adam from Eden onward. If God had 'imputed' (KJV) 'their trespasses against them' fully the full execution of death would have put an end to the human race. Now, since Calvary, it is clear why. The reconciliation in promise only (Gen. 3:15, the *protoevangelion*) became fulfillment at Calvary. There is a 'purpose and grace, which he [God] gave us in Christ Jesus before the ages began, and which now has been manifested through the appearing of our Savior Christ Jesus, who abolished death and brought life and immortality to light through the gospel' (2 Tim. 1:9, 10). In doing so God's grace brought salvation for 'all people' (Titus 2:11). I think it takes a remarkable degree of exegetical gymnastics to restrict 'all people' here to 'every kind of people' or 'elect people.' Paul made a *bona fide* offer of salvation to all and in God's name 'commanded all men everywhere to repent' and believe.

Calvary secured a reprieve on the penalty of eternal death for sin until the Judgment Day. Meanwhile, *because of Calvary*, execution is held in abeyance, 'not counting their trespasses against them' means God does not presently hold anything against sinners. '[T]he grace of God has appeared, bringing salvation for all people' (Titus 2:11). And 'whosoever will' may 'Come' (Rev. 22:17 KJV). The basis is the blood of Christ. The specific language of 1 Timothy 2:1-6 is helpful in resolving the obvious tensions of this doctrine. I think it points the way to avoidance of the error of the *universal redemption* doctrine of universalism and the error of some forms of *limited atonement* doctrine. I note: we are urged to pray 'for *all* [emphasis added] people [*anthropon*, male and female], for kings,' etc. These are both believers and unbelievers, elect and non-elect. 'This is good, and it is pleasing in the sight of God our Savior, who desires all people to be saved' (1 Tim. 2:1-4). It amounts to a kind of special pleading to suppose 'all people' in verse 3 to be only the elect when the whole human race is designated by the same Greek words in the first part of the syllogism (v. 2). Of course in verse 4 'who desires [ESV and RSV; 'Who will have' KJV, Gr. *thelo*] all people to be saved' has no reference to God's predestination, for which the usual verb is *proorizo*, or election (*ekloge*, *eklektos*) or purpose (several Greek nouns and verbs). Paul is speaking of God *ad hominem* (i.e. a human manner of speaking) as indeed we all must. Paul knew no more of God's mind in such matters than we do. He disclaimed such specifically (Rom. 11:33-35).

In John 12:27-34 we find Jesus early in the Passion Week predicting His imminent death and being 'lifted up [on the cross] from the earth' and somewhat enigmatically saying that 'when' that happens 'I... will draw all people to myself' (John 12:32). Up to that time He had spoken of the Father as the power which draws men to Christ in faith (John 6:44 and 65). Perhaps there is major reference here to some special enlightenment short of the call of Romans 8:28, 29 which renders one also sanctified and glorified. In view of the natural blindness of the children of Adam we may be sure no one ever came to saving faith unless in a supernatural way he is 'taught by God' (John 6:45). We have to be made willing to come by the new birth of Word and Spirit. This was not changed by the 'It is finished!' of Calvary. Yet now, after Calvary, from the ascended Son and the Father came the Spirit (Acts 1:1-5) just as the Baptist said (Matt. 3:11) and Jesus promised (John 14–16). That Spirit of the Son would now be diffused through the church through whose witness Christ would draw men to Himself. It is also a fact that preaching of the cross is the specific spear-point of the gospel which penetrates, woos and wins.

4. The Bible teaches that the victory that Christ won at Calvary delivered a permanent blow to Satan and all evil angels and spirits. It is a source of amazement to modern people – that is, to those few who take the trouble to discover it – how seriously Scripture takes the doctrine of satanic and demonic personal powers, especially their interference in worldly affairs. Daniel represents holy archangels Michael and Gabriel as in conflict with evil spiritual beings known as the prince of Persia and the prince of Greece, and they as delaying the arrival of the holy angel for three weeks (Dan. 8:16; 9:21; 10:13, 21). Paul speaks of evil spirits in such a way as to suggest a hierarchy organized to do Satan's work (Eph. 6:12; Rom. 8:38). That Christ's Calvary victory over them was manifested at His ascension (past), sitting at God's right hand (present) and Second Advent (future) is noted at Philippians 2:6-10; Colossians 1:20; 2:15; and 1 Peter 3:22; and elsewhere. Perhaps, as some competent exegetes suggest, the 'elementary principles of the world' (Gal. 4:3, 9; 'elements' KJV) should be understood as 'elemental spirits' (e.g. O. Cullmann, *The State in the New Testament*[4]). Several leading European theologians of the twentieth century, beginning with Martin Dibelius (*De Geisterwelt in Glauben des Paulus*, 1909), Karl Barth and O. Cullmann have supported the proposition that the 'powers that be' (Rom. 13:1 KJV) and 'rulers of this age' (1 Cor. 2:6, 8; 'princes of this world' KJV) are satanic spirits. They might not accept the New Testament as correct

---

4. O. Cullmann, *The State in the New Testament* (London: SCM Press, 1963), p. 77.

in asserting the existence of such unseen spirits, though ready to demythologize them into some human spiritual or psychic syndrome, personal or collective. In any case, they acknowledge the New Testament as teaching these things.

Martin Luther made much of Christ's victory over the devil at Calvary – as is well known. Calvin treats the subject somewhat at length.[5] John 12:31-33 seems to say Satan was judged at Calvary and Hebrews 2:14, 15 that the devil, as regards his 'power of death,' was destroyed 'through death,' i.e. Christ's. In that connection all of us must be thankful that Jesus 'brought life and immortality to light through the gospel' (2 Tim. 1:10). Hebrews 2:15 seems to say both saints and sinners before Jesus' death and resurrection were in bondage to fear of death. Likewise, though all men naturally 'fear death' believers in Christ have been delivered from 'bondage' to that fear. Because He died and yet lives so shall we.

Benefits for Christ Himself.

5. For Christ Himself the crucifixion was the last stage of the humiliation and the vestibule of the first stage of exaltation (if one accepts the burial as the first stage, see earlier discussion). When He committed His spirit into the hands of His Father we may be sure the 'joy that was set before him' (Heb. 12:2) began. There were many reasons for joy (Heb. 12:2), not least that His part of an 'eternal covenant' had been completed (Heb. 13:20). He had gained a prophetic vision of a numerous seed (Isa. 53:10; Ps. 72:15-17) – 'many sons' whom He would bring 'to glory' (Heb. 2:10). By the cross He earned a crown (Phil. 2:9; Isa. 53:11, 12; 1 Peter 1:10, 11).

6. The cross represented for our Lord a finished work. 'After making purification for sins, he sat down at the right hand of the Majesty on high' (Heb. 1:3). There is more in this sentence than the session as installation in a reign. His earthly life had been a ceaseless 'cross-bearing' from conception onward. 'The Son of Man came… to give his life a ransom' and at the end of that Passion it was all over. Now He could, as it were, sit down. The 'session' in heaven signifies the completed work of redemption. So there was a finality of Calvary for Christ Himself. '[W]hen Christ had offered for all time a single sacrifice for sins, he sat down at the right hand of God' (Heb. 10:12). '[H]e did this once for all when he offered up himself' (Heb. 7:27; cf. 1 Peter 3:18). There will be no second engagement.

The final, never to be repeated, never to be reenacted, never to be renewed character of the sacrifice of Calvary was in a large way the lynchpin of the Reformation of the sixteenth century – a corollary of justification by faith.

The teaching of Rome regarding 'the sacrifice of the mass' in the sixteenth century is still maintained by official authority to the present day. Rome both affirms and denies the finality of the cross in regard to human sin. 'The Papal Mass, A Sacrilege by which Christ's Supper Was Not Only Profaned But Annihilated': so is chapter 18 of Book IV of Calvin's *Institutes* entitled. The Roman Church has insisted to the present day that the bread and wine of the Eucharist are changed in substance to the veritable (i.e. real) body and blood of Christ. This is known as *transubstantiation* (change of substance). The 'accidents,' i.e. properties, remain those of bread and wine, hence they can be received and ingested as food. The bread is said to remain the body of incarnate God after the ceremony of the Mass is completed and may be (and frequently is) 'reserved' in a suitable receptacle ('the tabernacle') and elevated appropriately above or near the table ('altar') where the ceremony with the elements is conducted. This reserved sacrament is often formally adored by 'religious' personnel who address it and even pray to it. Many Roman Catholic sanctuaries have a special chapel where such a practice is perpetuated daily, even twenty-four hours a day. In Roman Catholic countries the sacramental elements are often borne in procession through the streets for the worship of crowds lining the way.

The one who performs the rite is called a priest precisely because the Mass is held to be a genuine sacrifice calling for a priestly (not a presbyterial) function. Hence, also the piece of furniture whereon the elements (i.e. the sacrifice of body and blood of Christ) are placed is called (and regarded as) an altar – a place of sacrifice. (Which is not to be confused with a communion table, or other surface sometimes metaphorically called an altar because gifts – offerings of money, food, flowers, fruits of harvest, Bibles, etc. – are placed there.)

Rome steadfastly perpetuates and defends the doctrine of the Mass. Masses are held to be meritorious for salvation of the offerer (priest) and attendees. Masses may be 'said' (performed) for the dead or living to aid in their

---

5. John Calvin, *Institutes of the Christian Religion i* (Philadelphia, PA: Westminster Press, 1960), I. 14, pp. 13–18.

salvation in some way. In large basilica-type church buildings there may be many altars with attending priests for each altar. The faithful pay for Masses to be said at these altars – especially for 'poor souls in purgatory.' This was a grievous offense to all the Reformers of the Reformation era and remains so to this day for any one sensitive to perversion of gospel purity.

These remarks are not intended to denigrate or condemn the believers in Christ who have been caught up in this system, which buries the gospel almost out of sight in unscriptural traditional observances. The Reformers regarded this feature of the papal church as the part which most severely vitiated the true gospel, making it, in the hands of zealots, an anti-gospel. This is why they chose the adjective 'evangelical' (good-news-preaching) as a name for their message and movement. They wished specifically to reject the notion of salvation by merit or even of gracious enablement to merit salvation. It is also why we must heartily reject the papal system grounded in the doctrine of repeated sacrifices and any cloying teaching or practice that distorts the Christian religion.

This discussion must not be extended, but I wish to emphasize the point that the offering of the body of Christ was a one-time event, plainly declared by Jesus Himself and competent apostolic authority never to be repeated. I will quote somewhat at length one of Calvin's pages as not likely to be improved upon and let the matter rest. Remember Calvin originally addressed much of what he had to say about the false sacrifice of the Mass to evangelical believers who were forced to worship clandestinely lest they be apprehended by the Inquisition. It was at a time when civil authority was daily killing those discovered to be evangelicals and at a time when Calvin was advisor also to the thousands of Reformed, evangelical believers in the Netherlands whom the Emperor and his chief general, the Duke of Alva, sought to exterminate. After citing affirmations of Christ's *once-only*, sufficient sacrifice (Heb. 9:26; 10:10, 14, 18, 26) he goes on to say:

> Christ also signified this by his last words, uttered with his last breath, when he said 'It is finished.' We commonly regard the last words of the dying as oracles. Christ, dying, testifies that by his one sacrifice all that pertained to our salvation had been accomplished and fulfilled. Are we to be allowed daily to sew innumerable patches upon such a sacrifice, as if it were imperfect, when he has so clearly commended its perfection? When God's Sacred Word not only affirms but cries out and contends that this sacrifice was performed only once and all its force remains for ever, do not those who require another sacrifice accuse it of imperfection and weakness? But to what purpose is the mass, which has been so set up that a hundred thousand sacrifices may be performed each day, except to bury and submerge Christ's Passion, by which he offered himself as sole sacrifice to the Father? Who, that is not blind, that it was Satan's boldness that grappled with such clear and open truth? Nor am I unaware of the tricks by which the father of lies is wont to disguise his fraud: that they are not varied or different sacrifices, but the same one often repeated. But such smoke clouds are easily dispersed. For in the whole discussion the apostle contends not only that there were no other sacrifices, but that this one was offered only once and is never to be repeated.
>
> Subtler men escape through a more secret chink – that it is not a repetition but an application. But it is just as easy to refute this sophism also. For Christ did not once for all offer himself up on condition that his sacrifice would be ratified by new oblations each day, but that the benefit of it should be communicated to us by the preaching of the gospel and the administration of the Sacred Supper.
>
> Thus Paul says, 'Christ, our paschal lamb, has been sacrificed' [1 Cor. 5:7], and he bids us feast [1 Cor. 5:8]. This, I say, is the means whereby the sacrifice of the cross is duly applied to us, when it is communicated to us to be enjoyed, and we receive it in true faith.[6]

Though Martin Luther also is on record with very extended remarks similar to those of Calvin, let us cite the confessional documents he inspired. The Lutheran Augsburg Confession (from Luther's time) rejected transubstantiation as well as any notion that the 'mass,' i.e. the Lord's Supper, was a sacrifice for sin, saying, 'The passion of Christ' is the sufficient oblation and sacrifice and citing Hebrews 10:10 adds, 'The Scripture also teaches that we are justified before God through faith in Christ, when we believe that our sins are forgiven for Christ's sake.' Then significantly, 'Now, if the mass do take away the sins of the quick and the dead [in purgatory]... then justification comes by the work of Masses, and not by faith; which the Scriptures cannot endure.'[7] As C. P. Krauth, perhaps the greatest American historian of Lutheran doctrinal developments, says of the Lutheran doctrine on this point (in the Augsburg Confession, tenth art.):

---

6. Calvin, *Institutes iv.* 3, p. 1432.
7. Philip Schaff, *Creeds of Christendom iii* (Grand Rapids, MI: Baker Books, 1966), p. 37.

> The body and blood of Christ cannot be reserved, laid up in monstrances, or carried in procession, any more than the Holy Ghost can be laid upon a Bible, or carried about in one… we worship Christ there ['at His table'] in no other mode than we worship Him everywhere.[8]

I have extended these quotations from standard sources of unquestioned authority for evangelical Protestants for a very pressing reason and beg the reader's attention and indulgence. Periodically waves of opinion among devout Protestants (and Roman Catholics) for rapprochement, or even 'healing of the breach,' rise high. On the personal level, Christian fellowship across the breach is taking place increasingly. On the personal level, I myself have been a part of this effort and approve heartily. Yet there has been no real movement at all in the papal hierarchy in this doctrinal area as recent Vatican documents, decrees and publications, including 'The New Catholic Catechism' of 1994, amply prove. There have been concessions toward the various kinds of liberal biblical criticism of the sort evangelicals must reject. In fact most Catholic biblical scholars of note today accept the documentary-development theories of Old Testament origins developed originally by Protestant, evolutionary Old Testament scholars over the past 200 years. Some of the most prominent negative New Testament critics of the left teach and write as Roman Catholics, as in some volumes of the *Anchor Bible* series. So though there is ample room on personal local levels for interaction and even co-operation and fellowship, the heart of the gospel is as much at stake today as in 'the breach' of the Reformation nearly 500 years ago.

Benefits for the Godhead as a Vehicle of Revelation.

7. Sound orthodox theology from Augustine of Hippo and Hilary of Poitiers to late Reformation times rejects all notions of suffering in the nature of the eternal 'God over all, blessed for ever' (Rom. 9:5); 'the One who is high and lifted up, who inhabits eternity' (Isa. 57:15); 'with whom there is no variation or shadow due to change' (James 1:17). The contrary assertion of 'the passibility of God' is almost entirely a modern notion. It was God the Son, according to the Scripture, not the Father God in heaven, who suffered in His human nature on Good Friday. Let us have none of the new Patripassianism.

Yet there was and is marvelous revelation of God in the cross. The cross made several explicit revelations about God. God was 'showing through' the supernatural darkness of the day and the rending of the veil. I shall present some of the scriptural evidences, summarize and attempt to draw some conclusions in a brief manner, even though books have been published on each.

(a) Calvary revealed the gracious purpose of God for sinners. Scripture says,

> [God] who saved us and called us to a holy calling, not because of our works but because of his own purpose and grace, which he gave us in Christ Jesus before the ages began, and which now has been manifested through the appearing of our Savior Christ Jesus, who abolished death [cross and resurrection] and brought life and immortality to light through the gospel' (2 Tim. 1:9, 10).

Take note: God's 'grace… now has been manifested through the appearing of our Savior.' The good news was dimly revealed in antiquity to Abraham (Gal. 3:8), but the chief revelation of Old Testament history and legislation is of God's holiness and truth. '[T]he law was given through Moses; grace and truth came ['came' is a very strong word in this context] through Jesus Christ' (John 1:17; cf. v. 14). The grace of God was present at every stage of Old Testament history, yet His holiness and righteous judgment often overshadow the grace. Think of the Great Flood; the death of Nadab and Abihu; the slaughter of Amelekites, Midianites and Canaanites; the Babylonian Captivity; and the story of Achan's execution. Quite to the contrary grace (in the sense of the unmerited favor to the undeserving) is prominent in everything about Jesus – incarnation, life, teaching, etc., but especially in His death. 'O the love that drew salvation's plan, O, the grace that brought it down to man, O, the mighty gulf that God did span at Calvary.'

(b) Calvary revealed the love of God. '[B]ut God shows ['commendeth' KJV; 'demonstrates' NAB] his love for us in that while we were still sinners, Christ died for us' (Rom. 5:8). The Greek word *sunistemi* (shows) has the root meaning of 'bring together' and by extension 'to demonstrate, show, bring out something' (Bauer, Arndt and Gingrich) 'render prominent' has been suggested. If ever the love of God was in doubt or obscure, the incarnation-for-immolation of the Second Member of the Godhead made it positive and plain (John 3:16).

---

8. C. P. Krauth, *The Conservative Reformation and Its Theology* (Philadelphia, PA: Lippincott, 1875), p. 622.

(c) Calvary revealed the righteousness of God. According to Romans 3:25 (KJV) and context God 'set forth [Christ Jesus] to be a propitiation through faith in his blood, to declare [Gr. *eis endeixin*, as a proof, demonstration of] his righteousness for the remission of sins that are past.' God's own personal righteousness in forgiving sins in previous ages without evident even-handed inflection of the penalties of law was 'justified' at Calvary. Substitutionary atonement (propitiation) enabled God righteously to carry out the penalties of His own law in forgiving sinners in ages before Christ's death. He simply remitted 'sins that are past, through the forbearance' looking ahead to the propitiation of sins at Calvary. So Calvary declares 'his righteousness at the present time… just and the justifier of the one who has faith in Jesus' (Rom. 3:26). Love of God for sinners meets His wrath at Calvary and nowhere else is fully explained. 'Mercy and truth are met together; righteousness and peace have kissed each other' (Ps. 85:10 KJV).

(d) Calvary revealed the wrath of God against sin and sinners. '[W]hy have you forsaken me?' (Matt. 27:46; Ps. 22:1) is explicable only as our Lord Jesus, once our sins were imputed to Him (2 Cor. 5:21), could not be spared the rod of divine abandonment. (See earlier discussions of atonement by vicarious sacrifice.)

(e) Calvary revealed the wisdom of God in providing a way to forgive sinners without relaxing the law of God or His justice in carrying out its penalties. As Romans 3:26 puts the matter, Christ became a propitiation through His blood 'To declare… at this time his righteousness: that he [God] might be [both] just, and the justifier of him which believeth in Jesus' (Rom. 3:26 KJV). 'Oh, the depth of the riches and wisdom and knowledge of God!' (Rom. 11:33).

8. Benefits of the Cross for Useful, Holy Living.

It is of great significance for a proper understanding of the nature of the Christian life that the first time Jesus in *literal language* spoke of His early death He immediately spoke of Christian discipleship in *figurative language* as taking up one's own cross and following Jesus (Mark 8:31; cf. vv. 34, 35). This is what He said: 'the Son of Man must suffer many things and be rejected by the elders and the chief priests and the scribes and be killed,' etc. Then after Peter tried to talk Jesus out of the whole repulsive notion Jesus went on to say to 'his disciples' in company with 'the people': 'If anyone would come after me [i.e. be a genuine disciple], let him deny himself and take up his cross and follow me.' Earlier He had said in connection with the first preaching mission of the Twelve, 'whoever does not take his cross and follow me is not worthy of me' (Matt. 10:38); then much later, en route to Jerusalem for the last time, 'Whoever does not bear his own cross and come after me, cannot be my disciple' (Luke 14:27).

> [W]hile he dwelt on earth… his whole life was nothing but a sort of perpetual cross… the reason: that it behoved him to 'learn obedience through what he suffered… why should we be exempt… since he submitted to it for our sake to show us an example of patience in himself.'[9]

The cross, in areas of the world ruled by Rome, was a symbol of social stigma and disgrace. For people in ancient Palestine who had seen a condemned criminal bearing each a cross and who had perhaps seen the same miserable man hanging in some public place the cross would have inspired terror as well. Any one seen bearing such a cross would have been on his way to public execution. No wonder therefore that the message of the cross, the central feature of the Christian proclamation, was a scandal to the Jews and foolishness to Gentiles! Yet the cross both in redemption and in Christian discipleship is both God's power and wisdom (1 Cor. 1:23, 24).

Our Cross and His Yoke.

'Take my yoke upon you… For my yoke is easy' (Matt. 11:29, 30). 'Whoever does not bear his own cross and come after me cannot be my disciple' (Luke 14:27).

A yoke usually joins two things, persons, animals. A yoke may have a bucket at each end, the burden on the carrier's shoulder; or it may rest on the necks of two oxen, the burden suspended between the mid-point of the yoke. In the case of persons, the figure is to share a burden as two oxen under a common yoke. Sometimes we are enjoined to cast all our care upon the Lord (1 Peter 5:7) but in the context of Matthew 16:29 Jesus means that the burdens of our life should be brought to Him where we share them with Him. There we find rest unto our souls. We still have the burden and with it Jesus' yoke – but the yoke is easy and the burden light. The key to this paradoxical teaching is to 'learn from me' the meekness He had. The 'meek' are the blessed 'for they shall inherit the earth.' Some suggest the burdens were the legalistic demands of the Scribes enforced upon common people. The Old

---

9. Calvin, *Institutes iii*. 8.1.

Testament ritual system was indeed described by Peter at the Jerusalem conference as 'a yoke on the neck of the [new, Gentiles] disciples that neither our fathers [Jews] nor we have been able to bear' (Acts 15:10). Of course Jesus did finish off that burden, though not the legalisms that we impose upon ourselves or upon others. It is likely Jesus was referring to the burdens of Hamlet's soliloquy – 'the slings and arrows of outrageous fortune... the heart-ache, and the thousand natural shocks that flesh is heir to... the whips and scorns of time.'

To take up this end of our yoke with Christ, in the sense of entering into the 'fellowship of his suffering, being made conformable unto his death' is no different essentially from bearing each his own cross as we follow Christ. As an old gospel song says, 'He always takes the heavy end and leaves the light to me'.

More specifically, to bear each his own cross means first, to enter into suffering *because* we are Christ's, i.e. suffering brought on specifically because we have taken His name and second, to accept the sufferings that Providence sends our way meekly, without bitterness. The Reformation era was a time of fierce persecution of evangelical believers in all of Europe, hence a large literature about cross-bearing, suffering for the Lord's sake and martyrdom arose. Until very recently those books were widely read among English-speaking peoples: Fox's *Book of Martyrs*, for example.

It was also a time when sickness and death were frequent visitors to nearly every family circle. Quite naturally an expositor like Calvin related much of his commentaries to willing acceptance of what Hamlet (Shakespeare) called 'the slings and arrows of outrageous fortune' as the refining chastisement of a loving Father God. The *Institutes* III.8.i and all of III.8.1–11, eleven pages in the Westminster Edition, develop this theme. Every generation has produced such literature for our profit.

I propose that what Christ said in a nutshell – as each disciple taking up his own cross as the way to Christian integrity, maturity, wholeness, holiness – is expounded and explained in four respects by Paul, one by John and one by the author of Hebrews.

(1) The righteousness of conformity to divine laws is 'fulfilled in us,' precisely because 'God... sending his own Son... for sin, he condemned sin in the flesh, in order that the righteous requirement of the law might be fulfilled in us' (Rom. 8:3, 4).

(2) Our standing as saints and to be presented to God some day 'holy and unblameable and unreproveable in his sight' (KJV) is precisely because 'he has now reconciled [us] in his body of flesh by his death' (Col. 1:22).

(3) Specifically, self-denial (or unselfishness) is enjoined by the fact that 'he died for all, that those who live might no longer live for themselves but for him who for their sake died and was raised' (2 Cor. 5:14,15).

(4) A biblical 'separation from the world' (a very unpopular item in our day of stepping to the world's tunes and conforming to its standards and styles) finds its support in Christ's cross: 'far be it from me,' Paul told the world-conforming Galatians, 'to boast except in the cross of our Lord Jesus Christ, by which the world has been crucified to me, and I to the world' (Gal. 6:14).

(5) The 'water and the blood' of Christ, who thereby Himself overcame the world, is our power of victory (1 John 5:4-6). This depends on a right doctrine of the cross. Christianity in integrity means the orthodox Christology of Nicea and Chalcedon *and* the vicarious satisfaction of divine justice at Calvary, i.e. propitiation of the divine wrath as well as expiation of the evil of sin. Nothing can set the conscience free from the accusation of conscience and consequent weakness at the emotional and ethical center unless the sinner, having been made aware of the debt of sin he owes to God, is also made aware the debt has been paid in full by the vicarious sacrifice of the God-man at Calvary. There is no Christian moral victory without conviction that 'Jesus paid it all.' (See previous comments on revelation at Calvary and discussion of reconciliation and propitiation.) Francis Pieper commenting on 'Christianity as the Absolute Religion' says, '[T]he Christian religion is absolutely perfect because it is not a moral code instructing men how to earn the forgiveness of sin themselves, but rather it is faith in that forgiveness which was gained through Christ's vicarious fulfillment of the Law and his substitutionary suffering of our punishment.'[10] Luther spoke often of this. As Calvin also remarked, our assurance that 'God remains kindly disposed and favorable to our works is not grounded in some nebulous belief in the loving character of God, but specifically the love of God manifested at Calvary.'

'God's unconditional love' may be an unfortunate expression. I think it is. Calvary proves God's love is great, but not unconditional at all. '[Y]ou hate all evildoers' (Ps. 5:5); 'The LORD is in his holy temple... his soul hates the wicked and the one who loves violence' (Ps. 11:4, 5). 'There are six things that the LORD hates...' (Prov. 6:16-19

---

10. Francis Pieper, *Christian Dogmatics i* (St Louis: Concordia Publ., 1950s), pp. 33–40.

– including a false witness and 'one who sows discord among brothers'). God does not love the reprobate, *as such*, at all and He loves no one unconditionally. Even the elect He loves conditional upon His grace, which for reasons known only to Him has not been equally extended to everyone on earth, granted the gospel is addressed to all without distinction. Let the unconvinced read the passages in Scripture about the eternal state of the lost and God's jealous anger over unrestrained and unpunished murderers, idolaters, fornicators, etc. See notes herein on 'sin to high heaven' in hamartiology.

(6) In the language of Hebrews 9:14, for one who in faith knows that the blood of Jesus Christ is enough to clear the record of all sin, the cross sets the conscience free for service to God. ' ...how much more will the blood of Christ, who through the eternal Spirit offered himself without blemish to God, purify our conscience from dead works to serve the living God.' Our human heritage provides two hands. If one must be employed to keep salvation intact the other will do little in the service of God or man on account of anxiety. 'Would you do service for Jesus your king? Would you live daily his praises to bring? There's wonderful power in the blood' (hymn by L. E. Jones).

The early Christians found that their crucified Lord was an obnoxious offense to the pagan world of their time. Paul speaks of 'the offense of the cross.' The cross therefore separated the Christians from the world of their time. Paul spoke of how by the cross 'the world has been crucified to me, and I to the world' (Gal. 6:14) – they became mutually irreconcilable. These expressions and others like Hebrew 13:12-14 assert this world is not our 'city' at all. The Lord expects us to go outside the city of the world to suffer outside the gate with our Lord.

These teachings must be balanced with other biblical teachings – we are to be *in* the world, not *of* it; to plant our vineyards, settle down, rear our families and seek the peace of our respective cities of residence, being salt and good savor and sweet odor in our journey to the eternal city.

It remains to be noted that the cross has opened the way of direct access in prayer, for we have 'boldness to enter into the holiest by the blood of Jesus' (Heb. 10:19 KJV).

19
The Doctrine of Atonement Before Anselm

In this chapter we shall see how through the centuries various aspects of the atonement by Christ's death on the cross were discerned by Christian teachers, yet all the while a doctrine of satisfaction by vicarious sacrifice was understood, even if dimly at times and often stated obscurely. In other words, the evangelical doctrine was never a novelty imposed upon the Scriptures. In every age it was at least partially understood.

I propose Anselm's work, especially his tract, *Cur Deus Homo?*, as the breaking point in sound interpretation of Christ's work of atonement, for several reasons. For one, he formulated and passed down to later generations the great idea of objective, finished accomplishment – a done deal as my lawyer says. For another, he saw that Scripture roots both 'the sending in the likeness of sinful flesh' and 'for sin' in the very nature of God. Anselm found both *holiness* and *justice* (righteousness) taking no back seat to His *love*. Further, as far as I can determine he was among the first scholastics to start with full approval of the ancient orthodox creeds and awareness of their incompleteness. His proposal of vicarious satisfaction of penal justice toward the infinite majesty of God, though needing some qualification, gave rational coherence to a theology of atonement. Evangelical theology has improved on Anselm but not rejected his accomplishments.

There is something of a consensus on this matter. 'In closing this brief skeleton of Anselm's theory of the atonement' said W. G. T. Shedd,

> It is evident that if his views and experience, as exhibited in the *Cur Deus Homo?* could have become those of the church... the revival of the doctrine of justification by faith in the Lutheran Reformation would not have been needed.... But the soteriology of Anselm, though exerting no little influence through his immediate pupils, did not pass into the church at large.[1]

This was because Britain and Normandy, where Anselm served, were then on the perimeter of Christendom. The city clergymen of Europe and the Roman bureaucrats were neither very pious nor interested in thoroughgoing theological reflection. J. L. Neve says, 'Anselm is gifted with genius.'[2] Shedd remarks of *Cur Deus Homo?* 'It is remarkable... bursting forth of a new spirit of inquiry, the dawning of a new era after five hundred years of stagnation and darkness.'[3] Geoffrey W. Bromiley claims Anselm's tract was 'epoch making.'[4]

---

1. W. G. T. Shedd, *The History of Christian Doctrine ii* (New York: Scribner, Armstrong and Co., 1872), p. 216.
2. J. L. Neve, *A History of Christian Thought i* (Philadelphia: Muhlenberg Press, 1946), p. 191.
3. Shedd, *op. cit.*, p. 273.
4. G. W. Bromiley, *Historical Theology* (Grand Rapids, MI: Eerdmans, 1978), p. 177.

During the first four centuries after the publishing of the last book of the New Testament the catholic (world-wide) church came to a consensus about the Person of Christ. This was expressed in the Apostles' Creed, the Nicene Creed and the Athanasian Creed. Yet little formulation of theology was directed to definition of Christ's work of redemption.

The Nicene Creed (AD 325, 381) simply says the Lord Jesus Christ 'for us men and for our salvation' 'came down from heaven, and was incarnate by the Holy Ghost of the Virgin Mary, and was made a man; and was crucified also for us under Pontius Pilate; he suffered and was buried; and the third day,' etc. The creed does not, however, say *how* those events in our Lord's career effected 'our salvation,' even though it states He came 'for …our salvation.'

In a very thorough treatment of 'the Pre-Nicene Theology' J. N. D. Kelly finds it 'useless to look for any systematic treatment either of man's lost condition, in need of redemption or of how redemption in Christ was brought about' among second-century writers. He notes 'while taking it for granted that men are sinful, ignorant and in need of true life, they never attempt to account for their wretched plight.'[5] They 'nowhere co-ordinate their main ideas or attempt to sketch a rationale of salvation.'[6]

The second century was a time of severe attacks upon the new faith from at least three quarters – Gnostic heretics, Judaism, and the pervasive, official and popular heathenism. The few of the second century who wrote to defend Christianity and whose writings are extant today wrote in the Greek language and are known to history as 'the Greek Apologists.' Of these the most important are Justin Martyr, Tatian and Athenagorus. They did not choose to treat doctrines in addressing their adversaries. Hence, 'These writers treat Christianity predominantly as a body of teachings relating to religion and morals.'[7] Their thoughts therefore on the work of Christ for fallen men were 'shot through with ambiguity.'[8] Kelly goes on to say, not until the third century, i.e. after AD 200, was there a beginning of a systematic doctrine of salvation, even 'the germ of a doctrine of substitution.'[9]

Salvation by Recapitulation – Irenaeus.

(Throughout the rest of this chapter 'Salvation' alternates with 'Atonement' and related words because the ideas were not clearly separated in early Christian times.)

Irenaeus of Lyon (AD 120–202) is known for his soteriology of *recapitulation*, also called *assimilation* and *imitation* of Christ. Passages usually cited are from *Against Heresies* (5.16.2 and 3; 2.22.4; 3.18.1 and 7; 3.16.2), a long treatise. Irenaeus engaged 'in a life-long struggle against the heresies that… came in, like locusts, to devour the harvests of the gospel.'[10] Irenaeus' idea of defense against heresies was defense and exposition of truth, such as is found in his famous work, *Against Heresies*, a book of 252 pages in ANF. In meeting the minds of his time, both pagan and Christian, Irenaeus enlarged upon the central mystery of the faith, the incarnation. God the Logos *assimilated* (accommodated) Himself to Adam (the human race) and in His life, from birth to death, recapitulated every stage of human life. This doctrine was based on a rather shallow exegesis of Paul's doctrine of the First and Second Adam. His notion never made much impression, even on Irenaeus himself, for, as he acknowledged. Jesus did not live through middle and old age and He was never a husband or parent. He called for *imitation* of Christ as our *example*. God *accommodates* to us; Jesus *recapitulates* Adam (us, all sinful men); He is our *example* whom we are to *imitate*.

Yet the energetic bishop must not be accused of anticipating the modernist heresy of salvation by following Christ's good example. For, in book 5, chapter 16, paragraphs 2 and 3, after stating the solidarity of the Logos both with God and man he adds that He, the Lord, manifested Himself by His Passion in which by His obedience on a tree (cross) He took away the effects of Adam's disobedience at a tree (in Paradise). He concludes, 'In the second Adam, however, we were reconciled, being made obedient even unto death. For we were debtors to none other but to Him whose commandment we had transgressed at the beginning' (*Against Heresies* XVI, 3, ANF 544). So Irenaeus apparently had at least an inkling of reconciliation (at-one-ment) by the death of Christ, after all. This is vicarious satisfaction in different words.

---

5. J. N. D. Kelly, *Early Christian Doctrines*, rev. ed. (San Francisco: Harper & Row, 1978), p. 163.
6. ibid., p 163.
7. G. P. Fisher, *History of Christian Doctrines* (Edinburgh: T & T Clark, 1927), p. 61.
8. Kelly, *Early Christian Doctrines*, p. 168.
9. ibid., p. 177.
10. A. C. Cox, in *Ante-Nicene Fathers*, ed. Roberts and Donaldson (American Edition, 1885, repr. Peabody: Hendrickson Publ., 1994), p. 309.

The relation of Jesus Christ to the Godhead and of the divine and human in His Person were matters of intense debate and careful definition in the early church, but the saving work – even though it was certainly the chief burden of evangelism and Christian nurture in the churches – was apparently never formally defined.

Savior.

However we explain the absence of an explicit soteriology, the church pervasively called Jesus *Soter*, Savior. We may be sure the meaning of that word was understood as something more profound than victor over Satan, teacher, prophet, fulfillment of Old Testament prophecies of Messiah or example, though all those ideas also were present in the writing of the apostolic Fathers.

The apostolic Fathers (the first writers after the close of the New Testament) failed 'to grasp the significance of the death of Christ.'[11] Even Justin (about AD 100–165), for example, says little or nothing about it. Yet as one of the most influential and most critical interpreters of Justin pointed out, 'It is equally certain that Justin's own faith was nourished more by that which the congregation confessed and taught concerning Christ its Lord than by that which he himself interpreted in a theoretical way.'[12]

Substitutionary Suffering.

Historians of the period quite regularly point out that the cross, interpreted as substitutionary suffering by reference to the prophecies of the Servant in Isaiah 42–53, especially chapter 53, was imbedded in the church's liturgy of the time. It could hardly be otherwise in view of the regular, frequent observance of the Eucharist (or Lord's Supper), always accompanied (as frequently still today) by liberal readings of the relevant words of institution, comments on the same in the Epistles and other Scripture. The language of the authors of the sub-apostolic period and on to Nicea (AD 325) reflects the liturgical language of the Supper and the story of Passion and cross.

Perhaps, as some say, the soteriology of Irenaeus, Tertullian and Clement of Alexandria did draw much from the prevalent Platonism in interpreting the Scriptures. Similarities to modern neo-orthodoxy's doctrine of salvation by the incarnation of the Son of God rather than by His sacrificial death are present in their writings. There was also an early appearance of what not long ago was called 'modernism.' 'The Logos assimilated himself to man and man to himself in his life and passion,' etc., etc. These notions have reappeared with differing emphases from time to time, but blessedly never were widely endorsed. It was probably more 'private speculation'[13] than church dogma. Yet the language of leading proponents shows 'that neither the teaching nor the example of Christ could be isolated from the message of the cross'[14] and according to Pelikan, there is reason to believe that the saving power of the suffering and death of Christ was more explicitly celebrated in the worship of the second century than formulated in the faltering, initial attempts at theologizing of the time.[15]

Satisfaction of Law and Justice.

Tertullian (AD 160–230) seems to have introduced the important word 'satisfaction' to Christian theological language, in a treatise on repentance. He did not, however, use the word in connection with the Calvary work of Christ. He probably derived the term and the idea it represented from Roman law (Tertullian had been a lawyer) 'where it referred to the amends one made to another for failing to discharge an obligation.' In one of Tertullian's treatises he spoke of God as One to whom in repentance 'you may make satisfaction' (*On Penitance* 7.14) and the desire to make satisfaction is a reason for confession (*On Penitence* 8.9). Though Tertullian did not use 'satisfaction' in explaining the Godward meaning of Christ's sacrifice on the cross he apparently introduced this heavily freighted word into the vocabulary of Christian theology. Furthermore, Tertullian understood what later was implied in 'satisfaction' saying in his treatise *On Modesty* (22.4), 'Who has ever redeemed the death of another by his own, except the Son of God

---

11. T. T. Torrance, *The Doctrine of Grace in the Apostolic Fathers*, repr. 1959, p. 37, cited by Jaroslav Pelikan, *The Christian Tradition, vol. i, The Emergence of the Catholic Tradition (100–600)* (Chicago: University of Chicago Press, 1971), p. 143.
12. Moritz von Engelhardt, *The Christianity of Justin Martyr*, Goettingen, 1878, cited by Pelikan, *Christian Tradition*, p. 143.
13. Pelikan, *Christian Tradition*, p. 141.
14. ibid., p. 146.
15. ibid.

alone? ...Indeed, it was for this purpose that he came – to die for sinners.' Only a little later than Tertullian, Hilary of Poitiers (AD 300?–367), a most competent and articulate theologian, became the first known to equate 'satisfaction' with the 'sacrifice' of Christ and to interpret the death of Christ as the 'act of reparation to God on behalf of sinners' (*Exposition of the Psalms*, on 53:12-13). Here in the translation of H. F. Stewart are the significant statements of one of the greatest of the early Christian theologians. Hilary said Jesus' suffering on the cross 'was intended to fulfil a penal function' and he received the 'penalty.' He relates the penalty to 'the sacrifices of the Law' and then interprets the work of Christ in these words,

> It was from this curse that our Lord Jesus Christ redeemed us, when as the Apostle says: 'Christ redeemed us from the curse of the law, being made a curse for us, for it is written: cursed is every one that hangeth on a tree [Gal. 3:13].' Thus He offered Himself to the death of the accursed that He might break the curse of the law, offering Himself voluntarily a victim to God the Father... offering to God the Father.[16]

This is the doctrine of satisfaction by substitutionary sacrifice many centuries before Anselm, Thomas and Calvin.

Sacrifice.

References to the death of Christ as a sacrifice appear among the apostolic Fathers. *The Epistles of Barnabas* (about AD 100) sees in the sacrifice of the red heifer, without blemish, slaughtered outside the camp, its blood sprinkled before the sanctuary, the flesh, blood and offal burned, its ashes mingled with water employed for purifying (Num. 17:1-22) a type of Christ's death.[17] He even has an incipient phraseology for imputation.

Cyprian of Carthage (d. AD 250) in his 63rd epistle was already calling ministers of the Word, priests and the elements of the Lord's Supper, oblations and sacrifices (ANF. 364, 365), so his reference therein to the death of Christ as a 'sacrifice' may be faint support for this term. I do not think it likely, however, as some do, that he derived the term from the 'liturgy of the altar' considering how the Old Testament ritual sacrifices were regarded widely as types of Christ's offering of His life to God. (In *Scorpiace* [*Antidote for the Scorpion's Sting*] Tertullian produces some shaky theology on the basis of the LXX rendering of Proverbs 9:2, praising martyrdom.)

Not much later Tertullian seems to assume everybody should understand the typical connection between many Old Testament people, institutions and events as well as prophecies of the Passion and death of Jesus.[18] He expounds on the typology of Christ in 'wood' and 'tree' in the Old Testament, which he invariably traces to the Lord's Passion. The wood Isaac carried typified Christ's cross. But unlike Isaac, for whom a ram was substituted, Christ was hung from His 'wood,' adding this important sentence: 'For him it behoved to be made a sacrifice on behalf of all Gentiles, who was led as a sheep for a sacrificial, victim.'[19] Of course the New Testament says 'Christ our Passover has been sacrificed for us' and it seems to me was quite sufficient grounds for the scripturally versed Fathers of the church to interpret the death of Christ as a sacrifice for sin offered to God. Historians who suppose a late date for New Testament writings find little there to explain the sacrifice interpretation in these early writers. Pelikan calls such descriptions of Christ's death as a sacrifice 'liturgical echoes,' a meaning derived from the Eucharistic liturgy of orthodox Christianity, which in turn, opponents of orthodox Christianity say borrowed from heathen language of sacrifice and the Jewish temple worship. In view of the dissemination of Gospels and Epistles before Cyprian and Tertullian, and perhaps before Barnabas, I see no need at all to find the source anywhere except in the New Testament.

Ransom.

This way of explaining the meaning of the Lord's death on the cross was common, being based on sayings of Christ (Matt. 20:28), Paul's use of the term in this way (1 Tim. 2:6) and the suggestive language of Isaiah 53:5, 6. The *Epistle to Diognetus* (about AD 130–150) uses this language in a gospel preachment worthy of George Whitefield, saying 'He Himself took on Him the burden of our iniquities, He gave His own Son as a ransom for us the holy One for transgression... capable of covering our sins [with] His righteousness... we, the wicked... O sweet exchange.'[20]

---

16. *Nicene and Post-Nicene Fathers ii*, ed. Schaff and Wace, 1890 (repr., Peabody: Hendrickson Publ., 1994), vol. 9, pp. 246, 247.
17. *Epistle of Barnabas* in *ANF i*, chap. 8, p. 142.
18. Tertullian, *An Answer to the Jews* in *ANF iii*, chaps. 10–13, pp. 164–172.
19. ibid., pp. 171, 172.
20. *Epistle to Deognetus*, chap. ix, in *ANF i*, p. 28 or Lightfoot, *The Apostolic Fathers* (New York: Macmillan, 1898), p. 501.

The writer of the *Epistle to Diognetus* does not say to whom the ransom was paid, but many over the second and third centuries, including Origen,[21] said it was paid to the devil. Yet, Gregory Nazianzen, while promoting the thoroughly biblical doctrine of the death of Christ as a payment for release or ransom, ridiculed the notion that it was paid to the devil. God the Father accepted the blood of the cross 'on account of the incarnation, and because Humanity must be sanctified by the Humanity of God' – in answer to the question, 'To whom was that blood offered which was shed for us, and why was it shed? ...the precious... Blood of our God and High priest and Sacrifice?'[22] In the brief chapter 22 he mingles ransom with sacrificial and victory metaphors, yet he obviously did not think of the atonement as any sort of ransom paid to the devil. Neither does any other widely accepted creed that has come to our attention over the span of centuries before the Reformation of the sixteenth century. This is quite amazing, for the Reformation for the first time made soteriology – how one can be saved and know one is for certain – the very center of the storm which swept Europe and propelled Luther, Melanchthon, Calvin, Cranmer and all the rest into the mighty shaking of 1517–1648.

Christus Victor (Victory Over All Enemies, His and Ours).

As Pelikan observes, modern Western Christians might see some formation of 'the orthodox doctrine of vicarious atonement' in these writers of the second and third centuries, 'but it is their emphasis on the saving significance of the resurrection of Christ that he will find most unusual.'[23]

Irenaeus and Origen were among the earliest advocates of the "Christus Victor" doctrine. This emphasis in the theology of many early Fathers that the victory over all enemies, Christ's and ours, at Calvary is sometimes called the classic theory of the atonement.[24] Yet this is an overstatement of its importance.

There is sufficient biblical evidence for this view that Gustaf Aulen's book (*Christus Victor*, 1969) has received favorable notice from even competent, conservative, evangelical quarters (Walvoord). Barth from a neo-orthodox perspective, Cullmann from his own unique perspective, and J. H. Yoder from a liberal pacifist outlook, have given this view currency in our era. They have found Scripture support chiefly in the promise of Genesis 3:15 concerning the crushing of the serpent's head and the bruising of the heel of the woman's seed and the supposed similar reference to the binding of the devil ('strong man') at Matthew 12:22-29.

Athanasius argues through chapters 21–25 of the *Incarnation of the Word* that the resurrection after a public death on a cross was intended by God's design to prove victory over death and the prince of the powers of the air.[25] Athanasius uses the figure of a good wrestler who lets his public foes choose his opponent (as Jesus' enemies chose a cross). 'He was to prove Conqueror of Death in all of its forms.... He defeated the "Prince of the powers of the air" in his own region.'[26] We now look to some of the outstanding theologians of the fourth to tenth centuries for clear statements of a doctrine of atonement.

Substitution and Satisfaction.

Athanasius (d. AD 373), of his time, the paramount exponent of orthodox Christology, composed nothing on the atonement, yet in his polemics with Arians he plainly expressed the *substitutionary* character of Christ's work on the cross. Shedd shows that in his writings on the Trinity he incidentally maintained 'the *expiatory* nature of Christ's work' and cites passages containing the substance of that doctrine of plenary satisfaction of divine justice 'by the theanthropic sufferings of Christ which acquired full scientific form in... Anselm, and which lies under the whole Protestant Church and [its] theology.'[27] Athanasius shows that the modern liberal notion that God *sovereignly* forgives any sin upon the sinner's repentance, without the need for any punishment, vicarious or otherwise (of which the story of the father's forgiveness of the prodigal son is supposed to be illustrative), was current in the fourth century. And Athanasius utterly rejected it, using language that Calvin might have used (and perhaps did use).

---

21. Origen, *Commentary on Matthew*, in ANF ix, Bk 16, chap. 8.
22. Gregory Nazianzen, *Second Oration on Easter* xxxxv.22 in NPNF vii, p. 431.
23. Pelikan, p. 149.
24. John Macquarrie, *Principles of Christian Theology*, 2nd ed. (New York: Charles Sribner's Sons, 1966, 1977), pp. 318–321.
25. Athanasius, *Incarnation of the Word*, chaps. 23–29, in NPNF iv, pp. 48–52.
26. Editor's summary of chaps. 24 and 25, NPNF iv, p. 49.
27. W. G. T. Shedd, *History of Christian Doctrine*, p. 242.

> Suppose that God should merely require repentance in order for salvation? This would not in itself be improper did it not conflict with the *veracity* of God. God cannot be untruthful, even for our benefit. Repentance does not satisfy the demands of *truth* and *justice*. If the question pertained solely to the *corruption* of sin, and not to the *guilt* and *ill-desert* of it repentance might be sufficient. But since God is both *truthful* and *just*, who can save, in this emergency, but the Logos who is above all created beings. He who created men from nothing could suffer for all and be their substitute. Hence the Logos appeared.... He saw how inadmissible it would be for sin to *escape the law*, except through a fulfillment and *satisfaction* of the law. [28]

In this quotation I have highlighted the ideas characteristic of the Anselmic-Protestant consensus: God's veracity and law must be honored in forgiveness; penalty must be paid; satisfaction (the key word) of justice must take place. There is no reference here to the divine majesty or infinity as in Anselm, or to the divine holiness as in Calvin, and the Protestant writings on the subject, but reference to God's veracity, law and justice (which are similar ideas).

Origen (born at Alexandria AD 185, d. AD 254) was a rare combination of great learning with little wisdom, deep piety with some truly weird behavior. The church is still greatly in his debt for his work on the text of the New Testament and in translation of the New Testament. His zeal to defend Christianity was unsurpassed. Though the greatest textual scholar of the ancient church, he went to such extremes the church finally denounced him as a heretic. He had a way of carrying good ideas to dangerous extremes. Yet even Origen was one of the many writers of the time who quoted Isaiah 53 to explain the connection between the death of Christ and the forgiveness of sin 'healed by the passion of the Savior.'[29]

Revelation.

That Christ came to reveal the one true God is a plain fact of Scripture. Passages in the writings of Origen, Gregory of Nyssa, Clement of Alexandria and others seem to refer to Christ's work as Revelator constitutes Him as the Savior; it is doubtful if they intended this to exclude His mission to deal with the guilt of sin.

Apparently Origen alone among the Fathers carried the idea of redemption by Christ to the extreme of universal salvation. He thought even the devil will ultimately be saved.

Churchgoers of those times, however, were not forming their theology by reading the erudite writings of the above-mentioned scholars. Their theology was formed by what they received from the Bible-readings and liturgy of worship services and catechisms. Popular theology then, even more than today, was so derived, because copies of the Bible were rare and printed study materials non-existent. Therefore, in spite of many rudimentary and confused ideas about Christ's work of redemption, the Bible-centered worship of the church insured widespread understanding that the death of Christ on the cross procured forgiveness of our sins.

Deliverance.

Little if any advance in putting together the biblical elements of a comprehensive summary of a doctrine of atonement is to be found in Augustine. Augustine's energetic mind, directed in part by his introspective nature (*The Confessions*) and the Pelagian controversy, was expended on the doctrines of man and sin. Yet he accepted and promoted what was best in his predecessors. Augustine developed no profound doctrine of atonement to compare with his accomplishments in many other areas. Even so, incidental comments here and there show unmistakably that he was convinced of atonement by vicarious satisfaction, though not well defined or free from inconsistencies. He did not always distinguish between the judicial side of redemption and the renewing work of Christ in our sanctification. He does not therefore advance beyond his predecessors and shares some of their confusion. Two of Augustine's best statements follow.

> For the devil, having deceived the woman, and through her brought about the downfall of the man was laying claim to all the descendants of the first man as sinners by the law of death; in a wicked desire to do harm, indeed, but none the less by a most equitable right. This power of his held good until he put to death the Just One, in whom he could show nothing deserving of death; but also because he was born without that lust [i.e. by

---

28. Athanasius, *The Incarnation of the Word*, chap. 6, Dorner's trans., quoted by Shedd, *History of Christian Doctrine ii*, pp. 242, 243, preferable to *NPNF iv*, pp. 39, 40.
29. Origen, *Against Celsus i*.54, 55, in Pelikan, *The Christian Tradition i*, p. 153.

> virgin conception], to which the devil had subjected those whom he had taken, so that whatever was born of it he would retain as if it were fruit of his tree; by a wicked desire to possess it indeed, but yet with a right that was not unfair. And so he is most justly compelled to let go those who believe in Him whom he put to death unjustly [Adam and all his descendants]; so that dying [in Christ's death] in this world they cancel the debt, living eternally they live in Him who paid for them [us] what He [Christ] did not owe.[30]

Augustine, like his predecessors, was overpersuaded of Satan's claims, but his emphases are justice, the holy character of divine law, substitution, and, in a strange way, the sinlessness of the Substitute.

Harnack once remarked that 'Whoever looks away from the formulas to the spirit will find everywhere in the writings of Augustine a stream of Pauline faith.'[31] This is apparent in the quote to follow. It is the clearest statement about Christ's redemptive work on the cross from Augustine I know of. He is answering the charge of Faustus the Manichaean that Moses stupidly cursed Christ.

> Christ has no sin in the sense of deserving death, but he bore for our sakes sin in the sense of death as brought on human nature of human sin. This is what hung on the tree; this is what was cursed by Moses [Deut. 21:23]. Thus was death condemned that its reign might cease and cursed that it might be destroyed. By Christ's taking our sin in this sense, in condemnation is our deliverance, while to remain in subjection to sin is to be condemned.[32]

These and other passages in his writings show indisputably that Augustine understood the work of Christ on the cross as a substitutionary satisfaction for the sins of mankind. He did not quite shake free from notions of deliverance from Satan and the demonic. The pervasive presence of idolatry, which Paul associates with worship of demons (1 Cor. 10), and the remarks of Jesus about Satan's being 'cast out,' and Jesus' awareness of the powers of darkness with the Hebrews chapter 2 teaching of deliverance from fear of death and 'him that has the power of death, that is the devil,' account for this. Theologians became aware that the overcoming of death (personalized or not) and power of the devil (whom Jesus said 'has nothing in me') are fruits or results of the atonement, not of the essence of it.

Salvation by a Penal Offering to Justice.

Gregory the Great (540–604), bishop of Rome and recognized as pope (590–604), is said to be like the double-headed Janus of Rome – looking back upon the patristic age and bringing it to an end while also in the midst of the collapsed civilization of antiquity, stepping out in the dark age that lasted until the beginnings of the revival of learning in the eleventh century. Though he preserved the Christological and Trinitarian consensus of the Ecumenical Councils – as medieval folk understood them – he also rendered official and almost unchallengeable many superstitions and practices of the popular culture.

Pope Gregory ruled the official thought of the Western church without serious challenge for the next 500 years. His theology is still dominant in the Roman Church – Trent and Vatican II notwithstanding.

Aptly described as 'a wise and energetic churchman, a shrewd politician, a lovable... shepherd of souls,'[33] his theology is 'a hodgepodge.'[34] He was not only a man *for* his time but *of* it and things did not change for 500 years. It may be laid to the kindness of divine providence that his writings echo an Augustinian doctrine of atonement, partially defective as it was. It was possible for people of western europe to hear the theology of Romans chapter 3 verses 24 and 25 at least on occasion and we may hope many thoughtful folk grounded faith and hope in the finished work of Christ on the cross.

It is a providence of God that Gregory carried into the medieval epoch a sound conception of the atonement so far as it had been stated up to his time. Gregory is the first outstanding representative of 'the hierarchical spirit which was now to mould and corrupt Christianity for a thousand years, we are naturally surprised to find in the writings of one whom some regard as the first pope, representations of the atoning work of Christ so much in accordance with the Pauline conception of it.'[35]

---

30. Augustine, *The Freedom of the Will*, iii.10, trans. C. M. Sparrow (University of Virginia Studies, Charlottsville, VA: University of VA Press, 1947), p. 112.
31. Cited by G. P. Fisher, *History of Christian Doctrine*, 2nd ed. (Edinburgh: T & T Clark, 1896, 1927), p. 180, from Harnack, *Dogmengeschichtechte ii. 71.*
32. Augustine, *Reply to Faustus the Manichaean, xiv.3*, in *NPNF*, 1st Series, 1, p. 208.
33. Juergen L. Neve, *History of Christian Thought ii* (Philadelphia, PA: Fortress Press, 1946), p. 173.
34. ibid., p. 173.
35. Shedd, ii, p. 263.

Gregory, though he aided and abetted the errors and abuses that much later brought on the sixteenth-century Reformation, was also a cogent advocate of the central doctrine of Scripture we describe as atonement by vicarious satisfaction. Among his voluminous writings is his *Moral Discourses of Job*, wherein he stresses that 'guilt can be extinguished only by a penal offering to justice. But it would contradict the idea of justice, if for the sin of a rational being like a man, the death of an irrational animal should be accepted as a sufficient atonement.' He follows, saying the sacrifice must be a man, a man unstained by sin. 'Hence the Son of God... assumed our nature without corruption... made himself a sacrifice for us... a victim without sin, and able both to die by virtue of its humanity and to cleanse the guilty, upon the grounds of justice' (Book XVII, 46). Gregory in thinking of 'justice' meant in the sense implied in vicarious satisfaction – i.e. divine justice. He does not say to whom the sacrifice was offered, but it seems to be implied it was to God, not to the devil as in some older theology.

So down through the generations of the 'dark ages' – and there was surely darkness enough – there were bound to be glimmerings, even shafts of the light of the gospel, in spite of ignorance, moralism, formalism, legalism, sacramentalism and corruption. It was received by those whose hearts were touched.

Of course the 'dark ages' were not entirely dark at any time. Wherever the Word of God is known, faith is apt to follow (Rom. 10:17); 'the entrance of thy work giveth light.' The ecclesiastical records of those centuries assure that matters of doctrine and Scripture interpretation were the subject of many synodical meetings and ecclesiastical decrees.

Atonement received some enlightened attention in the ninth century in the person of Gottschalk of Orbais (c. 806–868). (Gottschalk was a participant in a flurry of serious theological debate in ninth-century Europe. Chapter XI, 'Conflicts at Corbie' of G.W. Bromiley's *Historical Theology: An Introduction* provides a dependable summary of this important episode in the development of a theology of the atonement.) Through his studies of Augustine this monk (Benedictine), then a secular priest, discovered that the ecclesiastical system of the time had a near-Pelagian heart beneath a cloak of professed Augustinian beliefs. Augustine's views, drawn from Scripture, regarding the depravity of man, and the priority of the divine at all levels of salvation, led Gottschalk to a doctrine of unconditional (i.e. not based on foreseen faith) election and to propose that Christ died only for the elect. Gottschalk came to be a thoroughgoing Augustinian and in spite of suppression preached these views with enough success to receive prelatical rejection and martyrdom. He obviously viewed atonement as vicarious, penal satisfaction. The story of Gottschalk demonstrates that a doctrine of the atonement of Christ that satisfied God's justice and law fully was viable if not quite healthy in the darkest period.

Gottschalk aroused sufficient attention to the issues of election, grace and the nature of atonement that the practical Semi-Pelagianism of the Roman Church was made official in public pronouncements – from which it has never quite retreated. That is not to say there were not scholars who to a degree embraced true Augustinian views.

For these reasons Roman Catholics can never be certain of salvation, because no one can know when he has sufficient merit – additional to Christ's. Hence – at least in the past – their funerals lack the note of assurance and peace usual in funerals of devout Protestants. Alcuin and even Bede the Venerable are medieval English ecclesiastics who are said to have held similar notions of soteriology. Not surprisingly the career and writings of Gottschalk have been the subject of modern studies.[36] The seventeenth-century Jansenist movement within the Roman Church, whose most famous convert was Blaise Pascal (1623–1662), revived these features of doctrine promoted by Gottschalk.

Scholars speculate that where and when monasticism existed at its best, soteriological doctrines similar to those of Athanasius and Augustine may have been accepted. Be that as it may, during the eleventh century, the beginning of the age of scholasticism (i.e. formal school theology in the new universities and other centers of revived learning), a widespread interest in an adequate understanding of Christ's work of atonement arose. It may be that scholarship and speculation in the monastic period of 900 to 1100 were bypassed by devotional practice and piety, which in the Rule of Benedict of Nursia put nothing ahead of the love of Christ. Monastic writers vied with one another in promoting just that in literature still read today. Eventually theology caught up with this piety in 1098 when Archbishop Anselm, a Benedictine exiled from Canterbury, composed *Why God Became Man?* (or *Why the God-Man?*, – in the original Latin, *Cur Deus Homo?*).

---

36. See articles about Gottschalk's in *The Catholic Encyclopedia vi: An International Work of References on Constitution, Doctrine, Discipline and History of the Catholic Church* (New York: The Encyclopedia Press, 1907–1922), *vol. 6 and Britannica*, 11th ed., xii and bibliography of nineteenth-century studies.

Anselm's brief work 'read as an essay in... divinity... was a virtuoso performance with few rivals in the history of Christian thought' (Pelikan). Anselm's purpose was to produce a rationally organized and supported view of the Person and work of Christ that was in full harmony with the authority of Scripture and ancient dogma as well. He succeeded so well that his positive contribution, with one adjustment (divine holiness where Anselm put majesty) and one enlargement (active obedience of Christ), has not been superseded to the present.

Anselm was not alone at the time or without predecessors in godly endeavor to understand the work of Christ in redemption. Peter Damian, Bruno of Segni, Guilbert of Nogent and to a degree even Abelard (who challenged Anselm's view) created extant works which demonstrate that Anselm's *Why the God-Man?* was in part the fruit of common theological discussion. Both the piety of the time and speculative theology were synchronously at work and moving in the direction Anselm brilliantly expressed. Theology had treated the work of Christ as prophet, priest and king for a long time. It was in the dogmas (decrees of councils, synods, etc.) but now theologians sought 'to make explicit what had been implicit.'

20
The Resurrection of Christ I

Death and Resurrection Together.

We have already taken notice that the earliest preachers and writers of the ancient church had very little to say about the meaning of the death of Christ apart from His resurrection. This is already evident in the Acts and Epistles of the New Testament: 'Again and again the apostolic message calls our attention to both the crucifixion *and* the resurrection. The fact of the cross is followed by "the fact of the empty tomb."'[1] 'But God raised him from the dead' follows hard on His death and burial, 'they took him down from the tree and laid him in a tomb' (Acts 13:30). This 'but' announced the fact of Jesus' resurrection and explained to Paul's audience at Pisidia the reason why he and Barnabas were travelling around the world telling Jews: the old Mosaic epoch is now over; a new epoch now prevails when *real* forgiveness of sins can be preached – just as the prophets said (vv. 38-41). This is common evangelistic procedure in the book of Acts (Acts 2:23; 3:11 ff.; 4:10; 13:29). In Paul's address at Mars Hill in Athens, to a Gentile audience, he never even mentions the unique meaning of Christ's death but proclaims His resurrection as the proof of His message and God's demand for repentance (Acts 17:30-32). Peter's initial message to Gentile 'God-fearers' placed the death and resurrection side by side and, like Paul at Antioch of Pisidia, Peter mentioned the witness of Old Testament prophets saying, 'All the prophets testify about him' (Acts 10:43 NIV). Nevertheless 'They killed him by hanging him on a tree, but God raised him from the dead on the third day and caused him to be seen' (Acts 10:39, 40 NIV). Also like Paul, Peter made these events the ground of future judgment by the same Man (Acts 10:42; cf. 17:31).

Reduced to definitive gospel simplicity, the message of the physical resurrection of Jesus is a *sine qua non* for saving truth. As an event of first-century history it must be believed in the heart to be saved (Rom. 10:9) if Peter and Paul are to be credited with truth-saying. In parallel with 'that Christ died for our sins in accordance with the Scriptures, that he was buried,' the further statement 'that he was raised on the third day in accordance with the Scriptures' is part of 'the gospel… by which you are being saved' and 'in which you stand' (1 Cor. 15:1-4).

Resurrection and Ascension.

The scriptural connection of the *resurrection* with the *cross* is matched with a similar, if less highlighted, connection with our Lord's *ascension* from earth to heaven, as incarnate 'Son of Man.' In fact the prophecy of Christ as Son of Man in Daniel 7 is of the ascended Son of Man now 'coming' again, this time in judgment rather than in grace. Believers in former ages saw this clearly, as in the earliest form of what is called the Apostles' Creed (before AD 341), 'crucified under Pontius Pilate, and buried; the third day he rose from the dead; he ascended into heaven, and sitteth at the right hand of the Father; from thence he shall come to judge the quick and the dead' (Schaff, *Creeds of Christendom*, I, 47, 48).

Medieval Christianity paid more attention to the events of Christ's career in calendar, ritual and preaching than we moderns do. Pelikan points out 'it was characteristic of the piety and theology [of that time] ... that the resurrection of Christ was inseparable from His ascension into heaven.'[2] Though

> the cross and the crucifixion came to occupy a unique place... in which the plan of salvation achieved its fulfillment... one reason for rejecting what was taken to be Abelard's notion of the cross as primarily the decisive revelation of the love of God and the announcement rather than the achievement of redemption was that the resurrection performed this function of making known that the plan of salvation had been carried out by the crucifixion.[3]

In other words, if our salvation were to be dependent on a *demonstration*, then the Passion and death would be sufficient, no resurrection necessary.

For those who think (as some appear to do) that 'gospel' preaching came to an end early in the age of Constantine only to revive a thousand years later with the Reformation, or perhaps only with the Anabaptist wing of it, it comes as a correction to learn that some of the most justly revered names of the era were fervent preachers of the true gospel of grace. No doubt God was not in any Christian epoch without such evangelists. Certainly Bernard of Clairvaux was one of them. Peter Damian was another. They preached the evangel in a manner fitting to the time when most of their hearers were illiterate. Bernard emphasized the 'finished work of Calvary.' In a sermon on the Song of Solomon he said, 'the soul seeks the Logos but it had previously been sought by the Logos... "Our merits" are really "signs of a hidden predestination, and foretokens of future bliss." But "our merits" are not a basis for the divine act of justification, whose basis lies in God, not in man.' He remarks in another sermon on the *Song*: 'The righteousness of God consists in his not sinning, but the righteousness of man consists in his being forgiven of God.'[4]

Bernard's gospel ministry survives to the present day, as the following incident evidences. One sunny, comfortable day in May I happened to take a seat in one of the old carriages of the Chicago Transit Authority on Chicago's north side. I quickly found myself visiting with half a dozen Polish Catholic oldsters who were exchanging short religious tracts and printed poetry. They were a happy bunch, none at great remove from the end of life. They gave me copies of those tracts and poems – almost all by Bernard of Clairvaux. I was humbled but glad to discover the message of every one was the gospel of faith in what Christ the crucified and risen has done for us, *not* what we can do for Him.

These facts of the history of Christian thought suggest that though resurrection, ascension and enthronement on high are properly treated as stages of the one exaltation of Christ and, though the Calvary work was a finished work of substitutionary satisfaction for sin, His resurrection has an essential function in connection with the work of Christ as a unity. What was necessary and finished had necessary sequels if the finished purchase of redemption was to be carried into effect.

Apologetics of the Resurrection of Christ.

There is an abundance of modern, believing literature about Christ's resurrection. Much of it is apologetical literature, designed to refute attacks of unbelievers and half-believers. I myself have written and published in that connection with recent controversies. Yet the message of the resurrection of Jesus as it lies plainly in the Gospels provides its own attestation as an event of ancient history. The Gospel reports speak powerfully to the mind and heart of all who are willing to be convinced. The fact of the resurrection may profitably be preached to any audience without reserve.

In my experience, however, apologetics in defense of the resurrection must be handled with great care. There was a time when I taught apologetics – sometimes as much as three sections of thirty-plus students in 'Evidences' and as many more in 'Philosophy of Religion.' There was always some time spent defending the resurrection. It was worthwhile, of course, but I am still somewhat in shock from an incident in one of my classes. I had assigned to the

---

1. G. C. H. Berkouwer, *The Work of Christ*, trans. Cornelius Lambregtse (Grand Rapids, MI: Eerdmans, 1965), p. 180.
2. Jaroslav Pelikan, *The Christian Tradition iii, The Growth of Medieval Theology (600–1300)* (Chicago: University of Chicago Press, 1978), p. 153.
3. ibid., p. 133.
4. ibid., pp. 155, 156.

class the reading of a book on the subject of proofs of the resurrection by a renowned author. Then one day a young man in this class for seniors at Wheaton College showed up unannounced at my office, the book in hand. He sat down opposite me, and with tears, falteringly spilled out his anguish: 'I feel terrible. I never had any doubt of the resurrection of Jesus until I read this book.' Then I felt terrible too. He belonged in a course in Romans, rather than a course in apologetics.

The Resurrection As Gospel.

Belief 'that God raised him from the dead' is presupposed here and shall not be defended. The resurrection simply as reported is itself the central proof. For now, the task is to discuss what happened and what it means for our salvation, not to defend or explain the unique miracle of all time. The apostolic demand is not 'Defend the resurrection!' Quite the contrary, it is to believe it and to proclaim it – 'Remember Jesus Christ, risen from the dead... as preached in my gospel.' So the senior pastor at Ephesus on a preaching mission instructed his assistant left behind at Ephesus (2 Tim. 2:8). As J. Schep asserts:

> The resurrection provides the glorious evidence that Jesus is the Son of God (Rom. 1:4); it means the abolishment of death and the victory of life and incorruption (1 Tim. 1:10); it is the basis of the Christian faith and hope (1 Cor. 15:14 ff.; 1 Peter 1:3) and the guarantee of our future resurrection in glory (Rom. 8:11; 1 Cor. 15:20, 49; 1 Thess. 4:14).[5]

I. The Resurrection of Christ in Old Testament Typology and Prophecies.

In a rather subtle manner the New Testament declares that information about death and physical resurrection and related facts about personal immortality is obscure in the Old Testament. It comes in where Paul is writing the young interim pastor at Ephesus about the power of God and the gospel as antidote to 'a spirit... of fear' (2 Tim. 1:7). Then he goes on to say, God has 'saved us and called us to a holy calling, not because of our works but because of his own purpose and grace, which he gave us in Christ Jesus before the ages began, and which has *now been manifested* through the appearing of our Savior Christ Jesus, who abolished death and *brought life and immortality to light* [emphasis added] through the gospel' (2 Tim. 1:9, 10).

Robert B. Strimple draws out the meaning in an exceptionally well-composed essay:

> Many Christians have been puzzled by the meagerness of Old Testament revelation about what lies ahead for believers after they die, and many false teachers have taken advantage of this paucity of information to fashion elaborate tales of the shadowy world of hades and of Christ's "harrowing of hell" after his death...But attempts to establish a contrast between the afterlife of Old Testament saints and that of New Testament saints are misguided. The simple truth is that very little was revealed about the afterlife before our crucified and risen Savior conquered death and "brought to light" what had been previously shrouded in deep darkness. Praise God for the light that has burst forth from the empty tomb! Praise God for the bright beam of the gospel! The progressive nature of redemptive revelation is nowhere more clearly seen than here.[6]

In a sermon to Jews in the synagogue at Antioch of Pisidia Paul preached the 'good tidings' of Christ's resurrection as something 'written in the second Psalm' (Acts 13:33) and wrote to the largely Gentile church of Corinth that Christ was raised from the dead 'in accordance with the Scriptures' (1 Cor. 15:4). What were the 'Scriptures' Paul had in mind and what do they say?

Christ's Resurrection in Old Testament Types.

Let us first look at Old Testament types. A bit later we shall take note that the book of Hebrews *at length* discusses how Christ's past redemptive work and present ministry in heaven fulfill the elaborate ceremonial of the Old Testament - the *sanctuary*, *priests, sacrifices* and *rituals*. Early in this Christology we saw how these are said to be types, shadows, patterns, divinely instituted for that purpose. Those types, then, are not mere pictures of abstract truths,

---

5. J. A. Schep, *The Nature of the Resurrection Body* (Grand Rapids, MI: Eerdmans, 1964), p. 164.
6. Robert B. Strimple, 'Hyper-Preterism on the Resurrection of the Body' in *When Shall These Things Be? A Reformed Answer to Hyper-Preterism*, ed. Keith A. Mathieson (Phillipsburg, NJ: P & R Publishing, 2004), p. 239.

but of events now taking place in heaven. Our Lord would not be there except for resurrection, ascension and session at the right hand of God – all predicted in Old Testament types and prophecies. I do not doubt Paul had these typical institutions in mind in saying 'in accordance with the Scriptures.' Paul does not say much about the types of Christ's post-ascension work, but it occupies many verses in Hebrews.

Having said this, much alleged typology of the resurrection is unconvincing to modern minds, including my own. Some alleged types are Adam's awakening from sleep after 'anaesthesia and surgery' at the creation of Eve, deliverance of Isaac from the dead 'figuratively speaking' (Heb. 11:19; 'in a figure' KJV), the burning bush (Exod. 3) which was not consumed, Aaron's dry rod that budded, the release of a living bird at the ceremony of cleansing for plague of a house (Lev. 14:53). Some have 'discovered' a type of the three days in Genesis 22:4. Jesus told the Jews that Jonah was a 'sign' in that as Jonah was three days and three nights in the 'whale's belly' so He would be three days and three nights in the ground (i.e. buried). Yet Jesus did not say Jonah's experience was a symbolical prediction of His resurrection, that is, a type.

Christ's Resurrection in Old Testament Prophecies.

It must be acknowledged that the search for direct verbal predictions of Jesus' resurrection in the Old Testament has not discovered much outside the few passages cited in the New Testament. These, however, are very important.

We must distinguish between predictions of a future, final resurrection of the dead from prophecy of Christ's resurrection. As to the former, there is no doubt that in Jesus' time there was firm conviction of a resurrection 'on the last day' on the part of most Jews, apart from Sadducees (John 11:24; Acts 23:6-8). Paul quoted three Old Testament prophecies of Jesus' resurrection in his sermon at Pisidia – Psalm 2:7 (Acts 13:33); Isaiah 55:3 (Acts 13:34); and Psalm 16:10 (Acts 13:35).

There is disagreement over the first of these citations of Paul. Let us look closely. Having said just previously, 'God raised him from the dead,' Paul says, 'And we bring you good news that what God promised to the fathers, this he has fulfilled to us their children by raising Jesus, as also it is written in the second Psalm, "You are my Son, today I have begotten you"' (Acts 13:30, 32, 33). The ESV and RSV follow the division of thought in most editions of the Greek text. In this case the resurrection was God's proclamation of the sonship of Christ prophesied in Psalm 2:7. Romans 1:4, 'declared to be the Son of God in power according to the spirit of holiness by his resurrection from the dead,' falls in line with this common understanding.

There is another view, supported by the way the NIV punctuates Acts 13:33, which has 'raising up Jesus' refer to His birth and life rather than His resurrection. A period is placed in the middle of verse 33 after 'raising up Jesus.' 'As it is written in the second Psalm' is then made to introduce a new thought having no connection with the raising up of Jesus in the first part of the verse. '[R]aising up Jesus,' then, refers to His conception, birth and life, just as in verse 22 of the same chapter God 'raised up David to be their king' (ESV). Strangely, NIV reads 'made David their king' quite obliterating the connection, if any, with 'raising up Jesus,' and thus obscures what the Greek text really says.

In favor of the ESV/RSV/KJV (and many other Versions) which clearly declare the resurrection of Jesus was predicted in Psalm 2:7, I point out several pieces of evidence. *First*, is the fact that 'raised up' David (Acts 13:22) employs *egeirō* whereas in 'raising up Jesus' the word for the action is *anistēmi* the *usual* Greek word for raising someone from the dead in the Septuagint and New Testament (*per contra* Acts 3:23; 7:37). *Second*, the last part of verse 33 'as also it is written,' etc. disappears from Paul's evidence for anything. This is one bad result of the NIV shortening of New Testament Greek sentences to please modern readers. *Third*, the primitive church saw the fulfillment of the words of Psalm 2:7 in the resurrection of Christ. (See F. F. Bruce, *The Acts of the Apostles, The Greek Text with Commentary*, 1952, p. xix.) For history of views see J. P. Lange's *Volume on Acts*, pp. 250, 251. Luther favored the first view, Calvin the second.

The second and third Old Testament passages quoted as predictions of Christ's resurrection follow immediately after verse 33. We now quote Acts 13:34 and 35 and comment briefly.

'And as for the fact that he raised him from the dead, no more to return to corruption, he has spoken in this way, "I will give you the holy and sure blessings of David." [Isa. 55:3]. Therefore he says also in another psalm, "You will not let your Holy One see corruption [Ps. 16:10]."'

The importance and meaning of these prophecies are enhanced by the fact that they are part of a sermon Paul preached on a 'sabbath day' at the invitation of the leaders in a Jewish synagogue (Acts 13:13-16). The audiences were already well acquainted with the whole Tenak (or O.T.). So Paul addressed these Diaspora Jews with a view to showing how the Old Testament promises to David and other patriarchs had so far failed except that God had worked marvels in events connected with the death of Jesus. Further he made them aware that Jesus' death had been caused by the wicked, misguided actions of their own leaders up at Jerusalem not many years earlier.

The sense of Paul's argument is: 1) the resurrection of the Messiah-Jesus took place as was fully proven by witnesses to the event (v. 30). 2) The event showed that Jesus was the Son of God foreseen by the prophecy of Psalm 2:7. 3) The 'sure mercies' (v. 34 KJV), or Messianic blessing vouchsafed to and through David (as he goes on to say in v. 36) did not come to David who died and went to corruption in his grave. 4) These 'sure mercies' came to us living Jews in the One whom the Jewish leaders had killed, who was raised by God as prophesied in Psalm 16:10 and who never did see corruption and never will. 5) These 'sure mercies' (blessings) from 'this man' (v. 38) are forgiveness of sin and freedom ('from which you could not be freed by the law of Moses') (v. 39).

In speaking of 'sure mercies,' Paul quotes the Septuagint which has the words *ta hosia*, meaning pious, devout, supremely holy; in neuter plural here, mercies has the sense of 'the pledged bounties.' These sure mercies, or pledged bounties are, of course, every promise of salvation in connection with salvation through David's greater Son such as are found in the Immanuel prophecy of Isaiah 9–11.

> By David is meant Christ, as he often is called in OT prophecy, and by his mercies the blessings of the covenant of grace, which are in him; so called because they flow from the grace and mercy of God; and which being put into his hands are sure ['sure mercies']... and particularly through his resurrection from the dead; for had he died, and not risen again from the dead, the blessings... would not have been ratified and confirmed.[7]

A section of Peter's address on the Day of Pentecost employs a large part of Psalm 16 (vv. 8-11) as prophecy of Jesus' resurrection, His ascension (by implication, Acts 2:34) and enthronement (Acts 2:25-35). There are complications of translation from Hebrew to Greek and difficulties that puzzle interpreters to this day, but nothing could be plainer than the precise language of the prophecy applied to the fulfillment in Jesus' resurrection (Acts 2:29-35). And it was convincing as the flood of 3,000 public conversions at the end of the day shows.

Some scholars find a prediction of Christ's resurrection and of the 'many bodies of the saints who had fallen asleep were raised' of Matthew 27:52 in Isaiah 26:19 though others refer it to the resurrection of 'the last day.' Hosea 6:2 is also cited. Yet in all candor, if specific 'proof texts' of prophecy of the resurrection of Christ be sought, it must be said there are few to seize upon besides the ones already discussed here.

According to the Scriptures.

What one would not give for a transcript of Paul's lectures on the resurrection of Christ in Old Testament prophecy at Thessalonica! It was there he spoke in the synagogue for 'three sabbath days' and reasoning 'with them *from the Scriptures* [emphasis added], opening and alleging that it behooved the Christ to suffer, and to rise again from the dead' (Acts 17:2, 3 ASV). Of course the primary text must have been Isaiah 53, which is the paramount Old Testament passage on that subject.

Let us therefore see what, if anything, Isaiah 53 has to say about the resurrection of Christ, the causes and meaning of whose death it supremely expounds. Verses 10 to 12 speak of the Servant's reward (exaltation as opposed to humiliation) after the Passion. As important aspects of the Servant's reward, 'he shall see his seed, he shall prolong his days, and the pleasure of Jehovah shall prosper in his hand' (part of Isa. 53:10 ASV). I comment:

> The second element in His prosperity is to be great length of life... 'he shall prolong his days.' Great length of life, as among all ancient peoples, was among the Hebrews of Isaiah's time regarded as evidence of God's favor. Long life was promised for obedience to parents... (Exod. 20:12), as a reward for honest dealings (Deut. 25:15), and promise to the son who kept the commandments of the Lord (Prov. 3:2). In Jesus' case it was almost an insoluble mystery for three days between His death [at the age of about thirty-two or thirty-three] and His resurrection that God would give him 'length of days.' But the resurrection morning solved the mystery. This explains the Apostolic claim that His resurrection was 'according to the Scriptures.'[8]

---

7. John Gill, *Complete Body of Doctrinal and Practical Divinity i* (Grand Rapids, MI: Baker Books, 1978), p. 583.
8. Robert Culver, *The Sufferings and the Glory of the Lord's Righteous Servant*, pp. 112, 113.

There is a kind of epitome of Isaiah 53 in the last three verses of chapter 52. They introduce the whole poem of fifteen verses, five stanzas of three verses each. In a sense verse 13 of chapter 52 summarizes His entire future career as the Servant and the reward God will give Him. The Servant 'will act wisely' and as a result 'he will be raised' (resurrection) 'and lifted up' (ascension) 'and highly exalted' (the enthronement at the right hand of God). I have been fully persuaded of this understanding of Isaiah 53:13.[9] The NIV, cited above, is a quite exact rendition of the three words *yarum, nissa'* and *gavah m'odh*, as inflected in the text. The passage is at one with Isaiah 53:10-12, of course, but also with the exalted language of the several New Testament passages which speak of the Lord Jesus' exceeding great exaltation (Phil. 2:9-11; Eph. 1:20-23; etc.). These three expressions are *at least* 'a veiled reference' to Jesus' resurrection followed by ascension and enthronement. I doubt if Paul at Thessalonica would have failed to mention it to the folk who 'were persuaded and joined Paul and Silas' (Acts 17:4) after he alleged 'that it behooved the Christ... to rise again from the dead' (Acts 17:3 ASV).

II. The Fact of Jesus's Resurrection As Event in History.

Christology Without a Physical Resurrection?

The last century has furnished Christendom with several prominent writers of theology who think a Christology without the virginal conception of Jesus and without a genuine physical resurrection of Jesus is a more authentic Christianity than the orthodox teaching. Survival of the conscious personal spirit or 'continuity' is how to interpret the 'myth of bodily resurrection.' They have no following to speak of among the millions who publicly worship the Lord Jesus Christ on Sundays, but the amount of literature they have produced (and recent PBS specials) is amazingly large.

There are many who wish to associate themselves with historic Christianity, yet because of modern assumptions reject anything they think violates the authority of modern science. Many of these would properly be labeled neo-orthodox or Bultmannian. Let Emil Brunner speak for them. He has the distinction of a courteous spirit and understandability. Most of the distinctive marks of neo-orthodoxy appear in the following. It is theological double speak.

> Emphasis upon the Empty tomb led to the medieval conception of 'the resurrection body,' with its drama of the Last Day, and the opening of the graves, which has also been inserted into the Apostles' Creed (the main features of orthodox, biblical eschatology are not original with Christ and the New Testament)... Resurrection of the body, yes: Resurrection of the *flesh*, no! The 'Resurrection of the body' does not mean the identity of the resurrection body with the material (although transformed) body of flesh; but the resurrection of the body means the continuity of the individual personality on this side, and on that, of death.[10]

Brunner then in typical orthodox-sounding language with heretical meaning says 'Jesus Christ is Victor over death... Risen Lord... Christ... God-Man... could not remain subject to death.' But Jesus' victory 'is connected not so much with the fact of Easter as with the fact of Good Friday... for there the Incarnation of the Son of God – paradoxically – reached its climax [redemption by incarnation without satisfaction for sin].'[11] Similar thinking is to be found in the writings of many: Rudolph Bultmann;[12] Günther Bornkamm;[13] Paul Tillich.[14] Karl Barth is critical of Bultmann but in his discussion of Jesus' resurrection never seems plainly to affirm the reality of the resurrection of the flesh of Jesus.[15]

It has been in the line of my duties over the years to read many of these books and articles and to conduct courses that examined their ideas in some detail. But that has very little bearing on orthodox, evangelical Christian theology. I have no inclination whatsoever to spread their assertions or arguments further on these pages. 'The barkings of the ungodly ought, I repeat it, to be disregarded; for we see that the apostles were also assailed by these barkings' (Calvin on 1 John 4:2).

---

9. See Franz Delitzsch's rather brief survey of the history of interpretation, *Biblical Commentary on the Prophecies of Isaiah* (Edinburgh: T. & T. Clark, 1877), pp. 304, 305. See also Culver, *Sufferings*, pp.19–37.
10. Emil Brunner, *The Christian Doctrine of Creation and Redemption, Dogmatics ii* (Philadelphia, PA: Westminster Press, 1952), p. 372.
11. ibid., p. 372.
12. Bultmann, *Jesus Christ and Mythology*, p. 15, and *Theology of the New Testament i*. p. 45.
13. Gunther Bornkamm, *Jesus of Nazareth*, trans. Irene and Fraser McLuskey with James M. Robinson (New York: Harper & Row, 1960), pp. 183–185.
14. Paul Tillich, *Systematic Theology i* (Chicago: University of Chicago Press, 1951, 1963), p. 56.
15. Karl Barth, *Church Dogmatics iii*. 2, trans. G. W. Bromiley (Edinburgh: T. & T. Clark, 1936–1975), pp. 446–511.

Disregard the Barkings of the Ungodly.

An outstanding older author made this point in a different way. In the opening pages of a 300-page book about the resurrection of Jesus, William Milligan employed six pages to show why, in the first place, 'It is not my intention to make any appeal to those whose views of God and His relation to the world exclude the possibility of miracles,' and in the second place it is 'not my intention to discuss the authenticity... of any [portions of] Scripture which contain... the evidence of the fact before us.'[16]

To argue with those in whose eyes the miraculous and the historical exclude one another is a fruitless venture in theology. Debate with scholars who reject the authenticity and truthfulness of the New Testament reports never settles anything. '[T]hese are written' said John 'that you may believe' – speaking of 'signs' (miracles of meaning) which 'Jesus did... in the presence of the disciples.' Of himself John wrote: '[W]e know that his testimony is true' and that he wrote of 'That which was from the beginning... which we have seen with our eyes, which we have looked upon and have touched with our hands, concerning the word of life' (John 20:30, 31; 21:24; 1 John 1:1). We must trust the witnesses; otherwise we really know nothing at all about Jesus, or even if He ever lived.

While I heartily reject his lamentable opinion that the resurrection body of Christ was not 'of flesh,' George Ladd said truly: 'The witness of the New Testament is that an objective event took place in a garden outside of Jerusalem in which the crucified and entombed Jesus emerged from the grave into a new order of life.'[17] He not only came forth from the grave 'in the body in which he suffered and died but consorted with those who had been with him' beginning with the baptism of John (Acts 1:2). 'To them he presented himself alive after his suffering by many proofs, appearing to them during forty days and speaking about the kingdom of God' (Acts 1:3).

The Resurrection Appearances.

Samuel Andrews has summarized and indexed the appearances over those forty days in a brief and clear way.

> The number of our Lord's appearances after the resurrection during the forty days following... is generally said to be nine. Of these five were on the day of resurrection, one on the Sunday following, two at some later period, and one when he ascended... [F]ive were in Jerusalem, one in Emmaus, two in Galilee, and one on the Mount of Olives. If we to these add that to James, mentioned only by St Paul (1 Cor. 15:7), which was probably at Jerusalem, we have ten *recorded* [emphasis added] appearances. We may well believe that these were not all [the appearances]... 'appearing unto them by the space of forty days, and speaking the things concerning the kingdom of God,' clearly implying that the Lord met the apostles often for instruction.[18]

The Resurrection Story; Facts Attested.

The resurrection story is told by four Gospel authors, obviously independent of one another, without the slightest hint of any artful attempt to prove anything – only to report things seen and heard. Nor is there any sign they wrote to refute or anticipate beliefs or objections to belief, as a major part of the amazingly abundant current literature of New Testament studies (so-called) and negative Gospels criticism assumes. Nor did they write to stimulate the sort of celebrity-adoration prevalent in the colossal amphitheater cities as Ephesus ('Great is Diana of the Ephesians' Acts 19:28, 29 KJV) and Rome.

Many good scholars point to several facts attested by the Gospels which summarize the central fact of the resurrection. *First*, Jesus was dead. *Second*, the hopes of the disciples were also dead. *Third*, the disciples' discouragement and frustration was suddenly and abruptly transformed into confidence and certainty. A *fourth* fact is the empty tomb.

A *fifth* historical fact is the resurrection faith. The disciples believed that Jesus arose from the grave.

> They believed that their teacher and master, who was dead and buried, was alive again. They were confident that they saw him once again, heard his voice, listened to his [further] teachings, recognized his features. They believed his presence was not a 'spiritual,' i.e. nonmaterial 'ghostly' thing but an objective bodily reality. *This was the faith that created the church*. That which brought the church into being and gave it a message was not the hope of persistence of life beyond the grave, a confidence in God's supremacy over death, a conviction of immortality of the human spirit. It was belief in an *event* in time and space.[19]

---

16. William Milligan, *The Resurrection of Our Lord*, 4th ed. (London: Macmillan Co., 1901), pp. 2, 3.
17. George Ladd, *A Theology of the New Testament* (Grand Rapids, MI: Eerdmans, 1974), p. 319.
18. S. J. Andrews, *The Life of our Lord Upon the Earth*, rev. ed. (New York: Scribners, 1891), p. 596.
19. Ladd, *Theology of NT*, p. 320. (For a valuable sketch and summary of views of the resurrection as a fact of history see G. R. Habermas's 'The Resurrection of Christ,' *Evangelical Dictionary of Theology*, pp. 938–941; also initial guide to the literature at end of Habermas's article and Ladd, *Theology of NT*, p. 315.)

21
The Resurrection of Christ II

III. Six Features of the New Testament Witness to Jesus' Resurrection.[1]

Among the many features of the New Testament witness to Jesus' resurrection let us devote attention to several which ought to be noticed at least briefly to help us know what happened and what it all means.

1. In a remarkable rhetorical passage Scripture declares the enormous amount of power employed by God in raising Jesus from the dead. The resurrection of Christ called forth 'the surpassing [Gr. hyperbolical] greatness of His [God's] power' (*dunamis* 'dynamic'). This was 'in accordance with the working [*energeia* 'energy'] of the strength [*kratos*] of His might [*ischuos*] which He wrought [*ergeō*] in Christ, when He raised [*egeirō*] Him from the dead and seated Him at His right hand in the heavenly places' (Eph. 1:19, 20 my translation). There is no more fertile ground for exegesis of the wording of Scripture than these two verses. The resources of human language seem exhausted to express the 'surpassing greatness' of God's omnipotence in the event of the resurrection of Christ, exceeding even the energy required to create the world.

That the barrier between death and renewal of life had now been breached in anticipation of the resurrection of the 'last day' was marked by the resurrection of the bodies of many 'saints who had fallen asleep' after His resurrection (Matt. 27:52, 53).

2. Jesus came forth from the grave in the same body laid in the grave. The incarnation (in-flesh-ment) of the Son of God that began at the conception of Jesus is permanent. An incarnation without flesh is a contradiction of terms. That is why the grave was empty. That body was and is a permanent part of our Lord's human nature, in which He ascended to heaven and shall return, as the messengers of heaven rendered certain at the time of His ascension (Acts 1:10, 11). The ancient creeds make a special point (perhaps in response to Gnostic and Manichean heresies already prevalent) that His was a resurrection of 'the flesh' or 'in the same body' (in parallel with 'suffered in the flesh; and rose again').[2]

The literature and creeds of Christendom through ancient, medieval, Reformation and post-Reformation epochs echo and re-echo the doctrine of the resurrection, emphasizing the permanence and perfection of 'the flesh' of Christ. N. L. Geisler quotes Irenaeus, Tertullian, Justin, Athenagoras, Rufinius, Epiphanius, Cyril and Augustine among the ancient writers; Anselm and Aquinas of the medieval period; and seven modern creeds. (*The Battle For The Resurrection*, Updated Edition, Nashville: Thomas Nelson, 1992, pp. 51-63.) They all agree.

---

1. This chapter begins where the preceding chapter left off.
2. Creed of Ephiphanius AD 374, in Philip Schaff, *Creeds of Christendom I*, repr. (Grand Rapids, MI: Baker Books, 1966), p. 37.

I quote one of the plainest, Article 4 of the 'Thirty-Nine Articles of Religion' (Anglican) of 1562: 'Christ did truly rise again from death and *took again His body, with flesh bones, and all things pertaining to the perfection of Man's nature*; wherewith He ascended to Heaven, and there sitteth, until He return to judge all men at the last day' (emphasis added).

The leading modern exponent of this, the historic orthodox doctrine, is J. A. Schep.[3] He also wrote the articles 'Resurrection' and 'Resurrection of Jesus Christ' in *Zondervan Pictorial Encyclopedia of the Bible*. In the first article he wrote:

> The resurrection of the dead in a body of flesh is guaranteed by Jesus' resurrection in a body of 'flesh and bones,' with scars of his wounds visible, capable of being touched and of eating food (Luke 24:38-43; Acts 10:41). At His ascension Jesus did not discard this flesh-body, as is clear from Acts 1:11; Philippians 3:21; Revelation 1:17. Since the resurrected believers will be like the risen Christ (1 Cor. 15:49; Phil. 3:21; 1 John 3:2), they too will be raised in their bodies of flesh (cf. 1 Cor. 15:35-42). Only in this way is man saved in his totality, and able to live on a new earth (Isa. 65:17 ff.; 66:22; Matt. 5:5; Rev. 21:1-3).[4]

3. Not only did Jesus rise from the dead in the same body laid in the grave but that body in 'perfection' (completeness) as a part of His authentic human nature, is united with the God-man forever. In the New Testament Jesus is at every point after the resurrection a physical Being. He was present to the disciples in a structured figure of flesh and bones (Luke 24:39); He left behind no body; that is why the tomb was empty (Matt. 28:6). The Man Christ Jesus alive again was a body-soul unity; in that body-soul unity He ascended to heaven (Acts 1:10, 11). He is the Mediator in heaven now, still the *theanthrōpos* in His office as Great High Priest ministering on our behalf. His wounds will be visible and recognizable in that same body when He returns to earth (Acts 1:10, 11; Rev. 1:7).

An influential creed which predates the completion of the Nicene Creed (AD 324, 381), the Second Creed of Epiphanius, plainly says of the Lord Jesus Christ that He 'suffered in the flesh; and rose again; and went up to heaven in the same body, sat down gloriously at the right hand of the Father; is coming in the same body in glory.'[5]

The permanence of our Lord's human body was not a matter of great controversy among Christians at the time of the Reformation. Yet the French Confession of Faith prepared by Calvin and De Chandrieu, approved by Beza and approved at synods in 1559 and 1561, affirms it strongly: 'although Jesus Christ, in rising from the dead, bestowed immortality upon his body, yet he did not take from it the truth of its nature, and we so consider him in his divinity that we do not despoil him of his humanity.'[6] The Belgic Confession (1516) teaches the same: 'And though He hath not changed His human nature; for as much as our salvation and resurrection also depend on the reality of His body.'[7] The Thirty-Nine Articles of the Church of England, the Westminster Confessions, Baptist, Congregational, Methodist and others before 1800 confess the same.

4. The Bible itself makes confession of the permanent and complete humanity (i.e. infleshment, or incarnation), body and soul of the risen Son of God, the supreme test of orthodoxy. The two critical texts are plain in the King James Version, though exegesis of the Greek text enlarges and cements the meaning. They now follow: '...try the spirits.... Hereby know ye the Spirit of God: Every spirit that confesseth that Jesus Christ is come in the flesh is of God: And every spirit that confesseth not that Jesus Christ is come in the flesh is not of God...' (1 John 4:1-3). 'For many deceivers are entered into the world, who confess not that Jesus Christ is come in the flesh. This is a deceiver and an antichrist' (2 John 7).

In recent years these verses have become very important in dealing not only (as in ancient times) with acknowledged heresies such as Christian Science and the 'Jehovah's Witnesses' but errors arising in evangelical seminaries and books from the evangelical book business. I have been personally involved in some of the controversy generated thereby. For that reason I cite the words of an acknowledged scholar whose major contribution has been to this subject rather than my own, as follows:

---

3. J. A. Schep, *The Nature of the Resurrection Body* (Grand Rapids, MI: Eerdmans, 1964); unfortunately out of print as of this writing.
4. J. A. Schep, 'Resurrection' in *Zondervan Pictorial Encyclopedia of the Bible*, ed. Merrill C. Tenney (Grand Rapids, MI: Zondervan, 1969), chap. V, p. 74.
5. Schaff, *Creeds of Christendom ii*, p. 368, 369.
6. ibid., pp. 404, 405.
7. ibid., pp. 368, 369.

1. John does not say that Christ came into the flesh (which would refer to the historical fact of the incarnation) [i.e. the past event], but that he has come into the world *en sarki* (in the flesh; lit. in flesh), i.e. as one (the divine Word) clothed with flesh; one who is as truly human, man of flesh and blood, as he is divine. [footnote: The absence of the article emphasizes the quality: Christ adopted human FLESH.]

2. The perfect participle is used (*eleuthota*). This means, according to John, not only that Jesus Christ once came in the fullness of time as one clothed with flesh, but that thus He is *still present*. What happened at the incarnation has not been undone. He is a Christ who 'is come, who came and who abides in the flesh.' The last 10 words are quoted from A. Ross in the *New International Commentary*.[8]

Schep goes on:

In the second passage, 2 John 7, the anti-Christian deceivers are portrayed as men who 'confess not that Jesus Christ cometh in the flesh.' The expression 'in (the) flesh' is the same as in 1 John 4:2, but it is remarkable that the present participle has replaced the perfect participle. This is generally understood as a timeless present, having virtually the same meaning as the perfect of 1 John 4:2.

Some say, notes Schep, the phrase denotes the Second Advent, and that certainly is possible. 'In either case the consequence... is the same: Christ is still in the flesh.'[9] A thorough check of many critical commentaries plus two grammars (Robertson, Dana and Mantey) on the verbal and grammatical forms employed divulged little variation from Schep's sources. He is not mistaken. Any theory which claims that the glorified body of our Lord is immaterial or non-fleshly is not scriptural. And the judgment of Scripture is very severe – 'not of God,' 'of the world,' 'deceiver... antichrist.'

It is, of course, incorrect to say affirmation of our Lord's present incarnate state (in flesh, *en sarki*) during the forty days, at ascension and Second Advent, rests on two verses in John's Epistles. It rests on multitudes of texts and merges with other doctrines. If Jesus Christ is not today in flesh in heaven then the integrity of His incarnation has been forfeited. It would be strange to contend that He is still *incarnate* (from *in* plus *carnis*, the Latin for flesh) if He has no flesh. In such a case we have no true Mediator (1 Tim. 2:5).

From a certain point of view *incarnation* (Lat. *incarnatio*) is only a word. In this case it is a word with a history going back to the Latin theologians of the fourth century, and the Greek word it translates goes back to the very beginning. For *en sarki*, in flesh (1 Tim. 2:16) and 'became flesh' (John 1:14) fix the idea in language. It means complete human nature. In Scripture this figure of speech (synecdoche, a part put for the whole) is used for the whole man as when David says his flesh cries out for the living God. Would it not be strange to speak of Christ as incarnate God if He has no flesh?

This truth has inspired great poetry (unfortunately presently neglected by professional, lay and academic literature). Let us share a few precious lines from Robert Browning's poem, entitled *Saul*.

'Tis the weakness in strength that I cry for!/ My flesh that I seek/ In the Godhead!/ I seek and I find it, O Saul it shall be/ A face like my face, that receives thee; a Man like to me,/ Thou shalt love and be loved by forever;/ A hand like this hand/ Shall throw open the gates of new life to thee!/ See the Christ stand!' (*Saul*, lines 304–312).

5. The body of Christ's resurrection is 'the same' in identity as His crucified body but is in certain respects a changed body. The emphasis in the Gospels is far greater on the sameness than on the differences. Jesus seems to have exhausted the possible means for demonstrating the numerical identity of the 'new' body with the 'old.'

To this end Jesus 'showed' His 'hands and his side' to the assembled disciples on Easter Day (John 20:20) and a week later challenged Thomas to put his finger in the nail prints in His hand and put his hand on the site of the wound in His side (John 20:27, 28). To the same effect He prepared a meal of fish and bread for them, as reported in John 21:1-23. Note especially the expressions 'It is the Lord' (John 21:7) and 'They knew it was the Lord' (John 21:12). For the same reason He even ate a piece of broiled fish before them on Easter Day, asking for the food in order to demonstrate the reality of His physical presence among them. Luke says He 'he presented himself alive after his suffering by many proofs, appearing to them during forty days' (Acts 1:3). Proofs of what? The clear implication is proof of the reality of His physical presence in a living condition.

Some of the differences between the body nailed to the cross and the risen body that interpreters think they find are not necessarily true. There is no proof, for example, that Jesus did not enter the room of the assembled disciples by opening the 'locked' (John 20:19, 26) door. Even if locked, at this late date we do not know if it was the door to

---

8. Schep, *Resurrection Body*, pp. 71, 72.
9. ibid., p. 72.

the Upper Room, the door to the building or the gate to the enclosed court. Even if locked, Jesus, certainly, would have been up to the challenge of opening a lock that would have been easy for any skilled burglar. At any rate it seems as likely the disciples' 'fear of the Jews' and disconcerted condition of mind is the reason for the locked door's being mentioned in John's report, not that the risen Christ walked bodily through a stone wall or wooden door.

There is indeed an element of mystery about the way the risen Lord could suddenly appear and disappear. This has been discussed with various conclusions by Bible interpreters over the centuries. Passages pertaining to these mysterious appearances and disappearances are Luke 24:31, 36; John 20:19, 26. Calvin, commenting on John 20:19, would not deign to discuss the possibility of Jesus' body passing through stone walls or wooden doors; in comment on John 20:19 he pronounced the idea a 'childish trifling, which contains nothing solid, and brings along with it many absurdities.' Schep is correct in the following extended quotation:

> The fact is, however, that nowhere in the Gospels is it said that Jesus' body passed through closed doors. The only thing we are told is that he suddenly appeared while the doors were closed. It is certainly implicitly suggested that there was something mysterious and miraculous in his entering the room, but how he did enter is not mentioned at all...
> How did Jesus enter? Nobody knows, and the numerous suggestions made by commentators are all mere guesses. We do not even know whether 'the doors' mean only the outer door of the building itself, or the inner door to the room where the disciples were gathered, though the former interpretation seems more plausible.[10]

Paul writes much about the changes in our bodies at the resurrection, in 1 Corinthians 15. They will be 'like his glorious body' (Phil. 3:21), hence Paul's description of our resurrection bodies is applicable to Jesus' body. 'A description of the one is therefore a description of the other.'[11]

Transformation.

By the word 'must' in 1 Corinthians 15:53 he shows some change will be necessary for deceased believers as well as for translated, living ones. 'This perishable body *must* put on the imperishable and this mortal body must put on immortality.' This is required to enter the new 'eschatological' world of perfection and glory (1 Cor. 15:47-49). We are even now being transformed morally in preparation (2 Cor. 3:18). We may now ready ourselves in varying degrees (Dan. 12:3; 1 Cor. 3:14, 15; 2 Cor. 9:6). The great chapter 15 of 1 Corinthians shows that we, as frail and mortal, cannot enter that new world without being adapted to it ahead of time, becoming no longer frail but strong, no longer mortal but immortal, no longer humiliated but glorious. The transformation of our bodies will occur at the Second Advent of Christ (1 Thess. 4:16, 17; 1 Cor. 15:50-54). This is not in any way to deny 'the resurrection of the flesh' – the usual phrase in the creeds – objectionable as the phrase has become to some.

Glorification.

The crucified body of Christ was raised a 'glorious body.' 'There can be no doubt,' says J. A. Schep, 'that according to the New Testament the body in which our Lord appeared to his disciples *during the forty days between the resurrection and the ascension* was a glorified body of flesh.'[12] He is making the point the glorified body was *flesh*, and that the flesh was glorified during the forty days. He acknowledges that not all good scholars agree but stands by the statement.

Three main views have been taken as to the time our Lord's body became glorified. The *first* and most common is that the glorification took place at the moment of resurrection but that the glory was veiled during the forty days and no longer. Paul was confronted with the fully glorified Christ on the Damascus road as also was John on Patmos. Among famous authors who agree is William Milligan, who said,

> [T]he Glorification of Jesus began at His Resurrection, not at His Ascension... and when... 1 Timothy 3:16 gathers together six parts of 'the mystery of godliness,' he does not say 'received up *into* glory,' but 'in glory,' – the glory was already there.[13]

---

10. ibid., p. 141.
11. C. A. Hodge, *Systematic Theology ii*, repr. (Grand Rapids, MI: Eerdmans, 1970), p. 628.
12. Schep, *Resurrection Body*, p. 145
13. William Milligan, *The Resurrection of Our Lord*, 4th ed. (London: Macmillan Co., 1901), pp. 16, 17.

Another truly great theologian wrote of the resurrection body of Christ:

> It was raised very glorious, of which his transfiguration... was an emblem and pledge: and though he did not appear in so much glory immediately after his resurrection, and during his stay with his disciples, before his ascension, they not being able to bear the lustre of his countenance it really had; yet now, being crowned with glory and honour, his body is a glorious one, according to which the bodies of the saints will be fashioned, at the resurrection of the just, Phil, 3:21.[14]

The second view, advocated notably at the present time by Millard Erickson, is that it came about in two stages, the resurrection and ascension.

> God is in a different dimension of reality, and the transition from here to there requires not merely a change of place, but of state. So, at some point, Jesus' ascension was not merely a physical and spatial change, but spiritual as well. At that time Jesus underwent the remainder of the metamorphosis begun with the resurrection of his body.[15]

C. A. Hodge's treatment of Christ's resurrection occupies only four pages of his great three-volume *Systematic Theology*. He insists on a real resurrection of the 'flesh' of Christ, in which also He ascended. Yet his treatment of the subject is sketchy. He ventures the appearances were 'preternatural' and that 'it appears from the transfiguration of Christ that His body while on earth, was capable of passing from one state to another without losing its identity. Such was the state of our Lord's body during the forty days... It then, passed into its glorified state.'[16] This very briefly stated and almost wholly undeveloped opinion is apparently about the same as Millard Erickson's.

The third view, advocated by several nineteenth-century theologians, is that the glorification occurred progressively between the resurrection and the ascension. Among the best known are Julius Mueller and the commentators on the New Testament, Godet and Meyer.

There is no evidence I know of, for either the second or third views. There is no trace of stages, two or gradual, in the record. We know that during His years on earth His glory, while inherent to the divine nature, was veiled, only occasionally partially disclosed (e.g. John 2:11 at Cana and more obviously at the Transfiguration).[17]

Limitations.

The limitations of our Lord's human nature, including a material body, were not erased by resurrection and ascension, whatever new powers it may have. He is still locally present in only one place at a time; He was not ubiquitous or omnipresent in the human nature before or after resurrection. 'He is not here, for he has risen, as he said. Come see where the Lord lay' (Matt. 28:6). There is no proof that His body levitated from the tomb or passed through grave clothes like a vapor. He certainly did not appear unclothed before the female witnesses or on the way to Emmaus, etc. The wrapping of His head He removed, perhaps folded it and laid it in an orderly manner where John later noticed it (and the grave wrappings likewise John 20:7). He appeared twice to the disciples in a closed room (Luke 24:36; John 20:19, 26), but it is gratuitously assumed He passed *through* the walls or the closed door. He may have simply opened the door, something even burglars and magicians are good at. 'To conclude from the mysterious and miraculous features that since the resurrection the Lord's human nature partakes of the divine omnipresence seems unwarranted.'[18]

This exegetical oddity (omnipresence or ubiquity of the risen body of Jesus Christ) is sometimes brought forth to support the Lutheran form of the 'Real Presence' doctrine of the Lord's Supper. Jesus had a way of appearing and disappearing without His entrance or exit being observed even during His years of ministry, whether by natural or supernatural means we do not know. Skillful 'operators' on a purely natural level (magicians, prestidigitators, etc.) do seemingly similar things. He walked on water, supernaturally, during His days of *natural human existence*. He passed through crowds unrecognized to escape injury. He also stilled storms while in a local, natural body.

---

14. John Gill, *Complete Body of Doctrinal and Practical Divinity i*, repr. (Grand Rapids, MI: Baker Books, 1978), p. 587.
15. Millard J. Erickson, *Christian Theology* (Baker Books, 1985), p. 778.
16. Hodge, *Systematic Theology ii*, p. 628.
17. See Milligan's discussion, *The Resurrection of Our Lord*, pp. 16, 17 and 244.
18. Schep, in *ZPEB v*, p. 82.

6. His resurrection body is immortal in the sense of never dying, incapable of dying. In this case *immortal* should not be considered the opposite of *mortal* as usually understood. Mortal as understood ordinarily ('all men are mortal') means subject to death. In the normal course of events every man is mortal, destined to die – 'The living know that they will die... says the preacher.' It is appointed unto man once to die.' This 'appointment' is the punishment for original sin. '[D]eath spread to all men, because all sinned' (Rom. 5:12). But Jesus was not under the curse of death at all until He voluntarily assumed it. He did that as man in solidarity with our race. In the sense that 'it is appointed unto man once to die and after that the judgment' Jesus was not mortal, i.e. subject to death.

Some theologians assert that in assuming solidarity with the human race He became locked into all our liabilities, including, death and return to the ground. No sentence of Scripture says so. If it were true then from conception onward He was mortal in the same sense we all are. To the contrary, at various points of His spoken record He seems clearly to state He voluntarily undertook, as man, the task of dying in our place, in obedience to His Father's will and in accordance with His declared purpose (Matt. 20:28).

He was not Man in any sense until the incarnation took place, though some even find a *subsistence* (as opposed to *existence*) of the human Jesus in the *Logos* from eternity past and man's creation in the image of that subsistence. 'The God-man subsisted in heaven before the world.... Christ was the Son of Man in heaven, secretly before God, before he became the Son of Man openly in the world.'[19] Though not without precedents, this view is highly speculative and as far as I can see is not supported by any direct affirmation of Scripture unless one assumes, as Pink and many of the ancient Fathers, that 'Wisdom' in Proverbs 8 is no less than the pre-incarnate Logos rather than as elsewhere in Proverbs an hypostasization of the (feminine gender) Hebrew word *hokma* for wisdom.

He was totally free from sin except as He assumed ours. So He was not 'mortal,' even though He was capable of death and did die. But after resurrection He said 'I am he that liveth, and was dead; and, behold, I am alive for evermore' (Rev. 1:18 KJV).

IV. The Theological Meaning of the Resurrection of Christ.

Though godly and learned scholars have written at great length concerning the theological meaning of Christ's resurrection, the matter can be stated in fewer words, and satisfactorily, mainly in the words of Scripture.

A sound theology at this point will avoid two errors. The one might be termed the orthodox zealot's error, viz.: the resurrection of Jesus is important chiefly for its value as evidence for the truth of Christianity. This did not begin with the fundamentalist movement of the twentieth century. It has been characteristic of too much preaching throughout the modern era. It seems to be regarded as though it were an addition to redemption rather than as an integral part of the work the Father had in mind when He 'sent the Son to be the Saviour of the world.' It is not incorrect, but inadequate. The other is the liberal or Modernist error, that Christianity can exist quite apart from dependence on the *event* of the physical resurrection of the body of Jesus; we can have Jesus as example and teacher (prophet) and lord (king) but He did not die as a sacrifice for sin as the mythologizing Gospel writers and Paul suppose and there really was no resurrection of the flesh – for which this line of thought has proposed a number of weak and mutually contradictory alternate theories.

The Meaning of Christ's Resurrection for Redemption.

In the first place, Scriptures show that Christ submitted to death as the penalty of sin, and by His resurrection from the grave *gave proof* that the penalty of sin was exhausted (see Rom. 4:24; 6:9, 10; 8:3, 10, 11; Gal. 3:13).

In the second place, the resurrection is the specific factual basis, whether addressed to heathen skeptics or unconvinced Jews, for the imperative mood in gospel proclamation: to heathen 'intellectuals', 'God... now he commands [*apaggellō*, to announce, notify, command] all people [*anthrōpoi*, members of the human race, male or female, child or adult] everywhere to repent, because he has fixed a day, on which he will judge the world in righteousness by a man whom he has appointed; and of this he has given assurance to all by raising him from the dead' (Acts 17:30, 31). To unconvinced Jews, Peter at the first Pentecostal preachment, reported the resurrection event, with extensive 'proof' from Old Testament prophecy which ended with this: 'Therefore let all the house of

---

19. A. W. Pink, 'His Glory as the Son of Man' from *Gleanings in the Godhead*, repr., in *Free Grace Broadcaster #162*, Fall, 1997, pp. 26 and 28.

Israel know for certain that God has made Him both Lord and Christ' (Acts 2:36 NASB). The spectacular results are well known. The same technique was followed in all teaching and preaching reported in the book of Acts (Acts 2:24-33; 3:12-15; 10:34-43; 13:22-30; 17:30, 31; 23:6; 24:21; 26:23).

The Meaning for God Himself.

Romans 6:4, 'Christ was raised from the dead *by* [emphasis added] the glory of the Father' (*dia* with genitive, instrumental case), is to be matched with Philippians 2:11 '*to* [emphasis added] the glory of God the Father' (*eis* with accusative of purpose). This means God's attributes and perfections are manifest in the resurrection. He was not overtaken by events. The event fulfilled the prophecies and types and came together at the right time: 'what,' as Paul told Agrippa, 'the prophets and Moses said... that the Christ must suffer and [be]... the first to rise from the dead' (Acts 26:22, 23 RSV). God is seen to be true and faithful to His promises, also gracious, wise, just and benevolent, able to finish what He starts (see 1 Peter 1:21).

The Meaning for the Son of God.

(a) The resurrection was, for Him, the fulfillment of the Father's commandment, willingly assumed and obeyed. 'For this reason the Father loves me, because I lay down my life that I may take it up again. No one takes it from me, but I lay it down of my own accord....This charge have I received from my Father' (John 10:17, 18). The two parts of His mission, to lay down His life and to take it up again may not be separated. Resurrection was 'not a mere consequence' of laying down His life but with the life which followed 'the true goal of that race which he was to run' (Milligan, p. 124).

(b) The resurrection was God's answer to our Lord's most anguished prayer petitions and relief of the most deeply felt anguish – for One who is 'life' and 'prince of life.' It has been pointed out that the true rendering of 'Father, save me *from* [emphasis added] this hour' (John 12:27) employs *ek*, 'out of,' not *apo* 'away from.' Hence, the prayer is for deliverance from death *after He would be in its power*, not from dying itself. The point is important enough to quote the scholarly source:

> ...when we observe this the whole aspect of the prayer is changed. It is not the same prayer to avoid the bitterness of divine wrath as in Matthew 26:39 and parallels. Hence, Our Lord prayed... that he might pass through it to a glorious deliverance – in the context of John 12:27, wheat is sown... not for death but for the harvest for the sake of which Jesus came to that hour.[20]

(c) Through resurrection Jesus was proclaimed 'both Lord and Christ.' This is the force of Peter's final words at Pentecost, beginning at Acts 2:32, 'This Jesus God raised up' and concluding 'therefore... God has made him both Lord and Christ' (Acts 2:36).

(d) As first born of the dead God has declared Him Head of the church and King of creation. This is set forth in exalted, dramatic prose at Colossians 1:16-18; Ephesians 1:19-23; and Hebrews 1:1-3.

(e) He also was 'declared to be the Son of God with power, according to the spirit of holiness, by the resurrection from the dead' (Rom. 1:4 ASV). There is a convergence of scholarly opinion that, in this place, 'spirit' (lower case 's') lies in balanced contrast with 'according to the flesh,' i.e. human nature, in verse 3. Hence, 'spirit of holiness' designates the divine nature of Christ. The article 'the' has no basis in the Greek text. The phrase could properly be rendered 'a spirit of holiness' – no reference to the Third Person of the Godhead. Everyone of His time and place knew Jesus to be a descendant of King David. Even the blind knew it and addressed him as 'Son of David' (Matt. 12:27; see 15:22; 20:30, 31; Mark 10:47, 48; Luke 18:38, 39). The crowds proclaimed him Son of David at the 'Triumphal Entry.' Yet there is no evidence any one was convinced of His divine sonship until late in his ministry Peter made his great confession (Matt. 16:16), and Thomas did not believe it until a week after Easter he was convinced 'by sight' of the reality of our Lord's resurrection (John 20:24-29). So the resurrection made known to all the universe that the humble carpenter of Nazareth was also 'the Son of God in power,' as several sermons in the book of Acts claim and the Epistles and Apocalypse repeatedly proclaim.

(f) The resurrection was the Father's answer to Jesus' prayer for restoration of His power and glory with the Father (John 17:5). There is a significant conjunction of statement in 1 Peter 1:11 and 21 relative to Christ's resurrection, previous Passion and subsequent glory. Verse 21 states how that God 'raised him from the dead and gave him glory'

---

20. Milligan, *Christian Theology*, pp. 124, 125.

and verse 11, that the prophets of old knew of 'the sufferings of Christ and the subsequent glories.' Passages such as Isaiah 53:10-12 and Philippians 2:8, 9 speak first of His obedience and suffering, then after a 'therefore,' that God rewarded Him with glory and honor. Peter supplies the link between them. The resurrection was necessary for Him to enter into the glory He rightly deserved and concerning which He prayed: 'glorify your Son.... Father, glorify me in your own presence with the glory that I had with you before the world existed' (John 17:1, 5).

(g) The resurrection *and* ascension were necessary to the later special Advent and effusion of the Holy Spirit that constituted the believers a church, the body of Christ. These are the reasons for the forty days of meetings with Jesus and the ten more of tarrying of Acts 1:1 ff.: 'it is to your advantage that I go away, for if I go not away, the Helper will not come to you. But if I go, I will send him to you.' (John 16:7)

The Meaning for God's Own People.

As joined with the death of Christ His resurrection is the very heart of redemption and the whole plan of salvation. Beyond this, Scripture calls our attention to several aspects of meaning of the resurrection for us. There are several special particulars.

First, 'the surpassing greatness of His power toward us who believe' is measured by 'the working of the strength of His might which He brought about in Christ, when He raised Him from the dead' (Eph. 1:19, 20 NASB). As noted earlier in this chapter, Paul seems to have searched the Greek language for the most superlative terms available to characterize the power turned loose for our benefit when God raised Jesus from the dead. Four of them come across to our language as *hyperbolic* ('*surpassing*'), *dynamite, dynamic* ('*power*') and *energy* (*working*). In Philippians 3:10 Paul prays that he may know Christ both in fellowship with His suffering (daily cross-bearing) but also in the power of His resurrection. In this way all the blessings of the whole plan of salvation (or the covenant of grace, if one prefers that form of expression) are hinged to the resurrection of Christ. I shall not attempt the daunting project of examining all the blessings here. That belongs to the next section of systematic theology, subjective soteriology.

Second, He was 'raised for our justification' (Rom. 4:25). This is followed immediately by reference to the benefits that accrue to every believer justified 'by faith' (Rom. 5:1-5). Reformation Christianity in the Augustinian tradition rejoices to proclaim that these benefits are not attainments to be achieved *en route* to justification on the Judgment Day, but already secured by faith in Christ's work certified as finished not only on account of His sixth saying from the cross ('It is finished!') but by the victory of the resurrection (Rom. 1:4). Every sin past, present and future has already been forgiven. The justified are possessors of the imputed righteousness of our crucified, risen and ascended Savior. Beginning with 'peace with God' (another name for reconciliation), we have access, standing, joy in hope, joy in suffering, endurance (which one must have to be saved, Matt. 24:13), experienced character, no disappointment in God's love and finally God's Holy Spirit.

Third, since 'It is God who justifies' (Rom. 8:33) there is none to condemn us. Christ that died and who has risen again is making intercession for us (another benefit of the resurrection). Therefore nothing any one can think of now or ever shall separate us from the love of God in Christ Jesus our Lord (Rom. 8:34-39).

Fourth, we are already 'risen with Christ' (Col. 3:1 KJV). From the divine point of view our salvation began with union with Christ in election and foreknowledge, then continues onward in Him or with Him onward to glory. It is all by grace alone and has us, from this perspective, already sitting together with Christ in His 'session' at the right hand of God (Eph. 2:5, 6). The Letter to Colossians, however, brings us down to earth by exhorting believers who accept this state of affairs, at the present time, to think about our 'standing' in our present 'state' and to set our affections up there where Christ is presently enthroned in present fact. 'If then you have been raised with Christ, seek the things that are above, where Christ is, seated at the right hand of God,' etc. (Col. 3:1-3), knowing His destiny is also ours (v. 4). This is the highest kind of motive for holy living (v. 5 to the end of the Epistle).

Fifth, for believers, Christ's resurrection is the sufficient ground of our own hope of resurrection ('Because I live, you also will live' John 14:19).

Finally, the resurrection body of Jesus Christ is the pattern of the believer's resurrection body in eternity up ahead. 'For the Lord himself will descend from heaven with a cry of command, with the voice of an archangel, and with the sound of the trumpet of God. And the dead in Christ will rise first' (1 Thess. 4:16), 'who will transform our lowly body to be like his glorious body' (Phil. 3:21); and 'Just as we have borne the image of the man of dust, we shall also bear the image of the man of heaven' (1 Cor. 15:49). Our hearts are comforted because 'we know that when he appears we shall be like him, because we shall see him as he is' (1 John 3:2).

22
The Ascension of Christ

In most Christian circles, where we discuss what teachings our denominations or theological parties have in common, the ascension receives little notice. At an early stage of the sixteenth-century Reformation, however, the nature and qualities of the body of the ascended Christ became a matter of very serious difference between Reformed and Lutherans. Luther and Lutherans since his day define the 'the real presence' of Christ as bodily presence, in and with the elements of the Lord's Supper. The body is said, by virtue of union with the divine nature, to be ubiquitous, that is, present where and whenever the words of institution are properly pronounced over the elements of the Eucharist, or the Lord's Supper. In the time of Calvin and Melanchthon (Luther's colleague) they and others like-minded desperately wished to overcome this difference and with great regret gave up on the matter. Strict and unrelenting Lutheranism, in disagreement both with Roman Catholicism and Protestantism in general on the mode of the presence of Jesus' flesh and blood in the Eucharistic meal, has pursued its separate way on this matter to the present day. This colors many pages of Lutheran books of theology. It has also produced a rather severe separatist Lutheran outlook toward other Christians. Living as I do in the ocean of Lutheran Christendom in America's upper Midwest I have been made acutely aware of this regularly.

The sixteenth-century debate from Calvin's side is reported in large part in *Tracts Containing Treatises on the Sacraments*, Volume II of the Tracts, trans. by H. Beveridge, Edinburgh, 1849, recently reissued. For the history of the Lutheran doctrine see C. P. Krauth, *The Conservative Reformation and Its Theology*. For a more recent orthodox Lutheran presentation see Francis Pieper in *Christian Dogmatics*, pp. 323–330,[1] as well as many other places throughout discussion of Christology and sacraments, likewise J. Th. Mueller.[2]

The ascension of Christ, like His resurrection, has been impossible for the theology of liberalism to accept. There are several explanations proposed by those who reject the plain sense of Scripture as to why the narrative, brief as it is, appears on the pages of the Bible. These need not detain us at this stage of discussion but all should be put on notice that denials and perversions of the orthodox, biblical doctrines of our Lord's resurrection *and* ascension now frequently occur in otherwise orthodox settings. This commonly has gone unnoticed by church groups and their schools. There consequently have been some irruptions of severe controversies on account of this aberration.

---

1. Francis Pieper, *Christian Dogmatics ii* (St Louis: Concordia Publ., 1951), pp. 323–330 and on 'The Communicated Omnipresence,' vol. ii, pp. 66 ff.
2. John T. Mueller, *Christian Dogmatics* (St Louis: Concordia Publishing, 1955), pp. 295–309.

In our seminaries systematic theology is usually taught by professors trained in the history of doctrines and in the exegetical basis of them. They understand the necessary connections of the several *loci* of doctrines. This, lamentably, in this age of striving for academic respectability, is not uniformly the case among professors in all departments. In which case it is not uncommon for the current inheritance from neo-orthodoxy (halfway back to orthodoxy from liberalism) to be taught in the New Testament department in regard to our Lord's resurrection and ascension. The professor may never have taken a course in theology and be quite unaware he is planting a strange seed. In this way unsteady Christology (with good intentions) is passed on to the people of our churches and thereby theological instability and susceptibility to 'every wind of doctrine.' The literal, bodily ascension of Christ as taught in the ancient creeds and the evangelical creeds and confessions of the Reformation era is grounded in the Scriptures, especially Luke 24:50 and 51 and Acts 1:6-11. It is as genuine a part of 'the catholic faith' as any teaching. Vincent of Lerins' criteria of '*ubique, semper, ab omnibus* (everywhere, always, by all or universality, antiquity, consensus) are fully met by this doctrine. Along with Good Friday, Easter and Pentecost Sunday, Ascension Day is still observed in the ritual calendar of our Lord's last weeks on earth. What does Scripture demand that we believe?

The Fact of the Ascension.

There are several points generally acknowledged as true by a fair reading of Scripture with minor shades of difference. The church has believed, confessed and taught the following:

1. The ascension of Christ was expected by Christ and foretold by Him. Most of the information is in John's Gospel.

At His last attendance at the Feast of Tabernacles, Jesus spoke of a coming flow of 'rivers of living water' (John 7:38), about which John comments, that Jesus was referring to 'the Spirit' and adds, 'as yet the Spirit had not been given, because Jesus was not yet glorified' (John 7:39). John's comment is inexplicable apart from the ascension story, even though John did not say 'Jesus ascended,' he seems to have assumed it.

In the next chapter Jesus 'said to them [i.e. to the temple crowd] again "I am going away, and you will seek me, and you will die in your sin. Where I am going, you cannot come"' (John 8:21). John reports that even though this obvious reference to Christ's departure for heaven was misunderstood completely by the temple throng, 'As he was saying these things, many believed in him' (v. 30).

2. The Upper Room Discourse furnishes three distinct prophecies of the ascension. They are oblique, not understood till later, being explained like very much of biblical prediction only by fulfillment. The three are 'Yet a little while and the world will see me no more' (John 14:19); 'You heard me say to you, 'I am going away,' etc. (John 14:28, 29); and 'But now I am going to him who sent me,' etc. (John 16:5). These sayings do not refer to Jesus' death but to a departure of the Man, Jesus, as going on a journey. How John remembered these fine turns of cryptic phraseology is explained only by the special work of the Spirit, to 'bring to your remembrance all that I have said to you' (John 14:26).

Certain parables of Jesus near the end of His life pointedly allude to His 'departure.' In the Parable of the Talents the Lord of the house is 'a man travelling into a far country' (Matt. 25:14 KJV). In the Parable of the Pounds 'A nobleman went into a far country' (Luke 19:12) precisely to indicate our Lord's absence from earth in heaven.

A Question: Is the Ascension Anticipated in the Old Testament?

The stories of Enoch, Elijah and Moses are not quite parallel, though one acquainted with the Old Testament cannot help but be reminded of them. Several 'Royal Psalms,' which treat the elevation of 'David' or his Son to universal authority, imply the session at the right hand of the Father and by implication the ascension, and may be involved in Paul's 'in accordance with the Scripture' in 1 Corinthians 15:1-5. Some of these Psalms are 2, 18, 20, 21, 45, 61, 72, 89 and 110. Some good interpreters have found rather fanciful (according to contemporary thinking) connections between Old Testament Psalm texts and the ascension. Psalm 47:5 says 'God has gone up with a shout, the LORD with the sound of a trumpet'. John Gill suggested that since Jesus will come again with shout and trumpet (1 Thess. 4:16), perhaps the ascent of Immanuel (God with us) is predicted in the Psalm. Psalm 110:1 implies the ascension by speaking of the session at God's right hand as Peter showed (Acts 2:34, 35). (I find no *necessary* connection with the ascension of Christ in any of these Psalms or Daniel 7:13, 14 and Micah 2:13 which are sometimes cited.)

Another Question: Were There Two Ascensions?

One on Easter or shortly thereafter and another later? There was a time when popular exposition of the Bible was more affected by assumptions based on Old Testament types than today. This goes back at least to Puritan times in Britain and America. Without endorsing the view, the Scofield Bible reports how the supposed typology of the Day of Atonement (Lev. 16) required the ascension of Christ to present the blood of His Calvary sacrifice in heaven shortly after emerging from the tomb. It is supposed He had not yet ascended to make this presentation, when He commanded Mary 'Touch me not; for I have not yet ascended to my Father' (John 20:17 KJV), but He had ascended and returned when later He invited disciples to touch Him.[3] Commentators have ruminated over the problem in every age as far back at least as Augustine and Chrysostom.[4] John F. Walvoord points out that Hebrews 9:12 says Christ entered into the holy place 'through' (*dia* with the genitive) His own blood not 'with' it as though He carried it to heaven.[5] There is no suggestion in Scripture that the blood of Christ ever was transported anywhere beyond the cross itself. This question has been warmly discussed in pulpit and lecture over the years, but not now for a generation because 'typology' has fallen out of favor. (Actually the tense of the Greek verb [present imperative] with the negative implies that Mary was already touching Jesus physically. He is saying, 'stop hanging on to me.' This is reflected in the ESV 'Do not cling to me' or RSV 'Do not hold me.') Among the many published treatments of the critical verse ('Touch me not; for I am not yet ascended to my Father... I ascend unto my Father,' etc., John 20:17 KJV) Everett F. Harrison stated the sum of good scholarship briefly and I think well. I quote in part:

> [Jesus] was already glorified [when Mary met Him on Easter morning]. He belonged now to the heavenly realm, even though he was willing to tarry for a time to meet with his friends. *I am not yet ascended.* The implication was that Mary would not be able to touch Jesus in some sense after the Ascension, i.e. she would touch him by faith in the blessed life of the Spirit. The closeness of that new relationship is attested by the fact that he spoke of his followers as *brethren* (cf. the anticipation of this in Matt. 12:49). Even in the intimacy of the new order, however, Christ retained his own special relationship to God the Father. *My Father* is the language of deity; my God is the language of humanity.[6]

In Ephesians 4:8-10, Paul quotes Psalm 68:18 and applies it to the ascension of Christ. Paul's version of the Psalm quoted is unique to him: 'When he ascended up on high, he led captivity captive, and gave gifts unto men' (Eph. 4:8 KJV). A comparison of the passages raises several difficulties. The greatest one is that the Psalm says when the Lord ascended 'the high mount' he *received* gifts *among men* not that he gave gifts to *men* as Paul renders it. The Hebrew O.T. and the Greek O.T. (LXX) agree in this reading. Why does Paul use *edoken*, 'he gave,' rather than *elabes*, 'you took' as in the LXX? The Apostle has recast the passage.

The Psalm cited is a song of triumph perhaps, as some scholars think, when the Ark was brought up the hill of Zion in ceremonial procession. Therefore as a Messianic Psalm, Alford's comment seems adequate; 'Every part of that ark, every stone of that hill, was full of spiritual meaning. Every note struck on the lyres of the sweet singers of Israel, is but part of a chord, deep and world wide, sounding from the golden harps of redemption.'[7] He adds 'Christ received, upon his ascension, gifts for men; [but] he received them in order to give them.' This may explain the shift from second person ('thou didst receive') to third person ('he gave').

The Ascension of Christ Described As an Historical Event.

One does not read far in recent literature about the exaltation of Christ at His ascension to learn that there is presently a movement away from acceptance of the literal truth of what the record in Acts 1:9-11 says and the rest of the New Testament writers directly or indirectly accept. The alternative views are not always clearly stated, but out of the welter of opinions these emerge. I shall not enlarge upon them greatly.

a) The ascension is a parabolic sort of action, something like Jesus' cursing of the fig tree, performed to teach believers who must continue to live in a realm of time and space that Christ would no longer be visibly present with

---

3. *Scofield Bible*, pp. 1141, 1142.
4. See survey of views in J. P. Lange, *A Commentary on the Holy Scriptures: Critical, Doctrinal and Homiletical, – Matthew,* trans. Philip Schaff (New York: Charles Scribner & Co., 1870), pp. 610, 611.
5. John F. Walvoord, *Jesus Christ Our Lord* (Chicago: Moody Press, 1969), pp. 220, 221.
6. Everett F. Harrison, 'The Gospel According to John,' in *The Wycliffe Commentary* (Chicago: Moody Press, 1962), p. 1119.
7. Henry Alford, *The New Testament for English Readers*, repr. (Chicago: Moody Press n.d.), p. 1229.

them. The real departure of the risen Christ for that other dimension took place at the moment of the resurrection. Murray J. Harris presented this view, prevalent among neo-orthodox theologians, in two books, *Raised Immortal* (1983) and *From Grave to Glory* (1990). In the latter he supports the idea that the Lord may have returned from heaven to earth to enact the ascension reported in Luke 24 and Acts 1.[8] He writes:

> The ascension vividly dramatized Christ's earlier exaltation to God's right hand. It was a parable acted out for the benefit of the disciples as a visible and historical confirmation of a spiritual reality.[9]

b) The ascension is the report of a tradition only, a tradition which had developed among Christians of the first and second generation to explain Jesus' absence among them. Both views a) and b) were common among neo-orthodox writers.

c) The ascension story is a myth. This view has taken various forms from Straus (*The Life of Jesus*) to Bultmann. The resurrection of a dead body has never taken place, so neither has the ascension. I cite Emil Brunner as a clear example. Emil Brunner, in his later work, clearly relegated the 'forty days' and the ascension to unhistorical tradition. He wrote of these two parts of Luke's testimony (Luke 24; Acts 2):

> [O]nce more we stand at a point where theology must have courage to be ready to abandon the ecclesiastical tradition. For Paul the Exaltation of Jesus is identical with his Resurrection.... While the exaltation of Christ and his session at the Right Hand of God belong to the fundamental *keryma* of this witness in the New Testament, the exaltation as 'Ascension' plays no part in the teaching of the Apostles.[10]

d) F. F. Bruce held that Jesus ascended to heaven immediately from grave to glory in a 'body of glory.' He goes on to say,

> The resurrection appearances, in which He condescended to the disciples temporal conditions of life, even giving so far as to eat with them, were visitations from that exalted and eternal world.... What happened on the fortieth day was that this series of visitations came to an end with a scene which impressed on the disciples their Master's heavenly glory![11]

To the contrary, throughout the New Testament the ascension from Olivet is assumed and referred to as quite as much a happening at the end of Jesus' earthly career as His birth at Bethlehem at its beginning and His crucifixion outside the wall of Jerusalem at the climax. The book of Hebrews could never have been written if the author along with people addressed had not believed Jesus had bodily ascended to heaven and was there exercising royal authority and presently carrying on a ministry of intercession.

Objections to the ascension are really more severe than those offered to the resurrection. Why so? The resurrection involves the great miracle of restoring life to a dead body. The ascension involves the miracle of apparent suspension of the law of gravity – perhaps a greater miracle. Both are rejected by anyone who denies the supernatural altogether. The ascension seems to its objectors also to require two errors of fact: *first* that the cosmos is stacked in layers, with the heaven where God dwells being far above earth; whereas really 'up' changes direction from any given spot as the earth rotates. *Second*, the ascension of the material body of Jesus requires a 'space,' for the body to occupy, hence presumes that heaven is a place in a space of some kind. These two 'problems' puzzle us all, of course. The two are really the same. Do God, the angels and 'the spirits of the righteous made perfect' (Heb. 12:23) reside in a different dimension (as many orthodox acknowledge), a dimension perhaps unrelated to space, or, is there a region in space where, with the risen Christ, Elijah, Enoch and Moses dwell? The Bible says heaven shall come down to earth and that Christ shall reign here over His people (Isa. 65, 66; Rev. 21, 22). Jesus said He would go away 'to prepare a place' (John 14:2). I refer the reader to the last volume of this series, eschatology, the portion on heaven and the final destiny of the redeemed.

Peter Toon, a contemporary British orthodox theologian, has given the church a thorough presentation of the ascension and its meaning. On the point of heaven as a *place* he has written:

> Evangelicals have traditionally believed... that heaven is both a place and a state... on heaven being a place, not primarily because they did not have a modern, post-Einstein view of cosmology, but because the Scriptures

---

8. Murray J. Harris, *From Grave to Glory* (Grand Rapids, MI: Zondervan, 1990), pp. 178–183.
9. ibid., p. 423.
10. Emil Brunner, *The Christian Doctrine of Creation and Redemption, Dogmatics ii*, trans. Olive Wyon (Philadelphia, PA: The Westminster Press, 1952), p. 373.
11. F. F. Bruce, *Commentary on the Book of Acts,* rev. (Grand Rapids, MI: Eerdmans, 1988), p. 129.

require such belief (e.g. Deut. 4:36; 12:5, 11, 21; 26:15; Acts 1:11; 3:21). Heaven, as the dwelling place of God, the holy angels, and saints, was seen as 'above' the starry heavens. Thus Christ has passed through the physical heavens and has been raised 'higher' than them (sic, they) (Heb. 4:14; 7:26; 9:11, 23, 24). In insisting that heaven is both a state and a place, Christianity has usually been careful to deny any knowledge of its particular and specific characteristics or of its precise relation to the physical universe.[12]

Lutheran theology embraces a rather special view of Jesus' ascension. And, since there are about 60 million Lutherans in the world – including a major fraction of them in the American north central section – Christian charity would require that we try to understand them in this matter. The problem relates in part to the rather technical matter of whether there is *communion* of properties in the incarnate Son or *communication* of properties between the divine and human natures.

In the Lutheran confessional documents and in most Lutheran works of doctrinal theology as well as pastoral preaching (there are some exceptions), the attributes of the divine nature omniscience, omnipresence and omnipotence are said to be communicated to the human nature. In most orthodox theology, Reformed and other, it is understood the attributes of both natures are communicated to the one Person, not the natures one to the other. This means that if the Spirit of Christ, i.e. His Person, is present in the Eucharistic elements, then His body and blood are also – hence Lutherans insist (as noted several times earlier in these pages) on the *real presence*, by which they mean the flesh and blood of Christ in, with or under the bread and wine. It remains to be said some Lutheran theologians make it a point to deny human attributes are communicated to the divine nature. To most non-Lutherans this seems like a partial rejection of the Definition of Chalcedon of 451 ('without mixture' of the two natures) and a partial acceptance of the Eutychian party condemned at that Council. Shedd provides an excellent discussion.[13] Lutheran theologians tend to be very defensive – and write at great length – about this matter as we have noted earlier.

Charles Hodge's final thought on the subject of the 'place' (John 14:2) to which Jesus went when he 'was lifted up, and a cloud took him out of their sight' (Acts 1:9) says about as much as it is possible for us time-and-space-bound mortals to say. Heaven means:

> the place where God dwells, where the angels and the spirits of the just are congregated; whence Christ came, and to which he has returned. He told his disciples that he went to prepare a place for them (John 14:2). In this sense the word is used when the Bible speaks of God as our Father 'in Heaven'; or of heaven as his throne, his temple, his dwelling place. If Christ has a true body, it must occupy a portion of space. And where Christ is, there is the Christian's heaven.[14]

Summarizing and Concluding.

1) In all such matters of fact and meaning we mere human beings are limited to such knowledge of ultimate matters as God has seen fit to reveal. If some of His revelation is accommodated to human limitations of understanding, so be it. We are unable to think of non-spatially related substance in any clear way. Let us accept that: a) the Bible represents heaven, as we have seen, as the '*place*' of God's special manifestation. In Solomon's great dedicatory prayer he proposes, 'But will God dwell indeed with man on the earth? Behold, heaven [of birds, clouds] and the highest heaven [stellar spaces] cannot contain thee; how much less this house which I have built' (2 Chr. 6:18 RSV). Wise people of ancient times knew the Creator of time and space is not 'contained' there. Yet Solomon goes on to speak of a 'heaven thy dwelling place' from which God answers prayers. Wherever and whatever this heaven is, it is the place of *God's special manifestation* as opposed to the whole creation, where He is *generally manifest*. We can say no more.

2) Our Lord's leaving the disciples and scenes of earth is described as an ascent to heaven with clouds; and 'he went up.' He is said elsewhere to have 'passed through the heavens' (Heb. 4:14). Paul implies a plurality of heavens, to the third of which He, 'this man was caught up.' This third heaven he equates with Paradise (2 Cor. 12:1-4). How he knew it was Paradise – thence Jesus and the repentant thief arrived at death (Luke 23:43) – he does not say. He reports that there he 'heard things that cannot be told, which man may not utter' (2 Cor. 12:4) and presumably saw sights indescribable, quite like what John the Revelator says of his transport to heaven (Rev. 4:1). Though John rather plainly

---

12. Peter Toon, 'The Meaning of the Ascension of Christ,' 2nd of four articles on Christ's Ascension in *Bibliotheca Sacra*, vol. 140 (Oct.–Dec. 1983), p. 291.
13. W. G. T. Shedd, *Dogmatic Theology ii* (Grand Rapids, MI: Zondervan, 1969), pp. 323–327.
14. Charles A. Hodge, *Systematic Theology ii*. 630–635.

indicates he was 'in the Spirit' (Rev. 1:10; 4:2), which we may suppose means he never physically left the Isle of Patmos. Concerning Paul's remarkable experiences, he plainly states he does not know and cannot say if he was in the body or out of it. If Paul could say nothing reportable about heaven and John does not say he was literally there, at this distance from them and in want of further dependable revelation we best say no more about the geography of heaven.

3) In condescension to our inability to conceive of such a place, the Bible persistently represents 'heaven and earth' as opposed realities, upward and downward. The last two chapters of the Bible teach that after the resurrections and judgments with which the present order shall end a new Jerusalem will come down from God out of heaven. In an important manner therefore we may expect that the earth and heaven will no longer be polar opposites. It is not said the tabernacle of men will be with God, but the other way around. The souls of martyrs presently in heaven, near to God, are dissatisfied with their disembodied condition, for they cry 'how long' (Rev. 6:9-11).

4) Joseph Seiss, a prolific, widely read and learned Lutheran writer of a century and more ago, insisted that heaven is a place, however mysterious for the present, where human beings in physical bodies will feel at home. We are each, he said, 'a being who is not mere spirit – who knows only to live in a body.... Did men but learn to know the difference between a Paradise of sense and a Paradise of sensuality... that there was a material universe before sin was' and shall endure after sin is washed away from it, etc.[15] Heaven is normally a topic of eschatology, yet in thinking about our Lord's ascension one must form some clear idea about the destination of His ascension. Our conception cannot be as distinct and precise as one might wish, for though the heaven of God to which the Son of God returned is previous to the material creation, it is nevertheless 'true that our Lord returned to the Father not as he came, but forever united with human nature, the Word made Flesh.'[16] H. B. Swete states the obvious: heaven must be a place 'user-friendly' for our Lord and all the redeemed, whose physical bodies are permanently restored to them.

5) Let us observe that the Apostle Paul regarded the ascension ('taken up in glory,' 1 Tim. 3:16) as part of the mystery of Christ. When we are caught up to heaven at His coming, as He was at His ascension, we probably still will not fully understand, any more than we fully understand the appearance of firmness composed of innumerable atomic and sub-atomic particles of the whole periodic table of the elements.

The Importance of the Ascension.

The ascension of Christ is mentioned by Paul, as just observed, in his great summary of the mystery of Christ (1 Tim. 3:16). As we have seen, Jesus made a point of predicting it several times. The ascension furnishes a pattern of how the Lord shall appear 'the second time... unto salvation' (Heb. 9:28 KJV).

The ascension of Christ, says the author of Hebrews, marks the second of three 'appearances' of Christ in the flesh and in history – two of these appearances past and one yet future: 'Christ has entered, not into holy places made with hands... now to appear in the presence of God.' He also 'appeared once for all... to put away sin by the sacrifice of himself.' In the future He 'will appear a second time [on earth]... to save those who are eagerly waiting for him' (Heb. 9:24-28).

The church has professed belief in the ascension of Christ in its official creeds and confessions from the beginning. The 'Apostles Creed' places 'he ascended into heaven' between 'he arose from the dead' and 'sitteth on the right hand of God.' The most ecumenical in spirit of the Reformation documents, the Heidelberg Catechism, devotes four questions and answers to it. In the sketch to follow here, the great theological significance of the ascension will stand out.

The Theological and Practical Meaning of the Ascension of Christ.

As for Christ Himself: 1.) It marked the end of His career of redemption for, 'After making purification for sins, he sat down at the right hand of the Majesty on high' (Heb. 1:3) where the inhabitants of heaven worship Him as conqueror of sin and death (Rev. 5 ff.). 2.) There at the 'right hand of' Father He has put all things under His feet and has made Him the head over all things (Eph. 1:17, 22) as reward for His redemptive suffering (Acts 2:34-36; Phil. 2:9-11; Isa. 53:12). 3.) The ascension enabled Him to be inaugurated into the high priestly work He now exercises in the heavenly sanctuary (Rom. 8:34; Heb. 7:24, 25; 9:11, 24-26), as Hebrews describes at length (Heb. 8:1-6), 'exalted above the heavens' (Heb. 7:26).

---

15. Joseph A. Seiss, *Lectures on the Apocalypse*, 3 volumes (Philadelphia, PA: Approved Book Stores, 1865). (Reprint: Grand Rapids, MI: Zondervan, 1964), *loc. cit.* Rev. 21 ff.
16. Henry B. Swete, *The Ascended Christ: A Study in the Earliest Christian Teaching* (London: Macmillan, 1916), pp. 8, 9.

Millard J. Erickson's widely used textbook of theology provides only a brief treatment of the resurrection of Jesus and that as a stage of His exaltation.[17] He asserts that after the resurrection but before ascension His body 'was something of a resuscitation, such as that of Lazarus, rather than a true resurrection as will be the case for us.' He has already stated, 'the body that he had at the point of resurrection was yet to undergo a more complete transformation at the point of the ascension. It was yet to become a "spiritual body."' He goes on to say, 'So, at some point, Jesus' ascension was not merely a physical and spatial change, but spiritual as well. At that time Jesus underwent the remainder of the metamorphosis begun with the resurrection of his body.' Shortly, after brief attention to the absence of pain and presence of praise and glory in the ascended state this statement, strange to this reader, appears: 'There is a difference in another respect as well. For now Jesus is the God-man.' One must ask, has not our Lord been 'the God-man' from the first moment of incarnation? He affirms 'a continuing incarnation,' but 'His [humanity] is not of the type that we have, or even the humanity that he had while he was here.' These ideas are not presently usual in evangelical theology and differ in several ways from the discussion to follow here. H. L. Martensen, an influential Danish theologian set forth similar views,[18] as did Charles Hodge.[19]

Again, let not the misbelieving, unbelieving and half-believing academic, critical scholars of our times deceive any one about the permanence of our Lord's complete human nature, including His body of 'flesh.' Once more J. A. Schep speaks timely warnings in this connection.

> But all these and other changes which the ascension brought about have nothing to do with a change in Jesus' resurrection-body. It is in his risen, incorruptible, and immortal body of flesh that Jesus Christ in heaven exercises his all-embracing authority and performs his heavenly ministry as the exalted King, Priest and Prophet of the Church. Undoubtedly, his exalted position in heaven implies the possibility that he can display supernatural glories and appear in a splendour of light. So he appeared to Paul on the Damascus road (Acts 9:3), and so he will come at the end of the ages (Mark 8:38; 13:26; Matt. 24:30). But this gives us no right to regard the body of our risen and exalted Lord as being changed into a body consisting of some light-substance or glory. Much less does the manner in which he revealed himself to John in a vision (Rev. 1:13ff.) give any ground for such a conclusion.[20]

As for believers: the ascension made it possible for Christ to send the Holy Spirit in His several special office works – agent to complete revelation of 'all the truth' to the Apostles (John 16:12–14; 15:26, 27), agent to convict men of their need of forgiveness of sin (John 16:8, 9), agent of regeneration (John 3:5–8), to be the believers' Comforter (John 14:16, 17 KJV) and Intercessor (Rom. 8:26, 27), and, of course, to unite believers into a universal *ekklēsia* (Matt. 3:11; 1 Cor. 12:13 ff.) and much more.

The ascension also assures us that we have a sympathetic Advocate in heaven, 'For Christ has entered… into heaven itself, now to appear in the presence of God on our behalf' (Heb. 9:24 also see Heb. 4:14-16). In a strange way His absence from us and presence with the Father enables us to perform greater works in Jesus' name than if He were here in the flesh (John 14:12). In heaven our Lord has opened access for each of us even today in prayer 'by the new and living way which He opened for us… through his flesh' and actual entrance to heaven at last 'where Jesus has gone as a forerunner' (Heb. 6:20). Contemplation of the fact that our Lord has ascended to heaven should produce many spiritual benefits: especially, strong interest in heaven and heavenly things – seeking 'the things that are above, where Christ is, seated at the right hand of God' (Col. 3:1); great assurance, for now we have a 'hope set before us. We have this as a sure and steadfast anchor of the soul, a hope that enters into the inner place behind the curtain, where Jesus has gone as a forerunner on our behalf' (Heb. 6:18-20).

When in the next chapter we assess the practical import of the ascension and heavenly life of the incarnate Son of God the truly amazing importance of our Lord's passing into the invisible world, in the flesh, bodily, will be apparent.

This is all ground for assurance of a joyous eternal future, peculiar to evangelical Christian faith.

> Just as a captain casts his anchor, so the soul of the believer casts his anchor, and just as the captain does not put his ultimate trust in his anchor but in the anchor ground, so the believer does not put his trust in his hope but in the ground of his hope, namely the promises of God which have been fulfilled by the forerunner and which will still be fulfilled.[21]

---

17. Millard J. Erickson, *Christian Theology* (Grand Rapids, MI: Baker Books, 1985), pp. 776–779.
18. H. L. Martensen, *Christian Dogmatics*, 1864, p. 172, as cited by Toon, in *Bibliotheca Sacra*, p. 199.
19. C. A. Hodge, *Systematic Theology*, p. 628.
20. J. A. Schep, *The Nature of the Resurrection Body* (Grand Rapids, MI: Eerdmans, 1964), p. 165.
21. Grosheide, *Commentary on Hebrews*, p. 187, as quoted by G. C. Berkouwer, *The Work of Christ*, trans. C. Lambregtse (Grand Rapids, MI: Eerdmans, 1965), p. 208.

23
Enthroned in Heaven at God's Right Hand

Like everything else related to the New Testament message about Christ, the beginnings of the enthronement, or session doctrine, are found in the Old Testament either by preparation or prophecy, i.e. 'in accordance with the Scriptures' (1 Cor. 15:3, 4). The primary Old Testament passage is Psalm 110, though Psalms 2, 45 and 72 as well as every other text relating to the royal, Messianic office are related to the subject.

Christ's enthronement took place in heaven. It was not witnessed by human eyes on earth. Our knowledge of the session at God's right hand rests, first, upon two announcements by the new leader of the Apostles, Peter, by name. Second, upon the assumption through the rest of the New Testament that the enthronement had taken place.

The Fact of the Session at God's Right Hand.

The apostle Peter was God's revelatory agent in making the fact known. The amazing phenomena of Pentecost had taken place early in the day – before 'the third hour' (Acts 2:15), about 9 o'clock. So 'Peter, standing up' as new spokesman for the apostolic college launched into a discourse to explain the amazing phenomenon of the tongues-speaking and how everyone understood in the language in which he 'was born.' Peter's audience numbered several thousands of Jews representative of 'every nation under heaven' (v. 5). It was an auspicious occasion for an announcement of cosmic meaning.

The announcement was introduced as the scriptural explanation of the events in Jerusalem early that morning.

> This Jesus God raised up, and of that we all are witnesses. Being therefore exalted at the right hand of God, and having received from the Father the promise of the Holy Spirit, he has poured out this that you yourselves are seeing and hearing. For David did not ascend into the heavens, but he himself says,
> 'The Lord said to my Lord, Sit at my right hand, until I make your enemies your footstool.' Let all the house of Israel therefore know for certain that God has made him both Lord and Christ, this Jesus whom you crucified (Acts 2:32-36 ESV).

This is nothing less than official Christian interpretation of Psalm 110 as a prophecy of the enthronement of Christ which had now already taken place in heaven. It constitutes the very first example of a Christian theologian making a theological statement on the basis of Scripture interpretation. Peter told those Jewish listeners not only what had happened at the session but what it all meant, and did so in connection with Bible interpretation, as we shall see.

Many years later Peter wrote another report, of fulfilled prophecy as it were, speaking of 'the resurrection of Jesus Christ, who has gone into heaven and is at the right hand of God' (1 Peter 3:21, 22).

Hebrews presents the session more by way of reflection on accepted fact among the readers than as announcement. It was well known to them and a basis for exhortation.

The nearest thing to an 'eyewitness' testimony to the session is by Stephen, the first Christian martyr. At the close of his address to the Jewish council, Stephen 'full of the Holy Spirit, gazed into heaven and saw... Jesus standing at the right hand of God' (Acts 7:55; see v. 57). Whether risen from the throne and standing in response to the threatened atrocity about to take place, as some think, or more likely, to receive Stephen's spirit to heaven we cannot know. Any comment is speculative.

Also Jesus prophesied of the session and His eschatological coming (the *parousia*) when under oath in the high priest's court: 'But I tell you, from now on you will see the Son of Man seated at the right hand of Power and coming on the clouds of heaven' (Matt. 26:64). This was an outright claim to be the fulfillment of Daniel 7:14 and of Psalm 110:1. Peter no doubt was thinking of the connection in proclaiming 'this Jesus' whom the Jews before him had crucified 'God has made... both Lord and Christ' as we noted in Acts 2:36.

Through the epistles of Paul and Peter and the book of Hebrews the event of enthronement on high is already, within a generation of Jesus' death, a matter of settled Christian knowledge and belief among the Christian assemblies of the Empire and is employed as grounds for Christian doctrine, comfort and admonition. This was no myth made up by the 'creative Gentile Church' in imitation of some late Gnostic myth as some practitioners of redaction criticism would have us believe.

The Old Testament Background.

One can imagine how Jesus might respond to our incredulity about such unlikely events as the visible ascent of a Man up through the atmosphere and then out of sight to the very throne of God. Modernist theology rejects the factuality of the session altogether. Admittedly all of us must recognize that we are not on familiar ground. There is not much to be said except that Christian faith accepts what little the inspired documents say about Jesus' ascension and enthronement. Even Paul said it was not possible to describe heaven's language, geography and furniture, so to speak (2 Cor. 12:1-4). Might Jesus not say of the modern critics, 'O foolish ones, and slow of heart to believe all that the prophets have spoken. Was it not necessary that the Christ should suffer these things *and enter into his glory?*'

That 'was it not necessary' includes His session and the prophecy of it in Psalm 110 and 2. 'The LORD says to my Lord: 'Sit at my right hand, until I make your enemies your footstool' ...Rule in the midst of your enemies.... The Lord is at your right hand; he will shatter kings on the day of his wrath.' Peter's phraseology is clearly recognizable in later New Testament references to the session. Here at the fountain are the chief revealed elements of Christ's kingly reign, a beginning in which He is declared King and a reign which takes place at first 'in the midst of... enemies' but which will later triumph openly over all other sovereignties.

Initial Appropriation of Power.

The appropriation by Christ of His kingly power, won by death and resurrection, took place at His session at the right hand of the Father. This appropriation of power gives us the chief significance of the session. It marks the beginning of the reign of Christ. This is the meaning assigned, again by the Apostle Peter: 'Jesus Christ... has gone into heaven and is at the right hand of God with angels, authorities, and powers having been subjected to him' (1 Peter 3:21, 22).

This reign, as Psalm 110 says, is 'in the midst' of enemies and will progress until all of them are under His feet (Ps. 110:1). Although Jesus' reign is presently acknowledged on earth only by Christians, it will be enforced and become visible at His Second Coming. He will not only reign but rule as King of kings and Lord of lords (Rev. 5:6-14; 11:15; 19:11-21; Zec. 12-14).

This 'coming' (*parousia*) of Christ is described in part as securing justice for the poor, meek and needy: 'with righteousness he shall judge the poor' (Isa. 11:4a; and many similar passages). Yet in the passages cited in the New Testament in reference to the session, the context speaks of the exercise of coercive power. This is true both in the prophecy of Psalm 2 and in the vision of Patmos (compare Ps. 110:6 and Ps. 2:9 with Rev. 19:11 and Ps. 2 as a whole with Rev. 19:11-21). At that time will occur the resurrection of the righteous dead (Rev. 20:1-5), to be followed by Christ's millennial reign (Rev. 20:4-6), if our understanding of the sequence of events prophesied in Revelation 19 and 20 is correct. Then ensue the resurrection and judgment of 'the rest of the dead' and their final judgment (Rev. 20:7-15), including presumably also all wicked angels, demons and Satan. This will be succeeded (who knows how long?) by a merging of the reign of Christ with that of His Father, 'For he must reign until he has put all his enemies under his feet' (1 Cor. 15:23-25; Phil. 2:9-11). (The above remarks are not intended to persuade on moot points of biblical eschatology among believers but as enforcing the literal assumption of royal, governmental power.)

The church's present relation to the reign of Christ from the Father's right hand and share in it are mentioned at Ephesians 1:20-23; 4:15; 5:23; and Colossians 1:18-20. Many rightly observe that the Christian confession, 'Jesus Christ is Lord,' is an acknowledgment of this reign and that this doctrine brings about inevitable collision whenever 'Caesar' seeks to replace Christ as the object of ultimate allegiance. Much of the preceding paragraphs is adapted directly from a Bible dictionary article by the present author entitled 'The Work of Christ.'[1]

Christ's Present Reign As King.

One's understanding of the present reign of Christ has significant bearing on how one interprets the numerous passages of Scripture which speak of 'the kingdom of God,' or 'of heaven'; and terms like 'eternal life,' 'treasure in heaven' and related ideas; also on how to interpret the New Testament in relation to Christ's present and future reign at God's right hand.

Let us address this matter, taking as starting point the Lord Jesus Christ's words about the first preaching mission of the twelve Apostles: 'And proclaim as you go, saying, "The kingdom of heaven is at hand"' (Matt. 10:7).

Question: Was there a Postponed Kingdom of Power?

A commonly held theory holds that Jesus specifically meant, 'I am offering you the kingdom. Accept it and all the Old Testament promises about a coming reign of Messiah on earth will ensue immediately. Reject it and I will withdraw the offer and present it on another day. Meanwhile I will substitute a different program, the church, a unique new thing.'

It is difficult to deny that there was a legitimacy in the obvious expectation of a visible, physical reign of the promised 'Messiah of David' in the pious hearts of those who truly expected the Christ to come in their generation and who recognized Jesus of Nazareth to be that Person. Many saintly people were aware of the clear Old Testament prophecies of the reign of Him 'that is to come.' Among these prophecies were the very passages (Pss. 2 and 110) Peter used in announcing the enthronement of Christ. John also (Rev. 19:11) announced the Second Advent, this time as 'King of Kings and Lord of Lords' on earth. There are many similar Old Testament promises such as Psalm 72; Isaiah 2:1 ff.; Micah 4:1-5; Amos 9:11-15; and Jeremiah 31:31-34 are only sample texts which appear in Christmas liturgy and preaching and other 'high days' in the Christian year. Jeremiah frequently spoke of this future kingdom when a descendant of King David would 'execute justice and righteousness in the land' at a time when 'Judah will be saved, and Israel will dwell securely' (Jer. 23:5-8).

Let us acknowledge that the angel Gabriel rightly strengthened this expectation in Mary's heart when he affirmed to her 'amazement' 'the Lord God will give to him the throne of his father David' (Luke 1:32). The throne of David was not a throne in heaven as certain rather strident opponents of any doctrine of a future reign of Christ on earth seem to think, for David's throne is certainly not at God's right hand in heaven. That wise and gentle young lady reflected quite a literal understanding of Gabriel's announcement in her 'Magnificat' several weeks later (see Luke 1:46-55). She took the announcement literally, not to disregard features that speak of the spiritual quality of Messiah's kingdom as well. The same literal expectations are present in the 'Benedictus' of Zechariah (Luke 1:69-74), with the spiritual aspect present also. Jesus did not rebuke the mother of James and John for looking ahead to an earthly kingdom in which her two sons might have prominent positions, but for her selfish desires (Matt. 20:20-23).

In view of Jesus' plain prediction that His Apostles would in the future 'eat and drink at my table in my kingdom, and sit on thrones judging the twelve tribes of Israel' (Luke 22:30) it is not surprising that some of the disciples, in the last moments before the ascension, asked Jesus if He would 'at this time restore the kingdom to Israel' (Acts 1:6). Further it is not true, as it is often said, that the Lord rebuked that expectation. Rather Jesus informed the disciples

---

1. *Young's Bible Dictionary* (Wheaton: Tyndale House Publ., 1984), pp. 122–136.

(cf. Matt. 24:36-43 and parallels) that 'It is not for you to know times or seasons that the Father has fixed by his own authority' (Acts 1:7). This hope was neither morally nor factually defective only deficient of information which Jesus immediately supplied (Acts 1:7, 8).

The Old Testament predictions of Messiah's coming and of His kingdom do not present any clear delineation of or distinction between His two Advents. The Old Testament prophets therefore were puzzled by their own predictions of 'the sufferings of the Christ [at the First Advent] and the subsequent glories' (1 Peter 1:11). Even up till the events of Acts 10 and 11 Peter himself did not catch on to the distinct character of the present epoch of world evangelism to intervene before the coming of Christ in His 'kingly power' (Luke 23:42; Rev. 11:15), i.e. in His *manifest glory*.

But God knew and progressively revealed this in apostolic times to Apostles (John 16:12-16) and they have made clear to us in the New Testament Scriptures, which they wrote, what could not be clarified to Mary, Zechariah, the mother of Zebedee's children, and the disciples, not even Peter, without the passing of several years, much growth in spiritual perception and special revelation in the visions of Acts 10:1-16, to Cornelius and to Peter respectively.

No, their pious expectations of Christ's manifest kingdom and glory in a visible rule over the earth were not, as such, mistaken. The invisible reign of Christ from heaven now intervening was known to God and made known to them and us when the time was ripe. Nothing at all on God's predestined and foreknown schedule was postponed.

There is a better way of looking at the matter than the postponed kingdom idea on the one hand or, on the other, denial of any future reign of Christ on earth at all – a view that many think is fully compatible with the conviction that the church is unique and new, not simply a new Israel or a substitute heir of Israel's promises.

This can be seen by looking at 'kingdom' in the context of New Testament usage where 'kingdom' usually signifies kingly rule rather than territory. It means 'reign' in most of the contexts. 'The kingdom' is God's kingship working salvation, 'His government as a living and powerful Divine action, revealing itself in ever new forms of self-manifestation, in the course of many dispensations and periods' (George Ladd). Although the reign of God will ultimately take visible form on earth, it is not simply a future kingdom, millennial or otherwise.

By virtue of special calling and election and through a series of covenants Israel became a chosen people, an elect nation in special relation to Jehovah. In Scripture the Old Testament rule of God in Israel is sometimes termed the 'kingdom' of God. But that kingdom as a special sphere of God's saving action was taken away from the nation of Israel because of their unbelief (Matt. 21:43) and given to others. The new 'nation' producing the 'fruits' of the kingdom (Matt. 21:43) is no particular nation at all, but all of the nations, i.e. the Gentiles. During the present age, the church, the instrument of extension of God's reign in saving power, is called 'the kingdom of God.' The eternal heavenly kingdom that sinners will *not* inherit is also called 'the kingdom of God' (Gal. 5:21). In the parables of the kingdom (Mark 4; Luke 8; Matt. 13) the sphere of Christian profession, i.e. Christendom, is called the kingdom of heaven, as is commonly acknowledged.

Thus every member of the body of Christ belongs to the kingdom and every true citizen of the kingdom belongs to the church. Every true Christian believer is a citizen of that kingdom (Eph. 2:19; Phil. 3:20; Col. 1:13). Even those who are Christians only by profession are referred to by Christ as being in the kingdom (Matt. 7:21; 13:41; 22:11-14). Yet sometimes the New Testament acknowledges only the genuine believers as members of that spiritual kingdom (John 3:5). Both the *true* and the *professing* church can be referred to as the kingdom of God if it is kept in mind that this is not a permanent arrangement.

In the future, members of the true church will 'inherit' the kingdom of glory and power (Matt. 25:34; cf. 1 Cor. 6:10; Gal. 5:21; Eph. 5:5); they will enter into it (Acts 14:22). It is the goal of the present earthly pilgrimage to which they have been called (1 Thess. 2:12) and it is their reward (2 Thess. 1:5). If the future kingdom of God, when He is 'all in all' (1 Cor. 15:25-28), is thought of as the perfected kingdom of God, the church will be a sphere within that larger sphere. The idea of 'the kingdom' is so fluid in the New Testament that in one chapter, Matthew 19, the kingdom is roughly equated with 'eternal life' (v. 16), 'treasure in heaven' (v. 21), 'enter[ing] the kingdom of heaven' (v. 23), 'enter[ing] the kingdom of God' (v. 24), 'be[ing] saved' (v. 25) and 'inherit[ing] eternal life' (v. 29) – all with no sense of inconsistency with 'the regeneration,' a future visible reign of Christ from a throne (v. 28).

These ideas have a common core: Jesus' royal rights to every man's worship in a world He owns, won by His redemptive career. This is manifest in many related ideas and, of course, in the words whereby the Bible presents them. Any one who throws away some of these so as to make one idea or term regulative for all the rest does not understand the reign of Christ from His throne in heaven or the New Testament message about the kingdom of Him who is 'Lord and Christ.'

I have developed my thinking on this subject more fully in several other books: *Daniel and the Latter Days*, Chicago: Moody Press, 1977, pp. 112–114; 'The Work of Christ,' in *Young's Bible Dictionary*, Wheaton, IL: Tyndale, 1984, pp. 134, 135; *A Greater Commission*, Chicago: Moody Press, 1984, pp. 53-60.

This evidence forms a basis for affirming that the gospel of grace as found in Romans 1:16-17; 1 Corinthians 15:1-8; and throughout the New Testament is accurately described as the good news of the kingdom of God. It seems evident that Paul so understood it (see Acts 20:24-25; 28:31; see also pp. 58 and 59). There *is* a reign of God in the here-and-now, God's present kingdom of grace in the church, but there also *will be* a future manifest kingdom and hence Christians can be 'fellow workers for the kingdom of God' (Col. 4:11). (The preceding five paragraphs are adapted from the author's book *A Greater Commission*, pp.14 and 15.)

I treat the matter of the kingdom of God and the church much more at length in the later section of this book entitled, 'Ecclesiology or the Doctrine of the Church.'

The Present Reign of Christ and the Christian Gospel.

I have elsewhere expounded the thirteenth chapter of Matthew (with parallels in Luke 8 and Mark 4) as a 'seminar' on the subject of principles of the mission of world evangelism (*A Greater Commission*, pp. 40–113). In this discourse seeds are emblematic of the Christian gospel. Jesus once specified 'The seed is the word of God' (Luke 8:11) and that the work of the missionary is to sow the 'good seed' (Matt. 13:24, 27). Jesus also specified that the gospel seed is 'the word of the *kingdom*' (Matt. 13:19) thus showing how receiving Christ as Savior involves acknowledging His reign or Lordship (Rom. 10:9, 10).

Thirty-five years later Paul's understanding of the Word that was to be preached was no different – even though articulated more fully on the basis of completed redemption (and completed revelation, John 16:7-15). Near the end of his third journey in an address of great pathos to the elders of the church of Ephesus he declared: '…I have gone preaching *the kingdom of God* [emphasis added]' (Acts 20:25 KJV), 'to testify to the *gospel of the grace of God* [emphasis added] (v. 24). It consisted of 'testifying both to Jews and to Greeks [i.e. Gentiles] of *repentance* towards God and *faith* [emphasis added] in our Lord Jesus Christ' (v. 21). What Jesus spoke of in general terms, Paul spoke of in specifics (this paragraph adapted from Culver, *A Greater Commission*, pp. 62, 63).

Calvin, without any chiliastic expectation nevertheless had a marvellously inspiring way of distinguishing between the present and future aspects of His kingdom – the present kingdom of grace in the earth and His future reign over the universe. Specific comments will be found in his Commentaries on Psalm 2:8; 21:8; 25:57; 45:16; 72:8; 110:2; Matt. 12:31; 16:10; John 13:31. I cite a few lines from his comments on 'thy kingdom come' the second petition of 'the Lord's Prayer':

> Therefore God sets up his Kingdom by humbling the whole world, but in different ways. For he tames the wantonness of some, breaks the untameable pride of others. We must daily desire that God gather churches unto himself from all parts of the earth; that he spread and increase them in number; that he endow them with gifts; that he establish a lawful order among them; on the other hand, that he cast down all enemies of pure religion; that he scatter their counsels and crush their efforts. From this it appears that zeal for daily progress is not enjoined upon us in vain, for it never goes so well with human affairs that the filthiness of vices is shaken and washed away, and full integrity flowers and grows. But its fullness is delayed to the final coming of Christ when, as Paul teaches, 'God will be all in all' [1 Cor. 15:28].[2]

What inspiring encouragement to Christian nurture of every sort, personal and family witnessing, missionary evangelism, and pastoral preaching!

Christ the Head of the Present Kingdom of Grace.

Though the Lord Jesus Christ reigns from His throne in heaven, part of His realm is on earth in the here-and-now. That rule is the present 'kingdom of grace,' both in individual believers and collectively in the church – a church of which a familiar hymn explains: 'Yet she on earth hath union/ With God the three in one/ And mystic sweet communion/ With those whose rest is won.'

---

2. John Calvin, *Institutes of the Christian Religion III*, ed. McNeil, trans. and ed. Battles (Philadelphia, PA: Westminster Press ed. ii, 1960), 42, p. 905.

So the larger number of the Lord's kingdom of grace are in His presence in heaven. As to the members of this kingdom still living on earth, our relation to Christ the King is conditioned by the fact we are vitally united with Him and already 'in Him,' even 'raised with Christ.' In this relation:

1. He is 'the head of the body,' the church and 'pre-eminent' (Col. 1:18). Therefore 'we are to grow up in every way into him who is the head, into Christ' (Eph. 4:15). There is a practical domestic implication: 'Wives, submit to your own husbands, as to the Lord. For the husband is the head of the wife even as Christ is the head of the church, his body, and is himself its Savior' (Eph. 5:22, 23).

2. As Head of the church, His body, He is our constant 'Savior' (Eph. 5:23) and we are therefore 'safe,' 'and no one will snatch them out of my hand' (John 10:28). In that security none shall 'condemn' us (Rom. 8:33, 34), none 'shall separate us from the love of Christ' (Rom. 8:35, 39), nor shall any overcome us, because 'we are more than conquerors through him who loved us' (Rom. 8:37).

3. As the Head of the body Christ is our 'Master and Lord' (John 13:12-14 KJV). This also has practical implications within that portion of the church that is still on earth, for example, for the wealthy class: 'Masters, treat your slaves justly and fairly, knowing that you also have a Master in heaven' (Col. 4:1; cf. Eph. 6:8, 9).

4. Finally, this truth should direct all Christian thought, life, affection and interest heavenward, as it is written, 'If then you have been raised with Christ, seek the things that are above, where Christ is, seated at the right hand of God. Set your minds [affections] on things that are above, not on things that are on earth. For you have died, and your life is hidden with Christ in God' (Col. 3:1-4).

Some Clarifications and Cautions.

Immense areas of theology are opened up in connection with the inauguration of the reign of power and grace at the enthronement, or session of Christ. Some brief statements, therefore, must be made about some of them and some cautions issued.

1. The inauguration of Christ as King at His session has reference only to the installation of the *theanthrōpos,* God-man, as Ruler of His mediatorial kingdom. As Second Person of the triune God He has been from all eternity, and remains, Almighty King of creation. Of Him the Psalms say, 'The LORD reigns, he is robed in majesty... Your throne is established from of old; you are from everlasting... O judge of the earth' (Ps. 93:1, 2; 94:2). His inauguration is anticipated in Jesus' post-resurrection proclamation: 'All authority in heaven and on earth has been given to me' (Matt. 28:18).

2. There is a difference of opinion with respect to the idea of a future reign of Christ on earth. Revelation seems plainly to state that we 'saints' 'shall reign on the earth' (Rev. 5:10). Revelation 20 would lead us to expect this in a future millennium after a resurrection of the righteous dead (premillennialism). But many evangelical theologians hold that the reign of Christ with His saints is during the present age and takes place in heaven (amillennialism). The same theology says there is to be no future national restoration of Israel. Yet Jesus promised the disciples, 'Truly, I say to you, in the new world, when the Son of Man will sit on his glorious throne, you who have followed me will also sit on twelve thrones, judging the twelve tribes of Israel' (Matt. 19:28). I have not thought it proper to enter a full-scale discussion of the matter here. I do this in connection with ecclesiology (the church) and eschatology (last things). *My Daniel and the Latter Days*[3] treats the subject from a standpoint similar to what has come to be called 'historic premillennialism,' i.e. without the presuppositions of dispensationalism. Many treatises are available. A fair introduction to the major views is presented by Louis Berkhof.[4] He himself defends amillennialism which he deems to be 'the most widely accepted' and 'the prevalent view in Reformed circles'[5] but fairly presents what he calls 'Premillennialism of the Past,' 'Premillennialism... of the Present' (dispensationalism) and 'Postmillennialism.'

I do not regard his refutation of premillennialism as adequate. Nevertheless it seems best to reserve my further discussion to later *loci* of theology.

---

3. Robert D. Culver, *Daniel and the Latter Days* (Chicago: Moody Press, 1954, rev. 1977, and rev. by author and republished as *The Earthly Reign of Our Lord With His People,* 1998).
4. Louis Berkhof, *Systematic Theology* 2nd rev. ed. (Grand Rapids, MI: Eerdmans, 1941), pp. 406–411; 708–719.
5. ibid., p. 708.

24
The Present Heavenly High Priestly Work of Christ our Lord

Except for groups with direct roots in the Reformation of the sixteenth century and who still observe the Christian year, most Protestants hear little about our Lord's ascension and enthronement in heaven at God the Father's right hand after the 'forty days' (Acts 1:3). Similarly, pulpit and theology have not often up to the present said much about the present work of Christ in heaven.

Perhaps this is because we know very little of the unseen world of 'the city of the living God, the heavenly Jerusalem' where Jesus serves still as 'the mediator of a new covenant' as Hebrews 12:22-24 describes it. Perhaps modern preoccupations with material realities – assumed and genuine – have made heaven too far away to be interesting.

Yet we know our Lord in heaven does not spend His time (Is there time in heaven?) merely receiving praise from the 'innumerable company of angels' and 'the general assembly and church of the firstborn' (Heb. 12:22, 23 KJV) who dwell there, to the neglect of His permanent work as Mediator.

The truths of Christian faith form a consistent system, which means Christ's work has integral connections with every locus of doctrine. His work goes on in the church as well as for her: being present in all church life and assemblies, the vital source of all true church life, the Head who rules in all her normal activity. '[A]part from me you can do nothing' is no less true now than when Jesus spoke the words. However, to avoid unnecessary lengthening of this book and to avoid unnecessary repetition we reserve such topics for ecclesiology, later on in the order of systematic theology.

The theme of the present heavenly high priestly work of our Lord Jesus Christ is unique to the book of Hebrews. That ministry, as such, is mentioned nowhere else in the Bible. Paul, quite remarkably, never once calls Christ a priest, nor does Peter, who even speaks of ordinary Christians as 'a royal priesthood.' The book of Revelation, though it refers to 'us' as 'priests unto… God' and presents Jesus as the '[sacrificial] Lamb of God,' never once refers to Him as a priest. Hence, however valid and useful to theology dissection of Christ's mediatorial work into prophet, priest and king, that is not precisely how the New Testament authors present it. Only the book of Hebrews (chaps. 2–10, where it is the major theme) describes the present activity of Christ as that of our heavenly High Priest.

Since only the author of Hebrews speaks specifically of our Lord's present ministry in heaven as our Great High Priest it seems only sensible to view the subject as he viewed it. This present treatment will therefore be a consideration of a biblical theology of nine chapters of Hebrews.

High Priest More Than a Metaphor.

The New Testament appropriately employs much metaphorical language in conveying the Person and work of Christ. He is 'light' and 'the living bread' – but only in figure. When, however, His attackers heard Him refer to Himself as 'a *man* [*anthrōpos*] [emphasis added] who has told you the truth' (John 8:40) they had to take Him literally, as do we. He was 'every inch a man.' He also said, 'I am the vine,' and Paul that He is 'head' of every human being (1 Cor. 11:3), 'head' of the church (Eph. 5:23), etc., but each of these is a figurative expression. When the author of Hebrews speaks of Christ as priest or High Priest throughout the first ten of thirteen chapters of his book, we may concede he is making some concession to human custom and understanding; yet the sense is close to literal. He is more literally a priest than light, a vine or living water.

As he proceeds, the author of Hebrews himself explains his ideas of what a true priest of God is as he portrays Christ's present work in that capacity.

The present task must be to learn how the author of Hebrews, himself, regards Christ as High Priest and how he portrays His work in that capacity. Useful as the rubric, 'prophet, priest and king' is to theology, it does not provide either a key to understanding Hebrews or a template for explaining the present work of Christ in heaven as uniquely formulated in the Epistles to the Hebrews.

The Unique Religious Culture of the Epistle.

The religious and cultural atmosphere of the Epistle to the Hebrews is different from any other book of the New Testament. We are here in the world of Old Testament biblical religion – not of post-biblical Judaism and its rabbinical regulations. Scholars point out that the standpoint is even previous to the temple of Solomon, because the assumed situation of the ritual actions is the encampment of the twelve tribes in the wilderness around the Tabernacle. The rituals are performed by the sons of Aaron under a lawfully constituted high priest, not the politically appointed Sadducees of New Testament times and on to the destruction of the second temple.

Hence, no sacrificial or hierarchical (priest rule) precedents from the heathen priesthoods of the Roman world enter the thought-world of Hebrews. The first readers probably were Hebrews who from birth had been nurtured to regard the pagan priests, their rituals, sacrifices and temples with revulsion – 'abominations of the Gentiles.' Perhaps Paul, whose readers included a majority, perhaps, of converted Gentiles, did not feel his Gentile readers would be able to understand Jesus' present work as a priestly ministry without telling them more about the Old Testament background than his rather brief letters allowed him to say. So perhaps he never referred to Jesus as priest or High Priest for that reason.

The Old Testament Hierarchical Background.

The use which the author of Hebrews makes of the Levitical institutions (the Tabernacle and its furniture, priests, rituals, etc.) goes far beyond mere parallels of the sort modern anthropologists think they find between religious forms in different religions. F. Delitzsch well said:

> But surely the Old Testament high-priesthood, and its sacrifices, were for the sacred writer something far more than mere *illustrations*; on the contrary, they were types [symbolic prediction] of a future reality, and preliminary forms of its manifestation, being as closely connected with that reality as the shadow with the body by which it is cast.[1]

1. The Tabernacle Complex.

Seen from above, the Tabernacle complex would have been seen as a rectangular tent within a rectangular curtained court on an east-west axis. The dimensions of the court were 100 cubits (c. 150 ft) long and 50 cubits (c. 75 ft) wide. The Tabernacle, which was set in the west half of the court, was 10 cubits (15 ft) by 30 cubits (45 ft). Entrance to the court was through a curtained opening at the east and could be entered by lay worshippers and priests. Immediately ahead lay a large, bronze-covered, square altar where almost all sacrifices, slain or otherwise, were offered. After passing the altar, and to the north (right hand), was a large bronze tank, basin-shaped. Here there were facilities for

---

1. Franz Delitzsch, *Epistle to the Hebrews i* (Edinburgh: T. and T. Clark, 1887), p. 141, n.1.

the priests to wash themselves and for the required washings of certain sacrifices. Then immediately ahead at about the mid-point of the court was the curtained opening to the sanctuary, or Tabernacle. The tent had a large front room 15 ft by 30 ft and a second room 15 ft by 15 ft, the two separated by a heavy veil which kept the innermost room in darkness.

Upon entering the tent, to the left stood a seven-branched lamp-stand whose oil lamps were tended by priests and kept burning perpetually. To the right the light shone on a small rectangular table on which were constantly displayed twelve loaves of unleavened bread changed once each week. Immediately ahead was a small altar whereon incense was burned at stated intervals.

Beyond the heavy veil, which shut off the innermost 'holy of holies,' no one ever entered except the high priest and he only on one day a year, the autumnal 'day of atonement' (Heb. *Yom Kippur*). The room was empty except for a wooden, gold-covered chest (Ark) in dimension about 27 inches tall (the height of our desks and tables) about 45 inches long and 27 inches wide. Thereon lay a lid of the same materials, called a mercy-seat (Heb. *kapporeth*, place of propitiation), surmounted with gold cherubs, one at each end with wings extended so as to meet over the mid-point of the mercy-seat. Within the Ark were the two tables of the Ten Commandments, the pot of manna and Aaron's rod which budded.

The high priest typified the Lord Jesus Christ as our Great High Priest and His ministry on the annual Day of Atonement. This is featured in Hebrews. He wore special holy garments and bore many emblems representative of various aspects of the many rituals. These matters occupy lengthy portions of Exodus and Leviticus plus portions of Numbers and Deuteronomy. We shall introduce the few pertinent details only as the author of Hebrews does so in presenting the priesthood of Christ. Since the author of Hebrews concentrates on the priestly aspect of the Lord's work, he says much about Christ's death and exaltation to heaven but little about His resurrection. The Old Testament priestly ritual of the annual sin-offering on the Day of Atonement focused first upon the slaying of the victim in the court of the temple and subsequent presentation of the blood in the innermost room of the sanctuary. As F. F. Bruce says:

> In the antitype of these two moments [slaying the victim and presentations of the blood] were seen to correspond to the death of Christ on the cross and His appearance at the right hand of God. In this pattern the resurrection, as generally proclaimed in the apostolic preaching, finds no separate place.[2]

2. The Priesthood of Aaron As Typical of Christ's Priesthood.

The author of Hebrews also assumes acquaintance by his readers with the sacred literature about priests who served at the Tabernacle – who they were, their qualifications and what they did. Also, and very important to the Christology of the book, though Christ is priest of the order of Melchizedek, not of Aaron, Hebrews does not hesitate to draw typical parallels from Aaron's priesthood to Christ's priesthood. Melchizedek was typical of Christ in one way, Aaron in another way.

The Special Call to Priesthood.

'For every high priest chosen from among men,' says our author, 'no one takes this honor for himself, but only when called by God, just as Aaron was' (Heb. 5:1a, 4). He is referring to God's directive to Moses: 'Then bring near to you Aaron your brother, and his sons with him, from among the people of Israel, to serve me as priests – Aaron and Aaron's sons...' (Exod. 28:1; cf. 1 Chr. 23:13). Moses also was a priest, called to be such by God. Of Moses' priestly work it is said he served in God's 'house as a servant, to testify to the things that were to be spoken later' (Heb. 3:5). His service, like Aaron's, was only 'a shadow of the good things to come' (Heb. 10:1).

So also Christ 'did not exalt Himself to be made a high priest' (Heb. 5:5), i.e. did not appoint Himself in a pretentious manner, but to the contrary, the LORD God appointed Him. The author of Hebrews demonstrates this by recourse to two acknowledged Messianic prophecies: 'You are my Son; today I have begotten you' (Ps. 2:7) and 'You are a priest for ever after the order of Melchizedek' (Ps. 110:4).

Thus Moses' special call and priestly service, as well as Aaron's, pointed ahead to Christ's special call, God's special 'Apostle,' or minister plenipotentiary and 'High Priest of the religion we profess' (Heb. 3:1 NEB).

---

2. F. F. Bruce, *The Epistle to the Hebrews* (Grand Rapids, MI: Eerdmans, 1964), p. 1, vi.

The Special Ordination and Purification Ceremonies for Aaron and Sons.

Most of four long chapters (Exod. 29, 40; Lev. 8, 9) describe in great detail how Moses was to install (ordain KJV) Aaron and his sons in the priestly office. The entire congregation in the wilderness were to be gathered 'at the entrance of the tent of meeting' with the five men (Aaron and his four sons, Nadab and Abihu, Ithamar and Eliezer) to be installed. Moses himself washed their entire bodies to symbolize their moral cleansing. Then came investment with official garments, followed by anointing with specially prepared oil.

After that Moses performed an elaborate ritual slaughter of an unblemished young bullock. The five ordinands first laid their hands on the animal's head. Whereupon Moses slaughtered it as a sin-offering, sprinkled the horns of the Great Altar with the blood and executed the rest of the complicated ritual (Exod. 29; Lev. 9).

Then the basic ritual was repeated with a ram, except that this time Moses placed some of the blood on the tips of the five right ears of the five men, the thumbs of their five right hands and the great toes of their five right feet (Lev. 8:22-24).

There was much more, which need not concern us here. Leviticus 8:30 ff. seems to indicate the men spent a whole week at the Tabernacle, the bloody rituals being repeated each day. And apparently the Tabernacle and furnishings were similarly consecrated at the same time.[3]

Next, according to Leviticus, Aaron made sin-offerings, peace offerings and burnt offerings for himself as priest and 'for the people' (Lev. 9: 7). Only after that did Moses accompany Aaron into the Tabernacle 'and when they came out they blessed the people.' Only then a 'fire came out from before the LORD and consumed' the pieces of flesh and fat on the altar (Lev. 9:23, 24). The rituals were now in operation.

Points of Contrast Made by the Author of Hebrews.

1) In the first place, no such purification ceremonies were appropriate for Christ's installation. His installation was wholly by Jehovah's decree. He was already the 'Lord' (Ps. 110:1). True, He 'offered himself' to God, but not for purification of self, for He was already 'without blemish' (prefigured by the absence of physical blemish in the animals) (Heb. 9:14).

Further, Such a high priest meets our need – one who is holy, blameless, pure, set apart from sinners (Heb. 7:26 NIV) – because He was 'made in the likeness of sinful flesh and for sin' and 'numbered himself with the transgressors.' Our author sums up, 'The high priests made by the Law are men in all their frailty, but the priest appointed by the oath [of the LORD, Ps. 110:4] which supersedes the Law is the Son, was made perfect [in the school of suffering where He learned obedience, Heb. 5:8] now for ever' (Heb. 7:28 NEB).

2) In the second place, Aaron's sons inherited their office by physical descent. Christ came to His High Priestly office by virtue of the LORD's solemn oath (Ps. 110:4). Our author says this made Christ's priesthood perpetual. The somewhat periphrastic rendering of the NEB makes the matter clear: 'There was no oath sworn when those others were made priests; but for this priest an oath was sworn' (Heb. 7:21 NEB).

3) In the third place, Christ's priesthood is perpetual, as Scripture says of Him:

> The Lord has sworn and will not change his mind, "You are a priest for ever" [Ps. 110:4]. How far superior must the covenant also be of which Jesus is the guarantor! Those other priests are appointed in numerous succession [one generation after another], because they are prevented by death from continuing in office; but the priesthood which Jesus holds is perpetual, because he remains for ever... he is always living... (Heb. 7:21-25 NEB).

So in contrast to Aaron's priesthood Christ's was by divine oath and it was eternal whereas Aaron's was by physical descent and interrupted at each generational change.

Our Great High Priest's Preparation in the Outer Court for Service in Heaven.

On the Great Day of Atonement Aaron carried out the ritual ceremonies (described in Levi. 16) which the author of Hebrews employs to explain the High Priestly ministry of Christ. The author is selective. Not everything in Aaron and his priestly work is typical. Some does not apply at all. And some seems to be implicitly included even though unmentioned in Hebrews.

---

3. Philo, 'Life of Moses,' ii. 136 ff. (*The Works of Philo*, pp. 502, 503). See bibliography.

Upon entering the outer court with the proper materials for sacrifice he moved to the altar and killed a 'bull for a sin offering for himself.' Then representing himself and the people he entered the holy place and on into the holy of holies to perform the service of God before the Ark.

So our Lord first is seen in Hebrews preparing to do His High Priestly work in heaven: 'He is the radiance of the glory of God and the exact imprint of his nature, and he upholds the universe by the word of his power. After making purification for sins, he sat down at the right hand of the Majesty on high' (Heb. 1:3). The priestly work was to be done in heaven, but before He ascended there as eternal Son who shared with us our 'flesh and blood' (Heb. 2:14) He offered sacrifice, not *for* Himself as Aaron did, 'But… he has appeared once and for all at the climax of history to abolish sin by sacrifice of himself' (Heb. 9:26 NEB).

Four aspects of Christ's Person and career appear with emphasis and in close connection in the early part of Hebrews: the *incarnation*, the *sacrifice*, the *ascension* and the *session*. 1) *The Incarnation*. In all the New Testament it has its most detailed presentation (nature and purposes of it) in Hebrews 2:5-18. This is to show that 'he had to be ['it behoved Him to be' KJV] made like his brothers in every respect, so that he might become a merciful and faithful high priest in the service of God… For because he himself has suffered when tempted, he is able to help those who are being tempted' (Heb. 2:17, 18). 2) *Sacrifice*. 'After making purification for sins… suffering of death… taste death for everyone… to make propitiation for the sins of the people' (1:3; 2:9a; 2:9b; 2:17). 3) *Ascension* and 4) *Session*. '[S]at down at the right hand of the Majesty on high… Sit at my right hand' (1:3, 13). Thus Hebrews starts off showing how our Lord by virtue of who He is and what He did at the cross prepared Himself for His High Priestly work in heaven.

An Interruption: the author interrupts his theme by a lengthy direct address to his 'holy brothers,' first readers of the Epistle (3:1–4:13), charging them to *consider* the superiority of Jesus, the Apostle and High Priest of their confession, to heed His voice, to encourage one another and to rest in His promise. Then he resumes the theme of our Lord's present priestly work at Hebrews 4:14.

Moving On from Altar Sacrifice to Sanctuary Service.

The Old Testament Type.

> After completing the sacrifice of the altar, Aaron shall take a firepan full of coals from upon the altar before the LORD, and two handfuls of finely ground sweet incense, and bring inside the veil [of the first chamber]. And he shall put the incense on the fire before the LORD, that the cloud of incense [in the inner chamber] may cover the mercy seat that is on the ark of the testimony, lest he die. Moreover he shall take some of the blood of the bull [of the sin-offering for himself] and sprinkle it with his finger on the mercy seat on the east side; also in front of the mercy seat and in front… seven times (Lev. 16:12-14 NEB).

Then Aaron was instructed to slaughter 'the goat of the sin offering which is for the people, and bring its blood inside the veil, and do with its blood as he did with the blood of the bull, and sprinkle it on the mercy seat and in front of the mercy seat' (Lev. 16:15 NEB). So after the high priest had slaughtered one animal to propitiate for his own sins he took the blood into the holy of holies where he sprinkled it *at* and *on the* propitiatory (mercy-seat) and again a second similar performance with the goat slaughtered for the sins of the people.

The New Testament Antitype.

Following the typology of these opening ritual actions of *Yom Kippur* our author says, 'Having then a great high priest, who hath passed through the heavens' (Heb. 4:14 ASV), 'through court after court of the spiritual precincts, the Tabernacle not made with hands, until He reached the presence-chamber of God. There, in the inmost sanctuary, He now ministers.'[4] 'For Christ has entered, not into holy places made with hands, which are copies of the true things, but into heaven itself, now to appear in the presence of God on our behalf' (Heb. 9:24). It would be a mistake to suppose the author proposes a literal structure of successive areas and rooms in heaven overarching earth where they found earthly shape in Israel's Tabernacle and temple. Nor does he ever say Jesus literally bore the blood of Calvary above to a heavenly altar. Our author claims no special knowledge of heavenly geography or architecture. He is employing 'earthly things,' as Jesus did (John 3:12), to help us understand 'heavenly things,' related to Christ's present priestly ministry. We call this analogy.

---

4. Henry B. Swete, *The Ascended Christ: A Study in the Earliest Christian Teaching* (London: Macmillan & Co., 1916), p. 37.

The NEB is somewhat a paraphrase, but very plain:

> Nor is he there to offer himself again and again, as the high priest enters the sanctuary year by year with blood not his own. If that were so, he would have had to suffer many times since the world was made. But as it is, he has appeared once and for all at the climax of history to abolish sin by the sacrifice of himself (Heb. 9:25, 26, see 23-28).

The author of Hebrews lets us know our Lord now also occupies a throne at God's right hand even though ministering in heaven's temple's inmost precincts, as we shall see. He finds no problem in harmonizing the two spatial figures nor should we. What should interest us is in that place, remote from us just now, the throne is a throne of grace and the ministry in the sanctuary are both 'on our behalf.' Hebrews at this point is not prescribing elaborate new duties for believers to perform, rather informing us of how Jesus our 'great high priest' is presently working in heaven for our benefit.

Aspects of the Great High Priest's Work.

What Does a High Priest Do?

Theologians properly turn to Scripture to find several normal priestly functions – more than the author of Hebrews makes use of in his exposition: to offer sacrifice, to make intercession, to bless people.[5] H. B. Hacket points out 'the duties described in Exodus and Leviticus are the same as those recognized in… Chronicles… [and those] the prophet Ezekiel sees in the Temple of the future.' These duties were to care for the Tabernacle vessels, to assist the high priest, watch over the perpetual fire on the great altar, to feed the lamp of the outer chamber, offer the stated daily sacrifice. 'These were the fixed, invariable duties.' Higher ethical duties were to teach the people and to bless them at every solemn meeting.[6]

The author of Hebrews, however, has his own list of the priestly duties of Old Testament priests, not necessarily all the duties discoverable to theologians. He finds each one perfectly fulfilled in Christ. He also finds in each a reason for the necessity of the priesthood of Christ and of the supplanting of the priesthood after the order of Aaron by the priesthood of One 'after the order of Melchizedek.'

He Has Made the Required Propitiation.

As High Priest he has already made propitiation for the sins of the people. 'Wherefore it behooved him in all things to be made like unto his brethren, that he might become a merciful and faithful high priest in things pertaining to God, to make propitiation for the sins of the people' (Heb. 2:17 ASV).

This is the first direct mention in the entire Bible of Christ as a priest or High Priest. It appears early in Hebrews immediately after the most extensive specific biblical discussion of the incarnation and its purposes. The last-mentioned purpose is to that He 'helps the offspring of Abraham.' Here Abraham stands representatively for all believers (Gal. 3:7). Yet the author is still thinking in Hebrew terms.

The rest of Hebrews on through chapter 10 explains how, as High Priest, the incarnate Son gives that help. God had determined to solve the problem of sin in the world and did so following a pattern He had set in the Old Testament Tabernacle and the 'things pertaining to God' dealt with there. Everything about the sanctuary had to do with removal of the sin of people, which is the obstacle to 'the chief end of man… to glorify God and enjoy Him forever.'

The author is thinking of the 'things pertaining to God' (Heb. 2:17; 5:1 KJV) in the rituals of Tabernacle and altar. The readers were not only acquainted with the Exodus and Leviticus manual of procedures but some perhaps had participated in the rituals before conversion to Christ. In the wilderness setting, where everyone was in walking distance from the altar, many adults must have been in or near the court of the altar many times each month. The prescribed sacrifices and purification rituals required it. Three times a year every male adult was required by statute to appear 'before the Lord' (Exod. 23:14, 17) at the central sanctuary no matter where in 'the Land' his residence was. Even sexual copulation, birth of babies, sickness, under certain circumstances, required an offering for sin at the altar. The word *kapper* (atonement, expiation, propitiation, cover, in our Versions and regular forms of *hilaskomai*, propitiate, expiate in the Greek O.T.) appears over and over again. The ritual rules were 'a yoke… that neither' the Hebrews who read this letter nor 'our fathers… have been able to bear' (Acts 15:10).

---

5. W. G. Moorehead, 'Priest', in *International Standard Bible Encyclopedia iv*, ed. Orr (Grand Rapids, MI: Eerdmans, 1939, 1943), pp. 2439, 2440.
6. H. B. Hackett, 'Priests,' *Smith's Dictionary of the Bible iii* (New York: Hurd & Houghton), pp. 2581, 2582.

The most noted official, head and responsible director of all this ritual slaughter 'to put away sins,' was the head of the clan of the sons of Aaron called 'the high priest' (Lev. 21:10; Num. 35:25; many times in Hebrews). Thus by a bold stroke this author begins his exposition of Christ as the fulfillment of the typology of the Old Testament rituals of propitiatory bloody sacrifices.

The central ideas of propitiation, expiation and reconciliation have been dealt with in our chapter, 'The Vocabulary of Atonement' and it shall not be repeated here. Let us restrict our thoughts simply to how the book of Hebrews expands the matter.

The author interrupts his thought to exhort his readers ('holy brothers' 3:1) directly (chaps. 3 and 4) and then hastens on to point out that the religious services of the priest included 'both gifts and sacrifices' (voluntary or votive offerings and required ones). He notes that this was a never-ending process. The sacrifices went on from year to year, generation to generation (10:1). As one generation of priests died off another took its place. But the ceremonies were only 'a copy and shadow' of heavenly realities (8:5). The Tabernacle was 'a figure for the time then present' (9:9 KJV). These 'fleshly' ordinances had been imposed 'until the time of reformation' (Heb. 9:10), that is to say, the new Christian era.

'[I]t is impossible for the blood of bulls and goats to take away sins' (10:4). 'But when Christ appeared as a high priest... by means of his own blood... securing an eternal redemption' (9:11, 12). His sacrifice accomplished *genuine* propitiation and expiation, *actual* removal of the guilt of sin and its defilement which the rituals of the altar only typified and by their repetition testified to their own inadequacy except as they fulfilled the divine command and pointed ahead to a better arrangement.

'The blood of Christ' sets the heart of the believer free from self-accusation. The forgiven sinner is now free from guilt in any formal sense. Therefore, not only is the record clean but the 'conscience' is cleansed, freed from frantic effort to please God with 'dead works' but rather to serve the living God in grateful freedom.

How does Hebrews relate Christ's sacrifice to the present service of our Great High Priest? 'What have you done for us lately' is the question. Our author finds answers in the typology of Aaron's acts on the annual *Yom Kippur*.

He Has Introduced a New Covenant or Law or Covenant System.

As High Priest 'after the order of Melchizedek' 'The Lord' has replaced the obsolete 'law' or covenant which was founded on the Levitical priesthood. This accomplishment merits first mention because it encompasses all the other priestly duties now being carried out by Christ as High Priest. It is basic to all He now does from His 'place' in heaven. Our author states this as follows:

> Now if perfection had been attainable through the Levitical priesthood (for it is on this basis that the people were given the Law), what further need would there have been to speak of another priest arising, in the succession of Melchizedek, instead of the succession of Aaron. For a change of priesthood must mean a change of law (Heb. 7:11, 12 NEB).

Thorny problems of Greek syntax underlie this clear, somewhat periphrastic rendering, but it essentially agrees with how Delitzsch, Meyer, Bruce and most commentators construe the sense. The Levitical priesthood was the basis that supplied operational structure for the entire covenant system of Mosaic law. The mediatorial work of priests was necessary to make every ritual, every feast and festival, every sacrifice – the very structure of Israelite society – work. Yet, David in Psalm 110:1-6, several hundred years after the Levitical system began, announced that the even earlier priesthood of Melchizedek, who lived in Abraham's time (Gen. 14:17-20), would supersede the temporary regime of the Levitical priesthood. 'If God had intended the Aaronic priesthood to introduce the age of perfection, the time when man would enjoy unfettered access to Him, why should He have conferred on the Messiah priestly dignity of His own – different from Aaron's and by implication superior to Aaron's?'[7]

Our author points out several types and parallels between the Levitical system and the new one, but at this point he is spelling out contrasts. This begins with the choice of a Greek word rendered 'another', another priest (7:11). The word is *heteros*, another of a different kind, not *allos*, another of the same kind. More differences are pointed out in verses to follow.

The most comprehensive ('necessity' ASV) change connected with a new order of priesthood is this, namely 'a change in the law' we are discussing (7:12). In this case 'law' refers to a basic structure of religious observances, not a new moral order. The Levitical priesthood was as necessary to make the Mosaic religious system work as

---

7. Bruce, *Hebrews*, pp. 143, 144.

the central sanctuary. When, as happened visibly in AD 70, the temple disappeared, so did the visibly constituted priesthood. God had replaced them both forty-plus years earlier when our Lord ascended to heaven and took up His mediatorial ministry in the 'tabernacle, which the Lord pitched, and not man' (Heb. 8:2 KJV). If the priesthood of Aaron was designed for a temporary purpose, to be terminated when the new dispensation arrived, so also the law that the priesthood executed. F. F. Bruce comments, 'So by his own independent line of argument our author reaches the same conclusion as Paul: the law was a temporary provision, "our tutor to bring us unto Christ"' (Gal. 3:24).'[8]

Paul argued that the law of Moses served to make sinners aware of their sins but was powerless to produce justification before God. Hence, the very failure pointed to Christ. Hebrews argues in a different way that the Levitical sacrificial system, in its failure really to remove guilt for sin, pointed to Christ whose sacrifice does. Each was thinking of the whole law, though Paul's argument rested on the *moral* element in the law and Hebrews on the *ceremonial* element.

The new 'law' of Christ (Heb. 7:11, 12) has more effective moral power because its priesthood rests not on 'a system of earth-bound rules' (7:16 NEB) but upon the power of the new Priest's 'indestructible life' (7:16). Paul says much the same thing (Rom. 5:9, 10).

He Prays for His People.

As Mediator of a new 'Law,' or new 'covenant' (as the author of Hebrews more frequently calls it) *it is our Lord's priestly service to pray for his people*: 'he is able to save to the uttermost those who draw near to God through him, since he always lives to make intercession for them' (Heb. 7:25). The Lord's intercessory work for His people is not a major New Testament theme, for it is mentioned specifically only twice; yet it is important as the following shows.

Melchizedek 'priest of God Most High' in whose order of priesthood the risen Christ serves, prayed blessings on Abraham and brought forth 'bread and wine' (Gen. 14:18-20). In the prophecy of Psalm 2, the LORD directs the Son: 'Ask of me, and I will make the nations your heritage' (Ps. 2:8). The final sentence of the 'Golden Passional' of Isaiah 53 joins our Lord's atonement with His intercession: He 'was numbered with the transgressors; yet he bore the sin of many, and makes intercession for the transgressors.' For the wicked people who crucified Jesus He prayed, 'Father, forgive them, for they know not what they do' (Luke 23:34) and in the Upper Room He prayed for all the disciples and those to be won through their word (John 17:15-21).

It is beyond the scope of this treatment to treat the Old Testament types fully as does John Gill,[9] yet one outstanding type cries for attention.

> [T]he high-priest going into the most holy place, with the names of the children of Israel on his breastplate, and bearing their judgment before the Lord, and taking away the sin of the holy things, typified Christ as the representative, in heaven, of his people; appearing in the presence of God for them, presenting his sacrifice for the taking away of their sins, even of their most solemn services.[10]

We are reminded that although our Lord's priesthood is of Melchizedek, not Aaron, yet the ritual of the Levitical sanctuary 'throws light,' by typology, 'upon the Lord's priestly ministry in heaven.'[11] No passage of the Bible specifically says it was a duty of priests to make intercessory prayer for the people of Israel. As the numerous examples show, it was probably too obvious to require special command. Well known examples of priests who were also intercessors are Moses (Exod. 32, 33), Aaron (Num. 16:41-50), Samuel (1 Sam. 7:5; 12:19, 23), Ezra (Ezra 9:1-10), and Jeremiah, a priest, who constantly throughout his book is praying to God for the wayward nation.

Though it does not call Christ a priest, Romans, like Hebrews, says Christ is presently 'at the right hand of God' where He is 'interceding for us' (Rom. 8:34) placing that word, intercession, quite strategically between our justification (8:33) and our perseverance (8:35 ff.), for both are assured by His unending intercession.

We earthbound sinners wonder if our Lord prays 'out loud,' sometimes prostrate (Matt. 26:39) 'with loud cries and tears' (Heb. 5:7) as during His life on earth. In answer: it would be 'inconsistent with his state of exaltation.'[12] He does not pray to deflect God's wrath, for God is already propitiated. Nor is our High Priest engaged in any court-of-law-like

---

8. ibid., p. 145.
9. John Gill, *Complete Body of Doctrinal and Practical Divinity i* (Grand Rapids, MI: Baker Books, 1978 repr. of 1839 edition), pp. 612–614.
10. ibid., p. 614.
11. Swete, *Ascended Christ*, p. 40.
12. Gill, *Complete Body*, p. 615.

procedures, though He is represented in Scripture as Advocate, One who pleads our case as Counsellor at law. These questions arise from our human, earthbound orientation. It is enough to know that he *appears in the presence of God* for us (Heb. 9:24), that His 'blood and righteousness' have already procured our justification and sanctification, that His wounds are ever in heaven as evidence that redemption's price has been has been paid already (Rev. 5:6). His prayers were typified by the sweet smoke of the incense accompanying every presentation of the blood in Aaron's time. The prayers of God's people (Rev. 8:3, 4; Heb. 13:15; 1 Peter 2:5) are said to be the 'sweet incense' of the Christian epoch and are welcomed by the Father. Our prayers are offered with His, for His Spirit interprets them (Rom. 8:26).

There are additional benefits for believers from our ascended Lord in heaven, which apparently could have no specific typical counterpart in Aaron's priesthood. This is not surprising since the Old Testament priests were only human mediators of God's mercy on earth. Our Mediator is the *theanthrōpos* in heaven.

As Priest He Hears our Prayers.

The presence in heaven of a High Priest who was tempted and tried in every way His people are, illuminates the Christian understanding of prayer. The joy of hope in lifting hearts and hands to heaven is greatly enlarged over previous epochs. The author of Hebrews explains:

a. In heaven there is now a 'new' understanding of human needs. 'For we do not have a high priest who is unable to sympathize with our weaknesses, but one who in every respect has been tempted [tried, tested] as we are, yet without sin.' (Heb. 4:15). A Christian's child may then be taught to pray, as soon as the child does anything with understanding, as in Luther's Cradle Hymn, knowing Jesus too was once a baby. The child's grandmother with her last breath may pray confidently as Jesus did, 'Into your hands I commend my spirit,' or as Stephen, Christ's first martyr, 'Lord Jesus, receive my spirit.' Whether God now knows more about our feelings and infirmities than before Christ's Passion may be debated, but there is no question believers have more assurance 'He understands and cares.'

b. We now have an 'advocate' in heaven. Advocate is not the word employed in Hebrews, but the idea is prominent: 'For Christ has entered, not into holy places made with hands, which are copies of the true things, but into heaven itself, now to appear in the presence of God on our behalf' (Heb. 9:24). The priests made entrance into the first 'holy place' every day, but into 'the holiest' only on the Great Day of Atonement (*Yom Kippur*).

On that one day a year he actually entered beyond the veil to stand before the mercy-seat (place of propitiation) and exited at least three times – first with coals from the great altar whereon he put sweet incense 'that the cloud of the incense may cover the mercy seat ...so that he does not die' (Lev. 16:12, 13). His second was with blood of a slain bullock, a 'sin offering... atonement for himself and for his house' (Lev. 16:11). The third was with the blood of a goat slain as a sin-offering 'for the people' (Lev. 16:15) and, if Jewish tradition is correct, he entered and exited a fourth time to retrieve the vessels of the incense. According to Leviticus 16:15-17 these (and many other rituals of the day) were to make atonement not only for the uncleanness of the priests and the people but also for the sanctuary itself inasmuch as it remained among the people 'in the midst of their uncleannesses.'

Aaron and his successors in office entered the inmost chambers of the earthly sanctuary only one day of the year. In contrast, Christ our High Priest is now continually advocating our cause in the heavenly sanctuary. As the author of Hebrews several times reminds us, his readers, the offering of Christ was once and for all time, never to be repeated, its value infinite for propitiation, expiation and reconciliation. 'Who shall bring any charge against God's elect?' (Rom. 8:33). '[I]f anyone does sin, we have an advocate [*paraclete*] with the Father, Jesus Christ the righteous' (1 John 2:1). The Holy Spirit is 'another Helper [*paraclete*]' (John 14:16). Hence we have one divine Advocate in heaven and another (*allos*, of the same kind) on earth.

He Is Permanently 'The Lamb of God.'

The ascended Christ remains the 'propitiation for the sins of the people' (Heb. 2:17). It is always right to exclaim as John the Baptist did, 'Behold, the Lamb of God, who takes away the sin of the world!' (John 1:29). Hebrews devotes several chapters to what 1 John 2:2 (NKJV) states in a single short sentence: 'And He Himself is the propitiation for our sins.' It follows the acknowledgment that even though sin no longer has dominion over us, if we think we have no sin, 'we deceive ourselves' (1 John 1:8). It is for believing, forgiven sinners that 'He is the propitiation for our sins.' John departs from the more common omission of the word 'to be' in 1 John 2:2 where 'is' is *estin*, present tense, not past tense. John is emphasizing that Jesus is today and every day the propitiation for our sins. He is relating present sins of believers to our present Advocate: 'if anyone does sin, we have an advocate with the Father' (1 John 2:1).

Aaron day by day regularly and once a year on *Yom Kippur* made repeated 'propitiation for the sins of the people.' In our Lord's present appearance as our Advocate with the Father He pleads our case on the ground of His one and only act of propitiation, as our author says: 'For Christ has entered, not into holy places made with hands... but into heaven itself, *now to appear* [emphasis added] in the presence of God on our behalf' (Heb. 9:24) as our Advocate.

The author of Hebrews goes on plainly to say that Christ did not, like Aaron's repeated sacrifices, 'offer himself repeatedly' for 'then he would have had to suffer repeatedly since the foundation of the world. But as it is, he has appeared once for all at the end of the ages to put away sin by the sacrifice of himself' (Heb. 9:26).

It is a 'plain contradiction to the emphatic teaching of this epistle' (F. F. Bruce) to teach that Jesus is eternally offering Himself in heaven with the corollary teaching that in the Mass (Lord's Supper) His sacrifice is 're-offered' or 're-presented' or 're-enacted' by human priests on earth. The Roman Church is in plain conflict with Scripture on this point. (Anglican authors have pursued exposure of this error. See Swete, op. cit., N. Dimock, *Our One High Priest On High: The Present Sacerdotal Function of Christ in Heaven. What it is Not and What it is*, 1910.)[13] This rare book is a priceless, scholarly, condensed treatise (only eighty-eight pages). It demolishes Roman Catholic claims of scriptural support for their claims of valid sacrifice in the Roman Mass. Calvin's scornful rejection of papal *non-sequiturs* on the subject are about as up to date as Vatican II and its defenders.[14] A sample:

> When God's Sacred Word not only affirms but cries out and contends that this sacrifice was performed only once and all its force remains forever, do not those who require another sacrifice accuse it of imperfection and weakness.... Nor am I unaware of the tricks by which the father of lies is wont to disguise his fraud: that these are not varied or different sacrifices, but the same one often repeated.... Subtle men escape through a more secret chink – that it is not a repetition but an application.[15]

Is Jesus Advocate-Intercessor for All Mankind?

It is true that Jesus said 'I am praying for them [Apostles]. I am not praying for the world.... I do not ask for these only, but also for those who will believe in me through their word [believers through the Christian era]' (John 17:9, 20). Yet in 1 John 2:1, 2, John says our Advocate with the Father 'is the propitiation for our sins, and not for ours only but also for the sins of the whole world.'

I have proposed in chapter 16 that there is a special reference of Christ's propitiatory work to the elect only. Careful theology says that as full *redemption* this aspect of atonement is *particular*, for elect only. Particular election implies particular redemption, redemption effected, not merely made available. Yet as reconciliation, a truce in God's enmity for sin and sinners has been effected at Calvary. Execution of sentence has been delayed. '[I]n Christ God was reconciling the world to himself, not counting their trespasses against them' (2 Cor. 5:19), apparently not one person left out. The world is operating in an armistice. John says the propitiation is *peri holou tou kosmou*. *Peri* with the genitive (of the whole world) as here, with most 'verbs and expressions [means] with regard to, with reference to, etc'[16] John does not say Jesus' propitiation was in the stead of (*anti*) the sins of believers and unbelievers *in this text*, but that what He did took adequate care of the sin problem of all the world for now. In this sense Jesus is 'the Savior of all people' though 'especially of those who believe' (1 Tim. 4:10). Let us refer again to 1 Timothy 2:6, which I translate, '[Christ Jesus] gave himself a substitutionary ransom [*anti-lutron*] for the benefit, or advantage [*huper*] of all.' It certainly seems reasonable to interpret Paul as meaning that there is a divinely designed benefit for all men in the substitutionary ransom provided by Christ that is temporary, that opens the door of salvation even to those who refuse to go through the door. Hence the atonement is in one respect particular redemption, in another, world reconciliation.

In this sense Christ is at present in heaven the Advocate, or Guarantor, that the truce is still effective for the whole world. When He returns to the earth the truce will be over and will end with fiery judgments.

---

13. N. Dimock, *Our One High Priest On High: The Present Sacerdotal Function of Christ in Heaven. What it is Not and What it is*, intro. H. C. G. Moule (London: Longmans, Green & Co. 1910).
14. John Calvin, *Institutes of the Christian Religion iv*, ed. McNeil, trans. and ed. Battles (Philadelphia, PA: Westminster Press ed. ii, 1960), 18.2–18.
15. ibid., 18.3
16. Walter Bauer, *A Greek-English Lexicon of the New Testament and Other Early Christian Literature*, trans. and adapted from 5th German ed. by W. F. Arndt and F. W. Gingrich (Chicago: University of Chicago Press, 1957), *sub peri*, p. 650.

PART 1
THEOLOGY PROPER
Introduction and Doctrine of God

PART 2
ANTHROPOLOGY
Man as Created

PART 3
HAMARTIOLOGY
Man as Sinner

PART 4
CHRISTOLOGY
Person and Work of Christ

PART 5
SOTERIOLOGY
Salvation Applied

PART 6
ECCLESIOLOGY
Church Local and Universal

PART 7
ESCHATOLOGY
Last Things, Personal and Universal

BIBLIOGRAPHY

SCRIPTURE INDEX

GENERAL INDEX

Preface

The subject of this book has been of great interest to this author as a preacher since his earliest faltering efforts as a pulpit evangelist. Now, after taking courses in the subject in theological schools and teaching 'salvation' in the context of a whole theological system, I find it as attractive as ever. Yet this book is no theological memoir. I shall try to convince the reader of the truth of the doctrine of salvation (*soteriology*) presented and to do so with the breadth, balance and scriptural insight exemplified by a Calvin or Whitefield, the conviction of a Spurgeon or Wesley, and the clarity of a Warfield. These pages will not read like ruminations. Matters of eternal life are too critically important to aim at anything less than what a messenger told Cornelius about Peter's message: 'a message by which you will be saved, you and all your household' (Acts 11:14).

A sound theology of the classroom must be theology of the gathered assembly also. If I seem to be excessively 'dogmatic' it is only because I wish to be clear, economic in use of language and as brief as consistent with completeness. If the intelligent, devout, adult, believing reader or listener cannot understand it, the logic propounded is defective, the formulation of the matter obscure or otherwise incompetently presented. Apart from clear presentation, the best argument in the world is always obscure and thereby ineffective. On the contrary the most convincing argument for truth is often a clear presentation in and of itself.

Theology is to be preached. 'Until I come', said the great itinerant Apostle to his assistant at Ephesus, 'devote yourself to the public reading of Scripture, to exhortation, to teaching ["doctrine" KJV]' (1 Tim. 4:13). The Epistles specially addressed to the preacher in a pastoral setting (1 and 2 Tim. and Titus), ring the changes on the importance of regular proclamation of sound doctrine. Paul is so unafraid of doctrinal certainty that he once recommended 'the *form* [emphasis added] of sound words' (2 Tim. 1:13 KJV). Doctrine is the central feature of Paul's only specific mention of training of pastors (2 Tim. 2:2). Our thoughts, then, as writers of theology and as students are no less bound to Jesus Christ and the Christian revelation than as pastors and preachers.

This book is first *exegetical*. The fruits of study of the Bible in its original languages will be on display, though not the procedures. It is *traditional* in the sense that tradition is the history of exegesis through the ages (J. Pelikan, *The Christian Tradition*). It is *theological* before *philosophical*. I intend that sound logic, the principles of analysis and synthesis, and the usual categories of all good philosophy shall be employed, although I make no commitment to any metaphysics or theory of knowledge (*epistemology*) except the common-sense realism one finds in the Bible and common people everywhere. We must look beyond mere appearances of reality but be careful not to abandon our senses and the restraints of logic and disciplined intuitions in doing so.

The structure of theology (as most theologians, even the least traditional, find it) will be employed – not out of deference to tradition but to orderly thinking. We cannot do without logic: soteriology (salvation) *belongs* after anthropology (man), hamartiology (sin) and Christology (redemption), in that order, and before ecclesiology (church) and eschatology (last things).

One must use some technical terms related to the study of biblical languages and of the history of thought. This preface has already used more than will appear in some of the chapters to follow. Explanations and definitions will usually accompany first use. Part of theological education consists of exposure to the special terms of the discipline and the special use of common expressions. 'Anthropology', for example, was a special term of theology, long established, before social science tried to take it away from us.

With due fellow feeling for some feminist concerns, I still think it is simply wrong to write 'they' when the antecedent is a singular noun, nor can I bring myself to give up some use of the generic he, him and his when appropriate – though I make some effort to find other modes of expression in order to avoid injury to sincere feelings. This usage is common to every one of the several European and Semitic languages most of us know anything about. Technical writings today still employ these generic, masculine pronouns pretty much as though radical feminism had never taken over the Modern Language Association.

Documentation I do lightly – to support arguments, give credit to sources, but not as a full guide to the literature of soteriology. 'Get to the point' takes priority, even though background must not be neglected.

In addition to several English Versions of the Bible I employ a few translations of my own. If there is some reason for doing so the Version being quoted will be indicated.

1
Introduction to the Doctrine of Salvation

'I wish you'd worry less about my soul and more about the house I live in.' The words are those of a thin small black boy who appeared in a political cartoon in the Minneapolis Star. He is pictured, with school book and ruler tucked under his frail arm, as he looks up to a grotesquely caricatured Senator Everett Dirksen glowering down over his glasses while he holds in his hand, resting on an ample paunch, his 'school prayer amendment'. This occurred at a time when social welfare legislation and the loss of 'religion in the schools' were high in public interest. The cartoon says eloquently: mankind's present needs, that is, our physical welfare, are more important than any future salvation of our souls. It also suggests that the Christian religion does not have much to do with human welfare, whether individual or collective, in the present life.

The chief defect of this line of thinking is not in its interest in human social welfare but like most pronouncements emanating from universities and popular social commentators these days, it is shallow, unaware of what human condition in the world and before God really is. The true shape of human situation and thereby knowledge of our needs is set forth in two Christian doctrines: creation and fall.

Already the reader of this page has been encouraged to think beneath the appearance of things – for even though on warm spring days the world seems lovely to the healthy and the young, mature adults know such days are rare in most climates.

'[W]hat is man'? David sang of him that God 'made him a little lower than the heavenly beings and crowned him with glory and honour. You have given him dominion over the works of your hands; you have put all things under his feet' (Ps. 8:4-6). These verses are a poetic summary of the teachings of Genesis, chapters 1 and 2, about the greatness of mankind by creation. As one of the great evangelical creeds says:

> After God had made all other creatures, he created man, male and female (Gen. 1:27), with reasonable and immortal souls (Ps. 8:5, 6; Luke 23:43; Matt. 10:28), endued with knowledge, righteousness, and true holiness after his own image (Gen. 1:26; Col. 3:10; Eph. 4:24), having the law of God written in their hearts (Rom. 2:14, 15), and power to fulfil it; and yet under a possibility of transgressing, being left to the liberty of their own will, which was subject to change.[1]

These matters were considered earlier in *anthropology*, the doctrine of man. They cannot be treated fully here except to add that all human greatness – in art, science, industry, social relations, all our deepest yearnings and passions – root in our marvellous createdness. We are creatures formed by God in His own likeness.

---

1. *Westminster Confession* IV. 2.

Since the foregoing is pleasing to contemplate and on the surface apparently consonant with the way things really are, it is easy to accept as the whole truth – which it is not. The same book of Psalms has another page wherein after a lovely peroration on the marvels of creation suddenly there intrudes this startling sentence: 'Let sinners be consumed from the earth, and let the wicked be no more' (Ps. 104:35). Mankind did not remain as they originally were. They became 'sinners', deserving to be 'consumed from the earth'. The same Confession of Faith cited above goes on to say:

> Our first parents, being seduced by the subtlety and temptation of Satan, sinned in eating the forbidden fruit (Gen. 3:13; 2 Cor. 11:3; Gen. 3:1-14)… By this sin they fell from their original righteousness and communion with God (Gen. 3:7, 8; Gen. 2:17), and so became dead in sin (Rom. 5:12; Eph. 2:3), and wholly defiled in all the faculties and parts of soul and body (Gen. 6:5; Jer. 17:9; Rom. 3:10-19; Rom. 8:6-8; Ps. 58:1-5). [2]

The doctrine expressed in this typical evangelical confession was treated earlier in the doctrine of sin, *hamartiology* from a Greek word for sin.

As we shall now immediately explain, the doctrine of sin (*harmartiology*) is a central issue of any doctrinal formulation of a doctrine of salvation (soteriology) that in a serious, sincere manner seeks to be fully biblical and Christian.[3]

There are many other doctrines that produce a gulf of distance between Buddhism or Islam, for example, and Christianity. But to the extent that there are differences of teaching in regard to aspects of soteriological (salvational) doctrine among orthodox Christian believers those differences mainly arise from differences in the way they understand the condition of man as sinner. It would be pleasant to avoid discussion of these differences but a serious study of Christian doctrine may not do so. All agree that a fall took place, that when the Gospel first strikes one's ear, the ear is the receptor for an invariably sinful heart, i.e. understanding, vitiated – as the old theologians say – by sin. Granting that this is important and far enough to go with our research and formulation under certain conditions (let us say co-operative evangelism), it is not far enough to enable us to understand lost people or saved people, nor that we truly understand all that salvation is, nor what God had to do to bring us to Himself.

Traditionally, the orthodox Roman Catholic view of 'original sin' is about as follows. When it is said that God created man in His 'image' (Gen. 1:26) that means man, like God, has powers of reason, moral capacity, aesthetic and scientific appreciation, and similar '*natural*' capacities – though not to the degree or perfection that God has, of course. The fall did not affect these. They remain fully intact both in your favourite novelist or the teacher of your Bible class or George Washington, the same as in Adam and Eve after the fall. When it is said God made man in his 'likeness' (Gen. 1:26) it means that in addition to natural capacities '*supernatural*' gifts were granted Adam – such as holy will, love of God, righteous inclinations, etc. When the fall took place these supernatural gifts, and only these, were affected. They were lost. So according to Romanist doctrine, men today are as able to reason *rightly* in all things as were their first parents, even though apart from divine grace they cannot love God. Their reasoning powers are intact as ever even if their moral and spiritual faculties are not sound.

Evangelical (i.e. Protestant), orthodox doctrine of all varieties has generally held that man's *lostness*, his depravity, to use the harsher word, is much more serious. All parts have suffered debilitating injury by the fall, both body and soul: emotions, intellect and will. They have not ceased to exist, of course, but they have all suffered 'vitiation', again to use the old fashioned theological term. This is what is meant by 'total depravity'. We do not mean, for example, that such relatively good things as mother love or filial piety do not exist among unbelievers. It means that even mother love and filial piety are to a *serious* degree affected by the fall. God does not have His rightful place in thinking or loving or feeling or working. So far, so good. No informed evangelical Protestant disagrees.

There are many Protestants, however, who think the Scriptures carry the doctrine of sin and the fall a stage further. The fall of the race not only seriously injured all parts of man, but from a certain biblical point of view, *fatally*. If so, then when the gospel is preached, it is heard by people who are not only *sick* in sin but '*dead* in trespasses and sins'. If God is going to save such sinners He will do much more than simply provide the Savior and tell us about Him. He will also *do something* to dead hearts to enable them to respond favourably. In the Bible, quite differently from common figurative use in our language, the 'heart' is represented as the seat of understanding, of knowledge,

---

2. *Westminster Confession VI*, 1, 2.
3. What follows through the rest of this chapter is a non-technical summary of *Hamartiology, the Doctrine of Sin* treated at length earlier in this volume.

of discernment. It is not merely the seat of emotions. So, for example, 'believe in your heart' (Rom. 10:9) means in the mind. In theological-biblical discourse 'head knowledge' is not in contrast with 'heart knowledge'. The 'bowels' or 'kidneys' are often put for emotions in Scripture, but rarely if ever the heart. The heart stands for the whole 'inner man'. 'Heart, in fact, is associated with what is now meant by the cognitive, affective and volitional elements of personal life.'[4]

When the doctrine is stated thus, believers generally, after a bit of reflection, agree, for the following texts are quite plain as to man's helplessness in the lost condition: 'For the word of the cross is folly to those who are perishing' (1 Cor. 1:18); 'The natural person does not accept the things of the Spirit of God, for they are folly to him, and he is not able to understand them because they are spiritually discerned' (1 Cor. 2:14); and in referring to the former condition of believers, '…dead in the trespasses and sins in which you once walked, following the course of this world… sons of disobedience – among whom *we all* once lived in the passions of our flesh, carrying out the desires of the body and the mind, and were by nature children of wrath, like the rest of mankind. But God… even when we were dead in our trespasses, made us alive' (Eph. 2:1-5).

These passages clearly say we all are born without power to obey God, to love God, to want to love God, unable even to have any inclination to do so. Hence, God must take the initiative not only in providing the Savior but also in getting people to receive Him. At this point some not negligible differences have surfaced. Some seem willing simply to ignore the above texts and to assume that people can be persuaded of their need for the Savior, much as they can be persuaded to go to Fort Lauderdale or San Diego for a winter vacation or to buy Bayer's rather than some less expensive brand of aspirin. There are sentences in Charles Grandison Finney's *Lectures on Revivals* which read like that. Yet even Finney gave a large place to prayer in winning the lost, so he wasn't always a hardliner on the point of 'plenary ability'. Others have asserted, on what appears to be very weak evidence, that though all men are conceived totally depraved, unable in their own power to turn to God, immediately after the soul comes to consciousness, in a supernatural way, God restores the power of completely competent use of the reason in spiritual matters and power of free choice. Those who say God does this as a matter of *justice* were mainly among those followers of Arminius, a sixteenth–seventeenth century Dutch theologian, who came to be called Remonstrants. Those who say God does this as a matter of *grace* (certainly much more in harmony with sound doctrine) are usually influenced by the thought of John Wesley. Those who are convinced Paul in the passages cited above is describing the condition of all people of any time of life until God moves individually (particularly) and personally to enlighten them are commonly called Calvinists, though, as Dr G. C. H. Berkouwer in his book on *Election* shows, at the present time most evangelical thinkers of all stripes accept the *present* inability of all men to turn to Christ except in response to special personal activity of the Holy Spirit ordinarily operating through the Word. Another writer, Dr James I. Packer (*Evangelism and The Sovereignty of God*), has pointed out that when evangelicals of any theological stripe pray for the conversion of sinners they assume that God must enlighten the sinner's darkened mind before he can repent and believe.

Another very important teaching of Scripture is also basic. Sinful people, for whom the Savior did and does His saving work, are sinners in need of salvation because of their heart condition, previous to and quite apart from individual acts of sin. Put as an aphorism: people commit sins because they *are* sinners, not in order to *become* sinners. Quite apart from arguments about the fall of man there is a large number of texts which teach or imply that men are congenitally wicked, i.e. they are so conceived and born. To take one example, the sin of theft, proscribed in the eighth commandment (Exod. 20:15), develops out of the sin of covetousness, proscribed in the tenth commandment (Exod. 20:17). And why does covetousness arise so easily and quickly in human hearts? Let Paul answer: 'But sin, taking opportunity through the commandment, produced in me coveting of every kind' (Rom. 7:8 NASB). There is an immediate resentment against the revealed law (i.e. will) of God when the sinner learns of it. Paul is aware of a 'sin that dwells within me' (Rom. 7:17), which is innate (inborn), not produced by acts of sin but rather producing them. See all of the seventh chapter of Romans and James 1:14, 15. Men are guilty and deserving of eternal death (see Rom. 5:12-19) on this account more than for the many overt sins, major and minor, which they actually commit.

An interesting quotation from Martin Luther will serve to enforce this matter:

> These two sayings are true: 'Good, pious works never make a good, pious man, but a good, pious man does good, pious works. Evil works never make an evil man, but an evil man does evil works'. As Christ says: 'A bad

---

[4]. O. R. Brandon, 'Heart' in *Evangelical Dictionary of Theology*, ed., W. Elwell (Grand Rapids, MI: Baker Books, 1984), p. 497; see Gordon Clark, *The Doctrine of Man* (Jefferson: The Trinity Foundation, 1984), pp. 78–88.

tree bears no good fruit, a good tree bears no bad fruit'. Now it is obvious that the fruit does not bear the tree, nor do the trees grow on the fruit, but again the trees bear the fruit, and the fruit grows on the trees. Now as the trees must be there before the fruit, and the fruit makes the tree neither good nor bad, but the trees make the fruit, so must man first be pious or evil in his person before he does good or evil works. And his works do not make him good or evil, but he does good or evil works.

The discourse of Jesus cited here by Luther will be found at Matthew 7:15-20. This line of argument may seem obvious or even simplistic. Yet the point made is not generally understood. Several major theological works devote many pages in demonstration of two things: 1) that men commit sins because their hearts are wicked not the other way around; 2) that an evil disposition is more culpable and blameworthy than the evil deeds which give expression to it.[5]

Evil intentions, desires, purposes, dispositions are therefore the chief reason why 'the wrath of God is revealed from heaven against all ungodliness and unrighteousness of men' (Rom. 1:18). Though men commit all manner of wickedness, their prior and more blameworthy characteristic is that 'they did not see fit to acknowledge God' and they have a 'debased mind to do what ought not to be done' (Rom. 1:28). God judged the world by a flood in Noah's time, not simply because people were doing many wicked things but because 'all flesh had corrupted their way' (Gen. 6:12); because 'the intention of man's heart is evil from his youth' (Gen. 8:21).

Mankind's catastrophe in sin is pervasive, manifold and complete. They are without love of God, without desire to learn to love God or choose Him. This is why salvation must be manifold – cleansing, restoring, recreating all that man is, body and soul; past, present and future. This is why if any human being is ever to be saved God must take the initiative not only in providing salvation but in applying it – why salvation must be God's work – entirely, wholly, completely. God will not let man present any merit for it, work any co-operation with it or claim any credit for it. Salvation is of the Lord.

Synergism (from Greek, to work with) or 'co-operationism' is the name the Reformers, Luther and Calvin gave to the theory that God provided and offers salvation, but that the sinner co-operating with the promptings of Word and Spirit, comes to God for salvation. They insisted on the contrary that God chose him, finds him and brings him – as Jesus Himself says in John 6:40, 44, 65. Many balked at this doctrine when Jesus announced it: to which He responded, 'This is why I told you that no one can come to me unless it is granted him by the Father. After this many of his disciples turned back and no longer walked with him' (John 6:65, 66).

This is not the place to introduce all the scriptural reasons why each individual member of the human race is blameworthy (culpable, guilty) for his disposition to flee from God and 'to work all manner of unrighteousness'. The evidence, however, is overwhelming. For two reasons major theological works on the doctrine of sin (*hamartiology*) by evangelical authors almost invariably devote their keenest strokes to this aspect of the subject. In the first place, the evidence (as noted above) is overwhelming both in Scripture and practical experience; because in the second place it arouses the sharpest disagreement in every mind not won over already 'to receive' the 'engrafted word with meekness'.

The student will therefore be prepared to understand that salvation, while simple enough as preached in the gospel – 'everyone who calls on the name of the Lord will be saved' (Rom. 10:13) – is very complex. To illustrate, a man with a match rifle laid across a sandbag, prone on the ground, sighting it carefully at a target 500 yards away does a very simple thing to shoot the rifle. He simply squeezes the trigger. But behind the creation of that seemingly unremarkable event are hundreds of years of scientific refinement in the compounding of gunpowder, the casting of bullets, the fashioning of cartridges, the shaping of the barrel, rifling of the same, etc. The chemistry, physics and dynamics of detonation of cap and powder, treated scientifically, fills thousands of pages of books, while hundreds of people spend much of their time seeking to understand and improve it. The mysteries of thermonuclear physics are even remotely involved. So to squeeze a trigger is a relatively simple act (if you also neglect the human part of the equation), but the firing of a rifle in such a way as to hit a target (and we haven't mentioned ballistics and windage) is bafflingly complex. It can, however, be explained if teachers of the subject are both informed and skillful and if learners are intelligent, interested and patient. It is the purpose of the present study to explore in some detail, compactly, biblically and as scientifically as possible, just what happens when a lost man is saved. It has been a topic of interest for a long time and in strange places, for Peter said not only ancient Hebrew prophets but also angels in heaven (of all places) have desired to 'look into' it (see 1 Peter 1:10-12).

---

5. Among the several available the one which convinced me and recently all the students in several classes preparing to be 'biblical counselors' is A. H. Strong's discussion in *Systematic Theology* (Valley Forge: Judson Press, 1907), pp. 552–557.

2
What Salvation Is

In this chapter we must clear the ground for later topics by doing a number of things. First we shall make some definitions and draw some distinctions. Then we shall discuss some theories and opinions about how salvation is conveyed to mankind and how it is appropriated by them. We seek to derive our doctrine from Scripture and to bring our convictions to the judgment of Scripture. After that we shall observe how each person of the triune God worked in providing our salvation, noting particularly the prominence of the Second Person, the Son of God, in redemption. Finally preliminary attention will be directed to the two salient features of evangelical theology of salvation, namely: grace and faith.

Distinctions and Definitions.

Objective and *subjective* salvation. By objective salvation is designated those things which exist in God's great providence which have made possible our personal redemption. Everything which relates to the Savior's person and work, securing for us atonement for sin, redemption of our persons, eternal life with God, is sometimes designated 'objective soteriology' (salvation), sometimes the 'doctrine of redemption', sometimes 'the person and work of Christ'.

'Subjective soteriology' designates the actual occurrence in the sinner of the fruit of all Christ's work. This is salvation in the narrow, 'proper' sense. When we speak of being 'saved', 'born again' or of having become a 'believer' we are thinking of what relates to an individual human subject, hence, 'subjective'. Sometimes good authors refer to these two major divisions of the subject as 'the provision of redemption' and 'the application of redemption' and this does not exhaust the number of theological and scriptural terms.

Important Words and Concepts in the Original Languages of the Bible.

The manner of speaking about salvation and the terms employed, quite apart from the quaintness of English terms used for centuries in the language of prayer, devotion, worship, preaching and doctrine, are in many cases very common terms: 'calling' and 'assurance', for example. Others are terms mainly used only in specialized professions or trades, 'justification', from printing and law, being an example. Some are very rarely used outside of Christian doctrinal discussion – 'sanctification' being one. It seems there is no practical way to change this vocabulary of salvation. The same situation prevailed when certain Greek words regularly used to translate the Old Testament Hebrew Bible into Greek were employed to write the New Testament. The New Testament can be read with some understanding by almost any one, but to make it read like the daily newspaper is to betray it. Some of its mysteries must be explained by the advanced teacher (see Acts 8:26-39, especially v. 31). There are aspects of the New Testament which cannot be fully understood without recourse to the Old, not only its narrative but its legal, poetic and prophetic language, even vocabulary and syntax.

(*Paraphrases* of the Bible may be very useful but they should not be employed in establishing doctrines and in the proper sense are not *translations* or *Versions*. The latter word as used of Bible translations should always be spelled with an initial capital letter, as Version in King James Version. The Living Bible, for example, was published as a Paraphrase of the Bible not a 'Version'.)

A large number of these terms are concentrated in a single passage, Psalm 72:12-15, a prophecy of the saving work of God's Christ, our Lord Jesus. We shall treat each briefly, concentrating finally on the single most important of them. These words are deliver (v. 12), spare and save (v. 13), redeem and be precious (v. 14), live (v. 15), (all references to ASV) – six terms in all.

Deliver. The Hebrew word (*nitsel*) in secular context means to move away from threatened danger or to extricate from it when once involved. The Greek Bible uses a word (*hruomai*), which appears over and over again in the New Testament as the term for our salvation in Christ as well as in secular contexts. When Jesus is mockingly challenged to ask God for deliverance from the nails and spikes of His cross this is the word used (Matt. 27:43); Peter uses it of the rescue of Lot from Sodom's destruction (2 Peter 2:7); Paul of escape from 'every evil deed' (2 Tim. 4:18). Examples of its use to signify the sinner's rescue from sin, its punishments, pollution and power will be found at Romans 7:24; 11:26; 2 Corinthians 1:11 (three times in one verse); Colossians 1:12, 13, '...the Father... has delivered us from the domain of darkness'. The last text is an example of rescue from harm or oppression already existing while still another, 1 Thessalonians 1:10 ('Jesus... delivers us from the wrath to come'), is from threatened danger in the future. This word emphasizes that salvation is a true 'rescue operation' in which drastic emergency measures, so to speak, must be undertaken.

Spare. (Ps. 72:13 KJV and ASV, 'He shall spare... and shall save the souls of the needy.') The Hebrew word *ḥus* means to withhold an act of destruction or injury when it is easily possible – and usually with cause – to inflict it. Thus God's eye or His hand is said to spare (or have compassion on) the needy sinner (Neh. 13:22; Jon. 4:10). The results when God does not spare (*pheidomai*, Gr.) may be seen by reading 2 Peter 2:4, 5 ff., viz. '...God did not spare angels when they sinned... he did not spare the ancient world, but preserved [saved] Noah...' Here spare is a synonym for save.

Redeem. (Ps. 72:14 KJV and ASV, 'He shall redeem their soul'.) The word is *ga'al*, a very special one, designating what in customary law a benevolently inclined kinsman does for some member of his family when he is in distress of any sort. Its essential, primary meaning is to *act the part of a kinsman* (Ruth 3:13; Num. 5:8). What should a kinsman do? He should *buy back* forfeited family real-estate (book of Ruth, especially 4:4 ff.). He should *avenge*, i.e. bring legal punishment by the best means available, when a kinsman is murdered (avenger, Deut. 19:6, 12 *et al*). He should seek to *vindicate* his kinsman in court when that kinsman is unjustly charged (Job 19:25 ASV margin). In salvation, Jesus, our kinsman (see Heb. 2:14 ff.) does all these things and more, everything a loving, strong, dutiful kinsman could possibly be expected to do.

Be precious. Hebrew *yaqar*, to be dear, esteemed, precious. (Ps. 72:14 KJV and ASV '...precious shall their blood be in his sight'.) The idea, as later developed in the New Testament, is that the lost sinner is important to the Savior. He is not consigned to the trash bin but picked up for special attention and care.

> For while we were still weak, at the right time Christ died for the ungodly. For one will scarcely die for a righteous person – though perhaps for a good person one would dare even to die – but God shows his love for us in that while we were still sinners, Christ died for us (Rom. 5:6-8).

Live. Hebrew, *ḥayah*, to live or come alive. The exact syntax of the Hebrew here is obscure. Exegetes have puzzled over what the rendering should be, whether 'They shall live' or 'He shall live'. The ASV 'and they shall live' (Ps. 72:15) is at least possible. At any rate salvation is everywhere in the New Testament the impartation of a new kind of life on the true spiritual level where there was only deadness before. In the Old Testament see Ezekiel 3:18; 13:18, 19; and 18:27. Though the present life is emphasized in much of the Old Testament, these passages 'illustrate the way the

Old Testament prophet refuses to divorce physical from spiritual life'.[1] The Christian who has taken only the very first steps in understanding Scripture truths knows how prominent this aspect of salvation is. (See the many texts on salvation as eternal life, John 3:16; 5:24; etc.)

Save. Hebrew, *yasha'* (Ps. 72:13 'And the souls of the needy he will save' ASV). 'Souls' in these citations should be understood in the modern sense of persons. 'Save' is the most comprehensive term for God's complete work on behalf of sinners. The Hebrew word is the root of the names Hoshea, Hosea, Jehoshua and Joshua – Jehovah Saves – and, of course, in Greek dress this name becomes Jesus, which explains the angel's announcement, 'you shall call his name Jesus, for he will save his people from their sins' (Matt. 1:21). The root word *yasha'* with its derivatives in Hebrew and, as cognate words in related languages such as Arabic and Syriac demonstrate, means 'to be broad, ample, spacious'. Gesenius asserted, 'To the Hebrews broad space, wide room is the emblem of liberty, deliverance from dangers and straits; as on the other hand narrowness of space, straits, is put for difficulty, distress, danger.'[2] The sense of self-help, self-rescue from distress or imprisonment is absent from the Hebrew word *yasha'* (to save). One must think of a *first* person who is victim of a *second* person or thing being saved (rescued) by the agency of a *third*. 'The thought is neither that of self-help nor of co-operation with the oppressed. The help is such that the oppressed would be lost without it.'[3] Foerster in an article of fifty pages has shown that *sōtēr* (Greek for saviour) appears infrequently in the New Testament, and then very often in quotations of the *Septuagint* (OT in Greek).[4] It is also used sparingly of Christ in writings of the post-apostolic Fathers. Among much other valuable information, Foerster suggests that the infrequency may be due to the fact that since the emperor (and many mythical beings) was called *sōtēr*, the Christians avoided confusion by avoiding the term – even though the word fits our Lord exactly. Says Foerster: 'Nowhere in Christian writings does there seem to be any point of contact with *sōtēr*, as part of the style of imperial Rome, not even by way of antithesis.'[5]

A large amount of space here would be required fully to develop the biblical materials on this subject. Let us be content (1) to affirm that 'salvation', related of course to the word save, is the most comprehensive term for the subject of this division of systematic theology; (2) to recall that the name Jesus (Hebrew Jehoshua) means Yahweh (the LORD) saves – Matthew 1:21, 'you shall call his name Jesus, for he will save his people from their sins' (cf. Luke 1:31; 2:21); (3) to observe that Scripture adds 'that the Father has sent his Son to be the Saviour of the world' (1 John 4:14); and that (4) 'the living God', Himself, 'is the Saviour of all people, especially of those who believe' (1 Tim. 4:10).

Just as *save* is employed widely in connection with health (heal), political and civil oppression (rescue, deliver, set free), etc., in common discourse in English, so the equivalent expressions in Hebrew and Greek were used in the ancient world. In addition, at the time Jesus lived and the New Testament was being written the words *save*, *salvation* and *saviour* achieved very special meanings in civil-political society and in the mystery religions developing in the Roman world. New Testament and historical scholars have had great interest in these and related terms from Roman and Hellenic civilization of the time. As a result save *(sōdzō)*, saviour *(sōtēr)* and salvation *(sōtēria, sōtērion and sōtērios)*, all of which appear in the New Testament (especially numerous are save and salvation), have come in for great attention by scholars.

This scholarly energy, much of it directed against the integrity of the New Testament writings, has not always been fruitful for understanding save, salvation and savior in the New Testament and even less in constructing a sound theology of salvation, for a simple reason, viz.: from the beginning of the New Testament to its end (Matt. 1:21–Rev. 21:24) the idea is linked to the Old Testament history and promise. The first chapter of Matthew introduces 'the coming one' of Old Testament prophecy as named Jehovah (or *Yahweh* or the LORD) Saves, for such is the meaning of the name, Jesus. During His post-resurrection ministry Jesus Himself declared that the gospel of salvation through Him was the theme of every page of the Hebrew Bible (Luke 24:26, 27, 44-48). There is not a plain hint from Gospel or Epistle that the concept of save, salvation, savior owed a whit to Roman, Greek or other culture, though it may well be that pagan enemies of the Christians did find a false connection. For, since the emperor was beginning to be

---

1. E. M. B. Green, *The Meaning of Salvation* (London: Hodder & Stoughton, 1965), p. 13.
2. William Gesenius, *A Hebrew and English Lexicon of The Old Testament*, trans. E. Robinson, 26th ed. (Boston: Houghton, Mifflin & Co., 1891), sub. *Yasha*, p. 435.
3. Fohrer, 'The stem *yasha'* in the Old Testament' *TDNT*, vii, p. 973.
4. Foerster, '*sōdzō, sōtēria, sōtēr, sōtērios*', *TDNT* viii, pp. 965–1024.
5. ibid., p. 1019.

called *Sōtēr* (Savior) in eastern portions of the empire where the New Testament and Christian proclamation claimed 'no other' than Jesus to be the Savior of the world, the doctrine of salvation (*sōtēria*) by Christ the Savior (*Sōtēr*) brought the whole Christian movement into collision with the Roman world of the day. For this reason from time to time Christians were persecuted and slain in great numbers as subversive of public order.[6]

Comprehensive Character of Salvation.

When a believing man receives salvation from God he receives much more than he could possibly initially understand – a multitude of blessings, which he only gradually understands and appreciates. He becomes initially vividly aware that God has spared him the dreadful punishments everywhere denounced over unrepentant sinners. He is aware that having fled to the LORD for refuge, 'The name of the LORD is a strong tower; the righteous man runs into it and is safe' (Prov. 18:10); that 'Since... we have now been justified by his blood... shall we be saved... from the wrath of God' (Rom. 5:9; cf. 1 Thess. 5:9; John 3:17). This accounts in part for the profound relief and deep peace so evident in the lives of new believers. As they read the Bible further, however, they learn that in the salvation received, God 'has blessed us.... with every spiritual blessing' (Eph. 1:3) and that God's 'divine power has granted to us all things that pertain to life and godliness' (2 Peter 1:3).

(1) So the salvation that every true believer possesses *includes all the blessings one shall ever need*. There is no call for agonizing prayer or seeking for further blessings and degrees of grace, even though there may be struggle enough in the disciplines of grace whereby we enter into these blessings. The divisive doctrine that there is a further stage of present-day salvation whereby those Christians who attain it live on a different level of perfection and access to God will be treated in later chapters.

(2) Salvation is comprehensive *as to time* also. There is a *past* aspect. '[H]e chose us in him before the foundation of the world' (Eph. 1:4). There also came a moment in every believer's past when God 'saved us and called us' effectively (2 Tim. 1:9). There are *present* aspects wherein God is now saving us (1 Cor. 1:18 Gr. 'being saved') and there are instances wherein Scripture speaks of our salvation as a *future* goal (Rom. 13:11; 1 Peter 1:5; Rom. 5:9, 10). Sometimes all three aspects will appear together as in Hebrews 9:24-28 (observe 'now to appear... appeared... will appear a second time... to save' vv. 24, 26, 28).

(3) Another matter comes in for greater emphasis nowadays than in former times of less emphasis on the values of human physical and temporal existence, namely that in the Bible it is the whole man who is to be saved, not merely his 'soul', narrowly defined. When the Bible speaks of the 'soul' as safe or saved we should usually think of the whole being rather than his *psychē* (soul) or *pneuma* (spirit). In 1 Thessalonians 5:23 Paul specifies that at the last, believing men shall be saved 'completely' and specifies spirit and soul and body. Of course Christians sometimes suffer psychic disorders and all of us will die physically if Jesus does not come first, but we do nevertheless have the certain promise that 'salvation is nearer to us now than when we first believed' (Rom. 13:11), that though we may now 'groan within ourselves' (KJV) we may confidently await 'the redemption of our bodies' (Rom. 8:22, 23). We are at liberty, therefore, to think today of our loved ones who may be deranged or depressed or chronically confused as they shall be in the day of their resurrection.

As seen earlier the word 'save' (Gr. *sōdzō*) and salvation (*sōtēria*) in the New Testament in the context of physical illness means to be made whole; in case of insanity, to be made sane; in danger to be rescued; in prison to be set free. So the Gospel writers, knowing Jesus came indeed 'to seek and to save that which is lost' – and every kind of 'lost' – sometimes seem deliberately to impart ambiguous, or perhaps comprehensive, meaning to the word save. A familiar case is the story of the woman with 'an issue of blood' recorded by all three Synoptic Gospels. There must be some special importance for church and ministry about the story. It must contain the essential Christian preachment – which the form critics call the *kērygma* (Paul's word for 'preaching' that *saves*, 1 Cor. 1:21). See the story at Mark 5:25-34 (or parallels in Luke 8:43-48 and Matt. 9:20-24). At the close of the story Jesus, in the hearing of an enormous crowd, pronounced to and over the chronically ill woman [author's translation]: 'Daughter, thy faith has saved [*sesōken*] thee. Go in peace [another word for wholeness] and be healthy of thy plague' (a common word for the stroke of sin in the Old Testament). All the theology of Isaiah 53 should be entered here. Among the many writers who have drawn this lesson from Mark 5:34, perhaps the following puts it best:

---

6. Among the several scholarly works treating the idea of salvation in the New Testament and the gospel which proclaims it, the volume by Green *Meaning of Salvation* is heartily recommended here.

What particular usefulness did such a story have for church work which led to its incorporation in the Gospel?... The story, like so many in Mark, is plain *kērygma*, and makes a marvellous sermon illustration for evangelistic preaching. Here is a woman with a disease which makes her ceremonially impure and increasingly weak physically. She has tried all the remedies that she knows, and was nothing bettered but rather grew worse. She hears of Jesus; she comes to Jesus in simple (if superstitious) faith that he can cure her or, as Matthew and Mark put it, that she could be 'saved' (Mark 5:28; Matt. 9:21). She was assured by Jesus that her faith had 'saved' her, and she went out into a new life of peace and wholeness. We have here a paradigm of Christian conversion in the apostolic church.[7]

The Triune God, the Author of Salvation.

The pre-eminence of Christ as author of salvation is declared by a number of New Testament texts. He is 'the founder and perfecter of our faith' (Heb. 12:2). Jesus Himself said, 'I am the way, and the truth, and the life. No one comes to the Father except through me' (John 14:6) and Peter, filled with the Holy Ghost, proclaimed, 'there is salvation in no one else, for there is no other name under heaven given among men by which we must be saved' (Acts 4:8, 12). Jesus is the only name whereby to be saved (Acts 4:12), the one true vine from which comes life (John 15:1-4), apart from whom we can do nothing (John 15:5).

Yet there is great emphasis in Scripture on the fact that each Person of the Godhead was involved in effecting our redemption. The industrious reader will find this woven into Paul's marvelous peroration of redemption in Ephesians 1:1-14 (see especially vv. 3, 5, 7, 13). Another such passage is Titus 3:4-6. The formula that salvation is *of* the Father (as Planner), *through* the Son (as Mediator) and *by* the Holy Spirit (as Applier) is fairly consistent through the Scriptures wherever the subject is raised. The Father sent the Son (1 John 4:14; John 1:17); the Spirit proceeds into the world from the Father and the Son (John 14:26; 15:26; 16:7).

The Method by Which Salvation Is Brought to Men.

This rubric may seem confusing at first but it will soon be seen that a vital truth is at stake. Some people seem to think that salvation is conveyed by the environmental influences of early life, e.g. many suppose the *influence* of catechisms, meetings, denominational slogans, religious exercises, etc. secure this salvation. Paul refers to such false trust in Philippians 3:4-8. Others either implicitly or overtly trust their family or national *heritage* – sometimes in ignorant rejection of the true meaning of their ancestral faith. I think of the many to whom I preach who I suspect of having little more depth to their religion than the sacred precincts of the building familiar from childhood. God has said, 'who has required of you this trampling of my courts?' (Isa. 1:12). We recall God's demand by the prophecy of Isaiah when we observe crowds at church suppers and festivals but scarcely a pew full at meetings for prayer. Isaiah said, 'Bring no more vain offerings; incense is an abomination to me. New moon and... the calling of convocations... solemn assembly... my [God's] soul hates... even though you make many prayers, I will not listen...' (Isa. 1:13-15). The Old Testament prophets from Isaiah to Malachi inveigh against this. John 1:12, 13 specifically rejects such notions.

There are, however, only four formal theories known to the present author, views defended by doctrinal authorities. One holds salvation to be conveyed by an experience, something that happens in the heart through the direct operation of God without any means whatsoever. People of this persuasion – which goes technically by the name of 'mysticism' – are fond of giving their listeners a precise year, month, day, hour and minute when 'I was there when it happened and I ought to know'. There are both predestinarian and 'free will' varieties of this view. As we shall see, this outlook contains more than a germ of truth, but it is not an adequate explanation of the operation of God in bringing salvation to us.

Another view, Roman Catholic (and other) sacramentalism, holds that when the water of baptism is applied (with intent to baptize, and whether by ordained priest or layman) the guilt of original sin is removed and in the case of infants, if they die soon thereafter, salvation is complete. Four other rites of religion are necessary to save older persons.

A third view holds that in the case of infants the gospel is 'preached' to the heart of an infant by his baptism and that the heart of the infant truly hears and responds in faith at that moment and the infant is saved. So far as I know this doctrine is taught only by certain Lutherans. Regretfully, this author must firmly reject all three of these views in favour of what he is convinced the Bible distinctly teaches, in agreement with the vast majority of evangelical Christian scholars and lay believers of all ages.

---

7. E. M. B. Green, *The Meaning of Salvation*, p. 113.

The question of infant salvation is, of course, a problem which neither the Bible, itself, nor reflection upon the subject has fully answered. Every thoughtful Christian must be concerned about it. That baptism, however, is not the pole about which the question revolves is coming more and more to be acknowledged. This will be treated later in these pages.

The biblical teaching is simply that salvation is brought to sinners through the sole instrumentality of a message (the gospel) – this message, however phrased, being that God has effected a deliverance through His Son, that this message has its source in the Holy Scriptures and is governed wholly by the Holy Scriptures; it is addressed through the understanding to the heart, which is the seat of decision; that the understanding is enlightened by the Holy Spirit who also enables the heart to respond in faith. This matter also will be dealt with more at length later in connection with the doctrine of faith.

Let us close for now with some rather extensive Scripture quotations that clearly and distinctly teach that the gospel is God's sole means of conveying salvation to sinners.

Faith follows hearing the gospel: 'So faith comes from hearing, and hearing through the word of Christ' (Rom. 10:17); 'In him you also, when you heard the word of truth, the gospel of your salvation, and believed in him, were sealed with the promised Holy Spirit' (Eph. 1:13).

The gospel itself is the appointed means: 'For I am not ashamed of the gospel, for it is the power of God for salvation to everyone who believes' (Rom. 1:16); the Spirit sent Peter to Cornelius, and the Spirit told Cornelius, 'Send men to Joppa, and call for Simon, whose surname is Peter; Who shall tell thee words [*hrēmata*, the spoken word, i.e. the gospel], whereby thou and all thy house shall be saved' (Act 11:13, 14 KJV). Starkly put, but correctly, there is an important sense in which we are *saved by words*.

The gospel, itself, has power (the Spirit of God accompanying) to produce the new spiritual life of the saved: after speaking of redemption by the 'precious blood of Christ' (1 Peter 1:18-20) and of his readers' faith, Peter concludes that they are 'born again, not of perishable seed but of imperishable, through the living and abiding word of God…And this word is the good news [gospel] that was preached to you' (1 Peter 1:23, 25). Finally, in this connection another text of Scripture advises that men 'receive with meekness the engrafted word, which is able to save your souls' (James 1:21 KJV).

C. A. Hodge, refuted by contemporary Robert Dabney, insisted that the Word, or gospel, accompanies but is not instrumental in opening the heart to believe. Hodge insisted God, by a sovereign act of omnipotence, opens the heart first, then the Word enters savingly. Dabney insisted that the Word is the instrument of opening the heart. It is a technicality which others have addressed, some favourably, some unfavourably. I think it may be a fruitless discussion. The Bible does clearly say 'faith comes from hearing, and hearing through the word of Christ' (Rom. 10:17). The problem of the relation of Word and Spirit in regeneration and faith will recur again and again in following chapters, never achieving full solution.

All of God, All by Grace, All Through Faith.

The three ideas in this heading have already appeared in the foregoing discussion. They deserve special note as characteristic features of the biblical way of salvation. It is of interest that even those denominations that assign a prominent place to the meritoriousness of good works as a procuring cause, formally endorse these ideas. Throughout the medieval period the papal church claimed to be a religion of grace and faith. The canons and decrees of the Council of Trent give formal service to the same. A sharp difference of interpretation of both grace and faith is glaringly exposed. Hence it is evident that the biblical meaning of grace and of faith is supremely important to a sound doctrine. This matter also will be discussed later in these pages in connection with grace and faith.

3
Ordo Salutis, or the Order of Salvation

In this chapter we consider several truths related to the whole scope of subjective soteriology, i.e. the actual effectuation in and for the sinner himself of all the fruits possible through Christ's finished work of redemption. We shall first consider just what the various elements of this 'personal' salvation are. Then come some minor but important controversies related to the logical and possibly chronological order of these elements. When Latin was still the language of scholarly discourse the term for this topic was *ordo salutis*. After that we focus on two aspects: grace and union with Christ which, as we shall see, are involved throughout at every stage, process, event or action.

The Aspects of Personal Salvation and Their Order.

Think for a moment of the terms you have heard in sermons or have read in the Bible when salvation was being discussed. Words such as conversion, born-again, justification, repentance, regeneration, faith, grace, sanctification come to mind. Quite a list can be assembled. Classes of mine have in five minutes volunteered two dozen or more. Upon refinement some turn out to be synonyms for one another – new birth, regeneration, born-again for example. Some turn out to be subdivisions of others, i.e. acceptance of Christ being an aspect of faith; others have special overlapping relation – repentance and faith being the negative and positive sides of conversion. Some of the words are common everyday terms (faith); some are common to Scripture but rare elsewhere (sanctification); some are common but have rather narrow significance in Christian doctrine (perseverance). Not one, however, was specially invented as a peculiarly theological word. Good understanding of biblical doctrine does not usually require many special words, rather a thoughtful pursuit of the meaning and relationships of words people everywhere use. Some of them acquire a special, restricted meaning in the Bible and its doctrines. Christianity must be a 'faith' of the common man or it loses its genius. Our Savior was a carpenter by trade and several of the founding apostles were fishermen. For the most part the sublime and profound ideas in New Testament teachings are written in the language of fishermen, farmers and tradesmen – people, however, who 'went to church' regularly. They were not strangers to the language of biblical, religious devotion, because they had already been immersed in the vocabulary of the Old Testament and of the synagogue worship of Judaism. Throughout Christian history sincere, practicing Christians have learned that language – not from newcomers to faith but from advanced practitioners. If this is to continue then we must stop having one set of meetings for those with 'contemporary' tastes and another set of meanings for those for whom the practice of prayer and devotion, public and private, has already been learned. Since sin is manifold in its harmful effects in mankind – affecting everything that is human – salvation must also be manifold in its aspects and effects. St Peter writes that we are given 'all things that pertain to [eternal] life and godliness' (2 Peter 1:3). It should not be surprising then, that an analysis of the subject in Scripture should find many topics for consideration.

Furthermore, since the human malady of sin is 'systemic' the remedy must be systemic. One need not understand all of salvation to receive salvation's benefits, but every wise 'scribe who has been trained for the kingdom', is like the good householder who 'brings out of his treasure what is new and what is old' (Matt. 13:52). If he does so he will have his treasures previously classified and stored in order to bring them out for use as needed for his guests and others who call at his door for help. So also it is helpful as wise stewards of 'stored' doctrinal treasures to have them 'classified' and 'filed' according to topic and scriptural sources.

John Murray puts the matter in another way. God is generous in everything he has done for the sustenance and comfort of man and beast. He cites Psalm 104 where the poet praises God that He has made the earth teem with good things for all: 'These all look to you, to give them their food in due season' (v. 27); 'wine to gladden the heart of man, oil to make his face shine and bread to strengthen man's heart' (v. 15); 'O Lord, how manifold are your works! In wisdom have you made them all; the earth is full of your creatures' (v. 24). Murray adds: 'The provision which God has made for the salvation of men is even more strikingly manifold.'[1] Murray is saying a discussion of the 'parts' in the 'order' of salvation is necessary to do justice to the amplitude of salvation by God through Christ.

This amplitude is not immediately apparent to convicted sinners like the Philippian jailor who asked, 'what must I do to be saved?' (Acts 16:30). For him it is sufficient for the moment to answer, 'Believe in the Lord Jesus, and you will be saved'. This particular husband and father needed to know that the same offer extended to his whole household: 'and your household' (Acts 16:31). The jailor's faith could not do vicariously for his wife, children, extended family and retainers. Each must do his own believing. Later on, such folk, if faith is genuine, will wish to know what the precious gift of eternal life cost someone else, and how they, 'dead in trespasses and sins', ever came to desire the gift of salvation of whose benefits they were not only ignorant but thoroughly indisposed to desire – 'For the word of the cross is folly to those who are perishing' (1 Cor. 1:18).

As shall be seen, the order in which one conceives these aspects of the application of redemption decides which system of theology one adheres to, with great effect on the type of piety developed. Though there is a common quality to the piety of all Christian groups, the views that are adopted in this area of doctrine have profound effect on preaching and devotional practice.

The form of the arrangement below, while not fully original with me, first appeared in the present form in my lectures at Wheaton College about 1954. I have been flattered to see it copied exactly in a presently widely used textbook of systematic theology in evangelical seminaries and colleges.

The Ordo Salutis or Arrangement of Doctrines in Soteriology

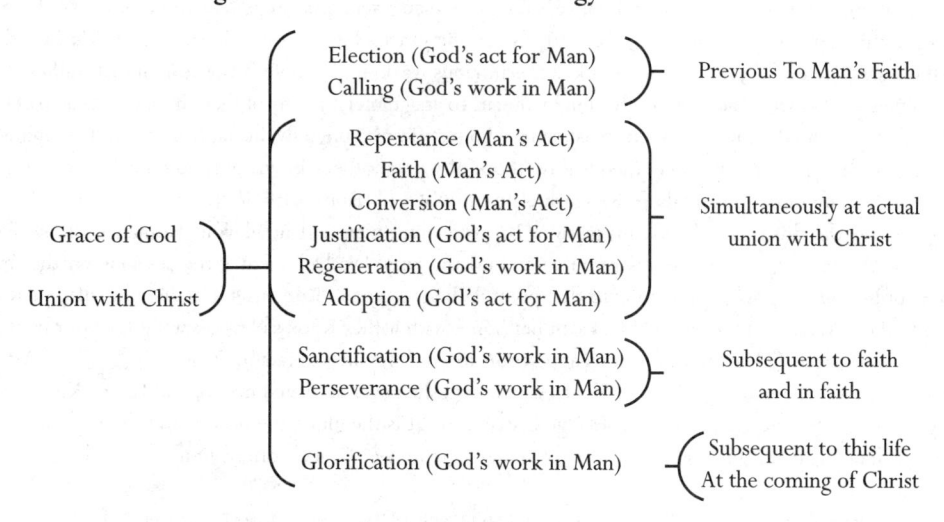

Grace of God
Union with Christ

- Election (God's act for Man)
- Calling (God's work in Man)
  — Previous To Man's Faith

- Repentance (Man's Act)
- Faith (Man's Act)
- Conversion (Man's Act)
- Justification (God's act for Man)
- Regeneration (God's work in Man)
- Adoption (God's act for Man)
  — Simultaneously at actual union with Christ

- Sanctification (God's work in Man)
- Perseverance (God's work in Man)
  — Subsequent to faith and in faith

- Glorification (God's work in Man)
  — Subsequent to this life
  At the coming of Christ

---

1. John Murray, *Redemption: Accomplished and Applied* (Grand Rapids, MI: Eerdmans Publ., 1955), p. 79.

'It is the glory, the power, and the preciousness of the Protestant doctrine that it makes the salvation of sinners a matter of grace from the beginning to the end.'[2]

This outline (called, in technical theology, *ordo salutis*, order of salvation) is mainly a logical order, though there are chronological aspects.

Charles Hodge explains:

> Logical order and chronological succession are different things… the order of nature and order of time are not to be confounded. Many things are co-instantaneous which nevertheless stand in a certain logical, and even causal relation to each other. Christ commanded the man with the withered arm to stretch forth his hand. He immediately obeyed, but not before he received strength. He called to Lazarus to come forth from the grave; and he came forth. But this presupposes a restoration of life. So God commands the sinner to believe in Christ; and he thereupon receives Him as his Savior; though this supposes supernatural power or grace.[3]

The form of the chart indicates that all of applied salvation, from election by God in eternity past on to final glorification, is by God's grace. While no argument is here presented in proof of this assertion the following passages of Scripture will persuade the reverent, industrious student: Romans 5:15, 20, 21; Ephesians 2:8; Romans 11:5; Galatians 1:15; Acts 18:27; 20:24; Titus 3:5; Romans 5:2; Ephesians 1:7; 1 Thessalonians 2:16; 2 Timothy 2:1; 2 Corinthians 12:3, 9; Ephesians 3:8; Hebrews 12:28; 1 Peter 3:19; 1 Corinthians 15:10. These passages show individually that one or another of the listed aspects (or some part of it) takes place by virtue of the grace of God. The essential working of divine grace is treated more at length in the next chapter.

Likewise there is a connection of every aspect of salvation with Christ's life. All Christian salvation is 'in Him'. The precise nature of this union whether forensic or vital will be discussed shortly. For the moment we only cite some of the texts that affirm the union. They relate to many aspects of ordo salutis: Romans 6:1-11; 7:4; Ephesians 2:10; Romans 8:1; Ephesians 1:6; 2:13; Romans 6:4; 1 Corinthians 1:4, 5; 6:53-56; 1 Corinthians 10:16-18.

Some Important Distinctions Within the 'Order of Salvation'.

The outline of the order of salvation, with accompanying qualifying remarks, distinguishes three things as to the character of each of the eleven events or processes in the central column (election to glorification) involved in Christian salvation. Some are God's *act for* man while others are God's *work in* man. And while certain are man's *act*, none is man's *work*. Works are meritorious (they call for wages). Human acts are not meritorious. We think of such an event as a divine appointment, or thought, or forgiveness of sin, as an act. It is not a work, producing effects in the external world of things. A work, however, is an effect-producing event, as for example, God's call whereby through Word and Spirit He reaches into the heart of a sinner and draws him to Himself. All works are, of course, acts, but not all acts are works.

Three items – repentance, faith and conversion – are man's acts. Man repents and believes. God cannot and will not do his repenting and believing for him, though by grace God does enable some so to do. Yet, though in official Roman Catholic dogma faith is a work, a meritorious work, in the Bible faith has no merit: rather faith is the abandonment of the whole project of salvation by merit. To assign merit to any of these human acts is to deny grace: 'And to the one who does not work but trusts him who justifies the ungodly, his faith is counted as righteousness' (Rom. 4:5; cf. 1-3); 'And if by grace, then is it no more of works: otherwise grace is no more grace. But if it be of works, then is it no more grace: otherwise work is no more work' (Rom. 11:6, 7 KJV).

I once had the difficult task of counseling a Baptist young man and his devout Roman Catholic fiancée in preparation for marriage. The sessions came to an end this way: We had spent three sessions on the first three chapters of Romans. We went peacefully to that point. When we got to Romans 4:1-5 the young lady demanded a Roman Catholic Version of the Holy Bible. I sent her home with Father Knox's New Testament. At our next meeting she firmly announced, 'This cannot mean what it seems to say. I'm going to talk to Father_____'. With that the sessions ended and the marriage never took place – though she never returned my copy of Father Knox![4]

Again the insight and clarity of C. A. Hodge instruct us: 'It is the glory, the power, and the preciousness of the Protestant doctrine that it makes the salvation of sinners a matter of Grace from beginning to end.'[5]

---

2. Charles Hodge, *Systematic Theology iii*, originally published 1871–1873 (Grand Rapids, MI: Eerdmans Publ., 1970), p. 174.
3. ibid., p. 173.

If the reader does not immediately understand these distinctions let him keep an open mind to the proposition that no right preaching of gospel Christianity is possible without them. Pray for help and read all the texts and this part of this discussion again. These things come by spiritual vigor coupled with a sound mind. Fuzzy, good feelings can be no substitute for 'the spirit of a sound mind'.

No construction of *ordo salutis*, including the one suggested here, should be regarded as wholly adequate. *Justification* is the imputation of Christ's righteousness to the one who has *faith*, yet faith is the act of one who has been effectively *called* and to whom sufficient spiritual life and discernment have been imparted (that is *regenerated*) to *repent* and *believe*. This conflict has borne the fruit of endless controversies, which do not appear fully capable of being settled.[6]

It seems obvious that regeneration cannot be separated either in logic or chronological succession from repentance and faith, which constitute conversion. Which of the spokes of a wheel starts first? Of course when the cart moves ahead all the spokes move together and do so simultaneously. The ray of light and the ray of heat arrive at the same time. Sensation and perception even though they occur simultaneously – for example, seeing this printed word and perceiving it as printed word – occur simultaneously, yet the sensation is the cause of the perception even though they occur simultaneously.[7]

The problem of *ordo salutis* or 'the order of grace in the application of redemption' has figured importantly in Protestant theology, especially in the period of Lutheran scholastic orthodoxy (seventeenth century) and to a lesser degree among the Reformed (the rest of us).

For Luther, faith was a prerequisite for baptism. He took one of his famous immovable positions on Mark 16, 'whoever believes and is baptized will be saved'. It was one of his decisive theses that sacraments save only when they are received by faith.[8] At first (and as late as four years after proposing the famous *Theses of 1517*) he declared the required faith was the faith of the believing sponsors of the infant at baptism. A year later he modified his 'stand' – 'Baptism helps no one and is to be administered to no one [infant or adult] unless he believes for himself.'[9] As a result Luther began to teach that the infant over whom the baptismal formula is pronounced and water applied in the name of the triune God does truly believe.[10] He made only feeble effort to prove this from texts that so affirm. Rather, Luther argued, since the kingdom of God welcomes children and to enter that kingdom one must be 'born again of water' (John 3:8), interpreted as baptism, then the Scripture enjoins that little children are to be baptized. 'He is certain that children believe because infant baptism is right and valid – and for no other reason.'[11]

Many have written of the evolution of Luther's thought in this area. The great Reformer's thought developed as he sought pastorally to teach assurance of salvation to his own people. A recent friendly discussion shows how Luther's response to Anabaptist rejection of baptismal regeneration figured in the development of his thought.[12]

When I have asserted these facts of Lutheran baptismal doctrine to students in theology classes – almost all evangelical but non-Lutheran – their faces fall in incredulity. I always carry copies of orthodox Lutheran authors (usually Mueller or Pieper) and follow my assertion by reading the appropriate pages. A corollary of infant baptismal faith is the Lutheran doctrine of baptismal regeneration. This introduces severe problems in aspects of the order of salvation, for the Reformers all insisted faith comes by the special work of the Holy Spirit ordinarily through the Word addressed to the understanding.[13] How can the gospel be understood by an infant? Lutheran theologians usually refer to the case of John the Baptist, who, still in his mother's womb, recognized the presence of the yet unborn Jesus in the womb of his mother (Luke 1:41). Luke, however, does not say the unborn child recognized Jesus, only that the appearance of the mother with Child *in utero* coincided with the 'leap' in the womb of Elizabeth.

---

4. Shortly afterward, the girl married a 'Catholic' man of Mexican nationality. But after several years the centripetal forces of incompatible cultures and spread of educational backgrounds shattered the marriage. I don't know the details, but now many years later the 'Baptist boy' and the 'Catholic girl' married and seem to have lived happily ever after.

5. Hodge, *Systematic Theology*, p. 174.

6. A. A. Hodge, *Outlines of Theology* (Grand Rapids, MI: Eerdmans, 1860, 1957), p. 517.

7. A. H. Strong, *Systematic Theology* (Old Tappan, NJ: Revell, 1907), p. 793.

8. Paul Althaus, *The Theology of Martin Luther* trans. R. C. Schultz (Philadelphia, PA: Fortress Press, 1966), p. 364; cf. p. 348.

9. ibid., p. 349, as cited by Althaus from *Luther's Works*, ed. J. Pelikan and H. T. Lehmann (Philadelphia, PA: Fortress Press, 1955), pp. 32, 14.

10. ibid., p. 365; see also Francis Pieper, *Christian Dogmatics ii* (St. Louis: Concordia Publ., 1951), pp. 448, 449; also John T. Mueller, *Christian Dogmatics* (St. Louis: Concordia Publ., 1955), p. 498.

11. Althaus, *Theology of Martin Luther*, p. 365.

12. 'Was Luther An Evangelical?' by Carl Trueman, *The Practical Calvinist: An Introduction to the Presbyterian and Reformed Heritage*, ed. P. A. Lillback (Ross-Shire, Scotland: Mentor/Christian Focus , 2002), pp. 131–148.

13. J. A. Dorner, *History of Protestant Theology Particularly in Germany ii*, trans. G. Robinson and S. Taylor (Edinburgh: T & T Clark, 1871), p. 155.

J. A. Dorner traced the history of accommodating the schema of any sort of evangelical 'plan of salvation' when infant baptism is thought to follow faith and to confer regeneration. Dorner insists Lutherans have always believed that before saving grace changes a man's heart from death to life he is enslaved by sin, that *liberatum arbitrium* (freedom of will) 'must first be bestowed, to make repentance and faith (*conversio*) possible, and that *then* [emphasis added] faith receives justification'. Lutheran scholastic theology turned handsprings through the scholastic era of the theologians Chemnitz, Gerhard, Scherzer, Calovius, Koenig, Beier, Calixtus, Hollatz. A chief problem was how the system works in the case of baptized (regenerate and justified) Lutherans who fell away, lost their grace of baptism and then repented as adults. On the one hand, in order to give prominence to the distinctly Reformation doctrine of justification there was developed a doctrine of pre-temporal justification by God as a foundation for the whole process of application of redemption. On the other hand some held that all the several stages of the process exist simultaneously.[14]

To keep the allegiance of almost any group of thoughtful people, a religious faith must maintain some semblance of structure wherein tenets of belief fall in consistent logical order. Lutherans to this day have the same problem their namesake had in constructing a stable *ordo salutis*, precisely because of the somewhat incompatible wedding of baptismal regeneration of infants with a doctrine of the spiritual impotence of the unregenerate mind and of a faith that comes by hearing and hearing by the Word of God.

Among Protestants other than Lutherans, the matter of an *ordo salutis* took a somewhat different course, chiefly because few if any connected regeneration with baptism, whether of infants or those who reach the 'age of discretion'.

The developments in soteriology had to do mainly with the place of election in relation to the decrees of God and the rise – more than a generation after Calvin's death – of a developing system of 'Covenant theology' known also to later generations as Federal theology.

The fully developed covenant (Federal) theology, for many like me who while recognizing certain values in covenant theology do not adhere to it, seems to be speculative, scholastic over-refinement of what is otherwise already plain in the Scriptures. It seems remote from the scriptural simplicity of Calvin's *Institutes of the Christian Religion*. Yet when it appeared in its first major development it was formulated as a correction to the growing Reformed Scholasticism. It was a reaction toward a theology drawn from Scripture rather than philosophical speculation. As a system of anthropology and soteriology it was first fully elaborated by a German named Cock (Lat. *Cocceius*) (1602–1669), professor first at Bremen, then Franecker and finally Leyden in the Netherlands. It has been said he invented a biblical theology that gave proper attention to the progress of revelation in the Bible and was perhaps the earliest post-Reformation theologian to find 'room... for a classification of history [in the Bible] into great periods or ages, governed by different principles'.[15] Thus the modern recognition of dispensations or epochs of time in the 'plan of salvation' is seen correctly to have become important to Protestant theology not first in '*dispensationalism*' but in *covenant* theology. Both are variant forms of the recognition of epochs not only in biblical history but in the divine administration of the same.[16]

---

14. ibid., pp. 155–165.
15. ibid., pp. 31–44.
16. Strong, *Systematic Theology*, pp. 612–616; also J. McClintock and J. Strong, 'Federal Theology' in *Cyclopedia of Biblical, Theological and Ecclesiastical Literature iii* (Grand Rapids, MI: Baker Books 1968–1970), pp. 515–520 (excellent); Robert Dabney, like Charles Hodge a Presbyterian and contemporary with him, thoroughly refuted Hodge's Federal theory of imputation. Robert Dabney, *Lectures in Systematic Theology*, first published 1878 (Grand Rapids, MI: Zondervan, 1972), Lecture xxix, pp. 337–351. This note could be enlarged, but further pursuit of this in-house debate among evangelicals in this venue would be a distraction.

4
The Doctrine of Grace

I. Meaning and Use of the Bible Term Grace.

The word for grace in the Greek New Testament is *charis* (pronounced car-ees). It appears at least 125 times, sometimes translated thanks, liberality, favour and such like. In general Greek literature of ancient times and in non-salvational references in the New Testament, it has as wide a range of meanings, as does grace in modern English (elegant living, pleasing decorative pieces; rhythmic, pleasing motion, etc.).

With reference to Christian salvation, however, *charis* (grace) always has the narrow technical meaning of *the unmerited favour of God*. We have already quoted Romans 4:4, 5 and 11:6 to show how grace and works-merit are utterly incompatible in the salvation event. To these add: 'For by grace you have been saved through faith. And this is not your own doing; it is the gift of God, not a result of works...' (Eph. 2:8, 9). As we have already seen, every aspect of salvation, even men's acts of repentance and faith are by the grace of God.

The matter may be further amplified, for in Scripture grace is declared to be an *attitude* of God in sending salvation (Titus 2:11), a *gift* of God imparted to believers (Eph. 4:7) and a *power* of God working in believers (1 Cor. 15:10). Grace as unmerited favour is a name not only for God's method in salvation but the very realm of salvation. The latter is an extension of the former.

1) Specifically, grace is the method of God – apart from and in spite of all human merit or de-merit and work or lack of it – whereby on the basis of redemption and upon the occasion of faith God saves sinful men. We shall have numerous occasions to advert to this, especially in connection with the doctrines of faith and justification, for sinful people are 'justified by his [God's] grace as a gift, through the redemption that is in Christ Jesus' (Rom. 3:24).

2) Grace is also the very realm wherein believing sinners, entering by faith, live out their earthly existence and shall abide forever. They have access to God by faith 'into this grace'; they 'stand' (Rom. 5:2) and shall 'continue in the grace of God' forever (Acts 13:43). It is not an exaggeration to say that in Paul's writings grace becomes a synonym for Christianity.

Two issues connected with grace, which have occupied some of the best efforts of some of the finest Christian thinkers, now come before us.

II. Grace and Law (or Law and Gospel).

Salvation has to do with deliverance from sin – its pollution, power and penalty; and sin is 'transgression of the law' (Gr. *anomia*, lawlessness, 1 John 3:4). Some treatment of what is meant by law is therefore appropriate. The following classic definition and explanation is helpful and submitted with approval:

> 'Moral Law' is that declaration of God's will which directs and binds men, in every age and place, to their whole duty to him. It was most solemnly proclaimed by God himself at Sinai, to confirm the original law of nature, and correct men's mistakes concerning the demands of it. It is denominated perfect (Ps. 19:7), perpetual (Matt. 5:17, 18), holy (Rom. 7:12), good (Rom. 7:12), spiritual (Rom. 7:14), exceedingly broad (Ps. 119:96). Some deny that it is a rule of conduct to believers under the Gospel dispensation; but it is easy to see the futility of such an idea; for as a transcript of the mind of God, it must be the criterion of moral good and evil. It is also given for that very purpose, that we may see our duty, and abstain from everything derogatory to the divine glory. It affords us grand ideas of the holiness and purity of God; without attention to it, we can have no knowledge of sin. Christ himself came, not to destroy, but to fulfil it; and though we cannot do as he did, yet we are commanded to follow his example. Love to God is the end of the moral law as well as the end of the Gospel. By the law, also, we are led to see the nature of holiness and our own depravity, and learn to be humbled under a sense of our imperfection. We are not under it, however, as a covenant of works (Gal. 3:13), or as a source of terror (Rom. 8:1), although we must abide by it, together with the whole preceptive word of God...[1]

Some exponents of dispensational outlook claim to be in formal disagreement with this common Protestant outlook, but in actual life-practice and preaching are in full conformity with it. It should not be a matter of important disagreement.

The situation is further clarified when we see the whole Bible, with due attention to dispensational distinctions, under the categories supplied by 2 Timothy 3:16: '...is breathed out by God and profitable for teaching, for reproof, for correction, and for training in righteousness... [to make us] equipped for every good work'. Paul, who certainly was no legalist, found it useful to lead people to Christ, i.e. to show them that they are helpless and condemned, utterly hopeless without grace (Gal. 3:19-22), and he found law's righteous standards to be useful goals for Christian living (Rom. 8:4). Paul frequently brought 'the Law', that is the Old Testament Scriptures, especially the Pentateuch, to bear on Christian duties by such expressions as 'also says the Law' or 'Moses says' or 'the Scripture says' and similar ways of making the law relevant either as statute or mere information or as duty.[2]

The law of God is proclaimed in all parts of the Bible, that is, in the sense of the holiness of God expressed as the standard of all true goodness: 'but as he who called you is holy, you also be holy in all your conduct [manner of living ASV], since it is written, "You shall be holy; for I am holy"' (1 Peter 1:15, 16; cf. Lev. 20:7).

If this, however, were the sole emphasis of Scripture we would be utterly cast down, under condemnation and without hope. So beginning with the same chapter wherein man's first sin appears (Gen. 3) the gleams of divine grace appear also. The God of all true law who drove them from the garden precisely as He said He would, came seeking Adam, calling, 'Where are you?' graciously provided the clothing of animal skins and delivered the first promise of the coming Redeemer, the 'seed of the woman' (Gen. 3:9, 15).

When it is more appropriate, a fuller discussion of the 'proper uses of the Law' will be introduced. Understandably an important matter to the Reformers and the early Reformation churches, hence lengthy sections of their documents treat the subject. The Lutheran *Formula of Concord* (Art. VI, 'Of the Third Use of the Law',)[3] sets forth the Lutheran view of the proper service of the law, both for unbelievers and for believers. Calvin's remarks in the *Institutes of the Christian Religion* are in essential agreement. Any one who considers all Calvin has to say on the subject will know for certain that he proclaims Gospel freedom from the law together with announcement of the importance of knowing God's revealed moral will as set forth in all parts of the Bible. His views are pretty well summarized in Book I, Chapter XI. The *Westminster Confession*, Chapters XXI, 'Of the Law of God' and Chapter XXII 'Of Christian Liberty, and Liberty of Conscience' (edition of Free Church of Scotland, XIX; XX in Presbyterian Church U.S.A. Edition) are in the main a model of sound doctrine worthy of the attention that many generations of preachers in preparation were asked to apply to it.

---

1. J. McClintock and J. Strong, *Cyclopedia of Biblical, Theological and Ecclesiastical Literature vol. v* (Grand Rapids, MI: Baker Books, 1968–1970), pp. 283, 284.
2. B. B. Warfield, *The Inspiration and Authority of the Bible* (Philadelphia, PA: Presbyterian & Reformed Publ., 1958), pp. 299–348.
3. Philip Schaff, *The Creeds of Christendom, iii*, 6th ed. rev. and enlarged (Baker Book House, 1966), pp. 130–135.

In the Scriptures even God Himself requires of Himself that He act in accordance with moral law – which is of course His own holiness, to be defined as His own 'self-affirming purity'.[4] On this view of what the divine holiness is, there is no problem of supposing that God brings Himself to a standard. Most of the English and literature courses listed on my college transcript were taught by a learned gentleman (Levi Leedy Garber of Ashland College) who was also a debate coach. If someone had proposed the question: Is something right or wrong because God says so, or, does God say so because it is wrong? (medieval scholastics debated this question.) – Professor Garber would have instantly pronounced, 'Not a debatable question'. Of course God has a standard of right and wrong. He Himself is the standard. As a holy God He affirms His own moral purity and His own character defines what 'moral' is. This ancient 'problem' frequently dragged out is a pseudo-problem.

It is helpful, in understanding the relation of law to grace in assessing Christian duties, to be fully aware that there is a rather broad range of reference wherein Scripture speaks of 'law'. This is true of *torah*, the Old Testament Hebrew word and *nomos* the Greek word to translate *torah* in the ancient Greek translation (*Septuagint*) and consistently in the New Testament.

1. *Torah* is the moral instruction by parents. Proverbs 1:8 pairs the *torah* (law) of one parent with the *musar* (instruction) of the other.

2. It seems to be the whole divine revelation in Psalm 1:2, though perhaps the whole of written Scripture of the time.

3. In John 10:34 Jesus cites Psalm 82:6 as from 'your law' (that is the Bible of 'the Jews', our Old Testament). So the whole Old Testament is 'the law'.

4. Frequently 'the law' is matched with 'the prophets' or 'Psalms' and the *Torah* of Moses, the Pentateuch (Luke 24:44; cf. Matt. 11:13).

5. Sometimes as in Psalm 19:7 (cf. Ps. 23:3) *torah* of the LORD seems to be an element in the written Scripture parallel with other elements such as testimony, precepts, commandments and ordinances. In it God brings comfort to the soul. This has overtones of good news not bad news. Let us recall that the same twentiethth chapter of Exodus that says God visits the punishment of fathers upon children to the third and fourth generation (Exod. 20:59) adds that He shows mercy unto thousands (Exod. 20:56). Among David's terms for elements in the law in Psalm 19:7–9, 'commandments' is not a comprehensive term for the whole either of the Pentateuch or the whole of the Old Testament.

6. In some cases in the New Testament 'the law' designates the ritual-ceremonial code (Heb. 10:1) embedded in the last four books of the Pentateuch.

7. Both Jesus and the writers of the Epistles frequently are thinking of the Ten Commandments as 'the Law', elaborated by the prophets (Matt. 22:36-40). Jesus says the decalogue may be summarized as duty to love God (the first four 'words') and duty to love man – one's 'neighbor' (the last six 'words'). When Paul says: 'therefore love is the fulfilling of the law' he specified love of God and love of neighbor and is referring specifically to the decalogue (Rom. 13:8-10).

The foregoing show that in some important sense 'the law' of God has relevance to Christian life 'under grace' as Paul characterizes the relation, even if 'we are not under law' (Rom. 6:15). Let us conclude that (1) the Christian has no covenant obligation to any part of the particular legislation laid down by Moses for the conduct both of national-religious and personal life such as Israel had, but (2) as 'training in righteousness' the whole of Old Testament Scripture remains both *for* us and *to* us. Whatever it reveals of God's will for men in general and believers in particular gives light to our path (Ps. 119:105) today, the same as it did when the unknown author of Psalm 119 sang 176 verses of praise to 'the law of the Lord... testimonies... commands... precepts... statutes... judgments... [God's] word... ordinances' and asked the LORD, 'Open my eyes, that I may behold wondrous things out of your law' (Ps. 119:18).

The Reformation discovered only three 'uses of the Law'. Robert Dabney, whose profound knowledge and practical wisdom enlightened Presbyterians of the American South during their most troubled years of the nineteenth century found five. God, he said, 'cannot but reveal Himself as He is... these precepts are the inevitable expression of a will guided by immutable perfections. It is therefore impossible that any dispensation, of whatever mercy or grace, could have the effect of abrogating righteous obligation over God's saints'.[5] His five points are:

First, the law must, under every dispensation, be the authoritative declaration of God's character. *Second*, the law convicts us of our need of Christ. *Third*, 'The great end, the believer's sanctification, can only be attained by giving

---

4. A. H. Strong, *Systematic Theology* (Valley Forge, PA: Judson Press, 1907), p. 268.
5. Robert Dabney, *Lectures on Systematic Theology* (Grand Rapids, MI: Zondervan, repr. 1972), p. 353.

him a holy rule of conduct.' *Fourth*, as published today, 'its precepts' 'instruct conscience' 'even of the unrenewed' and thus 'lay a foundation for a wholesome civil society'. *Fifth*, 'The publication of the Law is preparatory for that use which God will make of it in the Judgement Day... preparing to close the mouths of the disobedient in that day.'[6]

III. An 'Age of Grace'?

Is it legitimate and truly wholesome, in spite of the presence of both 'law and gospel' in both Testaments, to speak of the present age as 'the age of grace'? By all means, yes. Let us organize our reasons why, around a most pertinent text, Titus 2:11. 'For the grace of God has appeared, bringing salvation for all people'.

The actual 'appearance' of the grace of God had been *long in coming*. Grace began to operate when the God of our first parents spared them after their first sin in Eden. Both of them deserved to die, and except for the plan in the mind of God for the appearance of His grace they would have died. Later God gave a law through Moses to test and prove that grace is the only possible method of human salvation. Finally, when the grace of God came, thousands of years of human history had passed by.

The time of the 'appearance' of God's grace is no mystery. It appeared with the coming of our Lord Jesus Christ. John tells us this:

> And the Word became flesh and dwelt among us, and we have seen his glory, glory as of the only Son from the Father, full of grace and truth... And from his fullness we have all received, grace upon grace. For the law was given through Moses; grace and truth came through Jesus Christ (John 1:14-17).

Paul is even more specific that grace was first made fully manifest in the coming of Jesus Christ. He refers to God 'who saved us and called us to a holy calling, not because of our works but because of his own purpose and grace, which he gave us in Christ Jesus before the ages began, and which now has been manifested through the appearing of our Saviour Christ Jesus' (2 Tim. 1:9, 10).

Of course the grace of God existed and operated long before the birth of Jesus. Grace has always been the only method devised by God for the salvation of undeserving sinners. But – and this is the chief significance of the texts of Scripture just quoted – *grace never became most prominent as God's method* of dealing with sinners *until Jesus came*. The paramount facts about God, known to the people with whom God had evident dealings in those ancient days were His holiness, His wrath on sin and the righteousness of His law. Witness the forty years of wandering, the slaughter of Midianites and Canaanites and seventy years of captivity. Grace is not mentioned 'by name' in the Bible till in connection with Noah at the end of the first great epoch of human history. That the Old Testament saints, however, were fully aware of the grace of their God is evident both in their poetry (Pss. 32, 51, 130, 136) and their Prophets (the book of Hosea, for example). Nevertheless, the Old Testament narrative is in some respects a very grim tale and ends on a very discouraging note. See Nehemiah 13:23-31, perhaps later in time of completion than the last chapter of Malachi.

But everything about the coming of the Lord Jesus Christ manifests the grace of God. Grace with mercy and love are present in every incident connected with the coming of the Son of Man. God's grace *is in the plan of the incarnation* of the Son. The apostle Peter states that before the world was made, it was foreordained that the Son of God should become the 'Lamb of God' slain for the sins of the world (1 Peter 1:18-20).

Grace was always present *in the teaching of Jesus*. A *prodigal* insulted his father's generosity and concern by demanding his inheritance. After the granting of the wicked request and his turning a deaf ear to the father's importunate pleading he left home. In the city he squandered his money on 'wine and revelry' – devouring (as his brother said) his father's living with prostitutes – till at length he found himself penniless, hungry, sick and alone. In misery he repented and returned to his father's house. Upon his approach the gracious father ran down the road to meet him, kissed him, and restored him to a position of respect in the home. Jesus said that heaven is like that father – always rejoicing to receive a repentant sinner back home. A *wicked publican* (tax collector) truly repentant, 'beat his breast saying, God, be merciful to me, a sinner'. Jesus said, 'I tell you, this man went down to his house justified'. An *adulterous woman*, taken in the very act of the scarlet sin, was told by Jesus to 'go and sin no more'. Again, Jesus said, 'the Son of Man came to seek and to save the *lost*' (Luke 19:10, emphasis added). Truly grace was always prominent in the teaching of Jesus.

---

6. ibid., pp. 353, 354.

The grace of God was likewise paramount in the *life of Jesus*. If ever there was a nation that deserved the holy fire of the wrath of God it was the Israel of Jesus' day. They were thieving, murderous, stiff-necked, willful and mean. In the city of Jerusalem there lived the worst of them all, and in that city, their capital, He was to be falsely accused and condemned to die. Yet, 'when he saw the crowds, he had compassion on them, because they were harassed and helpless, like sheep without a shepherd'. And, when He looked on Jerusalem, He wept over the city because He foresaw the fierce judgments about to break upon it. The grace of God was, indeed, prominent in the life of Jesus.

It is one thing to teach grace as a doctrine; it is quite another to live graciously! We have all known some people who have gone so far as to make a hobby of the doctrine of grace – not always presenting it in balance with some other facts of biblical truth. People of this type sometimes, however, are quite ungracious in their dealings with others, even with others who agree with them in their special doctrines. It is a fine thing to teach that God saves men freely in spite of their merit of condemnation; it is even nobler to treat other sinners as God treats them – with compassion and grace.

To behold the crowning manifestation of the grace of God for sinners, of course, one should look neither at Christ's birth, teachings, nor life, but rather at His death. 'Behold, the Lamb of God, who takes away the sin of the world!' (John 1:29). Remember that grace is God's favor to men in spite of their meriting His disfavor. At Calvary is seen the sin of mankind, placed on the spotless Son of God. There, in the midst of the supernatural darkness of the day, when even nature seemed to turn her face from the horrid spectacle (darkness for several hours), is seen the full measure of the wrath of God which sinners deserve to bear throughout eternity, future in a fearful hell, exhausted upon the sinless Son of God. 'For our sake he made him to be sin who knew no sin, so that in him we might become the righteousness of God' (2 Cor. 5:21).

This is at least part of what is meant in the sayings that 'the grace of God has appeared, bringing salvation' (Titus 2:11). 'The Law was given by Moses, but grace and truth came by Jesus Christ.'

> Oh, the love that drew salvation's plan!
> Oh, the grace that brought it down to man!
> Oh, the mighty gulf that God did span at Calvary!
>   (*At Calvary* by William R. Newell).

We saw earlier in the discussion of the *Fall of Man* and the *Doctrine of Sin* that human nature in its entirety was 'vitiated' or corrupted by the Fall. Not only did the Fall affect the body, leading to physical death, but the soul, including our rational (thinking) and moral (conscience) powers was tainted. As Chrysostom wrote in comment on 2 Corinthians 2:14, we are not able to think in a fully correct way about common matters, much less the 'things of the Spirit of God'. This outlook is expressed in the order of salvation *(ordo salutis)*. God must not only provide salvation but cause one (any one who believes) to desire to be saved. God is initiator. It starts with the effective call with which, as Jesus said, the Father brings us to Christ. Thus grace – unmerited favour – is necessary at the start. Otherwise nothing would start.

IV. Grace in Roman Catholic Theology.

Roman Catholic theology also holds to salvation by grace, but not by grace alone, and it does not conceive of grace in the same way evangelical (i.e. Protestant) theology does. This is why earliest 'Protestants' called themselves evangelicals. In Roman theology: 1) the grace of God does enable sinners to repent and believe but not 'mere' grace as the Reformers understood Paul to mean; 2) grace does not impart salvation to believing sinners but divine grace (acknowledged to be unmerited favor of God) enables believing sinners to merit salvation available only because of the infinite merit of the redemption wrought by Christ. This grace is mixed with merit in this system. The Decree on Justification of the Council of Trent, Session VI adds human merit to the merit of Christ in achieving personal salvation. [7] Justification is said to be a growing process of gaining merit by the assistance of grace. Canon 24 on justification says:

> If anyone shall say, that justice [Justification] received is not preserved and also not increased in the sight of God through good works but that those same works are only the fruits and signs of justification received, but not a cause of its increase let him be anathema. [8]

Canon 1., transposed to an affirmative form of statement says divine grace is a process in which good works (not grace) increase the amount of justification. [9] Grace is involved as enablement to gain merit for final justification.

In Roman theology grace is *infused* into us to enable us, if we use it rightly, to merit salvation. The Reformers

---

7. H. J. D. Denzinger, *The Sources of Catholic Dogma*, trans. R. J. Deferrari (St Louis: B. Herder Co., 1957), paras. 792a–810.
8. ibid., para. 834.
9. ibid., para. 811.

heartily rejected this common perception as utterly unscriptural and the Council of Trent, while it tried to find a place for grace, only exacerbated the differences from evangelical doctrine.

Throughout Roman theology of salvation it is assumed that in the Fall, though Adam lost the gift of 'likeness' of God, given subsequent to creation in the divine 'image',[10] the rational powers and moral capacity – including undiminished freedom of the will – are intact and unimpaired. Freedom of the will in Tridentine dogma means freedom unspoiled by sin. We have the same power to choose either good or evil that Adam had before the Fall.

Rome sees how important this view of the Fall is to its system. Therefore at every point in its system, original righteousness in our first parents (i.e. moral likeness to God) is defended as a supernaturally added gift and as such ('in our likeness') could be forfeited and was withdrawn when Adam disobeyed. Man's natural mental powers (including free will, uncorrupted as such) remain in full integrity. To see how Rome insists on this, it is enough to read how Rome treated those who, like Cornelius Jansen (d. 1638), denied it, or to examine Ludwig Ott (*Fundamentals of Catholic Dogma*) and the anathemas of *The Council of Trent*.[11] The Catholic Encyclopedia places Jansenism along with Protestant doctrine in the category of heterodox doctrine.[12]

Yet Rome seems to think grace has something to do with bringing the sinner to faith in Christ. This is said not to be mere *sufficient* grace – which everyone who ever lived has – but *efficient* grace. If I understand the complicated explanations (and I have consulted Aquinas, the Canons and Decrees of more than one Council, and the deliverances of popes) of what is *sufficient* grace for everyone, in the case of the 'elect' it is also *efficient* grace. After all, Romanists know and cite the same Scripture passages Calvinists quote. This is a different route to about the same results Arminians and some Wesleyans attain. Arminians found *restoration* of power to come to Christ in divine *fairness*; the Wesleyans in divine *grace* achieved by the atonement. They all three essentially say God helps but the choosing power as well as duty is rooted in what we all are by a grace (infused) which everyone has in equal amounts. In each case grace and human 'free' will are said to co-operate in coming to faith. Luther condemned this view, Melanchthon adopted it, though waveringly – and history named it synergism.

Rome, in fact, has a very elaborate accounting for grace in its system – much of it derived from the university scholars of late medieval times. This was the scholasticism so fiercely rejected by all the Reformers.

J. Pohle, author of an extensive article on grace in Rome's theology says grace is 'the pillar on which the majestic edifice [!] of Christianity rests in its entirety'.[13] In the course of his exceedingly closely reasoned article, reference is made to *actual* grace, *sanctifying* grace, *healing* grace, *illuminating* grace, *mediate* grace, *strengthening* grace or the grace of inspiration. Pairs of graces are brought forward with a flurry of distinctions regarding how grace is related to free will. *Preventing* grace is said to precede 'the free determination of the will' and *co-operating* grace to follow it. The Thomists have *efficient* grace succeed in leading to faith because of God's infallible prescience or foreknowledge. This lame explanation of election and foreknowledge was rejected by predestinarian Jansenists. And there is dogma concerning 'the state of nature' and 'the *state* of grace'.

I recite these (and there are more) distinctions about grace not to clarify what one should believe but to show how complicated the task is for a system to affirm grace as unmerited favor while at the same time holding that, though saved by grace, one must also merit salvation: that though the merits of Christ are the ground of faith, one must also build a treasury of his own merits as well. Rome wishes to have it both ways. Hence, in the preaching of some (at least some of the time), salvation is wholly by grace through faith on the ground of redemption (Christ's merit) while others preach and their hearers (sadly) believe little differently from a pious Muslim as to the relation of works of merit to eternal salvation. In Rome's theology salvation is not mediated to sinners by a message but by efficacious ceremonies called sacraments, baptism as a minimum. This, however, may not literally always be the case, for, says Rome, if one should desire to have the benefit of the sacrament there is a 'baptism of desire' – no priest, no water, only earnest desire.[14]

Roman Catholic theologians, however, have not given uniform support to official dogmas of 'infused' grace. In Reformation and immediate post-Reformation times there were reversions to the voices of earlier pre-Reformation evangelical preachers: Jan Huss (1369–1415) martyred for his views of faith and grace, for example, Bernard of

---

10. W. G. T. Shedd, 'Tridentine Theory of Original Sin', *A History of Christian Doctrine* (ed. Of 1872 reprinted Minneapolis: Klock & Klock Christian Publ., 1978), pp. 140–149.
11. Ludwig Ott, *Fundamentals of Catholic Dogma*, trans. L. P. Lynch (Rockford: TAN Books and Publ., 1974), pp. 106, 224, 240, 246.
12. *Catholic Encyclopedia: An International Work of Reference on Constitution, Doctrine, Discipline and History of the Catholic Church vol. vi* (New York: Catholic Encyclopedia Press, 1907–1922), p. 710.
13. ibid., p. 689.
14. Ludwig Ott, *Fundamentals of Catholic Dogma*, pp. 311, 313, 314, 356, 114.

Clairvaux (1090–1153), and Hugh of St Victor (d. 1140). All three lived in times when, if one did not attract too much attention, there was considerable liberty of doctrinal expression, especially in preaching. But after the Council of Trent (1545–1563) and following the invigoration achieved by the Inquisition there was more insistence on toeing the line. Grace therefore – always in salvation only as a partner of good works in salvation – was (and remains) a problem for the Roman Church.

At this point a discussion of Jansenism, Molininism, the flight from Augustinian, Thomism and the post-Reformation Roman Catholic Councils would be appropriate but difficult to achieve without writing a small book. Louis Berkhof's summary of 'The Doctrine of Grace in the Church', though in general terms, is accurate and helpful.[15] To see the Roman Catholic view from its own side, see Ludwig Ott, *Fundamentals of Catholic Dogma*' on 'The Mystery of Predestination' and the index to the same on Molinism and Jansenism.[16]

V. Grace in the Theology of Dispensationalism.

That system of evangelical theology known as dispensationalism provided the atmosphere in which many older American evangelical pastors and professors took their first steps in theology – an inconsistency not worked out of the system related to how law is related to grace. Professor Alva J. McClain, a moderate dispensationalist, was also a thoroughgoing Calvinist in soteriology. In one of his lectures I once heard him say of his friend Louis Sperry Chafer's writings: 'Some of the things Chafer has written almost seem to say Old Testament people were saved by keeping the Law.' Then he added that Chafer couldn't possibly mean it. McClain was referring, I feel sure, to the following from Chafer's *Major Bible Themes* (1927) written before the latter's multi-volumed *Systematic Theology*. Chafer is expounding 'The Biblical Meaning of the Word Grace':

> This word, which in salvation truth has but the one meaning of unmerited favour, represents a divine method of dealing with men which has obtained from Adam until the present time, *except for the intrusion of the law system which was in force in the time between Moses and Christ* [emphasis added].[17]

This sentence seems to say from Moses to Christ grace did not save but law-keeping did.

The author follows by interpreting Exodus 19:3-25 as a record of how Israel 'passed from a grace relationship into a law relationship... God proposed the law to them, but did not impose the law on them... which law the people accepted'.[18]

That Chafer had not yet thought the problem through shows up seventeen lines farther on, on the facing page, where he says what looks to many of his embarrassed successors as a direct contradiction:

> God saves sinners by grace, and there is no other way of salvation offered to men... It is also necessary that every obligation be cancelled, and to this end salvation has been made an absolute gift from God.[19]

The same incongruity appears in the notes of the *Scofield Bible* on Exodus 19 and 20. This is not the case in the *New Scofield Bible* of 1967.

The problem is an aspect of the larger question of the relation of the Old and New Testaments. Scholars who espouse the dispensational scheme of biblical interpretation over recent years have gone divergent, if not quite separate, ways in treating this and related problems.

Darrel L. Bock, who is one of several who call themselves Progressive Dispensationalists, in 1994 identified three and perhaps four varieties of dispensational thought.[20] This has splashed over into the larger pool of literature on new forms of 'Covenant Theology'.[21] There is much ferment in this area of thought – an area through which I myself passed long ago and was reflected in my books *Daniel and the Latter Days*, *A Greater Commission* and *The Life of Christ*, and several articles read to the Evangelical Theological Society.[22]

---

15. Louis Berkhof, *Systematic Theology*, 2nd rev. ed. (Grand Rapids, MI: Eerkmans, 1939, 1979), pp. 428–431.
16. Ott, *Fundamentals of Catholic Dogma*, pp. 242, 243.
17. L. S. Chafer, *Major Bible Themes* (Chicago: The Bible Institute Colportage Association, 1927), p. 150.
18. ibid.
19. ibid., p. 151.
20. Darrel L. Bock, 'Charting Dispensationalism', *Christianity Today*, 12 Sept. 1994, pp. 26–29.
21. The Journal *Sounds of Grace* (5317 Wye Creek Drive, Frederick, MD), ed. John G. Reisinger, and the volume *New Covenant Theology* by Tom Wells and Fred G. Zaspel published *New Covenant Media* at the same address.
22. Robert D. Culver, *Daniel and the Latter Days* (Chicago: Moody Press, 1954, 1977), repr. under *The Earthly Reign of Our Lord With His People* by author, 1999); Robert D. Culver, *A Greater Commission* (Chicago: Moody Press, 1985, repr. 1999 by author); Robert D. Culver, *The Life of Christ* (Grand Rapids, MI: Baker Books, 1976), *The Earthly Career of Jesus, the Christ* (Ross-Shire, Scotland: Mentor/Christian Focus, 2002).

5
The Doctrine of Union with Christ

Though 'nothing is more central or basic than union and communion with Christ' according to John Murray, it is equally true 'this mystery of Christ's union with the devout is by nature incomprehensible'.[1] It is so much so that God 'shows its figure and image in visible signs best adapted to our small capacity', according to Calvin.[2] The importance of this union is clear in plain statements by Jesus such as 'I am in you and you in me' and 'apart from me you can do nothing'. Eating and drinking the emblems of our Lord's body and blood in the recurring ordinance of the Lord's Supper brings home the importance of this union to those who observe the ordinance 'with the understanding also'.

It is not quite correct to describe the union of the believer with Christ as an experience. It is rather a truth to be made known and by faith embraced. As stated by the learned preacher-missionary, L. L. Legters:

> When a person begins to apprehend what it means to be united to the Son of God and what he has through this union, he will at once realize that his spiritual growth depends upon a clear understanding of truth rather than an experience.[3]

That Bernard of Clairvaux preached and wrote of the benefits of this union is cited by Calvin.[4] Calvin was only one of many Protestant leaders to see the necessity of first knowing this truth, then of reflecting upon it and feeling in our hearts the comfort and power to be drawn from it. (Calvin discusses this union in over fifty paragraphs throughout the *Institutes* as well as in the *Commentaries*.)

For these reasons wise theology and fruitful response to the revelation of this 'mystery, which is Christ in you, the hope of glory' (Col. 1:27) do not treat it as an 'intellectual puzzle' to be explained. Like the mystery of the incarnation (1 Tim. 3:16), and of the church as the body of Christ (Eph. 5:32), we must humbly seek to master as much as scripture makes known about it and apply the same to our lives individually as individual believers (1 Cor. 6:17-20) and corporately (1 Cor. 3:16, 17) as members of His body, the church.

---

1. John Murray, *Redemption Accomplished and Applied* (Grand Rapids, MI: Eerdmans Publ., 1955), p. 161.
2. John Calvin, *Institutes of the Christian Religion iv*, ed. J. T. McNeil, trans. and ed. by F. L. Battles (Philadelphia, PA: Westminster Press, 1960), art. 17.1
3. L. L. Legters, one of the founders of the Wycliffe Translation Mission, *Union With Christ* (Philadelphia, PA: Pioneer Mission Agency – forerunner of Wycliffe Translators, 1933).
4. Calvin, *Institutes iii*, 2.25.

False Notions of the Union.

Some utterly false notions about the presence of the divine – whether person or essence – in every person are abroad and imbedded deeply in some religious movements. 'New Age'-isms bid their hapless seekers to find God within themselves. The same appears in the romantic and nature English poets in greater and lesser degree. William Wordsworth (1770–1850, Poet Laureate), for example, could hold in tension the notion that human mind could be spelled with a capital M, as a name for God's presence in man, but also 'Nature's self, which is the breath of God', also of human 'Powers, forever to be hallowed' along with orthodox faith in God's 'pure Word by miracle revealed'.[5]

'Union with Christ' in salvation must also be distinguished from the *logos* doctrine of universal presence of Christ in several theologies ancient and modern; also from the true doctrine of the immanence of God in all His creation. Scripture does say God is immanent in all creation (e.g. Ps. 139:1-10) and 'In him we live and move and have our being' (Acts 17:28). There is a divine efficiency that interpenetrates everything in all creation for God 'works all things in all' (1 Cor. 12:6 NASB) and Christ is said to 'fill all in all' (Eph. 1:23). But the scriptural doctrine that God's elect are 'in Christ' and He in them must be understood as different and special. This is rightly said to be:

> a union of life, in which the human spirit, while then most truly possessing its own individuality and personal distinctness is interpenetrated and energized by the Spirit of Christ, is made inscrutably but indissolubly one with him and so becomes a member and partaker of that regenerated, believing, and justified humanity of which he [Christ] is the head.[6]

Identification with Christ or Forensic Union in God's Counsel and in Redemption – to Be Distinguished from Vital, Spiritual Union.

We have already noted that every aspect of the application of redemption is by grace and is 'in Christ'. From the standpoint of the eternal counsels of God and appointment of the Father, God 'chose us *in him* [emphasis added] before the foundation of the world' (Eph. 1:4). Before Jesus came we were already 'in Christ' for his name was to be called Jesus because He would 'save *his people* from their sins' (Matt. 1:21). From this heavenly point of view, that union is as ancient as eternity past, presently prevails, and, according to Romans 8:11 and 18-25, will never end. Yet as the last quotation above indicates, the union is actually effected together with regeneration and faith. It is in this sense that union with Christ ('The Mystical Union', as some tradition calls it) has a place in *ordo salutis*.

We may, therefore, correctly affirm that in the broad sense salvation has its origin in union with Christ in the mind of God. We were not elected one by one in isolation either from one another or from the Son of God. Rather, 'he chose us *in him* [emphasis added] before the foundation of the world' (Eph. 1:4). This union is previous to all else in the 'order of salvation', even to election. Not literally, of course, but in God's reckoning, in the history of procurement of salvation we were present 'with Christ' in His death, burial, resurrection, ascension, exaltation and seated at the right hand of power (Rom. 6:1-11; Eph. 1:7; 2:1-6; Col. 3:3, 4). As John Walvoord suggests, perhaps this relationship is better designated as 'identification with Christ' rather than union with Him.

'Hence', says John Murray:

> we may never think of the work of redemption wrought once for all by Christ apart from the union with his people which was effected in the election of the Father before the foundation of the world… we may never think of redemption in abstraction from the mysterious arrangements of God's love in wisdom and grace by which Christ was united to his people and his people were united to him when he died upon the accursed tree and rose again from the dead.[7]

As elect believers in Christ we have been identified with him at every stage of His redemptive work. We are said to be *crucified* with Him (Gal. 2:20), we *died* with Him (Col. 2:20), we were *buried* with Him (Rom. 6:4), *made alive* and *raised up* with Him (Eph. 2:5, 6). Presently we are positionally *seated with Him in the heavenlies* (Eph. 2:6).

---

5. Wordsworth, *The Prelude*, Book v, line 45; lines 17, 20, 21, 22.
6. A. H. Strong, *Systematic Theology* (Valley Forge, PA: Judson Press, 1907), p. 795.
7. John Murray, *Redemption Accomplished and Applied*, p. 162, 163.

We are ideally and *de jure* complete in Him, as it is written, 'And ye are complete in him' (Col. 2:10 KJV), defective and immature as *de facto* we are just now. As I look at myself and those I love with our syndromes of mental and physical defects – especially as for ten years I daily watched a precious wife deteriorate before my eyes, yet beholding her wavering but unfailing trust in God, I tried each day to see her as God presently beholds and shall bring to pass when we behold one another in the resurrection of the last day and the Marriage Supper of the Lamb for which the bride shall have made herself ready.

The Effected Union of Believers with Christ.

Now as to *inception of the relationship*, the *actual* union with Christ occurs in the history of each believer. Exactly when is known to God but not necessarily in each case to us. The hymn writers have it right. There is a moment, however, when 'silently how silently the wondrous gift is given, when God imparts to human hearts' the gift of life 'in Christ'. 'I once was lost but now am found, was blind but now I see.' Believers are reminded that even though 'he chose us *in him* [emphasis added] before the foundation of the world' (Eph. 1:4), as Paul wrote, the same people were once 'dead in the trespasses and sins' (Eph. 2:1). 'But God… even when we were dead in trespasses, made us alive together *with Christ* [emphasis added] (by grace you have been saved)' (Eph. 2:4, 5 KJV). This happened in God's time. In another Epistle Paul points out that 'God is faithful, by whom you were called into the *fellowship* [emphasis added] of his Son' (1 Cor. 1:9). This call is more than an invitation, rather a summons, like the Lord's 'cry of command', the archangel's 'voice' and 'the trumpet of God' on the day of our future resurrection (1 Thess. 4:16). It brings the one 'dead in the trespasses and sins' to life. Jesus spoke of this spiritual call and resurrection in John 5:24, 25, connecting this event with hearing the Word, believing it and passing from death to life.

From our human point of view – another point of view also to be found in Scripture – the call of God is an invitation like the one in Revelation 22:17, 'let the one who desires take the water of life without price' or Isaiah 55:1, 'Come, everyone who thirsts, come to the waters… without money', etc. John the 'Revelator's' version of the invitation appears to paraphrase Isaiah's. Many of us are familiar with the 'invitation hymn' and moments for 'decision' at the end of church services and evangelistic meetings. Many 'come to Jesus' in such a setting. Yet in whatever setting one comes, upon reflection guided by Scripture, one must know he or she was *brought to Jesus*, even though the mind moved the legs to respond to the call to 'come forward' or perhaps to apply for Christian baptism.

How Is the Union Effected.

The union is effected wholly by the Holy Spirit – One who is also called 'the Spirit of Christ' (Rom. 8:9). Similarly, 'Whoever abides in the teaching has both the Father and the Son' (2 John 9; cf. John 10:38). Therefore, though in some mysterious sense the members of the Godhead cannot be separated, in another sense they must be distinguished as to peculiar office. Throughout the Gospels and the first chapter of Acts the 'coming' of the Spirit is a promise. John 7:37-39 brings this into clear focus: '…Now this he said about the Spirit, whom those who believed in him were to receive, for as yet the Spirit had not been given, because Jesus was not yet glorified'. That complete glorification was future still when the risen Jesus last appeared to the disciples. They were promised, however, it would not be 'many days from now' (Acts 1:5). During His last evening before crucifixion, Jesus spoke at length of this future event.

Let us not confuse the clear teaching by supposing some single covenant of which Old Testament and New Testament are only two administrations. He plainly said that as believers, before the closing events of His life on earth, the Spirit had already been '*with* [emphasis added] you' but when He should come the Spirit 'shall be *in* [emphasis added] you' (John 14:17).[8] Further, it was necessary for Jesus to leave as to His personally incarnate self, otherwise the Old Testament stage of revelation and salvation history would remain in effect. He who had always been with His people and already 'dwells with you' (John 14:17) by the special coming of the Holy Spirit would not come in this way until the *incarnate* Son should depart for heaven. Here are Jesus' words: 'I will come to you' Jesus said (John 14:18). But it would be a 'spiritual coming' for He had just said: 'Nevertheless… it is to your advantage that I go away, for if I do not go away, the Helper will not come to you. But if I go, I will send him to you'

---

8. There is some textual evidence that 'shall be' (*estai*) should be 'is' (*esti*). Bruce Metzger, *A Textual Commentary* on *The Greek New Testament* (New York: United Bible Societies, 1975), p. 295, states: 'A majority of the Committee interpreted the sense of the passage as requiring the future *estai*, which is adequately supported . . . ' Authorities still are not in full agreement.

(John 16:7). The event of Pentecost was a scheduled, epochal, 'dispensational' event. The relation of believers then living and of all future believers was changed and improved. Together with the events of the previous fifty days it was and remains the hinge of salvation history.

The gift of the Spirit to the redeemed was quite as essential to the plan of redemption as the gift of the Son, as N. B. Harrison said:

> [T]he two gifts are likened to the unfolding of the Father's plan. Of the Son it is said, 'When the fullness of the time was come, God sent forth his Son... to redeem... that we might have the adoption of sons' (Gal. 4:4, 5). And when He had accomplished redemption, and men could be brought as sons into his family, then [and only then, not before] 'God sent forth the Spirit of his Son' (Gal. 4:6) to make this an experimental reality.[9]

Near the end of that momentous day Peter publicly explained the amazing event by tracing it to the fact that Jesus, of whose death they were the cause and whose resurrection was well known had been 'by the right hand of God exalted' (Acts 2:33 KJV), had just now that very day 'poured out this that you yourselves are seeing and hearing' (Acts 2:33).

The Nature of the Individual Believer's Union with Christ.

There is nothing spectacular about initiation of this union. There is no shaking of the house or mighty wind. Though sometimes there is great inward commotion, more often there is an immense tranquillity, both of mind and body. This leads us to consider what Scripture has to say about the nature of the union. In what does it consist and with what consequences?

It Is a Spiritual Union.

Spiritual (a) in the Pauline sense, constituted and controlled by the Holy Spirit; (b) as opposed to physical or natural; (c) as opposed to a moral union of love or sympathy; (d) as opposed to union of essence; or (e) as opposed to sacramental union as held by Roman Catholic dogma and some Lutherans. Let us consider each of these points briefly.

a) The Pauline sense. Paul said, 'You, however, are not in the flesh but in the Spirit, if in fact the Spirit of God dwells in you' and 'Anyone who does not have the Spirit of Christ does not belong to him' (Rom. 8:9). Also, in Ephesians 3:16 Paul affirms that we receive strength 'with power through his Spirit in your inner being' and in verse 17, 'that Christ may dwell in your hearts through faith'. So as the 'spiritual body' of the resurrection is a body of flesh and bone empowered and directed by God's Spirit, a 'spiritual' person is one so directed and controlled by the Spirit (1 Cor. 2:13, 15, 16; see also 1 Cor. 12:13; 1 John 3:24; 4:13). A spiritual union is a union of the believer's spirit with Christ in virtue of the indwelling Spirit of Christ.

b) It is not that natural creaturely connection every human being has with the Creator by virtue of each being God's creation and object of preservation and providence. People everywhere are vaguely aware of this *concursus* inasmuch as Paul spoke of this as already known to the pagan Greeks at Athens – 'In him we live and move and have our being as even some of your own poets have said' (Acts 17:28, 29), 'in him all things hold together' (Col. 1:17).

c) It is not a natural union such as various philosophers propose. In the view of G. W. Hegel (1770–1831): 'Spirit... signifies not a metaphysical ghost, but that totality which is realized in each individual thing.'[10] In several varieties of personalism from the *logos* philosophy of Heraclitus (480–410 BC), Anaxagoras (500–430 BC) and Protagoras (480–410 BC) the 'reason' or *logos* in each of us is a fragment of the divine *logos* (reason, word, logic, mind) which permeates every man – on to Rudolph Lotze (1808–1881) for whom the universe is a connected whole, by individual miracles, with the Monad.

d) It is not a union of mere sympathy, common love or loyalty, such a unity as the first believers of Jerusalem are said to have had: '[T]he company of those who believed were of one heart and soul... they had everything in common' (Acts 4:32). Nor is it like the union of soldiers who go through a long series of battles together, a nation that unites against some common enemy, such as the British displayed in World War II. The unity of believers in Christ in the Upper Room discourse is of a far deeper sort, illustrated (not identical with) by the inter-participation

---

9. Norman B. Harrison, *His Indwelling Presence* (Chicago: Moody Press, 1928), page number lost.
10. 'Philosophy of Hegelianism', in *Twentieth Century Philosophy*, ed. D. D. Runes (New York: Philosophical Library, 1943), p. 168.

of the Father and the Son: 'That they all may be one; as thou, Father, art in me... that they also may be one in us' (John 17:21 KJV).

e) Nor is it a union of essence or substance. There is a streak of this false doctrine in Eastern Orthodoxy whereby the mystical tendency in oriental (i.e. Eastern) thought grasps the phrase 'partakers of the divine nature' (2 Peter 1:4) and develops out of it an ascetic, mystical theology. Salvation reaches climax, it is said, in *enosis* (union) with God or *theosis* (deification).

In the context of 2 Peter 1:4 the ascent of the soul is not *mystical* but practical and ethical, from root in faith developing through virtue knowledge, temperance, endurance, godliness and brotherly kindness to love (1 Peter 1:5-7). The 'partaking of the divine nature' issues from 'God's precious and very great promises' (2 Peter 1:4). The purpose of the promises, says Peter, is for us to have 'escaped from the corruption that is in the world because of sinful desire' (2 Peter 1:4). The 'promise' relates not to a 'beatific vision' as climax to a life of moral and spiritual effort or self-denial but to the experience of the new birth, viz.: 'if anyone is in Christ, he is a new creation' (2 Cor. 5:17); 'we are his workmanship, created in Christ Jesus' (Eph. 2:10). Though there is a 'mystical union' and some speak correctly of 'identification with Christ' in His death, burial, resurrection, etc., meaning a forensic union, yet as L. Berkhof warns, it is a 'dangerous error' to assert it is 'a union of essence, in which the personality of the one is simply merged into that of the other'.[11] The union Jesus described in John 14:23, 'we [the Son and the Father] will come to him and make our home with him', is entirely beyond our ability to explain – like all supernatural events.

The ascent is not to the solitary beatific vision of asceticism but to love of both man and God as a climax to growth in the company of other people. Nor is it a sacramental union, wherein by an ecclesiastical ceremony such as baptism or by consuming the *emblems* of our Lord's body and blood, faithful believers receive direct spiritual nourishment from the real presence of Christ's body and blood, whether in or with the elements (some Lutheran doctrine) or their real presence by mystic transformation of the elements (as in Roman Catholic doctrine). Both theories lack the support of Scripture and contradict the fact that the physical body of Christ is in heaven, where His local physical presence shall remain, as Peter said, 'until the time for restoring all the things about which God spoke by the mouth of his holy prophets' (Acts 3:21).

It Is a Supernatural or Mystical union – If Properly Defined.[12]

We relate the idea of mystical to the word mystery in the New Testament, not to mysticism. 'Mystical' is shorthand for something which 'no eye has seen, nor ear heard, nor the heart of man imagined... revealed to us through the Spirit' (1 Cor. 2:9, 10). The specific scriptural basis usually cited is Colossians 1:24-29. Parallel texts in two of Paul's other letters (Eph. 3:1-10 and Rom. 16:25-26) should be read with the Colossians text. The mystery in each of the three passages has to do with something unknown in former ages – that sometime in the future (the present age) Jews and Gentiles would be undifferentiated as members of one body and that therefore a mission was mounted to let all the peoples of the whole world know about it. Hence 'Christ in you' (Jews and Gentiles individually as saved persons and collectively as the church or body of Christ) is the mysterious (till now) union.[13] L. Berkhof modifies this explanation: 'Subjectively the union between Christ and believers is effected by the Holy Spirit in a mysterious and supernatural way, and for that reason is generally designated as the *unio mystica* or mystical union.'[14] A. H. Strong prefers to call it 'an inscrutable union', cautioning, 'If we call it mystical at all it should be only because, in the intimacy of its communion and in the transforming power of its influence, it surpasses any other union of souls we know, and so cannot be fully described or understood by earthly analogies.'[15]

The mystery of this union of the believer individually and of the church collectively – both the living and the dead – has some of the same indescribable mystery about it as the union of Father and Son in the Trinitarian relationship. I well remember my own puzzlement when I first heard the doctrine preached as a young adult. The

---

11. Louis Berkhof, *Systematic Theology* 2nd rev. ed. (Grand Rapids, MI: Eerdmans Publ., 1938, 1979), p. 401.
12. There is a long history of the notion of mystical union with God or Christ supposed to be superior to the union with Christ which all believers have. For a start, read D. D. Martins short article '*Unio Mystica*' in *Evangelical Dictionary of Theology*, ed. W. Elwell (Grand Rapids, MI: Baker Books, 1984, 1991), p. 1126.
13. The above explanation of appropriation of the term 'mysterical' in this connection agrees with John Murray's thoughts (*Redemption Accomplished and Applied*, p. 166 ff.).
14. Berkhof, *Systematic Theology*, p. 447.
15. Strong, *Systematic Theology*, p. 801.

preacher was no less than L. L. Legters one of the founders of what became Wycliffe Translators and the related enterprises now putting the Bible in dozens of languages around the world. He dragged a large leafy grapevine to the pulpit, tried to tear it apart and could not, explaining the unique intertwining of branches with the main stock. Then turning to John 17 (the union of Father and Son) and John 15 (the Parable of the Vine and Branches) he drew the lesson: 'Without me you can do nothing' (John 15:5).

Yet neither Legters or any other theologian can explain this union[16] In addition to these two analogies Scripture also compares the union to that of the holy temple of God. Believers are the stones of which it is built; Jesus Himself is 'the chief corner stone'; 'apostles and prophets' were its foundation and God Himself its resident (Eph. 2:20-22; 1 Peter 2:4, 5). The union is like the connection of a body of many members with its head (1 Cor. 12:2) and like that of husband and wife who are 'one flesh' (Rom. 7:4; Eph. 5:22-33).

Yet, as must be acknowledged by all, we only know by biblical revelation that the union exists; it is true for me only as I believe. Yet like all truth partaking of heaven and God, 'though now we see him not, yet believing, we rejoice with joy unspeakable'.

James Montgomery Boice commented on these illustrations as follows:

> In each of these cases the central idea is the same: *permanence*. Because Jesus is the foundation and is without change, all that is built upon him will be permanent also. Those who are Christ's will not perish but will endure to the end.[17]

Because of the danger of being understood in the context of ascetic mysticism, the term 'mystical union' should not be used, I think, unless with careful explanation. I have introduced the 'mystical' only to inform the reader how, when the term is met in discourse, one should understand the term. For us it has none of the connotation found in asceticism and mysticism as an approach to salvation.

It Is a Vital Union.

That is another way of saying it is an organic union. One member of such a living body has organic, that is, reciprocal, relation to every other member-organ as well as to the whole. 'God gave us eternal life, and this life is in his Son. Whoever has the Son has life' (1 John 5:11, 12). In Christ's body one is not a replaceable part but of the essence, not merely juxtaposed to one another with Christ the chief engineer and architect. Christ works 'on' us from within, as the lifeblood, so to speak, of each of our spirits. We have 'come to fulness of life in him' (Col. 2:10 RSV).

It Is a Complete Union.

This union is a *complete union* of the believer's whole being, body and soul, with his Lord. When the Spirit of God indwells me He dwells in all of me. This truth is the basis of one of Paul's most earnest exhortations. Many of the Corinthian believers had each harmed himself (not the church, *per se*) – as in our time, the loose mores of the ambient heathenism had found answer in the lusts of the flesh with the result of fornication (sexual immorality) in more than one Corinthian Christian. Paul addressed forty-eight verses in the heart of the first Epistle to this problem and brought forth this: 'Every other sin that a man can commit is outside the body; but the fornicator sins against his own body. Do you not know that your body is a shrine of the indwelling Holy Spirit, and the Spirit is God's gift to you? You do not belong to yourselves; you were bought with a price. Then honour God in your body' (1 Cor. 6:18-20 NEB). Earlier it is said, 'Your bodies are limbs and organs of Christ' (1 Cor. 6:15 NEB). Theft or murder or covetousness, etc. as the text says, of course, are pollutions of the spirit of man but have no debilitating effect or pollution of the body, but one can be a virgin only once. Unlawful sexual intercourse takes away unsullied purity of another sort forever – forgivable, but not restorable from the human side. David became an adulterer and then a forgiven one, and history has never forgotten the fact. Therefore the union of Christ with all of me or of you is a strong restraint against fornicating. The text of 1 Corinthians 6 provides much more of both comfort and threat for our age of the church.

The Union Is Permanent.

It remains to be said that the union is permanent. The union of the Corinthian fornicator with a temple prostitute did not end his union with Christ any more than Peter's thrice denial of Christ ended his ties to the Lord. He showed

---

16. Legters, *Union With Christ*, chap. v, 'Scriptural Illustrations of Our Union'.
17. James M. Boice, *Foundations of the Christian Faith* (Downers Grove: InterVarsity Press, 1986), p. 395, commenting on 'The Mystery of the Union'.

up at the Upper Room on Easter evening with the other Ten. Judas had no spiritual connection and ended up in the city dump and incinerator.

There is, by the Spirit of Christ, a permanent connection with the One who 'lives and reigns' above, whose life is both with us and in us. As a result, Paul argues, '[I]f, while we were enemies, we were reconciled to God through the death of his Son, much more, being reconciled [He holds nothing against us] shall we be saved his life' (*en tē dzōe autou*) (Rom. 5:10 ASV marg.). The argument is from the greater to the less: Before we came to Christ – long before – He died for us. It stands to reason, therefore, that now alive and able, He will rescue us again and again from our sins and backslidings. For, '[I]f anyone does sin, we have an advocate with the Father, Jesus Christ the righteous' (1 John 2:1).

It seems just to argue that we should give our bodies good care while we live and when we die our bodies should be interred in the ground (not cremated as in Roman custom) in something of the dignified posture of sleep. For there is no clear evidence the Holy Spirit resigns His residence in our bodies even in death. The Christian outlook is that the deceased Christian still sleeps 'in Jesus' (1 Thess. 4:14 KJV). The 'dead in Christ' (1 Thess. 4:16) shall rise. The believers in the Christian cemetery at Salonica of old, says the Bible, are 'asleep'; they are 'the dead in Christ' and they 'sleep in Jesus'. Christians through the ages have usually adjusted whatever funerary practice of their ancestors to these comforting facts and have interred their dead bodies, as the Jews before them, in the posture of sleep awaiting the shout, trumpet of God (1 Thess. 4:16) and the voice of the archangel on the resurrection morning.

Let this chapter end with a singular benefit of the believer's union with Christ.

> All self-effort toward transformation of character is futile. The vile pictures hung upon the walls of memory by indulgence in illicit imaginations, in obscenity, in habits of profligacy; the remorse that lingers from animosities, jealousies, ugly self-seekings – how have men sought in vain to purge their souls of these! How many suicides tell the tale of hopeless effort to be free from their relentless lashings. No, it is only the Holy Spirit of God who, coming into the life, can impart purity of mind and holiness of heart, where sin had wrought its havoc. To set sin's captives free – this He has power to do; this He delights to do.[18]

---

18. Harrison, *Indwelling Presence*, p. 22.

6
The Doctrine of Election

Let us make clear at the outset that the doctrine designated 'election' is of persons to salvation rather than, as certain writers would incline us to believe, of groups (Israel, for example) to the privilege, if desired, of being saved, or of people in general to hell or to heaven.

First consideration is now directed to a sort of 'neutral' statement and evaluation – not from traditional enemies of the doctrine nor from controversial advocates, but from the venerable 'Thirty-Nine Articles of Religion', published by the Church of England Convocation of 1562 but resting on Archbishop Cranmer's *Articles* of 1549. Minor changes were made up to 1571. 'Since 1571 no change whatever has been made in the text of the thirty-nine articles.'[1] Leading Reformers, refugees from the Continent, influenced their formulation – John Lasko, Martin Bucer, Peter Martyr, as well as the writings of Luther, Melanchthon, Calvin and others. These articles, the basic creed of the Church of England, were published nearly a century before the Calvinistic creeds usually cited in English speaking lands such as the Westminster Confession of the Puritan Revolution in Britain and earlier than the Savoy Declaration of Congregationalists in England (1658) and the several Baptist and Congregational confessions of Colonial American Baptists, Congregationalists and Reformed, all Augustinian-Calvinists and predestinarian.

Article XVII of the Thirty-Nine Articles of 1562, 'Of Predestination and Election', consists of three paragraphs. The first really treats both election and calling. I shall here quote only the first half of the article – on election – and reserve the second half for the chapter on calling. The second paragraph treats the values of the doctrine of election and the third offers advice on how to receive the doctrine. I shall quote that later. The source of the following is from Gibson's volume, pages 459 and 465.

> Predestination to life is the everlasting purpose of God, whereby (before the foundations of the world were laid) He hath constantly decreed by His counsel secret to us, to deliver from curse and damnation those whom he hath chosen in Christ out of mankind, and to bring them by Christ to everlasting salvation as vessels made to honour.

Anglican scholars say, 'The sources of the article… are thought to be to some extent in the writings of Luther… and the language of the last paragraph… to Melanchthon. Still more important… is it to notice that the description of predestination [in our terms, election] is to a very great extent couched in the language of Holy Scripture…Rom. viii and ix and Eph. i, and the correspondence is even closer in the Latin than in the English.'[2]

---

1. Edgar C. S. Gibson, *The Thirty-Nine Articles of the Church of England Explained with an Introduction*, 8th ed. (London: 1912), p. 47.

It will be news to some that all the first line of Reformers – Lutheran, Reformed, Church of England – endorsed a strong doctrine of election. Major controversy about it and rejection by a small segment waited at least two generations after 1517 (Luther's 95 Theses). It was already a near-universally held Reformation doctrine for nearly a generation before Calvin (who was only about eight years old when Luther sounded the watch cries of the Reformation in 1517) produced the first form of the *Institutes* in the 1530s.

It will help to remove misconceptions which hinder fair treatment if some care is taken to clarify what the doctrine of election is not and in what context of ideas it is presented in Scripture before addressing ourselves to definition and elaboration.

Election is strictly a salvational (soteriological) term. In connection with the doctrine of God and His works, the Bible presents a doctrine of what are styled 'decrees'. God is presented as in charge of history, planning it, overtaken by no surprises, including man's free choices and what philosophers call contingency. But this, though related, is not the same as the doctrine of election. Further, though 'predestination' sometimes means the same as decrees, sometimes it is used to designate God's purposes regarding fallen men only (whether elect or not); it is only rarely used as applying only to the believing, or elect. Hence, there is a much greater breadth of meaning to 'decree' and 'predestination' as used by theological writers than to 'elect' and 'election'. These two latter terms are used (twenty-one times) in the New Testament as follows:[3] *Eklegō* (to elect), twice of God's choice of the Jewish people (Acts 13:17); of Mary's choice of the 'better part' (Luke 10:42); finally, in the largest number of cases of God's choosing (election) of individuals to everlasting life (John 15:16 – perhaps belonging to one of the first category above – 1 Cor. 1:27, 28; Eph. 1:4; James 2:5). *Eklogē* (election) appears only seven times: once of choice to the apostolate (Acts 9:15); once abstractly to 'the election of grace' (Rom. 11:7); but in every other case of God's act of choosing His people to salvation (Rom. 9:11; 11:5, 28; 1 Thess. 1:4; 2 Peter 1:10). A linguistic analysis of related terms could be introduced, but sufficient has been presented to show that 'elect' and 'election' are in the New Testament uniformly used for *benign* choice. Hence it will always be incorrect biblically speaking to speak of God as 'electing' someone to hell. The Bible simply never says it. To repeat, election is a *soteriological* term and should be used only in connection with salvation, not with damnation, which is its opposite.

Some further qualifications and cautions will be helpful in resolving problems and irrelevant objections.

a) Election is a revealed truth of Scripture not a philosophically derived notion. Calvin, for example, approached the teaching from Scripture in all writings wherein he discussed it. Election was not a philosophical presupposition of his teachings, not a point of *departure* in theological formulation, but of *arrival* in submission to scriptural theological formulation.

b) It is a biblical teaching not a sectarian dogma, for election was in the Bible long before any one made either a 'hobby' or a 'whipping boy' out of it. One is commanded to believe it. Try to understand it without 'yes, but'. Biblical texts which establish the truth will be discussed later.

c) It must not be associated with certain pagan or philosophical notions such as *kismet*, *Islam*, *karma*, *Moira* or *fate*. These notions from several ethnic religions have far different bases and are really antithetical to the doctrine of God's gracious election.

d) An all-wise, gracious, loving, Father-God is the author of election – One more wise, gracious and loving than any human being can hope to be. Some objectors appear to conceive of themselves as more gracious than the God of the Bible. They suppose their own hearts to be more compassionate than the heart of the Father who sent His only Son to die for us while we were yet sinners.

e) In seeking to understand election we must not seek to shave off its troublesome difficulties. Such efforts lead to the same kinds of errors which similar efforts with regard to the Trinity or two natures of Christ always create.

It must be 'swallowed whole'. The Nicene Creed swallows the doctrine of the Trinity 'whole' as the Definition of Chalcedon does the Theanthropic Person of Christ. Unitarians of all sorts are only tearing apart the indivisible.

f) It is misleading and a disservice to the whole counsel of God to make election the 'spearpoint' of one's teaching. Contrary to common opinion, no truly great teacher of the past – certainly neither Augustine or Calvin, who sometimes are falsely so charged – ever did so. True, both wrote somewhat at length about election but only to clarify and defend it scripturally and logically.

---

2. ibid., pp. 459 and 465.
3. I am citing the analysis of A. A. Hodge, *Outlines of Theology* (Grand Rapids, MI: Eerdmans Publ., 1957), p. 215.

It is true that Calvin, who in ignorant secular circles is blamed for imposing fatalism on the city of Geneva and all else he influenced, taught a *soteriological* doctrine of election. He also drew from Scripture and the logic of election to salvation a doctrine of 'non-election', which is about what he meant by anything he said about 'damnation' and 'reprobation'. Actually he recommended acceptance of the 'mystery of His will' and no speculation at all about the unrevealed counsels of God. This is the judgment of some of the most careful, comparatively recent, scholarly treatments of Calvin's life and doctrine. I recommend Wilhelm Niesel's chapter 'God's Eternal Election' in *The Theology of Calvin*.[4] and François Wendel, *Calvin* on 'Predestination'.[5] Victor Monod, in a remark quoted by Mitchell Hunter, was precisely correct, in my opinion, in saying that Calvin's doctrine of election (or predestination) is 'a point of arrival not of departure'.[6]

Calvin did not begin his system of theology with the doctrine of 'predestination'. In fact he shunned such a thing. The following lines from the very first paragraphs of Calvin's formal treatment establish the absence of any centrality of election over other aspects of Christian doctrine. He continues after warnings against undue 'curiosity' and leaving 'no secret to God':

> First, then, let them remember that when they inquire into predestination they are penetrating the sacred precincts of divine wisdom. If anyone with carefree assurance breaks into this place he will not succeed in satisfying his curiosity and he will enter a labyrinth from which he can find no exit. For it is not right for man unrestrainedly to search out things that the Lord has willed to be hid in himself, and to unfold from eternity itself the sublime wisdom, which he would have us revere but not understand that through this he also should fill us with wonder. He has set forth in his Word the secrets of his will that he has decided to reveal to us. These he decided to reveal in so far as he foresaw that they would concern us and benefit us.[7]

The sixty-eight pages on election in the *Institutes* (III, 21–24) are devoted not to speculation but to scriptural demonstration and answers to objections. Those sixty pages are recommended to all who either wish to learn about the scriptural doctrine or about the real Calvin.

g) Statements of the doctrine must not go to logical extremes to which the biblical texts lend no specific endorsement. Logical extremes have led to affirmation of tritheism instead of the Holy Trinity and dual personality or some other monstrosity rather than our one Lord Jesus' two natures. The mysteries must be accepted.

h) Election must not be stated or understood in such a way as either to deny complete human responsibility for evil actions or the duty to choose Christ, nor in such a way as to empty the biblical warnings of their force.

i) It bears repetition: election is first, last and always, in Scripture, a soteriological term.

Statement of the Doctrine.

The seventeenth article of the Church of England's Articles has already been given. I defer to a Lutheran at this point:

> Election is the eternal act of God with respect to all who are saved, by which, out of pure grace and for Christ's sake He purposed to endow them in time with the spiritual blessings of conversion, justification, sanctification, and preservation unto eternal life.[8]

Mueller adds: 'This definition embraces all divine truths which Scripture presents in connection with the doctrine of eternal election', and so it does. Note he makes of it entirely a soteriological doctrine.

The Biblical Evidence.

1. First there are direct categorical statements. Let us quote several with brief comments and give references for others. 'God hath from the beginning chosen you to salvation through sanctification of the Spirit and belief of the truth' (2 Thess. 2:13 KJV). '[H]e chose us in him before the foundation of the world... having been predestined according to the purpose of him who works all things according to the counsel of his will' (Eph. 1:4, 11, see context). 'And when the Gentiles heard this, they began rejoicing and glorifying the word of the Lord, and as many

---

4. Wilhelm Niesel, *The Theology of Calvin*, trans. H. Knight (Philadelphia, PA: Westminster Press, 1956), pp. 159–181.
5. Francois Wendel, *Calvin, The Origin and Development of His Thought*, trans. P. Mairet (New York: Harper & Row, 1963), pp. 263–284.
6. A. Mitchell Hunter, *The Teaching of Calvin*, 2nd ed. (Westwood: Revell, 1950), p. 94.
7. John Calvin, *Institutes of the Christian Religion iii*, ed. J. T. McNeil, trans. and ed. by F. L. Battles (Philadelphia, PA: Westminster Press, 1960), art. 21.1.
8. John Theodore Mueller, *Christian Dogmatics* (St. Louis: Concordia Publ., 1934), p. 585.

as were appointed to eternal life believed' (Acts 13:48). There have been objections raised to the relevance of these clear statements, but they still boldly stand there, saying clearly that each believer was elect... chosen... predestined in eternity past.

Romans 8:28-30 identifies in a single *exclusive* group 1) those who 'love God', 2) 'the called', 3) those God foreknew, 4) predestined, 5) sanctified, 6) justified, 7) glorified. There is a single circle, so to speak.

love God
the called
the foreknown
the predestined
the sanctified
the justified
the glorified

Some would create a situation that Paul here specifically rejects.

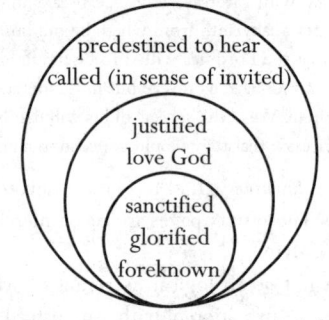

predestined to hear
called (in sense of invited)
justified
love God
sanctified
glorified
foreknown

2. Among other texts directly teaching this doctrine are 2 Timothy 1:9, 'who saved us and called us to a holy calling, not because of our works but because of his own purpose and grace, which he gave us in Christ Jesus before the ages began', and 1 Peter 1:1, 2, 'elect... according to the foreknowledge of God the Father, in the sanctification of the Spirit, for obedience to Jesus Christ and for sprinkling with his blood'.

3. Many biblical statements imply the doctrine. Examples are Matthew 1:21 wherein it is said Christ came to save 'his people'; Acts 18:10 wherein Paul is informed by God, before the evangelization of Corinth, 'I have many in this city who are my people'; and Jesus' prayer of John 17:2, that he may 'give eternal life to all whom you [the Father] have given him'. This list could be extended indefinitely.

Election and its corollary, effective calling, are also necessary inferences from the developments connected with Jesus' sermon on the bread of life to the crowd assembled in and outside the synagogue of Capernaum (John 6:24-59). The topic was suggested by the feeding of the 5,000 the preceding day (John 6:1-14). The crowd was, at first, frantic to catch His every word, but they were dull of heart and entirely missed the point when He announced, 'I am the bread of life; whoever comes to me shall not hunger, and whoever believes in me shall never thirst' (v. 35). Then, discerning that the crowd had nary a glimmer of His meaning, He said, 'you have seen me and yet do not believe' (v. 36).

In the following report of the sermon high points, at least four times, in varying language, Jesus specifically brought forth sovereign divine choice, and thereby occasion to explain, not why some believed but why the foolish crowd did not. They had already *disbelieved*, He says, and these are the reasons why 'All that the Father gives me will come to me [divine sovereignty], and whoever comes to me I will never cast out [human duty and privilege]' (v. 37).

Then after explaining the incarnation as 'the Father's will' He puts the fact of election and calling in that relation, adding '[T]his is the will of him who sent me, that I should lose nothing of all, he has given me' (v. 39).

The record goes on to say, 'so the Jews grumbled about him' on account of His momentous claim to divine origin; to which He responded, again stating that God is sovereign in personal salvation: 'Do not grumble among yourselves. No one can come to me unless the Father who sent me draws him.' To the negative remarks about why many do not believe He adds an affirmative: 'Everyone who has heard and learned from the Father comes to me' (v. 45). This is special calling, a calling that effects willing faith.

As mere nominal disciples always do when faced with the challenge of their own corrupt hearts and the offense of the cross, His followers now began to desert Him. Before they departed, however, Jesus reminded them of something the Old Testament prophets often said: that faith is a spiritual gift through the Word of God (see v. 63). And with an oblique reference to Judas, the traitor in the midst, Jesus concluded His sermon, saying: 'I told you that no one can come to me unless it is granted him by the Father' (John 6:65). Again as at the Nazareth synagogue and still today, 'After this many of his disciples turned back and no longer walked with him' (John 6:66).

When as a young theology student, wavering in acceptance of the doctrines of election and calling, it was Professor McClain's patient exposition of this passage which turned my heart and head forever to vigorous embrace of the biblical truth of divine election and calling. I pray the same for any reader patient enough to follow what I have written above.

The Ground of Election.

'God votes for you; the Devil votes against you; you have the deciding vote' – it is an attractive explanation, but really a denial of election.

'God elected those whom he saw by their own power of choice would believe'. This is attractive but utterly mistaken as to the powers of fallen men (1 Cor. 1:18; 2:14; Eph. 1:1-3). This is the Arminian-Wesleyan view.

The Lutheran *Formula of Concord* (sixteenth century) is wholly scriptural in affirming:

> The predestination, or eternal election of God, extends only over the godly, beloved children of God, *being a cause of their salvation*, which He provides as well as disposes what belong thereto. Upon this [election] our salvation is founded so firmly that the gates of hell cannot overcome it, John 10:28; Matthew 16:18.[9]

The esteemed Lutheran scholar John Theodore Mueller comments further:

> God's eternal election of grace did not take place in view of man's foreseen final faith, but rather embraced this faith together with the whole way of salvation [all elements in *ordo salutis*], such as conversion, justification, sanctification, and final preservation. Hence the believer is not elected because of his foreseen faith; on the contrary, he has become a believer in time because of his eternal election to salvation. In other words, a person is brought to saving faith in time just because God from eternity has graciously elected him to salvation.[10]

He goes on to cite Acts 13:48; Ephesians 1:3-6 and Romans 8:28-30 cited above. The Presbyterian A. A. Hodge expresses the same in brief:

> It is self-evident that the same actions cannot be both the grounds upon which election rests and the fruits in which election is said to result. Since the Bible teaches that 'faith', 'repentance', and 'evangelical obedience' are the latter [i.e. fruits]; they cannot be the former [i.e. grounds]. The Scriptures do so teach in Ephesians 1:4.[11]

Hodge cites in addition 2 Thessalonians 2:13; 1 Peter 1:2; Ephesians 2:10.

It should be observed that Scripture specifically denies that God's choice follows ours (John 15:16). 'You did not choose me, but I chose you', etc. It is important to acknowledge that most of the Lord's remarks to the Eleven in the Upper Room and *en route* to Gethsemane related to the apostles directly rather than to believers at large. He was addressing them as they upon whom the church should be founded (Eph. 2:20). Yet John 15, the Parable of the Vine and the Branches seems to relate to 'disciples' (v. 8) at large, all the 'Master's' (John 13:13, 14 KJV) 'servants' and 'friends' (John 15:12-15). So, it seems likely in verse 16, 'You did not choose me', etc., Jesus has reference to their call to be disciples as well as later to be one of only twelve apostles. There is a difference of opinion among exegetes on the question.

Nor do human acts of 'willing' underlie the initial conferral of divine mercy: God's 'mercy' or 'compassion' 'depends not on human will or exertion, but on God, who has mercy... So then he has mercy on whomever he wills, and he hardens whomever he wills' (Rom. 9:15, 16, 18). Nor are foreseen human events of any kind conditional to the divine decree. Second Timothy 1:9 focuses in on this, speaking of God 'who has saved us and called us to [or "with", ESV margin and KJV] a holy calling, not because of our works [doing, choosing, willing] but *because of* ["according to" KJV; emphasis added] his own purpose and grace'.

---

9. *Formula of Concord*, Epit. XI, 4, Schaff, *The Creeds of Christendom, vol. iii*, p. 166.
10. Mueller, *Dogmatics*, p. 587.
11. A.A. Hodge, *Outlines*, p. 219.

The Bible states positively that election is wholly of grace, based on God's good pleasure, will and purpose, not ours. As in Elijah's time there are thousands of saints alive – a 'remnant, chosen by grace. But if it is by grace, it is no longer on the basis of works; otherwise grace would no longer be grace' (Rom. 11:5, 6). (See also Eph. 1:5, 6, 11; 2 Tim. 1:9; John 15:16, 19; Matt. 11:25, 26; Rom. 9:10-18.)

Election is likewise said to be 'according to' God's knowledge or foreknowledge. Note: it is not on the basis of prescience (knowledge ahead of time) but in harmony, in consonance with it. When we read in 1 Peter 1:1, 2 that believers are 'elect... *according to* the foreknowledge of God the Father [emphasis added]' the Greek *kata*, rendered 'according to', presents a picture of parallel, harmony. It would be diagrammed like this:

```
foreknowledge        elect
```

Not like this with election *based on* (which is *not* what the Greek word means) foreknowledge.

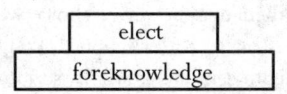

```
    elect
foreknowledge
```

Likewise Romans 8:29 affirms that God 'foreknew' *those whom* 'he also predestined'. Again, God did two things, He predestined and He foreknew, but the texts do not say one is based on the other. The basis is, as pointed out above, God's 'good pleasure... purpose... counsel... will' (Eph. 1:5, 6, 11).

Before moving on to other aspects of a doctrine of election, let the reader confront the many plain passages of Scripture quoted above. They make their own demands for acceptance in the plain English vernacular in which they stand. If swallowed whole, just as they stand, they will strengthen the whole body of truth. Election is a truth 'to humble the pride of man, to exalt the grace of God in salvation, and to promote real holiness in heart and life'.[12] A famous British preacher-scholar said in a sermon: 'The Bible teaches us to believe, God has been pleased from all eternity to choose certain men and women out of mankind, whom by his counsel secret to us, He has decreed to save by Jesus Christ. None are finally saved except those who are thus chosen' (from a sermon by the nineteenth-century Anglican bishop, J. C. Ryle, one of the best evangelistic preachers and writers of his century).[13]

This truth is so strong and important that the New Testament frequently refers to the saved as 'elect', 'the elect', 'God's elect', etc. In short, 'God's eternal Election is the first link in that chain of a sinner's salvation of which heavenly glory is the end. None ever repent, believe, and are born again, except the Elect.'[14]

'The days' of the great tribulation, 'for the *sake of the elect* [emphasis added],... will be cut short' (Matt. 24:22). In those days, if it were possible 'false prophets' would deceive '*the elect*' (Mark 13:22 [emphasis added]). '[W]ill not God give justice to *his elect*' (Luke 18:7, emphasis added)? And of 'those who are in Christ Jesus' (Rom. 8:1) the rhetorical question of Paul was 'Who shall bring any charge against God's *elect*' (Rom. 8:33, emphasis added). For Peter true believers scattered about the East were '*elect* [emphasis added]... according to [not on the ground of] the foreknowledge of God the Father, in the sanctification of the Spirit' (1 Peter 1:1, 2), whom he urged to make their 'calling and *election* [emphasis added] sure' (2 Peter 1:10).

God converts, renews, sanctifies and ultimately glorifies only the elect. Though we must do all our own repenting and believing, these human acts would be impossible to any 'sinner by choice and an alien by birth' (a choice line from an old gospel song, *The Child of a King*) apart from the regenerating work of the Spirit, who, as Jesus said, like the wind, moves where it wishes and no man can say whence it comes or whither it goes (John 3:8). As Jesus suggested to Nicodemus, he ought to have understood this as a 'teacher in Israel', acquainted with the prophecy of the dry bones (Ezek. 37). First, God 'will cause breath to enter into you, and ye shall live': only then do the dry bones stand 'upon their feet'.

It might weary the reader to introduce discussion of the numerous other texts – none denying the duty of every one to repent and believe the gospel – which either directly or by necessary inference teach that our choice of God, without any exceptions, is preceded by His choice of us with efficient grace to respond favourably. So I end the recitation here. The evidence is not a trickle but an avalanche.

---

12. On the masthead of *Free Grace Broadcaster* (2603 W. Wright St, Pensacola, FL, #173), Summer 2000.
13. J. C. Ryle, *Old Paths* (Edinburgh: Banner of Truth Trust, 1999, repr. of 1878), p. 461.
14. ibid., p. 461.

The Purpose of Election.

An examination of some of the relevant passages reaps the following fruit of teaching. Believers have been chosen by God 'to the praise of his glory' (Eph. 1:11, 12); to 'show forth the praises' of the One who called them (1 Peter 2:9 KJV); to live holy blameless lives (Eph. 1:4); to be fully sanctified, i.e. 'conformed to the image of his [God's] Son' (Rom. 8:28, 29); to 'go and bear fruit' (John 15:16). It is hence, an error to think of election apart from the high and holy ends which God had in mind when He did it.

The success of the plan of redemption could not be guaranteed – as all God's eternal counsels are – apart from divine initiative at every stage of the plan (*ordo salutis*). On account of sovereign election, God knew from the beginning who would populate heaven and a renewed earth. '[T]he Lamb' was 'slain' from 'the foundation of the world' (Rev. 13:8) and the inhabitants are 'those who are written in the Lamb's book of life' (Rev. 21:27). These facts of Scripture in no wise encourage any one to presume on God's grace in this regard, because divine sovereignty and human responsibility are juxtaposed in many a biblical declaration, perhaps never more starkly than in this verse: 'But God's firm foundation stands, bearing this seal: "The Lord knows those who are his", and, "Let everyone who names the name of the Lord depart from iniquity"' (2 Tim. 2:19).

Biblical Defence of the Doctrine of Election.

Anything so palpably contrary to what sinners would like to think – 'I am the master of my fate; I am the captain of my soul' (*Invictus* by E. Henley) – has always had its objectors. But the Bible never excuses God for His apparent playing of favourites. God is not a democratic 'chairman of the board', but a mighty king. The Holy Scriptures were written long before 'Liberty, Equality and Fraternity' became eighteenth-century watchwords.

Hence, it is no surprise that the sovereignty of God in electing 'whom he will' is defended, already within the Bible, against its gainsayers. Note also the Lord's answer to the 'unfair practices' complaints in the parable (Matt. 20:1-16); 'Am I not allowed to do what I choose with what belongs to me? Is your eye bad because I am good?' (v. 15 ESV margin). The reader will find Jesus defending God's right of sovereign choice – even preferring the relatively less good – from the facts of history and Jewish experience, even granting grace to a pagan widow in need of help, assisting a pagan soldier in need of healing, while passing over many equally needy Israelites (Luke 4:25-27). The citizens of Nazareth supposed their 'national election' to privilege as 'chosen people' qualified them to special treatment in every realm, including, one may suppose, personal salvation. Their soon-to-be most noted son reminded them, not so. God may choose Gentile widows for favour over Jewish widows and healed Syrian lepers over 'many lepers in Israel'. The response of the townsmen was not unlike the reception the doctrine sometimes receives today – even by some ill-informed Christians: 'When they heard these things, all in the synagogue were filled with wrath. And they rose up and drove him out of the town' (Luke 4:25-29).

This same insistence on salvation by grace *from start* to finish was essentially what made the religion of the Reformers of the early sixteenth century obnoxious to Rome which neither then nor now is able to see grace as God's way in salvation rather than an infusion of ability to merit what God can only give away 'without money and without price'.

We want human *needs* to dictate action, even God's action. This makes good socialist theory and is invincible political propaganda in times like ours, but God intends to be sovereign and let His own counsel stand; His will, grace and purpose decide. The same sort of defense of election is presented by Paul in the case of Jacob and Esau (Rom. 9:11, 12, see context). Jacob preferred the legitimate firstborn Esau, but God did not. Ultimately the Bible appeals to God's sovereign right. Read Paul's remarks about the potter and his clay (Rom. 9:19-23) and reflect again on the parable of Matthew 20:1-16.

Again, remember the situation starts with a race universally under divine wrath and bound for hell unless God intervenes. '[T]he wrath of God remains on him' (John 3:36); 'by nature children of wrath' (Eph. 2:3) is God's analysis of our character. God is to be praised that He has chosen some; why He did not choose everyone is His business, not ours. All about us lie evidences that God does not treat all men equally. He lets one child be born in a home where the mother is a drunkard and whose father was a visitor of the night in search of pleasure only; another in the same town is born to responsible, moral Christian parents who care for the child's every spiritual and physical need. Bangladesh and Somalia perish for hunger while America wallows in plenty. None has any choice as to what home or country is his birthplace.

Practical Spiritual Values of Election.

Simple as taught in Scripture but difficult for natural man to believe, some of the remaining genuine qualms of Christians may be allayed by attention to some values of election for the Christian life.

A. First mention goes to the comfort and encouragement it provides believers. Number XVII of the Anglican *Thirty-Nine Articles* quoted, in part, earlier, adds:

> As the godly consideration of predestination and our election in Christ is full of sweet, pleasant, and unspeakable comfort to godly persons, and such as feel in themselves the working of the Spirit of Christ, mortifying the works of the flesh and their earthly members, and drawing up their mind to high and heavenly things, as well because it doth greatly establish and confirm their faith of eternal salvation to be enjoyed through Christ, as because it doth fervently kindle their love toward God, so, for curious and carnal persons, lacking the Spirit of Christ, to have continually before their eyes the sentence of God's predestination, is a most dangerous downfall, whereby the devil doth thrust them either into desperation, or into wretchedness of most unclean living no less perilous than desperation. [Our ancestors took long sentences in stride.]

The practical spiritual benefit of being confident they were chosen and kept secure by God – guaranteed by Jesus' promise 'they shall never perish' – is perhaps more appreciated by believers when severely persecuted. In Reformation times evangelicals in France and Bible printers (such as Wycliffe) were being beheaded and burned. Dissidents from the Roman religion held their meetings in secret and pastors were on the run. Hence:

> To a persecuted Protestant in Paris it must have been an unspeakable consolation to feel that God had a plan of salvation for him, individually, from all eternity, and that nothing that priest or king could do could frustrate the divine purpose on his behalf. Nor was it less a source of strength to one profoundly conscious of his own sinfulness to feel that his salvation was based on the unshakable rock of the decree of God Himself.[15]

Scripture never uses the word 'reprobation' – sometimes used by theologians ancient and modern for a proposed or supposed decree of damnation. But Scripture does speak frequently of God's hardening of hearts (e.g. the heart of Pharaoh, Exod. 7:13 and about a dozen times in Exodus). There are many in every age that blaspheme God in outrageously blasphemous ways as well as relentlessly pursue any who stand up to them. These will come to a spectacularly appropriate end. 'How long, O Lord?' is an echoing cry of those persecuted for righteousness' sake from the second Psalm to the martyrs under the altar of heaven after the breaking of the fifth of the seven seals (Rev. 6:9, 10; cf. Isa. 6:11) – 'O Sovereign Lord, holy and true, how long before you will judge and avenge...?' This also is within God's plan and purpose: 'For the scripture says to Pharaoh, "For this very purpose I have raised you up, that I might show my power in you, and that my name might be proclaimed in all the earth"' (Rom. 9:17). Pharaoh may have thought of that while drowning in the Red Sea. Similar statements relate to Eli's reprobate sons (1 Sam. 2:25) and the degenerate populace of Isaiah's time (Isa. 6:9-11 quoted three times in the New Testament).[16]

B. This doctrine exalts God, as the Scriptures clearly indicate He should be exalted. God decreed the existence of the world; He created it; He preserves it; He is governing it (providence). Election fits that biblical portrait of God and adds something to admire.

C. It compels some humility, for it 'pulls the rug' from beneath any man who thinks he can challenge or contest God. He who at the beginning 'spoke, and it came to be' (Ps. 33:9) will also have the last word – not only at the death of every unrepentant sinner but when the books are opened on the Judgment Day.

D. It adds a motive for evangelistic and pastoral work, as Paul says very forcefully in his final Epistle, near the end of a long life of energetic, effective, if oft-times painful, service in those very matters: 'Therefore I endure everything *for the sake of the elect* [emphasis added], that they also may obtain salvation' (2 Tim. 2:10). That intrepid apostle understood well what some advocates of this doctrine sometimes tend to forget: God who ordains ends also ordains all the means to those ends.

Paul, who is perhaps the most ardent practitioner of a planned programme of missionary evangelism of the New Testament reports, is for certain, except for Jesus Himself, also the firmest expositor of the doctrine of election. We have already introduced many of Paul's statements of election. Let us also lay beside these statements some of the great missionary evangelist's expressions of zeal to persuade, first his brethren in the flesh, the Jews, and then 'the Gentiles' to whom he turned several times after being convinced that for now the minds of Jews were hardened to

---

15. Williston Walker, *John Calvin, The Organizer of Reformed Protestantism* (New York: G. P. Putnams & Sons, 1909), p. 418.
16. Calvin, *Institutes iii*, 24.14.

the gospel. As for the Jews he told the church in Rome: 'I have great sorrow and unceasing anguish in my heart. For I could wish I myself were accursed and cut off from Christ for the sake of my brothers, my kinsmen according to the flesh' (Rom. 9:2, 3). As for the Gentiles – the heathen world sunk deeply in corruption – perhaps the eighteenth chapter of Acts explains his 'predestinarian zeal' best: after testifying without avail to the Jews, 'when they opposed and reviled him, he shook out his garments and said to them, "Your blood be upon your heads! I am innocent. From now on I will go to the Gentiles."... And the Lord said to Paul one night in a vision, "Do not be afraid, but speak and do not be silent... for I have many people in this city."' Paul was aware that even before they are converted, the Lord has already designated in His eternal counsels exactly who are His, their names already written in the book of life. Consequently, 'he stayed a year and six months, teaching the word of God among them' (Acts 18:5-11 RSV). To the numerous body of believers brought to Christ by that vigorous campaign of evangelism, Paul later contributed the largest section of the epistolary literature of the New Testament – 1 and 2 Corinthians.

Scriptural Modes of Preaching and Teaching Election.

See Calvin on the 'Right manner of preaching divine predestination'[17] and Augustine.[18]

Good theological writing has devoted large attention to how the doctrine of election should be presented. It is, of course, a mistake to make it the leading topic of any sustained programme of instruction or preaching. Nothing, it seems, is more likely to further alienate the mind already darkened by sin and if inclined to accept it as true, to drive to despair rather than faith for salvation. What follows here will be brief abstracts rather than extended exposition.

1. Teach election in its biblical contexts. Mueller has some very helpful advice from an orthodox, creedal Lutheran perspective.[19] J. C. Ryle asserts, 'It is one of Satan's chief devices to make the Gospel odious by tempting men to distort it. Perhaps no part of Christian Theology has suffered so much damage in this way as the doctrine of personal election.'[20] Though I would not do so in a controversial situation, as a pastor I have consistently explained the doctrine in the course of Bible exposition (Rom. 9; Matt. 13; Eph. 1, 4, etc.).

2. Couple the doctrine of election with the universal offer of salvation. Here Jesus Himself is our best example. Matthew 11:25-27 is as strong a statement of special calling and election as to be found in any sermon. Yet it is immediately followed by Jesus' most tender offer of salvation: 'Come to me, all who labour and are heavy laden... and you will find rest for your souls' (vv. 28, 29). The sixth chapter of John is another such example of Jesus' method.

3. Usually, as in Scripture, bring out the doctrine of election after the offer of salvation has been made and hearers have decided for or against the Saviour. We have already seen how Paul did just that in Corinth. Near the end of the epiphany of Isaiah's call (Isa. 6:9, 10) God made known to him that preaching the Word to hardened sinners would (apart from a special call and election) only harden them. This passage is quoted five times in the New Testament to similar effect (Matt. 13:14, 15; Mark 4:12; Luke 8:10; John 12:40; Rom. 11:8), and similar language appears at Psalm 119:70 and Jeremiah 5:11. The New Testament quotations are all given as explanation of why hearers were rejecting the gospel. I discuss this more particularly in a book on theology of missions.[21]

4. Set forth the duty of evangelism with God's wisdom and the sovereignty of His election and the responsibility of man to respond in faith not as in any wise an intellectual problem or intrinsically mysterious.

Divine election is of the same order of truth as the existence of God.

Common Objections to and Questions About Election.

These objections and questions are as old as the Bible itself. Some are both raised and answered there. The book of Habakkuk, for instance, raises and responds to an aspect of whether God is *fair* or consistent in electing, judging and sparing. In Romans 9:14 Paul rhetorically questions if God was *righteous* in electing Jacob and rejecting Esau. His answer is simply *mē genoito* ('let it not be'), a bad question deserving no answer. Verse 19 voices complaints that God is *arbitrary* and impossibly *overbearing*, simply a *bully*. Paul in a sense says, 'Be quiet! Who do you think you are?' (v. 20).

---

17. ibid.
18. Augustine, *Nicene and Post-Nicene Fathers v*, ed. P. Schaff and H. Wace, 1890 (Peabody: Hendrickson Publ., 1890, repr. 1994), p. 540 ff.
19. Mueller, *Dogmatics*, p. 589 ff.
20. Ryle, *Old Paths*, p. 469.
21. Robert D. Culver, *A Greater Commission* (Chicago: Moody Press, 1985, repr. 1999 by author), pp. 74–78.

Teachers and preachers who saw election as a clear, biblical doctrine throughout church history met considerable reluctance among their audiences. No questions or objections or answers are new. Opponents of election in Augustine's time were not the heretics (Pelagians) but the Semi-Pelagian orthodox. The ground is pretty well covered in his *Treatise on the Predestination of the Saints*.[22] Calvin dignified five more or less standard objections of his time by devoting eighteen pages to them.[23] A. H. Strong – whose Calvinistic, non-covenantal, Infralapsarian, *Systematic Theology* has been continuously in print for 100 years, after continuous refinement over the long life of the author, has the best summary of five main objections and answers I know of.[24]

Dr Robert Reymond has a long section on election in relation to decrees (long a sort of Reformed playground of opinion) but does not address challenges to the whole idea of individual election: an excellent treatment.[25] Perhaps Dr Reymond hesitated to launch into such a tedious and lengthy task. Buswell makes some memorable remarks about 'reprobation' and 'double predestination'.[26] Millard Erickson, whose treatment of election, though brief, is strongly affirmative ('Grace is absolutely necessary.... In our Calvinistic scheme there is no basis for God's choice of some to eternal life other than his own sovereign will'),[27] has no section on objections.[28]

If, as logic compels, one must include the damnation of the non-elect in the decrees and give it the name of reprobation, then as several (especially well put by W. G. T. Shedd)[29] suggest, we must regard election as an efficacious decree and reprobation as a permissive decree. The discussion by that prince of scholastic Calvinism, F. Turretin (1623–1687), is in his *Institute of Elenctic Theology I*.[30] He is Infralapsarian. God is not the *author* of sins though He is the one who sustains all creation, including sinners and their father the devil plus all the angels that fell and left their first state.

Some objections to personal election call for very brief notice. I intend no disrespect to the unnamed objectors. Their arguments are as old as Pelagius and his disciple Celestius and the ancient Semi-Pelagians. Most of them can be found in a 1970 book by a Baptist minister named Robert Shank.[31]

1. Some Arminians and Wesleyans as well as Karl Barth say 'Election is simply for believers to be "in Christ" who is God's elect'.[32] It is of course true the saved of every age before and after Christ are 'in him' as Ephesians highlights. Yet the doctrine of particular election is securely locked into the many passages which clearly say the same as Luke observed: Acts 13:48 – 'And when the Gentiles heard this, they began rejoicing and glorifying the word of the Lord, and as many as were appointed to eternal life believed.'[33]

2. Also, some Arminians and Wesleyans say divine election relates not to individuals but to national preference, to Israel *per se* as represented by 'Jacob I loved', etc., in Romans 9:6-13.[34] This was developed at length by Wesley's great orthodox systematizer, Richard Watson.[35] I judge their lengthy arguments all crash on Paul's plain statements in Romans 9 that 1) the election stands not of works but of God who calls (v. 11) – not applicable to a nation *per se* and 2) that (v. 16 KJV, cf. ESV margin) election 'is not of *him* [a person, emphasis added] that willeth, nor of him [a person] that runneth'. The people of a nation usually have not one will (or opinion) but many; nor do they expend

---

22. Augustine, *Treatise on the Predestination of the Saints – NPNF v*, pp. 497–519.
23. Calvin, *Institutes iii*, 23. 1–14, Westminster Ed., pp. 941-964.
24. A. H. Strong, *Systematic Theology* (Old Tappan: Revell, 1907), pp. 464–502.
25. Robert L. Reymond, *A New Systematic Theology of the Christian Faith* (Nashville: Thomas Nelson Publ., 1998), pp. 464–502.
26. J. Oliver Buswell, *A Systematic Theology of the Christian Religion ii* (Grand Rapids, MI: Zondervan Publ., 1962, 1971), pp. 154-156.
27. Millard Erickson, *Christian Theology* (Grand Rapids, MI: Baker Books, 1985), p. 928.
28. Louis Berkhof does not introduce election, as I do here and A. H. Strong *et al*, as an aspect of soteriology but in connection with decrees. His treatment, however, is sound, including a limited discussion of the question of the order of decrees as in a characteristic Calvinist scholasticism. As readers of these pages know this author has not found the question of God's decrees a necessary part of systematics but rather an over-refinement, incapable of solution and more fruitful of controversy than sound teaching, and a waste of energy. There is more substance to the 'five points of Calvinism' (not of Calvin but of his scholastic successors). As those who have read the previous section of this volume on Christ's work of redemption know I regard the TULIP as a structure to which I give reluctant assent because it became a necessary development in consequence of the hypercalvinism of Beza and others and the inevitable reaction of Arminius and the Dutch Remonstrants of late sixteenth century after the death of the far more moderate, biblical and balanced scholar, John Calvin 1509–164.
29. W. G. T. Shedd, *Dogmatic Theology i* (Grand Rapids, MI: Zondervan Publ., 1969), p. 405 ff.
30. Francis Turretin, *Institutes of Elenctic Theology i*, trans. G. Giger, ed. J. T. Dennison, Jr (Phillipsburg: P and R Publ., 1992), pp. 206–211, 341–373.
31. Robert Shank, *Elect in the Son: A Study of the Doctrine of Election* (Springfield: Westcott Publ., 1970), p. 240.
32. ibid., p. 242.
33. Turretin, *Elenctic Theology*, pp. 206–211.
34. R. Shank, *Election*.
35. Richard Watson, *Theological Institutes* (New York: Lane & Sandford, 1850), chap. 26, in which he devotes twenty-six pages to Romans 9–11.

effort in 'running'. National will is never one but of several opinions or wills nor the effort of 'running' (Gr. *trecho*. *fig*. 'exert oneself to the limits of one's powers in an attempt to go forward, to strive to advance' Romans 1:16). The emphasis is entirely upon the effort that a *person* makes.[36]

3. An interesting variation of 'group' election proposes that Romans 9 refers to 'ecclesiastical' privilege, just as Israel was elected to the privilege of 'opportunity of obtaining salvation… as the Jews of old were God's chosen people' so now 'every baptized member of the church [not necessarily saved] is one of God's elect'. Second Peter 1:10 is cited. The only truth I see in this view is that often the Scriptures, Old and New Testaments, address the Israelite or 'Christian' hearers on the basis of their profession, not strictly their spiritual condition.[37]

4. It is objected that election is unjust to those not included. Answer: election deals not simply with creatures, but with sinful, guilty and 'condemned already' (John 3:36) creatures. God therefore is to be praised for His mercy in saving any at all. God can say to any, saved or otherwise, 'Friend, I am doing you no wrong… Am I not allowed to do what I choose with what belongs to me?' (Matt. 20:13, 15). There is something to be said for a parent treating each child the same, but a sovereign ruler is not obliged to treat condemned rebels alike. God is not an egalitarian and never heard of 'the declaration of human rights' when forming His counsels.

5. It is objected that individual election represents God as partial. Answer: these objections, usually by those who propose that election relates not to particular persons but to national or ecclesiastical privilege, would relate as well to this sort of election as to particular election. But Scripture bases election not only in His sovereignty but also in His wisdom and mercy. In electing, scripture is, as we have seen, without regard to earthly privilege or station (Ps. 44:3; Isa. 45:1, 4, 5, 25-27; Luke 4:25-27).

6. It is objected that election of some people no more worthy than others is arbitrary. Answer: to the contrary, Scripture bases God's electing of sinners in His freedom, will and wisdom. That we do not know His reasons does not mean He does not have adequate reasons. Let us remember election is only of condemned sinners. God is not to be charged with anything wrong because He does not extend the grace of election and calling to all. We do not know all His reasons but we know some of them: a) to provide example that no sinner is beyond reach of His mercy (1 Tim. 1:16); b) to provide witnesses and martyrs (Acts 9:15, 16). Paul could be a witness to one class of folk, Peter to another. In any case the ultimate reasons lie in God's providence and grace, not in what we are in ourselves. Beyond these reasons – as every teacher of biblical doctrine worth his salt knows – there remains what Scripture calls 'the mystery of his will'.

A Postscript.

Somehow the false impression is abroad that election is a denominational speciality peculiar to Presbyterians and Reformed theologians. Historically, the most numerous defenders of the doctrine in America have been Baptists, now in a state of recovery! The latter are only very recently reawakening to this their heritage. Besides A. H. Strong, whom I have cited frequently on this and related subjects, James Pedigree Boyce of Southern Baptist Seminary (Louisville, KY) brilliantly expounded the doctrine to several generations of pastors trained there. His great work, *Abstract of Systematic Theology* (1887), has recently been republished by Presbyterian and Reformed Publishers. I recommend it highly.

---

36. Bauer, Arndt, Gingrich, *Greek–English Lexicon of New Testament* (Chicago: University of Chicago Press, 1957), trecho, p. 833.
37. See Gibson, *39 Articles*, pp. 465–469. John Gill had met these views in his time and answered briefly and as well as any available today – John Gill, *The Complete Body of Doctrinal and Practical Divinity i* (Grand Rapids, MI: Baker Books, repr. of 1795, 1978), pp. 257, 258.

7
The Doctrine of Calling

The doctrine of calling is closely connected with the doctrine of election 'those whom he predestined [elected] he also called' (Rom. 8:30). Calling is God's initial act of doing something in the sinner to effect the salvation prepared for him 'from the foundation of the world'. Like election, calling is something in which the sinner has no active part. The initiative is all God's. This affinity perhaps explains why John Murray, in a book on salvation places effectual calling first, before regeneration, and never treats election, so important to most Calvinists.[1]

Calling is also closely connected with regeneration, as we shall see. Because the *special* call, which comes only to those whom both Paul and Peter call 'the elect' is identical with the initiation of regeneration.[2] Though the divine call to sinners is an invitation – 'Come to me, all who labour and are heavy laden' (Matt. 11:28), for example – it is more than an invitation, for the call actually *brings* the elect to Christ. If left to themselves by the Spirit of God they would never come at all. The 'heart of man is deceitful above all things' and deceives itself more than any others. The affinity between effectual calling and regeneration in the mind of good scholars explains why Louis Berkhof has a separate short chapter on general and external calling followed by a chapter on regeneration and effectual calling, not distinguishing the one from the other.[3]

It is important that this be well understood, for otherwise spiritual pride will be generated among believers, especially new ones. Clarence, forty-two years of age, married, father of two, long-time worker in a foundry, was a new believer and a transformed man when I became his pastor in my first charge after seminary. When given opportunity he would 'give a testimony', sometimes saying something like this: 'When I heard evangelist (name) preach I knew right away I was a lost sinner and had the sense to accept the Savior. I've been explaining this to the guys at the foundry and they are all too stupid to accept Christ too.' Clarence soon learned 'the rest of the story', that it was not any superior wisdom of his own that enabled him to see himself as in need of the Savior and why he had the will to believe. He quickly grew in faith and knowledge and 'in grace', not 'into grace'. He taught an adult Bible class for many years until well past eighty years of age.

The Bible distinguishes between a general invitation, a call of God that invites all who hear to come, and the special call which actually brings sinners to salvation. It is chiefly with the latter we are concerned here, but the former requires attention also.

---

1. John Murray, *Redemption: Accomplished and Applied* (Grand Rapids, MI: Eerdmans Publ., 1955, 1973), pp. 7 and 88–94.
2. A. H. Strong, *Systematic Theology* (Valley Forge, PA: Judson Press, 1907), p. 793.
3. Louis Berkhof, *Systematic Theology*, 2nd rev. ed. (Grand Rapids, MI: Eerdmans Publ., 1939, 1979), Contents, p. 12.

The General Call.

Some theologians speak of an *external* call or invitation as opposed to an *internal* call, others of a *general* as opposed to *special* call. For good reason the latter is to be preferred as shall be explained. Let us state the doctrine: Scripture speaks of a call of God which invites all who hear to come to Christ for salvation. For clarity's sake some more specific distinction should be made.

1. This call should be distinguished from the natural light Scripture describes in such passages as Psalm 19:1-6 and the first two chapters of Romans and elsewhere. There is no promise or grace in this 'general revelation'. The 'light of nature' tells something of divine benevolence as shown in 'rains from heaven and fruitful seasons, satisfying... hearts with food and gladness' (Acts 14:17), but it is an ambiguous message, complicated by natural disasters, which to the natural mind might suggest divine wrath, more than divine grace. True, God is nowhere 'without witness', but nowhere with a saving gospel witness unless a messenger is present to speak it. It is said 'if the heathen only live up to the light they have' they will be saved. But the light is never lived up to. Such statements do not reflect an understanding of the fearful effects of original sin on the understanding and will of every member of our fallen race.

2. This call is to be distinguished from any real or supposed strivings or restraining or constraining general work of the *Logos* or Holy Spirit. J. O. Buswell writes, '[A]lthough I cannot cogently prove it from Scripture, I postulate that the convicting work of the Holy Spirit is absolutely universal in the human race in all ages and in all areas.'[4] He cites Micah 5:2 and John 1:9. Buswell asserts (again without proof), that before any one's death one receives opportunity to respond to a valid offer of salvation. A. H. Strong defines the general call as 'to all men through God's providence and Spirit'.[5] But as he develops the subject later it is clear he sees no saving gospel in these influences. He does not agree with Buswell really.

3. As a call to salvation, this general call is only to those who actually learn the gospel through some mode of external proclamation. The gospel is a 'preachment', 'it pleased God through the folly of what we preach [*keryma*, proclamation] to save those who believe' (1 Cor. 1:21). This is the missionary theology of Romans 10:13-17 where Paul says 'everyone who calls on the name of the Lord will be saved' but adds 'they' cannot call or believe on 'him of whom they have never heard'; they cannot 'hear without someone preaching' for 'faith comes from hearing, and hearing through the word of Christ'.

4. Though universally valid, this call never has been universally proclaimed in any age. It is true that Isaiah, speaking for the LORD, proclaimed to the heathen whom he had been reproving for their idolatry: 'Turn to me and be saved, all the ends of the earth! For I am God, and there is no other' (Isa. 45:22). Does this say that a call has been issued and heard by all people without exception? I suggest three views of this matter:

a) One might take the view that God intended for Isaiah's generation to go to the nations as Jonah did to Nineveh. This was certainly not the case, for Jonah's commission to preach to the Gentiles has no Old Testament precedent or subsequent example.

b) Rather, God is saying, 'If you in the remotest parts of a pagan world want to achieve salvation by worshiping a god, then, look to me, for I am the only God.

c) It is a declaration of a future intention. For reasons we may only speculate about, God delayed proclamation outside Israel (see Matt. 10:5) until the events of Acts 8 and 10 (the Samaria and Cornelius episodes). Paul declared at Athens (Acts 17:29-31) that now God 'commands all people everywhere to repent', whereas previous ages of 'ignorance' God 'overlooked' (*huperidōn*, nom. sing. 2nd aor. part. *Huperoraō*?, overlook, disregard) (v. 30). That God did not leave Himself anywhere 'without witness' (Acts 14:17) does not mean there is a *gospel* witness in every area of the planet. The universal witness is the light of nature, the message of Psalm 19 and Acts chapter 14. Benevolence everywhere revealed? Yes (Acts 14:15-17). Grace and rest for the conscience? No.

Hence it seems *the general call to be saved by grace through faith goes only as far as human means have promoted it and shall promote it* – hence the prediction: 'you will be my witnesses... to the end of the earth' (Acts 1:8) and implied command 'to take the Gospel along, making disciples as you go' (Matt. 28:18) and even to 'send' missionaries – 'How are they to preach unless they are sent?' If God makes special cases of 'calling' – as He did to Paul on the Damascus Road and perhaps several of the Twelve – who can deny or forbid it? We cannot count on it as relief from the duty to 'proclaim the gospel to the whole creation' (Mark 16:15).

---

4. James O. Buswell, Jr, *A Systematic Theology of the Christian Religion ii* (Grand Rapids, MI: Zondervan Publ., 1962, 1971), p. 160.

5. A. H. Strong, *Systematic Theology*, p. 791.

5. The general call of God in salvation is addressed to all mankind who hear, whether numbered among the elect or not. Election is particular: 'The Lord knows those who are his' (2 Tim. 2:19). But this invitation is addressed broadly. Isaiah, whose oracles and sermons frequently anticipate the coming gospel age, cried: 'Come, everyone who thirsts, come to the waters; and he who has no money, come, buy and eat!… without money and without price' (Isa. 55:1). The last chapter of the New Testament echoes the same 'everyone' with 'let the one who desires take the water of life without price' (Rev. 22:17). Jesus's invitation, 'Come to me, all who labour', etc. (Matt. 11:27-30), does not say 'All you elect may come', though some advocates of what they suppose to be Calvinistic theology argue He meant just that (R. C. Sproul, for one). It seems a mistake to me to suppose His compassion on the multitudes (Matt. 9:36) and appeal to His disciples to view them as a field ripe for harvest (John 4:35, 36) had only the elect in view. His words in John 7:37, 'If anyone thirsts', would have found response only in those 'chosen' in Him from the foundation of the world and drawn by the Father and given to Christ (John 6:39, 44, 45, 64, 65). It is equally true, as Jesus added, 'whoever comes to me I will never cast out' (John 6:37).

6. This general call may be *successfully* resisted even though God's Spirit 'strive with men' and may be fatally rejected, as in the Parable of the Marriage Feast (Matt. 22:16) and as the pathos of 'O Jerusalem… how often would I have gathered thy children… and ye would not' (Matt. 23:37 KJV) sadly reflects. No doubt some of the Palestinian Jews who heard Jesus' invitations and who were seen in the field of people 'ripe for the harvest' heard Stephen say: 'you always resist the Holy Spirit' (Acts 7:51). Nevertheless, God says in every age, 'Today, if you hear his voice, do not harden your hearts' (Heb. 4:7 referring to Ps. 95:7, 8).

7. People who hear are held responsible for rejecting this proclaimed call of God. (And if not addressed by the divine invitation how can they be held responsible for rejecting it?) When I preach the gospel I will speak with the authority the divine Author of salvation confers on all His servants. I will speak earnestly as Paul did, even threaten them as Jesus did ('See, your house is left to you desolate'). As Stephen, I may even rebuke them: 'You stiff-necked people' (Acts 7:51) and 'persuade others' as Paul did (2 Cor. 5:11). I (or you) may even deliberately frighten 'others'… to 'save with fear' (Jude 23 KJV). I myself should not be shy or afraid of their faces (Jer. 1:8). The preacher may rightly say with Paul, 'I magnify my ministry… and thus save some' (Rom. 11:13, 14). I 'have become all things to all people [elect or otherwise], that by all means I might save some' (1 Cor. 9:22). If the ones I seek to save happen to be son or daughter I may go to my grave in grief if they do not respond to God's call, but I will not cease to pray they will respond.

It is significant that in the Parable of the Marriage Feast (Matt. 10) the ones who utterly and finally rejected the invitation were also severely and finally punished for despising it. The invitation is based on a redemption sufficient for all.

The Effectual, Special Call (Also Called an Internal, Spiritual Call).

We have had occasion many times in these studies to observe that man is alienated from the life of God and dead in sin. Therefore, if he is to be saved God must make the first move – something to cause 'us Greeks' who see only foolishness in 'the word of the cross' to see any sense in the cross of Christ (1 Cor. 1:18). This first move is the effectual call, sometimes quite accurately designated as 'illumination'. The latter term is accurate only if it is understood the soul (or understanding or reason) is illuminated, delivered from darkening, not the Word or the gospel. Some well-catechized, nominal Christians and atheistic scholars understand quite well both the sense of Scripture passages and evangelical theology. Their problem is that they dislike both. The gospel was a stumbling-block to some of the Jews of Paul's time and 'folly to Gentiles', precisely because they did 'get the drift' of Paul's teaching. Agrippa was informed by Paul but not persuaded (Acts 26:2, 3, 27-29). The cross is too bruising of pride to be welcomed apart from a change introduced within but wrought by 'power from above'.

Some unbelieving 'Jews and Greeks' handle the text quite objectively, having nothing to gain or lose wherever they come out in interpretation. A fairly recent commentary on the Hebrew text of the early chapters of Genesis by an Israeli Jew, unencumbered by two centuries of 'Christian' efforts to harmonize geology or evolution or some form of 'creationism' with the text, succeeds very well in extracting the intended meaning. As for the truth of the chapter and the wisdom of an evangelical theology of creation our contemporary scholarly 'Jews and Greeks' may not have a clue, or if they do may disregard it.

Poets, artists, mystics and even scientists speak of moments when influences and information are so brought together in the mind that all comes into clear focus. Then out comes a memorable poem, work of art, perhaps a new theory of 'natural selection' or 'a unified theory' of all material existence. Borrowing a term from Scripture and theology, some describe such a moment as an *epiphany*, Greek for a disclosure or unveiling. In the New Testament *epiphany* often designates the sudden glorious Second Advent of Christ and in ecclesiastical history His First Advent as in the January 6 'feast of epiphany'.

The internal, special call is not ordinarily an epiphany of this sort. Neither does it consist of a deduction or induction drawn from premises or evidences, nor is it simply the effect of hearing truth, but a change of the heart that makes it friendly to the truth. It may occur as a sudden overwhelming experience like Paul's or it may seem to develop toward a climax as with John Wesley and John Newton. In the case of many it occurs in childhood at a period of time so early one cannot remember and may seem to be a gradual development.

That there is a special call that not only invites the sinner but also brings him to salvation rests on no single particular scriptural statement, but is the assumption of the writers of the New Testament. A frequent name for believers or 'the elect' is 'the called' or 'called in Christ Jesus', etc. 'The called' would not distinguish God's people from any one else who had ever heard the gospel if only a general invitation were intended. In Romans 8:28, 29, those 'called' are the same as those who love God, foreknown and predestined by God and sanctified. In 1 Cor. 1:26 the 'calling' is something that came to 'brothers', not all the crowds (first of Jews and then of Gentiles, Acts 18:1-11) who heard Paul and his associates, Silas and Timothy, preach at Corinth. This call came only to those who responded with repentance and faith. Let us take note of several features of this effectual internal call.

1. The reasons for this call have nothing to do with human acts of will or works of faith whether foreseen or otherwise. Rather it is 'a holy calling, not because of our works but because of his own [God's] purpose and grace, which he gave us in Christ Jesus before the ages began' (2 Tim. 1:9).

2. It is a supernatural event like the creation of sight in the man blind from birth (John 9). In that case Jesus appears to have employed a means – a plaster of clay and spittle plus the water of a pool. We shall consider later if the Word (truth) is a means or only an accompaniment of special calling.

3. In any case this call is 'effectual'. All who receive it are among the elect. They are *brought* to Christ even though they also come to Him as invited in a general call. For them the call is special. 'Everyone who has heard and learned from the Father', Jesus replied to His objectors, 'comes to me' (John 6:45). Further 'No one can come to me unless the Father who sent me draws him' (John 6:44).

4. Everyone so called comes freely, un-coerced and willingly, because the call restores the original normal desire to love God, and freedom from bondage to sin. God is at work in them 'both to will and to work' (Phil. 2:13). They are like Lydia whose heart 'The Lord opened... to pay attention to what was said by Paul' (Acts 16:14). The Word is ineffective in and by itself to bring to 'belief, trust and commitment' until the heart is changed, i.e. until the effective 'call' comes. They are 'taught by God' (1 John 2:27; 1 Thess. 4:9) immediately by an inward work of the Spirit before they come to Jesus (John 6:45).

'You shall know the truth and the truth shall set you free' is a true saying in the context of John 8:2, but it is not truth itself that frees those in bondage until received as truth. In realms of personal life where inborn prejudice exists the truth about sin and grace staring one in the face does not in and of itself find a place in the center of being where commitments occur.

5. Finally, though the effective call of God is certain as to its success in bringing the called to final perfection (1 Thess. 5:22-24), each person so called has responsibility to pursue that final goal, being 'zealous to confirm your call and election' (2 Peter 1:10 RSV). '[C]hosen and faithful' go together (Rev. 17:14). As in every aspect of application of redemption, divine sovereignty and grace relieve no one of the responsibility of the 'great commandment' to love God with one's whole being. Failure to do so is the primary universal sin. If God is, He must be worshiped. The 'first and great commandment' is not optional.

How God Extends the Special Call and Makes it Effective.

At this point our discussion moves to the difficult question of how the Word (truth, gospel) as means and the divine Spirit as agent join in producing the effectiveness of the special call. Some of the same mystery accompanies the first creation and most supernatural and miraculous events. The wind blew across the Red Sea when the waters were parted, for example. Did the wind part the waters or was it a mere accompaniment? The story does not say the wind had anything directly to do with it. As frequently celebrated by Israel's poets and prophets (Ps. 78:12, 13, for example) it is referred to as a sign or wonder brought about by God's power. The presence or absence of means is of no interest to the narrators. Again – how does God extend the special call and how does He make it effective?

Let us begin an answer with an important passage relating to the subject, the opening verses of the First Epistle to the Thessalonians. Paul and associates address 'the church of the Thessalonians in God the Father and the Lord Jesus Christ' (v. 1 RSV). These 'chosen' (v. 4) have produced evidence of salvation by their work of *faith*, labour of *love* and steadfast *hope* [emphasis added] (cf. 1 Cor. 13:13) 'in our Lord Jesus Christ'. Hence Paul writes, '[W]e know, brothers loved by God, that he has chosen you, because our gospel came to you not only in word, but also in power and in the Holy Spirit and with full conviction' (1 Thess. 1:4, 5). The missionaries proclaimed the Word of God in the hearing of these Thessalonian people. The preached Word came with power in the Holy Spirit.

I think this is as near as we come to Paul's sense of the relation of the proclaimed Word with power when it comes to a group and of the Holy Spirit in the effective call of the chosen. To some of the hearers the Word is foolishness to be mocked, to others not a matter important enough to decide now (Acts 17:32). To a few the message comes with 'power', in 'the Holy Spirit and with full conviction', such as 'Dionysius the Areopagite and a woman named Damaris and others' (Acts 17:34).

The same elements of Word, power and Spirit are present in Paul's next letter to the believing folk at Thessalonica. In 2 Thessalonians 2:13 (KJV) Paul says 'God hath from the beginning chosen you to salvation' – saved 'through sanctification of the Spirit and belief of the truth'. In this case an effective change of heart such as Lydia's whose heart 'The Lord opened' (Acts 16:14) accompanied by 'belief in the truth'. He goes on to say, 'To this he called you through our gospel' (2 Thess. 2:14). It is not entirely clear that the Word, also called the Word of truth, was an instrument of calling but it was involved. The Spirit changed their hardened, heathen (idol worshipping, 1 Thess. 1:9) hearts to softened, believing hearts. They did not choose to change their 'evil heart of unbelief' – to be transformed at the depraved seat in the heart of man where moral habits reside and decisions are made – God did.

The Scriptures elsewhere make two categorical statements about the causes of effective calling (regeneration in its initiation). One says we are born again by the proclaimed Word of God, the gospel, as for example: 'you have been born again, not of perishable seed but of imperishable, through the living and abiding word of God… this word is the good news [gospel] that was preached to you' (1 Peter 1:23, 25). So 'the word' is said to be 'living and active, sharper than any two-edged sword, piercing… discerning' (Heb. 4:12). Further, God says His 'word' is 'like fire… and like a hammer that breaks the rock in pieces' (Jer. 23:29).

Another set of passages says the transformation of the heart is caused by the Holy Spirit (or Christ, or the Father). Everyone is familiar with Jesus' counsel to Nicodemus to this effect (John 3:5, 8). It is probable that in 'born of water and the Spirit' (John 3:5), water stands for the Word as in Jesus' words to the woman at Sychar, in the very next chapter (John 4:13).

Francis Turretin (1623–1687) of the theological academy at Geneva, a century after Calvin, produced a large systematic theology in scholastic style (much like Thomas Aquinas'), recently published in an English translation. Turretin devotes a long section to the question of the relation of Word and Spirit in special calling. The various views of the subject are canvassed thoroughly in relation to what he says has been the orthodox doctrine.

Yet his conclusions are very reserved. His first proposition states:

> The Ways of the Lord in grace as well as in nature are inscrutable. Nevertheless if we cannot understand the reason and the how of those things which God has willed to conceal from us, the thing itself and the fact, which has been plainly revealed to us, is not on that account to be denied by us.[6]

His last sentence on the subject, many pages later reads: 'There are innumerable things, the truth of which cannot be denied by anyone and yet their mode can evidently be understood by no one.'[7]

John Gill also comments with similar reserve:

> The instrumental cause, or rather means of effecting vocation, is the ministry of the word. Sometimes, indeed, it is brought about by some remarkable providers, and without the word; but generally it is by it: 'Faith comes by hearing and hearing by the word of God.' Christ stands in the gospel ministry, at the door of men's hearts, and having the key of the house of David he opens the heart by his power and grace, and lets himself in; and in this way, and by this means, the Spirit and all his grace, are received; men are called to grace and glory by the gospel, Gal. 1:6; 2 Thess. 2:14.[8]

---

6. Francis Turretin, *Institutes of Elenctic Theology ii*, trans. G. Giger, ed. J. T. Dennison, Jr (Phillipsburg, NJ: P & R Publ., 1992), p. 521.
7. ibid., p. 542.
8. John Gill, *The Complete Body of Doctrinal and Practical Divinity ii* (Grand Rapids, MI: Baker Books, repr. of 1795, 1978) vol. i, p. 149.

The Blessings of Effectual Calling.

This is a topic expounded at length in pastoral sermons and sermonic literature, fruitful for edification of believers. The following is a summary of John Gill's treatment.

1. Out of ignorance, a state of great and gross darkness, into marvelous and surprising light (1 Peter 2:9). But in effectual calling, the eyes of their understanding are opened and they are made light in the Lord. When Paul was called by grace a light surrounded him and there fell from his eyes as it had been scales, as a token of inward enlightenment.

2. Out of bondage worse than Egyptian bondage into glorious liberty: 'brethren, ye have been called unto liberty' (Gal. 5:13 KJV), while seeking righteousness and life by law, a spirit of bondage.

3. From fellowship with men of the world 'called into the fellowship of his Son Jesus Christ our Lord' (1 Cor. 1:9) and with others similarly delivered where there will be upward growth instead of downward.

4. God 'has called you to peace' (1 Cor. 7:15) whereas in a state of nature there is 'no peace for the wicked' (Isa. 48:22) because 'the way of peace they have not known' (Rom. 3:17).

5. God has 'not called us for impurity, but in holiness' (1 Thess. 4:7), 'to glory and virtue' (2 Peter 1:3 KJV).

6. 'Into the grace of Christ' (Gal. 1:6).

7. From the kingdom of Satan into 'his kingdom and glory' (1 Thess. 2:12).[9]

Summary and Conclusions.

I have presented what I believe to be a biblically correct view of calling, first thought through, expounded and defended by Augustine, then recovered by the sixteenth-century Reformers and the chief representatives of evangelical theology. Through the ages four other views have been taken; these are:

The Pelagian

This (which called forth Augustine's definitions of grace and faith) is outright rejection of any doctrine of inward grace in calling and regeneration. Pelagians ancient and modern do not believe man has anything so wrong with his heart and will that exposure to Scripture truth and persuasion cannot overcome. According to Pelagius, a fifth-century British monk, and a certain Celestius, his disciple and chief propagandist:

> The grace of the Holy Spirit is not absolutely, but only relatively necessary to holiness; it renders its attainment easier... Regeneration [or calling] does not consist in the renewal of the will by an internal operation of divine efficiency, but in the illumination of the intellect by the truth, the stimulation of the will by the threatenings of the law, etc... God's grace is designed for all but man must make himself worthy of it by honest striving after virtue [God helps those who help themselves].[10]

The Semi-Pelagian.

This acknowledges the necessity of divine grace – not restored ability of the will but only special assistance. To receive this assistance one must first desire to be free from sin, to turn away from sin, and to desire God and holiness. If one does this one may expect God's help.

As developed in the church first in North Africa in the early fifth century and – in spite of professed allegiance to Augustinism – as it has prevailed in the Latin Church thence onward, Semi-Pelagianism teaches:

> Freedom of the will, in the sense of power to do good, is not wholly lost, but it is very much weakened. Man in his present condition is morally diseased. The imputation [guilt for] of original sin is removed in baptism, and without baptism no one attains salvation. Owing to his morally diseased and weakened condition, man needs the assistance of divine grace, in order to the practice of holiness, and the attainment of salvation. The moral freedom of man, or his power to do good, *works in connection with divine grace*. The two things are not to be separated from each other... predestination to salvation or to perdition depends on the use man makes of the remainder of his freedom.[11]

So it has been correctly asserted – Pelagianism says man is morally *well*, Semi-pelagianism that he is *sick*, Augustinism that he is *dead*.

---

9. ibid., pp. 125–127.
10. W. G. T. Shedd, *A History of Christian Doctrine ii* (Minneapolis: Klock & Klock Christian Publ., first published 1872, 1978), pp. 96, 97.
11. ibid., pp. 109, 110.

Arminianism.

As set forth in the works of Jacob Arminius (1560–1609) this was closer to Augustinian-Reformation theology of special-internal calling than Semi-Pelagianism, for Arminius accepted original sin and the deadness of the heart of man toward God and holiness. He differed in that he declared the moral center had been restored by Christ's atonement to the degree that without further divine aid it is within the power of every man to repent and turn to God. If God had not done this he would be unjust. So Arminius rooted this restoration in justice. John Wesley affirmed the same restoration but based it upon God's grace not on justice, hence he was closer to views of the leading Reformers and the churches descended from them.

A well-balanced Tyndale New Testament Lecture (British Inter-Varsity sponsored) by Francis Davidson made this insightful comment on the Arminian position on special calling.

> This position refuses to distinguish between *common grace*, the operations of the Holy Spirit, universal in greater or lesser degree to all, and *efficacious grace*, which achieves its end in the conversion of the sinner. It is left to the moral ability of man to accept Christ and so escape eternal loss. The death of Christ is thus a fearful venture of God, uncertain as to its issue. On this view, God puts Himself at the mercy of something outside of Himself, since the divine foreknowledge, supposed to be its safeguard, is merely contemplative and not executive.[12]

Anglican thinking has tended to be Arminian (except at the very first), outside the Puritan party within the Church of England before the Puritan revolution. Gibson's comments on the Seventeenth Article (election, calling, perseverance) are Arminian. He criticizes Augustine for failure to balance the Scripture statement of predestination and election with those which employ not only human duties but ability to perform them and concludes on the 'Augustinian scheme': 'It is right in asserting that predestination is to life, and that the ground of it is inscrutable by us; wrong in denying that sufficient grace is given to all, and that salvation lies in the power of all men.'[13]

It is not wise to attribute any distinctive doctrine to the Church of England (Anglican, Episcopal). Says Jaroslav Pelikan: 'The Church of England – Lutheran in its intellectual origins, Catholic in its polity, Reformed in its official confessional statements [Arminian frequently in interpretation of the same], radical in its Puritan outcome, and, according to the old saw, "Pelagian in its pulpit, but Augustinian in its prayer book"'.[14]

---

12. Samuel Davidson (former professor in the seminary of United Original Secession Church of Scotland), *Pauline Predestination* (London: The Tyndale Press, 1945), p. 28.
13. Edgar C. S. Gibson, *The Thirty-Nine Articles of the Church of England Explained with an Introduction*, 8th ed. (London: Methuen & Co 1912), p. 489.
14. Jaroslav Pelikan, *The Christian Tradition: A History of the Development of Doctrine iii, Reformation of Church and Dogma 1300–1700* (Chicago: Universityof Chicago Press, 1984), p. 2.

8
The Doctrine of Regeneration

Meaning and Theological Employment of 'Regeneration'.

In the Bible, regeneration and the Greek word it translates are used only twice. Readers of several recent English Versions of the New Testament will miss the scriptural origin of 'regeneration' present to everyone familiar with the King James Version and its revisions. The word renders *paliggennesia*, which does literally mean 'again born'. The New International Version renders it literally – 'rebirth' at Titus 3:5 but furnishes an interpretation, not a translation at Matthew 19:28, the only other occurrence of *paliggennesia*: 'the renewal of all things'. Here, as in many aspects of theological discourse, the biblical origin of some of what otherwise might be thought to be invented, technical terms is lost on the reader. It is well to know that regeneration began its career in our tongue as a name for a religious event (*Oxford Historical Dictionary*) perhaps in Wycliffe's translation of the Bible, not as what happens when a starfish loses a leg or a chameleon a tail. Modernity has co-opted and thereby diminished the usefulness of many words that formerly had distinct religious-theological-biblical meaning.

Regeneration first appears as the word Jesus used to designate that still future time promised by the prophets – 'the regeneration when the Son of Man shall sit on the throne of his glory' (KJV; ESV also paraphrases 'in the new world') when His apostles shall 'sit upon twelve thrones, judging the twelve tribes of Israel' (Matt. 19:28) a verse critical to millennial interpretation. The prophets had much to say of it, connecting it with the Messianic age. Peter seems to have connected it with the times of restitution of all things the prophets had predicted and to follow the Second Advent (Acts 3:21). In this case regeneration is *cosmic renewal*.

'Regeneration' appears a second and last time in the New Testament as one of Paul's terms for the renewal of souls: 'not by works done in righteousness, which we did ourselves, but according to his mercy he saved us, through the washing of regeneration [*paliggennesia*] and renewing of the Holy Spirit' (Titus 3:5 ASV). Except for those who teach baptismal regeneration, most evangelical theology understands 'renewing of the Holy Spirit' as either an explanation of 'washing of regeneration' or as appositive – 'even the renewing of the Holy Spirit'. 'Washing of regeneration' is something that happens in the hearts of all like those new believers at Thessalonica when they 'turned to God from idols to serve the living and true God' (1 Thess. 1:9).

Some other New Testament designations of this transforming event are: to be 'born again' (1 Peter 1:3), 'created... in true righteousness and holiness' (Eph. 4:24), to be given life by the Son (John 5:21), to be 'called...

out of darkness into his marvellous light' (1 Peter 2:9) or 'brought from death to life' (Rom. 6:13), or 'a new creation' (2 Cor. 5:17), 'born again' or 'anew' (John 3:3, 7) becoming partakers of the divine nature (2 Peter 1:4) or God's 'workmanship, created in Christ Jesus' (Eph. 2:10). There are others. This idea is pervasive in the New Testament *patently* and, as we shall see, *latently*, in the Old Testament.

There is considerable uncertainty among us who teach theology as to whether Jesus meant 'born again' or 'born from above' (John 3:3) where He used the words *gennēthē anōthen*. Nicodemus understood 'born again'. Perhaps the scholars who suggest Jesus was purposely ambiguous are correct. Jesus did not rebuke His visitor's idea of a second or again-birth, but wished Nicodemus to understand what the Old Testament clearly teaches, that the prophesied new birth of the nation of Israel and necessarily of the individual people who would then compose the reborn Israel would be spiritual not physical. It would be caused by the Spirit of God, who is sovereign in method, means and timing.

So *gennēthē anōthen* and *paliggenesia* are near precise equivalents. Each word employs the same Greek root word for bearing a child, one in noun form (Matt. 19:28) and the other the verb form (John 3:3, 4, 5, 8). *Palin* unambiguously means again, another time; *anō* usually means above, but even so, perhaps *once more* is the sense of *above* in the Greek mind. The transition is natural. There is no question that the new- or again-birth Jesus intended is caused by divine power ('from above', if one so understands *anō*) for Jesus specifies a birth by water '*and* the Spirit' established in John 3:8.

'Regeneration' has been employed in a broad sense and in a narrow sense in Protestant theology. John Gill observes: 'Regeneration may be considered either more largely, and then it includes... effectual calling, conversion and sanctification; or more strictly... then it designs [designates] the first principle of grace infused into the soul.'[1] Calvin, James I. Packer notes, sometimes 'used the term "regeneration" to cover man's whole subjective renewal, including conversion and sanctification'.[2] For example, Calvin can 'interpret repentance as regeneration, whose sole end is to restore in us the image of God... all but obliterated through Adam's transgression'.[3] Yet he also held to the doctrine we designate regeneration by the narrow sense of the word.[4]

J. P. Boyce treated regeneration and conversion together – 'unquestionably so intimately associated that it is difficult to separate them and point out distinctions between them'. He explains:

> The Scriptures connect the two under the one idea of the new birth, and teach that not only is regeneration an absolute essential in each conversion, but that in every intelligent responsible soul conversion invariably accompanies regeneration... the Scriptures also teach that regeneration is the work of God, changing the heart of man by his sovereign will, while conversion is the act of man turning towards God with the new inclination thus given to his heart.[5]

After rejecting any regenerating power in baptismal 'washing' (Titus 3:5) Calvin goes on to say, 'It is therefore the Spirit of God who regenerates us, and makes us new creatures; but because his grace is invisible and hidden, a visible symbol of it is beheld in baptism.'[6] In comment on 2 Timothy 2:11, Calvin says: 'Our salvation begins with regeneration, and is completed by our perfect deliverance, when God takes us away from the miseries of this mortal life.'[7] See E. M. B. Green, *The Meaning of Salvation*.[8]

Regeneration as the awakening of the soul to life at the beginning of the application of redemption (Titus 3:5) is not as remote from regeneration at the cosmic renewal as it might seem. Our salvation as sinners is not complete renewal until the resurrection of our fully sanctified souls at the coming of the Lord (1 Thess. 5:23, 24). The complete deliverance of the remotest particle of the cosmos (*ta panta* 'all things' and 'the heavens and the earth') is scheduled for the same occasion. Paul found comfort for us all in bringing the full regeneration of the elect into future connection with full renewal of all creation. He sets this comprehensive vision of a completed redemption

---

1. John Gill, *The Complete Body of Doctrinal and Practical Divinity, vol. ii* (Grand Rapids, MI: Baker Books, repr. of 1795, 1978), p. 107.
2. J. I. Packer, 'Regeneration', in *Evangelical Dictionary of Theology*, ed. W. A. Elwell (Grand Rapids, Mi: Baker Books, 1984), p. 925.
3. John Calvin, *Institutes iii.3.8*, ed. J. T. McNeil, trans. and ed. by F. L. Battles (Philadelphia, PA: Westminster Press, 1960).
4. Calvin, *Institutes iii*.3.6–14.
5. James Pedigree Boyce, *Abstract of Theology* (Philadelphia: American Baptist Publication Soc., 1878).
6. Calvin, 'Commentary on Titus 3:5', in *Commentaries on the Epistles to Timothy, Titus & Philemon* (Edinburgh: 1856), p. 334.
7. ibid., p. 217.
8. E. M. B. Green, *The Meaning of Salvation* (London: Hodder & Stoughton, 1965), p. 231.
9. Packer, in *EDT*, p. 925.

in a remarkable flight of exaltation. 'I consider that the sufferings of this present time are not worth comparing with the glory that is to be revealed to us. For the creation waits with eager longing for the revealing of the sons of God' (Rom. 8:18, 19). Creation was subjected by the Creator to 'futility' (ESV and RSV) ('corruption' KJV), presumably in connection with man's fall (Gen. 3). This 'connection' may be subject to degradation of energy and misuse on account of sin, suffering the same along with the sufferings of mankind. In the future, when our 'regeneration' in the larger sense is complete at the 'redemption of our bodies' the order of nature ('the creation') also shall be delivered from its 'bondage to decay'. This seems to approximate Paul's expectation designed to give us 'hope' (vv. 24 and 25). Packer hints at such a connection in a short article:

> The noun 'regeneration' (*paliggennesia*) occurs only twice. In Matthew 19:28 it denotes the eschatological 'restoration of all things' (Acts 3:21) under the Messiah for which Israel was waiting. This echo of Jewish usage points to the larger scheme of cosmic renewal within which that of individuals [refers to Titus 3:5] finds its place.[9]

In modern preaching and systematic theology, however, regeneration is employed only with reference to the spiritual life of individual believers. This will be our only focus in this chapter.

A statement of Jesus to Nicodemus, the inquiring night visitor to Jesus during His first public ministry at Jerusalem, suggests that a good place to start the discussion of the idea of regeneration (renewal, spiritual cleansing and rehabilitation), is the Old Testament. Jesus had said, 'unless one is born again he cannot see the kingdom of God'. To which the shy, aristocratic night visitor responded, 'How can this be?' (John 3:9 RSV). To this the Master teacher rejoined, 'Are you the teacher of Israel and yet you do not understand these things?' (John 3:10). The clear implication is that any good teacher of the Hebrew Scriptures should know that Messiah's kingdom would be preceded by Israel's repentance and purification, that the nation would be purified in the hearts of its members as an aspect of the restoration of 'the kingdom to Israel' (Acts 1:6).

Paliggennesia (Regeneration) in Pre-Christian Literature.

Non-biblical Vocabulary of Renewal.

Paliggennesia, rendered 'regeneration' in both its New Testament appearances, like almost all theological religious New Testament terms, had a previous history in Greek culture. Briefly, it 'first seems to have acquired significance in Stoicism' (viz. Acts 17:18). In Stoicism its significance was first, the renewal of the world after a future *ekpurosis* (holocaust, purification of the world by fire). In a fragment of a pagan writer preserved in Augustine's *City of God* (22.28) '*paliggennesia* is used for the new birth of individuals in a new period of the world, and this (new birth of individuals) is accepted as the general Greek usage'.[10] Though used by ancient mystery religions, they followed Jewish and Christian usage.[11] When the word passed from Stoicism to Judaism its meaning changed. It is no longer a repetition of old existence but 'an existence in which righteousness dwells'. In Philo and Josephus, both of whom use the word, though it refers to a future world, it 'is filled with a new religious content'. A passage in Cicero, however, 'shows that even toward the end of the first century BC a present experience could be called *paliggennesia*'.[12]

So when the word appears in John's report of Jesus' conversation with Nicodemus its freight of individual transformation connected with a new principle of life 'had long since been used by the educated'.[13] Yet the same could be said of Jesus' reference to the coming New World, the kingdom of righteousness and peace connected with the Parousia in Matthew 19:28. (See also 22:30 'in the resurrection' and similar references at Mark 10:30 and Luke 18:30 'in the age to come'.)

A sentence from the thorough work of James V. Bartlet in *HDB* shows how close Jesus' assumptions about the future were to the national expectation of a national 'birth-again', i.e. restoration. National restoration is a sense

---

10. This is quoted and cited from Buechsel in *Theological Dictionary of the New Testament, vol. i*, ed. G. Kittel and G. Frederich, trans. G. W. Bromiley (Grand Rapids, MI: Eerdmans, 1964–1976), pp. 686, 687.
11. ibid., p. 689.
12. ibid., pp. 688, 689.
13. ibid., p. 689.

found in Josephus (Ant. XL iii.9) *"he anaktisis kai paliggennesia tēs patridos"* ["the new creation and regeneration of the fatherland"]; and this in the fuller sense of the Messianic renewal of Palestine'.[14] Bartlet's 8,000 word article is an abundant source (Contract 2½ columns in *The Anchor Bible Dictionary*).

Regeneration in Biblical History and Prediction.

In Old Testament History.

Theology which takes the 'higher critical' views of Old Testament literature and history finds no evidence of holiness in an ethical sense much before the pre-exilic prophets. Passages in the Pentateuch that relate to our subject of spiritual renewal, such as I will soon introduce, are supposed to come from the same epoch as the eighth-century prophets. On the word of Jesus, however, we accept what is evident anyway, that there are no compelling reasons to believe Abram, Isaac and Jacob were incapable of understanding a high level of ethical religion, however incomplete divine revelation may have been at the time. Recently my wife lifted her eyes from reading Genesis 32:22-32, where Jacob met God, left the encounter with a new name and a new limp, muttering, 'Peniel, for I have seen God face to face, and my life is preserved'. Then she asked, 'Do you think this is when Jacob was converted?' I said, 'Yes I do think so, as numberless old-fashioned preachers have declared.' Conversion is sequel to regeneration. If this is 'narrative theology' let us have more.

It does seem clear, however, that spiritually the sons of Jacob scarcely rose above a coarse level of moral and spiritual outlook. The records of the time do not say anything specific about a personal level of fellowship with God. True, God spoke to Jacob and Joseph in dreams, but He also spoke to Pharaoh and eminently to a Philistine pagan king (Gen. 20:6, 7; 41:1 ff.).

Further, though the thousands of the nation of Israel in Egypt were redeemed by the blood of the Passover lamb, those same thousands showed slight evidence of personal regeneration. They, everyone twenty years old and upward, died, many in unbelief, and their 'carcases' as Numbers 14:29 (KJV) indignantly puts it, were buried in the sands of the wilderness. Whatever one may think their theology of the 'Abrahamic Covenant' and of righteousness by faith may have been, it did not seem to 'take' with them.

Yet Moses' sermons to the next generation, delivered at the very borders of Canaan, breathe the spirit of religion of the heart. Much of the legislation earlier announced by him implies a heart to love God, His truth and a desire for His fellowship among those for whom the legislation was designed.

There are passages in Moses' sermons at the border of Canaan, which shape some of the New Testament language about regeneration. Moses speaks of a renewed heart to be effected in the hearers at that time, as in Deuteronomy 10:12-22, especially the following: '[T]he LORD set his heart in love on your fathers and chose their offspring after them… Circumcise therefore the foreskins of your heart, and be no longer stubborn' (Deut. 10:15, 16). With an important variation, in a later address at the border of Canaan, Moses spoke later of how God would effect such an inward spiritual renewal (Deut. 30:1-10), especially the following: 'And the LORD your God will circumcise your heart and the heart of your offspring, so that you will love the LORD your God with all you heart and with all your soul, that you may live' (Deut. 30:6).

In the first paragraph the preacher exhorts the hearers themselves to circumcise their hearts but in the second he promises that the LORD will circumcise their hearts. In both cases obedience to God's will as expressed in the law is an accompaniment. Whether as consequence or as cause is obscure.

In any case the story of Old Testament Israel describes many obviously sincere people who approached the ideal of the circumcised heart set forth above. There are of course the prophets and David whose heart-love for God has such intensity that he is described as a man after God's own heart (1 Sam. 13:14; see also Ps. 119:10 and many passages pronouncing persons blessed). The devout people who inhabit the first two chapters of Luke had each the circumcised heart as much as any person ever has – Mary, Joseph, Elizabeth, Zacharias, Simeon, Anna. It has been argued that John was regenerate in the womb or he would not have responded (leaped KJV) as he did to the presence of his likewise *in utero* Lord (Luke 1:41), though this is a rather broad 'leap' of logic, if the pun may be pardoned. And there are Simeon and Anna. We should not neglect the Magi whom mysteriously God had invited to search out the Savior of the world.

---

14. James V. Bartlet, 'Regeneration', in *Hastings Dictionary of the Bible, iv* (New York: Charles Scribner & Sons, 1909), p. 214.

These evidences – and much more – demonstrate that whether called regeneration or not, there were some, even innumerable multitudes, who were 'born again' before Jesus uttered the memorable words of John 3. Let us not forget about Melchizedek, Job and Moses' father-in-law who had passed from death to life through the immediate activity of the Holy Spirit.

I shall argue in the last chapter of this study of soteriology that there is no salvation except through Christ, and that other religions, far from being ways to salvation, are without exception obstacles to faith in the one true God. Yet it has always been true that the Spirit, like the wind, moves on whom and where He will, but also *when* He will.

Regeneration in Old Testament Promise.

Regeneration has an organic doctrinal development in the whole Bible far too extensive in detail to develop on these pages. I and everyone who writes on the subject is debtor to the comprehensive article, 'Regeneration', by James Vernon Bartlet,[15] Prof. of Church History, Mansfield College, Oxford University.

Much of Old Testament history and ritual is acknowledged by the New Testament to be typical of realities rather than the realities themselves as later revealed and explained in the New Testament. Paul, for example, employed the Red Sea crossing and wilderness wanderings as metaphor for Christian verities only partially partaking of permanent Christian realities (1 Cor. 10:1, ff.). Hebrews traces predictive symbolical connections (i.e. typical connections) between the Old Testament ritual shadows and New Testament realities. Among these are national election as a shadow of personal election. However, the passages concerning a national renovation, renewal, require the personal, spiritual renovation of the members of the nation.

In Jeremiah 31:17-20 the LORD says to Ephraim, leading tribe of the apostate northern kingdom, 'There is hope for your future' (v. 17), and goes on to describe a future chastening, repentance, divine mercy and permanent change of heart. '[T]his is the covenant that I will make with the house of Israel after those days, declares the LORD: I will put my law within them, and I will write it on their hearts... they shall all know me, from the least of them to the greatest' (Jer. 31:32-34). The reader will recognize that New Testament writers borrow these texts specifically to describe the New Testament experience of regeneration and incorporation into God's family of non-Israelites (Heb. 8:8-12). These writers treat the passage as a prediction of the regeneration of persons in this age as well as the coming age of the cosmic regeneration specified by Jesus in Matthew 19:28.

The same can be said of Jeremiah 32:38-40 especially, 'I will put the fear of me in their hearts, that they may not turn from me' (v. 40). The same may be said of Ezekiel's several prophecies of future spiritual renewal: Ezekiel 11:19, 20, especially v. 19, 'I will give them one heart, and a new spirit I will put within them. I will remove the heart of stone from their flesh and give them a heart of flesh'. Also Ezekiel 36:24-30, especially verses 26 and 27: 'I will give you a new heart, and a new spirit I will put within you. And I will remove the heart of stone from your flesh and give you a heart of flesh. And I will put my spirit [Holy Spirit?] within you', etc. See also the conclusion of the prophecy of restoring life to Israel's dry bones, chapter 37, especially the last verse (v. 14): 'And I will put my Spirit within you, and you shall live, and I will place you in your own land. Then you shall know that I am the LORD; I have spoken and I will do it, declares the LORD.'[16]

These are features of Old Testament prediction of and preparation for the New Testament teaching of regeneration. These Old Testament verities are without a shadow of a doubt, it appears to me, what Jesus had in mind when He sent Nicodemus back to his lodgings in a mood to rethink all his pharisaical presuppositions about the true religion of Israel as opposed to the official Judaism of the Palestinian synagogues. 'Are you the teacher of Israel and do not know about the necessity of being born again to enter the promised Messianic kingdom?'

Regeneration in the New Testament Presentation.

a) Jesus' public teaching phrased the doctrine in the context of particular incidents. Jesus once called a child out of the crowd and said, 'unless you turn and become like children, you will never enter the kingdom of heaven' (Matt. 18:3). In response to the grumbling objections of Pharisees and other 'experts' to the welcome Jesus put out to 'publicans and sinners', He told the story of the redemption of a prodigal son whose father twice pronounces at

---

15. ibid., pp. 214–221.
16. ibid., pp. 214–216.

the denouement, 'this your brother was dead, and is alive; he was lost, and is found' (Luke 15:24, 32). When Peter made the great confession the Lord informed him he had not simply thought it up, but that God had made his heart know it (Matt. 16:17).

The parable of the four kinds of seeds of which only one manifest 'an honest and good heart, and bear fruit' (Luke 8:15) exposes regeneration in action. To these let us add all the evidence of the sixth chapter of John that faith is always taught by God.

Of course the primary teaching about regeneration is Jesus' response to Nicodemus to which we have referred and to which we shall turn later.

b) The word of James is still Jewish (James 1:1) and the Christian assembly still a 'synagogue' (James 2:2). James was interested, like his Old Testament prophetic predecessors in 'the collective quickening traceable to the divine initiative rather than the individual – though the latter is implied in the exhortation to receive the "inborn word" (the implanted word which is able to save your souls, James 1:21)'.[17] James, the practical man, throughout his Epistle is addressing chiefly those who were already members of the persecuted 'sect of the Nazarenes' and of how regeneration of the heart will be manifest in observable manner of behavior. 'Of his own will he brought us forth by the word of truth, that we should be a kind of firstfruits of his creatures' (James 1:18). He is aware that the true believer may be seated beside a merely nominal one (see James 2:1), but the two will show their true colours in the way they endure trials, bridle their tongues, show respect of persons or not, how they use God's name in passion (curse or blessing), manifest meekness of wisdom, how they use money, and in concern for lapsed believers.

c) Peter, though an apostle to the circumcision and expressing much of his doctrine in metaphors drawn from the Old Testament, by the time he wrote his Epistles fully understood the doctrine of regeneration, as fully as Paul and John, though expressed in somewhat different language. Indeed, some of the most striking statements of the doctrine of regeneration are in the first chapter of each of Peter's Epistles, e.g. 'You have been born again' (1 Peter 1:23) and 'you may become partakers of the divine nature' (2 Peter 1:4).

Peter's expressive 'partakers of the divine nature' has been interpreted by various amateur theologians and by the entire Eastern church throughout Christian history as deification, *theosis* (Gr.), almost as though we partake of Christ's divine nature just as He partook of ours. Despite some incautious language by perfectly orthodox teachers and preachers the *theosis* doctrine has never been held by informed evangelical people. Jaroslav Pelikan observes that even 'Jonathan Edwards repeatedly quoted 2 Peter 1:4 to prove that "the grace which is in the hearts of the saints is of the same nature with the divine holiness", adding the proviso that this would be only "as much as" is possible for that holiness to be, which is infinitely less in degree… not to be taken to mean "that the saints are made partakers of the essence of God, and so are 'Godded' with God."'[18]

d) 'St Paul's unique experience of the gospel as the power of God in the soul, and as an essentially present Salvation, marks an epoch in the New Testament doctrine of regeneration.'[19] Paul's experience of the spiritual illumination and quickening which he later called 'the washing of regeneration' was unique. Neither he nor Luke, his biographer, tired of relating it. Paul developed 'the gospel that I proclaim among the Gentiles' (Gal. 2:2) not by thinking it up or by borrowing, but 'by revelation'. He 'conferred not with flesh and blood' (Gal. 1:16 KJV) in developing that proclamation (*kerygma*). That Peter learned some of what he knew from Paul, is clear from the Acts narrative and the second chapter of Galatians – as that impulsive converted fisherman acknowledged (Gal. 2; 2 Peter 3:14, 15). Though justification may be the *center* of Paul's emphasis, regeneration is no less important. If Jesus declared the *necessity* of regeneration Paul explained why it is necessary.

e) Hebrews affirms but does not develop the idea of individual regeneration. The Epistle brings the promised national regeneration in Jeremiah (see Heb. 9:6 ff. and 10:15-18) to bear on the importance of perseverance in full acceptance of the Christian revelation in the work and words of Jesus. The author is zealous to prevent apostasy of the converted.

f) John, the affectionate disciple, contributes to the idea of regeneration not only Jesus' pivotal words on the subject (John 3:3 ff.) but, from an aged pastor's heart, informs those willing to be taught as little children how regeneration works out in life and how it may be verified in others and in the self (1 John).

---

17. ibid., p. 217.
18. Jaroslav Pelikan, *The Christian Tradition: A History of the Development of Doctrine vol. v, Christian Doctrine and Modern Culture* (Chicago: University of Chicago Press, 1989), p. 163.
19. Bartlet, in *Hastings Dictionary of the Bible*, p. 220.

The Nature of Regeneration As Revealed.

I shall not repeat what was said about effective calling, the initiation of regeneration, all of which applies here. Nor can any one *explain* anything that is as such an immediate work of God. Let us come quickly to a definition and enlargement of the definition. In this section I acknowledge debt to B. B. Warfield.

Definition.

Warfield defined regeneration as the 'radical and complete transformation wrought in the soul (Rom. 12:12; Eph. 4:23) by God the Holy Spirit (Titus 3:5; Eph. 4:23), by virtue of which we become "new men" (Eph. 4:24; Col. 3:9), but in knowledge and holiness of truth created after the image of God (Eph. 4:24; Col. 3:10; Rom. 12:2)'.[20] This definition, though analytical, is also scriptural in language and more 'doxological', i.e. related to worship, than theoretical. It is useful as an index to the categories of the following discussion.

Let us keep in mind as we proceed that the characteristics of the effectual call, all carry over to regeneration, of which the call is only the initiation. We have already learned that 1) the person who is the subject of regeneration, though becoming active, is a receptor (passive) in regeneration. One receives Christ after gaining discernment and power to do so. 2) As in the paradigmatic case of Saul of Tarsus, effectual call and regeneration may not be successfully resisted. The poem of 'The Hound of Heaven' is true; God's Spirit pursues us, not we Him. 3) There may be preparation in one's inner experience (as in Saul's case). Was his conscience accusing him and not excusing as he pursued his way to Damascus? Likely so, but regeneration in the narrow sense is instantaneous. 4) It is a complete work. One can neither be somewhat pregnant or somewhat regenerated. 5) It is permanent. Said Jesus: 'I give them eternal life, and they will never perish' (John 10:28). This latter point will be discussed further as an aspect of assurance and perseverance.

1. Regeneration is wrought... 'by God'. God and God alone is the author of the new birth. In John 1:12, 13 we read: '...children of God, who were born, not of blood nor of the will of the flesh nor of the will of man, but of God'. James 1:18 states: 'Of his own will he brought us forth'. See also Ephesians 1:19, 20; 2:10; 1 Peter 1:3; 1 Corinthians 3:6, 7. This is in contrast with the views of certain Protestant leaders who have held that man co-operates with God in his own regeneration. This view, known as 'synergism', was belatedly advocated in the sixteenth century by Philip Melanchthon (Lutheran), in the seventeenth century by Jacobus Arminius, and in the eighteenth century by John Wesley. Yet, happily, none of the three was consistently synergistic, each rejoicing to give all the glory to God and anxious to pray for God to act in converting sinners. None succeeded in squaring his view with Scripture.[21]

2. It is a change wrought 'in the soul'. Sometimes we like to say the Word of God is empowered or illuminated and, understood as figures of speech, correctly. Yet the Word is always the same Word. As truth, it is not subject to change. The power or enlightenment involved in conversion of sinners is within the sinner not within the Bible. His mind (soul) is enlightened (special calling, prevenient grace) so that he can understand the gospel and his enfeebled will – really dead as regard to God – is strengthened to enable him to turn toward God. It would be quite as correct to say the change is in the sinner's heart. This is what is meant by 'new creation' (2 Cor. 5:17) and new 'nature' (2 Peter 1:4), a 'new heart' (Ezek. 36:26) and new 'spirit of your mind' (Eph. 4:23).

We must, however, guard against supposing that some new 'substance' is added to the soul. Certain well-meaning Christians have argued that natural man has two parts alive – body and soul – and a third part dead – spirit. They have said that when the Spirit of God comes in He takes the place of the dead spirit, etc. This is near enough to the truth to be dangerous. It reminds us of Apollinaris (condemned at Constantinople, AD 381) who tried to explain Christ's nature as two-thirds man (body and soul) and one-third divine *logos* (spirit, *pneuma*). True, the Spirit of God indwells the believer at regeneration, not to make him a divine being (the 'union with Christ' idea is pressed almost to this extreme sometimes), but to change the governing disposition. Man has the 'faculty' of love before regeneration. By regeneration it is redirected, away from improper love of self to a proper love of the self and of God.

3. Does the Spirit of God employ any instrument in effecting regeneration? This question has been discussed earlier in connection with effective calling, but must be raised again here.

---

20. B. B. Warfield, *Biblical and Theological Studies* (Philadelphia, PA: Presbyterian & Reformed Publ., 1952), p. 351. I note that J. I. Packer's article on 'Regeneration' in *EDT* employs Warfield's definition.
21. A. H. Strong, *Systematic Theology* (Valley Forge, PA: Judson Press, 1907), pp. 815–817.

There are those who suppose, resting on a misunderstanding of John 3:5 and Titus 3:5, that baptism effects regeneration in infants. We would contend that according to Scripture the water of baptism is not the instrument of regeneration but only its sign or ritual symbol. Many will agree, therefore, that baptism ought to follow regeneration, that only those showing credible evidence of new birth ought to be baptized. Those evangelical teachers who advocate baptism of those who by reason of infancy cannot believe (Lutherans excepted) often assign a quite different meaning to water baptism, such as a 'sign of the covenant of grace' or a 'promise of the parents' or 'dedication' of the infant by the parents or all three. Confessional Lutheranism affirms that infant baptism *is* believers' baptism, that not palpably, but none the less genuinely, the 'little ones' do believe. With A. H. Strong we strongly assert to the contrary that:

> Not external baptism, but the conscientious turning of the soul to God which baptism symbolizes saves us (1 Peter 3:2, the answer of a good conscience). Texts like John 3:5, Acts 2:38, Colossians 2:12, Titus 3:5 are to be explained upon the principle that regeneration, the inward change, and baptism, the outward sign of the change, were regarded as only different sides or aspects of the same fact, and either side or aspect might therefore be described in terms derived from the other.[22]

It is correct to say that the Word of God, pricking the graciously enlightened conscience (special calling) moves the man to turn to God. We do not know exactly how, two texts are especially pertinent: '...love one another earnestly from a pure heart, since you have been born again, not of perishable seed but of imperishable, through the living and abiding word of God... And this word is the good news that was preached to you' (1 Peter 1:22, 23, 25) and '...precious and very great promises, so that through them you may become partakers of the divine nature' (2 Peter 1:4).

4. Evidence of the new birth. There is small Scripture authority for demanding of one's self or of another professed believer some proof of regeneration based upon subjective feelings at a certain time and place, though at certain times in Protestant history men have thought otherwise. There are, however:

a) Certain internal evidences, designated by Scripture, whereby we may make our own 'calling and election sure' (2 Peter 1:10). They are true belief in Christ (1 John 5:1), true love for Christ (John 8:42) and the witness of the Spirit (Rom. 8:16; 1 John 3:24). Our spirits will also receive assurance from the Spirit as we understand the scriptures. True love of Christian brethren (1 John 3:14) is both an internal affection and as manifested, an observable evidence. If we believe that God has direct access to our minds, then the witness of the Spirit may be in the form of a subjective feeling of assurance. Much has been written on the subject and many disagreeing opinions expressed. We need greater assurance than our volatile feelings supply. The regenerate man delights in God's law (Rom. 7:22; Ps. 1:2).

b) Certain external evidences, designated by Scripture as 'credible evidence' of regeneration in other people than ourselves. They are practical righteousness (1 John 2:29), observable love of others (1 John 4:7), Christian victory over the world, i.e. lack of defeat by it or conformity to it (Rom. 12:1, 2; cf. 1 John 5:4), and observable discontinuance of sinful ways (1 John 5:18; 3:9).

To make one's 'calling and election sure' as Peter says (2 Peter 1:10) is a very important matter for every Christian. A later chapter of Soteriology will treat the subject more at length under the topic of 'Christian Assurance of Personal Salvation'.

Regeneration Expounded.

Let us further expound regeneration more in the mode of a pulpit homily, guided by the London scholar-pastor, John Gill, much abbreviated. (Excluded by law, as a non-conformist, from the universities, John Gill was self-taught. Over a long life while continually serving a Baptist church in London he mastered the biblical languages and the languages of European scholarship. He was probably the only Gentile in Britain who could read the Talmud in the original Aramaic and Hebrew. His writings on all branches of theology are largely phrased in the very language of Scripture. His works, including the *Body of Divinity*, which I have adapted in the following are again recommended – not for the hyper-Calvinism at occasional junctures, but for the transparent, orderly, understandable theological and biblical integrity.)

---

22. ibid., p. 821.

What Regeneration Is, or What Is Meant by Regeneration?

1. It is to be 'born again' (John 3:3, 7), which presupposes a prior birth of sinful parents and in their image, the second of God and in His image.

2. It is to be 'born from above' as John 3:3 and 7 may be translated but, if not so translated, it is certainly implied in John 3:27; James 1:17; 18 and 1 Peter 1:3, 4. This of course indicates that God Himself causes regeneration and by that event we become His children.

3. It is commonly called 'the new birth' in theological discourse because it produces 'newborn infants' (1 Peter 2:2). The regenerate person is variously said to be a 'new creature', a 'new man' with a new spirit, new understanding with new desires, new delights and new joys.

4. They have been made alive (Eph. 2:1). Christ is their resurrection and life. The new man has new eyes (the eyes of faith); new ears, they hear the Word in a manner they never heard it before (Matt. 13:16, 17); also new hands, to handle the Word of life and to work with; and new feet to flee to Christ the new city of refuge. New ability to pray to God. There are in the regenerate man (which shows he is alive spiritually), cravings for spiritual food as a newborn infant craves the mother's breast and a spiritual taste (see Ps. 19:10-14).

5. Christ is formed in the heart (Gal. 4:2), His image stamped there 'after the image of its creator'. They have been predestined to be conformed to the image of Christ (Col. 3:10; Rom. 8:29).

6. They have become partakers of the divine nature (2 Peter 1:4) – not of God's essence, for we are mere creatures of God. But in regeneration there is that wrought in the soul which bears a resemblance in spirituality, holiness, goodness, kindness, etc., and is therefore so called. The moral image of God restored.

7. Various other terms express regeneration where those born-again are said to be 'begotten again'. God's 'seed' is said to 'remain in him – and others'.

What Are the Causes or 'Springs' of Regeneration?

1. The efficient cause, of course, is not man. Scripture makes a special point of this. The natural man sees no need of it and does not want it (1 Cor. 2:14). They, as Jesus said, who think they are whole physically see no need of a physician – so it is in the spiritual realm. Nicodemus' wonderment at the notion shows how even a sincere, religiously informed, intelligent man could not even understand the notion by his own native but unrenewed powers.

2. The regeneration of a sinner is a 'creation' in the sense of bringing something new (not a new substance but a renewal of disposition) into existence, which is only God's to do. Spoken of a resurrection from the dead – as soon might dead bodies quicken themselves, as men, dead in sin, raise themselves up to a spiritual life. It is something done to us, not by us or even with our co-operation. Like all else, even our acts such as repenting, believing, turning to God (conversion), regeneration is a gift.

3. Scripture expressly denies regeneration to be of *men*: not of the blood, or circumcision, the blood of ancestors, even the most holy (John 1:12, 13). Those who in Jesus' time boasted of being of Abraham's seed were unable even to give the idea a friendly ear.

4. The efficient cause is God only, hence we read 'who has been born of God' and 'everyone who is born of God' (John 1:13; 1 John 3:9; 5:1, 4). In this the *Father* begets us again (1 Peter 1:3 KJV). The *Son*, who is the resurrection and *the life* is the one of whom we are born (1 John 2:28, 29). But the Holy Spirit is the author or agent (as expounded earlier).

5. The instrumental cause of regeneration is the Word of God and the ministers of it. Gill makes a point of including the ministers of the Word as a properly and scripturally instrumental cause of regeneration citing 1 Corinthians 4:15: 'For though you have countless guides in Christ, you do not have many fathers. For I became your father in Christ Jesus through the gospel.' Further, Paul speaks of Onesimus as one whom he had 'begotten in my bonds' (Philem. 10 KJV). Gill is as unable as any other theologian to explain just how the Word as Scripture or gospel is an instrument, for as God immediately spoke the original universe into being so He creates life (speaking it into being) before the Word as message exerts any power.[23]

---

23. Gill, *Doctrinal and Practical Divinity* vol. i, p. 115.

The Subjects of Regeneration.

They are neither good angels who have no need of it, nor evil angels for they are granted no share in it. John the Baptist said God could raise up sound, good children out of stones (Matt. 3:9; Luke 3:8) but He chose to operate thus on 'rational creatures' whom He regenerates. He does so not with all but such among mankind as are called and separated from the rest of the world of whom Peter speaks as 'born again to a living hope' and first described by Peter as 'elect... according to the foreknowledge' (1 Peter 1:1-2, 3). Regeneration's chief seat is the spirit or soul yet its influence is extended to the whole man, a fact to which Christians should give special attention (Rom. 12:1,2) and through the Spirit put to death the deeds of the body of sin (Rom. 6:12, 13).

The Effects of Regeneration Are Four.

1. The principal effect, perhaps an accompaniment, in any case not possible without new life, is participation (as all the first Reformers insisted) in repentance, faith, conversion and sanctification. Arminian and Semi-Pelagian theology puts faith ahead of regeneration in the order of salvation. But this supposes that men in the state of nature can initiate repentance and faith or at least co-operate with the Spirit in creating faith. Augustinians interpret 1 John 5:1 to say 'whosoever believeth that Jesus is the Christ *has been already* born of God'. Love of the brethren (1 John 3:14), and all the fruit of the Spirit (Gal. 5:22, 23), develop out of regeneration not into it.

2. Enjoyment of all spiritual blessings follows upon regeneration. These blessings take place only 'in Christ Jesus' which union *in history* occurs at the moment of regeneration. The regenerate have been loved by 'an everlasting love' (Jer. 31:3). '[T]herefore', says the LORD, 'with loving kindness have I drawn thee' (Jer. 31:3 KJV). They have been 'chosen in Christ before the foundation of the world', but this is not known by them till the gospel comes (special calling) not in word only, but in power, and in the Holy Spirit.

> Justification was a sentence conceived in the mind of God from eternity; was pronounced on Christ, and his people in him, when he rose from the dead; but is not known to those interested in it, till the Spirit of God reveals the righteousness of Christ from faith to faith, and pronounces upon it the sentence of justification in the conscience of the believer; until he is born again, he has no knowledge of this blessing, no comfortable perception of it, nor can he... nor have that peace and joy which flow from it.[24]

3. The third effect is a fitness and capacity for performance of good works – see such passages as Ephesians 2:10; 4:24; 2 Timothy 2:21; Hebrews 9:6; Romans 8:8; Ezekiel 36:37; and Philippians 4:13.

4. Regeneration makes us 'fit' or 'meet' to enter the kingdom of God – whether one thinks of that kingdom as (in part) a true Christian assembly of believers or the future kingdom of glory. This was the main point of Jesus' response to Nicodemus' inquiries (John 3:3, 5). At the coming judgment which introduces the future kingdom the unregenerate – the 'tares' or 'weeds' – will all be taken out and burned (Matt. 13:24-30; 23:15; 21:31, 43; see also 1 Cor. 6:9; Luke 12:32; Matt. 25:34).

It is hoped the reader who has followed carefully through the preceding adaptation of some theology of the Puritan-Baptist Paracelsus of the eighteenth century will see the value of minute and thorough mastery of the English Bible is necessary for a careful and complete theology. The Puritans did not resource their theology by 'surfing the net'. They made their minds the net by prolonged, careful, resourceful study until the Bible was part of id, ego and superego. Only then were they ready to write systematic theology.

We turn next to the acts of the elect, called and regenerate in conversion. In this they alone are active. They do all the repenting and all the believing.

---

24. ibid., p. 118.

9
The Doctrine of Conversion

A few terms of theology are special and rare in ordinary speech. Conversion and convert is not one of them. When contesting football teams change ends of the field and goalposts – a complete reversal of direction – it is called a conversion. This is strictly consonant with biblical and theological usage. To 'convert' from being a Protestant to being a Roman Catholic is not quite the same, I judge – a big change but not necessarily a complete reversal. Even so, this word conversion/convert is not in our vocabulary every day. Except in football or chemistry perhaps, we are more apt to speak of a reversal or to reverse directions. Nevertheless, the idea is prevalent, though we say convert or conversion infrequently in social intercourse.

So it is in theology. John Wesley once remarked, 'Conversion is a word I very seldom use, because it rarely occurs in the New Testament.'[1] The word conversion (or convert) occurs only fourteen times in the KJV – in recent translations usually translated 'turn' or 'return' or similar. The idea of a spiritual-moral reversal of direction – conversion – is endemic in the Bible from the LORD's appeal to Cain (Gen. 4:7) to that tender appeal to all in the last chapter of the Bible (Rev. 22:17). In formal theology 'conversion' usually simply designates the turning of a sinner from sin, death and the devil to holiness, life and communion with God. The idea is a simple one. Every time the turn of a sinner back to God is commanded, discussed or reported, the subject of conversion is before the reader.

The Hebrew and Greek Words for Conversion.

The word for this turning in the Hebrew Old Testament is usually *shuv* (or *shuvav*) which appears hundreds of times, usually with no theological connection, as for example, 'Abraham *returned* [emphasis added] to his place' (Gen. 18:33). It can be used either for turning *away* from God or of turning *to* God. It has no inherent theological sense. The Greek (*Septuagint*) translation of Jesus's time usually rendered *shuv* and its synonyms with a form of *strephō* (turn) or, more commonly, *epistrephō*, a strengthened, more emphatic word for turning or returning. It occurs 579 times in the *Septuagint*, about three-fourths of the time translating *shuv*. *Apostrephō*, literally turn away from, is another variation of *strephō*, usually having spatial (from here to there) rather than theological importance. A few times it means 'to be converted' (John 3:8; Zec. 1:4; Isa. 30:15 *et al*) but sometimes both apostasy and conversion in the same text (Ezek. 18:21 and 24).

---

1. John Wesley, 'Letter to Bishop Lavington', *Works, v*, p. 368 as cited in John McClintock and James Strong, *Cyclopedia of Biblical, Theological and Ecclesiastical Literature ii*, first published, 1895 (repr. Grand Rapids, MI: Baker Books, 1968–1970), p. 495.

In the New Testament the idea of conversion or to turn away from sin, death and the devil to holiness, life and God is commonly conveyed by these same words, sometimes in the language of an Old Testament text where the biblical thought originated. The prophets were preachers of repentance for sins, urging the people of Israel and Judah to return to God from their chronic apostasies. Compare, for example, Jesus' explanation of why His hearers were not converted (Matt. 13:15) by quoting Isaiah 6:10; see also John 12:40; Romans 11:26; Acts 3:26; cf. Isaiah 59:20, 21.

Special Importance of Conversion in Evangelical Devotion and Practice.

Conversion has always been of great importance to Protestant evangelical 'religion'. Biographies of our leaders will say of a theologian or other leader, 'He was converted at such and such an age', a datable event. This deserves some enlargement, especially for the benefit of twenty-first-century folk who aspire to be teachers and preachers or publicists. We need to be convinced of the importance of that personal change of thought, affection and life our Protestant evangelical Fathers all called 'conversion' and which we must have or be 'false witnesses of Christ'. John Wesley (born 1703), a paramount evangelical of evangelicals – both *evangelical* and fervently *evangelistic* – though the offspring of generations of godly ancestors 'was not to experience his "religious" conversion until 1725'.[2] Another random example: a certain William Clough, 'an English Wesleyan minister was born... May 30, 1799. He was converted in his 16th year'.[3] The outstanding Puritan theologian, John Owen (born 1616), a precocious child, acknowledged his early 'motive' for study was ambition for eminence and power in the Church of England. In the progress of his studies he was awakened by the Spirit of God to higher thoughts and aspiration,[4] as his later life demonstrated. Poignantly (for me at least) an editor of the volume you are reading stated to me at our first meeting, 'I was converted in a Plymouth Brethren Assembly', while only months earlier the 'Brethren' senior pastor in Nassau, the Bahamas, who had invited me to his pulpit made a point of telling me, 'I was converted through the ministry of a Mennonite missionary.'

Members of Protestant groups who were baptized as infants and perhaps (or perhaps not) confirmed at onset of adolescence, are not always conscious of the necessity of that event of turning from sin to holiness, death to life, Satan to God. Luther certainly was aware of the necessity of conversion and both Zwingli and Calvin wrote of their conversions. This unpleasant fact was rather spectacularly thrust before 'ecumenical' churchmen and others a few decades past – not by a Baptist or independent revivalist, but by Emil Brunner, probably most effective spokesman of and to the ecumenical movement in America. In his book, *The Misunderstanding of the Church*, 1953, prepared for and addressed to the World Council of Churches, he denounced what he called the 'Constantinian System'. In the third volume of Brunner's *Dogmatics*, which he wrote about a decade later, he said:

> Conversion to Christ is not a real possibility within the Constantinian church situation, since there everyone [in the parish] is a baptized Christian. This is why conversion is hardly mentioned there. This at once becomes clear when comparison is made with the Free [i.e. non-state] Churches of America. Here the concept of conversion is central. It is... the historical reality which has kept the concept of conversion true to its Biblical sense.[5]

Brunner adds, therefore: 'Europe... is to be seen as a missionary situation', and he rebukes the 'typical' European theologian because 'he presupposes Infant Baptism as the normal beginning of life in the church while the pietists (who, like Wesley, Finney, Spurgeon, Moody, etc., are also the great evangelists of modern times) take as their starting point the new situation, that the attachment of the great masses of the population to the Church is *only fictional* [emphasis original].'[6]

Therefore, as I shall try to expound more fully at the end of this chapter, conversion is as important to the experience and ministry of every minister of the Word and genuine Christian witness as birth to a baby or oxygen to a fire. Without it we are nothing in the kingdom of God and, Jesus said, destined to be cast out of it and, like weeds in the wheatfield at harvest time, to be removed from the field and burned in fire where 'there will be weeping and gnashing of teeth' (Matt. 13:36-42). Matthew, whose controlling purpose in writing seems (in part at least)

---

2. J. I. Packer, in *Evangelical Dictionary of Theology*, ed. W. A. Elwell (Grand Rapids, MI: Baker Books, 1984), p. 1163.
3. McClintock and Strong, *Cyclopedia, xi*, p. 990.
4. ibid., *vii*, p. 493.
5. Emil Brunner, *Dogmatics iii: The Christian Doctrine of the Church, Faith, and the Consummation*, trans. D. Cairns and T. H. L. Parker (Philadelphia, PA: Westminster Press, 1962), p. 276.
6. ibid., p. 276, see also p. 107.

to have seen the future of missionary evangelism, took care to promote the necessity of genuine conversion for every Christian witness, reports this from Jesus' mouth: 'On that day many will say to me, "Lord, Lord, did we not prophesy in your name, and cast out demons in your name, and do many mighty works in your name?" And then will I declare to them [as Judge], "I never knew you; depart from me, you workers of lawlessness"' (Matt. 7:22, 23).

The Nature of Conversion – What Is it?

1. Conversion viewed from the human point of view is the act of a sinner who turns from sin to the Savior but which viewed from the divine side is regeneration. Conversion is something the redeemed sinner himself does, but never prior to God's work of regeneration in his heart. There must be acceptance of the synchronism if not full understanding of it.

2. There is 'something to do' in conversion. If it were not so, the amazing plethora of appeals to sinners to 'turn', 'return', 'repent', 'turn back', etc., would not appear in both Testaments. Neither would there be demands to do so such as Peter's: 'Repent and be baptized every one of you in the name of Jesus Christ for the forgiveness of your sins' (Acts 2:38). The hearers wanted to know, 'What shall we *do*?' Answer: repent. Nor was this duty of repentance laid only on Jews as some early dispensational writers said. (A contrast is supposed with Paul's answer to the Philippian jailor's question in Acts 16:31). There had indeed been a time when few Gentiles heard the call to repentance, simply because the 'fullness of time' when God 'sent forth his Son' (Gal. 4:4) had not yet arrived. Heretofore God had not extended the command to Gentiles, but now says the apostle of the Gentiles: '[B]ut now he [God] commands all people everywhere to repent' – and He threatens dire consequences if they do not (Acts 17:30, 31).

3. There are two aspects of the act of the sinner in spiritual conversion for salvation – as in every form of conversion, or turning about. It may with propriety be said there are two aspects of one act – one is a negative aspect of turning away and the other the positive aspect of turning toward. The first is named repentance and the second faith. When 'the [pursuing] hound of heaven' finally catches up with the fleeing object of pursuit the pursued turns around and runs in the direction from which he fled away.

Again Peter helps us. Peter's second sermon (Acts 3) was to a crowd of 'people' who 'ran together' to Peter and John at Solomon's portico. Not to waste the opportunity to preach to an interested audience 'the apostle of the circumcision' began by delivering the bad news of how corrupt they all were at heart and how wickedly they had acted in killing 'the Author of life'. Then he spoke of how God had ruled and overruled in fulfillment of prophecy. The preacher never got to finish his sermon, because he was interrupted by the court police (Acts 4:1). He did, however, make a closing announcement: 'God, having raised up his servant [Jesus], sent him to you [Jews in Palestine] first, to bless you by turning every one of you from your wickedness' (Acts 3:26) – *apostrephein* (to turn or convert) *apo tōn ponēpiōn humōn* (from your wickedness). What wickedness, specifically? Primarily, what happened on Good Friday: 'But you denied the Holy and Righteous One, and asked for a murderer to be granted to you' (Acts 3:14). The international Jewish crowd assembled several weeks earlier to participate in Passover Week had stayed over for Pentecost and days following. They needed to repudiate their opinion of Jesus and what they had done to him seven weeks earlier. That is when 'as they were speaking' the police stopped the sermon. Let every sinner acknowledge, 'we hid as it were our faces from him; he was despised, and we esteemed him not... But he was wounded for our transgressions... bruised for our iniquities' (Isa. 53:3, 5 KJV). This is the repentance, the negative side of conversion.

Peter also helps us see faith as the positive aspect of what we *do* when we are converted. He had been ministering 'to the saints that lived at Lydda' where the chief airport of the state of Israel is now located. There, after another remarkable healing which caught the community's attention, Peter (presumedly) preached again. This time, 'all the residents of Lydda and Sharon saw' the healed paralytic 'and they *turned to the Lord*' [emphasis added] (Acts 9:35) – *epestrepsan epi ton kurion*. In conversion, like love and marriage, 'You can't have one [turning from Satan] without the other [turning to the Lord]'.

These two aspects (or elements) in repentance for salvation are both apparent in many other passages. Romans 6:11, 'So you also must consider yourselves dead to sin and alive to God in Christ Jesus'; Colossians 3:3, 'For you have died, and your life is hidden with Christ in God'; 1 Thessalonians 1:9, 'how you turned to God from idols'; Acts 26:18, 'turn from darkness to light and from the power of Satan to God, that they may receive forgiveness of sins'. 'To turn' here is *epistrepsai* and should be understood actively, to convert or to turn, not to *be converted* or to *be turned*, emphasizing the regenerate sinner's active part in conversion.

4. The Scriptures recognize both the human and the divine aspects in sinners' turn to God. They both convert and are converted. It seems best to think of the divine act (or work) as regeneration and the human acts of repentance and faith as conversion. The King James Version of Jeremiah 31:18 (v. 17 Heb.) is vivid in expressing both the human and divine movement in conversion: 'turn thou me, and I shall be turned'. The eight English words, two clauses, are only two words in the Hebrew, *shuv*, the word for reversing direction in each case. The first is in *hiphil*, the causative stem of the Hebrew verb, *hashiveni*, 'turn thou me!' Then, immediately follows in the *qal*, *wea'shuvah* 'And I shall be turned'. Conversion is no works-righteousness, meritorious, synergism of God and man. They move together but God initiates it by regenerating the will or disposition. Again, in KJV of Jeremiah 31:18, 19 (vv. 17, 18 Heb.) Ephraim says, 'Surely after that I was turned [by God], I repented; and after I was instructed [by God], I smote upon my thigh'.

The place of the divine and the human and their respective parts in conversion is to be decided squarely in consequence of the doctrine of sin. If the Fall rendered us all dead toward God, inclined away from Him at the center – our disposition or will, as well as intellect – then the initiative must be God's. The beginning of turning must be God's sovereign act, His choice not ours. Disagreement over this issue has broken out in every period of vigorous evangelism or reflective thought. This representation of the divine and the human side of conversion will seem scripturally, logically and theologically correct if we call to mind the following. *First*, that all the universe, 'the heavens and the earth' of Genesis 1:1, is preserved and governed (providence) by God – 'In him we live and move and have our being'. This is true in evil acts and thoughts quite as much as in good acts and thoughts and whether of angels or men or demons. Theology calls this the divine *concursus*. *Second*, though in our natural state 'we have all gone out of the way' and 'there is none righteous, no not one' God can and does penetrate our spirits by His spirit without destroying any faculty of volition, rather by setting it free to make right choices. We may not be aware of who is working within and exactly what is happening. If we are ever to convert or to be converted we must will (choose) to turn to God and do so without external coercion. We probably know nothing of God's part in the 'turn thou me and I shall be turned' transition, though much earnest prayer for us may have been effectually lifted by many who love God even more than they love us.

Among recent writers who have seen this clearly was Emil Brunner. Extract some (not all) of the existential dialectical orientation from chapter 20 'Conversion' of the 3rd Volume of his *Dogmatics* and the truth about conversion remains. I extract a few choice lines about the event of conversion:

> And when that happens God becomes present in me and I become present in God. Therefore here also the temporal moment of 'before' and 'after' is transcended. *Before* the event the call of the preacher is unambiguously imperative: 'Repent, be ye reconciled, believe in the Lord Jesus' (Acts 2:38; 2 Cor. 5:20; Acts 16:31) or 'Accept the invitation to the feast and make no excuses' (Luke 14:16ff), or 'Open the door to Him who knocks, and desires to come in unto thee and to sup with thee' (Rev. 3:20). *After* the event the word is: 'It is a pure gift. He alone has done it' (Rom. 5:1). *In* the event however, both elements are present in unity.[7]

Also Brunner urges:

> The task of the missionary is, above all… to proclaim the Word of repentance, because only through heart searching,… coming to his own frontiers does man become ready for the message of forgiving grace… Therefore in the New Testament as a missionary document the call is always 'Repent and believe'. But for the theologian, who sees the whole thing in retrospect, the order is reversed. For he knows that this *shub*, radically understood can only reach its goal in the strength of the assurance of Christ… 'Before' and 'after' become irrelevant where we have to do with the center, with the God who lays claim to us… the new life is effected on the one hand only through the repentance of man, and on the other only hand only through the act and speech or the speech and act of God. Both are true: We must repent, and it is God alone who creates the new life.[8]

Per contra for a vigorous advocacy of the Arminian-Semi-Pelagian view of the subject, see Norman Geisler's, *Chosen But Free*.[9]

5. To list the results of conversion in a comprehensive way is not feasible, in as much as faith is an element of conversion and faith opens the door to everything in salvation. If, however, we direct attention to what Scripture traces specifically to conversion several wonderful benefits are spelled out. Among these benefits are:

---

7. ibid., pp. 283, 284.
8. ibid., pp. 282, 283.

a) The converted's *sins are blotted out*. Peter had charged his Jewish audience with guilt for the rejection and crucifixion of their Messiah but exhorted them to 'Repent... and be converted, that your sins may be blotted out' (Acts 3:19 KJV). Later Paul spoke of 'forgiveness of sins' (Acts 26:18) as a result of conversion to Christ.

b) As a result of conversion, Peter added, 'that *times of refreshing may come from the presence of the Lord* [emphasis added]' (Acts 3:19). Some of my teachers thought that meant a re-offer of the visible kingdom of Old Testament prophecy in times of Messiah and the immediate return of Christ. Others of similar dispensational persuasion said it meant simply the spiritual blessings that accompany personal salvation (Rom. 5:1 ff. *et al*). We cannot doubt that the audience, composed exclusively of observant Jews being addressed by a Christian, but observant Jew, all fully aware of the special Old Testament predictions of wonderful blessings in the Messianic age, would have thought in those terms. The 'times of Messiah' were already in process. The kingdom of grace had been inaugurated. Therefore I think they are correct who say that Peter was promising the spiritual 'Refreshing' (*anapsuxis*, respite, as in Exodus 8:15 the only Septuagint occurrence of this word) which Christians were already enjoying.[10]

'The "times of Refreshing" are distinguished from the "restitution of all things" of verse 21, and would seem to be, as it were, the gracious preludes of the great consummation. The souls of the weary would be quickened by the fresh breeze of morning; the fire of persecution assuaged'. Israel as a nation did not repent, and therefore hatred and strife went on to the bitter end without refreshment (AD 70). For every church or nation or family, those 'times of refreshing come as a sequel of true conversion, and prepare the way for a more complete restoration' (at the resurrection).[11]

Conversion does not deliver us from trials in this world. Like Bunyan's Mr Pilgrim, it sets us moving toward the Celestial City with spiritual blessings at every stage of the way – no trial being more than is common to man and such as by God's grace man can bear (1 Cor. 10:13).

c) The converted also have a great future '*inheritance*' among other saints. In Paul's brief report of his conversion and call he was commissioned to proclaim to Gentiles a conversion from 'darkness to light' and 'from the power of Satan to God, that they may receive... a place [*kleron*, lot] among those who are sanctified by faith' in Christ. This 'lot' is correctly interpreted further by Paul in Colossians as 'a share in the inheritance of saints'. This is a promise of results that ought to entice any sinner who hears of it to turn from his idols to serve the living and true God (1 Thess. 1:9). And so the benefit of a future inheritance has been set forth by evangelists through the centuries. It is one of the motives for repentance – 'the goodness of God [that] leadeth thee to repentance' (Rom. 2:4 KJV).

d) A *new spiritual discernment* results from the change of direction and inner transformation. This is the meaning of the several 'from darkness to light' passages in the New Testament. Having referred to the blindness of the unsaved Jewish hearers of the law as having a veil over their minds, Paul says, 'But when one turns to the Lord, the veil is removed' (2 Cor. 3:16). Only God knows when the new discernment breaks through. Many nominally religious folk who, christened as infants and instructed for 'confirmation', will tell you 'It didn't mean a thing' until truly converted at a later time. The same, of course, can be said of some children in Baptist homes who always attended church, Sunday School, and as a matter of course or custom 'made confession' and were immersed in water 'in the name of the Father, and of the Son and of the Holy Ghost' – at about the same age as Lutheran children are confirmed and are admitted to 'first communion'.

e) Holding in mind that conversion is the obverse side of regeneration, two texts say the experience opens *new hopes and promises*. After conversion the Second Advent becomes more than a vague teaching about how the world will come to an end. '[Y]ou turned to God... to wait for his Son from heaven' (1 Thess. 1:9, 10) – said to be a 'blessed hope... and the glorious appearing' of the Saviour (Titus 2:13 KJV) for 'When Christ who is your life appears, then you also will appear with him in glory' (Col. 3:4). This is, of course, a great 'comfort' (2 Thess. 2:16, 17).

---

9. Norman Geisler, *Chosen But Free* (Minneapolis: Bethany House Publ., 1999). Dr Geisler attempts to put faith and repentance prior to regeneration. He asked me to review the manuscript before publication privately, which I did, seeking to dissuade the author from publishing it. Dr Geisler is not 'easily entreated' on this issue.

10. See F. F. Bruce, *The Book of Acts*, rev. ed. (Grand Rapids, MI: Eerdmans Publ., 1988), pp. 83, 84.

11. E. H. Plumptre, 'The Acts of the Apostles', in *Ellicott's Commentary on the Whole Bible vi*, (Grand Rapids, MI: Zondervans, repr. 1954), p. 19.

Some Questions and Problems and Observations About Conversion.

1. In my treatment of the order of 'aspects' (Brunner) or 'elements' (Strong) in election, effectual calling, regeneration, repentance, faith and conversion, I have insisted: 1) repentance and faith are negative and positive aspects of one act of conversion. 2) Regeneration is the same event viewed as God's work of beginning to apply redemption to a sinner. 3) That the initiative for it all comes from God alone who has power to cause the sinner even to desire rescue from his lost condition. 4) That divine initiative (Emil Brunner's felicitous expression) first takes hold in 'illumination' of the soul or first planting of spiritual life, which first planting, from the perspective of entering the kingdom (John 3:3 ff.), is regeneration. It is important that God's 'role' as solely the one who saves be preserved if our outlook is to be evangelical and truly Protestant. Nothing a sinner can 'do' is a meritorious 'work'. Paul defends the grace principle with these words: 'Now to the one who works, his wages are not counted as a gift but as his due' (Rom. 4:4) and 'So too at the present time there is a remnant, chosen by grace [we did not choose God; He chose us]. But if it is by grace, it is no longer on the basis of works; otherwise grace would no longer be grace' (Rom. 11:5, 6).

Thomas Oden is correct in asserting 'Repentance in one sense goes before faith, in another sense accompanies faith, and in still another sense issues from and follows faith.'[12] It *follows* faith in the sense that one must believe there is a God to whom to convert (Heb. 11:6); for faith itself contains this intellectual element of *assensus*, 'I believe *that*'. Repentance *accompanies* faith in the sense that turning to God is the same *act* as turning away from God's enemy Satan. It *precedes faith* in the sense that the initial *awakening* of new life in effectual calling finds the sinner in his corruption from which he must turn. He cannot take his hate for God along with him into faith. He must repent of his aversion to God's holiness.

2. *What is the place of confession in conversion?* First, let us consider that initial confession 'unto salvation' in the words of the classical text, Romans 10:8-10: '(that is the word of faith which we preach): that if you confess with your mouth the Lord Jesus and believe in your heart that God has raised Him from the dead, you will be saved. For with the... mouth confession is made unto salvation' (Rom. 10:8-10 NKJV). This was, Paul says, what he preached to those who needed to 'be saved' (v. 9). Let us change the word saved to 'converted'. In the context of evangelism they refer to the same event. The content of the confession in conversion in this bit of apostolic wisdom is 'the Lord Jesus' or as the English Standard and Revised Versions have it, 'Jesus is Lord'. This must be accompanied with acknowledgment that God has raised Jesus from the dead.

In the case of the raw heathen who makes this confession on the first presentation of the gospel and in a short time (in the middle of the night in the case of the Philippian jailor), to say 'Jesus is Lord' would mean simply to believe, I suppose, 'all authority in heaven and earth' is given 'to this Jesus'. We must presume, I think, that Paul or Silas explained that Jesus died on a certain day and three days later was raised from the dead by God. In this case the man made his confession by receiving baptism in 'the same hour of the night'. The missionaries had little time, I judge, to explain the Christian meaning of *theos* (God), a word familiar to the jailor. (He may like most Roman soldiers have cursed by the *theoi*.) How could Paul or Silas have traced its meaning through Scripture back to the 'God of Abraham, of Isaac and of Jacob'? It is doubtful the two missionaries made a case with the bewildered jailor for the identity of the Son of God of the Gospels with the LORD (Jehovah) of the Old Testament, though as the jailor participated in the life and ministries of the Philippian church it would have been fully explained to him there at a later time (as the second chapter of Paul's letter to the Philippians explained profoundly). The jailor, after that night grew – not *into* faith, but *in* faith and *the* faith as well.

Other texts show that when people confessed Christ in baptism the confession was accompanied by 'confessing their sins'. If they have no sin they have no need either of Christ or forgiveness (Mark 2:17). John the Baptist required it (Matt. 3:6). Again, baptism being the mode of confession, Peter proclaimed to his Jewish audience, 'Repent and be baptized every one of you... for the forgiveness of your sins' (Acts 2:38). In submitting to baptism, a ritual cleansing, one is confessing sin and sins. Like believing in the heart, therefore, repentance must be in the heart, otherwise baptism has no value as 'confession... made unto salvation' (Rom. 10:10 KJV).

There is one case in the New Testament where we have absolute certainty the confession was from the heart and that the person was truly saved (converted). It is the one known to all as the case of the penitent thief on the cross.

---

12. Thomas C. Oden, *Systematic Theology ii: Life in the Spirit* (San Francisco: HarperCollins Publ., 1992), p. 102.

When was the 'malefactor' converted? When in his heart he acknowledged, 'We are receiving the due reward of our deeds' and made this confession to the one on the other side who died cursing everything and everybody. The penitent in heart also believed 'in his heart' and acknowledged 'Jesus is Lord' and addressed the Savior that way. 'Lord, remember me when thou comest into thy kingdom' (Luke 23:42 KJV).

What knowledge is implied in that poignant confession-question? No one knows for certain. Did 'Lord' mean to him the 'God of Abraham, of Isaac and of Jacob'? Minimally he knew Jesus to be the Messiah, for that is implied 'In thy kingdom'. (The Greek has in (*en*) not into (*eis*) at Luke 23:42. RSV correctly interprets *en tē basileia* as 'in your kingly power'.) Perhaps he was Jewish, a backslidden son of a synagogue somewhere and knew much more, but that is by no means certain.

Other scriptural incidents and texts demonstrate beyond a doubt that a faith that sincerely confesses Jesus as Lord to God is saving faith. 'Look and live' is all there is time for sometimes at the end of a wasted life or in life's extremity. The children of Israel were dying in threatening numbers by snakebite when 'Moses made a bronze serpent, and set it on a pole; and if a serpent bit any man, he would look at the bronze serpent' (which Moses had set on a pole) and he would live. Jesus used this incident to illustrate 'saving faith', promising: 'as Moses lifted up [on a pole] the serpent in the wilderness, so must the Son of Man be lifted up [on a cross], that whoever believes in him may have eternal life' (John 3:14, 15). 'Look and live!' it is our privilege to say to sinners in any condition of awareness. Pastors who minister to the dying on the brink of eternity (as it has been my privilege to do several times) have witnessed that 'look and live' in the squeeze of a hand, flutter of an eyelid, a slight nod of the head, or a murmured 'yes', as we read 'the Word of Life' and asked, in the looming presence of death (like Jesus' at Bethany), 'Do you believe this?'

There is another kind of confession – that confession which is public acknowledgment of Jesus as opposed to denying Him. There were leading Jews like Nicodemus who came to Jesus by night to avoid publicity (John 12:42, 43) who 'did not confess it [belief in Him], so that they would not be put out of the synagogue'. See also 2 Timothy 2:12 and Matthew 10:32, 33. In view of the Matthew 10:33 statement ('but whoever denies me before men, I also will deny before my Father who is in heaven') we well understand Peter's distress of mind when he 'wept bitterly' (Matt. 26:75). From the stories of Peter who manifest weakness rather than outright unbelief, and of Judas, who manifest outright rejection at heart, we know that only God knows fully the meaning of our words either of confession or of denial.

John Foxe (1517–1587), author of *The Book of Martyrs* (1,082 pages in a one-volume edition), tells the enduring story of the innumerable confessors whose confession of Christ cost them their lives. In Britain many died trying to bring the Bible into print in the common language. Others died for even owning a copy. The Roman Church's Inquisitions exacted the price of martyrdom from thousands over the centuries. They are the subjects of Foxe's book. The reward of martyrdom is a prevalent theme of the book of Revelation. In this twenty-first century of the Christian era, martyrdom as the price paid for confessing Christ 'before men' is a continuing story.

Closing Thoughts: a Converted Pulpit and Pastoral Ministry.

The true prophets denounced the false prophets in Old Testament times. A thoroughly discouraged Jeremiah proclaimed to his backslidden generation, 'An appalling and horrible thing has happened in the land: the prophets prophesy falsely, and the priests rule at their direction; my people love to have it so, but what will you do when the end comes?' (Jer. 5:30, 31). We see the same 'appalling' situation in congregations throughout Christendom today. Amos' prophecy has found another fulfilment in our own day – '"Behold the days are coming," declares the Lord GOD, "when I will send a famine on the land – not a famine of bread, nor a thirst for water, but of hearing the words of the LORD"' (Amos 8:11). At the present moment there are innumerable towns, villages and rural communities where there are many church buildings in which religious services are held but where, if there is even a preacher in the pulpit on a Sunday, there is no word from God that a prophet or apostle would recognize as such. Amos described this poisonous atmosphere too: 'They shall wander from sea to sea, and from north to east; they shall run to and fro, to seek the word of the LORD, but they shall not find it' (Amos 8:12).

The situation has many causes, but the immediate cause is lack of a pulpit and pastoral ministry that is both converted and committed knowledgably to the truth. The damage was so severe in Jeremiah's time that a majority preferred the prevailing spiritual darkness – 'my people love to have it so'.

The reader of this page, if a minister of the Word or a minister in preparation, should be challenged to examine his own heart to see if the evidence of a genuine conversion is there. Why do you seek the 'office of overseer' (1 Tim. 3:1)?

10
The Doctrine of Repentance

Except for the doctrine of justification there is none for which the Reformation contributed greater understanding than the doctrine of repentance. The Reformers rescued repentance for sin from doing penance for sins. The true biblical doctrine had long been perverted from its evangelical bearings by incorporation into the system of salvation by sacraments. Baptism was thought to remove all guilt for original sin – not on the occasion of the contrite sinner's faith but *ex opere operato*, by the very act of sacramental applications of water on the infant offspring of Catholic parents – i.e. *baptism*.[1]

This has not changed to the present. The Catechism of 1994 in the section on 'The Seven Sacraments of the Church' states: 'Through Baptism we are freed from sin and reborn as sons of God; we become members of Christ, and incorporated into the church and made sharers in her mission: "Baptism is the sacrament of regeneration through water in the word."'[2]

In another sacrament, called *penance* or *confession*, sins committed afterward were to be made known to a priest; then the priest, employing powers conferred by the priest's bishop in the sacrament of *ordination*, was thought to forgive the sins confessed. The priest in this scheme of things confers *absolution*, not declaratively in the sense of 1 John 1:9, but judicially, as a judge. Penance was then (and so still today) held to consist of *contrition* (genuine sorrow for sin), *confession* to the priest and *satisfaction* for sins committed. This satisfaction is not that wrought by Christ on the cross but some onerous work imposed by the priest to whom confession is made, supposed to satisfy divine justice for the sins committed. These acts of satisfaction are thought to effect two things, *expiation* of guilt for past sins and *discipline* of the spiritual life. Current Roman Catholic manuals stress the discipline aspect rather than expiation.

The occasion for Luther's posting the Ninety-Five Theses, 31 October 1517, was this perversion of repentance as 'doing penance' and the outrageous customs accompanying it by which the ecclesiastical engine gathered money for the Pope's building projects. Rome's system has not retreated from penance as a sacrament whereby forgiveness is brought up to date. The priest still concludes '*the rite of penance*' with: 'I absolve you from your sins in the name of the Father, and of the Son, and of the Holy Ghost'.[3] Dr Geoffrey W. Bromiley has written:

---

1. A current standard handbook of Roman Catholic doctrine states: 'The sacrament... is more than a sign. It does not only remind us of the sacrifice of Calvary, or merely point to the interior and invisible action of Christ, but it does actually convey what it indicates', Jelsma Van Doornik and Van De Lisdon, *A Handbook of the Catholic Faith* (San Francisco: Ignatius Press, 1994).
2. ibid., p. 312, para. 1213.

Quite apart from the obviously non-scriptural nature of this whole system, five main evils may be seen in it: (1) it misunderstands the problem of post-baptism sin; (2) it deflects from the atonement; (3) it promotes related errors such as purgatory, masses, indulgences and invocation of saints; (4) it creates legalism and formalism; and (5) it gives rise to the moral evils of the confessional. The Reformers cut through the whole falsification of theory and practice by insisting that what the New Testament demands is not penance but penitence or repentance, though they saw a real value in the restoring of true discipline and of course the private counselling of those troubled in conscience as individually required.[4]

The Reformation era is customarily said to have ended with the Peace of Westphalia, 1648, when the Wars of Religion ended – as in the standard textbook, *The Reformation Era: 1500–1650* by Harold J. Grimm.[5] But doctrinal reform was extended in Britain on the subject of the divine and human in salvation, especially the nature of divine grace, the nature of regeneration, repentance, faith, justification and sanctification. The 'Puritan divines' of Britain and British America continued to refine the evangelical meaning well into the eighteenth century on both sides of the Atlantic.

William Haller, who has done as much as any man to recover awareness of the Puritan heritage in all English-speaking lands, says on the first page of the text of one of his several books on the Puritans:

> [A]s a concerted and sustained enterprise of preachers for setting forth in the pulpit and the press [books and other literature] a conception of spiritual life and moral behavior… Puritanism… was not incompatible with any given ecclesiastical system, episcopalian, presbyterian or congregational so long as its promoters were left free to preach. *It is in fact nothing but English Protestantism in its most dynamic form, and before it had run its course, it had transfused in large measure the whole of English life* [emphasis added].[6]

These people, led by intelligent, devout, university-educated preachers, were among the most morally earnest, biblically informed and theologically literate people who ever lived.[7] They pondered, reflected and compared (with earnestness painful for our flippant generation even to hear about) the nature and relationships of effectual calling, regeneration, repentance and faith. They debated whether the Word of God is a means or an accompaniment or catalyst in producing repentance, whether repentance or faith precedes in conversion. There seems to be nothing to say which they did not say.

My own professors of theology taught me some of the ripest thinking about these matters, even though they did not say that was what we were getting. Long afterward, when I began to teach seminary courses, I was made acquainted with the true Puritan history through the Puritan writers. What the reader is perusing here is the same as I received except I am notifying readers of some of my unpaid debts. Some of the Puritans (especially some eighteenth-century British Baptists) were Supralapsarians and I am Infralapsarian – if we must enter that realm of academic excess and over-refinement. Some of them seem almost to have left evangelism of the lost world out of the number of Christian duties. If there is no place for human works of righteousness in gaining salvation there is nevertheless something to *do*, action to take. God commands both repentance (Acts 17:30) and faith (Mark 1:15) as well as conversion (Acts 3:19).

I am not sure that one can ever state satisfactorily whether faith is prior to repentance or vice versa in conversion. Surely we should back off and acknowledge they all happen together. One will not turn away from sin unless he already knows in his heart that 'he that comes to God must believe that (i.e. have faith as assent to fact) He is and that He is a rewarder of those who diligently seek Him'. On the other hand no one will believe as long as one's attention is fixed on sin, Satan and the enticements of the world. Furthermore, none is able to enter the kingdom except he be born of the Spirit (John 3:5, 8) and the Spirit moves to produce new birth when and upon whom He will. The Spirit does not *find* faith. He creates it by 'quickening', which means giving life.

---

3. *The Rite of Penance*, a four-page folder, prescribed order published by Publication Office, U. S. Catholic Conferences, Washington D. C., 1974, 1986.
4. *Baker's Dictionary of Theology*, ed. E. F. Harrison (Grand Rapids, MI: Baker, 1960), p. 400.
5. Harold J. Grimm, *The Reformation Era: 1500–1650*, 2nd ed. (New York: Macmillan, 1954, 1973).
6. William Haller, *Liberty and Reformation in the Puritan Revolution* (New York: Columbia University Press, 1955), p. xi.
7. J. I. Packer, *A Quest for Godliness: The Puritan Vision of the Christian Life* (Wheaton: Crossway Books, 1990), 367 pages; entire book, especially the 'Introduction' and 'Afterword'.

The *sola deo* origin of faith, repentance, conversion and regeneration is joyfully celebrated in the hymn-song:

> I know not why God's wondrous grace
> To me He did impart,
> Nor how believing in His Word
> Wrought peace within my heart.
>
> I know not how the Spirit moves
> Convincing men of sin,
> Revealing Jesus in God's Word,
> Creating faith in him.
>
> (Stanzas 2 and 3 of 'I Know Not Why God's Wondrous Grace' by Daniel W. Whittle, 1840–1901).

I intrude once more with this seeming diversion about our Puritan predecessors for several reasons. First, so the reader will understand why those from that age of martyrs (many early Puritans were burned, hanged and beheaded for their faith) should be consulted.[8] Second, to help the same reader to accept a fact, unwelcome to any one not taught by the Spirit of God, that salvation is wholly a divine rescue operation, not merely of people in great need, screaming for help, but who must by the immediate work of the Spirit be made willing to be rescued. 'To humble the pride of man, to exalt the grace of God in salvation and to promote real holiness in heart and life.'

Definition of Repentance.

Theologians of immediate post-Reformation times were acutely aware of the importance of a sound, biblical definition of repentance. Doing 'penance' in the papal system had thoroughly perverted the meaning of the biblical doctrine and dislocated it in the way of salvation. It is hard to improve on the following:

> Repentance unto life is a saving grace (Acts 11:18), whereby a sinner, out of a true sense of his sin (Acts 2:37), and apprehension of the mercy of God in Christ (Joel 2:13), doth, with grief and hatred of his sin turn from it unto God (2 Cor. 7:11; Jer. 31:18, 19; Acts 26:18), with full purpose of, and endeavor after, new obedience (Ps. 119:59).[9]

The Greek and Hebrew Words.

As will be seen, repentance or some aspect of it, is frequently indicated by several English words which in turn translate several different Hebrew and Greek words, each with more than a shade of difference in meaning.

In the Old Testament there are mainly two words translated 'repent' in our English Versions. One, *naḥam*, usually in simple passive (*Niphal*) form, is most frequently used of God's repenting (thirty-five times, at least) of which Genesis 6:6 (KJV) is the first example – 'And it repented the LORD that he had made man'. Some recent translations render, the Lord 'regretted' or 'was sorry'. The essential idea is emotional in sense. I think 'regret' is the best English translation. Yet usage shows that *contemplated* changes in action or treatment of another are indicated (see 1 Sam. 15:29; Ps. 110:4; Jer. 4:25). It is used only about five times of man's repentance. This word is regularly translated by *metanoeō* and *metamellomai* (see below on New Testament Greek words).

---

8. Conservative evangelical theology never quite forgot its debt to the English and American Puritans. George Park Fisher in his *History of Christian Doctrine* (Edinburgh: T. & T. Clark, 1896, 1927), chapters vii and viii gives a sketch of an overview and the best Calvinist authors of the nineteenth century pay their respects, but the learned intelligentsia of the universities hated what little they knew of them. Perry Miller wrote: 'There is a pronounced disposition in America to resent the suggestion that the colonial leaders (for that matter, also the architects of the American Constitution) were intellectuals. In the vicinity of Boston [Harvard] one can encounter an aversion that amounts to settled hostility against any account implying that the founders of New England were primarily occupied with religious ideas, and even more against the supposition that they gave their days and nights to abstract speculation... The New Englanders were correct in claiming they were not followers of John Calvin, because they honestly believed that they were reading the Bible with their own eyes. Yet in the historical perspective, their way of interpreting the Bible must be called Calvinist'. Perry Miller in the 1964 reissue of *Errand to the Wilderness* (Cambridge: Belknap Press of Harvard University Press), preface to chapter iii, 'The Marrow of Puritan Divinity', pp. 48, 49.

9. This statement is the answer to Question 87 of *Westminster Shorter Catechism*, 'What is repentance unto life?'

The second Hebrew word is more basic to formation of the New Testament doctrine. It is *shuv*, as observed in the preceding chapter on conversion, a term related to volitions or choices and resultant action. Hence it may be rendered convert or conversion (of which repentance is a part): the Greek Old Testament regularly renders it by *epistrephō*. But it also is translated to backslide – a reverse, of conversion, as several times in Jeremiah 3, verses 6, 11 and 12 – through a special doubling of the last consonant of the Hebrew word *shuv* to *shuvav*. This word (*shuvav*) is employed to make the backslide idea clear in verses 14 and 22 of Jeremiah 3. (KJV translates 'backsliding' in Jeremiah 3; ESV uses 'faithless'.)

In the New Testament the word *metamellomai* corresponds to the Hebrew *naḥam* and *metanoeō* somewhat to *shuv* (the equivalence is not invariable). Of these four words *metanoeō* (and the corresponding noun *metanoia*) is most important, for when used of 'repentance unto salvation' it gathers up the significance of the others. A roster of texts referring to saving repentance will display that *metanoeō* is usually the New Testament word employed – almost sixty times. Hebrews 12:17 is an interesting exception to soteriological use, referring as it does to Jacob's repentance, not Esau's. In this case the narrow sense, to change one's mind, to reverse a decision, is paramount in *metanoeō*. *Metamellomai* is used only six times (Matt. 21:29, 32; 27:3; 2 Cor. 7:8; Heb. 7:21) but only once (Matt. 7:32) in salvational reference. So *metanoeō* is the word to study.

The theology of repentance among good writers makes no distinction between scriptural statements of or relating to the repentance of long-time believers and the person who is making initial repentance in initial conversion. The psychology of repentance, if we mean the processes of the moral faculties, or, better, the moral activities of the soul, are not different in kind or cause. Hence theologians who know the Bible well will turn to Psalms 51 and 32, the repentance of David, a 'man after God's own heart' (1 Sam. 13:14; Acts 13:22) to illustrate biblical repentance, whether of saint or sinner. The same may be said of Peter's repentance when as a true disciple he was 'converted' (Luke 22:32) from a backslidden condition in which he three times denied Christ.

Three Elements of Repentance.

As we shall note later of faith, there are three elements discernable in the 'repentance that leads to life' – the negative turn away from sin.

1. There is a *change (turnabout) of thinking* concerning sin, a change of opinion. When the preachers whom we meet on the pages of the New Testament call for repentance they do so after substantial efforts to persuade men's mind that their previous opinions about religious truth and the good life are both erroneous and sinful (see e.g. Acts 2:38; 8:22; 17:30). David's repentance was preceded by Nathan's visit (2 Sam. 12; cf. superscriptions to Ps. 51 and Ps. 32:3-5), which made his mind aware of what his conscience was telling him. This is to say the change must be accompanied by the rational process of learning as well as a purely spiritual event.

The pattern of the preaching of repentance by the Old Testament prophets is illustrated by Jeremiah's sermons to the citizens of Jerusalem and environs in the early years of the young prophet's association with the youthful King Josiah, a genuinely repentant believer and reforming king. God commissioned the prophet 'to pluck up and to break down, to destroy and to overthrow' (four negatives) as well as 'to build and to plant' (two positives) (Jer. 1:10). As the young *navi* (Hebrew word for prophet) set out to fulfill his commission he first cried 'in the ears of Jerusalem' concerning their wholesale departure from their covenanted moral obligations.

He pressed home knowledge of their sins. He used the metaphor of marital unfaithfulness, employing embarrassingly graphic language (like a mare ass in heat (Jer. 2:24) 'on every high hill and under every green tree you bowed down like a whore' (Jer. 2:20)). She went looking for partners in adultery, i.e. idolatry, and breaking the laws to which at Sinai they had made covenantal consent. They even had licentious tricks to teach the whores (Jer. 3). The desperately backslidden situation in the country, Jeremiah said, was through and through: 'the prophets prophesy falsely, and the priests rule at their directions; my people love to have it so' (Jer. 5:31).

The young preacher addressed their minds with knowledge of divine judgment: 'but what will you do when the end comes?' (Jer. 5:31). After reminding them in the vivid language of sexual lust (Jer. 5:7, 8) he exclaims, 'Shall I not punish them for these things? declares the LORD; and shall I not avenge myself on a nation such as this?' (v. 9). The punishment will be withdrawal of any authentic priestly or prophetic ministry to them (vv. 10-13) – a famine 'of hearing the words of the LORD' as an earlier preacher (Amos 8:11) denounced on Israel.

The prophet repeatedly makes known divine appeals for repentance: 'Return, faithless [backsliding KJV] Israel… I will not look on you in anger, for I am merciful, declares the LORD; I will not be angry for ever…And I will give you shepherds after my own heart, who will feed you with knowledge and understanding' (Jer. 3:12, 15). Repentance is preceded by understanding of divine ways.

The whole prophecy then becomes set in a context of divinely *scheduled* spiritual regeneration and repentance of the people after judgment (Jer. 3:15-18). The experiences of national Israel and the revelations concerning her become transformed into prophecies of individual experiences and truth for individuals in the New Testament revelation – so much so that New Testament authors employ the Old Testament texts in that way. We have already taken note of this in the chapter on regeneration in our Lord's words to Nicodemus.

The Bible simply does not support the irrationalism of existential philosophy wherein authentic existence is achieved by a 'leap into the dark'. Authenticity of being is achieved in part when sin is no longer seen as desirable or 'fun', but for what it is (Ps. 51, David's prayer of repentance). This is called 'knowledge of sin' and it comes by exposure of the mind to God's law (Rom. 3:20; Gal. 3:19-22). Hence true evangelistic preaching will devote some of its best effort to propounding God's standards. Again, the Reformers saw this plainly and acted accordingly as have authentic evangelists and Christian teachers in every epoch. An Old Testament example of such preaching is the preaching of Jonah. The writing prophets of the Old Testament made repentance their major theme as did also John the Baptist, the last of their line (Matt. 11:9-13; 3:1-12).

Experience of sin does not teach us 'knowledge of sin' in this sense; it only hardens our hearts. Nor is it repentance to call one's self harsh names, nor is overdone self-depreciation. As a pastor I have been first reader of two suicide notes which were self-depreciating to the point of black despair. Not every negative change of thinking (it may be called remorse, regret, sorrow) is in itself saving repentance. 'The sorrow of the world worketh death' (2 Cor. 7:10 KJV) – as the suicides of King Saul and of Judas illustrate. Judas decided he should not have betrayed Jesus for money (Matt. 27:4). 'I have sinned' was acknowledged by still hard-of-heart Pharaoh (Exod. 9:27), by vacillating Balaam (Num. 22:34) and an insincere Saul (1 Sam. 15:24), as well as by remorseful Judas. Pronounced by Jesus, 'son of destruction' (John 17:12), Judas repented in this sense only (Matt. 27:3 KJV; better 'seized with remorse' NIV; or simply 'changed his mind' ESV; *metamellomai* is used).

There is reason to lament the strange disparagement of the whole project of knowing truth among 'intellectuals'. In this they mimic their remote pagan ancestors whom God 'gave up' precisely because they 'refused to retain God in their knowledge' and became vain in their imaginations. Carl F. H. Henry, founding editor of Christian Today magazine in an article entitled 'The Crisis of Our Time' showed what current readers of college textbooks really want to know:

> …a special sale catalog came in the mail from a large American publisher of… university textbooks. Among the 1000 listings… only one title was premarked 'sold out.' What volume, you ask, was in such special academic demand? The title believe it or not, was 'Understanding the Female Orgasm.'

He goes on to say:

> An impenitent generation, the Apostle Paul tells us, receives its "due penalty," divine recompense proportionate to its own priorities. To suppress knowledge of God will skew right and wrong with devastating final consequences.[10]

Two more changes must accompany change of thinking.

2. There is a related *turnabout of feeling* concerning sin, an emotional change, 'sorrow for sin as committed against goodness and justice, and therefore hateful to God and hateful in itself'. Let the inquirer read Psalm 51 and note how this element predominates in many lines (vv. 1, 2, 10, 14). In this experience, David found that what sudden passion esteemed delightful became a 'groaning all day long' (Ps. 32:3). He discovered God did not relieve him of his burden until he acted on his feelings of regret and his self-accusation: 'I said, "I will confess my transgressions to the LORD", and you forgave the iniquity of my sin' (Ps. 32:5); after that came 'shouts of deliverance' (Ps. 32:7).

Paul calls this saving repentance 'godly grief' (or 'sorrow' KJV) (2 Cor. 7:10). The same apostle calls the mere feeling of sadness 'the sorrow of the world' and goes onto say it produces 'death' (2 Cor. 7:10). Compare the case of Judas and numerous suicides of people who have seen the fruitlessness of their own wicked lives as well as the bitterness and malaise

---

10. Carl F. H. Henry, *'The Crisis of Our Time', The Evangelical Beacon*, (October 30, 1979), p.4.

of many others who never end their own lives (Hamlet's famous soliloquy: 'Thus conscience doth make cowards of us all'). When saving repentance is ripe enough its subject ceases thinking mainly of the deadly consequences of sins, or of the harm to others, and especially ceases excusing himself or blaming childhood miseducation and heredity. (All parents do make mistakes in the rearing of their children.) One rather, in 'godly sorrow', discerns a) that all transgression is of *God's* laws – to sin (the Greek and Hebrew words for sin often have the narrow meaning of neglect or failure) is to come short of God's holiness; b) that he himself is personally responsible – guilty and blameworthy – no other human person, not the devil and certainly not God; c) that sins of any sort are inwardly defiled and defiling; d) this means one has a new feeling for God's interests. His newly informed conscience now directs him to think upon God and His interests. He sees God as spurned and rejected, that the sinner, God's creature, has failed his Maker and ought not to have done so.

3. A redirection of the will occurs. Knowledge of sin in one's self leads to a change of thinking which in turn leads to change of feeling and that to a redirection of will. Hence we speak of three elements – intellectual, emotional and volitional. The first two must be followed by the third. Again, the great repentance Psalm (51:5, 7, 10; cf. Jer. 25:4, 5) furnishes basic scriptural evidence. This decision will be decisive, thoroughgoing, permanent, described by Paul in relation to penitents of the church at Corinth: 'ye were made sorry after a godly manner… For godly sorrow worketh repentance to salvation *not to be repented of* [emphasis added] (2 Cor. 7:9, 10 KJV).' The will now takes on a totally new direction.

'Will' in theology touched by Reformation theological thinking includes much more than the faculty of the soul for making decisions. When we say the will takes a *totally* new direction in repentance, the repentance is viewed in relation to the comprehensive change called conversion which includes faith as well as repentance. This is spelled out in an essay by a minister of the Church of Scotland at Leith:

> In the moment of regeneration the Holy Spirit implants all spiritual and saving graces in the heart of the elect sinner, and among others faith and repentance. He implants at the same instant the root or principle of saving faith and of true repentance. He gives these two graces together and at once in respect of time; and therefore, though in our conception of them, they are to be distinguished, yet they are never to be separated from each other. The principle of faith in the regenerate soul, that is the capacity of acting faith is not in point of time before that of repentance, nor is the principle of repentance before that of faith. Every true believer in principle is at the same time a true penitent, and every true penitent in respect of principle is a genuine believer. An impenitent believer and a penitent unbeliever, are characters which have no existence but in the vain imaginations of some men.[11]

In the sense employed here 'will' has reference to the basic disposition of the soul. In 'natural man' (1 Cor. 2:14 KJV) the will is selfish. It was made so by the fall of our race. '[T]he mind that is set on the flesh is hostile to God, for it does not submit to God's law; indeed, it cannot' (Rom. 8:7). I have dealt with this matter at length in *Anthropology*, the doctrine of man, and elsewhere previously in this volume. Please refer to the work of W. G. T. Shedd and of A. H. Strong on the will of fallen man.[12] Our will is corrupt. It is even more wicked than our deeds which the will directs us to perform.

This third element, the change of will in repentance involves the first two. This element of change, unlike the other two, will immediately be manifest in a changed manner of life. There are works 'in keeping with repentance' which shall follow (Matt 3:8). Paul, in a remarkable passage, mentions all three elements as part of his message wherever he had gone – Damascus, Jerusalem, Judea and among the nations. He is addressing his captor Festus and the visiting King Agrippa: 'I… declared [i.e. made intellectually aware] first to those in Damascus, then in Jerusalem and throughout all the region of Judea, and also to the Gentiles, that they should repent [the emotional element, for this at least is reasonable to suppose in the context] and turn to God, performing deeds in keeping with their repentance [the volitional element]' (Acts 26:19, 20).

Further Factors in Repentance.

As is very frequent in the various aspects of salvation, repentance, though wholly man's own act, is also God's sovereign gift, His work in man. Most of the passages on repentance (with which we are familiar) emphasize that man, himself, must repent. Let one serve as an impressive example: 'God… now… commands all people everywhere

---

11. The quotation is from a chapter in *Evangelical Repentance* by John Colquhoun, 1748–1827, a minister of the Church of Scotland at Leith. My source is a booklet published by Chapel Library, 2603 W. Wright St, Pensacola, FL 32505. This source republishes a large amount of hard to find Puritan and more recent literature of similar theological outlook. They invite new subscribers.
12. W. G. T. Shedd, *Dogmatic Theology, ii*, 'The Human Will' (Grand Rapids, MI: Zondervan, 1969), pp. 115 ff.; A. H. Strong, *Systematic Theology* (Valley Forge, PA: Judson Press, 1907), pp. 504–513.

to repent' (Acts 17:30). The speaker (Paul) goes on to threaten judgment. Yet saving repentance is God's sovereign gift of grace as Peter unmistakably asserted: 'God exalted him... to give repentance to Israel' (Acts 5:31). This giving of repentance was no mere opening of the gate to salvation to Israel. It had already been open for 2,000 years. The conferees at a Jerusalem meeting of leaders 'glorified God, saying, "Then to the Gentiles also God has granted repentance that leads to life"' (Acts 11:18). If these two texts be denied relevance as having some dispensational rather than personal reference, the same is not possible on any ground for the following Pauline counsel to young pastor Timothy: 'And the Lord's servant must... be... kind to everyone.., patiently enduring evil, correcting his opponents with gentleness. *God may perhaps grant them repentance* [emphasis added] leading to a knowledge of the truth, and they may escape from the snare of the devil' (2 Tim. 2:24-26). Note the divine and human aspects both present in this citation. The divine Author of Scripture finds no contradiction between God's sovereign bestowal ('God may grant', etc.) and human action ('they may escape', etc.) in the same act of repentance. Neither should we.

Motives for repentance are numerous. Scripture mentions or suggests several. Fear of judgment to come was cited by Paul (Acts 17:30, 31) and employed at least once by him with partial success (with Felix, Acts 24:24, 25). It is clear that this motive, though important in arresting attention, does not in itself constitute, or lead to, repentance. Men must turn to God and heaven as well as *away from* sin and hell! Hence, the value of repentance 'for the forgiveness of sins' (Luke 3:3). Furthermore the 'goodness and forbearance' of God, together with His 'longsuffering' tend more to break the hardened shell of the sinner's heart, for 'the goodness of God [Gr. kindness as opposed to harshness] leadeth thee to repentance' (Rom. 2:4 KJV). In the last of the seven messages to the seven churches of Asia of the Apocalypse, professed believers are warned that if they do not repent God will bring severe providential chastening upon them (Rev. 3:19) and Jesus earlier said that if people do not repent they will perish (Luke 13:1-5).

Sometimes claims are made for dispensational distinctions with regard to repentance. One of the editors of the Scofield Bible, for example, used to claim that repentance was a Jewish message only, that Gentiles are only to have faith. This nowadays turns up only among ultra-dispensationalists. There is a fragment of truth to it. The Jewish people addressed by Peter (Acts 2) had taken a wrong attitude toward Jesus, even though they professed belief in the one true God, the God of Israel. When the sermon convinced them of their error in rejecting their Messiah and brought conviction of guilt for what they had done to Jesus seven weeks earlier, they asked Peter, 'what shall we do?' Thereupon they were told to 'repent' – of their *wrong assessment of Jesus* (Acts 2:37, 38). Faith was not mentioned specifically but is certainly the central feature of the command to be 'baptized every one of you in the name of Jesus Christ'. As a matter of patent fact, therefore, repentance has a high priority rating among all Bible prophets and preachers from Enoch and Noah to the two martyr witnesses of those 1,260 last days of Revelation, chapter 11, and from the sixth chapter of Genesis to the last chapter of Revelation. It would take us far afield to show this – though any industrious student can do so with the assistance of a concordance.

Perhaps the reader will now be more fully prepared than at the beginning of this chapter to understand that repentance as a negative act of the sinner, joined with an accompanying (not necessarily subsequent) positive act, called faith, together constitute conversion. Sometimes in the New Testament repentance is overtly associated with faith: 'repentance towards God and of faith in our Lord...' (Acts 20:21); and sometimes with conversion: 'repent ye therefore and be converted' (Acts 3:19 KJV). Repentance, faith and conversion are not stages in a process; they are aspects of a single step. In walking one picks up a foot, sets it down again, and the body moves forward, yet the several acts belong together and are inseparable, constituting one step. It is important as well as interesting to observe that Scripture, viewing an event of saving response to the gospel, from one aspect, may call it repentance, from another, faith, viz. Jonah 3:5 reports, so 'the people of Nineveh believed God. They called for a fast'; but Jesus says, 'The men of Nineveh... repented at the preaching of Jonah' (Matt. 12:41). Yet when faith and repentance are mentioned together repentance is usually put first (see Matt. 21:32; Mark 1:15; Heb. 6:1).

Concluding Reflection.

For a generation or so – since the horrors of Second World War days – repentance has been a neglected teaching. Perhaps the general helplessness of the human race under threat of population-destroying atomic fission bombs and then hydrogen bombs, later the AIDS epidemic and more recent terrorist episodes has made us feel sinful humanity had been frightened enough. Man's mental confusion and spiritual alienation from himself and others may unconsciously have suggested the priority of preaching to social or psychological needs which for many years has been the regular fare in many pulpits. Sometimes social and psychological needs – all temporal – have seemed to take precedence over eternal life with God in the city He has prepared. These worthy, but comparatively paltry matters, really hinge on conversion, of which repentance is an aspect. Perhaps we shall approach closer to meeting human social and psychological needs if we give consistent attention to this overriding spiritual matter: human beings are sinners, rebels against their Maker. 'Repent, therefore and believe the gospel'.

11
The Doctrine of Faith: Linguistic Factors and Specific Elements

There are a large number of terms rather special to Christian doctrine and liturgy. Until recently these words were treated with respect for their place in the prevailing religion of the culture. Within the memory of older people, however, many of these words have been borrowed (prostituted?) by a backslidden, secular, but literate, culture. So a fine word like charismatic, for example, no longer reserved for a spiritual gift imparted to a Christian by the Spirit of God, is applied to any popular leader of people movements, whether good or evil. This is where 'litany', 'gospel', 'born again' (since Jimmy Carter) and many others have gone: and where the word 'faith' seems to be going. Dictionaries of the Standard English language reflect a deflation of value over the past century similar to the loss in value of our money. In 1900 a nickel would buy about the same as a dollar in 2000. The 1915 Funk and Wagnalls *Desk Standard Dictionary* provided a distinctly Christian sense to the *first meaning* of faith, 'A firm conviction of truth of what is declared by another, simply on the ground of his truth or faithfulness... belief and trust exercised toward God and Christ.' By 1947 *The American College Dictionary* (Random House) listed a considerably weakened Christian definition as the *eighth meaning* and labeled it *theological,* i.e. a narrow meaning.[1] Nowadays, the confidence of Bristol-Meyers or General Motors in the integrity of their product (or of their customers) is more commonly understood as 'faith' than the Christian understanding.

Christians too are not consistent even in religious use of the word faith – 'faith-healing', for example, may be what goes on at 'charismatic' religious revivals of a certain sort. In 'faith-based charities', faith is flattened out to mean simply 'religious'.

In these circumstances a careful examination of the biblical meaning of faith is a necessary preliminary to formal exposition of the doctrine of saving faith.

Since *faith* (the noun) and the correlate verb *believe* are now used in ordinary discourse about all subjects, both in the Bible and out of it, it has a broad range of application which must be given some consideration preliminary to discussion of the specific act of saving faith.

---

1. Webster's New World Dictionary, 3rd ed., 1988, happily recovered some of the original religious meaning.

The Hebrew and Greek Words.

We shall at this point confine our remarks to the words for faith and to believe in the original languages of the Bible. Since the New Testament advances very far beyond the Old, though building on the Old Testament words, we shall narrow the field of inquiry quickly to the New Testament Greek verb *pisteuō* and its correlate noun *pistis*. The Old Testament Hebrew word *he'emin*, 'to believe' (causative active of *'aman*, to be firm) does not tell us much in itself, even though the doctrine of faith is prevalent in the Old Testament history (and doctrine) of salvation. Paul's historical references (Rom. 4; Gal. 2–4) and chapter 11 of Hebrews demonstrate that. In the Greek Old Testament the Hebrew word *he'emin* (*hiphil* of *'aman*) is rendered by *pisteuō*. This latter is the term (with *pistis*, faith) regularly used in the New Testament to designate that religious relationship of trust in God through Christ which people enter, in response to the preaching of the gospel.

In classical usage *pisteuō* means (Liddell and Scott *Greek-English Lexicon*) a) to believe, trust, trust in, rely on a person or thing; b) to comply or obey; and c) in certain constructions, 'to believe that, feel sure or confident that a thing is, will be, has been', 'to dare to do a thing'; d) with dative and infinitive, to trust to someone information which he will keep in confidence, to entrust something to another, and, passive, to have committed to one.

In the *koinē* (common) Greek of the New Testament there is a very wide range of usage. Joining the noun *pistis* and the cognate verb *pisteuō* together, the following categories of meanings emerge.

1. Apparently by virtue of the fact that the several Hebrew nouns and adjectives derived from Hebrew *'aman* (and meaning faithfulness, fidelity, etc.) are in the Greek Old Testament rendered by *pistis*, our term *pistis* does very occasionally signify faithfulness. It is used thus of God's faithfulness (Rom. 3:3) and of man's (Matt. 23:23; Gal. 5:22; Titus 2:10). The meaning of Hebrew *'emuna* (an inflected form of *'aman*) in Habakkuk 2:4 (whether human religious faith in God or God's faith) is in dispute, as is Paul's use of *pistis* which translates Habakkuk at Romans 1:17. There is growing weight of opinion that *pistis* means faithfulness in Romans 1:17.[2] This use, however, has only indirect relation to saving faith.

2. By what one good writer calls an occasional 'natural transition', 'the faith' (*hē pistis*) signifies the truths of Christianity, the body of truth believed.[3] Thus Paul was said to preach 'the faith' he once destroyed (Gal. 1:23); Paul refers to the Christian life as 'obedience to the faith' (Rom. 1:5 KJV) and another New Testament author urged that men 'contend for the faith that was once for all delivered' (Jude 3). (See also 1 Timothy 4:1, 6 and possibly James 2:14.) Beginning about AD 180 this sense, what Christians believe, was phrased in Latin *regula fidei*, rule of faith. This was well understood in that early epoch when New Testament Scripture had not fully replaced recollection (passed down by word of mouth, tradition) of what the Apostles had taught. Churches known to be places where one of the Apostles ministered were regarded as special custodians of the apostolic faith. Shortly the *rule of faith* became a canon truth, 'the official church teaching which is in complete harmony with scripture and is a summary of it'.[4]

3. The most common use is of the act of belief or the state of believing someone or something to be true, authentic, real, worthy. Most of the New Testament appearances of *pisteuō* and *pistis* are involved.

4. Perhaps hardly to be dissociated from 3) is the use of the word faith (*pistis*) as a name for the religion of the New Testament. Taking faith as the outstanding characteristic of gospel religion, Paul by metonymy, putting a significant part for the whole, at least twice employs this 'dispensational' significance, saying, 'Now before faith came, we were held captive under the law' (Gal. 3:23); 'But now that faith has come, we are no longer under a guardian' (Gal. 3:25).[5]

The General Meaning of the Act of Faith (*Pistis* and *Pisteuō*).

In a common secular sense, but by reduction of the Christian sense, the New Testament writers will occasionally employ the word to indicate simple mental assent to facts. More than once the Gospels will use the word for the

---

2. W. B. Wallis, *Journal of the Evangelical Theological Society*, vol. 16, no. 1 (1973), pp. 17–24, for an evangelical scholarly assessment.
3. J. I. Packer, 'Faith', in *Evangelical Dictionary of Theology*, ed. W. A. Elwell (Grand Rapids, MI: Baker Books, 1984), p. 400.
4. M. E. Osterhaven, *EDT*, p. 961. See J. N. D. Kelly, *Early Christian Doctrines*, rev. ed. (San Francisco: Harper, 1978), pp. 39–44.
5. The extended discussion of the Greek and Hebrew words for faith in the Bible is excellently traced out in *Theological Dictionary of the New Testament vi*, ed. G. Kittel and G. Frederich, trans. G. W. Bromiley (Grand Rapids, MI: Eerdmans, 1964–1976), pp. 174–228 by none other than Rudolph Bultmanm. Minus the now somewhat passé 'Acts of God' theology and Bultmann's own special theories of revelation and eschatology it is as complete and useful a presentation of the biblical words, both Hebrew and Greek as available. See esp. pp. 208–217 on 'Specific Christian Usage: The Relation of Christian Faith to that of the Old Testament.' In his own strange way he concludes that in the New Testament 'Now for the first time faith is religion and believers are Christians.'

temporary, impulsive response to Jesus' word and work (John 2:23 contrast v. 24; John 8:30, 31 contrast vv. 44, 45). (The folk at Jerusalem who witnessed some unspecified miracles believed in the shallow intellectual sense that they attributed some degree of validity to Jesus as a preacher, but they disbelieved in any full sense.) This is a case of the common diffuse employment of words of very special meaning and it happens every day in all languages.

A special sense, recognized by many scholars, is the attitude or expectation sometimes called faith, which occasioned special miracles from the Son of God during His days on earth. Nazareth was not a scene of many of His miracles: 'And he did not do many mighty works there, because of their unbelief' (Matt. 13:58), to which Mark adds: 'And he could do no mighty work there, except that he laid his hands on a few sick people and healed them. And he marvelled because of their unbelief' (Mark 6:5, 6). Many place His words about the faith that moves mountains, etc. (Luke 17:5, 6; Matt 17:19, 20; Mark 9:24; cf. 1 Cor. 12:9; 13:2), in this category. It is worthy of note that none of the 'faith' generated by Jesus' miracles nor the 'faith' calling forth His miracles was genuine saving faith (cf. John 12:37-41; cf. Isa. 53:1 ff.; also Matt 7:22 ff.). Nor does *saving* faith ask for miracles (2 Cor. 5:7).

Another unmistakably different sense is faith, the special gift of faith, to certain believers. It is a gift to be used in the edifying of the churches (1 Cor. 12:9 is an unmistakable case, perhaps Phil. 1:29 is another). Every Christian apparently has some 'measure of faith' (Rom. 12:3) of this kind. It enables those who have it in prominent degree to lead others in difficult exploits of evangelism and of church enlargement; and all need it in the harsh moments of life, especially those hard moments when we are leaving 'the land of the living' to meet a God and Christ whom we have never yet seen (see 1 Peter 1:8).

There is finally (and most prevalently in the New Testament) the act of believing in Christ for salvation.

The Specific Nature of Saving Faith.

In modern times faith has been wrongfully 'rationalized' and 'psychologized', just as in the medieval period it was 'legalized' and ruined by reduction to mere assent to facts.

Negatively, a saving faith is not merely a rational act, intellectual assent to words or propositions. Alexander Campbell, a founder of Disciples of Christ and The Christian Church, and some of his followers, have made faith along with repentance and baptism, steps to regeneration. It is supposed to be simply belief in the truth. If that were all faith is, of course faith would not be enough to save. The definition of faith at the Roman Catholic Council of Trent, wherein the evangelical doctrines were anathematized, practically equates faith with intellectual assent to truth only. As earlier noted, sometimes the New Testament does dignify mere assent to truth with the words faith and believe, but always makes clear that salvation is not involved. The case of Simon Magnus, who 'believed' but whose 'heart' was 'not right' (Acts 8:13, 18-31), is illustrative of this as well as the cases in the opening paragraph of the previous paragraphs above. (See also John 12:42, 43.)

Nor is faith a work of meritorious value for procurement of salvation, as in the Roman system. There are Roman Catholic confessional and theological documents which seem to support a proper biblical view but the ideas are overlaid with the teaching that grace is infused into the baptized, enabling them by various virtues and works, including faith, to merit salvation. Romans 4:4, 5, 16 and 11:6 specifically deny such a perverse interpretation. One of the great gains of the Reformation was clarification of this matter.

Schleiermacher's 'feeling of dependence' theory of faith – the psychologizing and emotionalizing of faith – is unscriptural as well.

Positively: there are at least three historically useful threefold analyses of the elements of saving faith. There is one, stemming from post-Reformation orthodoxy, which speaks of *notitia* (a knowing, conception, notion), *assensus* (agreement, admission of reality) and *fiducia* (trust, confidence, reliance, assurance). This analysis is more related to confessional controversy than to strict biblical study.

A. H. Strong improves this analysis by finding (1) an '*intellectual* element', recognition of the historical truth of the facts of Scripture but also of God's revelation therein as to man's sin and need for a Saviour; (2) an '*emotional* element', inward awakening and assent to the revelation of the grace of Christ as needed and applicable to one's soul; (3) a '*voluntary* element', trust in Christ first *as Lord* (involving surrender, as guilty, to Christ's Lordship) and *as Christ* (reception and appropriation of Christ for pardon and spiritual life).[6]

6. A. H. Strong, *Systematic Theology* (Valley Forge, PA: Judson Press, 1907), pp. 836–840.

A third analysis, not in disagreement with the two above described, but simpler, more exact and understandable, joins linguistic to theological analysis:

a) Saving faith is primarily and simply the divinely appointed way for man to receive salvation, including all attendant blessings, from God. '[W]hat must I do to be saved?' the trembling jailer cried. 'Believe in the Lord Jesus, and you will be saved' was all that Paul replied (Acts 16:30, 31). It is understood that man cannot make this response without divine enablement (see the doctrine of calling above), as Paul says elsewhere, '…no one can say "Jesus is Lord" except by the Holy Spirit' (1 Cor. 12:3).

b) This act of a person in saving faith, though simple, is a comprehensive act of the whole person, certainly involving all that one is. This is what is meant by the analysis into intellectual, emotional and volitional elements. One must 'believe in your heart' (Rom. 10:9, 10). This does not mean 'heart' as opposed to 'head' as some well-meaning but very harmful interpretation has it, but means *at the very center of being*, involving the *whole person*. The implied contrast is between heart-faith and mere lip profession, not heart and intellect! 'This people honors me with their lips, but their heart is far from me' as the ancient prophet reported (Matt. 15:8; cf. Isa. 29:13).

c) The first element, not to be neglected, is, indeed, *intellectual* assent – to the facts of biblical history and of redemption provided. This is sometimes called historical faith. This being true a correct evangelism will devote prime emphasis to the facts of biblical history (creation, fall, sin, examples of human situation, etc.) not hastening too overtly or quickly to the emotional. The content of every recorded sermon in Acts will amply justify this emphasis. We have already seen how intellectual assent to proposed statements, facts, etc., is a not uncommon meaning of *posteuō-pistis* (believe-faith).

d) A second element in saving faith is *appropriation* – of Christ as Lord and Savior. There is proof that such is the case in a very clear text which must now be discussed somewhat at length:

> He came unto his own, and they that were his own received him not. But as many as received him, to them gave
> he the right to become children of God, even to them that believe on his name: who were born, not of blood,
> nor of the will of the flesh, nor of the will of man, but of God (John 1:11-13 ASV).

The passage begins by reporting God's past offer of Himself to His own (the Jewish people) in the Person of the Word become flesh (1:1-3; cf.14). His own people did not 'receive him'. The Greek word 'receive' does not convey the more passive idea of admission, acknowledgment, etc. (in the Greek *dexomai*, often to receive a guest, 1 Cor. 2:14; Heb. 11:31), but is the strong active term *lambanō*. Though it is occasionally used as 'a colloquialism' in the sense of receiving (or taking) into one's home (Arndt and Gingrich, *Lexicon*) the usual sense is active appropriation of something. With the negative here it means rejection. Isaiah 53:1-3 by way of prediction, tells how and why. The middle and later chapters in all the Gospels tell the sad story of His rejection by way of history. But certain people did 'receive him'! The Greek tense (2nd aorist, active) points to an historic moment when it happened or happens and the sense is active – 'take… take in the hand, take hold of, grasp' (Arndt and Gingrich, *Lexicon*). *Elabon*, aorist active of *lambanō*, emphasizes an almost aggressive movement, which already in the simple present tense can mean to seize upon something. While He yet dwelt among men in His flesh, some seized upon Jesus so vigorosly and decisively they ultimately died in His service. We know some of them as the Twelve Apostles. The Gospels' narrative of their initial declarations of discipleship, of their faith in Him, and their growth in faith and knowledge instructs us in what it means to 'receive' Christ.

This active appropriation, in the same verse, is said to be faith: 'as many as received him… even to them that believe on his name'. *Believe* is present tense. The ones who believe (and keep on believing) are the ones who have appropriated Christ, i.e. believed 'on his name', for 'there is salvation in no one else, for there is no other name under heaven given among men by which we must be saved' (Acts 4:12).

The New Testament provides a number of vivid figures for appropriating Christ, some of them startling or even repugnant to contemporary people, but not to ancient people. It is being drawn by the Father to eat Christ's flesh; to drink his blood (John 6:35, 44, 54); to eat the bread of life (John 6:35); to drink the 'water of life' (John 4:14).

e) A third element in saving faith is *commitment* to Christ. Arndt and Gingrich give to 'entrust something to someone' as a third meaning of *pisteuō* and they list Luke 16:11; Romans 3:2; Galatians 2:7; 1 Thessalonians 2:4; 1 Timothy 1:11; Titus 1:3; 1 Corinthians 9:17 as furnishing examples – which, indeed, they do. A striking example is furnished by John 2:23, 24, viz. the miracles had produced a shallow assent to Jesus' claims, for which John employs *pisteuō*: '…many believed in his name when they saw the signs that he was doing'. Then he adds: 'But Jesus on his part did not entrust [commit KJV] himself [*episteuen auton*] to them, because he knew all people'. Thus the shallowest (assent to facts) meaning of *pisteuō* and the deeper (commitment to someone or something) are both exemplified in a single text. There are other words for commitment, and one of these is used parallel to *pisteuō* in another striking text, rendered poignant by the fact that the author expected soon to be executed: '…because I know whom I have believed [*pisteuō* in perfect tense], and am convinced that he is able to guard what I have entrusted to him for that day' (2 Tim. 1:12 NIV). 'What I have entrusted' (committed KJV) renders *tēn parathēkēn mou*, my deposit (property committed to another for safekeeping), in this case all that Paul was, body and soul. Here, to believe is to commit one's self to the care and support of another. And that is exactly what a contrite sinner does, having been convinced in mind that Jesus is, indeed, the Savior, and having received the Savior to himself – he commits himself, his hopes, ambitions and things to Jesus. This element of faith becomes very prominent in living the Christian life (as seen in 1 Peter 4:19, 'So then, those who suffer according to God's will should commit themselves to their faithful Creator and continue to do good' NIV).

When this aspect of faith is being emphasized, the New Testament frequently (though not invariably) employs *pisteuō* with the preposition *eis* (into) or *en* (in) followed by the noun indicating the object of faith. Or, the dative case may be employed. These features are not, however, invariable, and caution must be used in coming to doctrinal conclusions on the basis of them (cf. *eis* in John 3:16 with same in John 2:23).

As we have already seen, both in common English discourse and in Scripture, when a non-religious setting is the context, faith-belief (*pistis-pisteō*) frequently denotes mere intellectual assent to truth. As far as careful exegetes can determine James is the only New Testament writer so to employ the word in connection with salvation (James 2:14-26). Verse 24 seems to deny justification *sola fide* (by faith alone): 'You see that a person is justified by works and not by faith alone.' B. B. Warfield – along with many careful exegetes – points out that James does not intend in the least to say works are part of the payment we must make in order to be saved:

'James earlier had said "a sound faith lies at the very basis of the Christian life" (James.1:3), and is the condition of all acceptable approach to God (James 1:6; 5:15)'. Let my reader look up these verses to be convinced. The great New Testament and theology professor-writer continues: 'It is not faith as *he* [James] conceives it which he depreciates, but that *professed* faith [James 2:14 – "if someone *says* he has faith"] which cannot be shown to be real by appropriate works' and so differs diametrically from Abraham's faith (James 2:23) and from the faith of Christians. Evidently many of the recent Jewish accessions to the church had brought ideas of faith in the Judaism of the time along with them.

The defective faith of the new Jewish converts whom James is addressing is also diametrically opposed to James' own understanding, says our Princeton author, Warfield, and he cites James 2:1 and 1:3.[7] Even demons give intellectual assent (historical faith) to the existence of God. James says they 'believe – and shudder' (2:19). But a Christian faith is much more than that. James agrees with Paul: 'faith working through love' (Gal. 5:6). James' exhortation to faith and examples of faith and non-faith are quite like Paul's (see 1 Tim. 5:8, 10; 6:18; 2 Tim. 3:17; Titus 2:7, 14; 3:14, 18) and Peter's (1 Peter 2:12) and that found in Hebrews (10:24).

Temporary Faith.

The notion of a genuine faith, but not a saving faith, seems to be validated by Luke 8:13. Jesus is explaining the meaning of the Parable of the Seed and Four Soils and explains the rocky soil where the seed sprang up but it 'withered away, because it had no moisture' (Luke 8:6). Jesus explained, 'And the ones on the rock are those who, when they hear the word, receive it with joy. But these have no root; *they believe for a while* [emphasis added], and in time of testing fall away' (Luke 8:13). 'Believe' translates the usual word for the kind of believing that saves. '[A] while' translates *kairos* (season, specific or appropriate time) and the same word is translated 'time' (of testing, temptation) later in the verse. So, quite literally here is the biblically endorsed notion of a sincere but shallow, uncommitted, temporary faith. It obviously lacks the element of commitment.

It would be hazardous to say this is hypocritical faith, for both the text and observed behaviour of the folk for whom doing what feels good at the time and doing it with zest ('with joy' Luke 8:13) shows how sincere but volatile (i.e. 'for a while') their state of mind can be.[8]

---

7. All of B. B. Warfield's comments in *Biblical and Theological Studies* (Philadelphia, PA: Presbyterian & Reformed Publ., 1952), pp. 415, 416, are apropos, but many readers of our times have been weaned away from the compound and complex sentences of yesteryear by changes in society at large.

8. I have discussed this at length in Robert D. Culver, *A Greater Commission* (Chicago: Moody Press, 1984, new ed. by author, 1996), p. 69.

This faith, it is safe to say, is not saving faith, though some elements of saving faith – with reservations – are present.

> Such an one is *without root in his inner being* [emphasis in original], i.e. he is destitute of that faith (Eph. 3:16f.) which, as a power in the heart, is fitted to maintain and foster the life that has momentarily awakened by means of the word.[9]

Some theologians turn to Hebrews 6:1-8 as divine commentary on the temporary faith of 'the ones on the rock' (Luke 8:13). Warfield expands at great length on the subject.

It seems to this writer that the seed that 'fell among thorns' (Luke 8:7) does not represent temporary faith. Jesus does not say 'they were saved for a while'. I have written in a book of the theology of missions:

> It would be pressing the details too far to insist on a special meaning for lack of fruit from the good seed planted in this soil rather than destruction of the seed and death of the plant as in the first two kinds of soil. It seems doubtful that Jesus meant to say some soil produces believers who endure but never bear fruit. Without being doctrinaire about it, it seems best to regard Jesus as saying that there is too much competition for interest in some peoples' lives for the gospel seed ever to lodge in their hearts long enough for [saving] faith to come.[10]

Some Biblical Refinements of Saving Faith.

There are several refinements to our understanding of faith in salvation which the Bible furnishes, some of great encouragement to believers in the critical moments of life. Romans, chapter 4, furnishes several, as now follows.

a) Faith is in contrast to *law-works* in salvation (Rom. 4:14, 15). Law of any kind among fallen men in a moral universe leads to condemnation. '[T]he law brings wrath'. Paul is referring to Moses' law, but except by changing the verbal 'coin' of discourse (as some do when they point out that *torah* [law] means instruction and then say gospel as instruction is law), no law-works of any kind can do anything to save. To say the gospel is God's law of salvation is true enough, but confusing, and really ought to be proposed only with great care not to be misunderstood. Paul does say God's gospel does not operate lawlessly. Law may promote the sinner's consciousness of need for gracious salvation, but it points elsewhere than to itself for rescue. Law in Galatians is not the same in meaning as in Proverbs 1:8, where the *torah* of a parent does indeed mean instruction.

b) Faith looks to *the past* as furnishing the *promises of God*, on which promises faith rests. This was not only true of Abraham's faith, which is cited by Paul as an example (Rom. 4), but of all saving faith, for in this regard 'Abraham… is the father of us all' who believe (Rom. 4:16). The connection between promise and faith is a frequent theme of Scripture, occupying much of Galatians chapter 3 (especially verses 19-25) and the eleventh chapter of Hebrews, wherein the patriarchal promise of God is clarified, being clearly specified as not merely a promise of earthly blessedness but of heavenly blessedness also – immortality and eternal life (especially Heb. 11:11-16; cf. Rom. 4:17). How this does refute and chasten a lot that is being said today about the Old Testament perspective of faith – 'earthly only… no true eschatological perspective… no immortality', etc.! Jesus 'opened their minds to understand the Scriptures' (Luke 24:45). The Old Testament must always be allowed to speak for itself, of course. Yet, it is correct to say our Lord made 'the Scriptures' of the old covenant a Christian book on the afternoon and evening of Easter Day (Luke 24:25-27 and 44-48).

c) Faith is closely related to *hope*, though not identical with it. 'In hope he [Abraham] believed against hope' (Rom. 4:18); 'For in this hope we were saved. But hope that is seen is no hope at all. Who hopes for what he already has? But if we hope for what we do not yet have, we wait for it patiently' (Rom. 8:24, 25 NIV). This hope is not mere optimism, as in 'newspaper theology', but confident expectation. Abraham, Paul's example of true saving faith in this connection, was 'fully convinced that God was able to do what he had promised' (Rom. 4:21). The sense is not that hope is a legitimate object of faith but those who genuinely have saving faith have hope also, i.e. sure expectation – a form of certainty – that what God has promised He will perform.

d) Closely related to hope in connection with faith is the *unseen element* in faith's object and support. Scripture declares: 'we walk by faith, not by sight' (2 Cor. 5:7). Does this mean, then, that faith itself is merely an intangible something in the mind? By no means. The teaching is that faith for eternal salvation cannot ultimately be directed

---

9. H. A. W. Meyer, *Critical and Exegetical Commentary on the New Testament i* (New York and London: Funk & Wagnalls, 1884), p. 266.
10. Culver, *Greater Commission*, pp. 69, 70.

toward any of the tangible things about us, religious articles, holy precincts, special people, not the beautiful leather cover of a 'Holy Bible', nor even the paper and ink which convey John 3:16! This may be at once the most elusive and the most difficult feature of biblical religion. Israel always wanted a visible image to trust rather than a spiritual Jehovah who intransigently refused to make Himself visible and who would allow no visible representation of Himself whatsoever. It took 1,000 years of biblical history to get the point across, for the Israelites never quite got over addiction to worship of idols until the exile of the sixth century BC. Yet, Abraham travelled toward a land he had not yet seen, 'not knowing where he was going' (Heb. 11:8) but trusting the divine promise, Moses, 'By faith... endured as seeing him who is invisible' (Heb. 11:27). So it is with true faith today: 'Though you have not seen him, you love him. Though you do not now see him, you believe in him and rejoice with joy that is inexpressible and filled with glory, obtaining the outcome of your faith, the salvation of your souls.' (1 Peter 1:8, 9).

e) Faith's involvement with *promises* of and *hope* in an *invisible* God imparts a certain *desperate quality* to saving faith – certainly not complete freedom from attacks of uncertainty and doubt. 'When nothing whereon to lean remains; When strongholds crumble to the dust; When nothing is sure but that God still reigns; That is the time to trust!' The book of Job illustrates this well. Many a faithful pastor has read passages of Scripture such as Psalm 23 to the dying, only to find their desperation turn to quiet confidence, that what God has promised He is fully able to perform (Rom. 4:21).

In the next chapter we will enter what might seem to be complicated intellectual territory – *faith* as a 'theological construct'. It does sound somewhat formidable. Yet it is all about a very simple thing, the act of a sinner in giving up the project of self-redemption by one's own effort and receiving salvation as a gift from God through Christ. In an important book entitled *What Is Faith?*, a great New Testament scholar with a profound grasp of 'the whole counsel of God' wrote two-thirds of the way through this famous book:

> And faith in one sense is a very simple thing. We have been engaged, indeed, in a sort of analysis of it; but we have been doing so, not in the interests of complexity, but on the contrary, in order to combat the false notions by which simplicity is destroyed.[11]

He goes on to say no one consciously or unconsciously understands or articulates the 'mysterious... chemistry of the soul, and a whole new world of thought' in the 'experience of faith that seems as simple as the falling of a leaf' and concludes with the thought:

> Certainly, at bottom, faith... simply means that abandoning the vain effort of earning one's way into God's presence we accept the gift of salvation which Christ offers so full and free. Such is the 'doctrine' – let us not be afraid of the word – such is the 'doctrine' of justification through faith alone.[12]

---

11. J. Gresham Machen, *What Is Faith?* (New York: Macmillan, 1925, 1927), pp. 180, 181.
12. ibid., p. 181.

12
The Doctrine of Faith: The Theological Construct

In the preceding chapter the main features of the formal doctrine were discussed – the words for faith in the original languages, the general meaning of the act itself and the specific nature of *saving* faith. In this chapter we shall consider 1) some questions about how God acts in producing faith, i.e. how it comes to arise in sinners' hearts; 2) the relationship of faith with reason; 3) some refinement of the teaching of Scripture on the identity of the precise object of saving faith; 4) the relation of faith with knowledge; 5) what it means to confess faith in Christ; 6) the scriptural manner in which the confession should be made; 7) some further correlation between confession, repentance and faith; and 8) further implications for evangelism.

The Origin of Saving Faith: What Are the Bases and Causes of Saving Faith?

The Place of Evidences, Proofs, Arguments.

A lively debate has been going on throughout the Christian era as to the place of evidence, proofs, arguments, etc., in producing saving faith. To come immediately to issues, granting the doctrine of special calling (or call it efficient grace) that God must enlighten and quicken sinners before they can believe for salvation, do we have any information on how we are enlightened and quickened? How does God act in causing faith to arise? How does the Holy Ghost persuade? It seems it really should be possible to give a scriptural answer. And, it seems probable that much of the debate has been at least partially unnecessary and perhaps also irrelevant.

In the *first place*, in Scripture, we are directed to give 'reasons' for the faith we already have, i.e. we are to testify to it and defend it logically. We are not called upon to explain *how* we helpless sinners gained discernment and power to believe. There is considerable mystery about that which the Bible never fully dissolves. Isaiah's famous challenges are for unbelievers to defend their unbelief, and the arguments in the great passage are God's own not ours (see Isa. 40–46, especially 41:21-29). On the other hand, believers are advised to 'be ready always to give an answer to every man that asketh you a reason of the hope that is in you with meekness and fear' (1 Peter 3:15 KJV). I must, therefore, be prepared to plainly explain 'why I hope in Christ' rather than to prove 'why you ought to share this hope'. My reasons may not be yours, yours might seem inadequate to me. In any case no spur of the moment impulse is a 'reason', nor is it a merely inherited opinion. Parents and teachers may supply reasons better than mere tradition or peer pressure to profess faith. The faith must be real, an 'in you' faith.

In the *second place*, answering the questions put by unbelievers – sincere or otherwise – while not expressly any part of evangelism (i.e. preaching the good news), if the reasons are cogent and adequate may 1) make the unbeliever appear quite foolish to himself and others and 2) may remove what he thinks are obstacles to faith. The Bible everywhere insists that there are no genuine, objective obstacles to faith, for the ultimate obstacles to faith root in the darkening of the mind due to sin. All of us find this embarrassing to discuss with unbelievers, but in very sober fact it is the uniform biblical position. Yet, for example, the man who tells himself that he cannot accept the gospel of the Bible because its histories are unreliable may be quite shaken up by a good lecture on archaeological evidences of the historical accuracy of the book of Acts. So God can use certain 'evidences' in evangelism. Even though only the Holy Spirit who moves sovereignly can open the heart to faith, He may use any means He chooses.

Thirdly, and specifically, we must reject the empirical approach, for faith is not the product of sense experience *as such*, however impressive in confirming faith. We have already observed the superficiality of faith aroused by seeing miracles and have noted the case of Simon, the magician of Samaria, in that regard (see Acts 8:9-24). Furthermore, says John, though 'he [Jesus] had done so many signs before them' the generation who witnessed them all 'did not believe in him' because 'they could not believe' as they had eyes that could not see and ears that could not hear (John 12:37-40). All the passages cited in the previous chapter, showing how the object of our faith is the invisible, apply. Something beyond mere human faculties in 'the state of nature' must bring it to pass: not 'flesh and blood' but the God and Father of the Lord Jesus (Matt. 16:17). A generation suckled and brainwashed on the so-called scientific method has difficulty at this point – especially if they happen to be recent graduates of the university, for nowadays even human consciousness and man's soul are there assumed to be fully subject to purely empirical explanation. The laws and forces which erode mountains, rust iron pipes, produce atomic decay, are assumed to be no more 'natural' than the ones that constitute mother love and religious conversion.

Fourthly, the Bible also rejects purely rational explanations for faith's origin. Though the Bible throughout assumes the rational aspect of the soul of man and pervasively appeals to men's reasoning powers, it clearly teaches that reason's reasons *in fallen man* will lead away from faith not toward it. Kant's famous 'Critique of Pure Reason' may have been reasonable enough, but it excluded some of the data available, and hence produced a defective conclusion. Outside of purely logical and mathematical deductions and what philosophical logic calls tautologies (definitions) there is little that any human reason can establish with absolute certainty without help from experience or divine revelation. Of course $4 + 4 = 8$ either on the earth, under it in hell or in heaven above. Paul plainly says that faith does not 'stand' in the 'wisdom of men' and insists that the world's wisdom does not know anything accurately about God (see 1 Cor. 2:1-5 and 1:21; Eph. 4:17 ff; and Rom 1:18 *ad fin*).

Finally the same negative judgment must be placed on historical proofs (see Acts 26:26-28). People will simply reject the historical proofs – even of the resurrection of Jesus. That did not keep either Paul (Acts 17) or Stephen (Acts 7) from citing history to support his message to unbelievers.

For over 200 years now (since Napoleon's campaign in Egypt) archaeology has given Bible believers great encouragement. This is because archaeology has proven that many unbelievers' charges of errors in the Bible (for example the existence of Hittites and more recently the existence of David) have been proven false charges. Also, archaeology has demonstrated the accuracy of many biblical, geographical, social and political statements – notably Luke's geographical references and cultural references. This has not been decisive 'proof' that the Bible is true as revelation of God and the way to be saved – only that the Bible is a very good history book – if that is how you wish to read it. Furthermore, the mouths of insistent, learned opponents have not been stopped. They are the *minimalists* among recent 'experts'. Their mouths will be stopped only by conviction of truth by God Himself (Rom. 3:19).

Though it is not correct to say that God may not employ empirical arguments, rational arguments and historical proofs to address us, it is incorrect to say they *as such* produce faith. The Bible makes very clear several things about how faith arises in human hearts.

The Instrumentality of the Word of God.

This question of the use of truth or the Word as means was raised in connection with effective calling, the beginning of regeneration. It arises again at every stage of the application of redemption. We must, in due respect to the inability of the natural man, affirm the primacy of divine working, taking the initiative at each stage or aspect.

Yet we puzzle over and again whether God employs a means. David wrote, 'The law [*torah*] of the Lord is perfect, converting the soul' (Ps. 19:7 KJV). Here *torah* or law must mean instruction as the parallel *stichoi* in Proverbs 1:8 suggests. It is not the 'commandment' of God that converts. Paul makes that plain – by the law in the sense of commandment, he says, 'I died'. '[C]onverting' is a participle of *shuv*, the usual Hebrew word for conversion or repentance. So by the *Word*, *truth*, *instruction*, the *kerygma* (the foolishness of preaching), 'God chose to save them that believe'. Peter's declaration to the effect we are 'born again…through the… word of God' (1 Peter 1:23) seems to be plain enough that regeneration, and with it faith, have some dependency on hearing the Word of God, normally spoken (conveyed by whatever means) by an agent – angel or man or the Lord Himself as in Paul's case. Yet, there was an inward *illumination* (special call) within Saul of Tarsus' soul that *enabled* him to see what none others present saw and heard with understanding (Acts 9:3-7; 22:6-11). What others detected only as meaningless sound, Paul, the author of all those statements about communicating the message (Word, preachment, truth, etc.), also was aware of the presence of special illumination of the mind by divine power in his own and other cases.

The Puritans, John Owen to Samuel Hopkins, dealt with this problem. They were utterly opposed to the notion that mere hearing of the Word is sufficient to produce regeneration and consequent faith, for the same reasons I have repeatedly brought forward in this study. They insisted the event was not one with any necessary accompanying feeling – such as the 'praying through' technique. 'We have no way to determine what is the cause of the ideas and sensations of our hearts, whether we are influenced by the Spirit of God or by a wicked spirit, but by considering their nature and tendency, whether they are such as the scripture tells us are the fruits of the Spirit' (Samuel Hopkins, 1721–1803, student under Jonathan Edwards and Connecticut pastor, in a sermon on John 1:13).[1]

Recall remarks in the first chapter on how salvation is conveyed to sinners and the place of the gospel itself, or the Word of God. 'So belief cometh of hearing, and hearing by the word of Christ' (Rom. 10:17 ASV). 'Truly, truly, I say to you, whoever hears my word and believes him who sent me has eternal life… an hour is coming, and is now here, when the dead [in sin] will hear the voice of the Son of God, and those who hear will live' (John 5:24, 25). '[H]ear' is used in a common New Testament sense of the 'hearing with faith' in these passages (Gal. 3:2; see also Acts 18:8) – i.e. 'to hearken'. In such a case saving faith is based upon God's testimony, not man's, God's testimony concerning His Son (1 John 5:7, 9, 13). This suggests that God takes the message of the Bible and if not by means of 'truth' or 'the Word', then supernaturally working with the Word by His Holy Spirit (John 16:7-11; Rev. 22:17) produces faith in human hearts (cf. Ps. 19:1-6 with 19:7-14 regarding the necessity of more than natural revelation to convert the soul).

The Agency of the Holy Spirit in Producing Faith.

The inquiring student will find helpful counsel from John Calvin.[2] The heading to his major section on this matter reads: 'Scripture must be confirmed by the witness of the Spirit. Thus may its authority be established as certain, and it is a wicked falsehood that its credibility depends on the judgment of the church'. This was Calvin's way of repudiating the claims of the papal church that the New Testament was created by church authority and that only the papal hierarchy has knowledge and authority to interpret the Bible. The same may be said of the opinion that the Bible's authority must wait for empirical, rational or historical proofs.[3] Hence, as Paul has said, 'faith' must 'not rest in the wisdom of men, but in the power of God' (1 Cor. 2:5). This doctrine is congruent with the many affirmations of Scripture that 'the new heart' or 'new spirit' in the saved is the creation of God (Ps. 51:10; Exod. 11:19; 36:26; John 1:13; 3:1-8). *Saving faith, then, is man's response to hearing the Word of God under the influence (life-giving power) of the Holy Spirit.* God does not do men's believing for them, nor does He infuse any supposed grace of faith into them, for faith is always completely a human faith. Yet in the sense indicated in this paragraph it is thoroughly correct to say that saving faith, without means or by whatever means, is a divine gift.

Ephesians 2:8 reads, 'For by grace you have been saved through faith. And this is not of your own doing; it is the gift of God'. In the portion, and this is 'not of your own doing', 'this' translates *touto* which is neuter gender.

---

1. My source is Edward Hindson, *Introduction to Puritan Theology, A Reader* (Grand Rapids, MI: Baker Books, 1976), p. 183. His source is Volume 3 of *The Works of Samuel Hopkins* an 1852 publication. See Hindson, p. 4.
2. John Calvin, *Institutes of the Christian Religion i*, ed. J. T. McNeil, trans. and ed. by F. L. Battles (Philadelphia, PA: Westminster Press, 1960), chap. 7 and scattered throughout all four books.
3. ibid., i. 7.4, pp. 78–81.

Commentators have differed as to the antecedent noun whether faith (*pisteōs*), the nearest and hence most likely (in absence of contrary fact), or grace (*chariti*) or salvation by grace which has been previously discussed and is present in the word saved (*sesōsmenoi*). Among the ancients, Chrysostom appears to assume faith (*pisteōs*) even though a feminine noun and not in gender agreement with *touto* (that) is the antecedent, therefore 'the gift of God'. He says:

> 'And that not of ourselves'. Neither is faith, he means, 'of ourselves'. Because had He not come, had He not called us, how had we been able to believe? for 'how', saith he, 'shall they believe, unless they hear?' So that the work of faith itself is not our own. 'It is the gift', said he, 'of God'.[4]

Chrysostom's first language was Greek – of which he was a master and surely understood the rules for agreement of pronouns and antecedents. Abraham Kuyper cites seven classical passages (five from Plato and one each from Xenophon and Demosthenes) where the same phenomenon occurs. He insists, therefore, it is faith itself which, in this passage, is the gift of God. The 'ancient rendering', he says, 'cannot be anything else but correct'.[5]

This does not make the Bible anti-intellectual, nor does Scripture advise us to deny the evidence of sense experience and of history. Jesus appealed to *empirical* proofs when He directed Thomas to touch the wounds in His body (John 2:27-29). John assures his readers that he is reporting what he had 'heard' in company of the apostles, what he had 'seen' with his 'eye', what he had 'looked upon' and his 'hands' had 'touched' (1 John 1:1), and Peter makes a big point of asserting that he and the other apostles were 'eyewitnesses' of the events of redemption (2 Peter 1:16-18). There is historical research and confirmation within the New Testament record itself (Luke 1:1-4; cf. John 14:26). Securing eyewitness testimony is an important aspect of all historical study. Such 'proofs' are employed by Scripture to convince the minds of men. John 20:30, 31 thus distinctly affirms. Paul has much to say about the importance of the 'understanding' in the exercise of religious faith, though he never suggests that faith accepts no mysteries. Faith, understanding God's directives, accepts many things with the faculty of understanding which are not fully understood (cf. 1 Cor. 13:2; 14:13-16).

Existential doctrine, defining faith as a leap into the dark, a decision without data on which to base decision, could not be farther from biblical religion. One wonders how Karl Barth could ever have made his early pronouncements in this regard in a *Commentary on Romans*, of all books! Perhaps his later doctrine regarding the witness of the Holy Spirit is to be regarded as his more settled opinion.

It is important to keep in mind that although one must distinguish between the Word as *instrumental cause* of faith and the Spirit as *agent*, the two cannot be separated in the origin of saving faith in the heart of sinners. Attention to what has been called the psychology of conversion will help.

The Psychology of Conversion.

The biblical writers employed what we now call psychological terms to explain why some read or hear the gospel without ever truly coming to saving faith while others have the 'hearing of faith' and are spiritually renewed. We have already thought about this in the chapter on effectual calling. Let us now think of the problem in relation to the *Testimonium Spiritus Sancti*, the witness of the Holy Spirit – a biblical and theological phrase once widely discussed – in 1959 revived and ably presented by Bernard Ramm.[6] The speech and literature of most languages, including the Bible, use the eye and ear as metaphors for the mind ('I *see* what you mean', 'I *hear* what you are saying'). Though sight and hearing are physical functions, eyes and ears (as all five organs of sense) are the organs of perception of the external world, on a deeper level, for which the only right word seems to be 'spiritual', people may not truly attain understanding of what they are seeing and hearing, and perceive in a superficial way.

The capacity of everyone is to some degree limited by one's 'framework of plausibility'. The same has been called the paradigm of reality. These frameworks or paradigms within which human beings unconsciously assume anything real must be positioned are created by the atmosphere of influence from our earliest hours of existence onward and we find it difficult to escape from them. I once, for example, had great difficulty convincing a woman

---

4. 'The Commentary and Homilies of John Chrysostom', in *Nicene and Post-Nicene Fathers ii*, ed. P. Schaff and H. Wace, 1890 (Peabody: Hendrickson Publ., repr.1994), p. 67.
5. Abraham Kuyper, *The Work of the Holy Spirit*, trans. H. De Vries (Grand Rapids, MI: Eerdmans, 1941), pp. 407–414.
6. Bernard Ramm, *The Witness of the Spirit* (Grand Rapids, MI: Eerdmans, 1959).

who was at the same boarding house with my wife and me at Grenoble, France, that I was the Professor in whose apologetics class she had sat a few weeks before at Wheaton College. She could not focus on the evidence of my physical likeness in jeans and sweater in a scruffy dining room across the table. I was not wearing a suit and standing behind a desk. Similarly, a devout gentleman whose world is Islam is not going to find the world of the triune God of Christianity anything he even wishes to contemplate, much less embrace. It does not fit his framework of plausibility.

Jesus, quoting Isaiah 6:9, 10 said, 'Hearing you will hear and shall not understand, and seeing you will see and not perceive; for the hearts of this people have grown dull. Their ears are hard of hearing, and their eyes they have closed, Lest they should see with their eyes and hear with their ears, lest they should understand with their hearts and turn, so that I should heal them' (Matt. 13:14, 15 NKJV; see Mark 8:18).

On the other hand Jesus also said the 'pure in heart' shall 'see God'; those 'born from above' shall 'see the kingdom of God' (John 3:3); 'the 'hour is coming, and is now here, when the [spiritually] dead will hear the voice of the Son of God, and those who hear will live' (John 5:25).

The impairment of our spiritual powers of perception is, of course, part of the curse of death caused by the Fall. All the doctrine of sin and its results are apropos this deadness toward spiritual things. The sad fact is that 'the natural man receives not the things of the Spirit of God'. It is not necessary to restate the entire dreary litany of the sad effects of original sin.

In a supernatural way, not verifiable absolutely by the ordinary methods of empirical science, so-called, God's Spirit employs the Word in a special way to restore spiritual capacity. It should not be called a *revelation* in any strict sense, though when it happens, newly converted folk often feel that it is and say so. More properly, it is *illumination*, first of the mind or understanding after the image both of the originally created First Adam and of the Last Adam. What was once a stumbling-block (1 Cor. 1:23) and foolishness (1 Cor. 1:18) 'now appears to the man whose perception has been restored as "the power of God" (1 Cor. 1:18); "the wisdom of God" (1 Cor. 1:24) "a secret and hidden wisdom of God" (1 Cor. 2:7) and as "the mind of Christ (1 Cor. 2:16)"'.[7]

The matter should not be complicated by supposing two witnesses of the Spirit – one to the Word (though in another connection the Spirit witnesses to the Word) and one to the mind, recreating 'the spirit of understanding' and 'the eyes of your mind being enlightened'. The action is one. The Word is always the same. God is always *talking* there and always says the same thing.

God's voice ceases to be 'background noise' when the Word is accompanied by the action of the Spirit. When the Spirit enters into the heart with the Word to assure the truth of the gospel, its relevancy and the urgency of the message thus engenders the response of faith. This movement of the Spirit may be called 'special' or 'effectual calling' from one perspective. As regards the heart's perceiving the truth of the Word preached or read it is properly denominated the witness of the Holy Spirit.

Faith, Knowledge and Reason.

The preceding discussion of the origin of saving faith will suffice here for the philosophers' disjunction of faith and reason. There is a much more relevant intramural discussion among Christian thinkers, leaders and writers as to the relation of faith and knowledge. Calvin clearly taught that assured knowledge of Christ is the first part of saving faith. Many later Calvinists have disagreed, saying in effect such knowledge is prior to and a cause of faith though not a part of it.

The medieval scholastics, refining earlier misunderstandings of faith, distinguished *fides informis*, unformed faith (simple right beliefs, credence, orthodoxy) from a more admirable faith formed by love, *fides caritate formata*, i.e. right belief working through the supernaturally added grace of love. Faith of both kinds was held to be meritorious. What is more pertinent to the question of the relation of faith and knowledge was a certain distinction between the two, still maintained as follows: if the layman, who knows nothing of the doctrinal content of the gospel and the Bible, merely trusts the ordained minister of the church (priest) in matters of religion, he is, according to the doctrine of the medieval church, a Christian and worthy to receive all church rites. This is called implicit faith (*fides implicita*). Hence a pagan Mexican Indian who trusts the priest of the Roman Church and obeys him in matters of sacraments may be saved, even though he knows nothing of the doctrines of true religion. The priest must have explicit knowledge of the details of doctrine, *fides explicita*.

7. ibid., p. 37.

Today, when efforts toward rapprochement with Romanism are taking place, particularly on local community level, we do well to know what we are doing. Calvin, who had recently escaped the cloying scholasticism of the late medieval church, saw the necessity of an intellectual content in saving faith. Calvin gives an extended treatment of so-called implicit faith.[8] Against the notion that for faith to save, it is enough simply to trust the priest, or other favorite 'evangelist', he asserts that faith involves knowledge. The notion of implicit faith obscures a sound understanding of how to be saved, 'Bedecking the grossest ignorance with this term, they ruinously delude poor, miserable folk'.[9] He goes on to say that, properly understood, there is such a thing as implicit faith – in two respects. First as to true believers, 'We certainly admit that so long as we dwell as strangers in the world there is such a thing as implicit faith; not only because many things are as yet hidden from us, but because surrounded by many clouds of error we do not comprehend everything.' That is, we believe what we know God has revealed to us and trust Him for more in the future.[10] Second, those who come to saving faith do not always do so in a flash. 'We may also call that faith implicit which is strictly nothing but the preparation of faith.'[11] In Christ's day on earth many 'believed' who, caught up into wonderment by the miracles, 'did not advance further'. Yet others like the 'official' of John 4:46-53 went on from preparatory faith to full, abiding, saving faith.[12]

The Reformers all rejected these specious, unbiblical notions and connected saving faith with the preaching of the Word in order to the hearer's understanding of saving truth as a precondition of faith. There is a necessary preparation for faith. Paul called it 'the word of faith, which we preach' (Rom. 10:8 KJV) and went on to explain that people must know something of their own need and the provision which God has made in Christ. (See Romans 10:9-17; 1 Corinthians 15:1 ff.) It is not quite correct to say that faith has a 'content of knowledge', for faith is an act not a creedal statement, though what some mean to say by such remarks is correct. Though no one comes to faith in possession of a complete 'soteriology', true faith, though faltering and weak, acts on what the 'believer' knows. Faith is not knowledge but an act based on at least a little knowledge of its object, to which we now give attention.

The Object of Saving Faith.

Saving faith is not faith in faith, or faith in formulae as such. The true object of saving faith is ultimately God Himself in the Mediator, Jesus Christ. John 5:24 ('whoever... believes him who sent me') so indicates as does also Romans 4:5 and other texts. These must all be understood in the light of the fact that Christ is God 'manifested in the flesh' (1 Tim. 3:16; cf. John 14:9; 1:1-13, 14). So Christ, Himself, is the focus of saving faith – but not the 'Christ of faith' created by liberal-modernist theology or the 'Christ of the early Church's witness' of Bultmannism, rather the Christ promised to the patriarchs (Gen. 3:16; 12:1-2; 49:10; 2 Sam. 7), predicted by the prophets (Isa. 7:14; 9:1-12; 52:13–53:12; Micah 5:2; Pss. 16, 72, 110, etc.), indeed, by *all* the Hebrew Scriptures (Luke 24:27, 44-46; Acts 3:24); born at Bethlehem in the fullness of time (Gal. 4:4), interpreted as Savior in the Epistles, etc. – the Christ of the Bible. This is the heart of the saving gospel whether preached to Gentiles (Acts 17:18; Col. 1:27) or Jews (1 Cor. 1:23).

This faith, for Old Testament believers, it must be admitted, was as explicit as God and Scripture directed, but partially implicit as far as faith in Jesus (of Nazareth) Christ was concerned. (See Gal. 3:8 which says Gen. 12:1 ff. is 'the gospel'.) They believed God; they believed God's promise according to His Word; the promise was Messiah, Seed of the woman, Son of David, Son of God.

It is not incorrect to unite the Scriptures with their Author as sharing in this dignity of being the object of saving faith, for although some earnest but misguided Christians have sought to find a saving message of divine grace in nature or the constitution of man as 'inner light' or as conscience, the effort has been unsuccessful. The God of faith and the Christ of faith are the God and Christ of the Bible. Neither church nor tradition and certainly not the light of nature or the moral constitution of man offer a sure hope of eternal life. The classical handbooks of systematic theology usually contain several pages on the question of possible faith among the heathen (Socrates?) without missionaries.[13] In view of the doctrine of Romans 10:13, 14, 17, Hodge is surely correct when he asserts that calling upon Christ 'implies faith; faith implies knowledge: knowledge implies objective teaching. "Faith cometh by hearing,

---

8. Calvin, *Institutes iii.*, chap. 2, through sections 2–5.
9. ibid., 3.2.
10. ibid., 3.4.
11. ibid., 3.5.
12. ibid, 3.5.

and hearing by the word of God"... There is no faith, therefore, where the gospel is not heard; and where there is no faith, there is no salvation'.[14] (The last chapter of this section considers at length the currently pressing controversy whether Christ can be found savingly in non-Christian religions.)

Confession of Faith in Christ.

From the opening words of the 'Apostle's Creed', 'I believe' (Latin *credo*) comes from the word 'creed'. Hence a 'creed' in the best sense is a personal confession of faith.[15] It is to be regretted that since faith has been frequently over-intellectualized (right statement of doctrine) and, since many modern people know that formal creeds are sometimes associated with sacerdotal religion (salvation by forms and ceremonies), many are prejudiced against formal confessions and creeds. Yet we do well to remind ourselves that 'extemporaneous' or 'spontaneous' testimony (witness, confession) is likewise capable of being a public 'act', spoken only because it is expected. Much that goes for spontaneous witness is about as unrehearsed as a coached recitation of Macbeth's soliloquy in an elocution contest.

The earlier confessions of faith in the New Testament are mainly very simple: 'You are the Christ, the Son of the living God' (Matt. 16:16); 'Lord, remember me when thou comest into thy kingdom' (Luke 23:42 KJV); 'I believe that Jesus Christ is the Son of God' (Acts 8:37 KJV, omitted in some ancient MSS and therefore marginal in ESV). Then they become somewhat longer, though simple still (Rom. 10:9). Certain New Testament statements thought to be derived from ancient hymns or 'creeds' seem like public group confessions (Phil. 2:5 ff.; 1 Tim. 3:16) though it is far from certain they really ever were recited in churches before becoming a part of Scripture. The nearest thing to a list formulated as essential beliefs is 1 Corinthians 15:1 ff.

The baptismal formula (Matt. 28:19, 20), however, may tell us more than all these supposed 'creeds'. In the New Testament, initial confession is with the 'mouth' (Rom. 10:10) and it is by presenting one's self for and in baptism (Acts 16:15, 30-34). The early converts presented themselves at the water and were baptized in the name of the Father and of the Son and of the Holy Spirit, thereby making public announcement of faith in Christ. We are told that oral confession often preceded. Modern taste (necessity?) has asked for 'walking up front', 'raising of the hand', 'going to the inquiry room', 'praying through at the altar' or 'giving a testimony' – and other things. Initial confession in the New Testament – the restoration thereof greatly to be desired – was spontaneously oral (Peter and the repentant thief) or oral in response to question followed by baptism. Confession was of Christ as Savior and Lord, no distinction being made between the one (Lord) and the other (Savior) (all the examples clearly involve Christ's Lordship), and one was not considered a disciple until baptism had occurred.[16] The churches rather quickly adopted policies of extended instruction before baptism and of expecting some evidence of a changed life (fruits of repentance and faith) before baptism.

After several decades new believers, yet unbaptized, were required to sit or stand separately from members. Special portions of the liturgy were designed for them and they even were excluded from certain parts of the service until after baptism. 'The liturgy of the catechumens' (those being catechized) was a regular feature of the developing system. Later, when baptism of the infant offspring of Christian parents became general practice, the catechizing took place (usually in early adolescence) after 'christening'. That was followed by 'confirmation' vows (in place of earlier adult baptismal vows), 'first communion' and full church membership. Note that oral confession of Christian faith at 'confirmation' is required in this still widespread tradition before admission to the full privileges of church membership.

No separation of baptism from admission to local church membership, nor any church membership apart from the church's ordinance of baptism, apparently was made until modern post-Reformation times and the rise of religious pluralism in American and European communities.

When Christianity comes to a formerly wholly pagan culture, presenting oneself for public baptism is still the event which to the general (pagan) public, even family and friends, unites the new Christian with the fellowship of believers in Christ and disunites him in many ways (especially heathen initiation and puberty rites, superstitions,

---

13. See A. H. Strong, *Systematic Theology* ii, (Valley Forge: Judson Press, 1907), pp. 842–844 and Charles Hodge, *Systematic Theology ii*, originally published 1871–1873 (Grand Rapids, MI: Eerdmans Publ., 1970), pp. 646–675. Many popular and scholarly articles issuing continually.
14. Hodge, *Systematic Theology i*, p. 648.
15. The ancient so-called Apostles' Creed was intended as a personal statement of one's personal belief, a pre-baptismal confession. As recited in group worship it has value for worship only as 'What I believe' not merely 'what this denomination stands for', the shift from 'I' to 'we' is regrettable.
16. Robert D. Culver, article 'What is the Church's Commission?', in *Bibliotheca Sacra*, July–September, 1968.

spiritism, etc.) from the surrounding culture. Hindu and Muslim families care little, we are told, how much their members attend meetings and lectures of Christians. But baptism is another matter. There the tensions begin, often leading to rupture and ultimately to other conversions – as Jesus promised (Matt. 10:34-42).[17]

How Much and How Strong Must Saving Faith Be?

Is faith ever mixed with doubt? On a superficial level the Bible seems to be at odds with itself on the question whether true faith is ever mixed with 'honest doubt' – or at least lack of full confidence. On the one hand is James' blunt statement about a fatal kind of doubt. In one's prayers, he seems to say, doubt is the very opposite of faith. '[L]et him ask in faith, with no doubting, for the one who doubts is like a wave of the sea that is driven and tossed by the wind' (James 1:6). Such a doubter is 'double-minded... unstable in all his ways' and 'must not suppose that he will receive anything from the Lord' (vv. 7, 8). On the other hand we find the Lord generously rewarding the most timid sort of faith, e.g. the simple touch of His garment, and everyone knows that doubting Thomas had a thoroughly sceptical mix in his faith. Several 'heroes' of faith in Hebrews 11 are equally famous for the failures (doubts) mixed in with faith. One thinks of Abram's slippery slide to Egypt and Gerar – both on account of faith sadly mixed with doubt in the form of lack of confidence.

Alfred, Lord Tennyson (1809–1892) succeeded Wordsworth as Poet Laureate in the Victorian Age. It was a time when all the forces of a ripening 'Enlightenment' were converging to weaken or to destroy faith in a unique, saving revelation. Tennyson (with Bryant) became for me, first as a boy and ever since, the greatest single extra-biblical support of true saving faith against doubt as I too have wrestled with native scepticism and 'the heartache, and the natural shocks/ That flesh is heir to' while 'yet believing' (1 Peter 1:8 KJV). I have recited 'Crossing the Bar' at the grave of many to the amazing comfort of many, and lines from 'In Memoriam' in funeral services of many. It is precisely the recognition of the timid presence of something like doubt – perhaps it is only awe and trembling in presence of mystery (Otto's *tremendum*). At any rate I vibrate 'in sync' with these lines from Tennyson's 'In Memoriam' (to Arthur Hallan, his recently deceased dear friend):

> Strong Son of God, Immortal love,
> Whom we, that have not seen thy face
> By faith, and faith alone embrace,
> Believing where we cannot prove.

and from Tennyson's 'Crossing the Bar':

> For tho' from out our bourne of Time and Place
> The flood may bear me far,
> I hope to see my Pilot face to face
> When I have crossed the bar.

and finally from section 96 of 'In Memoriam':

> You tell me, doubt is Devil-born.
> I know not. One [a deceased friend] indeed I knew
> In many a subtle question versed,
> Who touched a jarring lyre at first,
> But ever strove to make it true;
>
> Perplexed in faith, but pure in deeds,
> At last he beat his music out,
> *There lives more faith in honest doubt,*
> *Believe me than in half the creeds.*

Grant some rhetorical excesses and poetic, allusive obscurity. Acknowledge that as a poet he dared express in the great poem what we orthodox rightfully repress, a hope that everyone will be saved – 'And faintly trust the larger hope'. Yet the faith of Thomas before the Sunday after Easter and of Mark between Acts 15 and 2 Timothy 4:11 was more like that of Tennyson's friend, Arthur Hallam, than the confidence of the author of the following:

---

17. Robert D. Culver, *A Greater Commission* (Chicago: Moody Press, 1985, new ed. by author, 1999), chap. 6.

'I... am persuaded that he is able to keep that which I have committed unto him against that day' (2 Tim. 1:12 KJV) and 'I am now ready to be offered, and the time of my departure is at hand.... I have kept the faith' (2 Tim. 4:6, 7 KJV).

It seems to me that we should observe the following feature: of faith in relation to doubt.

a) We first come trembling to Christ. As Charlotte Elliott said for most of us, 'Just as I am, though tossed about With many a conflict, many a doubt, fightings within and fears without, O Lamb of God I come'. Let us think of the despairing jailer of Acts 16, of the dying thief on the cross, even of Saul of Tarsus himself at the beginning of his journey of faith (Acts 9). Even as eighty-year-old Moses, when he caught sight of divine reality atop Mt Sinai thought 'so terrifying was the sight that Moses said, "I tremble with fear"' (Heb. 12:21).

b) Faith though small and weak, only slightly informed of the truth at first, grows, as noted above. Sometimes it even grows 'abundantly' (2 Thess. 1:3).

c) Steady confidence or trust is an aspect of mature faith only. The many exhortations of Scripture to increase believers' confidence demonstrates that desirable as full trust is, we sinners do mix it with doubt and need to be encouraged to 'lift your drooping hands and strengthen your weak knees' (Heb. 12:12). '[W]e beseech you, brethren, that ye increase more and more' in all virtues (1 Thess. 4:10 KJV). This encouragement came from a busy evangelist who was writing back to a very newly formed assembly of believers (Acts 17).

d) Increase of faith is a matter of prayer by and for Christians. Luke reports the Twelve faced with the formidable task of forgiving chronic offenders, says 'The apostles said to the Lord, "Increase our faith"' (Luke 17:5), and a newly convinced disciple, 'I believe; help my unbelief!' (Mark 9:24).

e) The Lord put greater emphasis on the authenticity of one's faith than the size of it. He did not say, 'If you have faith as a mountain you can move a mustard seed', but the other way around.

f) As B. B. Warfield points out, 'Jesus deals with notable tenderness with those of "little faith", and His apostles imitated Him.'[18] Indeed Jesus used 'little faith' (with big doubts) as occasion to teach big faith with smaller doubt (Matt. 6:20, 30; 14:31; 16:8; 17:20; Luke 12:28; 17:5; Mark 9:24).

To quote Warfield again:

> The *effects* of faith not being the immediate product of faith itself but of that energy of God which was exhibited in raising Jesus from the dead and on which dependence is now placed for raising us up with Him into newness of life [Eph. 3:19, 20] would seem to depend directly on the fact of faith, leaving questions of its strength, quality, and the like more or less, to one side.[19]

On Confessing Jesus As Both Lord and Christ.

'Lordship salvation' is an expression that first began to be heard in the last years of the twentieth century. It is a pejorative term used mainly by folk caught in the down-draught of expiring hyper-dispensationalism and others still holding on to the two-stage doctrine of sanctification in the waning holiness movement that swept Britain and America a century ago. They think they discern a doctrine of salvation by works encrypted in preaching that one must believe and confess Jesus Christ as Lord as well as Savior. The folk who tag the rest of us with 'lordship salvation' think of themselves as preserving the pure doctrine of salvation 'by grace alone' in denying that valid confession of Christ includes acknowledging Him as *Lord* of life as well as *Savior* of the soul.

The early church did not think so. In receiving Christian baptism they acknowledged, 'Jesus Christ is Lord' — and that was precisely why they were persecuted. Because Caesar (who couldn't have cared less about what they believed with respect to a 'spiritual' Savior) insisted that the Roman Emperor is lord.

The late A. W. Tozer met the problem and this is some of what he had to say about it.

> We have all heard the tearful plea made to persons already saved to accept Christ as Lord and thus enter into the victorious life.
> Almost all deeper life teaching is based upon this fallacy, but because it contains a germ of truth its soundness is not questioned. Anyway, it is extremely simple and quite popular, and in addition to these selling points it is also ready-made for both speaker and hearer and requires no thinking by either. So sermons embodying this heresy abit of verbal over kill are freely preached, books are written and songs composed, all saying the same thing; and all saying the wrong thing, except, as I have said, for a feeble germ of truth lying inert at the bottom.

---

18. B. B. Warfield, *Biblical and Theological Studies* (Philadelphia, PA: Presbyterian & Reformed Publ., 1952), pp. 426, 427.
19. ibid., p. 426.

Now it seems odd that none of these teachers ever noticed that the only true object of saving faith is none other than Christ Himself; not the 'saviourhood' of Christ nor the 'lordship' of Christ, but Christ Himself. God does not offer salvation to the one who will believe on one of the offices of Christ, nor is an office of Christ ever presented as an object of faith. Neither are we exhorted to believe on the atonement, nor on the cross, nor on the priesthood of the Saviour. All of these are embodied in the person of Christ, but they are never separated nor is one ever isolated from the rest. Much less are we permitted to accept one of Christ's offices and reject another. The notion that we are so permitted is a modern day heresy, I repeat, and like every heresy it has had evil consequences among Christians. No heresy is ever entertained with impunity. We pay in practical failure for our theoretical errors.

It is altogether doubtful whether any man can be saved who comes to Christ for His help but with no intention to obey Him. Christ's saviourhood is forever united to His lordship. Look at the Scriptures: 'If thou shalt confess with thy mouth the Lord Jesus, and shalt believe in thine heart that God hath raised him from the dead, thou shalt be saved... for the same Lord over all is rich unto all that call upon him. For whosoever shall call upon the name of the Lord shall be saved' (Rom. 10:9-13). There the Lord is the object of faith for salvation. And when the Philippian jailer asked the way to be saved, Paul replied, 'Believe on the Lord Jesus Christ, and thou shalt be saved' (Acts 16:31). He did not tell him to believe on the Saviour with the thought that he could later take up the matter of His lordship and settle it at his own convenience. To Paul there could be no division of offices. Christ must be Lord or He will not be Saviour.

There is no intention here to teach that the earnest believer may not go on to explore ever-increasing meanings in Christ, nor do we hold that our first saving contact with Christ brings perfect knowledge of all He is to us. The contrary is true. Ages upon ages will hardly be long enough to allow us to experience all the riches of His grace. As we discover new meanings in His titles and make them ours we will grow in the knowledge of our Lord and in personal appreciation of the multifold offices He fills and the many forms of love He wears exalted on His throne. That is the truth which has been twisted out of shape and reduced to impotence by the doctrine that we can believe on His saviourhood while rejecting His lordship.[20]

Several years earlier, James Orr, the famed author of *The Christian View of God and the World*, editor of the *International Standard Bible Encyclopaedia*, teacher of generations of seminary students in his numerous writings, tells how sound teachers of late Reformation times answered this error.

> They pointed out that acceptance of Christ in faith is acceptance of the *whole* Christ – of Christ in *all* His *offices*, and for *all the ends* of His work – for sanctification as well as for justification – and that holiness, being the end of pardon, for anyone to think of accepting Christ for forgiveness, while refusing to own Him as Lord, is only thereby to show that he has not yet attained a glimpse of what true faith means.[21]

An author who flourished as chaplain to Stonewall Jackson and influenced for good theology in the American South was Robert Dabney. In his *Lectures in Systematic Theology* he addressed this same tempest in a teapot, saying:

> The selfishness and guilty conscience of man prompt him powerfully to look to the Saviour exclusively as a remedy for guilt, even when awakened by the Spirit. The first and most urgent want of the soul, convicted of its guilt and danger, is impunity [from punishment]. Hence the undue prevalence, even in preaching, of that view of Christ which holds Him up as an expiation only... [receiving] Him in His priestly office!... The man who is savingly wrought upon by the Holy Ghost, is made to feel that his bondage to corruption is an evil as inexorable and dreadful as the penal curse of the law. He needs and desires Christ in his prophetic and kingly offices, as much as his priestly. His faith *receives Him as He is offered in the gospel* [emphasis added]; that is, as a 'Saviour of His people from their sins'.[22]

Distinction between receiving Jesus as Lord from Jesus as Saviour is a false distinction but a real red herring – apologies to President Harry Truman.

Some Implications of the Doctrine of Faith.

If faith is man's response to hearing the Word of God under the influence of the Holy Spirit, if the Spirit must prepare the heart of a sinner, then several conclusions about what is important follow.

---

20. From 'No Saviourhood Without Lordship' an excerpted passage from *The Root of Righteousness* by A. W. Tozer in '*The Fellowship of Concerned Mennonites*', vol. xvii, no. 1 (Harrisburg, VA , Jan./Feb. 2002), p. 8.
21. James Orr, *The Progress of Dogma*, first published in 1901 (Grand Rapids, MI: Eerdmans Publ., 1952), p. 272.
22. Robert L. Dabney, *Lectures in Systematic Theology* (Grand Rapids, MI: Zondervan Publ., 1878, repr. 1992), pp. 664, 665.

a) Proclamation of the Word of truth is of ultimate importance for the church. If people are to be saved, repent, be justified by faith and sanctified, then, by whatever means available, they must be given the good news.

The importance of proclaiming the good news accounts for the central place of public reading of Scripture and of preaching over all other aspects of public worship, once the Reformation and kindred movements, before and after, approximately restored the primitive pattern. Donald Bloesch devotes 37 of the 265 pages of *Essentials of Evangelical Theology*, Volume One, to a chapter on 'The Primacy of Scripture'.[23] Thirty-three of the 300 pages of his second (and last) volume constitute a chapter on 'The Cruciality of Preaching' by prophets and preachers who are conceived as, in an important sense, 'the mouthpieces and instruments of the Word of God'.[24] As to proper public worship, Bloesch writes:

> Reformed worship is centerd about preaching and hearing of the Word of God. We are here using the word *Reformed* in its widest sense to include the whole of Protestantism, the hallmark of which is the appeal to the authority of the Bible over the church tradition and mystical experience. This kind of spirituality was most clearly identifiable in the Reformation and in early Calvinism and Puritanism.[25]

There is more to say, of course. The emotional *high point* of worship may be a ritual act or a song. In Calvin's thought the *culmination* of the public service of worship ought to be the prayer. Recent writers call attention to the fact that in contemporary evangelical churches the whole atmosphere of the biblical 'solemn meeting' and 'sacrifice of praise' has been lost in mood music, light entertainment and catchy sermonizing rather than expounding the Word and attention to 'the public reading of Scripture... exhortation... teaching ["*doctrine*" KJV]' (1 Tim. 4:13), and corporate praise and prayer. Part of this may be simply the effect of the frivolous, entertainment-seeking of the television age, part the free church fear of liturgy (which has to be learned to be enjoyed and appreciated), and part, very regrettably, to the emphasis on the talents and personality of the preacher rather than the worship of God.

Yet the fact remains, as Paul enjoined the 'interim pastor' at Ephesus: 'Until I come [back], devote yourself to the public reading of Scripture, to preaching and to teaching [or "doctrine"]' (1 Tim. 4:13 NIV).

b) Prayer for the Holy Spirit's power to accompany the Word is equally important. There are many scriptural injunctions in this regard.

We live in a time when the surrounding culture leads us to suppose that no problems are solved by truth as such. Objective, eternal truths, authoritatively announced, are as out of style today as knee-breeches and bustles – especially among the products of the modern university. Somehow we must not let our minds be conformed to the world (Rom. 12:1 ff.) in this regard. But our current evangelical 'in' style of talk, shows that we are never the less conformed. Apostles did not 'share their faith' or 'make rapport'; they vigorously proclaimed a message and did so with authority. They were not mere authority figures but authorities. As preachers adhere closely to apostolic doctrine they share apostolic authority.

Again, the meetings of the churches for prayer are generally out of style also. This is a day of going and doing, of activity. The mid-week prayer meeting has largely been lost in the contest for a slot in the weekly schedule when people are free to attend. Everything else seems more important.

The old time mid-weekly prayer routines are not sacred, nor are the time-worn methods of proclaiming the Word, but proclamation and prayer are at the heart of the Savior's programme for His church. They dare not be laid aside. If we have scheduled them out we must again schedule them in. The forms may change, but the essentials must not be neglected and lost. Whole church prayer (Acts 4) has been scheduled out. If ever we prevail in this sick world we must schedule whole church prayer back in.

In the village culture of the ancient churches, people walked to church for two evening meetings between Sundays, for prayer, reading of Scripture (many could not read and few owned a Bible) and mutual encouragement. These days of meeting were called 'Station Days' – Tuesday and Thursday.

Two important observations remain: 1) that Christian faith – the faith that saves – can and does grow, gaining strength as the reliability of its object and the authenticity of the faith itself are verified in life. After a little time a vital faith is stronger than at first. This implies gaining more knowledge of divine things and experience in biblical

---

23. Donald Bloesch, *Essentials of Evangelical Theology, i* (San Francisco: Harper & Row, 1978, 1979), pp. 51–87.
24. ibid., *ii*, p. 72.
25. ibid., p. 87.

living. Of one group of young believers, left behind after only brief apostolic ministry by their evangelist, it is written, 'your faith is growing abundantly' (2 Thess. 1:3) and James notes how trials strengthen faith (James 1:2 ff.; cf. 1 Peter 1:7; and 2 Peter 3:18). Compare also the trembling faith of Saul of Tarsus described in the ninth chapter of Acts with the magnificent certainty of trust and commitment of the same man a generation later as set forth by his own hand in 2 Timothy (especially 1:12 and 4:6-8; cf. Ps. 34:8). 2) Faith, the first virtue, is itself the fountain from which arise all other Christian virtues. This is the teaching of 2 Peter 1:5-7, which may be paraphrased:

> ...applying all diligence, in your faith supply moral excellence, and in your moral excellence, knowledge; and in your knowledge, self-control, and in your self-control, perseverance, and in your perseverance, godliness; and in your godliness, brotherly kindness, and in your brotherly kindness, Christian love.

13
The Doctrine of Justification by Faith

Background to this Critical Evangelical Truth.

The *fact* that God forgives believing sinners, reckons them righteous and treats them as righteous, is a central feature of the doctrine of salvation from righteous Abel (see Heb. 11:4) through Abraham (Rom. 4:3) and on through Jesus' sayings and parables (Luke 18:4) to the Epistles of Paul and on to the last chapter of Revelation (Rev. 21:19).

Justification as a formal doctrine is first expounded in Paul's Epistles. This doctrine was the most critical feature of the Protestant revolt against the medieval church of the sixteenth century and remains today the indigestible surd which the Roman Church cannot swallow and the evangelical church can never yield.

'Justification by faith' is plain enough in the Bible but the teaching was early obscured by moralism and sacramentalism. Nevertheless, the Spirit of Truth did not fail to illumine minds to this truth through the Middle Ages (Bernard of Clairvaux, for example) though full clarification and emphasis awaited the reforms of the sixteenth century.

Some touching lines from Anselm of Canterbury (1033–1109) who wrote in a very dark period, show the 'dark ages' were not wholly dark. He is addressing God in 'A Meditation on Redemption':

> I was on slippery footing because I was weak and prone to sin. I was on the downward road to the chaos of hell because in our first parents I had descended from justice [righteousness] to injustice (and injustice leads down to Hell)... the unbearable burden of God's judgment was pushing me down... Being thus destitute of all help, I was illumined by You and shown my condition. You taught all these things to others on my behalf, and later You taught these same things to me even before I inquired...You removed the sin in which I had been conceived and born. You also removed the condemnation of my soul... You gave me the name Christian, which derives from Your own name; through Your name I confess, and you acknowledge, that I am among the redeemed. You stood me upright... You made me confident of my soul's salvation, for which You gave Your life... You who cause me to ask [for reception 'into the inner chamber of Your love'], cause me also to receive.[1]

As A. H. Strong says after quoting different passages by the medieval archbishop, these expressions 'give us reason to believe that the New Testament doctrine of justification by faith was implicitly, if not explicitly, held by many pious souls through the ages of papal darkness'.[2]

---

1. Anselm 'A Meditation on Human Redemption', in *Anselm of Canterbury I: Monologion, Proslogion, Debate With Janielo*, trans. by J. Hopkins and H. Richardson (Toronto and NY: The Edwin Mellen Press, 1974–1976), pp. 143, 145.
2. A. H. Strong, *Systematic Theology* (Valley Forge: Judson Press, 1907), p. 849.

It is important to know how the doctrine came first to be clearly understood and stated by those early Protestants who devoted so very much thought and prayer as well as literary energy to justification by faith. Hundreds of Reformed, evangelical believers died for confessing this faith in the Reformation era in many lands of Europe. We, their heirs, owe them at least to become acquainted with how they defined this doctrine that defined them in their own consciences and in the eyes of their enemies.

Discussions after Luther's first bold announcements of 1517 quickly led to a Lutheran consensus and were given permanent form in *The Formula of Concord of 1576*. Excerpts from this lengthy creedal document assert:

> By unanimous consent... it is taught in our churches... that sinners are justified before God... alone by faith in Christ, so that Christ alone is our righteousness.[3]
>
> We teach... the whole Christ... in his sole, most absolute obedience which he rendered to the Father even unto death, as God and man... thereby merited for us the remission of all our sins and eternal life.[4]
>
> For he bestows and imputes to us the righteousness of the obedience of Christ; for the sake of that righteousness we are received by God into favour and accounted righteous.[5]
>
> [W]e... recognize Christ... and confide in him:... for his obedience's sake we have by grace the remission of sins, are accounted righteous... and attain eternal salvation.[6]

The theology of Lutheranism came into minor but regrettable disagreement with Reformed theology after the initial impulses of the Reformation passed. There is little difference to be found in Calvin. Differences developed in discussion of *atonement*, whether particular (as in Reformed theology or universal as in Lutheran) and the distinction between *active* obedience (Jesus' sinless life of doing the Father's will) and *passive* obedience of Christ (passion and death), both involved in imputation. Yet essential agreement that justification is by grace through faith on the ground of Jesus' work of redemption remained. The *Westminster Confession* is still standard for all orthodox Presbyterians. *The Formula of Concord* is still standard for orthodox Lutherans.

The *Heidelberg Catechism* (1563) has been standard for instruction of the children in Reformed churches for over 400 years now. A 1963 translation of *Question 60* reads, 'How are you righteous before God?' *Answer*: 'Only by true faith in Jesus Christ. In spite of the fact that my conscience accuses me that I have grievously sinned against all the commandments of God, and have not kept any one of them, and that I am still ever prone to all that is evil, nevertheless, God, without any merit of my own, out of pure grace, grants me the benefits of the perfect expiation [better, *satisfaction*] of Christ, imputing to me his righteousness and holiness as if I had never committed a single sin or had ever been sinful, having fulfilled myself all the obedience which Christ has carried out for me, if only I accept such favour with a trusting heart.' *Question 61* reads, 'Why do you say that you are righteous by faith alone?' *Answer*: 'Not because I please God by virtue of the worthiness of my faith, but because the satisfaction, righteousness and holiness of Christ alone are my righteousness before God, and because I can accept it and make it mine in no other way than by faith alone.'[7] This unsurpassed catechism for children states the matter of justification in language any one who wants to know can understand.

The *Westminster Confession*, standard for generations of Puritans, Presbyterians, Congregationalists and Baptists in Great Britain, Ireland and America is more formal, but it has the advantage of precision and brevity. Chapter XII, art. i, 'Of Justification' reads:

> Those whom God effectually calleth, he also freely justifieth: not by infusing righteousness into them, but by pardoning their sins, and by accounting and accepting their persons as righteous; not for anything wrought in them, or done by them, but for Christ's sake alone; not by imputing faith itself, the act of believing, or any other evangelical obedience to them, as their righteousness; but by imputing the obedience and satisfaction of Christ unto them, they receiving and resting on him and his righteousness by faith; which faith they have not of themselves, it is the gift of God.[8]

---

3. *The Formula of Concord of 1576*, Art. iii, Philip Schaff, *The Creeds of Christendom*, vol. iii, pp. 93–180.
4. ibid., art. iii, i.
5. ibid., art. iii, ii.
6. ibid., art. iii, iv.
7. *The Heidelberg Catechism*, 400th Anniversary Edition – 1563–1963, trans. by Allen O. Miller and M. Eugene Osterhaven (Philadelphia and Boston: United Church Press, 1963), pp. 61–63.
8. *Westminster Shorter Catechism in Confession of Faith of the Presbyterian Church in the U.S. together with The Larger Catechism and The Shorter Catechism* (Richmond: John Knox Press, 1861, 1944), chap. xii, art. i, 'Of Justification'.

Notable both for breadth and accuracy is the summary by James Orr, who along with Philip Schaff, did more than any other theologian to make Americans aware of the sound part of European theology.

> The chief points in the doctrine of justification at the Reformation [were] (1) that justification is of God's free grace and not of works; (2) that it is through faith alone; (3) that it includes the forgiveness of sins and the pronouncing of the sinner righteous before God; (4) that it is to be distinguished from the internal change we designate regeneration and sanctification, and does not proceed on the ground of this change; (5) that it is nevertheless not a mere amnesty, but has its ground in the perfect righteousness of Christ, and the atonement made by Him for sin; and (6) that it is instantaneous and complete, an act of God never to be repeated, – these cardinal points on which all the Reformers were at one, were then fixed, I believe, beyond the power of future to recall.[9]

This fine statement co-ordinates with James Orr's thesis, which is hardly contestable, that doctrines of Christianity, always present latently in the Scriptures, have been given full and correct form at distinct junctures of Christian history – beginning first with Christology, then Theology (Trinity), Anthropology, and after that, in Reformation times, Soteriology including Justification.

Justification by Faith Through the Scriptures.

The 'seed plot' of this doctrine, for which the name is justification, is Genesis 15:6 (KJV), where it is said of Abraham: 'And he believed in the LORD; and he counted it to him for righteousness.' This text becomes the classical citation for the great expositions of justification in the New Testament (Rom. 4:3, 9, 22; Gal. 3:6; James 2:23). Three great themes of salvation, constituting the chief elements of the doctrine of justification, are here: belief (faith), imputation and righteousness. In an Appendix to this chapter, suggesting a translation of Genesis 15:6 different from the standard translations, the seed of Paul's doctrine of imputed righteousness is seen really to be in this verse. God did not, as the verse *seems* to say, accept faith in lieu of righteousness, but *imputed* righteousness to Abraham on the basis of his faith.

To trace the development of the doctrine through Scripture is too large a task for the present project. Suffice it to say that the Old Testament prophets *knew about it* and connected it with Messiah (Isa. 43:23-26; 45:21-25; 53:11). Without using the word, *Jesus announced* justification (John 5:24) and the *Gospels teach* it (John 3:18; Luke 18:9-14). It is the *special theme* of Romans and Galatians.

Historically speaking, the doctrine of justification – properly distinguished from sanctification and connected with faith – became important in the growth of Christian understanding of doctrine at the time of the Reformation. The Reformers emphasized regeneration and union with Christ too, for a fair reading of their writings shows how incapable the beginning of faith and of a life of faith they knew sinners to be apart from union with Christ and a new birth. The eighteenth-century revivals did by no means first clarify this teaching as it is often claimed. Indeed, there are not wanting informed persons who would affirm that the early Wesleyans, for all their emphasis on the need for new birth, were not fully aware of man's need of special awakening grace before faith can exist in the sinner's heart. Of course the book of Romans was read throughout the centuries by many. Yet one of the sad facts of Christian history is that the pure evangelical teaching of the New Testament and of the apostles was compromised in sub-apostolic and patristic ages by retreat into moralism, legalism and sacramentalism. Even the golden-tongued Chrysostom, and Augustine, mighty of pen for the doctrine of grace, were tainted by these errors.

The meaning of 'justification' or 'justify' in salvation will be treated at length below. The bare word is a forensic term, that is, related to law and courts where it means essentially to declare not guilty, as opposed to guilty. It is implicit that treatment as free from guilt (free from civil restraint – jail – and release from punishment) is a part of the idea also.

The Hebrew *tsadheq* (in *hiphil*) and Greek *dikaioō* in human civil matters mean the same (see Exod. 23:7; Deut. 25:1; Job 27:4; Ps. 143:2; Isa. 5:23; 2 Sam. 15:4; Prov. 17:15) as also in connection with God's acts in religious matters (1 Kgs. 8:32; Isa. 53:11).

In each of these texts the *hiphil* form of the Hebrew word is used and in the *Septuagint* (Greek) is rendered by *dikaioō*. The King James Version consistently reads some form of 'justify'. That the meaning of the word justify is to *declare* righteous, rather than make righteous is unmistakable in Deuteronomy 25:1. It reads in the KJV, 'If there be a controversy between men, and they come unto judgment [into court RSV], that the judges may judge them; then they

---

9. James Orr, *The Progress of Dogma*, first published in 1901 (Grand Rapids, MI: Eerdmans Publ., 1952), pp. 268, 269.

shall justify ["acquit" and "acquitting" RSV and ESV] the righteous, and condemn the wicked.' This puts justification out of the realm of moral or spiritual improvement and into the realm of legal determination of the moral standing of the subject before the law and declaration of the same. In the Roman Church justification – reduced from the scholastic verbiage attached to dogmatic statements about it – is the same as sanctification in the sense of moral perfection or improvement. Protestants believe in moral improvement too. Sanctification is the cart that follows the horse (justification), not the other way around.

The Greek *dikaioō* does not appear in strictly civil connection in the New Testament, but in secular literature it was commonly (though not extensively) used in the above civil sense.[10] The Greek Old Testament renders *tsadheq* by *dikaioō* and is quite uniformly 'a forensic term… constantly used in the sense of "to pronounce righteous", "to justify, to vindicate"'.[11] In the New Testament this is uniform.

Justification, when used technically, relates to legal status; it is to receive a favourable verdict. Sometimes the sense of declare righteous appears in non-legal situations, but the extended sense is the same (as when men justify God or vindicate Him; Luke 7:29, where 'make righteous' simply will not do; see also Rom. 3:4; Ps. 51:4). Justification therefore is related in civil situation to civil laws and in religious matters to divine laws.

The Special Vocabulary of Justification.

It would not be a diversion at this point to explore all the evidence of Scripture and of ancient languages and culture to show how justification and by it every aspect of biblical beliefs are constituted in an important way with righteousness before the law; also that justification is never to be made righteous but to be declared so. There was little of the democratic feeling in most ancient societies that laws for men proceed from men. Rather laws, including civil as well as moral and religious proceed from the gods (or God) to men, the creatures, in ancient thought. This was quite as prevalent among Israel's neighbours and the Greco-Roman world of New Testament times as in Israel.

The first element of the English word justification is Latin *jus*, which means law. Similarly, the first element in the Greek word *dikaioō* means legal punishment. Our leading authority, with abundant proofs furnished, states that in the New Testament '*dikē*' is found only three times, and always in the sense of 'penal justice' or 'punishment'.[12] The Textus Receptus has *dike* also at Acts 25:15. 'Popular [heathen] belief is reflected in Acts 28:4…Though Paul has escaped the sea, he is a marked man now overtaken by the goddess *Dikē*, personified [divine justice]. In the other instances the word conveys the inherited Jewish [and biblical] view of eternal judgment, as in 2 Thess. 1:9.'[13]

Five New Testament and Septuagint (Gr. OT) words have the element *dikē* (pronounced 'dee-kay') as an initial syllable. All relate to righteousness before the law and all are related to the doctrine of justification. This merits attention to the essential connection with *dike* as divine justice as law – throughout a forensic (legal) idea proper to courts of law. These words are *dikaios* (righteous); *dikaiosunē* (righteousness); *dikaioō* (justify, declare righteous); *dikaiōma* (1. ordinance or 2. righteous act or 3. sentence of justification); *dikaiōsis* (justification in sense of acquittal); and *dikaiokisia* (quality of righteous judgment). This last word does not appear in the New Testament and in the Old Testament only at Hosea 6:5 as rendering of *mishpat* in a rare variation of the LXX text. Let us look at each of the five New Testament words in relation to justification in salvation.[14]

1. *Dikaioō* uniformily means *the forensic act* of declaring righteous before the law. The only place in the KJV of the Bible where this word or its Hebrew equivalent might possibly mean to make righteous or turn to righteousness is Daniel 12:3. Yet even here, '*turn many* [emphasis added] to righteousness' probably should be (as the hiphil of *tsadheq* certainly allows) 'cause many to be justified'. James A. Montgomery comments here on 'the Hiphil of *tsadheq*' that the customary sense is legal and means 'declaring innocent' and suggests comparison with Isaiah 53:11,[15] where the usual rendering (as KJV) is 'shall… justify many'. James 2:21, 23, 24 are not exceptions. As we shall have occasion to note, James was correcting a false view of faith not a false view of righteousness, viz. 'Can that kind of faith which produces no righteous works truly be directed toward Jesus as Savior and Lord?'

---

10. *Theological Dictionary of the New Testament ii*, ed. G. Kittel and G. W. Bromiley (Grand Rapids, MI: Eerdmans Publ., 1964), pp. 211–214.
11. *TDNT ii*, p. 212.
12. *TDNT ii*, p. 181.
13. *TDNT ii*, ibid.
14. See Strong, *Systematic Theology*, pp. 350–354 for a very helpful treatment of these words, but without the input of *TDNT* which is to be consulted. I am in debt to both for this effort to point up the distinctive sense of each word in relation to justification by faith.
15. James A. Montgomery, *Daniel, International Critical Commentary* (New York: Charles Scribners Sons, 1927), p. 472.

2. *Dikaios*, the *quality of being righteous* – before God and God's law – is the constant Old Testament and New Testament understanding. The LXX uses the word somewhat differently from the Greek world's use. 'The fundamental belief in God links it firmly to the judgment of God.'[16] It gets 'a new application to the sphere of salvation in the NT'.[17] In common usage, of course, the word was used to describe one who conformed to whatever standard of morals the speaker held.

3. *Dikaiosunē* (translated righteousness) is moral uprightness, absence of guilt. In context of salvation it is the gift of God by imputation, as in many texts in Paul's Epistles. He contrasts the defective, false *dikaiosunē* (righteousness) which comes by keeping rules (Rom. 10:3 KJV) 'going about to establish their own righteousness' with 'the righteousness of God', 'the righteousness which is of God by faith' (Phil. 3:9 KJV). This righteousness was called an 'alien righteousness' by the old Protestant theologians because it is Christ's righteousness obtained through our Mediator's life of *active obedience* to God's law and His *passive* obedience of willingly accepting the passion and death. This righteousness is proper to Him for He secured it, but *alien* to us in that it is His righteousness imputed to us when we believe (Rom. 4:1-8).

4. *Dikaiōma* the *accomplished fact* of being justified in contrast to being condemned, no longer subject to penalty as in Romans 5:16-18 where it refers first to our 'justification' (v. 16) and to Christ's 'act of righteousness' (v.18). Sometimes it can refer to a righteous sentence as in Romans 1:32, or to acquitted righteous deeds as in Revelation 19:8.

5. *Dikaiōsis* is used only twice in the New Testament and seems to refer to the *procurement process* in our justification (Rom. 4:25, the resurrection of Christ and Rom 5:18, His whole life of righteousness).

The Soteriological Doctrine.

The soteriological doctrine now to follow will be developed in relation to seven rubrics, each furnished with a basic text of Scripture: 1) Author (Rom. 8:33); 2) Agent (Gal. 2:17); 3) Method (Rom. 3:24); 4) Basis (Rom. 5:9); 5) Means or Instrument (Rom. 3:28); 6) Fruit (Rom. 5:1-11); 7) Evidence (James. 2:24).

1. The *author* of justification is God. At Galatians 3:8 Paul, interpreting the Old Testament, affirms, '…the Scripture, foreseeing that God would justify the Gentiles ["heathen" KJV]' and adds that God in saying, 'In you shall all the nations be blessed' 'preached the gospel beforehand to Abraham' (Gal. 3:9; cf. v. 8; and Rom. 3:25; 8:33). God is now justifying believing 'heathen'.

God is 'the Judge of all the earth' (Gen. 18:25) and will 'do right' – Hebrew *mishpat*, judgment. Ultimately the verdict on a man is God's business to declare. There is hence an eschatological aspect to justification. God will not reverse a verdict, thus Jesus' strong statement about every true believer in 'him who sent me' – that he 'has eternal life. He does not come into judgment, but has passed from death to life' (John 5:24). As 'Judge of all the earth' the Creator's justification of believers has first, the aspect of verdict or sentence (not guilty, righteous) and secondly executive public action whereby the person vindicated receives treatment due (see Isa. 45:24, 25; 50:7-9). All the biblical materials which are appropriately discussed under the doctrine of divine judgment are properly introduced here. Calvary, where was shed the precious blood and where He bore the stroke in the place of those to whom the stroke was due was the scene of the first eschatological, 'general' judgment. 'The Lord has laid on him the punishment of us all'.

2. The *agent* of justification is Jesus Christ. The phrase 'justified by… Christ' is employed by Paul (Gal. 2:16, 17). The words of Jesus explain why the Second Person of the Godhead must be the actual justifier, viz. 'The Father… gave him authority to execute judgement, because he is a son of man' (John 5:26, 27 NASV margin and ASV, see also 19-26). The KJV, RSV and ESV have 'the Son of Man' but the ASV cited (*a* son, not *the* son) is correct. The Semitic idiom means a member of the human race – not in appearance only, but in very nature. True, the Son of God as man shall in wrath yet 'judge among the heathen', thereby littering the twilight of the present age 'with the dead bodies' (Ps. 110:6 KJV; cf. Rev. 19:11-18); but for now, as judge of believing 'heathen' (Gal. 3:8, 9) our Lord publishes the executive decree in heaven's courts, 'Treat this man as righteous'. An examination of Hebrews 2:9-18 will help explain just why he undertook the Father's plan and became a man; to justify believing sinners was an important

---

16. Schrenk, *TDNT ii*, p. 185.
17. *TDNT ii*, p. 187.

part of it. Even during the days of His earthly ministry we find Him proclaiming release to captives, forgiving sins and declaring men justified before God (Luke 4:18; Matt. 9:2, 56; Luke 18:14), meanwhile affirming that he 'came' that sinners might be called to repentance and be forgiven. When contrite sinners of every class and of any time of life and of every age of Christian history come to repentance and faith their confession is always amenable to the memorable words of Charlotte Elliott's hymn: 'Just as I am, without one plea,/ But that *thy* blood was shed for me,/ And that *thou* bidd'st me come to *thee*,/ O *Lamb of God*, I come! I come!... Just as I am, *thou* wilt receive, /Wilt welcome, pardon, cleanse, relieve;/ Because *thy* promise I believe,/ O *Lamb of God*, I come!'

3. The *method* of justification is by free grace: 'Being justified freely by his grace' (Rom. 3:24 KJV – ESV has 'justified by his grace as a gift'). All aspects of salvation are by God's grace, yet in a unique, striking way, justification, for God to declare the *ungodly* righteous, manifests divine grace. Paul graphically portrayed this, viz. 'Now to the one who works, his wages are not counted as a gift but as his due. And to the one who does not work but trusts him who justifies the ungodly, his faith is counted as righteousness' (Rom. 4:4, 5); also '...for all have sinned and fall short of the glory of God, and are justified by his grace as a gift, through the redemption that is in Christ Jesus' (Rom. 3:23, 24).

As previously noted (Introduction) grace is so contrary to fallen man's way of thinking about reality, so capable of perversion or misunderstanding, that it has always been under attack by those who supposed themselves to be the defenders of public morality and true religion. Paul was 'slanderously' accused of teaching 'why not do evil that good may come?' (Rom. 3:8; cf. 6:1). The Galatian legalists sought to improve on his doctrine by adding the rite of circumcision. We have commented already on the slippage from the teaching of salvation by grace alone in the early centuries. The Roman Church rejects complete justification by grace alone without meritorious works to the present day.

Yet the essential idea of justification by grace alone is simple. Grace is unmerited favour. It is granted 'freely' (Greek *dōrean*), i.e. as a gift – without charge – rendered 'without a cause' (John 15:25), 'without paying for it' or 'for nought' (KJV) (2 Thess. 3:8). Isaiah spoke of this 'righteousness' of the LORD as procured 'without money and without price' (Isa. 55:1; see connection with the last verse of chapter 54). The Bible never says that God has paid no price, but it forbids human beings even to try to pay for justification or to try to earn or merit part of it. This is a unique feature of biblical religion, for no other is a religion of pure grace.[18]

4. The *basis* of justification is the satisfaction rendered to divine law when Christ died in the sinner's place on the cross. There God made Him to be sin for us that we might be made the righteousness of God in Him (2 Cor. 5:21). '[W]e have now been justified by his blood' (Rom 5:9). Readers will know that this aspect of the work of Christ is fully treated in an earlier locus of theology.

A problem arises: some inquire how God can do something in the area of ethics, that is, of righteousness, which He condemns in others – 'Woe to those who call evil good... who put darkness for light... who put bitter for sweet' (Isa. 5:20). Yet God 'justifies the ungodly' (Rom. 4:5). The problem may be reduced to three elements: one of anthropology, one of the law of God, a third of theology proper. a) All men are sinners, guilty of breaking divine law. The possibility therefore of justification by law-keeping would be possible only among a class of people that has not a single member on earth. b) The moral law of God is non-relaxable and invariable: 'whoever keeps the whole law but fails in one point has become accountable for all of it' (James. 2:10); 'For God shows no partiality. For all who have sinned without the law will also perish without the law, and all who have sinned under the law will be judged by the law' (Rom. 2:11, 12). c) God is perfectly and incorruptibly just and holy. His name is holy. Holiness is his 'fundamental attribute' (Strong). If He is loving or merciful it will be with holy love and holy mercy. He will not break His holy law, which is the reflection or extension of His own holy will and nature. Look steadily at these facts and justification seems impossible. Modern writers, from Socinus (1539–1604) to C. H. Dodd and W. Echrodt, older contemporaries, have sought to remove justification from its legal-forensic, biblical setting to place it wholly in the realm of divine love, or mercy, or sovereignty, but the Bible does not allow it, hence the doctrine defended herein, especially the Pauline exposition, has been maintained steadily through the Reformation era and to the present only by the very committed evangelicals.

The liberal-Modernist, with (I suppose) genuine exasperation, asks, 'Why don't you rigid ideologues admit that God simply finds it easy to forgive people out of pure love and mercy without reparations or punishments?'

---

18. Unconvincing claims to the contrary have appeared in journals of social science and of anthropology. Unfortunately I have mislaid the references.

We assert that never in the Bible is man's need or his character, or legal obedience, or human ceremonies (circumcision or baptism) or God's love or His sovereignty or mercy brought forward as the true bases of divine forgiveness. It is wholly on the ground of that satisfaction rendered to divine moral law by Jesus Christ when He died in our place for our sins. This is set forth in some detail at Romans 3:20-26. Here is Paul's theodicy – if we may use the word – for the righteousness of God in forgiving sin from Eve and Adam onward.

I quote the NKJV, because it preserves *propitiation*, the correct rendering of *hilasterion* in v. 25:

> But now the righteousness of God apart from the law is revealed, being witnessed by the Law and the Prophets, even the righteousness of God, through faith in Jesus Christ, to all and on all who believe... through the redemption that is in Christ Jesus, whom God set forth as a propitiation by His blood, through faith, *to demonstrate His righteousness, because in His forbearance God had passed over the sins that were previously committed*, to demonstrate at the present time His righteousness, that He might be just and the justifier of the one who has faith in Jesus (Romans 3:21-26 with the indicated ellipsis [emphasis added]).

Paul seems to be asserting that up to now (v. 21) the righteousness of God in forgiving sin (justifying sinners) could be in question. The prophets preached justification by faith but didn't explain the ground of remitting deserved punishments. The threats of divine judgment seem to have failed. God did not seem to carry through with His own rules. David didn't die for his adultery. The judgment of the Canaanites and the exile of the two kingdoms were long delayed. Since the propitiation by Christ's blood took place we can now understand how God 'had passed over' the sins of former ages. 'At the present time', Paul is saying, we understand how God can 'be himself righteous' in former ages and now also be the 'justifier' of him that has faith in Jesus.

Long before Jesus died God was justifying the saints of old – Abel, Abraham, Moses, etc. – yet without palpable basis in law and righteousness. Reason as well as revelation acquiesces in acknowledging 'The blood of bulls and goats can never take away sin'. When, however, Jesus died, God vindicated Himself, for He then became *publicly* 'just [Himself] and the justifier of the one who has faith'. He did it 'freely' – without a cause in us but at great expense to Himself for ' . . . it was the will of the Lord to crush him' (Isa. 53:10); 'But... he was crushed for our iniquities; upon him was the chastisement that brought us peace' (Isa. 53:5); 'shall my righteous servant justify many; for he shall bear their iniquities' (Isa. 53:11 KJV).

5. The *means*, or human instrument, of justification is faith. This is the burden of whole books of Scripture (Romans and Galatians) and numerous smaller sections.

As to the nature and meaning of saving faith, the reader is referred to the chapters on the doctrine of faith. It is significant in the present connection to show how decisively God makes faith the single requirement from man. It is the only 'work of God' acceptable (John 6:29), the supreme duty of man (Heb. 11:6), the root out of which grow all other virtues, with love the beautiful flower (2 Peter 1:5-8). Righteousness is repeatedly said to be received by faith (usually as opposed to any other human means; Rom. 3:21, 22; 4:5, 11, 13, 21, 22; 9:30; 10:6; Gal. 5:5; Phil. 3:9; Heb. 11:7); justification, the imputation of righteousness, likewise (Acts 13:39; Rom. 3:25, 26, 28, 30; 4:5; 5:1; Gal. 3:14, 24); as also the contrite sinner is just (or righteous) by faith (Rom. 1:17; Gal. 3:11; Heb. 10:38; 11:4). There is not even a biblical hint of the specious notion that faith is a work whereby righteousness is earned or a virtue accepted by God instead of righteousness. Faith is not the ground of justification any more than of election (as some affirm).

Faith as the way by which the sinner receives the Savior and salvation is illustrated by many metaphors and similes as well as examples and illustrations. To believe in Christ for salvation is like eating food (John 6:35, 36) or drinking water (John 4:13, 14) or like looking toward the serpent in the wilderness as believing Israelites did (John 3:14, 15). Sometimes it is to step out on a promise as Abraham did (Heb. 11:9-18) or to act decisively in response to divine warnings as Noah did (Heb. 11:7). It is to confess one's self to be a hopeless sinner and throw one's self on the mercy of the God who covers sin, carries off transgression and imputes no guilt to the contrite (Ps. 32; cf. Rom. 4:5-8). Faith is the hand of the heart, which receives righteousness by receiving Christ. We may ponder the faith by which God justifies sinners, analyze it, and even write theology courses and books about it, but when it happens it will always be a warm, simple, personal event and, like true love, prolonged forever. It is reverent as a child's gaze at the sky, sincere as a mother's kiss, genuine as a true lover's declaration.

6. The *fruit* of faith, rather, of justification by faith, is everything God has for us in salvation. This is the climax of Paul's great treatment of justification in Romans:

> Therefore, having been justified by faith, we have peace with God through our Lord Jesus Christ, through whom also we have obtained our introduction by faith into this grace in which we stand; and we exult in hope of the glory of God. And not only this, but we also exult in our tribulations, knowing that tribulation brings about perseverance; and perseverance, proven character... because the love of God has been poured out within our hearts through the Holy Spirit who was given to us (Rom. 5:1-5 NASB).

Paul develops one of the items, 'love of God', on through verse 11, after which a new aspect of his doctrine is introduced.

Paul's clear doctrine is that when God declares a sinner righteous and proceeds to treat him so, there is included in justification immediate conferral of every blessing in Christ. 'Peace with God' – cessation of all hostility with fatherly benevolence is immediately ours, for 'we have' it. We have immediate 'introduction' or 'access' (KJV and ESV) to God and by grace we have approved standing with Him. Confident 'hope' replaces enervating fear. Henceforth even life's seeming hard blows (tribulations) are seen to be God's loving hand developing endurance, character and stronger hope, for we see the overruling 'love of God', not wrathful punishment in what Henley in his *Invictus* might call the 'bludgeonings of chance' or Shakespeare's Hamlet 'the slings and arrows of outrageous fortune'.

Especial attention should be directed to 'the Holy Spirit who was given to us' (v. 5). It is the clear teaching of the whole New Testament that the gift of the Holy Spirit belongs to all believers, that they have the gift of the Spirit from the first moment of faith and that they have this gift in full measure (John 3:34) – hence there is no command and *rightly no precedent* for 'waiting' for the Spirit to baptize believers. View the evidence. John prophesied that Jesus would baptize men 'in the Holy Spirit and fire' (Matt. 3:11 NASB margin). The fire will come in due season at the Second Advent (cf. Mal. 3:2-5; 4:1-5; 2 Peter 3:10). Meanwhile let us attend to the promise of Jesus' baptizing 'in the Holy Spirit' adumbrated by John's baptizing 'in water'.

Well along in Jesus' ministry He had not yet 'given' the Spirit and would not do so until 'glorified' (John 7:39). On the last night with His disciples the 'baptizing' was still future and had to remain so until redemptive history had moved on through Jesus' ascension to the Father (John 14:16-18, 26; 15:26, 27; 16:7-13). One utterance of Jesus is specific on this point, viz. 'Nevertheless, I tell you the truth: it is to your advantage that I go away, for if I do not go away, the Helper will not come to you. But if I go, I will send him to you' (John 16:7). After He ascended, the apostles, by Jesus' instruction (Acts 1:4, 5), waited at Jerusalem to 'be baptized with the Holy Spirit not many days from now'.

That coming of the Holy Spirit was to be as epochal, dispensational, as once-for-all as any other of the acts of redemption. A few days later He did come; the second chapter of Acts describes it as it happened (Acts 2:1-13) and in retrospect afterward (v. 33). Paul, decades later, would write of no similar waiting, not of a so-called second blessing, but of how 'in one Spirit were we all baptized into one body, whether Jews or Greeks, whether bond or free; and were all made to drink of one Spirit' (1 Cor. 12:13 ASV margin) and in Romans 5:5, quoted above, that we Christians all have as fruit of justification – part and parcel with it – the Holy Spirit and love of God shed abroad in our hearts as faith's best flower (cf. 2 Peter 1:5-7).

7. The *evidence* of justification is good works. This is the sense of James 2:14-26. Let us begin a brief examination of this passage, seat of controversy with some who reject salvation by grace through faith alone, with verse 18. 'But someone will say, "You have faith and I have works." Show me your faith apart from your works, and I will show you my faith by my works.' If a proof text is desired, James 2:18 supports the proposition that good works are evidence of the faith that saves (cf. v. 14).

But there is a problem: James concludes, 'You see that a person is justified by works and not by faith alone... For as the body apart from the spirit is dead, so also faith apart from works is dead' (vv. 24, 26). The theology of the Roman church argues from these verses that the merit of good works done in the state of grace are a cause of salvation.[19]

James is not, however, in his famous statement, thinking either of faith or of justifying faith in precisely the same sense Paul uses the two words. As to faith, for Paul, to have faith includes not only intellectual assent to certain truths but also trust and commitment as discussed earlier in this chapter. Only the first element, intellectual assent, is involved in James' statements about some folks' faith. His entire treatment of the subject is to show 'that [kind of] faith' cannot save him (v. 14 ASV). Even the demons have that kind of faith 'and shudder' (v. 19).

---

19. Ludwig Ott, *Fundamentals of Catholic Dogma*, trans. L. P. Lynch, 4th ed. (Rockford, IL: TAN Books and Publ. 1960), p. 354.

As to how Paul on the one hand and James on the other employ the word justification, a recent article by C. Ryan Jenkins says:

> Paul's concern was the sinner's basis for justification with God (i.e. the basis for his legal standing with God), while James' concern was to refute antinomianism by showing that one's true conversion will be 'justified' objectively by works. Paul was writing of a forensic *declaration* of righteousness that a sinner achieves only through faith, and James was writing of a universal *demonstration* of righteousness that is accomplished by works. James sought to show that a person who possesses faith in Christ will be justified (i.e. vindicated as a true Christian by his or her works...).[20]

James has the same doctrine of justification before God and God's law as Paul's. He even, as Paul, quotes Genesis 15:6 in that connection (James. 2:23). Of course faith which is unaccompanied by regeneration and fruits of righteousness here and now is 'dead' – i.e. not genuine. Genuine faith will vindicate the believer before his neighbor and bring glory to God (Matt. 5:16; 1 Peter 2:12).

Further comments: 1) James is not correcting or contending with Paul, because James wrote (in conservative scholarly opinion) before Paul did and likely before the conference over which James presided (Acts 15). 2) James is reproving both legalism and antinomianism among Jewish people who had joined the church and were producing no signs of true conversion. Any one interested enough to examine the book knows this to be true. 3) The language of the whole passage hinges on the 'if a man say' (v. 14). The KJV and ASV preserve the conditional mode, which Americans, to our loss of precise communication, do not use much any more. James is speaking hypothetically. 4) The kind of faith James belittles is the kind which shows respect of persons, preferring the wealthy over the poor (James 2:1-13), ignores and reproaches needs of the destitute (2:14, 15), does not control the tongue (chapter 3), manifests a worldly spirit (chapter 4), and has all its treasure on earth rather than heaven (5:1-6). 5) There is a doctrinal unity of Scripture – called the *analogy of faith*. The Bible teaches plainly throughout that justification is by faith alone, without works as earlier parts of this chapter demonstrate. James does not do otherwise.

Questions and Observations.

1. Why is there such variety of expressions – justification by *God*, by *Christ*, by *grace*, by *blood*, by *faith*, by *works*? Robert Haldane answers:

> The divine wisdom is admirable in the manner in which the Scriptures are written. It is not without design that inspiration varies the phraseology respecting justification. Each variety is calculated to meet a different abuse of the doctrine. The human heart is so prone to self-righteousness, that the very doctrine of faith has been made to assume a legal sense. Faith is represented as a work, and the office assigned to it is not merely that of the medium of communicating righteousness, but is made to stand itself for a certain value, either real or supposed. Had inspiration never varied the expressions, and always used the phrase *justified by faith*, though there would have been no real ground to conclude that faith is in itself the ground of justification, yet evidence to the contrary would not have been exhibited in the manner in which it is held forth by varying the diction.[21]

Haldane goes on to show how each of the several expressions serves a useful and necessary purpose.

2. How is justification related to regeneration, union with Christ, etc.? A. A. Hodge and some others have thought justification is 'an eternal act', that faith only puts the believer subjectively in possession of a blessing already his. Louis Berkhof has provided a useful discussion, in four tight pages, under the topic 'The Time of Justification'.[22] He is in agreement with the following sensible verdict of James Orr.

> But the true view would seem to be that regeneration, in the full sense, can as little be said to precede justification, as justification to precede it; for it is the same supreme act which unites us to Christ for our justification in which regeneration is spiritually completed. *What does precede faith, and beget it, is the exhibition of God's gracious disposition and His promise of salvation in Christ* [emphasis added]. We err, it seems to me, in endeavoring to separate the factors in a process all the elements of which are *reciprocally* conditioning. As well

---

20. C. Ryan Jenkins, 'Faith and Works in Paul and James' in *Bibliotheca Sacra*, no. 633 (Jan.–Mar., 2002), p. 64.
21. Robert Haldane, *Exposition of the Epistle to the Romans* (New York: Robert Carter 1847, reprints up to 1970), p. 196.
22. A. A. Hodge, *Outlines of Theology* (Grand Rapids, MI: Eerdmans Publ., 1957), pp. 517–520.

might we ask whether, in the apprehension of truth, the act of intellect precedes the possession of the truth, or vice versa. For clearly, unless in some sense the truth were already within the mind's ken, it could not be grasped by it [the truth]. The psychological process in which God reveals His Son to the soul is too subtle and swift-glancing for our categories of before and after.[23]

A Note On Translation of Genesis 15:6.

The last clause of Genesis 15:6 reads, 'and he [God] counted it to him [Abraham] as righteousness' (ESV); 'and he [God] counted it to him [Abraham] for righteousness' (KJV); 'and he reckoned it to him for righteousness' (ASV); 'He reckoned it to him as righteousness' (NASB); 'he credited it to him as righteousness' (NIV); 'the LORD counted that faith to him as righteousness' (NEB). These renderings are ambiguous at best and perhaps (unless doctored in transit through the reader's mind) even grievously in error.

There are three complete quotations of this clause in the Greek New Testament, two by Paul and one by James. All agree essentially in wording (Rom. 4:3; Gal. 3:6; James 2:23). There are also four partial quotations of it in Romans 4:4, 5, 6, 9. Paul quotes the verse (Gen. 15:6) to teach that saving faith means actually to give up one's effort to earn or deserve grace. It is trusting in God's mercy alone. God imputes righteousness to those who have such faith. Each of the three complete quotations cites the text of the ancient Greek Version (the Septuagint), this clause, exactly. A fair rendering of the Septuagint (*elogisthē autō eis dikaiosunēn*) is 'it was counted to him for [or unto] righteousness'.[24] There lies the problem. For, the Hebrew would literally read, 'he imputed it [lit. *her*] to him [masculine pronoun], righteousness [femine noun]'. The Hebrew text is short and simple, only five words, as follows: *wehe'emin bayhwh wayaḥsheveha lo tsedhaqah*. Is it possible that here is a case where the pronoun *it* (her) (really a suffix on 'imputed', viz. '*imputed it*') is in apposition to the noun righteousness? They agree essentially in gender and number and, I propose, are then both in direct objective relation to the verb. Thus: 'he imputed it [that is], righteousness, to him'. In such a case faith is not a 'substitute for' or 'as good as' or 'in lieu of' as several of the Versions, even the Septuagint suggest. The Septuagint and these Versions all seem to treat Abraham's believing as the antecedent of the pronoun 'it' (pronominal suffix) rather than 'righteousness'.

As is well known to students of Hebrew, there are precedents for the latter. Gesenius-Kautzsch-Cowley *Hebrew Grammar* says of feminine suffixes like this one, they are 'referring back to a whole statement' and cites verses at Genesis 15:6 as well as Exodus 10:11 and Job 38:18 (122. q). Evidence of such usage is enlarged and explained in a longer paragraph (135. p).

But this is not all. There are other sections of Gesenius-Kautzsch-Cowley where syntactic-grammatical constructions in the Hebrew Bible that are similar to or the same as the one in Genesis 15:6b are discussed. Some of these the same G.K.C. *Grammar* explains as *permutation* or an *appositive*, accusative suffixes (135. 1, p. 425). Among these are Exodus 2:6, 'she saw *him*, the child' [emphasis added]; Leviticus 13:57, 'thou shalt burn *it*, that which has in it the plague' [emphasis added]; 1 Kings, 19:21, 'he boiled *them*, the flesh'[emphasis added]. Among other examples are: 1 Kings 21:13; 2 Kings 16:15; Jeremiah 9:14; 31:2; Ezekiel 3:2; Ecclesiastes 2:21. Careful search might produce many more examples in the Hebrew Bible and in cognate literature.

Because it is a very familiar passage Exodus 2:6 is impressive as a parallel with 'he imputed *it*, righteousness to him' (Gen. 15:6b). The parallel is exact, viz. 'When she [Pharaoh's daughter] saw *him*, the child', etc. The NASB margin handles the clause in this manner: 'when she saw it, the child'.

And there is more evidence of the appositive pronoun suffix, also called a proleptic suffix. Let me cite a scholar whose fame and authority as a master of the languages of biblical antiquity command respect. Psalm 64:8 (v. 7 in English) would literally read, 'they shall cause *it* to stumble, their tongue'.[25] Franz Delitzsch calls *it* a proleptic suffix and cites Exodus 2:6 which we have considered above, along with Job 33:20 ('so that his life abhoreth bread') where he writes the suff(ix) '...is taken in anticipation of the following object' (*wezihamattu hayyatho lehem*).[26] He comments on a similar use of a pronoun suffix in Job 29:3, 'the suffix may, according to the syntax, be taken as an anticipatory statement of the object'.[27]

23. Orr, *Progress of Dogma*, p. 274.
24. L. C. L. Brenton in *Septuagint With Apocrypha: Greek and English*, trans. L. C. L. Brenton (London: Samuel Bagster & Sons, 1851; Grand Rapids, MI: Zondervan reprint, n.d.).
25. Franz Delitzsch, *Commentary on Job, i* (Edinburgh: T & T Clark, 1871), pp. 222, 223.
26. Delitzsch, *Commentary on Job, vol 2*, p. 226.
27. ibid., p. 118.

To draw a conclusion: these several parallels (and there are several more) do not *prove* that the feminine, singular pronoun suffix (it or her) to the verb 'he imputed' is an apposition or anticipation of the feminine word 'righteousness'. But they show that such is reasonable and syntactically possible. In such a case the employment of Genesis 15:6 by Paul to prove imputation of Christ's righteousness is rendered more understandable and certainly not far-fetched. Perhaps Paul was thinking of the Hebrew text even as he quoted the Greek translation to his Gentile readers. If so he was thinking 'He [God] imputed her [or it], that is, righteousness, to him'. It does make grammatical-syntactic sense and it clarifies Paul's use of Genesis 15:6 as proof text for justification by faith.[28]

---

28. I read a paper with a much more complete treatment of the problem entitled, '*The Righteousness of the First Hebrew: Reconsidering Imputation in Genesis 15:6*' at the annual meeting of the Evangelical Theological Society, 16 November 2000. It is available from the author.

14
The Doctrine of Adoption

Where Does Adoption Belong in *Ordo Salutis*?

There is wide difference among good theologians as to where this doctrine should be placed among the aspects of individual (personal) salvation. These teachers are not in disagreement as to anything essential in the doctrine of salvation, rather as to how narrowly adoption should be conceived and how related to other aspects of salvation, such as regeneration and justification. Lutheran theologians[1] I have consulted expound on believers' access to the Father and other benefits of sonship to God but do not mention adoption *per se* as having anything to do with it. It is 'beneath their radar'. Dr Robert Reymond, a contemporary Presbyterian, quite to the contrary, begins *not* with specific attention to the very few references to *huiothesia* (adoption) but with the noun son (*huios*), child (*teknon*) and little child (*paidion*). Then he says, 'all three [indicate] the filial relationship the Christian sustains to the Father by virtue of God's adoptive act (*huiothesia*) (Rom. 8:15, 23; Gal. 4:5; Eph. 1:15…)'.[2] He correctly asserts adoption is a forensic act and brings passages in Ephesians which speak of God as the believers' Father into the range of adoption and says, 'I suggest that just as Romans is Paul's treatise on justification so Ephesians is in a special sense Paul's treatise on the Fatherhood of God and the doctrine of adoption.'[3]

Others arrange themselves in-between. I know of others widely separated in time and denominational connections who have held adoption is an aspect of justification and give good account of their opinion. Francis Turretin's sixteenth topic is justification. The fourth Question: 'Does justification consist only in the remission of sins? Or does it embrace also adoption and the right to life? The former we deny and affirm the latter'. He devotes four pages to proof and nails it all down in Question VI later.[4] A. H. Strong (Baptist, died about 1920), though he was in no wise dependent on Turretin (Reformed), agreed and set forth a very appealing discussion to which we will shortly advert.[5]

---

1. Francis Pieper, *Christian Dogmatics* (St. Louis: Concordia Publ., 1950–1957) and John T. Mueller, *Christian Dogmatics* (St. Louis: Concordia Publ., 1934).
2. Robert L. Reymond, *A New Systematic Theology of the Christian Faith* (Nashville: Thomas Nelson Publ., 1998), p. 759.
3. ibid., p. 760.
4. Francis Turretin (1623–1687), *Institutes of Elenctic Theology i*, trans. G. M. Giger and ed. J. T. Dennison, Jr (Phillipsburg, NJ: Presbyterian & Reformed Publ., 1994), pp. 656–660, 666–669.
5. A. H. Strong, *Systematic Theology* (Valley Forge, PA: Judson Press, 1907), pp. 856–859.

John Murray (Presbyterian, 1898–1975) held that though not separable from justification and redemption, adoption is distinct from them.[6] Murray was a partial defector from covenant theology, yet like many others, not merely Calvinist but consistently 'covenantal' in persuasion, tends to cite texts which speak of the believer as a child (*teknon*) of God as well as a son (*huios*) as both referring to the believer's status as adopted son. (So in Murray's article 'Adoption' in *Baker's Dictionary of Theology*.) He contends the terms are interchangeable in Paul's thought, citing Romans 8:14-17, but does not, in my judgment, sustain the point.

Of recent reference literature, the essay that speaks most clearly of a *theology of adoption*, is by Addison Leitch.[7] It is interesting to me that in the bibliography he placed first A. H. Strong's treatment. I have found both Strong and Leitch to be convincing and valuable theologically. The following is indebted to both.

Roman Catholic authors, for whom divine grace is an undeserved infusion of power to earn whatever salvation we get, tend to define adoption or sonship as 'brought about by the indwelling in our soul by the "Spirit of God"'.[8]

The Background of Paul's Doctrine of Adoption Not Jewish but Roman.

Paul was a Roman citizen who found in the Roman legal custom of *huiothesia*, conferral of adult sonship on male offspring (or sometimes other males) at a certain age, an idea and term to describe how he who is already by regeneration a *teknon* (child) of God has conferred upon him the legal privileges of adult membership in the household of God. There was no comparable Jewish custom, and modern customs, where adoption is of the offspring of others, provide no parallel. Hence Scripture is our only real source of understanding what Paul meant, for he doubtless employed only a few features of the Roman observance. He makes nothing, for example, of the Roman ceremony whereby adoption (*huiothesia*) was conferred.

Many point out as does P. H. Davids that there is no adoption law in the Old Testament and notes that possible examples 'which do occur are from outside Israelite culture (Eliezer, Gen. 15:1-4; Moses, Exod. 2:10; Genubath, 1 Kings 11:20; Esther, Esther 2:7, 15) and that problems of the infertile wife were not solved by adopting other people's children, etc.'[9] William E. Brown refers to the 'adoption metaphor' in several texts of the Old Testament.[10] It seems to me, however, as for the Old Testament, it is more correct to say with E. Heinlein on 'Adoption – In the Old Testament' the examples even of Moses and Esther are not of adoption at all, for 'the context merely implies that Moses and Esther were protégé's of their respected benefactors'.[11] It should also be pointed out that Old Testament passages which speak of God as Father and Israel as God's son have nothing to do with a relationship with individual persons, but of the collective Israel, the covenant nation. The declaration to David and Messiah, 'You are my Son' (Ps. 2:7) is unique and certainly offers no precedent for Paul's use of the adoption idea to explain the special relation of believers to God as Father.

Main Features of Paul's Doctrine of Adoption.

Old Testament believers, while justified by God (Rom. 3:24, 25; 4:1-22; Gal. 3:1-22), were not granted *huiothesia* (adoption) which believers, 'not under law but under grace', now have. This is explained by Paul in a long section – Galatians 3:23–4:7. They had the benefit of a *national* adoption (Rom. 9:4) which brought them a certain privilege and intimacy with God which no other nation had. This seems to be what Paul had in mind in speaking of his 'kinsmen according to the flesh: who are Israelites; whose is the adoption [*huiothesia*], and the glory, and the covenants, and the giving of the law, and the service of God, and the promises... of whom is Christ as concerning the flesh' (Rom. 9:3-5 ASV). Until redemption took place after Jesus came in 'the fullness of time' (Gal. 4:4) they were kept under the Mosaic law as their '*tutor*' (Gr. *paidagogos*).

---

6. John Murray, *Redemption: Accomplished and Applied* (Grand Rapids, MI: Eerdmans Publ., 1955), pp. 132–133.
7. Addison Leitch, 'Adoption', in *The Zondervan Pictorial Encyclopedia of the Bible*, ed. M. C. Tenney (Grand Rapids, MI: Zondervan, 1975), pp. 61–63.
8. E. Heinlein, 'Adoption in the New Testament', in *The Catholic Encyclopedia: An International Work of References on Constitution, Doctrine, Discipline and History of the Catholic Church, i* (New York: Catholic Encyclopedia Press, 1907–1922), p. 147.
9. P. H. Davids, 'Adoption', in *Evangelical Dictionary of Biblical Theology*, ed. W. Elwell (Grand Rapids, MI: Baker Books, 1984), p. 13.
10. Wm. E. Brown, 'Adoption' in *Evangelical Dictionary of Biblical Theology*, ed. W. Elwell (Grand Rapids, MI: Baker Books, 1996), p. 11.
11. E. Heinlein, 'Adoption – In the Old Testament', in *The Catholic Encyclopedia vol. i*, p. 147.

Adoption is: 1) God's sovereign bestowal (Eph. 1:5 NASB 'sons') – something not required by justice but wholly gracious; 2) received by faith of the regenerate sinner (Gal. 3:26 NASB); 3) based on the redeeming work of God's 'Son' (Gal. 4:4-6); and 4) for the purpose of glory to God (Eph. 1:5 NASB).

Adoption confers on the believer 1) new freedom from fear (Rom. 8:15) and hence 2) through the Holy Spirit great boldness to come to God who is both our 'natural' Father by regeneration (John 1:12, 13) *and* our 'legal' Father by adoption (Gal. 4:6; Rom. 8:15). Divine adoption also includes promise of 3) future conferral of the divine family name (Rev. 21:7; cf. 3:12) and to become 4) joint heirs with Jesus Christ (Gal. 4:7; cf. Rom. 8:17-19).

Our sonship with God (adoption, *huiothesia*) will be gloriously manifest at the Second Advent of our Savior, at which time our adoption will be consummated by resurrection of our mortal bodies, for adoption in spirit only would be a defective sonship. In that day we shall be 'like him' (Rom. 8:23; 1 John 3:1, 2). The whole creation is said to be awaiting this time, groaning to be delivered likewise from its bondage to corruption (Rom. 8:19-22).

In Galatians the doctrine is set forth as an antidote to all forms of enslaving legalism; in Ephesians and Romans as part of a hope-engendering expectation and as a means of present Christian victory.

Addendum on Adoption As an Aspect of Justification.

I am here presenting some of the rich harvest of the practical import of adoption when viewed, if not as an aspect of justification, then as related to it. A. H. Strong points out:

> Justification is more than remission or acquittal. These would leave the sinner simply in the position of a discharged criminal – law requires a positive righteousness also. Besides deliverance from punishment, justification implies God's treatment of the sinner as if he were, and had been, personally righteous. The justified person receives not only remission of penalty, but the rewards promised to obedience.[12]

Scriptural evidence for this teaching seems to be decisive. It follows from the active obedience of Christ wherein he earned the rewards of righteousness as in His passive obedience He won the remission of our sin and sins. Some of the passages relevant are John 3:16; Romans 5:1 ff; and 2 Corinthians 5:21. In the Parable of the Prodigal Son there is a parallel. After receiving the prodigal as forgiven of his sin 'against heaven and before you [father]', the father directed, 'Bring quickly the best robe, and put it on him, and put a ring on his hand, and shoes on his feet. And bring the fattened calf and kill it, and let us eat and celebrate. For this my son was dead, and is alive again; he was lost, and is found' (Luke 15:22-24). '[T]his grace', Paul says elsewhere, is a position 'in which we stand' as a permanent state (Rom. 5:2).

'This restoration to favour', Strong goes on to say, 'viewed in its aspect as the renewal of a broken friendship, is denominated reconciliation; viewed in its aspect as a renewal of the soul's true relation to God as a father, it is denominated adoption'.[13]

It is in a passage on fruits or 'inclusion' of justification that Paul asserts 'we have now received reconciliation' (Rom. 5:11).

It was the same Abraham who was justified by faith who then became 'the friend of God'. This title was given to Abraham because of his close intimacy with God and his faithfulness (2 Chr. 20:7; James 2:23; Isa. 41:8). The friend of the king was a high court official, the king's confidant and advisor (Gen. 26:26; 1 Kgs. 4:5). Abraham was not only forgiven but rewarded with unique access to God's friendship and fellowship – one to whom God even confided future plans for Abraham's wicked neighbours (Gen. 18:16-33). The Lord did not depart Abraham's camp until 'he had finished speaking to Abraham'.

In human courts there can be acquittal but no restoration to the normal rewards of rights and privileges of lawful behaviour. In justification there is both acquittal and restoration. A convict may serve his term in 'the pen' to pay for his crime but when he leaves he does so with the burden of disgrace and loss of social acceptance. He finds it difficult to find employment, a place to live, and he is likely to be without friends, perhaps even without accepting family. As a result he may go back to a life of crime and return to the penitentiary. In the court of Calvary God not only secured remission for sins of the past, but secured a life of friendship with God and of consort with other forgiven sinners here and now. 'Blessed is the one whose transgression is forgiven, whose sin is covered. Blessed is the man against whom the LORD counts no iniquity... Many are the sorrows of the wicked, but steadfast love surrounds the one who trusts in the LORD' (Ps. 32:1, 2, 10).

---

12. Strong, *Systematic Theology*, p. 856.
13. ibid., p. 857.

15
The Doctrine of Sanctification: Linguistic Factors and Past Positional Aspects

It will be necessary to clear the ground by taking careful note of the use of the Hebrew and Greek words used in connection with 'sanctification' (and kindred terms such as sacred, sanctify, holy, holiness, hallow, hallowed, dedicate, devoted, etc.). After that the distinction between past (or positional) sanctification, which falls into the category of God's declarative *acts*, and present and future sanctification which are divine *works* in believers, must be given further attention. A sound theology, we repeat, must maintain a distinction between God's *works*, His *acts* and *human* acts in salvation – there can be no works of sinners effective to produce salvation.

The Words Employed for Sanctification in Old and New Testaments.

It will not be necessary to press any difference between the Hebrew and the Greek words, for it is acknowledged that the Greek New Testament follows the usage furnished by the Septuagint (Greek) translation of the Old Testament Hebrew words.

A group of Hebrew words (verb, noun, adjective) that are from a root composed of the consonants Q, D and SH are mainly involved. That the idea involved is not immediately apparent will be obvious by examining a few cases where this basic root form, *qadhash*, is employed. Examples from the KJV are: God 'sanctified' the seventh day (causative form of the verb, *qadhash*, Gen. 2:3); the burning bush at Horeb was on 'holy ground' (adjectival form of *qadhash*, Exod. 3:5); a 'whore' (noun feminine form of *qadhash*, Deut. 23:17); a male 'prostitute' (masculine noun form of *qadhash*, 1 Kgs. 14:24 ESV); God is 'holy' (*qadhosh*, Isa. 6:3) as are also His people (Lev. 11:44, 45) as well as first-born of man and beast (Exod. 13:2); the central house of worship is a 'Sanctuary' or 'holy place' (*Miqdash*, a noun formed from the same root, Exod. 15:17 and dozens of other texts), an angel ('holy one', Dan. 4:13 Aramaic) and the 'saints' (7:18); the law, the city of Jerusalem, etc., are holy. New Testament use parallels this amazing but only partial listing.[1]

The Meaning of *QDSH* in its Varieties of Forms and Uses.

Some authorities speak of two main uses – secular and religious – others of three – cultic, religious and ethical. The latter proves to be more exact and more helpful in analysis for purposes of biblical doctrine. The treatment in *The Theological Dictionary of the New Testament*, usually very helpful, is rendered defective by a developmental theory

---

1. Two qualifications: 1. scholars derive the verb *qadhash* from the corresponding noun, hence a denominative verb; 2. the negative idea in *herem*, 'devoted', is not strictly relevant.

tied to Wellhausian source analysis. Brown, Driver and Briggs Lexicon does a better job. If we had all the evidence from ancient extra-biblical usage, a strictly secular use whereby anything set apart for any special purpose would be holy (*qadhosh*) might conceivably appear. But the Bible and our present non-biblical sources do not seem to furnish such.

The following categories of use rather clearly emerge in Scripture.

(1) A Pagan Cultic Use.

Modern research into Near-Eastern antiquity as well as the Bible itself pretty well shows that the Hebrew language of the descendants of Abraham after they left Haran and came to Canaan was Canaanite. Hebrew has preserved 'the language of Canaan' (Isaiah 19:18). It is more surprising to know – as research has demonstrated – that the vocabulary of 'religion' and worship and even theology – though not the doctrines – of Canaan is somewhat the same as we find in the Pentateuch. We should not be surprised, though we are. In no case is this more difficult to accept than the words for holy and holiness. QDSH, with various vowels, prefixes, infixes and suffixes designated the gods and goddesses, temples and temple services of Canaan's pagan religious cult. It meant simply – dedicated. It had no specific moral connotation. Even today there are houses and people 'dedicated' to horrible immoral religious practices.

So we read in Deuteronomy 23:17 KJV (Heb., v. 18), 'There shall be no whore [Heb. *qadheshah*, female prostitute, holy woman] of the daughters of Israel, nor a sodomite [Heb. *qadhesh*, male prostitute, holy man] of the sons of Israel.' This understanding of the words is confirmed by the fact that another common word for a female prostitute is *zonah*, a female who commits fornication,[2] is used in Genesis 38:15 to designate the same woman who is three times called a *qadheshah* – 'Harlot' in verses 21 and 22 KJV. (The ESV reflects this by using 'cult prostitute' in both the Deuteronomy and Genesis references.) No moral sense either of good or evil is in the words, even though deeply imbedded in a corrupt religious culture.

So just as such words for ritual, temple, sacrifice – even god – share the same root-meaning in whatever system of religion they are used, so with words for holy, holiness and related ideas. In Canaan they apparently had no moral or (as we think of it) spiritual connotation.

Quite to the contrary, in the speech and literature of Moses and all of the 'holy scriptures' (2 Tim. 3:15 KJV), these words have almost infinite ethical (and other) value, for which I seem to find no term to describe except sanctity and sanctify – English words derived from another pagan (Latin) language of a pagan people.

As an adolescent first reading through the Bible I came across these references to 'harlot' and 'sodomite' in Deuteronomy. Puzzled and, of course, interested, I found out what the second (sodomite) meant in a dictionary. I had heard about the first from some boys at school. Not long afterward I read *The History* by the ancient Greek, Herodotus, where he says maidens in Babylon served a term as temple prostitutes before they were allowed to marry. Many years later I have, as a pastor, experienced great difficulty in convincing older Christians that in any circumstances such customs could prevail anywhere and that I must be in error in saying women and men who did such things could be called holy women and holy men. This is because, it is safe to say, quite correctly, in Christian context, holy, sanctified, consecrated, etc., bear the force of moral purity. In old-fashioned homes this is driven home to children at every opportunity by good parents.

I, therefore, in addressing some of the tender spirits, now cite from acknowledged authority how important a place temple prostitution held in ancient heathen (it is the only right word) societies, even esteemed to be meritorious in that it supported the maintenance of the religious institution.

> Among the ancient nations of the East, with the exception of the Jews, prostitution appears to have been connected with religious worship, and to have been not merely tolerated but encouraged. From the Mosaic ordinances and the narrative of the Old Testament it is clear that the separation of the Jews as the chosen people, and the maintenance of their faith, were always felt by Moses and by the later prophets to be chiefly endangered by the vicious attractions *of the religious rites practiced around them* [emphasis added]. The code of sexual morality laid down in the book of Leviticus is prefaced by the injunction not to do after the doings of the land of Egypt, nor after the doings of the land of Canaan, where all the abominations forbidden to the Jews were practiced; and whenever the Israelites lapsed from their faith and 'went awhoring after strange gods', the

---

2. Francis Brown, S. R. Driver, Charles A. Briggs, *A Hebrew and English Lexicon of the Old Testament* (Boston, New York and Chicago: Houghton, Mifflin and Co., 1906), sub *zonah*, p. 275.

transgression was always associated with licentious conduct. In Egypt, Phoenicia, Assyria, Chaldea, Canaan and Persia, the worship of Isis, Moloch, Baal, Astarte, Mylitta and other deities consisted of the most extravagant sensual orgies, and the temples were merely centers of vice. In Babylon some degree of prostitution appears to have been even compulsory and imposed upon all women in honour of the goddess Mylitta [as noted above in Herodotus]. In India the ancient connection between religion and prostitution still survives. [It was the same, says the author, in Greece, but there was no temple prostitution in Rome which had its Vestal Virgins.][3]

(2) In Biblical Religious Use.

In the revealed religion of the Old Testament, things such as animals for sacrifice, houses and fields (Lev. 27:14, 16), the tabernacle or temple and its furniture (Lev. 8:10, 11), even the gold of the temple (Matt. 23:17, 19) are holy. The central idea is set apart for God. The same is true of persons set apart to God such as the first-born (Exod. 13:2) and the priests (Exod. 28:41).

A comparison of Exodus 13:2 above with Exodus 30:30 will show that to be sanctified (or holy) to God is to be specially His as a possession and whose service He may command. In the first passage that which is 'Consecrate[d] to me', says the LORD to Moses, 'is mine'. In the second, of Aaron and his sons, 'consecrate them, that they may serve me'.

(3) Holy in an Ethical-moral Sense.

This applies only to persons not to things, and arises from the biblical cultic-ritual uses. Here is how: since God's character is pure from sin, people belonging to Him must likewise be pure from sin. They must be of a character with their Lord. Certain of *Baal's* servants, priests and priestesses could be sodomites and whores (to employ the straightforward King James diction) but not the LORD's. Their character and activities were of a piece with the gods they served. Robert Dabney remarks somewhere that the heathen could behave badly without fear of their gods because 'their gods were criminals'. This is not to deny that late Greco-Roman philosophy (not to be distinguished from science as understood at the time) became ashamed of their mythical deities, even though the philosophers' personal lives were hardly better than their ancestors' and the gods they worshiped.

An examination of Ezekiel 37:23 with verse 28 will illuminate this matter. Verse 23 predicts a time when Israel 'shall not defile themselves anymore with their idols, nor with their detestable things, nor with any of their transgressions, but I will deliver them from all their dwelling places [or 'all the backslidings' ESV margin] in which they have sinned, and will cleanse them. Then they shall be My people, and I will be their God' (NKJV). In such time God's 'dwelling place [tabernacle KJV] shall be with them' (v. 27). The prophecy then connects all this ethical improvement with holiness: 'then the nations will know that I am the LORD who sanctifies [QDSH] Israel'. The idea of separation or set apartness is paramount, but it is with respect to moral *and* religious matters.

Peter is exhorting his readers to abandon their 'former lusts' (1 Peter 1:14 KJV) inasmuch as 'He who called you is holy [in moral sense], you also be holy in all your conduct, since it is written [Lev. 11:44, 45; 19:2; 20:7], "You shall therefore be holy, for I am holy"'. Then he adds that they had not been 'redeemed with *corruptible* [emphasis added] things, like silver and gold' and that 'the precious blood' was of 'a lamb without blemish and without spot' (1 Peter 1:15-19 NKJV). This places the highest emphasis possible upon holiness as a term indicating moral purity and holds it up not only as a fundamental attribute of God but as His highest demand upon His people.

Throughout the New Testament the ethical aspect of the idea of holiness or sanctification is usually intended when this word group appears. This is nowhere more clearly displayed than in the writings of Paul. In an important passage Paul says:

> For this is the will of God, your sanctification: that you should abstain from sexual immorality; that each of you should know how to possess his own vessel in sanctification and honour, not in passion of lust, like the Gentiles who do not know God; that no one should take advantage of and defraud his brother in this matter, because the Lord is the avenger of all such, as we also forewarned you and testified. For God did not call us to uncleanness, but in holiness (1 Thess. 4:3-7 NKJV).

---

3. This quotation on Prostitution in the 11th ed. of *Encyclopeida Britannica* Vol. 22, p. 458, is about one-third of a column of a thirteen-column article, fine print, by Arthur Shadwell, M.A., M.D., L.L.D., a British public health expert. I should add that at the time this edition of Britannica was published the writers were usually at least nominal Christians and the chattering elite were not yet systemically opposed to orthodoxy in faith and predisposed to find everything good in pagan societies, ancient and modern. A more recent book by Jack Finegan, *Myth and Mystery: An Introduction to the Pagan Religions of the Biblical World* (Grand Rapids, MI: Baker Books, 1989), has a single sentence which only obliquely refers to the licentiousness of Canaanite religion and nothing at all about the others, except to say the gods and goddesses behaved the same way their worshippers did.

(4) Christian Doctrinal Use.

Christian doctrinal use employs both the religious 'set apart to God' idea and the ethical 'pure, conformed to the righteous character of God' idea. The sense of separateness is paramount. In some texts the idea to make holy, i.e. to sanctify, does not contain the sense of purify (see passages wherein God sanctifies Himself [Ezek. 38:23], or His name [Ezek. 36:23], or His Son [John 10:36], etc.). In these passages the sense of apartness is always primary, while the ethical is secondary.

Past or Positional Sanctification of Believers.

Even in elevated common English, one of the nuances of sanctify, or to make holy, is to declare set apart for someone or something or some purpose. We are familiar with this in ceremonies conducted to dedicate lands or buildings. An example is Lincoln's Gettysburg Address: 'In a larger sense we cannot dedicate, we cannot consecrate, we cannot hallow this ground.' Rich men sometimes create gardens, parks or fine public buildings by decrees of dedication in a last will and testament. There is a section of the book of Hebrews that lifts up this sense of consecration (men dedicate; God consecrates) and makes an important doctrine of it. The same is true of the larger number of passages, mainly Pauline, wherein regenerate sinners are called 'sanctified' and 'saints' – the former employing the verb *hagiadzō*, the latter the noun *hagios*.

Examples of such New Testament references to past, positional sanctification of believers, a much-neglected aspect of sanctification, must now be read. Because it preserves the distinction between singular and plural number important to the sense of the passage in second person pronoun the American Standard Version of 1901 will be cited.

> ...that they may receive remission of sins and an inheritance among them that are sanctified by faith (Acts 26:18).

> Paul... unto the church of God which is at Corinth, even them that are sanctified in Christ Jesus, called to be saints, with all that call upon the name of our Lord Jesus Christ in every place, their Lord and ours (1 Cor. 1:1, 2).

> Paul and Timothy... to all the saints in Christ Jesus that are at Philippi, with the bishops and deacons (Phil. 1:1).

> But of him are ye in Christ Jesus, who was made unto us wisdom from God, and righteousness and sanctification, and redemption (1 Cor. 1:30).

> Know ye not that ye are a temple of God, and that the Spirit of God dwelleth in you? If any man destroyeth the temple of God, him shall God destroy; for the temple of God is holy, and such are ye (1 Cor. 3:16, 17).

> Or know ye not that the unrighteous shall not inherit the kingdom of God?... And such were some of you: but ye were washed, but ye were sanctified, but ye were justified in the name of the Lord Jesus Christ, and in the Spirit of our God (1 Cor. 6:9, 11).

> Or know ye not that your body is a temple of the Holy Spirit which is in you, which ye have of God? and ye are not your own; for ye were bought with a price: glorify God therefore in your body (1 Cor. 6:19, 20).

> By which will [God's will, v. 7] we have been sanctified through the offering of the body of Jesus Christ once for all. And every priest indeed standeth day by day ministering and offering oftentimes the same sacrifices, the which can never take away sins: but he, when he had offered one sacrifice for sins for ever-sat down... For by one offering he hath perfected for ever them that are sanctified (Heb. 10:10–12, 14).

> Wherefore Jesus also, that he might sanctify the people through his own blood, suffered without the gate (Heb. 13:12).

These pieces of information from the Word of God enable us to make at least eight affirmations about positional sanctification.

1. There is, indeed, *a past declarative act of God* whereby all Christian believers have been rendered holy. The statements that they 'are [or have been] sanctified' (perfect, passive participle) in Acts 26:18 and 1 Corinthians 1:1 above say this. The event is placed in the past by the perfect tense. 'By this the church of God is distinctly characterized

as Christian... composed of persons who are sanctified; i.e. separated from the mass of sinful humanity, the world, and devoted to the exclusive service of the true God.'[4] Hebrews 10:10, stating 'we have been sanctified' tells the same story and 'you were sanctified' (1 Cor. 6:11) is in the historical aorist tense. Indeed part of our sanctification is a fact of history.

2. Past sanctification has been *conferred by Christ* (1 Cor. 1:30 'Christ Jesus... made... sanctification'; Heb. 10:10 'sanctified through the offering of... Jesus Christ'; Heb. 13:12 'Jesus... in order to sanctify the people'). Past sanctification is pre-eminently the work of the Son, though Father and Spirit are not excluded (see John 17:6 and last phrase of 1 Cor. 6:11).

Robert L. Reymond in his *A New Systematic Theology of the Christian Faith* and before him, John Murray in *Systematic Theology*, Volume II, propose the category of 'Definitive Sanctification'. It is based on the several New Testament affirmations that believers have been united with Christ in His death, burial and resurrection (Rom. 6:2, 6, 18; 7:4-6; 1 Peter 2:24; 4:1, 2). To these I would add Galatians 2:20 (RSV): 'I have been crucified with Christ; it is no longer I who live, and the life... I now live in the flesh I live by faith in the Son of God, who loved me and gave himself for me.' Dr Reymond summarizes:

> [E]very Christian, the moment he becomes a Christian, by virtue of his union with Christ, is instantly constituted a 'saint' and enters into a new relationship with respect to the former reign of sin in his life and with God himself, in which relationship he ceases to be slave to sin and becomes a servant of Christ and of God. And the Christian is to take this breach with sin, constituted by his union with Christ, as seriously as God does and stop 'presenting the members of his body as instruments of unrighteousness' and start 'presenting himself to God as one alive from the dead, and his members as instruments [or servants] of righteousness to God' (Rom. 6:13, 19). He has Paul's own assurance that 'sin will not lord it over him' (Rom. 6:14).[5]

John Murray's treatment is similar. He like Reymond cautions that the sainthood of every believer is not sinlessness.[6]

These writers, it seems to me, are making somewhat the same point I have made in the last previous paragraph much more at length, except that they relate it to union with Christ rather than a declarative act of God. Perhaps, like the declarative act of justification, it is correct to say the declaration is made on the ground of our union with Christ in His death, burial and resurrection.

3. Past sanctification is *by faith*. In Acts 26:12-23 Paul recites the story of his Damascus Road conversion, that is, how he came to believe. In Paul's narrative, Jesus, Himself, promised an 'inheritance among those who are *sanctified* [emphasis added] by faith in me' along with the '*forgiveness* [emphasis added] of sins' (Acts 26:18 NKJV). Hence past sanctification is no more a matter of meriting salvation than is justification. Immediately upon coming to belief one has the privilege to sing, 'Now I belong to Jesus... not for the years of time alone, but for eternity'.

4. Past sanctification constitutes the believer a 'called saint' (1 Cor. 1:2) or as NASB puts it, 'sanctified in Christ Jesus, saints by calling'. The passage (1 Cor. 1:2) cited employs a form of the Greek verb for 'sanctify' while the word saints is the noun for holy persons or things. Here we have connections with the doctrines of calling and the doctrine of the church, for called saints are part of a 'mustered' group (A. Deissmann), an *ek-klēsia*, a called-out group. Thus sainthood is the status of every Christian believer by virtue of having been so called or designated, by his Lord. A local church is a collection of 'saints' in a given place, directed and served by their own 'overseers ["bishops" KJV] and deacons' (Phil. 1:1).

5. Past sanctification is the present possession of all believing sinners. Every one of the texts cited above either directly affirms or indirectly implies it. The 'sanctified' and 'saints' of Corinth and Philippi are the entire local assembly of genuine believers. The insincere are addressed on the basis of their profession – what would be theirs if they were genuine. Sanctification creates no class of elite Christians.

6. Past sanctification, being a declarative act of God, has been perfectly done, complete, finished for each believer. There is no process about it. All God's 'acts' as such are so. They cannot be less. It took place 'once for all' (Heb. 10:10). This sanctification can be no more partial or process than election or justification.

---

4. *loc. cit.* C. F. Kling on 1 and 2 Corinthians in John Peter Lange, *A Commentary on the Holy Scriptures: Critical, Doctrinal and Homiletical*, trans. P. Schaff (New York: Charles Scribner & Co., 1870).

5. Robert L. Reymond, *A New Systematic Theology of the Christian Faith* (Nashville: Thomas Nelson Publ., 1998), pp. 758, 759.

6. John Murray, *Collected Writings: Selected Lectures in Systematic Theology* vol. ii (Edinburgh: Banner of Truth Trust, 1977), p. 281.

7. Past sanctification does not rest in any degree whatsoever upon what men do or ought to do. It has consequences in their lives, but rests upon no act of man except saving faith. There is a clear parallel, if not typology, in the action of Moses in sprinkling the blood of the Sinai covenant upon the people (Exod. 24:8), thus bringing them into bonds of that covenant, and the action of God in 'sprinkling with his [Jesus'] blood' (1 Peter 1:2). Moses, for God, did the sprinkling; the people did not do it. (See remarks under 8, below.)

8. In past sanctification we believers are set apart for God, being directed thereby to obedience to God, holiness of life. (See 1 Peter 2:9; Exod. 19:6; Lev. 19:2; 20:7.) Hebrews 13:12 says Jesus shed His blood to sanctify the people and Hebrews 10:29 speaks similarly. Peter (1 Peter 1:2) is thinking of Moses at Sinai (Exod. 24:8) and writes of 'sanctification of the Spirit, for obedience to Jesus Christ and for sprinkling with his blood'.

> The Old Testament type on which the expression is founded is no other than the making of the covenant related in Exodus 24:8…This is clear from Heb. 9:19… and 12:24… Accordingly, by [sprinkling of the blood of Jesus Christ] is to be understood the ratification of the covenant relation grounded on the death of Christ.[7]

Peter is perhaps thinking of continued obedience on the basis of that relation. This means that though positional sanctification is, indeed, wholly by God, it calls for response in personal holiness or obedience. See Leviticus 19:2; 20:7; 1 Peter 2:9 as well as 1:1, 2. There is a certain double meaning of *hupakoē* (obedience). It can mean faith *per se* or the obedience that springs from it. Either gives good sense at 1 Peter 1:2. The identification of obeying with believing is exemplified in the case of Abraham as cited at Hebrews 11:8, 9.

This eighth proposition provides a definition and summary of the doctrine of past or positional sanctification. The following chapter will lead on into discussion of present and future aspects of sanctification.

Paul's argument with certain carnally inclined believers at Corinth is based on an extension of the doctrine. Just as God took up His residence in the tabernacle (Exod. 40) and the temple (2 Chr. 7) consecrated to Him, so the Spirit of God has taken up His residence in the believer's body individually (1 Cor. 6:19). It is therefore utterly incongruous for a man to use God's own temple for intercourse with a harlot. Similarly (yet distinctly) the church as a local group has been taken over by God to be used as His temple. Those in the Old Testament era who perpetrated injury or pollution of the sanctuary, even inadvertently (Paul is thinking of Lev. 10 and the deaths of Nadab and Abihu, Aaron's eldest sons), were destroyed immediately. It is therefore dangerous to harm Christ's church, His collective body on earth, by any kind of disruptive action (1 Cor. 3:16, 17). (Also this is a severe threat to all enemies of the church of Christ, her detractors and persecutors.)

The Idea of the Holy is the title of a important book by Rudolph Otto (1869–1937), a very insightful German theologian. The subtitle captures his theme: 'An Inquiry into the non-rational factor in the idea of the divine and its relation to the rational'.[8] Otto was orthodox except for being limited by some acceptance of the 'higher criticism of his day'. He, for example, met the test of 1 John 4:2 and affirmed the bodily resurrection of Jesus. He was not opposed to Christian employment of rational powers in the exercise of faith any more than Paul in the first chapters of 1 Corinthians, but as the translator of Otto's book, quoting Pascal, says in his preface to the book, he thinks 'If one subjects *everything* [emphasis added] to reason our religion will lose its mystery and its supernatural character. If one offends the principles of reason [as rationalists perceive them] our religion will be absurd and ridiculous… There are two equally dangerous extremes, to shut out reason [on the one hand] and to let nothing else in [on the other].'

Otto's term for the holiness of God is the *Mysterium Tremendum*. The idea of the holy is, to interpret Otto, the presence of wonder in the presence of overwhelming mystery. Once when my younger son Keith was about five years old I took him for a little fishing trip, just for him, to a place on Sandusky Peninsula – about ten miles from the parsonage where we lived at Fremont, Ohio. For about an hour before sunset we fished from a rowboat on the lazy river. Then as the sun was sinking, the air still, the surrounding marsh beginning to grow dim to the eye, we rowed slowly and then let the boat drift. All was silent except for the mournful sound of a waterfowl. As I watched my precious, slender, little boy, he too stopped making sounds, though he had been remarkably expressive when he had caught a fish an hour earlier. As we drifted his little legs began to shake as he braced himself on the sternboard. Then trembling, he looked up to me and said in words his father cannot forget, 'Papa, I think I would say something, but it would make too much noise!' That was wonder mixed with many emotions, including both admiration and

---

7. J. E. Huther, *Meyer's Commentary on the New Testament*, The First Epistle of Peter, p. 206.
8. Rudolph Otto, *The Idea of the Holy*, trans. J. W. Harvey (New York: Oxford University Press, 1958), 252 pages.

fear before a mysterious presence, which might be either friendly or threatening or both. That experience of my little boy (now several times a grandfather) of both admiration and wonder before a mystery he perceived to be both admirable and desirable in the extreme, but perhaps also threatening, illustrates perfectly Otto's thesis that there is an aspect of deity which transcends and eludes comprehension in simply rational or ethical language about Him.

Otto invented a language to describe the elements in this kind of holiness. Though the rational and ethical are important to holiness, Otto desired to emphasize that there is more beyond them. Holiness minus the moral and rational he defines as the *numen* or *numinous* and he coined the expression *Mysterium Tremendum* to capture the essence of the *numinous*. This he reduces further to three aspects: 1) *awfulness*, that in God which inspires fear – as in the children of Israel before Mt Sinai. Not only did the mountain quake but so did the people. They feared not merely God's wrath but simply His tremendous special presence there. 2) The tremendum is also *majesty* – as when the LORD spoke to Job and displayed His presence to Job, and to Isaiah in the temple. We see ourselves as contingent and God as absolute. 3) The *tremendum* is also energy, a 'living fire' in Scripture language.

Otto also sums up the *Mysterium Tremendum* as the 'Wholly Other'. God is a Being of a different kind (and here he calls on Bible doctrine) yet of a similar kind. He sees Christ the Mediator as the bridge to us.

Though one cannot approach God's *tremendum*, we are fascinated with Him anyway. This element in his analysis of the *numinous* in God, therefore, Otto denominates *fascinans*, that which creates in us the feeling of *dread*. Like Isaiah we do cry 'I am undone'.

But God has not left us there (as Islam has done with God). We, like Moses, first glimpse the burning bush, then 'turn aside to see'; then spend the rest of our lives pressing forward and retreating and forward again.

In his book, Otto relates his thesis to biblical doctrine and religious practice. He finds it reflected in Mosaic laws regarding clean and unclean, for example. At a high point Otto affirms:

> [T]he God of the New Testament is not less holy than the God of the Old Testament, but more holy. The interval between the creature and Him is not diminished but made absolute; the unworthiness of the profane in contrast to Him is not extenuated but enhanced. That God none the less admits access to Himself and intimacy with Himself is not a mere matter of course; it is a grace beyond our power to apprehend, a prodigious paradox. To take this paradox out of Christianity is to make it shallow and superficial beyond recognition.[9]

A question to which there may be no answer: 'Be ye holy, for I am holy'. Does this aspect of holiness, *saintliness*, to make it human, attach to believers whose lights, Peter says, are to shine in the world? Some of it attached to Moses when he descended from the mount (Exod. 34:30). The violation of it killed Nadab and Abihu. As old age advances saints closer and closer to entrance of the holy city not yet descended from God out of heaven, does some of it rest on their heads as it did on Moses? Is that what the statute means which says: 'You shall stand up before the grey head and honour the face of an old man, and you shall fear your God: I am the LORD' (Lev. 19:32)? I observe, in the Torah, civil judges are called *elohim*, gods, or God, to which the admonition of Scripture relates, 'Love the brotherhood. Fear God. Honour the emperor' (1 Peter 2:17).

There is a frequent verb in the Hebrew Bible, *ḥaram*, which appears only in the causative stems (*hiphil* and *hophal*), with one odd exception (Lev. 21:18 where it may be a homonym) uniformly meaning 'to destroy utterly'. The corresponding noun, *ḥerem*, appears six times only, five in Leviticus and Numbers and once in Ezekiel, meaning 'devoted' or 'dedicated' but the remaining thirty-two times is rendered cursed, accursed or curse from Deuteronomy 7:26 to Malachi 4:6 (Heb. 3:4). This is an example of what grammarians call polar meanings. *Barakh* in Hebrew is such a verb usually translated 'to bless' but sometimes the very opposite, as in Job's wife's infamous outburst: 'Curse God and die'. In the case of *barakh*, it appears the ones who used it in their own language (Canaanites and neighbours) meant to call upon God in a formal way. The same word would serve the purpose whether pronouncing or denouncing, whether 'bane or blessing, pain or pleasure'.

Something of the same sort seems to be the case with *ḥerem*, the cognate noun in the Hebrew Scriptures. Leviticus 27 speaks of the custom whereby a man 'shall sanctify unto the LORD some part of a field of his possession' (Lev. 27:16 KJV). The usual word QDSH inflected here *yaqdish* (Hi, m.s. impf.) to declare set apart, i.e. to sanctify, is used. In the Year of Jubilee the field should be still 'holy' (*qodesh*) to the LORD as a field devoted (*ḥerem*) (Lev. 27:21). In this case the thing 'devoted' is not devoted to destruction but to preservation as a property from which the LORD receives the income. Thus the idea emerges of *ḥerem*, devoted either to divine use or to utter destruction.

---

9. ibid., pp. 56, 57.

It is not our Western way of thinking about important matters, but the people, then as now, indigenous to the Near East agree with the Hebrew mode, and we had better learn to appreciate how they think. Arabic is closely related to Hebrew and this word *ḥaram*, *ḥerem* is commonly used in Arabic. In Arabic it means to prohibit from ordinary use. 'Harem' the special quarters for Muslim wives (not to be trespassed) is a form of the word as *ḥaram* the Arab-Muslim name for the Jewish temple area in Jerusalem where there are several 'holy' Muslim shrines and a mosque.

This aspect of holiness is one we need to relearn. Let us think of the holy by its name 'the sacred' and recall that in any stable home, nation, state or society, the *truth* is sacred – 'you shall not bear false witness' or the courts cannot operate. The marriage-bed is sacred too, for 'Marriage is honourable in all, and the bed undefiled, but whoremongers and adulterers God will judge' (Heb. 13:4 KJV). We should not let the prissy conventions of contemporary translators wash these glaring, sharp-edged declarations out of our Bibles, even if we do not like to read them out loud. 'Our God is a consuming fire'. 'Let all the earth keep silence before him!' says the Bible. Therefore approach Him in prayer – even at youth 'events' 'with reverence and godly fear' and dress up to meet Him when you go to church!

Rightful authority, whether human or divine, has a certain holiness about it, because it is divinely given. Jude felt constrained to warn of 'filthy' people who 'speak evil of dignities' citing Michael the archangel who, reserving some respect even for the devil, simply said, 'The Lord rebuke thee' (Jude 8–10 KJV). There is a chattering class, endemic today, who seem to speak evil of any one as often as they can – at least so it seems, the so-called 'media' of public communications of what pretends to be news.

16
The Doctrine of Sanctification: Present and Future Aspects

Present, or progressive sanctification, is what most evangelical theologians mean by the doctrine of sanctification. There is a good reason for this, even though seeming neglect of the past 'definitive' or positional sanctification of believers is to be regretted. As a distinct doctrine, 'sanctification' lacked careful definition until the Reformers recovered faith from medieval neglect and misunderstanding. Medieval thinking about faith seldom escaped conceiving of faith as a good work or a virtue employed in the use of sacraments and performance of good works. Bellarmine, apologist for the canons and decrees of the Council of Trent, never could understand why 'by faith alone' 'should exclude works but not faith since faith was after all a good work as well'.[1]

As G. C. H. Berkouwer points out, though Luther's ardent heart and vigorous prose sometimes betrayed his sound insights and convictions by incautious language, he was unwavering in uncompromising insistence that justification must be distinguished (not separated) from sanctification. Justification is at the beginning. Good works, which accompany salvation, follow. These good works are not meritorious either, for though the Christian does them and they please God, good works do not produce the favor of God. Rather they are the fruit of growth in divine grace, by grace, in holiness of character.

For most of a century after 1517 there was debate (seldom dialogue) between the parties of Protestant Reformation, first with the lingering medieval mindset of the Roman theological hierarchy, then with the counter-Reformation as climaxed in the Council of Trent (1545–1563) and the Apologies (defence and explanations) for the canons and decrees of the Council which followed. The Roman Church at Trent formally excluded the teaching of Romans 3 and 4 and 11 that good works have nothing to do with justification before God as also did Robert Bellarmine (d. 1621), chief apologist for the Tridentine definition and anathemas.

Positional sanctification, or what Murray and Reymond call 'definitive' sanctification, or perhaps finished sanctification, is not to be found in Calvin, Turretin, Gill, Charles Hodge, A. A. Hodge or Strong. Perhaps they thought of the Scriptures relating to the believer's holy standing as only another way of looking at justification. Interestingly, some Lutheran dogmaticians view sanctification as having a wider sense, whereby:

> [S]anctification embraces all acts of divine grace by which the Holy Spirit turns a person from sin to holiness [which]… in its wider sense includes every work of God by which he separates a sinner from the lost and

---

1. G. C. H. Berkouwer, *Faith and Sanctification*, trans. J. Vriend (Grand Rapids, MI: Eerdmans Publ., 1952), p. 38.

condemned world... bestowal of faith, justification, sanctification in its narrow sense, or the inward change in man by which he becomes holy, his preservation in faith to the end, and his final glorification on the day of judgment.[2]

Luther, himself, viewed the matter in this fashion.[3] Mueller goes on to define sanctification in 'its narrower, or strict, sense' as 'the inward spiritual transformation of the believer, which follows upon, and is inseparably joined with, justification'. This 'narrow sense' is present sanctification.

If we think of sanctification as growth in moral likeness to God, improvement of character, fulfilling the ethical norms of Scripture in heart and life it must be acknowledged that the people of the early Reformation were deeply concerned with it, even though they did not produce volumes of theology with sections on 'present sanctification'. Berkouwer shows how, for example, the Heidelberg Catechism (first published in 1563 for the instruction of children) made these moral interests very prominent. He notes:

> The Heidelberg Catechism declares at the very outset, that our comfort in life and death is that we are saved through the blood of Jesus Christ and that by the Holy Spirit he assures us of eternal life and makes us heartily willing and ready, henceforth to live unto him...[4]

Berkouwer goes on to say:

> In numerous Lord's Days [the Catechism sections are divided by this device] the new life comes to the surface: in being governed by Word and Spirit, in sharing, the anointing of Christ and in the fulfilment of his three-fold office, in being free from the evil lusts of the flesh through the sacrifice and death of Christ, in being raised to a new life through the resurrection of Christ, in receiving the Spirit as an earnest, in the communion of the saints and our duties to our fellow members, and in the life-long battle against our sinful nature.[5]

The author documents each statement to the *Heidelberg Catechism*. This wonderful primer of doctrine by Zacharias Ursinus and Caspar Olevianus, published nearly four and a half centuries ago, was the primary instrument for instruction of children among Reformed Europe and is still a standard for New World denominations emerging from those roots.

Rome's partisans of the time accused the evangelicals of teaching antinomianism and moral licence in denying saving merit to good works.

John Calvin produced a theology of progressive sanctification and demonstrated it in his own life. Book III of the final edition of *The Institutes of the Christian Religion*, issued not long before the author's death in 1564, has five chapters (vi–x) specifically related to the moral-spiritual development of the regenerate person's soul, respectively entitled: vi. 'The Life of the Christian Man: and First, by What Arguments Scripture urges us to it', vii. 'The Sum of the Christian Life: The Denial of Ourselves', viii. 'Bearing the Cross, a Part of Self-denial', ix. 'Meditation on the Future Life', x. 'How We Must Use the Present Life and its Helps'.[6]

It is not, therefore, correct to say, as one sometimes hears it said, that the sixteenth-century Protestants discovered justification by faith but had no interest in sanctification, which had to wait for the eighteenth-century Awakening to discover it. Quite to the contrary, the same spiritual forces which again made publicly prominent salvation by the unmerited favour of God, based upon the blood of Christ and received by faith, assigned as much importance to development of holiness in Christian life as to justification. The Roman Church had made the attainment of high morality the business of the 'religious' – monks, nuns and non-secular clergy – while the parish priest and common run of baptized folk limped along morally (and immorally) at a lower level, compensated for by confession, penance, purgatory and masses for the dead. The highest goal was thought to be the 'beatific vision' of God attained by a schema of ascetic practices and several systems of mystical ascent. The Reformation decisively swept all of that away and put in its place essentially the doctrine and practice of progressive sanctification held by most evangelical bodies of Christians today. Where sincerely, believingly and knowledgably followed, it has produced a type of piety quite different from that of the Roman Catholic communities. This is most manifest at funerals. Times are changing

---

2. John Theodore Mueller, *Christian Dogmatics* (St. Louis: Concordia Publ., 1934), p. 384.
3. *Large Catechism iii*, 40, 41, cited by Mueller.
4. Berkouwer, *Faith and Sanctification*, p. 39.
5. ibid, p. 30.
6. John Calvin, *Institutes of the Christian Religion, i*, ed. J. T. McNeil, trans. and ed. by F. L. Battles (Philadelphia, PA: Westminster Press, 1960), pp. 684–719.

somewhat, for some Roman parishes have borrowed a good bit of the Protestant outlook on Christian assurance. But the very most sincere Roman Catholic Christian, if convinced of official teaching, is condemned as a heretic if he thinks or says he knows he is saved – for who can know how much saving merit he has accumulated? During my first pastorate, Mrs Culver and I attended the funeral of the elderly neighbour blacksmith, father of many children. After the mass, the priest's homily offered little comfort – for Jake had not attended church very often. The oldest son fainted and had to be assisted from the chapel. The family (all adults) wept through the sermon. My maternal grandfather died a non-observant Roman Catholic. His devout sister (mother of a nun) and another sister (a nun, sister superior) must have used all the papal devices – masses, prayers for application of the merit of many saints, etc., for rescue of Grandpa from wherever his soul went.

Let us, therefore, in pursuit of an honestly biblical-evangelical doctrine of sanctification, follow on with more than a mere nod of respect for that which the Reformers of the sixteenth century has transmitted to us from their fresh examination of apostolic Scriptures. I pray the previous remarks will nudge, if not propel, us toward humble acceptance of desperate need, as forgiven sinners, for the purifying of our hearts, enlightenment of our understanding and cleansing of our way. Let us, like John Bunyan's 'Pilgrim', progress toward the 'heavenly city' with a desire for it deeper than grudging acceptance that 'the living know that they shall die'.

> Whatever kind of tribulation presses on us, we must ever look to this end: to accustom ourselves to contempt for the present life and to be aroused thereby to meditate upon the future life. For since God knows best how much we are inclined by nature to a brutish love of this world, he uses the fittest means to draw us back and to shake off the sluggishness, lest we cling too tenaciously to that love. There is not one of us, indeed, who does not wish to seem throughout life to aspire and strive after heavenly immortality. For it is a shame for us to be no better than brute beasts, whose condition would be no whit inferior to our own if there were not left to us hope of eternity after death. But if you examine the plans, the efforts, the deeds of anyone, there you will find nothing else but earth. Now our blockishness arises from the fact that our minds, stunned by the empty dazzlement of riches, power, and honours, become so deadened that they can see no farther. The heart also, occupied with avarice, ambition, and lust, is so weighed down that it cannot rise up higher. In time, the whole soul, enmeshed in the allurements of the flesh, seeks its happiness on earth. To counter this evil the Lord instructs his followers in the vanity of this present life by continued proof of its miseries.[7]

With this paragraph Calvin began a chapter of his great work which treats what today theologians call the doctrine of sanctification. It does not find most of us readers where we are presently in our thinking, but where we shall 'sure as death and taxes' sometime be, barring sudden end of life.

It is the glory of Luther and the other Reformers of the sixteenth century that they proclaimed justification as the beginning of Christian life, sanctification the process of moral improvement as justified sinners, and glorification as its consummation. Berkouwer says:

> It was about this 'mystery of Christ' (Col. 4:3) the Reformers spoke when they discussed *Sola-fide* [by faith alone] and sanctification. They spoke to an age in which there was great eclipse of the Gospel, a time of great unrest. They spoke sharply and – it is no wonder – sometimes faultily. But they did give the essence of the Gospel back to the people. This is clear from their own words but also from the words of the opposition. The Council of Trent minced no words in its repudiation of *Sola-fide*. For this *Sola-fide* and *this* ground of sanctity could not be tolerated by those who loved the Roman doctrine of grace and penance, and this is the conflict [which remains to the present hour].[8]

The importance of continuing, present, moral improvement may be derived from New Testament prayers, affirmations, exhortations, etc. Let us take special note of several.

> [A]nd may the Lord make you increase and abound in love... so that he may establish your hearts blameless in holiness before our God... (1 Thess. 3:12, 13).

> For this is the will of God, your sanctification: that you abstain from sexual immorality; that each one of you know how to control his own body in holiness and honour, not in the passion of lust like the Gentiles who do not know God (1 Thess. 4:3-5).

---

7. Calvin, Institutes iii. 9.1.
8. Berkouwer, *Faith and Sanctification*, p. 44.

> For God had not called us for impurity, but in holiness (1 Thess. 4:7).
> Now may the God of peace himself sanctify you completely (1 Thess. 5:23).
> Strive for peace with everyone, and for the holiness without which no one will see the Lord (Heb. 12:14).

The last of these texts makes personal holiness, a holiness to be pursued, something 'without which no one will see the Lord'. Can we, then, doubt its importance?

The *subject* of sanctification is the entire man. We live in a time of exaggerated emphasis on the importance of a person's body and mind and needs related to the physical and psychic. Theologians have tended to follow along – to the extent that it is no longer fashionable to speak of saving *souls* and some like to insist that a person is an animated body rather than, as formerly, an embodied soul (or spirit). So caution must be urged lest we simply conform our thinking to current fads and thinking of the contemporary world.

Without proposing a technical anthropology – analysis of man's parts – a Christian person does have a spirit which goes to be with God when one dies and one has a psychic side, the seat of emotions and a body of flesh. Now, sanctification is concerned that God 'sanctify you completely... whole spirit and soul and body... blameless' (1 Thess. 5:23). The order is significant:

> As apostasy began in the pneuma [spirit], and affected the other parts of human nature, sanctification begins in the *pneuma* and passes throughout the soul and body. A man can control his physical appetites, in proportion as he has a vivid spiritual perception of God and divine things. The intuition of the *pneuma* restrains the appetites of the *psyche* [soul] and *soma* [body]. If spiritual perception be dim, the bodily appetite is strong.[9]

Regeneration, without making the human spirit perfect, does impart spiritual life, a new nature out from which, by God's grace, betterment of the thought-life, feelings and use of the body will grow. 'Sanctification is that continuous operation of the Holy Spirit, by which the holy disposition imparted in regeneration is maintained and strengthened.'[10]

The corrupt center of every human being born into this present evil world is in desperate need of inner renewal. The 'natural person' (1 Cor. 2:14) behaves badly but his bad behaviour is only surface exposure of the unseen root of his problem. Paul well puts 'a base mind' before 'improper conduct' (Rom. 1:28 RSV). Sophisticated, sinful leaders of the 'cool' crowd 'oppose the truth' because they are 'men of corrupt mind' (2 Tim. 3:8 RSV). For those who impute corruption to others 'nothing is pure' because 'their very minds and consciences are corrupted' (Titus 1:15 RSV). They read their own motives into the minds of their betters. They 'live... in the futility of their minds' (Eph. 4:17 RSV), says the unsparing apostolic psychological 'analyst', Dr Paul. He asserted that all of us were 'Gentiles' (i.e. heathen) at heart before renewal in regeneration. He traces 'the ignorance that is in them' to 'hardness of heart'.

But renewal of the heart has taken place (Eph. 4:23, 24). Though once 'unrighteous... immoral... idolaters... drunkards... revilers... swindlers', Paul assures the Corinthians believers, 'you were washed, you were sanctified, you were justified in the name of the Lord Jesus Christ and by the Spirit of our God' (1 Cor. 6:9-11).

Though this inward 'enlightenment' was 'the light of Christ', the detergent a 'washing of regeneration', a 'renewal of the Holy Spirit' and the 'seed incorruptible' the new believer is not sinless, for 'If we say we have not sinned, we make him a liar, and his word is not in us' (1 John 1:10).

The renewed heart – the 'new nature' – becomes the signal center for improvement of every part of the regenerate sinner. See Romans 12:1, 2. *Full* 'redemption of the body', however, must await the resurrection; the motions of sin still are there in all of us.

The *agent* in effecting sanctification is the Holy Spirit, who takes residence in the believer when he is born, again. He 'will be in you' (John 14:17). Jesus warned, 'apart from me you can do nothing' (John 15:5; cf. v. 3) and it is He who through the Holy Spirit of Christ dwells within us. See also 2 Timothy 1:14; Colossians 1:27-29. This is the fact behind Paul's assertion that 'love, joy, peace, patience, kindness, goodness, faithfulness, gentleness, self-control' are 'the fruit of the Spirit' (Gal. 5:22, 23; cf. 24-26) and of the promise that '...he which hath begun a good work in you [regeneration] will perform it [sanctification] until the day of Jesus Christ [glorification]' (Phil. 1:6 KJV).

Good theologians of every persuasion are careful to point out that though the sinner is not active in regeneration,

---

9. W. G. T. Shedd, *Dogmatic Theology ii* (Grand Rapids, MI: Zondervan Publ., 1969), p. 554.
10. A. H. Strong, *Systematic Theology* (Valley Forge: Judson Press, 1907), p. 869.

for we are wholly 'born of God', yet we are commanded to co-operate with God's Spirit in sanctification. Believers are to 'Strive for peace... and... holiness' (Heb. 12:14); they must not be conformed to this world but be renewed (Rom. 12:2). They are urged to 'walk by the Spirit' (Gal. 5:25), 'to live self-controlled, upright, and godly lives' (Titus 2:12). Historically, no group has been more sensitive than Lutherans to the error of any human 'cooperation' – synergism – with God in justification. Yet for four centuries their Formula of Concord has proclaimed.

> As soon as the Holy Ghost... has begun in us this His work of regeneration and renewal [sanctification], it is certain that through the power of the Holy Ghost we can and should co-operate... from the new powers and gifts which the Holy Ghost has begun in us in conversion [2 Cor. 6:1 is cited].[11]

W. G. T. Shedd (who served both Congregational and Presbyterian schools) remarks: 'The believer co-operates with God the Spirit in the use of the means of sanctification'.[12] (He cites 1 Cor. 16:13; Eph. 4:22, 23; 6:18, 19; Phil. 2:12, 13; Eph. 2:9 should be added.)

The *Pattern* of the holiness to which Christians aspire is the holiness of God Himself. Both Old and New Testaments emphasize that our holiness has respect to God's holiness. 'I am the LORD your God; sanctify yourselves and be ye holy, for I am holy... I am the LORD that brought you up out of the land of Egypt, to be your God; ye shall therefore be holy, for I am holy' (Lev. 11:44, 45). They were 'positionally' holy as a people collectively and had at Sinai entered into covenant to accept the arrangement. The elaborate ceremonies and special statutes regulating many aspects of life that had no specific reference to morals constantly called attention to this holiness – how they trimmed their beards and handled corpses, for example.

Their holiness related also to moral purity as the decalogue and the rules that enlarged it show. The New Testament relates the same sort of holiness to believers of our dispensation and provides the same 'pattern': 'as he who called you is holy, you also be holy in all your conduct, since it is written, "You shall be holy, for I am holy"' (1 Peter 1:15, 16).

In the New Testament the moral implications of our being children of a holy Father are relative to several practical duties. The chief one is to be 'perfect' as God is 'perfect' (Matt. 5:48). The perfection of God consists in the fact that He is utterly conformed to His own nature as God. We, created in the image of the Creator, but fallen and now redeemed and partially restored, should as far as possible bring our level of thought and deed up to the level of purpose God had for each of us when He created us. This is the correct understanding of a misused aphorism: 'to thine own self be true'. Romans chapter 7 and 8 report the apostle Paul's struggles with that standard (pattern) of sanctification.

A specific characteristic of the divine holiness is to bestow mercy upon one's enemies. 'The disciples are being exhorted to bestow loving kindness upon their enemies and the reason is that God himself is kind to the unthankful and to the evil.'[13]

Murray points out that we must take into consideration the distinction between man and God and the distance we are from Him. There is a 'total discrepancy between God as God and man as man, between God as Creator and man as creature, between God as sovereign and man as dependent'.[14]

> Our proper concern with the law of God as the criterion of right and wrong, or with the revealed will of God [Holy Scripture] as the norm of what is well-pleasing to God, or even conformity to the image of Christ must not prevent us from appreciating what underlies all of these, and gives them validity and sanction... man is made in the image of God and nothing less than the image of God can define the restoration which redemption contemplates.[15]

Many things are mentioned by Scripture as the *means* or causes of sanctification. In light of what 2 Timothy 3:16 says of the sanctifying quality of Scripture and Romans 8:28 of how 'all things' are employed by God for the good of 'those who are called' the means of sanctification are illimitable. Though not strictly parallel or commensurate there are five means or causes of sanctification which may justly be mentioned together.

a) Like all of salvation, our sanctification is 'by grace... through faith' (Eph. 2:8, 9). Further, the gift of the Holy Spirit, rendering the person positionally holy and producing fruit in good works, is to lead to 'cleansing' of 'hearts by faith' (Acts 15:9).

---

11. Mueller, *Christian Dogmatics*, pp. 386, 387.
12. Shedd, *Dogmatic Theology ii*, p. 555.
13. John Murray, *Collected Writings: Selected Lectures in Systematic Theology ii* (Edinburgh: Banner of Truth Trust, 1977), p. 305.
14. ibid., p. 306.
15. ibid., p. 306.

But sanctification is a duty as well as a product of grace. Regeneration is a grace, but is never enjoined upon men as a duty, even though Jesus told Nicodemus one will never enter the kingdom of God without new birth. We progress in sanctification, growing in character as we 'take up the shield of faith... with all perseverance' (Eph. 6:16, 18). We 'work out' our own salvation (Phil. 2:12), 'cleanse' our 'hands' (James 4:8), following 'peace... and... holiness' (Heb. 12:14) as we all are commanded to do. But it is all done in faith knowing that God is working in us (Phil. 2:13). 'Though the weakest faith perfectly justifies, the degree of sanctification is measured by the degree of the Christian's faith, and the persistence with which he apprehends Christ in the various relations which the Scriptures declare him to sustain us.'[16] (Strong rightly cites Matt. 9:29; Luke 17:5; Rom. 12:2; 13:14; Eph. 4:24; 1 Tim. 4:7.) Anything not performed in faith is less than fruitless for sanctification, 'For whatever does not proceed from faith is sin' (Rom. 14:23).

b) There are, secondly, the appointed *ordinances, offices and services of the church*. Sanctification cannot be carried out in isolation from other believers or from the community of faith. 'Saints' are served by deacons and ruled (as to church order) by bishops or elders (Phil. 1:1).

> We ask you, brothers, to respect those who labour among you and are over you in the Lord and admonish you, and to esteem them very highly in love because of their work. Be at peace among yourselves. And we urge you, brothers, admonish the idle [or 'disorderly' or 'undisciplined' ESV margin], etc. (1 Thess. 5:12-14).

> Obey your leaders... for they are keeping watch over your souls (Heb. 13:17).

The stated meetings of the church must not be neglected (Heb. 10:22-25) nor the ordinances of baptism and the Lord's Supper, both being means of grace to promote our sanctification (Rom. 6; 1 Cor. 11).

If believers are to grow by the 'sincere milk of the word' (1 Peter 2:2 KJV) they must frequent the place where the word is publicly read, preached and expounded. After all, through much of Christian history, many if not most believers were illiterate. Even for the literate, it is written, 'There are some things in them [Paul's letters, see 2 Peter 3:15] that are hard to understand, which the ignorant and unstable twist to their own destruction' (2 Peter 3:16). This is why we are warned not to neglect 'to meet together, as is the habit of some, but encouraging one another, and all the more as you see the Day drawing near' when 'The Lord will judge his people' (Heb. 10:25, 30). The Lord Jesus, Himself, when He ascended 'gave' to the church 'apostles and prophets' who launched the church, 'evangelists' (missionaries?) who spread it as well as 'pastors and teachers' who each week offer their services 'for the building up of the body of Christ'. There is no proper growth in grace and knowledge of the truth in private isolation. A good book by a famed author, Dietrich Bonhoeffer, sets forth in detail the ambience of 'progressive sanctification'.[17] All these matters are to be discussed later in connection with ecclesiology, the doctrine of the church including its ordinances, offices and services to believers.

c) There is, thirdly, the *Holy Scriptures*. Believers are made clean 'through the Word' which Jesus has spoken (John 15:3 KJV); sanctified through God's 'truth' in His 'word' (John 17:17 KJV). Jesus washes by the 'washing of water with the word' (Eph. 5:26; cf. John 13:4-10). Scripture compares the Word to a mirror, which, looked into, reveals sin (James 1:23, 24); it is compared also to a probe which discovers improper foreign matter (Heb. 4:12, 13). These actions direct the genuinely regenerate to confession both of inborn sins and acts of sin (1 John 7:7-9; cf. Isa. 53:6; 1 John 2:1-5; see also Luke 22:60-62). Hence the pastoral minister of the Word is a great benefit to the believing flock (1 Peter 5:1 ff.), for through this ministry men are transformed into the image of Christ (2 Cor. 3:18). See also Revelation 1:3 for the blessed power of the proclaimed (or publicly read) Word in a church setting. This is a part of b), with its ordinances and services of the church.

There is a poignant, acted parable of our Lord Himself washing His regenerate disciples, i.e. cleansing from the defilement accrued from day to day. The thirteenth chapter of John narrates how 'during' the Last 'Supper' Jesus arose from reclining at the table, 'girt himself about' with a 'towel', took a 'basin' and a pitcher of water and began to wash the disciples' feet – one disciple after another. When He came to Peter, that vigorous ex-fisherman (or as in some districts, a 'waterman'), declined to be washed, exclaiming, 'You (i.e. the master not the servant, whose normal task it is to pour water on the feet of newly arrived guests), shall never wash my feet.' After that the Lord promised a future enlightenment when Peter and the rest would understand the little ritual of cleansing, cryptically stating: 'What I am doing you do not understand now, but afterward you will understand' – i.e. when

---

16. Strong, *Systematic Theology*, p. 873.
17. Dietrich Bonhoeffer, *Life Together*, trans. J. W. Doberstein, (London: SCM Press, 1954).

the Spirit had come as the new revelator. Then Jesus, speaking obliquely, added the point of the parable, 'If I do not wash you, you have no share with me'. Whereupon Peter, the incurable enthusiast, asked that not only his feet 'but also my hands and my head'. In response, Jesus explained, 'The one who has bathed does not need to [be washed], except for his feet, but is completely clean' (with regeneration and justification and all that pertains). The washing of sanctification, the continuing need of every Christian, is effected by many means, especially the same Word which was the seed of regeneration.

At various moments in the church's long history some groups of believers have taken the words of Jesus literally, 'if I then, your Lord and Teacher, have washed your feet, you also ought to wash one another's feet. For I have given you an example, that you also should do just as I have done to you'. In several smaller Christian denominations a rite of feet washing – men of men, women of women – is conducted along with the Lord's Supper, at stated intervals but not weekly. Though these folk frequently interpret the acted parable as one in humility, the *Lord's* pronouncement about it makes it a symbolic act of daily cleansing – the Reformed doctrine of progressive sanctification. Professor Alva J. McClain always concluded on this matter with this adroit charge to his class of students for the ministry: 'Brethren pour out plenty of the water of the Word into the basin and do not move too quickly to exhortation. Let the Lord himself do the washing.'

Since essentially finishing my writing of this chapter, I took another look at an old standard Baptist textbook of systematic theology – probably out of print for more than a century – by James Pedigru Boyce. He is still remembered at the school where he taught generations of pastors in training. He is summarizing on the absolute centrality of the divine truth of Scripture as 'the primary means which the Spirit uses for our sanctification'. I abbreviate a section wherein Boyce shows that essentially *all* the instruments for producing our sanctification are in and through the Scriptures.

There are twelve sorts of relevant Scripture passages showing Scripture itself to be the instrument of sanctification; I abbreviate: such passages as 1) connect spiritual life with truth (John 6:63; 8:32); 2) teaching truth promotes obedience (Ps. 119:50, 93); 3) ascribe quickening power to the Word of God; 4) usefulness in preventing sin (Ps. 119:104); 5) cleansing from sin (Ps. 119:9; 1 Peter 1:22); 6) produces hatred of sin (Ps. 119:104); 7) power to lead to salvation (2 Tim. 3:15-17); 8) 'all things that pertain to life and godliness' through 'the knowledge of God and of Jesus our Lord' (2 Peter 1:2, 3); 9) growth in grace due to greater knowledge (Heb. 5:12-14); 10) weakness is traced to an infant level of knowledge (1 Cor. 3:1-3); 11) the Word of God as 'sword of the Spirit' (Eph. 6:17); 12) all the gifts for ministry of divine knowledge are 'For the perfecting of the saints' (Eph. 4:11-16 KJV).

There are other means of sanctification, but the Word is primary. The other means are all secondary and contributory to 'the Word' or 'divine truth'. 1) Divine providence must be apprehended by divine instruction in the Word. 2) Prayer is effective 'only through the believer's apprehension of divine truth'. 3) Association of believers 'must be connected with the recognition of divine truth' if sanctification of those who meet together. 4) The ministry of pastors and teachers is of course effective for sanctification only as the divine truth of the Lord is conveyed and apprehended. 5) The ordinances of baptism and the Lord's Supper do not convey grace as Rome teaches nor even serve as signs or seals (this is a Baptist speaking) but as visibly conveying symbolized truth to the recipients.[18]

d) *Prayer* is a fourth means of sanctification. This was Jesus' promise (John 14:13, 14). It is, however, greatly to be regretted that this democratized, individualistic age has practically voided the scriptural emphasis that the prayers by which we grow in grace are pre-eminently prayers of the church, with our Christian brethren, rather than prayers of the closet. Note the emphasis of Acts 2:42 and almost every recorded prayer in the book of Acts. Even the martyr saints in heaven pray in concert (Rev. 6:9-11)! Hence we have here another of the church's services and ordinances.

e) There is finally the *providential divine chastening* in the life experience of believers. Tribulation works patience; patience, experience; and experience, hope (Rom. 5:3, 4). *Our* sufferings enable us to be consoled by *Christ's* sufferings and to comfort others (2 Cor. 1:4-6). Every experience, pleasant or unpleasant, is God's Fatherly attention to our Christian discipline (Rom. 5:1-11; Heb. 12:1-17) so that we may triumphantly assure ourselves

---

18. I am citing James Pedigru Boyce, Joseph-Emerson-Brown Professor of Systematic Theology in the Southern Baptist Theological Seminary *Abstract of Theology* (Philadelphia, PA: American Baptist Publ. Society, 1887, repr. Pillipsburg, NJ. Nashville: Presbyterian & Reformed Publ.), selections from pages 417–421.

that 'for those who love God all things work together for good, for those who are called according to his purpose', leading to becoming morally 'conformed to the image of his [God's] Son' (Rom. 8:28, 29). Struggle cannot be absent from the life of any growing Christian. 'Sure I must fight, if I would reign; Increase my courage, Lord, I'll bear the toil, endure the pain, supported by thy Word' (hymn by Isaac Watts).

It has been assumed and stated already, but bears repeating, that this present sanctification is a *gradual process* not an instantaneously accomplished divine act such as election or justification.

> ...the whole body of sin is destroyed (Rom. 6:6, 14), and the several lusts thereof are more and more weakened and mortified (Rom. 8:13; Gal. 5:24; Col. 3:5), and they more and more are quickened and strengthened, in all saving graces, to the practice of true holiness, without which no man shall see the Lord.[19]

The life of Jacob, wherein a believing sinner (Heb. 11:21) was changed from a supplanter to a prince with God, is a grand illustration. 'And we all, with unveiled face, beholding the glory of the Lord, are being transformed into the same image from one degree of glory to another. For this comes from the Lord who is the Spirit' (2 Cor. 3:18). Yes, '...Though our out nature is wasting away, our inner nature is being renewed day by day' (2 Cor. 4:16; cf. Isa. 40:28-31).

The moral improvement of sanctification is not to be completed in the present life, but after the end of life. There is no promise that the sin nature will ever be eradicated in the present life. He who affirms otherwise deceives himself (John 1:8, 10). That the blessed apostle Paul himself was aware of this in himself is plain: 'Not that I have already obtained this [likeness to Christ (Phil. 3:10)] or am already perfect; but I press on to make it my own, because Christ Jesus has made me his own' (Phil. 3:12). It seems certain his acknowledgment of sin as a 'law' (principle) working in his members (Rom. 7, especially vv. 18, 23) was of his then present condition. We do not have a great deal of information about it, but it seems certain that when at death a Christian departs 'to be with Christ' 'in paradise' (Luke 23:43; cf. Phil. 1:23) his sin nature is truly eradicated, for heaven is the scene of 'the righteous made perfect' (Heb. 12:23). Furthermore, there can be no sin in His presence there.

Future Sanctification.

We have earlier stated that sanctification is of the entire person: body, soul and spirit as Paul says (1 Thess. 5:23) – it appears that complete sanctification will take place in two stages. The first stage occurs at death when a Christian departs to be with Christ, in paradise 'that is far better' (Phil. 1:23; cf. Luke 23:43). His sin nature is eradicated, for heaven is the scene of (as just noted) 'the righteous made perfect' (Heb. 12:23). Furthermore we may safely assume that there can be no sin in the presence of God in the glory.

When we are made complete men again at the resurrection, then also will be completed the sanctification of the body. This is part of what Paul means when he says the Lord Jesus Christ shall 'fashion anew the body of our humiliation' (Phil. 3:21 ASV). Yes, our bodies, while precious to us, are 'our humiliation'. If one has ever contemplated a corpse, especially of anyone very dear, the state of death seems not only unfortunate, but as we say, shameful. Dead bodies would normally soon be put out of sight even if they did not decay! Paul elsewhere, after referring to the fact that all creation including mankind, here below, is in bondage to corruption, speaks of the 'revealing' of the sons of God as connected with the 'redemption of our bodies' and of a deliverance from bondage to corruption (Rom. 8:19-23). This strongly suggests the resurrection and complete sanctification of the body. Passages such as 2 Thessalonians 4:13-18 and 1 Corinthians 15:51-57 promise resurrection and transformation of our bodies at our Lord's return. John informs us that the sight of Christ, Himself, shall be a transforming experience, making us completely 'like him... as he is' in respect of our souls and bodies (1 John 3:1, 2).

We are further assured that the very faithfulness of God is our guarantee of the fulfillment of these blessed promises: 'He... is faithful; he will surely do it' (1 Thess. 5:24; cf. v. 23).

This hope is one of the greatest of all encouragements to Christian perfection here and now, for Peter writes, 'Therefore, beloved, since you are waiting for these, be diligent to be found by him without spot or blemish, and at peace' (2 Peter 3:14; cf. 11-13) and John states that 'everyone who thus hopes in him [i.e. hope in Christ of the future transformation] purifies himself as he [Christ] is pure' (1 John 3:3).

---

19. *Westminster Shorter Catechism in Confession of Faith of the Presbyterian Church in the U.S. together with The Larger Catechism and The Shorter Catechism* (Richmond: John Knox Press, 1861, 1944), chap. XV. i.

The Second Advent of Christ As Moving Believers to Purity of Life.

This aspect of the Christian hope has been twisted out of shape so many times in Christian history and in the twentieth century so sensationalized by zealous practitioners of pulpit and press art that at the present time some shy away from preaching on the topic or the texts which clearly say the Christian should have steady awareness of this future, consummating event. A sampling of the numerous passages follows, beginning with the most graphic:

> But the day of the Lord will come like a thief, and then the heavens will pass away with a roar, and the heavenly bodies will be burned up and dissolved, and the earth and the works that are done on it will be exposed. Since all these things are thus to be dissolved, what sort of people ought you to be in lives of holiness and godliness, waiting for and hastening the coming of the day of God... (2 Peter 3:10-12).

The author having drawn out the lesson in preparation for the consummation of the age — whether the readers live to experience it or not — goes on to paint a picture and to state a promise.

> But according to his promise [Isaiah 65, 66; the Olivet discourses of Matt. 24, 25; Mark 13; Luke 21] we are waiting for new heavens and a new earth in which righteousness dwells (2 Peter 3:13).

> Therefore, beloved, since you are waiting for these, be diligent to be found by him without spot or blemish, and at peace [among yourselves] (2 Peter 3:14).

On the last day of the Lord's public ministry (and in the preceding weeks) Jesus spoke often and at length about His coming again and how His disciples should be preparing for it by active attention to their moral-spiritual condition and to fruitful living. I cite only one of His last-day-of-ministry admonitions to this effect. He had spoken at length of the course of the age intervening before His return (Luke 21:5-19 with parallels in Matt. 24:1-14 and Mark 13:3-13) and of how He would come. 'And then they will see the Son of Man coming in a cloud with power and great glory' (Luke 21:27). This, Jesus said, should encourage the disciples, for 'when these things begin to take place, straighten up and raise your heads, because your redemption is drawing near' (Luke 21:28). The redemption to which Jesus directed their hope is the completion of sanctification by transformation of living bodies of believers or resurrection and transformation of 'the bodies of the saints' as described in 1 Thessalonians 4:13-18 and 1 Corinthians 15:51-58.

There is both warning and hope in this future promise: 'But watch yourselves lest your hearts be weighed down with dissipation and drunkenness and cares of this life, and that day come upon you suddenly like a trap' (Luke 21:34; cf. Matt. 24:38 ff.; Mark 13:32 ff.). Jesus knew how easily the human heart lapses into spiritual lethargy in times of ease and plenty. He also knew how prone we are to despair in times of persecution, illness and disappointment. So His coming also offers hope. His future coming, which though no one knows when it will take place, is precisely important for holiness on that account. This is spelled out in many of the Lord's parables and sayings.

A few weeks before His final entrance to Jerusalem when as He said, 'the Son of man shall be lifted up' and 'glorified' by crucifixion — bringing his earthly career to an end — He devoted many sessions with disciples to 'exhortation to vigilance'.[20] They were intended both to deliver believers from anxiety and to spur them to morally correct, fruitful living. The entire twelfth chapter of Luke might be quoted to this effect, but the most focused is verses 35-48, from which the following lines are selected. He compares His return to events after a marriage celebration.

> Stay dressed for action and keep your lamps burning, and be like men who are waiting for their master to come home from the wedding feast, so that they may open the door to him at once when he comes and knocks. Blessed are those servants whom the master finds awake when he comes. Truly, I say to you, he will dress himself for service and have them recline at table, and he will come and serve them. If he comes in the second watch, or in the third, and finds them awake, blessed are those servants! But know this, that if the master of the house had known at what hour the thief was coming, he would not have left his house to be broken into. You also must be ready, for the Son of Man is coming at an hour you do not expect (Luke 12:35-40).

Under the heading, 'The Saints Will Reign With Christ', J. O. Buswell pursues this subject at some length, discussing several more of the pertinent tests I have referred to above.[21]

---

20. Harold Lindsell's expression in *Harper Study Bible, Revised Standard Version* (New York: Harper and Row, 1964), p. 1557.
21. J. O. Buswell, *A Systematic Theology of the Christian Religion ii* (Grand Rapids, MI: Zondervan Publ., 1962, 1971), pp. 353–361.

Glorification.

That eternity will be a time of activity and further personal spiritual growth seems scriptural, though there is scant direct teaching on the subject. One elder writer contends that even after deliverance from every taint of sin 'probably there is no such thing as bringing the divine life to such completion that no further progress is possible to it... If an end of the progress of the divine life... is possible, it lies far beyond the reach of human thought'.[22] Perhaps! Yet a special occasion at which the sons of God shall be 'revealed' (Rom. 8:19; 'manifestation' KJV) is fixed at the Second Advent, the transformation and translation of living believers and the resurrection and translation of those who 'are asleep', as noted under future sanctification above.

This doctrine of 'glorification' is not highly developed in Scripture. We do have further statements in the context of sanctification, such as Colossians 3:4, 'When Christ who is your life appears, then you also will appear with him in glory'. This text apparently is our strongest support for a distinct 'doctrine of glorification'. Up to now the believer is a frequent object of secret or overt scorn. It does 'not yet appear' what he 'will be'. True, he is spiritually already risen with Christ, but his 'life is hidden with Christ in God' (Col. 3:3). The world does not know about this and in times like the present era such notions are thought to be anti-social – too heavenly minded to be any earthly good. Hence, misunderstanding, enmity, even scorn, is sometimes the believer's lot in life. But the hidden life with God is real. It shall be vindicated. Christ, Himself, shall come – the now rejected and ignored Savior. When He comes it will be in power and great glory and all the holy angels with Him, 'When Christ who is [now *incognito*] your life appears, then you also will appear with him in glory' (Col. 3:4). There is encouraging agreement among the believing commentators on Colossians that this verse should be interpreted and applied as has just been done.

A book (*The Doctrine of Glorification* by Dr Bernard Ramm) seeks to enlarge the doctrine, even somewhat re-aligning all of soteriology in relation to glorification. I judge the book to be suggestive and helpful but not definitive. My judgment is that glorification may be regarded as an extension or enlargement of future sanctification. We shall not only be entirely freed from sin, but also in glorified bodies manifestly vindicated before the whole creation.

---

22. Wm. Newton Clarke, *An Outline of Christian Theology* 8th ed. (New York: Chas. Scribner's Sons, 1900), p. 417.

17
The Doctrine of Perseverance

Assurance is a biblical word important to the doctrine of salvation. It refers to the inward conviction which genuine believers have that their salvation is certain. It refers primarily to the subjective state of the believer rather than to any objective matter that may be the basis of the 'conviction'. There is a Greek verb, *plēroforeō*, which has the sense of to convince fully (Arndt and Gingrich *Lexicon*) and is so used at Romans 4:21, '[Abraham was] fully convinced ['persuaded' KJV] that God was able to do what he had promised'. The cognate noun, *plēroforia*, means 'full assurance, certainty' (Arndt and Gingrich) and has this clear meaning the four (only) times it is used in the New Testament (1 Cor. 2:2; 1 Thess. 1:5; Heb. 6:11; 10:22). When the gospel came to the Thessalonians, Luke relates, 'some of them [Jews] were persuaded and joined Paul and Silas, as did a great many of the devout Greeks and not a few of the leading women' (Acts 17:4). A few months later, Paul the evangelist on that mission reminded the same folk, 'our gospel came to you… with full conviction [*plēzoforia*]' (1 Thess. 1:5). The teaching is that the gospel promise, when it was believed by these folk, carried this inward certainty with it.

The Christian doctrine that those who are truly saved may know that they are saved is designated as assurance (Col. 2:2; Heb. 6:11; 10:22).

The certainty of the objective truth of the gospel in 1 Thessalonians 1:5 ('with full conviction'; 'in much assurance' KJV) in the minds of the hearers rested objectively on the manner in which it was delivered by Paul and his party: 'not only in word but also in power, and in the Holy Spirit… you know what kind of men we proved to be among you for your sake'. The Thessalonians were fully persuaded of the truth of the message, of its power and of the presence of the Holy Spirit with both message and messengers by something in the manner of life of the messengers of the gospel. We shall examine the doctrine of Christian assurance further in the next following chapter.

Perseverance is a related but different doctrine: that those who truly believe are saved with an everlasting salvation which can never be lost, though the term itself has reference to the permanence of saving faith. Though employed by Him in reference to a specific time of trial for believers, Jesus' statement applies: 'But the one who endures to the end will be saved' (Matt. 24:13). In this respect perseverance is sanctification viewed from the perspective of the believer himself while *preservation* designates the work of God in sanctification, keeping the believers in a state of belief. *Security* is another name given this group of ideas — sometimes referring to inward subjective assurance, sometimes to the objective certainty on which it rests, or to both.

Christians are admonished to strive for this inward assurance of salvation as a means to final perseverance: 'Therefore, brethren, be the more zealous to confirm your call and election, for if you do this you will never fall' (2 Peter 1:10 RSV). They are also frequently warned against falling away. These numerous warnings of Scripture are frequently cited by opponents of the doctrine of perseverance as arguments against it while proponents regard them as indispensable means to the goal of perseverance (Rom. 14:15; 1 Cor. 8:11; 2 Peter 2:20-22; Heb. 10:26-31 are examples).

The Roman Catholic position has been that no one on earth can know for certain that he is saved. Doctrines of mass, purgatory, contrition, satisfaction – among others – presuppose that full assurance of salvation is impossible. Their concept of merit does not allow otherwise. No one can know for certain he has accumulated enough merit. The early Reformers on all sides asserted that the believer can know that he *is* (at this moment) saved. Belief in perseverance and assurance among evangelical Protestants is a constant source of amazement to earnest, serious-minded Roman Catholics. 'No one can know with a certainty of faith, which cannot be subject to error, that he has obtained the grace of God.'[1] Luther, Melanchthon, Calvin and the English Reformers believed in assurance, as did John Wesley and his followers.[2] See also selections from creedal statements from A. A. Hodge.[3] Even today the question: 'Are you saved?' or 'Have you been born again?' calls for a Yes or No answer.

The Protestant agreement about *present* assurance does not carry over to perseverance, that is, to the doctrine that those once genuinely believing, regenerated and justified will infallibly persevere until the end.

The Lutheran confessions reject certain statements of perseverance, though the statements rejected are hardly phrased the way any Reformed/Calvinist would put them. Defined as in the Lutheran *Formula of Concord or Apology of the Augsburg Confession*, Calvinists also would reject the doctrine. The *Augsburg Confession*, art. XII, however, specifically rejects the doctrine that the gift of the Holy Spirit, with justification, cannot be lost. Hence, though Lutheran dogma affirms election, it is of only those believers who persevere. Some truly saved believers are said to be *temporary* believers and do not, it is affirmed, persevere.[4] Yet election is said to be the *cause* of faith. This puzzles most non-Lutherans who learn of it; perhaps it puzzles Lutherans also.

Part of Article XVI of the final form of the Thirty-Nine Articles of the Church of England speaks to the matter of perseverance:

> After we have received the Holy Ghost we may depart from grace given and fall into sin, and by the grace of God we may arise again and amend our lives, and therefore they are to be condemned which say they can no more sin as long as they live here.

E. C. S. Gibson reports: 'At the Hampton Court Conference of 1604 a suggestion was made that after the statement that we "may depart from grace given", there should be added the qualifying words, "yet neither totally nor finally"', and comments, 'no notice was taken... and the sober statement remained unqualified'.[5] The later influence of Arminianism on Anglican theology did not detract from belief in *present* assurance, but it did prevent endorsement of the doctrine of perseverance.

In English-speaking lands, especially recently, controversy over this doctrine has been mainly between Wesleyans (the immediate successors to Arminius in the low countries, the Remonstrants, soon abandoned the evangelical beliefs of Arminius), on the one hand, and Calvinists on the other.

The controversy is fairly quiet today. Most American Protestantism (Presbyterian, Congregational, Baptist, Episcopalian, even Methodism) is descended from Calvinist origins. Hence, in America, except for the late-coming Lutherans, the debate must be treated as intramural. Most American Protestants were loyal to the Calvinistic *Westminster Confession* for many generations and the Thirty-Nine Articles of the Episcopalians (Anglicans) has a strong Calvinistic emphasis in all the articles. It is interesting in this connection that Charles G. Finney – strong advocate of 'free will' and other Wesleyan-Arminian tenets – strongly advocated the perseverance doctrine, devoting about one-eighth of his work, *Systematic Theology*, to it. Theological reasons for the disagreement really root in the question

---

1. 'Canons and Decrees of Council of Trent' in H. J. D. Denzinger, *The Sources of Catholic Dogma*, trans. R. J. Deferrari (St. Louis: B. Herder Co., 1957), session 6, chap. 9, para. 802.
2. John McClintock and James Strong, *Cyclopedia of Biblical, Theological and Ecclesiastical Literature i*, first published, 1895 (repr. Grand Rapids, MI: Baker Books, 1968–1970), p. 485.
3. A. A. Hodge, *Outlines of Theology* (Grand Rapids, MI: Eerdmans, 1860, 1957), pp. 479, 481.
4. John T. Mueller, *Christian Dogmatics* (St. Louis: Concordia Publ., 1955), p. 585 ff.
5. E. C. S. Gibson, *The Thirty-Nine Articles of the Church of England Explained with an Introduction*, 8th ed. (London: Methuen & Co., 1912), pp. 455, 458.

of whether 'natural man' has a *free* will or an *enslaved* will. If free, then there is no compelling need for election and calling; but, if natural man's will, like all the rest of him, is sinful and therefore 'vitiated', or impaired, then no one comes to Christ in faith except God take the initiative to choose and bring him. We have already given reasons why we must affirm that man's will is enslaved and thereby support for belief in God's choosing (election) and bringing (calling) a people out from among the world of sinners.

Sustained assurance must ultimately rest on one's being convinced of God's preservation together with our perseverance. Evidence for one is evidence for the other.

Definition of Perseverance.

Three Cautions.

1) As with most biblical teachings there is a human side and a divine; God preserves us so that we may persevere. Our success depends on His; we 'work out your [our] own salvation' but only 'with fear and trembling' knowing that God 'works in you [us], both to will and to work for his good pleasure' (Phil. 2:12, 13) and the same balance is found in many texts bearing on perseverance/preservation (Jude 21; cf. 24; 2 Tim. 2:19; 1 John 3:9).

2) The true doctrine (not the caricature often rejected by opponents of the supposed doctrine) means that the believer is kept in faith and obedience, partial and temporary lapses notwithstanding. It means that final apostasy does not take place, that sins committed in moments of neglect of the means of grace will be repented of rather than continued in. Those who live scandalous lives have no basis for assurance and are not to be received as Christians by the churches (Heb. 10:26 ff.; Phil. 3:18-20; Eph. 5:5, 6).

3) God secures the final salvation of all who are truly converted, as with all aspects of gracious salvation. This He does by continuous operation of His sanctifying power *here* and *now* in order that *finally* I shall enter into heaven, still singing 'Nothing in my hand I bring/simply to thy cross I cling'.

These three cautious statements (1, 2, 3 above) will be found to accord with the two articles on perseverance and assurance in the *Westminster Confession*, a document very careful, biblical and cautious in diction and tone on this subject (see chapters XIX and XX, chapter XVIII 'Of Good Works' is also helpful).

At this point I address the large number of Protestant readers whose denominational connection is Baptist or 'Baptistic'. Many groups knowingly or unknowingly originated in that wing of Puritan Calvinism which did not call itself Presbyterian or Reformed and did not receive state endorsement as the Presbyterian Church in Scotland or Congregationalist in New England. The Baptist Churches of America were formed at first out of the New England Puritan Congregational establishment and were suppressed by the latter for a long time. (My own eight times great grandparents Culver and offspring helped in founding the very first Baptist Church in Connecticut near New London. They are buried in the Wightman Baptist Cemetery nearby.) Their doctrinal differences from their Puritan brethren and ancestors, however, related almost exclusively to the nature, polity and structure of the local church and its relation to civil authority. Hence, they early identified themselves doctrinally with their inherited Calvinism and were acceptive of the Westminster Standards. The Free Will Baptists were an early but still later development. So when New World Baptists distinguished themselves from British General Baptists (non-Calvinist), some took the name *Particular* Baptists, i.e. they affirmed particular, personal, individual election and effectual calling as well as particular redemption. In America 'Regular Baptists' in northern and western states generally followed the New Hampshire Confession of 1833 (see Schaff, *Creeds of Christendom,* vol. iii, pp. 742–748). It is a 'clear and concise statement… in harmony with' older Reformation Confessions but 'expressed in milder form'. In Article XI *The New Hampshire Confession* affirms 'of the Perseverance of the Saints':

> We believe that such only are real believers as endure unto the end; that their persevering attachment to Christ is the grand mark which distinguishes them from superficial professors; that a special Providence watches over their welfare; and they are kept by the power of God through faith unto salvation.[6]

An early *Confession of Faith of Baptist Churches* (Southern), Art. 16 reads: 'Those whom God hath accepted in the Beloved, effectually called and sanctified by his Spirit, shall certainly persevere therein to the end, and be eternally saved.'[7]

---

6. As cited by Philip Schaff, *Creeds of Christendom* vol. iii, 6th ed. (Grand Rapids, MI: Baker Books, 1966), p. 146, and by McClintock and Strong, *Cyclopedia* vol. i, p. 656.
7. McClintock and Strong, *Cyclopedia* vol. i, p. 657.

James Pedigru Boyce taught the same doctrine of total depravity and unconditional election as in the Westminster and Continental Reformed Confessions. His *Abstract of Theology* has twelve pages on 'Final Perseverance of the Saints', which he defines at length as follows. I cite his definition here as the historic, common view among educated, New World Baptists and as enlightening to the readers of this book, most of whom are apt to associate such doctrines with Presbyterians, Reformed and Puritan Congregationalists. Here are the words of this eminent Baptist authority:

> The doctrine of the final perseverance of the saints teaches that those who are effectually called of God to exercise of genuine faith in Christ will certainly persevere unto final salvation. This is not taught of a class of mankind in general, as something that will usually be true of the persons composing that class, but of each individual in it, – so that not one will finally apostatize or be lost; but each will assuredly persevere and be saved.
>
> This fact is explicitly taught in the word of God, which sets it forth as due to the purpose and power of God and the grace which he bestows, and not to any excellence or power in the believer. Indeed, such is stated to be the weakness of man that, if left to himself, he would assuredly fall, against the danger of which he is constantly warned; a danger to which even the best instructed and most sanctified are liable, and which is evidenced by the sins which are committed, which are often of a most heinous character, sometimes extending to actual denial of the faith, and backsliding from God; showing that but for God's mercy and grace, final apostasy would occur. But, from the danger thus due to himself he is rescued by the power and grace of God, who, by his watchful preservation, keeps guard over his unworthy children, preventing their total estrangement from him, and bringing them finally unto the salvation he has designed for them. In so doing, however, he does not act independently of their co-operation, but leads them unto salvation through their own perseverance in faith and holiness.[8]

Many of the young men in my classes preparing for ministry in 'Baptistic' churches and several doctoral students in interdenominational seminaries were utterly unaware of their church's organic descent from Puritan Calvinism. Most of them had been taught to affirm 'eternal security' but had never been informed of its logical-biblical connection with divine grace in personal election and calling to overcome the total inability of man to repent and believe apart from restored ability through awakening grace. The particularity of Christ's work on the cross is, of course, a logical *sequitur*, though as pointed out in the doctrine of the work of Christ, there is also a doctrine of world-reconciliation (2 Cor. 5:19).

Direct Scriptural Evidence.

Taught categorically in many passages, none is more direct and unambiguous than one of the discourses of Jesus:

> My sheep hear my voice, and I know them, and they follow me. I give them eternal life, and they will never perish, and no one [Greek here and below means 'none, nothing' – certainly not 'any *man*' as in KJV] will snatch them out of my hand. My Father, who has given them to me, is greater than all, and no one is able to snatch them out of the Father's hand. I and the Father are one (John 10:27-30).

Jesus speaks firstly, in relation to what God has done or is doing: *election* – 'my sheep... I give'; *calling* – 'hear my voice' (cf. John 6:37, 44); *divine foreknowledge* – 'I know them'; *sanctification* – 'they follow me' (see John 17:6); *regeneration* – 'I give them eternal life'. He also introduces the force of who and what God is: *veracity* – 'they will never perish' (the Greek is striking, *ou mē apolōntai eis ton aiōna*, they shall not never perish into eternity). Our Saviour speaks similarly in His discourse on the bread of life: 'And this is the will of him who sent me, that I should lose nothing of all that he has given me, but raise it up on the last day' (John 6:39).

In a class by itself is Romans 8:30-39. In an earlier chapter attention has been called to the fact that a certain limited group of persons, none added or subtracted, is the subject throughout. The persons ultimately 'glorified' are exactly the same persons as those 'justified' and 'called' and 'predestined'. Paul's high-flown language is simply a rather rhapsodic way of stating the doctrine of preservation (security). The author asks four rhetorical questions, each designed to demonstrate that saved men are securely saved forever. There is question number one: 'Who can be

---

8. James Pedigru Boyce, *Abstract of Systematic Theology* (Philadelphia, PA: American Baptist Publication Society, 1887, repr. Phillipsburg, NJ: Presbyterian & Reformed Publ. n.d.), pp. 525, 526.

against us?' Since God is for us, No one! Number two: 'Who bring any charge against God's elect?' Since the divine Judge has justified every one of them on the basis of the blood of His Son, again the answer is, No one! Number three: 'Who is to condemn?' If God has justified the elect, No one! Number four: 'Who shall separate us?' to which after a 'bill of particulars', viz. of all conditions (death, life), all authorities (angels, rulers, powers), all time (present time, time to come), all space (height, depth), all conditions (tribulation, distress, killed, etc.), and finally like a lawyer in a summation – 'anything else in all creation', the answer is again, Nothing! No one!

It is difficult to imagine more direct and definitive statements than these three great texts. The same teaching is found throughout the New Testament (see Rom. 11:29; cf. 1 John 5:9; 1 Cor. 1:8, 9; 13:7, 13; Eph. 4:30; cf. 1:13; Phil. 1:6; 2 Thess. 3:3; 2 Tim. 1:9, 12; 1 Peter 1:5; Jude 1). The present writer has felt for many years that his duty is clear: to affirm the above stated doctrine on the basis of these clear texts, whatever objections might be raised. He was convinced long before he knew about systems in theology.

Support by Other Doctrines.

Actually to show how perseverance is consonant with and required by other doctrines will seem to some to be a weakening of the case. Such it would be *if* the doctrine were based on these other doctrines. Such, however, is not the case. It is helpful to see that perseverance fits comfortably, consistently, supportingly in the other aspects of Scripture teaching. A few suggestions will be made to demonstrate this connection.

1. Perseverance is supported by the doctrine of the divine attributes. This is rendered specific by the following: 'The name of the Lord is a strong tower; the righteous man runs into it and is safe' (Prov. 18:10; cf. Ps. 33:21). God's name stands for Himself, what He is when manifest in His attributes. Hence we find the security of the justified guaranteed by God's providence (Rom. 8:28), His faithfulness (1 Thess. 5:24), His immutability (Heb. 6:17-20; cf. Mal. 3:6), His power (1 Peter 1:5; Matt. 19:25, 26), His love (Rom. 8:39; John 17:23) and His holiness (John 17:11).

2. Perseverance is supported by the various aspects of the doctrine of Christ: His deity (John 10:28-30), life, etc. (see 1 John 5:11, 12; Heb. 1:10-12; 2 Tim. 1:12; John 13:1; Eph. 3:18, 19; Rom. 8:39; Rom. 4:25; Eph. 1:19, 20; Heb. 7:25; Col. 3:4), as also by the doctrine of the Holy Spirit who indwells us and has sealed us.

3. There is hardly an aspect of soteriology from election to glorification that is not employed in some passage of the New Testament to give believers assurance and thereby support for the doctrine of perseverance. The following may be profitably examined: John 6:37; Rom. 8:28; Rom. 6:5, 8; cf. 1 Cor. 6:17; Rom. 8:33; 1 John 3:9; Heb. 12:5-11, especially good; Heb. 10:10, 13; Rom. 8:29, 30; see also John 5:22, 24.

Objections to the Doctrine.

Many objections are very sincerely offered. Of course no doctrine firmly and fairly taught by Scriptures ought, for any reason whatsoever, to be abandoned. Yet objections raised sincerely by believers ought to raise the question whether or not the Scriptures truly say what we think they do. Hence attention is here directed to some of the more impressive objections. Some objections arise from failure to hear exactly what the doctrine is. These questions can only be returned without answer or if the objector is inclined to listen, by clarifying the teaching.

The rational objections are mainly three: (1) that perseverance (security) is *inconsistent with free will* – that a man who by free will comes to Christ can surely in just the same way leave Him. Answer: this is based in part on a misunderstanding of freedom. The Bible teaches that while men who come to Christ come freely, in the sense that their wills are un-coerced, yet their wills must be set free by God's Spirit before they can choose to come. '[E]veryone who commits sin is a slave to sin' (John 8:34) hence 'No one can come to me unless the Father... draws him' (John 6:44). Therefore, the problem with freedom and perseverance is exactly the same as with election and calling on the one hand and supposed plenary ability of the will on the other. The quarrel is really with the doctrines of sin and of grace.

Baptists of recent generations seem to have forgotten much of their Puritan-Calvinist heritage, but not the doctrine of perseverance (or 'eternal security'). They forget there is a 'Free Will Baptist' denomination which long ago arose in protest, not specifically against the perseverance doctrine but against 'the Bondage of the Will' which Luther clearly saw to be the point in man's fallen condition from which he needs deliverance before he can exercise 'free will'. Scripture teaches that no person of Adam's race would 'will' to be holy, or have a will to be rescued unless God touches his heart first. Far and away the most ambitious effort of a Baptist scholar of recent times to overthrow the doctrine of perseverance is Robert Shank's *Life In the Son: A Study In The Doctrine of Perseverance*. I judge it to be a failed effort, though impressive, simply because Shank does not accept what Scripture teaches about the effect of the Fall on the whole body, soul and spirit of man. Man's will is un-coerced by God, but certainly neither free nor unpredictable: 'There is none that seeketh after God.' Shank lets this cat out of the bag near the end of his book, asserting:

> All theologians to the contrary notwithstanding, the Scriptures declare that, with respect both to the saved and the lost, God takes fully into account the *faculty of spiritual initiative* [emphasis added] and decision with which he endowed man in creation. He has respect for his own creation.[9]

Shank seems to have forgotten about the Fall of man and its effects on the whole being including a depraved will.

Samuel Fisk, a conservative Baptist and former professor at Western Baptist Bible College in a 1973 book[10] sought to prove that though God is sovereign, He limited His sovereignty to the extent that within limits even fallen mankind have free will. His book seeks a 'balanced approach' affirming, he says, both divine sovereignty and human freedom. He quotes some theologians whom I know taught the bondage of the will of human beings to sin (as Jesus plainly said) as teaching 'free will'. He comes close to achieving his goals but fails, as does Shank, to come to terms with the effects of the fall, including the moral disposition of the whole of each sinner. It is the will precisely that must be changed first and no one is able quite to take the initiative apart from awakening grace. Mr Fisk does not list 1 Corinthians 2:14 or Romans 7 or Jeremiah 17:9 or any of the texts affirming total depravity in his Scripture index.

(2) That perseverance *encourages men to presume on God's grace*, to turn it 'into lasciviousness'. Answer: this objection is really against the doctrine of *sola gratia* (by grace alone) rather than specifically against perseverance. Romanists have made this charge against wholly gracious salvation since the sixteenth century, even stating it at great length in the Tridentine decrees.[11] Paul resisted the same charge and called it slander, however sincerely offered (Rom. 3:8; 6:1, 2). This doctrine is, in the New Testament, always firmly locked into solid denial of this line of thinking either by friends of the doctrine or foes, viz. 'But God's firm foundation stands, bearing this seal: "The Lord knows those who are his", and, "Let everyone who names the name of the Lord [cf. Acts 4:12] depart from iniquity"' (2 Tim. 2:19).

(3) That it *tends toward slacking of effort* in good works and growth in Christian grace. This objection is supposedly grounded in human psychology. To the contrary, however, 'It is notoriously untrue that confidence of success inspires timidity or indolence' according to A. H. Strong.[12] The tortoise and hare fable does not come out of the Bible, and in any case is inapplicable. Such a perversion would in no case reflect the regenerate heart's aspirations. The 'punch line', the best illustration I ever heard of the true relation of security to Christian effort, was shouted by a telephone line crew foreman to a timid new hired hand trying to work on a crossbar forty feet above ground but who refused to trust his spurs and leather safety belt: 'Hey up there! Lean back in your belt and trust it so you can work with both hands'.[13]

There are many classes of biblical texts that are thought to be obstacles to acceptance of the doctrine of perseverance. These have been bruited about for generations, sometimes profitably, sometimes not. There are dozens of these texts. If the Bible teaches perseverance clearly in John 10 and Romans 8, then these other texts, correctly understood, will not contradict it. Most can be legitimately interpreted in a manner consistent with perseverance (note: not explained away!) on one of the following grounds: (1) *lip profession is being put in opposition to heart faith*. For example, 2 Peter 2:1 does not affirm that teachers who surreptitiously introduce false teaching lose their salvation thereby. They are rather 'false prophets' at heart to start with. They were insincere professors of true religion all the time. There are many texts of this type. (2) Some treat the subject of *loss of reward for service rather than loss of salvation*. First Corinthians 9:27, 'lest… I myself should be disqualified' ('a castaway' KJV; Greek *adokimos*,

---

9. Robert Shank, *Life in the Son: A Study of the Doctrine of Perseverance*, 2nd ed. (Springfield, MO: Westcott Publ., 1968), p. 339.
10. Samuel Fisk, *Divine Sovereignty and Human Freedom* (Neptune, NJ: Loizeaux Brothers Publ., 1973).
11. Denzinger, 'Canons of the Council of Trent 1545–1563', in *The Sources of Catholic Dogma*, Chapters ii–vi, para. 804–843, pp. 253–261.
12. A. H. Strong, *Systematic Theology* (Valley Forge, PA: Judson Press, 1907), p. 884.
13. As related of himself as the aspirant rooky by Prof. Alva J. McClain to successions of classes in his systematic theology course 'Salvation and the Christian of Life.'

disapproved) simply cannot be made to teach that Paul, the author of Romans 8, was fearful of losing his salvation. It should rather be connected with his words about rewards and loss of rewards for Christians earlier in the same Epistle (1 Cor. 3:12-15).

Warnings and exhortations are issued which are *thought to imply the contingency* that some truly regenerate can and do fall away. There are six or seven such in the book of Hebrews. Personally, I think several of these to be addressed to Jewish readers who are being warned of the peril to their souls in any return to Judaism and hence fall into the category already suggested of warning against false profession. Galatians is in large part a similar sort of argument. A. H. Strong makes five points about the 'commands to persevere and warnings against apostasy'.

> (a) They show that some, who are [only] apparently regenerate, will fall away [Matt. 18:7; 1 Cor. 11:19; 1 John 2:19]. (b) They show that the truly regenerate, and those who are only apparently so, are not clearly distinguishable in this life [Mal. 3:18; Matt. 13:25, 47; Rom. 9:6, 7; Rev. 3:1]. (c) They show the fearful consequences of rejecting Christ, to those who have enjoyed special divine influences but who are only apparently regenerate [Heb. 10:26-29]. (d) They show that the perseverance of the truly regenerate may be secured by these very commands and warnings [1 Cor. 10:12]. (e) They do not show that it is certain or possible, that any truly regenerate person will fall away. [He cites Spurgeon: 'The believer, like a man on shipboard, may fall again and again on the deck, but he will never fall overboard'.][14]

Many theologians would add another point, possibly the most important, that the warnings, exhortations and promises are, under God, the very appointed means, whereby God preserves the believing saint and whereby he perseveres.

Those who have embraced this doctrine in a knowledgeable way have found it helpful to piety and genuinely an aid to that rest spoken of in Scripture as birthright of the children of God (Heb. 3:12–4:11). The writer well remembers the permanent effect for Christian joy and steady faith in the life of his father when at about thirrty-eight years of age he came to be convinced of perseverance through a series of sermons by the local pastor. This is not to say piety cannot and does not flourish among evangelical believers who see the matter differently. Like every truth, it is capable of perversion even by its friends with invariably unhappy results. This is not because there is something wrong with the doctrine but because there is much wrong with human beings.

14. Strong, *Systematic Theology*, pp. 884–885.

18
The Doctrine of Assurance

Assurance may be defined as a valid, subjective, inward certainty in the heart of the believer that one is now at this moment truly 'saved', that his 'sins are forgiven', his 'name written in heaven', that he now has 'eternal life'.

Whether or not this state of matters can ever be changed by loss of salvation is not here under consideration. That is the subject of the preceding chapter. Rather, the biblical support for such inward certainty and how it relates to Christian life is now our interest.

This assurance is the specific subject of three New Testament texts, which authenticate the existence of such an immense benefit for joy and happiness in any circumstances.

The first is Colossians 2:2 where Paul says he desires that the readers, whom he has not yet met 'may be encouraged, being knit together in love, and attaining to all the riches of the full *assurance of understanding* [emphasis added], to the knowledge of the mystery of God, both of the Father and of Christ, in whom are hidden all the treasures of wisdom and knowledge' (Col. 2:2, 3 NKJV). It seems clear that understanding God, Father and Son, and the treasure of truth about Him is our only source of assurance. The Holy Scriptures, of course, are the objective source of this understanding by which we come to 'full assurance'.

The second and third texts are in the Epistle to the Hebrews. In the earlier the author has warned the readers against apostasy (Heb. 6:1-8) followed by expressing confidence they were truly 'saved' (v. 9) and that a just God was aware of their exemplary, fruitful lives. So as Paul 'desired' for the Colossians' 'assurance of understanding', this author says 'we desire that each one of you show the same diligence to the full *assurance of hope* [emphasis added] until the end' imitating 'those who through faith and patience inherit the promises' (Heb. 6:11, 12 NKJV). Hope in the sense of confident expectancy is a necessary companion of any joy in living a life of joy. In context here, such full assurance of hope is an accompaniment of energetic 'faith and patience' (*makrothumia*, endurance, steadfastness). The text seems to say that believers who are indolent, lacking 'things which accompany salvation', will not enjoy the benefit of 'full assurance of hope', but that they who are in heart tending to the business of working at their Christian profession may enjoy that immense benefit.

Later in the Epistle it is said believers have 'confidence to enter the holy places by the blood of Jesus by the new and living way… and since we have a great priest' are encouraged to 'draw near' that holy place with a true heart in '*full assurance of faith* [emphasis added]' (Heb. 10:19-22). 'Confidence' ('boldness' KJV; Greek *parrēsia*) is 'fearlessness, especially in the presence of persons of high rank'.[1] This boldness (*parrēsia*) is something for one to 'hold fast' (Heb. 3:6). The passages in Hebrews suggest that this confidence or boldness to come to God, as sons to a Father, is diminished or even lost, if not held fast. Both the assurance and the boldness are to be maintained by the usual 'means of grace' (see Heb. 10:23-39). 'Therefore do not throw away your confidence [*parrēsia*], which has a great reward' (v. 35).

Other considerations show that full assurance of understanding, hope and faith; inward, subjective certainty of forgiveness, peace with God and present possession of eternal life is normal for true Christians, even though not invariable.

1) Paul spoke confidently of such remarkable assurance among the new believers at Thessalonica, not long after their conversion and formation into a congregation. He took note of their ceaseless work of *faith*, labour of *love* and the enduring perseverance of their *hope* 'in the sight of God' the Father (1 Thess. 1:3 KJV). So strong was the evidence that an *apostle*, no less, claimed to 'know' their 'election of God'. Such language coming from a local booster for 'our side' – for example, the local pastor – would not be definitive. But this pronouncement of an apostle of Christ on the steadfast conduct (v. 7) even under persecution (v. 6; cf. Act 17:1-15) of these new Christians should lend great support to the doctrine that even less than mature believers may have subjective certainty of salvation. Paul knew they were 'elect' (KJV; 'chosen' ESV) – or so he said – and presumably so did they.

2) John the Apostle early came to be known as *ho theologos*, 'the theologian', or 'the divine', in the sense of expert in doctrine. It was this theologian who near the end of his first Epistle declared his purpose (one of several purposes): 'I write these things to you who believe in the name of the Son of God that you may know that you have eternal life' (1 John 5:13). Immediately he adds: 'And this is the confidence (*parrēsia*) that we have', etc., again, as Hebrews and Paul, connecting inward assurance of salvation with boldness – *plēroforia* with *parrēsia*. This certainty of heart regarding one's salvation is a repeated message in 1 John, connected with joy (1 John 1:4), not sinning (1 John 2:1 ff.), passing from death to life and love of brethren (3:14), the gift of the Spirit (3:24; 4:13), boldness on Judgment Day (4:17), keeping Christ's commandments (several), and victory over the world (5:4). Altogether, the picture drawn by the book is of a confident faith, boldness toward God as Father, all associated with a certain sonship (the *huiothesia* or adoption of Romans 8 and Galatians 4). It is not a careless, flippant approach to God or life but a joyful one. There is a balance between awareness that 'our God is a consuming fire' and 'the name of the LORD is a strong tower: the righteous man runs into it and is safe'.

The doctrine of *full assurance* (*plēroforia*) accompanied by *boldness* (*parrēsia*) of access to and complete acceptance by God is simply a way of characterizing 'the adoption' of which we read in Romans 8:15, 16 and Galatians 4:5, 6. As discussed earlier in connection with adoption (chapter 14), we have a *natural* relation to God by regeneration whereby we are *tekna* (offspring, children, those born of God). In adoption we also have the *legal* standing of sons (*huiothesia*) whereby the privileges of heirship with Christ are ours. We are not mere slaves or servants in the household. 'For you did not receive the spirit [not the Holy Spirit, but inward state of mind Godward] of slavery to fall back into fear, but you have received the spirit of sonship' (Rom. 8:15 RSV) 'whereby we cry, Abba, Father' (Rom. 8:15 KJV). This places us somewhat in the position of Abraham, but a bit more familiar with God, for though he was 'the friend [confidant] of God' we may, so to speak, take the privilege of children with Abba, 'Papa'. This is not one whit disrespectful, but simply, with assurance, going about our lives prayerfully resting in the love of God from which there will never be any separation (Rom. 8:37-39) and no reversal of the verdict of exoneration of any sin and imputation of righteousness. Such a son as this may fail in duties, but if so, as Father to sons, God will chasten him. Quoting Proverbs 3:11, 12, it is written:

> 'My son, do not regard lightly the
> discipline of the Lord, nor be weary
> when reproved by him. For the Lord
> disciplines the one he loves, and chastises
> every son whom he receives.'

---

1. William F. Arndt and F. Wilbur Gingrich, *A Greek-English Lexicon of the New Testament and Other Early Christian Literature*, a translation and adaption of Walter Bauer's German Work, 4th ed. (Chicago: University of Chicago Press, 1957), sub *parrēsia*, p. 636.

> It is for discipline that you have to endure. God is *treating you as sons* [emphasis added]. For what son is there whom his father does not discipline? If you are left without discipline, in which all have participated, then you are illegitimate children ['bastards' KJV] and not sons (Heb. 12:5-8).

As though to prevent our presuming on the Father-son relationship, the author reminds us that the respect our earthly fathers expected is also required by God (Heb. 12:9).

Galatians 4:4-6 is in the midst of an enlightening discourse on the difference between the subjection of Old Testament people as slaves, both nationally and individually, to the 'elementary principles [or "elements" KJV] of the world' (Gal. 4:3). These 'elementary principles' seem to be identical with the detailed regulations on life and worship (Gal. 4:10) the Old Testament people lived under. They had no freedom to dress as taste preferred, eat what they liked, or even to plan their own schedule of work and holiday. They were not 'free from the Law'. But, it is written, 'when the fullness of time had come, God sent forth his Son, born of woman, born under the law, to redeem those who were under the law, that we might receive adoption as sons' (Gal. 4:4, 5).

As in Romans 8:15, this 'adoption' (*huiothesia*, placing as a son) provides a unique *assurance* (*plēroforia*) that all is right between the forgiven sinner and God. One has boldness (*parrēsia*) or confidence in the Father's eagerness for them to enjoy His confidence. 'And because ye are sons, God sent forth into our hearts the Spirit of his Son, crying, Abba Father' (Gal. 4:6 Alford's trans.). Paul goes on, as in the texts cited above, to base on this an exhortation never to turn back to a legalistic understanding of how helpless sinners are saved.

These passages are not obscure in meaning. They say a person who has sincerely repented of his sins and placed his trust in Christ for eternal life has evidence of his regeneration in his own repentance and faith and has every right to the privileges of adoption, in full confidence that he need not be afraid of God. For God has declared him to be a beloved son with privileges of access. He may rightly say to his soul: Soul be at rest. Your sins have been forgiven; the blood of Christ is sufficient. Your name is written in the Lamb's Book of Life; eternal life is now yours and will not be taken away from you. Your Saviour has said, 'My sheep hear my voice… and they shall never perish, and no one shall snatch them out of my hand. My Father, who hath given them unto me, is greater than all; and no one is able to snatch them out of the Father's hand' (John 10:27-29 ASV).

As I shall explain more fully later, John Wesley, founder of the Methodist movement and leader of the Great Awakening in Britain of the eighteenth century, had a strong doctrine of assurance. Indeed he and followers among the numerous branches of evangelical Christianity who have been influenced by Wesleyan thinking, have made *present* assurance of salvation the goal of great exercises of prayer and devotion. In Wesleyan holiness movements the attainment of this assurance is by 'praying through'. For that purpose the 'altar rail' and kneeling shelf was placed at the front of many a Methodist (or other Wesleyan) house of worship. This was also an emphasis of the 'camp meetings'. The idea is to supplicate God for the experience of *feeling saved*, saved with certainty, accompanied by joy and often expressed by shouts of praise. This was (at least until recently) merged with a second spiritual experience – entire sanctification. At a holiness meeting I and several family members attended (in a tent) a good while ago a brother and sister sang a duet, the chorus: 'The holiness people stand/ for two definite works of Grace./ Entire sanctification is God's will'. The same system of theology rejects the possibility of full assurance that one will 'stay saved'. The doctrine of perseverance as certain for the genuinely regenerated and justified is rejected.

Richard Watson, the acknowledged faithful interpreter of Wesley, forerunner of the theologies of John Miley[2] and Henry Orton Wiley,[3] after advocating present assurance as desirable and possible, makes this caution and disclaimer:

> This doctrine has been generally termed the doctrine of assurance, and perhaps the expressions of Paul – 'the full assurance of faith', and 'the full assurance of hope', may warrant the word. But there is a current and generally understood sense of this term among persons of the Calvinists persuasion, implying, that the assurance of our present acceptance and sonship, is an assurance of our final perseverance, and of our indefeasible title to heaven: the phrase, a comfortable persuasion, or conviction of our justification and adoption, arising out of the Spirit's inward and direct testimony, is to be preferred; for this has been held as an indubitable doctrine of Holy Writ by Christians, who by no means receive the doctrine of assurance in the sense held by followers of Calvin.[4]

---

2. John Miley, *Systematic Theology* (New York: Hunt and Eaton, 1892).
3. Henry O. Wiley, *Christian Theology* (Kansas City: Nazarene Publishing House, 1940).
4. Richard Watson, *Theological Institutes ii*, 29th ed. (New York: Nelson & Phillips, 1850), pp. 270, 271. Mr. Watson (1781–1833) produced the standard, though not official, interpretation of Wesley's theology of Methodism. It is a major work, praised by Charles Hodge and I observe that Thomas Oden favourably cites *Theological Institutes* by Watson in his *Systematic Theology iii: The Living God i, The Word of Life ii, Life in the Spirit iii* (San Francisco: Harper Collins, 1992), the latest thorough and scholarly evangelical systematic theology by a Methodist.

Assurance Supported by Two Witnesses.

The normal state of assured peace of heart for a Christian is described in Paul's 'Joy Letter' to the Philippians. 'Rejoice in the Lord always... Be anxious for nothing, but in everything by prayer and supplication, with thanksgiving, let your requests be made know to God; and the peace of God, which surpasses all understanding, will guard your hearts and minds [thoughts] through Christ Jesus. The things which you learned and received and heard and saw in me, these do, and the God of peace will be with you' (Phil. 4:4, 6, 7, 9 NKJV).

As I write these verses they stimulate the preacher and pastor in me to write at least two sermons of exposition. They not only characterize assurance as the peace of God keeping the heart and mind (v. 7) but the God of peace within each one who meets the conditions. Do you wish to have this normal state of absence of anxiety? Does not the text say 'Rejoice in the Lord always.... Be anxious for nothing'. Some of the Puritan churches had an 'anxious seat'. How does one get off this seat where so many of us sit? There is a practical answer and a theological answer.

The verses just cited (Phil. 4:8, 9) provide the practical answer:

Address prayers and supplications with thanksgiving to God: let your requests be made known to Him. Do so formally. Do not try to be nonchalant, however unafraid. There is also a 'with reverence and awe' (Heb. 12:28) aspect of devotion. Each of these terms signals habits of devotion. People who think about their anxieties rather than to love the Lord their God with all soul, spirit, body and mind will not have the peace of God in heart. Get acquainted through the Bible with what a saintly man like Paul taught. Recall what you 'received' when you believed, then go on to see how the man lived who here says 'the things you heard and saw in me, these things do'. These will all be supplied by the appointed means – Bible reading, attendance at classes, sermons, reading the right literature. They will never come from hours seated before a television. If one fills the mind with nothing but what the world is pushing toward one the mind will never be aware of 'the God of peace' within.

Christian assurance is supported by two witnesses by whom assurance is made possible.

The first witness is the Holy Spirit, who speaks directly to the heart of the believer. The Revised Standard Version rendering of Romans 8:15b and 16 speaks plainly to this effect: 'When we cry, "Abba! Father!" it is the Spirit himself bearing witness with our spirit that we are the children [*tekna*, offspring] of God'. Most translations make a break between the verses and the Greek syntax seems to support that; but as Henry Alford, who led the way to joining the verses, asserts: 'This verse [v. 16], being without any conjuction coupling it to what went before, is best understood to refer to the same as the preceding, and the assertion to concern the same fact as the last verb, "*we cry*", grounding that fact on an act of the indwelling spirit Himself.'[5] This way of joining the verses together in one sentence is supported by the way Paul treats the doctrine of adoption in the Galatian Epistle: 'And because you are sons, God has sent the Spirit of his Son into our hearts, crying, "Abba! Father!"' (Gal. 4:6).

It appears to be the teaching of Paul here that there is an *immediate* communication of the Holy Spirit to the believer's own spirit inspiring 'filial' (meaning, proper for a son, as the older theologians say) confidence. In context, the whole triune God is present in this assuring of our hearts. The Spirit is 'the Spirit of his Son' (Gal. 4:6). He, Himself, delivers the assuring message, when the Spirit cries in and with our hearts 'Abba! Father!' This immediacy of the voice of the Spirit in assuring the heart merges exactly with the immediacy of the work (voice) of the Spirit in effectual calling and regeneration. Jesus spoke of the new birth as a mystery. 'So then is every one that is born of the Spirit'. Though Jesus says we are born of 'water and the Spirit' – the water a metaphor for the Word (see also 1 Peter 1:23), it is by no means clear that the Word is the instrument by *means* of which the Spirit effects regeneration; rather the Word, as someone says, is a catalyst. Most seed (of the Word) falls on hard or rocky or thorny ground and produces no fruit (Matt. 13). The good ground in the parable was made 'good' first by the *special* (not general as Arminians think) work of the Spirit in the individuals' hearts who hear the Word, understand it and bear fruit (Matt. 13:23). Further, Paul speaks in the second chapter of 1 Corinthians of the human spirit as the point of connection in man where the impartation of divine wisdom occurs (1 Cor. 2:10-16).

There was immense interest in the subject of assurance and all the texts referred to here (and elsewhere in Scripture) in the times of the Puritans of the seventeenth and eighteenth centuries. Assurance was an important goal of about everything 'religious' the devout Puritan did.[6]

---

5. Henry Alford, *The New Testament for English Readers*, repr. (Chicago: Moody Press n.d.), p. 908.
6. It would take us far afield here to introduce that mighty literature but we shall have somewhat of an introduction to it shortly.

The most extensive extant Bible exposition from Christian antiquity is the homilies of John Chrysostom. He was both praised and persecuted on account of his faithfulness as expounder of plain biblical truth. His skill in making biblical truth clear to his hearers caused him much trouble because both his friends and his enemies knew exactly what he meant to say. His simple comments on Romans 8:16 and Galatians 4:6 in relation to assurance derived from the witness of the Spirit are an example of his skill and bear repeating here. Commenting on Romans 8:16 and the passage in Galatians 4:6 he has put the sense in plain words, thus:

> God hath sent forth the Spirit of his Son into our hearts crying Abba Father [Gal. 4:6]. And what is that, 'Spirit beareth witness with spirit?' The Comforter, he means, with that Gift [of adoption], which is given to us. For it is not of the Gift alone that is the voice [saying Abba Father] but of the Comforter also who gave the Gift, He Himself having taught us through the Gift so to speak. But when the 'Spirit beareth witness; what farther place for doubtfulness? For if it were a man, or an angel, or an archangel, or any other such power that promised this, then there might be reason in some doubting. But when it is the Highest Essence that bestoweth this Gift, and 'beareth witness' by the very words he bade us use in prayer, who would doubt any more of our dignity [as able to say Abba Father]. For not even when the Emperor elects anyone and proclaims in all men's hearing the honour done him, does anyone venture to gainsay?[7]

There is a second witness. 'The Spirit himself bears witness *with* [*sunmarturei,* emphasis added] our spirit that we are children [born ones] of God' (Rom. 8:16). Observe the witness is not *to* our spirit but *with*. Not every Greek scholar agrees there is the second witness, the *human* witness of the redeemed soul, but the Greek *sun* prefix (meaning with) to *marturei*, in the opinion of many, requires that the human spirit witnesses to itself saying 'Soul take thine ease' – not because like the rich fool 'you have much goods laid up for many years' but because your name is certainly 'written in heaven' (Luke 10:20).

We have already in exploration of Philippians 2:1-7 and 11-13 taken note of the devotional practice necessary to be aware and certain 'the God of Peace' is in our heart. When fully aware, then 'the peace of God will keep your hearts and mind through Christ Jesus'. It seems correct to infer that one's own heart confirms the Spirit's witness by inference. In this respect, assurance is an induction.

The Puritans thought so. James I. Packer has written that 'Romans 8:16... speaks of two witnesses giving evidence together, the Holy Spirit corroborating the testimony of our spirit.' He goes on to say:

> The Puritans identified 'our spirit' with the Christian's conscience, which, with the Spirit's aid, is able to discern in his heart the marks which Scripture specifies as tokens of the new birth and to conclude from them that he is a child of God. The Spirit 'writes first of all graces in us, and then teaches our consciences to read his handwriting'. Without the Spirit's aid, man can never recognize the Spirit's handiwork in himself; 'if he do not give in his testimony with them, your graces will have no witness at all'. Sometimes the Spirit's help here is given in full measure; sometimes, however, to chasten us for sin, or to try our faith for a time, this help is partly or wholly withdrawn; and because the Spirit is not always active to enable us to know ourselves to the same degree, the witness of our spirit inevitably fluctuates: 'A man shall find the same signs sometimes witness to him, and sometimes not, as the Spirit irradiates them.' We must recognize that God is sovereign here, to give more or less assurance in this way as he pleases.[8]

Modern secular historians have spread abroad a wholly gratuitous theory – repeated as fact – that the Puritans conducted a desperate effort to obtain assurance of election – not through the witness of the Spirit or inward confidence based on peace of conscience, but in effort toward material success – or financial gain. It is a variation of the thesis of Max Weber, floated first in a lengthy two-part essay (1905–1906) in *Archiv für Socialwissenschaft* published in English as *The Rise of Protestantism and the Spirit of Capitalism*. I have dealt with it in a lengthy note in my book *Civil Government: A Biblical View*.[9] The view came in for fatal refutation by H. M. Robertson, Albert Hyma and others. Ernst Troeltsch in his *The Social Teaching of the Christian Churches*, two large volumes in English, 1931, original German, 1911, gave an excellent account of them, Calvinists all, including European and American Puritans, but

---

7. John Chrysostom, *Homilies on the Acts of the Apostles and the Epistle to the Romans in Nicene and Post-Nicene Fathers*, First Series vol. xi, ed. by P. Schaff (American Editor, 1886, repr., Peabody, MA: Hendrickson Publ., 1994), p. 442.
8. James I. Packer, *A Quest for Holiness: The Puritan Vision of the Christian Life* (Wheaton: Crossway Books, 1990), pp. 183, 184.
9. Robert D. Culver, *Civil Government: A Biblical View* (Edmonton, Canada: Canadian Institute for Law, Theology and Public Policy, 2000), pp. 111, 112.

though he refers very briefly to Weber in his massive work – over a thousand pages thoroughly documented – he apparently found no support for this theory of Puritan assurance-of-election-by-material-success. Many years have passed since I read the volumes and one can forget, but the index does not turn up the slightest evidence of Weber's really slanderous notion. Winthrop Hudson, eminent Baptist theologian and historian, said of capitalist economic opportunists, who in the seventeenth century 'went awhoring' after unearned riches, that they 'represented the infiltration of a spirit which the convinced Puritan did not hesitate to label pagan and antichristian… The victory of the spirit of capitalism in a very real sense meant the defeat of Puritanism.'[10]

Many Puritan theologians have left us their views on interpretation of Romans 8:16 and Galatians 4:6 about the witness of the Spirit and the witness of our own spirits. They were variations of a single view. All of them regarded it as a fruit of faith, though not necessarily of the essence of faith, for they, like the distraught father of the afflicted son and like us today, often 'said with tears, Lord I believe; help thou mine unbelief' (Mark 9:24 KJV). There are levels of strength in assurance as well as of faith. Jesus put a high value on 'faith as of a grain of mustard seed'. Some, as Calvinists today, thought the sealing of the Spirit was something like circumcision or baptism which in some Reformed thinking are 'seals' and 'signs' of our acceptance with God.

John Owen, the paramount early English Puritan theologian, regarded the gift of the Holy Spirit at the moment of faith as Himself the seal of our redemption. He reminds us that Paul does not say the Holy Spirit is the sealer, but is Himself the seal (Eph. 1:13; 4:30; 2 Cor. 1:21). He wrote: 'God's sealing of believers… is his gracious communication of the Holy Ghost unto them… to enable them unto all the duties of their holy calling, evidencing them to be accepted with him… and asserting their preservation unto eternal salvation'[11] Sealing, no more than adoption, is not a post-conversion event. Assurance will develop as a consequence of our apprehension of the Spirit who 'shall be in you' from conversion onward. The sealing Paul refers to in Ephesians 1:13 was already past to all his readers.[12]

The Puritans' concern for assurance prevailed no less in the eighteenth century than in the seventeenth, especially among those of the Scottish Presbyterian Secession of 1733. Ebenezer and Ralph Erskine, two leaders of that movement, are memorialized in Erskine Theological Seminary in South Carolina, which trains ministers for the Associate Reformed Presbyterian Church in the U.S.A. The writings of these men, which have been republished recently, manifest the continuing importance in devotion of assurance of salvation. A 2001 reprint by Christian Focus Publications of *Beauties of Ebenezer Erskine* has chapter titles such as 'How we are to know whether we be among the sealed servants of God' (three pages), 'Marks of our belonging to God's house or family' (ten pages). It would be fair to say that half the book is to offer assistance to troubled Christians in evoking the right means to finding and keeping assurance of their own personal salvation.[13]

I close discussion of assurance with a fact of Christian history pleasant to contemplate. John Wesley shared with the Puritans great concern for personal assurance of salvation in the context of a holy life. The Puritans were not 'puritanical'. *Puritan* and *puritanical* are terms, deliberately pejorative, hung on some of the greatest Christians who ever lived, by their contemporary enemies, the worldlings of established churches wherein had developed all the inevitable evils of formalism, sacerdotalism and conformity with the world. The New England 'transcendentalist' Emerson and backslidden Yankees such as Nathaniel Hawthorne, slandered them by making some backslidden New England Yankee church members to be typical of all the Puritan inhabitants of New England. Recent secular historians have come to see this as our upside-down view of religion in Britain and America. I cite Edmund Morgan's biography of John Winthrop, first governor of Bay Colony. These are the opening paragraphs of the 'Author's Preface':

> The Puritans of New England are not in good repute today. Authors and critics who aspire to any degree of sophistication take care to repudiate them. Liberals and conservatives alike find it advantageous to label the measures they oppose as Puritan. Whatever is wrong with the American mind is attributed to its Puritan ancestry, and anything that escapes these assaults is smothered under a homespun mantle of quaintness by the lovers of the antique. Seventeenth-century Massachusetts has thus become in retrospect a preposterous land of witches and witch-hunters, of tall-crowned hats whose main sole virtue lay in their furniture [as in the Travelling Antique Show].

---

10. Winthrop Hudson in 'Puritanism and the Spirit of Capitalism', *Church History* 18 (March, 1949):15.
11. John Owen, *Works iv*, p. 401, as cited by Packer in *Quest for Holiness*, p. 188.
12. See Packer, *Quest for Holiness*, chap. 11, 'The Witness of the Spirit in Puritan Thought', pp. 179–189.
13. Ebenezer Erskine, *The Beauties of Ebenezer Erskine*, selected by Samuel McMillan, intro. Joel R. Beeke (Ross-Shire, Scotland: Christian Heritage/Christian Focus, 2001), pp. 616, plus liii.

It is not likely that this vision will ever be wholly dispelled. We have to caricature the Puritans in order to feel comfortable in their presence. They found some answers to some problems we would rather forget. Their very existence is therefore an affront to our moral complacency, and the easiest way to meet the challenge is to distort it into absurdity, turn the challengers into fanatics.[14]

The Jewish Heritage Foundation in 1962 sponsored the publication of *The Puritan Heritage: America's Roots in the Bible*, by two Jewish scholars, Joseph Gael, author of several books and government official, and Ben Siegel, a prolific author of the California State Department of Language Arts. Out of this popular but scholarly and thoroughly researched book, I cite one relevant paragraph:

> Some modern commentators (among them, Allen Tate and Robert Penn Warren) view Emerson as the prime source of the secularism that dominated post-Civil War New England. Randall Stewart has declared Emerson to be 'the arch-heretic of American literature, and Emersonianism the greatest heresy. By no dint of sophistry can he be brought within the Christian fold… and [Emersonianism] has done more than any other doctrine to undermine Christian belief in America'. For many moderns, then, Emerson symbolizes the nineteenth century's shift from a God-centerd to a man-centerd America.[15]

The book points out that not only Thoreau and Hawthorne but the darling of the university professors' courses in *American Literature*, Walt Whitman, were really political-religious activists determined to destroy the Puritan Heritage and to replace it with secularism, the religion of man the measure of all things.

A tiny minority in the world of the universities of America have been producing a literature of correction, which I have tried to keep abreast of, beginning with William Haller and Perry Miller. Among more recent scholars, two have helped me most to relate the Puritans to the theology of Wesley and the Wesleyans. One was published jointly by the Institute of Early American History and Culture of Williamsburg, VA and the College of William and Mary and the Colonial Williamsburg Foundation, by Charles E. Hambrick-Stowe,[16] and second, a published Ph.D. Thesis (Princeton University) by Robert C. Monk.[17]

The relevance of this research is apparent in the opening paragraph of the preface in the first book:

> Historians have long treated New England Puritanism as an intellectual and social movement. At heart, however, Puritanism was a devotional movement, rooted in religious experience. This book deals with the form, content, and spiritual impact of the worship and private devotional activity of seventeenth-century New Englanders.[18]

The same could be said of the Wesleyan-Methodist phenomenon as taught and practised – a devotional movement, rooted in religious experience. Robert Monk says early on, in the 'Introduction' to *John Wesley, His Puritan Heritage*:

> The resemblance between Wesley and the Puritan ethics has been commonly recognized, especially the similarity of their teachings concerning the outward manifestations of the Christian life… In the eyes of many of his contemporaries he revived the spirit and practice of Puritanism.[19]

He elaborates the similarity, even dependency of Wesley on Puritan antecedents. Though Anglican John Wesley rejected attempted identification with nonconformist (i.e. Puritan) practices, the similarity was obvious. After citing several recent studies relating Wesley's ideas to Moravians, Anglicans, Eastern Fathers and Luther, Monk says:

> The majority of these studies… take note, to a greater or lesser degree, to the similarity between Wesley and the Puritan tradition… [those] concerned with showing Wesley's affinity with Calvin or Luther… do not give sufficient attention to the fact that… Wesley depends on the English form of the tradition, Puritanism.[20]

---

14. Edmund Morgan, *The Puritan Dilemma* (Boston: Little, Brown & Co., 1958), p. xi. Among Edmund Morgan's books is *The Puritan Family* (New York: Harper & Rowe, 1966).
15. Joseph Gaer and Ben Siegel, *The Puritan Heritage: America's Roots in the Bible* (New York: Mentor Books, 1964), p. 195.
16. Charles E. Hambrick-Stowe, *The Practice of Piety: Puritan Devotional Disciplines in Seventeenth-Century New England* (Chapel Hill, NC: The University of NC Press, 1982, 1988).
17. Robert C. Monk, *John Wesley, His Puritan Heritage* (Nashville: Abingdon Press, 1966).
18. Hambrick-Stowe, *Practice of Piety*, p. vii.
19. Monk, *John Wesley*, p. 15.
20. ibid.

This should not be surprising, says Monk, for though Charles Wesley's father was an Anglican priest, two of Charles Wesley's great-grandfathers were Puritans and a grandfather of Wesley's mother was a Puritan.[21] Some were of note in their time. Independency (usually Puritan) and Puritan views among his Anglican ancestors was common.[22]

Personal assurance of one's own salvation among zealous, devout Christians is – if not always, at the critical moment of death – a paramount concern. It undergirds the quiet 'peace of God, which… guard your hearts and your minds' (Phil. 4:7) of the devout in the daily life of the believer. At this point every devout Wesleyan and every devout Puritan (Calvinist) meet. Monk found that Wesley and the Puritans display a striking similarlity in their concern for the practical application of the Christian gospel to the daily life of the believer. This becomes the burden of the whole book, which he outlines in a paragraph.[23] The decisive evidence was 'Wesley's use, recommendation, and abridgement of Puritan literature'.[24] Wesley was the publisher of a whole library of literature for disciplined reading by the members of his societies. A major number of the titles were by Puritans.[25]

Finally, it is to be observed that, as Monk points out in pages 78–95, precisely in the doctrine of 'The Witness of the Spirit', Wesleyanism and Puritanism, as I have approvingly described it, were essentially at one. As a final word on the matter I quote Monk's first paragraph in the section, 'Assurance – the Witness of the Spirit'.

> The experiential religious life has at its center an awareness of being accepted by God through the grace offered in the gospel – a knowledge that what the gospel says and promises is actually true for *me*. Such a personal awareness not only is a rational deduction from these promises but also, of far greater significance, springs from contact with God in which he makes known to the believer the reality of this acceptance.[26]

This consciousness of being accepted is part of the doctrine of assurance, prominent and nearly identical in the theology both of Wesley and the Puritans. Dr Robert C. Monk's assertions in this paragraph are fully documented by references both to such Puritan leaders as Baxter and Thomas Goodwin and to the Journals and other works of John Wesley.

---

21. ibid., p. 17.
22. ibid., pp. 24, 25.
23. ibid., pp. 25, 26.
24. ibid., p. 26.
25. ibid., pp. 31–66.
26. ibid., p. 78.

19
Salvation Through Christ Alone

In expressing what one believes to be the truth of God on the topic of this and the next following chapter the caution of Augustine on a different but difficult question should be observed: '[I]t would seem that we might bear with considerable patience our ignorance of secrets that lie in the earth and heavens.'[1]

Likewise Calvin frequently warned against the kind of curiosity which demands that God in Scripture furnish an answer, saying in one place we may be 'titillated by an immoderate desire to know more than is lawful... trifling and harmful questions repeatedly flow forth'.[2]

It is hardly contestable that the apostles, eleven of whom suffered death at the hands of adherents of other 'religions' believed in the depths of their hearts, as one of them famously declared, 'there is salvation in no one else'. Early on and frequently since it has seemed to a few Christians there might be exceptions to the rule or perhaps even more than one way to be saved. Yet it would be false both to Scripture and Christian history to say any community of orthodox Christians ever denied the exclusive claims of Christ or that there is only one 'way of salvation'. This one way is not Christendom, i.e. 'Christianity' as a social phenomenon, even though the Roman Church in earlier times claimed the 'one holy, catholic and apostolic church' is the organization that submits to the papal hierarchy and that outside this *unum sanctum* there is no salvation. In recent times, as we shall briefly observe below, some liberal (really apostate) Christian writers have rejected the apostolic exclusivity and found salvation, they think, in several 'high' religions (Buddhism, Islam, etc.). Some otherwise orthodox, evangelical writers think there may be saving revelation and divine grace in the teachings of these 'ethnic' religions and implicit (if not explicit) faith in Christ among sincere followers of these systems of thought and practice. Recently some scholarly writers have invented names for these departures from the historic 'exclusivism'. The ones who think all religions equally true and false are called *pluralists* and the ones who think Christ may be found in other than biblical faith, *inclusivists*.[3]

---

1. Aurelius Augustine, *The Enchiridion on Faith, Hope and Love*, ed. H. Paolucci and analysis A. Von Harack (Chicago: Henry Regnery Co., 1966), end of chap. 16.
2. John Calvin, *Institutes of the Christian Religion ii*, ed. J. T. McNeil, trans. and ed. by F. L. Battles (Philadelphia, PA: Westminster Press, 1960), chap. 25.10.
3. There is a considerable amount of overlapping in this and the next chapter with a chapter in eschatology about perversions and denials of the doctrine of eternal punishment of the lost.

History.

For about 300 years American Protestants were spared the strain of loving acceptance of neighbors of a different 'religion' without accepting also the neighbors' religion as of equal validity with biblical, orthodox Christian faith. At first there were not even large numbers of Roman Catholic or Jewish people in the usual local mix. Now that has changed for any one alert to what is going on in the wider culture of Western civilization.

Almost the whole of Christendom has been infiltrated with immigrant peoples who bring their world-views, including their religions, with them. This has forced a consideration of the truth-claims of Islam, Buddhism, Hinduism (to say nothing of Roman Catholicism, Judaism and Eastern Orthodoxy) upon Protestant believers, not least those who call themselves evangelicals.

America has been called a 'melting pot', meaning that its character as a culture is a mix of all the cultures brought to these shores. This is not entirely true, however. In fact it is more false than true. Will Herberg, in a well-known book, *Protestant, Catholic, Jew* (1955), pointed out that the cultural character of the land has always been prevailingly both British and Protestant. He shows (what no informed scholar denies) that the culture was British, including language, institutions and religion. Those of the various European cultures became 'Yankees' too in a few generations, except for their religion. That part of their particular ancestral culture remained as the chief, single feature that still identified them with ancestral culture. Through the generations we have learned to live with this. Later immigrations of all these European people brought some form of Christianity to their new country.

The colonial culture, however, not only reflected a Christian world-view, but a Protestant world-view, and, as has been convincingly shown, the prevailing outlook was Calvinistic in tone from Nova Scotia to Georgia. So we had a fairly uniform British – slightly modified – culture, even though there were sectional and even neighbourhood islands of less assimilated culture.

To what extent will a constitutional government formed by and reflecting a biblical-Christian world-view accommodate clashing outlooks? Shall we now put the month of Ramadan in the civil calendar? Time will tell. The Western world already has developed a high level of *pluralism*, i.e. acceptance of the existence of other than 'native' cultures. If this be 'multiculturalism' it is now a fact of life. Strong movements within our culture seek to promote a variety of cultures, including manner of living (plural marriage, homosexual marriage, etc.) and moral standards each of equal value and rightness and call it 'multiculturalism'. When church leaders plan religious meetings where readings from the *Koran*, the *Vedas*, the Jewish and Christian Scriptures, prayers and sermons by 'clergy' of Islam, Hinduism, Judaism, etc., occur, they are not promoting mere peaceful acceptance of the right of people to live together in the same civil community with respect for contrary religious beliefs, but religious syncretism – properly labelled 'the perennial heresy'.

There is intense pressure from many quarters for Christians to accept all 'religions' as equally true. Most of the old standard works of theology have no chapters on the subject of this chapter, though they contain comments on the great commandment – 'Him only shalt thou serve' and the unique claims of Christ. Beginning, however, with such volumes as Hendrik Kraemer's *The Christian Message in a Non-Christian World* [4] and especially W. A. Visser 't Hooft's *No Other Name*,[5] the uniqueness of Christ and of salvation through Him and no other has been vigorously promoted as the only defensible Christian view. They have asserted the same insistence on the absolute and exclusive claims that brought down on Christians the wrath of both rulers and denizens of the Roman Empire in the first centuries of our era.

The Roman Church at Vatican II gave careful – if not quite satisfactory – attention to this matter, after several of its theologians, eminently Karl Rahner's *Theological Investigations* (vol vi, 1966), raised the subject. It was he who provided Romanist theology with the interesting term 'anonymous Christians' for presumed 'saved' folk among followers of other religions.

Rahner went beyond asserting that divine *revelation* is present in religions such as Islam and Buddhism to say that divine *grace* leading to eternal *salvation* is available also. The 'saved' among such religions he called 'anonymous Christians' and the striking term caught on.[6] Volume vi of Rahner's *Theological Investigations* is exerpted in *A*

---

4. Hendrik Kraemer, *The Christian Message in a Non-Christian World* (London: Harpers, 1938).
5. W. A. Visser 't Hooft, *No Other Name* (Philadelphia, PA: Westminster Press, 1963).
6. Karl Rahner, *Theological Investigations* v (London: Darton, Longman & Todd, 1966), pp. 115–134. Also *Theological Investigations* vi, pp. 390–395. The series was issued progressively beginning in 1961. Rahner did not complete the planned work.

Rahner Reader edited by G. A. McCool[7] who comments on Rahner's view that 'Through... implicit faith, men who have never accepted or even encountered Christian revelation become, not just anonymous theists, but anonymous Christians.'[8]

Even some atheists, according to Rahner, may be saved as *atheists*.[9] These atheists are persons of 'inculpable inability to understand or accept the formulated doctrine of the Christian religion... Pastorally we should deal with contemporary atheists on the assumption that they are anonymous Christians'.[10]

A majority of prelates at Vatican II in early 1960s endorsed the 'ecumenical' modernity prevalent at the time, going as far as possible toward accommodation of every human thought and group without relinquishing the distinctives of papal Christianity. They, however, refused to go as far as Rahner and the World Council of Churches (New Delhi 1961, at about the same time). Ecumenist Claude Nelson was the Protestant respondent to 'The Declaration on the Relations of the Church to Non-Christian Religions' in the first English edition of *The Documents of Vatican II*.[11] His response reflects no interest in the question of salvation through Judaism or Islam, etc., only in developing better inter-religious relations.

The Council had been instructed by Pope John XXIII, who summoned it, to seek what Christianity has in common with other religions. Pius XII had been severely criticized for perceived anti-Jewish policy, hence 'Pope John's deletion of a word [conversion] from the Good Friday prayer for Jews and Pope Paul's extensive revision of the prayer (now 'for the Jews' instead of 'For the conversion of the Jews', etc.)'.[12] So while encouraging dialogue (not debate or conversion) in this particular document, the Council nevertheless almost but not quite rejected the suggestion of some Roman Catholic theologians that all religions have saving power for their members. Here is the critical paragraph.

> The Catholic Church rejects nothing of what is true and holy in these religions [Hinduism, Buddhism, other religions]. She has a high regard for the manner of life and conduct, the precepts and doctrines which, although differing in many ways from her own teaching, nevertheless often reflect a ray of truth which enlightens all men. Yet she proclaims and is duty bound to proclaim without fail, Christ who is the way, the truth and the life (John 1[4]:6). In him, in whom God reconciled all things to himself (2 Cor. 5:18-19), men find the fullness of their religious life.[13]

On 21 November 1964, Vatican II adopted *Lumen Gentium* (light of the nations). The document is rife with slippery qualifications both before and after the following acknowledgment of saving power *through Christ* in any religion:

> Finally, those who have not yet received the Gospel... Those who, through no fault of their own, do not know the Gospel of Christ or his Church, but who nevertheless seek God with a sincere heart, and, moved by grace, try in their actions to do his will as they know it through the dictates of their conscience – those too may achieve eternal salvation. Nor shall divine providence deny the assistance necessary for salvation to those who, without any fault of theirs, have not yet arrived at an explicit knowledge of God, and who, not without grace, strive to lead a good life. Whatever good or truth is found amongst them is considered by the Church to be a preparation for the Gospel and given by him who enlightens all men that they may at length have life.[14]

The Council found support, they thought, in Thomas Aquinas who said: 'Those who are unbaptized, though not actually in the Church, are in the Church potentially [Aristotle again]. And this potentiality is rooted in two things – first and principally in the power of Christ, which is sufficient for the salvation of the whole human race; secondly, in free-will.'[15]

Recently from within professed 'evangelicalism' challenges have come to the exclusive claim that salvation is through Christ alone; or if through Him alone, then it is proposed that belief in Christ may be implicit, not explicit, *via* sincere allegiance to some other lord, savior, sage or proposed way of salvation.

---

7. G. A. McCool (ed.), *A Rahner Reader* (New York: Seabury Publ., 1975), pp. 211–220.
8. ibid., p. 211.
9. Rahner, *Theological Investigations, vol. ix*, pp. 146–156, excerpted by McCool, *Rahner Reader*.
10. McCool, *Rahner Reader*, p. 220.
11. *The Documents of Vatican ii*, ed. W. M. Abbott (New York: Guild Press/America Press, 1966), pp. 669–671.
12. *Documents of Vatican ii*, pp. 660–668.
13. *Vatican Council ii*, ed. by Austin Flannery, *vol. i* (Northport, NY: Costello Publ., 1996), p. 736.
14. ibid., pp. 367, 368.
15. Thomas Aquinas, *Summa Theologica iii*, trans. by Fathers of the English Dominican Province (Westminster, Maryland: Christian Classics, 1911, 1981), Question 8, Article 3, Reply 1.

J. I. Packer responded to the new inclusivism of the Roman Church in a lecture at Dallas Theological Seminary about twenty years before it burst out in evangelical circles, including the Evangelical Theological Society. He said – and I quote the first two and the last three sentences of the lecture:

> Suppose that when the Philippian jailor asked Paul what he must do to be saved, Paul had said, 'Be diligent in your present religion, whatever it is', would this have been an adequate answer? Luke, at any rate would hardly have thought so, for the speeches and sermons which he records in Acts link salvation exclusively with the name of Jesus and faith in his person and lordship (cf. 2:38; 4:12; 5:31; 10:43; 13:23, 38, 39; 16:31; 26:15-23; 28:23-28).... It thus appears that the case for other forms of faith beside Christianity is forlorn indeed. Without Christ we are without God and without hope. Non-Christian religions exhibit much that is noble and many insights that are true, but they do not exhibit saving grace. So far as the way of salvation is concerned, 'believe on the Lord Jesus Christ' really is the last word.[16]

Let us try to respond to the growing problem: *first* by separating out the two main questions involved, *then* providing a scriptural answer to each in so far as Scripture addresses it and, finally, suggesting how we as believers, scholars and churchmen ought to treat people – believers and others – caught up in the errors of syncretism. The questions are: 1) Does the Bible and historic, orthodox Christianity teach that salvation is exclusively through Christ and no other? 2) May Christ be encountered without being identified and proclaimed in other religions than biblical Christianity and thereby salvation made available for sincere adherents to these other religions? Our response should be no even-handed approach to balancing light and darkness, truth and error. A clear line, if possible, must be drawn. In process we shall not enlarge greatly on the proposals and arguments of advocates of contrary views. There is easy access to their literature elsewhere. The Bible and Christian history speak plainly. Let us for now let the matter rest there for purposes of a theology of salvation that is 'biblical, historical and systematic'.

Does the Bible and Historic Christianity Teach that Salvation is Exclusively Through Christ and No Other?

Since writing this section of the chapter I have had the privilege of reading Daniel B. Clendenin's excellent book on how 'Christianity Encounters World Religions' (the subtitle of his book *Many Gods, Many Lords*). He devotes the last two chapters (5 and 6) to the question I have just now stated. The fifth chapter, 'Old Testament Faith and the World Religions' pays more attention to the fact that there were many before the call of Abraham and afterward who did not share in the Abrahamic covenant of promise who though 'aliens and pagans [who] were not beyond the pale of the saving presence and activity of God... God elected his unique people, so it would be foolish to think we can approach him however we might choose. But notable exceptions were not too uncommon'.[17] He has shown how God made Himself known to Abel, Enoch, Noah, Melchizedek, Jethro and others. Beyond this he modestly declines to generalize. The sixth and last chapter entitled 'The New Testament Documents: Chronicles of Disbelief' shows how in stark reality it was the exclusive claims of Christianity in a pluralistic Roman world that distinguished biblical religion then and must do the same in our world today. Thirteen pages of select bibliography close the book. There is a complete absence of intellectual arrogance and strict submission to the *plain* texts of Scripture in this book.

The answer I shall present to this question has been stated currently by others: '[E]xcept perhaps in very special circumstances, people are not saved apart from explicit faith in Jesus Christ, which presupposes that they have heard about His salvific work on their behalf'.[18]

Let those who regard the Bible highly take note of Paul's very relevant remarks about those religious teachers who mixed fatal errors with acknowledged truth: 'there are some who trouble you and want to distort the gospel of Christ. But even if we or an angel from heaven should preach to you a gospel contrary to the one we preached to you, let him be accursed' (Gal. 1:7, 8; cf. v. 10). The author of that statement had no interest in promoting mutuality

---

16. J. I. Packer, 'The Way of Salvation, Part IV: Are Non-Christian Faiths the Way of Salvation', *Bibliotheca Sacra*, vol. 130, no. 518, April–June, 1973, pp. 110–116.
17. Daniel B. Clendenin, *Many Gods, Many Lords* (Grand Rapids, MI: Baker, 1995), p. 117.
18. R. Douglas Geivett and W. Gary Phillips, 'A Particularist View: An Evidentialist Approach', in *Four Views on Salvation in a Pluralist World*, ed. D. L. Okholm and T. R. Phillips (Grand Rapids, MI: Zondervan, 1996), p. 214.

of understanding or comity of dividing the turf with any gospel but his own, which he claimed to have received from Christ by immediate communication (Gal. 1 and 2). He goes on to insist the proper test to be applied is not whether some truths are present but if there is error in the mix of proclaimed doctrine and if the message is conveyed *first* by a properly certified apostolic messenger (Gal. 1:11–2:9). Consider the source!

The Scriptural Evidences.

Let us juxtapose two 'inspired' comprehensive statements: first, is the promise of the God of Abraham, Isaac and Jacob (Gal. 3:8) at the very beginning of the specifically soteriological narrative. The call of Abraham (Gen. 12:1-3) ends with a promise that was also a prediction: 'and in you shall the families of the earth shall be blessed'. Every informed student knows the prediction-promise was clarified to show that 'in you' (*bekha*, singular) was meant to refer to Abraham's descendants through many generations and ultimately to Christ, Himself (Gal. 3:16 and Gen. 13:15; 17:8, *et passim*). The 'seed' line of blessing to 'all the families of the earth' did not even include all of Abraham's offspring but only those through his wife Sarah's only son Isaac (Heb. 11:17; Rom. 9:7) and Isaac's younger son Jacob (Rom. 9:10-13).

The second passage is the pronouncement of Jesus at the Well of Sychar to a woman who professed to believe salvation available through a competing and partially contrary religion, 'of Samaria'. To the point of this chapter and the diverting question of the woman Jesus declared: 'You worship what you do not know; we [Jews] worship what we know, for salvation is from the Jews' (John 4:22).

The *prima facie* meaning of these texts is that the only salvation available anywhere to anybody, certainly the only salvation of interest to Scripture and its faithful readers, is through the line of chosen people which terminated upon Jesus Himself, elsewhere in the New Testament designated 'the Savior of the world' (John 4:42) and 'the Saviour of all people' (1 Tim. 4:10). A bit later in the conversation of Jesus with the Samaritan woman (we may imagine with great pathos) she wistfully spoke, saying, 'I know that Messiah [the Christ] is coming' (John 4:25), to which Jesus responded, 'I who speak to you am he' (John 4:26).

Everything falling between Genesis 12:3 (the call of Abraham) and John 4:26 falls in line saying not only, 'Salvation is from the Jews' but from a particular Jew. He is the only Saviour of mankind.

Let us see this starkly as it really is in the narrative of the Old Testament, beginning with Abraham's *chasse* into Egypt and Philistia (Gen. 12). Not only is salvation through a particular family but till the fullness of time (Gal. 4:4) in a particular portion of earth's surface – a 'land of promise' as well as sons of promise and a particular promised Son. Let the reader think of how the LORD at the Exodus not only annihilated the armies of Pharaoh but also judged all the gods of Egypt (Exod. 12:12); think also of the absolute rejection of any saving power in the elaborate rituals and idolatries of Canaan and divine revulsion even from their names.

Think also of the disasters in what Visser't Hooft calls 'the first wave of syncretism' with the nature-fertility worship of the Mother Goddess of Babylon and Damascus (2 Kgs. 23:7-11; Jer. 7:18; 44:17; Ezek. 8:14). The prophets Jeremiah (2:20) and Ezekiel (16:15 ff.) were not concocting allegories when they compared the Israel of that time to a whore. Says Visser't Hooft:

> It is inadequate to describe the prophetic protest against this syncretism as a moral protest. It is far more. It is the refusal in the name of the living God who calls men by their name and demands their personal response, to let men become playthings of the dark, arbitrary forces of nature, the denial of the idea that man's ultimate destiny is to adjust himself and let himself be integrated with the unending circular process of life and death represented by nature.[19]

Think also of the permanent annihilation by God of the northern kingdom of Israel (2 Kgs. 17:5-23) because they thought they could find some 'grace' and 'rays of revelation' (to borrow the language of Vatican II) in the idols, rituals and doctrines of the religions of their neighbours. Then turn attention to the Babylonian captivity, precipitated by Jewish flirtation with 'all the [religious] abominations of the nations' (2 Chr. 36:14, and context). See also Daniel's prayer of confession of the abomination of religious syncretism (Dan. 9:1-19) and Ezra's similar prayer (Ezra 9:1-15). See also how 'the Israelites separated themselves from all foreigners and stood and confessed their sins [chiefly of religious syncretism] and the iniquities of their fathers' (Neh. 9:1-38, especially v. 2).

---

19. Visser't Hooft, *No Other Name*, p. 13.

Let us pass lightly over inter-testamental times during which the constant temptation was to accept *religious* elements first from the ambient culture (Samaritan and degenerate Judaism) of the restored community (Ezra, Nehemiah) then from Greek paganism (1 and 2 Maccabees). The heroes of faith celebrated in the eleventh chapter of Hebrews are not they who found 'elements of grace', 'sanctification' and 'rays of revelation' in ethnic religion but they who not only resisted that mixing of beliefs which the scientific study of religion calls syncretion but fought it to the death (Heb. 11:34-38). The Epistles of Paul, Peter, John and Jude bristle with resistance to the notion of saving truth or any presence of the authentic Saviour in the mystery religions, pagan cults and philosophical currents of first-century antiquity. Resistance to such was the very occasion for the writing of much of this New Testament literature. In the book of Revelation, the believers and their leader at Pergamos are commended by the One who 'has the sharp two-edged sword' saying, 'I know where you dwell, where Satan's throne is. Yet you hold fast my name, and you did not deny my faith even in the days of Antipas my faithful witness, who was killed among you, where Satan dwells' (Rev. 2:12, 13). These Christians who had suffered deeply from pressures to find enough truth in a satanic cult somehow 'to get along' with it, are reproved for even allowing in their company some who held 'the doctrine of Baalam and Balak' which mixed idolatry with fornication (Rev. 3:14), also the presently unknown 'doctrine of Nicolaitans' (perhaps the same as Baalamism, as the Greek syntax suggests.[20] The comments on Revelation 3:14-16 by a godly Anglican bishop speak directly to the dangers that come from allowing any saving element in non-Christian religion. (How elitist this would sound in current debate!) He speaks distinctly:

> The simplest meaning of the passage seems to be that the temptation to which the Israelites were exposed, is used to illustrate the temptations of the Pergamene Church... in the same Antinomian [ism] [unrestrained by moral laws]... a tendency... very early seen (Rom. 6:4; Gal. 5:13; Jude 4) and is not extinct now... a vague, unavowed, unrealised idea that the Atonement has made sin less fatal, that sin indulged and persisted in, may yet not work death.[21]

The moral perils inevitably attached to a syncretic Christianity in this passage called for the very most severe denunciation and punishments by the risen and glorified Lord Jesus Christ. It was to this particular church, Pergamos, that the glorified Jesus reveals Himself as 'him who has the sharp two-edged sword' and threatens to use it on them.

What Texts of Scripture Plainly Say Salvation Is Through Christ and No Other?

The faith of the Old Testament was Christian in a preparatory sense, as is well understood, but this became clear only in the New Testament. We bring attention, therefore, to New Testament Scripture statements which plainly, in context, declare that salvation is by faith in Christ alone and in no other. Many before us have cited these texts for the same reason we are employing them now. After attention to what these texts say we shall briefly note how some, who do not welcome what these clear passages say, respond to them. Because most discussion of these verses has been in terms of the Authorized (or King James) Version, I shall quote several in that translation. I shall cite three verses from the third chapter of John first.

> John 3:16 – 'For God so loved the world, that he gave his only begotten Son, that whosoever believeth in him should not perish, but have everlasting life.'

> John 3:18 – 'He that believeth on him is not condemned: but he that believeth not is condemned already, because he hath not believed in the name of the only begotten Son of God.'

> John 3:36 – 'He that believeth on the Son hath everlasting life: and he that believeth not the Son shall not see life; but the wrath of God abideth on him.'

John's Gospel characteristically speaks immediately and plainly both to mind and feeling. It is always hard to miss the thrust of John's meanings. Exegesis may therefore be bypassed to exposition and application (see John 20:30, 31; 21:25). No one knows whether the section from verse 13 onward to 21 wherein two of these three verses lie was spoken to Nicodemus or is elaboration by John. Nor is it plain whether John the Baptist or John the Apostle

---

20. Robert H. Mounce, *New International Commentary on the New Testament – Book of Revelation* (Grand Rapids, MI: Eerdmans Publ., 1977), p. 98.
21. Bishop Boyd Carpenter in *Ellicott's Commentary on the Whole Bible viii*, ed. C. J. Ellicott (Grand Rapids, MI: Zondervan, 1954), pp. 543, 544.

spoke the words of verse 36. It makes no difference to knowledge and faith because 'the scripture says' – to employ Paul's trenchant phrase – is the same as 'God says'.[22] Let all Christians therefore heed the caveat that when Scripture speaks in these three verses, God is speaking and thereafter there really is no more to say. If there is no more to be said, why keep on protesting?

The way to 'have everlasting life' and 'not perish' is to 'believeth in him [Christ]' (John 3:16). Any one who does not so believe 'is condemned already' (John 3:36) and shall certainly 'not stand in the judgment' future (see Ps. 1:5). This is 'because he has not believed in the name' (John 3:18; see Acts 4:12).

Contrariwise the one who 'believes him' is not condemned now or ever (John 5:24). Later, Jesus, in conspicuous display of authority, declared, 'Truly, truly, I say to you, whoever hears my word and believes him who sent me has eternal life. He does not come into judgement, but has passed from death to life' (John 5:24). In this saying it is apparent that to hear the word of the gospel is prerequisite to believing on the One who is the Savior. It is this text (and similar texts) which still gives impulse, as it did in late apostolic times, to preach Christ where He has not yet been named (Rom. 15:20).

John 3:36 adds the stark and awful fact nobody wishes to face, for it is spoken by the One from whose presence in the Last Judgment, in this same Apostle's vision, 'earth and sky fled away, and no place was found for them' (Rev. 20:11): 'he that believeth not the Son shall not see life; but [to the contrary] the wrath of God abideth on him' (John 3:36). The absence of life is death. 'Death and Hades [hell] were thrown into the lake of fire. This is the second death' (Rev. 20:14).

No 'artful dodger' who once walked the earth and shall come to this judgment will find a place to hide in that great day of God Almighty (Rev. 16:14). No crafty theologian who seeks to explain away plain passages of Scripture by creative exegesis based on wistful surmises – suspended on strained explanations of obscure texts or inferential nonsequiturs – will furnish any help from the side of an attorney for the defence. As is rather well known, one of America's first great theologians (Jonathan Edwards) was rather insistent on the theology of this paragraph and helped spark a great revival, the waves of whose influence are still felt today. Where today is the LORD God of Jonathan Edwards? I doubt if there are any Edwards-like, in the serried ranks of inclusivist theologians and the still bolder pluralists.

The theology of the third chapter of John strengthens the nerve of aggressive missionary evangelism. To dilute it in any way is to 'cut the nerve' in missions, to borrow the phrase of Herbert Kane, the late missiologist. John Sanders, perhaps the most articulate and persuasive contemporary 'inclusivist', attempts throughout his book[23] to refute this charge. It does get his attention! Near the close he proposes four reasons for missionary evangelism even on inclusivist – 'wider hope' – presuppositions. They are: 1) 'that Jesus commanded us to go and preach the gospel to all people', 2) 'Motivation for missions also arises from the desire to share what we cannot hold inside ourselves', 3) 'God wants to bring the fullness of eternal life into the lives of all people now' 4) to engage the forces of evil in the world – 'to save people from… a life of rebellion against God'.[24] Such motives as these hardly explain the zeal of the apostles or any others in the age-long missionary enterprise.

Charles Hodge, in discussing 'the external call', entitled a section, 'The Call to Salvation is only Through the Gospel'. He has quoted Romans 10:14 and concluded with these almost transfixing sentences:

> Invocation implies faith; faith implies knowledge; knowledge implies objective teaching. 'Faith cometh by hearing, and hearing by the word of God' (Rom. 10:17). There is no faith, therefore, where the gospel is not heard; and where there is no faith, there is no salvation.
>
> This is indeed an awful doctrine. But are not the words of our Lord also awful, 'Wide is the gate, and broad is the way, that leadeth to destruction, and many there be which go in thereat; because strait is the gate, and narrow is the way, which leadeth unto life, and few there be that find it'? (Matt vii: 13, 14). Is not the fact awful which stares every man in the face, that the great majority even of those who hear the gospel reject its offers of mercy? Facts are as mysterious as doctrines. If we must submit to the one, we may as well submit to the other. Our Lord has taught us, in view of facts or doctrines which try our faith, to remember the infinite wisdom and rectitude of God, and say, 'Even so Father; for so it seemed good in thy sight'. The proper effect of the doctrine that the knowledge of the gospel is essential to the salvation of adults, instead of exciting opposition to God's word or providence, is to prompt us to greatly increased exertion to send the gospel to those who are perishing for lack of knowledge.[25]

---

22. See B. B. Warfield, *The Inspiration and Authority of the Bible* (Philadelphia, PA: Presbyterian & Reformed Publ., 1958), pp. 299–348.
23. John Sanders, *No Other Name: An Investigation into the Destiny of the Unevangelized* (Grand Rapids, MI: Eerdmans Publ., 1970).
24. ibid., pp. 284, 285.
25. Charles Hodge, *Systematic Theology ii* (Grand Rapids, MI: Eerdmans Publ., 1970), pp. 648, 649.

The case against 'inclusivism' and 'pluralism' might be rested here, yet there are many other plain texts and several will be introduced.

John 14:6 – 'I am the way, the truth, and the life: no man cometh unto the Father, but by me' (KJV).

At some juncture in the last hours of Jesus with His apostles, Jesus phrased this answer to a question expressed by Thomas about the way to God. Geivett and Phillips point out that this 'I am' statement identifies Jesus equally with the *way*, the *truth* and the *life*. He claims not merely to *know* but to *be* these three. Say these authors, 'Since he adds that "no one" (*oudeis*) comes to the Father except by this way, we infer that anyone who wants to come to the Father must find that way that uniquely leads to the Father, namely, Jesus himself.'[26] The definite article preceding each of the three (way, truth, life) seems to say there is only one way, one truth, one life, that other claimants are spurious and to be heartily rejected.

Later in that last evening Jesus offered special intercessory prayer for those already in His fold of salvation, those who had already received His 'word' (John 17: 6, 8). A little later he said to the Father, 'I do not ask for these only, but also for those who will believe in me through their word' (John 17:20). 'This implies a direct link between the future salvation of those who are not of his immediate Jewish fold (10:16) and the explicit proclamation of the apostolic word.'[27] In other words, availability of salvation depends, from the human perspective, on hearing the apostolically authentic gospel. Such a conclusion leads immediately to the next text we shall examine, Romans 10:9-17.

Romans 10:9-17.

That which is implicit in the preceding text is explicit here – not only is Jesus Christ the only Savior, but in order to believe on Him savingly one must first 'hear' the message about Him. Again for its stark, literal realism and, at this point, textual faithfulness, I cite the familiar King James Version. The ellipses are of verses 10 and 15b-16.

> That if thou [singular] shalt confess with thy mouth the Lord Jesus, and shalt believe in thine heart that God hath raised him from the dead, thou shalt be saved... for the scripture saith, whosoever believeth on him shall not be ashamed [Isa 28:16; 49:23]. For there is no difference between the Jew and the Greek: for the same Lord over all is rich unto all that call upon him. For whosoever shall call upon the name of the Lord shall be saved. How shall they call on him in whom they have not believed? And how shall they believe in him of whom they have not heard? And how shall they hear without a preacher? And how shall they preach, except they be sent? as it is written, How beautiful are the feet of them that preach the gospel of peace, and bring glad tidings of good things!... So then faith cometh by hearing and hearing by the word of God.

Little comment seems necessary. I call on pluralists and inclusivists in their debate with exclusivists to note the outright claim of this portion of Scripture that hearing the gospel is an assumed necessary preliminary to believing on Christ, presumed throughout to be the only Savior. Paul has previously in the same Epistle doused every hope of eternal life and righteousness before God apart from the redemptive work of Christ and faith alone as the way of human appropriation of the same.

Also the same should note (1) that the apostolic author regulates his doctrine by relevant Scriptures then existing ('For the scripture saith', v. 11, and 'as it is written', v. 15, 'For Isaiah says', v. 16). Where are the direct, positive affirmations of Scripture in arguments of the near-inclusivism of Alister McGrath, 'A Particularist View: A Post-Enlightenment Approach'?[28] The same is to be asked of Clark H. Pinnock, whose arguments for 'An Inclusivist View' rest on inferences not derived from the truly relevant texts cited here.[29] (2) The exclusive claims for Christ and the necessity of hearing the gospel in this passage are an important support for the author's appeal for assistance in a project of missionary evangelism proposed later in the Epistle.[30] One can hardly imagine anyone holding withered exclusivist convictions regarding the necessity of knowing 'the name' of Christ ever writing the book of Romans. I shall say more about this shortly.

---

26. Geivett and Phillips, in *Four Views on Salvation in a Pluralist World*, p. 236.
27. ibid., p. 237.
28. ibid., pp. 177–180.
29. ibid., pp. 95–123.
30. Robert D. Culver, *A Greater Commission: A Theology for World Missions* (Chicago: Moody Press, 1984 and reissued by WIPF & Stock, Eugene, OR, 2001), pp. 119–131.

Acts 4:12 'And there is salvation in no one else; for there is no other name under heaven that has been given among men by which we must be saved' (NASB).

Peter, in the temple court, had just performed the first apostolic miracle (Acts 3:1-11) in 'the *name* [emphasis added] of Jesus Christ [Messiah] of Nazareth' (v. 6). He had addressed the crowd of Jews attracted by the healing, not only stating that 'his *name*' had made the miracle happen but that Jesus was the Messiah of Israel's hope and of scriptural prophecy. He had previously identified Jesus as the promised Messiah (Acts 2:36). Then having been arrested and haled before the Jewish court, the court inquired 'By what power or by what *name* [emphasis added] did you do this?' (Acts 4:7). This is the setting of Peter's response to the court's inquiry – a response for which 'the Holy Spirit' filled him. It was no mere human testimony, for God had borne witness by raising Jesus from the dead (Acts 3:13-18). (I am addressing readers for whom divine testimony is both possible and important.) He proceeded not only to declare, 'by the name of Jesus Christ of Nazareth... whom God raised from the dead' did the miracle take place, but further: 'there is salvation in no one else' (v. 12). Let us focus on v. 12 and note how 'particularistic' it really is.

1. 'Jesus Christ of Nazareth', is the One who saves. Before a Jewish audience Peter, by the Holy Spirit, produced a summary interpretation of the Old Testament and of Jewish history. All the weight of hope and prophecy of 'the coming one' says Jesus is the Christ, the Son of Man, Suffering Servant, Son of God, Son of David, the Seed of Abraham through whom not only Israel but all the families of the earth would be blessed. There are not two of Him, nor a multitude of Immanuels, Avatars, etc. Only one. 'Are you the one who is to come?' (Matt. 11:3) was the Jewish question and 'salvation is from the Jews' (John 4:22) was a limitation defined by Jesus Himself.

2. 'The name'. The Bible nowhere hints that salvation is available through 'natural light', or, hints or surmises of reflective minds. Rather salvation is made available through announcement of 'the Name'. Peter and John (cf. Acts 3, 4) knew the names of the gods and saviors of the religions of their time – as did Paul at Mars Hill. Yet they insist that the biblical revelation that terminated on One named Jesus of Nazareth describes the only authentic Way, that the God who saves is the 'God of Abraham, the God of Isaac, and the God of Jacob' (Acts 3:13).

Space fails here to bring all the weight of the thinking of the people of the Bible and theology derived from it, to the importance of 'the Name' here and in many parts of Scripture. To curse the name was to be promptly punished by death (Lev. 24:11-23). On the other hand all the energy that flowed into the crippled man when he was healed is also connected to the One in whose *name* he was healed and the 'God who raised him from the dead'. There is 'no other name under heaven given among men whereby we must be saved'. This seems in context to be a *proclaimed* name, a name not simply pronounced as in an incantation or magical formula, but with explanation, that is to say, the gospel. 'Jesus Christ' and 'the name' are interchanged sometimes (Acts 5:41; 9:34; 3 John 7). I cite Geivett and Phillips:

> Philip identifies the gospel expressly with 'the name of Jesus Christ' (Acts 8:12, 35). Paul's vocation is to carry Jesus' name to Gentiles as well as to Jews (Acts 9:15; cf. 9:27). Indeed he indicates a definite preference for conducting his ministry among those who did not know the name of Christ, as though it is urgent that this name be known as a condition for salvation (Rom. 15:20)... the persecutors of the early church properly and routinely associated the message of salvation preached by the church with 'the name of Jesus' (Acts 4:17-30; 5:28-33, 40; 26:9).[31]

These authors conclude 'that "name" refers to the focus of God's universal redemptive plan in the person and work of Jesus Christ, who must be the object of *explicit* faith by those who want to be saved'.[32] We shall return to this thought.

The first occurrence of 'believe on the name' in the New Testament follows the first miracle performed by Jesus, His first cleansing of the temple and His performance of miracles at the Passover during the feast, viz. 'Many believed on his name'. This expression, 'into the name', has Jewish (not Hellenistic) origin.[33] Further, 'To believe in His name' (John 2:23), says Bietendorf, 'is to believe in his Messianic mission, to believe in Him as the Christ, as the only begotten Son of God, 3:18.' This belief, Bietendorf adds, arises in response to proofs of His power, manifesting

---

31. Geivett and Phillips, in *Four Views on Salvation in a Pluralist World*, p. 232.
32. ibid., p. 232.
33. Bietendorf in *Theological Dictionary of the New Testament* vol. v, ed. G. Kittel and G. Frederich, trans. G. W. Bromiley (Grand Rapids, MI: Eerdmans, 1964–1976), art. '*onoma*', p. 275.

'God's power in His acts'.[34] This only samples the evidence of Scripture that saving faith comes in response to reliable information about who Christ is and what He came to do. As demonstrated in chapter 2, salvation is conveyed by a message.

There is no such information furnished by 'natural light', only by authentic revelation. It is important that, *from the standpoint of Scripture*, *apokalupsis* (revelation) is a specially divinely caused event, not an inference drawn from nature or a surmise of the thoughtful mind. Strictly speaking, 'general revelation' is an oxymoron. According to Romans 16:25, 26, Paul's 'gospel and the preaching of Jesus Christ' was a 'mystery that was kept secret for long ages' but now in Paul's own time became a revealed mystery through the prophetic writings and only then 'made known to all nations'.

It seems clear to this reader of the Bible that 'the nations' knew nothing implicit or explicit about 'the name' by faith in whom and in no other way, they might be saved. This is the way the common run of believers have usually understood the breathless expectancy of the pious remnant of true believers at the time of the Advent (Mary, Zacharias, Elizabeth, Simeon and Anna [Luke 1, 2]. Even our hymns say the same.

Romans 16:25, 26.

From Paul's point of view, reliable information about salvation through Christ was not transparent even to the people of the Old Testament. If partially opaque to the Hebrew contemporaries of Moses and the prophets, then the heathen world was more seriously deprived. The nativity hymn has it right that until after Christ came the world was 'in sin and darkness lying'. The message of salvation was simply not generally available.

I refer to Paul's closing words of the Epistle to the Romans. The Greek text is very difficult, yet the translators of the Revised Standard Version (1946) seem to have it right and I cite the verses with little further comment.

> Now to him who is able to strengthen you according to my gospel and the preaching of Jesus Christ, according to the revelation of the mystery which was kept secret for long ages but is now disclosed and through the prophetic writings is made known to all nations, according to the command of the eternal God, to bring about the obedience of faith (Rom. 16:25, 26 RSV).

The word 'nations' in this passage is the plural of *ethnos* often translated 'gentiles' or 'heathen'. Depending on context (modern pluralist sensitivities notwithstanding) either of these translations may be appropriate. In the just-cited passage, heathen – the nations as alienated from God and 'without God in the world' – would not be inappropriate. The saving gospel, according to this passage was a mystery, not fully disclosed anywhere until disclosed through Christ, His apostles and evangelists. The world's peoples are to be brought to 'obedience to the faith' only through the apostolic channels.

The presupposition of the whole enterprise of Christian world evangelism has not been that there is a world full of the culturally deprived, or of the illiterate, or of the needy, as such, but of fallen humanity, estranged from their Creator and blind to their condition. They shall remain without hope, without Christ and without God in the world unless evangelized. The hymns of that enterprise composed since the explosion of Protestant evangelical missions at the end of the eighteenth century presuppose it. I cite a few lines:

> 'What though spicy breezes/ Blow soft o'er Ceylon's isle;/
> Though every prospect pleases,/ And only man is vile?/
> In vain with lavish kindness/ The gifts of God are strown;/
> *The heathen in his blindness*/ Bows down to wood and stone.'
> (Lowell Mason, 1792–1872, *From Greenland's Icy Mountains*).

'Are the heathen lost?' – the perennial question seems to be answered, Yes, unless and until they hear and 'obey', to use Paul's occasional term for 'believe' the gospel. The destiny Paul contemplated for those who do not come to the 'obedience of faith' is plain, but no less appalling on that account as the following text uniquely clarifies.

2 Thessalonians 1:5-10.

In this passage, for which space does not allow minute exegesis, Paul is comforting the new believers he had hurriedly left behind in the city now known as Salonika. They had recently suffered severe persecution from both Jews and Gentiles in their native city. In such a case even the martyrs in heaven justly call for vindication saying, 'O Sovereign

---

34. ibid.

Lord, holy and true, how long before you will judge and avenge our blood' (Rev. 6:10). Paul in a certain sense answers their question in his comfort of the Thessalonian Christians. He says God will grant them 'rest' and explains the time of this vindication. It will be:

> [W]hen the Lord Jesus is revealed from heaven with his mighty angels in flaming fire, inflicting vengeance on those who do not know God and on those who do not obey the gospel of our Lord Jesus. ['How shall they believe in him of whom they have not heard?'] They will suffer the punishment of eternal destruction, away from the presence of the Lord and from the glory of his might, when he comes on that day to be glorified in his saints, and to be marvelled at among all who have believed (2 Thess. 1:5-10).

Let the reader take this theology of vindication as well as of salvation seriously. Let the newly minted theological modifiers of evangelical theology include this text in their supposed new 'paradigm'. Their argument seems to be not with an outmoded conservative model of evangelicalism but with plain Scripture teaching.

This chapter began with warnings against speculation based in curiosity about matters on which God has not spoken in Scripture. I close it with insistence that we swallow whole what God has clearly revealed. If there are exceptions or qualifications to be made, let us wait for further revelation rather than try to tell God what He ought to have said so we could sleep better at night.

The next chapter will address the question raised earlier in this chapter: May Christ be encountered in a saving way, without being specifically identified, in other religions?

20
Is Christ Present in Non-Christian Religions?

May Christ be encountered in a saving way, without being specifically identified, in other religions? To sharpen the point of the question, granting that salvation is through Christ alone and that the gospel of Christ must be heard to be believed, is it possible to hear this message in non-Christian religions? To assert that Christ may be encountered for salvation in other religions is currently sometimes called 'inclusivism'.

This is not the same as 'pluralism', exemplified by such writers as John Hick (contemporary), Ernst Troeltsch (a century ago) and Friederich Schliermacher (two centuries ago) which says that there are many ways to salvation (however defined), each valid.

There are few if any who take the Bible seriously who agree. Leslie Newbigin spoke as an aggressive, articulate evangeliser from within the World Council of Churches. He well said on the last page of his book, *The Gospel in a Pluralist Society*:

> As we confess Jesus as Lord in a pluralist society, and as the Church grows through the coming of people from many cultural and religious traditions to faith in Christ, we are enabled to learn more of the length and breadth and height of the love of God (Eph. 3:14-19) than we can in a monochrome society. But we must reject the ideology of pluralism. We must reject the invitation to live in society where everything is subjective and relative, a society which has abandoned the belief that truth can be known and has settled for... 'truth for you' but not truth for me. For one thing, I doubt whether such a society can long sustain its integrity in the face of those who have a firm commitment to some vision of truth.[1]

Newbigin was referring to the rising, strident assertions of Islam – the Revolution in Iran, etc. – which he foresaw as exploiting the self-inflicted multiculturalism of the West. We see that more plainly after 11 September 2001. Newbigin made the same point at greater length in 'Religion for the Marketplace', a chapter in *Christian Uniqueness Reconsidered: The Myth of a Pluralistic Theology of Religions*.[2]

Biblical Christians of every persuasion have known and contended all along that multiculturalism (pluralism) in matters of religion is impossible. The Scriptures treated earlier in the last previous chapter (the history of the whole Bible; John 3:16-18 and 36; John 14:6; Acts 4:12; Rom. 10:4-17) are well known and convincing. The current crop

---

1. Leslie Newbigin, *The Gospel in a Pluralist Society* (World Council of Churches Publication Geneva and Grand Rapids, MI: Eerdmans Publ., 1989), p. 244.
2. Leslie Newbigin, 'Religion for the Marketplace', in *Christian Uniqueness Reconsidered: The Myth of a Pluralistic Theology of Religions*, ed. Gavin D'Costa (Maryknoll: Orbis Books, 1990), pp. 135–148.

of pluralists have every one of them abandoned all the unique claims of Christ and of the Bible as both truthful and of binding authority as well or they would not be pluralists. Some honest critical scholars outside orthodoxy see this plainly as, for example, the well-known John B. Cobb. In an essay, 'Beyond Pluralism', he points out that though the teachings of Buddhism, Confucianism, even Communism and Christianity, overlap somewhat in limited areas, they are thoroughly incompatible in what may be of central importance to each. It is not clear, he says, that they even share a central essence of some kind which might rightly be called 'religion'. He closes:

> I see no a priori reason to assume that religion has an essence or that the great religion traditions are well understood as religious, that is, as traditions for which being religious is the central goal. I certainly see no empirical evidence in favour of this view. I see only a scholarly habit and the power of language to mislead. I call for a pluralism that allows each religious tradition to define its own nature and purposes and the role of religious elements within it.[3]

Theology of the newspaper pundits and commentators, as well as organizers of gatherings to get the support of 'religion', for some cause or other assume there to be some essence, some valid core which is the same in every religion. Cobb had this to say about people who cherish this delusion:

> [A]mong those who assume that religion has an essence there is no consensus as to what the essence may be. Even individual scholars often change their mind. The variation is still greater when scholars represent diverse religious traditions. Yet among many of them the assumption that there is an essence continues unshaken in the midst of uncertainty as to what the essence is.[4]

Back more precisely to our topic – Granting all the exclusive claims of Christ and the Bible, may not God reveal Christ 'incognito' in other religions? Perhaps somewhat as Jesus did when on earth to the blind man of John chapter 9 – only after an interval of time saying, 'It is he who is speaking to you', i.e. Messiah, the Savior, 'Behold your God' (Isa. 40:9; John 9:37). By extrapolation from Matthew 25:40, 45 where Jesus is said to identify Himself with the poor, and the saved with those who show mercy on the poor as fit for heaven, this idea is sometimes promoted, as by Clark Pinnock.[5] Almost as an aside Dr Pinnock puts the position of 'inclusivism' quite plainly:

> Everyone must eventually pass through Jesus to reach the Father, but there is more than one path [other religions] for arriving at this place. Is this not the stuff of Christian testimony – how one came to know him? One can get to that place from many points on the compass. All the paths that lead to God end up at Jesus, but they do not all start with him.[6]

Dr Pinnock's chapter runs parallel to his 1992 book.[7] Both the book and the essay cited above represent 'musings' as noted by Alister McGrath[8] and are characterized by 'vagueness'.[9] Pinnock sometimes tries to speak as one of the evangelical crowd and about as often from an assumed superior position somewhere in space where he makes belittling comments on the fundamentalists. This has been the case with Dr Clark Pinnock for as long as I have known him – and for several years his office door was about six feet from mine. He has also during that time changed from a Calvinist posture to an Arminian posture, and from a radical leftist activism to a more conservative social outlook.[10] Hence his musings and wandering thoughts shall not be treated at length here. With some searching one can find that he argues for possible salvation (maybe) in other religions from 1) the presence of God in the whole world, 2) divine sovereignty, 3) the alleged saintliness of many non-Christians, 4) 'God's love' said to be the essence of the Holy Trinity, and 5) inferences from many Scripture texts and stories that do not relate to the subject. His 'essay' soars with a polemic that is 'frequently vague', employing analogies also frequently vague.[11]

---

3. John B. Cobb, Jr., 'Beyond Pluralism', in *Christian Uniqueness Reconsidered*, p. 84.
4. ibid., p. 84.
5. Clark Pinnock, 'An Inclusive View', in *Four Views on Salvation in a Pluralist World*, ed. D. L. Okholm and T. R. Phillips (Grand Rapids, MI: Zondervan, 1996), p. 119.
6. ibid.
7. Clark Pinnock, *A Wideness in God's Mercy: The Finality of Jesus Christ in a World of Religions* (Grand Rapids, MI: Zondervan Publ., 1992).
8. Alister McGrath in *Four Views on Salvation in a Pluralist World*, in Okholm and Phillips, op. cit., p. 132.
9. Alister McGrath in *Four Views on Salvation in a Pluralist World*, in Okholm and Phillips, op. cit., p. 133.
10. There are many teaching Bible and doctrine in theological schools today who bypassed a seminary education on the way to their doctorates and some were allowed to omit systematic study of theology. Perhaps Dr Pinnock is one of them. Perhaps this explains why he has had trouble making up his mind about a long list of theological, social and political questions. He has discovered, embraced and discarded several systems of thought on his intellectual and religious pilgrimage. He has related the details in somewhat entertaining fashion in several venues. See Clark H. Pinnock, 'A Political Pilgrimage', *Eternity* magazine, October, 1984, pp. 26–29 and an essay in Ronald B. Nash's symposium on *Liberation Theology* (Milford: Mott Media, 1984), 260 pages.

A sarcastic remark about German philosophers might apply to the arguments of those who as believers in the plenary inspiration of the Bible find evidence in the Bible for ways to Christ in non-biblical religions:

> We Germans suffer from no lack of systematic books. No nation in the world surpasses us in the faculty of deducing from a couple of definitions whatever conclusions we please, in most fair and logical order.[12]

Gerald R. McDermott is a quite different writer whose respect for fellow 'evangelicals' is plain and who sets out to find evidence of saving revelation in other religions. He defines his terms and states his evangelical theological presuppositions. Though I appreciate his frankness I do not share his admiration for Karl Barth's method and theology and think he finds more support for his idea in Jonathan Edwards than is there. At the end he finds no evidence that there is saving divine revelation in these religions but argues:

> that there is both biblical and theological grounding… for their notion of learning about God from non-Christians… I have found in the religions confirmation of familiar Christian doctrine, confirmation that enables us to see those doctrines with new vigour or application.[13]

The author teaches at Roanoke College, Salem, VA.

Dr McDermott is not likely to be followed by many believers in search for what they already know in potentially dangerous sources. He himself does not recommend his excursion into these religions for immature Christians.

Salvation of the Unevangelized in Historical Protestant Theology.

It is commonly said and written that the sixteenth-century Reformers had no interest in evangelizing any one, only in re-establishing a sound church with truly biblical doctrines. Granting that the first generations following 1517 had their hands full with these tasks and staying alive long enough to do them, it is not quite true that reaching the lost was not of interest to them. Their interest in 'the lost' was first in the lost near at hand who were perceived rightly to be trusting in 'ordinances' (see Epistles of Paul to Galatians and Colossians) and ceremonies, rather than in the unmerited favour of God who saves wholly by grace on the occasion of faith in Christ, a faith which comes only with exposure to truth. The Reformers were not unlike Paul and the other apostles who went first (and in Peter's case at least) almost always to 'the lost sheep of the house of Israel'. Further, on the side of the Roman Church, Columbus thought of himself as a missionary to the 'Indians'[14] and ere long the Puritans of the seventeenth century were motivated not only by desire to set up a commonwealth where they could raise their families Christianly, but perceived a part of their 'errand to the wilderness' to be to evangelize the natives of the New World.[15]

There has been frequent cautious acknowledgment from earliest times of the possibility that some who never hear the gospel from any human sources nevertheless do learn of Him and are saved. Most orthodox Lutherans have not accepted this but it has been steadily affirmed by leading Calvinist-Reformed, though with cautious reserve.

Luther asserted that man has the moral capability to produce a kind of righteousness that meets the demands of civil law. This righteousness preserves civil order and makes the world go around and Luther praised men for it. This kind of righteousness is to be found among 'heathen' and 'Turks' (i.e. Muslims). It was the virtue taught and,

---

11. Phillips and Geivett, in *Four Views on Salvation in a Pluralist World*, pp. 133–139.
12. W. G. T. Shedd, *Dogmatic Theology ii* (Grand Rapids, MI: Zondervan Publ., 1969), p. 703.
13. Gerald R. McDermott, *Can Evangelicals Learn From World Religions: Jesus, Revelation and Religious Traditions* (Downers Grove, IL: InterVarsity Press, 2000), pp. 207, 208.
14. I have been impressed by materials furnished by Peter Marshall and David Manuel in their book, *The Light and the Glory* (Old Tappan: Fleming Revell, 1977). Chapter one 'Christ Bearers' pp. 29–48 and page 17. They later document the horrible atrocities against the Indians of the New World but give full credit to the well-known zeal of Roman Catholic missionaries to evangelize the Indians and their relative success. *Death Comes to the Archbishop*, a novel by Willa Cather, illustrates the movement. What is not so well known is that their missions extended along the coast of the Gulf eastward into what is now our Deep South.
15. I am unable at the moment to document this except to refer to Perry Miller's volume *Errand Into the Wilderness* (Cambridge: Harvard U. Press, 1956). A missionary motive was not primary in the Puritan Plantation in New England, but it was cited as a reason for the colonizing of the New World. Very early, consistent effort was made to evangelize neighboring Indians, with some success. There were Indian members of the colony churches and separate Indian churches and communities of Indians. One of these proved decisive in assisting the colonists to survive the massacres of whites in King Philip's War. Marshall and Manuel in *The Light and the Glory* describe and document this assertion. Jonathan Edwards, for example, for an interval in his career served as resident missionary pastor of a small congregation of Indians and his daughter's fiancé, David Brainerd, served valiantly in an effort to evangelize Indians of New Jersey, a frontier territory of the time.

to some degree, found in Aristotle and Cicero. But this will not stand up in the court of heaven for God judges by higher standards (Rom. 2 and 4).[16] To this day strict Lutheran theology castigates 'Calvinists' for their opening up other possibilities for salvation outside the regular course of hearing a 'preacher'.[17]

The Westminster Confession, reflecting opinion going back to Calvin himself, states:

> Since there is no other way of salvation than that revealed in the gospel, and since in the divinely established and *ordinary method of grace* [emphasis added] faith cometh by hearing the word of God, Christ hath commissioned his church to go into all the world, etc.[18]

The language implies clearly that there may possibly be *extra*-ordinary methods whereby grace can operate.

At this point it would be fruitful, space allowing, to introduce all of W. G. T. Shedd's rundown of the subject over seven pages wherein the bulk of historical footnotes in fine print exceeds the main text's bulk. He begins with the following sentences:

> It does not follow… that because God is not obliged to offer pardon to the unevangelized heathen, either here or hereafter, therefore no unevangelized heathen are pardoned. The electing mercy of God reaches to the heathen. It is not the doctrine of the Church that the entire mass of the pagans, without exception, have gone down to endless impenitence and death. That some unevangelized men are saved, in the present life, *by an extraordinary exercise of redeeming grace in Christ* [emphasis added], has been the hope and belief of Christendom. It was the hope and belief of the elder Calvinists, as it is of the later.[19]

One of the earliest 'elder Calvinists', converted by reading writings of the first line of Reformers – and a very strict one who early opposed the Lutheran doctrine of ubiquity – was Hieronymus Zanchius (1516–1590). After remarking that many nations had never heard the gospel he asserted: 'It is not indeed improbable that some individuals in their unenlightened countries may belong to the election of grace, and the habit [inward heart disposition involving repentance] of faith may be wrought [by the Spirit] in them.'[20] Shedd also cites the Second Swiss Confession which after the remark that the ordinary mode of salvation is by the instrumentality of the written Word, adds: '*Agnoscionies, interim, deum illuminare posse homines etiam sine externe ministerio, quo et quando velit: id quod ejus potentae est.*'[21] (I translate, 'Meanwhile, we acknowledge it to be possible for God to illuminate men even without an outward ministry, at what place and whatever time he wills: this is that which is His power.')

A. A. Hodge carefully distinguishes this alleged power and disposition of God to reveal Himself specially as He wills from the Roman doctrine of implicit faith (lately expounded in Vatican II canons) by which a man is said to exercise faith in a truth of which he knows nothing. For example, if one believes the church's local priest he embraces all the priest and his church stand for.[22] Shedd was a zealous preacher as well as a supporter of missionary evangelism. He did not allow anything to obscure the duty and privilege to evangelize, saying:

> This extraordinary work of the Holy Spirit is mentioned by the Redeemer [Shedd has referred to Matt. 8:11; Luke 13:30; Matt. 8:5-10 and reference to the heathen saints Ruth, Tamar, Rahab; Isa. 66:2; Matt. 5:3; Matt. 21:31] to illustrate the sovereignty of God in the exercise of mercy, not to guide His church in their evangelistic labour. His command is, to 'preach the gospel to every creature'…The law of missionary effort is, that 'faith cometh by hearing, and hearing by the word of God', Rom. 10:17.[23]

Calvinists have Calvin himself to thank for this outlook. In comment on Romans 10:14, 'how shall they call on him of whom they have not heard' he wrote:

> No other word has he mentioned here but that which is preached, because it is *the ordinary mode* [emphasis added] which the Lord has appointed for conveying his word. But were any on this account to contend God cannot transfer to men the knowledge of himself, except by the instrumentality of preaching, we deny that to

---

16. See Paul Althaus, *The Theology of Martin Luther*, trans. R. C. Schultz (Philadelphia, PA: Fortress Press, 1966), pp. 143, 144.
17. Francis Pieper, *Christian Dogmatics i* (St. Louis: Concordia Publ., 1950–1957), pp. 125–127; Peiper, *Christian Dogmatics iii* , pp. 247, 248.
18. *Westminster Shorter Catechism in Confession of Faith of the Presbyterian Church in the U.S. together with The Larger Catechism and The Shorter Catechism* (Richmond: John Knox Press, 1861, 1944), chap. x 'of the Gospel', para. iv.
19. Shedd, *Dogmatic Theology ii*, p. 706.
20. ibid., p. 708.
21. ibid., p. 707.
22. A. A. Hodge, *Outlines of Theology* (1860, repr. Grand Rapids, MI: Eerdmans, 1957), pp. 467, 468.
23. Shedd, *Dogmatic Theology ii*, pp. 710, 711.

teach this was the Apostle's intention; for he had only in view *the ordinary dispensation of God* [emphasis added], and did not intent to prescribe a law for the distribution of his grace... But as Paul does not treat here the lawful call of anyone, it would be superfluous to speak at large on the subject. It is enough for us to bear this only in mind, that the gospel does not fall like rain from the clouds, but is brought by the hand of man wherever it is sent from above.[24]

Likewise, Sir Norman Anderson, in one of the most thoroughly informed and biblical volumes on this subject cites cases where God brought saving knowledge to those whom God's Spirit had brought a genuine effective call without previously being evangelized.[25]

This old concession shares some texts and thought with recent 'inclusivists', some of whom outrightly reject orthodox understanding of Trinitarian inner relationships and divine attributes (as Clark Pinnock and John Sanders) but none of their heterodoxy and spirit. A competent theologian of Reformed pedigree and conviction courteously but firmly points this out very recently. I refer to the last chapter of Robert E. Reymond's *Systematic Theology*, 'Downgrade trends in Contemporary Evangelical Eschatology'.[26] I shall reserve my own further remarks on this pesky diversion for the department of last things, or eschatology.

The Project of Christian Apologetics Is to Defend the Exclusive Claims of Christ.

The second-century Christian apologists (Aristides, Justin, Tatian, Athenagoras, *et al*) made a poor beginning from our point of view. They made what they deemed to be necessary concessions in order to make their point that Christians deserved to be tolerated. Irenaeus (*Against Heresies*) was concerned mainly to refute stupid but attractive heresies, though he did not shrink from stating and defending the sole existence of the one God of Scripture and of His incarnate Son the only Savior.[27]

Properly the task of Christian Apologetics has been precisely to defend the claim that Christ is indeed the one and only Savior of the world. His certification as such by His resurrection from the dead is paramount in the apostolic writings of the New Testament and in every sermon recorded in the book of Acts.

In a recent, excellent article approaching the question of this chapter and with essentially the same data, Klaas Runia points out that higher critics of the Gospels who deny the resurrection of the 'flesh' of Jesus have little to say to those who will listen. 'For a Reformed church and a Reformed Theologian this view is utterly unacceptable.'[28] For such theologians, 'The resurrection of Jesus on the third day after his death is not an "idea" that one can accept or reject.'[29] He goes on to show how the resurrection verifies 'the miracle of reconciliation' by His death on the cross and 'the miracle of the incarnation'.[30] The same points have been made by Christian missionaries in their daily work, by pastors in their pulpits and about every quotable orthodox author since Irenaeus in his 'Against Heresies' 1,800 years ago.

In view of these strictures against even the cautious 'wider hope' of some Reformed theologians, I share Klaas Runia's reluctance even fully to endorse the historic Reformed concessions toward special cases wherein God may have revealed Himself in a saving way to founders and followers of other religions. We know God apparently savingly revealed Himself without any presently human messenger at least once – to Abraham (Gen. 12:1 ff.; cf. Acts 7:1, 2).

Herman Bavinck is ambivalent: 'Even Hendrik Kraemer, who regarded all other religions as 'endeavors for self-redemption', wrote in his last book that he did not mean to say that 'the other religions are erroneous in their totality and in every respect'.[31] Another missiologist, J. Verkuyl, is quoted as speculating that God may have been involved somewhat in the writing of the *Vedas* and even the *Koran*.[32] Runia concludes – and I with him:

---

24. Calvin, *Commentaries on the Epistle of Paul to the Romans*, trans. John Owen (Edinburgh, 1849), pp. 398, 399.
25. Sir Norman Anderson, *Christianity and World Religious* (Leicester: InterVarsity, 1980), chap. 5.
26. Robert E. Reymond, *A New Systematic Theology of the Christian Faith* (Nashville: Thomas Nelson, 1998), pp. 1067–1093.
27. Irenaeus, *Against Heresies* ii, 28; iii.1–5.
28. Klaas Runia, 'Why Christianity of All Religions?' *Evangelical Review of Theology*, vol. 22, no. 3 (July 1998), p. 256.
29. ibid., p. 256.
30. ibid., pp. 257–260.
31. ibid., p. 262.
32. ibid., pp. 262, 263.

I am not so sure whether we have the right to be so expansive, but I do know that if it is possible that people of other faiths may be saved, they most certainly will not be saved by their own religiosity, by their own religious experiences and rites, but only because the Spirit of Christ was active in their lives and because by his work the secret of Christ became manifest in them too.[33]

Members of the Evangelical Theological Society have been close observers of the development of the 'inclusivist' view among a small number of members who have published articles in the *Journal of the Evangelical Theological Society* and lengthy books reviewed in the *Journal*. Though one hesitates to generalize in such matters, it seems fair to observe that the same theologians who have been rather stridently promoting their 'inclusivism' have also promoted a reduction in our understanding of God's essential (i.e. of His being) attributes of omniscience and omnipotence. In order not to extend these remarks to greater length I refrain here from providing the names, though some of them appear earlier in this chapter.

Addendum.

Finally, since completing the manuscript I have read once more a sermon by B. B. Warfield entitled 'False Religions and the True' – twenty-one pages in length. In it he calls to our attention that Paul at Athens addressed the most 'religious' city in the Greek world. There were gods and goddesses to be worshiped scattered in abundance throughout the city. The devotion of the people was far from assuring him that some might have been led to saving repentance and faith. To the contrary, their zeal for religion greatly offended him as an affront to the true God who is repelled rather than approached by their zeal. Though all people have an innate impulse to worship, it takes a course at a diameter (180 degrees) away from the one true God. Up to the coming of the 'God approved' Man, God let the nations go on in their ignorance, '*but now*' commands them to repent of their sins and acknowledge the One true God and His Man through whom alone there is forgiveness. Further there is full 'assurance' (proof) of the utterly valid authority of the demand for repentance in that God raised the Man from the dead, the one who is the Savior.

Paul used the word '*deisidaimonesterous*' (more fear of gods than other Greeks) to describe the Athenians' religion. They believed that there is a universal something in every religion (god, goddess, etc.) which might lead to blessedness here and hereafter. Warfield closed with an appeal to the hearer who might have such a multiculturist, inclusivist opinion:

> How easy it is to mistake the currents of mere natural religious feelings, that flow up and down in the soul, for signs that it is well with us in the sight of God. Happy the man who is born with a deep sensitive religious nature! But shall that purely natural endowment save him?.... Not because you are sensitive and easily moved to devotion, not because your sense of divine things is profound or lofty; not because you are like the Athenians, by nature 'divinity-fearing'; but because, when the word of the Lord is brought to you, and Jesus Christ is revealed in your soul, under the prevailing influence of the Holy Ghost, you embrace Him with a hearty faith – cast yourself upon his almighty grace for salvation, and turning from your sins, enter into a life of obedience to Him – can you judge yourself a Christian…. How instructive that when Paul himself preached in '*deisidaimonistic*' Athens, where religiosity ran riot, no church seems to have been founded. We have only the meagre result recorded that 'there were some men that clave to him and believed, among whom also was Dionysius, the Areopagete and a woman named Damaris, and others along with them'. The natively religious are not, therefore, nearer to the kingdom of God.[34]

Harold A. Netland, who currently teaches at Trinity Evangelical Divinity School, directly addressed religious pluralism in his book, *Dissonant Voices: Religious Pluralism and the Question of Truth*. Growing up in the home of Christian missionaries in Japan, he early faced the problem of religious pluralism: all religions possess religious validity. He proposes that this proposition ought to be addressed in detail. Further, taking his doctoral programme under guidance of the notorious John Hick, he is equipped to know what the problems are and how modern scholarship addresses the problem. So he patiently traces out the beliefs and resultant practices of four major

---

33. Bruce Nichols, writing in the same issue of *Evangelical Review of Theology*, vol. 22, no. 3 (July 1988), 'Is Jesus the Only Way to Go?', p. 242, cites what he thinks may have been such a case in the story of Bilquis Sheikta, a high-born Muslim and influential lady of Pakistan. For it remains true for all times and all people: 'There is salvation in no one else, for there is no other name under heaven given among men by which they must be saved.' (Runia, in *ERT*, vol. 22, no. 3), p. 263.

34. B. B. Warfield, 'False Religions and the True' in *Biblical and Theological Studies* (Philadelphia, PA: Presbyterian & Reformed Publ., 1952), p. 519.

religious traditions: Hinduism, Buddhism, Islam and Shintoism with regard to three basic questions which religions address. These are: 1) What is the nature of the religious ultimate? 2) What is the nature of the human predicament? 3) What is the nature of salvation/enlightenment/liberation?[35]

Though I cannot review his book here, Netland shows not with broad strokes of pen but in detail how these four religions, while in some broad aspect do have some similarity, in details of central beliefs and practice are at odds with one another. He is always reserved in statement. His first summary contains these statements:

> The common assumption that all religions ultimately are teaching the same things in their own culturally conditional ways is *primie facie* untenable. Not only are they not all saying the same things, but the particular issues addressed in the various religions are not necessarily the same.[36]

Then citing W. A. Christian's book, *Oppositions of Religious Doctrines: A Study in the Logic of Dialogue Among Religions*, Netland adds:

> Christian says that the recent popular views that beliefs of the major religions are all mutually consistent and that all religions say basically the same thing 'seem very implausible and certainly much current talk in aid of these views is loose and sentimental'. Surely the burden of proof is with those who would maintain the contrary.[37]

As participant in the enterprise of Christian missionary tactics, Netland does not shrink from acknowledging failures to extend the practitioners of other religions and the culture the respect due them as human and bearers of the divine image but he goes on to show that pluralism is in demonstrable ways inconsistent with facts.

The notion of pluralistic equivalency of all religions first became prevalent not in twentieth-century liberalism but in the Enlightenment or Age of Reason of the eighteenth century. It is ironic that the eighteenth century which at its end produced the modern Protestant Christian missionary movement also produced the notion that all religious doctrines are true for someone somewhere. 'As nothing is more irreligious than to demand general uniformity in mankind, so nothing is more unchristian than to seek uniformity in religion.'[38]

The story of the rise of unbelief as 'Enlightenment' has been told many times – perhaps best by Reinhold Niebuhr in chapters I–IV of the first volume of his book *The Nature and Destiny of Man*.[39]

Harold O. J. Brown specifically brought the story up to date in *'The Heresy of the Enlightenment'*, chapter 19 of his book, *Heresies*. It remains to be said – what seems most of the time to be forgotten – that the apostasy that says all religions are equally (or almost so) true also asserts or implies all religions are equally false.

---

35. Harold A. Netland, *Dissonant Voices: Religious Pluralism and the Question of Truth* (Grand Rapids, MI: Eerdmans, 1991), p. 36.
36. ibid., p. 111.
37. ibid.
38. Friederich Schleiermacher, *On Religion: Speeches to its Cultured Despisers*, as cited by Harold O. J. Brown in *Heresies* (Garden City, NY: Doubleday, 1984, repr. Peabody, MA: Hendrickson Publishers, 2000), p. 395.
39. Reinhold Niebuhr, *The Nature and Destiny of Man: A Christian Interpretation* vol. i (New York: Charles Scribner's Sons, 1941, 1961).

PART 1
THEOLOGY PROPER
Introduction and Doctrine of God

PART 2
ANTHROPOLOGY
Man as Created

PART 3
HAMARTIOLOGY
Man as Sinner

PART 4
CHRISTOLOGY
Person and Work of Christ

PART 5
SOTERIOLOGY
Salvation Applied

PART 6
ECCLESIOLOGY
Church Local and Universal

PART 7
ESCHATOLOGY
Last Things, Personal and Universal

BIBLIOGRAPHY

SCRIPTURE INDEX

GENERAL INDEX

1
The Critical Importance of the Doctrine of the Church

The purpose of this opening chapter is to convince the reader of two propositions: (1) the *church* is of supreme importance to God; and (2) the *doctrine of the church* is of critical importance to a correct understanding of Christianity, to a healthy spiritual life of every believer and to the propagation of Christianity.

I. The Importance of the Church to God.

Paul's Vigorous Assertions.

1. The preeminence of the church in God's scheme of things could hardly be stated more vigorously than in several texts from the Epistle to the Ephesians. With moving rhetorical power Paul says in the closing verses of chapter 1 that God (the Father) has designated Christ as Lord of all creation 'and appointed him to be head over everything for the church, which is his body, the fullness of him who fills everything in every way' (Eph. 1:22, 23 NIV).

Later he goes on to say that though God's justice and wisdom in providence may have been 'hidden for ages in God who created all things,' it is His purpose that 'through the church the manifold wisdom of God might now be made known to the principalities and powers in the heavenly places' (Eph. 3:9, 10 RSV).

Further on, he says, the church was from eternity so cherished by the Son that He 'loved the church and gave himself up for her' (Eph. 5:25 NIV). As for the Holy Spirit's interest in the church, Paul explains that members of the church are 'sealed with the promised Holy Spirit' (Eph. 1:13), and that by virtue of Christ's reconciliation through that Spirit, we all have 'access… to the Father' (2:18), and that the Spirit is the spiritual presence in us that brings forth 'fruit… in all that is good and right and true' (5:9). In this way Paul's stately diction gives transcendent importance to the church.

As a supervisor of pastors Paul declared 'the church of the living God' to be nothing less than 'the household of God' and the 'pillar and buttress of truth' (1 Tim. 3:15). In such cases, if theologies are interested in 'truth,' they hardly dare ignore the importance of the church in God's system of theology.

2. At the present moment 'the assembly of the firstborn' has a prominent place in heaven where millions of her members dwell in 'the city of the living God, the heavenly Jerusalem' with 'angels,' 'God, the judge of all,' and 'the spirits of the righteous made perfect [O.T. saints?]' (see Heb 12:22-24). The church therefore, even in heaven, has a special place 'near to the heart of God' (to borrow a line from a hymn).

These texts become important to several aspects of the *doctrine* of the church. For they serve to emphasize the importance of the church, *as such*, to God and His plan of things. They also cause us to realize how important it is to understand what the church is, our place in it, as well as our responsibilities and privileges.

3. There are many other hints that the church is far more important among the facts of our faith and the teachings of biblical religion than unreflective readers of the Bible might suppose. Some of these facts are outstanding, suggesting why 'church' as doctrine has a special focus in the scheme of divine truths. The following are only selections out of the many.

The church has a very large place in the kingdom of Christ (of God, of heaven) as it develops from the Gospels through the Epistles and the Apocalypse. In that connection Paul claims that revelation of the peculiar nature of the church was a climax of special revelation, first made known fully to him and then to other Apostles (Eph. 3:1-5), and that the building of a church was the reason why Jesus chose and trained Apostles (Eph. 2:19-22). The church was a matter of growing revelation in the New Testament, which Jesus with great emotion first announced to Peter at Caesarea Philippi and enforced with some of the strongest language in the Bible (Matt. 16:18-20). The church of God is said to be 'our mother' (Gal. 4:26), giving biblical ground to the ancient dictum that 'outside the church there is no salvation.' In the last book of the Bible the risen, glorified Christ is seen holding the 'angels' of representative churches in His hands (a place of special care) and Himself standing in the midst of the 'candlesticks' of representative churches, advising, correcting, judging, warning and cheering them on to victory (Rev. 1–3).

4. These are impressive features of the church, thrilling to contemplate. Cantatas and oratorios have been composed on these themes to charm Christian audiences and capture the devotion of musicians 'at church.' Much more sobering are two further pieces of the picture to engage time, talent and even life itself. First, the present age between Pentecost and Second Advent is preeminently, in God's stewardship of the fullness of the ages of history, the period of world evangelism (Matt. 16:13-20; Eph. 1:10-30). It is to be a time of proclaiming redemption to every kindred, tongue, tribe and nation at great cost to Christians (that is, the church in the world) of every generation (Rev. 5:9-14, 21, 22). It is the time first indicated by Jesus' strong language: 'I will build my church, and the gates of hell shall not prevail against it' (Matt. 16:18). Second, the church itself is the sole vehicle of evangelism, nurture and instruction by which the program of church-building is to take place. Organized churches within the great church are the scene of this amazingly varied action whereby the church simply by being the church carries out God's redemptive providence for the present age.

This theological importance of the church is given powerful artistic statement in Samuel Stone's famous hymn lines:

> The church's one foundation
> Is Jesus Christ her Lord;
> She is His new creation
> By water and the word:
> From heaven He came and sought her
> To be His holy bride;
> With His own blood He bought her,
> And for her life He died.

II. The Importance of the Doctrine of the Church.

The doctrine of the church (ecclesiology) is also vigorously expressed and expounded in the New Testament. Definition of the nature of the church as found in the Bible must await later treatment. For the moment let us assume there is such a thing and that we all have a provisional, working understanding of what the church is.

1. The church has allegedly failed. The Saturday editions of the daily papers lament the failures of 'the church' with wearying regularity. 'The church' fails to be relevant to people's needs and lacks force in social action, they say in a thousand ways. Frequently some anti-religious critic from without the church or some spokesman within it will lay all the world's present problems with race, poverty, crime and moral decline at the door of the church. Some in the religious press have charged that the church has departed from biblical integrity as though there really was no authentic church in the world today.

Of course, if the church which is 'failing' is the one, holy, catholic and apostolic church of the ancient creeds and of the sublime perorations of Paul's letter to the Ephesians (Eph. 1:18-23; 2:18-22), then the heavens have come unstuck!

Some of the harshest judgments against the twentieth-century church arose in precisely those quarters one might least expect severe criticism. But when the World Council of Churches was only five years on its way, Emil Brunner, in a sincere effort to give some expert advice to the new pilots of the Good Ship *Oikoumenē* (World Council of Churches, organized in 1948 [leaders adopted the ancient sail-ship as a symbol of the World Church]), wrote in 1953:

> It is a... fact that dogmatists and church leaders often pay but small attention to the results of New Testament research, and are only too ready to bridge the gulf between then and now by a handy formula such as that of development or by appealing to the distinction between the visible and the invisible church, and thus give a false solution to this grave and distressing problem. But while many theologians and church leaders are able to quieten their consciences by such formulae, others are so much the more painfully aware of the disparity between the Christian fellowship of the apostolic age and our own 'churches' and cannot escape the impression that there may perhaps be something wrong with what we now call the church.[1]

From the Roman Catholic direction, Hans Küng, a very gifted writer and theologian, wrote several books in protest against what he conceived to be the nearly utter lack of integrity of his own church as the biblical church of Christ. If space allowed, one could easily introduce many even more severe indictments of the empirical, 'visible' church from Roman Catholic authors who, quite out of step with Roman Catholic history, of late have turned critical of their own organized communion.

2. Neglect and evasion of what seem to be the church's own organs of service, evangelism and instruction by some of its most active members calls for renewed thinking about this subject. The churches have normal channels for gathering and nurturing their youth, yet strong organizations of evangelical aegis not infrequently attract our youth away from 'church-sponsored' programs into other programs apparently authorized quite independently of what we understand to be churches. Missionary work, in homelands and foreign countries, revival and renewal movements, relief organizations, and publishing of Christian literature are fields where these organizations proliferate. We have even borrowed the Greek preposition para (meaning 'extra,' 'beside') to invent 'parachurch' as a name for them. Are these parachurch entities competitors with the church? Are they arms of the church which like the church sometimes suffer from misdirection? Are they symptoms of malfunction of organized churches, perhaps even instruments of renewal?

3. A long period of neglect by American Christians renders the doctrine of the church now acutely in need of attention. Dr J. Oliver Buswell wrote as long ago as 1963:

> I must testify that in my opinion American fundamentalism for three quarters of a century, with its faithful emphasis on individual regeneration and purity of evangelical doctrine, has neglected the doctrine of the church. This has been true in two ways. The doctrine of the purity of the visible church has been neglected.... Secondly, we have neglected the doctrine of the unity and fellowship of believers.[2]

Alfred Kuen (1971) observed similarly:

> The Christian of the first century would never have conceived of his Christian life other than in communion with his brothers and sisters in the church.... The Robinson Crusoe Christian does not exist. During the first centuries of Christianity the church became progressively so important that one finally thought 'Outside the church – no salvation.' The Catholic overvaluation of the church was followed by the Protestant overemphasis of individual salvation. The church has little place in Protestant theological research from the sixteenth to the nineteenth century.[3]

Agreed! Not only so, in ignorance of what the church of Christ is (for Christ is still her head, the Holy Ghost her life, the Word of God her food and saints her members), evangelical Christianity in general has not infrequently rejected, wounded and shunned her true mother, the church,[4] in shameful ways. She is, however, still her mother. Those who remember the anti-churchism that frequently accompanied the revolts against apostasy (some real, some only alleged) in the denominations a few decades ago will know whereof we speak.

---

1. Emil Brunner, *The Misunderstanding of the Church* (Philadelphia: Westminster, 1953), pp. 5, 6.
2. J. Oliver Buswell, *A Systematic Theology of the Christian Religion* (Grand Rapids: Zondervan, 1971), Vol. ii, p. 226.
3. Alfred Kuen, *I Will Build My church* (Chicago: Moody Press, 1971), p. 10.
4. 'But the Jerusalem above is free, and she is our mother' (Gal 4:26).

4. There is a far more important reason, in no wise growing out of the accidents of history, why the doctrine of the church has critical importance, if not centrality, in the structure of Christian theology. I mean to say that it is in the empirical body of believers (call it organism, organization or institution) that Christianity (and theology) becomes manifest in concrete visible forms. The view which a group of believing Christians holds of the nature of the church will mightily affect the way in which its forms develop, i.e. the manner in which Christians organize themselves, the way they evangelize, their co-operation (or lack of the same) with other groups of believers with similar beliefs (or of different beliefs) and the kind of rites they observe. One's ecclesiology, of course, does not exist apart from and unqualified by the rest of one's theological schema, Christology, for example – for some go so far as to say the church as 'body of Christ' is a continuation of the incarnation. Yet, in a way unique among doctrines, and by whatever path ecclesiology develops, the doctrine of the church is the doctrine which above all others forces Christianity out in the open in social and structural forms which the world can see and which other Christians can see.

Let us cite, willy-nilly, some striking examples. The Roman Catholic Church holds that the visible church through the pope, Christ's vicar, and by means of apostolic succession from Him through Peter, archbishops, bishops, local clergy, and similar, is the embodiment of Christ on earth. This has imparted a sanctity to the empirical organization which through the centuries has been both the tactical competitive strength of Romanism and the weakness which has sometimes made it seem to some Christians 'the mother of harlots.' If the organized church is Christ Himself, then certainly the church can do no wrong.

Further, ritual ceremonies and calendar events (saint's days, Marian years and the like) within the organized body have a sanctity that no true Protestant would think of ascribing to services and calendar of observances in his own 'church.' Hence liturgy becomes all-important in public worship. Things are done to be *seen*; for this, appropriate *setting* is to be provided – hence the magnificence of traditional Roman Catholic Church architecture and the grandeur of the ritual, the awe in the pious heart when the priest elevates the 'host' while the waiting congregation bow in reverent worship of Christ's very body and blood in the visible sacrament.

Now all this may seem like a sorry joke at best or systematic blasphemy at worst to the sons and daughters of the Reformation – but there can be no doubt about this: Roman ideas about the nature of the church, its ministry and its ordinances have totally affected its visible forms: architecture, furniture, ritual and worship. Consider these words of Karl Adam:

> If I should ask a dying Christian uttering his last prayer, 'Why do you believe in Christ?' it may well be that his eyes will come to rest upon the priest, who is the witness of Christ most near to him. And the priest will refer to his bishop, and the bishop to the *successio apostolica*, the long series of episcopal witnesses of faith leading back to Peter and John. At the end of the succession stands Peter, with the disciples. In their midst stands Jesus himself. Thus across space and time the *successio apostolica* has brought me into the midst of the community of disciples and face to face with the Lord. My situation, in my heart and towards Christ, is now the same as the Apostles. By means of the succession of bishops, I have reached the same plane as the Apostles. This is not a question of any subjective experience or personal whim, but the concrete, visible reality of Christ's witnesses, from Peter down to the priest standing at the Christian's death-bed. The *objective reality of the whole church* [emphasis added] embraces me. For the sick man offers his dying prayer as a member of Christ's body, not in lonely isolation. The entire strength – vast, objective, holy – of all the members of Christ all over the earth is praying with him, through him. The entire *Ecclesia orans*, embracing earth and heaven, here and beyond, comes to meet me in the dying man's prayer. His act of faith is no more difficult than St. Peter's at Caesarea Philippi. For through the all-embracing Catholic church he has attained the same historical and religious feeling for Christ as Peter had for his divine master. The distances of time and space do not exist for him. Like Peter, he stands before Christ and hears his question: 'But who do you say I am?' The *reply* is not denied him; no one can take it from him. Thus far the Christian's act of faith is something completely personal. *But that he should be in position to make this act of faith*, that he should be objectively and subjectively directed toward the mystery, this *he has from the testimony of the church alone* [emphasis added].[5]

This lengthy quotation, from one of the most effective spokesmen for Roman Catholicism of the twentieth century, placed the ecclesiology of the church of Rome in true (and admittedly grand) perspective.

---

5. Karl Adam, *The Christ of Faith* (New York: Mentor Omega Books, 1962), p. 28.

At the opposite pole, Baptist ecclesiology regards a local church as 'that smaller company of regenerate persons who in any given community, unite themselves together in accordance with Christ's laws...'[6] Note that in this definition of the *esse* of the church, regenerate church membership and obedience to Christ's laws are included. On this basis some Baptists have argued that the only true *churches* in the world are Baptist churches and others similarly constituted of regenerated persons obeying Christ's laws, specifically, adult believer's immersion and congregational polity. To call a Presbyterian local group a 'church,' then, is not a matter of accuracy but only of 'courtesy.'[7] Further, since the ordinance of the Lord's Supper is held to belong to the local church, unimmersed people, who by definition of the church cannot be church members, are excluded, hence many Baptist churches practice 'close' communion. It is partly out of a background such as this that Southern Baptists have persisted in staying *out* of ecumenical and other inter-church organizations. They are not unfriendly, nor do most Baptists deny the catholicity of the church.[8] Rather they feel an essential principle of ecclesiology is at stake.

5. The practical importance of ecclesiology also shows up in questions about interdenominational co-operation. The following example cites Lutheran convictions, but strict Baptist views might illustrate the same problem.

The late Dr Walter Maier – of the world-wide radio broadcast of the Lutheran Church, Missouri Synod known as 'The Lutheran Hour' – was invited to address an interdenominational Bible conference gathering. It was to be at the grounds of a famous Bible conference in a tabernacle dedicated to the memory of a famous popular evangelist. One could hardly imagine a more 'unchurchly' setting from Dr Maier's point of view – interdenominational, fundamentalist sponsorship, popular gospel music, a Baptist moderator, a Presbyterian organist and so on. Now, as Philip Schaff once wrote, the Missouri Synod Lutherans are the most Lutheran Lutherans in all the world. At the time of this incident Dr Maier was certainly their best-known spokesman, heard the world around through 'The Lutheran Hour' broadcast. As the story was told, Dr Maier expressed interest in speaking but was unable to address the conference on account of a Missouri Synod, Lutheran Church view of inter-church co-operation. According to this view there are orthodox church bodies and heterodox ones. Brotherly relations should be maintained only with orthodox bodies. Orthodoxy is pure Scripture doctrine, which in view of the perspicuity of the Bible, can be known certainly. Recently Missouri Synod Lutheran leaders place more emphasis on the Reformers' distinction between fundamentals and non-fundamentals and find thereby inter-church co-operation easier to accept. At any rate, Dr Maier did address the conference after a Lutheran pastor was secured to preside at the meeting and present the speaker, i.e. when, in effect, the meeting became a Lutheran gathering with those in general doctrinal unity performing all essential functions of a church meeting except the listening.

The Missouri Synod view is set forth by Dr Francis Pieper, a leading doctrinal authority, as follows:

> Congregations and church bodies must be divided into two classes according to their doctrine.
>
> It is God's will and command that in His church His Word be preached and believed in purity and truth, without adulteration. In God's church nobody should utter his own, but only God's Word (1 Peter 4:11). Chaff and wheat do not belong together. All 'teaching otherwise' is strictly forbidden. 1 Timothy 1:3: 'As I besought thee to abide still at Ephesus when I went into Macedonia, that thou mightest charge some that they teach no other doctrine.' It is important to point out again and again that in all Scripture there is not a single text permitting a teacher to deviate from the Word of God or granting a child of God license to fraternize with a teacher who deviates from the Word of God....
>
> The distinction between orthodox and heterodox bodies and congregations is based on this divine order. A congregation or church body which abides by God's order, in which therefore God's Word is taught in its purity and the Sacraments administered according to the divine institution, is properly called an orthodox church.... But a congregation or church body which, in spite of the divine order, tolerates false doctrine in its midst is properly called a heterodox church.... All children of God should be earnestly concerned to see how real and serious this difference between the church bodies is, because indifference as to the Christian doctrine is rampant today among professed Christians.[9]

Again, these Christians take their position on co-operation or non-co-operation on an *ecclesiological* principle. These facts demonstrate that lack of love and understanding are not really the causes of non-co-operation at all. It is in doctrine, especially in ecclesiology, that the obstacles to visible church unity arise.

---

6. A. H. Strong, *Systematic Theology* (Old Tappen, NJ: Revell, 1907), p. 890.
7. ibid., p. 891.
8. A minority of Baptists deny the existence of the Universal church, e.g. H. E. Dana, *The Christian Ecclesia* and B. H. Carroll, *Ecclesia* – The Church.
9. Francis Pieper, *Christian Dogmatics* (St Louis: Concordia, 1953), Vol. III, p. 422.

Still another enlightening instance is the group of Christians known as Plymouth Brethren. They lay great emphasis on the spiritual nature of the church and insist consistently on the wholly non-sacerdotal character of church offices. It is fair to say it is basic to their ecclesiology that 'the church is an exclusively spiritual body, destitute of all formal organization, and bound together only by the mutual relation of each believer to his indwelling Lord.... Those believers who chance to gather at a particular place, or to live at a particular time constitute the church of that place or time.'[10] This view, similar to that of orthodox Quakers, though not carried out with Quaker consistency, has produced among the Brethren a distinct, though elusive visible shape. As oppressing officials in Catholic Spain used to find to their embarrassment, and more recently communist police in many countries, it is hard to deal with a 'church' that has no edifice at all, employs no clergy, never even receives a public offering of money, and which may meet in one part of town on the first Sunday morning in August, in another on the second Sunday. This is really an 'invisible church'!

These examples (and they could be greatly extended) are sufficient to demonstrate that we cannot be judged in error when we assert ecclesiology is of unique importance because doctrinal commitments here determine in a large measure the visible shape that Christianity will assume among those Christian believers with whom those views prevail.

6. Another facet of ecclesiology, related to the immediately foregoing, one not as widely recognized, is the effect ecclesiology wields on the practice of evangelism and Christian mission.

Kenneth Scott Latourette[11] points out that as early as the fourth quarter of the second century the case for apostolic succession of bishops and the theory of the church later espoused officially by the Roman Church was forcefully spelled out by one of Christendom's most able spokesmen, Irenaeus, bishop of Lyons.[12] Even earlier the clergy-laity distinction developed and other features of the naive view that the organized hierarchy is the church *per se* began to develop.[13] The bishop speaks for the church because he is the church[14] and can therefore open and shut its doors of entrance. How did (and does) this affect missionary work and evangelization of pagans? Let the same author tell the story.

> The precise course of the conversion of Armenia has been hopelessly beclouded by legend. The great missionary was one Gregory, to whom the designation Illuminator was added because of his successful labours. Gregory seems to have been of the Armenian aristocracy and to have become a Christian while in Caesarea in Cappadocia, a region in which Christianity early made marked progress. Returning to Armenia and seeking to propagate his new faith, Gregory encountered persecution. Then he won the king, Tradt, Tirdat or Tiridates by name. Why the king became a Christian we can only conjecture, but with the consent of his nobles he supported Gregory. The compliant population rapidly moved over to the new faith. Many of the shrines of the pre-Christian paganism were transferred, together with their endowments, to the service of Christianity, and numbers of pagan priests or their sons passed over into the body of Christian clergy. Some were made bishops. Gregory, obtaining episcopal consecration at Caesarea, became the head of the Armenian church and was followed in the post by his lineal descendants.[15]

Now granting that this is an extreme case, straining even the episcopal authority papal ecclesiology later associated with Roman Christianity, this is not out of keeping with the kind of approach employed many times later by the Roman Church – including missions to the Indians in the Americas. Richard Fletcher, an historian of the University of York in England, traces in detail how the Saxons and others of continental Europe were 'evangelized' by military force in the age of Charlemagne.[16] Try to imagine how different the story of evangelism in Armenia would have been if Gregory had derived all his theology, except ecclesiology, at Our Lady of the Pines Seminary but had studied his ecclesiology at Southern Baptist Theological seminary – voluntary association, regenerate membership, spiritual unity, believer's baptism and all the rest. To think about the difference is to close the argument.

---

10. A. H. Strong, op. cit., p. 895.
11. Kenneth Scott Latourette produced more than 300 articles and about thirty books. The best known are the seven volumes of *A History of the Expansion of Christianity* (1937–1945) and *A History of Christianity*, 1,515 pages in first edition (1953). He was a Baptist of moderately conservative theological persuasion.
12. Kenneth Scott Latourette, *A History of Christianity* (New York: Harper & Bros., 1953), p. 131.
13. ibid., pp. 131–133.
14. ibid., pp. 182–185.
15. ibid., p. 79.
16. Richard Fletcher, *The Barbarian Conversion: From Paganism to Christianity* (New York: Henry Holt & Co., 1998, chap. 7, 'Campaigning Sceptres, the Frankish Drive to the East,' pp. 193–227).

7. The bearing of ecclesiology on practice is quite as readily apparent, upon reflection, in *efforts toward union of denominations* – in the ecumenist terminology of our time, 'Christian unity' or 'Christian community.' This has long been recognized by leaders within the ecumenical movement – to their consternation and despair. The painful awareness of the problem there stimulated the production of a veritable library of books and articles among the ecumenically minded theologians. This stimulated others in the same direction. In fact, this forced wedding of ecclesiology with ecumenics more than anything else has made it necessary that at least some theologians of every Christian denomination and persuasion devote 'primetime' to the topic of the church. What is the church? What is the nature of her ministry and her ordinances?

Throughout Christian history people of varying beliefs about many aspects of doctrine have managed somehow to 'stay together.' But what people *think* about the church shapes what people *do* as churches. So not only mutual understanding but agreement as well must be achieved in ecclesiology or else on some of the most important levels of church life Christians of varying views must continue to function separately. It simply will not do to agree to disagree and then move into the same house.

To take only one aspect of the problem, consider the church's ministry and its relation to the essence of the church. The Roman Church finds the *esse* of the church in Christ *via* the apostolic succession and thereby necessarily through the pope, as we have already seen. The Anglican theologian usually finds it by way of apostolic succession, but through the episcopate (bishops).

The church has *invisible* unity in the Holy Spirit, as E. L. Mascall once wrote. There *visible* organ of this unity, said Mascall, is the Universal Episcopate whereby all bishops are apostles. This body of apostles = bishops is composed of living bishops on earth and those deceased in heaven, never losing a member by death!

This seems so strange to most Protestants that it is not always accepted, even by some Episcopalians. Yet let this representative, competent Anglican speak:

> It would be... surprising if there were no visible organ by which the church's unity is expressed and maintained.... Such an organ is, I would suggest, to be found in the Apostolate, instituted by Christ in the Twelve and expanded through the centuries into the universal Episcopate. It is, I think, noteworthy that the patristic tradition lays primary stress upon the Episcopate as the link between the local and the universal church....[17]
>
> I would maintain, then, that as a visible reality in the historic order, the church's unity is established in our Lord's institution of the Apostolate, which is continued in the universal Episcopate, the bishop is the link between the local and the universal church.... The diocese, gathered around its bishop, is thus not merely a *part* of the church of God, but it is its full manifestation in a particular place. Like the cell in a living organism, it is a coherent organic entity, yet it lives only because it coheres in the whole body. Like the sacramental Body of Christ in the Eucharist, the mystical Body of Christ which is the church is not divided into portions of its extension in space and time; it is *tota in toto, et tota in aliqua parte* [all in all and all in the various parts].[18]

Contrast this with a Baptist view of the ministry wherein the 'bishop' is no different from an 'elder' and both are merely designations of simple 'ministers' chosen by the congregation. The Presbyterian minister, while distinguished from a lay elder, is not thought to be a sacerdotal person in whom any mystical bond of church unity exists.

Thus, so far from finding universal Christian unity in the ministry, the church's spiritual unity promises to remain 'invisible' for a long time! Churches at the present time cannot even consistently recognize one another's ministry!

Baptism (whether adult, infant, sprinkling, pouring, immersion, etc., and whether conveying regeneration, accompanying regeneration or merely symbolizing it), the Lord's Supper with the theories of Christ's presence, and other problems of church practice and policy are a hornet's nest of painful insects aboard the Good Ship *oikoumenē*.

Thus the time has come when study of the church is thrust upon us. There are those in certain denominations which have inner differences (or indifferences) on these issues who will not wish to go along on this tour of investigation. A *modus operandi* has developed: 'Let well-enough alone!' These practical churchmen are not entirely wrong. As long as no plain command of Christ is being disobeyed we can live and let live – together. On the other hand if our quest should lead us to demonstrable truth, truth has a way of seizing pious hearts and welding them together in spite of past sentiments. This kind of unity will be far more deep and steady than any program based on mere compromise.

---

17. E. L. Mascall, *Corpus Christi* (London: Longmans, Green & Co., 1953, 1957), p. 13.
18. ibid., pp. 19, 20.

8. There has been no time in the history of the last 1,500 years, when the community of believers which we call the church has been more critically important to mankind. The breakdown of the natural communal life of people around the whole world has ripped mankind out of the commonality of existence among other men with whom and to whom they counted for something, and has brusquely dropped them in rude and rushing crowds where they count for nothing.

> One phase of the breakdown has been the dissolution of the ties which bound men and women to the natural communities of family, village, or working group, to which they had belonged.... Civilization has witnessed a sort of atomizing process.... [A man] becomes a sort of replaceable unit in the social machine. His nearest neighbors may not even know his name. He is free to move from place to place, from job to job, from acquaintance to acquaintance, and – if he has attained a high degree of emancipation – from wife to wife. He is in every context a more and more anonymous and replaceable part, the perfect incarnation of the rationalist conception of man. Wherever civilization has spread in the past one hundred years it has carried this atomizing process with it. Its characteristic product in Calcutta, Shanghai, or Johannesburg is the modern city into which myriads of human beings, loosened from their old ties in village or tribe or caste, like grains of sand fretted by water from an ancient block of sandstone, are churned in the whirlpool of the city.[19]

This has been true on all social and economic levels. There are few Americans today who know much about a permanent and stable community wherein one grows up and lives out his earthly existence among aunts and uncles, grandparents, cousins, and school-day friends and then is buried in the family plot in the community cemetery. For most of us outside very old rural areas this is something we know about only because our parents or grandparents have told us about it or something we have read about in novels and history books. 'Village' life is just about gone in America. In fact, in the western states the very word 'village' is not used by natives except as a quaint, affected name for places somewhere else. In the East, as a kind of fossil word, it is used without affectation, though there are not very many true villages there either, just joints and clefts in the seaboard megalopolis.

In such a situation it is natural that people should long for some sort of real community, for one cannot be human without it. It is especially natural that Christians should reach out after that part of Christian doctrine which speaks of the true, God-given community, the church of Jesus Christ.

All of modern, civilized life – urban, suburban and rural – has conspired to take us out of any satisfying form of commonality of being and living. The modern type of church has thoughtlessly (albeit learnedly, lovingly, anxiously and professionally) joined in the process of disintegration of human society. This has been accomplished by rationalizing: over-departmentalizing its worship and nurture; over-professionalizing its leaders and clergy; and running people to exhaustion with too many meetings, too many supplements to the Sunday church bulletin, too many 'opportunities' and 'counseling' them to death. This is presently being noticed and criticized by discerning critics whom we shall have occasion to notice later in this section.

Modern life has relentlessly attacked true social community at every level except the economic. Here we seem to be tied together in a growing, world-wide conjugal complex that threatens to crush the very soul out of human existence. Later pages of this book will take further note of this unhappy development.

Though decades have passed since the slogan was coined by ecumenists, it is still true that 'Now is the time for the church to be the church.' But what is the church? That is one of the chief questions this section of this volume seeks to answer.

A comment by Nathan Hatch of Notre Dame University gives this chapter real moral relevance. He raised the question, 'Do evangelical concepts of leadership and authority derive from the church or from the market place?' He answers:

> The evangelical movement is amazingly dynamic: entrepreneurial, decentralized, and given to splitting, forming, and reforming....
>
> The tendency is for us to anoint as leaders those who build a mass following in the free religious market. The thorny problem is that these leaders are not necessarily wise churchmen. They are more likely to be those who assume prominent political roles or who build mass special-purpose ministries. To the extent that this is the case, we allow the market to set the terms of church leadership.
>
> The long-term question for evangelicals is what kind of shepherds we will follow, whether we will follow leaders whose interest is the well-being of the church itself, men and women who are theologically savvy, historically informed, and committed to seeing the church prosper in all of its dimensions and for all of its people.[20]

---

19. Leslie Newbigin, *The Household of God* (New York: Friendship Press, 1964), pp. 3, 4.
20. Nathan O. Hatch, *Wheaton College Alumni Magazine* (Summer, 1999), pp. 10, 11.

2
Defining Ecclesiology

I. Church Is a Doctrine.

The historic creeds of the undivided ancient church, accepted by almost all Christians to the present hour, demonstrate that there is a common, consensual core of beliefs among all Christians, always and everywhere. One of the earliest references to doctrinal consensus (by Cyprian of Carthage, AD 250) says, 'I believe in the forgiveness of sins, and eternal life through the holy church.'[1] The 'Apostles' Creed' adds 'catholic' to the formula and the 'Nicene Creed' (325, 381) adds 'one,' viz.: 'one holy, catholic and apostolic church.'[2] Church, therefore, is as much a *bona fide* doctrine of historic Christianity as the doctrine of the holy Trinity or the incarnation.

II. Marks of the Church.

Not every group of believers is aware of this early and enduring consensus, but wherever Christians do become aware they will likely agree there is a church of which they are a part and that there is only *one* church, in some important sense: *holy*, as distinct from the world; *catholic*, as including true believers everywhere of every age from the apostles onward; and *apostolic*, in the sense of founded by apostles and as faithfully teaching and living out apostolic doctrines. Much more than this is of course affirmed and with varying emphasis and understandings.

These 'notes' or marks of the church are not empirically derived nor are they immediately observable in local churches. The marks themselves have to be defined rather carefully. We need to be reminded that though revelation gives us much information about the church, she is at least partly under the category of mystery in the Bible (Rom. 16:25; Eph. 1:9; 3:3-9; 5:32). Paul once connects the church with the revealed mystery of the incarnation (1 Tim. 3:14-16). In Revelation 1–3 the churches are seven lamps with Christ in their midst, whose 'angels' are in Christ's right hand (Rev. 1:12, 13, 20).

The church and its marks, however, may be discerned by biblically informed and spiritually sensitive people in thousands of assemblies where believers around the world gather every week. Where there is no *unity* with Christ and other Christians there is only *schism*; where no *holiness*, only *sham religion*; where no *catholic* faith, *apostasy*;

---

1. Philip Schaff, *The Creeds of Christendom* II (Grand Rapids: Baker Books, 1966), pp. 20, 55.
2. ibid., p. 59.

where not *apostolic*, then *unscriptural*. Lacking any discernable connection with the church of Scripture and history and propagating teachings contrary to apostolic Scripture it cannot be a church of Christ. If any of the marks is obscured or missing the assembly needs reformation (in the sixteenth-century sense of revival and restoration). This is precisely why the leaders of the Reformation at first labored to revive and restore the medieval church to its beginnings in the apostolic *ekklēsia*. Prevented from that, they set out sadly to find living space in Europe for evangelical churches. The results are well known.

In point of fact, as Emil Brunner correctly states:

> There are three classical 'definitions' of the church, each of which contains an answer to the question about the basis of the church. The church is the Company of the Elect, the Body of Christ, the Communion of Saints (*coetus electorum, corpus Christi, communio sanctorum*).[3]

These of course are Christian 'definitions,' though not comprehensive, scientific or sociological definitions. Each implies the church is a peculiar (particular) people different from all others. They are 'the company of the elect' because only they (not the entire world) are chosen in Christ and Christ is God's elect; they are 'the communion of saints' because God has declared them so and are a communion even though scattered abroad (as Peter says, 1 Peter 1:1, 2). 'The body of Christ' is a metaphor employed particularly by Paul with special reference to its being the functionary of Christ as Savior of mankind. Yet each 'definition' (or perhaps only characterization or designation) includes those who have been 'graduated' to heaven – and as 'the company of the elect' some yet unborn. These concepts have been incorporated into very precious hymns, as in Samuel Stone's *The Church's One Foundation*:

> Yet she on earth hath union
> With God the three in one
> And mystic sweet communion
> With those whose rest is won.

Calvin conferred importance on 'the communion of saints.' He points out, 'This clause, though generally omitted by the ancients, ought not to be overlooked, for it very well expresses *what the church is*' (emphasis added).[4]

III. Marks Do Not Define the Church As Such.

It is a mistake, I think, to suppose that the church may be defined simply by discussing her unity, holiness, catholicity and apostolicity. What is this church which wherever present possesses those characteristics? The critical questions remain to be answered.

Having said this, is it true that 'the adjectives "one holy, catholic, apostolic" are terms specific enough to describe the essential nature of the church'?[5] Hardly. It is a bit like saying of the place where I live, that it is made of bricks, glass, wood and steel without specifying further that it is a house not a barn, a residential structure not a warehouse, and so on. The definition says nothing of how the church is distinct from a club or a mob, or what it is in which the four marks inhere. These four adjectives designate *differentia* but no *major genus*.

Perhaps it is better to say these 'notes' or 'properties' are means by which, whatever the nature of the one society of Christ may be, it may be recognized by these marks. The Roman Catholic Church does not understand the notes (marks, properties) as Protestant evangelicals do, but she has it right as to what they are and what they do: 'conspicuous characteristics which distinguish it from all other bodies and prove it to be the one society of Jesus Christ.'[6] They 'indicate essential features.'[7] Rome thinks that she alone possesses these features authentically, hence, only as a matter of courtesy, not of fact, calls other Christian groups churches. Such added 'marks' or 'notes' as invisibility and exercise of discipline came into use as marks by the Reformers of the sixteenth century. Therefore, useful as the notes are in discussing the church, we must have many more categories. This does not mean that a theologian may not arrange

---

3. Emil Brunner, *The Christian Doctrine of the Church, Faith, and the Consummation, Dogmatics*: Vol. III, trans. D. Cairnes and T. H. L. Parker (Philadelphia: Westminster Press, English Trans. 1962), pp. 22, 23.
4. John Calvin, *Institutes of the Christian Religion*, IV, trans. F. L. Battler (Philadelphia: Westminster Press, 1960), p. 3.
5. R. L. Omanson, 'The church,' *Evangelical Dictionary of Theology* (Grand Rapids: Baker), p. 233.
6. A. J. Schulte, 'church,' *The Catholic Encyclopedia*, III, p. 758.
7. *The Catechism of 1994*, p. 811.

further *sub loci* of ecclesiology under the four notes and proceed with comprehensive treatment as does Thomas Oden.[8] The Roman Church at the Council of Constance (1414–1418) specifically condemned John Wycliffe's 'error' of saying that the church is an article of faith only if by *church* is meant the gathering of the elect.[9]

An illustrative example will help to clarify the point that the four notes of unity, holiness, apostolicity and catholicity do not define what the church is. Water is a clear, odorless liquid which freezes at 32 degrees Fahrenheit, vaporizes at 212 degrees Fahrenheit (at sea level) and in a vertical column 32 foot tall equals the weight of earth's atmosphere. These are the *properties* of water. A property is 'any trait or attribute proper to a thing… any of the principal characteristics of a substance.'[10] Note all of them in the case of water are directly observable to the senses without chemical analysis. Yet by chemical analysis we discover that each water molecule is composed of two atoms of hydrogen and one of oxygen. The compound H_2O is not similar to either hydrogen or oxygen. We might even try to define water by how it may be used – to wash or cook with, to swim in, to navigate the whole earth, to sustain life by drinking it, and similar. An adequate definition of water turns out to be quite a difficult matter, yet any animal or man recognizes it quickly (in pure form) when he drinks it or dips a part of his body in it. Whether we define water by properties or chemical analysis or what it does or can do, defining its identity is no simple matter.

This study from this point onward is entirely in response to that question: What is the church – both what it is and what it ought to be, its *esse* and its *bene esse*? We shall consider first the words *church* and *ekklēsia* – the New Testament Greek word which it invariably translates. Then after introducing several distinct but related ideas, *the Kingdom of God* and Israel (and metaphors and synonyms), then the two main aspects of the subject, the church *universal* and the church *local*, are to be introduced and explained. The treatment then moves on to nine topics related to the church universal: its foundation, establishment, relation to Israel and the kingdom of God, essential nature and the like, unity, gifts, mission, purposes, and destiny. After that the church local will be discussed: its nature, organization and government, offices, ordinances, and worship.[11]

It was my original plan to treat modern church union (ecumenical) movements but that would have enlarged this volume beyond reasonable size. It was that movement among 'foreign' mission fields in the nineteenth century that sparked intense interest in the nature of the church and a growing awareness of the importance of defining and clarifying every aspect of the subject. Soon there were journals wholly dedicated to research and discussion of narrowly defined aspects of the church and countless books, monographs, pamphlets and sermons. A special vocabulary was created to discuss the subject – for which the comprehensive term is ecumenism. Whatever one thinks of it – for good or ill – the ecumenical movement cannot yet be counted out.

IV. The Church Both an Aspect of and a Doctrine of Christianity.

The church of Christ is both an aspect of and a doctrine of Christianity. Christianity is sometimes thought to be the same entity as 'the church.' A different and better way of looking at the matter is to see Christianity as (1) the culmination of a *history of redemption* in the life and work of Jesus Christ who was born of a virgin, as the creed says, lived, died, was resurrected and ascended to heaven, and so forth. Christianity is also (2) a *system of doctrines* by which the Holy Scriptures and its expositors through the centuries interpret that redemptive history. The *church* is one of those doctrines. The church is also (3) *the multitudes of people* who have embraced the redemption in history and now live out their faith on earth and in heaven. And it is correct to say the church is (4) a society, the *institutional expression* of the redemption, the doctrines and of the people. It has a visible aspect which has had an ongoing history that people who are not even part of it, or who even reject it, can recognize at least in part. This study will ignore none of these four features of 'the church' but will focus on the second – the church as a doctrine of Christianity.

V. How to Approach Definition and Description of the Church.

Depending on presuppositions and goals, one of three different approaches – with modifications and crossovers – may be followed. Every group claiming to be a Christian church (or *the* Christian church) acknowledges Jesus

---

8. Thomas Oden, 'Life in the Spirit,' *Systematic Theology*, III (San Francisco: Harper Collins, 1992, 1996).
9. *The Church Teaches: Documents of the Church in English Translation*, ed. by Gerald Van Ackeren (Rockford, IL: TAN Books, 1973), p. 77.
10. Webster's New *World Dictionary*, 3rd ed.
11. In another book I have discussed the relations of the church to civil governments ('church and state'), to society and to civilization, to sects and denominations of Christians. See R. D. Culver, *Civil Government, A Biblical View* (Edmonton, Alberta, Canada: Canadian Institute for Law, Theology, and Public Policy, 2000).

Christ as founder of the church and that the church of Jesus Christ has some unique, vital connection with Him. Any 'church' which is orthodox in any meaningful sense finds in the New Testament its authority for doctrine and practice, but some do not regard the New Testament as the only authority. Some regard their structure as identically continuous with the church of the apostles, some acknowledge themselves as discontinuous and claim only to restore the essential features of the apostolic church.

Let us cite first the Roman Catholic approach. Though I simplify somewhat, the Roman Church claims that its visible organizational structure as such is the church. The esse of the church inheres in the structure. Let J. L. McKenzie, an eminent post-Vatican II Roman theologian, state the matter:

> In Roman Catholic belief, the hierarchical structure of the church is the bearer of the sacred power which Jesus Christ committed to that group of his disciples who are called apostles.... Just as no one but Jesus could confer this authority on the apostles, so no one but the apostles could transmit the authority to successors.[12]

McKenzie goes on to point out that this apostolic authority primarily includes the 'sacred power of the priesthood' or 'the power of orders' to administer the means of saving grace, the sacraments, and secondly, 'the power to rule' or 'jurisdiction.' As we observed in chapter 1 of this section these powers as thought to be discovered in Scripture, in tradition and traced through history to the present, are essentially the doctrine of the church.

At the opposite end of the scale are 'Pilgrim church' theories. They see the 'visible' or historic churches of Christendom as discontinuous with the apostolic church. They agree with McKenzie that the Roman aspect of the church began approximately with the conversion of Emperor Constantine but think of the 'true church' as a 'Pilgrim church' whose written history of faithfulness to apostolic, New Testament origins is largely lost from written documents. Roman (and Eastern Orthodox Christianity as well) are both *formally* apostate, though Christians were and are present in both.

A passage from a fine book by a convinced 'Christian Brethren' author tells in graphic, but not extreme, form how this approach to ecclesiology works.

> One day I resolutely put aside all my books, I took my New Testament and there underlined all that concerned the church; then I picked out and classified on cards what I had found. What a joy it was to see roughly outlined and gradually taking shape a living picture of the primitive church... the church according to the plan of God.[13]

Mr Kuen goes on to acknowledge enlightenment (influence?) from other churchmen and scholarly Christian sources, but insists on the validity and adequacy of what he found by inductive study of the Bible – the primitive apostolic church, still today the true church – though he does not attempt definition.[14]

The Roman Church acknowledges an invisible church of the 'elect' within the visible church of the hierarchy but both are aspects of the one, holy, catholic and apostolic church of which the Roman is the true and only structure, complete with the pope, who is Christ's vicar on earth. For the Pilgrim church theologian the hierarchy represents the apostate church.

In between these approaches fall the several efforts at definition and restoration of the authentic first-century church as set up by Christ and His Apostles attempted by Protestant Reformers on the continent and Anglicans and Puritans in Britain.

All the Reformers at first seem to have seen enough of New Testament authenticity in the Roman Church to regard it as still a church and as reformable (i.e. capable of being restored). They brought the 'Scripture only' principle to bear on their ideas of the church. And, since a visible church, however rudimentarily structured, involved practice (assembling, preaching, presbyters, baptisms, the Lord's Supper and much more), they were compelled to decide what was authentically apostolic and what was not. This quickly drew the attention of the Roman hierarchy who then drove the aspirant Reformers out of the medieval church. The Reformers were committed to historic orthodoxy and biblical authority; hence they were driven to weigh what they found in the Roman Church of the time against Scripture and, finding it wanting, they endeavored to construct something authentically apostolic.

---

12. J. L. McKenzie, *The Roman Catholic Church* (Garden City, NY: Image Books, 1971), pp. 22, 23.
13. A. F. Kuen, *I Will Build My Church* (Chicago: Moody Press, 1971), p. 12. Mr Kuen, a professor at a State Teachers College in France, was trained in theology at a Plymouth Brethren school in Switzerland.
14. ibid., p. 11.

As in the whole range of doctrine, the Reformers did not attempt to erase 1,500 years of church history and theology in constructing ecclesiology. They were not able quite to break free from the cloying influence of the state-church notion – or, better stated, the territorial church. They did not cut free from the wholeness of post-Constantinian Christendom wherein there was no room for the Christian *ekklēsia* as simply a voluntary association. For them baptism in infancy remained the door of entrance both to church and civil commonwealth.

Yet Zwingli and Luther at the beginning, followed shortly by Calvin, all sought to find in the Scriptures a doctrine of the church. Brunner observes,

> The [Roman] Catholic doctrine of Baptism... is unambiguously sacramental; salvation is imparted in an event which makes no personal claim on the man, which works automatically and mechanically, *ex opere operato*.... it remains a matter of indifference whether it is an infant who is baptized or a man capable of answering the word in faith.... Luther's new knowledge of the personal character of faith as trust in the grace offered in Jesus Christ was bound to crack this whole sacramental structure.[15]

For present purposes it will not be necessary to report in detail how Luther came to conclusions similar to modern 'free church' doctrine of the church but receded from them. Similarly Zwingli found that his own principles of *sola scriptura*, taken seriously by 'the radicals,' i.e. the Anabaptists of Zurich, led to a church of voluntary associates, and the leaders of Zurich were not prepared to break with the territorial (or Constantinian) principle and later joined others in formation of territorial churches throughout Switzerland. This system was already established in Switzerland when Calvin came to Geneva in 1536.

Yet all the Reformers agreed that the pattern of the visible assemblies of the Christian *ekklēsia*, like all doctrine and practice of Christianity, should be derived from Scripture only. Further, they agreed that historical patterns should be corrected by Scripture. They aimed to judge the 'fathers' by the Scriptures, not the other way around.

The rise of the modern ecumenical movement produced a torrent of literature on this subject. We shall attend to some of it later in two chapters on the nature of the local church and of the universal church.

VI. Ecclesiology Addresses the 'Visible' Church.

The churches as they exist on earth have many flaws. Yet, the New Testament addresses these assemblies as churches – even 'the churches of Galatia' which Paul knew to have removed from grace to another gospel (Gal. 1:1-6) and the 'seven churches' of the province of Asia, one of which was about to be spewed out of the Lord's mouth (Rev. 2, 3). The *ekklēsia* at Ephesus (where Timothy ministered, in Paul's absence, with other elders and deacons) the Apostle declared to be 'the house of God.' This was not because God's residence is there as it is in the Tabernacle and first temple, but because the *ekklēsia* assembled is where the Word is preached, where by the foolishness of a preached message God has chosen to save, and where Christian worship takes place, without which true Christian nurture cannot be normal. The visible, professing church is not only 'the house of God' but also 'the church of the living God, the pillar and ground of the truth' (1 Tim. 3:15 KJV). For this reason believers must not forsake the practice or neglect 'to meet together' (Heb. 10:25), where they must also 'See that you [they] do not refuse him who is speaking' (Heb. 12:25).

We know very little about 'the church triumphant' of the present and future in heaven. Hebrews 12:22-24 says there is an 'assembly of the firstborn' in heaven, called 'Mount Zion and... the city of the living God' where also are 'innumerable angels in festal gathering... God, the judge of all,' other 'spirits of the righteous made perfect' and 'Jesus, the mediator.' The passage furnishes a field day for commentators. What is plain and relevant here is that the bulk of the New Testament is addressed to believers on earth, most of it in their capacity as members of local churches. Further the 'churches' and 'church' of Matthew 16 and 18, the Acts, and on through Revelation is the church on earth as it exists visibly. There is validity to distinctions between church visible and invisible, but the distinction does not mean the same to every theologian who employs it.

VII. Ecclesiology Is a Big Subject.

This church, Galatians 3:20 notwithstanding, is the mother who on earth has mediated motherhood for us all for all our lives from first spiritual awakening to the end of life.

---

15. Emil Brunner, *Dogmatics*, III (Philadelphia: Westminster Press, 1952), p. 52, 55.

Paul, in a passage (Gal. 4:21-31) where he is speaking somewhat in the oriental mode of undefined but understood metaphor, says: 'But the Jerusalem above is free, and she is our mother' (Gal. 4:26). The Roman church thinks the idea of 'mother church' refers to the papal edifice. I recommend Calvin's exposition:

> The Jerusalem which is *above*, or heavenly, is not contained in heaven; nor are we to seek for it out of this world; for the church is spread out over the whole world, and is a 'stranger and pilgrim on the earth' (Heb. 11:13). Why then is it said to be from heaven? Because it originates in heavenly grace; for the sons of God are born... by the power of the Holy Spirit. The heavenly Jerusalem, which derives from heaven, and dwells above by faith (Phil. 3:20; Col. 3:1-4) is the mother of believers. To the church, under God, we owe it that we are 'born again, not of corruptible seed, but of incorruptible' (1 Peter 1:23), and from her we obtain the milk and food by which we are afterward nourished. Such are the reasons why the church is called the mother of believers. And certainly he who refuses to be a son of the church in vain desires to have God as his Father; for it is only through the instrumentality of the church that we are 'born of God' (John 3:19), and brought up through the various stages of childhood and youth, till we arrive at manhood.[16]

Calvin has much to say of this in the first chapters of Book IV of the *Institutes*. It is not without significance that Calvin, who lived at a time when 'the church' was as corrupt and divided as it ever has been, devoted 510 pages (Westminster Ed.), roughly one-third of the pages of the *Institutes*, to 'the Holy Catholic church' – 'The External Means or Aids By Which God Invites Us Into the Society of Christ and Holds Us Therein.'[17]

VIII. Many Sources Go Into an Adequate Ecclesiology.

The Bible does not anywhere define the church. Captions such as we have already considered – 'company of the elect,' 'communion of saints,' 'body of Christ,' and others such as 'community of faith' and 'household of faith,' 'the new Israel,' some biblical, some not – are only designations. The *ekklēsia* is introduced by name in the Gospels only in the phrase 'I will build my church' (Jesus to Peter, Matt. 16:18) and 'tell it to the church... listen... to the church' (Matt. 18:17). We may be sure the disciples did not yet understand these predictions, though later they did (John 16:12-14). The next time we hear of *ekklēsia* is at Acts 2:47 (KJV), where some time following the effusion of the Spirit it is said 'the Lord added to the church daily.' The church is, of course, the group of 120 plus about 3,000 (Acts 1:15; 2:41). It was something new, formed supernaturally into a unique entity on the Day of Pentecost. In Matthew 16 and 18 it was a future entity. After Pentecost it was an existing entity. Yet no verse of Scripture tells us specifically what it was and is.

The rest of the New Testament assumes an understanding of the *ekklēsia* by the readers, yet also by bits and pieces gives information on every aspect of its nature, services, mission, ministry, government and destiny. At all points therefore our studies must begin with Scripture and end with Scripture. Yet no one comes to research the Bible without previous knowledge of and experience in the church – unless one wishes to reject one's previous Christian life along with one's mother. So though I must judge what I already know of my mother-church from living in and with her it is not necessary for me to repudiate her. This means simply that my views of the church have been inescapably affected by my experience in the bosom of the church. Further, I am not the first to attempt the daunting task of extracting from the Bible what it has to say about Christ's church. Others have been doing so for centuries. We may not neglect to learn from them. This 'history of exegesis' is how Jaroslav Pelikan rightly identifies tradition. Also, the church for the past century and on to the present has attracted the serious attention of many Christian scholars. Though I am not able to give credit to each from whom I have learned, this book owes a debt to each of them, for ecclesiology has been a topic of special interest to me since an article I wrote on the subject was published many years ago and which article had much to do with my being invited to begin a career as a professor of theology.

Let us 'launch out into the deep.'

---

16. Calvin, *Commentary on Galatians and Ephesians*, trans. W. Pringle (Edinburgh: Calvin Translation Society, 1854), pp. 140, 141.
17. Calvin, *Institutes* (Westminster Ed. of 1960), pp. 1009–1524.

3
The Words 'Church' and *Ekklēsia*

I. The English Word 'Church' and Its Meaning.

There are probably few members of civilized society today who are unfamiliar with the word 'church' or its equivalent in their own language, for 'church' is a part of Western civilization, which has now extended its influence almost everywhere. In the language of eastern (Slavic) and northern (Germanic) Europe and of the British Isles the words of common speech for 'church' show their relationship to our English word, all being some variation of the K-R-K form with which we of Anglo-Saxon culture are familiar in 'church' or its Scottish variant 'kirk.' In the Romance languages, however, the word is almost invariably similar to the French 'eglise,' usually featuring an initial 'e' followed by a 'c,' 'k,' or 'g,' then an 'i' followed by some appropriate vowel and finally an 's.' We have a form of it in several adjectives – [ecclesi]astic, [ecclesi]ology, etc. For some, the explanation of these facts may suggest the boredom of seventh grade language class, for others, the romance of an archaeological expedition. In either case, the very heart of the Christian doctrine of the church is involved in the unscrambling of this philological anagram.

Most Christians and their ministers devote small effort to questioning what their church is and even less to the meaning of the word in their own language – to say nothing of the ancient languages of the Bible. 'Church' is, after all, a matter of daily experience. 'I go to church; I am a member of the church; my church is Methodist; our church is located at the corner of First Street at Broadway. Of course I know what church means! It is a big thing in my daily life.' What will emerge, however, from a minimum of reflection on this hypothetical quotation is that though used four times, 'church' means something different in each of the four cases – a meeting, a society, a denomination, a building used for worship. This is just a start.

In this chapter the aim is to clarify the whole theological project by definition and limitation of the goals through clarifying terms. If the terms are not clarified with utmost care the following study will inevitably be conducted in an atmosphere of ambiguity – as indeed is the case in all too much theological discussion. It is this prevalent 'low visibility' which calls for the whole effort at a comprehensive statement of the Christian doctrine of the church. Attention will first be directed to the very devious history of the English word. Then, the use of that word in our English Bible must be considered briefly. After that I shall devote more extended attention to the New Testament Greek words underlying the translations and their connection, if any, with Old Testament usages. The impatient or casual may not relish this kind of intellectual excursion, but it is essential in the early stages of this study if any persuasive statement of the Christian doctrine of the church is to be spelled out.

It is an historical question almost wholly within the domain of philological experts. A fairly large number of monographs and research abstracts bearing on the subject has been produced in the last century and more, sparked by the pioneer work in language history by Jacob Grimm.[1] Some of the relevant material will be found summarized in *Theological Dictionary of the New Testament*.[2] Of far greater importance, comparatively up-to-date and not likely ever to be superseded, is the article 'church,' extending to eleven columns, about 11,000 words total, in *The Oxford English Dictionary*.[3] My discussion at this point is especially indebted to these 'authorities' — if such a word ever can be used today.

As for the word 'church' in Anglo-Saxon (=English) speech, it is as old, at least, as the written language, though varying somewhat in pronunciation and spelling. In fact, the realities for which the word has stood have had a strong formative influence at all stages of the history of the British Isles since shortly after the beginning of the Christian era. The heathen Angles and Saxons possessed the word before they settled in Great Britain because they had become acquainted with the buildings and cultural features of Greek Christian and Latin Christian communities through their travels and raids (see below). Also Christian missions and merchant settlements had provided some acquaintance. All branches of the German and Slavic linguistic groups thus took over the word 'church.' As early as the time of the Emperor Carcalla in the third century, the Goths, a Germanic tribe, came into conflict with the Roman Empire in the lower Danube Valley. In the next century, when after the time of Constantine Christians were erecting edifices for worship everywhere in the Empire, the Goths plundered Thrace and Moesia (in the Greek-speaking East), and elsewhere. Meanwhile the Goths were in contact with other German tribes and passed this word *church* along. So even before they were Christianized, these German tribes had become acquainted with buildings used for Christian worship, in the Greek language called *kuriakon doma*, the Lord's House. *Kuriakon* is an adjective derived from *kurios*, Lord, employed in the New Testament only twice, in the phrases 'the Lord's supper' (1 Cor. 11:20) and the 'Lord's day' (Rev. 1:10).

Although this representation of the case has been disputed it can be said that 'there is now general agreement among scholars in referring it [church] to the Greek word *kuriakon*, properly an adjective, "of the Lord, *dominicum* [Latin], *dominical*" (from *kurios*, Lord), which occurs from the 3rd century at least, used substantively (supply *doma* [house], or the like) = "house of the Lord" as a name of the Christian house of worship.'[4]

Nor is this identification based on recent speculation or scholarly guesswork. The article goes on to report that: 'Of this the earliest cited instances are in the *Apostolical Constitutions* (II, 59), before 300, the edict of Maximinus (303–13), cited by Eusebius (Eccl. Hist. ix, 10) before 324, the Councils of Ancyra 314 (Canon 15), Neo-Caesarea 314–23 (Canon 5), and Laodicea (Canon 28). Thenceforward it appears to have been in fairly common use in the East: e.g. Constantine named several churches built by him *kuriaka* [plural] (Eusebius *De Laud*, Const xvii).'[5]

As will be seen, the New Testament Greek word *ekklēsia* (assembly, congregation, etc., and translated church) though it never has the sense of building or edifice in the Bible did very early come to be used of buildings for Christian worship, along with *basilikon*, a common name for important public buildings before Christian times. These words passed into Latin from Greek as ecclesia and *basilica*.[6] From the Latin then, which had borrowed *ekklēsia* from Greek Christian use, spelling it *ecclesia*, the word passed into the Romance and all Celtic languages. Thus, though English does not use the Greek noun *ekklēsia* in the sense of 'building,' the Celtic dialects of Great Britain in the pre-Anglo-Saxon epoch picked it up and have preserved it: in Old Irish as *eclais*, Gaelic as *eglais*, Welsh as *eglwys*, Cornish as *eglos*, etc. Thus, from the Roman conquerors of Britain, even before their being Christianized, the native Celts were taught to call a building used for Christian worship an *ekklēsia*, so to speak, while the Germanic, Angles and Saxons, and likely also the Jutes, Danes and Norwegians, who came later, still as pagans, had learned to call such a building by the word *kurikon* (abbreviated from *kuriakon doma*), i.e. 'church.'

Thus it is that from the standpoint of the informed and perceptive English-speaking Christian who desires to introduce some semblance of verbal consistency in doctrinal discourse, the whole subject of ecclesiology has been

---

1. Jacob Grimm, *Geschichte der deutschen Sprache* (Leipzig: 1848, 3rd ed., 2 vols., 1868).
2. *Theological Dictionary of the New Testament*, Vol. III, art. '*Ekklēsia*.'
3. *Oxford English Dictionary*, Vol. II (Oxford: The Clarendon Press, 1971, 1975).
4. ibid., p. 402. A lengthy discussion in a footnote on pages 531, 532, *Theological Dictionary of the New Testament*, Vol. III., art. *ekklēsia* goes over this same ground and leads to similar conclusions.
5. ibid., p. 403.
6. See art. 'Basilica,' p. 198, *A Dictionary of Greek and Roman Antiquities*, William Smith, London, 1882 and art. 'Ecclesia,' *Latin-English Lexicon*, Freund, Andrews, New York, 1862 and *ekklēsia* TDNT, Vol. III.

made obscure by the very history of our language, whereby a word first properly applied to a building of stone and wood became the common word also for the body of believers who worship there. It is not only ironic but confusing to learn that historically speaking, the English word 'church' refers *primarily* to a building dedicated to Christian worship of God and only secondarily to the people who meet there regularly for such purpose. This has been, is, and shall remain a cause of confusion, embarrassment and not a little injury to the cause of truth. The confusion is as old as the English language and will doubtless persist as long as and wherever English is spoken. Use of the word 'church' for pagan temples has even been dignified by its appearance in Tyndale's Bible Version of 1526–34 at Acts 19:37 ('neither robbers of churches [i.e. pagan temples], nor yet despisers of your goddess') and perpetuated until this very day in the Authorized Version.

The English word 'church' finds many uses in our culture. It is commonly used as (1) a synonym for a religious denomination or sect – hence the Lutheran church, the Presbyterian church and the like, even though the most rudimentary knowledge of the biblical doctrine of the church renders such use objectionable, to say the least. It is also commonly used for (2) a Christian congregation meeting in some particular place. This sometimes gets very much confused with the previously mentioned use and the one to be mentioned next. For example, an independent congregation in Williams Bay, Wisconsin long known as 'The Gospel Tabernacle,' from the wooden building in which it met, almost had a split over a change in name when a move to another building was contemplated.

Another use is (3) of a building where a Christian congregation meets. As seen in the above discussion of etymology, this is the oldest use of the word 'church' in the English language. A highly improper, but nevertheless prevalent, further use is (4) to apply the word to any building used for religious purposes, even to mosques, synagogues and pagan temples. A *Life* magazine article, for example, referred to the Buddhist temples of Bangkok as churches. Sometimes all the Christian congregations in a geographical area, or even in the whole world, are called 'the church.' 'Church' is also popularly employed for (5) the chief worship service of a Christian congregation, as opposed to auxiliary meetings (as in 'I attended church last Sunday, but was absent from Sunday School'). Finally, by abstraction (6) Christianity in any or all times may be referred to as 'the church,' as in the term 'church history.'

II. The Word *Ekklēsia* in the New Testament.

As further study will show, there are many words and figures of speech for Christ's church in the New Testament. Yet the common and special word is *ekklēsia*, derived from *ek*, out of, and *kaleō*, to call. Hence the basic significance of 'called out' is derived. How much emphasis should be placed on this etymological meaning is difficult to say. Etymology does support the emphasis Scripture places on the spiritual separateness of the body of believers from the world in which they live. It has suggestive connection with 'elect' (Greek *eklektos*), emphasizing that the church are the chosen, the saved. Decisive information about what the word *ekklēsia* meant to the authors who wrote the New Testament and the Greek-speaking readers will be found only by examining how they used the word, according to an axiom of linguistics that usage determines meaning.

Before looking at the New Testament usage we should observe that there were at least two pre-Christian associations, and a possible third, which had already been named *ekklēsia*, long before Jesus and Paul employed the word for a Christian community.

There was, firstly, the Old Testament assembly of Israel, for which the usual Hebrew word is *qahal*, rendered frequently in the LXX by *ekklēsia*. *Ekklēsia* appears about a hundred times in the Greek Old Testament. Almost every time it is a translation of the Hebrew word *qahal* or the verbal equivalent of it. It is easy to make too much of this fact, interesting though it is. There is no consistent use indicating that every time *qahal* (= *ekklēsia*) appears, the same entity is being described. A mob in the streets, the prophets as a group, the elders in session, the leaders of Judah or of Israel gathered together – any gathering of people may be called an *ekklēsia* in the Greek Old Testament rendering of *qahal*. This word definitely is not the name for the national or spiritual people of God in the Old Testament. There were as many '*ekklēsia*' as there were gatherings. In each case the *ekklēsia* comes into existence on the occasion of gathering and dissolves with the dissolution of that gathering. See such illustrative examples as Deuteronomy 4:10; 9:10; Judges 21:8, and similar. True, sometimes there is reference to the '*ekklēsia* of Israel' or 'of the Lord.' We do not know what Hebrew or Aramaic word Stephen actually used and which by Luke was rendered *ekklēsia* (church) at Acts 7:38. He is alluding to Deuteronomy 9:19 where it refers to a special assembly, not a continuing social organization rendered 'day of *assembly*' (KJV, AV, RSV, NIV).[7] There is very slim support, however, for the concept of a continuing organ or body known as the *ekklēsia* in the Greek Old Testament. The one text wherein this word appears in a New Testament quotation of the Old Testament (Heb. 2:12; cf. Ps. 22:23) offers no support at all for the supposition the word *ekklēsia* may be used theologically to weld the Old Testament people of God into some organic or conceptual union with the New Testament people of God. The question of the connection between Old Testament Israel and New Testament *ekklēsia* will have to be settled on other grounds. Many recent authors assume but do not demonstrate this connection.

I base these conclusions in part on personal examinations of all the occurrences of *ekklēsia* in the *Septuagint*, employing the *Concordance to the Septuagint* of Hatch and Redpath in searching them out. Those who may wish the judgment of a recognized authority in the area will find my interpretation of the data confirmed by K. L. Schmidt's article *Ekklēsia*.[8] Schmidt writes, 'In the LXX *ekklēsia* is a wholly secular term; it means "assembling," whether in the sense of the act of assembling or of those "assembled".'[9]

Though without special religious content, this word was nevertheless available to Jesus and the Apostles and to the first Christians. Though *ekklēsia* is sometimes used in the LXX as equivalent to *sunagogē* (synagogue), by the time of Jesus that word had distinctly Jewish connections which made it unsuitable as a name for the church of Jesus Christ.

In the second place, there was the use of *ekklēsia* as a name for a secular gathering in the Greek city states. When the citizens of a Greek city gathered, an *ekklēsia* came into existence. When it was dismissed, except for a vague nominal sense, the *ekklēsia* dissolved until called into existence again. There is again only one New Testament example of this use – i.e. three occurrences in one passage, Acts 19:32, 39, 41. (In verses 32 and 41 *ekklēsia* is used of an informal spontaneous community gathering, in verse 39 of a formally convened legal assembly.) I have discussed this somewhat at length elsewhere.[10]

Some have suggested that the cultic societies prevalent in the Greco-Roman world of the first century may have been designated by the word, *ekklēsia*. It has been advocated that this indeed is the immediate precedent for the distinct Christian use of *ekklēsia*. Yet though advocated by a few of the learned for three-quarters of a century, the view has now no known advocates.[11] This is not to say that it may not have been used by one or another of the mystery cults as a name for their meetings, though less likely of the cult itself. Indeed, the idea, 'business meeting,' might be rendered (and was so rendered) *ekklēsia* by any social group of the ancient Greek-speaking world.

The most valuable gain from this excursion is to make one aware that if we are to discover what the word *ekklēsia* means for definition of the church we will have to search the New Testament itself. The first-century preachers and missionaries referred to a local body of Christian believers as an *ekklēsia*. The New Testament documents use the word quite prevalently in the same way. Just why, we likely can never know. But they used many other terms of designation as well. Some attention must be given to all of these in due time.

The word *ekklēsia* appears 115 times in the New Testament. After the Gospels, which do not use the word except for two occurrences in Matthew (16:18 and 18:17), the word appears in all books except 2 Timothy, Titus, 1 and 2 Peter, 1 and 2 John, and Jude. The *idea* is present in these books also though the *word* may be missing. Nevertheless, since the idea is represented by this word an overwhelming number of times our study may not omit *ekklēsia*. We shall, however, pass over the usual tedious tracing of the word book by book and come immediately to a summary of the findings.

Two types of use of *ekklēsia* are not significant for our study. As previously noted, our word is used in one passage of the assembly of the citizens of a Greek city (Acts 19:32, 39, 41) and twice of the meetings of the Israelites in Old Testament times as at Hebrews 2:12 (whether in a synagogue type of setting or of some national 'synod' is hard to say) where Psalm 22:22 is quoted and at Acts 7:38 where Stephen refers to assembled Israelites as 'the *ekklēsia* in the wilderness.' He clearly is thinking of the assembly at Mount Sinai not of the continuing nation of Israel.

---

7. See TDNT, III, 504.
8. TDNT, III, pp. 527–529.
9. ibid., p. 527.
10. R. D. Culver, *Civil Government, A Biblical View* (Edmonton, Alberta: Canadian Institute for Law, Theology, and Public Policy 2000), pp. 222–227.
11. TDNT, III, Schmidt, p. 513.

A third use is interesting and relates to the church of Christ but is not related to the essential nature of the church in the New Testament. This is of an event, the local group of believers gathered for worship (or business as the case might be, cf. 1 Cor. 5:4). Occurrences are limited to 1 Corinthians 11:18; 14:19, 34. The New English Bible conveys this sense quite precisely: 'I am told that when you meet as a congregation you fall into sharply divided groups,' etc. (11:18); 'In the congregation I would rather speak five intelligible words,' etc. (14:19); 'As in all congregations of God's people, women should not address the meeting' (14:34). In this last reference, though, 'congregations' is in Greek the plural of *ekklēsia* (a case of the fourth use; see below) – it is the recurrence of the word *ekklēsia* in 'address the *meeting* [emphasis added]' only that furnishes the example of the third use. In this sense an *ekklēsia* comes into existence at about 11:00 o'clock Sunday morning and goes out of existence about an hour later.

This usage is usual in the Septuagint. There, a meeting or assembly of select persons (or of all) of Israel was called an *ekklēsia*; the total people as such were never so called, as far as I can determine. For the total people *ekklēsia* is not the way the idea is represented. The whole nation is 'all Israel' or 'all Judah,' or some such combination of words. In the New Testament, as we shall see, an advance was made, for the New Testament people as such are called the *ekklēsia*.

A fourth use is of the permanent group, the believers in Christ associated into a unit of permanent fellowship in a given locality. They are an *ekklēsia* whether listening to a sermon together on Sunday or sleeping in their beds in their various homes on Saturday night. There are approximately ninety occurrences of this sort in the New Testament. In this sense the word is often plural, as in Romans 16:16, where reference is made to 'churches of Christ' and 1 Thessalonians 2:14, *viz.* 'churches of God in Christ Jesus that are in Judea.' More frequently the single 'house church,' characteristic of the apostolic epoch, is so designated. Examples are, 'the church in their house' (Rom. 16:5), and 'Gaius, who is host to me and to the whole church' (Rom. 16:23). The plural as well as the singular in reference to the single local churches appear together in 1 Corinthians 16:19; 'The churches of Asia send you greetings. Aquila and Prisca, together with the church in their house, send you hearty greetings.'

Finally *ekklēsia* is used of what theologians have come to call the church universal. Opinions vary somewhat as to how many times this is the sense, but most scholars allow twenty-five or twenty-six. True, a minority of Baptists and a few others have sought to eliminate the very idea of the universal church from the New Testament, but their arguments have not prevailed. A work by Dale Moody, a prominent Southern Baptist professor,[12] appears to have laid this spook to rest in the Southern Baptist Convention. Outstanding and hardly questionable references are 1 Corinthians 10:32; Hebrews 12:23; and Ephesians 5:25.

It must be added that in some scriptural texts the author seems to merge both the local and universal concepts. This is quite natural, considering the relation between the universal and local church. An example of this apparent merging is at Acts 20:28. Addressed, as it is, to local elders – 'Pay careful attention to yourselves and to all the flock, of which the Holy Spirit has made you overseers' – one would suppose the 'flock' to be the local assembly or *ekklēsia*. Yet he continues, 'to care for the church of God, which he obtained with his own blood.' Who can say that Paul's sweep of thought did not include also the same whole body of Christ of which the same Apostle wrote in Ephesians 5:25-27? 'Christ loved the church and gave himself up for her... that he might present the church to himself' and so on.

It is only with the church local and universal that this study is concerned.

Scholars have pondered which is primary theologically. Is the application of *ekklēsia* to the church local a constriction of the idea of universal *ekklēsia*, or is the idea of church universal an extension of the more simple notion of the local *ekklēsia* or assembly? Hold in mind the previous usage in the Greek world, where an *ekklēsia* was always local, and the post-biblical use among Jews (an item we have not yet herein presented) where it is a very close synonym for a local synagogue. Schmidt asserts: 'Parallel discussion of *ekklēsia* and *sunagogē* makes it plain... that the two words mean much the same and often correspond to the same Hebrew word.'[13] It seems close to certain that the word *ekklēsia* is primarily the local assembly and that its use to designate the universal church is a secondary extension of the primary meaning.

A notable author, Adolph Deissmann wrote in this vein:

> The first scattered congregations of Greek-speaking Christians up and down the Roman Empire spoke of themselves as a '(convened) assembly'; at first each congregation was so called, and afterwards the whole body of Christians everywhere was spoken of collectively as 'the (convened) assembly.' That is the most literal

---

12. Dale Moody, *Christ and the Church, An Exposition of Ephesians, etc.* (Grand Rapids: Eerdmans, 1963).
13. *TDNT*, Vol. III, 'qahal,' p. 528.

translation of the Greek word *ekklēsia*. This self-bestowed name rested on the certain conviction that God had separated from the world His 'saints' in Christ, and had 'called' or 'convened' them to an assembly, which was 'God's assembly,' 'God's muster,' because God was the convener.[14]

F. J. A. Hort, of the galaxy of conservative orthodox scholars who in many ways brought evangelical biblical scholarship up to and into the twentieth century, wrote what many regard as the seminal work for all subsequent study of the biblical *ekklēsia*. He pointed out that the history of the New Testament shows how a small incipient *ekklēsia* (church) of twelve Apostles became 120 and then a single ethnic congregation at Jerusalem. Only as they caught the notion that the new *ekklēsiae* (plu.) which formed in other parts of a Jewish holy land, and then finally after a struggle with the idea of more *ekklēsiae* outside the Jewish nation and territory, did they fully see that the many were one *ekklēsia*, the larger being fully present in each authentic *ekklēsia* or local church.[15]

With this groundwork of understanding we are prepared further to focus this study, of which the church universal and the church local are the two foci.

---

14. Adolph Deissmann, *Light From the Ancient East*, tr. L. R. M. Strachan (London: Hodder and Stoughton, 1927) p. 112.
15. F. J. A. Hort, *The Christian Ecclesia: A Course of Lectures on the Early Conceptions of the Ecclesia* (London: Macmillan & Co., 1898).

4
Metaphors, Images and Ideas Related to the Church

Like the Trinity of the Godhead and like the incarnation, the church is a New Testament 'mystery,' as Paul says: 'This mystery is profound, and I am saying that it refers to Christ and the church' (Eph. 5:32; cf. 1 Tim. 3:16). Hence, though the New Testament speaks at great length and in minute detail about many aspects of the church (members, officers, ordinances and the like) no text of Scripture defines the church in formal categories. Some of the same transcendent element which belongs to the Godhead and to the incarnation belongs to the church as well.

Theologians have different ways of calling attention to this fact. Strong emphasizes the 'transcendent element in the church'.[1] J. V. L. Casserley in an important work speaks of 'the mystery' of the church, explaining correctly that 'like all singulars the church is incapable of definition. We can enter into and expound the heart of the mystery but we cannot define its limits.'[2]

This element of 'transcendence' is profoundly present in many New Testament references to the Christian *ekklēsia*, or church: 'I will build my church, and the gates of hell shall not prevail against it' (Matt 16:18); 'he... gave him as head over all things to the church, which is his body, the fullness of him who fills all in all' (Eph. 1:22, 23); 'so that through the church the manifold wisdom of God might now be made known' (Eph. 3:10). These and other amazingly grand statements (e.g. Heb. 12:23) are almost in a class with what the Bible says about Christ or God Himself. The incorporation of both natural branches (believing Israelites) and wild branches (Gentiles) into the olive tree of God's grace and favor (Rom. 11:17) is said by Paul to speak of the wisdom and knowledge of God, both unsearchable and past finding out (Rom. 11:37). The unity of the church with Christ, though illustrated by the union of husband and wife, is said to be 'a great mystery' (Eph. 5:32 KJV).

Yet God has said much about Himself in Scripture — enough that chapters in great books of theology rightly expound God's person, His attributes and works. Metaphors and other verbal images for God are abundant, each contributing valid information. So it is with the church.

Metaphors and Images of the Church.

A distinction must carefully be made between metaphors for the collective entity, the church and metaphors for individual disciples of Christ who compose the church. When, for example, Jesus said of His disciples, 'You are the

1. A. H. Strong, *Systematic Theology* (1907), p. 890.
2. J. V. L. Casserley, *Christian Community* (Longmans, 1960), p. 19.

salt of the earth' there is no reference at all to the collective entity, the *ekklēsia* (assembly) as such. When authors of New Testament books frequently address fellow disciples as believers or ambassadors for Christ or saints these terms have no specific significance in defining the church. When, however, Peter exhorts his readers throughout the 'dispersion' as 'a holy nation' (1 Peter 2:9) the metaphor clearly designates the collective *ekklēsia* or church.

In a very widely influential book,[3] P. A. Minear found ninety-six 'analogies.' Yet all except less than a score are really metaphors for individual Christians rather than the church as such.

Further, in the New Testament the church has an undefined, but certain, relation to 'the kingdom of God [of Christ, of heaven]' and to the Old Testament people of God, Israel, Abraham's seed. Church, kingdom, Israel and people of God are viewed by some as identical, only viewed from different perspectives. Some others insist Israel and church have no connection at all, being in sequence two distinct kinds of collectives with different connections with God's kingdom. Discussion of these questions has been controlled, at least in larger part, by interests seemingly remote, such as the proper form of church government and whether infants should be baptized or not.

Among recent writers Robert Saucy treats the metaphors as defining *indicia* of the church.[4] Another selects only 'the people of God,' 'the body of Christ' and 'the temple of God' for comment and handles the church in relation to Israel and to the kingdom as special problems.[5] Thomas Oden writes of 'the metaphorical logic of Ecclesiology,' briefly expounding seven such metaphors while treating kingdom and Israel in other connections.[6]

There are two important purposes served by some brief but careful preliminary attention to these topics right at this point, before later specific, extended chapters on the nature of the church. In first place, the scholar must rid himself of the prevalent unconscious notion that without faith and revelation one already knows anything at all of that entity, the Christian *ekklēsia*, which is so grandly represented in the New Testament. In some respects it is as far from authentic perception by the unregenerate or shallow believer as the mystery of the holy Trinity – the *perchōrēsis*, the procession of the Holy Spirit, and the begetting of the Son. The resort of the Bible to figures, analogies, metaphors and images demonstrates as much. In the second place, employment of such Old Testament terms and ideas as Abraham's seed, Israel, holy priesthood, chosen people, holy nation, Zion and Jerusalem for New Testament entities has obscured for many the actual distinctions. 'We're marching to Zion' or 'O Zion haste thy mission high fulfilling' in beloved hymns or St Peter's extended metaphors such as 'a chosen race, a royal priesthood, a holy nation' (1 Peter 2:9) do not mean that the church is truly an Israel, a Zion, thus in any literal sense a mere extension of an Old Testament entity. There is a theological disagreement here that should be recognized early, even if settlement must come later.

Metaphors of the Church.

Peter liked to 'stir up' the 'pure minds' of his readers 'by way of remembrance' (2 Peter 3:1 KJV). He required them to think of themselves (likely Gentile readers) as 'exiles of the dispersion' to compare themselves with the Jews of the dispersion (1 Peter 1:1). He assumes they know written revelation, the Old Testament, the reading of which we know consumed a major portion of time in every Christian assembly of the period. No less than for Paul the Holy Scriptures are 'profitable… for training in righteousness' (2 Tim. 3:16). His Epistles are laced with Old Testament allusions, figures, citations and doctrinal assumptions. In his first Epistle Peter begs his readers to think of themselves individually as 'strangers and exiles' (Heb. 11:13) similar to Abraham (cf. Heb 11:9). At 1 Peter 2:5-11, 17, Peter instructs them as a collective entity. For that entity he uses seven different figures drawn from the Old Testament – several of them more widely used in the Old Testament as figures of speech than as literal references. They are (1) 'a spiritual house,' (2) 'a holy priesthood,' (3) 'a chosen race,' (4) 'a royal priesthood,' (5) 'a holy nation,' (6) 'a people for his own possession' (v. 9) and (7) 'the brotherhood'.

Though Paul is thinking of the individual believer's body as 'the temple of the Holy Spirit' in his admonition against fornication at 1 Corinthians 6:19, in an earlier chapter the church collectively is (8) 'God's temple' (1 Cor. 3:16, 17). To the Ephesians Paul expounded the unity of the *ekklēsia* under the figure of (9) 'one new man' (Eph. 2:15). In several texts the *ekklēsia* collectively is called (10) 'one flock' (John 10:16), 'little flock' (Luke 12:32), and similar.

---

3. Paul A. Minear, *Images of the church in the New Testament* (Philadelphia: Westminster Press, 1960).
4. Robert Saucy, *The Church in God's Program* (Chicago: Moody Press, 'The Nature of the church,' 1972), pp. 19–56.
5. Millard J. Erickson, *Christian Theology* (Grand Rapids: Baker, 1985), pp. 294–297.
6. Thomas Oden, *Life in the Spirit* (San Francisco: Harper Collins, 1992), pp. 294–297.

Upon reflection one must admit that even the Greek word *ekklēsia*, (11) 'assembly,' is a metaphor drawn from Greek *politeia* (political life). The church is (12) 'his body,' i.e. 'the body of Christ.' So prevalent in the Epistles and so important in extended explanations is this designation that it seems almost to pass from metaphor to literal reality (see 1 Cor. 12:13 ff.). Yet it is truly another metaphor, however amazingly realistic it seems in many ways. It will be our chief resource in understanding *The Essential Nature of the Church Universal* (chapter 10).

The universal, God-sponsored, human practice of marriage furnishes the image of the collective *ekklēsia* as (13) 'the bride' of Christ. This is explicit in the last book of the New Testament (Rev. 21:2, 9; 22:17) and implicit in Paul's discourse on Christian marriage in Ephesians 5:22-33, and several other New Testament texts. This relation is in large part an eschatological figure pointing to special events at the Lord's Second Advent when the *ekklēsia* as 'espoused wife' shall be joined to her husband furnished with special nuptial garments of white and shall celebrate the union at 'the marriage supper of the Lamb.' These images will furnish a major source of such information as we have regarding *The Destiny of the Church* (chapter 14 of this study).

Finally, the church is (14) 'the fellowship' or *koinōnia*, a word which does perhaps pass from the status of metaphor of human association to real – if intangible, perhaps ineffable – sharing, which the *ekklēsia* collectively has in the very life of God (Acts 2:4; 2 Peter 1:4). Yet *koinōnia* too is first of all a Greek word for community (intimate sharing) on the level of the purely human. It is not an Old Testament word. Hatch and Redpath report it only once in the whole Old Testament, at Leviticus 6:2, where it means something like partnership in a matter of material things.[7] In the Greek world, however, as Hauch points out, words of the group *koinon* were applied 'to the most varied relationships' including sacral speech and rituals where it was thought to be an 'inward reception of mysterious divine power in eating and drinking.'[8] In biblical Judaism, however, although the idea of 'fellowship' with God in various contexts is not absent, the idea of permanent participation of a group of human beings in the life of God is largely a matter of predictions of the future – Immanuel, 'God with us,' for the future in a consummate sense (incarnation, church, the new Jerusalem). It remained for the Hellenist, Dr Luke, author of two of the largest books of the New Testament, to employ the very Greek term *koinōnia* for that vital intimacy of reborn people, with one another and with God, by the Holy Spirit, which is normal for a healthy body of local believers in Christ, the New Testament *ekklēsia*:

> And they devoted themselves to the apostles' teaching and fellowship [*kai tē koinōnia*], to the breaking of bread and the prayers (Acts 2:42).

The communion service both enhances and celebrates the *koinōnia* of believers in unity with Christ. In the eating of the Eucharistic bread the symbolism of the 'one loaf' (1 Cor. 10:16) eaten by all believers speaks of their *koinōnia* (communion, common participation) in the benefits of His death on their behalf. So also with the one 'cup' of which Jesus instructed, 'all of you drink of it.' In this way they exercise their own 'body life' as *ekklēsia* and symbolize their collective existence as drawn from and subsisting in Christ. The (15) 'one loaf' then becomes still one more clear New Testament metaphor for the church. This is vivid in the Greek text of 1 Corinthians 10:16, 17: 'The loaf which we break [and eat], is it not a fellowship (*koinōnia*) of the body [the broken body] of Christ? because there is one loaf, we who are many (*hoi polloi*) are one body, for we all partake (*metechomen*, have together) out of (*ex*) the one loaf.'

Questions and Problems.

Church, Israel, Kingdom.

There are three interrelated matters that will be examined at length later in this study. The reader should be aware of them at this stage of discussion, namely the relation of the church to Israel and to the kingdom of heaven (of God) and the time of the beginning of the church. If the church began at some point after the Ascension of Christ it is not specifically an extension of the people of God known as Israel, however many parallels may be drawn, or analogies, for our instruction (see 1 Cor. 10:11 ff.). Parallels drawn by New Testament passages between the Old Testament people and the New Testament people of God, the members of the church are then just that – parallels, analogies, types. Further, Jesus spoke often of the kingdom of God in such a way as clearly to indicate that it was a present

---

7. Edwin Hatch and Henry A. Redpath, *A Concordance to the Septuagint and the Other Greek Versions of the Old Testament* (Including the Apocryphal Books), 3 vols., (Graz, Austria: Akademische Druck, U. Verlagsanstalt, 1954), p. 775, col. 1.
8. Hauch, *TDNT*, III, p. 798 ff.

reality as he was speaking; that in the future His disciples and their converts would be witnesses to the kingdom as members of it; that the coming of the kingdom of God in some sense is a wholly future eschatological event to 'come' at the Second Advent. So these three biblical ideas, the inauguration of the church, the relation of Israel to the church and of the kingdom to the church have to be addressed.

No one can doubt that in some way true believers in revealed biblical religion before the coming of Christ have an intimate spiritual relation to New Testament believers after Pentecost. That does not necessarily mean that the New Testament church of Gentiles and Jews should be called an Israel and consequent application of all Israel's promises and warnings directly to the Christian *ekklēsia*, dear to New England Puritan theology. Both Israel and church are, however, in many biblical texts, placed within the kingdom of Messiah. How shall we sort this out? There are consequences for many departments of church doctrine, practice and spiritual formation. We cannot here trace out the origins and history of the several answers biblical interpreters have supplied. At this point let us note only how the subject appears in the New Testament narrative and reserve extended discussion to chapter 6 below, *The Foundation for the church*.

The Gospels report Jesus as referring to the church, as such, only twice, each time as something in the future, *viz.*: 'I will build my church' (Matt. 16:18 KJV) and 'tell it unto the church' (Matt. 18:17 KJV). Then after Jesus' Ascension and period of waiting in Jerusalem for the promised baptism of the Holy Spirit (Acts 1:4, 5), as Jesus commanded, the promised baptism in the Holy Spirit did occur (Acts 2:1 ff.; cf. 1 Cor. 12:13 ff.). That this constituted them one body, the Christian *ekklēsia* is the understanding apparently not only of Paul (1 Cor. 12:13 ff.) but of the author of Acts 2:47 for there (at least in the *Textus Receptus* reflected in KJV) the first appearance of the word *ekklēsia* as a name for the whole body of believers occurs after Matthew 18:17, *viz.*: 'And the Lord added to the church daily such as should be saved' (KJV). The vast majority of readers on the basis of this simple narrative evidence have (perhaps naively) understood that the Christian *ekklēsia* was predicted by Christ for the future and came into existence on that great Day of Pentecost of Acts 2. That 'Day' appears in theological writing of about every shade of opinion as 'the birthday of the church.' This is hardly negated by the revised Greek text which omits *ekklēsia* from Acts 2:47. Nor does this mean that the people who formed the Christian *ekklēsia* of Jerusalem had no special status during the days of waiting – the 120 of Acts 1. They were certainly 'the church in expectation.'

Though some enthusiastic advocates of Reformed theology assert the *ekklēsia* is 'Spiritual Israel' or the 'New Israel,' the Bible never in any text says so as does one enthusiastic partisan book title which announces, *The Church is Israel Now*. No less presumptuous, it seems to me, was the frequent assumption of the optimistic liberalism of early and mid-twentieth century that enlarging church membership or promoting 'world peace' was what Jesus was talking about in His parables of the kingdom. It is equally indefensible to assume that the coming of the kingdom of heaven is uniformly and precisely the fulfillment of Old Testament promises to Israel in a future millennium.

The Church Militant, Expectant, Triumphant.

Tradition has spoken of 'three phrases or aspects of the church's being,' thought to have a biblical basis – the *church militant*, the *church expectant* and the *church triumphant*. The biblical basis is thought to be 1 Corinthians 13: church militant under the category of faith (struggling, warring, but believing and faithful); under the category of hope (expectant) – living in 'an atmosphere of serene hope… all anxiety banished from their lives'; triumphant, under the category of 'absolute love,' i.e. God's love, the ultimate victory in the coming kingdom of God. Though this suggestive explanation by Anglican J. V. Langmede Casserley[9] is attractive other explanations of this ancient tradition have been proposed.

The Church Visible and the Church Invisible.

This distinction and its importance in Protestant-evangelical theology is not generally understood and is commonly severely criticized as though the Swiss Reformers who articulated it believed an absurdity of two universal churches in the world. After the Reformation epoch, reading of Calvin's ecclesiology declined until recently, hence the world forgot what he (the Reformer who best articulated the distinction) really meant. The New Testament from Matthew 18 onward fully supports what he had to say. In fact a lengthy section of Rufinus' *Commentary on the Apostles' Creed*[10] powerfully makes this very distinction. Hold in mind that Calvin was trying to help truly believing,

---

9. Casserley, op. cit., pp. 16, 17, 19.
10. NPNF, ii, Vol. 3, pp. 558, 559.

converted people of his time understand that in addition to the organized, widely corrupted, professing church, there was the 'church of the living God, pillar and ground of truth.' Calvin used the accepted definitions of the church of 'St. Cyprian and St. Augustine' and repeats 'in accord with general tradition and with Luther, that the church is our mother and that apart from her there is no salvation.'[11] He clarifies the biblical distinction in the following:

> Holy Scripture speaks of the church in two ways. Sometimes by the term 'church' it means that which is actually in God's presence, into which no persons are received but those who are children of God by grace of adoption and true members of Christ by sanctification of the Holy Spirit.... Often however, the name 'church' designates the whole multitude of men spread over the earth who profess to worship one God and Christ.... In this church are mingled many hypocrites who have nothing of Christ but the name and outward appearance.... Such are tolerated for a time either because they cannot be convicted by a competent tribunal or because a vigorous discipline does not always flourish as it ought.
>
> Just as we believe that the former church, *invisible to us*, is *visible to the eyes of God alone* [emphasis added], so we are commanded to revere and keep communion with the latter which is called 'church' in respect to men.[12]

Calvin quickly moves on to show how by certain marks the true church may be recognized.

This does not mean that in Calvin's view we are to 'keep communion' with every organization which calls itself a church, for there are marks by which the partially hidden existence of God's true church in a local assembly may be recognized. The true Christian *ekklēsia* may be recognized in the human assembly with its leading structure, members and the like. 'Sometimes the church is able to survive only in a hidden state, that the church should not be utterly extinguished. God always preserves a hidden seed, for there must always be a church in the world.'[13]

So the distinction between visible church and invisible church is, properly understood, a very important, necessary, practical matter. The Roman Church of the sixteenth century, of course, vigorously rejected it, holding that the existing, visible hierarchical structure is the one church outside which there is no salvation. Peter was appointed to be the 'visible foundation' of the one church. The Roman Mass is 'a visible sacrifice,' the hierarchy and priests are a visible structure of administration. 'The rejection of the hierarchy inevitably [among Albigenses, Waldenes, Hus, Reformers] led to the doctrine of the invisible church.'[14] Vatican II and the *New Catechism* have made some concessions and modifications in the way the matter is stated.

The Communion of Saints.

Though not employed much recently among British and American evangelicals this expression is biblical, finding expression in some early forms of the tenth article of the Apostles' Creed.[15] 'I believe... in the holy catholic church' follows, 'the communion of saints.' In the Roman church the communion of saints is an aspect of doctrine of the Mass, *viz*.: 'The faithful are fed by Christ's holy body and blood to grow in communion of the Holy Spirit....'[16] Among Protestants, 'the communion of saints' should be understood almost in the same sense as 'the invisible church' except that emphasis is placed upon universality, including saints departed to be with Christ and all the saved of every dispensation (epoch), perhaps even holy angels. A precious hymn sung frequently (and perhaps only half understood) conveys the idea of the invisible aspect of 'the communion of saints':

> Yet she on earth hath union
> With God the Three in One
> And mystic sweet communion
> With those whose rest is won.[17]

---

11. Francois Wendel, *Calvin* (New York: Harper and Row, 1963), p. 294. See I Tim. 3:15; Gal. 4:26.
12. Calvin, *Institutes*, Book IV. i. 2, (Westminster ed.), pp. 1021, 1022.
13. Calvin, *Commentary on Ezekiel*. Vol. II, trans. T. Myers (Edinburgh: 1850), 16:53.
14. Ludwig Ott, *Fundamentals of Catholic Dogma* (Rockford, IL: TAN Books, 1960, 1974), p. 301. See art. 'church,' VI. 'The Necessary Means of Salvation,' *The Catholic Encyclopedia*, Vol. III, pp. 752–754.
15. Henry S. Bettenson, *Documents of the Christian Church*, 2nd ed. (Oxford U. Press, 1963), p. 24.
16. *Catechism of 1994*, #948.
17. *The Church's One Foundation*, S. J. Stone, 1864.

The Pilgrim Church or the Believers' Church.

The origin of this good name for the Christian *ekklēsia* and authority for using it is Hebrews 11:13 and 1 Peter 2:11. The former refers to saints of old as strangers and pilgrims on the earth, while Peter addresses his Christian readers as sojourners (temporary residents) and beseeches them as sojourners and pilgrims, to abstain from fleshly lusts. In context these passages are addressed to believers in their capacity of disciples (followers) of Christ. 'The children of God, wherever they may be, are only guests in the world' (Calvin on 1 Peter 2:11).

Yet the 'left wing of the Reformation' (Roland Bainton) – also called 'the Believers' church' or 'Radical Protestantism' (G. F. Williams), including first Anabaptists and then many other persecuted believing groups, including New England Baptists and Quakers – have taken these verses to themselves as special for themselves (not without reason).

The Roman Church has long since, and still to the present, sought to attract to itself the title 'Pilgrim church.' *The Catechism of 1994* anomalously applies to the Roman Church Augustine's references to the patient suffering of the pre-Constantinian church to show that 'The [Roman] church progresses on her pilgrimage amidst this world's persecutions and God's consolations… and… will not be perfected in glory without great trials, etc.'[18]

Though the Roman Church has furnished some martyrs since 1517 it is *per se* hardly the persecuted pilgrim church. Ask the thousands of martyrs (Albigensians, Cathari, Huguenots, victims of Bloody Mary in Britain and the Inquisition) about that. The Roman Church insisted that the hierarchical structure is of the essence of the church and could therefore hardly escape bearing the role of persecutor of the pilgrim church. Yet the Word of God was preserved in written form by people within the fold of the Roman Church, and throughout the Middle Ages there are not wanting many who possessed faith, hope and love toward Christ. The 'invisible' church was present in the 'visible' – precisely the point Zwingli and Calvin wished to make. In recent times many believers in Christ of common persuasion continue to be 'slain for the testimony of Jesus' in Marxist, pagan and Islamic areas of the world.

It is beyond the scope of this book to trace out the history of efforts – sometimes under duress of persecution, sometimes with encouragement of the civil community – to form what Max Weber first called 'The Believers' church.'[19] For trustworthy coverage of the subject see G. G. Westin,[20] Franklin Littell,[21] Donald F. Durnbaugh.[22]

Durnbaugh describes a group formed by Alexander Mack (1708), in the Palatine district of Germany as upholding the pilgrim church ideal. They called themselves simply Brethren; by their critics, Dunkers, i.e. 'dippers', because they practiced baptism of believers by trine immersion. They were severely persecuted by Lutheran and Reformed as well as by the Roman Catholic clergy and several governments. A Lutheran pastor in 1713 (E. G. Gruber) challenged the Dunkers' first printed record of beliefs. To this Mack replied in words which truly are a statement of the pilgrim church ideal:

> We maintain… that at all times God has had His church which always observed the true baptism and ordinances. This, however, was always hidden from unbelievers and often consisted of but few members. Despite this the gates of hell could not prevail against the church of the Lord Jesus. It can also be proved from the histories that God has caused His ordinances to be revealed as a witness to the unbelievers at all times.[23]

The last sentence in the quotation is the theme of many volumes of Mennonite, Brethren (Dunker) and Baptist literature. Above-mentioned books will lead the interested reader into this truly vast realm.

---

18. *Catechism of 1994*, #769.
19. Max Weber, *The Protestant Ethic and the Spirit of Capitalism*, trans. T. Parsons (New York: Scribners, 1958), pp. 144, 145.
20. G. Westin, *The Free Church Through the Ages*, trans. V. A. Olson (Nashville: Broadman Press, 1958).
21. Franklin Littell, *The Free Church* (Boston: Star King Press, 1957).
22. Donald F. Durnbaugh, *The Believers' Church* (New York: Macmillan, 1970).
23. Quoted from Alexander Mack, Jr.. in Durnbaugh, ibid., p. 124.

5
The Twofold Aspect of the Church, Universal and Local

The Scriptures distinguish between the universal church and the local assembly, but the New Testament consistently refers to either by the word *ekklēsia*. They are obviously not the same entity nor entirely different and the history of attempts to define and relate the two is part of the history of orthodoxy, schism and heresy. The differences of opinion have been not only between large groups such as Roman Catholics and Protestants (though the disagreement there is well-nigh absolute) but between Protestant denominations and within them. The Protestant differences are, of course, less.

The distinction between the church universal and the church local was introduced in connection with the meaning of *ekklēsia* in the New Testament It would be easy simply to move on to discuss the two in the manner of biblical exegesis, without reference to the profoundly different ways in which Christian groups and teachers have understood both, especially the church universal.

The Roman Catholic Church, as we will show shortly, does not admit that any outside the pale of their own hierarchically structured society, all in obedience to Peter's successor and Christ's vicar, the Roman pontiff, are within the one, true, holy, catholic and apostolic church. The papal church claims to be the *one* authentic church. By 'catholic' they mean inclusive of every member of the church. This hierarchical structure is 'the mystical body of Christ.' At any time there are three parts of this body. Ott says, '"mystical body of Christ" means communion of all those made holy by the grace of Christ. This includes the faithful on earth; those in the place of purification [purgatory] who are not yet completely justified; and the perfectly justified in heaven... the militant, the suffering and the Triumphant church.'[1] The pope has jurisdiction over all those on earth, the church militant. Until recent times all who claimed to be Christians and outside the Roman fold were called by various deprecatory names, the mildest being schismatics and heretics, and were denounced as dangerous and worthy of elimination by death. (As evidence, refer to all those anathemas which conclude many of the decress of the Council of Trent and what the Roman Church actually did in pre-Reformation times and the Reformation epoch. Pope John Paul II has publicly apologized for the blood letting.) In recent times this has changed. That is to say, though the exclusive claims have not been renounced, it is allowed that Protestants and some others may be 'separated brethren.' The new stance seems to be quite sincere and it started before Vatican II in the 1960s. There has been growing a better feeling, with manifold rapprochement in varying degrees from almost all parties. Yet still, as I shall show – decisively I

---

1. Ludwig Ott, Fundamentals of Catholic Dogma (Rockford, IL: TAN Books, 1960, 1974), pp. 270, 271.

think – however defined, the official theology (dogma) is that only the Roman Church is Catholic (universal). Rapprochement did not begin suddenly with Vatican II, even though to the general public it seemed to be so. The volume *Man's Disorder and God's Design*,[2] prepared in anticipation of the 'ecumenical' founding council of 1948, reports early efforts of Roman Catholic clergy to establish fraternal relations with 'schismatics and heretics' (= Protestants). See also Rouse and Neill's *History of the Ecumenical Movement*.[3]

The New Testament use of *ekklēsia* is not limited to the universal church and local churches but these are the senses that relate to the present topic. As we saw in chapter 4, in the Greek world an *ekklēsia* was a local assembly of people – whether of a city or some other civic, geographical, social or religious unit. In the New Testament an *ekklēsia* is a company of people united by faith in Christ who meet together regularly to hear apostolic doctrine, to share mutual life (fellowship), for worship (the breaking of bread), prayer, mutual encouragement, praise and service (Acts 2:42-47).

This New Testament use will be elaborated in chapter 15 below. Sometimes the *ekklēsia* is the whole church, that is, all believers everywhere. No doubt the clearest statement of the catholic or universal church is Paul's: 'so we, though many, are one body in Christ, and individually members one of another' (Rom. 12:5). Paul was no member of the local church at Rome, but he says 'we' referring to Christians at home and everywhere else.

Thus far there is much agreement among all orthodox parties. It is summed up in the Nicene Creed (AD 325, 381): 'And [I believe] in One Holy Catholic and Apostolic church.'[4] These four 'notes' or 'marks' of the church in the article of the Creed ('I believe in the church') refer, as Calvin observed, 'not only to the visible church… but also to all God's elect, in whose number also are included the dead.'[5]

The Reformers rejected the notion that the true church is an ecclesiastical organization *as such*. They distinguished the visible, i.e. the earthly organized church, from the invisible, the company of elect, regenerate, believers. Yet they asserted that wherever the local assembly was an authentic *ekklēsia* of genuinely saved people, the one, holy, catholic and apostolic church, was present.

> The Roman church, *per contra*, asserts the unity of Rome includes all the notes of the church…. the church is a world-wide corporation, whose existence is to be forced upon the notice of all, willing or unwilling. Formal visibility is secured by those attributes which are usually termed the 'notes' of the church – her Unity, Sanctity, Catholicity, and Apostolicity…. Without this formal visibility, the purpose for which the church was founded would be frustrated.[6]

Pope Boniface VIII (1294–1303) in his Bull, '*Unam Sanctum*,' November 18, 1302 asserted the visible 'spiritual' power of church is supreme over 'earthly powers,' that the Roman Church is 'the one, holy, Catholic church, and… apostolic… outside which there is no salvation.'[7] Recently, the late learned and articulate Roman Catholic theologian, Hans Urs von Balthasar asserted:

> The Catholic church is not one church amongst others, she is the single source from which they have come, the point of convergence of all the churches that have split off from her. Only when joined [publicly and visibly] to the Catholic [i.e. Roman] church can they plunge into the ocean of eternity.[8]

At the time of the Reformation the Roman Church had claimed for a thousand years to be the one true catholic church. John McKenzie of the University of Notre Dame University asserts: 'The jurisdiction of the Roman Catholic Church is organized in such a way that there is no place on earth not subject to some Episcopal authority; there are some interesting and complex rules that govern ecclesiastical actions on shipboard, which have been adapted to aircraft.'[9] The Church of Rome, it was assumed, both then and now, is the one and only church. Present-day Roman theologians acknowledge Rome did not immediately become the site of the 'vicar of Christ,' but it was Christ's purpose from the beginning and was predicted in the Old Testament.

---

2. *Man's Disorder and God's Design*, Vol. (Part) I (New York: Harper & Bros., n.d.,), pp. 169–176.
3. Ruth Rouse and S. C. Neill, *History of the Ecumenical Movement* (Philadelphia: Westminster Press, 1954), pp. 593–596 *passim*.
4. Philip Schaff, *Creeds of Christendom ii* (Grand Rapids: Baker Books n.d., rep. 1966), p. 59.
5. Calvin, *Institutes*, Book iv, 1.1.
6. W. H. W. Fanning, 'Church,' *The Catholic Encyclopedia*, III, p. 753.
7. Heinrich Denzinger, *The Sources of Catholic Dogma* (St Louis: B. Herder, 1957), paras. 468, 469.
8. Hans Urs von Balthasar, *In the Fulness of The Faith: On the Centrality of the Distinctively Catholic*, trans. G. Harrison (San Francisco: Ignatius Press, 1988), p. 123.
9. John McKenzie, *The Roman Catholic Church* (New York: Image Books, 1971), p. 65.

Thomas Aquinas spoke for what innumerable pages in Denzinger (*The Sources of Catholic Dogma*) and even the *Cathechism of 1994* say. He first quotes an ancient sermon: 'If He had chosen the great city of Rome [instead of Bethlehem and Nazareth], the change in the world would be ascribed to the influence of her citizens. If He had been the son of the Emperor, His benefits would be attributed to the latter's power,' etc. Aquinas then, citing 1 Corinthians 1:27, goes on to say, 'And therefore, in order the more to show His power, He set up the head of His church [the succession of popes said to be Peter, then Clement, Linus, Anacletus and onward] in Rome itself, which was the head of the world, in sign of His complete victory, in order that from that city the faith might spread through all the world; according to Isaiah xxvi. 5,6; "The high city He shall lay low... the feet of the poor, i.e. of *Christ* [emphasis added], shall tread it down; the steps of the needy, i.e. of the Apostles Peter and Paul."'[10] By virtue of the perpetual authority of the papal successors, the authority of Peter as Christ's vicegerent on earth and of the bishops as successors of the other Apostles, this monarchical, ecclesiastical organization has jurisdiction in matters doctrinal, spiritual and moral over the whole earth. God has two 'swords' – the secular (civil rulers) and spiritual (the papal church), but the spiritual has precedence over the secular. Recent, post-Vatican II Roman authors acknowledge these teachings of the medieval Roman Church and yield little of such claims for today. It is important in the present ecumenical climate that we all know this.

J. L. McKenzie, Professor of Theology at the University of Notre Dame, observes: 'It was not until the Second Vatican Council that any official Roman document recognized the modern secular religiously pluralistic state as a legitimate form of society.'[11] McKenzie further acknowledges:

> After the French Revolution [1789–1799], the established church in most of Europe became a charming anachronism rather than a reality, but as far as the Roman church is concerned, it has been preserved as an ideal from which existing practice is a deviation, and indeed as an ideal which a kindly Providence might be hoped to restore.[12]

McKenzie[13] also acknowledges that the theological pronouncements of the Second Vatican Council have really not changed the Roman Church's heart on this subject, only the manner of speaking about it to the church's skittish members, lay and clerical, and to the rest of us.

That McKenzie speaks not only a scholarly opinion but the continuing official point of view is demonstrable by paragraph #870 of the *Catechism of 1994* which is in turn a direct quotation of paragraph #8 of '*Lumen Gentium*' (or 'Dogmatic Constitution of the church'), the first section of the Documents of the Second Vatican Council.

> The sole church of Christ which in the Creed we profess to be one, holy, catholic and apostolic... [elipsis in the Catechism] subsists in the [Roman] church, which is governed by the successors of Peter and by the bishops in communion with him. Nevertheless, many elements of sanctification and of truth are found outside its visible confines.[14]

The Council plainly in almost all parts of the *Documents* desired to extend a friendly, welcoming hand to all professing Christians, even calling them 'separated brethren.' Yet, the invitation is without any discernible variation or exception to 'come home to Mother church,' the historic Roman establishment. A flood of recent literature makes this plain. Evangelicals find much in post-Vatican II orthodoxy to agree with, even to admire. Yet, insistence on papacy and the hierarchical structure in obedience to the Roman pontiff is now (or at least should be) as much an obstacle to any Protestant agreement to joining of ecclesiastical forces as ever. Sacraments, Mariolatry, orders (the sacerdotal priestly hierarchy), the Mass (Eucharist), penance (confessional), adoration of images, relics, intercession of saints and other features of the Roman religion are lesser obstacles.

Several renowned liberal Roman Catholic scholars have renounced or explained away orthodox doctrines (of mankind, the fall, the Person of Christ, the Trinity) which orthodox Protestants do share with historic Roman Catholicism (examples are Küng, Schillebeecks, Teilhard). But these scholarly writers are not in good standing with the hierarchy. Others – of whom perhaps the best example is Hans von Balthasar – in good standing and mainly

---

10. St Thomas Aquinas, *Summa Theologica*, trans. English Dominican Fathers, Christian Classics (Philadelphia: Westminster Press, 1981), Pt. III, Q. 35, art. 8.
11. McKenzie, op. cit., p. 151.
12. ibid., p. 151.
13. ibid., pp. 151–153.
14. *Catechism of the Catholic Church*, authorized English trans. of Latin text of 1994 (San Francisco: Ignatius Press, n.d.), p. 230.

orthodox, strongly affirm every feature of the Roman religion which orthodox Protestants do not and cannot approve. Von Balthasar, in a 1988 translation of his 1975 small German work (*Katholisch*),[15] treats most of the items of Roman belief objectionable to Protestants in such a way as to make them acceptable to skeptical laymen of his own denomination and to evangelical Protestants. Yet he yields not an inch to eliminating the essential historic Roman dogmas and practices. 'One, Holy, Catholic Apostolic' still means the same as ever, even if now spoken with a genuinely friendly smile and an honestly friendly heart. Significant theological movement is not likely to come from the Roman Church, it appears. The deadlock seems likely not to go away.

Several decades have now passed since the Second Vatican Council. Many acts of 'reconciliation' have taken place both on matters of broad consequences as, for example, reception of several former Anglican/Episcopal priests into Roman priesthood, common declarations between two different Anglican bishops and popes Paul VI and John Paul II.[16] Hence, we all want to know, do Rome's exclusive claims still hold? Even during the age of scholasticism, at the time of the early Renaissance, when some accepted Roman claims were being challenged, the scholastic authors attempted to support the papal supremacy over the 'church' and over kings and emperors as well. They assembled arguments from Scripture, patristic authors, and even the history and literature of ancient Greece and Rome. True, official Rome has renounced the extremes of the Inquisition. But did the Roman Church abandon any of her claims over the church and claim to be the sole one, holy, catholic and apostolic church? The answer must be, No. Some lesser prelates have acted as though it were so; some theologians have thought so; many laymen felt so.

The Vatican Congregation for Divine Worship set the matter straight in the Declaration, *Mysterium Ecclesiae*, June 24, 1973, less than ten years after the close of the Council. This official *Declaration* rebuked their *avant garde* theologians 'who have obscured catholic doctrine' and are 'opposed to Catholic faith even in fundamental matters'.... These offenses, they say, are especially grievous in relation to 'the ministerial priesthood,' 'truths concerning the mystery of the church.'[17] The document acknowledges 'separated brethren,' and 'ecclesial communities which are joined by an imperfect communion.' They acknowledge 'truly Christian endowments' by these communities 'derived from our common heritage.... But at the same time... through the gift of God's mercy they belong to that church which Christ founded and which is governed by the successors of Peter [popes] and the other Apostles [bishops], who are the depositories of the original Apostolic tradition, living and intact, which is the permanent heritage of doctrine and holiness of that same church.'[18]

The claim is here asserted, in undiminished dogmatic form, that the episcopal hierarchy under the pope and over the priests, and they over all lay people, is the church universal, visible, structured, papal, one, holy, catholic and apostolic – this and no other. Some distinctives such as the infallibility of the pope and the magisterium are given a 'spin' less offensive to Protestants in *Mysterium Ecclesiae*. Many other features of Romanism rejected by the Protestant Reformation are restated throughout the Vatican II and post-conciliar documents in a manner more acceptable to us. Many are trimmed of what Calvin and Luther called superstition (especially penance and purgatory, indulgences, prayers to the Virgin Mary and other saints) but Rome's dogmatic structure remains intact right where it was at the close of the Council of Trent, at the heart of the Roman system.

The foregoing presentation is not a digression. The purpose has been twofold: first, to demonstrate that though most Christians of every persuasion affirm a universal church, there is need to discover as exactly as possible what this universal (catholic) church is; second, to make the reader fully aware of the magnitude of the difference between accepted Protestant understanding (for all their minor variations) and that of the Roman Church from which the sixteenth-century evangelicals were driven out. Interestingly, among many other things John Owen, the Puritan rector of Oxford during the interregnum and acknowledged peer of theologians of the time, said this in answer to the Roman charge of schism:

> [S]ome of our divines... say they did not *voluntarily* forsake the communion of the church that then was, but being necessitated by the command of God to reform themselves... they were driven out by bell, book, and candle [instruments of the Roman liturgy, ecclesiastical rules and civil magistracy]; which is a strange way of being schismatic.[19]

---

15. Von Balthasar, op. cit.
16. *The Vatican Collection of Vatican ii and Postconciliar Documents* (new rev. ed.. 1982, 1998 Vol. II), pp. 183–189.
17. ibid., p. 428.
18. ibid., p. 429.
19. John Owen, 'Of Schism,' *Works*, 16 vols. (London: Banner of Truth Trust, repr. 1965, 1970), p. 169.

He goes on to say: '[T]hey forsook not the communion of the church, but the *corruptions* of it, or the communion of it in its corruption, not in other things wherein it was lawful to continue communion with it.'[20] Some of the corruptions to which Owen alludes have been acknowledged by Roman authorities over the centuries since – many of the corruptions of practice, if not the clutter of false doctrines, accumulated over the millennium and more before 1517.

The pre-Reformers, among them (and in this order) John Wycliffe (1320–1384), Jon Hus (1369–1415) and William Tyndale (1494–1536) drew from Scripture a doctrine of the wholly spiritual nature of the universal or catholic church. This teaching first pronounced by Wycliffe and later Hus, was rightly discerned to be totally destructive of the Roman establishment which had grown up after the end of the persecution by the Roman Empire.

John Wycliffe was a leading scholar of Oxford (then two centuries old). Already before his time the glaring corruptions of Rome had created widespread anti-papal feelings in Britain. Wycliffe translated the whole Bible into the English language of the time (Chaucer's *Canterbury Tales* are contemporary). French terms of the Norman conquerors had now coalesced with Anglo-Saxon language-structure to form a new stage of English which has essentially survived to the present. Into that language Wycliffe translated the whole Bible. Yet before the age of printing it went only as far as the translator and his disciples could take it in manuscript. They preached the gospel far and wide – bringing the Fathers, Councils and the Popes to the bar of scriptural judgment and as far as the papal view of the church was concerned found it false and pernicious. As to the church, Wycliffe and his Lollard followers:

> viewed the church not as the visible Catholic [Roman] church, or organized community of the hierarchy, but as Christ's Body and Bride, consisting of the whole number of the elect, having *in the visible world*, only its temporary manifestation and pilgrimage, its home, origin, and end being in the invisible world, in Eternity. Salvation... is not dependent on connection with the official church or the mediation of the clergy.... The ground of the church, Wycliffe taught, was the divine election.[21]

Wycliffe's doctrine of the church universal, with later refinement, and some variation, became the heart of the Reformation doctrine and of all evangelicals since.

John Wycliffe lost his post as leading scholar at Oxford University for his efforts and escaped execution by papal forces only by retirement. Hus (national hero of Bohemia) was burnt at the stake (by the Council of Constance, supposed to be a reforming council) on account of his successful efforts, and Tyndale (whose first *printed* translation of the Bible in English was his worst offense) got himself executed by strangling by papal agents.

What followed in the teaching of Luther, Calvin and even Anabaptists was already worked out by these heroic people. The details belong to church history and the history of Christian thought.[22]

The New Testament speaks of the church on earth in two importantly different ways. The word *ekklēsia* is not always employed. Passages which refer to believers collectively as the body of Christ, the bride of Christ, His flock, the saints and similar expressions refer to the 'one, holy, catholic [universal] church.' When Paul addressed 'all the saints in Christ Jesus who are at Philippi, with the overseers and deacons' (Phil. 1:1) or the believers (or *ekklēsia*) at so and so's house, and similar, we rightly assume a local, organized (in some sense) church is designated. The rest of this ecclesiology will be devoted to details of nature, mission, offices, functions, origin and destiny of the church in these two aspects: universal and local.[23]

The idea of the church universal is never precisely defined. Yet it is everywhere assumed. The Lord 'gave himself up for her' (Eph. 5:25) not 'them.' 'Christ is the head of the church' (Eph. 5:23) not 'the churches' and 'savior of the body' not the 'bodies' (Eph. 5:23 KJV). The one body, Spirit, hope, Lord, faith, baptism; one God and Father of all (believers); and 'the unity of the Spirit' (Eph. 4:3-6), like innumerable other passages, are meaningless unless all true believers in Christ – living and dead – are organically connected by union with Him in one vital unity.

---

20. ibid., p. 169.
21. E. H. Broadbent, *The Pilgrim church*, 2nd ed. (London & Edinburgh: Pickering and Ingles, 1935), p. 120.
22. There is a significant literature relating to the Paulicians, Cathari, Albigensians, Waldensians and others who saw these truths and acted on them in the era between the establishment of hierarchical Roman Christianity and the Reformation.
23. At several points in the following chapters three questions initially surface, the second depending on how the first is answered. (1) What is the relation of the church of the New Testament Apostles and prophets to the saints of the Old Testament? (2) When did the church come into existence? Another follows, presenting the 'newness' of the New Testament church and Pentecost, its birthday. (3) Are the Old Testament people ever incorporated into a single 'people of God'? These questions will be addressed in chapters 8 and 9 below, 'The Relation of the church to Israel and the Kingdom of God.'

There have been evangelical groups who acknowledging the unity in Christ yet have denied the present existence of a universal church. It has never been an emphasis of Protestant congregationalists [=independents]. The advancing frontier of settlement in America produced a minor stream of such thought.... In colonial days Baptists had experienced persecution at the hands of the Congregational state church [in Massachusetts and Connecticut]. As a result these Baptists had come to fear the concept of the universal church, for with it they associated state-churchism.[24]

The tendency issued in a book by Dr J. B. Graves, a prominent Baptist,[25] gave the name *Landmarkism* to the most exclusivist stream within American Baptist belief and practice. In a later book[26] this influential author, in harmony with the then prevalent postmillennialism, equated the church and the kingdom of Christ. The church, he said, is an organized visible organization, earthly and local. The local church is always a single congregation which one enters by professing regeneration. Baptism by immersion (only) is the door of entrance. The Lord's Supper is restricted to members of one local church only – never extended even to Baptist visitors or guests. Though far from universal or even widely known among Baptists today, the stream of thought still flows.[27] This stream of thought continues in a small minority of Baptist teachers and writers and congregations. R. V. Clearwaters, of Central Convervative Baptist Seminary (Minnneapolis), held that the only church on earth today is a local church. The universal church has no present existence, ideal or real. He said, 'the universal church... has never been assembled or had a meeting. It is a prospective church.'[28] Several Baptist congregations in the U. S. Southeast actively promote their own brand of Landmarkism.[29]

This view is quite the opposite of the English evangelicals of the late sixteenth and seventeenth centuries who were the 'Fathers' of the Protestant groups of the English-speaking world. Briefly, these Puritans both within the state church (Anglican) party and those who sought freedom from the state church as Independents (Congregationalists), Baptists, Quakers and Presbyterian (initial majority), and others, believed intensely that every truly regenerate believer is a member of the church catholic. They believed that the church catholic is not the mere sum total of the elect but the body of Christ, the bride in preparation for wifehood; that the church though *invisible* to people on earth (inasmuch as only 'the Lord knoweth them that are his') achieves visibility through the churches (we now call them denominations), even in the papal system from whose subservience they wished to be freed; and that every believer, if possible, should associate himself with a local church.[30]

These principles were embodied in part by the archetypal Anglican authority Richard Hooker,[31] even though he thought the episcopal system was best. They are embodied in full and in detail in the prime spokesman for English Puritan theology, John Owen, in his work, *Of Schism* and *A Review of the True Nature of Schism*.[32] We in the modern world, at least for now, feel little threat from the Roman Church – at least not of the sort that came with the Inquisition, the Spanish Wars, the attempted Conquest of the Netherlands, and the attacks on Protestant Britain from 1588 (the Spanish Armada) to 1745 when Bonnie Prince Charlie, encouraged by France, led his armies down from Scotland to within a few days' march of London. I quote an interesting paragraph to this effect from Father Richard John Neuhaus, while he was still a Lutheran minister.

> In America, the threat has been handled by the constitutional nonestablishment of religion and by the Roman Catholic church's theological legitimation of democratic pluralism, including religious pluralism. Vatican II says this about the one, holy, catholic, and apostolic church we profess in the Creed: 'This church, constituted and organized in the world as a society subsists in the Catholic church, which is governed by the successor of Peter and by the bishops in union with that successor, although many elements of sanctification and of truth can be found outside of her visible structure.' Dulles observes: 'The substitution of the term "subsists" in... for the term "is'... in previous drafts [at the Vatican II Council] on the church is one of the most significant steps taken by Vatican II.[33]

---

24. R. G. Torbet, 'Larkmarkism,' *Baptist Concepts of the Church*, ed. W. S. Hudson (Philadelphia: Judson Press, 1959), p. 172.
25. J. B. Graves, *An Old Landmark Reset*, (1854). Publisher not indicated.
26. J. B. Graves, *Old Landmarkism: What is It?* (1880). Publisher not indicated.
27. R. G. Torbet, *Baptist Concepts of the church*, pp. 170–195.
28. R. V. Clearwaters, *The Local church of the New Testament* (Minneapolis., MN: Central Conservative Baptist Press, 1954), p. 8.
29 The same and similar statements are made by W. C. Hawkins and W. A. Ramsay (*The House of God*, Simpson, SC: Hallmark Baptist church, n.d., p. 48). And in a companion book by the same authors (The Nature of the Church On Earth, n.d.). These books are recent expressions of Baptist Landmarkism. Another equally conservative and similarly 'restorationist,' a representative of the Plymouth Brethren, says the opposite: 'The Local church [is] an expression of the church as a whole,' A. P. Gibbs, *Scriptural Principles of Gathering* (Kansas City: Walterick, n.d.), pp. 3, 19.
30. Peter Toon, *Puritans and Calvinism* (Svengel, PA: Reiner Publications, 1973), especially chap. iii, 'The Cromwellian church.'
31. Richard Hooker, *Of the Laws of Ecclesiastical Polity* (eight 'books' published between 1594 and 1662).
32. John Owen, *The Works of John Owen*, Vol. xiii (rep. Banner of Truth Trust, 1976), pp. 90–275.
33. Richard John Neuhaus, *Freedom for Ministry* (San Francisco: Harper & Row, 1984), p. 43.

This was not the opinion of the Curia which met previously to the Council and except for the perceived benefits to be gained by giving in slightly and the persuasive arguments of a few – notably J. C. Murray, an American priest – the defense of Trent by Bellarmine (died 1621) might still remain official as it did for over 400 years.

Nor do evangelical Protestants deny 'elements of sanctification and the truth' in the 'visible structure' of the papal church, then and now. We all know about Luther's confessor Johann von Staupitz and of course there was Mother Theresa!

A Biblical Theology of the Universal Church.

With growing clarity from Wycliffe onward there was and is practical agreement that biblically the one, holy, catholic and apostolic church may be taken in two ways. In Owen's words again:

1. ...the *mystical body* [or sometimes *invisible body*] of Christ, his elect, redeemed; justified, and sanctified ones throughout the world; commonly called the *church catholic militant*.
2. ...the universality of men throughout the world *called* by the preaching of the word, visibly professing and yielding obedience to the gospel; called by some *the church catholic visible*.[34]

The first we often call the 'true church,' or 'invisible church,' or even 'the mystical body of Christ.' The second is nowadays more often called *the professing church*, some of whom are merely nominal or even hypocrites. This apparently is the meaning intended at Acts 9:31: 'So the church throughout all Judea and Galilee and Samaria had peace' (RSV). Most recent translations have 'church' rather than 'churches,' as in the *Textus Receptus* and KJV. Some theologians prefer to call this the *historical* church.

Our present interest is obviously in the 'true' church, the body of Christ, 'the church of the firstborn whose names are written in heaven.' The church as such did not come into concrete existence until the advent of the Spirit as described in Acts 2 (as most agree, and as we shall try to demonstrate). Every true believer since that effusion of the Spirit anywhere and everywhere is a member of the church. This is plain in the manner Paul addressed the Corinthians: 'To the church of God that is in Corinth, to those sanctified in Christ Jesus, called to be saints together with all those who in every place call upon the name of our Lord Jesus Christ, both their Lord and ours' (1 Cor. 1:2).

Among the first to notice this decisive testimony to the fact of one universal (catholic) church was John Chrysostom (337–407), chief pastor at Antioch of Syria and later at Constantinople. He commented on this verse:

> He [Paul] calls it... the church 'of God,' it is united, and is one, not in Corinth only, but also in all the world: for the church's name (ekklēsia: properly *assembly*) is not a name of separation, but of unity and concord. 'In every place, both theirs and ours' – For although the letter be written to the Corinthians only, yet he makes mention of all the faithful that are in all the earth; showing that the church throughout the world must be one, however separate in divers places... so those in different places, if they have not different lords but one only [the Lord Jesus Christ]... the One Lord binds them together.[35]

The mystical catholicity came out in a practical orthodoxy which produced everywhere among believers a recognizably similar response to Caesar's claims as well as distinctive morality. This aroused social resentment and government persecution of the ancient church.

Though members of a universal body of believers, the 'saints,' as Paul called them, are all members of local churches. There are no unregenerate in the 'mystical' or 'invisible' body, but there are varying numbers of merely nominal Christians in the local churches where these believers meet. Unbelievers also attend their assemblies (1 Cor. 14:23). Some of them become accepted baptized members, among them surreptitious 'enemies of the cross of Christ' (Phil. 3:18), 'false brothers' (Gal. 2:4), savage wolves (Acts 20:28, 29). They creep in (Jude 4) with bad motives. Some depart, to the improvement of the church (1 John 2:20), but some stay and will not be manifest till the Judgment Day (2 Tim. 3:9). Viewed in its world-wide aspect, this professing church is 'catholic' or universal.[36]

There is no evidence that this church ever had an 'ecumenical' structure. There was a unity of doctrine in the early centuries. The Epistles witness to the importance attached to that orthodoxy by the Apostles. In early church literature the word 'catholic' was frequently used simply to mean orthodox. Having surveyed the evidence, Jaroslav Pelikan asserts:

---

34. Owen, op. cit., p. 124.
35. John Chrysostom, *Homily I*.1,2 (NPNF, 1st Series, XII.3). p. 3.
36. John Gill, *Complete Body of Divinity* II, new ed. (Grand Rapids: Baker Books, 1978), pp. 559–568.

What did characterize primitive Christianity was a unity of life, of fidelity to the Old Testament, of devotion, and of loyalty to its Lord, as he was witnessed to in the Old and New Testament. Heresy was deviation from that unity; and as that unity came to be transposed into the languages of creed and dogma from that of testimony and proclamation, heresy was seen as an aberration from 'the pattern of sound words which you have heard.'[37]

One of the very most excellent pieces of literature coming from the ancient church is the *Apology* of Tertullian (AD 145–240?), a North African lawyer turned preacher, theologian and apologist. It is addressed to 'Rulers of the Roman Empire.' Throughout he treats the Christian 'race' as a uniform element in the Roman world. He claims 'to exhibit the peculiarities of the Christian society' (xxxix., opening sentence). Christians, he says, acknowledge all mankind as 'brethren... by the law of common mother nature,' but there is a special oneness of 'mind and soul' among all Christians. Such a 'community' is one of mutual care for one another, sharing earthly goods and about all else except their wives – in which they differ, he says, markedly from the rest of Roman society. 'We are,' he sums up, 'in our congregations just what we are when separated from each other... as a community what we are as individuals.'[38]

This community is the professing church of the time throughout the world – with all its warts and defects – a catholic *ekklēsia*.

This church is the subject of the next several chapters.

---

37. Jaroslav Pelikan, *The Christian Tradition*, Vol. I (Chicago: U of Chicago Press, 1971) p. 70.
38. Tertullian, *Apology*, xxxix (ANF iii) pp. 46, 47.

6
Foundation for the Church

Inasmuch as in the counsels of God the church was always a very special focus (Eph. 1:3-13; 3:21), the church has a pre-existence, not in the sense of Aristotle's potentiality or Plato's eternal forms, but in God's eternal purpose. This is somewhat as when we say the electric light bulb was only an idea in Edison's mind until October 21, 1879, when he succeeded in making an incandescent lamp (an electric lightbulb) which then transformed civilization in a manner almost inconceivable. By 'foundation for the church' we mean those preparations, specifically for the church, which came to being in the sphere of human history before the appearance of Jesus Christ.

There is difference of opinion about when the church actually (as opposed to in idea only) began. The chief differences appeared in post-Reformation times with two developments. The first, which appeared among certain Calvinists, is that the history of salvation should be interpreted within a scheme of certain divine and divine-human covenants, hence 'Covenant Theology.' The second appeared in Britain and America after about 1830. This scheme relates to all human history (not just of salvation) to seven or eight distinct epochs. Of these the church of the present age is not the ultimate but penultimate or ante-penultimate 'dispensation.' We shall be taking note of these systems of evangelical thought as we precede. The disagreement over the time of origin, hence, dispensationalism of the church is in part only a war of words – a *logomachy* – as some contemporary participants seem now to acknowledge.

Practically speaking, though no one doubts the Lord has had 'a people' from Adam, Abel, and onward to Elizabeth, Zacharias, Joseph and Mary, there is also agreement that the church *as such*, as the body of Christ, the bride of Christ, specially 'all baptized into one body' in the Holy Spirit, began the Day of Pentecost as described in the second chapter of Acts. All agree the church was not present *in this sense* at any previous moment of time. Though some speak of the people of God in Old Testament times as 'church,' yet even they begin church history with the book of Acts, not Genesis 4 or 12 or Exodus 25.

Foundation for that church was forming throughout Old Testament times (as the biblical record shows) however dimly perceived at the time, just as the foundations of the United States were forming in North America no later than the landing of the Pilgrims at Plymouth, Massachusetts in 1620 – 169 years before the Union of thirteen 'states' under a written constitution took place in 1789.

Let us take brief note of (1) certain *intimations* of less or greater specificity; (2) *types* of the church; and (3) *preparations*.

1. Intimations of the Church in the Old Testament.

One searches the Old Testament in vain for plain-out predictions of the formation of a body or bride of Christ with the special lineaments we shall be examining. Yet, as we can all see now from our perspective, there are *intimations* that their fulfillment takes place in the church.

First in importance is doubtless the promise to Abraham at the time of his initial call: 'I will bless those who bless you... and in you all the families of the earth shall be blessed' (Gen. 12:3). At this point the Genesis account turns abruptly from general human history to Hebrew history. Abraham and his physical descendants are the cynosure from here to the end of the Bible. The promise rather quickly was enlarged to include a numerous progeny and their perpetual title to the Land of Canaan (Gen. 13:14-17). The language is definite to this effect. The promise did not take the formal quality of a covenant until later in the striking ceremony of Genesis 15. The promise (which came first) and the covenant were confirmed no less than twelve times over 215 years of the family's residence in Canaan to the several patriarchs Abraham, Isaac and Jacob.[1] Usually the promise of the Land of Canaan is prominent but we observe the promise of blessing to all the human families on the earth was initially present and was repeated later – notably to Jacob as he fled to Padan Aram from his brother, Esau, after Isaac pronounced 'May he [God Almighty] give [you] the blessing of Abraham' (Gen. 28:1-4). At Bethel God repeated, 'in you and your offspring shall all the families of the earth be blessed' (Gen. 28:14).

Reverent interpretation has always connected this with the *protevangelion* of Genesis 3:15 and crushing of the serpent's head (Gen. 3:18) and the lineal physical descent of Christ the Savior (Gen. 1:21) from Abraham (Matt. 1:1-25). Evangelical commentators nowadays do not draw specific connection between the *protevangelion* (Gen. 3:15) and specific events in Messiah's career, but rather that this is the 'first good news' – 'the announcement of a prolonged struggle, perpetual antagonism, wounds on both sides, and eventual victory for the seed of the woman. God's promise that the head of the serpent was to be crushed pointed forward to the coming of Messiah and guaranteed victory.'[2]

Second in importance are the several notices in several parts of the Old Testament that God's saving grace was intended all along to be extended to Gentiles, that 'all the peoples of the earth may know your [Jehovah's] name and fear [worship] you, as do your people Israel, and that they may know,' and so on.[3] The language of one of Israel's ritual Psalms prays that God's 'way' and 'saving power' be known 'among all nations' (Ps. 67:1-4). Isaiah 56:6-8 (RSV) states that 'foreigners' will 'join themselves to the LORD' and in language cited directly by Jesus (Mark 11:17) says 'My [God's] house shall be called a house of prayer for all the nations.' It is predicted of the Servant of the LORD (whose atoning death is explained in Isa. 53) that He will establish his 'justice' in foreign places outside Israel (42:4) and He who will be a 'covenant of the people [Israel]' will also be 'a light to the nations.'

These and other Old Testament intimations are set within the cultural-religious ambience of the Mosaic revelation, limited perhaps to the perspectives of the time. Jews of the time scarcely understood the real force of these predictions – a world-wide offer and acceptance of salvation. There is no hint here of a body of saints baptized in one Holy Spirit into one Body, yet they reveal the love of God for all mankind and provision of a Savior and implied proclaimed offer of salvation to every family kindred, tribe and nation.

Third in importance, Paul hinged his effort to persuade the church at Rome to help him shift his efforts to evangelize Gentiles from the eastern regions of the Roman Empire to the west (Spain) on a direct appeal to authority to the Old Testament. He draws from passages in all three major divisions of the Hebrew Bible (Old Testament): the Torah (five books of Moses), the Prophets and the Writings. Jesus, he says, ministered only to Jews because of God's special promises of a Jewish Messiah (Rom. 15:8), but this was in order that (since rejection by Jews led to His atoning death) 'the Gentiles might glorify God for His mercy' (i.e. participate in gracious salvation, Rom. 15:9 NKJV). Then he goes on to cite a chain of four verses to prove the point (Ps. 18:49; Deut. 32:43; Ps. 117:1; and Isa. 11:10, all cited immediately below from NASB):

> As it is written,
> 'THEREFORE I WILL GIVE PRAISE TO THEE AMONG THE GENTILES AND I WILL SING TO THY NAME.'
> Again he says, REJOICE O GENTILES WITH HIS PEOPLE.

---

1. Gen. 12:1-3; 13:14-17; 15:1-21; 17:1-21; 18:1-15; 22:11-18; 27:27-29; 28:10-17; 31:3; 32:24-29; 46:1-4; 48:15–49:27.
2. Kyle M. Yates, Sr., 'Genesis,' *The Wycliffe Bible Commentary* (Chicago: Moody Press, 1962), p. 8.
3. 2 Chron. 6:32-33 from Solomon's prayer of dedication for the temple at Jerusalem.

> And again,
> 'PRAISE THE LORD ALL YOU GENTILES, AND LET ALL THE PEOPLES PRAISE HIM.'
> Again Isaiah says,
> 'THERE SHALL COME THE ROOT OF JESSE,
> AND HE WHO ARISES TO RULE OVER THE GENTILES,
> IN HIM SHALL THE GENTILES HOPE.'

Before another audience Paul appealed to Isaiah 49:6: 'I have made you a light for the Gentiles, that you may bring salvation to the ends of the earth' (Acts 13:47).

After these citations of Old Testament authority for a gospel mission to the remote, Gentile west, Paul appealed for three benefits from the Roman Christians to help him on his mission to the West. He desired their *friendship* – he called it 'company' (v. 24) – their *material support*, 'helped on my way,' and their 'prayers' (v. 30).[4]

Though Paul found proof of the church's missionary commission to evangelize Gentiles as well as Jews in the Old Testament he found nothing there about the special nature of the church. As we shall see, this came as a special revelation to Paul and other apostles. It is obscurely present in the Old Testament. Even the apostles themselves did not see things that way at first.[5] The Lord had to stand Peter on his head – as reported in the vision of the sheet let down from heaven, his visit to Cornelius at Caesarea, and his subsequent convincing report to the reluctant Jerusalem church, before even the apostles saw a Jew-Gentile, 'both one,' church (Acts 10:1-11:18; Eph. 2). Only then did they acknowledge, 'God has also granted to the Gentiles repentance to life' (Acts 1:18 NKJV).

2. Types of the Church in the Old Testament.

This is not the proper venue for a debate about types in biblical interpretation. Long ago as a professor of Old Testament I came to see what Stanley Gundry rightly says is 'that one point of agreement' among evangelical, orthodox interpreters: 'that the essence of a type is that it is in some sense predictive, every bit as predictive as a verbal utterance of predictive prophecy.'[6] The ark of Noah – favorite of preachers from John Chrysostom to Billy Graham – hardly qualifies as a type in this restricted sense. We can be certain of at least one. The evidence for divine intention as a type (= prediction by symbol) is clear in this case: the 'tabernacle' (or 'tent' Exod. 40:19 *passim*), 'the house of God' (Judg. 18:31 *passim*) and (much less frequently) 'the temple (*hekal*) of the LORD' [Jehovah], (1 Sam. 1:9 *passim*). This structure was God's official 'residence'; it was there that Moses came when the LORD wished to talk with him (Lev. 1:1 *passim*), where the entire worship system had its seat and center. God's presence 'filled' it, as numerous passages say (Exod. 40:34-38). Many features of the structure and the priestly service were types of New Testament realities (antitypes), but it was the house (*beth*) itself (*ohel* or tent, then *hekal* or temple) which is a type of the New Testament church. This is marked with remarkable doctrinal and practical significance in 1 Corinthians 3:16, 17. I quote the passage in the KJV because the necessary distinction between plural ye (nom.) and you (accus.) and singular thou (nom.) and thee (accus.) is preserved in translation from the Greek text.

> Know ye not that ye are the temple of God,
> and that the Spirit of God dwelleth in you?
> If any man defile [or corrupt] the temple of God,
> him shall God destroy [corrupt];
> for the temple of God is holy,
> which temple ye are.

Paul did not mean to say each person is God's temple. The Jerusalem temple played no significant role in the life of Gentile Christian churches; so he could freely make a figurative contrast: God's sanctuary was no longer a material building but was rather the collection of people among whom God's Spirit dwells.[7]

---

4. Verse 24, see C. R. Barrett, A *Commentary on the Epistle to the Romans* (New York: Harpers, 1957), p. 229; C. E. B. Cranfield, *Critical and Exegetical Commentary on the Epistle to the Romans*, Vol.. 32:2 ICC (Edinburgh: T and T Clark, 1979), p. 769; and R. D. Culver, *A Greater Commission* (Chicago: Moody Press, 1976, 1996), pp. 129, 130.

5. H. R. Boer, *Pentecost and Missions* (Grand Rapids: Eerdmans, 1961), pp. 15–27. And Culver, op. cit., pp. vii–xv.

6. Stanley Gundry, 'Typology as a Means of Interpretation,' *Journal of the Evangelical Theological Society* XII, 4), p. 237.

7. W. F. Orr and J. A. Walther, *I Corinthians: The Anchor Bible* (Garden City, NY: Doubleday & Co., 1976), p. 174.

The sense is as follows: the believers, not only at the Corinth congregation but everywhere, are a temple (Gr. *Naos*), the room where the idol god in a Greek temple was set up, corresponding to the 'most holy place' in the Old Testament 'house of God,' where the ark of testimony and the *shekinah* (glory presence of God) were located. Just as Jehovah dwelt in the 'most holy place' of old so now the Holy Spirit of God indwells His whole church, rendering it a 'holy temple in the Lord.' In Ephesians 2, after showing Jews and Gentiles since Calvary (vv. 13-18), from only 'one body' he shifts the figure to citizenship; then to a household (v. 19); and finally to a whole 'building fitly framed together [which] groweth unto an holy temple in the Lord: In whom ye [plural again] also are builded together for an habitation of God through the Spirit' (vv. 21 and 22 KJV).

Back to 1 Corinthians 3:17 (KJV) – 'If any man defile [harm or destroy] the temple of God, him shall God destroy [harm or defile].' God destroys, as in the case where He took the lives of Nadab and Abihu when they ignored the inviolability of divine regulations for temple service (Lev. 10), and when similarly 'God smote' Uzzah for violating the sanctity of the ark (2 Sam. 6:6, 7), though that poor man had every good intention to 'save' the ark from falling. So those who violate the sanctity of Christ's church by gossip, sectarian division, slander and the like, rebuked in the previous section of Paul's Epistle, will be judged in just proportion to the harm they have done to the church, the 'habitation of God through the Spirit.' This is a kind of divine *lex talionis*. Bengel calls it *talione justissima*, i.e. of a most just punishment similar and equal to the injury.[8]

The general trend of these comments will be both supported and amplified by most standard commentaries: older (Lange, Hodge, Meyer, Wordsworth, Alford) or more recent (Sauer, Bruce, Lindsell); even the somewhat liberal Orr and Walther in *The Anchor Bible Commentary* on the Corinthian Epistles.

The reliance of Paul on the house of God of old as type of the church is too obvious to be doubted by those who believe in any sort of typology of New Testament entities in the Old Testament. What convinced Christian can doubt that the type was of divine intention – a predictive prophecy in symbolic form? Like all types (and many verbal predictions), however, the connection between type and antitype could not be perceived clearly by people contemporary with the type. That could not happen until fulfillment, and even then often only by further revelation.

> In this indwelling of the Holy Spirit in the church lies its dignity and its responsibility. Through this great fact they become the dwelling-place of God in history, one point of contact between eternity and time, the anticipation of the great and true perfection, 'Behold the tabernacle of God is with men' (Rev. 21:3).[9]

3. Preparation for the Church in the Old Testament.

All of the plan of redemption, of course, from eternity past, has reference to the church as *preparing* for its creation, hence truly 'foundation.' The entire history of the Messianic nation – call, selection, growth, training, discipline and judgment, from Abraham to Joseph and Mary – which produced Jesus Christ, Lord of the church, is foundational. We press on to the actual establishment of the church.

In the next several chapters I seek to show that even though Jesus plainly said that He was 'not sent except to the lost sheep of the house of Israel,' God's design was the founding of the church. God's plan and purpose involved rejection of Jesus by Israel. One thinks of Joseph's rejection by his brothers. They could have received him with his father's (Jacob's) message of goodwill up north in Dothan (Gen. 37:12-27), but they did not. Instead they delivered him over to death, then changed their minds and sold him into slavery in Egypt. Later when their murderous intent was exposed to the world, Joseph, their intended victim, wise in the ways of providence, told them, 'it was not you who sent me here, but God… to preserve life' (Gen. 45:5, 8), and later, 'you meant evil against me, but God meant it for good… that many people should be kept alive' (Gen. 50:20). So Jesus' death at the hands of wicked men to whom He offered Himself as king was 'according to the definite plan and foreknowledge of God' (Acts 2:23). And, though I do not quite agree completely with my wise old professor in working out the details, I cannot improve on his judgment that this fact

> does not in the least detract from its moral and historical reality…. There remains the philosophical problem, of course, but this is nothing new; it being only an aspect of the wider problem of Divine Sovereignty and

---

8. J. A. Bengel, *Gnomon Novi Testament ii* (Tubingen, 1850), p. 110.
9. Erich Sauer, *From Eternity to Eternity* (Grand Rapids: Eerdmans, 1957), p. 38.

Moral Responsibility. And for this there is no completely rational solution which does not end by affirming one and denying the other. But the Word of God teaches the reality of both. And if perhaps we shall never wish to give up the search for an answer to the problem, a Christian attitude of intellectual humility will help in some degree to alleviate our uneasiness as we continue the quest.[10]

We may be sure that whatever in the eternal counsels of the Father Christ came to do, He 'prosperously effected' (2 Chron. 7:11 KJV, cf. Ps. 45:4). At the end of life He could report to the Father, 'I... [have] accomplished the work that you gave me to do' (John 17:4).

Just how great that was must be appreciated if one is to grasp firmly the dimensions of His preparatory work in founding the church. In the Christology section of this Systematic Theology (see above, Part 4: Christology: The Person and Work of Christ), chapter 2, 'Preparation for the Coming of Christ,' I set forth in some detail how Old Testament history and prophecy prepared for the coming of Christ as Savior of mankind and LORD of the church.[11] The whole Old Testament is involved, some Messianic by way of preparing the historical setting as found in Israel when Messiah arrived; some by calling for the ethical ideal (Pss. 1 and 5) of a holy and just Man, never attained except when Jesus came; others by heralding the distant *parousia*, i.e. personal presence of God (the incarnation) (Micah 1:3; Pss. 50:3; 94:1 and 96:13); others speaking of a King whose universal realm shall extend to the ends of the earth (Pss. 45 and 72 are examples). Still others provide particular types of Christ's person, experience and redemptive work in the life experience of prominent Old Testament personages. Among these some passages, like Psalm 22, describe experiences of the typical person in an exaggerated (hyperbolic) way, while others are direct predictions in typical objects (as the Tabernacle-temple) or the Passover sacrifice. Finally in the highest and most direct level are direct, verbal predictions such as the place of Jesus' birth (Micah 5:2) or of His rejection and sufferings for the sake of His church (Isa. 53; cf. Eph. 5:25; Acts 20:28).

We have spoken of types of Christ as such, and of prophecies of the salvation of Gentiles in the Old Testament a bit earlier. In the above we are thinking in a more general way of how the Old Testament predicts the manner in which provision in Christ for the redemption, calling and creation of the body of Christ is unfolded in Old Testament prophecy. A feature of this aspect of the subject is how our LORD fulfilled the law. This important subject is a matter of ongoing difference of opinion among sober, believing scholars. If pursued in detail here it would distract from pursuit of a comprehensive doctrine of the church. Let us therefore move on to the narrative of actual establishment of the Church.

---

10. A. J. McClain, *The Greatness of the Kingdom* (Grand Rapids: Zondervan, 1959), p. 320.
11. Also in 'The Old Testament as Messianic Prophecy,' Bulletin of *Evangelical Theological Society*, VII, #3, Summer, 1964, pp. 91–96 and in *The Life of Christ* (Grand Rapids: Baker, 1976), pp. 18–24.

7
The Establishment of the Church

In several previous chapters we have seen that God has always had the creation of the body of Christ, the church of the first-born, the temple of the living God, in His plans. Further, though the church *per se* is never named or described in the Old Testament, the Gospels do show Jesus fully aware of His mission to found and to build a church. Paul cited and interpreted several Old Testament passages as predicting the extension of the gospel to the world of Gentiles. We have also seen how the New Testament writers point to types of the church in the Old Testament. So none can deny that the church has always been at the 'omega point' (to borrow a phrase from Pierre Teilhard de Chardin) of God's plan for the fullness of consummation of all things. This is the particular emphasis of Ephesians 1–3. The church, then, was no improvisation or backup position in case the first plan failed. Calvary was not a failure of plans but the very *sine qua non* of their success.

In a general way most students of the Word agree to this. Yet that we hold strictly to it is necessary if we are properly to interpret the New Testament narrative relating to the creation (establishment, inauguration) of the church.

For the present let us defer consideration of the relation of the church to Old Testament Israel and the kingdom of God and some related issues to the next chapters. For clarity's sake we must think of the church as an entity brought into existence – fresh and new – after the close of the epoch of 'the old covenant' (2 Cor. 3:14; Heb. 8:6-13). Jesus said: 'The Law and the Prophets were until John [the Baptist]; since then the good news of the kingdom of God is preached' (Luke 16:16). For now let us accept a common-sense opinion stated well by W. E. Garrison (who certainly had no dispensationalist inclinations) whom I shall quote somewhat at length. He notes that some people presuppose:

> (a) a 'people of God' at however early a stage in history may be called the church, and (b) that at any later stage it can still be called an Israel. This is a loose use of language. There is no justification for making 'church' and 'Israel' synonyms for 'people of God' under all circumstances. The linguistic link is provided for by the use of the *ekklēsia* both in the Greek Version of the Old Testament and in the New Testament. The link is weak, however, because the word is used with different meanings. In the Greek Old Testament *ekklēsia* (like the Hebrew *qahal* which it generally translates) means only an assembly or meeting which ceases to exist when the meeting breaks up [C. F. Keil says in his famous *Commentary* that 'the congregation (Heb. *qahal*, Gr. *ekklēsia*) of Israel' was never the entire population anyway, but only the elders who represented them]; in the New Testament it means a continuing entity.... The phrase 'new Israel' has no New Testament support, nor was it

used by any of the early fathers in reference to the church. It came into use only after the church had lost its free voluntary character and had taken on some of the characteristics of the Hebrew 'people of God'... when the church had made its alliance with the government... and virtually co-extensive with the community... and had committed its religious and administrative functions to a priesthood....The rootage of Christianity in Hebrew history is deep, and undoubtedly a continuing process of God runs through both. But the church was a new thing. It is the body of Christ and the fellowship of those who are committed to him. No religion before Christianity ever had a church.[1]

We shall return to this important matter in the next chapter. It is true that Jesus limited His personal (as opposed to redemptive) ministry to national Israelites who inhabited ancient Palestine, and sent the Twelve only 'to the lost sheep of the house of Israel' (Matt. 10:6). Yet this was subordinate to His redemptive ministry for all mankind and ultimately for 'the church.' Several oft-cited, golden texts make the point: 'the Son of Man came not to be served [as Israel's royal Messiah] but to serve, and to give his life as a ransom for many' (Matt. 20:28; cf. Mark 10:45). When Paul addressed the elders of the church at Ephesus he spoke of them as overseers of God's 'flock' appointed by the Holy Spirit 'to care for the church of God, which he obtained with his own blood' (Acts 20:28). So we know for whom the Son of Man gave 'his life as a ransom' – 'the church of God.' More of this later, but these impressive texts should lead us to expect the creation of 'the church of the living God' to be on God's program for the Son from the beginning of His life and career. The following paragraphs are intended to show, in the language of the New Testament records, how this 'plan for the church' was carried out. We observe the following.

I. The Appearance and Certification of Jesus As Both the Promised Christ and Lord of the Church.

This is the meaning of the Gospels' narrative of the coming and career of Jesus of Nazareth in Peter's speech to the assembled Gentiles in Caesarea Maritima, at the house of the Roman centurion, Cornelius (Acts 10:34-43). The speech opens with Peter's new understanding that Jesus was sent by God to be 'Lord of all' in 'every nation' even though 'the word' was first sent to Israel and was preached 'throughout all Judea, beginning from Galilee after the baptism that John proclaimed.' Peter alludes to some difference in Jesus' message, the 'word that he sent to Israel,' from 'the baptism that John proclaimed' (vv. 34-37).

Peter reports what Jesus did and what happened to Him, not what He said, 'God anointed Jesus of Nazareth with the Holy Spirit and with power. He went about doing good and healing all who were oppressed by the devil, for God was with him' (v. 38). Peter is saying this means Jesus established Himself not merely as an outstanding rabbi, but as Savior and Lord of all (v. 36) and the one 'appointed by God to be judge of [all] the living and the dead' (v. 42) (not to deny His prophetic office as Teacher). Jesus' dominion is universal, Peter said, being Lord of all – which includes the ordering of times, seasons and epochs. He goes on to mention Jesus' death 'by hanging him on a tree' and how 'God raised him on the third day' (v. 40). Peter makes no mention of the redemption wrought by Christ's death and resurrection – a point Peter emphasized later in teaching the believers 'of the dispersion' throughout the world chosen by 'God the Father, in the sanctification of the Spirit' (1 Peter 1:1, 2) 'ransomed... with the precious blood of Christ' (1 Peter 1:18, 19).

But at Caesarea – where Peter is describing a change of epochs in God's ordering of salvation history from preparatory stages to realization in a new thing of world-wide, supranational proportions – he does not call this new thing a church, though no doubt the meaning of what Jesus solemnly announced to him ('I will build my church') at Philippi several years before (Matt. 16:18, 19) now began to stimulate Peter's sometimes sluggish rate of perception.

Then Peter moves on to tell Cornelius and company how the Holy Spirit empowered Jesus for His mission and rendered it to certain apostolic 'witnesses' (v. 39) that Jesus was the authentic Messiah. He cites the anointing 'with the Holy Spirit' (at His baptism) and 'with power' (*dunamis*, a word both for authority and for a miracle, of which Jesus performed many). He refers to Jesus' miracles of 'healing' and casting out of demons ('all... oppressed by the devil' [v. 38]). Then he speaks of Jesus' resurrection after crucifixion. Only those 'chosen by God as witnesses, who ate and drank with him after he rose from the dead' saw Him after God 'made' the risen Savior 'to appear.'

This is the authentic primitive *kerygma* the liberal New Testament scholars have sought for a century.

---

1. Winfred Ernest Garrison, *A Protestant Manifesto* (New York, Nashville: Abington-Cokesbury, 1952), pp. 94, 95.

This amazing discourse has more Old Testament connections than is immediately obvious. The tests of authenticity of a messenger of God (*nabhi*, prophet), set forth in Deuteronomy 18:9-22 and chapter 13, were all met by Jesus as reported in the Gospels. This is pointedly noticed in Peter's speech to Cornelius' household. The authenticating marks are evident: an Israelite who spoke in Jehovah's name, who performed authenticated miracles, and made authenticated predictions of the near future, and conformed to the Mosaic revelation, are all present in Jesus' story. Peter concluded his discourse, as Calvin said, with

> three things, [1] that it is the proper office of Christ to reconcile men to God when their sins are done away; [2] that we have remission of sins by faith; [3] that this doctrine is not new or of late invented, but that it had all the prophets of God since the beginning of the world to bear witness of it.[2]

'To him all the prophets bear witness' does not mean that a particular text in each Old Testament book of prophecy, or every oracle or sermon in the historical books and Pentateuch, predicts the coming of the Savior and the remission of sins for 'everyone who believes in him.' There is a much deeper connection here with God's promise to Abraham and Abraham's example of justification by faith and by faith alone (Gen. 15:6; cf. Rom. 4:1-6). Every true prophet directly or indirectly called the people of Israel to faith in the promise of God to Abraham. They were the ones to whom the oracles of God were committed (Rom. 3:1, 2), and from whom as 'according to the flesh [i.e. His human nature], is the Christ' (Rom. 9:5). For quite some time before Peter was specially sent to Caesarea, Cornelius had been 'a devout man who feared God with all his household' (Acts 10:2). That is to say, he was already a believer in the Word of God and the God of the Word – a sincere Gentile in possession of hearty faith in the revelation most of the contemporary Jews only professed to understand and believe. He was not unlike the little circle of Jews (Mary, Joseph, Zachariah, Elizabeth, Simeon, Anna) who 'waited for the consolation of Israel' about forty years earlier. He was already one of Abraham's spiritual children in the sense of Galatians 3:6-9 – 'those of faith… are the sons of Abraham.'

Cornelius and his household, all justified by faith, were an earnest of the great church universal of every kindred and tribe and nation. He trusted 'the gospel [preached] beforehand to Abraham' (Gal. 3:8). All the prophets had called the people of Israel back to the righteousness imputed to those who have genuine faith, manifest in what theologians like to call 'evangelical obedience.'

Peter's witness to the appearance and certification of Jesus as Christ and Lord was used to open the door of the church to these Caesarean Gentiles. Immediately the same Spirit who baptized the waiting Jewish believers at Jerusalem into the 'one body' (cf. Acts 2:1-4 with 1 Cor. 12:12, 13) now united this household of Gentile believers into that one church, for 'while Peter was still saying these words [*ta hrēmata*] the Holy Spirit fell on all those heard the word [*ton logon*].' They all listened to the words and understood the message of the words.

I have cited the Cornelius incident (Acts 10) before citing the Pentecostal 'birthday of the church' because Peter's message at Caesarea interprets the Gospels' narratives in relation to the appearance and certification of Jesus of Nazareth (Acts 10:30) as LORD of the church, not merely as the 'king of Israel,' as Nathanael, the sixth Jew to adhere to Jesus, seems to have thought (John 1:49). Yet on the earlier occasion, Peter had made some of the same points. For example, he said 'Jesus of Nazareth' was 'a man attested to you by God with mighty works and wonders and signs which God did through him in your midst' (Acts 2:22 RSV) – Jesus appeared as One sent of God and as fully accredited by the proper means.

Hebrews 2:1-4, likely written near the end of the apostolic age, points out that the message of salvation spoken by the Lord Jesus was confirmed to the second generation of believers (that is those evangelized by the Apostles) by signs (*sēmeious*) and wonders (*terasin*) and diverse miracles (*dunamesin*) performed by the apostolic preachers (Rom. 15:17-19). These are the same special terms employed in the Gospels to identify Jesus' supernatural works of healing, feeding the 5,000, walking on water and the like. They confirmed the message of Jesus and His Messiahship even though very few of the generation who heard Jesus believed Him (John 12:37-41). The signs wrought later by the Apostles, after the special work of the Holy Spirit at Pentecost and subsequently in and through the Apostles, proved more persuasive. So the great Apostle to the Gentiles explained in his letter to the church at Rome, concerning 'what Christ has accomplished through me to bring the Gentiles to obedience – by word and deed, by the power of signs and wonders, by the power of the Spirit of God – so that from Jerusalem

---

2. Calvin, *Commentary on the Acts of the Apostles*, Vol. i (Edinburgh: 1844), p. 448.

and all the way around to Illyricum I have fulfilled the ministry of the gospel of Christ' (Rom. 15:18-20). Paul's campaign of evangelism was appropriate and successful only because an epochal change had been inaugurated, the epoch of the Spirit. The same Spirit who after Pentecost united all believers into one church was now also for the first time in history convicting people *everywhere* of sin, righteousness and judgment (John 16:8-10) through the Word.

II. The Choice of the Founders of the Church, Their Instruction and Qualifications.

I have reference, of course, to those companions of our Lord who 'accompanied us during all the time that the Lord Jesus went in and out among us... from the beginning' of His ministry,[3] known as Apostles.[4]

Jesus was apparently the first religious leader – or for that matter, any kind of leader – to call His chief agents *apostles*. One might expect some precedent in the Old Testament, but there is none. *Apostolos*, derived from the usual Greek verb (*apostello*) to send someone away, is almost identical in meaning to the Hebrew word *shaluah*, one sent, used dozens of times. But *apostolos* translates *shaluah* only once (1 Kings 14:6). This occurrence might just possibly be the one linguistic source of our word Apostle as the New Testament uses it. Jesus, who likely spoke to His disciples in Aramaic, would have said *shaliah*, the Aramaic form of the word.

Let us look at the single occurrence of *Apostolos* in the Greek Old Testament, the *Septuagint*.[5]

King Jeroboam's son Abijah was sick, so the king 'sent' (*shalah*) his wife, disguised as someone else, to inquire of the aged prophet Ahijah if the boy would recover. Ahijah, though blind by reason of age, penetrated the disguise, and informed the poor woman, that he too had been officially 'sent' (by God) with a message and command, saying 'I am sent to thee with heavy tidings' (1 Kgs. 14:6 KJV). '[S]ent' is Hebrew *sha-lu-ah*, a *qal* passive participle of the ordinary word 'to send.'[6]

III. Founders of the Christian *Ekklēsia*.

This probable connection of *shaliah* with *apostolos* makes it appropriate that Jesus should choose the Twelve and name them 'apostles' (Luke 6:13) immediately prior to *sending them out* on their very first preaching mission, a mission to Israel only (Matt. 10:5, 6; cf. v. 2). Yet it is hardly possible that in choosing them and authorizing them as ministers plenipotentiary (as we shall see), Jesus had anything less than their future as founders of the church in mind. Ephesians expounds the doctrine of the church in a special way. The teaching in Ephesians 2 is that the eternal purpose of God toward the consummation of history in a church composed of Jews and Gentiles, the veritable 'household of God' (Eph. 2:19), is 'built on the foundation of the apostles and prophets' (Eph. 2:20). This seems decisive to the effect that this is precisely why Christ established the 'office,' chose twelve men to fill the office and trained them to fulfill their office.

The initiative in becoming a *disciple* came partly from the people who became disciples – and there were multitudes of them. Other Jewish rabbis had *disciples* (*mathētēs*, learner, follower) too. The initiative for becoming one of Jesus' Apostles, however, came entirely from the Master Himself: 'he called his disciples and chose from them twelve, whom he named apostles' (Luke 6:13; cf. Matt. 10:1 ff.; Mark 3:14 ff.); 'You did not choose me, but I chose you and appointed (*ethēka*) you' (John 15:16). Though, as fair-minded commentators agree, 'Jesus is undoubtedly addressing himself to all Christians... as John 15:27 makes clear, Jesus' words here are directed to those who have been with him from the beginning. That apostles, "ones sent" are particularly in mind in the "I chose you" of verse 16 is suggested by what follows.'[7] C. K. Barrett suggests that the Greek verb may reflect 'Heb. *samak*, to lay [hands] on, ordain, the verb-used in later Judaism of the ordination of a scholar or rabbi. *Samak/epitithenai* are used respectively

---

3. Acts 1:21, 22; John 15:27.
4. Matt. 10:1-3; Luke 6:13-16; John 15:27; Acts 1:21, 22.
5. Hatch and Redpath, *Concordance to the Septuagint*, sub. *Apostolos*, i, p. 145.
6. The ancient Aramaic translation of the Bible (*Syriac Peshitta*) uses *shaliah* to translate *apostolos* throughout the New Testament. This word (also in Aramaic, the spoken language of Jesus and His circles) slightly modified from *shaluah* to *shaliah* is the common word in rabbinical Hebrew for an official messenger authorized to act for the sender. Amazingly, 1 Kings 14:6 is the one occasion in the entire *Septuagint* (ancient Gr. trans. of the Old Testament) that the word *apostolos* (apostle) is used. Though this incident and the rabbinical *shalliah* provide possible background for this use of the word, they are no precendents for the *Apostolate* of twelve select men for Jesus: it was entirely without precedent, as far as scholars can determine.
7. R. E. Brown, *The Gospel of John, Anchor Bible II* (Garden City, NY: Doubleday, 1970), pp. 683, 684.

in the Hebrew MT and LXX of Numbers 6:10 for the ordination of Levites and in Numbers 27:18 for Moses' commission of Joshua.'[8]

Mark says that Jesus' initial purpose in constituting twelve of His disciples as Apostles was threefold (Mark 3:14 15). The *first* was 'that they might be with him.' This was surely with a view to instructing them fully as missionary founders and instructors of the church by oral (preaching) and written (New Testament Scripture) means in the period after His Ascension: *viz.* 'teaching them to observe all that I have commanded you... to the close of the age' (Matt. 28:20 RSV).

The *second* purpose, that 'he might send them out to preach,' was completed in part when they returned from their first mission to announce to Jews then living in northern Palestine the presence of the promised Messianic King and His kingdom (Matt. 10:5-7; cf. Luke 8:1-10). They did so as ministers plenipotentiary (Matt. 10:40).

The *third* purpose – to have miraculous powers – was similar to the Lord's purpose in using such powers, *viz.* to provide credentials as divinely certified heralds of the arrived king and kingdom. Similar powers were temporarily granted to seventy messengers whom Jesus later sent out (Luke 10:1-17).

These purposes, including the miraculous powers, were permanently attached to the Apostles, and only to them. The Twelve certainly failed later in many ways. They even briefly 'forsook him and fled' as did all the disciples.

> Yet the discourses of Jesus with the Twelve, especially the Upper Room Discourse of John 13–18, do clearly imply that their Lord was addressing the Twelve as accredited plenipotentiaries for an age about to begin at Pentecost [Acts 2], however sad their temporary lapse[s] may have been. Further, the several promises and charges given by Jesus to the apostles during their years with him compel us to believe that from the moment of their first commission Jesus constituted them the first chronologically in the church to be founded. Likewise, as the 'founders' of the church they were its first teachers (Matt. 16:18-19 cf. John 20:19-23; Eph. 2;20; see also Matt. 19:28; Luke 22:28-30).[9]

At this point it is important to point out that Jesus designated the Apostle Peter to a unique place among the Twelve in the founding of the church. I shall seek to show that the LORD used him in a special way to constitute the church a new and unique entity.

It is too much to assume that every reader will be familiar with the circumstances which led up to Jesus' near ecstatic announcement to Peter in the region about Caesarea Philippi – territory mostly populated by heathen, high on the southwestern slopes of Mt Hermon. Let me therefore summarize thirteen pages (137–149 of *The Earthly Career of Jesus, the Christ*[10]). Jesus had definitely turned away from addressing the Jewish inhabitants of Palestine months before. The tetrarch Herod Antipas, having just lynched John the Baptist, was now perceiving Jesus as a threat (Mark 6:14-29; Matt. 14:1-12; Luke 9:7-9). The Pharisees and their scribes, angry with Him and offended from the first (John 2:13-21), now sought to kill Him. The population both of Judea and Galilee had shown themselves quite uncomprehending of the repentance required by His kingdom. Besides, he needed extended time alone with the Twelve to do *what could be done* before 'He the Spirit of Truth' should come and history would enlarge their understanding. Time was required to deposit in their minds the truths the Spirit would later bring to remembrance (John 14:26) and explain (John 16:12-14).

Jesus created the opportunity to instruct the Twelve and to impart as much information about the future as was possible by retreating from Jewish territory to an unclean land, northwest Canaan (Phoenicea) as far as Sidon (Matt. 7:24–8:10; Matt. 15:31-38). After an unsuccessful, brief foray back into Galilee (Mark 8:10-25; Matt. 15:39 ff.) the party of thirteen headed for pagan lands again, 'the borders of Caesarea Philippi.' All this must have been done in part to show by the very road they traveled (among Gentiles) that a new epoch in salvation history and of God's dealing with the human race was about to dawn. Just before the retreat to Phoenicia, Mark, hinting at a break with the Mosaic epoch, parenthetically notes: 'Thus he [Jesus] declared all foods [kosher or not] clean' (Mark 7:19). So the stage was set for Jesus' pivotal announcement about a future church, a church in which Peter would carry out a very special mission (Matt. 16:13-19).

Many ingenious explanations of the passage containing these announcements have been proposed. Albright and Mann comment: 'There is no passage in the Gospels more discussed than this.'[11] It would require a long chapter to

---

8. C. K. Barrett, *The Gospel according to St. John* (London: SPCK, 1962), p. 339. As cited by Brown, ibid., p. 684.
9. R. D. Culver, 'Apostles and Apostolate in the New Testament,' *Bibliotheca Sacra*, Vol. 121 (April–June, 1977), p. 135.
10. Christian Focus Publ., 2002.
11. W. F. Albright and C. S. Mann, *Matthew: The Anchor Bible* (Garden City, NY: 1981), p. 197.

name and describe the various opinions. Many of the differences derive from views brought to the passage about (1) the time of the origin of the church (was it entirely future?); (2) the nature of the church (i.e. what constitutes for believers, Jewish or Gentile, a church?); and (3) the 'rock' on which Jesus said 'I will build my church' (is it Peter himself, Peter's confession ['thou art the Christ, the Son of the living God'], 'Peter confessing' or perhaps not Peter at all but Christ Himself?).

In addition, if, as I am convinced, Peter is the rock (whether *petra* or *petros*), what are the 'keys of the kingdom of heaven' and what is bound or loosed by him in heaven and earth? Further, when and how did Peter use these keys and did he pass this mighty power on to any one else – to the papal succession, as the Roman Church claims? To elders as rulers of a local church?[12]

Salient points of Jesus' announcement in the order they appear are as follows. Peter had already prophetically been renamed *Kephas* by Jesus when He first summoned him to discipleship (John 1:42; Mark 3:16). Jesus now discloses why He had called Simon a *kephas* (Gr. *Petros*) from the beginning.

1. Simon Barjona, now named Rock, was sovereignly chosen by the Father in heaven to receive the revelation of Jesus the Messiah. The conviction did not develop out of unusual insight.

2. Peter (also Simon and *Kephas* or Rock) is the name Christ gave this man. The word *petros* (as in our petrify and petroglyph, which mean, respectively, to turn to rock and rock-writing) has no article, hence 'Thou art Rock.' He was not 'Rock' before Jesus met him but simply Simon, a name passed down from one of Jacob's twelve sons (Simeon). Peter was not 'naturally' a rock-like man, any more than Moses had all the qualities of leadership before the LORD met him at the burning bush. There were, however, 'born in' qualities which could be 'petrified' (see the case of Jeremiah, Jer. 1:5; Gal. 1:15).

3. As Rock, Peter will be *tautē tē petra*, literally, 'this, the stone,' on which Christ will build His *ekklēsia* (church). Twice in Matthew 7:24 this word *petra* is used for the foundation rock on which one would build a permanent house, likewise, twice in Luke 6:48. Our equivalent in English would be 'bedrock.' Peter is presented in the Gospels and Galatians as possessing less than the steady character of rock. No other apostle seems to have so much unsteadiness reported – one of the 'weak things' chosen to 'confound the wise.' Nevertheless, throughout the period of the birth and first steps of the new community, the Christian *Ekklēsia*, Peter is the prime character of the story, as we shall see. To a lesser degree the same is true in the Gospels' reports of the apostolic nucleus (e.g. Matt. 10:2; 14:28-31; and our text). 'The interest in Peter's failures and vacillations does not detract from this pre-eminence; rather it emphasizes it.'

4. Peter as Rock also received from Christ 'the keys of the kingdom of heaven.' He was thereby designated Christ's vizier, steward or chamberlain in admitting people to the new community of Messiah. It was an office like Joseph's (Gen. 41:40-44; 45:8). To get to Pharaoh one had to get by Joseph first. I think Isaiah 22:15-25 is probably the specific Old Testament background. A certain Shebnah who was 'over the house' of David (vv. 15, 22) and had the 'office' and 'station' (v. 19), also had a special 'robe,' 'girdle' and 'the key of the house of David' (v. 22) was borne on his shoulder. (See 2 Kings 15:5.) In Christ's time this steward of the house had a key sometimes heavy enough to be borne on the shoulder – the heavy doors of palaces swung in stone sockets (see Isa. 9:6, 7; Isa. 22:22). As appears later on, Peter functioned in this office no less than three times, each time opening the door of the church to a new class of people, progressively admitting believers in God through Christ into the church, here called both church and the kingdom of heaven. We shall shortly attend to this matter.

Peter would never have any special authority to admit people to salvation. Every preacher of the gospel has that. Rather, Peter's authority is that of an *oikonomos*, manager of a household or steward (Luke 12:42; 16:1, 3, 8; Rom. 16:23) responsible to the master (owner). 'The authority in question is that of a house-steward, who is empowered to determine who are and who are not to be admitted to the household over which his master has commissioned him to preside.'[13]

I add: the power of Peter described here relates to the whole church universal, which power Peter exercised as described in Acts 2; 8; and 10. Similar language in Matthew 18 relates to the power a local assembly of believers has to include and to exclude from that local *ekklēsia*. The Matthew 18 account does not say anything of extending Peter's powers. It relates to a different situation entirely, on a different plane.

---

12. For a brief statement of why Peter's confession that Jesus is 'the Messiah' requires a community of Messiah, i.e. no church, no Messiah, see Albright and Mann, ibid., p. 197.
13. H. A. W. Meyer, *The Gospel of Matthew* (New York: Funk & Watnall's, 1884), p. 299.

5. In exercising his office Peter would be 'loosing' and 'binding' publicly and visibly on earth what God had already loosed and bound beyond human vision, in heaven. The sense is that the events are associated with Peter's use of the keys at Jerusalem in forming the first *ekklēsia* of 3,000 Jews (Acts 2), the second of a group of newly converted half-Jews at Samaria (Acts 8), the third of a large household of Roman Gentiles at Caesarea (Acts 10). Peter later assigned this significance to 'the keys of the kingdom' given exclusively to him (Acts 15:7). Space forbids marshaling all the evidence for this interpretation of Matthew 16:19 and 'the keys.'[14] Roman Catholic theology and exegesis, of course, insists that Peter, the Rock, was the church's representative of Christ on earth, and after him, in lineal descent, each bishop (pope) of Rome has full jurisdiction over all the church on earth. This jurisdiction is also over all princes and governors. Though the latter is not emphasized today, Rome has not plainly withdrawn the claim. This may be documented in the Documents of Vatican II and subsequent official pronouncements. (These sources do not usually attempt to prove from Scripture that Peter's 'jurisdiction' was passed on to succeeding popes.) The power of the keys 'designates authority to govern... the church.'[15]

> Christ appointed the Apostle Peter to be the first of all the Apostles and to be the Visible Head of the whole church by appointing him immediately and personally to the primacy of jurisdiction.[16]
> According to Christ's ordinance, Peter is to have successors in his Primacy over the whole church and for all time.[17]

These quotations from a current standard textbook for instruction of priests supports the perpetual jurisdiction of the pope primarily on Matthew 16:17-19, the passage presently under discussion. Insofar as the post-Vatican II Roman Church finds 'marks of authenticity' ('sanctification') among Protestants, Eastern Orthodox and others it claims right of government by the pope over them too.

Rome relates what is clearly the power of the local assembly to govern itself set forth by Jesus (Matt. 18:18) to 'all the Apostles,' i.e. Roman bishops.[18]

Rome had difficulty at the time of the Reformation in finding support for the succession of Peter's power in the successive popes and likewise for apostolic succession in the bishops of the hierarchy. The Roman Church has simply assumed the authority of Apostles promised by Jesus (John 14—16) resides in the church's hierarchy and rests their practice upon dogmatic pronouncements. Karl Adam, who combined great learning with marvelous felicity of expression, frankly admitted that the exegetical basis of papal succession from Peter is not present in Matthew. He acknowledged the 'Roman primacy' was 'subject to some development.'[19] It seems to this reader of Karl Adam's famous book that he resorts to Roman Catholic feeling alone, not to historical or biblical proofs.

Note On Binding and Loosing.
Most Versions of the binding and loosing by Peter in Matthew 16:19 are essentially alike – indicative mood, future tense. In the Greek, however, *dēsēs* (bind) and *lusēs* (loose) are both subjunctive active – 'you may bind' and 'you may loose,' not necessarily future, but certainly conditional. The clauses about heaven are not simple future passive ('shall be bound... shall be loosed') but future, perfect passive – *estai dedemenon*, 'will have been bound'; *estai lelumenon,* 'will have been loosed.' This tense and mood are very rare in ancient Greek. Authorities usually cite only three occurrences in the New Testament and two in the Old Testament LXX. Why the scholars who gave us our Versions and our commentaries take no notice of these facts, I do not know. There is no precise correspondence between Greek tenses and English tenses. Yet about as precise as possible a rendering is the one found in the *The Anchor Bible*:[20] 'Whatever you bind on earth will have been bound in heaven, and whatsoever you release on earth will have been so released in heaven.' This is how the Latin Vulgate translates it also – Latin and Greek having quite similar tense systems. Is this important? Yes. 'It is certainly unsafe... to proceed upon any other supposition than

---

14. Among the many authors who support this view in whole or part I cite among exegetes W. F. Albright and C. S. Mann, Matthew, *The Anchor Bible*, pp. 195-198; Lange's *Commentary on Matthew*, p. 298; Alford, *New Testament for English Readers in loc.*; Strack-Billerbeck, *Kummentar Zum Neven Testamentum*, I, pp. 736–7, who show how fully the passage reflects the *Housverwalter* (German), *oikonomos* (Greek), steward (English) in Jewish and Old Testament customary usage. Among biblical theologians: G. E. Ladd, *Theology of the New Testament* (1974, 1991), pp. 340–348. For a full survey of other views see A. Kuen, *I Will Build My church* (Chicago: Moody Press, 1971), pp. 109–117.
15. *Catechism of 1994*, English ed., para. 553.
16. Ludwig Ott, *Fundamentals of Catholic Dogma* (Rochford, IL: TAN. 1960, rep. 1974), p. 282.
17. ibid., p. 282.
18. ibid., p. 280.
19. Karl Adam, *The Spirit of Catholicism* (New York: Doubleday Image Books, 1954 and onward), pp. 96–101.
20. *Matthew*, op. cit., p. 193.

that the New Testament writer used the tense which would convey just the idea he wished to express.'[21] The idea here seems plain. Heaven did not promise to certify and enforce whatever Peter and successors might decree true or demand of the church; rather that Peter as steward of God's new household (the Christian *ekklēsia*) would act at God's pleasure not his own, and admit or exclude precisely those whom heaven had already admitted or excluded. We see him admitting in Acts 2; 8; and 10. We see him refusing Ananias and Sapphira (Acts 5) and Simon Magus (Acts 8).

The New Testament, outside of the ministry of Paul, does not tell much of the particular deeds of the Apostles beyond Jerusalem in founding churches. I have published a book showing that Jesus supplied them with specific principles and methods for their mission.[22] We owe a debt to Eusebius of Caesarea, Palestine, who gathered up a narrative of their work shortly after the Council of Nicea (AD 324) in his *Ecclesiastical History*, available in several English editions. All we know of Christian antiquity demonstrates the early church universally regarded the Apostles as authoritative messengers of Christ who, together with certain New Testament prophets, founded the first churches, furnished them with the canon of New Testament Scripture and established the *ekklēsia* firmly in all the world (see Mark 16:19,20; Col. 1:6; 1 Peter 1:1). The church of Jesus Christ is at its very heart not only one, holy and catholic, but veritably apostolic. There has been no personal power on earth equal to theirs since except as present in the Holy Scriptures which they left behind. Similar language about binding and loosing occurs at Matthew 18:18. Roman Catholic apologetics and dogmatics claim this text for the bishops of the church as successors to the apostolic Twelve, without textual support, because it relates wholly to a local *ekklēsia* 'gathered together' in prayer and exercising discipline over its members.

IV. The Instruction and 'Inspiration' of the Apostolic Founders.

The twelve men chosen by Jesus were already initiated and practicing Palestinian Jews. They already had received the best the synagogue had to offer. They were no strangers to any part of the Old Testament revelation, as the way Jesus addressed them constantly demonstrates.

Men worthy to be first members of the church, to serve as special agents in the great harvest of souls, must be prepared of God. The Twelve had individually long awaited 'the consolation of Israel'; several had heard John the Baptist and, as he insisted, had 'prepared the way of the Lord' in their own hearts by repentance. When the Baptist cried: "'Behold, the Lamb of God!" ...they followed Jesus' (John 1:36, 37). Later when Jesus said, 'Follow me, and I will make you fishers of men' (Matt. 4:19) the record says they left all and did just that. When called to be Apostles some had already been following the Baptist for quite a while and all had been Jesus' disciples from six months to more than a year.[23] Full instruction had to await the redeeming death of Christ, His resurrection, post-resurrection ministry in the 'forty days' and the special advent of the Holy Spirit. Yet Jesus had filled their several years in His company with instruction and conditioning for the coming epoch, some of it very specific, pertaining to their specifically apostolic work of missionary evangelism (Matt. 10 and 13). What they received was all intended directly or indirectly for the believers in the about-to-be formed church.

Portions of His discourses would have no relevance until after Christianity began to be widespread, late in the Apostles' lives and even after their death (e.g. Matt. 10:18). Among His last admonishments to them was to teach disciples among 'all nations... all that I have commanded you' (Matt. 28:19, 20). Jesus' parables and proverbs, warnings and promises became the commonplaces of early instruction of believers. The Christian preachers of the first centuries whose teachings, sermons and sayings have come down to us were occupied heavily with what Jesus had spoken – not all of it in the canonical Gospels. As a safeguard of 'the doctrine' Paul 'exhorted' Timothy to point people to Jesus' work, saying: 'Teach and urge these things. If anyone teaches a different doctrine and does not agree with the sound words of our Lord Jesus Christ and the teaching that accords with godliness, he... understands nothing' (1 Tim. 6:2-4).

Some features of the church and kingdom were revealed to the Apostles – and to certain prophets – only after redemption was finished and after the effusion of the Holy Spirit.

---

21. Harvey Dana and Julius Mantey, *Manual Grammar of the Greek New Testament* (New York: Macmillan, 1927, 1955), p. 177.
22. *A Greater Commission: A Theology of Missions* (Chicago: Moody Press, 1984).
23. Robert D. Culver, *The Earthly Career of Jesus, the Christ* (Ross-Shire, Scotland: Mentor/Christian Focus, 2002), pp. 67–69, 105–108.

It is an educational axiom that people understand *answers* well only after they have asked related *questions*, i.e. education cannot run ahead of personal development. Therefore it should be no surprise that on that last night with the Twelve (and only the Twelve), He said to Peter that he was not yet ready to understand the significance of that striking feet-washing incident in Chapter 13 of John. Later in the evening He said to them all (now only Eleven), 'I have yet many things to say unto you, but ye cannot bear them now' (John 16:12).[24]

During the forty days of Jesus' post-resurrection ministry Jesus spoke, evidently at length, to them of 'things pertaining to the kingdom of God' (Acts 1:3 KJV). The Apostles even then were not ready for all the incipient church would need to know. Jesus had explained in His 'Upper Room Discourse' (John 14–16) in some detail to those who 'have been with me from the beginning' (John 15:27) that after 'the Spirit of truth' should come He would cause them to remember what Jesus had been saying to them over the months of their association. He, the Spirit, would explain what Jesus had meant. He would also show them 'things to come' and the revelation would be a complete revelation (John 16:13). In a future chapter we shall see how the specific nature of the church became a matter of special treatment vouchsafed to 'holy apostles and [N.T.] prophets' (Eph. 3:1-5). Though Paul is the apostle who reports the matter most fully and, as an 'out of season' (1 Cor. 15:8) Apostle received some special treatment, it was by no means an exclusively Pauline revelation. This also will come in for fuller treatment. Likewise we must put on hold several features of the doctrine of the Holy Spirit which relate to the inauguration of the church. At a critical moment well along in His ministry Jesus spoke the words which are the key to distinguishing old covenant believers from the church, new covenant believers:

'On the last day of the feast, the great day, Jesus stood up and cried out, "If anyone thirsts, let him come to me and drink. Whoever believes in me, as the Scripture has said, 'Out of his heart will flow rivers of living water.'" [to which John adds:] Now this he said about the Spirit, whom those who believed in him were to receive, for as yet the Spirit had not been given, because Jesus was not yet glorified' (John 7:37-39).

The new relation of believers to God is to be constituted by a new 'giving' of the Holy Spirit. Jesus' last word on that subject came in His last hours with the Apostles: 'You know him, for he dwells with you [*par' humin*] and will be [*estai*] in you [*en humin*]' (John 14:17).

These passages seem clearly to say that even exemplary believers before Pentecost – think of the eleventh chapter of Hebrews – did not have that *indwelling* presence of the Spirit which was first experienced by the disciples of Christ on the Day of Pentecost (Acts 2).

Ascertaining the time and manner of the actual inauguration of the church requires ascertaining the nature of the church. This is deeply involved with ascertaining the relation of the church to Israel and the kingdom of God (or of heaven). To these matters we now turn our attention.

---

24. Lloyd Perry & Robert D. Culver, *How to Search the Scriptures* (Grand Rapids: Baker Books, 1967, 1979), p. 66.

8
The Church in Relation to Israel

In this chapter several related controversial subjects must be introduced. They have to do mainly with the degree of continuity between the epoch before Calvary and after it. All Protestant evangelicals agree there has never been but one way of salvation from Abel onward and that there are important differences between some formal duties of believers in the several epochs – as before Abraham, and from Abraham to Moses, and from there on to Christ's death and resurrection. All agree that Calvary, Easter and Pentecost brought changes in duties and observances. The controversies relate to the precise continuities, discontinuities and new elements introduced by the last of these transitions – the Mosaic to the Christian.

For many centuries the name in theology for these epochs has been *dispensation*, which translates the Greek word *oikonomia* (1 Cor. 9:17; Eph. 1:10; 3:2; Col. 1:25), also stewardship (Luke 16:2, 3, 4). The word *economy* (as in capitalist, socialist, mercantile or mixed economy) is the anglicized Greek word, with somewhat the same meaning as 'dispensation.' So we should not shrink from the word, dispensation, even if one is not a 'dispensationalist.' Presbyterians, after all, do not refuse to speak of 'baptism' simply because Baptists have disagreements with them on the mode of baptism, nor do Baptists refuse to speak of presbyters.

Some questions arising from these circumstances follow. Is the church a continuation of Israel? If so, to what extent do the Old Testament promises and predictions regarding the national Israel apply to the transnational church of Christ? Further, to what extent do the religious observances of the 'seed of Abraham' (previous to Moses), and circumcision in particular, have parallel in the church (in baptism)? To what extent, if any, should the Mosaic rules for civil life (say on incest or punishment of adultery or murder) be applied in civil settings today? These and many more are all tough strands in one Gordian knot. I shall neither cut the Gordian knot as Alexander did, nor attempt to loose all the strands, nor report all I have written and said elsewhere about the issues, except as it relates to the subject at hand.

Many will be learning what these and related questions mean after some of the proposed answers have been provided – not the best way to learn, but there is no help for it, for we dare not pass this by. Most Protestant theologians, beginning with Luther and 'Reformed' even before Calvin, have discussed these issues, sometimes with anguish. These questions have been and continue to be formative in several strands of theology *within*, not necessarily *between*, denominations or the several branches of evangelical Christianity. They embarrass many efforts toward united evangelical action.

Only orthodox, believing Christians have any serious interest in these questions and problems. They should therefore be debated amicably.

Why, one often hears, can't we all just lay aside these theological quarrels and simply begin working together in promotion of the kingdom of God? This, of course, is pure naiveté, for there is no more divisive question, especially among theologians, than the precise meaning of the kingdom of God. We need not wait for full agreement on exactly what Jesus meant by 'the kingdom of heaven' to start co-operating as Christians. Yet a consistent and feasible doctrine of the church must recognize the problem and adopt some procedure, however tentative, in applying Old Testament teaching regarding Israel and the kingdom to the church.

If the church of the New Testament is a continuation of Israel of the Old Testament under new forms and ordinances (sacraments), certain definite results in biblical interpretation and church practice follow. On the other hand, if the church is a different kind of entity, a spiritual rather than natural body, and had a definite beginning in a different epoch of God's stewardship of the eons ('fulness of times,' Eph. 1:10 KJV), then somewhat different results will follow.

In view of the amount of literature treating these questions it will be necessary to narrow the field of inquiry to manageable size without doing injustice to the subject matter.

1. The investigation should not be restricted to any portion of the Bible; it must include it all. The objection of several premillennialists that too much discussion of the subject ignores the whole Old Testament – as if when John the Baptist first mentioned the kingdom of heaven (Matt. 3:2) it was a new idea – is as obviously valid as the sunshine, for even the immediate context directs the reader (and John's listeners) back to Isaiah's prophecies of the coming reign of Messiah (cf. Matt. 3:3 with Isa. 40:3-5). Any scholar who has before his mind the specific details of passages like Zechariah 12-14 will not likely find it easy to dismiss a national future for Israel in times of Messiah's Second Advent. Similarly, the investigation cannot end with the Synoptic Gospels, or with John, for the theme is carried directly from the last chapters of Luke (23:38) to the first chapter of Acts (Acts 1:3-6) by the common author of both books, and on through the New Testament. The kingdom (reign) of God in general, especially in the history of Israel leading to her Messiah (Anointed King), is the reigning idea of Old Testament law, history, poetry and prophecy. The Old Testament says, 'the King is coming,' the New Testament says, 'the King has come and will come again.'

2. A reverent believing approach will insist on consistency in our doctrine of church-Israel-kingdom. This is simply to say, for example, that we shall not indulge in the liberalist penchant for pitting Peter against Paul or Gospels against Epistles.

Aspects of kingdom theology in Scripture there certainly are, but not differing doctrines.

3. To achieve the consistency we seek we must work from the canonical texts of the Gospels as they are. Source criticism, form criticism, redaction criticism and several varieties of approach among recent devotees of 'Gospels research' and 'the search for the historical Jesus' have seemed to say that readers must know in advance about Q, M, L, and other supposed source documents and scholarly opinion about the 'creative community' and the like. Even W. G. Kümmel, a leading New Testament critic of rather moderate opinions, has said in print,

> In the *oldest* tradition of Jesus' message, to be ascertained by critical methods, we meet with the Jesus whose *historical* message alone confirms the correctness of the apostolic message. To set forth this the oldest message is therefore not only a historical task, but one that is theologically indispensable and no historical mistake.[1]

He apparently thinks that we must all become committed adherents to and masters of form criticism – his specialty – before being qualified theologians. No sort of criticism has yet shown the apostolic witness as it appears in the Gospels to be less than authentic report of 'the things said and done' by Jesus. Competent evangelical criticism, to say nothing of the internecine warfare of the liberal critics themselves, has removed any necessity for acting on Kuemmel's advice.

4. Neither shall we expect interpretive help from the dialectical approach of neo-orthodoxy. While granting a legitimate place for *paradox* as a pedagogical device and for *mystery* in revelation of truths too manifold for human reason quite to explain, it is not permitted of us to find the Bible-teaching self-contradictory. We cannot have the church, Israel and kingdom be the same part of the time and different part of the time *in precisely the same respect* – any more than God can be one and three in precisely the same respect.

---

1. W. G. Kümmel, *Promise and Fulfillment* (Naperville, IL: Alec Allenson, 1957), p. 105.

The Hermeneutics of Israel-church Identity.

The Old Testament, Isaiah through Malachi, predicts at great length and in considerable detail a coming kingdom of God on earth in which a restored nation of Israel, in her land, under Messiah, will be delivered spectacularly from all her enemies and will enjoy many visible benefits – spiritual, political, social and material. These blessings are all dependent on Messiah's coming and directly or indirectly involve Israel's repentance previous to national restoration. There really is surprisingly little disagreement as to what the prophecies of national Israel say and mean in context. Exegetes of every opinion regarding the connection of these prophecies to the New Testament church go amicably on their way discussing the grammar and syntax and share space in co-operative commentaries. Yet, having decided what the prophecies mean, then a large number say the subjects to whom they apply are not the physical descendants of Abraham ('seed of Abraham according to the flesh') but all 'the children of Abraham by faith.'

Accurate and charitable assessment ought to acknowledge that all parties to the debate espouse what used to be called the 'literal sense' of these prophecies. 'The issue among evangelical interpreters is not over the validity of grammatical or literal exegesis.'[2] All informed, believing parties in our time agree that sound interpretation of the Bible takes into consideration (1) the symbolical aspects of most words, indeed of all language; (2) the *genre* of literature (narrative, poetry, apocalyptic, wisdom and the like); and (3) rhetorical methods and devices; as well as (4) authorial intent.

Several important orthodox, believing groups who accept the above old Protestant approach do not expect literal *fulfillment* of what the prophecies concerned literally say of the future of Israel and the Messiah in an earthly kingdom of God on earth. At the risk of some oversimplification I will here state the chief theories as nearly as I can formulate them from the writings of their advocates.

1. One school of thought supposes the prophecies of Israel's glorious future as a national entity in times of Messiah *never were intended by God to be understood literally*, even though the prophets who spoke and wrote them may have thought so. The prophecies were intended to capture the interest and approval of ancient Israelites by means which people of the time could understand. The prophecies were designed to rebuke sins and inspire moral life, holy purpose, sublime thoughts. Christians today should employ the same prophecies in the same way. One would have to research the literature accompanying the International Sunday School lessons of the period before World War II to document this outlook. The temper of the times in and out of church was optimistic. Millions of Christians were convinced 'The Great War' of 1914–18 would be the last one. About halfway between World War I and World War II school teachers told our eighth grade class that there would never be another war. The great prophecies of Israel's future in times of the Messiah were to be fulfilled simply by successes of Christian evangelism. Sunday School lessons were selected from 'rosy tinted' passages like Isaiah 2:1-4; 11:1 ff.; and similar passages in other Old Testament prophetic books. This was typical of a whole *genre* of nineteenth and early twentieth-century devotional commentary on the Bible.

2. A second view is more rooted in serious exegetical and doctrinal study. The prophets' rebukes of Israel and predictions of judgment for her sins were intended to be understood literally, but the predictions of Israel's glorious future and world dominion in times of the Messiah relate immediately to the church of the present Christian epoch and are to be interpreted symbolically. This was how the Spirit of God intended the prophecies to be understood. A prestigious, conservative *Commentary by the Bishops and Other Clergy of the Anglican Church* at the turn of the nineteenth century to the twentieth on Isaiah 2:2 declares the 'mountain of the Lord's house' is 'the mountain which God will establish for His household, church; the antitypical Zion… The prophecy began to be fulfilled in John 12:20-32 ("I, if I be lifted up from the earth, will draw all men unto Me"…).'[3] This outlook was most prevalent in the 150 years after 1790, the great modern missionary epoch, promoted widely in sermons, literature and many hymns still sung today, 'O, Zion Haste thy Mission High Fulfilling,' for example.

It is significant, however, that many serious commentaries paid little attention to this wholesale symbolizing, paying minute attention rather to the literal sense of the text, impossible of applicability to the present-day church in any sure way whatsoever.

---

2. Bernard Ramm, *Protestant Biblical Interpretation: A Textbook of Hermeneutics*, 3rd ed. (Grand Rapids: Eerdmans, 1970, 1990), p. 243.
3. *Commentary on the Whole Bible including the Apocrypha by the Bishops and Other Clergy of the Anglican Church*, Vol. v (London: 1898), p. 38.

Furthermore, these same symbolizing interpreters uniformly applied many texts literally to Israel and the Messiah, e.g. Micah 5:2 as literal prediction of the place of Jesus' birth, but Micah 4:1-5 to the success of the church in world-wide missionary work.

Lange's Commentary (a very valuable late nineteenth-century set of many volumes) on Zechariah says of the very detailed picture of Jewish Jerusalem and land of promise in chapters 12–14: '[T]he Prophet here passes from the old to the new form of the church, he refers to the kingdom of God on earth after appearance of Messiah, and describes its trials and triumphs.'[4] Similarly Thomas Laetsch on Zechariah 12:2, 'I will make Jerusalem a heavy stone,' etc.: 'Judah... Jerusalem... both being types of the New Testament church.'[5] Nevertheless, many of these same authors insist certain passages in these prophecies must be interpreted literally – Zechariah 9:9 of the Messiah's triumphal entry riding a donkey colt; 11:12, 13 of Jesus' betrayal for thirty pieces of silver and purchase by the money of a potter's field; 12:10 of the piercing of the nails in Jesus' hands and the spear in His side; and 13:7 of the smiting of Christ ('the shepherd') and scattering of the disciples. The New Testament writers, as we know, interpreted these verses literally. But the rest of these chapters, they say, is figurative of the church of the New Testament. This class of interpreters thinks they find support in precedents set by Jesus Himself and the New Testament writers (Apostles). A. J. McClain rightly called this 'eclectic' (selective) interpretation: literal when it suits one's system, figurative when it does not.

In this outlook on prediction of the kingdom of God, Israel and the church are nearly precise equivalents. There is to be no physical, earthly kingdom of Christ on earth for the kingdom of God is a spiritual affair only. The disciples' question (Acts 1:6-7) about restoration of 'the kingdom to Israel' was wholly mistaken – not about the time ('at this time'... 'not for you to know times') – but was mistaken as to fact. There never is to be such a kingdom.

E. P. Clowney bases his discussion on the principle that not only the Old Testament predictions regarding Israel relate to the church but also the institutions (temple, priests, Levites, sacrifice and similar) and whole national structure relate directly to the church in greater way than to ancient Israel. He holds that the restoration of Israel takes place in the Christian dispensation, that is, 'the very fulness of the blessing transcends the form of the covenant which is restored.... The outward symbols of the old covenant are so intensified with the fulness of the glory of the new covenant that they are transfigured and transformed.' He cites passage after passage of Old Testament predictions of Israel's restoration 'in the latter days' in development of his doctrine of the church.[6]

3. Another approach, similar in results but very different in theory, avers that the promises of a future earthly kingdom for Israel under the Messiah were intended indeed to be fulfilled literally. Yet, it is asserted, since the promises were conditional upon Israel's obdience, when Israel proved obdurately unfaithful, even rejected and crucified Him 'that should come,' the Messiah, the promises were all transferred to the church and are therefore to be 'spiritualized,' i.e. interpreted metaphorically. This differs from #2 only in saying the promises were transferred from disobedient Israel to the church and transformed from literal to symbolical, says C. D. Provair, a more recent postmillennial writer:

> A verse which demonstrates the transition quite clearly is Matthew 21:34, which reads, 'Therefore I tell you that the kingdom of God, will be taken away from you [Jews] and given to a people [church of present epoch] who will produce its fruit.'[7]

4. An important Methodist scholar, F. C. Eiselen of Garret Biblical Institute, proposed that the promises to a failed and defunct Israel were all transferred to a better Servant of the Lord, Jesus the Christ, and should be adjusted accordingly. Though different in rationale, this is similar in result to views #2 and #3. Eiselen asserted:

> [W]ith the cutting off of Israel the promises, based upon the assumption that the nation would prove faithful, became of no effect. Hence all elements of Messianic prediction connected with the nation Israel, such as the final exaltation of the nation, the permanence and unique place of Zion should be eliminated from all Christian expectation concerning the nature and character of the true kingdom of God.[8]

---

4. *Lange's Commentary*, The Minor Prophets, 1874, p. 89.
5. Thomas Laetsch, *The Minor Prophets* (St Louis: Concordia Publishing House, 1956), on Zech. 12:2, p. 479.
6. E. P. Clowney, *The Doctrine of the Church* (Philadelphia: Presbyterian & Reformed Pub. Co., 1969), pp. 24–31.
7. C. D. Provair, *The Church is Israel Now* (Valecito, CA: Ross House Books, 1987), p. 1.
8. F. C. Eiselen, *The Minor Prophets* (New York: 1907), p. 399.

He further argues:

> [I]t is a legitimate inference from the conditional character of all prophecy, that if at some future time, through its own fault, the nation should prove incapable of carrying to completion its mission, some other 'Servant' must take its place, if God still desires to carry out his original purposes. The later history of Israel shows that through disobedience it cut itself off, as a nation, from God and from its place in his plan of redemption. As a result its place became vacated, and another 'servant' had to be found. This other 'servant,' Christians believe was Jesus the Christ.[9]

These comments follow Eiselen's exposition of Micah 4:1-6 (parallel to Isa. 2:1-4). Regarding 'fulfillment' of this and similar prophecies he says it will probably 'never be fulfilled' literally, but 'in spirit and in essence... when the Spirit of God or the Spirit of Jesus comes to be the dynamic of individual and national life and conduct everywhere.'[10]

This view, common among some Presbyterians and Reformed writers, is well stated by R. O. Zorn.[11]

These views all agree in rejecting any literal application of Old Testament prophecies of a future repentant and restored nation of Israel under their Messiah in an earthly reign of Christ over all people. The explanations vary slightly but results are about the same.

Paul's argument in Romans 9–11, which climaxes at 11:25, 26, says: 'a partial hardening has come upon Israel, until the fullness of the Gentiles has come in. And in this way all Israel will be saved.'

It can hardly be that *Israel* in this definition means the *church*, as some would have it, for such involves an unlikely redundancy, *viz.* 'all the saved shall be saved.' Hence, many who reject a literal application of Old Testament prophecies of national Israel's repentance and restoration see here a prophecy that sometime in the future there will be a mass conversion of Jews to Christianity. They will simply become a part of the church as the original disciples did and as multitudes of Jews through the ages have done. Marvin Olaskey points out: 'Many Jews, particularly in Spain and Portugal during late medieval times, publicly converted.... Some particularly in Germany during early modern times, sought baptism for economic or civic gain. But hundreds of thousands over the centuries experienced true, God-given conversion.'[12]

Let us further observe that non-literal applications of the prophecies are rarely based on the form or grammatical sense of the Old Testament passages but upon putative 'interpretations' of the Old Testament in the New Testament. Here is where the debate lately seems to center. The many parallels between the people of the old covenant and of the new covenant which all Christians acknowledge are lifted up to 'prove' the identity of Israel and church. Writings presently emanating from Ligonier Ministries (R. C. Sproul) and several centers of Reconstruction Theology frequently follow this line. Perhaps the most sophisticated proposals and New Testament exegesis of this view is by E. P. Clowney, *The Doctrine of the Church*.[13] Perhaps the most systematic and cogent in brief form is 'The church in the Different Dispensations' by L. Berkhof.[14] Charles Hodge gives fuller treatment of infant baptism, in which he argues, 'The church under the Christian dispensation is identical with that of the old.'[15] A widely distributed essay by the renowned Dr Francis Schaeffer is influential among evangelical Presbyterian folk at present.[16]

It should be added that the article 'Israel' by G. Van Groningen in *Evangelical Dictionary of Biblical Theology* and 'Israel and Prophecy' in *Evangelical Dictionary of Theology* are both friendly to a non-literal interpretation of Old Testament prophecies of a future for national Israel.

Response to Non-literal Interpretations of Prophecies of Israel.

1. The New Testament never says the church is a new Israel, even though many parallels are drawn. How else could 'all scripture be profitable' to us for 'instruction in righteousness'? These parallels in no wise imply identity. I totally agree with what R. L. Saucy wrote about this:

---

9. ibid., p. 399.
10. ibid., p. 398.
11. R. O. Zorn, *Church and Kingdom* (Philadelphia: Presbyterian & Reformed Publ. Co., 1962), pp. 44–46.
12. *World* magazine (March 27, 1999), p. 38.
13. Clowney, op. cit.
14. Louis Berkhof, *Systematic Theology* (Grand Rapids: Eerdmans, 1941, 1979), pp. 570–572.
15. Charles Hodge, *Systematic Theology iii* (Grand Rapids: Eerdmans, reprint 1970), pp. 546–557.
16. Francis Schaeffer, *Baptism* (Wilmington, Delware: TriMark Publishing, 1976).

> The NT never confuses Israel and the church... the term Israel retains its reference to that people which came physically from the loins of Abraham [and Gentiles who like Ruth, the Ethiopia eunuch, and the like became proselytes]. After the beginning of the church Israel is still addressed as a national entity... demonstrating the fact the church had not taken this term for itself ([Acts 3:2,] 3:12; 4:10; 5:21, 31, 35; 21:28). Paul's prayer for 'Israel' (Rom. 10:1 cf. 11:1) and his references to Israel throughout... Romans 9–11 concern his 'kinsmen according to the flesh' (9:3). If Israel were a reference to the church, the reference to Israel's 'blindness in part... until the fulness of the Gentiles be come in' (11:25) would be meaningless.[17]

I have before me a list of thirty-one Old Testament passages which are quoted in the New Testament in such a way as to imply parallels between Israel of old and Christian believers and are said by some to teach that the church has inherited the name and position of Old Testament Israel. I have another list of fifty-four texts which speak of Israel, its covenant with God and the various designation (children of Abraham, kingdom of God, chosen and the like), of Jerusalem, Zion and similar which these same authors say the New Testament applies directly to the church. These texts were drawn mainly from the books listed in the note, especially from the first listed.[18]

These passages are not decisive singly or collectively. They are beside the point. It is specious to claim the New Testament authors are in any sense saying all the prophecies and covenants with Israel are transferred to the church. I refer to two of my books.[19]

2. It is readily granted here that all Christians are saved in the same way Abraham was, by grace through faith, and in that sense are spiritual children of Abraham. Yet Paul, who presses this point throughout Romans and Galatians, never says the church is an 'Israel.' 'The seed of Abraham' is an expression used in two (or more) distinct ways in the Bible. Paul's poignant use of it is an example of reference to Abraham's seed by natural descent: 'has God rejected his people? By no means [*mē genoito*, may it never happen now or ever]! For I myself am an Israelite, *a descendant of Abraham, a member of the tribe of Benjamin* [emphasis added]' (Rom. 11:1). Paul is proud to have been 'circumcised on the eighth day,' to be 'of the people of Israel... a Hebrew of Hebrews' (Phil. 3:5). He plainly accepts the then present integrity of the Jewish nation as 'his [God's] people' still. He echoes multitudes of Old Testament passages where 'offspring of Abraham' is equated with 'children of Jacob' (Ps. 105:6) – 'Israel... Jacob, whom I have chosen' (Isa. 41:8), to 'your people Israel' God gave 'this land... for ever.' They are 'the descendants of Abraham your [God's] friend' – a special friendship never to cease (2 Chron. 20:7).

3. Several texts are cited in the literature to prove Israel is now the church, the church a 'new Israel,' part and parcel of only one people of God. The chief texts cited are Galatians 6:16; Romans 2:20 ff.; Romans 9:25, 26 with Hosea 1:10; 2:23. It is not difficult to show these texts make no such assertions. I shall treat each briefly.

Galatians 6:16.

'And as for all who walk by this rule, peace and mercy be upon them, and upon the Israel of God.'

Galatians was addressed to a church whose members were preponderantly Gentile. The burden of the Epistle is to correct the error that a Gentile must in effect become a proselyte Jew, by circumcision, as part of becoming a Christian. The discussion closes with a pronouncement in the preceding verse, saying, neither circumcision nor lack of it avails anything (Gal. 6:15).

Paul pronounced a blessing on the whole group, saying 'as for all who walk by this rule, peace and mercy be upon them' (v. 16); but there were some Jews in the Galatian church too. Hence, he adds 'and upon the Israel of God.'

This understanding fully meets the grammatical requirements of the passage if the translation is closely literal and adds no interpretive flourishes; KJV, NKJV, NAB, Luther's Bible and other strictly literal Versions conform to the same rendering.

In such a case 'the Israel of God' is not an alternate name for all the Gentile Christians in Galatia 'who walk by this rule.' They are Christian Jews, 'Israelites according to the flesh' who have received their Messiah and are now within the Christian *ekklēsia*.

---

17. R. L. Saucy, *The Church in God's Program* (Chicago: Moody Press, 1972), pp. 71, 72.
18. Charles D. Provair, *The Church is Israel Now* (Valecito, CA: Ross House Books, 1987); Raymond O. Zorn, *Church and Kingdom* (Philadelphia: Presbyterian & Reformed Publ. Co., 1962); Herman Ridderbos, *The Coming of the Kingdom,* trans. H. de Jongate (Phila.: P & R Publ., 1962); M. J. Wyngaarden, *The Future of the Kingdom in Prophecy and Fulfillment* (Grand Rapids: Baker, 1955); O. T. Allis, *Prophecy and the Church* (Phila: P & R Publ., 1945, 1964).
19. R. D. Culver, *Daniel and the Latter Days*, rev. ed. (Chicago: Moody Press, 1977).

Several recent Versions read the translators' theory of Israel-church identity into the verse. The New International Version does so by changing the word order. In NKJV, and ESV quoted above, 'and upon the Israel of God' (as in the Greek) is an afterthought, the author getting every Christian under the blanket of his blessing of 'peace and mercy'. But NIV changes the order, 'and' to 'even,' resulting in 'Peace and mercy to all who follow this rule, even to the Israel of God.' The REV, 1992, successor to NEB meddles with syntax and instead of translating the Greek makes a statement of the translator's theology of church-Israel identity, as follows: 'All who take this principle for their guide, peace and mercy be upon them, the Israel of God.'

Calvin gave Protestant currency to the opinion that 'the Israel of God' is a 'name' for 'children of Abraham by faith,' 'all believers whether Jews or Gentiles' (*Commentary*, 186.7), even though the Latin Version of Galatians 6:16 follows the Greek order as also KJV.[20]

I have given space to this discussion in order to make the reader aware of a possible bearing of the expression 'and upon the Israel of God' to the question of Israel-church identity. Most treatments of the passage seem to reflect views the interpreter brings with him. Yet by no means whatever can the text be made to say the church has now replaced Israel, the natural seed of Abraham, and that the church has inherited Israel's promises.

Dr Saucy at greater length has brought to bear the evidences for understanding the expression as Paul's designation for natural-born Jews ('Israel according to the flesh') who are also children of Abraham by faith, circumcised in heart as well as in flesh,[21] as in Romans 2:28: 'he is not a Jew who is one outwardly, nor is circumcision that which is outward in the flesh' (NKJV).

The sense of Romans 2:28 is plainly, as the rest of the chapter from verse 17 onward, about Jews 'according to the flesh.' Educated in Jewish Scripture and lore, Paul has been talking to male, circumcised Jews in particular. Any one not circumcised physically who yet obeys the law (Torah of Moses) will condemn any Jew who has the written code and circumcision if he is a lawbreaker (v. 27). The sense of verse 28 applies the thought only to Jewish, natural descendants of Abraham and is hence irrelevant to the question of alleged transfer of the name and divine promises of God from Israel to church. In the same article cited earlier, Gutbrod closes his treatment of *Ioudaios* (Jew) in Paul's writings thus: 'This does not mean that the name *Ioudaios* is taken from Jews and transferred to some concept of a Jew apart from national membership of the Jewish people.'[22]

Romans 9:6.

'For they are not all Israel, which are of Israel' (KJV).

Romans 9:6 likewise relates only to people who are already natural-born Israelites, Paul's 'kinsmen according to the flesh... Israelites... according to the flesh' (vv. 3-5). Among these people (called Jews in chap. 2, Israel in chaps. 9–11), (1) some are only 'of Israel' in the sense that they are physical offspring of Abraham like Esau mentioned as the one God 'hated' (six and seven verses farther along); and (2) some of these Jews are truly 'Israel' (v. 6), true 'children' (*tekna*) in the spiritual sense. In verse 8 'Israelites,' some natural offspring of Abraham, are called '*children* [emphasis added] of the flesh.' They may or may not be spiritual '*children* [emphasis added] of God,' of whom 'our father Isaac' (v. 10) is an example and 'Jacob' whom God 'loved' (v. 13) is another example. These spiritual children are 'children of the promise' and 'counted for the seed' of promise, as Jacob, a physical Israelite was, and Esau, his twin Israelite, was not.

In these verses, as in all of Romans 9:1-13, the only people under discussion in particular or in principle are Jews. Any one, Jew or Gentile, may be a spiritual child of Abraham (Gal. 2:6-9) in direct spiritual line with all Old Testament believers from Abel on through all the faith heroes of Hebrews 11. But only a Jew of the natural line of Abraham can be an 'Israelite indeed' (John 1:47) in the sense Paul specifies in Romans 9:1-13 unless he was by natural descent 'of Israel' (v. 6). This passage is irrelevant to the question of Israel-church identity.

Romans 11:16-24.

1. It is affirmed by some that Paul's 'parable' of the olive tree teaches that the Gentiles have been adopted into Israel, the Israel which is to inherit all the Old Testament promises. The 'good olive tree' (v. 24 KJV) is said to be Israel. Believing Gentiles (v. 13), 'branches' of 'the olive tree which is wild by nature' (24), as Christians (church) have been grafted into Israel, the good olive tree. Hence now church is Israel and Israel is church. But is the good

---

20. Calvin, *Commentary on Galatians and Ephesians*, trans. N. Pringle (Edinburgh: Calvin Translation Soc., 1854), pp. 186, 187.
21. Saucy, op. cit., pp. 71–73.
22. *TDNT*, III, p. 382.

olive tree Israel in the 'parable'? The text does not say so. It says 'his people' (v. 1). 'Israel' (vv. 7, 11) are 'natural *branches'* (v. 21) (not trunk) of a 'holy root' (v. 16) and 'olive tree' (vv. 17, 18). What is the holy root and olive tree? Neither Israel nor the church, but the place of God's special favor. It has to do with the promise 'in thee shall all the nations... be blessed' in God's initial revelation to Abraham.

A bit later (vv. 25 and 26) Paul concludes that the blessedness of Israel is temporary (cf. 8, 10). They will be grafted back into the good olive tree (v. 24) 'when the fullness of the Gentiles has come in' (v. 25). At that time 'all Israel will be saved' (v. 26). In this case Israel cannot be (as some would have it) the church of saved Jews and Gentiles for that is a redundancy, like saying all the saved will be saved.

There is no name of evangelical commitment more respected in Old Testament theology than that of G. F. Oehler, who has been read to the present by generations of seminary students. He clearly states at the close of a section of his *Old Testament Theology* that 'especially on the ground of Romans 11:25 ff. "the predictions of the prophets which speak of the glories of Israel in the latter days [are not] abrogated" nor are they spiritually fulfilled to the Christian church.'[23]

This profound climax to Paul's great essay on the place of Israel in the plan of God does not therefore conclude by saying the church has been grafted into Israel, hence a 'New Israel,' or that Israel and church are now convertible terms.

Some theologians in several denominations, including Roman Catholics but especially in Reformed-Presbyterian circles, have come to define much of their whole theology in terms of 'covenant.' In a common form of this teaching *redemption* began in a *covenant* between God the Father and the Son; mankind's probation and fall in Eden took place in a 'covenant of works' between God and Adam. Salvation took place in a 'covenant of grace' (patterned on Abraham's case). The covenant with Abraham was furnished with a 'sacrament' or 'sign-seal,' the circumcision of every male participant ('Abraham's seed') in the covenant of grace. The later covenant with 'Abraham's seed' (Moses and 'the Law,' David and his 'house') did not change the covenant of grace (or of salvation) with Abraham. It is held that the ritual and sacrificial requirements of the Mosaic law came to an end with Christ. Christ Himself assumed all the Davidic features of the covenant and presently occupies a Davidic throne in heaven. The Abrahamic covenant is said to prevail still with a change in sacrament-sign-seal only. Whereas circumcision of infant sons or male proselytes was the outward sign in Old Testament times in ancient Israel, baptism of infants (or adult converts to Christ) is the sign of the 'covenant of grace' since Christ came.

In Galatians 3 Paul does indeed say (v. 6) that the Galatian Gentiles received imputed righteousness by faith, the same way Abraham did, and are in some sense 'sons of Abraham.' But, *per contra* Hebrews 11 says that Abel, Enoch and Noah 'obtained' such righteousness by faith (vv. 4-7) and then that Abraham 'by faith' sojourned (vv. 8 ff.). Hence it might be said Abraham was a child of Abel, Enoch and Noah. They three, saved by faith, certainly were not 'children of Abraham.' We today are as much children of Abel, Enoch and Noah as of Abraham. Furthermore, Abraham was certainly no Israelite spiritually or physically, for Israel (=Jacob) was Abraham's grandson. Abel, Enoch and Noah received no sacramental 'sign' such as circumcision in order to be part of a society of God's children. No mention of any special 'covenant' of works, grace or anything else, appears in this story in Genesis or any subsequent passage of Scripture. Nor is any group of believers said to be a 'church.'

Which leads to the conclusion that outside the elect nation of Old Testament Israel the idea of 'covenant' is of limited application as a vehicle of theology – whether of the doctrine of salvation or of the church. As for children of believers – whether christened or not, the offspring of Baptists, who baptize believers only, are no less 'covenant children' than the offspring of Lutheran or Presbyterian parents, who cause their infant children to be baptized by any one of several modes. Even Calvin, who spoke occasionally of God's promises of salvation by grace through faith on the ground of redemption by Christ, never constructed a system of theology based on covenants, even though such a theology did develop among the third and fourth generations of his followers – based apparently on suggestions of some of Calvin's Reformed contemporaries. There has always been a healthy section of Calvinists (Presbyterians, Congregationalists, Baptist and others) who either ignored or rejected the distinctive features of what has come to be called 'covenant theology.' Some practice infant baptism, some do not.

2. While the 'covenant' support for infant baptism is widespread, even among Reformed and Presbyterians it is far from uniform. James Orr (1844–1913), renowned Scottish Presbyterian pastor, scholar, editor of encyclopaedias,

---

23. G. F. Oehler, *Old Testament Theology*, trans. G. E. Day (New York: Funk & Wagnalls, 1883), p. 494.

author of books of theology and apologetics still read and highly regarded, outrightly rejected covenant theology, saying that it sought to 'read back practically the whole of the New Testament into the Old,' created 'an artificial scheme' not based on Scripture and gave theology an increasingly 'stiff and artificial shape.'[24]

Infant baptism is more commonly defended simply on the ground of 1) ancient practice; 2) household baptisms reported in the New Testament; 3) mention of children in Acts 2:39; 4) the blessing of children by Christ (Mark 10:13 ff.); and 5) Jesus' speaking of 'these little ones which believe in me' (i.e. infant baptism can then be believer's baptism). Whether or not these grounds are valid is not my point here. I intend merely to point out that one need not accept an Israel-church identity and supporting covenant theology to be a loyal Methodist or Presbyterian and as such to accept and to practice infant baptism. In other words, there should be no creedal loyalty involved in one's decision on this issue. In my opinion they who insist otherwise do so against the facts and err greatly.

3. Related to the above is the fact that Christians of every evangelical denomination, some of them influential theologians, have been premillennarians – accepting a future thousand years of Christ's reign on earth, with His people, both Israel and the church. During this reign they expect the promises distinct to national Israel to be fulfilled. Among these whose names come to mind quickly are Lutherans, Joseph Seiss (preceptor of generations of prophecy students in his Lectures on the Apocalypse) and G. N. H. Peters, author of 2,000 pages of the three-volume *The Theocratic Kingdom* (a Kregel reprint of 1952). John Gill (1697–1771) was the greatest English Hebraist of his time, a premillennarian Baptist, yet also advocate of covenant theology. The justly famous Charles Spurgeon was Baptist, premillennial and convinced Reformed-covenant in theology. Gordon Clark, Francis Schaeffer, Barton Payne and J. O. Buswell, all Presbyterians, were covenant-premillennial in theology. The relevance is that there is no *necessary* opposition between premillennialism with its hope of a future distinct place of Israel and any particular denominational connection or baptismal practice or theory of convenants or dispensations.

4. During the first three centuries of the church, with the apparent sole exception of Origen, the believers and their teachers uniformly understood the Old Testament prophecies about Israel in their literal sense and expected them to be fulfilled in a future millennium. They were *chiliasts*, or as we now say *millennialists* or *premillennialists*. The thousand years of the reign of saints (Rev. 20; cf. Dan. 7), following the Second Advent of the Son of Man (Dan. 7; Rev. 19), spoke plainly to them of the time of fulfillment of the multitude of predictions (such as Zech. 12–14) speaking of Messiah's (or the LORD's) coming to rescue Judah, Jerusalem, the house of David and the like from attack by assembled armies of the world and prophecies of a world wherein swords would be beaten into plowshares and even nature would take on new benevolence (Isa. 35).

The apostolic age knew nothing of a spread of the church which would bring in the conditions described in the prophecies of Israel's future and the world's perfection. The writings of Paul and of John propagate rather hope of a speedy return of Christ to judgment and establishment of a new order. There is no evidence that they regarded the devil as presently bound and Christ reigning *over the earth*. They knew the Lord Jesus Christ was reigning in heaven at God's right hand, but it seems never to have occurred to any of them before Augustine that such was a fulfillment of Revelation 20 or the Old Testament prophecies of Messiah's kingdom over Israel extending over all the earth.[25]

This uniform opinion of the first three centuries should give pause to the simple equation of Israel and church which volatilizes the Old Testament and New Testament promises of a future restoration of Israel, *as such*, and transfers fulfillment of the prophecies to the church, *as such*.

---

24. James Orr, *The Progress of Dogma* (Grand Rapids: Eerdman Publ. rep., 1952), pp. 303–304.
25. See G. N. H. Peter's *The Theocratic Kingdom of Our Lord Jesus, the Christ*, Vol. i, props 69–78, (Grand Rapids: Kregel Publ., 1957), pp. 433–555.

9
The Church in Relation to the Kingdom of God

Announcements of the new presence of 'the kingdom of God' (or 'of Heaven') by John the Baptist appear on the earliest pages of the Gospels. John's preparatory work was followed soon by Jesus' presence on the national scene of Israel, repeating and enlarging John's announcement. But what came out three or four years later after Jesus' Ascension was not a visible kingdom in Palestine but the beginning of a world-wide church. The apparent paradox of these hard facts does not seem to have concerned the church's teachers for about two and a half centuries. The early church teachers were almost all chiliasts, i.e. they believed in a future millennium (Rev. 20) when the kingdom of God would be established on earth. These promises both to Israel (repentant and restored) and the resurrected saints of all ages would be fulfilled. They all would have expected to '[come] to life' (Rev. 20:4) and 'reign on the earth' (Rev. 5:10) 'with Christ for a thousand years' (Rev. 20:4).

That, however, was not the end of the matter. In the fourth century Augustine conceived of the church as the present kingdom of God on earth. Though he did not envision the organized church of his time it was not long before the developing papal church took over the idea and has not really parted with it to the present day, though lately with some scholary dissent among the learned class. The Roman Catholic Church claims still to be the visible kingdom of God on earth.

Jesus Himself never defined the kingdom of God nor does any New Testament passage do so. Jesus seems to have spoken of it on the reasonable assumption that His hearers, schooled by the Palestinian synagogues, already knew, or thought they knew, what the kingdom of God would be, as described in the Torah, Nebhiim and Kethuvim. This remains true even though Jesus was constantly correcting their pre-understandings and misunderstandings as He explained its authentic character, its present and future aspects and conditions for participating in it. That they misunderstood is evident when they tried by force to make Him king (John 6:15).

Study of the kingdom of God in the New Testament in recent times has profited from several sources. Even the most liberal critic today knows that the kingdom of heaven of the New Testament is not simply the prevalence of the ethics of Jesus in the world or mere love of God and mankind in the heart within. Just before and after 1900 several scholars captured scholarly attention by publishing research proving (they thought) that for the Jesus of the Gospels, the kingdom of God was only an eschatological idea that had been 'realized' or 'inaugurated.' Full report and documentation of this research is impossible here.[1]

Meanwhile, among evangelical, orthodox scholars 'kingdom' theology has developed along several courses. Views diverge on certain important points. Candor compels us to admit that much discussion of this topic among evangelical scholars has been what Paul called *logomachia*, wars of words. He warned against it as 'to no profit' (1 Tim. 6:4; 2 Tim. 2:14 KJV).

One group of writers, pretty much in continuity with the chiliasm of the ancient church, finds much Old Testament prophecy of the Messiah and His kingdom fulfilled in Christ Himself, His ministry and redemptive work, and in the church which He founded, but look for a future repentance and restoration of Israel who, with the church of resurrected saints, will reign with Christ during a further millennial kingdom. This outlook has come to be called historic premillennialism.

Another group, only partially in continuity with ancient chiliasm, teaches that the kingdom of God was offered by Jesus to the Jews. Since they rejected it, crucifying their rightful King, the offer was withdrawn and the kingdom postponed until the Second Advent. Hence, A. J. McClain refers most if not all references to the kingdom of God in the New Testament to the millennium. This is 'consistent eschatology' of a sort. At the Second Advent God will give Israel repentance and will restore the nation and advance them to the conditions predicted in Old Testament prophecies of Israel in times of the Messiah. Views of the relation of Israel to church in the millennium are not uniform. Most advocates of this view develop a scheme of the history of God's dealing with mankind around seven or eight epochs called dispensations, hence the view is often called 'dispensational premillennialism.' Most New Testament passages referring to the kingdom of heaven are said to refer to the millennial age. A. J. McClain even insists the 'keys of the kingdom' in Matthew 16:19 will be used only in 'the future when this kingdom shall have been established on earth'.[2] The 'gospel of the kingdom' and the 'gospel of the grace of God' are different messages.[3]

Another contemporary group of orthodox evangelicals agree that though 'all Israel shall be saved,' i.e. shall repent in large numbers and become members of the church, the promises of the Old Testament regarding Israel's restoration to the holy land and hegemony under the Messiah will never happen, except in a 'spiritual' manner in Christ Himself and in the church. Most advocates of this view accept the name amillennialism. There are significant differences among proponents of each of these views. There is some variety in each and some overlapping, and I have not described postmillennialism. My book *Daniel and the Latter Days* deals at length with millennial views.[4]

It is interesting to find the same standard hymns, expressing each and all of these hopes, sung in churches of all these persuasions. 'Jesus Shall Reign,' for example, a versified Psalm 72, represents the church itself as fulfilling prophecy of God's kingdom and is in about every hymn book.

Out of these discussions arise several questions. One I have treated already in chapter 8, 'The Church in Relation to Israel.' I contended there that while the New Testament inevitably finds many parallels between God's Old Testament people, Israel, and His New Testament people, the church, they are never identical in Scripture. The wholly Israelite Apostles and pre-Pentecost group of Jerusalem disciples were the incipient church, yet the church is not an Israel and Israel is not a church.

I myself began to withdraw from the second of the views noted above almost as soon as I received the full form of it in the seminary lectures of one of moderate dispensationalism's most competent and convincing advocates. Through preparing lectures on ecclesiology, first in Trinity Theological Seminary and then Wheaton College Graduate School, a good while ago and on to the present, I came to understand that the scriptural evidence leads to considerable modification of that view. Some would say rejection of it. Briefly: from the beginning of the New Testament in Matthew to the end in Revelation, the church is presented as fulfilling certain aspects of Old Testament kingdom prophecy, without being its sole fulfillment; other aspects of the kingdom, especially its distinctly Israelitish, visible, Zion-centered features, await the coming age for their fulfillment.

This view requires no special hermeneutical rule to 'spiritualize' selected portions of Old Testament (amillennialism) or to multiply entities and distinctions to excess (multiple resurrections, gospels, groups). It does

---

1. Inquiring students may consult articles about Harnak, Dodd, A. Schweitzer and 'Eschatology,' 'Realized Eschatology,' 'Enaugurated Eschatology' and 'Kingdom of God' in recent encyclopaedias of theology or of the Bible to gain further background and bibliography. Also any of the works of G. Ladd, especially his article 'Kingdom of Christ, God, Heaven' in *Evangelical Dictionary of Theology*. The literature is quite overwhelming. See also R. D. Culver, *The Life of Christ*, index 'kingdom of Christ,' 'God' and 'Heaven,' p. 291, Excursus 13, pp. 246–247; *A Greater Commission*, Appendix A., pp. 155–159; 'Rhetorical Allegories Among the Parables of Jesus,' pp. 103–124; *New Testament Essays*, G. T. Meadors, Winona Lake, IN: BMH Books, 1991.
2. Alva J. McClain, *The Greatness of the Kingdom* (Grand Rapids: Zondervan, 1959), p. 329.
3. ibid., p. 332.
4. *Daniel and the Latter Days* (Chicago: Moody Press, 1954, 1977) reprinted by author as *The Earthly Reign of Our Lord With His People*, 1999.

not confine fulfillment to a single moment. The prophecies were comprehensive in their reference and the fulfillments manifold – including aspects of the present age So Paul argued for Gentile evangelism in Romans 15:8-12 on the ground of 'the promises made to the fathers' (v. 8 NKJV). Nor do we attempt to divorce the rather clear 'kingdom of heaven' connections of the church's missionary task and message as exemplified in Paul and the apostolic literature from Acts through Revelation.

I. A Change in Message?

Let us first address a crucial question: Is there New Testament evidence of an essential change in Jesus' message and that of the Apostles after it became evident that the Jewish nation was rejecting Him? Specifically, was there a shift from kingdom message to church message? Is the 'gospel of the kingdom' something different from the gospel of the grace of God? We may rightly assume such a sharp juncture would not be subtly introduced but clearly marked in a 'perspicuous' Bible. Without citing every reference to the kingdom, sufficient texts at proper junctures supply a clear answer.

1. The 'forerunner,' John the Baptist, presented Jesus as a King, the 'Coming One' (*ho erchomenos*), fulfilling the prophecies of the coming of Messiah's kingdom. John called for Israel's repentance in order to participate in the kingdom about to appear, just as the prophecies required. The texts speak plainly.[5] This plain fact seems to be the place where a search must start.

2. Jesus began His ministry by introducing a message like John's. Matthew's account, 'when he [Jesus] heard that John had been arrested, he withdrew… and lived in Capernaum,' in fulfillment of the Immanuel prophecy of the coming Prince who would reign from David's throne in a kingdom which would never end (Matt. 4:12-17; cf. Isa. 9:6-7). 'From that time,' Matthew says, 'Jesus began to preach, saying, "Repent, for the kingdom of heaven is at hand"' (Matt. 4:17). He then began to gather His disciples (later Apostles).

3. After several months Jesus sent out the twelve Apostles to preach the kingdom gospel to the 'lost sheep of the house of Israel,' charging them, 'proclaim as you go, saying, "The kingdom of heaven is at hand"' (Matt. 10:1-7). As is well recognized, Matthew highlights Jesus' descent from David (Matt. 1) and birth at King David's city, Bethlehem (2:1-12), said to be in fulfillment of the Immanuel prophecy (1:22, 23; Isa. 9:6, 7) of a Davidic Christ to reign as King forever, as a Prince of Peace.

Jesus' commission to the Twelve on their first mission sounds an eschatological note (Matt. 10:23; cf. 24:29, 30) connecting this kingdom with the future coming of the Son of Man (Matt. 26:63-65; cf Dan. 7:14 and context). Yet, His words of commission show that Jesus clearly foresaw the rejection of His message and Himself (Matt. 10:14-16). He also foresaw the spread of His gospel and His church when His Apostles would appear not only before Jews and synagogues (v. 17) but Gentile governors and kings (Matt. 10:18-22). His gospelizing vision was by no means limited to the possibility of an immediately-to-be founded, visible Jewish kingdom. He clearly foresaw rejection of the gospel which He, John and the Apostles preached (Matt. 10:16-22). It was to be expected that the Jews would be the first to hear, being the natural 'children of the kingdom' (Matt. 8:12 KJV) even though not spiritually worthy. Long after the Ascension and Pentecost the policy of 'to the Jews first' (or perhaps *especially*) continued (Acts 13:5, 14, and onward; cf. Rom. 1:16): 'It was necessary that the word of God be spoken first to you [Jews]' (Acts 13:46).

4. During His post-resurrection ministry to the disciples – 'forty days… speaking about the kingdom of God' (Acts 1:3) – the kingdom of God was still His main thrust. It would seem that with the inauguration of the church immediately to take place (Acts 2), and the long age of the church to ensue, He would not be giving information about a millennial kingdom at least 1,900 years in the future – or any alternate kingdom of God. After all, the church would be formed by the effusion of the Holy Spirit in a matter of less than a week and Jesus had fixed their attention on the Spirit's coming[6] to complete the inauguration of the church.

Expositors who are convinced that the Messianic kingdom of God is in no wise established in the church say that Jesus was discussing the universal kingdom 'as including the Mediatorial [Messianic] Kingdom and the Church'[7]

---

5. See Matt. 3:1-3; 11:3 ff.; 3:13-17; John 1:19-35.
6. Acts 1:4, 5; cf. Matt. 2:11; John 14:16-18.
7. Alva J. McClain, *The Greatness of the Kingdom*, p. 425.

or perhaps 'the *Ekklēsia*... then regarded as the saved Jewish "remnant" of Old Testament prophecy.' Maybe so, but it is doubtful. It is hard to define precisely what aspect of God's kingdom Jesus had in mind. The fact the Apostles, like a swarm of bees in their hive, clung to Jerusalem and exercised a 'Jews only' ministry for long after those forty days and Pentecost, suggests that whatever He said about their coming mission of world-evangelism (Acts 1:8) they did not yet relate what He said to evangelizing Gentiles or to the formation of a Spirit-baptized body composed of Gentiles and Jews (Eph. 2). However that may be, the subject of discourse apparently continued to be that which John, Jesus and the Twelve had proclaimed – however incompletely – 'the kingdom of God.' We know that He drew the substance of His remarks from the Old Testament 'Law... Prophets and... Psalms' (Luke 24:44) suggesting that the future Jewish aspect of that kingdom was not absent, and accounting for the fact that on the very last of the forty days the Apostles still believed in a future restored Jewish kingdom (Acts 1:6). Whatever Jesus may have said during the forty days about the kingdom of God did not revise that opinion. The time had not arrived to explain what Peter learned at Caesarea (Acts 10) in the house of Cornelius and which Paul (and other Apostles and prophets) later learned 'by revelation' (Eph. 3:1-6; Rom. 16:25, 26).

5. Persecution drove many disciples (but no Apostles) away from the Jerusalem congregation in a short time, among them a vocal and zealous 'deacon' named Philip (Acts 6:5; 8:3-5) who 'went down to the city of Samaria [whose residents were quasi-Jews] and proclaimed to them the Christ.' Philip's preached gospel, accompanied with certifying 'miracles' (Acts 8:6 KJV), was so convincing that 'they believed Philip' and 'were baptized, both men and women' – as Christians, not as Jewish proselytes. This was in response to the fact that 'he preached good news about the kingdom of God' (v. 12). This is all the record says of Philip's *kerygma*. Plainly, in this first case of Christian evangelism beyond 'Jerusalem and all Judea' the gospel message was 'the kingdom of God.' It should appear, I think, clear to the candid reader of Acts that the author intended his readers to understand that the Christian gospel is a gospel of the kingdom of God. The assertion that this message was about God's universal kingdom or an eschatological Jewish kingdom far in the future[8] seems far from likely. Some will think it grotesque.

6. Near the very close of Paul's three great missionary journeys that intrepid evangelist made a comprehensive statement regarding his preached message (Acts 20:17-35) from his 'first day' in 'Asia' and presumably anywhere else. He consistently proclaimed 'at all seasons' (v. 18 KJV) as he preached publicly and privately in homes (v. 20) both to 'Jews' and 'Greeks [Gentiles]' (v. 21). As to content, he characterized his message as either 'the gospel of the grace of God' (v. 24) or 'proclaiming the kingdom' (v. 25) – comprehensively characterized as 'the whole counsel of God' (v. 27), a 'ministry... received from the Lord Jesus' (v. 24). Those determined to remove the kingdom of God connection of the Christian *ekklēsia* (to some of whose elders the lengthy statement was addressed, v. 17) may wish to separate out the kingdom elements from this comprehensive summary of Paul's gospel. I have literature in my library which would say that the repentance message was just for Jews, the faith message for Gentiles: seeing the kingdom as message for Israel's future, the grace message for Gentiles – salvation by 'the gospel of the grace of God.' A. J. McClain again does not treat this plain text. This passage appears on only one of the 556 pages of his book where verse 25 is simply listed as one of seven references in Acts to the universal kingdom of God. Those who insist that the kingdom of God of Old Testament prophecy (Messianic or mediatorial kingdom) has no fulfillment in the church are embarrassed by all the references to that kingdom in the book of Acts, apparently as referring to the church and its gospel.

At a stage of my life when I was considering the possibility that the church has some important connection with the prophesied kingdom of the Son of Man on earth this text was decisive in forming my view expressed in this chapter. I have found it to be decisive also for most students in my classes in ecclesiology in several seminaries over the years.

It is claimed that Peter made a 're-offer of the kingdom' to the Jews in his address to them in Acts 3 and that, when the Apostles themselves still had no clear awareness of the body of Christ composed of Jews and Gentiles alike baptized into one Spirit (Eph. 2; 1 Cor. 12), the preachers were only gradually shifting to a church gospel. This in essence is Dr McClain's position.[9] As I have shown above, this can scarcely apply to Paul's speech to the Ephesian elders. Furthermore, it was Luke who wrote Acts, Luke who was Paul's constant companion through many of his missionary journeys and present with Paul as he faced martyrdom at the very last (2 Tim. 4:11). He certainly was under no misapprehension of Paul's doctrine of the church – or of Peter's and John's. Luke apparently saw no

---

8. ibid., p. 425.
9. ibid., pp. 389–430.

inconsistency between the church as part of the kingdom of Old Testament promise and its essential character as a new body of Christ with a special new relation to the Godhead by virtue of a new relation to the Holy Spirit. Ephesians 2–3 and 1 Corinthians 12 had probably long been delivered to the churches when Luke wrote the last lines of the last chapter of the Acts of the Apostles. Only the Pastoral Epistles likely were composed at a later time than the first Roman imprisonment.

7. The last verse of Acts leaves Paul in prison at Rome, long after his work of evangelizing the eastern 'parts'.. Rome of the Empire was over (Rom. 15:18-23). At this late date Paul is still majoring on the kingdom of God – perhaps during the same general period of time when he wrote about the church in the Ephesian and Colossian letters: 'He lived there two whole years at his own expense, and welcomed all who came to him, proclaiming the kingdom of God and teaching about the Lord Jesus Christ…' (Acts 28:30, 31).

8. Onward throughout the New Testament Epistles and the Revelation, the kingdom of Christ (or of God or of heaven or 'his kingdom') is presented as the realm in which Christians live. How this relates to the persistent theme of a future kingdom of glory on earth is well put by George Ladd. As the gospel is preached throughout the world, he writes, 'two things always happen: some men are loosed while others are bound. Some believe and receive the message. They are delivered out of the power of darkness and transferred into the Kingdom of the Son of God's love (Col. 1:13); that is, they enter the kingom of God because they receive its blessings. Furthermore, they are assured of an entrance into the future Kingdom of God when Christ comes in glory.'[10]

These facts lead to the conclusion that from the first of the New Testament epoch, beginning with Jesus' opening sermons in Galilee on until the end of the present age, the Christian message to the world is the gospel of the grace of God. The same is the gospel of the kingdom (Matt. 24:14). There was never any essential change of message, though the message came to be more perfectly revealed, better understood and more clearly articulated as time passed by. It is not to be distinguished in content from the gospel of 'repentance and forgiveness of sins' which 'should be proclaimed in his name to all nations' (Luke 24:47) authorized by the risen Christ on Easter Day.

II. A Change in Plan?

Does the inauguration of the church represent a change of plan on the part of Jesus? That is, was an external earthly kingdom of Old Testament prophecy offered by John, Jesus, the Twelve and the Seventy for Jews only, and upon rejection of the Messiah and that kingdom by the Jewish nation was the kingdom offer withdrawn and a different plan (the church) introduced?

This chapter began by taking note that the gospels begin with vigorous proclamations of the kingdom of God that had just drawn near and then 'in the midst.' The proclamations were accompanied by demands for Israel's repentance as necessary for entrance into that kingdom. Yet by the midpoint of Jesus' career He is speaking of building a church (Matt. 16:17-19). The book of Luke, which carries the reader deepest into the post-resurrection narrative, pointedly beckons on to the inauguration of the church (Luke 24:47-49). We know that the nation of Israel did decide to meet none of the requirements of the kingdom and rejected the King. It seems reasonable, therefore, to some careful and rational scholars, to assume the withdrawal of the kingdom plans and introduction of an alternate 'backup' mode. Though not a matter of difference between denominations, Yes and No answers to this question divide a large amount of academic theology.

To give an affirmative answer, 'Yes, there was a change of program,' is not to give up on God's eternal decrees, for any theologian with a little skill at his art can explain that all change in God is on the level of 'revelation' or 'procedure' not of essence. It will be better to consult Scripture to discover what, in fact, were the Savior's goals in this matter. In order to limit the study to manageable size let us restrict inquiry mainly to Matthew, where the issue arises most sharply.

1. Matthew connects his narrative at numerous stages with the Servant prophecies of Isaiah 42–53. This seems to start with an allusion to Isaiah 53:8, 'stricken for the transgression of my people,' at Matthew 1:21, 'He will save his people from their sins.' As I show in Part IV, Christology, chapter 13, 'The Passion and Death of Jesus,' Isaiah 52:13–53:12, concern throughout with our Lord's atoning death, is scarcely ever fully out of sight in Matthew's Gospel. Hence we can say that the rejection of our Lord by His people Israel and His redemptive death on Calvary for the sins of mankind was in God's plan for His Son from eternity. He is 'the Lamb slain from

---

10. George Ladd, The Gospel of the Kingdom (Grand Rapids: Eerdmans, 1959), p. 116.

the foundation of the world' (Rev. 13:8 KJV; cf. 1 Peter 1:18-20). The venerable Authorized Version of Isaiah 53:10 reads, 'Yet it pleased the LORD to bruise him,' but this pleasure of God is the same plan of God which Paul mentions as the 'the good pleasure of his will… which he hath purposed in himself… the purpose of him who worketh all things after the counsel of his own will' (Eph. 1:5, 9, 11 KJV). Hence the death of Christ for the sins of our race was his eternal pleasure, plan, purpose, will.

Before the Jews officially rejected Him He spoke of how He, 'the bridegroom,' would be 'taken away from them' (Matt. 9:15). He knew already that 'the Son of Man [would] be three days and three nights in the heart of the earth' (Matt. 12:40, i.e. slain and buried).

2. Similarly, the rejection of Jesus' disciples and their gospel of the kingdom by their contemporaries, with subsequent persecution, was known to Jesus from the beginning of His ministry and predicted by Him (Matt. 10:16-23). In His inaugural sermon, Jesus held out the prospect of their being 'persecuted for righteousness' sake' (Matt. 5:10), of being reviled and slandered (5:11).

3. The purpose of His mission was not to bring civil tranquillity, domestic peace and cessation of all conflict. 'Think not,' He said, 'that I am come to send peace on earth: I came not to send peace, but a sword. For I came to set a man at variance against his father, and the daughter against her mother, and the daughter in law against her mother in law: And a man's foes shall be they of his own household' (Matt. 10:34-37 KJV). Jesus positioned these warnings among a set of instructions that fit only the long ages of the church after the rejection and crucifixion of Christ, when evangelism would advance through frequent family disruption.[11] It becomes clear that Jesus came in the first place to bring to pass exactly what did come to pass, not to set up a Zion-centered, external world-government – something His last address (Matt. 24–25) clearly placed at a future time after 'this gospel of the kingdom will be proclaimed throughout the whole world as a testimony to all nations' (Matt. 24:14).

4. Early in His ministry, after a peculiarly impressive demonstration of faith by a Gentile (the Capernaum Roman army officer of Matt. 8:1-10), He hinted at what during the last week He forecast plainly – the temporary setting aside of the Jews, the natural 'children of the kingdom,' with Gentiles being brought into 'the kingdom of heaven.' The Parable of the Vineyard and the Husbandmen (Matt. 21:33-44) traces this transfer to Old Testament prediction (Matt. 21:42-44). This does not read like the circumstances of any change of plan.

5. In His very closing hours before being arrested in Gethsemane Jesus declared His death to be necessary – that is, His rejection by Israel and death by their instigation – to fulfill the Scriptures. The incident is familiar – 'How then should the scriptures be fulfilled, that it must be so?' – and is not of moral necessity, but *dei genesthai*, necessity grounded in Old Testament Scriptures, expressing the purpose of God to send His Son to be the Savior of the world. On Easter Day He explained to two disciples on the road to Emmaus thus: 'Behooved it not the Christ [of whom 'the prophets have spoken] to suffer these things…. And beginning from Moses and from all the prophets, he interpreted to them in all the scriptures the things concerning himself' (Luke 24:25-27 ASV).

Jesus clearly presented Himself as the Messiah of Israel, albeit never by direct claim. And He said that the kingdom of God was 'at hand,' i.e. had arrived. That the Messiah had no intention at that time to introduce the glorious reign of a final scion of the house of David is equally plain in the humble manner of His coming and the 'image' (as we now in journalistic idiom say) projected by the non-regal way He lived and behaved all His years in the presence of the Israel of Palestine. In the first of his several books on the kingdom of God, George Ladd perceptively wrote:

> It is difficult to see how Jesus could have offered to Israel the earthly Davidic kingdom *without the glorious Davidic king* [Ladd's emphasis] who was to reign in that kingdom. The very fact that he did not come as the glorious King, but as the humble Savior, should be adequate evidence by itself to prove that his offer of the kingdom was not the outward, earthly kingdom, but one which corresponded to the form in which the King himself came to men.[12]

With withering logic Philip Mauro demonstrated from the testimony of John the Baptist, Jesus Himself and other New Testament witnesses that 'having come into the world to die for sinners' He could not and did not go 'about telling His hearers that He had come to restore again the Kingdom to Israel [at least not at that time, it should be added].'[13]

---

11. See R. Culver, *A Greater Commission*, pp. 36–39.
12. George Ladd, *Crucial Questions About the Kingdom of God* (Grand Rapids: Eerdmans, 1952), p. 117.
13. Philip Mauro, *God's Present Kingdom* (New York: Revell, 1919), pp. 192–208.

6. The final words of Matthew indicate clearly that all of Jesus' teaching ('commanded you') from day one onward was designed for the present age of the kingdom of God, not a future age of visible kingdom glory on earth (Matt. 28:19, 20). In other words, all of Jesus' teaching in the Gospels was intended for the instruction for a minority *ekklēsia* of humiliation, not a universal kingdom of glory such as the prophets predicted and Jesus confirmed for a more distant future.

We may conclude therefore, as already stated above: 'From the beginning of the New Testament in Matthew to the end of Revelation, the church is presented as fulfilling certain aspects of Old Testament kingdom prophecy without being sole fulfillment. Other aspects of the kingdom, especially its distinctly Israelitish, visible, Zion-centered features await the coming age of their fulfillment.'

Advocates of the doctrine that Jesus began with proclamation of an earthly Jewish kingdom and upon rejection shifted to a different program altogether – the church – are not agreed as to when in His career and at what point in His teaching the shift came. Anything before the shift is detached from any direct application to the present age of the church. Philip Mauro insightfully inquired long ago:

> We would simply raise at this point the question whether the difficulty our friends have in agreeing as to where the supposed 'break' occurred may not perhaps be due to the fact that there was no break at all? If so, then all the conflicting groups would be correct in so far as they deny the existence of any 'break' where the other parties say it occurred.[14]

The above proposition and arguments arose out of my own early theological pilgrimage away from rather strict 'postponed kingdom' doctrines made almost universal among fundamentalists in my childhood and youth. I was not influenced directly by other dissenting theologians of the time but my own reflections as I studied for lectures as a professor of Old Testament with a strong interest in New Testament and theology as well as for the pastor's pulpit. We were not very specialized in those days. But at the same time others were devoting some of their energy to the same problems and were coming to similar conclusions. They came from many layers and sections of what was still self-designated as orthodox fundamentalist opinion. L. E. Maxwell, principal of Prairie Bible Institute,[15] and Robert McQuilkin, president, Columbia Bible College, are representative of those who saw a weakening in the moral force of Christianity if large portions of the Gospels and Acts, the commandments and all promises and predictions of the Old Testament and New Testament through Acts, relate primarily to national Israel and a future earthly kingdom of God. Others were George Ladd[16] (of fundamentalist Baptist origins and graduate of Gordon Divinity School followed by graduate university studies) and C. R. Ludwigson[17] (raised a Lutheran, later independent) who taught this subject at Wheaton College and later as president of Trinity Seminary.[18] I wrote *Daniel and the Latter Days* before 1952, though in its first form the book was not published until 1954. There were others – enough that these authors found a receptive market for their arguments far and wide, and modified the accepted dispensational fundamentalism of the time and onward. In Britain and on the continent of Europe several authors developed 'premillennialism' (Sauer, Lang, Pache, and others) along lines much more like the historic premillennialism of the eighteenth and nineteenth centuries.[19]

A Positive Assessment of Transitions and Stages of Kingdom Revelation in the New Testament.

With regard to the transitional stages and progress within the New Testament, upon which several dispensational distinctions have been built, it may be better to think of revelational stages. This is mainly what some dispensational writers appear to mean, in part, by the distinctions they make.

---

14. ibid., p. 19.
15. L. E. Maxwell, *Crowded to Christ* (Grand Rapids: Eerdmans, 1950), with McQuilkin's foreword to Maxwell's book.
16. Ladd, *Crucial Questions About the Kingdom of God*.
17. C. R. Ludwigson, *A Survey of Bible Prophecy* (Grand Rapids: Zondervan, 1951, 1975).
18. Later known as Trinity Evangelical Divinity School.
19. I would direct the reader who is forming an opinion on this difficult matter to consider the irenic writings of Erich Sauer, *From Eternity to Eternity* (Grand Rapids: Eerdmans, 1954), pp. 171–178, still available and applicable, or C. R. Ludwigson, *A Survey of Bible Prophecy* (Grand Rapids: Zondervan, 1951, 1975), pp. 169–182, and then more technical books and articles. See George Ladd, 'Kingdom of Christ,' 'God,' 'Heaven,' in Elwell, *Dictionary of Theology*, and pp. 607–611 for a survey of the subject and basic bibliography. See A. J. McClain, *The Greatness of the Kingdom*, 1959, p. 556, presently available at BMH Books, P. O. Box 554, Winona Lake, IN 46590, for a superb presentation of the postponed kingdom (dispensational) view and very full theological bibliography.

At this juncture it will be helpful to observe in what light T. D. Bernard's Bampton Lectures put the evident differences of procedure and message in the various parts of the New Testament. He observed, firstly, that the teaching of our Lord in the Gospels does, indeed, contain the substance of all Christian doctrine but does 'not bear the character of finality.' Secondly, the teaching of Jesus in the Gospels follows a 'visibly progressive course, but on reaching its highest point [the Last Supper Discourse] announces its own incompleteness' and declares another epoch of revelation to come (John 16:12-14).[20] He says, 'There was nothing then on the lips of the preachers of the Gospel [i.e. the Apostles and contemporaries] but what had begun to be spoken by its first preacher, and in following to their utmost the words of the Apostles we are still within the compass of the words of the Lord Jesus.' A comparison of John 3:14, 15, on the topic of faith, redemption and personal salvation, with the book of Romans will strongly support this assertion. The latter develops ideas both explicit and latent in the former. A comparison of John 8:35, 36 on the subject of faith and freedom with Paul's Epistle to the Romans will do the same. Bernard observes further that Jesus' direct teaching during the time of His earthly ministry was not perspicuously and systematically presented. Firstly, as to form, Jesus commonly used the Hebraic parable and proverb – which, as is well known, was frequently employed to obscure the truth from the unworthy (Matt 13:10-17).[21] The Epistles, on the other hand, are in sections, models of forensic and rhetorical method. Secondly, as to method, Jesus' discourses were usually related to 'chance' and occasion – a visit from John's disciples, the question of a rich young ruler, a snare set by Pharisees and Sadducees, a bit of bad news like the execution of John, the tragic collapse of a building, or a question from one of His own disciples. Later portions of the New Testament, though sometimes arising out of a pressing missionary emergency, often take the form of extended systematic treatises on doctrine and practice. Thirdly, as to substance, Jesus' teachings 'bear a double character… firstly clearing, restoring, perfecting of truth already known; and it is, secondly, the revealing of a mysterious economy which has not yet been divulged.'[22]

Historical development of the kingdom of God theme is plainer in Matthew, I judge, than in the other Gospels. I propose (and am far from alone in this[23]) that the 'problem' may be worked out in that book by observing the following.

1. Both John and Jesus initially announced that the kingdom of Old Testament prophecy had arrived in the Messiah. It was now present among the people of Palestine. John's announcement is recorded in Matthew 3:1-12. Jesus' announcement (Matt. 4:17) was verbally the same as John's. His message squarely rested on Old Testament prophecy of the kingdom.

> The real and most profound explanation of the presence of the kingdom is to be sought in the person of Jesus himself. The secret of the presence of the kingdom lies in Jesus' victory over Satan [Luke 11:18-20; Matt. 12:25-28], in his unlimited miraculous power [Matt. 4:23; 9:35; 11:2-5], his unrestricted authority to preach the gospel [Matt. 11:5; Luke 16:16; Luke 4:17-21], in his pronouncements of blessedness [Matt. 5:3 ff. and Luke 6:20 ff.] and bestowal of salvation [Luke 12:32; 22:29; Matt. 21:43 et al] upon his people. There can be no doubt that we are confronted here with the messianic, Christological character of the kingdom of heaven and the entire fulfillment which Jesus proclaims as a present reality is based on the fact that he himself is the Christ [proclaimed so at baptism, transfiguration, et al].[24]

2. From the time of His baptism, in His early public ministry, Jesus went about all Galilee teaching in Jewish synagogues at Sabbath services and preaching the kingdom of God, furnishing the supernatural signs of the arrival of the kingdom (Matt. 4:23-24) which readers of the prophets had a right to expect and a duty to acknowledge (cf. Matt. 11:1-6). Jesus responded to those who denied the presence of the kingdom by saying: 'If it is by the Spirit of God that I cast out demons, then the kingdom of God has come upon you.'

3. Both John and Jesus asserted that repentance for sin and faith (i.e. conversion, personal spiritual regeneration) were necessary for entrance into this kingdom then present (Matt. 3:6-8). John threatened severe judgment for trust in mere Jewishness instead of repentance (Matt. 3:9-12). The punishments threatened were eschatological – 'unquenchable fire' (Matt. 3:12).

---

20. Cf. my remarks in Perry and Culver, *How to Search the Scriptures*, 1967, 1979, pp. 67–69.
21. Also see my article, 'The Difficulty of Interpreting Old Testament Prophecy,' *Bibliotheca Sacra*, July, 1957.
22. All the ideas since the last previous note are from *The Progress of Doctrine in the New Testament*, Bampton Lectures of 1865 by Thomas Dehany Bernard (Grand Rapids: Zondervan, repr. n.d.), pp. 72–77.
23. See Ludwigson, *A Survey of Bible Prophecy*, pp. 78–82.
24. Herman Ridderbos, *The Coming of the Kingdom* (Philadelphia: Presbyterian & Reformed Publ. Co., 1962), pp. 81, 82. This quotation summarizes the first ninety-seven pages of this great book.

4. Citizens of the kingdom would be regenerate folk, living according to the divine will and laws (Matt. 5–7), seeking 'first the kingdom of God and his righteousness' (Matt. 6:33).

5. Some aspects of Christ's kingdom were and remain incompletely revealed. Certain 'mysteries of the kingdom of heaven' were made known to the circle of loyal disciples (Matt. 13:11 KJV) but not repeated to us.

It is important to note that the New Testament concept of mystery (Greek, *mustērion*), which in secular literature usually refers to something essentially unknown, is first introduced in connection with preaching the gospel of the kingdom, the seed of the Word of God (Matt. 13:11).

> Biblical mysteries are truths of a religious sort, known to God from eternity, but known to men simply and exclusively because God has revealed them. Paul used the word in that sense in Romans 16:25, 26 and Ephesians 3:3. Since a supernatural opening of the mind is necessary to understand some of these things, the New Testament mystery often takes on the added sense of truth explained only to initiates [see 1 Cor. 5:12, 13].[25]

These 'mysteries' were made known in parables (Matt. 13 KJV; Mark 4; Luke 18) but were only partly understood then and now. They have to do with principles of evangelism over the long church age to come. All eight of the 'seminar of parables' relate to this missionary program. Matthew 10, which in chronological order followed the seminar of kingdom parables, told them and succeeding generations what procedures to follow in the age-long mission of world evangelism. These chapters are inexplicable without specific, planned intention on the part of Jesus as instruction for the church of Christian believers throughout the age in which we live.

6. In formal statements such as Matthew 5:3, 6, 10, 11; 10:15-25, Jesus foretold that His disciples in the future would mourn, hunger and thirst for righteousness' sake, be as sheep in the midst of wolves, scourged in synagogues (as Paul was), and brought into judgment in front of Gentile magistrates for Jesus' sake. Before the heavenly kingdom of peace could come to earth there would be a long time of 'not peace, but a sword' when the spiritual and moral good of the kingdom would be in stubborn conflict with intractable evil, as several of the parables plainly imply – especially of the wheat and tares.

7. At the 'end of the age' (Matt. 13:40 NIV; there is much manuscript evidence for 'this age') – the present age – the 'regeneration' of the world will take place (Matt. 19:28, 29 KJV) with Christ and His saints in charge (Rev. 5:10; 20:1-6).

8. The special Jewishness of Jesus' first proclamations and limitation of His life and ministry to the Land of Israel and its people is to be accounted for by the simple fact that the redemptive events of Gospel history had to transpire among Jews and at their city to provide salvation in a spiritual kingdom. This was the divine plan for the Lamb slain from the foundation of the world. This explains, in part, why John and Jesus and the Apostles as well never went into any 'way of the Gentiles.'

Beginning at Romans 15:8 and through verse 14 Paul gives his own version of this argument in explaining the urgency of the church's assisting him in a mission to Gentiles in Spain in particular. This passage, perhaps the most complete systematic biblical argument for world evangelism, hinges on the Old Testament kingdom promises voiced in the whole *TENAK*, the Hebrew Bible of *Torah* (Law), *Neviim* (Prophets) and *Kethuvim* (Holy Writings). 'Christ,' he says, 'became a servant to the circumcised [the nation of Israel only] to show God's truthfulness, in order to confirm the promises given to the patriarchs [Abraham onward].' Then he carries a statement of a more ultimate purpose, a world-wide offer of divine mercy to Gentiles as well, adding, 'and in order that the Gentiles might glorify God for his mercy.'

He clinches the point by quoting first from the *Kethuvim*, 'Therefore I will praise you among the Gentiles' (Ps. 18:49); then from the *Torah*, 'Rejoice, O Gentiles, with his people' (Deut. 32:43); and lastly from the *Nevi'im*, 'The root of Jesse will come [house of David], even he who arises to rule the Gentiles; in him will the Gentiles hope' (Isa. 11:10).[26] These comments apply equally to Matthew 10:5-7; John 10:16; and Romans 9:4, 5. See also Isaiah 56:3-8 and many other Old Testament predictions elaborating the 'promise to the patriarchs that in Abraham all the families of the earth shall be blessed' (Gen. 12:3).

9. The term 'kingdom of heaven' as employed by Jesus displays an area of equivalence with eternal life, treasure in heaven, the kingdom of God and 'the regeneration' of the world which have several present and future aspects of the kingdom of Christ in this world.

---

25. R. D. Culver, *A Greater Commission* (Chicago: Moody Press, 1984), p. 75.
26. See chapter 14 above, and my discussion of this passage in *A Greater Commission*, pp. 123–126.

A story in Matthew 19 displays the point. Jesus had just spoken of celibate living 'for the sake of the kingdom of heaven' (v. 12); whereupon there were brought to him 'little children' of whom He declared, 'to such belongs the kingdom of heaven' (v. 14). The first of these two references to the kingdom of heaven seems to indicate simply the sphere of God's spiritual-moral interests on earth, the second the sphere of salvation – not an essentially different thought.

Then follows (Matt. 19:16-30) the incident of the rich young ruler (cf. Luke 18:18 ff.; Mark 10:17 ff.). The man asked how to have eternal life (v. 16). Jesus told him how but called the 'life' (v. 17) to be obtained 'treasure in heaven' (v. 21). Then, addressing 'his disciples,' Jesus spoke of this eternal life or treasure in heaven as entering into 'the kingdom of heaven' (v. 23); and as entering 'the kingdom of God' (v. 24); again as inheriting 'eternal life' (v. 29). He also spoke of the Apostles as 'in the new world [regeneration, KJV, *paliggenesia*, Gr.] when the Son of Man will sit on his glorious throne, you who have followed me will also sit on twelve thrones, judging the twelve tribes of Israel' (v. 28). This last scarcely has primary reference to the church – in which case one should wonder which tribe one belongs to!

There is quite sufficient basis in this text alone to understand that the kingdom of heaven has plain reference sometimes to the era of Messiah's reign on earth in the future predicted by the prophets of the Old Testament and sometimes to a living hope of Israel in Jesus' time. In view of this passage how can we think of the disciples' question of Acts 1:6 as stupid? Yet, there is also plain and, I think, unmistakable reference, in the expression 'kingdom of heaven' or 'kingdom of God,' to the eternal life the believer has now – to heaven above where his 'treasure' is even now.

10. There is an understood overlapping of the future (supernatural and eschatological) with the present (natural and worldly) in the above language, making it appropriate to speak of the reign of Christ by the Spirit in the hearts, lives and mutual connections of believers in the church as the kingdom of God, and even of the professing church as the kingdom of Christ (or of God). Calvin made the discerning comment on John 17:2, 'So then, the kingdom of Christ extends, no doubt, to all men; but it brings salvation to none but the elect, who with voluntary obedience follow the voice of the Shepherd; for the others are compelled by violence to obey him, till at length he utterly bruise them with his iron sceptre.'[27]

The personal accredited presence of the Son of David, the Messiah of Old Testament prophecy, rendered the kingdom of heaven, in an eschatological sense, present on earth. He invaded Satan's kingdom, casting out the demons who got in His way or who ruled the lives of victims He chose to deliver (Matt. 12:22 ff.), declaring to Satan's Jewish friends, 'if it is by the Spirit of God that I cast out demons, then the kingdom of God has come upon you' (Matt. 12:28). Shortly afterward Jesus proclaimed '[a] greater than Jonah is here' (Matt. 12:41) and '[a] greater than Solomon is here' (Matt. 12:42). The works (miracles, signs, power) following His baptism that accompanied Him and His official representatives, the Apostles, and some others, were directly a sign to that generation that God's kingdom of power was (and still is) present on earth (see Heb. 2:3, 4). These blessings (see Luke 4:16-19) were proclaimed early by Jesus (Luke 4:16-21) and cited later by Him (Matt. 11:1-6) as evidence that the King of Israel (John 1:49) was present in the Person of Jesus of Nazareth. To the same effect are the comments of K. L. Schmidt of Basel:

> That the *ekklēsia*, too, is an echatological entity is proved by the eschatological events [miracles as prophesied] of the self-witness of Jesus as Son of man and the institution of the Lord's Supper. But the *basileia tou theou* and the *ekklēsia* are not the same. They are not the same in the primitive community which certainly regarded itself as the *ekklēsia* but which continued the proclamation of the basileia. Nor are they the same in the preaching of Jesus, who promises [the kingdom of God] to his *ekklēsia*. ['Fear not, little flock, for it is your Father's good pleasure to give you the kingdom' (Luke 12:32)] In this sense the post-Easter *ekklēsia*, too, regarded itself as eschatological. In this sense the individual [believer] is to be understood eschatologically as a justified sinner [who has passed from death to life].[28]

Hence the age to come (see Matt. 19:28) has already broken into the present age with the Advent of Messiah; believers in the Messiah (Old Testament predictions included Gentiles also in His benevolent reign) have already entered Messiah's kingdom and already participate in some of the blessings of that properly future kingdom. They now 'have eternal life' (John 3:16); they already have 'passed from death to life' (John 5:24). Their 'life' now already 'hidden with Christ in God' (Col. 3:3) and shall 'appear with him in glory' when 'Christ… appears' (Col. 3:4). They even now may be 'transformed' (Rom. 12:1, 2) if not yet translated, and have even 'tasted… the powers of the age to come' (Heb. 6:5).

---

27. Calvin, *Commentary on John* vol ii (Edinburgh, 1847), pp. 165, 166.
28. K. L. Schmidt, *TDNT*, III., p. 522.

When Jesus said that the kingdom of heaven is like a seed sown in the field of the world or in the heart of hearers (Matt. 13:38; 19; Mark 4:15), that kingdom is obviously in the here-and-now of this present world. Similarly, when Jesus informed 'one of the scribes… "You are not far from the kingdom of God"' (Mark 12:28, 34) the tense is not future but present. Contrariwise, Jesus spoke a parable 'because they [the Passover crowds] supposed that the kingdom of God was to appear immediately' (Luke 19:11) and in the parable spoke of going to 'a far country' to 'receive… a kingdom' (Luke 19:12; see also Matt. 22:1-4; 25:14). This places the 'also-kingdom' in a future time.

Though these observations may appear novel and strange to some and like a brilliant discovery to others, they are neither strange nor new ideas. The present spiritual aspects and future spiritual, visible and glorious aspects of the kingdom of God have been obvious to Bible readers always, I judge. Let me cite first a personal anecdote and then a bit of rabbinic theology.

In the period of prevalence of 'postponed kingdom' theory among conservative evangelicals, at the tender age of about sixteen, I was asked to teach a class of boys my own age. It was a time before radio and television had robbed our homes of extensive Bible reading, so the boys knew something of Scripture. Our thirteen-week quarter was on Matthew. Lesson material from Union Gospel Press resolutely argued that the kingdom of Matthew's Gospel is the future visible, earthly reign of Christ. My best friend argued me down each Sunday, though I gamely followed Robert McQuilkin's 'notes on the lesson.' My friend, Norwood, had seen both the present and future plainly, without any special pleading, in the King James Version before his unbiased vision.

Solomon Schechter, late head of the Jewish Theological Seminary of America, is perhaps the most widely known to American Gentiles of interpreters of rabbinic theology. His *Aspects of Rabbinic Theology* is about as near to systematic theology as Judaism gets. It seeks to summarize and systematize major concepts of the Talmud and devotes three of the eighteen chapters to 'The Kingdom of God – Invisible, Universal and National.' I cite first the summary on the subject by Louis Finkelstein, another famous Jewish scholar, in the lengthy introduction. He held that in eastern Europe of the nineteenth century the society of the good early years of the Judaism in the Diaspora was restored, saying:

> In this rejuvenated ancient world… The spirit of man was far more real than his body; mastery of Torah and compliance… far more urgent and important than success in any aspect of mortal life. The kingdom of God was at once *distantly future and immediately present* [emphasis added]. It was distant in the sense that the vast majority lived outside it [remember the scribe 'not far from the kingdom']. It was present in the sense that one spent almost all one's life [i.e. that of a true Jew] within it. Every Jew 'accepted' each day 'the yoke of the Kingdom of Heaven,' and a moment later prayed that this Kingdom might through a miracle be realized on earth in the future.[29]

This was the best sort of Jewish piety in Palestine when Jesus addressed its crowds of curious people. Space does not allow me to show that Jesus was in almost every respect a true Jewish rabbi, employing many rabbinical and popular Jewish forms of expression, trains of thought, patterns of speech and accepted *weltanschauung*. For one example, most of what Christians call the 'Lord's Prayer' (Matt. 6:9-13) evidently previously existed in the earliest forms of what became the Jewish Prayer Book. '"Our Father, who is in heaven" is one of the most frequent ways of addressing God in the Jewish Prayer Book and the subsequent liturgy.'[30] Almost every member of the prayer can be found in the oldest rabbinic literature, the prayer book and the liturgy. If, as seems likely, these ideas of the kingdom of God derive from the days of Hillel and Shammai and the earlier Diaspora schools, then we may rest assured that Jesus' teachings of a present kingdom of God in and among godly people and their association, as well as a future visible-earthly kingdom of glory on earth, were not *per se* thought strange. In such case the fluidity of terminology we have discovered in Matthew 19 – life, eternal life, heaven, treasure in heaven, kingdom of heaven (or of God) – would have seemed quite unremarkable – along with a reference on the same plane of thought to a future reconstitution (regeneration, *paliggenesia*) when the Messiah would reign with His saints over the reconstituted 'twelve tribes of Israel' (Matt. 19:28).

Schechter shows that the kingdom of hope of post-biblical Judaism always embraced future hope of fulfillments, spiritual and national, as well as universal spread of the same blessings to the whole world.[31]

---

29. Solomon Schechter, *Aspects of Rabbinic Theology: Major Concepts of the Talmud* (New York: Schocken Books, 1961), p. viii.
30. ibid., pp. 54, 55.
31. ibid., pp. 97–115.

The Ascended Christ's Present Reign at the Father's Right Hand.

1. The Fact.
The nature of this event prevents any 'this-worldly' eyewitness report. Yet the New Testament provides revelation both of the fact itself and the meaning of it.

With reference to the fact, Jesus predicted it (Matt. 26:64) during His trials before Caiaphas; Peter in the first Christian sermon announced that Jesus had been exalted to the right hand of God (Acts 2:23); Stephen in his dying moments saw Jesus at the 'right hand of God' (risen from His throne to receive to glory the first Christian martyr, Acts 7:56). Through the New Testament the event is related to Christian doctrine, comfort and admonition (see the paragraphs to follow).

2. The Predictions.
As in the case of other aspects of Messiah's work the Ascension is regarded as predicted in prophecy, prophecy which shaped the very language by which the whole subject is treated in the New Testament. That prophecy is Psalm 110: 'The LORD says to my Lord: "Sit at my right hand, until I make your enemies your footstool." ...Rule in the midst of your enemies!.... The Lord is at your right hand; he will shatter kings on the day of his wrath.' This phraseology is clearly recognizable in New Testament references to the Ascension. Here at the fountain are the elements of Christ's Kingly reign – a beginning in which He is declared King and a reign which takes place at first 'in the midst of... enemies' but which shall later triumph openly over all other sovereignties.

3. The Salvational Meaning.
Viewed from the viewpoint of redemption, the session at the Father's right hand was a signal that redemption was a finished work. By one sacrifice – once and for all – He had finished His work (Heb. 10:11-13). Thus the seated Savior is a ground of assurance to the Christian of full forgiveness. It completes setting the conscience free (Heb. 1:3; 12:2).

4. The Inauguration of Christ's Reign.
The appropriation by Christ of His Kingly power, won by death and resurrection, took place at His session at the right hand of the Father – and it is this which gives it great significance. It marks the beginning of the reign of Christ. This is the meaning assigned at 1 Peter 3:21, 22, 'Jesus Christ... has gone into heaven and is at the right hand of God, with angels, authorities, and powers having been subjected to him.' This reign, as Psalm 110 says, is 'in the midst' of enemies and will progress until all of them are under His feet (vv. 1, 2, 5; cf. Ps. 8:4-6; Heb. 2:6-9).[32]

5. The Consummation of Christ's Reign.
That reign, presently invisible and acknowledged on earth only by Christians, will become visible at His second coming as King of kings and Lord of lords (Rev. 5:6-14; 11:15; 19:11-21). At that time will occur the resurrection of the righteous dead (Rev. 20:1-5), to be followed by Christ's millennial reign (Rev. 20:4-6). Then ensue the resurrection and judgment of 'The rest of the dead' and their final judgment (Rev. 20:7-15), including presumably also all wicked angels, demons and Satan. This will be succeeded – who knows how long? – by a merging of the reign of Christ with that of His Father, 'For he must reign until he has put all his enemies under his feet' (1 Cor. 15:23-25; see also Phil. 2:9-11).

6. The Church's Present Share in Christ's Reign.
The Church's present share in and relation to the reign of Christ from the Father's right hand is mentioned at Ephesians 1:20-23; 4:15; 5:23 and Col. 1:18-20. It has been observed that the Christian confession, 'Jesus Christ is Lord' is an acknowledgment of this reign and that this doctrine brings about inevitable collision whenever 'Caesar' seeks to replace Christ as the object of ultimate allegiance. God's Son will allow no competitors.[33]

---

32. There is no scriptural evidence for the claims of some that at Christ's session He fulfilled all the promises of Old and New Testaments of the Messiah's reign from the 'throne of David.' Passages cited (e.g. Acts 8:32-36) say nothing of the sort. David's throne is on earth, not in heaven.

33. I read *The Gospel of the Kingdom* by G. H. Lang after completing this chapter and was pleasantly surprised. Almost every proposal of mine was anticipated long ago by Mr Lang, who first wrote his small book about seventy-five years ago. G. H. Lang, *The Gospel of the Kingdom* (reissued Miami Springs, FL: Schoettle Publ. Co., 1988).

10
The Essential Nature of the Church

Early in these pages it was pointed out that divine revelation in the New Testament supplies copious information about the church and numerous figures (vine and branches, body of Christ, household of God, and similar), yet it is never defined. Paul calls the church a 'mystery' – something we know only because God reveals it and only as much as He reveals – several times (Rom. 16:25; Eph. 1:9; 3:3-9; 5:22). Jesus referred to His *ekklēsia* by name only twice and in the future tense (Matt. 16:18; 18:17). The society of believers is called 'the church' (*ekklēsia*) in Luke's history only after she had existed as an *ekklēsia* for quite some time (Acts 5:11).[1] Yet in those early days the Christian *ekklēsia* was a concrete visible reality which the unconverted Saul of Tarsus could identify and persecute (Acts 8:1, 3; 1 Cor. 15:9). There was a church at Jerusalem before it had deacons or elders or a permanent place of worship, and the *ekklēsia* in Crete evidently existed for a brief period without pastors or other officers – perhaps with no formal organization at all (Titus 1:5-7 ff.). The church was there, but what was it? The problem is ours, certainly not theirs.

Why We Have the Problem.

Though the church Fathers wrote much about the local churches and the whole 'body of Christ,' they do not anywhere define her. Why? Let an acknowledged modern Eastern Orthodox authority on doctrine and history explain:

> The Fathers did not care so much for the *doctrine* of the church precisely because the glorious *reality* of the church was open to their spiritual vision. One does not define what is self-evident.[2]

Florovsky goes on to point out this omission prevailed until 1489 when the first systematic treatise on the church was composed by Cardinal de Turracremata.[3]

---

1. 'Church' is not in Acts 2:47 in better texts.
2. George Florovsky, 'The church: Her Nature and Task,' *Man's Disorder and God's Design* in the *Amsterdam Assembly Series* prepared for first World Council of Churches Assembly 1948 (New York: Harper, n.d.). Four books bound in one volume - Book i, p. 43.
3. ibid.

Reformation Attempts.

The Roman Church of the sixteenth century, however, claimed to be the one true church, sole dispensary of the means of salvation. When Luther (and before him the fifteenth-century 'pre-reformers') broke with a 'church' he deemed to be a spiritual harlot, he found it necessary to explain to himself and his disciples just what a true church is. He struggled with the problem and formed tentative statements on how to recognize the church of any particular place but did not produce a formal definition, though he thought he 'knew it when he saw it.' We will get back briefly to Luther and Lutheran thought on the matter.

By Calvin's time, a generation later, the nature of the church, its ministry and sacraments (ordinances) were matters of confessional controversy. Church teachers and doctrinal authorities have attempted from then to now to state what the church is, and with some success. There is more agreement than immediately apparent in the variety of wordings. It has well been said that the nature of the church 'can be rather depicted and described than properly defined.'[4]

Missionary and Ecumenist Interest.

Many forces in the world and the churches of Christendom conspired to make the period from the beginning of the modern missionary movement (1790+), culminating in the organization and the formation of the World Council of Churches (1948), and with diminishing force on to about 1970, a time of great effort to forge some visible unity of all churches in Christendom. This demanded a common understanding of what the church *as such* is – in a word, the essential nature of the church, the subject of this chapter. Early on, many evangelicals led the search and research, though ultimately liberal forces took control of the organized ecumenical movement. The works by Rouse and Neill referred to above, and the *Amsterdam Assembly Series*, *Man's Disorder and God's Design* (New York: Harper, 1948), record the effort to 1948. Numerous bibliographies guide the scholar to the literary remains of the largely failed organizational effort. Many of the best hours of my life were spent reading these materials. I will not attempt summary or report save to sketch what I believe to be the two important formulations in a few paragraphs. The first is the chapter by Florovsky noted earlier from 1948 and the second from T. M. Lindsay, *The Church and the Ministry in the Early Centuries*.

Wherever there is a genuine local assembly of regenerate believers, the universal church of the first-born, whose names are written in heaven, is also present. In the main, therefore, the following remark of T. M. Lindsay applies: 'And we are definitely taught by the very ways in which St. Paul uses the word "church" to see the church Universal in the individual Christian community.' He cites 1 Corinthians 10:32; 11:22; 12:28; Acts 20:28 (as probably); and 1 Timothy 3:5, 15 (as perhaps).[5]

A World Council of Churches Definition.

Florovsky eschews definition (as earlier observed here) as being impossible, but sets forth what he asserts can be *apprehended* (not his word) within the worshipping church.

Ekklēsia, claims this Eastern Orthodox author, lays emphasis on 'the ultimate unity of the Chosen People... a sacred whole' existing from the beginning 'as a corporate whole.'[6]

'Christianity means a "common life"... united not only among themselves, but... one – in Christ.' This makes real community possible 'in Him.' Florovsky cites Colossians 2:7, 'rooted and built up in him.' Believers are 'born anew in Him,' 'baptized' by the 'one Spirit... into one body' (cites 1 Cor. 12:13). She is not a mere 'human society,' but rather a 'Divine Society... intrinsically not of this world' or 'this eon... but of the age to come.'[7]

This orthodox scholar refines the One-In-Christ idea saying, as a 'peculiar people... the *ekklēsia*, is a *sacramental community*.' He states the Latin *communio sanctorum* as neuter gender in the ancient formula, hence not communion of saints but of *holy things*, that is the 'two "social sacraments" [baptism and Eucharist],' and finds the right administration of the sacraments belongs to the essence of the church. Yet strangely this scholar of Eastern Orthodoxy, which

---

4. ibid., p. 44.
5. T. M. Lindsay, *The Church and the Ministry in the Early Centuries* (Minneapolis: James Family Publ. repr., 1977, original in early twentieth century), p. 18.
6. Florovsky, op. cit., pp. 44, 45.
7. ibid., pp. 46, 47.

regularly baptizes infants (by true immersion), adds, 'Baptism is to be preceded by repentance and faith. A personal relation between an aspirant and his Lord must be first established by the hearing and the receiving of the Word, the message of salvation.' Perhaps Florovsky is thinking of adult converts only. This seems to say the uniting essence of the church lies in the rites of baptism and the Lord's Supper observed by all Christendom. Though he draws close parallels between the Israel of old and the *ekklēsia* he regards the church as a 'new Christian existence' (45). Florovsky asserts:

> Strictly speaking the Messianic Community gathered by Jesus the Christ was not yet the church, before His Passion and Resurrection, before 'the promise of the Father' was sent upon it and it was endued with power from on high... still *sub umbraculo legis* [under the umbrella of the law].... Pentecost was the mystical consecration, the baptism of the whole church (Acts 1:5). [8]

He goes on to say, 'By the Spirit we are united with Christ and constituted into His Body.' Body is more than a metaphor, rather a summary of faith and experience. The church as His body is said to be 'the extension of the incarnate life of the Son,' carefully avoiding saying it is an extension of the incarnation *per se*. He quotes the Fathers Chrysostom, Augustine and Hilary, a modern Lutheran (A. Nygren), and a Roman Catholic (K. Adam) in support.[9] This seems to say the church began at Pentecost and that its essence was created by the events of that day.

The unity of the church of Christ in the Spirit, he says, is through the apostolic succession of the 'ministers.' 'Pentecost is continued and made permanent in the Church by means of the Apostolic Succession.'[10] It began as an apostolic community and continues. 'Ministry [priesthood] is... an indispensable, constitutional or *structural* feature... They are acting not only in the "persona" of the church, as primarily in the person of Christ. The local priest in celebrating the eucharist with the people builds the unity of the local church. The bishops secure the same for the whole church in the world.' In the episcopacy Pentecost becomes universal and continuous. This seems to say the essence of the church is preserved by apostolic succession of the church's official ministry, i.e. clergy.

Florovsky makes the point that there is a 'symphony' of the holy Trinity reflected in the church. He cites John 17:21, 23. Yet the church he affirms, is more Christ-centered (Christological) than Spirit-centered (pneumatological). He closes by saying the church has 'as it were, a double life, both in heaven and on earth.' The heavenly life (eschatological) is 'only an anticipation.'[11]

This brief excursion into some of the best 'ecumenical' ecclesiology will be a novel experience for many readers. It reveals that the special significance of Pentecost was not invented by modern dispensationalists, nor the indispensability of 'sacraments, rightly administered' invented by the Lutheran and Reformed, even though Luther and Calvin gave this view currency in Reformation Christianity to the present.

It is reassuring to find that Florovsky, speaking knowledgably of modern historical and theological research and, presumably, for Eastern Orthodoxy, found the essence of the church at Pentecost in the coming of the Holy Spirit to dwell not only *with* the waiting 120-plus (including the Twelve) but now to be in them forever. He rightly affirms that to that time the 'little flock' of 'remnant Israel' were *sub umbraculo legis* (under the umbrella of) the legal dispensation. He did not learn that from American dispensationalists either. According to Hebrews 7 and 8 that old umbrella was not perpetuated in a new Christian administration but was permanently disposed of – more later.

Florovsky's sacramental theology is similar to the Roman Church's inherited teaching. Even in the Roman system the significance of Pentecost to 'the essential nature of the church' is not lost.[12] Also see L. Ott.[13]

T. M. Lindsay (chap. 1, 'The New Testament Conception of the Church') does not define the New Testament church in terms of essence (what a thing is) but descriptively, as does the book of Acts and the Epistles. He deals with 'characteristics.' First, 'The church of Christ... is a *fellowship* with Jesus Christ; that is the divine element in it. It is a fellowship with the brethren; that is the human element in it' (p. 6). He calls attention to the fact the church is a society: 'union with Christ which is the deepest of all personal things, always involves something social.' The 'call' to be saved seldom comes except in company of believers.[14]

---

8. op. cit., pp. 48, 49. He cites Matt. 3:11 and Luke 3:16.
9. op. cit., pp. 50, 51.
10. op. cit., p. 51.
11. op. cit., p. 54.
12. *The New Cathechism* (San Francisco: Ignatius Press, 1994) see para. 1096, p. 280.
13. Ludwig Ott, *Fundamentals of Catholic Dogma* (Rockford, IL: TAN, 1960, 1974), p. 274, first complete para.
14. Lindsay, op. cit., p. 7.

'The second characteristic... is that [the church] is a unity.'[15] He means the world-wide church on earth at this point. Lindsay showed that 'this unity of the church of Christ in the mind of St. Paul was something essentially spiritual.'[16] He explains:

> [I]n the unity of the Christian church, something which ties implicitly in the unformed faith of every believer, that in personal union with Christ there is union with the whole body of the redeemed, and that man is never alone either in sin or in salvation.... And because the Unity of the church of Christ is a primary verity of the Christian faith, it can never be adequately represented in any outward polity... never an earthly throne, but must always be that heavenly place where Jesus sits at the Right hand of God.[17]

He goes on, quoting Ignatius: 'Where Jesus Christ is, there is the *whole* church' and adds:

> The congregation at Corinth was, in the eyes of Paul... not a Body of Christ, for there is but *one* Body of Christ; not part of the Body of Christ, for Christ is not divided; but *the* Body of Christ in its unity and filled with the fulness of His powers [see Lindsay's exegesis of 1 Cor. 12:27, pp. 14, 15].... In every Christian society... our Lord has placed 'gifts' or charismata, which enables the church to perform its divine functions; and all the spiritual actions of the tiniest community [a house church] – Prayer, Praise, Preaching, Baptism, the Holy Supper – are actions of the whole church of Christ.[18]

It was at this point where, without saying so, Lindsay struck the essential nature of the church – a body of redeemed people in union with the risen, exalted and ascended Christ, baptized by Him in the Holy Spirit into one body, as we shall see.

Lindsay found three further 'outstanding elements in the New Testament conception of the church of Christ': (1) *visible community*; (2) *authority* from Christ for oversight and discipline of its members; and (3) 'Lastly, the church of Christ is a *sacerdotal* society – a *ministering* priesthood of all believers not a *mediating* priesthood.'[19] His treatment is enlightening, but does not bring us precisely to the point of this chapter, 'the *essential* nature of the church.' Think of the church in its essential nature as *having* visibility, authority and a holy ministry, not *being* visibility, authority and holiness. These matters call for attention when we come to discuss the local church.

I shall spare the reader further modern views of the essence of the church – what it is by definition. Some include a form of baptism in the essence or a theory of ordination to the office of bishop or priest or alleged right administration of sacraments. Most of these distinctions in my judgment might best be applied to the *bene esse*, that is well-being, not the *being* essence of the church. Acts 2:42 tells us the newly constituted church 'devoted themselves to the *apostles' teaching* and *the fellowship*, to the *breaking of bread* and the *prayers* [emphasis added].' These four elements of her life – sound doctrine, vital sharing with one another, common worship and united prayer – were and are of the *bene esse* (well-being) of the church, but they are not the church; they are vital signs of the church.

The New Testament Conception of the Church.

Let us come to focus on that which constituted Jesus' waiting disciples, the church of Jesus Christ.

> Although it provides no definition or detailed description of the church, the New Testament does use various terms which, by direct implication and by rich and varied symbolism, provided materials for understanding the nature of the church universal and local. Most of the information available, of course, deals with the details of the function and of the conduct of churches as local organizations.[20]

It must be added that the dependence of the church for its very existence upon the ministry of the Holy Spirit and on the career of the Son of God are important considerations.

The teaching of the New Testament regarding the nature of the (universal) church may be summarized in two propositions. The first now follows.

---

15. ibid., p. 10.
16. ibid., p. 13.
17. ibid., pp. 13, 14.
18. ibid., pp. 14, 15.
19. ibid., pp. 21–37.
20. W. O. Carver, *What is the Church?* ed. by Duke McCall (Nashville, TN: Broadman, 1958) p. 5.

I. *The church is a body of believers in Christ created by the Holy Spirit, who imparts His own eternal life to each believer-member and who is Himself, in a distinct and special way, the bond of vital unity between the members themselves and of all with Christ.* This teaching is set forth in Paul's rather full presentation of the subject of the nature of the church in 1 Corinthians 12.

The chapter begins with discussion of the gifts of the Holy Spirit among the 'brethren' (v. 1 KJV). These brethren are 'the church [*ekklēsia*] of God that is in Corinth ...sanctified in Christ Jesus, called to be saints together with all those who in every place call upon the name of our Lord Jesus Christ' (1 Cor. 1:2). They have been divinely enabled to say, 'Jesus is the Lord... by the Holy Spirit' (v. 3; cf. 12:3 KJV). To each believer is given some manifestation of the presence of the Spirit in his life by some one or more gifts (vv. 4-11). Then Paul moves on to state that there is a unique and profound unity among these Spirit-enabled Christ-believers. 'For as the body is one, and hath many members, and all the members of the body, being many, are one body; so also is Christ. For in one Spirit were we all baptized into one body, whether Jews or Greeks, whether bond or free; and were all made to drink of one Spirit' (1 Cor. 12:12, 13 ASV).

In verse 12, ending with 'so also is Christ,' the figure of the human body is introduced. It is one body with many parts (members). The unity in diversity and diversity in unity of the human body are the ideas of interest to Paul.

He points out that there was a then past act whereby all the believers ('we all') were united together into one body ('baptized into one body'). It was an historically past event. The word baptized (Greek *ebaptisthēmen*) is aorist passive (not perfect as the KJV suggests). Note also that according to the ASV rendering believers are baptized *in* (Greek *en*) the 'one' Holy Spirit, not *by* Him. As we shall see, this points back to the Pentecostal event (I would not lay emphasis on the charismatic experience of the 120 but on the filling of the house by the Spirit). We are at liberty to affirm that all believers everywhere, when they become believers, enter into the same event. All Christians are joined to Christ's body in the same way. There is only one Spirit. Through vital union with Him believers are constituted one divinely universal, spiritual body just as the natural body of man is a natural vital union through the natural life within it.

> The church properly speaking had its birthday on the day of Pentecost, for the church is composed of all of those who by one Spirit [better, *in* one Spirit] have been baptized into one body [by Christ, Matt. 3:11] (1 Cor. 12:13), and this baptizing work of the Spirit began on the day of Pentecost [Acts 2].[21]

Furthermore, all believers are made to participate in the life of Christ. Above in verse 12, the body itself (i.e. the church) is called 'Christ' – 'so also is Christ.' This is because all the life in the church is Christ's own. He is the spiritual progenitor of them all (cf. Heb. 2:10, 13). Thus by the well-known water-of-life figure (John 3:5; 4:10, 13, 14; 1 Cor. 10:4) Paul says 'we... all were made to drink of one Spirit.'

Now, there is no doubt that in 1 Corinthians 12 'the body' is 'the church.' This is the sense from the beginning of the chapter, though the word 'church' is not used there. At verses 27 and 28, however, the text is explicit: 'Now you are the body of Christ and individually members of it. And God has appointed in the church first apostles, second prophets,' and so on. That Paul is thinking specifically of the church universal rather than the local church is indicated not only by the exchange of *body* and *church* here, but also by the character of the Pentecostal event referred to in verse 13, by the grandeur of the general conception of the passage, and also by his reference to 'apostles.' The Apostles were given to the whole church everywhere – even that part of it already in heaven (which, by this time had received at least one Apostle, James). There is no evidence that Corinth had any of these Apostles resident when Paul wrote the Epistle to the church there or indeed had ever had them, as the church local at Corinth is not the specific referent. The Cephas party (1 Cor. 3:22) was not built on Peter's residence there.

The 'body of Christ' metaphor for the church has been periodically pressed toward a 'high ecclesiology,' making the metaphor something close to an ontological statement. This happened in the Anglo-Catholic movement of the nineteenth century and again in the flood tide of the world church or ecumenical movements of the mid-twentieth century. Gustaf Aulen wrote (in 1948, at the time of the organization of the World Council of Churches): 'Therefore, when the church is called the Body of Christ, this expression is not to be understood merely as figurative. This word visualizes in a very concrete way that Christ and the church are a unity.'[22] Karl Barth at that time resisted the notion.[23]

---

21. G. E. Ladd, *The Gospel of the Kingdom* (Grand Rapids: Eerdmans, 1959), p. 117.
22. Gustaf Aulen, 'The Church in the Light of the New Testament' in *Man's Disorder and God's Design: The Amsterdam Assembly Series*, Vol. I (New York: Harper & Bros., n.d.), p. 19.
23. Barth, *Church Dogmatics* IV, Part 2, pp. 600–604.

Likewise many Roman 'Catholics and Orthodox... see 1 Corinthians 12:27 as more than mere metaphor and particularly as a simple statement of reality proving that the relationship of the church and Christ should be seen more in terms of identity.'[24]

This idea is prominent in some recent writings of Roman theologians who insist Christ mediates salvation through the church and her sacraments – sacraments provided by a priestly hierarchy at whose head is Christ's vicar, the pope.[25] Robert Saucy has thoroughly canvassed the subject in the above-named article.

II. *The formation of the church by the special work of the Holy Spirit was the culmination of a process of revelation and of history, all of which lie in the record and history of the New Testament.*[26]

The story begins with Matthew 3:1-17, the preparatory ministry of John and the inauguration of Jesus as the Messiah of God. The baptizing forerunner commands repentance, demands fruits of righteousness, and promises a Messiah of both grace and judgment. The Messiah comes, and is baptized by John in an act of dedication to His coming ministry of redemption. Then, before the forty days of temptation and while still in the baptismal waters, the Spirit visibly descends from heaven upon Him and henceforth leads and empowers His entire ministry. The sevenfold enduement of the 'rod out of the stem of Jesse,' promised by Isaiah (11:2 and 42:1 ff. KJV), having taken place, He is 'led up' (Matt 4:1) henceforth in a special way by the Third Person of the Godhead. Of course the Spirit had always been with Him on earth (*vid*. Luke 1:35) but this outstanding event at Jesus' baptism, emphasized in each of the four Gospels (Matt. 4:13-17; Mark 1:1-11; Luke 3:21, 22; John 1:29-34) as fulfillment of the prophecies, was something special.

John the Baptist made the first announcement of Jesus's future special bestowment of the Spirit upon certain people – presumably those prepared for it – as follows: 'I baptize you with water for repentance, but he who is coming after me is mightier than I, whose sandals I am not worthy to carry. He will baptize you with (Gr. *en*, in) the Holy Spirit and with fire' (Matt. 3:11; Mark 1:8; Luke 3:15-17).[27] Such is the promise. The Holy Spirit baptizes no one. Jesus baptizes. Jesus is the agent. The Spirit is the 'element' in which Jesus baptizes. The symbolism is derived from immersion in water.

Many months later the promise of the baptism of believing people in the Spirit was still unfulfilled, though Jesus did add His own promise of the same. 'On the last day of the feast [Tabernacles, John 7:2], the great day, Jesus stood up and cried out, "If anyone thirsts, let him come to me and drink. Whoever believes in me, as the Scripture has said, 'Out of his heart will flow rivers of living water'" (John 7:37, 38). These are Jesus' words. There follows a bit of inspired apostolic 'Biblical theology' interpreting Jesus' words. 'Now this he said about the Spirit, whom those who believed in him were to receive, for as yet the Spirit had not been given, because Jesus was not yet glorified' (John 7:39). This is exceedingly plain. John's promise of the baptism in the Holy Spirit, reaffirmed and amplified by Jesus, had to do with a unique and totally unprecedented conferral of the Holy Spirit on believers in Christ which could not take place until after Jesus' redemptive ministry of death, burial, resurrection and Ascension had been accomplished. Jesus' 'hour' was yet future as He said only a few days earlier (John 7:6, 8). Up to the time of the Last Supper His hour had not come – as several notices in the Gospels relate. But beginning with the Last Supper His time had come (*vid*. John 13:31, 32). The Ascension climaxed His 'time' or 'hour.' Pentecost came a few days later (Acts 1:5; 2:1).

We have the example of the New Testament itself in applying many Old Testament references to the Spirit of God and His work to the Third Person of the Trinity.[28] The Spirit was the Author of faith then as now (2 Cor. 4:13; cf. Ps. 116:10). He gave the temple ritual to Moses (Heb. 9:8) and spoke through all the Old Testament prophets (Matt. 22:43; Mark 12:36; Acts 1:16; 20:25; Heb. 3:7; 10:15). Saints were aware of His presence with them (Ps. 51:11). One cannot conceive of the regeneration necessary to enter the kingdom of God (John 3:3, 5, 7) back then apart from enlightenment and empowering of the souls, then as now 'dead in trespasses and sins.' He was in the world and with mankind then as now, though 'not yet' doing His present special office work.

---

24. Mark Saucy, 'Evangelicals, Catholics and Orthodox Together: Is the church the Extensions of the incarnation'? *Journal of the Evangelical Theological Society*, Vol. 43, no. 2, June 2000, pp. 193, 194.

25. Ratzinger, Dulles, von Balthasar and others, popularized by Richard John Neuhaus.

26. This is not to neglect the fact that preparation for these events is, in part, what the Old Testament was all about. We treated this idea earlier in connection with the chapter on the Old Testament Foundation for the Church.

27. Presumably unrepentant and unbelieving people are to be baptized in judging fire in connection with the Second Advent; believers on the other hand, in connection with the First Advent are to be baptized in the Holy Spirit. This, of course, was not apparent to the Baptist and his audience.

28. B. B. Warfield, 'The Spirit of God in the Old Testament,' *Biblical and Theological Studies* (Philadelphia: Presbyterian Reformed, 1952), pp. 129–130. Charles Hodge, *Systematic Theology I* (Grand Rapids: Eerdmans, repr. 1970), p. 477.

A. H. Strong illustrated the matter well. He points out that the Holy Spirit is 'eternal' (Heb. 9:14) and wrought in Old Testament times. Yet:

> Before Christ, the Holy Spirit was not yet (John 7:39), just as before Edison electricity was not yet. There was just as much electricity in the world before Edison as there is now. Edison has only taught us its existence and how to use it. Still we can say that, before Edison, electricity as a means of lighting, warming [instant communication]... had no existence. So until Pentecost, the Holy Spirit, as the revealer of Christ [and whose presence within each believer unifies and constitutes the *ekklēsia* of Christ] 'was not yet.'[29]

F. Meyrick and H. B. Smith, from an Anglican perspective, find the same significance for Pentecost:

> The Day of Pentecost is the birthday of the Christian Church. The Spirit, who was sent by the Son from the Father, and rested on each of the Disciples, combined them once more into a whole – combined them as they had never before been combined, by an internal and spiritual bond of cohesion. Before they had been individual followers of Jesus, now they became his mystical body, animated by his Spirit. The nucleus was formed. Agglomeration and development would do the rest.[30]

Now note the progress. Perhaps in the Upper Room, perhaps on the way to Gethsemane (John 18:1), Jesus gave the 'promise of the Father' (Acts 1:4; 2:33) in some detail – greatly advancing the information supplied by John the Baptist and his own striking utterance in John 7:37-39. The first and most significant paragraph is John 14:16-18: 'And I will ask the Father, and he will give you another [Gr. *allon*, another of the same kind] Helper, to be with you for ever, even the Spirit of truth [of great significance since these Apostles were to be the special bearers of new revelation (John 16:12, 13)], whom the world cannot receive, because it neither sees him nor knows him. You know him, for he dwells with you [Gr. *par' humin*, beside, or alongside you] and will be in you [*en humin*, in, or inside you]. I will not leave you as orphans; I will come to you.' It is possible that 'will be' (*estai*) should be 'is,' present tense (*esti*). As Alford and Westcott agreed in their commentaries on John in either case the sense is future. It is pointed out by more recent writers, including Max Zerwick and Macy Grosvenor,[31] that the sense is future in either case, if present tense, a 'futuristic present.' It is parallel with 'I will not leave you as orphans' immediately following. Recent Versions preserve the futuristic translations (NIV, RSV, etc.).

This also is not obscure. As believers in the one true God through the Scriptures, such as Elizabeth (Luke 1:41), Zacharias (Luke 1:67), Simeon (Luke 2:26) and others, they 'knew' the Holy Spirit. He had been 'with' them. Now a deeper relationship was to be theirs. The Spirit of God was going to be 'in' them in some special sense no believer could know until some future time after Jesus had gone away, as the text plainly states and exegetes of every stripe remind us. This special coming of the Holy Spirit, inasmuch as in a mysterious way the triune Godhead cannot be divided, was to be a coming of Christ, for he said of it, 'I will come to you' (John 14:18). As just now stated, some of the problems of the local 'presence' of Persons of the Godhead either in heaven 'with the Father' or on earth 'with you' and of their identity, which inevitably arise at this juncture, belong to the mysteries of the Persons of the Trinity and of the two natures of Chirst and are hence, though matters of revelation and of faith, not fully explicable. They are by definition biblical *mysteries*.

No argument from those who might wish to over-press the continuity between the old and new covenants or of the continuity of the people of God under each of the covenants may ignore or bypass these facts. The relation of the Holy Spirit to the Christian believers post-Pentecost is not in every respect the same as it was before that event.

Jesus spoke very much of the future descent of the Spirit during the last night with His disciples. Yet, since for our present purpose no particular doctrinal advance was made, we cite the references and pass on. They are all in John – 14:25-28; 15:26, 26; 16:7-15. Then at an Easter evening appearance, to the startled Apostles and perhaps other disciples, Jesus made a dramatic pronouncement, *viz*.: 'he breathed on them, and saith unto them, Receive ye the Holy Spirit' (John 20:22 ASV). This Easter evening pronouncement has a cryptic flavor. The Greek text might be translated 'receive Holy Spirit' (no 'the'). This, like the twofold pronouncement of peace, was something special, just for those frightened ten believers in that room – Judas and Thomas being absent. Pentecost was yet nearly seven weeks in the future. For those momentous but tedious days of waiting they needed staying power that

---

29. A. H. Strong, *Systematic Theology*, p. 317.
30. 'Church,' ed. H. B. Hackett *Smith's Dictionary of the Bible I* (New York: Hurd & Houghton), pp. 453, 454.
31. Zerwick & Grosvenor, *Grammatical Analysis of the Greek New Testament* (Rome: Biblical Institute Press, 1981), pp. 330, 331.

even the strongest of them had not yet demonstrated. 'To enable them, Jesus imparted "a Holy Spirit" (John 20:22, *pneuma hagion*) the power of new life from the risen Savior. This was necessary to create in them the proper conditions for the descent of the Holy Spirit in the special way He came at Pentecost. The Spirit conferred was the [risen] Christ's Spirit, the Holy Spirit as dwelling in Him.... The conferral of the Spirit in John 20:22 might be conceded to have been preliminary to Pentecost in the same sense that the descent of the Spirit at Jesus' baptism was preliminary to the mighty work of the Spirit of God some years later.'[32] The view of John 20:22 which I have summarized here[33] follows the lead of B. F. Westcott in his famous commentary on the Gospel of John.[34]

We should not be surprised then to read how that shortly before His ascension and only a few days before the Feast of Pentecost, 'And while staying with them he [Jesus] ordered them [the disciples] not to depart from Jerusalem, but to wait for the promise of the Father, which, he said, "you heard from me; for John baptized with water [Gr. suggests 'administered water baptism'], but you will be baptized [in] with the Holy Spirit not many days from now"' (Acts 1:4, 5).

Jesus here comes full circle back to the prophecy of John the Baptist with which we started: 'he will baptize you with the Holy Spirit' (Mark 1:8).

The fulfillment, when it came, was, then, climactic – and let us now return to the proposition with which these recent paragraphs began: *The formation of the church by the special work of the Holy Spirit was the culmination of a process of revelation and of history, all of which lie in the record and history of the New Testament*. Pentecost was as decisive and epochal and essentially unrepeatable an event as the birth of Jesus, His resurrection or His Ascension. 'When the day of Pentecost arrived ["fully come" KJV], they were all together in one place. And suddenly there came from heaven a sound like a mighty rushing wind, and it filled the entire house where they were sitting' (Acts 2:1-2). The believers present were all 'immersed' in the Holy Spirit, so to speak. The filling of the house was *accompanied by* (not identical with) a special filling of each disciple. These momentous spiritual events were accompanied by outward signs – to convince the disciples of the reality of fulfilled promise. This was complete fulfillment of the Father's promise (John 14–16) noted reflectively by Jesus (Acts 1:4, 5). The Spirit of God 'came.' He does not need to come again. Further, it was as truly unique and epochal as any event of redemptive history – the giving of the law at Sinai, the crossing of the Jordan or the 'It is finished!' of Calvary. Paul reflecting on it could then say, 'In one Spirit were we all baptized into one body' – thus our first proposition above: *The church is a body of believers in Christ created by the Holy Spirit ,who imparts His own eternal life to each believer-member and who is Himself, in a distinct and special way, the bond of vital unity between the members themselves and of all with Christ*.

This is as far as the specific topic 'The Nature of the Church in the New Testament' might need to take us except for two things: (1) a whole Pandora's box of theological problems concerning the relationship of the church, its ministers, Apostles and members, its revelation, and its forerunner, John, to the Old Testament dispensation, its people of God, its procedures and its prophecies; and (2) the fact that teaching on the church is amplified throughout the later books of the New Testament.

The first matter, the relation of the church to Israel, has been treated in another chapter. Observe, however, that the conclusions attained above were reached wholly without resort to assumptions about either dispensations or covenants. Further, I think that although John the Baptist was the last of the Old Testament prophets, the program of Jesus from the time of His baptism and temptation onward to His Ascension was one of church foundation, and that He never at any time changed His approach or plan because of His rejection by Israel. His Apostles were chosen in the first place to be founders of the church. Those who like to discuss theology in connection with party labels will observe that this presentation is representative neither of dispensationalism nor of covenant theology. I have chosen quite deliberately not to move within those categories. My opinions about them have been expressed elsewhere in this book.

With regard to the fact that the nature of the church receives amplification throughout the Epistles and Revelation we note the following.

First Corinthians 12 is basic to this subject. A. J. McClain was the first to call to this writer's attention that it presents at least six features of the body of Christ, the church. Note that in this chapter there is a mysterious

---

32. R. D. Culver, *A Greater Commission* (Chicago: Moody Press, 1985), p. 140.
33. Adapted from my *A Greater Commission*, pp. 139, 140.
34. B. F. Westcott, *The Holy Bible ... Commentary*, NT, Vol. II, p. 295.

identification of Christ with the whole body – that the head is not Christ, but rather believers who are ears, nose, mouth and the like compose the head. In certain other passages Christ Himself is represented as the head of the body. This is, of course, because 'body' is a metaphor not a literal entity, even though it does stand for a literal group of persons in real spiritual union. These six features are as follows.

1. *Organic Unity* (vv. 12, 13). The church may or may not be externally organized. In either case it is inwardly ordered by a life – the life of God's Spirit. The unity of the universal *ekklēsia* is not a goal to be attained, it is a fact to be acknowledged. This unity is not concocted or artificial. It was created at Pentecost and shall never dissolve. It includes believers living and dead – the church triumphant as well as the church militant.

> Yet she on earth hath union
> with God the three in one
> And Mystic sweet communion
> with those whose rest is won.

Though there is great difference of opinion on the subject, I find no compelling reason to exclude Old Testament believers, now deceased and in heaven, from this union with Christ. Yet see Hebrews 12:23, 'to the assembly of the firstborn… and to the spirits of the righteous made perfect.' The language distinguishes but does not necessarily separate. This unity may be obscured by schism, sinned against by sectarianism, denied by ignorance, but it cannot be diminished or destroyed.

2. *Diversity* (vv. 14-20). There are as many members as there are genuine believers. They differ among themselves in abilities and characteristics, but as each is true to the law of his own individual being (as redeemed by Christ) and lives out the life of the Spirit of God (Gal. 5:22-26; 2:20), he will serve Christ effectively and with joy in his own inimitable and unduplicable way.

3. *Universality* (v. 13). Wherever there is a Christian the great church of Christ is present by virtue of the vital union of all the parts. There are no Christians who have no share in the Spirit of God (Rom. 8:9; also 1 Cor. 12:7). This is without respect to the social, educational or economic situation of the believer.

4. *Mutuality* (vv. 21-27). Every member receives from and imparts to every other member of the body. In some degree, however ignored or unrecognized, the body is entirely affected by the spiritual health-situation of each member. None lives or dies, rejoices or grieves to himself. This is quite apart from certain similar statements which might be made about the common humanity of all mankind everywhere. This is not socialism, egalitarianism or humanitarianism. It is spiritual union in its practical mutual relationships.

5. *Visibility*. This is not to say that the universality of the church is visible to the world. It isn't even clearly visible to the genuine members who, sadly, do frequently question and harass one another. But it is the church alone which, shining as a light in the world, makes Christ spiritually visible to men. His is the Spirit animating the body which is His church (v. 12). It is not true that Christ or His mother are seen or have been seen at Fatima or Lourdes or even at St Peter's in Rome. Rather Christ is seen everywhere and anywhere that Christians live out their distinctly Christian union with Him. Read Philippians 2:14-16 and also 2 Corinthians 10:4, 5, especially if you are concerned about relating the visible church to the world's visible problems.

Karl Barth put an interesting spin on the question of the visibility and invisibility of the church – this time one of his inevitable paradoxes seems useful.

> Like Israel in the Old Testament, the Christian community is not just a people in world-occurrence but *this* people. It is just as essential [essential nature, that is] to it to be *this* people as to be *a* people. And it is just as essential to it to be not merely *visible* as *one* people among many but also *invisible* as to *this* people, i.e. to be a phenomenon which cannot be comprehended and therefore known by all in empirical and rational terms. As *this* people it might well be a magnitude which is totally unknown to all. Hence it is both visible and invisible in one essence.[35]

6. *Spirituality*. The entire twelfth chapter of 1 Corinthians deals of course with our spirits and God's Spirit, their relations and activities. With effects in the world of 'men and things… roots and grubs and fishin' worms' the church is not seen with the same sort of eye that counts ballots or calculates the effect of a true statement about sin on a national senatorial election.

Further, in relation to God, the church is His *temple*. In relation to Christ the church is a *temple* of which He is cornerstone; a *virgin* by whom Christ is Beloved; a *bride* for whom He is the Groom; a *city* of which He is Chief

---

35. Karl Barth, *Christian Dogmatics*, iv, 3, Second Half (Edinburgh: T and T Clark), p. 726.

Citizen; a *people* of whom He is LORD; a *flock* of which He is Shepherd; a *family household* of which He is Firstborn; a *new man* of whom He is Creator; an *elect race* of whom He is Progenitor; a *royal priesthood* of which He is High Priest; an *inheritance* of which He is the Heir.[36] Paul Minear devoted 300 pages to discussion of these twelve and eighty-four other images of the church, ninety-six in all, to be found in the New Testament.[37]

In the 'heavenly Jerusalem' the church is '*firstborn* [emphasis added]' in distinction from 'innumerable angels in festal gathering… God, the judge of all… the spirits of the righteous made perfect, and… Jesus, the mediator' (Heb. 12:22-24).

Finally, in relation to the whole created universe she is *preeminent* as Paul reveals in the great paean of prayerful praise with which we presently close, Ephesians 1:17-23.

Supplementary.

Note #1.

I append a note on this important subject. Neo-orthodox theologians have had their own way of conceiving the essential nature of the church. Karl Barth makes some interesting remarks on the nature of the church, despite his theories of universal salvation by covenant. Christ, he says, 'is the man in whose person God has… elected and loved from all eternity the wider circle of humanity as a whole, but also with a view to this wider circle, the narrower circle of a special race, of His own community within humanity.' This, he says, is the Christian *ekklēsia*. He makes the point that though the 'Christian tradition' has an 'aetiological narrative' to explain the origin of the Lord's Supper there is none for the church as such, and explains: 'The reason why the establishment of the community [*ekklēsia*] by Jesus Himself could not emerge as a definite and distinctive event in the Gospel tradition is rather that this is the theme of the whole Gospel narrative as an account of Jesus, the whole of the Gospel narrative as an account of Jesus necessarily being an account of the birth of the Christian community, of the development, corresponding to and consummating the unification of the twelve tribes of Israel in the exodus from Egypt, of the people of God of the last time which has been inaugurated with the coming of Jesus Christ.' Written in opposition to the background of a continental theology which held Jesus never founded or intended to found an *ekklēsia*, this complicated sentence is helpful. Yet in all his lengthy chapter,[38] I find no awareness of any connection with the nature and founding of the church in John's promise of a baptism in the Spirit and the events of Acts 2. Barth found paradoxes in every aspect of theology, and ecclesiology was no exception.

Note #2.

Views of the nature of the church vary so widely *in many details* that a modest-sized book would be necessary to present them. The largest section of my files on ecclesiology is under 'The Essential Nature of the church.'

---

36. References in Scripture to the above will be found, in order at Eph. 2:20, 21; 2 Cor. 11:2; Eph. 5:26-42; cf. Rev. 21:9; Rev. 21:9, 10; cf. Rev. 22:1; Titus 2:14; 1 Peter 5:2-4; Eph. 2:10; cf. Col. 1:18; Eph. 2:15; 1 Peter 2:9; cf. 1 Cor. 15:45-48; 1 Peter 2:9; cf. Heb. 4:14; Eph. 4:18.
37. Paul Minear, *Images of the Church in the New Testament* (Philadelphia: Westminster Press, 1960).
38. Karl Barth, op. cit., 'The Holy Spirit and the Sending of the Christian Community'.

11
The Unity of the Church

As we have noticed several times, much New Testament teaching about the church is by means of metaphors, parables and various other figures. This is true also of the unity of the church. In much recent and current treatment of the church's unity, however, the body figure has been overworked to the neglect of other New Testament approaches. The unity of the church is not the first thrust of the body figure (1 Cor. 12), but rather diversity of gifts.

The Unity in Ephesians 2 and 4:4-6.

At Ephesians 4:4-6 (again in the passage where gifts of Christ to the church are going to be discussed) Paul announces the oneness of the church in a series of strictly propositional statements. The nature of the church, her gifts and her unity are aspects of one subject.

In this opening of the practical section of his Epistle Paul brings to bear the meaning for life of the fact of the reconciliation of Jew to Gentile 'through the cross' (Eph. 2:16) and mutual 'access by one Spirit unto the Father' (v. 18 KJV). Christ has made 'both one' (v. 14), creating 'one new man' (v. 15). This oneness is something that never existed before. Whatever continuities exist between the old dispensation and the new, the 'new man' or 'one body' is a fresh creation. Israel had a *national* unity, with a plethora of divine benefits, but never had there been a unity in spiritual life and inward religion. The Old Testament story plainly shows that the majority of Old Testament Israelites were unbelieving and disobedient throughout most of their national history. Jesus pointed this out vividly on several occasions. Stephen was murdered for doing the same. Up to 3 million disobedient and unbelieving Israelites still lie in the dust of the forty-year trek through the wilderness. In verses 19-22 Paul says the people of this new entity are *fellow citizens* with holy beings and are of the *household* of God – two very understandable human analogies.[1]

This new establishment has precedent and preparation in Moses and the Old Testament prophets, though Paul does not mention that here as he does elsewhere. Rather the new household has a new foundation – Apostles and prophets of the New Testament epoch, both present in the *ekklēsia* in its formative years. They not only planted the churches but were its resident, spiritual authorities and produced the canon of Scripture.

---

1. Who are the 'saints' of fellow citizenship? Perhaps Abel and Enoch, pre-Israelites, for many of them lived before Abraham, as well as Abraham, Moses and others. Not because in an Abrahamic covenant which frequently gets overworked in relation to unity of the church, but because they had faith and were holy.

In Ephesians 4 the Apostle employs the newly created unity as ground for Christian lives of humility, meekness, long-suffering and mutual love among members of the *ekklēsia* on the ground of its own essential unity. This unity is sevenfold, as we shall try to expound in a moment, but first take note that 'body' here has almost escaped from figure to literal – as when we today speak of any group of people with some important commonality as a body, for instance the upper body (or house) of congress. No real vital community is implied. This sort of ambiguity is inescapable and too much should not be made of it. Yet in many New Testament passages 'the body' comes close to being a synonym for *hē ekklēsia*, the church.

The translations obscure the fact that Paul introduced the seven unities of the church very abruptly and with the apparent assumption that the Ephesian church (or wherever else) would know why. 'There is' (v. 4) is not in the Greek text. It is as though he simply flashed a picture before the eyes of the church to remind them of something they well knew but must keep ever before their consciousness. Omitting the supplied words, the striking passage reads:

> [O]ne *body*,
> and one *Spirit*,
> even as ye are called in one *hope* of your calling;
> One *Lord* [Jesus],
> one *faith* [once for all delivered],
> one *baptism*,
> One *God and Father* of all, who is above all, and through all, and in you all (Eph. 4:4-6 KJV, [emphasis added]).

In this passage the word 'one' is used seven times, probably with symbolical sense of fullness or completeness, as the sevenfold spiritual endowment of Messiah, 'the Branch' in Isaiah 11:2, and sevenfold description of God's voice in Psalm 29.

Though Paul says something about gifts to every believer in Ephesians 4:7, the presentation of the unity moves immediately on to gift of specially endowed persons to the whole church ('into the lower parts of the earth,' v. 9) for its inward perfection and completion as the one 'body of Christ' (vv. 12, 16). The one body, Spirit, hope, faith, baptism, Lord and Father have organic connection from within, a true uni-verse: one-many which is a one. In the next chapter, on the gifts of God to the church, this will be discussed in some detail.

In an interesting way R. E. Brown, citing E. Käsemann, points out how the doctrine of the unity of the church seems to have special connection with the great church at Ephesus.[2] Besides the Epistle to the Ephesians there is the fact that Ephesus is the most likely site of the composition of the fourth Gospel where in chapters 15 and 17 in Jesus' last discourse and prayer He emphasized Christian unity. One might say the same of 1, 2 and 3 John. Did the youthful 'beloved disciple' John hear these things in the Upper Room and recall them at Ephesus fifty to seventy years later (John 14:22) to record them in these chapters? Further, the Ephesian congregation manifested some of the virtues which alone arise within the community of love (Rev. 2:1-7) and merited the risen Lord's praise (Rev. 2:2, 3). Further, the importance of 'the faith' and a common 'form of sound words' is central to the first two of Paul's pastoral letters, both addressed to Timothy, an 'interim' pastor at Ephesus. Both Apostles framed their messages on unity to encourage the unity of the Spirit in the bond of peace as something already possessed and to be made manifest in conduct.

The Unity in the Allegory of the Vine and the Branches.

The allegory (or metaphor: 'I am the vine; you are the branches') in John 15:1-16 stresses the connection of Christ the vine stock with the branches for Christian fruit-bearing.

Christ Himself in the metaphor is 'the true vine' (*hē ampelos hē alēthinē*). It can scarcely be doubted He intended to bring before these eleven orthodox Jews the many Old Testament passages which represented (metaphorically) Israel as a vine, God's vine, but *in each case* as faithless and disobedient, deserving of punishment (Ps. 81:8-16; Isa. 5:1-7; Jer. 3:21; Ezek. 15:19; Hos. 10:1). The disciples are not about to become the 'true vine,' as some would have it, in contrast to the old rebellious one, but if they abide in unity with Christ the vine they will be fruitful Christians.

---

2. R. E. Brown, *Anchor Bible: The Gospel According to John*, chaps. 13–21, Vol. 26a (Garden City, NY: Doubleday, 1966, 1970), p. 778.

Let us not try to empty the Lord's stern warnings of fearful consequences of breaking the unity: 'If anyone does not abide in me he is thrown away like a branch and withers; and the branches are gathered, thrown into the fire, and burned' (v. 6). The truth propounded relates to useful service for Christ's Father by the *geōrgos* (literally 'earth-worker'), farmer, husbandman (KJV) (v. 1). Good vinegardeners know about 95 per cent of each year's growth must be cut away each winter. 'The fruit is always borne on fresh growth.' Those interpreters who point out that the thrust of the parable is *good* fruit-bearing not *salvation* are surely correct. The lesson is an exhortation to keep our personal communion and community with Christ vital and vigorous: 'Abide in me, and I in you... He that abideth in me, and I in him, the same bringeth forth much fruit: for without me ye can do nothing' (John 15:4, 5 KJV). The 'you' and 'ye' of KJV in this passage translate second person plurals not singulars.

There is a connection between this allegory of unity in the coming *ekklēsia* imbedded in the Last Discourse (John 14–16) and the same theme in the High Priestly Prayer of John 17, especially verses 20-24, so we turn to this.

The Unity in Jesus' Prayer for the Eleven Apostles and the Future *Ekklēsia*.[3]

John likely composed his Gospel during the reign of Domitian (AD 81–96), ignoble brother of Titus, his noble predecessor. Persecutions by Nero (AD 54–68) were limited mainly to Rome itself and were sporadic. Domitian, 'who was hungry for divine honours' carried persecution to many parts of the empire including the province of Asia where John lived at the time he wrote, if traditions are correct. Here believers were first invited, then compelled on pain of severe sanctions, even death, to say 'Caesar is Lord.' Domitian, the then reigning Caesar, was king of the *oikoumenē* ('civilized' world) and chief magistrate of the *kosmos* (organized-by-Satan) – 'the world' mentioned often by Jesus in John's Gospel (about seventy-five times, only fifteen times in all the Synoptics). In John, Jesus says the world is wicked, ruled by Satan, against God, against His Son and out to kill Him; it hates the disciples and will do all it can to deceive them and to destroy them.

The solemnity, intimacy and depth of this chapter have made it a subject of intense study in all ages, beginning with the early Fathers and – sadly – the heretics. In recent generations every new kind of higher criticism, positive and negative, has worked it over. I have read everything immediately accessible to me from Bengel and Calvin from Reformation times on through Meyer, Alford, Westcott, Schaff and others of the nineteenth-century surge of evangelical scholarship; Hoskins, Schnackenburg, R. E. Brown, Morris, Barrett and other recent writers who usually employ the recent forms of criticism in a positive way. It has seemed apparent to me that nothing in these mountains of research and resulting decisions helps us understand the text except to call attention to the Gospel history (Synoptics and John 1–16), especially Jesus' own previous discourse about the promised Paraclete, and the faith of the first Christians. I do not think the beliefs of any of the 'Hellenistic church,' 'Jewish church,' or any social or religious movement of late first century modified John's language in reporting what Jesus said to His Father. I take special note that R. E. Brown (*Anchor Bible*, Vol. 29a, *John*), though he frequently opens the possibility that this or that phrase arose out of some contemporary Christian concern or current of opinion in some sector of Greco-Roman society, rarely commits himself to such and usually interprets the text as it stands, usually drawing quite orthodox (and sometimes non-Roman) conclusions.

Similarily C. K. Barrett[4] and Leon Morris,[5] like Alford and Westcott who wrote before the riot of twentieth-century Gospels criticism, both treat the text of John's Gospel with respect for its authorial genuineness and for its textual integrity as a report of Jesus' prayer. Sir Edwin Hoskins[6] and Rudolph Schnackenburg[7] follow about the same policy.

After all, Jesus laid great emphasis here on the integrity of the Father's words (both *hrēmata* and *logi* are employed) which were given to Him and imparted by Him to the Apostles and they to us. Most people sense this as they read and reflect on the Gospel of John.

In His prayer of John 17, the only extended prayer of Jesus whose contents we know at length, Jesus reminds the Father that He had manifested God's name to these eleven men 'which thou gavest me [*aor.* tense, a past definite act] out of [*ek*] the world' (v. 6 KJV). Now Jesus prays the Father to preserve their Christian integrity (against the

---

3. John 17:20-25.
4. Charles K. Barrett, *The Gospel According to John* (London: SPCK, 1962).
5. Leon Morris, *The Gospel According to John* (Grand Rapids: Eerdmans, 1971).
6. Sir Edwin Hoskins, *The Fourth Gospel* (London, 1947).
7. Rudolph Schnackenburg, *The Gospel According to John*, 3 vols., English trans. (New York: Seabury, 1979).

'evil one' as they go out into the world, vv. 15-17). He speaks of the 'word' and 'the truth' brought by the Son from the Father to the Eleven and them to the world.

John introduced the theme of the world's ignorance of the Savior and rejection of Him at the beginning of the Gospel: 'He was in the world, and... the world did not know him' says the author (John 1:10). Now, in these last seven verses of His prayer we hear Jesus explaining to us *via* a private petition to the Father how the world will come to 'believe' on Jesus and to 'know' Him and His Father. It is to be through manifest unity of the believers of the *ekklēsia*. Let us see what Jesus said about it. For some reason Jesus went over the ground twice – and few would regard this as a copyist's mistake. It must have been His most earnest plea to the Father and thereby for us as well.

It is not feasible to discuss much not specifically related to our theme of unity though we cannot avoid very brief reference to issues related to the mysterious unity of the Godhead, the extent of the atonement and even the order of salvation (*ordo salutis*).

From the standpoint of the prayer (1) there is going to be a company of believers won by the apostolic 'word.' (2) Jesus prayed for this yet-to-be *ekklēsia*. (3) He prayed specifically for their manifest unity. (4) He spoke of a pattern for their manifest unity in the unity of the Father and the Son. (5) The manifest unity of the believers in the *ekklēsia* has brought some of the world to knowledge that the Son was sent by the Father and to *know* that God loves the *ekklēsia*.

1. There is going to be a company of believers won by the apostolic word. 'I do not pray for these [the Eleven] only, but also for those who believe in me through their word' (v. 20 RSV). '[T]hese' are the eleven faithful Apostles, the subject of His prayer through verses 6-19. Earlier in the evening in His discourse on the vine and branches He had said that unity with Himself would glorify the Father in that 'you bear much fruit, and so prove to be my disciples' (John 15:8 RSV). That fruit is partly love, as our passage makes plain. That will have effect (vv. 20, 23) in the world. As Calvin discerningly noted, '"through their word" expresses admirably the power and nature of faith, and at the same time is a familiar confirmation to us that our faith is founded on the Gospel taught by the apostles.'[8]

2. Jesus prayed for this future *ekklēsia*.

'[T]hose who will believe in me through their word' (v. 20) looks to the future. The many present tenses in the prayer 'I am coming to you' (v. 11), 'now I am coming to you' (v. 13), are all futuristic presents. Every new believer from that moment on till Gabriel sounds his horn is included in His prayer. 'All subsequent faith would take place through the Apostolic word [spoken or inscriptured]' (Alford).

'[T]heir word' had been received from Christ both as *hrēmata* (meaningful sounds, v. 8) and logos (expression of idea, v. 14), as He had received the same from the Father (v. 14). This is an important connection for unity between sound words of doctrine (1, 2 Tim.) and the unity of the church, both visible unity and spiritual. This word of the Father, both the idea and the human words which expressed them, issued in formal statements and a true 'apostolic succession' of sound doctrine (2 Tim. 2:2), which have helped anchor the church to the Word down through the centuries.

A contentious problem arises in verse 9. Did Jesus ever pray for the people of the world, or did He not? Jesus had prayed for the Eleven: 'I am praying for them. I am not praying for the world but for those whom you have given me' (v. 9). Yet it is not clear that Jesus is here excluding the world from interest in His prayers. He did (as we shall see) pray for 'the world' – several times in this case 'the world' as lost and against God is in His thoughts. His concern is the incipient church. The RSV rendering makes plain what most exegetical commentaries (Bengel to Father Brown) point out: Jesus is saying, in effect, '*at this critical moment* I am not praying for the world.' His concern of the moment was the small group of disciples (seed of the church and the future Christian *ekklēsia*). Calvin, himself, does not quite come through as a Princetonian Calvinist in his comments on this passage. He adopts the language of the paradox of Isaiah 6:9, 10, quoted several times in the New Testament. In his comments on 'that the world may believe that you have sent me' (v. 21) and 'that the world may know that you sent me' (v. 23) he affirms the love of God even for the reprobate – quite unseemly for a 'Calvinist'![9]

It is this future company of 'all his people' who are the subject of verses 20-24. They are soon to emerge from the waiting little 'flock' (Acts 1:12-15; cf. Luke 12:32) as the *ekklēsia* to which first 3,000, then 2,000 more and millions on through the ages were gathered.

---

8. Calvin, Commentary, *John*, Vol. II, trans. W. Pringle (Edinburgh: Calvin Translation Society, 1847), p. 182.
9. ibid., pp. 183–186.

3. Jesus' prayer for the future *ekklēsia* was for our unity, a oneness corresponding in some manner to the unity between the Father and the Son: 'that they may all be one, just as you, Father, are in me, and I in you, that they also may be in us' (v. 21). The request is repeated in similar language in verse 22, except that the second time 'The glory,' which the Father had given the Son, He in turn has given to the disciples as a means to their unity. I fail to see any connection between this glory and either His 'Gloria Unitgeniti' (uncreated glory),[10] or the glory of the cross as such, rather 'for them the true glory lay in the path of lowly service wherever it might lead them... The apostles are right with God... They have the true Glory'[11] – in other words, His moral glory. In this path tangible, empirical, visible unity occurs.

In what respect is the unity of the *ekklēsia* parallel with the unity of Father in Son and Son in Father? There are opposite errors. E. L. Mascal in his *Corpus Christi* argued that as the Holy Spirit is the bond of unity in the *ekklēsia*, so is the bond that renders the holy Trinity a unity.[12] But the comparison is of *ekklēsia* to God, not the other way around. Ancient Arians made the same procedural error with opposite results when they claimed that, as the bond that unites believers is moral only, so the bond of Father and Son is moral only.

As Calvin points out, the Fathers went to ridiculous lengths in refuting the Arian view. He proposed modestly that the oneness of Father and Son was in the Son's mission and message as Mediator. Throughout the chapter, Calvin says, 'When Christ affirms that he is one with the Father, he does not speak simply of his Divine essence, but that he is called one, as regards his mediatorial office, and in so far as he is our head.'[13]

J. F. Randall wrote a long, technical book in an effort to explain the comparison and the unity.[14] He cites the various opinions: unity of purpose; harmonious existence together; like husband and wife; achieved through the divine image in man; unity in the Eucharist; and the like. 'Sooner or later,' R. Brown correctly states, 'most authors say that it is a union of love.'[15]

This unity has to be evident to the world, otherwise it could not help produce belief and knowledge among unbelievers. This points to the 'fellowship' (Gr. *koinōnia*) which characterized the Jerusalem *ekklēsia* and has characterized every healthy local church since that day and in an apparent degree in the world-wide *ekklēsia*, as we all feel when we meet true believers of any hue or culture or organized community. This is ably expressed and defended by Raymond Brown.[16]

4. The effect of the evident unity of the *ekklēsia* (both invisible and spiritual) by the Holy Spirit, visible to the world through their love upward to God as well as inward to one another and outward toward lost people, brings the world to knowledge that the Father sent the Son and that some would believe in the same: 'that the world may believe that thou hast sent me' (v. 21 RSV); 'so that the world may know that thou hast sent me and hast loved them even as thou hast loved me' (v. 23 RSV). There is a whole theology of mission and evangelism here and questions that ask for answers. For example, 'hast loved them' – the believers or the world? Though most assume without comment that it is the believers, it is grammatically and syntactically possible that it is the world (as in John 3:16). At least one important modern author (J. H. Bernard in ICC, *John*) thought so.[17] In context it is more likely the Father's love for believers is intended. That Christian love for God, fellow believers and for lost mankind, in the *koinōnia* of the *ekklēsia*, is key to letting the world know and bring some to faith is a familiar theme in the New Testament. Wescott, after referring to the ultimate summation of 'all things' (= heaven and earth) in God (1 Cor. 15:28), and to 'every knee' bowed to the Son, relates this goal to the oneness of the church. He well says:

> This end... is to be brought about by the spectacle of the disciples.... The unity of disciples, therefore, while it springs out of a direct relation to Christ, must have some external expression that it may affect those outside the church.[18]

---

10. J. A. Bengel, *Genomon Novi Testamenti* (Tuebingen, 1850), p. 464.
11. Morris, op. cit., p. 735.
12. E. L. Mascal, *Corpus Christi: Essays on the Church & the Eucharist* (London: Longman's, Green & Co., 1953, 1957), p. 9.
13. Calvin, op. cit., p. 183.
14. J. F. Randall, *The Theme of the Unity in John 17:20-23* (Louvain Univ., 1962).
15. Raymond E. Brown, *The Anchor Bible: The Gospel According to John*, 2 vols. (Garden City, NY: Doubleday, 1966, 1970), p. 776.
16. ibid., pages 774–779.
17. Morris, op cit., p. 736.
18. B. F. Westcott, *The Holy Bible ... Commentary, NT*, Vol. II, p. 246.

Its importance is overwhelming. The church is in retreat wherever apparent moral and spiritual unity are missing. (See 1 John 1:3, 6, 7; 2 Cor. 9:13; 1 Peter 2:12.) The vigor with which Roman Catholic author Raymond Brown elaborates and supports this truth is both refreshing and amazing.[19]

Unity a Mark of the True Church.

Though the early Christians simply assumed the church and their incorporation in it, never attempting a definition as far as we know, they found it useful, perhaps necessary, to agree on four marks which are necessarily present in the true church. Of these the church's unity is the first mark. They were given permanent statement in the Nicene Creed (AD 325, 381): 'We believe... in one, holy, catholic and apostolic church.'[20] This creed has been honored by continuous use in instruction and worship to the present. Whatever the church may be, as such (and there is some disagreement as we have seen), there is only one church, the mystical body of Christ, the bride, the household of God, that is, the universal church, not of all professors but all who are elect, true believers, whose 'names are written in heaven.'

The 'one' church is not anything distinct from holy, catholic and apostolic. As understood by evangelical Protestants – and I think by the survivors of the late Roman persecutions who gave the creed its first form in AD 325 – there is only *one* church both in the world below and in the world above, *holy* because it is in union with Christ who is holy, *catholic* in that it leaves no true disciple out anywhere in the whole wide world, and *apostolic* in that it teaches truly (if imperfectly) what the original Apostles passed down to the churches immediately through oral teaching and mediately through their inspired writings in the ministries of the 'pastors and teachers' of the *ekklēsia* everywhere.

The point of emphasis in this chapter is that the holy, catholic church in the world, in spite of our inherited patterns of thinking about Christian groups (sects, denominations, societies, customs, observances) other than the one we belong to – officially or only by folk custom – is truly a unity.

Defined and Expressed by Necessity in the First Centuries.

The concept of unity was defined out of necessity imposed by heresies and schisms.[21]

In recent times the unity of the *ekklēsia* has been of great interest both to advocates of the so-called ecumenical movement and its opponents. The growth of heresies in the immediately pre-Nicene (325) period compelled the church to care for unity of doctrine. A millennium afterward, the Reformation seemed to shatter the unity. Efforts to restore formal communion between all evangelicals and 'Papists' in the first generation after 1517 was a dismal failure. The same must be reported of sixteenth-century efforts to secure formal communion if not orgainizational unity between Lutheran and Reformed.

The unity was expressed well in the late second century by Irenaeus of Lyons (130–200). I cite Danielou's comment and translation of *Against Heresies* (v. 20.1):

> The bond of unity in every sphere is given great emphasis in a passage such as the following: 'For they (the Gnostics) are all very much later than the bishops to whom the Apostles handed over... all the churches. Hence the aforesaid heretics, since they are blind to the truth, are bound to wander out of the way, taking now one road, now another; and for this reason the traces of their teachings are scattered abroad without any harmony or sequence [no systematic theology!]. But the path of those who are from the church, circling the whole world, and possessing a firm tradition from the apostles, enables us to see that all have one and the same faith, since all teach one and the same God and Father, and believe the same dispensation of the Incarnation of the Son of God, and know the same gift of the Spirit, and meditate on the same precepts, and preserve the same form of organization as regards the church, and look for the same coming of the Lord, and affirm the same salvation of the whole man, both soul and body.[22]

This describes *in nuce* the emphatic, real and felt spiritual and largely still-visible unity of the church of the early centuries. After Christianity became the state church both in the Byzantine east and the Roman west, though an awareness of unity in Christ, of sorts, remained, there were times when there was more faith among those called

---

19. Brown, op. cit.
20. H. Denzinger, *Sources of Catholic Dogma* (St Louis: B. Herder Co., 1957), para. 36, p. 36; NPNF, 2nd Series, para. 14, p. 163; Henry S. Bettenson, *Documents of the Christian Church*, 2nd ed. (New York: Oxford Univ. Press, 1963), p. 37.
21. See Pelikan, *The Christian Tradition i*, pp. 69, 70, 117, 118, 159, 160, 309–312 for recent scholarly authority.
22. Jean Danielou, *Gospel Message and Hellenistic Culture* (Philadelphia: Westminster, 1973), pp. 150, 151. A slightly different rendering appears in ANF, i, pp. 547, 548.

sectarians, heretics, schismatics and similar than in the hierarchy, the monasteries and the neglected lay members of the geographical parishes. The true whole church was visible only to God, even though we may be sure that the believers in and out of the official, legally recognized 'church' were drawn to one another as always in the Christian *ekklēsia*.

Christian Unity Degenerated to Christendom.

In western Europe, Latin (Roman) Christianity became the folk religion of largely unconverted masses. Eastern Europe and large sections of the Near and Middle East and North Africa (before Islam) became nominally Christian (Eastern Orthodoxy as well as Armenian, Coptic Assyrian and other groups). There is, of course, no godly spirituality in mere nominal profession of Christianity.

This was Christendom and it remained so into modern times. During this period, while there was some awareness of unity in Christ among some, there was small effort toward union except as the 'Christian' secular states sought to conquer one another. There was little reflection on the doctrine of the church except as the Roman papacy sought to increase its hegemony and from time to time issued increasingly bold claims to be the *una sancta*. In his bull *Unam Sanctam of 1299*, Boniface VIII (pope, 1294–1303) declared that 'it is altogether necessary to salvation for every human creature to be subject to the Roman Pontiff' (Latourette, 487). And outside this church 'there is no salvation nor remission of sin' (Denzinger, 468, p. 186). The same claim was brought up to date on July 29, 1896, when Leo XIII issued an encyclical on 'the Unity of the Church' which declares: 'When the divine Founder decreed that the church be one in faith, and in government, and in communion, He chose Peter and his successors [bishops of Rome] in whom should be the principle and as it were the center of unity.'[23]

In Reformation Times.

When the Reformers were expelled from the church, so-called, they were compelled to reflect on the doctrine of the church and her unity. What is the church and in what does the unity consist? They defined the unity of the church in response to the universal claim of the Roman Church and under the pressure of their circumstances when civil magistrates and ecclesiastical authorities were trying to kill them. They found it helpful to distinguish between the visible church and the invisible church. By this distinction they claimed no affinity with the notion that the church has no organization or buildings or special officers, rather with Paul's comment about distinguishing true believers from false professers: 'The Lord knows those who are his' and 'Let every one who names the name of the Lord depart from iniquity' (2 Tim. 2:19 RSV).

In Post-Reformation Times.

Protestantism broke up into many Christian 'denominations,' i.e. distinct Christian groups having a name and organization and perhaps some doctrines distinguishing themselves from others.[24] Some famous scholars (e.g. E. Troeltsch) like to refer to the main branches of Protestantism as 'churches' and to the rest of us as 'sects.' In the Reformation era earnest efforts to draw all the orthodox evangelicals together failed because centrifugal forces overcame centripetal and continued to do so until the rise of the 'ecumenical movement.' Whatever gain or loss for the cause of the kingdom of Christ was brought about by the dissolution of the medieval form of Christendom and subsequent rise of the denominations and recent parachurch movements, there are compelling reasons for recovering unity of some sort. No one has given this problem more serious thought with positive recommendations than the late Lesslie Newbigin.[25] In the four points now to follow I have incorporated some of Newbigin's wisdom from several of his books.

Reasons for Recovering 'Unity.'

First, in the modern epoch came the breakdown of the medieval synthesis we call Christendom. Christianity had become the folk religion of western Europe – with the Bible story and events of Jesus' life, death, resurrection and similar woven into the very texture of civil, educational, family, as well as religious life. The Reformation did not modify that much, except that the 'denominations' now defined unity in relation to diversity. But the Renaissance and Reformation set in motion secularizing forces which, gradually and consummating in recent memory of living people, placed the church again in a largely secular and newly semi-pagan world.

---

23. Denzinger, op. cit., p. 495.
24. *Evangelical Dictionary of Theology*, 'denomination' and 'denominational.'
25. Lesslie Newbigin, *The Household of God* (New York: Friendship Press, 1964).

In the changed situation we Christians have been compelled by the non-Christian forces in government, law, education, business and competing social forces (psychology, which eliminates the psyche, for example) to ally ourselves with one another. We have been compelled to think again of our oneness in Christ and to act it out. We must realize that whatever comity between civil and religious community may have existed when our denominations and their creeds were formed, it no longer exists. In this changed atmosphere it is not only scriptural but rational to cease defining our denominations and local churches in contrast with other such groups but to discover how to express our acknowledged unity in Christ and to cultivate some humility.

Further, the atomizing of the stability and community of the older culture brought about by the industrial revolution and subsequent technical and communications advances means that the local churches individually and the world-wide community of believers have immensely greater opportunities.

> It is natural that men should long for some sort of real community, for men cannot be human without it. It is especially natural that Christians should reach out after that part of Christian doctrine which speaks of the true, God-given community, [a word formed from Latin for *with* and one-ness], the church of Jesus Christ.[26]

The second reason for recovering unity is that the experience of Western missionaries and the new churches established in parts of the world outside Christendom over the past two centuries has demonstrated acute need for Christian unity and community.

In our country, one's church membership may require only superficial contact with other members of our church between Sundays, for 'church' may be only one of several of one's associations. This, however, is not the case in Hindu, Muslim, Buddhist or primitive pagan cultures. There, publicly submitting to Christian baptism requires a radical break with the local culture, often even with immediate family. The new believer is not so much one who has joined a new club as born into a new community and a different family. That new community and family must provide the solidarity (unity) of a real family.

Further, the church in a culture foreign to its nature must provide for its people avenues for personal and corporate life extending beyond 'what goes on at church.' It may even need to provide the new believer with a new way to earn a living, a way to get education and medical attention. These are all to a great degree corporate, not individual, functions.

Third, the church in a totally non-Christian society must undertake the moral and social discipline of the new believers. This is a function of the church as a social unity. This takes time. We note that Paul did not always ordain elders and deacons immediately after a church was formed in a heathen (if we may still use that ancient Anglo-Saxon word) society (Titus 1).

> The removal of the convert from the sphere of the traditional discipline of caste, community or tribe, puts on the church the responsibility of seeing to it that this is replaced by a new kind of social discipline… because without this the church's witness to the non-Christian world becomes hopelessly compromised… [hence] the sharpest necessity arises for rethinking traditional attitudes from the Christendom background.[27]

In this regard, churches of the several denominations located in the same area have felt compelled to acknowledge and respect the disciplinary authority of churches of other missions. This of course ought to prevail in the sending churches also. Yet, as it is today, a person placed under censure in the local Baptist church may escape embarrassment simply by joining the Methodist church across town, or even a Baptist church of another association.

In the fourth place, as a by-product of the modern missionary movement, came the ecumenical movement. This is a misnomer because *oikoumene* is a Greek word for the inhabited earth or the 'civilized' part of it – in the New Testament, the Roman world (Luke 2:1). It has come to stand for the impulse in all branches of the Christian church toward friendly co-operation if not formal union.

As painfully pointed out by an 'ecumenist,' Dr E. O. Smith, in the *Ecumenical Review*,[28] most evangelical groups declined to participate in either the World Council of Churches or the National because of certain legitimate concerns.[29]

---

26. ibid., p. 4.
27. ibid., p. 7.
28. E. O. Smith, *Ecumenical Review* (Vol. xv, no. 2, Jan. 1963).
29. The nineteenth century beginnings of the ecumenical movement in mainly evangelical missionary circles, later the *Faith and Order* organization, did address important doctrinal matters. That history is too large a subject for us to tackle here. It is correct to say that the *History of the Ecumenical Movement*, Rouse and Neill (1954, 822 tightly packed pages, which took me a whole summer to digest) presents it fully in honest and usually favorable light. They do not omit the warts.

Smith reminded his colleagues that the evangelicals have stayed out for legitimate reasons. I summarize:

1. They feel the 'ecumenical' churches have not maintained purity of doctrine and are therefore more to be shunned than joined in any sort of unity. 'The enemy of the church has no place within the church' (John 3:17; 2 John 9, 10).[30]

2. They feel they should not join with churches which make no effort to insure genuine conversion among members.

3. They feel the parochial and sacramentarian orientation of some 'ecumenical' churches is inconsistent with biblical norms.

4. The indifference to discipline among 'main-line' Protestants and Roman Catholics manifests indifference to doctrine also, hence they suspect insincerity in the several orthodox-appearing statements issued by World and National Councils.

5. The emphasis of the ecumenical movement seems almost entirely on organizational unity having no basis in shared unity in the bonds of the Spirit, of the truth, and of new birth and faith.

6. The inclusivism of the World Council of Churches seems to imply a doctrine of universal salvation, especially since many of the ablest 'ecumenical' theologians past and present are Universalists.

7. And finally, a point Smith did not see, millions of biblically oriented evangelicals (and even some biblically oriented Roman Catholics) find an oppressive, false church organized on a world-scale under a final, personal pseudo-Christ predicted in many passages of the Bible. They therefore want no part of what in their opinion might be a large-scale foreshadowing, preparatory for that event.

During the period of the growing strength of World and National Councils many mergers of denominations took place. The Methodists and the Evangelical United Brethren denominations came together as the United Methodist church, for example. Three of the several Lutheran 'churches' are now one, and so on. COCU, Council on Church Union (frequently lampooned by C. F. H. Henry in the early years of *Christianity Today* magazine), promoted a merger of all denominations. But the wind went out of the bag in the period after about 1970. The latent unbelief of many of the leaders and lack of biblical-spiritual forces could not resist the rising tide of moral delinquency in an increasingly paganized society. The mainstream denominations in the WCC and NCC are the ones now no longer discussing church union but ordination of homosexuals and struggling for any sort of integrity as churches. The ecumenical movement, for now at least, is the mouse that first barked, then roared and now scarcely squeaks.

Evangelicals have produced their own brands of 'ecumenicity,' taking the form of innumerable trans-denominational church organizations and movements, as well as several not very inclusive organizations whose goal has been to show a united evangelical face to the world and to be mutually helpful. None is doing well at producing a 'united' *ekklēsia* at this writing, however well the oneness Jesus spoke of (John 17) persists.

Older standard orthodox works have had little to say about the unity of the church. I note A. H. Strong, for example, had little to say of the unity in his *Systematic Theology* yet had some fine ideas about it expressed in a sermon, 'Christian Truth and Its Keepers,' preached in 1868,[31] in which he found denominational divisions helpful, no peril to the church's unity, but rather as aids in fulfilling the diverse tasks of the church in evangelism and nurture of believers. There is no section on the unity in Charles Hodge's three volume *Systematic Theology*, yet he eloquently defined and applied the doctrine in a sermon preached several times but not published till 1958.[32]

The ecumenical movement produced more literature on the subject than any one could possibly read in a lifetime. Partly in response to that enterprise, now expiring, evangelical writing on the church is also paying attention to the first of the four 'marks of the church': unity, holiness, catholicity and apostolicity. Thomas Oden's laudable passion to acquaint our generation of preachers with knowledge of Christian history has a fine section on the first mark. Says he: 'Every particular expression of genuine faith in Christ participates in the one, holy, catholic church, the communion of Saints.'[33]

Addendum.

For various reasons over a period of years ending about 1985 there was a small burst of scholarly and popular writing on the problem of church unity, both of doctrines and of formal-informal fellowship. Robert Brindsmead in an

---

30. This is the heart of the continuing fundamentalist-modernist controversy – by whatever name.
31. A. H. Strong, *Philosophy and Religion* (1888), pp. 238–244.
32. Charles Hodge, 'The Unity of the church,' *Eternity* magazine, June, 1958, pp. 20–28.
33. Thomas Oden, *Systematic Theology: Life in the Spirit iii* (1992), p. 314.

outstanding article in an ephemeral journal (*Verdict, A Journal of Theology*) characterized the problem as 'The Gospel versus the Sectarian Spirit.'[34] He pointed out, 'In recent years, a number of scholars have challenged the myth of an ideal [unity] early church,' citing Walter Bauer,[35] James D. Dunn,[36] Peter Toon[37] and Robert Wilken.[38] Brindsmead thanks the ecumenical movement for making us conscious of the 'scandal of a divided Christian church.' From the exasperatingly 'brief and vague' New Testament reports he says:

> We could even speak of different theological or spiritual emphases in the primitive church... authentic apocalyptic, enthusiastic and pietistic elements... great diversity. Even Peter and Paul could not work harmoniously together... Neither... Paul and Barnabas.

The consultation of Acts 2:17-25 (Toon remarks) issued an acceptance of differences of culture among new and old groups of Christians with resultant styles of worship and congregational activity, and with common commitment to Scripture in general and the gospel in particular.[39]

Brindsmead's truly great article (now apparently lost from sight except for files like mine) cannot be fully summarized. He notes Lutherans in Reformation times needed the corrections of Calvinists (and *vice versa*), while both needed the corrections and contributions of Anabaptists for whom neither could speak a kind word. The great churches as zealous sects have now lost their zeal. According to Robert McAfee Brown:

> There is an assurance in the faith of the sectarian that more sophisticated Protestants... do not even begin to attain... a willingness to go to the four corners of the earth and preach the sectarian gospel to every creature, that makes the missionary program of organized Protestantism look puny in proportion to the vaster resources [no longer true in the twenty-first century] available to it. Denominational Protestants [the 'mainline' now 'sideline'] must be grateful that the sectarians [i.e. evangelical groups] are witnessing to these things.[40]

Some other unusually helpful thoughts on Christian unity coming from that epoch will be found in a few paragraphs by Edward John Carnell[41] and two early articles by Carl F. H. Henry, as editor of *Christianity Today*.[42]

Church unity and church union were themes prevailing in both scholarly and popular journals for two or three decades following the inauguration of the World Council of Churches at Amsterdam in 1948.

The last year of the twentieth century brought ecumenist efforts to remarkable conclusions if not consummation. Pope John Paul II met with Eastern Orthodox Patriarch Teocist in Romania, May 7–9, 1999. Another first was the 'Joint Declaration on the Doctrine of Justification' issued by the Vatican and the Lutheran World Federation. This was supposed to announce agreement. Apparently it set aside the Protestant Reformation and declared it all really a theological mistake. A similar accord was arrived at by 'The Anglican-Roman Catholic International Commission' which seems to acknowledge the primacy of the Roman pope. There was also in America an agreement between the Evangelical Lutheran Church in America with its 5.2 million members and the Episcopal Church with its 2.3 million members to enter into full communion. Nine Protestant denominations comprising the Consultation on Church Union agreed among themselves to deepen their relationship by the year 2002.

Multiculturalism and political correctness are acids eating away at the distinctive claims of Christianity within every orthodox, believing persuasion. There is also a deep and growing desire for a community of action and mutual recognition between Eastern Orthodox, conservative Roman Catholic and Evangelical Protestants. Several new, well-edited journals are promoting this enterprise. These folks find their unity in the ancient creeds and the authority of the Bible and necessity for sincere repentance and faith for salvation. These seemingly ineradicable doctrinal barriers which prevent formal ecclesiastical unions are proving no insuperable obstacle to mutual acceptance on the personal level. How far this friendly exchange will go is hard to say.

---

34. Robert Brindsmead, *Verdict*, Vol. 4, no. 3, March, 1981, pp. 8–16. Published at Fallbrook, CA.
35. Walter Bauer, *Orthodoxy and Heresy in Earliest Christianity* (Philadelphia: Fortress Press, 1971), cited by Brindsmead.
36. James D. Dunn, *Unity and Diversity in the New Testament: an Inquiry into the Character of Earliest Christianity* (Philadelphia: Westminster Press, 1977), cited by Brindsmead.
37. Peter Toon, *The Development of Doctrine in the Church* (Grand Rapids: Eerdmans, 1978), cited by Brindsmead.
38. Robert Wilken, *The Myth of Christian Beginnings: History's Impact on Belief* (Garden City, NY: Double Day & Co., 1972), cited by Brindsmead.
39. Brindsmead, op. cit., pp. 10, 11.
40. Robert McAfee Brown, *The Spirit of Protestantism* (Oxford: Oxford Univ. Press, 1961), p. 212, as cited by Brindsmead, p. 12.
41. Edward J. Carnell, *The Case for Biblical Christianity* (Grand Rapids: Eerdmans, 1967), pp. 14–17.
42. Carl F. H. Henry, 'The Perils of Independency,' *Christianity Today*, Nov. 12, 1956, pp. 20–23, and 'The Perils of Ecumenicity,' Nov. 16, 26, 1956, pp. 20–22. Both republished by Millard J. Erickson, ed., *The New Life: Readings in Christian Theology* (Grand Rapids: Baker Books, 1979), pp. 341–353.

12
The Gifts of Christ to the Church

The church has received two sorts of divine gifts for her health and growth. Paul is our sole source of specific information about them. He discusses the first, gifts of ability to each member in Romans 12:3-8, and the second, gifts of specially authorized and qualified people in Ephesians 4:7-17. This chapter treats both.

I. Divine Gifts of Ability to People in the Church.

Paul expressed deep concern in two Epistles regarding Christians living together in harmonious unity within each congregation, building (edifying) one another up in mutual service and manifesting all the Christian graces.

In Romans 12:3-8 he discusses this matter dear to his heart and essential to the well-being of the churches. Such health of the church, he says, is brought about by proper exercise of certain gifts of God, called *charismata* (sing. *charisma*), to every individual of the church. *Charisma* is obviously related to *charis*, Greek for grace. He uses this word sixteen times, often a name for special gifts (natural or supernatural) to Christians to use in service to one another. Recent secular journalism has pounced upon this 'rare and late word'[1] and, knowing nothing of divine *charisma*, calls personal magnetism, leadership ability, *charisma*. In Paul's Epistle *charisma* is a special ability imparted (naturally or supernaturally) to a Christian for service to others in the body of Christ, certainly not power to induce popularity. Paul mentions seven *charismata*, obviously not an exhaustive list, in verses 6-8: prophecy, service, teaching, exhorting, giving money, helping and acts of mercy. The gist of his exhortation is to get on with humble, but faithful, exercise of these and other gifts within the 'one body in Christ.'

His instructions about gifts in a lengthy second passage (1 Cor. 12–14) is in response to a previous inquiry by the Corinth church. One cannot avoid noticing Paul's concern about misuse of the opportunity provided by the recurring weekly assembly of plain Christian folk for people who only want opportunity to sound off before an audience or have some private idea or agenda to promote or mistake their own thoughts and feelings for the voice of God.

In their inquiry the Corinthians had called the more spectacular manifestations in their assembly 'spirituals' (*pneumatikos*, sing.), a term not learned from Paul but from pagan sources. It appears thousands of times in the literature of ancient Greece and has no necessary connection with the Holy Spirit, Third Person of the triune God.[2]

---

1. Hans Conzelmann *TDNT*, IX, p. 402.
2. Hauck and Kasch, *TDNT*, VII, pp. 332–451. One of the largest entries in nine volumes.

Paul uses *pneumatikos* only twice with reference to 'gifts' (1 Cor. 12:1 and 14:1). For Paul the gifts are not of the Holy Spirit specifically, but of 'God' the Father (Rom. 12:3) or of Christ (Eph. 4:7 ff.). It may be that Paul only condescended to use the term 'spirituals' for gifts because the Corinthians had used it in their previous inquiry (cf. 7:1 with 12:1). We may be sure that whatever false pagan notions regarding 'spirituals' and spirituality the Corinthians had in mind in questioning Paul he corrected in his answer (1 Cor. 12–14). There were many there who liked to be seen and heard exercising what they only assumed were gifts of God. Paul conferred a judgment of charity in calling all these exercises 'gifts,' *charismata*, but used the occasion to instruct his readers on how to sort out the genuine from the inauthentic, the show-offs from earnest servants of Christ. Every exercise of alleged gifts should 'edify' (build up) the church (14:4, 5 NIV): 'Let all things be done for building up [edification]' (14:26), 'decently and in order' (14:40).

Throughout these two sections (Rom. 12; 1 Cor. 12–14) the *charismata* are to individuals to use in service to one another to build up the church. Nowhere is there slightest suggestion that any particular *charisma* is attached to an office such as elder, bishop, pastor or deacon. Throughout Paul's discussion the gifts are of abilities in the 'spiritual' realm to individual believers. Even when Paul mentions apostles, prophets and teachers 'appointed in the church,' and similar (1 Cor. 12:28), he does so in context of seeking the 'higher gifts' (12:31), a scale of values, not grades of honor or authority in the congregations.

II. Divine Gifts of People of Ability and Authority to the Church.

We shall now examine at some length the passage, Ephesians 4:7-16, wherein the great planter of churches throughout the eastern half of the Roman Empire wrote of Christ's gift of certain people to the church at large and to the congregations individually. These specifically designated leaders (for want of a better term) were to enable the believers of the congregations to provide the services necessary for mutual help and building the whole body, internally among themselves and externally through mission to the lost world about them.

There are several problems of grammar and syntactical connection in the passage. Paul can argue like a Roman lawyer at times (Rom. 1–4, for example). Yet, here his Epistle reads like 'a rapid conversation' taken down in shorthand. Discontinuous clauses 'pour in full stream, sentence hurrying after sentence and phrase heaped upon phrase with an exhuberance that bewilders us.'[3] Scholars have come to a fair consensus on what the Apostle said and meant. I shall try to avoid the technicalities behind interpretation as much as possible.

Even in the abbreviated and simplified treatment to follow the argument will be trying to a reader unaccustomed to exegetical discourse. The general sense is 'perspicuous' but difficulties of interpretation, in which much variety of church polity, government and mission are rooted, loom in almost every word. The Summary and Conclusions at the close of this chapter may well be read before tackling the exegesis in pages 890–897 intervening.

In our passage (Eph. 4:7-16) gifts are designated neither by the rare word *charisma* nor by the exotic term *pneumatika*, but by the very common words *dōrea* and *dōron*, both rendered gift and apparently derived from *didōmi*, to give. Their quality as 'gifts' rather than native abilities or 'talents' is emphatic.

Verse 7 seems to introduce gifts as though another treatment of *charismata* to individuals were to follow. I do not think that is what the Apostle meant by his words: 'But grace was given to each one of us.' 'But' (*de*) connects the sentence to God's 'all and in all' in verse 6. 'The grace' (*hē charis*) 'was given' (*edothē*, first aorist passive) – not 'the graces' (*charismata*). To the contrary the '[one] grace was given' in some past incident. The text does not say that each one of us received an individual gift but 'the gift.' We each share the benefits of the one gift.

What was the incident? When 'the gift' was 'given'? This was the giving which took place at our Lord's Ascension, described generally in verses 8-10 and in detail in the very long sentence, verses 11-16 – apostles, prophets, evangelists, pastors and teachers. The gift was comparable to the gift of Christ: 'according to the measure of Christ's gift.'

What is 'the gift of Christ'? There are three possibilities in the grammar: (1) the gift to Christ; (2) the gift Christ gave (or gives); or (3) the gift which is Christ Himself. Commentators mention the 'gift to Christ' as possible but reject it as not fitting the context or for other reasons. Most older commentators and theologians opt for the gift which Christ gave, subjective genetive – Alford, Meyer (Calvin is noncommittal, as also Bengel), Ellicott, *et al.* They

---

3. G. G. Findlay, *Ephesians, Exposition of the Bible*, Vol. vi (Hartford, CT: 1907), p. 63.

connect this with *charismata* and *pneumatika* of Romans 12 and 1 Corinthians 12–14. When reason is supplied they cite 'he [Christ] gave gifts to men' in verse 8. It may be that Christ's gifts are in Paul's mind, but if so I think not of abilities to each Christian (Rom. 12; 1 Cor. 12–14) but of the persons to follow in Ephesians 4:11-16. Among some recent writers the gift is Christ Himself, the Father's gift (2 Cor. 9:15, God's 'inexpressible gift'). 'The gift of Messiah is the measure' (M. Barth, II, xvii). In this case then the Father's generosity is the measure of the Son's generosity in His conferrals on the church which each member now enjoys. I shall not reproduce the convincing argument for this view of the verse to be found at length in Marcus Barth's, *Ephesians*.[4] The chief supporting text cited is Romans 8:32. At any rate, in view of the fact that Paul introduces Christ's gift of men who have certain functions and prerogatives with *dio legei*, 'on this account,' 'it says' (or 'he says,' v. 8) tends to the conclusion that verse 7 has reference to the gifts of 11-16, not the gifts of Romans 12 and 1 Corinthians 12–14.

The point of verses 8 and 9 is to provide scriptural precedent if not authority for the revelation (found nowhere else in the New Testament) that Christ endowed the church with an operating constitution at the time of His Ascension: 'When he ascended... he gave gifts to men' (v. 8); 'He... also ascended far above all the heavens.... And he gave,' etc. (vv. 10, 11).

Paul's ponderous and somewhat obscure language should not obscure the fact he is introducing a profound revelation – the operating constitution of the church for propagation and governance, no less, to be presented in verses 11-17.

1. The Time of Conferral of the Gifts.

It was at the time of Christ's Ascension – and session. 'When he ascended... he gave gifts to men.... And he gave...' (Eph. 4:8 and 11). Verses 9 and 10 are parenthetical (Ellicott). The functioning leaders are not sent out by Christ from time to time. The language clearly says certain saints known and called from eternity were conferred upon the church from a throne in heaven at the beginning of the 'church age.' Paul, for example, plainly says he was called by Christ and the Father before he was born (Gal. 1:1, 15), to be an Apostle, the first in the list of gifts. According to Ephesians 4:10 this is no less the case with every evangelist, pastor or teacher. This casts an aura of great solemnity in the appointment, support and acceptance by the church of all those designated in this passage. Their charge came from God before the churches were formed in which they serve. The little band who witnessed the event of Christ's ascent from Olivet could not have been aware of this aspect of that event, but we are aware and, hence, there is laid on us enormous responsibility for discerning acknowledgment, godly response to and proper treatment of the evangelists, pastors and teachers who serve Christ in our churches.

2. The Author Who Conferred the Gifts.

The emphatic (third pers. sing. pronoun *autos*) appears twice: 'He himself [and no other (Alford)] who descended is also the one who ascended' (v. 10), '...and he *himself* gave some,' etc. (v. 11). The names, number, function, purpose, etc., of these gifts comes on quickly. Again, however, the awful import of these gift-men of the ascended Lord's appointment must not be lost upon us. They are very special.

We search in vain to find these 'offices' in operation in the earliest chapters of Acts, except for the Apostles themselves. Years passed before one of the number of disciples, for example, became an evangelist (Acts 8:5; cf.; 21:8) and much later any pastor or teacher. The time for them to be fully recognized in the churches would be soon enough – later in the apostolic age, as seen in the Epistles. We do not know anything of how the Lord made this structure of affairs known but the Lord Jesus Christ who 'gave' also 'made known' as soon as the church moved out into the Gentile world and began founding churches.

It seems to be the clear assumption of the New Testament that the gifted men necessary for continued propagation and governance would appear among the churches, if not fully in each church. More on this later in Chapters 18 and 19.

3. The Number of the Gifts.

'And he gave the apostles, the prophets, the evangelists, the pastors and teachers' (Eph. 4:11 ESV). 'And he gave some, apostles; and some, prophets; and some, evangelists; and some, pastors and teachers' (Eph. 4:11 KJV). It is hard to be brief because the longest article I have ever written for an encyclopaedia was on 'Apostle,' and some extensive research has been on prophets and prophecy. Every item here is the subject of immense literature.[5]

---

4. Marcus Barth, *The Anchor Bible, Ephesians*, II (Garden City, NY: Doubleday, 1974), pp. 429, 430.
5. R. D. Culver, 'Apostle and Apostate in the New Testament' published fully in *Bibliotheca Sacra* (April–June, 1977, #534), pp. 131–143. Digested in *Encyclopedia of the Bible*, Vol. I (Baker), pp. 131–133.

As to the number of such 'offices', there is difference of opinion whether this list is exhaustive or not. A somewhat similar list in 1 Corinthians 12:28-30 does not distinguish carefully between gifts to men and men as gifts. That list also differs in omitting evangelists and pastors, so it probably does not bear on the question of the number of the gifts of Christ at His Ascension.

Pastors and teachers, as indicated by the grammar of the Greek text, are almost certainly one office (as shall appear). Reference to elders and bishops (or overseers) also relate to the same office. The gradations of 'clergy' as developed in the growing hierarchy of the third and fourth centuries are not founded on this passage.

The list does not include deacons and deaconesses as described in the pastoral Epistles (1, 2 Tim.; Titus) because the gifts are to the universal church. Apostles moved around in exercise of their office. Each one could say 'The world is my parish.' Some prophets moved about too as presumably also did most (missionary) evangelists. We have the example of Philip the Evangelist (Acts 8). As a matter of fact, most pastors also move from church to church over time. Each of these terms should be interpreted according to the limited meaning in the text. In this sense the list is intended to be exhaustive, as shall appear as we consider the names of the 'offices' and their functions.

4. The Names of 'Offices' and Their Functions.

'...the apostles, the prophets, the evangelists, the pastors and teachers.' Each of these, whether four or five, has to do with proclamation of the word, usually publicly.

> In short, the government of the church, by the ministry of the word, is not a contrivance of men, but by appointment made by the Son of God.... To Christ we owe it that we have ministers of the gospel, that they abound in necessary qualifications, that they execute the trust committed to them. All, all is his *gift*.[6]

In the same context Calvin correctly remarks:

> When men are called by God[to a particular office], gifts are necessarily connected with offices. God does not confer on men the mere name of Apostles or Pastors, but also endows them with the gifts, without which they cannot properly discharge the office.[7]

Apostles. According to Ephesians 2:19-22, 'the household of God,' i.e. the church, is 'built on the foundation of the apostles and prophets' (v. 20). The Greek uses the article 'the' (Gr. *tōn*) before 'apostles and prophets,' showing that they are considered a unit, hence both had to do with the foundation of the church. As far as the book of Acts is concerned, God used an Apostle, Peter, first to take the gospel to Gentiles, and Paul, another Apostle, was the one who further led in founding congregations in eastern parts of the Empire. Early traditions trace founding of churches in other regions to other Apostles. This was the claim of orthodox Christians everywhere in a few decades. The ancient church assigned special prominence to apostolically founded congregations. Further, these twelve men were the ones upon whom Jesus laid the duty and promise of recollection and record of what He had taught them (John 14:25, 26; 15:26, 27; 16:13-15). Paul asserts earlier in Ephesians that revelations were made not only to him but to other 'holy apostles and prophets' (Eph. 3:5). The earliest test of authentic New Testament Scripture was apostolicity. The writing of Holy Scripture, the New Testament, was a major part of their founding ministry enduring until today. Apostles were chosen by Christ Himself (Matt. 10 and parallels) and 'sent' with His authority as 'ministers plenipotentiary' both in establishing churches and writing 'Scripture' (see 1 Peter 3:15, 16). It should be added that 'apostles' is used here in the narrow sense of those witnesses of the resurrection of Christ specially commissioned by Him (see 1 Cor. 9:1; 15:7). (See footnote.[8])

Prophets. There is considerable evidence for the existence of prophets of a lesser sort of 'inspired' status than the ones Paul here designates Apostles (similarly in 1 Cor. 12:28). As seen above in Ephesians 3:5, prophets were associated with the Apostles in reception of important divine revelation of the sort to be incorporated into Scripture. Romans 16:25, 26 informs us that a certain mystery which had been kept secret through 'times eternal' (ASV) 'for long ages' (RSV) is 'manifest[ed]' (*phanerōthentos*) now (*nun*, at this time) 'by the scriptures of the prophets' (KJV, so also ASV). This seems to many interpreters to say that 'now' the 'Scriptures' of prophets of Paul's time disclose some mystery unknown (or not fully known) previously. If so, Paul is designating the writings of certain contemporary prophets as 'Scripture' just as Peter (2 Peter 3:15, 16) called Paul's writings 'Scripture.'

---

6. Calvin, *Commentary on Galatians and Ephesians* (Edinburgh: Calvin Translation Society, 1854), at Eph. 4:11, p. 278.
7. ibid., p. 277.
8. Culver, op. cit., pp. 131–143.

Acts 11:2; 13:1; and 15:32 report the presence of 'prophets' (*prophētai*) in the Jerusalem congregation and the Antioch congregation. They are associated with 'teachers,' however, not Apostles. These prophets assisted local churches in seeking guidance from God in practical matters of life and mission. Acts 21:10 tells of Agabus who in the manner of some Old Testament prophets warned Paul of imminent dangers if he finished his journey to Jerusalem – which warning Paul ignored. These folk are in continuity with the saintly Anna (Luke 2:36) and other godly folk of pre-New Testament times – the disciples of Elijah and Elisha and Isaiah – who possessed superior piety and powers of insight and who advised God's people. They were not channels of 'the oracles of God' for all time. Several Old Testament characters who made *false claims* to such powers and closeness to God are called prophets, as a matter of courtesy or perhaps simply to take note of their claims (e.g. Jer. 5:31; 14:14; 23:21). This class of prophets continued on for many decades into the future after the end of the apostolic age.[9]

But prophets associated with Apostles in writing Scripture – and we know not what else – were special, probably deriving their authority from the Apostles with whom they were, by apostolic choice, associated. Luke, associated with Paul and author of about 20 per cent of the New Testament, would certainly qualify.

In 1883 a newly discovered copy in Greek of a very ancient Christian manual self-described as the 'Teaching [*didachē*] of The Twelve Apostles to the Nations' was published. Scholars assigned it to the late first or early second century, though in the century since a somewhat later date is preferred by many. It is a window on practices of Christians in the sub-apostolic period. This document clearly presupposes the distinction made here between the special apostles and prophets, authorized by Christ 'himself' (*autos*, Eph. 4:10, 11), and the presence among the churches of a lesser grade of spokesman for the gospel and biblical teaching. The lead sentence clearly designates 'the twelve apostles to the nations,' while sections 11–13 instruct how to test claims of itinerant 'apostles and prophets,' what credibility to assign them, and how to entertain them. The best brief assessment of the *Didachē* I have found is by Robert M. Grant.[10] New translations and editions are available.

We may be sure that the Lord supplied the 'gifts' of founders as needed and ceased to do so when no longer needed. In the special sense that the Twelve and Paul were 'apostles' they were never replaced. The 'gift' was not withdrawn but because man is mortal they died and were not replaced. They wrote the New Testament Scriptures and launched the good ship *ekklēsia*. The same is true of New Testament founding prophets. Papal claims for perpetuation of apostolic powers, of Muslim and Mormons for 'latter day' reappearance of such powers, are unsupportable either in Scripture or in history.

Evangelists (Gr. *Euangelistēs*). It is difficult to know for certain exactly what is meant by an *euangelistēs*. He is obviously one who publishes the good news of Christ's salvation; but in what capacity? Neither Scripture nor history furnishes a clear answer. In one New Testament passage, God is an evangelist who 'preached the gospel beforehand to Abraham' (Gal. 3:8 RSV). So also did angels at Christ's birth (Luke 2:10), likewise Apostles; and so ought every Christian. Yet only three times does the apparently technical designation of the gift of evangelist to the whole church appear in the New Testament: (1) 'Philip the evangelist' (Acts 21:8); (2) Paul instructing Timothy to 'do the work of an evangelist' (2 Tim. 4:5); and (3) in our text, Ephesians 4:11. We know that Philip could preach and baptize (Acts 8) but was subject to Peter as Timothy likewise was subject to Paul. All the twelve Apostles were missionaries, of course.

In my judgment those scholars are correct who assert that *in this passage* the Apostle 'desires to mention all the principal offices, whereby Christ had provided for the spiritual edification of the church universal… (1) the evangelists were inferior to the apostles… (2) they were travelling missionaries, preaching the Gospel to those unacquainted with it, yet sometimes with a settled place of abode, as Philip [Acts 21:8] at Caesarea, and Timothy at Ephesus. Thus they were officers acting for the whole Christian community, not for a single church…. (3) They were charismatically endowed.'[11] Massie calls attention to the *charisma* (special gift of the Lord) conferred on Timothy (1 Tim. 4:14; 2 Tim. 1:6). Evangelists are not mentioned in the second century *Didache* or in any of the apostolic Fathers, which supports the opinion that in the sense intended here, they like Apostles and prophets, belonged to the founding era only. Later writers (Eusebius, fourth-century church historian) called the early missionaries 'evangelists.' Chrysostom omitted *evangelists* in comments on Ephesians 4:11. Eusebius called itinerant

---

9. D. E. Aune reports modern scholarship on the subject of prophecy in early church and early centuries. My conclusions seem to be compatible with his findings. D. E. Aune, *Prophecy in Early Christianity & the Ancient Mediterranean World* (Grand Rapids: Eerdmans, 1983), pp. 194–201.
10. Robert M. Grant, *Twentieth Century Encyclopedia of Religious Knowledge*, Vol. I (Grand Rapids: Baker, 1955), pp. 357, 358.
11. J. Massie, 'Evangelist,' *Hastings Dictionary of the Bible*, Vol. I, pp. 795, 796.

missionary preachers 'evangelists' and that custom prevails today. The Apostle Paul frequently called himself (and other itinerant missionary-proclaimers) a preacher (*kērux*, 1 Tim. 2:7; 2 Tim. 1:11), the gospel a preached message (*kērygma*, 1 Cor. 1:21; 2 Tim. 4:17), and what they did was to preach or proclaim as a herald (*kērusso*), used about sixty times in the New Testament, often of missionary proclamation. Romans 10:8-15 demonstrates that for Paul the 'foreign missionary,' sent from some 'home base,' was a *kērux*, preacher, not an '*euangelistes*' (evangelist).

Pastors and Teachers. In Greek, the words pastor (or shepherd), flock and feed are related, as in English pastor and pasture are related. J. Jeremias notes:

> Only once in the New Testament are congregational leaders called shepherds, namely, in the list of officers in Ephesians 4:11. The absence of the article before *didaskalous* [teachers] which follows (*tous de poimenas kai didaskalous*) shows that the pastors and teachers form a single group, obviously because they both minister to the individual congregation.[12]

The congregation as a flock and leaders as shepherds is superbly treated by Jeremias.[13] See Jeremias' summary of the New Testament use of the work of leading the local church.

Paul's Epistles never again use the word 'pastor' (*poimen*) but he exhorted the presbyters (elders) of the *ekklēsia* at Ephesus (Acts 20:28 KJV) to care for 'the flock'.

In the Greek language the words for *flock, feed a flock* of sheep and *shepherd* are variations of the same root word. So though the New Testament never again calls the leaders of a church pastors (shepherds) it becomes clear that Paul attached the shepherding function to the local elders (*presbuteroi*) or overseers, bishops (*episkopoi*). In Acts 20:17 he called the presbyters of the *ekklēsia* of Ephesus to meet him at Miletus. There he declared these presbyters had been positioned as overseers of the flock and that it was their duty to feed (*poimainō*) the *ekklēsia* (20:27, 28 KJV). It seems clear therefore, pastor, presbyter and overseer are only one office. If, as suggested above, *eangelistēs* (evangelist), like apostle and prophet, was a temporary gift, the pastor-elder-overseer is the only 'gift' still in operation. This is not to say that we do not still have those who evangelize. (See also 1 Peter 5:2.)

In a later chapter on church offices and government this matter will be discussed further.

5. How the Gifts Function in the Church.

The pertinent verse – Ephesians 4:12 – is composed of three prepositional phrases, as follows: 'for the perfecting of the saints, for the work of the ministry, for the edifying of the body of Christ' (KJV). In RSV and KJV, which are similar, in each phrase the preposition is 'for,' and each is preceded by a semi-colon or a comma. In such case the gifts function to do three things: 'for the equipment of the saints, for the work of ministry, for building up the body of Christ'; and each is apparently a different effect of the functioning of the gifts, presently only the pastor-teacher. But this is not the best understanding of Ephesians 4:12.

The Greek text varies the prepositions, *viz.*: '*pros* (with accusative meaning, to or toward) the equipment of the saints'; '*eis* (unto, often indicating purpose, or goal) the work of ministry.' In such case there should be no comma after 'saints' and now read 'toward the equipment of the saints unto the work of ministry.' The third phrase like the second begins with *eis*. So in one continuous progress from beginning to end we have *a single purpose* or *telos*, goal-directed construction (with or without a comma after 'ministry'): 'toward the equipment of the saints unto the work of ministry, unto the building up of the body of Christ.' In this manner all the gifts were given by Christ (including pastors of churches) to equip 'the saints' to do the work of ministry, thereby to build up ('edify' KJV) the body of Christ. Meyer's *Commentary* was one of the first of modern times to propose this understanding. It has become the prevailing scholarly consensus.[14]

Markus Barth discusses this problem at great length and concludes that 'a decision on the two interpretations cannot be made by quibbling about such trifles as the changes of prepositions or the appropriateness of a comma. Rather the whole context and all parallels of [Eph.] 4:12 provide at least four reasons' for the *telic* meaning (one purpose, not three). I summarize his 'four reasons.'

1. The 'grace' given to saints (4:7) elsewhere in the New Testament (Eph. 3:2, 7; Rom. 1:5; 1 Cor. 15:10; Phil. 2:12, 13) 'does not terminate and die in the recipient but makes him an active servant' ... '*Katartismos* ("equipment"), denotes preparation for a job.'[15]

---

12. J. Jeremias, 'Poimēn,' *TDNT*, VI, pp. 302–497.
13. ibid., p. 498.
14. H. A. W. Meyer, *Critical & Exegetical Handbook to the Epistle to Ephesians*, trans. M. J. Evans (New York: Funk and Wagnalls, 1884), pp. 454–460.
15. Markus Barth, op. cit., p. 480.

2. Throughout the passage (Eph. 4:7-16) all saints, 'not only apostles, prophets, evangelists and teaching shepherds are called recipients of grace from on high... interest is focused upon the mutual contact of all members.'

3. He argues (with less cogency, I think) that though Ephesians 4 has the universal church in mind, close parallels in 1 Corinthians 12, which relates to the local congregation, show 'the common good' must be present in Ephesians 4.

4. He seems here to say that a democratic structure of the church requires a *telic* interpretation.[16]

His third and fourth arguments I think are indecisive and he does not need them. In reaction against the hierarchical and mixed free and state church systems of Europe he seems to argue from assumptions of democracy in church and state rather than specifically scriptural truth.

6. The Ultimate Goals of the Gifts.

These verses – Ephesians 4:13-14 – conduct the reader to another of Paul's high literary-doctrinal climaxes. The prepositions *eis*, five times, and *mechri,* leading off at the beginning, are forward-, goal-, destiny-related words; *hina*, the strongest term in the language for purpose, points to the goals for the gifts Christ gave the universal church, concretely desirable, even if not present in every local assembly. The goal in time is the *parousia*, the 'appearing' of Christ at His Second Advent. This Advent might not be such an obviously leading idea in Ephesians as in the Thessalonian Epistles, yet these verses point to that 'one far off' yet impending '*event* toward which the whole creation moves.' In 'until we all attain' (RSV), the author chose a verb (*katantaō*) which signifies movement, usually toward a predetermined goal, 'downhill' with increasing momentum, arriving at a destination (Acts 16:1; 18:19, etc., eight times), 'upon whom the ends of the world have come' (1 Cor. 10:11 KJV; cf. Phil. 3:11). '[W]e all' – all Christians – are swept up, consciously or not, in this movement toward this 'blessed hope and glorious appearing of the great God and our Savior, Jesus Christ.' Meanwhile along the way we partially attain to the goal, we 'follow after' (Phil. 3:12-14 KJV). Moral excellency in mutual relations in unity of the one body was the ideal besought in introducing the subject of gifts of leaders to the church (4:1-6). Now in the denouement the goal is to be attained when we meet a 'Man,' 'the Son of God,' 'the perfect man,' 'the Messiah' (*tou Christou*) (Eph. 4:13).

For present purposes it is important and sufficient to summarize the goals as follows.

1. First, *unity* – 'until we all come to meet the unifying faith and knowledge of the Son of God' (Eph. 4:13 M. Barth trans. in *Anchor Bible*).

In comment on John 17:21 ('that they may all be one') and here on Ephesians 4:13, 'all attain to the unity of the faith,' Calvin clearly sees the cosmic dimension both of alienation and of unity of mankind.

> The ruin of the human race is, that having been alienated from God, is also broken and scattered in itself [he might have cited the tower of Babel confusion]. The restoration of it, therefore, on the contrary, consists in its being properly united in one body, as Paul declares the perfection of the church to consist in *believers being joined together in one spirit*, and says *that apostles, prophets, evangelists, and pastors were given that they might edify and restore the body of Christ, till it came to the unity of faith*; and therefore he exhorts believers to *to grow into Christ, who is the head, from whom the whole body* [is] *joined together... to edification* (Calvin's emphasis throughout) (Eph. 4:3, 11-16).[17]

Calvin acknowledged the unity has been attained only imperfectly and why so, and commenting on 'in the unity of the faith' (Eph. 4:13) he explains:

> The unity does reign, I acknowledge, among the sons of God, but not so perfectly as to make [even] them *come together*. Such is the weakness of our nature, that it is enough if every day brings some nearer to others. [That we shall] never really reach until this garment of flesh, which is always accompanied by some remains of ignorance and weakness shall have been laid aside.[18]

If there was an 'ecumenist' among the Reformers it was Calvin.[19] Yet already in 1548, when the above was published, failure of his efforts at reconciliation of Lutherans and Reformed had convinced him it would not take place short of heaven.

---

16. ibid., pp. 480–484.
17. Calvin, Vol. II, p. 183.
18. Calvin, *Epistle to the Ephesians*, p. 283.
19. See 'Serving for Unity and the Ensuing Debate,' chap. 7, *The Writings of John Calvin*, Wulfert de Greef, trans. Lyle D. Bierma (Grand Rapids: Baker, 1993).

2. Second, *maturity* – 'unto a full-grown man, unto the measure of the stature of the fulness of Christ' (4:13 ASV).

This ideal of maturity which the author states here as a goal he demands elsewhere. Paul's Greek is quite 'politically incorrect': 'Watch ye, stand fast in the faith, quit you like men, be strong' (1 Cor. 16:13 KJV). '[Q]uit you like men' translates a single Greek word, *andrizo*, meaning simply to behave as an adult male should – with normally expected courage. '[B]e strong' also is proper to adult male mankind (Liddell & Scott, *Lexicon*). The opposite is *holigopseucheō*, to be faint of heart. The ancients thought that an adult male should have control of his emotions, to be brave in face of threats, not given to *hysteria* (a Greek word for suffering in the womb, a female organ). This outlook is not absent from Scripture (Isa. 3:4, 12 compares civil rule by women to rule by children). When a woman of outstanding courage saw her seven brave sons brutally executed 'she bore it bravely… her woman's thought fired by a manly spirit.'[20] The celebrated heroes of the inter-testamental centuries (Heb. 11:33 ff.) behaved like real men even though perhaps a majority of them may have been women, as likewise did the Christian martyrs of every age. The standard of such maturity, says Marcus Barth, is 'the Perfect Man, the perfection of the Messiah, who is the standard of manhood.' Barth adds: 'The term *anēr* used here to denote the perfect "man" does not mean "mankind" (as Greek *anthrōpos* and Hebrew '*adam* often do) but "adult man" in contradistinction to woman and child.'[21]

3. Third, *stability*, 'that we may no longer be children, tossed to and fro by the waves and carried about by every wind of doctrine, by human cunning, by craftiness in deceitful schemes' (Eph. 4:14). Later in his career as Apostle Paul wrote to insure sound doctrine in the instruction of pastors (2 Tim. 2:2) and demanded of his pastoral assistant, 'Keep a close watch on yourself and on the teaching' (1 Tim. 4:16), 'Until I come, devote yourself to the public reading of Scripture, to exhortation, to teaching [*didaskalia*]' (1 Tim. 4:13). The only gift of God to the church in Ephesians 4:11 of which it can be said with certainty it is present today is the one called 'pastors and teachers.' We are of divine intention bound to acknowledge these gifts of God, our pastors and teachers as critical if not indispensable to stable lives of Christians and stable churches. This matter comes in for more extensive treatment in chapters 18 and 19 on 'Church Offices and Ministry.'

Church history is inseparable from the history of doctrines – their definition, disputes about them, heresies and orthodoxy. Imperfectly expressed as it may be in our time, there is in truth a consensual core of orthodox Christian doctrine, as Thomas Oden has competently contended in the 'Epilogue' to his *Systematic Theology*.[22] The people of the churches through the centuries have had a share in passing on 'the teaching' (1 Tim. 4:16), but especially before the printing of Bibles, and general literacy shortly thereafter, the doctrinal views of people of the churches have been dependent on the work of the 'pastors and teachers' – God's gifts for the 'building up' of the church.

4. Fourth, *growth* (Eph. 4:15, 16). The flight of rhetoric in this climactic of peroration about Christ's gifts to the church exceeds any possibility of adequate exposition. Paul defines the mission of the church as to produce inward and outward growth: 'but maintaining the truth in love, may grow up into Him in all things; which is the head, even Christ, from whom the whole body, fitly framed together and compacted by every joint of its supply, according to the effectual working in the measure of every part, maketh increase of the body, unto the building thereof, in love.'[23]

Paul made an art of mixing figures effectively in clarifying an idea. 'This recurrence to the companion metaphor of building reminds us that the reality which St. Paul is endeavoring to illustrate is more than a physiological structure. The language derived from the body's growth needs to be supplemented by the language derived from the building of the sacred shrine of God. The mingling of the metaphors helps us to rise above them.'[24]

In verse 12 (KJV) he speaks of 'the edifying of the body of Christ' as the purpose of the four gifts. 'Edify' (related to edifice, a building) renders *oikodomeō*, to build a house. But it is a body, Christ's body, the *ekklēsia* that is to be 'house built.' The idea is that the body of Christ should be enlarged. Peter speaks of the church as a 'spiritual house' (1 Peter 2:5).

The mixed figure carries over into verse 15 and 16. '[G]row up in every way into him who is the head, into Christ.' This appears to mean simply that the 'unity of the Spirit' (v. 3), which we already have, must grow 'into

---

20. 2 Macc. 7:20, 21 Revised English Bible with Apocalypus.
21. op cit., p. 441.
22. Thomas Oden, *Systematic Theology* (San Francisco: Harper Collins, 3 vols., 1994), vol. iii, pp. 473–502.
23. Trans. of J. A. Robinson, *St. Paul's Epistle to the Ephesians*, 1939, pp. 131, 132.
24. J. Armitage Robinson, *St. Paul's Epistles to the Ephesians* (London: Macmillan, 1939), pp. 144, 145.

Christ' with whom we are already united. A parallel with sanctification is suggested. Positional holiness should lead to growth in practical improvement in holy conduct, so the perfect 'unity of the Spirit' in Christ is something to 'keep' and to 'grow into.' If we are 'eager to maintain' (v. 3) and 'speaking the truth in love' (v. 15) we will each 'grow' into Christ – as a novice progressively feels more at home in his job and improves his perfomance as he conscientiously 'keeps on keeping on.' This is inward spiritual growth of the members of the body and is the primary mission of the church: to nourish her own.

Back in verse 12 the purpose of the gifts of 'pastors and teachers' is to equip the 'saints' for the work of ministering. As the passage proceeds it becomes clear that the ministering is to one another. Pastors who would like to find direct command to evangelism and mission here (I among them) must look elsewhere in Paul's Epistles – as we shall do in the next chapter. Yet any congregation functioning in the harmony and mutual edification descibed in Ephesians 4:7-16 is a 'city set on a hill' attractive to all around. The evident love of believers one for another in the centuries of Roman persecution did result in the *external* growth as the body 'builds itself up in love.'

Summary of Exegesis of Ephesians 4:7-16 and Conclusions

This passage of Holy Scripture furnishes the church knowledge of the necessary leadership and authority from her beginning to the second advent. At the time of His ascension Christ gave the church her workmen who would found the church throughout the world, provide authoritative guidance through the New Testament Scriptures which they wrote, and shepherd the flocks scattered through the world.

1. The gifts were not conferred from time to time as churches multiplied. Rather certain saints, qualified and authorized, known to God from all eternity, were conferred on the universal church at her beginning. They were to appear among the churches as the movement spread. It is the duty and privilege of the believers in the church to acknowledge and to respond to these apostles, prophets, evangelists, pastors and teachers. The churches accept and confirm this leadership and authority, but do not confer it.

2. Paul emphasizes that Jesus Himself appointed these agents of His and that they are bearers of His word. They are His agents in the work of equipping of saints for ministry resulting in growth of the body of Christ.

3. Two of the gifts, probably three – apostles, prophets and evangelists – are now a part of history, though their finished work is still with us. *Apostles* and *prophets* with the aid of missionary *evangelists* founded the churches in scattered corners and at the centers of the ancient world, the church universal being present in each assembly. They also gave the church her constitutional document, the New Testament. The *pastors* and *teachers* continue the work as they preach the gospel, feed their flocks on the true Word of Christ and take oversight of her corporate life. The pastor-teacher is also called minister, elder (presbyter) and overseer (bishop) in the New Testament.

4. Further, as to the names and functions of the four offices – *Apostles* had ambassadorial authority from Christ, unique to that group of twelve men, specifically authorized to found the church and provide the scriptures for that continuing household of God (Eph. 2:19-22). Certain *prophets*, such as Mark and Luke, not only assisted the apostles but received revelation and wrote scripture. Other lesser prophets, in an age before the New Testament was written and collected, exercised their gifts in local churches. *Evangelists* obviously proclaimed the good news. Like Philip (Acts 8:4-6; 21:8), they were pioneer missionaries. They are not mentioned after the apostolic age, though prophets are.

5. These agents and messengers function then and now to 'edify' (KJV) or 'equip' (ESV) saints 'for the work of ministry for the building up of the body of Christ' so that when each part and member is operating properly, the whole body grows, building itself up in love.

6. The ultimate goals of Christ's gifts of able, authorized leaders are the *unity* of the church, her *maturity*, *stability* and *growth*.

13
The Mission of the Church in the World

Students in theological seminary usually are required to take a course in mission(s), entitled something like 'Philosophy of Christian Missions,' 'Theology of Missions' or 'Missiology.' For many years of the twentieth century the usual textbook was *The Progress of World Wide Missions* by R. H. Glover, an historical survey, not a biblical or theological survey. More recently books such as G. W. Peter's *A Biblical Theology of Missions* (1972) and J. H. Kane's *Christian Missions in Biblical Perspective* (1976) have sought to bring the whole Bible to bear on the subject of world evangelism, greatly to the gain of the readers. A whole literature, academic departments and specialized schools have sprung up making 'missiology' a field of study as adjunct to the practice of evangelism at home and abroad.[1]

In this chapter we shall limit our thought to (1) how the churches in the New Testament record came to understand their duty to evangelize the world; (2) how they and the church of the first three centuries carried out this duty; (3) the grounding of this mandate for 'making disciples' among all nations; (4) Paul's understanding of the logical mandate for sending preachers of the Word (Rom. 10:13-17); (5) Paul's understanding of the *Old Testament mandate* both for *going* and *sending* (Rom. 15:8-12); (6) *principles* for disciples in the mission of world evangelism (Matt. 13); and (7) *practice* for disciples in the mission of world evangelism.

1. How the Church in the New Testament Record Came to Understand Their Duty to Evangelize the World.

Neither the twelve Apostles nor any disciples became missionaries either to Jews outside the neighborhood of Jerusalem or to the heathen world for several years after Jesus' Ascension. Jesus had said early in His ministry that He was sent 'only to the lost sheep of the house of Israel' (Matt. 15:24). Paul called Jesus Himself 'a servant to the circumcised' (Rom. 15:8). In their first preaching mission Jesus commanded the Twelve, 'Go nowhere among the Gentiles and enter no town of the Samaritans' (Matt. 10:5).

---

1. I have referred frequently in this book to my own modest contribution to that development in several papers read at academic gatherings, articles and sermons and *A Greater Commission: A Theology of Missions* (Chicago: Moody, 1984), revised and reissued as *A Greater Commission: The Broad Range of Scriptural Mandate for World Evangelism* (Clayton, CA: Witness, Inc., 1996) also available from the author. I shall refer to it several times in this chapter.

Nothing Jesus said later seems to have modified the disciples' acceptance of that limitation for their own lives and ministry. They defined their growing church in relation to Judaism. To outsiders they looked like a sect of Judaism (Acts 2–7). We today are puzzled at the reluctance of the group at Jerusalem to move out into the world to preach the good news and to establish new congregations. It seems to us that given the resurrection, the Ascension and Pentecost there should have been an immediate push outward. But Luke's narrative in Acts is careful to show that something quite different happened.

Several years passed before the first expansion took place. Philip's evangelistic foray into Samaria (Acts 8) was to 'half Jews' among whom Jesus once lodged (John 4), and the Ethiopian eunuch (Acts 8) was probably a proselyte Jew.

Several changes in the disciples themselves had to take place before missionary evangelism of the world could begin.

The first involved immense reversal of deeply held opinions. They had to become aware that the Lord's redemptive work had been intended for the entire human race. It is obvious that they and their leader (Peter) interpreted Jesus' sayings about being a 'ransom for many' (Matt. 20:28) and the 'whoever believes in him may have eternal life' (as in John 3) as promises to Jews and those who would become Jews (proselytes) first. In Acts 10 and 11 Luke carefully explains how that change began. Acts 15 and Galatians show how slowly full realization that Judaism was defunct took place.

The second change related to the church at Jerusalem, which was composed mainly of very provincial and parochially minded people – the Apostles not excepted – who needed a vast increase of intellectual perception of the meaning of revelation in Jesus' words and a full understanding of His work of redemption. Jesus had said it would be so[2] and human psychic processes being what they are it could not happen in a moment.

The third change was that the disciples had to lose both their social dependence on one another and similar attachment for the familiar scenes of the Savior's short sojourn among them, and the fourth was that they were in acute need of inward power and inspiration to get them up and move them out. The meaning of the events of Pentecost were not then as clear to them as they are now to us.

These changes may have begun feebly as they reflected on Jesus' last words to them (Luke 24:45-47; Acts 1:8) about being His witnesses 'to the end of the earth.' Yet even after Pentecost Peter still thought their preaching was to be only to 'the people,' *ho laos*, the Jewish people.[3]

Acts 10 and 11 carefully narrates how the Lord miraculously explained the end of an old covenant and the beginning of a new one first to Peter and then through him to the reluctant leaders of the Jerusalem church.

Concurrently, or nearly so, the Lord Himself revealed to an obscure Jewish Christian, named Ananias, in Damascus that the name of Christ was now to be borne before Gentiles and that a presently dazed young Jewish aristocrat named Saul was to be the leading instrument in Gentile evangelism (Acts 9:15). Meanwhile other disciples became active evangelists in Phoenicia, Cyprus and Antioch of Syria, but at first only to Jews and then Greeks (Acts 11:19, 20). Not many months later Paul and Barnabas set off on the first formally commissioned campaign of Christian missionary evangelism (Acts 13:1 ff.).

It is important to recognize that Paul never refers to any command of Jesus to evangelize Gentiles. He drew his mandate from a different source. He never had been a part of the Jerusalem community of believers. Matthew, Mark and Luke may not have written during his lifetime, hence it is entirely possible he never was informed of Jesus' so-called Great Commission sayings spoken during His post-resurrection ministry, however we interpret them.

Why then did Paul feel constrained to devote his life to evangelize the Gentile world? He clearly was not aware of any commission that commands, 'Go and preach the gospel in unevangelized places; if you cannot go send someone else.' The disciples at Jerusalem clearly did not interpret Jesus' sayings reported in Matthew 28:19, 20 and Acts 1:8 that way. Even those first scattered by persecution evangelized no Gentiles.

It is clear Paul recognized only two sources of his missionary mandate. The first part was a special revelation from God delivered by Ananias at Damascus (Acts 9:10-19): 'he is a chosen instrument of mine to carry my name before the Gentiles and kings and the children of Israel' (v. 15). Perhaps Paul received special direct revelations on the matter (Gal. 1:11-22). The second part he derived from the written Scriptures at the time, the Old Testament,

---

2. John 16:12-14; 14:25, 26; 15:26, 27.

3. See article on 'Laos' by Strathmann in TDNT, IV, pp. 29–57; H. R. Boer, *Pentecost and Missions* (Grand Rapids: Eerdmans, 1961), p. 39; Culver, *A Greater Commission*, chap. xv.

as he and Barnabas explained to a large audience at Antioch of Pisidia (Acts 13:14, 44-47), quoting Isaiah 49:6, 'For so the Lord has commanded us, saying, "I have made you a light for the Gentiles, that you may bring salvation to the ends of the earth."'(Acts 13:47). Later he would enlarge that scriptural mandate (Rom. 15:3-9) and also argue from common-sense reason that missionary evangelists must be sent (Rom. 10:14-17). We shall look at these very important passages regarding the mission of the church to the Gentile world later in this chapter.

2. How the Church of the First Centuries Carried Out Their Mission of World Evangelism.

Though, as we have seen, the first Christians were not quite aware that a new epoch in world-wide redemption and of universal offer of salvation had begun, once the true state of affairs struck home a zeal took over that had no precedent and has never been surpassed. The first three centuries lived up to Roland Allen's trenchant characterization of events as 'The Spontaneous Expansion of the Church.' Though not without specific missionary organization and propaganda, the church did not sponsor a missionary society; it *was* a missionary society. There was no limit on their ambitions, goals and zeal. Less than thirty years after the Ascension and only a little more than a decade into his formal mission in the eastern Mediterranean lands, Paul wrote to Rome in the west, 'from Jerusalem and all the way around to Illyricum [Albania] I have fulfilled the ministry of the gospel of Christ' (Rom. 15:19, 20).

Justin Martyr (AD 110–165) wrote:

> There is no people, Greek or barbarian or any other race by whatsoever appellation or manner they may be distinguished, however ignorant of art or agriculture, whether they dwell in tents or wander about in covered wagons, among whom prayers and thanksgivings are not offered, in the name of the crucified Jesus, to the Father and creator of all things.[4]

Tertullian (AD 160–240), North African preacher, churchman, and theologian, wrote many times of the spread of 'God's school,' reporting that the Christians were more numerous than the emperor's soldiers and if all were to resort to arms could defeat his armies! And, Tertullian claimed, this missionary success had occurred in a short time. Christians, he claimed, were 'a race that covers the whole world! We are but of yesterday, and we have filled… cities, islands, forts, towns, exchanges, yes! and the [army] camps, tribes… palace, senate, forum [Paul had converts in "Caesar's household"]. All we have left to you is the [pagan] temples [which of course no Christian would enter].'[5]

Eusebius of Caesarea (AD 266–340), first great church historian, in one of his best paragraphs, traces this zeal and technique – that led to the Christianization of the Empire – back to the work of the Apostles.

> Disciples of such men [the Apostles] built up churches where foundations had been previously laid in every place by the apostles. They augmented the means of promulgating the gospel more, spread the seeds of salvation far and wide…. Afterward leaving their country, they performed the office of evangelists to those who had not yet heard… they also delivered to them… the holy gospels.[6]

Eusebius goes on to say that these missionaries who immediately followed the Apostle-evangelists appointed pastors and arranged for the nurture of new believers.

3. The Grounding of the Mandate for Making Disciples of All Nations by Being Disciples in a Greater Commission.

The only imperative in the Greek text of Matthew 28: 19, 20 is 'make disciples' (*mathēteusate*, mistranslated 'teach' in KJV). 'Go ye therefore' (KJV) in the Greek text is *poreuthentes oun*, better rendered 'as ye go' or literally 'having gone' (not preferred by the learned). The passage assumes what had already actually taken place (see quotations of Paul, Justin Martyr, Tertullian and Eusebius in preceding paragraphs). Christians were scattered throughout the known world and there, both by life and death, both by discreet silence and winsome words, they made disciples, not neglecting to baptize and teach in the process.

---

4. As quoted by Robert Hall Glover, *The Progress of World-Wide Missions*, rev. and enlarged by J. Herbert Kane (New York: Harper & Row, 1960), p. 21.
5. Tertullian, *Apology 37.3-4*, ANF, III, p. 44. See also 1.7 ANF III, pp. 23, 24.
6. Eusebius, *Ecclesiastical History 3.37*, trans. Isaac Boyle (Grand Rapids: Baker, 1850, 1969), p. 123.

As I seek to demonstrate elsewhere,[7] the so-called 'Great Commission' of Matthew 28:19, 20 sets forth a program of disciples making disciples by being disciples. Neither going nor sending, but *being* disciple-makers wherever we are is the evangelistic program for each Christian. Every evidence from antiquity shows that it was the witness of the Christians to holiness, purity of life, love for one another (as seen in chap. 11) and for their neighbors which gave the church of the early centuries victory over satanic forces and brought Christianity to victory.

4. The Pauline Mandate for Special Sending of Missionary Evangelists.

Paul's mandate is in part based on common-sense argument. The logic of his argument is so transparently correct that it scarcely needs comment except to approve it as correct. No translation improves on the accurate, starkly literal KJV. The great Apostle of the Gentiles had been expounding on divine sovereignty in election (Rom. 9). Now in Romans 10 he is emphasizing 'the word of faith that we proclaim' (v. 8), and there follows the familiar words about confessing with the mouth, believing in the heart to salvation (Rom 10:9, 10). Then follows:

> For whosoever shall call upon the name of the Lord shall be saved [quoting Joel 2:32]. How then shall they call on him in whom they have not believed? and how shall they believe in him of whom they have not heard? and how shall they hear without a preacher? [Paul called himself a *kerux*, preacher not an evangelist.] And how shall they preach, except they be sent? (Rom. 10:13-15).

It is rare for Paul to use a purely logical (or common sense) argument to enjoin a practical Christian duty, but he does it here. If salvation comes by faith and faith is produced only by hearing the gospel then it is the duty of Christians to *send* preachers to proclaim the gospel to those who have never heard.

'If the Gentiles could not believe in the Lord without hearing of him, unless he was declared to them, then it follows from the prophecy above quoted [Joel 2:32], that preachers must be sent to them....This quotation was... calculated to produce the strongest conviction... of the duty of preaching the gospel to the Gentiles.'[8] There is no plainer statement of the mandate for mission in all of literature, biblical or otherwise. Some must go with the gospel to the people who have not heard it yet and others must send them.[9]

How did Paul lead into this argument? By showing his Jewish readers that their theological father, Moses, had taught that righteousness comes only by faith (vv. 5-9), then that the prophet Joel (2:32) had taught the same (Rom. 10:13).

How did he further defend the logical argument? By showing that the Old Testament, all three parts of it – Law, Prophets, Writings – teach salvation only by faith, a faith in response to hearing the Word of God (Rom. 10:16-21).

These five verses present the contrasting responses of hearers of the good news. There is another Jew *versus* Gentile contrast: glad faith on the part of many Gentiles as opposed to increasingly sullen rejection by Jews. These verses also show how Paul unfailingly relied on the Old Testament to support Christian doctrines.[10] F. Gode's comment is applicable:

> Paul has done what we do or should do in every sermon: 1st. Disentangle from the temporary application, which is the strict sense of the text, the fundamental and universal principle which it contains; 2nd. Apply fully this general principle to the circumstances in which we are ourselves speaking.[11]

5. The Mandate for Some to Go and Others to Send.

The mandate is based squarely on Old Testament teachings. This is the form of argument Paul employed in persuading the believers at Rome to help send a missionary, in this case Paul himself, on his way to evangelize heathen Spain (Rom. 15:8-13).

---

7. Culver, 'What is the church's Commission'?, *Bulletin of Evangelical Theological Society* (#10, Spring 1967) and *Bibliotheca Sacra*, July 1968; *A Greater Commission*, pp. 149–154.
8. Robert Haldane, *Exposition of the Epistle to the Romans* (first published in London, 1839, then Edinburgh through numerous printings and by Moody Press of Chicago repr. up to 1970). My copy is a New York printing of 1847, p. 524.
9. Culver, *A Greater Commission*, pp. 119–122.
10. See Culver, *A Greater Commission*, p. 120–122. The reader should compare v. 15 with Isaiah 52:7 and Nehemiah 1:15; verse 16 with Isaiah 53:1; verse 18 with Psalm 19:4; verse 19 with Deuteronomy 32:21; verse 20 with Isaiah 65:1 and 42:6, 7; verse 21 with Isaiah 65:2. The connections may seem obscure to us but not to Paul's Jewish readers, who had heard the Hebrew Bible and its Targums read at synagogue and in the home and were acquainted with Jewish lore.
11. F. Gode, *A Commentary on the Epistle to the Romans*, trans. T. W. Chambers (Grand Rapids: Zondervan, 1956) p. 582.

First Paul disposed of the problem imposed by the fact Jesus Himself ministered directly only to Jews. With a bold stroke he simply declared that Jesus limited His ministry to Jews because truly the promise of salvation was first promised to Abraham, Isaac and Jacob. 'For I say that Christ has become a servant to the circumcision on behalf of the truth of God to confirm the promises given to the fathers [Abraham, Isaac, Jacob, etc.]' (Rom 15:8 NASB).

The force of Romans 15:8 is to say there was an historic reason why Jesus' personal ministry was solely to Jews, and that it furnished no precedent.[12]

Then he proceeded again (as in Rom. 10) to quote from all three parts of the Hebrew *Tanach* – *Torah* (Law), *Neviim* (Prophets) and *Kethuvim* (Writings) – to show that the Old Testament Scriptures predicted a time when all the peoples of the world, both Jew and Gentile, would rejoice in Messianic salvation. Verse 9 quotes Psalm 18:49; verse 10, Deuteronomy 32:43; verse 11, Psalm 117:1; and verse 12, Isaiah 11:10.

He makes three points. The first (v. 8) is that although the presentation of Christ to Israel was the fulfillment of many promises – beginning at Genesis 12:1-3 – extension of the benefit to Gentiles was a matter of sheer mercy: 'and in order that the Gentiles might glorify God for his mercy. As it is written, "Therefore I will praise you among the Gentiles"' (Rom. 15:9, citing Ps. 18:49).

This does not quite fully explain why Providence withheld a saving gospel from the heathen world until the beginning of the Christian mission (see Acts 17:23-31). It does affirm that God had a merciful purpose in the delay. We are not allowed to suppose ourselves more wise or compassionate than God.

The second point is that it had been God's intention right along to receive praise from the majority section (Gentiles) of the race rather than from a small tribe (Israel). This is the thrust of each of the quoted texts. 'And again it is said, "Rejoice, O Gentiles, with his people [Rom. 15:10 quoting Deut. 32:43]." And again, "Praise the Lord, all you Gentiles, and let all the peoples extol him [Rom. 15:11 quoting Ps. 117:1]."' The nations (Gentiles, heathen) are going to rejoice with Israel, God's people (v. 10). All the peoples (v. 11) shall praise God. Peoples, Gentiles, tribes, families must rejoice with Israel in praise of the one true God. This is why pioneer missionaries become linguists and have led in reducing hundreds of dialects to writing in order to produce Bibles in the languages of 'the peoples.' Jesus had this truth in mind when He predicted, 'this gospel of the kingdom will be proclaimed throughout the whole world as a testimony to all nations [Gentiles, heathen], and then the end will come' (Matt. 24:14).

The third point is that 'the Gentiles' shall have hope in Christ. 'And again Isaiah says, "The root of Jesse will come, even he who arises to rule the Gentiles; in him will the Gentiles hope"' (Rom. 15:12 quoting Isa. 11:10). This hope arrived when 'the Root of Jesse... arises to rule the Gentiles' (v. 12). They who formerly were 'strangers to the covenant of promise, having no hope and without God' (Eph. 2:12) have been 'brought near by the blood of Christ' (Eph. 2:13) and must be informed by preachers sent for that very purpose.

Thus Paul concludes his statements of the mandate for a Christian, world-wide mission of evangelism.

6. Principles for the Church's Mission of World Evangelism.

Jesus Himself expounded these principles in a lengthy discourse of eight parables (Matt. 13 and Mark 4:21-29) shortly before He sent the Twelve out on their first mission of preaching (Matt. 10).[13] Two long chapters of the Bible predict the course of this age in the language of symbolism. Each begins with the time the spokesman lived and each ends with the consummation of the present age. The former, Daniel 2, predicts the course of dominant national succession under the figure of a statue with a head of gold, breast and arms of silver, belly and thighs of bronze, legs of iron and feet of iron mixed with clay.

The coming judgment and establishment of the eternal reign of Messiah is represented by a stone that smashes the image. Jesus prophetically called this period of time 'the times of the Gentiles' (Luke 21:24).

Matthew 13 (with some supplementing from Mark 4 and Luke 8) is the other long chapter predicting the course of this age. In it Jesus refers to 'the kingdom of heaven' (Matt. 13:11 and throughout the chapter; in Mark 4; and Luke 8, 'the kingdom of God'). That kingdom is plainly the sphere in which people would profess to be Christians, acknowledging Him at least with the lips as Lord and Christ. This is a matter of some controversy but, with variation

---

12. I discuss that matter at length in my two books, *A Greater Commission*, pp. 123, 124 and *The Life of Christ*, pp. 103–105.
13. The actual chronology supplied by Mark 3:13-19; 4:1-34; and 6:7-13 as well as Luke 6:12-16; 8:4-18; and 9:1-6 shows that chronologically Matthew 13 falls before Matthew 10.

in emphasis, most serious students agree that Jesus was speaking of the response people will make to the preached gospel (the *kērygma*) and what preachers should do about it after the disciples came to understand the world-wide intent of the gospel and began their world-wide mission.

In the latter part of the middle year of Jesus' ministry of three years the shape of the future was falling into place. The disciples' minds needed to be prepared for the disappointments of failed expectations of a visible kingdom restored to Israel (Acts 1:6, 7). Otherwise they would never be ready to be Apostles in the founding of an *ekklēsia* within a kingdom of grace in the age to follow. Matthew 13 furnishes a lengthy report of how Jesus began that preparation in a series of eight 'parables of the kingdom' (one reported only by Mark). Though Jesus provided some interpretation of the parables (vv. 10-23, 36-43) – enough that the disciples thought they understood them all (v. 51) – yet it is certain these parables were among the words of Jesus the promised Spirit would call to their 'remembrance' and 'show the meaning' only in later years (John 14:26; 16:12-14).

Extended treatment of these eight parables will be found in many works of exposition and commentary. A summary of my own treatment in *A Greater Commission* now follows. Jesus spoke, in order:

1. Of four kinds of soil for the seed of the Word of God (Matt. 13:3-9, 18-23) showing how people will respond to the gospel in different ways, only a minority with hearty, enduring faith.

2. Of a man who sowed seed in a field and patiently waited for harvest, not interfering with growth (Mark 4:26-29; not in Luke or Matt. 13). It explains the utter dependence of the human messenger upon the inner working of the Word and Spirit to produce conversion of the evangelized. In the words of 1 Corinthians 3:7, 'So neither he who plants nor he who waters is anything, but only God who gives the growth.'

3. Of a field sowed with wheat in which tares (a noxious weed that looks like wheat) were sown (Matt. 13:24-30, 36-43). The devil sows his own seed along with the good seed in the same field. The field is not the church but the world, where the tares must be left undisturbed by violence until the Judgment Day and when God's own angels will make separation.

4. Of a very small seed, the mustard seed, and its phenomenal growth (Matt. 13:31, 32). There will be a surprising world-wide extension of the professing church with mixed results of good and bad.

5. Of leaven in a bowl of meal (Matt. 13:33). The gospel works quietly, unseen and with spectacular results. The mustard seed and the leaven teach us: *do not despise the day of small things* (Zech. 4:10).

The next two parables speak of two different ways in which people come to awareness of God's truth in the gospel and acceptance of the message. Jesus spoke:

6. Of a hidden treasure (Matt. 13:44). Some people are overtaken by the truth – it comes with a flash – and are so overcome by it they are willing to give all for it.

7. Of a pearl of great price (Matt. 13:45, 46). Other people seem to find Christ and the meaning of His Word after painful searching.

8. Of a drag-type of fishnet that gathered both good and bad fish, which had to be sorted (Matt. 13:47-50). There will be many hypocrites among those who profess to believe the gospel preached by the messengers. They will stay in this sphere of Christian profession until the judgment at the end of this age; the bad fish (hypocrites) will be sorted out and severely judged.

There is a singular note of finality about Jesus' discourse: 'When Jesus had finished these parables, he went away from there' (Matt. 13:53). Then He picked up his baggage and left the scene. He had said all the disciples were then prepared to hear about the progress of the kingdom in the world. These were the principles which should guide missionary evangelism, both revealed and concealed in eight vigorous parables. The church has ignored them to her defeat in aborted attempts at evangelism and violated them to her defeat in countless efforts at 'church growth.' Whatever else we think we learn about that subject it ought to be rigorously adjusted to our Lord's own philosophy of mission, if we may use such an expression.

7. Practice in the Mission of World Evangelism.

Earlier in this chapter we have paid attention to the missionary setting of Matthew's Gospel, citing Irenaeus (AD 180, *Against Heresies* 3.1.1). In ancient oriental fashion Matthew states his missionary theme at (or near) the end of his book (28:19, 20) – like Ecclesiastes 12:13, 14 and John 20:30.

From the very beginning Matthew marshaled his materials toward the announcement of the mission of world evangelism. Believers are, so to speak, to take the gospel along and by it making disciples as they go out among 'all nations.' This they did, beginning with the persecutions after the martyrdom of Stephen (Acts 8:1). Several times Matthew quotes Jesus regarding the value of 'souls.' He reports the angel's saying that Jesus 'shall save his people from their sins' (1:21). At least a dozen times apart from chapters 10 and 13 the 'soul-winning,' missionary theme is introduced, directly or subtly. On the very first day of public ministry after the temptation, Jesus' invitation was, 'Follow me, and I will make you fishers of men' (4:19). A reading of the following partial listing shows that Matthew sustained the missionary theme throughout – 5:29, 30; 8:11; 9:35-38; chapter 10; 11:25-30; 12:46-50; chapter 13; 18:9-14; 19:28-30; 21:42, 43; 24:13-14; 25:31-46; 26:13; 28:16-20.

Matthew 9:35-38 has no parallel in the other Gospels:

> And Jesus went throughout all the cities and villages, teaching in their synagogues and proclaiming the gospel of the kingdom and healing every disease and every affliction. When he saw the crowds, he had compassion for them, because they were harassed and helpless, like sheep without a shepherd. Then he said to his disciples, 'The harvest is plentiful, but the labourers are few; therefore pray earnestly to the Lord of the harvest to send out laborers into his harvest.'

These verses, mirroring Jesus' tender concern to minister to the multitudes and to preach the good news to them, are a preface to the unique following chapter on the future of the Christian mission of evangelism. He speaks of the vast harvest field, ripe for harvest. We cannot doubt that all the mission fields of all the age then to follow, in which we all must live as responsible missionary disciples, were in the scope of His vision.[14]

Matthew 10, after introducing (by pairs) the names of the twelve Apostles (vv. 1-4), falls into three parts: (1) verses 5-15, practice by the Twelve in the mission from which they would return in a few weeks (compare Mark 6:30 and Luke 9:10); (2) verses 16-23, relates primarily to practice in the mission while it was still mainly Jewish and in the environs of Jerusalem; (3) verses 24-42 relate primarily to practice in the mission of world evangelism to the end of the age in which we live.

Older modern writers (e.g. Alford, Edersheim, Ellicott) agree with this structure of the chapter and bring evidence to support it. More recently W. Hendriksen stated, 'A single reading of the charge shows that from verse 16 to the end the One who addresses the Twelve is predicting the future. He is describing what is going to happen when the church brings Christ's message to those lost in sin.'[15] These authors call attention to how Jesus divided the sections with the emphatic 'Truly, I say to you' in verses 15 and 23.

What can we learn about true laborers in the harvest of souls from verses 1-4 about the twelve chosen first messengers? Briefly, there are four things. First, *twelve is a very significant symbolic number*, the usual numerical emblem for Israel of the Old Testament people of God. There were twelve sons of Jacob and twelve 'tribes of Israel,' twelve representative stones on the 'breastplate' of Aaron's 'ephod,' and much else (see Lev. 24:5; Num. 1:44; 7:3, 84; Matt. 19:28; Luke 22:30; James 1:1; Rev. 12:1). Twelve also is an emblem of the New Testament people of God. So it is not surprising to see the name of 'the twelve apostles of the Lamb' written on the twelve foundations of the coming city (Rev. 21:14) as well as the names of the twelve tribes of Israel on the twelve gates (Rev. 21:12, 13). It may be that when saints of both dispensations are represented together it is by twice twelve, the twenty-four elders of Revelation 4:4, 10, 11 and 5:8-10.

The fact that two pairs of the Twelve were brothers, they and others were fishermen, some were cousins of Jesus, two were friends, and all except one (Judas) lived in the same neighborhood (Galilee) shows that *familial* and *community relationships* foster Christian association in leadership.

The close association of the Twelve as disciples for several years in apprenticeship, testing and training as well as indoctrination shows the *importance* of some *preparation* for leadership. When the time came to serve they were no novices (cf. 1 Tim. 5:22).

The fact that Jesus chose twelve obscure, very ordinary common people suggests the *significance of insignificance*. No special mental cast, intellectual attainments, no splendid prizes of university scholarships or worldly advantage is necessary to be one of the fishers of men. They were all 'out of the loop' of the elite; all are unlettered men, like Jesus Himself.

---

14. Culver, *A Greater Commission*, pp. 3, 4.
15. Wm. Hendriksen, Matthew: *The New Testament Commentary Series* (Grand Rapids: Baker, 1973), p. 446.

I. The First Mission: Application Then and Now (Matt. 10:5-15).

The field for this first mission was restricted 'to the lost sheep of the house of Israel' (v. 6). In addition to what might be called 'dispensational' reasons, there was the problem of the parochial and nationalistic (anti-Roman) state of the disciples' minds. These twelve Jewish Apostles-to-be were not ready for any ministry to despised 'sinners of the Gentiles.' Jesus sometimes spoke of 'other sheep' of a different fold (John 10:16) but the Apostles were not ready to understand that, much less accept it.

Several matters of strategy and message follow.

First, begin your missionary evangelism among those you are best fitted by personal history to communicate with – 'Go nowhere among the Gentiles.'

Second, begin your witness where you are, near at hand. Any one who aspires to be a missionary to unknown people in a strange culture should be proven able among his own people in a culture he understands.

Third, the principle of grace – 'freely ye have received, freely give' (v. 8 KJV). '[F]reely' translates *dorean*, meaning as a gift, no charge. This is how the Spirit offers salvation (Rev. 22:17 KJV) and how justification of sinful people must take place (Rom. 3:24) – a revolutionary, utterly strange idea wherever the good news is preached, which requires the very most careful explanation and emphasis.

Fourth, to preach the kingdom demand (v. 7) of repentance and faith is essentially the demand the gospel makes in every age, including ours (Rom. 10:9, 10).

Fifth, the thrust of verses 9 and 10 is simply 'Go as you are.' New converts, at least initially, without going anywhere are usually very effective witnesses, according to points 1 and 2 above. Soul-winning effort can begin without any necessary material preparation.

Sixth (vv. 11-13), the gospel will be received for salvation only by prepared hearts. They manifest their preparation by hospitality (in many forms) to the messenger. This preparation is the Holy Spirit's function, not ours.

Seventh, there will be some painful negative results even of competent faithful proclamation (vv. 14, 15). When overtly rejected by Jews, Paul and Barnabas did indeed shake off the dust of their feet and move on (Acts 13:50, 51). It is important to note, however, that these twelve preachers were addressing an already partially hardened Jewish population to whom 'much' had already been 'given,' likewise with Paul and Barnabas mentioned above. This is hardly true of every audience and it is worth noting that one of the two missionaries of Acts 13:50, 51 returned to preach again in the same area. The field was not permanently abandoned. They did not 'dialogue' with blaspheming Jews any more than Elijah did with the prophets of Baal (1 Kgs. 18:40).

II. Mission Practice After Pentecost but Before the Dispersion of the Apostolic Church at Jerusalem (Matt. 10:16-23).

As noted earlier, 'Truly, I say' in verses 15 and 23 sets this section apart from the first and third sections. There are no strict parallels to this passage in the other Gospels. Jesus' statement that it is 'the Spirit of your Father speaking through you' (v. 20) suggests the Pentecostal effusion of the Spirit will have occurred when these practices become applicable. Experiences of persecution by governors and kings mentioned here were mainly after AD 70. Good writers on this section propose three considerations which render it applicable to all Christian times. (1) Since the passage is predictive prophecy a feature of many biblical predictions becomes applicable, *viz.* such prediction usually lays emphasis more on kinds of events than on specific occurrences. The Olivet discourse is predictive of the whole age and there Jesus repeats much of this section – cf. Matthew 10:19-22 with Mark 13:9-13 and Luke 21:12-19. (2) Further, in the Bible, the past and present are often a figure ('type') of the future; and, (3) of special importance, Jesus required His Apostles to pass on His commandments as binding on future generations of believers (Matt. 28:20).

I devote a long chapter in *A Greater Commission* to this passage's instructions on missionary evangelism for today. The emphases of the passage are as follows.

a. The sender of every true evangelist is Christ Himself (v. 16a). The sense of the Greek text is, 'Beloved, I, myself, send you forth.'

b. The enemies of the witness will be wicked men 'as sheep in the midst of wolves' (v. 16b; cf. 17 'Beware of men'). The Lord's enemies were also compared to animals – bulls, dogs, lions and similar (Ps. 22).

c. The evangelist's approach will be nonviolent and wise: 'be wise as serpents and innocent as doves' (v. 16c).

d. The evangelists can expect both religious leaders and public government officials to oppose them, even to persecute them (vv. 17-18); they will go before councils and synagogues, governors and kings, for 'a testimony' both to Jews and Gentiles.

e. The chief resources of messengers of Christ under attack are all spiritual (vv. 19-20). Their defense is only God Himself.

f. The most crushing blows against the messengers will come from those unconverted among their own extended family groups (vv. 21, 22). Jesus Himself was opposed at first by His own brothers (John 7:1-6), and the congregation of His home town were the very first to attempt to assassinate Him (Luke 4:29). Jeremiah narrowly escaped a plot against his life mounted by his own village and family (Jer. 11:18-21). Ezekiel aroused only tolerance and amusement among his own (Ezek. 33:30, 31). Though family and kinship *can* be of great help to the messenger if they are converted, they *may*, if the messenger is the only believer, be his most dangerous enemies.

g. Sometimes the proper response to life-threatening persecution is flight: 'When they persecute you in one town, flee to the next' (v. 23a). Paul and his associates in missionary evangelism followed this plain advice frequently (Acts 13:14–14:21; Acts 16:12–18:18; Acts 19). So Jesus' words were both instruction and prediction of what actually happens over and over.

Jesus's puzzling comment, 'you will not finish going through the cities of Israel until the Son of Man comes' (v. 23 NASB), is interpreted variously. It may properly be regarded as Christ's very first prediction to His Apostles that His coming as Prophet, Healer, Teacher and crucified Redeemer was to be followed by another coming in power and unveiled glory. He had hinted at such a thing earlier (Matt. 7:21-23). The very language of Jesus' sentence seems to be shaped by Daniel 7:13, 14, which speaks of a coming in power and glory. Some propose that the whole section relates to the great tribulation after the rapture of the church. Many more propose that the coming of the Son of Man took place providentially, not personally, when Caesar's armies came to Jerusalem and destroyed it. The evidence for the latter is impressive. (See Matt. 22:1-8, especially v. 7.) That the Roman 'coming' was an *immediate fulfillment*, a foreshadowing of ultimate fulfillment at the Second Advent, appeals to many.[16] One can hardly avoid thinking of this passage's fulfillment in Paul's life as persecuted missionary ('but the Lord stood by me'). The Lord comes again and again to stand by His own in the crises of life.[17]

III. The Age-long Mission: the Disciples' Relation to Christ (Matt. 10:24-33).

There is a shift from *Apostles* to *disciples* suggesting a time after the Apostles' decease.

a. Conflicts on the mission (vv. 24, 25). In a threefold relation to Christ the Christian missionary will serve and suffer. As (1) *disciples* of a *Master*, apprentices, they cannot be relieved of experiencing what He did, nor as (2) *servants* of a LORD. As (3) *members* of the household of Christ the *House-Master* they share His experiences.

b. Duties on the mission (vv. 26, 27). It is a shallow exegesis to refer to 'covered' as to sins and 'revealed' as to the judgment. In context Jesus is saying simply that what the disciples heard Him say in the privacy of their years of uninterrupted communion with Him and instruction by Him is to be preached as publicly as possible. It is their duty even if threatened by death. They should 'Beware of men' but 'have no fear of them' (v. 26; cf. 17). '[P]roclaim on the housetops' (v. 27) means, give the gospel the widest possible distribution, as preachers from then till now, and as translators, printers and colporteurs from Ulfilas to Kenneth Pike, have understood.

c. The section continues with *encouragements in mission* (vv. 28-31) and *warnings on mission* (vv. 32, 33).

IV. The Age-long Mission: the Disciples' Relation to Others in the Mission (10:34-42).

This long discourse of Jesus relates more specifically than any comparable section to the right practice of missionary evangelism by the church. Lamentably it has not figured largely in the literature of missiology.

Christians within the Roman Empire succeeded in evangelizing it in less than three centuries. This was not because they were organized to 'go, and to send,' but because they as Christians simply behaved as Christians as set forth in the Scriptures discussed in this chapter and followed examples of apostolic activity.

Slavic and Germanic Europe was still largely unreached by the gospel when the emperor convened the first Ecumenical Council at Nicea (AD 325). England did not embrace Christianity until AD 627 and the last of the Baltic regions late in the fourteenth century.

---

16. Alford, *New Testament for English Readers*, p. 71.
17. Culver, *A Greater Commission*, pp. 27–29.

How Europe became the major part of 'Christendom' must remain an untold story here. Once civil government undertook to expand Christendom – the realm where people rest on Sunday and go to church as a matter of obedience to civil law – many atrocities against truly biblical-Christian evangelism took place. A fair history of what happened, as far as it can be determined, together with an evaluation, is in *The Barbarian Conversion: From Paganism to Christianity* by Richard Fletcher,[18] a professor at the University of York in England.[19]

---

18. Richard Fletcher, *The Barbarian Conversion: From Paganism to Christianity* (New York: Henry Holt & Co., 1998), 562 pages.
19. This chapter organizes and summarizes my volume, *A Greater Commission: The Broad Range of the Scriptural Mandate for World Evangelism*, 176 pages, available from the author. Formerly published as *A Greater Commission: A Theology for World Missions* (Moody Press, 1984).

14
The Present Purposes of God for the Church and Her Destiny

I. The Present Purposes of God for the Church.

In his exposition of Revelation 2 and 3, John Stott says:

> The New Testament supplies us with much information concerning our Lord's purposes for His church. We may glean from some of His own words as recorded in the Gospels, from description of the primitive church given us in the Acts, and from the epistles to various churches in the rest of the New Testament just what is His plan for the church which is His body.[1]

Though Stott does not put it just this way, the purposes might be summed up as sanctification of believers in love, suffering, truth, holiness, reality, opportunity and wholeheartedness – as revealed in the messages of Christ to the seven churches (Rev. 2, 3). The church is designed to be the vehicle in which they are developed and expressed.

Calvin put it another way: '[W]e need outward helps to beget and increase faith within us, and advance it to its goal, God has added… aids…. And in order that the preaching of the gospel might flourish, he deposited this treasure in the church.'[2] He goes on to explain that he is speaking of the church in the world. It is invisible in the sense that the church of true believers is spiritual, 'a church beyond our ken. For here we are not bidden to distinguish between reprobate and elect – that is for God alone, not for us to do' (*Institutes* IV. 1.3). The church is also often invisible to the wicked in times of persecution, able to survive only in a hidden state: 'God miraculously keeps his church as in hiding places' – he cites the 'seven thousand in Israel' of 1 Kings 19:18. It is, of course, visible in the extent that believers are visible and known publicly, even if tares and wheat are not fully distinguishable. The 'possessing church' lies within the 'professing church.'

This church is always today. It is catholic. Its members are in every 'denomination' or no denomination. Yet they do constitute on earth a 'communion of saints,' the 'body of Christ on earth,' all being 'united in Christ' and 'dependent on one head.' This church in which we 'believe' is joined to the deceased saints now in heaven. This 'fact' therefore 'belongs to the realm of faith' but should be real to us by faith no less than if it were clearly visible. The presence of hypocrites in the church should be of concern but not dismay us.[3] (We shall discuss church discipline a bit later.)

---

1. John Stott, *What Christ Thinks of the Church* (Downers Grove, IL: InterVarsity Press, 1958), p. 9.
2. Calvin, *Institutes*, trans. F. L. Battles (Philadelphia: Westminster Press), iv, 1.1.
3. Calvin's treatment, *Institutes*, iv, chap 1 (pp. 1011–41) is unequalled.

This understanding of the church in which God's purposes must be realized was shared by most early Protestants:

> Wherever we see the Word of God purely preached and heard and the sacraments administered according to Christ's institution, there, it is not to be doubted, a church of God exists. For his promise cannot fail: 'Wherever two or three are gathered in my name, there I am in the midst of them.'[4]

The views of Luther and early Lutherans were not essentially different. Rouse and Neill demonstrate this.[5] Article VII of the *Augsburg Confession* (German trans. of 1540) affirms: 'But the church is the assembly of all believers, in which the Gospel is purely preached and the Sacraments administered according to the Gospel.'[6] For Calvin, discipline of open sin in the church was very important, though apparently he thought it was for the *well*-being of the church not an invariable mark of the church. Many early Anabaptists thought it was of the *esse* (Wendel, *Calvin*, Harper ed. of 1963, pp. 296–301). The 1560 Presbyterian *First Scots Confession* (art. XVIII) adds as a third mark of a church, 'Ecclesiastical discipline uprightly ministered as Goddis Worde prescribes, whereby vice is repressed and vertew nourished,'[7] as does also the Reformed *Belgic Confession* (1561).[8]

This is the church for which Paul gave rules for appointment of bishops and deacons (1 Tim. 3:1-13) and told Timothy 'how thou oughtest to behave thyself' in 'the church [on earth as well as heaven] of the living God, the pillar and ground of the truth' (1 Tim. 3:15 KJV) and which 'is our mother' (Gal. 4:26).

Let me emphasize that it is this continuing earthly body of saints (though their commonwealth is in heaven) for whom God has purposes and a destiny – we who preach sermons, teach Sunday School, listen, socialize, witness, rear our families, go to work and to school are the topic under consideration. At this point theology becomes hope and duty, practice and expectation. Every purpose of God for the church calls for some specific personal response from each believer and from every local congregation.

1. The First Divine Purpose Is Service.

That is, the church is the paramount instrument through which our Lord accomplishes His designed work in the present world. This is a comprehensive category which includes all the rest.[9]

Christ Himself gave to the church the Apostles, prophets, evangelists of the past and the 'pastors and teachers' of today 'to equip the saints for the work of ministry' (Eph. 4:11, 12). Chrysostom's comments on the meaning and lessons of the church as 'the fulness of Him that filleth all in all' occupy about seven columns of tight print,[10] relating it to 'riches of the glory of His inheritance in the saints.'

In a way no expositor or exegete, from Jerome[11] and Chrysostom to the latest in the present flood of commentaries, has ever quite fully expounded the way that God the Father has a plan 'to unite all things in him [Christ], things in heaven and things on earth' (Eph. 1:10) and that plan has 'put all things under his [Christ's] feet and gave him as head over all things to the church, which is his body, the fullness of him who fills all in all' (Eph. 1:22, 23). J.A. Robinson captures the sense well:

> In some mysterious sense the church is that without which the Christ is not complete, but with which He is or will be complete.... Even now in the imperfect stage... the church is that through which Christ lives on and works on here below on earth.... His feet and hands no longer move and work in our midst.... But St. Paul affirms that He is not without feet and hands on earth: the church is His Body. Through the church, which St. Paul refuses to think of as something separate from Him, He still lives and moves among men... as the church grows toward completion, the Christ grows toward completion... if we may use the language of our own great poet [Tennyson] – [the Christ] 'that is to be.'[12]

---

4. iv., 1.9, first paragraph.
5. Rouse and Neill, *History of Ecumenical Movement* (Philadelphia: Westminster Press, 1954), pp. 27–35.
6. Philip Schaff, *Creeds of Christendom*, III (Grand Rapids: Baker Books, 1966), pp. 11, 12.
7. ibid., p. 462.
8. ibid., p. 4.
9. *The Roman Catholic Catechism of 1994* makes this point in para. 737 and 760 with citations from Hermas, Aristides, Justin, Tertullin, Epiphanius, Clement of Alexandria.
10. NPNF, Vol. xiii, pp. 62–64.
11. I do not have easy access to Jerome's fine comments in a complete translation. Robertson (see note 11) fills a page (61) with quotation of Origen's excellent treatment, quite in harmony with the view that I have taken of the amazing last phrases of Ephesians 1:22, 23, 'the church, Which is ... fulness of him that filleth all in all.'
12. J. Armitage Robinson, *St. Paul's Epistle to the Ephesians* (London: MacMillan, 1939), pp. 57, 59.

Let us note some specific practical ways in which the church in union with Christ does His work on earth today. I think the first of the two most important is that it is in the church, *per se*, where most sinners who are saved, come to be aware of their sins and receive forgiveness of their sins. So it was on the Day of Pentecost at the close of Peter's sermon and likewise for most of us – remembering of course that the church sends missionaries and evangelists and that Christian fathers and mothers are associated with and strengthened in their local churches. The second most important way is that it is in the church, in its integral ministries of teaching, preaching, administering ordinances, providing the support of a praying fellowship, that sanctification of believers takes place. Jesus prayed, 'Sanctify them in the truth; your word is truth.' The church has preserved, printed, distributed, explained the Word. Jesus gave Himself for us that He might sanctify and cleanse it with the washing of water by the Word. Our spots and wrinkles (Eph. 5:27) are removed that Jesus may present 'himself a glorious church.' His church's ministries are precisely engineered for that purpose.

Also, thirdly, it is only in the church as a public organism, that the consistent provision of apostolic doctrine, the special fellowship, the worship and the prayers essential for normal Christian life occur (Acts 2:41-47). Here the gifts of the Spirit act together for mutual betterment (1 Cor. 12:12 ff.) and in this union with Christ and believers we experience both the power to bear fruit and the pruning discipline if we do not (John 15:1 ff.).

Children of Lutheran parents are taught that God 'calls, gathers, enlightens, and sanctifies the whole Christian church on earth, and keeps it... in which Christian church He daily and richly forgives all sins to me and all believers.'[13] A. H. Strong taught generations of Baptist preachers, 'The church, like the family and the state is an institution of divine appointment... its necessity is grounded in the social and religious nature of man.'[14] He points out the community and 'communion' of the first congregation in Acts was not for the community of mankind in general, but only for the church, and approves the statement that it is 'the duty of all good men to become identified with the visible church.'[15]

The *Westminster Confession* is outstandingly clear, 'Unto this catholic visible church, Christ hath given the ministry [pastors and teachers], oracles [the Bible], and ordinances of God [baptism, the Lord's supper], for the gathering and perfecting of the saints, in this life, to the end of the world: and doth by his own presence and Spirit, according to his promise make them effectual thereunto.'[16]

Perhaps the most thoroughly orthodox pronouncements of the World Council of Churches came from the Evanston 1954 Assembly. On the point of present topic at the close of a good discussion of the mission of the church is this summary: 'All this means that the function of the church is, in the last analysis, to be both the instrument of God's purpose in history and also the first realization of the life of His kingdom on earth.'[17]

On the same point, but with his usual colorful flair, the late Lesslie Newbigin says of the local church in one of his last books that it is a 'hermeneutic of the gospel'; if 'true to its calling, it becomes the place where men and women and children find that the gospel gives them the framework of understanding, the "lenses" through which they are able to understand and cope with the world.'[18] Such a 'community,' he says, will be one of 'praise, reverence, thanksgiving, involvement in neighborhood, priesthood in the world, a social order of mutual concern and of hope.'[19]

Thomas Oden, whose research in patristic literature has greatly enriched our recent theological literature, quotes Irenaeus (*Against Heresies* 8.24.1): 'Where the Spirit of God is, there is the church and every kind of grace,'[20] and comments himself, 'To elect to live without the grace offered in the church is like a neonate refusing nourishment from the mother's breast.'[21] One might add, with Calvin, that the church in this sense is chief external support of our faith and 'mother of us all.' Calvin insisted on the indispensability of the church on earth as God's instrument

---

13. Luther's *Small Catechism* Sect. I, art. 3.
14. A. H. Strong, *Systematic Theology* (Old Tappen, NJ: Revell, 1907), p. 892.
15. ibid., p. 894.
16. Chap. xvii, III.
17. Report of the Advisory Commission on the Main Theme of the Second Assembly of the WCC, 'Christ, the Hope of the World.' This appeared in the book *The Christian Hope and Task of the Church*, 1954, p. 19. Many of the reports at Evanston in 1954 were framed by orthodox evangelical believers, still a force in the new WCC. I attended several sessions.
18. Leslie Newbigin, *The Gospel in a Pluralistic Society* (Grand Rapids: Eerdmans, 1989), pp. 222, 227.
19. Developed on pp. 227–233.
20. Thomas Oden, *Life in the Spirit* (San Francisco: Harper Collins, 1992, 1996), p. 281.
21. ibid., p. 281.

for Christian sanctification. In developing this thought he quotes both Cyprian and Augustine and says that 'our weakness does not allow of our being withdrawn from school until we have been pupils [in the church] for the whole course of our lives.'[22] Luther wrote similarly in his *Large Catechism* explanation of the third article of the creed.

Charles Colson, responding to the personal moral failure of the president of a conservative college which disclaims religious connection, concluded a short article [23] with the sentence: 'Without the help of the living Christ even the most powerful among us is potentially nothing more than the next moral embarrassment waiting to happen.' A former student advisee of mine, now for thirty-five years a pastor, published a reply propounding the proposition that 'no man can be good without a vital connection to that functioning biblical community called "a church."'[24]

2. A Second Divine Purpose Is for Manifestation of Christ's Glory.

His moral glory was manifest to all with eyes to see when He was present on earth in the flesh (John 1:1, 14), even though His divine glory was then almost wholly veiled. Now the church is His body on earth – not an incarnation but a spiritual union of people in natural flesh, a spiritual body which manifests His moral excellencies on earth.

The universal church, chiefly visible in local churches, is not an end in itself, but as Strong says, it 'exists for the sake of the kingdom.' Its unity is 'that of the kingdom' – and is 'internal.' It 'is not coming with signs to be observed' (Luke 17:20), but consists in 'righteousness and peace and joy in the Holy Spirit' (Rom. 14:17).

Ephesians explicitly asserts that it was the 'counsel' of God's 'will' that those who hope in Christ 'have been destined and appointed to live for the praise of his glory' (Eph. 1:11, 12 RSV). In an earlier chapter we found in John 17 that a manifest spiritual unity is a sign to a lost world that God sent His Son and leads both to knowledge of Him and faith.

Jesus said, 'As long as I am in the world, I am the light of the world' (John 9:5). Our Lord presently is seen only in heaven. During the long absence the 'children of God without blemish [!] in the midst of a crooked and perverse generation… shine as lights in the world, holding fast the word of life' (Phil. 2:15, 16 RSV).

> Jesus bids us shine
> With a clear pure light,
> Like a little candle
> Burning in the night.
> In this world of darkness
> We must shine,
> You in your small corner
> And I in mine.[25]

Paul said, 'Christ shall be magnified in my body, whether it be by life or by death' (Phil. 1:20 KJV). The Greek *megalunthēsetai* (pass. fut.) literally means 'shall be made great.' The magnifying glass makes great to the eye of the observer whatever it is focused on. This very aptly suggests how Christ is to be made great in the eyes of an unbelieving world – by the lives and deaths of believers. The intense love of the ancient Christians for one another was what attracted the attention of the denizens of the Empire to Jesus, and their steadfast faith in face of death made Christ great in the eyes of millions. This is what brought victory: 'this is the victory that has overcome the world' (1 John 5:4); 'The blood of the martyrs is the seed of the church.'

3. A Third Divine Purpose Is to Exhibit Both the Wisdom and Grace of God.

A third divine purpose is to *exhibit* to heaven and earth both the *wisdom* of God in devising a plan to save fallen man and God's grace. The doctrine is specifically developed in exalted Pauline prose, *viz*.:

> To me, the very least of all saints, this grace was given, to preach to the Gentiles the unfathomable riches of Christ, and to bring to light what is the administration [dispensation, stewardship] of the mystery which for ages has been hidden in God who created all things; so that the manifold [*polupoikilos*, varied beyond measure, TDNT] wisdom of God *might now be made known through the church* to the rulers and the authorities in the heavenly places. This was in accordance with the eternal purpose which He carried out in Christ Jesus our Lord (Eph. 3:8-11 NASB, emphasis added).

---

22. *Institutes* IV. 1.4. See F. Wendel, *Calvin*, p. 294.
23. Winter 1999–2000.
24. Rev. Michael Braun of Montvale, NJ 07645.
25. An old children's hymn by Susan Warner.

In former times Gentiles knew a little about God, but only a little. Through Moses and the prophets of Israel God progressively made known much more, but not quite everything. The 'principalities and powers' of the heavenly regions knew more than men, but perhaps because of their knowledge had more questions. Proverbs praises the wisdom of God in creation and many other things but does not address the problem of why an omnipotent, omniscient and holy God allowed the entrance of sin into the world in the first place and apparently after the Great Flood had done nothing 'cosmic' to prevent a seeming repeated victory everywhere of sin and sinners over righteousness and the people of God. Further, Israel never got a handle on the reason(s) why the LORD out of pure grace had chosen them as His peculiar people. For a while even Jewish members of the nascent church (Acts 1:1-9) seemed unaware that 'God sent his Son to be the Savior of the world.' With hindsight we see more of God's wise purpose in Old Testament times. (See earlier discussions of divine decrees, preservation and providence in the doctrine of God and such passages as Genesis 45:5; 50:19, 20; Psalm 73; Habakkuk; and even the book of Job.)

Nevertheless the Old Testament history was itself a mystery, seeming to end in failure, one which even Mosaic and prophetic revelation did not explain fully. God spoke in those times in bits and pieces ('many parts,' Heb. 1:1) and in many ways ('many manners,' Heb. 1:1), puzzling even to God-fearing people (Acts 8:30-34). But Christ 'the wisdom of God' (1 Cor. 1:24) created the church. Hence 'now' God's wisdom has been made known to holy angels and other supernatural beings through the church.

'The *mystery* is defined twice over. First, it consists in the fact that in Christ Jesus through the gospel, the Gentiles are co-heirs and co-incorporated and co-partners in the promise (v. 6); and secondly, it is the unsearchable riches of Christ (v. 8). The latter phrase gathers to a point what is diversely expressed in the former.'[26]

In the passage 'the mystery' which the church makes known is something Paul preached to the Gentiles (Eph. 3:8), the unfathomable riches of Christ, that God invented and prepared by managing history since eternity past (v. 9) yet kept secret during those ages (v. 9). God's purpose in this management of history was expressly so that the church might make known God's wisdom by demonstration (v. 10). The church in Ephesians is the church universal, invisible to people in the sense only that 'the Lord knows those who are his' but visible to all in its teachings, institutions, assemblies and history.

The fact that in the church all this wisdom is 'made known' does not mean the sin-perverted wo.ld recognizes any wisdom in it. The world by its own wisdom does not know God (1 Cor. 1:21). The present post-Christian world has rejected both the church and her God as having anything specific to teach it. The Peace Corps, for example, gets far more favorable rating as an agency for world betterment than Christian missionaries; the 'wisdom' of the anthropologists berates the changes wrought by missions as harmful. At the present moment the mighty among worldly educators are seeking by any means available to direct the boys and girls away from any specific influence of the church. The state has competence (wisdom) but the church has none.

II. The Destiny of the Church.

Simply and comprehensively stated, the destiny of Christ's church on earth is to be presented to Christ at the time of His return from heaven. He said to the nascent *ekklēsia* of twelve Apostles, 'And when I go and prepare a place for you, I will come again and will take you to myself' (John 14:3 RSV). The idea of taking the church, a bride, is only suggested here; it is explicit in the equally tender words of Ephesians 5:25-27:

> Husbands, love your wives, as Christ loved the church and gave himself up for her, that he might sanctify her, having cleansed her by the washing of water with the word, so that he might present the church to himself in splendor, without spot or wrinkle or any such thing, that she might be holy and without blemish.

The presentation of the church by Christ, to Himself, as a pure bride, not only loved by Him and pure but serviceable (if we may allow the word), prepared by useful habits to be a 'good wife' – this is clearly implied by Jesus in His Parable of the Marriage Feast (Matt. 22:1-14) and Parable of the Ten Virgins (Matt. 25:1-13). The texts say that the virgins went out to meet the bridegroom (v. 1) not the groom and the bride.[27]

The bride is the church in her collective unity, the contrasted characters (wise and foolish)

---

26. G. A. Lindsay, *Ephesians: Exposition of the Bible [Expositors Bible]* (American Edition, 1907), p. 42.
27. Some interpret the passage as though it said the virgins are 'the Jewish remnant' who will go out to meet 'the bride' (raptured church) and the groom (Christ) 'at the end of the Tribulation.' Home A. Kent, Jr, *Wycliffe Bible Commentary* (Chicago: Moody Press, 1962), p. 974.

of the members of the church are represented here by the virgins as [in the Parable of the Marriage Feast, Matt. 22:1-14] by the guests who were invited; and for this reason, probably, the bride herself is not introduced as part of the imagery of the parable [of chap. 22].[28]

It is impossible to be sure to what extent earthly human customs reported in Jesus' parables are emblems of heavenly events and truths. But the same language found in Paul's exhortation (Eph. 5:25-28) and in Jesus' Parable of the Wedding Feast and the Parable of the Ten Virgins is carried over in the book of Revelation. There is a connection between 'the marriage supper of the Lamb' for which 'his Bride has made herself ready' (Rev. 19:6-9) and the triumphant return of Christ (Rev. 19:11-21). The 'supper' evidently occurs immediately before the Second Advent of Christ though a strict succession of events is not supplied. Later in the book of Revelation the eternal home of the redeemed is described as 'the holy city, new Jerusalem, coming down out of heaven [to earth] from God, prepared as a bride adorned for her husband' (Rev. 21:2) while a few verses farther on the Revelator says that an angel invited him to see 'the Bride' now the 'wife of the Lamb' and again 'showed me the holy city Jerusalem coming down out of heaven from God' (Rev. 21:9, 10).

Thus the Bible stimulates emotive and imaginative response to expectation of the Christian church as a collective body in which we will participate as individuals. The parables of Matthew 22 and 25 (and several others) enjoin spiritual watchfulness. The 'postmillennium' passages (Rev. 21, 22) stimulate joyful expectation, while the Revelation 19 passages remind us that while we as members of 'the bride' will be without spot and clean, our 'outward garments' will only be as adequate and resplendent as we by 'righteous deeds' prepare them here and now (Rev. 19:8 RSV). Our 'underwear' will be perfect, Christ's imputed righteousness, our visible clothing only as good and as much as we industriously prepare before 'that day.' The judgment of believers at 'the judgment seat of God' (Rom. 14:10) and several other matters relating to the church's future at the *parousia* belong to eschatology in systematic theology and will be treated in that connection.

Meanwhile further brief attention should be directed to how the *ekklēsia* should be advised as to its place in the world as the present eon of the cosmos (*aiōn tou kosmou*) moves toward the Advent of Christ and how we as members of Christ's *assembly* on earth should think and act in view of the Advent.

The church will continue to be formed gradually until the last elect saint has been born spiritually into the kingdom of heaven. (See chap. 13, above, 'The Mission of the Church in the World.') Jesus' last words to the disciples at the moment of His Ascension were not (as often supposed) a command, but a prediction: 'you will be my witnesses in Jerusalem and in all Judea and Samaria, and to the end of the earth' (Acts 1:8). Six weeks before He had said, 'And this gospel of the kingdom will be proclaimed throughout the whole world as a testimony to all nations, and then the end will come' (Matt. 24:14). Whatever expectations believers in every age have for the 'imminent' end of the age, the end is not scheduled until world evangelism – as God sees it – is complete.[29]

It is to be a quiet procedure as far as the Lord is concerned. Just as the ancient temple was built of 'stone prepared at the quarry, so that neither hammer nor axe nor any tool of iron was heard in the house while it was being built' (1 Kgs. 6:7), so of all the 'members' of the ever enlarging *unam sanctum* it is said in Scripture, 'you yourselves like living stones are being built up as a spiritual house' (1 Peter 2:5). 'How silently, how silently, the wondrous gift is given; when God imparts to human hearts, the glories of his heaven.'

---

28. C. J. Ellicott, *Commentary*, Vol. vi (Grand Rapids: Zondervan, repr. 1954), p. 152.
29. We have already traced the process by which the Jerusalem church composed only of Jewish Christians came to realize that evangelization of the world, both Jews and Gentiles, is the Christian mission. The final stage in that process of education is the judicial decision of the conference of Acts 15:1-29. What James pronounced as 'my sentence' (KJV) or 'my judgment' (ESV), translates *krinō*, to announce a judicial decision. This was James in his capacity of presiding officer of the assembled Apostles and elders announcing official consensus. The church knew already that the ends of the world were to be evangelized; now they must acknowledge that every man, woman and child was to be the object of evangelization.

15
The Nature of the Local Church

I. The Distinction Between Universal and Local.

An earlier chapter of this book established the presence, in the New Testament, of a clear distinction (but not separation) between the church universal and the church local. Most of that chapter, however, related to the basis in Scripture for a doctrine of the universal church and extended discussion of how the idea is entertained in the Roman Church and in churches of the Reformation as well as recent times.

Let us recall that out of the about 115 times the word *ekklēsia* appears in the New Testament at least ninety refer to the local church (or churches) and a few more to meetings of the local *ekklēsia*. Emphasis on the local *ekklēsia* is furthered by the fact that authors of several Epistles addressed a single local church or a geographical group of local churches[1] rather than the church at large *directly* or individuals *indirectly*. There is therefore no lack of biblical information regarding the local church, even though no passage expressly defines it.

A very small but significant minority of nineteenth-century Baptist leaders and their followers denied the present existence of the universal church (as we noted in chap. 5 above, p. 28). They thought the only church in the New Testament is the local church, usually explaining apparent universal references such as 'Christ loved the church' and similar (Eph. 5:29) as generic use of the word, as when say 'the farmer tills the soil,' where both farmer and soil are generic, not any particular tiller of the soil or piece of ground. In the twentieth century, H. E. Dana, an important Baptist scholar, competently if not successfully, wrote a book asserting that the idea of a universal church is foreign to the New Testament.[2]

More recently, R. V. Clearwaters, a Baptist pastor and seminary head, wrote that 'the universal church' has no present existence on earth or in heaven. It will come into existence when those believers yet to be born and others now dead receive glorified bodies and are assembled by Christ. The universal church 'is a prospective church.'[3]

II. Definitions of the Local Church.

It is more difficult than it seems at first glance to define what is meant by the generic term 'the local church' or a specific 'local church.' No one who has interest in the topic will deny that such exist; the problem is of including

---

1. Romans, 1 and 2 Corinthians, Galatians, Ephesians (probably), Philippians, Colossians, 1 and 2 Thessalonians, even the book of Revelation.
2. H. E. Dana, *The Christian Ecclesia* (Nashville: Sunday School Board of the Southern Baptist Convention, 1956).
3. R. V. Clearwaters, *The Local Church in the New Testament* (Minneapolis: Central C. B. Press, 1954), pp. 4, 5.

enough in the definition to distinguish a local church from some other religious society while not including elements which exclude genuine local churches. Thomas Oden, a Methodist, for example, defines 'a local or individual church' as 'a company of those who are united in any given place in faith in Christ for worship, proclamation and worship.'[4] The definition is true as far as it goes, but it would eliminate migratory people, who do not remain in one place, and it appears to say that a group of Christians on vacation at let us say Estes Park, Colorado for a day or a week might constitute themselves a 'local or individual church.'

Richard Watson, the first and perhaps greatest systematizer of Methodist doctrines, would add *visible* and *permanent* and prefers *society* to company and adds to his definition 'bound to observe certain rites and to obey certain rules,' concluding, 'the existence of *government* in it is necessarily supposed.'[5] Earlier on the page Watson affirms, 'The church of Christ... consists of all who have been *baptized* in the name of Christ, and who thereby make a visible *profession* of faith in his Divine mission, and in all the *doctrines* taught by him and his apostles.' Thus we have in the contemporary Methodist Oden, a minimal definition, and in the early Methodist Watson, a maximal definition. (All italic type is the present author's emphasis.)

III. Denominational Distinctives in the Definition of the Local Church.

Baptist A. H. Strong's definition in more crisp language agrees with Watson's but qualifies the definition with 'according to Christ's laws,' under which he specifies what mode of baptism (immersion) and the form of government (congregational). Where either of the latter is missing, claims Strong, a Baptist should only out of courtesy call the society (say Episcopal) a church.[6] Not all Baptist authorities agree.

Lutheran F. Pieper's definition adds the Lutheran interpretation of the sacraments of baptism (not the form) and the real presence of Christ's body and blood in the 'sacrament of the altar' and says non-Lutheran congregations are churches, to be sure, but 'heterodox churches.' He specifies 'the Roman Catholic church, the Eastern Catholic church and the Reformed church with its many subdivisions' as heterodox churches.[7]

The *Westminster Larger Catechism* of the Presbyterian Church adds its own distinctive. Reflecting this Catechism, *The Book of Church Order* of the Presbyterian Church in America (P.C.A.) says that 'the visible church... consists of all those who make profession of their faith in the Lord Jesus Christ, *together with their children*' and further, 'It is according to Scriptural example that the church is divided into many individual churches.' The Presbyterian Church in America acknowledges that 'all of these [denominations] which maintain the Word and Sacraments in their fundamental integrity are to be recognized as true branches of the church of Jesus Christ.'[8] Presbyterians have their own way of organizing each local congregation but they do not make these matters of the essence of a local church.

Another view, held by a small minority but prevalent and persistent through the centuries, is summarized by the titles of books on the subject of the church issued in the twentieth century: *The Pilgrim Church;*[9] *The Churches of God;*[10] *The Believers' Church.*[11] A. F. Kuen (*I Will Build My Church*) does not embody the idea in the title, but quotes Tertullian's definition as his own, 'Where there are two or three people, even laymen, there is a church.'[12] The immense literature by modern advocates of the pilgrim church view is cited in these books. Students of church history will recognize the 'restorationist impulse' in nineteenth and twentieth-century forms.

The basic idea common to these restorationists is that Jesus provided a formal pattern for the local church in Matthew 18:20: that wherever there are two or three Christians gathered for worship a local expression of the church universal exists. Many would add that in every such local group all the gifts of the Spirit necessary to teach and lead the congregation are present. Broadbent is typical: 'A church... in the New Testament sense of the word, is, from the moment of its beginning, when two or three are gathered in the name of the Lord Jesus [alluding to

---

4. Thomas Oden, *Life in the Spirit* (San Francisco: Harper Collins, 1992), p. 282.
5. Richard Watson, *Theological Institutes,* Vol. II, ed. J. McClintock (New York: Nelson and Phillips, 1850), p. 572.
6. A. H. Strong, *Systematic Theology,* 29th Printing, pp. 890, 891.
7. Francis Pieper, *Christian Dogmatics,* III (St Louis: Concordia Publishing House, 1953), pp. 422, 423.
8. Part I, chap. 2 of Committee for Christian Education of the Presbyterian Church in America (1020 Monticello Ct., Montgomery, Alabama, 1976), pp. 4, 5.
9. E. H. Broadbent, *The Pilgrim Church* (London: Pickering & Inglis, 2nd ed. 1935).
10. G. H. Lang, *The Churches of God,* English trans., (London: Paternoster, 1959).
11. D. F. Durnbaugh, *The Believers' Church* (London: Macmillan, 1970).
12. A. F. Kuen, *I Will Build My Church,* trans. from French, Ruby Lindblad (Chicago: Moody Press, 1971), p. 51.

Matt. 18:20 as definition of a local church], on the same foundation as the oldest established church, having the same Centre, the same principles... and draws its supplies from the same source.'[13] The Plymouth Brethren will be recognized in the above, yet many in several denominational circles subscribe in principle (see Broadbent's and Kuen's references). Actually I have seen this understanding of the nature of the local church innocently assumed by many among interdenominational groups, composed of members of denominations which reject it – InterVarsity gatherings, city-wide evangelistic 'crusade' meetings, seminary convocations, even a reunion of my own extended family at a mountain retreat.

Two hundred years ago, in the wake of the Great Awakening in Britain, John Wesley did not recognize the meetings of believers for prayer, testimony, instruction and mutual edification as proper churches, advising attendance at the local Anglican churches to receive communion, and so on. Many similar examples exist among Christianized immigrant folk in America who came to faith when evangelized in America and formed new assemblies rather than take communion in an atmosphere of what they felt was 'dead orthodoxy.' To these folk the definition of a local Christian *ekklēsia* became – and remains – important. These are some of the folk Ernst Troeltsch called founders of 'sects' rather than 'churches.' An example is the Evangelical Free Church of America.

Troeltsch did not express any disapproval of sects as opposed to churches. It was for him only a matter of definition. A church (as opposed to a sect) he said, is 'conservative... accepts the social order and dominates the masses... desires to cover the whole of life of humanity.... The sects... are comparatively small groups... aspire after personal inward perfection... and personal fellowship between members of each group.... they work upwards from below.'[14]

IV. What Constitutes a Local Church After the New Testament Pattern?

We all know that a church is a group of Christian people, that they meet together regularly for several purposes, that they observe certain rites and rituals (formal or informal), and that they have certain requirements (formal or informal) for membership and to some degree or other have standards of behavior (explicit or implicit). How much of this is the essence and how much simply universal human features of any limited society? In absence of direct statements we are compelled to rely on precedents set in the Acts and Epistles and inferences.

I propose to define a 'particular' or 'individual' church as a group of mutually acknowledged Christian believers in any place associated permanently together for purposes of doctrinal instruction, mutual vital communion (*koinōnia*), worship and for prayer. Though other features will be present, these constitute the necessary elements of a normal local church. Let us attend to the details.

1. 'A group.' How many are required to form a genuine *ekklēsia*? Are the 'two or three' of Matthew 18:20 sufficient? Probably not. Examination of the context indicates Jesus intended to argue from the lesser to the greater when He said, 'Where two or three are gathered together in my name, there am I in the midst of them.' He had just been speaking of the discipline of delinquent members of 'the church' (vv. 15-19) and of the authority of the church to proceed against the delinquent in a manner recognized in heaven. In verse 18 Jesus is saying, to paraphrase as an argument – if I am present in the midst of a small meeting of two or three I am no less present in the larger meeting of the local *ekklēsia*. Long ago John Gill took note that the revered Tertullian thought that two or three might constitute a church, yet Gill firmly rejected the idea, arguing as follows: two or three are sufficient to meet, to pray together and to edify one another, but not to conduct a 'church' 'judicial process' such as described immediately before. There are an offended party and an offending party. That makes two. Then there are 'one or two others' (v. 16) taken into the process. That makes a possible four. Then, notes Dr Gill,

> If reconciliation cannot be made, the matter must be brought before the church, which must consist of a greater number than the parties before concerned; and which it should seem cannot be less than six more, and in all ten; which was the number of a [synagogue] with the Jews and a church organically considered or as having proper officers, seems to require more; the church at Ephesus was begun with twelve men or thereabouts, Acts 19:7.[15]

---

13. Broadbent, op. cit., pp. 397, 398.
14. Ernst Troeltsch, *The Social Teaching of the Churches*, trans. O. Wyon, Introduction by Richard Niebuhr (New York: Harper & Row, 1911, 1961), p. 331. See pp. 331–372.
15. John Gill, *Complete Body of Divinity*, vol. II (repr. Grand Rapids: Baker Book, 1978), p. 562.

As usual, the devout, amazingly learned, Baptist pastor, Dr John Gill (1697–1771) was correct.

It is objected that there were churches in Crete before the groups had officers (elders, Titus 1:5). Yet Paul indicates that until they had elders they were 'defective' churches (Titus 1:5). Paul seems to reserve for himself and Titus some authority less than apostolical to bring them up to the standard of being 'full-fledged' *ekklēsiae*. They were incipient churches yet without strength (or was it authority?), independent of outside help, to form themselves into a 'standard' church of the New Testament pattern. Hence it seems right to affirm that a meeting of two or three Christians cannot constitute a church and act with Christ's authority. I have been present when a single female adult believer assumed authority by virtue of the presence of Christ in and with her to cure a relative of the 'demon' of a certain kind of psychic difficulty. It didn't work out and I do not hesitate to affirm the lady had no such authority. She had been deceived by other self-deceived zealots.

2. 'Mutually acknowledged professed Christian believers.' A Christian church must be constituted of people who publicly acknowledge that Jesus Christ is Lord and all that implies. A Buddhist must renounce Buddhism and a Muslim, Islam. Syncretism has no home in Christianity. So before admission to a church one must confess that Jesus Christ, and He alone, is Lord and Savior. This he must do to the satisfaction of fellow believers in the *ekklēsia*. This, of course, is utterly inconsistent with the parish system whereby all the 'christened' residents of a specified geographical area constitute a local church. The Reformers struggled with this fact. Luther, much against his wishes, accepted the 'reality' of a true church within the parish church and even thought of organizing meetings for it; Calvin expelled from residence all in the parish who would not meet the standards for a public evangelical Christian. Luther's policy persists in strict Lutheran parishes to the present hour, with slight modification. Among Calvinist churches both the parish (Reformed on the continent; Presbyterian in Great Britain) and gathered church came to exist rather quickly, especially in Britain and America (Congregational and Baptist).

3. 'Associated permanently together.' They are a society in the best sense of that word. When one purchases a ticket for a journey on an ocean liner he may find himself associated with frivolous pleasure seekers, immoral revelers and covetous thieves along with zealous evangelists and missionaries as well as quiet retirees and noisy children. But no one on the ship's roster is committed to any common purpose except a comfortable ride to the destination and then it will all be over. In the church the ties last as long as life. A church is, to use Bonhoeffer's phrase, 'Life Together.' Peter addressed the readers as 'sojourners of the dispersion' almost as if they were practitioners of Judaism in a local synagogue (1 Peter 1:1) but ends his letter referring to 'elders' of 'the flock of God' (1 Peter 5:1, 2 ff.; and to Jesus as chief Pastor, v. 4).

In the ancient world people associated themselves in all sorts of permanent organizations – burial and cemetery associations, traders and skilled workers, banking and finance. More to the point, the Jews in dispersion had formed local associations (synagogues) for carrying on their religion and for mutual encouragement as aliens in a pagan culture. The Jerusalem believers had this example before them and, as Jews, quite unconsciously, we may presume, carried the same sort of associations into their practice of Christianity. Modern scholarship, both Jewish and Christian, has thoroughly researched this matter.[16] This is an ongoing matter among scholars.

There came to be a church at Samaria (Acts 8); after that among Gentiles at Antioch (Acts 13) and elsewhere. In somewhat less than forty years the Jerusalem congregation moved *en masse* to Pella in Transjordan to escape the impending destruction of their city. They were the same church as they migrated and after they settled in a new location.

4. 'In any place.' In New Testament times most people walked where they wished to go. This prevailed among those of limited means until the twentieth century was well advanced. It is three miles from Batavia, Illinois to Geneva, Illinois. In 1894 the Swedish Baptists of Geneva formed a separate congregation and constructed a small house of worship simply because they did not like to walk six miles in order to participate in the 'assembly' – *ekklēsia* – at Batavia. So most congregations outside of towns until very recently were quite small. A group may form anywhere to create a Christian *ekklēsia*. It is evident from a casual reading of the last chapter of Romans that a large city might have numerous more or less permanent assemblies, each with its own elders (= bishops) and deacons (Phil. 1:1).

5. 'For purposes of doctrinal instruction, mutual vital communion worship and for prayer.' This statement rests on the description of the constant practice of the first, apostolically led, assembly at Jerusalem (Acts 2:41, 42) and the correct assumption that if the Word is sufficient guide for Christian practice then the practices of the apostolic churches, especially the first one at Jerusalem, provide some guidance.

---

16. As guide see Commentary on Acts by F. F. Bruce in *New International Commentary* as well as the Strack-Billerbeck *Commentar Zum Neven Testamentum* Vol. II.

The immediately following verses suggest some additional functions of a normal, healthy congregation. They cared for one another's needs. The way they did it proved not to be practical, for they disposed not only of the financial income of their investments but the principal from which the income was derived and soon became so impoverished that collections were taken among Christians far and wide to aid them. Yet the example of mutual concern speaks loudly still. The succeeding chapters tell of their fervent witness to fellow Jews in the concourse which was the temple. Jews from the local province and of the *Diaspora* (see Acts 2:5-11) passed through the temple courts daily, so there the Jerusalem Christians gave their witness daily (Acts 2:44, 45).

V. Relation of Local and Universal and Both to Christ.

'The Evangelical Creeds' – as the third volume of Schaff's *The Creeds of Christendom* designates them and as most evangelical theology emphasize – harbor local, visible churches, some unconverted people, and are all too frequently tragically alienated from one another to some degree. They are nevertheless 'the external and visible form in which the universal church manifests itself on earth. There is no other way for this manifestation to come to pass' (A. J. McClain, unpublished notes by a student). The local church may be distinguished from the universal, but not separated.

The universal church was fully contained in one local church at Jerusalem numerically for a short while. The local made the universal visible insofar as spiritual things are ever visible. The local, which was imperfect in ways soon evident in the behavior of some (Ananias and Sapphira, for example, for there were certainly others) did make the invisible visible in a limited way.

The two are distinguishable in thought and word, yet wherever the local church is there also is the universal. This accounts for Paul's statement at Galatians 1:13 where he said of his persecution of the Jerusalem believers and intended persecution of believers at Damascus, 'I persecuted the church of God.' This occurrence of *ekklēsia* seems clearly to refer to the universal (not generic) church which had members both in Jerusalem and Damascus (Acts 9:1-2).

These local churches are not swallowed up in the universal. The only 'offices' in the church universal on earth were the Apostles and prophets (probably also evangelists) of the first generation.[17] Since then all the offices are local: bishops (= elders, pastors and deacons). Researchers have convinced scholars even of churches which are formed into episcopal districts or dioceses and governed by the diocesan bishop (or other prelate) that this is what the New Testament reflects in every reference to these offices. Roman Catholic dogma does not acknowledge this but many scholars of the Roman Church do. They defend both the governmental jurisdiction of the hierarchical structure and the doctrinal jurisdiction of the magisterium, or teaching office of the hierarchy.

The only 'officers' of the church universal are the members of the Trinity and they are directly accessible without mediation to each local congregation. The congregations everywhere are 'the churches of Christ' (Rom. 16:16) and 'the churches of God' (1 Thess. 2:14) and are supervised not by provincial prelates or district superintendents but by the Holy Spirit (Acts 13:1-3). The Antioch church did not consult any prelate at Jerusalem before deciding the unique (to that time) project of formally launching an 'overseas' mission project. This does not mean that the churches were not connected, for they were, and even united in many respects, but it does mean that they were independent of one another in governance.

This means that the emphasis of the New Testament on the local church is *vital*, that is, essential to the very life (Lat. *vita*) of Christianity. The local church is not merely a branch of a world organization; it is not a man-made affair of little consequence. It is of such value to God and so essential to His work on earth that when a local congregation compromises truth (Rev. 2:14-16) or degenerates into immorality (Rev. 2:20-23) or lapses into indifference (Rev. 3:15-17) God will repudiate the group as a genuine *ekklēsia*, even though they continue 'to hold services' (Rev. 2:5; 3:16).

VI. Membership in the Church.

While the New Testament never declares that local church membership is mandatory for every believer in Christ, it assumes so. If, for example, Aquilla and Priscilla were Christians and lived in Ephesus they were members of an *ekklēsia* there and when they moved back to Rome they had a church in their own house. At the beginning, to become a baptized believer was to be added to the church (Acts 2:47; cf. 5:11; 7:38; 8:1 and 3) – in the context of the first eight chapters of Acts, the church local as well as universal.

---

17. A case may be made that churches seem to regard pastors also as 'officers' of the church universal.

The early chapters of Acts make no mention of a weekly meeting of the local *ekklēsia*: 'Every day they continued to meet together in the temple courts. They broke bread in their homes and ate together' is a correct interpretive rendering of the Greek (Acts 2:46 NIV). Soon, however, like post-exilic Jews everywhere, they met weekly for worship and other religious exercises, but on the first day of the week (1 Cor. 16:1, 2; Acts 20:7; Rev. 1:10) not on the Jewish seventh-day Sabbath. Jewish Christians may also have attended Sabbath synagogue meetings.[18] That they met *weekly* for worhsip distinguished Christians from all their neighbors except Jews, for the heathen, then and now, approached their temples singly or by families. That they met *on the first day* distinguished the *ekklēsia* from the Jewish *synagogue* though the Greek words could apply to either gathering. Regular gathering for worship is an essential *sine qua non* for the church by definition.

Attendance at the weekly meeting (and other meetings), however, did not completely distinguish a believer and member of the local *ekklēsia* from an unbeliever, for non-believers were sometimes present in their weekly gathering (1 Cor. 14:23, 24), and there were false believers as well. As we all know, today, members in a crowd at a given church on Sunday morning may be outnumbered by regular attendees who are not local members. In the ancient church it was not attendance but submission to public water-baptism in the name of Christ which made a local believer a member of that local congregation. As far as the church was concerned, baptism had to be preceded by repentance and faith (Acts 2:38; 16:30-33; 9:1-19; cf. 22:16). Baptism remains today, in lands outside the range of historic Christendom, frequently the signal for persecution as one who has chosen to move *spiritually* from natural family to a Christian association.

VII. Did the Churches Have Membership Rolls?

Was membership in a local church informal, simply the number of Christians who in a locality met regularly as an assembly? Or was membership formal with a roll of particular names – preserved orally or written? After development of the geographical parish system everyone born in the parish, of professed Christian parents, was automatically enrolled.

In any case it is clear that the first church (or its leaders) knew who were and were not members. Even during the first days of waiting for the promised visitation of the Spirit (Acts 1:4, 5) the number of local believers was known to be 'about 120' (Acts 1:15). There was a 'list' – whether written down on parchment or not. Justus and Matthias were known to be on the list (Acts 12:23). Years later Luke knew from some permanent source there were added around 3,000 new believers (Acts 2:41) and later 'the number of the men came to be about five thousand' (Acts 4:4). In the latter case 'men' is *andron*, grown males, in typical Old Testament biblical fashion omitting women and children in a census or numbering of a group of people (e.g. Exod. 12: where 'men' renders *ragli haggibborim*, i.e. male foot soldiers). Luke knew how many and what sex. The instruction to 'the multitude' as 'brethren' to search out seven men of good reputation to serve the neglected widows (Acts 6:1-3) clearly implies certain knowledge of who 'belonged' to the 'multitude' and who did not (Acts 6:1-5). Among a non-literate society this would not imply a written list, but these people were literate Jews and a roll is therefore not excluded.

This was a congregation of Jews who from very ancient times were familiar with formal registers of membership – especially membership in the priestly family of Aaron. The first eight chapters of 1 Chronicles consists of family registers necessary to reinstate Levites and Priests in the restored system of worship. In the close of this register of names, the author tells the readers where he got the information for the new register. He says 'these are written in the Book of the Kings of Israel. And Judah' (1 Chron. 9:1). Ezra 2:59 says some returning from exile could not establish their membership in Israel even though they had returned. Further, certain who claimed to be of priestly families 'sought their registration among those enrolled in the genealogies, but they were not found there, and so they were excluded from the priesthood as unclean.' In view of this it seems likely that a congregation of literate Jews under Jewish leadership would have made an official list of their members.

A clearer indication of a roll with names of members is 1 Timothy 5:9 where regarding indigent widows Paul instructs, 'Let a widow be enrolled,' etc. If a catalog of widows was kept then surely also one for all members. 'Be enrolled' translates *katalegesthō*, from *katalego*, a word which usually means to write in a list or catalog, according to standard lexicons.[19] But the Ephesian congregation to which the instruction first applied was a very large one, mainly Gentile. It is doubtful such people would have relied on anything less than a written list.

---

18. Philip Schaff, *History of the Christian Church* Vol. I (Grand Rapids: Eerdmans, 1960), p. 478.
19. The word occurs only here in the New Testament.

We also know that written messages and names of messengers were passed between apostolically founded churches.[20] These men had been authenticated as members of local congregations. Paul knew Epaphras was 'one of you' (Col. 4:12).[21] Paul's way of writing things down partially accounts for the fact we have fourteen of His epistles in the Bible. It is doubtful that names of Pauline church members would not have been kept in a list. The utter flexibility of membership averred by Quakers and several groups of 'Brethren' does not seem to fit.

VIII. Duties of Membership.

Recent books of theology usually either ignore this topic or devote less than a paragraph to it. The likely reason is that the task of describing and defining is thought to be the task of the pulpit not the theology professor's chair. It is certainly true that all of theology has direct bearing on conduct. Yet rules for conduct are part of theology in Scripture. The first published textbook of systematic theology was a set of ten duties of membership in the commonwealth of Israel – the Ten Commandments engraved on two tablets of stone. The summaries of doctrine in most Reformation creeds and catechisms include the Decalogue. The first great work of evangelical systematic theology, Calvin's *Institutes*,[22] devotes many pages to theological explanation and specific exposition of the Ten Commandments. Let us observe that the doctrine of God in the first commandment is followed by three stating duties to God, followed by six stating duties in relation to mankind. These duties are part of doctrine. But Calvin considered the Decalogue under the locus of God, theology proper, not of the church.

Some separation and placement of topics must be made. Members of Adam's race have certain duties simply as beings created by God, for God and in His image. All human beings are God's servants. Their chief end is to glorify Him. The fact they are disobedient servants does not cancel the obligations. This is not formally an aspect of ecclesiology as such.

Christians take upon themselves the individual obligation to learn the commands of Christ and to do them (Matt. 28:20). It is a responsibility directly between the believing saint and his Lord (Rom. 10:9, 10). This is a lifelong project, never complete.

Further, each believer is also a member of the whole body of Christ, the church universal and, properly, of a local church. It is only one's duties as a part of the body of Christ, and of the local *ekklēsia* in particular, which are of concern to ecclesiology.

The earliest post-New Testament writings, called *The Apostolic Fathers* (about AD 95–100), were deeply concerned about duties of believers as believers and as members of the *ekklēsia*. The chief burden of *Clement to the Corinthians* (ca. AD 95) was proper recognition of elders and rebuke of rebellion against them. The whole Epistle (twenty-eight tight columns in ANF) rebukes envy of leaders, demands repentance, and encourages humility and submission to their presbyters. The Epistle of Polycarp to the Philippians (ca. AD 130), addressed to a church as a church, consists simply of a series of exhortation to virtue and attendance to duties – as deacons, youth, virgins, presbyters and similar. As he is winding down Polycarp makes plain his main concern for conduct of believers in their relations within the church:

> Stand fast, therefore, in these things, and follow the example of the Lord, being firm and unchangeable in the faith, loving the brotherhood [1 Peter 2:17], and being attached to one another, joined together in the truth, exhibiting the meekness of the Lord in your intercourse with one another and despising no one. When you can do good, defer it not, because 'alms delivers from death' [from the apocryphal Book of Tobit 4:10; 12:9]. Be all of you subject to one another [1 Peter 5:5].[23]

In a time of revival this aspect of ecclesiology accompanies renewal of the churches. The eighteenth-century 'Awakenings' in Britain and America exemplify this partnership of a theology of duties of churchmen with expansion and revived health of the church. I cite three examples.

Wesley thought of his works as within the realm of the Church of England. He was an highly educated, ordained Anglican clergyman and regarded the Methodist 'societies' of the Wesleyan movement raised up throughout Britain as within that church; even though they did, even in his lifetime (in America), evolve into congregations of a separate

---

20. Acts 18:27; Rom. 16:1, 2; 1 Cor. 16:10, 17; 2 Cor. 12:17, 18; Eph. 6:21, 22; Phil. 4:18 *et al.*
21. See Gill, II, p. 617.
22. Calvin, *Institutes* II, chap. 8.
23. *Epistle of Polycarp to the Philippians*, Chap x, ANF I, p. 35.

denomination. Wesley rightly thought that these congregations of regenerate people needed a doctrine of the Christian life to guide development of personal holiness toward perfection and the health of each congregation. Entrance to a 'society' did not require my religious rite, for most Britons were christened already with the record already inscribed in a parish roll somewhere. Wesley's 'general rules' for the societies were thirty-three in number. The Ten Commandments, the Sermon on the Mount and the ethics of the Epistles are 'indexed' under three heads: (1) 'By doing no harm by avoiding evil of every kind'; 2) 'by doing good'; 3) 'by attending on all the ordinances of God.'[24]

Contemporary with Wesley and the rise of Methodism was John Gill, perhaps the most-learned Baptist, historical, linguistic and theological scholar who ever lived, also a London pastor, honored by the University of Aberdeen with a doctor's degree in a time when Baptists were excluded from English universities. Though freshly published in a new printing by Baker Book House (1978), Gill's Body of Divinity (1,400 pages) is lamentably not widely read in this hasty age. His ecclesiology has a section 'Of the Duties of Members of a Church to Each Other.'[25] Though different in form it is similar to Wesley's 'Rules.' I close this chapter with some of Gill's best thoughts.

Since a church is united by mutual agreement certain duties necessary for the effectiveness of the agreement and the glory of God follow.

1. The principal duty is 'to love one another.' This is (1) the royal command of Christ as King in His church (John 13:34; 15:12, 17); and (2) Christ's example (John 13:34; 15:12; 1 John 3:16). (3) As a brotherhood they should love one another (1 Peter 2:17; 3:8) as 'members one of another' (1 Cor. 12:13-27). (4) Mutual love is evidence of discipleship (John 13:35); and (5) makes being a Christian in a 'church-state' 'pleasant' and 'comfortable.' He cites Psalm 133; Galatians 5:15; 1 Peter 4:8 and 1:22.

2. 'It is incumbent on church-members' to 'keep the unity of the spirit in the bond of peace' (Eph. 4:3-6) with regard to affection (Phil. 2:2), opinions (1 Cor. 1:10, 11) and doctrines (Eph. 4:5, 13; Phil. 1:27). He emphasizes zeal for wisdom. We should with one consent and one mind glorify God – Gill cites numerous passages.[26]

3. 'It is a duty of church members to sympathize with one another' – there is half a page on this with citation of the example of Job's three friends who called to comfort him when he was sick, also 1 Corinthians 12:26; 1 Thessalonians 4:14; and Galatians 6:2. Members should sympathize with one another in all conditions and circumstances. For all the rather spare language (Gill never rhapsodizes or even decorates with adjectives), one sees the heart of a loving pastor here.

4. They should share with one another in all their natural needs. It is a proof of genuine love for one another (Rom. 12:13; Gal. 6:10; 1 Cor. 16:1, 2; 1 John 3:17). They should also share in spiritual comfort, praying, teaching *and admonishing*. The last is necessary and obligatory, however reluctant one may be to correct the conduct of a brother or a sister.

5. They should watch over one another (Heb. 12:15), and bear with one another.

6. They should pray for one another (Eph. 6:12).

7. On the delicate matter of mixing with the world and worldly people Gill puts up a strong argument (as Wesley did also) for separation. Alluding to several Old Testament and New Testament passages he says:

> It becomes church-members to separate themselves from the men of the world, and not to touch things which are defiling; they are in a church state, which is a garden enclosed; they are a separated people and should dwell alone, and not be reckoned among the nations, or the vain people of a carnal world; they... should not be unequally with men if... ignorant, lawless, disobedient, dead, profane... with whom they can have no profitable communion; and indeed from all such in their own societies [Wesley's word also] who walk disorderly they are directed to withdraw themselves.[27]

Dr Gill goes on to explain this does not mean that 'they are to have no commerce nor correspondence... in civil things' but not 'to keep up' familiar or intimate relations with them.

If church members are to separate themselves from the men of the world they are to associate themselves closely and regularly with one another as they did in the very first church (Acts 2:42) and were admonished later to do, not to forsake the assembling of themselves together (Heb. 10:25). In their assemblies there must be no respect of persons; they are in honor to prefer one another and 'condescend to men of low estate' (Matt. 20:26, 27;

---

24. The Commemorative Edition of the Book of Discipline of the United Methodist Church (Nashville, 1984), pp. 68–71.
25. John Gill, op. cit., pp. 568–573.
26. Zech. 3:9; Rom. 15:6; Prov. 17:14; Phil. 2:3; 1 Cor. 11:16; Phil. 2:1, 2; and 2 Cor. 13:11.
27. John Gill, op. cit., p. 572.

Rom. 12:10, 16). They should be careful to keep the ordinances 'as they were delivered' (an allusion to 1 Cor. 11) and to be examples to one another.

The concerns of this sobering evangelical Protestant theology of the eighteenth century are strikingly similar to the 'theology of the congregation' we found in the apostolic Fathers cited earlier. Though hardly a description of the average Protestant congregation in North America today it remains an ideal – modified by the history of the congregation and their teachers. These ideals prevailed through evangelical Protestant America until radio and television, now the Internet, brought the world into almost all our homes.

One of the greatest historians of the church in America was the late William Warren Sweet, a Methodist scholar of the University of Chicago and Garrett Biblical Institute (Methodist theological seminary in Evanston, Ill.). He researched the minutes of business meetings of very early Baptists, Presbyterians, Congregationalists and Methodists over a period of fifteen years (1931–1946), and published results in four volumes of *Documents of Early American Church History* and as *Religion on the American Frontier*. I read several of these volumes when my daughter, Lorraine, brought them home for assignments in church history at Bethel College. Sweet demonstrates by actual quotation of hundreds of pages from those eighteenth and nineteenth-century congregational minutes that the most common topic of business was maintenance of standards of behavior through discipline of members: not putting others down, but doing exactly what Gill, as reported above, sets forth as duties of church members, including the duty to admonish one another.

Present preoccupation with church growth and pandering (I fear) to tell people what they want to hear, makes this sort of theologizing hardly popular. Perhaps soon God will raise up a popular and forceful exponent of this dreadfully needed theology.

16
The Form of the Church: Organization and Governance

Most people who attend the meetings of a church unquestioningly accept the organization on the local level about the same way they accepted the organization of the family of which they were a part, first as infants. The theory of government is not apparent. Differences in 'style' of worship seem independent of theoretical types of organization. This, of course, suggests that however we think we are organized, some deeper-than-visible principle (superintendency of the Holy Spirit?) may be operating *in spite of defective organization* rather than because of biblically sound organization, assuming there is a prescribed form.

No statement anywhere in the New Testament provides specific instructions on how the church local should be organized and governed. If there is an 'apostolic' pattern it will be discovered in the precedents set by the apostolic missionaries who founded and organized churches and in inferences drawn from apostolic (chiefly by Paul) instructions to their official representatives. In addition, inferences may be drawn from certain incidents such as the conference between the Jerusalem and the Antioch church (Acts 15) and Paul's address to the Ephesian elders (Acts 20), and incidental expressions such as 'those who ... are over you' (1 Thess. 5:12) and 'them that have the rule over you' (Heb. 13:17 KJV), and others (see 1 Peter 5:1-5).

At different junctures of history earnest Christians, often persecuted and at risk of life and limb, have interpreted these data differently, as the names (1) 'Episcopal,' (2) 'Congregational,' (3) 'Presbyterian' and (4) 'Brethren,' with some qualifying adjective, indicate. *Episcopal* means government of congregations of a geographical area (*diocese*) from top down by bishops; *Congregational* means government of congregations independent of any authority outside the local members; *Presbyterian*, though recognizing congregational authority, delegates that authority to a plurality of elders who are 'connected' to elders of a district or presbytery and the presbytery to a synod and the synod to a General Assembly; *Brethren* is the commonest name for several groups who are independent, as in Congregationalism, and sometimes governed by elders as Presbyterians, but have (or so intend) no elder or minister who is chief officer as the rector or vicar (Episcopal) or minister, pastor (Presbyterian and Congregational). Baptists are presently the most well-known practioners of congregational government. There has been a significant number of zealous, evangelical believers who, theoretically at least, reject any local organization except the existence of elders. They reject any organizational connections between congregations altogether.

These facts render it advisable to devote serious prime attention to organization of a local church and its government in apostolic churches.

That the churches of the New Testament had connection with one another and communications is evident from the story of the expansion from Jerusalem to Samaria and Antioch and elsewhere in Acts 8–12. Some sort of co-operation and connection is explicit in the mutuality of all the churches of Pauline establishment as seen in Paul's Epistles to them – as well as with churches of unknown origin (Romans). The General Epistles (Hebrews; James, 1; 2, 3 John) are addressed to every church in the world. Yet there is not even the glimmer of world-wide (universal) organization or any headquarters of government. Scholars of about every denomination, including many highly placed scholars of denominations who might wish it were otherwise, acknowledge this state of evidence.

I. The Fact of Organization.

Though Jesus never provided any 'organizational chart,' or even named any officer of the church except Apostles – who were not really local officers or functionaries *as such* – His words about settling disputes (Matt. 18:15-20) suppose some rudimentary local organization at least. Though no New Testament passage commands organization, evidence of its presence is convincing. A. H. Strong found fourteen kinds of evidence for organization[1] and my seminary professor, who greatly appreciated Strong's ecclesiology, found two or three more. Organization is implied in the New Testament presence of (1) stated meetings (Acts 20:7; Heb. 10:25); (2) choosing of officers (Acts 6:5; 6:3); (3) the presence of officers – bishops and deacons – with ordinary 'saints' (Phil. 1:1); (4) leaders whose authority was to be obeyed (1 Thess. 5:12; Heb. 13:17); (5) the presence of elder-pastors (1 Peter 5:2); (6) instructions for corporate (the whole *ekklēsia*) discipline of members (1 Cor. 5:4-13); (7) instructions for systematic collection of moneys (1 Cor. 16:1, 2; Rom. 15:26); (8) letters of recommendation (Acts 18:27; 2 Cor. 2:3, 9); (9) uniform 'rites' and 'ordinances' (1 Cor. 11); (10) uniform qualifications for offices (1 Tim. 3; Titus 2) – and more.

These features of organization developed over a period of several years among churches which were instructed by the authority of Christ and the Spirit through the Apostles. The learned and devout Baptist John Gill, who wrote over two centuries ago, was one of several who have argued as follows. Jesus specified that the promised Holy Spirit would guide the Apostles into *all the truth* (John 16:13). That truth would certainly include how Jesus, who loved the church and died for her, wanted her to be organized and governed.[2] Similar statements appear in writings of other denominations. But, did those original Apostles ever provide an inspired, written manual of church government? Most certainly they did not. Though the Pastoral Epistles have much to say about the church office of elder or bishop and of deacon, what they say relates to a form of government already in operation in churches established by the Apostle Paul and his assistants and converts. Acts and Revelation also have something to say about messengers (or angels) of the churches and heavenly 'elders.' If we accept all the New Testament books as genuine, originating in the apostolic age, we can draw inferences as to the forms of government which emerged during that period, but not everyone draws the same inferences. We have reason to know that the sub-apostolic Christians esteemed the spoken work of those who heard the Apostles speak more than written documents. They did not everywhere in every area of the world have all the New Testament canon, though by Irenaeus' time (late second century) in Gaul that vigorous writer was citing every book of the New Testament except Hebrews, Philemon, 2 Peter, 2 and 3 John, Jude, and Revelation. He may have known them too. He simply had no reason to quote them in Writings, which have come known to us. Earlier, in the time of transition to the sub-apostolic age (AD 85–125, which includes the writings of Ignatius, first-known patristic advocate of local government centered in a bishop *and* elders), the Pastoral Epistles may not have been sufficiently dispersed to be read in every church.

The Jerusalem church quickly grew to enormous proportions, including Gentiles unacquainted with any previous form of biblical religion and numerous indigent people. These thousands of people formed a distinct community, not merely a segment of the population who meet regularly for worship. Their religious concerns are described quickly in Acts 2:42 ff. But in addition there was work to be done: (1) the special instruction of new believers; (2) the gathering of funds and their administration to care for the poor and perhaps to support some of the leaders; (3) general guidance of the community in a time of persecution and the stress of poverty; and (4) discipline of erring members. We see all this happening in Acts 1–9. And though we find evidence of the same in all the churches, the way the Jerusalem church did these things was only in a limited degree a pattern for all churches everywhere.

---

1. A. H. Strong, *Systematic Theology*.
2. John Gill, *Complete Body of Divinity* II (Grand Rapids: Baker Books, repr., 1978), p. 559 ff.

II. The Apostolic Pattern of Church Organization.

There was an element present in the Jerusalem church that somewhat distorts the picture – the presence of Apostles. We would have to know how the Jerusalem church was governed after there were no Apostles remaining there to get a clear picture of polity in that apostolically founded church. Peter exercised discipline (Ananias and Sapphira, Acts 5) on his own authority. Apostles *told* the church to choose seven men (deacons?) to 'serve tables' and care for 'business' (Acts 6:1-5 KJV) and Apostles 'prayed and laid their hands on them' (v. 6). Nothing like that happened again in the New Testament record. We must consult what apostolically founded churches did, as reported in the New Testament. We also desire to know how the Apostles (specifically Paul) set up the government of local churches and what indirect and directly stated information can be gathered from the Epistles and Revelation.

That the Apostles did not control all the inner workings of the early Jerusalem church in detail is suggested by the fact that even Peter had to give account of his actions at Caesarea (Acts 10) to 'brethren' who had been opposed to what he had done (Acts 11:1-4, 18 KJV), not only to the other Apostles. Shortly after, 'the church which was in Jerusalem' (not just its Apostles or other officers) 'sent forth Barnabas' on an investigative mission to Antioch (Acts 11:22 KJV). It is not said to be a disciplinary mission. And only a little later we first are informed there were 'presbyters' (or elders) in the Jerusalem church who received the charitable gifts of the church from Antioch (Acts 11:30). After that at the new *ekklēsia* at Antioch, 'the Spirit,' probably through one of the prophets present (Acts 13:1), said 'Separate me Barnabas and Saul' (v. 2 KJV). The message was to the church not *from* it. The church obeyed by renewed fasting and prayer and then laid hands on them and 'they [the church] sent them away' (vv. 2, 3).

Barnabas and Saul (also briefly Mark) began their 'work' at Cyprus, but though there were some victories for the gospel, apparently no church was founded in Cyprus. Back on the mainland to the north at Antioch of Pisidia (Acts 13:14-50) they preached the gospel, making some disciples, and then moved on to Iconium, Lystra, Derbe and environs.

The two missionaries, with their new disciples, suffered severe persecution by Jews and then by Gentiles also in Iconium and Antioch. So they moved on to Derbe where they worked and waited (14:20) until, as W. M. Ramsay suggests, there was a change in officers in the cities where they had been.[3]

At this point something of great importance for our understanding of apostolic church organization occurred. Paul and Barnabas returned to the places (Lystra, Iconium and Antioch, Acts 14:21-24) where they had made numerous disciples in the preceding months for the purpose of confirming 'disciples' (13:52; 14:20, 22) and organizing the churches. To this point the Acts record has informed us about elders, perhaps deacons (Acts 6), of messengers sent by churches, meetings for prayer, preaching, and business but nothing else of congregationally organized structure for governance.

Sir W. M. Ramsay, after thorough preparation in the necessary languages and thorough geographical, archaeological and literary research, wrote a corpus of literature on Paul's life and work – still valued today, though ignored by present reigning critical scholarship. He showed that Luke in writing Acts regularly followed certain principles, which Ramsay sets forth.[4] (1) Luke was acquainted with Paul's letters – 'he was in Paul's company when he wrote them – and consciously provided historical background for them' (p. 16 *passim*). (2) 'Luke's style is compressed,' providing only an 'uncolored recital of important facts in briefest possible terms' (p. 20). He leaves out any detail not necessary to his purpose (p. 17). (3) 'Luke had studied the sequence of events carefully, and observes it in his arrangement minutely,' but after carrying one thread of the narration forward he 'goes back in time to pick up another thread' without saying he is doing so (p. 18). (4) He lets facts speak for themselves (p. 21). (5) He employs 'first case' of each feature of the mission work to indicate what was normal procedure in all subsequent cases (p. 21).

These principles bear directly on the meaning of Acts 14:21-23. *First*, Luke does indeed let the facts speak for themselves (v. 21); *second*, his style is compressed, with little or no interpretation, 'uncolored recital of important facts in briefest possible terms' (p. 20); *third*, his narrative is chronological, though he will carry one thread to a point and return to pick up another (v. 18); *fourth*, of supreme importance, when he reports what Paul did in the 'first case is intended to be typical of the way… of all later cases' (p. 121).

Let us hold in mind as we read the critical passage that this is the first and only place in all the New Testament that we are told how an Apostle organized a church. Its very brevity tells us much. It was not complicated.

---

3. W. M. Ramsay, *St. Paul the Traveller and Roman Citizen* (New York: Putmans, 1897, and many reprints), p. 120.
4. ibid., pp. 14–20.

They returned to Lystra and to Iconium, and to Antioch, confirming the souls of the disciples, exhorting them to continue in the faith, and that through many tribulations we must enter into the kingdom of God. And when they had appointed for them elders in every church (*kat' ekklēsia*), and had prayed with fasting, they commended them to the Lord on whom they had believed (Acts 14:21-23 RV, RSV).

Let the following be noted.

1. There was a sizeable group of 'disciples' in each place. (See Acts 13:42, 48, 52; 14:20.) There was no mere two or three gathered in the name of the Lord. Evidently in Cyprus, where the two missionaries made only a very few disciples, they apparently organized no church.

2. The fundamental element in organization of a church is the installation of elders. Paul instructed Titus to 'set in order the things that are lacking,' specifically to 'appoint elders in every city.' Evidently this was not a novel procedure, but a settled policy, for it was 'as I [previously] commanded you' (Titus 1:5 NKJV). Paul does not say, 'In every *ekklēsia* appoint elders,' but 'in every city' (*kata polin*). The group of believers in a city were not an *ekklēsia* until they had properly installed elders. William Ramsay sagely observed:

> It is probable that in [Paul's] estimation, some definite organization was implied in the idea of a church; and until the brotherhood in a city was organized, it was not in the strictest sense a church. In this passage [Acts 14:21-23] we see that the fundamental part of church organization lay in the appointment of Elders (*presbuteroi*). In [Acts] 13:1 we found there were prophets and teachers in the Antiochian [i.e. of Syria] church... nothing is said about appointing them, but the reason indubitably is that prophets and teachers required divine grace, and could not be appointed by men: they were accepted when grace was found to have been given them.[5]

3. How elders were selected is a matter of some uncertainty. Authorities[6] show 'appointed' (v. 23) could mean either election by the group or designation by Barnabas and Paul.

> The term (*cheirotonesantis*, from *cheirotoneō*) is by no means certain in meaning; for, though originally it meant to elect by popular vote (show of hands), yet it came to be used in the sense *to appoint* or *designate* (e.g. Acts 10:41). But it is not in keeping with our [Ramsay's] conception of the precise and pragmatically accurate [mode of] expression of Luke, that he should in this passage have used the term... unless he intended its strict sense.... It must, I think, be allowed that the votes and choice of each congregation were considered; and the term is obviously used in that way by Paul, 2 Corinthians 8:19.[7]

It remains to be said (1) that Paul's instructions to Titus make certain that *elder* (presbyter) and *bishop* (overseer) designate the same office, the former the title of office and the latter the duties or functions (Titus 1:5 and 7, where the words are used interchangeably). Further, (2) Luke supplies no details about how 'candidates' were brought forward, neither does Titus 1:5 ff. It appears that one could present himself for the office (1 Tim. 3:1) and, in Paul's exhortation at Miletus (Acts 20:28), it also appears that the Holy Spirit makes men bishops. Probably the process of choosing candidates was informally conducted, even as in small churches today. The missionaries emphasized that 'through many tribulations [such as Paul and Barnabas had endured in their towns] we must enter into the kingdom of God' (Acts 14:22). It certainly would have crossed people's minds that local church leaders would become marked for persecution, hence seekers for power and attention would hardly have applied for election to office. The same qualifications Paul later set forth in 1 Timothy 3 and Titus 1 would have been applied in securing candidates for the office.

III. Source of the Apostolic Pattern.

An acknowledgment is in order: what most call 'the apostolic pattern' – and I have concurred up to this point – is by a few scholars called 'the pattern in Pauline churches,' i.e. not necessarily in every church. Bruce L. Shelley reflects this outlook, when he writes:

> The churches in Asia Minor [also Greece], under Paul's oversight, probably adopted a style of leadership based on a plurality of elders (Acts 14:23).
> Jerusalem retained a loyalty to the family of Jesus and looked to Christ's half brother, James, as a Christian counterpart of the ruler of the synagogue (Acts 15:13). James was succeeded by another half brother, Simeon.

---

5. ibid., pp. 120, 121.
6. *TDNT*; Liddell and Scott; Bauer, Arndt & Gingrich.
7. Ramsay, op. cit., p. 122.

We also know that Titus and Timothy, while not Apostles, assumed a kind of superintendent's role toward some of the congregations under Paul's oversight (Titus 1:5 and Philippians 2:19-24). Church history, as well as the New Testament, teaches us that the church can and has survived changing times and cultures by adapting its basic message and mission to changing forms [of government].[8]

Dr Shelley, who is a church historian and an evangelical Baptist, goes on to say that the nature of the church and its mission are revealed in the New Testament, but not a 'rigid pattern of government for all local churches,' adding: 'But the Gospel of Christ and the Spirit's presence are more important than the particular forms in which they find expression.'[9]

Furthermore, as many good scholars have noted, the Pastoral Epistles do not announce a formal constitution according to which every church must be built. Rather, Paul is writing about an already existing reality. The fact of organized churches precedes the regulations Paul sets forth.

Lindsay, who contended the Pauline pattern was practically universal, wrote in a similar spirit:

> Without any apostolic sanction, in virtue of the power lying within the community and given to it by the Master, the church of the second century effected a change in its ministry quite as radical, if not more so, as that made by the Reformed church in the sixteenth century, when it swept away medieval excrescences, restored the bishops to their ancient position of pastors of congregations, and vested the power of oversight in councils of greater and lesser spheres of authority [Presbyterian pattern]. What was within the power of the Christian people of the second century belongs to it always when providential circumstances seem to demand a change in the organization, for the ministry depends upon the church and not the church on the ministry.[10]

Paul asserted more than once that the union of Gentiles and Jews as 'fellow heirs' and 'fellow members' of the body was a 'mystery' revealed first in time to him and other 'holy apostles and prophets' of that time (Eph. 3:4, 5). But the New Testament has no record of any similar special revelation of exactly what form the assemblies (*ekklēsiae*) were to take, how to be organized and governed as societies. The form evidently was in large part derived from the inheritance of custom in which every orthodox Jew of the time grew up – the synagogue.

Perhaps beginning as early as the exile of Ezra, certainly for several centuries before Christ, Jews of Palestine and the Diaspora had formed local societies for worship; instruction of youth; and other social, civil and religious purposes. Both the assembly and the building where it met were called by the Greek word, a *sunagōgē* (synagogue), though primary reference at first was to the assembled people – from Greek *sun* (with, together) and *agō* (to lead or bring). (*Sunagō* is used at Matthew 2:4 and more than forty times in the New Testament for 'assemble, bring together.') *Ekklēsia* has the meaning of 'called out.' Hence the two words, like repentance and faith, represent two aspects of one thing, one negative, the other positive. Once in the New Testament (James 2:2) a Christian assembly is called a synagogue. In the Greek Old Testament *ekklēsia* often refers to gatherings of representatives of 'all Israel,' but seldom, if ever, of the nation itself or of local gatherings.

So it is very likely that Paul used the term *ekklēsia* for a gathering together (*sunagōgē*) consistently for the new entity, the local Christian assembly, thus avoiding confusion with the assemblies of Judaism by making a distinction in nomenclature. Paul himself may have been chief influence in giving this name to the church. Luke, author of Acts, uses the word *ekklēsia* in his history down to Acts 14:22 but never in the speech of any Christian. *Ekklēsia* is always Luke, the historian's, word. Matthew is the only Gospel writer to use *ekklēsia* (Matt. 16:18 and 18:17). He does so twice but only in Jesus' speech. But we do not know what the Aramaic word He employed was – perhaps *kenishta*, related to *keneseth*, a good Hebrew word for Old Testament gatherings and the word modern Israelis use for their national parliament.

Three-fourths of the about 110 times *ekklēsia* is used in the New Testament it is by Paul or Luke, his friend and biographer. All the others (except James 5:14) wrote *after* Paul had done his work. And James also called the Christian assemblies a *sunagōgē*.

These facts are well known to scholars and most scholars competent to have an opinion think it more than likely, close to a certainty, that Paul, an upper-class Jew, raised in the synagogue at Tarsus and educated in the system of the synagogue at Jerusalem, carried useful and appropriate features of synagogue governance and worship into the Christian *ekklēsia*.

---

8. Bruce Shelley, *The Church: God's People* (Wheaton, IL: Victor Books, 1978), pp. 50, 51.
9. ibid.
10. T. M. Lindsay, *The Church and the Ministry in the Early Centuries* (Minneapolis: The James Family, repr. 1977), p. 210.

It is, of course, possible that Paul and other Christians collaborated in deciding whether *ekklēsia*, *sunagōgē* or some other should be adopted. If so, reasons suggested by Wolfgang Schrage in the *Theological Dictionary of the New Testament* might have been decisive.

Schrage says that the word 'synagogue' in New Testament times had come to mean the building more than the Jewish congregation and was hence unsuitable for the fledging churches, but he asserts:

> Above all... the synagogue was very closely bound up with the *nomos* [law] and *paradosis* [rabbinical tradition]... This alone makes it easy to see why *sunagōgē* could not be used in self-designation by a community to which the central position of the Law expressed in the name *sunagōgē* had become suspect because it [the people of the church] knew it was constituted not by Moses and observance of the Law, but by the eschatological Christ event.[11]

In a similar way Protestants in general and evangelicals in particular prefer terms like 'world-wide church' or simply 'the church' to either 'catholic' or 'ecumenical,' either of which is technically applicable for the whole visible church.

Further, each of the Twelve was a Palestinian Jew. Post-biblical Jewish sources about Judaism in the time of Jesus and the book of Acts are not contemporary, while the Gospel's accounts are contemporary. From the Gospels we know that many Jewish communities, probably all, in Palestine had synagogues (buildings), synagogue organization and government and regular services for worship, instruction in the Law and the Prophets, education of children and other social purposes. Many scholars today think it likely that the Palestinian synagogues developed from the *ma amadoth*, (literally *places of standing*). These 'were divisions of the people... which were intended to correspond to the twenty-four courses of the priests.'[12] Each *ma amad* (singular) assembled to hear reading of Scripture passages being synchronously read by its priests at the temple. Jewish tradition in the *Mishna* (*Taanith* IV. 2) traces the custom back to Moses' command at Numbers 28:2, as Bowker explains.[13] It seems therefore quite inevitable that some synagoue custom and practice should be deeply ingrained into these twelve orthodox 'children of the synagogue' (including Mathias) and should have been carried by them into the Christian *ekklēsia*.

In stark contrast, none of the personnel (Levites, priests and similar) or ritual practices appears at all in the primitive Christianity of the New Testament. They sang the Psalms, not because some of them were part of the developed temple ritual, but because they were in their Bible and were a part of the synagogue worship to which they were accustomed and – it is right to say – socialized.

But the first Christians finally were cut loose from the theology and fellowship of the synagogue by the events of Acts 10 and 11 and onward to the conference between Antioch and Jerusalem (Acts 15:6-32). The leading members were still all Jewish and former members of the synagogues and preserved synagogue learning and many of its social practices. It was inevitable that the *ekklēsia* should preserve the best of the synagogue.[14]

When the Dead Sea Scrolls first came to public attention in 1947 and for more than fifteen years thereafter, there was great interest in discovering what effect their contents might have on our understanding of Christian origins and the early church. The excitement of the time – in which I participated as a young professor of Old Testament and theology – produced a number of very radical theories: too much to report here. In the decades since, however, scholarship – particularly swayed in opinion by Christian presuppositions – has not found direct connections between Qumran and its literature with the New Testament literature and the church. They do, however, find that many forms of expression of Jewish piety at Qumran paralleled Jewish-Christian forms of expression in the churches at Jerusalem and elsewhere. Citing Millar Burrows of Yale – one of the first to examine the scrolls and who gave years to their study – James C. VanderKam observes:

> [T]he more convincing resemblances were to be seen in matters such as communal structure (12 nonpriests in the Qumran council parallel the 12 apostles) forms of worship (baptism, [sacramental] meal), practices (community of goods), doctrines (dualism of light and darkness, a righteousness conferred by grace),[15] etc....[16]

---

11. Wolfgang Schrage, *TDNT*, Vol. vii, p. 829.
12. John Bowker, *The Targums and Rabbinic Literature* (Cambridge: Cambridge Univ. Press, 1969), p. 9.
13. ibid., note 1, p. 10.
14. The synagogue developed as a way for the Jewish people to continue their worship of God in want of the temple – either by reason of distance from it while the temple remained standing or because it had been destroyed (as for several generations after 586 BC and perpetually since AD 70). In New Testament times there were synagogues wherever there were Jews.
15. I disagree with VanderKam here. The Qumran people thought they made atonement without propitiating sacrifice through their acts of meritorious piety.
16. James C. VanderKam, *The Dead Sea Scrolls Today* (Grand Rapids: Eerdmans, 1994), pp. 161, 162.

VanderKam continues, directly quoting Burrows:

> For myself I must go further and confess that after studying the Dead Sea Scrolls for Seven years [he wrote in the late 50s] I do not find my understanding of the New Testament substantially affected. Its Jewish background is clearer and better understood, but its meaning has neither been changed nor significantly clarified.[17]

William White, Jr, trained at Westminster Seminary and holding a doctorate from a great Jewish university, summarizes in an important article, entitled *Synagogue*: 'The most important legacy of the first century synagogue was the form and organization of the apostolic church.'[18] Prof. James Hadley of Yale similarly, in another thorough article, said, 'The synagogue... was the order with which the first Christian believers were most familiar, from which they were most likely to take the outlines or even the details, of the worship, organization, government of their own society.'[19] J. L. Drumwright, Jr, writes, 'It was required that any community that contained ten males above 12 years of age support a synagogue.'[20]

There is supreme importance to this fact, for each synagogue (assembly) was an independent unit, not created or sponsored or governed by a central authority, though there was a commonly held understood constitution, both written and customary. It was governed by its own elders chosen by the people themselves. The elders had powers derived from custom and delegated by the people.

IV. Church Organization and Government Onward from Apostolic Times.

Summary of the Apostolic Age.

Government in the churches of the apostolic age was by a college of elders – always plural, though we do not know how many. The people themselves decided who was qualified according to the stiff qualifications (1 Tim. 3:1-7; Titus 1:5-9) and installed them. After being installed these elders were those that 'are over you' and 'them that have the rule over you.' The people who chose them were obliged to 'respect' them, 'to esteem them very highly,' 'Obey ... and submit to them' (1 Thess. 5:12; Heb. 13:17 KJV). These elders are also called overseers (or bishops) and pastors. Their authority, in the New Testament, is always held jointly, though there was a division of labor among them. Deacons had no ruling authority.

This pattern was already in retreat at the beginning of the second century. Ignatius, bishop of Antioch, martyred at Rome AD 110, wrote letters to his own congregation and to many others in seven presently acknowledged genuine Epistles. These letters clearly indicate that Ignatius was fully aware he was urging a change, owing to the exigencies produced by heresies and persecution. Careful reading of the letters shows that some of the churches addressed had a single bishop and a college of elders while others had the older college of bishops (=elders) and no president. '[E]very Christian community ought to have at its head a bishop, a... session of elders, and a body of deacons... to whom, jointly and severally obedience is due.'[21] That this soon became *kath' holou* (i.e. *catholic*) is conceded by scholarly writers generally. Lindsay, quoted here, goes on to say, 'There is not a trace of sacerdotalism in the sense that the Christian ministry is a special priesthood set apart to offer a special sacrifice.'[22] He adds, 'There is no apostolic succession in any form whatsoever,' and 'there is no trace of diocesan rule' (Lindsay, 197). Again, this is a near unanimous consensus among scholars who hold to the genuineness of the New Testament books, and whether advocates of government by bishops of territorial dioceses or not.[23]

---

17. ibid., see also John J. Collins, *The Scepter and the Star: The Messiahs of the Dead Sea Scrolls and Other Ancient Literature* (New York: Doubleday, 1995) p. 270. Adela Yarbro Collins, *Cosmology and Eschatology in Jewish and Christian Apocalypticism* (London: E. J. Brill, 1996), p. 261. John J. Collins, *Apocalypticism in the Dead Sea Scrolls* (London & New York: Routledge, 1997), p. 187.
18. Wm. White, Jr, Zondervan *Pictorial Encyclopedia of the Bible*, p. 556.
19. James Hadley, 'Synagogue' in *Smith Dictionary of the Bible*, Vol. iv, p. 3133.
20. J. L. Drumwright, Jr, 'Synagogue' in *Wycliffe Bible Encyclopedia*, Vol. II, p. 63.
21. T. M. Lindsay, op. cit., p. 196.
22. op. cit., p. 196.
23. Perhaps the best summary of supporting historical evidence for this consensus was written by Philip Schaff in his *History of the Christian Church*, Vol. I, 488 ff. T. M. Lindsay's *The Church and the Ministry in the Early Centuries*, cited frequently here has convincingly summarized the evidence of Scripture and history. Alexander Strauch, *Biblical Eldership: An Urgent Call to Restore Biblical Church Leadership* (Littleton, CO: Lewis and Roth, 1988, 288 pages) practically exhausts the subject, including useful practical suggestions for implementing the restoration of the New Testament order in churches of any evangelical denomination.

It is plain to be seen that some variety of the threefold ministry (pastor, elders, deacons) is what prevails today in Protestant churches – with varieties everywhere. The one designated 'the pastor' or 'senior pastor' has a board of advisors or associates (Baptist deacons, Presbyterians elders, Episcopal wardens and vestrymen) and a third layer of lay officials who care for property, superintend 'alms' or charities, finances, and similar. There are many varieties.

The essence of the change was simply that in a church of the apostolic age the ruling body in every congregation was a session of elders without a 'president' or 'superior,' while by mid-second century the ruling body became a session with a president.[24] Without retreating from his 'Brethren' insistence on perpetuating the New Testament pattern, Alexander Strauch has published a very helpful book both on the New Testament pattern and how approximation can be achieved within existing polities.[25]

A. H. Strong produced what is perhaps the most persuasive 'modern' defense of strict independency and congregational government. He expresses preference for a single elder, or pastor, rather than plurality, arguing that the only reason for more than one in apostolic times was the large size of a congregation – in spite of the fact that most New Testament references to local church elders are in plural number: 'a plural eldership is natural and advantageous only where the church is very numerous and the pastor needs assistants in his work: and only in such cases can we say that New Testament example favors it.' James, he thinks, was 'pastor' of the Jerusalem church. He finds direct scriptural support for one elder or bishop for each congregation in the fact that several passages refer to 'the bishop' in singular number (1 Tim. 3:2; Titus 1:7) but to 'deacons' in plural number (1 Tim. 3:8, 10, 12). So too, each of the seven churches of Revelation 2 and 3 had but one 'angel,' interpreted as pastor.[26] So this Baptist did not think that the threefold ministry (pastor-bishop, elders, deacons) was a change from the New Testament pattern. He evidently had not carefully read the scholarly sources he cites. There was indeed a change from practice in the apostolic age, fully effected by the end of the second century.

Modern Anglicans, not all of whom readily accept that there was a change, explain it as a natural development in absence of any direct dominical or apostolic commandment to the contrary. Ignatius' 'earnestness implies apostolic sanction. Episcopacy must have originated before the apostles had all passed away; and its strength in Asia cannot be explained without some encouragement from St. John,' according to Gwatkin.[27] He goes on to propose, among other things, that perhaps several 'vicars – apostolic' like Timothy might have remained at their posts after their apostolic superiors died.

Good scholars have suggested four reasons why churches enacted the change.

First, J. B. Lightfoot (an Anglican bishop) suggested in his famous *Commentary* on Philippians[28] that it first appeared in Asia Minor in order to have a single voice in each congregation to speak for all. In a society already accustomed to one-man rule in secular affairs, this arrangement helped to stand up to the temptations of persecution and false teaching very prevalent in the East, according to Lindsay.[29]

Second, W. M. Ramsay suggested that perhaps when an elder was assigned oversight as a supervisor (Gr. *episkopos* =bishop) of any special duty and did well, he might continue permanently and come to represent the church to outsiders.[30]

Third, Lindsay points out that (as at the Last Supper) only one should preside and that one, if he presided repeatedly, would easily become *the* bishop. He who presided at this highest position of worship would be regarded with special respect.[31]

Fourth, my own opinion regarding the modification is as follows.

1. We know from evidence of Acts and the Epistles that organization and governance in the first congregation were not invariably followed in other New Testament churches. To give an example, Peter by his own authority denounced and judged Ananias and Sapphira, but Paul enjoined the churches as such to take charge of discipline.

---

24. See Lindsay, 205.
25. Strauch, ibid.
26. A. H. Strong, *Systematic Theology*, pp. 915, 916.
27. H. W. Gwatkin, a Cambridge professor of Ecclesiastical History, 'Church Government in the Apostolic Age,' *Hastings Dictionary of the Bible*, Vol. I, p. 441.
28. J. B. Lightfoot, *Commentary on Philippians*, 1881, 6th ed., p. 206.
29. Lindsay, op. cit., pp. 206, 207.
30. Ramsay, *The Church in the Roman Empire*, 1893, p. 367 ff.
31. Lindsay, op. cit., p. 208.

2. The Pauline instructions regarding plurality of elders ('elders in every city,' and the like) neither forbid nor prescribe that one should preside and lead.

3. The presence of a 'chief executive officer,' subject to the will and authority of the body of people whom he leads develops in almost every group as a natural (in the good sense) tendency. Thus there was 'the ruler of the synagogue' (*ho archi-sunagōogos*, Luke 13:14; Acts 18:8).

4. To be 'pastors and teachers' was and is a special gift of Christ to the church (Eph. 4:11). But some elders were 'teachers of the Word and doctrine' and some were not.

5. We also know that in early post-apostolic times the presiding elder-bishop-pastor might not be a teacher of the congregation.

It seems, therefore, that in developing the threefold ministry the churches acted not only obediently but probably wisely. They modified the form of local church organization *within the parameters of New Testament precedent and instruction*.

It is beyond the present project to trace how local church independence with co-operation within the church according-to-the-whole (*kath' olikos, katholic*) devolved into territorial episcopal dioceses and thence to primacy and jurisdiction of the bishop of the diocese of Rome. ('Diocese' is derived from *dia* plus *oikeo* 'to manage all the house… to conduct the affairs of a state,' Liddell and Scott, *Lexicon*.) The whole idea was borrowed from imperial Roman government administration, and after legal establishment was imposed upon the churches of the Roman Empire.

Standard works on ecclesiology usually dismiss the 'Plymouth Brethren' and other earlier and later groups who have sought to perpetuate the most primitive apostolic pattern. Current leaders and writers of the 'Brethren' and related authors insist that wherever a group of believers come into being the gifts of pastor-teacher will be present among them, along with other gifts as needed, but that there should be no single person (pastor, minister) who heads the congregation and who wields any special authority. Ordination to 'the Ministry' is said not to exist.[32] The similar views of Watchman Nee and Witness Lee of 'The Little Flock,' important among Chinese Christians everywhere, are available in the thesis of James Cheung at Trinity Evangelical Divinity School library where the literature of the movement is listed and summarized, as noted earlier.[33]

These authors all seek to demonstrate from the New Testament the same picture of apostolic church order set forth earlier in this chapter and now widely acknowledged. They also argue that (1) the primitive order was uniform through all the ancient churches; (2) that it was designed to be permanent, operative in every culture; and (3) that departure from strict independence to any formal organized 'connectionalism' is both wrong and damaging to the church. There is no room for Christ-approved development or expediency in determining the form of church organization and government after the death of the Apostles.

History provides numerous examples of groups disgusted with the rigid and sterile structure of the church who have withdrawn and claimed to worship and serve God without any structure save the Bible and impulses of the Holy Spirit.

Shelley remarks: 'History shows how rapidly these movements developed their own forms, their own distinctive customs, beliefs, and organizational structure and forms of government.'

---

32. See *The Pilgrim Church* by E. H. Broadbent (London: Pickering and Inglis, 1935); A. Strauch, *Biblical Eldership*, 2nd ed. (Littleton, CO: Lewis & Roth, 1988); D. L. Norbie, *New Testament Church Organization* (Chicago: Letters of Interest n.d.); and A. F. Kuen, *I Will Build My Church*, trans. Rudy Lindblad (Chicago: Moody Press, 1971).

33. Mr Cheung's book was suppressed after threats of legal action from some leaders of the movement.

17
Church Polity: Theories of Church Government

It is customary to say that there are three theories of church polity or government: *Episcopal*, *Presbyterian* and *Congregational*. In practice, however, presently and through the centuries, there has been both a moderation of the differences with borrowing of one from another and elevation of some distinct feature or mutation to a point the name no longer applies exactly. And one sort, say of episcopal government, may be utterly unlike any other of the category.

Episcopal.

Very early, the prevalent episcopal system in the eastern portion of the church in the Roman Empire, the organized church, became closely attached to the government of the emperor (the current Caesar). This form of church government has been called *Caesaro-Papism*, though nominally episcopal. Similarly, but in a different way, the western (Latin, Roman) part of the Empire became subject to the bishop of the diocese of Rome. This developed over many centuries. The system is rightly called *Papal* or *Papist* (formerly the standard word among Protestants), i.e. subject to the supreme authority of the Papa (Father) or universal bishop of Rome. And there came to be two Roman theories: Gallicanism and Ultramontanist views. The latter ascribes the pope's power to direct authority from Christ and from the pope to the bishops. The former holds that the bishops get their authority directly from Christ, the same as the pope does. Gallicanism has lost badly in modern times.

When the papal church of England cut loose from the papal court and became a national, English, episcopally governed church three or more theories developed within the system. (1) Erastianism, in which the king of England is head of the church in the same way the Roman pontiff is head of the papal church. (2) The *high church*, which maintains the divine right of episcopacy and that such is of the esse, very existence, of the church. (3) The *low church* party treat episcopacy as a matter of usefulness, not required by Scripture as necessary to the being of the church. In *Methodism* the bishops and district superintendents are each merely one presbyter-pastor who has been selected for a fixed term to supervise the churches of an area. In *Methodism*, episcopacy 'is neither diocesan nor hierarchical, but itinerant and presbyterial.'[1]

---

1. D. S. Schaff, 'Episcopal church,' *Schaff-Horzog Encylopadeia of Religious Knowledge*, Vol ii, p. 746.

It is therefore reasonable to say what is called *episcopal* is not one theory and practice but several (episcopacies). It is also true that in recent times, especially in North America, popular democratic sentiment has penetrated every system to the degree that both presbyterian and congregational features appear in the government of most denominations, not least Anglicans and Episcopalians and not excluding the Roman Church, for good or ill.

When Anglican-Episcopalian scholars explain the origin of their system several explanations come forth.

1. The 'high church' explanation goes like this. The order of bishops is a continuation of the apostolate. When Jesus remained on earth He was governor of the church. He kept them near Himself to teach them how to teach and govern others, so to be qualified as bishops of the church later. In the interval between His resurrection and Ascension He explained their future duties as bishops and imparted special authority to them as apostle-bishops to discharge duties implied. Matthew 28:19, 20 and John 20:21, 22 are said to be directed to Apostles only. Soon after the Ascension they received extraordinary gifts, as Jesus promised, and they began to employ those powers not only as teachers but rulers over those gathered by their preaching. They ordered the inauguration of the diaconate (Acts 6) and ordained deacons by laying hands on the men chosen. Later Paul ordained presbyters. He also ordained Timothy and Titus in the office of 'jurisdiction' as well as of teaching (2 Tim. 1:6), thus imparting the apostolic powers of jurisdiction. These men were set over the presbyters whom they, with Paul, ordained to the ministry. Titus in Crete, as an archetypical bishop, had authority over all orders of Christians in Crete, including power to reject and expel heretics. Through these words and acts of Paul we are made 'aware that there would be continual occasion… for the exercise of that authority over pastors and teachers which the apostles had derived from the Lord Jesus.'[2]

2. There is no official 'other' explanation, but some Episcopalian authors, with a more contextual and historical interpretation of relevant materials of Scripture and history, assert (as pointed out earlier here) that the earliest 'constitution' of the church was modeled after the religious community from which the believer came, the synagogue. The synagogue order was modified to conform to the spirit and nature of the new community – the Christian *ekklēsia*. The 'rulers' of the synagogue were elders (*presbuteroi*) and subsequently also in the new *ekklēsia*. The theory of these writers is that in Gentile churches the more applicable and familiar name *episcopos* (bishop) was employed. Not in New Testament record but in New Testament times – when John at least was still active and influential – the threefold ministry of bishop, elders and deacons was adopted. Ignatius pled for it and he was contemporary with John, it is said. From this, in order to meet exigencies of the third and fourth centuries, the church rightly and almost universally adopted the episcopal system of local churches governed by presbyters (nowadays called priests), supervised in their diocese by a bishop. This understanding leans heavily on the principle of expediency in absence of direct scriptural command.

3. Anglican confidence in episcopal government by diocesan bishops in apostolic succession was badly shaken by some research of its own best scholars in the nineteenth century.[3]

4. Interestingly in the great *Langes' Commentary* (ten vols. on the New Testament), the German author of the volume on 1 Timothy argues that Timothy and Titus were diocesan bishops, and the elders they ordained were local presbyters. The American translator (E. A. Washburn, an Episcopal rector) inserted a rebuttal, saying as follows. (1) The situation reflected in the New Testament was a *plastic* stage when church government was forming. (2) The episcopal government was a development, a legitimate change from the college of elders or bishops, strictly local. (3) Diocesan episcopacy is not described in the New Testament but it began in the time of the apostles and must have had their sanction. (4) There is utter silence about how the change came in patristic writing: it came without opposition, silently (contradicted, says Lindsay, by the controversial, strident tone of Ignatius' *Epistles*, advocating episcopacy). (5) There is acknowledgment that it is wrong to import the 'fixed order of a later age' to interpretation of the situation when 1 Timothy was written.[4]

Presbyterian.

Presbyterian church government, of course, means government by elders. This we have seen was the prevalent system in the apostolic churches on display in the New Testament. The system now known as presbyterial is the same, with important differences. It arose in well-defined form among Calvinist groups in Reformation times. In

---

2. McClintock and Strong, Vol III, art. 'Episcopacy,' pp. 262, 263.
3. F. J. A. Hort's Bampton Lectures, *The Christian Ecclesia*; J. B. Lightfoot, *Saint Paul's Epistle to the Philippians*; Edwin Hatch's Bampton Lectures, *Organization of Early Christian Churches*.
4. E. A. Washburn on The Two Epistles to Timothy, trans. of Van Oorterzee in Vol. VIII of *Langes' Commentary*, 1870, pp. 36, 37.

Scotland it developed in opposition to both the papal form of episcopacy and Erastian Anglican government by bishops backed up by the king's army. The story is heroic but out of place here. In the presbyterian government of churches in the British Isles and English-speaking nations, also in the Netherlands and France and lesser districts of Europe, government of each local church is by a college of elders called a session (or consistory) and their 'teaching elder' or pastor. The elders are elected by the people, the minister-pastor, also an elder (presbyter), is chosen by the session and confirmed by the presbytery.

The persecuted evangelical Waldenses maintained many evangelical doctrines through late medieval times and on into Reformation times. Some were enlisted by G. Farel, Calvin's predecessor at Geneva. They readily accepted the Reformed outlook in polity, having employed a three-office polity (bishop, presbyters, deacons) among their local churches. So in the Waldenseans this sort of presbyterial polity continued from antiquity through the middle ages.[5]

In presbyterianism the pastor is not a member of the local church but of the presbytery, composed of a lay elder and the pastor from each church in a presbytery (district). Actions of the local church session are subject to review of the presbytery. Above the presbytery is the synod made up of an equal number of ministers and lay elders chosen by each presbytery (or classis). The presbyteries (not the synods) also send equal numbers of ministers and lay elders to the highest level government, the General Assembly.

The General Assembly is not considered as of the essence of this form of government. In America, for example, up to 1788 there was only the Synod of New York and Philadelphia. This gave place to four synods and 'the General Assembly,' which met for the first time in 1789.[6]

The duties, prerogatives and procedures to carry them out for each office and 'court' are set forth in some detail in a constitution for the denomination, called *The Book of Church Order*.

This method of linking local congregations to a presbytery and presbyteries to synods and to a General Assembly is called 'connectionalism.' It is employed to distinguish it from the congregational theory, which endorses 'independency.' It is held, 'The principle of mutual accountability, depending and submission among the churches is taught at several places in Scripture.'[7] Connectionalism is also characteristic of Methodist polity, though a much larger supervision of local churches and districts by superintendents and bishops takes place among Methodists than among Presbyterians. There is enough similarity, however, that, in spite of some serious differences between Presbyterianism, Calvinism and the Wesleyan Arminianism of Methodism, a single pastor may serve two churches, one a Methodist church in one town and a Presbyterian church in another.

As shall appear shortly, Baptist advocates of congregational polity make statements about mutual accountability, dependence of one Christian group upon another, and submission that imply informal, spiritual 'connectionalism.' In practice, Baptist churches frequently connect themselves together in 'association' with more solidarity than most modern Presbyterians (or Reformed) ever dreamed of. The same can be said of Lutheran churches, which in America are not state-connected and have local congregational government.

In former times the presbytery held title to local church properties but in some of the newer evangelical Presbyterian denominations in America the congregation, whether incorporated or not, owns the local church properties.[8] The local churches have full control over the disbursement of their moneys and 'The superior courts of the church may receive moneys or properties from a local church only by free and voluntary action of the latter.'[9] Discussions go on at the various Presbyterian Church of America levels moving further in congregational directions, and there are 'Independent Presbyterian Churches' (perhaps an oxymoron?) as well as large congregations which do not submit to normal Presbyterian jurisdiction. These modifications, of course, have evolved out of disputes within the several mainline Presbyterians and withdrawals of congregations to form new presbyteries, synods and general assemblies – in effect new Presbyterian denominations.

Though Presbyterians of Reformation times thought they were restoring the New Testament pattern quite exactly, this is not the case today, though they hold their system to be closer to the New Testament than episcopacy *or* congregationalism.[10]

5. See McClintock & Strong, Vol. x, p. 855 and Vol. viii, p. 513.
6. *Presbyterian Law for the Local church*, published by United Presbyterian Church, 6th ed., p. 15.
7. Robert L. Reymond, *A New Systematic Theology of the Christian Faith* (Nashville: Thomas Nelson, 1998) on 'Presbyterian Connectionalism,' p. 901.
8. *Book of Church Order of the Presbyterian Church in America*, 1976, pp. 40, 41, paras. 26-6 through 26-8.
9. ibid.
10. R. Reymond, op. cit., pp. 896–906.

There is another presbyterian, 'small p,' development. Some congregations in many denominations nominally congregational-independent have adopted government by local elders and their pastor. The motives seem to be chiefly two – to suppress the rising and endemic strife in American local churches and to give pastors some protection against rising levels of dissidence in our churches. I myself wrote the new constitution of a congregationally governed church which moved to government by elders and the pastor – a long time ago. At that time the motive was to conform the church to what was esteemed to be the New Testament pattern. We really became more like a late second-century church with threefold ministry (local bishop, college of elders, and deacons) than the strictly Pauline pattern.

Official documents of American Presbyterianism are quite modest in their statements about their form of government. Even before there was a General Assembly, the Synod of New York and Philadelphia drew up 'the Preliminary Principles of the Presbyterian Form of Government.'[11] There are eight of them, which I summarize.

1. God alone is Lord of the conscience, hence no religious or civil authorities may rightly coerce 'private judgment... in all matters that respect religion.'

2. Every 'particular church' or union of churches 'is entitled to declare' terms of admission and systems of internal government.

3. The 'blessed Savior... hath appointed officers... and it is incumbent upon these officers, and upon the whole church to exercise discipline... observing... the rules contained in the Word of God.'

4. '[T]ruth is in order to goodness... there is an inseparable connection between faith and practice, truth and duty.'

5. '[A]ll who are admitted as teachers [must] be sound in faith.' They acknowledge that 'there are truths and forms with respect to which men of good character and principle may differ.'[12]

6. Scripture provides the sole authority of officers and of rules of government; yet the individual 'society' must elect the ones who hold the offices and enforce the rules.

7. All church power is 'by delegated authority, [and] is only ministerial and declarative... The Holy Scriptures are the only rule of faith and manners.' All synods and councils may err. Councils really must not make laws but as 'fallible men' carry out scriptural laws already made.

8. No civil authority should ever be called upon to enforce ecclesiastical decisions and discipline.

I present this to expose readers convinced of congregational polity, and who may not realize in how many points historic Presbyterianism – in America, purged from any dependence on or union with any form of civil government – is similar to their own. Baptists rightly make much of the necessity of a 'regenerate membership' to make congregational government operate aright, yet the same is true of Presbyterianism, implied in the above eight 'principles.' Presbyterians, in deference to the Westminster Confession, include children of believers in the church membership but do not claim that they are yet regenerate and of course children do not vote in electing elders.

Congregational.

Congregational polity means two things: (1) independency or autonomy of each local church as opposed to being part of a bishop's diocese (episcopal); and (2) democracy, wherein each member of voting age has a share in government. Advocates are quick to point out independency is in no manner opposed to co-operation and mutual fellowship with other congregations and genuine Christians everywhere. Further, democracy does not mean that no delegation of authority to representatives takes place; rather that all persons and small groups (committees) to whom authority is committed are agents of the congregation, responsible to the congregation.

A local church thus cannot be controlled by any authority outside itself. It may and should associate itself freely with other congregations, conferences and similar. Yet in such associations it must retain power to withdraw and cannot, in congregationalism, give up its own sovereign independence.

Advocates hold that all prerogatives, duties and functions directed to the local church in the New Testament require congregational independency and democracy. What follows is the heart of the evidence.

---

11. My source is *Presbyterian Law for the Local Church*, 6th ed., rev. 1960, ed. Eugene Carson Blake, pp. 16–18.
12. A charitable outlook on denominational differences on church government!

1. *Admonitions to preserve unity* of behavior and action are addressed to local churches, not districts or dioceses and the like.[13] Passages in 1 Corinthians, for example, relate to breaches of unity in Corinth and not between Corinth and Athens or Thessalonica, or in the church universal. All the passages relate to people who live close to one another in a village or town, not to dispersed churches in a district or diocese. The address at the beginning of the Epistle shows that Paul designed the instruction for any congregation in any place (1 Cor. 1:2).

2. Similarly, *charges to preserve pure doctrine and practice* are addressed to local churches. This is particularly the case in the words of Christ, by John, to the 'angels' of the 'Seven Churches of Asia' (Rev. 2–3). These words come in each case to a whole local church and imply the duty of each person in it to respond appropriately and to take personal responsibility within the church to bring the entire congregation to appropriate obedience.

3. The first church was charged by all the Apostles present to *choose and install its own officers* (Acts 6:1-6).

As noted about Presbyterianism, godly advocates wish to be strictly scriptural in their form of government, 'Holy Scripture the only rule of faith and manners' (*Form of Government of 1789*, paragraph 7).[14] Congregationalists agree, but add that church government, directed by Scripture, is a monarchy of Christ through the Spirit who indwells each member equally. 'In ascertaining the will of Christ... and in applying his commands... the Holy Spirit enlightens one member through the counsel of another, and as the result of combined deliberation, guides the whole body to right conclusions... unity... intelligent and willing' (Strong, 903).[15]

Advocates of congregational polity assert that when it functions properly, each member not only is 'indwelt' by the Spirit but 'filled' by Him, hence church government is a spiritual function. It is not as in American political elections an expression of each voter's private opinion, but of the 'mind of the Spirit' (Rom. 8:27; 11:34), 'the same mind and the same judgment' (1 Cor. 1:10; 2 Cor. 13:11), 'the mind of Christ' (1 Cor. 2:16).

This is because from the beginning they were 'all filled with the Holy Spirit' (Acts 2:1-4). As they continued the first church formed 'their own company' (KJV) and were 'all filled with the Holy Spirit' (Acts 4:23, 31). In the Antioch church half a generation later the Holy Spirit through the congregation separated Barnabas and Saul for their work through congregational action (Acts 13:2, 3). The activities of a well-ordered church according to 1 Corinthians 12 are all expressions of the power of the Spirit working through gifted people.[16]

4. The local church at Corinth had the duty to *observe and to guard the ordinance* of the Lord's Supper (1 Cor. 11:17-34). Paul addresses the church as a whole ('in giving you this charge,' v. 17 ASV), not its leaders. See also verse 2: 'I praise you... even as I delivered them to you.' There is no evidence here that serving communion or performing a baptism was wholly at the discretion of the pastor, even though history furnishes many examples where pastors rightly refused to serve communion to the unworthy and paid the price of dismissal. Calvin himself is a well-known example. Jonathan Edwards is another.

5. The local church – not a district, presbytery or officer – has the duty and authority to *judge its own members*. In 1 Corinthians 5:1 ff., Paul directed the Corinthian congregation to deal decisively in a case of scandalous immorality and he enlarges on the same in chapter 6.

6. The local church has the duty and authority to *settle quarrels among its own members*. In 1 Corinthians 6, Paul addresses the congregation as a whole: 'Dare any of you' (ASV) 'do you not know,' etc. The only ecclessiastical court evidently is the local church *itself*. Paul did not himself appoint a judge or discipline committee but he did direct the church itself, not an outside court of inquiry to look after matters.

This does not mean, advocates of congregationalism point out, that the church, by its authority, may not appoint a small committee or even one man to deal with a problem of discipline. In some cases known to me the problem is so severe the church felt helpless to solve its own problems, and so called in a committee from 'conference' to help. (This reveals a connectionalism, in fact, if not theory.) In each case the move did not prevent disaster.

It should be said that Presbyterians have time-tested rules for dealing with such crises and seem to use them effectively. Baptists and other congregational groups usually do not. When they improvise within the crisis situation the results are often unsatisfactory to the desperate folk who try to deal with it and may call for help. They have no rules or precedents.

---

13. Rom. 12:16; 1 Cor. 1:10; 2 Cor. 13:11; Eph. 4:3; Phil. 1:27; Phil. 2:2-4; 1 Peter 3:8.

14. ibid., p. 17.1

15. Comment on *epi to auto* in Acts 1:15; 2:1, 44, 47.

16. Advocates of governance by elders, however, might point out that one of the gifts of the Spirit is 'governments' (1 Cor. 12:28 ASV, 'administrators,' RSV) the Greek *kubernēseis* is derived from *kubernaō* to steer a ship. Hence *kubernēsis*, 'in general, a guiding, directing, government [of a *polis*, city]' (Liddell and Scott, *Lexicon*). So, perhaps the Spirit's government may be through elders that rule after all (1 Tim. 5:17), with the delegated authority of 'the whole church.'

7. Finally, the one New Testament case involving one congregation's relations with another (Acts 15:1-35) seems to imply *voluntary consultation and co-operation* not a pre-established organized 'connection.'

Some advocates of episcopacy find evidence for episcopal authority in the action of James of Jerusalem, half brother of Jesus, who seems to them to make the decision: 'Brothers... my judgment is...' (Acts 15:13, 19). Also they propose that the decisions of James as a bishop were rendered not only to the delegation from Antioch but to churches elsewhere as rules to be obeyed because they were issued from a sort of inter-diocesan conference.

The instance, however, is not one of a general gathering of pastors around a bishop or anything of the sort, but of a problem which arose in the Antioch congregation because 'some men' from Judea, presumably the Jerusalem church, came to Antioch and taught the Antioch 'brothers' (Acts 15:1) that circumcision of Gentiles was necessary for their salvation. This was contrary to the teaching and practice of the Antioch church and their missionaries, Paul and Barnabas. So 'the brothers' sent a delegation headed by Paul and Barnabas to go up to Jerusalem 'to the apostles and the elders' about this question. When they arrived, however, it was 'the church *and* the apostles and elders' who received them. Though the Apostles and the elders 'considered this matter' in session (v. 6), Peter addressed the 'brothers' (v. 7) and 'the assembly,' i.e. the whole church were present and listened (v. 12).

James rendered an opinion. 'My judgment is' (v. 9) translates *krinō*, for which the first meaning is '*separate, distinguish*, then select, prefer' (Bauer, Arndt, Gingrich, who cite Rom. 14:5, 'prefers one day,' etc), and even to make a judicial decision (Liddell and Scott, *Lexicon*). James' opinion was accepted as correct by 'the apostles and the elders, with the whole church [at Jerusalem]' (v. 22) who as a group (by what means we are not told) composed a letter. It began, 'The brothers, both the apostles and the elders, to the brothers,' etc. (v. 23). The letter was carried back to Antioch (v. 30) where it was read in the church who 'rejoiced because of its encouragement' (not *orders* or *bull* or *decree*, v. 31).

This decision set a precedent, of course, and it is clear that apostolic authority stood behind it, but the occasion was a matter of difference between certain members of two local churches, not an ecumenical gathering of bishops or even of ruling and lay elders. Even the Apostles appear as members of the Jerusalem church, respected, but not in charge of a local assemblage. Paul and Barnabas had been the focus of the controversy to start with (Acts 15:1, 2). After being vindicated, Paul set off again, at Derbe, joined by Timothy whose 'father was a Greek'! So as they went on their way they 'gave over' (*paredidosan*) the 'decisions' (*dogmata*) of the Apostles and elders (Acts 16:4). These decisions, of course, confirmed for the church catholic what Paul had already established in every church he founded.

Restorationist Views.

Restorationist is the usual designation for numerous groups, beginning in early Reformation times, who claim to restore precisely what they deem to have been the New Testament or Pauline pattern. Some groups have sought and thought they found a *form* of association, and organization in the Bible, and sought with some success to imitate it in detail. Most of these groups would be classified by Ernst Troeltsch as sects rather than churches. In their beginnings they rejected the authenticity of the professing church, which they regarded as 'fallen.'

In America, however, there are so many groups, denominations and independent churches which fall into this category (whether they are aware of it or not), and their members so numerous, that it would be a serious mistake to omit them in a treatment of church polity.

Systematic theology commonly neglects this category of views, partly because restorationists are characteristically anti-creed and disinterested in formal theology, hence they have not been publicized in the mainstream religious press. Yet in America and around the world at the present time, millions of Christians including, we hope, many readers of this book, belong to groups who hold this view.

Under this rubric may be included many who are referred to by scholars as Free Church, Believers' Church, Gathered Church, or even more narrowly self-designated as *The* Christian Church, *The* Church of God, Church of *The* Nazarene, or simply Friends or Brethren, and similar. I include them under the umbrella of *restorationist* because each began consciously in withdrawal from the prevalent form of the church existing where the founders lived to form a community of believers committed to a form of church organization and government which they thought to be the New Testament pattern. Some were also fugitive from oppressive ecclesiastical *regimes*. An early example is 'the Unity of the Brethren' (Hussites of late 1400s in Bohemia); earlier examples are Waldensians and Albigensians.

From the first stages of the Reformation in continental Europe there were those whom R. Bainton called the left wing of the Reformation and G. H. Williams the Radical Reformation, but whose enemies labeled them Anabaptists. They style themselves Brethren, Mennonites, Hutterites, Amish and the like. These people came to notice initially at Zurich. At first they accepted the leadership there of Zwingli, but because the government of the church was an aspect of local civil government, regarding every christened person (which included everybody) as a church member, these brave souls withdrew to form their own (unlawful) assemblies of 'believers only.' These brave folk recently had been baptized as confessed believers. As the movement developed they consciously sought to reestablish the New Testament pattern and did succeed in a measure. They and their defenders among mainline Protestant scholars have produced a very large literature in recent generations. Their distinctive doctrines and practices are adequately discussed in the writings of Franklin Littell, Roland Bainton, G. H. Williams in the United States; E. A. Payne and P. T. Forsyth of Great Britain; as well as J. H. Yoder (Mennonite), D. F. Durnbaugh (Dunker or Church of the Brethren) and others.

In the Britain of the seventeenth century, restorationism is usually called non-conformity or simply the Puritan revolt. The relevant point here is that out of the Puritan movement came English Presbyterians, Quakers, Baptists, Congregationalists and others. At first their objective was mainly to separate their churches from government control and episcopally required architecture, furniture, priesthood and liturgy. All thought of themselves as determined to restore church worship and government to the pattern perceived to be discovered in the New Testament. What came out of it all was exported to America as Presbyterian, Quaker, Baptist, Congregational and (to a degree) even early Episcopal denominations. Recent scholarship has recovered the fact that colonists in America before 1775 were as much fearful that King George III would be coaxed into appointing a bishop to control the churches in America as they were offended by the encroachments of parliament on their liberties as Englishmen. This has been thoroughly researched and reported by Carl Bridenbaugh.[17]

Restorationist efforts of early nineteenth-century America gave the country such diverse ecclesiastical phenomena as the Mormons, who are governed by 'Apostles,' and 'Disciples of Christ' or 'Church of Christ.' The latter began as a movement to restore New Testament simplicity of doctrine, life and government to Presbyterian churches and then to Baptist churches. This movement, which grew to a large 'denomination' (though they reject the term), was founded by Alexander Campbell (1788–1866).

During the same period in Britain two important contradictory Restorationist movements developed. 'One was the Tractarian or Oxford movement led by John Keble, Edward Peese, and John Henry Newman,' who assayed to call Anglicanism back to its pre-Reformation heritage and the writings of the early church Fathers. They were determined to rescue their church from state-sponsored interference. This movement persists to the present day.[18]

In another direction, in early nineteenth-century Britain, reaction against restrictive Acts of Parliament against dissenters and Roman Catholics, produced (at first) some small groups of members of the established church who met at hours when there were no services in the state church to study the Bible for prayer and instruction. Some were clergymen.

Among them were those who came to be known as Plymouth Brethren. They deserve more than a footnote in a chapter on church government. Many of the Brethren would be recognized as outstanding Christians in any age: George Mueller of Bristol, founder of orphanages and famous example of the principle of faith in mission; S. P. Tregelles, Hebrew scholar, exegete, translator of Gesenius' *Lexicon*; G. W. Wigram, creator of concordances of Scripture in Hebrew and Greek; Sir Robert Anderson of Scotland Yard, and keen writer and evangelical scholar; F. F. Bruce, professor, scholar and commentator; H. A. Ironside; C. H. Mackintosh; and many other preachers, pastors, scholars. To this number might be added the name of Watchman Nee, founder of the very similar 'Little Flock' of China.

No man prescribes polity for 'the Brethren' but there are several treatments of church constitution and ministry by their best authors. Of these the best in my estimation is G. H. Lang.[19]

The early history of the movement revolves in major part around the lives of four English citizens – A. N. Groves, George Mueller, Robert Chapman and John Nelson Darby. Their story as told in some detail by E. H. Broadbent[20] starts off with this paragraph:

---

17. Carl Bridenbaugh, *Mitre and Scepter, Transatlantic Faiths, Ideas, Personalities, and Politics, 1689–1775* (New York: Oxford University Press, 1962).
18. D. F. Durnbaugh, *The Believers' Church* (London: Macmillan, 1970), p. 161.
19. G. H. Lang, *The Churches of God: Their Constitution, Government and Ministry* (London: Paternoster, 1959), p. 190.
20. E. H. Broadbent, *The Pilgrim Church* (London: Pickering and Inglis, 2nd ed., 1935), pp. 347–385.

> In the early part of the 19th century a number of people were impressed by the importance as well as by the possibility of a return to the teachings of Scripture, not only in respect of questions of personal salvation and conduct, but also as regards *the order and testimony of the churches* [emphasis added].[21]

Most recently the 'Brethren' have taken note of their own history and ecclesiological views in a symposium, *Understanding the Church*,[22] and another symposium, *New Horizons in Mission*.[23]

Durnbaugh (Dunker, or Church of the Brethren) asserts of these English Brethren, 'they were the most rigorously consistent in their primitivism, the most evangelistic, and have certainly had the most influence upon modern life of all these [nineteenth-century British Restorationist] bodies.'

Time fails to sketch their history. They have always worked quietly; never promoting their 'non-organization' (the term seems correct), yet missionaries of these Brethren have served inostentaciously but effectively in about every corner of the planet up to now. Many of them make a point of keeping no lists, rolls or statistics, but informed sources indicate there are about 500,000 Brethren in Britain, Germany, America, Canada, New Zealand, Belgium and the Netherlands.[24]

Two incidents illustrate why they almost defy identification to most people. I once asked Walter Liefeld (a 'P.B.') when we were fellow teachers at a seminary, 'How do you choose elders in your assemblies?' He paused, pursed his lips, then cautiously answered only this much, 'My elder may not be the same man as your elder.' Again, in a two-weeks tour group were a middle-aged farm couple, members of an 'assembly' in a rural Iowa town. The husband simply could not explain what church 'denomination' they were a part of. If he knew the term 'Plymouth Brethren' he would not use it. The Lutherans, Baptists and Presbyterians in our party could not figure them out, though obviously devout, godly church people. When I interposed a brief, friendly explanation the brother seemed much pleased, but I think it was the first time he had ever heard his own 'denomination' explained.

Another personal contribution: the brother who preached to us in the small community, pioneer church (central Washington state) was publicly only identified as Mr Elder from 'the assembly' in Yakima. Yet, when as a college sophomore I attended a Plymouth Brethren 'Gospel Hall' the brother who seemed to be in charge invited me to preach at the evening service several times, though not at the morning service where the Lord's Supper was observed.

These Brethren (at least some of them) seem to teach that the only real, permanent *ekklēsia* is the universal one, of which every true believer is a member. Whenever believers meet for worship there is an *ekklēsia*. Wherever a somewhat permanent group of believers meet regularly – even if all are new believers – God has already supplied to that continuing *ekklēsia* all the gifted people they need to function as a true New Testament church, including 'pastors and teachers.' Broadbent emphasizes this over and over. Several 'members' (there is no 'roll') may preach at a single service and no one is 'the' pastor. Reading in recent journals of the Brethren manifests several evidences of a change in thinking. (1) An awareness that pastoral care has been missing because no one knows precisely to whom to go for pastoral care. 'Pastor' is a gift and dissociated from the 'elder,' as office, not a gift. Are elders pastors or rulers? There is uncertainty. (2) They are coming to draw inferences from the fact their founders were almost all former clergymen trained in theology and disciplined scholars, hence they were able to give form and content to the movement and to lead it. (3) A felt need of trained leadership has brought about some acceptance of the presence of a designated preacher-teacher in the assembly. (4) Regrets over a lost generation or two of young people has led many to wonder if their 'present distress' does not call for drastic change. Not all accept D. L. Norbie's confident affirmation: 'Today throughout the world there are thousands of assemblies where the individuals are fervent, where there is exercise of spiritual gifts [in sufficient power to provide pastoral leadership and care]… and where the apostolic assembly government is followed in detail.'[25]

Conclusions and Suggestions.

1. The New Testament provides no specific command or teaching providing details of how the Christian *ekklēsia* should be governed.

---

21. ibid., p. 347.
22. Compiled and ed. J. M. Vogl and J. H. Fish III (Neptune, NJ: Loizeau, 1999), 235 pages.
23. Edited by Farez Marzoni, Union Cristiana Edizioni Bibliche, Casella Postale 45-04022-LT Italy.
24. Durnbaugh cites sources, p. 172 note 37.
25. *New Testament Church Organization* (Chicago: Letters of Interest, n.d.), p. 73 (Open Plymouth Brethren).

2. There is, however, what appears to be a consistent precedent: a polity in which elders, without a single president, rule and deacons serve the congregation.

3. During the second century many assemblies adopted the plan of government by elders who chose a president. Even earlier there were elders who gave much time to teaching the Word and who were at least partially supported by the church. This appears in Paul's letters.

T.M. Lindsay observes, 'During the last decades of the second and throughout the third century... [almost] every Christian community had at its head a single president who is almost always called the bishop. He presided over the session of elders, over the body of deacons, and over the congregation.'[26] Most aspects of the church's life revolved about the local pastor-bishop, as in a Presbyterian congregation when the pastor presides over elders, or a Baptist church where he presides over deacons who 'share in the spiritual oversight' (as very many local constitutions say). There are similarities within the local Episcopal parish in America.

4. Most local church government today is similar to the pattern described above in point 3.

5. No present system precisely reproduces the New Testament pattern – whatever it may have been.

6. The reason is that all our present forms of organization and governance are historically conditioned. We tend to interpret every Scripture passage about rule, pastor, elder, bishop, deacon, deaconess and the like out of our cultural horizon. Read the qualification for elder to a Baptist and it describes for him his pastor, to a Presbyterian, one of the members of the session, to an Episcopalian, one of the clergy who are in charge, to a Roman Catholic, his parish priest.

7. A common form of congregational government among American churches is by a board composed of deacons, trustees, Sunday School superintendent and perhaps some others, presided over perhaps by the pastor, or perhaps by an elected 'moderator.' Of these the only office besides pastor subject to the spiritual qualifications enumerated by Paul in 1 Timothy 3 and Titus 1 is that of the deacon. The trustees may have no spiritual attainments at all, but are esteemed to be capable handlers of money and properties; the moderator may be one esteemed simply to have ability to stand before a body of people with dignity, and so on. He may be a pushy type who has promoted himself successfully. The result in this case is rule by the spiritually incompetent.

Sometimes country church government tends to be somewhat in charge of a strong-minded lady or two who settle important matters on the telephone with calls to other women in the church before the congregational meeting takes place.

8. Hence ideas about church government have tended to reflect ideas current in the time and place (cultural environment) where the church is located. This is true whatever the theory: government of a church in China will reflect the Chineness reverence for elders and ancestors; a congregational church in a working-class district may have features of government that look like a local unit of a labor union; in an old-fashioned rural district of independent-minded farmers the government will reflect the dead-level democratic feeling of such people – whatever the pastor, the presbytery, the bishop or the district superintendent may think.

9. The mind of the Spirit may be in charge under any of the historical systems – as history demonstrates. Likewise His mind may also be unknown, submerged or overwhelmed in any such system. Correction toward the normal and right is possible where a 'settled minister' or pastor of wisdom can lead, and a session, consistory, board of elders (by whatever name) – who meet the qualifications of Titus 1 and 1 Timothy 3 – work things out and then present decisions with reasons for them to a well-instructed congregation.

10. These matters will be considered from a somewhat different perspective when we discuss the *offices* of the church, its *ordinances* (sacraments) of baptism and the Lord's Supper, and its *worship* in following chapters.

---

26. T. M. Lindsay, *The Church and the Ministry in the Early Centuries* (Minneapolis: The James Family, repr. 1977), p. 204.

18
Church Offices and Ministry, I
Preliminary Matters

1. Extraordinary and Ordinary.

Theology distinguishes between extraordinary and ordinary officers of the church. The extraordinary are the *Apostles*, strictly defined, directly empowered by Christ as His ministers plenipotentiary; *prophets* of the New Testament (possibly also the sub-apostolic era); and *evangelists* such as Philip, Mark, Timothy and Titus, special missionary agents of Apostles. It is doubtful if the evangelist, mentioned three times in the New Testament – prominently in Ephesians 4 – refers to the missionary or evangelist of today.

2. Office, Function, Ministry.

It is doubtful if any New Testament Greek word corresponds exactly to a present-day understanding of 'office.' Two Greek words are so translated in the KJV: *diakonia* (Rom. 11:3 once only), *praxis* (Rom. 12:4 once only). The former is normally rendered *service, ministry, ministration, administration,* and the latter *deed* or *work* (in the sense of acting). These are words for what people do, not their 'official' position. The word which covers all people do in and for the church is *diakonia*, ministry. There is no term in the Greek New Testament corresponding exactly to our idea and word 'office.' As 'the apostle of the Gentiles,' said Paul, 'I magnify mine office' (Rom. 11:13 KJV); but the newer translations rightly correct *office* to *ministry* (*diakonia*) – again what Paul did, not a position he held.

Nevertheless the New Testament does provide specific qualifications or requirements for being Apostles, elders and deacons and specifies their duties and functions. Prophets and evangelists are also mentioned though no New Testament qualifications are supplied. Also certain honors and prerogatives are mentioned. The Old Testament has much to say about requirements to be a true prophet of God. In modern conception all so designated are 'officers' of the church and we shall herein employ the term without defending it further – even though strictly speaking an equivalent term for 'office' does not seem to occur in the Greek New Testament. In constructing a doctrine of church office, therefore, 'the only course… is to find out what the New Testament teaches respecting persons endowed with particular gifts and discharging the corresponding functions in virtue of which they are set apart and distinguished from others… distinguished by specific functions.'[1]

---

1. John Murray, *Collected Writings*, Vol. II (Edinburgh: Banner of Truth Trust, 1977), p. 357.

3. Temporary and Permanent Offices.

At this point we should be reminded that the New Testament enumerates 'functions, and persons exercising them, which no longer obtain in the church of Christ' (Murray, p. 358). This is the case with Apostles and prophets, upon whom the foundation of the church was laid[2] (Eph. 2:20), and probably also with the 'evangelists' of Ephesians 4:11, for (to repeat) it is doubtful if that word has direct reference to those who now carry out special 'crusades' (now 'missions'), 'campaigns' or 'festivals' of evangelism. It seems likely that the word *euaggelistēs*, applied only to Philip (Acts 21:8) and Timothy (2 Tim. 4:5) and said to be a 'gift' (Eph. 4:11), also belonged to the epoch of revelation and founding of the church (Murray, Berkhof). They, like Apostles and prophets, were 'gifts' to the whole church, even though Timothy did for a time serve as a sort of presiding local elder at Ephesus. In the case of Philip, after he 'evangelized' Samaria and, in effect, Ethiopia (Acts 8), he apparently settled down in Caesarea to raise a large family (Acts 21:8).[3]

We may then join the tradition of Protestant theologians in speaking of the New Testament offices of Apostles, prophets and evangelists as *Extraordinary Offices* and the offices of elder and deacon as *Ordinary Offices*, normally present in every local church.[4]

Questions arise as to the number of offices in the apostolic churches. Were all elders also teachers? Were there some teachers who were not elders? Was it required that all elders be 'apt to teach'? More importantly, was the office of presbyter (elder) only a ruling office or did it imply pastoral work as well? Was one *episkopos* (bishop) or elder designated as the president of the college of elders (*presbuteroi*) already in the churches of Timothy and Titus – apostolic churches? Or was there strictly plural leadership?

4. Biblical Sources.

Some of these questions and others will be addressed in the discussions of this chapter. The precise form of the 'primitive Christian ministry' was a subject of intense study for several decades beginning in the mid-nineteenth century. The nineteenth-century discovery of the AD 100 (plus or minus) *Didache* or *Teaching of the Twelve Apostles* stimulated renewed attention to previously known pieces of Christian writing (*Epistles of Ignatius*, *Shepherd of Hermas*, *Epistle of Clement to the Corinthians* and others) coming from earliest times. As noted in the previous chapter we know that by about AD 175 there was usually a bishop in each local *ekklēsia*, a college of elders and a college of deacons – a threefold ministry. Most now agree that there were only two offices – elders (also called presbyters and pastors) and deacons – in the first century. Literary evidence is still lacking as to how the change came. Jerome (fourth century) made the bold and startling assertion, that though diocesan bishops were by then in charge everywhere, that bishops and elders were originally the same.[5]

It is a fact now generally (though not unanimously) recognized by theologians of all shades of opinion, that in the language of the New Testament the same office in the church is called indifferently 'bishop' (*episkopos*) and 'elder,' or 'presbyter' (*presbyteros*).[6]

Respected evangelical scholars who are convinced there were three offices in the time covered by the New Testament (to AD 95) argue as follows.[7]

(1) 'It is certain that the church had officers who discharged functions not discharged by ordinary Christians… [hence] a distinction… between clergy and laity.' First Thessalonians, probably the first book of the New Testament to be written, distinguishes three functions 'exercised by a few with regard to the many' – [1] 'them which labor among you,' [2] 'and are over you in the Lord,' [3] 'and admonish you' whom the believers were told to 'esteem… very highly in love for their work's sake' (1 Thess 5:12, 13 KJV).

(2) Late in the New Testament era, 3 John 9, in the incident about Diotrophes, 'seems to show that [there was] not only ecclesiastical government but ecclesiastical government by a single official.'

---

2. See chapter 6, above, 'Foundation for the church.'
3. J. Massie, 'Evangelist,' *Hastings Dictionary of the Bible*, Vol. I, pp. 795–797.
4. Louis Berkhof, *Systematic Theology* (Grand Rapids: Eerdmans, 1979), p. 585; H. Harvey, *The Church: Its Polity and Ordinances* (Philadelphia: American Baptist Publication Society, 1879), pp. 66, 69.
5. W. A. Jürgens, ed. and trans., *The Faith of the Early Fathers*, 3 vols. (Collegeville, MN: The Liturgical Press, 1979), Vol. II, p. 194.
6. J. B. Lightfoot, *Saint Paul's Epistle to the Philippians*, 4th ed., repr. ed. (New York: Macmillan and Co., 1894), p. 95.
7. This has been condensed from Alfred Plummer's treatment of *The Pastoral Epistles in An Exposition of the Bible*, Vol. vi, Hartford, Conn.: 1908, pp. 412–416.

(3) In-between 1 Thessalonians and 3 John, Hebrews 13:17 exhorts, 'Obey your leaders and submit to them.'

(4) First Clement, from about the last decade of the first century, seems to describe the same situation. Further in 1 Clement, 'three things come out very clearly.' [1] There is 'a clear distinction between clergy and laity.' [2] 'This distinction is not temporary agreement but is the basis of a permanent organization.' [3] A person who has been duly promoted to the ranks of the clergy as a presbyter or bishop (the two titles being here synonymous, as in the Epistle to Titus) holds that position for life. Unless he is guilty of some serious offense, to depose him is no light sin.

(5) To these three 'certainties' may be added the following. [1] There is a regularly organized clergy with gradation of rank. [2] 'Each local church is constitutionaly governed by one chief officer... who received the title of bishop.' [3] 'There is no trace of belief or even suspicion, that the constitution of these local churches had ever been anything else.' In the time of, say, AD 180–200 'Christians were fully persuaded that the episcopal [without dioceses] form of government had prevailed... from the Apostles' time to their own.' They were as convinced of this as that there were only four authentic Gospels.

The Pastoral Epistles became very important in the restoration of the churches of Europe in the sixteenth and seventeenth centuries. Church reforms of offices and ministry received their first boost in England during the short reign (1547–1553) of the pious boy known to history as Edward VI. During this period (1548) Calvin wrote his commentary on the Epistles to Timothy. Reformed people on the continent had high hope for reform of the church in England. Calvin, therefore, dedicated the commentary to Edward Seymour, Duke of Somerset, guardian and regent for the boy king. In a few lines of the dedication Calvin showed how important the Pastorals were then thought to be to decent church order:

> Now since in order to restore the English church, which... had been miserably corrupted by the shocking wickedness of Popery, you employ your strenuous efforts under the direction of your king, and for that purpose have many Timothys under your charge, neither they nor you can direct your holy translations in a more profitable manner than by taking the rule laid down by Paul for your pattern. For there is nothing in them that is not highly applicable to our times, and hardly anything that is necessary in the building of the church that may not likewise be drawn from them.[8]

Then, refering to the *Commentary*, Calvin added, 'I trust that my labour will, at least, afford some assistance.'

In employing the Pastoral Epistles as authoritative guidance for a doctrine of church offices, a serious matter of interpretation sometimes arises in unexpected ways. To whom do the charges to Timothy apply?[9]

As long as ordination sermons have been preached and charges to ordinands have been given the charges of Paul to Timothy as a public person have been read as charges to pastors rather than to a board of elders or of deacons on the one hand or to Timothy alone as apostolic legate or archetypal diocesan bishop. Context shows which charges were intended to be strictly personal – e.g. 'Do thy diligence to come shortly unto me' (2 Tim 4:9 KJV); 'Let no one despise you for your youth' (1 Tim. 4:12) – though there are applications to pastors and people in each text. My memory is green of the moment when a solemn, white-haired minister took me by the right hand, looked me straight in the eye and recited, 'Take thou authority in the church of God... preach the word,' etc. (see 2 Tim. 4:1-5). It happened at my ordination many years ago but it still rings in my ears.

Customary preaching and 'pastoral theology' somewhat naively applies everything addressed to Timothy in his public capacity to the office of elder-pastor-bishop, as well as all Paul says specifically about elders.

We are not without guidance in this matter from the author himself in 1 Timothy 3:14 and 15. The author says he may or may not soon get back to Ephesus where Timothy is standing in for him; but if delayed, 'I write so that you will know how one ought to conduct himself in the household of God... the pillar and support of truth' (v. 15 NASB). The marginal reading – 'how one ought to conduct himself' – agrees with the King James Version: 'how

---

8. Calvin, *Commentary on the Epistles to Timothy, Titus, and Philemon*, English trans. 1866, the 'Dedication,' p. xi. See Wulfert DeGreef, *The Writings of John Calvin*, trans. L. D. Bierma (Grand Rapids: Baker Books, 1993), p. 97.

9. I came in to visit an adult Bible class in a church I recently served – a class taught by rotation among five or six members of the class. On this day they were trying to figure out how to apply 1 Timothy 4:11 ff. ('Command and teach these things,' etc.) to themselves and no one seemed to know. They should have taken a cue from 'let no one despise you for your youth' (v. 12). I spoke up and pointed out that 1 Timothy is primarily a private letter to an 'interim pastor' about his duties in that capacity and that the text should tell them what to expect of a good pastor rather than of a Bible class of farmers, business men, their wives and the high school teacher who was presiding that Sunday morning. There were scattered exclamations of 'Oh!' Everyone seemed relieved that each was not obliged to command and exhort and teach doctrine as well as to read.

thou oughtest to behave thyself.' The Greek form of the verb for 'conduct yourself' is an infinitive and is amenable to either rendering. The NIV has, 'how people ought to conduct themselves.' A literal rendering would be like the KJV – 'I write in order that thou [second person singular] may know how it is necessary [*dei*, strong necessity] in the house of God to behave one's self.' Behave one's self is a reflexive present participle. The 'people' of NIV is not in the Greek text at all.

Luther, Calvin, Melanchthon, Beza and most commentators to the present have understood Paul to be instructing 'thee' (Gr. *soi* dat. sing.), that is, Timothy, pastor and overseer of the *ekklēsia* at Ephesus. Paul in 1 and 2 Timothy is telling that timid leader how *he* ought to behave in the *ekklēsia*. Calvin is representative: 'By this mode of expression he commends the weight and dignity of the office; because pastors may be regarded as stewards, to whom God has committed the charge of governing his house.'[10] This includes specific charges (like 2 Tim. 4:1 ff.) and rules for elders, deacons, which Paul directed Timothy to pass on to the *ekklēsia*. I think older Versions and interpreters are correct and the new Versions very mistaken. If we accept the new translations (how 'people,' NIV, 'ought to behave in the church,' etc. or how 'one,' RSV, etc.), the force of the thought of the Pastorals (1 and 2 Tim. especially) as specifically about the pastoral office is thereby weakened though not destroyed.

How thou oughtest to behave thyself in the house of God (KJV), then, applies to Timothy in particular. 'The explanatory *soi* [Gr. to thee] has this degree of weight' (Van Oosterzie, *en loc, Lange's Commentary*) though 'the expression has a general sense also' (ibid.). The infinitival verb '*anastrephesthai* [to behave one's self] means not Christian life in general, but the life of the Christian officer, which belongs to Timothy and his fellow-*episcopoi* [overseers]. The scene... of this [behavior] is the Christian community at Ephesus and elsewhere' (ibid.). On this understanding of the whole Pastoral corpus the rest of this chapter proceeds.

'[I]n the household of God, which is the church of the living God, a pillar and buttress of truth' (1 Tim. 3:15): relates the behavior of church officers, described in the Pastorals, both to the local church which Timothy served, and in the church *as a whole* (catholic). Locally, at Ephesus, for the 'living God' is a contrast with the heathen worship of the famous statue of Diana at Ephesus.[11]

The grand language, 'pillar and foundation of truth,' indicates the whole church in the world, the only realm on earth where 'the truth' as opposed to 'truths' of every sort is preserved and propagated. (Jesus Himself is 'the truth,' John 14:16.) This is one of the several passages in the New Testament where reference to church catholic and church local cannot be sharply distinguished.

5. The Relation of Offices to Spiritual Gifts.

The 'gifts' of special abilities to members of the local *ekklēsia* (1 Cor. 12:4-11, 27, 28 and Rom. 12:3-8) and 'offices' of the local church are not exactly the same, but neither are they unrelated. Among those gifts are 'helping' (*antilēmpseis*), and 'administrators' (*kubernēseis*) (1 Cor. 12:28 RSV). The first word, 'helping' refers to helping others, works of mercy which elsewhere in the New Testament are done for the body corporate by 'the seven' of Acts 6, deacons, deaconesses and widows. The second word referred originally to steering a ship, but in common use later to 'guiding, directing, government,'[12] and is often translated 'rule.' The cognate *kubernētēs* is rendered 'the pilot' (of a ship, Acts 27:11 NIV) and 'captain' (of a ship, Rev. 18:17 NIV). This certainly is a gift necessary for the office of elder as set forth in the Pastorals at length.[13]

It bears repetition that though the Apostles, prophets and evangelists of Ephesians 4:11 are no longer with us, the pastor-teachers are. Important to this discussion is that the pastor-teachers are men whom Christ at the time of His Ascension 'gave' to the church down through all its history. The Pastorals connect the office of elder-bishop with the 'gift' of pastor-teacher. Hence, as we shall see, pastoral authority does not flow entirely from the church which chooses the pastor as their leader. His appointment is from Christ. 'he [Christ *Himself* (*autos*)] gave' (Eph. 4:11).

---

10. Calvin, *The Epistles to Timothy, Titus and Philemon* (Edinburgh: Calvin Translation Society, 1856), p. 89.
11. 'Ecclesia Dei viventis opponitur fano Dianae Ephesiorum *Vita Dei*, fundamentum *spei nostrae*' ('the church of the living God is in contrast to the sanctuary of Diana of the Ephesians'). 'The Life of God, the foundation of our hope,' J. A. Bengel, *Novi Testamenti*, 3rd Latin ed., Vol. II (Tuebingen, 1850), p. 354.
12. Liddell and Scott, *Lexicon*.
13. How this particular Greek word migrated into computer jargon as 'cybernetics,' I would like to know.

Further, in the Ephesian passage, the pastor-teacher is a gift to the whole church. This suggests that men who hold the pastoral office, though they have authority in only one local *ekklēsia* at a time, may be accepted as pastors anywhere in the *diaspora* as Peter describes the whole church in the world (1 Peter 1:1). This is indeed the way matters have stood throughout church history. This group is a gift to the whole church. We can't get along very long without them.

Scholars have noted that in the list of gifts in 1 Corinthians 12:28 Paul thinks of 'teachers' as persons God gave to 'the church' (universal) along with apostles and prophets and enumerates teachers as 'thirdly.' 'After this' (*epeita*) indicates a separation from the ability-gifts following. The inference has been drawn (rightly it seems to me) that some teachers have a catholic (whole-church-in-the-world) function, if not office. Throughout church history, there have been itinerant teachers (*didaskaloi*) who traveled about from church to church. The *didachē* and other early Christian literature refer to these men with approval and appreciation. T. M. Lindsay points out that these men were not necessarily the pastor-teacher, but 'wise men and scribes', whom Jesus promised (Matt. 23:34), and that Paul was emphasizing their presence at Romans 12:7 and 1 Corinthians 12:28. They were very important to the catholicity of the church's doctrine, for they were itinerants and traveled from church to church, being honored and heeded.[14]

> It is evident, at least when we get beyond the apostolic period, that many gifted men, whose services were appreciated, went from church to church teaching and preaching, and that without any pretension to the prophetic gift. Justin Martyr and Tatian, well known apologists of the second century, were wandering teachers of this kind.[15]

There was a time in living memory, before mothers came home at day's end from working somewhere else, and the members of our churches became so over-scheduled that there is no time to attend meetings such as 'Bible Conferences,' when traveling teachers had a very great influence for good. I myself was guided toward the pastoral ministry by such men and engaged in such ministry up until the present disinterest set in. We now use recorded (CD, cassette) lectures of assorted types for various local church settings.

There have also been teachers (examples: Augustine, Anselm, Aquinas, Calvin, Luther, Owen, Gill, Watson, Baxter) whose shadows lengthen on to the present hour. These teachers have been given to the whole church. There have been hundreds of scholarly and saintly men who in their time may or may not have held a presbyter's office in a local church but who shaped orthodox, evangelical theology enduringly far and wide for the whole church, the pillar and ground of truth. There might not have been an enduring church except for this kind of teaching of the whole church. In the sense we use 'office' in ecclesiology there are only two church offices – elder or bishop and deacon. There are, however, several special 'ministries' which will call for some attention here.

The Office of Elder.

Elders Among Ancient People.

The Greek word *presbuteros* (Eng. presbyter, elder) meant either an aged person or a ruling officer in some unit of society. Equivalent words exist in every language of antiquity related to the Bible – indeed in most languages to the present. Elders were important civic and religious figures in Israel of the Old Testament period and on to Jesus' time. Güenther Bernkamm has provided a very complete survey and discussion from beginning in Israel and in the church to the time of Hippolytus (AD 170–236).[16]

A College With President?

In the preceding chapter we set forth the view that the churches of the New Testament were governed by a college of elders, of whom some labored in 'the word and doctrine' and some did not. We add here that all elders should be 'apt to teach' at least their own families. Deacons do not share in government except as members of the assembly. They are not required to be teachers (1 Tim. 3:8-10). As pointed out in the chapter above, it is certain that in Ignatius' time (the end of the first century) in many churches, one elder was chairman of the college of elders. It is possible that the arrangement began in apostolic times. By the late second century only the presiding elder of

---

14. T. M. Lindsay, *The Church and the Ministry in the Early Centuries*, repr. (Minneapolis: The James Family, 1977), pp. 103–109.
15. ibid., p. 105.
16. Güenther Bernkamm, *TDNT*, Vol. vi, pp. 651–683.

the local college of elders was called bishop (*episcopos*, overseer). This bishop had authority only in his own local congregation, though it should be borne in mind that likely all the congregations in a city and immediate area were one church. The New Testament reflects such an arrangement (Rom. 1:7 and chap. 16; Phil. 1:1; and the address of Christ to seven *cities* in the Roman province of Asia in Rev. 2–3). This arrangement has been pretty much standard throughout Christendom outside papal and episcopal denominations and to a degree in even those denominations to the present. Groups such as the (Plymouth) Brethren, who have thought of themselves as having no single person as overseer or pastor, have implicitly in practice had the same structure. (See the preceding chapter.) This development seems almost inevitable, as history shows. 'Everybody's business is nobody's business.' 'Who's in charge here?'

Special Duties of Church Elders.

Duties As Indicated by Names.
The several names assigned this office say much.

(1) From time immemorial *elders* in civil society have had representative capacity as legislators and judges. They do not always do much outside their collective work in conferring with one another on matters brought before them. Such apparently was the case with elders in Israel from Egypt onward.

(2) *Bishop*, Greek *episcopos*, meaning overseer (Anglo-Saxon), supervisor (Latin), plainly suggests the man in charge, who sees that things get done. Once Jesus is called 'Bishop of your souls' (1 Peter 2:25 KJV).

(3) *Pastor* is another defining name. Peter, as a presbyter himself, wrote that presbyters should 'tend the flock of God' (1 Peter 5:1, 2 ASV). When Paul called the Ephesian elders (*presbuterous*, Acts 20:17) to meet him at Miletus he exhorted them to 'Pay careful attention to... all the flock [*poimniō*], of which the Holy Spirit has made you overseers [*episkopous*], to care for [*poimainein*, take to pasture] the church [*ekklēsia*] of God, which he obtained with his own blood' (Acts 20:28).

This makes plain that the elder is a *pastor*, a form of the Greek word for shepherd. In the Greek Version of Psalm 23:1 shepherd is a form of this same word. Hence we know that 'pastor' is a very important name for this office, derived from Scripture. Of the four gifts of the ascended Christ 'For the perfecting of the saints' the shepherd (pastor)-teacher is the only one still in the church today (Eph. 4:11, 12 KJV), as we have frequently noted.

Having myself grown up on a ranch where I herded sheep I recommend what Robert Reymond well says, 'I have often thought that pastors would benefit greatly from reading some books on what sheep are like, what their needs are, and what is involved in feeding them.'[17]

There are false shepherds who seek to harm the flock (Jude 12). Perhaps they do less damage in aggregate than lazy shepherds!

(4) Paul addressed pastor Timothy as a *man of God* (1 Tim. 5:11) (an honor shared with the prophet Daniel).

(5) He also called Timothy a *minister of Christ* (1 Tim. 4:6).

Presbyter, Supervisor, Minister, Pastor, Man of God are all biblical designations of this office in the church. What are the duties of such men? Many of the duties are defined by the names. As *presbyters* they are to weigh affairs of church administration with wisdom, as *overseers* to tend to details of operation or see to it that someone else does so. There are many different models of how elders can truly 'oversee' in modern churches. As *pastor* the elder's chief task as indicated by 'pastor-teacher' in Ephesians 4:11 and to 'Feed the flock of God' (1 Peter 5:1, 2 KJV) is to instruct the church. As *ministers* of Christ they serve as He served, not themselves but Christ, as present in His people. 'In as much as ye did it unto these, ye did it unto me.' As *men of God* (1 Tim. 6:11), elders are to measure up to the qualifications of office set forth in passages under the next heading, 'being examples to the flock' (1 Peter 5:3 KJV).

Duties as Indicated by Commands and Exhortations.
Thinking specifically of the whole college of elders seen in Acts and the Pastorals, 1 Thessalonians 5:12, 13 sets forth three ways in which elders ministered in a Pauline church. 'But we request of you, brethren, that you appreciate those who diligently *labor* among you, and *have charge over you* in the Lord and *give you instruction,* and that you esteem them very highly in love because of their work' (1 Thess. 5:12, 13 NASB, emphasis added).

---

17. Robert Reymond, *Systematic Theology* (Nashville: Thomas Nelson, 1998), p. 898.

1. The elders 'diligently labor' (1 Thess. 5:12 NASB) among the assembly; 'diligently labor' (*kopiaō*) means to work hard and it can be 'physical, mental or spiritual to the point of weariness' (Bauer, Arndt, Gingrich, *Lexicon*). A. Strauch devotes a whole chapter to discuss elders as 'hard working men.'[18]

2. Elders 'have charge over' the *ekklēsia*; in the language of 1 Thessalonians 5:12 (NASB), 'are over you' (NIV). The Greek word is *proistamenoi*. In the Second Vision of the *Shepherd of Hermas*, about AD 160,[19] the author refers to 'the presbyters who preside over the *ekklēsia*' (*hoi presbuteroi hoi proistamenoi tēs ekklēsias*). The word for 'over you' or 'have charge over' is the same in Hermas as in 1 Thessalonians 5:12.[20] So evidently for the first 100 years of the church, elders were in charge of the church's meetings and superintended their public affairs.

3. They 'give you instruction' (NASB). The KJV 'admonish' is closer to the Greek *noutheteo*, frequently rendered *warn*, something different from teaching, for Colossians 1:28 speaks of *warning* (*noutheteō*) and teaching. There is a negative quality. It has a sharp edge, something which the self-assertive and super-democratic atmosphere of our times pastors scarcely dare to do today (see 2 Tim. 4:2, 'reprove, rebuke, and exhort').

4. According to Hebrews 13:17 the same elders 'watch over your souls' and are accountable to God to do it well. It is implicit that they also watch against harm to the flock by insiders or outsiders who teach false doctrine or seduce morals (Acts 20:17, 28-31). This suggests prayer for the flock as well as attention to the 'souls' of members of every time of life, including the aged and children. James clearly says 'elders,' not 'the elder,' may be called upon to pray for the sick (James 5:14).

5. 'Let him call for the elders of the church' (James 5:14) suggests the proper procedure in observance of the rites and ordinances of the church and its worship. 'This... does not imply any exclusive authority in the elder. All believers are priests and can therefore lead in such matters if the need should arise. But since God is a God of order, and He has ordained the office of the eldership, the presiding function should be committed to the elders in all ordinary cases where that is possible. The church, however, is never dependent upon any official clerical class in its functions. The church is always greater than any office it creates.'

These remarks by A. J. McClain in lectures I attended as a student echo the thinking of the founders of the churches of the sixteenth-century Reformation. Luther's views are to be found summarized with full documentation from Luther's writings by P. Althouse.[21] Calvin had much to say about the validity of a special ministry of presbyter, bishop, pastor, mininster, but also said, '[I]t is clear that every member of the church is charged with the responsibility of public edification according to the measure of [God's] grace, provided he perform it decently and in order.'[22] Like Luther he based this teaching on the universal priesthood of believers.

Gradual Development of the Office.

The New Testament writings come from different stages in the development of the New Testament church. The above sources cited for duties of elders (1 Thess. and James) are probably from about the end of the sixth decade of the first century, Hebrews possibly before AD 64. Acts, cited for the origin of the offices of deacon and elder, describes very early government of the Jerusalem church (Acts 6 onward). If the angels (or messengers) of the seven churches in Revelation 2 and 3 were elder-pastors or 'ministers' of those churches, they reflect a situation at the very end of the apostolic age – according to late dating of Revelation. It is reasonable to assume that there was some development during that time. What prevailed in the Jerusalem church in the forties or even Antioch in the fifties or Ephesus in the sixties were not quite the same and certainly not the same as thirty years later when Revelation was written on a prison island and Clement of Rome wrote his famous epistle to the Corinthians. L. Berkhof has very helpful suggestions on this subject from which this paragraph has profited.[23]

In the early days at Jerusalem there was no place for the 'pastors-and-teachers' of Ephesians 4:11 because Apostles, prophets and evangelists were their ministers. By the time (before AD 46) of the visit of Barnabas and Saul, bearing financial assistance from Antioch, the Jerusalem church had elders (Acts 11:30) who administered

---

18. Alexander Strauch, *Biblical Eldership* (Littleton, CO: Lewis & Roth, 1988), pp. 101–110.
19. *Visions of the Pastor of Hermas* II. 4,1 ANF, Vol. II, p. 12.
20. Bauer, Arndt, Gingrich, *Lexicon sub proistemi*, p. 714.
21. P. Althaus, *The Theology of Martin Luther*, trans. R. C. Schultz, 1966, 'The Office of the Ministry,' pp. 323–328. See also F. Pieper's comments, 'The Relation of the Public Ministry to the Spiritual Priesthood of All Christians,' in Francis Pieper, *Systematic Theology* (St Louis: Concordia Publishing, 1950), pp. 440–443.
22. Calvin, *Institutes*, IV. I.12 and note 22.
23. L. Berkhof, *Systematic Theology*, p. 586.

the aid but most likely neither governed nor taught since the Apostles, prophets and evangelists were still there. They may have 'ruled' the church in the sense of conducting its business. Their work at that time seems to overlap that of deacons. With the passing of time the teaching of doctrines came to be the particular duty of elders who were teachers, hence 'pastors' in the sense used by 1 Peter 5:1. 2. There were elders, 1 Timothy 5:17 tells us, who specialized in 'word and doctrine' and were to receive monetary support (v. 18). Near the close of Paul's life (perhaps AD 67) he directed the creation of schools for the training of ministers for teaching of the doctrines Paul had disseminated in the church at Ephesus (2 Tim. 2:2). He thereby created a class of *official teachers* of the church as well as *teachers of teachers* which surely meant they were among those elders we meet in Titus and 1 and 2 Timothy.

Forces Working for Change.

Already in late apostolic times there were present other forces which gradually in the next century brought about the development of the college of presbyters with a president to whom later the title *episcopos* (bishop) was reserved. T. M. Lindsay in a justly praised magisterial work reported four suggestions of scholars as to what those forces were.

The first was that rising temptations from multiplying heresies and trials from persecution 'probably' led to the feeling that resistance to both would be strengthened by a more thorough unity. 'One man can take a firmer grip on things.... What is the business of many is often the work of none.'[24]

Secondly, he cites W. M. Ramsay,[25] who proposed that the 'overseer = presbyter' who did his work well would likely become permanent in that work. 'The elder who had oversight' of 'correspondence with other... churches and the reception and entertainment of delegates [which was a feature of *ekklēsia* already in New Testament times]... naturally became a very important man... thus gradually one of the... elders came to stand forth as the *episcopus par excellence*' (Lindsay, pp. 207, 208).

Thirdly, he highlights Justin Martyr,[26] who describes a typical weekly meeting for worship. At this service there was a 'president who verbally instructs' and who at the time of distribution of the elements of the communion (Eucharist) 'offers prayers and thanksgivings.'[27] 'This man,' says Lindsay,[28] 'is clearly the anticipation of the later [local] bishop.'[29]

Fourthly, '[T]he need for one authority in doctrinal matters led to the selection of one man, and to placing on him the responsibility of seeing that the members of the congregation were not tempted away from the true faith by irresponsible teachers, who offered themselves to instruct the community.'[30]

To these suggested causes for the prevalence of the office of a single 'pastor' or 'bishop,' in the sense that we find it in writings of second and third centuries and generally up till Nicea I, add some possible reasons why the development, if it was a development, took place.

1. Timothy himself was the pastor with unique authority in the Ephesian church. True, this was in part because he was a special emissary of an Apostle there. Yet the church through history has regarded instructions to him *in his public capacity* as instruction for all pastors. It is doubtful if after he ceased to serve there (he left at least briefly to be with Paul in his last days, 2 Tim. 4) there was no successor in his office. There evidently was no such person at Philippi as yet at about the same time but, if I am correct, a precedent had been set which became widely accepted before long.

2. There seems to be no express biblical reason why each elder should have an equal share of authority in plural eldership. It is within the power of any local congregation to designate one elder as leader, *the pastor*, or the senior pastor, as has become the fashion, and the others to 'assist him in spiritual oversight of the church.'

3. There is an irresistable impulse in every group to desire and to have a chief officer of some sort. This existed in ancient Israel before King Saul when elders ruled. True, it was a 'natural' impulse, not a godly consensus that asked for a king for a C.E.O., but they already had such an officer of a different kind, Samuel by name, and before him a variegated succession of 'judges.' Does history furnish clear proof of exception to this state of affairs?[31]

---

24. Lindsay, op. cit., pp. 206–207.
25. W. M. Ramsay, *The Church in the Roman Empire*, 5th ed. (London: Hodder & Stoughton, 1893), p. 307 ff.
26. Justin Martyr, *Apology I*, p. 67.
27. I am citing ANF, Vol. I, pp. 185, 186.
28. Lindsay, op. cit., p. 208.
29. To which I add, a rather plain picture of Protestant pastors of every denomination from 1517 onward.
30. Lindsay, op. cit., pp. 209, 210. Though T. M. Lindsay wrote almost a hundred years ago, he wrote after historical and biblical scholars of high competence had thoroughly investigated the evidence recovered from antiquity and summarized it.
31. *Shophet*, the Hebrew word translated 'judge,' and *dun* [doon] refer to rule, governance, not simply rendering judicial decision.

4. Groups such as the Plymouth Brethren, and Little Flock of China, at first desired to have no local chief officer, preacher or pastor. They seemed to be unconscious of the fact that even at early stages of development they had just such local leaders, whose names we know. Among these 'Brethren' were Darby, Mueller, Groves, B. W. Newton and many more; among the 'Little Flock' Watchman Nee himself and several others. This was pointed out in a research paper presented to me in 1970 by a student in my class at Trinity Evangelical Divinity School.[32] Among the many assemblies of the Brethren today a local single-man-preacher-overseer, with a college of elders, exists. There has been 'felt need,' that is to say, an 'impulse' for change. 'Open Brethren' in a recent international consultation gave recognition to this 'new' arrangement.

5. The New Testament does not say how many elders a church should have. It is common for seminal churches to exist for awhile, as in Crete (Titus 1:5), without any elders. Paul directed Titus to 'appoint elders in every town' – not every church. Does this mean that the groups of Christians in these towns were not full-fledged churches? Evidently so. Some churches in every time may have only one male adult member. I have served as interim pastor where there was not a single person who met the qualifications for eldership set forth in Titus 1 and 1 Thessalonians 3.[33]

---

[32]. *The Concept of Pastor in Brethren Thought* by O. Rex Major. Dr Major has recently put in my hands new literature of the Brethren and a tape of Ken Fleming's address at an international conclave of Brethren church leaders at Rome in 1996 and a book, *New Horizons in Mission*, which contains the papers read at that gathering. The address by Ken Fleming reports that presently there are 'Four Types of Leadership' (*New Horizons*, p. 134) among 'Open Brethren.' There is acceptance of government by a board of elders of which one is a salaried full-time 'pastoral worker' (*New Horizons*, p. 135).

[33]. Very early in my ministry as a pastor I became intensely interested in a biblical 'job description' of my duties as a pastor, because I had come to the conviction that simply to preside over the local consensus, in a denomination where rather uninformed American rural traditions prevailed, was not the right thing to do. My duties as a pastor, stated clearly in ordination vows, were not matched with adequate support from a college of mature, qualified elders and deacons elected to be my support. The church board consisting of all the chief elected officers – including deacons and deaconesses – rarely if ever came up to the biblical standards either for deacons or elders, certainly not to be *episcopoi* (overseers) and *presbuteroi* (mature judges).

19
Church Offices and Ministry, II

Choice, Installation, Term of Service of Elders.

1. The office may be sought by any 'man.' '[I]f any man aspires to the office of overseer [bishop], it is a fine work he desires to do' (1 Tim. 3:1 NASB). If we may paraphrase what follows immediately, 'All right, but these are the stiff requirements' (vv. 2-7). 'Aspire' implies 'diligently seek' (Heb. 11:6 KJV). This encourages a young man who aspires to pastoral ministry to present himself to his church and to ask the church's direction in educational preparation, or for a mature, prepared man to submit an application, as is common.

2. The precedent set by Paul's instruction to Titus (1:5) and the actions he and Barnabas took at Lystra, Iconium and Antioch (Acts 14:21-23) in appointing elders (perhaps by securing elections in each church) suggests that the initiative may come from the church itself, the missionary who established the congregation, or even the congregation or mission organization who sponsored the missionary. This also is common in both denominational and independent missions.

3. In the case of established churches, in any case, the church itself should do its best to be sure that the candidate meets the qualifications. At this point the custom arises of having ministers – recognized as such by other churches and groups – share in examining the candidate for ordination.

4. Mutual recognition of 'ordained' ministers is both a fact and a necessity. Official lists formed by ministerial associations, presbyteries, dioceses and the like may or may not be involved. Baptists in general, for example, recognize Methodist or Presbyterian 'ordination' and the converse is true. In congregational government the ordaining church cannot legislate for another, nor can a conference or denominational authority legislate for the church. Baptist and Congregationalist custom is to call for examination of the candidate's fitness, usually by a committee of pastors, or pastors and laymen of neighboring churches invited by the ordaining church. Then ministers of other churches should share in the act of ordination if the ordination is to be recognized in those churches. There are various denominational ways of securing this approval.

5. The usual way of choosing an elder is by vote of the congregation. We know 'the whole multitude' chose the 'seven' – usually regarded as deacons (Acts 6:1-6 KJV). If deacons should be elected by the congregation where they serve, certainly elders should be also. As noted earlier, the Greek word translated 'appointed' or 'ordained' in

Titus 1:5 and Acts 14:23 in usage came to mean to designate, by whatever method, but originally probably to elect by show of hands. It seems not inconsistent with Luke's and Paul's language to assume that newly planted churches might initially have an elder, or elders, appointed by some sponsoring church agency or missionary founder(s).[1]

Nothing is said in Scripture about length of term of the office. 'Apostles' were a gift to the universal church for the lifetime of the bearer of the office. Why then should not 'pastors and teachers' also be such for their lifetimes? This can be said: up until recent times (when society has become very mobile) pastors frequently held office in the same local church for life.[2] Ambrose was bishop (pastor) of Milan for twenty-three years – till his death in AD 397 at about fifty-seven years of age. In 1720, at the age of about twenty-three, John Gill became pastor at Horsleydown, near London, and remained there as pastor till his death fifty-one years later. Augustine remained bishop of Hippo from the moment the people seized him at a regular worship service and elected him to succeed the aged and not very competent Valerius. He remained at his post to the end of his life thirty-five years later.

Of course an ordained minister is pastor of a church only if installed after accepting a proper invitation. If for any reason he leaves that position, by custom he retains the *title* of 'elder' or 'pastor' and in the denominational group is regarded as an elder without *office* and without authority in any congregation until invited and installed again – not unlike military titles and titles of office in legislatures and the judicial system of most countries.

Not everyone who has one of the spiritual gifts suitable for public ministry is installed as an elder or other official person in a church. All, of course, should and many do exercise their 'gift' to the limit, without let or hindrance as long as they do not claim officially to represent a local church. Many modern missionary enterprises, for example, are staffed largely by unordained but highly trained people – Campus Crusade, Wycliffe Translators and New Tribes Mission are examples. Would Bill Bright have been more effective as facilitator and promoter of campus evangelism if he had been recruited at a theological seminary and ordained by a Presbyterian or Baptist church instead of moving from the world of business into a tremendously important evangelistic missionary movement? Not likely. I suspect the intelligent and pious farmer's wife, teacher of the class of adolescent boys and girls in my home church, and who first pointed me toward a lifetime in ordained ministry, might have been spoiled by three years in a seminary followed by formal ordination!

The Authority of Elders, Pastors and Teachers.

As set forth above in chapter 12, 'The Gifts of Christ to the Church' (Eph. 4:7-17), the pastor-teacher (along with Apostles, prophets and evangelists at the first age of the church) is a person *given* to the church. He performs his work locally, but receives his authority from Christ for the building up of the church. His authority to teach the local assembly is a 'given,' as we say in mathematics and logic, which the churches are bound to recognize and accept if they elevate him to the office. The assembly is exhorted to weigh his worthiness and competence carefully (1 Tim. 3:1-10; Titus 1:5-11) and instructed to provide adequate material support for him and his family as far as they are able (1 Tim. 5:17, 18; Gal. 6:6-8).

We have seen that pastoral authority proceeds from Christ, not a church. A church which calls a man to be their pastor is not obligated to install any particular candidate for the office of pastor-teacher. Though they should check the prospective minister's doctrinal beliefs against their received doctrine, and both against Scripture, the people of a church should not ordinarily attempt to tell their pastor how and what to preach. The wise pastor, on the other hand will adjust his teaching, his manners and strategy to meet his people where they are as he brings them where they ought to be, being careful to separate his own cultural-familial baggage from the faith once for all delivered.

Spiritual authority of pastors, as both a 'gift' of the ascended Christ to the church (Eph. 4:7 ff.), and as one to whom authority has been delegated by a church, was considered seriously by the Reformers. Luther saw the two sources clearly, but thought that times, customs and circumstances rightly could affect the form of church government and the offices.[3] His views spread widely through his writings and have been worked out by Paul Althaus[4] and Francis

---

1. *Per contra*, as we have earlier noted, some restorationists insist that God plants in every new *ekklēsia* all the *gifts* necessary to be a fully operating *ekklēsia* immediately.
2. My seven-times great-grandfather Culver, I discovered recently, helped found the first Baptist church in Connecticut in the year 1709. A visit to that church's cemetery near Old Mystic discovered a monument to three successive generations of Wightmans who successively led that congregation as pastors for 120 years – pastorates of forty years each.
3. Francois Wendel, *Calvin 'Sacraments'* trans. P. Mairet (New York: Harper & Row, 1963), p. 302, note 24.
4. Paul Althaus, *The Theology of Martin Luther*, trans. R. C. Schultz (Philadelphia: Fortress Press, 1966), pp. 312–318.

Pieper.[5] Calvin also saw the two sources of ecclesiastical power. His understanding of the form of government, the number of offices, and their powers, was modified somewhat, as he revised his writings, though to the end he sought to discover biblical precedents and directives. During his 'exile' at Strasburg he learned much about church order from Bucer. The ultimate source of authority, whether of pastors, teachers or the 'lay' *ekklēsia*, is from Christ, drawn *from* Scripture, *through* the local church's election, and by the Holy Spirit: about the same as Luther's views.[6] I recommend Calvin's summary of his own views as both ponderable and wholesome.

> I approve only those human constitutions which are founded upon God's authority, drawn from Scripture, and, therefore, wholly divine.... I mean that the Lord in his sacred oracles faithfully embraced and clearly expressed both the whole sum of true righteousness, and all aspects of the worship of his majesty... therefore, in these matters the Master alone is to be heard. But because he did not will in outward discipline and ceremonies to prescribe in detail what we ought to do (because he foresaw *that this depended upon the state of the times, and he did not esteem one form suitable for all ages*) [emphasis added], here we must take refuge in those general rules which he has given, that whatever the necessity of the church will require for order and decorum should be tested against these. Lastly, because he has taught nothing specifically, and because these things are not necessary to salvation, and for the upbuilding of the church these things ought to be variously accommodated to the customs of each nation and age, it will be fitting (as the advantage of the church will require) to change and abrogate traditional practices and to establish new ones... not rashly.... But love will best judge.[7]

There is a small measure of truth in the common pronouncement of speakers at seminars that authority of office and respect for office must be earned. This certainly is true for retention of authority and respect. Under the church's biblical constitution, the church at Ephesus has 'tested those who call themselves apostles and are not, and found them to be false' (Rev. 2:2) and we all are to 'test the spirits' of those who claim to be spokesmen for God (1 John 4:1 ff.; see also Acts 20:28 ff.; 2 Cor. 11:10-15). Yet, he who deliberately challenges a faithful pastor's right to do his job, solemnly conferred at his ordination, and accepted at his installation, has much to answer for in the last day.

Dignity, Responsibilities, Compensations of Elders.

As to *dignity*: Jesus, Himself, is 'Shepherd [pastor] and Bishop [overseer] of your souls' (1 Peter 2:25 KJV). Peter, leader of the Apostles, referred to himself in addressing elders as a 'fellow elder' (1 Peter 5:1) and John similarly (2 John 2). Church members are exhorted to recognize the dignity of the office and therefore of holders of this office.[8]

As to *responsibilities*: an elder is a 'steward of God' (Titus 1:7 KJV). Stewards work under the shadow of the coming of the Lord, when account must be given (1 Cor. 4:1-5) and when they shall each receive appropriate praise or blame. One should be cautious therefore in seeking or accepting this office in the church.

As to *compensations*: the New Testament has much to say of rewards for each Christian as a steward of all God has provided, but special promises of rewards for good stewards of the 'manifold grace of God' (1 Peter 4:10 KJV), for elders as well as every 'Paul or Apollos or Cephas' (1 Cor. 3:21-23; 4:1-5). In all these passages the subject is the public ministers of the gospel and shepherds of the flock of God. Peter sets up a doctrine of a special 'unfading crown of glory' as reward for faithful pastors and how to earn it – not as money-grabbers or attention-seekers but as humble and cheerful examples to the 'charge alloted' to them (1 Peter 5:1-4).[9]

Qualifications for the Office of Elder or Bishop.

Elder designates office or position in a local church; *bishop* (overseer) designates function, what an elder is supposed to do. Hence qualifications for office must be defined as corresponding to the duties of office. Let it be repeated that functions and duties more than position are involved in New Testament terms for what we have come to call 'office.' No Greek word for 'office' is ever in the New Testament used to designate an elder or deacon and only once of an Apostle (*hupēretēs*, 1 Cor. 4:1) where it is rendered 'minister(a)' in KJV, 'servant(a)' in ESV.

---

5. Francis Pieper, *Christian Dogmatics*, Vol. III (St Louis: Concordia Publishing, 1950) pp. 439–462.
6. See *Institutes* IV.8.8-II and all of IV.I-II, IV.I0.30 and especially IV.3. 1-9. The last should be required reading for every church constitution committee!
7. Calvin, *Institutes*, IV. Lo.30.
8. 1 Thess. 5:12, 13; Heb. 13:7, 17, 24; Gal. 6:6, 7; *et al.*
9. Material and financial support of pastors and missionaries is discussed in the next chapter.

As far as the New Testament is concerned, we qualify for church membership by repenting of our sins and confessing Christ as Lord in Christian baptism. We thereby set out on the journey toward perfection. The candidate for eldership must have demonstrated to the church a high degree of attainment on that journey, as set forth in 1 Timothy 3:1-7; Titus 1:5-9; and, by inference, in 1 Peter 5:1-4. Commenting on these passages a revered authority says:

> In taking a general view of ministerial qualifications... if the ministry is a spiritual work a corresponding *spiritual character* seems to be required in its administrators.... The Scripture justly insists that ministers should be 'holy' – in a peculiar sense men of God.[10]

Titus 1:5-9 relates that Titus was left behind by Paul, at the end of some unreported mission of evangelism in Crete, to organize churches there, appointing elders in each 'city.' It would have taken Titus an extended period of time. The newly formed Christian groups had only recently escaped the moral ravages of an admittedly extraordinarily corrupt society (Titus 1:12, 13). Yet Titus was instructed to appoint as an elder only a man who 'hold[s] firm to the trustworthy word as taught, so that he may be able to give instruction in sound doctrine and also to rebuke those who contradict it' (Titus 1:9). The new elder must be 'able to teach' (1 Tim. 3:2) and 'not be a recent convert' (1 Tim. 3:6). Furthermore he was to 'Lay hands hastily on no man' (1 Tim. 5:22 ASV), that is, take time to review the man's record and character. At least a cursory acquaintance with Christian doctrinal and ethical standards plus maturity are biblical requirements for this office. Titus must have toured the Island of Crete systematically to produce such a corps of church elders – parallel in every particular with the situation in the recent mission fields of the past two centuries.

Thus the existence of a valid ministry of pastors and teachers cannot be apart from some program of education for 'the ministry' – under whatever cultural, political and physical situations exist where the churches are located. Churches would therefore seem to have a right in lands like our own to require educational preparation for a candidate for the ministry. Further it seems proper that students aspiring for ministry should be subject to proof of moral competence before admission to schools for ministers. Where possible their churches should aid them financially on their long way to election, ordination and installation.

A newly appointed young pastor should not be hobbled with heavy debts incurred in many years of post-high school studies. Many of the moral qualifications and traits of leadership can be developed by the proper kind of education. For example, the fine sermons my family hear from week to week are by a middle-aged pastor who had to receive special education to overcome stammering. Not all elders are pastors. More are simply local church leaders (in some churches called 'ruling elders'). A. R. Hay writes, 'Let us note what is not required of an Elder. It is not stated that he must have the gift of preaching.' First Timothy 5:17 is cited.[11]

I leave for other venues a full discussion of the qualifications set forth in the texts at the head of this section. Commentaries treat them fully.

At the present time enormous changes are taking place among the churches in regard to 'the ministry' and the pastorate. That there should be no 'ordained' pastors at all is a vague idea circulating along with conflict over ordination of women and even of practicing homosexuals. I have been called upon to teach pastoral theology several times of late. My preparations have made me acquainted with some interesting literature of the subject – old and new. Thomas Oden – as is his fashion and unique contribution – supplies thirty-four pages of bibliography of the subject from the earliest Fathers to the present.[12] Richard J. Neuhaus, while still a Lutheran minister, wrote a book which, as supplementary reading, shook up my class of anti-liturgical but very conservative evangelicals with arguments from an historic liturgical outlook.[13] If, however, the same logic-chopping, Scripture-wresting hermeneutics Oden uses in his chapter, 'Women in the Pastoral Office,' had been the norm through the rest of his book it would be useless for instruction of evangelical pastors. From the perspective of the Plymouth Brethren, Alexander Strauch provides a cogent, scholarly 'Urgent Call to Restore Biblical church Leadership' in *Biblical Eldership*.[14] Strauch makes good use of the best scholarly research. George Bromiley treats *Christian ministry* with

---

10. Charles Bridges, *The Christian Ministry* (Edinburgh: Banner of Truth, 1830, 1976), p. 26.
11. A. R. Hay, *The New Testament Order for Church and Missionary* (256 Oak St, Audubon, NJ: New Testament Missionary Union, n.d.), p. 237.
12. Thomas Oden, *Pastoral Theology* (San Francisco: Harper & Row, 1983).
13. R. J. Neuhaus, *Freedom for Ministry* (San Francisco: Harper & Row, 1984).
14. Alexander Strauch, *Biblical Leadership* (Littleton, CO: Lewis & Roth, 1988).

due regard for scriptural norms and historical perspectives.[15] Special mention should be made of two chapters: 'Theology as Aptitude' and 'The Attainment of Theological Aptitude' by F. Pieper;[16] *The Christian Ministry*[17] and *The Reformed* [regenerated] *Pastor*[18] are classics every pastor should know. Any Baptist seeking an older Baptist authority for government of the local church by a plurality of elders should read Harvey, *The Church*.[19]

The Office of Deacon.

It is hard to say how the custom arose among Baptists and similar groups of Protestant believers of making the *diaconate* a 'ruling office' – in other words, to make them elders in fact. Innumerable local church constitutions have a line which says 'the deacons shall assist the pastor in spiritual oversight of the church.' Unhappily, A. H. Strong, (outstanding and very competent) defends that arrangement in the face of all the historical evidence (especially the *Didachē*) coming to light in his time (Hatch, Harnak, Lindsay, *et al*) and contrary results of biblical studies (J. B. Lightfoot, *Commentary on Philippians*). Harm is mitigated if the deacons chosen truly meet the requirements of 1 Timothy 3:8-13; yet there is distortion of the pastoral office when the descriptions of the elder's office are applied to *the* pastor only and thereby the pastor is expected to wield all the authority of the elder's office and perform all the tasks. This has led to prevalent congregational anarchy in many churches of our time as well as to pastoral dictatorship in others. It helps explain Strong's rueful comment that 'Every pastor is a potential pope.'

A Baptist contemporary of Strong, Professor H. Harvey of the Baptist seminary at Hamilton, New York – very competently, from the evidence of Scripture, history and archaeology – was demonstrating that the church of the New Testament and of antiquity, at least till Nicea (325), was ruled by a college of local elders, a true presbytery, with their pastor (or pastor-teacher), now called the bishop, and that deacons performed what he called 'secular duties.'[20] Harvey discovered and explained how Baptists had abandoned the primitive ruling presbytery. He notes:

> The earlier Baptist confessions of faith – those of 1643 and 1689 – recognize the plural eldership. The discipline adopted by the Philadelphia Association in 1743 presents it in the modified form of a ruling eldership, in which form it still exists in the English churches.[21]

Then after noting the change to 'spiritual oversight' by pastor and deacons he says of government of elders:

> There is serious reason to doubt whether an institution which rests on what seems the uniform example of the apostles can rightfully be set aside; as also whether, in the absence of such a guiding and conserving body within it, our church organization is not essentially weakened, alike in the purity and power of its church-life and in the wisdom and steadiness of its evangelizing efforts.[22]

He goes on to say that ruling elders are adapted to provide continuity 'in worship and ordinances amidst pastoral changes.'[23] The present writer can attest from both happy and painful experiences that the matter is precisely as Harvey says.

The qualifications for serving in the deacon's office are set forth only in one passage – 1 Timothy 3:8-13. If we regard the Seven of Acts 6:1-6 as deacons then we are instructed that deacons do not occupy themselves with 'the word of God and prayer' but 'serve tables' and take charge of the needy members such as 'widows.' Further, at verse 11 of 1 Timothy 3, in the midst of a paragraph apparently wholly relating to the *diaconate*, Paul says, 'Women must likewise be dignified, not malicious gossips, but temperate, faithful in all things' (ASB). If intended to refer to Christian women in general, the sentence is extraneous to the subject of the paragraph. The Greek *gunaikas* (acc. plu of *gunē*), apart from context, would be translated simply 'women'; in context it cannot easily be so understood. So the NASB margin comments 'either deacons' wives or deaconesses.' This is moot in theological literature. For several reasons I, with many, assert that Paul is referring to female servants (deaconesses) of the church.

15. George Bromiley, *The Christian Ministry* (Grand Rapids: Eerdmans, 1960).
16. *Systematic Theology* I, pp. 46–51, 186–190.
17. Charles Bridges, Edinburgh: Banner of Truth Trust, 1830, 1976.
18. Richard Baxter, Carlisle, PA: Banner of Truth Trust, 1656, 1979.
19. H. Harvey, *The Church* (Philadelphia: American Baptist Publication Society, 1879), p. 74 ff.
20. ibid., pp. 66–104.
21. ibid., p. 76.
22. ibid., p. 77.
23. op. cit., p. 77.

1. The qualifications both for elders and deacons in 1 Timothy 3 include 'husband of one wife' (3:2, 12) but say nothing about elders' wives as such. Why should this be brought up in the case of deacons if not in the case of elders?

2. Paul, who just previously had said 'I do not permit a woman to teach or to exercise [or usurp, KJV] authority over a man' (1 Tim. 2:12), would have had no reason not to include females in the deacon's office, where many of the duties require the sensibilities and abilities which most women have more than men do.

3. There is elsewhere a reference to a female servant (or deaconess) – 'I commend to you our sister Phoebe, a servant of the church at Cenchreae' (Rom. 16:1). *Sister* is the feminine form of the word for *brother*; *servant* is the word in 1 Timothy 3:8 rendered *deacon*, in accusative singular form here either masculine or feminine. Hence it would be fully justified to translate *diakonon*, in Romans 16:1, as deaconess. It is therefore possible that '*gunaikas*,' women (1 Tim. 3:11), should be understood as referring to 'female-deacons,' or better deaconesses.

4. The mention of 'husband of one wife' (v. 12) after *gunaikos* in verse 11 as a kind of separate entry indicates that the subject is not the same in each case.

5. Among the earliest parts of *Apostolic Constitutions*, the 'deaconess' (*hē diakonos*) appears as one who, after deacons, should be honored.[24] Says Beyer, whatever construction we place on the reference to Phoebe (Rom. 16:1) and 'women' in 1 Timothy 3:11, 'It is indisputable… that an order of deaconesses did quickly arise in the church.'[25]

Here again all passages relating to the organization, government and officers of the New Testament *ekklēsia* relate to a system (probably not in fixed form) already in operation. No passage describes or prescribes the system. We are a bit like curious neighbors looking in on a party at a neighbor's house. We learn much in parts and pieces but the whole escapes us. For this reason it behooves theologians to be modest in making pronouncements in this area of the doctrine of the church.

---

24. *The Apostolic Constitutions* II.26, ANF VII, p. 388.
25. *Diakonos'* TDNT, II, p. 93.

20
Church Discipline

Positive discipline of Christian believers by instruction and nurture was a major reason for the very existence of local New Testament churches. Discipline as action to correct wrong behavior was a lesser but important concern. The latter stands out in all records of the church in the first three centuries – a time when the church endured the pervasive tug of heathenism's morals and manners, but in vital struggle against that tug and tow. The purity of the lives of the Christians impressed their pagan neighbours and, in the opinion of scholars – favorable to Christianity and unfavorable, ancient and modern – was one strong factor in winning multitudes for Christ in the centuries leading up to the legalization of Christianity.

Leaders of the sixteenth-century Reformation clearly saw restoration of church discipline as a *sine qua non* for raising the level of morality among their people, likewise good order in the churches as a means to well-ordered individual Christian lives. Though they distinguished imputed righteousness (justification) from sanctification (personal holiness) they knew that the two stand together, not in opposition. Luther was very concerned to correct the morals of the German people and was himself a model of balanced behavior – as he saw it from his somewhat acculturated perspective. As the evangelical movement gained strength, forces of history, which cannot be separated from divine providence, placed what Krauth called *The Conservative Reformation*[1] under partial control of the various civil governments of Germany and Scandinavia. Thereby the church lost power to do as much as its best leaders wished to do in calling professed Christians to account for bad behavior. This began rather early in Luther's career as a Reformer.

Calvin's leadership was always directed toward improvement of moral life of the church – often, as in his Geneva – limited by the inability of the church completely to act without interference from the civil authorities. Calvin was forced to leave his pastoral charge at Geneva and the city for three years because, in part, of government meddling in control of access to the Lord's Supper. After refinement of views during his stay 'in exile' at Strasbourg he returned as convinced as ever of the need for church discipline. He felt 'whatever might produce disorder in the church and be a scandal to its members thus reflected upon and affronted Christ' (Wendel, p. 298). Hence, he thought, 'discipline is indispensable if a church has any desire to preserve its character as the church of Christ' (Wendel, p. 299). Neither Calvin nor the Calvinist wing of the Reformation has thought discipline to be of the essence of the church but as necessary for its well-being – not the *esse* but the *bene esse*.

---

1. *The Conservative Reformation and its Theology as represented by the Augsburg Confession and in the History and Literature of the Evangelical Lutheran church* (Philadelphia: Lippincott, 1875), 840 pages, is still the most thorough polemic for orthodox Lutheranism in America.

The Reformation folk who came to be called Anabaptists rather fiercely defended the integrity of the local church by severe ecclesiastical discipline of members.

As for early American churches, examination of congregational records reveals intense concern about the moral life of members and their scandal-free reputation among neighbors. This is evident in congregational records – Baptist, Methodist, Presbyterian, Congregatonal – less so among Anglicans.[2]

Discipline such as the church of the first centuries practiced did not arise first in the 'churches' (à la Troeltsch) but in the 'sects' – the unity of the Brethren, Anabaptists, Quakers, Baptists, Separatist Puritans. Donald F. Durnbaugh remarks:

> It is known that the Reformed tradition added to the marks the church maintained by the Lutherans – the word truly proclaimed and the sacraments truly admiminstered – the mark of discipline. John Knox... likened the exercise of church discipline to the quarantine of a disease.... A somewhat different attitude was expressed by the Anabaptists, who saw the practice of discipline as a means of restoration of the wayward brother.[3]

Durnbaugh has a superb section on 'church discipline' (pp 220–225). A church is of course a place where justified sinners meet *en route* to entire sanctification, not having yet attained it. There is no place in a biblically constituted assembly for the hopeless statement of the United Church of Canada:

> Like most of the larger Protestant churches it follows a middle way.... It makes little attempt... to discriminate between true believer and nominal Christian.... The church, like the children of Israel, is a mixed multitude (Exod. 1:38).[4]

Discipline, of course, is related to the noun *disciple* – one who learns. To repeat: positive discipline as teaching and nurture (Acts 2:42 ff.) is a major reason for the very existence of local churches. Discipline as measures taken to correct wrong behavior is a lesser, but important concern. The latter is necessary to the former.

Duty to Discipline.

The New Testament enjoins corrective discipline as a solemn duty *of the local church* with strong language in five books, in at least seven passages.[5] Elders figure prominently in the Matthew passage and Timothy (the pastor in the last reference), but the other five are addressed to the congregations. It is everyone's duty to act.[6]

The language in each passage is severe, insisting that some kinds of behavior cannot be tolerated in a Christian assembly and commanding that the church *as such* take notice of it and take due action to eliminate it. To carry out these commands is always disagreeable. Even where procedures are defined by church constitutions and bylaws or a denominational Book of Order, discipline tends to be neglected so long as it fails its biblically intended purposes and even sets the members to quarreling amongst themselves. Pastors who run away from facing their duty in this regard simply run into more trouble farther along.

The Necessity of Discipline.

The word *urgency* might be more appropriate today than necessity, for contemporary congregations are doing little to reintroduce serious church discipline. Considering our Lord's words both of threat for neglect of discipline and praise for attending to it (Rev. 2–3), the urgent tone of Daniel E. Wray is justified:

> Today, the church faces a moral crisis.... Her failure to take a strong stance against evil (even in her own midst), and her tendency to be more concerned about what is right, has robbed the church of biblical integrity and power... the church has sometimes erred in this matter of discipline, but today, the problem is one of outright neglect.[7]

---

2. W. W. Sweet, *Documents of Early American History and Religion on the American Frontier*. Also C. E. Hambrick-Stowe, *The Practice of Piety: Puritan Devotional Disciplines in 17th Century New England* (Chapel Hill: U. of NC Press, 1982, 1988).
3. Donald F. Durnbaugh, *The Believers' Church* (New York: Macmillan, 1970), p. 221.
4. ibid. pp. 220, 221.
5. Matt. 18:15-18; 1 Cor. 5:1-13; 6:1-10; 2 Cor. 2:5-7; 7:8-12; 2 Thess. 3:6-15; 1 Tim. 5:19-24.
6. In a parallel way when, after due legal process, someone of the nation of Israel was convicted of the sin of absolute apostasy, it was the duty of the entire community in which he lived to stone him (Deut. 13:10; Lev. 20:2; 24:16).
7. Daniel E. Wray, *Church Discipline* (Carlisle, PA: Banner of Truth Tract, 1978), p. 1.

When a congregation moves with biblically informed procedures and with right motives – 'doing nothing from partiality' (1 Tim. 5:21; James 3:17), and 'without respect of persons' (1 Peter 1:17 KJV; James 2:1, 3, 9) – good results may be expected. When we offer conversion to Christ with no cost of discipleship we offer cheap grace – a travesty on 'pure religion and undefiled,' however large a crowd of shallow professors of religion may regularly assemble for stated services. The severities of discipline are necessary for:

1. The purity of the church where the impure conduct arises. Paul rebuked the evident 'glorying' of the Corinth church over their tolerance of a fornicator among their members (1 Cor. 6:2, 6). His rebuke took the form of a simple similitude where the church is compared to a lump of dough wholly leavened by a tiny amount of yeast (leaven). Continuing the figure, he urged discipline: 'Cleanse out the old leaven that you may be a new lump' (1 Cor. 5:7).

2. The personal salvation of the diciplined member. Discipline is applied in order 'that he may be ashamed' (2 Thess. 3:14) and 'that his spirit [that of the disciplined man] may be saved in the day of the Lord' (1 Cor. 5:5; see 3:15).

Discipline of flagrant sins of immorality among church members in the form of rebuke, correction, and even severance from the church (excommunication) and shunning is present or implied on about every page of the two Epistles to the Corinthians. Paul's entreaties become mixed with threats near the end of the second letter. He informs them he is about to visit them to set things straight. He fears he will find 'quarreling, jealousy, anger, hostility, slander, gossip, conceit, and disorder' (2 Cor. 12:20). And he rather expects to be affronted by 'impurity, sexual sin and debauchery' (2 Cor. 12:21 NIV). If these fears are justified, he warns, 'On my return I will not spare those who sinned earlier' (2 Cor. 13:2 NIV). In other words, Paul will hold court and bring up to date any discipline neglected by the church and its leaders between his second and third visits (2 Cor. 13:1).

We today are not threatened by a personal scolding and visitation by an outraged apostle but we shall be held to account of our stewardship in respect to apostolic – that is scriptural-discipline of the sins of wicked talk (2 Cor. 12:20 above) and sinful acts (2 Cor. 12:21 above).

Offenses that Call for Discipline.

What are the offenses which call for disciplinary action by church officers and people? Most of them fall into three categories in the passages cited above.

1. Two (Matt. 18:15-17 and 1 Cor. 6:5-6) relate to *difficulties between members*. In the one case the offense is a 'trespass,' KJV ('sins,' RSV), of one brother against another (Matt. 18:15) – not simply a disagreement, but a real wrong, as calling of witnesses (Matt. 18:16) implies and the language of verse 15 requires. The other case is one of disagreement between two members about some moot matter.

2. A second kind of offense is simple *failure to conform* to reasonable standards of social behavior in any society, such as living off the generosity of other believers instead of working for a living (2 Thess. 3:6-14). This particular offense is also mentioned and severely condemned in non-biblical early church literature (the *Didache.* 5).[8] The church is to be no haven for trashy people who will not work.

3. Gross sins and crimes against any high standard of morality such as incest, fornication, greed (covetousness), idolatry, corrupt speech, drunkenness, robbery – some subject to civil penalties – are to be judged in the church by the church (1 Cor. 5:1-13; 2 Cor. 12:21).

4. There are oblique references to other types of cases with which Paul and others dealt in unique ways. He speaks of two men (Hymenaeus and Alexander) who have renounced good conscience and whom he had delivered to Satan, 'that they may learn not to blaspheme' (1 Tim. 1:20). Paul denounces one who likely is one of the same men – a certain Alexander the coppersmith who did Paul 'great harm,' adding that 'the Lord will repay him according to his deeds… he strongly opposed our message' (2 Tim. 4:14, 15).

These men appear to have been associated somehow with the congregation at Ephesus. In some unspecified way, in opposing Paul's message, they 'blasphemed,' i.e. spoke against the dignity of truth or against God Himself. These offenses were not simply bad thoughts but public scorn of the truth of the Word of God and personal attacks against the integrity of Paul the messenger. Many pastors have suffered from such outrages. Paul does not demand that the church at Ephesus come to his defense but he pointedly called it to the pastor's (Timothy's) attention.

---

8. 'Let every apostle, when he cometh to you, be received as the Lord; but he shall not abide more than a single day, or if there is need, a second likewise; but if he abide three days he is a false prophet,' *Didache.* 5, J. B. Lightfoot, *The Apostolic Fathers* (New York: Macmillan, 1898), p. 233.

5. Foolish troublemaking is another type of offense calling for disciplinary action by the congregation. The people who behave this way are misguided fools who must not divert the church from the 'good... excellent and profitable' to the 'unprofitable... worthless' and divisive (Titus 3:8-11). They must be compelled to keep quiet (v. 10).

6. Purveyors of false doctrines are to be dealt with harshly. The entire Epistle of Jude in vivid language, unparalleled elsewhere in the New Testament, makes the point.

Procedures in Discipline.

1. Where applicable, each Christian has a duty to his brother to call the offender's attention to his offense and lovingly seek change for the better. This is to say, notice and report of offending behavior or a wrong state of affairs should begin with someone who is suffering from the bad behavior or noticing the wrong. This, of course, can lead to tattling and other childish acts which are in themselves wrong. If the accuser is required to face the accused then there will be a few frivolous charges. Yet, as all 'whistle blowers' know, a degree of courage is required to initiate investigative and corrective action of a social group. 'Brethren, if a man be overtaken in a fault, ye which are spiritual, restore such an one... lest thou [singular number] also be tempted' (Gal. 6:1 KJV). '[G]o and tell him his fault between thee [singular] and him alone' (Matt. 18:15 KJV).

Some contend that the aggrieved person is obliged to start this proceeding and 'becomes an offender if he fails to do so.' Harvey cites Leviticus 19:17, 'Thou shalt not in any wise rebuke thy neighbor, and not suffer sin upon him.'[9] This is very difficult to do, but where carried out in love has great possibility of success. 'Faithful are the wounds of a friend; profuse are the kisses of an enemy' (Prov. 27:6). 'Oil and perfume make the heart glad, and the sweetness of a friend comes from his earnest counsel' (Prov. 27:9).

2. When personal attempts at correcting a brother fail one has not completed responsibility, for the Lord went on to say, 'if he will not hear thee [again singular], then take with thee one or two more.. And if he shall neglect to hear them, tell it unto the church' (Matt. 18:16, 17 KJV). This was spoken before a single church had been organized after the usual pattern. Later, such a matter would have been presented to the elders of the church. As in sickness, one calls for prayers of friends and family and then if the illness is life threatening 'Let him call for the elders of the church, and let them pray over him' (James 5:14), so in cases where one cannot get a personal wrong righted or knows of grievous behavior, let him present the matter to the elders of the church. Not every congregation has competent elders, nor can every wrong be righted. If the elders cannot solve the problem either they or the complainant should take the matter 'to the church.'

3. The next step is for the church (or the elders, it would seem) to make a careful investigation to establish the facts. If charges are made or serious questions of conduct alleged or suspected, clear proof is necessary. The severe case of 'sexual immorality' at Corinth (1 Cor. 5:1) was apparently already a public scandal that could not be denied. Action, not investigation, was in order. In case of serious charges against an elder (in this case an elderly man or woman, 1 Tim. 5:19), no charge was to be accepted as true, 'except' (*ektos ei mē*, a very strong adversative connection) 'on the evidence of two or three witnesses,' quoted from Deuteronomy 19:15. This brings to bear the legal requirements of Mosaic civil law. For Paul this provision was of great importance in church courts – for courts they really are. He cites Deuteronomy 19:15 again at 2 Corinthians 9:9 in a specific case. Jesus Himself cited the same law in His only recorded reference to church disputes (Matt. 18:16). Nothing should be received in evidence in a church court that would not stand up in a Mosaic court of law: 'The judges shall inquire diligently, and if the witness is a false witness and has accused his brother falsely, then you shall do to him as he had meant to do to his brother. *So you shall* [emphasis added] purge the evil from your midst' (Deut. 19:18-19).

4. The evidence must be brought before the whole church acting in official session 'with the power of our Lord Jesus' (1 Cor. 5:4) to declare the 'punishment, which was inflicted of many' (2 Cor. 2:6 KJV). Punishment is to 'deliver ... to Satan' (1 Cor. 5:5 and 1 Tim. 5:20). The realm of Satan is apparently the pagan world ('let him be to you as a Gentile,' Matt. 18:17). Excommunication – cut off from fellowship – is the way this has come to be understood.

5. Repentance and restoration with renewed fellowship is the last stage of successful discipline of erring brethren. Whether 2 Corinthians 2:6-11 refers to the disciplined *fornicator* of 1 Corinthians 5:1 ff. or not, the procedure of repentance, restoration and renewal set forth there applies.

---

9. H. Harvey, The Church: Its Polity and Ordinances (Philadelphia: American Baptist Publishing Society, 1879), p. 89.

The church during the centuries of Roman persecution was more than vigorous in applying discipline and stern in providing restoration only after lengthy probation. The Montanist, Novatian and Donatist 'heresies' arose because rigorists opposed restoration without extremely long, extensive probation before even partial restoration. These controversies ran on for centuries. Sad to say, in medieval times a legalistic discipline became a matter of regular private confession to a priest and prescribed formal acts of contrition. There is an enormous literature on the subject.[10]

The principle of salvation by grace through faith without works (Rom. 4:4, 5; 11:6) was obscured in almost all patristic thought. After the sub-apostolic age this lamentably happened nowhere more than in discipline. Penance, came to be thought of as a means of merit, the key to salvation, especially in the East. I cite the following for the benefit of contemporary churchmen who may feel 'queezy' about severe church discipline. It is from a letter of Gregory of Neo-Caesarea to another pastor in Pontus (northern Asia Minor) about AD 260. There were four grades of penitents who by five stages attained restoration and admission to the communion: 'the "weepers"... stand outside the door of the church, beseeching the faithful to intercede for them; the "hearers" are placed in the narthex [vestibule]; the "kneelers" kneel within the nave amid the standing congregation; the "costanders' join normally... with others except that they cannot take communion.'[11] After many years in this graded process the penitent is fully restored and can take communion. This system of public penance spread through Anatolia (now called Asia Minor) and was practiced in parts of the West as late as AD 488.[12]

Biblical discipline calls for excommunication only in severe cases where folk are unresponsive to lesser measures. Paul directed the Thessalonian church to 'keep away from any lazy brother who refused to work and to keep accepted rules' (2 Thess. 3:6), especially the specific instructions 'in this letter' (2 Thess. 3:14 RSV). In 1 Corinthians 5:11 the instruction is to refuse even to eat with a professed Christian who engaged in gross sins. The believers are *not* to cut such people off from communication – complete social ostracism – for Paul goes on to say, 'Do not regard him as an enemy, but warn him as a brother' (2 Thess. 3:15). With delinquent but not totally alienated folk such treatment effected in a loving way is a powerful instrument for good.

Notes and Cautions Regarding Biblical Discipline in the Church.

1. The need arises quickly in a new church if it has been formed of recent converts from the surrounding culture, and very difficult to effect without a substantial core of biblically and doctrinally informed members. This accounts for the severe need at Corinth when the church moved out and away from evangelizing the Jews and God-fearers of the synagogue and began to draw Gentile people, who brought with them into the new fellowship only a partially formed biblical, ethical and world view.[13] An independent missionary who established a chain of churches across the Island of Hispaniola (Haiti and Dominican Republic) reports in his autobiography that before long he had to preside at the discipline of every single pastor on account of sexual immorality.[14] There are innumerable examples. The same remarks hold true of great influxes of members in mass revivals. In some ways every new convert from the surrounding culture is a new problem of discipline unless he is quickly and thoroughly instructed.

2. Proper discipline cannot take place unless the congregation are both regenerate and instructed to a high degree. If they are not the members will neither understand nor approve of proper action – whether undertaken by deacons, elders, a board or the pastor. The effort will fail. A wise pastor's strategy will begin with careful instruction in general biblical standards and on the subject of biblical discipline. This will require a long-term, quiet but skillfully conducted program of instruction in Christian conduct and biblical discipline by the pastor and other teachers (see Titus 2:1-15; 2 Tim. 4:1-5).

3. A successful strategy is not to wait until a crisis arises – above all, not to precipitate a crisis until the congregation is ready to do the right thing without disruption of the unity of the church (if possible). We are enjoined to be 'wise as serpents, harmless as doves,' and to lead a 'quiet and peaceable' life as far as possible. After a

---

10. J. T. McNeill, *A History of the Cure of Souls* (New York: Harper & Row, 1951), Chap. V, 'Discipline and Consolation in the Age of the church Fathers'; K. S. Latourette, *A History of Christianity*, first ed. (New York: Harper and Brothers., 1953), Chap. VII, 'Admission, Worship and Discipline in the Community,' pp. 193–220.
11. McNeill, p. 96.
12. McNeill, p. 96.
13. See Acts 18:1-11 and compare 1 Corinthians 5 and 6.
14. Florent D. Toirac, *A Pioneer Missionary in the Twentieth Century* (Nappanee, IN: Evangel Press, 1988), an autobiography.

pastor has preached on 1 Corinthians, a chapter a week, then likewise the Thessalonian Epistles, discipline will come to be seen as a part of the whole scheme of biblical truth about the beliefs and life of a healthy church. There is then hope of doing the right thing without disruption.

4. There is much else that can be done from the pulpit to head off crises of discipline before they arise. Most children can be convinced that parental discipline is for their own benefit and the same may be said of church discipline if the pastor is supported at all by elders or other acknowledged teachers and leaders.

Consider what these passages prescribe and promise. 'Till I come [wrote Paul to the pastor at Ephesus], give attendance to [public] reading [of the Scriptures], to exhortation, to doctrine' (1 Tim. 4:13 KJV). The KJV here translates *paraklēsis* correctly as exhortation. The sense is to stand beside – literally in private, figuratively from the pulpit – encouraging the people to keep the commands of Christ. Note the connection with Bible-reading and doctrinal instruction. A more severe form of pulpit and pew discipline follows.

'I did not cease night or day to admonish everyone with tears' (Acts 20:31, Paul to the elders of Ephesus). '[W]e proclaim, warning everyone and teaching everyone' (Paul, Col. 1:28) – *noutheteo* (warn) sometimes gets translated 'admonish,' as in 2 Thess. 3:15 KJV, 'admonish him [the delinquent man] as a brother.' Warnings and admonitions delivered many times by many people besides the pulpit preacher over a long period will have good effect.

'[R]ebuke them sharply, that they may be sound in the faith' (Titus, the organizer of the churches of Crete, Titus 1:13). See also 2 Timothy 4:2: 'in season and out of season; reprove, rebuke.' In context the latter passage is rightly characterized as preventive discipline.

D. F. Durnbaugh's section on 'Church Discipline' in Free Churches is helpful for churches of any tradition outside the State Churches of the Old World. He tells how discipline has been exercised peacefully and effectively in the past, how it can be done and ought to be done today.[15]

John Gill, though not fully in agreement with conclusions in this chapter on church discipline, has an excellent, full treatment from a Baptist perspective, 'Of the Discipline of a Church of Christ.'[16]

W. W. Sweet's several works on early American church history, especially *Documents of Early American Church History*, also entitled *Religion on the American Frontier*, decisively demonstrate that discipline of members was a major concern of the churches of America in the first generations.[17]

---

15. Durnbaugh, op. cit., pp. 220–225.
16. John Gill, *A Complete Body of Divinity*, Vol. II, repr. (Grand Rapids: Baker Books, 1978), pp. 607–620.
17. See also Durnbaugh, pp. 17, 223.

21
Public Meetings for Worship in the Church

A timeless characterization, if not definition of public worship, appears in David's psalm at the inauguration of services at the newly set up 'tent' for the recently returned ark (1 Chron. 16:28-30).

> Ascribe to the LORD, O families of the peoples,
> ascribe to the LORD glory and strength!
> Ascribe to the LORD the glory due his name;
> bring an offering, and come before him!
> Worship the LORD in holy array [i.e. proper garments];
> tremble before him, all the earth (RSV).

These three couplets are central to a poetic ritual delivered to 'Asaph and his brethren' to employ in public services at the inauguration of the new tent sanctuary. The Mosaic and Davidic ritual forms became defunct when the temple veil was rent, the earth quaked and darkness came over the land as Jesus was dying. Yet the essence and meaning of all public worship of the one true God remain intact, as David the prophet-king set them forth here.

1. Public worship is duty and privilege of all mankind – 'O families [plural] of the peoples' (v. 28) – not *people* (singular), and 'all the earth' (v. 30). 'Messianic hopes' explain this language.[1] The three couplets are partially, for that reason, timeless.

2. Group worship is the subject. The occasion (16:1-6) and plural form of all the imperative verbs so indicate. Similarly, of the central event of church worship, the communion of cup and loaf, and citing 1 Corinthians 10:17, Dom Gregory Dix says, 'All Eucharistic worship is of necessity and by intention a *corporate action* – "Do this"' (*poieite*, plural). The blessed bread is broken that it may be *shared*.'[2]

3. The LORD (Jehovah, KJV), the God of Revelation, the God of Abraham, Isaac and Jacob is the only proper object of worship (Deut. 5:6, 7; 6:4-9; 1 Cor. 8:4-6).

4. Worship is ascribing (Heb. *yadah*, give, set, place) to God, Himself.

5. Worship is ascribing God honor (*kavodh*, weight, heaviness, as the Latin *gravitas*, dignity, importance, seriousness – Freund-Andrews, *Lexicon*). This means levity will be absent from our most worshipful moments.

---

1. J. K. F. Keil, *Chronicles* (Grand Rapids: Eerdmans, repr. 1875), p. 212, see John 4:22, 23.
2. Dom Gregory Dix, *The Shape of the Liturgy* (London: Dacre Press, 1978 [repr. of 2nd ed. of 1945]), p. 1.

6. Worship is to set on God the importance, honor, weight due to His name (v. 29). As usual in the Old Testament, 'name' stands for character and attribute.

7. Worship is accompanied by an offering (Heb. *minḥah*). This was not a bloody offering for atonement but a grain offering, a gift or tribute. Such offerings will be something of value when they 'cost' the offerer something (see Jesus' comments on 'the widow's mite,' Mark 12:41-43).

8. Worshippers properly 'come before' God (v. 29) in public worship with bodies clothed appropriately for the occasion ('in holy attire,' v. 29 REB). This would have been special vestments for Asaph and the singers. For us it should be as we think proper to stand before the Supreme Dignity, Creator and Redeemer. Attire will vary with times and culture but special occasions call for special attire.

9. The element of *fear*, in the usual sense, is not absent in true worship: 'tremble before him, all the earth' (v. 30) – 'let us offer to God acceptable worship, with reverence and awe, for our God is a consuming fire' (Heb. 12:28). It is not abnormal for fear of the consequences of refusing God the 'glory due his name' (v. 29) to move one to rise early on Sunday morning!

Worship of the living God is the duty and privilege of every rational being. Ordinary people know in their heart that God exists. And, if God exists, He must be worshipped. The principle appears first in Genesis 3 in the worship of Cain and Abel. The Bible is a book for mankind; it addresses our awareness of God from 'In the beginning, God created' (Gen. 1:1) to 'Amen' (Rev. 22:21). The normal response of our awareness is in English called *worship* (contracted from *worth-ship*). Fallen creatures that we are, we may deny, suppress or pervert our awareness as in atheism, secularism, and various forms of idolatry of the self or of a created object (Rom. 1:18-32). When, however, the Scriptures represent the best example of a pious worshipper, he is not one of the covenant people but a Gentile, God's 'servant Job,' of whom God says 'that there is none like him on the earth, a blameless and upright man, who fears God and turns away from evil' (Job 1:8 and 1:1). God adds later that 'He still holds fast his integrity' (Job 2:3).

To be one who *fears God* is the technical language of the Old Testament for a true worshipper of the one true God, and to be a *servant* of God is to be at God's beck and call. A God-fearing servant is not necessarily someone under the Mosaic covenant or the Abrahamic, for Job is a Gentile and so were all the pious friends who visited him. As God's uniquely exemplary worshipper Job is 'perfect' (*tam*, complete, mature), 'upright' (*yashar*, straighforward), he persists in 'integrity' (*tummah*). This is acknowledged by Job's wife (2:9), by God (2:3) and claimed by Job himself, calling God to witness to it (Job 27:5 and 31:6).

These moral qualities accompanying true worship are ideals in the New Testament as well. See for examples of the same the aged Simeon (Luke 2:25) and Anna (Luke 2:36-38).

Ancient paganisms did not connect *eusebeia* (piety toward the gods) with moral purity, for the gods, themselves, were conceived to engage in immoral thoughts and deeds. Nevertheless, all the New Testament terms for piety, religion and worship of the true God are from the language of Greek paganism, *via* the Greek translation of the Old Testament (LXX). This is even true of the words for attitudes of the heart such as fear (Gr. *eulabeia*, Heb. 12:28) and awe (*deos*, Heb. 12:28). Worshippers of God are 'devout' (*eulabēs*), as the aged Simeon (Luke 2:25), the thousands of Jews who came from all the world to observe Pentecost (Acts 2:5) and the men of the first church who bore the martyred Stephen to his burial (Acts 8:2).

Whether called pious, God-fearing or devout, the foregoing characterizes the kind of people to be found in honest Christian public worship in local churches and the general character of biblical worship in any age. These terms *per se*, however, have only indirect reference to the *forms* which the worship of the local worship should take. The forms should be friendly to piety, fear of God and devotion. It is not uncommon to read or hear that the New Testament provides no specific guidance to forms of worship. I think otherwise. There is no command such as 'see that you make' all 'after the pattern for them, which is being shown you on the mountain' (Exod. 25:40). Yet examples are found in the New Testament; data are furnished and detailed instructions both general and specific. They are spread throughout. In addition to this, we know of some of the synagogue patterns which the first 5,000 believers, every one a child of the synagogue, carried over into the newly formed *ekklēsia*.

The Forms of Public Worship in Apostolic Times.

1. Group worship follows some agreed-upon 'order' (see 1 Cor. 11:34 KJV) or 'traditions' (1 Cor. 11:2), otherwise disorder, for which another name is chaos, prevails. A problem of order in worship was one of the reasons Paul wrote the first letter to the Corinthians (see all of 1 Cor. 11 and 14). Though Free Church folk tend to depreciate

ritual, for which another word is 'liturgy,' every regular group observance from family meals to the crowning of kings falls quickly into a recurring order of observances. This is quite as much the case with Mennonites and Pentecostalists as with Lutherans and Episcopalians. The order of service may or may not be printed on paper. It may simply be a habit of procedure as it was before mimeograph machines gave us the Sunday bulletin. A few of us still remember.

2. The common good must be served in group worship not individual preference – 'for the common good' (1 Cor. 12:7 NIV). An individual at church may wish to sound off in an unknown tongue a hymn he has composed, a revelation or interpretation he thinks important, but for good order 'Let all things be done for building up' of the church (1 Cor. 14:26).

3. Rituals must be vehicles for the expression of true sentiments, thoughts and feelings of common people at worship. They should not be fad-driven. They may be led by 'experts,' but the aged and very young, the weak as well as the strong, must be included. Psalm 23 and the Lord's Prayer have stood the test of time in every kind of public Christian meeting precisely because they met this test.

4. Liturgy – a fixed order – may become so habitual that there is a tendency for form to replace feeling. The Old Testament prophets denounced and bewailed this in their day as Jesus did in His. '[H]aving the appearance of godliness, but denying its power' (2 Tim. 3:5).

5. The form of the liturgy itself is not sacred, though Roman and Eastern Orthodox churches call the Mass (really the liturgy of the Lord's Supper) 'the sacred liturgy.'

> Within the limits of dignity worthy of the presence of God… we should be free at any time to set aside or change our stated ritual under the leadership of the Holy Spirit. Table manners, yes; but not the rigid type that stifles the intimate fellowship of the family of God.[3]

As late as Paul's last journey to Jerusalem Jewish Christians observed some customs associated with the temple (Acts 20:16; 21:23, 26 ff.), and the first believers made use of the temple courts for fellowship and testimony (Acts 2:46; 3:1 ff.). Yet as W. D. Maxwell, a widely acknowledged Reformed liturgical scholar, says:

> The Temple worship left little [permanent] mark upon Christian worship, and this principally for two reasons. First, the great majority of the Jews of the Dispersion had never seen the worship of the Temple, and, even in Palestine the real home of Jewish worship… was in the synagogues; while to the Gentile Christians the Temple and its worship meant little. Secondly, forty years after the death of our Lord, the Temple was destroyed by the Romans and never rebuilt; the synagogues remained.[4]

To this should be added: the Christians knew that the specific ritual forms associated with the 'old' Mosaic covenant were now defunct – as Acts 15 and the whole of Hebrews make plain. There was therefore no inclination among the first generations of Christians to introduce any elaborate permanent rituals, observances, postures and set forms. There had to be *forms*, of course, but not temple forms where God was conceived as specially present in a building (John 4:24). When Christianity developed the forms we associate with the Roman Mass (what Gregory Dix calls 'The Liturgy'), some of the forms were drawn from pagan examples with which the then nominally Christian public was familiar and from the architecture, priesthood, actions and paraphernalia described in connection with the Mosaic ritual law and the elaborate functions of Davidic invention described in 2 Samuel, 1 Chronicles and the Psalms. Recent defenders of organs, drums, dance and similar in Christian worship do not quote precedents in Acts or the Pastorals but in the Psalms.[5]

I have already stated that in my view there is no New Testament demand that government of the local church must in every particular exactly mirror the patterns we discover or think we discover in the New Testament. Yet those patterns harmonize with principles which we also must observe. The same is true of the content of worship to a degree. Once we see the Pastorals as addressed to pastors who lead the church, there are significant instructions on the form and content of the churches' public 'worship – i.e. meetings of the *ekklēsia* as the church of the living God.'

---

3. Bruce L. Shelley, *The Church: God's People* (Wheaton, IL: Victor Books, SP Publications, 1978), p. 75.
4. W. D. Maxwell, *An Outline of Christian Worship* (Oxford: Oxford University Press, 1936, 1958).
5. Dix on developments to AD 125, p. 736, and on Thomas Cranmer's Reformed interpretation of the Supper, p. 649. Dom Gregory Dix, *The Shape of the Liturgy*, 1978.

I. A Recurring Weekly Assembly on 'the Lord's Day.'

'[L]et us consider how to stir up one another to love and good works, not neglecting to meet together, as is the habit of some' (Heb. 10:24, 25 RSV). 'The Bible attributes the origin of the Sabbath to God's example in creation.'[6] The custom of every seventh day (Sabbath is Hebrew for a 'seven') did not occur in any other nation of antiquity. Though in Old Testament law the Sabbath was not a day of assembly but of cessation of labor and family observances, after the destruction of the temple (586 BC) it was natural that devout people used it for group religious observances, that is, the synagogue. The Jewish Christians continued the custom of weekly gathering for religious observances. 'The prayers' (*tais proseuchais*), to which they gave 'constant attention' (*proskaterountes*, Acts 2:42), is the word used regularly for group prayer in synagogue meetings. Perhaps they thought of themselves as forming a new synagogue (see Acts 6:9).[7] Ancient pagans had recurring gatherings in connection with seasonal festivals but no frequent regularly recurring gatherings like the Jewish Sabbath observance. In ancient paganisms a man or woman (or possibly a family) went alone to the shrine of the god with a gift or sacrifice. At the entrance this was presented to a priest who conveyed it to the presence of the image of the deity. To this day the Chinese bring their cooked pork to the local temple on festive occasions and then return home to eat it. We find the first Christians meeting daily (Acts 2:46) but when Paul wrote 1 Corinthians the chief meeting was on 'the first day of every week' (1 Cor. 16:2). John's reference to 'the Lord's day' (Rev. 1:10, *kuriakē hēmera*, 'a day belong to the Lord') is likely to the first day of the week. The eschatological term, 'the day of the LORD' (*hēmera tou kupiou*), is quite different in the Greek. In a very thorough treatment Paul Jewett concludes:

> In all subsequent Patristic usage the term 'Lord's Day' refers to Sunday, and there is no reason to suppose that Revelation 1:10 is an exception to this rule.... it is hard to conceive how the author of the Apocalypse could look upon his vision as pertaining exclusively to the final 'day of the Lord' in light of the epistolary portion with which the work begins, anchoring it clearly in the historical situation in which he was writing.[8]

George L. Gibson points out how Jewish believers not only took note of the resurrection of the Lord on Sunday but that 'Christ appeared five times to disciples, and after an interval of a week appeared again,' that 'the Pentecost of Christian significance fell on Sunday.' Paul at Troas met those who came together 'On the first day of the week... to break bread' (Acts 20:7): took collection on 'the first day of every week' (1 Cor. 16:2). He goes on to say that 'the evidence pours in from all sides that Sunday was the main Christian Day for prayer, teaching, and the Lord's Supper.'[9]

II. Public Reading of Scripture.

'Till I come, attend to the public reading of scripture' (1 Tim. 4:13 RSV). This was the central feature of the synagogue service. It was followed by an oral translation of the Hebrew Scriptures into the common language of those present (a *Targum*) and, if someone competent to provide it was present, also by an exposition of the portion read from the prophets. Jesus performed the reading on the occasion described in Luke 4:21 ff. at Nazareth and Paul later at Antioch (Acts 13:15 ff.). Paul charged Pastor Timothy, 'Until I come, devote yourself to... reading' and to be diligent in the matter (1 Tim. 4:13, 15). The only clear verbal picture of a Christian assembly at worship presents a single 'blessed' reader before a group who are equally 'blessed' in hearing and keeping 'the words... written' and read (Rev. 1:3). At first, when there was as yet no written apostolic literature, recitation of the words of Jesus or of His Apostles by those who 'heard him' (Heb. 2:3 KJV) was a feature of the service, but before long, apostolic letters were read as Scripture (Col. 4:16; 2 Peter 3:15, 16; Rev. 1:3). Then came Gospels, Acts and all the rest of a story belonging to the growth of the New Testament canon.

In many modern churches this essential aspect of a complete worship service is scandalously neglected because 'liturgy' has crowded it out of the service by what current fancy deems important. The synagogue always read the Law and Prophets. Traditional liturgy, official or only customary for 1,500 years, has included readings from the Psalms, other Old Testament passages, an Epistle and a Gospel – sometimes special reverence for the Gospel-reading marked by the worshippers' standing. In many ages of the church, the members' only exposure to Scripture was through the public readings at church worship, for Bibles were scarce and the members illiterate. Nowadays

---

6. C. C. Ryrie, 'Sabbath' in *Wycliffe Bible Encyclopedia*, Vol.II, p. 1493.
7. Ralph P. Martin, *Worship in the Early Church* (Westwood, NJ: Fleming H. Revell C., 1964), pp. 18, 19.
8. Paul Jewett, *The Lord's Day* (Grand Rapids: Eerdmans, 1972), p. 59.
9. George L. Gibson, *The Story of the Christian Year* (Nashville: Abingdon, 1945), p. 71.

ignorance of Scripture prevails because for many reasons reading of the Bible has simply fallen out of fashion for multitudes of believers – all the more reason for recovering this part of ancient liturgical practice.

III. Designated Leaders.

'I write so that you may know how to conduct yourself in the house of God, which is the church of the living God' (1 Tim. 3:15 NAB margin).

One would have to assume each local church about the Empire had designated people to lead their services. Paul addressed Timothy as one presiding at meetings for worship, charged him as to how he ought to 'behave thyself' (KJV) – in the house of God, which is the church. Archippus was evidently the man in charge at Colosse (Col. 4:17). This does not mean that in government of the churches before the second century the threefold system (bishop, elders, deacons) prevailed, but that when churches met in worship there would ordinarily be one of the elders who directed the service. We have little record of the age from the last decade of the first century on to the mid-second century except Pliny's letter (to Emperor Trajan AD 112), the letter of Clement of Rome to the Corinthians (AD 96) and the *Didachē* (AD 130-140?). None of the three speaks of any single man who regularly presided at meetings of worship. However, as Justin Martyr is 'writing from Rome some seventy years after the death of St. Paul, we may be sure that the worship he describes is not far removed from Apostolic practice.'[10] At the time of the Lord's Supper, states Justin: 'Having ended the prayers we salute one another with a kiss. There is then brought to the president of the brethren bread and a cup,' and so on.[11] Says the editor of the translation: 'This expression may quite literally be translated, 'to the one of the brethren who was presiding.'

IV. Corporate Prayers and Praise.

'[T]hey devoted themelves to... the prayers' (Acts 2:42). See also 1 Timothy 2:1-8 where the public meeting seems to be Paul's intention. Heaven's Praise of God (Rev. 5:9, 10; 7:11, 12) is mirrored in the meeting of the churches.

The Gospels furnish no examples of the Lord leading the group of disciples in prayer or instructing them in the art of group prayers. He frequently prayed alone with the disciples attending or looking on from some distance. John had instructed his disciples in the art of prayer (Luke 11:1). Nevertheless one day, after Jesus had ended a prayer of His own, one of the disciples asked: 'Lord, teach us [not *me*] to pray' (Luke 11:1).

Jesus responded, 'When you [not 'thou,' singular] pray, say: "Our Father," etc. (Luke 11:1-4; cf. Matt. 6:7-13). In the accounts (you [*plural*]), us, our, we, etc.) group prayer is assumed. It was a true instinct that for most of the church's history the principles of this prayer has been used for all true Christian prayer, private or public, and the actual words used as a form to be participated in orally by all believers present in a service of Christian worship. The setting in Matthew 6 is how to pray in the synagogue or other occasion of corporate worship (Matt. 6:1-6).

> The prayer which Jesus gave to His disciples is not designed for the individual but for the corporate worship of the community (Matt. 6:9 ff; Luke 11:2 ff). It is a prayer not of an individual but of a people, whose sense of peoplehood is expressed in the plural pronouns 'our' and 'us.' It is the corporate prayer of a people whose first concern is not for themselves but for the political [in a specially defined sense] leadership of God in the world.[12]

The book of Acts reports that 'the prayers' were an essential element in the first worship along with 'the apostles' teaching and fellowship' and 'the breaking of bread' (Acts 2:42; cf. 1:14).

The first recorded meeting of a local church for prayer took place when Peter and John were released from detention by the Jerusalem synagogue (Acts 4:23-30). Let us take note of features of that narrative pertinent to prayer as an aspect of worship. There was a special note of urgency not usually present and the meeting was not an ordinary worship service, yet, it is instructive for worship in the *koinōnia* as assembled for worship.

1. The prayer was public in the sense that the 'many' (Acts 13:48; Rom 8:14) believers were present, but private in the sense that only believers were there, all sympathetic with the purposes of the *ekklēsia*. Peter and John had returned to *idios* (Gr.), 'their own company' (Acts 4:23 KJV). The phrase captures the sense quite exactly. They were by profession and, in fact, genuinely of 'the fellowship,' for persecution would have sifted out mere sympathizers and uncommitted converts from bare, rocky or thorny soil (Matt. 13:18-22). The collective church is, as such, most

---

10. Maxwell, op. cit., p. 11.
11. Justin, *ANF*, Vol. I, p. 185.
12. M. C. Lind, *Biblical Foundations for Christian Worship* (Scottdale, PA: Herald Press, 1973), pp. 39, 40, citing G. Delling, *Worship in the New Testament*, 1963, p. 29 ff.

truly itself on such occasions. Some churches of the first centuries came to exclude all except baptized, confessing believers from the chamber where the Eucharist, high point of worship, occurs. Prayer in connection with the Lord's Supper will be treated further in a following chapter.

2. They addressed their prayers, collectively, directly to 'God,' the 'Lord.' Though the word 'Father' does not appear, He is the 'God and Father,' for in this prayer Jesus is the 'his Christ' and 'holy child' (or servant). There are both the '*tremendum*' of Isaiah 6 and John 17 and the '*fascinans*' (to employ R. Otto's language in *The Idea of the Holy*). Yet there is also an implicit awareness of Christ's full deity as anointed and ascended King, as the allusions to Psalm 2 show.

3. The near-complete burden of the prayer is to praise God in His works of creation (Acts 4:24b), revelation (vv. 25-27), providence and decrees (v. 28).

4. Their petitions are few and short, first simply that God would take notice of their plight, secondly that the believers would be enabled to speak 'your word' boldly, and that God would act to promote the interests of Jesus and His people with manifest power.

Prayer and praise, corporate and private, is a major theme in the New Testament too large for further development here. Ralph Martin adequately develops the subject, incorporating the findings of twentieth-century scholarly literature.[13]

V. Urgent Preaching.

'Till I come, attend... to preaching' (1 Tim 4:13 RSV).

'[P]reaching' or 'exhortation' (KJV) are the renderings most English Versions give *paraklēsis*. If there is a word for the Protestant Sunday morning sermon in the New Testament this is it. Like the word *sōtēria*, salvation, which often has such a very ordinary meaning as *rescue* from a shipwreck, so 'ordinary usage... of *parakalein* [verbal form] in Acts 28:20 simply means "to call for," "to summon" in 28:14, "to invite" in 16:39... to exhort... to beseech... to ask.'[14] But with reference to 'the New Testament event of salvation' this word 'occurs... for exhortation by the Word proclaimed in the power of the Holy Ghost.... [T]he address does not proceed from the person who seeks help but from one who speaks with almighty power in the name of God. Thus *parakalein* is used for the wooing proclamation of salvation in the apostolic preaching.'[15]

This word is used of missionary preaching (2 Cor. 6:1; 1 Thess. 2:3). 'We are reminded of Acts 9:31 where the Palestinian community is increased by *hē paraklēsei tou hagiou pneumatos* [the exhortation of the Holy Ghost].'[16]

Parakalein in the sense of urgent preaching is used for Peter's sermon at Pentecost (Acts 2:40) and John the Baptist's preaching (Luke 3:18) and teaching (Luke 3:10-14). 'The same term is used in Hebrews for the "word of exhortation" (13:22) to men of long standing in the faith, though in danger of growing weary.'[17]

The preaching (NIV, RSV) or exhortation (KJV) Paul had in mind in his charge to pastors (1 Tim. 4:13) is not mere moralizing, for it has reference to Christ's saving work on the cross and the urgent necessity for the hearers to make decisions on the spot. This quality of urgency in appeal is fully consistent with pastoral comfort and encouragement. Through Barnabas ('son of consolation') 'much people was added unto the Lord' at Antioch (Acts 11:24 KJV) where this partner with Paul 'exhorted [*parekalei*] them all' (Acts 11:23) and 'taught a great many people' (Acts 11:26). Two early 'prophets' in the church, Judas and Silas by name (Acts 15:22), imparted 'consolation,' and 'exhorted [*parakalesan*] the brethren... and confirmed them' (Acts 15:32 KJV). People who can do this are a gift to the church (Rom. 12:8). Not every person who attends a service is articulate enough or sufficiently informed in divine things to give public exhortation.

Among the features of the public services of worship in the *ekklēsia* the sermon, therefore, is of great importance. During the dark ages of the Western churches of Europe parish priests were so prevailingly ignorant of the Scriptures that the memorized liturgy of the Mass was about all they could produce. The evangelical Reformation restored the Bible to the people and put it again at the center of worship by way of public reading and urgent preaching by a competent preacher.

---

13. Ralph Martin, *Worship in the Early Church* (Westwood, NJ: Fleming H. Revell Co., 1964), pp. 28–38.
14. Schmitz, *Macological Dictionary of the New Testament*, Vol. v, p. 793.
15. ibid., p. 793, 794, 795.
16. ibid., p. 795.
17. ibid., p. 795.

VI. Offerings.

The Lord Himself had much to say about proper stewardship. Present purposes limit our treatment to that subject as related to worship in public meetings of the Christian assembly.

We know from indirect evidence in the Epistles that the believers brought gifts of food to the assemblies. Part of the food was eaten in connection with the *agapē* or *love feast*, a meal of fellowship, and in the Eucharist, which accompanied the *agapē*. The food was deposited outside the room for worship and brought to the room by a deacon (minister) with some ceremony at the appropriate time. We also know from earliest reports that the amounts of food gathered were deliberately in excess of the amount consumed. The overplus was distributed to elders and others whose services to God in the church were rewarded somewhat in this way (Gal. 6:6, 7).

Offerings of money also were brought to the weekly meetings for worship, and to that we direct our attention.

The first churches – and onward for over 150 years – owned no buildings specially dedicated to Christian worship. Nor was there at first a 'clergy' whose livings were fully supported by the church, as came to be the case later. Hence New Testament instructions and precedents, though applicable today, are more so in principle than practice.

Paul argued for support of ministers like himself, his party of helpers and ministers of the Word (Apostles, prophets, evangelists, pastors) everywhere in several ways.

1. Paul argues on principle and Scripture that though he and Barnabas are partially self-supported,[18] it is proper to provide financial support to the ministry (1 Cor. 9:6); 'If we have sown spiritual things among you, is it too much if we reap material things from you?' (v. 11). He argues by analogy with the financial support of the Old Testament priests – 'Do you not know that those… who serve at the altar share in the sacrificial offerings?' (v. 13). He cites some otherwise unknown saying of Jesus: 'the Lord commanded that those who proclaim the gospel should get their living by the gospel' (v. 14). Perhaps he is thinking of Jesus' instructions to the twelve apostles on the brink of their first preaching mission (Matt. 10:9-15). Those who are 'taught the word' should share their wealth with those who teach – for their own sakes (Gal. 6:6, 7).

2. It is fair to conclude from these passages and 1 Timothy 5:17, 18 that in Paul's time some local pastors (elders, bishops) were supported in whole or part by their churches. Paul, in other places, sets forth the principle that established churches should raise money to support missionary evangelism and church-planting. In the Philippian Epistle it is clear that the Philippians sent special messengers carrying funds to him as he pioneered the gospel at Thessalonica (Phil. 4:14-19). We know the messenger's name (Epaphroditus). He gives religious significance to their 'gifts' as parallel to Old Testament 'fragrant offering[s]' and 'sacrifice' acceptable to God (Phil. 4:18).

3. Missionaries and those who were their emissaries and assistants, Paul said, should be fully supported – at least while engaged in their missionary tasks: 'Do your best to speed Zenas… and Apollos on their way; see that they lack nothing' (Titus 3:13). This will teach the Cretan Christians to be 'fruitful' (Titus 3:14). John much later urgently recommended the same, inasmuch as such people are wholly dependent for livelihood on the church. Further he said that it enables the church people to be 'fellow workers for the truth' (3 John 5-8). Paul did not hesitate to instruct Philemon, a wealthy Christian, to 'prepare a guest room for me' in his own house where the church also met (Philemon 1, 2, 22).

4. Members of the churches who were of necessity in a state of chronic need – widows and others – were supported in whole or part by their churches. First Timothy 5:5-16 presumes such a custom and regulates it.

5. The churches also engaged in what today is called Christian philanthropy – financial aid to support believers in other places. The first evidence is emergency relief raised by the church at Syrian Antioch for the Jerusalem church in time of famine (Acts 11:27-30). Paul's efforts to raise money throughout the area of his work to relieve the poverty of the Jerusalem congregation is evidenced in several letters (Rom. 15:26; 1 Cor. 16:1-4; 2 Cor. 9:12). This liberality was to be extended not only to fellow believers but 'to everyone' as they were able (Gal. 6:10).

In the *oikoumenē* (inhabited world) of the New Testament a money-economy prevailed. Christians, as everyone else, rightly worked in that world to earn money to buy food, clothing, shelter and other needs of civilized living. They brought some of the fruit of their labor in the form of money to the recurring weekly service of Christian worship (1 Cor. 16:1-4). The Gospels as well as the Epistles have much to say about that stewardship. As for weekly offerings at the service of worship the giving was to be regular and systematic.

---

18. 1 Cor. 9:6; cf. 1 Thess. 2:9; 2 Thess. 3:6-10; Acts 18:2, 3.

The current competitive solicitation of contributions from every Christian household in North America through the mail for every good cause is a recent phenomenon. This new development is part of the junk-mail phenomenon. It completely bypasses the churches. This phenomenon has rendered necessary that first the biblical claim of the church (1 Cor. 16:2) be kept in mind as we Christians decide what to do with the Lord's money placed at our personal disposal.

VII. Doctrine: Teaching it and Confessing it.

As observed very early in this book of theology, doctrines interpret redemptive events. Christian lives and the church itself express in vital organic fashion commitments to those doctrines. Constant attention to the Apostles' doctrine (Acts 2:42) is one of the main features of the very essence of the local church. Doctrine, then, of inner necessity becomes from the beginning a major feature of authentic worship in the local church, essential to the integrity of the local assembly as an *ekklēsia* of Jesus Christ, its preservation as such, and its extension into the world about it as well. Congregations are never more truly at worship than when their souls are captured by the depth of meaning of redemption or of God's holiness, as those truths are effectively conveyed from the pulpit. Earlier in this chapter, in discussion of *paraklēsis* – exhortation, urgent preaching, in connection with 1 Timothy 4:13 – these thoughts were broached. But more should be noted at least briefly.

1. Doctrine is a part of an evangelistic proclamation of truth. When Paul met pagan Greek minds at the Areopagus in Athens he did not trace the points of the usual evangelistic tract – 'four things' of some sort. He announced a doctrine of God: one true, supreme, personal deity who decreed all, created all, sustains and rules all, by decrees, creation, preservation and providence (Acts 17:23-28). He added some Christology, 'Jesus and the resurrection' (Acts 17:18), soteriology (demand for repentance, v. 30), and some eschatology – the coming Judgment Day and resurrection of the dead (v. 31). When he addressed heathen audiences anywhere (Acts 14) he made similar proclamations. When he addressed Jewish audiences it was no different – apostolic doctrine (teaching) was the bill of fare. Relying on the basic doctrines of Christianity as distinct from Judaism 'as was his custom' (Acts 17:2), Paul preached biblical doctrine on three successive Sabbaths at 'a synagogue of the Jews' at Thessalonica; 'he reasoned with them from the Scriptures, explaining and proving that it was necessary for the Christ to suffer and to rise from the dead, and saying, "This Jesus, whom I proclaim to you, is the Christ."' So it was at Antioch of Pisidia (Acts 13:14-52), at Corinth (Acts 18:4, 5, 11) and at Ephesus, where his broad doctrinal thrust was 'the kingdom of God' (Acts 19:8). Later, in the summary of his preached doctrines that he provided for the elders gathered at Miletus, he particularized the doctrines taught: repentance and faith (Acts 20:21); the gospel of grace (Acts 20:24); the kingdom of God (Acts 20:25); and 'the whole counsel of God' (Acts 20:27). These were the themes taught for over two years in a rented hall (Acts 19:9, 10), which drew them to Christ and which melded them into the great church of Ephesus. Christian pulpit proclamation anywhere at any period of history should ever be the same.

2. It is the task of the overseers (bishops), teaching elders and pastors of the churches, at all the gatherings of the whole local *ekklēsia*, vigorously and carefully to proclaim *tē didachē* (the doctrine, Acts 2:42 KJV), *tē didaskalia* (the teaching, what is taught, 1 Tim. 4:13). The elders of the church must 'feed [*poimainein*] the church' (*ekklēsia*) which the Lord purchased with His own blood (Acts 20:28 KJV). The content of 'the doctrine' was uniform in content among all the Apostles and spread from Rome to Cappadocia (Rom. 1:7; 1 Peter 1:1; 2 Peter 3:14, 15). The basic theology of Paul, Peter, John, James, the author of Hebrews is one theology; whatever the emphasis or occasion of each might be, it was uniform through all the churches (1 Cor. 11:16). When a few years later the term 'catholic' (*kat'holikos*, according to the whole, universal) and still later 'orthodox' came to be employed, this uniform set of teachings (or beliefs) is what was meant. In the New Testament it is said to be 'the standard of teaching' (Rom. 6:17 RSV), 'the words of the faith and of the good doctrine' (1 Tim. 4:6) and 'the pattern of the sound words' (2 Tim. 1:13). These Pauline expressions are matched by 'the faith that was once for all delivered to the saints' (Jude 3), 'the truth that you have' (2 Peter 1:12), 'salvation... declared at first by the Lord... attested to us by those who heard' (Heb. 2:3). It was in large part to preserve the integrity and limits of this sacred deposit that the Epistles and Gospels were written.

A revival of emphasis in preaching doctrine as indispensable truth is perhaps the most acute need of the churches of our time. Several recent widely publicized events are only a minute part of evidence that present-day evangelical Christians, including seminary professors, pastors and people, are not only ignorant of some of the basic moral teachings which distinguish Christianity from any other faith or confession, but also somewhat resentful of efforts to correct the ignorance. Discussion of causes of this declension would take us far afield, but these remarks seem necessary. (1) The state of denial in schools and churches must be resisted and corrected; (2) the replacement of Bible and theology (doctrines of Christianity) in schools for the ministry by so-called *practical*, how-to-feel and how-to-do-it courses must be reversed; and (3) the surge of denial of realities by fixation on perceptions must be reversed.

So important to Paul was the saturation of the church with doctrine that he spoke of it in line after line of the Epistles to Timothy under such titles as doctrine, the commandment, sound doctrine (opposed to vain jangling), the faith, the truth, the mystery of the faith, the words of the faith, a pattern of sound words, good doctrine and the doctrine. He opposes the same to fables, vain jangling, no understanding, being contrary to sound doctrine, doctrines of demons, lies and hypocrisy, profane and old wives' fables, questions and strifes about words, perverse disputings, opposition of science falsely so-called, erring concerning the truth, and resisting the truth. Christian pastors must teach, preach and exhort with all long-suffering and doctrine, to hold faith, to teach no other doctrine. The doctrine is a treasure to be guarded against perversion, neglect and denial as well as a deposit or treasure to be guarded. Let all earnest Christians pray to God that He raise up, as of old – as I have treated at length earlier in this book – a generation of teachers who will train up another generation of teachers in order that they be able to pass on the treasure (2 Tim. 2:1, 2).

VIII. Recital of Beliefs in a Creed?

Recital of a creed, as also of the Lord's Prayer, implies at least some rudimentary formal liturgy. Hence, I have placed this rubric in this text with a question mark. 'It is fashionable at present for students [i.e. scholarly writers of the New Testament] to find liturgy everywhere.'[19] To explore whether certain passages in Paul's letters were first creeds recited or sung in public worship in a stage before the Epistles and Gospels were written would take us far beyond the scope of this chapter. It seems to me that clear evidence is lacking. Yet it is hard for me to doubt, recalling Paul's reference to 'the form of sound words' and the like, that repetition of teachings about divine acts of redemption, and the like, in prescribed forms, would have been employed, as now, to combining pedagogy with worship among people who knew none of Old Testament background of the biblical world-view.[20]

IX. Music.

'*A priori*, we would and should expect that a movement which released so much emotion, and loyalty, and enthusiasm, would find expression in song.'[21] This statement seems correct, yet the New Testament is almost completely silent as to the use of music in the public worship of the *ekklēsia*. The Revelation speaks of songs of worship in heaven (Rev. 5:9; 14:3; 15:3). Paul in parallel sections of Ephesians and Colossians recommends 'addressing one another in psalms and hymns and spiritual songs, singing and making melody to the Lord with all your heart' (Eph. 5:19 cf.; Col. 3:16). In context, however, such singing expresses one's being filled with the Spirit, *personally*. The subject of the chapter is personal Christian life. The singing indicated seems like what farmers used to do when following a team of horses across the otherwise silent fields and children playing – before radio and television taught mankind to listen to music rather than to make some of their own, as Paul advises. The one mention of music 'in the church' (1 Cor. 14:19, 34) seems to be at 1 Corinthians 14:26 where he rebukes excesses in bringing too many individually composed psalms, doctrines, tongues, revelations and interpretations to the assembly gathered for worship.

The Jewish believers probably brought the singing or chanting of Psalms from synagogue to church, but this helps us little as to whether or how Psalms may or may not have been sung in the New Testament services of worship. The scholar who has exceeded all others in research and readable writing on this matter has said:

> The Jewish synagogue service, which was the root from which the apostolic synapsis [gathering before the Lord's Supper] sprang, consisted of public readings from the scripture, the singing of Psalms, a sermon and a number of set prayers. Rabbinic scholars are in disagreement as to whether the prayers came first or last in the synagogue of the first century AD.[22]

---

19. C. F. D. Moule, *Worship in the New Testament* (Richmond, VA: John Knox Press, p. 1961, 1967), p. 7.
20. I recommend R. Martins, Chap. 5, 'Early Creeds and Confessions of Faith,' *Worship in the Early Church*, pp. 53–65 for a balanced treatment of the question and evaluation of scholarly writing on the subject. The literature is extensive.
21. A. B. McDonald, *Christian Worship in the Primitive Church* (Edinburgh: 1934), p. 112, as cited by Martin, p. 40.
22. Dom Gregory Dix, op. cit., p. 37.

The earliest description, by a Christian, of the 'order of service,' is Justin's *First Apology* (about AD 155). Justin describes in some detail the weekly meeting 'on the day called Sunday.' He mentions, in order, reading 'memoirs of the apostles or the writings of the prophets, then the president verbally instructs [pastor's sermon]... then we all rise together and pray... bread and wine mixed with water are brought'[23] and the Eucharist follows. Strangely, it seems to us, Justin mentions no music. The evident reason for no mention may have been that there was no music and for good reason. In those times of persecution the Christians might not have wished to call attention to themselves by enthusiastic singing of Psalms or hymns or spiritual songs. Later when public practice of Christianity was lawful and prevalent, various kinds of music were interspersed throughout.

These facts may account for the difficulties in every period of substantial change with regard to church music. We simply are left without direct scriptural guidance. It appears to be possible to worship God with His approval with vocal music or without it, accompaniment by musical instruments or without them. No one has produced convincing evidence that any music except the human voice was employed in church worship of apostolic times. If music is to be an aspect of worship one rule will prevail: like all else in the liturgy of worship, the design is to thank God, to praise and glorify Him, not merely to please our culturally determined habits of listening or undisciplined personal preferences. Music in services of the church has always been a matter of question. In times of rapid cultural change like our own, music in church is both a question and a whole bundle of problems – none of them of easy solution and certainly beyond this writer's competence.

Excursus: Church Architecture and Furniture As a Reflection of Doctrine.

The next four chapters relate to observance of the ordinances of baptism in water and of the Lord's Supper at the Lord's table, both of which should take place in the midst of the assembled believers. They are part, therefore, of public services of worship. They will be observed usually in connection with the features of worship treated in this chapter: weekly assembly; the public reading of Scripture; corporate prayer and praise; preaching; offerings; teaching of doctrine and confessing the same; and perhaps music, vocal and instrumental.

All of these functions have been wonderfully well conducted in architectural settings of the crudest sort – caves, barns, warehouses and small residences. Yet the churches in certain periods of history constructed houses of worship which were antithetical to the formula of 'when you come together' in Paul's instruction for the 'eucharistic' observance and all else that takes place in corporate worship. Church architecture and arrangement of furniture for the congregation at worship are therefore indirectly important aspects of a sound doctrine of the church.

The house a man builds for himself makes a statement about the man himself and what he thinks is important to him. The house a Christian congregation builds ought to make a statement about their theology of worship – especially the place of 'the public reading of Scripture' (1 Tim. 4:13), of preaching the Word and of sharing together at the Lord's table.

The Tabernacle in the wilderness and the temple of Solomon and the second temple which succeeded it were entered only by priests. The inner chamber where the LORD dwelt and where the *shekinah havodh* appeared was forbidden to any except the high priest, who made several entrances and exits on the Day of Atonement. The people (laity) could bring gifts and sacrifices to the Great Altar but that was completely out of doors in a court before the sanctuary (holy building). 'Coming together' came to be a part of synagogue worship but was never regularly a part of temple worship.

The first Christian congregations usually met in the homes of believers. There is little information as to the part of the house used. Authorities differ. It must have varied greatly. In times of persecution it would have been conducted as quietly as possible, probably in an inner room. The synagogue, with which the Jewish Christian converts were familiar, was essentially a place for reading the Hebrew Scriptures and hearing the same with accompanying translation (Talmud) and prayers, plus comments by those esteemed competent to so speak. The room was usually a wide rectangle with a reading desk near the center. There were seats for some but folk in the East knew then as now how to sit comfortably on the floor and to rise without difficulty.

Hence some of the earliest structures for Christian worship provided a large round, octagonal or square room. The foundations of the Church of the Ascension (fourth century) atop the Mount of Olives show an octagonal building and the earliest part of the Church of the Holy Sepulchre in Jerusalem (fourth century) is a circle. In each, the table for the Lord's Supper was in the center, around which the people gathered and from which the Word was read, the sermon preached and the elements of the Supper received by the people.

---

23. *ANF*, Vol. I, p. 186.

The figures are representations not exact plans.

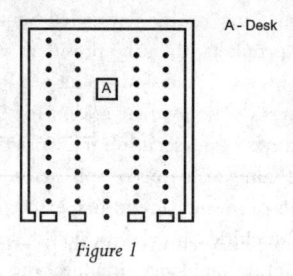

Figure 1

Figure 1 is of the main room of a typical ancient synagogue. The first Christians, being Jews, were familiar with it and, as we have seen, carried over much they remembered from it into Christian worship. They gathered around the reading desk, standing or likely seated on the floor as Eastern people do yet today at home and (Muslim) in Mosques. When Jesus 'stood up to read' in the Nazareth synagogue, 'and there was given to him the book of the prophet Isaiah' (Luke 4:16, 17 RSV), this likely would have happened at the desk and he would have likely risen, not from a chair, but from the floor. When 'the eyes of all in the synagogue were fixed on him' (v. 20) that would have been from four directions. The male Jews of Nazareth were not in front of Him but all around Him with perhaps the females looking down on Him from galleries.

The early Christians met in homes and rented halls as well as synagogues (e.g. Acts 8:7, 8; 19:8-10). We do not know if worship was conducted in the courtyard of the homes of wealthy believers or in rooms of houses. Archaeologists and other scholars have no uniform opinion.

When free to construct buildings specially for Christian worship, sometimes under government auspices and at government expense, it is noteworthy that the shape of the main room was more like the Jewish synagogue than either a Roman-Greek pagan temple or the Jerusalem temple. The central room of the Church of the Holy Sepulchre (dedicated AD 335) at Jerusalem, *Figure 2*, was circular.[24]

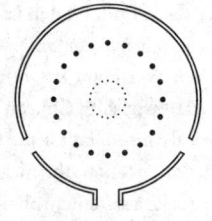

Figure 2

The Church of the Ascension (about AD 373) on top of the Mount of Olives is octagonal (*Figure 3*).[25] This was carefully pointed out by the Arab guide when I first saw the foundation in 1960.[26]

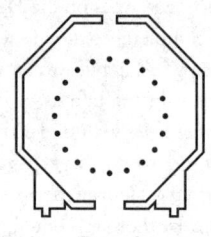

Figure 3

Beginning in the fourth century, external form and inside arrangements evolved differently – especially between the Orthodox East and the Latin Catholic West. In the West, the Roman basilicas (*Figure 4*) – that is, government buildings – were adapted for Christian worship. Some of the buildings had formerly been used for the worship of the emperor and pagan deities (before Constantine). The church made some changes in the furniture and arrangement

---

24. Jack Finegan, *Light From the Ancient Past*, Vol. I, 2nd ed., 1969, pp. 526–531.
25. Figures 2 and 3 are adapted from Andre Bieler, *Architecture in Worship*, Philadelphia: Westminster Press, 1965, p. 11.
26. See Finegan, pp. 535-537.

Figure 4

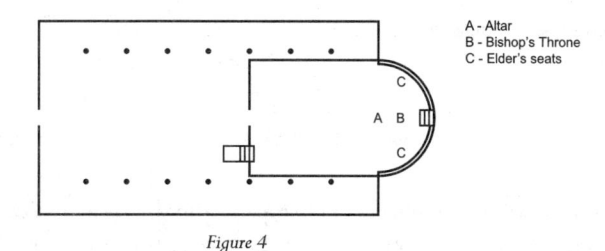

of it but the basilica style persisted until modern times in the West. The place of the judge in the civil court was replaced by the bishop's chair. Only clergy were to step up on the platform. To the right and left of the bishop's chair were rows of seats for the elders (presbyters). The communion table became an altar and was set in various places in the building. Later the main altar replaced the bishop's chair. Roman theology called for many Masses, so as cruciform buildings (*Figure 5*) developed, altars were placed in the transepts and elsewhere.

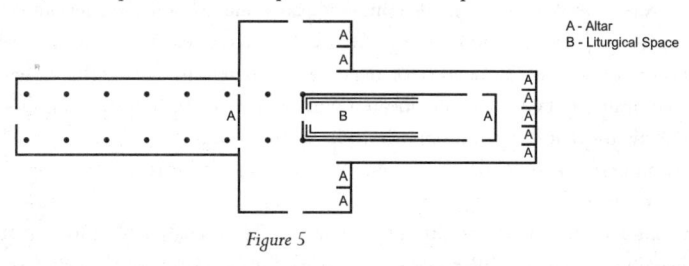

Figure 5

When the Reformed congregations took over these buildings, they tended to leave the west (entrance) end of the nave empty as well as the apse and choir and to set the pulpit desk high in a central part of the nave or trancept and the communion table in the center or near the center with pews arranged to face the pulpit – where the Word is read and preached – from three directions. The changes at Geneva where Farel, then Calvin, and associates and successors ministered, serve as an example (*Figure 6*).

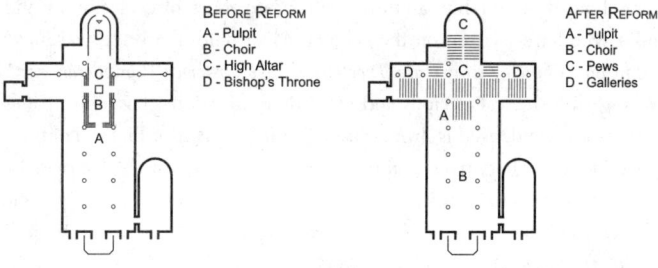

Figure 6

They set an elevated pulpit near the intersection of nave and transept and at the front of the nave, all around the preacher. Most of the nave was left empty. A table was set in a central position only when the Eucharist was to be observed.

When the Reformed constructed buildings of their own, they tried to let their evangelical theology dictate their architecture. An early Reformed congregation in Amsterdam worshipped in a wide rectangular room with the pulpit centered against a long wall (*Figure 7*).

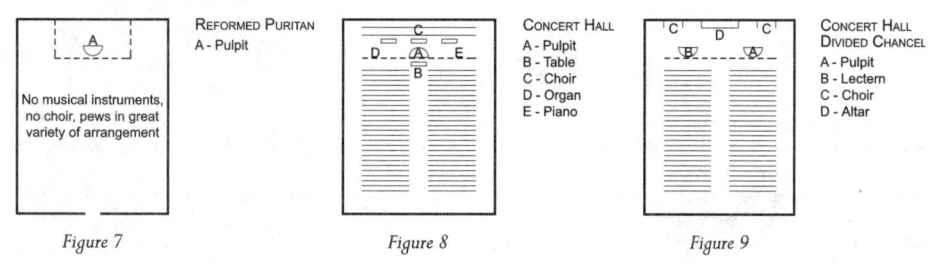

Figure 7   *Figure 8*   *Figure 9*

The Reformation impulses in theology and corresponding church architecture were not sustained. Andre Bieler (of the faculty of the University of Geneva) wrote of the eighteenth century:

> Reason prevailed over faith and secular culture triumphed. During the following century Christian sanctuaries [sic. Chapels] were turned into concert halls with vast organs and galleries and into lecture halls with a podium.[27]

Bieler is speaking particularly of the situation in Europe, but there was more than an echo on the west side of the North Atlantic. In new structures a platform was placed across one end of the room with choir seats and chairs in imitation of a concert hall, the pulpit center in front on the platform and communion table below in front (*Figure 8*). This style presently exists in thousands of older church buildings and many new ones. Some have the 'divided chancel' (*Figure 9*) variation. We make them work, but I must somewhat cynically remark, that if there is a center aisle, it is great for fancy church weddings, but less than best for communicating the Word and observing 'communion' as 'when ye come together therefore into one place' (1 Cor. 11:20 KJV).

During the seventeenth century in Britain, Anglicans and the Puritan denominations wrestled together for control of the existing church buildings. Only after 1689 were dissenting groups free to follow their own course in constructing houses of worship. In various forms, the Puritan denominations (including Presbyterians) built to have the pulpit and communion table centrally located with seats as close to pulpit and table as possible and often with ranks of pews facing one another from opposite sides of the room.

After the London fire of 1666 Sir Christopher Wren, architect for reconstructing public buildings, 'wrote of the necessity "in our reformed Religion... that all who are present can both hear and see. In contrast with the churches of the Roman Catholics ours are to be fitted for Auditories" thus enabling "all to hear the Service, and both to hear distinctly, and see the Preacher."'[28] Wren was successful, for the chapel of the usual Anglican (Episcopal in U.S.A.) church provides somewhat friendly facilities for hearing the preacher and receiving the communion (as 'when you come together') if employed correctly together with the liturgy of the Book of Common Prayer. I supply the following drawing of a cross section of a small Anglican church (*Figure 10*). Absent is the centrality and visibility of the communion table.[29]

Though I am no authority on church architecture, my experience in helping to guide several congregations in construction of new houses of worship, and my studies as teacher of ecclesiology and pastoral duties, have driven me to consult those who have written on the subject. Most helpful are the writings of James F. White, especially his *Protestant Worship and Church Architecture: Theological and Historical Considerations*. He provides eleven pages of bibliography covering all historical periods and most denominations. There are pages of diagrams of architecture and furnishings. Crisp and condensed is *Architecture in Worship* by Andre Bieler. He traces the origins of the medieval structures which excluded the laity from real participation, shows how the Reformation adapted to those buildings and built better ones, and addresses the current 'architectural problems' of the present – as of 1965. A third which adds a different dimension is by George L. Gibson, *The Story of the Christian Year*, with illustrations by the author,[30] as does a fourth, *Ecclesiastical Terms*, Frederick L. Eckert.[31]

---

27. Andre Bieler, *Architecture in Worship* (Philadelphia, PA: Westminster Press, 1965), p. 71.
28. Christopher Wren, London: 1950, p. 320, as quoted by James F. White, *Protestant Worship and Church Architecture: Theological and Historical Considerations* (New York: Oxford U. Press, 1964), p. 95.
29. *Cross Section of a church* from Frederick L. Eckel, Jr, *A Concise Dictionary of Ecclesiastical Terms* (Boston, MA: Whittemore Associates, Inc., 1960), pp. 32, 33. *Communion Table*, Eckel, p. 20; *Altar*, Eckel, p. 5.
30. New York, Nashville: Abington Press, 1945.
31. Boston: Whittemore Associates.

ECCLESIOLOGY 6.21

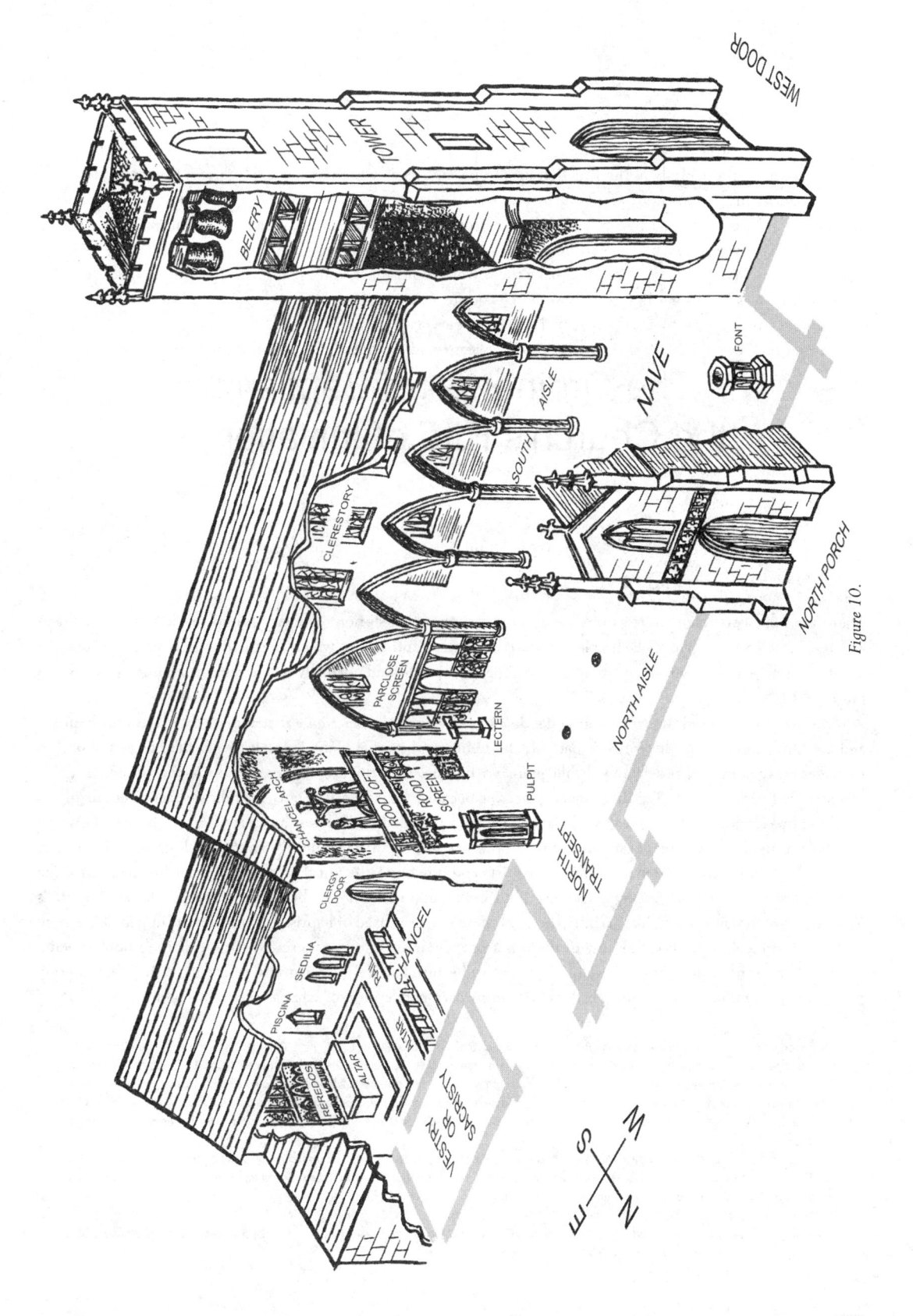

Figure 10.

22
The Ordinance of Baptism: the Church's Rite of Initiation, I

There are only two religious rites observed, almost without exception, in every group of churches – baptism and the Lord's Supper. We shall discuss the initiatory rite, baptism, by which normally one is initiated into the visible church, and the continuing rite of the Lord's Supper, observed normally in Christian assemblies at recurring intervals.[1]

We have already used the words *rite* and *ordinance* and suggested *observance* as names or categories for baptism and the Lord's Supper. In the Western part of Christendom the usual name is *sacrament*. In the Eastern churches *mystery* is more common. A very few dislike *ordinance* because they think it suggests legalism (they cite Col. 2:14, 20; Heb. 9:1, 19). A large number reject *sacrament* because for some it seems to indicate sacramentalism, or salvation by religious rites. The early Christians frequently called these rites 'mysteries.' Even though the word 'mystery' is used in the Bible, evangelical Protestants are largely unacquainted with this ecclesiastical usage, and it seems both misleading and inappropriate. Baptists and most non-liturgical groups prefer 'ordinance,' since the Lord 'ordained' the rites.[2] Presbyterians use both *sacrament* and *ordinance*[3] but seem to prefer sacrament.[4] It is generally agreed that though, like 'Trinity,' none of these words is used of baptism or the Lord's Supper in the New Testament, under proper controls any of them is a proper designation of these two sacred rites (a non-specific term). In using the commonest, *sacrament*, 'we have to be sure to give it a scriptural reference rather than merely give it a vague and loose definition, or feed into it our own conception of what a sacrament ought to be.'[5]

---

1. A minority of evangelical Christian groups regard the washing of 'the saint's feet' (John 13:14, 15; 1 Tim. 5:10) as commanded by Christ to be an adjunct to the ordinance of the bread and wine. Some of them regard the Lord's Supper (the Last Supper cf. 1 Cor. 11:20-22, or love feast of Jude 12) as being a full meal also to be perpetuated. So among these folk – more numerous than might be supposed – some accept 'eucharist' (= thanksgiving, 1 Cor. 11:24; Luke 22:17, 19) as the proper name for the rite of the bread and wine and 'the Lord's Supper' (love feast) as a full meal. Eucharist is unambiguous and through the remainder of this discussion I shall use it frequently as a proper name for the ordinance of loaf and cup.
2. Millard Erickson, *Christian Theology* (Grand Rapids: Baker, 1985), p. 1094; A. H. Strong, *Systematic Theology* (Old Tappen, NJ: Revell, 1907), p. 930; Harvey, *The Church* (Philadelphia: American Baptist Publ., 1879), p. 105; G. W. Bromiley, *Sacramental Teaching and Practice in the Reformation Churches* (Grand Rapids: Eerdmans, 1951), p. 11.
3. *Westminster Shorter Catechism*, Q 92.
4. The subject is adequately discussed in Smith's *Dictionary of Greek and Roman Antiquities* (London, 1882), pp. 659–663 sub *Jusjurandum*; also McClintock and Strong, *Cyclopedia*, vol. ix, p. 212.
5. Bromiley, op. cit., p. 12.

Only by degrees through the centuries did 'sacraments' come to be distinguished exactly from the many ritual observances in various provinces of the church. In the twelfth century Hugh of St Victor counted thirty 'sacraments.' In 1437 a decision of the Council of Florence for the first time gave the authority of the church to a suggestion of Peter Lombard (twelfth century) that the number of sacraments should be fixed at seven, *viz.*: baptism, confirmation, Eucharist, penance, extreme unction, orders and matrimony.[6] How two simple rites comanded by Christ came to be called *sacraments* and *mysteries* and multiplied to seven and corrupted by superstitious magical ideas is too long to report further here.[7]

Definition of an Ordinance, or Sacrament.

James Montgomery Boice provides a summary of how *ordinance* and *sacrament* relate by defining 'sacraments' as '*ordinances* instituted by Christ' and proceeds to define sacraments as 'divine ordinances instituted by Christ... in which material elements are used as visible signs of God's blessing... are means of grace... by reminding the believer of what they signify[8]... [and] are seals, certifications or confirmations of the grace they signify.' John Murray adds, 'to be observed perpetually.'[9] The father of them all is Calvin, who provides two somewhat tentative definitions.[10] Like Luther and Zwingli his emphasis was on limiting the number to the two truly set forth in the New Testament rather than the seven of tradition and Roman dogma.

The Roman Church never clearly defined the criteria by which they came to the number of seven. The record shows that they held the sacraments were all commanded by Christ, though in different ways. He Himself was baptized and commanded His 'stewards of the mysteries' (1 Cor. 4:1), i.e. the Apostles, to baptize. He participated in the Eucharist and commanded its continuing observance. The power of the keys being imparted to Peter, the apostolic college and thereby the church, had power to institute the rest with guidance and power of the promised Paraclete.[11] A standard textbook of Roman Catholic theology states: 'Holy Scripture attests that Christ immediately instituted... Baptism, Eucharist, Penance and Consecration [ordination]. The other Sacraments "were in existence in apostolic times," being instituted by apostles as "ministers of Christ and dispensers of the mysteries of God" (1 Cor. 4:1) cf. 1 Corinthians 3:5.'[12] *The Cathechism of 1994* confirms this teaching.[13] *The Council of Trent* pronounced anathema on any one who says that there are less or more than seven or that Christ did not institute all seven.[14]

Though they do not agree in all particulars of form and meaning of the church's sacraments there are few if any evangelical Protestant theologians who would quarrel seriously with the following proposed criteria by which a sacrament (ordinance) should be defined. A sacrament is (1) a sensible physical action or use of materials; (2) performed with formal spiritual intent; (3) commanded clearly and personally by Christ while on earth in His flesh; and (4) of universal and perpetual obligation in the church. I add that (5) each of these qualifications must be plainly derived from plain statement in the New Testament and no other precedent or authority. (6) Further, the New Testament must define their purposes and meanings. As we proceed it will be seen each of these points is applicable and important.

1. A sacrament, or ordinance, is a sensible physical action or use of materials. If it is a sacrament you can see it, hear, smell, taste or touch it. The most real facts do not fall in this category. The God revealed in nature is invisible (Rom. 1:20). 'What no eye has seen, nor ear heard, nor the heart of man imagined... God has prepared for those who love him' (1 Cor. 2:9). Contrariwise, baptism is a spectacle which attracts viewers; the water is cold or warm; the one baptized comfortable or uncomfortable; the bread of communion is leavened or unleavened; and the wine either sweet or fermented. There are specified actions and manipulated objects essential to the ordinance. Wine is not used in baptism nor plain water in the Eucharist.

---

6. *ISBE*, Vol. iv, 2636.
7. D. P. Ridder 'Sacrament,' McClintock & Strong, *Cyclopedia*, Vol. ix, pp. 212–218.
8. James M. Boice, *Foundations of the Christian Faith* (Downers Grove, IL: InterVarsity Press, 1986), pp. 495–497. Similar statements by modern Reformed or Presbyterians will be found in Buswell, the Hodges and Berkhof.
9. John Murray, *Collected Writings*, Vol. II (Edinburgh: Banner of Truth Trust, 1977 onward) pp. 366, 367.
10. Calvin, *Institutes*, IV 14.1.
11. F. C. Coneybear, 'Sacrament,' *Britannica*, 11th ed., Vol. xxiii, p. 977.
12. Ludwig Ott, *Fundamentals of Catholic Dogma*, 4th ed., trans. Patrick Lynch (New York: Herder and Herder, 1960), p. 337.
13. Paras. 113, 1117, 1210.
14. Henry Denzinger, *The Scources of Catholic Dogma* (St Louis, MO: Herder Book Co., 1954, 1957), para. 844, p. 262.

Because these ordinances are sensible physical acts it is possible for thoughtless and unbelieving – even superstitious people – to participate in them. Unlike the temple rites of old, God does not strike the ministering priest dead for carelessness in the ritual as He did Nadab and Abihu in the old dispensation.

2. The ordinances are performed with formal, spiritual intent. Baths are administered to people unable to bathe themselves; bread is broken and wine consumed all the time; but since no specific formal religious intent is involved, bathing and eating meals are not, as such, of spiritual value nor are they so intended. In the first Christian baptisms on record there were certain specific events – repentance (Acts 2:38) and belief (Acts 8:12, 37). In the first 'Lord's Supper' there was first a special prayer, then special instruction – symbolic action and explanation of the symbolism (Luke 22:17-20). Bathing the baby is sometimes called a 'ritual' and precious family meals at special occasions 'sacramental,' but this is hyperbole. Because of the formal, spiritual intent the ordinances should be guarded carefully against misuse, misunderstanding and pollution by disorder or hypocrisy (1 Cor. 10, 11).

3. An essential characteristic of a church ordinance is that it be sovereignly authorized, personally and directly by our Lord Himself. Since Christ 'is the head of the body, the church' (Col. 1:18), it 'follows logically that from the day of Pentecost when the church was formed... the church should obey her sovereign Lord. It is therefore fitting that the Lord of the church should not have delegated to any other, even to an apostle, the sacred task of instituting ordinances for the church.'[15]

Jesus did therefore deliberately and with great solemnity introduce both the Lord's Supper and the ordinance of baptism, each in a unique way. There is surprisingly little reference to baptisms by Jesus and His disciples before the Day of Pentecost. Instructions for the apostolic mission of Matthew 10 do not include baptizing converts. The only reference to their baptizing is at John 3:22 ff. and 4:1. We do not know if Jesus baptized again those of His Apostles who had been John's disciples. It seems very unlikely. Nor do we know if any members of the Jerusalem church of Acts 2:1 ff. had previously been baptized by Jesus or an Apostle during their pre-Calvary ministries. Inferences based on this 'non-information' are risky. We do know that when Jesus in His resurrection body was with His followers in Galilee He solemnly announced, 'All authority in heaven and on earth has been given to me,' following which He commanded the disciples to take the gospel of salvation with them wherever they might go among 'all nations' and that they should make disciples by baptizing and teaching (Matt. 28:18-20).[16]

As for the Lord's Supper He chose the solemn occasion of His last meal with the Twelve, probably a last Passover Feast, to institute the ordinance. Of the eating of the bread He commanded, 'Do this in remembrance of me' (Luke 22:19; 1 Cor. 11:24). Of the cup, He said, 'Do this, as often as you drink it, in remembrance of me' (1 Cor. 11:25).

4. The church was obligated by the Lord's command to observe His ordinances everywhere (universally) and always (perpetually): among 'all nations' 'to the end of the age' and 'until he comes' (Matt. 28:19, 20; 1 Cor. 11:26). The churches initially understood this. There were no unbaptized, full members in the churches until many decades had passed – not until legalism and sacramentalism had interfered with the plain gospel of grace and changed perception of baptism from a symbol of regeneration and renewal to a means of the same, and the Eucharist to continuation of that work. Then many postponed baptism to near the end of life, supposing baptism secured the forgiveness of all past sins.

5. Each of these qualifications of an ordinance must be derived from plain statements of the New Testament and no other precedent or authority. This we have already noted is true of baptism and the Eucharist. Such is not the case for any of the five extra rites of the Roman and Eastern Orthodox churches – confirmation, penance, ordination (orders), extreme unction and matrimony. The Reformers of the sixteenth century heartily rejected them all as ordinances, per se. The Council of Trent responded with 'anathema' to any one who 'shall say that the sacraments of the New Law were not all instituted by Christ... or that there are more or less than seven.'[17] Ludwig Ott, 'The Institution and Seven-fold Nature of the Sacraments,'[18] and *The Cathechism of 1994*,[19] steadfastly reaffirm the claim, asserting unrecorded sayings of Christ preserved in tradition, the inspiration of the Paraclete, the divine authority of the hierarchy, and adding inferences based on 1 Corinthians 4:1 and 3:5.

---

15. Herman A. Hoyt, 'How Can One Determine a church Ordinance,' *Brethren Missionary Herald* magazine, April 15, 1961.
16. See Chap. 13 above, 'The Mission of the Church in the World.'
17. Denzinger, op. cit., para. 844, p. 262.
18. Ott, op. cit., pp. 336–341.
19. Paras. 113, 1117, 1210.

6. Though it might not at first be thought necessary to say it, it does remain to be emphasized: the purpose, effects, authority, and meanings of baptism and the Eucharist must be defined by the New Testament. Anything more or less than Scripture plainly says will obstruct the intentions of our Lord to some degree or even pervert the ordinance to something harmful to faith and salvation. One should not therefore assert as dogma that baptism removes the effects of original sin or that it effects regeneration either of adults or infants. By building a chain of irrelevant texts about water, children, baptism, the washing of regeneration and the like, the New Testament can be construed to say such things; but when the texts which truly relate directly to baptism are consulted no such interpretation springs forth naturally. There is, of course, room for some difference of opinion as to how the truly relevant texts should be interpreted.

Views of the Ordinance of Christian Baptism.

A reader of the present generation is not likely to be as well acquainted with the different views of the mode, meaning and proper subjects of baptism as previous generations of Protestants. Yet the differences persist even though the polemical exchanges are now less strident. Even so, my reading of a considerable amount of Protestant debate over the past three centuries left the impression of courtesy between most contestants – except where decimation of congregations was involved (as in the Campbellite incursions to Baptist and Presbyterian congregations from 1827 onward for forty years).

Points of Agreement.

There are many points of agreement by almost all. Baptism consists in the application of water to the ordinand's body – at least to the head. It is a mode of confessing Jesus Christ as Savior and Lord and was commanded by Him as a mark of discipleship. The obvious symbolism has some reference to cleansing from sin. To a degree this agreement extends to views of the apostolic mode of baptism. Though himself a defender of sprinkling and pouring, Anglican G. D. Bromiley acknowledges that 'Immersion was fairly certainly the original practice and continued in general use up to the [late] Middle Ages. The Reformers agreed that this best brought out the meaning of baptism as a death and resurrection.'[20] It is a simple matter to document this assertion.

Luther at first affirmed immersion as the original mode. Zwingli did likewise. Calvin's concession on the matter is well known, but it bears repeating:

> But whether the person being baptized should be wholly immersed, and whether thrice or once, whether he should only be sprinkled with poured water – these details are of no importance, but ought to be optional to churches according to the diversity of countries. Yet the word 'baptize' means to immerse, and it is clear that the rite of immersion was observed in the ancient church.[21]

Lumpkin observes, 'Lutheran and Reformed confessions condemned the Anabaptists both for rejecting infant baptism and for what they called rebaptism, not for practicing immersion, which all accepted.'[22]

Yet all three also strenuously affirmed that other modes were proper. The movements they began still largely practice aspersion or affusion. The churches of the Reformation, Lutheran and Reformed, including Anglican, Presbyterian and offshoots of the English Reformation (Congregationalists, Methodists) prevailingly practice sprinkling (aspersion) or pouring (affusion). Sprinkling had become the practice of the Roman Church from which the Reformation churches were separated and they did not change the form of baptism they received. In the lands of the Reformation every person born was christened as an infant. He was registered in the local church as a member of the community, both civil and religious, no distinction being made. When Europe divided into Roman Catholic and Protestant states the principle prevailed that the religion of 'the prince' (ruler) was to be the religion of his subjects. All the princes had been christened as infants, knew nothing else and approved nothing else.

Opposition arose contemporarily with Zwingli and Luther among people (later called Anabaptists) who thought that the Reformation principle of *sola scriptura* (the Bible alone) required baptism of believers only. They were

---

20. G. W. Bromiley, 'Baptism,' *Evangelical Dictionary of Theology*, p. 113.
21. Calvin, *Institutes*, IV. 15, 19. See documentation in William Lumpkin, *A History of Immersion* (Nashville: Broadman, 1963), pp. 21, 22. For Luther see *The Holy and Blessed Sacrament of Baptism*, 1519 (Works of Martin Luther, I., 56). For Zwingli, S. M. Jackson (ed.), *The Latin Works and the Correspondence of Huldrich Zwingli*, 'Commentary on Epistle to the Romans' (New York: G. P. Putman's Sons 1912–29, iv, 420.
22. Wm. Lumpkin, *A History of Immersion* (Nashville: Broadman, 1963), p. 24.

persecuted unmercifully by the rulers of Europe – Roman Catholic, Lutheran and Reformed. A century later in Britain (probably independently of the continental advocates of believers-only baptism), in the independent wing of the English Puritan Revolution, similar views arose leading to the formation of the Baptists who baptize only by immersion and believers only – i.e. no infants.[23]

Several scholarly treatments follow a similar approach, akin to the method of 'biblical theology.' I shall follow the analytic method in order to come quickly to conclusions. I would like to lead the reader to consider: (1) the origins of baptism (how it came to be practiced universally in the church); (2) its place in the life of the believer and the church; (3) its symbolism and theological meaning; (4) the effects of baptism (what does it do?); (5) its proper subjects (i.e. who should be baptized); and (6) the preferred mode – dipping, pouring, sprinkling or moistening.

The Origins of Baptism: How it Came to Be Practiced Universally in the Church.

C. F. D. Moule expresses common scholarly agreement among those who address the practice in the apostolic period.

> In the New Testament it is fair to say, Baptism is assumed as the way of entry into the Christian church. It is taken as a matter of course in (to cite only some of the passages) Acts 2:38, 41; 9:18; 10:47; 19:3; Rom. 6:13; 1 Cor. 6:11 (apparently); 12:13; Gal. 3:27; Eph. 4:5; Col. 2:12; Titus 3:5; Heb. 6:2 (perhaps), 4 (probably); 1 Peter 3:21.... In some of the passages just addressed, it is simply assumed that Christians, as such, must have been baptized; and the same is at least implied in others.[24]

Old Testament Background.

The Bible first introduces ritual washing in water in connection with priestly preparation for ministration at the Tabernacle. The story starts with the 'pattern' of the brazen 'laver' or tank of water shown to Moses 'in the mount' (Exod. 30:17-21; cf. 25:9). Does any one doubt the ritual washing of the priest's hands spoke to them symbolically of the holiness of God and of both ritual purity and moral purity of the priests who conducted His service (see Exod. 40:12-15; Lev. 8:5 ff.; Num. 8:5-8)? Other passages command vigorous washing of lay people in water (see especially Exod. 19:10), their offerings, their dwellings and similar in connection with solemn worship. In the Psalms (51:7; 24:3, 4) and the Prophets (Isa. 1:16; Ezek. 36:25; Zech. 13:1) the marks of spiritual cleansing are symbolized by washings in water. Isaiah, Jeremiah and Ezekiel made much of washing with water in their metaphors of Israel's future cleansing, renewal and restortion (Isa. 4:2-6; Ezek. 36:37; Jer. 33). These passages must have been in Jesus' mind when He reminded Nicodemus that as a teacher in Israel he ought to know what it means to be born of 'water and the Spirit' (John 3:5-10).

We do not know where dipping spiritually renewed people in a pool or stream as a sign of repentance and with reference to sin's cleansing began. 'We may safely assert there is no mention of proselyte baptism in Old Testament or in the Apocrypha.'[25] There is no clear evidence that proselytes to Judaism were baptized in pre-Christian times.[26] R. Martin seems to assume proselyte baptism was practiced 'in the first centuries BC and AD' and cites two British authors, but no proof.[27] This is the usual unproven assumption.

Emil Schürer shows that earliest written Jewish sources say full proselytes took a bath of purification upon embracing Judaism. If it was a self-washing as his citations indicate, this illustration is hardly specifically a 'baptism' as in the New Testament and Christian practice.[28]

Since discovery of the first seven Dead Sea Scrolls and their publication some scholars have proposed that the stepped pools at Qumran were for ceremonial purifications, i.e. self-immersions, and that John the Baptist derived

---

23. Baptism has been grossly neglected in recent decades. Three times I have served congregations for a lengthy interim pastorate and one five-year pastorate where many who professed to be Christians – even large numbers of them – had never been baptized at any age by any form or mode. To lead them to meaningful baptism I have offered a weekly class taking them simply first to John's practice, then to the baptism of Jesus by John, thence to Jesus' command, after that, to apostolic practice, and finally to the meaning of baptism as explained by Paul and Peter. Finally we also discussed references to 'born of water and the Spirit,' 'washing of regeneration' and the like. The first time I did this I baptized twenty-seven members of the congregation in the baptistry of the neighboring Baptist church.
24. C. F. D. Moule, *Worship in the New Testament* (Richmond, VA: John Knox Press, 1961, 1967), p. 47.
25. A. Plummer, 'Baptism,' *Hastings Dictionary of the Bible*, Vol. I, p. 239.
26. ibid.
27. Ralph Martin, *Worship in the Early Church* (Westwood, NJ: Revell, 1964), pp. 90, 91.
28. Emil Schürer, *A History of the Jewish People in the Time of Jesus Christ*, 2nd div., Vol. II (repr. Peabody, MA: Hendrickson Publ., 1998), pp. 319–324.

his practice from Qumran. Further that Christian practice was derived from John's. But the purification (baptism) at Qumran was a daily ritual for the spiritually elite who shared a special meal, not a once for all rite and in both John's and Christian baptism the candidate is immersed by a minister, not by self-immersion. Earlier scholars, as noted above, traced the baptism of John to earlier and contemporary proselyte baptism. Research of Douglas J. Culver, Ph. D. in Hebrew studies finds no solid proof of proselyte baptism before the rise of Christianity. He cites Baron: 'The problem is inextricably complicated by uncertainty in dating' – i.e. of 'early [Jewish] baptist sects' and the practice of ritual immersions. (See George Ladd [29] and Adela Warbro Collins.[30]) Collins concludes:

> Christian and rabbinic baptism both have their ultimate roots in the ritual washings of Leviticus. Both came to function as rituals of initiation. The major difference is the relation of this ritual to eschatology [i.e. Is Jesus the promised Messiah?].[31]

There are pools for water storage at Qumran that look like baptistries, but not every competent archaeologist agrees they were used for baptism. Josephus in a famous passage says the Essenes in times of Pharisees and Sadducees 'when they have clothed themselves in white veils, they then bathe their bodies in cold water. And after their purification is over they meet together,' etc. (*Wars of the Jews, II*, 8.5). In this case each bathed himself. There is quite a large literature about proselyte baptism in Judaism and Oepke thinks 'it is hardly conceivable that the Jewish ritual should be adopted at a time when baptism had become an established religious practice in Christianity.'[32] Yet the record suggests that late Judaism might have copied Christianity in this regard, rather than the other way around. The frequent assertion that sectarian baptism was established practice before John appeared on the scene seems far less than certain. The amount of literature seems more weighty than the evidence.[33]

John's Practice and Jesus' Example and Approval.

Where the earliest Gospel opens there is John, the son of Zachariah, baptizing 'in the wilderness' and preaching 'a baptism of repentance for the forgiveness of sins' (Mark 1:4). Five verses farther on Jesus Himself 'came from Nazareth of Galilee and was baptized by John in the Jordan' – not 'for the forgiveness of sins' but to fulfill all righteous requirements any ordinary human servant of God should meet (Mark 1:8).[34] On any basis of judgment, therefore, baptism is an important component of Jesus' entrance into public life and inauguration of His work of redemption. There is no doubt whatsoever that in taking the place of a sinner in an ordinance that came later clearly to symbolize His death (Matt. 20:22; Luke 12:50), Jesus had already set His face to go to Jerusalem to accomplish His 'departure' (Gr. *exodos*) there (Luke 9:31, 53). It is therefore correct to say that just as our Lord's public baptism marked the moment of public embarking on His public career of redemption so public baptism marks the beginning of the believer's public career as a member of Christ's body on earth.

The other Gospels have no strict parallel to the command to baptize of Matthew 28:19. Yet Luke, in his narrative, goes right on from the Ascension and the disciples' continuing in Jerusalem to report the baptisms which took place a few days later. It seems obvious that Jesus all the while was observing and approving baptisms by His disciples. This is supported by the fact that in preparing the disciples for His coming Passion He referred to it figuratively as a baptism (Mark 10:38, 39; Luke 12:50). Perhaps these baptizers and the people they baptized – including the 120 (Acts 1:15) – performed the baptisms on the Day of Pentecost.

The Command of Jesus.

As noted earlier, the Gospels of Mark and Luke nowhere say that Jesus commanded any one either to baptize or to be baptized. The Gospel of John almost incidentally reports that though Jesus Himself performed no baptisms (John 4:1, 2), His disciples baptized many (John 3:25, 26). Yet at His meeting with a crowd of many disciples in Galilee (Matt. 28:1 ff.) after the resurrection He commanded those disciples to make public Christians of all nations (disciples) by baptizing and teaching them (Matt. 28:19, 20 RSV, NIV). Carrying out the command to baptize began on the Day of Pentecost (Acts 2:38, 41). It seems a correct judgment that the Apostles (including Matthias,

---

29. George Ladd, *The Theology of the New Testament* (Grand Rapids: Eerdmans, 1974, 1991), pp. 40, 41.
30. Adela W. Collins, 'The Origin of Christian Baptism,' chap. 7, *Cosmology and Eschatology in Jewish and Christian Apercalypticism* (Leiden: E. J. Brill, 1996), pp. 219–238.
31. Collins, op. cit., p. 238.
32. Oepke, 'Bapto,' TDNT, Vol. I, p. 535.
33. *per contra* see Martin, op. cit., pp. 89, 90 and references.
34. I discuss this more at length in *The Life of Christ*, Baker, 1987, pp. 67–69.

Acts 1:22-26) and many others previously baptized by John the Baptist and Jesus' disciples would have performed those baptisms. There is no hint that any 'rebaptisms' took place. From that day to this, even the world has come to understand that baptism in a public display of repentance from sin and faith in Christ is the normal way believing sinners take their public stand forever with Him.

Church Practice in the New Testament and Beyond.

The practice of administering baptism to every new believer continued onward throughout the expansion of the church, as seen in Acts.[35] When Paul, freshly converted en route to Damascus, arrived at that city he was promptly instructed ('teaching them' Matt. 28:20), and after that baptized and then instructed some more. Throughout the rest of the New Testament the general silence on the subject – except by way of reflection on the matter (1 Cor. 1:13, 14, 16; 10:2), or building upon it (1 Cor. 12:13; Gal. 3:27), or arguing from it (1 Cor. 15:29), or interpreting it (Eph. 4:5; 1 Peter 3:21) – simply assumes that every member of the body, baptized 'into one spirit' within the body of Christ, has also been properly baptized in water in 'the name of the Lord,' or in 'the name of the Father and of the Son and of the Holy Spirit.' The use of 'in the name of the Lord' rather than the Trinitarian formula has many proposed explanations. It probably means 'by the Lord's authority' as opposed to pagan gods or Jewish formulas.[36]

---

35. See Acts 8:12, 13, 16, 36, 38; 9:18; 10:47, 48; 16:15, 33; 18:8; 19:3, 5.
36. See note by R. L. Saucy, *The Church in God's Program* (Chicago: Moody Press, 1972), p. 193.

23
The Ordinance of Baptism: the Church's Rite of Initiation, II

I. The Proper Subjects of Baptism.

The question of the proper subjects is not unrelated to the meaning and the mode of baptism. We shall, however, at this stage simply consult the New Testament as to who was baptized and with what requirements. Robert Reymond has recently approached the topic, conveniently listing in textual order every one of the eleven 'actual baptisms' in the New Testament.[1] We shall briefly examine each reference in search of an answer.

Acts 2:37-41.

On the Day of Pentecost Peter addressed 'Jews, devout men from every nation' (Acts 2:5). '[M]en' in this case translates *andres*, plural of the regular noun for the male of our race – not boys or females. At the conclusion of the sermon 'they were cut to the heart, and said to Peter and the rest of the apostles, "Brothers, what shall we do?" And Peter said to them [to these adult males], "Repent and be baptized" ....So those [adult males] who received his [Peter's] word were baptized.... And they [adult males] devoted themselves to the apostles' teaching...' and so on. Can any one doubt that the people baptized that day – 'three thousand souls' – were male adults? It would be precarious to say absolutely that there were no women present, but worship at the stated festivals three times a year was a male duty. The Old Testament is very specific about this (Exod. 23:17; Deut. 16:16). True, sometimes for Passover at least (1 Sam. 1:3, 21) in the land of Israel, the whole family went along and also probably to the Feast of Tabernacles (see John 7:17). At any rate the only ones within the sweep of the text's attention are adult male Jews. The reference 'to you and your children' means their descendants, not offspring present on the occasion.

These men were already 'devout' believers in the one true God. As believers they needed to repent of their disbelief in 'Jesus of Nazareth' (v. 22) and publicly to acknowledge their adherence to Jesus as Messiah by baptism. In this case baptism was an act of confessing faith – parallel to 'confess with your mouth' (Rom. 10:9).

Acts 8:12-17.

This describes the results of the first preaching of the good news of Christ away from Jerusalem: at Samaria in central Palestine, where a clan of mixed Jewish-Gentile ancestry and an heretical form of Judaism lived. The significant reference to baptism says, 'But when they believed Philip as he preached good news about the kingdom of God and

---

1. Robert L. Reymond, *A New Systematic Theology of the Christian Faith* (Nashville: Thomas Nelson, 1998), p. 193.

the name of Jesus Christ, they were baptized, both men [*andres*, adult males] and women [*gunaikes*, adult females]' (v. 12 RSV). The passage goes on to say that one of those who believed was a sorcerer named Simon, 'Even Simon himself believed, and after being baptized he continued with Philip' (v. 13 RSV). The passage is a fertile one for many doctrines, but in relation to the question of the proper candidates for baptism it is clear that Philip baptized only those adults, of either sex, who believed and were prepared publicly to confess the same in water baptism. This was all in response to the fact that 'Philip went down to the city of Samaria, and proclaimed to them the Christ,' with accompanying evidence of authority (Acts 8:4-8 RSV).

This passage shows that adults who believe in God and were prepared publicly to declare their faith in Christ are proper subjects of baptism.

Acts 8:35-38.

The scene is on the road which descends from Jerusalem southwest to Gaza – part way through a 'wilderness' (uninhabited) area (v. 26). The same Philip has explained to a traveling, royal officer of Jewish faith the reference of Isaiah 53:7, 8 to Christ. Philip 'told him the good news,' evidently also raising the possibility of baptism. The Western text of Acts preserves a valid report of what we shall see was already standard baptismal procedure, as reported in Acts 8:37 (KJV). The question was, 'what doth hinder me to be baptized?' The answer: 'If thou believest with all thine heart thou mayest.' Again the subject was a person of the age of mental competence who voluntarily requested baptism after having been persuaded by the truth of the Word. So 'they both went down into the water, Philip and the eunuch, and he baptized him.'

We shall return to this passage in discussing the apostolic mode of baptism.

Acts 9:18 and 22:16.

After his marvelous conversion from persecution of Christ to deep faith in Christ on the road to Damascus (Acts 9:1-9) the Apostle-to-be was led on to that city. After three days, still blind from the meeting with Christ on the road and still fasting, Ananias, 'a disciple,' visited him, 'And laying his hands on him he said, "Brother Saul, the Lord Jesus who appeared to you on the road by which you came, has sent me that you may regain your sight and be filled with the Holy Spirit." And immediately something like scales fell from his eyes and he regained his sight. Then he rose and was baptized, and took food and was strengthened' (Acts 9:17-19 RSV). Later, reflecting on these events, Paul filled out the narrative. After receiving his sight back Ananias urged, 'And now why do you wait? Rise and be baptized, and wash away your sins, calling on his name' (Acts 22:16 RSV). Again, much here cries for comment on many topics of doctrine, but as regards the proper candidate for baptism, here is a young adult Jew who first received the truth about Jesus as Savior and himself as sinner, who repented his past behavior of persecuting Jesus, committed himself without reserve to Jesus, and when invited to do so, confessed his new faith in baptism – here described as washing away his sins. We shall return to this text also when considering the meaning of baptism.

Up to this point advocates of 'believers' baptism' and of 'infant baptism' find only a little to disagree about. The normal pattern is to hear the gospel, then to believe it, then to confess faith in Christ in baptism. In the next three instances – the households of Cornelius of Caesarea (Acts 10:44-48), of Lydia at Philippi (Acts 16:13-15), and the Roman jailor of the same city (Acts 16:30-34) – advocates of infant baptism think that they find ground for the baptism of the infant offspring of believing parents. All readily agree that in the case of adult members of the three groups the procedure was the same as above: first hearing the gospel, then believing, and after that baptism. When faith only is mentioned repentance is implied and when repentance only, faith is implied. They are the negative and positive aspects of one movement of the soul. They are two sides of one thing.

Acts 10:44-48.

The interested reader may examine the cited passages. Let us take note only of the aspects related to the subject of baptism. In the case of Cornelius, the centurion of Caesarea, he 'was expecting' Peter and his party 'and had called together his relatives and close friends' (Acts 10:24). Shortly after he arrived 'Peter opened his mouth' and spoke what scholars like to call 'the primitive *kērygma*,' or preached gospel (Acts 10:34-43). While Peter was still speaking 'the Holy Spirit fell on all who heard the word' (Acts 10:44) astounding the believing Jews in Peter's party of travelers that Gentiles had received the Holy Spirit – which they knew to be the 'sign' or 'seal' of their redemption. In view of the fact they had already witnessed the sign or seal[2] of the Spirit's effusion, Peter declared that baptism, the public rite of initiation into the church, could not be withheld from them. He therefore

---

2. 2 Cor. 1:22; Eph. 1:13; 4:30, cf. 2 Tim. 2:19.

'commanded them' (who heard the Word) and on whom 'the Holy Spirit fell' 'to be baptized in the name of Jesus Christ' (v. 48). It seems clear that those baptized were a group of adults gathered from several families for this occasion (cf. 10:27), all competent to hear the Word with understanding and to respond in faith.[3]

Acts 16:13-15.
This passage presents the same succession of events in connection with baptism – hearing the Word, believing, confessing in baptism.[4]

Many advocates of infant baptism have argued, inasmuch as the 'woman named Lydia, from the city of Thyatira, a seller of purple goods' and 'a worshiper of God' (a proselyte, or, one convinced of Judaism) 'was baptized, and her household as well' that, if not infant children of her own, then children of her servants (slaves), would have been baptized. In such case the faith would have been that of Lydia or of the slave parents, not of the infants. The text, however, makes no mention of children (infants). No mention is made of a husband; even in a patriarchal society where there is no husband she speaks as head of the house; hence, no offspring of Lydia is present. The narrative is very condensed, so though 'she was baptized, and her household as well' (v. 15), it is to be expected that, as in the case of the jailor, later in the chapter, Paul and Silas first 'spoke the word of the Lord to him and to all who were in his house' (Acts 16:32), and all the household believed.

Acts 16:30-34.
The jailor gave the two missionaries opportunity to speak 'the word of the Lord to him and to all who were in his house.' He had already been told he should 'Believe in the Lord Jesus, and you will be saved, you and your household' (v. 31). No one will likely claim that the jailor's faith would save any one else apart from that person's own belief in 'the Lord Jesus.' Paul and Silas obviously meant that the household had the same privilege of access that the jailor had, and that is why the household, 'all who were in his house,' was apparently gathered together to hear 'the word of the Lord.' Whether 'house' in each case means a building or the people – jailor, his family and retainers – makes little difference. As most scholars agree, whether they advocate infant baptism or not, the narrative assumes that all the persons involved are of responsible age, probably adults.

The next three texts relate to baptisms at Corinth when Paul and Silas had their next extended ministry.

Acts 18:8; 1 Corinthians 1:14; and 1:16.
The first text speaks of another household who became Christians: 'Crispus... believed in the Lord, together with his entire household. And many of the Corinthians hearing Paul believed and were baptized.' Does it not seem here again that a man, his household and many neighbors were first evangelized by the gospel messengers, then they believed and confessed the Lord in baptism? By theologizing from Old Testament analogies to circumcision, and the covenant which circumcision sealed, some find ground for infant baptism in this passage – as in the jailor, and Lydia and Cornelius stories. Robert Reymond, a firm believer in infant baptism on the basis of this analogy and covenant, warns:

> I would counsel that the paedobaptist should not put much weight on these 'household baptisms,' for even if he could convince the antipaedobaptist that in these cases the believer's household was baptized on the basis of the believer's faith... he cannot prove that any of these households had infants or small children in them.[5]

The baptism of certain disciples early in Paul's time at Ephesus (Acts 19:5) furnishes no evidence for this part of our inquiry into the subject of baptism.

Perhaps the most important work to promote the legitimacy of infant baptism in a hundred years was Joachim Jeremias', translated and published in English in 1960 as *Infant Baptism in the First Four Centuries*.[6] A famous scholar, he sought to employ the historical sources to vindicate infant baptism. He derived his evidence from the New Testament, documents of history of the first four centuries and surviving inscriptions – especially inscriptions of Christian burials. Earlier, Oscar Cullmann had written in defense of infant baptism. Though himself an advocate of the present practice of infant baptism, Kurt Aland, of the German University of Münster, produced a point-by-point refutation of Jeremias.[7] At about the same time G. R. Beasley-Murray produced a very comprehensive volume.[8]

---

3. On 'in the name of Jesus' see Robert L. Reymond, *A New Systematic Theology of the Christian Faith*, 1998, pp. 926–927.
4. See Reymond, p. 942.
5. ibid., p. 943.
6. Joachim Jeremias, *Infant Baptism in the First Four Centuries* (London: SCM Press, 1960).
7. Kurt Aland, *Did the Early Church Baptize Infants?*, trans. G. R. Beasley-Murray (London: SCM Press, 1963).
8. G. R. Beasley-Murray, *Baptism in the New Testament* (London: Macmillan, 1963).

Karl Barth may have done most to stir up this new scholarly literature on an old subject by, as the world's most famous Reformed theologian, writing in fierce repudiation of infant baptism.[9] The same wave of interest produced Anglican C. F. D. Moule's statement 'that there is no direct evidence' for infant baptism 'in the New Testament,' that inferences based on household baptism and Jesus' blessing of little children are quite inadequate. He used these conclusions to propose anew that in the case of baptized infants the laying on of hands (confirmation) 'was integral to baptism' (Acts 19:5) – in connection, of course, with preparatory instruction.[10]

Defense of Infant Baptism by Protestant Non-Lutheran Evangelicals.
About all that can ever be said on this matter was said by the first generations of Reformed theologians – Zwingli, Bucer and contemporaries and stated shortly thereafter by Calvin in the fourth book of the *Institutes*, chapters 14–16.

All the Reformers, beginning with Luther, struggled with two things. First, they knew from the evangelical promises of Scripture that justification is wholly by faith. They knew that baptism is an act of faith, a confession of faith. Each of the Reformers had been baptized as an infant before he could exercise his own faith. All the adherents of the Reformation had similarly been christened, and as pastors they baptized the infant offspring of their adherents. The apparent disconnection with faith had to be explained somehow. Second, beginning immediately, growing numbers of Christians renounced infant baptism and brought persuasive arguments against it. They were called Anabaptists – 'again-baptizers.'

Calvin's doctrine of baptism was thoroughly free of sacramentalism. To be sure, some of his language seems to assign to the act of baptism what rightly belongs to faith. But the suspicious reader should grant to Calvin the same consideration he grants to Ananias who urged Paul, 'Rise and be baptized and wash away your sins' (Acts 22:16). Here Ananias simply merged the symbol with the fact symbolized, as is not infrequent in discourse of any kind.

It seemed obvious to opponents of infant baptism (as Calvin stated) that 'infant baptism has arisen not so much from a clear mandate of Scripture as from a decree of the church.'[11] He promised to show that 'the fact is far otherwise.'[12] He did not in his mature teaching claim that in some way infants can have faith (as Luther did), or that parents' or sponsors' faith suffices, or that baptism is required in view of future faith (as some others of the time were saying).[13] Early on, he had been content to say that God could call the elect to 'enter by faith into eternal life' at whatever age God chooses, but felt unsure of that argument, as shown by immediate appeal to another route of proof, namely Jesus' saying that it is the will of God that 'little children' should 'come' to him (Matt. 19:14).[14]

In the final edition of *Institutes*, Calvin strove mightily to prove – against persistent Anabaptist attacks at Geneva – that God had instituted infant baptism. He rather grandly introduces the argument.[15] The editors of the Westminster edition of 1960 summarize Calvin's argument through the next six paragraphs: 'Infant baptism, considered in relation to what it typifies, corresponds to circumcision and is authorized in the covenant with Abraham.'[16] The covenant is the same. The promised salvation is the same. Only the symbols – i.e. the outward ceremonies, circumcision and baptism – are different. The chief arguments of Charles Hodge (nineteenth-century Presbyterian), Berkhof (*Systematic Theology*), Buswell (*A Systematic Theology of the Christian Religion*), John Murray (*Christian Baptism*), Francis Schaeffer (*Baptism*) and Robert Reymond (*A New Systematic Theology*), are essentially the same. Calvin buttresses the main argument by appeal to Jesus' receiving and blessing little children (Matt. 19:13-15).[17] He bristles at the obvious question, 'What is the connection with baptism?' and answers in a way satisfactory, I think, only to those who wish him to be correct.

He devotes many pages to answering objections to the supposed analogy between baptism and circumcision[18] and dealing with other problems raised (17–31). At the end of this discussion he proposes one final reason for perpetuating the custom of infant baptism. The baptism of their own children (and presumably of others from time

---

9. Karl Barth, *The Teaching of the Church Regarding Baptism*, trans. E. A. Payne (London: SCM Press, 1965).
10. C. F. D. Moule, *Worship in the New Testament* (Richmond, VA: John Knox Press, 1961, 1967), p. 50.
11. Calvin, *Institutes*, IV. 8.16.
12. ibid.
13. Francois Wendel, *Calvin: His Origins and Development of His Religious Thought* (New York: Harper and Row, 1950, 1963), p. 324.
14. ibid., p. 384.
15. Calvin, op. cit., 16.1.
16. ibid., p. 1324.
17. Calvin, *Institutes*, IV. 16, 7-9.
18. ibid., 16.10-16.

At the beginning of the sixteenth century, Europe had been blighted for centuries by the utterly false dogma that baptism is only the first of seven sacraments which actually confer salvation or some aspect of it and that the only agency from whom to receive these sacraments is the Church of Rome.

Having learned anew that salvation is by faith alone, the sixteenth-century evangelicals understood the blessings of baptism are the very blessings of that faith in Christ which baptism confesses. Further, even the 'magisterial' Reformers (we now say 'mainline'), though they granted the legitimacy of infant baptism against the protestations of Anabaptists, were compelled to think of baptism as it is spread on the pages of the Bible which everyone now was reading. The New Testament was written by the very apostolic evangelists (Peter, Paul, John) whose preaching had produced the believers whose baptisms these writers administered and explained on those New Testament pages. Let us leap backward before the centuries of Protestant controversy for an introduction to the subject of the blessings of Christian baptism. The quoted words in the next paragraphs are from John Calvin.

1. Baptism formally initiates us 'into the society of the church.'[32] This is clearly indicated by the sequence of events in the reports of baptisms in Acts. At the end of Peter's first sermon, and presumably over the next hours, 'they that gladly received his word [i.e. they believed it] were baptized and the same day were added [obviously to the group who earlier in the day were baptized by the Spirit into a body] about three thousand souls.' At Caesarea, baptism of Cornelius and his company certified publicly that they had 'received the Holy Spirit just as we have' (Acts 10:47, 48). Further, the command to baptize at Matthew 28:19, 20 specified that making a disciple is by baptizing and teaching. Early generations accepted this without question. Baptism is the public 'certificate,' so to speak, that one is by religious profession a Christian, a member of the church of his locality with all the benefits appertaining – and, of course, in a sinful world, all the risks as well.

2. 'Baptism was given us by God primarily to strengthen our faith in him.'[33] This should be coupled with the fact that when we receive baptism faith is strengthened thereby. The very act of submitting one's body to the hands of the minister to submerge us in water and draw one out again is an exercise in faith of a sort. Baptism in the ancient stone baptistries was of necessity, because of the short length of the pool, in kneeling posture as the head was bowed and moved forward into the water – the classic oriental posture of reverent worship or of submission.[34] Going through the motions of submission or of its opposite is, from a purely psychological point of view, strengthening to the state of mind it intended to mirror.

3. 'Baptism... was given by God... to serve as our confession before men.'[35] Calvin said that was true of the sacrament of *Eucharist* also, for when we walk into the place of assembly and publicly receive the elements in the company of the believers who have 'come together' in the church (1 Cor. 11:17, 18, 20), we tell the world to whom we belong – to Christ and 'the church, which is his body' (Eph. 1:22, 23).

4. More important for the new believer, his baptism is an experiential certificate that his sins are forgiven. 'The first thing that the Lord sets out for us is that baptism should be a token and proof of our cleansing ... like a sealed document to confirm to us that all our sins are so abolished, remitted and effaced that they can never come to his sight, be recalled, or charged against us. For he wills that all who believe be baptized for the remission of sins.'[36] The Reformers generally – against the doctrine of the Mass, of penance and of purgatory – held before their people that the forgiveness certified in baptism covered not only sins of the past but all sins present or future: as Luther declared in his early work *The Babylonian Captivity of the Church* (see Wendel, p. 320) and as Calvin goes on to say.

> We are not to think that baptism was conferred upon us only for past time so that for newly committed sins committed after baptism we must seek new remedies of expiation in some other sacraments.... [He then refers to the error of some early church people in this regard who postponed baptism till death was imminent and goes on to say:] We are once for all washed and purged for our whole life [not by water but by the blood of Christ]. Therefore, as often as we fall away we ought to recall the memory of our baptism and fortify our mind with it.[37]

---

32. Calvin, *Institutes*, IV, 15.1.
33. ibid., 14.1., trans. Wendel, p. 318.
34. These relics of antiquity are spread all over the world of ancient Christendom. The one perhaps most frequently seen by tourists is at the site of the basilica of Mt. Nebo — visited by Pope John Paul II in 2000. I examined it in 1962 and again in 1976. Harvey, op. cit., pp 152–162, provides details of measurements, examples of ancient baptistries, mosaics and catacombs.
35. Calvin, op. cit., 14.1.
36. ibid., p. 1304.
37. ibid., IV.15.3.

5. Baptism furnishes the believer with an object-lesson affirming our union with Christ in His death and resurrection. It must not be construed merely to admonish us to follow Jesus' example of self-denial, or death to sinful desire, but that, as we go under the water, we symbolize Jesus' death and our union with Him in it. In emerging from the water we picture to ourselves our union with Him in resurrection and His divine life (see *Institutes*, IV.15.5). Sometimes here the language of Calvin seems to suggest that baptism effects this union but elsewhere it is clear that he means that just as we are justified by faith in Christ, so by faith we know that we are united with Christ in death and resurrection, that 'to live is Christ' (Phil. 1:21).

6. We must also point out that baptism reminds us that in union with Christ we are presently guaranteed a share in all the good things He gained by death and resurrection. Somehow medieval theology, as well as the perennial drift toward salvation by human merit and accomplishment, have hidden this plain truth of Romans 5 and 6 and of Philippians 2. My memory is fresh of the first time I heard it unfolded to me at a Bible conference when at the age of fourteen I was already a baptized believer. I have found that when preaching to audiences in mid-America, where various strains of legalism and sacramentalism have taken hold, much care should be taken to explain what baptism is and is not, what baptism does effect and does not effect. It sometimes seems impossible to eradicate the ancient error of Christendom that sinners can be saved by a ceremony, even one instituted by Jesus our Lord. This problem is about as acute in Baptist and similar groups as among those which practice infant baptism. I remember all too well a question asked by a young woman named Marian in our church at Fremont, Ohio. I had just conducted a ceremony of dedication of a newborn infant at the Sunday morning worship service. I had explained that we were not conferring salvation in part or whole on the baby. 'But pastor, would Norma's baby go to heaven if she died even if it hadn't been blest?' Errors old, deep and prevalent die hard!

A Postscript

With regret I close this brief treatment of the subjects of baptism and the mode of administration. Denominational works of systematic theology usually devote large space to these matters. In past generations great public debates over the subjects and mode of baptism were attended by crowds. Many of these debates were recorded by a stenographer and published. These books sit on back shelves of church and school libraries today. More recently, with less heat and more research, a scholarly debate has risen in books and journals. I have for many reasons (chiefly to avoid enlarging this book) determined not to proceed further into this world of controversy here.

24
Worship at the Lord's Table, I

Chapter 21, on 'Public Meetings for Worship in the church,' said little about the ordinance of 'the Lord's Supper,' reserving that important topic for special treatment. Baptism normally occurs but once in a believer's lifetime; the Lord's Supper is a continuing ordinance which Jesus clearly indicated should be observed frequently. Furthermore, in this ordinance, worship of God in Christ reaches a depth and height not ordinarily equaled elsewhere at any other time. Thus we first associated the Supper rather than baptism with worship even though these two are the only Christian rites properly called ordinances or sacraments.

Late in the Reformation era *The Westminster Confession* (chap. 31, Arts. 1–8) and *The Thirty-Nine Articles of Religion* (Arts. 28–31) formulated a basic Protestant-evangelical theology of the Eucharist for English-speaking evangelicals. Neither refers specifically to the Lutheran doctrine of the Supper, though Westminster specifically denies the Lutheran doctrine that wicked people actually receive 'the thing signified' in the bread and wine. Both reject the Roman doctrine of Transubstantiation. Though both call the Supper a 'sacrament' they do so without any idea that the elements confer saving grace. The discussion to follow here is rather fully oriented to the few biblical materials on the subject, but does not reject these important historic documents of primitive evangelical theology. They rendered permanent until this day important gains of the Reformation of the sixteenth century.

Names of the Ordinance.

Not everyone agrees that the ordinance is properly called 'The Lord's Supper,' for many think the one occurrence (1 Cor. 11:22) designates the meal ('love feast,' Jude 12) at which the churches of ancient times observed the Eucharist. Yet, in most present-day circles, the Lord's Supper is the commonest name and it is not likely to be dislodged. Paul also called it 'the communion' (*koinōnia*, 1 Cor. 10:16 KJV) probably because it is the most meaningful ritual act of the church, which is itself the *koinōnia* (a word which means mutual participation, Acts 2:42). The 'Supper' was understood to be received from the Lord Himself as host, hence 'the Lord's table' and 'the cup of the Lord' (1 Cor. 10:21 NIV). The earliest designation was 'breaking of bread' (Acts 2:42; 20:7). This Supper is opposed to the *koinōnia* of devils (1 Cor. 10:20). Further, it is the 'communion [*koinōnia*] of the body of Christ' (1 Cor. 10:16 KJV). Another common name has always been 'eucharist' (Gr. *he eucharistia*, 'the thanksgiving') echoing Luke 20:19 and 1 Corinthians 11:23, 24, where it is said that at the Last Passover 'Jesus... took bread, and... [gave] thanks,' and so on. Though some are uncomfortable using the word 'eucharist' because it is perceived to have overtones of the Roman Catholic Mass and of sacramentalism, Eucharist (thanksgiving) is a perfectly unambiguous term as far as the scriptural setting is concerned. This term clearly designates the bread and cup as distinct from the then customary meal, or love feast. Moreover, in this rite, believers do communally give thanks to God for His 'inexpressible gift' of Jesus our Lord (2 Cor. 9:15).

Origin and Institution by Christ.

Not the Supper itself but the interpretation of it by Paul has been traced by certain historians to heathen, Hellenist memorial feasts familiar to the Gentile believers and to Paul.[1] Other critical writers reject this view.[2] Yet form criticism and historical studies have produced no convincing evidence that Paul, our only source of a theology of the Lord's Supper, drew any of his ideas about it from any source except the Lord, either through other Apostles or direct revelation of Christ Himself. He did not, of course, have the Gospel's reports, because at least in present form they had not yet been written.

Modern scholarship has gone through waves of opinion as to whether the occasion of the institution was indeed 'the last passover' or a last Jewish supper of a different kind, perhaps a *kiddush* or a *chaburah*. The former was a supper-ceremony held by a family or brotherhood in preparation for a larger celebration, the latter a fellowship-meal frequently held.[3]

Such theories really raise as many problems as they try to solve. There are real problems with the Gospel accounts as to the day of the Supper and the crucifixion a few hours later, not particularly relevant to the institution of the Eucharist. Christian tradition fixes attention to the fact that the Passover is the feast mentioned. Joachim Jeremias supplies perhaps the most decisive word and he favors the Passover.[4] Whatever the case may be, we know that Jesus took elements of Old Testament ritual familiar to twelve Jews and transformed their meaning. On the other hand it can be truly said that He took the commonest elements of any Near East meal and employed them as the most holy emblems of the central message of the gospel, namely: 'Christ Jesus died to save sinners.'

There are five accounts of the Supper – each Gospel and Paul (1 Cor. 11), though John does not mention the institution of the Eucharistic rite. Writing about twenty-five years after that evening Paul said: 'the Lord Jesus the same night in which he was betrayed took bread: And when he had given thanks, he brake it, and said, Take, eat: this is my body, which is broken [broken is not in the best Gr. texts] for you: this do in remembrance of me. After the same manner also he took the cup, when he had supped, saying, This cup is the new testament in my blood: this do ye, as oft as ye drink it, in remembrance of me' (1 Cor. 11:23-25 KJV). I remark:

1. Paul's discourse, just quoted, is the fullest scriptural account, containing most elements of the other accounts of the actions of our Lord and the actual words of institution (Luke 22:19, 20; Mark 14:22, 23; Matt. 26:26, 27).

2. Jesus' actions and words were deliberate, intended to model a rite to be regularly observed among His disciples (if not quite fully yet a church) until the future return of Christ in His kingdom: 'until it is fulfilled in the kingdom of God.... until the kingdom of God comes' (Luke 22:16, 18; cf. Mark 14:25; Matt. 25:29). Further, 'Do this, as often as you drink it' (1 Cor. 11:25 and parallels) uses the present imperative of *poieo*, to do, the appropriate mood and tense for repeated future action. '[A]s often.... as often' (1 Cor. 11:25, 26) indicates many future observances of the rite.

The writers of the Gospels present the story of the Last Supper as the setting for the Eucharistic rite which Christians everywhere were then, at least a generation later, observing. This rite already had been continuously observed at Corinth from the beginning of the church in that city but needed an historical explanation to give meaning. If the tradition had not received authentic written form in the apostolic age the church Fathers later would not have been able to say, as they did, that the church had the same teaching and rites everywhere – that is, it was *kat'holikos*, Catholic, according to a whole.

---

1. Hans Lietzmann, *Mass and Lord's Supper*, 1926 and others since.
2. Ernst Käsemann, *Essays On New Testament Themes* (Philadelphia: Fortress, 1942), p. 120 ff.
3. The best discussion of the problem I know of is in *The Shape of the Liturgy* by Dom Gregory Dix, the chapter on 'Eucharist and Lord's Supper' (London: Dacre Press, 1945, 1978), pp. 48–102, conclusions stated p. 95. Dix on p. 95 favors the *chaburah* but in a note 1, p. 50 acknowledges that 'the question is not yet finally settled,' as Jeremias notes (p. 31). Wm. D. Maxwell, in his widely read book (*An Outline of Christian Worship, Its Development and Forms*, 1936, 1958) disseminated the *kiddush* view through several generations. It went through at least seven printings.
4. Joachim Jeremias, *The Eucharist Words of Jesus* (New York: Macmillan, 1955), pp. 1–60.

To define and enlarge the meaning of the Eucharistic rite and of the events of the day of crucifixion was an *apostolical* function not a *dominical* function. Doctrinal explanation was to take place only after the Lord's Ascension and the affusion of the Spirit – as we have had occasion frequently to note (John 14:25, 26; 15:26, 27; 16:12-15). Paul is the only Apostle who put in canonical writing what the Spirit taught in regard to the meaning of Eucharistic acts and words of Jesus at the Last Supper. Treatment of that subject here will therefore mainly take the form of exposition of what Paul had to say, with some references to the Synoptic texts and John 13–16.

Let us attend preliminarily to the following.

1. Paul founded the church at Corinth, continuing there long enough (eighteen months, Acts 18:11) with some of his best assistants (Aquila, Priscilla, Silas, Timothy) to ground the church in authentic doctrine and practice, leaving behind an active (hyperactive? 1 Cor. 14) congregation. He claimed no originality for the form and texture of his 'ecclesiology.' His *doctrine* was 'what I also received' (1 Cor. 15:3 RSV). Conduct and procedures instituted were the deposit of the same tradition which he had received and which were prevalent in all the churches (1 Cor. 11:2; cf. 14:34; 11:16).

2. He wielded full authority from the same Christ who instituted the church and its practice to command obedience to His rules (1 Cor. 14:37, 38). He therefore wrote to confirm old instructions, to clarify and to apply them as well as to institute new ones. He did not hesitate lovingly to assert his authority as above texts and the tenor of both Corinthian Epistles clearly mainfest. They bristle with Paul's awareness of responsibility to set things 'in order' (1 Cor. 15:40; 11:33).

3. First Corinthians 10 and 11 supplement Eucharistic practices and interpretation already given. The Lord's Supper had no doubt been observed at Corinth from the founding of that *ekklēsia* by Paul several years earlier. The instructions of the chapters are also corrective. We do not know precisely what liturgical procedures Paul introduced. In 11:23 he says he 'received' the words of institution 'from the Lord' and 'delivered to you.' This is careful language. He claims no originality whatsoever. He is not, however, claiming a special revelation. Presumably it was what he saw as a new Christian being practiced at Damascus, Antioch and Jerusalem. There was an apostolic tradition about such things to which he refers in a special way in introducing the rules about modest attire for presence at communion (1 Cor. 11:13). In the former he uses the technical term for teachings passed down from earlier authority. '[Y]ou... maintain the traditions [Gr. *Paradoseis*] even as I have delivered [Gr. *Paredōka*] them to you' (1 Cor. 11:2 RSV). At the end he says he will later 'set in order' (Gr. *Diataxomai*) (1 Cor. 11:34 KJV). Paul was insistent on 'order' and 'decency' (1 Cor. 14:40) in public worship.

Buechsel's brief remarks[5] sum up: 'For Paul Christian teaching is tradition (1 Cor. 11:2; 2 Thess. 2:15; 3:6 cf. 1 Cor. 11:23; 15:1-11), and he demands the churches should keep to it, since salvation depends on it (1 Cor. 15:2). He sees no antithesis between pneumatic [spiritual] piety and the high estimation of tradition. The essential point for Paul is that it has been handed down (1 Cor. 15:3), and that it derives from the Lord (11:23). A tradition initiated by himself or others is without validity.'

4. Modern criticism – source, literary, form, redaction and the like – has been busy for several generations, seeking to establish which parts of the Synoptic and Pauline reports of the words of institution and interpretation are genuinely 'the eucharistic, words of Jesus,' and exploring the related question whether the Last Supper was a Passover supper or something else. Jeremias' bibliography of the latter topic starts with a book by John Lightfoot in the year 1686 and seven densely packed pages later takes us up to the publication of his own book, *The Eucharistic Words of Jesus* of 1955. There has been a blizzard of papers and books as spin-offs from The Jesus Seminar. In the midst of chaff some of this literature is serious, fruitful scholarship. And I for one have profited from reading some of it – see my *A Greater Commission*[6] and *The Life of Christ*[7] and 'Rhetorical Allegories Among the Parables of Jesus?' in *New Testament Essays*, ed. G. T. Meadors.[8] Yet all our doctrines must be derived from the canonical Scriptures as the text has come to us from antiquity. In this, textual criticism has been of some direct aid in establishing an authentic text and it is that text with which the exegetes and theologians must work, not the waves of scholarly opinion as to sources, redactions, trajectories, genre and similar which hypothetically produced the Gospels' text.

---

5. TDNT, Vol. II, pp. 172, 173.
6. Moody Press, 1984, pp. 153–163.
7. Baker Books, 1976, 1991, 'passim.'
8. Winona Lake, IN: BMH Books, 1991, pp. 103–124.

The Order of the Lord's Supper and its Meaning.

There is an 'order' for the continuing memorial rite to which both Scripture and custom have given the name the Lord's Supper. As we have noted, the rite is conducted at 'the Lord's table' (1 Cor. 10:21 NIV) indicating that He owns the table. It is conducted in the spiritual precincts of the 'churches of Christ' (Rom. 16:16) whose angels 'testify... for the churches' (Rev. 22:16) and which meets to worship on 'the Lord's day' (Rev. 1:10; Acts 20:7; 1 Cor. 16:2). There is still great liberty within the customary table etiquette of every ethnic, tribal or family group for the serving of food and drink, but only with due respect for the table etiquette and ceremony of the Lord whose Supper it is, i.e. the prescribed 'order' of the scriptural sources. Paul, as we have seen, received the order for the Supper from 'the Lord' via those Apostles which were 'before me' (Gal. 1:17) and the practice (tradition) of churches founded by them. We do not need to know why of all these custodians of 'the tradition' none except Paul gave specific instructions and interpretation in canonical New Testament writings. Nor do we know why Paul did so, only to rebuke the undiscerning error of Christians eating at the 'table of demons' (1 Cor. 10:14-33) and to correct disorder at 'the table of the Lord' (1 Cor. 10:21; 11:17-34). In either case, whether lack of discernment or the disorder, the results were 'not for the better but for the worse' (1 Cor. 11:17).

We shall consider first, *What the Ordinance of the Lord Supper is* (1 Cor. 11:17-23), secondly, *What It Means* (vv. 24-26a), and thirdly, *How the Ordinance Should be Observed* (vv. 26b-30).

I. What the Ordinance is (1 Cor. 11:17-23).

A Coming Together of the Local Ekklēsia.
The Lord's Supper is a coming together of the local *ekklēsia*. The Supper also occasions the coming together, the reason for gathering. This is the sense of verses 17-20, *viz.*: 'when you come together' (v. 17); 'when you assemble as a church [*ekklēsia*]' (v. 18 RSV); 'When you meet together' (v. 20 RSV).

In these verses *ekklēsia* refers to the gathering, a gathering of the church specifically to observe 'the Lord's supper' (v. 20).[9]

1. This is a unique feature of Christianity. Even in the Judaism of Paul's time and to the present the chief ordinances and rituals took place in family and home, though synagogue meetings were important. Meetings at the Tabernacle-temple were required only of adult males three times a year. Neither did the pagans of antiquity gather together for worship in their idol temples. Rather, people came to the porch or portal of the building with their offerings and requests and were met there by a priest or servant of the place. He then took their gift or sacrifice within and performed prescribed rituals within. The people who came to the door then went away. There were religious aspects of public gatherings for civic purposes but they were not usually designed specially for worship of the god or for mutual encouragement or expression of religious feelings, as in a gathering of the Christian *ekklēsia*. The ancient Roman world took notice of the strange 'come[ing] together' (v. 18) and 'meet[ing] together' (v. 20 RSV) of the Christians and wondered what was going on – nothing good, it was said. On account of this 'peculiarity', the Christians became suspects of conspiracy and sedition, leading rather quickly to severe persecution. It is our identifying characteristic. Even today the population as a whole seems to regard Christians simply as people who go to church on Sunday.

The efforts of Christians before the 'edict of toleration' (AD 313) to find places to meet for fellowship, instruction and worship at the Lord's table without interference required great ingenuity. Latourette places this in perspective.[10] See the source of this information in Eusebius.[11] This testifies to the importance of this indispensable feature of the church's worship.

2. Since it is a 'come[ing] together' of all the *ekklēsia* the 'clergy' cannot observe the Eucharist by themselves. The practice of celebrating 'mass' by a priest, who himself eats the Eucharistic bread and drinks the wine, with no participants, is a travesty of 'communion.' Throughout Roman Catholic history to the present, Masses are performed for various purposes – to accumulate merit for the dead so to release their souls from purgatory, and similar, and may be paid for by concerned relatives of the dead. This custom resulted in endowed altars which produced regular

---

9. In chapter 3 above we saw that this gathering of the members into one place is one of the meanings of *ekklēsia*, as in 1 Corinthians 14:28, 33, 34.
10. Kenneth S. Latourette, *A History of Christianity* (New York: Harper & Brothers, 1953, 1971), p. 92.
11. Eusebius, *Church History* IX, pp. 9, 10; NPNF, Vol. I, pp. 363–367.

income for the church. Before he renounced the stipend, the young John Calvin was supported in his studies by the income generated by Masses said at several altars.[12] The same 'come[ing] together' discourages – if it does not prohibit – private communion.

3. In such a 'come[ing] together,' at its best, there will be participation by all those assembled. First Corinthians 14 does not seem to describe a meeting to observe the Eucharist, but the obvious congregational participation by attending believers should not be uncharacteristic of the solemnity of the Eucharist. The scholarly consensus on 'Do not quench the Spirit. Do not despise prophecies' (1 Thess. 5:19, 20) seems to be that the subject of the verses is the church's meetings for worship. In any case, wholesome worship should strike a balance (certainly not the same in every assembly nor always at exactly the same level) between 'decently and in order' (1 Cor. 14:40) on the one hand and, on the other, 'Do not quench the Spirit. Do not despise prophecies' – spontaneous unrehearsed expressions (1 Thess. 5:19, 20).

4. As a coming together for *koinōnia* (mutual participation, 1 Cor. 10:16; 11:17, 20) the Eucharist *at its best* requires certain features of church architecture once the house church is outgrown. Church architecture should promote mutuality of participation by having all 'liturgical' actions (reading of Scripture; breaking bread; pouring wine; speaking words of prayer, blessing and benediction) in full view of all attendants. Also participants should not be isolated from one another by seating arrangements.

The ancient Roman 'court house' or basilica-style of edifice adopted in the early centuries promoted all the errors of communal worship possible, ending up with a partially physical spectacle hidden in mysterious, almost unseen, ritual. Activities of the leaders (priests) came to be centered at an 'altar' hidden behind a screen in a small extension of the building called an apse. The Roman Church is presently engaged in controversy about moving the 'altar' (for 'the sacrifice of the mass') to somewhere near the worshippers and in plain view. The Reformed-Presbyterian-Puritan people brought the 'communion table' out into the 'nave' (main room) of the church edifices they inherited and arranged the pews or chairs about in various configurations. Under the influence of the Enlightenment (eighteenth-century) and later Revivalist impulses the familiar Protestant 'concert stage' appeared with table, chairs, pulpit, lectern, choir and baptistry all in plain view straight ahead, but farther and farther from 'the back row' of the assembled church (gathering).

There is no way yet discovered whereby a room adapted specifically for worship within biblical lines can be quite what modern people seem to want for weddings, drama, Christmas programs, and the like. The diagrams at the end section of chapter 21 above illustrate both good and bad arrangement. There is no conflict between a room set up for speaking and hearing the preached Word (1 Cor. 1:21) and worship at the Lord's table, but the same is not true of that form of modern drama known as the church wedding – which ought to tell us something about this late twentieth-century development and about how the popular culture affects the tastes and the real interests of many 'modern' Christians.

Leaders in public worship should be able to have eye contact with the assembled people and the worshippers should not be able to isolate themselves in the pew, looking vaguely far ahead to preacher and choir. Public address (electric) systems can promote this architectural delinquency so that worshippers have little more 'come[ing] together' than if they were listening to a religious broadcast at home. Some churches have, with some success, put the 'co' (which means *with*) back in 'communion' by setting the service around tables in a fellowship hall.

To sum up, church architecture both reflects and teaches theology. It either facilitates preaching and hearing the Word and promotes Eucharistic worship at its biblical best or hinders it. The figures at the end of chapter 21 illustrate these points.[13]

It should be added that the physical setting of valid worship is of only relative importance. I cite with approval two trenchant statements – the first from theoretically the least formal in worship of modern Christian groups.

> Nor is any building required for [worship] though such may be of great convenience to a company of believers in bad weather. The size, cost and architectural design of such a building has *nothing whatever to do with the worth*, or otherwise of worship.[14]

Mr. Gibbs is associated with the Plymouth Brethren.

---

12. Francois Wendel, *Calvin*, trans. P. Mairet (New York: Harper & Row, 1950, 1963), p. 17 and documentation.
13. A surge of studies in styles and content of worship took place mid-twentieth century as an aspect of the ecumenical movement – at first quite strong among mission-minded evangelicals.
14. A. P. Gibbs, *Worship, The Christian's Highest Occupation*, 2nd ed. (Kansas City: Walterick, n.d.), p. 239.

The second was a representative of the ecumenical movement when that movement was strong, inspiring serious study of worship theory, style, setting and the like in an effort to find a common denominator for everyone.

> A Protestant missionary points out that 'Catholic' worship, whether Roman or Anglo-Catholic, has great attraction for the primitive African, and for Christians of the first generation. The services in the churches founded by 'Evangelical' or non-episcopal churches in the West, usually reflect affairs in the Home church, only on a 'simpler' level. The revivalist fire which once gave this kind of worship its real power has died out, and in too many places the result is respectability – and dullness. 'Is it any wonder' writes a missionary from West Africa, 'that our Christians say, under their breath, or openly "what a weariness it is"!'[15]

A 'Supper' Peculiarly 'the Lord's.'

The Eucharist is a 'supper' peculiarly 'the Lord's' (1 Cor. 11:20). The God of Israel spoke of the Sabbath as 'my Sabbaths' (Exod. 31:13; Lev. 19:3, 30; 26:2) and 'the LORD's Sabbaths' (Lev. 23:38). The Sabbath was given by God even though 'for man' (Mark 2:27). He is 'lord of the Sabbath' (Luke 6:5). Though the first day of the week (1 Cor. 16:2) is not called the Sabbath, it is specially designated 'the Lord's day' (Rev. 1:10). In the latter case 'Lord's' is not the usual possessive form of the noun *kurios*, but the adjective *kuriakos*, 'belong to the Lord.' This word is used only twice in the New Testament (as discussed in chapter 4 of this section) – of the Lord's Supper (1 Cor. 11:20) and the Lord's day (Rev. 1:10). Both are His and precious but, like the Sabbath, designed also for mankind's benefit.

Jesus, then, is the host at the supper. The table is 'the Lord's table.' The elements of the Supper – common foods of common people – have been given to the Lord by the Lord's people for the Lord's use. In the beginning, these were large contributions of food for a common meal, the excess food being distributed to needy folk.

This, then, is not at all like pagan worship, in which the god lived in his *naos* (sanctuary) deep within the temple (*hieron*) where his (or her) statue stood and where only priests could enter.

So the problem of the proper name for the 'meeting place' arises. Is the building where 'the Lord's people' eat 'the Lord's supper' properly 'the Lord's house,' i.e. a sanctuary? Our English Protestant ancestors said, No! 'Sanctuary' properly designates the place where the god of a heathen temple lives or, as in the Old Testament house of God, the place where God was specially manifest. '[T]he LORD is in his *holy temple*' says Habakkuk (2:20). The Greek Old Testament renders the word 'temple' as *naos* – 'place of God's residence.' But did not Jesus lay all that aside (John 4:24)? God's place of special residence on earth is now in the hearts of the people who worship Him, not in a house of wood or stone. The Roman Church claims that the leftover bread from last Sunday's Mass, reserved in the 'tabernacle' over the 'altar' of the 'sacrifice of the mass,' is God incarnate. One should genuflect before 'it.' So the name 'sanctuary' fits the part of the building where the 'altar' is situated in the place where the god is.

'Sanctuary' does seem to express the reverence which devout Christians feel for the place where they regularly meet for worship. Yet, if our church's architecture should reflect and teach sound theology, so also should our vocabulary of church architecture. Hence a question arises: What is the appropriate name for the room in which 'the Lord's people' gather as guests at 'the Lord's table' to eat 'the Lord's Supper,' the same room where other acts of corporate worship take place? It has become customary (and church architects uniformly employ it) to call it 'the sanctuary.' Is this desirable? Again, our English-speaking Protestant ancestors said, No! Why?

Frederick L. Eckel defines sanctuary for Anglicans as 'holy place,'[16] writing, 'The area around an altar or portion of the chancel behind the altar rail; the main room for worship in evangelical [i.e. now liturgical] churches.' Elsewhere he notes that the evangelicals do not have a solid-sided 'altar' in the style of the ancient stone altars where fire burned on the top, but a 'communion table' with legs and 'In Remembrance of Me' inscribed on the front apron.

Objection to 'sanctuary' is that it is a relic of ancient pagan temples, where the god dwelt in the eastern end in a recession called an apse (in basilican style) and where real blood sacrifice took place on an altar. For the ancient Athenian worshipper of the *parthenos* (virgin) Athena at the *Parthenon* (residence of the virgin), the east chamber where she dwelt was indeed a 'holy place' (that is, sanctuary, Gr. *naos*). The Tabernacle of the Old Testament and the various temples which replaced it were properly called sanctuaries (holy places) because the God of Israel did indeed choose to dwell there (2 Chron. 6:1; Hab. 2:18-20; cf. Heb. 8:1 ff.). At the present time there is said to be

---

15. Olive Wyon, 'Evidences of New Life in the Church Universal,' *Man's Disorder and God's Design* (The Amsterdam Assembly Series, 1948, i), p. 113.
16. F. L. Eckel, Jr, *A Concise Dictionary of Ecclesiastical Terms* (Boston: Whittemore Assoc., 1960), p. 53.

such a 'sanctuary... the true tabernacle' in heaven (Heb. 8:2 KJV), but none on earth except the believers (singly and collectively) themselves.

'Sanctuary' also helps perpetuate the utterly false notion that a real sacrifice takes place in the Eucharist. In such case it is proper to call the communion table an altar. The substance of bread and wine are 'transubstantiated' into Christ's flesh and blood. When leftover portions are kept over the altar in a small cupboard ('tabernacle' of His presence) the incarnate God is present in the area. Hence worship is properly directed toward it by genuflection (a rather intricate partial bow and kneeling motion). In this sphere of thought, the area about the 'altar' in the depths of the chancel is indeed a 'sanctuary,' for God does dwell there in the flesh of the sacrament.

A sounder theology holds that the assembly of Christians constitutes a sanctuary where God dwells (1 Cor. 3:16, 17) – whether the believers be assembled or dispersed to work, play, school or home. Paul tells us that God will avenge with destruction any who desecrate (the opposite of consecrate) this sacred place, saying: 'Anyone who destroys [harms] God's temple will himself be destroyed [harmed] by God, because the temple of God is holy; and you are that temple' (1 Cor. 3:17 REB).

The church meets in a 'meeting house' or 'chapel,' or even a 'church,' for that word, in a Christian setting, was first used of the meetinghouse – a *kuriakon*, the house belonging to the Lord (see chap. 4 above). 'Church house' also has good precedent. Every one of these terms sadly may at present sound quaint or queer to ears accustomed to 'sanctuary.' Yet, of them all 'chapel' is apparently the one most historically and doctrinally correct for the room where the local church regularly meets for worship.

This extended discussion is important chiefly to stimulate reflection on what is truly the holy place where on earth God dwells in special residency – the Christian *ekklēsia*.

I am particularly indebted to several authors in these remarks about church architecture and Christian worship. Among them are James F. White,[17] Andre Bieler,[18] F. L. Eckel, Jr,[19] J. D. Robertson,[20] James F. White,[21] Richard Spielmann,[22] and T. A. Stafford.[23] A large literature of worship is currently being published. I have not found it related to issues treated in this section.

The Church Itself, Uniquely at Worship.

The ordinance of the Lord's Supper is the church itself, uniquely at worship (1 Cor. 11:22). Paul says that to think lightly of the Eucharist and to humiliate the poor who are attending is to 'despise *the church of God* [emphasis added].' The local church gathered about the Lord's table, worshipping her Lord, is in a special way never more fully an organic fellowship (*koinōnia*) than in these moments. Is it truly a church when dispersed to their homes? Yes, but uniquely so in the moments of Eucharistic observance. They are never more a communion of saints in a most heightened level of communion. There is a vertical communion with the Lord as 'in remembrance' of Him we partake of the symbols of His body and blood, a horizontal communion with the other members of His body – communion not to be described but felt. We are truly a new kind of people. Formerly estranged Jews and heathen – strangers from the covenants of promise, having no hope and without God – now all brought near together 'by the blood of Christ.' In Him we are 'one new man' (Eph. 2:11-22). This is deeply felt in the solemn moments when we share the emblems of our Lord's dying in our place to create this blessed, worshipping community. There can be little doubt that godly folk feel in their hearts this nearly 'unspeakable' feature of their worship. This partially explains the exceeding sinfulness of casual participation, 'not discerning the Lord's body' – the literal one, the corporate one, the Eucharistic one, each in one way or another a feature of the ordinance.

A very helpful presentation of this aspect of the Eucharistic observance clearly written and fully researched is the chapter 'The Lord's Supper as Communion,' by Fred D. Howard.[24]

Finally, the Eucharist is a unique participation in something tangible and which Jesus gave us before He departed from us and left us behind. It allows us, in a manner of speaking, to be in the Upper Room with Him and the Twelve

---

17. James F. White, *Protestant Worship and Church Architecture: Theological and Historical Considerations* (New York: Oxford Press, 1964).
18. Andre Bieler, *Architecture in Worship*, trans. D. & O. Elliott (Philadelphia: Westminster Press, 1965).
19. Eckel, op. cit.
20. J. D. Robertson, *Minister's Worship Handbook* (Grand Rapids: Baker, 1974).
21. James F. White, *New Forms of Worship* (Nashville: Abingdon, 1971).
22. Richard Spielmann, *History of Christian Worship* (New York: Seabury Press, 1966).
23. T. A. Stafford, *Christian Symbolism in the Evangelical Churches* (Nashville: Abingdon, 1842).
24. Fred D. Howard, *Interpreting the Lord's Supper* (Nashville: Broadman, 1966), pp. 45–69.

to receive something from the visible, personal presence of Jesus. The powers of imagination must be employed to make this true for each worshipper; and, like all such measures, must be controlled by 'the understanding' (1 Cor. 14:13-19 KJV). If certain sacerdotalists have made too much of this feature, perhaps some unbending, no nonsense, rationalistic brethren have made too little. This concept collides squarely with twelve o'clock boredom and hungry haste to hear the last 'amen' before we rush home for dinner after church on 'Communion Sunday.' In the next chapter we consider what the Eucharist means and how it should be observed, concluding with historical views in both pre-Reformation times onward to the present.

25
Worship at the Lord's Table, II

II. What the Ordinance Means (1 Cor. 11:24-26).

The meaning of our Lord's words, 'This is my body' and 'the new covenant in my blood,' has not been absent in foregoing discussion of the Eucharist. Now we focus on what these terse sentences mean – not emphasizing the divisive controversies about the meaning over the past five centuries. We shall train our attention on four of Paul's expressions, together with a part of Luke's report of Jesus' instructions.

Mutual Participation in Christ Himself.

The Eucharist symbolizes mutual participation in Christ Himself. Mutuality and participation are both suggested. '[W]hen he had given thanks, he broke it [the loaf], and said, "This is my body which is for you"' (1 Cor. 11:24). '[A]nd they all drank of it' (Mark 14:23 KJV). The best texts do not include 'broken.' Though one naturally is reminded of the bruises, cuts and piercing of His body on the cross this is not the point to be made. Rather it was that the redemption was *for His people* (Matt. 1:21). 'It is finished!' 'By his stripes we have been healed.'

Luke reports: 'And he took a cup, and when he had given thanks he said, "Take this, and divide it among yourselves"' (Luke 22:17). The received text of Luke 22:19, 20 adds, 'divide it among yourselves' and 'my body which is given for you.' Matthew says, 'Drink of it, all of you' (Matt. 26:27), and Mark, 'and they all drank of it' (Mark 14:23). However the textual problem is explained, a common participation of everyone – presumably even Judas – is as emphatic as anything in the passages which describe incidents at the Last Supper. Mutuality with one another in participation – for which the usual word is 'communion' in our language – is the first significance.

There is no extension of the incarnation to the disciples' bodies or the church – an idea promoted vigorously in ecumenical circles. A few years ago at a time the scholars of the World Council were promoting this idea, Lesslie Newbigin – one of their best scholars – emphasized the reality of the church as the body of Christ but stressed that it is not scripturally correct to speak of the mystical body of the Lord, the church, as the extension of the incarnation.[1] As a metaphor, the 'extended incarnation' figure is useful in childrens' songs such as 'Christ has no home but yours to do his work today,' but without metaphysical overtones.

---

1. Leslie Newbigin, *The Household of God* (New York: Friendship Press, 1964), p. 298.

Commemoration of Jesus Christ.

The Eucharist signifies commemoration of Jesus Christ. Luke, alone (among the Gospels) includes, 'Do this in remembrance of me' (Luke 22:19) in connection with the cup, while Paul has it in connection with both cup and loaf. At this point, connection with the Passover symbolism emerges. Howard cites the following from Edward Beckersteth's *Treatise on the Lord's Supper*:[2]

> One was instituted the night before the deliverance from Egypt; the other the night before our deliverance from our iniquities. One commemorated redemption from the bondage of sin. One pre-figured, by shedding of blood, the redemption of Christ: the other would exhibit, by striking emblems, a redemption already [after the crucifixion] accomplished.[3]

We should recall that just as the Passover was a joyous feast – a thanksgiving festival – so is the Eucharist. It is quite normal for both solemnity and joy to be present at the peak when important rites are observed. Ask the bride's mother after the wedding.

The Inauguration of a New Covenant.

The Eucharist signifies the inauguration of a new covenant to take precedence over the Mosaic covenant. This is patent in the Lord's words: 'This cup is the new covenant in my blood' (1 Cor. 11:25). Luke says nothing of a new covenant; Mark reports, 'This is my blood of the covenant' (14:24); Matthew's report connects the shed blood with 'the covenant' and both with the 'many' and 'the forgiveness of sin' (Matt. 26:28). Jeremias argues convincingly – from (1) the abundant evidence of Isaiah 53:11, 12 and Zechariah 9:11; (2) Jewish Targums; and (3) the history of interpretation – that Jesus is referring to Isaiah's prophecy of the atoning death of the Servant, and that Jesus thought His death would have atoning effect.[4] The 'old' covenant with which the 'new' is in contrast is the Mosaic covenant. That covenant, though gracious in ultimate purpose, was strictly a legal covenant, as Galatians and Hebrews explicate. If Passover produces joy, how much more the communion of the bread and cup!

The contrast between 'old' covenant and 'new' in Galatians is not between two administrations of one covenant of grace, nor between two administrations of an Adamic or Abrahamic covenant. I agree with the following excerpt from a book by John G. Reisinger:

> God had a *gracious purpose* in putting the nation of Israel under the law as a covenant, but that fact cannot change the law covenant into a covenant of grace. The law, as a covenant, was intended to be the 'needle that pierced the conscience so that the thread of the gospel could follow and heal.' However, to be able to accomplish that ministry the law had to have the teeth of a true legal covenant with the power of life and death. If the Decalogue could not make men feel lost in sin and condemned by God, then how could it 'prepare the sinner for the gospel.'[5]

An Impressive Preachment of the Gospel.

The Eucharist presents an impressive preachment of the gospel. '[Y]e proclaim the Lord's death' (1 Cor. 11:26). It is tied to the memorial aspect: 'It is a dynamic declaration of the gospel by an object lesson.'[6]

During His ministry Jesus executed more than one acted parable – the cursing of the unfruitful fig tree as an example (Luke 19:45-48).[7] The broken bread and poured-out wine serve as a commentary on Isaiah 53:5, 'he was wounded for our transgressions; he was crushed for our iniquities; upon him was the chastisement that brought us peace, and with his stripes we are healed.' Only as understood as memorial and preachment, rather than as 'medicine of immortality' or somehow *ex opero operato* (automatically conferring some grace), does it preach the gospel. Here, as in baptism, nothing good comes of the ordinance without being accompanied by the word of proclamation. The presiding churchman, whether Brethren elder, Presbyterian minister, Baptist pastor or Anglican priest, has the duty to explain to the participating congregation, and the seeking or unbelieving, what is taking place.

---

2. Edward Bickersteth, *Treatise on the Lord's Supper* (New York: Thos. Stanford, 1815), p. 17.
3. Fred D. Howard, *Interpreting the Lord's Supper* (Nashville: Broadman Press, 1966), p. 39.
4. Jeremias, op. cit., pp. 146–152.
5. Appendix No. 3, Covenant Theology's 'Two Administrations Of One Covenant' in *Abraham's Four Seeds* (Sound of Grace. POB #185, Webster, NY: 14580), p. 81.
6. Howard, op. cit., p. 44.
7. Culver, *Life of Christ*, pp. 217, 218; Edersheim, *Life and Times of Jesus* II, pp. 374, 375.

A Mutual Expression of the Church's Hope and Christ's Glorious Second Advent.
The church at communion mutually express 'their blessed hope and the glorious appearing' of the Savior at the Second Advent: 'ye do shew the Lord's death till he come' (1 Cor. 11:26 KJV – the conditional sense of 'come,' rather than 'comes,' preserved in KJV, is unfortunately lost in recent Versions). The Lord also spoke of how the memorial rite expressed His own hope for that event when He would again for the first time in the coming, manifest kingdom of God again drink the fruit of the vine (Mark 14:25; Luke 22:16; Matt. 26:29); 'therefore,' says the Messiah, 'my heart was glad, and my tongue rejoiced; my [entombed] flesh also will dwell in hope' (Acts 2:26).

Actually Jesus' expectation of a feast in the coming kingdom is based squarely on the 'Little Apocalypse' (Delitzech) of Isaiah 24 and 25 (and 65:13), specifically 25:6-8: 'On this mountain the LORD of hosts will make for all peoples a feast of rich food, a feast of well-aged wine… of aged wine well refined.' The prophet goes on to predict that in this 'mountain' (kingdom) the veil of sin will be universally removed, death 'swallow[ed] up' forever, all tears wiped away and 'the reproach of his people' taken away.

The 'eschatalogical' reference of the Supper only picks up where the Old Testament literature leaves off.

Throughout this discussion I have omitted the background in the Passover Feast and other New Testament 'suppers' lest the chapter become a book. There are at least six other biblical 'suppers' with symbolic significance. Alfred P. Gibbs calls them the suppers of 'gospel proclamation' (Luke 14:16-24); 'of spiritual fellowship' (Rev. 3:20); 'of believers' appreciation' (John 12:1-8); 'of nuptial celebration' (Rev. 19:9); 'of just retribution' (Rev. 19:17); and the Last Passover itself as 'of typical consummation' (Luke 22:7-18).[8]

Says Eduard Schweizer, 'The Lord's Supper… is the anticipation of the messianic banquet which is to come and therefore should be celebrated in eschatological jubilation.'[9] After citing the above Isaiah passages, as well as 1 Enoch 62:145; 2 Enoch; Apocalypse of Baruch 42:5 (pseudepigraphal Jewish literature), Schweizer concludes:

> Thus it is certainly the Jewish background which shaped the early Christian Lord's Supper. The use, in Acts 2:46 ['with glad… hearts'] of the typical concept of eschatological 'bliss' to describe the frame of mind of the early church at the breaking of bread makes clear how strong this… motif was. It is unrestrained joy and songs of praise which characterized the Lord's Supper, and not under any circumstances a funeral sobriety clothed in penitence and remorse.[10]

The passages cited above and Schweizer's remarks give us, both those who lead communion services and those of the joyful communion, something to aim for.

III. How the Ordinance Should Be Observed (1 Cor. 11:26b-30).

Let us take brief notice of five points which Paul makes.

1. Observe the Eucharist Expectantly (v. 26 KJV), 'till he come'.
The future prospect of the Second Advent, prominent in every aspect of our salvation, should save observance of this ordinance from a maudlin preoccupation with details of the Passion. The note of good cheer (John 16:33; Acts 23:11) should help us as we consider the next point.[11]

2. Observe the Eucharist in a Worthy Manner (v. 27).
What does 'an unworthy manner,' and 'guilty of profaning the body and blood of the Lord,' mean? Many authors rightly point out that no one is personally worthy and no forgiven sinner is guilty of the shed blood of Christ. Rather, the faults of the Corinthians pointed out earlier, and again in verses 33 and 34, were firstly in lack of consideration of other believers at the table and flippant regard for the meal (love feast) at which the observance of the Eucharist took place. Secondly, there was a 'failure to recognize practically the symbolism of the elements, and hence the treatment of the supper as a common meal.'[12] To bring unrepented-of sins of various seriousness to the Lord's table, as it were, is to partake in an unworthy manner, says Calvin, and will result in various degrees of divine chastisement. No particular sin, repented of, excludes one from the fellowship of the Lord's table.[13]

---

8. Alfred P. Gibbs, *The Lord's Supper* (Kansas City: Walterich, 1963).
9. Eduard Schweizer, *The Lord's Supper According to the New Testament* (Philadelphia: Fortress, 1967), p. 3.
10. ibid.
11. A. H. Strong, *Systematic Theology*, p. 960.
12. ibid., p. 951.
13. Calvin, *Commentary, Corinthians ad loc cit.*

3. Observe the Ordinance with Self-examination (v. 28).

'Let a person examine himself.' It is a right impulse and wholesome that the service book of Lutheran churches schedules the responsive reading of Psalm 51 early in the liturgy for the Lord's Supper. The same right judgment has put Psalm 51 among the responsive readings of most standard hymn books, available for use where (as in my own case) there is no prescribed liturgy. It speaks to the heart by way of self-examination, leading to repentance and confession to God. This is not, in my opinion, as widely observed as it should be in 'free' churches.

All the Reformation churches gave proper emphasis to self-judgment before communion. It is not even today neglected in evangelical groups descended from those churches. The Christian Reformed in their Psalter Hymnal of 1976 has two suggested forms for 'celebration of the Lord's supper.' Immediately following the reading of 1 Corinthians 11:23-29, the minister's suggested sermon expounds the 'Let a person examine [or prove] himself' clause – five columns of very penetrating exposition and application to specific sins of thought, word and deed. The sermon may be delivered a week before the observance.[14]

The sermon begins: 'In fellowship with these words and in fellowship with the church universal... let each of us, therefore, consider his sin and guilt, against which the wrath of God is so great that He has punished it in His beloved son,' and so on. I add: let us pray that the church named here never loses this treasure of faithful adherence to this word and that all will learn to do better!

In the earliest post-New Testament reports of communion gatherings, after extensive reading of appropriate Scriptures from all parts of the Bible, a deacon or bishop exhorted the assembly to bring their lives up to standard. There was, sadly, a developing legalism accompanying this emphasis. Standards were high and rigidly enforced in times of persecution, but tended to be relaxed in time of peace with secular authorities.

At this point in the text of 1 Corinthians 11 a question arises: Did Paul also teach us Christians to submit to one another's judgment (or of church elders or deacons) as to fitness to receive the Supper? He says, 'But if we [plural] judged ourselves truly, we would not be judged. But when we are judged by the Lord, we are disciplined so that we [plural] may not be condemned along with the world' (1 Cor. 11:31, 32). Verses 28 and 30 use singular verbs, indicating self-examination. It is tempting to suppose mutual judgment of believers by believers in a formal way is indicated, but there is not sufficient basis for that in this verse. However, believers are encouraged (as we noted in our chapter on discipline) to recognize 'faults' and to take discreet action (see Gal. 6:1, 2). In any case, the first generations of Christians made attendance at the Lord's table more a privilege than a right. Very early in Christian history a liturgy for the weekly observance developed and in it this element was faithfully observed. As early as the *Didache* any non-baptized (in times of persecution baptism was a dangerous step to take) were excluded (*Didache* IX. 5); confessing transgressions came before breaking bread (XIV.1). Before communion all not yet baptized were excluded from the room: 'but let the door be watched, lest any unbeliever, or one not yet initiated, come in.'[15] The Christians of the first centuries were people of their time, hence *some* of this 'fencing of the table' was overdone and some of their reasons were partially superstitious.

'Fencing the table' is the old ecclesiastical term for protecting the table fellowship of the Lord's Supper from disturbance by unbelieving and wicked people engaging falsely in communion. Some groups of earnest believers conduct visitation of all families by elders to prepare and qualify them for communion. Some Lutheran pastors issue written tickets of eligibility. It now consists usually simply in issuing Paul's warnings (1 Cor. 11:27-32) from the pulpit or by the presiding elder at the table. Most deem this sufficient. There have been occasions, however, when a minister or group *publicly* excluded wantonly immoral people from the Lord's Supper. There is a long history among the Reformed churches, beginning with the Strasbourg pastors in the 1530s, of admitting no one to communion except the faithful who have previously presented themselves to the pastor or his 'vicar.' They also made instruction in a catechism obligatory for children, who were not allowed to come to communion until instructed specifically.[16]

---

14. *Liturgy of the Christian Reformed Church* (Grand Rapids: Board of Publications of the Christian Reformed Church, 1941, 1976), pp. 143–148.
15. *Apostolic Constitution*, ii.57, ANF, VII, p. 57.
16. Francois Wendel, *Calvin* (New York: Harper & Row, 1950, 1963), p. 61.

Concluding Questions.

1. The Doctrine of the Mass – How Did it Develop?

At the time of the Reformation, observance of the Eucharist was understood as an occasion for solemn worship of the body and blood of Christ present in the elements. The Mass did not usually provide opportunity for lay people to 'eat… this bread' and to 'drink ye *all* of it.' Mass was not a communion between the saints present. The service was not even called a communion, but a Mass. The Lord's table was called an altar. The enactment was not regarded primarily as a memorial but as a sacrifice of blood and flesh, and the official of the church who pronounced the words of 'transubstantiation' and who himself consumed a portion of the elements was named and regarded as a sacrificing priest – not primarily a minister of the Word.

In response to the Protestant Reformation the Roman Church assembled the Council of Trent (1545–1563) which in its thirteenth Session made dogma of accumulated beliefs and practices of previous centuries of evolution of *Mass* and related doctrines. Denzinger's 'Systematic Index' (*The Sources of Catholic Dogma*) devotes three fine print, double columns of 'Systematic Index' to the topics 'The Real Presence; the Sacrament, Communion; the Sacrifice of the Mass' (39–41). The index itself summarizes the doctrine.

Louis Berkhof summarizes Trent's decrees about the Eucharist briefly:

> Jesus Christ is truly, really, and substantially present in the holy sacrament…. seated at the right hand of God does not exclude the possibility of His substantial presence in several places simultaneously. By the words of consecration the substance of bread and wine is changed into the body and blood of Christ. [Transubstantiation is the accepted name for this doctrine. The origin is obscure, but it was adopted in documents of the Fourth Lateran Council in 1215.] The entire Christ is present under each species [bread, wine] and under each particle of each species. Each one who receives a particle of the host receives the whole Christ. He is present in the elements even before the communicant receives them. In view of this presence, the adoration of the host [Latin, hostia, sacrificial victim] is but natural. The sacrament effects 'an increase of sanctifying grace, special actual graces, remission of venial sins, preservation from grievous [mortal] sin, and the confident hope of eternal salvation.'[17]

How did this dogma that the Eucharistic rite is a sacrifice of the blood and body of Christ arise in the soil of the apostolic Christianity of the Gospels and Epistles? Though the notion arose in seminal form at least as early as the fourth century it was not to become dogma for several centuries.

Historical and theological scholars have proposed at least six causes, some rooted in the mindset of all ancient peoples where the church first took root and some events in the first five centuries of our era.

The first cause is the acknowledged ancient habit of sometimes referring to a rite or other symbol as though it were the truth or divine act signified. Paul himself puts such words in the mouth of Ananias: 'Rise and be baptized and wash away your sins' (Acts 22:16). Paul knew he had been regenerated, released from sin's penalties and declared righteous days before when he was met by the glorified Christ, and presumably so did Ananias. Of a piece with the same is the way New Testament authors refer to Christian dedication as a 'living sacrifice' (*thusia*) as opposed to a slain sacrifice (Rom. 12:1); evangelistic labor as being 'offered' (*spendomai*, offer a libation) upon the sacrifice (*thusia*) and as service (*leiturgia*), service as a priest (Phil 2:17); a gift for support for a missionary as 'a fragrant offering, a sacrifice' (Phil. 4:18). They also exhort to 'offer' (*anapherō*, to bring a sacrifice) the 'sacrifice [*thusian*] of praise to God' (Heb. 13:15). Untaught and ignorant people (unknowingly) as well as the informed and perverse (knowingly) could use such sacrificial language of the gifts brought to the *Agapē* feast and the *Eucharist* which accompanied it. Ignatius of Antioch, *en route* to a martyr's death, wrote, 'The eucharist is the flesh of our Savior,' and of the 'breaking of the one bread, which is the medicine of immortality.'[18] Tertullian and Cyprian agreed, though Clement of Alexandria and Origen thought that the Lord's Supper fed the soul with the divine Word. They did not see it as essentially an act of worship.

About the middle of the second century several Christian authors (the 'apologists') sought (1) to defend Christianity against misrepresentation by heathen writers and current rumors which attacked the church and (2) also

---

17. Louis Berkhof, *Systematic Theology*, 2nd rev. ed. (Grand Rapids: Eerdmans, 1939, 1979), pp. 646, 647.
18. Ignatius, *To the Ephesians*, XX.2 ANF, i, p. 57; see also Ignatius, *To the Smyrnaeasn*, VII, ANF, Vol. I, p. 89; J. Kurtz, *Church History*, Vol. I, #36.4, p. 205.

tried to address the Roman government in a way to deflect persecution. In doing so, the apologists accommodated their language to the understanding of their opponents enough to somewhat undermine their own biblical bases. Thus they 'set a bad example for succeeding generations.'[19] Sadly, they also represent the early drift away from the plain gospel of grace toward moralism and legalism as well as sacramentalism.

A second cause is that the church took to its bosom a few, then a majority, of people still heathen at heart. This happened during long periods free from persecution and particularly after Christianity became tolerated, then legal, then required of everyone on pain of severe punishment (fourth century). They were accustomed to religion whose center was an impressive sanctuary on whose altars sacrificial rites were effected by officially designated priests with elaborate vestments. It was natural for these unconverted and untaught people to nudge interpretation in the direction it went.[20]

A third cause is that Christians were already denizens of an advanced heathen civilization. Many of them were technically trained in its religious theories and vocabulary. This constantly nudged the church toward ideas of priesthood and sacrificial interpretations. 'The idea that a priestly mediation between sinful men and a gracious [or malevolent] deity had been so deeply implanted in the religious consciousness of pre-Christian antiquity, pagan as well as Jewish, that a form of public worship without a priesthood seemed almost as inconceivable as a religion without a god.'[21] This frame of mind led to 'the idea... not sharply and clearly defined... yet widespread and profound conviction that the Lord's Supper was a supremely holy mystery, spiritual food indispensable to eternal life, that the body and blood of the Lord entered into some mystical connection with the bread and wine, and placed the believing partaker of them in true and essential fellowhip with Christ.... Gradually... the theory prevailed of a sacramental memorial celebration of the sacrifice of Christ[22]... [as] that of an unbloody but actual repetition of the same.'[23]

Gregory of Nyssa exemplifies the results of this tendency. He was thoroughly educated in pagan philosophy and one of the most prolific writers among the Fathers. As G. W. Bromiley points out, Gregory argued that Jesus used bread and wine in daily nourishment. They became His flesh-and-blood body in which God dwelt, in a sense identical with them. When believers consume the Eucharist God enters into them and thereby humanity shares in deity and immortality.[24]

The fourth cause is the heresy of docetism, denial of the authentic existence of material things, which brought about orthodox reaction, lending support to materialists' views of the Eucharist. Without introducing details about docetism, we observe that it was so widely spread, and both aggressive and persuasive in prevalent Neo-platonism, that fears of docetism and its twin dualisms (both metaphysical and ethical) ruled out for many any possibility of a spiritual feeding on Christ in worship at the Eucharist which was not also feeding on real body and blood – even if not clearly defined. It remains to be said that Gregory's doctrine was a seed of the later standard Eastern Orthodox understanding of salvation as *enosis*, union with God.

The fifth cause is that, from another quarter, 'the Old Testament Bible of Jesus and the Apostles' came a pattern – albeit misused – for the rise of a sacerdotal class and worship through sacrifice. I do not refer to Judaism, from which the church quickly separated itself. Until the books of the New Testament were collected and widely distributed as Scripture, the Scriptures read in all the public services (2 Tim. 4:14) and for private devotion (2 Tim. 3:14-17) were 'the Law, the Prophets and the Writings,' the same as in synagogue worship. They treasured the 'tradition' of Jesus' 'words' (1 Tim. 6:3) and of the apostles (2 Peter 3:14-16) but they did not have all of it yet in written form in the days of the apostolic Fathers (to AD 150). They found Christ 'in all the scriptures,' but they also read there of a system of ritual religion with priests, sacrifices and sacred festivals. Much of this – especially before Augustine wrote on distinguishing the covenants – was brought over also in a day before Christians had leisure to develop theological acuity. Anders Nygren points out that 'primitive Christianity succeeded only with the help of the Old Testament in making any sense of... the *Agapē* of the cross.... It involved a risk' – the risk of legalism and sacerdotalism.[25]

---

19. Jürgen Neve, *A History of Christian Thought*, Vol. II (Philadelphia: Fortress Press, 1946), p. 49.
20. Gibbon, *The Decline and Fall of the Roman Empire*, chap. 27 on the Age of Theodosius; Kenneth Latourette, History of Christianity (New York: Harper, 1953), p. 201.
21. J. H. Kurtz, *Church History*, vol. 1 (New York: Funk and Wagnall Co., n.d.) #34.4, p. 192.
22. Kurtz, #36.5, p. 209.
23. Kurtz, #38.3, p. 368.
24. Geoffrey Bromiley, *Historical Theology* (Grand Rapids: Eerdmans, 1978), pp. 144, 145.
25. Anders Nygren, *Agape and Eros*, trans. P. S. Watson (New York: Harper & Row, 1953), pp. 254, 255.

Other writers point out that, even though the New Testament expressly taught that the Old Testament institutions of sacrifice and priesthood had been abolished and replaced by a spiritual priesthood of every believer (Heb. 4:16; 1 Peter 2:5, 9; Rev. 1:6), sacerdotal ideas prevailed and very early the churches 'relapsed' into 'the Old Testament standpoint.'[26]

A sixth cause was that the leaders of the church, after the apostles disappeared from the scene – we may theorize also before the Epistles to Romans and Galatians were universally distributed and read – quickly lost a keen sense of the doctrine of salvation by grace alone, faith alone, Christ alone, apart from any human merit or any religious rite of God or man.

Anders Nygren traced these two antagonistic movements in Christian thought Christian history under the *motifs* of *Agapē* (salvation is wholly from God who reaches down and rescues sinners) and *eros* (salvation is attained by mankind's striving upward to God). Of the sub-apostolic age he summarizes: 'The center of gravity has changed; love is no longer [as in the New Testament] God's way to man, but man's way to God.'[27]

Anders Nygren traces through Christian theological history the doctrine of divine love (*agapē*, saving mankind by grace alone) as opposed to salvation by mankind's aspiration for God (*eros*) and keeping rules (*nomos*). Regarding the apostolic Fathers, first writers after the Apostles, Nygren makes several points. As early as the *Didachē* and 1 Clement the sayings of Jesus about love have become the way to be saved. However, 'it is not,' Nygren says, 'the Way of Agape, whereby the Divine love in its groundless compassion finds a way to the sinner and freely gives him salvation, but the directly opposite way, by which man, through exercising so sublime a love finally reaches perfection.'[28] He continues, 'This is not to deny that there are passages where the full message of *Agapē* [grace alone] appears.'[29] He cites Ignatius, *II Clement*, *Shepherd of Hermas*.[30] He adds, 'such observations in no way alter the impression of legalistic modification in the Apostolic Fathers.'[31]

These same Fathers, as L. Berkhof observes,[32] used the language of then current religious philosophy to defend Christianity against heresies and government intrusion. Nygren shows that in calling the Christian way 'the true philosophy' and 'the new law' these Fathers meant 'the true *faith* and a new *covenant*,' with proper biblical connotations. But the terms came to be used in ways which borrowed the notion of mystical ascent to God by human striving from the prevalent Neo-platonism and idea of Christianity as a 'nomism' – salvation by law-keeping.

These seeds grew like the mustard seed of Jesus' parable, in the mouths and pens of lesser churchmen, into the utterly perverted doctrines of 'transubstantiation' and 'the sacrifice of the mass.' By gradual stages – but not without some resistance – in common opinion and clerical ritual practice, material change in the elements to Christ's body and blood, and the Eucharist as a sacrifice, came to be accepted. These teachings became official dogma first in the *Canon of the Mass* issued by Pope Gregory I (ca. AD 600). It was an age of naive realism.[33] In the following four centuries fierce controversies over the 'real presence' developed among a few theologians (Radbertus, Hrabanus and Ratramus in the ninth century; Berengar in the eleventh century resisted Transubstantiation).[34] All sought a patristic consensus but could find none. The age of scholasticism generally accepted Transubstantiation and sought to explain it in harmony with clashing metaphysical theories of the time. All the niceties of the scholastic distinctions were firmly and universally rejected by the Protestant Reformers.

2. Post-Reformation Views of the Manner of Christ's Presence in the Eucharist.[35]

Before Rome gave formal statement of all the accumulated errors of Eucharistic doctrine at Trent, the Reformers repudiated the most egregious – transubstantiation and sacrifice. They pointed out that the latter plainly contradicts the New Testament insistence on the all-sufficiency of Christ's single, once-for-all, unrepeatable sacrifice.

---

26. Kurtz, I, p. 193; see also Latourette, op. cit., J. N. D. Kelly, *Early Christian Doctrines*, rev. ed. (New York: Harper & Row, 1978), pp. 193–199.
27. Nygren, op. cit., p. 259.
28. ibid., p. 259.
29. ibid., p. 261.
30. ibid., pp. 260, 261.
31. ibid., p. 262.
32. Berkhof, op. cit., p. 645.
33. Neve, op. cit. I, p. 159.
34. Neve, op. cit. I, pp. 156–164; Pelikan, *The Christian Tradition*, Vol. III (Chicago: U. of Chicago Press, 1978), pp. 184–229.
35. As noted earlier, Paul called this ordinance not only the Lord's Supper but also *Eucharist* (thanksgiving), *koinōnia* (communion) and *eulogia* (blessing).

Rome insists that when the priest pronounces, 'This is my body' in the liturgy of the Mass, the bread and wine miraculously become the body and blood of Christ. The elements, they must and do acknowledge, look, feel, taste and smell the same as before, but the 'substance' (or essence) is changed.[36]

But let the following be noted. (1) In intimate discourse with His disciples Jesus made many statements similar to this one, of clear symbolical intent – saying, 'I am' the 'way,' 'truth,' 'life,' 'light of the world,' 'the vine,' 'the door,' and similar (John 14:6; 8:12; 15:1; 10:7). This is another such. (2) The Romish view has Jesus in His living body say that the bread is His (slain) body, the wine His (shed) blood, many hours before the crucifixion, a strange contradiction. Scripture gives no authority for saying that the words pronounced will signal a miracle of Transubstantiation. (4) The procedure denies the same testimony of the senses which verified the resurrection of Jesus' body from the dead. What looks, tastes, smells, feels like bread is bread, the same as a body which looks, feels, sounds and behaves like Jesus is Jesus. (5) Supposed proof from John 6:54 ff. about the necessity of eating Jesus' flesh and drinking His blood to gain eternal life misses the point of the passage. The benefits of Messiah's coming are primarily spiritual, not material. The audience was a crowd who had already rejected that message. He therefore used a familiar Jewish rabbinical figure for receiving the teachings of a teacher or even of Messiah.[37] Is it reasonable to suppose that Jesus was explaining a Christian rite (Eucharist) to a hostile audience who had already rejected Him and would later join in demand for His crucifixion?

Martin Luther and the Lutheran View.

There is no sacrifice and no change in substance of the elements. Nevertheless, in some unexplained, miraculous way the whole Christ, divine and human, spirit and body, flesh and body is present with, in, under the elements. So the communicants, whether true believers or false Christians, masticate the body and blood. Jesus' body is at the right hand of God – which has no local presence anywhere. Lutheran scholars (Krauth, *The Conservative Reformation*) affirm that the right hand of God is as much 'in this room' as anywhere. This doctrine of the 'ubiquity' of Christ's body led Luther to make statements which deny any materiality to the glorified body either of Christ or of the saints. Berkhof comments, 'It really makes the words of Jesus mean, "this accompanies my body."'[38] Not all orthodox Lutherans are particularly enthusiastic about this teaching. It is an improvement on the Romish view of the matter. Lutherans are not taught to worship the sacraments.

Reformed Views.

Protestants of the sixteenth century defined this doctrine against the Roman institution and teachings. This sometimes resulted in extreme statements by some of the Reformers – a subject too complicated to treat here. Calvin, commenting on 1 Corinthians 11:23-25, says 'Would to God… we could bury… in perpetual oblivion the unhappy contests that have tried the church in our time as to the meaning of these words ["This is my body," etc.].' On that phrase in verse 24 he concludes, 'I lay it down, then, as a settled point, that there is here what is usual in connection with Sacraments, in which the Lord gives to the sign the name of the thing signified.'[39] This is about as close to Zwingli's view as words can speak. In the *Institutes* Calvin hedges toward some obscure participation of communicant with the body and blood. In my judgment, the present body of Christ is not intended. In the only reference to the 'material substance' of His resurrection body Jesus spoke of it as 'flesh and bones as you *see* that I have.' So the resurrection body of the Lord was composed still of 'flesh and bones' – whether of blood also we have no evidence.

Let us bury the volumes of wearisome debate from that era (I see them grinning from my library shelves) – Lutheran, Reformed, Roman Catholic, and later Anglican and Puritan – in the 'perpetual oblivion' Calvin spoke of – if only temporarily. How is that for an oxymoron!?

---

36. Biblical ground is found in literal sense of 'It is…' and the several statements of Jesus in John 6:51-58 about the necessity of eating His flesh and drinking His blood to receive eternal life.
37. See Strack-Billerbeck, *KZNTTM*, II, p. 485 and J. Lightfoot, *Commentary on the New Testament from the Talmud and Hebraica*, Vol. III, Hendrickson, 1997, pp. 304–309.
38. Berkhof, op. cit., p. 653.
39. Page 377 coalesced with footnote #2 of *Calvin's Commentary, Corinthians i* (Edinburgh: Calvin Translation Society, 1848).

PART 1
THEOLOGY PROPER
Introduction and Doctrine of God

PART 2
ANTHROPOLOGY
Man as Created

PART 3
HAMARTIOLOGY
Man as Sinner

PART 4
CHRISTOLOGY
Person and Work of Christ

PART 5
SOTERIOLOGY
Salvation Applied

PART 6
ECCLESIOLOGY
Church Local and Universal

PART 7
ESCHATOLOGY
Last Things, Personal and Universal

BIBLIOGRAPHY

SCRIPTURE INDEX

GENERAL INDEX

1
Introduction to Eschatology

1. The Word 'Eschatology.'

'Eschatology' has an interesting sound. After theology students hear the word they like to use it. It rolls off the tongue easily.[1] It is a modern word invented by theologians which apparently wasn't even in our language until about 160 years ago.[2]

It is a fortuitous choice, created no doubt by some scholars who noticed that the word *eschatos* occurs about fifty times in the New Testament for such finalities as the resurrection of the dead (John 6:39, 40, 44, 54; 11:24), the judgment of the 'last day' (John 12:48), and the 'last day' of history (John 11:24, 28) as well as 'last days' or 'times' of the present age (2 Tim. 3:1; James 5:3; 1 Peter 1:5, 20; 2 Peter 3:3). Scholars point out that in Jewish literature read by Jews in Jesus' time 'the eschaton' (Gr. *ton eschaton*) was very commonly used for death. In *Ecclesiasticus* or *The Wisdom of Sirach*, very widely read, for example: 'Whoso feareth the Lord, it shall go well with him at the last [*ep' eschaton*] and shall find favour in the day of his death' (Eccles. 1:13; and many times more). So also in classical Greek.[3]

It should be of great comfort to Christian believers that Jesus, Himself, is 'the last one.' So Christian eschatology ends with Christ in His glorious return. He likewise is the first One. This was pointed out to John the Revelator more than once by Jesus Himself. The eighth verse of the Prologue to Revelation reads: '"I am the Alpha and the Omega [first letter to last letter]," says the Lord God, "who is and who was and who is to come, the Almighty."' So there is an *eschatos*, last One, to meet us, not just an *eschaton*, last thing. The coming is not merely of a time, but of a Person (see John 1:1-14; and cf. Rev. 22:13, where Jesus interprets Rev. 1:8). As Job put the matter, 'Whom I shall see for myself, and mine eyes shall behold, and not another' (Job 19:27 KJV).

2. Medieval Last Things and 'the Theology of Hope.'

Before the awakening of biblical theology in the Reformation of the sixteenth century, medieval theology reduced the last things to four – death, judgment (or purgatory), heaven and hell. Since these four things are all after this life is over (and beyond present reportable experiences) and therefore new, theology of the time called our 'last

---

1. The *ch* sound in eschatology does not quite correspond to any sound in ordinary English, so we use the *k* sound as in *ch*aracter, *Ch*ristmas, etc.
2. The Oxford English Dictionary, Vol. E, p. 793 finds it first in the writings of a certain G[eorge?] Bush in the year 1844!
3. Herodotus, *Histories*, VII, 107, Liddell & Scott, Lexicon sub *eschatos*.

things' the 'newest' things, for which the term was *novissimus*, Latin superlative degree of the adjective *novus*, 'new.' So death was not thought of as the last or end of anything but as the beginning of all things new. In some ways this does express a more biblical outlook than 'last things,' death being the entrance to heaven, the presence of Jesus and the angels, who carry believers, however humble, to Abraham's bosom (Luke 16:22), and friends who have gone ahead (Luke 16:9). The 'theology of hope' was expounded by Jürgen Moltmann, and disciples in the 1960s and as late as 1995.[4] The theology of hope, however, owes more to Marxist sources than to any roots in any past epochs of Christian thought. In this theology, eschatology is not the last chapter but the first, through which every department of Christian life and doctrine is to be given meaning.[5] The Bible, lamentably, does not speak with authority and finality to these theologians, many of whom were associated with 'liberation theology,' a doctrine of civil revolution along 'christianized' Marxist (Communist) lines.

3. The Antithetical Structure of the Biblical Doctrine of Last Things.

By 'antithetical' I mean this as opposed to that, or cold as opposed to heat. With reference to 'last things' – a phrase we have to learn – we usually think in terms of antithesis and speak of 'here and hereafter.' Paul was thinking in this non-technical way of last things when he wrote, 'For now we see in a mirror dimly, but then face to face. Now I know in part; then I shall know fully, even as I have been fully known' (1 Cor. 13:12). This is the language of all of us before we study theology and it is quite in touch with reality, both human and divine. It turns out this is also quite in keeping with several uniquely biblical ways of presenting last things in antithetical relation to the present life.[6] Important aspects of a true biblical view of the earthly, natural ambience of our present lives as contrasted with the heavenly, super-natural character of the future life are exposed in several striking expressions.

We see it in 'now in this time' versus 'in the world [age] to come' as in Mark 10:30 KJV: 'he shall receive an hundredfold now in this time… and in the world to come eternal life' (see also Luke 18:30). Similar is 'in this world [age]' versus 'in the world [age] to come' as in Matthew 12:32 KJV: 'Whosoever speaketh against the Holy Ghost, it shall not be forgiven him, neither in this world, neither in the world to come.' The author of Hebrews, addressing Jewish minds, steeped in Old Testament ways of thinking, assumes this same contrast when he speaks of how his believing readers now 'have [already] tasted of the heavenly gift, and were made partakers of the Holy Ghost, And have tasted the good word of God [i.e. the gospel],' and have also tasted 'the powers of the world [age] to come' (Heb. 6:4, 5 KJV).

This way of contrasting the now age with the coming age was not derived directly from the Old Testament but from inter-testamental times and the Jewish apocryphal and pseudepigraphal[7] literature it produced. As we have seen, Jesus employed this outlook. The Old Testament, of course, had other ways of representing the last things, as we shall see.

4. The Contrast Between the Present Age and the Age to Come Partly Broken.

One way of making this point is to observe that when the promised Messiah of Israel arrived in the person of the God-man, God was now 'with flesh.' As the King James Version of Hebrews 2:11 has it, both the sanctifier (God) and the sanctified (we sinners) are 'all of one.' But we are only on the way to becoming fully 'sanctified,' and as far as the invisible world is concerned, we 'walk by faith, not by sight' and 'endure as seeing him who is invisible.'

Another way of taking note of this is to observe that when the Messianic King arrived, the kingdom became present and remains so in the regenerate and in the other Comforter, the Holy Spirit.

Still another is to appreciate that 'whoever believes in the Son of God has eternal life.' We have 'passed from death to life' eternal – partakers of the powers of the world to come (John 3:36; 5:24; Heb. 6:5).

---

4. *Das Kommen Gottes*, Jürgen. Moltmann, 1995, English trans. by Margaret Kohl, *The Coming of God* (Minneapolis: Augsburg Fortress, 1996), 390 pages.
5. See S. M. Smith's article 'Theology of Hope' in *Evangelical Dictionary of Theology*, pp. 532–534, 'New Theology,' No. 5 and Moltmann's *The Coming of God*.
6. I am partially indebted to *Studies in Eschatology*, classroom lectures of John Murray (1898–1975) at Westminster Theological Seminary, printed but not published, n.d.
7. These two words, in order, mean 'hidden' and 'falsely assigned authorship.' After the last canonical Old Testament book was written, beginning about 200 BC, devout Jews produced a number of writings on religious subjects. Some of these are among the thirteen (or fourteen) books included in some printed English Bibles between Malachi and Matthew. Some are not. They tell us much about the religious ideas current among Jews in Jesus' time, ideas from the first and second centuries BC.

There are forms of New Testament interpretation which seem to say that this 'realized' or 'inaugurated' eschatology is all or nearly all that the New Testament doctrine of last things means. This, of course, is possible only by distorting some statements of Jesus about Satan's fall from heaven (Luke 10:18), and the judgment as having taken place 'already' (John 3:19), and ignoring threats and promises of a future *parousia* (coming, presence) of Christ with all His holy angels, resurrection of all the dead and judgments according to works. To borrow an overworked phrase, this theology magnifies 'already' while it nullifies 'not yet.'

Emil Brunner's comment on this interpretation of the New Testament gives a sort of dogmatic form and immense notice among scholars to this proposal of C. H. Dodd (*The Parables of the Kingdom*, 1936). Brunner correctly comments:

> The conception of 'realized eschatology' is right inasmuch as it correctly apprehends where the centre of gravity of primitive Christian faith lies, in the events which have already happened in Jesus, in the grace of God's presence in the Holy Spirit already bestowed.... But it is wrong in not doing sufficient justice to the messanic character of the existence of the believing Ecclesia, which is shown also in its expectation of the fulness of revelation in the coming of the Lord in glory.[8]

5. Prediction and Fulfillment.

The subject of last things in the New Testament must be understood, as indeed the Jewish authors of the New Testament did understand it, as enlargement of and fulfillment of both prophecy and history in the Old Testament. The expression 'that it might be fulfilled,' which was spoken by such and such a prophet, or 'as the scripture says,' is frequent in the Gospels when they explain the meaning of Jesus' life and work. Jesus Himself trained them to think that way by His own explanations of His mission. In two episodes with His disciples He explained that all His work and program had been predicted throughout the Old Testament (Luke 24:25-27, 44-47). As I have indicated, several times earlier in these studies, Jesus discerned these prophecies in all parts of the Hebrew Bible. He saw not only His sufferings, death, resurrection, ascension and present reign in heaven 'written in Moses, and in the prophets and in the Psalms' but also the preaching of 'repentance and forgiveness of sins and in his name among all nations' in the present age. He also saw His coming kingdom and visible glory written there. Readers should check this out against the passages cited above from Luke 24 if not already convinced of these facts.

Throughout His ministry, but especially at the last, Jesus spoke, sometimes plainly, sometimes obliquely, of features of His future coming predicted or foreshadowed in the Old Testament. Scholars have not to the present day organized all these materials into a 'system' demonstrable to every interested believer, and I shall not attempt to do so here, but it is feasible in a few paragraphs to come to terms with some leading ideas, i.e. verbal vehicles by which Old Testament revelation spoke of 'the last things.'

The Bible of the first Christians was the Old Testament. They saw their own 'religion' as in continuity, under a new covenant, with Old Testament religion. They, of course, saw the Hebrew Bible from a new perspective supplied by Jesus' life, work and teaching. Hence they did not hesitate to interpret from the standpoint of fulfillment, partially already in Christ, and to await further fulfillment more fully in 'the latter days' and ultimately in 'the day of the LORD.'

To state this important matter differently: when Jesus spoke of 'eternal life,' 'the last days,' 'the day of the Lord' and other topics of eschatology He was using terms familiar to devout Jews such as the Apostles were. They understood these and other such terms and teaching within the framework of Jewish religion of the time. The paradigm, to borrow a grammatical term, had been furnished, within which such language was relevant. The chief source both of the ideas and the patterns was the Old Testament books of prophecy (our Major and Minor Prophets). Among the most important eschatological terms and revelant ideas were 'the latter days' and 'the day of the LORD.' We must therefore know what Isaiah, Joel and company meant when using such language to learn what Jesus and the apostolic writers meant by them and how we should understand Christian eschatology.

6. The Latter (or Last) Days.

The first Christian sermon was by Peter on the Day of Pentecost when early in the day the effusion of the Spirit took place. To explain the day's events Peter took as his text an Old Testament prophecy of 'the last days' found in Joel 2:28, 29, one of the early Minor Prophets: 'And in the last days it shall be, God declares, that I will pour out my

---

8. Emil Brunner, *The Christian Doctrine of the Church, Faith and the Consummation*, Dogmatics, vol. iii, trans. David Cairns (Philadelphia: Westminster Press, 1962), pp. 399, 400.

Spirit on all flesh, and your sons and your daughters shall prophesy, and your young men shall see visions, and your old men shall dream dreams; even on my male servants and female servants in those days I will pour out my Spirit, and they shall prophesy' (Acts 2:17, 18). Peter went on to cite Joel's prophecy of events connected with 'the day of the Lord,' but as Gurdon C. Oxtoby says, in a book on prediction and fulfillment in the Bible:

> The original prophecy of Joel was a poetic description of the Day of the Lord.... But Peter, picking up the phrase 'pour out my Spirit,' finds the Pentecost experience involves exactly that.... Peter does not claim that now is the Day of the Lord. He makes no parallel with the part of the passage that mentions wonders and signs.... The pouring out of God's Spirit is sufficient for him to claim what the prophet stated has now been realized.[9]

It is apparent Peter thought that 'the latter days' of Joel had set in. It is also evident that he thought the day of the Lord to be in the future (2 Peter 3:10 ff.).

It is important therefore to examine the Old Testament meaning of this striking, recurring phrase, 'in the last [or latter] days' as it relates to last things. As we shall see, 'latter' interprets the Hebrew *acharith* as well as translates the word, because 'latter' tends to indicate not only the absolute end or full consummation, but also many events leading up to it – precursors to the final 'Coming of God,' the last act of 'He that cometh.'[10]

This expression 'latter [last] days' appears fourteen times in the Old Testament, scattered from the first book (Gen. 49:1) through Deuteronomy, Numbers, Isaiah, Jeremiah, Ezekiel, Daniel, Hosea and Micah.[11]

In the first passage, Jacob as a prophet, is calling his sons together, 'that I may tell you that which shall befall you in the last days' (Gen. 49:1 KJV). Most of the twelve following oracles, one for each of the twelve sons, relates to their future settlement in Canaan, but the prophet's vision reaches to the times of Messiah, as in verse 10: 'The scepter shall not depart from Judah, nor the ruler's staff from between his feet, until tribute comes to him ['until Shiloh come,' KJV]; and to him shall be the obedience of the peoples.'

A diversion seems important. The word 'Shiloh' in Genesis 49:10 is one of the most mysterious words in the Bible. Not only is the meaning obscure, but there is a real question whether the original Hebrew is one word or three.

It could be explained as three words as follows: the Hebrew relative pronoun (who, which, whose, etc.) is sometimes one simple 'sh' symbol; the sign of possession is sometimes the 'l' symbol; and the pronoun 'him' is symbolized by 'oh.' So, Shi-l-oh could possibly mean 'that which is his,' or 'whose it is.'

The word 'Shiloh' could also possibly be simply the name of the ancient city of Israel of that name, so often mentioned, and for many centuries a seat of government and worship.

Also, it might be a word derived from a relative of *shalom*, peace. In such a case the word could probably mean 'peacemaker' or 'tranquilizer,' a reference to the Messiah (see Isa. 9:6, 'Prince of Peace'). At an earlier time this was the most common view of the word, but it has no specific support in the Scripture, even though there are some feasible reasons for adopting it.

The view outlined above – that it means 'whose it is' – makes sense in the context. It was adopted in an ASV marginal translation, viz. 'The sceptre shall not depart from Judah, nor the ruler's staff from between his feet, till he come whose it is,' etc. and supported in ESV quoted above.

This rendering, supported by a similar Hebrew construction at Ezekiel 21:27, gives the passage a rich Messianic interpretation to the effect that Judah would produce the line of kings in Israel, and that this line of kings would finally present the sovereignty to the One whose it properly is, our Lord Jesus Christ.

The rulership of Israel, and the whole universe also, is His properly for several reasons. It is His by right of creation (John 1:3), by right of redemption (Rev. 5:9) and by right of inheritance (as the last of the line of David, Luke 1:31, 32; 2 Sam. 7:12-16). It is His as the first-born of all creation by the Father's appointment (Heb. 1:4-13).

Gabriel seems to relate this prophecy to the first parousia of Christ when he announced to the virgin of Nazareth: 'And the Lord God will give to him the throne of his father David, and he will reign over the house of Jacob for ever, and of his kingdom there will be no end' (Luke 1:32-33). The whole section on Judah (Gen. 49:7-9) for the first

---

9. Gurdon C. Oxtoby, *Prediction and Fulfillment in the Bible* (Philadelphia: Westminster Press, 1966), pp. 33, 34.
10. There are volumes of literature usually categorized as Old Testament theology which trace these ideas through the Hebrew Scriptures. This does not seem to be the place to lengthen this discussion by introducing the history and present state of the subject.
11. Deut. 4:30; 31:29; Num. 24:14; Isa. 2:2; Jer. 23:20; 30:24; 48:47; 49:39; Ezek. 38:16; Dan. 2:28; 10:14; Hos. 3:5; and Mic. 4:1.

time in biblical history and prophecy announced (albeit obliquely) the future-anointed dynasty of David, greatly to be enlarged in an extensive revelation to King David (2 Sam. 7) as well as in the Major and Minor Prophets. The significance reaches even to the future beyond Judgment Day. 'Forever' is a long time in the future, as David did not fail to comment on: 'for a great while to come' (2 Sam. 7:19).[12]

Onward through most of the Old Testament oracles about 'the latter days' both the near and the farthest earthly future are explicitly within the range of the prophet's vision, and when not explicit, implicit. Gustav F. Oehler is correct to say: 'But in prophetic diction, properly so called, *acharith* [latter, last] is... the time of the consummation of redemption (Hos. 3:5; Isa. 2;3, with Mic. 4:1; Jer. 48:47; Ezek. 38:16).'[13] In each of these passages the word *acharith* is used for 'last' or 'latter.'

In prophecies of 'the latter days' two major themes presume a prior condition, chronic in ancient Israel and her kings, of guilt for disobedience to the terms of their several covenants.[14] The two themes (1) of future judgment both of Israel and the nations and (2) future redemption 'are repeated and interwoven as highly charged eschatological warnings and promises that often refer to historical events just past or soon to come, as well as to the long-range messianic age.'[15]

Judgment and redemption, sometimes in the period of time when the prophet spoke, but always with eschatological overtones, sometimes with greater emphasis on the *eschaton*, are chief themes in prophecies of the latter days. Hosea, contemporary with Isaiah (cf. Hos. 1:1 with Isa. 1:1), foresaw Israel's guilty idolatry bringing on 'many days,' now stretching out into almost 2,000 years without either a valid Jewish civil government ('without king or prince') or a valid, biblical worship ('without sacrifice or pillar, without ephod or household gods,' Hos. 3:4) – no king, no priest or temple. Yet this is not to be permanent, for 'in the latter days' there will be repentance, recovery and redemption, for 'Afterwards the children of Israel shall return and seek the LORD their God, and David their king [in the Person of the Messiah], and they shall come in fear to the LORD and to his goodness in the latter days' (Hos. 3:5).

Some insist that we must find fulfillment of these prophecies in the small remnant of Israel who became the first Christians, or the church of both Gentiles and Jews. There is no doubt that the prophecies of the latter days began to be fulfilled with the Advent of Christ. This is apparent not only in Peter's sermon at Pentecost, noted above, for Hebrews 1:1, 2 places God's speaking through 'a Son' (as opposed to through prophets as of old) in the epoch of 'these last days'. Yet the theology of the author of Romans 9–11 does not say merely some Jews are going to become Christian believers and thereby a part of the church; rather, 'God has not rejected his people whom he foreknew' (Rom. 11:2); 'And in this way all Israel will be saved' (Rom. 11:26). If, as some insist, by 'Israel' Paul here simply meant all saved people, the sentence conveys no information; it would be a nonsense tautology: 'and in this way all saved people will be saved.' I, with many, am convinced that Israel will yet again en masse seek the Lord and David their king in the latter days as many chapters in the Old Testament Prophets declare.[16]

I do not doubt that these prophecies find germinal fulfillment in past and present but await fulfillment in the *eschaton*. The rule, as I see it, is: 'Prophecies with comprehensive future reference will have manifold fulfillment.'

Sometimes writers on this feature of biblical prediction and fulfillment define it as double fulfillment. If, however, the prediction had comprehensive reference to more than one future, similar event, then there is not double fulfillment but only one full, i.e. complete, fulfillment. Many informed devout interpreters of every age of the church have struggled with this problem, none more earnestly than the English Puritans of the early seventeenth century, in their struggles with the monarchy and the established church. Robert Manton, whose life spanned those turbulent years, in 1642 wrote the following about fulfillment of Joel's prophecy of the effusion of the Spirit on the Jews in the latter days and what Peter meant in relating it to the events of Pentecost. It is, Manton wrote,

> as if he had said, My brethren, these are not the effects of wine, but of the Spirit of God, which is now poured out on the first fruits of the Jews, as a pledge and assurance of that bountifull effusion of it, which (as Joel hath said) shall one day happen to the whole Nation. And this is what S. Peter meant, it may thus appear: first because the chief and most remarkable effect of the Spirit in the Apostles, at this time, was the gift of tongues,

---

12. See Jer. 17:25; 23:5; 33:15, 17; 36:30; Isa. 55:3; cf. Acts 13:34.
13. Gustav F. Oehler, *Theology of the Old Testament*, trans. George E. Day (New York: Funk and Wagnalls, 1883), p. 489.
14. ibid.
15. R. G. Gruenler, 'Last Days, Day' in EDT, p. 619.
16. I have devoted many pages to this matter in *Daniel and the Latter Days* and its successor *The Earthly Reign of our Lord with His People* with many pages of documentation and bibliography, but do not press the matter at this juncture.

of which the Prophet makes no mention: and secondly, because as the Prophet revealed, so he repeats this pouring out of the Spirit, as a contemporary event with the wonders which shall be shown, in the heavens and in the earth before the great and terrible day of the Lord comes. Which day can no way be referr'd to the first coming of Christ, when he came to save sinners, not to destroy them.[17]

7. The Day of the LORD.

The day of the LORD has attracted the interest and attention of every teacher or writer of Old Testament theology and serious exegesis. Every serious Bible dictionary or encyclopaedia of theology has a scholarly article on the day of the LORD. Let us take note that it appears apparently as a fully developed idea on the pages of the Old Testament, but only in the Prophets. Yet they employ it as a widely held, apparently well-defined expectation. The prophets only purified and clarified this hope of Israel. Among the many theories of the origin of the idea I cite as likely that of Walter Eichrodt, as summarized by John Bright:

> For the future, Israel trusted in the coming of the Day of Yahweh. The origin of this concept, first mentioned in Amos 5:18-20 but already an entrenched popular hope in the eighth century is obscure and debated. The probability is that as Israel recalled in the cult the great days of Yahweh's victories in the past... the expectation grew of a coming day par excellence when Yahweh would intervene in Israel's behalf and make his promises to the patriarchs actual. Though all the fundamentals of Israel's faith... were still held, all were prostituted.[18] Later on Amos and Isaiah, while retaining the idea changed it radically, making it a messianic hope.[19]

These views, now widely endorsed, are approved here, as following treatment shows.

The word, 'day,' among ancient Hebrews sometimes had a special meaning. Decisive events in one's own history may be called 'the day of... trouble' (Ps. 77:2; and twelve more times in the Old Testament); the time of Jerusalem's siege and demolition, 'the day of Jerusalem.' '[T]he day of Midian' (Isa. 9:4) was the battle where Gideon and reassembled hosts of Ephraim slaughtered the hordes of the threatening Midianites and brought the severed heads of Oreb and Zeeb, the two 'princes of Midian,' 'to Gideon across the Jordan' (Judg. 7:24, 25; cf. Isa. 10:26). This essentially Hebraic manner of speaking has come over to us in 'the Lord's day,' the recurring weekly hours which for Christians belong to the worship of the Lord Jesus. 'The Lord's Supper' reflects the same manner of thinking. The sacrament is not for our nourishment but 'to show forth the Lord's death,' i.e. to honor Him, 'till he come.'

The most characteristic verbal designation of the whole of the wind-up of human history is 'the day of the LORD'. The ancient Hebrews and their Semitic neighbors (Arabs, Syrians, Assyrians) to this day employ graphic, frequently physical, images in ordinary conversation. The greatest battle is 'mother of all battles,' a great mountain is a 'mountain of God,' and similar.

As in the case of 'the latter days' which meets us in the first Christian sermon, so 'the day of the LORD' appears in the New Testament as a conception already familiar to the Jewish readers of the letters of the Apostles. Paul reminds readers of this Old Testament expectation at the end of the present age in 1 Corinthians 5:5; 2 Corinthians 1:14; 1 Thessalonians 5:7; and 2 Thessalonians 2:2 (ASB, RSV, NIV). It will be, said he, their time of meeting Christ and giving final account. Peter says that the day of the LORD will introduce a renovation of the world, resulting in a new heaven (2 Peter 3:10-13).

So the day of the LORD comes into the New Testament as an exclusively eschatological expression, and so it is regularly in the Old Testament, though not exclusively so in the Old Testament. Delling reminds us that 'from time to time the possibility has to be considered that expectation of a day of Yahweh applies to an event in Israel's history which though it is of supreme importance does not imply the inauguration of the last time.'[20] He cites as examples Ezekiel 34:12. So the greatest of all events in the future, bringing history to consummation, is 'the day of the LORD.'[21]

---

17. Robert Manton, *Israel's Redemption* or *The Prophetical History of Our Saviour's Kingdom on Earth*, etc., London, 1642. R. Manton was a minister, M.A., Wadam College in Oxford. The research of Douglas J. Culver for his doctoral thesis at New York University, published as *Albion and Ariel, British Puritanism and the Birth of Political Zionism*, New York: Peter Lang, 1995, turned up Manton's book, of which I have a University microfilm copy.
18. John Bright, *A History of Israel* (Philadelphia, PA: Westminster Press, 1959), pp. 243, 244.
19. ibid., pp. 244, 245, 281.
20. Delling, hemera, TDNT, II, p. 944.
21. As always in this book I have avoided both the artificial transliteration of Jehovah, the four letters of the name of Israel's national God, and the very uncertain, scholars' attempt to recreate the name as Yahweh. The 'h' represents a sound not ordinarily vocalized in English and both the 'a' and the 'e' are uncertain for we do not know if the word had a causative verbal inflection or a simple, nor if it was pronounced after an Arabic

This formula, 'the day of the LORD' appears at least twenty times in the Old Testament – always and only in the Major and Minor Prophets. 'In that day', also a frequent term in these prophetical writings, often refers to the same – a time when God vindicates Himself by judging or defending His people through great works, which even the heathen must recognize as divine in cause, 'the day of the LORD.' Since it was a breaking through of the invisible, supernatural order into the visible world it partook of eternity and was an anticipation of the consummation.

An examination of 'that day,' 'day of God,' 'day of the LORD' passages in any exhaustive concordance abundantly justifies characterization it as the day of the LORD's vindication. The good people longed for such a day as this because in that day they saw vindication of their own steadfastness in face of oppression and as both judgment of their tormentors and as vindication of God's honor. This explains some of David's outbursts, as for example: 'Do I not hate those who hate you, O LORD?' (Ps. 139:21; cf. 22-24).

This 'day' has regard to the fact God created all things according to His pleasure and for His own glory. 'All things' includes all mankind, whether they are now good or evil. 'The chief end of man is to glorify God, and enjoy him forever.' This being the case, certain Israelites of the prophet Amos's time had it all wrong when they thought the day of the LORD was solely for their advancement. They had supposed the day was coming because 'God is on our side.' Amos set them right as follows: 'Woe unto you that desire the day of the LORD! to what end is it for you? the day of the LORD is darkness, and not light [i.e. 'to you,' though not for everyone]. As if a man did flee from a lion... and a serpent bit him...' (Amos 5:18, 19 KJV). God declares Himself fed up with their religiosity and noisy rituals (Amos 5:21-24). And because they had mixed their proper Jewish observances with pagan ones they will go into captivity – which brings us to observe that the day of the LORD in its usual eschatological dimension included divine settling up of accounts with both Israelites and Gentiles and had three dimensions, as now follow.

I. Discrimination.

In spite of the distortion of the word and its meaning in public thinking currently and for half a century, there is a proper place for discrimination both by God and man.

1. God will 'in that day' discriminate between the righteous and unrighteous in Israel. We have already seen this in Amos 5:18-24. Malachi's brief prophecy focuses on this theme throughout the four chapters. Though he takes special umbrage at their religious functionaries, the Levites and priests (Mal. 1:1–2:17), no one of any class escapes notice (3:1-12). But God will not paint all with the same brush, for of those 'who feared the LORD and esteemed his name.... "They shall be mine, says the LORD of hosts"' (3:16-17). '[T]he sun of righteousness shall rise with healing in its wings' (4:2) and Elijah shall come again to convert many (4:5, 6). Such are the last words of Old Testament Scripture.

2. In the eschatological 'day of the LORD' God will discriminate between Israel and the nations. 'And in that day... Egypt shall become a desolation and Edom a desolate wilderness, for the violence done to the people of Judah, because they have shed innocent blood in their land. But Judah shall be inhabited for ever, and Jerusalem to all generations. I will avenge their blood, and I will not clear the guilty, for the LORD dwells in Zion' (Joel 3:18a, 19-21 RSV). This divine notice of Israel's persecution by her neighbors and settling up in judgment is not a small part of the day of the LORD or of any other day, for that matter (Isa. 14:1; and especially Obad. 15-21). The severe language of Isaiah 34:1-17 is unmatched with respect to God's 'day of vengeance, a year of recompence for the cause of Zion' (v. 8). God will discriminate between righteousness and unrighteousness through the whole earth. Malachi 4:1 seems to have such a universal reference. Isaiah 13:6-16 twice threatens a looming 'day of the LORD' (vv. 6 and 9) 'to make the land a desolation and to destroy its sinners from it' (v. 9). Presumably 'sinners' in this passage means unrepentant sinners. The poetic character of this passage (shaking heaven, darkened celestial lights, a quaking earth and the like) is notice that not quite everything is to be taken literally.[22]

As a result of discrimination between every appearance of righteousness and unrighteousness, two further features are characteristic of 'that day'.

---

manner or according to the manner of the Massorites of seventh to ninth centuries AD. It seems best to follow the precedent of the KJV and RSV which uniformly render the 'tetragrammaton' *the* LORD, all capital letters.

22. Early in study of this subject, I became convinced that such language, carried over into 2 Peter 3:10 ff. – fervent heat, dissolving elements – has to do with something far short of annihilation of the natural order. 'Briefly, as I have considered the possibilities, it seems that the cosmic disturbances in 2 Peter 3:10 [and elsewhere in Scripture] shall consist of a limited renovation involving ... such changes in the realms of inanimate material, of vegetable, animal, and human life as are necessary to produce conditions which the prophets declare shall prevail during the coming kingdom age' (from my book *Daniel and the Latter Days*, p. 194). It also seems to me the evidence is that this occurs immediately with the Second Advent (parousia). 'Appendix I, The Time and Extent of the Coming World Dissolution,' in the book, pp. 188–200.

II. Salvation.

Though this salvation for the whole earth is promised, salvation for Israel and their Land is prominent in most texts. The 'salvation' includes perfection not only of the saved but thorough 'regeneration' of the natural order (to use Jesus' term, Matt. 19:28; 'new world' in RSV). Let the reader turn to Isaiah chapter 2 or 11 or 35:1-10 and gather one's own impressions and apply them as widely or as narrowly to converted Israel or all the redeemed (as Rev. 21, 22 seem to do). 'And the ransomed of the LORD shall return and come to Zion with singing; everlasting joy shall be upon their heads; they shall obtain gladness and joy, and sorrow and sighing shall flee away' (Isa. 35:10). With this paean of joy, Isaiah concluded the first 'book' of his great volume of sixty-six chapters.

III. Judgment.

Retributive judgment – though with chastening effects for some, not all – is prominent. Perhaps this corrective element is due to the historical situation then prevailing. For the writing prophets were always called to serve when moral conditions were generally low and political situations precarious. So 'in wrath' God would 'remember mercy' (Hab. 3:2). Three statements seem to characterize what judgment will be like in the day of the LORD.

1. The retributive element is most prominent, especially as it relates to 'all the nations' (Obad. 15 RSV), but which in the more spiritually accurate, though now less politically correct, KJV is, 'For the day of the LORD is near upon all the heathen: as thou hast done, it shall be done unto thee: thy reward shall return upon thine own head.' '[H]eathen' is a word no one seems to want to use any more. The retributive element is present every time the judgments of the day of the LORD is mentioned. Eschatological judgment will not improve people's souls: 'The wicked shall be turned into hell, and all the nations [heathen] that forget God' (Ps. 9:17 KJV).[23]

2. The judgments of the day of the LORD will be universal in scope. As seen from the particular perspective of Joel they will rest chiefly on 'all you surrounding nations' (Joel 3:11). Yet he reports: 'the LORD has spoken' and follows with this address: 'Proclaim this among the nations,' and then follows what reads like a world-wide summons to a final showdown in 'the Valley of Jehoshaphat' (Jehovah judges) near Jerusalem. This theme is picked up in Revelation and connected with a final battle of Antichrist's world-order against Christ and His world-order (Rev. 14 and 19). Isaiah says 'the day of the LORD is near' (Isa. 13:6) 'to make the land a desolation' (v. 9) and promises to 'punish the world for its evil' (Isa. 13:11). Earlier in a so-called 'little apocalypse' (Isa. 24, 25) there is a longer formal announcement of a final, universal judgment 'On that day' (24:21).

At this juncture let us advert to the previous point, that the day of the LORD introduces a perfect eternal state of perfect human and earthly felicity. The judgment is to be followed by a new and perfect day when 'on this mountain [new kingdom] the LORD of hosts will make for all peoples a feast of rich food, a feast of well-aged wine, of rich food.... And he will swallow up... the covering that is cast over all peoples, the veil that is spread over all nations. He will swallow up death for ever; and the Lord God will wipe away tears from all faces' (Isa. 25:6-8). In these two chapters (Isa. 24, 25) there is a miniature of everything in the Apocalypse, where the voice of divine revelation reaches its highest point and leaves off.

When Will the *Eschaton*, or the Day of the Lord, Come?

This Old Testament question translates to a serious continuing present question, debated, sometimes bitterly, among schools of theology – even in recent denominational statements of faith. It is a complex question. Is the *parousia*, the Second Advent of Christ, something to be expected at any moment? How should signs of His coming figure in our expectation? I propose that the situation of devout believers awaiting the First Advent is quite parallel, if not quite identical, with our situation regarding the Second Advent.

---

23. The Hebrew word goi (plu. goiim) has four translations in KJV – nation, heathen, people, Gentile. (1) When God promised Hagar regarding her son, Ishmael, 'I will make him a great nation' – a group united by a common ancestry is obviously correct. 'Nation' is related to Latin natus, born. (2) When (much rarer) in Leviticus 25:44 and 26:33, 38 and 45 the neighbor worshippers of false gods are called goi, the KJV is correct to render 'heathen' – people commonly distinguished by false worship, usually idolatry and accompanying immorality. (3) Rarely as at Joshua 3:17; 4:1; 5:6, 8; and 10:13 the KJV renders goi as 'people,' with regard to the fact they were simply a band of folk crossing a river, forming an army and the like having in common a civil-religious social connection. (4) 'Gentiles' alternates with nation(s) in KJV renderings in the Major Prophets. (eg. Isa. 42:1, 6 where Messiah will 'bring forth judgment ... and ... light to the Gentiles'). 'Gentiles' is always spelled with initial capital. The root of the English word (Latin, *gentiles*) means races or nations. 'The threat of contamination by paganism in the Greek period led the Jews to adopt a rigorous exclusive attitude toward non-Jews' (R. K. Harrison, 'Gentiles' in *ZPBE II*, p. 697, Harrison's article is highly recommended).

The day of the Lord did not arrive with the Advent of Jesus the Messiah and the events of Pentecost, though, as we have seen, certain aspects of 'the last days' did. Our Lord's second parousia which introduces the day of the Lord is still future. There are two facts about the time of the coming day of the LORD usually explicitly present in the prophecies.

1. The day of the Lord is future. It is future the first time the expression appears in the Bible (Isa. 2:12). Over and again Isaiah uses the phrase, 'in that day,' to identify a future day. Isaiah 12 is a song to be sung when the perfect redemption of mankind and their earthly environs shall have been effected. Let us examine a short passage from Isaiah's Immanuel oracle (Isa. 7–12).

> In that day the root of Jesse shall stand as an ensign to the peoples [not Israel alone]; him shall the nations seek, and his dwellings shall be glorious. In that day the Lord will extend his hand yet a second time to recover ... his people, from Assyria, from Egypt, from Pathros, from Ethiopia, from Elam, from Shinar, from Hamath ... from the four corners of the earth (Isa. 11:10-12 RSV).

This seems to be a future 'latter days' day of the LORD, of regathering and salvation (see chap. 12, below), then far in the future, as it is still today. The 'second time' implies the return from Babylon, as the 'first time.' The Exodus was not a 'time to recover his people' from 'Assyria ... Egypt ... Pathros' and similar. The sons of Israel became a 'people' first in Egypt, hence the Exodus was not a 'recovery' but an 'escape.'[24] Isaiah telescopes the near future (the doom of Babylon) with the remote eschatological future, in the prophecy of Isaiah 13. Here, though 'the day of the LORD is near', it is not present but future, as the prophet goes on to say: 'as destruction from the Almighty it will come' (Isa. 13:6). Joel likewise sees no dimension of depth in his picture of the day of the Lord, but there is remote future, then as now in his oracle.[25] It is to be admitted that sometimes a 'day of the LORD' seems to be in what is now long ago, but close examination of such passages will show the prophet sees elements of the near action of God in judgment and salvation similar to the final showdown of history. To my Old Testament students I say when we come to these passages – as professors and previous scholars have said to me – 'The prophets frequently associate future events similar in kind but widely separated in time. The dimension of depth is absent from the prophets' vision of the future.' So Joel saw in the plague of locusts already devastating the country, a harbinger of the day of the Lord (Joel 1:15) as well as a threatening army of foreign invaders (2:20) close at hand, the effusion of the Spirit 'afterward' (2:28, cited by Peter in Acts 2), a final judgment of Israel's heathen enemies (Joel 3:1-16) and everlasting blessing in the final future (3:17-23). The best-known example of this element of depth (hidden to contemporaries) in Old Testament prediction is Isaiah's prophecy of the virgin (Isa. 7:14) which, as most modern, conservative scholars agree, had a partial, initial fulfillment in the prophet's own child (cf. Isa. 7:14-17 with 8:1-4; and Matt. 1:18-24).

2. The day of the Lord is always presumed to be drawing near, in some sense impending or imminent. Let Ezekiel furnish an example, where the prophet says that the day of the Lord or the time of Messiah is drawing near or has drawn near: 'Thus says the Lord GOD: "Wail, "Alas for the day!" For the day is near, the day of the LORD is near' (Ezek. 30:2, 3 twice in verse 3). The prophet goes on to speak of the coming conquests of Nebuchadnezzar in language which has eschatological color. Zephaniah, contemporary of Jeremiah, uses the same language ('is near') in his first chapter, twice in one verse: 'Be silent before the Lord GOD! For the day of the LORD is near' (Zeph. 1:7); 'The great day of the LORD is near, near and hastening fast' (v. 14). The Hebrew word *qaruv* (a passive participle of the ordinary word for drawing near and bringing near in other forms) is rendered 'near' in each case. 'Hastening fast' employs the strongest language available for swift movement. They are all threatening expressions in context of judgment. This word is used ten times in the Old Testament, including the above quoted passage, ascribed to the day of the Lord – Joel 1:15; 2:1; 3:14; Obadiah 15; Zephaniah 1:7, 14 (twice); Isaiah 13:6; Ezekiel 30:3 (twice).

It seems to me that the saints of Luke 2 – Zacharias and Elizabeth, Simeon and Anna, Joseph and Mary, and others 'looking for the consolation of Israel' – saw the bright (salvation) side of this situation. Though amazed by what happened when angels announced the Messiah's arrival, or when they actually met Him, as Simeon and Anna (and later Philip and Nathanael, Peter, James, and John), they were not surprised.

---

24. Robert D. Culver, *Daniel and the Latter Days* (Chicago: Moody Press, 1977), or *The Earthly Reign of Our Lord with His People* (by author, 1998), pp. 80–82.

25. Too much must not be made of the 'tense' (or state) of the verb, but in Isaiah 13:6 as in Joel 1:15, where there is similar lack of depth and telescoping of the future, the word is 'shall come' *yabho'*(*kal* imperfect), first masculine singular from *bo'*, to come.

So, it seems, as believers throughout the Christian dispensation have witnessed conditions or events which they thought might be harbingers of the *parousia*, they would have been amazed but not surprised if Jesus had returned in glory. His coming has not been unexpected in any generation. We shall have more to say about this matter in later chapters.

Now, after personally surviving the 'experts' on prophecy and their mutual criticisms, their 'lo heres' and 'lo theres,' I know no more than Philip did, before Jesus actually appeared in his presence with marks of the anointing, which one must have to be 'the anointed' – which is what *Christos* or Messiah means. I shall later describe what Paul and others seem to say are precursors of the *parousia* (coming) or day of the LORD. Paul distinctly describes them as such, when, in 2 Thessalonians 2:1 ff., he strongly denounces unjustified propaganda that the day of the Lord has arrived, or is about to arrive. Yet, we must avoid any denial that He might come 'soon,' or 'quickly' (see Rev. 1:1, 3; 22:20). We shall know for certain soon enough and plainly enough – as obvious as a flash of lightening from horizon to horizon. We should be watching in the sense of tending to godly business every day and all day long, for the 'master of the house' may 'come in the evening, or at midnight, or at cockcrow, or in the morning.'

2
Death, Mortality and Immortality

Quite understandably, death and its sequels are of pervasive and timeless interest. About everything that could possibly be derived from Scripture, from philosophy and from experience has been said many times over. Of course science – some of it 'falsely so-called' – continues its efforts to solve the mystery of death. There is a Protestant form of the Christian view of death and the intermediate state. Let those with interest in the history of it read Charles Hodge.[1] A. H. Strong has digested and summarized the arguments for the Protestant view – rational, teleological, ethical and historical.[2] I am looking at about fifty books arranged on or near my desk, all related to this subject. In order adequately to treat the doctrine of death and not too briefly I shall follow fairly closely the outline of the subject furnished by my professor, Alva J. McClain, whose careful biblical approach served me well all those years before I became acquainted with more recent essays, symposiums, and monographs, as well as some very old ones, not least Calvin's exposé of the soul-sleep error of Reformation times (Psychopannychia, available in English in the Beveridge translation of Calvin's Tracts).[3]

A scriptural understanding of the nature of death in mankind depends in part upon a scriptural understanding of the nature of mankind. The converse also is true. In treatment of the doctrine of mankind (Anthropology) we devoted chapter 4 to 'The Non-Physical Aspects of Man's Nature,' and as subtitle, 'The Soul, Its Distinct Features and Functions' and early in the chapter promised, 'When these studies reach Eschatology, in connection with the doctrine of death and the intermediate state, a fuller account must be given.' I also cited J. O. Buswell's affirmation of 'Man's two-fold Being' and quoted his cautiously stated definition of the same, here repeated in part. He says, it is 'obvious' (and I add that the wearisome volumes and columns of so-called biblical theology of recent generations to the contrary, will never erase the obvious)

> that according to the Bible man is both a material and non-material entity, both body and soul, and that these two aspects of man are not only logically distinguishable, but separable, so that at death the non-material man goes into the realm of the unseen...[4]

---

1. Charles Hodge, *Systematic Theology III* (Grand Rapids: Wm. B. Eerdmans, 1970), pp. 713–733.
2. A. H. Strong, *Systematic Theology* (Valley Forge, PA: Judson Press, 1907), pp. 982–991.
3. Tracts Relating to the Reformation, Volume III, Edinburgh, 1851.
4. J. O. Buswell, *A Systematic Theology of the Christian Religion I* (Grand Rapids: Zondervan, 1962), p. 237.

This is the plain assumption of the Bible throughout and has been the near unanimous opinion of every branch of the church and its orthodox theologians. Augustine was not quoting his Platonist professors when he equated 'the death of the body' with 'the separation of the soul from the body' and characterized death as 'violent sundering of the two elements, which are conjoined and interwoven in a living being... bound to be a harsh and unnatural experience.'[5] He was expressing what Jesus Himself believed when He in the words of Psalm 31:5 made His last prayer to God, 'Father, into your hands I commit my spirit!' (Luke 23:46).

Thomas Oden is right when he remarks:

> What was being committed and received? Surely not the body only, for it was soon to die. Nor was it merely his breath in a literal sense, for what difference could that last portion of air make? Rather it was the living spirit (pneuma) as distinct from the body that was being committed to God in death (Luke 23:46). James assumed that 'the body without the spirit is dead' (James 2:26).[6]

We shall say more about these matters later.

At the present moment, however, we observe the professional, elite theologians of the European university faculties, along with many leading lights of the biblical theology movement, have said the exact opposite. Perhaps among these scholars the most nearly orthodox and one whose interest in eschatology and 'a theology of hope' qualifies him to speak, is Jürgen Moltmann. In a chapter on 'Cosmic Eschatology, The Future of Creation,' he says:

> The world of the living, of the earth, the solar system, our galaxy and the cosmos is the condition for our human world too, for it is in this world that our human world is imbedded. Because there is no such thing as a soul *separate from the body* [emphasis added], and no humanity detached from nature – from life, the earth and the cosmos – there is no redemption for human beings either without the redemption of nature.[7]

For these theologians, soul (mind, consciousness, memory) is a function of the nervous system only. Moltmann holds that at death, though a believer sleeps in Jesus, he goes out of existence until resurrection in a restored newly-created body – into a new heaven and earth. This is an improvement, of course, on the evolutionary theology of liberalism and fits neatly both into post-Freud psychology and neo-orthodox theology. These theologians regard the Bible as valuable testimony to the religious insights and experiences of those who wrote the Bible. They then bring their own educated competence (as they understand it) to the theological task and seek to confirm only as much of the Christian theological consensus (historical orthodoxy) as passes muster with the educated consensus of the Enlightenment and the succeeding post-enlightenment of today. They find some evidence of belief in the separable existence of human souls in the beliefs of some people in the Bible, but deny that the existence of souls is a matter of divine revelation which speaks with authority.[8] What are the biblical grounds for believing in the existence of a human soul in each member of our race? I shall try to be brief. We make no claim for a natural immortality of the soul. As the church Fathers and Reformers explained, the soul along with all else of creation is a contingent thing, dependent at each moment on the providence and preservation of God, specifically of Christ, in whom all things hold together. We do assert, however, that for good reason the Old Testament somewhat obscurely and the New Testament very plainly teach that 'after God had made all other creatures, he created man, male and female, with reasonable and immortal souls.'[9]

It is well known that the ancient Egyptians believed in the existence of the soul which exits the body at death, appears before deity in judgment, and is assigned to a 'heaven' or a 'hell.' It was a national obsession. Their best minds as well as the resources of the realm were devoted to this perception of human existence. Moses, author of the first five books of the Bible, 'was instructed in all the wisdom of the Egyptians, and he was mighty in his words and deeds' (Acts 7:22). It would therefore be surprising if no evidence of belief in an immaterial 'substance' or 'entity' – the soul as an aspect of human nature – would appear in the first five books (Pentateuch) of the Bible. Archaeology of the nineteenth century poured a flood of light on ancient Egypt's preoccupation with the survival

---

5. Augustine, *City of God*, XIII, 6, trans. Henry Bettenson (Baltimore: Penguin Books, 1972), p. 515.
6. Thomas Oden, *Life in the Spirit* (San Francisco: Harper Collins, 1992), p. 381.
7. Jürgen. Moltmann, *The Coming of God: Christian Eschatology*, trans. Margaret Kohl (Minneapolis: Fortress Press, 1996), p. 260.
8. Though I shall not review it here, any one who has kept up on recent 'biblical theology' has been thoroughly exposed to this 'monism' as regards human nature. See the volumes *Grave to Glory* and *Raised Immortal* by Murray Harris, for example.
9. *Westminster Confession* of 1647.

of souls. It is therefore 'inconceivable that the people of Israel should have lived so long among the Egyptians, and observed their elaborate Ritual of the Dead, and not to some extent become possessed of the idea of immortality, or that... Moses should have left them ignorant of a doctrine which he knew so well.'[10] Joseph, son of Jacob (longtime prime minister of Egypt) had his father's body embalmed in accordance with Egyptian custom (Gen. 50:1, 2). Whatever his reasons may have been, Joseph (and his eleven brothers) would not have been ignorant of the reasons for the Egyptian customs they carried out. It was expected the *Ka* or soul would become associated with supreme gods and perhaps return from time to time to inhabit the mummified corpse.

Christian exegesis has always found the doctrine of a 'future life' of an immortal soul affirmed in the Psalms. In the late twentieth century, however, discovery of the Ras Shamra (ancient Ugarit) tablets on a headland of the North Syrian coast has vastly enlarged our understanding of the literary form and vocabulary of the Psalms. The reader is directed to the introductory chapters of the three volumes of *The Anchor Bible* on the Psalms, written by Mitchell Dahood, Professor of Ugaritic at the Pontifical Institute in Rome. I visited the site of Ugarit in 1962 and had a brief conversation with Father Dahood in about 1970 shortly after he finished his work on the Hebrew Psalms. Ultimately he found a clear doctrine of immortality of the soul and future resurrection of the body in more than forty texts.

Traditional Christian interpretation has always found belief in immortality and resurrection in Psalm 16:10; 17:15; 49:14, 15; 73:25, 26; as well as in Hosea 12:14; Isaiah 36:19; Ezekiel 37; Job 19:25-26; and Daniel 12:2.

2 Maccabees 7 witnesses the firm faith of the Maccabean martyrs in immortality and the first five chapters of the apocryphal *Wisdom of Solomon* are entirely devoted to the subject of rewards and punishments in an after-death existence of immortal souls.

These beliefs were not new when they appear so prominently in these later records, but, as Dahood and other writers now show, such beliefs were already present among the Canaanites of Ugarit long before the Israelites settled in among them in the southern reaches of Canaanite culture and religion. The texts in the Psalms and a few other Old Testament books where Dahood (now deceased) found everlasting life beyond the grave are listed and quoted on pages XLV to LII of *The Anchor Bible: Psalms*, Vol III.[11]

Old Testament scholarship has been slow in accepting the obvious in Dahood's (and more recent authors') work. Jürgen Moltmann either ignores or is unaware of the sweeping change that has come, for his *The Coming of God* cited above in this chapter takes no notice whatsoever of it. Evangelical scholars as well have been tardy in gaining this awareness.

The subject of this chapter is never absent from human consciousness or sub-consciousness. This fact is specifically recognized in the Scripture text which says the Son of God partook of our 'flesh' – human nature – 'that through death he might ... deliver all those who through fear of death were subject to lifelong slavery' (Heb. 2:14, 15). Even believers are not delivered from fear of death, only delivered from bondage to that fear. Among mankind in general this angst is inseparably connected with accusations of conscience and responsibility to God for moral conduct, inasmuch 'as it is appointed for man to die once, and after that comes judgment' (Heb. 9:27).

Whether we think of death as the last event (*eschaton*) of the present life or as first event (*novissimum*) of existence beyond the event itself, physical death raises many more questions. My sister Eleanor, a retired teacher of children, who knew she was soon to die of cancer, asked me for a Christian book about heaven; Job wanted to know 'If a man die, shall he live again?' 'Will we know one another in heaven?' is a frequent inquiry. I do not recall any anxious persons asking for information about hell.

The word 'death' and the idea of it are not always employed in a literal theological sense in Scripture. In a plain metaphor for poison the prophets of Gilgal exclaimed, 'there is death in the pot' (2 Kgs. 4:40), and of physical dangers Paul wrote that he was 'in deaths oft[en]' (2 Cor. 11:23 KJV). Death is personified: 'Death and Hades were thrown into the lake of fire' (Rev. 20:14; cf. v. 13; and 1 Cor. 15:54, 55). '[P]ut to death' the first time it appears (Gen. 26:11) and nearly forty times in Old and New Testaments, is the judicial expression for capital punishment.

After we have discussed the nature and causes of physical death, which is the main focus of this chapter, we shall reflect on its meaning and what one's response should be to the dread fact that 'it is appointed for man to die once' (Heb. 9:27).

Theologically, in relation to the experience of human beings, death (as also the verb 'die' and the adjective 'dead') designates three related but nevertheless distinct experiences or states.

---

10. William Wright, *Life and Immortality* (London: Religious Tract Society, n.d.), p. 35.
11. Mitchell Dahood, *The Anchor Bible: Psalms* Vol. III (New York: Doubleday & Co., 1970).

The first is a condition, the condition of everyone by (fallen) nature, i.e., by reason of descent from the natural head of our race, who lost life for all of us. This is spiritual death, and is the specific teaching of Romans 5:12-19, elaborated at Ephesians 2:1, 5, 12 and 4:17-19. It consists essentially in alienation from the life of God. The remedy for this condition is to become united with the life of God through union with His Son (Eph. 2:5, 6). This matter has been treated at length in several earlier parts of this study.

The second is an event, the event which terminates physical life in the human body, physical death. '[I]t is appointed for man to die once' (Heb. 9:27). Both in Scripture and in all human verbal expression, *death*, *die* and *dead* usually mean physical death. 'Wretched man that I am! Who will deliver me from this body of death?' (Rom. 7:24). This is the subject of the present study. James 2:26 defines the event: 'the body apart from the spirit is dead.' It introduces each one who dies into a state called 'death' – the essence of which is separation of body and spirit, for which the universal remedy will be resurrection of all (1 Cor. 15:20; Rev. 20:12, 13).

The third is an event and state called the second death, mentioned only 'by name' in Revelation 20:14 and 21:8 where it is set in contrast with the life eternal (Rev. 21:9–22:5. This topic will be considered later in connection with the eternal destiny of the unsaved. Second death apparently will involve perpetuation of spiritual death (alienation from God) as well as a repetition of physical death after the 'resurrection of... the unjust' (Acts 24:15), also called by Jesus 'the resurrection of judgment' (John 5:29). It is without remedy – a truly immedicable woe.

Observe further that in Scripture death of any kind is not essentially annihilation (see later on eternal punishment) but (1) separation, (2) cessation of normal activity and (3) destruction (the rendering inoperative) of normal capacity.

I. The Nature of Physical Death.

1. Constitutionally, as a human being, normally existing as an ensouled body or stated otherwise (either is correct) an embodied soul, death is a radical rupture – a parturition of body from soul (or spirit). It should be noted that, though no doubt phrased in the customary idiom of the ancient Hebrews, more than folk opinion is involved in the first biblical description of the event of death – of Rachel in childbirth – the Scripture says, literally as in KJV, 'and it came to pass, as her soul was in departing, (for she died) ...' (Gen. 35:18). The text is straightforward Hebrew narrative – *wayehi betse'th naphshah ki methah*. The word for soul here is *nephesh* (life, soul, mind, person), not *ruaḥ* (breath, wind, spirit). *Nephesh* never means breath – hence, it is erroneous to translate, in twentieth-century medical idiom, 'as she breathed her last' (as NIV and others). This misfired 'dynamic equivalence' utterly misrepresents what Scripture says.

In a psalm of trust in his God to be his Savior both here and hereafter, David prayed to the LORD 'Into your hand I commit my spirit [*ruaḥ*, also breath or wind]' (Ps. 31:5; cf. v. 1). *Ruaḥ* is the word for the divine Spirit (Gen. 6:3), known in the New Testament as Third Person of the Godhead. The human spirit departs the body when one dies, though in this case the more usual word would be *nephesh*, soul (Ps. 78:39).[12] It is the word Job used for a 'ghost,' a 'disembodied being.'[13]

Robert Martin-Achard, in a remarkably complete work on this subject, says of the Old Testament theological assumptions about death:

> When a Israelite dies, his breath or spirit, *ruaḥ*, is withdrawn. It is not in fact a possession freely and eternally at man's disposal, it has only been lent to him, it belongs to God and so it is quite natural that, in the hour of death it should revert to its owner, Gen. 2:7; Ps. 104:29; Job 34:14 f.[14]

In our Lord's final prayer to the Father, as He was about to pronounce, 'It is finished,' He expressed Himself in David's phraseology: 'Father, into your hands I commit my spirit' (Luke 23:46). Matthew says, 'Jesus cried out again with a loud voice and yielded up his spirit' (Matt. 27:50), and John, 'he bowed his head and gave up his spirit' (John 19:30). Stephen later, at the moment of death, saw Jesus and said, 'Lord Jesus, receive my spirit' (Acts 7:59).

---

12. Calvin translated 'and he remembered that they were flesh: a spirit that passeth, and returneth not.' Calvin's translator argues: 'Dr Adam Clarke translates, "the spirit goeth away, and it doth not return." ....He considers the translation... "a wind that passeth away, and cometh not again [KJV]" to be a bad one, and that it may be productive of error; as if when a man dies, his being were ended, and death an eternal sleep.' John Calvin, *Commentary on the Book of Psalms*, Vol. III (Edinburgh, 1847), p. 254.
13. *BDB*, sub *ruaḥ*, p. 925.
14. Robert Martin-Achard, *From Death to Life: A Study of the Doctrine of the Resurrection in the Old Testament*, trans. J. P. Smith (Edinburgh: Oliver & Boyd, 1960), p. 31.

All these considerations furnish prima facie support for the assertion that death in human beings is not simply a permanent shutting down of functions of the body, with resulting dissolution, but, as noted above, a radical rupture, a parturition of body from soul (or spirit). James puts the same this way, 'the body apart from the spirit is dead' (James 2:26).

2. As to the physical side of mankind, death is an event, the cessation of life (indefinable but marked by activity) in the body (marked by recognizable signs) ushering the soul into a new state of existence. Everyone is familiar to some degree with signs of death, varying in degree by the amount of acquaintance with death in others. Common knowledge, medical science and law have different standards of judgment as to how and when death has certainly occurred. The body ceases to move, rigor mortis stiffens the joints and flesh after a few hours and, rather quickly, except for the undertaker's intervention with embalming, the corpse becomes corrupt and repulsive to any in its neighborhood. As Martha, 'the sister of the dead man,' said to Jesus, 'Lord, by this time he stinketh: for he hath been dead for four days' (John 11:39 KJV). Yet that is not the only reason for prompt burial. The presence of an exposed corpse is very depressing inasmuch as it reminds us starkly of our own mortality.

Scripture has two ways of expressing the fact of physical death. James says, 'the body... is dead.' Jesus said in His famous exchange with the Sadduces, 'And as for the resurrection of the dead, have you not read what was said to you by God: "I am the God of Abraham, and the God of Isaac, and the God of Jacob"? He is not God of the dead, but of the living' (Matt. 22:31, 32), that is, they live as spirits with God. Following Jewish custom He even referred to paradise, the 'third heaven' where God is specially present (2 Cor. 12:1-4), as 'Abraham's Bosom' (Luke 16:23). In such a case one may say biblically that the body is dead, but the spirit of the deceased is alive. On the other hand, though Jesus obliquely referred to Lazarus' death as 'Our friend Lazarus has fallen asleep,' He went on to say 'plainly, "Lazarus has died"' (John 11:11, 14). In such case it is not the body that is said to be dead, but the person. In the Old Testament the latter is the invariable manner of speaking, for revelation regarding the future life was obscure. It was Christ 'who... brought life and immortality to light through the gospel' (2 Tim. 1:10).

3. Comprehensively considered, physical death is something which happens to the entire person, the whole man.[15] Though, as we have just noticed, some texts speaking from a limited point of view refer to the body's dying, other passages speaking more comprehensively say the man, the whole man, dies. 'The beggar died.... the rich man also died.' Rachel 'died.' God told Adam, 'You shall surely die.' Eight times in Genesis 5 it is written, 'and he died.' 'You are dust, and to dust you shall return' (Gen. 3:19), and from all appearances to his sons, who (we may assume) buried Adam, the whole of Adam was placed in the ground. Yet the same Bible, no longer speaking the language of appearances, sometimes views the deceased as dead in body, but consciously existing ('alive') in soul/spirit. Thus Peter says of the Lord as 'being put to death in the flesh but made alive in the spirit' (1 Peter 3:18), and Paul says that 'our outer nature is wasting away [already], our inner nature is being renewed day by day...' (2 Cor. 4:16).

More about the state of body and soul after death will follow in connection with the 'intermediate state.'

II. The Causes of Physical Death.

1. Physical death, of course, is brought about by a multitude of material events and physical causes. These may be natural or otherwise, i.e. brought about by homicide. The medical profession, the keepers of public records of population and the news media, analyze and report the natural causes. The Bible takes cognizance of the same. Some passages cite human frailty as a cause, as Psalm 103:15, 16. Others speak of old age (e.g. Ps. 90:9, 10). Physical hazards are mentioned, such as the tower of Siloam which 'fell and killed' eighteen people (Luke 13:4)

---

15. The view that man is wholly and only a material being with a supremely complicated neuro-physical system whose functions account for consciousness, memory, character and the like is now often called physicalism. Those who also deny any creative intelligence (God) in bringing such marvelously complex beings as we are and any permanence beyond death (Denis Diderot of the 'Age of Reason,' Richard Dawkins, contemporary, and many others) are sometimes now called reductionist physicalists. Those who attempt to merge biblical Christian commitment with physicalism may call their view non-reductive physicalism. *Whatever Happened to the Soul: Scientific and Theological Portraits of Human Nature* (3 eds., 9 authors, Minneapolis: Fortress Press, 1998) seeks to explain why physicalism – i.e. materialistic monism – is the correct view of human nature, as opposed to dualism, body-soul, a physical substance and an immaterial substance. The editors' summary finds eternal life only in the re-created resurrection body. It is a serious book, setting forth 'Christian' monism of human nature in up-to-date scientific language. It is friendly to 'faith' but, as the editor acknowledges, hard to harmonize with the New Testament.

and how Ahaziah fell through a second-story lattice, causing fatal injury (2 Kgs. 1:2 ff.). Disease is also frequently the cause of death on the pages of Bible history: a King Herod died of one disease (Acts 9:37) and Abjah, son of King Jeroboam, of another (1 Kgs. 14:1-18). Plagues, famines, wars causing multiple deaths are part of all history, including biblical. The first physical death reported in Scripture was a homicide (Gen. 4:8). Foolish risk-taking is another frequent cause of death – 'the wicked... dies for lack of discipline, and because of his great folly he is led astray' (Prov. 5:22-23). The harlot's 'house is the way to Sheol, going down to the chambers of death' (Prov. 7:27).

2. The primary, i.e. originating cause, of physical death is sin – both original sin and personal sin. The former is taught explicitly in Romans 5:12-21, 'Therefore, just as sin came into the world through one man, and death through sin, and so death spread to all men because all sinned' (v. 12), stated in similar language later in the passage: 'many died through one man's trespass' (v. 15); 'For the judgment following one trespass brought condemnation' (v. 16); 'because of one man's trespass, death reigned through that one man' (v. 17); 'one trespass led to condemnation for all men' (v. 18); 'by the one man's disobedience the many were made sinners' (v. 19); 'sin reigned in death' (v. 21).

In a particular case Jesus almost spoofed the notion that a man's affliction by blindness was punishment for his own or his parent's sin (John 9:1-3). It is nevertheless true that 'the wages of sin is death' (Rom. 6:23) and every sin increases mortal danger: wisdom cries, 'he that sinneth against me wrongeth his own soul: all they that hate me love death' (Prov. 8:3, 36 KJV). Sexual license is the way to death and hell (Prov. 7:1-27).

Every major Christian group – Roman Catholic, Protestant, Eastern Orthodox – has taught that in some sense 'the fall of Adam, as the divinely appointed head of the race... brought this evil [when he first sinned] not only upon himself but upon all his posterity.'[16]

Repeatedly the Bible drives this truth home – every human death, either physical or spiritual, is punishment, the penalty applied by God for sin. Genesis 2:17 makes this plain. The Old Testament does not say much more about it but the New Testament makes much of the Adamic connection. The imputation of guilt for Adam's sin applies to everyone, infants to elders. Infants, of course, cannot suffer death for personal sins – only for original sin. On the one hand, 'sin when it is fully grown brings forth death' (James 1:15); on the other hand we are born 'dead in the trespasses and sins' (Eph. 2:1).

Pelagians of Augustine's time asserted that Adam was mortal at his creation, that like all earthly, created living things he was liable to death whether he sinned or not. Socinians of Reformation times and later Unitarians and liberalism generally since Schleiermacher – who reinterpreted most Christian doctrines to accommodate the age of reason – have agreed. Herman Bavinck wrote:

> When Pelagius, Socinus, Schleiermacher, Ritschl and a number of other theologians and philosophers separate death from its connection with sin, they are led by a defective insight between *ethos* [Gr. the customary, usual] and *physis* [Gr. nature]. Misery and death are not absolutely always consequences of punishment of great personal transgression (Luke 13:2; John 9:3); but that they are connected with sin, we learn every day. Who can number the victims of mammonism, alcoholism and licentiousness? Even spiritual sins exercise their influence on corporal life; envy is a rotteness of the bones (Prov. 14:30). This connection is taught us in a great measure, when it placed the not yet fallen man in Paradise, where death had not yet entered, and eternal life was not yet possessed and enjoyed; when it sends fallen man, who, however, is destined for redemption, into a world full of misery and death; and at last assigns to the wholly renewed man a new heaven and a new earth, where death, sorrow, crying, or pain shall no longer exist (Rev. 21:4).[17]

3. Satan, whom Jesus labeled a 'murderer [man-killer] from the beginning' (John 8:44), is an agent of death among mankind, in some not fully understood way. Hebrews 2, in a unique discussion of the divine purpose of the incarnation, says that it was 'that through death he might destroy the one who has the power of death, that is, the devil' (Heb. 2:14). Perhaps the book of Job explains this in part. Behind the natural agents which killed Job's children was the devil, who with God's permission destroyed them (Job 1:12, 18 19). It was Satan who accused (slandered) Job in God's presence and 'incited me [God] against him to destroy him without reason' (Job 2:3). Satan has the 'power of death' (Heb. 2:14) only within divine providence, though he is a very dangerous being – as a roaring lion seeking to devour (1 Peter 5:8).[18]

---

16. Lorraine Boettner, *Immortality* (Grand Rapids: Eerdmans, 1956, 1973), p. 13.
17. Herman Bavinck, 'Death,' *International Standard Bible Encyclopedia*, Vol. ii, ed. James Orr (Grand Rapids: Eerdmans, 1943), p. 813.
18. Compare 1 Chron. 21:1 with 2 Sam. 24:1.

4. Ultimately God Himself is the cause of death inasmuch as He imposed it on humankind as the only fitting penalty for sin. It is for this reason that limits must be placed on expectations of lengthening human lives indefinitely. The scriptural and national evidence for death as the judicial penalty for sin, rather than simply the way nature gets rid of one generation to make room for succeeding generations, is overwhelming, as assembled by A. H. Strong,[19] with modification. I refer the reader to these pages, though I have here abbreviated Strong's summary.

The original threat, 'you shall surely die' (Gen. 2:17) and 'to dust you shall return' (Gen. 3:19), is introduced obviously as punishment. Allusions to the threat confirm its penal quality, e.g. Numbers 16:29 – concerning the punishment of Korah's rebellion – speaks of common deaths as the visitation of 'the fate of all mankind,' where *paqadh* (visitation) means judicial, penal visitation or punishment. Caleb, though a godly man, was esteemed by his daughters as one who 'died for his own sin' (Num. 27:3). This shows that ancient Israelites understood the connection of physical death with punishment for sin. The prayer of Moses (Ps. 90:7-9, 11 KJV) shows that he understood death to be a punishment for sin, for the Psalm declares that in dying we are 'consumed' by God's 'anger,' 'troubled' by divine 'wrath' in view of 'our iniquities' and are passing away 'in' divine 'wrath.' Hezekiah's praise to God for a brief extension of life acknowledges that in such extension God had 'cast all my sins behind your [his] back' (Isa. 38:17).

The most significant human death is of course the death of Jesus, the 'man of sorrows, and acquainted with grief' (Isa. 53:3). Though Isaiah's prophecy predicted that Jesus would die at the hands of those who esteemed Him to be worthy of execution for His own sins (sabbath-breaking and blasphemy), the prophecy says, 'Yet it was the will of the Lord to crush him; he has put him to grief' (Isa. 53:10).

In cosmic perspective of the divine counsels, it is not incorrect to say that God killed Jesus, just as He does every other human being – not because Jesus was a sinner but because 'For our sake he [God] made him to be sin' (2 Cor. 5:21).

The New Testament is more specific, tracing all death of mankind to Adam's transgressions, as we have seen earlier (Rom. 5:12-21), and even says that people everywhere know at least certain sins deserve the punishment of death – 'they know God's decree that those who practice such things deserve to die' (Rom. 1:32). See also 1 Peter 4:6; 1 Corinthians 15:21, 22; and Romans 8 which draws the connection of death with divine punishment several times (8:3, 10, 11). The doctrine of redemption (atonement) specifically presupposes the same throughout the New Testament.

A Question.

If physical death is punishment for sin why do believing, forgiven sinners die like everyone else? If death is a penal evil why does God inflict it on those He has absolutely justified?

Let us start by reminding ourselves that 'for those who love God all things work together for good' (Rom. 8:28) and that nothing 'will be able to separate us from the love of God' including 'death' (Rom 8:38, 39). This means death is a means of our complete sanctification. It is not an invariably necessary means, because Enoch and Elijah were taken to God's presence without death and all believers who survive until Jesus comes at the *parousia* will be translated and completely sanctified without experiencing physical death. Further, death and a supposed subsequent purgatory in order to complete satisfaction for sins – either venial or mortal, as in the Roman eschatology – is a wholly unscriptural notion. It is certain that death of believers is compatible with God's work of vicarious redemption. For reasons of His own God sees fit not to give His people every benefit until the right time, on a schedule for our best interest, as 'wholesome and sanctifying chastisement.'[20] What are these benefits?

Let Robert Dabney explain. 'From the earliest day' the prospect of death 'begins to stir the sinner's conscience,' and serves 'to humble the proud soul, to mortify carnality, to check pride, to foster spiritual mindedness.'[21] He adds:

> It is the fact that sicknesses are premonitions of death, which makes them active means of sanctification. Bereavements through the death of friends form another class of disciplinary sufferings.... And, when the closing scene approaches, no doubt in every case where the believer is conscious, the pains of its approach,

---

19. A. H. Strong, op. cit., pp. 656–658.
20. R. L. Dabney, *Lectures on Systematic Theology*, first published, 1878 (Grand Rapids: Zondervan, 1972), p. 819.
21. ibid., p. 819.

> the solemn thoughts and emotions it suggests, are all used to ripen the soul rapidly for heaven.... we shall see that all other chastisements put together, are far less efficacious in checking inordinate affection and sanctifying the soul.... A race of sinners must be a race of mortals; Death is the only check... potent enough to prevent depravity from breaking out with a power which would make the state of the world perfectly intolerable.[22]

This is strong language about the moral restraint of death on evil in general and chastisement of believers for their sanctification, but it finds support in the words of Peter: 'Beloved, do not be surprised at the fiery trial when it comes upon you to test you, as though something strange were happening to you. But rejoice insofar as you share Christ's sufferings, that you may also rejoice and be glad when his glory is revealed' (1 Peter 4:12, 13; see also 14-19 and Phil. 3:7-10).

III. The Meaning of Death.

As I write, the news magazines and popular television and newspapers are recounting the deaths of June 6, 1944, on the beaches of Normandy, as well as memorializing the deaths in New York City, September 11, 2001. Hence, aside from Scripture, the question arises, what does death mean to mankind in general?

In the first place, it is the ultimate sacrifice for one's kin or nation. Though forgotten or even despised as false idealism by a few cynics or professed elite thinkers, this is so obvious to all who love life and place and admire courage, that nothing further needs to be said. Exemplified in the famous speech of Patrick Henry – 'Is life so dear or peace so sweet as to be purchased at the price of chains of slavery?' – it is also scriptural (John 15:13): 'Greater love has no one than this, that someone lays down his life for his friends.' Secondly, it is an extreme tragedy. Whether the grim reaper arrive in one's infancy, youth, maturity or extreme old age, death is a tragic end. As philosophers have been wont to say, it takes a long life to learn how to live, hence to take away life just when one is prepared to perform well seems wrong. Death is associated with tears, mourning, earth, dust and ashes, as Job reflected at great length.

The Scriptures assert death's tragedy to be an inevitability (Eccles. 2:15, 16; 3:1, 2, 19; 9:5). When one puts down an unwanted kitten or slaughters a sheep or chicken one is reminded that we must die too: 'For the fate of the sons of men and the fate of beasts is the same; as one dies, so dies the other. They all have the same breath, and man has no advantage over the beasts' (Ecc. 3:19 RSV). On a summer day I put down a sick kitten with a blow to the back of the head in the sight of my late wife. She wept profusely. In a few weeks she also died and I wept. In a short time you and I shall shut down all operations and leave behind all our possessions. The place that knew us shall know us no more. Those who love us shall weep. Tragic, is it not?

Considered in view of its tragic aspect, death is both a curse – which of course is primary (Gen. 3:17-19) – and a dreadful enemy, the last to be destroyed, as Paul said (1 Cor. 15:25, 26).

Aside from the Christian hope, death remains also a mystery – even more mysterious, however, in pre-Christian times. Though Job was confident he would 'see God... on my side' (Job 19:26, 27 ASV; 'for myself' KJV) after death, resurrection of the body was not revealed to him. Job 19:26 probably should be rendered 'yet without my flesh' (mibesari, the m prefix is ambiguous, either 'out from' or 'away from'). Earlier he raised the question, 'If a man dies, shall he live again?' (Job 14:14), followed by an eagerly embraced glimmer of hope that he might live again. There is more sure hope for a tree, that 'cut down' sometimes sprouts again, than for a man who 'lies down and rises not again; till the heavens are no more he will not awake' (v. 12). Yet he asks God to remember him in the grave at some future time (v. 13). It was Christ Himself, who for us has 'brought light and immortality to light through the gospel' (2 Tim. 1:10).

Perhaps the most severe sadness about death, both for those about to die and family and friends who survive them, is the consequent complete exclusion from all social connections which have given meaning to life. A standard Old Testament expression, which often means death by execution, is to be 'cut off from people' (see many examples in Lev. 7, 17, 19, 20). It meant this for the LORD's Servant-Messiah who was 'cut off out of the land of the living [people]' (Isa. 53:8 KJV), as leprous King Uzziah was excluded from the temple premises – 'excluded from the house of the LORD' (2 Chron. 26:21). The Sweet Singer observed sadly, 'As for man, his days are like grass... for the wind passes over it... and its place knows it no more' (Ps. 103:15-16, see Job 20:9; 24:20).

22. ibid., p. 819.

To the unsaved, 'having no hope and without God in the world' (Eph. 2:12), death takes on many different faces. Obviously not all view it in exactly the same way. Paul, assuming momentarily a hedonist outlook, exclaimed, 'Let us eat and drink, for tomorrow we die' (1 Cor. 15:32). Qoheleth ('the preacher') says the same in various ways (e.g. Eccles. 3:16-22): this life is the only one you have so enjoy it to the full. But it is also, for those without a sure hope, a complete and final deprivation, making this life an unprofitable enterprise. You came into the world naked and so shall you leave it. 'This also is a sore evil.... Life is a striving for wind.' Many people of a more stoic (i.e., ancient stoic) outlook thought of death as a welcome escape from life, i.e. life not of joy and happiness but of intolerable evils and hardships. There are situations in which death as an end to excruciating pain is viewed as welcome relief (see Rev. 9:1-6). In one of his moods Job thought this way (Job 3:20-22). Believers under stress (like Job) may speak in this vein, though the Apostle also under great stress was ambivalent on the point (Phil. 1:23-26). For the person who does not have assurance of hope in Christ, the 'fear of death' is a 'bondage' (Heb. 2:15) from which few are ever quite delivered, because whatever one's profession one cannot evade an innate conviction that death is only a precursor to divine judgment (Heb. 9:27; cf. Rom. 2:3).

As for the Christian, even one who has grown in grace and has counted his blessings, there is a lingering 'fear of death' even though 'delivered' from 'bondage' to the fear of death (Heb. 2:14, 15), and 'free... from the law of sin and death' (Rom 8:2). Satan's power has been nullified (Heb. 2:14, 15), but faith must embrace the announcement of the same each day. '[W]e walk by faith, not by sight' (2 Cor. 5:7) and for now we 'see in a mirror dimly' (1 Cor. 13:12). Yet faith, even though it does not fail, is stronger at some times than others, otherwise we would not be advised to exhort one another in faith (Heb. 3:13). '[L]ife and immorality' have truly been 'brought... to light through the gospel' (2 Tim. 1:10) and we are encouraged to walk in the light. That light has robbed death of some of its mystery. We are free to enter fully into assurance and certainty from our natural feelings of horror of death, for as Paul assured the wavering Corinthian believers, 'all things are yours, whether... life or death or the present or the future, all are yours; and you are Christ's; and Christ is God's' (1 Cor. 3:21-23 RSV). He has assured us today that nothing will ever separate us in death or life from God and His love (Rom. 8:1, 2, 38, 39).

The Outlook of Old Testament Believers on Death and the Future Beyond the Grave.

The inter-testamental literature and other Jewish sources have indirect but not decisive bearing on this question, just as their bearing on New Testament faith is indirect. The apocryphal book known as *The Wisdom of Solomon*, for example, has immortality, judgment, future rewards and punishments as major themes, and the Gospels as well as other Jewish sources demonstrate there was general acceptance of the teachings we have been reviewing, among Jews of Jesus' time. No Old Testament passage, however, plainly teaches such beliefs, though they might be assumed by the writers.

The principle of progressive revelation would lead us to infer that special revelation (or revelation as opposed to what used to be called 'natural light') began with Abraham's very special call, and further that his faith responded to much less revealed truth than subsequent generations. Moses would have known more than Abraham, David more than Moses and Isaiah, and Daniel more than David.

Israel's history and religious beliefs, as reconstructed in the mold of modern criticism, imposes an evolutionary literary growth of the Old Testament, before attempting a history of Israel's religious beliefs. Gerhard Von Rad, a prestigious representative of the liberal critical approach, is typical and explicit on this matter.[23] He is not sure there ever was an Abraham; and even if we were certain, we do not really know for certain what his beliefs were. Rather, we read in the Genesis account what the priestly (P) writer, or the 'Yahwist historian' writing over a thousand years later, wished to project back into Abraham's (or Moses' or Gideon's or Samuel's) time.

---

23. Gerhard Von Rad, *Old Testament Theology*, 2 vols, trans. D. M. G. Slatker (Edinburgh: Oliver and Boyd, 1962, 1965). Though Gerhard Von Rad published *Theologie des Alten Testaments* in 1957 and the English translation in 1962 it seems still to be the leader in its field outside strictly evangelical orthodox circles. When I last taught Old Testament theology – a special course at Bethel Theological Seminary in 1977 – it was dominant. He wrote under the immediate influence of Barth and in the tense atmosphere of the decade following World War II in Germany, favorable to the paradoxes and dialectic of Krisis (neo-orthodox) theology. As W. Brueggemann says in his introduction to the 1962 edition, 'Von Rad is not free of nineteenth century positivism' (v.i. p. xxvi). He tried to reconstruct the history of Israel's religious traditions, with his own 'fix' of layers and strands in the 'Hexateuch' (Genesis–Joshua), on the basic JEDP documentation structure of nineteenth-century criticism, modified by 'form criticism' and a Barth-like resort to paradox. The 'evangelical' element is his emphasis on the 'witness' or 'credo recitals' of Deuteronomy 1:20-24 and Joshua 24:1-13, together with rightful recognition of the 'mighty acts of God' in the Exodus from Egypt and settlement in the promised land. I make this too brief diversion because every reader should be aware of both the errors and great values, as textual commentator, of G. Von Rad. Post-moderns, multiculturalists and pluralists are said to resort to his pronouncements too.

According to the usual portrayal, the early Hebrews had no individual expectation of a soul's existence after death, only at most a shadowy presence of some sort in an equally shadowy *sheol* (translated *grave*, *hell*, *pit*, etc., in English Bibles). Their interest was only in long life, a prosperous, mature age, and a numerous and prosperous line of descendants. In very recent times this critical orthodoxy has been modified somewhat by the supposed concept of 'corporate personality,' by which the following verdict on the Hebrew mindset on death emerged. I am citing the summary of Milton McC. Gatch, an Episcopalian scholar whose book has been widely read among students and clergy. I quote at length: 'It is not possible,' he says,

> to speak in individual terms of Abraham, for the Hebraic mind does not conceive of the situation as we do. There is no way to separate Abraham from the clan he produces. Even his personality is indistinct from that of the tribe. Thus, one can only speak anachronistically of his death as an end since, even dead, Abraham continues to be an important aspect of the corporate personality. Such is the meaning of... 'he was gathered to his kin' [Gen. 25:8]... The man who dies becomes... a name in the genealogical list; and as such he never ceases to be a part of the continuing story of the People.
>
> This frame of mind made quite inconceivable the question of an afterlife and probably contributed to the fact that Hebrew thought never developed a notion of a soul or life-force which is separable from historical man... Personality and identity are terms which attach not to persons but to the People; thus, when one dies, personality and identity are not disrupted, for the People continues. Only the possibility that one's line [of descendants] may not be fruitful gives rise to anxiety in the face of death.[24]

A few pages later Dr Gatch asserts that when the early church Fathers assumed 'a doctrine of the soul' they were 'unlike the biblical writings.'[25]

This outlook, though common among critical writers, has met many strong challenges – as we have suggested in chapter 1, above, where this subject was preliminarily raised. The corpus of liberal-critical literature which has arisen on this subject is too large to report here, except for a striking repartee between Oscar Cullman, an eminent New Testament scholar of the University of Basil, and Harry A. Wolfson, a Professor of Hebrew Literature and Philosophy at Harvard University. Cullman, in a lecture, 'The Immortality of the Soul or the Resurrection of the Dead' (Ingersoll Lecture, Harvard University for 1955),[26] strenuously asserted that the Bible has no doctrine of immortality of the soul. The Bible has only the doctrine of bodily resurrection after an interim of nothingness. The whole man goes out of existence at death: 'The soul can be killed. There must be resurrection for both; for since the Fall the whole man is "sown corruptible".'[27] Jesus was so thoroughly afraid to be alone in Gethsemane because He shrank from the nothingness of death. This, Cullman contrasts with Socrates' serene confidence in the hour of his death – serene and hopeful because he had a Greek doctrine of immortality of the soul.

A year later Harry A. Wolfson gave the Ingersoll lecture. He easily demonstrated that Cullman not only had the facts wrong but had misconstrued them. The Jews of Jesus' time believed in immortality *and* resurrection. The early church Fathers were of the same mind. I quote a few lines and press on to other matters.

> With regard to immortality ... the Fathers knew that the Platonic conception of immortality is not exactly the same as the scriptural conception of it. ... This distinction between the Platonic and the scriptural conception of immortality is constantly stressed by the Fathers. One of the first ... Justin Martyr ... says, 'I pay no regard to Plato,' and... argues, evidently against Plato's conception of immortality, that, if the soul lives, 'it lives not as being itself life, but as partaking of life,' and this because 'God wills it to live, and hence it will cease to live whenever he may please that it shall live no longer, for it is not the property of the soul to have life in itself as it is the property of God.'[28]

He adds, with documentation, that 'the same view is expressed also by Irenaeus, Tatian, Theophilus, Arnobius, Lactantius and others.'[29] Though he gives a rather derogatory explanation of every view taken by the Fathers regarding the origin of human souls, Wolfson correctly agreed:

---

24. Milton McC. Gatch, *Death: Meaning and Mortality in Christian Thought and Contemporary Culture* (New York: Seabury Press, 1969), pp. 37, 38.
25. ibid., p. 52.
26. Oscar Cullman, Harry A. Wolfson, Werner Jaeger and Henry J. Cadbury, ed. Krister Stendahl, *Immortality and Resurrection, Death in the Western World: Two Conflicting Currents of Thought* (New York: Macmillan Co., 1965), pp. 9–53.
27. ibid., p. 28.
28. Harry Wolfson, ibid., p. 57.
29. op. cit., p. 57.

> However the nature of the soul is described by us, whether as corporeal or as incorporeal, and however the origin of the soul conceived of by us, whether as created with the body or as pre-existent or as inherited, the soul is unlike the body and is not an inseparable part of the body. It can therefore survive the body.[30]

The Old Testament does not have much to say by way of positive statement about death, 'the afterlife' and the state of the soul when life in the body ends. In the next chapter, 'The Intermediate State,' we shall attempt a synthesis of the materials. At this point, however, some conclusions should be made. In drawing conclusions we acknowledge that there are no positive statements in the Old Testament such as James and Paul make on the subject. Most of the biblical data express only the thoughts of ordinary people and customary expressions; some are mere expressions of feeling. Hence not all should be interpreted as revealed truth. Ecclesiastes is in a special class of texts, for the author through most of the book assumes a skeptical, sometimes cynical, 'under the sun' philosophy, though in the final chapter he speaks straightforwardly, about death and its issues.[31]

Sometimes a poet expresses dread (almost like a post-enlightenment existentialist's 'concept of dread') of death as he laments over his backslidden state or mourns in repentance; for no Old Testament believer had sufficient revelation on the forgiveness of sin in the future redemptive work of Christ. The author of Psalm 88, for example, did not understand Isaiah 53:4-6 as Philip explained it to the eunuch (Acts 8:27-39) and as we deeply appreciate. Some of the Psalms seem almost to find no hope for now or the future. Though one Psalmist knows of God's present unfailing forgiveness and trusts to dwell in the house of the Lord forever, another questions God's faithfulness after destruction of the body or if God's loving kindness will be declared in the grave (Ps. 88:11). Perhaps the author, his conscience awakened by God's law, was not equally assured by atoning sacrifice of animals 'which,' as he must have sensed, 'can never take away sin.' Those sacrifices really made 'remembrance again of sins every year.' The 'remission of sins' in those times 'through the forbearance of God' was validated when 'God… put forward' Christ Jesus 'as a propitiation' (Rom. 3:24-26) but that was dimly known, if at all, beyond the future's horizon. Sometimes, it seems clear, the poet is thinking that one's praise of God proclaimed in one's living body will cease when once the body is still in death. This is David's lament in Psalm 6:4, 5 (5, 6 in Hebrew): 'Turn, O LORD, deliver my life; save me for the sake of your steadfast love. For in death there is no remembrance [made] of you; in Sheol who will give you praise?' Even with the light of the New Testament revelation we believers sometimes share these gloomy feelings. And poetry, even biblical poetry at its best, is by definition 'literature, emotional and concrete in content, rhythmical in form.' We read these Psalms today (sometimes in united worship) with some of the ancients' fervor and feeling; and many struggling with severe, life-threatening disease or injury are no less fervent than good King Hezekiah when he pled with God for a few more years.

For reasons we do not know and have no right to demand, the Old Testament does not provide full information on the saints' expectations. We are not, however, dependent either on the critical biblical theologians or speculation, because the New Testament has its own biblical theology of the Old Testament. It is first of all Christological. We must not be 'foolish ones, and slow of heart to believe all that the prophets have spoken' for it was 'necessary that the Christ should suffer… and enter into his glory' as Jesus explained to the wondering pedestrians of the Emmaus road (Luke 24:23-27). Once we see the Old Testament this way our hearts will burn as Jesus opens to us the Scriptures (Luke 24:32).

The patriarchs had a 'theology of hope' far brighter than the current theologians of that school suppose. Theirs was a sure expectation of life with God in an intimate fellowship with Him – though not yet restoration of their bodies. These remarks are not dependent on indistinct or tenuous inductions from obscure texts, for they rest on the inspired comments of the holy author of the book of Hebrews. Let the author of Hebrews explain. Abraham and Sara, as Noah, Enoch and Abel before them, 'all died in faith, not having received the things promised, but having seen them and greeted them from afar, and having acknowledged that they were strangers and exiles on the earth. For people who speak thus make it clear that they are seeking a homeland. If they had been thinking of that land from which they had gone out, they would have had opportunity to return. But as it is, they desire a better country, that is, a heavenly one' (Heb. 11:13-16).

Their 'hope' was not only earthly but also heavenly. They knew that their eternal destiny was not the grave nor was their only immortality in survival of family or nation. Hebrews goes on to say that Abraham 'considered that

---

30. op. cit., p. 76.
31. Ecclesiastes is an inspired account, in part, of a cynical outlook on life.

God was able even to raise... from the dead' and that Moses believed in an 'invisible' realm (Heb. 11:19, 23-27). He traces the belief of others from Abel to the martyrs of the second century BC that they had a future beyond death – in heaven as well as earth – and permanent survival of personal self-consciousness in a place near God in heaven.

It must be acknowledged that there are few passages in the Hebrew Bible relating directly either to immortality or the 'resurrection of the flesh' as in the ancient creeds. One wonders, Why? Perhaps, as Jesus explained about another matter, they were not yet ready to receive it. Having been saturated with the utterly false preoccupation of their Egyptian rulers with death for 430 years and living alongside the Canaanite culture, with its elaborate mythology of gods and deified men, the topic would have led to more severe backsliding and apostasy than did occur. There is a parallel in the gospel age: the New Testament says nothing directly about the salvation of infants in general or specifically of those who die in infancy. How many Christian mothers in desperate circumstances, or seeing their young likely to be seduced by home or community circumstances, might have slain their babies if some verse of the New Testament were plainly to say, 'All infants who die are saved and go immediately to heaven.'

The episode of Jesus' exchange with the Sadducees during His last week (Matt. 22:23-33; cf. Acts 23:8) demonstrates that denial of the permanent existence (not the sort of natural immortality which only God has, 1 Tim. 6:16) of the human soul after death of the body was exceptional in the Israel of Jesus' time. The same inference may be drawn from Jesus' earlier Parable of the Rich Man and Lazarus. It also manifests a common belief in some sort of separation of the wicked from the righteous in the world of the dead immediately following death.

Resurrection of the body will be treated here shortly, but at this point it is relevant to note that the bodily translation of Enoch and of Elijah imply enduring human life in an invisible realm. First Samuel 2:6 says that 'The LORD kills and brings to life; he brings down to Sheol and raises up' and Daniel 12:2 specifically predicts a bodily resurrection of the righteous dead (at least). Psalm 16:8-11 expresses David's faith in deliverance of his soul from Sheol (perhaps the grave). Passages such as Hosea 13:14; Isaiah 25:6-8; and 26:19-21 relate the prophets' expectation of resurrection of the body after an 'interim' (perhaps millennium) not described. The great thirty-seventh chapter of Ezekiel prophesies about Israel's future national resurrection as the resurrection to physical life of a 'valley of dry bones.' This has bearing on faith in personal resurrection, as J. A. Schep has said:

> Although this passage does not refer to resurrection of the dead... the question arises, is this symbolic language not inexplicable unless one assumes that the prophet and his people were familiar with the conception of a bodily resurrection of the dead as an eschatological event.[32]

Our attention next turns to the question of the present condition of those who have passed through death into that invisible world. Resurrection of their bodies is an event still future. Where are they now and in what condition?

---

32. J. A. Schep, *The Nature of the Resurrection Body* (Grand Rapids: Eerdmans, 1964), pp. 56, 57.

3
Where Are the Dead Now and What Is Their Condition?: the Doctrine of the Intermediate State

Christians have always believed that after death there will be resurrection of all the dead followed by judgment and heaven for the saved as well as hell for the lost – to put the matter starkly. The sequence between death and resurrection is plain enough in Scripture, but much mystery exists with regard to the time, place and condition of the soul between death and resurrection. We have seen that despite intense attack in the last several generations against the existence of the soul and its permanent, conscious existence after death, it remains the conviction of almost everyone. So widespread, enduring and strong is this conviction among pagans, Jews, Christians and secularists – to say nothing of the major non-Christian religions – that some say 'it is so knitted into human consciousness that it cannot be repressed without denying our fundamental humanity.'[1] If so, it has the forensic force of a consensus gentium, i.e., common consent of the (human) race.

In such a case it is no wonder that in the presence of death – particularly of kin or friend – we have urgent questions about where the souls of the dead are, what might be their condition and for how long. If death is looming and one sees the grim reaper coming near, the question may occupy frantic attention. Several of Jesus' parables build on that fact.

'Intermediate state' is not a biblical expression, but it is a good name for the biblical doctrine, designating the state of the soul (or spirit) between the events of death and resurrection. We know that people die. We know that there is a resurrection coming for all the dead (John 5:28) and that it will be in connection with the future, Second Advent of the LORD. The interval between, when the bodies of the dead have 'returned to their dust' and their spirits are somewhere else, is an intermediate period. Hence theology has appropriately coined the term, 'the intermediate state.' Those who affirm future resurrection but deny existence of a soul separate from the body deny also, of course, such an 'intermediate' state. In such a case, nothing is nothing. There is no state at all except non-existence.

Before proceeding, some humble acknowledgments and cautions are appropriate. The first is that the subject is wrapped in much mystery. Revelation has provided so little that the theologian has few resources to consult. 'The New Testament places emphasis on the eschatological developments at the end, and leaves many things connected with the intermediate state in darkness.'[2] The poets have responded to the mystery in two ways: the imaginative, with elaborate geography of the places of the dead as Dante's *Purgatorio, Inferno* and *Paradiso;* and the reflective, with sad-hopeful lyrics such as John Donne's,

---

1. Thomas Oden, *Life in The Spirit* (San Francisco: Harper Collins, 1993), p. 377.
2. Gerhardus Vos, 'Hades,' *International Standard Bible Encyclopedia*, Vol. ii, p. 1315.

> Death be not proud, though some have called thee...
> One short sleep past, we wake eternally,
> And Death shall be no more, Death, thou shalt die![3]

Such meager information as the Bible furnishes must be interpreted with great caution. Among the cautions the interpreter should observe are these:

1. A sharp distinction should be made between the expressed opinions of the people who appear on the pages and in the narratives on the one hand and revealed biblical truth on the other. Not everything they say is 'gospel truth' or revelation of any kind. A New Testament example is the disciples' belief in ghosts. The fact that ten disciples in an upper room 'were startled and frightened and thought they saw a spirit' (Luke 24:37) or that when 'they saw [Jesus] walking on the sea they thought it was a ghost' does not mean that souls of the departed really walk about. I found that all my class of Chinese students at a seminary in China assumed as a matter of course that souls prowl around cemeteries for awhile after burial of their bodies. Beliefs of this kind are hard to shake, for they are rooted deep in the subconscious. Death is such a rude and implacable intruder that strong group-opinion about death, long held, of whatever origin (let the psychologists of the subconscious have their field day!), are not fully erased by Christian revelation. The superstitions of pagan Europe did not disappear when Christianity replaced the heathen religions. They are still alive and well even in sophisticated circles.

It seems to me therefore that Job's opinions about Sheol – whether the grave or some postmortem residence of the soul – do not necessarily relate to reality. It is certain that the ancient Near and Middle East had an elaborate mythology about an unseen world, peopled by quarrelsome gods, who exercised some control over the destiny of human souls and where elite men and women were assigned to places of joy or torment.

The beliefs of faithful adherents of the LORD, in the Old Testament, express much bewilderment in the face of death yet have confidence that they will not be separated from God's care and love in the realm of death. The learned and pious G. F. Oehler surveyed all evidences of beliefs about the life of the soul after death among the Psalms. He found many possible expressions of optimistic expectations of something like 'The Father's House' of John 14 (Ps. 16:10; 17:15; 48:14; 49:15; 68:20; 73:24, 26; among others). Especially impressive is the use of the same verb *laqach*, 'he will receive me' (Ps. 49:15), also used in Genesis 5:24 for the translation of Enoch. Yet Oehler's closing sentences on personal eschatological hope in this part of the Bible show how little doctrine can confidently be constructed on expressions either of despair or of confident hope by Old Testament people. After quoting 'My flesh and my heart may fail, but God is the strength of my heart and my portion for ever' (Ps. 73:26), Oehler goes on to say that these words

> express the confidence of the Psalmist that even if his heart fails in death, his communion with God cannot be dissolved. Still, even in these passages we have (as Delitzsch well observes) no direct word from God for this hope to lean on; they do but express the postulate of faith, that for the just, existence must issue in glory and in the permanent possession of communion with God. How this is to be realized cannot, however, be shown. Hence the triumph of faith over death and the grave is accompanied by the complaint, so strongly and incisively expressed in Psalm 88 [e.g. 'Is your steadfast love declared in the grave, or your faithfulness in Abaddon? Are your wonders known in the darkness, or your righteousness in the land of forgetfulness?' vv. 11, 12] that the seals of death and Sheol remain as yet unbroken.[4]

Dr Oehler found nothing more of specific revelation about life of the soul beyond the grave in the rest of the Old Testament though he pointed out that the believers are assured that God's justice would prevail there. He found in Job 19:25-27 a conviction that after death God will manifest Himself to Job and continue in communion with Him.[5]

I am in agreement. I do not regard much of anything said of Sheol, in the narrative and poetry of the Old Testament, as specifically revelational in character.[6] Further, as regards the references to Hades (the Greek translation of Sheol in the LXX and New Testament) even as employed by Jesus in Luke 16:23 – 'in Hades, being in torment, he lifted up his eyes' – no one knows what Aramaic word Jesus used. The Greek word Luke used, 'Hades,' literally

---

3. John Donne, 1st, 13th and 14th lines of his Sonnet, *'Death,'* 1633.
4. Gustav Friederich Oehler, *Theology of the Old Testament*, trans. Geo. E. Day (New York: Funk and Wagnalls, 1883), p. 560.
5. ibid., pp. 564, 565.
6. More about this later.

means 'the unseen.' Let us take it to mean just that, the unseen world, wherever the souls of the wicked dead are in God's universe. I agree with the learned and faithful theologian, W. G. T. Shedd, that a compartmented underworld, where both righteous and wicked go at death, has, as Paul said of the 'many "gods" and many "lords"' of the Greeks, 'no real existence' (1 Cor. 8:4-6). I do not think we should bring any of that Greek and Near-Eastern mythology to our theology of the intermediate state. If we were to do so we would have to organize 'the other world' like the civil society of ancient Babylon into tribes, and according to Babylonian court protocol. See also Isaiah chapter 14 and Ezekiel 32:17-32.

2. Several New Testament passages (such as Heb. 11:16) inform us that Old Testament saints desired a 'heavenly' country, a 'better' place, a 'city' (Gr. *polis*, a civil community), and one of them at least (Moses) understood that both present afflictions and sinful pleasures are temporary; that there is 'reward' and 'recompense' in the future (Heb. 11:23-26); and that they understood there would be a resurrection (Heb. 11:35; cf. v. 19). This all means that the Old Testament does not tell us all of what the believers of the time knew from God and believed, any more than we know everything Jesus said to the Apostles which is unrecorded. C. H. Hodge's remarks are very helpful:

> We have in the New Testament an inspired, and, therefore, an infallible commentary on the Old Testament scriptures.... We have then in the New Testament the most explicit declarations, not only that the doctrine of a future state was revealed in the Old Testament, but that from the beginning it was part of the faith of the people of God.[7]

3. The Old Testament is now a Christian book, made so by the fulfillment of its prophecies and completion of its narratives. Jesus declared it so (Luke 24:25-27, 44-47). It is proper to read it in the light of New Testament revelation and history, but not to read the New Testament into the Old Testament.

4. Jesus by His life, death, teaching, resurrection and Ascension has 'brought life and immortality to light' but as far as factual information in literal, descriptive language is concerned, the New Testament reveals only a little more than the Old Testament. David knew he would 'dwell in the house of the Lord forever' after traveling through 'the valley of the shadow of death.' We know more about that 'house of the Lord' because Jesus said 'many rooms' are being prepared there for us (John 14). We expect to be met by the Lord when we pass through the door but we know only a few things about the ambience and furnishings of God's world beyond that door. It is incorrect to apply descriptions of the eternal future state to the present heaven. We know who is there – the living God, angels, the church triumphant, the Judge of all and Jesus (Heb. 12:21-23).

Alfred, Lord Tennyson, Britain's poet laureate, put it this way in the fourth stanza of his memorable 'Crossing the Bar':

> For though from out our bourne of time and place
> The floods may bear me far,
> I hope to see my Pilot face to face
> When I have crossed the bar.

Several Views of the Intermediate State.

Roman Catholic Teaching of Different Destinations.

Roman dogma insists there are (or have been) five different immediate destinations for the souls of mankind at death: *limbus patrum, limbus infantum* (or *puerorum*), purgatory, heaven and hell. Three of these were rejected wholly by the Reformers, and Protestants still vigorously reject them to this day. The three rejected by all Protestants should at least be understood as Roman Catholics are taught to believe.

1. *Limbus Patrum*, according to a standard Roman Catholic authority, is 'The Limbo of the Fathers; a place and state of rest wherein the souls of the just who died before Christ's ascension were detained until he opened Heaven to them: referred to as "Abraham's bosom" (Luke 16:22) and "Paradise" (Luke 23:43).'[8] The article cites also Ephesians 4:9 and 1 Peter 3:18-20. As explained by Ludwig Ott, 'the heart of the earth' (Matt. 12:40), where he says Jesus' soul was during the 'three days', is the location of *Limbus Patrum*. Acts 2:24 is said to refer to Jesus' deliverance (resurrection) from hell (= Hades = *limbus patrum*). Paul's reference to a descent of the Lord to 'the

---

7. Charles H. Hodge, *Systematic Theology III* (Grand Rapids: Eerdmans, 1970), p. 714.
8. *The Catholic Encyclopedic Dictionary*, ed. Donald Atwater, 3rd ed. (New York: Macmillan, 1961), sub 'Limbo,' p. 293.

lower parts of the earth' (Eph. 4:9) and a preaching by Christ 'to the spirits in prison' and the testimony of ancient 'tradition' are cited. 'The purpose of the descent into Hell, according to the general teaching of the theologians, was freeing of the just in Limbo by the application of the fruits of Redemption.'[9] Views of some modern evangelicals are similar – as for example the footnotes in the Scofield Bible to which we will advert shortly.

2. *Limbus Infantum* (or *limbus puerorum*) – 'the Limbo of children.' 'It is of faith that all, children and adults, who leave the world without the Baptism of water, blood or desire, and therefore in original sin, are excluded from the vision of God in heaven. The great majority of theologians teach that such children and unbaptized adults, free from grievous actual sin, enjoy eternally a state of perfect natural happiness, knowing and loving God by the use of their natural powers.'[10] This doctrine meshes with the Roman view that original sin did not deprave (vitiate) 'the image of God' (defined as rational faculties) but is intact without being affected by and toward sin. Taken according to the above quotation, the heathen are not really 'lost' and John 3:36 does not really mean what it says. Non-faith is implicit faith if one has not sinned egregiously.

3. Purgatory. The doctrine of purgatory, together with the 'sacrament' of penance (confessional) and 'sacrifice of the mass,' is the economic engine which for centuries financially supported the vast hierarchical structure and the institutions of the papal church. Rome's teaching regarding purgatory is not in every respect uniform. First dogmatically shaped by Gregory the Great (c. AD 600), the twenty-fifth Session of Trent asserted: 'that there is a Purgatory, and that the souls there detained are helped by the suffrages [prayers for the souls of the departed] of the faithful, but principally by the acceptable sacrifice of the altar [special, designated, private Masses, by priests paid to perform these Masses].' Though the Roman doctors find a vague connection of this doctrine with Matthew 5:26; Matthew 12:32; and 1 Corinthians 3:12-15, 'The main proof for the existence of the cleansing fire lies in the testimony of the Fathers.'[11] Also citing the Apocrypha, 'according to 2 Maccabees 12:42-45, the Jews prayed for their fallen on whom had been found donaries of the idols, that their sins might be forgiven them. Then they sent twelve thousand drachmas of silver to Jerusalem for sacrifice to be offered in expiation.'[12]

This complicated doctrine has been a modern embarrassment, and is stated in very vague language in recent dogmatic deliverances on the subject. The Catechism of 1994 does not even speak of a place called purgatory, affirming only that 'The Church gives the name PURGATORY to this final purification of the elect, which is entirely different from the punishment of the damned.'[13]

John McClintock and James Strong comment that 'it is well known that Roman Catholic principles are of great elasticity in their application, so that there is always some way for the Church of getting out of difficulties.'[14]

Rome believes that 'those souls gathered round Jesus and Mary in Paradise... share with the holy angels in the exercise of divine power... when they intercede for us.'[15]

We must however rejoice that bishops of a Synod of Rome, on May 11, 1979, issued the following in an important elaboration of the last statement of the Apostles' Creed, 'I believe in the life everlasting.' It is third of seven paragraphs.

> The Church affirms that a spiritual element survives and subsists after death, an element endowed with consciousness and will, so that the human self subsists. To designate this element the Church uses the word 'soul,' the accepted term in the usage of Scripture and tradition. Although not unaware that this term has various meanings in the Bible, the Church thinks that there is no valid reason for rejecting it; moreover, she considers that the use of some word as a vehicle is absolutely indispensable in order to support the faith of Christians.[16]

4. Believers who have attained a state of perfection go immediately to heaven. There are classes among these. Some are 'beatified' and some not. The Medieval Schoolmen distinguished three classes of 'the blessed.'[17]

5. All unbaptized (though there is a 'baptism of desire' in lieu of water baptism), and those who subsequent to baptism lose the grace of baptism through mortal sin and die unreconciled to the church, go immediately to hell.

---

9. Ludwig Ott, *Fundamentals of Catholic Dogma*, 4th ed. (Rockford, IL: TAN Books, 1974) pp. 191, 192. Thomas Aquinas, *Summa Theologica* III.52.5.
10. *A Catholic Dictionary*, ibid.
11. Ott, op. cit., p. 484.
12. Ott, op. cit., p. 483.
13. *Catechism of 1994*, para. 1031, see 1030–1032, pp. 268, 269.
14. McClintock and Strong, *Cyclopedia* Vol. V, 'Limbo,' p. 435.
15. Vatican Council II, vol. 2, *More Postconciliar Documents*, new rev. ed., ed. Austin Flannery, O.P. (Northport, NY: 1982), pp. 394, 395.
16. ibid., p. 502.
17. op. cit., p. 502.

Doctrine of Soul Sleep.

I have referred in an earlier chapter to some of the forms the doctrine of Soul Sleep takes in a number of modern advocates.[18] Oscar Cullmann asserted non-existence of the person between death and resurrection and thought he had proved it.[19] Henry Wolfson thought that Cullmann was greviously in error, that Jesus 'believed his soul was immortal' and that, beginning with Justin Martyr, the Fathers – against Plato's conception of natural, intrinsic immortality – believed the soul lives on because (quoting Justin Martyr) 'God wills it to live… for it is not the property of the soul to have life in itself as it is the property of God.'[20] Jaeger's article is almost wholly without reference to Scripture and operates on non-theistic principles, and Cadbury makes no commitments.[21]

Seventh Day Adventists and other biblically oriented but not strictly orthodox believers have their own brand of 'Soul Sleep' doctrine. They were comforted greatly by Cullmann's essay (and many similar by activists of the biblical theology 'movement'). In Calvin's day the doctrine of Soul Sleep (*psychopannychia*) was strong in some Anabaptist circles. His first major evangelical writing was to examine everything the Bible says on the matter. There have been few advances on Calvin's survey and apologetic for orthodox doctrine.[22] I regard the positive treatment to follow as sufficient response to this error.

Immortality and Resurrection As Evolved Doctrine.

A third view I call, for want of a better name, immortality and resurrection as evolved doctrine. I have in mind a sort of half-believing acceptance of the survival of personality and identity with memory. There are beliefs precious to the heart of all Christians supported by biblical scholars who, taking a low view of Scripture, nevertheless give some credence to the historic teaching. All scholars in the symposium above fall in this category.[23]

The 'Waiting Chamber'.

Before my own version of how Protestant orthodox theology has interpreted the scriptural evidence we should look at an ancient view popularized by the Scofield Reference Bible, graphically illustrated by the chart lectures of numerous teachers, and presented in eclectic but systematic form by Herman A. Hoyt[24] and in summary fashion by H. C. Thiessen of Wheaton Graduate School of Theology.[25] This scheme (unawares, I think) borrowed from two sources: the Roman Catholic *limbus patrum* dogma and eighteenth and nineteenth century Semitic scholarship.

J. O. Buswell describes the view simply as 'a persistent notion, rather definitely coupled with Greek Mythology on the one hand and leading into the Roman Catholic doctrine of purgatory on the other, that before the time of Christ the saints who died were not admitted to the blessed presence of God in heaven, but were kept in a… waiting chamber, and that only since the time of Christ [i.e. His Ascension] has it been true that those who die in the faith go immediately to heaven.'[26]

Sheol, it is said, lies at the center of the earth,[27] citing Matthew 12:40, 'three days and three nights in the heart of the earth.' It is divided into two compartments, one not specifically named (though perhaps Gehenna) but a place of punishment, and another called Abraham's bosom or paradise. Luke 16:23-31 and 23:43 are said to demonstrate this and to explain why Sheol-Hades must have been every soul's destination at death. Between the compartment there was 'a great gulf fixed,' visualized horizontally.

---

18. Oscar Cullmann, Henry Wolfson, Werner Jaeger and Henry J. Cadbury, *Immortality and Resurrection, Death in the western World: Two Conflicting Currents of Thought* (New York: Macmillan Co., 1965).
19. ibid., pp. 9–53.
20. ibid., p. 57.
21. See note 26, page 1027.
22. Calvin entitled his book: *Psychopannychia: A Refutation of the Error Entertained by Some Unskillful Persons, Who Ignorantly Imagine that In the Interval Between Death and The Judgment The Soul Sleeps, Together With an Explanation of the Condition and Life of The Soul After This Present Life*, Vol. iii, Tracts by Calvin, trans. Henry Beveridge (Edinburgh: Calvin Translation Society, 1851), pp. 413–490.
23. A thorough work from the same point of view is Robert Martin-Achard, *From Death to Life: A Study of the Development of the Doctrine of Resurrection in the Old Testament*, trans. John Penney Smith (Edinburgh & London, 1960). These authors naturally do not bring to bear passages of Old Testament interpretation in the New Testament such as Peter's interpretation of Psalm 16:9-11 (Acts 2:25 ff.) and Paul's (Acts 13:35-37) and Hebrews 11:13 ff. A more trustworthy source is George E. Ladd's, *A Theology of the New Testament*, chap. 19 'Eternal Life' and chap. 24 'Resurrection' (Grand Rapids: Eerdmans, 1974, 1991). See also the brief article and bibliography 'Immortality' by Julius Scott in *Evangelical Dictionary of Biblical Theology*.
24. Herman A. Hoyt, 'The Intermediate State' in *The End Times* (Chicago: Moody Press, 1969), pp. 34-48.
25. H. C. Thiessen, *Introductory Lectures in Systematic Theology* (Grand Rapids: Eerdmans, 1949, 1966), pp. 488, 489.
26. J. O. Buswell, *A Systematic Theology of the Christian Religion*, Vol. ii (Grand Rapids: Zondervan, 1971), pp. 318, 319.
27. Hoyt, op. cit., pp. 44, 45.

Christ is said to have delivered paradise to heaven at the time of His Ascension (Eph. 4:8, 9 is so interpreted). At this time there was a 'reorganization of the intermediate state.'[28] While in Hades Jesus literally 'preached even to those who are dead' (1 Peter 4:6), pronouncing doom to the lost, and deliverance for the saved (1 Peter 3:18, 19; Luke 4:18).[29] Henceforth the souls of saints go immediately to be with Christ in heaven – 'The gates of Sheol-Hades were barred to entrance of any saved soul thereafter[30]....The wicked... still go to Sheol-Hades at the time of physical death and are there kept "under punishment unto the day of judgment" (2 Peter 2:9).'[31] It should be observed that for convenience I have cited Dr Herman Hoyt. This view, however, with variations, has a long history and is still widely held. In extreme form advocates find no less than six destinations for spirits, wicked and good, human or demons or angels.

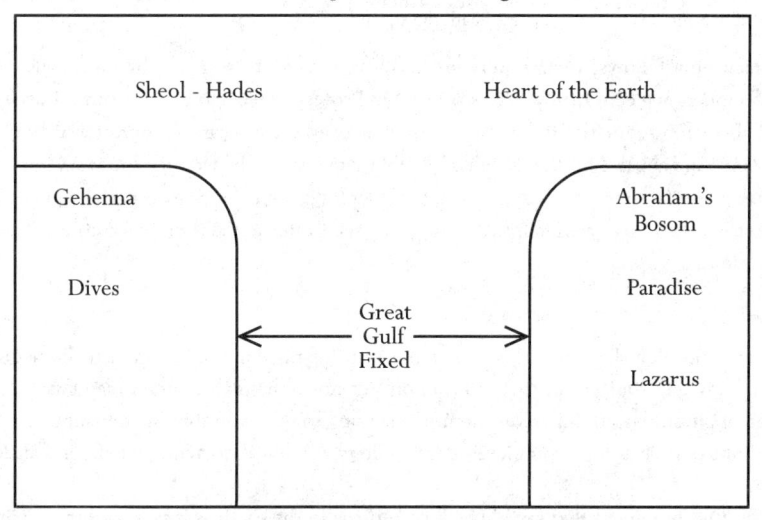

```
         Sheol - Hades              Heart of the Earth

         Gehenna                      Abraham's
                                       Bosom

         Dives                        Paradise
                          Great
                       ← Gulf →
                          Fixed
                                      Lazarus
```

Clarence Larkin, a draftsman who graphically expounded the system, had in addition to heaven: (1) Tartarus for fallen angels only (he cites 2 Peter 2:4 and Jude 6); (2) the underworld abyss ('bottomless pit') where certain demons are kept and Satan shall be imprisoned for a thousand years (Rev. 9:1, 2; 20:1 ff.); (3) paradise, for Old Testament saints (now empty); (4) hell or Hades, the present abode of souls of wicked dead; and (5) the lake of fire or Gehenna, the final hell (Matt. 25:41; Rev. 19:20; 20:10, 14, 15).[32]

This view was very familiar to many early twentieth-century evangelicals, however bizarre it may seem to most current Bible students.

Though very ancient and persistent, both in the Roman form of *limbus patrum* and in the Protestant form, orthodox Protestant theology among almost all writers (many of whom we cite with reverence) thoroughly reject it. It was never the doctrine of Calvinist evangelical orthodoxy.[33]

Shedd is plain: 'A pagan underworld containing both Paradise and Hades, both the happy and the miserable, like the pagan idol is "nothing in this world." There is no such place.'[34] Again Shedd says:

> The creeds, Lutheran and Reformed rejected the 'compartments in the underworld' idea. It was reintroduced by 18th and 19th century writers like Lowth in England and Herder in Germany. [Both pioneered modern research into Hebrew poetry.] They contend the Old Testament prophets like surrounding nations regarded metaphysical separation of body and soul as impossible and thought of dead men as being in the grave wholly.[35]

---

28. Hoyt, op. cit., p. 45.
29. Hoyt, op. cit., p. 45.
30. Hoyt, op. cit., p. 45.
31. Hoyt, op. cit., p. 47.
32. See chart, 'The Spirit World,' *Dispensational Truth*, 1918, enlarged 1920 and many printings, by author, 2802 No. Park Ave., Philadelphia, PA, between pp. 95 and 96.
33. John Calvin, *Institutes II*.16.8–12; Francis Turretin, *Institutes of Elenctic Theology II*,(Grand Rapids: Baker Books, 1981), pp. 356–364; Charles Hodge, *Systematic Theology III*, op. cit., pp. 733–747; W. G. T. Shedd, *Dogmatic Theology II* (Grand Rapids: Zondervan Publ., 1969), p. 595; A. H. Strong, *Systematic Theology* (Valley Forge, PA: Judson Press, 1907), pp. 707, 708; Buswell, op. cit., pp. 318, 319.
34. Shedd, op. cit., p. 595.
35. Shedd, op. cit., p. 595.

If Hades, which means 'the unseen,' is understood without mythological baggage, it rightly stands for 'that mysterious realm where each [good and bad] shall take his chamber in the silent halls of death'[36] and rightly translates Sheol in the Hebrew Old Testament, but in the New Testament, as R. C. H. Lenski (Lutheran) rightly points out in comment on Revelation 20 and 21:

> Revelation uses *ho ha-i-des* as a name for the place into which 'the death' delivers the souls of human beings who are damned. Until the judgment day hell functions only for the souls of the damned and is termed 'hades' the unseen place. When hell is mentioned as receiving both the souls and bodies of the damned, Jesus calls hell, 'the Gehenna' and 'the Gehenna of fire,' and in Revelation 20:14, 15, the lake of fire, in 21:8 'the lake, the one burning with fire and brimstone, which is death the second.'[37]

The approach which now follows, though perhaps new and strange to some, is by no means original with me. It is essentially the much neglected (now less so) historic Protestant doctrine (with some Lutheran exceptions). I have presented the same, with the preceding discussion over many years to ministerial students with about unanimous acceptance and apparent relief. Much of the following will be by way of expository comment on passages of Scripture. I owe a special debt of gratitude to many theologians of the past, especially W. G. T. Shedd and to Robert Martin-Achard who have been helpful in the exegesis. I offer a series of propositions. There will be some unavoidable repetition.

First Proposition.
Both Old Testament and New Testament represent the state of mankind after death to be a disembodied state – that the human body and soul are normally in union but not indissoluble union (see chap. 2, above), for the radical parturition of physical death separates them. Everything to follow in this chapter supports this as a uniform assumption of Scripture. Eschatology completes anthropology. A biblical doctrine of mankind anticipates a biblical doctrine of death.

One prominent Old Testament text says, 'The dust returns to the earth as it was, and the spirit returns to God who gave it' (Eccles. 12:7). Job, in spite of wavering in exercise of faith, made public his confidence that 'after my skin has been thus destroyed, then from [whether 'away from,' i.e. disembodied or 'out from' i.e. in a resurrected body] my flesh I shall see God' (Job 19:26 RSV). Many more passages will be introduced later.

A few from the New Testament follow. 'Jesus… yielded up spirit' (Matt. 27:50); 'Jesus… said, "Father, into your hands I commit my spirit"' (Luke 23:46). Stephen's dying words were, 'Lord Jesus, receive my spirit' (Acts 7:59). Paul faced death with 'good courage' because he would 'rather be away from the body and at home with the Lord' (2 Cor. 5:8). His body was an earthly 'tent' to live in, to be replaced with a 'house… in the heavens' (2 Cor. 5:1, 2) and he knew that it was possible to be a conscious person 'in the body or out of the body' (2 Cor. 12:2). John the Revelator saw martyr souls in heaven, under divine protection (Rev. 6:9-11). This is not a complete list.

Further indirect but decisive evidence (some cited earlier) is as follows.

1. The prohibition of necromancy in several parts of the Old Testament. Whatever the Israelites of Moses' time thought about Sheol, where only the 'shade' of the deceased was supposed to go at death, they were forbidden to seek contact with departed spirits precisely because they did believe that the person endured as a soul after death separated it from the body. Otherwise the 'necromancer' (Deut. 18:11, literally, 'one who seeks after dead ones') would not have been forbidden. There would have been no temptation to seek after the dead. In King Ahaz's time (eighth century BC) the population of Jerusalem were warned against 'mediums' who 'enquire of the dead on behalf of the living' (Isa. 8:19).

2. As we have seen earlier, the mythologies of Israel's remote and near neighbors were peopled by disembodied souls (e.g. the *Gilgamish Epic* of Mesopotamia and the Baal myths of Ugarit).

3. Many Old Testament expressions of good hope for the future and of faith are inexplicable apart from belief in a future life of the soul with God. Abraham's faith, which was 'commended as righteous' (Gen. 12:3; 15:6) according to Hebrews, was meaningless if he was not expecting in the future to see and participate in the blessing of all families of the earth: 'These all died in faith… having acknowledged that they were strangers and exiles on the

---
36. Wm. Cullen Bryant, *Thanatopsis*.
37. R. C. H. Lenski, *The Interpretation of St. John's Revelation* (Minneapolis: Augsburg Publ., 1961), p. 75.

earth' (Heb. 11:13). The several Psalmists' prayers and aspirations are inexplicable in people who expected to end their existence with their last breath. David prayed, 'My flesh and my heart may fail, but God is the strength of my heart and my portion for ever' (Ps. 73:26), and 'my hope is in thy ordinances. I will keep thy law continually, for ever and ever' (Ps. 119:43, 44 RSV; see also Ps. 31:5). At the moment of death Jacob reported in to God, saying, 'I have waited for thy salvation, O LORD' (Gen. 49:17,18 KJV). At that moment he was hardly concerned about further rescue from perils of this world.

In this connection scholars have pointed out that Old Testament covenants with God and His promises do not provide anything to excite much joy if there is no future with God after death. God promised to be a 'God *to you, and to your descendants after you*. And I will give to you [emphasis added], and to your descendants after you,' etc. (Gen. 17:7, 8; cf. Exod. 6:7; Deut 35:3, 29 RSV). Calvin makes the point that these sentiments, promises and the like require belief in everlasting life and divine mercy to make sense.[38]

Second Proposition.

Both Testaments of Scripture teach that the intermediate state for the believer is one of conscious blessedness. At the Old Testament level this hope rested on unfinished revelation — especially regarding the remission of sins (see Rom. 3:21-26; Heb. 2:14-17). Only Jesus 'brought life and immortality to light through the gospel' (2 Tim. 1:10).

Some of the Old Testament expressions of this expectation follow. The mysterious Gentile Balaam of Pethor understood this, full of hope prophesying: 'Let me die the death of the righteous, and let my end be like his!' (Num. 23:10 RSV).

In addition to Psalm 16:9-10, cited several times earlier, Psalm 17:13-15 first prays for deliverance from the wicked 'whose portion is in this life,' then expresses confidence for life after death: 'As for me, I shall behold your face in righteousness; when I awake, I shall be satisfied with your likeness.' Psalm 49:10-15 deserves pondering clause by clause. The Sons of Korah observe wise and foolish both die and leave their wealth behind and 'Their graves are their homes for ever' — then this contrast: 'But God will ransom my soul from the power of Sheol [a context where, I think, Sheol means 'grave'], for he will receive me.' In Psalm 49 the psalmist, like the prophet Habakkuk, expresses unwavering faith that God is and will always be his salvation (see Hab. 3, especially v. 17). Asaph, in contrasting his own prospects with that of the wicked who are to be 'destroyed in a moment, swept away utterly by terrors' (Ps. 73:19 RSV), knows of himself that God does 'hold my right hand...' and will 'guide me... and afterward... receive me to glory. Whom have I in heaven but thee.... My flesh and my heart may fail, but God is the strength of my heart and my portion for ever' (Ps. 73:23-26 RSV).

Job 19:25-27 is in a class by itself. The Authorized Version (KJV) plainly has Job say 'Yet in my flesh shall I see God.' The Hebrew, *mibbesari*, can be translated that way, though literally it reads 'Yet from my flesh...' As often as not *mi* (abbr. of *min*) means the opposite, 'away from' or 'more than,' and similar. Barton Payne devotes several pages of his excellent volume of Old Testament theology to an extended and careful survey of development of the doctrine of the future life after death. In my judgment he is incorrect in saying that evangelicals insist on 'from my flesh' – implying resurrection of the body. In Job 14:12 ff. Job does express such a hope. Dahood translates Psalm 73:26, 'My flesh and my heart may waste away, O Mountain, but my heart and my body, God, will be eternal'[39] and in a note[40] translates the clause 'Refreshed by him, I will gaze upon God.' If confirmed by more study, this is an enormous breakthrough for the doctrine of the blessedness of the righteous dead in the Old Testament. In any case, Job will see God 'on my side,' vindicating his righteousness in the judgment when at last he 'stands upon the earth.'

The doctrine of resurrection, first latent and then specific, is taught in the Old Testament, and, while related, does not prove a doctrine of conscious personal blessedness after death for the Old Testament saints.

On that point let me cite the work of a respected Reformed scholar. Geerhardus Vos, in his influential work, *The Pauline Eschatology*, appends an important chapter on 'Eschatology of the Psalter.' Early he comments on Old Testament religion: 'A redemptive religion without eschatological interest would be a contradiction in terms. The orthodox interpretation of Scripture has always recognized this.'[41] Vos does not concede that the Psalmist's

---

38. Calvin, op. cit., 10.8.
39. Mitchell Dahood, *Psalms*, Anchor Bible II (Garden City, NY: Doubleday, 1965–1970), p. 187.
40. *ibid.*, 2nd note on v. 26, p. 196.
41. Geerhardus Vos, *The Pauline Eschatology* (Grand Rapids: Eerdmans, 1952), p. 325.

eschatological hope of 'enjoyment of Jehovah, the beatific vision of his face, the pleasures at his right hand, the perpetual dwelling with him in his sanctuary,' and similar was intended in any collective sense for the future of the nation of Israel as such.[42] He is convinced that these 'familiar passages' quoted from Psalms 16, 17, 49 and 73, 'where the confidence of uninterrupted fellowship with Jehovah is expressed, are based on the belief in a future blessed life after death.'[43]

Furthermore, says Vos, 'It is only through the gateway of eschatology that universalism [i.e., world-wide offer of salvation] and the missionary idea come in.'[44] The desire of the Psalmists projects itself into the future and breaks out into a direct missionary appeal conceived as addressed to Gentiles. Vos cites many Psalms.[45]

H. R. Mackintosh, R. H. Charles and many others, who accept the 'higher critical' late dating of the Psalms and the 'higher theology' of the Pentateuch, think that belief in personal immortality and a post-death blessed vision of God was a late development.[46] They would credit 'Yahwism' with gradually 'destroying the belief in the false life in Sheol and replacing it with hope for individual future post-mortem life springing from present fellowship with God.'[47]

As earlier noted, the New Testament explicitly discovers the doctrine of an intermediate state of conscious 'life' in the Old Testament. '[T]he Sadducees say that there is no resurrection, nor angel, nor spirit' (Acts 23:8) but Jesus – arguing from 'I am... the God of Abraham, the God of Isaac, and the God of Jacob' (Exod. 3:6, 16) and that 'He is not God of the dead, but of the living' – reasoned that the Sadducees were 'wrong, because you know neither the Scriptures nor the power of God' (Matt. 22:29-33). The Sadducees believed the Mosaic Pentateuch but had not discovered a conscious future of the soul after death there. Jesus did not find (at least He did not quote) a direct statement of the same.

What is only latent there and somewhat clearer in later Old Testament Scripture in the New Testament is 'taught with more or less distinctness in many passages.'[48] Among distinct references, first mention should go to Revelation 6:9-11, where, at the breaking of the fifth of the seven seals, John is showed the souls of the martyrs in heaven 'under the altar,' where they pray to God and 'rest,' each clothed in 'a white robe.' Revelation 7:9-17 pictures a multitude of those who endured great tribulation, of every nation, people, kindred and tongue, praising God in heaven. At Revelation 14:13 the Revelator 'heard a voice from heaven saying, "Write this: Blessed are the dead who die in the Lord from now on." "Blessed indeed," says the Spirit, "that they may rest from their labors, for their deeds follow them!"' In Jesus' Parable of the Rich Man and Lazarus, He says 'The beggar died and was carried to Abraham's bosom,' implying immediate migration of the soul to heaven. Accordingly Jesus promised the repentant thief, 'Truly, I say to you, today you will be with me in Paradise' (Luke 23:43). Two other New Testament texts locate paradise in heaven (Rev. 2:7; cf. Rev. 12:12; and 2 Cor. 12:4). Though, of course, paradise was a place on earth (the Garden of Eden), in Jesus' time, and in His and Paul's language, it is where Christ is – and with Him the believers 'in the heavenly places' (Eph. 2:6). There is a 'house not made with hands,' 'a building from God,' awaiting the believer 'eternal in the heavens' at death (2 Cor. 5:1), which Paul held forth as a motive for steady service at the present time. To 'be away from the body and at home with the Lord' reduces the doctrine to a formula (2 Cor. 5:8, 9). There is difference of opinion as to whether the house or 'tabernacle' is (1) heaven itself (cf. John 14:1 ff.), or (2) a temporary body of some sort, appropriate to residence in heaven until the resurrection of the body presently in the grave; or (3) a 'proleptical' reference to the resurrection body of the future. Some have even gone so far as to hold that after writing 1 Thessalonians 4:13 ff. and 1 Corinthians 15:51 ff. – wherein Paul definitely, as in common Jewish expectation, placed the resurrection at 'the last day,' i.e. the *parousia*, the Second Advent (John 11:13, 24; cf. Acts 24:15) – he changed his mind, and thought the moment of death to be the moment of resurrection – not, of course, of the dead body, but a non-material body.

Another explicit reference to departure of the believer's soul for heaven, at death, is Paul's poignant, but happy, problem as a prisoner of the Empire: 'For to me to live is Christ, and to die is gain.... I am hard pressed between the two. My desire is to depart and be with Christ, for that is far better' (Phil. 1:21, 23; cf. 22 and 24).

---

42. ibid., p. 349.
43. ibid., p. 349.
44. ibid., p. 347.
45. Pss. 57:8-11; 66:1-4; 67:2-5; 96:3, 7-13; 100:1-3; 108:3; 113:3, 4; 117:1, 2; 145:21.Vos, ibid., p. 347.
46. H. R. Mackintosh, *Immortality and the Future*, 2nd ed. (London: Hodder and Stoughton, 1917), 'Eschatology in the Old Testament and Judaism,' pp. 19 ff.
47. ibid., as Mackintosh quotes Charles, p. 31.
48. Charles Hodge, op. cit., p. 727.

Other New Testament facts bear on the question. Throughout John's Gospel, to believe on Christ is to have eternal life here and now. Can this eternal life be suspended or go out of existence during a 'soul-sleep' or 'soul-annihilation' between death and the future day of resurrection?

Third Proposition.

The Bible teaches that the intermediate state of the impenitent and unbelieving is one of misery in hell (or Hades). In the Old Testament Sheol, the pit or lowest *sheol*, is a place (or condition) to which the wicked, in distinction from the righteous, are sent at death. The texts involved would be meaningless if Sheol were 'merely a promiscuous underworld for all souls… no more a menace for the sinner than for the saint, and consequently a menace for neither.'[49] Against the person who 'forsook God which made him,' God says, 'a fire is kindled in mine anger, and shall burn unto the lowest hell [Sheol]' (Deut. 32:15, 22 KJV). The stupid man who turns aside to the harlot's house 'does not know that the dead are there; that her guests are in the depths of Sheol' (Prov. 9:18 RSV). This is an example of many such in Proverbs where Sheol is a place from which a 'soul' is delivered by righteousness. A 'life after death' gave meaning to careful discipline of children. 'Do not withhold discipline from a child…. If you beat him with the rod you will save his life from Sheol' (Prov. 23:13, 14 RSV). 'The wise man's path leads upward to life, that he may avoid Sheol beneath.' Sheol is equated in three texts with a destruction (*abaddon*) distinct from death: 'Sheol and destruction [*abaddon*]' (Job 26:6; Prov. 15:11; and 27:20). This frightening term, rendered *apollyon* ('perdition') in the Greek New Testament, is hell. Here the devil is destined to be (see Rev. 9:11). These texts have no threatening force specially for sinners if Sheol does not designate a place of punishment.

The New Testament has a great deal to say about the intermediate state of the wicked dead. The rich man of Luke 16:19 ff. dies and immediately is 'tormented' in hell (Hades). This Hades is then (1) a place of retribution and torment, and (2) the contrary of heaven ('exalted to heaven… brought down to Hades,' (Matt. 11:23). It is also (3) a kingdom of Satan, i.e. of evil (Matt. 16:18), and (4) the present residence of the wicked dead, later to be emptied into the final lake of fire (Rev. 20:12-14). Furthermore, (5) because of its frequent association with death in the New Testament, it is properly designated as eternal alienation from God. For the wicked, 'death and Hades' belong together (Rev. 1:18; 6:8; 20:13, 14).

These considerations lead to a synthetic conclusion that the traditional Protestant view is correct: that at death the souls of the wicked go to a place of torment (the nature of which has not yet been discussed here) and the righteousness to heaven and this, though dimly revealed in early Old Testament times, with nothing to the contrary, is a part of Old Testament revealed religion.

A comparatively recent treatment of progressive revelation regarding death, immortality and future life in the Old Testament by J. Barton Payne, goes into these matters in great detail and ends with this conclusion, which I fully endorse.

> The traditional Protestant position is to be maintained as: 1) The most simple, in holding to the hope stated in the Old Testament and New Testament (and nowhere denied) of a carrying to heaven immediately upon death for all believers. 2) The most Scriptural, in recognizing the paucity of revelation on Old Testament life after death and in rejecting hypothetical migrations [of O.T. Saints from Sheol-Hades to heaven at Christ's Ascension]. 3) The most consistent, in refusing the poor concepts of paganism and in maintaining the divine normativeness of the O.T. Scriptures.[50]

This position – as against the prevailing opinions of all my teachers and the scholars marshaled in seminary days – holds that, though revelation on the matter appeared slowly throughout the Old Testament, more was understood by the people, as Hebrews 11 and John 11 indicate, than was enscriptured. We acknowledge a common core meaning of Sheol in the Old Testament – the realm of death, the grave and the mystery of what follows.[51] 'Sheol' apparently is an infinitive of the verb *sha'al*, *to ask* and, as in most languages infinitives and participles may act as nouns, so it serves as a noun throughout the Old Testament. From the primary meaning of the place of the dead (always asking for more) come extended meanings. The first is 'grave' (where the body decomposes[52]). The underground

---

49. Shedd, op. cit., p. 636.
50. J. Barton Payne, *The Theology of the Older Testament*, topic 30 'Life After Death' (Grand Rapids: Zondervan, 1962, 1976), pp. 443-463 and Appendix G, pp. 527-529.
51. ' …But that dread of something after death, —/The undiscovered country, from whose bourn/No traveller returns – puzzles the will, /and makes us rather bear those ills we have /Than fly to others that we know not of' (Shakespeare, *Hamlet* iii.1. lines 78-82.
52. Job 17:13, 14; Ps. 88:3; Gen. 42:38; 1 Sam. 2:6; 1 Kgs. 2:6.

grave explains why saints 'go down to Sheol.' Secondly, 'The abstract meaning "DEATH" occurs twenty-one times – in Psalm 89:48 parallel to "sheol".'[53] The third is 'hell,' a place of punishment (Ps. 55:15), according to Payne, occurring twenty-four times.

On this basis the following can be concluded.

1. Luke 16:19 ff. (the rich man and Lazarus) does not represent a horizontal picture but a vertical one.

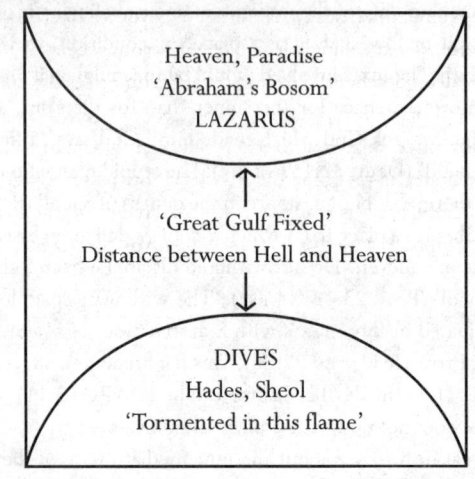

```
                Heaven, Paradise
                'Abraham's Bosom'
                    LAZARUS

                        ↑
                  'Great Gulf Fixed'
              Distance between Hell and Heaven
                        ↓

                        DIVES
                    Hades, Sheol
                'Tormented in this flame'
```

What elements of the story (or parable) are drawn from popular beliefs is hard to say. Calvin wisely remarks regarding the details:

> Souls have neither fingers nor eyes, and are not liable to thirst, nor do they hold such conversations among themselves as are here described to have taken place between Abraham and the rich man; but our Lord has here drawn a picture, which represents the condition of the life to come according to our measure of capacity.
>
> The general truth conveyed is that believing souls, when they have left their bodies, lead a joyful and blessed life out of this world, and that for the reprobate there are prepared dreadful torments, which can no more be conceived by our minds than the boundless glory of the heavens…[54]

2. From the Old Testament perspective, when a righteous man is said to 'go down to Sheol' at death it is the body, not the soul – as when Jacob said, 'I shall go down to Sheol to my son, mourning' (Gen. 37:35). Sometimes the whole thought of the realm of the dead, i.e. of Sheol, takes on features of the grave (Amos 9:2).

3. The hope of the saints in death, natural revulsion against it notwithstanding, was full of hope. See our earlier discussion. Some passages treated were Numbers 23:5, 10; Psalms 17;15; 49:14, 15; 73:25, 26. We must seriously regard Hebrews 11:13, which says that these saints regarded themselves as pilgrims and foreigners on earth, preferring a heavenly country.

4. First Peter 3:19, 20 describes a preaching of the pre-incarnate *Logos* on earth during Noah's time, not as a proclamation by Jesus in Hades during the 'three days' (Matt. 12:40). The article of the Apostles' Creed, 'He descended into hell,' seems to rest on the view that the disembodied Jesus spent time in a subterranean Sheol-Hades, and rests on 1 Peter 3:19, 20 so interpreted.

With regard to the creedal article, let the following be observed.

A. The most ancient form of the creed did not contain this article.

B. The first ecumenical creeds, Nicea (AD 325) and Constantinople (AD 381), do not contain this article.

C. Some of the early statements of faith have 'descended into Hades' but, omitting 'and buried,' understand the descent as 'burial.'

D. Except in some Lutheran theology, most Protestants, following Calvin,[55] have interpreted the *descensus ad infernum* 'as a figurative expression of the unutterable suffering of Christ in his humanity [human nature].'[56]

---

53. Payne, op. cit., p. 528.
54. John Calvin, *Commentary on a Harmony of the Evangelists, Matthew, Mark and Luke*, Vol. ii, trans. Wm. Pringle (Edinburgh: 1845), pp. 188, 189.
55. Calvin, *Institutes* II.16.8–12.
56. Donald G. Bloesch, 'Descent into Hell' (Hades) *Evangelical Dictionary of Theology*, p. 314.

Those who do think that Jesus descended to Hades and preached 'to the spirits' (souls of the dead) have no agreement as to the persons addressed, the message preached, the purpose of it or the results. The reader who would like a quick survey of the proposals should read the old standard, *Lange's Commentary*.[57] Herman Wits (Witsius), a Dutch theologian and early exponent of the Federal (Covenant) theology, is reported to have said, 'There are almost as many dissertations concerning the Descensus as there are flies in the heat of summer.'

A thorough and convincing extended advocacy of the view advocated here is to be found in W. G. T. Shedd's *Dogmatic Theology*.[58] Francis Turretin, an exceedingly learned and devout successor to Calvin at Geneva, also presents a convincing advocacy of the view defended here.[59] A. H. Strong summarizes the view and evidence for it.[60] See also Geerhardus Vos' 'Eschatology.'[61]

5. Several passages of Scripture often supposed to teach a descent of Christ to Sheol-Hades or the *limbus patrum* are fully amenable to the view defended here. Some of these will now be examined.

First Peter 4:5, 6 (NKJV) says that Christ 'is ready to judge the living and the dead. For this reason *the gospel was preached also to those who are dead* [emphasis added]....' Geerhardus Vos comments,

> For explaining the reference to 'the dead' [in v. 5] the connection with the preceding verse is fully sufficient. It is there stated that Christ is 'ready to judge the living and the dead.' The 'living and the dead' are those who will be alive and dead at the parousia. To both the gospel was preached, that Christ might be the judge of both. But that the gospel was preached to the latter in the state of death, is in no way indicated. On the contrary the telic clause, 'that they might be judged according to men in the flesh,' shows that they heard the gospel during their lifetime, for the judgment according to men in the flesh that has befallen them is the judgment of physical death. If a close connection between the passage in chapter three and that in chapter four did exist, this could only serve to commend the exegesis which finds in the earlier passage a gospel-preaching to the contemporaries of Noah during their lifetime, since, on that view, it becomes natural to identify the judgment in the flesh with the Deluge.[62]

This is better than to suppose the 'dead' of verse 6 means 'spiritually dead,' for 'the living and the dead' in verse 5 clearly means *physically* dead. A shift to *spiritually* dead seems unlikely.

Though Matthew 12:40 says, 'so will the Son of Man be three days and three nights in the heart of the earth,' that in no wise means that the soul of Jesus went to Sheol-Hades (the Roman *limbus patrum*) somewhere near the center of our planet. '[H]eart of the earth' means simply the grave, not a deep, deep subterranean cavern. It is an Hebraic-Aramaic expression, translating to Greek what Jesus said in Aramaic. Similarly, Tyre, located on a shore and an island offshore, is said to be 'in the midst of the sea' (Ezek. 26:5). Tyre's ships sailed the surface of the oceans (it had no submarines). As a seafaring nation its 'borders are in the heart of the seas' (Ezek 27:4, 26, 32; 28:2). When in fulfillment of this prediction Alexander's army scraped the part of Tyre on shore into the shallow shore water (Ezek. 27:27) it was 'into the heart of the seas.' After Pharaoh and his army were drowned, Miriam sang of the 'heart of the sea' as where it happened (Exod. 15:8). It should also be said that the language of Scripture nowhere reflects a world-picture (*weltbild*) in which earth is a planetary sphere with a heart or center downward from every spot on its surface. The heart of the earth in Scripture simply means under ground. All graves are underground but near the surface, covered with earth-fill in our times usually, but in Jesus' time usually in a cavern cut in bedrock, with an opening closed by a single stone. In Joseph's tomb Jesus' body lay 'in the heart of the earth.' Similarly, in Scripture birds fly 'in the midst of heaven' (Rev. 19:17 KJV). Poets still speak like that.

Ephesians 4:7, 9 (KJV) says that 'Christ... descended first into the lower parts of the earth.' Even in antiquity this was understood by some wise Fathers as referring to the incarnation, not a descent to Sheol-Hades. I discussed that at some length earlier (in Part 6: Ecclesiology) in connection with 'Gifts of Christ to the church' and in connection with the incarnation (in Part 4: Christology).

---

57. *Lange's Commentary, Epistles General of Peter*, G. F. C. Fronmüller, trans. J. S. Mombert, 1872, 'Excursus on the Descensus Ad Infernos,' pp. 67-71.
58. Shedd, op. cit., pp. 603–609, especially extended footnotes on pages 606–609.
59. Turretin, op. cit., Q. XV, para. 12, pp. 360, 361.
60. A. H. Strong, op. cit., pp. 707, 708.
61. G. Vos, op. cit., p. 992.
62. G. Vos, 'Eschatology,' ibid., p. 992.

Fourth Proposition.

The condition of the unsaved in their present disembodied state is one of conscious torment. This has already been partly established by previous considerations in this chapter. In addition, let the following be said.

1. '[T]he Lord knows how to rescue the godly from trials, and *to keep the unrighteous under punishment* [emphasis added] until the day of judgment, and especially those who indulge in the lust of defiling passion and despise authority' (2 Peter 2:9, 10). This is very specific and scarcely needs comment.

2. As in the general outlook of the Old Testament, so in the book of Revelation, for the wicked, 'Death' is followed by 'Hades' (Rev. 6:8; 20:13, 14). Taken futuristically, and granted any literal meaning at all, Hades is inhabited by those who only after a future judgment will be turned into the lake of fire. This is the Hades where the wicked rich man of the parable of Luke 16 (Dives in the Latin Bible) was 'in anguish in this flame' (v. 24). Like 'the angels when they sinned' they are 'kept until the judgment' (2 Peter 2:9 and context). A change comes after 'the thousand years were ended' when all 'the dead, great and small' will stand before God for final judgment (Rev. 20:11-15). 'Death and Hades gave up the dead who were in them'; they are judged and are 'thrown into the lake of fire.'

This scheme of things was partly foreseen in outline by the prophet Isaiah in what Delitzsch called 'the Little Apocalypse' (Isa. 24:27): 'On that day the LORD will punish the host of heaven, in heaven, and the kings of the earth, on the earth. They will be gathered together as prisoners in a pit; they will be shut up in prison, and after many days they will be punished' (Isa. 24:21, 22 RSV). I have treated this more at length elsewhere.[63] Franz Delitzsch commented, 'What the apocalyptist of the New Testament describes in detail in Revelation 20:4, 20:11 sqq., and 21, the apocalyptist of the Old Testament condensed.'[64]

Fifth Proposition.

The condition of the righteous dead in their present, disembodied, intermediate state, while not one of complete blessedness, is nevertheless 'far better' than that of living saints. 'Blessed are the dead who die in the Lord,' says the Scripture (Rev. 14:13). Though theirs is not a state of complete happiness, they 'sleep in Jesus' (only as to their bodies, whose usual reclining posture in the grave is obviously indicated). They are 'with Christ' and 'them also which sleep in Jesus will God bring with him' (1 Thess. 4:14, 15 KJV) – their souls, not their bodies, of course, for only their bodies are in their graves, 'and the dead in Christ shall rise first' (1 Thess. 4:16). Our best information is derived from several scriptural sources:

1. *Jesus' words to the thief*: 'in Paradise' (Luke 23:43) brings a very pleasing prospect. Paradise is a Persian word: not nature as such, but a formal garden – calm, verdured, with splashing water. It is introduced in the Old Testament in the Song of Solomon 4:13 as an orchard; in Nehemiah 2:8 and Ecclesiastes 2:5 as a park or forest. In Revelation 2:7 overcomers are promised 'to eat of the tree of life, which is in the paradise of God.'

2. *Paul's numerous statements*: 'to... be with Christ,' which 'is far better'; 'away from the body and at home with the Lord'; 'clothed... with our house which is from heaven, ; 'the time of my departure [release, loosening of moorings] has come' (Phil. 1:21-23; 2 Cor. 5:1-9 KJV; 2 Tim. 4:6). At 2 Corinthians 12:1-4, in language of mystical thought, he describes paradise, the third heaven, as a realm of 'things that cannot be told, which man may not utter.'

3. *The book of Hebrews*: What it says throughout of heaven – its occupants, temple, temple furniture and the like – is in terms parallel to the Old Testament temple, priests and ritual, but in Hebrews 12:22, 23 the present inhabitants, divine, angelic and human, are classified as 'innumerable angels in festal gathering... the assembly of the firstborn who are enrolled in heaven... God, the judge of all... the spirits of the righteous made perfect, and... Jesus, the mediator of a new covenant.' Then, as though to account for the 'firstborn' and 'spirits of the righteous,' the writer adds 'the sprinkled blood that speaks a better word than the blood of Abel.' A considerable challenge both to the exegete and poet, as well as the artist!

4. *Insights from Revelation 6:9-11 and 7:9-17*: Some clear facts and cautious inferences yield the following. (a) The righteous dead are in heaven. (b) They are conscious and resting. (c) They are robed. The robes (both of the martyr souls and the multitude) suggest an answer to Paul's desire not to be 'unclothed,' i.e. disembodied. Some cover for the soul (implied in 'clothed') is provided. (d) Some of them are 'under the altar' (here Revelation matches Hebrews), suggesting special care of martyrs. (e) They have capacity for speech and emotion. (f) They are blessed, for as Revelation 14:13 confirms, 'Blessed are the dead who die in the Lord.'

---

63. Robert D. Culver, *Daniel and the Latter Days* (Chicago: Moody Press, 1977), pp. 57, 58.
64. Franz Delitzsch, Biblical Commentary on the Prophecies of Isaiah, loc. cit. See also F. C. Jennings, Studies in Isaiah (New York: Loizeaux, 1950), p. 288.

Such revelation as the Bible furnishes about the home and condition of saints in the span of time between death and resurrection is scanty. The imaginations of Christians of every race, temperament, social level and degree of culture has been stimulated to supply the want of information with imaginative creations – lyrics, songs, painting, architecture. These lie deep in culture everywhere in Christendom and they grow with each new generation. Surely God intends it to be so. To empty the lyrics of hymn books of every element of imagination not strictly supported by factual statements of Scripture would gut the hymns and songs of their power and beauty. To ask the poets to quote a verse for every line would put them out of business – from 'Ring them bells' to Kipling's *L'Envoi*.

Postscript.

An article by Robert G. Rayburn[65] properly brands as 'common errors' – not topics for debate among evangelicals – four teachings 'respecting the abode of the soul after death.' They are as follows. 1. 'The doctrine that the souls of both the righteous and the wicked sleep between death and the resurrection... 2. The doctrine that the intermediate state is one of further probation... 3. The doctrine taught by the Church of Rome that souls at peace with the church but not perfectly pure at death... must undergo a period of purging before they are permitted to enter... heaven... 4. Finally there is the error of the doctrine of annihilationism... no conscious existence of the wicked after death [or the judgment].'[66] These errors are not 'evangelical' doctrines, and this writer is one among many who questions the wisdom of the growing acceptance of those advocating one or more of these false doctrines in otherwise evangelical organizations.

---

65. The late Robert G. Rayburn was President of Covenant Theological Seminary, St Louis, Missouri.
66. Robert G. Rayburn, 'Intermediate State,' Wycliffe Bible Encyclopedia, Vol. i, (Chicago: Moody Press, 1975), pp. 851, 852.

4
The Doctrine of the Resurrection of the Dead I: Its Main Features and Unique Position in Biblical Religion

The name for the doctrine and title of this chapter is drawn from Paul's defense of his preaching before Governor Felix at Caesarea: 'there will be a resurrection of both the just and the unjust' (Acts 24:15). Paul frequently used this and similar language for that wonderful event (whether two events or only one). In John 5:29 Jesus spoke of 'the resurrection of life' and 'the resurrection of judgment.'

No one in recent decades has seen more clearly and written more effectively – and at length – on the subject of the resurrection of the dead and of the connection thereof with the resurrection of Jesus Himself, than J. A. Schep. I quote from one of his lesser works on the subject as an epitome of this chapter.

> The resurrection of the dead in a body of flesh is guaranteed by Jesus' resurrection in a body of flesh and bones; with scars of His wounds visible, and capable of being touched and of eating food (Luke 24:38-43, Acts 10:41). At His ascension Jesus did not discard his flesh-body, as is clear from Acts 1:11; Philippians 3:21; Revelation 1:17. Since the resurrected believers will be like the risen Christ (1 Cor. 15:49; Phil. 3:21; 1 John 3:2), they too will be raised in their bodies of flesh (cf. 1 Cor. 15:35-42). Only in this way is man saved in his totality, and able to live on a new earth (Isa. 65:17 ff.; 66:22; Matt 5:5; Rev. 21:1-3).[1]

Wolfhart Pannenberg draws the same connection between Jesus' resurrection and ours, with the added notion that certainty of the revelation of God and way of salvation in Scripture and Christian teaching rests first on Jesus' resurrection and finally on ours. This theme runs throughout Pannenberg's work. In two prolix and complicated Germanic sentences he states this recurring theme:

> Just as our understanding of eternity the Easter event is not merely the basis of the knowledge that Jesus of Nazareth even in his earthly form was the eternal Son of God, but also decides that he was this by giving retrospective confirmation, so the deity of the God whom Jesus proclaimed is definitively manifested by the eschatological consummation of his kingdom and the conflict between atheism and belief is finally settled thereby with repercussions for all eternity, for talk about God by its very nature implies the concept of eternity. Furthermore the resurrection of Jesus is definitively and irrefutably decided only in connection with the eschatological resurrection of the dead, with all the implications for the person of Jesus Christ that the Church already confesses on the basis of the conviction that the Easter message is true.[2]

---

1. J. A. Schep, 'Resurrection' in *Zondervan Pictorial Encyclopedia of the Bible* (Grand Rapids: Zondervan, 1975), p. 74.
2. Wolfhart Pannenberg, *Systematic Theology*, Vol. i., trans. Geoffrey W. Bromily (Grand Rapids: Eerdmans, 1991), p. 331. For similar affirmations see pages 442, 314ff., 306ff., 264–265.

The Apostle Paul, who also liked long sentences, came more quickly to the point when he wrote, 'Christ Jesus... was declared to be the Son of God in power according to the Spirit of holiness [the divine nature] by his resurrection from the dead' (Rom. 1:1-4); and also, 'Now if Christ is proclaimed as raised from the dead, how can some of you say that there is no resurrection of the dead? But if there is no resurrection of the dead, then not even Christ has been raised. And if Christ has not been raised, then our preaching is in vain and your faith... is futile and you are still in your sins' (1 Cor. 15:12-14, 17).

The Best Good News to Mortal Men, Yet a Perennial Stumbling Block.

'No doctrine of the Christian faith,' says St Augustine, 'is so vehemently and so obstinately opposed as the doctrine of the resurrection of the flesh.'[3]

Resurrection of the body of flesh, though the best news sinners destined to death and judgment forever can hear, always has been nevertheless an offense to many. The resurrection of Jesus threatened the Jews of Jerusalem and Judea, for it authenticated the Messiah they had rejected. The cross and empty tomb both offended Greek 'wisdom' about the nature of man and the soul (1 Cor. 1:17-2:14; cf. Acts 17:32). Simple reference to the resurrection of Jesus as 'assurance to all' caused Greeks to mock Paul's gospel for it was then as still today 'against the wisdom' of men, even though it also attracted some (Acts 17:31-34).

In our times leading neo-orthodox scholars, though assigning great importance to 'the Easter event,' nevertheless have rejected 'the resurrection of the flesh' (as the ancient creeds have it). Emil Brunner, for example, in a book entitled 'Eternal Hope' could say on the one hand that except for what he called an Easter event 'the knowledge of Jesus would not have reached us.... the tiny flock of Christ's disciples filled and conquered the world... solely and exclusively because Jesus Christ showed himself as the Risen One,' etc.[4] On the other hand, he said that the idea of resurrection was a pagan import to Israel[5] and, citing R. Bultmann, asserts that 'Paul's experience and testimony [as well as Gospel records] do not show that a dead man was raised to physical life.'[6] Brunner spoke of 'the manifold discrepancy' of the 'Easter reports' as supporting the neo-orthodox (dialectical) assumption of an infinite qualitative gulf between our space-time world and the eschatological (i.e. supernatural) world. So the resurrection of Jesus was nothing that can be reported in space-time language.[7] He had no explanation for the empty tomb.

As for the resurrection of 'the last day' Brunner makes the following points. (1) 'The resurrection of the individual is in the New Testament plainly to be understood as personal immortality.'[8] (2) The body of our resurrection is a 'spiritual corporality' – 'a paradoxical idea.' However (3), even though 'I, this specific non-interchangeable man, am to rise again... the flesh will not rise again' whatever the creed says.[9] (4) Two things must be demarcated: (a) 'the transient element, the flesh, is not to take part in the resurrection,' but (b) 'the individual person who is a special thought in the mind of God will not be excluded from eternity.'[10] It is a very small leap from these statements to Barth's apparently final opinion that our 'resurrected' state in eternity will be as a loved thought in God's mind – the only heaven Jesus went to such great effort to purchase and to prepare and all we will ever get.

The heretical aspect of such views as these arose early in Gnosticism and among the followers of Marcion.[11] Tertullian argued against these assertions and similar, with evidences and arguments employed by the orthodox ever since. 'The proof that Tertullian had the gnostics in mind has been supplied by the discovery at Nag Hammadi of the so-called Letter to Rheginos.'[12] The errors have reappeared recently among liberals, neo-orthodox and their successors, even among some evangelicals who seem not to understand the provenance of their perversion and denials of Christ's resurrection.[13]

---

3. Augustine's second sermon on Psalm 89. See *The Catholic Encyclopedia* Vol. xii, p. 794.
4. Emil Brunner, *Eternal Hope*, trans. Harold Knight (Philadelphia: Westminster, 1954), p. 143.
5. ibid., p. 142.
6. ibid., p. 144.
7. ibid., p. 144.
8. ibid., p. 148.
9. ibid., p. 149.
10. ibid., p. 149.
11. Tertullian's 'Masterpiece,' *De resurrectione*, early 3rd century.
12. J. Danielou, *The Origins of Latin Christianity* (Philadelphia: Westminster Press, 1997), p. 395.
13. See, e.g. Murray Harris, *Raised Immortal* (Grand Rapids: Eerdmans, 1985), pp. 44, 53-58; *From Grave to Glory* (Grand Rapids: Eerdmans, 1990), pp. 351, 376, 390–392, 404, 405, 423; with reference to the believers' resurrection, *Raised Immortal*, pp. 44, 123, 124, 126, 127. For further reaction to Harris's view see Norman Geisler, *The Battle for the Resurrection* (Nashville: Thos. Nelson, 1989); Robert Culver, *A Wakeup Call* (Clayton, CA: Witness, Inc., 1993).

The Biblical Vocabulary of Resurrection of the Flesh.

A subject as ancient as this and so furiously debated over the past two centuries has generated an enormous apologetical literature, too much to investigate further here. We shall seek to keep as close to Scripture itself as possible through this study.

In the King James Version – whose terms have furnished vocabulary for discussion of 'resurrection' – the expression is used forty-two times, always translating *anastasis* – a standing up. It is a technical term for restoration of life to a dead person in the New Testament, though in non-biblical literature it had this and metaphysical uses. The idea of a corpse reclining in death, rising to the feet and looking abroad is the action indicated. *Rise, risen, rose, arose* and *rising* frequently translate *anistēmi*, which is the verbal equivalent of *anastasis* (above). This is illustrated at Acts 12:7, where an angel struck the sleeping Apostle Peter and said, 'Arise up' (KJV), 'Get up' (RSV). Sometimes these English words translate *egeiro*, usually of Jesus' resurrection. It is sometimes transitive-active in meaning (so *raise*, Acts 4:10, 5:30), sometimes intransitive-active (*rise*, 1 Cor. 15:29). The idea of a human body at rest or deceased rising to the feet is implied whenever applicable to resurrection. Another group of related words for resurrection are *live, liveth, alive, make alive* (revive, quicken), which need no explanation. '[F]irstborn of the dead' (Rev. 1:5) and 'brought again from the dead' (Heb. 13:20) also refer to our Lord's resurrection.

Though in Jesus' language the spiritually 'dead' who 'hear the voice of the Son of God… will live,' i.e. receive new birth (John 5:25), regeneration is not ever called a resurrection, though some would equate 'This is the first resurrection' (Rev. 20:5, 6) with 'this is regeneration.'[14]

In addition to these specific terms for resurrection of the dead, in many contexts such words as *live, lives (liveth), alive* and *make alive (quicken)* imply resurrection.[15] '[C]ome out' is used at John 5:29. Jesus as the first to have complete resurrection to unending, glorified life is called 'firstborn from the dead' (Col. 1:18 KJV).

Orthodox Jews of Jesus' time believed in a future resurrection of the righteous dead. If they, along with Abraham, Isaac, and Jacob, and other saints of the past, were all to share in the blessings of the reign of Messiah, a resurrection would be necessary, according to Emil Schürer,[16] the great historian of Jewish life and beliefs in Jesus' time. R. H. Charles' pioneering work is still a resource for all who examine the subject. He says: 'According to all the Jewish literature of the century [first AD] save the Apocalypse of Baruch and 4 Ezra, there was to be a resurrection of the righteous only.'[17] Charles also argued at great length that the doctrine of personal, individual resurrection was indigenous to Israel. I quote a few lines at the close of his study of 'eschatologies of the individual and of the nation' as follows:

> Thus when the doctrine of the blessed immortality of the faithful is connected with the coming Messianic kingdom, the separate eschatologies of the individual and of the nation issue finally in their synthesis: the righteous individual, no less than the righteous nation, will participate in the Messianic kingdom, for the righteous dead of Isaiah will rise to share therein.[18]

Strack and Billerbeck, in an excursus on John 5:28,[19] say, in preliminary remarks, which translate, 'The pre-Christian Jewish literature has identified the Days of Messiah *yemoth hammashiach* with the future world *olam habba*. The messianic period serves as the time of absolute completion of salvation; accordingly it brings also the resurrection of the dead.'[20] They go on to show that Daniel 12:2 was the fountain of the teaching, but the obscurity of the text led to various interpretations – not only before Christ came but among later rabbis.

It is important to recognize that no heathen source of the idea of resurrection in Israel or the biblical doctrine of resurrection needs be conceded. There is a prevalent critical assumption that the notion came from Zoroastrianism, a religion of Persia, and that the Jews picked up the idea there during exilic and post-exilic times. No one however has found any direct or indirect link. It is true that early Zoroastrianism – about seventh century BC – had a conception of 'eschatology.' Noss remarks, 'According to Zoroaster's teachings, a general resurrection will take place at the end

---

14. More about this later.
15. See, e.g. Rev. 20:4, 'and they came to life and reigned.'
16. Emil Schürer, *A History of the Jewish People*, Second Div., Vol. ii, pp. 130–137.
17. R. H. Charles, *Eschatology: The Doctrine of a Future Life in Israel, Judaism and Christianity* (New York: Schocken Books, 1963), p. 358.
18. ibid., p. 130.
19. 'Allgemeine oder teilweise Auferstehung der Toten' (General or Partial Resurrection of the Dead).
20. Strack & Billerbeck, Vol. iv. 2., p. 1166.

of the present world order.'[21] It is also true that Cyrus, Darius I and Xerxes were Zoroastrians. These three figure in the last three Minor Prophets, Ezra, Nehemiah, and Esther, as well as Daniel. Yet the government 'aid' for the returning Jews was to restore the Jewish religion and temple on its home ground for the worship of the territorial god whose name – and probably little more – Cyrus knew. The faith of the people of the restored commonwealth became Palestinian Judaism and, while cultural accretion occurred from the Hellenization of the Near East, there was only resistance to foreign religion among the most faithful.

Martin-Achard, who devoted exhaustive research to these matters, says that though

> Iranian [Persian] influence on the formation of the Old Testament belief in the resurrection must not be either exaggerated or denied… Zarathustra's [Zoraster] followers did not hand over an entirely unknown idea to the Jews; it is incorrect to speak of borrowing here and even questionable to say, as H. Birkland does, that the decisive factor in formation of the Jewish belief came from the Persian religion. The Iranian doctrine helped the Jews to adopt a conception whose essential elements had already been provided by their own tradition.[22]

E. R. Bernard adds: 'At the most such belief among their foreign rulers did no more than stimulate the home-born expectation of resurrection in the breast of Israel.'[23]

A whole school of Old Testament exegetes and theologians have sought the origin of Israel's late doctrine of resurrection in the Near Eastern beliefs and annual ceremonies of the dying (in the fall) and resurrecting (in the spring) god – Baal, Tammuz, and similar (cf. Ezek. 8:14). Martin-Achard cites J. Peterson,[24] 'The idea of dying and rising God, so dear to the agricultural peoples, was incompatible with the nature of Yahweh,' and adds, 'The Living God does not need to be born.'[25] Brief attention to this basis in Old Testament Scripture now follows.

Resurrection in the Old Testament.

There is no Old Testament divine pronouncement of the resurrection comparable in fullness to statements of the unity of God or that God created the heavens and the earth. What we do have is (1) a series of promises which, to be fulfilled in a manner meaningful to the saints, requires a resurrection in the Messianic age; (2) a saintly awareness of the living God and of their life in Him which led to expectation of a cure from the loss of life in the tragedy of death; (3) examples of bodily translation of saintly people from earth to heaven; (4) several examples of return from physical death to physical life; and (5) many expressions of hope for a future restoration of life (in the flesh) and several prophecies of a resurrection of the righteous – the *hasidim*, true intimates of God.

1. There is a series of promises to the people of God, which, to be fulfilled in a meaningful manner, requires a resurrection in the times of Messiah. The promises to Abraham and his seed furnish the structure for all of Genesis after chapter 11. Over and over God spoke to the three patriarchs in language like this: 'all the land which thou seest [the Land of Canaan], to thee [singular] will I give it, and to thy seed [descendants] for ever' (Gen. 13:15 KJV). God challenges Abram to check out the promised land by walking through it (see vv. 14-18). Similar forms of the promise with much enlargement are found throughout Genesis.[26] All are reports of theophanies or oracles of the highest order of Old Testament religious expression. Among others, not only was David promised an eternal 'house' or dynasty (2 Sam. 7:1-28), also that the people Israel would be the LORD's forever (v. 24). Augustine's comments on Psalm 89:4, that David's 'seed will I establish forever,' makes this point.[27] David claimed to speak for God as a prophet: 'The Spirit of the LORD speaks by me; his word is on my tongue' and his psalm is a divine 'oracle' (2 Sam. 23:1, 2). Later prophets seem to predict that David will himself occupy his throne in times of the Messiah. '[B]ehold, days are coming,' prophesied Jeremiah of coming times of the Messiah, when 'they shall serve the LORD their God and David their king, whom I will raise up for them' (Jer. 30:3, 9). '[R]aise up' here is *aqim*, a form of *qum*, which, though used hundreds of times for any act of rising, is here 'causative' (*hiphil* – i.e. God will cause David to rise from the dead). This word is one of three Hebrew words for resurrection from the dead in Isaiah 26:19 to be considered shortly.

---

21. John B. Noss, *Man's Religion*, 3rd ed. (New York: Macmillan, 5th printing, 1974), p. 343.
22. Robert Martin-Achard, *From Death to Life* (Edinburgh: Oliver & Boyd, 1960), p. 195.
23. E. R. Bernard, 'Resurrection' in Hastings' *Dictionary of the Bible,* Vol. iv, p. 232.
24. *Israel*, Vol. iii-iv, 1926, p. 442.
25. Martin-Achard, ibid., p. 208.
26. Genesis 12:1-3; 15:1-21; 17:1-21 and ff.; 18:1-15; 22:11-18; 27:27-29; 28:1-11; 31:3; 32:24-29; 46:1-4; 48:15-49:27.
27. Augustine in NPNF, Vol. viii, 2nd Series, p. 430.

2. There is the saints' awareness of the living God and of their life in Him, which led to expectation of a cure for loss of life in the tragedy of death. Jesus surely was not the first to think that 'God is not the God of the dead but of the living.' If God was David's 'refuge [and], my portion in the land of the living' (while hiding in a cave, as says the superscription of Ps. 142:5), and he could say that in 'the valley of the shadow of death, I will fear no evil, for you are with me' (Ps. 23), then even in the grave his 'flesh also dwells secure' (Ps. 16). That hope was shared by Job, who in a flash of faith cried out, 'Oh that you would hide me in Sheol, that you would conceal me until your wrath be past, that you would appoint me a set time, and remember me!' (Job 14:13-15).

3. There are examples of bodily translation of godly people without death from earth to heaven. The instances, of course, are Enoch and Elijah. Such is the natural sense of Genesis 5:24, 'Enoch walked with God, and he was not, for God took him,' and is so explained at Hebrews 11:5. So also it is with Elijah (2 Kgs. 2:11), a case where literally God made 'winds' His 'messengers' and fire and flame His 'ministers' (Ps. 104:4). Jews who believing, as we know they did, in a judgment of the 'last day' would have expected something of this sort first.

4. There are several Old Testament examples of miraculous resuscitations, returns from death to life. Murray Harris rightly points out that there are six such in the Old Testament. Three are in the Elijah-Elisha cycle of narrative: the son of the widow of Zarephath (1 Kgs. 17:17-24), the son of a Shunammite woman (2 Kgs. 4:18-37) and the man cast into the grave of Elisha (2 Kgs. 13:20, 21). Though not examples of resurrection to 'eschatological' (transformed) bodies (as in the prophecy of Daniel 12:2), 'they demonstrated that Yahweh's power extended to the grave and could revive even the dead.'[28]

5. There are a few expressions of confidence in a future restoration to physical life. The godly Hannah, mother of Samuel, celebrating the birth of her prayed-for infant Samuel, sang 'The LORD kills and brings to life; he brings down to Sheol and raises up' (1 Sam. 2:6). Join this to the Song of Moses (Deut. 32): 'See now that I, even I, am he, and there is no god beside me; I kill and I make alive; I wound and I heal' (Deut. 32:39).

Granted that both quotations are from poetry where hyperbole (literary exaggeration) is a common figure of speech, the passages seem to indicate belief that God can and may indeed raise the dead to deathless life, if not in every case, in some cases. In this class seems to fall Job's expression of confidence, in Job 19:23-27. Von Rad makes this statement: 'Everyone who reads the book must see in the two passages, Job 16:18 ff. and 19:23 ff., the climax of Job's struggle. Nowhere else does such a certainty and consolation infold him as here. Nevertheless these passages are not to be called the solution, for the dialogue does not of course end here.'[29]

6. And finally, there are several apparently plain prophecies (inspired predictions) of a future resurrection of the holy people (or *hasidim*), intimates of the LORD and His obedient servants. Scholars from earliest times have examined these passages minutely. We cannot here trace the history of exegesis, but results support the claim made at the head of this discussion that the firm belief of the Jews of Jesus' time was based on Old Testament revelation, not mere wishful thinking or borrowing from Persian rulers or Canaanite neighbors. The prophetic passages are in Hosea, Isaiah, Ezekiel and Daniel.[30]

I shall discuss the passages which appear to predict a future resurrection of the dead – whether of the righteous, or of righteous Israelites, of Gentiles, of all – in the order they appear in the English Bible. Some good scholars, e.g. Burton Scott Easton, find only 'two certain passages... Isaiah 26:19 and Daniel 12:2.'[31] Though he discusses several more, Murray Harris adds only Isaiah 53:10-12 and Daniel 12:2 and 13 to Easton's 'certain passages.'[32] Barton Payne adds Hosea 6:2 and 13:14 as well as Isaiah 24:22.[33]

We shall briefly consider each.

---

28. Murray Harris, *From Grave to Glory* (Grand Rapids: Zondervan, 1990), p. 49.
29. Gerhard Von Rad, *Old Testament Theology*, Vol. i, trans. D. M. G. Slatker (Edinburgh: Oliver and Boyd, 1962, 1965), pp. 415, 416.
30. Coming to the Old Testament as we do from the brilliant light of the New Testament on the resurrection from the dead we wonder why the Old Testament in general and the prophets in particular say so little about it. Von Rad derives this near silence from 'Jahvism's tendency to destroy myth in all its forms [which] was not abandoned in its understanding of death... this mysterious world is [contrary to the religions of Israel's neighbors] divested of its sacral character' (Von Rad, ibid., p. 350). He shows that Israel did not derive its 'understanding of the world and of man from the surrounding culture. For the Old Testament view was rather one which needed the constant support of Israel's faith to re-establish and maintain it in the face of the temptations offered by an environment where the determining factor was myth' (Von Rad, *ibid*., p. 351).
31. Burton Scott Easton, 'Resurrection' in ISBE iv, p. 2563.
32. Murray Harris, op. cit., p. 66.
33. Barton Payne, *Theology of the Older Testament* (Grand Rapids: Zondervan, 1962, 1976), p. 460.

There is a class of scholars who, though they apparently have an honest commitment to an orthodox Christology and faith in salvation through Christ's death and resurrection, find almost no genuine prediction of anything in the Old Testament. Yet they find it valuable to faith. R. Martin-Achard is typical in his conclusions on Psalm 16:9-11, which both Peter and Paul quote as prediction of Christ's resurrection (Acts 2:25 ff. and 13:35). His thoughts on the subject follow:

> There is no question of a resurrection here.... This Psalm [post-exilic, not Davidic] is speaking neither of the immortality of the faithful, nor of his translation into the Beyond; the *hasid* is not really concerned about what will happen after death, his sole interest is in praising his chiefest good: Yahweh, God of Israel.
>
> The real question of Psalm 16 is that of communion with the Living God; the writer sees no end to this; he does not trouble his mind, because it depends on God.... After Easter the faith of the psalmist became the great certainty that the Church has to proclaim to the world.[34]

Christ made the whole Old Testament a Christian book when He taught the disciples to interpret 'in all the Scriptures' and 'beginning with Moses and all the Prophets' (Luke 24:27) and in 'the Psalms' (Luke 24:44) things 'concerning himself' (Luke 24:27). 'Then he opened their minds to understand the Scriptures' and 'that... Christ should suffer and on the third day rise from the dead' (Luke 24:45, 46). Of course, not all the Old Testament is Messianic in a direct sense. Evangelical scholars distinguish five or more levels of messianic prophecy, as I have set forth at length in an earlier publication.[35]

Psalm 16:9-11, seen as a prediction, not merely a hope.[36] In Acts 2:24-31 and 13:34-37, first Peter then Paul quote Psalm 16:10 as a prophecy of the resurrection. They had every right to do so for David, whose experience and words they report, was a person typical of Christ. Franz Delitzsch placed this Psalm in the category of indirectly Messianic, or Messianic by hyperbole. The Psalmist described his feelings in such a way that 'he was raised above his own individuality and time, and uses regarding himself hyperbolic [i.e. legitimately exaggerated] expressions which were not to become full historical truth until they became so in Christ.'[37] Let the reader check out how Peter and Paul interpreted the Psalm as prediction of Christ's resurrection. Peter was especially convincing. It became, if it had not been before (and that is not certain), part of the basis on which Jews just before Jesus would have come to believe in resurrection of the dead.

Isaiah 24:1–27:13. This passage predicts, from an Old Testament perspective, the consummation of history – that which the book of Revelation (*Apokalupsis*, English, 'apocalypse') presents through the eyes of a Christian seer with a final perspective. Two parts of this section seem to speak of a future resurrection, both of the righteous and unrighteous. They are not stated in such a way that a doctrine of resurrection could be established, but are certainly suggested. I deal with the entire passage in *Daniel and the Latter Days*.[38] Let us look more closely at two portions of this passage.

Isaiah 24:21-23. 'On that day the LORD will punish the host of heaven, in heaven, and the kings of the earth, on the earth. They will be gathered together as prisoners in a pit; they will be shut up in a prison, and after many days they will be punished. Then the moon will be confounded and the sun ashamed, for the LORD of hosts [armies] reigns on Mount Zion.'

To come quickly to the point – 'the shutting up of wicked kings in a "pit"' or "prison," later to be "visited" in times when Messiah reigns in Zion.' The visitation described, according to uniform Hebrew usage, can be for either deliverance or judgment. This passage suggests the 'resurrection of judgment' of which Jesus spoke (John 5:29).[39]

Isaiah 25:8. 'He will swallow up death for ever, and the LORD GOD will wipe away tears from all faces, and the reproach of his people he will take away from all the earth; for the LORD has spoken' (RSV).

---

34. Martin-Achard, op. cit., pp. 152, 153.
35. Robert D. Culver, *The Life of Christ* (Grand Rapids: Baker, 1976, 1991), pp. 18–24.
36. Also see 2 Sam. 22:2, 3.
37. Franz Delitzsch, *Biblical Commentary on the Psalms*, I (3 vols., Edinburgh: Clark, 1871, 1893), p. 93.
38. Robert D. Culver, *Daniel and the Latter Days* (Chicago: Moody Press, 1977) or The Earthly Reign of our Lord With His People (available from author, 1998), p. 57 ff.
39. See Culver, ibid., p. 58. See also C. Von Orelli, *Prophecies of Isaiah*, pp. 142, 143.

This will be in the time the divine Savior for whom Israel has waited (v. 9) has come and has set up a feast of reconciliation 'for all peoples' (v. 6). From a New Testament perspective that is the *parousia*, the Second Advent. Portions of this verse are quoted in Paul's resurrection chapter, 1 Corinthians 15 (v. 54), and in Revelation 7:17 and 21:4. Though every line asks for comment, we press on. Jewish people of Jesus' time had got the message, we may be sure.

Isaiah 26:1, 19. 'In that day [when God has brought messianic rest] this song will be sung in the land of Judah...

> Your dead shall live;
> Together with my dead body they shall arise.
> Awake and sing, you who dwell in dust;
> For your dew is like the dew of herbs;
> And the earth shall cast out the dead (nkjv).

Liberal critical authors find a plethora of figures drawn from Canaanite myth in the passage and, of course, if some of the language of that culture was in the mind of Isaiah he may have used it. Yet Von Rad's dictum that Hebrew religion and language was steadily against these scholars' opinions is valid. The language of dead bodies arising, awakening and singing, dwellers in dust rising as fresh as morning dew, the earth to which innumerable Adams have returned giving up her dead, all speak of literal resurrection – whether also transformation is not said. In context it is not a general resurrection. 'My dead bodies' (perhaps God's or perhaps the prophet's) suggests the resurrection of the righteous dead only.

Isaiah 53:10-12. It is the fashion of modern Old Testament scholarship to detect four 'servant songs' in Isaiah 42–53. Jesus applied portions of them as predictions of Himself. New Testament interpretation of the meaning of the death of Christ does so in the fourth and last of these 'songs,' Isaiah 52:13–53:12.[40] These fifteen verses constitute a poem of five stanzas of three verses each. The first verse (53:10) of the last stanza promises compensation and reward for the Servant's suffering and vicarious death. Three benefits accrue to Him. They are the very rewards characteristic of successful work in ancient Hebrew society: (1) numerous family ('he shall see his offspring'); (2) a long life ('he shall prolong his days'); and (3) successful accomplishment of life's purposes ('the will [plan, pleasure] of the Lord shall prosper in his hand'). This is the sequel to being killed (v. 8), assigned a grave in a potter's field 'with the wicked' (v. 9) yet buried in the tomb a 'rich man' (v. 9).

The Old Testament people who read these lines must have wondered how one martyred by his contemporaries (v. 8) could enjoy these three benefits, especially the prolonging of 'his days.' Like Abraham, who 'considered that God was able even to raise him from the dead' (Heb. 11:19), they might have considered just that possibility. Any Jew of Jesus' time and for long before would have been prepared for the full New Testament revelation of the resurrection of the dead. I have discussed these verses in Isaiah at length elsewhere.[41]

Two passages in Hosea help lay a foundation for the doctrine of resurrection as found in Jewish expectation in Jesus' time, as well as among the inter-testamental saints and their literature (Apocrypha and pseudepigrapha). Hosea, who prophesied in the northern kingdom, was contemporary with Isaiah, who addressed the southern kingdom shortly before and after the turn of the eighth to seventh centuries bc. For present purposes we may be brief. Scholars no less than lay readers find Hosea's oracles difficult to relate either to historical or literary context and his Hebrew is extremely difficult, due to lack of grammatical connections. Yet what he has to say about resurrection is important as background to Jewish expectations of Jesus' time and the New Testament doctrine.

Hosea 6:1-3 quotes some unidentified person, perhaps God, perhaps the prophet or some group of Israelites, expressing perhaps sincere repentance, perhaps presumptuousness:

> Come, let us return to the Lord; for he has torn, that he may heal us; he has stricken, and he will bind us up...
> that we may live before him. Let us know, let us press on to know the Lord; his going forth is sure as the dawn;
> he will come to us as the showers, as the spring rains that water the earth (rsv).

The 'spring rain' and 'the showers' are of course associated with the revival (apparent restoration to life) of nature after winter. The verbs unambiguously assert resurrection, being the same as was used in Isaiah 26:14 and 19 and

---

40. The centrality of the prophecy of Isaiah 52:13–53:12 to New Testament interpretation is demonstrated in this work in connection with 'Part 4: Christology, specifically Christ's death as a substitutionary sacrifice. There are dozens of New Testament references and allusions.
41. Culver, *The Sufferings and the Glory of the Lord's Righteous Servant* (Eugene, OR: Wipf and Stock Publ., 2001), pp. 109–114.

Daniel 12:2. Yet the revivals, living before God, are national, not personal. The northern kingdom was being threatened with an extinction which soon came. Someone (perhaps a pious remnant) hopes that beyond the extinction there will be a restoration, as the prophet had graphically predicted earlier (probably) in chapters 2 and 3. Though details of the three verses invite technical comment, the value of the passage is plain for present purposes. The Hebrews of the eighth century BC were already acquainted with the idea of physical resurrection and had language to express it.[42]

Hosea 13:14 – 'Shall I ransom them from the power of Sheol? Shall I redeem them from Death? O Death, where are your plagues? O Sheol, where is your destruction?' (RSV).

On this reading in context the questions imply that the LORD 'expresses despair over an unrepentant people who refuse to allow him to spare them the pains of exile.'[43] Death and Sheol are invited to come to destroy Ephraim (northern kingdom of Israel). But the Hebrew question mark (letter h) is not present. So a 'jussive' (I would) or indicative mood (I will) is more likely (as in KJV, ASV, NIV). The KJV language, which renders the Hebrew well, is partly reflected in 1 Corinthians 15:54, 55, where Paul employs it for the climax of a chapter on the resurrection of the body. The KJV reads, 'I will ransom them from the power of the grave; I will redeem them from death: O death, I will be thy plagues; O grave, I will be thy destruction.'

In any case, whether threat or promise, the passage (from God's mouth, so to speak) 'demonstrates that death is Yahweh's servant and that resurrection is therefore not impossible.'[44]

Ezekiel 37, a prophecy of restoration of dry bones to life, in a valley of dry bones, is a prediction purely of national restoration, though the notion of physical resurrection is the vehicle of expression. This again demonstrates the presence of the idea among sixth-century Jews.

Daniel 12:2, 3 (and 13) specifically predicts a limited future resurrection of the righteous and possibly of the unrighteous in unambiguous language. I reserve treatment for a later connection.

I think the Old Testament itself has demonstrated for us that though some of the modes of expressing resurrection from the dead may have been derived from the Near East culture of the time, the idea of resurrection of the flesh was contra-mythical in Israel, and that the idea arose from their revealed faith. It is a unique feature of biblical religion in details as we shall develop them in following pages.

The New Testament Doctrine of the Resurrection of the Dead.

Resurrection of the Essence of Christianity.

Though the resurrection of Christ and the resurrection of the righteous dead are not mentioned on every page of the New Testament, the Christian Testament and the religion of the same would be pointless without them.

J. E. Fison, an unusually outspoken Anglican prelate, put the case this way.

> The distinctive biblical perspective is focused on no continuance of a psychological something within us, called the soul, but rather on the incomprehensible miracle which affects the whole of us. Resurrection and not immortality is the Christian faith here and now and the Christian hope hereafter. From the beginning of creation to the end of time the Christian faith is a materialistic faith. The eschatological focus of Christian thinking as well as the eucharistic focus of Christian worship is not upon an immaterial state of being or upon some spiritual experience but upon a meeting of embodied man, with embodied God and with embodied fellow men and even with embodied nature. Out of the final meeting will come a transformation affecting not only men but nations [Isa. 11:1-9; Rom. 8:18 ff.]. There is no hint of pie in the sky when you die; there is no strategic withdrawal from the body and from the world. On the contrary, in and through the embodied meeting [the resurrection day] is offered the hope of the transformation of the human body and of the material world.[45]

This is orthodox affirmation a pole apart from the liberalism and neo-orthodoxy of Fison's day when – as Brunner was asserting – 'resurrection is mere personal survival.' Fison's vigorous, if reserved, prose is exceeded in force by the Apostle's fierce rebuttal of denial of eschatological re-embodiment, not only of Christ but of believers in particular and of all mankind in general.

---

42. Francis I. Anderson and David N. Freedman, *Hosea, The Anchor Bible* (New York: Doubleday, 1980) is excellent on technical data of this verse. Author accepts the data on the future life in Psalms provided by Ugaritic research of Dahood and his disciples.
43. M. Harris, op. cit., p. 65.
44. M. Harris, op. cit., p. 66. F. I. Anderson, op. cit., is excellent on technical problems of the verse.
45. J. E. Fison, *The Christian Hope: The Presence and the Parousia* (London: Longmans, Green & Co., 1952), p. 50.

It is uncertain whom Paul had in mind when he wrote, 'Now if Christ is proclaimed as raised from the dead, how can some of you say that there is no resurrection of the dead?' (1 Cor. 15:12). Were they former Sadducees and now members of the congregation at Corinth? Former heathen Epicureans who did not leave their peculiar denial of the worth of the flesh behind? Former ascetical Essenes or denizens of Qumran? Was it nascent Gnosticism? Or just some philosophically inclined believers, lately come over from the Stoa or Academy at Athens? Whoever they were, the consequences of the denial had to be addressed, as Paul proceeded to do in *1 Corinthians 15*.

A. Paul characterizes their objection as a denial of resurrection of the dead in principle. (1) In such a case the gospel Paul 'preached' (v. 12 KJV) is false, and (2) Christ did not rise from the dead (v. 13). (3) In consequence of such a denial of Christ's resurrection the Corinthians' faith in Christ is vain (*kenos*, empty) (v. 14) and (4) Paul and his fellow missionaries, Apollos, Silas, Timothy, Peter, Priscilla and Aquila, are misrepresenting God and are false witnesses (v. 15).

B. As further consequence of the logical subversion of Christ's resurrection (vv. 14, 17) not only is 'your faith… futile (Gr. *mataia*, groundless, fallacious) but your sins are still unforgiven by God (v. 17) and the believers who had already died have 'perished,' never to be met again at the future return of Christ (v. 18; see vv. 51-55).

C. Such a 'this-life-only' outlook only increases the misery of the professed Christians who adopt it: 'If in this life only we have hoped in Christ, we are of all people most to be pitied [most miserable, KJV]' (v. 19). Yet there are moments and sometimes long periods of doubt and spiritual depression, when just such a paragraph as this, even for some great saints, is helpful to turn our thoughts away from self to Christ, who said 'Because I live, you also will live' (John 14:19).

Resurrection in the Life and Teachings of Jesus.

Jesus performed several 'resurrections' in the sense of resuscitations, among many other miracles of His power and 'authority on earth to forgive sins' (Matt. 9:6). He called attention to this miracle in response to John's question about His Messiahship (Matt. 11:5). It was His own resurrection in a deathless body, however, that He set forth as a 'sign' (John 2:19-20; Matt. 12:32-40). And during His ministry Jesus confirmed His power and authority as 'the one who is to come' (Matt. 11:3), i.e. the promised Messiah, by raising the dead (Matt. 11:5), among whom were a certain widow's son (Luke 7:12-15), Jairus' daughter (Luke 8:41, 42, 49-56), and, famously, Lazarus of Bethany (John 11:41-44). These were restorations of natural life, not eschatological resurrection and transformation, of which Jesus' own resurrection was to be the very first, 'the first fruits of those who have fallen asleep' (1 Cor. 15:20 RSV).

Though Jesus assured us, 'Because I live, you also will live' (John 14:19), He did not provide many details or any theological construct as to the nature of the resurrection body, its characteristics and powers. We must turn to the entire New Testament for that.

Specific Reference of 'Resurrection' Is to the Human Body.

When redemption is the subject of Scripture teaching, it is the whole of man which is redeemed – body and soul. Body as well as soul are redeemed (Rom. 8:23), but the word 'resurrection' is always, without exception, of the body, never the soul. Jesus did speak of regeneration as the dead hearing the voice of the Son of God and living (John 5:25), and a bit later of a certain parallel with resurrection of 'all that are in the graves,' but for good reason He did not call regeneration a resurrection. As J. A. Schep says, orthodox Jews of Jesus' time

> believed strongly in the resurrection of the body of flesh…. Consequently, when Jesus spoke of resurrection and the apostles taught the resurrection of the body, there was no sense in emphasizing the fact the resurrection-body would consist of flesh.[46]

According to Jesus 'all who are in the tombs' on the last day 'will hear his voice and come out' either to 'the resurrection of life' or 'the resurrection of judgment' (John 5:28, 29). For the saved, the resurrection will be in a changed and glorious body (Phil. 3:2; 1 Cor. 15:49). We are told nothing of the nature of the bodies of those raised for judgment (John 5:29), who 'did not come to life until the thousand years were ended' (Rev. 20:5).

---

46. J. A. Schep, *The Nature of the Resurrection Body* (Grand Rapids: Eerdmans, 1964), pp. 184, 185.

Hence from here on our discussion will relate almost entirely to the resurrection of the saved. The resurrection of Jesus Himself was of 'the temple of his body' (John 2:19-22) and His resurrection is to be the pattern of ours, 'like his glorious body' (Phil. 3:21), for, 'we know that when he appears we shall be like him, because we shall see him as he is' (1 John 3:2). Therefore both ancient and modern evangelical (Protestant) creeds say that in the same body in which Jesus suffered and died He arose and is going to come again. It therefore is with resurrected bodies, as such, that resurrection is concerned.[47]

The Extent of the Resurrection.

The Old Testament speaks clearly and unmistakably of physical resurrection of the dead in only two passages, Isaiah 26:19 and Daniel 12:2. The latter is in an eschatological setting of tribulation (v. 1) and eternal rewards (v. 3). English translations usually seem to teach a general resurrection of both righteous and wicked dead, but neither the Hebrew text nor the commentators agree that resurrection of the wicked is contemplated in Daniel 12:2. My own opinion, which I have defended in several earlier works, is that Daniel's informer is speaking only of the resurrection of 'many' righteous, probably Israelites, at a remote future time.[48] We earlier called attention to expressions of Jewish belief in a future resurrection, but less than clear revelation of resurrection in the Old Testament.

References to future physical resurrection in Jewish inter-testamental literature (mostly of martyrs or of righteous only) do not speak with such authority as to require discussion here.

The New Testament, as seen earlier, promises physical resurrection of both the righteous and unrighteous (Acts 24:15; John 5:29; Rev. 20:12). We pursue the subject further in the next chapter.

---

47. We must not enter into the vast field of New Testament criticism and liberal reconstruction of this matter. Schep is a good guide both as to limiting the project to what the canonical texts say and drawing out their meaning. G. C. H. Berkouwer, 'Resurrection' in *The Return of Christ* (Grand Rapids: Eerdmans, 1972), pp. 170–210 does the same in brief fashion. The two works by Murray Harris are valuable because they explore the field but should be used with caution: *Raised Immortal: Resurrection and Immortality the New Testament* (1983) and *From Grave to Glory* (1990). Dr Harris concludes 'the believer's resurrection body will come from heaven, not the grave,' Raised Immortal, p. 44 and 'dead persons are raised, not impersonal corpses' (ibid., p. 133).

48. C. F. Keil essentially agrees, *Commentary on Daniel*, pp. 481, 482 as also S. P. Tregelles, *Remarks on the Prophetic Visions in the Book of Daniel*, p. 168; Barton Payne, *The Theology of the Older Testament*, pp. 461, 462. See my *Daniel and the Latter Days*, rev. ed., 1977, pp. 183–187; also 'Daniel' in *The Wycliffe Bible Commentary*, 1962, p. 798; *Histories and Prophecies of Daniel*, 1980, pp. 186, 187.

5

The Doctrine of the Resurrection of the Dead II: Time and Order of the Resurrection of the Dead

At this point in our study of last things a persistent question which arose acutely in the fourth century calls for attention. Jesus said, 'The hour is coming when all who are in the tombs will hear his voice and come forth, those who have done good, to the resurrection of life, and those who have done evil, to the resurrection of judgment' (John 5:28, 29 RSV). Most Christian teachers before Augustine (fourth century) were much agreed that the Lord here specified two future times of resurrection for two different groups of people, the earlier for saints ('those who have done good') at the *parousia* (coming), *apocalupsis* (revelation) and *epiphaneia* (manifestation) of the Lord Jesus. These are the three most common New Testament words for the 'come again' (John 14:3) of Jesus (cf. Acts 1:11). They expected a later resurrection (after a thousand years) of 'those who have done evil, to the resurrection of judgment' (RSV) or 'damnation' (KJV). These were held to be the same as 'a resurrection of both the just and the unjust' (Acts 24:15).

These Fathers of the church found the view of the future filled out plainly in Revelation 19–20. There Christ comes with the armies of heaven to conquer and incarcerate 'the beast and the false prophet' and 'the dragon' (Satan). Then follows a scene where enthroned 'saints' (cf. 20:4, 'those to whom the authority to judge was committed' with 1 Cor. 6:3) and martyrs come to life and reign 'with Christ for a thousand years' (Rev. 20:4). The next verses say 'This is the first resurrection' – seeming to imply a second resurrection – of the unrighteous, for the verse also says, 'The rest of the dead did not come to life until the thousand years were ended.... Blessed and holy is the one who shares in the first resurrection!' Another resurrection of 'the rest of the dead' – the wicked dead, it would seem – is detailed in verses 11-14.

This is a very unsophisticated approach and seems to have prevailed through the first three Christian centuries. During the fourth century persecutions ceased, Christianity prevailed and was becoming not only official but popular. Christian leaders began to doubt their earlier opinion that Rome was the Antichrist to be destroyed before the 'Second Advent.' Augustine (354–430) reinterpreted the thousand-year reign of saints as of the present age by deceased saints in heaven, and the 'first resurrection' as personal regeneration. Emphasis came to be placed on the 'hour' of John 5:28 ('[the] hour is coming') as literally a very short time and not two separate eschatological resurrections, but one called 'the general resurrection' to be followed by a 'general judgment.' The older view was known as 'chiliasm' (Gr. thousand-ism), now usually 'premillennialism,' the newer view, 'amillennialism.' The latter view prevailed in the church until premillennialism was revived somewhat in Reformation times by 'left wing Protestants' and then became popular in several modified forms in the nineteenth century.

The development and present forms of millennial interpretations are very complicated. I have presented them in their simplest historic form simply to lay out the background of the question of two eschatological resurrections, and shall now proceed to sketch first the view that there will be two future resurrections, first, of 'the just,' and, second, of 'the unjust.' After that we shall present the view that there is to be only one resurrection. The reader who is uninitiated to this subject should know that there is immense literature on it, that it is imbedded deeply in certain prevalent systems of evangelical theology, and that these differences cross denominational lines.

The View of Two Future Resurrections.

We shall first examine two chief passages which furnish a framework for the doctrine, called 'historic premillennialism', then supporting texts, after that linguistic evidences, and finally a summary.

Revelation 19:11-20.

Some attention has just now been devoted to these climatic verses.[1] Near the beginning of the book of Revelation, John writes, 'Behold, he is coming with the clouds, and every eye will see him, every one who pierced him' (Rev. 1:7 RSV). This counts strongly for a futuristic interpretation of the book of Revelation. On that basis the climax falls at 19:11, where the seer sees heaven opened and forthwith follows the termination of Antichrist's persecutions of the believers by destruction of the earthly forces of Satan, followed, as we have seen, by a coming to life of saints and martyrs – 'those who have done good' (Rev. 20:4-6; cf. John 5:29) to a 'resurrection of life.' Then after 'the thousand years are ended' comes a vision of a judgment scene to which 'the rest of the dead' are summoned by resurrection from every conceivable place of disposal of their dead bodies (Rev. 20:11-14).

S. P. Tregelles (1813–1875) is perhaps best known for his work and leadership in preparing a critical list of manuscripts of the Greek New Testament and his translation of the Gesenius Hebrew Lexicon. What is not so well known is his strong exposition and defence of historic premillennialism. He quotes Revelation 20:1-4 and comments:

> This is not only a vision, but also an explanation. John is taught what the thrones with certain sitting on them meant. They are the faithful in Christ in general (i.e. the whole family of faith from Abel onward), and one special class, those suffering for the witness of Jesus; and the glory given to them is explained to be the first resurrection. This is in full accordance with ... 1 Cor. 15:23, where the order of the resurrection is taught: 'Every man in his own order: Christ the firstfruits; afterward (i.e. next in order), they that are Christ's at his coming.'[2]

Premillenarians insist that, granting the presence of much symbolism in Revelation 20 (key, chain and the like), the flow of thought requires a literal series of events. Otherwise we are left to pure subjectivism, i.e. to make the story fit what we bring to it. If we draw our doctrine from the text it teaches two future resurrections – one of the saved at Christ's coming and another of those who are not His a thousand years later. Some of contrary opinion say the first resurrection is spiritual (i.e., regeneration as in John 5:25, not physical as in John 5:29). Famous comments by a great, devout scholar bear repeating:

> As regards the text itself, no legitimate treatment of it will extort what is known as the spiritual interpretation now in fashion. If in passages where two resurrections are mentioned, where certain *psuchai edzesan* (souls lived) at the first, and the rest of the *nechroi edzesan* (dead lived) only at the end of a specified period after the first – if in such a passage the first resurrection may be understood to mean spiritual rising from the grave – then there is an end of all significance of language, and Scripture is wiped as a definite testimony to anything.[3]

1 Corinthians 15:1-28.

I cite KJV here, and refer especially to verses 22-24. This is part of the longest continuous treatment of the resurrection of the dead in the Bible.

Let us see how Paul's discourse on resurrection leads up to the matter of resurrection of all the dead.

1. In verses 1-5 Paul states all the elements of the saving 'gospel' which 'I preached' – of which the last is Christ, who died and was buried, 'rose again the third day.'

---

1. I have published a more complete treatment of this and the other texts to follow in *Daniel and the Latter Days*, rev. ed. (Chicago: Moody Press, 1977), and a further rev. ed. entitled *The Earthly Reign of Our Lord with His People* (self-published).
2. S. P. Tregelles, *The Hope of Christ's Second Coming*, 5th ed. (London: The Sovereign Grace Advent Testimony, 1986), pp. 29, 30.
3. Henry Alford, *Greek Testament with a Critically Revised Text* 4:732–733.

2. '[H]e was seen of Cephas, then [*eita*, after that] of the twelve' (v. 5).

3. 'After that [*epeita*, it interchanges with eita in Greek] he was seen of above five hundred' (v. 6).

4. 'After that [*epeita*], he was seen of James; then [*eita*] of all the apostles' (v. 7).

5. 'And last of all he was seen of me also.' In verses 8-11 the Apostle declares how he saw the risen Christ and explains the meaning of the event.

It is easy to see that *eita* and its enlarged form *epeita* are interchangeable and mean 'after that' with reference to succession of events and passage of time, not 'at the same time' or 'immediately after.' The 'five hundred' of verse 6, for example, saw the risen Christ several weeks after the Twelve (v. 5) saw Him. The length of time designated by *eita* or *epeita* will depend on what series is being described. Events in atomic fission occur quickly 'after that,' but in growing a seed into a crop of wheat, weeks are involved.[4] (See Mark 4:26-29, 'first the blade, then [*eiten* = *eita*] the ear, after that [*eiten*] the full corn in the ear.')

6. Paul proceeds to set forth the absolute essentiality of Christ's resurrection to Christianity (vv. 12-19). We treated these verses earlier. From this point onward Paul assumes the resurrection of Christ really took place. In verses 20-28 he explains that not all dead men will rise at the same time – even though 'all that are in the graves,' as Jesus said, shall in a future 'hour' come forth at the sound of the 'voice' of 'the Son of man' (John 5:27-29). Paul reveals that there are three stages in the resurrection process, one already complete (of 'Christ the firstfruits') followed by two more in the future. Let us trace his thought.

i. Christ '[became] the firstfruits of them that slept' (v. 20). '[S]lept' is a euphemism for death and burial in a sleep-like posture. Paul is asking us to think in terms of order of events. No one ever before Jesus arose from the dead in a living glorified 'eschatological' body. So He was *aparchē*, 'from-beginning,' the first one. Others are to follow.

ii. Man (Adam) brought death and Man (Christ) brought resurrection (v. 21).

iii. 'For as in Adam all [the whole race of mankind] die, even so in Christ shall all be made alive' (v. 22). The subject of the whole of our race continues. Most commentators agree that in this passage 'in Christ' includes the human race as a whole. The phrase does not designate believers only (as so often in Ephesians and elsewhere). It is defined by the parallel with 'in Adam' as in Romans 5:9 ff. The entire human race is in Adam.

iv. 'But everyman in his own order [*tagma*]' (v. 23). All sources agree that the word *tagma* does not mean position in a series, as in ranking honors students who are placed first, second, third and so on in their class. Rather a whole group, cohort, body, collection of people is designated. There are three such groups in the resurrection, as appears: Christ the firstfruits, they that are Christ's and the end group.

'Christ the firstfruits,' is the first rank, a group of one only. '[A]fterward [*epeita*, not 'at same time,' but *after an interval*] they that are Christ's at his coming.' This is the resurrection of a second *tagma* or group or rank, those who are Christ's – everyone from our first parents on to the last saint to die before Jesus' return. In 1 Thessalonians 4:15 'the coming' (*tēn parousian*), *parousia* meaning 'coming,' refers to the time of resurrection and to the translation of the saved ('rapture') and the judgment of the Antichrist (2 Thess. 2:8). Both of these events occur at the *parousia*, which takes us directly to Revelation 19:16-21 (the destruction of 'the beast' and 'the false prophet,' evidently followed by (or co-ordinate with) the 'first resurrection' of Revelation 20:1-5.

v. 'Then [*eita*, afterwards] cometh the end' (v. 24). After the resurrection of 'Christ's' people a third *tagma* (rank) will be raised from the dead. Taking Revelation 20 as guide, this will be the wicked dead who face the judgment of the great white throne '[after] the thousand years are expired (Rev. 20:7, 11). If this is not the case then Paul seemed to promise a resurrection schedule for every 'man' in 1 Corinthians 15:22, 23, but left out the wicked dead in his schedule. Admittedly it is possible that he left them out for some reason. If so Revelation 20 includes them in the schedule.

These are the chief passages of Scripture on which contemporary advocates of two future resurrections rest their view.

Supporting Texts for Two Future Resurrections.

The clearest Old Testament text teaching a doctrine of resurrection of the dead is Daniel 12:1-2, which reads:

> And at that time shall Michael stand up, the great prince who standeth for the children of thy people [Daniel's people, Israel]; and there shall be a time of trouble, such as never was since there was a nation even to that

---

4. Bauer, Arndt & Gingrich, *Greek-English Lexicon*, sub *eita*.

same time: and at that time thy people shall be delivered, every one that shall be found written in the book (Dan. 12:1 ASV).

Commentators almost unanimously agree that this is eschatological, describing the great tribulation of the Last Days, and most agree that it relates primarily to Israel, presumed to exist as a national entity. The passage goes on to make the first clear reference to a partial resurrection of the dead, of the righteous only: 'And many of them that sleep in the dust of the earth shall awake, some to everlasting life, and some to shame and everlasting contempt' (Dan. 12:2 ASV).

S. P. Tregelles asks, 'If language of this verse be not declaratory of a resurrection of the dead, actual and literal, is there any passage of Scripture at all which speaks of such a thing as a resurrection?'[5] To what resurrection does it refer? It takes place at or near the time of the great tribulation and of deliverance of the nation of Israel. Who are included? 'Many, not all,' C. F. Keil insisted, quite against what he as an amillennialist might have wished 'all [is] a meaning, *rabbim* (many) cannot have.'[6] Further, says this great scholar, the word *min* must mean some, not all the 'sleepers' in the dust, that 'the angel has it not in view to give a general statement regarding the resurrection of the dead.'[7]

So it is not only premillennarians who regard Daniel 12:2 as teaching a future resurrection which includes saints only. This lends support to the above interpretation of 1 Corinthians 15 and Revelation 20 as teaching two future resurrections. I quote from an earlier work of mine which is part of a five-page discussion of Daniel 12:1, 2:

> The Hebrew of the passage permits and, according to many of the best authorities, demands a translation favoring this view. The translation, brought to the attention of the English reading public by Tregelles[8] and advocated before him by Jewish commentators Saadia Haggon (10th century) and Aben Ezra (12th century)... as given by Tregelles, it is: 'And many from among sleepers of the dust shall awake; these shall be unto everlasting life; but those the rest of the sleepers, those who do not awake at this time, shall be unto shame and everlasting contempt.'[9]

It should be admitted by advocates of the two future resurrections view that supporting 'proof' is absent, but there are certain specific expressions which seem to favor the view. The ones usually cited are 'a better resurrection' (Heb. 11:35), 'the resurrection of the just' (Luke 14:14). There are also passages which seem to separate a resurrection of the righteous from a resurrection of the unrighteous, as in John 5:28, 29 (ESV): 'for an hour is coming when all who are in the tombs, will hear his [Son of Man's] voice and come out, those who have done good to the resurrection of life, and those who have done evil to the resurrection of judgment.' This passage seems to speak of two resurrections but it may also be construed to refer to two results of one. If two, then the 'hour' must be understood as indicating simply a long period of time. It proves nothing either way. Like Hebrews 11:35 and Luke 14:14 (cited above) 1 Thessalonians 4:13-20 describes a resurrection of saints only and locates it in time at the Second Advent. If there is to be a general resurrection of all at one time why no mention of a resurrection of the 'unjust' in these important passages? There is no evidence of being raised for a discriminating or penal judgment there. The souls of those who have gone 'to be with Christ' come 'with him' to rejoin their freshly resurrected bodies. There is no evidence of a resurrection of the unsaved here at all, however one accounts for it.

Linguistic Evidence for Two Future Resurrections.

Paul refers to his own future resurrection in a peculiar way as attaining unto 'the resurrection of the dead' (Phil. 3:11). A rare Greek word for 'resurrection' appears only here in the New Testament – *exanastasis*, literally, 'the-out-from-resurrection.' 'Of the dead' translates *ek nekrou* 'out from dead.' The best Greek texts are clear. Paul is contemplating not a resurrection 'of' the dead, but an *out-resurrection* 'from among the dead' (see Alford and Meyer *in loco*).

Whenever the New Testament reports or claims a resurrection 'from the dead' (not 'from death') the usual expression is 'risen from the dead' (Gr. *ek nekrou*; the first occurrence relates to, the supposed resurrection of John the Baptist in Matt. 14:2). In such case John would rise from among the many dead who did not also rise. It is not from death (*thanatos*) but 'out from among dead people.' *Ek nekrōn* is usual for the resurrection of Jesus – 'out from

---

5. S. P. Tregelles, *Remarks on the Prophetic Visions in the Book of Daniel*, 7th ed. (London: Sovereign Grace Advent Testimony, 1965), p. 168.
6. C. F. Keil, *Biblical Commentary on Daniel*, p. 482.
7. ibid., p. 481.
8. Tregelles, op. cit., pp. 162 ff.
9. Culver, op. cit., p. 186.

among the dead' (Matt. 17:9). But when the possibility of resurrection in general is contemplated and the Sadducean denial of the same – 'touching the resurrection of the dead' – the Greek does not supply *ek*, out of *tou nekrōn*. The words mean 'of the dead,' not 'out from the dead.' Throughout the New Testament the future resurrection of the righteous is designated as an *ek nekrou* resurrection, 'out from the dead ones.' In 1 Corinthians 15:12 the resurrection of Christ is *ek nekrōn*, 'out-resurrection,' but resurrection as a general event is *anastasis nekrōn*, 'resurrection of dead ones.'

To summarize: premillennalists affirm 'the teachings of two resurrections is a clear assertion of Scripture and the teaching of a single resurrection must pass over several important passages.'[10] If, as almost all agree, the resurrection at the end of the millennium (Rev. 20:4-15) is literal, so is the first. 'Two literal bodily resurrections are demanded.'[11] Other passages throughout the New Testament suggest or presuppose a first resurrection unto life and a second to damnation (John 5:29). Jesus spoke of 'the resurrection of the just' (Luke 14:14) and in Luke 20:35 of a resurrection 'from among dead ones' as a goal for believers – not a general resurrection of all.

Paul as a Pharisee believed in a future resurrection of the dead (Acts 23:6), but he personally hoped to attain to a special resurrection of the righteous, which he carefully designated *tēn exanastasin tēn ek nekrōn*, the out-resurrection from among the dead ones (Phil. 3:11). At His coming they that are Christ's shall rise from the dead (1 Cor. 15:23) and afterward at 'the end' of a time unspecified (by Paul), the rest of the dead 'shall rise,' as Revelation 20 teaches. This view claims to rest its case on explicit affirmation of Scripture, not on any manipulation of texts.[12]

The View of One Future Resurrection.

Another way of designating the one future resurrection view is amillennialism – i.e. denial of any long period (the thousand years of Rev. 20) between a first resurrection of the just and a second of the unjust. In the course of writing and lecturing on this matter over a good many years I have encountered a very large amount of amillennial (and postmillennial) theological and exegetical literature denying two resurrections and affirming one. I have brought much of it up to date in text and notes of *The Earthly Reign of our Lord With His People* (1998).

Perhaps the fairest, most comprehensive and convincing advocacy of this view was set forth by Geerhardus Vos, Professor of Biblical Theology at Princeton Theological Seminary.[13] My own brand of premillennialism, or chiliasm, finds much support in evidence Vos brings forth 'that a hard and fast distinction between a Messianic kingdom and the ultimate kingdom of God cannot be carried through in Paul'.[14] I have argued at length that the cosmic changes described in (for example) Isaiah 65 and 66 and 2 Peter 3:10, 11 introduce the Messianic (or millennial) age rather than conclude it and that the Messianic age is an initial stage of the eternal, not preliminary to it.[15]

Postmillennialists of the past such as Daniel Whitby (1638–1726)[16] affirm the Great Commission and other texts as showing that the gospel will continue to work like leaven in the bowl of dough until the whole world professes Christianity and then the second Advent, a general resurrection and a general judgment will take place. In recent times this view has been defended by Lorraine Boettner[17] and J. Marcellus Kik.[18] Contemporarily, articles asserting that it is God's program to win the world for Christ and to establish biblically based civil government everywhere appear regularly in *Chalcedon*, organ of the Reconstruction Movement,[19] and in its official statement of beliefs. *(Faith for All of Life* is the new name of this magazine.)

It is acknowledged by most exegetes and theologians that a literal interpretation of Revelation 20 plainly extracts two future resurrections – first, one of the godly and a later one, of the ungodly. A prominent (amillennial) exponent of one general resurrection well wrote:

10. George Ladd, *The Blessed Hope* (Grand Rapids: Eerdmans, 1956), p. 81.
11. ibid., p. 81.
12. A strong summary statement of evidence for two future resurrections quite apart from the thousand years of Revelation 20 was published in 1866 in Edinburgh and inserted by the American editor of Lange's *Commentary on Revelation*, last line on p. 353 and top half of p. 354. Though now over 125 years old, this lengthy work is exceedingly valuable, especially on account of the additions by the American editor, E. R. Craven.
13. Geerhardus Vos, chap. 9, 'The Extent of the Resurrection' and chap. 10, 'The Question of Chiliasm,' *The Pauline Eschatology* (Grand Rapids: Eerdmans, 1952), pp. 215–260.
14. ibid., p. 260.
15. Robert Culver, *Daniel and the Latter Days*, rev. ed. 1977, pp. 41–65.
16. Daniel Whitby ended his life as an Arian, and during his orthodox phase really 'invented' postmillennialism.
17. Lorraine Boettner, *The Millennium* (Philadelphia: Presbyterian & Reformed Publ., 1970).
18. J. Marcellus Kik, *An Eschatology of Victory* (Philadelphia: Presbyterian & Reformed Publ., 1971).
19. The Reconstruction Movement, P.O. Box 158, Vallecito, CA 95251-9989.

> The most prominent line of cleavage among interpreters is between those who, with due allowance for figures of speech, take the vision literally, and those who consider it a symbol. The former see here a description of events that must come to pass substantially as written, at some future time: The latter understand it to be a symbolical presentation of some spiritual truth, or of events that happened long ago.[20]

In modern times those who take the one-resurrection view are either postmillennialists or amillennialists – to employ the theological jargon.

> Postmillennialism is that view of the last things which holds that the kingdom of God is now being extended in the world through the preaching of the gospel… that the world eventually is to be Christianized.[21]

Boettner adds that after this takes place the Second Coming will occur, to 'be followed immediately by the general resurrection, the general judgment, i.e. heaven… hell.'[22] First expounded by Daniel Whitby in his orthodox phase, it was popular in the eighteenth and nineteenth centuries among all denominations, but in recent times only by a few.[23] The downward moral trends, civil strife, social disintegration and wars of the past century have been unkind to any optimistic view of the course of the future leading up to the Second Advent.[24] Almost all other 'orthodox' theology, formal or popular, expects not only an Antichrist and great tribulation near the end of the present age but also apostasy of the church and a fearfully destructive war. More on this later.

Several varieties of theological opinion properly labeled amillennial hold that Revelation 20 describes only one future physical resurrection, not the one described in verses 1-4 but the one presupposed by the judgment scene of verses 11-13, where John 'saw the dead, great and small, standing before the throne, and books were opened. Then another book was opened, which is the book of life. And the dead were judged by what was written in the books, according to what they had done' (v. 12).

Amillennial theology, beginning with Augustine, has proposed several explanations of Revelation 19:11–20:15 to do away with any reference to two future physical resurrections. Augustine's thought comes to focus on this point as follows:

> So are there two resurrections – the one, the first and spiritual resurrection, which has place in this life, and preserves us from coming into the second death; the other the second, which does not occur now, but in the end of the world, and which by the last judgment shall dismiss some into the second death, others into life which has no death.[25]

This form of amillennial theology, held through the Middle Ages by the Roman Church, has developed some variations, but consistently remains fixed on Augustine's notion that the resurrection of Revelation 20:1-4 is spiritual, i.e. regeneration of every true believer, and the 'second' resurrection is one of all, both good and evil, for a general judgment. For Augustine the 'reign' of saints is in the church on earth today.

Most contemporary evangelical, Protestant, amillennial scholars adopt Augustine's essential view of resurrection but think that the 'reign' of saints is in heaven 'with Christ.' Some Roman theologians now agree. The influential mid-twentieth century works by W. Hendriksen, O. T. Allis, G. L. Murray and Floyd Hamilton employed a 'recapitulation' or 'parallelistic' interpretation of the Apocalypse (book of Revelation).[26] In this view, for a seventh (and last) time the book of Revelation in chapters 20–22 goes over the course of the present age onward to the consummation. Anthony Hoekema, following Hendricksen, says:

---

20. Albertus Pieters, *Studies in the Revelation of St John* (Grand Rapids: Eerdmans, 1950), p. 282.
21. Loraine Boettner, 'Postmillennialian' in *The Meaning of the Millennium, Four Views*, ed. Robert G. Clouse (Downers Grove, IL: InterVarsity Press, 1977), p. 117.
22. ibid., p. 117.
23. See A. H. Strong, *Systematic Theology* (Valley Forge, PA: Judson Press, 1907), pp. 1014, 1045; Lorraine Boettner, *The Millennium* (Philadelphia: Presbyterian & Reformed, 1970); Marcellus Kik, *An Eschatology of Victory* (Philadelphia: Presbyterian & Reformed, 1971); Articles in *Chalcedon*, journal of Reconstruction, regularly posts its postmillennial creed and publishes articles in support. A very favorable and convincing brief summary of arguments in support of a postmillennial interpretation of Revelation 20 is two columns by E. R. Craven (American ed.) in John Peter Lange, *The Revelation of St John*, trans. (Elvina Moore, New York, 1874), p. 353.
24. See Boettner's essay cited earlier and my *Daniel and the Latter Days*, pp. 203–208 for details of the view, its history and further evaluation.
25. Augustine, The City of God, 20.6. His full treatment is found in chaps. 6–13.
26. W. Hendriksen, *More Than Conquerors: An interpretation of the Book of Revelation* (Grand Rapids: Baker Books, 1944); O. T. Allis, *Prophecy and the Church* (Philadelphia: Presbyterian & Reformed Publ., 1964); G. L. Murray, *Millennial Studies* (1948); Floyd Hamilton, *The Basis of Millennial Faith* (Grand Rapids: Eerdmans, 1942).

Chapters 20–22 comprise this last of the seven sections of the book of Revelation and therefore do not describe what follows the return of Christ. Rather, Revelation 20:1 takes us back again to the beginning of the New Testament era.[27]

Hoekema interprets the verse, 'they lived [or came to life] and reigned with Christ a thousand years' (Rev. 20:4), not as regeneration of believers (as many amillennialists do) but simply a way of describing the joy of dead saints (at present disembodied souls) now 'living and reigning with Christ in heaven.'

At least four other modern amillennial theories have appeared, with varieties of each, but the theory that most of the book of Revelation has already been fulfilled, and that the thousand years are the present age, has growing support today. This is called a preterist or 'Realized Millennium' view. There are many varieties of this view. A very competent report and evaluation of these theories of the millennium and attending events is chapter 4, 'The Fourth Last Thing' in David J. MacLeod's *The Seven Last Things*. He brings the discussion up to date.[28]

The Body of the Resurrection.

The previous discussion has shown that God intends to bring about the resurrection of all human dead – whether at one time or two (or several, as one form of premillennialism holds). The wicked dead, however, are raised only to be judged, each as a complete man, body and soul, and then to experience a 'second death,' presumably physical, for they will not be restored to spiritual life. In their resurrection they will still be spiritually 'dead in trespasses and sins.' Perhaps for this reason Scripture says nothing of the nature of their resurrection bodies. Therefore all that follows immediately here relates to those who participate in what may be called the resurrection of the just unto life everlasting.

The Bible tells us little about the intermediate state and few concrete details of the eternal states of heaven and hell. Because our Lord became a resurrected man and for forty days visited with and enlightened the apostolic agents of New Testament revelation, we know much more of the nature of the body of the resurrection. Further, a large part of 1 Corinthians 15 is devoted especially to the nature of the resurrection body. These sources and other biblical data enable us to know certainly two facts: (1) the body of the resurrection is to be a body of flesh, the same flesh laid in the grave; and (2) the flesh-body of the resurrection shall be changed in certain specified ways. We shall address these matters and follow with acknowledgment of some variations of understanding of the above and respond to some denials of the resurrection of our bodies of flesh.

I. The Very Same Flesh-body Laid in the Grave.

The body of the resurrection is to be the very same flesh-body laid in the grave. This is the way the first Christians understood the Scriptures. Irenaeus (AD 120–202) in the first extensive, Christian, apologetical treatise, explains that among the universally held beliefs of Christians 'dispersed throughout the whole world... received from apostles and their disciples was faith in the resurrection from the dead, and the ascension into heaven in the flesh of the beloved Jesus Christ' and His coming again 'to raise up anew all flesh of the whole human race.'[29] The twelfth article of the earliest well-known creed, *The Old Roman Creed*, forerunner of *The Apostles' Creed*, affirms, 'The resurrection of the flesh.'[30] Though in most minds (quite correctly) body and flesh mean about the same, even in ancient times there were, as today, false teachers who affirmed the body of the risen Christ was spirit, not flesh, in substance, hence the creedal insistence on 'resurrection of the flesh' of Christ as pattern of our resurrection bodies.

The Apostles' Creed as recited today sometimes reads 'the resurrection of the body.' It seems this appeared for the first time in certain liturgies in 1552 (documented by J. A. Schep).[31] J. N. D. Kelly showed that the phrase 'resurrection of the flesh' occurred in liturgies and creeds around all the Roman world at the end of the second century, as cited by Schep. He informs us that 'the entire early Church, in the West and in the East alike, publicly confessed belief in the resurrection of the flesh.'[32] He adds that this prevailed almost without exception through Reformation times.[33]

---

27. Anthony Hoekema, 'Amillennialism,' chap. 4 in *The Meaning of the Millennium: Four Views*, ed. Robert G. Clouse (Downers Grove, IL: InterVarsity Press, 1977), pp. 59, 60.
28. David J. MacLeod, *The Seven Last Things* (Dubuque, IA: Emmaus College Press, 2003), pp. 131–178.
29. Irenaeus, *Against Heresies*, I.10, ANF i, p. 330.
30. Henry Bettenson, *Documents of the Christian Church*, 2nd ed. (New York: Oxford Press, 1963), p. 34.
31. J. A. Schep, *The Nature of the Resurrection Body* (Grand Rapids: Eerdmans, 1964), p.322. Schep cites J. T. Darragh, *The Resurrection of the Flesh*, pp. 224 ff.
32. ibid., p. 221.
33. ibid., p. 221. See extensive documentation in works of J. N. D. Kelly, H. B. Swete and Philip Schaff, *The Creeds of Christendom*.

Just as Jesus' resurrection was an historical event in the world of space and time 'on the third day' so ours will be in a coming 'last day' or 'hour.' Norman L. Geisler writes, 'Regardless of the supernatural nature of the event, the resurrection of Jesus was [as ours shall be] as much a part of history as was His incarnation before His death.'[34]

Biblical evidence for the correctness of this view and for the value of its perpetuation is of several sorts.

1. The believer's resurrection body will be like the resurrection body of Christ in every respect. Jesus took extreme measures to demonstrate beyond cavil or doubt that His was a body of 'flesh and bone.' That He omitted mention of blood does not mean for certain that it was absent from the hands and side exposed to Thomas or the lips and tongue which masticated the food at Emmaus and the lakeside.[35]

According to Philippians 3:20, 21 'we await a Savior, the Lord Jesus Christ, who will change our lowly body to be like his glorious body, by the power which enables him even to subject all things to himself' (RSV). The same is stated as ground of cheerful hope for God's children now: '[and] it does not yet appear what we shall be, but we know that when he appears we shall be like him, for we shall see him as he is' (1 John 3:2 RSV). It is hard to quarrel with the evident relevance of these passages to the resurrection body. Second Corinthians 3:18 seems relevant too, though not all agree: 'And we all, with unveiled face, beholding the glory of the Lord, are being changed into his likeness from one degree of glory to another' (RSV). Interpretations which would make this a physical change going on now must be rejected as foreign to the Bible. Granting that a moral and spiritual growth in Christlikeness is described, is that all? Is there an 'eschatological element'? It is suggested the 'to another' refers to the honor (or splendor, Gr. *endoxos*) of the believers' resurrection bodies, in this context, a form of Christlikeness.[36] In the context of 1 Corinthians 15:35-50 – all about 'how' and 'what kind of body' in the resurrection – there seems surely to be a reference to the resemblance of our resurrection bodies to Christ's body in verse 49: 'Just as we have borne the image of the man of dust, we shall also bear the image of the man of heaven.' Though there is apparent reference to the whole range of one's life, the context (as many observe) requires reference also to the believer's resurrection body.

2. It is implied by the biblical doctrine of mankind, that our whole being was created 'very good'; that the body of man was fashioned from earth, likewise good; that redemption of man involves advancement to immortality of body as well as soul. To be normal again as social creatures among other social creatures, to work and serve God day and night, requires the resurrection of a useable body adapted to the soul with which it was concreated.

3. There really is no other way in the New Testament context, without twisting the meaning of language, to interpret the primary statements. It is true to say that neither Jesus nor the Apostles, in so many words, declared 'the resurrection body will be composed of human flesh.' They did not need to. Orthodox Jews of the time, as scholars versed in rabbinical apocryphal and apocalyptic literature acknowledge, firmly believed in the resurrection of the flesh. How else would the Jews of the time have understood Isaiah 26:19, 'Thy dead shall live, their bodies shall rise' (RSV) or Daniel 12:1-3? This was the doctrine rejected by the heterodox Sadducees. All Paul's hate-filled Jewish hearers, both Sadducees and Pharisees, understood well (Acts 23:6) when he claimed to be on trial 'with respect to the hope in the resurrection of the dead' (see also Acts 24:15). So we must understand Jesus' own comments on the subject. Why talk about coming out of tombs if not in the bodies deposited there (John 5:28, 29), as Mary's hope and Lazarus' 'come forth' demonstrate (John 11:24, 43, 44 KJV).

4. It was for the Jews of Jesus' time, as for us today, a legitimate inference from the translation of Enoch and Elijah. These two events are described at Genesis 5:22-23 and 2 Kings 2:1-18. Both these gentlemen were taken to heaven – as the natural sense of Genesis 5:24 (cf. Heb. 11:5) reads and 2 Kings 2:11 specifically states. Their flesh, blood and bones went to heaven – with what modificications we do not know. Not only did Jesus ascend in a body of 'flesh and bones' (Acts 1:9; Luke 24:39) but as 'this same Jesus,' He 'shall so come [again] in like manner' (Acts 1:11 KJV).[37]

5. Resurrection of the fleshly body is anticipated in the prophecies of the Messianic kingdom in both Testaments. In an outstanding apocalyptic vision of the messianic age, Isaiah 25:8 proclaims that the LORD of hosts 'will *swallow up death* [emphasis added] for ever, and the Lord GOD will wipe away tears from all faces, and the reproach of his people he will take away from all the earth; for the LORD has spoken' (RSV). Further on in Isaiah's apocalyptic vision

---

34. Norman L. Geisler, *The Battle for the Resurrection* (Nashville: Thomas Nelson, 1989), p. 64.
35. The evidence is overwhelming. See Part 4: Christology: Person and Work fo Christ, chapters 19-20.
36. Schep, op. cit., p. 184; G. Kittel, TDNT II, pp. 254, 255 and others.
37. See my discussion above of Jesus' Ascension and present residence in heaven as incarnate (enfleshed) God in treatment of the Ascension in Part 4 of this book.

of the future of Israel and the world in times of Messiah and just before proclamation of a final burst of divine wrath (Isa. 26:19-21) the prophet announces to Israel's elect saints: 'Thy dead shall live, their bodies shall rise. O dwellers in the dust, awake and sing for joy!' (RSV) Many scholars, even those who expect no future millennial reign and restoration of a converted nation of Israel, agree with this explanation of the passage.[38] These prophecies were addressed to the faithful remnant of Israel in Isaiah's time. He is saying that these dear folk, many of them martyrs, perhaps including the prophet himself, would in and through resurrection participate in the earthly glory and blessing of the Messianic age, merging into an eternal state (see Isa. 65, 66). Paul rightly quoted these verses to explain his own revealed doctrine of resurrection of the body of flesh. Says Schep:

> Paul is correct, therefore, when he writes that the saying of Isaiah 20:8 will come to pass when those who died in Christ are raised imperishable, and when believers who are alive when Jesus returns are changed to glory and immortality (1 Cor. 15:54). 'The veil of mourning' (v. 7) 'spread over the nation' is of course in context grief over deaths of loved ones (See 2 Sam. 15:30; Jer. 14:1-4; Esther 6:12; Eccles. 12:8; Amos 5:16).... Understood this way as a prophecy within the framework of a moving description of the eschatological feast that the Lord will 'make unto all people' (v. 6), verse 8... [it describes] the great deliverance from death and its consequences, as Yahweh will grant it to his people all over the world.[39]

In 1983 Murray J. Harris asserted, 'The identity between the physical and spiritual bodies can scarcely be material or substantial or physical unless we believe Paul and the early Christians took over without modification a crassly materialistic view of resurrection....'[40] He proposed that the 'identity of the resurrection body with the natural' is 'personal' only. 'There are two dwellings but only one occupant.'[41] In a later book (*From Grave to Glory*) he stated, 'From this standpoint the new body is qualitatively and numerically distinct from the old body.'[42] Along with numerous statements of this sort these large books also contain many orthodox sounding statements. To enter into extended debate on paper with these two books would take us far afield. They seem to have persuaded few of the apparent inconsistencies of outlook.

Wherein the identity of the natural body with the resurrection body lies is hard to establish. I shall remark briefly on the matter later, but the Scriptures are clear that the identity is in the body itself not in the 'person,' as Harris has it, who occupies the body.

II. The Saints' Resurrection Bodies Will Be Changed.

In a manner similar to the change in our Lord's resurrection body, the saints' resurrection bodies will be changed.[43] The most relevant Scripture is Philippians 3:21, 'who will change our lowly body to be like his glorious body,' in the context of 1 Corinthians 15:51, 52: 'Lo! I tell you a mystery. We shall not all sleep [in death], but we shall all be changed, in a moment, in the twinkling of an eye, at the last trumpet. For the trumpet will sound, and the dead will be raised imperishable, and we shall be changed' (RSV). The operative words obviously are *change* and *changed*.

In Philippians 3:21 Paul simply affirms what we have seen already in several texts – that the resurrection bodies of saints will be like Christ's resurrection body and that this obviously will require some changes. He explains elsewhere that this will be the case both for deceased saints at the *parousia* and those living at the time. Further, Paul seems to imply no difference in the human body of the incarnate (enfleshed) Son of God in heaven today from that body during the 'forty days' when He was 'appearing to them.' Who can say how this fits with the manifest deity of the appearance of the glorified Christ when He first made Himself known to Saul of Tarsus (Acts 9:1-9) and when He appeared to John on Patmos (Rev. 1-3)? His body, even before death and resurrection, made some temporary changes for, 'as he was praying, the appearance of his face was altered, and his clothing became dazzling white' and presumably likewise so did 'Moses and Elijah' who 'appeared in glory' with Him (Luke 9:29-31).

The whole matter is explained (as fully as in our present state we mortals can know) by the Apostle Paul in response to two questions by a 'foolish person': 'How are the dead raised? With what kind of body do they come?'

---

38. G. C. Berkouwer, *The Return of Christ*, trans. James Van Oosterom (Grand Rapids: Eerdmans, 1972), pp. 116, 175–179, 186. Schep, op. cit., pp. 51–56,
39. Schep, op. cit., p. 52.
40. Murray J. Harris, *Raised Immortal* (London: Marshall, Morgan & Scott, 1983), p. 126.
41. ibid., p. 126.
42. Murray J. Harris, *From Grave to Glory* (Grand Rapids: Zondervan, 1990), p. 22.
43. Here again I ask the reader to refer to the portions of this work relating to Jesus' resurrection and Ascension.

(1 Cor. 15:35; cf. v. 36). One derives the impression that Paul was more than a little disgusted with the questions. Why otherwise would he call the questioner a fool (v. 36)? He seems to think he is explaining the obvious. Jesus was known to scold His disciples for inattention, stupidity and poor memory (Mark 8:11-21; Matt. 16:1-12). Once He called their incredulity 'hardness of heart,' and 'upbraided' them for it. I shall therefore enter into no minute exegesis of this passage. Paul intended to use language plain enough for anyone who wants to know what he meant. Cultural distance from the world of Paul and ancient Corinth poses no serious obstacle.

In verses 36-38 there is an assumed parallel between planting a seed in soil and placing a dead human body in the grave. Each kind of seed appears to rot in the soil. There is also an assumed parallel between the plant that grows from the rotting seed and the body which shall come forth from the grave at the resurrection. In each case with seeds 'God gives it a body as he [God] has chosen, and to each kind of seed its own body' (v. 38). There are as many kinds of bodies as there are kinds of seeds.

In verse 39 he expatiates on the varieties of flesh which compose bodies – of men, of animals, of birds, of fish. Then he makes the non-technical observation that just as among the various earthly (terrestrial) bodies each has an excellence (glory) peculiar to itself, so likewise have the ones in the skies above (celestial) – sun, moon and stars. Further, the earthly ones as a group differ from the ones in the sky as a group (vv. 40, 41).

Then returning to the seed-plant metaphor he says, 'So it is with the resurrection of the dead.' '[W]hat you sow is not the body that is to be' (v. 37) in verses 42-44. The corpse 'sown' (i.e. buried) is perishable, but raised imperishable; buried in dishonor, but raised in glory; buried weak, raised powerful; buried a physical body, but raised a spiritual body. He affirms the existence of each kind of body (v. 44). Because the bare translation of the terms 'physical' and 'spiritual' have a cultural and linguistic context not apparent to us today we must return to this matter. However explained, Paul is not denying that the body of the resurrection has 'flesh and bones' as Jesus' resurrection body did. As regards the 'nature' or attributes of the resurrection body, it will be imperishable, honorable, glorious, strong and spiritual.

Verses 45-47 bear directly on a single point – in the resurrection 'we shall also bear the image of the man of heaven' (v. 49). He explains the cause of this 'change' by contrasting 'the first man Adam' – whose progeny we all are – with 'the last Adam.'[44] The First Adam 'became a living being' (v. 45), i.e. he received such life as he had and Adam passed the same on to us who are all 'in Adam' (vv. 22, 27). The KJV faithfully indicates (as RSV does not) that the text of verse 45 says simply 'the last Adam [was made] a life giving spirit.' As pre-incarnate Logos, the Lord made the First Adam and gave Adam life. Now as incarnate Logos He gives life, spiritual and physical. But perhaps Paul means he 'became' a life-giving spirit and if so, as Alford asks, 'When?' and comments: 'That his resurrection state alone is not intended, is evident from the words "from heaven" (*New Testament for English Readers, en loc*).[45] Verse 47 calls Adam 'the man of dust', recollecting Adam's condemnation to death in 'unto dust shalt thou return' (Gen. 3:19 KJV). All the human beings of whom he is head are physically dead or shall become so: 'so also are those who are of the dust.' After this comes the happy conclusion that in the resurrection we who believe will no longer bear Adam's death mark but in our resurrection flesh will 'bear the image of the man [Christ] of heaven' (v. 49).

Verses 50-58 summarize, repeat, emphasize and apply what the apostolic author has already written. The only new information is that it will all happen 'in a moment, in the twinkling of an eye, at the last trumpet' (v. 52). G. C. H. Berkouwer wisely cautions:

> This reality is assumed into the sphere of our expectation and consolation, without any effort to satisfy our desire for it to be imaginable.... The same applies to Romans 8:29, where Paul talks about the predestination of the elect, 'to be conformed to the image of his Son.'[46]

Even after our resurrection and transformation take place we will not understand much more about it, I think, just as essentially I know little about my present natural body. Even though I am perfectly at home in it. I do not need to know more than I do. I like it here.

Two Misused Texts.

First Corinthians 15:44 reads: 'It is sown a natural body; it is raised a spiritual body. There is a natural body, and there is a spiritual body' (KJV). There are several other ways to translate the verse as the Versions testify, but the

---

44. Not a second, for there will be no further Adams 'as being the last head of humanity' (Alford).
45. William Milligan, Erich Sauer and Klaas Schilder are in agreement with Schep, that Christ became a life-giving spirit 'when, as the reward for his atoning death, he received the promised Spirit in His resurrection and ascension' (Schep, p. 76). Matthew 28:18 does connect Jesus' 'all power' with His resurrection ministry and Peter's pronouncement (Acts 2:33) with Jesus' Ascension.
46. G. C. H. Berkouwer, op. cit., p. 194.

essential sense does not vary. Neo-orthodox authors, as I pointed out early in this chapter, have used this one of the several Pauline antitheses (1 Cor. 15:42-44) to do away with any physical resurrection at all. Brunner, as we saw, thought that survival of the person and whatever changes take place in the personal spirit at death constituted the 'resurrection.' It would take several pages to document the departures from an orthodox view of the resurrection, which ground or support their views on Paul's statement, 'it is raised a spiritual body.'

What does 'spiritual' mean? What is 'a spiritual body'? The answers are not far away. The antithesis of spiritual (Gr. *pneumatikon*) is natural (*psuchikon*). Let us start with 'natural' (Gr. *psuchikon*). *Psuchikos* is used six times in the New Testament. Earlier in this same Epistle it is said that 'The natural person does not accept the things of the Spirit of God' (1 Cor. 2:14). Here also, in context, 'natural' is in contrast with 'spiritual': the spiritual man. 'The spiritual person judges all things' (1 Cor. 2:15). The spiritual man dwells in a body quite as fleshy as that of the natural man. The natural (*psuchikos* = soulish) is directed by the 'desires of the body and the mind' (Eph. 2:3) while the spiritual is directed by the Holy Spirit through a renewed mind. In James 3:15, the KJV renders *psuchikos* 'sensual,' i.e. controlled by appetites not God's Spirit. In Jude 19 'sensual' (*psuchikos*) is defined as not having 'the Spirit.' So the opposite of spiritual is being 'devoid of the Spirit', not to be directed by the Spirit. Therefore the spiritual is to be filled and directed by the Spirit.

Psuchikos is employed twenty-five times in the New Testament and in no single case does it designate something composed of spirit. Never in the New Testament does it mean something ethereal, airy or of refined substance. The article on *pneuma-pneumatikos* (over a hundred pages in *TDNT*, VI) in brief comment says that *pneumatikos* means to be controlled by the Spirit of God (*TDNT*, VI, p. 437). The idea is control, not substance or matter.

In English the usual antithesis to 'natural' is 'supernatural.' While this is not precisely the contrast Paul has in mind, it is close. RSV renders *pneumatikos* as 'supernatural' at 1 Corinthians 10:4. Whatever 'spiritual' (*pneumatikos*) means, it is not immaterial. Alford, who is to be trusted in such matters, commenting on our verse, quotes Theophylact with approval: 'A spiritual body is one rich with the working of the Holy Spirit, and administered in all things by Him.'[47]

1 Corinthians 15:50 reads: 'Now this I say, brethren, that flesh and blood cannot inherit the kingdom of God; neither doth corruption inherit incorruption' (KJV). This passage has been the chief scriptural 'proof text' for erroneous views of the resurrection from early Christian times on to the present. Irenaeus opens a very competent lengthy treatment of the importance of the resurrection of the flesh with these lines: 'Among the other [truths] proclaimed by the apostle [Paul], there is this one, that flesh and blood cannot inherit the kingdom of God. This is [the passage] which is addressed by all the heretics in support of their folly, with an attempt to annoy us, and to point out that the handiwork of God [i.e. the human body] is not saved.'[48] He then devotes eight chapters to defense of the doctrine of the resurrection of the flesh. One chapter develops the theme that 'Unless the flesh were to be saved, the Word would not have taken upon him flesh of the same substance as ours: from this it would follow that neither should we have been reconciled by him.'[49] This church Father saw what some evangelicals today cannot seem to discern, that the resurrection of our flesh is a correlate of the incarnation, which to deny and carry to its logical conclusion is a heresy.

The facts are apparent to any one who cares to look into the matter more than casually. Besides 1 Corinthians 15:50 ('flesh and blood cannot inherit the kingdom of God'), the expression 'flesh and blood' appears in four other passages in the New Testament. They 'form a single conception... a semitic wordpair.'[50]

I shall sketch Scheps's five-page discussion of the expression. When Jesus said to Peter, 'flesh and blood has not revealed this to you' (Matt. 16:17), he writes, 'Jesus cannot possibly have meant that the substance of flesh and blood could give any revelation.' He was not thinking of the human body.[51] The article on 'flesh and blood' in *TDNT* shows that the term in then-current rabbinic vocabulary always denoted the whole man with all his functions, with particular emphasis on man's earthly condition as a frail and perishable creature in contrast to the eternal and Almighty God.[52] Hence 1 Corinthians 15:50 does not mean 'the body of resurrected saints cannot be a body of flesh,' as certain scholars claim, for four reasons (I drastically abbreviate).

---

47. Henry Alford, *New Testament for English Readers*, p. 1081.
48. Irenaeus, *Against Heresies*, V.17; *ANF*, I, p. 531.
49. *ANF* I, p. 541.
50. Joachim Jeremias, New Testament Studies, Feb., 1965, p. 152 as cited by Schep, op. cit., p. 201.
51. Schep, op. cit., p. 201.
52. Schep, op. cit., p. 202.

1. Such a meaning contradicts what Scripture says of Jesus' resurrection body of flesh (and bones), the body He now has in heaven.

2. It contradicts what Paul himself says elsewhere in 1 Corinthians 15 and Philippians 1:21.

3. It misrepresents the meaning of the expression, 'flesh and blood,' in Jewish literature of the time and in Galatians 1:16 and Ephesians 6:12.

4. It is foreign to the context, especially the verses immediately following, where Paul explains sufficiently for our present pilgrimage, the kind of change 'necessary for man to enter the new world.'[53]

The notion that personal existence and personal responsibility for 'deeds done in the flesh' endure beyond the crisis of one's death, and that public accounting to God with consequences to follow, is deeply planted in human consciousness in every place and in every age:[1] this is on record in long ago ages, in records as disparate as the

---

53. Schep, op. cit., pp. 203, 204.

6
The Doctrine of Judgment

Akkadian *Gilgamish Epic* (at least as early as seventh century BC) and the Egyptian *Book of the Dead* (fifth and sixth dynasties, before 2000 BC). Though presently suppressed in the world of what goes for journalism it remains deeply imbedded in human consciousness.

This future accounting, with consequences in reward for good deeds and punishment for bad ones, is the judgment of the biblical record. 'Therefore the ungodly shall not stand in the judgment' (Ps. 1:5 KJV) is an early biblical reference to such a 'grand assize.' The Old Testament refers to a heavenly council where God holds court (Ps. 82:1): 'God has taken his place in the divine council; in the midst of the gods [angels] he holds judgment [*Mishpat*, often the place or convening of a judicial court].'[2]

There will be a final special convening of such a court but not of such a council (Rev. 20:11-15; cf. Matt. 25:31 ff.). As we shall see, there is considerable variety in the manner Scripture represents such a presently incomprehensible event of cosmic proportions.

The Sum of the Doctrine.

The entire doctrine of judgment is summed up in two short verses in the book of Hebrews: 'And just as it is appointed for man to die once, and after that comes judgment, so Christ... [was] offered once to bear the sins of [the] many' (Heb. 9:27, 28a).[3] The notion of 'once' (*hapax* Heb. 9:26, 28 KJV) and 'one' (*mia* Heb. 10:12, 14 KJV) are opposed to 'often' (*pollakis* Heb. 9:25, 26 KJV). 'Once' and 'one' pervade chapters 9 and 10 (9:7, 12, 26, 28; 10:10, 12, 14 KJV). The idea governs the verses quoted above. There once was a particular past day of judgment when Jesus was judged (punished) for 'the many' (Isa. 53:6 and 12). There is also a future day appointed for every human being after death. Though Jesus did say that 'whoever hears my word and believes... does not come into judgment' (*krisin* John 5:24),

---

1. See discussion in Part 1: Theology Proper, Chapter 4. Why People Do Believe in God.
2. I have previously cited the great work of Mitchell Dahood on Psalms who comments on this: 'The proposed exegesis assumes a rather advanced concept of resurrection and immortality, but there is ample basis in the Psalter for this supposition,' *Psalms I, 1–50. Anchor Bible* (New York: Doubleday, 1965), p. 4, 5.
3. Among the several competent exegetical commentaries on these verses, Franz Delitzsch in his *Commentary on the Epistle to the Hebrews* (Edinburgh: T. & T. Clark, 1887) has not been excelled. He brings his unsurpassed mastery of Old Testament language and sacrificial liturgy to the text with reverence for sound orthodoxy. I am indebted particularly to his exegesis of this passage.

His authorized messenger, Paul, elaborated the statement with: 'we shall all stand before the judgment seat of God' (Rom. 14:10 RSV) and 'we must all appear before the judgment seat of Christ; that every one may receive the things done in the body, according to that which he hath done, whether it be good or bad' (2 Cor. 5:10 KJV).[4]

Human Awareness in Conscience.

It is deeply written in the conscience of mankind that, as 'the Preacher' (*Qoheleth*, Eccles. 1:1, 2) said: 'God will bring every deed into judgment, with every secret thing, whether good or evil' (Eccles. 12:14). In enjoying youthful pleasures to the full, 'know that... God will bring you into judgment' (Eccles. 11:9). For this reason old age may be a time of anxious conscience about early misbehavior ('Remember not the sins of my youth... O LORD' Ps. 25:7) and may be why unchaperoned 'dating' and co-educational colleges for eighteen year olds, much less 'co-ed dorms,' may be very bad ideas. The same David was most concerned about sins undiscerned by himself (Ps. 19:12) and accounts for his prayer that 'the meditation of my heart [phantasies] be acceptable in thy sight' (Ps. 19:14 KJV).

Emil Brunner, who in his lifetime sought manfully to bring the liberal wing of Protestantism at least partway back to biblical orthodoxy, thought deeply on these matters and expressed them in a chapter on 'The Last Judgment.' He speaks of world history as existing under the 'category' of the long-suffering of God. Yet 'one day the saturation point will be reached and it will be necessary to terminate the provisional period.' He goes on to say, 'The vague surmise or intuition – a surmise widespread among many peoples who know nothing of the Christian revelation – that one day all secrets must be disclosed, that a time of final retribution and reckoning must come, is thus in harmony with the divine will as it is revealed in Christ.'[5]

This natural feeling is enhanced in the regenerate heart, but may be very feeble among the unregenerate. Abraham was quite fearful for his life among such people: 'There is no fear of God at all in this place, and they will kill me because of my wife' – i.e. to steal her from him (Gen. 20:11). Paul was constrained by 'the terror of the Lord' as well as 'the love of Christ' to live and work for God (2 Cor. 5:11, 14 KJV). The preaching of both law and grace stirs to life innate awareness of a coming day of judgment, as when Paul 'reasoned about righteousness and self-control and the coming judgment [and], Felix [the Roman governor] was alarmed' (Acts 24:25). On the other hand, when the 'gospel came... not only in word, but also in power... and with full conviction' (1 Thess. 1:5) those who are 'chosen' and believing (1 Thess. 1:2-4) can wait for God's 'Son from heaven' knowing He 'delivers us from the wrath to come' (1 Thess. 1:3 and 10).

Interim Judgments.

The final judgment is not the only judgment of God on good or evil works of mankind. Scripture presupposes that history reflects the righteous judgment of God, even though not apparent at every point of time. When Abraham protested to divine beings en route to destroy the 'cities of the plain' he was aware of this: 'Shall not the Judge of all the earth do what is just? (Gen. 18:25). As One whose 'kingdom rules over all' (Ps. 103:19) the course of the world constantly carries out what theology has called His 'providential judgments.'

The book of Proverbs regularly states and presupposes such, as for example 'Whoever closes his ear to the cry of the poor will himself call out and not be answered' (Prov. 21:13; cf. 29:9). The captivity of Israel to Babylon, the destruction of Jerusalem by the Romans, and similar, are said specifically to be divine judgments, but they were not eschatological judgments. Each person who suffered or was rewarded in these matters has yet to face God's throne in the judgment after 'the resurrection on the last day' (John 11:24). Likewise the very entrance of Jesus into the world and the proclamation by His messengers was 'For judgment... that those who do not see may see, and those who see may become blind' (John 9:39; cf. Matt. 13:14-17). There are eternal consequences in providential judgments but they are not final judgments. These judgments are part of the control God exercises over the world in order that human society does not destroy itself and that orderly civil life might be possible. God 'has established his throne for justice' (Ps. 9:7); hence the prophet says, 'When your judgments are in the earth, the inhabitants of the world learn righteousness' (Isa. 26:9). Since Calvary, the world has been 'reconciled to God': a temporary truce

---

4. The syntax of this verse is very difficult. 'It is the final judgment of all believers that is in view here, not a universal judgment ... and the issue is not salvation or damnation (as in 2:14; Rom. 2:5-11, etc.) but whether, as a Christian, one has been committed to the Lord.' Paul Furnish, *II Corinthians: The Anchor Bible* (New York: Doubleday, 1984), p. 305.

5. Emil Brunner, *Eternal Hope* (Philadelphia: Westminster Press, 1954), p. 176.

declared (2 Cor. 5:9-21), final judgment delayed. Nevertheless God is not mocked. Whatsoever a man sows he shall reap (Gal. 6:7), not because of any built-in justice in the world but because 'the Lord is the avenger' of everyone who 'defraud[s]' his brother 'in any matter' (1 Thess. 4:6 KJV). The Scriptures of both Testaments plainly teach that there will be a future final judgment for every person whether Jew or Gentile, pagan or Christian, when Jesus comes again. We have already quoted some of the passages. Some additional texts say that God will come 'to judge the earth... the world in righteousness' (Ps. 96:13) and 'God will bring every deed into judgment... whether good or evil' (Eccles. 12:14). Details of the principles God will follow in that judgment are set forth in Romans 2 and other places. Paul told a heathen audience that God 'has fixed a day on which he will judge the world in righteousness by a man whom he has appointed; and of this he has given assurance to all by raising him from the dead' (Acts 17:31).[6]

Necessity of a Final Judgment.

1. A public event, such as a final Judgment Day, is a moral necessity for more than one reason. Emil Brunner pointed out: 'The God who reveals himself in Scripture... does not occupy an attitude of indifference beyond good and evil' and goes on to say: 'This non-neutral positive purposefulness is so consistently and piercingly the Biblical idea of God that we cannot be surprised that the thought of judgment penetrates unequivocally every section and layer of Holy Scripture.'[7]

2. For another reason, the threats of conscience which do restrain evil actions would not exist, or if they existed would not have force, if in the heart there were no lingering fear that God will bring every deed into judgment.

3. Further, some sort of divine judication is necessary to adjust the rewards life here gives to the greedy and ruthless, as well as the unjust sufferings of the pious, the poor and the defenseless, whose cause the Lord promises to take up sometime, somewhere.

The Law and the Prophets state it and the Psalms celebrate it: 'The LORD sets the prisoners free; the LORD opens the eyes of the blind... lifts up those who are bowed down... loves the righteous... watches over the sojourners... upholds the widow and the fatherless, but the way of the wicked he brings to ruin' (Ps. 146:7-9). Yet this is not evident anywhere in the wide world now or at any other time – except to the eyes of faith. God's justice awaits public vindication on the day of judgment. Habakkuk 2 raises this problem, as well as Psalm 73, and also the cries of the martyrs of Revelation 6:9-11. The necessity for a public vindication of God's righteousness is so plain that the most obtuse must recognize that it awaits the Great Day of the Almighty up ahead. Then and only then will there be public answer to the cry, 'Where were you, God, when I needed you?'

4. In all of the periods of a person's life from infancy to old age there is a sense of responsibility for what one thinks and does. The same is true of every human collectivity from partnerships and family businesses and social collectivities to national governments and armies. Apart from belief in a future judgment this sense lacks strength to enforce its dictates. Emil Brunner said,

> Only the thought of judgment gives to the thought of responsibility its ultimate seriousness, and thus makes clear the relationship between God and man. Apart from the prospect of divine judgment, man may repeatedly misunderstand his freedom as freedom in responsibility, as absolute indetermination, and such a misunderstanding of his own being spells his own sin and death.[8]

5. Jesus enforced the necessity of spiritual preparedness for Judgment Day in a series of parables and pronouncements, among them Matthew 25:31-46. It is surely a mistake to put this 'judgment of the nations' at Jesus' return in a schedule of preliminary end-time events. Let us take a closer look.

'When the Son of Man comes in his glory, and all the angels with him' (Matt. 25:31) introduces the time of judgment. But it is not necessary to suppose the next words, 'then he will sit on his glorious throne,' and following takes place immediately. 'When the Son of Man comes [Gr. *hota de elthē*]' might more literally be rendered 'When the Son of Man has come [*elthē*, a second aorist subjunctive].' Then (*tote*) indicates what follows but not necessarily immediately. When Luke wanted to indicate immediate action with *tote* he prefixed *eutheos* and this is translated 'immediately after' (Acts 17:14). J. O. Buswell's careful interpretation treats the passage as gathering together all the events of the *Parousia* in what he calls 'cosmic perspective,' and I think he is right.[9]

---

6. See also Luke 10:14; Jude 14, 15.
7. Brunner, op. cit., pp. 173, 174.
8. Brunner, op. cit., p. 178.

The form of the parable-like vignette is similar to a parable or allegory. It seems meant to teach spiritual preparedness for that Return which could happen at any time, as in the Parables of the Ten Virgins (vv. 1-13), and of the Talents (vv. 14-30). The 'sheep on his right' and 'the goats on the left' has given rise to a valid but eccentric (off-center) view of the purpose of this dominical presentation of the coming final judgment. The orderly mind of J. E. Fison, a devout Anglican scholar, lays out the Lord Jesus' point of the panorama, which certainly was neither to produce morbid introspection, nor to frighten sinners into a rush to repentance, nor to describe the opening act of the millennium. Rather the passage, like much New Testament teaching regarding the 'last judgment,' is to jolt the complacent church member. The New Testament presentation, Fison says, 'is not to spring a surprise on the post pagan souls outside the pale of the church, but upon the complacent ecclesiastical souls whose entire confidence is based upon the fact that they are well within [the church].'[10]

Contrariwise, there are others who are well aware of their peril.

> For they see only too clearly the abiding significance of the fact that 'judgment must begin at the house of God' (1 Peter 4:17). All the last judgment does to them when it is devoid of any living connection with Jesus himself is to cut the nerve of certainty and hope and joy and to kill the inspiration for creative and adventurous living by inspiring a perpetual, morbid and scrupulous introspection.[11]

Contrariwise, I add, for the instructed believer who is also spiritually and emotionally healthy, in the New Testament the Advent of Christ is a 'blessed hope,' a 'glorious appearing,' for which one has 'eager expectation' (Titus 2:13). It bespeaks invitation to the joy of a wedding feast (Rev. 19:6-9).

One Final Eschatological Judgment: One, Two or Many?

All Christians agree that every person, angel or man, who ever lived, will come to a final judgment. Those convinced that there is to be a resurrection of the righteous dead and translation of living saints before a thousand-year reign of Christ on earth, to be followed by the resurrection of the ungodly following that millennium, believe there are to be two future, final, eschatological judgments. Most are convinced that the first is 'at the judgment seat of Christ,' referred to in 2 Corinthians 5:10 and Romans 14:10, and the second that is described in Revelation 20:10-15.[12] Some schools of thought have refined and expanded the doctrine of two resurrections and two judgments in harmony with their understanding of end-time events to distinguish several resurrections and judgments. This outlook has been popularized by recent, widely read Christian fiction. This view was carefully expressed in the very useful *Introductory Lectures In Systematic Theology* by H. C. Thiessen.[13] In Dr Thiessen's book (the standard at Wheaton College for several generations of juniors) 'there are at least seven future judgments.'[14] These are elaborated, with Scriptures related, as follows. (1) The judgment of believers (Rev. 14:10; 2 Cor. 5:10; 1 Cor. 3:11-15; 4:5; Matt. 25:14-30; Luke 19:11; Matt. 20:1-16). (2) The judgment of Israel during the great tribulation (Jer. 30:7; Rev. 7:1-8; 12:6; 13:17; Ezek. 20:33, 34; Mal. 3:2-5). (3) The judgment of Babylon (Rev. 17:1–19:5) during the great tribulation. (4) The judgment of the beast, the false prophet and their armies (2 Thess. 2:7-10; Rev. 16:12-16; 19:19-21; Zech. 12:1-9; 13:8–14:2). (5) The judgment of the nations on the basis of their treatment of the Jews (Matt. 25:31-46; Joel 3:11-17; 2 Thess. 1:7-10; Acts 17:31, see comments p. 463). (6) The judgment of Satan and his angels (Rev. 2:7-9, 13-17; Matt. 5:41; Matt. 8:29; Luke 8:31). (7) The judgment of the unsaved dead (Rev. 20:11-15; 21:5; and other passages).[15] Thiessen's arrangement is similar to that of the Scofield Bible of 1909, 1919, 1945, replicated in many early twentieth-century evangelical publications. Herman Hoyt[16] adds a resurrection and judgment of tribulation, saints and martyrs, a judgment of God and Magog, and another of angels – though as 'categories' rather than distinct events.

This eagerness to schedule every aspect of end-time events in a schema has not been shared by every recent premillennial scholar. Erich Sauer, for example, found two future resurrections in Scripture and only two judgments: 'The Judgment seat of Christ for believers and the Great White Throne judgment of unbelievers.'[17]

---

9. J. O. Buswell, *A Systematic Theology of the Christian Religion*, Vol. ii (Grand Rapids: Zondervan, 1963), pp. 417–423.
10. J. E. Fison, *The Christian Hope* (London: Longmaus, Green & Co., 1952), p. 249.
11. ibid.
12. C. R. Ludwigson, *A Survey of Bible Prophecy* (Grand Rapids: Zondervan, 1975), pp. 115–126; 65–68.
13. H. C. Thiessen, *Introductory Lectures In Systematic Theology* (Grand Rapids: Zondervan, 1949 and many repr.), 574 pages.
14. ibid., p. 498.
15. ibid., chap. 45, 'The Judgments' pp. 496–505.
16. Herman A. Hoyt, *The End Times* (Chicago: Moody Press, 1969), pp. 217–222.
17. Erich Sauer, *From Eternity to Eternity* (Grand Rapids: Eerdmans, 1957), chap. 11, pp. 78–80.

Paul developed the doctrine of resurrection in some detail, even a 'schedule' of three 'orders' of the resurrection – Christ the first-fruits, then they that are Christ's at His coming, and after that 'the end' resurrection. But there is no such schedule of judgments, though he knows of the 'judgment seat of Christ' (2 Cor. 5:10) or 'of God' (Rom. 14:10), and he speaks of those who store up wrath for themselves on the day of wrath when God's judgment will be revealed (Rom. 2:5) and develops principles of judgment (Rom. 2). George Ladd, an historic premillenarian, noted Paul's passing references to judgment and a day of judgment in Romans 13:2; 1 Corinthians 11:32; Romans 3:6; 1 Corinthians 4:5; 2 Thessalonians 2:12; and 2 Timothy 4:1 and comments: 'In some way not explained to us, the saints are to assist God in the judgment of the world, even to the point of judging angels (1 Cor. 6:2, 3).'[18]

Will Saints Ever 'Come into Judgment'?

Jesus said, 'he who hears my word and believes him who sent me has eternal life; he does not come into judgment, but has passed from death to life' (John 5:24 RSV). Jesus said the same thing in various ways, including some parables. Paul in various ways declared the judgment of those justified by faith, by blood, by grace, by Christ, a matter of past history at the cross. We need fear no future 'wrath of God.' 'Since, therefore, we have now been justified by his blood, much more shall we be saved by him from the wrath of God… while we were enemies we were reconciled to God' (Rom. 5:9, 10 ESV).

In an important treatise, Geerhardus Vos, Professor of Biblical Theology at Princeton Seminary, asserted that 'justification… is to Paul virtually a judgment by way of anticipation.'[19] But this, says Vos, does not mean that believers do not need to think about judgment, for many passages in Paul's letters to Christians remind them of coming judgment where 'salvation' and 'non-salvation' (Rom. 2:2, 3, 6; 3:6, 8; 5:16; 1 Cor. 5:13; 6:2; 2 Cor. 2:9; 2 Thess. 2:12; 1 Tim. 3:6; 2 Tim. 4:1) are discussed.[20] Though Vos thinks in terms of only one future resurrection and judgment he asserts that, 'with Paul the judgment is an event that will make discrimination as to future rank and enjoyment in the life to come between individual Christians. The differences established may and will be great, but the range covered by them lies within the realm of salvation.'[21]

This judgment is scheduled to take place at Christ's appearing (*epiphaneia*) when a 'righteous judge' will assign 'crown[s] of righteousness' and many other awards (2 Tim. 4:8). Though already, in justification, declared righteous – acquitted – before God, being regarded by the Judge as 'in Christ,' we must nevertheless 'all appear before the judgment seat.'[22] It holds no threat of damnation for those in Christ for 'There is… no condemnation for those who are in Christ Jesus' (Rom. 8:1-39). Yet there will be loss of rewards which can only be gained in the present life by proper stewardship of God's gifts of abilities, of time and of strength through the Spirit (1 Cor. 3:12-15). I have already tried to show that we should not think of this scene as taking place at the Last Judgment, described as before 'a great white throne' (Rev. 20:11-15) following the millennium. Believers will not stand before God to be judged by Him in that grand assize, because they are to be associated with God in Christ at that judgment in some unspecified way. Paul says, 'the world is to be judged by you' (1 Cor. 6:2), including angels (1 Cor. 6:3).

There is nevertheless a certain threat of possible grievous loss of 'what might have been.' Think of the severe conclusions to Jesus' parables and several warnings about careless stewardship. Paul warned servants to be obedient to 'earthly masters with fear and trembling, with a sincere heart, as you would Christ, not by the way of eye-service, as people-pleasers, but as servants of Christ, doing the will of God from the heart… as to the Lord… knowing that whatever good anyone does, this he will receive back from the Lord.' In some way we will get back what we did. Then he warns masters to 'do the same… and stop your threatening, knowing that… there is no partiality with him [God]' (Eph. 6:5-9; see also Col. 3:24, 25). At God's *bēma* (both podium of reward and seat of justice) we will get back what we gave in life, in some undisclosed way, not involving loss of salvation, so says the same author elsewhere (1 Cor. 3:10-15, especially v. 15). John A. Sproule seems therefore correct on the basis of the above in concluding that 'believers will be rewarded for lives of faithful service and obedience…. However there is strong evidence

---

18. George Ladd, *A Theology of the New Testament* (Grand Rapids: Eerdmans, 1974, 1991), p. 565.
19. Geerhardus Vos, *The Pauline Eschatology* (Grand Rapids: Eerdmans, 1952), p. 271.
20. ibid.
21. ibid.
22. I find no great significance in Paul's use of *bēma* for this seat, for both judges at games and at judicial courts were seated on a *bēma*, or throne set on a podium, ordinarily. See I Corinthians 16:12 where Gallio occupied a *bēma*.

that believers, at the judgment seat of Christ, will suffer some kind of chastisement for slothful, careless lives. This involves more than simply the loss of reward. Concerning the details, the Bible is silent.'[23]

The Word of God makes more of this matter than we preachers do. It warns plainly of severe loss if present opportunities are lost and present duties neglected. Here are some more of them in the stark severity of the King James Version: 'And now, little children, abide in him; that, when he shall appear, we may have confidence, and not be ashamed before him at his coming' (1 John 2:28); 'behold, I come quickly; and my reward is with me, to give every man according as his work shall be' (Rev. 22:12); 'Knowing therefore the terror of the Lord [not of hearers but of preachers], we persuade men' (2 Cor. 5:11). See also Revelation 2:7, 10, 17, 26-28; 3:2-5, 10-12, 18-21. Leon Morris makes the point that

> Believers may have confidence in the judgment. Though believers, like all the rest of mankind, face judgment, they do not face it in the same way. The New Testament attitude is not one of cowardly shrinking from it but of anticipation in mingled joy and solemnity... the dawn of the kingdom more than the doom of the world.[24]

Morris cites Romans 8:33; Hebrews 6:10; Jude 24; and 1 John 4:12.

The Certainty of Final Future Judgment.

There is analogy between human tribunals and the divine one yet future, but not strict similarity of process or court scene. An omniscient God will require no investigative procedures. The books which shall be opened will not require time to read for memory and all else will be 'open' to public knowledge. There will be no preliminary motion to dismiss charges.

The 'literary' court of world judgment set up in the first three chapters of the Epistle to the Romans summarily dismisses objections to a final Judgment Day, saying: 'Let God be true though every man be false ... if our wickedness serves to show the justice of God, what shall we say? That God is unjust to inflict wrath upon us? (I speak in a human way.) By no means! For then how could God judge the world?' (Rom. 3:3-6 RSV). Similarly Hebrews 6:1 ff. puts 'eternal judgment' among 'the principles of the doctrine of Christ' (Heb. 6:1, 2 KJV).

As for the Old Testament, the sentence of death for sin on the first man and the race of mankind in him was the actual beginning of eschatological judgment. Henceforth 'the living know that they will die' (Eccles. 9:5). The prophets declare the future 'day of the LORD' or 'that Day' or 'the great and awesome day of the LORD' (Mal. 4:5) that will burn 'like an oven, when all the arrogant and all evildoers will be stubble. The day that is coming shall set them ablaze, says the LORD of hosts.... But for you who fear my name, the sun of righteousness [the Messiah] shall rise with healing in its wings. You shall go out leaping [frolic] like calves from the stall' (Mal. 4:1, 2).

Jesus certainly endorsed the conviction of future divine judgment already present among His audience: 'It shall be more tolerable for Sodom and Gomorrha in the day of judgment, than for that city [which spurned His messengers]' (Mark 6:11 KJV). In John 5:22 and 27 ff. Jesus assumed His duties as the prophesied Messiah to be the Judge at the final reckoning and said something specific about it in Matthew 25:31 ff. The communion ordinance He founded was designed in part to speak to hearts of the importance of getting ready for the coming of the kingdom of God over all the earth, calling for self-judgment 'that we may not be condemned along with the world' (1 Cor. 11, especially vv. 28-32).

The Gospels are filled with statements about the coming of God's kingdom. Liberalism of the past was designed to take the threat of judgment out of that *parousia* of the Son of Man by treating the kingdom simply as the reign of good ethics in human hearts. More recently (and more seriously) some New Testament scholarship would make the *parousia* of Christ and His kingdom entirely something of the present. 'Realized Eschatology' is the name for this partially true but essentially fractional address to the whole truth.[25]

It is correct to say that the certainty of the judgment in a world created by God is guaranteed by the nature of the Creator, who is omniscient and omnipotent as well as holy. Emil Brunner was almost right about many aspects of theology. Even though there is in the New Testament 'variety of testimony,' he saw clearly that it is necessary to

---

23. J. A. Sproule, 'Judgment Seat' or 'Awards Podium,' *Grace Theological Seminary Journal*, Vol. 13, No. 1, Spring, 1974, p. 5. Two recommended books which treat this serious matter have the same title, *The Judgment Seat of Christ*. The older work is by D. M. Parton (republished by Bethany Fellowship Press, Minneapolis, n.d.). The newer work is by L. Sale-Harrison, 4th ed., New York, 1938.

24. Leon Morris, *The Biblical Doctrine of Judgment* (London: The Tyndale Press, 1960), p. 71.

25. C. H. Dodd in *The Parables of the Kingdom* (London, 1935) and *The Apostolic Preaching and Its Development* (1944, 1980) gave the world this interpretation of Jesus' doctrine of the kingdom. It was early answered (with due appreciation for its positive contributions) by many New

emphasize – as the one consistent and basic factor implied through it all – the conviction that the conception of judgment flows necessarily from a recognition of the holiness of God. God is He who takes His will (i.e. law) in absolute seriousness, He who is not mocked (Gal. 6:7).[26] Writing when the existentialist doctrine of freedom as autonomous self-will had not yet borne fruit of disaster and gone stale, he denounced the 'absolute determinism' of 'atheistic existentialism,' which found no place for the holiness of God or the creaturely responsibility of mankind. In thinking 'about judgment' we must 'recognize God seriously as God, and man as man. If there is no last judgment, it means that God does not take His own will seriously.'[27]

Principles of Divine Judgment.

In the scene of the Last Judgment (Rev. 20:12) it is said, 'books were opened.' Not 'the books' as later in the verse, but books indefinitely, books such as registers of what people say, do and think (Ps. 56:8; Isa. 65:6 and context; Mal. 3:16; Deut. 32:34; Matt. 12:37). For 1,500 or more years these books have been interpreted as a symbol of the divine omniscience or of 'a certain divine power, by which it shall be brought about that everyone shall recall to memory all his own works, whether good or evil.'[28] In Daniel's vision of the judgment, likewise the 'judgment [was set], and the books were opened' (Dan. 7:10).

Five Books.

What books? Scripture suggests five records, 'books' available and publicly exposed on that day.

1. The book of divine omniscience. When 'the messenger of the covenant' comes, before whom none 'can stand,' then 'I [the LORD] will draw near to you for judgment. I will be a swift witness...' (Mal. 3:2, 5). No investigative research. An omniscient and willing witness will be there.

2. The book of divine remembrance – this book might also be called – of 'those who feared the LORD... a book of remembrance was written before him of those who... esteemed his name' (Mal. 3:16).

3. The book of human conscience. Romans 2:12-15 shows that apart from special revelation, some of the righteous requirements of God are 'written on their hearts, while their conscience also bears witness and their conflicting thoughts accuse or perhaps excuse them on that day when... God judges the secrets of men by Christ Jesus' (Rom. 2:14-16 RSV).

4. The book of divine providence. The goodness of God in His providence toward mankind (Acts 13:15-17) was designed to 'lead... to repentance' (Rom. 2:4) but 'man' (2:3) has presumed 'on the riches of his kindness and forbearance and patience,' storing up 'wrath... on the day of wrath...' (Rom. 2:3-5).

5. The book of God's Word, spoken and written. Jesus said, 'the word that I have spoken [and written in the Bible] will judge him on the last day' (John 12:48).

6. The book of life. Alford writes, 'Those books and the book of life bore independent witness to the fact of men being or not being among the saved: the one by inference... the other by inscription or non-inscription of the name in the list. So the books would be as it were the vouchers for the book of life.'[29]

Evidence, however, must be weighed by judge or jury. The principles or rules of evidence, relevance of circumstances, and the like are no less important in the Last Judgment than in human courts. What are the 'rules' supplied by Scripture for that grand assize?

The standard as in human courts will be law. There are several kinds of law acknowledged in courts: customary or common-law (the way things have been done in this particular jurisdiction); judge-made laws or legal precedents; positive enactments of legislatures; and, where a government has a religious commitment, what is esteemed divine law. In the Last Judgment, of course, it will be divine law, whether inscriptured or not. As was shown in the sections of this volume on mankind and sin, God's law is simply the expression of His will, which flows from His nature. He is ever true to Himself. This will has been expressed in conscience, and 'common grace' by prophets who received revelation in many ways, some of which is written down in Scripture. (See above, Part 1: Theology Proper.)

Testament scholars. The theological errors were answered notably by J. E. Fison, *The Christian Hope, The Presence and the Parousia* (London, 1952), chaps. 3–6. I have relied on Fison's work frequently in this volume.

26. Emil Brunner, op. cit., p. 173.
27. Brunner, op. cit., p. 179.
28. Augustine, *City of God* XX.14, NPNF First Series, 2, p. 434.
29. Henry Alford, *NTER*, p. 1931.

The Standards of God's Law.

1. In the first place, because so frequently mentioned, is the complete absence of what in the KJV is designated 'respect of persons,' and in recent translations 'partiality.' All God's judgments are so.[30] Jesus made this the point in more than one of His parables.

2. God will judge according to the standard of the law, but 'not as that law has been ignorantly conceived of by each, but as it has been more or less clearly, revealed by the Judge Himself to each severally.'[31] According to Romans 2:12-15 the heathen who had no written revelation shall be judged by the law 'written' on the heart ('natural light' in old terms, 'general revelation' in the newer). Those who have known the light of scriptural law will be judged by that in accordance with the whole will of God made known and the privileges and responsiblities there. This is the point in the parable of the 'faithful and wise steward' (Luke 12:41-48) where some are punished with 'a light beating' others with 'a severe.' 'Everyone to whom much was given, of him much will be required, and from him to whom they entrusted much, they will demand the more' (Luke 12:47, 48).

3. Judgment will be 'according to truth' (Rom. 2:2) – truth as to the law of God and truth as to actual facts in right relation. 'Circumstances alter cases.' Paul put this first in the order of principles in Romans 2.

4. '[T]o each one according to his works' (Rom. 2:6) is second of Paul's stated principles. All of Romans 2:6-13 should be read, especially by complacent Christians, 'For it is not the hearers of the law who are righteous before God, but the doers of the law who will be justified.' Let us thank God for our Lord Jesus who took the strokes of the law in our place – as the author of Romans 2 carefully explained in the two next following chapters of Romans.

5. Though perhaps covered in point 3 above, Paul also mentions 'that day when... God judges the secrets of men by Christ Jesus' (Rom. 2:16). 'Therefore do not pronounce judgment before the time, before the Lord comes, who will bring to light the things now hidden in darkness and will disclose the purposes of the heart. Then each one will receive his commendation from God' (1 Cor. 4:5). David's concern about 'hidden faults' – hidden even from himself – should be a concern of all.

Concluding Questions.

1. How can justified (acquitted) believers be judged by their works? A. A. Hodge's paragraph applies: 'The saints will not be acquitted on the ground of their good deeds, but because their names are found "written in the book of life," or the book of God's electing love and on the ground of their participation in the righteousness of Christ.'[32] Their good deeds will be publicly cited as evidence of their faith which is the instrument of their justification by faith (Phil. 4:3; Rev. 3:5; 13:8; James 1:22-25; 2:14-18).

2. What is the final purpose or *telos* of eschatological judgments? It is the same as the *telos* of God in all creation and in His providence as well as His eternal plans for all creation, the manifestation of His own glory. Ephesians 1:1-12 makes plain that this was the purpose of the Father, 'the purpose of him who works all things according to the counsel of his will' (v. 11). This is His purpose in the church as well (Eph. 3:9, 10), and in His government (providence) of nations (Rom. 9:17, 22, 23). And it is the duty of Christians to adjust their own goals in life to God's goal, that is, His glory. Enforcement of laws is as necessary to an orderly universe as to any well-ordered human society.

It is therefore proper to say, uncomfortable as the idea may be to modern denizens of this planet, that final judgment has the same *telos* – God's glory. I am not here on earth to attain personal fulfillment. Paul says explicitly in Romans 9 that the redeemed are forever 'vessels of mercy' prepared beforehand to make known the riches of God's glory, and that the lost, as 'vessels of wrath,' will exhibit God's righteous wrath and make His power known. God will necessarily thus unveil the secrets of men to make known their real character in order to make final disposition of them. This is true whether there be one final judgment or several.

Other aspects of the doctrine of divine judgment will now follow as we consider the final state of the lost and of the saved.

---

30. Deut. 10:17; 2 Chron. 19:7; Rom. 2:11; Eph. 6:9; Col. 3:25; Prov. 24:23; 28:21; Col. 2:16; James 2:1, 3, 9; 1 Peter 1:17.
31. A. A. Hodge, *Outlines of Theology* (New York: R. Carter & Brothers, 1860), p. 574.
32. A. A. Hodge, *The Confession of Faith* (London: Banner of Truth Trust, 1964), p. 302.

7
The Final Destiny of the Unsaved, I

The doctrine of the dreadful destiny of the lost is an unpleasant shadow across biblical doctrine. So it is not very remarkable that the surveys of religious opinion, frequently reported in the press, will relate that of the same church people, who by strong majority believe in God, immortality, the divinity of Jesus and heaven, many dissent from a belief in hell. Yet that doctrine stands behind and enforces the need for the incarnation of the Son of God, His sinless life, and especially His substitutionary atonement and present ministry of intercession. It also sustains the common moral life of mankind and is indispensable to any strong apostolic fervor in Christian missions and evangelism.

In an earlier period of growing national wealth, accompanied by a decline in biblical faith and Christian living, the then Roosevelt Professor of Systematic Theology in Union Theological Seminary, New York City, William Greenough Thayer Shedd (1820–1894), wrote near the end of his life:

> The recent uncommon energy of opposition to endless punishment... synchronized with great... breaches of trust, uncommon corruption in mercantile and political life, and great distrust between man and man. Luxury deadens the moral sense, and luxurious populations do not have the fear of God before their eyes. Hence, luxurious men, recalcitrate at hell and 'kick against the goads.' No theological tenet is more important than eternal retribution to those modern nations which like England, Germany and the United States, are growing rapidly in riches, luxury and earthly power. Without it, they will infallibly go down in that vortex of sensuality and wickedness that swallowed up Babylon and Rome. The bestial and shameless vice of the dissolute rich... is a powerful argument for the necessity and reality of the lake which burneth with fire and brimstone.[1]

Dr Shedd's great exposition of the doctrine of divine punishment is not widely read today. Among the greatest informers of the lecture desk in theology today is the *Church Dogmatics* of the late Karl Barth. Barth is more widely read by professors than by students, for whom one would hardly dare assign such voluminousness! Though he probably would not acknowledge it, Barth's universalism appears in his treatment of Christology and Soteriology. Yet significantly, it is in one of the volumes on reconciliation (IV, 1) that his most extensive development of this subject appears – over a hundred pages of it. It is the old universalism in new dress. Barth did not believe anyone would be finally lost and ultimately perish. Presumably his views have now been clarified.

---

1. W. G. T. Shedd, *The Doctrine of Endless Punishment* (New York: Charles Scribner's Sons, 1886), pp. 158, 159.

Only a step behind Barth in importance, and far more readable and widely read in America since the arrival in America in English dress of *The Mediator* in mid-twentieth century, is Emil Brunner. His three-volume *Dogmatics* was widely used in Protestant theological schools, including some which up to very recently were strongly fundamentalist. What did this teacher of teachers say? Having resolved the issue into the usual paradoxes of the school of neo-orthodoxy, adding the inevitable denial of propositional statements of theological truth, he affirmed both universal salvation and eternal damnation, merging both in what he understood is the personal dimension of theological truth.[2] Other theologians have managed to say, 'I do not know,' with less flourish. How different the clear statements of the Bible!

Five Propositions.

I shall summarize what I have confirmed to be the biblical doctrine in connection with five propositions. After that, theories which deny the biblical doctrine will be discussed briefly. Finally a conclusion will be suggested. The five propositions now follow:

1. The state of the lost in their final punishment is death.
2. The measure of the final punishment is deeds done in life.
3. The nature of the final punishment is torment.
4. The duration of the final punishment is everlasting.
5. The place of the final punishment is hell, also called the lake of fire and Gehenna.

When I first assembled this outline, late on a cold northern Ohio night, alone in a small church basement room with concrete walls, my feet cold, my hands numb, alone in the great building, my dear wife and two small sons snug in bed two miles away, the stillness undisturbed save for the hiss of the gas heater and the annoying clack of the ancient typewriter, I shrank from every word I wrote. Even now in greater comfort there is no greater pleasure in the task, for the very atmosphere of this lovely autumn Sabbath seems deadly with the weight of the sinner's doom. Yet we approach it with the interest and respect due to all of God's revelations. What His Word teaches clearly we accept in faith even if the heart staggers and the mind reels. Just what does the Bible clearly say?

> For if we sin wilfully after we have received the knowledge of the truth, there remaineth no more sacrifice for sins, but a certain fearful looking for of judgment and fiery indignation, which shall devour the adversaries. He that despised Moses' law died without mercy under two or three witnesses: Of how much sorer punishment, suppose ye, shall he be thought worthy, who hath trodden under foot the Son of God, and hath counted the blood of the covenant, wherewith he was sanctified, an unholy thing, and hath done despite unto the Spirit of grace? For we know him that hath said, Vengeance belongeth unto me, I will recompense, saith the Lord... It is a fearful thing to fall into the hands of the living God (Heb. 10:26-31 KJV).

I have cited the above text in the stark simplicity of the Authorized Version to prick the conscience, thereby impelling us, if possible, to see the matter through. For similar reasons I now present some of the strongest words on the subject, two statements from the lips of the Savior of mankind, with the additional purpose of laying part of a scriptural groundwork for the doctrine to be developed later.

> [I]f thy hand offend thee, cut it off: it is better for thee to enter into life maimed, than having two hands to go into hell, into the fire that never shall be quenched. And if thy foot offend thee, cut it off: it is better for thee to enter halt into life, than having two feet to be cast into hell, into the fire that never shall be quenched: Where their worm dieth not, and the fire is not quenched. And if thine eye offend thee, pluck it out: it is better for thee to enter into the kingdom of God with one eye, than having two eyes to be cast into hell fire: Where their worm dieth not, and the fire is not quenched (Mark 9:43-48 KJV).

> As therefore the tares are gathered and burned in the fire; so shall it be in the end of this world. The Son of man shall send forth his angels, and they shall gather out of his kingdom all things that offend, and them which do iniquity; And shall cast them into a furnace of fire: there shall be wailing and gnashing of teeth (Matt 13:40-42 KJV).

These are only a sampling of the many passages of Scripture which set forth the destiny of the lost. We now turn to an analysis of the biblical doctrine.

---

2. Emil Brunner, *Dogmatics* III (Philadelphia: Westminster Press, 1962), pp. 420–424.

I. The State of the Lost in Their Final Punishment Is Death.

Scripture clearly teaches that although it is 'appointed unto men once to die,' all men will also experience an 'eschatological' resurrection, i.e. a restoration of physical life, as a part of the divine program of the consummation. As seen in the previous chapters on the resurrection of the dead, though there is difference of opinion as to whether the unsaved shall rise from the dead at the same time the saved do, there is no difference among orthodox theologians about the fact of a resurrection to condemnation. Jesus spoke plainly of a physical resurrection of the lost for judgment: 'the hour is coming, in the which all that are in the graves shall hear his voice, And shall come forth; they that have done good, unto the resurrection of life; and they that have done evil, unto the resurrection of damnation' (John 5:28, 29 KJV).

It was given to John the Revelator to see a vision of the Last Judgment. He reports:

> And I saw a great white throne, and him that sat on it, from whose face the earth and the heaven fled away; and there was found no place for them. And I saw the dead, small and great, stand before God; and the books were opened: and another book was opened, which is the book of life: and the dead were judged out of those things which were written in the books, according to their works... And death and hell were cast into the lake of fire. This is the second death (Rev. 20:11, 12, 14 KJV).

This plain passage, together with Jesus' parable-like 'sheep and goats' prophecy of Matthew 25, has shaped generations of Christian imagination of 'the last judgment.' We presently focus on one last detail of Revelation 20:14: 'This is the second death.' Many other passages, beginning with Genesis 2:17, connect all human death with sin as its invariable penalty. But what is death?

There are three conditions which the Bible calls death. Each one consists of a separation, or alienation, of what normally should be in union. We are familiar with one of them as physical death.

Technical discussions aside for the moment, when the Apostle Paul dies he not only, like Adam, returns to the ground from which he was taken (Gen. 2:17; 3:19), but he also departs to be with Christ in heaven, which is far better (Phil. 1:21-24); he is 'absent from the body' and 'present with the Lord' (2 Cor. 5:8 KJV). That which is present with the Lord when a believer dies is a 'soul' (Rev. 6:9 ff.; 20:4). Some recent theology, seeking an orthodox basis for shifting the chief emphasis of the church from spiritual matters to social ones sometimes over-emphasizes an alleged 'indissoluble unity' of man – spiritual and physical. To the contrary, while man is normally such a unity, the unity was disturbed and in part destroyed by sin at the beginning and is fully ruptured at physical death. Anthropology must come to terms with eschatology! '[T]he body apart from the spirit is dead' (James 2:26) and from another point of view, when the body goes to dissolution and the spirit goes to God, the man is dead even though his spirit has departed to Paradise or Hades.

Spiritual death is alienation of man from his creator-God. God had threatened this too (Gen. 2:17), and it occurred upon the occasion of the original sin (Gen. 3:8 ff.). Spiritual death is the present condition of all men apart from a new birth for 'we all' are 'dead in the trespasses and sins... by nature children of wrath... alienated from the life of God' (Eph. 2:1, 3; 4:18), and that because of our connection natural and federal with Adam (Rom. 5:12-21); hence 'sin reigned in death.'

But what will the 'second death' be? I think the simplest explanation, the literal one, probably is the correct one. In their final judgment men shall stand before God in physical bodies. What the capacities of those bodies may be, we are not told, but we are told that in the judgment men will be physically alive. Their condemnation to everlasting banishment from God's presence is perpetuation of spiritual death – alienation forever from their Creator, in whom alone is life. Cast into a 'lake of fire,' punished with 'everlasting destruction,' they shall die physically again, existing forever in the state of permanent disembodiment. There are competent interpreters who treat the expression figuratively (and there certainly are figurative elements in the book of Revelation). Yet there is no clear biblical parallel to such use of 'second' as indicating something like 'consummate degree' or 'ultimate.' Besides being the literal sense of the phrase, punishment in a disembodied state during final eternity is parallel to, and rendered feasible by, such punishment of the wicked during the state intermediate between death and the final judgment, in a disembodied state. Though his body was in a grave somewhere, Dives, the 'rich man,' was 'in anguish in this flame' (Luke 16:24)! Before proceeding onward, let us put ourselves on notice that death is not the same as extinction, cessation of existence or annihilation. In the Bible, dead men exist – and consciously so – quite as truly as living men. In Jesus' familiar story of the rich man and Lazarus, when 'The poor man died' he was carried by the angels to 'Abraham's side' and the rich man also having died and being buried, 'in Hades, being in torment, he lifted up his eyes' (viz. Luke 16:19 ff.). Both men continued to exist as men. Think also of Jesus' words to the repentant thief and of Paul's expectation.

Passages which refer to a dead man as being buried (and there are lots of them) are only employing the common manner of speaking the Bible usually employs. They do not deny the common scriptural teaching that life is one mode of human existence, death another. It will be helpful to know that 'destruction' in 'the way... that leads to destruction' (Matt. 7:13) is a verbal form of the same word rendered 'destroy' in the place where Jesus speaks of God's power to 'destroy both soul and body' in Gehenna (Matt. 10:28). So extinction of being is not what the 'destruction' of death means. The word for destruction or destroy in each of the passages just cited is always a form of *apollumi* (verb) or *apoleia* (noun). The use of this term by the happy father in Jesus' story of the prodigal son will help us to see what the true sense of the word is. After the prodigal had come home again the father declared, to the elder brother, 'your brother was dead, and is alive; he was lost [*apollumi*], and is found' (Luke 15:32). Specifically, to be lost (or destroyed) is the opposite of being found, not the opposite of existence.

Destroyed things, in the biblical sense (as in most discourse in English), are rendered useless, out of order, wasted, unable to perform the normal part in ongoing existence; they are not rendered extinct or annihilated. So when the wicked are said to be destroyed in hell, as several texts in one way or another do say, the meaning is that they are put out of order, wasted, made useless there, but not extinct.

II. The Measure of Final Punishment Is Deeds Done in Life.

The terms of this sentence are suggested by extracts from Paul: 'God's righteous judgment... will render to each one according to his works' (Rom. 2:5, 6) 'For we must all appear before the judgment seat of Christ, so that each one may receive what is due for what he has done in the body, whether good or evil' (2 Cor. 5:10). Also there is one from Peter to the effect that judgment is to be 'in the flesh the way people are' (1 Peter 4:6).

The simple teachings captured in the rubric above signify that what people do is of eternal consequence, their deeds bearing directly on their final eternal condition and that all the deeds of consequence for that final state are performed in the 'here and now.' Eternal destiny is settled here and now without opportunity for revision of the record or change of destiny after death.

It is the uniform teaching of the Bible that God has scheduled a 'time' or 'day' or 'hour' of final judgment. In this chapter our interest is not how that judgment relates to the redeemed, but to the lost. As we found in studying the doctrine of judgment, the basis of God's verdict on that day will be what people have done. We are assured that divine law will be the formal basis, laws about deeds (see Ps. 1:2, 6). The second chapter of Romans assures its readers that the judgment of God accords to truth (v. 2), that God will decide without partiality (v. 11; cf. 1 Peter 1:17), and that He shall uncover 'the secrets of men' (v. 16) in doing so. All this however is in specific relation to people's actions, for the passage focuses on deeds, referring to the wicked as those who 'because of your hard and impenitent heart... are storing up wrath for yourself on the day of wrath when God's righteous judgment will be revealed. He will render to each one according to his works: ... wrath and fury... tribulation and distress for every human being who does evil' (Rom. 2:5, 6, 8, 9). An impressive array of passages could be added.[3] The words which people speak are specifically joined with the deeds they do as being together the works to be judged, i.e. words are a species of works, for, as Jesus Himself said, the Son of Man shall not only 'repay each person according to what he has done' (Matt. 16:27) but that 'on the day of judgment people will give account for every careless word they speak' (Matt. 12:36; cf. Jude 15).

These things being true, several further aspects of the doctrine of judgment appear. There is not a large amount of revelation on the subject but enough to allow several firm statements. Here are some of them.

Though sin is a habit which, if unchanged by personal salvation in Christ, will persist in hell forever, consignment to that dread place is on the basis of deeds performed in the here and now, done 'in the body,' as 'men in the flesh.' Though the continuing wicked thoughts of people in hell may provide some justification for the unending punishment which the Bible denounces, Scripture says nothing about it. People's words and deeds in the present life are the crucial ones.

---

3. See Eccles. 12:14; Ps. 28:4; Prov. 24:13; Jer. 25:14; John 3:18-21; 1 Tim. 5:24, 25; Rev. 2:2, 5, 9, 13, 19, 23, 26; 3:1, 2, 8, 15; 20:12, 13.

Judgment according to deeds, on logical grounds, demands grades and degrees of punishment, though a firm basis for a doctrine of proportionate rewards (for the righteous deeds of righteous people) and punishments is based primarily on texts which affirm it rather than on logic. In a former age, when Christian doctrines (as opposed to the present preoccupation with feelings only) was thought to be a fit subject for lyrical expression, the first important American poet, a Puritan, of course, wrote a poem of judgment and hell which still turns up in symposiums of American literature. Michael Wigglesworth – preacher, physician, poet of New England (1631–1705), famous as a poet throughout Puritan America[4] and to a lesser degree in England as well – was pastor of a single church at Malden for forty-nine years, till his death in 1705. Our present interest is in his 'The Day of Doom,' America's first significant poem. Early in the long semi-epic the composer prays:

> The God of Heaven grant
> These lines so well to speed
> That thou the things of thine own peace
> Through them may'st better heed;
> And may'st be stirred up
> To stand upon thy guard,
> That Death and Judgment may not come,
> And find thee unprepared.

As the imaginary description of Judgment Day moves on, the least hell-deserving are represented as being brought before the bar of God and there hear Him say:

> A crime it is; therefore in bliss
> you may not hope to dwell;
> But unto you I shall allow
> the easiest room in Hell.

Now we must admit that Wigglesworth's lyric does not fall on appreciative ears today, even among those in agreement with his high Calvinism. And though we have no firm biblical teaching affirming various 'rooms in hell' corresponding to the 'many mansions' of 'the Father's House,' the idea of graduation of punishments, as affirmed above, is a logical correlate of the doctrine of judgment and has a sufficient biblical basis. In the law of Moses, for example, some crimes were punishable by fines, some with flogging, a few with banishment and a very few by death. In a statement about the judgment, Jesus affirmed 'that servant who knew his master's will but did not get ready or act according to his will, will receive a severe beating. But the one who did not know, and did what deserved a beating, will receive a light beating' (Luke 12:47, 48). Similarly Sodom, famous of old for sin, and Tyre and Sidon, two wicked pagan cities, will find affairs 'more bearable' at 'the day of judgment' than will the towns of Palestine which received the benefit of the Savior's ministry (Matt. 11:20-24; Luke 10:12-15).

Modern theories of penology, based on correction of offenders, deterrence of offenses in society and protection of society, have little if any place in a rationale for such statements about punishments. In the biblical view, sinners are offenders against divine laws, which in turn are expressions of justice which finds its root in the divine character and will. Deserved punishment should be inflicted only because it is right to do so.

This explanation of law and justice is true on all levels. It is the clear teaching of Scripture that when punishment is just, then and only then is it either preventive or corrective. In the final punishment, while there likely is some benefit by way of isolating incorrigibly wicked souls from the rest of God's creation, they are put forever beyond the reach of correction. People fear light because their deeds are evil and they fear exposure. Because they resist correction here and now they must be punished hereafter – not because they are proper subjects of improvement but because their deeds were evil! For such people life itself becomes day by day a preparation for final punishment, just as other people's lives are a daily promise of future glory. 'While there are people whose offenses are so obvious

---

4. With the decline of orthodoxy in the heirs of New England Puritanism some of them (Hawthorne, Emerson, *et al*) slandered their ancestral theology. Puritans were aware of the orthodox, biblical doctrine of hell but were not generally preoccupied with it. For example, Thomas Boston, a Scot of the Puritan era (1676–1752), produced a widely read, substantial work on *Human Nature in its Fourfold State* (1720, repr. London: Banner of Truth Trust, 1964). Of the 500 pages of the book only thirty pages deal with 'Hell.' Lamentably, Jonathan Edward's famous sermon on 'Sinners in the Hand of an Angry God' is the only part of his voluminous writings most people know about. Not only were the Puritans not puritanical, they were not morbid about life or death or, as forgiven sinners, either unconcerned or preoccupied with the terrors of hell.

that they run before them into court [judgment], there are others whose offenses have not yet overtaken them. Similarily, good deeds are obvious, or even if they are not, they cannot be concealed forever' (1 Tim. 5:24, 25 NEB). People today are inclined to scoff at any anxious thought about such things – which makes for bad life adjustment, they say – but this is not the biblical wisdom of Moses, the man of God in Psalm 90:7-12:

> For we are brought to an end by your anger;
> by your wrath we are dismayed.
> You have set our iniquities before you,
> our secret sins in the light of your presence.
> For all our days pass away under your wrath;
> we bring our years to an end like a sigh.
> The years of our life are seventy,
> or even by reason of strength eighty;
> yet their span is but toil and trouble;
> they are soon gone, and we fly away.
> Who considers the power of your anger,
> and your wrath according to the fear of you?
> So teach us to number our days
> that we may get a heart of wisdom.

Serious contemplation of the many passages like this one will make it clear that all people ought to consider death and eternity now. They should 'seek the LORD while he may be found.' It is good for believers to temper their presently touted joie de vivre with sober contemplation of their coming meeting at a judgment seat of Christ (Rom. 14:10; 1 Cor. 3:13-15; 2 Cor. 5:10). Contemplation of the future life in heaven has always been a Calvinist emphasis, beginning with Calvin himself; it is an important aspect of biblical Christianity. There is a frightening possibility that if our pastoral efforts are completely successful in getting people's anxieties quieted and their lives well adjusted, the same people will some day slip peacefully into perdition. Rather let us set before them *A Serious Call to a Devout and Holy Life*.[5]

Punishment according to deeds is possible only because the judge is to be an all-knowing and all-wise God. He will be fully aware of mitigating circumstances of every sort. No, there is no promise, as the somewhat sub-biblical song has it, 'He'll understand and say, "Well done,"' but rather, 'He'll understand and see that what is done is right.' As everyone ought to know, to break the commandments of God is wrong, but not all acts of law-breaking, though culpable, are equally blameworthy. Even human law and jurisprudence recognizes the principle: 'Circumstances alter cases.'

Hence, in civil law there are several degrees of murder, from premeditated ('in the first degree'), punishable by death, to homicide by preventable accident, which is punishable by fine or short-term imprisonment, and similar. This same feature is to be found in Mosaic law, as noted earlier. So there are the varying degrees of blameworthiness noted in Luke 12:47, 48; Matthew 11:20-24; and Luke 10:12-15, also observed earlier. One of the circumstances God will take into consideration will be the degree of knowledge of divine law involved. 'Ignorance is no excuse,' but it is an ameliorating circumstance. God also knows the hidden hereditary weaknesses individuals carry, the faulty training they have had, the perverted misdirections of conscience, quirks of disposition and the effects of training and environment. These all affect the record of the deeds of personal beings, responsible before their Creator for every deed. Otherwise God's judgment could not be wholly just when the time comes to 'render to each according to his works.'

There are consequences for evangelism in this New Testament point of view. We must work to save people now, for 'night is coming, when no one can work' (John 9:4). Yet, while laboring to save the lost from hell's danger, we must be careful lest the perils of our closeness to them and our intimate dealings with them do not destroy our power and willingness to proclaim and counsel, as Jude puts it, 'There are some doubting souls who need your pity; some you should snatch from the flames and save; there are others for whom your pity must be mixed with fear; hate the very garment that is contaminated with sensuality' (Jude 22, 23 NEB margin). 'There are grave dangers to the soul in aggressive evangelism! Be aggressive! Yet be on your guard!' Jude seems to say.

---

5. William Law, *A Serious Call to a Devout and Holy Life* (reprint, Grand Rapids: Eerdmans, 1966).

III. The Nature of the Final Punishment of the Lost Is Torment.

The amount of information furnished on this aspect of the subject by the Scriptures, though small, is very impressive. Acknowledging at the start that many of the expressions are obviously figurative, the general sense of the passages on this subject is frighteningly clear. I shall present first an elaboration of the texts which form the basis of the above proposition and then try to sketch out details of the subject as far as the Scripture gives us leave to do so.

The nearest thing to a direct, complete statement about the nature of final punishment is a passage which treats the destiny of the followers of Antichrist (the 'first beast' of Rev. 13), as follows.

> If any man worship the beast and his image, and receive his mark in his forehead, or in his hand, The same shall drink of the wine of the wrath of God, which is poured out without mixture into the cup of his indignation; and he shall be tormented with fire and brimstone in the presence of the holy angels, and in the presence of the Lamb: And the smoke of their torment ascendeth up for ever and ever: and they have no rest day nor night, who worship the beast and his image, and whosoever receiveth the mark of his name (Rev. 14:9-11 KJV).

The phrases 'shall be tormented,' 'their torment' and 'no rest day or night' capture the idea of the essential nature of the punishments of hell. The verb (*basanidzō*, to torment), though used in non-biblical Greek of torture in judicial examination, has no such special sense in any biblical text. Its primary sense is any severe pain, whether physical (see Rev. 12:1, of childbirth) or mental (see 2 Peter 2:8, Lot's mental distress at the sins of Sodomites). The corresponding noun (*basanismos*) here means the pain of being tortured. It is as simple as that. In the case of the rich man in Hades (Luke 16:23) and his 'being in torment' (*basanois*, sing. *basanos*, a related word of similar meaning) is employed. Being in 'torment' uses the word *huparchōn*, a strong word meaning 'existing,' emphasizing the permanence of the torments. When the rich man later says 'I am tormented', a different Greek word (*odunaō*) is employed but it means essentially the same. So the idea is still simple – exactly the same as the English word 'torment' means. It is appropriate to add that the passive voice, 'they shall be tormented,' points to God, as is frequent in similar biblical constructions (see Isa. 53:5 of Messiah's sufferings), as the agent in bringing the torment about. God will be acting there no less than He was when the LORD 'laid on him the iniquity of us all' and 'it was the will of the LORD to crush him.' Though in divine providence and human history Pilate, Herod, the Roman soldiers, the Sanhedrin and assembled Jewish people killed Jesus (Acts 2:23; 3:14; 4:27), it was God Himself who delivered the stroke which 'laid on him the punishment due us all' (Isa. 53:6 author's translation).

There are several ways by which the torments of hell are represented. A number of passages say that the wicked will be punished with fire – 'the unquenchable fire… thrown into hell… where… the fire is not quenched' (Mark 9:44-48). The rich man in Hades claims that he is 'in anguish in this flame' (Luke 16:24) and the passage cited from Revelation 14:10, 11 speaks of 'fire and sulphur' as well as 'smoke.' Once Jesus speaks of hell as the 'eternal fire prepared for the devil and his angels' (Matt. 25:41).

On the contrary, other passages speak of hell as a dark place (unlike flames of fire). Jesus says that the unprofitable servant (all people are supposed to be God's servants) shall be cast into 'outer darkness' (Matt. 25:30) as also unfaithful sons of the kingdom, to the accompaniment of 'weeping and gnashing of teeth' (Matt. 8:12). Similarly, for false prophets, such as Balaam, 'the gloom of utter darkness has been reserved' (2 Peter 2:17). One thinks of the blackness of interstellar space – a truly mind-numbing thought.

A related idea is that the place for wicked spirits is an abyss (i.e. a deep, or as in Rev. 20:1, 2: KJV, a bottomless pit). Satan's minions swarm out of it (Rev. 9:2, 11). The leaders of the horde are called Abaddon and Apollyon, forms of the Hebrew and Greek words, for 'perishing,' 'loss,' 'perdition,' 'destruction' (see earlier comments herein on 'destruction'). This place is the home of demon spirits (see Luke 8:31 where the deep is 'abyss'). The torment is also said to be an undying worm (Mark 9:47, 48; cf. Isa. 66:24). The wicked, false prophets are destined to be forever 'wandering stars' (Jude 13) – one thinks of the comets and asteroids of outer space.

Finally, this punishment is said to be submission to God, even if compelled, on the part of infernal spirits 'under the earth' (Phil. 2:10) and an 'eternal punishment' (Matt. 25:46) – i.e. a punishment belonging to eternity, whatever in specific that may be.

Let me propose some feasible interpretations of these – at least mainly – figurative terms. Holding in mind that having experienced a 'second death' (and hence being disembodied spirits as in their state between first death and the resurrection for judgment) some of the terms seem quite understandable. The eternal fires may be remorse, for

'Of all the sad words of tongue or pen, the saddest are these: "It might have been."' The darkness has been equated with exclusion from God's presence forever; the wandering to everlasting loneliness; and the abyss of endless descent, to the utter hopelessness of hell. The lost are 'without hope' even now. Imagination fails when one thinks of the hopelessness of eternity without Him.

The developing Enlightenment which came to be called 'modernism' intruded upon the thinking even of the orthodox in the late eighteenth century; hence arose an extensive literature, furious as well as reasonable, in defense of the orthodox historic doctrine. In the year 1881 a small volume of 150 pages by a scholarly American pastor, Rev. John W. Daley (*The Hereafter of Sin: What it Will Be; Answers to Certain Questions and Objections*), summarized about all that ever has been said or can be said by way of interpreting the expressions, literal and figurative, regarding the 'nature' of 'future retribution.' He made nine points. Further retribution will consist of the following.

1. *Consciousness of personal blame.* He cites Matthew 25:46; Luke 16:25; several theologians; and the painful admissions of Lord Byron.

2. *A deep and abiding sense of shame.* He quotes Jeremy Taylor; and refers to Ecclesiastes 12:14; Matthew 12:36; Mark 4:22; Luke 8:17; and 12:2, 3.

3. *Remorse of conscience.* He quotes Dorner and Martineau and the 'famous scene' of Lady Macbeth 'endeavoring to wash an imaginary blood-stain from her hand' – 'Out damned spot!'

4. *The withdrawal of good and saving influences* – of which the lost will be aware. He cites Matthew 25:29; and Luke 8:18; and exegetes Trench, Meyer, Lange, Murphy, and Taylor. All the brakes have now failed. He cites Psalm 81:13; Romans 1:24-28; Mark 3:29; and Revelation 22:11.

5. *Consciousness of a self-perpetuating tendency for moral character.* The only movement is downward. Habit has taken over forever. He refers to many literary and doctrinal authorities and, of course, to Jeremiah 13:23.

6. *A conviction of the hopelessness of their condition.* In Dante, there is the message, 'All hope abandon, ye who enter here,' over the gate of hell. He cites Luke 16:26; Matthew 22:13; 25:41; the chasm between Abraham's bosom and Hades in Luke 12; and Isaiah 57:20, 21.

7. *The raging of unholy and unsatisfied passions and desires.* We leave behind all objects of desire, 1 Timothy 4:7 (his longest section).

8. *The miserable 'society of that dark world.'* 'Companionship may prove to man the greatest blessing or the greatest curse.' Adam needed the society of Eve. Outside the heavenly Jerusalem are only those described in Revelation 21:8 and 22:15 as incorrigibly evil.

9. Last and most burdensome: *an unfailing sense of the displeasure of the Almighty.* John 3:36, 'The wrath of God remains on him.'

Among his concluding lines are the words: 'These, as we gather from Scripture and reason are some of the ingredients of that cup of woe which the finally impenitent must drain to the dregs. We say "some" for there may be others of which we have no knowledge "…the wages of sin."'[6]

I know Christians whom I would like to count as friends who are mightily upset about anything other than a literal-material interpretation of the phrases and sentences just now discussed. If they have a formula wherein fire and darkness, worms and a bottomless pit, disembodiment and a tongue tormented by flame, with consistency, logic and good sense can be interpreted literally, we shall all be willing to let them be our teachers, but I think they shall not succeed and are obviously on the wrong track. As many utterly devout and godly teachers have observed, when the subject matter of revelation transcends anything of direct human experience, when even direct analogies break down, God teaches us by symbols and figures. The literal realities represented by the symbols will be immeasurably more meaningful than the symbols. Hence to employ the symbols is in no wise to degrade or depreciate the realities.

In *Four Views of Hell*, Dr John Walvoord – a longtime friend – was assigned the first essay, 'The Literal View.' For some reason he surveys the whole doctrine of the final state of the unsaved – views, history of the doctrine, objections and the like – and devotes only two-thirds of his last page to the main question, 'Is the fire of eternal punishment to be understood literally?' In refutation of 'The Metaphorical View' he adamantly refuses to budge, though he does not explain how Dives (the rich man of Luke 16), in a disembodied state in 'hades,' could suffer physical pain from literal, material flame. It is apparent that Dr Walvoord is trying (valiantly but ineffectively,

---

6. John W. Daley, *The Hereafter of Sin: What it Will Be; Answers to Certain Questions and Objections* (Andover, Mass., 1881), pp. 1–63.

I think) to protect 'literal' or grammatico-historical interpretation of the predictive parts of the Bible. Most of his four-page rebuttal of metaphorical interpretation of 'the fire' of hell is, as he says, to prove 'the metaphorical view requires a non-literal interpretation of prophecy.'[7]

Scripture employs figurative language no less in describing the eternal home of the blest than the final 'place' of the damned. 'Why?' asked Thomas Boston, the pastor of Ettrick, Scotland in the time of the prevalence of Puritanism, 'Why are the things of another world represented to us in an earthly dress?' He answers, 'because the weakness of our capacities... requires it; it being always supposed that the things of the other world are in their kind more perfect than those by which they are represented.' As to why hell is represented in so many different ways in Scripture, the worthy scholar-pastor says that 'the reason of it is plain; namely, that hereby what of horror is wanting in one notion of hell, is supplied by another.' Similarly 'heaven's happiness' is 'represented under the various notions of a treasure, a paradise, a feast, a rest' and similar.[8]

IV. The Duration of the Punishment of the Lost Is Everlasting.

Such is the plain sense of several clear statements of Jesus, who said more about it than any biblical prophet or writer. We have had occasion to note His warnings against the place where the 'worm does not die and the fire is not quenched' (Mark 9:47, 48) and of hell's 'eternal fire' (Matt. 18:8) and of 'eternal punishment' (Matt. 25:46). We have also seen how the terrible smoke of the torment of Antichrist's followers goes up 'for ever and ever' (Rev. 14:11).

Now, at this point those who wish to expect something like universal salvation of all people, restitution of most of the wicked or their utter annihilation, usually start to talk about Greek words. Some of them do not do so very knowledgably, but they do make a show of scholarship. And since their messengers are often at the front door seeking to peddle books and supposed Bible translations supporting their doctrines, it seems necessary here to devote some space to the meaning of the terms used in Scripture for the everlasting duration of the final punishment of the wicked. I will try to be as non-technical as possible.

The New Testament words for 'everlasting' are chiefly one noun (aiōn, often translated 'world' or 'age') and one adjective (*aiōnios*) derived from it. In the New Testament these words are arranged in essentially three ways to express 'everlasting' – be it life, death, punishment, the life of God, or whatever. The simplest idiom (adj., *aiōnios*) I shall render 'aiōnion,' the more complicated combination 'unto ages' or 'unto the ages,' as the case may be, and the most complicated 'unto ages of ages' or 'unto the ages of the ages,' as the case may be.

These standard expressions for endless futurity in the New Testament are used firstly of the endless life of God or of Christ, viz. 'the everlasting God' (the aionian God, Rom. 16:26 KJV), 'Christ remains for ever' (Christ remains unto the age, John 12:34), 'I am alive for evermore' (I am alive unto the ages of the ages, Rev. 1:18).

They are employed, secondly, of the believer's eternal life: viz. 'but have eternal life' (but have aionian life, John 3:16 and forty-four times in John alone); 'eternal salvation' (aionian salvation, Heb. 5:9); 'eternal redemption' (aionian redemption, Heb. 9:12); 'he will live for ever' (he will live unto the age, John 6:51); 'and they will reign for ever and ever' (and they shall reign unto the ages of the ages, Rev. 22:5).

Two of these standard expressions are used to set forth the contrast between the everlasting and the temporal: viz. 'For the things that are seen are transient [lit., for a season], but the things that are unseen are eternal [aionian]' (2 Cor. 4:18); 'God... has called you to his eternal [aionian] glory,' etc. (1 Peter 5:10); 'they were prevented... from continuing... but he... continues for ever [unto the age]' (Heb. 7:23, 24).

These are the very same standard expressions used by Scripture to designate the everlasting duration of the punishment of the wicked. *Aiōnian*, for example, appears in the phrase 'eternal punishment' at Matthew 25:46 and, most significantly again, in the same verse of the believer's everlasting life. Jude 13 employs *unto (an) age* in the phrase 'the gloom of utter darkness... for ever,' and in John 10:28 the phrase 'will never perish' literally translates *unto the ages* as 'never.' In Revelation 14:17 (which I have cited several times) *unto ages of ages* is translated 'forever and ever,' while in Revelation 19:3 ('The smoke from her goes up for ever and ever') the same English words translate *unto the ages of the ages*, the fullest and strongest of the expressions.

---

7. John F. Walvoord, Wm. Crockett, Zachary J. Hayes, Clark H. Pinnock, *Four Views on Hell*, ed. Wm. Crockett (Grand Rapids: Zondervan, 1996), pp. 78–81.
8. Thomas Boston, *Human Nature in its Fourfold State* (London: The Banner of Truth Trust, first printing, 1720, 1964), p. 4.

We conclude therefore the following: (a) in a context of the life of the redeemed or the punishment of the lost these expressions must mean endless time. (b) The very variety of usage (three main categories, with minor variations of two, making five in all) indicate effort to exhaust the possibilities of the language for expression of endlessness. If we were to translate the English Bible into the common Greek of the first century we would have to employ them. (c) Though these Greek words do sometimes refer to periods of limited time – limited by the nature of the things connected (e.g. the epoch of the gospel in Matt. 28:20 where 'world' is *aiōn*) – the context will always make this clear (see Matt. 12:23 also, where 'world' is *aiōn*). (d) Qualitative distinctions may sometimes be indicated by 'eternal' (*aiōnios*, *aiōn*, etc.) but in such cases it is not because quality is in any manner inherent in the meaning of such words. Rather, as in all languages, words can be drawn away from their normal sphere of use into uses not strictly proper to them, especially when the language lacks proper words for such meanings. Such a case may be the use of 'eternal' in 2 Corinthians 5:1 which refers in a puzzling manner to the resurrection body as now 'eternal in the heavens.' There is no reason at all for making a rare or even non-existent sense the prevalent one.[9]

V. The Place of the Final Punishment Is Hell, Also Called the Lake of Fire and Gehenna.

The word 'hell,' found often in Scripture as a name for the place wherein the wicked go immediately after they die, is also the commonest English translation of other terms for the place wherein they are to be punished forever. The English word 'hell' translates several Greek and Hebrew words, but does so quite adequately, for the right idea is conveyed by it. Though the old Saxon word *helan*, from which it is derived, means 'to cover' (hence, *hell*, the covered or unseen world of the dead), 'it has been so long appropriated in common usage to the place of future punishment for the wicked, that its earlier meaning has been lost sight of.' This common meaning is the one the translators of the Authorized Version (1611) convey when sometimes they use it in the Old Testament to render *Sheol* and in the New Testament to render *Hades* and *Gehenna*. True, frequently as in Luke 16, the 'hell' (or Hades) is to be emptied into the place of final punishment (Rev. 1:12, 13), the distinction, however valid, is not very important. What English-speaking people mean by 'hell' when they thoughtfully use the word is what the biblical words mean also.

Among the Jews when our Lord walked among men, a common name for this place was evidently 'Gehenna.' It appears twelve times in the New Testament and, except for James 3:6, only in the speeches of the Savior of men, Himself (Matt. 5:22, 29, 30; 10:28; 18:9; 23:15, 33; Mark 9:43, 45, 47; Luke 12:5). The practice of translating this word by 'hell,' which in utterly unambiguous fashion refers to the place of final punishment of the wicked, is older than the Authorized or King James Version of 1611 and is quite properly continued by recent scholarly translators. NEB, for example, does so consistently.

At this point, an interesting, if somewhat horrifying, story about words and geography is appropriate and seems necessary. When the Land of Canaan was apportioned to the twelve tribes under Joshua, the border between Judah and Benjamin was run just south of Jerusalem 'by the valley of the son of Hinnom.' This valley was very near a south gate of Jerusalem (Jer. 19:2). Though originally just an ordinary patch of real estate (as it is now again and has been for centuries), its proximity to Jerusalem and relative isolation, owing to the fact of its being a rather narrowly confined ravine, made it a convenient center for a particularly heinous form of apostate religious cult-practice in ancient Israel.

Here two apostate kings, both under the influence of Syrian and Mesopotamian religion, carried out human sacrifice – the burning of infants to the worship of Moloch (also Moleck, Milcom, Malcham, Melcom), a fire god, specially honored by the Ammonites. The above-mentioned kings, Ahaz and Manasseh, made their children to 'pass through the fire' to Moloch in this ravine (or valley) before idols and altars erected therein at a place called 'Topheth' (or Tophet) (2 Kgs. 16:3; 2 Chr. 28:3; 2 Kgs. 23:10; 2 Chr. 33:6; see also Jer. 7:31, 32). Archaeology of Carthage has turned up acres of the cemetery or Tophet for the infants sacrificed at that colony of Canaan in North Africa. So now we know what the word *Tophet* means.

---

9. Mention should be made of the claims that *aiōn* (age, eternal) and derivitives refer to quality rather than quantity – especially as applied to 'eternal life' (*dzōēn aiōnion*, John 3:16). *TDNT* does not recognize such a meaning in its long article. Robert W. Yarbrough says that the terms relate 'especially to the quality of life in this age, and to both the quality and duration of life in the age to come' (*EDBT*, 'Eternal Life, Eternality, Everlasting,' p. 209). Yet throughout the article he treats the terms only as indicating duration, and demonstrates that time and eternity have connection, rejecting the Thomist notion that 'eternity is a motionless, changeless state, remote and qualitatively distinct from time... The Old Testament like the New Testament resists this time-eternity dualism' (ibid.).

Josiah put an end to these wretched ceremonies (2 Kgs. 23:10-14), but they were shortly thereafter briefly revived (Jer. 11:10-13; Ezek. 20:30; cf. Jer. 7:32; 19:11). In late times, according to Jewish sources, when the Jewish people were cured of idol-worship, the defiled gully was used as a city dump for Jerusalem with fires constantly smoldering there. It served also as a place for disposal of corpses of beasts and unwanted, unclaimed human corpses. It has been said that Jesus' body would have ended up there had not friends lovingly provided otherwise (Isa. 53:9 ASV).

This place, it is affirmed, furnishes the imagery for the terrible description of the eternal punishment of apostates found in Isaiah 66:24: 'And they shall go out and look on the dead bodies of the men who have rebelled against me. For their worm shall not die, their fire shall not be quenched, and they shall be an abhorrence to all flesh.' This vivid manner of referring to hell developed further during the inter-testamental period and later, as is easily traceable in the apocryphal and pseudepigraphal literature. When Jesus lived, the words 'ge-hinnom' (Gr., 'Gehenna') meant hell, the place of eternal loss and retribution as regularly and certainly as 'Waterloo,' the place of Napoleon's defeat, means defeat, or to 'cross the Rubicon' means not Caesar's act at all but any important irrevocable commitment, or 'Munich' means appeasement, and so on. Significantly, in a similar manner 'Paradise' – a Persian word for 'garden' – came to be the name for 'Heaven,' the eternal home of the redeemed. When one visits Jerusalem today (unless the Israelis have made some unexpected topographical changes!) a short walk from the 'dung gate' can take one to the site of that strange, infamous property of Hinnom (belonging to some Canaanite farmer of long ago?). The persistent notion that the 'Akeldama' of the story of Judas (Acts 1:18, 19) was in the valley of Hinnom cannot be far from correct. There is (or was) a tumbledown Orthodox monastery there – inhabited the last time I visited it, several years ago, by a single ragged monk and a few scrawny chickens.

The passage describing this place as the 'lake of fire' will be quoted without further comment: 'Then Death and Hades were thrown into the lake of fire. This is the second death, the lake of fire. And if anyone's name was not found written in the book of life, he was thrown into the lake of fire' (Rev. 20: 14, 15).

Does the Doctrine Have a Practical Importance?

It is most significant that Gehenna, what we would today call a city dump, the place of discarded, corrupt and useless things, is the biblical name most frequently used by Jesus for hell. Hell is the place of discard, of uselessness, of abandonment, of eternal destruction; hell is the final smoldering trash-heap of the universe. The doctrine of hell has great importance for the moral life of the mankind. Jesus spoke of hell many times, always by way of supporting some moral imperative.

Some striking language in a tract I selected from a literature rack in an Episcopal church, renders this poignantly:

> For this reason, then, I believe that hell has a very practical importance in our Christian lives. Most of us treat life entirely too lightly. We say, 'What difference does it make what I do or choose or think?' Hell reminds us it does make a difference. Life is earnest... every day we choose between life and death, every hour we look toward God or toward destruction, we stand between heaven and hell. This is why Jesus had such an offensive earnestness as he looked at Gehenna: 'If thy hand offend thee, cut it off, if thy foot offend thee, cut it off, if thine eye offend thee, pluck it out.' Did he mean to mutilate our bodies? Not at all. He meant that what our hand may choose, our foot may do, our eye may see, can take us moment by moment on the road either to heaven or to hell. That's how important our decisions are in this life; they determine character and character stands for all eternity.[10]

Robert Peterson proposes two reasons for 'such terrible doctrine: to provide believers with powerful motivation for evangelism, and to make us grateful to him who redeemed us by suffering the pains of hell for us.'[11]

---

10. *The Meaning of Hell* (Boston: Whittemon Associates, n.d., no author's name).
11. Robert Peterson, 'Eternal Punishment' in *EDBT*, p. 313.

8
The Final Destiny of the Unsaved, II

Some Perversions and Denials of the Scriptural Doctrine.[1]

The perversions and denials of the scriptural doctrine which here concern us are those made in the name of Christian truth. The ingenious efforts to expound these ideas have created an enormous literature which to cite and document here is impossible. D. A. Carson has competently addressed the problem of pluralism, but acknowledges some limitations to this expanding character of the present spirit of the age in a book of 600-plus pages.[2] His chapter on the subject of this chapter is entitled, 'Banishing the Lake of Fire.' After sketching some of what I call perversions and denials and suggesting answers, he wisely concludes his chapter with this paragraph:

> Despite the sincerity of their motives, one wonders more than a little to what extent the growing popularity of various forms of annihilationism and conditional immortality are a reflection of this age of pluralism. It is getting harder and harder to be faithful to the 'hard' lines of Scripture. And in this way evangelicalism itself may contribute to the gagging of God by silencing the severity of its warnings and by minimising the awfulness of the punishment that justly awaits those untouched by his redeeming grace.[3]

How much more direct and convincing the biblical passages which affirm the doctrine!

How does one explain the singular persistence among Bible-honoring Christians of doctrines which fly in the face of some of the strongest language in the Bible? Universalism, also called restorationism and *apokatastasis* from Peter's remarks (Acts 8:21), the doctrine that all sinners will ultimately be saved and annihilationism, the doctrine that the incorrigibly unrepentant will cease to exist, as well as the Post-Mortem Evangelism teaching, have been consistently, unanimously and invariably rejected by every orthodox body of Christians in the history of our faith. Donald G. Bloesch gingerly advocates the possibility of conversion after death, describing it as Post-Mortem faith and repentance. In his *Essentials of Evangelical Theology* (otherwise quite traditional orthodoxy) he proposes that repentance and faith may arise in sinners after death and that God will not withhold mercy even then. He cites

---

1. Many of the topics discussed in this chapter receive much fuller treatment in Part 5: Soteriology, chap. 20, 'Salvation Through Christ Alone' and chap. 21, 'Is Christ Present in Non-Christian Religions?'
2. D. A. Carson, *The Gagging of God: Christianity Confronts Pluralism* (Grand Rapids: Zondervan, 1996).
3. ibid., p. 536.

as scriptural warrant, Isaiah 26:19; John 5:25-29; Ephesians 4:8, 9; 1 Peter 3:19, 20; and 4:6.[4] These opinions have never wanted earnest advocates (scholarly and unlearned), making every conceivable appeal to Scripture, to antiquity, to reason, to dogma and to sentiment.

Roots in Feelings of Sympathy.

It is safe to say that distaste for the scriptural teaching of everlasting punishment of the lost finds its chief support in natural human feelings of sympathy and in native common sense. As to the former, I cite a striking example. Robert Browning, 'the preacher's poet,' tells how in the year 1856, while visiting Paris, he stepped into a city morgue where he saw three corpses laid out, each a suicide by drowning in the Seine. One, he theorized to be a disappointed politician, the second an anarchist and the third a gambler disappointed at cards. Then the tenderhearted poet wrote:

> It's wiser being good than bad;
> It's safer being meek than fierce;
> It's fitter being sane than mad.
> My own hope is, a sun will pierce
> The thickest cloud earth ever stretched
> That after Last returns the First,
> Though a wide compass round be fetched;
> That what began best, can't end worst,
> Nor what God blessed once, prove accursed.

These lines from 'Apparent Failure' do not state a doctrine, they only express what Browning called 'my own hope.' Tennyson, whose life, like Browning's, spanned most of the Victorian era, devotes many lines of his grandest poem, 'In Memoriam,' to meandering expressions of similar thoughts, closing with the famous fainthearted sentiment:

> I stretch lame hands of faith, and grope,
> And gather dust and chaff, and call
> To what I feel is Lord of all,
> And faintly trust the larger hope.

Browning's 'my own hope' and Tennyson's 'faintly trust the larger hope' furnish the tone of most 'evangelical' advocacy of restorationism and second chance (a few) and annihilationism (some in every age). Browning and Tennyson were among the most learned poets of the great Victorian epoch; both were intelligent and articulate and both were earnest Christians. Neither ever wrote a learned treatise advocating universal salvation, yet their mutual tenderness of heart, not well-balanced by steady awareness of biblical teachings, brought forth these dainty, inchoate expressions. It has ever been so, for the greatest dangers in this quarter do not arise from the Unitarian-Universalist churches but from the ever-present natural human sympathy for people who suffer, certainly stronger among the regenerate than among the unregenerate. Aside from the biblical revelation, universal salvation is a doctrine our hearts find it easy to believe.

Roots in Common Sense Rationalism.

The sentiment which responds favorably so readily to 'the larger hope' finds a strong ally in common sense. It is true that the orthodox Christian doctrine is supported everywhere by the poignant pricks of conscience (what rationalist's conscience declares with certitude that there cannot be a hell?), yet reflective people cannot help but wonder how a finite person, a mere speck in the ocean of created reality, can possibly commit any act of evil which calls for punishment in torments which last forever.

Charles Hodge (contemporary with the above poets), a firm supporter of the orthodox doctrine, compares it, in this respect, with the doctrine of salvation by God's free gift rather than by works, viz.:

> Rationalists say that it is very impolitic [non-strategic] for Christians to represent the everlasting punishment
> of the wicked as a doctrine of the Bible. This is undoubtedly true. And so Paul felt that it was very impolitic to
> preach the doctrine of the cross. He knew that doctrine to be a stumbling-block to the Jew and foolishness to

---

4. Donald A. Bloesch, *Essentials of Evangelical Theology* vol. ii(San Francisco: Harper & Row, 1978, 1979), pp. 224 and 227.

the Greek. He knew that had he preached the common sense doctrine of salvation by works, the offence of the Cross would have ceased. Nevertheless, he knew that the doctrine of Christ crucified was the wisdom of God and the power of God unto salvation. He knew that it was not his business to make a Gospel, but to declare that Gospel which had been taught him by the revelation of Jesus Christ.[5]

The Mood of Modern Denials.

These characteristics of mankind have assured a perennial opening for doubt, if not rejection, of the truly frightful biblical doctrine, in every age of the church. The past four centuries have developed a climate of general intellectual, social and religious outlook which has rendered acceptance of the biblical teaching even more abhorrent than in previous centuries, even among Christian people. Mention could be made of the growth of skeptical, naturalistic, mechanistic ways of looking at everything. This, however, should not be a strong factor where people are genuinely Christian. There are some other influences, very powerful because people are unconscious of how they have taken possession of us. I take note of two: the prevalent humanism (often called humanitarianism) and pragmatism.

By humanism I mean that progressive shift of focus in our system of values which has been ever away from the glory of God, biblically understood, to the comfort, health, longevity and personal growth of man, secular man, temporally related, apart from his God-relatedness. By progressive and now accelerating degrees the proper love of neighbor has come to be to regard one's neighbor primarily in his temporal, social connections rather than in relation to God and with regard to his eternal destiny. In such a case it becomes hard to suppose that God, who presumably also puts such great emphasis on man's present comfort and happy adjustment, can ever consign any human being to everlasting torment. I am aware that several contemporary 'evangelical' theologians and their disciples will react very negatively to these assertions, but does not such reaction demonstrate how desperately this point needs to be made, if we are to remain truly biblical and Christian?

J. I. Packer, in connection with a related topic, made some telling comments as to the confused state in evangelical churches produced by this kind of thinking. His remarks were written before the false notion of God's 'universal salvific will' had gained currency among us and in that sense are somewhat predictive. The situation is worse now than when he wrote over forty years ago. I quote somewhat at length.

> There is no doubt that Evangelicalism today is in a state of perplexity and unsettlement.... If we go to the root of the matter, we shall find that these perplexities are all ultimately due to our having lost our grip on the biblical gospel. Without realizing it, we have... bartered away that gospel for a substitute product.... The new gospel conspicuously fails to produce a deep reverence, deep repentance, deep humility.... The subject of the old gospel was God and his ways with men: the subject of the New is man and the help God gives him.... Thus we appeal to men as if all had the ability to receive Christ at any time; we speak of His redeeming work as if He had done no more in dying than make it possible to save ourselves by believing; we speak of God's love as if it was no more than general willingness to receive any who will turn and trust; and we depict the Father and the Son, not as sovereignly active in drawing sinners to himself but as awaiting in quiet impotence 'at the door of our hearts for us to let them in.'[6]

By pragmatism I have no reference to the theories of William James, rather the growing and amazingly prevalent, peculiarly American conviction, that what produces desired results must necessarily be true. 'If it ain't broke, don't fix it' and 'If it works it must be right.' The time has come when even in strictest evangelical circles it takes a great deal of courage strenuously to promote an idea or doctrine simply because it is biblical, right and true, quite apart from 'church growth' considerations. It often seems that effects on the feelings, responses, generosity, and good feelings of the public or constituency must come first. This now extends even to theories of Bible translation. It is part of the 'success ethic' of our time and the American nation. It tends to be the most prominent consideration in the choice of every kind of leader, not only in business and politics, where it might justly be expected, but also in selection of Christian college presidents, pastors and other church leaders.

---

5. Charles H. Hodge, *Systematic Theology*, Vol. iii (reprint, Grand Rapids: Eerdmans, 1970), p. 877.
6. J. I. Packer, 'Introductory Essay,' in *The Death of Death in the Death of Christ* by John Owen, 1959 repr. of the 17th century work (Edinburgh: Banner of Truth Trust), pp. 1, 2.

1. Universalism, Also Called Restorationism and Apocatastasis.

I must limit discussion of this ancient error to a few paragraphs. As already noted, it has an ancient lineage, beginning among Christians probably with Clement of Alexandria (c. 155–220). His brief remark was: 'For all things are arranged with a view to the salvation of the universe.'[7] Origen of Alexandria, the first Christian scholar of eminence (c. 185–254), was the first to give the doctrine of universal salvation 'systematic' exposition.[8] Clement supposed all punishment to be remedial and grounded his Universalism on that. Origen, his pupil and successor, argued on the ground of never-ending freedom of the will, here or hereafter, and the power of truth ultimately to prevail, that all would ultimately be saved. Origen, however, had frequent second thoughts on the subject, as Pierre Batifol points out.[9] Universalism was condemned in several councils and synods of late antiquity, though some brave souls ventured to believe it privately and to teach it publicly. 'Universalism almost wholly disappeared during the period known as the Dark Ages, although there are occasional glimpses... in the mutilated records which the papal Church has permitted to descend to us.'[10]

Varieties of Universalist Doctrine.

Since Reformation times there have never been wanting a few sincere, otherwise orthodox advocates (and some thoroughly heterodox) of universal salvation. Since not really based on clear scriptural grounds, there has been no uniform Universalist doctrine. Three commonest shades of Universalist doctrine are proposed. (1) Sinners are punished for all their sins in this life and when they die go immediately to heaven, or, with a soul-sleep twist, they all die and at the general resurrection go to heaven. (2) More commonly, there is a real hell to which all unreconciled to God go for punishment. All punishment is held to be remedial, hence a sort of purgatory. After an indefinite period they are purified and then go to heaven. (3) More commonly all, including the devil, will attain apocatastasis (Gr. for restoration, Acts 3:21), though some exclude him. In reading about this subject I have found no uniformity in detail. Most, like the poets quoted earlier, are very indefinite – as to a degree, it must be acknowledged, all of us are when Scripture does not speak decisively about a topic of curious interest.

Modern Advocates.

During the seventeenth and eighteenth centuries Universalism attracted a number of advocates in Britain and America – notably canon F. W. Farrar (1831–1903), in whose 1877 book *Eternal Hope* he somewhat timidly advocated universal salvation (mentioned earlier). Universalism took sufficient hold in northeastern United States in the late eighteenth century for a formal organization of Universalist churches with a statement of belief, in Winchester, New Hampshire in 1803. The second article of their 'Profession of Belief' was 'that there is one God, whose nature is love... who will finally restore the whole family of mankind to holiness and happiness.' Though at first somewhat biblically rooted, the Universalist church quickly wandered away from most recognizably historic Christian doctrinal commitments. They later merged with the Unitarian church, also restorationist. Their beliefs have spread and are now widely held by mostly liberal Protestants of many denominations.

In the past 100 years many notable liberal theologians have held some form of apocatastasis doctrine.[11] I say 'liberal' advisedly, for the Report of the Evangelical Alliance Commission correctly concluded that 'a universalist stance... is not an option for evangelicals.'[12]

I have already said something of Karl Barth's views. He denies the charge of Universalism, yet says all human beings are elect in Christ who is God's elect.[13] He argues from the unity of the race in Christ by the incarnation[14] and affirms Christ's death was 'the death of all' whether they know it or not and whether they agree or not.[15] He

---

7. Clement, *The Stromata or Miscellanies*, Book VII, chap. 11, *ANF* II, p. 525.
8. Origen taught salvation of all souls through transmigration and the Sibylline oracles, mid-second century, taught salvation of all through prayers of the saints.
9. Pierre Batifol, 'Apocatastasis,' *The Catholic Encyclopedia*, Vol.i, pp. 599, 600.
10. 'Universalists' McClintock and Strong *Cyclopedia*, Vol. x, p. 658. This condensed article provides an excellent brief survey of the history of the subject (pp. 657–665).
11. G. C. H. Berkouwer, 'Apocatastasis?' in *The Return of Christ* (Grand Rapids: Eerdmans, 1972), pp. 387–423.
12. ACUTE, *The Nature of Hell* (London: Evangelical Alliance Commission, 2000), p. 121.
13. Karl Barth, *Church Dogmatics II*, Part 2, p. 167.
14. Barth, *Church Dogmatics IV*, Part 1, p. 53.
15. ibid., p. 295.

also argues for universal salvation from the doctrine of an everlasting covenant which includes every sinful being in its scope. Yet he falls short of dogmatizing, he says, because it would seem to limit God's freedom. 'God does not owe eternal patience and therefore deliverance.'[16]

In the next two paragraphs I am indebted to several researchers, especially Larry E. Dixon. C. H. Dodd, whose New Testament studies gave the world 'realized eschatology,' taught that 'in the end no member of the human race is left outside the scope of salvation.'[17] More spectacular were the publications by J. A. T. Robinson (1919–1985), made famous by his *Honest to God* book. He insisted in articles and books that the very necessity of the nature of God demands and will result in not one sinner left in hell.[18]

Nels Ferré, however, was perhaps the most aggressive and most famous proponent of universal salvation of the twentieth century. He cut quite a swath for a few years following 1950. He too based his argument for salvation of all on what he conceived to be God's nature and attributes.[19] He was perfectly clear that his views were in no wise scripturally derived. That being the case, the purposes of this chapter are fully served by ignoring what he had to say. He understood 'God is love' as definitive of God's nature to exclusion of other attributes. As a fellow Baptist and Swede, Dr Millard Erickson pays special attention to Ferré. His treatment is worth reading by any one interested in pursuing this heresy.[20]

Proposed Bases and Arguments for Universalism.

Whatever the real reasons may be for adhering to Universalism (apocatastasis, restorationism), the usual arguments proposed are based on misconstrued Christian doctrines and misinterpreted (i.e. out of context) biblical texts.

A. The proposed doctrinal bases are mainly (1) God's love, and (2) God's atonement, or, one could say, (1) the attributes of God, and (2) the work of Christ.

(1) God's love, in one way or another understood as overwhelming or including all other attributes, is the attribute of God on which universalism rests its case against historic Christian orthodoxy. This argument, of course, pays scant attention to the fact that God's love is not unconditional, unless the word is carefully defined. It is true God loves the unlovely; but it is also true, as the Psalmist said, 'You hate all evildoers' and His love is conditioned by His own justice, holiness and all His other attributes. God's love is not absolute, which seems to be what advocates of Universalism mean by unconditional.

Robinson wrote, in an article where he cites Origen as precedent: 'Christ, in Origen's old words remains on the Cross as long as one sinner remains in hell… a statement grounded in the very necessity of God's nature. In a universe of love there can be no heaven which tolerates a chamber of horrors, no hell for any which does not at the same time make it hell for God. He cannot endure that – for that would be the final mockery of his nature – and he will not.'[21] Carl F. H. Henry, founding editor of *Christianity Today*, in the first volume of the magazine, was getting on top of the then flourishing Universalism current in the likes of Barth, Brunner (yes, Brunner), Ferré, Dodd, Robinson and others. I shall not here refute these authors' presentation of divine love, save to say that it does not relate love satisfactorily to holiness and justice and neglects the decrees and works of God. These authors are reincarnate today in the spin placed on what Clark Pinnock called 'the unconditional love of God' by 'inclusionists' in soteriology and annihilationists and second-chance theorists. When I used to hear Clark Pinnock preach it thirty years ago I wondered how far it would go. Now I know.

John Sanders, another contemporary advocate of inclusivism, is more cautious, speaking of 'God's radical love.'[22] This is in debate, but in an earlier work Sanders devotes several pages to show what he calls 'God's universal salvific will' is a 'theological axiom,' an 'essential truth.'[23] He seeks to show, among other examples, that God loved Pharaoh

---

16. Barth, *Church Dogmatics*, IV, part 3, pp. 477, 478.
17. C. H. Dodd, *New Testament Studies* (Manchester: Univ. Press, 1953), p. 123 as cited by Larry Dixon, *The Other Side of the Good News* (Wheaton, IL: Scripture Press, 1992), p. 42.
18. J. A. T. Robinson, *In the End God* (London: James), p. 38, 102, 103, and 'Universalism: Is It Heretical?' *Scottish Journal of Theology II* (June, 1949), pp. 143, 144 as cited by Larry Dixon, ibid., pp. 45–47.
19. Nels Ferré, *The Christian Understanding of God* (NY: Harper Bros., 1951) as cited by Larry Dixon, ibid., pp. 47–58.
20. Millard Erickson, *Christian Theology* (Grand Rapids: Baker, 1985), pp. 1018–1020. Dr Larry Dixon likewise pays special attention to Ferré's multiple heresies in many books, op. cit., pp. 47–58.
21. Cited by G. C. H. Berkouwer, 'Universalism,' in *Christianity Today*, Vol. i, #16, May, 13, 1957, p. 5.
22. Gabriel Fackre, Ronald H. Nash and John Sanders, *What About those who Have Never Heard?* (Downers Grove, IL: InterVarsity Press, 1995), pp. 26–31.
23. John Sanders, *No Other Name: An Investigation Into the Destiny of the Unevangelized* (Grand Rapids: Eerdmans, 1992), pp. 25–31.

and God sought to save him and the Egyptians through the plagues, but failed. This same sort of thinking has since led both Pinnock and Sanders to reject the attribute of divine omniscience and to put limits on His sovereignty and omnipotence. In this they are quite logical.

I close on this aspect of the subject with the prime affirmation of the alleged basis of Universalism and its refutation in an old standard:

> The ultimate restoration of all sinners to happiness and the favor of God is maintained by universalists on the ground that the final exclusion of any soul from heaven would be contrary to the illimitable love of God; that the wrath of God is only exercised against sin.... This supposes a distinction between sin and the sinner which is without foundation in the Holy Scriptures, but is contradictory to their statements. We are nowhere told, as regards a future state, that God's wrath against sin will only continue so long as sin remains, but the sinner himself who dies impenitent will be eternally punished.[24]

(2) A doctrine of universal atonement by Christ's sacrifice is asserted. There are several places in Scripture where something like a universal 'reconciliation' is affirmed. Older Universalists cited Colossians 1:19-20 and similar passages such as 2 Corinthians 5:19-21. They argued that Christ's death made absolute reconciliation for all sin and every sinner and if there is a hell it must be temporary to bring those sent there to repentance.

There were and are many varieties of this sort of doctrine for there are no scriptural controls for them anyway. Karl Barth and disciples connect this doctrine also with the incarnation whereby simply becoming one with the race as a whole, in Christ we are all redeemed and certainly elect, plus the rest of the *ordo salutis*. We shall not pursue these matters here. Let the positive doctrine be sufficient refutation.

B. Misinterpreted and wrongly applied Scripture texts are employed to support Universalism. I will cite and discuss a few typical examples, such as Psalm 103:8, 9 ('He will not... keep his anger for ever') and Isaiah 57:16 ('I will not... be always wroth' KJV). These passages have to do with God's treatment of His people who have disobeyed, not the unrepentant reprobate. John 12:32 states, 'I... will draw all people to myself.' This remarkable statement cannot mean merely 'Gentiles and Jews' or 'the elect' or 'all who believe,' said B. F. Westcott. Christ in His incarnate life, death, resurrection and Ascension has had an unusual drawing power through His own story in the New Testament Scriptures and the Holy Spirit, that 'other Advocate' who 'convicts the world' of sin, righteousness and judgment. But if He 'draws' all He does not effectually 'bring' all.

First Timothy 2:4-6 states that God 'desires all people to be saved... one mediator between God and men... gave himself as a ransom for all.' It has been thought by Universalists (and contemporarily by Clark Pinnock, John Sanders and others) that these verses teach 'God's universal salvific will' toward all people, hence the likelihood of a general rescue as well as a general redemption at the cross, which effects salvation for all. But God's purpose, for reasons He has never revealed, is not to save all as Romans 9 and numerous other texts reveal, and He has given each the power of making final choices – not quite 'free' will, but certainly uncoerced choices. Some choose to go to their 'own place.' Jesus died, according to 1 Timothy 2:6, 'as a ransom for [on behalf of] all': not 'in the place of all.'

Philippians 2:10 and other passages which affirm that God at last will be 'all in all,' and similar are Universalist super proof texts. Yet Philippians 2:10 omits the usual Pauline 'under the earth.' And besides, many passages, Old Testament and New Testament, insist finally that God will bring forced submission, not willing obedience. The demons in Christ's time on earth recognized Christ as their nemesis, not their Savior. So similarly with Colossians 1:19, 20; 2 Corinthians 5:19, 20; Ephesians 1:9, 10. They cite 1 Corinthians 15:22, 'in Christ shall all be made alive' as teaching universal salvation. Yet in context the subject is resurrection of the physical bodies of all who have died; some 'made alive' will enter the future kingdom of God while some will be cast into the lake of fire. After all, the same Jesus who said something about drawing all people to (toward) Himself also plainly spoke of resurrection of all people, some of them to 'the resurrection of judgment' (John 5:29 RSV), and said, 'he who does not obey the Son shall not see life, but the wrath of God rests upon him' (John 3:36 RSV).

Let me add some excerpts from Scripture – all of which, if the reader cares to check, are genuinely relevant to the subject. They are truly chilling thoughts for any who entertain false Universalist hopes: 'shall... be destroyed, and that without remedy'; 'When a wicked man dieth, his expectation shall perish'; 'hath never forgiveness'; 'the wrath of God abideth on him'; 'Whose end is destruction'; 'good for that man [Judas] if he had not been born'; 'sorrow not, even as others which have no hope' (Prov. 29:1; 11:7; Mark 3:29; John 3:36; Phil. 3:19; Matt. 26:24; 1 Thess. 4:13 KJV).

---

24. 'Universalism,' in McClintock and Strong *Cyclopedia* Vol. x, p. 656.

The Universalist doctrine is equally a menace to morality, both private and civic, and the end of sufficient motivation for missions and evangelism. Imagine the Apostles giving their lives to evangelize a world which was already saved forever without their labors! The armies of missionaries might have stayed at home and waited for Gabriel to notify the heathen of their salvation at the resurrection.

2. Annihilationism or Conditional Immortality.

The rubric calls for clarification. Annihilation means to be brought to non-existence. Conditional immortality is the name for the view that the soul of man is neither 'naturally immortal' nor granted immortality (deathlessness) by God in creation; but that immortality is the gift of God to the saved only. In relation to the present topic, there are theologians and groups who teach that after the resurrection and judgment of the lost they will be annihilated by God – either immediately or after a term of punishment in hell. The saved will, after resurrection, be granted immortality (eternal life) and live forever with God. Their eternal life (immortality) is conditional upon their faith, repentance, conversion and the divine grant of immortality.

This view is frequently connected with the doctrine of 'soul sleep' (or *psychopannychia* in the Latin/Greek of Reformation times): that if the soul, or center, of consciousness exists apart from the body as instrument of consciousness, it is inoperative (unconscious) between death and the resurrection, but brought back into existence by resurrection. Among modern denominations Advent Christian and Seventh Day Adventists make this distinctive of their groups. It gained some notoriety, though not general acceptance, in the nineteenth century among a few Anglican clergyman.[25] In recent years, as noted earlier in connection with the intermediate state, Oscar Cullmann revived the notion in scholarly circles.

In 'evangelical' circles – as indeed among orthodox Christians everywhere in every age – these notions are not only rejected but frequently condemned. Calvin wrote his first[26] sizeable book of doctrine (*Psychopannychia*) to disprove and condemn it. In the first form of the Articles of Religion of the Church of England, the fortieth article read, 'They which say the souls of those who depart hence do sleep being without all sense, feeling or perceiving till the Day of Judgment, do utterly dissent from the right belief disclosed to us in Holy Scripture.' The founding documents of the Evangelical Alliance made immortality of the soul a test of orthodoxy, i.e. of evangelical faith. It remained so until recent modification in response to rise of 'conditional immorality' in the teaching of one or two prominent evangelicals. Anyone interested will find the story in *The Nature of Hell*[27] and in recent issues of the *Journal of the Evangelical Theological Society*. In the Society, many of the same persons promoting conditional immortality (annihilation of the unsaved rather than eternal punishment) are also prominent in promoting the notion that God is somewhat less than omniscient and omnipotent. The situation is too fluid to summarize.

At any rate, it is clear that though Universalism offers no strong challenge to the received orthodox (and biblical) teaching of everlasting punishment and has no prominent advocates who influence orthodox evangelicals, this is not true of Roman Catholics, for whom the late Pope John Paul II may be quoted in mild support of Universalism. Since Cullmann's Immortality or Resurrection, there has been some scholarly 'evangelical' pressure toward 'soul sleep' and more toward conditional immortality, or annihilation of the wicked dead after the judgment. Though the topic was raised in the period 1941–1982,[28] the issue was thrust into the midst in 1988 by no less an evangelical stalwart than John Stott in his *Evangelical Essentials: A Liberal-Evangelical Dialogue*[29] and other publications shortly thereafter.

It was not long until the somewhat theologically peripatetic Professor Clark Pinnock challenged the orthodox doctrine with some deliberately provocative statements and shortly thereafter some ancient arguments to go with them in *A Wideness in God's Mercy*.[30] The bait did get attention; for said he:

---

25. The lengthy book, *Hades and the Intermediate State of Man*, by H. Constable, Prebendary of Cork, was republished in America by the Advent Christian Publication Society.
26. Though not published first.
27. *The Nature of Hell*, A Report of the Evangelical Alliance's Commission, London, 2000.
28. See Robert A. Peterson, 'A Traditionalist Response to John Stott's Arguments for Annihilationism,' *Journal of the Evangelical Theological Society*, Vol. 37, no. 4, December, 1994, p. 553.
29. John Stott, *Evangelical Essentials: A Liberal-Evangelical Dialogue* (Downers Grove, IL: InterVarsity, 1988), pp. 312–320.
30. Clark Pinnock, *A Wideness in God's Mercy* (Grand Rapids: Zondervan, 1992), p. 217.

> I consider the concept of hell as endless torment in body and mind an outrageous doctrine, a theological and moral enormity, a bad doctrine which needs to be changed. How can a Christian possibly project a deity of such cruelty and vindictiveness.... Surely a God who would do such a thing is more like Satan than like God.... Surely the God and Father of our Lord Jesus Christ is no fiend; torturing people without end is not what our God does.[31]

The above was two years before the book, *A Wideness in God's Mercy,* was published.

Professor Pinnock condensed his arguments in a 1996 symposium, Four Views on Hell, Zondervan, 1996, in which he was well answered by the other three writers, John Walvoord, William Crockett and Zachary Hayes. Clark Pinnock had once held to scriptural inerrancy but later conceded to a self-described flexible outlook. He had once been a high Calvinist, then an Arminian, an associate of the young social radicals of the 60s and 70s, then a social conservative, so theologians tended to shrug him off. But then came John Stott's announcement (1988, as above) and a clutch of British advocates of the doctrine of annihilation of the unsaved.

In my judgment both annihilationism and its sometimes partner, conditional immortality, are best refuted simply by asserting the positive scriptural doctrine as I have done in the last previous chapter and, as in the main, Walvoord and Crockett do in the above-mentioned symposium-debate. Good point-by-point rebuttals of annihilationism have been very competently produced, of which the ones I have found most helpful are a paper by Harold O. J. Brown in which he concluded Pinnock simply 'sidesteps the question of truth' in favor of his own feelings and says of *A Wideness in God's Mercy,* '...the book is a kind of exercise in wishful thinking – compassionate and thoughtful wishful thinking, but wishful thinking nevertheless.'[32] Robert Peterson, cited earlier, is complete, well documented and devastating. Perhaps the most thorough airing of the controversy is *The Nature of Hell*, a report of a commission working group (David Hilborn, Faith Forster, Tony Gray, Philip Johnston and Tony Lane) of the Evangelical Alliance in Britain, cited earlier in this chapter.

The Theory of Eschatological Evangelism.

This is also called postmortem evangelism (Gabriel Fackre) and other designations. In the last two chapters on soteriology in this volume I discussed, (1) whether Christ is the only way to salvation and (2) whether Christ may be found as Savior, though unnamed, in other religions. I did not discuss the proposition of a few 'on the fringes of Christianity,' as Millard Erickson refers to them, who propose that death does not mark the final border of opportunity to hear and believe.[33]

As noted earlier even Donald Bloesch, who certainly is not on the fringe of Christianity, hesitantly proposes this view, not wishing, he says, 'to build fences around God's grace' so as to 'preclude that some in hell might be translated into heaven.'[34] In other writings he condemns any notion that one can be saved apart from hearing and believing the gospel.[35] Sanders gives this view very favorable description[36] and without committing himself sees 'many strengths in the concept of eschatological evangelism.'[37] Clark Pinnock in a tentative probe says that 'Scripture does not require us to hold that the window of opportunity is slammed shut at death' and proposes perhaps 'babies... who die in infancy' and a 'post-mortem encounter' for those who in life wanted 'to love God' but 'had not heard of Jesus,' and so on.[38]

Gabriel Fackre, however, is not tentative. Among current defectors from strict historic doctrine that death closes the door of opportunity, he most aggressively, under the banner of 'Divine Perseverance,' has proposed his view in several works but spelled it out fully in debate with inclusivist John Sanders and orthodox restrictivist Ronald Nash in a 1995 book quoted earlier: *What About Those Who Have Never Heard?: Three Views on the Destiny of the Unevangelized.*

---

31. This was published somewhat obscurely in a journal, *Criswell Theological Review*, April 2, 1990, pp. 246, 247, cited by Robert Peterson, 'Eternal Punishment' in *EDBT*, p. 553.
32. Harold O. J. Brown, 'Contra Augustum,' a review of *A Wideness in God's Mercy* read at a Midwest sectional meeting of the Evangelical Missiological Society at Grace Seminary, Winona Lake, IN, March 20, 1992.
33. Millard Erickson, *How Shall They Be Saved: The Destiny of Those Who Do Not Hear of Jesus* (Grand Rapids: Baker, 1996), p. 159.
34. Bloesch, op. cit., p. 225.
35. John Sanders, *No Other Name: An Investigation Into the destiny of the Unevangelized* (Grand Rapids: Eerdmans, i952), p.189.
36. ibid., pp. 177–214.
37. ibid., p. 283.
38. Pinnock, op. cit., p. 171.

This view on the 'fringe of orthodoxy' achieved undeserved respectability by the commentary of G. F. C. Fronmueller, a German pastor, on *The Epistles General of Peter* in the large *Lange's Commentary* series. Though several current writers assign the comments to Lange he did not write it. Fronmueller did and said in comment on 1 Peter 4:6:

> Holy Scripture nowhere teaches the eternal damnation of those who died as heathens or non-Christians; it rather intimates [cautious language!] in many passages that forgiveness may be possible beyond the grave, and refers the final decision not to death but to the day of Christ, Acts 16:31; 2 Timothy 1:12; 4:8; 1 John 4:17. But in our passage [1 Peter 4:6] as in 1 Peter 3:19, 20, Peter by divine inspiration clearly affirms that the ways of God's salvation do not terminate with earthly life, and that the Gospel is preached beyond the grave to those who have departed from this life without a knowledge of the same.... The divine truths contained in this passage may be abused against the cause of missions and the necessity of a holy life.[39]

Scripture references alleged to support this view, in addition to 1 Peter 3:18-20 and 4:6 cited above, are Isaiah 26:14; John 5:25-29; and Ephesians 4:8, 9 (by Bloesch). Fackre finds support in John 10:16; 5:25; 1 Corinthians 15:19; Ephesians 4:8, 9; and even Matthew 12:40; Romans 10:7; Philippians 2:10; and Revelation 1:18; 5:13; 21:25.

It is significant that except for 1 Peter 3:18-20 and 4:6, the texts cited by different authors in support of postmortem evangelism (Fackre's 'Divine Perseverance') are not the same. Any reference to an offer of salvation to souls after death is obtained only by strained, often ridiculous, exegesis. I select for example Jesus' mention of 'other sheep... not of this fold' in John 10. In context Jesus is referring plainly to the change from the Jewish fold to a world-wide offer of salvation, as the history of Acts 1–15 relates, and so forth. As Ronald B. Nash points out, 'great violence to the text' is required to support such a doctrine (*Is Jesus the Only Savior*, p. 98).

Ephesians 4:8, 9 describes the descent of the Second Person of the Godhead to the earth at the incarnation and return to heaven, not a descent to a realm of spirits of antediluvians.

I have discussed the meaning of 1 Peter 3:18-20 and 4:6 in connection with other theological loci, especially the intermediate state and Christology. At this point I would direct the reader to several recent and older authors.[40]

In greater depth of exegesis, Charles Hodge expounds both passages in relation to the creedal statements showing how unlikely there is any reference in 1 Peter to Jesus' preaching to either Old Testament saints or the lost in the unseen world.[41]

It has seemed to me and to several others who would have desired to keep this discussion brief, that the matter of any trip of Jesus' spirit to a prison of departed spirits during the three days His body lay in Joseph of Arimathea's tomb is specifically excluded by Jesus' promise to the dying thief (Luke 23:43) 'today you will be with me in Paradise.' If Jesus was with the thief (who died hours later) our Lord must have been in Paradise for some time, beginning immediately after He proclaimed His work 'finished' and, having committed His spirit to His Father's hands, 'gave up the spirit.' The human spirit of the temporarily disembodied incarnate Person is not ubiquitous. If He as human spirit was in Paradise He was not with any 'spirits in prison.'

I close on the subject of a supposed postmortem evangelism by quoting two famous authorities who will likely still be read when the current buzz has receded from memory, and a proposal from another great author of an earlier time. First, James Orr says regarding

---

39. Fronmueller in *Lange's Commentary* (New York: Scribners, 1872), p. 275.
40. Millard Erickson furnishes a careful but thorough investigation of these passages in his recent volume on 'the destiny of those who do not hear of Jesus.' op. cit., pp. 164–173. Larry Dixon on 'Confronting Contemporary Challenges to Jesus' Teaching on Hell.' op. cit., pp. 111–119. They relate the topic to current controversy. Ronald H. Nash in *Is Jesus the Only Savior?* (Grand Rapids: Zondervan, 1994) is mainly concerned about pluralism and inclusionism but raises the question of postmortem evangelism as set forth by John Sanders, Joseph Leckie, George Lindbeck (non-evangelicals) and evangelicals Gabriel Fackre, Donald Bloesch, John Lawson and Wayne Grudem. He asserts, 'The position is widely taught in Southern Baptist colleges and seminaries.' In pages 150–158 he discusses 'What About Salvation After Death?' devoting major attention to 1 Peter 3:18-20 and 4:6 as the only possibly relevant Scripture texts.
41. Charles Hodge, *Systematic Theology* III (Grand Rapids: Eerdmans, reprint 1970), pp. 618–625. See also pp. 616–618 where he discusses other Scripture texts alleged to support a preaching by Jesus in hell. Also A. H. Strong, *Systematic Theology* (Valley Forge, PA: Judson Press, 1907), pp. 707, 708 from the same epoch, both in connection with Christology. Louis Berkhof, 'The Intermediate State Not a State of Probation' in *Systematic Theology*, 2nd ed. (Grand Rapids: Eerdmans, 1979), pp. 692–694. Robert Reymond more recently defended the doctrine that death closes the door of opportunity and helps the reader face the evident biblical truth that God's 'salvific will' is not best described as universal (as we are being told) but 'by divine arrangement' only to those 'who actually hear the gospel': *A New Systematic Theology of the Christian Faith* (Nashville, TN: Thomas Nelson, 1998), pp. 673–678. All the recent writers cover the same ground pretty much as the older writers cited. The arguments pro and con do not change, hardly even the form or statement.

the hypothesis of an extended probation and work of evangelization beyond death. This theory labors under the drawback that, in marked contrast with Scripture, it throws the larger part of the work of salvation into the future state of being. It is, besides, apart from the dubious and limited support given it by the passage in Christ's preaching to 'the spirits in prison' (1 Peter 3:19, 20) destitute of Scriptural support.[42]

I give now an extract from Geerhardus Vos's article 'Eschatology of the New Testament.'

> The New Testament does not teach that there is any possibility of a fundamental change in moral or spiritual character in the intermediate state.... The only passages that can with some semblance of warrant be appealed to in this connection are 1 Peter 3:19-21 and 4:6.... The context is not favorable to the view that an extension of the opportunity of conversion beyond death is implied; the purport of the whole passage points in the opposite direction, the salvation of the exceedingly small number of eight of the generation of Noah being emphasized (3:20). Besides this it would be difficult to understand why this exceptional opportunity should have been granted to this particular group of the dead, since the contemporaries of Noah figure in Scripture as examples of extreme wickedness. Even if the idea of a gospel-preaching with soteriological purposes were actually found here, it would not furnish an adequate basis for... the broad hypothesis of a second probation for all the dead in general or for those who have not heard the gospel in this life... because the generation of Noah had the gospel preached to them before death.[43]

On 1 Peter 3:19 and 4:6 Geerhardus Vos goes on to say that the two passages may have 'had no connection in the mind of the author' and points out:

> For explaining the reference to 'the dead' the connection with the preceding verse is fully sufficient. It is there stated that Christ is 'ready to judge the living and the dead.' 'The living and the dead' are those who will be alive and dead at the parousia. To both the gospel was preached, that Christ might be the judge of both. But that the gospel was preached to the latter in the state of death is in no way indicated. On the contrary the telic clause 'that they might be judged according to men in the flesh,' shows that they heard the gospel during their lifetime, for the judgment according to men in the flesh that has befallen them is the judgment of physical death. If a close connection between the passage in [1 Peter] ch. 3 and that in ch. 4 did exist, this could only serve to commend the exegesis which finds in the earlier passage a gospel-preaching to the contemporaries of Noah during their lifetime, since, on that view, it becomes natural to identify the judgment in the flesh with the Deluge.[44]

AN ADDENDUM.

The nineteenth century was a time of debate among learned Protestant divines over the fate of the lost in general and the possibility of salvation of the heathen, apart from hearing the gospel. In 1889 a book was published entitled *That Unknown Country*.[45] Professor A. J. McClain spoke approvingly of the book when I was a student in his class. So when I discovered a copy I bought it and have read much of it. I do not recall anything I have read in the spate of literature raised by recent controversy not said many times in that book, wherein famous British, European and American scholars, preachers and prelates expressed their arguments from every possible angle, and the views of the theologians of the past from Justin Martyr to Joseph Cummings (Methodist, President of Northwestern University at the time) are set forth. I write this to make readers aware of this treasure of theological literature; also to report that whatever the views taken by the authors of articles in that book, most agreed that taking the Bible for what it says, it teaches a doctrine of everlasting punishment – whether of banishment from the presence of God; mental suffering symbolized by fire, worm, brimstone and the like; irremedial loss of all hope and joy; loss of personal awareness but everlasting empty existence; and so forth.

The question of the destiny of 'those who have never heard' has been raised in this my book, in the parts on Christology and soteriology and should be mentioned again here. My own view coincides with the usual consensus of orthodox theologians:

---

42. James Orr, article 'Punishment' in *The International Standard Bible Encyclopaedia*, Vol.. iv ((Grand Rapids: Eerdmans, 1943), p. 2503.
43. Geerhardus Vos article 'Eschatology of the NT' in *ISBE*, Vol. ii, p. 992.
44. ibid., p. 992.
45. C. A. Nichols (Editor), *That Unknown Country, or What Living Men Believe Concerning Punishment After Death Together with Recorded Views of Men of Former Times, The Whole Field Explored, Every Source of Wisdom, Past and Present, Made Tributary to the Theme: Man's Final Destiny, A Standard Book for All Time*, published in Springfield, Mass.: 1889, 959 pages.

> As to the heathen... who have missed the way of life... we can safely leave to God the justification... of his own government of the world; but we must take careful heed that we do not be more merciful and wise than he to whom sin, as long as it continues to be sin, is thoroughly damnable.[46]

If there is salvation for the unevangelized, God has not spoken clearly about it in His Word. As another wisely said, it is one of God's many secrets.

Current discussion of the 'fate of the heathen' seems unaware the subject was rather fully canvassed in the nineteenth century. Many substantial, orthodox authors were convinced that 'implicit saving faith' on the part of heathen does exist by virtue of special divine grace in general revelation. They found authority for their view in the Parable of the Judgment of Sheep and Goats (Matt. 25:31-46). I quote the new edition of *The Expositors' Bible*.

> Kindness to the poor comes in, not as in itself the ground of the division, but as furnishing the evidence or manifestation of that devotion to God as revealed in Christ, which forms the real ground of acceptance and the want of which is the sole ground of condemnation. True it is that Christ identifies Himself with his people, and accepts the kindness done to the poorest of them as done to Himself; but there is obviously implied, what is elsewhere in a similar connection clearly expressed, that the kindness must be done in the name of a disciple. In other words, love to Christ must be the motive of the deed of charity.
>
> While there is no encouragement here for those who hope to make up for the rejection of Christ by deeds of kindness to poor people, there is abundant room left for the acceptance at the least of those who had no means of knowing Christ, but who showed by their treatment of their fellow-men in distress that the spirit of Christ was in them. To such the King will be no stranger when they see him on the throne; nor will they be strangers to Him. He will recognize them as His own; and they will recognize Him as the very King of Love for whom their souls were longing.... To all such will the gracious words be spoken 'Come, ye blessed of My Father; but they too, as well as all the rest, will be received not on the ground of works as distinguished from faith, but on the ground of a real though implicit faith which worked by love and which was only waiting for the revelation of their King and Lord to make it explicit, to bring it out to light.[47]

Ethnos, the word in plural form rendered 'nations' in Matthew 25:32, is frequently, in appropriate contexts, translated 'Gentiles' or 'heathen,' or even occasionally 'peoples.' If we were to read in English that the subjects of the judgment were 'all the heathen' it might make some sense to accept the above argument as correct. No less famous an authority of orthodox credentials than Denney, took the words this way. He outrightly rejected all notions of future probation and universal salvation but wrote this:

> In the 25th chapter of Matthew our Lord expressly gives, in pictorial form, a representation of the judgment of the heathen. All nations – all the Gentiles – are gathered before the King; and their destiny is determined, not by their conscious acceptance or rejection of the historical Saviour, but by their unconscious acceptance or rejection of Him in the persons of those who needed services of love. Those who acknowledge the claim of a brother's need prove themselves the kindred of Christ and are admitted to the Kingdom; those who refuse to acknowledge it prove themselves children of another family and are shut out. This is unquestionably Christ's account of the judgment of the heathen, and it does not square with the idea of a future probation. It rather tells us plainly that men may do things of final and decisive import in this life, even though Christ is unknown to them. I frankly confess that this is the only view of the matter which seems to me to keep the ethical value of our present life at its true height.[48]

Recently Thomas Oden, quite as tentatively as the above-quoted authors, under the umbrella of 'prevening grace,' presents a similar argument. His whole discussion is well worth reading. I select the following of his concluding remarks. Citing pre-Mosaic Old Testament saints, 'pious Jews of every generation' and 'Gentiles who have not heard,' he affirms, 'All humanity is offered sufficient prevenient grace to enable each to respond rightly to probational opportunities' (a Wesleyan doctrine). He suggests perhaps 'in meeting these situations they might have developed a general or inchoate predisposition for faith such as [ascribed]... to Abel (Heb. 11:11).' Later on Dr Oden concludes: 'Though such an argument is speculative, venturing beyond clear scriptural definition, at the very least it provides a way by which Christian teaching may keep the question open as to the destiny of the benighted.'[49]

---

46. Johann J. Van Oosterzee, *Christian Dogmatics*, Vol. ii, p. 458.
47. Sir W. Robertson Nicoll, ed., *The Expositors Bible* (London: Hodder & Stoughton, n.d.), pp. 372, 373.
48. James Denney, *Studies in Theology, Lectures Delivered in Chicago Theological Seminary* (London: Hodder and Stoughton, 1895), p. 243.
49. Thomas Oden, *Life in the Spirit: Systematic Theology* III (San Francisco: Harper, 1992), p. 449.

9
Heaven, the Eternal Home of the Redeemed

D. L. Moody published a small book, *Heaven and How to Get There* in 1880. My 1908 edition was printed after 350,000 copies had already been sold. Dozens of books on heaven appeared in late Victorian and in Puritan times, but not many specifically on the topic in the twentieth century as Wilbur Smith's extensive bibliography shows.[1]

But if scholarship has neglected the theme, interest in heaven has not waned among the ill, the aged and the devout of every time of life. Though death has been masked under many euphemisms, the Christian doctrine of heaven is of compelling interest when one faces death up close, as all of us inevitably, and sooner than we would like, must do. Early Protestants were familiar with death. In Calvin's time hundreds of evangelicals (Hugenots) in France were being martyred for their faith. Families prepared their own dead for burial, dug the graves and were present as the coffins were lowered into the ground. Funerals were frequent, for medical science had not yet learned how to handle plagues, the perils of childbirth, epidemics, infections and the like. Hence early Protestant writers had much to say about heaven as a present hope of all believers. Calvin's *Institutes* has many pages about heaven as a hope and the values of contemplation of heaven.[2] At the time Wilbur M. Smith published *The Biblical Doctrine of Heaven*, we both taught at Trinity Evangelical Divinity School. In a special lecture he challenged the scholars with these remarks: 'A most interesting theme in the area of English literature, would be a critical study of those great classics of the seventeenth century. Setting forth the blessedness of the life to come, e.g. *The Invisible World Discovered to Spiritual Eyes*, by Joseph Hall (1574–1656); *Of the Blessed State of Glory Which the Saints Possess After Death*, by Thomas Goodwin (1600–1679); *The Saints' Everlasting Rest*, by Richard Baxter (1615–1691), a work of some 460,000 words!; *The Holy*

---

1. Wilbur Moorehead Smith, *The Biblical Doctrine of Heaven* (Chicago: Moody Press, 1968), pp. 289–301. Smith says, 'As far as I know, this is the only comprehensive bibliography in English on the subject of Heaven that has been attempted' (p. 289) and follows with a list of about 200 books. Klaas Schilder's *Heaven – What is It?* (Grand Rapids: Eerdmans, 1950) and Peter Kreeft's *Heaven, The Heart's Deepest Longing* (New York: Harper & Rowe, 1980) are useful. Schilder treats the subject from a biblical-theological angle; Kreeft from the standpoint of 'the heart's hunger' but does try also to be biblical-theological. He is a disciple of C. S. Lewis, whose many books of Christian apologetics argue for the existence of God. Many of these works argue for the existence of God – the God of the Bible – from the nature of man, the anthropological argument. Such is Kreeft's argument for heaven. Since the God of the Bible 'dwells' in heaven, it may rightly be said Lewis and the numerous school of writers he exemplifies are all writing about heaven. They only lead to a biblical theology of heaven; but they do not create one. The literature bearing on *ouranos* and related Greek terms in the New Testament and Septuagint is overwhelming in magnitude. Two authors, Traub and von Rad, devote nearly fifty pages in Vol. v of *TDNT*, with 386 footnotes, most referring to other works on the words *shamayyim*, *ouranos* and *ouranios* in the literature of Jewish and Greek antiquity.

2. Calvin, *Institutes of the Christian Religion* III, 9. See R. S. Wallace, *Calvin's Doctrine of the Future Life* II, chap iv.

City or The New Jerusalem, by John Bunyan (1628–1688); *A Discourse Relating to the Expectation of Future Blessedness*, by John Howe (1630-1705); and *A Discourse Concerning the Happiness of Good Men*, by William Sherlock (1647–1707).'[3]

In this chapter we shall discuss first the meaning of the words for the eternal home of the saints in the Bible, and heaven as God's dwelling place, then what heaven offers believers up ahead and what the inhabitants of heaven will do. We close with John's vision of heaven in the book of Revelation.

Biblical Words for the Eternal Home of the Saints.

The Hebrew word *shamayim*, which is in the first verse of the Bible and appears an uncountable number of times, is of unknown derivation. In a general way the Hebrews of Old Testament times thought of heaven as everything in the skies overhead, beginning (1) with the air where the clouds and birds fly and the winds blow; (2) extending to the '*rachia* of heaven' (rendered 'firmament,' perpetuating the LXX mistake – *stereoma*, firm, hard, the stereo in stereophonic) or expanse, where sun, moon and stars follow their courses; and (3) beyond that to the heaven of heavens of God and His angels. Gerhard von Rad makes the comment regarding biblical expressions that add 'waters under the earth' to 'heaven above' and 'the earth beneath' as in Exodus 20:4: 'It seems that there never was a sacrally canonized view of the world in Israel. The basis of this surprising fact is to be sought in the complete absence of a myth uniting and quickening [giving life to] the elements. Only occasionally do we find fragmenting mythical ideas, and these are rather used with poetic freedom as ancient ways of making things vivid.'[4]

In the Old Testament 'the heavens' (always plural in Hebrew, perhaps indicating immensity) also refers to the place of God's dwelling. This is literally 'the heavens of the heavens' rendered 'highest heaven' (1 Kgs. 8:27 RSV) and 'the heaven of heavens' (Deut. 10:14 RSV). More about this later.

This word is regularly translated *ouranos* in the ancient Greek translation (Septuagint, LXX) and thus comes into the New Testament in quotations of the Old Testament. Many times heaven or heavens is simply the part of the creation which is non-earth, as 'heaven and earth' indicates (Gen. 1:1; Exod. 20:11; Acts 4:24; Rev. 14:7). Sometimes 'and the waters' is added to distinguish earth as dry land from oceans, lakes, springs and similar.

The New Testament adds nothing to the meaning of the word *ouranos* as such, though very much to the meaning of heaven. Heaven (*ouranos*) is still (1) the air space over the earth where birds and clouds fly (Matt. 8:20; 24:30); and (2) the region of sun, moon and stars, as in Genesis 1:14 ('Let there be lights in the expanse of the heavens') and Genesis 1:16 (see Acts 7:42 and Heb. 11:12). There is also a higher heaven from whence Christ came down at the incarnation, as we have seen, and to which Paul was caught up (2 Cor. 12:2), and to which the risen, incarnate Christ returned 'now to appear in the presence of God on our behalf' (Heb. 9:24).

The derived term, *ta ouriania*, 'the heavenlies,' sometimes seems to mean (1) the region where God and the angels dwell (Eph. 1:2, 20; 2:6); (2) the unseen spirit-world of good angels (John 3:12; cf. Heb. 2:14; Dan. 8:15; ff. and the doctrine of angels generally); as well as (3) the world of unseen evil spirits (Eph. 6:12; Rom. 8:38; Dan. 10:10-14; Jude 8, 9).

Other Designations of Heaven.

The speakers in the story of the Bible and the didactic texts refer to heaven more frequently without employing the name 'heaven' for the 'place' (we shall say more about this). Two figures of speech, where an important part of heaven is put for the whole (*metonymy*), are (1) God's 'throne,' as in Matthew 5:34 ('Do not take an oath... by heaven, for it is the throne [seat of power] of God,' cf. Jer. 14:21; and Isa. 6:1; and Rev. 4:2 ff.); and (2) 'the glory of God' (Acts 7:55 and 1 Tim. 3:11). The hope of heaven is the same as 'the hope of glory' (Col. 1:27).

Six other designations in various ways, without using the word, indicate heaven as the place of God's 'special manifestation' as theologians say, or more simply, 'dwelling.'

Heaven is (1) God's dwelling or tabernacle (Heb. 8:2; 9:11); (2) His sanctuary (Heb. 8:2; 9:8, 12); (3) His habitation (Ps. 33:14, cf. Isa. 63:15); (4) His tent (Ps. 61:4); (5) His house (Ps. 65:4; John 14:2); and (6) God's temple. This last term calls for a bit of explanation. The Hebrew language borrowed an Akkadian (Babylonian-Assyrian) word, Egal, for a great house – be it palace, citadel or temple – and modified it to hekhal.[5] Though the

---

3. Wilbur M. Smith, lecture, Trinity Evangelical Divinity School, 1965.
4. *TDNT*, V, p. 503.
5. It would clarify things if only this one word were translated 'temple'. NIV is very confusing in 2 Samuel 7, where the whole point of the passage hinges on a consistent rendering of *beth* as house.

most magnificent edifice in Israel at the time was only a very special 'tabernacle,' it might occasionally be called an hekhal (1 Sam. 1:9). This word was usually reserved for the first or second temple at Jerusalem (1 Kgs. 6:3, 5, 17, 33) and occasionally for the temple in heaven (2 Sam. 22:7; Isa. 6:1). The ideas of the heavenly and earthly seem to merge.[6]

Heaven Primarily God's Home Not Man's.[7]

The above considerations introduce the fact that in three-fourths of the Bible, i.e. the entire Old Testament, heaven is scarcely, if ever, said to be or intended to be the eternal home of a redeemed people. David might exclaim, 'Whom have I in heaven but you?' (Ps. 73:25) and 'If I ascend up into heaven, thou art there' (Ps. 139:8 KJV). Lack of revelation did not prevent David's composing a liturgical prayer which exclaims, 'Let me dwell in your tent for ever! Let me take refuge under the shelter of your wings!' (Ps. 61:4). Yet, the Psalmist had no more expectation, so far as we know, of going to heaven very soon, any more than '[to] make my bed in hell' (Ps. 139:8 KJV). I know of no Old Testament passage which specifically says that any Old Testament saint expected to 'go to heaven when I die,' though it may be inferred perhaps from hope to 'dwell in the house of the LORD for ever' (Ps. 23:6) and the unusual ascension of Elijah (2 Kgs. 2:11), and the translation of Enoch (Gen. 5:25; Heb. 11:5). Von Rad is surely correct in affirming, 'Whenever the Old Testament refers to rapture it always has in view heavenly chambers… set in a state of perpetual nearness to God.'[8]

Not only in the Old Testament, but to a high degree also in the New Testament, heaven is God's dwelling place, manifest there in a manner nowhere else: He 'who is high and lifted up, who inhabits eternity, whose name is Holy' (Isa. 57:15). 'The heaven, even the heavens, are the LORD's; but the earth hath he given to the children of men' (Ps. 115:16 KJV).

Does not this indicate that already before the fall the earth was designed as mankind's home indefinitely into the future? And does this not coincide with Revelation 21 and 22, in which heaven comes down to earth where 'God will be with them and they shall be his people'? We greatly err when we ignore the biblical emphasis on the Ascension of Christ in a physical body and of our coming back with Him to earth, after resurrection, in glorified but physical bodies, to inhabit an earthy (not etherial) earth. A large incubus of medieval, mystical, neo-Platonic, ascetic thinking has carried over among many Christians into modern times.

The future hope of 'the people' of Israel, and of every godly Israelite, lay more in 'God with us' than 'we with him.' That was the symbolism of God's tabernacle-house-temple at the center of the camp or Land of Israel. Isaiah's prophecy of Immanuel (chaps. 7–12) is all about 'God-with-us' – which is what 'Immanuel' means. The same is cast in an eschatological setting in chapter 60: 'Your people shall all be righteous; they shall possess the land for ever… that I might be glorified' (Isa. 60:21 RSV). Revelation 21 borrows language from this and other late chapters of Isaiah to describe the eternal home of all saints of the earth, on the earth, in enhanced Christian terms. Ezekiel's prophecy of a future temple for Israel with gates (Ezek. 48:31-34) is enhanced into 'the tabernacle of God… [which is with [all] men.' And 'He will dwell with them, and they will be his peoples,' [plural] (Rev. 21:3).

This is not the end of the story however. God was not ready to reveal clearly that the blessed dead go immediately to be with Christ until Christ returned there, as we shall see.

In several interesting passages of Scripture God is seen to preside over a court composed of angels and perhaps other sentient, rational beings. It appears as some kind of court in the first two and last chapters of Job. There are references to the LORD of hosts (armies) sitting above the cherubim (1 Sam. 4:4; 2 Sam. 6:2; Pss. 80:1 and 99:1).

---

6. W. M. Smith, 'Heaven,' *ZPEB*, III, pp. 61, 62.

7. Scholasticism (late medieval theologians and followers) speculated that since God 'in the beginning of the world' created the 'heavens and the earth' His so-called dwelling place before that was not in heaven and there was no created 'place' where He dwelt. Similarly, though the created universe displays God's glory (Pss. 19, 103; Rom. 1) there has always been an 'uncreated' glory of God which creation only mirrors. In other words, God was glorious before creation took place, when creation was only in His purpose. The glory displayed in nature is not that uncreated glory. (See the article 'Glory' in *The Catholic Encyclopedia*, Vol. vi, pp. 585, 586.) The heavens 'declare' that glory but are not per se the glory. Some Christian mystics through the ages and to the present have conceived of multiple layers of heavens through which by various practices and moral attainments those both pious and industrious in religious exercises many ascend to the goal of beatific (blessed) vision of the essence of God. There have been numerous decrees of popes and councils defining these matters – utterly without authority or precedent in the Bible. Recently Romanist theologians have pretty much laid aside these speculations and have, like Protestants, interpreted the biblical language about seeing God 'face to face' simply as 'living joyfully and everlastingly in the immediate presence of God' (J. Van Engen, 'Beatific Vision' *EDT*, p. 131) without speculating as to how the invisible essence of God can ever be viewed except as seen in the incarnate Second Person.

8. *TDNT*, V, p. 508.

In the last of these passages His reign from a heavenly throne is over 'all the peoples' (the Hebrew word is *amnim*, plural) including Israel (cf. all of Pss. 93–100). The prophet Micaiah 'saw the LORD sitting on his throne, and all the host [army] of heaven standing beside him on his right hand and on his left' (1 Kgs. 22:19). It is said elsewhere that these armies of angels are sent out to do God's bidding. For example, 'the LORD sent an angel' to turn back Sennacherib (2 Chron. 32:21) and on numerous other occasions of Scripture story. Angels (of which there are thousands, Ps. 68:17) are not sent forth generally and willie-nillie but, specifically, are 'all ministering spirits sent out to serve' (Heb. 1:14). This means that, in an utterly non-Platonic sense, everything that happens on earth, especially to His people, is controlled, even directed by heaven, a thought connected of course with many things, including our opinions about prayer, God's knowledge of the future and control of it. '[T]he Most High rules the kingdom of men' (Dan. 4:32; cf. Joel 3:11 and the doctrine of providence) and He has 'thousands upon thousands' of powerful agents available to do His bidding (Ps. 68:17 RSV).

At the Incarnation the Son of God 'Came Down From Heaven' and at the Ascension Returned.

Having said all this, heaven is the place whence came the Son of God from the Father, where He had been 'at the Father's side' (John 1:18) 'before the world existed' (John 17:5). Repeatedly in John 6 Jesus says that He had 'come down from heaven.' He ascended there again to be with the Father at His 'right hand' (Heb. 1:3; 8:1; 10:12; 12:2; 1 Peter 3:22). Believers on earth are presently 'in Christ' (Eph. 1) and we are told to set our affections there 'where Christ is, seated at the right hand of God' (Col. 3:1-3). We pray to 'Our Father in heaven' (Matt. 6:9) and at death, like the repentant thief, we expect to be with Christ 'in Paradise' (Luke 23:43). Therefore for now, and until the consummation, heaven is our natural home. 'The hope that sustains us is laid up for us in heaven (Col. 1:5).'[9] So we, like Stephen, in dying, pray 'Lord Jesus, receive my spirit' (Acts 7:59) while through our lives we acknowledge 'our commonwealth is in heaven,' and from it we 'await a Savior, the Lord Jesus Christ' (Phil. 3:20 RSV). So heaven is central to the eternal future of the redeemed, even though heaven, it seems, shall some day come down to earth. These facts lead to a familiar question.

Is Heaven a Condition or a Place?

Our answer to this question will not be determined by literalizing the anthropomorphic figures for God and metaphors for heaven, but by our understanding of the nature of Jesus' body at resurrection, Ascension and Second Advent. The 'flesh' in which He arose, ascended and in which He will return is the same as ours in the resurrection.

In effect we answered this question in discussion of the resurrection and Ascension of our Lord and of the resurrection body of the saints. I shall not here repeat the clear biblical doctrines that Jesus arose in the same body of flesh and bone (perhaps of blood also) as that laid in the tomb and that we too shall experience 'the resurrection of the flesh' as the earliest, authentic form of the Apostles' Creed has it.[10] 'Flesh' was to correct the Gnostic notion that Christ's body which arose and our 'spiritual bodies' of the resurrection will be immaterial. Current errors call for re-emphasis of these points.

Since Jesus arose in a physical body now in heaven, then heaven has dimensions of a sort commensurable with physical existence. The best literature related to this question, cited by many defenders of physical resurrection, both Christ's and ours, is, unfortunately out of print – J. A. Schep, *The Nature of the Resurrection Body*. Schep points out that the Ascension of Christ furnishes the deciding answer to the question – recognized by many orthodox scholars.[11]

Many recent liberal and neo-orthodox scholars and some evangelicals who were influenced by them deny this connection.[12] Schep refers to several who regard heaven not as a local place but 'a state of blessedness' (W. Barclay,

---

9. W. M. Smith, op. cit.
10. Henry Bettensen, *Documents of the Christian Church*, 2nd ed. (London: Oxford Univ. Press, 1963), p. 33, 34; Philip Schaff, *The Creeds of Christendom* vol. i (Grand Rapids: Baker Books, n.d., repr. of the 1919 ed.), p. 50.
11. J. A. Schep, *The Nature of the Resurrection Body* (Grand Rapids: Eerdmans, 1964), chap 5, 'The Body of our Exalted Lord,' pp. 145–179.
12. Murray Harris in two books, *Raised Immortal* (England: Marshall, Morgan & Scott, 1983) and *From Grace to Glory* (Grand Rapids: Zondervan, 1989) insists that the physical body of the risen Christ was non-physical – 'that after his resurrection his essential state was one of invisibility and

A. M. Randy, J. G. Davies), and several to the contrary (A. Kuyper, K. Schilder and even Karl Barth). He makes the point that even though we need not accept the Hebrew notion of a three-storied universe or seven heavens ('safely left to the Rabbis,' K. Schilder), 'this does not imply that heaven is no place at all.'[13] Further, the human nature of Christ partakes of creaturehood and creatures have no existence at all except in relation to space and time.

> Even spirits, who have no physical body that can be measured, cannot be omnipresent. As creatures they must be somewhere in space, though they do not occupy a measurable part of space. According to scripture their [the holy angels?] usual dwelling place is heaven, which is a part of God's creation [see Gen. 1:1] where they worship God, whose throne is in heaven and who from there [a created heaven], rules the universe and blesses his people (e.g. Ps. 103:19-21; Isa. 62 ff.; Heb. 8:1; 12:2; Rev. 4:2 ff.).[14]

The presence of the glorified, complete manhood of Christ (body and soul and spirit) in heaven renders certain that it is a place friendly to the flesh of holy human beings. The surpassing insight of H. B. Swete in his amazingly illuminating study, *The Ascended Christ: A Study in the Earliest Christian Teaching*, furnishes the following on the relation of this teaching to the fulfillment of God's original purposes for mankind in God's creation. After citing Hebrews 2:5 ff., which quotes Psalm 8:6 ff. on 'the supremacy of man over the rest of creation,' Swete enlarges:

> Modern knowledge has almost indefinitely extended the limits of this control, making man master of natural forces the very existence of which was unknown to Biblical writers, or in some instances to the last generation; and it is not improbable that the coming years will witness [writing before 1910!] an enormous enlargement of such powers. But in Jesus Christ humanity has already entered upon the fulness of its inheritance: whatever can be done by human nature which from the first was free from sin and has now been perfected in all its powers is within the reach of the glorified manhood of our Lord. How far such a nature may carry its control over the physical world we have no means of judging. Moreover, it is to be remembered that the glorified humanity is, so far as manhood can be this, a perfect medium for the self-expression of the Divine Word. The personal force which lies behind the forces of Nature, carrying them on to the accomplishment of their destiny, works through the human mind and will of the ascended Christ, so far as the human in its perfected state is able to respond to the divine.[15]

B. F. Westcott spoke to those who think there is no place for a complete humanity, body and soul in heaven, when in a time of intense controversy with dogmatic Enlightenment agitation, he wrote:

> At one time the logical development of His true divinity leaves room only for a shadow of manhood, as unsubstantial as the phantom which already usurped His place [in early Gnosticism]. At another time the loving portraiture of his true humanity places Him before us as a man among men as a part among parts; and not, according to His own self-chosen title as the Son of man in whom all the separate endowments of sex and race and age co-exist in absolute harmony.... The forms of Nature, so to speak, are revealed to us in the Bible as gathered together and crowned in man and the diversities of men as gathered together and crowned in the Son of man; and so we are encouraged to look forward to the end, to a unity of which every imaginary unity on earth is a phantom or symbol, when the will of the Father shall be accomplished and He shall sum up *all things* in Christ [emphases added] – all things and not simply all persons.[16]

Such a future of nature and of mankind in the biblically prescribed order of things means precisely that heaven as well as earth be 'places' friendly to and compatible with whole human persons, body and soul, or for now, of disembodied saints. To isolate man, complete man, at any time now or ever 'from the realm committed to him is a doctrine of heathen philosophy and not of Judaism or Christianity.'[17] The same argument I have pursued above is stated succinctly by Klass Schilder:

therefore immateriality' (*From Grave to Glory*, p. 53, see also pp. 53–57), that the Ascension was a parable acted out for the benefit of the disciples, for the Ascension actually occurred at the moment of resurrection (*Grave to Glory*, p. 423; see *Raised Immortal*, p. 92). These pages remind one of Paul Tillich's distinction (an advanced case of unbelief) between the ultimate and penultimate. For rebuttal of these views see Norman Geisler, *The Battle for the Resurrection*, Nashville: Thos. Nelson, 1989 and N. Geisler, *In Defense of the Resurrection* (Nashville, Thomas Nelson 1992) and R. D. Culver, *A Wakeup Call* (Clayton, CA: Witness Inc., 1993).

13. Schep, op. cit., p. 159.
14. op. cit., pp. 159, 160.
15. H. B. Swete, *The Ascended Christ: A Study in the Earliest Christian Teaching* (London: Macmillan, 1916), pp. 28, 29.
16. B. F. Westcott, *Christus Consummator* (London: Macmillan, 1886), in his second section 'The Incarnation and the Creation,' pp. 102, 103. (In this age of short sentences and short attention span it is to be noted that these remarks are part of sermons preached in Westminster Abbey while the author was Canon of Westminster in 1885 and 1886. Let his remarks not be pearls cast before swine.)
17. Westcott, ibid., p. 133.

Let us note the historical relationship of Christ, Adam, and the last day. In the center of history Christ ascended from earth to heaven, *bodily*. The glorified body of Christ was received into heaven, and appeared at the right hand of the Father, who is upon His throne surrounded by angels who 'behold' His face. In all this, the 'physical' gives the exegete something concrete to hold to in the interpretation of figurative language.... We cannot escape implication of transition from one state with *preservation of the physical* and therefore of *space* [all emphases original]. *In* this sense also the dwelling place of God would then have come to men. And turning to the end of history, we read again of a moment of time... which will bring man into a different state, again with the preservation of the physical. Man will inhabit the new earth – and also heaven – physically. Heaven also, because heaven then will unite itself with earth [Rev. 22:1 ff.].[18]

It is important to note that the Apostle Paul had a glimpse of the Paradise of God above (2 Cor. 12:1-10) and was able to disclose nothing of what he saw and heard there, and revealed that he had the experience only after about fourteen years had passed. He desired not to boast and seems to suggest – in opinion of some interpreters – that he had already experienced a severe 'thorn in the flesh' on account of it. How this holy restraint contrasts with some today, including the abysmally ignorant and learned, who claim trips to heaven to report what Paul plainly declares is 'unspeakable' and 'not lawful.' Charles E. Hambrick-Stowe, in a thorough study of the devout, but hard-nosed New England Puritans, records that

> Since Puritans believed that the goal of devotional practices was union with Christ, a union that was expressed in mystically erotic imagery from the Song of Songs and Jesus' parable of the ten virgins, opening the record [of deep spiritual experience in devotion to Christ] was as improper as publishing an account of one's sexual experiences in marriage.[19]

That pioneer of common sense in the doctrine of heaven, Joseph A. Seiss, expounded at length on the theology of Revelation 22, of which I quote a small portion. He has noted that many believers seem anxious to put off going to heaven as long as possible, and proposes that

> The reason is heaven has no substance, no reality, for the soul to take hold on. It is nothing but a world of shadows, of dim visions of blessedness with which it is impossible for a being who is not mere spirit – who... knows only to live in a body – to feel any fellowship or sympathy with.... Did men but learn to know the difference between a Paradise of sense and a Paradise of sensuality.... There was a material universe before sin was, and ... a material universe will live on when sin shall have been clean washed away from the entire face of it.[20]

One need not subscribe to Islam's notions of a heaven of sensual extravagance catering to male erotic pleasures to accept what the Scriptures say of the final state of the redeemed in a real place, including a renewed earth, where truly risen and glorified whole human beings will truly be 'at home' and able to fulfill the mandate given the first man before the fall which brought about the ensuing disaster. That disaster crimped, twisted and misdirected every one of us 'from ... youth' onward (Ps. 129:1) because of our being conceived in sin, born in iniquity (Ps. 51:5), our hearts 'deceitful above all things, and desperately sick' (Jer. 17:9).

What Heaven Offers Those Who Attain it Now.

We are urged by Jesus to rejoice that our names are 'written in heaven' and when some country villager asked Him, '[W]ill those who are saved be few?' He said to the whole mixed crowd, 'Strive to enter through the narrow door' (Luke 13:23, 24). In the last chapter of the Bible Jesus pronounced a blessing on those 'that do his commandments, that they may have right to the tree of life, and may enter in through the gates into the city [the New Jerusalem come from heaven to earth]' (Rev. 22:14 KJV; cf. 21:2). What specifically does Holy Scripture tell us about the blessedness of heaven now and when the dwelling of God is with mankind? I can only sketch some answers and leave it to the interested reader to explore the texts.

---

18. K. Schilder, *Heaven: What Is It?* (Grand Rapids: Eerdmans, 1950), pp. 32, 33.
19. Charles E. Hambrick-Stowe, *The Practice of Piety: Puritan Devotional Disciplines in Seventeenth-Century New England* (Chapel Hill, NC: Univ. of NC Press for Institute of Early American History and Culture, Williamsburg, VA, 1982, 1988), p. 189.
20. J. A. Seiss, *Lectures on The Apocalypse* (Grand Rapids: Zondervan, 1964). I regret that I have lost the page number.

Because these expressions have captured the hearts of believers in all conditions of life, whether in sickness or health, joy or sorrow, youth, middle life or old age – but especially in sickness, sorrow and old age – they appear in hymns, poetry and the liturgies ministers use to minister in those border areas (what Tillich called the *grenz*) of transition: sickness, death and other sad seasons. They are sweet 'to sinner's ears.' I acknowledge the help of some old writers, especially J. P. Boyce.[21]

We shall take note of expressions which are stated with reference (1) to the condition where grace found us; (2) to new possessions as opposed to old; (3) to a contrast with former oppression and scorn; (4) to Christ; (5) to rewarding activities; (6) to how the place called heaven is described and characterized; and (7) to how the Lord announces our entrance to the eternal home of the redeemed.

Most of these expressions, imbedded in the language of devotion and worship, have been derived over 350 years from the Authorized or King James Version and I therefore quote it in this section.

1. The future state is said to be salvation. '[N]ow is our salvation nearer than when we believed' (Rom. 13:11; also 1 Thess. 5:9; 2 Tim. 2:10). We are delivered 'from every evil work ... unto his heavenly kingdom' (2 Tim. 4:18); rescued from sufferings such as hunger and thirst, tears and pain (in many passages, e.g. Rev. 7:16, 17); and relieved from toil in rest ('they may rest from their labours, Rev. 14:13).

> We shall rest
> And faith we shall need it;
> Lie down for an eon or two
> Till the Master of all good workmen
> Shall put us to work anew (Kipling).

We shall have a comfortable environment, no night (Rev. 21:25; 22:5) and no filth (Rev. 21:27), and good company as opposed to bad (Rev. 21:8 and 22:15).

2. With reference to new possessions as opposed to old ones, we shall receive complete knowledge ('know as we are known,' no longer 'in part' 1 Cor. 13:12), and several possible crowns: 'of life' (Rev. 2:10); of righteousness (2 Tim. 4:8); and of glory (1 Peter 5:4). We shall also gain several precious emblems of victory: 'a white stone ... and a new name' (Rev. 2:17) and 'white raiment' (Rev. 3:5).

3. In contrast to former oppression and scorn there will be many desirable distinctions such as to 'sit with' Christ 'in [H]is throne' (Rev. 3:21) and to receive from Christ 'power over the nations' (Rev. 2:26) and privileged to 'walk with me [Him] in white' (Rev. 3:4).

4. In relation to Christ, the saved shall 'always be with the Lord' (1 Thess. 4:17), where 'they may behold [His] glory.' Christ will be 'glorified in his saints' (2 Thess. 1:10) and they shall 'enter thou into the joy of the Lord' (Matt. 25:21, 23 KJV).

5. Heaven will provide not only rest but rewarding activities which are said to be reigning (2 Tim. 2:12), judging (Matt. 19:28), serving God (Rev. 7:15; 22:3), praising Him (Rev. 14:2, 3; 15:3, 4; 19:5, 6) and praying (Rev. 6:9-13; 7:11, 12).

6. The place called heaven is also described and characterized as 'paradise,' i.e. a beautiful, cultivated garden (Luke 23:43; 2 Cor. 12:4; Rev. 2:7); a beautiful city, both 'holy' and 'great' (Rev. 21:10-27). It is the 'Jerusalem which is above' (Gal. 4:26) 'come down to earth' (Rev. 3:12; 21:2); a place of 'many mansions' in the 'Father's house' (John 14:2).

7. The Lord Himself is represented by Scripture as rendering a favorable verdict, sentence or proclamation establishing permanent entrance to heaven and all it offers them. Let us savor some of these supremely encouraging sentences and phrases. The 'sheep' on the Lord's right hand in the judgment hear Him say, 'Come, ye blessed of my Father, inherit the kingdom prepared for you from the foundation of the world' (Matt. 25:34), and at the close of this parable-prophecy, 'the righteous [go] into life eternal' (v. 46). In the parable of the 'wheat and tares' the 'householder' (Matt. 13:27) says to the reapers (angels), 'gather the wheat into my barn' (Matt. 13:30) and 'Then shall the righteous shine forth ... in the kingdom of their Father' (Matt. 13:43).

---

21. James Pedigru Boyce, *Abstract of Systematic Theology* (Philadelphia: American Baptist Publication Society, 1878), pp. 472–477. Dr Boyce is still remembered at Southern Baptist Seminary of Louisville, KY as professor of systematic theology and his Abstract has been recently reprinted by Presbyterian & Reformed.

A particularly thrilling sentence comes from the Parable of the Talents, where the lord says to each of the good servants, 'thou hast been faithful over a few things, I will make thee ruler over many things: enter thou into the joy of thy lord' (Matt. 25:21, 23).

From the Bible itself we learn how to respond to all this beauty of thought and language. In the hour of his death the first Christian martyr breathed out this prayer, 'calling on God and saying, "Lord Jesus, receive my spirit"' (Acts 9:59), not unlike the Lord Jesus Himself who near the end of His Passion cried out with loud voice and declared, 'It is finished' (John 19:30). And in the words of Scripture (Ps. 13:5), 'he said, Father, into thy hands I commend my spirit: and having said thus, he gave up the ghost' (Luke 23:46). How many devout folk have whispered those same poignant words in the hour of death! I so used them once myself after about forty minutes pinned under an overturned Farmall H tractor with no help in sight, though I thought I heard the distant wail of an approaching ambulance.

The great Christian poets of Britain and America were saturated with these biblical themes and phrases about the eternal home of the redeemed and their entrance to it. One theme not yet mentioned is the blessed prospect of a first meeting with Jesus face to face. Alfred, Lord Tennyson drew on that for the best lines in what may be his best short poem, *Crossing the Bar*:

> For tho' from out our bourne of time and place
> The floods may bear me far,
> I hope to see my Pilot face to face
> When I have crossed the bar.

Though Presently Unseen, Heaven Is the Most Real of All Great Realities of Faith.

Even in the world of time and space where we presently live out our days, the passing of time only makes more emphatic the truth that things we cannot see or sense in any other way are the very most real and enduring. When the atom bombs exploded on two cities of Japan in 1945 we were rudely brought to attention that a theoretical, tiny 'thing' with a nucleus of a proton and planetary particles called electrons (or something like it) is not only real but important. Gravity, or mass attraction, is a name for some universal physical force never given a name till Sir Isaac Newton announced it along with centrifugal and centripetal (and who knows what more?) forces, which are all invisible but decisively affect every molecule from that in the ink I now spread on this yellow lined sheet to the most remote galaxy. Yet no one has quite seen or exposed the What and How about them.

The highest values of the Christian faith, though invisible to the eye, are blessedly real: God, the Holy Spirit, faith, hope, love, eternal life – 'Jesus Christ: Whom having not seen, ye love; in whom, though now ye see him not, yet believing, ye rejoice with joy unspeakable and full of glory: Receiving the end of your faith, even the salvation of your souls' (1 Peter 1:7-10 KJV/RSV; see also 2 Cor. 4:18; Heb. 11:1).

Heaven, however inadequate or even misconceived our perception of it, is repeatedly clothed with more reality than the present scene of earthly life. This is the message of Hebrews 6–9, of which the following select quotations are very encouraging examples. This profound book speaks of believers as heirs of God's promise, and of 'two unchangeable things' of God, in which it is 'impossible for God to lie' and of this as both our 'refuge' and 'encouragement.' Hebrews continues:

> We have this as a sure and steadfast anchor of the soul, a hope that enters into the inner place behind the curtain [in heaven], where Jesus has gone as a forerunner on our behalf, having become a high priest for ever (Heb. 6:7-20).

The writer dwells at length through Hebrews 7 on that heavenly high priesthood and continues the theme in Hebrews 8:

> Now the point in what we are saying is this: we have such a high priest, one who is seated at the right hand of the throne of the Majesty in heaven, a minister in the holy places, in the true tent [or, tabernacle, ESV marg.] that the Lord set up, not man (Heb. 8:1, 2).

Of the Tabernacle of Moses and accoutrements he says:

> They serve [as] a copy and shadow of the heavenly things (Heb. 8:5).

Of heaven and its 'good things,' he states that they are 'greater and more perfect... not made with hands, that is, not of this creation' (Heb. 9:11). The Mosaic rites are 'copies of the heavenly things' where 'Christ has [now] entered, not into holy places made with hands, which are copies of the true things, but into heaven itself, now to appear in the presence of God on our behalf' (Heb. 9:23, 24).

These are matters not of logical inference, natural light or of human insight, but of divine revelation available and applicable to faith which 'walks' but 'not by sight,' useful for believers in all of life but specially encouraging 'as the morning breaks' at life's end 'and the shadows fly away.'

Treasure, Inheritance and Rewards in Heaven.

Jesus admonished, 'but lay up for yourselves treasures in heaven, where neither moth nor rust destroys and where thieves do not break in and steal' (Matt. 6:20) and that thereby our hearts may already be in heaven. Christians are truly 'future oriented.' Earlier in the day He had said the '[b]lessed' who suffer persecution and slander for righteousness' sake and 'for my sake' should 'Rejoice... for your reward is great in heaven' (Matt. 5:11, 12). There is therefore nothing derogating to service in and for Christ's present kingdom done in hope of treasure and rewards for the same. Beyond 'treasure' and 'rewards' up ahead, Paul writes eight times of our inheritance here and in heaven as well as of God's inheritance in us (Eph. 1:18; also Heb. 9:15; and 1 Peter 1:4).

Without being technical, it is ordinarily true that treasure which is inherited comes as a gift or bequest upon the death of someone else, while rewards are conferred upon those who earn them. We may think of inheritance and rewards both as treasures.

Let us speak first of rewards.[22] A quick search of the Bible in a concordance reveals many rewards and the conditions for receiving them. The Bible recognizes that it is entirely righteous and wholesome for believers, whose salvation is already assured by faith in Christ, to work for rewards. These rewards will come when Jesus returns from heaven as the last chapter of written revelation, spoken by Jesus Himself, declares: 'Behold, I am coming soon, bringing my recompense with me, to repay everyone for what he has done' (Rev. 22:12). As for the Twelve, Jesus promised, 'Truly, I say to you, in the new world [regeneration, KJV; Gr. *palengennesia*], when the Son of Man will sit on his glorious throne, you who have followed me will also sit on twelve thrones, judging the twelve tribes of Israel' (Matt. 19:28). This places the time of formal awarding of these earned treasures after the first resurrection, though there is much difference of opinion as to what 'the regeneration' may be.

This kind of life and service is important to us precisely because Jesus made so very much of it from the beginning to the end of His ministry. The theme begins in the Sermon on the Mount and continues to the last chapter of Revelation. Rewards shall be given for Christian hospitality (Matt. 10:41, 42; cf. Mark 9:41), for love even for enemies, 'expecting nothing in return' (Luke 6:35 RSV). The messages of Christ to the seven churches of Asia (Rev. 3–4) furnish several awards. For those 'who have not soiled their garments, and they will walk with me in white, for they are worthy' (Rev. 3:4). Their names will remain in 'the book of life' (3:5) and Jesus will 'confess' each one's name 'before my Father and before his angels.' He says, 'The one who conquers, I will make him a pillar in the temple of my God. Never shall he go out of it, and I will write on him the name of my God, and the name of the city of my God... and my own new name' (3:12).

That every such reward is not automatically distributed to everyone who attains that kingdom, Jesus warns: 'I am coming soon [1,900 years ago!]. Hold fast what you have, so that no one may seize your crown' (3:11). 'The one who conquers, I will grant him to sit with me on my throne' (3:21).

Those who win 'the victory' of faith (1 John 5:4) will 'eat of the tree of life, which is in the paradise of God' (Rev. 2:7) and to those who are 'faithful unto death [i.e., die for their faith],' says our Lord, 'I will give you the crown of life' (2:10), also 'some of the hidden manna, and... a white stone, with a new name written on the stone that no one knows except the one who receives it' (2:17).

The promises to the Apostles (Matt. 19:28) that they would sit on thrones and judge seems to be extended to all who 'overcome.' I quote more at length:

> The one who conquers and who keeps my works until the end, to him I will give authority over the nations, and he will rule them with a rod of iron, as when earthen pots are broken in pieces, even as I myself have received authority from my Father. And I will give him the morning star (Rev. 2:26-28).

---

22. I am indebted here to Wilbur M. Smith, *The Biblical Doctrine of Heaven* (Chicago: Moody Press, 1968).

Efforts of Christian antiquarians, linguists, and authorities in Jewish and Roman antiquities have filled shelves of theological libraries with results of their searches for the specific meaning of some of the mysteries of these seven short letters to the seven churches of Asia – 'new name,' 'morning star' and the like – and the millennial or non-millennial significance of ruling 'with a rod of iron'. This must not obscure the obvious. Precious indeed shall be the awards for purity of life and dedicated stewardship of God's gifts. They are worth working and waiting for.

Several of Jesus' parables place this giving of rewards at the time of His return 'after a long time': the Parables of the Faithful and Wise Steward (Luke 12:41-47; Matt. 24:45-51); of the Pounds (Luke 19:11-28); of the Laborers in the Vineyard (Matt. 20:1-16); and of the Talents (Matt. 25:14-30).

R. C. H. Lenski says, commenting on Jesus' response to the rich young ruler ('one thing you lack, go sell... and give to the poor and you shall have treasure in heaven'):

> It would be the grossest perversion of this word of Jesus to have it mean that by selling and giving away his entire wealth the man would receive... this treasure in heaven. This treasure is the unmerited pardon of God. For the other side of the one thing the man yet lacked, the one thing that always goes with contrition, is the true and saving faith in Christ.[23]

As for our inheritance in heaven, it is a curious fact that such is first mentioned in Paul's address to the elders at Miletus on his third missionary journey (Acts 20:32), when Paul appears to be passing on something Jesus told him audibly at the Damascus Road encounter (Acts 9:3-6), but reported only in his defense before King Agrippa and Governor Festus at Caesarea. In each case it is an inheritance among the 'sanctified by faith.' An inheritance comes to the receptor only after the death of the 'testator' (see Heb. 9:16, 17). In which case apparently the testator is our Lord Himself and the testament or inheritance is the same for each believer – life everlasting, 'For God so loved the world, that he gave his only Son, that whoever believes in him should not perish but have eternal life' (John 3:16) and 'Whoever believes in the Son has eternal life' (John 3:36). It is manifest that we cannot exhaust this theme.

The Inhabitants of Heaven and Their Occupations and Preoccupations.

The only comprehensive statement of Scripture as to who dwells in heaven reflects both biblical history and fresh revelation. The author of Hebrews is trying to get his Jewish-Christian readers to shake free of the limited horizon of the old covenant background. The horizon is no longer the summit of gloomy height, Mt Sinai:

> But [now] you have come to Mount Zion and to the city of the living God, the heavenly Jerusalem, and to innumerable angels in festal gathering, and to the assembly [*ekklēsia*] of the first-born who are enrolled in heaven, and to a judge who is God of all, and to the spirits of just men made perfect, and to Jesus, the mediator of a new covenant, and to the sprinkled blood that speaks more graciously than the blood of Abel (Heb. 12:22, 23 RSV).

We saw earlier that the Old Testament informs of the court of heaven, with God on the throne surrounded by seraphim, cherubim and other angels (assuming all these celestial beings are rightly called angels). Daniel was given to know that a Son of Man would come from that glory presence and be given an eternal kingdom (Dan. 7:9-14) in which the 'wise shall shine like the brightness of the firmament; and those who turn many to righteousness, like the stars for ever and ever' (Dan. 12:3 RSV). They do so as members of the church of the first-born and spirits of the just made perfect (but not yet resurrected) now in heaven – as Hebrews 12:22, 23 says. God, innumerable joyful angels, the *ekklēsia* of Christ and spirits of just men (Old Testaments saints, whether distinct from the *ekklēsia* or not) – all shining like stars of the sky – and Jesus Himself, are the present list of 'those who dwell in heaven' (Rev. 13:6; cf. 12:12).

What do they do there? What occupies their time and effort and preoccupies their thoughts? I shall answer first by a sketch derived from the sense of Scripture and conclude with what John the Revelator saw and heard in Revelation 4 and onward.

A quick check of a dozen general treatments of systematic theology in English turned up only one which offered even a minimal treatment of the activities of the saints in heaven. An exception is Millard Erickson's last chapter, where he addresses 'Our Life in Heaven: Rest, Worship and Service,' developing these themes on the basis of appropriate passages.[24] The same is not true of larger treatment in books and monographs on the final state of

---

23. R. C. H. Lenski, *Interpretation of the Gospel of Luke* (Columbus, OH: 1944), p. 41 as cited by Smith p. 176.
24. Millard Erickson, *Systematic Theology* (Grand Rapids: Baker Books, 1985), pp. 1229–1231.

the redeemed. Wilbur M. Smith, whom I have profitably cited several times, devotes twelve pages to 'Occupations of the Redeemed in Heaven,' which are found to be worship, service, authority, fellowship and learning.[25] Chapters 12 to 14 of Smith's volume relate the book of Revelation to heaven, including the heavenly activities of saints.

I shall freely mine the exposition of my friend, Dr Smith, of activities of saints in heaven, as well as my own previous studies in connection with ecclesiology.

Worship is the primary activity of saints in glory. Reading the New Testament furnishes not a single verse that certainly prescribes music in public worship. Authorities do not think the ancient synagogue furnished any example of music in the weekly Sabbath services. Yet Dr Smith rightly says of heavenly worship: 'Much of this worship will be conducted within the framework of music.'[26] He cites several passages to demonstrate the claim, but most of them say nothing of song or music, though in Revelation 'each' of the twenty-four elders has a harp (Rev. 5:8) '[a]nd they sang a new song' (Rev. 5:9, 10). Later we find them 'playing on their harps' (Rev. 14:2) and still later 'those who had conquered… with harps of God' (Rev. 15:2). 'And they sing the song of Moses, the servant of God, and the song of the Lamb' (Rev. 15:3). A prophecy of Isaiah says in the future kingdom of Messiah: 'the ransomed of the LORD shall return and come to Zion with singing; everlasting joy shall be upon their heads' (Isa. 35:10). I suspect when John reports various heavenly groups 'saying with a loud voice' (Rev. 5:12; 19:1) we should understand chanting, giving voice in unison, not singing.

Service to God is another activity of saints in heaven. It is said of 'the holy city… coming down out of heaven from God' (Rev. 21:2), that 'the throne of God and of the Lamb will be in it, and his servants will worship him' (Rev. 22:3). 'Servant' (Gr. *doulos*) is a term Paul applied to himself frequently. It means bond-slave. As created and redeemed – 'bought with a price' – believers are God's (1 Cor. 6:19-20) and obligated not only to 'glorify God' here on earth but also to 'serve him' (KJV) forever (Rev. 22:3) in heaven. The word for service has no relation to slave labor as such, but to ministry of various sorts, especially religious service. The ritual which the Levitical priest exercised in the Jewish temple was a *leiturgia* (Luke 1:23; Heb. 9:21), hence the exercises of Christian worship in public worship are called a liturgy, obviously the Greek word in English dress. It is a good word, whether designating what Quakers do in worship of God, or high church Anglicans, or Baptists – though we like to fancy our 'order of worship' as 'non-liturgical.' Though not always a religious term, it is obviously so in Revelation 22:3. So it seems that we shall participate in regular, if not formal, 'liturgies' in heaven just as we do here. Why should we not?

Perhaps there will be service in the form of work. The word for 'servant' in the Old Testament, is *ovedh*, one who does work. May we connect this with prophecies of the Messianic kingdom, when each on his own farm 'shall sit every man under his vine and under his fig tree' (Micah 4:4)? Why not? Because Rudyard Kipling's great poem *L'envoi* (a not fully scriptural gem) fires my imagination and, I pray, my readers'. I expose the reader to 12 lines once more.

> When Earth's last picture is painted, and the tubes are twisted and dried,
> When the oldest colours have faded, and the youngest critic has died,
> We shall rest, and, faith, we shall need it – lie down for an aeon or two,
> Till the Master of All Good Workmen shall put us to work anew!
>
> And those that were good will be happy: they shall sit in a golden chair;
> They shall splash at a ten-league canvas with brushes of comets' hair;
> They shall find real saints to draw from – Magdalene, Peter, and Paul;
> They shall work for an age at a sitting and never be tired at all!
>
> And only the Master shall praise us, and only the Master shall blame;
> And no one shall work for money, and no one shall work for fame;
> But each for the joy of the working, and each, in his separate star,
> Shall draw the Thing as he sees It for the God of Things as They Are!

Exercise of Government. I choose another venue for discussion of whether or not Christians shall reign with Christ over a millennial earth. Whatever one's view of that, it must accommodate the fact that Jesus made promises to the Apostles and spoke parables which seem plainly to say that, sometime in the future, 'in the new world,

---

25. W. M. Smith, op. cit., pp. 190–201.
26. Smith, op. cit., p. 199.

when the Son of Man will sit on his glorious throne, you who have followed me will also sit on twelve thrones, judging the twelve tribes of Israel' (Matt. 19:28). Further, Jesus made many statements which seem designed to stimulate such expectations among hearers steeped, as they were, in Old Testament prophecies of a glorious future on earth for a restored and repentant Israel. It is no wonder that they still had such hopes right up until Jesus' Ascension (Acts 1:6). In the Parable of the Pounds the king 'When he returned' gave 'authority over ten cities' to one servant and 'to be over five cities' to another (Luke 19:15, 17, 19). In the Parable of the Talents Jesus twice prophesies of good servants, 'You have been faithful over a little; I will set you over much' (Matt. 25:21, 23). According to the Revelation certain highly honored saints in heaven expect to join in a future reign, for they cry out, 'and you [the Lamb] have made them a kingdom and priests to our God, and they shall reign on the earth' (Rev. 5:10).

No doubt we of every millennial persuasion have many surprises in store as to how exactly these dominical and heavenly sayings will be fulfilled. Yet wielding of some sort of governing authority must be in prospect for at least some 'overcomers.' Wilbur M. Smith calls attention to the several New Testament references to our future 'inheritance' (Luke 20:32; Eph. 1:11, 14; 5:5; Col. 1:12; 3:24; Heb. 9:15; 1 Peter 1:4) and the promises to Abraham and his seed that he would be 'heir of the world' (Rom. 4:13). Though our unearned inheritance, he acknowledges, is 'first of all spiritual, immaterial, involving eternal life, righteousness, etc.,'[27] he asks, 'Is there not something more here?'[28] He cites the promise to Christ in Psalm 2:8, 'I will make the nations your heritage, and the ends of the earth your possession' and notes that we are 'fellow heirs with Christ' (Rom. 8:17).

Growth in Knowledge. 'Ever learning yet never coming to the knowledge of the truth.' Truths without the truth has become the sad result of secularized academic pursuit in what used to be called Christendom. But when 'we are in him who is true' (1 John 5:20) and 'see him as he is' (1 John 3:2) learning will take on a new interest. There will be access to new worlds of truth to explore. The original mandate for our race, both to fill and to subdue the earth, as well as to exploit it for human benefit (Gen. 1:28, 29; 9:3), now no longer cursed but renewed (Isa. 65:17-25; Rom. 8:18-23; Rev. 21–22), will no doubt now be fully implemented.[29] This of course does not apply to the present occupations of saints in the presence of Christ in heaven. While it is 'far better' there, as Paul assures us (Phil. 1:23), it has an interim character, of hopeful expectation of the coming day of God when they shall receive their glorified, resurrection bodies and find some wrongs righted (Rev. 6:9-11; Ps. 73; Jer. 12:1-4; Hab. 1:1-4 *et al*). Consider also that we will have the Lord Jesus, the Master Teacher, as our 'professor.'

Finally, there will be fellowship with all 'of the righteous made perfect.' The present state of believers may or may not include such fellowship. The Bible, all agree, has very little to say about the state of souls between death and the resurrection. The promises of future glory relate to our resurrection at Christ's coming. 'God considers it just… to grant relief to you who are afflicted… when the Lord Jesus is revealed from heaven' (2 Thess. 1:6-7). This promise is in a context of correcting false hope and false views brought on by uninformed speculation (see 2 Thess. 2:1 ff.) At the close of a celebration of the faith of saints of the past, Hebrews 11:40 seems to say that they with 'us' shall all 'be made perfect' at some future time. Consider the cautious remarks of John Calvin on this subject in his comments on 'when the perfect comes' in 1 Corinthians 13:10:

> 'Perfection,' says he [Paul], 'when it will arrive, will put an end to everything that aids imperfection.' But when will that perfection come? It begins indeed at death, for then we put off, along with the body, many infirmities [Calvin was chronically sick]; but it will not be completely manifested until the day of judgment…. Hence we infer, that the whole of this discussion is ignorantly applied to… the intermediate [state].[30]

Stephen M. Smith, with good reason, therefore ends a fine article on the intermediate state with cautions against transferring what the Bible teaches about our eternal state to our situation between death and resurrection. Having earlier cautioned that 'Salvation is never the extrication of the soul from the body for participation in etherial bliss,'[31] he says:

---

27. Smith, op. cit., p. 193.
28. ibid., p. 193.
29. Perhaps I will finally be able to fill in the blanks in our family genealogical chronicles!
30. John Calvin, *Commentary on the Epistles of Paul to the Corinthians*, vol. i, trans. John Pringle (Edinburgh, 1848), p. 428.
31. Stephen M. Smith, 'Intermediate State' in *EDT*, p. 562.

The intermediate state remains an area of inevitable concern for Christians both for practical pastoral reasons and as part of the meaning of salvation. However it should remain clear that the hope of the Christian focuses on the parousia of Christ and the new creation. Speculation on the intermediate state should never diminish the certainty which flows from the cross or the hope in the new creation.[32]

Heaven in Revelatory Visions of the Bible.

As we saw early in this discussion, heaven, the dwelling place of God, from which the Son of God came, returned to, and shall come again, is not ordinarily visible to the inhabitants of earth. Yet several prophets ('formerly called a seer,' 1 Sam. 9:9) were privileged in some mysterious way both to see the heaven of God and to hear it. Paul had such a remarkable experience, but was not allowed to describe it. He is unsure, he says, whether he was in the body or out of it (2 Cor. 12:1-5). Many prophets received revelation by the channel of dreams and visions (Num. 12:6 *et al*). The word of the LORD came in many other manners to many prophets (Heb. 1:1). Some of them, 'in the Spirit' or better 'in spirit' as opposed to 'in flesh' or 'in body,' were 'brought in the visions of God' apparently to the heaven of God. They are Isaiah, Ezekiel, Daniel and John the Revelator.

Isaiah, in his much homiletically overworked sixth chapter tells how he beheld the LORD on his throne 'high and lifted up' and spoke further of a temple, and seraphim (Isa. 6:1-4); whether the temple is heavenly or the one in Jerusalem is obscure.

Ezekiel simply says, 'I saw visions of God' and reports that 'the hand of the LORD was upon him' (Ezek. 1:1, 3) and forthwith, right from his house in Babylon, he beheld an elaborate enactment of worship by the inhabitants of heaven (Ezek. 1:4 *ad fin*).

Daniel at first only interpreted the dreams, or apparitions of others (Dan 2:36 ff.; 4:8 ff.; 5:13 ff.); but later, though in 'a dream and visions of his head as he lay in his bed' (Dan. 7:1) he beheld 'the Ancient of days' (i.e. the Eternal God) in an elaborate judgment scene in heaven on a throne, and the granting of an eternal kingdom to 'one like a son of man' (Dan. 7:9-13).

John's experience starts at verse 10 of his first chapter with a visitation by the risen Christ in revelatory and ruling mode and at chapter 4:1 moves on through a door to the throne room of heaven – all while he was 'in the Spirit on the Lord's day' (Rev. 1:10 onward).

I shall not go into the details of these revelatory passages, but we should try to grasp both what we should and should not derive from them as to the eternal destination of the righteous. Let us make some relevant observations.

1. There are both similarities and differences in these several representations of heaven and its inhabitants. God always rules from a throne, but only in John's vision is there a rainbow about it. There are 'living creatures' close to the throne in each case, but above it in Isaiah's vision, beneath it in Ezekiel's. In Daniel, these beings are evidently hidden among the throng (Dan. 7:10) or perhaps identical with the 'wheels' of 'burning fire' and beside the throne in Revelation 4:6. A comparison shows similar features of these 'beings' displayed in different ways. This suggests another observation.

2. These vivid pictorial scenes were designed by their divine and human authors, for pastoral reasons, to prick consciences and to stimulate both interest and imagination. The stories have made their impact through the generations, leading to fear of God, conviction of sin and reverent worship as well as other benefits. The impressions are mostly direct, straight to the heart and mind, when read aloud (as first intended) to an assembled group of worshippers.[33]

3. They are not descriptions of heaven, and those who dwell there. They are symbolical representations, crafted to fit the historical and revelatory context when enacted. There is therefore considerable material unique to each, as well as much that is similar in all the visions. I shall not dwell on this save to say it calls for great reserve in interpretation.

4. Great care as well as caution must characterize our effort to distinguish literal and figurative elements. At one time my teaching assignments, as well as my preaching, caused me to assemble dozens of books on Daniel,

---

32. ibid., p. 563.
33. When our youngest was about five years old, we were reading Revelation, a chapter a day. I had just concluded, 'they had hair as the hair of women ... teeth of lions ... tails like unto scorpions,' etc. (Rev. 9:8-10), when the little girl sprang from her chair and exclaimed, 'Daddy, when we finish Revelation, let's read it again. This is exciting!'

Revelation, Isaiah and Ezekiel. Every author struggled with this problem. All, of course, try to distinguish the literal from the symbolical; also the doctrinal from the revelatory framework. Lest any of us be 'exalted above measure' by the successes we think we have attained in such projects I quote G. H. Lang's opening remarks in a truly insightful commentary on Revelation.

> To employ figurative speech is a native characteristic of the human mind. It is more marked in some minds than in others, and in some races than in others. The oriental is very prone to it, the westerner less so, as result perhaps of the mechanical and mathematical habit of mind induced by modern industry and science. It is a regrettable loss, and especially it disenables the ordinary westerner from penetrating into the deeper and higher truths taught in the Bible, this Book being preeminently oriental in style and tone, and beautiful by reason of its richness in figurative language. It is highly needful that the western mind should immerse itself in the Bible manner of speech and endeavor resolutely to form the habit of speaking pictorially.[34]

Lang quickly warns against wholly symbolical and wholly literal interpretation, though he concludes, 'Doubtless it is safer to incline rather to a literal rather than a figurative sense, but always with the large reserve and latitude that human speech is a blend of direct and symbolic language.'[35]

5. The four heavenly scenes (Isa. 6; Ezek. 1; Dan. 7; and John in Rev. 4 ff.) are scenes both of worship and of judgment. They tell us nothing about our 'Father's house' where Jesus is preparing many 'abiding places.'

These prophets promise a glorious future for God's people in the coming kingdom of God (Ezek 40–48; Dan. 7:27, 28; Rev. 21, 22), when heaven has come down to earth and all the judgments are past (Rev. 21, 22). They therefore relate more to the eternal state than the intermediate state. Revelation adds a little about our present and future state whether 'in the body' or 'absent.' Our prospects are superb: 'the Lamb' has 'ransomed' us and made us 'a kingdom and priests' to our God, and we 'shall reign on the earth' (Rev. 5:10) – whether in the millennium of chapter 20 or the eternal state of chapters 21 and 22, granting they are to be distinguished. Martyrs for Christ's sake have a special place of protection under heaven's altar while they wait for vindication (Rev. 6:9).

Of the same sort of encouragement is the whole of chapter 7 of Revelation, an interlude before breaking of the seventh seal. As John looked toward earth from his 'door opened in heaven' he sees history pause while 144,000 out of 'every tribe of the sons of Israel' are given a protective seal against the divine judgments of 'the great tribulation' coming on the world – perhaps 'it represents the complete number of Jews who are children of Abraham by faith... who will turn to God during the closing days of the present age.'[36]

This literary interlude seems also to indicate a pause in the processes of judgment of the final great tribulation which will be the birth pangs of the coming kingdom of God. Before the most severe tribulations of them 'who dwell on earth' (Rev. 13:8), on 'the great day of their [God's] wrath' (Rev. 6:17), John sees a worshipping multitude before the august throne 'and before the Lamb.' Whether the scene should be interpreted as of only those who 'are coming out of great tribulation,' three and a half times or forty-two months or 1,260 days in length (Rev. 11:2; 12:14; 12:6; 13:5; Dan. 9:27; 12:7, 11, 12) or if there is a projection of the interpreting elder's mind (see Rev. 7:13-14) into the future beyond all resurrections and judgments is hard to say. Scholars differ.

This is the most complete picture anywhere in Scripture of glorified saints in heaven and their participation in their activities. Though every phrase makes allusions to Old Testament passages and incidents from Genesis 13:5 to Zechariah 2:17, as well as the prophetic addresses of Jesus in the Sermon on the Mount and the Olivet discourse, we leave that for a later portion of this book. Let the reader seek to absorb both the grand scale and the exquisite beauty of this glittering picture of saints in heaven before the throne of God, in the presence of their Redeemer and every other living creature – all the denizens of the future home of the redeemed. I cite the Revised Standard Version of Revelation 7:9-17.

> After this I looked, and behold, a great multitude which no man could number, from every nation, from all tribes and peoples and tongues, standing before the throne and before the Lamb, clothed in white robes, with palm branches in their hands, and crying out with a loud voice, 'Salvation belongs to our God who sits upon

---

34. G. H. Lang, *The Revelation of Jesus Christ: Select Studies*, 2nd ed. (London: Paternoster, 1948), p. 17.
35. ibid., p. 23.
36. Harold Lindsell, note on Rev. 7:4-8 in *Harper Study Bible, RSV*, p. 1871.

the throne, and to the Lamb!' And all the angels stood round the throne and round the elders and the four living creatures, and they fell on their faces before the throne and worshiped God, saying, 'Amen! Blessing and glory and wisdom and thanksgiving and honor and power and might be to our God for ever and ever! Amen.'

Then one of the elders addressed me saying, 'Who are these, clothed in white robes, and whence have they come?' I said to him, 'Sir, you know.' And he said to me, 'These are they who have come out of the great tribulation; they have washed their robes and made them white in the blood of the Lamb.

'Therefore are they before the throne of God,
and serve him day and night within his temple;
and he who sits upon the throne will shelter them with his presence.
They shall hunger no more, neither thirst any more;
the sun shall not strike them, nor any scorching heat.
For the Lamb in the midst of the throne will be their shepherd,
and he will guide them to springs of living water;
and God will wipe away every tear from their eyes.'

10
The Second Advent of Christ and Related Events

Advent is a venerable Christian word embedded in liturgies, creeds, hymns and theological writing.[1] In the first place it refers to the coming of Jesus the promised Messiah and all events related to that coming, especially the birth narratives of Matthew and Luke. Hence we call Christmas 'Advent Season.' There is going to be a Second Coming. Jesus many times promised His disciples – as also throughout the New Testament – that He will come again. The Nicene Creed (325/381) confesses that the 'Lord Jesus Christ… cometh again with glory to judge the quick and the dead.' This is the Second Advent, or, as some prefer, 'The Return of Jesus Christ.'[2] In theology and history some groups which make the return, or 'second coming,' of Christ their major emphasis, are called Adventist – as Seventh Day Adventist and Advent Christian denominations. In the following discussion Second Advent, Second Coming and return are used interchangeably.

The Second Advent is sometimes employed as a comprehensive caption for all of eschatology – as for example Berkouwer's *The Return of Christ*. This is quite feasible, for every feature of individual eschatology – death, intermediate state, resurrection, judgment, and finally hell or heaven – at some point focuses on the return of the Lord in glory.

'Comings' of Christ in the New Testament.

Modern interpreters of the New Testament have discovered valid references to several 'comings' of Christ after His death. Some of these 'discoveries' have led to systematic theories of the Second Advent and formation of enduring Christian sects. There is a certain validity and importance to each of these 'comings.'

1. There was a physical Advent in Jesus's resurrection. At the Last Supper Jesus said to the Twelve, 'I will come to you. Yet a little while, and the world will see me no more, but you will see me' (John 14:18, 19). A short while later the same evening He repeated, 'A little while, and you will see me' (John 16:16). The Apostles were mystified by His words, but on the two following Sundays the mystery of this 'I will come' was cleared up. The Christian gospel, of course, was born out of this 'advent' (1 Cor. 15:1 ff.).

---

1. The word Advent came into all languages of Christendom via Latin when all its literature was in Latin. It means the same as the Greek *parousia*, translated 'coming' in the New Testament, either of Christ's first coming, arrival, approach, drawing near or His Second Coming.
2. Title of G. C. Berkouwer's volume on eschatology.

2. The 'coming' of the Holy Spirit fifty days later was a coming of Christ. This also was stated to the Twelve early in the evening of Jesus' Passion. '[W]e [the Father and I] will come to him and make our home with him [the one who loves Jesus]' (John 14:23). Later, Jesus spoke of the Paraclete who will 'come to you' (John 16:7). According to Harold DeWolf, the coming of God's rule in the individual heart, what all call 'regeneration' ('come into my heart Lord Jesus'), is a sort of Second Advent.[3]

3. Some have interpreted John 14:3, 'I will come again and will take you to myself,' as Jesus coming to every believer at death to take him to a 'mansion' or 'place' that is 'prepared' in 'the Father's house.' This is not usually intended to foreclose on an eschatological coming of Jesus.

4. The destruction of Jerusalem and slaughter of its inhabitants by the Roman armies in AD 70 was a 'coming' of God in judgment. Most interpreters find this obliquely set forth in Jesus' Parable of the Wicked Tenant-farmers (Matt. 21:33-45; Mark 12:1-12; Luke 20:9-19) and very plainly in the Parable of the Marriage Feast (Matt. 22:1-4; Luke 14:15-24), both given on the Lord's last day of public ministry in the capital city, Jerusalem. In the latter parable the Jews of the city understood these parables to be 'against them' (Mark 12:12). They heard Him say '[t]he king' (in this case, God) was angry and sent His troops (Vespasian's army, it turned out) and destroyed their city (Matt. 22:7). Preterist (past-fulfillment) interpreters of the Olivet discourse (Matt. 24:1–25:46; Mark 13; Luke 21) think that this is the whole subject of these passages, and specifically that 'then will appear in heaven the sign of the Son of Man' (Matt. 24:30) has no reference to the future 'coming' Christ, only to His providential coming in AD 70. Matthew 24:34 is often cited in proof. Evangelical preterists do not deny that other passages promise a now still future 'Second Advent.' Advocates of this preterist theory seem to be growing in number today.[4]

5. It seems correct to speak of many critical events at different times in church history as 'comings' of Christ in judgment, distinct from His future eschatological coming. Several times in the messages to the 'seven churches of Asia' (Rev. 2–3), Jesus threatens, 'I will come' and do such and such in judgment on the church (Rev. 2:5, 16; 3:3). There is however no confusion of Christ's comings in providential judgment or in special deliverances with His parousia in power and glory (Rev. 2:25; 3:11).

6. Many providential events may be said to be comings of Christ. H. A. W. Meyer interpreted Matthew 26:64 ('from now on you will see the Son of Man seated at the right hand of Power and coming on the clouds of heaven') as continual and sustained 'comings' of the now glorified Christ in sovereign manifestation of His 'power' in many events of history. He cites several European Protestant scholars in agreement.[5]

7. An eschatological Second Advent of Christ at the end of the present age is the subject of this section of this volume. The New Testament does not in every case – especially in Jesus's own 'apocalypse' of the Olivet discourse (Matt. 24–25; Mark 13; Luke 21) – distinguish precisely between the eschatological *parousia*, His Advent at the end of the age and some of the other comings mentioned above. Therefore it seems that the student of theology should be made aware of the above non-eschatological 'comings.'

I know of no orthodox, evangelical interpreters of the Bible who do not find large portions of the New Testament – as well as the Old Testament – which predict an eschatological Second Advent of Jesus to raise the dead, to judge the dead and the living (as the ancient creeds affirm) to be followed by renewal of the heavens and the earth. Yet there has been considerable variety of opinion throughout much of Christian history as to the precise order of events and the spacing of them. Over the centuries three major strongly held and rather precisely defined views of these matters have developed among orthodox Christians. There are also some other views of the Second Advent. The three main views will be briefly examined shortly in this study.

A Pre-Christian Connection.

The doctrine of a Second Coming of Christ at the end of the present age to bring a close to ordinary history by supernatural intervention is a generally acknowledged New Testament teaching. Jesus is the One who introduced

---

3. Harold DeWolf, *A Theology of the Living Christ* (New York: Harper, 1953), pp. 302, 303.
4. In my judgment it is correct to say, 'If it were not for Matthew 24:14 and Mark 13:10 [which prophecy preaching the gospel to all the nations before the end] it would be easy [better, feasible] to bring the entire prophecy of Matthew and Mark within the limits of a single generation.' W. A. Brown in 'Parousia' in *HDB*, III, p. 676 rt. col.
5. H. A. W. Meyer, *Critical and Exegetical Commentary to the Gospel of Matthew*, trans. F. Crombie & W. Stewart (New York: Funk & Wagnalls, 1884), p. 482.

it. He hinted at it over the months of ministry and in the very last days before His Passion taught the doctrine in parables (which we shall briefly examine) that were understood only afterward and He gave a lengthy discourse (the Olivet discourse of Matt. 24, 25; Mark 13; and Luke 21) which plainly and in some detail promises a future Advent.

Yet Jesus also has made plain to present readers of the Bible (if not immediately to the original disciples) that His First Advent did not completely fulfill Old Testament prophecy of Messiah and many other features of Old Testament prediction. Especially plain are His remarks on the Easter evening (Luke 24:25-27) and on the first Sunday after Easter: 'And he said unto them, These are the words which I spake unto you, while I was yet with you, that all things must be fulfilled, which were written in the law of Moses, and in the prophets, and in the psalms, concerning me. Then opened he their understanding, that they might understand the scriptures, And said unto them, Thus it is written, and thus it behoved Christ to suffer, and to rise from the dead the third day: And that repentance and remission of sins should be preached in his name among all nations, beginning at Jerusalem' (Luke 24:44-47 KJV). These announcements helped them understand that Jesus the Christ was also the Suffering Servant of Isaiah 53 and the God-forsaken One of Psalm 22. Jesus had promised that the Holy Spirit will 'declare to you the things that are to come' (John 16:13), and so the Holy Spirit did. Over the next few years the Apostles received much further revelation about a Second Advent of Christ as King of kings and Lord of lords. He came once in humiliation; He shall return in glory.

Peter, who heard Jesus make such limited explanation of the two comings as the disciples were then prepared to hear, makes precise reference to them in his first Epistle, the first being 'the sufferings of Christ' and the second 'the subsequent glories' (1 Peter 1:10-12). In Peter's second Epistle he developed the Second Advent theme at length (2 Peter 3:1-15). Even the writing prophets, though they foresaw both humiliation and glory and had the order right, did not distinquish two Advents. Peter's first Epistle is mainly concerned with 'the suffering,' both of Jesus in His First Advent and of His disciples through the generations (see 1 Peter 2:13-25); his second Epistle is concerned mainly with the Second Advent (see especially chap. 3). Already there were 'scoffers' (2 Peter 3:3) in the church who denied any such supernatural intervention as Peter talked about, when 'the heavens will pass away with a roar, and the heavenly bodies will be burned up and dissolved' (2 Peter 3:10).

It is legitimate therefore, with New Testament hindsight, to seek out the evidence of foresight of a Second Advent in the Old Testament. W. A. Brown well said that the doctrine of a future parousia had its origin in Jesus' prophecy of His own return, but adds:

> Nevertheless, it is not without preparation in the past. It has its parallel... in the prophetic anticipation of the day of the Lord (e.g. Amos 5:18; Isa. 2:12; 13:6; Joel 1:15; 2:1; Zeph. 3:8) – that great day when Jehovah shall be manifested as the Judge and Saviour of Israel.... Many features of the New Testament doctrine are anticipated in the Old Testament. Thus the warlike imagery of Revelation 19:11 ff. finds parallels in Isaiah 13:4; 34:6; Jer. 16:10, etc. The connexion of the resurrection of the dead with the deliverance and judgment of the living is made in Daniel 12:1-3. The great convulsions of 2 Peter 3:10 have their anticipation in Isaiah 34:4. The signs in the heavens predicted in Matthew 24:29 and parallels are foretold in Isaiah 13:10 ff., Joel 3:15, 16, etc. The renewal of nature prophesied in Isaiah 65:17 reappears in Revelation 21:1 (cf. Rom. 8:21; 1 Cor. 7:31). Most striking is the parallel in Daniel 7:13ff., where the seer has a vision of one like unto a Son of Man coming with the clouds of heaven to receive dominion and glory, and a kingdom that all the peoples, nations, and languages should serve him [as Rev. 19:11-21; and 22:5; also 1 Cor. 15:25 plainly say].[6]

Special credit is due the research of R. H. Charles and successors in inter-testamental studies, who have demonstrated that in the late Old Testament period, the apocalyptic writings (or pseudepigrapha) found friendly lodgement in the hearts of many truly pious Israelites, lifting the hope from a merely worldly triumph of the nation of Israel (though they did not give that up) 'till the hopes of the righteous were transferred from a kingdom of material blessedness to a spiritual kingdom, in which they were to be as the angels [as Jesus agreed] and become companions of heavenly hosts. This partial transference of the hopes of the faithful from the material world took place about 100 BC.'[7]

---

6. W. A. Brown, 'Parousia' in *Hasting's Dictionary of the Bible* III, p. 675.
7. R. H. Charles, *Eschatology: The Doctrine of a Future Life In Israel, Judaism, and Christianity* (New York: Schocken Books repr. 1963 of the 2nd ed. of 1913), p. 179. Dr Charles was not only an eminent scholar but an Anglican preacher who wore himself out from time to time in his combined pastoral and scholarly efforts. I sympathize. R. H. Charles, in another very large work, carried inter-testamental connections too far. The 'Apocalyptic' pseudepigraphal writings were hardly 'the parent of Christianity' as he says in *The Apocrypha and Pseudepigrapha of the Old Testament* (Oxford, 1963 repr. p. 1). See Leon Morris's comment, *Apocalyptic* (Grand Rapids: Eerdmans, 1972), p. 9. If any books were 'parent of Christianity' they were the Law, the Prophets and the other writings of the Old Testament.

Around the time John the Baptist and Jesus were born there were people waiting for this kind of 'consolation for Israel.' Some of them became parents of John and of Jesus; others became His supporters in ministry as well as disciples and followers.

The Two Comings in Old Testament Prediction.

Believing scholars generally agree that prediction of two comings of Christ are latent in the Old Testament, but there is no uniform interpretation as to which relate to the Second Coming and how. Most agree, for example, that Genesis 3:15 is a *protevangelion* (first preaching of the gospel). Satan will, at the cross, bruise the heel of the 'seed' of the woman and the 'seed' will crush the serpent's head. The heel-bruising refers to the success of the devil's seed in crucifying the woman's 'seed' but not destroying Him, for He arose from the dead. Satan's program of death – physical and spiritual – for all mankind was potentially destroyed, for Jesus' death 'destroy[ed] him that had the power of death, that is, the devil' (Heb. 2:14 KJV; cf. Luke 10:18; John 12:31).

Yet Satan still prowls about 'as a roaring lion' (1 Peter 5:8 KJV) and deceives billions as effectively as he did Eve (1 Tim. 3:6; 2 Tim. 2:21). '[T]he whole world is in the power of the evil one' (1 John 5:19 RSV). So the serpent's head is still not fully crushed. That will happen only in an eschatological event (1 Cor. 15:24) when the devil will be 'cast into the lake of fire' (Rev. 20:10 KJV).

The plainest case of this age-long temporal span, hidden away in a single Old Testament passage, probably is Isaiah 9:6, 7. 'For to us a child is born, to us a son is given' (v. 6a) obviously applies to Jesus's first advent as an infant who grew up as a Son both of God and of man. The passage continues, 'And the government shall be upon his shoulder,' and so on to the verse which ends 'The zeal of the LORD of hosts [armies] will do this' (v. 7b). The latter begins its fulfillment at Jesus' return in power and glory as set forth in Revelation 19:11 ff. and other passages.

This dual character of the first Old Testament prediction of Christ and of Isaiah's vision of 'a Son' is characteristic of many other Old Testament predictions. This is not 'double fulfillment' but simply two distinct elements, each fulfilled separately.

The largest single passage in which these two comings lie unlabeled, so to speak, in the prophecy, but distinguishable from our New Testament viewpoint may be Isaiah 52:13–53:12. In this 'golden passional,' as Franz Delitzsch called it, the Lord's suffering and death is followed by the prediction that God 'will divide him a portion with the great, and he shall divide the spoil with the strong' (Isa. 53:12 RSV). Isaiah 61:1, 2 is cited by Jesus as being fulfilled as far as 'to proclaim the year of the LORD's favor' (Isa. 61:2a) at Nazareth, about AD 30, but not 'the day of vengeance of our God' (Isa. 61:2b). (Read Luke 4:16-20 to see how our Lord did it.) Some object to this understanding of Luke 4:16-20, but I think to do so is to deny the obvious. Another example is Zechariah 9:9, 10. Verse 9 is a specific prophecy of that Palm Sunday when Jesus presented Himself to the Jewish people, 'mounted on a donkey' (Matt. 21:1-5). Verse 10 looks far into a time, still future today, when 'he shall speak peace unto the heathen: and his dominion shall be from sea even to sea, and from the river even to the ends of the earth' (KJV).

Though most conservative commentators recognize this feature of Old Testament predictions, there is disagreement as to how much of some of the predictions remains unfulfilled. Many are inclined to place fulfillment of all prophecies of a kingdom of Messiah in the present age while many others place at least some of them in the future. If the church, as some say, has replaced Israel in fulfillment of the Old Testament prophecies of Israel's future blessedness in times of a Messiah, then the great mass of Old Testament prophecy is being fulfilled now. If so, most of these prophecies have little if any specific literal reference. How, for example, should we interpret Zechariah 12–14 KJV, which describes a future rescue of embattled Israelites in the Land when 'the LORD comes.... And his feet shall stand in that day upon the mount of Olives' and 'they shall look upon me whom they have pierced' and 'the inhabitants of Jerusalem' shall receive 'the spirit of grace'? See Zechariah 14:1-4 and 12:9, 10 and compare the verses with Revelation 1:7, which seems to apply this passage to the time when 'Jesus Christ... is coming with the clouds, and every eye will see him, even those who pierced him, and all tribes of the earth will wail on account of him' (Rev. 1:1, 7). While dissolving these Old Testament prophecies into a 'spiritual' (wholly non-literal) fulfillment might seem reasonable enough in principle, such transformation is very difficult in detail, as the strivings of spiritualizing commentators, who choose not to skip the hard verses, adequately demonstrate. They simply do not know what to do with the details. This is not to say advocates of literal (i.e. grammatico-historical) interpretation, both in meaning and reference, do not have problems with a restored temple worship, and the like.

These two lines of prediction have puzzled Jewish rabbis before and since Jesus' First Advent. Emil Schürer says that the semi-official Targum of Jonathan refers the prophecy of Isaiah 53 to the Messiah on the whole, but denies application to Messiah of just those verses which treat of the sufferings of the servant of God.[8] He adds, 'In not one of the numerous works [of Jewish interpretation] discussed by us have we found the slightest allusion to an atoning suffering of Messiah.'[9] John 12:34 shows how wholly foreign such an idea was to Jewish thinking of Jesus' time and we know how utterly the disciples at first rejected the notion (Matt. 16:22; Luke 18:31-34; 24:21). It is true that the Qumran sect (of the Dead Sea Scrolls) may have expected two Messiahs and perhaps even one who would be violently killed. The Qumran community may have thought of themselves as, in their suffering, being *maskilim* – the wise ones (Dan. 12:10) – and would 'accumulate merit sufficient to make propitiation for their erring fellow-countryman.'[10] Such a Messiah as Jesus Christ of the four Gospels, however, was no more present in that community's expectation than anywhere else in Judaism. Both in the pseudepigrapha and at Qumran there was possibly a rare rabbinical expectation of two Messiahs – one priestly, one Davidic (discussed in scholarly literature now for fifty years) – but no expectation of two Advents of one Messiah. Even Jesus' Jewish disciples took quite a while before figuring out the puzzle. The puzzle was first publicly explained by Peter many weeks after Jesus' resurrection and Ascension:

> But what God foretold by the mouth of all the prophets, that his Christ would suffer, he thus fulfilled. Repent therefore, and turn again, that your sins may be blotted out, that times of refreshing may come from the presence of the Lord, and that he may send the Christ appointed for you,[11] Jesus, whom heaven must receive until the time for restoring all the things about which God spoke by the mouth of his holy prophets long ago (Acts 3:18-21).

There is a lesson here for us all who conscientiously, in the fear of God, try to interpret the unfulfilled prophecies of Scripture. If prophecies of the First Advent of Christ could only be partially understood until after fulfillment, even by the best devout minds, it is likely true that no interpreter of yet unfulfilled prophecy today, or any school of interpretation, has a lock-hold on all the certainites of the future. We will likely all be as surprised as Peter (who tried to talk Jesus out of His determination to embrace the Passion, Matt. 16:22) was when prediction of 'the sufferings of Christ' became history (1 Peter 3:8-12). Though we have enough information to formulate a 'theology of hope' we must still 'walk by faith, not by sight.'

So it should be clear that though much Old Testament prediction awaits the Second Advent for fulfillment, the specific doctrine of a future parousia of Christ is, in a strict sense, a New Testament teaching. It originated in Christ Himself. At several points he made statements indicating that there was to be a future kingdom of Messiah in a definitely eschatological setting beyond His first presence on earth. He was not so plain or so well understood that the Apostles adopted it immediately. Poring over His words and bringing all the techniques of modern historical and literary research to the problem, scholars have put many interpretations on those words. It would be a diversion from present purposes to introduce theories of consistent eschatology, realized eschatology, inaugurated eschatology, and theories of Jesus' statements about the kingdom of God and kingdom of heaven. I have dealt with some of these matters in the first chapter of this present Part 7 of this book as well as in Part 6: Ecclesiology, and other sections. In the main, these theories divert the believing student away from the great and noble task of interpreting Scripture as truthful and consistent in all it teaches.

It is apparent the Second Advent, a topic extending from Genesis 3:15 through Revelation 22, is a big subject with numerous aspects and angles of approach.

We shall focus and limit our discussion of the Second Advent in this volume.[12] In this chapter, we shall examine what the Bible has to say plainly – and as much as possible without reference to controversies among orthodox, believing scholars – concerning the nature of the event itself, viewed as a moment of expectation. Though we do not

---

8. Emil Schürer, *A History of the Jewish People in the Time of Jesus Christ*, 2nd Division, Vol. ii, trans. John MacPherson (Edinburgh: T. and T. Clark, 1890), p. 186.
9. ibid., p. 186.
10. F. F. Bruce, *Biblical Exegesis in the Qumran Texts* (London: Tyndale Press, 1960), p. 58.
11. Some commentators and theologians of various schools of doctrine think verse 20 constitutes an offer by Peter (presumably with apostolic authority and by divine revelation) that if the assembled Jews in the assembled crowd would at that time repent and return to God (v. 19), God would cause their Christ to come down from heaven, that is, the Second Advent would occur. A better meaning of Peter's words must be sought in verse 21. Peter goes on to say that Jesus Christ will remain in heaven until *all* the Old Testament prophecies about the present age should be fulfilled. Jesus had said only days before that this would include evangelizing from Judea to the uttermost part of the world. The disciples did not even then know fully what that meant. Even Peter did not yet catch on. See Acts 10 and 11.
12. In *Daniel and the Latter Days* (rev. as *The Earthly Reign of Our Lord With His People*) and in *The Histories* and *Prophecies of Daniel* I discuss this topic in detail and at some length.

know the day or the hour there will be such a day and hour. In following chapters we shall view the Second Advent of Christ in relation to other aspects of the future of the world.

The Second Advent of Christ Viewed As a Single Future Event.

The doctrine of the Second Advent of Christ is not a sectarian specialty of some queer Christians. It is affirmed in the Apostles' Creed: 'From thence he shall come to judge the quick and the dead' and the Nicene Creed (381): 'And he shall come again, with glory to judge the quick and the dead; whose kingdom shall have no end.' This teaching, properly designated a dogma (official church doctrine), is an essential affirmation in that coherent body of truth which distinguishes Christianity from every other faith-system. The very spectacular nature of that possibly near event seemed a bit weird to me when I first heard it declared by a lay preacher, especially the 'rapture' as described in 1 Thessalonians 4:13-18. Yet I quickly came to understand it as pervading every aspect of the hope my parents and I had recently embraced. Though 'prophecy' of the Second Advent is not the only string on the theology harp,[13] it is as important as 'the crown of righteousness' is for those 'who have loved his appearing' and 'have kept the faith' (2 Tim. 4:7-8): those to whom Christ 'will appear a second time, not to deal with sin but to save those who are eagerly waiting for him' (Heb. 9:28).

The Moral and Spiritual Imperatives of the Second Advent.

Several of our Lord's last discourses and parables demanded spiritual watchfulness for His coming as a mark of spiritual preparedness. As Jesus and His disciples journeyed from Galilee toward His rendezvous with death He knew, of course, that the friendly crowds likewise journeying toward the Passover celebration would join with others of their nation in the cry 'Crucify him' in a very few days. He warned them of the dire results of spurning His 'reign.' As they came 'near to Jerusalem' (Luke 19:11) He warned them in the parable of the 'pounds' (minas): 'But as for these enemies of mine, who did not want me to reign over them, bring them here and slaughter them before me.' The words have an eschatological ring but they also have odour of the slaughter which would take place at Jerusalem in AD 70.

After entering the city and on through the last week Jesus repeated the warning in other parables of the 'husbandmen' or tenant farmers (Matt. 21:33-45), concluding: 'Therefore I tell you, the kingdom of God will be taken away from you.... And the one who falls on this stone [Christ Himself] will be broken to pieces; and when it falls on anyone, it will crush him' (Matt. 21:43, 44).

The Parable of the Wedding Feast (Matt. 22:1-14) climaxed with a warning for the Jews of His time who spurned Him at His First Advent which is no less applicable to careless, insincere Christians at His Second Advent. The grim warning is from the lips of the Savior Himself: 'cast him into the outer darkness' (Matt. 22:13).

This parable is transitional from warnings for the Jews of that long ago time, for those whose religious professions were insincere, to a series of warnings to Christians whose professions are insincere.

In the declining hours of the last day of His public ministry Jesus addressed several Apostles as they paused on the Mount of Olives enroute to lodging at Bethany. He spoke of the time of His Second Advent as immediately after a great tribulation, 'Immediately after the tribulation of those days.... Then will appear in heaven the sign of the Son of Man, and then all the tribes of the earth will mourn [see Rev. 1:7; cf. Zech. 12:10-14], and they will see the Son of Man coming on the clouds of heaven with power and great glory. And he will send out his angels with a loud trumpet call, and they will gather his elect from the four winds, from one end of heaven to the other' (Matt. 24:29-31; cf. Matt. 13:30, 41, 42 and context; also 2 Thess. 4:13-18 and 1 Cor. 15:51-53).

He goes on to say that the time was unknown to any one but the Father and that 'the Son of Man is coming at an hour you do not expect' (Matt. 24:44), therefore His servants should be ready at all times lest they be found to be hypocrites and be judged with the same Jewish hypocrites whom Jesus had reproached earlier in the day (Matt. 24:45-51).

---

13. A Baptist pastor in Fredericktown, Ohio, near my student pastorate, preached on the Second Coming and nothing else. For a period in the second third of the twentieth century, fundamentalists' interest in the Second Coming rose to a crescendo, together with the prophecies of Daniel and Revelation. There have been recurrences of this interest throughout Christian history due likely to the same forces – persecution of Christians and curiosity about the future, as well as general moral decay – which caused the first several generations of Christians to feel certain of the Lord's return in their lifetimes. More about this later in this chapter.

The lesson of the Parable of the Ten Virgins which followed (Matt. 25:1-13) is likewise about spiritual preparedness or watchfulness. Not that one be in tiptoe expectancy, but attending to the spiritual readiness: 'Watch therefore, for you know neither the day nor the hour' (Matt. 25:13).

The severity of our Lord's words about failure to be ready and watching extends to industry ('good and faithful servant' versus 'worthless servant') in the last of these parables, the Parable of the Talents (Matt. 25:14-30; contrast vv. 21, 23 with v. 30). The lesson seems to be that zeal and activity in tending to the Lord's interests on earth during His long absence is a mark of genuine faith in Christ, an indispensable element in preparedness.

In what may be the first canonical New Testament writing, the Epistle of James, the Lord's brother, put the Second Advent at the very heart of Christian, ethical motivation, saying: 'Be patient, therefore, brethren, until the coming of the Lord. Behold, the farmer waits for the precious fruit of the earth, being patient over it until it receives the early and the late rain. You also be patient [enduring]. Establish your hearts, for the coming of the Lord is at hand' (James 5:7, 8 RSV). This emphasis, coupled with severe warnings and exhortations, is strong in all the Epistles of the New Testament as well as Hebrews and Revelation.

The Second Advent is the central feature of the consummation of history in a world judgment. While not quite unique to Christianity,[14] belief in an 'end' of history was foreign to the culture of the Greco-Roman world. That civilization looked with scorn on the notion of a *telos* which involved resurrection and judgment. That civilization had no eschatology, only endless repetitions of cycles. This was an early cause of rejection of Christianity by the intelligentsia (Acts 17:32; 2 Peter 3:4). The early Christian apologists labored the point. They insisted that the world had a created beginning by the same God who would also bring it to His predestined *telos* (consummation).

Outstanding Characteristics of the Second Advent.

As explained by the Lord Jesus Himself, as well as angelic messengers and apostles, the Second Advent of the Lord will have the following characteristics.

1. Christ will come again visibly, just as He departed. At Jesus' Ascension 'while they were gazing into heaven as he went, behold two men stood by them in white robes, and said, "Men of Galilee, why do you stand looking into heaven? This Jesus, who was taken up from you into heaven, will come in the same way as you saw him go into heaven"' (Acts 1:10, 11 RSV). Whatever partial truth there may be in a spiritual coming at the believer's death or in the descent of the Holy Spirit, and so on, 'in the same manner as you saw him go' is as visible as a hot-air balloon ascent. 'For as the lightning comes from the east and shines as far as the west, so will be the coming of the Son of Man' (Matt. 24:27 RSV) shows how publicly visible His coming will be, as does also 'every eye shall see him' (Rev. 1:7 KJV), which removes the event from dreams, visions or a spiritual category. There will be no 'Lo, here ... or there' (Matt. 24:25 KJV; Luke 17:22) as with the false prophets of the Adventist movement of the 1840s and the Russellites (Jehovah's Witnesses), whose predictions even of a spiritual return failed to materialize.

2. He will return in Person. We have just taken note of Luke's report of how the two angelic messengers to the scene of the Ascension said 'this same Jesus' (KJV) would so come again. Paul was quite as specific: 'the Lord himself will descend from heaven' (1 Thess. 4:16 RSV). The Greek text is very specific: '*autos ho kurios... katabēsetai.*' *Autos* (the intensive pronoun) in this particular construction means 'himself,' 'herself,' 'itself,' and the like. 'The function of the intensive pronoun is to emphasize identity.'[15]

3. Jesus' Second Coming, though personal and visible like His first coming, is otherwise quite in contrast with the humble carpenter who, when they saw Him, '[there was] no beauty that we should desire him' (Isa. 53:1, 2), for Jesus will come again in glory. Jesus' petition to the Father (John 17:1-4) to regain His uncreated glory was answered at His Ascension. Three times Matthew quotes Jesus to the effect that He will come again in glory: 'in the glory of his Father' (Matt. 16:27); 'with... great glory' (Matt. 24:30); and 'in his glory' (Matt. 25:31).

The glory of God has several quite biblical senses. The glory which was the Son's 'before the world was' is the

---

14. There is a somewhat similar doctrine in Parsee (Zoroastrian) religion (See John B. Noss, *Man's Religions*, [New York: Macmillan, 1978] p. 343) as well as in the indigenous polytheistic religions of Celtic and Germanic Europe, both Celtic and Teutonic. Of course the Old Testament is the root of this aspect of Christian doctrine.

15. H. E. Dana and Julius R. Mantey, *A Manual Grammar of the Greek New Testament* (New York: Macmillan, 1927, 1955), p. 129. See as further examples Rom. 8:16, 26; 1 Thess. 4:9 in Dana and Mantey, ibid., p. 130. Also J. Gresham Machen, *New Testament Greek for Beginners* (New York: Macmillan, 1934), p. 53.

'essential' or 'uncreated glory' so mysterious that no one of the several sources I have consulted seems to know exactly what to say about it. Is it 'the sum of all His attributes'? In the above references to His coming in glory, the glory surely must be the same brightness of light as Isaiah and Ezekiel saw (Isa. 6; Ezek. 1).

This seems to be a necessary inference from the several accounts of the Transfiguration. Late in His ministry Jesus promised His disciples that 'some standing here who will not taste death until they see the Son of Man coming in his kingdom' (Matt. 16:28). The story of the Transfiguration immediately follows: Jesus 'was transfigured before them, and his face shone like the sun, and his clothes became white as light' (Matt. 17:2; see parallel in Luke 9:27-36). This must be when the prediction of seven days earlier occurred, of seeing 'the Son of Man in his kingdom' – Peter, James and John looking on as Moses and Elijah (denizens of heaven) conversed with our Lord. The parallel, Luke 9:32, says that 'they saw his glory.' So this is how the next time Jesus is seen on earth He will appear to all.[16]

4. Jesus will come again with power: 'and they will see the Son of Man coming on the clouds of heaven with power and great glory' (Matt. 24:30). The 'power' is *dunamis*, inherent might, connected with 'His coming at the commencement of the millennial reign to establish his kingdom'.[17] This is the event prophesied in Daniel 7:13, 14, which Jesus claimed for Himself at His interrogation by Caiaphas in Mark 14:61-64, asserting thereby to be the divine Messiah who would in the *eschaton* fulfill the Old Testament prophecies of the kingdom of God. This power is the authority of divinity and the might of omnipotence. It was possessed, but unused, except as willed by the Father in occasional miracles during His incarnate life on earth, but resumed after His resurrection (Matt. 28:18), and fully employed at His Second Advent, when he shall raise the dead, sit in judgment and reign until every enemy has been brought to submission (1 Cor. 15:24; John 5:25-29; Phil. 2:10, 11; Isa. 9:6, 7; 11:1–12:6).

5. He will come 'with clouds.'[18] Why is this important enough to receive Scripture notice? It should be remembered that Jesus departed with 'a cloud' and that in 'this way' He shall come again (Acts 1:11). The Apocalypse declares: 'Behold, he is coming with the clouds' (Rev. 1:7), echoing the high point of the Savior's Olivet discourse: 'and they will see the Son of Man coming on the clouds of heaven with power...' (Matt. 24:30) and the earlier prophecy, again, of Daniel 7:13, where one like a son of man comes before the Ancient of Days in heaven 'with the clouds of heaven.' What are these clouds and what do they mean?

It has been suggested that the 'ten thousands of his holy ones,' i.e. angels with whom the Lord shall come (Jude 14), are the cloud (= crowd). Much more likely is the rather well known Old Testament cloud as sign of the presence of deity. The cloud over Sinai not only signified that God was there but also served as protection for mortals against instant death. At least six times in the twenty-two New Testament occurrences of *nephelē* (cloud) it is used to indicate the presence of deity. For our topic it is important that several of these are in eschatological connection. (1) We have already cited the Transfiguration, when God spoke from a cloud (Matt. 17:5) in a species of pre-constitution of the eschatological kingdom, and (2) and the cloud over Sinai which may be the same as the cloud that followed the Israelite 'fathers' (1 Cor. 10:12); also (3) Jesus' Ascension (Acts 1:9), and (4) that 'he is coming [again] with the clouds' (Rev. 1:7; Matt. 24:30 and 26:64; with parallels in Mark 13:26; 14:62; Luke 12:54; and 21:27). Furthermore (5) a 'mighty angel' descends in a cloud in the midst of other eschatological events (Rev. 10:1), announcing 'the end' – some think the mighty angel to be none other than the Lord Himself. In the same book the two martyred and resurrected witnesses ascended to heaven in a cloud (Rev. 11:12).

I quote the language of the King James Version at 1 Thessalonians 4:13-18 because it is well embedded in Christian consciousness and vocabulary. '[T]he Lord himself shall descend from heaven with a shout... and the dead in Christ shall rise first: Then we which are alive and remain shall be caught up together with them in the clouds to meet the Lord in the air...' In the ancient Latin Version 'caught up' employs the verb *rapio*, hence the word 'rapture' for this opening event of the day of the Lord.

This language suggests natural clouds 'in the air' though perhaps the presence of deity as well. Oepke[19] observes: 'In the two rapture stories in the Old Testament (Enoch in Genesis 5:24; Elijah in 2 Kings 2:1 ff.) there is no express mention of a cloud.'

---

16. Many scholars suggest that the Transfiguration quite fully matches the situation when in the millennium a glorious Christ, resurrected saints (Moses and Elijah) and other men (the three Apostles) in natural life and bodies will mingle together. If it happened on 'a mountain' in Palestine where Jesus went to pray, why not in a renewed earth during a future millennium?

17. Henry Alford in *NTER*, p. 168.

18. Some of us can remember when country roads were unpaved and everything that moved came with clouds – of dust!

19. 'Nephelē,' *TDNT*, vol. ii, p. 905.

In my judgment the coming 'with clouds' indicate the divine presence and fulfillment of one of the several strands of Old Testament prophecy, that the denouement of history in the eschaton will be an occasion when 'the Lord whom you seek will suddenly come' (Mal. 3:1); 'behold, the LORD is coming out of his place, and will come down' (Micah 1:3). See also Psalm 50:3; Psalms 93; and 94. 'These constitute predictions of the deity of the coming Christ, a fact which the Jews never fully understood and which renders a large part of the Old Testament distinctly messianic and, in a certain sense, exclusively Christian.'[20]

6. He will come again accompanied by angels: 'all the angels with him, then he will sit on his glorious throne' (Matt. 25:31). Perhaps the 'ten thousands of his holy ones' with whom He shall come (Jude 14) are not a host of human saints but angels. They will not be a mere escort party, for there is sifting and sorting and harvesting to be done by angels. The weeds must be removed from the field of the world (Matt. 13:24-30). 'The Son of man will send his angels, and they will gather out of his kingdom all causes of sin and all evildoers...' (Matt. 13:41 RSV). There will be a kingdom to establish and these angels are to be the agents of effecting the same.

7. Jesus will return 'swiftly.' I have put 'swiftly' in quote marks because that is how it seems best to interpret places in the New Testament where Jesus Himself says, 'behold, I am coming soon' (Rev. 22:7 RSV), 'Surely I am coming soon' (Rev. 22:20 RSV) and John the Revelator says the events of his book 'must soon take place' (Rev. 1:1 RSV). In this text (Rev. 1:1) the word 'soon' translates *en tachei* which means 'with speed,' though also 'soon' or 'shortly'. The two other uses of 'soon' translate *tachu*, a related adverb meaning 'speedily' or 'soon,' as the several lexicons agree. Which is the meaning here? Will Jesus come after a short interval of time (soon) or when He comes will the event itself happen with speed (like lightning)? The words as such are capable of either meaning. It seems plain that the interval between the Ascension and the *parousia* is not intended. After all, the words were written 1,900 years ago and the Lord has not yet returned. Speed rather than a short interval is the first meaning assigned these words by Bauer, Arndt and Gingrich.[21] It must be the sense in these three passages as in Matthew 28:7, 8, where *tachu* appears twice and refers not to an interval of time, but is interpreted by the fact that the two Marys 'ran [not walked or strolled] to tell his disciples' that Jesus was risen. Many decisive events of history occur swiftly but are long in developing. The same will be the case in that most decisive event of the future.

James 5:7-8 and 1 Peter 4:7 define for every believer the lesson to be drawn from the sudden swiftness with which the *parousia* will occur and the solemn duty. James says that the believer should wait, just as the farmer, who sows in hope of harvest and patiently waits for the necessary rains from heaven to produce harvest, knows in God's time the harvest time will come. It will be through many uncertainties, rains sometimes fail and the poor husbandman must skimp on expenses, plant again and wait some more. Yet he has *makrothumia*, patience: literally, long patience or long mindedness. The farmer does not give up. James compares this patience to the 'steadfastness' of Job (James 5:11) and we all know how impatient Job was, though enduring and believing. We know the coming of the Lord, says James, 'has been' or 'is' (*ēggiken*, perfect tense) drawing near. The verb is cognate with the adjective *eggus* (near). The coming of the Lord has always been 'nearing' and remains so. James' exhortation calls for 'long patience' (James 5:7 KJV) (not tippie-toe excitement, so we won't be 'left behind').

Peter used the same word for 'drawing near,' *ēggiken* (1 Peter 4:7), for the divinely scheduled but to us unknown moment of our Lord's return. But Peter drew still another lesson. It relates to the believers' lives of prayer. 'The end of all things is at hand [*ēggiken*]; therefore be self-controlled and sober-minded for the sake of your prayers'. The end Peter intends is, of course, the future arrival of the King, Himself. 'The kingdom of this world' becomes 'the kingdom of the Lord and of his Christ.' We keep 'the end of all things' in mind as we watch and pray, 'Give us this day our daily bread' (we need it for 'long patience'), but we long and pray also, 'Thy kingdom come.'

Let these sayings of the Lord and two of His leading disciples rule both our theology of the Second Advent and our spiritual preparation for His appearing.

---

20. Robert D. Culver, *The Earthly Career of Jesus the Christ* (Scotland: Mentor/Christian Focus, 2003) p. 22.
21. Bauer, Arndt & Gingrich, *Greek-English Lexicon*, also Thayer, *Greek-English Lexicon*, and Liddell & Scott, *Greek-English Lexicon*.

11
The Time of the Lord's Return

When will the Lord return? There is no scriptural answer which satisfies mere curiosity. Long ago after I had finished my first series of sermons on prophecy and had then passed the seminary course in eschatology with a good grade, I might have answered the question with a more certain answer; but since then I have read the Bible some more and I am now less certain. In my opinion this is exactly what Jesus Himself intended (who said much about the time of His return), as well as the Apostles (who both spoke and wrote about it). More about this later. Let us view some of the biblical evidence and attempt some synthetic conclusions.

I. When asked by four of His disciples (Mark 13:3, 4) for a 'sign' of His promised return and the consummation of the present age, Jesus gave an answer that is both plain and obscure. The plain part of the answer should condition every other remark Jesus made: 'But concerning that day and hour no one knows, not even the angels of heaven, nor the Son, but the Father only' (Matt. 24:36). The Father sent the Son the first time at His own pleasure in 'the fullness of time' (Gal. 4:4) and the same will be the case when the Father sends the Son again. He will not consult the prophecy 'experts,' whether critical or evangelical, scholarly or popular.

Comparison of the three accounts (Matt. 24; Mark 13; and Luke 21) yields several then future events to transpire before Jesus' return. They are the destruction of Jerusalem, appearance of false Christs, severe persecution of Christians – especially those dwelling in or near Jerusalem – and a uniquely fierce time of tribulation such as never was before or ever will be, 'upon all who dwell on the face of the whole earth' (Luke 21:35). He said that 'the abomination of desolation spoken of by the prophet Daniel' (Matt. 24:15; cf. Dan. 9:27) would be placed in an end-time 'holy place,' i.e. the temple of Jewish worship and went on to say: 'Immediately after the tribulation of those days… will appear in heaven the sign of the Son of Man, and then all the tribes of the earth will mourn, and they will see the Son of Man coming on the clouds of heaven…' (Matt. 24:29, 30).[1]

Immediately after He had made known these many harbingers of the Second Advent, Jesus went on to issue a lesson and a warning designed to do away with any form of date-setting or of fanatical excitement about an immediate (perhaps an impending or imminent) appearance of the Lord from heaven.

---

1. Insofar as a partial fulfillment of the predicted events took place at the siege and fall of Jerusalem to the Roman armies in AD 70, 'this generation' (v. 34) did not 'pass away, until all these things' took place. This verse is, of course, the spear-point of preterist interpretation.

(1) Jesus drew 'The Lesson of the Fig Tree' (Matt. 25:32-35 ESV rubric) from the fact that in Palestine the fruit of the fig tree appears very shortly after the leaves develop. (This explains the acted parable of Matthew 21:18-20.) The similitude does not provide another sign of the Lord's return but a lesson in how to interpret all the things He said earlier in response to the request for a sign of His coming again and related events. Leaves on the fig tree ('and all the trees' cf. Luke 21:29) do not appear overnight nor do figs spring to full size and ripeness. But the latter does follow the former. 'So also,' Jesus explained, 'when you see all [note, not simply one or two] these things, you know that he is near, at the very gates' (Matt. 24:33). The Greek text is not quite so vivid. 'Very' is not present, or any equivalent idiom – *engus estin epi thurais*. 'Drawing near upon the gates' is more the tone of the expression. The notion that 'he' or 'it' is presently to walk through the city portals is not required, but rather approaching, getting closer but still out of sight – 'we walk by faith, not by sight.' The lesson is: think of our Lord's return as approaching, perhaps very near, but not certainly so. This has been the mindset of God's people through the generations, generally speaking. The tiptoe excitement induced by the 'left behind' literature of recent generations is not the élan of sober Christian fathers, mothers, children and their pastors. (See Titus 2:1-13 KJV.)

(2) Jesus' warning (Matt. 24:36 and parallel Mark 13:32) further conditions the previous language about a 'sign' and precursors of the future Advent: 'But concerning that day and hour no one knows, not even the angels of heaven, nor the Son, but the Father only.'

It has occurred to me that this verse is best explained by Galatians 4:4: 'But when the fullness of time had come, God sent forth his Son.' Then as now the Father decides when to send the Son incarnate into the world of men. We know that a circle of devout but obscure believers were expecting it to happen (Simeon, Anna, Zacharias and Elizabeth, Joseph and Mary). One of them had special information about it. One of them (Simeon of Jerusalem) was specially informed that he would live to see the Lord's Christ (Luke 2:26). All were very quiet about it. Think what a sensation Simeon might have created if he had published and distributed a book about what 'had been revealed to him by the Holy Spirit' (Luke 2:26) in the manner of one of the current 'prophecy' novels of evangelical pop theology.

The rest of the discourse on our Lord's return in Matthew 24:7–25:30 is all about being watchful and ready when Jesus comes, at whatever time of our lives, whatever the time of day, and under whatever exigencies of health or illness, peace or prosperity, war or poverty.

As pointed out earlier, there are several dominical parables to the same effect. This line of evidence (and there is more of it) seems plainly to say that true faith and loyal service to Christ, who presently is at the right hand of the Father, rather than preoccupation with the time of the Advent, is our proper habit of thinking about the Second Advent.

II. Some New Testament passages seem to say that His return would be then far in the future. Crowds accompanied Jesus as He slowly progressed toward Bethany and Jerusalem. Luke tells us that he spoke a parable 'because he was near to Jerusalem, and because they supposed that the kingdom of God was to appear [with Jesus as Messianic King] immediately. He said therefore, "A nobleman went into a far country to receive a kingdom and then return"' (Luke 19:11, 12 RSV). The parable thus introduced has much more to say about how we should behave while the Lord is away in heaven. The words 'far country' correct the notion that the interval between Jesus' departure and return (as we now can see clearly) would necessarily be short. Similarly, a few days later in the Parable of the Talents, the man who distributes his property 'went away' (Matt. 25:15) and 'after a long time the master... came and settled accounts' (25:19). In the Parable of the Ten Virgins 'the bridegroom was delayed.' In each of these cases the passing of considerable time before the coming of Christ 'in his kingdom' is integral to the message. What is a long time? To a small child on Christmas morning, waiting for father and mother to arise and open packages of gifts, fifteen minutes is a long time. For a ninety-year-old man, most of a century seems a short time. On the above evidence a century, a millennium, or more or less is not only possible but likely.

III. According to Scripture – both Old Testament and New Testament – certain recognizable events will occur before Jesus comes again to bring the present age to a close. These are of two sorts.

First are events somewhat tangential to the matter – not intended primarily as related to the time of Second Advent but impinging on it nevertheless. In this category are (a) the days of waiting for the promise of the Holy Spirit (Acts 1:4, 5), and (b) the death of Peter in old age (John 21:18, 19). Of greater relevance (c) is the destruction of Jerusalem and with it the end of temple and Torah and the beginning of the Diaspora (dispersion) of Palestinian

Jews (Luke 21:20-24). There is not space here to trace out all the scriptural information found in the three accounts of our Lord's last formal discourse (on the Mount of Olives) found in Matthew 24; 25; Mark 13; and Luke 17; and related Old Testament passages such as Hosea 3:4, 5. The latter text says that 'the children of Israel shall dwell many days' without a civil commonwealth and without the historic sacrifical system but later 'shall return and seek the LORD their God, and David their king, and they shall come in fear to the LORD and to his goodness in the latter days.' The judgments on Jerusalem (AD 70) which began the present sad epoch are clearly forecast by Jesus in the Olivet discourse as preceding the second advent.[2]

The destruction of Jerusalem and dispersion of the Jews, including the numerous Christians of Jewish ancestry before, during and after the lengthy siege is specifically said by Jesus to precede His Second Advent. In prospect of this looming catastrophe Jesus warned the Jewish Christians to flee Judea and Jerusalem (Luke 21:21), which they did – to Pella far to the north in trans-Jordan in the valley below the present city of Irbid in the Kingdom of the Jordan. Luke's report of Jesus' grim forecast of the future of Jerusalem should be read in entirety (Luke 21:20-28). I quote verses most pertinent to the matter of the long delay of the Second Advent.

> But when you see Jerusalem surrounded by armies, then know that its desolation has come near. Then let those who are in Judea flee to the mountains, and let those who are inside the city depart, and let not those who are out in the country enter it, for these are days of vengance, to fulfill all that is written' (Luke 21:20-22).

Among the 'all that is written' in the Old Testament were many prophetic oracles, written after the first destruction and diaspora (586/585 BC), of a prolonged desolation of Jerusalem. Some predicted it would lie desolate for a long time before Messianic renewal. One such is the prophecy of Hosea 3:1-5. The prophet Hosea had redeemed his wayward, enslaved wife and prevented any further unlawful sexual intercourse with her and determined not to resume the lawful married relation with her for a long time, designated as 'for many days' (Hosea 3:3). This symbolic action was, in authentic prophetic technique, a symbolic prediction of Israel's future, when they would endure a long period of time without valid ritual temple worship (owing to destruction of the temple) and without pagan ritual and priestly ministration as well. This describes Israel in world-wide dispersion since AD 70. Hosea, however, predicted Israel's repentance and resumption of right relation with the LORD under a Davidic (anointed, Messianic) king. The desolate condition initiated by the Roman armies was to last for 'many days' (Hosea 3:4).

And so it came to pass. The land and the city fell into the hands of Gentiles – Romans, Byzantines, Persians, Arabs, Crusaders, Arabs again; then in times remembered by people living today, by Turks and then the British (after 1918); then shortly after World War II, some of the land and city was turned over to the 'Israeli.' As of now, it is hard to say who is treading down Jerusalem, Jews or their irate Arabic-speaking Muslim neighbors.[3] Whatever the outcome of the recent turmoil, Daniel's prophecy, echoed by Jesus, still holds true: 'And after the sixty-two weeks, an anointed one shall be cut off [crucified] and shall have nothing. And the [Roman] people of the prince [Antichrist] who is to come shall destroy the city and the sanctuary… and… Desolations are decreed' (Dan. 9:26).

It is true, Jesus' predictions of the destruction of temple and city are not clearly distinguished from events in connection with the Second Advent in Jesus' Olivet discourse, but they became distinguishable, as they certainly became evident to Christians when forty-plus years later the horrible climax to Jewish intransigence took place.

We should also mention (d) Jesus' instructions to the Apostles for their first mission (Matt. 10) in which there is much which related, not alone to the immediate mission to Israel which lasted a few weeks, but also to the apostolic age of the church and later ages.[4] For example, few if any Christians, whether missionaries or not, were not 'dragged before governors and kings for my [Jesus'] sake' for several decades (Matt. 10:18).

Instructions for church discipline in Matthew 18 (e) seems to assume a future for the church for some time into the future. The same is true of Jesus' remarks about the church spoken near Caesarea Philippi in response to Peter's great confession (Matt. 16:18).

---

2. The preterist interpretation of the Advent in the Olivet discourse will be treated briefly later in this book.

3. Most of the residents of pre-1948 Palestine, west of the Jordan, were not ethnic Arabs.

4. I have discussed this at length in *The Life of Christ* (Grand Rapids: Baker, 1976), pp. 149–151; *The Earthly Career of Jesus the Christ* (Scotland: Mentor/Christian Focus, 2003); and also in my book *A Greater Commission* (Chicago: Moody Press, 1984), where I treat Matthew 9:35-10:42 as specific instruction to the church in its age-long mission of world evangelism. Alford in his *New Testament for English Readers*, treats Matthew 10 as a preview of evangelism through the several stages of the present age., pp. 65–75.

Four Specific Events to Precede the Parousia.

More directly, several specific, important events are to precede what one of the disciples called 'your coming [*parousia*] and of the close of the age' (Matt. 24:3). The position of the article before 'your coming and end of the age' shows they thought of that as one event and Jesus did not correct their opinion. Jesus said many things about His coming again and the end of the age in that discourse and clearly declared at least one important goal to be completed before His return. Paul added two more. Let us take preliminary notice of all of them.

1. The evangelization of all the nations before Jesus' return, when 'this gospel of the kingdom will be proclaimed throughout the whole world as a testimony to all nations, and then the end will come' (Matt. 24:14; parallel Mark 13:10).[5] Jesus said more about this just before His Ascension, predicting (not commissioning!) Christian witness 'to the end of the earth' (Acts 1:8) and 'that repentance and forgiveness of sins should be proclaimed in his name to all nations' (Luke 24:47). It seems unlikely that twenty-five or thirty years later Paul intended to say, in the Epistle to the Colossians, that the mission had already been completed (Col. 1:6, 23). He refers to 'the word of the truth, the gospel, which has come to you, as indeed in the whole world...' (Col. 1:5, 6). And again Paul asserts, 'the hope of the gospel... has been proclaimed in all creation under heaven' (Col. 1:23). E. Earl Ellis, a first rate New Testament scholar, comments on 'to every creature' (KJV, i.e. 'whole creation'): it 'may be a reference, as the context would admit, to the cosmic scope of the proclamation (cf. 2 Peter 3:9). If Paul is here speaking of the Roman citizenry, he may be allowed a hyperbole inevitable to a "born" evangelist.'[6]

Nor do I accept as reasonable or scriptural the notion I was taught in the footnotes of the first Bible I owned (and the opinion of a diminishing number of scholars today) that all this relates to a preaching different from the gospel of grace in a period after the rapture of the church.[7] That such a campaign of evangelism will be conducted by the 144,000 Israelite elect of Revelation 7 is without any contextual basis at all.

This great task of world evangelism is the goal of history as announced to Abram: 'in thee shall all families of the earth be blessed' (Gen. 12:3b KJV). The same is implied by passages such as Matthew 8:11; Luke 2:32; Romans 9:24-26; and the many Old Testament prophecies of Messiah as light to the nations, as the one in whom the Gentiles would come to trust. In the Romans passage Paul interprets Old Testament prophecy as embracing the winning of the Gentiles to Christ. These are events which most will find it difficult to place in any prophetic schedule after the *parousia* of Christ.

Most candid readers of Jesus' plain words about the evangelization of the world before His return will, I think, agree with J. O. Buswell, who devotes several paragraphs to the subject. He takes note that Mark simply says 'the gospel' not the 'gospel of the kingdom' must be preached, and similar, and concludes: 'Certainly the chief business of the church is the preaching of the Gospel in all the world for a witness to all nations. No man can judge when God will count the task completed; but when God sees it completed, then the end will come.'[8]

2. The revelation of Antichrist, called 'the man of lawlessness' and 'son of destruction' (2 Thess. 2:3) by Paul is clearly scheduled to be 'revealed' before the *parousia* (coming) of Christ – also designated our being 'caught up together... to meet the LORD' (i.e. the resurrection and translation of saints, 1 Thess. 4:13-18). Paul puts these events also before 'the day of the Lord' (2 Thess. 2:2). This is what the passage seems plainly to say. It has been read that way from remote Christian antiquity. Only with development in modern times of the theory of two phases of the *parousia* did many earnest folk see it otherwise. I do not personally see how an informed person can firmly assert a 'rapture' of the church before the revelation of Antichrist, in view of this passage – though I am aware of how the seeming plain sense is reversed by some earnest, informed people. They do so, I think, because of the complicated system they bring to the passage rather than what they find in it. More on this problem in the next chapter.

3. The same is true of the 'falling away' or apostasy of which Paul speaks in the same second chapter of 2 Thessalonians. The falling away and the revelation of Antichrist are joined as though they are aspects of the same event – 'that day shall not come, except there come a falling away (apostasy) first, and that man of sin (lawlessness) be revealed' (2 Thess. 2:3 KJV).

---

5. An important system of contemporary evangelical theology relates this evangelistic program to a time of the rapture of the church. The 'gospel' is the news that the visible reign of Christ is to begin soon. 'Verse 14 has specific reference to the proclamation of the good news that the kingdom [postponed since the Jews rejected it and crucified the King] is *again* [emphasis added] at hand.' *The New Scofield Reference Bible*, p. 1033 note
4. See also H. A. Hoyt, *The End Times* (Chicago: Moody Press, 1969), pp. 147, 155–157.
6. *Wycliffe Bible Commentary*, eds. Charles F. Pfeiffer & Everett F. Harrison (Chicago, IL: Moody Press, 1962), p. 1339.
7. I have treated this view with respect but with contrary evidence in these studies in connection with Part 6, on the doctrine of the church as also in another book, *A Greater Commission*.
8. James O. Buswell, Jr, *A Systematic Theology of the Christian Religion*, II (Grand Rapids: Zondervan, 1962), p. 367.

In a moment of exasperation over the faithlessness of most people of the time our Lord exclaimed: 'Nevertheless, when the Son of Man comes, will he find faith on earth?' (Luke 18:8). Does this not suggest that for all the victories of Christian evangelism and 'church planting' there will be a time of acute abandonment of proclamation of 'the faith' (as the Greek text of Luke 18:8 has it) as far as Christendom has spread immediately before 'the Son of Man comes'?

A later chapter will take up the great apostasy in more detail. It will suffice for now to say that the earliest Christian writers to comment on our Lord's return agreed generally with the foregoing points. Chief among these was Irenaeus, whose writings are held in high regard. His remarks on these aspects of eschatology are found in his justly famous book, *Against Heresies*.[9]

4. There will be what Jesus called 'great tribulation' for the Lord's people immediately before the Lord's return. Whether this is to be equated with 'the great tribulation' of Revelation 7:14, will receive some attention later. That this season of the world's history will be one of extreme distress for believers, perhaps also for the whole world, is clearly indicated in each of the three Synoptic reports. Having just spoken of 'people fainting with fear and with foreboding of what is coming on the world,' Jesus drew connection to His return, saying: 'Now when these things begin to take place, straighten up and raise your heads, because your redemption is drawing near' (Luke 21:26, 28). Mark is even more specific (if that seems possible). Having spoken of 'that tribulation,' Jesus proceeds to connect it with His coming to gather the saints: 'And then they will see the Son of Man coming in clouds.... And then he will send out the angels and gather his elect...' (Mark 13:24, 26, 27). Matthew's report is like Mark's. He quotes Jesus as predicting, 'Immediately after the tribulation of those days.... Then will appear in heaven the sign of the Son of Man... and they will see the Son of Man coming on the clouds of heaven.... And he will send out his angels with a loud trumpet call, and they will gather his elect from the four winds, from one end of heaven to the other...' (Matt. 24:29, 30, 31).

How shall we put these indications of the time of our Lord's coming again together? Are they capable of synthesis into an airtight position? These New Testament statements which relate to the time of our Lord's return leave us in somewhat the same situation which prevailed in late pre-Christian times among thoughtful, informed believers. They knew that the Messiah was coming, as all the Scriptures in one manner or another indicated. They could not know how prophecies of the seed of David, the Son of Man, the Suffering Servant, 'that prophet' and the universal King, were to be related to the renewal of creation in a new heaven and a new earth. The several elements seemed to lack coherence. Their rabbis disagreed among themselves. They did form theories of how to integrate it all. No scheme turned out to be wholly correct. Yet much they knew for sure – enough to be ready for His appearance if their hearts were right. Their experience should teach those who 'love his appearing' to be humble as to how we interpret some of the details. Though our present-day Christian 'rabbis' disagree, let them still stay on comfortable speaking terms. We shall try to follow our own advice as we proceed through further aspects of the doctrine of our Lord's return.

How Jesus Interpreted Daniel's Prophecy of Christ and Antichrist.

Early in our Lord's Olivet discourse about His Second Advent He announced a sure, immediate precursor of the closing events of the present age, saying: 'So when you see the abomination of desolation spoken of by the prophet Daniel, standing in the holy place [i.e. the Jewish temple] (let the reader understand),' a 'great tribulation' would immediately follow (Matt. 24:15, 21). He continued:

> Immediately after the tribulation of those days the sun will be darkened, and the moon will not give its light, and the stars will fall from heaven, and the powers of the heavens will be shaken. Then will appear in heaven the sign of the Son of Man, and then all the tribes of the earth will mourn, and they will see the Son of Man coming on the clouds of heaven with power and great glory. And he will send out his angels with a loud trumpet call, and they will gather his elect from the four winds, from one end of heaven to the other (Matt. 24:29-31).

Thus Jesus connected the great tribulation, the resurrection and translation of 'the elect,' and His Second Coming (Dan. 12:1, 2; Jer. 30:1-7). These things He declared would all immediately follow 'the abomination of desolation spoken of by the prophet Daniel.' If therefore 'the reader' is to 'understand' (Matt. 24:15), at least a rudimentary knowledge of several chapters of Daniel (Dan. 2; 7; 9; 11:36–12:13) is required. The key to that series of predictions as they relate to 'the sign of the Son of Man,' His coming, the tribulation and the gathering of the elect (Matt. 24:30, 31; 1 Thess. 4:13-18; 2 Thess. 2:1 ff.) is Daniel 9:27, I now quote as in the New American Standard Bible of 1963.

---

9. Irenaeus, *Against Heresies*, Book V, chapters 30–36.

> And he [the prince that shall come, of v. 26] will make a firm covenant with the many for one week, but in the middle of the week he will put a stop to sacrifice and grain offering; and on the wing of abominations will come one who makes desolate [marg. 'causes horror'], even until a complete destruction, one that is decreed, is poured out on the one who makes desolate (Dan 9:27).

It appears that we owe New Testament recognition of the future fulfillment of this week of years to Jesus, Himself. He definitely removed 'the abomination' spoken of by the prophet Daniel from the past, present or immediate future to a more remote future time. He also appears to acknowledge the division of the seven years into two equal parts, for He affirms Daniel's words about the predicted sacrilege 'in the middle of the week.'

Further, the person who shall perform this act of desecration is a prince of 'the [Roman] people' who destroyed 'Jerusalem and its sanctuary' (AD 70, v. 26). So it is Jesus Himself who places the seventieth week of Daniel's prophecy of seventy weeks (Dan 9:27) in the future, immediately preceding the Second Coming of 'the Son of Man.'

The two halves of this week (probably of seven 360-day years) appear many times in the Old and New Testaments. To begin with the first reference and then consecutively to read each occurrence in literary order is quite an eye opener for the skeptically inclined, even if lightly read. I present these passages here for several reasons: first, to demonstrate the prevalence of the idea through Scripture and thereby, secondly, to open minds to the possibility that Scripture prediction specifies some details about end-times and thirdly, to open up some vistas of revelation among serious-minded readers and students. Here is some of the biblical material.

'[A]nd they [Daniel's holy people] shall be given into his hand until a time and [two] times and half a time' (Dan. 7:25 ASV).

'[F]or one week: and in the midst of the week [of years] he shall cause the sacrifice and the oblation to cease; and upon the wing of abominations shall come one that maketh desolate' (9:27 ASV).

'[T]he children of thy people; and there shall be a time of trouble, such as never was since there was a nation... How long shall it be... he held up his right hand and his left hand unto heaven, and sware by him that liveth for ever that it shall be for a time [two], times, and a half' (Dan. 12:1-7 ASV).

'And from the time that the continual burnt-offering shall be taken away, and the abomination that maketh desolate set up; there shall be a thousand and two hundred and ninety days [three and a half years plus thirty days]' (Dan. 12:11, ASV).

'Blessed is he that waiteth, and cometh to the thousand three hundred and five and thirty days' (Dan. 12:12 ASV).

Observe here that Jeremiah spoke of 'the time of Jacob's trouble' with accompanying specification of unique and terrible suffering, out of which he (Jacob = Israelites) would be saved (Jer. 30:4-7 ASV), and that each of the Synoptic Gospels reports Jesus as speaking of 'the abomination of desolation, which was spoken of through Daniel the prophet' (Matt. 24:15 ASV; cf. Mark 13:14; Luke 21:20). Then follows in the book of Revelation: 'And the court which is without the temple leave without, and measure it not; for it hath been given unto the nations [Gentiles]: and the holy city shall they tread under foot forty and two months' (Rev. 11:2 ASV). 'And I will give unto my two witnesses, and they shall prophesy a thousand two hundred and threescore days' (Rev. 11:3 ASV). 'And the woman fled into the wilderness, where she hath a place prepared of God, that there they may nourish her a thousand two hundred and threescore days' (Rev. 12:6 ASV). 'And there were given to the woman the two wings of the great eagle, that she might fly into the wilderness unto her place, where she is nourished for a time, and times, and half a time, from the face of the serpent' (Rev. 12:14 ASV). '[A]nd there was given to him [the beast = Antichrist] a mouth speaking great things and blasphemies; and there was given to him authority to continue forty and two months... to make war with the saints' (Rev. 13:5-7 ASV).

To read these verses thoughtfully and consecutively at a single sitting is a disturbing experience if you have been led to believe that a seven of years, significant to biblical predictive prophecy, is a bizarre thing, of interest only to sectarian fanatics.

Daniel arranged his chapters in such a way that this consummately evil opponent of Christ and His people (both Israel and the church) is progressively introduced. Chapter 2 is a prophecy of the succession of empires from Daniel's time on till the Advent of the Son of Man to judge and rule the world. He tells of Nebuchadnezzar's dream of a great metallic image – the head of gold, the breast and arms of silver, the belly and thighs of bronze, the legs of iron, its feet of iron mixed with clay. Daniel interpreted these stages as four empires which history determined to be the Babylonian, succeeded by the Medo-Persian, then the Grecian empire of Alexander, succeeded by the Roman. In the only actions of the dream a divinely cut stone strikes the image on its weak feet (iron mixed with clay), the image crashes, the fragments are blown away, to be followed by the establishment on earth by 'the God of heaven,' of a kingdom which shall never be destroyed.

I have argued that the kingdom envisioned is the future millennial kingdom (*Daniel and the Latter Days*, pp. 131–134, and *Wycliffe Commentary*). This view implies, say some, a revival in end-times of the Roman Empire. My own opinion is that culturally, in law and literature, Western civilization is almost a living, breathing extension of the Rome of the Caesars, Seneca, Cicero, Roman law and all the classical Latin literature on which even the education of children in Europe and America was based until very recent times.

Chapter 7 of Daniel goes over the same ground from a divine outlook. The succession of kingdoms is not a statue of a rational man but a succession of violent, snarling, non-rational, brute beasts. The first, a winged lion, represents Babylon; the second, a bear, represents Medo-Persia;[10] the third is a swift leopard with four wings and four heads. It represents the Greeks (Alexander) who swiftly, about 330 BC, brought down the Persian Empire. Upon his death the area was divided into four jurisdictions represented by the four heads. The Jews of the second century suffered greatly from one of those four 'heads' (Syria), as prophesied in Daniel 8 and reported in several books of the Apocrypha, especially 1 and 2 Maccabees. The fourth (Roman) beast is an unnatural monster: 'It devoured and crushed and trampled down the remainder with its feet; and it was different from all the beasts that were before it, and it had ten horns' (Dan. 7:7 NASB). That is exactly what transfer of the center of the gravity of world rulership did when the ruling culture moved from East (Oriental) to West (Occidental). The process is still going on. Example: even the Chinese and Japanese have given up their robes for Western garb. Will Iran, Afghanistan and Pakistan follow? This is partly what the war on terrorism (the West) and *jihad* (the East) is about.

But Daniel 7 particularizes and enlarges on a little horn (v. 8) which 'came up among them [the ten horns]... before which three of the first horns were plucked up by the roots.' Yet, though, the fourth 'beast' lived on awhile. The little horn becomes the ruler of all. 'He shall speak words against the Most High, and shall wear out the saints [holy people] of the Most High... and they shall be given [by God, of course] into his hand for a time [year], times, and half a time' (Dan. 7:25).

Three years later Daniel received a vision (Dan. 8:1) of developments in the second (Medo-Persian) and third (Grecian) periods. In this, the division of Alexander's dominions into four, one of which was Syria, is the burden of revelation. The king of Syria is represented by a 'little horn' who in history turned out to be an aggressor named Antiochus (Epiphanes, the magnificent). He sought to seduce the Jews, then under his rule (second century BC), to abandon worship of Jehovah and to adopt Grecian social and religious customs. He brought temple ritual practice to a stop, desecrated the temple and began enforcing paganism. In his war with the Jews which followed this 'little horn' was defeated. The revealing angel ended his explanation with the promise, 'he shall become great. Without warning he shall destroy many. And he shall even rise up against the Prince of princes [high priest?] and he shall be broken – but by no human hand' (Dan. 8:25). Further details of this king's nefarious career are supplied in early verses of Daniel 11.

The prophecy provides such specific details that when Antiochus (the little horn) began the depredation of 168–165 BC, the Jews could hardly fail to recognize him.

Many interpreters of the 'little horn' of chapter 8 (I think rightly) have seen in him a type or foreshadowing of the final 'little horn' (of chap. 7), and the prince that shall come of Daniel 9, the one who creates the abomination of desolation of Matthew 24:15, the one Paul names the 'man of lawlessness' (2 Thess. 2:3) 'whom the Lord Jesus will kill with the breath of his mouth' (2 Thess. 2:8).

The theological literature read by the earliest church Fathers was chiefly the Old Testament. They were well acquainted with the picture of the future painted by Daniel in particular. Hippolytus (AD 170–236) in his *Treatise on Christ and Antichrist*, laid out for one Theophilus a detailed exposition, concentrating on Daniel.[11] He treated Daniel chapters 2, 7, 9, 11 and 12 essentially as I have summarized above. Moreover he regarded the first sixty-nine weeks of Daniel's prophecy of seventy weeks, determined on Daniel's people and city of Jerusalem, as terminating on the Christ. Further, he taught that the seventieth week is future and belongs to the period immediately before

---

10. Daniel began his career with the lion, ended with the bear.
11. Hippolytus, *Treatise on Christ and Antichrist* in ANF, Vol. v, pp. 204–219.

Christ's return, that its division into two parts of forty-two months, 1,260 days, or three and a half years is real not allegorical. The church, he said, will be persecuted by Antichrist and will go through the great tribulation. Let the reader confirm this report by reading Hippolytus' treatise, which is easily available and the sixteen pages may be read in one sitting. A sample from chapter 64 near the end of the *Treatise on Christ and Antichrist* provides the sense and tone of Hippolytus's exposition of prophecies of the course of the world and of end-times.

> These things, then, being to come to pass, beloved, and the one week being divided into two parts, and the abomination of desolation being manifest then, and the two prophets [Rev. 12] and forerunners of the Lord having finished their course, and the whole world finally approaching the consummation, what remains but the coming of our Lord and Saviour Jesus Christ from heaven, for whom we have looked in hope.[12]

This Father of the church then employs the language of Scripture (Luke 21:28, 18; Matt. 24: 27, 28, 31) to show that the Second Advent comes near or at the end of that seventieth week of Daniel.[13] He ends his treatise by quoting in full the description of 'the rapture' (1 Thess. 4:13 ff.) and quotes Titus 2:13 as summarizing the Christian hope.

Historic premillennialists will feel quite at home in all of Hippolytus's treatise on Christ and Antichrist. The same is generally true also of *The Epistle of Barnabas* IV, Justin Martyr (*Dialogue with Trypho the Jew*, lii, lxxx, cx), *The Shepherd of Hermas* (Fourth Vision), *The Teaching of the Twelve Apostles* and Irenaeus in the last part of the Fifth Book of *Against Heresies*. It is evident that Hippolytus's ideas were passed down from his teacher, Irenaeus. Irenaeus is said to have been taught by Polycarp and he by the Apostle John. This chain of tradition is very important to the establishment of a very early distribution of the whole New Testament canon (see C. R. Gregory's *Canon and Text of the New Testament*).[14] Jerome (AD 340–420), perhaps the greatest of translator and Bible commentator of Christian antiquity, quite untypically refrained from publishing any opinion of his own on the meaning of Daniel 9:24-27, the prophecy of the 69 plus 1 weeks. Instead he presented at length the interpretation of seven others, of whom three (Africanus, Apollinarius of Laodicia and Hippolytus) affirmed 'that the final week will occur at the end of the world (*Jerome's* commentary on Daniel, trans. Gleason L. Archer, Grand Rapids: Baker Book House, 1958, pp. 94-108.)

'The Seventy Weeks' prophecy is the chief basis for the commonly held (but little understood) teaching that there will be seven years of the 'Great Tribulation,' at the end of which Jesus will come again. Some more recent schools of thought have placed His coming to rapture the church at the beginning of the week (pre-tribulationism), the middle (mid-tribulationism), or even later in the week, just before the eschatological wrath of God announced by the sounding of the seventh trumpet and subsequent seven bowls of wrath in the midst of the week (seven) of years (pre-wrathism).

Literature on the Time of the Lord's Return.

There is an enormous amount of literature – ancient, recent and contemporary – on these aspects of eschatology, but few major works of systematic theology have extented treatment. It was a major concern of L. S. Chafer's multi-volume *Systematic Theology* and J. O. Buswell favored the church with a large section on the Second Advent, the millennium and related matters.[15] I acknowledge a certain debt to the latter work which appeared in early years of my ministry. In his major volume, Millard Erickson furnished merely a chapter of twenty pages on 'Millennial and Tribulational Views,' providing only a single sentence relating to the seven years: 'In theory, all premillennialists hold that there will be a great disturbance of seven year's duration… prior to Christ's coming,'[16] but reserved full treatment with exegesis of relevant Scripture for a subsequent volume (wisely, I think). I follow a similar technique except that I refer the reader to volumes and articles which were published previously to this present work of systematic theology. With respect to the seventy weeks of Daniel 9 and the futurity of the seventieth week see *Daniel and the Latter Days*, also *The Earthly Reign of our Lord with His People* (pp. 144–169), *The Histories and Prophecies of Daniel* (pp. 147–161), and in the *Wycliffe Commentary* (pp. 792–795).

---

12. ANF, Vol v, p. 218.
13. ibid., p. 218.
14. C. R. Gregory, *Canon and Text of the New Testament* (Edinburgh: T. & T. Clark, 1907), pp.146–154.
15. J. Oliver Buswell, *A Systematic Theology of the Christian Religion*, Vol. II (Grand Rapids, MI: Zondervan, 1971), pp. 346–538.
16. Millard J. Erickson, *Christian Theology* (Grand Rapids, MI: Baker Books, 1985), pp. 1205–1225.

12
Precursors to the Day of the Lord: The Great Tribulation, the Great Apostasy and the Revelation of the Man of Sin

There are passages in the New Testament which provide partial perspective on the course of the present age leading up to consummation in the Second Advent. The felt need we all have is expressed in the disciples' question, 'what will be the sign of your coming and of the close of the age' (Matt. 24:3). Paul surely is thinking of the same in 2 Timothy 3:1-7, which begins, 'But understand this, that in the last days there will come times of difficulty' and ends with prediction of growing moral decline and doctrinal deviation of 'men corrupted in mind,' presumably at the parousia. Similarly in Peter's second epistle he says, 'scoffers will come in the last days with scoffing, following their own sinful desires. They will say, "Where is the promise of his coming?"' (2 Peter 3:3). He then launches into a vigorous discourse on events at the parousia (2 Peter 3:4-17). These scoffers are to be expected before that consummation. Jesus rebuked every request for a 'sign' of His authority as Messiah (John 2:18; Matt. 12:38-45), but He gave a long discourse in response to the disciples' interest in some 'sign' of His promised return. He refused to respond to mere curiosity, but He did provide information relative both to the disciples' interest and ours. His answer fills several long chapters in each of the Synoptic Gospels (Matt. 24; Mark 13; Luke 21).

There is a large number of devout teachers who insist that in the Olivet discourse Jesus addressed the Apostles as Jews, or even 'a future Jewish remnant' after the rapture – an opinion without any direct support in the language of any of the three reports (Matt. 24; Mark 13; Luke 21) and dependent on doubtful inferences from other passages of Scripture.

Matthew 24:14 (KJV) reads, 'And this gospel of the kingdom shall be preached in all the world for a witness unto all nations; and then shall the end come.' A note on this verse in the Scofield Reference Bible declares: 'Verse 14 has specific reference to the proclamation of the good news that the kingdom is again at hand by the Jewish remnant.' Scofield insisted that this 'remnant' would arise after the rapture of the church. Homer A. Kent, Jr. comments on the gospel of the kingdom as 'the good news of salvation in the Messiah, with the emphasis that the Messianic kingdom is about to be established. This message will go into all the world during the tribulation through the efforts of the two witnesses (Rev. 11:3-12) and the sealed remnant of Israel (Rev. 7).'[1]

An extended response to the idea would point out that the Olivet discourse in detail parallels quite exactly the teaching of every other section of the New Testament regarding the course of the age and its consummation, hardly intended only for Jews. Several authors have demonstrated this. It is a commonplace of New Testament biblical

---

1. Homer A. Kent, Jr, in *Wycliffe Bible Commentary*, p. 972.

theology. When Paul delivered the classic passage on the resurrection and translation of believers, he prefaced it with: 'this we declare to you by a word from the Lord [*en logo kurio*]' (1 Thess. 4:15). 'By a word from the Lord' is close to the usual Pauline designation for what Jesus Himself had taught while on earth, as distinguished from what Paul, himself, had received later 'by revelation' (Gal. 1:12; 2:1, 2; Eph. 3:3) or expressed as personal counsel (1 Cor. 7:25 ff.; cf. 7:12). Paul had ample opportunity to learn Jesus' teaching from the Apostles and their immediate associates. Barnabas took him as a new believer to Jerusalem, possibly precisely to mingle with the Apostles (Acts 9:27, 28). Luke reports another time Paul consorted with the Apostles at Jerusalem (Acts 15:4) and, in Galatians 1:18, Paul reports that he once 'went up to Jerusalem to visit Cephas and remained with him fifteen days.' In an excellent article Marvin J. Rosenthal observes:

> It is certainly reasonable to understand that when Paul spent time with Peter and other Apostles, the major topic of conversation would have been the Lord and His teachings.
>
> From Peter and the other Apostles, Paul would have heard what the Lord Himself taught concerning His second coming and the end of the age, particularly His Olivet Discourse, which He shared with His Apostles shortly before His crucifixion.[2]

Rosenthal demonstrates the amazing identity of teaching by pairing the discourse of Matthew 24 with 1 Thessalonians 4 and 5. The conclusion: the Olivet discourse is as much for believers of this age, whether Jews or Gentiles, apostles or common believers. The elect who are 'raptured' after 'the tribulation of those days' are the same as 'the elect' in other parts of the New Testament. This issue is canvassed well by J. O. Buswell in his chapter, 'The Olivet Discourse and Collateral Scriptures.'[3]

C. Henry Waterman, a professor of New Testament at Wheaton College Graduate School, demonstrated the full dependence of Paul's teaching regarding the Second Coming of Christ in the Thessalonian Epistles on the teaching of Jesus in the Olivet discourse. I list his twenty-four correspondences: (1) the use of the word *parousia* for the Second Coming; (2) it will be 'the Lord himself'; 3) He will come 'from heaven,' (4) accompanied by angels, (5) heralded by a loud trumpet sound; (6) those who endure or are alive and remain are translated; (7) He will come 'with clouds'; (8) the waiting believers will 'meet the Lord'; (9) the subject of the time of His coming is introduced by almost exactly the same words (cf. 1 Thess. 5:1, 2 with Matt. 24:36 – *peri de tōn*, 'concerning the'); (10) both relate the *parousia* to 'the day of the Lord'; (11) He will come 'like a thief in the night,' (12) bringing sudden destruction; (13) the sudden coming is compared to 'labor pains'; (14) there is no escape for the unprepared; (15) believers compared to sons of light; (16) Christians are urged to 'watch'; (17) there is warning against danger of sleeping, and (18) warning against the danger of drunkenness; (19) believers are destined to receive salvation rather than wrath; (20) Jesus will come in power and glory; (21) the saints will be gathered together; (22) the apostasy will precede the day of the Lord; (23) the Antichrist will be revealed before the coming of Christ; and (24) the gospel will be preached far and wide first.

Waterman concludes (I abbreviate):

1. The Olivet discourse in oral or written form is the source of Paul's teaching.
2. Close verbal resemblances point to a written rather than an oral source.
3. Paul's materials are parallel more to Matthew than to either Mark or Luke.
4. Where there is no verbal resemblance to Matthew the thoughts are parallel.
5. Papias (whose life overlaps the Apostles' lives) mentions the Logia (sayings) which he says Matthew composed in Hebrew (Aramaic), probably a collection of Jesus' sayings and discourses. This might have been Paul's source.[4]

If this is true, Paul applied Jesus' teachings in the Olivet discourse directly to the believers at Thessalonica, and we should apply Jesus' teachings directly to Christians, whether Jew or Gentile, now or in the future.

New Testament expectation of the *eschaton* (the last time) or the *telos* (consummation) focuses on the Second Advent. Several aspects of this overture to the *eschaton* are to be stages in the consummation of evil, the last gasps of the serpent's seed,. They are, so to speak, harbingers of Christ's coming in the clouds with power and great glory accompanied by angels – precursors to the parousia and the day of the Lord, constituting movements in an overture to the main event.

---

2. Marvin J. Rosenthal, 'By the Word of the Lord' in *Zion's Fire* magazine, vol.i. 14, No. 6, Nov.–Dec. 2003, p. 5.
3. J. Oliver Buswell, *A Systematic Theology of the Christian Religion*, Vol. ii (Grand Rapids, MI: Zondervan, 1971), pp. 393–395.
4. C. Henry Waterman, 'The Sources of Paul's Teaching on the 2nd Coming of Christ in 1 and 2 Thessalonians' in *Journal of the Evangelical Theological Society*, Vol. 18, no. 2, Spring 1975, pp. 105–113.

From the earliest times of which we have record Christians found (1) the great tribulation, (2) the apostasy and (3) the revelation of the Man of Sin in the oral apostolic tradition (before the collection of apostolic Scripture) and in the writings of the Apostles. Though not a part of the consummation, these three events are prelude to the consummation. We therefore attempt here to report and clarify – as far as present knowledge enables us – what Scripture says of these three matters.

Enter these waters gingerly, for there is great difference of opinion about some biblically obscure aspects of 'prophetic' subjects, accompanied, too frequently, with unjustified insistence and more harsh judgment than seems justified. Many years ago James Graham (who wrote tellingly, if a bit too fiercely, on these topics) wisely observed, 'Prophecy… cannot be popularized. Neither is it so simple nor the order so clearly defined that the events can be listed like a high school commencement program.'[5]

A backward look on Old Testament prophecies of the first parousia of the Savior from the standpoint of their fulfillment illuminates this matter. Generously explained, both by the events and the apostolic explanations, all seems reasonably clear. 'Unfulfilled prediction is designedly less clear than that which has been completed. If we see fulfilled prophecy of the first advent quite plainly, we can see the unfulfilled prophecy of the second Advent only in the manner of "men as trees walking" [Mark 8:24]. Its general contours can be discerned and as the events draw closer, the lines are more clearly defined, though some of the details remain obscure. The course of events convinces us that our redemption draweth nigh, yet the day and the hour knoweth no man, and the prophecies are always elastic enough that we cannot apply them with absolute precision to any specific person or event.'[6]

Biblical predictions usually will have a true but obscure reference to future events. Jesus' predictions of His resurrection are typical examples. In giving a 'sign' (Matt. 12:40), He did not plainly say, I will die, my body will be buried and three days later emerge alive again. Rather He made an enigmatical reference to Jonah's experience in the 'great fish' and indicated He would have a similar experience in the 'heart of the earth'. He earlier predicted His resurrection in connection with His cleansing of the temple (John 2:18. 19) in a manner which neither the Jewish antagonists nor the disciples present understood until after fulfillment (Easter), and then only upon steady reflection (John 2:22). 'If this obscurity were not initially present, prophecy might actually produce its nonfulfillment through the efforts of those who might wish to oppose it, or its evidential value might be destroyed by bungling efforts of too-helpful friends who would try to bring it to pass.'[7]

If I am correct, the future events discussed in this chapter belong to the final years of the present age though they have been developing ever since the fall. They will come to climax as immediate precursors of the return of Christ. There is a very respectable number of earnest Bible students in about every evangelical group who believe there will be a preliminary descent of Christ to the air seven (or three and a half) years before His return to earth to rapture the church. Neither the title of this chapter nor ensuing remarks is intended to denounce that possible interpretation of the scriptural information. I once held similar opinions based on what I heard at church and in the literature recommended, especially the notes in my first copy of the Holy Scriptures, the *Scofield Reference Bible*, bought at the age of fourteen years and my only Bible until I entered seminary nine years later.

Though exposition of biblical prophecy invites speculation, treatment here will try to avoid it. A. W. Tozer, of an older generation, wrote:

> Shortly after the close of the first World War, I heard a great Southern preacher say that he feared the intense interest in prophecy current at the time would result in a dying out of the blessed hope when events had proved the excited interpreter wrong. The man was a prophet, or at least a remarkably shrewd student of human nature, for exactly what he predicted has come to pass.[8]

Tozer was right several times over.

---

5. James Graham, *Watchman, What of the Night?* (Los Angeles: Ambassador for Christ, n.d.), p. 5.
6. ibid., pp. 6, 7.
7. Robert D. Culver, 'Were the Old Testament Prophecies Really Prophetic' in *Can I Trust My Bible*, in a symposium by eight authors (Chicago: Moody Bible Institute), p. 99.
8. A. W. Tozer, *Born After Midnight*.

The Great Tribulation.

The name of the event was furnished by one of the twenty-four elders whom John saw seated about the throne of God in the Revelator's initial vision of 'what must soon take place' (Rev. 1:19). It is during an interlude before the breaking of the 'seventh seal': the elder's explanation identified the glorified 'great multitude... from every nation' tribe, people and tongue, saying, 'These are the ones coming out of the great tribulation [Gr. 'the tribulation, the great one']. They have washed their robes and made them white in the blood of the Lamb' (Rev. 7:14).

Immediate, previous connection of the great tribulation with the Second Advent seems clearly stated in the Lord's great eschatological discourse about His return at the end of the age:

> Immediately after the tribulation of those days the sun will be darkened, and the moon will not give its light, and the stars will fall from heaven, and the powers of the heavens will be shaken. Then will appear in heaven the sign of the Son of Man, and then all the tribes of the earth will mourn, and they will see the Son of Man coming on the clouds of heaven with power and great glory (Matt. 24:29, 30).

This tribulation will be unique in human history. In Mark's report of the Olivet discourse Jesus warned, 'For in those days there will be such tribulation as has not been from the beginning of the creation that God created until now, and never will be' (Mark 13:19).

Though, as we shall see, there is some special reference to Israel in Old Testament prophecies of this uniquely distressful period (Jer. 30:4-11; Dan. 12:1), it will be world-wide in scope. The ones saved out of it (apparently while it is going on) are of every nation (Rev. 17:13), and again in the description of it in the Revelation it is the whole living human race who suffer its ravages. In Jesus' message to the Philadelphian church He spoke of it as 'the hour of trial that is coming on the whole world, to try those who dwell on the earth' (Rev. 3:10).

The language of all the above passages seems to reflect Old Testament prophecies which relate these trials in a special way to the nation of Israel, still in rejection of their Messiah at that future time. Let us look at portions of some of them. The first contemplates a restoration (Jer. 30–31) far exceeding anything that happened in the post-exilic period following 536 BC.

The restoration will be permanent – 'It shall not be uprooted or overthrown any more for ever' (Jer. 31:40). Before that however:

> These are the words that the LORD spoke concerning Israel and Judah: "Thus says the LORD: We have heard a cry of panic, of terror, and no peace. Ask now, and see, can a man [*zakar*, male] bear a child? Why then do I see every man [*gever*, male person] with his hands on his stomach like a woman in labor? Why has every face turned pale? Alas! That day is so great there is none like it; it is a time of distress for Jacob [*tsarah*, distress, anguish]; yet he shall be saved out of it" (Jer. 30:4-7).

The passage goes on to say that this unprecedented time of anguish will terminate with what can only be called conversion and permanent restoration of the entire nation of Israel in times of Messiah (Jer. 30:8–31:40).

The prophecies of Jeremiah were well known to Daniel (see Dan. 9:20). So the revelation given to him on the subject of future unique distress for Jacob was no surprise. Note both the similarity of the revelation vouchsafed to him and the advance in detail, but strictly in eschatological context. I cite the text in ASV:

> And at that time shall Michael stand up, the great prince who standeth for the children of thy people; and there shall be a time of trouble [*tsarah*, as in Jer. 30:7 above], such as never was since there was a nation even to that same time: and at that time thy people shall be delivered, every one that shall be found written in the book. And many of them that sleep in the dust of the earth shall awake, some to everlasting life, and some to shame and everlasting contempt. And they that are wise shall shine as the brightness of the firmament; and they that turn many to righteousness as the stars for ever and ever (Dan. 12:1-3).

At this point it is important to point out (in whatever manner one thinks these predictions of Israel's conversion, restored relation and new covenant with the LORD should be interpreted) this trouble is not located in any past historical situation but just previous to the *eschaton*. Here are all the main events of eschatology: a resurrection of the dead, a judgment when the books are opened (see Rev. 20:12, 15), and rewards, both for good and for evil. It meshes quite exactly with Jesus' specification that 'Immediately after the tribulation of those days... they will see the Son of Man coming on the clouds of heaven' (Matt. 24:29, 30).

These plain to a point but still somewhat enigmatic statements, along with the terrors of Revelation 6–19, went into general Christian awareness very early. The *Epistle of Barnabas* (written, says Lightfoot, before AD 132) is rife with references to the prophecies of Daniel, the Revelation and the Olivet discourse. It refers even to the shortening of the days of the great tribulation.[9] 'Barnabas' seems to entertain no doubt that the Christians he addresses might be involved in that time of great stress. *The Shepherd of Hermas* (before AD 150) has these lines: 'Blessed are ye, as many as endure patiently the great tribulation that cometh, and as many as shall not deny their life. For the Lord swore concerning his Son, that those who denied their Lord should be rejected from their life, even they that are about to deny him in the coming days.... But thou, Hermas, hast had great tribulation of thine own,' etc.[10] These ancient Christians obviously thought it possible that they might suffer this predicted 'great tribulation' and felt they should get ready for it.

Irenaeus in Book V of *Against Heresies* very plainly taught that Christians of his own or some future generation would enter the great tribulation and encounter Antichrist (the man of lawlessness of 2 Thess., the beast of Rev.). Among many passages, perhaps the strongest is: 'But he [John, author of Rev.] indicates the number of the name [the Beast, Antichrist, 666] now, that when this man comes we may avoid him, being aware who he is.'[11]

This awareness of prophesied 'perilous times,' 'trouble,' 'travail,' was already present in late pre-Christian Judaism. Borrowing Jeremiah's pungent expression (rendered 'travail with child' above, Jer. 30:6) they speak of the 'birth pangs of Messiah.' So Jesus was not introducing something entirely new.

Raphael Patai is a renowned contemporary Jewish scholar. In *The Messiah Texts*, where he records Jewish Messianic teaching through the ages, he writes:

> Once the idea became entrenched that the coming of Messiah will be preceded by greatly increased suffering, and that even the beginning of the messianic era itself will be an age of trials and tribulations, apocalyptic fancy went to work elaborating in gruesome detail what would happen at the onset of the days of the Messiah[12]... Both the people and its religious leaders continued to hope for the coming of the Messiah, much like a woman who hopes and waits for the birth of her child, even though she knows that she will have to go through severe pangs of childbirth before she can enjoy the pleasures of motherhood.[13].... (There was even a Talmudic tradition of seven years.)[14]

Of course these thoughts were derived from such Old Testament passages as Jeremiah 30; Daniel 7 and 9; Zechariah 12–14; and others.

At about the same time the birth pangs preliminary to birth of the Messianic age were being discussed at Qumran by the teachers of the people of the Dead Sea Scrolls.

In every epoch of perceived persecution of Christians or of expected persecution, devout believers have wondered if the predicted great tribulation were impending or even present.

This, as far as I can determine, has never changed except that an influential movement, which originated in Britain early in the nineteenth century, captured wide attention in recent decades, and is promoted throughout the world, holds that all believers will be removed from earth to heaven before the great tribulation begins. This is a modification of the premillennialism (or millennialism) of the early centuries and of common understanding among all millennial views – as we shall see. It requires a considerable readjustment of historic premillennial interpretation of the book of Revelation, the Olivet discourse, and Paul's treatment of the *parousia* in 1 and 2 Thessalonians.

I ordinarily do not use the word 'rapture' as a short designation of the resurrection of the righteous dead and their translation with the righteous living at our Lord's return, because in our time many who read that word 'rapture' will bring to it a whole complex of popular end-time scheduling which may or may not be scriptural. The teaching of 1 Thessalonians 4:13-18 has great capacity for spectacular enlargement by creative imagination. Several series of fictional books and movies, built on the words 'one shall be taken and the other left,' have captured evangelical readers in recent generations. Presently a whole series of movies and novels employ the 'left behind' theme. When 'rapture of the church' is read the result is just as the American West of pioneer times is imprinted on minds by

---

9. J. B. Lightfoot, ed. J. R. Harmar, *The Apostolic Fathers* (London: Macmillan, 1898), p. 271.
10. ibid, pp. 408, 409.
11. Against Heresies, Vol. v, 30.4.
12. Raphael Patai, *The Messiah Texts* (Detroit, MI: Wayne State Univ. Press, 1988), p. 95.
13. ibid., p. 96.
14. ibid., p. 104.

Gary Cooper and John Wayne movies, more than by memory of the elders, and bona fide historical literature. The public in general (including naive and theologically neglected church folk) bring a prophetic 'schedule' and supposed spectacular end-time events at the 'coming' of the Lord, its precursors and sequents, to the subject. Distortion of the doctrine by spectacular imagination has created a prophetic paradigm for which, even if correct in part, has been accepted without knowledge of the basis for it. How many, for example, could supply biblical support for 'seven years of tribulation'? Most would not know even the chapters of the Old Testament and New Testament to consult. So I try to avoid the word which triggers a partly fictitious paradigm of prophecy.

Yet nothing has dislodged this conviction of the first Christians that just before our Lord's return there would be a period of intense persecution of believers in Christ. Usually this is discussed in the very terms of the Olivet discourse, Revelation 7; Daniel 12; and Jeremiah 30; as well as Paul's 'perilous times' and Peter's 'last days.' There have been three waves of interest and attempts to relate current events to this aspect of prophecy in my lifetime. The first was during the decade of the 1930s, when there was the rise of fascism (Mussolini) and Italian subjection of Libya and Ethiopia (see Dan. 11:36), plus in the United States of America, the New Deal efforts at centralized control (the National Recovery Act and the Blue Eagle). The second was in the late 1960s, when Hal Lindsey's writings hit the market. The third was the now recent (though much chastened) popularity of the 'Left Behind' books and films.

Concurrent with the popular 'rapture' excitement, serious study with scholarly control has proceeded steadily. There are dozens of monographs on deposit in seminary libraries and hundreds of journal articles. Results have been incorporated in volumes of systematic theology by competent evangelical authors. Even biblically oriented Roman Catholic scholars such as Vincent P. Miceli, S. J., have become interested. Father Miceli produced a scholarly work covering the subject.[15] Before we proceed let us emphasize that the topics of this chapter, weird as they may seem at first exposure and distasteful to nominal Christians, and even 'turned off' by some evangelical believers, are authentic main features of Christ's own revelation about the future of the human race.

The second and third topics should be introduced together.

The Great Apostasy and the Revelation of the Man of Sin.

These two end-time events are introduced together as aspects of the period of time known as the great tribulation which we have just previously discussed. Paul's 'eschatological discourse' found in his two Epistles to the new congregation of Thessalonica assumes and supplements Jesus' Olivet discourse on the time of His coming. As we have seen, they should be studied side by side. Paul's 'discourse' starts at 1 Thessalonians 4:13 and continues through 2 Thessalonians 2:11. He had taught the Thessalonian congregation about these matters when he was with them founding the congregation (see Acts 17:1-9; cf. 2 Thess. 2:5). The letters were probably written within a year while Paul was missionizing Corinth (Acts 18:11).

In the earlier letter he wrote a message of comfort, assuring them that at Jesus' coming their believing dead would be restored to life and, together with living believers, would be transformed and rise to 'meet the Lord in the air' (1 Thess. 4:13-18). Meanwhile unhealthy fanaticism and speculation (never quite absent from discussion of biblical predictions) had broken out. Hence the second Epistle carries a message of correction.

Some at Thessalonica were agitating fellow believers with the notion that 'the day of the Lord' was about to occur. Some felt so sure, they had stopped daily labor to earn a living (2 Thess. 2:2; cf. 3:5-15). Paul counseled 'patient waiting' (2 Thess. 3:5 KJV). Paul's teachings had been misconstrued and even falsely represented, perhaps by forged letters and perhaps even denied by 'spirit or word' – i.e. prophetic utterances, perhaps spoken or written by members of the local church (2 Thess. 2:2). So the great evangelist and teacher, in a rather severe mood, wrote a second letter to set things straight. He explained how the 'rapture,' the apostasy and the revelation of Antichrist really are connected and in what order. Paul sets forth the order in which the tribulation, the apostasy and the revelation of the Man of Sin were to take place. Here are his own words. I cite the KJV with one textual correction ('Lord' for 'Christ' in v. 2) because it furnishes the classic terms in which the discussions and controversies have been conducted over several generations.

---

15. Vincet P. Miceli, *The Antichrist* (Harrison, NY: Roman Catholic Books, 1981).

> [1] Now we beseech you, brethren, by the coming [arrival, *parousia*] of our Lord Jesus Christ, and by our gathering together unto him [the 'rapture'], [2] That ye be not soon shaken in mind, or be troubled, neither by spirit, nor by word, nor letter as from us, as that the day of the Lord is at hand. [3] Let no man deceive you by any means: for that day shall not come, except there come a falling away first, and that man of sin be revealed, the son of perdition; [4] Who opposeth and exalteth himself above all that is called God, or that is worshipped; so that he as God sitteth in the temple of God, shewing himself that he is God. [5] Remember ye not, that, when I was yet with you, I told you these things? [6] And now ye know what withholdeth [is restraining, RSV] that he might be revealed in his time. [7] For the mystery of iniquity [*anomia*, lawlessness, RSV] doth already work: only he who now letteth [restrains, RSV] will let [do so, RSV] until he be taken out of the way. [8] And then shall that Wicked be revealed, whom the Lord shall consume with the spirit of his mouth, and shall destroy with the brightness of his coming: [9] Even him, whose coming [*parousia*, arrival, as of Christ's Second Advent in v. 1] is after the working of Satan with all power and signs and lying wonders, [10] And with all deceivableness of unrighteousness in them that perish [are perishing]; because they received not the love of the truth, that they might be saved. [11] And for this cause God shall send them strong delusion, that they should believe a lie: [12] that they all might be damned who believed not the truth, but had pleasure in unrighteousness (2 Thess. 2:1-11).

A principle which should guide in interpreting any piece of literature, especially in interpreting biblical prediction, is that stray or incidental statements delivered in another connection must not take precedence over statements of an author made specifically regarding the subject he is treating. In this case the subject was a question (v. 2): Has the day of the Lord arrived yet, i.e. at the time of Paul's writing? Is it already here? The Greek, *enestēken hē emera tou kouriou*, rendered 'the day of the Lord is at hand' (KJV) requires some special attention, as now follows.

Does the word *enestēken* mean 'has arrived' or 'is at hand, about to appear'? The KJV 'is at hand' is changed to 'has arrived' in most recent Bible Versions and the preponderance of modern scholarship favors arrival resulting in presence rather than proximity. It is true that in several of the six times of the employment of some form of *enestēken* in the New Testament it means to have arrived and be present (in Rom. 8:38, e.g. things present as opposite things to come). Yet in some others the RSV renders it 'impending' (1 Cor. 5:26) and in 2 Timothy 3:1 RSV renders the future tense as 'will come.' Lexicons furnish both 'to stand close upon, to be at hand, impend' (as KJV reflects) and 'to be present' (as RSV and others).

There is a respectable school of thought which proposes that some were worried the Parousia and 'rapture' had already happened and they all at Thessalonica had been left behind. Thirty-five years ago Dr John Walwoord proposed this theory to me when he was visiting me in my office at Wheaton College. He became the most notable advocate of it. Literature supporting the view is now plenteous.

However we translate – whether the day of the Lord is about to happen ('at hand,' KJV) or 'has come' (RSV and many scholars) – the notion that the Thessalonians thought that the day of the Lord, i.e. the rapture, had taken place and they had been 'left behind' seems quite implausible, for at least one compelling, simple reason. It is unreasonable to suppose that they thought the 'rapture' had occurred and all the congregation, including their elders and others who had endured much persecution for the Lord's sake (1 Thess. 1:13-16), had been 'left behind.' Did they suppose that Paul himself and perhaps Silas and Timothy (Acts 18:5), all of whom probably kept in communication with Thessalonica, had missed the rapture too? Verses 1 and 2 show that Paul and perhaps his assistants were in regular communication. That is how he, Paul, would have known of false and perverted teachings being promoted at the scene of his ministry back in Thessalonica.

In any case, therefore, it seems clear that Paul is saying, the day of the Lord will not come until after the *he apostasia* (KJV 'the falling away'; RSV 'the rebellion') – that day shall not arrive except the *apostasia* comes first.

What does *he apostasia* (the apostasy) mean? 'Apostasy' is an anglicized form of the Greek word. We have already briefly examined the word in chapter 10 above, under the subject of the time of the return of Christ.

In the New Testament and the Greek Old Testament (Septuagint) as well as in other *koine* (i.e. common Greek of New Testament times) the term invariably has the meaning of *departure* or *rebellion* in the sphere of politics or religion. Many years ago, when a highly regarded evangelical author[16] proposed that in 2 Thessalonians 2:3 *apostasia* means departure (of the saints), i.e. rapture of the church, one of the most able senior students in our seminary wrote his graduation thesis on this subject,[17] demonstrating to everyone's satisfaction that the word does not mean

---

16. E. Schuyler English, 'Rethinking The Rapture' in *Our Hope* magazine, Vol. 56 #6, December, 1949.
17. Kenneth Teague, whose monograph is on deposit at the library of Grace Theological Seminary, Winona Lake, IN.

physical departure of any sort in actual usage, but political or religious defection from a previously held position – what Christian theology has always meant by apostasy (see article 'apostasy,' in *The Catholic Encyclopedia* Vol. 1), abandonment of the Christian faith. The word appears over forty times in the Septuagint in various forms, always in the sense of defection, not physical removal. The New Testament simply (as with most Greek words of doctrinal significance) took over the meaning in Hellenistic (*koinē*) Greek from the Septuagint. It is true that *aphistēmi*, the verbal relative of *apostasia*, often bears the meaning of physical, spatial removal but at the time Paul wrote, not the noun *apostasia*. The reality of apostasy occured regularly in Israel's history which, as I. H. Marshall states,

> was one of continual apostasy as the people deliberately turned away from the God who redeemed them out of Egypt, and followed false gods and sinful ways.... In the New Testament apostasy occurs when men turn aside from following Jesus (John 6:66 ff.)... in falling away from faith under persecution (Matt. 24:9-13), denying the deity of Jesus (1 John 2:22), living a life of open sin that denies the faith (2 Peter 2:20). It is characteristic of the last days (2 Tim. 2:3; 1 Tim. 4:1; 2 Tim. 3:1, 5; 4:3).[18]

Paul, however, in 2 Thessalonians 2:3 is not pointing to apostasies in general but *the* apostasy (*hē apostasia*), an already prophesied apostasy. He is not making a fresh revelation, for Paul is very careful to distinguish what he might have received as special revelation, as a prophet (Apostle), from what he knew from Jesus' teaching as passed on in the Christian tradition, which later was written down in the Gospels (see Gal. 1:11-24 and 1 Cor. 7:10, 12, 25). The origin of Paul's teaching about the apostasy and the man of lawlessness is Jesus' Olivet discourse (Matt. 24; 25; Mark 13; Luke 18). In that discourse Jesus said much about the great apostasy and the tribulation which would occasion it.

First He warned against going 'astray' (Matt. 24:5) at the time of 'the close of the age' (v. 3) and spoke of a succession of earlier false Christs (v. 5; cf. Luke 18:8, 'when the Son of Man comes, will he find [the] faith on earth?'), and of potentially alarming wars and rumors preliminary to 'the end' (v. 6). He told also of widespread devastating famines and earthquakes (v. 7). Jesus continues:

> Then they will deliver you up to tribulation, and put you to death; and you will be hated by all nations for my name's sake [religious persecution and martyrdom]. And then many will fall away [KJV, be offended, Gr. *skandalisthēsontai*], and betray one another, and hate one another. And many false prophets will arise and lead many astray [KJV, and shall deceive many]. And because wickedness [*anomia*, lawlessness] is multiplied, most men's love will grow cold (Matt. 24:9-12 RSV).

Mark 13:22 adds: 'False christs... will... lead astray, if possible, the elect.'

Some of the very earliest Christian writers saw identity of subject between these verses spoken by Jesus and prophecy of great tribulation in the sense of religious persecution, religious falling away from Christ (apostasy) and revelation of the man of lawlessness by Paul in 2 Thessalonians 2:3 ff. Jesus says that 'lawlessness' shall be multiplied and Paul identifies the cause as 'the man of lawlessness,' thus connecting *the* apostasy with the supreme apostate, the final Antichrist (Antichrist is subject of later consideration in these pages) or the man of lawlessness. The connection is cemented when Jesus goes on to inform His questioners that all this will come to climax in a certain act of sacrilege (abomination of desolation, KJV) taking place 'in the holy place' (v. 15). Prophecy of the abomination of desolation and the wicked ruler of the end-times who installs it starts at Daniel 7:8, 'another horn, a little one,' then on through chapter 7, continuing as a 'prince who is to come' (Dan. 9:26) and a 'king' who 'shall do as he wills' (Dan. 11:36-45), and on to the 'abomination' of the Olivet discourse (Matt. 24:15). John knew about this rambunctious, big-mouthed, persuasive character and introduced him to his readers as one they already knew about: 'antichrist is coming' (1 John 2:18 cf. 4:3), and the 'beast rising out of the sea' (Rev. 13:1 onward). There is every reason to unite these references with the 'man of lawlessness' (cf. 2 Thess. 2:3). Later we shall take more notice of this monstrous enemy to come. Let us now turn our attention to what Paul has to say about what and who is holding up the arrival of this Antichrist.

What and Who Restrains, the *Parousia*, and the Man of Lawlessness.

Paul expands on the career of this man, but does so in a manner that raises several questions and leaves several either unanswered or only partially so. 'Do you not remember that when I was still with you I told you these things?' (2 Thess. 2:5). He evidently told them when he was still at Thessalonica and before he wrote 1 Thessalonians that

---

18. I. H. Marshall, 'Apostacy,' *ZPEB* I, p. 216.

this monstrous person would appear. What any Bible student would give to have a transcript of those sermons! But we do not have them, though if God, the providential Manager of such things, intended for us to know what Paul said it would have been in our New Testament.

There follows another important item of information along with another question for us: 'And you know what [neuter gender, a thing not a person] is restraining him [the man of lawlessness] now so that he may be revealed in his time' (v. 6). There will come a proper time for revelation of this man. After he is revealed Jesus will come. The believers at Thessalonica knew what this thing was (or is) but we do not.

There follows another pair of predictive pieces of information, with a question: 'For the mystery of lawlessness is already at work. Only he who [masculine gender, a person] now restrains it [the mystery of lawlessness] will do so until he is out of the way [*ek mesou genētai*, becomes out of the middle]' (v. 7). Most expositors rightfully agree that this means removal of some person, and now holding back a surge of lawlessness, from the scene of action. Alternative views have not found general acceptance. The identity of the thing restraining a surge of lawlessness by the man of lawlessness, and the person who does the same, as well as the relation of the two, have been vigorosly explored and discussed from Christian antiquity to the present. There is a crowd of commentators and a plethora of literature to advise us.

One of the most thorough and penetrating has come from an unexpected quarter, an article by a European scholar in the *Journal of Biblical Literature*. Roger D. Aus, who lived in Germany, published his 'God's Plan and God's Power; Isaiah 66 and the Restraining Factors of 2 Thess. 2:6, 7.'[19] He produced impressive evidence – too technical to present here. Thoroughly versed in the Hebrew Bible and its Greek translation (Septuagint), Aus found all verbal and doctrinal elements of 2 Thessalonians 2:1-11 in the Old Testament: in Daniel 11 and 12; in Ezekiel 28; and especially in Isaiah 66:3-7, 9, 15 and 18-21. The passage (2 Thess. 2) also, Aus thinks, reflects Matthew 24:14 and anticipates Revelation 17–19. The person who restrains, *ho katechon* (2 Thess. 2:7), is God Himself, who is in absolute control and the thing which restrains is God's plan – His project of evangelizing all the world (Matt. 24:14). That which is removed or taken away (*ek mesou genētai*, 2 Thess. 2:7) is the same as the mystery of lawlessness. 'The mystery of lawlessness in v. 7a is the subject of *genētai* in v. 7b... That is, evil or lawlessness which has not yet reached its peak. Only then when it is most intense and apparent to all, will God cease His restraining, the Messiah will come, and the decisive battle between the lawless one and the Lord Jesus takes place.'[20]

Aus refers in this article to his larger works on the subject in two other European scholarly journals. Would I had time and means to pursue them! But perhaps someone will open up this channel of very competent research, reported in footnotes to the article. Aus concludes his article with a summary as follows:

> The above interpretation of the *katechein* motif in 2 Thess 2:6-7 does not solve all the difficulties inherent in the text. There are too many variables in these verses to obtain any absolute certainty. Nevertheless, the solution offered above has two major arguments in its favour. First, it means that *To Katechon* [the thing which restrains] and *ho katechōn* [the person who restrains] are intimately related. God, he who now restrains the Day of the Messiah, does so because of his plan or will that the gospel first be brought to all men. Secondly, it is based on an OT text, Isaiah 66, which is employed elsewhere in 2 Thessalonians. The author then employed imagery from the same OT chapter for his description of the restraining factors in 2:6, 7.[21]

I treat the topics of this chapter at length in *Daniel and the Latter Days* and in the successor volume, *The Earthly Reign of Our Lord With His People*.[22]

Though Paul, in my opinion, clearly settled the matter of the order of the tribulation, the apostasy and the man of lawlessness, this chapter must close with some mysteries of biblical prediction unresolved. This is as it should be, because the Bible itself leaves them so. It is profitable for us not to be wise beyond that which is written and to be cautious and humble in speculation.

True religion must always protect its mysteries. The sort of religion that one can easily figure out before being initiated into it is of no more use to the healthy minded person than a novel whose plot can be figured out by careful scrutiny of the dust jacket. The permanent appeal lies in the mysteries.

---

19. Roger D. Aus in *Journal of Biblical Literature*, 96, 4, Dec. 1977, pp. 537–553.
20. ibid., p. 551.21. ibid., p. 553.
22. Robert D. Culver, *Daniel and the Latter Days* (Chicago: Moody Press, 1977), pp. 66–77. Now available from author in revised form with a new title. See also R.D. Culver, *The Histories and Prophecies of Daniel* (Winona Lake, IN: BMH Books, 1980), 191 pages.

The same is true of other important aspects of human life. For example, it is doubtful if any other social arrangement is more important to the race than marriage. Everybody is interested in some features of marriage. In recent times when sexual experiences have been emphasized as important to happiness (or fun, pleasure, fulfillment) a large number of people have apparently been led to suppose that sex is the only feature of marriage they need to know about in order to be fully successful and happy – with or without entering into marriage vows and covenants.

In a similar manner a considerable number of people who have only casual interest in Christian worship and doctrines have an insatiable appetite for what is popularly called 'prophecy.' And, though theologically illiterate, insist on being supplied a schedule of future events which neither Daniel nor Paul nor John the Revelator, not even the Son of God Himself, could produce. Scripture reminds these folk and other earnest seekers that the promise is not to those with the most defensible timetable for end-time events but to all of them 'that love his appearing.'

13
The Thousand Years of Revelation 20

The words *chilia etē*, a thousand years, appear six times in Revelation 20:2-7. Pseudo-Latin renders the words as 'millennium' after the analogy of biennium, and the like. It is not news to readers that there is much difference of opinion among orthodox scholars and believers about the place of these 'thousand years' in Christian doctrine. A full treatment would require reference to the structure of Revelation, especially with regard to the succession of seven seals broken, seven bowls of wrath poured out and seven trumpets sounded. At this point I propose simply that we read Revelation 20 continuously with chapter 19. The vision of chapter 19 begins with 'After this [Gr. *meta tauta*, literally, after these things] I heard' and continues with 'Then I heard' (v. 6) and 'Then I saw' (v. 11), 'Then I saw' (v. 17) and 'Then I saw' (20:1) followed by 'Then I saw' (20:4). This successions of events John heard and said are set off from John's previous narrative and visions by 'After this' (*meta tauta*) at the beginning of chapter 19. They seem therefore all to be connected with the beginning of chapter 20, each a successive event in one vision. Let the reader consider that as we now read, beginning with the last phrase of chapter 19:

> ...and all the birds were gorged with their flesh. [20:1]Then I saw an angel coming down from heaven, holding in his hand the key to the bottomless pit [Gr. abyssos] and a great chain. [2]And he seized the dragon, that ancient serpent, who is the devil and Satan, and bound him for a thousand years, [3]and threw him into the pit, and shut it and sealed it over him, so that he might not deceive the nations any longer, until the thousand years were ended. After that he must be released for a little while.
> [4]Then I saw thrones, and seated on them were those to whom the authority to judge was committed. Also I saw the souls of those who had been beheaded for the testimony of Jesus and for the word of God, and who had not worshipped the beast or its image and had not received its mark on their foreheads or their hands. They came to life and reigned with Christ for a thousand years. [5]The rest of the dead did not come to life until the thousand years were ended. This is the first resurrection. [6]Blessed and holy is the one who shares in the first resurrection! Over such the second death has no power, but they will be priests of God and of Christ, and they will reign with him for a thousand years.
> [7]And when the thousand years are ended, Satan will be released from his prison [8]and will come out to deceive the nations that are at the four corners of the earth, Gog and Magog, to gather them for battle; their number is like the sand of the sea. [9]And they marched up over the broad plain of the earth and surrounded the camp of the saints and the beloved city, but fire came down from heaven and consumed them, [10]and the devil who had deceived them was thrown into the lake of fire and sulfur where the beast and the false prophet were, and they will be tormented day and night for ever and ever. (Rev. 20:1-10).

It should be apparent that the natural (normal) sense of this passage is that the predicted future events of chapter 20 are subsequent in time to those of chapter 19. But are there reasons, not apparent, to the contrary? There have been interpreters, both learned and devout, since at least Augustine's time (354–430), who think that John's story starts over again (as, some suppose, several times before) at 20:1, and relates to a situation long past or perhaps to the present time, or of spiritual realities which have no relation to earthly history.

No less an authority than H. B. Swete in his work on the Apocalypse, pronounced by Wilbur Smith the best ever, says, as he begins his exegesis of chapter 20: 'It must not... be assumed that events now to be described chronologically follow the destruction of the Beast and the False Prophet and their armies [of chap. 19].'[1]

What evidences support this outlook? We shall say more of this later, but now note only that some who think John's vision starts over again with events at the beginning of the present age (1) say that the restraint put on the devil by the cross of Christ (Matt. 12:26-29; Heb. 2:14; John 12:31; 16:13) is identical with the imprisonment of the devil in Revelation 20:1, 2; (2) 'They came to life' (Rev. 20:4) is individual regeneration, as described by Jesus (John 5:25-27); (3) 'and reigned with Christ for a thousand years' (Rev. 20:4) is to be explained as believers presently in the heavenlies reigning there with Christ (Eph. 3:19-23 *et al*).

What evidences support the view that the events of chapter 20 – the imprisonment of the devil for a thousand years, the resurrection of saints and martyrs, and their reign with Christ for a thousand years – follow the return of Christ described in the preceding chapter?

1. For thousands of ordinary readers the natural reading of Revelation 20, to which I have already called attention in introducing this chapter, continues the narrative with no flashbacks. If there were no editorial division between chapters 19 and 20 this would be even more apparent.

2. The narrative of chapter 19 seems unfinished. Two members of the wicked trinity – the beast and the false prophet – have been disposed of properly; now the narrative follows, chronologically, unless there is contrary evidence in the text, to dispose of the third and most enduring nefarious member, the devil himself. This is how Henry Alford (1810–1871), no less an authority than his younger contemporary, H. B. Swete cited earlier, handles the text. Alford begins his comments on chapter 20: 'The next enemy now remaining is the Arch-fiend himself....'[2]

3. The antecedent subject of the verb *ekathisan* (they sat) in verse 4 cannot be found in context except in the host of saints, 'the armies of heaven,' who accompany Christ to the battle of 19:17-21 and who share the rewards of victory. Opponents say many verbs lack subjects in this book. I have not found this assertion plausible. This, however, is not the end of the matter.

It is not surprising therefore that chiliasm (belief in the thousand-year reign) was widely spread, if not universal, in the first three centuries. They interpreted Daniel 2, 7, 9 and 11–12 in relation to this future thousand years. It may well be that this thinking was influenced toward a literal future fulfillment by Jewish apocalypse (another very large subject), but that hardly accounts for the way educated and sophisticated Christians such as Justin or Irenaeus, both scholars conversant with classical Greek literature, were convinced of thoroughgoing millennialism and vigorously propagated it. Philip Schaff, whose authority as church historian has hardly been exceeded, wrote: 'The most striking point in the eschatology of the ante-Nicene age is the prominent chiliasm, that is, the belief of a visible reign of Christ in glory on earth with the risen saints for a thousand years, before the general resurrection and judgment.'

Schaff cites as examples 'Barnabas,' Papias, Justin Martyr, Irenaeus, Tertullian, Methodius, and Lactantius.[3] Hippolytus should be added, as outstanding.

Schaff was no advocate of millennialism, hence, this is not a tendentious report. Adolph Harnack held no admiration for Christian orthodoxy, much less the notion of a future 'millennial reign'. Yet his article 'Millennium,' retained through several editions of *Britannica*, forcibly declares belief in a future much like that of Jewish apocalypse 'shorn of its sensual attractions.' was prevalent among early Christians.[4]

Harnack says:

> Amongst the early Christians (50–150)... a fixed element [was] (1) the notion that a last terrible battle with the enemies of God was impending; (2) the faith in the speedy return of Christ; (3) the conviction that Christ will judge all men, and (4) will set up a kingdom of glory on earth.[5]

---

1. H. B. Swete, *The Apocalypse of John* (New York: Macmillan, 1907), p. 259.
2. Henry Alford in *NTER*, p. 1997.
3. Philip Schaff, *History of the Christian Church*, Vol. ii (Grand Rapids: Eerdmans rep. 1973), p. 614.
4. Adolph Harnack, 11th ed., *Britannica*, Vol. 18, 1911, p. 462.

He remarks of Justin Martyr's millenarian views:

> That a philosopher like Justin, with his bias towards an Hellenic construction of the Christian religion, should nevertheless have accepted its chiliastic elements is the strongest proof that these enthusiastic expectations were inseparably bound up with the Christian faith down to the middle of the 2nd century.[6]

Yet millennialism (chiliasm, premillennialism) did not entirely hold the field. Over-ardent premillenarians do well to take note of all Justin Martyr (110-165) had to say in his *Dialogue With Trypho* about millennial expectations. Toward the end of chapter 80 he wrote:

> I and others who are right-minded [orthodox] Christians on all points, are assured that there will be a resurrection of the dead and a thousand years in Jerusalem which will then be built, adorned and enlarged [as] the prophets Ezekiel and Isaiah and others declare.[7]

He acknowledges, however, earlier in the chapter that not all the 'right-minded' (= orthodox, Catholic) agreed on this millennial prospect, and that he had been acknowledging the same over a period of time, as follows:

> I admitted to you [Trypho, the Jew] that I and many others are of this opinion, and [believe] that such will take place, as you assuredly are aware; but on the other hand, I signified to you that many who belong to the pure and pious faith, and are true Christians, think otherwise.[8]

Jean Cardinal Danielou, without peer among twentieth-century historians of very early Christian doctrine, has a long chapter on millenarianism. He says that the doctrine is of

> an earthly reign of the Messiah before the end of time.... It seems hard to deny that it contains a truth which is a part of the common stock of Christian teaching, and which occurs in 1–2 Thessalonians, in 1 Corinthians and in the Revelation of John [and] is to be found as early as Ezekiel [and, he goes on to say, in several apocryphal books].[9]

Danielou thinks that the doctrine, though very widely accepted, may not have been accepted universally or consistently, for he points out that as ardent a millenarian as Irenaeus was willing to apply some of Isaiah's prophecies of a renewed heaven over a reconciled earth to the church age[10] and remarks, 'It is worthy of note that neither Clement of Rome nor Hermas make any allusion to millenarianism – indeed, with the latter the emphasis is placed on the times of the church as immediately preceding the final judgment [i.e, amillennialism].'[11]

In fairness one should add that only a few Fathers before AD 150 wrote anything now extant about an earthly reign of Christ. W. J. Grier takes advantage of this fact to refute the verdict that the early Church was fully millenarian. He also claims that Origen's argument against chiliasm prevailed and that 'Lactantius was the only man of note in the fourth century who still held the system.'[12]

While the church remained a persecuted minority in the pagan world of the Roman Empire it was easy for Christians to see themselves as candidates for deliverance from a great tribulation by the return of Jesus to be followed by a thousand years when they would 'live and reign with Christ.' When, however, the Roman government became their protector and then sponsor, it seemed unpolitic, if not incorrect and false, to regard that government and its emperor as the beast (Antichrist). Thus a reversal took place and for more than a thousand years millennialism (premillennialism, chiliasm) almost disappeared.

Though there is some evidence Augustine (354–430) borrowed it from North African Donatist schismatics, it was he who first fully articulated the new views. He grew up in Roman Africa, more Latin than Italy itself, and in his magnum opus, reinterpreted Revelation 20 for both the Western and Eastern church and formulated the roots both of postmillennialism and amillennialism.

---

5. ibid., p. 461.
6. ibid., p. 462.
7. Justin Martyr, *ANF*, Vol. i, p. 239.
8. ibid., p. 239.
9. Jean, Cardinal Danielou, *The Theology of Jewish Christianity: A History of Early Christian Doctrine Before the Council of Nicea*, trans. John A. Baker (Philadelphia: Westminster Press, 1964/1978), p. 377.
10. ibid., p. 386.
11. ibid., p. 386.
12. W. J. Grier, *The Momentous Event: A Discussion of Scripture Teaching on the Second Advent* (London, Banner of Truth Trust, 1970), p. 27.

Augustine on the Thousand Years.

Augustine's views on eschatology, among many other subjects, are set forth in *The City of God*, the result of thirteen years of labor (AD 413–426).[13] The part which relates to the millennium is book 20, chapters 4 to 15.[14] It is safe to assert that until this section of Augustine's great work is mastered one cannot fully appreciate the millennial discussions which have followed since his day. It is almost, if not wholly true, that all amillennial and postmillennial systems have been postscripts to *The City of God*.

Having read the entire section in *The City of God* several times over many years, I do not feel that it can be positively asserted that Augustine was convinced that the thousand years should be taken literally. He seems to say so, but he is not unequivocal. His nearest approach is in chapter 10. There he seems to say that the millennium may be either the last thousand years before the consummation, into which the present age falls, or it may be the entire period of the world's history, called a thousand years because 1,000 as the cube of 10 would be 'the number of perfection to mark the fullness of time.'[15] He seems to lean toward the first of the two possiblities. But, in either case, whether he thought the thousand years to be literal or a figure, he believed the term stood for a real period of time, whether one thousand or 6,000 years.

At any rate, he believed the whole present age to be in the millennium and that the termination of the present age and of the millennium would be approximately synchronous. It also appears that he followed the Septuagint chronology (it is believed that he did not know Hebrew) and thought that the 6,000 years of human history to be well in progress when the present dispensation began. He also evidently believed that at the end of 6,000 years of history, Christ would come again and end the current age.[16] He specifically rejected the idea that the millennium is a future age after the close of the present dispensation.

Later he makes it clear that he feels the millennium refers to the course of the church in the world, and the reign of saints to be a present situation on earth (the organized church), except insofar as the unity of the church living and dead involves a secondary reference to the saints in heaven as well.

His views of matters related to the millennium are clarified as he goes on to give his views on the rest of Revelation 20.

'The first resurrection' (Rev. 4–6) he holds to be a spiritual resurrection – the same as that 'resurrection' or 'regeneration' described in John 5:26, 27. It is the same as personal salvation. It is participated in only by the saved; as he says, 'In the first resurrection none have a part save those who shall be eternally blessed.'[17]

The second resurrection described in Revelation 20 is a physical resurrection of all people, according to Augustine. He speaks of it as a resurrection 'of judgment,'[18] almost as a premillennialist, but he goes on to clarify his statement and show that he means only that the saints, all of whom participate in spritual regeneration (the first resurrection), shall not be 'judged' (damned) in this second or physical resurrection at the consummation, even though they do participate in the same resurrection. He concludes:

> So are there these two resurrections, – the one the first and spiritual resurrection, which has place in this life, and preserves us from coming into the second death; the other the second, which does not occur now, but in the end of the world, and which by the last judgment shall dismiss some into the second death, others into that life which has no death.[19]

On the binding of Satan, he asserts that it has regard to the nations (as Rev. 20 says) but that this means 'no doubt, those among which the church exists.' Later he clarifies this to mean that Satan will not be able to seduce the elect of the church militant. This binding took place at the beginning of the present age when Christ first bound the 'strong man' in order that He might 'spoil his goods' (he cites Mark 3:27). This binding he seems to conceive of as a judicial act of God rather than of some specific historical event such as the death of Christ, the founding of the church, the work of the first missionaries, and similar.

---

13. A more up-to-date introduction and translation which I have found useful is Augustine: The City of God, trans. Henry Bettenson (who has provided much such literature) ed. David Knowles (Penguin Book) Middlesex England, 1972, LIII + 1095 pages. The last three books contain Augustine's eschatology.
14. This may be read in *The Nicene and Post-Nicene Fathers*, Second Series, Vol. 2, trans. Marcus Dods.
15. Augustine, The City of God, 20.6.
16. ibid., 20.7.
17. ibid., 20.6.
18. ibid., 20.6.
19. ibid., 20.8.

On the loosing of Satan (Rev. 20:7-9), he writes that it refers to the revived ability of Satan to seduce the non-elect of the church visible. He seems to relate the biblical references to a final great tribulation, the great apostasy and the Antichrist to the 'little season' during which Satan is to be loosed. This he places at the end of the present age but before the consummation (i.e. before the 'general resurrection' judgment, and so forth).[20] He leaves the problem as to whether the 'little season' is within the thousand years or immediately afterward an open question.

These are the main features of Augustine's view. It bears repeating that his views are of the utmost importance to present-day millennial discussions, for about every orthodox ammillennial or postmillennial view since Augustine has embodied some of the main features of his view. Indeed, the very passages of Scripture which Augustine used in support of his arguments appear often in contemporary amillennial literature.

To recapitulate the main features of Augustine's view: the thousand years is an expression, whether figurative or literal he is not certain, standing for a literal period of time. The millennium (Rev. 20:2-5) relates to the present age. Either this age is the millennium or is contained in it; approximately, the present age and the millennium terminate synchronously. The reign of the saints (Rev. 20:4) is during this age and it is on earth through the appointed leaders (clergy, and the like) of the visible church. The first resurrection (Rev. 20:4, 5) is spiritual and is the regeneration of the individual believers whereby they become members of the body of Christ, that is, of the kingdom of God. The second resurrection (Rev. 20:12-14) is physical and refers to the resurrection of all people at the consummation. The binding of Satan (Rev. 20:2) consists of Satan's being deprived of any ability to seduce the elect. The loosing of Satan (Rev. 20:7 ff.) consists of revived ability to seduce the non-elect. The 'little season' (Rev. 20:3) will come at the end of the current age when the Antichrist, the great tribulation, the apostasy and so on, will come. This will be followed by a general resurrection and a general judgment (Rev. 20:11-14).

It remains to be added that, in the main, Augustine's view is, and has been, the view of the Roman Catholic Church.[21]

Christianity world-wide, at present, is possibly as much allied with Augustinian post- and amillenarian exegesis as with premillennialism. In the next chapter we shall consider what scholars and ordinary Christian folk since Reformation times have come to believe about the millennium and associated events.

---

20. ibid., 20.13.
21. A note in the offical Roman Catholic Bible in English (The Holy Bible Douay-Rheims Version) on Revelation 20:3 reads: 'The souls of the martyrs and saints live and reign with Christ in heaven, in the first resurrection, which is that of the soul to the life of glory.'

14
Recent and Current Views of 'The Millennium': Postmillennial, Amillennial, Premillennial

First off, it must be acknowledged that many, perhaps most, Christians have no clear, well-articulated conception of the thousand years. A great deal of reading and reflection is required even to ask meaningful questions. One competent, and later famous writer, whom I heard lecture on the book of Revelation said it was a 'cryptic letter' from the 'concentration camp' on Patmos and when first read to the seven churches was also furnished with a key which was irretrievably lost.[1]

In the American Midwest where I live there is a 'fifth Gospel' – the Gospel according to Martin Luther. The Christians here learn nothing at church about the millennium, the Augsburg Confession has already pushed it out the church door, even though some leading advocates of millenarian thought since Reformation times have been Lutherans. Among them Joseph Seiss and George N. H. Peters were nineteenth-century Americans, and it was J. A. Bengel, a German Lutheran scholar, who is credited with making the word 'millennium' respectable in Europe in the eighteenth century.[2]

As we proceed to present postmillennialism, amillennialism and premillennialism several notices are in order. (1) The discussion will be kept as closely to Revelation 20 as possible. (2) There are varieties of each view, which, though they do not render generalizations impossible, require some caution in generalizing. (3) Though some reference to historical backgrounds is necessary,[3] I will pass over medieval and Reformation times, except as necessary to explain views as expressed in the nineteenth and twentieth centuries. (4) With due respect to Swedenborgians, Russellites (Jehovah's Witnesses), Church of God (Armstrongism), Seventh Day Adventists, their millennial views do not come within the limits of this survey. (5) There are varieties of opinion in each category. Hence the course followed will be to describe each view as set forth by a leading advocate(s).

Postmillennial Views of the Millennium.

Postmillennialism is of comparatively recent origin. Several of the best advocates of the view attribute its origin to Daniel Whitby (1638–1726), an English Arminian theologian who near the end of his life adopted Arian views of the Godhead. A. H. Strong, for example, writes: 'Our own interpretation of Revelation 20:1-10, was first given, for substance, by Whitby.'[4]

---

1. See E. M. Blaiklock, *The Seven Churches* (London: Marshall, Morgan & Scott, n.d.).
2. Joseph Seiss, *Lectures on the Apocalypse* and George N. H. Peters, *The Theocratic Kingdom* were 19th century Americans. J. A. Bengel in *Exposition of the Apocalypse and Gnomon of the New Testament*, made the word millennium respectable in Europe in the 18th century.

One of the best-known statements of the postmillennial position is that of A. A. Hodge. With his customary force, skill and brevity, Hodge presented the case as follows:

> What is the Scriptural doctrine concerning the millennium?
>
> 1st. The Scriptures, both of the Old and New Testament, clearly reveal that the gospel is to exercise an influence over all branches of the human family, immeasurably more extensive and more thoroughly transforming than any it has ever realized in time past. This end is to be gradually attained through the spiritual presence of Christ in the ordinary dispensation of Providence, and ministrations of His church.
>
> 2nd. The period of this general prevalency of the gospel will continue a thousand years, and is hence designated the millennium.
>
> 3rd. The Jews are to be converted to Christianity either at the commencement or during the continuance of this period.
>
> 4th. At the end of these thousand years, and before the coming of Christ, there will be a comparatively short season of apostasy and violent conflict between the kingdoms of light and darkness.
>
> 5th. Christ's advent, the general resurrection and judgment, will be simultaneous, and immediately succeeded by the burning of the old, and the revelation of the new earth and heavens.[5]

Hodge, then, was convinced that the 'one thousand years' is a literal period of a thousand years, and that they will run their course in the latter portion of this present age.

However, David Brown, certainly the most voluminous writer in support of postmillennialism, took a slightly different view. He wrote:

> One remark, however, I must request the reader to bear in mind... I attach no importance, in this argument, to the precise period of a thousand years. It occurs nowhere in Scripture but in one solitary passage. There are reasons for taking it definitely and literally; but to some these reasons appear slender. They think it means just a long indefinite period; agreeing with us, however, as to its being yet to come.[6]

There are variations in the minor points among postmillenarians but most would agree on the general scheme of Hodge above. Another orthodox and scholarly advocate of postmillennialism was A. H. Strong. I cite his views as characteristic of most orthodox postmillennial doctrine.

> The binding of Satan is presumably the restraint put on the devil by the ultimate prevalence of Christianity throughout the earth – when Jew and Gentile alike became possessed of Christianity's blessings.[7]
>
> The first resurrection (Rev. 20:4-6) is not a preliminary resurrection of the body, in the case of departed saints, but a period in the latter days of the church militant, when, under special influence of the Holy Ghost, the spirit of the martyrs shall appear again, true religion be generally quickened and revived, and the members of Christ's churches become so conscious of their strength in Christ that they shall, to an extent unknown before, triumph over the powers of evil both within and without.[8]

The resurrection is only of 'the spirit of sacrifice and faith,' and the statement of Revelation 20:5 (ASV) that 'The rest of the dead lived not [again] until the thousand years should be finished' means only that the 'spirit of persecution and unbelief shall be, as it were, put to sleep.'[9]

Strong feels that the release of Satan (Rev. 20:7) for 'a little season' indicates that

> at the close of this millennial period, evil will again be permitted to exert its utmost power in a final conflict with righteousness. This spiritual struggle, moreover, will be accompanied and symbolized by political convulsions, and by fearful indications of desolation in the natural world.[10]

---

3. For complete coverage of views through the Christian centuries see LeRoy Edwin Froom, *The Prophetic Faith of the Fathers*, 4 vols., about 4,000 pages (Washington D.C.: Review & Herald, 1950). This work is unique and valuable.
4. A. H. Strong, *Systematic Theology* (Old Tappan, NJ: Fleming Revell, 29th printing of the 1907 ed.,1974), p. 1014.
5. A. A. Hodge, *Outlines of Theology* (Grand Rapids: Eerdmans, 1957), p. 568 ff.
6. David Brown, *Christ's Second Coming: Will It Be Premillennial?* (New York: Carter, 1879), pp. 27, 28.
7. A. H. Strong, op. cit., p. 1008.
8. ibid., p. 1013.
9. ibid., p. 1013.
10. ibid., p. 1009.

Thus the 'little season' is the great tribulation period. The destruction of Satan, Gog and Magog, the general resurrection, and the general judgment of the great white throne are held to be at the Second Advent, sometime after the close of the millennium.

It should be seen that postmillennialists have not generally held that the Second Advent closes the Millennium, for in Strong's view, the 'little season' is said to intervene. It is after the millennium, but how long after is not declared.

It needs to be added that many advocates have been of the opinion that neither the church nor the world may be conscious of either the beginning or the close of the millennium. Brown makes this clear:

> Let no one suppose I expect that the beginning and end of this period will be so clearly discernible as to leave no room for doubt on any mind. On the contrary, I think there can hardly be a doubt that it will follow the law of all Scripture dates in this respect – of Daniel's 'seventy weeks,' and of the 'twelve hundred and sixty days' of Antichristian rule. The beginning and end of the former of these periods [the seventy weeks of Dan. 9] is even yet a matter of some controversy.[11]

The period during which postmillennialism was at its height of acceptance was the latter half of the nineteenth century and during the first quarter of the twentieth century. It was an era of optimism, belief in progress, congenial to the premillennial view. Among the great theologians of this era, Strong, C. A. Hodge, A. A. Hodge and C. A. Briggs were postmillenarians. Postmillennial writers of the more popular sort were Albert Barnes (Commentaries on the New Testament) and David Brown, to mention only a few. James H. Snowden (*The Coming of the Lord*, 1919) and B. H. Carroll (*The Book of Revelation*, 1916) are among the most recent thoroughgoing postmillennial orthodox writers. During the 'golden age' of American Protestant Modernism, which came to an end with World War II, Modernists adopted a kind of postmillennialism to which earlier doctrinally orthodox advocates would have given no approval (e.g. Rall, *Modern Premillennialism and the Christian Hope*). It was based more on the theory of evolution and humanism than on any interpretation of the Bible and need not occupy our attention here. The present heirs of Modernism, the neo-orthodox and neo-liberal people, are scarcely more optimistic about the course of the present era than premillenarians and so are not inclined to postmillennialism.

Fifty years ago postmillennialism had few strong, vocal advocates. This, however, is not true today. Lorraine Boettner's *The Millennium* (1957) disturbed the quiet. It has nearly 400 pages of exposition and defense of postmillennialism. Boettner speculated that 'Life in the Millennium will compare with life in the world today in much the same way that life in a Christian community compares with that in a pagan or irreligious community.'[12] Marcellus Kik has produced essays in support of the doctrine. Another writer, like Boettner and Kik, of strongly Reformed background and persuasion, tries to draw too much theological water from the present reign of Christ 'in the midst of… [his] enemies' (Ps. 110:2). I refer to the redoubtable and inimitable late R. J. Rushdoony, founder of the Christian Reconstruction movement. Andrew Sandlin, upon whom Dr Rushdoony's mantle seemed to fall for awhile, outlines the Reconstruction arguments for postmillennialism in *A Postmillennial Primer*.[13] Being Calvinists all, and holding a strong and sound doctrine of man's fallenness, it seems surprising that they would expect human depravity ever to yield such results. I quote here my remarks in another publication:

> Peter announced that at Jesus' session at the Father's right hand, He was proclaimed, 'Lord and Christ' (Acts 2:33, 36). It is argued [as Reconstructionists] that it is right, therefore, to expect His Lordship to be effected in the present age by the work of evangelism and instruction. It is a form of postmillennialism, though not of the usual type. Most of the advocates of this approach are of strong Reformed background, especially the admirers of Kuyper, Dooyweerd, and Rushdoony. Elements of this approach will also be found in the writings of Dietrich Bonhoeffer (especially in *Ethics*), and Oscar Cullmann.[14]

In fact one cannot quite keep up with the postmillennial literature of the Reconstruction movement, especially in their well-edited magazine, *Chalcedon* (now *Faith for All of Life*).

---

11. Brown, op. cit., p. 28.
12. Lorraine Boettner, *The Millennium*, 4th ed. (Philadelphia: Presbyterian & Reformed), p. 19.
13. Andrew Sandlin, *A Postmillennial Primer* (Valecito, CA: Chalcedon Foundation, 1997), 50 pages.
14. Robert D. Culver, *Civil Government, A Biblical View* (Edmonton, AB: Canadian Institute for Law, Theology & Public Policy, 2000), p. 207.

Mid-twentieth century, Lorraine Boettner spoke up for postmillennialism when it was in eclipse in his book *The Millennium*.[15] Later Robert Clouse chose Dr Boettner to defend this view in a symposium of four authors.[16] J. Marcellus Kik affirmed that enemies of Christ 'could be completely vanquished if the Christians of this day and age were as vigorous, as bold, as earnest, as prayerful, and as faithful as Christians were in the first centuries and in the time of the Reformation.'[17]

Though in order to be brief as possible I have not traced post-Reformation optimism about a successful spread and victory of Christianity which has since come to be called postmillennialism, but readers should know that the Puritan movement both in Britain and America had a broad streak of this outlook. The researches of Haller and Becker, and others in Puritan history, show clearly that the men who led the Puritan migration from Britain and many New England clergy before 1776 thought that the millennial situation might be brought about first in the 'New World.' More enlightening on this score is *Puritans, the Millennium and the Future of Israel, Puritan Eschatology 1600–1660* (ed. Peter Toon, London: James Clark, 1970). Chapter II, 'The Latter-Day Glory,' by Toon, illustrates from writings of the time the birth of hope that the 'Thirty Years War' then raging on continental Europe might introduce the millennium.

Many 'secularized versions of millennialism' owe much to liberal Protestant postmillenarianism. Hanz Schwarz comments: 'The idea of the kingdom of God in America, a country which is not just called the New World because it was discovered late' is a secularized version of millennialism – of course in its post-form.[18]

Amillennial Views of the Millennium.

In the preceding chapter we observed how Augustine reframed Christian understanding of the course of the present age, making the church age the time of the thousand years. So when theologians decided to call this denial of a millennium after Christ's return amillennialism, a misunderstanding was introduced, because most who deny a future post-Advent millennium agree that the Second Advent is 'post' some sort of 'millennium in the present age.'[19]

1. A Modified Augustinian View.

The most aggressive and, in my opinion, most cogently presented form of amillennialism among evangelicals for several generations accepts Augustine's interpretation with one major change and some minor shifts.

The 'thousand years' is a figurative expression designating the course of the present age from the death of Christ to the Second Advent. The reference is to the reign of the saints with Christ in heaven.

It will be seen at once that this is an Augustinian view modified. The major change is that the reign of the saints in the millennium is said to take place in heaven rather than on earth, as in the view of Augustine. An important minor shift is that recent amillennialists have clearly broken with the idea that the millennium is to be taken as a literal designation of a literal length of time. Instead of setting any particular date, precise or approximate, for the end of the millennium, the length of the millennium is simply conceived to be the length of the present age not of the age of the human race. Some adjustment of this kind was inevitable in amillennialism when once AD 1000 was passed.

An able representative of the school was William Hendriksen, whose views are set forth in his book, *More Than Conquerors: An Interpretation of the Book of Revelation*. Following the 'recapitulation' or 'parallelistic' method of interpreting the Apocalypse, he believed that with Revelation 20 the prophecy returns to the beginning of the present age. The 'order of events' has the following 'sequence.' He says, 'Christ's first coming is followed by a long period during which Satan is bound; this in turn is followed by Satan's little season; and that is followed by Christ's second coming, that is, His coming unto judgment.'[20] Concerning the binding of Satan, he writes: 'This work of

---

15. Lorraine Boettner, *The Millennium* (Philadelphia: Prebyterian & Reformed Publ.).
16. Robert Clouse, ed., *The Meaning of the Millennium: Four Views* (Downers Grove, IL: InterVarsity Press, 1977).
17. J. Marcellus Kik, *An Eschatology of Victory* (Philadelphia: Prebyterian & Reformed, 1970), as cited by Boettner, op. cit., p. 119.
18. Hanz Schwarz, *On the Way to the Future* (Minneapolis: Augsburg Publ., 1972), p. 154.
19. Amillennial and amillenarian are evidently recently coined words. While the *Oxford English Dictionary* traces premillennial back to 1846, it does not even have an entry for amillennial. Advocates do not approve the name. I employ the word only as a convenience to 'label' those who do not fall under the categories commonly understood as pre or post millennial.
20. William Hendriksen, *More Than Conquerors: An Interpretation of the Book of Revelation*, (Grand Rapids: Baker, 1944), p. 222.

binding the devil was begun when our Lord triumphed over him in the temptations in the wilderness.' Then, after citing and discussing a number of texts (Matt. 4:1-11; Luke 4:1-13; Luke 10:17, 18; John 12:20-32; Col. 2:15; and Rev. 12:5 ff.), he asserts that the 'binding and casting out or falling of Satan is... associated with the first coming of our Lord Jesus Christ.' He thinks that it consists of reducing Satan's power to keep the nations from the light of divine revelation and the saving gospel – almost unrestricted till Jesus came. Satan has been so bound that Christ may, in this age, draw people of every nation unto Himself.[21]

This school of amillennial theology dissociates itself completely from the postmillennial optimism which expects a kind of literal millennium in this age. It also rejects the aggressive stance of the reconstructionism or dominion theology of Rushdoony and disciples. Hendriksen makes it clear that he believes that the binding of Satan is only in certain limited respects. The imprisonment (or binding) has respect to earth and living people; the reign of saints has respect to heaven and dead believers.

The first resurrection is the 'translation of the soul from this sinful earth to God's holy heaven' at the death of the believer.[22] The second resurrection, according to Hendriksen, is the resurrection of the bodies of all people at the consummation. The 'little season' during which Satan is loosed is related to a coming time of apostasy, tribulation and the like, at the end of this age, and just before the consummation.

These confident expressions of Protestant amillennialism, skillfully articulated mid-twentieth century by O. T. Allis,[23] G. L. Murray,[24] Floyd Hamilton,[25] Wm. Hendricksen[26] and others became standard for much of evangelical Reformed and Presbyterian Christianity in America. Dr Robert Reymond of the Presbyterian Church in America later set it forth briefly in his volume of systematic theology.[27]

2. The Millennium As a Form of 'Apocalyptic Comfort'.

In a long chapter G. C. Berkouwer cautiously introduces about every serious theory of the millennium and decides among none of them. He concludes: 'So the important choice is not between interpreting the millennium as a feature of church history and interpreting it as something to be awaited at the end of history. Rather, it is the choice between *apocalyptic comfort* [emphasis added] and a strictly chronological account. Apocalyptic comfort is not spiritualization... it is a view of reality seen in eschatological perspective in the last days.'[28] Is this something like 'doxological language'? Elsewhere in his chapter Berkouwer seems to allow credence to the modified Augustinian view. At least Robert Reymond thinks so.[29]

3. The Millennium As a Figurative Expression.

The millennium is a figurative expression whereby the present age is viewed from the standpoint of how much it is enjoyed by saints in heaven, now in the disembodied intermediate state. This was B. B. Warfield's view and except that it was phrased by a noted scholar whose expositions of other Christian doctrines are justly and famously regarded as very valuable, it is doubtful it would have made much of an impression. Warfield set this forth in the last chapter of a posthumous collection entitled *Biblical Doctrines*.

4. The Millennium As an Idea of Completeness or Perfection.

The millennium is a figurative designation of the idea of completeness or perfection. William Milligan in the section on 'Revelation' in *The Expositor's Bible* promulgated this idea, adopted later by A. Plummer in a commentary on 'Revelation' in the multi-volumed *The Pulpit Commentary*. Milligan proposes the notion only as a suggestion as follows: 'The Thousand years... express no period of time.... They embody an idea, and that idea whether applied to the subjugation of Satan or to the triumph of the saints is the idea of completeness or perfection.'[30]

---

21. ibid.
22. ibid., p. 222.
23. Oswald T. Allis, *Prophecy and the Church* (Philadelphia: Presbyterian & Reformed, 1945).
24. George L. Murray, *Millennial Studies* (Grand Rapids: Baker, 1948).
25. Floyd E. Hamilton, *The Basis of Millennial Faith* (Grand Rapids: Eerdmans, 1942).
26. William Hendriksen, *More Than Conquerors: An Interpretation of the Book of Revelation*, 3rd ed. (Grand Rapids: Baker, 1944).
27. Robert Reymond, *A New Systematic Theology of the Christian Faith* (Nashville: Thomas Nelson, 1998), p. 1063.
28. G. C. Berkouwer, *The Return of Christ* (Grand Rapids: Eerdmans, 1972), p. 315.
29. ibid., p. 307. See Reymond's comment in his book, op. cit., p. 1063.
30. William Milligan, 'The Book of Revelation' in *The Expositor's Bible*, W. R. Nicoll, ed. (Grand Rapids: Eerdmans, 1943), p. 913.

5. The Preterist School of Millennial Doctrine.

The preterist school of millennial doctrine holds that the millennium refers figuratively to 'a great epoch in history' (H. B. Swete). The conquest of the devil and reign of saints refer to the long past triumph of Christianity which began with the victory of Christianity over paganism in European history and continues to the present. This has been the opinion of several contemporary scholars.

This view was advocated notably by Henry Barclay Swete in *The Apocalypse of St. John*, 2nd ed., 1907 and later, in America, by Albertus Pieters in *Studies in the Revelation of St. John* (1943, 1950), among orthodox scholars.

Most contemporary amillennialists, as pointed out earlier, draw a sharp break between chapters 19 and 20, but, like premillennialists, the advocates of the preterist form of amillennialism recognize that the first resurrection, the binding of Satan and the thousand years follow the defeat of Antichrist related in chapter 19. They (quite correctly in my opinion) do not think John started to tell his story all over again at Revelation 20:1. In respect to most of the details of the prophecy their views are similar to the postmillennial scheme. Details of interpretation are very similar to those of David Brown and B. H. Carroll, postmillennialists. In fact, except that this system finds the fulfillment of the prophecy of the binding of Satan and the first resurrection in the past, the preterist view would have to be called postmillennial.

Swete thinks that the millennium began with the breakup of the beast ('Roman world power') and the false prophet ('pagan system of priestcraft and superstition'). This is followed by a long period of 'Christian supremacy during which the faith for which the martyrs died would live and reign.' The war with Gog and Magog to follow is the recrudescence of evil at the end of the present age.[31]

> The binding of Satan is the divine restraint put upon the devil so that he was unable any longer to 'deceive the nations,' that is, to bring about a restoration of that paganism.
> The three and half years stand for the period of struggle with paganism, and the thousand years for the succeeding period of uninterrupted triumph of Christianity over it.[32]

On second thought, this may be the most satisfactory of all varieties of amillennial interpretations. It has the least inconsistency and has regard to the place of Revelation 20 in the order of events in the book of Revelation.

John Calvin, though he never wrote a commentary on Revelation, shows a definite leaning toward a preterist interpretation of Daniel's predictions of the victory of Christ over the nations. Of the dream-image of Daniel 2 he says, 'The image perished when the Roman empire was broken up.'[33] Similarly, in commenting on Daniel 7:27, he asserts that the giving of the kingdom to the people of the saints:

> was partially fulfilled when the Gospel emerged from persecution… thus Daniel or the angel does not predict here occurrences connected with the advent of Christ as Judge of the world, but with the first preaching and promulgation of the Gospel, and the celebration of the name of Christ.[34]

Then he uses something of a double-fulfillment technique (not common among current Augustinian interpreters) and applies it also to the 'final completion' of Christ's reign. He does not like it that Rabbi Abarbinel thought this 'spiritualizing' to be foolish.

6. A Different and Distinct Preterist View: 'Realized Millennialism'.

A different and distinct preterist view of the millennium has been proposed by Jay E. Adams, known for writing on many theological subjects. His modest-sized book, *The Time is at Hand*, effectively employs the long standard interpretive methods and arguments of amillennialism, with a bit of flair. He responds to several recent premillennial writers who he rightly feels have moved away from the garden varieties of premillennialism of the past several years, such as J. O. Buswell[35] and George Ladd.[36] Adams thinks my *Daniel and the Latter Days* offers a more feasible brand of premillenarian teaching. However this may be, Dr Adams has done us the favor of summarizing his own preterist (he calls it 'realized millennialism') doctrine of the millennium:

---

31. Henry Barclay Swete, *The Apocalypse of St. John. The Greek Text with Introduction, Notes and Indices,* 2nd ed. (London: Macmillan, 1907), p. 266.
32. Albertus Pieters, *Studies in the Revelation of St. John*, p. 301.
33. John Calvin, *Commentaries on the Book of the Prophet Daniel*, Vol. i, p. 167.
34. ibid., Vol. ii, p. 74.
35. J. O. Buswell, *Systematic Theology*, Vol. ii (Grand Rapids: Zondervan, 1971), pp. 424–538.
36. George Ladd, *The Blessed Hope* (Grand Rapids: Eerdmans, 1956).

1. The book of Revelation is largely fulfilled. It is written about things which would take place shortly after its writing.

2. It deals with the persecution of believers under Judaism and Rome and predicts God's judgment upon these enemies of the church. Its purpose, therefore, is to strengthen and encourage believers in time of trial. This is an important fact from the homiletic viewpoint.

3. The kingdom of God was set up in the days of the Roman empire, and through preaching the gospel, broke the latter in pieces. The kingdom is the fifth kingdom promised by Daniel.

4. The millennium, like the book of Revelation, is realized. It is coeval with the so-called church age, and coextensive with the time of the world-wide kingdom of God which has replaced the world-kingdom of Satan.

5. The kingdom is not, and never was intended to be, a golden age.... The golden age of Scripture is perfect... and... will emerge after the general judgment.

6. The 1000 years of Revelation 20 refer to the 'church age' during which the martyrs first are given the special privilege of 'living and reigning' with Christ, which all believers will enjoy during the eternal state.[37]

Dr Adams asserts of Revelation 20: 4, 6:

> That the reign of Christ and the martyrs is in heaven is the only sensible construction to place upon the passage. Nothing is said about the earth.... Then too, everywhere else in Revelation, thrones are mentioned as being in heaven. Christ too is said to be there.[38]

I have withheld extensive evaluation of these views but must comment that certainly Dr Adams ought to direct his attention to Revelation 5:9-10, wherein saints, on thrones set in heaven, surely enough, proclaim to their Lord, the Lamb: 'Worthy are you to take the scroll and to open its seals, for you were slain, and by your blood you ransomed people for God from every tribe and language and people and nation, and you have made them a kingdom and priests to our God, and they shall reign on the earth.' Perhaps Adams should look over all the evidence, not just selected passages. Adams relates that the book is essentially a transcript of lectures he gave at Covenant Theological Seminary at a time when prominent premillennial theologians (J. O. Buswell, R. Laird Harris) were leaders there. One wonders about how they reacted and what has become of premillennialism at that school in the decades since.

(A new, thoroughly erroneous preterism contends that the events the Bible associate with the Second Advent of Christ [the parousia], including resurrection and judgment, have already happened at the time of the destruction of Jerusalem in AD 70. The movement and the literature which promotes it are thoroughly exposed and answered in a recent volume published by Presbyterian & Reformed Publishing [*When Shall These Things Be? A Reformed Response to Hyper-Preterism*, ed. Keith A. Mathison (Presbyterian & Reformed Publishing, Phillipsburg, NJ, 2004)].)

7. Approaching the Apocalypse As a Whole.

Finally, over the years several thoughtful scholars have approached the Apocalypse as a whole, paying attention to the way transitions are indicated by 'I was in the Spirit,' as well as the 'after these things,' indications of shift of subject, and the many 'and I saw' or 'and I heard' suggestions of movement and continuity. One must ignore most of the chapter divisions to do this. One such is Verner Eller, who at the time he wrote was an ordained minister in the Church of the Brethren, teaching at LaVerne College (CA). He found a break in thought not at the end of Revelation 19, where the first two of the unholy trinity of beast, false prophet and dragon (devil) are put in the lake of fire, and the beast's army fed to the birds, but at the end of Revelation 20:3, with Satan in custody and under protective custody in 'the abyss.' So he observes that, now the bad actors are well in hand, the narrative turns to the good ones – dead and living. The devil is imprisoned for a thousand years; the good people, now all 'come to life,' reign for a thousand years, after which the evil people (all raised from the dead) are sentenced to the lake of fire (Rev. 20:4-15). Though I do not endorse all of Eller's exposition I think his book[39] has never received quite the

---

37. Jay E. Adams, *The Time Is At Hand* (Philadelphia: Presbyterian & Reformed, 1970), pp. 105, 106.
38. ibid., p. 90.
39. Verner Eller, *The Most Revealing Book of the Bible: Making Sense Out of the Bible* (Grand Rapids: Eerdmans, 1974).

attention it deserves. It cuts through established systems, hence it must overcome initial resistance. I understand his problem, having gone through the same myself more than once.

Premillennial Views of the Millennium.

Louis Berkhof, not an advocate of the view but a keen observer and a very competent theologian, formally described premillennialism (millennialism, chiliasm) as commonly held by chief advocates before several competing forms of the doctrine were introduced in late nineteenth century. These views are fervently held by multitudes of evangelical Christians today.

> The coming advent of Christ... is near and will be visible, personal, and glorious... preceded... by certain events such as the evangelization of all nations, the conversion of Israel, the great apostasy and great tribulation, and the revelation of the man of sin. Dark and trying times are therefore still in store for the Church, since she will have to pass through the tribulation. The second coming will be a single... event, but will be accompanied by several others bearing on the church, on Israel, and on the world. The dead saints will be raised and the living transfigured, and together they will be translated to meet the coming Lord. Antichrist and his wicked allies will be slain, and Israel... will repent, be saved, and restored to the Holy Land. Then the Kingdom of God, predicted by the prophets, will be established in a transformed world.... Gentiles will turn to God in great [numbers].... A condition of peace and righteousness will prevail.... After the expiration of the earthly rule of Christ the rest of the dead will be raised up... followed by the last judgment and the creation [or renovation] of a new heaven and a new earth.[40]

Whenever millennialism of this sort has arisen, believers, not necessarily scholars, thought that they derived it essentially from chapters 2 and 7 of Daniel and portions of chapters 8–12, Paul's Epistles to the Thessalonians, and the nineteenth and twentieth chapters of Revelation. With due allowance for normal figures of speech and the prevailing symbolism of Daniel and Revelation, they have accepted what these chapters (especially Rev. 19–20) seem to say about how this age will end.

There are other impressive reasons for a simple, non-technical literalism in interpreting these chapters, derived from what Jesus Himself and those associated with Him said about the future. Observe:

1. First, the Old Testament contains the story of the kingdom of God on earth under the conditions caused by the fall. This kingdom, as given form in a succession of patriarchs, kings, priests and prophets, is sometimes called the Mediatorial Kingdom of God. Promises of a coming Messiah (anointed King) are frequent in that story. Many passages in the prophetical books predict in detail features of a coming visible, earthly reign of Messiah, as well as the conversion and restoration of Israel.

2. John the Baptist, Jesus' forerunner, announced that the King and His reign had arrived and that the people of Israel should therefore prepare to meet Him by repentance (Matt. 3:10).

3. Jesus was the promised King. He was reserved in public acknowledgment that He was the Messianic king, but He represented His gospel as the Word of the kingdom and the Apostles as its messengers, with entrance to the kingdom variously stated as by repentance, or faith, or new birth. At that stage of history and on to the present moment the kingdom of Christ on earth has been definitely a spiritual affair – though not without important beneficial effects in every department of the lives of people and nations. The many parables of Jesus about the message of the kingdom (Matt. 13) and instructions to the corps of preachers (Matt. 10), as well as numerous passages, insure that the church, considered as professed believers in Christ (Messiah), is a present form of a spiritual kingdom of God (or of heaven). But one must ask, 'Is this kingdom wholly and forever only a spiritual affair?'

4. Quite to the contrary, nowhere in the New Testament is the promised visible earthly kingdom denied; nor was the disciples' expectation of the same reproved or denounced by Jesus. Early on, Jesus almost casually announced to His disciples, 'many [Gentiles] will come from east and west and recline at table [presumably on earth, for heaven is neither east nor west] with Abraham, Isaac, and Jacob in the kingdom of heaven' (Matt. 8:11). Jesus encouraged Peter, somewhat disconsolate over 'poor pay' in discipleship, this way: 'Verily I say unto you [plural], That ye which have followed me, in the regeneration when the Son of man shall sit in the throne of his glory, ye also shall sit upon twelve thrones, judging the twelve tribes of Israel' (Matt. 19:28 KJV).

---

40. Louis Berkhof, *Systematic Theology*, 4th ed. (Grand Rapids: Eerdmans, 1979), p. 709.

Perhaps these apparently plain references to a future reign of our Lord *on earth*, in which disciples are associated with Him, might be understood in some metaphorical, spiritual sense as applying to spiritual salvation in the present age. If so, why does Jesus add 'and [not 'that is'] shall inherit everlasting life' (Matt. 19:29 KJV)? Jesus apparently did not equate sitting on thrones with possessing eternal life. The disciples did not understand these promises as metaphors when spoken by Jesus, nor a few months later during the 'forty days,' for they asked if He would at that 'time restore again the kingdom to Israel.' Their question was quite in order. Jesus had just reiterated His previous promise that the Holy Spirit would soon be poured out upon them. They also knew that several Old Testament prophecies predicted the outpouring of the Spirit, and, coupled with Israel's repentance, would usher in the earthly Messianic kingdom, with Israel 'the head' not the 'tail' in the world (Isa. 32; 44:1-5; Ezek. 36, 37; Deut. 28:13), and with 'David... king over them' (Ezek. 37:24). A further reason was that Jesus neither modified nor rebuked their expressed hope, but rather implied that the restoration of the kingdom to Israel was for another time, and turned their thoughts away from any earthly future kingdom to the missionary program within the present spiritual kingdom of heaven (Acts 1:6-8; cf. all of Matt. 13).

5. According to the vision of John the Revelator, certain highly honored beings in heaven (the twenty-four elders) still have expectation to join in a future reign of Christ on earth. They express their hope in the opening heavenly throne scene as part of a 'new song,' which concludes: 'and you [Christ the Lamb] have made them a kingdom and priests to our God, and they shall reign on the earth' (Rev. 5:10). Their understanding of a reign of saints was all to be in the future and to take place not in heaven, as some claim, but 'on the earth.'

6. At the grand climax of the book of Revelation, the Advent of the Word of God with the armies of heaven, the beast and his armies already cast into the lake of fire, and the resurrection of believers now having occurred, it is said of these now resurrected saints, 'they will be priests of God and of Christ, and they will reign with him for a thousand years' (Rev. 20:6). If we may speak of a geography of the kingdom over which they shall reign a thousand years, it shall occupy 'the four corners of the earth' (Rev. 20:8). Of course it seems entirely proper that special mention by way of eminent honor (Rev. 20:4) should be made of the beheaded martyrs (even in heaven they now pray for vindication and deliverance, Rev. 6:9-11) who lost their lives 'for the word of God and for the witness they had borne.' *Martyr* is the Greek word for *witness* and it is for this reason the word came into language as a name for those who give up their lives because of their witness for Christ.

7. The specifically biblical-Christian understanding of the coming resurrection of believers made the idea of a future time when the risen Christ 'reigns on Mount Zion and in Jerusalem, and his glory will be before his elders [risen glorified saints]' (Isa. 24:23) seemed quite a normal thing for Christians to accept. The Fathers and the early creeds were consistent in affirming that Jesus ascended to heaven in a body of flesh and shall come again in 'the same body,' likewise that believers shall rise again in a body like His. They knew that Jesus in His resurrection body companied with His disciples in their natural bodies for forty days and it seemed to them not grotesque that such associations should occur during a coming 'regeneration' of human environment and society in a future renovated millennial world. Even heaven itself (as pointed out carefully by H. B. Swete in *The Ascended Lord*) is at the present time a place of friendly environment for the human body of Jesus, a place where, in the future, risen saints in bodies of flesh shall feel at home. All Christians, not only premillenarians, should share this expectation and usually do so unless seduced away from it.

For these reasons and quite apart form any other influences, the millennial hope of many through the ages of the church and to the present hour, seems quite justifiable. There seems to be nothing fantastic or weird about it. Admittedly some, both ancient and recent, have distorted the millennial hope in some weird ways.

Many justly honored names, some famous scholarly writers of modern times (post-Reformation), mainly before the beginning of the twentieth century, adhered (with some variation) to chiliastic views. Among them are Mede, Bengel, Gill, Auberlen, F. Delitzsch, Bernard, Godet, Hofmann, J. P. Lange (editor and writer in the famous commentary series), Stier, Van Oosterzee, Samuel Andrews, Ellicott (editor of the commentaries), Guinness, T. Zahn, W. G. Moorehead, B. W. Newton, Trench, Tregelles, Alford, Duesterdick (in Meyer's *Commentary*) and Meyer himself. Some of these are still widely read today and their views are cited in current scholarly literature.

Ideas of a future millennial reign of Christ after the Second Advent and associated matters, should stand on their own feet without distortion or support from presuppositions such as are sometimes found in some 'covenant' theology and some 'dispensational' theology today. (I put these words in quote marks because, though each system has a distinctive view of biblical history and of doctrines, each has a place for biblical covenants and periods of divine government, i.e. dispensations.) In competent hands neither is without an important handle on systematic theology though each has been overzealously championed by some to the distortion of mutually acknowledged truths. Neither outlook is by inherent necessity either contrary or favorable to the ancient millennial hope.

One matter of importance has been excluded from discussion: the precise time-relation of the resurrection and translation of believers (the so-called rapture of the church) to the coming great tribulation, for two reasons.

1. While the millennium rests on what most millenarians hold to be clear Scripture texts, the 'Rapture debate' depends on inferences from Scripture passages which primarily treat other subjects. Some supposedly direct affirmations of a pre-, post- or mid-tribulational rapture are irrelevant.

2. Though the firmness with which competing views (pre-, mid- and post-tribulational) of the coming resurrection and translation of believers is sometimes advocated suggests otherwise, the Scriptures indicate that God may have rendered this problem incapable of full solution until He gives more light. There is always danger in going beyond that which is written, especially in speculative matters and in biblical prediction. In a famous passage which we have already discussed, Paul clearly asserts that readers of his Epistles had access to knowledge on this matter which he saw fit never to commit to writing. After referring to Jesus' Second 'coming' and the 'gathering together' of saints at that time, and speaking of the revelation of the man of lawlessness, the Antichrist, Paul writes, 'Do you not remember that when I was still with you I told you these things?' (2 Thess. 2:5). The Thessalonian believers were told these things, but we have not been told — at least not fully — as they were. He adds, 'And now ye know that which restraineth... only there is one that restraineth now' (2:6, 7 ASV). True, of the people who heard Paul at Thessalonica, he could say, 'now ye know.' We, however, have our theories but do not know for certain because there is no record of what he 'told' the believers at Thessalonica. In fact, there is hardly a New Testament text which has more thoroughly mystified interpreters. Since this is true, then this seems to be how God intended and intends to let the matter rest for awhile. Does this not suggest that we should be willing to leave the matter where God left it? I say this even though, as I understand the Word of God, the great tribulation will be among precursors to the coming. As indicated many times in the course of these chapters, there is a degree of built-in, divinely-intended obscurity in most biblical, prophetic predictions, especially those delivered in the form of visions. Did not the LORD make this plain when He said to Aaron and Miriam: 'Hear my words: If there is a prophet among you, I the LORD will make myself known to him in a vision, I will speak with him in a dream. Not so with my servant Moses; he is entrusted with all my house. With him I speak mouth to mouth, clearly, and not in dark speech' (Num. 12:6-8 RSV).

15
The Future Eternal State

When God created mankind, male and female, He put them in an earthly setting. There 'God blessed them. And God said to them, "Be fruitful and multiply and fill the earth".' Further, 'The heavens are the Lord's heavens, but the earth has he given to the sons of men' (Ps. 115:16 RSV). And though the saved of every age have a 'heavenly hope,' and at present 'our citizenship is in heaven' (Phil. 3:20), it seems apparent in Scripture, in the final state, that redeemed humanity will again call earth their home. In the final vision of the Apocalypse John 'heard a loud voice from the throne saying, "Behold the dwelling place of God is with man. He will dwell with them, and they will be his people, and God himself will be with them"' (Rev. 21:3). In its present fallen state of 'bondage to corruption,' earth is no proper permanent home for God's regenerate children, so at death they 'depart and be with Christ' in heaven which 'is far better' (Phil. 1:23) – but not permanently.

The kingdom of God of which Old Testament prophets spoke, announced by John, Jesus and the Apostles, includes heaven, of course, but ultimately is to be formally and permanently established on earth also. Its final state is a new heaven and a new earth. The Old Testament prophets predicted its establishment in a world from which the disordering effects of the fall have been removed and replaced by a new cosmic order (numerous passages in Isaiah, Jeremiah, Joel, Amos). Jesus spoke of this change as a 'regeneration' (Matt. 19:28). Peter spoke of it as 'new heavens and a new earth in which righteousness dwells' (2 Peter 3:13). Peter was carrying forward Old Testament prophecy, including the two promises of the same in Isaiah 65 and 66, as also the Apocalypse elaborated in John's vision of the descent of the Lamb's wife from heaven to dwell in a new Jerusalem under a 'new heaven' upon a 'new earth' (Rev. 21:1, 2, 9, 10). These references – together with Paul's unprecedented and unrepeated declaration that our Lord will yield up this kingdom to God the Father after the last enemy, death, has been destroyed (1 Cor. 15:24-28) – will occupy our attention for the rest of this chapter and will bring this journey through the loci of systematic theology to a close.

The doctrine of the future visible reign of God in a new world, a renovated earth under a 'new heaven,' has its roots in Old Testament history and prophecy. The picture drawn in Revelation 21 and 22 of the final development of the history and fulfillment of the prophecy is, in almost every detail, connected by the author (John) to specific Old Testament texts. He does not formally base his remarks about the new heaven come down on earth to Old Testament Scripture. He simply employs the language and the symbols about the kingdom employed by prophets (chiefly Isaiah) to describe the 'new regime.'

The prophetic picture of the kingdom's future in times of Messiah, after 'the day of the LORD' has arrived, is hard to harmonize fully with itself. This is because even though the prophets predicted absolute holiness and perfect reconciliation of mankind, God and nature, they also imply that some of the imperfections of our present fallen world will persist. For example, the same Isaiah who predicts complete victory over death 'on that day' (Isa. 25:9), also seems to say that, though the length of human life will be greatly extended, sinners will be present among the people, and physical death will still occur (Isa. 65:20). A temporary reign of Christ with His people for a thousand years after the resurrection of the saved, followed by the second resurrection (and judgment) of the lost, to be succeeded by the eternal state, provides a feasible explanation. In such a case the mixed condition is millennial; the perfect one is the eternal state. Those who reject a post-Advent, temporary reign of Christ have other explanations, chiefly based on progressive revelation.[1]

George Eldon Ladd, who gave this subject as exhaustive an examination as any, declared:

> Whatever [the] historical background… we must still ask the question of its theological significance in the New Testament. Here we are shut up to inferences, for the New Testament nowhere explains the need for the temporal kingdom except to indicate that in some undisclosed way it is essential to the accomplishment of the reign of Christ (1 Cor. 15:24 ff.).[2]

I find myself now, after a long life of reflecting on the biblical materials, very reluctant to say much about the eternity to come. It seems presumptious to do so. Hence I present the relevant passages and comment as seems justified. The description of the final state in Revelation 21 and 22, of course, specifically employs only the elements in the prophecies predicting perfection.

The Final Future State Is the Kingdom of the Father.

After speaking of the order of the resurrections in 1 Corinthians 15:22-24, Paul's thought continues:

> [24]Then comes the end, when he delivers the kingdom to God the Father after destroying every rule and every authority and power. [25]For he must reign until he has put all his enemies under his feet. [26]The last enemy to be destroyed is death. [27]'For God has put all things in subjection under his feet.' But when it says, 'All things are put in subjection under him,' it is plain that he is excepted who put all things under him. [28]When all things are subjected to him, then the Son himself will also be subjected to him who put all things under him, that God may be everything to every one (1 Cor. 15:24-28 RSV).

The Son was aware, as he spoke in parting words to the disciples, that all power had been given Him in heaven and earth (Matt. 28:18), but He had yet to employ that power to clear the creation of death, 'the last enemy.' Such ultimate benefit had to await the Last Judgment when not only that unholy trinity – the beast, the false prophet and the devil (Rev. 20:7-10) – but every other unreconciled enemy has been disposed of, removed from God's world. After that, creation shall take the form originally designed in God the Father's eternal counsels, including those features which even evils, both material and moral, were designed to effect (see Eph. 1:9, 10). In that coming epoch creation will have been delivered from its present bondage to corruption into the liberty proper to it (Rom. 8:19, 20).

George E. Ladd well says in comment on Romans 8:19-23:

> The final restoration includes the very material world… While Paul does not develop this truth of the redemption of nature, there is a profound biblical theology underlying it. The redemption of the natural world from evil and decay is the corollary of the redemption of the body. The prophet constantly described the establishment of God's kingdom in terms of a redeemed world (Isa. 11:6-9; 65:17-25); and the New Testament shares the same theology.[3]

It is also apparent that the Son of God, eternally begotten of the Father, shall within the created order of things take the subordinate position which is a mark of the essential Trinity. This passage seems to suggest that the subordination of the Son to the Father is to be affirmed not only of the economic (functional) Trinity but of the essential Trinity,

---

1. It is interesting to read the debate between the amillenarian translator, George E. Day, and millenarian Gustav F. Oehler, the author of *Theology of the Old Testament* (NY: Funk & Wagnalls, 1883). I shall not repeat the debate here.
2. George Eldon Ladd, *A Theology of the New Testament* (Grand Rapids: Eerdmans, 1974, 1991), p. 631.
3. ibid., p. 567.

what the Godhead is in and of itself. The final, eternal age to come is to be the time of the Father's unmediated authority; the millennium of the Son's unveiled and manifest authority and glory; the present is the time of the 'Son's veiled reign and hidden glory.'[4]

The New Heaven and the New Earth.

The Apocalypse strikingly introduces the future eternal state in continuity ('And I saw,' Rev. 21:1 KJV) with the preceding vision of the final judgment of the wicked (Rev. 20:11-14). 'Then I saw a new heaven and a new earth; for the first heaven and the first earth had passed away, and the sea was no more' (Rev. 21:1 RSV).

Peter makes the only other New Testament reference to a new heaven and a new earth as a summation of previous remarks about 'the day of the Lord' which will come like a thief. Then 'the heavens will pass away with a roar, and the heavenly bodies will be burned up and dissolved, and the earth and the works that are done on it will be exposed' (2 Peter 3:10). Then after a warning he concludes: 'But according to his promise we are waiting for new heavens and a new earth in which righteousness dwells' (2 Peter 3:13).

Peter to a degree (2 Peter 3:13), and John overwhelmingly in the last two chapters of the Apocalypse, are both borrowing language from the prophecies of Isaiah and interpreting the same. Both 2 Peter and the Revelation are extracting ideas and language from two passages in Isaiah where that evangelic prophet spoke in a context which (if one believes in a future millennium) sounds inescapably millennial.

Both passages, Isaiah 65:17-25 and 66:18-23, should now be read to get the full flavor of the remarkable projection of the final future of our world. In the first passage the LORD promises: 'For behold, I create new heavens and a new earth, and the former things shall not be remembered nor come into mind' (Isa. 65:17). The passage proceeds to place 'Jerusalem to be a joy' in this 'new earth,' a renovated new world where no one weeps; where if one dies at 100 he will be a 'child' (long life); where a spiritual condition enables answered prayers; and where a natural environment allows even animals to be reconciled one to another (Isa. 65:18-25).

Isaiah's second reference to 'the new heavens and the new earth' (Isa. 66:22, 23) likewise compares the same to the permanent restoration of Israel:

> For as the new heavens and the new earth that I make shall remain before me, says the LORD, so shall your offspring and your name remain. From new moon to new moon, and from Sabbath to Sabbath, all flesh shall come to worship before me, declares the LORD.

This again raises the question of the millennium and its relation to the eternal state. I am among many who think the only way the many predictions of Israel's future national regeneration and restoration can find complete fulfillment is in a literal fulfillment. For this the millennium provides an appropriate time. Because I have written elsewhere at length on this subject it seems appropriate here to say little more about it.

I argue,[5] 'The closing days of the present age shall witness the restoration of Israel to the land and the conversion of the nation, to be followed in the millennium by fulfillment of the Old Testament covenant promises distinctive to that nation.' Later in the same volumes I contend, 'that as to time the new heavens and new earth anticipated by Peter and the other prophets are to appear at the beginning of the Millennium, and that in nature and extent the conflagration which introduces the new heavens and new earth shall consist of a strictly limited renovation rather than annihilation of the existing natural order.'[6]

Through the Christian centuries theologians no less than lay readers of the Bible have wrestled with the problem. It is not a problem any more severe than the predictions of 'the sufferings and the glory' of Christ were to the Old Testament prophets in interpreting their own divinely supplied oracles predicting Messiah's 'sufferings' and 'glory' (1 Peter 1:10-12). How could the same reigning Savior also be a Suffering Servant? We should take notice of the fact that the special place of Israel in the divine scheme of the future extends even into the eternal future state. For though the walls of 'the holy city Jerusalem coming down out of heaven from God' (Rev. 21:10) have 'twelve foundations, and on them were the twelve names of the twelve apostles' (Rev. 21:14) the wall itself has twelve gates, 'and on the gates the names of the twelve tribes of the sons of Israel were inscribed' (Rev. 21:12).[7]

---

4. ibid., p. 630.
5. In *Daniel and the Latter Days* (1977) and revised as *The Earthly Reign of Our Lord With His People* (1998), pp. 87–100. Same page in each ed.
6. My arguments (pp. 188–200, both eds.) follow rather closely the work of George N. H. Peters, *The Theocratice Kingdom*, three large volumes, 1854, republished 1957.
7. Chapter 9 above, 'Heaven, the Eternal Home of the Redeemed' is relevant and appropriate at this point.

Let these remarks conclude with the plain apostolic application of the message of the new creation in which we hope to dwell forever:

> But the day of the Lord will come like a thief, and then the heavens will pass away with a roar, and the heavenly bodies will be burned up and dissolved, and the earth and the works that are done on it will be exposed.
>
> Since all these things are thus to be dissolved, what sort of people ought you to be in lives of holiness and godliness, waiting for and hastening the coming of the day of God, because of which the heavens will be set on fire and dissolved, and the heavenly bodies will melt as they burn! But according to his promise we are waiting for new heavens and a new earth in which righteousness dwells (2 Peter 3:10-13).

THE END

PART 1
THEOLOGY PROPER
Introduction and Doctrine of God

PART 2
ANTHROPOLOGY
Man as Created

PART 3
HAMARTIOLOGY
Man as Sinner

PART 4
CHRISTOLOGY
Person and Work of Christ

PART 5
SOTERIOLOGY
Salvation Applied

PART 6
ECCLESIOLOGY
Church Local and Universal

PART 7
ESCHATOLOGY
Last Things, Personal and Universal

BIBLIOGRAPHY

SCRIPTURE INDEX

GENERAL INDEX

Bibliography

Abernathy, G. L. & T. A. Langford, *Philosophy of Religion: A Book of Readings*, New York: Macmillan, 1962.

ACUTE, *The Nature of Hell*, London: Evangelical Alliance Commission, 2000.

Adam, Karl, *The Christ of Faith*, New York: Mentor Omega Books, 1962.

Adam, Karl, *The Spirit of Catholicism*, New York: Doubleday Image Books, 1954 onward.

Adams, Jay E., *The Time Is At Hand*, Philadelphia, PA: Presbyterian & Reformed Publ., 1970.

Adams, J. L., *Paul Tillich's Philosophy of Culture, Science and Religion*, New York: Harper & Row, 1965.

Adeney, Walter F., *The Greek and Eastern Churches*, Clifton, NJ: Reference Book Publishers, 1965.

Aland, Kurt, *Did the Early Church Baptize Infants?*, trans. G. R. Beasley-Murray, London: SCM Press, 1963.

Albright, W. F. & C. S. Mann, *The Anchor Bible, Matthew*, Garden City, NY: Doubleday, 1981.

Alford, Henry, *The Greek Testament*, rev. text by E. F. Harrison, 4 vols., Chicago, IL: Moody Press, 1958.

Alford, Henry, *The New Testament for English Readers*, Chicago: Moody Press, n.d., repr. of the 18th ed.

Allis, Oswald T., *Prophecy and the Church*, Philadelphia, PA: Presbyterian & Reformed Publ., 1945, 1964.

Allison, C. Fitzsimons, *The Cruelty of Heresy: An Affirmation of Christian Orthodoxy*, Harrisburgh, PA: Morehouse Publishing, 1994.

Althaus, Paul, *The Theology of Martin Luther*, trans. Robert Schultz, Philadelphia: Fortress Press, 1966.

Anchor Bible Dictionary, The, 6 vols., David Noel Freedman, Editor-In-Chief, New York: Doubleday, 1992.

Andersen, Francis I. and David N. Freedman, *The Anchor Bible, Hosea*, New York: Doubleday, 1980.

Anderson, Sir Norman, *Christianity and World Religions*, Leicester, England: InterVarsity Press, 1980.

Anderson, Sir Robert, *The Silence of God*, Grand Rapids, MI: Kregel Publications, n.d.

Andrews, Samuel J., *The Life of Our Lord Upon the Earth*, rev. ed., New York: Charles Scribner's Sons, 1891.

Anselm of Canterbury, 4 vols., ed. and trans. Jasper Hopkins & Herbert Richardson, Toronto & New York: The Edwin Mellen Press, 1974-1976.

Ante-Nicene Fathers, ed. Alexander Roberts and James Donaldson, 10 vols., American ed., 1885, repr., Peabody, MA: Hendrickson Publ., 1994.

Aquinas, St Thomas, *Summa Contra Gentiles*, Book One: *God*, trans. C. Pegis; Book Two: *Creation*, trans. J. F. Anderson; Book Three: *Providence*, trans. Vernon J. Burke; Book Four: *Salvation*, C. J. O'Neil, London: Univ. of Notre Dame Press, 1975.

Aquinas, St Thomas, *Summa Theologica*, complete English ed. in 5 vols., trans. Fathers of the English Dominican Province, Westminster, Maryland: Christian Classics, 1911, 1981.

Aquinas, St Thomas, *Commentary on Saint Paul's Epistle to the Ephesians*, trans. M. L. Lamb, Albany, NY: Magi Books, 1966.

Armbruster, C. J., *The Vision of Paul Tillich*, New York: Sheed & Ward, 1967.

Arminius, James, *The Works of Arminius vol. II*, trans. James Nichols, Buffalo, NY: Derby, Miller and Orton, 1853.

Attwater, Donald, *The Catholic Encyclopaedic Dictionary*, 3rd ed., New York: Macmillan, 1961.

Augustine, Aurelius, *Confessions*, Middlesex, England: Penguin Books, 1970.

Augustine, Aurelius, *The City of God*, trans. Henry Bettenson, Introduction by David Knowles, Baltimore, MD: Penguin Books, 1972.

Augustine, Aurelius, *The Enchiridion on Faith, Hope and Love*, ed. Henry Paolucci and Analysis by Adolph Von Harack, Chicago: Henry Regnery Co., 1966.

Augustine, Aurelius, *Exposition of Certain Propositions from the Epistle to the Romans*. Publication data lost.

Augustine, Aurelius, *The Freedom of the Will*, trans. C. M. Sparrow, Charlottsville: Univ. of Virginia Press, 1947.

Aune, D. E., *Prophecy in Early Christianity & the Ancient Mediterranean World*, Grand Rapids, MI: Eerdmans, 1983.

Baillie, Donald M., *God Was in Christ: An Essay on Incarnation and Atonement*, New York: Charles Scribner's Sons, 1948.

Baillie, John, *The Idea of Revelation in Recent Thought*, New York: Columbia Univ. Press, 1956, 1958.

Baker's Dictionary of Theology, ed., Everett F. Harrison, Grand Rapids, MI: Baker Books, 1960.

Baker Encyclopedia of the Bible, 2 vols., ed. Walter A. Elwell, Grand Rapids, MI: Baker Books, 1996.

Barnhouse, Donald G., *The Invisible War*, Grand Rapids, MI: Zondervan, 1965.

Barrett, Charles K., *The Gospel According to St. John*, London: SPCK, 1962.

Barrett, Charles K., *A Commentary on the Epistles to the Romans*, New York: Harpers, 1957.

Barth, Karl, *Church Dogmatics*, 13 vols., trans. G. W. Bromiley, Edinburgh: T. & T. Clark, 1936–1975.

Barth, Marcus, *The Anchor Bible, Ephesians, vol. II*, Garden City, NY: Doubleday, 1974.

Barth, Karl, *The Teaching of the Church Regarding Baptism*, trans. E. A. Payne, London: SCM Press, 1965.

Bauer, Walter, *Orthodoxy and Heresy in Earliest Christianity*, Philadelphia, PA: Fortress Press, 1971.

Bauer, Walter, *A Greek-English Lexicon of the New Testament and Other Early Christian Literature*, trans. and adaption from the 5th ed. by W. F. Arndt and F. W. Gingrich, Chicago: U. of Chicago Press, 1957.

Bauman, Louis S., *Three Unclean Spirits Like Frogs*, Long Beach, CA: self-published, 1936.

Bavinck, Herman, *The Doctrine of God*, trans. Wm. Hendrickson, Grand Rapids, MI: Baker Books, 1951, 1983.

Baxter, Richard, *The Reformed Pastor*, Carlisle, PA: Banner of Truth Trust, 1656, 1979.

Beasley-Murray, G. R., *Baptism in the New Testament*, London: Macmillan Publ., 1963.

Behe, Michael, *Darwin's Black Box: The Biological Challenge to Evolution*, New York: Free Press, 1996.

Bengel, J. A., *Gnomon Novi Testamenti II*, 3rd Latin edition, Tübingen, 1850.

Berger, Peter L., *The Sacred Canopy: Elements of a Sociological Theory of Religion*, Garden City, NY: Doubleday, 1967.

Berkhof, Hendrikus, *The Doctrine of the Holy Spirit*, Atlanta, GA: John Knox Press, 1977.

Berkhof, Louis, *Systematic Theology*, original copyright 1939, 4th Edition, Grand Rapids, MI: Eerdmans, 1979.

Berkouwer, G. C. H., *Divine Election*, Grand Rapids, MI: Eerdmans, 1960.

Berkouwer, G. C. H., *Faith and Sanctification*, trans. John Vriend, Grand Rapids, MI: Eerdmans Publ., 1952.

Berkouwer, G. C. H., *General Revelation*, Grand Rapids, MI: Eerdmans, 1955, 1971.

Berkouwer, G. C. H., *Man: The Image of God*, Grand Rapids, MI: Eerdmans, 1962.

Berkouwer, G. C. H., *The Person of Christ*, trans. John Vriend, Grand Rapids, MI: Eerdmans, 1954.

Berkouwer, G. C. H., *The Providence of God*, trans. L. B. Smedes, Grand Rapids, MI: Eerdmans, 1972.

Berkouwer, G. C. H., *The Return of Christ*, Grand Rapids, MI: Eerdmans, 1972.

Berkouwer, G. C. H., *Studies in Dogmatics, Sin*, Vol. 5, Grand Rapids, MI: Eerdmans, 1971.

Berkouwer, G. C. H., *The Work of Christ*, trans. Cornelius Lambregtse, Grand Rapids, MI: Eerdmans, 1965.

Bernard, Thomas Dehany, *The Progress of Doctrines in the New Testament* (Bampton Lectures of 1865), Grand Rapids, MI: Zondervan, repr. n.d.

Bertocci, Peter Anthony, *Introduction to the Philosophy of Religion*, Englewood Cliffs, NJ: Prentice-Hall, 1951, 1961.

Bertocci, Peter Anthony, *The Person God Is*, London: George Allen & Unwin Ltd., 1970.

Bettenson, Henry S., *Documents of the Christian Church*, 2nd ed., New York: Oxford Press, 1963.

Biblical and Theological Studies, ed. Samuel Craig, Philadelphia, PA: Presbyterian & Reformed Publ., 1952.

Bickersteth, Edward, *Treatise on the Lord's Supper*, New York: Thomas Stanford, 1815.

Bickersteth, Edward, *The Trinity*, Grand Rapids, MI: Kregel Publ., 1965.

Bieler, Andre, *Architecture in Worship*, trans. D. & O. Elliott, Philadelphia, PA: Westminster Press, 1965.

Blaiklock, E. M., *The Seven Churches*, London: Marshall, Morgan & Scott, n.d.

Bloesch, Donald, *Essentials of Evangelical Theology*, 2 vols., San Francisco, CA: Harper & Row, 1978, 1979.

Boer, H. R., *Pentecost and Missions*, Grand Rapids, MI: Eerdmans, 1961.

Boettner, Lorraine, *The Reformed Doctrine of Predestination*, Philaelphia, PA: Presbyterian & Reformed Publ., 1968. First publised in 1932.

Boettner, Lorraine, *The Millennium*, Philadelphia, PA: Presbyterian & Reformed Publ., 1957, 1972.

Boice, James M., *Foundations of the Christian Faith*, Downers Grove, IL: InterVarsity Press, 1986.

Bonhoeffer, Dietrich, *Creation and Fall*, trans. John C. Fletcher, New York: Macmillan, 1937, 1959.

Bonhoeffer, Dietrich, *Life Together*, trans. J. W. Doberstein, London: SCM Press, 1954.

Bornkamm, Guenther, *Jesus of Nazareth*, trans. Irene and Fraser McLuskey with James M. Robinson, New York: Harper and Row, 1960.

Boston, Thomas, *Human Nature in its Fourfold State*, earliest printing, 1720, repr., London: Banner of Truth Trust, 1964.

Bourke, Vernon J., *Augustine's Quest of Wisdom*, Milwaukee, WI: Bruce Publ., 1945, 1947.

Bowker, John, *The Targums and Rabbinic Literature*, Cambridge: Cambridge Univ. Press, 1969.

Bowne, Borden P., *Theism*, Comprising the Deems Lectures for 1902, New York: American Book Co., 1902.

Boyce, James Pedigru, *Abstract of Theology*, Phillipsburg, NJ: Presbyteran & Reformed Publ., n.d. (Repr. of Philadelphia ed. by American Baptist Publication Society, 1878.)

Bray, Gerald, *The Doctrine of God*, Downers Grove, IL: InterVarsity Press, 1993.

Bridenbaugh, Carl, *Mitre and Sceptre; Transatlantic Faiths, Ideas, Personalities, and Politics*, 1689–1775. New York: Oxford University Press, 1962.

Bridges, Charles, *The Christian Ministry*, Edinburgh: Banner of Truth, 1830, 1976.

Bridges, Charles, *Exposition of Psalm CXIX*, 17th ed., New York: Robert Carter & Bros., 1861.

Bright, John, *A History of Israel*, Philadelphia, PA: Westminster Press, 1959.

Broadbent, E. H., *The Pilgrim Church*, 2nd ed., London & Edinburgh: Pickering and Ingles, 1935.

Bromiley, Geoffrey W., *The Christian Ministry*, Grand Rapids, MI: Eerdmans, 1960.

Bromiley, Geoffrey W., *Historical Theology*, Grand Rapids, MI: Eerdmans, 1978.

Bromiley, Geoffrey W., *Sacramental Teaching and Practice in the Reformation Churches*, Grand Rapids: Eerdmans, 1951.

Brown, David, *Christ's Second Coming: Will It Be Premillennial?*, New York: Carter, 1879.

Brown, Francis, S. R. Driver, Charles A. Briggs, *A Hebrew and English Lexicon of the Old Testament*, Boston, New York and Chicago: Houghton, Mifflin and Co., 1906.

Brown, Harold O. J., *Heresies*, Garden City, NY: Doubleday, 1984, 1988, repr., Peabody, MA: Hendrickson Publishers, 2000.

Brown, Raymond E., *The Anchor Bible: The Epistles of John*, Garden City, NY: Doubleday, 1982.

Brown, Raymond E., *The Anchor Bible: The Gospel According to John*, 2 vols., Garden City, NY: Doubleday, 1966, 1970.

Brown, Robert McAfee, *The Spirit of Protestantism*, London: Oxford Univ. Press, 1961.

Bruce, Alexander Balmain, *The Humiliation of Christ*, 2nd ed., New York: George H. Doran, n.d. First published in 1876 as Cunningham Lecture.

Bruce, F. F., *Biblical Exegesis in the Qumran Texts*, London: Tyndale Press, 1960.

Bruce, F. F., *Commentary on the Book of Acts*, rev., Grand Rapids, MI: Eerdmans Publ., 1988.

Bruce, F. F., *The Epistle to the Hebrews*, Grand Rapids, MI: Eerdmans, 1964.

Bruce, F. F., *Jesus and Christian Origins Outside the New Testament*, London: Hodder & Stoughton, 1974.

Brunner, Emil, *The Christian Doctrine of the Church, Faith, and the Consummation, Dogmatics*, Vol.III, trans. David Cairns, Philadelphia, PA: Westminster Press, 1962.

Brunner, Emil, *The Christian Doctrine of Creation and Redemption, Dogmatics*, Vol.II, trans. Olive Wyon, Philadelphia: Westminster Press, 1952.

Brunner, Emil, *The Christian Doctrine of God, Dogmatics I*, trans. Olive Wyon, Philadelphia: Westminster Press, 1950, 1974.

Brunner, Emil, *Eternal Hope*, trans. Harold Knight, Philadelphia, PA: Westminster Press, 1954.

Brunner, Emil, *God and Man*, trans. David Cairns, London: SCM Press, 1936.

Brunner, Emil, *The Mediator: A Study of the Central Doctrine of the Christian Faith*, trans. Olive Wyon, Philadelphia, PA: Westminster Press, 1947.

Brunner, Emil, *The Misunderstanding of the Church*, Philadelphia, PA: Westminster, 1953.

Bultmann, Rudolf, *Faith and Understanding*, London: SCM Press, 1969.

Bultmann, Rudolf, *Jesus Christ and Mythology*, London: SCM Press, 1958.

Bultmann, Rudolf, *The Presence of Eternity: History and Eschatology*, New York: Harper and Brothers, 1957.

Bultmann, Rudolf, *Theology of the New Testament*, 2 vols., London: SCM Press, 1956.

Bunyan, John, *The Pilgrims Progress*.

Burrows, Millar, *The Dead Sea Scrolls*, New York: Viking, 1955.

Burrows, Millar, *More Light on the Dead Sea Scrolls*, New York: Viking, 1958.

Bush, George, *Notes on Genesis*, Minneapolis, MN: Klock & Klock Christian Publ., 1976.

Buswell, J. Oliver, *A Systematic Theology of the Christian Religion*, 2 vols. bound into 1, Grand Rapids, MI: Zondervan, 1962, 1971.

Calvin, John, *A Harmony of the Gospels: Matthew, Mark and Luke, I*, trans. A. W. Morrison, ed. D. W. Torrance & T. F. Torrance, Grand Rapids, MI: Eerdmans, 1972.

Calvin, John, *A Harmony of the Gospels: Matthew, Mark and Luke, II*, Trans. T. H. L. Parker, ed. Torrance & Torrance, Grand Rapids, MI: Eerdmans, 1972.

Calvin, John, *A Harmony of the Gospels: Matthew, Mark and Luke, III & The Epistles of James and Jude*, trans. A. W. Morrison, ed. Torrance and Torrance, Grand Rapids, MI: Eerdmans, 1972.

Calvin, John, *Commentary on Ezekiel*, vol. ii, trans. T. Meyers, Edinburgh, 1850.

Calvin, John, *Commentary on Galatians and Ephesians*, Edinburgh: Calvin Translation Society, 1854.

Calvin, John, *Commentary on Philippians*, Grand Rapids, MI: Eerdmans, 1949.

Calvin, John, *Commentary on the Acts of the Apostles, Vol. I*, Edinburgh: Calvin Translation Society, 1844.

Calvin, John, *Commentary on the Book of the Prophet Daniel*, 2 vols., trans. Thomas Myers, repr. Grand Rapids, MI: Eerdmans, 1948.

Calvin, John, *Commentary on the Catholic Epistles*, trans. & ed. John Owen, Edinburgh: Calvin Translation Society, 1855.

Calvin, John, *Commentary on the Epistle of Paul to the Corinthians*, vol. i, trans. John Pringle, Edinburgh: Calvin Translation Society, 1848.

Calvin, John, *Commentary on the Epistle of Paul to the Romans*, trans. John Owen, Edinburgh: Calvin Translation Society, 1849.

Calvin, John, *Commentary on the Epistles to Timothy, Titus & Philemon*, Edinburgh: Calvin Translation Society, 1856.

Calvin, John, *Commentary on The Gospel According to John*, trans. Wm Pringle, Edinburgh: Calvin Translation Society, 1847.

Calvin, John, *Commentary on the Psalms I*, Edinburgh: Calvin Translation Society, 1845.

Calvin, John, *Commentary on the Psalms IV*, trans. James Anderson, Edinburgh: Calvin Translation Society, 1847.

Calvin, John, *Commentary Upon the Book of Genesis*, trans. John King, Edinburgh: Calvin Translation Society, 1847.

Calvin, John, *Institutes of the Christian Religion*, 2 vols., ed. John T. McNeil, trans. and ed. Ford L. Battles, Philadelphia: Westminster Press, 1960.

Calvin, John, *Tracts Relating to the Reformation*, trans. from the original Latin by Henry Beveridge et al, 3 vols., Edinburgh: Calvin Translation Society, 1844 onward.

Cargill, Thompson, *Political Ideas*, ed., D. Thompson, New York: Basic Books, 1966.

Carnell, Edward J., *The Case for Biblical Christianity*, Grand Rapids, MI: Eerdmans, 1967.

Carson, Alexander, *Baptism: Its Mode and Its Subjects*, Grand Rapids, MI: Baker Books, 1957.

Carson, D. A., *The Gagging of God: Christianity Confronts Pluralism*, Grand Rapids, MI: Zondervan, 1996.

Casserley, J. V. L., *Christian Community*, London: Longmans Press, 1960.

Cassuto, Umberto, *A Commentary on the Book of Genesis, Part One*, trans. Israel Abrahams, Jerusalem: Magnes Press, Hebrew Univ., 1944, 1978.

Catechism of the Catholic Church (of 1994), English trans. of the Catechism of the Catholic Church for the U.S., copyright 1994, United States Catholic Conference, Inc.–Libreria Editrice Vaticana, San Francisco: Ignatius Press, 1994.

Catholic Encyclopedia, The: An International Work of References on Constitution, Doctrine, Discipline and History of the Catholic Church, 16 vols., New York: The Encyclopedia Press, 1907–1922.

Cave, Sydney, *The Doctrine of the Person of Christ*, London: Gerald Duckworth, 1925.

Chafer, L. S., *Major Bible Themes*, Chicago, IL: The Bible Institute Colportage Association, 1927.

Chafer, Louis Sperry, *Systematic Theology*, 8 volumes, Dallas, TX: Dallas Seminary Press, 1948.

Charles, R. H., *Eschatology: The Doctrine of a Future Life in Israel, Judaism and Christianity*, New York: Schocken Books, 1963, repr. of the 2nd Edition of 1913.

Christian Hope and the Task of the Church, Report of the Advisory Commission on the Main Theme ("Christ the Hope of the World") of the Second Assembly of the World Council of Churches, 1954.

Church Teaches, The: Documents of the Church in English Translation, eds. Gerald Van Ackeren, S.J., Rockford, IL: Tan Books & Publ., 1955, 1973.

Clark, Gordon, *Reason, Religion and Revelation*, Philadelphia: Presbyterian & Reformed Publ., 1961, republished by Trinity Foundation in 1995.

Clark, Gordon, *The Biblical Doctrine of Man*, Jefferson, MD: Trinity Foundation, 1984, 2nd ed., 1992.

Clarke, William Newton, *An Outline of Christian Theology*, 8th ed., New York: Charles Scribner's Sons, 1900.

Clearwater, R. V., *The Local Church in the New Testament*, Minneapolis, MN: Central Conservative Baptist Press, 1954.

Clendenin, Daniel B., *Many Gods, Many Lords*, Grand Rapids, MI: Baker Books, 1995.

Clines, J. A., "The Image of God in Man" in *Tyndale Bulletin*, 1967.

Clouse, Robert, ed., *The Meaning of the Millennium: Four Views*, Downers Grove, IL: InterVarsity Press, 1977.

Clouse, Robert & Bonnidell Clouse, ed., *Women in Ministry: Four Views*, Downers Grove, IL: InterVarsity Press, 1989.

Clowney, E. P., *The Doctrine of the Church*, Philadelphia, PA: Presbyterian & Reformed Publ., 1969.

Cobb, John B., Jr and David Ray Griffin, *Process Theology*, Philadelphia: Westminster Press, 1976.

Collins, Adela Yarbro, *Cosmology and Eschatology in Jewish and Christian Apocalypticism*, Leiden: E. J. Brill, 1996.

Collins, John J., *The Scepter and the Star: The Messiahs of the Dead Sea Scrolls and Other Ancient Literature*, New York: Doubleday, 1995.

Collins, John J., *Apocalypticism in the Dead Sea Scrolls*, London & New York: Routledge, 1997.

Collingwood, F. I., *Man's Physical and Spiritual Nature*, New York: Rinehart & Winston, 1963.

Commentary on the Holy Scriptures, The: Critical, Doctrinal and Homiletical, 10 vols. (New Testament only), ed. John Peter Lange, trans. Philip Schaff, New York: Charles Scribner's Sons, 1870.

Commentary on the Whole Bible Including the Apocrypha, by the Bishops and Other Clergy of the Anglican Church, 13 vols., ed. F. C. Cook, London: John Murray, various dates.

Commemorative Edition of the Book of Discipline of the United Methodist Church, Nashville, TN: United Methodist Publ. House, 1984.

Concord, The Book of, The Confessions of the Evangelical Lutheran Church, trans. and ed. Theodore G. Tappert, in collaboration with Jaroslav Pelikan, Robert H. Fischer, Arthur C. Piepkorn, Philadelphia, PA: Muhlenberg Press, 1959.

Cox, L. G., *John Wesley's Concept of Perfection*, Kansas City, MO: Beacon Hill Press, 1964.

Craddock, F. B., *The Pre-existence of Christ*, Nashville, TN: Abington, 1968.

Cranfield, C. E. B., *Critical and Exegetical Commentary on the Epistle to the Romans*, ICC, Vol. 32:2, Edinburgh: T. & T. Clark, 1979.

Cullmann, Oscar, *The Earliest Christian Confessions*, trans. J. K. Reid, London: Lutterworth Press, 1949.

Cullmann, Oscar, *The Early Church*, London: SCM Press, Ltd., 1956, 1966.

Cullmann, Oscar, *The State In The New Testament*, London: SCM Press Ltd, rev. ed., 1963.

Cullmann, Oscar, Harry A. Wolfson, Werner Jaeger and Henry J. Cadbury, ed. Krister Stendahl, *Immortality and Resurrection, Death in the Western World: Two Conflicting Currents of Thought*, New York: Macmillan Co., 1965.

Culver, Douglas J., *Albion and Ariel: British Puritanism and the Birth of Political Zionism*, New York: Peter Lang, 1995.

Culver, Robert D., *A Greater Commission*, Chicago, IL: Moody Press, 1985, reissued Eugene, OR: Wipf and Stock, 2001.

Culver, Robert D., *A Wakeup Call*, Clayton, CA: Witness, Inc., 1993.

Culver, Robert D., *Civil Government, A Biblical View*, Edmonton, Alberta: Canadian Institute for Law, Theology and Public Policy, 2000.

Culver, Robert D., *Daniel and the Latter Days*, Chicago: Moody Press, 1954, 1977. Repr. under *The Earthly Reign of Our Lord With His People*, by author, 1999.

Culver, Robert D., *The Life of Christ*, Grand Rapids, MI: Baker Books, 1976. Republished as *The Earthly Career of Jesus, the Christ*, Fearn, Ross-shire, Scotland: Mentor/ Christian Focus, 2002.

Culver, Robert D., *The Peacemongers*, Wheaton, IL: Tyndale House, 1985.

Culver, Robert D., *The Sufferings and the Glory*, Moline, IL: Christian Service Foundation, 1958, republished Eugene, OR: WIPF & Stock, 2001.

Culver, Robert D., "Were the Old Testament Prophecies Really Prophetic?" in *Can I Trust My Bible*, a symposium by 8 authors, Chicago, IL: Moody Press, 1963.

Custance, Arthur C., *The Mysterious Matter of the Mind*, Grand Rapids, MI: Zondervan, 1980.

Custance, Arthur C., *The Seed of the Woman*, Brockville, Ontario: Doorway Publications, 1980.

Cyclopedia of Biblical, Theological and Ecclesiastical Literature, 12 Vols., John McClintock & James Strong, first published, 1895, repr., Grand Rapids, MI: Baker Books, 1968–1970.

Dabney, R. L., *Lectures on Systematic Theology*, Grand Rapids, MI: Zondervan, 1972, first published in 1878.

Dahood, Mitchell, *The Anchor Bible: Psalms*, 3 vols., Garden City, NY: Doubleday & Co., 1965-1970.

Dale, R. W., *Christian Doctrine*, London: Hodder & Stoughton, 1899.

Dana, Harvey E., *The Christian Ecclesia*, Nashville, TN: Sunday School Board of the Southern Baptist Convention, 1956.

Dana, Harvey E. and Julius Mantey, *A Manual Grammar of the Greek New Testament*, New York: Macmillan, 1927, 1955.

Daniel, Curt, *Biblical Calvinism: An Introduction to the Doctrine of Grace*, Springfield, IL: Reformed Bible Church, n.d.

Danielou, Jean Cardinal, *Gospel Message and Hellenistic Culture: A History of Early Christian Doctrine Before the Council of Nicea*, trans. J. A. Baker, Philadelphia, PA: Westminster Press, 1973.

Danielou, Jean Cardinal, *The Origins of Christianity*, Philadelphia, PA: Westminster Press, 1997.

Danielou, Jean Cardinal, *The Theology of Jewish Christianity: A History of Early Christian Doctrine Before the Council of Nicea*, trans. J. A. Baker, Philadelphia, PA: Westminster Press, 1964/1978.

Davidson, Francis, *Pauline Predestination*, The Tyndale New Testament Lecture, London: The Tyndale Press, 1945.

D'Costa, Gavin, ed., *Christian Uniqueness Reconsidered: The Myth of a Pluralistic Theology of Religions*, Maryknoll, NY: Orbis Books, 1990.

DeGreef, Wulfert, *The Writings of John Calvin*, trans. L. D. Bierma, Grand Rapids, MI: Eerdmans, 1993.

DeHaan, Richard W., "The Origin, Fall and Activity of Satan" in *Satan, Satanism and Witchcraft*, Grand Rapids, MI: Zondervan, 1972.

Deissman, Adolph, *Light From the Ancient East*, trans. L. R. M. Strach, London: Hodder and Stoughton, 1927.

Delitzsch, Franz, *Biblical Commentary on Job*, Vol. II Edinburgh: T and T Clark, 1871.

Delitzsch, Franz, *Biblical Commentary on the Epistle to the Hebrews*, Edinburgh: T. & T. Clark, 1887.

Delitzsch, Franz, *Biblical Commentary on the Prophecies of Isaiah*, 2 vols., Edinburgh: T. & T. Clark, 1857, 1877.

Delitzsch, Franz, *Biblical Commentary on the Psalms*, 3 vols., Edinburgh: T. & T. Clarke, 1871, 1893.

Delitzsch, Franz, *New Commentary on Genesis*, trans. Sophia Taylor, Edinburgh: T. & T. Clark, 1888.

Denney, James, *The Death of Christ*, rev. ed., London: Hodder & Stoughton, 1911.

Denney, James, *The Christian Doctrine of Reconciliation*, London: James Clarke & Co., 1959.

Denney, James, *Studies in Theology*, Grand Rapids, MI: Baker Books, 1976 (repr. of 1895 ed.).

Denton, Robert C., *A First Reader in Biblical Theology*, New York: Seabury, 1961.

Denzinger, Henry, *The Sources of Catholic Dogma*, trans. R. J. Deferrari, St Louis, MO: Herder & Herder, 1954, 1957.

DeVaux, Roland, *Ancient Israel*, trans. John McHugh, New York: McGraw-Hill, 1961 (there is a rev. newer ed.).

DeVaux, Roland, *Studies in Old Testament Sacrifice*, Cardiff: Univ. of Wales Press, 1964.

DeWolf, L. Harold, *A Theology of the Living Church*, New York: Harper & Brothers, 1953.

Dictionary of the Bible, A: Dealing With Its Language, Literature and Contents including the Biblical Theology, 5 vols., ed. James Hastings, New York: Charles Scribner & Sons, 1909.

Dimock, N., *Our High Priest: The Present Sacerdotal Function of Christ in Heaven, What it is Not and What it is*, Introduction, H. C. C. Moult, Longdon: Longmans, Green & Co., 1910.

Dix, Dom Gregory, *The Shape of the Liturgy*, London: Dacre Press, 1978 (repr. of 2nd ed. of 1945).

Dixon, Larry, *The Other Side of the Good News*, Fearn, Ross-shire, Scotland: Christian Focus, 2002.

Documents of Vatican II, The, with Notes and Comments by Catholic, Protestant and Orthodox Authorities, General Editor, Walter M. Abbott, S.J., Translation Editor, Joseph Gallagher, New York: Guilds Press, 1966.

Dodd, Charles H., *The Apostolic Preaching and Its Developments, With an Appendix on Eschatology and History*, Grand Rapids, MI: Baker Books, 1980.

Dodd, Charles H., *New Testament Studies*, Manchester, England: Manchester University Press, 1953.

Dodd, Charles H., *The Parables of the Kingdom*, Welwyn, Herts., England: James Nisbet & Co., 1935.

Donfried, K. P., ed., *The Romans Debate*, Peabody, MA: Hendrickson, 1991.

Dorner, J. A., *Divine Immutability: A Critical Reconsideration*, Minneapolis, MN: Augsburg Fortress Press, 1994.

Dorner, J. A., *History of Protestant Theology Particularly in Germany*, 2 vols., Edinburgh: T. & T. Clark, 1871.

Douty, N. F., *The Death of Christ*, Swengel, PA: Reiner, 1973.

Dunn, James D., *Unity and Diversity in the New Testament: An Inquiry into the Character of Earliest Christianity*, Philadelphia, PA: Westminster Press, 1977.

Durnbaugh, Donald F., *The Believers' Church*, New York: Macmillan, 1970.

Eckel, F. L., Jr, *A Concise Dictionary of Ecclesiastical Terms*, Boston, MA: Whittemore Assoc., 1960.

Edersheim, Alfred, *The Life and Times of Jesus the Messiah*, 2 vols., Grand Rapids, MI: Eerdmans, 1962.

Eichrodt, Walter, *Man in the Old Testament*, Chicago: Alec R. Allenson, 1951.

Eiselen, F. C., *The Minor Prophets*, New York: Eaton and Mains, 1907.

Eisenman, R. and Michael Wise, *The Dead Sea Scrolls Uncovered*, New York: Penguin, 1993.

Eller, Verner, *The Most Revealing Book of the Bible: Making Sense Out of Revelation*, Grand Rapids, MI: Eerdmans, 1974.

Ellicott, Charles John, ed., *Ellicott's Commentary on the Whole Bible*, 8 vols., Grand Rapids, MI: Zondervan, ed. of 1954.

Encylopedia Britannica, 11th ed., 28 vols, New York: The Encyclopedia Britannica Co., 1910–1911.

Erickson, Millard J., *Christian Theology*, Grand Rapids, MI: Baker Books, 1985.

Erickson, Millard J., *How Shall They Be Saved: The Destiny of Those Who Do Not Hear of Jesus*, Grand Rapids, MI: Baker Books, 1996.

Erickson, Millard J., ed., *The New Life: Readings in Christian Theology*, Grand Rapids, MI: Baker Books, 1979.

Ernest, Victor H., *I Talked With Spirits*, Wheaton, IL: Tyndale Publ., 1972.

Erskine, Ebenezer, *The Beauties of Ebenezer Erskine*, Fearn, Ross-shire, Scotland: Christian Heritage/Christian Focus, 2001.

Eusebius, *Ecclesiastical History,* trans. Isaac Boyle, Grand Rapids, MI: Baker Books, 1850, 1969.

Evangelical Dictionary of Biblical Theology, Walter A. Elwell, Grand Rapids, MI: Baker Books, 1996.

Evangelical Dictionary of Theology, ed., Walter A. Elwell, Grand Rapids, MI: Baker Books, 1984, 1991.

Exposition of the Bible (Expositors Bible), American ed., vol. vi., Hartford, CT: S. S. Scranton Co., 1907.

Fackre, Gabriel, Ronald H. Nash and John Sanders, *What About Those Who Have Never Heard*, Downer Grove, IL: InterVarsity Press, 1995.

Fairbairn, Patrick, *The Typology of Scripture*, 2 vols., 2nd ed., enlarged and improved, Philadelphia, PA: 1854.

Feinberg, John S., *No One Like Him*, Wheaton, IL: Crossway Books, 2001.

Ferre, Nels, *The Christian Understanding of God*, New York: Harper Bros., 1951.

Fichtner, John, *Theological Anthropology: The Science of Man in His Relation with God*, South Bend, IN: Univ. of Notre Dame Press, 1963.

Finegan, Jack, *Light From the Ancient Past: The Archeological Background of the Hebrew-Christian Religion*, Princeton, NJ: Princeton U. Press, 1969.

Finegan, Jack, *Myth and Mystery: An Introduction to the Pagan Religions of the Biblical World*, Grand Rapids, MI: Baker Books, 1989, 4th printing, 1993.

Finney, Charles G., *Lectures on Systematic Theology*, ed. J. H. Fairchild, South Gate, CA: Colporter Kemp, 1878, 1944.

Finney, Charles G., *Lectures on Revivals of Religion*, New York: Fleming H. Revell, n.d. reprint of 1888 edition.

Fisher, George P., *Grounds of Theistic and Christian Belief*, New York: Charles Scribner's Sons, 1888.

Fisher, George P., *History of Christian Doctrine*, 2nd ed., Edinburgh: T. & T. Clarke, 1896, 1927.

Fisk, Samuel, *Divine Sovereignty and Human Freedom*, Neptune, NJ: Loizeaux Brothers Publ., 1973.

Fiske, John, *Through Nature to God*, Boston and New York: Houghton, Mifflin & Co., 1899.

Fison, J. E., *The Christian Hope: The Presence and the Parousia*, London: Longmans, Green & Co., 1952.

Fitzmeyer, J. A., *Anchor Bible, The Gospel According to Luke I–IX*, New York: Doubleday, 1981.

Flannery, Austin, ed., *Vatican Council II*, 2 vols., Northport, NY: Costello Publ., 1996.

Flavel, John, *The Mystery of Providence*, London: Banner of Truth Trust, 1963.

Fletcher, Richard, *The Barbarian Conversion: From Paganism to Christianity*, New York: Henry Holt & Co., 1998.

Foh, Susan T., *Women and the Word of God: A Response to Biblical Feminism*, Phillipsburg, NJ: Presbyterian & Reformed Publ., 1980.

Frances, R. T., *Jesus and the Old Testament*, London: The Tyndale Press, 1971.

Froom, LeRoy Edwin, *The Prophetic Faith of the Fathers*, 4 vols., Washington D.C.: Review & Herald, 1950.

Fuller, B. A. G., *History of Philosophy*, 2 vols., rev. ed., New York: Henry Holt & Co., 1945.

Fundamentals, The, 4 vols., no ed. listed, Los Angeles: Bible Institute of Los Angeles, 1917.

Furnish, Paul, *The Anchor Bible: II Corinthians*, New York: Doubleday, 1984.

Gaer, Joseph and Ben Siegel, *The Puritan Heritage: America's Roots in the Bible*, New York: Mentor Books, 1964.

Garrett, J. L., *Systematic Theology: Biblical, Historical & Evangelical*, Vol. I, Grand Rapids, MI: Eerdmans, 1990.

Garrison, Winfred Ernest, *A Protestant Manifesto*, New York, Nashville, TN: Abington-Cokesbury, 1952.

Gaster, T. H., *The Dead Sea Scriptures*, rev. and enlarged ed., Garden City, NY: Doubleday & Co., 1964.

Gatch, Milton McC., *Death: Meaning and Mortality in Christian Thought and Contemporary Culture*, New York: Seabury Press, 1969.

Geisler, Norman, *The Battle for the Resurrection*, Nashville, TN: Thomas Nelson, 1989.

Geisler, Norman, *Chosen But Free*, Minneapolis, MN: Bethany House Publ., 1999.

Geisler, Norman, *Creating God in the Image of Man*, Minneapolis, MN: Bethany House Publ., 1997.

Geisler, Norman, *In Defense of the Resurrection*, Nashville, TN: Thomas Nelson, 1992.

Geisler, Norman, *Signs and Wonders*, Wheaton, IL: Tyndale House, 1988.

Gerstner, John, *Reasons for Faith*, New York: Harper & Brothers, 1960.

Gesenius, William, *A Hebrew and English Lexicon of the Old Testament*, trans. Edward Robinson, 26th ed., Boston, MA: Houghton, Mifflin & Co., 1891.

Gesenius' Hebrew Grammar, ed. and enlarged by E. Kautzsch, 2nd English ed., rev. by A. E. Cowley, Oxford: Clarendon Press, 1910.

Gibbon, Edward, *The Decline and Fall of the Roman Empire*, abridged by F. C. Bourne, New York: Dell Publ. Co., 1963, 1970.

Gibbs, Alfred P., *Scriptural Principles of Gathering*, Kansas City, MO: Walterick, n.d.

Gibbs, Alfred P., *Worship, The Christians Highest Occupation*, 2nd ed., Kansas City, MO: Walterick, n.d.

Gibbs, Alfred P., *The Lord's Supper*, Kansas City, MO: Walterick, 1963.

Gibson, Edgar C. S., *The Thirty-nine Articles of the Church of England*, explained with an Introduction, 8th ed., London: Methuen & Co., 1912.

Gibson, George L., *The Story of the Christian Year*, Nashville, TN: Abingdon Press, 1945.

Gilkey, Langdon, *Maker of Heaven and Earth: The Christian Doctrine of Creation in the Light of Modern Knowledge*, Garden City, NY: Doubleday & Co., 1965.

Gill, John, *Complete Body of Doctrinal and Practical Divinity*, 2 vols., first published 1795, repr., Grand Rapids, MI: Baker Books, 1978.

Gill, John, *Sermons and Tracts* in 6 vols., first published, 1814, repr., Choteau, MT: Old Paths Gospel Press, 1997.

Girdlestone, Robert B., *Synonyms of the Old Testament*, 2nd ed., Grand Rapids, MI: Eerdmans, n.d.

Glover, Robert Hall, *The Progress of World-Wide Missions*, rev. and enlarged by J. Herbert Kane, New York: Harper & Row, 1960.

Gode, F., *A Commentary on the Epistle to the Romans*, trans. T. W. Chambers, Grand Rapids, MI: Zondervan, 1956.

Godsey, J. D., *The Theology of Dietrich Bonhoeffer*, Philadelphia, PA: Westminster Press, 1960.

Gonzalez, Justo L., *A History of Christian Thought vol. I*, Nashville, TN: Abingdon Press, 1970.

Gore, Charles, *The Incarnation of the Son of God*, London: John Murray, 1891, 1903.

Graham, James, *Watchman, What of the Night?*, Los Angeles, CA: Ambassdor for Christ, n.d.

Grant, Robert M., *Gods and the One God*, Philadelphia, PA: Westminster Press, 1986.

Graves, J. B., *An Old Landmark Reset*, publisher not indicated, 1854.

Graves, J. B., *Old Landmarkism: What Is It?*, publisher not indicated, 1880.

Green, E. M. B., *The Meaning of Salvation*, London: Hodder & Stoughton, 1965.

Gregory, Caspar Rene', *Canon and Text of the New Testament*, Edinburgh: T. & T. Clark, 1907.

Grenz, Stanley, *Renewing the Center*, Grand Rapids, MI: Baker Books, 2000.

Grier, W. J., *The Momentous Event: A Discussion of Scripture Teaching on the Second Advent*, London: Banner of Truth Trust, 1970.

Griffith-Thomas, W. H., *Genesis: A Devotional Commentary*, Grand Rapids, MI: Eerdmans, 1946.

Grimm, Harold J., *The Reformation Era: 1500-1650*, 2nd ed., New York: Macmillan, 1954, 1973.

Grimm, Jacob, *Geschichte der Deutschen Sprache*, Leipzig, Germany: 1848, 3rd ed., 2 vols., 1868.

Haldane, Robert, *Exposition of the Epistle to the Romans*, New York: Robert Carter, 1847 and repr. up to 1970.

Haley, John W., *The Hereafter of Sin: What It Will Be: Answers to Certain Questions and Objections*, Andover, MA: Warren F. Draper, 1881.

Haller, William, *Liberty and Reformation in the Puritan Revolution*, New York: Columbia Univ. Press, 1955.

Hambrick-Stowe, Charles E., *The Practice of Piety: Puritan Devotional Disciplines in Seventeenth-Century New England*, Chapel Hill, NC: Univ. of NC Press for Institute of Early American History and Culture, Williamsburg, VA, 1982, 1988.

Hamilton, Floyd, *The Basis of Millennial Faith*, Grand Rapids, MI: Eerdmans, 1942.

Hamilton, Victor P., *The Book of Genesis*, Grand Rapids, MI: Eerdmans, 1990.

Hammon, N. G. L. & H. H. Scullard, Editors, *The Oxford Classical Dictionary*, 2nd ed., Oxford: Clarendon Press, 1970.

Harnack, Adolf, *What is Christianity*, New York: Harper & Rowe, repr. of 1900 English ed., 1951.

Harper Encyclopedia of Science, The, 4 vols., ed. James R. Newman, New York & Evanston: Harper & Row Publ., 1963.

Harris, Murray, *From Grave to Glory*, Grand Rapids, MI: Zondervan, 1990.

Harris, Murray, *Raised Immortal*, Grand Rapids, MI: Eerdmans, 1985.

Harris, R. Laird, *Man, God's Eternal Creation*, Chicago, IL: Moody Press, 1967.

Harrison, Norman B., *His Indwelling Presence*, Chicago, IL: Moody Press, 1928.

Hart, Julian N., *The Lost Image of Man*, America: Louisiana State Univ. Press, 1963.

Hartmann, Nicolai, *Ethics*, 3 vols., trans. Stanton Coit, New York: the Macmillan Co., 1932, 1962.

Harvey, H. *The Church: Its Polity and Ordinances*, Philadelphia, PA: American Baptist Publication Society, 1879.

Hatch, Edwin & Henry A. Redpath, *Concordance to the Septuagint and the Other Greek Versions of the Old Testament* (including the Apocryphal books), 3 vols., Graz, Austria: Akademische Druck, U. Verlagsanstalt, 1954.

Hatch, Edwin, *Organization of Early Christian Churches* (Bampton Lectures), London: Longmans, Green, and Co., 1901.

Hawkins, W. C. and W. A. Ramsay, *The House of God*, Simpson, SC: Hallmark Baptist Church, n.d.

Hawkins, W. C. and W. A. Ramsay, *The Nature of the Church On Earth*, Simpson, SC: Hallmark Baptist Church, n.d.

Hay, A. R., *The New Testament Order for Church and Missionary*, 256 Oak St., Audubon, NJ: New Testament Missionary Union n.d.

Heidelberg Catechism, The, 400th Anniversary Edition – 1563-1963, trans. Allen O. Miller and M. Eugene Osterhaven, Philadelphia and Boston, MA: United Church Press, 1963.

Heimert, Alan, *Religion and the American Mind From the Great Awakening to the Revolution*, Cambridge, MA: Harvard U. Press, 1966.

Hendriksen, William, *More Than Conquerors: An Interpretation of the Book of Revelation*, Grand Rapids, MI: Baker Books, 1944.

Hendriksen, William, *The New Testament Commentary Series*, Grand Rapids, MI: Zondervan, 1973.

Henry, Carl F. H., *Personal Idealism and Strong's Theology*, Wheaton, IL: Van Kampen, 1951.

Herberg, Will, *Protestant, Catholic, Jew*, 1955. *An Essay in American Religious Sociology*, Garden City, NY: Anchor Books, 1960.

Hick, John, *The Myth of God Incarnate*, Philadelphia, PA: Westminster Press, 1977.

Hilborn, David, Faith Forster; Tony Gray; Philip Johnson; Tony Lane; *The Nature of Hell*, Report of a Commission of the Evangelical Alliance, London, 2000.

Hirsch, E. D., *Cultural Literacy*, New York: Houghton Mifflin Co., 1988.

Hirsch, E. D., *Validity in Interpretation*, New Haven, CT: Yale Univ. Press, 1967.

Hirsch, E. D., *The Aim of Interpretation*, Chicago, IL: Univ. of Chicago Press, 1976.

Hindson, Edward, *Introduction to Puritan Theology, A Reader*, Grand Rapids, MI: Baker Books, 1976.

Hodge, A. A., *Outlines of Theology*, Grand Rapids, MI: Eerdmans, 1860, 1957.

Hodge, A. A., *The Confession of Faith*, London: Banner of Truth Trust, 1964.

Hodge, Charles A., *Systematic Theology*, 3 vols., Grand Rapids, MI: Eerdmans, repr. 1970.

Hodge, Charles A., *Commentary on the Epistle to the Romans*, rev. ed. of this work published in 1886, Grand Rapids, MI: Eerdmans, repr. 1947, 1993.

Hoeksema, Herman, *The Triple Knowledge: An Exposition of the Heidelberg Catechism*, Grand Rapids, MI: Eerdmans, Kregel, 1943.

Hooker, Richard, *Of the Laws of Ecclesiastical Polity* (8 "books" published between 1594 and 1662).

Hooykaas, R., *Religion and the Rise of Modern Science*, Grand Rapids, MI: Eerdmans, 1972.

Hope, Marvin H., *Job, The Anchor Bible*, New York: Doubleday and Co., 1965, 1980.

Hort, F. J. A., *The Christian Ecclesia: A Course of Lectures on the Early Conceptions of the Ecclesia*, London: Macmillan & Co., 1898.

Hoskyns, Edwin Clement, Sir, *The Fourth Gospel*, 2nd ed., London: Faber & Faber, 1947.

Howard, Fred D., *Interpreting the Lord's Supper*, Nashville, TN: Broadman Press, 1966.

Hoyt, Herman A., *The End Times*, Chicago, IL: Moody Press, 1969.

Hudson, Winthrop S., *Baptist Concepts of the Church*, Chicago, IL, Philadelphia, PA, Los Angeles, CA: The Judson Press, 1959.

Hunter, A. M., *The Teaching of Calvin: A Modern Interpretation*, Westwood, NJ.: Revell, 2nd ed., 1950.

Hurd, J. B., *The Tripartite Nature of Man*, Edinburgh: T & T Clark, 1868.

Huxley, Thomas H., *Man's Place in Nature*, Ann Arbor, MI: Univ. of Michigan Press, 1959.

International Standard Bible Encyclopedia, 5 vols., ed. James Orr, Grand Rapids, MI: Eerdmans, 1939, 1943.

Jaki, Stanley L., *The Origin of Science and the Science of Origins*, South Bend, IN: Regenery Gateway by arrangement with Scottish Academic Press, 1979.

Jeremias, Joachim, *The Eucharistic Words of Jesus*, New York: Macmillan, 1955.

Jeremias, Joachim, *Infant Baptism in the First Four Centuries*, London: SCM Press, 1960.

Jerome, *Jerome's Commentary on Daniel*, trans. Gleason L. Archer, Grand Rapids, MI: Baker Book House, 1958.

Jewett, Paul K., *The Lord's Day*, Grand Rapids, MI: Eerdmans, 1972.

Johnson, Phillip E., *Darwin on Trial*, Downers Grove, IL: InterVarsity Press, 2nd ed., 1993.

Josephus, Flavius, *The Life and Works of Flavius Josephus,* trans. William Whiston (*Life of Josephus, Antiquities of the Jews, Wars of the Jews*), Philadelphia, PA: John C. Winston, n.d.

Jurgens, W. A., ed. and trans., *The Faith of the Early Fathers*, 3 vols., Collegeville, MN: The Liturgical Press, 1979.

Käesemann, Ernst, *Essays On New Testament Themes*, Philadelphia, PA: Fortress Press, 1942.

Kallas, James, *Jesus and the Power of Satan*, Philadelphia: Westminster Press, 1968.

Kallas, James, *The Real Satan*, Minneapolis: Augsburg Publ., 1975.

Kane, J. Herbert, *The Progress of World-Wide Missions*, New York: Harper & Row, 1960.

Kegan, Robert, *The Evolving Self*, Cambridge, MA: Harvard Univ. Press, 1982.

Kegley, Charles and Bretall, ed., *The Theology of Paul Tillich*, New York: Charles Scribner's Sons, 1952, 1961.

Kegley, Charles, ed., *The Theology of Rudolf Bultmann*, New York: Harper & Row, 1966.

Keil, C. F., *Biblical Archaeology* (Antiquities), 2 vols., trans. Alex Cusin, Edinburgh: T & T Clark, 1888.

Keil, C. F., *Biblical Commentary on the Book of Daniel*, Grand Rapids, MI: Eerdmans Publ., 1947.

Keil, C. F., *Biblical Commentary on the Old Testament I*, Keil & Delitzsch, Edinburgh: T. & T. Clark, n.d.

Keil, C. F., *The Books of the Chronicles*, trans. Andrew Harper, Grand Rapids, MI: Eerdmans, repr. of 1875 edition.

Kelly, J. N. D., *Early Christian Doctrines*, rev. ed., New York: Harper Collins, 1978.

Kik, Jacob Marcellus, *An Eschatology of Victory*, Philadelphia, PA, Presbyterian & Reformed Publ., 1970.

Killen, R. Allan, *Ontological Theology of Paul Tillich*, Kampen: J. H. Kok, 1956.

Kimbro, Reginald C., *The Gospel According to Dispensationalism*, Toronto: Wittenberg Publications, 1995.

Klaren, M., *Religious Origins of Modern Science, Belief in Creation in Seventeenth Century Thought*, Grand Rapids, MI: Eerdmans, 1977.

Klausner, Joseph, *The Messianic Idea in Israel*, trans. W. F. Stinespring, New York: MacMillan, 1955.

Klein, Wm. W., C. L. Craig and R. L. Hubbard, Jr, *Introduction to Biblical Interpretation*, Dallas, TX: Word Publ., 1993.

Knight, Walter I., *Weird World of the Occult*, Wheaton, IL: Tyndale Publ., 1972.

Kraemer, Hendrik, *The Christian Message in a Non-Christian World*, London: Harpers, 1938.

Krauth, Charles P., *The Conservative Reformation and Its Theology* (as represented in the Augsburg Confession, and in the History and Literature of the Evangelical Lutheran Church), Philadelphia, PA: J. B. Lippincott, 1875.

Kreeft, Peter, *Heaven, The Heart's Deepest Longing*, New York: Harper & Row, 1980.

Kuemmel, W. G., *Promise and Fulfillment: The Eschatological Message of Jesus*, Naperville, IL: Alec R. Allenson, 1957.

Kuen, Alfred, *I Will Build My Church*, trans from French, Ruby Lindblad, Chicago, IL: Moody Press, 1971.

Kuhns, William, *Environmental Man*, New York: Harper & Row, 1969.

Kuiper, R. B., *Are Infants Guilty Before God*, Grand Rapids, MI: Zondervan, 1952.

Kurtz, Johann Heinrich, *Church History* 3 vols., trans. John MacPherson, New York: Funk & Wagnalls, n.d.

Kuyper, Abraham, *The Work of the Holy Spirit*, 3 vols. in 1, trans. Henri De Vries, Grand Rapids, MI: Eerdmans, 1941.

Ladd, George, *The Blessed Hope*, Grand Rapids, MI: Eerdmans, 1956.

Ladd, George E., *Crucial Questions About the Kingdom of God*, Grand Rapids, MI: Eerdmans, 1952.

Ladd, George E., *The Gospel of the Kingdom*, Grand Rapids, MI: Eerdmans, 1959.

Ladd, George E., *A Theology of the New Testament*, Grand Rapids, MI: Eerdmans, 1974, 1991.

Laetsch, Thomas, *The Minor Prophets*, St Louis, MO: Concordia Publ. House, 1956.

Lang, G. H., *The Churches of God: Their Constitution, Government and Ministries*, English trans., London: Paternoster Press, 1959.

Lang, G. H., *The Gospel of the Kingdom*, Miami Springs, FL: Schoettle Publ., 1988.

Lang, G. H., *The Revelation of Jesus Christ: Select Studies*, 2nd ed., London: Paternoster Press, 1948.

Lange, John Peter, *A Commentary on the Holy Scriptures The New Testament: Critical, Doctrinal and Homiletical*, 10 vols., trans. Philip Schaff, New York: Charles Scribner & Co., 1870.

Lange, John Peter, *A commentary on the Holy Scriptures: Critical, Doctrinal and Homiletical, The Minor Prophets*, trans. Philip Schaff, New York: Charles Scribner's Sons, 1875.

Lange, John Peter, *The Revelation of St. John*, trans. Elvina Moore, New York: 1874.

Langford, T. A., *Philosophy of Religion*, New York: Macmillan, 1962.

Latourette, Kenneth S., *A History of Christianity*, New York: Harper & Brothers, 1953.

Latourette, Kenneth S., *A History of the Expansion of Christianity*, 7 vols., Grand Rapids, MI: Zondervan Publ., 1953, 1971.

Law, Willam, *A Serious Call to a Devout and Holy Life*, repr., Grand Rapids, MI: Eerdmans, 1966.

Legters, L. L., *Union With Christ*, Philadelphia, PA: Pioneer Mission Agency, 1933.

Lenormant, Francois, *The Beginnings of History According to the Bible and the Traditions of Oriental People*, New York: Charles Scribner's Sons, 1891.

Lenski, R. C. H., *The Interpretation of St. John's Revelation*, Minneapolis, MN: Augsburg Publ., 1961.

Lenski, R. C. H., *The Interpretation of the Gospel of Luke*, Columbus, OH: 1944.

Leupold, H. C., *Exposition of Genesis*, Columbus, OH: Wartburg Press, 1942.

Lewis, C. S., *Miracles*, New York: Macmillan, 1945.

Lewis, Gordon & Bruce Demarest, *Integrative Theology*, 3 vols., Grand Rapids, MI: Zondervan, 1987, 1990 onward.

Life and Times Historical Reference Bible, The: A Chronological Journey Through the Bible, Culture and History by 13 scholars, Nashville, TN: Thomas Nelson, 1997.

Lightfoot, J. B., *The Apostolic Fathers*, New York: Macmillan, 1898.

Lightfoot, John, *A Commentary on the New Testament From the Talmud and Hebraica*, 4 vols., Oxford Univ. Press, 1859, repr., Grand Rapids, MI: Baker Books, 1979.

Lightfoot, John B., *Saint Paul's Epistle to the Philippians*, 4th ed., repr. ed., New York: Macmillan & Co., 1894.

Lind, M. C., *Biblical Foundations for Christian Worship*, Scottdale, PA: Herald Press, 1973.

Lindberg, D. C. & R. L. Numbers, *God and Nature: Historical Essays on the Encounter Between Christianity and Science*, Berkeley, CA: U. of Calif. Press, 1986.

Lindsay, G. A., *Ephesians: Exposition of the Bible (Expositors Bible)*, American ed., Hartford, CT; The S. S. Scranton Co., 1907.

Lindsay, T. M., *The Church and the Ministry in the Early Centuries*, Minneapolis, MN: James Family Publ. repr., 1977, original in early 20th century.

Lindsell, Harold, *Harper Study Bible, Revised Standard Version*, New York: Harper & Row, 1964.

Littel, Franklin, *The Free Church*, Boston, MA: Star King Press, 1957.

Liturgy of the Christian Reformed Church, Grand Rapids, MI: Eerdmans, 1941, 1976.

Livingston, J. C., *Modern Christian Thought*, New York: Macmillan, 1971.

Longenecker, Richard N., *The Christology of Early Jewish Christianity*, London: SCM Press, 1970.

Ludwigson, C. R., *A Survey of Bible Prophecy*, Grand Rapids, MI: Zondervan, 1951, 1975.

Lumpkin, William, *A History of Immersion*, Nashville, TN: Broadman Press, 1963.

Luther, Martin, *The Bondage of the Will*, trans. James I. Packer and O. R. Johnston, Grand Rapids, MI: Baker Book House, 1957/ 1994.

Luther, Martin, *Small Catechism*, St Louis, Mo.: Concordia Publ., ed. of 1943.

Luther's Works, ed. Jaroslav Pelikan and Helmut T. Lehmann, 55 vols., Philadelphia, PA: Fortress Press, 1955.

Machen, John Gresham, *Christianity and Liberalism*, Grand Rapids, MI: Eerdmans, 1923.

Machen, John Gresham, *New Testament Greek for Beginners*, New York: Macmillan, 1934.

Machen, John Gresham, *The Virgin Birth of Christ*, Grand Rapids, MI: Baker Books, 1967.

Machen, John Gresham, *What Is Faith?*, New York: Macmillan, 1925, 1927.

Mackintosh, H. R., *Immortality and the Future*, 2nd ed., London: Hodder and Stoughton, 1917.

MacLeod, David J., *The Seven Last Things: An Exposition of Revelation 19–21*, Dubuque, IA: Emmaus College Press, 2003.

MacNamara, Martin, *Targum and Testament*, Shannon, Ireland: Irish Univ. Press, 1968.

Macquarrie, John, *Principles of Christian Theology*, 2nd ed., New York: Charles Scribner's Sons, 1966, 1977.

McCall, Duke K., ed., *What is the Church?*, Nashville, TN: Broadman Press, 1958.

McClain, Alva J., *The Greatness of the Kingdom*, Grand Rapids, MI: Zondervan, 1959.

McCool, G. A., ed., *A Rahner Reader*, New York: Seabury Publ., 1975.

McDermott, Gerald R., *Can Evangelicals Learn From World Religions: Jesus, Revelation and Religious Traditions*, Downers Grove, IL: InterVarsity Press, 2000.

McDonald, A. B., *Christian Worship in the Primitive Church*, Edinburgh, 1934.

McGrath, Alister E., *Christian Theology, An Introduction*, 2nd ed., Oxford: Blackwell Publ., 1997.

McKenzie, John, *The Roman Catholic Church*, Garden City, NY: Image Books, 1971.

McNeill, J. T., *A History of the Cure of Souls*, New York: Harper & Row, 1951.

Man's Disorder and God's Design, The Amsterdam Assembly Series, (1 vol. ed. of 4 books including: I. The Universal Church in God's Design; II. The Church's Witness to God's Design; III. The Church and the Disorder of Society; IV. The Church and the International Disorder), prepared for First World Council of Churches Assembly, 1948, New York: Harper & Brothers, n.d.

Marshall, I. Howard, ed, *New Testament Interpretation*, Grand Rapids, MI: Eerdmans Publ., 1991.

Marshall, I. Howard, *The Origins of New Testament Christology*, Downers Grove, IL: InterVarsity Press, 1977.

Marshall, Peter and David Manuel, *The Light and the Glory*, Old Tappan, NJ: Fleming Revell, 1977.

Martin, Ralph P., *Worship in the Early Church*, Westwood, NJ: Fleming Revell Co., 1964.

Martin-Achard, Robert, *From Death to Life: A Study of the Doctrine of the Resurrection in the Old Testament*, trans. John P. Smith, Edinburgh: Oliver & Boyd, 1960.

Mascal, E. L., *Corpus Christi: Essays on the Church & The Eucharist*, London: Longman, Green & Co., 1953, 1957.

Mathison, Keith A., ed., *When Shall These Things Be? A Reformed Answer to Hyper-Preterism*, Phillipsburg, NJ: Presbyterian & Reformed Publishing, 2004.

Mauro, Philip, *God's Present Kingdom*, New York: Revell, 1919.

Maxwell, L. E., *Crowded to Christ*, Grand Rapids, MI: Eerdmans, 1950.

Maxwell, W. D., *An Outline of Christian Worship, Its Development and Forms*, London: Oxford Univ. Press, 1936, 1958.

Meadors, G. T., ed., *New Testament Essays*, Winona Lake, IN: Brethren Missionary Herald Books, 1991.

Meaning of Hell, The, Boston, MA: Whittemore Associates, n.d., no author's name.

Melanchthon, Philipp, *Melanchthon on Christian Doctrine, Loci Communes, 1555*, trans. Clyde L. Manschreck, Grand Rapids, MI: Baker Books, 1982.

Metzger, Bruce M., *A Textual Commentary on the Greek New Testament*, London–New York: United Bible Societies, 1975.

Meyer, Heinrich A. W., *Critical and Exegetical Commentary on the New Testament*, 11 vols., New York–London: Funk & Wagnalls, 1884.

Miceli, Vincent P., *The Antichrist*, Harrison, NY: Roman Catholic Books, 1981.

Miley, John, *Systematic Theology*, 2 vols., New York: Hunt & Eaton, 1892.

Miller, Perry, *Errand Into the Wilderness*, Cambridge, MA: Belknap Press of Harvard Univ. Press, 1956, 1964.

Milligan, William, *The Resurrection of Our Lord*, 4th ed., London: Macmillan Co., 1907.

Milligan, William, "The Book of Revelation" in *The Expositor's Bible*, ed., W. R. Nicoll, Grand Rapids, MI: Eerdmans, 1943.

Minear, Paul A., *Images of the Church in the New Testament*, Philadelphia, PA: Westminster Press, 1960.

Moberly, R. W. L., *The Old Testament of the Old Testament, Patriachal Narratives, Mosaic Yahwism*, Minneapolis: Fortress Press, 1992.

Moltmann, Juergen, *The Coming of God: Christian Eschatology*, trans. Margaret Kohl, Minneapolis, MN: Augsburg Fortress, 1996.

Monk, Robert C., *John Wesley, His Puritan Heritage*, Nashville, TN: Abingdon Press, 1966.

Montgomery, James A., *Daniel in International Critical Commentary*, New York: Charles Scribner's Sons, 1927.

Montgomery, John Warwick, *Evidence for Faith*, Dallas: Word Publ., 1991.

Moorehead, W. G., *Studies in Mosaic Institutions*, Dayton, OH: The Otterbein Publ. House, 1901.

Moody, Dale, *Christ and the Church, An Exposition of Ephesians*, Grand Rapids, MI: Eerdmans, 1963.

Morgan, Edmund, *The Puritan Dilemma*, Boston, MA: Little, Brown & Co., 1958.

Morgan, Edmund S., *The Puritan Family*, New York: Harper & Row, 1966.

Morris, Leon, *Apocalyptic*, Grand Rapids, MI: Eerdmans, 1972.

Morris, Leon, *The Apostolic Preaching of the Cross*, Grand Rapids, MI: Eerdmans, 1965.

Morris, Leon, *The Biblical Doctrine of Judgment*, London: The Tyndale Press, 1960.

Morris, Leon, *The Cross in the New Testament*, Grand Rapids, MI: Eerdmans, 1965.

Morris, Leon, *The Gospel According to John*, Grand Rapids, MI: Eerdmans, 1971.

Morrison, A. Cressy, *Man Does Not Stand Alone*, Westwood, NJ: Fleming H. Revell, 1944.

Moule, Charles F. D., *An Idiom Book of New Testament Greek*, Cambridge: Cambridge Univ. Press, 1959.

Moule, Charles F. D., *Worship in the New Testament*, Richmond, VA: John Knox Press, 1961, 1967.

Mounce, Robert H., *The New International Commentary on the New Testament, The Book of Revelation*, Grand Rapids: Eerdmans, 1977.

Mueller, John T., *Christian Dogmatics*, St Louis, Mo.: Concordia Publishing Co., 1934, 1955.

Murray, George L., *Millennial Studies*, Grand Rapids, MI: Baker Books, 1948.

Murray, John, *Collected Writings: Selected Lectures in Systematic Theology*, 4 vols., Edinburgh: Banner of Truth Trust, 1977 onward.

Murray, John, *Principles of Conduct*, Grand Rapids, MI: Eerdmans, 1957, 1971.

Murray, John, *Redemption: Accomplished and Applied*, Grand Rapids, MI: Eerdmans, 1955, 1965.

Nash, Ronald B., *Is Jesus the Only Savior?*, Grand Rapids, MI: Zondervan, 1994.

Nash, Ronald B., *Liberation Theology, A Symposium*, Milford, MI: Mott Media, 1984.

Netland, Harold A., *Dissonant Voices: Religious Pluralism and the Question of Truth*, Grand Rapids, MI: Eerdmans, 1991.

Neufeld, Vernon H., *The Earliest Christian Confessions*, ed., Bruce M. Metzger, Leiden, the Netherlands: E. J. Brill Publ., 1963.

Neuhaus, Richard John, *Freedom for Ministry*, San Francisco, CA: Harper & Row, 1984.

Neve, Jürgen L. and O. W. Heick, *A History of Christian Thought*, two vols., Philadelphia, PA: Muhlenberg Press, 1946.

Nevius, John L., *Demon Possession and Allied Themes*, Fleming H. Revell, Chicago: 1894.

New Catechism, A: Catholic Faith for Adults, Authorized Edition of the Dutch Catechism, New York: Herder & Herder, 1967.

New Testament Church Organization, Chicago, IL: Letters of Interest, n.d. (Open Plymouth Brethren).

Newbigin, Leslie, *The Gospel in a Pluralist Society*, World Council of Churches Publication, Geneva and Grand Rapids, MI: Eerdmans Publ., 1989.

Newbigin, Leslie, *The Household of God*, New York: Friendship Press, 1964.

Nicene and Post-Nicene Fathers, 1st series, 14 vols., ed. Philip Schaff, American ed., 1886, repr., Peabody, MA: Hendrickson Publ., 1994.

Nicene and Post-Nicene Fathers, 2nd series, 14 vols., ed. Philip Schaff and Henry Wace, 1890, repr., Peabody, MA: Hendrickson Publ., 1994.

Nichols, C. A., ed., *That Unknown Country: What Living Men Believe Concerning Punishment After Death Together With Recorded Views of Men of Former Times. The Whole Field Explored, Every Source of Wisdom, Past and Present, Made Tributary to the Theme: Man's Final Destiny, A Standard Book for All Time*, Springfield, MA: The C. A. Nichols Co., 1889.

Nichols, R. Hastings, *The Growth of the Christian Church*, Philadelphia, PA: Westminster Press, 1932.

Niebuhr, Reinhold, *Faith and History: A Comparison of Christian and Modern Views of History*, New York: Charles Scribner's Sons, 1949.

Niebuhr, Reinhold, *Man's Nature and His Communities: Essays on the Dynamics and Enigmas of Man's Personal and Social Existence*, New York: Charles Scribner's Sons, 1965.

Niebuhr, Reinhold, *The Nature and Destiny of Man: A Christian Interpretation;* Vol. I, *Human Nature*; Vol. II, *Human Destiny*, New York: Scribners, 1941, 1964.

Niesel, Wilhelm, *The Theology of Calvin*, trans. Harold Knight, Philadelphia, PA: Westminster Press, 1956.

Noll, Mark A. and David F. Wells, ed., *Christian Faith and Practice in the Modern World*, Grand Rapids, MI: Eerdmans, 1988.

Norbie, D. L., *New Testament Church Organization*, Chicago, IL: Letters of Interest, n.d.

Noss, John B., *Man's Religion*, 3rd ed., New York: Macmillan, 5th printing, 1974.

Nygren, Anders, *Agape and Eros*, trans. P. S. Watson, New York: Harper & Row, 1953.

Oden, Thomas, *Pastoral Theology*, San Francisco, CA: Harper & Row, 1983.

Oden, Thomas, *Systematic Theology*, 3 vols., *The Living God I, The Word of Life II, Life in the Spirit III*, San Francisco, CA: Harper Collins, 1992, 1996.

Oehler, G. F., *Theology of the Old Testament*, trans. G. E. Day, New York: Funk & Wagnalls, 1883; Grand Rapids, MI: Zondervan, n.d.

Oesterley, W. O. E. & T. H. Robinson, *Hebrew Religion, Its Origin and Development*, London: SPCK, 1930, 1944.

Okholm, Dennis L. and Timothy R. Phillips, ed., *Four Views on Salvation in a Pluralist World*, Grand Rapids, MI: Zondervan, 1996.

Orr, James, *The Christian View of God and the World* (1893), repr., Grand Rapids, MI: Eerdmans, 1947.

Orr, James, *The Progress of Dogma*, Grand Rapids, MI: Eerdmans, 1952, first published in 1901.

Orr, James, *The Virgin Birth of Christ*, New York: Charles Scribner's Sons, 1907, 1927.

Orr, W. F. and J. A. Walther, *The Anchor Bible: I Corinthians*, Garden City, NY: Doubleday & Co., 1976.

Ott, Ludwig, *Fundamentals of Catholic Dogma*, trans. L. P. Lynch, 4th ed., Rockford, IL: TAN Books and Publ., 1960, 1974.

Otto, Rudolph, *Naturalism and Religion*, trans. J. A. Thomson & Margaret R. Thomson, New York: G. P. Putnam's Sons, 1913.

Otto, Rudolph, *The Idea of the Holy*, trans. J. W. Harvey, New York: Oxford Univ. Press, reprint 1958.

Outler, Albert C., ed., T. C. Ogden & L. R. Longden, *The Wesleyan Theological Heritage*, Grand Rapids, MI: Zondervan, 1991.

Owen, H. P., *Concepts of Deity*, New York: Herder & Herder, 1971.

Owen, H. P., *Revelation and Existence: A Study in the Theology of Rudolf Bultmann*, Cardiff: University of Wales Press, 1957.

Owen, H. P., *Revelation and Existence: A Study in the Theology of Rudolf Bultman*, Cardiff, Wales: Univ. of Wales Press, 1951.

Owen, John, *The Death of Death in the Death of Christ*, Edinburgh: Banner of Truth Trust, 1959, repr. of the 17th century work.

Owen, John, *Works of John Owen*, 16 vols., London: Banner of Truth Trust, 1965, 1976.

Oxford English Dictionary, The Compact Edition, 2 vols., Oxford: Oxford Univ. Press, 1971.

Oxnam, G. Bromley, *A Testament of Faith*, Boston, MA: Little, Brown, 1958.

Oxtoby, Gurdon C., *Prediction and Fulfillment in the Bible*, Philadelphia, PA: Westminster Press, 1966.

Packer, James I., *Evangelism and the Sovereignty of God*, London: InterVarsity Press, 1961.

Packer, James I., *Knowing Man*, Westchester, IL: Cornerstone Books, 1978.

Packer, James I., *A Quest for Godliness: The Puritan Vision of the Christian Life*, Wheaton, IL: Crossway Books, 1990.

Pagolu, Augustine, *The Religion of the Patriarchs*, JSOTSS 277, Sheffield, England: Sheffield Academic Press, n.d.

Paley, William, *Natural Theology, or Evidences of the Existence and Attributes of the Diety*, Collected from the Appearances of Nature, Westmead, England: Gregg, 1970, repr. Originally published London: Printed for R. Faulden, 1802.

Pannenberg, Wolfhart, *Systematic Theology*. 3 vols., trans. G. W. Bromiley, Grand Rapids, MI: Eerdmans, 1991–1994.

Parton, D. M., *The Judgment Seat of Christ*, Minneapolis, MN: Bethany Fellowship Press, n.d.

Patai, Raphael, *The Messiah Texts: Jewish Legends of Three Thousand Years*, Detroit: Wayne State Univ. Press, 1979.

Payne, J. Barton, *The Theology of the Older Testament*, Grand Rapids, MI: Zondervan, 1962, 1976.

Pelikan, Jaroslav, *Christianity and Classical Culture*, New Haven, CT: Yale Univ. Press, 1993.

Pelikan, Jaroslav, *The Christian Tradition: A History of the Development of Doctrine*, 5 vols., Chicago: University of Chicago Press, 1971–1989.

Pelton, H. M., *A Study in Christology: The Problem of the Two Natures in the Person of Christ*, New York: Macmillan, 1922.

Perry, Lloyd and Robert D. Culver, *How to Search the Scriptures*, Grand Rapids, MI: Baker Books, 1967, 1979.

Peters, George N. H., *The Theocratic Kingdom of Our Lord Jesus, the Christ*, 3 vols., repr., Grand Rapids, MI: Kregel Publ., 1957.

Pfeiffer, Robert H., *Introduction to the Old Testament*, New York: Harper & Bros., 1941.

Philo, *The Works of Philo*, new updated ed., complete & unabridged in 1 vol., Peabody, MA: Hendrickson Publ., 1993.

Pieper, Francis, *Christian Dogmatics*, 4 vols., St. Louis: Concordia Publ., 1950–1957.

Pieters, Albertus, *Studies in the Revelation of St. John*, Grand Rapids, MI: Eerdmans, 1950.

Pike, Nelson, ed., *God and Evil*, Englewood Cliffs, NJ: Prentice Hall, 1964.

Pinnock, Clark, *A Wideness in God's Mercy: The Finality of Jesus Christ in a World of Religions*, Grand Rapids, MI: Zondervan Publ., 1992.

Pinnock, Clark, Richard Rice, John Sanders, William Hasker and David Basinger, *The Openness of God*, Downers Grove, IL: InterVarsity Press, 1994.

Piper, John and Wayne Grudem, *Recovering Biblical Manhood and Womanhood: A Response to Feminism*, Wheaton, IL: Crossway Books, 1991.

Pittinger, W. Norman, *The Christian Understanding of Human Nature*, Philadelphia, PA: Westminster Press, 1964.

Plantinga, Alvin, *The Nature of Necessity*, Oxford: Oxford Univ. Press, 1974.

Plummer, Alfred, *The Pastoral Epistles*, The Expositor's Bible, vol. VI, New York: A. C. Armstrong & Son, 1908.

Poe, Harry L. and Jimmy H. Davis, *Science and Faith: An Evangelical Dialogue*, Nashville, TN: Broadman & Holman, 2000.

Pope, Hugh, *Saint Augustine of Hippo*, Garden City, NY: Image Books, A Division of Doubleday & Co., 1961.

Pope, Hugh, *Protestant Biblical Interpretation*, 3rd rev. ed., Grand Rapis, MI: Baker Books, 1970.

Pope, Marvin H., *Job, The Anchor Bible*, New York: Doubleday & Co., 1965, 1980.

Practical Calvinist, The: An Introduction to the Presbyterian and Reformed Heritage, in Honor of D. Clair Davis, ed., Peter A. Lillback, Fearn, Ross-shire, Scotland, U.K., 2002.

Presbyterian Church of America, The Book of Church Order of, 1976 (publication data not supplied).

Presbyterian Law for the Local Church, 6th ed., rev. 1960, ed. Eugene Carson Blake. Office of the General Assembly, Division of Publications of the Board of Christian Education of the Presbyterian Church, USA.

Provair, C. D., *The Church is Israel Now*, Valecito, CA: Ross House Books, 1987.

Rahner, Karl, *Theological Investigations*, 12 vols., London: Darton, Longman & Todd, 1961, 1975; New York: Seabury Publ., 1974, 1975. These vols. were issued progressively.

Ramm, Bernard L., *The Christian View of Science and Scripture*, Grand Rapids, MI: Eerdmans, 1954.

Ramm, Bernard L., *Them He Glorified: A Systematic Study of the Doctrine of Glorification*, Grand Rapids, MI: Eerdmans, 1963.

Ramm, Bernard L., *Protestant Biblical Interpretation: A Textbook of Hermeneutics*, 3rd rev. ed., Grand Rapids, MI: Baker Books, 1970, 1990.

Ramm, Bernard L., *The Witness of the Spirit*, Grand Rapids, MI: Eerdmans, 1959.

Ramsay, William M., *The Church in the Roman Empire*, earlier ed., 1893, Grand Rapids, MI: Baker Books, 1954.

Ramsay, William M., *St. Paul the Traveler and Roman Citizen*, New York: Putmans, 1897 and many repr.

Randall, J. F., *The Theme of the Unity in John 17:20-23*, Louvain: Publications Universitaires de Louvain, 1965.

Rehwinckel, A. M., *The Voice of Conscience*, St Louis, Mo.: Concordia Publ., 1956.

Reisinger, John G., *Abraham's Four Seeds: An Examination of the Basic Presuppositions of Covenant Theology and Dispensationalism, etc.*, Frederick, MD: Sound of Grace. n.d.

Reymond, Robert L., *A New Systematic Theology of the Christian Faith*, Nashville, TN: Thomas Nelson, 1998.

Ridderbos, Herman, *The Coming of the Kingdom*, trans. H. de Jongate, Philadelphia, PA: Presbyterian & Reformed Pub. Co. 1962.

Rite of Penance, The, 4-page folder, prescribed order published by the Publication Office, U.S. Catholic Conferences, Washington, D.C., 1974, 1986.

Roberts, David E., *The Grandeur and Misery of Man*, New York: Oxford Univ. Press, 1955.

Robertson, A. T., *Harmony of the Gospels*, New York: Harper & Bros., 1950.

Robertson, J. D., *Minister's Worship Handbook*, Grand Rapids, MI: Baker Books, 1974.

Robinson, J. Armitage, *St. Paul's Epistle to the Ephesians*, London: Macmillan, 1939.

Robinson, John Arthur T., *In The End God*, London: James. n.d.

Robinson, H. Wheeler, *The Cross of the Servant*, 2nd book in the vol., *The Cross in the New Testament*, London: SCM Press, 1955, 1965.

Rouse, Ruth & S. C. Neil, *History of the Ecumenical Movement*, Philadelphia, PA: Westminster Press, 1954.

Runes, Dagobert D., *Twentieth Century Philosophy*, New York: Philosophical Library, 1943.

Rushdoony, R. J., *The Foundation of Social Order*, Philadelphia, PA: Presbyterian & Reformed Publ., 1968.

Ryle, J. C., *Old Paths*, Edinburgh: Banner of Truth Trust, 1999, repr. of 1878.

Sale-Harrison, L., *The Judgment Seat of Christ*, 4th ed., New York: 1938.

Sanders, John, *No Other Name: An Investigation Into the Destiny of the Unevangelized*, Grand Rapids: MI: Eerdmans Publ., 1992.

Sandlin, Andrew, *A Postmillennial Primer*, Valecito, CA: Chalcedon Foundation, 1997.

Saucy, Robert, *The Church in God's Program*, Chicago, IL: Moody Press, 1972.

Sauer, Erich, *From Eternity to Eternity*, Grand Rapids, MI: Eerdmans, 1954.

Schaeffer, Francis, *Baptism*, Wilmington, DE: TriMark Publ., 1976.

Schaff-Herzog, *Encyclopaedia of Religious Knowledge*, or *A Religious Encyclopaedia: or Dictionary of Biblical, Historical, Doctrinal and Practical Theology*, based on the Real-Encyclopaedia of Herzog, Plitt and Hauck, ed. Philip Schaff, 4 vols, New York: Funk & Wagnalls Co., 1891.

Schaff, Philip, *History of the Christian Church*, 8 vols, Grand Rapids, MI: Eerdmans, 1960.

Schaff, Philip, *Creeds of Christendom*, 3 vols., ed. of 1919, repr., Grand Rapids, MI: Baker Books, 1966.

Schechter, Solomon, *Aspects of Rabbinic Theology: Major Concepts of the Talmud*, New York: Schocken Books, 1961.

Schep, J. A., *The Nature of the Resurrection Body*, Grand Rapids, MI: Eerdmans, 1964.

Schilder, Klaas, *Heaven—What Is It?*, Grand Rapids, MI: Eerdmans, 1950.

Schliermacher, F. D. E., *The Christian Faith*, 2 Vols., New York: Harper & Row, 1963.

Schmidt, Wm., *The Origin and Growth of Religion, Facts and Theories*, trans. H. F. Rose, New York: Dial Press, 1935.

Schnackenburg, Rudolph, *The Gospel According to John*, 3 vols., English trans., New York: Seabury, 1979.

Schneider, Bernard N., *The World of Unseen Spirits*, Winona Lake, IN: Brethren Missionary Herald Books, 1975.

Schürer, Emil, *A History of The Jewish People in the Time of Jesus Christ*, 1st division, 2 vols., trans. John Macpherson; 2nd division, 3 vols., trans. Sophia Taylor & Peter Christie. These 5 vols. originally published at Edinburgh: T. & T. Clark, 1890. Repr., Peabody, MA: Hendrickson Publishers, 1998.

Schultz, Herman, *Old Testament Theology*, 2 vols., trans. J. A. Paterson, Edinburgh: T. & T. Clark, 1892.

Schwarz, Hanz, *On The Way to the Future*, Minneapolis, MN: Augsburg Publ., 1972.

Schweizer, Eduard, *The Lord's Supper According to the New Testament*, Philadelphia, PA: 1967.

Seiss, Joseph A., *Holy Types: The Gospel in Leviticus, A Series of Lectures on the Hebrew Ritual*, new ed., Philadelphia, PA: United Lutheran Publication House, n.d.

Seiss, Joseph A., *Lectures on The Apocalypse*, 3 vols., Philadelphia: Approved Book Stores, 1865, repr., Grand Rapids, MI: Zondervan, 1964.

Septuagint With Apocrypha: Greek and English, trans. Lancelot C. and L. Brenton, London: Samuel Bagster & Sons, 1851; Grand Rapids, MI: Zondervan repr., n.d.

Seventh-day Adventists Believe ... A Biblical Exposition of 27 Fundamental Doctrines, Hagerstown, MD: Review & Herald Publ., 3rd printing, 1989.

Shank, Robert, *A Study in the Doctrine of Perseverance*, 2nd ed., Springfield, MO: Westcott Publ., 1968.

Shank, Robert, *Elect in the Son: A Study of the Doctrine of Election*, Springfield, MO: Westcott Publ., 1970.

Shedd, Russell Phillip, *Man in Community* (A Study of St. Paul's Application of Old Testament and Early Jewish Conceptions of Human Solidarity), Grand Rapids, MI: Eerdmans Publ., 1964.

Shedd, W. G. T., *A History of Christian Doctrine*, 2 vols, New York: Scribner, Armstrong & Co., 1872; repr. Minneapolis, MN: Klock & Klock Christian Publ., 1978.

Shedd, W. G. T., *The Doctrine of Endless Punishment*, New York: Scribner's Sons, 1886.

Shedd, W. G. T., *Dogmatic Theology*, 3 vols., Grand Rapids, MI: Zondervan, 1969, repr. of 1884 ed.

Sheldon, Henry Clay, *System of Christian Doctrine*, Cincinnati & New York: Methodist Book Concern, 1903.

Shelley, Bruce, *The Church: God's People*, Wheaton, IL: Victor Books, 1978.

Silver, Abba Hillel, *Messianic Speculation in Israel*, Boston, MA: Beacon Hill Press, 1927, 1959.

Skinner, B. F., *Beyond Freedom and Dignity*, New York: Alfred A. Knopf, Bantam, 1972.

Skinner, John, *Genesis, ICC*, 2nd ed., Edinburgh: T. & T. Clark, 1910, 1950.

Smith, David, *The Days of His Flesh: The Earthly Life of Our Lord*, 8th ed., London: Hodder & Stoughton, 1910.

Smith, David L., *With Willful Intent: A Theology of Sin*, Wheaton, IL: Victor Books, 1994.

Smith, R. Payne, *Prophecy a Preparation for Christ*, Boston: Gould & Lincoln, 1870.

Smith, W. Robertson, *The Religion of the Semites*, Edinburgh: Adam & Charles Black, 1889; 3rd ed.

Smith, Wilbur Moorehead, *The Biblical Doctrine of Heaven*, Chicago, IL: Moody Press, 1968.

Smith, William, *Smith's Dictionary of the Bible*, 4 vols, rev. and ed. H. E. Hackett, New York: Hurd & Houghton, 1875.

Smith's Dictionary of Greek and Roman Biography and Mythology (3 vols.) plus vol. 4, *Greek and Roman Antiquities* and vols. 5 & 6 on *Greek and Roman Geography* by William Smith (also author-ed. of the 4th vol. *Smith's Dictionary of the Bible*), London: John Murray, 1853–1880, about 1,100 pages per vol. Amazingly complete, valuable.

Sontag, Frederick and John K. Roth, *The American Religious Experience*, The Roots, Trends, and Future of American Theology, New York, San Francisco, London: Harper & Rowe, 1972.

Spanner, Douglas, *Biblical Creation and the Theory of Evolution*, Exeter: The Paternoster Press, 1987.

Speiser, E. A. *The Anchor Bible: Genesis*, Garden City, NY: Doubleday, 1964.

Spielmann, Richard, *History of Christian Worship*, New York: Seabury Press, 1966.

Sproul, R. C., *The Cross of Christ*, Orlando, FL: Ligonier Ministries, 1989.

Spurgeon, C. H., *Metropolitan Tabernable Pulpit*, London: Banner of Truth Trust, 1965.

Spurrell, G. J., *Notes on the Hebrew Text of the Book of Genesis*, Oxford: Clarendon Press, 1887.

Stafford, T. A., *Christian Symbolism in the Evangelical Churches*, Nashville, TN: Abingdon, 1942.

Stalker, James, *The Life of Jesus Christ*, Chicago, IL: Henry A. Summer, 1881. Repr., Westwood, NJ: Fleming H. Revell, Co., 1949.

Stauffer, Ethelbert, *Jesus and His Story*, London: SCM, 1960.

Stott, John Robert W., *Evangelical Essentials: A Liberal-Evangelical Dialogue*, Downers Grove, IL: InterVarsity, 1988.

Stott, John Robert W., *What Christ Thinks of the Church*, Downers Grove, IL: InterVarsity Press, 1958.

Strack, Hermann L. and Paul Billerbeck, *Kommentar Zum Neuen Testament Aus Talmud und Midrasch*, 6 vols., München: C. H. Beck'sche Verlagsbuchhandlung, 1919.

Strauch, Alexander, *Biblical Eldership*, 2nd ed., Littleton, CO: Lewis and Roth, 1988.

Strong, A. H., *Philosophy and Religion*, New York: A. C. Armstrong & Son, 1888.

Strong, A. H., *Systematic Theology*, Old Tappan, NJ: Revell, 1907. Also Valley Forge, PA: Judson Press (many printings of the 1907 ed. are quoted in this vol.).

Sweet, William Warren, *Religion on the American Frontier*, New York: Cooper Square Publ., 1964.

Swete, H. B., *The Apocalypse of St. John*, The Greek Text with Introduction, Notes and Indices, 2nd Edition, New York: Macmillan, 1907.

Swete, H. B., *The Ascended Christ: A Study in the Earliest Christian Teaching*, London: Macmillan, 1916.

Taylor, E. L. Hebden, *The Christian Philosophy of Law, Politics and the State*, Chatley, NJ: Craig Press, 1966.

Taylor, E. L. Hebden, *Reformation or Revolution*, Chatley, NJ: Craig Press, 1970.

Taylor, Vincent, *The Person of Christ In New Testament Teaching*, London: Macmillan Co., 1958.

Tenney, Merrill C., *The Genius of the Gospels*, Grand Rapids, MI: Eerdmans, 1951.

Theological Dictionary of the New Testament, 10 vols., ed. Gerhard Kittel & Gerhard Frederich, trans. G. W. Bromiley, Grand Rapids, MI: Eerdmans, 1964-1976. Abbreviated to TDNT in this vol.

Theological Dictionary of the Old Testament, 2 vols, ed. Botterweck, G. Johannes and Helmer Ringgren, trans. John T. Willis, Grand Rapids, MI: Eerdmans, 1974, 2003.

Theological Wordbook of the Old Testament, 2 vols., R. Laird Harris, ed.; Gleason L. Archer, Jr and Bruce K. Waltke, associate ed., Chicago, IL: Moody Press, 1980. Abbreviated to TWOT in this volume.

Thielicke, Helmut, *Man in God's World*, ed. and trans. by John W. Doberstein, New York: Harper & Row, 1963.

Thiessen, H. C., *Introductory Lectures in Systematic Theology*, Grand Rapids, MI: Eerdmans, 1949, 1966.

Thistleton, Anthony, *The Two Horizons: New Testament Hermeneutics and Philosophical Designation with Special Reference to Heidegger, Bultmann and Willgenstein*, Grand Rapids, MI: Eerdmans, 1980.

Thornwell, James H., *Collected Writings*, vol. I, Edinburgh: Banner of Truth Trust, 1875, 1986.

Thurmer, John, Chancellor of Exeter Cathedral, *A Detection of the Trinity*, Exeter: The Paternoster Press, 1984.

Tillich, Paul, *Systematic Theology*, 3 vols., Chicago, IL: Univ. of Chicago Press, Vol. i 1951, Vol. ii 1957, Vol. iii 1963.

Toirac, Florent D., *A Pioneer Missionary in the Twentieth Century*, Nappanee, IN: Evangel Press, 1988.

Toon, Peter, *The Development of Doctrine in the Church*, Grand Rapids, MI: Eerdmans, 1978.

Toon, Peter, *Puritans and Calvinism*, Svengel, PA: Reiner Publications, 1973.

Toon, Peter, ed., *Puritans, The Millennium and The Future of Israel: Puritan Eschatology 1600 to 1660*, a collection of essays by 5 authors, Cambridge & London: James Clarke & Co. Ltd., 1970.

Torbet, R. G., *Baptist Concepts of the Church*, ed. W. S. Hudson, Philadelphia, PA: Judson Press, 1959.

Tregelles, S. P., *The Hope of Christ's Second Coming*, 5th ed., London: The Sovereign Grace Advent Testimony, 1986.

Tregelles, S. P., *Remarks on the Prophetic Visions in the Book of Daniel*, 7th ed., London: Sovereign Grace Advent Testimony, 1965.

Troeltsch, Ernst, *The Social Teaching of the Churches*, 2 vols., trans. O. Wyon, Introduction by Richard Niebuhr, New York: Harper & Row, 1911, 1961.

Trueman, Carl, *The Practical Calvinist: An Introduction Presbyterian and Reformed Heritage*, ed., Peter A. Lillback, Fearn, Ross-shire, Scotland: Mentor/Christian Focus, 2002.

Turretin, Francis, *The Atonement of Christ*, trans. J. R. Wilson, 1850, new ed., Grand Rapids, MI: 1978.

Turretin, Francis (1623–1687), *Institutes of Elenctic Theology* in 3 vols., trans. George M. Giger, ed. James T. Dennison, Jr, Phillipsburg, NJ: Presbyterian & Reformed Publ., 1992.

Twentieth Century Encyclopedia of Religious Knowledge, 2 vols., ed., Lefferts A. Loetscher, Grand Rapids, MI: Baker Books, 1955.

VanderKam, James C., *The Dead Sea Scrolls Today*, Grand Rapids, MI: Eerdmans, 1994.

Van Doornik, Jelsma and Van De Lisdon, *A Handbook of the Catholic Faith*, San Francisco, CA: Ignatius Press, 1994.

Van Oosterzee, Johann Jacob, *Christian Dogmatics* Vol. II, New York: Scribner, Armstrong & Co., 1874, 1878.

Vatican Council II: The Conciliar and Postconciliar Documents, 2 vols., new revised ed., General Editor, Austin Flannery, Northport, NY: Costello Publ. Co., 1975, 1996.

Venning, Ralph, *The Plague of Plagues*, London: Banner of Truth Trust, 1669, 1965.

Visser't Hooft, W. A., *No Other Name*, Philadelphia, PA: Westminster Press, 1963.

Von Balthasar, Hans Urs, *In the Fulness of the Faith: On the Centrality of the Distinctively Catholic*, trans. G. Harrison, San Francisco, CA: Ignatius Press, 1988.

Von Harnack, Karl G. A., *History of Dogma*, New York: Dover Publ., 1961.

Von Rad, Gerhard, *Genesis, A Commentary*, trans. J. H. Marks, Philadelphia, PA: Westminster Press, 1961.

Von Rad, Gerhard, *Old Testament Theology*, 2 vols, trans. D. M. G. Slatker, Edinburgh: Oliver & Boyd, 1962, 1965.

Vos, Geerhardus, *The Pauline Eschatology*, Grand Rapids, MI: Eerdmans, 1952.

Walker, Williston, *A History of the Christian Church*, New York: Charles Scribner's Sons, 1918.

Walker, Williston, *John Calvin, The Organizer of Reformed Protestantism*, New York: G. P. Putnam & Sons, 1909.

Walvoord, John M., *Jesus Christ Our Lord*, Chicago, IL: Moody Press, 1969.

Walvoord, John M., Wm. Crocket, Zachary J. Hayes and Clark H. Pinnock, *Four Views on Hell*, ed. Wm. Crockett, Grand Rapids, MI: Zondervan, 1996.

Ware, Timothy, *The Orthodox Church*, Middlesex, England: Penguin Books, 1963, 1972.

Warfield, B. B., *Biblical and Theological Studies*, Philadelphia, PA: Presbyterian & Reformed Publ., 1952.

Warfield, B. B., *The Inspiration and Authority of the Bible*, Philadelphia, PA: Presbyterian & Reformed Publ., 1958.

Warfield, B. B., *The Lord of Glory*, Grand Rapids, MI: Zondervan, n.d.

Warfield, B. B., *Perfectionism*, Philadelphia: Presbyterian & Reformed Publ., 1967.

Warfield, B. B., *The Person and Work of Christ*, Philadelphia, PA: Presbyterian & Reformed Publ., 1950.

Warfield, B. B., *The Plan of Salvation*, rev. ed., Grand Rapids, MI: Eerdmans, 1973.

Washburn, E. A. & E. Harwood, *The Two Epistles to Timothy*, trans. of J. J. Van Oosterzee in Vol. VIII of *Lange's Commentary*, New York: Charles Scribner, 1872.

Watson, Richard, *Theological Institutes*, 2 vols., 29th ed., New York: Nelson & Phillips, 1850.

Weaver, Richard, *Ideas Have Consequences*, Chicago, IL: University of Chicago Press, 1948, 1984.

Weber, Max, *The Protestant Ethic and the Spirit of Capitalism*, trans. T. Parsons, New York: Scribners, 1958.

Weinandy, Thomas G., *Does God Suffer?* Edinburgh: T. & T. Clark, 2000.

Weiss, Bernhard, *Life of Christ*, trans. J. O. Hope, 3 vols., Edinburgh: T. & T. Clark, 1883.

Wells, David F., ed., *Reformed Theology in America: A History of Its Modern Development*, Grand Rapids, MI: Baker Books, 1997.

Wells, David F., *The Person of Christ: A Biblical and Historical Analysis of the Incarnation*, Westchester, IL: Crossway Books, 1984, 1990.

Wells, Tom and Fred Zaspel, *New Covenant Theology*, 5317 Wye Creek Dr., Frederick, MD: New Covenant Media, 2002.

Wendel, Francois, *Calvin: The Origins and Development of His Religious Thought*, trans. Philip Mairet, New York: Harper & Row, 1950, 1963.

Wenham, Gordon J., *Word Biblical Commentary: Genesis 1–15*, Waco, TX: Word Books, 1987.

Westcott, Brook F., *Christus Consummator*, London: Macmillan, 1886.

Westcott, Brook F., *The Holy Bible with Commentary, New Testament*, Vol. II, *St. John – The Acts of the Apostles*, London: John Murray, 1899.

Westin, G., *The Free Church Through the Ages*, trans. V. A. Olson, Nashville, TN: Broadman Press, 1958.

Westminster Confession, The, or Confession of Faith of the Presbyterian Church in the U.S. together with *The Larger Catechism* and *The Shorter Catechism*, Richmond, VA: John Knox Press, 1861, with amendments through 1944.

Whatever Happened to the Soul: Scientific and Theological Portraits of Human Nature, 3 eds., 9 authors, Minneapolis, MN: Fortress Press, 1998.

When Shall These Things Be? A Reformed Response to Hyper-Preterism, edited by Keith A. Mathison, Phillipsburg, NJ: Presbyterian & Reformed Publ., 2004.

Whitcomb, John, *The Early Earth*, rev. ed., Grand Rapids, MI: Baker Books, 1972, 1986.

Whitcomb, John, *The World That Perished*, Grand Rapids, MI: Baker Books, 1988.

Whitcomb, John and Henry Morris, *The Genesis Flood*, Philadelphia, PA: Presbyterian & Reformed Publ., 1961.

White, A. D., *A History of the Warfare of Science with Theology in Christendom*, 2 vols., New York: Dover Pubs (1960), repub. of the first ed. "unabridged, unaltered" that appeared in 1896.

White, James F., *Protestant Worship and Church Architecture: Theological and Historical Considerations*, New York: Oxford Press, 1964.

White, James F., *New Forms of Worship*, Nashville, TN: Abingdon, 1971.

Whitehead, Alfred N., *The Concept of Nature*, Ann Arbor, MI: U. of Michigan Press, 1959, repr. of the book first published by Cambridge Univ. Press, 1920.

Whitehead, Alfred N., *Science and the Modern World*, New York: Macmillan, 1925.

Wiley, Henry O., *Christian Theology*, 3 vols., Kansas City, MO: Nazarene Publ., 1940.

Wilken, Robert, *The Myth of Christian Beginnings: History's Impact on Belief*, Garden City, NY: Doubleday & Co., 1972.

Willis, W. Waite, Jr, *Theism, Atheism and The Doctrine of the Trinity: The Trinitarian Theologies of Karl Barth and Jüergen Moltmann in Response to Protest Atheism*, Atlanta, GA: Scholars Press, 1987.

Wilson, J. A., *The Culture of Ancient Egypt*, Chicago, IL: U. of Chicago Press, Phoenix Books, 1951, 1960.

Wiseman, P. J., *New Discoveries in Babylonia About Genesis*, London: Marshall, Morgan & Scott, 1946.

Wolfson, Harry, *Immortality and Resurrection, Death in the Western World: Two Conflicting Currents of Thought*, New York: Macmillan Co., 1965.

Wray, Daniel E., *Church Discipline*, Carlisle, PA: Banner of Truth, 1978.

Wright, William, *Life and Immortality*, London: Religious Tract Society, n.d.

Wright, William K., *A History of Modern Philosophy*, New York: Macmillan, 1941.

Wycliffe Bible Commentary, ed., Charles P. Pfeiffer & Everett F. Harrison, Chicago, IL: Moody Press, 1962.

Wycliffe Bible Encyclopedia, 2 vols., ed, Charles F. Pfeiffer, Howard F. Vos and John Rea, Chicago, IL: Moody Press, 1975.

Wyngaarden, M. J., *The Future of the Kingdom in Prophecy and Fulfillment*, Grand Rapids, MI: Baker Books, 1955.

Zerwick, Max & Macy Grosvenor, *Grammatical Analysis of the Greek New Testament*, Rome: Biblical Institute Press, 1981.

Zimmerli, Walther and Joachim Jeremias, *The Servant of God*, London: SCM Press, 1941.

Zondervan Pictorial Encyclopedia of the Bible, The, 5 vols., ed., Merrill C. Tenney, Grand Rapids, MI: Zondervan, 1975. Abbreviated to ZPEB in this volume.

Zorn, R. O., *Church and Kingdom*, Philadelphia, PA: Presbyterian & Reformed Publ., 1962.

Zuck, Roy B., ed., *Vital Apologetical Issues*, Grand Rapids, MI: Kregel Publ., 1995.

PART 1
THEOLOGY PROPER
Introduction and Doctrine of God

PART 2
ANTHROPOLOGY
Man as Created

PART 3
HAMARTIOLOGY
Man as Sinner

PART 4
CHRISTOLOGY
Person and Work of Christ

PART 5
SOTERIOLOGY
Salvation Applied

PART 6
ECCLESIOLOGY
Church Local and Universal

PART 7
ESCHATOLOGY
Last Things, Personal and Universal

BIBLIOGRAPHY

SCRIPTURE INDEX

GENERAL INDEX

Scripture Index

GENESIS 173
1 .... 58, 142, 150, 155, 162, 163, 229, 231, 232, 233, 235, 240, 253, 325, 642
1–3 .... 13, 150, 229, 317
1–5 401
1:1 .... 12, 143, 144, 145, 147, 148, 149, 150, 153, 163, 231, 241, 242, 243, 325, 702, 963, 1097, 1100
1:1-2 .... 148, 288
1:1-3 .... 90, 147, 148, 149, 150, 151
1:1-25 249
1:1–2:4a 229
1:2 .... 147, 149, 150, 151, 154, 160, 163, 325, 475
1:3 .... 26, 149, 184, 243, 293
1:4a 148
1:6 293
1:9 293
1:10 191
1:14 .... 293, 1097
1:14-18 160
1:16 1097
1:20 .... 243, 293
1:21 .... 242, 243, 835
1:22 402
1:24 .... 240, 243, 293
1:26 .... 69, 110, 156, 230, 231, 241, 243, 244, 248, 249, 251, 254, 255, 287, 289, 351, 355, 642, 643
1:26-27 25
1:26-28 ...... 279, 401
1:26-29 229
1:26-30 256
1:27 .... 86, 141, 156, 231, 241, 243, 244, 248, 249, 252, 254, 255, 258, 279
1:28 .... 235, 244, 294, 299, 402, 514, 1107
1:29 .... 230, 287, 1107
1:30 230
1:31 .... 157, 161, 191, 234, 251, 276, 321
1:33 401
2 .... 31, 58, 139, 142, 229, 230, 231, 232, 233, 234, 235, 240, 253, 286, 288, 294, 295, 325, 378, 465, 642
2–3 305
2:1 .... 144, 152
2:1-3 .... 145, 159
2:1-4 141
2:2 .... 152, 192
2:2a 152
2:3 .... 94, 319, 747
2:4 231
2:4-25 .... 156, 288
2:4a 163
2:4b-25 ...... 163, 229, 231
2:5 .... 240, 244, 288
2:6 231
2:7 .... 26, 231, 233, 234, 240, 241, 242, 243, 244, 251, 252, 253, 258, 271, 272, 279, 295, 307, 317, 321, 326, 495, 514, 1021, 1076
2:8 .... 233, 284, 286, 287
2:8-15 285
2:8-17 284
2:9 .... 291, 306
2:10 287
2:10-14 284
2:11 .... 284, 285, 398
2:14 284
2:15 .... 157, 235, 286, 324
2:15-17 402
2:16 .... 298, 305, 306, 307, 309, 392, 402
2:17 .... 97, 258, 305, 306, 307, 309, 311, 317, 392, 402, 643, 1023, 1024, 1076
2:18 315
2:18 ff 307
2:18-20 233

SCRIPTURE INDEX

2:18-25......306	3:23..........288	6:6...........25, 26, 27, 103, 708
2:19..........231, 234, 295	3:24..........286, 306, 307	6:7...........26
2:21..........233, 295	3:27..........322	6:8...........27
2:21-23......234	4.............58, 234, 318, 378, 834	6:9...........49
2:21-25......157	4:1...........24, 127, 139, 244, 278, 446	6:11.........330, 375
2:22..........233, 244, 279, 295	4:1 ff.........230	6:12..........645
2:23..........279, 392, 401, 402	4:1-3.........401	6:17..........375
2:23-25......230, 235	4:1-15........13	7:2...........289
2:24..........141, 233, 240, 301, 315	4:2...........319	7:3...........289
2:25..........315	4:2-4.........288	7:6...........113
3.............31, 58, 157, 163, 178, 182, 211, 231, 286, 288, 303, 304, 305, 306, 317, 349, 369, 378, 416, 465, 658, 691, 963	4:3...........319	8:4...........284
	4:4...........317	8:21..........294, 361, 374, 645
	4:5...........319	8:22..........84, 101, 123, 194, 294, 302, 374
	4:6...........319	
	4:7...........95, 315, 319, 339, 699	9.............331
3:1............308	4:8...........319, 1023	9:1 ff.........375
3:1-5.........305, 308	4:9...........319	9:1-3.........230
3:1-6.........312	4:10..........316, 375	9:3...........288, 402, 1107
3:1-14........643	4:10-12......319	9:5...........330
3:1-15........173	4:11..........316	9:5-7.........330, 374
3:1b-3........309	4:12..........316, 416	9:6...........49, 248, 249, 253, 254, 256
3:2...........306	4:13..........95, 319, 341, 343, 345, 416	
3:3...........306		9:11..........294
3:4...........180, 309	4:14..........319, 375	9:18..........234, 244
3:5...........180, 309	4:15..........375	9:19..........234, 244, 401
3:6...........291, 305, 370	4:16..........319, 320	9:25-27......402
3:6a..........309	4:16-24......320	9:32..........401
3:6b..........309	4:17..........320	10............245
3:7...........290, 321, 643	4:19..........320	10:32.........135
3:7-10........256	4:20-22......320	11:2..........26
3:7-12........311	4:21..........158, 320	11:5..........26, 87
3:8...........643	4:22..........158, 320	12............434, 506, 784, 834
3:8 ff.........1076	4:23..........320	12–25.........14
3:8-13........308	4:24..........320	12–50.........1047
3:8–4:15....49	4:25..........244	12:1 ff........68, 726, 795
3:9...........658	4:26..........158, 319, 401	12:1-2........726
3:9-23........67	5.............378, 401, 1022	12:1-3........15, 431, 784, 835, 902, 1047
3:13..........643	5:1...........68, 244, 248, 249, 254	
3:14..........313	5:1-3.........278	12:1-4........14, 82
3:14-19......313	5:2...........68, 156, 240, 244	12:3..........428, 784, 835, 865, 1036
3:14-24......313	5:3...........395	12:3b.........1123
3:15..........305, 313, 316, 431, 585, 596, 658, 835, 1114	5:3-32........234	12:6..........14
	5:21-24......261, 262	12:7..........14, 263
3:15-19......402	5:22..........49	12:8..........14
3:16..........313, 314, 315, 403, 726	5:22-23......1061	12:17-19....346
3:16-19......163	5:24..........1031, 1048, 1061, 1118	13............434, 506
3:17..........157, 258, 314, 316, 321, 323	5:25..........1098	13:5..........1109
	5:27..........311	13:14-17....835
3:17-19......316, 1025	5:29..........314, 316	13:14-18....1047
3:17b-19a...316	6.............169, 260	13:15.........784, 1047
3:18..........288, 316, 323, 835	6–8...........330	14............14
3:19..........157, 242, 307, 317, 518, 1022, 1024, 1063, 1076	6:1-4.........174, 184	14:17-20....635
	6:3...........46, 260, 294, 1021	14:18.........56, 80
3:20..........244, 401	6:4...........174	14:18-20....434, 636
3:22..........110, 306	6:5...........263, 330, 361, 384, 643	14:19.........80, 144, 280, 487
3:22-24......307		Genesis (cont.)

1179

Genesis (cont.)
14:20 279
14:22 ....144, 487
15 ....434, 506, 835
15:1-4 745
15:1-21......835, 1047
15:6..........99, 735, 741, 742, 743,
              841, 1036
15:6b 742
15:7..........402
15:14-16 15
15:15 137
15:16 362
16 442
16:12 402
16:33 58
17:1..........56, 57, 90
17:1-8 57
17:1-21......835
17:1-21 ff ...1047
17:2..........80
17:7..........1037
17:8..........784, 1037
17:20 402
18 ....172, 442
18:1-15......835, 1047
18:1-33......26
18:2..........110, 170
18:8..........168
18:9-18......68
18:10-12 15
18:11-14 15
18:12 ....15, 57
18:12 ff......167
18:14 ....90, 126
18:16 110
18:16-33 746
18:17 68
18:18 68
18:18-21 443
18:20 375
18:23 95
18:25 ....80, 95, 106, 351, 566,
              737, 1067
18:33 ....68, 699
19 ....172, 247, 375
19:2..........110
19:3..........168
19:13 375
20:1-17......346
20:3..........30
20:6..........139, 199, 349, 373, 692
20:7..........506, 692
20:9..........346
20:11 ....30, 248, 263, 410, 1067
21:1..........15

21:2..........15
21:31 58
21:33 85
22:1..........369, 370
22:4..........604
22:11-18 ....835, 1047
22:12 451
22:16 103
23:4..........260
24:9..........57
25:1..........448
25:2..........448
25:25 450
26 ....346, 434
26:6-7 346
26:6-11......346
26:9..........346
26:10 ....263, 346
26:11 1020
26:26 746
27:27-29 ....835, 1047
28:1-4 835
28:1-11......1047
28:10-17 835
28:14 835
28:37 171
29:32-35 58
30:6..........58
30:8..........58
30:11 58
30:13 58
30:20-24 58
31:3..........835, 1047
31:13 56
31:19 55
31:24 373
31:25-35 14
31:30 55
31:32 55
32 442
32:1..........167
32:2..........167
32:22-32 692
32:24-29 ....835, 1047
34:7..........27
34:11 27
35:1-4 55
35:7..........110
35:11 ....57, 90
35:18 ....58, 272, 1021
37–45........195
37:12-27 837
37:23-28 137
37:35 1040
38 527
38:15 748

38:21 748
38:22 748
39 87
39:9..........263
40 87
41:1 ff 692
41:8..........272
41:40-44 844
42:38 1039
43:14 57
43:20 57
45:1-15......303
45:4-8 137
45:5..........195, 373, 837, 912
45:7..........195, 199
45:8..........195, 199, 837, 844
46:1-4 ....835, 1047
46:26 279
47:9..........260
48:3..........90
48:15–49:27 835, 1047
49 58
49:1..........1011
49:7-9 1011
49:10 ....431, 726, 1011
49:17 1037
49:18 ....260, 1037
49:24 27
49:25 ....56, 57
50:1..........1020
50:2..........1020
50:5-21......40
50:15-21 303
50:19 ....195, 373, 912
50:20 ....137, 195, 199, 303, 373,
              374, 837, 912
50:21 199

Exodus 542
1:38..........957
2:6............742
2:10..........745
2:16–3:1.....434
2:23..........374
3 ....207, 604
3:1-5.........95
3:1-22 54
3:1–4:17.....67
3:2............443
3:3-6.........67
3:5............747
3:6............1038
3:7............374
3:8............374
3:11..........15
3:12..........15

Scripture Index

3:13-15......450	19:16-20.....13	40............632, 752
3:13-16......449	20............235, 306, 663	40:12-15....980
3:14..........69, 84, 220	20:1-6.......375, 567	40:19.........836
3:16..........1038	20:2...........108	40:34-38....836
4:1.............15	20:4...........1097	
4:1-9..........81, 207	20:5...........392, 399, 400	**LEVITICUS**..........542, 547, 557
4:10............15	20:7............54	1–15.........344
4:11............254	20:9-11.......145	1:1.............836
4:14............15, 26	20:11.........319, 1097	2:11............557
4:24-26.......79, 182	20:12..........605	3:1.............557
4:27............15	20:15..........644	3:6.............557
4:28............15	20:17..........644	4...............342, 345
4:28-31.......81	20:56..........659	4–23...........342
5:2.............50	20:59..........659	4:1.............342
6:1-8..........54	21..............448	4:2.............272
6:2-9..........450	21:1-4.........502	4:22............342
6:3............84, 90	21:5............502	4:26............557
6:7............1037	21:6............448, 502	4:27............342
6:12............361	21:12..........198	5...............342, 345
7:3-5..........50	21:13..........198	5–7.............468
7:13............678	21:24..........312	5:17-19........409
7:17............50	21:25..........312	6:2.............822
8:15............703	21:30..........551	7...............1025
8:19............82	22:8............448	8...............632
9:16............211, 303	22:9............448	8:5 ff..........980
9:27............710	22:21-24.....375, 567	8:10............749
9:29............50	22:28..........448	8:11............749
10:1-2.........50	23:4............343	8:22-24........632
10:11..........742	23:7............735	8:30 ff........632
11:19..........723	23:14..........634	9...............632
12..............919	23:17..........634, 983	9:7.............632
12:5............521, 557	24:4-8.........551	9:23............632
12:6............464	24:8............550, 551, 752	9:24............632
12:12..........784	25..............834	10..............752, 837
12:40..........207	25:9............980	10:11...........506
12:41..........207	25:40..........963	11–15..........506
12:48..........362	28:1............631	11:44...........97, 747, 749, 759
13:2............747, 749	28:41..........506, 749	11:45...........747, 749, 759
14:17..........373	29..............632	12:2-6..........361
14:21..........195	30:17-21.....980	13:57...........742
14:30..........82	30:30..........749	14:53...........604
14:31..........15, 82	31:13..........996	15:7-33........361
15:8............1041	32..............636	16..............343, 344, 618, 632
15:17..........747	32:15..........505	16:11...........344, 637
16:22-30....235	32:18..........505	16:12...........637
17:2............369	32:31-35....505	16:12-14....633
17:8-16......400	33..............636	16:13...........637
18:1-27......434	33:11..........232	16:15...........344, 633, 637
19..............663	33:20..........45	16:15-17....637
19:1-25......15	34:5-7.........554	16:16...........344
19:3-25......663	34:6............56, 100	16:17...........344
19:4...........27	34:7............56, 566	16:21...........344
19:5...........245	34:10..........242	16:22...........344
19:6...........752	34:30..........753	16:29...........344
19:9-19......68	36:26..........723	17..............1025
19:10.........980	39:36..........549	

Leviticus (cont.)

1181

Levticus (cont.)
17–26........94
17:7..........184
18 375
18:22-30 375
18:24-30 567
19 1025
19:2..........749, 752
19:3..........996
19:15 120
19:17 959
19:20 551
19:30 996
19:31 188
19:32 753
20 1025
20:2..........957
20:7..........658, 749, 752
21:10 635
21:18 753
22 345
22:18-20 557
22:21 557
23:26-32 344
23:38 996
24:5 904
24:11-23 788
24:16 957
24:20 312
25:24 551
25:26 551
25:44 1015
25:51 551
25:52 551
26:2 996
26:33 1015
26:38 1015
26:45 1015
27 753
27:14 749
27:16 ....749, 753
27:21 753
27:28 96

Numbers 542, 547
1:44..........904
3:12..........551
3:46..........551
3:48..........551
3:49..........551
3:51..........551
5 344
5:8 647
5:31 344
6:1-21 342
6:7 342
6:9 342
6:10..........843
6:11..........342
6:23-26......506
7:3 904
7:84..........904
8:5-8..........980
12:1..........246
12:6..........1108, 1152
12:6-8 284
14:18 ....554, 566
14:26 299
14:29 ....197, 692
15:22-41 409
15:27 557
16:1-30......241
16:1-50......241
16:17 345
16:22 ....272, 277
16:28-30 241
16:29 1024
16:41-50 636
17:1-22......595
18:22 366
20:10-12 409
22:28 308
22:34 710
23:5 1040
23:10 ....1037, 1040
23:19 133
24 207
24–29........345
24:14 1011
27:3 1024
27:14 409
27:18 843
28:2 928
31:53 345
33:52 249
35:25 635
35:31-33 ....375, 567

Deuteronomy
1:17..........120, 448
1:20-24......1026
2:12..........135
2:14..........342
3:24..........90
4:5 80
4:8-13 68
4:10..........816
4:12..........249
4:30..........1011
4:33-35......51
4:34..........370
4:35..........80
4:36..........620
4:39..........65, 75
5:6 962
5:7 962
5:9 347
5:23-27......13
5:26..........71
6:4 ....13, 80, 81, 108, 110, 297
6:4-9..........962
6:5 ....108, 297
6:13..........141
6:16..........141, 284
7:6 245
7:7 127
7:8 51
7:9 51
7:9-11 101
7:19..........370
7:26..........753
8:2 199
8:3 141
8:7 285
9:10..........816
9:19..........817
10:12-22 692
10:14 1097
10:15 ....245, 692
10:16 ....361, 692
10:17 1073
10:20 141
11:12 27
12:5 620
12:10 342
12:11 620
12:21 620
13 ....82, 206, 207, 841
13:1 ff 16, 506
13:1-18......16
13:2 ff 208
13:10 957
14:22 285
16:3..........557
16:4..........557
16:16 983
18 206
18:9-14......80, 180, 189, 376
18:9-18......15
18:9-22......82, 207, 506, 841
18:11 ....259, 1036
18:12 189
18:15 ....16, 506
18:15-22 506
18:16 ....13, 68
18:18 ....16, 508
18:20 16
18:21 ....15, 16

18:22 ....15, 16	32:30 ....54, 55	**RUTH** 647
19:6 647	32:31 55	2:3 198
19:12 647	32:36 54	2:12 27
19:15 959	32:37-39 55	3:13 647
19:17 448	32:39 1048	4:4 ff 647
19:18-19 959	32:43 ....835, 865, 902	
19:20 26	32:48-50 197	**1 SAMUEL**
19:21 312	33:2 108	1:3 ....74, 983
19:45 198	33:10 506	1:9 ....836, 1098
21:1-9 ....375, 567	33:27 ....85, 108, 123, 193	1:21 983
21:5 506	34:6 172	2:6 ....1029, 1039, 1048
21:23 532	34:7 317	2:12 138
22:25 366	35:3 1037	2:25 ....138, 678
22:26 366	35:29 1037	3:2-4 151
23:4 ff 362		4:4 1098
23:13 430	**JOSHUA**	4:17 138
23:14 54	3:10 71	5:1-3 77
23:17 ....747, 748	3:11-17 71	6:5 249
24 392	3:17 1015	6:11 249
24:14 567	4:1 1015	7:5 636
24:14-15 375	4:23 51	8:1-5 409
24:15 567	4:24 51	9:9 1108
24:16 ....392, 400	5 171	9:15 506
25:1 735	5:6 1015	10:1 506
25:4 231	5:8 1015	12:19 636
25:15 605	5:13-15 167	12:23 ....349, 636
26:13 342	5:14 170	13:14 ....692, 709
26:15 ....96, 620	5:15 170	15:2 400
28 392	6:25 400	15:3 ff 400
28:13 1151	10:13 1015	15:11 133
29:3 370	12 171	15:24 710
29:29 71	14:6 123	15:29 ....133, 708
30:1-10 692	18:10 198	16:1 197
30:6 692	24:1-13 1026	16:14 173
30:14 71	24:2 ....14, 77, 106	16:14-16 184
30:20 108	24:3 80	16:16 173
31:29 1011		18:10 184
32 ....56, 57, 455, 1048	**JUDGES**	18:11 184
32:1-43 54	2 ....376, 567	19:9 184
32:3 ....54, 55	2:18 566	19:10 184
32:4 ....55, 56, 101	5:20 171	23:1-2 199
32:6 ....54, 56	7:24 1013	23:11-14 137
32:7 245	7:25 1013	23:12 88
32:8 ....57, 135, 245, 246	9:23 184	24:5 265
32:9 ....54, 245	9:24 184	25:22 148
32:10 27	11:27 566	25:31 265
32:11 27	13:2-25 26	25:34 148
32:12 ....27, 54, 56	13:3 168	28:7 188
32:15 ....55, 56, 101, 1039	13:6 ....26, 168	28:7-25 180
32:17 ....55, 82, 175	13:10 168	
32:17-19 55	13:11 168	**2 SAMUEL** 964
32:18 ....55, 56, 82, 101	13:18 443	2:6 100
32:19 54	13:19 168	6:2 1098
32:21 ....56, 901	13:22 26	6:6 837
32:22 1039	18:31 836	6:7 837
32:27 54	20:16 342	2 Samuel (cont.)
	21:8 816	

1183

2 Samuel (cont.)
7 .... 726, 1012
7:1-28 1047
7:12-13 475
7:12-16 1011
7:14 241
7:19 1012
7:24 1047
12 709
12:1-13 32
12:13 349
14:20 168
15–18 194
15:4 735
15:30 1062
16:10 372
17:14 195
19:21 260
22:2 1049
22:3 1049
22:7 1098
23:1 1047
23:2 1047
23:15 494
24:1 .... 302, 372, 1023
24:1-10 349
24:10 265
24:15 349

1 Kings
2:6 1039
4:5 746
6:3 1098
6:5 1098
6:7 913
6:17 1098
6:33 1098
8:27 .... 85, 87, 92, 1097
8:30 87
8:32 735
8:38 265
8:46 .... 408, 409
11:20 745
14:1-18 1023
14:6 842
14:10 148
14:24 747
16:11 148
16:24 57
17–18 14
17:17-24 1048
17:21 272
18 206
18:17-29 80
18:19 55
18:20-40 28
18:27 80
18:36 14
18:36-39 ..... 82, 200, 207
18:37 14
18:39 15
18:40 .... 16, 905
19:16 506
19:18 908
19:21 742
21:13 742
21:19 198
22 15
22:19 .... 171, 1099
22:19-23 184
22:22 .... 173, 183
22:23 .... 173, 183
22:34-38 198

2 Kings
1:1 342
1:2 176
1:2 ff 1023
1:6 176
2:1 ff 1118
2:1-11 261
2:1-18 1061
2:11 .... 1048, 1061, 1098
4:18-37 1048
4:40 1020
6:15 165
6:15-17 171
6:16 .... 165, 171
6:17 .... 168, 171, 374
8:22 342
9:27 287
13:20 1048
13:21 1048
15:5 844
16:3 1083
16:15 742
17:5-23 784
17:6-23 80
17:16 171
19:9 246
19:35 172
21:3 171
21:6 188
21:18 287
23:7-11 784
23:10 1083
23:10-14 1084
23:24 188

1 Chronicles 173, 964
1–8 919
1:32 448
9:1 919
16:1-6 962
16:28 962
16:28-30 962
16:29 963
16:30 .... 962, 963
21:1 .... 303, 372, 1023
23:13 631

2 Chronicles
2:5 .... 65, 83
6:1 996
6:18 .... 180, 486, 620
6:30 .... 173, 486
6:32-33 835
6:33 173
7 752
7:1 443
7:11 838
11:15 184
15:3 506
16:9 .... 27, 87
18:18-22 184
18:21 173
18:22 173
19:6 448
19:7 1073
20:7 .... 68, 746, 853
24:19 444
24:20 444
26:21 1025
28:3 1083
32:21 .... 199, 1099
32:31 373
33:6 1083
36:14 784
36:19-23 129
36:20-23 23

Ezra 785
1 129
1:1 23
1:2 23
2:59 919
2:63 508
9:1-10 636
9:1-15 784
9:5-15 409

Nehemiah 785
1 87
1:15 901
2:1 197
2:2 197
2:8 .... 284, 1042
7:65 508

9:1-38 784
9:2 784
9:6 192
9:13 235
9:14 319
9:17-21 103
9:20 107
9:27-32 103
13:22 647
13:23-31 660

Esther
2:7 745
2:15 745
6:1 197
6:12 1062

Job 173, 180, 373, 912
1 178
1–2 1098
1:1 .... 93, 167, 409, 434, 963
1:3 .... 93, 434
1:6 .... 113, 170, 171, 178, 179
1:7 179
1:8 .... 93, 179, 409, 411, 963
1:11 347
1:12 .... 179, 199, 374, 1023
1:18 1023
1:19 1023
2 178
2:1 .... 167, 171, 178
2:1-6 179
2:3 .... 409, 411, 963, 1023
2:5 347
2:6 .... 199, 374
2:7 174
2:9 .... 347, 963
3:20-22 1026
4:18 171
4:19 229
5:1 171
5:9 91
5:16 411
7:9 186
7:10 186
7:11 411
7:20 192
9:33 499
10:8-12 229
10:18 229
11:7 91
12:6 347
12:9 192
12:10 .... 192, 193, 197
13:26 347
14:4 384

14:5 136
14:12 1025
14:12 ff 1037
14:13 1025
14:13-15 1048
14:14 1025
16:18 ff 1048
17:13 1039
17:14 1039
19:23 ff 1048
19:23-27 1048
19:25 .... 56, 186, 647
19:25-26 1020
19:25-27 .... 1031, 1037
19:26 .... 186, 1025, 1036
19:27 .... 1008, 1025
19:29 343
20:9 1025
23:4 411
24:13 347
24:20 1025
26:6 1039
26:7 160
26:13 160
27:4 735
27:5 963
27:33 272
28:24 87
29:3 742
30:27 270
31:6 963
31:33 378
32:8 272
33:4 .... 108, 272
33:18 272
33:20 742
33:23 171
33:24 552
34:14 f 1021
34:15 317
37:5 197
37:10 197
37:16 90
38 .... 50, 142
38–40 91
38–41 74
38–42 302
38:1-7 170
38:2 74
38:4 152
38:6 170
38:7 .... 152, 167, 168, 170, 173, 180, 448
38:8 167
38:8-11 123
38:18 742

39 50
40:2 74
40:4 411
40:5 411
42 1098
42:1 90
42:2 .... 90, 127
42:6 .... 74, 362, 409

Psalms 173, 964
1 838
1:1 430
1:2 .... 352, 430, 659, 696, 1077
1:3 .... 136, 188
1:5 .... 786, 1066
1:6 .... 566, 1067
2 .... 503, 617, 623, 624, 625, 636, 967
2:6 .... 349, 507
2:7 .... 114, 490, 604, 605, 631, 745
2:8 .... 627, 636, 1107
2:9 624
4 364
5 838
5:5 .... 25, 99, 102, 590
5:9 409
6:2 270
6:4 1028
6:5 1028
6:9 347
7:9 270
7:17 57
8 .... 48, 83, 142, 229, 235, 250, 289
8:3 47
8:4 .... 228, 291, 294
8:4-6 .... 642, 868
8:5 .... 291, 294, 642
8:6 642
8:6 ff 1100
8:7-10 294
9:7 1067
9:10 58
9:17 .... 347, 1015
10:3 347
10:17 27
11:4 590
11:5 .... 102, 347, 590
11:7 99
13:5 1103
14:1 .... 30, 345, 408
14:1-3 408
14:2 408
14:3 .... 408, 523

Psalms (cont.)

Psalms (cont.)
14:4..........347
14:11 56
15 1040
16 ....726, 1038, 1048
16:8-11.......605, 1029
16:9-10......1037
16:9-11......1049
16:10 ....604, 605, 1020, 1031
17 ....1038, 1040
17:6..........27
17:13-15 1037
17:15 ....1020, 1031
18 617
18:6..........27
18:7..........409
18:30 ....90, 569
18:49 ....835, 865, 902
19 ....21, 35, 48, 1098
19:1..........38, 155, 159, 251
19:1-3 47
19:1-4 155
19:1-5 25
19:1-6 ....37, 683, 723
19:2..........38, 251
19:3..........38
19:4..........38, 901
19:5..........38
19:6..........38
19:7..........90, 101, 108, 658, 659, 723
19:7-9 ....541, 659
19:7-11......541
19:7-14......723
19:9..........51, 212, 400
19:10-14 697
19:11 409
19:12 ....25, 69, 339, 364, 373, 409, 1067
19:13 ....347, 373
19:14 ....56, 101, 1067
20 617
20:7..........507
20:9..........408
21 617
21:8..........627
22 ....139, 431, 533, 535, 838, 905, 1113
22:1..........589
22:22 817
22:23 817
22:30 487
23 ....455, 720, 964, 1048
23:1..........946
23:3..........659
23:4..........431, 532

23:6..........1098
24:1..........171, 449
24:3..........xv, 97, 980
24:4..........xv, 97, 980
24:8-10......449
25:7..........347, 373, 1067
25:57 627
27:1..........56
28:4..........1077
28:8..........507
29 ....125, 880
29:1..........170
29:2..........170
29:3..........374
31:1..........1021
31:5..........100, 1019, 1021, 1037
32 ....304, 362, 364, 660, 709, 739
32:1..........343, 746
32:1-5 32
32:2..........343, 345, 400, 746
32:3..........270, 710
32:3-5 709
32:5..........710
32:7..........710
32:10 746
33 142
33:6..........160, 243
33:6-8 229
33:9..........160, 243, 678
33:10 133
33:10-13 133
33:11 133
33:13-15 87
33:14 1097
33:21 769
34:7..........168, 172, 173
34:8..........xvi, 94, 108, 452, 732
34:15 200
35:11 ff......347
35:23 447
36:1..........410
36:5-6 91
36:5-7 194
36:6..........192, 448
36:9..........84, 108
37:1-7 347
37:20 347
38:3-5 413
38:4..........364
39:12 260
40 525
40:7..........490
40:8..........352, 490
41:6 ff 347
42:6..........272

44:3..........681
45 ....617, 623, 838
45:3-7 99
45:4..........838
45:6..........447
45:7..........102, 447
45:16 ....487, 627
46 382
47 97
47:4..........198
47:5..........617
47:7..........97
47:8..........96, 97
48:14 1031
49 ....1037, 1038
49:10-15 1037
49:14 ....1020, 1040
49:15 ....1020, 1031, 1040
50:3..........431, 838, 1119
50:6..........566
50:12 487
51 ....265, 362, 364, 660, 709, 710, 1002
51:1..........710
51:2..........710
51:3..........342, 553
51:4..........349, 553, 736
51:5..........347, 711, 1101
51:7..........711, 980
51:8..........270
51:10 ....242, 710, 711, 723
51:11 ....95, 874
51:14 710
52:5..........347
55:15 1040
56:8..........1072
57:4..........410
57:8-11......1038
58:1-5 643
58:3..........343, 345, 413
61 617
61:4..........1097, 1098
63:1..........33, 270
64:3..........410
64:4..........410
64:8..........742
65:4..........1097
66:1-4 1038
67:1-4 835
67:2-5 1038
68:5..........566
68:6..........157
68:17 ....171, 1099
68:18 618
68:20 1031
70:18 369

72 ....476, 503, 507, 617, 623, 625, 726, 838, 858	89:14 ....99, 101	100:3 108
72:1-17......300	89:18 101	102:1-13 85
72:7..........299	89:20-32 101	102:12........85
72:8..........299, 627	89:27 450	102:27.......133, 217
72:12 647	89:34 97	103............47, 1098
72:12-15 ...647	89:35 ....95, 97, 476	103:8 1090
72:13 ....647, 648	89:36 101	103:9 1090
72:14 647	89:37 101	103:13........73
72:15 647	89:48 1040	103:14........73
72:15-17 586	89:49 476	103:15........1022
72:16 ....294, 311	90 ....137, 145, 409	103:15-16 ..1025
73 ....100, 136, 210, 912, 1038, 1068, 1107	90:1 ....92, 145, 449	103:16........1022
	90:2...........85, 92, 142, 144, 145, 449	103:19........123, 197, 1067
73:1 94		103:19-21 ..1100
73:2 347	90:3 317	103:19-22 ..170
73:19 1037	90:3-12......136	103:20........171
73:23-26 1037	90:7 26	103:20-22 ..170
73:24 1031	90:7-9 1024	104............35, 47, 48, 58, 65, 145, 192, 193, 205, 322, 369, 653
73:25 ....1020, 1040, 1098	90:7-12	
73:26 ....33, 1020, 1031, 1037, 1040	90:8 ....347, 409	
	90:9 1022	104:1 47
75:6 197	90:10 1022	104:1-3.......73
75:7 197	90:11 1024	104:1-4.......193
76:10 ....139, 211, 303, 374	90:12 136	104:2 ....47, 48
77:2 1013	91:1 ....56, 57	104:3 ....47, 48, 73
78 ....376, 567	91:4 27	104:4 ....73, 169, 170, 1048
78:12 686	91:9 57	104:5 73
78:13 686	91:11-12 284	104:5-9.......193
78:39 1021	93 ....431, 1119	104:6 73
80:1 1098	93–99.........135	104:7 73
81:8-16......880	93–100.......1099	104:10-13 ..193
81:12 ....199, 373	93:1 628	104:10-15 ..322
81:13 ....199, 1081	93:2 628	104:14........205
82:1 1066	94 ....431, 1119	104:14-15 ..39
82:2 120	94:1 838	104:14-18 ..193
82:6 659	94:2 628	104:14-30 ..278
84:1 72	94:7-10......254	104:15........205, 653
84:2 ....33, 72, 261, 270	94:9-11......38	104:16........197
85:10 589	95:7 684	104:19-23 ..193
86:8 47	95:8 684	104:21........197
88 ....1028, 1031	95:10 26	104:24........47, 88, 155, 159, 441, 653
88:3 1039	96:3 1038	
88:11 ....1028, 1031	96:7-13......1038	104:24a 73
88:12 1031	96:10 135	104:24b 73
89 617	96:13 ....838, 1068	104:27........653
89:1 133	97:10 34	104:27-29 ..137
89:1-2 101	98:1 97	104:28........197
89:4 1047	98:2-9 97	104:29........197, 317, 1021
89:5 101	99:1 1098	104:30........152, 153, 268, 474
89:6 ....167, 170	99:1-3 96	104:31........47, 294
89:7 167	99:1-5 97	104:33........47
89:8 101	99:1-8 95	104:35........294, 322, 369, 643
89:9 123	99:5b 96	104:35a 47
89:9-13......101	99:6-9 97	105............195
89:11-15 145	99:9 95	105:6 853
	100:1-3.......1038	

Psalms (cont.)

1187

Psalms (cont.)
105:14.......507
105:15.......506, 507
105:16-23 ..195
105:17.......137
105:42.......95
106............15
106:1 103
106:12.......15
106:14.......373
106:15.......373
106:37.......175, 182
107:1 ....65, 93
107:2 300
107:4 ....343, 345
107:4-9......87
107:10-16 ..87
107:17-22 ..87
107:24-30 ..87
107:41.......157, 375
108............365
108:3 1038
108:8 300
108:15.......300
108:21.......300
108:31.......300
109:6 178
109:29.......278
110............507, 617, 623, 624, 625, 726, 868
110:1 ....110, 444, 617, 624, 632, 868
110:1-6......635
110:2 ....507, 627, 868, 1145
110:3 221
110:4 ....631, 632, 708
110:5 868
110:6 ....624, 737
111............100
111:7 100
111:8 100
113:3 1038
113:4 1038
113:5 514
113:6 ....514, 517
115............233
115:3 ....71, 127, 536
115:16.......157, 230, 233, 287, 1098, 1153
116:10.......874
117:1 ....835, 902, 1038
117:2 1038
118:22.......531
118:23.......531
119............260, 659
119:9 761
119:10.......692

119:15........155
119:18........659
119:19........260
119:43........1037
119:44........1037
119:50........761
119:59........708
119:64........103
119:70........679
119:90........133
119:91........133
119:93........761
119:96........658
119:104......761
119:105......659
119:119......380
119:137......99
119:176......345
121:5..........56
124:2..........199, 374
124:3..........374
127............315
128............315
129:1 1101
130............660
132:1 476
132:11.......476
133............921
135:6 ....127, 197
135:7 197
136............145, 660
136:11.......103
138:2 100
138:3 108
139............127, 145
139:1-4......87
139:1-5......198
139:1-10....665
139:2..........87
139:6..........88, 528
139:7..........108
139:7-10....86, 87
139:8 1098
139:13-16 ..229
139:15........87
139:16.......197
139:21.......34, 1014
139:22-24 ..1014
139:23........69
140:3..........409
142:5 1048
143:2..........735
143:10.......108
145:15.......103
145:16.......103
145:21.......1038

146:5 145
146:6 145
146:7-9......1068
147............145
147:4 87
148............142, 145
148:1 170
148:2 ....168, 170, 171
148:5 ....160, 168
148:8 196
150............300

PROVERBS................ 912
1:1-4..........442
1:7 ....347, 410, 442
1:8 ....249, 659, 723
1:16............410
2:9-11 442
2:14............347
3:2 605
3:3..............159
3:4..............159
3:11............773
3:12............773
3:19............74
3:20............74
3:22............159
3:27-31......159
4:16............347
4:18............317
4:23 ff 347
5:22............415
5:22-23......1023
6:16-19......364, 367, 590
6:32............349
7:1-27 1023
7:27............1023
8 ....142, 159, 441, 442, 517
8:3 1023
8:22............441
8:23............441
8:36............349, 350, 1023
9:2 595
9:4 347
9:7 ff..........347
9:18............1039
9:23............347
10:24 355
11:7............1090
12:10 ....100, 231
14:12 416
14:13 416
14:30 1023
15:4............410
15:11 1039
16:2............25

16:4 .... 160, 299
16:33 .... 88, 197
17:5 .... 374, 567
17:14 921
17:15 .... 400, 735
18:6-8 349
18:10 .... 56, 58, 649, 769
18:21 410
19:2 342
20:9 409
20:12 254
21:10 347
21:13 .... 374, 567, 1067
22:15 345
23:13 1039
23:14 1039
23:16 270
24:9 346
24:13 1077
24:23 1073
25:3 90
27:6 959
27:9 959
27:20 1039
28:21 1073
29:1 1090
29:6 349
29:9 1067
29:27 347
31 315

ECCLESIASTES
1:1 1067
1:2 1067
1:13 1008
2:5 .... 284, 1042
2:15 1025
2:16 1025
2:21 742
3:1 1025
3:2 1025
3:11 191
3:16-22 1026
3:19 1025
3:20 317
9:5 .... 1025, 1071
11:5 278
11:9 1067
12:13 260
12:14 260
12:7 .... 258, 272, 277, 317, 1036
12:8 1062
12:13 .... 350, 903
12:14 .... 72, 566, 903, 1067, 1068, 1077, 1081

SONG OF SOLOMON
2:15 287
4:12 287
4:13 .... 284, 287, 1042
7:10 315
8:1 57

ISAIAH 1048, 1153
1:1 1012
1:2 342
1:2 ff 347
1:3 74
1:12 650
1:13-15 650
1:16 980
2 .... 1012, 1015
2:1 ff 625
2:1-4 .... 503, 850, 852
2:2 .... 850, 1011
2:12 .... 1016, 1113
3 1012
3:4 896
3:9 347
3:12 896
3:13-15 448
4:2-6 980
4:3 108
5:1-7 880
5:15 347
5:20 .... 267, 347, 414, 738
5:21 267
5:23 735
6 .... 22, 171, 347, 967, 1109, 1118
6:1 .... 97, 449, 1097, 1098
6:1 ff 166
6:1-3 97
6:1-4 .... 97, 1108
6:3 .... 449, 527, 747
6:5 .... 13, 97, 348, 362, 413
6:5-7 97
6:8 .... 110, 449
6:9 .... 449, 679, 725, 882
6:9-11 678
6:10 .... 449, 679, 700, 725, 882
6:11 .... 449, 678
6:12 449
6:13 430
6:20-24 882
6:21 882
6:23 882
7–9 430
7–12 .... 1016, 1098
7:12 476
7:14 .... 51, 726, 1016

7:14-17 1016
8:1-4 1016
8:19 .... 72, 180, 190, 1036
8:20 190
9–11 605
9:1-12 726
9:4 1013
9:6 .... 80, 443, 450, 468, 494, 844, 859, 1011, 1114, 1118
9:6-7 859
9:6a 1114
9:7 .... 494, 844, 859, 1114, 1118
9:7b 1114
10:5 .... 199, 303, 374
10:5-7 130
10:6 374
10:7 .... 199, 374
10:26 1013
11 .... 97, 286, 1015
11:1 ff 107, 499, 850
11:1-9 1051
11:1–12:6 .. 1118
11:2 .... 74, 874, 880
11:4a 624
11:6-9 1154
11:8 108
11:9 290
11:10 .... 835, 865, 902
11:10-12 ... 1016
11:15 430
12 1016
13 1016
13–24 57
13:4 1113
13:6 .... 1014, 1015, 1016, 1113
13:6-16 1014
13:9 .... 1014, 1015
13:10 ff 1113
13:11 1015
13:21 184
14 .... 173, 174, 178, 184, 308, 1032
14:1 1014
14:12 .... 171, 308
14:12-14 ... 308
14:13 179
14:24 126
14:24-27 ... 130
14:26 74
14:27 .... 74, 126
16:8 .... 343, 345
19:18 748
20:6 1062

Isaiah (cont.)

Isaiah (cont.)

Reference	Pages
20:7	1062
20:8	1062
22:15	844
22:15-25	844
22:19	844
22:22	844
24	1001, 1015
24:1–27:13	1049
24:10	171
24:21	1015, 1042
24:21-23	1049
24:22	1042, 1048
24:23	487, 1151
24:27	1042
25	1001, 1015
25:6	1050
25:6-8	434, 1001, 1015, 1029
25:8	1049, 1061
25:9	1050, 1154
26:1	1050
26:5	828
26:6	828
26:9	1067
26:14	1050
26:19	605, 1047, 1048, 1050, 1053, 1061, 1086
26:19-21	1029, 1062
27:1	413
28:7	343, 345
28:16	250, 787
29:13	717
29:16	74, 229
29:18	16
29:20	347
30:15	699
32	1151
34:1-17	1014
34:4	1113
34:6	1113
34:8	1014
34:14	184
35	286, 288, 503, 856
35:1-10	1015
35:5	16, 82
35:6	16, 82
35:10	1015, 1106
36	129
36:19	1020
37	129
37:36	172
37:36-38	195
38:17	1024
40–46	721
40–53	16, 502, 533
40–66	69, 80, 88, 129, 416
40:3	534
40:3-5	849
40:9	792
40:10	69, 217
40:12-14	69
40:12-24	128
40:13	108, 128
40:15	171
40:18	128, 249
40:21	229
40:22	128
40:25	128
40:25–42:9	128
40:26	171, 193
40:27	128, 198
40:28	90, 198
40:28-31	145, 762
40:48	454
41:1-20	128
41:4	85
41:8	746, 853
41:21-24	12, 16, 128, 190
41:21-29	721
41:24	190
41:25	128
41:26	128
41:27-29	128
42–53	1050
42–53	448, 513, 533, 594, 861
42:1	107, 127, 274, 533, 1015
42:1 ff	504, 534, 874
42:1-4	499
42:1-6	533
42:4	534, 835
42:5	229, 277
42:6	533, 901, 1015
42:7	901
42:8	129, 375, 454
42:9	129
42:24	349
43:1-13	145
43:7	161, 299
43:23-26	735
43:25	453, 533
44:1-5	1151
44:2	229
44:6	80, 110, 449
44:6-17	12
44:7	80
44:9-20	72
44:21-45	129
44:22	90
44:24-26	145
45:1	128, 681
45:1-6	51, 80
45:4	681
45:5	80, 681
45:5-7	302
45:6	80
45:7	139
45:9	229
45:18	229
45:21-25	735
45:22	683
45:24	737
45:25	737
45:25-27	681
46:9	126, 130
46:9-10	16
46:9-11	87, 129
46:10	126, 130, 132
46:11	126
47:12-14	189
48:11	160, 299, 376, 454, 567
48:12-16	449
48:16	110
48:22	416, 687
49:6	533, 836, 900
49:23	787
50:4-9	502, 535
50:6	534
50:7	534
50:7-9	737
51:1	55
51:17	533
52:3	533
52:7	901
52:12–53:13	110
52:13	504, 513, 534, 606
52:13-15	513, 606
52:13–53:12	139, 504, 513, 531, 534, 556, 726, 861, 1050, 1114
52:14	513
52:15	534
53	313, 319, 343, 344, 431, 504, 533, 544, 556, 594, 597, 606, 636, 649, 835, 838, 1113, 1115
53:1	449, 517, 533, 534, 901, 1117
53:1 ff	716
53:1-3	16, 514, 717
53:1-12	502, 513
53:2	466, 517, 1117
53:3	534, 701, 1024
53:4	504, 533, 534, 556
53:4-6	1028
53:5	102, 534, 556, 595, 701, 739, 1000, 1080
53:6	343, 344, 345, 363, 409, 504, 534, 555, 556, 595, 760, 1066, 1080

53:7 .... 504, 529, 534, 543, 984	65:9 127	5:30 705
53:8 .... 556, 861, 984, 1025, 1050	65:13 1001	5:31 .... 705, 709, 893
53:9 .... 504, 534, 1050, 1084	65:17 .... 152, 242, 1113, 1155	6 185
53:10 .... 102, 373, 468, 531, 532, 533, 534, 556, 586, 605, 739, 862, 1024, 1050	65:17 ff 609, 1044	6:15 347
	65:17-25 .... 1107, 1154, 1155	7:12 347
	65:18-25 1155	7:18 784
53:10-12 .... 499, 605, 606, 615, 1048, 1050	65:20 1154	7:24 ff 347
	65:22 127	7:31 1083
53:11 .... 448, 487, 513, 534, 586, 735, 736, 739, 1000	65:24 199	7:32 .... 1083, 1084
	66 .... 286, 288, 416, 619, 763, 1058, 1062, 1136	8:4 ff 347
53:12 .... 294, 513, 533, 534, 556, 586, 621, 1000, 1066, 1114		8:7 349
	66:1 584	9:2 347
	66:2 794	9:4 347
53:12-13 595	66:3-7 1136	9:8 410
54:17 738	66:4 373	9:9 274
55:1 .... 666, 684, 738	66:9 1136	9:14 742
55:3 .... 604, 1012	66:13 108	10:1-11 72
55:11 127	66:15 .... 171, 1136	10:1-15 71
56:3-8 865	66:18-21 1136	10:10 .... 71, 145
56:6-8 835	66:18-23 1155	10:11 .... 71, 145
56:7 533	66:22 .... 609, 1044, 1155	10:12 .... 71, 160
57:15 .... 85, 87, 95, 96, 97, 108, 584, 588, 1098	66:23 1155	10:12b 159
	66:24 .... 1080, 1084	10:13 71
57:15-17 97		10:14 71
57:16 1090	JEREMIAH 1153	10:15 71
57:20 .... 416, 1081	1:5 .... 127, 197, 229, 243, 280, 844	11:10-13 1084
57:21 .... 416, 1081		11:18-21 906
58:9 199	1:8 684	11:20 270
58:11 .... 270, 287	1:10 709	12:1-4 .... 100, 1107
59:1 27	1:15 87	13:23 .... 246, 347, 1081
59:2 27	2:13 84	14:1-4 1062
59:7-8 410	2:20 .... 709, 784	14:7 349
59:20 700	2:24 709	14:14 893
59:21 700	3 709	14:20 349
60 1098	3:3 347	14:21 1097
60:21 .... 161, 299, 1098	3:6 709	15:1 408
61:1 .... 16, 82, 107, 1114	3:11 709	15:6 26
61:2 1114	3:12 .... 709, 710	16:1-9 136
61:2a 1114	3:14 709	16:10 .... 349, 1113
61:2b 1114	3:15 710	16:19 101
61:3 .... 161, 299	3:15-18 710	17:9 .... 263, 643, 770, 1101
62 ff 1100	3:21 880	17:25 .... 476, 1012
62:11 533	3:22 709	18 243
63:7-10 110	3:23 246	19:2 1083
63:9 103	4:4 361	19:11 1084
63:10 347	4:19 270	19:13 171
63:15 1097	4:22 347	22:1-4 448
63:16 56	4:23 229	23:5 1012
64:6 412	4:25 708	23:5-8 625
64:8 .... 56, 229	5:4 347	23:20 1011
65 .... 286, 288, 619, 763, 1058, 1062	5:7 709	23:21 893
	5:8 709	23:23 87
65:1 901	5:9 709	23:24 .... 86, 87, 108, 198
65:2 901	5:10-13 709	23:29 686
65:3 347	5:11 679	25:4 711
65:6 1072	5:25 416	

Jeremiah (cont.)

Systematic Theology

Jeremiah (cont.)
25:5 711
25:9 .... 129, 211, 303
25:11 129
25:12 129
25:14 1077
26:1 151
27:1 151
28 .... 15, 207
28:1 151
28:1-6 55
28:16 55
28:17 55
29:1 331
29:7 331
29:10 23
30 .... 1132, 1133
30–31 1131
30:1-7 1124
30:3 1047
30:4-7 .... 1125, 1131
30:4-11 1131
30:6 1132
30:7 .... 1069, 1131
30:8–31:40 . 1131
30:9 1047
30:24 1011
31:2 742
31:3 698
31:12 287
31:17 693
31:17-20 693
31:18 .... 702, 708
31:19 .... 702, 708
31:22 242
31:29 392
31:31-34 625
31:32-34 693
31:35-37 135
31:40 1131
32:17 .... 90, 126
32:38-40 693
32:40 693
33 980
33:6 100
33:8 341
33:15 1012
33:17 1012
36:3 341
36:30 1012
43 177
44:17 784
46–51 57
48:47 .... 1011, 1012
49:39 1011

Lamentations
1:20 270
4:2 229

Ezekiel 487, 1048
1 .... 1109, 1118
1–3 22
1:1 1108
1:3 1108
1:4-28 1108
1:26 249
1:28 249
2:4 108
3:2 742
3:18 647
8:1 108
8:3 108
8:14 .... 784, 1047
9:3 443
10:4 443
10:18 443
11:9 51
11:10 51
11:19 693
11:20 693
11:23 443
13:18 647
13:19 647
14:14 408
15:19 880
16:15 ff 784
18 392
18:1-20 391
18:2 392
18:4 97
18:20 .... 97, 391, 392, 401
18:21 699
18:23 392
18:24 699
18:27 647
20:9 299
20:30 1084
20:33 1069
20:34 1069
20:41 250
21:27 1011
23:14 249
24–32 57
26:5 1041
27:4 1041
27:26 1041
27:27 1041
27:32 1041
28 .... 173, 174, 178, 184, 308, 1136
28:2 1041

28:10-19 308
28:13 287
28:14 .... 179, 180
30:2 1016
30:3 1016
31:8 .... 287, 448
31:9 .... 287, 448
31:11 448
32:17-32 1032
33:30 906
33:31 906
34:12 1013
36 1151
36:21 299
36:22 299
36:23 750
36:24-30 693
36:25 980
36:26 .... 693, 695
36:27 693
36:37 .... 698, 980
37 .... 676, 693, 1020, 1051, 1151
37:14 693
37:23 749
37:24 1151
37:27 749
37:28 749
38:16 .... 1011, 1012
38:23 750
39:7 299
40–48 .... 503, 1109
43:2 444
47:1 285
47:8 285
47:12 285
48:31-34 1098

Daniel 1048, 1150
2 .... 902, 1051, 1124, 1125, 1126, 1139, 1148, 1150
2:11 95
2:28 1011
2:36 ff 1108
3 1051
3:17 .... 90, 197
3:18 197
3:26 57
4 .... 171, 434
4:1 1108
4:8 ff 1108
4:13 .... 167, 170, 747
4:17 .... 57, 71, 135, 170, 171
4:23 170
4:24 57
4:25 .... 57, 71

1192

4:32...........57, 71, 1099	10:6...........168	13:1..........317
4:34..........57	10:10-14....1097	13:14........1029, 1048, 1051
4:35..........71, 126, 133, 197	10:11.........409	
5:13 ff.......1108	10:12.........86	## JOEL 1153
5:18..........57	10:13..........86, 168, 171, 173, 184, 585	1:15..........1016, 1113
5:21..........57	10:14.........1011	2:1 ....1016, 1113
5:23..........192	10:19.........409	2:3 286
6..............71, 87	10:20.........171	2:13..........708
6:25-27.......71	10:21.........171, 585	2:20..........1016
6:26..........101	11 ....1126, 1136	2:27..........107
7...............442, 601, 856, 1109, 1124, 1126, 1132, 1135, 1139, 1150	11–12.........1139	2:28..........107, 1010, 1016
	11:1...........171	2:29..........1010
	11:36.........1133	2:32..........901
7:1 1108	11:36-45.....1135	3:1-16........1016
7:7 1126	11:36–12:13 1124	3:11..........171, 1015, 1099
7:8 ....1126, 1135	12 ....1126, 1133, 1136	3:11-17......1069
7:9 249	12:1 ....1053, 1057, 1124, 1131	3:14..........1016
7:9-13 1108	12:1-2 1056	3:15..........1113
7:9-14 1105	12:1-3 ....1061, 1113, 1131	3:16..........1113
7:10..........168, 249, 1108	12:1-7 1125	3:17-23......1016
7:13..........438, 442, 509, 617, 906, 1118	12:2...........1020, 1029, 1046, 1048, 1051, 1053, 1057, 1124	3:18a.........1014
		3:19-21......1014
7:13 ff 1113	12:3...........430, 611, 736, 1051, 1053, 1105	
7:14..........425, 426, 438, 509, 617, 624, 859, 906, 1118		## AMOS 1153
	12:7...........1109	1:1-2..........13
7:16..........171	12:10.........430, 1115	1:3 ....13, 57
7:18..........747	12:11.........1109, 1125	1:6 13
7:25..........57, 1125, 1126	12:12.........1109, 1125	1:9 13
7:27..........1109, 1148	12:13.........1048, 1051	1:11...........13
7:28..........199, 1109		1:13...........13
8..............362, 1126	## HOSEA 1048	2:1 13
8–12 1150	1:1 1012	2:3 57
8:1 1126	1:2 151	3:2 ....127, 345
8:8-11 362	1:10...........853	3:6 ....125, 139, 302
8:15 ff 1097	2:4 57	5:16..........1062
8:16..........168, 585	2:6 199	5:18..........1014, 1113
8:25..........1126	2:9 323	5:18-24......1014
8:27..........199	2:23...........853	5:19..........1014
9..............1124, 1126, 1127, 1132, 1139	3:1-5..........1122	5:21-24......1014
	3:3 1122	5:26..........249
9:1-3..........129	3:4 ....1012, 1122	6:8 274
9:1-19 784	3:5 ....1011, 1012, 1122	6:12..........347
9:2 23	4:8 555	8:11..........705, 709
9:3-19 413	4:9 185	8:12..........705
9:8 413	4:17...........199, 373	9:1-4..........87
9:9 413	5:5 347	9:2 1040
9:11..........342	6:1-3..........1050	9:11-15......625
9:14..........100	6:2 1048	
9:20..........1131	6:5 736	## OBADIAH 57
9:21..........168, 169, 585	6:6 284	15 ....1015, 1016
9:23..........409	6:7 ....296, 378	15-21 1014
9:24-27......1127	9:14...........57	
9:26..........535, 1122, 1125, 1135	10:1...........880	## JONAH 87
9:27..........1109, 1120, 1124, 1125	11:9...........449	1:1-3..........87
10:1...........171	12:14.........1020	1:17...........197
10:5..........168		Jonah (cont.)

1193

Jonah (cont.)
2 57
2:4 285
3:4 ....13, 30
3:5 ....13, 30, 712
3:8-9 13
4:7 197
4:10 647

Micah
1:3 ....430, 838, 1119
2:1 347
2:13 617
3:1-4 448
3:2 347
3:9 347
4:1 ....1011, 1012
4:1-5 ....625, 851
4:1-6 852
4:4 1106
5:2 ....47, 108, 196, 431, 443, 683, 726, 838, 851

Nahum 57

Habakkuk 912
1:1-4 1107
1:1-11 210
1:4 413
1:13 ....93, 374
2 ....100, 1068
2:4 715
2:11 323
2:18 243
2:18-20 996
2:20 ....96, 996
3 1037
3:2 1015
3:17 1037

Zephaniah
1:3 171
1:7 1016
1:14 1016
3:8 1113

Zechariah 173
1:4 699
2:17 1109
3:1 178
3:1 ff 180
3:2 178
3:5 347
3:9 921
4:10 903
7:12 107

9:9 ....851, 1114
9:10 1114
9:11 ....550, 1000
11:12 851
11:13 851
12–14 ....624, 849, 851, 856, 1114, 1132
12:1 ....272, 277
12:1-9 1069
12:2 851
12:9-10 1114
12:10 ....535, 851
12:10-14 1116
13:1 980
13:7 851
13:8–14:2 1069
14:1 ff 256
14:1-4 1114
14:4 444
14:5 171
14:20 96
14:21 96

Malachi
1:1–2:17 1014
1:2 573
1:3 573
1:10 564
1:11 564
2:10 56
2:17 30
3:1 ....170, 431, 442, 443, 554, 1119
3:1-12 1014
3:2-5 ....740, 1069
3:6 ....133, 217, 769
3:16 1072
3:16-17 1014
3:18 771
4:1 ....1014, 1071
4:1-5 740
4:2 ....1014, 1071
4:5 ....430, 1014, 1071
4:6 ....430, 753, 1014

Matthew 428
1 ....477, 859
1:1-25 835
1:2-17 470
1:6 475
1:16 475
1:17 475
1:18 ....470, 474, 477, 481
1:18-24 1016
1:18-25 430
1:19 477

1:20 ....171, 443, 469, 474, 475, 477, 481
1:21 ....55, 58, 333, 339, 463, 474, 481, 483, 547, 648, 665, 674, 861, 904, 999
1:22 859
1:23 ....474, 859
1:24 443
1:25 ....470, 474
2:1 ....284, 484
2:1-12 859
2:4 927
2:11 859
2:13 171
2:19-23 196
2:22 557
2:28 272
3:1-3 859
3:1-12 ....710, 864
3:1-17 874
3:2 849
3:3 ....108, 849
3:5 333
3:6 704
3:6-8 864
3:8 711
3:9 ....90, 698
3:9-12 864
3:10 1150
3:11 ....107, 535, 585, 622, 740, 871, 873, 874
3:12 864
3:13-15 525
3:13-17 ....107, 499, 859
3:15 517
3:16 ....111, 116
3:17 ....111, 504, 522, 533
4 ....309, 369, 496, 515
4:1 ....499, 874
4:1 ff 527
4:1-10 180
4:1-11 ....181, 1147
4:3 176
4:3-11 370
4:4 ....xv, 141, 284, 499, 515
4:7 ....141, 284, 499
4:8-10 455
4:10 ....141, 499
4:11 526
4:12-17 859
4:13-17 874
4:17 ....859, 864
4:19 ....846, 904
4:23 864
4:23-24 864
5–7 ....506, 865

5:3 ....794, 865	8:12 ....859, 1080	10:19-22 905
5:3 ff 864	8:20 1097	10:20 ....114, 905
5:5 ....609, 1044	8:24-26 496	10:21 906
5:6 865	8:29 ....183, 454, 1069	10:22 906
5:10 ....862, 865	8:31 184	10:23 ....529, 859, 904, 905, 906
5:11 ....862, 865, 1104	9:2 738	10:23a 906
5:12 1104	9:6 1052	10:24 906
5:13 181	9:12 411	10:24-33 906
5:16 741	9:13 ....284, 411	10:24-42 904
5:17 ....141, 431, 658	9:15 862	10:25 906
5:18 ....533, 658	9:20-24 649	10:26 ....189, 906
5:19 141	9:21 650	10:27 906
5:22 1083	9:29 760	10:28 ....189, 258, 272, 642, 1077, 1083
5:26 1033	9:32 185	10:28-31 906
5:29 ....904, 1083	9:33 185	10:29 ....87, 122, 194, 197
5:30 ....904, 1083	9:35 864	10:30 122
5:31-34 454	9:35-38 904	10:31 194
5:34 1097	9:35–10:42 .1122	10:32 ....705, 906
5:38 ....312, 454	9:36 ....502, 684	10:33 ....705, 906
5:39 ....312, 454	9:38 502	10:34-37 862
5:41 1069	9:56 738	10:34-42 ....728, 906
5:45 ....197, 452	10 ....684, 846, 865, 892, 902, 904, 978, 1122, 1150	10:37-39 454
5:48 ....90, 759		10:38 589
6:1-6 966	10:1 ff 842	10:40 843
6:6 56	10:1-3 842	10:41 1104
6:7-13 966	10:1-4 904	10:42 1104
6:8 ....56, 197	10:1-7 859	11:1-6 ....189, 864, 866
6:9 ....56, 87, 1099	10:2 ....842, 844	11:2-5 ....82, 864
6:9 ff 966	10:5 ....185, 503, 683, 842, 898	11:2-6 16
6:9-13 ....181, 867	10:5-7 ....843, 865	11:3 ....425, 429, 484, 788, 1052
6:11 197	10:5-15 ......904, 905	11:3 ff 859
6:12 345	10:6 ....185, 503, 564, 840, 842, 905	11:5 ....864, 1052
6:20 ....729, 1104		11:9-13 710
6:25 193	10:7 ....185, 187, 625, 905	11:13 659
6:25-34 191	10:8 ....185, 187, 189, 905	11:20-24 ....1078, 1079
6:26 ....193, 197	10:9 905	11:23 1039
6:30 ....197, 729	10:9-15 968	11:25 ....454, 676
6:33 865	10:10 905	11:25-27 ....426, 679
6:34 191	10:11 108	11:25-30 904
7:13 ....786, 1077	10:11-13 905	11:26 ....454, 676
7:14 786	10:14 905	11:27 ....75, 108, 452, 494
7:15-20 645	10:14-16 859	11:27-30 684
7:17 413	10:15 ....904, 905	11:28 ....454, 679, 682
7:18 413	10:15-25 865	11:29 ....454, 589, 679
7:21 626	10:16-22 859	11:30 589
7:21-23 906	10:16-23 ....862, 904, 905	12:8 ....284, 454
7:22 ....207, 701	10:16-42 904	12:9-45 206
7:22 ff 716	10:16a 905	12:15-21 504
7:23 ....207, 701	10:16b 905	12:16 454
7:24 844	10:16c 905	12:17-21 533
7:24–8:10 ..843	10:17 ....859, 905, 906	12:22 185
7:28 454	10:17-18 906	12:22 ff 866
7:32 709	10:18 ....529, 846, 1122	12:22-29 596
8:1-10 862	10:18-22 859	12:23 1083
8:5-10 794	10:19 529	
8:11 ....794, 904, 1123, 1150	10:19-20 906	Matthew (cont.)

Matthew (cont.)
12:24 176
12:24-27 184
12:25-28 864
12:26 176
12:26-29 1139
12:27 614
12:28 .... 189, 866
12:31 .... 347, 627
12:32 .... 1009, 1033
12:32-40 1052
12:34 352
12:35 352
12:36 .... 1077, 1081
12:38 200
12:38-40 16
12:38-45 1128
12:39 200
12:40 .... 17, 862, 1032, 1034, 1040, 1041, 1093, 1130
12:41 .... 712, 866
12:42 866
12:43 184
12:46-50 904
12:49 618
13 .... 426, 626, 627, 679, 775, 846, 865, 898, 902, 903, 904, 1150, 1151
13:3-9 903
13:10-17 864
13:10-23 903
13:11 .... 122, 426, 865, 902
13:11-16 426
13:14 .... 122, 679, 725
13:14-17 1067
13:15 .... 122, 679, 700, 725
13:16 697
13:17 697
13:18 178
13:18-22 966
13:18-23 .... 181, 903
13:19 .... 178, 182, 627
13:19-23 408
13:23 775
13:24 .... 10, 627
13:24-30 .... 698, 903, 1119
13:25 771
13:27 .... 627, 1102
13:30 .... 1102, 1116
13:31 .... 10, 903
13:32 903
13:33 903
13:36-41 181
13:36-42 700
13:36-43 903
13:38 .... 181, 182, 867

13:39 181
13:40 865
13:40-42 1075
13:40-43 529
13:41 .... 171, 455, 626, 1116, 1119
13:42 .... 171, 455, 1116
13:43 1102
13:44 903
13:45 903
13:46 903
13:47 771
13:47-50 903
13:51 903
13:52 653
13:53 903
13:54-57 476
13:57 506
13:58 716
14:1-12 843
14:2 1057
14:13 464
14:28-31 844
14:31 729
14:31-33 455
15:1 553
15:1-3 326
15:3 .... 342, 346
15:7 553
15:8 .... 326, 717
15:16 304
15:16-20 327
15:17 304
15:17-20 413
15:18 .... 352, 361
15:19 .... 263, 384
15:19-20 553
15:21-28 502
15:22 .... 189, 614
15:24 .... 564, 898
15:25-28 455
15:28 189
15:31-38 843
16 .... 812, 813
16:1-12 1063
16:8 729
16:10 627
16:13 .... 425, 466
16:13-18 420
16:13-19 843
16:13-20 801
16:13-21 534
16:14 466
16:15 425
16:15-17 494
16:16 .... 504, 507, 614, 727
16:16-19 448

16:17 .... 415, 426, 494, 504, 694, 722, 1064
16:17-19 .... 845, 861
16:18 .... 454, 675, 801, 813, 817, 820, 823, 840, 869, 927, 1039, 1122
16:18-19 843
16:18-20 801
16:19 .... 454, 840, 845, 858
16:21 .... 420, 504, 537, 539, 565
16:21-23 181
16:22 .... 536, 1115
16:23 536
16:27 .... 455, 1077, 1117
16:28 1118
16:29 589
17:1-9 534
17:2 1118
17:5 .... 116, 1118
17:9 1058
17:14-20 189
17:19 716
17:20 .... 716, 729
17:24-27 451
17:46 494
18 .... 812, 813, 844, 1122
18:3 .... 172, 694
18:7 771
18:8 1082
18:9 1083
18:10 .... 166, 167
18:15 .... 958, 959
18:15-17 958
18:15-18 957
18:15-19 916
18:15-20 924
18:16 .... 916, 958, 959
18:17 .... 813, 817, 823, 869, 927, 959
18:18 .... 845, 846, 916
18:20 .... 450, 497, 916
19 .... 626, 866, 867
19:3-6 .... 141, 315
19:3-8 .... 229, 235
19:4 .... 228, 240
19:4-6 .... 244, 283
19:5 228
19:8 315
19:12 .... 528, 866
19:13-15 986
19:14 .... 866, 986
19:16 .... 626, 866
19:16-30 866
19:16–20:16 525
19:17 .... 452, 524, 866
19:21 .... 626, 866

19:23 .... 626, 866	22:33 271	25:1-13 ...... 912, 1069, 1117
19:24 .... 626, 866	22:36-40 659	25:11 183
19:25 .... 90, 626, 769	22:37 .... 297, 350	25:13 1117
19:26 .... 90, 769	22:41-45 444	25:14 .... 617, 867
19:28 .... 626, 628, 689, 690, 691, 693, 843, 865, 866, 867, 904, 1015, 1102, 1104, 1107, 1150, 1153	22:41-46 110	25:14-30 .... 1069, 1105, 1117
	22:42 479	25:15 1121
	22:43 .... 107, 874	25:19 1121
	23 .... 406, 502	25:21 .... 1102, 1103, 1107, 1117
19:29 .... 626, 865, 866, 1151	23:15 .... 407, 698, 1083	25:23 .... 1102, 1103, 1107, 1117
20:1-16 ...... 677, 1069, 1105	23:17 749	25:29 .... 992, 1081
20:13 681	23:19 749	25:30 .... 1080, 1117
20:15 681	23:23 715	25:31 .... 166, 171, 1068, 1117, 1119
20:20-23 625	23:25-27 361	
20:22 .... 533, 981	23:32-38 400	25:31 ff 1066, 1071
20:26 921	23:33 1083	25:31-46 .... 454, 1068, 1069, 1095
20:27 921	23:34 945	25:32 1095
20:28 .... 273, 333, 420, 450, 463, 484, 502, 503, 509, 538, 551, 557, 564, 572, 595, 613, 840, 899	23:35 .... 399, 444	25:32-35 1121
	23:36 399	25:34 .... 626, 698, 1102
	23:37 .... 444, 684	25:40 792
	24 .... 763, 1113, 1120, 1122, 1128, 1129, 1135	25:41 .... 1035, 1080, 1081
		25:45 792
20:30 614	24–25 .... 862, 1112	25:46 .... 1080, 1081, 1082, 1102
20:31 614	24:1-14 763	25:64 1112
21–26 518	24:1–25:46 . 1112	26:24 1090
21–28 463	24:3 .... 1123, 1128, 1135	26:26 992
21:1-5 1114	24:5 1135	26:26-29 535
21:5 533	24:6 1135	26:27 .... 992, 999
21:13 533	24:7 1135	26:28 .... 550, 576, 1000
21:16 565	24:7–25:30 . 1121	26:29 1001
21:18-20 1121	24:9-12 1135	26:36-44 526
21:19 515	24:9-13 1135	26:38 .... 533, 534, 538
21:20 515	24:13 .... 529, 615, 765	26:39 .... 532, 533, 534, 538, 614, 636
21:29 709	24:14 .... 861, 862, 902, 913, 1112, 1123, 1128, 1136	
21:31 .... 698, 794		26:42 .... 532, 534, 538
21:32 .... 709, 712	24:15 .... 1120, 1124, 1125, 1126, 1135	26:44 .... 532, 538
21:33-44 862		26:52-54 .... 503, 538
21:33-45 .... 1112, 1116	24:21 1124	26:53 .... 168, 171, 373, 515
21:34 851	24:22 676	26:54 539
21:42-44 862	24:25 1117	26:63 534
21:43 .... 626, 698, 1116	24:27 .... 1117, 1127	26:63-65 859
21:44 1116	24:28 1127	26:63-66 448
22 913	24:29 .... 859, 1113, 1120, 1124, 1131	26:64 .... 438, 624, 868, 1118
22:1 912		26:65 438
22:1-4 .... 867, 1112	24:29-31 .... 1116, 1124	26:75 705
22:1-8 906	24:30 .... 622, 859, 1097, 1112, 1117, 1118, 1120, 1124, 1131	27:3 .... 709, 710
22:1-14 ...... 912, 913, 1116		27:4 .... 584, 710
22:7 .... 906, 1112	24:31 .... 455, 1124, 1127	27:7 552
22:10 525	24:33 1121	27:9 503
22:11-14 626	24:34 .... 1112, 1120	27:11-14 534
22:12 411	24:36 .... 169, 1120, 1121, 1129	27:12 534
22:13 .... 1081, 1116	24:36-43 626	27:12-14 529
22:16 684	24:38 ff 763	27:14 534
22:23-33 1029	24:45 382	27:19 .... 31, 523
22:29-33 1038	24:45-51 .... 1105, 1116	27:43 647
22:30 691	25 .... 763, 913, 1076, 1095, 1113, 1122, 1135	27:46 .... 500, 532, 589
22:31 1022		
22:32 1022		Matthew (cont.)

Matthew (cont.)
27:50 ....272, 1021, 1036
27:51 ....323, 504
27:52 ....605, 608
27:53 608
27:57-60 534
28:1 ff 981
28:2 171
28:5 171
28:6 ....171, 609, 612
28:7 1119
28:8 1119
28:9 455
28:10 455
28:16-18 455
28:18 ....126, 628, 683, 1063, 1118, 1154
28:18-20 978
28:19 ....65, 104, 107, 111, 535, 727, 846, 863, 899, 900, 901, 903, 933, 978, 981, 989
28:19-20 9
28:20 ....108, 497, 509, 727, 843, 846, 863, 899, 900, 901, 903, 905, 920, 933, 978, 981, 982, 989, 1083

MARK 428
1:1-11 874
1:1-12 107
1:1-20 476
1:2 442
1:4 ....525, 981
1:8 ....535, 874, 876, 981
1:9 525
1:9-11 111
1:13 526
1:15 ....707, 712
1:21-28 185
1:24 184
1:26 185
2:5-12 453
2:17 704
2:23 464
2:27 ....141, 996
3:13-19 902
3:14 ff 842
3:14-15 843
3:16 844
3:22 186
3:27 1141
3:29 ....1081, 1090
4 ....626, 627, 865, 902
4:1-34 902
4:12 679

4:15 867
4:19 355
4:21-29 902
4:22 1081
4:26-29 ......903, 1056
4:38 515
5:1-5 185
5:4 185
5:5 185
5:6-8 184
5:7 185
5:15 185
5:25-34 649
5:28 650
5:34 649
6:1 476
6:3 ....476, 478
6:5 716
6:6 716
6:7-13 902
6:11 1071
6:14-29 843
6:30 ....464, 904
7:1-4 326
7:11 550
7:14-15 327
7:14-23 365
7:18 304
7:19 843
7:20-23 352
8:10-25 843
8:11-21 1063
8:17 304
8:18 ....304, 725
8:24 1130
8:27 ....425, 426
8:27-31 534
8:28 168
8:31 ....531, 589
8:33 175
8:34 589
8:35 589
8:36 274
8:37 274
8:38 ....173, 622
9:1-10 534
9:9 504
9:12 531
9:13 548
9:14-29 189
9:17 ....184, 185
9:18 184
9:18-21 185
9:22 185
9:24 ....716, 729, 777
9:26 185

9:31 ....504, 531
9:39 207
9:41 ....72, 1104
9:42 377
9:43 1083
9:43-48 1075
9:44-48 1080
9:45 1083
9:47 ....1080, 1082, 1083
9:48 ....1080, 1082
9:49 548
10:6 ....228, 240
10:7 ....228, 240
10:13 ff 856
10:17 ff 866
10:18 ....93, 452, 524
10:30 ....691, 1009
10:32-34 531
10:33 533
10:34 533
10:38 ....532, 981
10:39 981
10:45 ....551, 557, 572, 840
10:47 614
10:48 614
11–15 518
11–16 463
11:17 835
12:1-12 1112
12:6 439
12:12 1112
12:23 992
12:25 168
12:28 ....110, 867
12:28-34 81
12:29 110
12:30 ....272, 273, 274
12:33 272
12:34 867
12:36 ....107, 874
12:41-43 963
13 ....763, 1112, 1113, 1120, 1122, 1128, 1135
13:3 1120
13:3-13 763
13:4 1120
13:9-13 905
13:10 ....1112, 1123
13:14 1125
13:19 1131
13:22 ....676, 1135
13:24 1124
13:26 ....622, 1118, 1124
13:27 1124
13:32 ....169, 451, 515, 1121
13:32 ff 763

Scripture Index

14:18-21 137	1:68..........220	4:19..........463, 502, 503
14:21 137	1:69-74.......625	4:21 ff 965
14:22 992	1:71............551	4:25-27.......677, 681
14:22-25 535	1:72............95	4:25-29.......677
14:23 999	1:73............95	4:29..........906
14:24 ....508, 576	1:76............57, 108	5:8 ....13, 348, 362
14:25 ....992, 1001	2 789	5:14..........506
14:27 503	2:1 ....335, 435, 436, 886	5:20..........533
14:49 503	2:1-5..........196	5:22..........451
14:50 531	2:1-7..........484	5:24..........499
14:61 ....216, 220, 534	2:5 474	6 464
14:61-64 ....425, 426, 1118	2:7 ....114, 450, 515	6:5 996
14:62 1118	2:8-14 171	6:12-16......902
15:5 534	2:10............893	6:13..........842
15:37 504	2:11............449	6:13-16......842
15:42-45 532	2:14............57	6:20 ff 864
15:46 552	2:15............308	6:35..........1104
16 655	2:19-24.......430	6:45..........352
16:15 ....462, 683	2:21............474, 648	6:48..........844
16:16 462	2:22-24.......361	7:12............114
16:19 846	2:25............963	7:12-15......1052
16:20 ....462, 846	2:25-38.......430	7:24..........170
	2:26............875, 1121	7:29..........736
Luke 428	2:28-32.......476	8 ....626, 627, 865, 902
1 ....477, 789	2:30............533	8:1-10 843
1:1 462	2:31............533	8:4-18 902
1:1-4..........476, 724	2:32............1123	8:5 242
1:3-80 430	2:36............893	8:6 718
1:11-20.......171	2:36-38.......963	8:7 719
1:15............474	2:38............551	8:10..........679
1:19............168, 169, 170	2:40............517	8:11..........627
1:23............1106	2:41-52.......518	8:12..........180
1:26............169, 521	2:52............451, 515, 517	8:13..........718, 719
1:26-38.......171	3:1 463	8:15..........694
1:26-56.......430	3:3 712	8:17..........1081
1:27............470, 474, 521	3:8 698	8:18..........1081
1:28............481	3:10-14.......967	8:26-39......188
1:28-35.......474	3:15-17.......107, 874	8:31..........1069, 1080
1:30............474	3:16............535, 871	8:36..........186
1:31............495, 497, 521, 648, 1011	3:18............967	8:41..........1052
1:31-33.......474	3:21............111, 874	8:42..........114, 1052
1:32............57, 475, 495, 497, 625, 1011	3:22............111, 874	8:43-48......649
1:32-33.......1011	3:23............463, 471	8:45..........515
1:34............127, 470, 474	3:23-38.......470	8:46..........515
1:35............57, 108, 111, 467, 469, 470, 474, 477, 480, 481, 517, 521, 527, 874	3:33............475	8:49-56......1052
1:41............655, 693, 875	3:38............113, 228, 448	9:1-6..........902
1:41-45.......476	4 369	9:7-9..........843
1:46............274	4:1-13 1147	9:10..........464, 904
1:46-55.......476, 625	4:3-13 370	9:21..........537
1:48............481	4:16............972	9:22..........504, 537
1:52............197	4:16-19.......866	9:27-36......1118
1:66............551	4:16-20.......1114	9:28-32......536
1:67-79.......476, 875	4:16-21.......107, 866	9:29-31......1062
	4:17............972	9:30..........534
	4:17-21.......864	9:31..........504, 523, 534, 536, 981
	4:18..........502, 503, 509, 738, 1035	Luke (cont.)

1199

Luke (cont.)
9:32 .... 523, 1118
9:37-42 ...... 186, 188
9:37-43 189
9:44 504
9:45 504
9:51 534
9:51 ff 535
9:51–19:27 .464
9:52 534
9:53 981
9:58 534
9:62 534
10:1-17 843
10:1-24 185
10:12-15 .... 1078, 1079
10:14 1068
10:17 .... 179, 185, 189, 1147
10:18 .... 179, 185, 1010, 1114, 1147
10:19 185
10:20 776
10:22 494
10:25-29 411
10:30-37 411
10:31 198
10:42 672
11:1 .... 409, 966
11:1-4 966
11:2 ff 966
11:9-13 254
11:11 557
11:13 409
11:14 185
11:17-26 187
11:18-20 864
11:29–24:53 463
11:32 13
12 .... 763, 1081
12:2 1081
12:3 1081
12:5 1083
12:6 198
12:7 198
12:14 382
12:28 729
12:32 .... 698, 821, 866, 882
12:35-40 763
12:35-48 763
12:40 513
12:41-47 1105
12:41-48 1073
12:42 844
12:47 .... 1073, 1078, 1079
12:48 .... 1073, 1078, 1079
12:50 .... 513, 981

12:54 1118
13 392
13:1-5 712
13:2 1023
13:4 .... 345, 1022
13:14 931
13:16 174
13:19 200
13:22 967
13:23 1101
13:24 1101
13:30 794
13:33 .... 506, 509
14:14 .... 1057, 1058
14:15-24 1112
14:16 ff 702
14:16-24 1001
14:27 589
15:11-32 564
15:12 309
15:13 309
15:18 384
15:19 384
15:22-24 746
15:24 694
15:32 .... 694, 1077
16 .... 261, 1042, 1081, 1083
16:1 844
16:2 848
16:3 .... 844, 848
16:4 848
16:8 .... 414, 844
16:9 1009
16:11 717
16:16 .... 839, 864
16:19 ff 1039, 1040, 1077
16:22 .... 166, 172, 184, 271, 1009, 1032
16:23 .... 184, 1022, 1031, 1080
16:23-31 1034
16:24 .... 1042, 1076, 1080
16:25 1081
16:26 .... 184, 1081
17 1122
17:5 .... 716, 729, 760
17:6 716
17:20 911
17:22 1117
18 1135
18:1 199
18:4 733
18:7 676
18:8 1135
18:9-14 735
18:13 555
18:14 738

18:18 .... 525, 1124
18:18 ff 866
18:19 524
18:30 .... 691, 1009
18:31 533
18:31-34 1115
18:38 614
18:39 614
19–22 518
19:10 .... 463, 502, 660
19:11 .... 867, 1069, 1116, 1121
19:11-27 439
19:11-28 1105
19:12 .... 617, 867, 1121
19:15 1107
19:17 1107
19:19 1107
19:42 514
19:45-48 1000
20:9-19 1112
20:19 991
20:32 1107
20:34-36 168
20:35 1058
21 .... 763, 1112, 1113, 1120, 1128
21:5-19 763
21:12-19 905
21:18 1127
21:20 1125
21:20-22 1122
21:20-24 1122
21:20-28 1122
21:21 1122
21:24 902
21:26 1124
21:27 .... 487, 763, 1118
21:28 .... 763, 1124, 1127
21:29 1121
21:34 763
21:35 1120
22:7-18 1001
22:15 .... 355, 532
22:15-20 535
22:16 .... 532, 992, 1001
22:17 .... 976, 999
22:17-20 978
22:18 992
22:18-20 521
22:19 .... 976, 978, 992, 999, 1000
22:20 .... 992, 999
22:27 533
22:28-30 843
22:30 .... 625, 904
22:31 181
22:32 .... 181, 709

Scripture Index

22:37	503
22:42	526
22:43	171
22:44	526
22:60-62	760
22:66-71	509
22:71	442
23:9	534
23:14	523
23:15	523
23:34	56, 636
23:38	849
23:41	348, 523
23:42	523, 626, 705, 727
23:43	258, 620, 762, 1032, 1034, 1038, 1042, 1093, 1099, 1102
23:46	273, 311, 513, 532, 1019, 1021, 1036, 1103
23:47	523
24	513, 619, 1010
24:21	551, 1115
24:23-27	1028
24:24-27	305, 429
24:25	7, 304, 513, 547
24:25-27	51, 88, 141, 429, 503, 719, 862, 1010, 1032, 1113
24:26	7, 513, 538, 547, 648
24:27	513, 538, 543, 648, 726, 1049
24:31	611
24:32	1028
24:36	611, 612
24:37	183, 1031
24:38-43	609, 1044
24:39	169, 609, 1061
24:41	169
24:42	169
24:43	642
24:44	659, 860, 1049
24:44-46	503, 538, 543, 726
24:44-47	51, 88, 141, 429, 1010, 1032, 1113
24:44-48	648, 719
24:44-49	7
24:45	7, 429, 513, 719, 1049
24:45-47	899
24:46	513, 1049
24:47	861, 1123
24:47-49	861
24:50	617
24:51	617

John

1	160, 441
1–16	881
1:1	21, 150, 304, 438, 441, 447, 475, 501, 517, 911
1:1-3	26, 52, 171, 378, 439, 441, 445, 717
1:1-5	142
1:1-12	145
1:1-13	726
1:1-14	486, 1008
1:1-20	126
1:2	192, 444, 475, 517
1:3	108, 160, 453, 486, 1011
1:4	434, 450
1:6	486
1:7-11	115
1:8	762
1:9	47, 359, 574, 683
1:10	115, 160, 486, 534, 762, 882
1:11	115, 439, 534
1:11-13	717
1:12	486, 650, 695, 697, 746
1:13	477, 486, 650, 695, 697, 723, 746
1:14	21, 51, 113, 114, 279, 405, 439, 445, 447, 466, 467, 476, 484, 486, 487, 494, 495, 496, 501, 512, 525, 588, 610, 717, 726, 911
1:14-17	553, 660
1:15	21, 439
1:17	100, 588, 650
1:18	45, 51, 113, 448, 487, 509, 1099
1:19-35	859
1:21	508
1:23	534
1:29	200, 319, 339, 521, 523, 534, 543, 547, 576, 637, 661
1:29-32	16
1:29-34	107, 499, 874
1:32-34	111
1:33	16
1:36	200, 846
1:37	846
1:42	844
1:45	423
1:46	509
1:47	854
1:49	507, 841, 866
2	464
2:11	612
2:13-21	843
2:13-22	16
2:13-23	464
2:18	17, 1128, 1130
2:18-22	534
2:19	17, 137, 452, 1130
2:19-20	1052
2:19-22	1053
2:20	17, 452
2:21	17, 736
2:22	17, 1130
2:23	715, 717, 718, 736, 788
2:24	451, 715, 717, 736
2:25	451
2:27-29	724
3	693, 786, 899
3:1-8	723
3:2-26	486
3:3	416, 690, 697, 698, 725, 874
3:3 ff	695, 704
3:4	339, 690
3:5	416, 626, 686, 690, 696, 698, 707, 873, 874
3:5-8	574, 622
3:5-10	980
3:7	690, 697, 874
3:8	108, 417, 426, 655, 676, 686, 690, 699, 707
3:9	691
3:10	691
3:11	490
3:12	633, 1097
3:13	426, 438, 439, 484, 490, 497
3:13-21	785
3:14	534, 538, 705, 739, 864
3:15	538, 576, 705, 739, 864
3:16	34, 102, 111, 112, 113, 114, 117, 261, 448, 537, 553, 554, 576, 588, 648, 718, 720, 746, 785, 786, 866, 883, 1082, 1083, 1105
3:16-18	791
3:17	333, 484, 577, 649, 887
3:18	47, 113, 382, 394, 735, 785, 786, 788
3:18-21	1077
3:19	813, 1010
3:22 ff	978
3:25	981
3:26	981
3:27	697
3:33	100
3:34	740
3:36	454, 553, 566, 581, 677, 681, 785, 786, 791, 1009, 1033, 1081, 1090, 1105

John (cont.)

1201

John (cont.)
4 899
4:1 .... 978, 981
4:2 981
4:6 515
4:8 .... 102, 552
4:9 .... 466, 537
4:10 .... 537, 873
4:13 .... 686, 739, 873
4:14 .... 455, 717, 739, 873
4:16 451
4:16-19 451
4:19 508
4:22 .... 412, 784, 788, 962
4:23 962
4:24 .... 56, 65, 66, 249, 252, 319, 964, 996
4:25 .... 508, 784
4:26 .... 508, 784
4:29 508
4:34 .... 352, 502
4:35 .... 464, 684
4:35-38 502
4:36 684
4:38 xi
4:42 .... 110, 784
4:46-53 726
5:17 .... 133, 191, 192, 502
5:18 .... 113, 426, 448
5:19 452
5:19-26 737
5:21 .... 108, 111, 454, 468, 690
5:21 f 456
5:21-27 456
5:22 .... 454, 495, 769, 1071
5:23 .... 111, 455
5:24 .... 84, 261, 648, 666, 723, 726, 735, 737, 769, 786, 866, 1009, 1066, 1070
5:25 .... 666, 723, 725, 1046, 1052, 1055, 1093
5:25-27 1139
5:25-29 ...... 1086, 1093, 1118
5:26 .... 84, 450, 737, 1141
5:26 f 456
5:27 .... 454, 487, 737, 1141
5:27 ff 1071
5:27-29 1056
5:28 .... 454, 495, 1030, 1046, 1052, 1054, 1057, 1061, 1076
5:29 .... 72, 454, 1021, 1044, 1046, 1049, 1052, 1053, 1054, 1055, 1057, 1058, 1061, 1076, 1090
5:30 .... 352, 456, 516

5:39 .... 51, 305
5:44 81
6 .... 477, 478, 496, 508, 1099
6:1 464
6:1-14 674
6:4 .... 451, 464
6:5 451
6:6 .... 69, 451
6:10 486
6:14 506
6:15 857
6:22-40 477
6:24-59 674
6:25-71 534
6:27 110
6:29 739
6:33 477
6:35 .... 455, 674, 717, 739
6:36 .... 674, 739
6:37 .... 415, 674, 684, 768, 769
6:38 .... 477, 526
6:39 .... 415, 674, 684, 768, 1008
6:40 .... 645, 1008
6:41 .... 444, 477
6:44 .... 263, 415, 417, 585, 645, 684, 685, 717, 768, 769, 1008
6:45 .... 415, 585, 674, 684, 685
6:51 .... 444, 455, 477, 484, 486, 1082
6:51-58 1006
6:52 477
6:54 .... 717, 1008
6:57 72
6:62 .... 438, 439, 490, 497
6:63 .... 675, 761
6:64 684
6:65 .... 415, 585, 645, 675, 684
6:66 .... 645, 675
6:66 ff 1135
7:1 464
7:1-6 906
7:2 874
7:3 331
7:4 331
7:5 531
7:6 .... 331, 874
7:7 .... 329, 331
7:7-9 760
7:8 874
7:14 464
7:15 517
7:17 .... 208, 983
7:18 208
7:22 983
7:28 108

7:37 .... 455, 684, 874
7:37-39 ...... 666, 847, 875
7:38 .... 617, 874
7:39 .... 617, 740, 874, 875
8 477
8:2 685
8:5 497
8:9 .... 40, 266
8:12 .... 434, 454, 478, 1006
8:13 .... 101, 439, 478
8:14 .... 101, 439, 478
8:16 101
8:18 .... 101, 478, 496
8:19 478
8:20 477
8:21 617
8:23 496
8:25 .... 478, 522
8:26 .... 496, 506
8:28 .... 101, 496
8:29 522
8:29-44 410
8:30 .... 617, 715
8:31 .... 478, 715
8:31-36 415
8:32 761
8:33 .... 478, 522
8:34 .... 196, 415, 769
8:35 .... 450, 864
8:36 864
8:37 478
8:39 .... 478, 522
8:40 .... 496, 630
8:41 .... 478, 522
8:42 .... 439, 696
8:44 .... 178, 180, 184, 304, 308, 715, 1023
8:45 715
8:46 .... 467, 522
8:48 .... 478, 522
8:50 .... 208, 477
8:57 463
8:58 .... 450, 496
9 .... 392, 685, 792
9:1-3 1023
9:3 1023
9:4 1079
9:5 .... 434, 911
9:33 505
9:37 792
9:39 .... 434, 1067
10 .... 770, 1093
10:1-18 535
10:4-6 455
10:7 1006
10:11 .... 108, 332, 455, 539

10:14-18 534	12:31-33 586	14:22 880
10:15 273	12:32 ....585, 1090	14:23 ....111, 668, 1112
10:16 ....787, 821, 865, 905, 1093	12:34 ....1082, 1115	14:25 ....892, 899, 993
10:17 614	12:37-31 514	14:25-28 875
10:18 ....398, 452, 456, 539, 614	12:37-40 ....426, 722	14:26 ....108, 111, 114, 121, 617, 650, 724, 740, 843, 892, 899, 903, 993
10:22 464	12:37-41 ....16, 35, 304, 449, 503, 716, 841	
10:25 ....206, 261	12:38 ....449, 533	14:28 ....456, 496, 617
10:26 261	12:40 ....449, 679, 700	14:29 617
10:27-29 774	12:41 449	14:30 ....185, 467
10:27-30 767	12:42 ....705, 716	15 ....468, 669, 675, 880
10:28 ....453, 455, 628, 675, 695, 1082	12:43 ....705, 716	15:1 ....881, 1006
	12:48 ....1008, 1072	15:1 ff 910
10:28-30 769	13 ....502, 847	15:1-4 650
10:29 455	13–16.........993	15:1-16......880
10:30 ....81, 111, 494	13–18.........843	15:3 ....758, 760
10:30-33 426	13:1 769	15:4 881
10:32-36 448	13:4-10......760	15:5 ....455, 650, 669, 758, 881
10:33-36 448	13:8 340	15:6 881
10:34 659	13:12-14 628	15:8 ....675, 882
10:35 ....141, 182	13:13 ....449, 675	15:12 921
10:36 ....456, 750	13:14 ....675, 976	15:12-15 675
10:37 206	13:15 ....127, 976	15:13 1025
10:38 ....51, 206, 666	13:16 127	15:16 ....672, 675, 676, 677, 842
11 1039	13:18 127	15:17 921
11:4 367	13:19 127	15:19 676
11:11 ....269, 1022	13:21 272	15:22-25 206
11:13 1038	13:21-30 137	15:24 207
11:14 1022	13:31 ....627, 874	15:25 ....503, 738
11:20-24 503	13:32 ....456, 874	15:26 ....111, 114, 121, 622, 650, 740, 875, 892, 899, 993
11:24 ....604, 1008, 1038, 1061, 1067	13:34 921	
	13:35 921	15:27 ....622, 740, 842, 847, 892, 899, 993
11:25 455	14 ....111, 1031, 1032	
11:25-44 453	14–16.........106, 585, 845, 847, 876, 881	16:5 617
11:26 455		16:7 ....111, 615, 650, 666, 1112
11:27 507	14:1 454	16:7-10......47
11:28 1008	14:1 ff 1038	16:7-11......723
11:35 496	14:2 ....451, 497, 619, 620, 1097, 1102	16:7-13......740
11:38 496		16:7-15......627, 875
11:39 1022	14:3 ....912, 1054, 1112	16:8 ....304, 622
11:41-44 1052	14:5 494	16:8-10......842
11:43 ....496, 1061	14:6 ....72, 108, 450, 451, 454, 650, 787, 791, 1006	16:8-11......409, 417
11:44 ....496, 1061		16:9 622
11:47-50 508	14:8-19......51	16:11 ....181, 185
11:52 508	14:9 ....450, 506, 726	16:12 ....6, 847, 875
12–18.........518	14:10 107	16:12-14 ....622, 813, 843, 864, 899, 903
12–21.........463	14:12 622	
12:1-8 1001	14:13 761	16:12-15 ....51, 993
12:20-24 538	14:14 ....454, 761	16:12-16 626
12:20-32 ....850, 1047, 1147	14:15 454	16:13 ....426, 847, 875, 924, 1113, 1139
12:23 539	14:16 ....111, 114, 622, 637, 944	
12:24 539	14:16-18 ....740, 859, 875	16:13-15 892
12:27 ....272, 538, 614	14:16–16:16 496	16:14 450
12:27-33 188	14:17 ....100, 108, 622, 666, 847	16:15 450
12:27-34 585	14:18 ....111, 666, 875, 1111	16:16 1111
12:28 ....116, 523	14:19 ....72, 454, 615, 617, 1052, 1111	
12:31 ....176, 185, 1114, 1139		John (cont.)

1203

John (cont.)
16:30 451
16:33 1001
17 ....333, 468, 479, 490, 514, 669, 880, 881, 887, 967
17:1 ....56, 456, 490, 615
17:1-4 1117
17:2 ....456, 674, 866
17:3 ....62, 81, 100, 452, 454
17:4 ....490, 838
17:5 ....56, 142, 145, 294, 299, 439, 441, 454, 456, 487, 490, 494, 496, 513, 514, 614, 615, 1099
17:6 ....751, 768, 787, 881
17:6-19 882
17:8 ....506, 787, 882
17:9 ....332, 340, 638, 882
17:11 ....769, 882
17:12 ....137, 503, 710
17:13 882
17:14 ....340, 882
17:15 182
17:15-17 882
17:15-21 636
17:15-26 181
17:16-18 330
17:17 ....108, 760
17:18 ....340, 456
17:20 ....332, 787, 882
17:20-24 881
17:20-25 881
17:21 ....667, 871, 883, 895
17:21-24 490
17:22 ....456, 883
17:23 ....769, 871, 882, 883
17:24 ....108, 142, 145, 332
17:25 108
18:1 875
18:36 507
18:37 507
18:38 31
19:1 496
19:6 448
19:7 ....448, 534
19:9 534
19:24 503
19:28 ....494, 496, 503, 515
19:30 ....273, 431, 504, 1021, 1103
19:34 535
19:35-39 455
19:36 503
19:37 ....503, 535
19:38-42 532
20:7 612

20:17 618
20:19 ....610, 611, 612
20:19-23 843
20:20 610
20:21 933
20:22 ....875, 876, 933
20:24-29 614
20:25 558
20:26 ....610, 611, 612
20:27 610
20:28 610
20:30 ....477, 484, 607, 724, 785, 903
20:31 ....454, 477, 484, 607, 724, 785
21:1-23 610
21:6 451
21:7 610
21:9 232
21:12 610
21:17 108
21:18 ....197, 1121
21:19 ....197, 1121
21:24 607
21:25 ....228, 785

Acts 812, 834
1 ....207, 513, 619, 823
1–9 924
1–12 459
1–15 1093
1:1 ff 615
1:1-5 585
1:1-9 912
1:2 607
1:3 ....607, 610, 629, 847, 859
1:3-6 849
1:4 ....107, 740, 823, 859, 875, 876, 919, 1121
1:5 ....107, 666, 740, 823, 859, 871, 874, 876, 919, 1121
1:6 ....625, 691, 860, 866, 903, 1107
1:6-7 851
1:6-8 1151
1:6-11 ....451, 617
1:7 ....626, 903
1:8 ....435, 475, 626, 683, 860, 899, 913, 1123
1:9 ....620, 1061, 1118
1:9-11 ....171, 618
1:10 ....608, 609, 1117
1:11 ....487, 608, 609, 620, 1044, 1054, 1061, 1117, 1118
1:12-15 882
1:14 966

1:15 ....813, 919, 936, 981
1:16 ....107, 874
1:18 ....836, 1084
1:19 1084
1:21 ....523, 842
1:22 ....523, 842
1:22-26 982
1:24-26 198
1:25 137
2 ....619, 712, 823, 832, 843, 844, 845, 846, 847, 859, 873, 878, 1016
2–7 899
2:1 ....874, 936
2:1 ff 823, 978
2:1-2 876
2:1-4 ....841, 936
2:1-13 740
2:2-4 116
2:4 822
2:5 ....623, 963, 983
2:5-11 918
2:15 623
2:16 107
2:17 1011
2:17-25 888
2:18 1011
2:22 ....137, 206, 483, 841
2:22-24 40
2:22-40 82
2:23 ....88, 127, 137, 139, 196, 303, 373, 374, 420, 513, 531, 601, 837, 868, 1080
2:23-36 504
2:24 1032
2:24-31 1049
2:24-33 614
2:25 ff 1034, 1049
2:25-35 605
2:26 1001
2:27 133
2:29 476
2:29-35 605
2:30 476
2:32 614
2:32-36 623
2:33 ....107, 667, 740, 875, 1063, 1145
2:33-36 487
2:34 ....605, 617
2:34-36 ......483, 621
2:35 617
2:36 ....614, 624, 788, 1145
2:37 ....708, 712
2:37-41 983
2:38 ....535, 696, 701, 702, 704,

Scripture Index

	709, 712, 783, 919, 978, 980, 981	
2:39	856
2:40	967
2:41	4, 813, 917, 919, 980, 981
2:41-47	910
2:42	4, 7, 761, 822, 872, 917, 921, 965, 966, 969, 991
2:42 ff	924, 957
2:42-47	827
2:43-47	4
2:44	918, 936
2:45	918
2:46	919, 964, 965, 1001
2:47	813, 823, 869, 918, 936
3	208, 701, 788, 860
3:1 ff	964
3:1-11	788
3:1–4:22	16
3:2	853
3:6	788
3:11 ff	601
3:12	788, 853
3:12-15	614
3:13	788
3:13-18	303, 788
3:14	108, 449, 523, 701, 1080
3:15	497, 523
3:17	137, 504
3:18	137, 429, 504
3:18-21	1115
3:19	703, 707, 712, 1115
3:20	1115
3:21	429, 450, 451, 497, 513, 620, 668, 689, 691, 703, 1088, 1115
3:22	506
3:23	604
3:24	429, 504, 726
3:26	700, 701
4	731, 788
4:1	701
4:4	919
4:7	788
4:8	650
4:10	601, 853, 1046
4:12	454, 650, 717, 770, 783, 786, 788, 791
4:13-18	16
4:17-30	788
4:23	936, 966
4:23-30	966
4:23-31	180
4:23-41	4
4:24	1097
4:24b	967
4:25-27	967
4:26	507
4:27	303, 507, 523, 1080
4:28	133, 303, 967
4:30	448
4:31	936
4:32	667
5	846, 925
5:1-11	366
5:2	175
5:3	110, 173
5:4	110
5:11	869, 918
5:12-42	4
5:19	172
5:21	853
5:28	7
5:28-33	788
5:30	1046
5:31	712, 783, 853
5:35	853
5:40	788
5:41	788
6	925, 933, 944, 947
6:1-3	919
6:1-5	919, 925
6:1-6	936, 954
6:3	924
6:5	860, 924
6:6	925
6:9	965
7	22, 529, 722
7:1	795
7:2	795
7:9-16	195
7:22	232, 414, 1019
7:35	505, 506
7:37	604
7:38	817, 918
7:42	550, 1097
7:51	107, 684
7:52	523
7:55	456, 487, 624, 1097
7:56	868
7:57	624
7:59	1021, 1036, 1099
8	683, 844, 845, 846, 892, 893, 899, 917, 942
8–12	924
8:1	869, 904, 918
8:2	963
8:3	869, 918
8:3-5	860
8:4-6	897
8:4-8	984
8:5	891
8:6	860
8:7	972
8:8	972
8:9-24	722
8:12	788, 978, 982, 984
8:12-17	983
8:13	716, 982, 984
8:16	982
8:18-31	716
8:21	1085
8:22	709
8:26	984
8:26-39	647
8:27	436
8:30-34	912
8:31	647
8:31-35	534
8:32	534
8:32-36	868
8:33	534
8:35	788
8:35-38	984
8:36	982
8:37	727, 978, 984
8:38	982
9	304, 729
9:1-2	918
9:1-9	984, 1062
9:1-19	919
9:3	622
9:3-6	1105
9:3-7	723
9:10-19	899
9:15	672, 681, 788, 899
9:16	681
9:17-19	984
9:18	980, 982, 984
9:27	788, 1129
9:28	1129
9:31	832, 967
9:34	788
9:35	701
9:37	1023
9:59	1103
10	626, 683, 841, 844, 845, 846, 860, 899, 925, 928, 1115
10:1	436
10:1-16	626
10:1–11:18	836
10:2	841
10:24	984
10:25	455
10:26	455

Acts (cont.)

Acts (cont.)
10:27 985
10:30 841
10:34 412
10:34-37 840
10:34-43 .... 104, 462, 483, 614, 840, 984
10:35 412
10:36 840
10:36-43 503
10:37-44 467
10:38 .... 174, 492, 503, 504, 840
10:39 .... 601, 840
10:40 .... 601, 840
10:41 .... 609, 926, 1044
10:42 .... 454, 601, 840
10:43 .... 429, 601, 783
10:44 984
10:44-48 984
10:47 .... 980, 982, 989
10:48 .... 982, 985, 989
11 .... 626, 899, 928, 1115
11:1-4 925
11:2 893
11:13 651
11:14 .... 640, 651
11:16 107
11:18 .... 708, 712, 925
11:19 899
11:20 899
11:22 925
11:23 967
11:24 967
11:26 .... 4, 483, 967
11:27-30 968
11:30 .... 925, 947
12:7 .... 133, 1046
12:7-10 ...... 168, 172
12:8 133
12:21-23 455
12:23 919
13 917
13:1 .... 893, 925, 926
13:1 ff 899
13:1-3 918
13:2 .... 108, 925, 936
13:3 .... 925, 936
13:4-12 180
13:5 859
13:12 7
13:13-16 605
13:14 .... 859, 900
13:14-50 925
13:14-52 969
13:14–14:21   906

13:15 ff 965
13:15-17 1072
13:16 436
13:17 672
13:22 .... 604, 709
13:22-30 614
13:23 783
13:26 436
13:27 .... 429, 504
13:28-41 504
13:29 601
13:30 .... 601, 604, 605
13:32 .... 114, 604
13:33 .... 114, 490, 603, 604
13:34 .... 604, 605, 1012
13:34-37 1049
13:35 .... 604, 1049
13:35-37 1034
13:38 .... 605, 783
13:38-41 601
13:39 .... 605, 739, 783
13:42 926
13:43 657
13:44-47 900
13:46 859
13:47 .... 836, 900
13:48 .... 674, 675, 680, 926, 966
13:50 .... 436, 905
13:51 905
13:52 .... 925, 926
14 969
14:3 208
14:11-14 455
14:15-17 683
14:15-18 245
14:16 .... 49, 198, 373, 434
14:17 .... 48, 49, 103, 434, 683
14:18 925
14:20 .... 925, 926
14:21 925
14:21-23 .... 925, 926
14:21-24 925
14:22 .... 626, 925, 926, 927
14:23 .... 926, 951
15 .... 208, 728, 741, 923, 964
15:1 937
15:1-29 913
15:1-35 937
15:2 937
15:4 1129
15:6 937
15:6-32 928
15:7 .... 845, 937
15:8 87
15:9 .... 759, 937
15:10 .... 66, 369, 590, 634

15:12 937
15:13 .... 926, 937
15:18 .... 108, 130
15:19 937
15:22 .... 937, 967
15:23 937
15:30 937
15:31 937
15:32 .... 893, 967
16 729
16:1 895
16:3 327
16:6 197
16:12–18:18   906
16:13 436
16:13-15 985
16:14 .... 436, 685, 686
16:15 .... 727, 982, 985
16:16 186
16:16-18 185
16:18 189
16:30 .... 483, 653, 717
16:30-33 919
16:30-34 .... 727, 984, 985
16:31 .... 653, 701, 702, 717, 730, 783, 985, 1093
16:32 985
16:33 982
16:39 967
17 .... 401, 436, 492, 722, 729
17:1-9 1133
17:1-15 773
17:2 .... 605, 969
17:3 .... 547, 605, 606
17:4 .... 436, 606, 765
17:14 1068
17:16 436
17:16-34 32
17:17 436
17:18 .... 691, 726, 969
17:18-31 28
17:19 7
17:22 .... 175, 182
17:22-25 245
17:22-28 30
17:22-31 .... 376, 433
17:22-34 49
17:23 192
17:23-28 969
17:23-31 902
17:24 135
17:24-28 246
17:26 .... 132, 135, 245, 398, 405, 434, 435
17:27 .... 46, 87, 434
17:28 .... 48, 49, 58, 87, 108, 192,

	245, 252, 268, 367, 448, 665, 667	20:25 ....627, 860, 874, 969
17:29 ....49, 108, 245, 252, 667	20:27 ....423, 457, 860, 894, 969
17:29-31 683	20:28 ....448, 490, 495, 497, 552, 584, 818, 832, 838, 840, 870, 894, 926, 946, 969
17:30 ....417, 434, 613, 614, 683, 701, 707, 709, 712, 969	20:28 ff......952
17:30-32 ....16, 601	20:28-31 947
17:31 ....97, 436, 454, 601, 613, 614, 701, 712, 969, 1068, 1069	20:29 ....457, 832
	20:30 457
17:31-34 1045	20:31 961
17:32 ....686, 1045, 1117	20:32 1105
17:34 ....167, 686	20:35 462
18:1-11......685, 960	20:36 423
18:2............968	21:8............891, 893, 897, 942
18:3............968	21:10 893
18:4............969	21:14 108
18:5............969, 1126	21:23 964
18:5-11......679	21:26 550
18:7............436	21:26 ff......964
18:8............723, 931, 982, 985	21:28 853
18:10 674	22:3............8
18:11 ....969, 993, 1133	22:6-11......723
18:12-17 435	22:16 ....919, 984, 986, 1003
18:19 895	23:1............40, 267
18:27 ....654, 920, 924	23:6............614, 1058, 1061
19 906	23:6-8 604
19:3............980, 982	23:8............1029, 1038
19:5............982, 985, 986	23:9............184
19:7............916	23:11 1001
19:8............969	24:14 429
19:8-10......972	24:15 ....1021, 1038, 1044, 1053, 1054, 1061
19:9............969	24:16 267
19:10 969	24:17 550
19:11-12 189	24:21 614
19:13 188	24:24 712
19:13-16 189	24:25 ....712, 1067
19:13-17 185	25:15 736
19:19 189	26:2............684
19:20 189	26:3............684
19:28 607	26:9............788
19:29 607	26:12-23 751
19:32 817	26:15-23 783
19:37 816	26:18 ....701, 703, 708, 750, 751
19:39 817	26:19 711
19:41 817	26:20 711
20 ....208, 923	26:22 614
20:7............919, 924, 965, 994	26:23 614
20:16 964	26:26-28 722
20:17 ....860, 894, 946, 947	26:27-29 684
20:17-35 860	26:28 483
20:18 860	27:11 944
20:20 ....423, 457, 860	28:2............416
20:21 ....423, 627, 712, 860, 969	28:4............736
20:24 ....423, 627, 654, 860, 969	28:7............416
20:24-25 627	28:9............208, 416

28:14 967
28:20 967
28:23-28 783
28:25 107
28:27-39 1028
28:30 861
28:31 ....627, 861

ROMANS 338, 739, 914, 924
1 1098
1–4.............890
1:1 406
1:1-3...........51
1:1-4...........1045
1:1–3:20 379
1:3 ....279, 458, 467, 476, 494, 614, 654
1:4 ....206, 458, 494, 603, 604, 614, 615
1:5 ....450, 715, 894
1:7 ....946, 969
1:10-13.......136
1:13 684
1:14 684
1:15-17.......51
1:16 ....503, 651, 681, 859
1:16-17.......627
1:17 ....715, 739
1:18 ....34, 46, 48, 407, 569, 645
1:18-23.......48
1:18-32.......38, 49, 722, 963
1:18–3:8a...407
1:18–3:9 411
1:18–3:20 ..434
1:18–3:26 ..538
1:18–3:31 ..406
1:19 ....35, 67, 155, 156
1:19 ff 156
1:19-25.......376, 567
1:19-32.......407
1:20 ....25, 33, 35, 46, 48, 67, 85, 155, 156, 304, 977
1:21 ....30, 298, 304
1:21-22.......34
1:24 ....48, 198, 373
1:24-28.......1081
1:25 ....91, 100, 216, 220, 346
1:26 ....48, 198, 216, 414
1:27 414
1:28 ....48, 304, 346, 373, 645, 758
1:28-32.......553
1:32 ....348, 376, 407, 737, 1024
2 ....794, 854, 1068, 1070, 1073

Romans (cont.)

Romans (cont.)
2:1-5 103
2:1-6 434
2:2 ....407, 1070, 1073
2:3 ....1026, 1070, 1072
2:3-5 1072
2:4 ....48, 103, 567, 703, 712, 1072
2:5 ....48, 567, 1070, 1077
2:5-11 1067
2:6 ....407, 1070, 1073, 1077
2:6-13 1073
2:8 1077
2:9 1077
2:11 ....407, 738, 1073, 1077
2:11-14 412
2:12 738
2:12-14 348
2:12-15 ....1072, 1073
2:12-16 ....40, 264
2:14 ....25, 264, 416, 642
2:14-15 ....156, 264
2:14-16 ....49, 1072
2:15 ....25, 32, 156, 264, 266, 416, 642
2:16 ....407, 1073, 1077
2:17-29 854
2:17–3:9a 407
2:20 ff 853
2:23 346
2:27 854
2:28 854
3 755
3:1 ....206, 841
3:1-20 379
3:2 ....564, 717, 841
3:3 715
3:3-6 1071
3:4 ....100, 736
3:6 1070
3:8 ....738, 770, 1070
3:9 ....407, 411, 412
3:9-19 407
3:9b 407
3:9b-20 406
3:10 408
3:10 ff 345
3:10-18 ....407, 408, 411
3:10-19 643
3:11 ....263, 407, 408
3:11a 408
3:11b 408
3:12 ....408, 523
3:12b 408
3:12c 408
3:13 ....409, 413
3:13-18 408
3:14 ....409, 413
3:15-17 410
3:16 407
3:17 687
3:18 410
3:19 ....81, 304, 340, 348, 363, 407, 412, 416, 566, 722
3:19a 411
3:19b 407, 411
3:20 ....407, 710
3:20-26 739
3:21 ....99, 739
3:21-26 ....538, 1037
3:21-28 99
3:21-31 379
3:21–5:11 393
3:21–5:21 99
3:22 ....411, 739
3:23 ....566, 738
3:24 ....552, 657, 737, 738, 745, 905
3:24-25 598
3:24-26 ....566, 1028
3:25 ....99, 199, 373, 536, 550, 552, 554, 555, 589, 737, 739, 745
3:26 ....99, 505, 536, 589, 739
3:28 ....737, 739
3:30 ....81, 739
4 ....14, 715, 719, 755, 794
4:1-5 654
4:1-6 841
4:1-8 737
4:1-22 745
4:1–5:11 379
4:3 ....733, 735, 742
4:4 ....657, 704, 716, 738, 742, 960
4:5 ....654, 657, 716, 726, 738, 739, 742, 960
4:5-8 ....343, 739
4:6 742
4:8 400
4:9 ....735, 742
4:11 739
4:13 739
4:14 ....511, 719
4:15 ....348, 719
4:16 ....716, 719
4:17 ....90, 150, 719
4:18 719
4:21 ....719, 720, 739, 765
4:22 ....735, 739
4:24 613
4:25 ....534, 615, 737, 769
5 ....303, 398, 401, 403, 566, 990
5:1 ....702, 739
5:1 ff 703, 746
5:1-5 ....615, 740
5:1-11 ....737, 761
5:2 ....654, 657, 746
5:3 761
5:4 761
5:5 740
5:6 ....414, 553
5:6-8 647
5:6-10 ....537, 553
5:6-11 740
5:8 ....34, 553, 555, 588, 859
5:8-12 859
5:9 ....553, 636, 649, 737, 738, 1070
5:9 ff 1056
5:10 ....509, 636, 649, 670, 1070
5:11 ....495, 546, 552, 566, 746
5:12 ....162, 234, 245, 247, 276, 280, 302, 303, 312, 339, 345, 380, 382, 383, 386, 393, 394, 398, 613, 643, 1023
5:12-19 ....241, 281, 304, 305, 349, 382, 392, 393, 396, 398, 468, 644, 1021
5:12-20 398
5:12-21 ....xvi, 283, 377, 378, 379, 380, 393, 394, 399, 406, 527, 1023, 1024, 1076
5:14 ....247, 309, 342, 384, 393, 558
5:15 ....382, 393, 654, 1023
5:15-17 403
5:15-19 398
5:16 ....382, 393, 404, 405, 737, 1023, 1070
5:16-18 737
5:17 ....307, 393, 405, 1023
5:18 ....247, 312, 363, 382, 393, 404, 405, 577, 737, 1023
5:19 ....162, 245, 380, 382, 393, 398, 517, 550, 563, 584, 1023
5:20 ....393, 654
5:21 ....394, 654, 1023
6 ....760, 990
6:1 ....738, 770
6:1-11 ....654, 665
6:2 ....751, 770
6:3 535
6:4 ....535, 614, 654, 665, 785, 987

6:5 769	8:18-23......583, 1107	9:10..........854
6:6 ....751, 762	8:18-25......665	9:10-13......784
6:8 769	8:19..........71, 691, 764, 1154	9:10-18......676
6:9 613	8:19 ff 335	9:11..........276, 672, 677, 680
6:10............613	8:19-22......322, 323, 746	9:11-29......138
6:11............701	8:19-23......762, 1154	9:12..........677
6:12............698	8:20..........316, 323, 1154	9:13..........554, 573, 854
6:12 ff 352	8:20-22......163, 379	9:14..........431, 679
6:13............690, 698, 751, 980	8:21..........316, 323, 1113	9:15..........675
6:14............751, 762	8:22..........649	9:15-18......200
6:15............659	8:23..........649, 744, 746, 1052	9:16..........581, 675, 680
6:17............969	8:24..........691, 719	9:17..........161, 211, 299, 303, 678, 1073
6:18............751	8:25..........691, 719	
6:19............751	8:26..........622, 637, 1117	9:18..........675
6:23............97, 307, 394, 395, 416, 1023	8:27..........622, 936	9:19..........679
	8:28..........131, 132, 138, 140, 585, 677, 685, 759, 762, 769, 1024	9:19-21......136
7................340, 362, 368, 406, 412, 759, 762, 770		9:19-23......677
		9:20..........127, 229, 679
7:4 ....654, 669	8:28-30......421, 674, 675	9:21..........127
7:4-6..........751	8:29..........114, 127, 248, 450, 585, 677, 685, 697, 762, 769, 1063	9:22..........161, 303, 373, 1073
7:8 ....354, 644		9:23..........161, 229, 1073
7:12............658		9:24-26......1123
7:14............658	8:30..........132, 682, 769	9:25..........853
7:17............644	8:30-39......768	9:26..........853
7:17-24......351	8:31..........535	9:30..........739
7:18............762	8:31-39......514	10 ....21, 901, 902
7:21............340	8:32..........102, 103, 535, 891	10:1..........853
7:22............352, 696	8:33..........615, 628, 636, 637, 676, 737, 769, 1071	10:1-3 200
7:22-24......415		10:3..........737
7:23............340, 762	8:34..........621, 628, 636	10:4-17......791
7:24............415, 647, 1021	8:34-39......615	10:5-9 901
7:25............340, 415	8:35..........628	10:5-10......71
8 ....583, 759, 770, 773, 1024	8:35 ff 636	10:6..........739
8:1 ....654, 1026	8:37..........628	10:7..........1093
8:1-39 1070	8:37-39......773	10:8..........726, 901
8:2 ....108, 312, 1026	8:38..........85, 166, 585, 1024, 1026, 1097, 1126	10:8-10......704
8:3 ....446, 468, 484, 547, 590, 613, 1024		10:8-15......894
	8:39..........85, 92, 145, 628, 769, 1024, 1026	10:9..........449, 458, 601, 627, 643, 704, 717, 727, 901, 905, 920, 983
8:4 ....590, 658		
8:6-8..........643	9................679, 680, 681, 901, 1073, 1090	
8:7 ....351, 352, 414, 711		10:9-13......730
8:8 ....352, 416, 698	9–11 ....122, 680, 852, 853, 854, 1012	10:9-17......51, 726, 787
8:9 ....111, 666, 667, 877		10:9a.........449
8:10............613, 1024	9:1 267	10:10 ....627, 704, 717, 727, 787, 901, 905, 920
8:11............603, 613, 665, 1024	9:1-3..........200	
8:13............762	9:1-13 854	10:11 787
8:14............966	9:2 679	10:11-17 47
8:14-17......745	9:3 ....556, 679, 853	10:12-15 200
8:15............744, 746, 773, 774	9:3-5..........745, 854	10:13 ....247, 645, 726, 901
8:15b 775	9:4 ....745, 865	10:13-15 901
8:16............696, 773, 775, 776, 777, 1117	9:5 ....57, 110, 216, 220, 446, 448, 490, 494, 497, 567, 588, 841, 865	10:13-17 ....683, 898
		10:14 ....417, 726, 786, 794
8:17............1107		10:14-17 900
8:17-19......746	9:6 ....771, 854	10:15 ....787, 901
8:18............71, 691	9:6-13 680	10:15b-16 ..787
8:18 ff 1051	9:7 ....771, 784	

Romans (cont.)

Romans (cont.)
10:16 ....534, 787, 901
10:16-21 901
10:17 ....34, 319, 417, 557, 599, 651, 723, 726, 786, 794
10:18 901
10:19 901
10:20 901
10:21 901
11 ....196, 755
11:1 ....853, 855
11:2 ....138, 1012
11:3 941
11:5 ....654, 672, 676, 704
11:6 ....255, 427, 654, 657, 676, 704, 716, 960
11:7 ....654, 672, 855
11:8 ....679, 855
11:10 855
11:10-13 127
11:11 ....342, 855
11:12 ....342, 346
11:13 ....854, 941
11:16 855
11:16-24 854
11:17 ....820, 855
11:18 855
11:21 855
11:24 ....854, 855
11:25 ....426, 852, 853, 855
11:25 ff......855
11:25-36 145
11:26 ....647, 700, 852, 855, 1012
11:28 672
11:29 769
11:33 ....71, 88, 91, 589
11:33-35 585
11:33-36 387
11:34 ....71, 936
11:34-35 91
11:36 ....160, 161, 299
11:37 820
12 ....890, 891
12:1 ....448, 696, 698, 758, 866, 1003
12:1 ff 731
12:2 ....90, 695, 696, 698, 758, 759, 760, 866
12:3 ....716, 890
12:3-8 ......889, 944
12:4 941
12:5 827
12:6-8 889
12:7 945
12:8 967
12:10 922

12:12 695
12:13 921
12:16 ....922, 936
13:1 ....135, 171, 334, 335, 373, 585
13:2 1070
13:4 266
13:5 266
13:8-10......659
13:11 ....649, 1102
13:14 760
14 376
14:1-23......267
14:2 327
14:3 327
14:5 937
14:10 ....566, 913, 1067, 1069, 1070, 1079
14:13 376
14:15 766
14:17 ....495, 911
14:21-23 376
14:23 ....339, 351, 760
15:3-9 900
15:4 ....429, 430
15:6 ....108, 921
15:8 ....835, 898, 902
15:8-12......898
15:8-13......901
15:8-14......865
15:9 ....835, 902
15:10 902
15:11 902
15:12 902
15:16 550
15:17-19....841
15:18 ....207, 499
15:18-20 842
15:18-23 861
15:19 ....207, 435, 499, 900
15:20 ....786, 788, 900
15:21 534
15:24 ....435, 836
15:26 ....924, 968
15:27 440
15:30 ....108, 836
16 946
16:1 ....920, 955
16:2 920
16:5 818
16:16 ....818, 918, 994
16:17 ....376, 377
16:23 ....818, 844
16:25 ....145, 789, 808, 860, 865, 869, 892
16:25-26 668

16:26 ....108, 789, 860, 865, 892, 1082

1 CORINTHIANS 338, 679, 914, 965
1 ....43, 575
1–2............564, 752
1:1 750
1:2 ....108, 408, 750, 751, 832, 873, 936
1:3 543
1:4 654
1:5 654
1:8 769
1:9 ....666, 687, 769
1:10 ....8, 921, 936
1:11 921
1:13 982
1:14 ....982, 985
1:16 ....982, 985
1:17 511
1:17–2:14 ..1045
1:18 ....16, 408, 415, 574, 575, 644, 649, 653, 675, 684, 725
1:21 ....7, 503, 575, 649, 683, 722, 894, 912, 995
1:21-25......156
1:23 ....589, 725, 726
1:24 ....441, 589, 725, 912
1:26 685
1:26-31......299
1:27 ....672, 828
1:28 672
1:29-30......255
1:30 ....750, 751
2 ....43, 575
2:1 535
2:1-5 722
2:2 ....112, 421, 509, 535, 765
2:3 112
2:5 723
2:6 ....412, 585
2:6-8 410
2:7 ....85, 92, 126, 725
2:8 ....449, 490, 495, 497, 585
2:9 ....69, 668, 977
2:10 ....69, 108, 668
2:10-16......775
2:11 ....69, 128, 272
2:12 ....69, 176, 178
2:12-14......412
2:13 667
2:14 ....16, 17, 124, 263, 267, 352, 359, 408, 414, 415, 574, 644, 675, 697, 711, 717, 758, 770, 1064, 1067
2:15 ....667, 1064

2:16 .... 667, 725, 936	6:19 .... 750, 752, 821	10:13 .... 197, 370, 703
3 517	6:19-20 1106	10:14-33 .... 440, 994
3:1 112	6:20 .... 552, 750	10:16 .... 550, 584, 822, 991, 995
3:1-3 761	6:53-56 654	10:16-18 654
3:2 112	7:1 890	10:17 .... 822, 962
3:5 .... 977, 978	7:5 181	10:18-21 81
3:6 695	7:7 528	10:20 .... 175, 182, 991
3:7 .... 695, 903	7:9 528	10:20 f 177
3:8 208	7:10 1135	10:21 .... 175, 182, 991, 994
3:10-15 1070	7:12 .... 1129, 1135	10:25 18
3:11 56	7:15 687	10:27 267
3:11-15 1069	7:20-24 136	10:28-33 267
3:12-15 .... 771, 1033, 1070	7:23 552	10:31 .... 161, 299
3:13-15 .... 566, 1079	7:25 1135	10:32 .... 818, 870
3:14 611	7:25 ff 1129	11 .... 462, 760, 922, 924, 963, 978, 992, 993, 1002, 1071
3:15 .... 611, 958, 1070	7:25-26 136	
3:16 .... 111, 664, 750, 752, 821, 836, 997	7:25-40 528	
	7:27 136	11:1 528
3:17 .... 664, 750, 752, 821, 836, 837, 997	7:28-31 136	11:2 .... 170, 963, 993
	7:31 1113	11:2-12 465
3:21-23 .... 952, 1026	8 .... 81, 267, 440	11:3 630
3:22 873	8:1-4 198	11:3-12 315
4:1 .... 575, 952, 977, 978	8:1-6 100	11:7 .... 156, 248, 254, 289
4:1-5 952	8:4 .... 81, 100	11:8 .... 228, 242, 244
4:5 .... 1069, 1070, 1073	8:4-6 .... 12, 18, 962, 1032	11:9 .... 228, 241
4:15 697	8:5 .... 81, 100, 440	11:10 241
5 .... 366, 960	8:6 .... 108, 112, 160, 212, 440	11:13 993
5:1 959	8:7 .... 40, 212, 267	11:16 .... 921, 969, 993
5:1 ff 936, 959	8:9 40	11:17 .... 936, 989, 994, 995
5:1-13 .... 957, 958	8:10 267	11:17-20 994
5:3 272	8:11 766	11:17-23 994
5:4 .... 818, 959	8:12 .... 40, 267	11:17-34 .... 936, 994
5:4-13 924	9:1 892	11:18 .... 818, 989, 994
5:5 .... 174, 366, 958, 959, 1013	9:6 968	11:19 771
5:7 .... 548, 557, 587, 958	9:9 231	11:20 .... 815, 974, 989, 994, 995, 996
5:8 .... 557, 587	9:11 968	
5:11 960	9:13 968	11:20-22 976
5:12 865	9:14 968	11:22 .... 870, 991, 997
5:13 .... 865, 1070	9:15 511	11:23 .... 991, 993
5:26 1126	9:17 .... 717, 848	11:23-25 .... 992, 1006
6 .... 936, 960	9:20 177	11:23-29 1002
6:1-10 957	9:22 684	11:24 .... 976, 978, 991, 999, 1006
6:2 .... 958, 1070	9:27 770	11:24-26 999
6:3 .... 169, 1054, 1070	10 .... 81, 462, 598, 978, 993	11:24-26a ... 994
6:5-6 958	10:1 56	11:25 .... 535, 978, 992, 1000
6:6 958	10:1 ff 693	11:26 .... 535, 978, 992, 1000, 1001
6:7 .... 346, 750	10:1-3 52	
6:9 .... 698, 750	10:1-4 440	11:26b-30 .. 994, 1001
6:9-11 758	10:2 982	11:27 1001
6:10 626	10:3 .... 56, 199	11:27-32 1002
6:11 .... 750, 751, 980	10:4 .... 56, 873, 1064	11:28 1002
6:15 669	10:4-9 439	11:28-32 1071
6:17 769	10:11 895	11:30 .... 366, 373, 1002
6:17-20 664	10:11 ff 822	11:31 1002
6:18 .... 180, 252	10:11-13 440	11:32 .... 1002, 1070
6:18-20 669	10:12 .... 771, 1118	

1 Corinthians (cont.)

1 Corinthians (cont.)
11:33 ....993, 1001
11:34 ....170, 963, 993, 1001
12 ....860, 861, 873, 876, 877, 879, 895, 936
12–14........889, 890, 891
12:1 890
12:1-3 426
12:2 669
12:3 ....415, 717, 873
12:4-6 111
12:4-11.......873, 944
12:6 665
12:7 ....877, 964
12:9 716
12:11 108
12:12 ....841, 873, 877
12:12 ff......910
12:13 ....667, 740, 841, 870, 873, 877, 980, 982
12:13 ff......622, 822, 823
12:13-27 921
12:14-20 877
12:21-27 877
12:26 921
12:27 ....872, 873, 874, 944
12:28 ....870, 873, 890, 892, 936, 944, 945
12:28-30 892
12:29 10
12:31 890
13 823
13:2 ....207, 716, 724
13:7 769
13:9 62
13:10 ....208, 1107
13:12 ....1009, 1026, 1102
13:13 ....367, 686, 769
14 ....963, 993, 995
14:1 890
14:2 xvii
14:4 890
14:5 890
14:13-16 724
14:13-19 998
14:14 492
14:15 492
14:19 ....492, 818, 970
14:23 ....832, 919
14:24 ....919, 1000
14:25 108
14:26 ....890, 964, 970
14:28 994
14:33 ....xvii, 170, 994
14:34 ....xvii, 818, 970, 993, 994
14:37 993

14:38 993
14:40 ....xvii, 170, 890, 993, 995
15 ....7, 401, 495, 611, 1052, 1057, 1060, 1065
15:1 ff 726, 727, 1111
15:1-3 503
15:1-4 601
15:1-5 ....617, 1055
15:1-8 627
15:1-11.......993
15:1-28.......1055
15:3 ....534, 539, 541, 547, 623, 993
15:4 ....603, 623
15:5 1056
15:6 1056
15:7 ....607, 892, 1056
15:8 ....426, 847
15:8-11.......1056
15:9 869
15:10 ....654, 657, 894
15:12 ....485, 1052, 1058
15:12-14 1045
15:12-19 1056
15:13 1052
15:14 1052
15:14 ff......603
15:15 1052
15:17 ....1045, 1052
15:18 1052
15:19 1093
15:20 ....603, 1021, 1052, 1056
15:20-28 1056
15:21 ....398, 495, 1024, 1056
15:22 ....378, 383, 395, 398, 1024, 1056, 1063, 1090
15:22-24 ....1055, 1154
15:23 ....1055, 1056, 1058
15:23-25 ....625, 868
15:24 ....1056, 1114, 1118
15:24 ff......1154
15:24-28 ....1153, 1154
15:25 ....334, 1025, 1113
15:25-28 626
15:26 ....312, 1025
15:27 ....289, 1063
15:28 ....160, 299, 627, 883
15:29 ....556, 982, 1046
15:32 1026
15:33 349
15:35 1063
15:35-42 ....609, 1044
15:35-50 1061
15:36 1063
15:36-38 1063
15:37 1063

15:38 1063
15:39 1063
15:40 ....993, 1063
15:41 1063
15:42-44 ....1063, 1064
15:44 1063
15:45 ....234, 241, 256, 468, 495, 1063
15:45-47 ....496, 1063
15:45-50 307
15:45-58 878
15:47 ....231, 233, 287, 307, 439, 1063
15:47-49 611
15:49 ....603, 609, 615, 1044, 1052, 1061, 1063
15:50 ....307, 575, 1064
15:50-54 611
15:50-58 1063
15:51 1062
15:51 ff......1038
15:51-53 1116
15:51-55 1052
15:51-57 762
15:51-58 763
15:52 ....1062, 1063
15:53 611
15:54 ....1020, 1050, 1051, 1062
15:55 ....1020, 1051
16:1 ....919, 921, 924
16:1-4 968
16:2 ....919, 921, 924, 965, 969, 994, 996
16:10 920
16:13 ....759, 896
16:17 920
16:19 818
16:22 ....108, 115

2 CORINTHIANS 679, 914
1:3 220
1:4-6 761
1:11 647
1:14 1013
1:21 777
1:22 984
2:2 451
2:3 924
2:5-7 957
2:6 959
2:6-11 959
2:9 ....924, 1070
2:11 ....178, 180, 186
2:14 661
2:14–3:4 273
3:13-15.......434

Scripture Index

3:14 839	10:5 .... 415, 877	2:1 1129
3:16 703	11:2 878	2:2 .... 694, 1129
3:17 109	11:3 .... 304, 308, 309, 643	2:3 327
3:18 .... 248, 611, 760, 762, 1061	11:10-15 952	2:4 832
4:2 267	11:12-15 185	2:6-9 854
4:3 185	11:14 .... 175, 180	2:7 717
4:4 .... 160, 175, 176, 178, 180, 185, 255, 329	11:14 ff 181	2:10 440
4:6 .... 90, 160	11:15 180	2:16 737
4:7 229	11:23 1020	2:17 737
4:13 .... 107, 874	11:31 220	2:20 .... 4, 448, 665, 751, 877
4:16 .... 762, 1022	12:1-4 .... 22, 286, 620, 624, 1022, 1042	3 719
4:18 .... 21, 1082, 1103	12:1-5 1108	3:1-22 745
5 575	12:1-10 1101	3:2 723
5:1 .... 269, 1036, 1038, 1083	12:2 .... 169, 1036, 1097	3:6 .... 735, 742, 855
5:1-9 1042	12:2-4 290	3:6-9 841
5:2 1036	12:3 654	3:7 634
5:7 .... 716, 719, 1026	12:4 .... 169, 620, 1038, 1102	3:8 .... 588, 726, 737, 784, 841, 893
5:8 .... 1036, 1038, 1076	12:7 .... 170, 175, 185, 186	3:9 737
5:9 1038	12:7-10 136	3:11 739
5:9-21 1068	12:8-10 185	3:13 .... 532, 555, 556, 595, 613, 658
5:10 .... 454, 1067, 1069, 1070, 1077, 1079	12:9 654	3:14 739
5:11 .... 684, 1067, 1071	12:12 207	3:15 506
5:14 .... 108, 556, 590, 1067	12:17 920	3:16 .... 313, 506, 784
5:15 590	12:18 920	3:19 .... 505, 506
5:17 .... 330, 668, 690, 695	12:20 958	3:19-22 .... 658, 710
5:18 552	12:21 958	3:19-25 719
5:18-19 782	13:1 958	3:20 .... 506, 812
5:19 .... 331, 333, 509, 551, 552, 575, 584, 638, 768, 1090	13:2 958	3:23 715
5:19-21 1090	13:11 .... 921, 936	3:23–4:7 745
5:20 .... 702, 1090	13:14 .... 107, 108, 111	3:24 .... 430, 636, 739
5:21 .... 102, 399, 467, 504, 521, 523, 532, 534, 543, 547, 555, 556, 589, 661, 738, 746, 1024	**GALATIANS** 338, 739, 914	3:25 715
	1 784	3:26 746
	1–4 99	3:27 .... 980, 982
6:1 .... 759, 967	1:1 891	4 773
6:16 298	1:1-6 812	4:1-7 517
6:36 523	1:4 .... 329, 331, 575	4:2 697
7:1 413	1:6 .... 686, 687	4:3 .... 585, 774
7:8 709	1:6-9 9	4:4 .... 3, 110, 428, 476, 479, 484, 517, 667, 701, 726, 745, 774, 784, 1120, 1121
7:8-12 957	1:7 783	4:4-6 .... 746, 774
7:9 711	1:8 .... 115, 783	4:5 .... 430, 517, 667, 744, 773, 774
7:10 .... 710, 711	1:9 115	4:6 .... 667, 746, 773, 774, 775, 776, 777
7:11 708	1:10 783	
8:9 .... 440, 484, 487, 511, 512, 514, 527	1:11-22 899	4:7 746
8:19 926	1:11-24 1135	4:9 585
9:3 511	1:11–2:9 784	4:10 774
9:6 611	1:12 1129	4:13 269
9:9 959	1:13 918	4:19 472
9:12 968	1:15 .... 197, 280, 654, 844, 891	4:21-31 813
9:13 885	1:16 .... 197, 694, 1065	4:22 476
9:15 .... 891, 992	1:17 994	4:24 476
10:4 877	1:18 .... 8, 1129	
	1:23 715	
	2 .... 694, 784	
	2–4 715	Galatians (cont.)

Galatians (cont.)
4:26.........801, 813, 824, 909, 1102
4:29.........476
5...............368
5:5............739
5:6............718
5:12..........114, 115
5:13..........687, 785
5:15..........921
5:17..........356
5:19..........361
5:21..........626
5:22..........698, 715, 758
5:22-26......877
5:23..........698, 758
5:24..........762
5:24-26......758
5:25..........759
6:1............342, 959, 1002
6:2............108, 921, 1002
6:6............952, 968
6:6-8.........951
6:7............101, 952, 968, 1068, 1072
6:10..........921, 968
6:14..........590, 591
6:15..........853
6:16..........853

EPHESIANS 338, 914
1................112, 679, 1099
1–3.............122, 839
1:1-3..........675
1:1-12........1073
1:1-14........650
1:2.............1097
1:3.............220, 649, 650
1:3-6..........112, 675
1:3-13........834
1:3-14........111
1:4.............145, 649, 665, 666, 672, 673, 675, 677
1:4-7..........333
1:5.............70, 71, 161, 299, 650, 676, 746, 862
1:5-11........126
1:6.............161, 299, 654, 676
1:7.............421, 537, 550, 584, 650, 654, 665
1:7-13a......112
1:8.............537
1:9.............70, 71, 299, 808, 862, 869, 1090, 1154
1:10...........298, 848, 849, 909, 1090, 1154
1:10-30......801
1:11...........70, 71, 90, 108, 126, 130, 131, 132, 197, 298, 673, 676, 677, 862, 911, 1073, 1107
1:12...........161, 677, 911
1:13...........650, 651, 769, 777, 800, 984
1:13b.........112
1:14...........112, 1107
1:15...........744
1:15-23......514
1:17...........621
1:17-23......878
1:18...........1104
1:18-23......802
1:19...........90, 608, 615, 695, 769
1:19-23......507, 614
1:20...........608, 615, 695, 769, 1097
1:20-23......606, 625, 868
1:21...........167, 169
1:22...........5, 126, 456, 621, 800, 820, 909, 989
1:23...........5, 456, 665, 800, 820, 909, 989
2.................836, 837, 842, 860, 879
2–3.............861
2:1.............180, 267, 273, 383, 387, 553, 574, 666, 697, 1021, 1023, 1076
2:1-3..........17, 532
2:1-5..........644
2:1-6..........665
2:2.............174, 176, 179, 180
2:3.............253, 316, 343, 351, 359, 363, 368, 394, 396, 416, 643, 677, 1064, 1076
2:4.............108, 666
2:5.............108, 311, 615, 665, 666, 1021
2:6.............615, 665, 1021, 1038, 1097
2:7.............575
2:8.............654, 657, 724, 759
2:8-10........299
2:9.............657, 759
2:10...........654, 668, 675, 690, 695, 698, 878
2:11-13......368
2:11-18......330
2:11-22......997
2:12...........902, 1021, 1026
2:13...........550, 584, 654, 902
2:13-18......837
2:14...........879
2:15...........821, 878, 879
2:16...........879
2:18...........112, 800, 879
2:18-22......802
2:19...........626, 837, 842
2:19-22......801, 879, 892, 897
2:20...........675, 842, 843, 878, 892, 942
2:20-22......669
2:21...........837, 878
2:22...........837
3:1.............197
3:1-5..........801, 847
3:1-6..........860
3:1-10........668
3:2.............848, 894
3:3.............865, 1129
3:3-9..........426, 808, 869
3:4.............484, 927
3:5.............892, 927
3:6.............912
3:7.............894
3:8.............452, 654, 912
3:8-11........911
3:9.............145, 299, 800, 912, 1073
3:9-11........132
3:9b-11......74
3:10...........74, 88, 161, 167, 173, 299, 537, 800, 820, 912, 1073
3:11...........74, 131, 133
3:14-19......791
3:16...........108, 667
3:17...........108, 667
3:18...........769
3:19...........452, 494, 729, 769
3:19-23......1139
3:20...........90, 729
3:21...........834
4.................454, 679, 880, 895, 941
4:1-6..........895
4:3.............895, 896, 897, 936
4:3-6..........830, 921
4:4.............880
4:4-6..........111, 879, 880
4:5.............8, 368, 921, 980, 982
4:6.............890
4:7.............657, 880, 890, 891, 894, 1041
4:7 ff..........890
4:7-16........890, 895, 897
4:7-17........889, 951
4:8.............539, 618, 891, 1035, 1086, 1093
4:8-10........618, 890
4:9.............539, 880, 891, 1032, 1033, 1035, 1041, 1086, 1093

4:10 .... 891, 893	6:11 ff 181	2:9 .... 513, 586, 615
4:11 .... 328, 891, 892, 893, 894, 896, 909, 931, 942, 944, 946, 947	6:11-18 181	2:9-11 .... 534, 606, 621, 625, 868
	6:12 .... 165, 167, 168, 173, 179, 585, 921, 1065, 1097	2:10 .... 334, 449, 455, 1080, 1090, 1093, 1118
4:11-16 ...... 761, 890, 891, 895	6:12-19 189	2:11 .... 334, 455, 458, 614, 1118
4:11-17 891	6:13 173	2:11-13 776
4:12 .... 208, 880, 894, 896, 897, 909, 946	6:13-18 166	2:12 .... 759, 760, 767, 894
	6:16 .... 175, 182, 760	2:13 .... 685, 759, 760, 767, 894
4:13 .... 895, 896, 921	6:17 .... 499, 761	2:14-16 877
4:13-14 895	6:18 .... 759, 760	2:15 911
4:14 896	6:19 759	2:16 911
4:15 .... 625, 628, 868, 896, 897	6:21 920	2:17 1003
4:16 .... 880, 896	6:22 920	2:19-24 927
4:17 758		3:2 1052
4:17 ff 722	PHILIPPIANS 914	3:4-6 8
4:17-19 ...... 532, 1021	1:1 .... 750, 751, 760, 830, 917, 924, 946	3:4-8 650
4:18 .... 253, 267, 311, 343, 408, 414, 553, 878, 1076		3:5 853
	1:6 .... 758, 769	3:7-10 1025
4:19 .... 267, 408, 414	1:9 102	3:9 .... 737, 739
4:22 759	1:12-14 197	3:10 .... 615, 762
4:23 .... 695, 758, 759	1:20 .... 4, 911	3:11 .... 895, 1057, 1058
4:24 .... 248, 249, 251, 297, 642, 690, 695, 698, 758, 760	1:21 .... 4, 990, 1038, 1065	3:12 762
	1:21-23 1042	3:12-14 895
4:26 566	1:21-24 1076	3:15 412
4:26-27 186	1:22 .... 451, 1038	3:18 832
4:27 181	1:23 .... 184, 355, 762, 1038, 1107, 1153	3:18-20 767
4:30 .... 103, 769, 777, 984		3:19 1090
5:2 548	1:23-26 1026	3:20 .... 626, 813, 1061, 1099, 1153
5:5 .... 626, 767, 1107	1:24 1038	
5:6 .... 185, 767	1:25 451	3:21 .... 609, 611, 612, 615, 762, 1044, 1053, 1061, 1062
5:8 414	1:27 .... 921, 936	
5:9 800	1:29 716	4:3 1073
5:11 180	2 .... 492, 990	4:4 .... 191, 775
5:12 180	2:1 921	4:5 191
5:16 198	2:1-7 776	4:6 .... 191, 775
5:18-20 111	2:2 921	4:7 .... 775, 779
5:19 970	2:2-4 936	4:8 .... 367, 775
5:22 .... 628, 869	2:3 .... 440, 921	4:9 775
5:22-33 ...... 669, 822	2:4 486	4:13 .... 108, 193, 698
5:23 .... 468, 625, 628, 630, 830, 868	2:4 ff 514	4:14-19 968
	2:4-11 440	4:18 .... 920, 968, 1003
5:25 .... 800, 818, 830, 838	2:5 514	4:19 197
5:25-27 ...... 818, 912	2:5 ff 727	
5:25-28 913	2:5-8 439	COLOSSIANS 914
5:26 .... 760, 987	2:5-9 .... 441, 446, 498	1 492
5:26-42 878	2:5-11 514	1:5 .... 114, 334, 1099, 1123
5:27 910	2:6 .... 251, 439, 487, 514	1:6 .... 334, 846, 1123
5:28-31 229	2:6-8 .... 511, 512, 525	1:8 108
5:29 914	2:6-10 585	1:10 248
5:32 .... 304, 427, 575, 664, 808, 820	2:6-11 486	1:12 .... 647, 1107
	2:7 .... 405, 443, 484, 487, 510, 511, 514, 515	1:13 .... 497, 626, 647, 861
6:1 97		1:13-15 490
6:5-9 1070	2:7 ff 527	1:14 .... 334, 497, 577, 584
6:8 628	2:8 .... 443, 484, 487, 514, 515, 563, 615	1:15 .... 248, 249, 255, 450
6:9 .... 628, 1073		1:15-20 440
6:11 .... 165, 175, 178, 179, 180, 308	2:8-10 255	Colossians (cont.)

1215

Colossians (cont.)
1:16 .... 108, 160, 161, 164, 168, 453
1:16-18 614
1:17 .... 192, 439, 453, 456, 667
1:18 .... 334, 450, 628, 878, 978, 1046
1:18-20 ...... 625, 868
1:19 .... 452, 583, 1090
1:19-20 1090
1:19-23 334
1:20 .... 323, 334, 550, 583, 585, 1090
1:22 590
1:23 .... 334, 1123
1:24-29 668
1:25 848
1:27 .... 108, 664, 726, 1097
1:27-29 758
1:28 .... 947, 961
2 492
2:2 .... 448, 494, 765, 772
2:3 .... 112, 451, 452, 494, 536, 772
2:7 870
2:8 .... 181, 185, 452
2:9 .... 51, 452, 456
2:10 .... 452, 456, 666, 669
2:12 .... 696, 980
2:13 .... 383, 387, 553
2:14 .... 181, 584, 976
2:15 .... 166, 169, 173, 179, 181, 584, 585, 1147
2:16 .... 431, 1073
2:17 .... 431, 558
2:18 .... 167, 169
2:20 .... 665, 976
3:1 .... 615, 622
3:1-3 .... 615, 1099
3:1-4 .... 628, 813
3:3 .... 665, 701, 764, 866
3:4 .... 615, 665, 703, 764, 769, 866
3:5 .... 354, 762
3:5–4:18 615
3:9 695
3:10 .... 251, 297, 642, 695, 697
3:11 450
3:16 .... 108, 970
3:24 .... 1070, 1107
3:25 .... 1070, 1073
4:1 628
4:3 .... 484, 757
4:11 627
4:12 920
4:16 965
4:17 966

1 THESSALONIANS ... 914, 942, 947, 1132, 1150
1:1 .... 686, 1134
1:2 1134
1:2-4 1067
1:3 .... 773, 1067
1:4 .... 672, 686
1:5 .... 686, 765, 1067
1:6 773
1:7 773
1:9 .... 71, 72, 100, 686, 689, 703
1:10 .... 647, 703, 1067
1:13-16 1126
2:4 717
2:9 968
2:12 .... 626, 687
2:14 .... 818, 918
2:14-16 400
2:16 654
2:18 .... 185, 197
3 949
3:5 176
3:12 757
3:13 757
4 1129
4:3-5 757
4:3-7 749
4:4-5 354
4:6 1068
4:7 .... 687, 758
4:8 72
4:9 1117
4:10 729
4:13 .... 1090, 1133
4:13 ff 1038, 1127
4:13-18 ...... 763, 1116, 1118, 1123, 1124, 1132, 1133
4:13-20 1057
4:14 .... 921, 1042
4:15 .... 1042, 1129
4:16 .... 169, 171, 611, 615, 617, 666, 1042, 1117
4:17 .... 171, 611, 1102
5 1129
5:1 1129
5:2 1129
5:7 1013
5:9 1102
5:12 .... 924, 929, 942, 946, 947, 952
5:12-14 760
5:13 .... 942, 946, 952
5:17 199
5:19 995

5:20 995
5:22-24 685
5:23 .... 273, 649, 690, 758, 762
5:24 .... 690, 762, 769

2 THESSALONIANS .. 914, 1132, 1136, 1150
1:3 .... 729, 732
1:5-10 .... 789, 790
1:6-7 1107
1:7-10 1069
1:9 736
1:10 1102
1:12 448
2 .... 1123, 1136
2:1 ff 1017, 1107, 1124
2:1-11 .... 1134, 1136
2:2 .... 1013, 1123, 1133, 1134
2:3 .... 185, 1123, 1126, 1134, 1135
2:3 ff 1135
2:3-6 374
2:5 .... 1133, 1135, 1152
2:6 .... 1136, 1152
2:6-7 1136
2:7 .... 374, 1136, 1152
2:7-10 1069
2:7-11 186
2:7-12 .... 180, 303
2:7a 1136
2:7b 1136
2:8 .... 1056, 1126
2:9 .... 175, 208
2:10 .... 175, 208
2:10-12 ...... 47, 372
2:11 .... 173, 183, 373, 1133
2:12 1070
2:13 .... 111, 673, 675, 686
2:14 .... 111, 686
2:15 1135
2:16 703
2:17 703
3:3 .... 181, 182, 769
3:4 181
3:5 1133
3:5-15 1133
3:6 960
3:6-10 .... 235, 968
3:6-14 958
3:6-15 957
3:8 738
3:10 235
3:14 .... 958, 960
3:15 .... 960, 961
4:13-18 ...... 762, 1116

SCRIPTURE INDEX

1 Timothy 640, 882, 892, 944, 948

1:3 804
1:6 552
1:9 .... 553, 701
1:10 .... 553, 603
1:10-11 8
1:11 .... 220, 717
1:15 .... 362, 412
1:16 681
1:17 .... 81, 85
1:20 958
2:1 461
2:1-4 585
2:1-5 331
2:1-6 585
2:1-8 966
2:2 585
2:3 .... 585, 967
2:4 461
2:4-6 1090
2:5 .... 333, 461, 499, 505, 506, 557, 610
2:6 .... 333, 461, 506, 595, 638, 1090
2:7 894
2:8 .... 237, 461
2:9-15 .... 229, 461
2:11 308
2:12 955
2:12-14 241
2:13 .... 228, 283, 465
2:14 .... 283, 304, 308, 309, 499
2:16 610
3 .... 924, 926, 940, 955
3:1 .... 705, 926
3:1 ff 10
3:1-7 .... 929, 953
3:1-10 951
3:1-13 909
3:2 .... 10, 930, 953, 955
3:5 870
3:6 .... 178, 180, 308, 953, 1070, 1114
3:7 .... 175, 178
3:8 .... 930, 955
3:8-10 945
3:8-13 954
3:10 930
3:11 .... 954, 955, 1097
3:12 .... 930, 955
3:13 552
3:14 943
3:14-16 808
3:15 .... 800, 812, 824, 870, 909, 943, 944, 966

3:16 486
3:16 .... 168, 304, 427, 461, 484, 487, 489, 494, 500, 525, 575, 611, 621, 664, 726, 727, 820
4:1 .... 177, 182, 184, 185, 186, 715, 1135
4:2 .... 40, 267, 414
4:3 327
4:6 .... 715, 946, 969
4:7 .... 760, 1081
4:8 72
4:9 685
4:10 .... 72, 333, 435, 638, 648, 784
4:11 ff 943
4:12 943
4:13 .... 269, 423, 640, 731, 896, 961, 965, 967, 969, 971
4:14 .... 269, 603, 670, 893
4:15 965
4:16 .... 670, 896
5:5-16 968
5:8 718
5:8-16 235
5:9 649
5:10 .... 718, 976
5:11 946
5:12 923
5:17 .... 936, 948, 951, 953, 968
5:18 .... 231, 948, 951, 968
5:19 959
5:19-24 957
5:20 959
5:21 .... 127, 173, 958
5:22 .... 376, 904, 953
5:23 .... 208, 272, 327
5:24 .... 1077, 1079
5:25 .... 1077, 1079
6:2-4 846
6:3 .... 462, 1004
6:4 858
6:8 487
6:11 946
6:13-16 445
6:15 .... 57, 81, 91, 220
6:16 .... 65, 75, 81, 168, 220, 1029
6:18 718
6:20 9

2 Timothy 640, 732, 882, 892, 944, 948

1:3 267
1:5 626
1:6 .... 893, 933
1:7 603

1:9 .... 126, 145, 333, 484, 585, 588, 603, 649, 660, 674, 675, 676, 685, 769
1:10 .... 333, 484, 585, 586, 588, 603, 660, 1022, 1025, 1026, 1037
1:11 894
1:12 .... 718, 729, 732, 769, 1093
1:13 .... xvii, 8, 9, 640, 969
1:14 .... xvii, 758
1:15 xvii
1:16 xvii
2:1 .... 8, 107, 654
2:1-2 .... 9, 970
2:2 .... 8, 9, 107, 640, 882, 896, 948
2:3 1135
2:8 603
2:10 .... 312, 678, 1102
2:11 690
2:12 .... 705, 1102
2:13 .... 90, 99, 101, 536
2:14 858
2:15 993
2:19 .... 677, 684, 767, 770, 885, 984
2:21 .... 698, 1114
2:22 180
2:24 534
2:24-26 712
2:26 .... 175, 208
3:1 .... 1008, 1126, 1135
3:1-7 1128
3:3 414
3:5 .... 964, 1135
3:6 993
3:8 758
3:9 832
3:13 185
3:14-17 1004
3:15 748
3:15-17 761
3:16 .... 51, 52, 141, 162, 182, 243, 658, 759, 821
3:17 .... 51, 52, 718
4 948
4:1 1070
4:1 ff 944
4:1-5 .... 943, 960
4:2 .... 947, 961
4:3 1135
4:5 .... 893, 942
4:6 .... 729, 1042
4:6-8 .... 136, 732
4:7 729

2 Timothy (cont.)

2 Timothy (cont.)
4:7-8 1116
4:8 .... 1070, 1093, 1102
4:9 943
4:11 .... 728, 860
4:14 .... 958, 1004
4:15 958
4:17 894
4:18 .... 647, 1102
4:20 .... 136, 208

Titus 640, 892, 948
1 .... 886, 926, 940, 949
1:2 .... 90, 99, 126, 145, 427
1:3 717
1:5 .... 917, 926, 927, 949, 951
1:5 ff 926
1:5-7 ff 869
1:5-9 .... 929, 953
1:5-11 .... 10, 951
1:7 .... 926, 930, 952
1:9 .... 8, 953
1:12 .... 247, 367, 953
1:13 .... 953, 961
1:15 .... 267, 413, 758
2 924
2:1-13 1121
2:1-15 960
2:7 718
2:10 715
2:11 .... 553, 560, 585, 657, 660, 661
2:12 759
2:13 .... 448, 703, 1069, 1127
2:14 .... 112, 551, 718, 878
3:3-6 553
3:4-6 650
3:5 .... 537, 654, 689, 690, 691, 695, 696, 980, 987, 988
3:8-11 959
3:10 959
3:13 968
3:14 .... 718, 968
3:18 718

Philemon 924
1 968
2 968
10 697
15 197
22 968

Hebrews 542, 635, 924, 947, 964
1 171
1:1 .... 46, 51, 429, 509, 912, 1012, 1108

1:1 ff 509
1:1-2 542
1:1-3 614
1:2 .... 46, 51, 85, 160, 429, 453, 1012
1:3 .... 2, 51, 90, 192, 255, 372, 453, 456, 586, 621, 633, 868, 1099
1:4-13 1011
1:5 .... 441, 490
1:5-12 85
1:6 .... 114, 450, 455
1:7 .... 169, 170
1:8 447
1:9 447
1:10 .... 160, 453
1:10-12 .... 450, 769
1:13 633
1:14 .... 167, 169, 170, 172, 1099
2 .... 466, 492, 598
2–10 629
2:1-4 .... 51, 206, 207, 499, 841
2:3 .... 866, 965, 969
2:3-4 208
2:4 .... 208, 866
2:5 ff 1100
2:5-18 633
2:6-9 868
2:8 289
2:9 .... 441, 462, 468, 484, 514
2:9-18 .... 27, 441, 468, 486, 737
2:9a 633
2:9b 633
2:10 .... 586, 873
2:11 1009
2:12 817
2:13 .... 468, 873
2:14 .... 174, 245, 405, 441, 468, 484, 586, 633, 1020, 1023, 1026, 1097, 1114, 1139
2:14 ff 647
2:14-17 1037
2:15 .... 136, 583, 586, 1020, 1026
2:16 .... 245, 462, 536
2:17 .... 484, 487, 529, 555, 633, 634, 637
2:17–10:39 634
2:18 .... 487, 496, 529, 633
3 635
3–10 .... 431, 558
3:1 .... 631, 635
3:1–4:13 633
3:3 453
3:4 .... 453, 753

3:5 631
3:6 773
3:7 .... 107, 874
3:12–4:11 771
3:13 .... 414, 1026
3:19 369
4 635
4:4-16 468
4:7 684
4:12 .... 51, 273, 384, 686, 760
4:13 .... 87, 88, 108, 384, 760
4:14 .... 462, 523, 620, 633, 878
4:14-16 .... 27, 487, 529, 622
4:15 .... 467, 472, 523, 527, 528, 637
4:16 .... 58, 1005
5:1 .... 548, 634
5:1-3 345
5:1a 631
5:4 631
5:5 .... 490, 631
5:6 434
5:7 636
5:8 .... 308, 525, 534, 563, 632
5:9 .... 308, 1082
5:10 434
5:12-14 .... 11, 761
6–9 1103
6:1 .... 712, 1071
6:1 ff 1071
6:1-8 .... 719, 772
6:2 .... 980, 1071
6:4 1009
6:5 .... 866, 1009
6:7-20 1103
6:9 772
6:10 1071
6:11 .... 765, 772
6:12 772
6:17 505
6:17-20 769
6:18 .... 65, 274, 427
6:18-20 622
6:19 274
6:20 622
7 .... 871, 1103
7:9 396
7:10 .... 279, 396
7:11 .... 635, 636
7:12 .... 635, 636
7:16 .... 72, 636
7:21 .... 632, 709
7:21-25 632
7:23 1082
7:24 .... 621, 1082
7:24-28 507

7:25 .... 181, 621, 636, 769	10:5-10 462	11:21 762
7:26 .... 462, 467, 499, 620, 621, 632	10:7 .... 352, 487, 526	11:23-26 1032
7:27 586	10:10 .... 587, 751, 769, 1066	11:23-27 1029
7:28 632	10:10-12 750	11:26 444
8 .... 871, 1103	10:11 557	11:27 720
8:1 .... 1099, 1100, 1103	10:11-13 868	11:31 .... 415, 717
8:1 ff 996	10:12 .... 548, 557, 586, 1066, 1099	11:33 ff 896
8:1-6 621	10:13 .... 334, 769	11:34-38 785
8:2 .... 558, 636, 997, 1097, 1103	10:14 .... 587, 750, 1066	11:35 .... 1032, 1057
8:3 564	10:15 .... 107, 874	11:39 536
8:5 .... 558, 635, 1103	10:15-18 695	11:40 .... 536, 1107
8:6 .... 499, 507	10:18 587	12:1 .... 504, 534
8:6-13 839	10:19 .... 550, 591	12:1-3 513
8:8-12 693	10:19-22 772	12:1-4 .... 371, 529
9:1 976	10:22 .... 267, 765	12:1-17 761
9:6 698	10:22-25 760	12:2 .... 462, 504, 513, 534, 586, 650, 868, 1099, 1100
9:6 ff 695	10:23-39 773	12:3 504
9:7 .... 345, 1066	10:24 .... 718, 965	12:5-8 774
9:8 .... 874, 1097	10:25 .... 319, 760, 812, 921, 924, 965	12:5-11 769
9:9 .... 431, 558, 635	10:26 .... 548, 563, 587	12:9 .... 272, 277, 279, 774
9:10 635	10:26 ff 767	12:10 97
9:11 .... 620, 621, 635, 1097, 1104	10:26-29 771	12:12 .... 729, 1105
9:12 .... 536, 550, 551, 618, 635, 1066, 1082, 1097	10:26-31 .... 348, 553, 567, 766, 1075	12:14 .... 758, 759, 760
9:14 .... 108, 267, 521, 547, 550, 584, 591, 632, 875	10:27 566	12:15 921
9:15 .... 499, 507, 1104, 1107	10:29 .... 551, 584, 752	12:17 709
9:16 1105	10:30 760	12:21 729
9:17 1105	10:31 71	12:21-23 1032
9:19 .... 752, 976	10:35 773	12:22 .... 168, 629, 1042, 1105
9:19-22 ...... 505, 550	10:38 .... 274, 739	12:22-24 .... 629, 800, 812, 878
9:21 1106	11 .... 14, 715, 719, 728, 785, 854, 1039	12:23 .... 5, 168, 247, 272, 450, 619, 629, 762, 818, 820, 877, 1042, 1105
9:22 .... 547, 584	11:1 1103	12:24 .... 499, 507, 584, 752
9:23 .... 431, 548, 558, 583, 620, 1104	11:1-3 155	12:25 812
9:23-28 ...... 557, 634	11:3 .... 35, 143, 150, 160, 243, 372	12:28 .... 58, 654, 775, 963
9:24 .... 431, 558, 620, 622, 633, 637, 638, 649, 1097, 1104	11:4 .... 318, 319, 733, 739	12:29 .... 56, 58, 98
9:24-26 621	11:4-7 855	13:4 754
9:24-28 ...... 621, 649	11:5 .... 1048, 1061, 1098	13:6 189
9:25 .... 634, 1066	11:6 .... 339, 704, 739	13:7 952
9:26 .... 547, 548, 583, 587, 633, 634, 638, 649, 1066	11:7 739	13:8 .... 450, 551
9:27 .... 312, 313, 1020, 1021, 1026, 1066	11:8 .... 14, 720, 752	13:12 .... 547, 584, 750, 751, 752
9:28 .... 621, 649, 1066, 1116	11:8 ff 855	13:12-14 591
9:28a 1066	11:9 .... 752, 821	13:15 .... 637, 1003
10:1 .... 431, 557, 631, 635, 659	11:9-18 739	13:17 .... 760, 923, 924, 929, 943, 947, 952
10:2 267	11:11 1095	13:20 .... 550, 586, 1046
10:3 557	11:11-16 719	13:24 952
10:4 .... 557, 635	11:12 1097	
10:5-7 .... 525, 538	11:13 .... 260, 813, 821, 825, 1037, 1040	JAMES 924, 947
	11:13 ff 1034	1:1 .... 694, 904
	11:13-16 .... 260, 1028	1:2 ff 732
	11:16 1032	1:3 718
	11:17 .... 114, 448, 784	1:6 .... 718, 728
	11:19 .... 604, 1029, 1032, 1050	

Hebrews (cont.)

Hebrews (cont.)
1:6-8 200
1:7 728
1:8 728
1:12-15 528
1:13 .... 90, 372
1:13-15 .... 370, 371
1:14 .... 309, 403, 528, 644
1:15 .... 309, 644, 1023
1:17 .... 57, 65, 90, 133, 217, 588, 697
1:18 .... 694, 695, 697
1:21 .... 274, 651, 694
1:22-25 1073
1:23 760
1:24 760
1:27 297
2:1 .... 694, 718, 958, 1073
2:1-13 741
2:2 .... 694, 927
2:3 .... 958, 1073
2:5 672
2:9 .... 346, 958, 1073
2:10 .... 363, 738
2:14 .... 715, 718, 740, 741
2:14-18 1073
2:14-26 .... 718, 740
2:15 741
2:18 740
2:19 .... 30, 81, 184, 718, 740
2:21 120
2:23 .... 68, 718, 735, 741, 742, 746
2:24 .... 718, 737, 740
2:26 .... 72, 272, 740, 1019, 1021, 1022, 1076
3 741
3:3-12 410
3:6 1083
3:8-10 49
3:9 .... 248, 249, 250, 253, 254, 256
3:14 185
3:15 1064
3:17 958
4 741
4:4 340
4:7 .... 180, 181
4:8 760
4:12 108
4:13-15 136
5:1-6 741
5:3 1008
5:7 .... 1117, 1119
5:7-8 1119
5:8 .... 566, 1117

5:11 .... 25, 1119
5:14 .... 927, 947, 959
5:15 718
5:16 342

1 PETER
1:1 .... 139, 674, 676, 752, 809, 821, 840, 846, 917, 945, 969
1:1-2 698
1:2 .... 127, 139, 550, 573, 674, 675, 676, 752, 809, 840
1:3 .... 220, 603, 690, 695, 697, 698
1:4 .... 697, 1104, 1107
1:5 .... 51, 649, 769, 1008
1:5-7 668
1:7 732
1:7-10 1103
1:8 .... 495, 716, 720, 728
1:9 .... 272, 720
1:10 .... 52, 513, 586
1:10-12 .... 645, 1113, 1155
1:11 .... 52, 107, 513, 531, 547, 586, 614, 615, 626
1:12 .... 169, 536
1:14 749
1:15 .... 97, 658, 759
1:15-19 749
1:16 .... 97, 658, 759
1:17 .... 120, 958, 1073, 1077
1:18 .... 575, 840
1:18-20 .... 651, 660, 862
1:19 .... 103, 200, 420, 521, 523, 550, 557, 584, 840
1:20 .... 103, 132, 200, 420, 538, 1008
1:21 .... 408, 614, 615
1:22 .... 696, 761, 921
1:23 .... 574, 584, 651, 686, 694, 696, 723, 775, 813
1:23-25 51
1:25 .... 651, 686, 696
2:2 .... 697, 760
2:4 669
2:5 .... 637, 669, 896, 913, 1005
2:5-11 821
2:7 .... 137, 531
2:8 137
2:9 .... 295, 677, 687, 690, 752, 821, 878, 1005
2:11 825
2:12 .... 718, 741, 884
2:13-25 1113
2:17 .... 753, 821, 920, 921
2:17-25 267

2:18-25 529
2:19 267
2:21 523
2:21-25 462
2:22 .... 499, 504, 523
2:22-25 344
2:23 504
2:24 .... 534, 556, 751
2:25 .... 504, 534, 946, 952
3 1094
3:2 696
3:5 95
3:6 449
3:8 .... 921, 936
3:8-12 1115
3:10 180
3:15 .... 23, 34, 501, 721, 892
3:16 .... 40, 892
3:18 .... 107, 271, 547, 556, 586, 1022, 1035
3:18 ff 519
3:18-20 .... 496, 519, 1032, 1093
3:19 .... 168, 654, 1035, 1040, 1086, 1094
3:19-21 1094
3:20 .... 1040, 1086, 1094
3:21 .... 624, 868, 982
3:22 .... 168, 585, 624, 868, 1099
4 1094
4:1 751
4:2 751
4:5 1041
4:6 .... 1024, 1035, 1041, 1077, 1086, 1093, 1094
4:7 1119
4:8 921
4:9 108
4:10 952
4:11 .... 161, 804
4:12 1025
4:13 1025
4:14-19 1025
4:16 483
4:17 1069
4:19 718
5:1 .... 917, 946, 948, 952
5:1 ff 760
5:1-4 .... 952, 953
5:1-5 923
5:2 .... 894, 924, 946, 948
5:2 ff 917
5:2-4 878
5:3 946
5:4 .... 917, 1102
5:5 920
5:7 589

Scripture Index

5:8 .... 173, 308, 1023, 1114
5:10 1082

2 Peter 924
1:1 448
1:2 761
1:3 .... 52, 649, 653, 687, 761
1:4 .... 668, 690, 694, 695, 696, 697, 822
1:5-7 .... 732, 740
1:5-8 739
1:10 .... 672, 676, 681, 685, 696, 766
1:12 969
1:16-18 .... 523, 724
1:21 .... 107, 108
2:1 .... 169, 552, 770
2:4 .... 168, 173, 174, 183, 184, 371, 647, 1035
2:5 ff 647
2:7 647
2:8 1080
2:9 .... 1035, 1042
2:10 1042
2:11 169
2:14 316
2:17 1080
2:18 371
2:20 1135
2:20-22 766
3 1113
3:1 821
3:1-15 1113
3:3 .... 1008, 1113, 1128
3:4 1117
3:4-17 1128
3:5 346
3:9 1123
3:10 .... 740, 1014, 1058, 1113, 1155
3:10 ff 1011, 1014
3:10-12 763
3:10-13 ...... 153, 1013, 1156
3:11 1058
3:11-13 762
3:13 .... 763, 1153, 1155
3:14 .... 694, 762, 763, 969
3:14-16 1004
3:15 .... 122, 694, 760, 892, 965, 969
3:16 .... 122, 333, 760, 892, 965
3:18 732

1 John 695, 880, 924
1:1 .... 439, 607, 724
1:1-3 477
1:2 .... 439, 450, 496
1:3 .... 108, 884
1:4 773
1:6 884
1:7 .... 550, 584, 884
1:8 .... 32, 409, 412, 637
1:8-10 412
1:9 .... 32, 100, 706
1:10 .... 409, 412, 758
2:1 .... 637, 638, 670
2:1 ff 773
2:1-5 760
2:2 .... 330, 333, 344, 388, 412, 509, 554, 555, 575, 577, 578, 637, 638
2:13 182
2:14 182
2:15 108
2:15-17 ...... 369, 528
2:16 370
2:17 4
2:18 1135
2:19 771
2:20 832
2:22 1135
2:23 115
2:26 185
2:27 685
2:28 .... 697, 1071
2:29 .... 696, 697
3:1 .... 412, 746, 762
3:2 .... 26, 412, 609, 615, 746, 762, 1044, 1053, 1061, 1107
3:3 762
3:4 .... 350, 658
3:5 484
3:6 412
3:7 185
3:8 308
3:9 .... 412, 696, 697, 767, 769
3:11 318
3:12 .... 180, 182, 318
3:14 .... 696, 698, 773
3:16 921
3:17 .... 370, 921
3:24 .... 667, 696, 773
4:1 ff 952
4:1-3 .... 175, 468, 609
4:1-4 .... 185, 186
4:2 .... 485, 606, 610, 752
4:3 .... 115, 485, 1135
4:4 181
4:7 696
4:9 113
4:10 .... 111, 554, 555
4:11 103
4:12 .... 103, 1071
4:13 .... 667, 773
4:14 .... 110, 333, 435, 501, 648, 650
4:17 .... 773, 1093
4:19 103
5:1 .... 108, 696, 697, 698
5:4 .... 696, 697, 773, 911, 1104
5:4-6 590
5:6 .... 108, 550
5:7 .... 100, 723
5:8 550
5:9 .... 723, 769
5:11 .... 450, 669, 769
5:12 .... 669, 769
5:13 .... 723, 773
5:14 200
5:16 .... 366, 367, 373
5:17 .... 350, 366, 367
5:18 .... 182, 696
5:19 .... 178, 180, 182, 309, 329, 340, 369, 1114
5:20 .... 62, 297, 448, 1107
5:21 448

2 John 880, 924
2 952
7 .... 468, 485, 609, 610
9 .... 666, 887
10 .... 235, 887
11 235

3 John 880, 924
5-8 968
7 788
9 .... 371, 942

Jude 924
1 .... 108, 769
3 .... 715, 969
4 .... 81, 785, 832
6 .... 167, 174, 184, 1035
8 .... 180, 181, 1097
8-10 754
9 .... 169, 172, 180, 181, 1097
11 318
12 .... 946, 976, 991
13 .... 1080, 1082
14 .... 166, 170, 171, 529, 1068, 1119
15 .... 529, 1068, 1077
19 1064
20 111
21 .... 111, 767

Jude (cont.)

Jude (cont.)

22 1079
23 1079
24 ....767, 1071

REVELATION 812, 914, 924, 1132, 1149, 1150

1–3 ....502, 801, 808, 1062
1–22 22
1:1 ....179, 1017, 1114, 1119
1:3 ....283, 760, 965, 1017
1:4 ....170, 179
1:5 ....114, 450, 584, 1046
1:6 1005
1:7 ....535, 609, 1055, 1114, 1116, 1117, 1118
1:8 ....85, 439, 449, 452, 496, 550, 1008
1:10 ....621, 815, 919, 965, 994, 996, 1108
1:12 ....808, 1083
1:13 ....808, 1083
1:13 ff 622
1:15 444
1:17 ....108, 449, 609, 1044
1:18 ....449, 496, 613, 1039, 1082, 1093
1:19 1131
1:20 ....172, 808
2 ....812, 908, 947
2–3 ....936, 946, 957, 1112
2:1-7 880
2:2 ....451, 880, 952, 1077
2:3 880
2:5 ....918, 1077, 1112
2:7 ....307, 1038, 1042, 1071, 1102, 1104
2:7-9 1069
2:8 449
2:9 ....451, 1077
2:10 ....181, 1071, 1102, 1104
2:12 785
2:13 ....451, 785, 1077
2:13-17 1069
2:14-16 918
2:16 1112
2:17 ....1071, 1102, 1104
2:18 108
2:19 1077
2:20-23 918
2:23 1077
2:24 175
2:25 1112
2:26 ....1077, 1102
2:26-28 ....1071, 1104

3 ....812, 908, 947
3–4 1104
3:1 ....451, 771, 1077
3:2 1077
3:2-5 1071
3:3 1112
3:4 ....1102, 1104
3:5 ....1073, 1102, 1104
3:7 286
3:8 ....451, 1077
3:10 1131
3:10-12 1071
3:11 ....1104, 1112
3:12 ....746, 1102, 1104
3:14 ....453, 785
3:14-16 785
3:15 ....451, 1077
3:15-17 918
3:16 918
3:17 414
3:18-21 1071
3:19 712
3:20 ....52, 702, 1001
3:21 ....274, 1102, 1104
4 ....170, 553
4 ff 1109
4–6 1141
4:1 620
4:1-11 509
4:2 ....249, 621
4:2 ff 1097, 1100
4:4 904
4:6 1108
4:9 ....71, 72
4:10 ....85, 297, 299, 904
4:11 ....145, 160, 161, 297, 299, 904
5 ....170, 553, 566
5 ff 621
5–22 541
5:1 249
5:1-14 509
5:5 453
5:6 ....523, 637
5:6-14 ....624, 868
5:8 ....249, 1106
5:8-10 904
5:9 ....247, 523, 584, 966, 970, 1011, 1106
5:9-10 1149
5:9-14 ....455, 801
5:10 ....628, 857, 865, 966, 1106, 1107, 1109, 1151
5:11 ....171, 311
5:11-14 300
5:12 ....171, 497, 523, 1106

5:13 ....523, 1093
5:21 801
5:22 801
6 ....261, 566
6–19 1132
6:1 453
6:5 453
6:7 453
6:8 ....1039, 1042
6:9 ....272, 274, 453, 678, 1109
6:9 ff 1076
6:9-11 ....180, 621, 761, 1036, 1038, 1042, 1068, 1107, 1151
6:9-13 1102
6:9-17 453
6:10 ....678, 790
6:15 13
6:16 13
6:17 1109
7 ....1109, 1123, 1128, 1133
7:1-4 453
7:1-8 1069
7:9 311
7:9-17 ....1038, 1042, 1109
7:11 ....966, 1102
7:12 ....966, 1102
7:13-14 1109
7:14 ....180, 1124, 1131
7:15 1102
7:16 1102
7:17 ....1050, 1102
8:3 637
8:4 637
9:1 1035
9:1 ff 177
9:1-6 1026
9:2 ....1035, 1080
9:8-10 1108
9:11 ....174, 1039, 1080
9:14 174
9:15 174
10:1 1118
11 712
11:2 ....1109, 1125
11:3 1125
11:3-12 1128
11:12 1118
11:15 ....181, 624, 626, 868
11:17-18 90
12 ....179, 180, 1127
12:1 ....904, 1080
12:1-4 180
12:4 184
12:5 ff 1147
12:6 ....1069, 1109, 1125

12:7	168, 173, 176	
12:7 ff	173	
12:7-9	176	
12:7-12	179, 180	
12:9	163, 173, 175, 176, 178, 180, 302, 308, 313, 329	
12:10	176, 180	
12:11	179, 180, 181, 584	
12:12	179, 1038, 1105	
12:13	179, 180	
12:14	1109, 1125	
13	335, 1080	
13:1 ff	1135	
13:2	186, 303	
13:5	1109	
13:5-7	1125	
13:6	1105	
13:7	303	
13:8	103, 126, 200, 303, 420, 547, 677, 862, 1073, 1109	
13:17	1069	
14	1015	
14:2	1102, 1106	
14:3	970, 1102	
14:4	552	
14:7	1097	
14:8	132	
14:9-11	1080	
14:10	1069, 1080	
14:11	1080, 1082	
14:13	1038, 1042, 1102	
14:17	1082	
15:2	1106	
15:3	509, 970, 1102, 1106	
15:4	108, 1102	
16:1-12	172	
16:3	274	
16:4-7	99	
16:12-16	180, 1069	
16:13	180, 183	
16:13 ff	177, 180	
16:14	183, 186, 786	
17:1–19:5	1069	
17:3-7	304	
17:5	426	
17:13	1131	
17:14	685	
17:17	303	
18:14	355	
18:17	944	
19	507, 625, 732, 856, 913, 1015, 1138, 1139, 1148, 1149	
19–20	1054	
19:1	1106	
19:3	1082	
19:5	1102	
19:6	90, 1102, 1138	
19:6-9	913, 1069	
19:8	737, 913	
19:9	1001	
19:11	624, 625, 1055, 1138	
19:11 ff	447, 1113, 1114	
19:11-16	445	
19:11-18	737	
19:11-20	1055	
19:11-21	624, 625, 868, 913, 1113	
19:11–20:15	1059	
19:15	243	
19:16	487	
19:16-21	1056	
19:17	1001, 1041, 1138	
19:17-21	1139	
19:19-21	1069	
19:20	1035	
20	233, 566, 625, 628, 856, 857, 1036, 1055, 1056, 1057, 1058, 1059, 1109, 1138, 1139, 1140, 1141, 1146, 1148, 1149	
20–22	284, 1059	
20:1	1060, 1080, 1138, 1139	
20:1 ff	1035	
20:1-3	172, 180	
20:1-4	1055, 1059	
20:1-5	625, 868, 1056	
20:1-6	865	
20:1-10	1138	
20:1-10	1143	
20:2	199, 306, 1080, 1139	
20:2-5	1142	
20:2-7	1138	
20:3	199, 1142, 1149	
20:4	274, 857, 1042, 1046, 1054, 1060, 1076, 1138, 1139, 1142, 1149, 1151	
20:4-6	625, 868, 1055, 1144	
20:4-15	1058, 1149	
20:5	1046, 1052, 1142, 1144	
20:6	1046, 1149, 1151	
20:7	1056, 1144	
20:7 ff	1142	
20:7-9	1142	
20:7-10	1154	
20:7-15	625, 868	
20:8	1151	
20:10	1035, 1114	
20:10-15	1069	
20:11	553, 786, 1056, 1076	
20:11 ff	1042	
20:11-13	1059	
20:11-14	1054, 1055, 1142, 1155	
20:11-15	532, 1042, 1066, 1069, 1070	
20:12	1021, 1053, 1059, 1072, 1076, 1077, 1131	
20:12-14	1039, 1142	
20:12-15	553	
20:13	1020, 1021, 1039, 1042, 1077	
20:14	311, 532, 786, 1020, 1021, 1035, 1036, 1039, 1042, 1076, 1084	
20:15	1035, 1036, 1084, 1131	
20:21	1042	
21	141, 286, 288, 619, 913, 1015, 1036, 1098, 1109, 1153, 1154	
21 ff	621	
21–22	325, 621, 1107	
21:1	1113, 1153, 1155	
21:1-3	609, 1044	
21:2	297, 822, 913, 1101, 1102, 1106, 1153	
21:3	298, 837, 1098, 1153	
21:4	220, 1023, 1050	
21:5	1069	
21:7	746	
21:8	364, 1021, 1036, 1081, 1102	
21:9	297, 536, 822, 878, 913, 1153	
21:9–22:5	1021	
21:10	878, 913, 1153, 1155	
21:10-27	1102	
21:12	904, 1155	
21:13	904	
21:14	536, 904, 1155	
21:19	733	
21:22	256, 536	
21:23	56, 536	
21:25	1093, 1102	
21:27	302, 536, 677, 1102	
22	141, 286, 288, 349, 619, 913, 1015, 1098, 1101, 1109, 1153, 1154	
22:1	306, 878	
22:1 ff	1101	
22:2	286, 306, 307	
22:3	536, 1102, 1106	
22:5	1082, 1102, 1113	
22:7	1119	
22:8	455	
22:9	455	
22:11	1081	
22:12	452, 1071, 1104	

Revelation (cont.)

Revelation (cont.)
22:13	449, 452, 1008	22:16	449, 468, 487, 994	22:20	1017, 1119
22:14	307, 1101	22:17	585, 666, 684, 699, 723, 822, 905	22:21	963
22:15	364, 1081, 1102	22:18-21	12		

PART 1
THEOLOGY PROPER
Introduction and Doctrine of God

PART 2
ANTHROPOLOGY
Man as Created

PART 3
HAMARTIOLOGY
Man as Sinner

PART 4
CHRISTOLOGY
Person and Work of Christ

PART 5
SOTERIOLOGY
Salvation Applied

PART 6
ECCLESIOLOGY
Church Local and Universal

PART 7
ESCHATOLOGY
Last Things, Personal and Universal

BIBLIOGRAPHY

SCRIPTURE INDEX

GENERAL INDEX

General Index

Page ranges in bold refer to the relevant major part of the work. Specific topics to do with the subject may be found in the subheadings. Where an author is cited only in a footnote, with no relevant quotation in the text, the reference is followed by 'n'.

Aa

Abelard, Peter   600
Abraham
  faith of   15
  friend of God   68, 746
  justified by faith   735, 742–43
  meanings of 'seed' of promise to   853
  at oaks of Mamre   79
  promise to, as intimation of the church   835 see also Israel, relation to the church
  role in development of worship   14
Absolute Being of God   91
absolution   706
Adam
  first Man   240–41, 290 see also mankind
  meaning of name   53
  racial presence in   234, 244–45, 401–04
  righteousness and divine image in   355
  sin of see fall of man; original sin
  see also Christology, Christ as 'last Adam'
Adam, Karl   803, 845
Adams, J. L.   425
Adams, Jay E.   1148, 1149
Adler, Mortimer   165
adoption
  and assurance   773–74
  doctrinal features   745–46
  place in order of salvation   744–45
  Roman background   745
adoptionism   111
Advent
  as first coming of Jesus   1111
  second see Second Coming
Aland, Kurt   985, 987
Alcuin   599
Alford, Henry (Dean of Canterbury)   444, 471, 475, 618, 775, 881
  and Antichrist   1139
  on faith through the apostolic word   882
  and fallen angels   174
  on judgment   1072
  and sin   350, 394, 412
  on two resurrections   1055
Allen, Roland   900
Allis, O. T.   1059, 1147
Althaus, Paul   19, 105, 498, 519, 561–62, 947
  and Lutheran ecclesiology   951
Ambrose, St.   67, 477, 951
amillennialism   858, 1054, 1058–60, 1141–42, 1146–50
  and approach to Apocalypse as a whole   1149–50
  figurative approach to   1147
  modified Augustinian view   1146–47
  preterist school   1148

'realised millennialism'   1148–49
Amyraut, Moses   399
analogical language   63, 224–25
   see also metaphors
Anaxagoras   39, 78, 667
ancestor-worship   76
Anderson, Norman   795
Andrews, Samuel J.   462–63, 607
angels
   activities and work   170–72, 1098–99, 1119
   of darkness   166, 173–75, 334, 585–86 see also demons
   epochs of activity   173
   hierarchy   169
   identity   167–68
   importance in scripture   165–66
   interest in passion and death of Christ   536
   Judaic beliefs in late pre-Christian era   166
   names   166, 168
   nature   168–69
   a neglected subject   164
   origin   168
   patristic and medieval angelology   167
   position in creation   169
   present at foundation of earth   152
   as representatives of the churches   801
   in service of Christ   171
   in service to God's people   172
   'the angel of the LORD'   442–43
   treatment by dialectical and existential theologians   165
Anglican Articles (AD 1553)   221
anhypostasia   472
animism   76, 79
annihilationism (conditional immortality)   1091–92
Annunciation   480, 521, 1011
Anselm, St.   35, 60, 83, 733
   and atonement   555, 563, 599–600
   and election   578
   faith and understanding   427
   and God's law   562
   impassibility   220
   and necessity of Christ's death   537
   ontological argument   41
   providential control of sin   139–40
anthropology (doctrine of man)   **227-335**
   beginnings of civilization   318–20
   concupiscence   354–57
   crisis in civilization   329–40
   death see death
   dichotomy theory   270–73
   gender problem   237
   historical nature of Genesis 1 and 2 narrative   141, 229, 231–33
   human spirit see spirit, of man
   mankind, the image of God see mankind, created in God's image
   mankind's original constitution and situation   230–31, 233–36, 240–42, 244, 284–92, 401–04

monism theory   269–70
non-physical aspects of human nature   258–67, 275–81
   see also soul
Old Testament texts of relevance listed   229
social control   330
soul see soul
theological study of   228–38
trichotomy theory   270–71, 273–74
   see also mankind
anthropomorphism   25–27, 56–57, 216, 252
   anthropopathism   26–27, 219, 225
   anthropopoiesis   26
   objections to   28
   see also analogical language; metaphors
Antichrist   1055, 1056, 1080
   persecution by   1127
   restraint of   1135–36
   revelation of   1123, 1133–35
antinomianism, evangelicals accused of teaching,   756
anxiety   191, 775
   see also assurance
apocatastasis see universalism
Apollinaris, Bp. of Laodicea   273, 492, 695
apologetics   xv, 23, 29
   and exclusivism of the gospel   795–96
   and prophecy   16–17, 429, 504
   and resurrection of Christ   602–03
apostasy   80, 771, 772
   as harbinger of Second Coming   1123–24, 1133–35
   original act of see fall of man
apostles
   and church organization   925–29
   doctrine   7–8
   as founders of the church   842–47, 892
   gift to the whole church   873
   ministries of instruction and inspiration   846–47
Apostles' Creed   104, 420, 465, 482, 727
   Christ's 'descent into hell'   518–19
   communion of saints   824
   death and resurrection   602, 1060
   Second Coming   1116
apostolic succession   803, 806, 845, 871
   in episcopal 'high church' teaching   933
Aquinas, St. see Thomas Aquinas, St.
archaeology   722
Archer, Gleason   375
arguments for existence of God
   anthropological or moral (from human nature)   40–41
   causal   36–38
   necessary postulate (Kant)   41–42
   ontological (idea of being)   41
   teleological (from design)   38–40, 155
   universal consensus   41
Arianism   75–76, 105, 447, 448, 883
   see also Arius
Aristarchus of Samosa   202

Aristotle   43, 78, 93
Arius   105, 115
   see also Arianism
Ark of the Covenant   79
Armbruster, C. J.   425
Arminius (Jacobus van Hermann)   125, 391, 573, 574, 579, 580
   and regeneration   695
   and sin   388–89
   and special calling   688
ascension of Christ   601–02, 616–17, 868
   as historical event   618–20
   idea of two ascensions   618
   importance and meaning of doctrine   621–22
   and nature of heaven   1099–1101
   possible O.T. anticipations   617
asceticism   203, 756
aseity (self-existence)   64, 83–84
assurance   32, 87, 696
   and boldness   773–74
   definition   765, 772
   of the human spirit   776–77
   normality of   773
   and perseverance   766
   and priestly work of Christ   772–73
   through understanding of scripture   772
   and witness of the Spirit   775–76 *see also* witness of the Spirit
Athanasius, St., Bp. of Alexandria   105, 119, 255, 446
   and Christ's victory   596
   and necessity of Christ's death   537
   and substitution   596–97
atheism   210, 212–14, 223, 782
Athenagoras   109, 174, 593
Athanasian Creed   465, 493
Athens, and pagan philosophers   28, 433–34
atonement
   biblical centrality   541
   blood of the covenant   550–51 *see also* Jesus, as 'Lamb of God'
   Christ's victory ('classical' theory)   596
   doctrine before Anselm   593–600
   extent   333, 572–82, 597
   fruit of God's love   103
   fulfillment of divine plan   547
   historic Christian consensus on doctrine   540–41
   offering or presentation   550
   particular and general aspects   575
   particular election   573–74
   penal substitution   555–58, 594–95, 596–97, 599 *see also* vicarious satisfaction
   plenary ability   574–75, 579, 582 *see also* free will, ability or inability of fallen man to turn to God
   principles of interpretation   541–43, 545
   propitiation (appeasement)   554–55, 567, 589
   ransom   333, 503, 551–52, 595–96
   reconciliation *see* reconciliation of the world
   redemption *see* redemption
   sacrifice   548–50, 555–58, 595 *see also* Jesus, as 'Lamb of God'
   saviourhood of Christ   594, 597
   setting in plan of salvation   574
   sin as the reason for   547
   unity of the two Testaments   543–45
   and universalism   1090
   use of the term   546–47, 552
   vicarious satisfaction   561, 568–70, 594–95, 596–97, 599
      see also penal substitution
   see also Day of Atonement
attributes of God   27, 60–65
   Absolute Being   91
   assigned to Christ   449–52
   eternity   84–85, 146
   faithfulness   101–02, 194
   goodness   93–94
   holiness *see* holiness
   immanence   92
   immensity   85–86
   immutability   63, 133
   impassibility *see* impassibility, doctrine of
   incomprehensibility   90–91
   infinity   91
   love   102–03
   mercy   103
   omnipotence   90
   omnipresence   86–87
   omniscience   87–89, 1072
   perfection   64–65, 90, 759
   reflected in man   27 *see also* mankind, created in God's image
   righteousness   99–100
   Self-consciousness   68–69
   Self-determination   69–71, 72
   Self-existence (aseity)   64, 83–84
   simplicity   63
   transcendence   92
   truth   100
Augsburg Confession   221, 562, 587–88, 766, 909
Augustine, St., of Hippo   33, 34, 43, 184, 597, 735
   and anthropology   238
   anti-Pelagian stance of   312, 380
   and awareness of sin   362
   on binding and loosing of Satan   1141–42
   and calling or regeneration   687
   on Christ's prayer in Gethsemane   526
   and church as kingdom of God   857
   and concupiscence   355
   on creation   153
   and death   1019
   doctrine of providence   203
   and election   680
   on eternity   84
   on evil angels   174
   and free will   262
   view of goodness   93
   and infant baptism   380
   on the millennium   1054, 1059, 1140–42

ministry of   951
on names of God   58
and necessity of Christ's death   537
on origin of soul   277
and original sin   380–81, 383
and pagan superstition   567
and particular election   573–74
and reconciliation   578
on resurrection   1045, 1059, 1141, 1142
on Self-existence of God   84
on spiritual substance   66–67
and trinitarian constitution of man   250
guidelines on Trinity   106, 112, 115–16, 119
and the unconscious realm   360
on vicarious sacrifice   555, 597
and virgin birth   477, 478, 522
Aulen, Gustaf   596, 873
Aus, Roger D.   1136

BBb

Baal, prophets of   15, 16
Bacon, Francis   204
Bahr, J.   305
Baillie, Donald M.   510, 511, 555, 567–68
Baillie, John   45
Bainton, R.   938
Balthasar, Hans Urs von   491, 827, 828–29
Bangs, Carl   388
baptism   871, 989
   Anabaptist views   979–80
   command of Jesus   981–82
   and confession   704, 727, 989 *see also* confession
   cultural and social break of   727–28, 886, 919, 982
   in the Holy Spirit   667, 740, 873, 874, 876, 1112
   infant *see* infant baptism
   John the Baptist   111, 499, 981
   nature and modes of   979–80, 987–90
   New Testament church practice   982, 983–86
   Old Testament background   980–81
   renunciation of Satan   181
   as a sacrament   706, 976–79
   symbolic meanings   988–90
Baptist Church   767
   communion (Eucharist)   804
   ecclesiology   804, 806, 831
Barnabus, Epistles of   595, 1132
Barnes, Albert   1145
Barnhouse, Donald G.   178
Barrett, C. K.   842–43, 881
Barrick, William D.   94
Barth, Karl   22, 43, 45, 878
   and angels   157, 165
   and atonement   554–55, 570–71
   Berkouwer on his treatment of divine love   103
   and body of Christ   873
   and Christ's victory   334, 596
   on election   680
   and faith   724
   and faithfulness to scripture   425
   and the future state   1045
   on God's being and perfections   64
   on holiness   98
   impassibility denied, by redefinition of trinitarianism   223
   against infant baptism   986
   influenced by Feuerbach   214
   on modes of God   63
   on the nature of the church   877, 878
   on omnipresence   86
   on 'powers' and 'rulers of this age'   585
   and relational nature of divine image   252
   on soul and body   268, 270
   and Trinitarian Christology   214–15
   and universalism   47, 1074, 1088, 1090
Barth, Marcus   891, 894–95
Bartlet, James Vernon   691–92, 693
Basil, St., 'the Great'   75, 119
Bauer, Walter   888
Baur, F. C.   461
Bavinck, Herman   59, 63, 795, 1023
   on God's aseity   64
Beasley-Murray, G. R.   985
'beatific vision'   668, 756
Beattie, D. R. G.   305
Bede, the Venerable, St.   478, 599
Behe, Michael   155
belief in God   29–34
   and saving faith   717 *see also* confession, of faith in Christ
   see also arguments for existence of God
Bellarmine, Robert   254–55, 755
Benedict, Rule of   599
Bengel, Johann Albrecht   122, 1143
Berger, Peter L.   164
Berkeley, George   22
Berkhof, Hendrikus   105
Berkhof, Louis   194, 401, 510, 511, 628, 1005
   and apologetics   xv n
   and calling   682
   and church ministry   947
   and creationism (of soul)   277
   and Eucharist   1006
   on identification with Christ   668
   and N.T. interpretations of O.T. prophecies   852
   on premillennialism   1150
   and will of God   70
Berkouwer, G. C. H.   103, 281, 304, 524–25, 563
   and humanity of Christ   468
   on loss of plenary ability   644
   on Lutheran distinction beween justification and sanctification   755, 756, 757
   and the millennium   1147
   on resurrection   1063

on sin   348, 350, 417
Bernard, E. R.   1047
Bernard of Clairvaux   119, 602, 662–63, 664, 733
Bernard, T. D.   864
Bernkamm, Güenther   945
Bertocci, Peter Anthony   427, 434
Beza, Theodore   572–73
Bible *see* scripture
biblical theology   xiii, 6, 21
Bickersteth, Edward   107–08, 1000
Bieler, Andre   974, 997
bishops *see* ministries and offices of the church, elders and bishops
Bleek, F.   444
blessedness of God *see* impassibility, doctrine of
Block, Ernst   214
Bloesch, Donald G.   731, 1085, 1092
Blomberg, C. L.   209
blood of Christ   584, 618
   see also cross of Christ
Bock, Darrel L.   663
body
   as abode of Holy Spirit   669–70
   of Christ *see* church, as body of Christ
   full redemption of   758 *see also* resurrection, doctrine of
   natural and spiritual   1063–65
Boehme, Jacob   118
Boettner, Lorraine   1058, 1059, 1145, 1146
Boice, James Montgomery   669, 977
Bonhoeffer, Dietrich   252, 304, 305, 760
Boniface VIII, Pope   827, 885
Bornkamm, Günther   606
Boston, Thomas   1082
Bourke, Vernon J.   116, 380
Bowker, John   928
Bowne, Borden P.   33
Boyce, James Pedigru   404, 681, 1102
   on perseverance   768
   on regeneration and conversion   690
   on sanctification   761
Bray, Gerald   30
Bridenbaugh, Carl   938
Bridges, Charles   260
Briggs, C. A.   1145
Brindsmead, Robert   887–88
Broadbent, E. H.   830, 915–16, 938–39
Bromiley, Geoffrey W.   592, 599, 706–07, 953–54, 979, 1004
Brown, David   1144, 1145, 1148
Brown, Harold O. J.   797, 1092
Brown, Raymond E.   366, 370, 447, 478, 497, 881
   on concept of sinlessness in John's Epistles   412
   and unity of the church   880, 883, 884
Brown, Robert McAfee   888
Brown, W. A.   1113
Brown, William E.   745
Bruce, A. B.   498

Bruce, F. F.   432, 441, 631, 636, 638, 938
   on ascension   619
   Messianic expectation   508
Brunner, Emil   22, 45
   on angels   165
   on ascension   619
   and atonement   554–55, 570
   on Christ and world history   433
   on conversion   700, 702
   and depravity of heart   408
   and ecclesiology   802, 809
   and faithfulness to scripture   425
   on holiness   98
   and the Last Judgment   1067, 1068
   on Luther's attack on sacramentalism   812
   The Mediator   500
   on 'realised eschatology'   1010, 1071–72
   rejection of virgin birth   471, 482
   on resurrection   606, 1045, 1064
   on universalism and eternal damnation   1075
Bruno of Segni   600
Bucer, Martin   671, 986
Buddha   79
Bultmann, Rudolph
   demythologization   176, 473, 571
   on John's Gospel   477
   re-interpretation of virgin birth   471
   and resurrection   606
Bunyan, John   4–5
Burnet, Gilbert   495
Burroughs, John (naturalist)   291–92
Burrows, Millar   432
Bushnell, Horace   98
Buswell, James Oliver   117, 221, 223, 318, 518
   and antiquity of human origins   232
   on the church   802
   on evangelism   1123
   on general call   47, 49, 683
   on intermediate state   1034
   on reigning with Christ   763, 856
   and Second Coming   1068, 1127, 1129
   and sinlessness (impeccability) of Christ   526
   on soul and body   259, 1018–19
   and Traducianism   281
   on universal work of the Holy Spirit   359

Cc

Caesarius, Bp. of Arles   493
calling
   blessings of   687
   general (external)   682–84
   Holy Spirit as agent   686
   special (internal, effectual)   684–86, 687 *see also* conversion; prevenient/preventing grace; regeneration; witness of the Spirit

Word as means of   686
see also election
Calvery *see* cross of Christ
Calvin, John   12, 64, 116, 275, 1001–02
   on angels   168, 169, 172
   on art and science   158
   and atonement   575–77
   on baptism   979, 986–87, 989
   on basis of Christian assurance   590
   on Christ and the world   575, 882
   and Christ's 'descent into hell'   519
   and church discipline   909, 917, 936, 956
   commentary on the Epistles to Timothy   943–44
   as commentator   43
   and communion of saints   809
   on concupiscence   355
   and conscience   266
   and the constitution of man   250–51
   and conversion   700
   and defining sacraments   977
   on delight and temperance   327
   on devils   183
   on divine purpose of creation   293–94
   and duties of man   920
   ecclesiology   823–24, 825, 908–09, 910–11, 947, 952
   and election   387, 672, 673, 680
   and Eucharist   616, 1001, 1006
   on faith and knowledge   725, 726
   and faith through the apostolic word   882
   and free will   262–63
   on gifts of office   892
   and grace through extra-ordinary methods   794–95
   on the heavenly Jerusalem   813
   on holiness   98
   on human and divine natures of Christ   495, 497
   on humiliation of Christ   514
   on idle curiosity   174
   on impassibility   220–21
   and infralapsarianism   388
   and the intermediate state   1040
   and 'Israel of God'   854
   on kingdom of God   627, 866
   lack of concern with classifying attributes of God   64, 86
   and Law's proper uses   658
   on man as image and likeness of God   70, 156, 252, 255
   on marks of God's glory in creation   65, 155
   and natural theology   35
   and necessity of Christ's death   537
   and need of metaphors   59
   and noetic effect of sin   415
   on obedience of Christ   517
   on once-only sacrifice of Christ   587, 638
   on the 'oneness' of the Father and the Son   883
   and origin of soul   277, 280–81
   and original sin   280–81
   on perfection   1107

   preterist view of Daniel's predictions   1148
   on propogation of life   153
   on providence   194, 203
   on purpose of the church   908–09, 910–11
   and regeneration   690
   on restraining grace   359
   on resurrection appearances   611
   on sacrifice   549
   and sanctification   756, 757
   and self knowledge   48
   on signs and wonders   208
   on sin   364, 379, 383
   and soul sleep   1091
   style of theological writing   457
   and the Trinity   106
   on union with Christ   664
   on unity of the church   895
   on vocabulary for theological matters   20
   on witness of the Spirit   723
   on worship and prayer   731
Cameron, John   399
Campbell, Alexander   716, 938
Camus, Albert   214
canons of Laodicea   167
Cappadocian Fathers   75–76, 119
   Macrina, the 'Fourth Cappadocian'   119
   on Wisdom and preexistence of Christ   441
   see also Basil, St., 'the Great'; Gregory Nazianzen; Gregory of Nyssa
Cappel, Louis   399
Carnell, Edward John   479, 888
Carpenter, William Boyd   785
Carroll, B. H.   1145, 1148
Carson, Alexander   988
Carson, D. A.   1085
Carthage, Council of (AD 418)   386
Carver, W. O.   572, 872
Casserley, J. V. L.   820
Cassuto, Umberto   150–51, 288, 301
Cave, S.   454
Ceasarea Philippi
   announcement concerning Peter and the church   801
   Peter's confession   425–27, 448, 534, 843–44
Chafer, Louis Sperry   663, 1127
Chalcedon, Council of (AD 451)   105, 167, 218, 219
Chalcedon, Definition of   105, 446, 465, 492, 672
   translation   118, 488–89
Chapman, Robert   938
charismata   889–90
Charles, R. H.   1038, 1046, 1113
Charnock, Stephen   222
chastening   761–62, 773–74, 1070–71
   providential events as 'comings' of Christ   1112
Cheung, James   931
children
   infant baptism *see* infant baptism

and the kingdom of heaven 866
chiliasm *see* premillennialism
Christ *see* Christology; incarnation of Christ; Jesus
Christian life 4
   assurance *see* assurance
   duties 760, 920–22
   and the Eucharist 1001–02 *see also* Eucharist (Lord's Supper)
   and experience xvi
   and growth 760, 896–97
   sharing in Christ's sufferings 590, 1025
   taking the 'yoke' of Christ 589–91
   worship *see* worship
Christology, person and work of Christ **419–638**
   ascension of Christ *see* ascension of Christ
   atonement *see* atonement
   attributes of God assigned to Christ 449–52
   authority to forgive sins 453
   Christ and non-Christian religions 791–95
   Christ as High Priest *see* priestly work of Christ
   Christ as 'last Adam', head of redeemed mankind 307–08, 468, 1063
   Christ as mediator 72, 461, 499–500, 609 *see also* mediation
   Christ designated as God 447–48
   cosmic dimensions of Christ 456, 565
   Deity of Christ 445–56, 496–97
   divine works of Christ 453–54
   economic subordination of Son (Vincent Taylor) 456, 1154–55
   enhypostasia 472
   enthronement of Christ *see* enthronement (session) of Christ
   existential 424–25
   glory of Christ 883–911
   human nature of Christ 461–68, 514, 515 *see also* incarnation of Christ
   impassibility *see* impassibility, doctrine of
   incarnation *see* incarnation of Christ
   Jesus as builder and supporter of the church 454
   Jesus as focus of saving faith 454, 704–05, 726–28, 780–90
   Jesus as Lord (ku-ri-os) 448–49, 729–30, 840
   Jesus as Son of God 448
   Jesus' role in answering prayer 454
   Jewish preparation for coming of Christ, in the Old Testament 428–33
   judgment powers given to Christ 454
   Messiahship of Jesus 426, 862
   names attributing deity to Christ 449
   objections to biblical doctrine 458
   passion and death *see* passion and death of Jesus
   Peter's confession 425–27, 448, 534, 843–44
   preexistence of Christ 438–44, 496
   principles of 457–59
   providential preparation of nations for coming of Christ 433–37
   resurrection of Christ *see* resurrection of Christ
   saving work of incarnate Son 500–509 *see also* salvation; soteriology
   Second Coming *see* Second Coming
   sinlessness (impeccability) of Christ 467–68, 499, 520–29
   Son of Man 425–26, 438, 613, 1116, 1118
   trinitarian (Barth) 214–15
   union of Christ's human and divine natures 468, 489–91, 492–500 *see also* enhypostasia
   ways of presenting 422–27
Chrysostom, St. John 552, 724, 735, 776, 832, 909
   on noetic effect of sin 661
church **799–1006**
   architecture 971–75, 995
   Baptist 767, 804, 806, 831
   as body of Christ 809, 871, 873, 876–77
   as bride of Christ 912–13
   Christ as Head 628
   as company of the elect 809
   congregational government 935–37
   criticism of 801–02
   defining marks 808–09, 915, 916–18
   destiny 912–13
   discipline 909, 917, 936, 956–61
   doctrine of the *see* ecclesiology (doctrine of the church)
   ecumenism *see* ecumenism
   episcopal government 930, 932–33
   governmental theory 932–40
   as guardian of the truth 800, 812
   and the Holy Spirit 800, 837, 873
   as household of God 800, 812
   importance of 800–801, 807
   initial establishment of 839–47
   Israel and the 822–23, 850–56
   Jesus proclaimed Lord of the 840–41
   kingdom of God and the 822–23, 857–68
   local congregations of believers 4–5, 760, 818, 827, 832–33, 914–22
   love of the Son for 800, 840
   members' gifts of ability 889–90 *see also* ministries and offices of the church
   membership 918–22 *see also* baptism
   metaphorical allusions 820–22, 877–78
   Methodist 357, 390, 920–21
   ministries *see* ministries and offices of the church
   mission 898–907, 968 *see also* proclamation of the gospel
   as mother of believers 812–13, 824
   nature of 809–13, 869–78, 918
   New Testament term and usage 816–19
   offices *see* ministries and offices of the church
   Old Testament foundations 835–38
   organization patterns 923–31
   'pilgrim church' 811, 825
   presbyterian government 933–35
   purposes of God in and for 908–12
   and 'reign' of saints 628, 868, 1059, 1141, 1142, 1146
   restorationist government 937–39
   as revelation of God's wisdom 74, 800, 911–12
   ritual 803

Roman *see* Roman Church
and sanctification   760
and sources of authority   811
as temple of God   836–37, 877
the term's history and uses   814–16, 927
traditional categories of Militant, Expectant and Triumphant   812, 823
unity of *see* unity of the church
universal (catholic) communion of saints   809, 822, 824, 826–32, 872, 877, 918
universal priesthood of believers   947, 1005
as vehicle of evangelism   801
visible and invisible   812, 823–24, 877, 908
worship *see* worship
see also ecclesiology (doctrine of the church)
circumcision   361
of the heart   692
civil government   135–36, 157, 299, 330, 331, 406
and church government   935, 938, 956
Clark, Gordon   64, 211, 251, 255, 856
on fall of man   263
and mind-body theories   271
and Traducianism   277, 281
Clearwaters, R. V.   831, 914
Clement of Alexandria, St.   174
on Christ as Revelator and Savior   597
and the Eucharist   1003
on philosophic learning   218
and soteriology   594
and trichotomy theory   273
Clement of Rome, Epistle of   109, 920, 942, 943, 966
Clendenin, Daniel B.   783
Clines, J. A.   250
Clough, William   700
Clowney, E. P.   851, 852
Cobb, John B. Jr   73, 792
Coelestius   386
Collingwood, F. I.   229
Collins, Adela Yarbro   981
Collins, John J.   432
Colson, Charles   911
common sense, use of   901
see also faith, and reason
communion
fellowship of the saints   809, 822, 824, 1107
with God   298
Holy Communion (Lord's Supper) *see* Eucharist (Lord's Supper)
Comte, Auguste   211
Concord, Formula of (AD 1576)   303n, 356, 498–99, 512, 519, 562–63
on election   675
on humanity of Christ   465
on imputed sin   396
on justification by faith   734
and Law's proper uses   658

on sanctification   759
concupiscence   354–57, 369–70
and sinlessness (impeccability) of Christ   528
concurrence/concursus   372–73, 702
confession
baptismal   704, 989
credal   970
of faith in Christ   425–27, 448, 534, 704, 727–30, 989
of humanity of Christ   468
of sins   704–05, 706
Confucius   79
connectionalism   934
conscience   40, 263–67, 349, 726, 1067, 1072
and awareness of God   32
place in regeneration   696
consecration *see* sanctification
Constance, Council of (AD 1414-18)   810
Constantinople, Council of (AD 381)   105
Constantinople, Council of (AD 553)   217
Constantinople, Council of (AD 680-1)   526
contrition   706
conversion
benefits   702–03
biblical terms   699–700
definition and nature   701–03
importance in evangelical tradition   700–701
psychology of   724–25
and regeneration   690, 701
and repentance   701
conviction
of salvation *see* assurance
of sins *see* knowledge, of sin
cosmic evolutionism (Teilhard de Chardin)   73
cosmological argument   36–38
Council of Carthage (AD 418)   386
Council of Chalcedon (AD 451)   105, 167, 218, 219
Council of Constance (AD 1414-18)   810
Council of Constantinople (AD 381)   105
Council of Constantinople (AD 553)   217
Council of Constantinople (AD 680-1)   526
Council of Ephesus (AD 431)   218
Council of Florence (AD 1437)   977
Council of Nicea (AD 325)   75, 104–05, 115
condemnation of Arius   115
Council of Orange, Second (AD 529)   303
Council of Reims (AD 1148)   64, 218
Council of Trent (AD 1545-63)   351–52, 356, 561, 563–64
on Eucharist   1003
and faith   716
on good works   755
on justification   661–62, 755
on seven sacraments   978
on sin   366, 367
covenant theology   280, 296, 397–98, 656, 663, 855–56
see also Federal (representative) theology
Cox, L. G.   353, 354

Craddock, F. R.   440
Craig, S. C.   354
Cranmer, Thomas   596, 671
creation   210, 284–92, 327
  as absolute beginning   145–47
  alternatives to doctrine of   143
  in anticipation of man   157
  completed   152–55
  corruption of   322–23, 328, 329–40
  cosmic benefits of cross of Christ   583–86
  divine intelligence in   73–74, 156
  fundamental to Christian world-view   145
  Genesis 1:1-3 translation and interpretation   147–51
  for God's glory   160, 161, 293–95, 298–300
  God's presence in   59
  goodness of   251, 321–22, 332
  grounded in God's faithfulness   101
  hope of renewal   690–91
  interpretive questions   162–63, 232–33, 282–84, 324–25
  language   243, 244
  of mankind *see* mankind
  mediate or immediate   161–62, 244
  Mesopotamian myths   148, 285–86
  method   159–62
  new   295, 668, 695, 1155–56
  out of nothing (*ex nihilo*)   143
  preservation *see* preservation
  and problem of evil   39–40, 162–63, 209–12, 328
  as revelation of Creator   24–25, 47–48, 62, 155–56, 160–61
  social expressions   157–59
  stability, due to God's plan   134
  supernatural events of   232
  theological sources for doctrine   141–42, 231–35
  by word of God   160
creationism (of soul)   276–78
Creator and His creation *see* creation
crisis theology *see* neo-orthodox theology
Crockett, William   1092
cross of Christ
  and Christian life   589–91
  cosmic benefits   583–86
  Jew and gentile reconciled through   879
  Pauline centrality of   421
  resulting benefits for Christ   586–88
  as revelation of God   588–89, 597
  as symbol   421, 540, 589
  see also passion and death of Jesus
crucifixion *see* cross of Christ
Cullmann, Oscar   532, 585, 985
  and Christ's victory   334–35, 596
  on creation   323
  and the soul   1027, 1034, 1091
culture   320
Culver, Douglas J.   475, 981
Culver, Robert D.
  Civil Government: a Biblical View   136, 157, 406, 776, 1145

Daniel and the Latter Days (reprinted as *The Earthly Reign of our Lord with His People*)   627, 663, 853n, 858, 1042n, 1049, 1058, 1126, 1127, 1136
The Earthly Career of Jesus, the Christ   843
A Greater Commission   627, 718n, 719, 846, 865, 901n, 902n
The Histories and Prophecies of Daniel   1127
The Life of Christ   663, 902n
The Nature and Origin of Evil   139n
The Sufferings and the Glory   514n, 556n
Cyprian, St., Bp. of Carthage   174, 595, 1003
Cyril, St., Patr. of Alexandria   218–19

Dd

Dabney, Robert L.   238, 363, 383, 391, 398, 489
  and Adam's 'probation'   402
  on death   1024–25
  on faith in Christ as Lord and Saviour   730
  on instrument of salvation   651
  on Law's proper uses   659–60
Dahood, Mitchel   283, 1020, 1037
Dale, R. W.   378
Daley, John W.   1081
Damian, Peter   600, 602
Dana, H. E.   914
Daniel, and prophecy concerning the Second Coming   902, 1124–27, 1139
Daniel, Curt   582
Danielou, Jean   218, 1140
Darby, John Nelson   938, 949
Darwin, Charles   326
David, throne of   1011–12, 1047
Davids, P. H.   745
Davidson, A. B.   171
Davidson, Francis   125, 688
Day of Atonement   344, 631, 632–33
Day of the Lord   1013–17
Dead Sea Scrolls, and the Qumran sect   179, 432, 442, 928, 1132
  ceremonial purifications   980–81
  expectation of priest-Messiah   508
  expectation of two Messiahs   1115
death   258, 302, 324
  causes   1022–24
  as consequence of the fall of man   311–12, 317, 384
  erroneous common beliefs   1043
  eschatological evangelism   1092–94
  God's people and   1024–25
  and the intermediate state   1030–43, 1108–09
  as last enemy   1153
  meaning of   1025–26
  nature of   1020–22
  and the nature of man   1018–21
  Old Testament outlook   1026–29
  second   1021, 1076–77, 1084 *see also* hell
  spiritual *see* spiritual death
  see also passion and death of Jesus; resurrection of Christ

Decalogue   78, 659, 920
DeHaan, Richard W.   178
deification (*theosis*)   668, 694
deism   77, 92, 520
Deissmann, Adolph   818–19
Delitzsch, Franz   148, 149, 277, 305, 313, 630
   and fallen angels   174
   on humiliation and exaltation of Christ   513
   and the 'Little Apocalypse' of Isaiah   1042
   on Messianic scripture   1049, 1114
   and nature   323
   on subordination of the woman   315
deliverance from Satan   598
   see also demons, exorcisms
Democritus   39, 154
DeMolina, Luis   88
demons
   evil character of   184
   existence in scripture   81, 176–77
   exorcisms   175, 185, 186, 189, 866 *see also* deliverance from Satan
   identity of   175, 182–84
   in Messiah's career   185
   and the occult   186, 190
   in Old Testament   184–85
   origin and fall   178, 183–84
   possession by   175, 186, 187
   powers and acts of   184–85
   recent and current interest in   187–90
   in scripture after resurrection of Christ   185
demythologization   176, 473, 571
Denney, James   549–50, 1095
Denton, Robert C.   283
Denzinger, Henry   351
depravity   399, 403, 408, 434, 643
   total   359, 416 *see also* original sin
   of will   352
Descartes, René   153
desire (concupiscence)   354–57, 369–70, 528
Devil *see* Satan
devils *see* demons
deWitte, W. M. L.   478
DeWolf, L. Harold   86, 88
dialectical materialism   211
dialectical theology *see* neo-orthodox theology
Diaspora, and the coming of Christ   436
Dibelius, Martin   585
Didache   893, 942, 945, 966, 988, 1002
Dimock, N.   638
Diognetus, Epistle to   595–96
discernment   703
discrimination   1014
   see also Last Judgment
dispensationalism   318, 663
   dispensational premillennialism   858
   see also kingdom of God, revelational stages

divine decrees, doctrine of   89, 672
Dix, Gregory   964, 970, 992n
Dixon Larry E.   1089
docetism   466, 1004
doctrine
   false   377
   as instruction   7, 846–47, 969–71
   and inter-church relations   804
   nature and source of   xv, 3
   public teaching and confession of   969–71
   teaching ministry   xvii–xviii, 7–11, 640, 896
   see also theology
Dodd, C. H.   8, 555, 738, 1010, 1089
Dordrecht, Assembly *see* Dort, Synod of
Dorner, I. A.   512
Dorner, J. A.   234, 396, 656
Dort, Synod of   573, 579
   second canon of   580–81
Dostoevski, Fyodor Mikhailovich   424
doubt   728–29
Drumwright, J. L. Jr   929
dualism   77, 143
Dunn, James D.   888
Duns Scotus, Johannes   538
Durnbaugh, Donald F.   825, 915, 938, 939
   and church discipline   957, 961
Dwight, Timothy   391
dynamism   76

EEe

earth
   as God's gift to mankind   1153
   kingdom of God on   1153
   new   1153, 1155
Ebhard, J. H. A.   188
ecclesiology (doctrine of the church)   **799–1006**
   definition and nature   808–13
   evangelism *see* proclamation of the gospel
   importance and varieties of   801–07
   see also church
Echrodt, W.   738
Eckel, Frederick L.   996, 997
Eckert, Frederick L.   974
Ecumenical Councils
   first (Nicea AD 325)   75, 104, 115
   second (Constantinople AD 381)   105
   third (Ephesus AD 431)   218
   fourth (Chalcedon AD 451)   105, 167, 218, 219
   fifth (Constantinople AD 553)   217
   sixth (Constantinople AD 680-1)   526
ecumenism   806, 810, 826–27, 886–88
   and ecclesiology   870–72
Eden, garden of   284–89
Edersheim, Alfred   190, 521
Edwards, Jonathan   98, 112, 224, 262, 407–08, 786

and church discipline   936
  on continuous creation   153
  on depravity and guilt   403
Egypt, plagues of   50–51, 81–82
Eichrodt, Walter   1013
Eiselen, F. C.   851–52
election   581, 671–73
  authored by God   672, 674
  biblical defence of doctrine   677
  biblical evidence   673–75
  in Christ   665
  and foreknowledge of God   573, 676
  objections to biblical doctrine   679–81
  particular   573–74
  practical effects of doctrine   678–79
  purpose   677
  teaching and preaching the doctrine   679
  terms relating to the elect   674
  see also calling
Elijah   14–15, 534, 536
Eller, Verner   1149–50
Elliott, Charlotte   729, 738
Ellis, E. Earle   543
Elohim *see* names of God
emanationism   143, 276
Emmaus, meeting on the road to   429
Emmons, Nathaniel   391
Empedocles   39
end times, doctrine of *see* eschatology (doctrine of last things)
Engels, Friederich   211
English, E. Schuyler   1134
enhypostasia   472
enlightenment *see* calling, special (internal, effectual)
enthronement (session) of Christ
  anticipation in Old Testament   623, 624
  as Head of the body   628
  initial appropriation of power   624–25
  New Testament proclamation   623–24
  and present reign as King   625, 627–28, 868
  theory of postponed kingdom   625–27
Ephesus, Council of (AD 431)   218
Ephesus, theological school   8, 9
Epicurus   210
Epiphanius, Second Creed of   609
Episcopacy *see* church, episcopal government
Erasmus, Desiderius   382, 388, 389, 520
Erastianism   932
Erickson, J. Millard   223, 256, 384, 458, 612, 622
  and anthropology   238, 368n
  and election   680
  and heaven   1105
  and imputed sin   404
  on objections to sinlessness of Jesus   524
  and universalism   1089
  writings on Second Coming   1127
Erskine, Ebenezer   777

Erskine, Ralph   777
eschatology (doctrine of last things)   **1007–1156**
  antithetical language of   1009
  Day of the Lord   1013–17
  death *see* death
  derivation of term   1008
  everlasting punishment *see* hell
  future eternal state   1153–56
  heaven *see* heaven
  judgment *see* Last Judgment
  medieval   1008–09
  postmortem evangelism   1092–94
  'realised'   1009–10, 1071–72 *see also* kingdom of God, revelational stages
  rejection of truth   372
  resurrection *see* resurrection, doctrine of
  Second Coming and preceding events *see* Second Coming
eternal life   72, 260–61
  assured by God's Self-existence   84
  power of Jesus to bestow   453
eternity   146
  of God   84–85
  timeless existence of Christ   496
Eucharist (Lord's Supper)   664, 996, 1013
  Baptist Church   804
  as commemoration   1000
  as communion   822, 997
  dominical instigation   535, 978, 992–93, 999, 1000
  as expression of hope   1001
  and inauguration of a new covenant   1000
  and liturgical setting   594
  and the 'Lord's Day'   996
  meal of fellowship   968, 996
  mutual participation in Christ   999
  names of the ordinance   991–92
  and the Passover   992, 1000
  Pauline interpretation and instruction   993, 994–97, 997, 1001–02
  and proclamation of the gospel   1000
  'real presence', Lutheran   490–91, 497, 498, 612, 616
  'real presence', non-Lutheran treatment of   512–13
  'reserved' bread   996–97
  Roman Mass *see* Mass
  as a sacrament   976–79
  sacrificial ideas (Roman) *see* Mass
  self-examination at   1002
  symbolic meanings   1000
Eunomius, Arian Bp. of Cyzicus   76
Eusebius   470, 846, 893–94, 900, 994
  on typology of prophet, priest and king   507–08
Eutyches   218
evangelism *see* mission; proclamation of the gospel
evangelists   893–94
evil
  deepening of   332
  origin of   162–63, 302

pollution of natural order   323
and predestination   137, 139
and the present world   329–32
problem of   39–40, 162–63, 209–12, 328
and providence   198–99, 303, 328
see also hamartiology; sin
evolutionary theory   39, 76, 210, 242–44, 326
   of History of Israel   544
   social Darwinism   210, 211, 368
   theistic   253
   see also cosmic evolutionism (Teilhard de Chardin)
exclusivism
   apologetics and   795–96
   biblical teaching   783–90
   and pluralism   780–81
   Roman Catholic teaching   781–83
existence of God *see* arguments for existence of God; belief in God
existentialism   214, 423–24, 1072
   'leap into the dark'   710, 724
   see also neo-orthodox theology
expiation   554, 706

F Ff

Fackre, Gabriel   1092, 1093
Fairbairn, Patrick   431, 558
faith
   and creeds   xvi, 727
   as divine gift   674, 723–24 *see also* election
   and doubt   728–29
   Holy Spirit as agent   723–24
   and hope   719
   implicit   725–26
   Jesus as focus of saving faith   454, 704–05, 726–28, 729–30
   justification by   3, 733–43 *see also* justification (imputed righteousness)
   and knowledge   725–26
   and law   719
   naturalistic interpretation   77
   nature of saving faith   716–18, 719–20
   presentation to non-believers   34
   and psychology of conversion   724–25
   and reason   xvi, 23–24, 34–35
   reasons for   721–22
   and repentance   704
   role of miracles and prophecy   15
   Roman Catholic teaching   716
   strengthening of   731–32
   temporary   718–19
   terms and definition   714–16
   through Word of God   722–23, 726–27
faithfulness
   as attribute of God   101–02, 194
   of God's work of preservation   194
fall of man   402, 702

act of apostasy   309–10
alienation   311, 1021
bibical narrative   305–10
curse on the ground   316, 322–24, 328
death   311–12, 725, 1023
probation   305–08, 401–02, 405
sanctions   312
sentence on the man   316–17
sentence on the serpent   313
sentence on the woman   313–16
temptation   306–09
use of Genesis 1-3   301–02, 305
see also original sin
family life   313–16, 318
   see also sex and marriage
Fanning, W. H. W.   987
Farel, G.   934
Farrar, F. W.   1088
fatherhood of God   56–57
fear
   of death   1026
   of God   410–11, 963, 1067
   of the Satanic   82
Federal (representative) theology   280, 295–96, 318, 384, 396–98, 404, 656
   see also covenant theology
Feinberg, John   211
fellowship *see* communion
Ferré, Nels   1089
fetishism   76, 79
Feuerbach, Ludwig   61, 213–14, 223
Fichter, Joseph   294
Finegan, Jack   148
Finney, Charles G.   391, 644, 766
Fisher, George Park   31, 32, 34, 120
Fisk, Samuel   770
Fiske, John   210n
Fison, J. E.   1051, 1069
Fitzmeyer, J. A.   474–75
Flavel, John   125, 201
Fletcher, Richard   907
Florence, Council of (AD 1437)   977
Florovsky, George   869, 870–71
Foerster, Werner   177, 179
Foh, Susan   314–15
foreknowledge of God   88, 138–39
   and election   573, 676
   and providence   194
   see also omniscience of God; predestination (decrees of God)
forgiveness
   assurance of   32
   and baptism   989
   Christ's divine authority of   453
   and vicarious satisfaction   569
Formula of Concord see Concord, Formula of (AD 1576)
Forster, Michael B.   205

Forsyth, P.T. 938
Fox, James J. 93
Foxe, John 705
free will 88–89, 261–63, 351–52, 415
   ability or inability of fallen man to turn to God 124–25, 137–38, 353–54, 391, 416–17, 767 see also atonement, plenary ability; prevenient/preventing grace
   and doctrine of perseverance 769–70
   meanings of 'will' 352
   and sovereignty of God 770
   see also predestination (decrees of God)
Fronmueller, G. F. C. 1093
funerals 258–59, 670, 756–57, 1096

GGg

Garrett, J. L. 393
Garrison, W. E. 839–40
Gatch, Milton McC. 1027
Gehenna 1077, 1083, 1084
Geisler, Norman 208, 385, 491, 608, 702
   on resurrection 1061
Geneva, and Reformation 106, 208, 387, 572, 673, 812
   interference from civil authorities 956
   see also Calvin, John
Gerstner, John 40
Gesenius, William 648
Gethsemane 526, 538, 562
Gibbon, Edward 4, 435
Gibbs, A. P. 995, 1001
Gibran, Khalil 92
Gibson, Edgar C. S. 467, 671, 688, 766
Gibson, George L. 965, 974
Gilkey, Langdon 145, 146–47
Gill, John 32, 98, 222, 305, 579, 617
   and Adam's 'probation' 401
   on calling and regeneration 686–87, 690, 696–98
   on fall of man 309–10
   and Federal theology 318, 404
   on Immanuel prophecy of Isaiah 9-11 605
   on local church 916–17, 921, 924, 961
   and millennialism 856
   ministry of 951
   on resurrection body of Christ 612
glorification of the body 764, 1062–65
   of Christ 611–12
   see also redemption, of the body
glory of Christ 883, 911
glory of God 761–62, 1117–18
   and judgment 1073
   purpose of creation 160, 293–300
   shekina 443–44
   see also glory of Christ
Glover, R. H. 898
Gnosticism 59, 1045
   beliefs about Jesus as Son of God 466

God
   of action 72
   attempts to define 60–61
   attributes see attributes of God
   being or substance of 61–63, 104–05
   belief in see belief in God
   biblical presentation 12
   death imposed by 1024
   doctrine **12–225**
   essence (being or substance) 61–63, 104–05
   existence see arguments for existence of God
   human awareness of 12–13, 30–33
   and intelligence 72–74
   as Judge 566
   the living God 71–72
   metaphorical sayings see anthropomorphism
   modes of subsistence (as three persons) 63, 120 see also Holy Trinity
   names see names of God
   the only God 14–15, 18 see also monotheism
   personal character of Godhead 67–68
   revelations of see revelation
   of scripture 68
   the Son see Christology; Jesus
   spiritual nature 66–67
   trinitarian nature see Holy Trinity
   unity of Godhead 75–82, 110, 111
   will 70–71, 160, 350–51
   worship of 13–14 see also worship
   see also Holy Spirit
Gode, F. 901
gods (idols) 81
   see also idolatry
Godsey, J. D. 304
Golgotha 562
Gonzalez, Justo L. 109
Gore, Charles 458, 485
gospel message 704, 840, 969
   identity of gospel of grace and gospel of the kingdom 859–61
   see also doctrine; proclamation of the gospel; Word of God
Gottschalk of Orbais 138, 578, 599
grace 359, 368, 704, 911–12
   definition 657
   dispensationalist view 663
   general and special (Calvin) 415
   'infused' 662
   in and through Jesus Christ 660–61 see also union with Christ
   and justification by faith 738
   and law 658–60
   mission practice and 905, 911–12
   present age of 660–61, 859–61
   prevenient/preventing 353–54, 359, 1095
   Roman Catholic teaching 661–63
Graham, James 1130
Grant, Robert M. 219, 893

Graves, J. B.   831
Great Commission   1058
  see also proclamation of the gospel
'great tribulation'   1116, 1124, 1127, 1131–33
Greco-Roman world, and the coming of Christ   435–36
Green, E. M. B.   647–48, 690
Gregory, C. R.   1127
Gregory I, St. ('the 'Great')   184, 598–99
Gregory Nazianzen (Gregory of Nazianzus, St.)   61, 75, 112, 119
  and ransom   596
Gregory of Nyssa, St.   75, 119, 597, 1004
Gregory Thaumaturgus, St., of Neo-Ceasarea   960
Grenz, Stanley   238, 240
Grier, W. J.   1140
Griffith-Thomas, W. H.   283
Grimm, Harold J.   707
Grounds, Vernon   564
Groves, A. N.   938, 949
Guilbert of Nogent   600
guilt   304, 312, 343–44, 346, 354, 362–63
  and original sin   382–84, 400–405, 1023 see also original sin, imputation theories
  Pauline doctrine   379, 411
Gundry, Stanley   836
Gwatkin, H. W.   930

H Hh

Hades   1034–36, 1039, 1041, 1042
Hadley, James   929
Hague, Canon Dyson   532
Haldane, Robert   322–23, 410, 741
Haller, William   707
hamartiology (doctrine of sin)   **337–417**
  divine control of sin   139–40, 372–74
  judgment and grace following the original sin   313–17
  original sin see fall of man; original sin
  sin see sin
  sinful acts   339–40, 364–71, 374–77
  temptation see temptation
  vocabulary of sin   339, 341–47
Hambrick-Stowe, Charles E.   778, 1101
Hamilton, Floyd   1059, 1147
Hamilton, Victor P.   305
Hare, John E.   210
Harnack, Adolph   4, 9, 218, 223, 520, 598
  on millennialism   1139–40
  on sin   389
Harris, Murray J.   269, 619, 1062
Harris, R. Laird   26
Harrison, Everett F.   618
Harrison, Norman B.   667, 670
Harrison, R. K.   182–83, 187–88
Hartt, Julian N.   229
Harvey, H.   954

Hatch, Nathan O.   807
Hawthorne, Nathaniel   778
Hay, A. R.   953
Hayes, Zachary   1092
healing   649–50
heart
  hardness of   449, 684, 710, 758
  renewal of   692, 758 see also regeneration; sanctification
heaven
  biblical terms related to   1097–98
  blessedness of   1101–02
  as God's home   1098–99
  as greatest reality of faith   1103–04
  life in   1105–07, 1109
  nature of   621, 1099–1101
  new heaven in final kingdom of God   1153, 1155
  in revelatory visions   1108–10
  the Son's descent from and return to   1099
  treasures of   866, 1104–05
Hegel, George W. F.   31, 132, 146, 667
Heick, O. W.   395
Heidegger, Martin   45
Heidelberg Catechism (AD 1563)   465, 531, 532, 756
  and ascension   621–22
  on divine purpose in creating man   295, 297–300
  on fall and depravity of man   303
  on justification by faith   734
Heinlein, E.   745
hell
  and annihilationism   1091–92
  Christ's 'descent'   518–19, 1033, 1040–41, 1093
  everlasting   1082–83
  final destiny of the unsaved   1075–84
  graduation of punishment   1078
  importance of doctrine   1084
  and the intermediate state   1039
  and the moods of humanism and pragmatism   1087
  Roman Catholic teaching   1033
  roots of objections to doctrine   1086–87
  second death   1076–77
  terms and metaphors for   1083–84
  torment of   1080–82
  and universalist objections see universalism
Helvetic Confession, Second   497
Helvetius, C. A.   210
Hendriksen, William   904, 1059, 1146–47
henotheism   77, 78, 79–80
Henry, Carl F. H.   42, 146, 253, 565, 888, 1089
  on suppression of knowledge of God   710
Heraclitus   78, 667
Herberg, Will   781
hermeneutics   xvii, 542, 559
  creation account   282–84
  Israel-church identity   850–52, 863
  mythology and allegory   304
Herod the Great   432

Hick, John   564, 791, 796
higher criticism   xvii, 544
　see also redaction criticism
Hilary of Poitiers, St.   221, 595
Hippolytus   1126–27
Hirsch, E. D.   542
history
　interpretation of   3–4
　of salvation see salvation history
Hobbes, Thomas   210
Hodge, A. A.   174–75, 221, 741
　on all events serving God's plan   131
　on election   675, 1073
　on Federal view of inputed sin   396–97
　and postmillennialism   1144
　on proclaiming the gospel   794
Hodge, Charles A.   63, 127–28, 153, 401–04
　and anthropology   238
　on ascension   620
　and atonement   577, 579, 584
　and church's identity   852
　and concursus   373
　and conscience   264
　and creationism (of soul)   277
　on defining God   61
　and eschatological evangelism   1093
　on everlasting punishment   1086–87
　and exclusivism of the gospel   786
　and Federal theory   398, 405
　and free will   261
　on future state   1032
　on imputation theories   385–86, 401
　on instrument of salvation   651
　on man's dominion   289
　on means of salvation   726–27
　on miracles   209
　on 'order of salvation'   654
　and postmillennialism   1145
　on resurrection   612
　on salvation as grace   654
　on sin   351
　and sinlessness (impeccability) of Christ   526
　and unity of the church   887
Hoekema, Anthony   1059–60
Hoekema, Herman   296
Holbach, P. H. T.   210
holiness
　in Canaan and pagan religion   97, 748–49
　concept in book of Genesis   95
　definition and meaning   96–97, 749
　as fundamental attribute of God   95–96
　God's goodness based on   94
　and knowledge of God   297
　laws as expression of   99, 350
　in liberal theology   98
　Mysterium Tremendum   98, 752–53
　and union with Christ   669
　see also sanctification
Holiness Code, 'H'   94
Holy Communion (Lord's Supper) see Eucharist (Lord's Supper)
Holy Spirit
　access to the Father through   800
　as agent of calling   686, 723–24
　as agent of creation (Pannenberg)   154
　as agent of sanctification   758–59
　at baptism of Jesus   499, 874
　and creation of the church   873 see also baptism
　epoch of   842
　fruit of   800
　gift of Himself to all believers   740
　and gift of union with Christ   666–67, 830, 873 see also baptism, in the Holy Spirit
　gifts of   208 see also charismata
　indwelling of   669, 752, 837
　as initiator of repentance and faith   417
　inspirer of scripture   xvi–xvii, 107
　knower of deep thing of God   69
　and the new covenant   693, 847, 874, 875
　and noetic effect of sin   415
　outpouring of (baptism with)   667, 740, 873, 874, 876, 1112
　preliminary impartation through Jesus' 'breathing'   875–76
　procession   121
　and proclamation of the Word   686, 765
　resistance to   684
　revelations of the future   1113
　sealing of   777, 800
　universal inner prompting   46–47
　witness of   723, 724–25, 774, 775–76 see also calling; prevenient/preventing grace; regeneration
Holy Trinity, doctrine of
　actions of individual Persons   114
　belief before Nicea AD 325   108–10
　champions of   119
　and Christ as 'firstborn'   114
　creative functions of each member   160
　defence against the Arians   75–76
　difficulties in formulations   75–76
　errors and denials   115
　eternal generation   114
　eternal procession (spiration)   114
　First Ecumenical Council   104
　and God's eternal independence   72
　illustrations and analogies   115–16
　modes of being   63, 120
　New Testament   110–12
　Old Testament preparation for   110
　reasons for belief in   106–08
　reasons for the name 'Son of God'   113
　relations of the three Persons   112, 118–19, 497–98, 1154–55
　repudiation of polytheism   76

'shield' of   117
term 'only begotten'   113–14
term 'persons'   105, 120–21
values of   117
vocabulary pointers   119–21
Hooker, Richard   831
Hooykaas, R.   134, 202–03, 204
hope
  expressed in the Eucharist   1001
  and faith   719
  of people of Israel   1098
  as vision of the future   763, 1028–29, 1036–37 see also heaven, in revelatory visions
Hopkins, Samuel   391, 723
Horkheimer, Max   214
Hort, F. J. A.   819
Hoskins, Sir Edwin   881
Howard, Fred D.   997, 1000
Hoyt, Herman A.   1034, 1035, 1069
Hudson, Winthrop   777
Hugh of St. Victor   663, 977
Hume, David   22, 39, 61
  and empiricism   213
  and presence of evil   210, 211
Hus, Jan   662, 830
Huxley, Thomas H.   326
Hyma, Albert   776
hypostatic union   489–91, 492–500

I Ii

idolatry   18, 49, 77
  not tolerated by holiness of God   99, 375–76
idols   18, 81
Ignatius of Antioch, St.   470, 872, 929, 930
illumination see calling, special; witness of the Spirit
image of God
  man as see mankind, created in God's image
  Roman Catholic teaching   351, 662
immanence of God   92
Immanuel (God with us)   51
immutability of God   63, 133
impassibility, doctrine of   133, 224, 567
  pre-Reformation theology   220
  Reformers of 16th and 17th centuries   220–21
  Reformation tradition, 17th and 18th centuries   221–22
  contemporary and recent theology   222–23, 500
  definition   216–17
  scriptural warrant   219–20
  Tertullian on   217
implicit faith   725–26
imputed righteousness see justification (imputed righteousness)
imputed sin see original sin
incarnation of Christ
  biblical terms related to   484
  first formulations of doctrine   483–84

humiliation-exaltation   512–19 see also kenosis doctrine
  implications of becoming a man   486–87
  O.T. prophecy of states of Christ   513
  passion and death see passion and death of Jesus
  personal identity not changed   488
  personal (theanthropic) union   489–91, 492–500
  practical importance of doctrine   486
  saving work of incarnate Son   500–509
  theological formulations of ancient church   485
  see also Christology; Jesus
inclusivism   780, 786, 791–96
  see also pluralism
infallibility   22
infant baptism   650, 700, 727, 855–56, 984, 985–87
  in Lutheran theology   655, 696
  and regeneration   696
  see also limbo
Infinity of God   91
infralapsarianism   388, 680
intercession
  corporate prayer   966
  of Jesus   636–37, 638
intuition, as basis for knowledge of God   32–33
Irenaeus, St., Bp. of Lyons
  and the Antichrist   1132
  and apologetics   795
  in chain of tradition   1127
  and Christ's victory   596
  defence against gnostic denial of Christ's humanity   467
  and ecclesiology   805
  and image and likeness of God   254
  and necessity of Christ's death   537
  and New Testament canon   924
  and original sin   380
  and premillennialism   1139, 1140
  and recapitulation   593
  on resurrection of the body   1060, 1064
  and soteriology   594
  on unity of the church   884
  on virtue of theological refinements   218
Ironside, H. A.   938
Isaiah
  and monotheism   80
  and predictive prophecy   128–29, 1114
  suffering servant prophecies   344, 533–34, 594, 605–06, 861–62, 1050, 1114
Israel
  Jewish rejection of Jesus and Gospel   835, 837, 859–63
  relation to the church   822–23, 850–56, 863

J Jj

Jacob, at Bethel   79, 80
Jaki, Stanley L.   134–35
Jansen, Cornelius   88, 662
Jaspers, Karl   45, 214

Jastrow, Morris   365
Jefferson, Thomas   520
Jehovah
　identity of Christian God with   75
　meaning *see* Tetragrammaton (YHWH)
Jenkins, C. Ryan   741
Jeremias, Joachim,   533, 894, 985, 987, 992, 993
Jerome, St.   54, 942, 1127
Jerusalem
　destruction of   1112, 1116, 1120, 1122
　as mother of the church   813
　new and heavenly   878, 913, 1153, 1155
Jesus
　attitude to matter   327
　attitude to scripture   7, 305, 429, 431, 862
　authentic humanity   464–66
　baptism   111, 463–64, 874, 981
　chronology of ministry   463–64
　death *see* passion and death of Jesus
　divine nature *see* Christology
　earthly life   462–63, 862
　exclusive claims   787
　genealogies   470–71, 475–76
　'Golden Rule'   79
　on grace   660
　on his return   763
　historical dogma on humanity of   465
　Jewishness of   867
　as 'Lamb of God'   132, 133, 344, 536, 637, 660–61, 861–62
　　see also atonement, blood of the covenant; sacrifice, and atonement
　as 'last Adam', head of redeemed mankind   468
　nativity narratives   474, 476–78
　normality of   465–66
　obedience   514–15, 517–18, 525
　passion and death *see* passion and death of Jesus
　person and work as the Christ *see* Christology
　on preservation of elect   768
　prophecies in O.T. relating to *see* prophecy, in preparation for the coming of Christ
　as revelation of God   51–52 *see also* revelation, in and through the Son of God
　and saving faith   454, 704–05, 726–28, 729–30 *see also* salvation
　on Second Coming   1112–13, 1115
　on sin   361
　sinlessness (impeccability)   467–68, 499, 520–29
　temptations of   370
　titles of *see* Christology
　virgin birth *see* virgin birth of Jesus
　see also incarnation of Christ
Jewett, Paul K.   511, 965
Jews, as a people *see* Israel
Job, and goodness   93
John of Damascus   184, 256
John Paul II, Pope   365, 826, 829, 888, 1091
John the Baptist
　baptism   111, 981
　call for repentance   859, 864
　and preexistence of Christ   439
John XXIII, Pope   782
Johnson, Phillip E.   156
Jonah, warning to Nineveh   13, 30
Josephus, Flavius   174, 436, 691
joy   191
Judaism, as seed-bed for coming of Christ   436
judgment
　and the Day of the Lord   1013–17
　destruction of Jerusalem   1112, 1116, 1120, 1122
　and God's control of history   1067–68
　and grace, following original sin   313–17
　last *see* Last Judgment
　as work of reigning saints   1070, 1104–05, 1106–07
Julian of Eclanum   380
Julius Africanus   470
justification (imputed righteousness)   99, 556, 561–62
　cross of Christ as basis of   738–39
　doctrine of 'justification by faith'   3, 733–43
　God as author of   737
　good works as evidence   740–41, 1073
　grace as method   738
　Jesus Christ as agent of   737–38
　relations with other blessings in Christ   741–42
　resurrection of Christ, and   615
　terms and definition   735–37, 741
　and translation of Gen. 15:6   742–43
Justin Martyr, St.   43, 167, 174, 470, 593, 1034
　and church ministry   948
　and millennialism   1139, 1140
　on world evangelism   900
　and worship   966, 971

K Kk

Kallas, James   178, 183
Kane, J. H.   898
Kant, Immanuel   20, 21–22, 32, 38, 39, 41
　defective conclusions on reason   722
　and essence of things   61
　necessary postulate argument   41–42
Kantzer, Kenneth S.   106
Käsemann, Ernst   880, 992n
Keble, John   938
Keil, C. F.   149, 558, 1057
Keller, Helen   46
Kelly, J. N. D.   217, 593, 1060
kenosis doctrine   510–12
　see also incarnation of Christ
Kent, Homer A.   1128
Kent, W. H.   540–41
kerygma *see* gospel message
Kierkegaard, Søren Aaby   223, 424

Kik, J. Marcellus   1058, 1145, 1146
Killen, Robert Allan   424
kingdom of God   627–28, 1071, 1119
   embodied in the Messiah   864, 866
   as final kingdom of the Father   1154–55
   hermeneutics of Israel-church identity   850–52, 863
   in the 'millennium'   1126
   new heaven and earth in future eternal state of   1153–56
   parables and   865, 903
   relation to church   822–23, 857–68
   revelational stages   863–68
Klausner, Joseph   442
Kleinknecht, H.   567
Knapp, George Christian   112
knowledge
   and faith   725–26 *see also* faith, and reason
   of God   24, 61–62, 297
   of good and evil   305–07
   growth in   1107
   of sin   710–11
Kraemer, Hendrik   781
Krauth, Charles P.   221, 381, 498, 587–88
   on imputed sin   396
'krisis' theology *see* neo-orthodox theology
Kuen, Alfred F.   802, 811, 915
Kümmel, W. G.   422, 849
Küng, Hans   802, 828
Kuyper, Abraham   159, 724

Ll

Lactantius   174
Ladd, George E.   458, 607, 861, 863, 1070, 1154
   on birthday of the church   873
Lang, G. H.   915, 938, 1109
Laodicea, canons of   167
LaPlace, Joshua   399
Larkin, Clarence   1035
Lasko, John   671
Last Judgment   566, 786, 790, 1066–67
   according to deeds   1077–79
   certainty of   1071–72
   and the Day of the Lord   1013–17
   everlasting punishment *see* hell
   and hell *see* hell
   necessity of   1068–69
   as one or two events   1069–70
   preparation for   1068–69, 1116–17
   principles of judgment   1072–73, 1077–79
   purpose   1073
   saints and the   628, 1070–71
   and standards of God's Law   1073, 1077
   see also judgment
'last things' *see* eschatology (doctrine of last things)
Latourette, Kenneth Scott   4, 805, 994
law of God
   definition   658–60
   as extension of His holiness   97, 99
   and grace   658–60
   Jesus' claim of authority over   454
   and judgment   1073
   and knowledge of sin   710–11
Lee, Witness   931
Legters, L. L.   664, 669
Leitch, Addison H.   511, 745
Lenormant, Francois   182
Lenski, R. C. H.   1036, 1105
Leo I, St.   218, 219
Leo XIII, Pope   885
Leupold, H. C.   148–49, 230, 243, 319
Lewis, C. S.   41, 73
Lewis, Gordon   223
Leydecker, Melchior   214
liberation theology   368
Lietzmann, Hans   992n
Lightfoot, J. B.   930
limbo   1032–33
Lindberg, D. C.   205
Lindsay, T. M.   870, 871–72, 927, 930, 940
   on pastors and teachers   945, 948
Lindsell, Harold   471
Littell, Franklin   825, 938
liturgy   731, 964, 1106
   and creeds   970
   and the cross of Christ   594
   and music   970–71
   Roman Catholic   803
Locke, John   22, 210–11
Lombard, Peter   97, 184
Longenecker, Richard N.   460
Lord *see* Christology, Jesus as Lord
Lord's Supper *see* Eucharist
'lordship salvation'   729–30
Lotze, Rudolph   667
love
   as attribute of God   102–03
   as climax of Christian growth   668
   as evidence of indwelling divine presence   103
   and its place in salvation   1005
   and knowledge of God   297
   'unconditional', not true to scripture   99, 590–91, 1089
Lowell, James Russell   97, 100
Ludwigson, C. R.   863
Luther, Martin   12
   on actions reflecting the heart   644–45
   and baptism   655, 696, 979
   The Bondage of the Will   382, 388, 415
   and Christ's 'descent into hell'   519, 562
   and Christ's victory over Satan   562, 586
   and church ministry   951
   and civil government   330, 331, 335
   and civil righteousness   793–94

and concupiscence   356
and conversion   700
on creation and preservation   203–04
on doctrine and experience   3
and doctrine of the Trinity   105
and ecclesiology   812, 870, 911, 917
and the Eucharist   1006
and free will   351
on holiness   98
on impassibility and suffering   220
and infant baptism   655, 696
and justification by faith alone   3, 561–62
on Mary's sinful nature   527
on miracles and love   207
on natural theology   156
Ninety-Five Theses, at Wittenberg   706
on obedience of Christ   517
and 'order of salvation'   655
on reality of devils   183
rejection of scholasticism   19
and Sacramentarian Controversy   512
and sanctification   755–56
and theology of covenants   397
and Traducianism   277
on work   158
see also Lutheran theology
Lutheran theology
on ascension   620
on atonement   562
on eucharistic 'real presence'   490–91, 497, 498, 620, 1006
on humiliation-exaltation of Christ   512–13 see also kenosis doctrine
on infant baptism   696
on justification by faith   734
on man's dominion   289
on noetic effect of sin   414
on original knowledge   234
on original sin   381, 396
on perseverance   766
on sanctification   755–56
see also Augsburg Confession; Concord, Formula of (1576); Luther, Martin

M Mm

Machen, John Gresham   3, 387, 720
  on virgin birth   470, 472–73, 480, 482
Mack, Alexander   825
Mackintosh, C. H.   938
Mackintosh, H. R.   1038
MacLeod, David J.   114, 1060
Macquarrie, John   45, 571
  Christology   425
  on creation   142
  on holiness   98
  impassibility denied, by redefinition of trinitarianism   223

on spiritual beings   165
treatment of virgin birth   471
MacRae, Allan   242
Macrina, sister of St Basil and Gregory of Nyssa   119
Maier, Walter   804
Malebranche, Nicholas   270
man of sin/lawlessness see Antichrist
Manichaeism   59, 179
mankind, man as created   **227–335**
  Adamic origin   240–42
  anthropological elements   268–74, 758 see also body; soul; spirit, of man
  conscience see conscience
  created in God's image   48–49, 156, 230, 248–57, 297, 351
  dominion   230, 256, 289–90, 299
  earth and environment   231, 233–34, 290, 302, 321–28
  evolution and creation   242–44
  fall see fall of man
  family life   313–16, 318 see also sex and marriage
  first life, in 'paradise'   284–92, 307
  food   230
  human depravity see depravity
  lines of family descent through Cain and Seth   319
  male labor as order of creation   157, 202, 235, 287–88
  Marxist views   368
  natural and spiritual nature   234, 325
  original equality of the sexes   230
  original powers and mission   290–91
  place in order of creation   291
  purpose of God in and for   231, 293–300
  separate races   245–47
  social order of primal man   156–59
  soul see soul
  unity of human race   234, 240–41, 244–45, 247, 401–04
  womanhood   313–16
  see also anthropology
Manton, Robert   1012–13
Marcel, Gabriel Honoré   424
Marcion   520, 1045
Marcus Aurelius   43
marriage   1137
  of God and His people   298
  as order of creation   157
  and sex   235, 251–52, 314–16, 528, 754, 1137
Marshall, I. H.   1135
Martensen, Hans L.   214, 622
Martin-Achard, Robert   1021, 1036, 1047, 1049
Martin, Ralph P.   965n, 967, 980
Martyr, Peter   671
Marx, Karl   31, 211
Marxism   368
Mary, mother of Jesus   474–75, 481, 527
  theotokos (God-bearer)   495, 496
  see also virgin birth of Jesus
Mascall, E. L.   806, 883
Mass   824, 964, 994–95, 996, 1003–06

canons on the   563–64
sacrifice of the   586–87, 638
see also Eucharist (Lord's Supper); transubstantiation
Mauro, Philip   862, 863
Maxwell, L. E.   863
Maxwell, W. D.   964
Mazlisch, Bruce   205
McCasland, S. Vernon   183
McClain, Alva J.   65, 170, 481, 505–06, 663
   on church eldership   947
   and death   1018
   on divine sovereignty and moral responsibility   837–38
   and 'eclectic' interpretation of scripture   851
   and kingdom of God   858, 859
   on likeness of God   256–57
   on washing with the Word   761
McClintock, John   1033
McCool, G. A.   782
McDermott, Gerald R.   793
McDonald, H. D.   293
McGrath, Alister E.   223, 787, 792
McKenzie, John L.   811, 827
McNeill, John T.   86
McQuilkin, Robert   863
mediation   461, 499–500
   function of mediator   505, 557
   mediatory offices of prophet, priest and king   506–09, 529
   in Paul's theology   505–06
Melanchthon, Philipp   19, 20, 64, 98, 512, 695
   and Christ's 'descent into hell'   519
   Common Places (*Loci Communes*)   562
   on creation, preservation and providence   204
   and soteriology   596
   see also Augsburg Confession
Mennonites   485
mercy   759
   as attribute of God   103
Messiah *see* Christology, Messiahship of Jesus
messianic expectation   428–33, 1114–15
   Dead Sea Scrolls and Qumran community   432, 508
   post-exilic   508–09
   see also prophecy, in preparation for the coming of Christ
metaphors
   necessity of   58–59
   scriptural use   56–57, 62–63
   see also analogical language; anthropomorphism
Methodism   357, 390, 920–21
Meyer, H. A. W.   477, 894, 1112
Meyrick, F.   875
Miceli, Vincent P.   1133
Miley, John   390, 774
Mill, John Stuart   213
millennium *see* Second Coming, and the thousand years of Revelation 20
Miller, Perry   397
Milligan, William   607, 611, 1147

Milton, John   308
Minear, P. A.   821, 878
ministries and offices of the church   xvii–xviii, 760, 930–31
   apostolic founders   842–47, 873, 892 *see also* apostolic succession; Peter, St., and church's 'rock' of foundation
   appointment of   950–51 *see also* ordination
   authority of   951–52
   biblical sources   942–44
   biblical terms for ideas of office, function and ministry   941
   deacons   930, 954–55
   elders and bishops   926, 929, 931, 945–49, 950–54, 959
   evangelists   893–94
   financial support   968–69
   modern denominational differences   806
   pastors and teachers   xvii–xviii, 894, 930, 944–45, 946, 951–52 *see also* teaching ministry
   Paul's teaching in Ephesians 4   890–97
   prophets   892–93
   purpose and function   894–97
   qualifications for   952–54
   relation of offices to spiritual gifts   944–45
   temporary and permanent   942
   women's   953, 955
miracles
   alleged post-New Testament occurrences   209
   apostles' powers of   843
   definition   205–06
   empiricist objection to   213
   and establishment of monotheism   81–82
   love and   207
   and preaching of the gospel   841, 866
   prophecy and   14–15, 50–51, 207
   providence and   205–09
   superstition and   203, 208
mission   898–907, 968
   see also proclamation of the gospel
modalism (heresy)   63, 115, 116
   Modalistic Monarchianism   27
Modernism   389–90
Molteau, A. Scott   186
Moltmann, Jürgen   1009
   impassibility   223, 491
   on redemption of soul and body   1019
monarchianism *see* patripassionism
Monk, Robert C.   778–79
Monod, Victor   673
monolatry   77
monotheism
   biblical authority   14–15, 80–82
   definition   77
   general arguments for   50, 78–79
   religious values   82
Montgomery, James A.   736
Moody, Dale   818
Moody, Dwight L.   1096
Moorehead, W. G.   557, 559

moral evil *see* hamartiology; sin
morality
   depravity *see* depravity
   and doctrine of hell   1084
   and holiness   97 *see also* sanctification
   and knowledge of God   13, 40–41, 72
   and responsibility   348–49
Morris, Leon   532, 547, 548, 555, 881
Morrison, A. Cressy   39
Moses
   at the burning bush   67
   faith of   15
   revelations through miracles   50–51
   the Shema   80
   song of   54–58, 245
Moule, C. F. D.   980, 986
Mounce, Robert H.   785n
Mueller, George   200–201, 938, 949
Mueller, John Theodor   234, 616, 755–56
   on election   673, 675, 679
   on man's dominion   289
Mueller, Julius   612
multiculturalism *see* pluralism
Murray, G. L.   1059, 1147
Murray, John   231, 234, 235, 584
   and adoption   745
   and calling   682
   against 'covenant of works'   296, 397
   and image of God   253, 254, 759
   and imputed sin   397
   on sacraments   977
   on salvation   653
   and sanctification   751
   on soul and body   258, 260
   on union with Christ   664, 665
   universal benefits from death of Christ   333
music   158, 801, 970–71, 1106
   see also worship, hymns
mystical union, true and false   668–69
   see also union with Christ, false notions

NNn

names of God   13, 14, 27, 53–58, 69, 84, 449
   necessity of   58–59
Nash, Ronald B.   1093
natural theology   35, 42–43, 47–48
   repudiated by Luther   156
   see also arguments for existence of God
nature   73–74, 101, 321–28
   new nature of man   695, 758
   uniformity of   134
   see also creation
necromancy   259, 1036
Nee, Watchman   931, 938, 949
neo-orthodox theology   xvi, 22–23, 44–45

angels   165
Christology   424–25
conditioned omniscience of Jesus   451
faith   724
human depravity   381–82
humanity of Christ   465
Jesus as teacher of authentic existence   521
re-interpretation of atonement   570–71
resurrection   606, 1064
transcendence of God   92
virgin birth   471
Neoplatonism   17, 59, 167
   effect on Augustine   67
Nestorius, Cyril's Epistle to   218–19
Netland, Harold A.   796–97
Neuhaus, Richard John   831, 953
Neve, J. L.   108–09, 379–80, 592
   on Pelagianism   387
   on Socinianism   389
Nevius, John L.   177
new birth *see* regeneration
new creation   295, 668, 695, 1155–56
new heaven and earth   1153, 1155
new nature, of man   758
   see also regeneration
Newbigin, Leslie   791, 807, 885–86, 910, 999
Newman, John Henry   938
Newton, B. W.   949
Newton, John   304, 685
Newton, Sir Isaac   38
Nicea, Council of (AD 325)   75, 104–05, 115
Nicea, Creed of (AD 325)   530
Nicene Creed (AD 381)   104, 105, 446, 465, 593, 672
   'filoque' clause   111
   impassibility   221
   one holy, catholic, and apostolic church   827, 884
   Second Coming   1116
   suffering and death of Christ   530
   translation   117–18, 488
   virgin birth of Jesus   470
Niebuhr, Reinhold   45, 210, 236, 408, 425, 797
Niesel, Wilhelm   673
Nietzsche, Friedrich Wilhelm   214
Nineveh, warning of Jonah to   13, 30
Norbie, D. L.   939
noumena   21
Novak, Michael   237
Numbers, R. L.   205
numinous, the   95, 98
Nygren, Anders   1004, 1005

OOo

obedience
   of Christ   514–15, 517–18, 525
   in resisting temptation   371

and sanctification   97, 752
occultism   82
Oden, Thomas   124, 126, 390, 582
   on creation theories   144, 153
   ecclesiology   810, 821, 910, 953
   on local church   915
   on prevenient grace and probational opportunities   1095
   on repentance   704
   on spirit and death   1019
   and substitutionary atonement   537
Oehler, G. F.   294, 304, 361, 855, 1031
Olaskey, Marvin   852
Old Roman Creed   470, 482, 1060
Olevianus, Caspar   297
   see also Heidelberg Catechism (AD 1563)
Olshausen, Hermann   478
omnipotence of God   90
   and humiliation of Christ   515
omnipresence of God   86–87
   and humiliation of Christ   515
omniscience of God   87–89, 1072
   and humiliation of Christ   515
O'Neil, A. C.   367
Oosterzee, Johann Jacob Van   1095
Orange, Second Council of (AD 529)   303
ordination   706, 953
   see also ministries and offices of the church, appointment of
Origen   43, 184, 219, 477, 528, 856
   and Christ's victory   596
   and the Eucharist   1003
   and image and likeness of God   254
   against premillennialism   1140
   and trichotomy theory   273
   and universal salvation   597
   use of Isaiah 53   597
original sin   303–05
   Augustinian teaching   380–81
   Calvinist views   280–81
   and death   1023
   Early Church's teaching   379–80
   imputation problems   382–84, 398–99
   imputation theories   385–93, 395–405
   Pauline doctrine   339–40, 378–79, 383, 393–94
   Reformation and later teachings   381–82
   Roman Catholic teaching   643, 662
   see also fall of man
Orr, James   115, 161, 730
   against 'covenant of works'   295–96
   on covenant theology   855–56
   and eschatological evangelism   1093–94
   on justification by faith   735, 741–42
   on sinlessness of Jesus   524
   on virgin birth   480, 481, 482
Ott, Ludwig   85, 86, 88, 242, 564, 662
   and creationism (of soul)   277
   and institution of sacraments   978

and limbo   1032–33
on mystical body of Christ   826
on Peter's primacy   845
Otto, Rudolph   32–33, 94, 95, 376
   on holiness   98, 752–53
Outler, Albert C.   353
Owen, John   700, 707, 723, 777, 829–30
   and ecclesiology   831, 832
Oxford movement   938
Oxtoby, Gurdon C.   1011

P Pp

Packer, James I.   644, 690, 691, 776, 783, 1087
Paley, William   39
panentheism   73, 89, 491
Pannenberg, Wolfhart   64
   on angels and demons   183
   on creation   153–55
   on man as image of God   252
   on New Testament basis for Trinity   75
   on omnipresence   86
   on resurrection   1044
   on sin   312
   on virgin birth   471–72
pantheism   28, 36, 70, 73, 77, 92
parables
   and the mysteries of God   865
   and the progress of God's kingdom on earth   903
paradise
   garden of Eden   284–89
   heaven as   1101, 1102
   promise of   286
   and the tabernacle   298
parousia see Second Coming
Parshall, Gerald   382
particular election   573–74
Pascal, Blaise   236, 424, 599
passion and death of Jesus   118
   and angels   536
   as atonement see atonement
   belong together as one subject   530–31
   cosmic implications see cross of Christ, cosmic benefits
   crucifixion see cross of Christ
   doctrinal importance   532–39
   emphasis in Epistles and Revelation   535–36
   emphasis in Gospels   463
   and importance of baptism and eucharist   535 see also baptism; Eucharist
   nature of His death   531–32
   necessity   536–39
   process of rejection   531
   specific predictions of Old Testament   535
   and suffering servant prophecies of Isaiah chapts 42-53   344, 533–34, 594, 605–06, 861–62, 1050, 1114
   and the world to come   536

Patai, Raphael   166, 442, 533, 1132
patripassionism   27, 115, 215, 223, 588
  'new'   491
Paul, Apostle
  and adoption   745–46, 773–74
  on body of Christ   873, 876–77, 879–90
  and Christ's gifts of ministries in the church, Ephesians 4   890–97
  and Christ's victory over principalities and powers   166
  on church's preeminence in plan of God   800, 801, 878
  on corruption   758, 762
  and the cross of Christ   421
  and doctrinal instruction   7–8, 9, 969–70
  and the Eucharist   993, 997
  and evangelizing gentiles   835–36, 865, 899–900, 901–02
  and exclusivism of the gospel   783–84, 787, 789–90
  on financial support for the ministry   968
  and freedom from legalism   327
  on grace   704
  on guilt   379
  on Israel   853–55
  and justification by faith   566, 737–41
  and man's dominion   289
  on preservation of elect   768
  on proclaiming the Word in the power of the Spirit   686
  on reconciliation   334
  and regeneration   694
  on rejection of truth   372
  on resurrection   1045, 1056, 1058, 1062–65, 1070
  on sanctification   749, 751, 752
  on Second Coming and preceding events   1129, 1133–36
  on sin   339–40, 361, 378–79, 383, 393–94, 406–11, 566
  style of theology   457
  and supernatural gifts   208
  universal inner law   48, 49
  on witness of the Spirit   775
Paul VI, Pope   829
Payne, E. A.   938
Payne, J. Barton   361, 558–59, 856, 1037, 1039
Peese, Edward   938
Pelagianism   312, 387, 473, 541, 568, 1023
  and calling or regeneration   687
  on imputed sin   386
  recent version   569
  see also Socinianism
Pelagius   138, 379, 386, 578, 687
Pelikan, Jaroslav   76, 110, 119, 135
  on apologists of creation   143
  on Christ's victory   596
  on Church of England   688
  and deity of Christ   458
  and doctrines of covenant   397
  and early Christian worship   594, 595
  on history of exegesis   564
  on impassibility   217, 218
  and paradoxes of theology   576
  on partaking of the divine nature   694
  and primitive Christianity   833
  and resurrection   602
  on Wisdom and preexistence of Christ   441
Pelton, H. M.   468
penal substitution   555–58, 594–95, 596–97, 599
  see also atonement; vicarious satisfaction
penance   706, 960
Pentecost   667, 876
  as birthday of the church   873
  as a coming of Christ   111, 1112
perfection
  of God   64–65, 90, 759
  of man   759 *see also* mankind, created in God's image
persecution   860, 862, 906, 1120, 1127
  and church leadership   926
  Roman Church and   825
  see also 'great tribulation'
perseverance
  and assurance   766
  Baptist doctrine   767–68
  based on grace   768
  definition   765, 767–68
  and divine attributes   769
  and heavenly rewards   1104–05
  Jesus as model   529
  objections to doctrine   769–71
  as patient endurance and watchfulness   1117, 1119, 1121
  scriptural evidence   768–69
  see also preservation
personhood   67–68
Peter Lombard   977
Peter, Apostle
  'binding' and 'loosing'   845–46
  and church's 'rock' of foundation   843–44
  confession at Caesarea Philippi   425–27, 448, 534, 843–44
  on day of Pentecost   667
  at house of Cornelius   840–41
  and the 'keys of the kingdom of heaven'   844–45
Peters, G. W.   898
Peters, George N. H.   856, 1143
Peterson, J.   1047
Peterson, Robert   1084, 1092
Pfeiffer, Robert H.   94, 182
Pharisees, view of matter   327
phenomena   21, 22
Philo   691
Pieper, Francis   8, 10, 63, 94, 352, 512
  Christology   491
  on churches   915
  on creation   142, 234
  on doctrine and ecclesiology   804, 952, 954
  on human and divine natures of Christ   498
  on man's dominion   289
  noetic effect of sin   414

on perfection of Chrisian religion   590
and sinlessness (impeccability) of Christ   527
and soul   277
on the Trinity   114
Pieters, Albertus   1059, 1148
Pink, A. W.   582
Pinnock, Clark H.   787, 792, 1089–90, 1091–92
Pius XII, Pope   782
Plantinga, Alvin, problem of evil   210
Plantinga, Cornelius, Jr   256
Plato   39, 78, 93
Pliny the Elder   134
Pliny's letter on the Christians to Trajan   966
Plotinus   17
Plummer, Alfred   8–9, 1147
pluralism   780–81, 791–92, 796–97
  see also inclusivism
Plymouth Brethren   805, 938–39, 946, 949
Pohle, J.   662
Polycarp, St., Bp. of Smyrna   109, 1127
  Epistle to the Philippians   920
polytheism   76, 77, 79–80
Porphyry   17
postmillennialism   1058, 1059, 1141–42, 1143–46
praise   300, 966–67
  see also worship
prayer
  heard and answered by Jesus   454
  intercession of Jesus   636–37, 638
  in light of Second Coming   1119
  meetings for   731, 966–67
  and praise   966–67
  and providence   199–200
  and sanctification   761
  'The Lord's Prayer'   182, 966
pre-existentialism   276
preaching   731, 967
  see also proclamation of the gospel
predestination (decrees of God)   351–52, 373
  biblical statements about God's plan   126–27, 131–37
  biblical terms related to   127
  certainty of fulfillment   133–34
  and civil government   135–36
  distinguished from soteriological election   124
  evil acts   137, 139
  exemplified in Paul   125
  length and circumstances of individual lives   136–37
  nations and   135
  offensive to secular mind   122–23
  and predictive prophecy   128–30
  providence   123–24
  sin   139–40
  values of doctrine   140
  see also election; free will
prediction *see* prophecy
premillennialism   858, 1054–55, 1058, 1132, 1150–52

dispensational   858
in early church   1139
preservation
  continuing work of   192–94
  and integrity of creation   193
  peculiar work of God the Son   192
  and perseverance   767, 768–69
  and sin   372–74
prevenient/preventing grace   353–54, 359, 1095
priesthood   871, 872, 1004
  of all believers   947, 1005
priestly work of Christ   529, 609, 629–30, 633–35
  as advocate   622, 637–38
  and assurance   772–73
  and inauguration of a new covenant   635–36
  intercession   636–37, 638
  Old Testament background   630–32
primo-geniture   114
problem of evil   39–40, 162–63, 209–12, 328
  see also theodicy
process theology   72, 73, 521
  creation considered unimportant   143
  against doctrine of omniscience   89
  rejection of doctrine of impassibility   223
procession, of Holy Spirit   121
Procksh, O.   95
proclamation of the gospel   686, 731, 765, 840, 913
  changes needed before gentile evangelization   899
  ecclesiology and evangelism   805
  eschatological evangelism   1092–94
  in the Eucharist   1000
  evangelism and doctrine of hell   1079
  evangelization of all nations to precede Second Coming   1123, 1128
  gentile evangelization   835–36, 899–907
  mission practice from Matthew's Gospel   903–06
  nature of 'Great Commission'   900–901
  Pauline mandate for mission   901–02
  principles for world evangelism   902–03
  see also gospel message
Profession of the Tridentine Faith (AD 1654)   465
prophecy   852, 859–61
  apologetic use   16–17, 429, 504, 841
  authenticity   15–16, 129–30, 206–07
  characteristics   17
  Israel and the church   822–23, 850–56, 863
  and the 'last things' (eschatology)   1010–17, 1113, 1124–27, 1130
  and miracles   14–15, 50–51, 206
  and omniscience of God   88
  pentecostal fulfillment   1010–11, 1012–13, 1112
  and predestination   128–30
  preexistent Christ in O.T. prophecy   441–43
  in preparation for the coming of Christ   305, 428–33, 503, 693, 1113–15, 1130 *see also* Isaiah, suffering servant prophecies

prophets
  of Baal   15, 16
  in the church   892–93
  O.T. prophetic office   15–16
propitiation (appeasement)   554–55, 589, 634–35, 637–38
  origin of doctrine   567
  see also atonement
Protagoras   667
protest atheism   210, 212–14, 223
Protestant Reformation see Reformation views, general
Provair, C. D.   851, 853n
providence   50–51, 123–24, 200–201, 205, 245–47, 372–74
  all-inclusiveness of   196–97
  angels and   171–72
  and chance   197–98
  and chastening   761–62
  Christ as director of   453
  David as example of (2 Sam. 15-18)   194–95
  and evil   198–99, 303, 328
  through free moral agents   196
  general and special   194
  and God's foreknowledge   194
  human effort required   200
  and hypothetical contingency   199
  Joseph as example of (Gen. 37-45)   195
  and judgment   1072
  and judgmental 'comings' of Christ   906, 1112
  through miraculous intervention   195, 205–09
  through natural processes   196
  prayer required   199–200
  preparation of nations for coming of Christ   433–37
  sin controlled through   139–40, 372–74
  and will of God   200
Pseudo-Dionysius   167
  see also Neoplatonism
psychopannychia (soul sleep)   1034, 1091
Ptolemy   463
purgatory   587, 1033
Puritanism   707–08, 723, 777–79
  ecclesiology   831
purity   749–50
  see also holiness; sanctification

Q Qq

quest for the historical Jesus   471
Quicumque see Athenasian Creed
quietism   200
Qumran, the community and its literature see Dead Sea Scrolls, and the Qumran sect

R Rr

racial unity   234, 240–41, 244–47, 401–04
Rad, Gerhard von see Von Rad, Gerhard
Rahner, Karl   223, 781–82
raising the dead   453–54

Ramm, Bernard L.   134, 724
Ramsay, W. M.   925, 926, 930, 948
Randall, J. F.   883
ransom   333, 503, 551–52, 595–96
rapture of the church   1118, 1124, 1127, 1129, 1133–34
  in popular imagination   1132–33
  and the preaching of the gospel of the kingdom   1128
Ras Shamra tablets   283, 1020
Rauschenbusch, Walter   98
Rayburn, Robert G.   1043
'realised eschatology'   1009–10
reason see common sense, use of; faith, and reason
reconciliation of the world   330–31, 332, 332–35, 552–54
  limits on   334–35
  promise and fulfillment   585
  and universalism   1090
  see also atonement
redaction criticism   463, 849
redemption
  and application of the atonement   581, 665
  of the body   758, 762
  finished work of God   2, 868
  price of   552
  promise of   313–17
  and sanctification   749
  see also atonement; salvation history
Reeve, J. J.   548
Reformation views, general see also under individual theologians
  assurance of salvation   766
  authority   811
  baptism   986
  disgust with scholastic controversies   64
  ecclesiology   812, 827, 885
  election   671–72
  Eucharist   1006
  the Holy Trinity   105–06
  natural theology   35
  original sin   381–82
  rejection of scholastic vocabulary   19
  rescue of doctrine of repentance   706
  return to biblical view of nature   203
  Sacramentarian Controversy   512–13
  saving faith   726
  soteriology of atonement   561–63, 596
regeneration
  and baptism   696
  in biblical history   692–93
  causes   697, 723
  definition and nature   695–97
  effects   698
  evidences   696
  New Testament teaching   693–94
  in non-biblical vocabulary   691–92
  prophesied in the Old Testament   693
  Puritans and   723
  theological meanings   689–91

of whole man   698
see also calling; conversion; prevenient/preventing grace; witness of the Spirit
Rehwinkel, A. M.   265, 349
Reims, Council of (AD 1148)   64, 218
Reisinger, John G.   296, 1000
renewal of the heart   692, 758
  see also regeneration; sanctification
repentance   13, 701
  biblical terms   708–09
  contribution of Reformation   706
  definition   708
  and faith   704
  feeling redirected   710–11
  as gift of God   711–12
  John the Baptist's call for   859, 864
  motives   712
  thinking redirected   709–10
  will redirected   711
  see also conversion
reprobation   678, 680
restorationism *see* universalism
resurrection, doctrine of
  biblical terms related to   1046–47
  body of flesh   1052–53, 1060–65, 1099–1101
  extent   1053
  idea of one future resurrection   1058–60
  idea of two resurrections   1054–58
  millennial interpretations   1054–55, 1058–60, 1138–52
  New Testament teaching   1051–65
  Old Testament outlook   1047–51
  order of events   1055–56
  relation of future resurrection to Christ's resurrection   1044, 1062–63, 1099–1101
  as stumbling block   1045
  see also resurrection of Christ
resurrection of Christ
  apologetics   602–03
  and ascension *see* ascension of Christ
  and Christian hope of resurrection   615 *see also* resurrection, doctrine of
  as Gospel   603
  as historical event   606–07, 1045
  limitations of His risen nature   612–13
  in O.T prophecies   604–06
  in O.T. typology   603–04
  physical body changed   610–11
  physical body glorified and immortal   611–12, 613
  physical body raised   608–10
  and power of God   608, 615
  proclaimed together with His death   601
  proclamation of Jesus as Lord and Christ   614
  and subsequent appearances   607, 847, 859
  theological meaning   613–15
revelation   23–24
  through the church   74, 800

and exclusivism of the gospel   788–89
and faith   716
general (through creation)   24–25, 47–48, 62, 142, 155–56, 160–61
through Holy Spirit   46, 69, 1113
and information   22–23, 44, 45
through man's original nature   48–49 *see also* mankind, created in God's image
Moses at burning bush   67
neo-orthodox views   22, 23, 44
original and direct   49
through scripture   23–24, 51–52, 62, 429
at Sinai   67–68
in and through the Son of God   51–52, 425–27, 429, 597
special (through providence and miracles)   24–25, 50–51, 206
Reymond, Robert L.   149, 296, 401, 680, 795
  on adoption   744
  and amillennialism   1147
  and baptism   983
  on sanctification   751
  and Traducianism   281
Ridderbos, Herman   853n, 864
righteousness
  as aspect of divine image in Adam   355
  as attribute of God   99–100
  imputed *see* justification (imputed righteousness)
  revealed at Calvery   589
Robertson, H. M.   776
Robertson, J. D.   997
Robinson, H. Wheeler   533
Robinson, J. A. T.   1089
Robinson, Joseph Armitage   909
rock, as metaphor for God   56, 57
Roman Church   46, 561, 729, 871–72
  apostolic succession   803, 806, 845
  assurance of salvation denied   766
  authority   811
  catholicity claims   826–29
  Christ's 'descent into the underworld'   519
  concupiscence   356
  ecclesiology   803, 805–06, 811, 824
  faith   716
  fall of man   662
  funerals   756–57
  grace   368, 661–63
  image of God   351, 662
  inclusivism   781–83
  on intermediate state   1032–33
  Mass *see* Mass
  piety   756
  as 'pilgrim church'   825
  priests   586–87
  rejection of justification by grace alone   738
  response to Reformers' soteriology of atonement   563–64
  seven sacraments   706, 977

sin   303, 365–66
transubstantiation   512, 587, 991, 997, 1005–06
Roman world, and the coming of Christ   435–36
Rosenthal, Marvin J.   1129
Rousseau, Jean Jacques   409
Runia, Klaas   795–96
Rushdoony, R. J.   104, 118, 1145
Russell, Bertrand   89, 411
Ryle, J. C.   676, 679
Ryries, Charles   238

Ss

Sabbath rest   192, 235, 288
  and the 'Lord's Day'   965, 996
Sabellianism   115, 116, 123
sacramental theology   650, 662, 871, 874
Sacramentarian Controversy   512–13
sacraments (ordinances)   976–79
  baptism *see* baptism
  Eucharist (Lord's Supper) *see* Eucharist
  seven defined by Roman Church   706, 977
sacredness *see* holiness
sacrifice
  and atonement   548–50, 555–58, 595 *see also* Jesus, as 'Lamb of God'
  human death as   1025
  and the Mass *see* Mass
  and worship   319
sainthood   751
saintliness *see* holiness
salvation   **639–737**
  adoption *see* adoption
  assurance of *see* assurance
  atonement *see* atonement
  biblical terms related to   646–49, 652
  calling *see* calling; regeneration
  through Christ alone   780–90 *see also* exclusivism
  comprehensiveness of   649–51
  conversion *see* conversion
  conveyance through infant baptism   650, 655
  and the Day of the Lord   1015, 1016
  dispensational view   663
  distinctions within 'order of salvation'   654
  election *see* election
  gospel message as instrument of   651, 901 *see also* gospel message
  by grace   657–63 *see also* grace
  healing   649–50
  identification with Christ *see* union with Christ
  involvement of the three Persons of the Godhead   650 *see also* union with Christ
  'justification by faith'   733–43 *see also* justification (imputed righteousness)
  'mystical' method of conveyance   650
  nature and character   646–51

new birth *see* regeneration
objective and subjective   646
perseverance *see* perseverance
recapitulation (assimilation/imitation of Christ)   593
regeneration *see* regeneration
sacramental method of conveyance   650, 662, 874 *see also* sacramental theology
sanctification *see* sanctification
saving work of incarnate Son   500–509
self-salvation as enemy of orthodox doctrine   579
of unevangelized   793–95 *see also* Christology, Christ and non-Christian religions
in union with Christ *see* union with Christ
see also soteriology (doctrine of salvation)
salvation history   3
  vs Greek theory of recurring cycles   135
  see also Israel, relation to the church; kingdom of God, revelational stages
sanctification
  and the community of faith   760
  complete (future)   762–64
  as duty   760
  'entire' (Wesleyan)   774
  Holy Spirit as agent   758–59
  positional (past, 'definitive')   750–54, 755
  progressive (present)   755–62
  second coming as motive for   763
  terms and meanings   747–50
  through the Word   760–61
Sanders, John   786, 1089–90, 1092
Sandlin, Andrew   1145
Santayana, George   79
Sartre, Jean-Paul   214
Satan   160
  as agent of death   1023
  Augustine's writings   598, 1141–42
  binding and loosing of   1141–42, 1146–47, 1148
  career and destiny   179–80, 313, 1055, 1114
  character   178, 308
  and the Christian   181–82
  Christ's victory over   181, 562, 585–86, 596
  delivery to   959
  and evil angels   173–75 *see also* demons
  existence in scripture   176–77
  fear of   82
  god of the present world   329
  and idea of ransom   596
  identity   176, 308
  origin and fall   163, 178, 302
  present activities and devices   180–81
  renunciation of   181
  as tempter   303, 308–09, 371
satisfaction   594–95, 596, 706
  see also penal substitution; vicarious satisfaction
Saucy, Robert L.   821, 852–53, 854, 874, 988
Sauer, Erich   324, 1069

Sauvage, G. M.   224
saving faith *see* faith
Sayers, Dorothy L.   116, 256
Schaeffer, Francis   852, 856
Schaff, Philip   105, 498, 511
  on premillennialism   1139
Schechter, Solomon   867
Schep, J. A.   603, 609–10, 611, 622, 1029
  on resurrection   1044, 1052, 1064–65, 1099–1100
Schilder, Klass   1100–1101
Schillebeecks, Edward C. F. A.   828
Schleiermacher, F. D. E.   xv n, 31, 79, 222, 716, 791
Schmidt, K. L.   817, 866
Schmidt, W.   50
Schnackenburg, Rudolph   881
Schneider, Bernard N.   172
Schultz, Herman   260–61, 295, 347
Schürer, Emil   166, 980, 1046, 1115
Schwarz, Hanz   1146
Schweitzer, Albert   427
Schweizer, Eduard   1001
science, and first cause   37
Scofield Reference Bible   318, 618, 663, 1034, 1069, 1128
scripture
  Bible 'created' over 1,500 years   243–44
  criticism   xvii, 544, 849
  historical nature of Genesis 1 and 2 narrative   141, 229, 231–33
  inspired by Holy Spirit   xvi–xvii, 107
  Jesus' attitude to   429, 431, 1010, 1049
  prediction and fulfillment *see* prophecy
  preexistent Christ in Old Testament   441–43
  public reading   965–66
  as Reformers' sole source of doctrinal and ecclesiastical authority   812
  relations of the two testaments   874, 1010, 1032, 1049 *see also* Israel, relation to the church
  reliability of the Gospels   459–60
  revelation through   22–23, 51–52, 62, 429
  and theological doctrine   xv, xvi–xviii
  see also Word of God
sealing of the Spirit   777
  see also witness of the Spirit
Second Advent *see* Second Coming
Second Coming   530, 624–25, 1015–17
  anticipated in the Eucharist   1001
  characteristics   1117–19
  as consummation of Christ's reign   868
  Daniel's prophecy and the   902, 1124–27, 1139
  harbingers   1016–17, 1120, 1128–35
  as motive for sanctification   763
  Old Testament anticipation   1113–15
  and presentation of church as bride   912–13
  and the 'rapture' *see* rapture of the church
  and related terms   1111
  and the several 'comings' of Christ   906, 1111–12

  spiritual preparedness for   1116–17
  teachings of Jesus   1112–13, 1115
  and the thousand years of Revelation 20   1138–52 *see also* amillennialism; postmillennialism; premillennialism
  time of   1120–27, 1134
Seiss, Joseph   621, 856, 1101, 1143
semi-Pelagianism   386–87, 687
Seneca, Lucius Annaeus   43
Septuagint   26, 505, 545, 605, 1135
  Genesis 1:1-3   147, 150
service   1106
Servitus   115
sex and marriage   235, 251–52, 314–16, 528, 754, 1137
Shank, Robert   680, 770
Shedd, W. G. T.   49, 63, 122, 351, 352, 500
  on Anselm   592
  and anthropology   238
  on Arminian theology   388–89
  on Athenasius   596
  on calling and regeneration   687
  on creation account   162
  on divine justice   569
  and humanity of Christ   468
  on imputed sin   396
  on original sin   380–81
  on particular atonement   581
  on Pelagianism   568
  on retribution and hell   1074
  on sanctification   758, 759
  on sin and predestination   139
  and sinlessness (impeccability) of Christ   499, 526
  and Traducianism   275, 277
  and trichotomy theory of Clement and Origen   273
  and the underworld   1032, 1035
  on the unevangelized   794
  and unregenerate will   711
shekina   443–44
Shelley, Bruce L.   926–27, 931, 964
Shelley, Percy Bysshe   85
Shema, the   80, 81
sheol   1027, 1031, 1034, 1036, 1039–40
Shepherd, Norman   252
Shepherd of Hermas, The   942, 1132
Siegfried, E. P.   144
signs and wonders *see* Holy Spirit, gifts of; miracles; Second Coming, harbingers
Silver, Abba Hillel   376
sin **337–417**
  and awareness of God   13, 362
  biblical terms related to   339, 341–42, 345–46
  blameworthiness   343–44, 360–62 *see also* guilt
  categories of offense   365–67, 374–77
  as cause of death   1023
  collective participation   344–45
  commission   342
  and concupiscence   354–57

culpability of   343–44, 345
doctrinal scheme of *see* hamartiology (doctrine of sin)
expansion of   332
forgiveness of *see* atonement; forgiveness
as inhuman   236
and loss of human authenticity   465, 710
man of *see* Antichrist
as moral evil   348–49, 358–63
noetic effect   408, 414–15
omission   342–43
opposition to will of God   349–51
original *see* fall of man; original sin
Pauline doctrine   339–40, 361, 378–79, 383, 393–94, 406–11
personal consequences   413–14
and predestination   139–40
present in God's creation   162–63
as a principle   340
providential control   139–40, 372–74
scriptures used against doctrine of universal sin   411–12
and sinful condition of soul, heart and mind   351, 358–63, 368, 408, 645
and sins   339–40, 364–71, 374–77 *see also* confession, of sins
and temptation *see* temptation
and theodicy   211–12
universality   344–45, 407–09
as voluntary transgression   353–54
Wesleyan teaching concerning sins of Christians   354
wrath of God as response to *see* wrath of God
see also confession; evil
Sinai, voice of God at   68
Skinner, John   301, 305, 313
Smith, Adam   211
Smith, David   177, 187
Smith, David L.   382, 391–93
Smith, E. O.   886–87
Smith, H. B.   64, 875
Smith, R. Payne   429–30, 432
Smith, Stephen M.   1107–08
Smith, W. Robertson   94, 182
Smith, Wilbur Moorehead   1096, 1106, 1107
Snowden, James H.   1145
Socinianism   105, 115, 541, 564, 568, 1023
against imputed sin   389–90
Socinus   738
Socrates   39, 49, 78, 79, 1027
view of goodness   93
sonship with God *see* adoption
soteriology (doctrine of salvation)   **639–797**
and anthropology   565
arrangement of doctrines (*ordo salutis*)   653–54, 655, 744–45
biblical terms related to   646–49, 652
definition   421
main concern of Reformation theology   561, 596
perseverance *see* perseverance

saving work of incarnate Son   500–509
see also salvation
soul
capacities   290–92
creationism   276–78
and death   1018–21 *see also* death, and the intermediate state
and dichotomy theory   270–73
Egyptian beliefs   1019–20
emanationism   276
features and functions   258–59
in funeral litergy   258–59
immortality of   1020, 1091
and monism theory   269–70
N.T. interpretation of O.T. ideas   259–60
O.T. theology   260–61
pre-existentialism   276
psychopannychia (soul sleep)   1034, 1091
Traducianism   277–81, 383–84, 402
and trichotomy theory   273–74
space   92
Spanner, Douglas   198, 328
Speiser, E. A.   147, 148, 149, 285, 313
Spielmann, Richard   997
spirit
and death   1021 *see also* spiritual death
of God *see* Holy Spirit
of man   268, 270–71, 272–74, 758, 776–77
spirits
and 'ghosts'   1031
in 'prison'   1093
see also angels; demons
spiritual death   311, 399, 532, 1021, 1076
Sproul, R. C.   312, 578, 579, 684, 852
Sproule, John A.   1070–71
Spurgeon, C. H.   318, 579, 584, 856
Spurrell, G. J.   149, 231
Stafford, T. A.   997
Stahlin, G.   567
Stoicism   691
Stone, Samuel   801, 809
Stott, John   908, 1091, 1092
Strauch, Alexander   930, 953
Strauss, David F.   187, 473
Strimble, Robert B.   603
Strong, A. H.   31, 63, 86, 88, 352, 404
and adoption   744, 746
on angels   165
and anthropology   238
on apriorism   235
on Calvinism   579
on chance and providence   198
on the church   910, 915, 924, 930
and cosmic dimensions of Christ   565
on creation   153, 161
and death   312, 1018, 1024
in defence of vicarious satisfaction   568

on divine love   102–03
on divine works of Christ   453
and doctrine of the Trinity   112
and election   680
on eternity   146
and 'Ethical Theory' of atonement by vicarious satisfaction   565
and faith   716
on Federal view of inputed sin   398
on general call   683
on general reconciliation   581
on grace working in the soul   359
on gulf between brute and man   291
on holiness   95, 98–99
on humiliation of Christ   516
on justification by faith   733
and kenosis   511
and nature   302
and necessity of Christ's death   537
on obedience of Christ   518
and pentecostal giving of the Spirit   875
and perseverance   770–71
and postmillennialism   1144–45
on preservation of evil people   194
on regeneration and baptism   696
on repentance and sin   362
on sacrifice   548–49
on sanctification   758
and sin   412
on soul and body   272
and theistic evolution   253
on theological order of treatment   124
and Traducianism   277
on tree of life   307
against trichotomy theory   274
and union of Christ's human and divine natures   468
on union with Christ   665, 668
and unity of the church   887
and unregenerate will   711
Strong, James   1033
substitutionary sacrifice *see* penal substitution; vicarious satisfaction
suffering
of Christ *see* atonement; passion and death of Jesus
of God, in Barth's Trinitarian theology   214
and God's impassibility *see* impassibility, doctrine of
and the problem of evil *see* problem of evil
superstition, and expectation of miracles   208
supralapsarianism   388, 397, 573
Swedenborg, Emmanuel   118
Sweet, William Warren   922, 961
Swete, Henry Barclay   1100, 1139, 1148, 1151
syncretism   783, 784, 917
   see also pluralism
synergism   387, 645, 662, 695, 759

Tt

tabernacle   298, 630–31
taboo   76
Talmud   545
Tatian   174, 593
Taylor, James   479
Taylor, Jeremy   112
Taylor, Nathaniel   391
Taylor, Vincent   456, 511, 548
   on humiliation of Christ   515–16
teaching ministry   7–11, 731
   see also doctrine; ministries and offices of the church, pastors and teachers
Teilhard de Chardin, Pierre   73, 828
temptation   211–12, 368–71, 403, 529
   and the fall of man   306–09
   Satan's role in   303, 306, 308–09, 371
Ten Commandments   78, 659, 920
Tennant, F. R.   212
Tenney, M. C.   463
Tennyson, Alfred, Lord   51, 728, 1032, 1086, 1103
Tertullian, Quintus Septimus Florens   174, 217, 477, 522, 1045
   on baptism   988
   on Christian community   833, 916
   and concupiscence   355
   on crucifixion   530
   and the Eucharist   1003
   and original sin   380
   and soteriology   594
   and Traducianism   278
   and typology   595
   on world evangelism   900
testimony of the Spirit (*testimonium Spiritus Sancti*) *see* witness of the Spirit
Tetragrammaton (YHWH)   13, 14, 54–55, 84, 449
   see also names of God
theanthropic union   489–91, 492–500
theism   77
theodicy   211–12, 302, 739
theology   xv, 2-11
   biblical *see* biblical theology
   biblical mandate   6–7, 9
   changing vocabulary   19–20, 22
   'covenant'   280, 397–98, 656, 663, 855–56
   definition and nature   2, 5, 20–21, 23–24
   and divine mysteries   427, 865
   education   xviii, 9
   federal   280, 295–96, 318, 384, 396–98, 404, 656
   'God-is-dead'   44, 424
   of hope (Moltmann)   1009
   liberal modern scholarship   150
   'liberation'   368
   Lutheran *see* Lutheran theology
   natural *see* natural theology
   neo-orthodox *see* neo-orthodox theology

opposition to 6
'process' *see* process theology
resources xv–xvi
Roman Catholic *see* Roman Church
sacramental 650, 662, 871, 874
see also doctrine; knowledge, of God
theophanies 26, 1047
'the angel of the LORD' 442–43
Theophilus of Antioch 143
theosis (deification) 668, 694
Thielicke, Helmut 331
Thiessen, H. C. 64, 138, 164, 270, 384, 1034
and judgment 1069
Thirty-Nine Articles of the Church of England (AD 1571) 465, 467–68, 527
on election 671, 678
on the Eucharist 991
and perseverance 766
Thistleton, Anthony 238
Thomas Aquinas, St. 35, 98, 184
on analogical language concerning God 224
on Church of Rome 828
on creation 153, 162
and election 578
and free will 70, 262
on God as supreme good 65
and image of God 252
on infusion of grace 255
and necessity of Christ's death 537
and need of metaphors 58–59
and parental derivation of souls 275, 277
and sin 366, 367
against Traducianism 278
and the unbaptized 782
Thomasius, Gottfried 510
Thoreau, Henry David 778
Thornwell, James H. 297, 401
Tillich, Paul 22, 23, 45, 465
Christology 423–25
on the demonic 176–77
and the numinous 98
and resurrection 606
and revelation 25
and task of theology 20, 346
time 84, 92, 142, 145–46
geological ages 163, 324–25
see also eternity
Timothy, doctrinal instruction 9–10
Toon, Peter 619–20, 888, 1146
Toplady, Augustus 582
Torbet, R. G. 831
total depravity 359, 416
see also depravity
Toynbee, Arnold 4
Tozer, A. W. 729–30, 1130
Tractarian movement 938

Traducianism 277–81
and original sin 383–84, 402
transcendence of God 92
and purity 96–97
Transfiguration 534, 536, 1118
transformation of the body 611
transubstantiation 512, 587, 991, 997, 1005–06
tree of life 306–07, 1104
Tregelles, S. P. 938, 1055, 1057
Trent, Council of (AD 1545-63) 351–52, 356, 561, 563–64
on Eucharist 1003
and faith 716
on good works 755
on justification 661–62, 755
on seven sacraments 978
on sin 366, 367
tri-theism 68
tribulation *see* 'great tribulation'; persecution
Trinity of God *see* Holy Trinity
Troelsch, Ernst 4, 776–77, 791, 885, 916
influence on Tillich 424
truth
as attribute of God 100
God as ground of 78, 100
and judgment 1073
as personal encounter 22
Turretin, Francis 70, 122n, 281, 578, 680, 686
and adoption 744
Tuttle, R. G. Jr 359
Tyndale, William 830
typology 558, 603–04, 618
of Christ as High Priest 630–35
of church 836–37
of sanctification 752

Uuu

Ungar, Merril F. 177
union with Christ 664
in baptism 990 *see also* baptism
call of God to 666
false notions 665, 668
through the Holy Spirit 666–67
mystery of 668–69
nature of 667–70
Unitarianism 72, 105, 389
see also Socinianism
unity of the church 872, 877
in allegory of the vine 880–81
defined against heresies and schisms 884–85
degeneration to Christendom 885
gifts for 895
Jesus' prayer for 881–83
in letter to the Ephesians 879–90
as mark of authenticity 884
recovery of 885–88 *see also* ecumenism

in Reformation onwards   885
see also church, universal (catholic) communion of saints
universalism   1074, 1085
　arguments   1089–91
　history   1088
　modern advocates   1088–89
Ursinus, Zacharius   297
　see also Heidelberg Catechism (AD 1563)
Ury, William   95

V Vv

Van Oosterzee, Johann Jacob   1095
Van Til, Cornelius   34, 43
VanderKam, James C.   432, 928–29
Vanderkooi, Garret   204
Vatican Council II   46, 208–09, 781–82
　ecclesiology   824, 828
Vaux, Roland De   543, 558
Verkuyl, J.   795
vicarious satisfaction   561, 568–70, 594–95, 596–97, 599
　see also atonement; penal substitution
Vincent of Lerins, St.   xviii
virgin birth of Jesus   467
　and authority of Bible   472
　belief of ancient church   469
　definition   469
　evidence   473, 474–79
　importance of doctrine   480–82
　in New Testament doctrine   479–80
　objections   470–74
Visser 't Hooft, Willem Adolf   781, 784
Von Rad, Gerhard   79, 147, 319, 1026, 1050, 1095
　on creation story   149, 150
　on heaven   1097, 1098
Vos, Geerhardus   558, 559, 1037–38, 1041, 1058
　and eschatological evangelism   1094
　and judgment   1070

W Ww

Waldensians   934, 937
Walvoord, John F.   431, 471, 618, 665, 1081–82, 1092
　on Christology   423
Ware, Timothy   387
Warfield, B. B.   107, 162, 438, 439, 446, 455–56
　on inclusivism   796
　on Paul and the earthly life of Christ   462
　and perfectionism   354
　and the reconciling of the world   575, 578
　on regeneration   695
　on saving faith   718, 719, 729
　on virgin birth   479
washing *see* sanctification, through the Word
watchfulness   1117, 1119, 1121
Waterman, C. Henry   1129
Watson, Richard   89, 124, 222, 390–91, 537, 582

on assurance   774
on election   680
on local church   915
Wesleyan doctrine   390–91
Watts, Isaac   582
Weber, Max   776, 825
Weinandy, Thomas   217, 219
Weiss, Bernard   469
Wells, David   423
Wells, David F.   521, 545
Wendel, Francois   495, 576, 673, 987
Wenham, Gordon J.   283
Wesley, Charles   390, 582, 779
Wesley, John   89, 125, 353, 390, 574
　and assurance   774, 777, 779
　on concupiscence   357
　and entire sanctification   774
　Evangelical Arminianism   390–91
　experience of God's call (conversion)   685, 700
　and local church   916, 920–21
　on prevenient and preventing grace   353–54, 359
　and Puritan background   778–79
　and regeneration   695
Westcott, B. F.   114, 876, 881, 883, 1100
Westin, G. G.   825
Westminster Catechism   298
Westminster Confession   61, 221, 303, 465, 467, 581
　on the Bible   xvi
　on the church   910
　on corruption of nature   356
　on 'covenant of works'   295
　on the Eucharist   991
　on greatness of God's creation of man   642
　on justification by faith   734
　on original sin   397–98, 643
　and perseverance   767
　and possible extra-ordinary methods of grace   794
　on soul of man   1019
Westminster Shorter Catechism   488
Westminster Standards   397–98
Westphal, Joachim   512
Whitby, Daniel   1058, 1059, 1143
Whitcomb, John   232
White, A. D.   204
White, James F.   974, 997
White, William, Jr   929
Whitehead, Alfred N.   89, 205
Whitman, Walt   778
Wigglesworth, Michael   1078
Wigram, G. W.   938
Wiley, Henry Orton   390, 774
Wilken, Robert   888
will
　depravity of   352
　freedom of *see* free will
　of God   70–71, 160, 350

redirected in repentance 711
Williams, G. F. 825
Williams, G. H. 938
Willis, W. Waite, Jr 213, 223
wisdom
    to be revealed in the church 74, 800, 911–12
    revealed at Calvery 589
    revealed in creation 73–74
    used in creation 159, 441–42
Wiseman, P. J. 231
witness of the Spirit 723, 724–25, 774, 775–76
    agreement of Wesleyanism and Puritanism 779
    together with that of human spirit 776–77
    see also assurance; calling; prevenient/preventing grace; regeneration
Witt, W. M. L. de 478
Wittenberg 3, 304
    Ninety-Five Theses 706
    see also Luther, Martin
Wolfson, Harry A. 1027–28, 1034
Word of God
    calling through 686, 722–23, 731
    creation through 160
    and judgment 1072
    proclamation in the power of the Spirit 686
    sanctification through 760–61
    see also gospel message; scripture
work 157, 202, 235, 287, 328
    horticulture and husbandry 320
    and the sentence of Adam 316, 322
    service as 1106
world
    Christian attitudes to 330–32
    as creation *see* creation
    as 'present evil age', ruled by Satan 329–32, 575, 881–82
    reconciliation *see* reconciliation of the world
    temptations of 309, 369–70
worship 318–19
    of ancestors 433
    of angels 167
    biblical atmosphere of 81
    buildings for 971–75, 995
    of Christ 455
    in church gatherings 915–16, 919
    of Creator 13–14, 297
    doctrinal teaching and confession 969–71

in heaven 1106
hymns 40, 297, 433, 582, 584, 858, 970–71 *see also* music
leaders 966, 995
on the 'Lord's Day' 965, 996
at the Lord's table *see* Eucharist (Lord's Supper)
offerings 968–69
prayer *see* prayer
preaching *see* preaching
public 731, 803, 962–71
reading of scripture 965–66
in spirit and truth 66
synagogues 927, 928, 933
see also liturgy; praise
wrath of God 48, 541, 553
    as background to atonement 566
    origin of doctrine 567
    revealed at Calvery 589, 661
    see also soteriology
Wray, Daniel E. 957
Wrede, W. 427
Wren, Sir Christopher 974
Wycliffe, John 810, 830
Wyon, Olive 996

Xx

Xenophanes 78

Yy

Yahweh *see* Tetragrammaton (YHWH)
Yarbrough, Robert W. 21n, 23–24
Yoder, J. H. 596, 938
Young, Edward J. 149

Zz

Zanchius, Hieronymus 794
Zimmerli, W. 533
Zinzendorf, Nicolaus Ludwig, Graf von 118
Zion, return to 1015
Zorn, R. O. 852, 853n
Zurich 812
Zwingli, Ulrich 356, 387, 397, 512, 979, 986
    and conversion 700
    and ecclesiology 812, 825, 938

Other books of interest

from

Christian Focus Publications

The Earthly Career of Jesus, the Christ

A Life in Chronological, Geographical and social context

Robert D. Culver

What's new about the life of Jesus? Sunday school lessons have drummed the stories into our heads, Christmas and Easter are now legends in the popular psyche and fortunes have been made writing that Jesus was everything that he said he wasn't!

Can we ever clear away the baggage from this most significant life or will the real Jesus remain frustratingly just out of reach?

This is a fresh, revealing investigation with scholarly backing. As you look beyond the clichés you will understand the true context of those familiar stories. Events and sayings will hit you between the eyes as you look upon an historic life with new understanding.

'Admirably fills the need for an up-to-date, well-arranged, and interestingly written life of Christ of moderate length... should be a standard textbook for many years to come. It is a superb production, masterfully organized and reverently written.'

Presbyterian Journal

'Some works on the life of Christ... emphasize the doctrinal aspects of the life of our Lord, others the historical, and still others the geographical. ...a balanced blend of all of these... If a person is choosing one book on this subject for his library, this should be the one.'

Calvary Review

'Many careful explanations and insights make this a worthy work for pastors and students... The inclusion of valuable recent historical and archaeological discoveries, and excellent indexes make this a useful and helpful study tool.'

Bibliotheca Sacra

ISBN 1-85792-798-2

A Compendious View of Natural and Revealed Religion

A Systematic Theology by John Brown of Haddington
Introduced by Joel R. Beeke

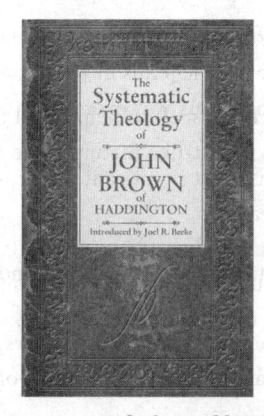

'Eighteenth Century Scotland produced many noted ministers, scholars and educators, but none greater, or so greatly loved in his own day or afterwards, as John Brown of Haddington'

Joel R. Beeke

John Brown (1722-1787) of Haddington was the leading minister in the Associate Synod during the formative years of eighteenth-century Scotland. He was a devout Christian, a gifted preacher, and a prolific writer of theology. He began life in obscure poverty, without advantage of wealth, position, title, or education. Yet God favored him with unusual gifts and an enormous capacity for hard work.

Brown taught himself Greek while working in the fields. He became a man of deep spiritual experience with skill in preaching the doctrines of free grace and piety. His last words, "my Christ," summarize his life and thought.

Brown was well-known as a theologian in his day but has since been overlooked, although recently a biography and some of his expositional work has been published. . His systematic theology, *A Compendious View of Natural and Revealed Religion*, is based on his seminary lectures and is notable for its evangelical eloquence and biblical centricity.

It contains more than 26,000 proof texts and numerous exegetical insights along with a consistent covenantal emphasis, experiential depth, and compelling applications. This single volume of Reformed systematic theology is rich in content and an indispensable tool for students, pastors, and professors of theology.

A new introduction to the life and writings of John Brown is provided by Joel R. Beeke and Randall J. Pederson.

ISBN 1-89277-766-5

Christian Focus Publications
publishes books for all ages

Our mission statement –
STAYING FAITHFUL
In dependence upon God we seek to help make His infallible Word, the Bible, relevant. Our aim is to ensure that the Lord Jesus Christ is presented as the only hope to obtain forgiveness of sin, live a useful life and look forward to heaven with Him.

REACHING OUT
Christ's last command requires us to reach out to our world with His gospel. We seek to help fulfill that by publishing books that point people towards Jesus and help them develop a Christ-like maturity. We aim to equip all levels of readers for life, work, ministry and mission.

Books in our adult range are published in three imprints.

Christian Focus contains popular works including biographies, commentaries, basic doctrine and Christian living. Our children's books are also published in this imprint.

Mentor focuses on books written at a level suitable for Bible College and seminary students, pastors, and other serious readers. The imprint includes commentaries, doctrinal studies, examination of current issues and church history.

Christian Heritage contains classic writings from the past.

Christian Focus Publications, Ltd
Geanies House, Fearn,
Ross-shire, IV20 1TW, Scotland, United Kingdom
info@christianfocus.com

For details of our titles visit us on our website
www.christianfocus.com